INTERMEDIATE ACCOUNTING

EDITION 14

K. FRED SKOUSEN, PhD, CPA
Brigham Young University

EARL K. STICE, PhD
Hong Kong University of
Science & Technology

JAMES D. STICE, PhD
Brigham Young University

South-Western College Publishing
Thomson Learning™

Australia • Canada • Denmark • Japan • Mexico • New Zealand • Philippines
Puerto Rico • Singapore • South Africa • Spain • United Kingdom • United States

Intermediate Accounting, 14e, by Skousen, Stice, and Stice

Team Director: Dave Shaut
Acquisitions Editor: Sharon Oblinger
Developmental Editor: Leslie Kauffman, Litten Editorial and Production, Inc.
Production Editor: Mark Sears
Production House: Navta Associates, Inc.
Marketing Manager: Dan Silverburg
Internal Design: Michael H. Stratton
Cover Design: Michael H. Stratton
Cover Photo: © 2000 TSM/Herrmann/Starke
Photo Researcher: Cary Benbow
Manufacturing Coordinator: Doug Wilke
Printer: RR Donnelley & Sons

Printed in the United States of America
1 2 3 4 5 03 02 01 00

For more information contact South-Western College Publishing, 5101 Madison Road, Cincinnati, Ohio, 45227 or find us on the Internet at http://www.swcollege.com

For permission to use material from this text or product, contact us by
• **telephone: 1-800-730-2214**
• **fax: 1-800-730-2215**
• **web: http://www.thomsonrights.com**

Library of Congress Cataloging-in-Publication Data
Skousen, K. Fred
    Intermediate accounting.—Ed. 14/K. Fred Skousen, Earl K. Stice, James D. Stice.
        p. cm.
    Includes bibliographical references and indexes.
    ISBN 0-324-01307-8 (alk. paper)
        1. Accounting. I Stice, Earl K. II. Stice, James D. III. Title.

    HF5635 .S5946 2000
    657'.044—dc21

This book is printed on acid-free paper.

Brief Contents

SKOUSEN STICE STICE

COUNTING WAS
MEHOW DETACHED
DAY WORLD OF
ACCOUNTING IS NO
AS A ONDARY
ACK ROO THAT
RDS FOR THE REAL
WITH ADVANCES
USING
ANAGE
INTO A VITAL
AN
CHIEVING THE
OF THE
THER IT BE SMALL
LTINATIONAL
ERA WHEN
ONSIDERED AS
FROM THE DAY
BUSINESS IS OVER.
LONGER THOUGHT
RY FUNCTION IN THE
IMPLY KEEPS
REAL BUSINESS OUT
ES IN TECHNOLOGY
TURES OF BUSINESS
TING HAS EVOLVED
URCE FOR
PORTANT PARTNER IN
AMENTAL GOALS OF
WHETHER IT BE
A MULTINATIONAL

ILLUSTRATED PREFACE

Out of the Backroom and into the Boardroom

Accounting is no longer the mysterious language of numbers, spoken only by a practiced few who do little in the way of communicating their knowledge with those outside of the accounting arena. Today, accountants are integral and vital resources in the structure of the world's leading corporations. Their ideas and skills are now thoroughly woven into the tapestry of management, and their ability to help an organization achieve significant and profitable goals is undisputed.

With a keen sense of the monumental changes taking place in the field, *Intermediate Accounting*, **Fourteenth Edition**, is an unparalleled resource that fully reflects the broadening definition of accounting today. From advances in technology to changing attitudes, *Intermediate Accounting* explores the essential concepts of the discipline—all with an engaging style that encourages students to read, think, and explore. Combined with an extensive supplements package, the *Intermediate Accounting* learning system prepares students for real-world business with real-world examples and exercises.

THE MISSING LINK

Intermediate Accounting takes an important step beyond the traditional balance sheet approach to show students how accounting principles are linked to the central activities of a business—operating, financing, and investing. This connection is made and reinforced throughout the text.

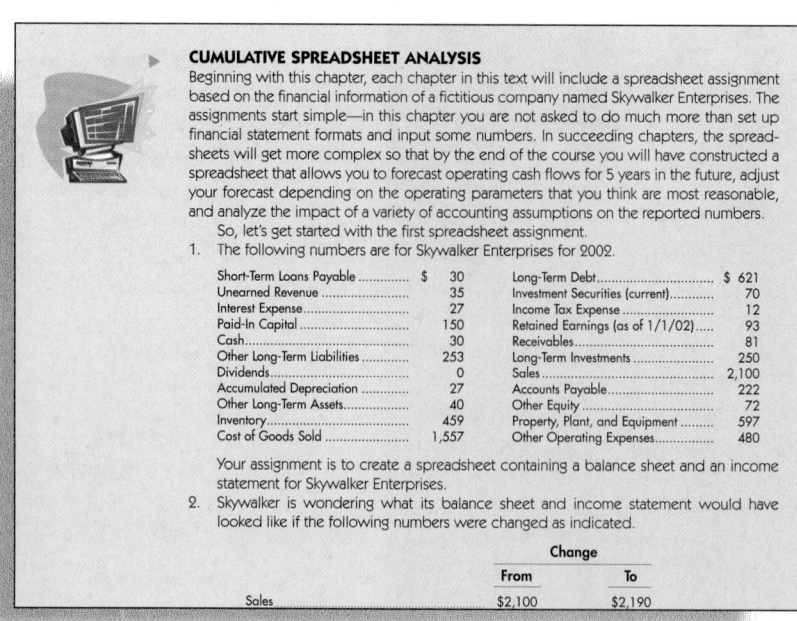

CUMULATIVE SPREADSHEET ANALYSIS

Beginning with this chapter, each chapter in this text will include a spreadsheet assignment based on the financial information of a fictitious company named Skywalker Enterprises. The assignments start simple—in this chapter you are not asked to do much more than set up financial statement formats and input some numbers. In succeeding chapters, the spreadsheets will get more complex so that by the end of the course you will have constructed a spreadsheet that allows you to forecast operating cash flows for 5 years in the future, adjust your forecast depending on the operating parameters that you think are most reasonable, and analyze the impact of a variety of accounting assumptions on the reported numbers. So, let's get started with the first spreadsheet assignment.

1. The following numbers are for Skywalker Enterprises for 2002.

Short-Term Loans Payable	$ 30	Long-Term Debt	$ 621
Unearned Revenue	35	Investment Securities (current)	70
Interest Expense	27	Income Tax Expense	12
Paid-In Capital	150	Retained Earnings (as of 1/1/02)	93
Cash	30	Receivables	81
Other Long-Term Liabilities	253	Long-Term Investments	250
Dividends	0	Sales	2,100
Accumulated Depreciation	27	Accounts Payable	222
Other Long-Term Assets	40	Other Equity	72
Inventory	459	Property, Plant, and Equipment	597
Cost of Goods Sold	1,557	Other Operating Expenses	480

Your assignment is to create a spreadsheet containing a balance sheet and an income statement for Skywalker Enterprises.

2. Skywalker is wondering what its balance sheet and income statement would have looked like if the following numbers were changed as indicated.

	Change	
	From	To
Sales	$2,100	$2,190

A new project in this edition, the **Cumulative Spreadsheet Analysis**, helps students build their understanding of this connection. Found at the end of Chapters 2–21, the assignment provides students with a chance to demonstrate and reinforce their understanding of the chapter topics. Each exercise requires them to create a spreadsheet that allows numerous variables to be modified and their effects to be monitored. Through this and other examples, students come to understand and appreciate the activities that attract customers, produce bottom-line results, and mean success or failure for companies and the people who run them.

Students using *Intermediate Accounting* take an important advantage with them into the world of business—they understand accounting in terms of operating, financing, and investing. These students are well prepared to work as managers in these functional areas, or as valuable teammates or advisors of those who do.

FORM FOLLOWS FUNCTION

The organization of *Intermediate Accounting* strongly reflects its focus on the activities of business. Building on the foundations of financial accounting (**PART 1**),

Brief Contents

PART 2 discusses business from the perspective of operating, financing, and investing and how accounting is intrinsically linked to each.

PART 3 covers additional business activities and disclosures. For instance, Chapter 17 consolidates topics dealing with employee compensation. Chapter 18 contains material on derivatives and the fair value of financial instruments.

PART 4 covers other dimensions of financial reporting including accounting changes, earnings per share, the impact of inflation and exchange rates, and financial statement analysis. Discussion of the time value of money is placed in an appendix, allowing instructors the flexibility of covering present value issues when they feel it is most appropriate.

Coverage of financial and accounting ratios is integrated throughout the text and summarized in the final chapter. For example, Chapter 3 includes efficiency, liquidity, and asset mix ratios in its discussion of the balance sheet; inventory turnover and days' sales in inventory are discussed in Chapter 8. These and many other ratios are tied together in the last chapter, but, consistent with the activities theme of the text, students do not need to wait until the end of the text to appreciate how accounting information is used by managers.

Based on input from instructors, we have significantly expanded the coverage of international issues throughout the text. As the business workplace becomes more global, it is essential that students comprehend how accounting practices differ from country to country. Nearly every chapter features a new section that discusses the international aspects of the relevant accounting topics. An IAS (International Accounting Standards) icon marks this new coverage. An international icon is shown in the end-of-chapter problem materials to highlight these important issues.

COMPREHENSIVE COVERAGE IN A STREAMLINED FORMAT

Intermediate Accounting accomplishes what was once thought to be impossible: comprehensive coverage of essential accounting topics in an efficient format that doesn't overwhelm students. Key topics are immediately recognizable—the more important the topic, the greater detail in which it is covered.

Where appropriate, chapters are divided into two main sections. The first section covers the central content of the chapter. The second section, "**Expanded Material**," deals with complexities, variations, alternatives, and exceptions. For example, the main part of Chapter 8 deals with the fundamentals of cost of goods sold and inventory. More complex methods such as LIFO pools and dollar-value LIFO are found in "**Expanded Material**," for use at the professor's discretion.

E X P A N D E D   M A T E R I A L

The flexible nature of "**Expanded Material**" allows professors to cover the essentials of an ever-expanding set of course material as well as to tailor the course to their own specific preferences and circumstances.

WHEN THE END IS REALLY THE BEGINNING...

As students come to the end of each chapter, they discover a rich set of learning material that goes beyond the ordinary to give them an opportunity to achieve true comprehension. Only *Intermediate Accounting* features such a diverse set of exercises and cases, all designed to take learning to a new level:

- 15-25 questions to help assimilate chapter content.
- Brief cases for homework or classroom discussion.
- Exercises to reinforce key concepts or applications.
- Problems that integrate several concepts or techniques.

DISCUSSION CASES

CASE 9–1

HAVE WE REALLY HAD A LOSS?
The Destro Company is experiencing an unusual inventory situation. The replacement cost of its principal product has been declining, but because of a unique market condition, Destro has not had to reduce the selling price of the item. Eric Dona, company controller, is aware that GAAP requires the valuation of inventory at the lower of cost or market. He considers market to be replacement cost, and he is concerned that to reduce the ending inventory to replacement cost will improperly reduce net income for the current period. Has an inventory loss occurred? Discuss.

CASE 9–2

BUT THEY WON'T BUY DUCKS ANYMORE!
The Bright-Lite Shirt Company buys wholesale sweatshirts, nightshirts, T-shirts, and other clothing items and, using a novel four-color processing system, imprints hundreds of designs on the items. The printed shirts are marketed widely to sports stores, department stores, col-

In addition to traditional questions, cases, exercises, and problems, each chapter's EOC includes **Competency Enhancement Opportunities** designed to cultivate the skills of critical thinking, communication, research, and teamwork necessary for accountants and other business professionals. The **Competency Enhancement Opportunities** include:

- Up to five "**Deciphering Actual Financial Statements**" problems that allow students to analyze actual financial statement data derived from recent annual reports.
- A **writing assignment** to be completed individually or in a group.
- A group **research project** that involves real world research, data collection, or interviews.
- A **debate** requiring two teams to argue the opposing sides of an accounting controversy.
- An **ethics assignment** that deals with ethical business behavior.
- A **cumulative spreadsheet analysis problem** that builds from chapter to chapter.
- An **Internet Search** assignment that provides practice in using the Internet to find specific information.

COMPETENCY ENHANCEMENT OPPORTUNITIES

▶ Deciphering Actual Financial Statements	▶ Ethical Dilemma
▶ Writing Assignment	▶ Cumulative Spreadsheet Analysis
▶ Research Project	▶ Internet Search
▶ The Debate	

Accounting is more than just doing textbook problems. This expanded competency material provides practice in critical thinking, oral and written communication, research, teamwork, and consideration of ethical issues.

▶ **DECIPHERING ACTUAL FINANCIAL STATEMENTS**
- **Deciphering 4–1 (The Walt Disney Company)**

Refer to the financial statements and related notes of THE WALT DISNEY COMPANY in Appendix A in answering the following questions.

1. Of Disney's three major segments—creative content, broadcasting, and, theme parks and resorts—which generated the most revenue in 1998? Which had the highest profit margin?
2. Disney's net income decreased from $1,966 million in 1997 to $1,850 million in 1998. Identify the major reasons for the decrease.
3. Does Disney generate most of its revenue within the United States or outside the United States? (Search the notes to the financial statements for additional information.)
4. How does Disney recognize revenue?
5. Does Disney expense its film and television costs using direct matching, systematic and rational allocation, or immediate recognition?
6. How does Disney expense its theme parks, resorts, and other property?

REAL WORLD...REAL UNDERSTANDING

Intermediate Accounting goes beyond numbers on a page to show students how accounting techniques and principles come into play in the real world. By incorporating numerous examples of accounting policies and procedures as practiced by real-world industry leaders, *Intermediate Accounting* gives students "**on-the-job experience**" in the classroom.

Each chapter opens with a specific real-world scenario that relates that chapter's content to students' future careers. Every chapter also features at least one boxed item relating to current business news that asks students to consider various policy and conceptual issues to address the company's situation or problem. Suggested solutions to the boxed items are included in the Solutions Manual.

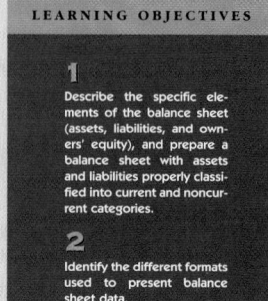

"Every man in uniform gets a bottle of Coca-Cola for 5 cents, wherever he is and whatever it costs." So said Robert Woodruff, Coca-Cola chairman, as American soldiers entered the fighting in World War II. By this time, Coca-Cola was such a part of American life that Coke also became part of the war machine. In 1943, General Dwight Eisenhower requested the necessary equipment and bottles to refill 10 million Coca-Cola's for soldiers in the European theater. Sixty-four bottling plants were operated under the direction of Allied Headquarters in North Africa during the war.

From its beginnings in Atlanta, Georgia, in which 1886 sales averaged nine drinks per day, to its worldwide presence, in which 1998 sales averaged 600 million servings per day, Coca-Cola

LEARNING OBJECTIVES

1 Describe the specific elements of the balance sheet (assets, liabilities, and owners' equity), and prepare a balance sheet with assets and liabilities properly classified into current and noncurrent categories.

2 Identify the different formats used to present balance sheet data.

Opening Scenarios—examples:

- Disney's Accounting Challenges (C 1)
- The Balance Sheet of Coca-Cola (C 3)
- Blockbuster Video: Garbage, Videos, and Depreciation Policy (C 13)
- The Turnaround of Home Depot (C 21)

▶ PHAR-MOR AND THE WORLD BASKETBALL LEAGUE

Michael "Mickey" Monus, former president of PHAR-MOR INC., a deep-discount drugstore chain, had a keen interest in sports. His interest was such that he purchased a share of the COLORADO ROCKIES major league baseball team and also founded the World Basketball League (WBL)—a league for players 6'7" and under. The Rockies did quite well financially, setting attendance records in their first season of play. Unfortunately,

Mr. Monus was forced to sell his interest in the Rockies because of financial difficulties touched off by the failure of the WBL. WBL players and referees rebelled in July 1992 because they hadn't been paid in two months. Monus tried to prop up the league, but it soon suspended operations.

During late July 1992, Phar-Mor received a tip that Monus had been transferring money from Phar-Mor to the WBL. Investigation revealed that the $10 million in Phar-Mor cash Monus had used in an attempt to sustain the WBL was just the tip of a large iceberg of accounting irregularities. Payments from large vendors to secure exclusive supply arrangements for a period of time were recorded as revenue at the time of receipt instead of being deferred and recognized over the period of the

arrangement. Inventory was overstated by $175 million by keeping items in the inventory records even after they had been sold and also by creating phantom inventory at selected stores. The stores were selected based on the auditor's plan to verify inventory at only a few stores—Mr. Monus and his accomplices allegedly found out which stores those were and made sure not to manipulate inventory in those stores. The resulting investigation resulted in Phar-Mor's filing for bankruptcy protection on August 17, 1992.

Monus faced a 129-count indictment filed by the U.S. attorney general's office. The first trial was declared a mistrial in June 1994. Monus was convicted on 109 felony counts in May 1995 and was sentenced to 20

Boxed Items—examples:

- Qualified Audit Opinions in China (C 1)
- Russian Accounting (C 2)
- Phar-Mor and the World Basketball League (C 4)
- Baseball Accounting (C 13)

Elsewhere are hundreds of examples, illustrations, and exercises featuring AT&T, Boeing, Nike, IBM, Wal-Mart, PepsiCo, and many other leading firms. Company names are highlighted in blue and are indexed at the end of the text.

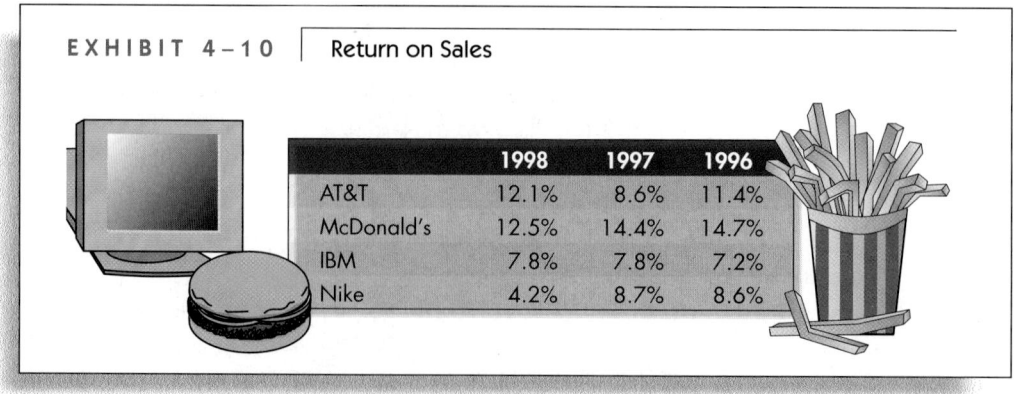

EXHIBIT 4-10 | Return on Sales

	1998	1997	1996
AT&T	12.1%	8.6%	11.4%
McDonald's	12.5%	14.4%	14.7%
IBM	7.8%	7.8%	7.2%
Nike	4.2%	8.7%	8.6%

STYLE AND SUBSTANCE

Students consistently complain that business textbooks, especially accounting texts, are dull, drab, and uninteresting to read. Not anymore. ***Intermediate Accounting***, **Fourteenth Edition**, with its bright, colorful, and graphic-rich layout, captures and maintains student interest. The consistent use of color, graphics, and icons sets this text apart from the crowd.

The dynamic layout is enhanced by **Margin Notes** and **Stop & Thinks**. Margin Notes emphasize additional points of interest and caution. Stop & Thinks provide critical thinking questions to stimulate student curiosity and class discussion.

Caution! When changes are made to retained earnings for prior-period adjustments, changes are also necessary to any prior-period income statements that are prepared in comparative format.

 STOP & THINK: Why do you think Kinross waits to recognize revenue from the sale of Kubaka gold until the gold is actually sold?

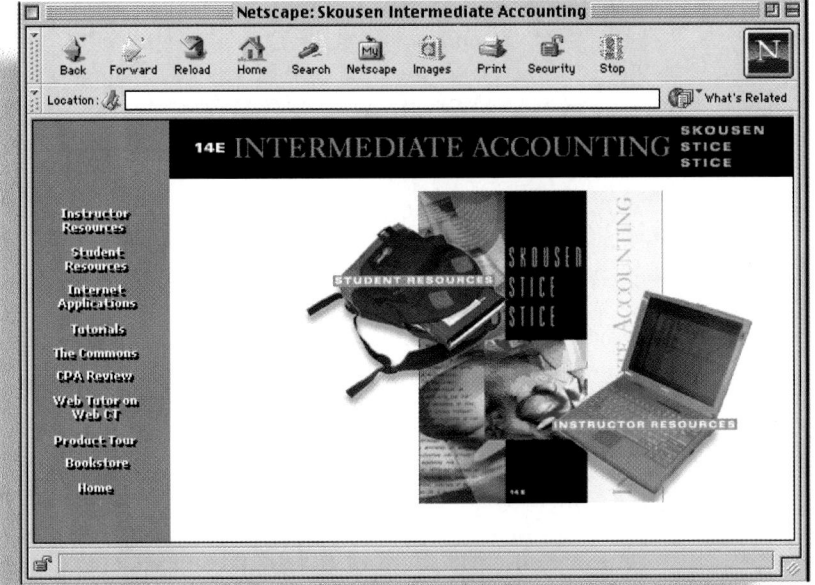

UNTANGLING THE WEB

With the Internet becoming an increasingly important part of business, it's essential that your students have the edge when it comes to using it on the job. ***Intermediate Accounting*** takes full advantage of the wealth of information available on the Internet through its product support site: http://skousen. swcollege.com. This content-rich site features numerous resources for both the instructor and the student. Instructors are able to download all of the supplemental material, access lecture outlines, and administer Internet assignments utilizing recently published source documents such as journal articles and updates. Students have access to links to accounting-related sites, PowerPoint slides, Net Work exercises and boxed items from the text, on-line tutorials, and CPA Review questions. From academic research to on-the-job exploration, this plugged-in text helps students learn about and fully exploit this important medium.

net work exercise

A wealth of financial information is available on the Internet. For instance, you can view Disney's most recent annual report by visiting Disney's Web site (**www.disney.com**) or by searching the SEC's on-line database EDGAR (**www.sec.gov/edgarhp.htm**).
Net Work:
1. What was Disney's net earnings for the most recent year?
2. Did net earnings increase or decrease from the previous year? By how much?

Each chapter directs students to World Wide Web sites that contain data relevant to the chapter's content. For instance, the **Net Work exercise** for Chapter 1 includes an assignment that involves EDGAR, the online database of the Securities and Exchange Commission.

GET CONNECTED

The **Fourteenth Edition** makes an astute use of technology, using it not simply for technology's sake, but for an enriching educational experience. Hundreds of teaching slides in Microsoft® PowerPoint® format can be used in on-screen lecture presentations, printed out and used as traditional overheads, or printed and distributed to students (3 or 6 to a page). This last option allows students to concentrate on the professor, rather than rushing to copy down the information or exhibit contained on each slide.

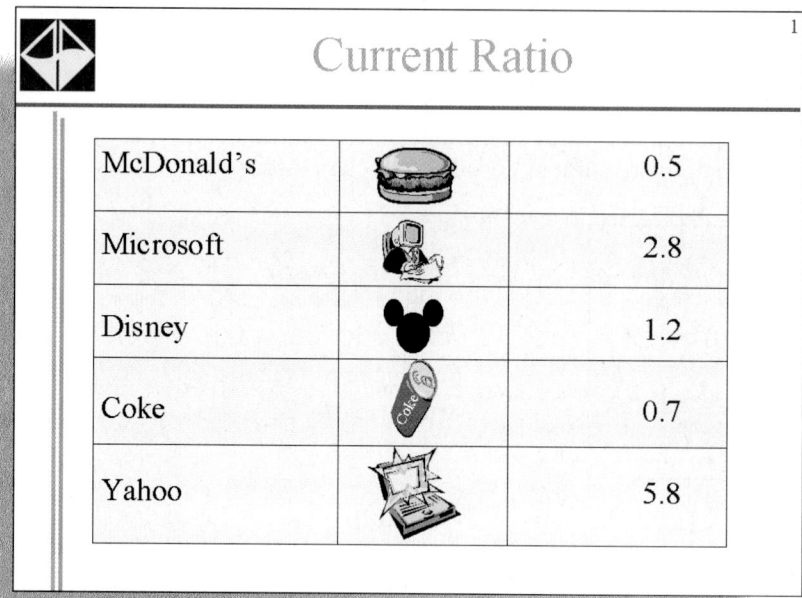

Short, but powerful, lecture videos bring the book's topics to life as the authors teach various topics covered in the text. Also available is Homework Assistant and Tutor (HAT) software, developed by Rayman Meservy of Brigham Young University. This Windows®-based software visually illustrates the relationship between accounting transactions and their impact on financial statements. In addition, Excel spreadsheet templates are available for solving selected end-of-chapter exercises and problems.

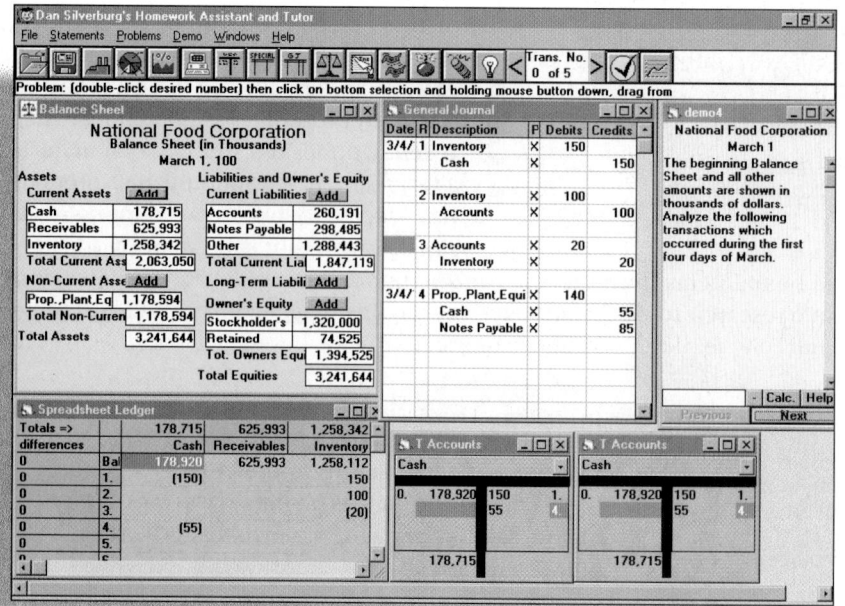

TAKE TEACHING AND LEARNING FURTHER

Intermediate Accounting's outstanding resource package of supplementary materials enhances the text's applied, real-world approach.

Available to Instructors

- **Solutions Manual**, prepared by Earl K. Stice and James D. Stice, Brigham Young University. This manual contains independently verified answers to all end-of-chapter questions, cases, exercises, problems, and Competency Enhancement Opportunities, plus suggested solutions to questions that accompany the boxed items and Stop & Think questions in the text.
- **Solutions Transparencies.** Acetate transparencies of solutions for all end-of-chapter exercises and problems are available to adopters.
- **Instructor's Resource Manual**, prepared by W. David Albrecht, Bowling Green State University. This manual contains objectives, chapter outlines, teaching suggestions and strategies, and topical overviews of end-of-chapter materials. It also features assignment classifications with level of difficulty and estimated completion time, suggested readings on chapter topics, and transparency masters.
- **Test Bank**, prepared by Larry A. Deppe, Weber State University. The revised and expanded test bank is available in both printed and computer versions. Test items include multiple choice questions and short examination problems for each chapter, along with solutions.
- **PowerPoint Slides**, prepared by C. Douglas Cloud, Pepperdine University. Selected teaching transparency slides of key concepts and exhibits are available in PowerPoint presentation software.
- **Spreadsheet Template Diskette**, prepared by Leslie Turner, Northern Kentucky University. Excel templates are provided for solving selected end-of-chapter exercises and problems that are identified in the text with a spreadsheet icon. The diskette may be ordered free of charge from South-Western College Publishing by instructors who have adopted the textbook.

Available to Students

- **Web Site** (http://skousen.swcollege.com). This content–rich site features PowerPoint slides, on-line tutorials, CPA Review questions, and links to accounting–related sites, as well as numerous features from the text.
- **INTACCT: Intermediate Accounting Tutor**, by D. Rama, University of Massachusetts–Dartmouth. This Internet-based tutorial provides students with reinforcement of key Intermediate Accounting concepts. Completely interactive, this product is the most advanced method to further enhance a student's understanding of *Intermediate Accounting* available on the market today.
- **Web Tutor on Web CT.** This on-line study guide is available to students through the Skousen/Stice/Stice product site http://skousen.swcollege.com. It is designed to provide students interactive assistance in applying the concepts proposed in the textbook. It does this through the use of self-testing questions, learning objectives, and tutorial assistance.
- **Homework Assistant and Tutor (HAT) Software**, prepared by Rayman Meservy, Brigham Young University. This Windows-based software visually illustrates the relation-ships among accounting transactions and the financial statements. It can be used to solve selected text exercises and problems. HAT is also an ideal classroom teaching aid.
- **Study Guide**, prepared by Sara York Kenny, International Finance Corporation. Each chapter of the study guide includes learning objectives, a study outline, self-testing questions, and study group activities. The Study Guide may be ordered directly from South-Western College Publishing on the Internet at http://accounting.swcollege.com.
- **Working Papers.** Forms for solving end-of-chapter exercises and problems are contained in a single bound volume and are perforated for easy removal and use.
- **Check Figures.** Key figures for solutions to selected exercises and problems are provided at the end of the text as an aid to students as they prepare their answers.

ACKNOWLEDGMENTS AND THANKS

Relevant pronouncements of the Financial Accounting Standards Board and other authoritative publications are paraphrased, quoted, discussed, and referenced throughout the text. We are indebted to the American Accounting Association, the American Institute of Certified Public Accountants, the Financial Accounting Standards Board, and the Securities and Exchange Commission for material from their publications.

We wish to thank the following faculty who reviewed manuscript and provided many helpful suggestions:

Charlene Abendroth	California State University, Hayward
Bruce Branson	North Carolina State University
David A. Cook	Calvin College
Alan H. Falcon	Loyola Marymount University
Richard Fern	Eastern Kentucky University
Inam Hussain	Purdue University
Anne C. Lewis	Edgecombe Community College
Sharon M. Lightner	San Diego State University
Paula Morris	Kennesaw State University
Mary Phillips	North Carolina Central University
Richard M. Piazza	University of North Carolina at Charlotte
J. Marion Posey	Pace University
Joe Sanders	Indiana State University
Victoria Shoaf	St. John's University
John J. Surdick	Xavier University

We also extend our thanks to the many instructors and students who have used *Intermediate Accounting* and volunteered their comments and suggestions.

Finally, we pay tribute to and recognize the significant contributions that our friend and former co-author, Jay Smith, has made to this textbook. While Jay is now retired and is making contributions to many other projects, his careful and scholarly work on eight previous editions of this text continue to provide a solid foundation upon which this fourteenth edition is built. We express our sincere appreciation to Jay and extend our best wishes to him.

K. Fred Skousen
E. Kay Stice
James D. Stice

Contents

Appendices

Indexes

About the Authors

K. FRED SKOUSEN

K. Fred Skousen, Ph.D., CPA, is the Advancement Vice President at Brigham Young University. He earned a bachelor's degree from BYU and master's and Ph.D. degrees from the University of Illinois.

Professor Skousen has been a consultant to the Financial Executive Research Foundation, the Controller General of the United States, the Federal Trade Commission, and to several large companies. The summer of 1969 he was a Faculty Resident on the staff of the Securities and Exchange Commission in Washington, D.C. The summer of 1973 he was a Faculty Fellow with Price Waterhouse & Co. in Los Angeles. Dr. Skousen currently serves on the Board of Directors of several corporations.

Professor Skousen taught at the University of Illinois and the University of Minnesota prior to joining the faculty at Brigham Young University. In 1970 he received the Distinguished Faculty Award for the School of Business Administration at the University of Minnesota. He was Visiting Associate Professor at the University of California, Berkeley, Spring Quarter, 1973, and Distinguished Visiting Scholar at the University of Missouri, Summer 1977. He received the College of Business Distinguished Faculty Award at Brigham Young University in 1975, the National Beta Alpha Psi Academic Accountant of the Year Award in 1979, and the 1980 Karl G. Maeser Research and Creative Arts Award at Brigham Young University. Professor Skousen was appointed to a nine-member National Commission on Professional Accounting Education in 1982. In 1983 Dr. Skousen was awarded the Peat Marwick Professorship at BYU. In 1984 Dr. Skousen was elected to AICPA Council, and in 1985 he received the UACPA Outstanding Faculty Award. From 1989 to 1998, Skousen held the J. Willard and Alice S. Marriott Chair and was Dean of the Marriott School of Management.

Dr. Skousen is the author or co-author of more than 50 articles, research reports, and books, including: An Introduction to the SEC, Intermediate Accounting, Accounting: Concepts and Applications, and Financial Accounting. He served as Director of Research and a member of the Executive Committee of the American Accounting Association from 1974 to 1976 and is a member of the American Institute of CPAs, the American Accounting Association, and is past-president of the Utah Association of CPAs.

Fred and his wife, Julie, have five sons, one daughter, and 13 grandchildren.

Left to right: Jim Stice, Fred Skousen, and Kay Stice

EARL K. STICE

Earl K. Stice is the PricewaterhouseCoopers Professor of Accounting in the School of Accountancy and Information Systems at Brigham Young University. He holds bachelor's and master's degrees from Brigham Young University and a Ph.D. from Cornell University. Dr. Stice has taught at Rice University, the University of Arizona, Cornell University, and the Hong Kong University of Science and Technology (HKUST). He won the Phi Beta Kappa teaching award at Rice University, and was twice selected at HKUST as one of the ten best lecturers on campus. Dr. Stice has also taught in a variety of executive education and corporate training programs in the United States, Hong Kong, and South Africa. He has published papers in the *Journal of Financial and Quantitative Analysis, The Accounting Review, Review of Accounting Studies,* and *Issues in Accounting Education,* and his research on stock splits has been cited in *Business Week, Money,* and *Forbes.* Dr. Stice has presented his research results at seminars in the United States, Finland, Taiwan, Australia, and Hong Kong. He is co-author of *Accounting: Concepts and Applications, 7th edition* and of *Financial Accounting: Reporting and Analysis, Fifth Edition.* Dr. Stice and his wife, Ramona, are the parents of five children: Derrald, Han, Ryan Marie, Lorien, and Lily.

JAMES STICE

James D. Stice is the Distinguished Teaching Professor of Accounting in the School of Accountancy and Information Systems (SOAIS) at Brigham Young University. He holds bachelor's and master's degrees from BYU and a Ph.D. from the University of Washington, all in accounting. He has been on the faculty at BYU since 1988. During that time, he has been selected by graduating accounting students as "Teacher of the Year" on numerous occasions, selected by his peers in the Marriott School of Management at BYU to receive the "Outstanding Teaching Award," and received the University's top award for teaching excellence, the Maeser Award, in 1999. Professor Stice has published articles in *The Accounting Review, Decision Sciences, Issues in Accounting Education, The CPA Journal,* and other academic and professional journals. In addition to this textbook, he has published two other textbooks: *Financial Accounting: Reporting and Analysis* and *Accounting: Concepts and Applications.* Professor Stice has also been involved in executive education for Ernst & Young, Bank of America, and IBM. Dr. Stice and his wife, Kaye, have seven children: Crystal, J. D., Ashley, Whitney, Kara, Skyler, and Cierra.

Photo Credits

For permission to reproduce the photographs on the pages indicated, acknowledgement is made to the following:

Page v   ©PhotoDisc, Inc.
Page vi   ©SWCP/Cary Benbow
Page xxix   Mark A. Philbrick/BYU
Page 1   ©SWCP/Cary Benbow
Page 2   ©Bruce T. Brown/Tony Stone Images
Page 11   ©Corbis/Richard T. Nowitz
Page 22   ©Corbis/Vince Streano
Page 25   ©Corbis/Charles O'Rear
Page 44   ©PhotoDisc, Inc.
Page 50   ©David Young-Wolff/Photo Edit
Page 60   ©PhotoDisc, Inc.
Page 98   ©PhotoDisc, Inc.
Page 106   ©PhotoDisc, Inc.
Page 114   ©Corbis/Vince Streano
Page 158   ©PhotoDisc, Inc.
Page 166   ©Corbis/Adamsmith Productions
Page 168   ©PhotoEdit
Page 177   ©Corbis/Reuters Newmedia Inc.
Page 222   ©PhotoDisc, Inc.
Page 225   ©PhotoEdit
Page 244   ©Corbis/Kenneth Rogers
Page 306   ©SWCP/Cary Benbow
Page 308   ©PhotoDisc, Inc.
Page 312   ©Myrleen Ferguson/PhotoEdit
Page 326   ©Corbis/Steve Raymer
Page 370   ©PhotoDisc, Inc.
Page 375   ©Bill Bachman/PhotoEdit
Page 387   ©Corbis/Jim Sugar Photography
Page 422   ©PhotoDisc, Inc.
Page 428   ©PhotoDisc, Inc.
Page 445   ©Bonnie Kamin/PhotoEdit
Page 488   ©PhotoDisc, Inc.
Page 490   ©Corbis/Joseph Sohm; ChromoSohm Inc.
Page 508   ©PhotoDisc, Inc.
Page 534   ©PhotoDisc, Inc.
Page 538   ©Tony Freeman/PhotoEdit
Page 543   ©Corbis/Lynn Goldsmith
Page 600   ©PhotoDisc, Inc.
Page 605   ©Corbis/Richard T. Nowitz
Page 676   ©PhotoDisc, Inc.
Page 682   ©South-Western College Publishing
Page 693   ©Corbis/Vince Streano
Page 738   ©PhotoDisc, Inc.
Page 742   ©SWCP/Cary Benbow
Page 752   ©PhotoEdit/Michael Newman
Page 792   ©PhotoDisc, Inc.
Page 797   ©Kevin R. Morris/Corbis
Page 802   ©Ed Eckstein/Corbis

Page 857   ©SWCP/Cary Benbow
Page 858   ©PhotoDisc, Inc.
Page 861   ©Rachel Epstein/PhotoEdit
Page 885   ©Kevin R. Morris/Corbis
Page 920   ©PhotoDisc, Inc.
Page 922   ©Gary A. Conner/PhotoEdit
Page 938   ©Michael Newman/PhotoEdit
Page 972   ©PhotoDisc, Inc.
Page 973   ©Royalty Free/Corbis
Page 1016   ©Michael Newman/PhotoEdit
Page 1048   ©PhotoDisc, Inc.
Page 1057   ©Darrell Gulin/Corbis
Page 1072   ©Roy Corral/Corbis
Page 1099   ©SWCP/Cary Benbow
Page 1100   ©PhotoDisc, Inc.
Page 1105   ©AFP/Corbis
Page 1140   ©PhotoDisc, Inc.
Page 1145   ©George Hall/Corbis
Page 1184   ©PhotoDisc, Inc.
Page 1187   ©Michael Newman/PhotoEdit
Page 1205   ©AFP/Corbis

part 1

Foundations of Financial Accounting

chapter 1
Financial Reporting

In 1923, two brothers, Walt and Roy Disney, founded the Disney Brothers Studio as a partnership to produce animated film features. Five years later, the Disney Brothers Studio released its first animated film with sound effects and dialogue, *Steamboat Willie,* featuring a soon to become famous mouse, Mickey. Pluto was introduced to American audiences in 1930 and Goofy was created just two years later. Walt Disney earned his first Academy Award in 1932 with the release of *Flowers and Trees,* the first full-color animated film. Donald Duck appeared on the scene in 1934, and in 1937 *Snow White and the Seven Dwarfs* was released accompanied by the first comprehensive merchandising campaign.

But Walt Disney's vision encompassed more than animated films. In 1952, Disney began designing and creating Disneyland, which opened on July 17, 1955. Beginning in the late 50s, the television shows *Disneyland* (which ran for 29 seasons under various names) and *The Mickey Mouse Club* were also successful Disney ventures. Although Walt Disney passed away in 1966, his influence is still felt around the world today. We have Disney theme parks in California, Florida, Paris, and Tokyo.

His company has expanded far beyond what even Mr. Disney could have foreseen. THE WALT DISNEY COMPANY is now involved in the ownership of television and radio stations; international film distribution; home video production; live theatrical entertainment; on-line computer programs; interactive computer games; telephone company partnerships; cruise lines; Disney Stores; newspaper, magazine and book publishing; and the convention business. In the past decade, the Disney Company has grown over 600%, culminating in its 1996 acquisition of AMERICAN BROADCASTING CORPORATION (ABC).

Disney paid $18.9 billion for ABC's net liabilities of $300 million (assets of $4.0 billion and liabilities of $4.3 billion). The excess of cost over the fair value of net assets was accounted for as goodwill to the tune of $19 billion. Since the acquisition, Disney's revenue mix has changed dramatically as illustrated in Exhibit 1–1. In addition to the issue of accounting for the acquisition and consolidation of ABC, Disney is also facing some other interesting accounting issues.

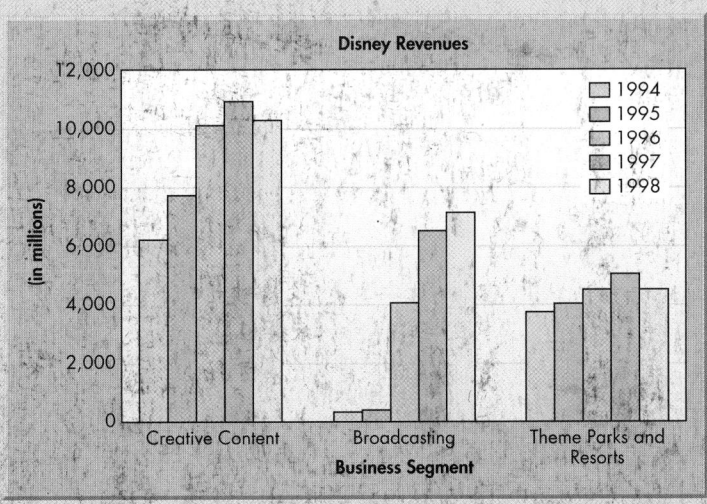

EXHIBIT 1–1 | Disney's Revenue Mix: 1994–1998

LEARNING OBJECTIVES

1
Describe the purpose of financial reporting and identify the primary financial statements.

2
Explain the function of accounting standards and describe the role of the FASB in setting those standards in the United States.

3
Recognize the importance to financial reporting of the SEC, AICPA, AAA, and IRS.

4
Realize the growing importance and relevance of international accounting issues to the practice of accounting in the United States and understand the role of the IASC in international accounting standard setting.

5
Understand the significance of the FASB's conceptual framework in outlining the qualities of good accounting information, defining terms such as asset and revenue, and providing guidance about appropriate recognition, measurement, and reporting.

6
Identify career opportunities related to accounting and financial reporting in the fields of public accounting, corporate accounting, financial analysis, banking, and consulting.

- In 1998, for example, Disney changed the way it computes earnings per share. Disney now reports a number called basic earnings per share, which was $0.89 per share in 1998, down from $0.95 in 1997. The FASB worked in concert with the International Accounting Standards Committee (IASC) in developing an earnings-per-share standard that is now used by most major companies around the world. That new standard was issued in 1997. In Chapter 19 we will discuss why a change was needed and why many companies report two EPS figures, and you will become proficient at the mechanics of that standard.
- In June 1998, Disney declared a 3-for-1 stock split that it accounted for as a stock dividend. In Chapter 11 we'll talk about the difference between the accounting for a stock split and a stock dividend and discuss why it is extremely difficult to look at Disney's 1998 financial statements and see any sign of this transaction at all.
- Disney is very active in managing the risks that it faces worldwide. Two of those risks that are discussed at length in the notes to Disney's financial statements are interest rate risk and foreign currency exchange risk. In Chapter 18 we will discuss how companies manage these risks and how derivatives are sometimes used to manage risk. We will also study the brand-new accounting rules that govern the area of accounting for derivatives.
- In its financial statement notes, Disney reveals that it has long-term noncancelable real estate leases that obligate it to make payments of $2 billion in the future. In Chapter 15 we will discuss the accounting rules that allow Disney to avoid reporting any obligation for these payments in the liability section of its balance sheet.
- Disney also reports that it has a $321 million obligation to provide postretirement health care benefits to some of its employees. That same note reveals that Disney employees hired after January 1, 1994, are not entitled to these benefits. In Chapter 17 we will discuss why some people think that the FASB is responsible for Disney (and many other U.S. companies) canceling retiree health care plans.

- Disney has a stock option plan that grants rights to buy shares of Disney stock to employees. The intent of the plan is to encourage Disney employees to work hard to increase the value of the company, thus benefiting themselves and the shareholders at the same time. The options granted to employees by Disney during 1998 had a value of over $200 million, and yet Disney was not required to report any compensation expense with respect to this stock option plan. Chapter 11 reveals how the U.S. business community, led by the high-tech companies, forced the FASB to back down from its attempt to require the value of these kinds of options to be reported as an expense.

The intricacies of accounting often result in differences of opinion as to what accounting methods are appropriate and the level of disclosure that should be required of companies. Arguments over appropriate accounting are a fact of life because accounting involves judgment. Before the financial statements of a company are released, the management of the company is likely to have some accounting disagreements with the independent auditor. If a company falters, outside analysts are sure to find accounting judgments with which, in retrospect, they disagree. If the FASB proposes a new accounting rule, it is certain that some business executives will proclaim the rule to be utterly absurd. This is not because managers are sleazy, conniving, and self-serving (although such managers certainly exist); it is because the business world is a complex place filled with complex transactions, and reasonable people can disagree about how to account for those transactions.

net work exercise

A wealth of financial information is available on the Internet. For instance, you can view Disney's most recent annual report by visiting Disney's Web site (www.disney.com) or by searching the SEC's on-line database EDGAR (www.sec.gov/edgarhp.htm).

Net Work:
1. What was Disney's net earnings for the most recent year?
2. Did net earnings increase or decrease from the previous year? By how much?

Your introductory accounting course gave you an overview of the primary financial statements and touched briefly on such topics as revenue recognition, depreciation, leases, pensions, deferred taxes, LIFO, and financial instruments. In intermediate accounting, all these topics are back, bigger and better than ever. But now, instead of getting an overview, you will actually get the nuts and bolts. Yes, some of these topics are complex—they are complex because the business world is a complex place. However, when you complete your course in intermediate accounting, you will be quite comfortable with a set of financial statements. In fact, you will probably find yourself skipping the statements themselves and turning directly to the really interesting reading—the notes.

Now is an exciting time to be studying accounting. Students have been learning double-entry bookkeeping for over 500 years. And now it will be your privilege to witness the transformation of financial reporting via the twin forces of internationalization and information technology. Over the next 10 to 15 years, the increased integration of the worldwide market for capital will inevitably force diverse national accounting practices to converge on appropriate global standards. This text will help you see how this process has already begun. In the longer term, the power of computers to create and analyze huge databases will change the very nature of accounting. Users will not learn about companies through a few pages of financial statements and notes but, ultimately, through on-line access to the raw financial data. It isn't clear what "accounting" will entail in the technological future, but it is certain that those professionals trained in the underlying concepts of accounting and in the importance of accounting judgment and accounting estimates will be best able to make the transition. This book is intended to prepare you for the future.

Describe the purpose of financial reporting and identify the primary financial statements.

ACCOUNTING AND FINANCIAL REPORTING

The overall objective of **accounting** is to provide information that can be used in making economic decisions.

> Accounting is a service activity. Its function is to provide quantitative information, primarily financial in nature, about economic entities that is intended to be useful in making economic decisions—in making reasoned choices among alternative courses of action.[1]

Several key features of this definition should be noted.

- Accounting provides a vital *service* in today's business environment. The study of accounting should not be viewed as a theoretical exercise—accounting is meant to be a practical tool.
- Accounting is concerned primarily with *quantitative* financial information that is used in conjunction with qualitative evaluations in making judgments.
- Accounting information is used in making decisions about how to *allocate scarce resources*. Economists and environmentalists remind us constantly that we live in a world with limited resources. The better the accounting system that measures and reports the costs of using these resources, the better decisions can be made for allocating them.
- Although accountants place much emphasis on reporting what has already occurred, this past information is intended to be useful in making economic decisions about the *future*.

---

1 *Statement of the Accounting Principles Board No. 4*, "Basic Concepts and Accounting Principles Underlying Financial Statements of Business Enterprises," New York: American Institute of Certified Public Accountants, 1970, par. 40.

> **Caution!** Remember that accounting information is only one type of information used in decision making. And, in many cases, qualitative data are more useful than quantitative data.

Users of Accounting Information

Who uses accounting information and what information do they require to meet their decision-making needs? In general, all parties interested in the financial health of a company are called **stakeholders.** Stakeholder users of accounting information are normally divided into two major classifications.

- **Internal users,** who make decisions directly affecting the internal operations of the enterprise
- **External users,** who make decisions concerning their relationship to the enterprise

Major internal and external stakeholder groups are listed in Exhibit 1–2.

EXHIBIT 1–2 | Major Internal and External Stakeholder Groups

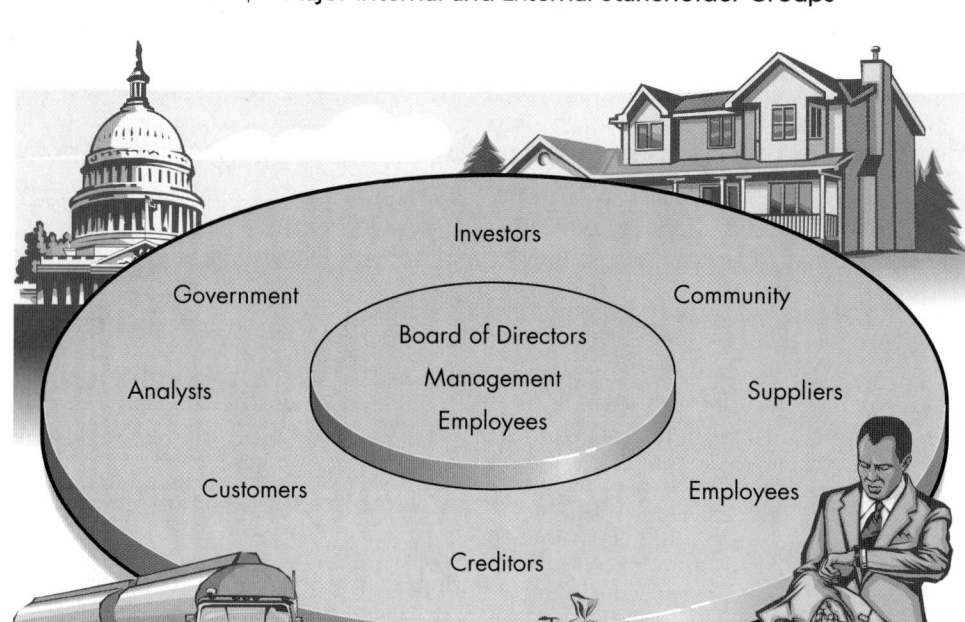

Internal users need information to assist in planning and controlling enterprise operations and managing enterprise resources. The accounting system must provide timely information needed to control day-to-day operations and to make major planning decisions, such as: Do we make this product or another one? Do we build a new production plant or expand existing facilities? **Management accounting** (sometimes referred to as managerial or cost accounting) is concerned primarily with financial reporting for internal users. Internal users, especially management, have control over the accounting system and can specify precisely what information is needed and how the information is to be reported.

Financial accounting focuses on the development and communication of financial information for external users. As a company grows and expands, it often finds its need for cash to be greater than that provided from profitable operations. In this situation, it will turn to people or organizations external to the company for funding. But these external users need assurances that they will receive a return on their investment. Thus, they require information about the company's past performance as this information will allow them to forecast how the company can be expected to perform in the future.

Companies compete for external funding as external users have a variety of investment alternatives. The quality of the accounting information provided to external users aids in determining (1) if funding is to be received and (2) the costs associated with that funding.

The types of decisions made by external users vary widely; therefore, their information needs are highly diverse. As a result, two groups of external users, creditors and investors, have been identified as the principal external users of financial information. **Creditors** need information about the profitability and stability of the enterprise to answer such questions as: Do we lend the money? And, if so, with what provisions? **Investors** (both existing stockholders and potential investors) need information concerning the safety and profitability of their investment.

Incentives

As mentioned, companies often need external funding if they are to compete in the marketplace. Thus, the managers of these companies have an incentive to provide information that will attract external funding. They want to present information to external users that will make it appear as though their companies will be profitable in the future.

In their pursuit of external funding, management may not be as objective in evaluating and presenting accounting information as external users would like. As a result, care must be taken to ensure that accounting information is neutral. Standards have been established and safeguards have been implemented in an attempt to ensure that accounting information is neutral and objective.

Financial Reporting

Most accounting systems are designed to generate information for both internal and external reporting. The external information is much more highly summarized than the information reported internally. Understandably, a company does not want to disclose every detail of its internal financial dealings to outsiders. For this reason, external financial reporting is governed by an established body of standards or principles that are designed to carefully define what information a firm must disclose to outsiders. Financial accounting standards also establish a uniform method of presenting information so that financial reports for different companies can be more easily compared. The development of these standards is discussed in some detail later in this chapter.

This textbook focuses on financial accounting and external reporting. The centerpiece of financial accounting is the **general-purpose financial statements:** balance sheet, income statement, and statement of cash flows.

The three major financial statements, along with the explanatory notes and the auditor's opinion, are briefly described below:

- The **balance sheet** reports, as of a certain point in time, the resources of a company (the assets), the company's obligations (the liabilities), and the net difference between assets and liabilities, which represents the equity of the owners. The balance sheet addresses the fundamental questions: What does a company own and what does it owe?
- The **income statement** reports, for a certain interval, the net assets generated through business operations (revenues), the net assets consumed (expenses), and the difference, which is called net income. The income statement is the accountant's best effort at measuring the economic performance of a company for the given period.
  - The **statement of cash flows** reports, for a certain interval, the amount of cash generated and consumed by a company through the following three types of activities: operating, investing, and financing. The statement of cash flows is the most objective of the financial statements because it is somewhat insulated from the accounting estimates and judgments needed to prepare a balance sheet and an income statement.

FYI: The cash flow statement is the youngest of the primary financial statements. It has been required only since 1988.

- Accounting estimates and judgments are outlined in the **notes to the financial statements.** In addition, the notes contain supplemental information as well as information about items not included in the financial statements. Using financial statements without reading the notes is like preparing for an intermediate accounting exam by just reading the table of contents of the textbook—you get the general picture, but you miss all the important details. Each financial statement routinely carries the following warning printed at the bottom of the statement: "The notes to the financial statements are an integral part of this statement."

- **Auditors,** working independently of a company's management and internal accountants, examine the financial statements and issue an **auditor's opinion** about the fairness of the statements and their adherence to proper accounting principles. The opinion is based on evidence gathered by the auditor from the detailed records and documents maintained by the company and from a review of the controls over the accounting system. Obviously, there is a motivation on the part of management to present the financial information in the most favorable manner possible. It is the responsibility of the auditors to review management's reports and to independently decide if the reports are indeed representative of the actual conditions existing within the enterprise. The auditor's opinion adds credibility to the financial statements. The types of opinions issued by auditors, along with their relative frequencies, are outlined in Exhibit 1-3.[2] As you can see, the audit opinion is almost always "unqualified."

EXHIBIT 1-3 | Relative Frequency of Audit Opinions

Types of Audit Opinions Relative Frequency For the Year 1998	Companies
UNQUALIFIED: Financial statements are in accordance with generally accepted accounting principles. They are consistent, and all material information has been disclosed.	5,978
UNQUALIFIED, WITH EXPLANATORY LANGUAGE: The opinion is unqualified, but the auditor has felt it necessary to emphasize some item with further language.	1,030
QUALIFIED: Either the audit firm was somehow constrained from performing all the desired tests, or some item is accounted for in a way with which the auditor disagrees.	6
NO OPINION: The auditor refuses to express an opinion, usually because there is great uncertainty about whether the audited firm will be able to remain in business.	2
ADVERSE: The financial statements are not in accordance with generally accepted accounting principles.	0
Total	7,016

SOURCE: Standard and Poor's COMPUSTAT. The database includes firms traded on the New York, American, and NASDAQ exchanges.

2 For an example of an actual audit opinion, see the auditor's report that accompanies the financial statements of The Walt Disney Company, reproduced in Appendix A at the end of the book.

 What other methods of communicating financial information to external users are available to the management of a company?

The financial statements and accompanying notes (certified by the auditor's opinion) have historically been the primary mode of communicating financial information to external users.

 Explain the function of accounting standards and describe the role of the FASB in setting those standards in the United States.

THE DEVELOPMENT OF ACCOUNTING STANDARDS

Consider the following situation:

A company decides to pay its managers partly in cash and partly in the form of options to buy the company's stock. The options would be very valuable if the company's stock price were to increase but would be worthless if the company's stock price were to decline. Because the company gives these potentially valuable options to employees, cash salaries don't need to be as high.

Should the value of the options be reported as salary expense or not? (You'll learn the answer to this surprisingly explosive question in Chapter 11.) One alternative is to let each company decide for itself. Users then have to be careful about comparing the financial statements of two companies that have accounted for the same thing differently. Another alternative is to have one standard accounting treatment. But who sets the standard?

Accounting principles and procedures have evolved over hundreds of years in response to changes in business practices. The formal standard-setting process that exists today in the United States, however, has developed in just the past 60 years. The triggering event was the Stock Market Crash of 1929. In the aftermath of the crash, many market observers claimed that stock prices had been artificially inflated through questionable accounting practices. The **Securities and Exchange Commission (SEC)** was created to protect the interests of investors by ensuring full and fair disclosure. The SEC was also given specific legal authority to establish accounting standards for companies desiring to publicly issue shares in the United States. The emergence of the SEC forced the U.S. accounting profession to unite and to become more diligent in developing accounting principles. This led over time to the formation of a series of different private-sector organizations, each having the responsibility of issuing accounting standards. These organizations, their publications, and the time they were in existence are identified in Exhibit 1–4. The SEC has generally allowed these private-sector organizations to make the accounting standards in the United States. These standards are commonly referred to as **generally accepted accounting principles (GAAP).** Remember, however, that the SEC retains the legal authority to establish U.S. accounting standards, if it so chooses.

EXHIBIT 1–4 | U.S. Accounting Standard-Setting Bodies

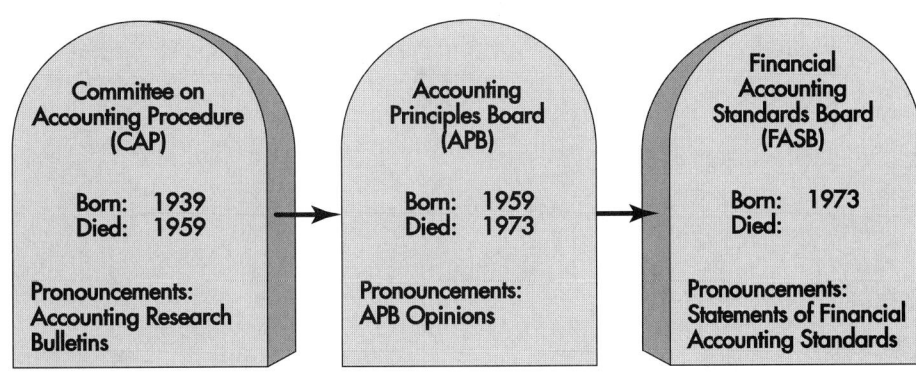

► QUALIFIED AUDIT OPINIONS IN CHINA

The need for external independent auditors arises because potential creditors and investors are naturally suspicious of the financial reports prepared by company managers. Managers have incentives to favorably bias the reported numbers such as to make it easier to get loans, to attract investors, and to increase their own bonuses and job advancement

opportunities. An independent auditor increases the reliance that external users can place on the management-prepared financial statements.

Before the 1990s, there was no need for external auditors in China. When all companies in China were owned by the state and managed by central planners in Beijing, company financial statements were viewed as confidential government documents not available to outsiders. There was no need for independent external auditors because there were no external financial statement users. The economic reforms of the 1980s resulted in decentralization of the ownership of the Chinese state-owned enterprises (SOE). The demand for external

audits of Chinese companies increased dramatically with the establishment of the Shanghai and Shenzhen Stock Exchanges, in 1990 and 1991, respectively.

In response to this demand for the independent certification of the financial statements of publicly traded companies, in 1995 the Chinese government adopted a more rigorous set of auditing standards to be followed by Chinese CPA firms. Before these standards were enacted, qualified audit opinions were rare and were not publicly announced. The first publicly announced audit qualification under the new standards was published in the *Shanghai Securities Journal* on February 15, 1996. [*Note:* In China, all listed companies are required to print

Financial Accounting Standards Board

The **Financial Accounting Standards Board (FASB)** is currently recognized as the private-sector body responsible for the establishment of U.S. accounting standards. The FASB was organized in 1973, replacing the **Accounting Principles Board (APB)**. The APB was replaced because it had lost credibility in the business community and was seen as being too heavily influenced by accountants. As a result, the seven full-time members of the FASB are drawn from a variety of backgrounds—professional accounting, business, government, and academia. The members are required to sever all connections with their firms or institutions prior to assuming membership on the Board. Members are appointed for five-year terms and are eligible for reappointment to one additional term. Headquartered in Norwalk, Connecticut, the Board has its own research staff and an annual operating budget around $20 million. The FASB receives about one-third of its operating funds through donations from the accounting profession and from businesses. The remaining two-thirds is generated through sales of publications and other services (e.g., a CD-ROM version of all the existing accounting standards).

> **FYI:** The annual salary of a member of the FASB is about $300,000.

Fund-raising for the FASB, as well as appointment of new Board members, is done by the **Financial Accounting Foundation (FAF)**. The FAF is an independent, self-perpetuating body that, like the FASB, is made up of representatives from the accounting profession, the business world, government, and academia. However, the FAF has no standard-setting power, and its members are not full time. The FAF serves somewhat like a board of directors, overseeing the operations of the FASB. In addition to funding and overseeing the FASB, the FAF is also responsible for selecting and supporting members of the **Governmental Accounting Standards Board (GASB)**. The GASB was established in 1984 and sets financial accounting standards for state and local government entities.

The Standard-Setting Process

The major functions of the FASB are to study accounting issues and to establish accounting standards. These standards are published as **Statements of Financial Accounting Standards**. The FASB has also issued **Statements of Financial Accounting Concepts**

their annual report and auditor's opinion in one of seven designated newspapers.] On this date, YANZHONG ENTERPRISES, a Shanghai-based conglomerate, revealed that its auditor, DA HUA CPA, had qualified the audit report for the 1995 financial statements. The reason for the qualification was that Yanzhong had misclassified investment gains and interest income as part of operating income and refused to revise the presentation. The reaction to this audit qualification was rapid and negative—the Da Hua CPA firm received many phone calls asking whether Yanzhong was on the verge of bankruptcy. Overall, for the ninety-six Chinese audit qualifications announced in 1996, 1997, and 1998, the average loss in company market value was 2% in the three days surrounding the qualification announcements.

QUESTIONS:

1. At the end of 1997, there were 105 CPA firms authorized by the Chinese government to audit the 740 listed companies. This is a large number of CPA firms competing for a small set of clients. What problems can be caused by this type of audit industry structure?

2. Exactly why would a company's stock price decline upon announcement that the company's financial statements have received a qualified audit opinion?

SOURCE:
Charles J. P. Chen, Xijia Su, and Ronald Zhao, "Market Reaction to Initial Qualified Audit Opinions in an Emerging Market: Evidence from the Shanghai Stock Exchange," Working paper, City University of Hong Kong, March 1999.

that provide a framework within which specific accounting standards can be developed. The conceptual framework of the FASB is detailed later in the chapter.

The FASB follows a standard-setting process that is open to public observation and participation. At any given time, the Board has a number of major "Agenda Projects" under way. For example, as of October 21, 1999, the FASB was engaged in 9 general agenda projects, including projects dealing with consolidations, asset impairment and disposal issues, and financial instruments.

For each major agenda project undertaken by the Board, a task force of outside experts is appointed to study the existing literature. When available literature is deemed insufficient, additional research is conducted. Subsequently, the Board issues a **Discussion Memorandum**, which identifies the principal issues involved with the topic. This document includes a discussion of the various points of view as to the resolution of the issues, as well as an extensive bibliography, but it does not include specific conclusions. Readers of the Discussion Memorandum are invited to comment either in writing or orally at a public hearing.

FYI: The FASB is quite scrupulous about holding all of its deliberations in public. In fact, since five (out of seven) votes are required to pass an FASB proposal, Board members are even careful not to discuss accounting issues at social occasions when five or more Board members are present.

After a Discussion Memorandum has been issued and comments from interested parties have been evaluated, the Board meets as many times as necessary to resolve the issues. These meetings are open to the public, and the agenda is published in advance. From these meetings, the Board develops an **Exposure Draft** of a statement that includes specific recommendations for financial accounting and reporting. An issuance of an Exposure Draft requires the approval of at least five of the seven FASB members.

After the Exposure Draft has been issued, reaction to the new document is again requested from the accounting and business communities. At the end of the exposure period, usually 60 days or longer, all comments are reviewed by the staff and the Board. Further deliberation by the Board leads to either the issuance of a Statement of Financial Accounting Standards (if at least five of the FASB members approve), to a revised Exposure Draft, or in some cases to abandonment of the project. As you can see, the standard-setting process is a political one, full of consensus building, feedback, and compromise.

Caution! This description makes the standard-setting process seem orderly and serene. It is not. As outlined later in the chapter, some people hate the FASB.

The final statement not only sets forth the actual standards but also establishes the effective date and method of transition. It also gives pertinent background information and the basis for the Board's conclusions, including reasons for rejecting significant alternative solutions. If any members dissent from the majority view, they may include the reasons for their dissent as part of the document. These dissents are interesting reading. For example, the dissent to Statement No. 95 on the statement of cash flows reveals that the Board members disagreed about a fundamental issue—whether payment of interest is an operating activity or a financing activity.[3]

The FASB also considers implementation and practice problems that relate to previously issued standards. Depending on the nature of a problem, the Board may issue a Statement of Financial Accounting Standards or an Interpretation of a Statement of Financial Accounting Standards. Problems that arise in practice are also addressed in Technical Bulletins prepared and issued by the staff of the FASB. The Bulletins, which are reviewed by the Board prior to being issued, provide guidance for particular situations that arise in practice.

EMERGING ISSUES TASK FORCE   The methodical, sometimes slow, nature of the standard-setting process has been one of the principal points of criticism of the FASB. There seems to be no alternative to the lengthy process, however, given the philosophy that arriving at a consensus among members of the accounting profession and other interested parties is important to the Board's credibility.

In an effort to overcome this criticism and provide more timely guidance on issues, in 1984 the FASB established the **Emerging Issues Task Force (EITF)**. The EITF assists the FASB in the early identification of emerging issues that affect financial reporting. Members of the EITF include the senior technical partners of the major national CPA firms plus representatives from major associations of preparers of financial statements. The EITF meets periodically, typically at least once every quarter.

As an emerging issue is discussed, an attempt is made to arrive at a consensus treatment for the issue. If a consensus is reached, that consensus opinion defines the generally accepted accounting treatment until the FASB considers the issue. The EITF not only helps the FASB and its staff to better understand emerging issues but in many cases it also determines that no immediate FASB action is necessary.

Abstracts of the FASB Emerging Issues Task Force are published periodically. The abstracts are identified by a two-part number; the first part represents the year the issue was discussed, and the second part identifies the issue number for that year. For example, among the consensuses reached in 1999 was 99-1, "Accounting for Debt Convertible into the Stock of a Consolidated Subsidiary." Although many of the issues are very specialized by topic and industry, the importance of the EITF to the standard-setting process cannot be overemphasized. Because discussions rarely last more than a day or two and a consensus is reached on a majority of the issues discussed, timely guidance is provided to the accounting profession without the lengthy due process of the FASB.

FASB SUMMARY   Remember this: The FASB has no enforcement power. Legal authority to set U.S. accounting standards rests with the SEC. FASB standards are "generally accepted," meaning that, on average, the FASB standards are viewed by the business community as being good accounting. However, the credibility of the FASB has fluctuated through the years as different issues have been resolved. For example, within the past ten

---

3 Three of the seven members of the FASB dissented to *Statement of Financial Accounting Standards No. 95.* Prior to 1991, a majority of the seven-member board (four members) was the minimum requirement for approval of an Exposure Draft or a final statement of standards. This requirement was changed to a minimum approval of five members, or to what has been referred to as a "super-majority." A number of close, 4–3, votes that resulted in standards not favored by many businesspeople led to strong pressure on the Financial Accounting Foundation to change the voting requirements. Although not favored by members of the FASB, the change was made in 1990.

years the business community has been outraged by proposed standards for accounting for deferred income taxes and for stock-based compensation. In both those cases (which are discussed in Chapters 16 and 11, respectively), the FASB was forced to significantly revise its initial proposal. The FASB's job has been described as a "balancing act" between theoretical correctness and practical acceptability.

Recognize the importance to financial reporting of the SEC, AICPA, AAA, and IRS.

OTHER ORGANIZATIONS IMPORTANT TO FINANCIAL REPORTING

In addition to the FASB, several other bodies impact accounting standards and are important in other ways to the practice of accounting. Some of these bodies are discussed below.

Securities and Exchange Commission

The SEC was created by an act of Congress in 1934. Its primary role is to regulate the issuance and trading of securities by corporations to the general public. Prior to offering securities for sale to the public, a company must file a registration statement with the Commission that contains financial and organizational disclosures. In addition, all publicly held companies are required to furnish annual financial statements (called a 10-K filing), quarterly financial statements (10-Q filing), and other periodic information about significant events (8-K filing). The SEC also requires companies to have their external financial statements examined by independent accountants.

> **FYI:** The first chairman of the SEC was Joseph P. Kennedy, father of the late President John F. Kennedy.

The Commission's intent is not to prevent the trading of speculative securities but to insist that investors have adequate information. As a result, the SEC is vitally interested in financial reporting and the development of accounting standards. The Commission carefully monitors the standard-setting process and responds to Discussion Memorandums and Exposure Drafts issued by the FASB. The Commission also brings to the Board's attention emerging problems that need to be addressed and sends observers to meet with the EITF.

When the Commission was formed, Congress gave it power to establish accounting principles as follows:

> The Commission may prescribe, in regard to reports made pursuant to this title, the form or forms in which the required information shall be set forth, the items or details to be shown in the balance sheet and the earning statement, and the methods to be followed in the preparation of reports in the appraisal or valuation of assets and liabilities . . . . [4]

The Commission has generally refrained from fully using these powers, preferring to work through the private sector in the development of standards. Throughout its existence, however, the Commission has issued statements pertaining to accounting and auditing issues. At present, SEC official statements are referred to as **Financial Reporting Releases (FRRs)**, which are accounting interpretations and policies the SEC uses in evaluating firms' disclosure practices. For example, in 1997 the SEC issued FRR 48 outlining rules on what information companies should provide about their outstanding derivative financial instruments. In addition, the SEC issues **Staff Accounting Bulletins (SABs)**, which are SEC staff interpretations and do not necessarily represent official positions.

Although the SEC is generally supportive of the FASB, there have been disagreements between the two bodies. One of the most public of these disagreements occurred in the

---

4 Securities Exchange Act of 1934, Section 13(b).

► Who Hates the FASB?

Some things in life are constant: Texans complain about the summer heat, Minnesotans complain about the winter cold, voters complain about Congress, and accountants and businesspeople complain about the FASB. In recent years, the FASB has been criticized for overly complex deferred tax accounting, market value accounting leading to more volatile earnings, postretirement benefit accounting that has significantly

increased reported liabilities, and difficult stock option accounting that many users think is unnecessary.

Criticisms of the FASB fall under two general headings:
1. The standards are too theoretical and too costly to implement.
2. The standards negatively impact companies' bottom lines.

The FASB has made a great effort to address the first concern. Proposed standards are often field-tested to ascertain how costly they will be to implement. Recent standards, such as Statement No. 115, which requires recording most securities at market value, have included explicit discussion of the expected costs and benefits of the standard. The Board also asks selected volunteer companies to field-test proposed standards to get an idea of how to minimize implementation costs. The Board views the standard-setting process as a balancing act—balancing the desire to make financial reporting technically and theoretically sound against the need to

late 1970s and concerned the accounting for oil and gas exploratory costs. The FASB issued a standard in 1977, and the SEC publicly opposed the standard; the FASB finally succumbed to the pressure and reversed its position in 1979. (See Statements No. 19 and No. 25 in the list of FASB Statements in Appendix B.) In recent years, the SEC and FASB have increased their efforts at behind-the-scenes coordination and consultation. Still, the two bodies are not in complete harmony. For example, the SEC has been impatient with the FASB's slow progress on improving accounting for derivative financial instruments. Often, the SEC establishes broad disclosure requirements in an area while the FASB deliberates about the specific accounting rules. In recent years, this was the pattern with stock-based compensation, environmental disclosures, and derivatives.

American Institute of Certified Public Accountants

The **American Institute of Certified Public Accountants (AICPA)** is the professional organization of practicing **certified public accountants (CPAs)** in the United States. The organization was founded in 1887, and it publishes a monthly journal, the *Journal of Accountancy*. [Note: Anyone interested in current developments in accounting should regularly read the *Journal of Accountancy.*] The AICPA has several important responsibilities, including certification and continuing education for CPAs, quality control, and standard setting.

The AICPA is responsible for preparing and grading the Uniform CPA examination. This examination is given simultaneously in all 50 states and the U.S. territories twice each year, in May and November. In addition to passing the examination, an individual must meet the state education and experience requirements in order to obtain state certification as a CPA. Most states now require CPAs to meet continuing education requirements in order to retain their licenses to practice. The AICPA assists its members in meeting these requirements through an extensive Continuing Professional Education (CPE) program.

The AICPA is also concerned with maintaining the integrity of the profession through its Code of Professional Conduct and through a quality control program, which includes a process of peer review of CPA firms conducted by other CPAs.

Prior to the formation of the FASB, accounting principles were established under the direction of the AICPA. Both the CAP and the APB were AICPA committees. Although the FASB replaced the APB as the official standard-setting body for the profession, the AICPA

avoid overly radical and costly changes in the current system.

Although business executives often oppose FASB standards in public by voicing practicality concerns, privately they are more worried about the standards' impact on reported performance. The 14,000-member Financial Executives Institute (FEI) has suggested that the FASB be abolished or that its staff and budget be cut and the body transformed into a part-time one. The FEI complains that the FASB is too slow and that its rules do not leave enough room for professional judgment in reporting results.

The FASB must continue to carefully walk the fine line between theory and practice in order to avoid the fate of its predecessors, the APB and the CAP.

QUESTIONS:

1. What reasons might a company have for opposing a new accounting standard?
2. What factors favor entrusting the setting of accounting standards to the SEC? to the FASB?
3. What do you think should be the FASB's most important consideration when setting accounting standards?

SOURCES:

Lee Berton, "Accounting Rules Board Is Under Fire as It Nears Decision on Two Key Issues," *The Wall Street Journal,* April 6, 1993, p. A2.

"A Visit to the FASB," *The CPA Journal,* January 1992, p. 40.

Roger Lowenstein, "Can FASB Be Considered Antibusiness?" *The Wall Street Journal,* March 21, 1996, p. C1.

continues to influence the establishment of accounting standards. The AICPA helps the FASB identify emerging issues and communicates the concerns of CPAs on accounting issues to the FASB. In addition, the AICPA frequently establishes the specialized standards that relate to particular industries. For example, in October 1998 the AICPA issued a proposed set of rules for the accounting by the producers and distributors of films. Also, with the blessing of the FASB, the AICPA occasionally tackles thorny accounting issues of more general interest. One example is the AICPA pronouncement on accounting for the forecasted costs of environmental cleanup.

American Accounting Association

> **FYI:** Ask your instructor if he or she is a member of the AAA.

The **American Accounting Association (AAA)** is primarily an organization for accounting professors, although over one thousand practicing professional accountants also belong to it. The AAA sponsors national and regional meetings where accounting professors discuss technical research and share innovative teaching techniques and materials. The AAA also organizes working committees of professors to study and comment on accounting standards issues. In addition, the AAA publishes a number of academic journals, including *The Accounting Review,* a quarterly research journal, and *Accounting Horizons,* which contains articles addressing many real-world accounting problems. In fact, *Accounting Horizons* is an excellent journal to read for more depth on intermediate accounting issues.

One of the most significant actions of the AAA is to motivate and facilitate curriculum revision. As the accounting profession changes, it is critical that accounting educators continually revise their curricula to keep pace with these changes. The AAA provides forums for educators to share ideas about changes in curriculum and rewards innovative curriculum revision efforts.

The AAA played a major role in the formation of the Accounting Education Change Commission (AECC) in the early 1990s. The AECC was formed to facilitate improvements in accounting education. This was done through the publication of reports and position statements urging a renewed commitment to quality classroom teaching by professors and through the funding of innovative curriculum restructuring projects at various colleges and universities in the United States. The AECC objective was to assist in the development of an educational environment that encourages curriculum revision. Having achieved this objective, the AECC was disbanded in the late 1990s.

Internal Revenue Service

Tax accounting and financial accounting are different, but the popular perception is that they are one and the same. Tax accounting and financial accounting were designed with different purposes in mind. In the THOR POWER TOOL case (1979), the Supreme Court stated:

> The primary goal of financial accounting is to provide useful information to management, shareholders, creditors, and others properly interested; the major responsibility of the accountant is to protect these parties from being misled. The primary goal of the income tax system, in contrast, is the equitable collection of revenue. . . .

Although this text on intermediate accounting is not a study of income tax accounting, the U.S. tax rules as administered by the **Internal Revenue Service (IRS)** will still be discussed from time to time. In most areas, financial accounting and tax accounting are closely related. For example, your study of leases, depreciation, and inventory valuation in this text will aid your understanding of the corresponding tax rules.

What Is GAAP?

With all of these different bodies (FASB, EITF, AICPA, and SEC) establishing accounting standards, what is GAAP? The Auditing Standards Board of the AICPA has defined GAAP in the context of the phrase included in the standard auditor's opinion: "present fairly . . . in conformity with generally accepted accounting principles."[5] The hierarchy of pronouncements is illustrated in Exhibit 1–5.

EXHIBIT 1–5 | What Is GAAP?

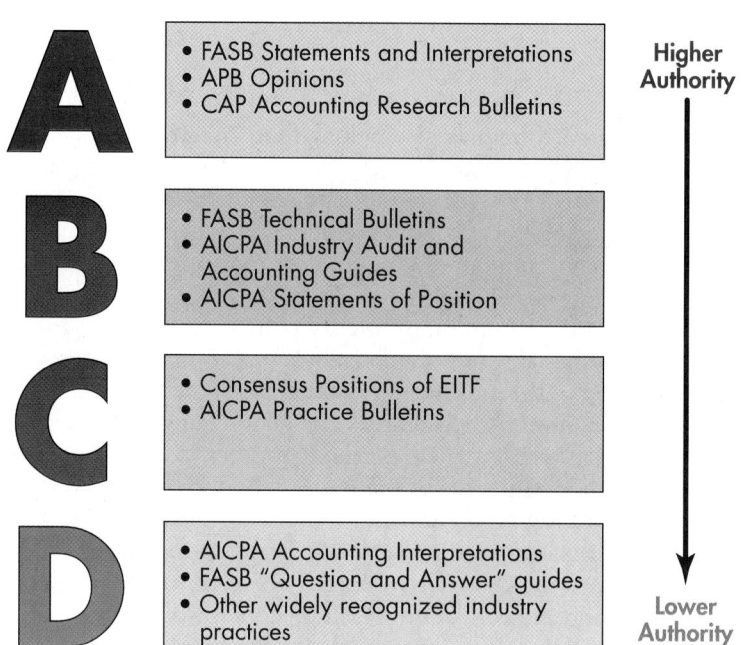

A
- FASB Statements and Interpretations
- APB Opinions
- CAP Accounting Research Bulletins

Higher Authority

B
- FASB Technical Bulletins
- AICPA Industry Audit and Accounting Guides
- AICPA Statements of Position

C
- Consensus Positions of EITF
- AICPA Practice Bulletins

D
- AICPA Accounting Interpretations
- FASB "Question and Answer" guides
- Other widely recognized industry practices

Lower Authority

---

5 *Statement of Auditing Standards No. 69,* "The Meaning of Present Fairly in Conformity With Generally Accepted Accounting Principles in the Independent Auditor's Report," New York: AICPA, December 1991.

net work exercise

Many influential accounting organizations have their own Web sites, including the SEC (www.sec.gov), the AICPA (www.aicpa.org), the AAA (www.rutgers.edu/Accounting/raw/aaa), and the IRS (www.irs.ustreas.gov).
Net Work:
Visit the IRS's Web site; locate and read the organization's mission statement.

For firms required to file financial statements with the SEC, the SEC rules and interpretive releases have the same authority as the standards listed in category A. The pronouncements in category A are of particular importance to auditors because Rule 203 of the AICPA Code of Professional Conduct specifies that an auditor must not express an unqualified opinion where there is a material departure from category A pronouncements.

Realize the growing importance and relevance of international accounting issues to the practice of accounting in the United States and understand the role of the IASC in international accounting standard setting.

INTERNATIONAL ACCOUNTING ISSUES

Divergent national accounting practices around the world can have an extremely significant impact on reported financial statements. And with the increasing integration of the worldwide economy, these accounting differences have become impossible to ignore. For example, to raise debt or equity capital, many non-U.S. firms, such as SONY, BRITISH AIRWAYS, and FIAT, list their securities on U.S. exchanges and borrow from U.S. financial institutions. The number of non-U.S. companies listed on the New York Stock Exchange (NYSE) has increased substantially in recent years. As of March 10, 1999, 452 foreign share issues were trading on the NYSE. In addition, many U.S. companies have listed their shares on foreign exchanges; for example, IBM's shares trade on the Tokyo Stock Exchange. U.S. companies also do substantial amounts of business in foreign currencies; as seen in Appendix A, DISNEY has significant amounts of business denominated in Japanese yen, French francs, German deutsche marks, British pounds, Canadian dollars, and Italian lira.

The international nature of business requires companies to be able to make their financial statements understandable to users all over the world. The significant differences in accounting standards that exist throughout the world complicate both the preparation of financial statements and the understanding of these financial statements by users.

International Differences in GAAP

As will be noted throughout this text, there are significant differences between U.S. GAAP and GAAP of other countries. The good news is that the fundamental concepts underlying accounting practice are the same around the world. As a result, a solid understanding of U.S. GAAP will allow you to quickly grasp the variations that exist in different countries. Throughout this book, we will include specific coverage of the areas in which significant differences exist in accounting practices around the world. One other piece of good news is that the demands of international financial statement users are forcing accountants around the world to harmonize differing accounting standards. Accordingly, the differences that currently exist will gradually diminish over time.

International Accounting Standards Committee

Just as the FASB establishes accounting standards for U.S. entities, other countries have their own standard-setting bodies. In an attempt to harmonize conflicting standards, the **International Accounting Standards Committee (IASC)** was formed in 1973 to develop worldwide accounting standards. This body now represents more than 142 accountancy bodies from 103 countries (including the United States). Like the FASB, the IASC develops proposals, circulates these among interested organizations, receives feedback, and then issues a final pronouncement.

The early standards of the IASC were primarily catalogs of the diverse accounting practices then used worldwide. Recent IASC projects have been more focused and innovative. For example, the substance of IASC decisions on improving earnings-per-share reporting was embraced by the FASB. In fact, the FASB and the IASC worked closely to develop compatible standards.

The accounting standards produced by the IASC are referred to as International Accounting Standards (IASs). IASs are envisioned to be a set of standards that can be used by all companies regardless of where they are based. In the extreme, IASs could supplement or even replace standards set by national standard setters such as the FASB. IASC standards are gaining increasing acceptance throughout the world. However, the SEC has thus far not recognized IASC standards and has barred foreign companies from listing their shares on U.S. stock exchanges unless those companies agree to provide financial statements in accordance with U.S. GAAP. Disclosure requirements in the U.S. are the strictest in the world, and foreign companies are reluctant to submit to the SEC requirement. This is a conflict that will be interesting to watch in the coming years: Will the SEC maintain a hard line and ultimately force U.S. GAAP on the rest of the world? Or will the IASC standards gain increasing acceptance and become the worldwide standard? We'll see.

 Consider these four organizations: FASB, AICPA, SEC, and IASC. Which one do you think will be making U.S. GAAP 20 years from now?

By the time you read this, the issue of how worldwide accounting standards are going to be set for the next 20 years may have been settled. In December 1998, the IASC published a discussion paper, "Shaping IASC for the Future," that proposes a restructuring of IASC operations in a bid to make the IASC standard-setting process more acceptable to the international business community. The FASB responded to this discussion paper in March 1999 with a description of its continuing reservations about the dominance of practicing accountants in the IASC structure. Although it is still uncertain who or what will be setting worldwide accounting standards in the future, this much is certain: Such standards will exist.

Understand the significance of the FASB's conceptual framework in outlining the qualities of good accounting information, defining terms such as asset and revenue, and providing guidance about appropriate recognition, measurement, and reporting.

A CONCEPTUAL FRAMEWORK OF ACCOUNTING

A strong theoretical foundation is essential if accounting practice is to keep pace with a changing business environment. Accountants are continually faced with new situations, technological advances, and business innovations that present new accounting and reporting problems. These problems must be dealt with in an organized and consistent manner. The **conceptual framework** plays a vital role in the development of new standards and in the revision of previously issued standards. Recognizing the importance of this role, the FASB stated that fundamental concepts "guide the Board in developing accounting and reporting standards by providing . . . a common foundation and basic reasoning on which to consider merits of alternatives."[6] In a very real sense, then, the FASB itself is a primary beneficiary of a conceptual framework.

In addition, when accountants are confronted with new developments that are not covered by GAAP, a conceptual framework provides a reference for analyzing and resolving emerging issues. Thus, a conceptual framework not only helps in understanding existing practice but also provides a guide for future practice.

Nature and Components of the FASB's Conceptual Framework

Serious attempts to develop a theoretical foundation of accounting can be traced to the 1930s. Among the leaders in such attempts were accounting educators, both individually and collectively as a part of the American Accounting Association (AAA). In 1936, the Executive Committee of the AAA began issuing a series of publications devoted to accounting theory, the last of which was published in 1965 and entitled "A Statement of Basic Accounting Theory." During the period from 1936 to 1973, there were several

6 *Statement of Financial Accounting Concepts No. 6, "Elements of Financial Statements,"* Stamford, CT: Financial Accounting Standards Board, December 1985, p. i.

additional publications issued by the AAA and also by the AICPA, each attempting to develop a conceptual foundation for the practice of accounting.[7]

While these publications made significant contributions to the development of accounting thought, no unified structure of accounting theory emerged from these efforts. When the FASB was established in 1973, it responded to the need for a general theoretical framework by undertaking a comprehensive project to develop a "conceptual framework for financial accounting and reporting." This project has been described as an attempt to establish a so-called constitution for accounting.

> **Caution!** Don't think that the conceptual framework is a useless exercise in accounting theory. Since its completion, the framework has significantly affected the nature of many accounting standards.

The conceptual framework project was one of the original FASB agenda items. Because of its significant potential impact on many aspects of financial reporting, and therefore its controversial nature, progress was deliberately slow. The project had high priority and received a large share of FASB resources. In December 1985, after almost 12 years, the FASB issued the last of six Statements of Financial Accounting Concepts (usually referred to as Concepts Statements), which provide the basis for the conceptual framework.[8]

The six Concepts Statements address four major areas.

1. *Objectives:* What are the purposes of financial reporting?
2. *Qualitative characteristics:* What are the qualities of useful financial information?
3. *Elements:* What is an asset? a liability? a revenue? an expense?
4. *Recognition, measurement, and reporting:* How should the objectives, qualities, and element definitions be implemented?

Objectives of Financial Reporting

Without identifying the goals for financial reporting (e.g., who needs what kind of information and for what reasons), accountants cannot determine the recognition criteria needed, which measurements are useful, or how best to report accounting information. The key financial reporting objectives outlined in the conceptual framework are:

- Usefulness
- Understandability
- Target audience: investors and creditors
- Assessing future cash flows
- Evaluating economic resources
- Primary focus on earnings

7 Among the most prominent of these publications were the following:
- Maurice Moonitz, Accounting Research Study No. 1, "The Basic Postulates of Accounting," New York: American Institute of Certified Public Accountants, 1961.
- William A. Paton and A. C. Littleton, "An Introduction to Corporate Accounting Standards, Monograph 3," Evanston, IL.: American Accounting Association, 1940.
- Thomas H. Sanders, Henry R. Hatfield, and W. Moore, "A Statement of Accounting Principles," New York: American Institute of Accountants, Inc., 1938.
- Robert T. Sprouse and Maurice Moonitz, Accounting Research Study No. 3, "A Tentative Set of Broad Accounting Principles for Business Enterprises," New York: American Institute of Certified Public Accountants, 1962.
- Statement of the Accounting Principles Board No. 4, "Basic Concepts and Accounting Principles Underlying Financial Statements of Business Enterprises," New York: American Institute of Certified Public Accountants, October 1970.
- Report of the Study Group on the Objectives of Financial Statements, "Objectives of Financial Statements," New York: American Institute of Certified Public Accountants, October 1973.

8 The six Concepts Statements issued by the FASB are:
  (1) Objectives of Financial Reporting by Business Enterprises.
  (2) Qualitative Characteristics of Accounting Information.
  (3) Elements of Financial Statements of Business Enterprises.
  (4) Objectives of Financial Reporting by Nonbusiness Organizations.
  (5) Recognition and Measurement in Financial Statements of Business Enterprises.
  (6) Elements of Financial Statements (a replacement of No. 3, broadened to include not-for-profit as well as business enterprises).

USEFULNESS The overall objective of financial reporting is to provide information that is useful for decision making. The FASB states:

> Financial reporting should provide information that is useful to present and potential investors and creditors and other users in making rational investment, credit, and similar decisions.[9]

UNDERSTANDABILITY Financial reports cannot and should not be so simple as to be understood by everyone. Instead, the objective of understandability recognizes a fairly sophisticated user of financial reports, that is, one who has a reasonable understanding of accounting and business and who is willing to study and analyze the information presented.[10] In other words, the information should be comprehensible to someone like you.

TARGET AUDIENCE: INVESTORS AND CREDITORS While there are many potential users of financial reports, the objectives are directed primarily toward investors and creditors. Other external users, like the IRS or the SEC, can require selected information from individuals and companies. Investors and creditors, however, must rely to a significant extent on the information contained in the periodic financial reports supplied by management. In addition, information useful to investors and creditors in most cases will be useful to other external users (i.e., customers and employees).

ASSESSING FUTURE CASH FLOWS Investors and creditors are interested primarily in a company's future cash flows. Creditors expect interest and loan principals to be paid in cash. Investors desire cash dividends and sufficient cash flow to allow the business to grow. Thus, financial reporting should provide information that is useful in assessing amounts, timing, and uncertainty (risk) of prospective cash flows.

EVALUATING ECONOMIC RESOURCES Financial reporting should also provide information about an enterprise's assets, liabilities, and owners' equity to help investors, creditors, and others evaluate the financial strengths and weaknesses of the enterprise and its liquidity and solvency. Such information will help users determine the financial condition of a company, which, in turn, should provide insight into the prospects of future cash flows.

PRIMARY FOCUS ON EARNINGS Information about enterprise earnings, measured by accrual accounting, generally provides a better basis for forecasting future performance than does information about current cash receipts and disbursements. Thus, the FASB states that "the primary focus of financial reporting is information about an enterprise's performance provided by measures of earnings and its components."[11]

Qualitative Characteristics of Accounting Information

The overriding objective of financial reporting is to provide useful information. This is a very complex objective because of the many reporting alternatives. To assist in choosing among financial accounting and reporting alternatives, the conceptual framework identifies the qualitative characteristics of useful accounting information. The key characteristics discussed below are:

- Benefits greater than cost
- Relevance
- Reliability
- Comparability
- Materiality

---

9 *Statement of Financial Accounting Concepts No. 1*, par. 34.
10 Ibid.
11 *Statement of Financial Accounting Concepts No. 1*, par. 43.

EXHIBIT 1–6 | Qualitative Characteristics of Accounting Information

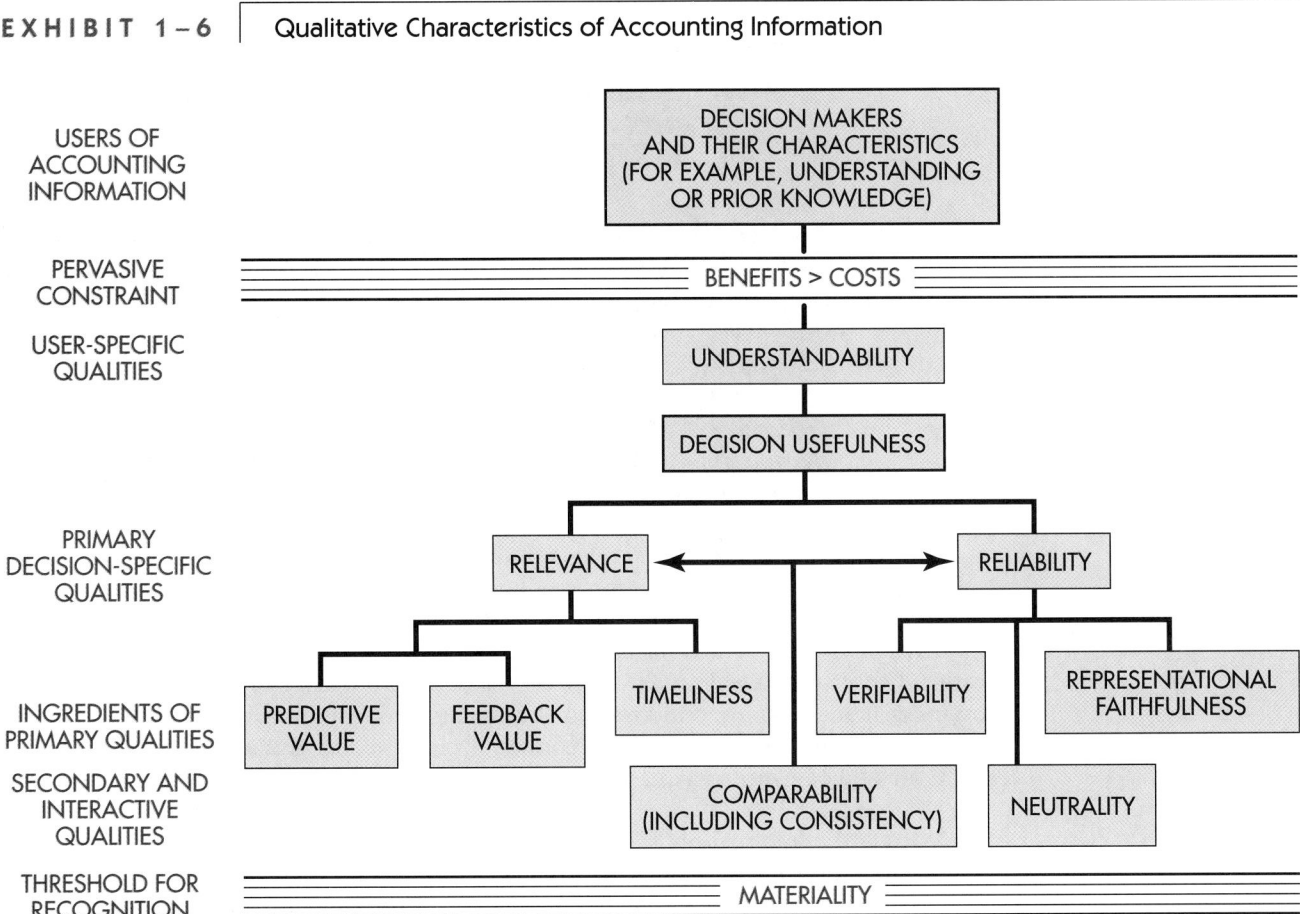

SOURCE: *Statement of Financial Accounting Concepts No. 2.*

The relationships among these characteristics and their components are illustrated in Exhibit 1–6.

BENEFITS GREATER THAN COST   Information is like other commodities in that it must be worth more than the cost of producing it. The difficulty in assessing cost-effectiveness of financial reporting is that the costs and benefits, especially the benefits, are not always evident or easily measured. In addition, the costs are borne by an identifiable and vocal constituency, the companies required to prepare financial statements. The benefits are spread over the entire economy. Thus, the FASB more frequently hears complaints about the expected cost of a new standard than it hears praise about the expected benefits. In the majority of its recent standards, the FASB has included a section attempting to describe the expected costs and benefits of the standard.

RELEVANCE   The FASB describes **relevance** as "making a difference." Qualities of relevant information are:

- Feedback value
- Predictive value
- Timeliness

Relevant information normally provides both **feedback value** and **predictive value** at the same time. Feedback on past events helps confirm or correct earlier expectations. Such information can then be used to help predict future outcomes. For example, when a company presents comparative income statements, an investor has informa-

The estimated cost of environmental cleanup represents a trade-off of relevancy over reliability.

tion to compare last year's operating results with this year's. This provides a general basis for evaluating prior expectations and for estimating what next year's results might be.

Timeliness is essential for information to "make a difference," because if the information becomes available after the decision is made, it isn't of much use. Financial reporting is increasingly criticized on the timeliness dimension because in the age of information technology, users are becoming accustomed to getting answers overnight, not at the end of a year or a quarter.

RELIABILITY   Information is reliable if it is relatively free from error and represents what it claims to represent. **Reliability** does not mean absolute accuracy. Information that is based on judgments and that includes estimates and approximations cannot be totally accurate, but it should be reliable. The objective, then, is to present the type of information in which users can have confidence. Such information must have:

- Verifiability
- Representational faithfulness
- Neutrality

Verifiability implies consensus. Accountants seek to base the financial statements on measures that can be verified by other trained accountants using the same measurement methods. **Representational faithfulness** means that there is agreement between a measurement and the economic activity or item that is being measured.

Neutrality is similar to the all-encompassing concept of "fairness." If financial statements are to satisfy a wide variety of users, the information presented should not be biased in favor of one group of users to the detriment of others. Neutrality also suggests that accounting standard setters should not be influenced by potential effects a new rule will have on a particular company or industry. In practice, neutrality is very difficult to achieve, because firms that expect to be harmed by a new accounting rule often lobby vigorously against the proposed standard.

Many of the hard decisions in choosing appropriate accounting practices boil down to a choice between relevance and reliability. Emphasizing reliability results in long preparation times as information is double-checked, and there is an avoidance of estimates and forecasts that cloud the data with uncertainty. On the other hand, relevance often requires the use of instant information full of uncertainty. A good illustration is information regarding expected environmental cleanup costs. Toxic waste cleanup takes years, and any forecast of the total expected cleanup cost is full of assumptions. These forecasts are not very reliable, but they are extremely relevant—ask any company that has ever purchased property without considering the potential environmental liabilities. As the world has filled with competing sources of instant information, the accounting standards have slowly moved toward more relevance and less reliability.

COMPARABILITY The essence of **comparability** is that information becomes much more useful when it can be related to a benchmark or standard. The comparison may be with data for other firms or it may be with similar information for the same firm but for other periods of time. Comparability of accounting data for the same company over time is often called **consistency**. Comparability requires that similar events be accounted for in the same manner on the financial statements of different companies and for a particular company for different periods. It should be recognized, however, that uniformity is not always the answer to comparability. Different circumstances may require different accounting treatments.

> **FYI:** In October 1998, a task force formed by the Big 5 international audit firms reported to the SEC on proposals intended to improve the consistency of practice with respect to audit materiality.

MATERIALITY **Materiality** deals with the specific question: Is the item large enough to influence the decision of a user of the information? Quantitative guidance concerning materiality is lacking, so managers and accountants must exercise judgment in determining whether an item is material. All would agree that an item causing net income to change by 10% is material. How about 1%? Most accountants would say an item changing net income by 1% is immaterial, unless the item results from questionable income manipulation or something else indicative of broader concern. Remember, there is no definitive numerical materiality threshold—the accountant must use his or her judgment.

WHAT ABOUT CONSERVATISM? No discussion of the qualities of accounting information is complete without a discussion of **conservatism**, which historically has been the guiding principle behind many accounting practices. The concept of conservatism can be summarized as follows: When in doubt, recognize all losses but don't recognize any gains. In formulating the conceptual framework, the FASB did not include conservatism in the list of qualitative characteristics (see Exhibit 1–6). Nevertheless, conservatism is an important concept. Financial statements that are deliberately biased to understate assets and profits lose the characteristics of relevance and reliability.

> **Caution!** Although the conceptual framework excludes conservatism from its list of qualitative characteristics, most practicing accountants are still conservative in their estimates and judgments.

Since the conceptual framework was formulated, the accounting standards have moved away from conservatism. For example, recognition of unrealized gains on financial instruments is now required, in contrast to the conservative lower-of-cost-or-market rule in existence when the conceptual framework was written. However, as pointed out by the FASB in Concepts Statement No. 2, there is still a place for practical conservatism. When two estimates are equally likely, the prudent decision is to use the more conservative number. This approach provides a counterbalance to the natural optimism and exaggeration of managers and entrepreneurs.

Elements of Financial Statements

The FASB definitions of the 10 basic financial statement elements are listed in Exhibit 1–7. These elements comprise the building blocks upon which financial statements are constructed. These definitions and the issues surrounding them are discussed in detail as the elements are introduced in later chapters.

Recognition, Measurement, and Reporting

To recognize or not to recognize . . . THAT is the question. One way to report financial information is to boil down all the estimates and judgments into one number and then use that one number to make a journal entry. This is called **recognition**. The key assumptions and estimates are then described in a note to the financial statements. Another approach is to skip the journal entry and just rely on the note to convey the information to users. This is called **disclosure**.

EXHIBIT 1–7 | Elements of Financial Statements

Assets are probable future economic benefits obtained or controlled by a particular entity as a result of past transactions or events.

Liabilities are probable future sacrifices of economic benefits arising from present obligations of a particular entity to transfer assets or provide services to other entities in the future as a result of past transactions or events.

Equity, or Net Assets, is the residual interest in the assets of an entity that remains after deducting its liabilities.

Investments by Owners are increases in equity of a particular business enterprise resulting from transfers to it from other entities of something valuable to obtain or increase ownership interests (or equity) in it. Assets are most commonly received as investments by owners, but that which is received may also include services or satisfaction or conversion of liabilities of the enterprise.

Distributions to Owners are decreases in equity of a particular business enterprise resulting from transferring assets, rendering services, or incurring liabilities by the enterprise to owners. Distributions to owners decrease ownership interests (or equity) in an enterprise.

Comprehensive Income is the change in equity of a business enterprise during a period from transactions and other events and circumstances from nonowner sources. It includes all changes in equity during a period except those resulting from investments by owners and distributions to owners.

Revenues are inflows or other enhancements of assets of an entity or settlement of its liabilities (or a combination of both) from delivering or producing goods, rendering services, or other activities that constitute the entity's ongoing major or central operations.

Expenses are outflows or other using up of assets or incurrences of liabilities (or a combination of both) from delivering or producing goods, rendering services, or carrying out other activities that constitute the entity's ongoing major or central operations.

Gains are increases in equity (net assets) from peripheral or incidental transactions of an entity and from all other transactions and other events and circumstances affecting the entity except those that result from revenues or investments by owners.

Losses are decreases in equity (net assets) from peripheral or incidental transactions of an entity and from all other transactions and other events and circumstances affecting the entity except those that result from expenses or distributions to owners.

SOURCE: *Statement of Financial Accounting Concepts No. 6,* pp. ix–x.

The recognition versus disclosure question has been at the heart of many accounting standard controversies and compromises in recent years. Two examples include:

- The business community absolutely refused to accept the FASB's decision to require recognition of the value of employee stock options as compensation expense. The FASB compromised by only requiring disclosure of the information (FASB Statement No. 123).
- The FASB has used disclosure requirements to give firms some years of practice in reporting the fair value of financial instruments (FASB Statement Nos. 105, 107, and 119). Some standards now require recognition of those fair values (FASB Statement No. 115).

The conceptual framework provides guidance in determining what information should be formally incorporated into financial statements and when. These concepts are discussed below under the following three headings:

- Recognition criteria
- Measurement
- Reporting

Most inventories are valued at historical cost—the cash equivalent price exchanged for the goods at the date of acquisition.

RECOGNITION CRITERIA　For an item to be formally recognized, it must meet one of the definitions of the elements of financial statements.[12] For example, a receivable must meet the definition of an asset to be recorded and reported as such on a balance sheet. The same is true of liabilities, owners' equity, revenues, expenses, and other elements. An item must also be reliably measurable in monetary terms to be recognized. For example, as mentioned earlier, many firms have obligations to clean up environmental damage. These obligations fit the definition of a liability, and information about them is relevant to users, yet they should not be recognized until they can be reliably quantified. Disclosure is preferable to recognition in situations in which relevant information cannot be reliably measured.

MEASUREMENT　Closely related to recognition is measurement. There are five different measurement attributes currently used in practice.

1. **Historical cost** is the cash equivalent price exchanged for goods or services at the date of acquisition. (Examples of items measured at historical cost: land, buildings, equipment, and most inventories.)
2. **Current replacement cost** is the cash equivalent price that would be exchanged currently to purchase or replace equivalent goods or services. (Example: some inventories that have declined in value since acquisition.)
3. **Current market value** is the cash equivalent price that could be obtained by selling an asset in an orderly liquidation. (Example: many financial instruments.)
4. **Net realizable value** is the amount of cash expected to be received from the conversion of assets in the normal course of business. (Example: accounts receivable.)
5. **Present (or discounted) value** is the amount of net future cash inflows or outflows discounted to their present value at an appropriate rate of interest. (Examples: long-term receivables, long-term payables, and long-term operating assets determined to have suffered an impairment in value.)

On the date an asset is acquired, all five of these measurement attributes have approximately the same value. The differences arise as the asset ages, business conditions change, and the original acquisition price becomes a less relevant measure of future economic benefit.

12 *Statement of Financial Accounting Concepts No. 5,* "Recognition and Measurement in Financial Statements of Business Enterprises," Stamford, CT: Financial Accounting Standards Board, December 1984, par. 63.

Current accounting practice in the United States is said to be based on historical costs, although, as illustrated, each of the five measurement attributes is used. Still, historical cost is the dominant measure and is used because of its high reliability. Many users feel that current replacement costs or market values, though less reliable, are more relevant than historical costs for future-oriented decisions. Here we see the classic trade-off between relevance and reliability. In recent years we have seen an increasing emphasis on relevance and thus a movement away from historical cost. Most financial instruments are now reported at market value, and the present value of forecasted cash flows is becoming a more common measurement attribute. In spite of this trend, the United States still lags behind other countries in the use of market values in financial statements. For example, many British companies report their land and buildings at estimated market values.

> **Caution!** You will be doing lots of present value calculations during your course in intermediate accounting. Check the batteries in your calculator.

REPORTING The conceptual framework indicates that a "full set of financial statements" is necessary to meet the objectives of financial reporting. Included in the recommended set of general-purpose financial statements are reports that show:

- Financial position at the end of the period
- Earnings (net income) for the period
- Cash flows during the period
- Investments by and distributions to owners during the period
- Comprehensive income (total nonowner changes in equity) for the period

The first three items have obvious reference to the three primary financial statements: balance sheet, income statement, and statement of cash flows. By the way, at the time the conceptual framework was formulated, there was no requirement to prepare a statement of cash flows. One of the early consequences of the completed conceptual framework was an increased emphasis on cash flow and the addition of the cash flow statement to the set of primary financial statements. The fourth reporting recommendation is typically satisfied with a **statement of changes in owners' equity.** Finally, a statement of comprehensive income is intended to summarize all increases and decreases in equity except for those arising from owner investments and withdrawals. **Comprehensive income** differs from earnings in that it includes unrealized gains and losses not recognized in the income statement. Examples of these unrealized gains and losses include those arising from foreign currency translations, changes in the value of available-for-sale securities, and changes in the value of certain derivative contracts. While the concept of comprehensive income has been discussed by the FASB for 20 years, it was finally operationalized in 1998. Beginning in that year, companies were required to provide, in at least one place, information relating to these unrealized gains and losses.

For financial reporting to be most effective, all relevant information should be presented in an unbiased, understandable, and timely manner. This is sometimes referred to as the **full disclosure principle.** Because of the cost-benefit constraint discussed earlier, however, it would be impossible to report all relevant information. Further, too much information could adversely affect understandability and, therefore, decision usefulness. Those who provide financial information must use judgment in determining what information best satisfies the full disclosure principle within reasonable cost limitations.

> **FYI:** These points are illustrated with the Walt Disney Internet Search question in the end-of-chapter material.

Two final points to remember are that the financial statements are just one part of financial reporting and that financial reporting is just one vehicle used by companies to communicate with external parties. Exhibit 1–8 illustrates the total information spectrum. In one way, this chart is somewhat misleading. Financial reporting is represented as four-fifths of the information spectrum, with other information comprising the other fifth. In reality, the proportions are probably reversed. In a world where on-line information is available 24 hours a day, the accounting profession faces the challenge of maintaining the relevance of financial reporting in the information spectrum.

EXHIBIT 1 – 8 | Total Information Spectrum

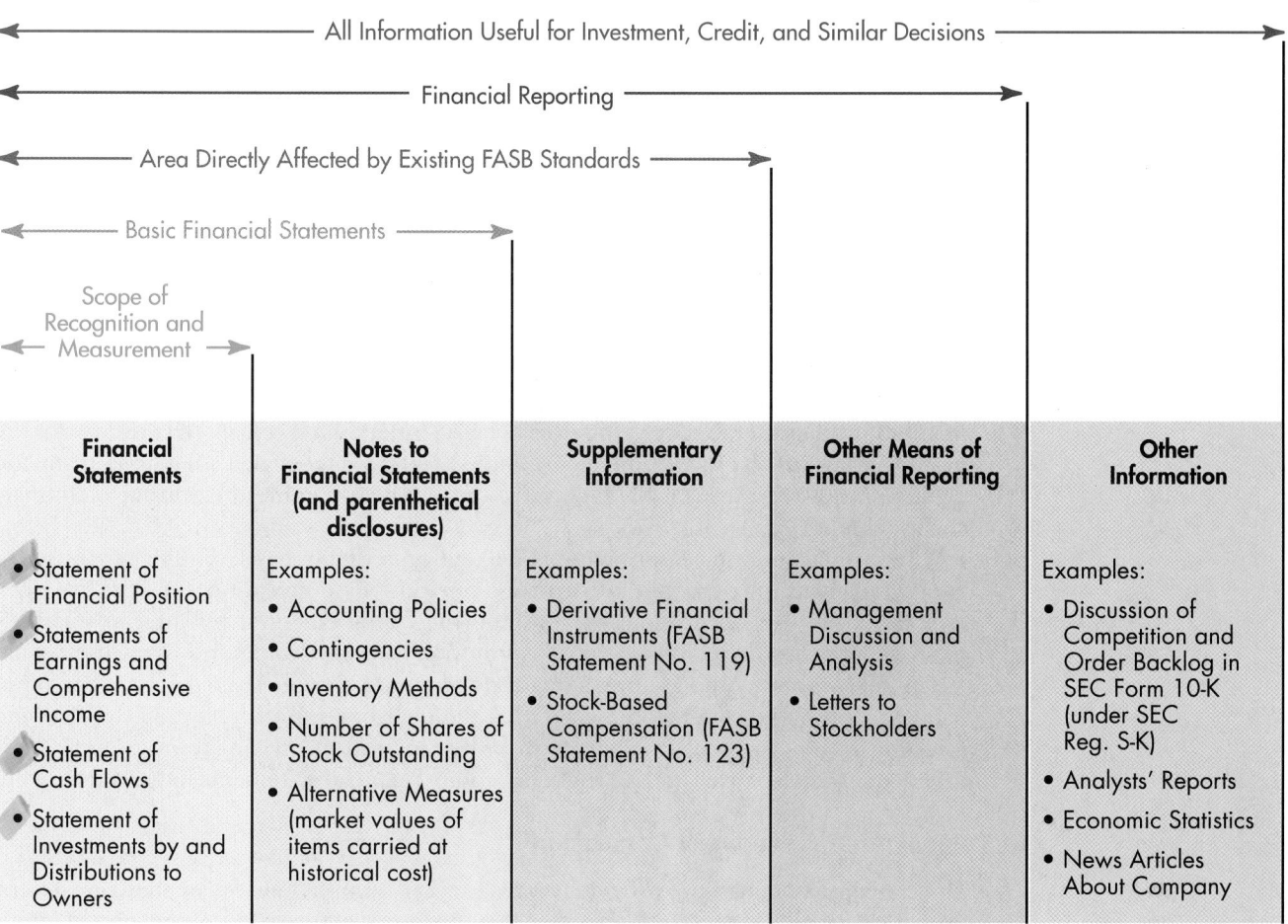

Recognition and Measurements in Financial Statements of Business Enterprises

← All Information Useful for Investment, Credit, and Similar Decisions →

← Financial Reporting →

← Area Directly Affected by Existing FASB Standards →

← Basic Financial Statements →

← Scope of Recognition and Measurement →

Financial Statements	Notes to Financial Statements (and parenthetical disclosures)	Supplementary Information	Other Means of Financial Reporting	Other Information
• Statement of Financial Position • Statements of Earnings and Comprehensive Income • Statement of Cash Flows • Statement of Investments by and Distributions to Owners	Examples: • Accounting Policies • Contingencies • Inventory Methods • Number of Shares of Stock Outstanding • Alternative Measures (market values of items carried at historical cost)	Examples: • Derivative Financial Instruments (FASB Statement No. 119) • Stock-Based Compensation (FASB Statement No. 123)	Examples: • Management Discussion and Analysis • Letters to Stockholders	Examples: • Discussion of Competition and Order Backlog in SEC Form 10-K (under SEC Reg. S-K) • Analysts' Reports • Economic Statistics • News Articles About Company

SOURCE: Adapted from *Statement of Financial Accounting Concepts No. 5.*

Traditional Assumptions of the Accounting Model

The FASB conceptual framework is influenced by several underlying assumptions, although these assumptions are not addressed explicitly in the framework. These five basic assumptions are:

- Economic entity
- Going concern
- Arm's-length transactions
- Stable monetary unit
- Accounting period

The business enterprise is viewed as a specific **economic entity** separate and distinct from its owners and any other business unit. Identifying the exact extent of the economic entity is difficult with large corporations that have networks of subsidiaries, and subsidiaries of subsidiaries, with complex business ties among the members of the group. The *keiretsu* in Japan (groups of large firms with ownership in one another and interlocking boards of directors) are an extreme example. At the other end of the spectrum, for small businesses it is often very difficult to disentangle the owner's personal transactions from the transactions of the business.

In the absence of evidence to the contrary, the entity is viewed as a **going concern**. This continuity assumption provides support for the preparation of a balance sheet that reports costs assignable to future activities rather than market values of properties that would be realized in the event of voluntary liquidation or forced sale. This same assumption calls for the preparation of an income statement reporting only such portions of revenues and costs as are allocable to current activities.

Transactions are assumed to be **arm's-length transactions**. That is, they occur between independent parties, each of whom is capable of protecting its own interests. The problem of related party transactions was at the hub of the 1994 strike by the major league baseball players. The players did not believe the numbers in the owners' financial statements because important reported transactions were between the baseball teams and other businesses controlled by the owners (e.g., television stations).

Transactions are assumed to be measured in **stable monetary units**. Because of this assumption, changes in the dollar's purchasing power resulting from inflation have traditionally been ignored. To many accountants, this is a serious limitation of the accounting model. In the late 1970s when inflation was in double digits in the United States, the FASB adopted a standard (Statement No. 33) requiring supplemental disclosure of inflation-adjusted numbers. However, because inflation has remained fairly low for the past 15 years, interest in Statement No. 33 died and it was repealed. Of course, many foreign countries with historically high inflation routinely require inflation-adjusted financial statements.

Because accounting information is needed on a timely basis, the life of a business entity is divided into specific **accounting periods**. By convention, the year has been established as the normal period for reporting, supplemented by interim quarterly reports. Even this innocent traditional assumption has come under fire. Many users want "flash" reports and complain that a quarterly reporting period is too slow. On the other hand, U.S. business leaders often claim that the quarterly reporting cycle is too fast and forces managers to focus on short-term profits instead of on long-term growth. Many other countries, like the United Kingdom, require financial statements only semiannually.

Conceptual Framework Conclusion

The conceptual framework provides a basis for consistent judgments by standard setters, preparers, users, auditors, and others involved in financial reporting. A conceptual framework will not solve all accounting problems, but if used on a consistent basis over time, it should help improve financial reporting.

The framework discussed in this chapter will be a reference source throughout the text. In studying the remaining chapters, you will see many applications and a few exceptions to the theoretical framework established here. An understanding of the overall theoretical framework of accounting should make it easier for you to understand specific issues and problems encountered in practice.

 If you were a practicing accountant faced with an unusual accounting question, how could you use the conceptual framework to help determine the appropriate accounting treatment? What other sources of help might be valuable?

Identify career opportunities related to accounting and financial reporting in the fields of public accounting, corporate accounting, financial analysis, banking, and consulting.

CAREERS IN FINANCIAL ACCOUNTING

If you are like most students who take intermediate accounting, you aren't taking this class as a general social science elective. You intend to pursue a career in an accounting-related field. This introductory chapter closes with a brief discussion of some of the careers in accounting. One piece of advice: The best career move you can make right now (in addition to taking this class, of course) is to get familiar with your school's job placement office. Ask them where the jobs are and what kind of candidates employers are hiring. Have them help you get started crafting a "killer" résumé. Find out about summer internships. The sooner you start gathering information and establishing a network of contacts, the better.

net work exercise

The Internet is a great source of career information. The Ohio State University has a Web site that deals specifically with accounting careers: (www.cob.ohio-state.edu/dept/fin/jobs).
Net Work:
Identify the different skills required of accounting graduates depending on whether their career path takes them to auditing, tax, financial, or management accounting.

The three major career areas in financial accounting are:

1. Public accounting
2. Company accounting
3. User (analyst, banker, consultant)

Public Accounting

Public accountants do not work for a single business enterprise. Rather, they provide a variety of services for many different individual and business clients. In essence, a public accountant is a freelance accountant, an accountant for hire. Public accountants practice either individually or in firms.

A CPA is a *certified* public accountant. As mentioned earlier in connection with the discussion of the AICPA, in order to become a CPA an individual must pass the CPA exam and satisfy education and work experience requirements that differ somewhat from state to state. One of the most significant (and controversial) developments in CPA licensing in recent years is the requirement adopted in many states that one must have 150 college credit hours (five years of full-time education) in order to become a CPA.

Traditionally, the most prominent role of CPAs has been as independent auditors of financial statements. Almost all large publicly held corporations are audited by a few large CPA firms. Listed in alphabetical order, the five largest firms (known as the Big 5) are ARTHUR ANDERSEN, DELOITTE & TOUCHE, ERNST & YOUNG, KPMG PEAT MARWICK, and PRICEWATERHOUSECOOPERS. Each of these firms is an international organization with many offices in the United States and abroad. Many small businesses are serviced by regional and local CPA firms, including a large number of sole practitioners. In these smaller firms, the role of auditing is often less important than the areas of tax reporting and planning and systems consulting. A CPA in a smaller firm is expected to be something of an accounting generalist, as opposed to the more specialized positions of CPAs in large regional and national firms.

Slow growth in the market for audit services has caused public accounting firms to earn an increasing share of their revenue doing consulting work. In fact, it has been suggested, only partly in jest, that the large accounting firms are becoming consulting firms that do a little auditing on the side. Increased consulting is both good and bad; consulting work typically is more profitable than is traditional audit service, but the practice of auditors doing consulting for the same clients they audit has caused some to question the independence of the auditor.

An important element of providing audit services is the financial liability an auditor bears when he or she gives an unqualified opinion about the financial statements of a company and that company subsequently goes bankrupt. The auditor liability crisis is discussed in detail later in this chapter.

Company Accounting

Public accountants move from client to client as accountants for hire. Of course, businesses also employ their own staffs of in-house accountants. A large business enterprise employs financial accountants, who are primarily concerned with external financial reporting; management accountants, who are primarily concerned with internal financial reporting; tax accountants, who prepare the necessary federal, state, and local tax returns and advise management in matters relating to taxation; and internal auditors, who review the work performed by accountants and others within the enterprise and report their findings to management. In smaller organizations, there is less specialization and more combining of responsibility for the various accounting functions.

Not all CPAs are public accountants. Individuals who start their careers in public accounting and become CPAs often leave public accounting after a few years and join the in-house accounting staff of a business. Typically the company they join is one of the clients they audited or consulted for as a public accountant. In fact, this is the most common career path for college graduates who start out working for one of the Big 5 accounting firms.

FYI: You might also consider a career as an accounting instructor. Ask your instructor what he or she thinks.

► PUBLIC ACCOUNTING AND LEGAL LIABILITY

In the early 1990s, the soaring cost of lawsuits threatened the financial viability of the public accounting profession. For example, during 1991, the then–Big 6 public accounting firms paid $477 million to settle and defend against lawsuits. This amount equaled 9% of total U.S. accounting and auditing revenues for these firms. And the amounts continued to climb. In November 1992, ERNST & YOUNG alone agreed to

pay $400 million to settle claims that it had improperly audited a number of failed savings and loan institutions. As of August 1992, it was estimated that the public accounting profession faced a total of $30 billion in damage claims.

Critics of public accounting hailed these judgments. Stephen Gillers, a professor of legal ethics at New York University, said: "This represents a new magnitude of exposure for professional firms. Now maybe we'll get auditors who audit." Defenders of the profession suggested that the large judgments against auditors were not a sign of negligence, but instead a sign that investors who had lost money were willing to bring suit against anyone with "deep pockets" to pay. These lawsuits were also encouraged by the mistaken public perception of an audit as a guarantee that the audited firm is solvent, well managed, and free of fraud.

Not surprisingly, as a result of these large judgments against auditors, audit fees increased sharply. Forty

percent of CPA firms operated without legal liability insurance because the premiums had skyrocketed, tripling since 1985 for some firms. In addition, because of the liability risk, some companies found it difficult to hire a public accounting firm willing to perform an audit. Companies having particular difficulty finding an auditor were small banks and companies preparing to issue stock for the first time.

The auditing profession addressed this liability crisis with the following actions:

- *Proportionate liability.* Auditors have historically been found jointly and severally liable for losses suffered by investors. Joint and several liability means that if the auditor is found 1% responsible for a $100 million loss but those responsible for the other 99% (i.e., the failed company's management and board of directors) are unable to pay, then the "deep pockets" auditor must come up with the whole $100 million. Proportionate liability would limit an auditor's

User (Analyst, Banker, Consultant)

Believe it or not, not everyone in the world wants to become an accountant. Many students take intermediate accounting in preparation for becoming a user of financial statements. Credit analysts in large banks are required to have a strong working knowledge of accounting in order to be able to evaluate the financial statements of firms seeking loans. Investment bankers and brokerage firms employ staffs of analysts to evaluate potential clients and to provide financial statement analysis services to customers. And, as mentioned above, the large CPA firms are doing an increasing amount of consulting work—not auditing a client but advising the client on how to improve operations. The consulting role of public accounting firms started as they advised clients on how to use computer technology in their accounting systems. These days, most consulting jobs require strong skills in information technology.

OVERVIEW OF INTERMEDIATE ACCOUNTING

This chapter has briefly described financial reporting and the accounting standard-setting process, has introduced the organizations (and their acronyms) that all accountants should know, has outlined the FASB conceptual framework (the "constitution" of accounting), and has discussed the major accounting-related careers. In the next four chapters, we will review everything you learned in introductory financial accounting, starting with the accountant's basic tools of analysis, the journal entry, and the T-account. The text then covers the accounting standards for the different aspects of a business: operations, investing, and financing. The text concludes with individual chapters on a number of important topics such as deferred taxes, derivative financial instruments, and earnings per share.

obligation to the appropriate share of the total loss. Congress passed a proportionate liability law called the Private Securities Litigation Reform Act in 1995. Class action attorneys attempted to circumvent this act by bringing suit under state laws, but President Clinton closed this loophole in November 1998.

- *Trade-off with the federal authorities.* The bill granting auditors proportionate liability also imposed an increased responsibility on auditors to report fraud they discover in the course of an audit. Auditors opposed this provision because, they explained, audits are not designed specifically to detect fraud. Be that as it may, the law now requires auditors to ensure that any illegal acts they discover are reported to the SEC within one business day.

- *Quasi-limited liability.* In the past, most CPA firms were organized as partnerships. In an ordinary partnership, all of the partners are legally liable for the damages caused by the actions of one partner. An alternative—made available in all U.S. states in 1994—is to organize as a limited liability partnership (LLP). In an LLP, each partner has unlimited liability for the general debts of the business but is not responsible for legal liabilities associated with the

negligent actions of other partners. All of the Big 5, and many other CPA firms, have organized as LLPs.

QUESTIONS:

1. The public mistakenly perceives an audit as a guarantee that the audited firm is solvent, well managed, and free of fraud. What assurance is actually given by an unqualified audit opinion?

2. Why might an audit firm shy away from auditing a small bank or a company preparing to issue stock for the first time?

3. As an investor, would you place more reliance on financial statements audited by a firm organized as an ordinary partnership or as an LP? Why?

SOURCES:

"The Liability Crisis in the United States: Impact on the Accounting Profession" (A statement of position by Arthur Andersen, Coopers & Lybrand, Deloitte & Touche, Ernst & Young, KPMG Peat Marwick, and Price Waterhouse), August 6, 1992.

Kelley Holland and Larry Light, "Big Six Firms Are Firing Clients," *Business Week,* March 1, 1993, p. 76.

John H. Cushman, Jr., "$400 Million Paid by S. & L. Auditors, Settling U.S. Case," *The New York Times,* November 24, 1992.

"News Report," *Journal of Accountancy,* February 1996, p. 13.

"Securities Litigation Reform Revisited," *Journal of Accountancy,* January 1999.

As mentioned at the start of this chapter, now is an exciting time to be studying accounting because things are changing so fast. For example, one of the biggest topics of discussion currently is the accounting for financial instruments. Twenty years ago the accounting for financial instruments was a minor topic. And the important point is that we really can't know what the important accounting issues will be 20 years from now. The best preparation for this unknown future is to learn the existing accounting rules, to understand how these rules arose, and to recognize the underlying concepts. That is the aim of this textbook.

REVIEW OF LEARNING OBJECTIVES

1 **Describe the purpose of financial reporting and identify the primary financial statements.** The purpose of financial reporting is to aid interested parties in evaluating the past performance of a company and in forecasting future performance. The information about past events is intended to improve future operations and forecasts of future cash flows.

Internal users have the ability to receive custom-designed accounting reports. External users must rely on the general-purpose financial statements. The five major components of the financial statements are:

- Balance sheet
- Income statement
- Statement of cash flows
- Explanatory notes
- Auditor's opinion

2 **Explain the function of accounting standards and describe the role of the FASB in setting those standards in the United States.** Accounting standards help accountants meet the information demands of users by providing guidelines and limits for financial reporting. Accounting standards also improve comparability of financial reports among different companies. There are many different ways of accounting for the same underlying economic events, and users are never satisfied with the amount of financial information they receive—they always want to know more. By defining which methods to use and how much information to disclose, accounting standards save time and money for accountants. Users also benefit because they can learn one set of accounting rules to apply to all companies.

The Financial Accounting Standards Board (FASB) sets accounting standards in the United States. The FASB is a private-sector body and has no legal authority. Accordingly, the FASB must carefully balance theory and practice in order to maintain credibility in the business community. The issuance of a new accounting standard is preceded by a lengthy public discussion. FASB adoption of a new Statement of Financial Accounting Standards is preceded by a Discussion Memorandum (identifying the principal accounting issues in question) and an Exposure Draft (initial draft of the new standard). The Emerging Issues Task Force (EITF) works under the direction of the FASB. The EITF formulates a timely expert consensus on how to handle new issues not yet covered in FASB pronouncements.

3 **Recognize the importance to financial reporting of the SEC, AICPA, AAA, and IRS.**

- *Securities and Exchange Commission (SEC).* The SEC has legal authority to establish U.S. accounting rules but generally allows the FASB to set the standards. To speed up the improvement of disclosure, the SEC sometimes implements broad disclosure requirements in areas still being deliberated by the FASB.
- *American Institute of Certified Public Accountants (AICPA).* The AICPA is a key professional trade organization of practicing accountants. The AICPA administers the CPA exam, polices the practices of its members, and sets some accounting standards, particularly those related to specific industries.
- *American Accounting Association (AAA).* The AAA is the professional trade organization of accounting professors. The AAA helps disseminate research results. The AAA also facilitates improvements in accounting education.
- *Internal Revenue Service (IRS).* Financial accounting is not the same as tax accounting. However, many specifics learned in intermediate accounting are similar to the corresponding tax rules.

4 **Realize the growing importance and relevance of international accounting issues to the practice of accounting in the United States and**

understand the role of the IASC in international accounting standard setting.

Because business is increasingly conducted across national borders, companies must be able to use their financial statements to communicate with external users all over the world. As a result, divergent national accounting practices are converging to an overall global standard.

The International Accounting Standards Committee (IASC) is an international body representing professional accounting bodies in 103 countries (including the United States). IASC standards are gaining increasing acceptance worldwide.

5 **Understand the significance of the FASB's conceptual framework in outlining the qualities of good accounting information, defining terms such as asset and revenue, and providing guidance about appropriate recognition, measurement, and reporting.**

The conceptual framework allows for the systematic adaptation of accounting standards to a changing business environment. The FASB uses the conceptual framework to aid in an organized and consistent development of new accounting standards. In addition, learning the FASB's conceptual framework allows one to understand and, perhaps, anticipate future standards.

The conceptual framework outlines the objectives of financial reporting and the qualities of good accounting information, precisely defines commonly used terms such as asset and revenue, and provides guidance about appropriate recognition, measurement, and reporting.

The key financial reporting objectives are:

- Usefulness
- Understandability
- Target audience of investors and creditors
- Assessment of future cash flows and existing economic resources
- Primary focus on earnings

Qualities of useful accounting information are:

- Benefits greater than cost
- Relevance: feedback value, predictive value, and timeliness
- Reliability: verifiability, representational faithfulness, and neutrality
- Comparability
- Materiality

Recording an item in the accounting records through a journal entry is called *recognition*. To be recognized, an item must meet the definition of an element and be measurable, relevant, and reliable.

The five measurement attributes used in practice are:

- Historical cost

- Current replacement cost
- Current market value
- Net realizable value
- Present (or discounted) value

A full set of financial statements includes a balance sheet, income statement, statement of cash flows, statement of changes in owners' equity, and statement of comprehensive income. As yet, comprehensive income is not used in practice, but it may come into use in association with the accounting for financial instruments.

6 **Identify career opportunities related to accounting and financial reporting in the fields of public accounting, corporate accounting, financial analysis, banking, and consulting.**

Public accounting is not just auditing. Public accounting firms provide an increasing amount of consulting and other customer services. In addition, since all companies have some financial reporting responsibilities, there are many financial accounting career opportunities in industry. Finally, jobs based on financial statement analysis require a detailed familiarity with financial accounting.

KEY TERMS

Accounting 5
Accounting periods 28
Accounting Principles Board (APB) 10
American Accounting Association (AAA) 15
American Institute of Certified Public Accountants (AICPA) 14
Arm's-length transactions 28
Auditor 8
Auditor's opinion 8
Balance sheet 7
Certified Public Accountant (CPA) 14
Comparability 23
Comprehensive income 26
Conceptual framework 18
Conservatism 23
Consistency 23
Creditors 7
Current market value 25
Current replacement cost 25
Disclosure 23
Discussion Memorandum 11
Economic entity 27
Emerging Issues Task Force (EITF) 12
Exposure Draft 11

External users 6
Feedback value 21
Financial accounting 6
Financial Accounting Foundation (FAF) 10
Financial Accounting Standards Board (FASB) 10
Financial Reporting Release (FRR) 13
Full disclosure principle 26
Generally accepted accounting principles (GAAP) 9
General-purpose financial statements 7
Going concern 28
Governmental Accounting Standards Board (GASB) 10
Historical cost 25
Income statement 7
Internal Revenue Service (IRS) 16
Internal users 6
International Accounting Standards Committee (IASC) 17
Investors 7
Management accounting 6
Materiality 23

Net realizable value 25
Neutrality 22
Notes to the financial statements 8
Predictive value 21
Present (or discounted) value 25
Recognition 23
Relevance 21
Reliability 22
Representational faithfulness 22
Securities and Exchange Commission (SEC) 9
Stable monetary units 28
Staff Accounting Bulletin (SAB) 13
Stakeholders 6
Statement of cash flows 7
Statement of changes in owners' equity 26
Statements of Financial Accounting Concepts 10
Statements of Financial Accounting Standards 10
Timeliness 22
Verifiability 22

QUESTIONS

1. Accounting has been defined as a service activity. Who is served by accounting and how are they benefited?

2. How does the fact that there are limited resources in the world relate to accounting information?

3. Accounting is sometimes characterized as dealing only with the past. Give examples of how accounting information can be of value in dealing with the future.

4. Distinguish between management accounting and financial accounting.
5. What five items make up the general-purpose financial statements?
6. Contrast the roles of an accountant and an auditor.
7. Why are independent audits necessary?
8. What conditions led to the establishment of accounting standard-setting bodies in the United States?
9. Describe the structure of the FASB. Where does the FASB get its operating funds?
10. What are the differences in purpose and scope of the FASB's Statements of Financial Accounting Standards, Statements of Financial Accounting Concepts, Interpretations of Statements of Financial Accounting Standards, and Technical Bulletins?
11. What characteristics of the standard-setting process are designed to increase the acceptability of standards established by the FASB?
12. (a) What role does the EITF play in establishing accounting standards? (b) Why can it meet this role more efficiently than the FASB?
13. How does the SEC influence the setting of accounting standards?
14. What is the AICPA? the AAA?
15. Explain the relationship between financial accounting rules and tax accounting rules.
16. Why is standard setting such a difficult and complex task?
17. According to Rule 203 of the AICPA Code of Professional Conduct, which set of accounting standards has the highest priority?
18. Why are differing national accounting standards converging to a common global standard?
19. What is the IASC? What is the SEC position regarding IASC standards?
20. List and explain the main reasons why a conceptual framework of accounting is important.
21. Identify the major objectives of financial reporting as specified by the FASB.
22. One objective of financial reporting is understandability. Understandable to whom?
23. Why is it so difficult to measure the cost-effectiveness of accounting information?
24. Distinguish between the qualities of relevance and reliability.
25. Does reliability imply absolute accuracy? Explain.
26. Define comparability.
27. Of what value is consistency in financial reporting?
28. What is the current numerical materiality standard in accounting?
29. What is conservatism in accounting? What is an example of conservatism in accounting practice?
30. Identify the criteria that an item must meet to qualify for recognition.
31. Identify and describe five different measurement attributes.
32. Briefly describe the five traditional assumptions that influence the conceptual framework.
33. What is the most common career path for a college graduate who starts out in public accounting?
34. What user careers require a knowledge of intermediate accounting issues?

DISCUSSION CASES

CASE 1–1

HOW SHOULD I INVEST?

Assume that you just inherited $1 million. You are aware that numerous studies have shown that investments in equity securities (stocks) give the highest rate of return over the long run. However, you are not sure in which companies you should invest. You send for and receive the annual reports of several companies in three growth industries.

In making your investment decision, what useful information would you expect to find in the following?

a. The balance sheet
b. The income statement
c. The statement of cash flows

CASE 1–2

THE ADVANTAGE OF INTERNAL USERS

Emilio Valdez worked for several years as a loan analyst for a large bank. He recently left the bank and took a management position with Positron, a high-tech manufacturing firm. Emilio prepared for his first management meeting by extensively analyzing Positron's external financial statements. However, in the meeting, the other managers referred to lots of information that Emilio hadn't found in the financial statements. In addition to using the financial statements, the other managers were also using computer printouts and reports unlike anything Emilio had seen in his years at the bank. After the meeting, Monique Vo, one of Emilio's associates, offered the following advice: "Emilio, you have to remember that you are an internal user now, not an external user." What does Monique mean?

CASE 1–3

WE AREN'T GETTING WHAT WE EXPECT.

Quality Enterprises Inc. issued its 2001 financial statements on February 22, 2002. The auditors expressed a "clean" opinion in the audit report. On July 14, 2002, the company filed for bankruptcy as a result of an inability to meet currently maturing long-term debt obligations. Reasons cited for the action include (1) large losses on inventory due to over-production of product lines that did not sell, (2) failure to collect on a large account receivable due to the customer's bankruptcy, and (3) a deteriorating economic environment caused by a severe recession in the spring of 2002. Joan Stevens, a large stockholder of Quality, is concerned about the fact that a company with a clean audit opinion could have financial difficulty leading to bankruptcy just 4 months after the audit report was issued. "Where were the auditors?" she inquired. In reply, the auditors contend that on December 31, 2001, the date of the financial statements, the statements were presented in accordance with GAAP. What is an auditor's responsibility for protecting users from losses? Are auditors and investors in agreement on what an audit should provide?

CASE 1–4

DOES LOBBYING IMPROVE THE QUALITY OF ACCOUNTING STANDARDS?

The "due process" system of the FASB encourages public input into the standard-setting process. Written comments are invited, public hearings are held, and proposed standards are often changed in response to this input. However, some observers have suggested that this process makes the setting of accounting standards less a technical exercise and more a political one. Parties are known to lobby for or against proposed standards according to their economic interests.

a. How would accounting standard setting be improved by eliminating lobbying?
b. How would accounting standard setting be harmed by eliminating lobbying?

CASE 1–5

HOW IMPORTANT ARE ECONOMIC CONSEQUENCES?

FASB Statement No. 106 requires companies to recognize a liability for their obligation to pay for retirees' health care. Prior to this rule, most companies recognized no liability for their health care promises to employees, although an economic liability certainly existed. Many companies used the adoption of the FASB rule as an excuse to cut retiree health benefits, claiming that the FASB had suddenly created this liability. Thus, it seems that FASB Statement No. 106 had an economic impact on retirees. Recognizing that accounting rules can have economic consequences, sometimes unintended and undesirable, should the impact on society be an important consideration for the FASB in setting accounting standards?

CASE 1–6

WHO NEEDS INTERNATIONAL ACCOUNTING?

Tom Obstinate is disgusted by all of the emphasis being put on international accounting issues. Tom plans to practice accounting in the United States, with U.S. companies, using U.S. GAAP. Accordingly, Tom sees no reason to know anything about the International Accounting Standards Committee or cross-national differences in accounting practices. Is there any merit in Tom's view? What might you say to Tom to get him to reconsider his position?

CASE 1–7

YOU NEED MORE EDUCATION!

For over three decades, accounting professionals, accounting educators, and accounting bodies have debated requiring more education for those entering the public accounting profession. In 1988, the AICPA passed a resolution mandating 150 college credit hours as a minimum educational requirement for all new members of its organization after 1999. This requirement placed added pressure on state legislators to pass new accounting legislation, and during the 1990s, an increasing number of states have passed the "150-hour rule." Some groups, however, oppose this move and argue that it is restrictive to entry of minority groups and that it will unnecessarily reduce the number of accounting graduates and put accounting educators "out of work" as students opt for less expensive educational alternatives.

Why does the accounting profession recommend more education for new accounting professionals? Why would some groups resist this move? As an accounting student, were you deterred in your decision to major in accounting because of the "150-hour rule"? Why or why not?

CASE 1–8

LET'S PLAY BY THE IRS RULES.

Little attempt is made to reconcile the accounting standard differences between the IRS and the FASB. These differences are recognized as arising from differences in the objectives of the two bodies. However, the existence of differences requires companies to keep two different sets of records in some areas: records that follow the FASB pronouncements and those that follow the IRS rules and regulations.

In many foreign countries, such as Japan and Germany, the financial accounting standards closely follow the tax rules established by the respective governments. What applies for taxes often applies for the balance sheet and the income statement as well.

Should the United States follow the practice of many foreign competitors? What are the advantages of merging accounting standards for taxes and financial reporting? What are the disadvantages? What would it take to change a system so deeply ingrained in the business fabric of either the United States or other countries?

CASE 1–9

CASH FLOW VS. EARNINGS

The FASB concluded in Concepts Statement No. 1 that investors and creditors are interested in an enterprise's future cash flows. However, the Board further stated that the primary focus of financial reporting is information about earnings. If an investor or creditor is interested in future cash flows, why isn't the focus on an examination of a firm's past cash flows? What are the limitations associated with using cash flows to measure the performance of an enterprise? Conversely, what are the risks to an investor or creditor of focusing solely on accrual-based earnings figures?

CASE 1–10

THE TRADE-OFF BETWEEN RELEVANCE AND RELIABILITY

The cable television industry is facing competition from companies using advanced technologies. The use of microwaves allows programs to be beamed, at low cost, to locations not accessed by cable. This technology, if successful, could eliminate the need for the current high-fixed-cost, physically intrusive cable systems. What information do cable companies need in order to evaluate the potential of microwave TV? What is a limitation associated with estimating demand for microwave TV? Why don't cable companies just wait and see if microwave TV is a success?

CASE 1–11

WHAT IS AN ASSET?

Conserv Corporation, a computer software company, is trying to determine the appropriate accounting procedure to apply to its software development costs. Management is considering capitalizing the development costs and amortizing them over several years. Alternatively, they are considering charging the costs to expense as soon as they are incurred. You, as an accountant, have been asked to help settle this issue. Which definitions of financial statement elements would apply to these costs? Based on this information, what accounting procedure would you recommend and why?

CASE 1–12

WHY DON'T WE USE CURRENT VALUES IN THE UNITED STATES?

Financial statements in the United States rely heavily on historical cost information, particularly in the valuation of land, buildings, and equipment. However, accounting standards in many other countries allow for fixed assets to be reported at their current values. As an example, DIAGEO (the British consumer products firm owning such brand names as Smirnoff, Johnnie Walker, J&B, Gordon's, Guinness, Pillsbury, Haagen-Dazs, and Burger King) provides financial statements using a current value basis to measure fixed assets. In its 1998 annual report, Diageo reported land and buildings with a current value of £1.425 billion. The assets' historical cost was £1.235 billion. Why do accountants in the United States focus primarily on historical cost figures? If the £1.425 billion figure is more relevant for investors and creditors, why don't traditional financial statements reflect current values? What are the risks to investors, creditors, and auditors of presenting current value information in the body of financial statements?

CASE 1–13

WHICH MEASUREMENT ATTRIBUTE IS RIGHT FOR BONDS PAYABLE?
Companies regularly obtain money through the issuance of bonds. The market value of bonds changes daily and on any given day is a function of many factors including economic variables, interest rates, industry developments, and firm-specific information. How should bonds be reported on the books of the issuer: At their market value on the balance sheet date? at their historical selling price? at their discounted present value? or at their eventual maturity value? For each of the above measurement attributes, identify and discuss the issues associated with each attribute.

CASE 1–14

BUT WE NEED ONLY ONE ACCOUNTING STANDARD—FAIRNESS.
In the 1970s, a leader in the accounting profession proposed that there really needed to be only one underlying standard to govern the establishment of generally accepted accounting principles. That standard was identified as *fairness*. Financial statements should be prepared so that they are fair to all users: management, labor, investors, creditors. As changes occur in society, financial reporting should change to fairly reflect each user's needs. Because the financial statements are the responsibility of management, such a standard would require management to determine what reporting methods would be fair. What advantages do you see to this proposal? What would be management's most serious problem in applying a fairness standard?

CASE 1–15

AND THEN THERE WERE FIVE!
The existence of just five large CPA firms that service virtually all of the major industrial and financial companies and thus dominate the accounting profession has led to criticism through the years.

a. What dangers do you see from the dominance of a few large CPA firms? What advantages?

b. During 1998, a merger between two of the large public accounting firms reduced the Big 6 to the Big 5. One reason offered for the merger is that it improved the ability of the merging firms to provide the broad array of consulting services that provide an increasing share of the revenues of the large accounting firms. What problems might intensify as public accounting firms earn an ever-larger share of their income from consulting?

EXERCISES

EXERCISE 1–16

ASPECTS OF THE FASB'S CONCEPTUAL FRAMEWORK
Determine whether the following statements are true or false. If a statement is false, explain why.

1. Comprehensive income includes changes in equity resulting from distributions to owners.
2. Timeliness and predictive value are both characteristics of relevant information.
3. The tendency to recognize favorable events early is an example of conservatism.

4. The conceptual framework focuses primarily on the needs of internal users of financial information.
5. The six Statements of Financial Accounting Concepts are considered part of "generally accepted accounting principles."
6. The overriding objective of financial reporting is to provide information for making economic decisions.
7. The term "recognition" is synonymous with the term "disclosure."
8. Once an accounting method is adopted, it should never be changed.

EXERCISE 1–17

CONCEPTUAL FRAMEWORK TERMINOLOGY

Match the numbered statements below with the lettered terms. An answer (letter) may be used more than once, and some terms require more than one answer (letter).

1. Key ingredients in quality of relevance.
2. Traditional assumptions that influence the FASB's conceptual framework.
3. The idea that information should represent what it purports to represent.
4. An important constraint, relating to costs and benefits.
5. An example of conservatism.
6. The availability of information when it is needed.
7. Recording an item in the accounting records.
8. Determines the threshold for recognition.
9. Implies consensus.
10. Transactions between independent parties.
    a. Cost-effectiveness
    b. Representational faithfulness
    c. Recognition
    d. Verifiability
    e. Time periods
    f. Unrealized
    g. Completeness
    h. Timeliness
    i. Materiality
    j. Predictive value
    k. Economic entity
    l. Lower-of-cost-or-market rule
    m. Phrenology
    n. Arm's-length transactions

EXERCISE 1–18

OBJECTIVES OF FINANCIAL REPORTING

For each of the following independent situations, identify the relevant objective(s) of financial reporting that the company may be overlooking. Discuss each of these objectives.

1. The president of Coventry, Inc., feels that the financial statements should be prepared for use by management only, because they are the primary decision makers.
2. Cascade Carpets Co. feels that financial statements should reflect only the present financial standing and cash position of the firm and should not provide any future-oriented data.
3. The vice president of Share Enterprises, Inc., believes that the financial statements are to present only current-year revenues and expenses and not to disclose assets, liabilities, and owners' equity.
4. Cruz Co. has a policy of providing disclosures of only its assets, liabilities, and owners' equity.
5. Marty Manufacturing, Inc., always discloses the assets, liabilities, and owners' equity of the firm along with the revenues and expenses. Marty's management believes that these items provide all the information relevant to investing decisions.

EXERCISE 1–19

APPLICATIONS OF ACCOUNTING CHARACTERISTICS AND CONCEPTS

For each situation listed, indicate by letter the appropriate qualitative characteristic(s) or accounting concept(s) applied. A letter may be used more than once, and more than one characteristic or concept may apply to a particular situation.

1. Goodwill is recorded in the accounts only when it arises from the purchase of another entity at a price higher than the fair market value of the purchased entity's tangible assets.
2. Land is valued at cost.
3. All payments out of petty cash are debited to Miscellaneous Expense.
4. Plant assets are classified separately as land or buildings, with an accumulated depreciation account for buildings.
5. Periodic payments of $1,500 per month for services of H. Hay, who is the sole proprietor of the company, are reported as withdrawals.
6. Small tools used by a large manufacturing firm are recorded as expenses when purchased.
7. Investments in equity securities are initially recorded at cost.
8. A retail store estimates inventory, rather than taking a complete physical count, for purposes of preparing monthly financial statements.
9. A note describing the company's possible liability in a lawsuit is included with the financial statements even though no formal liability exists at the balance sheet date.
10. Depreciation on plant assets is consistently computed each year by the straight-line method.

   a. Understandability
   b. Verifiability
   c. Timeliness
   d. Representational faithfulness
   e. Neutrality
   f. Relevance
   g. Going concern
   h. Economic entity
   i. Historical cost
   j. Measurability
   k. Materiality
   l. Comparability

EXERCISE 1–20

TRADE-OFF BETWEEN QUALITATIVE CHARACTERISTICS

In each of the following independent situations, an example is given requiring a trade-off between the qualitative characteristics discussed in the text. For each situation, identify the relevant characteristics and briefly discuss how satisfying one characteristic may involve not satisfying another.

1. The book value of an office building is approaching its originally estimated salvage value of $200,000. However, its current market value has been estimated at $20 million. The company's management would like to disclose to financial statement users the current value of the building on the balance sheet.
2. MMM Industries has used the FIFO inventory method for the past 20 years. However, all other major competitors use the LIFO method of accounting for inventories. MMM is contemplating a switch from FIFO to LIFO.
3. Stocks Inc. is negotiating with a major bank for a significant loan. The bank has asked that a set of financial statements be provided as quickly after the year-end as possible. Because invoices from many of the company's suppliers are mailed several weeks after inventory is received, Stocks Inc. is considering estimating the amounts associated with those liabilities to be able to prepare its financial statements more quickly.
4. Satellite Inc. produces and sells satellites to government and private industries. The company provides a warranty guaranteeing the performance of the satellites. A recent space launch placed one of its satellites in orbit, and several malfunctions have occurred. At year-end, Satellite Inc.'s auditors would like the company to disclose the potential liability in the notes to the financial statements. Officers of Satellite Inc. believe that the satellite can be repaired in orbit and that disclosure of a contingency such as this would unnecessarily bias the financial statements.

EXERCISE 1–21

ELEMENTS OF FINANCIAL REPORTING

For each of the following items, identify the financial statement element being discussed.

1. Changes in equity during a period, except those resulting from investments by owners and distributions to owners.
2. The net assets of an entity.
3. The result of a transaction requiring the future transfer of assets to other entities.
4. An increase in assets from the delivery of goods that constitutes the entity's ongoing central operations.
5. An increase in an entity's net assets from incidental transactions.
6. An increase in net assets through the issuance of stock.
7. Decreases in net assets from peripheral transactions of an enterprise.
8. The payment of a dividend.
9. Outflows of assets from the delivery of goods or services.
10. Items offering future value to an entity.

EXERCISE 1–22

ASSUMPTIONS OF FINANCIAL REPORTING

In each of the following independent situations, an example is given involving one of the five traditional assumptions of the accounting model. For each situation, identify the assumption involved (briefly explain your answer).

1. A subsidiary of Parent Inc. was exhibiting poor earnings performance for the year. In an effort to increase the subsidiary's reported earnings, Parent Inc. purchased products from the subsidiary at twice the normal markup.
2. When preparing the financial statements for MacNeil & Sons, the accountant included certain personal assets of MacNeil and his sons.
3. The operations of Uintah Savings & Loan are being evaluated by the federal government. During their investigations, government officials have determined that numerous loans made by top management were unwise and have seriously endangered the future existence of the savings and loan.
4. Pine Valley Ski Resort has experienced a drastic reduction in revenues because of light snowfall for the year. Rather than produce financial statements at the end of the fiscal year, as is traditionally done, management has elected to wait until next year and present results for a two-year period.
5. Colobri Inc. has equipment that was purchased in 1996 at a cost of $150,000. Because of inflation, that same equipment, if purchased today, would cost $225,000. Management would like to report the asset on the balance sheet at its current value.

EXERCISE 1–23

MEASUREMENT ATTRIBUTES AND GOING CONCERN PROBLEMS

One of the underlying assumptions of the accounting model is the going concern assumption. When this assumption is questionable, valuation methods used for assets and liabilities may differ from those used when the assumption is viable. For each of the following situations, identify the measurement attribute that would most likely be used if the company is not likely to remain a going concern.

1. Plant and equipment are carried at an amortized cost on a straight-line basis of $1,500,000.
2. Bonds with a maturity price of $2,000,000 and interest in arrears of $500,000 are reported as a noncurrent liability.
3. Accounts receivable are carried at $700,000, the gross amount charged for sales. No allowance for doubtful accounts is reported.
4. The reported LIFO cost of inventory is $300,000.
5. Investments in a subsidiary company are recorded at initial cost plus undistributed profits.

COMPETENCY ENHANCEMENT OPPORTUNITIES

▶ Deciphering Actual Financial Statements
▶ Writing Assignment
▶ Research Project

▶ The Debate
▶ Ethical Dilemma
▶ Internet Search

Accounting is more than just doing textbook problems. This expanded competency material provides practice in critical thinking, oral and written communication, research, teamwork, and consideration of ethical issues.

▶ DECIPHERING ACTUAL FINANCIAL STATEMENTS

• Deciphering 1–1 (The Walt Disney Company)

The 1998 financial statements for THE WALT DISNEY COMPANY are included in Appendix A. Locate those financial statements and consider the following questions:

1. How well did Disney do financially during the year ended September 30, 1998? (Hint: Look at the income statement.)
2. Comment on the level of detail in Disney's balance sheet. Should there be more balance sheet categories or fewer?
3. In 1998, was Disney's net cash from operations sufficient to pay for its investments in films, television, theme parks, resorts, and other property?
4. Look at the notes to the financial statements. There are 14 of them. Which ones seem to give you the most new information?
5. Find the auditor's opinion. Who is Disney's auditor? Was the 1998 audit opinion unqualified?

• Deciphering 1–2 (McDonald's Corporation)

The following information comes from the 1998 financial statements of MCDONALD'S CORPORATION. The financial statements were contained in McDonalds' annual 10-K filing with the SEC. This portion was extracted using the SEC's on-line database EDGAR (Electronic Data Gathering And Retrieval) accessible on the World Wide Web.

Franchise arrangements generally include a lease and a license and provide for payment of initial fees, as well as continuing rent, service fees, and royalties to the Company, based upon a percentage of sales with minimum rent payments. Franchisees are granted the right to operate a McDonald's restaurant using the McDonald's system as well as the use of a restaurant facility, generally for a period of 20 years. Franchisees pay related occupancy costs including property taxes, insurance, and maintenance. Beginning in 1998, franchisees in the United States generally have the option to own new restaurant facilities while leasing the land from McDonald's. In addition, franchisees outside the United States pay a refundable, noninterest-bearing security deposit. The results of operations of restaurant businesses purchased and sold in transactions with franchisees and affiliates were not material to the consolidated financial statements for periods prior to purchase and sale.

(In millions)	1998	1997	1996
Minimum rents	$1,440.9	$1,369.7	$1,350.7
Percent rent and service fees	2,026.9	1,836.3	1,689.7
Initial fees	58.7	66.3	75.4
Revenues from franchised and affiliated restaurants	$3,526.5	$3,272.3	$3,115.8

Future minimum rent payments due to the Company under franchise arrangements are:

(In millions)	Owned Sites	Leased Sites	Total
1999	$ 905.0	$ 670.6	$ 1,575.6
2000	887.8	660.3	1,548.1
2001	872.2	651.6	1,523.8
2002	854.1	638.0	1,492.1
2003	835.8	625.4	1,461.2
Thereafter	7,412.1	5,774.0	13,186.1
Total minimum payments	$11,767.0	$9,019.9	$20,786.9

This nearly $21 billion amount represents the future minimum payments McDonald's expected to receive from its franchisees as of December 31, 1998. Using the element definition from the conceptual framework, should this $21 billion be recorded as an asset in McDonald's 1998 balance sheet? Why or why not? If your answer is yes, what measurement attribute should be used in reporting the asset?

▶ WRITING ASSIGNMENT
• Should the SEC replace the FASB?
Imagine that you have been selected to compete with students from other universities in presenting a case considering whether the FASB should be abolished and its standard-setting role taken over by the SEC.

Prepare a one-page summary outlining the major arguments for and against the SEC replacing the FASB.

▶ RESEARCH PROJECT
• Where are the jobs?
Your group is to report (either orally or in writing) on the success of the job search by last year's accounting graduates from your college or university. Proceed as follows:
1. Find your school's placement office.
2. Identify yourselves and ask for an appointment.
3. As much as possible, find out the following about last year's graduates:
   a. What percentage went into public accounting?
   b. What percentage went on for further postgraduate study?
   c. What percentage got jobs locally?
   d. What were the average starting salaries?
4. Also, find out what current students can do to improve their job search.
5. Prepare your report.

▶ THE DEBATE

• Should the SEC allow use of IASC standards?
Historically, the SEC has refused to allow foreign securities to trade in the United States *unless* those foreign firms provide potential investors with financial statements prepared using U.S. GAAP. Many foreign firms and global financial analysts have suggested that the SEC should allow financial statements prepared using IASC standards to be substituted for U.S. GAAP statements. So far, the SEC has refused.

Divide your group into two teams.
1. One team is the SEC. Prepare a 2-minute oral argument supporting the SEC's refusal to accept IASC standards.
2. The other team is a foreign company wishing to have its shares traded on the New York Stock Exchange. Prepare a 2-minute oral argument seeking to convince the SEC to let your IASC-standard financial statements be substituted for U.S. GAAP statements.

▶ **ETHICAL DILEMMA**

• **Should you manipulate your reported income?**

Accounting standards place limits on the set of allowable alternative accounting treatments, but the accountant must still exercise judgment to choose among the remaining alternatives. In making those choices, which of the following should the accountant seek to do?

1. Maximize reported income.
2. Minimize reported income.
3. Ignore the impact of the accounting choice on income and just focus on the most conceptually correct option.

    Would your answer change if this were a tax accounting class? Why or why not?

▶ **INTERNET SEARCH**

There are a variety of ways to retrieve current financial information via Internet links. For example, the 1998 annual report for THE WALT DISNEY COMPANY is reproduced in Appendix A, but more recent data can be accessed by going to Disney's Web site at www. disney.com. Once you've gained access to Disney's Web site, answer the following questions.

1. Just looking at the menu of information available about Disney, how would you rate the importance of financial statement information to the average Web browser?
2. Companies often post their recent financial press releases in their Web site. Find Disney's earnings press release for the third quarter of the current or most recent year.
    a. What is the date on the press release? How many days elapsed between the end of the fiscal quarter and the release of quarterly earnings information to the press?
    b. Was it a good quarter or a bad quarter for Disney?
    c. Briefly describe any unusual accounting items mentioned in the press release.
3. Use Disney's "Fact Book" to find out when the Disney Brothers Studio was founded and when the original Disneyland opened for business.
4. Does Disney's Web site include a copy of Disney's most recent annual balance sheet? If so, describe what steps a person must follow to find that balance sheet.

chapter 2
A Review of the

Tom Clancy typed the first draft of his first novel, *The Hunt for Red October*, on an IBM Selectric typewriter while still holding down his full-time job as an insurance agent. The book was published in October 1984, and sales took off when it became known that the book was President Ronald Reagan's favorite. To date, Clancy has published a total of seven novels featuring the reluctant hero, Jack Ryan, and the stories have been so popular that Clancy now commands a record $25 million advance per book.

In *The Hunt for Red October*, Jack Ryan, who was trained as a historian, is a part-time analyst for the CIA. By the sixth novel in the series, *Debt of Honor*, a well-earned reputation for being a "good man in a storm" has landed Ryan, against his wishes, in the position of serving as the president's national security advisor. Jack Ryan's abilities are tested as an international crisis is touched off when a group of Japanese businessmen gain control of their government and determine that the only way to save the Japanese economy is through neutralization of U.S. power in the Pacific.

The first act of war against the United States is not an attack on a military target but instead is an attack on the bookkeeping system used by U.S. stock exchanges. A computer virus, injected into the program used to record trades on all the major U.S. stock exchanges, is activated at noon on Friday. The records of all trades made after that time are eliminated so that

> No trading house, institution, or private investor could know what it had bought or sold, to or from whom, or for how much, and none could therefore know how much money was available for other trades, or for that matter, to purchase groceries over the weekend. (Tom Clancy, *Debt of Honor*, page 312)

The uncertainty created by the destruction of the stock exchanges' bookkeeping records threatens to throw the U.S. economy into a tailspin and distract U.S. policy makers from other moves being made by Japan in the Pacific. Jack Ryan saves the world as we know it and restores the U.S. economy to sound footing by . . . well, it wouldn't be fair to say—you'll have to read the book. Suffice it to say that a key part of the restoration plan is the repair of the stock exchanges' bookkeeping system.

1

Identify and explain the basic steps in the accounting process (accounting cycle).

2

Analyze transactions and make and post journal entries.

3

Make adjusting entries, produce financial statements, and close nominal accounts.

4

Distinguish between accrual and cash-basis accounting.

5

Discuss the importance and expanding role of computers to the accounting process.

e|m

EXPANDED MATERIAL

6

Use special journals and subsidiary ledgers to process accounting information more efficiently and to provide additional useful information.

This example, though fictitious, makes a very good point: The business world in which we live and work would not be able to operate, for even one day, without a reliable method for recording the effects of transactions. A systematic method of recording transactions is necessary if companies such as IBM and General Electric (and even local music stores and Internet vendors) are to generate information with which to make sound business decisions.

This information is summarized in a variety of reports, which are prepared from accounting records, to assist users in making better economic decisions. Examples include:

1. General-purpose financial statements prepared for external user groups, primarily current or potential investors and creditors, who are involved financially with an enterprise but who are not a part of its management team.

2. Reports received by user groups within organizations, especially those in managerial positions, to assist them in planning and controlling the day-to-day operations of their organizations.

3. Tax returns and similar reports prepared to comply with Internal Revenue Service (IRS) requirements.

4. Special reports required by various regulatory agencies such as the Securities and Exchange Commission (SEC).

Each of these reports is based on data that are the result of an accounting system and a set of procedures collectively referred to as the *accounting process,* or the *accounting cycle.* While this process follows a fairly standard set of procedures that has existed for centuries, the exact nature of the *accounting system* used to collect and report the data will depend on the type of business, its size, the volume of transactions processed, the degree of automation employed, and other related factors. The various routines in each system are developed to meet the special needs of the business unit. Every accounting system, however, should be designed to provide accurate information on a timely and efficient basis. At the same time, the system must provide controls that are effective in preventing mistakes and guarding against dishonesty.

Historically, accounting systems were maintained by hand and referred to as manual systems. Such systems continue to be used effectively in many situations. In today's business environment, however, most companies use computers to collect, process, and analyze financial information. Has the computer changed the accounting process? It allows businesses to collect and analyze much more information and do it quickly, but the computer has not changed the underlying accounting concepts involved—debits still equal credits; assets still equal liabilities plus owners' equity.

The purpose of this chapter is to review the basic steps of the accounting process, including a brief review of debits and credits and the mechanics of bookkeeping. So get ready for a discussion of double-entry accounting, a system described by the German poet Goethe as "an absolutely perfect one."

OVERVIEW OF THE ACCOUNTING PROCESS

1

Identify and explain the basic steps in the accounting process (accounting cycle).

As you will recall from your Introductory Accounting class, the accounting process (or accounting cycle) consists of two interrelated parts: (1) the recording phase and (2) the reporting phase. The recording phase is concerned with collecting information about economic transactions and events and distilling that information into a form useful to the accounting process. For most businesses, the recording function is based on double-entry accounting procedures. In the reporting phase, the recorded information is organized and summarized, using various formats for a variety of decision-making purposes. The two phases overlap because the recording of transactions is an ongoing activity that does not cease at the end of an accounting period but continues uninterrupted while events of the preceding period are being summarized and reported. The recording and reporting phases of the accounting process are reviewed and illustrated in this chapter. The form and content of the basic financial statements are discussed in depth and illustrated in Chapters 3, 4, and 5.

The accounting process, illustrated in Exhibit 2–1, generally includes the following steps in a well-defined sequence:

EXHIBIT 2–1 | The Accounting Process

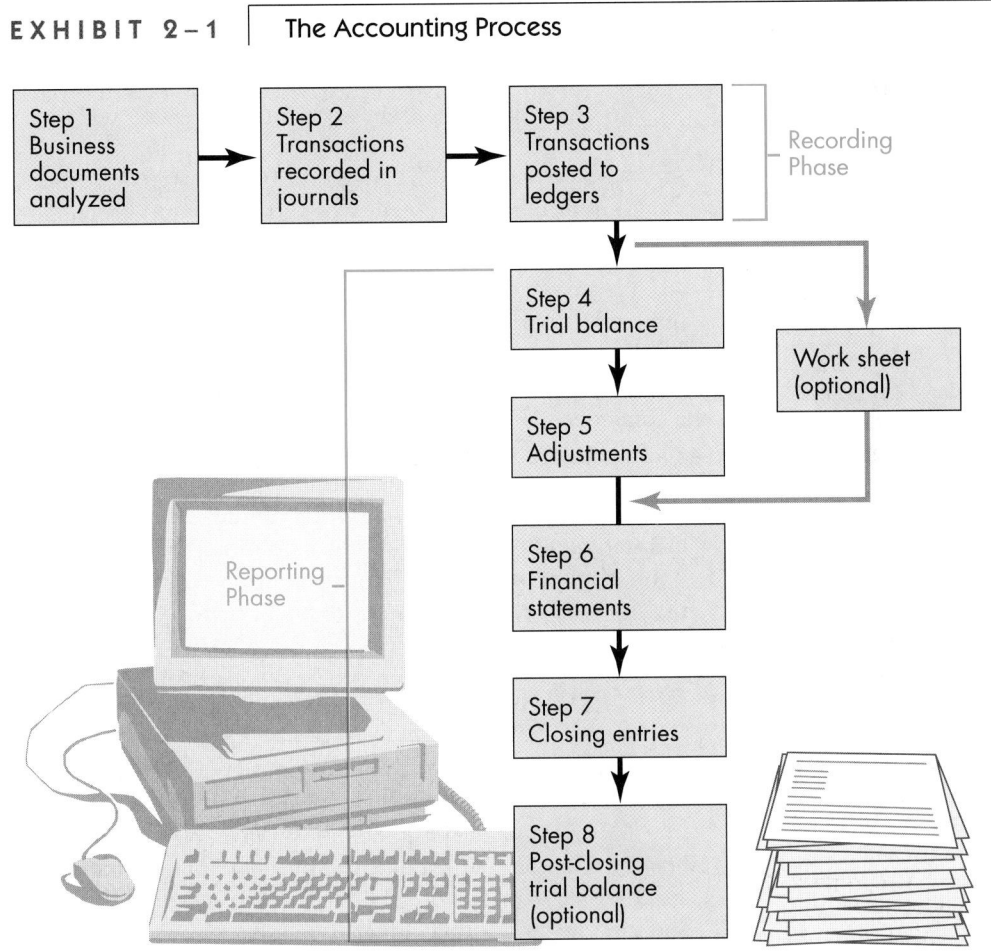

Recording Phase

1. Business documents are analyzed. Analysis of the documentation of business activities provides the basis for making an initial record of each transaction.
2. Transactions are recorded. Based on the supporting documents from Step 1, trans-

actions are recorded, using journal entries, in chronological order in books of original entry, or journals.

3. Transactions are posted. Transactions, as classified and recorded in the journals, are posted to the appropriate accounts in the general and, where applicable, subsidiary ledgers.

Reporting Phase

4. A trial balance of the accounts in the general ledger is prepared. The trial balance simply lists every account in the ledger along with its current debit or credit balance. This step in the reporting phase provides a general check on the accuracy of recording and posting.

5. Adjusting entries are recorded. Before financial statements can be prepared, all relevant information that has not been recorded must be determined and appropriate adjustments made. Adjusting entries must be recorded and posted so the accounts are current prior to the preparation of financial statements.

6. Financial statements are prepared. Statements summarizing operations and showing the financial position and cash flows are prepared from the information obtained from the adjusted accounts.

7. Nominal accounts are closed. Balances in the nominal (temporary) accounts are closed into the retained earnings account. This closing process results in beginning each accounting period with zero balances in all nominal accounts.

8. A post-closing trial balance may be prepared. A post-closing trial balance is prepared to determine the equality of the debits and credits after posting the adjusting and closing entries.

> **FYI:** As noted in Exhibit 2–1, an optional work sheet can be used for the reporting process. This work sheet has columns for the trial balance, adjustments, an adjusted trial balance, and the financial statements. All accounts, with their balances, are listed on the work sheet in the appropriate columns. Computer spreadsheets are often used to facilitate this process.

Before we get immersed in the details associated with the accounting process, it is important to remember that such functions as journalizing, posting, and closing are

 What is the difference between a bookkeeper and an accountant?

bookkeeping functions. You must be familiar with the mundane details of bookkeeping and know how to analyze transactions in terms of debits and credits, but you should not expect to spend your entire accounting career doing bookkeeping. As an accountant, you will spend a great deal of your time involved in designing information systems, analyzing complex transactions, aggregating data for the financial statements, and interpreting accounting results. A knowledge of the fundamentals of bookkeeping provides a foundation upon which these activities are based. These activities are vital to the management of an organization.

RECORDING PHASE

2

Analyze transactions and make and post journal entries.

Accurate financial statements can be prepared only if the results of business events and activities have been properly recorded. Certain events, termed **transactions**, involve the transfer or exchange of goods or services between two or more entities. Examples of business transactions include the purchase of merchandise or other assets from suppliers and the sale of goods or services to customers. In addition to transactions, other events and circumstances may affect the assets, liabilities, and owners' equity of the business. Some of those events and circumstances also must be recorded. Examples include the recognition of depreciation on plant assets, a decline in the market value of inventories and investments, or a loss suffered from a flood or an earthquake.

As indicated, the recording phase involves analyzing business documents, journalizing transactions, and posting to the ledger accounts. Before discussing these steps, the system of double-entry accounting will be reviewed, because virtually all businesses use this procedure in recording their transactions.

Double-Entry Accounting

As explained in Chapter 1, financial accounting rests on a foundation of basic assumptions, concepts, and principles that govern the recording, classifying, summarizing, and reporting of accounting data. **Double-entry accounting** is an old and universally accepted system for recording accounting data. Background on the origin of double-entry accounting is included in the box entitled "Luca Pacioli," shown later in this chapter. With double-entry accounting, each transaction is recorded in a way that maintains the equality of the basic accounting equation:

$$\text{Assets} = \text{Liabilities} + \text{Owners' Equity}$$

> **Caution!** Remember, debit does not mean good (or bad) and credit does not mean bad (or good). Debit means left and credit means right.

To review how double-entry accounting works, recall that a **debit** is an entry on the left side of an account and a **credit** is an entry on the right side. The debit/credit relationships of accounts were explained in detail in your Introductory Accounting course. Exhibit 2–2 summarizes these relationships for a corporation. You will note that assets, expenses, and dividends are increased by debits and decreased by credits. Liabilities, capital stock, retained earnings, and revenues are increased by credits and decreased by debits. Note that while dividends reduce retained earnings, they are not classified as an expense and are not reported on the income statement.

EXHIBIT 2–2 | Debit and Credit Relationships of Accounts

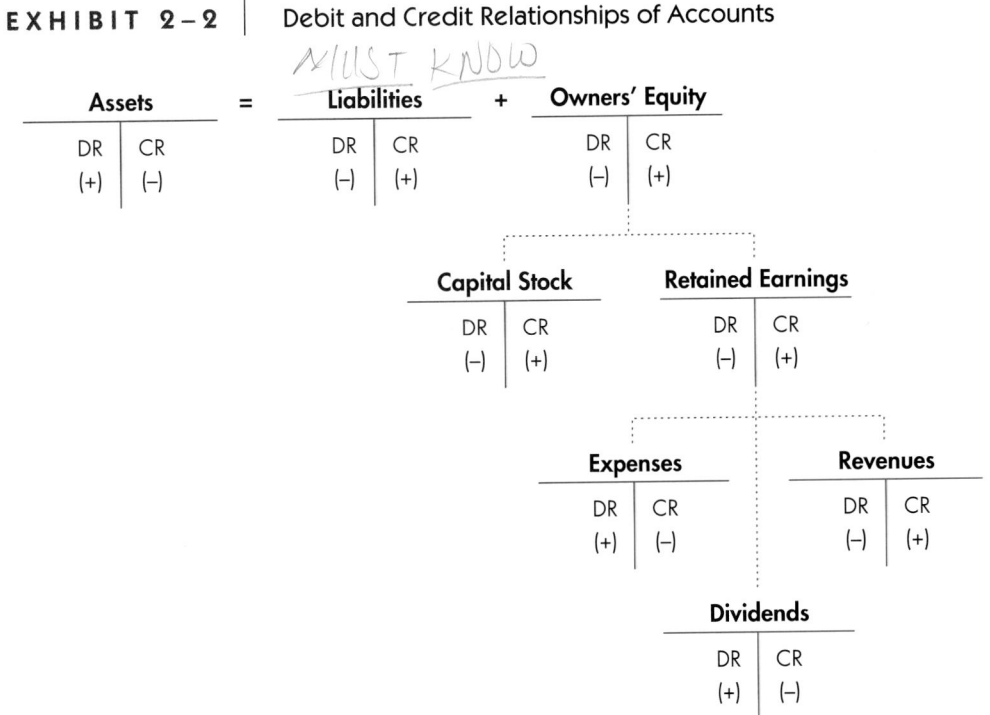

Journal entries provide a systematic method for summarizing a business event's effect on the accounting equation. Every **journal entry** involves a three-step process:

1. Identify the accounts involved with an event or transaction.
2. Determine whether each account increased or decreased (this information, coupled with the answer to question 1, will tell you if the account was debited or credited).
3. Determine the amount by which each account was affected.

Purchasing groceries at your local supermarket is a common example of a business transaction. Can you identify the accounts involved with this transaction?

This three-step process, properly applied, will always result in a correct journal entry. Note that this process is used whether the accounting is being done manually or with a computer.

To illustrate double-entry accounting, consider the transactions and journal entries shown in Exhibit 2–3 and their impact on the accounting equation. In studying this illustration, you should note that for each transaction, total debits equal total credits, therefore, the equality of the accounting equation is maintained.

To summarize, you should remember the following important features of double-entry accounting:

1. Assets are increased by debits and decreased by credits.
2. Liability and owners' equity accounts are increased by credits and decreased by debits.
3. Owners' equity for a corporation includes capital stock accounts and the retained earnings account.
4. Revenues, expenses, and dividends relate to owners' equity through the retained earnings account.
5. Expenses and dividends are increased by debits and decreased by credits because they reduce owners' equity.
6. Revenues are increased by credits and decreased by debits.
7. The difference between total revenues and total expenses for a period is net income (loss), which increases (decreases) owners' equity through the retained earnings account.

> **Caution!** Note in Exhibit 2–2 that dividends reduce retained earnings, but they are not classified as an expense and are not reported on the income statement.

With this brief overview of the accounting equation and journal entries, we are now ready to proceed through the steps in the accounting process.

Analyzing Business Documents

The recording phase begins with an analysis of the documentation showing what business activities have occurred. Normally, a **business document**, or **source document**, is the first record of each transaction. Such a document offers detailed information concerning the transaction and also assigns responsibility by naming the parties involved. The business documents provide support for the data to be recorded in the journals. Copies of sales invoices, for example, are the evidence in support of sales transactions; purchase invoices support purchase transactions; debit and credit memoranda support adjustments in receivable and payable balances; check stubs and canceled checks provide data concerning cash disbursements; and the corporation minutes book

EXHIBIT 2-3 | Double-Entry Accounting: Illustrative Transactions and Journal Entries

| Transaction | Three-Step Process | | | | Journal Entry |
	(1) Identify Accounts.	(2) Increase or Decrease?	(1) and (2) together indicate whether an account is debited or credited.	(3) By How Much?	
Investment by shareholder in a corporation, $10,000	Cash Capital Stock	Increase Increase	Asset ↑ = debit Owners' equity ↑ = credit	$10,000 $10,000	Cash 10,000 Capital Stock 10,000
Purchase of supplies on account, $5,000	Supplies Accounts Payable	Increase Increase	Asset ↑ = debit Liability ↑ = credit	$5,000 $5,000	Supplies 5,000 Accounts Payable 5,000
Payment of wages expense, $2,500	Cash Wages Expense	Decrease Increase	Asset ↓ = credit Expenses ↑ = debit	$2,500 $2,500	Wages Expense 2,500 Cash 2,500
Collection of accounts receivable, $1,000	Cash Accounts Receivable	Increase Decrease	Asset ↑ = debit Asset ↓ = credit	$1,000 $1,000	Cash 1,000 Accounts Receivable 1,000
Payment of account payable, $500	Cash Accounts Payable	Decrease Decrease	Asset ↓ = credit Liability ↓ = debit	$500 $500	Accounts Payable 500 Cash 500
Sale of merchandise on account, $20,000	Accounts Receivable Sales	Increase Increase	Asset ↑ = debit Revenues ↑ = credit	$20,000 $20,000	Accounts Receivable 20,000 Sales 20,000

Purchase of equipment: $15,000 down payment plus $40,000 long-term note	Cash
	Equipment
	Notes Payable
		Decrease
		Increase
		Increase
			Asset ↓ = credit
			Asset ↑ = debit
			Liability ↑ = credit
				$15,000
				$55,000
				$40,000
					Equipment 55,000
					  Cash 15,000
					  Notes Payable 40,000

Payment of cash dividend, $4,000	Cash Dividends	Decrease Increase	Asset ↓ = credit Dividends ↑ = debit	$4,000 $4,000	Dividends 4,000 Cash 4,000

supports entries authorized by action of the board of directors. Documents underlying each recorded transaction provide a means of verifying the accounting records and thus form a vital part of the information and control systems.

Journalizing Transactions

Once the information provided on business documents has been analyzed, transactions are recorded in chronological order in the appropriate **journals**. In some small businesses, all transactions are recorded in a single journal. Most business enterprises, however, maintain various special journals, designed to meet their specific needs, as well as a general journal. A **special journal** is used to record a particular type of frequently recurring transaction. Special journals are commonly used, for example, to record each of the following types of transactions: sales, purchases, cash disbursements, and cash receipts. A **general journal** is used to record all transactions for which a special journal is not maintained. As illustrated on the following page, a general journal shows the transaction date and the accounts affected and allows for a brief description of each transaction.

Special journals are illustrated and explained in the Expanded Material section of this chapter.

	GENERAL JOURNAL				Page 24
Date	Description	Post. Ref.	Debit		Credit
2002 July 1	Dividends	330	25,000		
	Dividends Payable	260			25,000
	Declared semiannual cash dividend on common stock.				
10	Equipment	180	7,500		
	Notes Payable	220			7,500
	Issued note for new equipment.				
31	Payroll Tax Expense	418	2,650		
	Payroll Taxes Payable	240			2,650
	Recorded payroll taxes for month.				

Posting to the Ledger Accounts

An **account** is used to summarize the effects of transactions on each element of the expanded accounting equation. For example, the cash account is used to provide detail for all transactions involving the inflow (debit) and outflow (credit) of cash. A **ledger** is a collection of accounts maintained by a business. The specific accounts required by a business unit vary depending on the nature of the business, its properties and activities, the information to be provided on the financial statements, and the controls to be employed in carrying out the accounting functions. The accounts used by a particular business are usually expressed in the form of a **chart of accounts**. This chart lists all accounts in systematic form with identifying numbers or symbols that provide the framework for summarizing business operations.

Information recorded in the journals is transferred to appropriate accounts in the ledger. This transfer is referred to as **posting**. Note that posting is a copying process; it involves no new analysis. Ledger accounts for Equipment and Notes Payable are presented at the top of the following page illustrating the posting of the July 10 transaction from the preceding general journal. The posting reference (J24) indicates that the transaction was transferred from page 24 of the general journal. Note that the account numbers for Equipment (180) and Notes Payable (220) are entered in the Posting Reference column of the journal.

It is often desirable to establish separate ledgers for detailed information in support of balance sheet or income statement items. The **general ledger** includes all accounts appearing on the financial statements, while separate **subsidiary ledgers** afford additional detail in support of certain general ledger accounts. For example, a single accounts receivable account is usually carried in the general ledger, and individual customer accounts are recorded in a subsidiary accounts receivable ledger. The general ledger account that summarizes the detailed information in a subsidiary ledger is known as a **control account**. Thus, Accounts Receivable would be considered a control account. Subsidiary ledger accounts are illustrated in the Expanded Material section of this chapter.

STOP & THINK What types of errors can occur in the posting process? Why is the computer so valuable in this particular phase of the accounting cycle?

Depending primarily on the number of transactions involved, amounts may be posted to ledger accounts on a daily, weekly, or monthly basis. If a computer system is being used, the posting process may be done automatically as transactions are recorded. At the end of an accounting period, when the posting process has been completed, the balances in the ledger accounts are used for preparing the trial balance.

GENERAL LEDGER

Account EQUIPMENT

Account No. 180

Date		Item	Post. Ref.	Debit	Credit	Balance
2002 July	1	Balance				10,550
	10	Purchase Equipment	J24	7,500		18,050

Account NOTES PAYABLE

Account No. 220

Date		Item	Post. Ref.	Debit	Credit	Balance
2002 July	1	Balance				5,750
	10	Purchase Equipment	J24		7,500	13,250

REPORTING PHASE

3 Make adjusting entries, produce financial statements, and close nominal accounts.

As noted earlier, the objective of the accounting process is to produce financial statements and other reports that will assist various users in making economic decisions. Once the recording phase is completed, the data must be summarized and organized into a useful format. The remaining steps of the accounting process are designed to accomplish this purpose. These steps will be illustrated using data from Rosi, Inc., a hypothetical merchandising company, for the year ended December 31, 2002.

Preparing a Trial Balance

FYI: A fundamental difference between the trial balance and the financial statements is that no external users ever see the trial balance. And most managers have never seen a trial balance. It serves as the basis for the preparation of the financial statements but is not an information source to either management or external users.

After all transactions for the period have been posted to the ledger accounts, the balance for each account is determined. Every account will have either a debit, credit, or zero balance. A **trial balance** is a list of all accounts and their balances. The trial balance, therefore, indicates whether total debits equal total credits and thus provides a general check on the accuracy of recording and posting. When debits equal credits in a trial balance, however, it is no guarantee that the accounts are correct. For example, a journal entry involving a debit to Accounts Receivable could have been incorrectly posted as a debit to the Notes Receivable account. The trial balance would indeed balance, but the accounts would be in error. Thus, a balanced trial balance provides no guarantee of accuracy. However, a trial balance that does not balance indicates that we needn't go further into the reporting phase of the accounting process. An error exists somewhere and must be detected and corrected before proceeding. If we elect to proceed without correcting the error, we have one guarantee—the financial statements will contain errors. The trial balance for Rosi, Inc., is on the next page.

Preparing Adjusting Entries

FYI: DISNEY's 1998 balance sheet included in its annual report does not balance. The preparers of that balance sheet transposed two numbers, and the result was a $9 (million) error. The balance sheet in the 10-K that was filed with the SEC (and is included in Appendix A of this text) does not contain the transposition error.

In order to report information on a timely basis, the life of a business is divided into relatively short time periods, such as a year, a quarter, or a month. While this is essential for the information to be useful, it does create problems for the accountant who must summarize the financial operations for the designated period and report on the financial position at the end of that period. Transactions during the period have been recorded in the appropriate journals and posted to the ledger accounts. At the end of the period, many accounts require adjustments to reflect current conditions. At this time, too, other financial data, not recognized previously, must be entered in the accounts to bring the

Rosi, Inc.
Trial Balance
December 31, 2002

	Debit	Credit
Cash	$ 83,110	
Accounts Receivable	106,500	
Allowance for Doubtful Accounts		$ 1,610
Inventory	45,000	
Prepaid Insurance	8,000	
Interest Receivable	0	
Notes Receivable	28,000	
Land	114,000	
Buildings	156,000	
Accumulated Depreciation—Buildings		39,000
Furniture & Equipment	19,000	
Accumulated Depreciation—Furniture & Equipment		3,800
Accounts Payable		37,910
Unearned Rent Revenue		0
Salaries and Wages Payable		0
Interest Payable		0
Payroll Taxes Payable		5,130
Income Taxes Payable		0
Dividends Payable		3,400
Bonds Payable		140,000
Common Stock, $15 par		150,000
Retained Earnings		126,770
Dividends	13,600	
Sales		479,500
Purchases	162,600	
Purchase Discounts		3,290
Cost of Goods Sold	0	
Salaries and Wages Expense	172,450	
Heat, Light, and Power	32,480	
Payroll Tax Expense	18,300	
Advertising Expense	18,600	
Doubtful Accounts Expense	0	
Depreciation Expense—Buildings	0	
Depreciation Expense—Furniture & Equipment	0	
Insurance Expense	0	
Interest Revenue		1,100
Rent Revenue		2,550
Interest Expense	16,420	
Income Tax Expense	0	
Totals	$994,060	$994,060

books up to date. This requires analysis of individual accounts and various source documents. Based on this analysis, **adjusting entries** are made, and financial statements are prepared using the adjusted account balances.

This part of the accounting process is illustrated using the adjusting data for Rosi, Inc., presented at the top of the next page. The data are classified according to the typical areas requiring adjustment at the end of the designated time period, in this case the year 2002. The accounts listed in the trial balance do not reflect the adjusting data. The adjusting data must be combined with the information on the trial balance if the resulting financial statements are to appropriately reflect company operating results and financial position.

ASSET DEPRECIATION   Charges to operations for the use of buildings, furniture, and equipment must be recorded at the end of the period. In recording asset depreciation,

---

Adjusting Data for Rosi, Inc.
December 31, 2002

Asset Depreciation:
    (a) Buildings, 5% per year.
    (b) Furniture and equipment, 10% per year.
Doubtful Accounts:
    (c) The allowance for doubtful accounts is to be increased by $1,100.
Accrued Expenses:
    (d) Salaries and wages, $2,150.
    (e) Interest on bonds payable, $5,000.
Accrued Revenues:
    (f) Interest on notes receivable, $250.
Prepaid Expenses:
    (g) Prepaid insurance remaining at year-end, $3,800.
Deferred Revenues:
    (h) Unearned rent revenue remaining at year-end, $475.
Income Taxes:
    (i) Federal and state income taxes, $8,000.
Inventory:
    (j) A periodic inventory system is used; the ending inventory balance is $51,000.

---

operations are charged with a portion of the asset's cost, and the carrying value of the asset is reduced by that amount. A reduction in an asset for depreciation is usually recorded by a credit to a contra account, Accumulated Depreciation.

STOP & THINK What benefits are there to accumulating depreciation in a separate contra account instead of crediting the asset account directly?

A **contra account** (or offset account) is set up to record subtractions from a related account. For example, Allowance for Doubtful Accounts is a contra account to Accounts Receivable. Certain accounts relate to others but must be added rather than subtracted on the statements; they are referred to as **adjunct accounts**. Examples include Freight-In, which is added to Purchases, and Additional Paid-In Capital, which is added to the capital stock account balance.

Adjustments at the end of the year for depreciation for Rosi, Inc., are as follows:

(a)	Depreciation Expense—Buildings	7,800	
	Accumulated Depreciation—Buildings		7,800
	To record depreciation on buildings at 5% per year.		
(b)	Depreciation Expense—Furniture & Equipment	1,900	
	Accumulated Depreciation—Furniture & Equipment		1,900
	To record depreciation on furniture and equipment at 10% per year.		

DOUBTFUL ACCOUNTS Invariably, when a business allows customers to purchase goods and services on credit, some of the accounts receivable will not be collected, resulting in a charge to income for bad debt expense. Under the accrual concept, an adjustment should be made for the estimated expense in the current period rather than when specific accounts actually become uncollectible in later periods. This practice produces a better matching of revenues and expenses and therefore a better income measurement. Using this procedure, operations are charged with the estimated expense, and receivables are reduced by means of a contra account, Allowance for Doubtful Accounts. To illustrate, the adjustment for Rosi, Inc., at the end of the year, assuming the allowance account is to be increased by $1,100, would be as follows:

(c)	Doubtful Accounts Expense	1,100	
	Allowance for Doubtful Accounts		1,100
	To adjust for estimated doubtful accounts expense.		

Throughout the accounting period, when there is positive evidence that a specific account is uncollectible, the appropriate amount is written off against the contra

► **LUCA PACIOLI**

The earliest systematic explanation of modern double-entry accounting is contained in a book on mathematics written in 1494. *Summa de Arithmetica, Geometria, Proportioni et Proportionalita* (Everything about Arithmetic, Geometry, and Proportion) was written by Luca Pacioli, a noted mathematician and a monk of the order of St. Francis. Pacioli was no obscure writer; he once collaborated on a book with Leonardo da

Vinci. The bookkeeping portion of *Summa* is called *De Computis et Scripturis* (Of Reckonings and Writings). Pacioli did not invent double-entry accounting; he simply provided an organized treatment of the "method of Venice," which had developed during the 14th and 15th centuries.

In most respects, the double-entry method explained by Pacioli is the same as that used today. One difference was the use of a third book—the

memorial—in addition to the journal and the ledger that we currently use. The memorial was the book of original entry. Because transactions occurred in a variety of currencies, and also because money was rarely worth its face value, amounts recorded in the memorial were converted to a common working currency before being entered in the journal. In addition, Pacioli didn't outline procedures for the production of periodic financial statements. Business

---

FYI: Tax law requires bad debts to be expensed in the year they are uncollectible (the direct write-off method). Thus, for tax purposes, estimating bad debts (the allowance method) is not allowed.

account. For example, if a $150 receivable were considered uncollectible, that amount would be written off as follows:

Allowance for Doubtful Accounts	150	
Accounts Receivable		150
To write off an uncollectible account.		

No entry is made to Doubtful Accounts Expense, because the adjusting entry has already provided for an estimated expense based on previous experience for all receivables.

ACCRUED EXPENSES During the period, certain expenses may have been incurred for which payment is not to be made until a subsequent period. At the end of the period, it is necessary to determine and record any expenses not yet recognized. In recording an accrued expense, an expense account is debited and a liability account is credited. The adjusting entries to record accrued expenses for Rosi, Inc., are:

(d)	Salaries and Wages Expense	2,150	
	Salaries and Wages Payable		2,150
	To record accrued salaries and wages.		
(e)	Interest Expense	5,000	
	Interest Payable		5,000
	To record accrued interest on bonds.		

ACCRUED REVENUES During the period, certain amounts may have been earned, although collection of cash is not to be made until a subsequent period. At the end of the period, it is necessary to determine and record the revenues not yet recognized. In recording accrued revenues, an asset account is debited and a revenue account is credited. The illustrative entry recognizing the accrued revenue for Rosi, Inc., is as follows:

(f)	Interest Receivable	250	
	Interest Revenue		250
	To record accrued interest on notes receivable.		

was seen as a succession of individual ventures (such as a voyage to trade textiles for spices), and the revenues and expenses for each venture were accounted for separately. Instead of a periodic closing of the nominal accounts, the profit or loss from an individual venture was transferred to the capital account when the venture was completed.

One notable feature of Pacioli's work is that it contains no worked-out examples; the topic of bookkeeping is dealt with strictly in the abstract. (Since Pacioli's day, quite a number of accounting students have unsuccessfully tried the same approach in preparing for accounting exams!)

SOURCES:
J. Row Fogo, "History of Bookkeeping," in *A History of Accounting and Accountants,* Richard Brown, ed., London: Frank Cass and Company Limited, 1968, pp. 93–170.
Henry Rand Hatfield, "An Historical Defense of Bookkeeping," *The Journal of Accountancy,* April 1924, pp. 241–253.

net work exercise

There's not much you won't find on the Internet. You can actually view a virtual history of accounting!
www.acaus.org/history/
Net Work:
1. The oldest discovered evidence of writing is a record of what?
2. In the century following its publication, Pacioli's work was translated into how many languages?

PREPAID EXPENSES   During the period, expenditures may have been recorded on the books for goods or services that are not to be received or used up currently. At the end of the period, it is necessary to determine the portions of such expenditures that are applicable to subsequent periods and, hence, require recognition as assets.

The method of adjusting for prepaid expenses depends on how the expenditures were originally entered in the accounts. They may have been recorded originally as debits to (1) an asset account or (2) an expense account. Both methods, if consistently applied, result in the exact same end result. Thus, both methods are equally correct. An individual company would choose one method or the other and apply it each period.

Original debit to an asset account.   If an asset account was originally debited (Prepaid Insurance in this example), the adjusting entry requires that an expense account be debited for the amount applicable to the current period and the asset account be credited. The asset account remains with a debit balance that shows the amount applicable to future periods. An adjusting entry for Prepaid Insurance for Rosi, Inc., illustrates this situation as follows:

(g)	Insurance Expense	4,200	
	Prepaid Insurance		4,200
	To record expired insurance ($8,000 – $3,800 = $4,200).		

Because the asset account Prepaid Insurance was originally debited, as shown in the trial balance, the amount of the prepayment ($8,000) must be reduced to reflect only the $3,800 that remains unexpired. The following T-accounts illustrate how this adjusting entry, when posted, would affect the accounts.

Prepaid Insurance					Insurance Expense			
Beg. Bal.	8,000				Beg. Bal.	0		
		Adj. (g)	4,200		Adj. (g)	4,200		
End. Bal.	3,800				End. Bal.	4,200		

► RUSSIAN ACCOUNTING

Were there accountants in the former Soviet Union? Absolutely. A Soviet-style centralized economy requires a sophisticated statistical database for use by central planners. A drawback of a unified information system like this is that it places a premium on ease of aggregation. All firms use a uniform chart of accounts, and accountants are reduced to filling in spaces in government forms instead of using individual judgment to account for unique circumstances. In this type of environment, accountants are, in practice, merely bookkeepers.

With the increase in Western joint ventures and the rise of homegrown Russian enterprises, accounting and accountants in Russia are evolving. One of the most fundamental changes is an increased focus on using accrual accounting to measure income. (The concept of accrual accounting is discussed later in this chapter.) According to Richard Lewis, partner in the Moscow office of Ernst & Young, "No one in the past was concerned about whether you made a profit. If you made one, it was likely to be taken away; whereas if you made a loss, you would be given money by the government." Formerly, revenues were recognized only when cash was received, partly because of the uncertainty of payment. In addition, bad debt expense was recognized only when there was absolutely no chance of recovering a debt.

Many Western accountants have been enlisted to

Caution! The original debit to an asset account makes more sense conceptually. Remember, however, that the account balances reported in the financial statements are what matter; the working balances that exist in the accounting records on a day-to-day basis are not as important.

Original debit to an expense account. If an expense account was originally debited (Insurance Expense in this example), the adjusting entry requires that an asset account be debited for the amount applicable to future periods and the expense account be credited. The expense account then remains with a debit balance representing the amount applicable to the current period. For example, if Rosi, Inc., had originally debited Insurance Expense for $8,000, the adjusting entry would be:

Prepaid Insurance	3,800	
Insurance Expense		3,800
To record prepaid insurance ($8,000 – $4,200).		

The following T-accounts illustrate the effect that this adjusting entry would have on the relevant accounts.

Prepaid Insurance				Insurance Expense		
Beg. Bal.	0			Beg. Bal.	8,000	
Adj.	3,800					Adj. 3,800
End. Bal.	3,800			End. Bal.	4,200	

Note that regardless of which method is used, the ending balance in each account is the same. In this example, using either method results in an ending balance in Prepaid Insurance and Insurance Expense of $3,800 and $4,200, respectively.

DEFERRED REVENUES Payments may be received from customers prior to the delivery of goods or services. Amounts received in advance are recorded by debiting an asset account, usually Cash, and crediting either a revenue account or a liability account. At the end of the period, it is necessary to determine the amount of revenue earned in the current period and the unearned amount to be deferred to future periods. The method of adjusting for deferred revenues depends on whether the receipts for undelivered goods or services were recorded originally as credits to (1) a revenue account or (2) a liability account.

explain the ins and outs of FIFO, LIFO, goodwill, and dividends to the Russians. However, not all assistance offered has been welcomed. Occasionally, consultants from the West have tried to sell complex systems to countries struggling to implement basic accrual accounting. As one Eastern European official put it: "You are trying to teach us how to make juice out of oranges. Instead, we need to learn how to make soup from potatoes." Even more blunt is the comment from a Russian accountant: "Accounts reflect our reality. Reality in Russia is very complicated."

central planning, to evaluate individual firm performance, and to provide data for taxation. In the United States, separate, though related, systems are used to accomplish these tasks. What advantages do you see in the old Soviet system? in the U.S. system?

2. Accountants in the former Soviet Union possessed little prestige. Why do you think this was so?

SOURCES:

Andrew Jack, "Working Russian Model Now in Need of Overhaul," *Financial Times*, July 31, 1992.

Alison Leigh Cowan, "Profit? Loss? A Primer for Soviets," *The New York Times*, September 22, 1990, p. 17.

Andrew Higgins, "At Russian Companies, Hard Numbers Often Are Hard to Come By," *The Wall Street Journal*, August 20, 1998, p. A1.

QUESTIONS:

1. In the former Soviet Union, a single accounting system was used to generate statistics for use in

Original credit to a revenue account. If a revenue account was originally credited (Rent Revenue in this example), this account is debited and a liability account is credited for the revenue applicable to a future period. The revenue account remains with a credit balance representing the earnings applicable to the current period. As indicated in the trial balance for Rosi, Inc., rent receipts are recorded originally in the Rent Revenue account. Unearned revenue at the end of 2002 is $475 and is recorded as follows:

(h)	Rent Revenue	475	
	Unearned Rent Revenue		475
	To record unearned rent revenue.		

The T-accounts given below illustrate the effect that this adjusting entry would have on the related accounts.

Unearned Rent Revenue				**Rent Revenue**		
	Beg. Bal.	0			Beg. Bal.	2,550
	Adj. (h)	475	Adj. (h)	475		
	End. Bal.	475			End. Bal.	2,075

Original credit to a liability account. If a liability account was originally credited (Unearned Rent Revenue), this account is debited and a revenue account is credited for the amount applicable to the current period. The liability account remains with a credit balance that shows the amount applicable to future periods. For example, if Rosi, Inc., had originally credited Unearned Rent Revenue for $2,550, the adjusting entry (along with affected T-accounts) would be:

Unearned Rent Revenue	2,075	
Rent Revenue		2,075
To record rent revenue ($2,550 – $475).		

Unearned Rent Revenue				**Rent Revenue**		
		Beg. Bal.	2,550		Beg. Bal.	0
Adj.	2,075				Adj.	2,075
		End. Bal.	475		End. Bal.	2,075

Adjusting entries for inventory depend on whether a periodic or perpetual inventory system is used.

Again, note that using either method results in exactly the same balances for the income statement and balance sheet accounts.

INCOME TAXES　When a corporation reports earnings, adjustments must be made for federal and state income taxes. Income Tax Expense is debited and Income Taxes Payable is credited. The entry to record income taxes for Rosi, Inc., is as follows:

(i)	Income Tax Expense	8,000	
	Income Taxes Payable		8,000
	To record income taxes.		

Note that the above entry assumes a single year-end accrual of income taxes. Most companies record income taxes quarterly when estimated payments are made to federal and state taxing authorities.

INVENTORY　The type of adjustment required for the inventory account depends on whether a periodic or a perpetual inventory system is used. When the periodic inventory system is used, physical inventories must be taken at the end of the period to determine the inventory to be reported on the balance sheet and the cost of goods sold to be reported on the income statement. When perpetual inventory records are maintained, the ending inventory and the cost of goods sold balances appear in the ledger. An adjustment is necessary with the perpetual method only to correct the recorded balances for any spoilage, theft, or bookkeeping errors that may have occurred, as determined by a physical count of the inventory. The inventory procedures for merchandising companies are reviewed in the following paragraphs. Accounting for inventories of manufacturers is explained in Chapter 8.

Periodic (physical) inventories.　When using the **periodic inventory system,** all purchases of merchandise on account during a period are recorded in a purchases account with the following journal entry:

Purchases	xxx
Accounts Payable	xxx
To record inventory purchases on account made during the period.	

At the end of the period, before adjustments are made, the inventory account still reflects the beginning inventory balance. The ending balance, based on a physical count, may be recorded in the inventory account by an adjusting entry. At the same time the

STOP & THINK Note that every adjusting entry made at the end of a period involves at least one balance sheet account and one income statement account. Why is that? Note also that one account is conspicuously absent from all adjusting entries. What account is that and why?

inventory account is adjusted, the balance in Purchases and related accounts, such as Purchase Discounts or Freight-In, are transferred to Cost of Goods Sold. In this way, the amount of Cost of Goods Sold is established through a single adjusting entry.

Using the method just described, an adjustment for Rosi, Inc., would be made to the inventory account by debiting it for $6,000 ($51,000 – $45,000), debiting Purchase Discounts for $3,290, crediting Purchases for $162,600, and debiting Cost of Goods Sold for the net amount, $153,310. This would increase Inventory to its ending balance of $51,000, close Purchase Discounts and Purchases, and reflect the amount of Cost of Goods Sold to be reported on the income statement. The adjusting entry would be as follows:

(j)	Inventory	6,000	
	Purchase Discounts	3,290	
	Cost of Goods Sold	153,310	
	Purchases		162,600
	To adjust inventory, cost of goods sold, and related accounts.		

The following T-accounts illustrate how the adjusting entry closes out the purchases and purchase discounts accounts, adjusts the inventory account to its ending balance, and establishes the amount of cost of goods sold.

Inventory

Beg. Bal.	45,000	
Adj. (j)	6,000	
End. Bal.	51,000	

Purchases

Beg. Bal.	162,600			
		Adj. (j)	162,600	
End. Bal.	0			

Purchase Discounts

		Beg. Bal.	3,290
Adj. (j)	3,290		
		End. Bal.	0

Cost of Goods Sold

Beg. Bal.	0	
Adj. (j)	153,310	
End. Bal.	153,310	

Perpetual inventories. When a **perpetual inventory system** is maintained, a separate purchases account is not used. The inventory account is debited whenever goods are acquired. When a sale takes place, two entries are required: (1) the sale is recorded in the usual manner, and (2) the cost of the merchandise sold is recorded by a debit to Cost of Goods Sold and a credit to Inventory. Accounting for the purchase and sale of inventory using a perpetual method are illustrated:

Inventory	xxx	
Accounts Payable		xxx
To record the purchase of inventory on account.		
Cash (or Accounts Receivable)	xxx	
Sales		xxx
Cost of Goods Sold	xxx	
Inventory		xxx
To record the sale of inventory using the perpetual method.		

At any time during the period, Inventory reflects the inventory on hand, and Cost of Goods Sold shows the cost of merchandise sold. At the end of the period, no adjustment is needed for inventory, except to adjust for spoilage, theft, or bookkeeping error, as noted earlier. Cost of Goods Sold would be debited and Inventory would be credited for the cost of any spoiled or stolen goods.

Preparing Financial Statements

Once all accounts have been brought up to date through the adjustment process, financial statements are prepared. How long does it take for large corporations to complete the accounting process to the point where financial statements are available? For December 31 year-end firms, financial statement preparation is usually completed in February. Some firms pride themselves on having their financial statements ready by the end of January. For example, the date of Disney's audit opinion for the fiscal year ended September 30, 1998, (a rough measure of when financial statement preparation is essentially complete) is November 19, 1998, an elapsed time of just seven weeks. For firms with publicly traded shares, the SEC requires the annual financial statements to be released within three months of fiscal year-end. The data used to prepare financial statements may be taken directly from the adjusted account balances in the ledger, or a work sheet may be used. Financial statements are prepared by determining which accounts go on which financial statement, appropriately listing those accounts, and summing to obtain totals.

Using a Work Sheet

An optional step in the accounting process is to use a **work sheet** to facilitate the preparation of adjusting entries and financial statements. The availability of computer spreadsheets, such as Microsoft Excel or Lotus 1-2-3, make the preparation of a work sheet quite easy. But remember that preparing a work sheet is not a required step. As indicated, financial statements can be prepared directly from data in adjusted ledger account balances.

When a work sheet is constructed, trial balance data are listed in the first pair of columns. The adjusting entries are listed in the second pair of columns. Sometimes a third pair of columns is included to show the trial balance after adjustment. Account balances, as adjusted, are carried forward to the appropriate financial statement columns. A work sheet for a merchandising enterprise will include a pair of columns for the income statement accounts and a pair for the balance sheet accounts. There are no columns for the statement of cash flows, because this statement requires additional analysis of changes in account balances for the period. A work sheet for Rosi, Inc., is shown on pages 64 and 65. All adjustments illustrated previously are included.

Closing the Nominal Accounts

Once adjusting entries are formally recorded in the general journal and posted to the ledger accounts, the books are ready to be closed in preparation for a new accounting period. During this closing process, the **nominal (temporary) account** balances are transferred to a **real (permanent) account**, leaving the nominal accounts with a zero balance. Nominal accounts include all income statement accounts plus the dividends account for a corporation. The real account that receives the closing amounts from the nominal accounts is Retained Earnings. Because it is a real account, this and all other balance sheet accounts remain open and carry their balances forward to the new period.

The mechanics of closing the nominal accounts are straightforward. All revenue accounts with credit balances are closed by being debited; all expense accounts with debit balances are closed by being credited. This process reduces these temporary accounts to a zero balance. The difference between the closing debit amounts for revenues and the credit amounts for expenses is net income (or net loss) and is an increase (or decrease) to Retained Earnings. Dividends are also closed at the end of each period. The closing of Dividends serves to reduce Retained Earnings. Thus, the closing entries for revenues, expenses, and Dividends may be made directly to Retained Earnings, as follows:

Revenues	xx	
Retained Earnings		xx
To close revenues to Retained Earnings.		
Retained Earnings	xx	
Expenses		xx
To close expenses to Retained Earnings.		

Retained Earnings	xx	
Dividends		xx
To close Dividends to Retained Earnings.		

The **closing entries** for Rosi, Inc., are presented below. Note that with the adjusting method illustrated for Inventory, Cost of Goods Sold is already computed. It can then be closed to Retained Earnings just like any other operating expense.

Closing Entries

2002			
Dec. 31	Sales	479,500	
	Interest Revenue	1,350	
	Rent Revenue	2,075	
	Retained Earnings		482,925
	To close revenue accounts to Retained Earnings.		
Dec. 31	Retained Earnings	441,710	
	Cost of Goods Sold		153,310
	Salaries and Wages Expense		174,600
	Heat, Light, and Power		32,480
	Payroll Tax Expense		18,300
	Advertising Expense		18,600
	Doubtful Accounts Expense		1,100
	Depreciation Expense—Buildings		7,800
	Depreciation Expense—Furniture & Equipment		1,900
	Insurance Expense		4,200
	Interest Expense		21,420
	Income Tax Expense		8,000
	To close expense accounts to Retained Earnings.		
31	Retained Earnings	13,600	
	Dividends		13,600
	To close Dividends to Retained Earnings.		

The following T-accounts (revenues and expenses have each been combined into one account for illustrative purposes) illustrate the effect the closing process has on the nominal accounts and Retained Earnings.

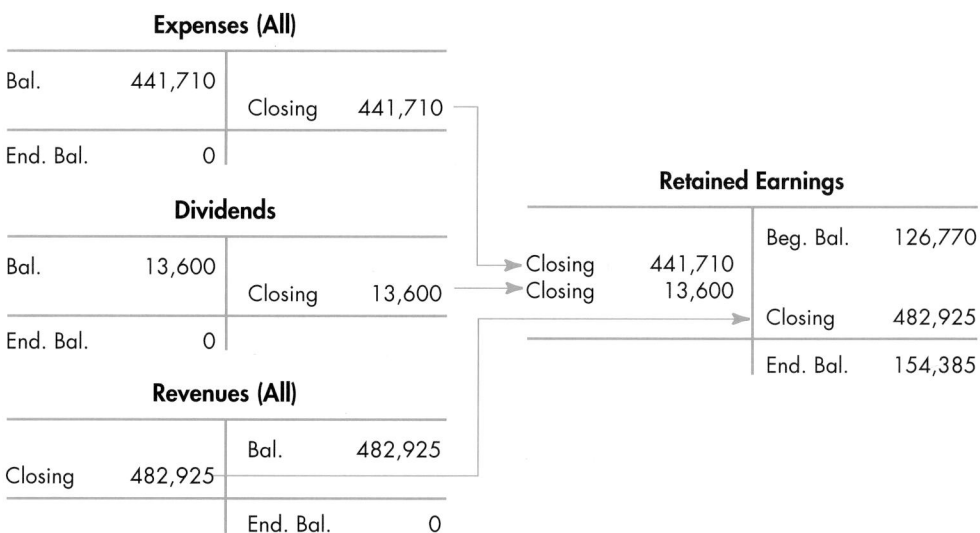

Preparing a Post-Closing Trial Balance

After the closing entries are posted, a **post-closing trial balance** may be prepared to verify the equality of the debits and credits for all real accounts. Recall that real accounts are only those accounts that show up on the balance sheet. The post-closing trial balance

	Account Title	Trial Balance		
		Debit	Credit	
1	Cash	83,110		1
2	Accounts Receivable	106,500		2
3	Allowance for Doubtful Accounts		1,610	3
4	Inventory	45,000		4
5	Prepaid Insurance	8,000		5
6	Interest Receivable	0		6
7	Notes Receivable	28,000		7
8	Land	114,000		8
9	Buildings	156,000		9
10	Accumulated Depreciation—Buildings		39,000	10
11	Furniture & Equipment	19,000		11
12	Accumulated Depreciation—Furniture & Equipment		3,800	12
13	Accounts Payable		37,910	13
14	Unearned Rent Revenue		0	14
15	Salaries and Wages Payable		0	15
16	Interest Payable		0	16
17	Payroll Taxes Payable		5,130	17
18	Income Taxes Payable		0	18
19	Dividends Payable		3,400	19
20	Bonds Payable		140,000	20
21	Common Stock, $15 par		150,000	21
22	Retained Earnings		126,770	22
23	Dividends	13,600		23
24	Sales		479,500	24
25	Purchases	162,600		25
26	Purchase Discounts		3,290	26
27	Cost of Goods Sold	0		27
28	Salaries and Wages Expense	172,450		28
29	Heat, Light, and Power	32,480		29
30	Payroll Tax Expense	18,300		30
31	Advertising Expense	18,600		31
32	Doubtful Accounts Expense	0		32
33	Depreciation Expense—Buildings	0		33
34	Depreciation Expense—Furniture & Equipment	0		34
35	Insurance Expense	0		35
36	Interest Revenue		1,100	36
37	Rent Revenue		2,550	37
38	Interest Expense	16,420		38
39	Income Tax Expense	0		39
40	Totals	994,060	994,060	40
41	Net Income			41
42				42

Inc.
Sheet
31, 2002

#	Adjustments Debit	Adjustments Credit	Income Statement Debit	Income Statement Credit	Balance Sheet Debit	Balance Sheet Credit	#
1					83,110		1
2					106,500		2
3		(c) 1,100				2,710	3
4	(j) 6,000				51,000		4
5		(g) 4,200			3,800		5
6	(f) 250				250		6
7					28,000		7
8					114,000		8
9					156,000		9
10		(a) 7,800				46,800	10
11					19,000		11
12		(b) 1,900				5,700	12
13						37,910	13
14		(h) 475				475	14
15		(d) 2,150				2,150	15
16		(e) 5,000				5,000	16
17						5,130	17
18		(i) 8,000				8,000	18
19						3,400	19
20						140,000	20
21						150,000	21
22						126,770	22
23					13,600		23
24				479,500			24
25		(j) 162,600					25
26	(j) 3,290						26
27	(j) 153,310		153,310				27
28	(d) 2,150		174,600				28
29			32,480				29
30			18,300				30
31			18,600				31
32	(c) 1,100		1,100				32
33	(a) 7,800		7,800				33
34	(b) 1,900		1,900				34
35	(g) 4,200		4,200				35
36		(f) 250		1,350			36
37	(h) 475			2,075			37
38	(e) 5,000		21,420				38
39	(i) 8,000		8,000				39
40	193,475	193,475	441,710	482,925	575,260	534,045	40
41			41,215			41,215	41
42			482,925	482,925	575,260	575,260	42

represents the end of the accounting cycle. The post-closing trial balance for Rosi, Inc., is shown below.

Rosi, Inc.
Post-Closing Trial Balance
December 31, 2002

	Debit	Credit
Cash	83,110	
Accounts Receivable	106,500	
Allowance for Doubtful Accounts		2,710
Inventory	51,000	
Prepaid Insurance	3,800	
Interest Receivable	250	
Notes Receivable	28,000	
Land	114,000	
Buildings	156,000	
Accumulated Depreciation—Buildings		46,800
Furniture & Equipment	19,000	
Accumulated Depreciation—Furniture & Equipment		5,700
Accounts Payable		37,910
Unearned Rent Revenue		475
Salaries and Wages Payable		2,150
Interest Payable		5,000
Payroll Taxes Payable		5,130
Income Taxes Payable		8,000
Dividends Payable		3,400
Bonds Payable		140,000
Common Stock, $15 par		150,000
Retained Earnings		154,385
Totals	$561,660	$561,660

ACCRUAL VERSUS CASH-BASIS ACCOUNTING

Distinguish between accrual and cash-basis accounting.

The procedures described in the previous sections are those required in a double-entry system based on accrual accounting. **Accrual accounting** recognizes revenues as they are earned, not necessarily when cash is received. Expenses are recognized and recorded when they are incurred, not necessarily when cash is paid. Accrual accounting provides for a better matching of revenues and expenses during an accounting period and generally results in financial statements that more accurately reflect a company's financial position and results of operations.[1]

Some accounting systems are based on cash receipts and cash disbursements instead of accrual accounting. **Cash-basis accounting** procedures frequently are found in organizations not requiring a complete set of double-entry records. Such organizations might include smaller, unincorporated businesses and some nonprofit organizations. Professionals engaged in service businesses, such as CPAs, dentists, and engineers, also have traditionally used cash accounting systems. Even many of these organizations, however, periodically use professional accountants to prepare financial statements and other required reports on an accrual basis.

Discussion continues as to the appropriateness of using cash accounting systems, especially as a basis for determining tax liabilities. The FASB, in Concepts Statement No. 1, indicates that accrual accounting provides a better basis for financial reports than does information showing only cash receipts and disbursements.

---

1 In Concepts Statement No. 6, the FASB discusses the concept of accrual accounting and relates it to the objectives of financial reporting. *Statement of Financial Accounting Concepts No. 6,* "Elements of Financial Statements," Stamford, CT: Financial Accounting Standards Board, December 1985.

The AICPA's position, however, is that the cash basis is appropriate for some smaller companies and especially for companies in the service industry. Until this issue is settled, accountants will continue to be asked on occasion to convert cash-based records to generally accepted accrual-based financial statements. The concepts involved are described and illustrated in Chapter 5, which explains the statement of cash flows.

COMPUTERS AND THE ACCOUNTING PROCESS

5

Discuss the importance and expanding role of computers to the accounting process.

As an organization grows in size and complexity, the recording and summarizing processes become more involved, and means are sought for improving efficiency and reducing costs. Some enterprises may find that a system involving primarily manual operations is adequate in meeting their needs. Others find that information-processing needs can be handled effectively only through the use of computers.

Companies requiring great speed and accuracy in processing large amounts of accounting data utilize computer systems capable of storing and recalling data, performing many mathematical functions, and making certain routine decisions based on mathematical comparisons. Early business computers were descendants of the scientific computers developed during World War II. Use of computers for accounting purposes was resisted initially because of concerns about high costs. To get a sense of how high the cost was in those early days, consider that it has been estimated that the cost of computing has been cut in half every three years since 1950. That means that to buy the same computing power that one could get for $1,000 in 1998 would have cost approximately $65,536,000 in 1950. Another concern with using those early computers for accounting purposes was reliability. Anyone who has experienced a hard disk crash on the reliable machines of today can appreciate the apprehension felt by accountants in 1950 who were asked to entrust the bookkeeping function to a roomful of vacuum tubes, wires, and punch cards.

Business computing in the 1960s was characterized by batch computing—all computer jobs were initiated from terminals located near the computer itself, and transactions were processed in batches. The 1970s saw the development of time-sharing arrangements where computers were accessed from remote locations and more on-line, real-time processing was done.

Technological advances in integrated circuitry and microchips led to one of the most significant phenomena of the 1980s—the development of personal computers (PCs). These compact, relatively inexpensive computers have changed the way in which many companies and individuals keep track of their business activities. These computers are being used for a variety of activities, including financial analysis, accounting functions, word processing, database management, inventory control, and credit analysis of customers. As uses have expanded, software packages have been developed to meet current and future demands. The impact of PCs is felt not only in business but also in education and in family life. Many colleges now require entering freshmen to purchase their own PCs for use in a variety of business, mathematics, and science courses. Exposure to computers, and especially the PC, is also very common in elementary and secondary school curricula.

This computer revolution has rapidly changed society and along with it the way business is conducted and, therefore, the way accounting functions are performed. The 1990s are referred to as the Decade of Networking—indicating that the PCs on people's desks in the 1980s have been and will increasingly be interconnected. The opportunities for information exchange will expand exponentially. However, despite their tremendous capabilities, computers cannot replace skilled accountants. A computer, for example, does not know the difference between inventory and supplies until someone (the accountant) specifies the accounts involved in the transaction. Instead of reducing the responsibilities

► WHY DOESN'T THE UNITED STATES GOVERNMENT USE ACCRUAL ACCOUNTING?

In February 1993, the Office of Management and Budget forecast that the budget deficit for the U.S. government for fiscal 1993 would total $332 billion. The deficit was projected to decrease to only $205 billion in 1996. This inability of the federal government to balance its budget prompted a flood of proposals, accusations, campaign slogans, and TV "infomercials." At the time, no one imagined that there

would be a budget surplus by 1998.

In the midst of the budget deficit despair years, one suggested remedy was that the U.S. government adopt accrual accounting. The cash basis used by the federal government makes no attempt to differentiate between operating expenditures, such as current period salaries, and capital expenditures, such as amounts spent on interstate highway construction. All cash expenditures are lumped together, the total is subtracted from total cash receipts, and the difference is called the deficit. Accrual accounting, it is claimed, would yield a more accurate picture of the government's financial health.

This call for accrual accounting by the federal government is not a new one. In 1975, ARTHUR ANDERSEN, the public accounting firm, assisted the U.S. government in preparing a prototype set of financial statements using accrual accounting. These financial statements are still prepared annually but are not widely publicized by the government. A look at the 1998 balance sheet reveals why this might be so. Total reported assets were $853 billion, while total liabilities were $6.987 trillion, resulting in a negative equity of $6.134 trillion. Thus far, the only national government to adopt the accrual basis for its official accounting system is New Zealand.

Some claim that the use of accrual accounting would make the reported federal budget numbers less subject to manipulation. One of the most blatant acts of manipulation occurred in 1987 when Congress ordered

of accountants, the existence of computers places increased demands on them in directing the operations of the computer systems to assure the use of appropriate procedures. For example, a poorly designed computer system may leave no document trail with which to verify accounting records. Although all arithmetical operations can be assumed to be done accurately by computers, the validity of the output data depends on the adequacy of the instructions given the computer. Unlike a human accountant, a computer cannot think for itself but must be given explicit instructions for performing each operation. Computers have certain advantages, for example, the accountant can be sure every direction will be carried out precisely. On the other hand, computers place a great responsibility on the accountant to anticipate any unusual situations requiring special consideration or judgment.

The question to be asked is this: If computers now take care of all of the routine accounting functions, why does an accounting student need to know anything about debits, credits, journals, posting, T-accounts, and trial balances? Good question. First of all, even though computers now do most of the routine work, the essence of double-entry accounting is unchanged from the days of quill pens and handwritten ledgers. Thus, the understanding of the process explained in this chapter is still relevant to a computer-based accounting system. In addition, with or without computers, the use of debits, credits, and T-accounts still provides an efficient and widespread shorthand method of analyzing transactions. At a minimum, all businesspeople should be familiar enough with the language of accounting to understand, for example, why a credit balance in the Cash account or a debit balance in Retained Earnings is something unusual enough to merit investigation. Finally, an understanding of the accounting cycle—analyzing, recording, summarizing, and preparing—gives one insight into how information flows within an organization. And great advantages accrue to those who understand information flow.

the Department of Defense to change its payday from the last day in September, which is the last day in the federal government's fiscal year, to the first day in October. Since the cash basis requires that expenditures be recognized in the period they are paid instead of when they are incurred, this simple delay in mailing out the paychecks reduced the reported deficit for fiscal 1987 by $1 billion.

The cash basis is certainly subject to some manipulation, but the same can be said of the accrual basis. If the federal government were to adopt the accrual basis, cash outlays would then have to be classified as capital expenditures or operating expenditures. For capital expenditures, lawmakers would be required to estimate depreciable lives, among other important variables. Imagine a Congress empowered to make accounting judgments—scary.

QUESTIONS:

1. The "equity" in the 1998 prototype balance sheet of the U.S. federal government was a negative $6.134

trillion. What aspects of the historical cost accounting model might have caused this prototype balance sheet to look worse than it really is?

2. How can Congress take advantage of cash-basis accounting to manipulate the reported deficit? How could Congress use accrual accounting to manipulate the reported deficit?

SOURCES:
"Clinton's Budget at a Glance," *The Wall Street Journal*, February 19, 1993, p. A4.
"Balancing the Government's Books," *The Economist*, January 25, 1992.
Charles A. Bowsher, "Commentary on the Federal Budget: Presenting and Facing the Facts," *Accounting Horizons*, June 1990, p. 96.
Financial Report of the United States Government—1998.

net work exercise

Visit the government's (**www.publicdebt.treas.gov/opd/opdhisto.htm**) Web site for an up-to-date estimate of the U.S. national debt.
Net Work:
What is the public debt to the penny as of today?

EXPANDED MATERIAL

6

Use special journals and subsidiary ledgers to process accounting information more efficiently and to provide additional useful information.

In recording transactions, companies use special journals in addition to the general journal. Special journals eliminate much of the repetitive work involved in recording routine transactions. In addition, they permit the recording functions to be divided among accounting personnel, each individual being responsible for a separate record. This specialization often results in greater efficiency and increased accuracy, as well as a higher degree of control.

Some examples of special journals are the sales journal, the purchases journal, the cash receipts journal, the cash disbursements journal, the payroll register, and the voucher register.

Sales on account are recorded in the *sales journal*. The subsequent collections on account, as well as other transactions involving the receipt of cash, are recorded in the *cash receipts journal*. Merchandise purchases on account are entered in a *purchases journal* or a *voucher register*. Subsequent payments on account, as well as other transactions involving the payment of cash, are recorded in a *cash disbursements journal* or a *check register*. A payroll register may be employed to accumulate payroll information, including payroll deductions and withholdings for taxes.

Column headings in the various journals specify the accounts to be debited or credited; account titles and explanations may therefore be omitted in recording routine transactions. A Sundry column is usually provided for transactions that are relatively infrequent, and account titles must be entered in recording such transactions.

The use of special journals facilitates recording and also simplifies the posting process, because the totals of many transactions, rather than separate data for each transaction, can be posted to the ledger accounts. Certain data must be transferred individually—data affecting individual accounts receivable and accounts payable and data reported in the Sundry columns—but the overall volume of posting is substantially reduced.

The format of a particular journal must satisfy the needs of the individual business unit. For example, with an automated or computerized system, the general journal, any specialized journals, and subsidiary ledgers may be modified or eliminated. Recognizing that modifications are necessary for individual systems, the following sections discuss a voucher system and illustrate some special journals that are commonly used with manual accounting systems.

VOUCHER SYSTEM

Relatively large organizations ordinarily provide for the control of purchases and cash disbursements through adoption of some form of a **voucher system**. With the use of a voucher system, checks may be drawn only upon a written authorization in the form of a *voucher* approved by some responsible official.

A voucher is prepared not only in support of each payment to be made for goods and services purchased on account but also for all other transactions calling for payment by check, including cash purchases, retirement of debt, replenishment of petty cash funds, payrolls, and dividends. The voucher identifies the person authorizing the expenditure, explains the nature of the transaction, and names the accounts affected by the transaction. For control purposes, vouchers should be prenumbered, checked against purchase invoices, and compared with receiving reports. Upon verification, the voucher and the related business documents are submitted to the appropriate official for final approval. When approved, the prenumbered voucher is recorded in a voucher register. The voucher register is a book of original entry and takes the place of a purchases journal. Charges on each voucher are classified and recorded in appropriate Debit columns, and the amount to be paid is listed in an Accounts Payable or Vouchers Payable column. After a voucher is entered in the register, it is placed in an unpaid vouchers file together with its supporting documents.

Checks are written in payment of individual vouchers. The checks are recorded in a check register, which is used in place of a cash payments journal, as debits to Accounts Payable or Vouchers Payable and credits to Cash. Since charges to the various asset, liability, or expense accounts were recognized when the payable was recorded in the voucher register, these accounts need not be listed in the payments record. When a check is issued, payment of the voucher is reported in the voucher register by entering the check number and the payment date. Paid vouchers and supporting documents are removed from the unpaid file, marked "paid," and placed in a separate paid vouchers file. The balance of the payable account, after the credit for total vouchers issued and the debit for total vouchers paid, should be equal to the sum of the unpaid vouchers file. The voucher register, while representing a journal, also provides the detail in support of the accounts payable or vouchers payable total.

ILLUSTRATION OF SPECIAL JOURNALS AND SUBSIDIARY LEDGERS

Assume that Central Valley, Inc., maintains the following books of original entry: sales journal, cash receipts journal, voucher register, check register, and general journal. As noted, the format of a particular journal must satisfy the needs of the individual business unit. Those presented for Central Valley, Inc., are illustrative only.

Sales Journal

The sales journal for the month of July 2002 appears as follows:

SALES JOURNAL					**Page 6**

Date	Invoice No.	Account Debited	Post. Ref.	Accts. Rec. Dr. Sales Cr.
2002				
July 2	701	The Chocolate Factory	✓	3,450
6	702	Huffman Company	✓	6,510
10	703	Stocks and Co.	✓	1,525
12	704	Bennet, Inc.	✓	4,860
15	705	The Chocolate Factory	✓	2,000
18	706	Ridnour Corporation	✓	5,940
20	707	Hillcrest Sales Co.	✓	1,910
23	708	Kirstein, Inc.	✓	7,650
27	709	Datamark Systems Inc.	✓	1,280
29	710	Fuller Distributing Co.	✓	2,925
31	711	Stocks and Co.	✓	2,100
				40,150
				(116) (41)

As illustrated, credit sales are recorded by debits to Accounts Receivable and credits to Sales. The sales invoice number provides a reference to the original source document for each transaction. Debits are posted to individual customers' accounts in the accounts receivable subsidiary ledger as indicated by a check (✓) in the Posting Reference column. The total sales for the month ($40,150) are posted to Accounts Receivable and Sales (accounts #116 and #41, respectively).

Cash Receipts Journal

The cash receipts journal for Central Valley, Inc., for July 2002 appears as follows:

CASH RECEIPTS JOURNAL						**Page 8**

Date	Account Credited	Post. Ref.	Sundry Accounts Cr.	Accounts Receivable Cr.	Sales Discounts Dr.	Cash Dr.
2002						
July 3	Hamilton Sign Co.	✓		5,650	113	5,537
7	DataMark Systems Inc.	✓		1,400	28	1,372
8	Sales	41	365			365
10	The Chocolate Factory	✓		3,450	69	3,381
11	Sawyer Co.	✓		2,735		2,735
14	Rohas, Inc.	✓		4,875		4,875
16	Milo Company	✓		920		920
17	Poynter Corp.	✓		6,100		6,100
21	Earnst Co.	✓		6,870		6,870
22	Tax Refund Receivable	120	5,780			5,780
25	Sales	41	440			440
29	Hillcrest Sales Co.	✓		1,900	38	1,862
31	The Chocolate Factory	✓		2,000		2,000
31	Notes Receivable	113	8,500			
	Interest Revenue	72	65			8,565
			15,150	35,900	248	50,802
			(✓)	(116)	(42)	(111)

The cash receipts journal records all receipts of cash. Collections of cash from previously recorded credit sales are posted in total as a credit to Accounts Receivable (account #116) and as debits to Sales Discounts (account #42) and Cash (account #111). The credits to Accounts Receivable are posted to the individual customer accounts in the subsidiary ledger as noted by the check (✓) in the Posting Reference column. Cash sales, for example, as shown for July 8 and July 25, are posted individually as a credit to Sales (account #41) and as a part of the total debit to Cash. Other transactions involving cash receipts, for example, the collection of a note receivable on July 31, are posted individually as credits and as a part of the total debit to Cash.

Voucher Register

As noted, the voucher register takes the place of a purchases journal, providing a record of all authorized payments to be made by check. A partial voucher register is presented below. For illustrative purposes, separate debit columns are provided for two accounts—Purchases and Payroll. Other items are recorded in the Sundry Dr. column. Additional separate columns could be added for other items, such as advertising, if desired. The total amount of each column is posted to the corresponding account, with the exception of the Sundry Dr. and Cr. columns, which are posted individually.

VOUCHER REGISTER

Date	Vouch. No.	Payee	Paid Date	Ck. No.	Accounts Payable Cr.	Purchases Dr.	Payroll Dr.	Account	Post. Ref.	Sundry Amount Dr.	Sundry Amount Cr.
31	7132	Security National Bank	7/31	3106	9,120			Notes Payable	211	9,120	
31	7133	Payroll	7/31	3107	1,640		2,130	FICA Taxes Payable	215		90
								Income Taxes Payable	214		400
31	7134	Far Fabrications			3,290	3,290					
31	7135	Midland Inc.			1,500	1,500					
31	7136	Nyland Supply Co.			5,550	5,550					
					55,375	24,930	2,130			33,645	5,330
					(213)	(51)	(620)			(✓)	(✓)

Check Register

A partial check register is illustrated below. It accounts for all the checks issued during the period. Checks are issued only in payment of properly approved vouchers. The payee is designated together with the number of the voucher authorizing the payment.

CHECK REGISTER

Date	Check No.	Account Debited	Voucher No.	Accounts Payable Dr.	Purchase Discounts Cr.	Cash Cr.
31	3106	Security National Bank	7132	9,120		9,120
31	3107	Payroll	7133	1,640		1,640
31	3108	Pat Bunnell	7005	1,500	30	1,470
				61,160	275	60,885
				(213)	(52)	(111)

General Journal

Regardless of the number and nature of special journals, certain transactions cannot appropriately be recorded in the special journals and are recorded in the general journal. A general journal with an illustrative entry during the month of July is illustrated below. This general journal is prepared in two-column format. Debit and Credit columns is provided for the entries that are to be made to the general ledger accounts.

GENERAL JOURNAL   Page 3

Date	Description	Post. Ref.	Debit	Credit
2002 July 31	Allowance for Doubtful Accounts	117	1,270	
	Accounts Receivable	116		1,270
	To write off uncollectible account.			
	(The Rit-Z Shop)			

Subsidiary Ledgers

Subsidiary ledgers provide the detail of individual accounts in support of a control account in the general ledger. Whenever possible, individual postings to subsidiary accounts are made directly from the business documents evidencing the transactions. This practice saves time and avoids errors that might arise in summarizing and transferring this information. If postings to the subsidiary records and to the control accounts are made accurately, the sum of the detail in a subsidiary record will agree with the balance in the control account. A reconciliation of each subsidiary ledger with its related control account should be made periodically, and any discrepancies found should be investigated and corrected.

As an illustration of the relationship of a general ledger control account to its subsidiary ledger accounts, the accounts receivable control account is shown. Three of the subsidiary accounts are also shown.

GENERAL LEDGER

Account: ACCOUNTS RECEIVABLE   **Account No.** 116

Date	Item	Post. Ref.	Debit	Credit	Balance
2002 July 1	Balance				9,200
31	Sales on account	S6	40,150		49,350
31	Collections on account	CR8		35,900	13,450
31	Write-off of uncollectible account (The Rit-Z Shop)	J3		1,270	12,180

ACCOUNTS RECEIVABLE SUBSIDIARY LEDGER

Name: Stock and Co.
Address: 546 South Fox Rd., Chicago, IL 60665

Date	Item	Post. Ref.	Debit	Credit	Balance
2002 July 1	Balance				1,000
10	Purchase	S6	1,525		2,525
31	Purchase	S6	2,100		4,625

Name: The Chocolate Factory
Address: 7890 Redwood Dr., Pittsburgh, PA 15234

Date		Item	Post. Ref.	Debit	Credit	Balance
2002						
July	2	Purchase	S6	3,450		3,450
	10	Payment	CR8		3,450	–0–
	15	Purchase	S6	2,000		2,000
	31	Payment	CR8		2,000	–0–

Name: The Rit-Z Shop
Address: 789 Cotton Drive, Phoenix, AZ 85090

Date		Item	Post. Ref.	Debit	Credit	Balance
2002						
July	1	Balance				1,270
	31	Write-off of uncollectible account (6 months old)	J3		1,270	–0–

REVIEW OF LEARNING OBJECTIVES

1 Identify and explain the basic steps in the accounting process (accounting cycle). The accounting process, often referred to as the accounting cycle, generally includes the following steps in well-defined sequence: analyze business documents, journalize transactions, post to ledger accounts, prepare a trial balance, prepare adjusting entries, prepare financial statements (using a work sheet or from the adjusted individual accounts), close the nominal accounts, and prepare a post-closing trial balance. This process of recording, classifying, summarizing, and reporting of accounting data is based on an old and universally accepted system called double-entry accounting.

2 Analyze transactions and make and post journal entries. Transactions are events that transfer or exchange goods or services between two or more entities. Business documents, such as invoices, provide evidence that transactions have occurred as well as the data required to record the transaction in the accounting records. The data are recorded with journal entries using a system of double-entry accounting. The journal entries are subsequently posted to ledger accounts.

3 Make adjusting entries, produce financial statements, and close nominal accounts. Adjusting entries are made at the end of an accounting period prior to preparing the financial statements for that period. Adjusting entries are often required to update accounts so that the data are current and accurate. Generally, the required adjustments are the result of analysis rather than based on new transactions. Once adjusting entries are journalized and posted, the balance sheet, income statement, and statement of cash flows can be prepared and reported.

At the end of each accounting cycle, the nominal or temporary accounts must be transferred through the closing process to real or permanent accounts. The nominal accounts (all income statement accounts plus dividends) are left with a zero balance and are ready to receive transaction data for the new accounting period. The real (balance sheet) accounts remain open and carry their balances forward to the new period.

4 Distinguish between accrual and cash-basis accounting. Accrual accounting recognizes revenues when they are earned, not necessarily when cash is received. Similarly, expenses are recognized and recorded under accrual accounting when they are incurred, not necessarily when cash is paid. Some organizations (and most individuals) use cash-basis accounting, which recognizes revenues when cash is received and expenses when cash is paid. The FASB has indicated that accrual accounting generally provides a better basis for financial reports, especially in reporting earnings, than does information showing only cash receipts and disbursements. However, the FASB and SEC both require a statement of cash flows to be presented along with an accrual-based income statement and a balance sheet as the primary financial statements of an enterprise.

5 **Discuss the importance and expanding role of computers to the accounting process.** Computers play an increasing role in today's business environment as well as society in general. In the past, many companies used manual systems to record, classify, summarize, and report accounting data. Today, most companies use computers and electronic technology as an integral part of their accounting systems. In the future, technological advances will continue to significantly impact the accounting process of recording and reporting data for decision-making purposes.

6 **Use special journals and subsidiary ledgers to process accounting information more efficiently and to provide additional useful information.** Some companies use special journals, in addition to the general journal, to record transactions. This specialization allows for a division of duties among accounting personnel and usually results in greater efficiency, increased accuracy, and a higher degree of control. The most commonly used special journals are: sales journal, cash receipts journal, purchases journal (or voucher register), and cash disbursements journal (or check register). Subsidiary ledgers provide the detail of individual accounts (e.g., accounts receivable subsidiary ledger) in support of a control account in the general ledger.

KEY TERMS

Account 52
Accounting process
    (accounting cycle) 46
Accounting system 46
Accrual accounting 66
Adjunct account 55
Adjusting entries 54
Business (source) document 50
Cash-basis accounting 66
Chart of accounts 52
Closing entries 63
Contra account 55
Control account 52

Credit 49
Debit 49
Double-entry accounting 49
General journal 51
General ledger 52
Journal 51
Journal entry 49
Ledger 52
Nominal (temporary) account 62
Periodic inventory system 60
Perpetual inventory system 61
Post-closing trial balance 63
Posting 52

Real (permanent) account 62
Special journal 51
Subsidiary ledgers 52
Transactions 48
Trial balance 53
Work sheet 62

Voucher system 70

QUESTIONS

1. What types of reports are generated from the accounting system?
2. What are the main similarities and differences between a manual and an automated accounting system?
3. Distinguish between the recording and reporting phases of the accounting process.

4. List and describe the steps in the accounting process. Why are these steps necessary? Are any steps optional?
5. Under double-entry accounting, what are the debit/credit relationships of accounts?

6. Distinguish between: (a) real and nominal accounts, (b) general journal and special journals, and (c) general ledger and subsidiary ledgers.

7. Explain the nature and the purpose of (a) adjusting entries and (b) closing entries.

8. As Beechnut Mining Company's independent certified public accountant, you find that the company accountant posts adjusting and closing entries directly to the ledger without formal entries in the general journal. How would you evaluate this procedure in your report to management?

9. Give three common examples of contra accounts. Explain why contra accounts are used.

Allowance for Doubtful accounts
Accum Depr
Purchasis Discounts

10. Payment of insurance in advance may be recorded in either (a) an expense account or (b) an asset account. Which method would you recommend? What periodic entries are required under each method?

11. Distinguish between the procedures followed by a merchandising enterprise using a periodic (physical) inventory system and one using a perpetual inventory system.

12. Describe the nature and purpose of a work sheet.

13. What effect, if any, does the use of a work sheet have on the sequence of the reporting phase of the accounting process?

14. The accountant for the Miller Hardware Store, after completing all adjustments except for the merchandise inventory, makes the following entry to close the beginning inventory, to set up the ending inventory, to close all nominal accounts, and to report the net result of operations in the retained earnings account.

Inventory (Dec. 31, 2002)	22,500	
Sales	250,000	
Purchase Discounts	2,500	
Inventory (Jan. 1, 2002)		25,000
Purchases		175,000
Selling Expenses		25,000
General and Administrative Expenses		18,750
Interest Expense		1,875
Retained Earnings		29,375

(a) Would you regard this procedure as being acceptable?

(b) What alternate procedure could you have followed to close the nominal accounts?

15. From the following list of accounts, determine which ones should be closed and whether each would normally be closed by a debit or by a credit entry.

Cash   Accounts Receivable
Rent Expense *C*   Land

Depreciation Expense *C*   Interest Revenue *D*
Sales *D*   Advertising Expense *C*
Sales Discounts *C*   Purchase Discounts *D*
Purchases *C*   Notes Payable
Freight-In *C*   Dividends *C*
Retained Earnings   Accounts Payable
Capital Stock

16. Distinguish between accrual and cash-basis accounting.

17. Is greater accuracy achieved in financial statements prepared from double-entry accrual data as compared with cash data? Explain.

18. What are the major advantages of computers as compared with manual processing of accounting data? *DO A LOT OF POSTING WORK BOOKKEEPING W*

19. One of your clients overheard a computer manufacturer sales representative saying that the computer will make the accountant obsolete. How would you respond to this comment?

20. What advantages are provided through the use of: (a) special journals, (b) subsidiary ledgers, and (c) the voucher system?

21. The Tantor Co. maintains a sales journal, a voucher register, a cash receipts journal, a check register, and a general journal. For each account listed below, indicate the most common journal sources of debits and credits.
(a) Cash
(b) Temporary Investments
(c) Notes Receivable
(d) Accounts Receivable
(e) Allowance for Doubtful Accounts
(f) Merchandise Inventory
(g) Land and Buildings
(h) Accumulated Depreciation
(i) Notes Payable
(j) Vouchers Payable
(k) Capital Stock
(l) Retained Earnings
(m) Sales
(n) Sales Discounts
(o) Purchases
(p) Freight-In
(q) Purchase Discounts
(r) Salaries Expense
(s) Depreciation Expense

DISCUSSION CASES

CASE 2–1

WHERE IS YOUR CASH BOX?

Consider the following account of a veterinarian attempting to hire his first bookkeeper:

Miss Harbottle, the prospective bookkeeper, paused at the desk, heaped high with incoming and outgoing bills and circulars from drug firms with here and there stray boxes of pills and tubes of udder ointment.

Stirring distastefully among the mess, she extracted the dog-eared old ledger and held it up between finger and thumb. "What's this?"

Siegfried trotted forward. "Oh, that's our ledger. We enter the visits into it from our day book, which is here somewhere." He scrabbled about on the desk. "Ah, here it is. This is where we write the calls as they come in."

She studied the two books for a few minutes with an expression of amazement that gave way to grim humor. She straightened up slowly and spoke patiently. "And where, may I ask, is your cash box?"

"Well, we just stuff it in there, you know." Siegfried pointed to the pint pot on the corner of the mantelpiece. "Haven't got what you'd call a proper cash box, but this does the job all right."

Miss Harbottle looked at the pot with horror. Crumpled cheques and notes peeped over the brim at her; many of their companions had burst out on the hearth below. "And you mean to say that you go out and leave that money there day after day?"

"Never seems to come to any harm." Siegfried replied.

"And how about your petty cash?"

Siegfried gave an uneasy giggle. "All in there, you know. All cash—petty and otherwise."

(Excerpted from: James Herriot, *All Creatures Great and Small*, 1972, St. Martin's Press: New York.)

Situations similar to the one described above are not unusual for small businesses. How does a business survive with such bad bookkeeping?

CASE 2–2

TO RECORD OR NOT TO RECORD

Explain why each of the following hypothetical events would not be recorded in a journal entry.

1. A famous and much-beloved movie star is secretly filmed by an investigative news team using your company's product when she in fact has an endorsement contract with your company's major competitor.
2. Two of your firm's top vice presidents have a bitter argument and will probably never speak to one another again.
3. Your company's chief research chemist is killed in a plane crash.
4. Because of unfavorable economic news, consumer confidence is shaken, and the stock market falls by 10%.
5. You, a small business owner, buy a sofa for your home. You pay with a check drawn on your personal, not your business, checking account.
6. Disney decides to build the next Walt Disney World near a large piece of property you own.

CASE 2–3

IS IT TIME TO REVOLUTIONIZE THE RECORDING OF BUSINESS EVENTS?

Jim Price and Elaine Bijard are taking an accounting systems course at their local university. They are intrigued with the rapid advances in technology and communication that are occurring in the computer world. Today's lecture was especially thought-provoking. Professor

Hansen stated that it is no longer necessary or even desirable to record business events in sequential order as has been traditionally done in accounting journals. The better approach is to capture all data related to a business event in a computer database, including accounting, marketing, and production data, and to prepare reports for many different users from a single source. The database would be a management information database, not just one for accounting reports.

Jim argues that such an approach would make it more difficult for accountants to keep control of input and ensure the integrity of their financial reports, but Elaine feels that the sooner the accountants recognize the potential, the better they can serve management's varied needs. What advantages and disadvantages do you see coming from a database approach to recording? How can Jim's objections be met?

CASE 2–4

WHEN CASH BASIS IS DIFFERENT FROM ACCRUAL

Alice Guth operates a low-impact aerobics studio. Alice has been in business for 3 years and has always had her financial statements prepared on a cash basis. This year, Alice's accountant has suggested that accrual-based financial statements would give a more accurate picture of the performance of the business. Alice's friend Frank Geller tells her that, in his experience, accrual-based financial statements tell pretty much the same story as cash-basis statements.

Under what circumstances would the cash basis and the accrual basis of accounting yield quite different pictures of a firm's operating performance? Under what circumstances would the cash basis and the accrual basis show approximately the same picture?

CASE 2–5

THE IMPACT OF COMPUTERS ON FINANCIAL REPORTING

Computers have drastically altered the way accounting records are maintained. Almost all businesses now keep at least some of their accounting records on computer. However, the most visible output of the accounting system, the financial information included in the annual report, is still prepared and disseminated the old-fashioned way—on paper. What types of changes in companies' annual reports are likely to occur over the next 10 to 15 years as a result of the increasingly widespread use of computers?

CASE 2–6

BUT I NEED MORE TIMELY INFORMATION!

Julie is successful in her position as a consultant for Worldwide Enterprises. She has selectively invested her money in stocks of several companies. She receives the annual reports and faithfully analyzes them as she was taught in her university accounting class. She is concerned, however, with the impact that events have on the financial reports between years. Julie understands that quarterly reports are available from the companies upon request, but she also understands that they are not audited and thus may not be reliable. She wonders if they can be trusted. Even quarterly reports might not be frequent enough. Wouldn't it be useful if she could use her computer and modem to interrogate the company's computer and obtain information anytime she wanted it?

She decides to write for advice to the chief accountant of the companies in which she holds stock. As chief accountant, how would you address Julie's concerns?

EXERCISES

EXERCISE 2–7

RECORDING TRANSACTIONS IN T-ACCOUNTS

Alaska Supply Corporation, a merchandising firm, prepared the following trial balance as of October 1:

	Debit	Credit
Cash	$200,000	
Accounts Receivable	21,540	
Inventory	32,680	
Land	15,400	
Building	9,000	
Accounts Payable		$ 9,190
Mortgage Payable		23,700
Common Stock		185,000
Retained Earnings		60,730
Totals	$278,620	$278,620

Alaska Supply engaged in the following transactions during October 2002. The company records inventory using the perpetual system.

Oct. 1 Sold merchandise on account to the Plough Corporation for $15,000; terms 2/10, n/30, FOB shipping point. Plough paid $200 freight on the goods. The merchandise cost $7,450.

5 Purchased inventory costing $8,350 on account; terms n/30.

7 Received payment from Plough for goods shipped October 1.

15 The payroll paid for the first half of October was $18,000. (Ignore payroll taxes.)

18 Purchased a machine for $10,400 cash.

22 Declared a dividend of $0.75 per share on 45,000 shares of common stock outstanding.

27 Purchased building and land for $150,000 in cash and a $250,000 mortgage payable, due in 30 years. The land was appraised at $150,000 and the building at $350,000.

1. Prepare T-accounts for all items in the October 1 trial balance and enter the initial balances.
2. Record the October transactions directly to the T-accounts.
3. Prepare a new trial balance as of the end of October.

EXERCISE 2–8

ADJUSTING ENTRIES

In analyzing the accounts of Loma Corporation, the adjusting data listed below are determined on December 31, the end of an annual fiscal period.

(a) The prepaid insurance account shows a debit of $4,800, representing the cost of a 2-year fire insurance policy dated July 1.

(b) On September 1, Rent Revenue was credited for $5,750, representing revenue from subrental for a 5-month period beginning on that date.

(c) Purchase of advertising materials for $2,475 during the year was recorded in the advertising expense account. On December 31, advertising materials costing $475 are on hand.

(d) On November 1, $3,000 was paid for rent for a 5-month period beginning on that date. The rent expense account was debited.

(e) Miscellaneous Office Expense was debited for office supplies of $1,350 purchased during the year. On December 31, office supplies of $250 are on hand.

(f) Interest of $428 is accrued on notes payable.

1. Give the adjusting entry for each item.
2. What sources would provide the information for each adjustment?

EXERCISE 2–9

ADJUSTING AND CORRECTING ENTRIES

Upon inspecting the books and records for Beardall Company for the year ended December 31, 2002, you find the following data.

(a) A receivable of $380 from Clarke Realty is determined to be uncollectible. The company maintains an allowance for doubtful accounts for such losses.

(b) A creditor, E. J. Stanley Co., has just been awarded damages of $2,200 as a result of breach of contract during the current year by Beardall Company. Nothing appears on the books in connection with this matter.

(c) A fire destroyed part of a branch office. Furniture and fixtures that cost $10,200 and had a book value of $7,800 at the time of the fire were completely destroyed. The insurance company has agreed to pay $6,500 under the provisions of the fire insurance policy.

(d) Advances of $1,150 to salespersons have been previously recorded as sales salaries expense.

(e) Machinery at the end of the year shows a balance of $18,460. It is discovered that additions to this account during the year totaled $4,460, but of this amount, $800 should have been recorded as repairs. Depreciation is to be recorded at 10% on machinery owned throughout the year but at one-half this rate on machinery purchased or sold during the year.

Record the entries required to adjust and correct the accounts. (Ignore income tax consequences.)

EXERCISE 2–10

RECONSTRUCTING ADJUSTING ENTRIES

For each situation, reconstruct the adjusting entry that was made to arrive at the ending balance. Assume statements and adjusting entries are prepared only once each year.

1. Prepaid Insurance:
   Balance beginning of year $5,600
   Balance end of year   6,400
   During the year, an additional business insurance policy was purchased. A 2-year premium of $2,500 was paid and charged to Prepaid Insurance.

2. Accumulated Depreciation:
   Balance beginning of year $85,200
   Balance end of year   88,700
   During the year, a depreciable asset that cost $7,500 and had a carrying value of $1,600 was sold for $2,400. The disposal of the asset was recorded correctly.

3. Unearned Rent:
   Balance beginning of year $11,000
   Balance end of year   15,000
   Warehouse quarterly rent received in advance is $18,000. During the year, equipment was rented to another company at an annual rent of $9,000. The quarterly rent payments were credited to Rent Revenue; the annual equipment rental was credited to Unearned Rent.

4. Salaries Payable:
   Balance beginning of year $42,860
   Balance end of year   34,760
   Salaries are paid biweekly. All salary payments during the year were debited to Salaries Expense.

EXERCISE 2–11

ADJUSTING AND CLOSING ENTRIES AND POST-CLOSING TRIAL BALANCE

Accounts of Pioneer Heating Corporation at the end of the first year of operations show the balances listed at the top of the next page. The end-of-year physical inventory is $50,000. Prepaid operating expenses are $4,000, and accrued sales commissions payable are $5,900. Investment revenue receivable is $1,000. Depreciation for the year on buildings is $4,500 and on machinery, $5,000. Federal and state income taxes for the year are estimated at $18,100.

	Debit	Credit
Cash	$ 39,000	$
Investment	50,000	
Land	70,000	
Buildings	180,000	
Machinery	100,000	
Accounts Payable		65,000
Common Stock		320,000
Additional Paid-In Capital		40,000
Sales		590,000
Purchases	280,000	
Sales Commissions	200,000	
General Operating Expenses	101,000	
Investment Revenue		5,000
Totals	$1,020,000	$1,020,000

1. Prepare the necessary entries to adjust and close the books, assuming use of the adjusting method for inventory.
2. Prepare a post-closing trial balance.

EXERCISE 2–12

ADJUSTING AND CLOSING ENTRIES AND POST-CLOSING TRIAL BALANCE

Below is the trial balance for Feigenbaum Company as of December 31.

	Debit	Credit
Cash	$ 58,000	$
Accounts Receivable	402,000	
Inventory	57,000	
Prepaid Expenses	54,000	
Land	65,000	
Plant and Equipment	1,167,000	
Other Assets	1,563,000	
Accounts Payable		147,000
Wages, Interest, and Taxes Payable		215,000
Unearned Revenue		33,000
Long-Term Debt		1,201,000
Other Liabilities		336,000
Common Stock		185,000
Retained Earnings		1,112,000
Dividends	139,000	
Sales		2,801,000
Interest Revenue		23,000
Costs of Goods Sold	1,565,000	
Selling, General, and Administrative Expenses	640,000	
Interest Expense	79,000	
Income Tax Expense	264,000	
Totals	$6,053,000	$6,053,000

Consider the following additional information:

(a) Feigenbaum uses a perpetual inventory system.
(b) The prepaid expenses were paid on September 1 and relate to a 3-year insurance policy that went into effect on September 1.
(c) The unearned revenue relates to rental of an unused portion of the corporate offices. The $33,000 was received on April 1 and represents payment in advance for one year's rental.
(d) Plant and Equipment includes $10,000 for routine equipment repairs that were erroneously recorded as equipment purchases. The repairs were made on December 30.
(e) Other Assets include $8,000 for miscellaneous office supplies, which were purchased in mid-October. An end-of-year count reveals that only $6,500 of the office supplies remain.

(f) Selling, General, and Administrative Expenses incorrectly includes $15,000 for office furniture purchases (Other Assets). The purchases were made on December 30.

(g) Inventory wrongly includes $6,000 of inventory that Feigenbaum had purchased on account but that was returned to the supplier on December 28 because of unsatisfactory quality.

Based on the information provided:

1. Record the entries necessary to adjust the books.
2. Record the entries necessary to close the books. Assume the adjustments in (1) do not affect Income Tax Expense.
3. Prepare a post-closing trial balance.

EXERCISE 2–13

ANALYSIS OF JOURNAL ENTRIES

For each of the journal entries below, write a description of the underlying event.

1. Cash	300	
Accounts Receivable		300
2. Accounts Payable	400	
Inventory		400
3. Cash	5,000	
Loan Payable		5,000
4. Cash	200	
Accounts Receivable	700	
Sales		900
Cost of Goods Sold	550	
Inventory		550
5. Prepaid Insurance	200	
Cash		200
6. Dividends	250	
Dividends Payable		250
7. Retained Earnings	1,000	
Dividends		1,000
8. Insurance Expense	50	
Prepaid Insurance		50
9. Inventory	600	
Cash		150
Accounts Payable		450
10. Allowance for Doubtful Accounts	46	
Accounts Receivable		46
11. Interest Expense	125	
Interest Payable		125
12. Wages Payable	130	
Wages Expense	75	
Cash		205
13. Accounts Payable	500	
Cash		490
Purchase Discounts		10

(handwritten notes: "DECLARED / CLOSING DIVIDENDS" next to 6 and 7; "LAST year didn't reverse" next to 12)

EXERCISE 2–14

ADJUSTING ENTRIES

The following accounts were taken from the trial balance of Cristy Company as of December 31, 2002.

Sales	$90,000
Interest Revenue	5,000
Equipment	46,000
Accumulated Depreciation—Equipment	12,000
Beginning Inventory	$20,000
Advertising Expense	2,000
Selling Expense	6,000
Interest Expense	1,000

Given the information below, make the necessary adjusting entries.

(a) The equipment has an estimated useful life of 9 years and a salvage value of $1,000. Depreciation is calculated using the straight-line method.

(b) Ending inventory is $28,000. Purchases for the year totaled $120,000. The adjusting method for inventory is used.

(c) $2,500 of selling expense has been paid in advance.

(d) Interest of $750 has accrued on notes receivable.

(e) $620 of advertising expense was incorrectly debited to selling expense.

EXERCISE 2–15

ADJUSTING ENTRIES

The data listed below were obtained from an analysis of the accounts of Noble Distributor Company as of March 31, 2002, in preparation of the annual report. Noble records current transactions in nominal accounts. What are the appropriate adjusting entries?

(a) Prepaid Insurance has a balance of $14,100. Noble has the following policies in force:

Policy	Date	Term	Cost	Coverage
A	1/1/02	2 years	$ 3,600	Shop equipment
B	12/1/01	6 months	1,800	Delivery equipment
C	7/1/01	3 years	12,000	Buildings

(b) Unearned Subscription Revenue has a balance of $56,250. The following subscriptions were collected in the current year. There are no other unexpired subscriptions.

Effective Date	Amount	Term
July 1, 2001	$27,000	1 year
October 1, 2001	22,200	1 year
January 1, 2002	28,800	1 year
April 1, 2002	20,700	1 year

(c) Interest Payable has a balance of $825. Noble owes a 10%, 90-day note for $45,000 dated March 1, 2002.

(d) Supplies has a balance of $2,190. An inventory of supplies revealed a total of $1,410.

(e) Salaries Payable has a balance of $9,750. The payroll for the 5-day workweek ended April 3 totaled $11,250.

EXERCISE 2–16

ANALYZING ADJUSTING ENTRIES

Computer Consulting Company uses the asset-and-liability approach in accounting for prepaid expenses and unearned revenues. Selected account balances at the end of the current and prior year are presented below. Accrued expenses and revenues are adjusted only at year-end.

	Adjusted Balances December 31, 2001	Adjusted Balances December 31, 2002
Prepaid Rent	$ 6,200	$3,600
Salaries and Wages Payable	1,900	4,500
Unearned Consulting Fees	16,400	6,400
Interest Receivable	650	1,800

During 2002, Computer Consulting paid $10,000 for rent and $50,000 for wages. $108,000 was received for consulting fees, and $2,400 was received as interest.

1. Provide the entries that were made at December 31, 2002, to adjust the accounts to the year-end balances above.

2. Determine the proper amount of Rent Expense, Salaries and Wages Expense, Consulting Fees Revenue, and Interest Revenue to be reported on the current-year income statement.

EXERCISE 2–17

CLOSING ENTRIES

An accountant for Jolley, Inc., a merchandising enterprise, has just finished posting all the year-end adjusting entries to the ledger accounts and now wishes to close the appropriate account balances in preparation for the new period.

1. For each of the accounts listed, indicate whether the year-end balance should be: (a) carried forward to the new period, (b) closed by debiting the account, or (c) closed by crediting the account. Assume Jolley uses a perpetual inventory system.

(a)	Cash	$ 25,000
(b)	Sales	75,000
(c)	Dividends	3,500
(d)	Inventory	7,500
(e)	Selling Expenses	7,900
(f)	Capital Stock	100,000
(g)	Wages Expense	14,400
(h)	Dividends Payable	4,000
(i)	Cost of Goods Sold	26,500
(j)	Accounts Payable	12,000
(k)	Accounts Receivable	140,000
(l)	Prepaid Insurance	16,000
(m)	Interest Receivable	1,500
(n)	Sales Discounts	4,200
(o)	Interest Revenue	6,500
(p)	Supplies	8,000
(q)	Retained Earnings	6,500
(r)	Accumulated Depreciation	2,000
(s)	Depreciation Expense	1,800

2. Give the necessary closing entries.
3. What was Jolley's net income (loss) for the period?

EXERCISE 2–18

CLOSING ENTRIES

Lennon's Tannery Corporation reports revenues and expenses for the period of $196,400 and $80,200, respectively. Give the remaining entries to close the books assuming the ledger reports Additional Paid-In Capital of $250,000 and Retained Earnings of $100,000. Dividends during the year amounting to $32,500 were recorded in a dividends account.

EXERCISE 2–19

DETERMINING INCOME FROM EQUITY ACCOUNT ANALYSIS

An analysis of Huffman, Inc., disclosed changes in account balances for 2002 and the supplementary data listed below. From these data, calculate the net income or loss for 2002. (Hint: Net income can be thought of as the increase in net assets resulting from operations.)

Cash	$21,000	increase
Accounts receivable	25,000	increase
Inventory	10,000	decrease
Equipment	70,000	increase
Accounts payable	5,000	decrease

Huffman sold 5,000 shares of its $5 par stock for $8 per share and received cash in full. Dividends of $15,000 were paid in cash during the year. Huffman borrowed $50,000 from the bank and made interest payments of $5,000. Huffman had no other loans payable. Interest of $1,000 was payable at December 31, 2002. There was no interest payable at December 31, 2001. Equipment of $20,000 was donated by stockholders during the year.

EXERCISE 2–20

ACCRUAL ERRORS

Loring Tools, Inc., failed to make year-end adjustments to record accrued salaries and recognize interest receivable on investments over the last 3 years as follows:

	2000	2001	2002
Accrued salaries	$25,000	$19,000	$32,000
Interest receivable	10,500	8,500	13,200

What impact would the correction of these errors have on the net income for these 3 years? Ignore income taxes.

EXERCISE 2–21

SPECIAL JOURNALS

Caddy's Inc. uses a general journal, sales journal, cash receipts journal, check register, and voucher register. For each transaction below, indicate the appropriate journal(s) or register to be used.

(a) Make a credit sale.
(b) Collect cash on an account receivable.
(c) Record doubtful accounts expense.
(d) Write a check for payroll expense.
(e) Purchase materials on account.
(f) Give a discount on a sale.
(g) Sell equipment on credit.
(h) Make a cash sale.
(i) Borrow $3,000 from the bank.
(j) Record adjusting and closing entries.
(k) Pay a supplier with a check.
(l) Record accrued interest payable.
(m) Sell truck for cash.
(n) Record depreciation expense.
(o) Pay back loan.

EXERCISE 2–22

VOUCHER REGISTER

On July 15, vouchers for payment of the following items were approved by the chief financial officer of Lorenz Company:

Amount	Payee	Purpose
$1,530	Outland Hardware	Payment for inventory received
4,000	Locker Bank	Repayment of loan principal
350	Thom Insurance	Payment in advance for insurance
8,790	Payroll	Gross pay = $10,000; taxes payable = $1,210
1,240	Better Electric	Last month's utilities
2,600	Rands Supply	Payment for inventory received
670	Frank Elsholz	Customer refund for sales return
1,210	U.S. Government	Remittance of taxes withheld
3,000	Thurston Howell	Advance on salary

Prepare a voucher register and record the approved vouchers described above. The last voucher prepared on July 14 had the number 1022. Lorenz uses a periodic inventory system.

EXERCISE 2–23

VOUCHER REGISTER AND CHECK REGISTER

All of the vouchers described in Exercise 2–22 were paid by check on July 16, starting with check number 439. A 2% purchase discount was taken on the payment to Rands Supply. Based on the information provided:

1. Complete the voucher register prepared in Exercise 2–22 showing the payment of the vouchers by check.
2. Prepare a check register and enter the checks paid on July 16.

EXERCISE 2–24

CASH RECEIPTS JOURNAL

Mandelbrot Graphics makes most of its sales on credit. Data from the October sales journal are given below:

Date	Invoice No.	Account Debited	Acct. Rec. (Dr.) Sales (Cr.)
10/2	9045	Franklin Printing	$3,275
10/8	9046	Simpson Company	2,350
10/15	9047	Midstate University	4,780
10/18	9048	Topper Oil, Inc.	565
10/24	9049	Julia Company	1,700
10/29	9050	Fractal Design	3,675

During November, Mandelbrot received payment for all of the credit sales made in October. Julia Company was given a 3% sales discount. Mandelbrot's cash sales during November totaled $380. In addition, during November Mandelbrot received full payment on a $5,000 note receivable, along with $450 in interest. Also, Mandelbrot received a $750 refund for an insurance policy that had been canceled. Prepare a cash receipts journal for Mandelbrot Graphics for November.

PROBLEMS

PROBLEM 2–25

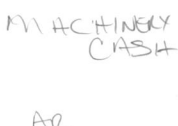

JOURNAL ENTRIES

Selfish Gene Company is a merchandising firm. The following events occurred during the month of May. (Note: Selfish Gene maintains a perpetual inventory system.)

May 1 Received $40,000 cash as new stockholder investment.

3 Purchased inventory costing $8,000 on account from Dawkins Company; terms 2/10, n/30.

4 Purchased office supplies for $500 cash.

4 Held an office party for the retiring accountant. Balloons, hats, and refreshments cost $150 and were paid for with office staff contributions.

5 Sold merchandise costing $7,500 on account for $14,000 to Richard Company; terms 3/15, n/30.

8 Paid employee wages of $2,000. Gross wages were $2,450; taxes totaling $450 were withheld.

9 Hired a new accountant; agreed to a first-year salary of $28,000.

9 Paid $1,500 for newspaper advertising.

10 Received payment from Richard Company.

12 Purchased a machine for $6,400 cash.

15 Declared a cash dividend totaling $25,000.

18 Sold merchandise costing $13,000 for $3,000 cash and $21,000 on account to Feynman Company; terms n/30.

19 Paid Dawkins Company account in full.

22   Company executives appeared on the cover of a national newsmagazine. Related article extolled Selfish Gene's labor practices, environmental concerns, and customer service.

23   Market value of Selfish Gene's common stock rose by $150,000.

25   Purchased a building for $15,000 cash and a $135,000 mortgage payable.

29   Paid dividends declared on May 15.

Instructions:

1. Record the preceding events in general journal form.
2. Which event do you think had the most significant economic impact on Selfish Gene Company? Are all economically relevant events recorded in the financial records?

PROBLEM 2-26

ACCOUNT CLASSIFICATION AND DEBIT/CREDIT RELATIONSHIP

Instructions: Using the format provided, identify for each account:

1. Whether the account will appear on a balance sheet (B/S), income statement (I/S), or neither (N)
2. Whether the account is an asset (A), liability (L), owners' equity (OE), revenue (R), expense (E), or other (O)
3. Whether the account is real or nominal
4. Whether the account will be "closed" or left "open" at year-end
5. Whether the account normally has a debit (Dr.) or a credit (Cr.) balance.

Account Title	(1) B/S, I/S, N	(2) A, L, OE, R, E, O	(3) Real or Nominal	(4) Closed or Open	(5) Debit (Dr.) or Credit (Cr.)
Example: Cash	B/S	A	Real	Open	Dr.

(a) Unearned Rent Revenue
(b) Accounts Receivable
(c) Inventory
(d) Accounts Payable
(e) Prepaid Rent
(f) Mortgage Payable
(g) Sales
(h) Cost of Goods Sold
(i) Dividends
(j) Dividends Payable
(k) Interest Receivable
(l) Wages Expense
(m) Interest Revenue
(n) Supplies
(o) Accumulated Depreciation
(p) Retained Earnings
(q) Discount on Bonds Payable
(r) Goodwill
(s) Additional Paid-In Capital

PROBLEM 2-27

ADJUSTING ENTRIES

On December 31, the Philips Company noted the following transactions that occurred during 2002, some or all of which might require adjustment to the books.

(a) Payment to suppliers of $2,900 was made for purchases on account during the year and was not recorded.

(b) Building and land were purchased on January 2 for $175,000. The building's fair market value was $120,000 at the time of purchase. The building is being depreciated over a 20-year life using the straight-line method, assuming no salvage value.

(c) Of the $34,000 in Accounts Receivable, 2.5% is estimated to be uncollectible. Currently, Allowance for Doubtful Accounts shows a debit balance of $460.

(d) On August 1, $40,000 was loaned to a customer on a 6-month note with interest at an annual rate of 12%.

(e) During 2002, Philips received $8,500 in advance for services, 80% of which will be performed in 2003. The $8,500 was credited to sales revenue.

(f) The interest expense account was debited for all interest charges incurred during the year and shows a balance of $1,100. However, of this amount, $600 represents a discount on a 60-day note payable, due January 30, 2003.

Instructions:

1. Give the necessary adjusting entries to bring the books up to date.
2. Indicate the net change in income as a result of the foregoing adjustments.

PROBLEM 2–28

ANALYSIS OF ADJUSTING ENTRIES

The accountant for Save More Company made the following adjusting entries on December 31, 2002.

(a)	Prepaid Rent	1,800	
	Rent Expense		1,800
(b)	Advertising Materials	1,700	
	Advertising Expense		1,700
(c)	Rent Revenue	900	
	Unearned Revenue		900
(d)	Office Supplies	1,000	
	Office Supplies Expense		1,000
(e)	Prepaid Insurance	1,050	
	Insurance Expense		1,050

Further information is provided as follows:

(a) Rent is paid every October 1.

(b) Advertising materials are paid at one time (June 1) and are used evenly throughout the year.

(c) Rent is received in advance every March 1.

(d) Office supplies are purchased every July 1 and used evenly throughout the year.

(e) Yearly insurance premium is payable each August 1.

Instructions: For each adjusting entry, indicate the original transaction entry that was recorded.

PROBLEM 2–29

ADJUSTING ENTRIES

The bookkeeper for the Irwin Wholesale Electric Co. records all revenue and expense items in nominal accounts during the period. The following balances, among others, are listed on the trial balance at the end of the fiscal period, December 31, 2002, before accounts have been adjusted:

	Dr. (Cr.)
Accounts Receivable	$152,000
Allowance for Doubtful Accounts	(1,000)
Interest Receivable	2,800
Discount on Notes Payable	300
Prepaid Real Estate and Personal Property Tax	1,800
Salaries and Wages Payable	(4,000)
Discount on Notes Receivable	(2,800)
Unearned Rent Revenue	(1,700)

Inspection of the company's records reveals the following as of December 31, 2002:

(a) Uncollectible accounts are estimated at 4% of the accounts receivable balance.

(b) The accrued interest on investments totals $2,200.

(c) The company borrows cash by discounting its own notes at the bank. Discounts on notes payable at the end of 2002 are $1,400.

(d) Prepaid real estate and personal property taxes are $1,800, the same as at the end of 2001.

(e) Accrued salaries and wages are $6,200.

(f) The company accepts notes from customers, giving its customers credit for the face of the note less a charge for interest. At the end of each period, any interest applicable to the succeeding period is reported as a discount. Discounts on notes receivable at the end of 2002 are $1,900.

(g) Part of the company's properties had been sublet on September 15, 2001, at a rental of $3,000 per month. The arrangement was terminated at the end of one year.

Instructions: Give the adjusting entries required to bring the books up to date.

PROBLEM 2–30

CASH TO ACCRUAL ADJUSTING ENTRIES AND INCOME STATEMENT

Gee Enterprises records all transactions on the cash basis. Greg Gee, company accountant, prepared the following income statement at the end of the company's first year of operations.

Gee Enterprises
Income Statement
For the Year Ended December 31, 2002

Sales		$252,000
Selling and administrative expenses:		
Salaries expense	$78,000	
Rent expense	45,000	
Utilities expense	29,000	
Equipment	30,000	
Commission expense	37,800	
Insurance expense	6,000	
Interest expense	3,000	228,800
Net income		$ 23,200

You have been asked to prepare an income statement on the accrual basis. The following information is given to you to assist in the preparation.

a.   Amounts due from customers at year-end were $28,000. Of this amount, $3,000 will probably not be collected.

b.   Salaries of $11,000 for December 2002 were paid on January 5, 2003. Ignore payroll taxes.

c.   Gee rents its building for $3,000 a month, payable quarterly in advance. The contract was signed on January 1, 2002.

d.   The bill for December's utility costs of $2,700 was paid January 10, 2003.

e.   Equipment of $30,000 was purchased on January 1, 2002. The expected life is 5 years, no salvage value. Assume straight-line depreciation.

f.   Commissions of 15% of sales are paid on the same day cash is received from customers.

g.   A 1-year insurance policy was issued on company assets on July 1, 2002. Premiums are paid annually in advance.

h.   Gee borrowed $50,000 for one year on May 1, 2002. Interest payments based on an annual rate of 12% are made quarterly, beginning with the first payment on August 1, 2002.

i.   The income tax rate is 40%. No prepayments of income taxes were made during 2002.

Instructions:

1.   Prepare adjusting entries to convert the books from a cash to an accrual basis.
2.   Prepare the income statement for the year ended December 31, 2002, based on the entries in (1).

PROBLEM 2–31

ADJUSTING AND CLOSING ENTRIES

Account balances taken from the ledger of the Builders' Supply Corporation on December 31, 2002, before adjustment, are listed below. Information relating to adjustments on December 31, 2002, follows:

(a)   The inventory on hand is $87,570. Inventory and related accounts are adjusted through Cost of Goods Sold.
(b)   Allowance for Doubtful Accounts is to be increased to a balance of $3,000.
(c)   Buildings are depreciated at the rate of 5% per year.
(d)   Accrued selling expenses are $3,840.
(e)   There are supplies of $780 on hand.
(f)   Prepaid insurance relating to 2003 totals $720.
(g)   Accrued interest on long-term investments is $240.
(h)   Accrued real estate and payroll taxes are $900.
(i)   Accrued interest on the mortgage is $480.
(j)   Income taxes are estimated to be 20% of the income before income taxes.

Cash	$ 24,000
Accounts Receivable	72,000
Allowance for Doubtful Accounts	1,380
Inventory, December 31, 2001	62,000
Long-Term Investments	15,400
Land	69,600
Buildings	72,000
Accumulated Depreciation—Buildings	19,800
Accounts Payable	35,000
Mortgage Payable	68,800
Capital Stock, $10 par	180,000
Retained Earnings, December 31, 2001	14,840
Dividends	13,400
Sales	246,000
Sales Returns	4,360
Sales Discounts	5,400
Purchases	138,480
Purchase Discounts	2,140
Freight-In	3,600
Selling Expenses	49,440
Office Expenses	21,680
Insurance Expense	1,440
Supplies Expense	5,200
Taxes—Real Estate and Payroll	7,980
Interest Revenue	660
Interest Expense	2,640

Instructions:

1.   Prepare a trial balance.
2.   Journalize the adjustments.
3.   Journalize the closing entries.
4.   Prepare a post-closing trial balance.

(Note: Although not required, the use of a work sheet is recommended for the solution of this problem.)

PROBLEM 2–32

ADJUSTING AND CLOSING ENTRIES AND POST-CLOSING TRIAL BALANCE

Kwon International Corporation
Unadjusted Trial Balance
December 31, 2002

	Debit	Credit
Cash	$ 22,500	$
Accounts Receivable	24,000	
Allowance for Doubtful Accounts		240
Inventory	45,300	
Equipment	210,000	
Accumulated Depreciation—Equipment		42,000
Accounts Payable		28,000
Notes Payable		80,000
Wages Payable		10,000
Income Taxes Payable		8,900
Common Stock		50,000
Retained Earnings		27,310
Sales Revenue		270,000
Interest Revenue		8,000
Cost of Goods Sold	171,250	
Wages Expense	28,000	
Interest Expense	1,500	
Utilities Expense	5,000	
Insurance Expense	2,000	
Advertising Expense	6,000	
Income Tax Expense	8,900	
	$524,450	$524,450

Data for adjustments at December 31, 2002, are as follows:

(a) Kwon International uses a perpetual inventory system.

(b) An analysis of Accounts Receivable reveals that the appropriate year-end balance in the Allowance for Doubtful Accounts is $700.

(c) Equipment depreciation for the year totaled $45,000.

(d) A recheck of the inventory count revealed that goods costing $4,300 were wrongly excluded from ending inventory. The goods in question were not shipped until January 3, 2003. A related receivable for $6,000 was also mistakenly recorded.

(e) Interest on the note payable has not been accrued. The note was issued on March 1, 2002, and the interest rate is 15%.

(f) The balance in Insurance Expense represents $2,000 that was paid for a 1-year policy on October 1. The policy went into effect on October 1.

(g) Dividends totaling $5,600 were declared on December 25. The dividends will not be paid until January 15, 2003. No entry was made.

Instructions:

1. Journalize the necessary adjusting entries. (Ignore income tax effects.)
2. Journalize the necessary closing entries.
3. Prepare a post-closing trial balance.
4. Can a company pay dividends in a year in which it has a net loss? Can a company owe income taxes in a year in which it has a net loss?

PROBLEM 2–33

PREPARATION OF WORK SHEET

Account balances taken from the ledger of Royal Distributing Co. on December 31, 2002, follow:

Cash	$ 35,000
Accounts Receivable	91,000
Allowance for Doubtful Accounts	1,800
Inventory, December 31, 2001	84,000
Long-Term Investments	27,500
Land	53,400
Buildings	112,500
Accumulated Depreciation—Buildings	26,780
Accounts Payable	47,300
Mortgage Payable	99,500
Capital Stock, $5 par	175,000
Retained Earnings, December 31, 2001	14,840
Dividends	9,670
Sales	359,000
Sales Returns	12,890
Sales Discounts	7,540
Purchases	159,000
Purchase Discounts	6,780
Freight-In	6,300
Selling Expenses	62,350
Office Expenses	38,900
Insurance Expense	14,000
Supplies Expense	4,800
Taxes—Real Estate and Payroll	9,500
Interest Revenue	550
Interest Expense	3,200

Information relating to adjustments on December 31, 2002, follows:

(a) The inventory on hand is $92,000. Inventory and related accounts are adjusted through Cost of Goods Sold.

(b) Allowance for Doubtful Accounts is to be increased by $2,000.

(c) Buildings have a salvage value of $7,500. They are being depreciated at the rate of 10% per year.

(d) Accrued selling expenses are $8,600.

(e) There are supplies of $1,250 on hand.

(f) Prepaid insurance relating to 2003 totals $4,000.

(g) Total interest revenue earned in 2002 is $1,400.

(h) Accrued real estate and payroll taxes are $2,340.

(i) Accrued interest on the mortgage is $1,780.

(j) Income tax is estimated to be 40% of income.

Instructions: Prepare a work sheet showing the net income and balance sheet totals for the year ending December 31, 2002.

PROBLEM 2–34

PREPARATION OF WORK SHEET AND ADJUSTING AND CLOSING ENTRIES
The following account balances are taken from the general ledger of the Whitni Corporation on December 31, 2002, the end of its fiscal year. The corporation was organized January 2, 1999.

Cash	$40,250
Notes Receivable	16,500
Accounts Receivable	63,000
Allowance for Doubtful Accounts (credit balance)	650
Inventory, December 31, 2002	94,700
Land	80,000
Buildings	247,600
Accumulated Depreciation—Buildings	18,000
Furniture and Fixtures	15,000
Accumulated Depreciation—Furniture and Fixtures	9,000

Notes Payable	$ 18,000
Accounts Payable	72,700
Common Stock, $100 par	240,000
Retained Earnings	129,125
Sales	760,000
Sales Returns and Allowances	17,000
Cost of Goods Sold	465,800
Heat, Light, and Power	16,700
Property Tax Expense	10,200
Salaries and Wages Expense	89,000
Sales Commissions	73,925
Insurance Expense	18,000
Interest Revenue	2,600
Interest Expense	2,400

Data for adjustments at December 31, 2002, are as follows:

(a) Depreciation (to nearest month for additions): furniture and fixtures, 10%; buildings, 4%.

Additions to the buildings costing $150,000 were completed June 30, 2002.

(b) Allowance for Doubtful Accounts is to be increased to a balance of $2,500.

(c) Accrued expenses: sales commissions, $700; interest on notes payable, $45; property taxes, $6,000.

(d) Prepaid expenses: insurance, $3,200.

(e) Accrued revenue: interest on notes receivable, $750.

(f) The following information is also to be recorded:
   (1) On December 30, the board of directors declared a quarterly dividend of $1.50 per share on common stock, payable January 25, 2003, to stockholders of record January 15, 2003.
   (2) Income taxes for 2002 are estimated at $15,000.
   (3) The only charges to Retained Earnings during the year resulted from the declaration of the regular quarterly dividends.

Instructions:

1. Prepare an eight-column work sheet. There should be a pair of columns each for trial balance, adjustments, income statement, and balance sheet.
2. Prepare all the journal entries necessary to record the effects of the foregoing information and to adjust and close the books of the corporation.

PROBLEM 2–35

USING SPECIAL JOURNALS

West Mountain Inc., a fruit wholesaler, records business transactions in the following books of original entry: general journal (J); voucher register (VR); check register (CR); sales journal (SJ); and cash receipts journal (CRJ). West Mountain recorded and filed the following business documents:

(a) Sales invoices for sales on account totaling $4,600.
(b) The day's cash register tape showing receipts for cash sales at $700.
(c) A list of cash amounts received on various customers' accounts totaling $2,930. Sales discounts taken were $30.
(d) The telephone bill for $60 payable in one week.
(e) Vendors' invoices for $5,000 worth of fruit received.
(f) Check stub for payment of last week's purchases from All-Growers Farms, $5,940. Terms were 1/10, n/30, and payment was made within the discount period.
(g) Check stub for repayment of a $10,000, 90-day note to Mercantile Bank, $10,300.
(h) A letter notifying West Mountain that Littex Markets, a customer, has declared bankruptcy. All creditors will receive 10 cents on every dollar due. Littex owes West Mountain $1,300.

Instructions:

1. Indicate the books of original entry in which West Mountain recorded each of the business transactions. (Use the designated abbreviations.)
2. Record the debits and credits for each entry as though only a general journal were used. Use account titles implied by the voucher system.

PROBLEM 2-36

USING SPECIAL JOURNALS

A fire destroyed Fong Company's journals. However, the general ledger and accounts receivable subsidiary ledger were saved. An inspection of the ledgers reveals the following information:

GENERAL LEDGER

Cash (Acct. No. 11)					
May 1 Bal.	8,200				
31	7,338				

Sales (Acct. No. 41)		
	May 31	5,050
	31	4,500

Sales Discounts (Acct. No. 42)	
May 3	12

Accounts Receivable (Acct. No. 12)			
May 1 Bal.	3,100	May 31	2,850
31	5,050		

ACCOUNTS RECEIVABLE SUBSIDIARY LEDGER

Customer A		
May 1 Bal.	290	
5	500	

Customer B			
May 1 Bal.	1,250	May 13	1,000
5	400		

Customer C	
May 2	1,450

Customer D			
May 1 Bal.	1,560	May 11	650

Customer E			
May 2	1,200	May 3	1,200
12	1,500		

Fong's credit terms are 1/10, n/30.

Instructions: Reconstruct the sales and cash receipts journals from the information given.

PROBLEM 2-37

VOUCHER AND CHECK REGISTERS

Prepare a voucher register and a check register for Bethe Company and record the following transactions. The last voucher used was #9847, and the last check used was #562.

June 1   Paid voucher #9846 (for office supplies from JOK Supplies), $560. No discount was taken. (Record this in the check register only.)

     2   Purchased inventory on account from Nimitz Company, $1,800; terms 1/10, n/30. Bethe uses the periodic inventory method.

     2   Received utilities bill from NiStar Electric for May, $985; terms 3/15, n/30.

     4   Paid voucher #9847 to the Archer Journal for advertising, $400. No discount was taken. (Record this in the check register only.)

     8   Paid Nimitz Company account in full.

     8   Authorized customer refund to Spruance Company, $1,150.

     8   Paid refund to Spruance Company.

June   9   Authorized payment of cash dividends previously declared, $2,500. (No voucher was prepared at declaration date.)

10   Received notice of mortgage payment due to ATP Financial, $5,000; $4,600 represents interest and $400 represents principal. Payment was authorized.

12   Paid utility bill.

12   Made mortgage payment.

13   Approved loan to Ken Nelson, an officer of the company, $6,000.

15   Disbursed loan to Ken Nelson.

15   Approved payroll: gross pay, $11,000; taxes withheld, $2,000; health insurance premiums withheld, $980.

15   Paid net payroll.

17   Signed a contract for a fire insurance policy with Halsey Casualty. The policy is for 1 year, costs $4,000, and goes into effect on June 18.

18   Paid for fire insurance.

19   Purchased inventory on account from Wainwright Company, $2,300; terms 2/10, n/30.

22   Paid cash dividend.

30   Approved payroll: gross pay, $11,500; taxes withheld, $2,200; health insurance premiums withheld, $980.

30   Paid net payroll.

30   Authorized and paid taxes withheld for June to U.S. government.

30   Authorized and paid health insurance premiums withheld for June to Unicare Insurance.

COMPETENCY ENHANCEMENT OPPORTUNITIES

▶ Deciphering Actual Financial Statements

▶ Writing Assignment

▶ Research Project

▶ The Debate

▶ Ethical Dilemma

▶ Cumulative Spreadsheet Analysis

▶ Internet Search

Accounting is more than just doing textbook problems. This expanded competency material provides practice in critical thinking, oral and written communication, research, teamwork, and consideration of ethical issues.

▶ **DECIPHERING ACTUAL FINANCIAL STATEMENTS**
• Deciphering 2–1 (Walt Disney Company)
The income statement and the balance sheet for THE WALT DISNEY COMPANY are presented in Appendix A. Reconstruct the company's adjusted trial balance as of September 30, 1998.

▶ **WRITING ASSIGNMENT**
• I am going to be an accountant—not a bookkeeper!
Some accounting students feel that the mechanics of accounting (journal entries and T-accounts) are for bookkeepers. Because these students are training to be accountants, they see no need to spend a great deal of time studying these mechanics.

In one page, explain why accountants must have a thorough understanding of journal entries and T-accounts even though these tools are mostly the domain of bookkeepers.

▶ **RESEARCH PROJECT**
• How have computers changed the accounting process?
Your group is to interview practicing accountants to determine how computers have changed the accounting process. Report back to the class either orally or in writing. Proceed as follows:
1. Identify two local companies—one large and one small.
2. Contact the accounting department of each company, identify yourself, and ask for an appointment with a member of the accounting staff.
3. In your interview, find out as much as you can about how computers influence the accounting process. Ask questions, such as:
   • Does the company use computerized accounting software?
   • If the company does not use a computerized software package, ask why.
   • Assuming the company uses some sort of accounting software, ask what the software does that cannot be done manually.
   • What benefits does the company realize as a result of using computerized accounting software?
▶ • Does the accounting software package produce more useful information than was (or would be) provided under a manual system? What are some examples?
4. Prepare your report.

THE DEBATE
• No more debits and credits!
Some accounting academics and professionals argue that debits and credits are relics from the 15th century. Advocates of this position feel that computer spreadsheets and accounting software packages have made debits and credits obsolete, and accountants should no longer have to be constrained by the use of these terms. For example, most popular computer financial software packages (like Intuit's Quicken and Microsoft's Money) allow users to create balance sheets and statements of cash flows without ever learning the terms debit and credit.
Divide your group into two teams.
• One team is to prepare a 5-minute oral presentation explaining why the use of the terms debit and credit are still useful.
▶ • The second team is to prepare a 5-minute presentation explaining why current computer technology allows us to do away with the terms debit and credit.

ETHICAL DILEMMA
• The art of making adjusting entries
Refer back to the section of the chapter entitled "Preparing Adjusting Entries." Who determines how long buildings and furniture and equipment are to last? Who determines the dollar amount of accounts receivable that are doubtful?
Suppose we were to change our asset depreciation on the buildings and the furniture and equipment from 5% and 10% to 4% and 8%, respectively. What would be the effect on net income? Would it increase or decrease? Likewise, suppose our estimate of the balance in Allowance for Doubtful Accounts was reduced to $1,000. What would be the effect on net income?
Answer the following: Is the adjusting entry process an exact science where accountants can determine exactly how well a company has done for a period? Or is accounting an
▶ art that requires significant judgment on the part of the accountant?
What are the dangers for the accountant when making an estimate in an area (like doubtful accounts) where significant judgment is required?

CUMULATIVE SPREADSHEET ANALYSIS
Beginning with this chapter, each chapter in this text will include a spreadsheet assignment based on the financial information of a fictitious company named Skywalker Enterprises. The

assignments start simple—in this chapter you are not asked to do much more than set up financial statement formats and input some numbers. In succeeding chapters, the spreadsheets will get more complex so that by the end of the course you will have constructed a spreadsheet that allows you to forecast operating cash flows for 5 years in the future, adjust your forecast depending on the operating parameters that you think are most reasonable, and analyze the impact of a variety of accounting assumptions on the reported numbers.

So, let's get started with the first spreadsheet assignment.

1. The following numbers are for Skywalker Enterprises for 2002.

Short-Term Loans Payable	$ 30	Long-Term Debt	$ 621
Unearned Revenue	35	Investment Securities (current)	70
Interest Expense	27	Income Tax Expense	12
Paid-In Capital	150	Retained Earnings (as of 1/1/02)	93
Cash	30	Receivables	81
Other Long-Term Liabilities	253	Long-Term Investments	250
Dividends	0	Sales	2,100
Accumulated Depreciation	27	Accounts Payable	222
Other Long-Term Assets	40	Other Equity	72
Inventory	459	Property, Plant, and Equipment	597
Cost of Goods Sold	1,557	Other Operating Expenses	480

Your assignment is to create a spreadsheet containing a balance sheet and an income statement for Skywalker Enterprises.

2. Skywalker is wondering what its balance sheet and income statement would have looked like if the following numbers were changed as indicated.

	Change	
	From	**To**
Sales	$2,100	$2,190
Cost of Goods Sold	1,557	1,650
Other Operating Expenses	480	495

Create a second spreadsheet with the numbers changed as indicated. Note: After making these changes, your balance sheet may no longer balance. Eliminate any discrepancy by increasing or decreasing Short-Term Loans Payable as much as necessary.

► **INTERNET SEARCH**

Let's go take a look at one of the most profitable companies around—MICROSOFT. The Internet address is www.microsoft.com. Once you have accessed Microsoft's Web site, complete the following exercises.

1. Locate Microsoft's "Shareholder Information" page. What information is contained at this site that would interest a Microsoft shareholder?
2. Find Microsoft's latest earnings press release. How well has the company done compared to last year?
3. Can you locate information on Microsoft's history? If so, identify the important events in the company's past.
4. Locate Microsoft's most recent annual report. In past years, readers have been able to download the financial statements into an Excel spreadsheet file. Do this. Once you have downloaded the files, call up your spreadsheet program and prepare a trial balance for Microsoft for the most recent fiscal period using the information you downloaded.

chapter 3
The Balance Sheet and Notes

"Every man in uniform gets a bottle of Coca-Cola for 5 cents, wherever he is and whatever it costs." So said Robert Woodruff, COCA-COLA chairman, as American soldiers entered the fighting in World War II. By this time, Coca-Cola was such a part of American life that Coke also became part of the war machine. In 1943, General Dwight Eisenhower requested the necessary equipment and bottles to refill 10 million Coca-Cola's for soldiers in the European theater. Sixty-four bottling plants were operated under the direction of Allied Headquarters in North Africa during the war.

From its beginnings in Atlanta, Georgia, in which 1886 sales averaged nine drinks per day, to its worldwide presence, in which 1998 sales averaged 600 million servings per day, Coca-Cola has grown to the point where it is now the most recognizable trademark on the planet—recognized by 94% of the world's population.

Pharmacist Dr. John S. Pemberton mixed the first kettle of Coca-Cola in his backyard in 1886. Frank Robinson, Pemberton's bookkeeper and partner, named the drink and came up with the unique script that is Coke's signature. Bottled Coke was first offered in 1894, and five years later, Joseph Whitehead and Benjamin Thomas purchased the exclusive rights to bottle Coca-Cola for $1. Within 20 years, 1,000 bottlers around the world were bottling Coke. In 1915, the contoured bottle that symbolizes Coca-Cola was developed, and its shape was finally granted a patent in 1977.

With Coca-Cola's remarkable success, one must wonder what company executives were thinking in 1985 when an historic blunder was made. In April of that year, the Company changed its secret formula, terminated the original Coke, and introduced "new" Coke. The public reaction was overwhelmingly negative, with consumers organizing and calling for the return of the original. After four months, the company reintroduced the original formula as "Coca-Cola Classic."

Today, about 7,000 soft drink servings from The Coca-Cola Company are consumed around the world every second of every day.

Owning the most valuable trademark in the world (Coke's market value in April 1999 exceeded $160 billion), one might expect Coca-Cola's balance sheet to contain a significant amount assigned to this asset. One look at the company's balance sheet (see Exhibit 3–1), however, reveals that virtually nothing is recorded on Coke's balance sheet related to its intangible assets.

As illustrated with the trademark example, Coke's balance sheet is interesting, as much for what it excludes as for what it includes. Consider the following additional items:

- Coke owns 42% of Coca-Cola Enterprises, a bottling company. Coca-Cola Enterprises has $18.7 billion in liabilities, none of which is reported in Coke's balance sheet. Coke also owns significant percentages of other bottlers who together report over $13 billion in liabilities, again none of which is reported by Coke.
- Coke estimates it owes current and former employees over $2 billion in pensions and other postretirement benefits. Where is that amount reported on the balance sheet?

1

Describe the specific elements of the balance sheet (assets, liabilities, and owners' equity), and prepare a balance sheet with assets and liabilities properly classified into current and noncurrent categories.

2

Identify the different formats used to present balance sheet data.

3

Analyze a company's performance and financial position through the computation of financial ratios.

4

Recognize the importance of the notes to the financial statements, and outline the types of disclosures made in the notes.

5

Understand the major limitations of the balance sheet.

EXHIBIT 3-1 | Coca-Cola's Balance Sheet

The Coca-Cola Company and Subsidiaries
Consolidated Balance Sheets
December 31, 1997 and 1998
(In millions except share data)

ASSETS

CURRENT ASSETS		
Cash and cash equivalents	$ 1,648	$ 1,737
Marketable securities	159	106
	$ 1,807	$ 1,843
Trade accounts receivable, less allowances of $10 in 1998 and $23 in 1997	1,666	1,639
Inventories	890	959
Prepaid expenses and other assets	2,017	1,528
TOTAL CURRENT ASSETS	$ 6,380	$ 5,969
INVESTMENTS AND OTHER ASSETS		
Equity method investments:		
Coca-Cola Enterprises Inc.	$ 584	$ 184
Coca-Cola Amatil Limited	1,255	1,204
Coca-Cola Beverages plc	879	–
Other, principally bottling companies	3,573	3,049
Cost method investments, principally bottling companies	395	457
Marketable securities and other assets	1,863	1,607
	$ 8,549	$ 6,501
PROPERTY, PLANT AND EQUIPMENT		
Land	199	183
Buildings and improvements	1,507	1,535
Machinery and equipment	3,855	3,896
Containers	124	157
	$ 5,685	$ 5,771
Less allowances for depreciation	2,016	2,028
	$ 3,669	$ 3,743
GOODWILL AND OTHER INTANGIBLE ASSETS	$ 547	$ 668
	$19,145	$16,881

LIABILITIES AND SHAREOWNERS' EQUITY

CURRENT LIABILITIES		
Accounts payable and accrued expenses	$ 3,141	$ 3,249
Loans and notes payable	4,459	2,677
Current maturities of long-term debt	3	397
Accrued income taxes	1,037	1,056
TOTAL CURRENT LIABILITIES	$ 8,640	$ 7,379
LONG-TERM DEBT	687	801
OTHER LIABILITIES	991	1,001
DEFERRED INCOME TAXES	424	426
	$10,742	$ 9,607
SHAREOWNERS' EQUITY		
Common stock ($.25 par value; authorized, 5,600,000,000 shares; issued, 3,460,083,686 shares in 1998 and 3,443,441,902 shares in 1997)	$ 865	$ 861
Capital surplus	2,195	1,527
Reinvested earnings	19,922	17,869
Accumulated other comprehensive income and unearned compensation on restricted stock	(1,434)	(1,401)
	21,548	18,856
Less treasury stock, at cost (994,566,196 shares in 1998; 972,812,731 shares in 1997)	13,145	11,582
	8,403	7,274
	$19,145	$16,881

- Coke has entered into derivative financial instrument agreements with a face (or notional) amount totaling over $4.2 billion. Where is that amount reported on the balance sheet?
- Coke has one of the most aggressive stock buyback programs of any company. The company has issued almost 3.5 billion shares, receiving about $3 billion for them. Yet the company has repurchased 29% of those shares back at a cost of over $13 billion. Why would the company do this, and what effect would these buybacks have on the company's value?
- A relatively new addition to balance sheets is the account "Accumulated other comprehensive income." What does this account represent?

Coke's balance sheet appears relatively simple—deceptively simple. While we are each comfortable with accounts such as cash, inventory, accounts payable, and reinvested earnings, the balance sheet becomes much more complex as a business gets more complex. It is important that we understand what the balance sheet tells us, what it does not tell us, and the role that the financial statement notes play in assisting us in interpreting the financial statements.

net work exercise

Check out Coke's Web site (**www.thecoca-colacompany. com**). Here you will learn interesting information about the company, its history, and its future.
Net Work:
1. What is an anchor bottler and how many does Coke have?
2. In what year was Diet Coke first introduced?

Coca-Cola's balance sheet, like the balance sheet of any company, lists the organization's accounting assets and liabilities. However, this does not mean that the balance sheet includes complete, up-to-date information about all of the organization's economic resources and obligations. As described in Chapter 1, the choice of how to include information in the financial statements is often a trade-off between relevance and reliability. The balance sheet has been criticized for being *too* reliable, with too many assets being recorded at historical cost instead of market value, and with many important economic assets (like Microsoft's management or Intel's market dominance) not being recorded at all. A characteristic of recent FASB statements is an effort to improve the relevance of the balance sheet.

Even with its limitations, the balance sheet is still *the* fundamental financial statement. In fact, the income statement and statement of cash flows can be thought of as simply providing supplemental information about certain balance sheet accounts—the income statement gives a detailed description of some of the yearly changes in retained earnings, and the statement of cash flows details the reasons for the change in the cash balance.

This chapter focuses on the strengths and limitations of the balance sheet and describes how companies report their assets, liabilities, and owners' equity. The chapter also introduces some financial ratios used to analyze the balance sheet, and it outlines the type of information contained in the notes to the financial statements.

ELEMENTS OF THE BALANCE SHEET

Twenty years after his victory at the Battle of Hastings in 1066, William the Conqueror commissioned a royal survey of all the property in England. The survey was described as follows by one of the defeated Anglo-Saxons:

> He sent his men all over England into every shire and had them find out how many hundred hides there were in the shire, or what land and cattle the king himself had in the country, or what dues he ought to have in twelve months from the shire. Also, he had a record made of how much land his archbishops had, and his bishops and his abbots and his earls, and . . . what or how much everybody had who was occupying land in England, in land or cattle, and how much money it was worth.

The survey thoroughly frightened the people of England, and it was called "Domesday [or Doomsday] Book" because it caused them to think of the final reckoning at the Last Judgment.[1]

Had the original Doomsday Book also included a listing of all the obligations, or liabilities, of the people of England, it would have comprised a balance sheet for England as of the year 1086. A **balance sheet** is a listing of an organization's **assets** and **liabilities** as of a certain point in time. The difference between assets and liabilities is called **equity**. Equity can be thought of as the amount of the assets that the owners of the organization can really call their own, the amount that would be left if all the liabilities were paid. The balance sheet is an expression of the basic accounting equation[2]:

$$\text{Assets} = \text{Liabilities} + \text{Owners' Equity}$$

The three elements found on the balance sheet were precisely defined in Chapter 1. These definitions are repeated in Exhibit 3–2.

EXHIBIT 3–2 | Definitions of Asset, Liability, and Equity

Balance Sheet

Asset:
Probable future economic benefit obtained or controlled by a particular entity as a result of past transactions or events.

Liability:
Probable future sacrifice of economic benefit arising from a present obligation of a particular entity to transfer assets or provide services to other entities in the future as a result of past transactions or events.

Equity:
Residual interest in the assets of an entity that remains after deducting its liabilities. In a business enterprise, the equity is the ownership interest.

SOURCE: *Statement of Financial Accounting Concepts No, 6, "Elements of Financial Statements," pars. 25, 35, and 49.*

1 Elizabeth M. Hallam, "Domesday Book Through Nine Centuries," Thomas and Hudson, 1986, pp. 16, 17.
2 In abbreviated form, the basic accounting equation can be expressed as A = L + E. This can be rearranged algebraically to yield E = A − L. Notice the similarity with Einstein's famous equation: E = mc². Researchers thus far have had no luck in finding an underlying connection that would unify the fields of physics and accounting.

These definitions contain several key words and phrases that are briefly discussed below.

- *Probable.* Contrary to popular belief, accounting is not an exact science. Business is full of uncertainty, and this is acknowledged by the inclusion of the word "probable" in the definitions of assets and liabilities.
- *Future economic benefit.* Although the balance sheet summarizes the results of past transactions and events, its primary purpose is to help forecast the future. Hence, the only items included as assets and liabilities are those with implications for the future.
- *Obtained or controlled.* Accountants have a phrase: substance over form, meaning that financial statements should reflect the underlying economic substance and not the superficial legal form. If a company economically controls the future economic benefits associated with an item, that item qualifies as an asset whether it is legally owned or not.
- *Obligation.* This term includes legal commitments as well as moral, social, and implied obligations. Again, the phrase "substance over form" applies.
- *Transfer assets or provide services.* Most liabilities involve an obligation to transfer assets in the future. However, an obligation to provide a service is also a liability. For example, having received your tuition check, your college or university now has a liability to you to provide top-notch education.
- *Past transactions or events.* Assets and liabilities arise from transactions or events that have already happened. Consider a company that promises in May to pay a student $4,000 for a summer internship starting in June. If the company declares bankruptcy, does the student get to collect the $4,000? No, because the transaction, the actual summer internship work, has not yet occurred.[3]

Assets include financial items such as cash, receivables, and investments in financial instruments. Assets also include costs that are expected to provide future economic benefits. For example, expenditures made for inventories, equipment, and patents are expected to help generate revenues in future periods. Most assets are measured in terms of historical cost. But, as mentioned in Chapter 1 and as outlined later in this chapter, some assets are measured in terms of replacement cost, market value, net realizable value, or discounted present value.

STOP & THINK Alternatively, an asset could be defined as everything legally owned by a company, and a liability defined as all legal obligations. What problems would arise from using these definitions?

Liabilities include obligations with amounts denominated in precise monetary terms, such as accounts payable and long-term debt. The amounts of other liabilities must be estimated based on expectations about future events. These types of liabilities include warranties, pension obligations, and environmental liabilities.

The total liability amount measures the amounts of the assets of the enterprise that are claimed by various creditors. Owners' equity measures the amounts of the total assets of the enterprise that remain and are thus claimed by the ownership group. Owners' equity equals the net assets of an enterprise, or the difference between total assets and total liabilities. Owners' equity arises from investment by owners and is increased by net income and decreased by net losses and distributions to owners. Other items that can impact owners' equity are outlined later in the chapter.

Classified Balance Sheets

Although there are no standard categories that must be used, the general framework for a balance sheet shown in Exhibit 3-3 is representative and will be used in this chapter.

---

3 Whether the transaction has already occurred is sometimes difficult to determine. For example, if the student signs a summer internship contract guaranteeing payment of $4,000 whether or not any work is done, then the contract signing itself might be viewed as creating an asset for the student and a liability for the company. This exact issue is important in determining the proper accounting treatment for long-term leases.

Balance sheet items are generally classified as current (or short-term) items and noncurrent (or long-term) items. How long is "current"? For most companies, "current" means "one year or less." Accordingly, assets expected to be used and liabilities expected to be paid or otherwise satisfied within a year are current items. When assets and liabilities are so classified, the difference between current assets and current liabilities may be determined. This difference is referred to as the company's **working capital**—the liquid buffer available in meeting financial demands and contingencies of the near future.

EXHIBIT 3–3 | Categories of a Classified Balance Sheet

ASSETS

Current assets:
    Cash
    Investment securities
    Accounts and notes receivable
    Inventories
    Other current assets, such as prepaid expenses

Noncurrent assets:
    Investments
    Property, plant, and equipment
    Intangible assets
    Other noncurrent assets, such as deferred income tax assets

LIABILITIES

Current liabilities:
    Accounts and notes payable
    Accrued expenses
    Current portion of long-term obligations
    Other current liabilities, such as unearned revenues

Noncurrent liabilities:
    Long-term debt, such as notes, bonds, and mortgages payable
    Long-term lease obligations
    Deferred income tax liability
    Other noncurrent liabilities, such as pension obligations

OWNERS' EQUITY

Contributed capital:
    Capital stock
    Additional paid-in capital
Retained earnings
Other equity, such as treasury stock (a subtraction)

The division of assets and liabilities into just two categories—current and noncurrent—is in some sense an arbitrary partition. Users of financial statements may desire a different partition. For example, some users exclude inventory when evaluating a company's working capital position. Users are certainly free to recast the balance sheet in whatever manner they wish. However, although there is some arbitrariness in the current/noncurrent classifications, its popularity among users as an indication of liquidity suggests that the classification does meet the test of decision usefulness.

Current Assets

The most common **current assets** are cash, receivables, and inventories. As depicted in Exhibit 3–4, the normal operating cycle involves the use of cash to purchase inventories, the sale of inventories resulting in receivables, and ultimately the cash collection of those receivables. In some industries, like lumber and shipbuilding, this normal operating cycle is longer than one year. When the operating cycle is longer than a year, the length of the operating cycle should be used in defining current assets and liabilities. In practice, almost all companies use the one-year period.[4]

E X H I B I T 3 – 4 | Operating Cycle

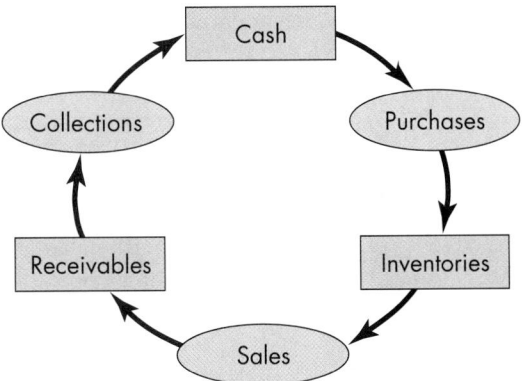

In addition to cash, receivables, and inventories, current assets typically include prepaid expenses and investments in certain securities. Prepaid items are a bit different from other current assets in that they are not expected to be converted into cash within a year. Instead, their expiration makes it possible to conserve cash that otherwise would have been required. Prepayments for periods extending beyond a year should be reported as noncurrent assets.

Debt and equity securities that are purchased mainly with the intent of reselling the securities in the short term are called **trading securities**. Trading securities are classified as current assets. Other investments in debt and equity securities are classified as current or noncurrent depending on whether management intends to convert them into cash within one year, or one operating cycle, whichever is longer.[5]

The reported amounts for current assets are measured in a variety of different ways. Cash and receivables are reported at their net realizable values. Thus, current receivable balances are reduced by allowances for estimated uncollectible accounts. Investments in debt and equity securities are reported, in most cases, at current market value. Inventories are reported at cost (FIFO, LIFO, etc.) or on the lower-of-cost-or-market basis. Prepaid expenses are reported at their historical costs.

Current assets are normally listed on the balance sheet before the noncurrent assets and in the order of their liquidity, with the most liquid terms (those closest to cash) first. This ordering is a tradition, not a requirement. Most utilities and insurance companies reverse the order and report their longer-lived assets first. In addition, foreign companies frequently start their balance sheets with their long-term assets.

> **Caution!** As illustrated with current assets, a balance sheet is not restricted to reporting historical cost.

---

4 In classifying items not related to the operating cycle, a one-year period is always used as the basis for current classification. For example, a note receivable due in 15 months that arose from the sale of land held as an investment would be classified as noncurrent even if the normal operating cycle exceeds 15 months.

5 *Statement of Financial Accounting Standards No. 115,* "Accounting for Certain Investments in Debt and Equity Securities," Norwalk, CT: Financial Accounting Standards Board, 1993, par. 17.

Some exceptions to the normal classification of assets should be noted. If management intends to use an asset for a noncurrent purpose, then that asset should be classified as noncurrent in spite of the usual classification. For example, cash that is restricted to a noncurrent use (e.g., for the acquisition of noncurrent assets or for the liquidation of noncurrent debts) should not be included in current assets. Similarly, land that is held for resale within the coming year should be classified as current. The overriding criterion is management intention.

Noncurrent Assets

Assets not qualifying for presentation under the current heading are classified under a number of noncurrent headings. Noncurrent assets may be listed under separate headings, such as "Investments," "Property, plant, and equipment," "Intangible assets," and "Other noncurrent assets."

> **FYI:** When an investment in another company represents majority ownership of that company, no single investment amount is reported in the balance sheet. Instead, all of the individual assets and liabilities of the other company are included, or consolidated, in the balance sheet.

INVESTMENTS Investments held for such long-term purposes as regular income, appreciation, or ownership control are reported under the heading "Investments." Debt and equity securities purchased as investments that management does not intend to sell in the coming year are classified as long-term investments. Acquisitions of the stock of other companies made in order to exert influence or control over the actions of those companies are accounted for using the equity method, which is explained in Chapter 14. These investments are classified as long-term investments. The "Investments" heading also includes other miscellaneous investments not used directly in the operations of the business, such as land held for investment purposes. Many long-term investments are reported at cost. However, more and more long-term assets are being reported at current market values. These deviations from cost will be discussed in later chapters.

Properties used in normal business operations, such as the printing press shown here, are classified as "property, plant, and equipment" on the balance sheet.

PROPERTY, PLANT, AND EQUIPMENT   Properties of a tangible and relatively permanent character that are used in the normal business operations are reported under "Property, plant, and equipment" or other appropriate headings, such as "Land, buildings, and equipment." Land, buildings, machinery, tools, furniture, fixtures, and vehicles are included in this section of the balance sheet. If an asset, such as land, is being held for speculation, it should be classified as an investment rather than under the heading "Property, plant, and equipment." Tangible properties, except land, are normally reported at cost less accumulated depreciation. If the current value of a tangible property is less than its depreciated cost, the asset is said to be impaired. Guidelines for when and how to recognize asset impairments are given in Chapter 13.

INTANGIBLE ASSETS   The long-term rights and privileges of a nonphysical nature acquired for use in business operations are often reported under the heading "Intangible assets." Included in this class are such items as goodwill, patents, trademarks, franchises, copyrights, formulas, leaseholds, and organization costs. Intangible assets are normally reported at cost less amounts previously amortized.

OTHER NONCURRENT ASSETS   Those noncurrent assets not suitably reported under any of the previous classifications may be listed under the general heading "Other non-current assets" or may be listed separately under special descriptive headings. Such assets include, for example, long-term advances to officers, long-term receivables, deposits made with taxing authorities and utility companies, and deferred income tax assets. Deferred income tax balances result from temporary differences between taxable income (the income subject to tax on the tax return) and income before taxes reported on the income statement. **Deferred income tax assets** arise when taxable income exceeds reported income for the period and the difference is expected to "reverse" in future periods. These assets are similar to prepaid expenses, but the computation and reporting of deferred income tax assets is much more complex (as will be explained in Chapter 16).

Current Liabilities

Current liabilities are those obligations that are reasonably expected to be paid using current assets or by creating other current liabilities. Generally, if a liability is reasonably expected to be paid within 12 months, it is classified as current. As with receivables, payables arising from the normal operating activities may be classified as current even if they are not to be paid within 12 months, as long as they are to be paid within the operating cycle, which may exceed 12 months.

In addition to accounts payable and short-term borrowing, current liabilities also include amounts for accrued expenses. Common accruals include salaries and wages, interest, and taxes. The current liabilities section also includes amounts representing the portion of the long-term obligations due to be satisfied within one year.

The current liability classification generally does not include the following items that normally would be considered current.

- *Debts to be liquidated from a noncurrent sinking fund.*   A **sinking fund** is comprised of cash and investment securities that have been accumulated for the stated purpose of repaying a specific loan. If the sinking fund is classified as a noncurrent asset, then the associated loan is also classified as noncurrent.
- *Short-term obligations to be refinanced.* If a short-term loan is expected to be refinanced, or paid back with the proceeds of a replacement loan, the existing short-term loan will not require the use of current assets even though it is scheduled to mature within a year. To reflect the economic substance of this situation, the existing loan is not classified as current as long as: (1) the intent of the company is to refinance the loan on a long-term basis, and (2) the company's intent is evidenced by an

► BALANCE SHEET TILT

Which is more important, the income statement or the balance sheet? During the middle part of the 20th century, accountants viewed the income statement as the premier financial statement. The balance sheet was just a holding tank for debits and credits that had not yet flowed through the income statement. The overriding accounting concept was matching: matching and reporting revenues and the related expenses

to compute periodic income. An income statement emphasis makes it possible for strange creatures to take up residence in the balance sheet. One example that persists to this day is LIFO inventory. A conceptual argument for LIFO is that it is a good technique for matching current costs with current revenues. The downside is that the LIFO inventory number on the balance sheet can be far less than the current value of the inventory.

In its conceptual framework project, the FASB rejected the primacy of matching and made the defini-

tions of an asset and a liability the central accounting concepts. The balance sheet can no longer be a home for stray debits and credits—balance sheet items must satisfy the definitions of assets and liabilities. Opponents have predicted from the beginning of the FASB's conceptual framework project that a balance sheet emphasis would lead to current value accounting and the inclusion of volatile unrealized gains and losses on the income statement. This prediction has come true.

The FASB's financial instruments project epitomizes

---

actual refinancing after the balance sheet date but before the financial statements are finalized, or by the existence of an explicit refinancing agreement.[6]

CALLABLE OBLIGATIONS Classification problems can arise when an obligation is callable by a creditor, because it is difficult to determine exactly when the obligation will be paid. A **callable obligation** is one that is payable on demand and thus has no specified due date. If the terms of an agreement specify that an obligation is due on demand or will become due on demand within one year from the balance sheet date, the obligation should be classified as current.[7]

A loan can become callable because the debtor violates the provisions of the debt agreement. Loan agreement clauses that identify specific deficiencies (e.g., missing two consecutive interest payments) that can cause a loan to be immediately callable are referred to as **objective acceleration clauses.** If these specific deficiencies exist as of the balance sheet date, the associated liability should be classified as current unless the lender has agreed to waive the right to receive immediate payment or the deficiency has been fixed (e.g., an interest payment made) by the time the financial statements are issued.

In some cases, the debt agreement does not specifically identify the circumstances under which a loan will become callable, but it does indicate some general conditions that permit the lender to accelerate the due date. This type of provision is known as a **subjective acceleration clause** because the violation of the conditions cannot be objectively determined. Examples of the wording in such clauses are, "if the debtor fails to maintain satisfactory operations . . . ," or "if a material adverse change occurs. . . ." If invoking of the clause is deemed probable, the liability should be classified as a current liability. If invoking of the clause is considered to be reasonably possible but not probable, only a note disclosure is necessary, and the liability continues to be classified as noncurrent.[8]

---

6 *Statement of Financial Accounting Standards No. 6,* "Classification of Short-Term Obligations Expected to Be Refinanced," Stamford, CT: Financial Accounting Standards Board, 1975.

7 *Statement of Financial Accounting Standards No. 78,* "Classification of Obligations That Are Callable by the Creditor," Stamford, CT: Financial Accounting Standards Board, 1983, par. 5.

8 *FASB Technical Bulletin, 79–3,* "Subjective Acceleration Clauses in Long-Term Debt Agreements," Stamford, CT: Financial Accounting Standards Board, December 1979, par. 003.

the conflict between the balance sheet and the income statement. Almost everyone agrees that reporting the current value of financial instruments makes for a better balance sheet. But many argue that including the associated unrealized gains and losses adds a distorting volatility to the measurement of net income. To settle the issue, the FASB has constructed a grand compromise called *comprehensive income* that essentially allows current values on the balance sheet and provides a separate place for reporting the unrealized gains and losses, leaving the income statement clean and pure.

QUESTIONS:

1. In your opinion, which is more important: the income statement or the balance sheet?

2. Why are companies concerned about earnings volatility?

3. What is the difference between net income and comprehensive income?

4. In your opinion, where does the statement of cash flows rank in terms of importance?

SOURCES:

Oscar S. Gellein, "Financial Reporting: The State of Standard Setting," *Advances in Accounting,* Vol. 3, 1986, p. 3.

L. Todd Johnson, Cheri L. Reither, and Robert J. Swieringa, "Toward Reporting Comprehensive Income," *Accounting Horizons,* December 1995, p. 128.

Statement of Financial Accounting Standards No. 130, "Reporting Comprehensive Income," Norwalk, CT: Financial Accounting Standards Board, 1997.

Noncurrent Liabilities

Obligations not reasonably expected to be paid or otherwise satisfied within 12 months (or within the operating cycle if it exceeds 12 months) are classified as noncurrent liabilities. Noncurrent liabilities are generally listed under separate headings, such as "Long-term debt," "Long-term lease obligations," "Deferred income tax liability," and "Other noncurrent liabilities."

> **FYI:** Large banks have entire "compliance" departments that verify whether borrowers are following the terms of their loan agreements.

LONG-TERM DEBT Long-term notes, bonds, mortgages, and similar obligations not requiring the use of current funds for their retirement are generally reported on the balance sheet under the heading "Long-term debt."

Long-term debt is reported at its discounted present value, which is initially measured by the proceeds from the debt issuance. When the amount borrowed is not the same as the amount ultimately required to be repaid, called the *maturity amount,* a discount or premium is included as an adjustment to the maturity amount to ensure that the debt is reported at its discounted present value. A discount should be subtracted from the amount reported for the debt, and a premium should be added to the amount reported for the debt.

When a note, a bond issue, or a mortgage formerly classified as a long-term obligation becomes payable within a year, it should be reclassified and presented as a current liability, except when the obligation is to be refinanced, as discussed earlier, or is to be paid out of a fund classified as noncurrent.

LONG-TERM LEASE OBLIGATIONS Some leases of property, plant, and equipment are financially structured so that they are essentially debt-financed purchases. The FASB has established criteria to determine which leases are to be accounted for as purchases, or capital leases, rather than as ordinary operating leases. In accounting for capital leases, the present value of the future minimum lease payments is recorded as a long-term liability. That portion of the present value due within the next year is classified as a current liability. The long-term lease obligation reported by some firms is often more interesting for what it doesn't include than for what it does include. For example, as of January 28, 1999, the present value of future minimum lease payments for capital leases for ALBERTSON'S, INC., a supermarket chain, was $168 million. At the same time, the present value of future minimum lease payments for operating leases (an amount not recognized in the balance sheet) was $576 million. Be patient; in Chapter 15 you will learn more about leases than you ever wanted to know.

DEFERRED INCOME TAX LIABILITY Almost all large companies include a **deferred income tax liability** in their balance sheets. This liability can be thought of as the income tax expected to be paid in future years on income that has already been reported in the income statement but which, because of the tax law, has not yet been taxed. The liability is valued using the income tax rates expected to prevail in the future when the income is taxed. However, since the liability is not reported at its present (discounted) value, some analysts disregard it when evaluating a company's debt position. The accounting for deferred income taxes is very complex and controversial and has been the subject of considerable debate.

OTHER NONCURRENT LIABILITIES Those noncurrent liabilities not suitably reported under the separate headings outlined above may be listed under this general heading or may be listed separately under special descriptive headings. Examples of such long-term liabilities are pension plans and obligations resulting from advance collections on long-term contracts.

CONTINGENT LIABILITIES Past activities or circumstances may give rise to possible future liabilities, although obligations do not exist on the date of the balance sheet. These possible claims are known as **contingent liabilities.** They are potential obligations involving uncertainty as to possible losses. As future events occur or fail to occur, this uncertainty will be resolved. A good example of a contingent liability is the cosigner's obligation on a co-signed loan. The cosigner has no existing obligation but may have an obligation in the future, depending on whether the borrower defaults on the loan.

> **Caution!** This description makes it sound like accounting for contingencies is cookbook simple. But the words "probable" and "possible" represent very complex concepts. For example, when exactly does a future event (such as a thunderstorm tomorrow) stop being "possible" and start being "probable"?

Contingent liabilities are accounted for according to the judgment of management about the probability of the contingent obligation's becoming an actual obligation. If a future payment is considered probable, the liability should be recorded by a debit to a loss account and a credit to a liability account. If future payment is possible, the contingent nature of the loss is disclosed in a note to the financial statements. If future payment is remote, no accounting action is necessary.[9]

A contingent liability is distinguishable from an **estimated liability**. An estimated liability is a definite obligation with only the amount of the obligation in question and subject to estimation at the balance sheet date. Examples of estimated liabilities are pensions, warranties, and deferred taxes. Some liabilities combine the characteristics of contingent and estimated liabilities. A good example is a company's obligation for environmental cleanup costs. In many cases, a company is not certain it is liable for environmental damage until the obligation is confirmed in the courts. However, even after the cleanup obligation is verified, estimating its amount is quite difficult—the cleanup typically extends over several years, the amount of the cost to be shared by other polluting companies is uncertain, and governmental environmental regulations can change at any time. If no reasonable estimate of an obligation can be made, it is not recognized as a liability in the balance sheet, but the nature of the obligation is disclosed in the financial statement notes. Chapter 18 contains more details on the accounting for contingent and estimated liabilities.

STOP & THINK The current/noncurrent classification scheme is only one way to split assets and liabilities into two groups. Can you think of any other basis that might be used to separate assets and liabilities into two groups?

---

9 *Statement of Financial Accounting Standards No. 5,* "Accounting for Contingencies," Stamford, CT: Financial Accounting Standards Board, 1975, pars. 8–13.

Owners' Equity

The method of reporting the owners' equity varies with the form of the business unit. Business units are typically divided into three categories: **proprietorships, partnerships,** and **corporations.**[10] In the case of a proprietorship, the owner's equity in assets is reported by means of a single capital account. The balance in this account is the cumulative result of the owner's investments and withdrawals as well as past earnings and losses. In a partnership, capital accounts are established for each partner. Capital account balances summarize the investments and withdrawals and shares of past earnings and losses of each partner and thus measure the partners' individual equities in the partnership assets.

In a corporation, the difference between assets and liabilities is referred to as **stockholders' (shareholders') equity** or *owners' equity.* In presenting the owners' equity on the balance sheet, a distinction is made between the equity originating from the stockholders' investments, referred to as **contributed capital** or **paid-in capital,** and the equity originating from earnings, referred to as **retained earnings.**

Most financial statement analysis calculations use total stockholders' equity and do not distinguish between contributed capital and retained earnings. However, for some purposes the distinction can be very important. Historically, companies could legally pay cash dividends only in an amount not exceeding the retained earnings balance. This legal restriction has been relaxed in most states, but the retained earnings amount is still viewed as an informal limit to cash dividend payments.

CONTRIBUTED CAPITAL Contributed (or paid-in) capital is generally reported in two parts: (1) **capital stock** and (2) **additional paid-in capital.** The amount reported on the balance sheet as capital stock usually reflects the number of shares issued multiplied by the par value or stated value per share. Historically, par value was the market value of the shares at the time of their issue. In cases where shareholders invested less than the par value of the stock, courts sometimes held that the shareholders were contingently liable for the difference if corporate resources were insufficient to satisfy creditors. Today, most stocks are issued with low or no par values; par value no longer has much significance.

The two types of capital stock are **preferred stock** and **common stock.** In general, preferred stockholders are paid a fixed annual cash dividend and have a higher likelihood of recovering their investment if the company goes bankrupt.[11] Common stockholders are the real owners of the corporation; they vote for the board of directors and have legal ownership of the corporate assets after the claims of all creditors and preferred stockholders have been satisfied. For accounting purposes, when a corporation has issued more than one class of stock, the stock of each class is reported separately.

Additional paid-in capital represents investments by stockholders in excess of the par or stated value of the capital stock. Additional paid-in capital is also affected by a whole host of diverse transactions such as stock repurchases, stock dividends, share retirements, and stock conversions. In a sense, additional paid-in capital is the "dumping ground" of the equity section.

---

10 In addition to these three general categories, there are many hybrids. Some of these are limited partnerships, S corporations, and limited liability companies (LLCs). In general, these organizations are taxed as partnerships but have some of the limited liability advantages of a corporation. All of the Big 5 accounting firms are organized as a limited liability partnership (LLP) to insulate uninvolved partners from client lawsuits directed at individual partners. According to IRS records, about 75% of U.S. businesses are organized as sole proprietorships. See Coopers & Lybrand, "Choosing a Business Entity in the 1990s," Washington, D.C., 1994.

11 In essence, preferred stock is an investment that has some of the characteristics of a loan—fixed periodic payment, no vote for the board of directors, and higher priority than common stock in case of bankruptcy liquidation. Increasingly, finance wizards are creating securities that combine characteristics of both debt and equity. The accounting question is where to put these creations. The SEC requires one such type of security, mandatory redeemable preferred stock, to be reported in the balance sheet in a separate section between liabilities and owners' equity. This has been called "mezzanine" treatment. Distinguishing between debt and equity is addressed more fully in Chapter 11.

RETAINED EARNINGS   The amount of undistributed earnings of past periods is reported as retained earnings. An excess of dividends and losses over earnings results in a negative retained earnings balance called a **deficit.** As detailed in Chapter 11, retained earnings can also be reduced as a result of stock retirements and the issuance of stock dividends. A sample of large positive and negative retained earnings balances for U.S. companies is given in Exhibit 3-5.

EXHIBIT 3-5 | Large Positive and Negative Retained Earnings Balances

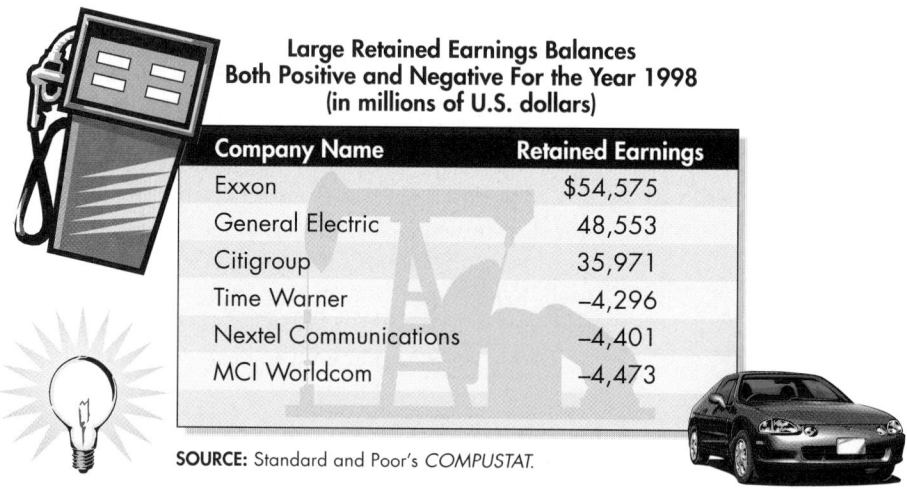

Large Retained Earnings Balances Both Positive and Negative For the Year 1998 (in millions of U.S. dollars)

Company Name	Retained Earnings
Exxon	$54,575
General Electric	48,553
Citigroup	35,971
Time Warner	–4,296
Nextel Communications	–4,401
MCI Worldcom	–4,473

SOURCE: Standard and Poor's *COMPUSTAT.*

Portions of retained earnings are sometimes reported as restricted and unavailable as a basis for cash dividends. This ensures that a company does not distribute cash dividends to shareholders to the extent that the ability to repay creditors or make other planned expenditures comes into question. Retained earnings restrictions can be part of a loan agreement or can be voluntarily adopted by a company (called an appropriation). These restrictions are usually disclosed in a financial statement note.

OTHER EQUITY   In addition to the two major categories of contributed capital and retained earnings, the equity section can include a couple of other items: treasury stock and accumulated other comprehensive income. These are described in detail in later chapters, but they are briefly discussed here.

> **FYI:**   For those interested in stock tips, buy the stocks of companies that announce treasury stock purchases. Those companies tend to outperform the market in the three to four years following the announcement.

Treasury stock.   When a company buys back its own shares, accountants call the repurchased shares **treasury stock**. Treasury shares can be retired, or they can be retained and possibly reissued later. When the shares are retained, the amount paid to repurchase the treasury stock is usually shown as a subtraction from total stockholders' equity. In essence, a treasury stock purchase returns funds to shareholders.

Accumulated other comprehensive income.   Beginning in 1998, the FASB required companies to summarize changes in owners' equity exclusive of net income and contributions by and distributions to owners. This summary, termed **other comprehensive income,** is typically provided by companies as part of their statement of stockholders' equity. The corresponding balance sheet item, reflecting the cumulative total of these items over the years, is titled accumulated other comprehensive income. The three most common components are certain unrealized gains and losses on investments, foreign currency adjustments, and certain unrealized gains and losses on derivative contracts.

Unrealized gains and losses on available-for-sale securities. Available-for-sale securities are those that were not purchased with the immediate intention to resell but also are not meant to be held permanently. These securities are reported in the balance sheet at their current market values. The unrealized gains and losses from market value fluctuations are not included in the income statement but are instead shown as a separate equity item.[12]

Foreign currency translation adjustments. Almost every U.S. multinational corporation has a foreign currency translation adjustment in its equity section. This adjustment arises from the change in the equity of foreign subsidiaries (as measured in terms of U.S. dollars) that occurs during the year as a result of changes in foreign currency exchange rates. These adjustments are discussed in Chapter 21.

Unrealized gains and losses on derivatives. A **derivative** is a financial instrument, such as an option or a future, that derives its value from the movement of a price, an exchange rate, or an interest rate associated with some other item. For example, an option to purchase a stock becomes more valuable as the price of the stock increases, and the right to purchase foreign currency at a fixed exchange rate becomes more valuable as that foreign currency becomes more expensive. As will be discussed in Chapter 18, companies often use derivatives in order to manage their exposure to risk stemming from changes in prices and rates. Some of the unrealized gains and losses from the fluctuations in the value of derivatives are reported as part of accumulated other comprehensive income.

INTERNATIONAL RESERVES The first thing one notices about the equity portion of the balance sheets of many foreign companies, particularly those from countries influenced by the British accounting tradition, is the extended description of the company's "reserves." In familiar terms, reserves are merely different equity categories similar in nature, depending on the reserve, to additional paid-in capital or to restricted retained earnings. Reserve accounting is very important because in many foreign countries the legal ability to pay cash dividends is strictly tied to the balances in various reserve accounts. Common reserve category titles are revaluation reserve, goodwill reserve, and capital redemption reserve. Reserves are discussed in more detail in Chapter 11, which is devoted to the equity section.

Offsets on the Balance Sheet

As illustrated in the preceding discussion, a number of balance sheet items are reported at gross amounts not reflecting their actual values, thus requiring the recognition of offset balances in arriving at proper valuations. In the case of assets, for example, an allowance for doubtful accounts is subtracted from the sum of the customer accounts in reporting the net amount estimated as collectible; accumulated depreciation is subtracted from the related buildings and equipment balances in reporting the costs of the assets still assignable to future revenues. In the case of liabilities, a loan discount is subtracted from the maturity value of the loan in reporting the loan at its discounted present value. In the stockholders' equity section of the balance sheet, treasury stock is deducted in reporting total stockholders' equity.

The types of offsets described above, utilizing contra accounts, are required for proper reporting of particular balance sheet items. In addition, accounting rules require some assets and liabilities to be offset against one another, resulting in just one net amount being reported in the balance sheet. For example, a company's pension obliga-

---

12   One never knows where controversy and compromise will rear their ugly heads. Accounting purists hoped to include these unrealized gains and losses in the income statement. Companies (particularly banks) fearful of the volatility that this would add to the income statement opposed the treatment. This equity item is the FASB's compromise.

This aerial shot of Disneyland shows some of the Walt Disney Company's noncurrent assets.

tion is offset against the assets in the pension fund, and only the net number goes into the balance sheet. Deferred tax assets and liabilities are also offset against each other.

The cases just described are the exceptions. The general rule is that assets, liabilities, and equities should not be offset when compiling the balance sheet. Offsetting, or netting, can significantly reduce the information value of the balance sheet. If offsetting were taken to its extreme, the balance sheet would be just one line, total equity, embodying total liabilities offset against total assets.

Identify the different formats used to present balance sheet data.

FORMAT OF THE BALANCE SHEET

When preparing a balance sheet, the order of asset and liability classifications may vary, but most businesses emphasize working capital position and liquidity, with assets and liabilities presented in the order of their liquidity. An exception to this order is generally found in the property, plant, and equipment section where the more permanent assets with longer useful lives are listed first. The balance sheet of THE WALT DISNEY COMPANY, reproduced in Appendix A, is an example of current assets and of current liabilities being listed first.

As mentioned earlier, in some industries, like the utility industry, the investment in plant assets is so significant that these assets are placed first on the balance sheet. Also, since long-term financing is so important in these industries, the equity capital and long-term debt obtained to finance plant assets are listed before current liabilities. To illustrate this type of presentation, the 1998 balance sheet for COMMONWEALTH ELECTRIC COMPANY is given in Exhibit 3-6. Commonwealth Electric was organized in 1850 and these days provides electricity service to Cape Cod and Martha's Vineyard.

As seen in the Commonwealth Electric illustration in Exhibit 3-6, balance sheets are generally presented in comparative form. With comparative reports for two or more dates, information is made available concerning the nature and trend of financial changes taking place within the periods between balance sheet dates. Currently, a minimum of two years of balance sheets and three years of income statements and cash flow statements are required by the SEC to be included in the annual report to shareholders.

EXHIBIT 3-6 | 1998 Balance Sheet of Commonwealth Electric Company

Commonwealth Electric Company
Balance Sheets
December 31, 1998 and 1997

	1998	1997
	(Dollars in Thousands)	
ASSETS		
PROPERTY, PLANT AND EQUIPMENT, at original cost	$566,477	$550,449
Less—Accumulated depreciation	182,345	174,488
	$384,132	$375,961
Add—Construction work in progress	2,544	4,010
	$386,676	$379,971
INVESTMENTS		
Equity in nuclear electric power company	$ 485	$ 519
Other	14	14
	$ 499	$ 533
LONG-TERM RECEIVABLE—AFFILIATE	$184,343	$ —
CURRENT ASSETS		
Cash	$ 3,584	$ 1,496
Accounts receivable—		
Affiliates	1,483	1,753
Customers, less reserves of $1,069 in 1998 and $2,044 in 1997	40,114	45,199
Unbilled revenues	6,096	9,162
Inventories, at average cost	2,669	2,578
Prepaid taxes—		
Property	3,153	3,043
Income	5,195	—
Other	1,192	1,771
	$ 63,486	$ 65,002
DEFERRED CHARGES		
Regulatory assets	$101,895	$ 70,112
Deferred tax asset	30,838	—
Other	1,618	3,601
	$134,351	$ 73,713
	$769,355	$519,219
CAPITALIZATION AND LIABILITIES		
CAPITALIZATION		
Common Equity—		
Common stock, $25 par value—		
Authorized and outstanding—2,043,972 shares wholly owned by		
Commonwealth Energy System (Parent)	$ 51,099	$ 51,099
Amounts paid in excess of par value	97,112	97,112
Retained earnings	36,984	31,993
	$185,195	$180,204
Long-term debt, less current sinking fund requirements	143,651	147,192
	$328,846	$327,396
CURRENT LIABILITIES		
Interim Financing—		
Notes payable to banks	$ —	$ 14,900
Advances from affiliates	40,350	5,315
	$ 40,350	$ 20,215
Other Current Liabilities—		
Current sinking fund requirements	$ 3,553	$ 3,553
Accounts payable—		
Affiliates	14,159	12,007
Other	26,370	32,826
Accrued taxes—		
Local property and other	3,343	3,299
Income	—	19,114
Accrued interest	3,751	3,811
Other	22,690	12,717
	$ 73,866	$ 87,327
	$114,216	$107,542
DEFERRED CREDITS		
Regulatory liabilities	$297,693	$ —
Accumulated deferred income taxes	—	50,283
Unamortized investment tax credits	6,224	6,696
Other	22,376	27,302
	$326,293	$ 84,281
COMMITMENTS AND CONTINGENCIES	—	—
	$769,355	$519,219

Format of Foreign Balance Sheets

Foreign balance sheets are frequently presented with property, plant, and equipment listed first. In addition, foreign balance sheets frequently list the current assets and the current liabilities together, and label the difference between the two as net current assets or working capital. This manner of reporting the current items reflects the business reality that a person starting a company needs to get long-term financing (long-term debt and equity) to finance the acquisition of long-term assets as well as to finance the portion of current assets that can't be acquired by incurring current liabilities. For example, if a company can acquire all of its inventory through credit purchases (accounts payable), and if the supplier will wait for payment until the inventory is sold and the cash collected, then no long-term financing is needed to purchase the initial stock of inventory.

An example of a typical foreign balance sheet is provided in Exhibit 3–7, which contains the March 31, 1998, balance sheet of BRITISH TELECOM-MUNICATIONS. In addition to the format difference already mentioned, this balance sheet also reflects several other differences between a U.S. balance sheet and the balance sheet of a foreign company. The most obvious of these differences is in terminology. However, with some thought and a little accounting intuition, one can deduce that the item "debtors" is what we would call "accounts receivable," "called-up share capital" is "common stock at par," and so forth. More substantive differences, which aren't apparent just from looking at Exhibit 3–7, arise from international differences in accounting methods. For example, the £90 million deferred tax liability (included in "provisions for liabilities and charges") is computed based on the deferred tax items that are expected to become payable in the foreseeable future. If British Telecommunications had used U.S. GAAP, an additional £30 million in deferred tax liability would have been recognized for items expected to become payable after this "foreseeable" time horizon. As another example, British Telecommunications excludes from its assets £3,603 million in goodwill. According to U.K. GAAP, this goodwill amount can be recorded as a direct reduction in equity, so British Telecommunications reports goodwill as a reduction from the £7,514 million reported as retained earnings, or "profit and loss account." The details of these differences, and many others, will be discussed in subsequent chapters. The important point to note here is that foreign balance sheets differ from U.S. balance sheets in both format and in the accounting methods used in computing the balance sheet numbers.

> **FYI:** BRITISH TELECOMMUNI-CATIONS (BT) is one of the leading telecommunications companies in the world. In addition to competing in the international telecommunications market, BT also provides local and national phone service in the United Kingdom. In November 1996, BT announced that it had agreed to merge with MCI, the U.S. long-distance company. In November 1997, BT and MCI agreed to cancel this merger, and MCI merged with WORLD-COM instead.

Analyze a company's performance and financial position through the computation of financial ratios.

BALANCE SHEET ANALYSIS

The purpose of classifying and ordering balance sheet items is to make the balance sheet easier to use. Look at Exhibit 3–8 on page 118 and compare the two balance sheets for the fictitious company Techtronics Corporation. The balance sheet on the left is just a list of assets, liabilities, and equities in alphabetical order, like a simple account listing. The balance sheet on the right uses the classification and ordering format described in the previous section. You decide which is easier to interpret.

The Techtronics numbers will be used to illustrate standard balance sheet analysis techniques. The simple techniques described in this overview will probably not help you to pick "winning" stocks and become a millionaire. But they are a start. It is said that Warren Buffett (worth about $29 billion at last count) picks his investments only after "a careful balance sheet analysis."[13]

STOP & THINK From the information in Exhibit 3–7, compute total assets for British Telecommunications as of March 31, 1998.

---

13 Robert Lenzner and David S. Fondiller, "The Not-So-Silent Partner," *Forbes,* January 22, 1996, p. 78.

EXHIBIT 3-7 | 1998 Balance Sheet of British Telecommunications

British Telecommunications
Balance Sheet
At 31 March 1998

	1998 (In millions of British pounds)
Fixed assets	
Tangible assets	17,252
Investments	1,708
Total fixed assets	18,960
Current assets	
Stocks	145
Debtors	3,387
Investments	731
Cash at bank and in hand	62
Total current assets	4,325
Creditors: amounts falling due within one year	
Loans and other borrowings	881
Other creditors	6,081
Total creditors: amounts falling due within one year	6,962
Net current liabilities	(2,637)
Total assets less current liabilities	16,323
Creditors: amounts falling due after more than one year	
Loans and other borrowings	3,889
Provisions for liabilities and charges	1,426
Minority interests	223
Capital and reserves	
Called-up share capital	1,603
Share premium account	892
Other reserves	776
Profit and loss account	7,514
Total equity shareholders' funds	10,785
	16,323

Balance sheet information is analyzed in two major ways.

1. Relationships between balance sheet amounts
2. Relationships between balance sheet and income statement amounts

In general, relationships between financial statement amounts are called **financial ratios.**

Relationships Between Balance Sheet Amounts

Financial ratios comparing one balance sheet amount to another yield information about the operating and financial structure of a business. Three examples, which are discussed below are liquidity, overall leverage, and asset mix.

LIQUIDITY The relationship between current assets and current liabilities can be used to evaluate the **liquidity** of a company. Liquidity is the ability of a firm to satisfy its short-term obligations. Many companies with fantastic long-run potential have been killed by short-run liquidity problems.

EXHIBIT 3–8 | Techtronics' Balance Sheet, With and Without Classification

Techtronics Corporation
Balance Sheet
December 31, 2002

WITHOUT CLASSIFICATION

Assets

Buildings and equipment (net of accumulated depreciation of $228,600)	$ 732,900
Cash	52,650
Intangible assets	165,000
Investments	128,000
Investment securities	67,350
Inventories	296,000
Land	76,300
Other noncurrent assets	37,800
Prepaid expenses	32,900
Receivables (less allowance for doubtful accounts)	363,700
Total assets	$1,952,600

Liabilities

Accounts payable	$ 312,700
Accrued expenses	46,200
Bonds payable	165,000
Current portion of long-term debt	62,000
Deferred tax liability	126,700
Long-term lease obligations	135,000
Notes payable—current	50,000
Notes payable—noncurrent	100,000
Other current liabilities	28,600
Other noncurrent liabilities	72,500
Total liabilities	$1,098,700

Stockholders' Equity

Additional paid-in capital	$ 375,000
Common stock	170,000
Retained earnings	308,900
Total stockholders' equity	$ 853,900
Total liabilities and stockholders' equity	$1,952,600

WITH CLASSIFICATION

Assets

Current assets:	
Cash	$ 52,650
Investment securities	67,350
Receivables (less allowance for doubtful accounts)	363,700
Inventories	296,000
Prepaid expenses	32,900
Total current assets	$ 812,600
Noncurrent assets:	
Investments	$ 128,000
Land	76,300
Buildings and equipment (net of accumulated depreciation of $228,600)	732,900
Intangible assets	165,000
Other noncurrent assets	37,800
Total noncurrent assets	$1,140,000
Total assets	$1,952,600

Liabilities

Current liabilities:	
Notes payable	$ 50,000
Accounts payable	312,700
Accrued expenses	46,200
Current portion of long-term debt	62,000
Other current liabilities	28,600
Total current liabilities	$ 499,500
Noncurrent liabilities:	
Notes payable	$ 100,000
Bonds payable	165,000
Long-term lease obligations	135,000
Deferred tax liability	126,700
Other noncurrent liabilities	72,500
Total noncurrent liabilities	$ 599,200
Total liabilities	$1,098,700

Stockholders' Equity

Contributed capital:	
Common stock	$ 170,000
Additional paid-in capital	375,000
	$ 545,000
Retained earnings	308,900
Total stockholders' equity	$ 853,900
Total liabilities and stockholders' equity	$1,952,600

A common indicator of the overall liquidity of a company is the **current ratio**. The current ratio is computed by dividing total current assets by total current liabilities. For Techtronics, the current ratio is computed as follows:

$$\text{Current ratio:} \quad \frac{\text{Current assets}}{\text{Current liabilities}} = \frac{\$812,600}{\$499,500} = 1.63$$

Historically, the rule of thumb has been that a current ratio below 2.0 suggests the possibility of liquidity problems. However, advances in information technology have enabled companies to be much more effective in minimizing the need to hold cash, inventories, and other current assets. As a result, current ratios for successful companies these days are frequently less than 1.0. Note that this is just a rule of thumb; proper evaluation of a company's liquidity involves comparing the current year's current ratio to current ratios in prior years and also comparing the company's current ratio to those for other companies in the same industry.

Minimum current ratio requirements are frequently included in loan agreements. A typical agreement might state that if the current ratio falls below a certain level, the lender can declare the loan in default and require immediate repayment. This type of minimum current ratio restriction forces the borrower to maintain its liquidity and gives the lender an increased assurance that the loan will be repaid. When **loan covenant** restrictions are violated, the lender usually waives the right to immediate repayment, sometimes in exchange for a renegotiation of the loan at a higher interest rate. Exhibit 3-9 contains the 1998 current ratios for selected companies. Note that YAHOO! and MICROSOFT have higher current ratios relative to the other companies. This is an indication of the need for liquidity in technology industries. As technology changes, companies in that industry need to be able to quickly adapt, and that ability requires liquidity. Note also MCDONALD'S low current ratio. At first glance you might think that 0.5 is dangerously low. Before jumping to that conclusion, think about what McDonald's current assets are. McDonald's does not have receivables relating to its sales of hamburgers because the cash is collected immediately. Also, the nature of McDonald's perishable inventory dictates that it not sit around for weeks (hopefully). Therefore, the "secret" for McDonald's low current ratio is its ability to turn over its current assets very fast.

EXHIBIT 3-9 | Selected 1998 Ratios

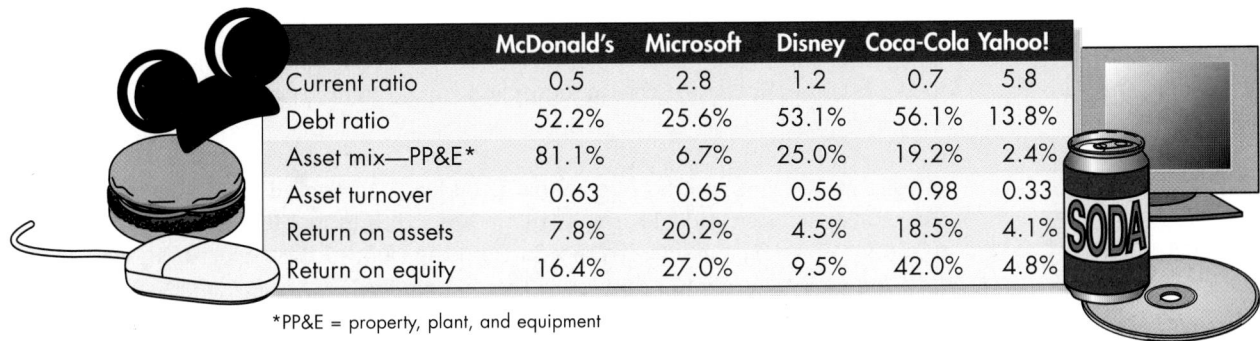

	McDonald's	Microsoft	Disney	Coca-Cola	Yahoo!
Current ratio	0.5	2.8	1.2	0.7	5.8
Debt ratio	52.2%	25.6%	53.1%	56.1%	13.8%
Asset mix—PP&E*	81.1%	6.7%	25.0%	19.2%	2.4%
Asset turnover	0.63	0.65	0.56	0.98	0.33
Return on assets	7.8%	20.2%	4.5%	18.5%	4.1%
Return on equity	16.4%	27.0%	9.5%	42.0%	4.8%

*PP&E = property, plant, and equipment

Another ratio used to measure a firm's liquidity is the **quick ratio,** also known as the **acid-test ratio.** This ratio is computed as total quick assets divided by total current liabilities, where quick assets are defined as cash, investment securities, and net receivables. For Techtronics, the quick ratio is computed as follows:

$$\text{Quick ratio:} \quad \frac{(\text{Cash + Securities + Receivables})}{\text{Current liabilities}} = \frac{\$483,700}{\$499,500} = 0.97$$

The quick ratio indicates how well a firm can satisfy existing short-term obligations with assets that can be converted into cash without difficulty. For a bank considering a three-month loan, or for a supplier considering selling to a company on short-term credit, the quick ratio yields information about the likelihood of being repaid. Techtronics' quick ratio indicates it has $0.97 in quick assets for every $1.00 in current liabilities.

A lender wants to lend on a short-term basis to a company with high current and quick ratios, thus ensuring repayment. However, maintaining an excessively high current ratio is an inefficient use of company resources. Having excess investment securities will increase a company's current and quick ratios, giving comfort to lenders, but the resources used to buy those excess securities might be better utilized by buying trucks or buildings, paying off debts, or if nothing else, returning the cash to the owners for their personal use. A common characteristic of almost all financial ratios is that a ratio that deviates too much from the norm, either above or below, is an indication of a possible problem.[14]

> **Caution!** A current ratio that is too high can also be an indication of trouble. Excess current assets, resulting in a high current ratio, can represent an inefficient use of resources. Cash management and just-in-time inventory systems are designed to keep current asset levels low.

OVERALL LEVERAGE Comparing the amount of liabilities to the amount of assets held by a business gives an indication of the extent to which borrowed funds have been used to **leverage** the owners' investments and increase the size of the firm. One frequently used measure of leverage is the **debt ratio,** computed as total liabilities divided by total assets. The debt ratio is frequently used as an indicator of the overall ability of a company to repay its debts. An intuitive interpretation of the debt ratio is that it represents the proportion of borrowed funds used to acquire the company's assets. For Techtronics, the debt ratio is computed as follows:

$$\text{Debt ratio:} \quad \frac{\text{Total liabilities}}{\text{Total assets}} = \frac{\$1,098,700}{\$1,952,600} = 0.56$$

In other words, Techtronics borrowed 56% of the money it needed to buy its assets. The higher the debt ratio, the higher the likelihood that some of the debt might not be repaid. The general rule of thumb is that debt ratios should be below 50%. Again, this varies widely from one industry to the next. A bank, for example, could easily have a debt ratio in excess of 95%.

See Exhibit 3–9; MICROSOFT and YAHOO! have the lowest debt ratios, with the other three companies each having more than 50%. As a general rule, companies in mature industries have a higher amount of debt than in newer industries because the proven track records of the companies make lenders willing to provide more debt financing.

ASSET MIX A large fraction of a bank's assets is in financial investments—either loans receivable or securities. Property, plant, and equipment (PP&E) comprise only a small fraction of a bank's assets. By comparison, the bulk of the assets of an electric utility is property, plant, and equipment. A company's **asset mix,** the proportion of total assets in each asset category, is determined to a large degree by the industry in which the company operates.

Asset mix is calculated by dividing each asset amount by the sum of total assets. For example, to determine what fraction of Techtronics' assets is buildings and equipment, perform the following calculation:

---

14 Working capital management involves making sure a company does not have excess resources tied up in the form of cash, receivables, and inventory. An example is a just-in-time inventory system. An excess $1 million in working capital implicitly increases finance charges by $100,000 per year if the interest rate on borrowing is 10%.

$$\frac{\text{Buildings and equipment}}{\text{Total assets}} = \frac{\$732,900}{\$1,952,600} = 0.38$$

Techtronics holds 38% of its assets in the form of buildings and equipment. To determine whether this proportion is appropriate requires looking at the comparable number for other firms in Techtronics' industry. We can tell, for example, that Techtronics is probably not an electric utility, since property, plant, and equipment are 50% ($386,676,000/$769,355,000) of the total assets of COMMONWEALTH ELECTRIC in 1998 (see Exhibit 3-6). Similar computations and comparisons can be done with any of the asset categories.

Not surprisingly, MCDONALD'S has a large amount of its assets invested in property, plant, and equipment as shown in Exhibit 3-9. It is also not surprising that MICROSOFT and YAHOO! have very little invested in these long-term assets. What is somewhat surprising is COCA-COLA's low level of investment in PP&E. As mentioned at the beginning of the chapter, however, many of Coca-Cola's bottling facilities are owned by subsidiaries and are not reported on Coca-Cola's balance sheet.

Relationships Between Balance Sheet and Income Statement Amounts

Financial ratios comparing balance sheet and income statement amounts reveal information about a firm's overall profitability and about how efficiently the assets are being used. For this discussion, the following income statement data will be assumed for Techtronics: sales, $4,000,000; net income, $150,000.

EFFICIENCY The balance sheet of Techtronics reveals that Techtronics has $1,952,600 in assets. Are those assets being used efficiently? A financial ratio that gives an overall measure of company efficiency is called **asset turnover** and is computed as follows:

$$\text{Asset turnover:} \quad \frac{\text{Sales}}{\text{Total assets}} = \frac{\$4,000,000}{\$1,952,600} = 2.05$$

Techtronics' asset turnover ratio of 2.05 means that for each dollar of assets, Techtronics is able to generate $2.05 in sales. The higher the asset turnover ratio, the more efficient the company is at using its assets to generate sales.

As indicated in Exhibit 3-9, COCA-COLA is far and away the most efficient of the five companies in using assets to generate sales. Every dollar of Coke's assets generates $0.98 in annual revenue.

Similar computations can be done for specific assets. The general principle is that in measuring whether a company has too much or too little of an asset, the amount of that asset is compared to an income statement item indicating the amount of business activity related to that asset. For example, evaluating the level of inventory involves comparing the inventory level to cost of goods sold for the year. Specific efficiency ratios for accounts receivable, inventory, and fixed assets will be described in the appropriate chapters later in the text.

OVERALL PROFITABILITY Techtronics' net income was $150,000. Is that a lot? It depends. If Techtronics is a small backyard computer-repair business, net income of $150,000 is a lot. If Techtronics is a multinational consumer electronics firm, net income of only $150,000 is terrible. To appropriately measure profitability, net income must be compared to some measure of the size of the investment. Two financial ratios used to assess a firm's overall profitability are **return on assets** and **return on equity.** Companies purchase assets with the intent of using them to generate profits. Return on assets is computed as follows:

$$\text{Return on assets: } \frac{\text{Net income}}{\text{Total assets}} = \frac{\$150,000}{\$1,952,600} = 7.7\%$$

Caution! A low ROE tells you only that a company is sick. Other financial ratios are the diagnostic tools used to pinpoint the exact nature of the illness.

Techtronics' return on assets of 7.7% means that one dollar of assets generated 7.7 cents in net income. As with all ratios, this number must be evaluated in light of Techtronics' return on assets in previous years and the ratios for other firms in the same industry.

Note from Exhibit 3-9 that MICROSOFT and COCA-COLA both stand out in terms of profitability, with DISNEY and YAHOO! bringing up the rear. The 20.2% return on assets earned by Microsoft and the 18.5% earned by Coca-Cola are unusually high.

One important factor not included when using return on assets to evaluate profitability is the effect of leverage. The stockholders of Techtronics did not have to invest the entire $1,952,600 needed to purchase the assets; they leveraged their investment through borrowing. Return on equity (ROE) measures the percentage return on the actual investment made by stockholders and is computed as follows:

$$\text{Return on equity: } \frac{\text{Net income}}{\text{Stockholders' equity}} = \frac{\$150,000}{\$853,900} = 17.6\%$$

Techtronics stockholders earned 17.6 cents for each dollar of equity investment. Computing return on equity is like taking a child's temperature—this one number is a summary indicator of the health of the entity. As a rule of thumb, companies with return on equity significantly below 15% are doing poorly. Companies with return on equity consistently above 15% are doing well.

Coca-Cola demonstrates how the effective use of debt can be of benefit to shareholders. In Exhibit 3-9 we see that Coca-Cola's shareholders earned a 42% return on their investment in 1998. Contrast that with Yahoo!'s return of 4.8%. Because Microsoft and Yahoo! have small debt ratios, there is a relatively small difference between each company's return on assets and its return on equity.

NOTES TO THE FINANCIAL STATEMENTS

Recognize the importance of the notes to the financial statements, and outline the types of disclosures made in the notes.

The basic financial statements do not provide all the information desired by users. Among other things, creditors and investors need to know what methods of accounting were used by the company to arrive at the balances in the accounts. Sometimes the additional information desired is descriptive and is reported in narrative form. In other cases, additional numerical data are reported. To interpret the numbers contained in the financial statements and make useful comparisons with other companies, one must be able to read the notes and understand the assumptions applied.

The following types of notes are typically included by management as support to the basic financial statements.

- Summary of significant accounting policies.
- Additional information (both numerical and descriptive) to support summary totals found on the financial statements, usually the balance sheet. This is the most common type of note used.
- Information about items that are not reported on the basic statements because the items fail to meet the recognition criteria but are still considered to be significant to users in their decision making.
- Supplementary information required by the FASB or the SEC to fulfill the full disclosure principle.

net work exercise

Using the SEC's on-line database EDGAR (**www.sec.gov/ edgarhp.htm**), find PepsiCo's most recent financial statements.
Net Work:
1. How many notes to the financial statements are there?
2. What types of information are disclosed in the notes?

These notes are considered to be an integral part of the financial statements and, unless specifically excluded, are covered by the auditor's opinion.

Before reading any further, turn to Appendix A, which contains the financial statements for THE WALT DISNEY COMPANY. Now find the notes to Disney's financial statements. Mark that spot in your book—those notes will be used to illustrate the points explained below.

Summary of Significant Accounting Policies

GAAP requires that information about the accounting principles and policies followed in arriving at the amounts in the financial statements be disclosed to the users. The Accounting Principles Board concluded in APB Opinion No. 22:

> . . . When financial statements are issued purporting to present fairly financial position, cash flows, and results of operations in accordance with generally accepted accounting principles, a description of all significant accounting policies of the reporting entity should be included as an integral part of the financial statements.[15]

Examples of the required disclosures of accounting policies include those relating to subsidiaries that have been included in the consolidated statements, depreciation methods (Is straight-line used?), inventory valuation method (FIFO, LIFO, or something else?), implementation of any accounting changes, and special revenue recognition practices. This information is usually included as the initial note or as a separate summary preceding the notes to the financial statements. The summary of significant accounting policies for DISNEY is presented in Note 1 in Appendix A.

Additional Information to Support Summary Totals

FYI: Financial statements in the United Kingdom are usually much more condensed than U.S. financial statements. For example, all current assets and current liabilities are often summed and reported as one net number. The details are given in the notes.

In order to prepare a balance sheet that is brief enough to be understandable but complete enough to meet the needs of users, notes are added that provide either quantitative or narrative information to support the statement amounts. For example, only summary totals for property, plant, and equipment and long-term debt are given in the balance sheet itself; the breakdown of these two items by category is usually given in the notes. Most large firms also have extended notes relating to leases, income taxes, and postemployment benefits. If a firm has entered into long-term leases, the length of the leases and the required future payments are outlined in a note. The income tax note identifies the major areas of difference between a company's financial accounting and tax accounting records. The tax note is also the place one has to look to find out what a company's actual income tax bill is. The postemployment benefit note describes a company's pension plan and plan for coverage of retiree medical benefits. Examination of this note reveals the large amount of information that underlies the single summary numbers recognized in the balance sheet. For illustrations, look at Note 6 (income taxes) and Note 7 (pensions) in the financial statements of DISNEY in Appendix A. Disney also includes notes detailing the summary totals for other assets (see Note 10) and borrowings (see Note 5).

Information About Items Not Included in Financial Statements

As discussed in Chapter 1, items included in the financial statements must meet certain recognition criteria. Even though an item might not meet the criteria for recognition in the statements, information concerning the item might be relevant to users. Loss contingencies are good examples of this type of item. As discussed earlier, if the probability of

---

15 *Opinions of the Accounting Principles Board, No. 22, "Disclosure of Accounting Policies,"* New York: American Institute of Certified Public Accountants, 1972, par. 8, as amended.

► Information Overload

"Important information is getting lost in a disclosure forest."

—Ray J. Groves, retired chairman of Ernst & Young

In 1994, the Jenkins Committee, a special committee of the AICPA, released a report entitled "Improving Business Reporting—A Customer Focus." One of the recommendations of the Jenkins Committee was that

some accounting disclosures be eliminated to cut down on what has been called "information overload." An informal survey of annual reports by Ray Groves of ERNST & YOUNG indicated that the amount of financial statement note disclosure had increased by 7.5% each year between 1972 and 1992. He forecast that by the year 2012, the financial statement notes in a typical annual report would average 72 pages. For many financial statement preparers, the time has come to say that enough is enough.

Does anyone want MORE disclosure? The Jenkins Committee report noted that "users have insatiable appetites for information." Areas mentioned in which

more disclosure is wanted include business segment information, leases, and intangible assets. How do companies feel about making additional disclosures? Clearly, companies don't like the cost of preparing additional information and the idea of potentially giving away strategic information to competitors. But companies also experience benefits from disclosure. By providing information to investors and creditors, companies make themselves less mysterious and thus reduce the cost they have to pay to obtain capital.

One suggestion for reducing information overload is to require a periodic, independent review of accounting standards with the goal of identifying the least useful

---

paying a contingent liability is estimated as "possible," or if the contingent liability is "probable but not reasonably estimable," the contingency should not be recognized but should be disclosed in the notes to the financial statements. The information provided should include as much data as possible to assist the user in evaluating the risk of the loss contingency.[16] Along these lines, most large companies have an interesting note describing the lawsuits outstanding against them.

Conceptually, disclosure should not be an alternative to recognition. In other words, if an item meets the recognition criteria given in Chapter 1, it should be included in the financial statements themselves and not just disclosed in a note. However, recall that the FASB's standard-setting process has been described as a "balancing act" between conceptual purity and business practicality. One of the tools in this balancing act is disclosure. Two examples are the accounting for stock-based compensation and for derivative financial instruments.

- In 1993, the FASB tentatively decided to require firms to recognize as compensation expense the value of stock options given to employees. This decision caused an angry uproar in the business community. After deliberation, the FASB decided to use note disclosure as a compromise—recognition of the stock option values is not required; the values need only be disclosed in a note (see DISNEY's Note 9 for details on its stock incentive plans).[17]
- With derivative financial instruments (e.g., options, futures, swaps, and other exotic financial contracts), the FASB responded to a public demand (backed by requests from the SEC) for more information about derivatives by requiring extensive disclosure.[18] This disclosure standard was a stopgap measure while the FASB studied the

---

16   Companies sometimes emphasize the importance of contingent liabilities by showing a category for them on the balance sheet with a zero balance and a reference to the contingent liabilities note. For an example of this treatment, see the balance sheet for Commonwealth Electric in Exhibit 3–6.

17   *Statement of Financial Accounting Standards No. 123,* "Accounting for Stock-Based Compensation," Norwalk, CT: Financial Accounting Standards Board, 1995.

18   *Statement of Financial Accounting Standards No. 119,* "Disclosure about Derivative Financial Instruments and Fair Value of Financial Instruments," Norwalk, CT: Financial Accounting Standards Board, 1994.

disclosures as candidates for elimination. A two-tier reporting process has also been suggested. Companies could produce a summary annual report for wide distribution, with the detailed disclosures made available only to those users requesting them. This summary annual report has been an option in the United States since 1986 but has never caught on. A third suggestion is that disclosures could be reduced if recognition were increased. For example, if all leases were recognized as capital leases, the amount of disclosure concerning leases could be cut dramatically. This option is unlikely to garner much support.

So, will disclosure increase or decrease in the future? In spite of all the talk of information overload, one force will almost certainly cause the amount of disclosure to increase—information technology.

QUESTIONS:

1. What are the costs of providing additional financial disclosures for a company? Which one of these costs do you think is most significant?
2. How would a summary annual report reduce information overload?
3. How will information technology cause the amount of disclosure to increase?

SOURCES:

"Disclosure Effectiveness," *Prospectus of the Financial Accounting Standards Board,* July 31, 1995.
Dennis R. Beresford and John A. Hepp, "Financial Statement Disclosures: Too Many or Too Few?" *FASB Status Report,* May 25, 1995, p. 7.
Robert K. Elliott and Peter D. Jacobson, "Costs and Benefits of Business Information Disclosure," *Accounting Horizons,* December 1994, p. 80.
Ray J. Groves, "Financial Disclosure: When More Is NOT Better," *Financial Executive,* May/June 1994, p. 11.

STOP & THINK In analyzing a company, do users care whether they get the information from the financial statements themselves or from the notes? From a user's standpoint, are recognition and disclosure the same thing?

issue further with the view of establishing a recognition standard (which was accomplished with FASB Statement No. 133). Derivative financial instrument disclosure is illustrated in Disney's Note 12 in Appendix A.

Supplementary Information

The FASB and SEC require supplementary information that must be reported in separate schedules. For example, the FASB requires the disclosure of quarterly information for certain companies. While the information in these notes is important to the users, it may not be covered by the auditors' opinion. A note that is not covered by the opinion is marked "unaudited."

Another category of supplementary information is business segment information. For companies with geographically dispersed operations, this segment information outlines the results for the different geographic segments. For example, COCA-COLA reports that less than one-third of its revenue comes from the United States. For firms with diverse product lines (such as PEPSICO, with substantial operations in soft drinks and snack foods), segment information for the different product lines is presented.[19] Note 11 for DISNEY in Appendix A includes information about the geographic distribution of Disney's revenues, operating income, and assets.

In addition to FASB requirements, the SEC also requires the disclosure of supplemental information about financial statement information for those publicly traded firms falling under the SEC's jurisdiction. For example, if the level of property, plant, and equipment is significant, the SEC requires a firm to provide details about changes in gross property, plant, and equipment and about changes in accumulated depreciation. The SEC also requires disclosure of the details of the changes in short-term borrowing and the average interest rate on short-term loans during the period.

---

19 *Statement of Financial Accounting Standards No. 131,* "Disclosures about Segments of an Enterprise and Related Information," Norwalk, CT: Financial Accounting Standards Board, 1997.

Subsequent Events

Although a balance sheet is prepared as of a given date, it is usually between one and three months before the financial statements are issued and made available to external users. For publicly traded companies, the SEC requires filing of the financial statements within 90 days of the fiscal year-end. During this time, the accounts are analyzed, adjusting entries are prepared, and for most companies, an independent audit is completed. During this "subsequent period," business doesn't shut down while the accountants huddle over the books. Business continues, and events may take place that have an impact upon the balance sheet and the other basic financial statements for the preceding year. Some of these events may even affect the amounts reported in the statements. These events are referred to in the accounting literature as **subsequent events** or **post-balance sheet events.** This subsequent period is illustrated in Exhibit 3–10.

EXHIBIT 3–10 | Subsequent Event Interval

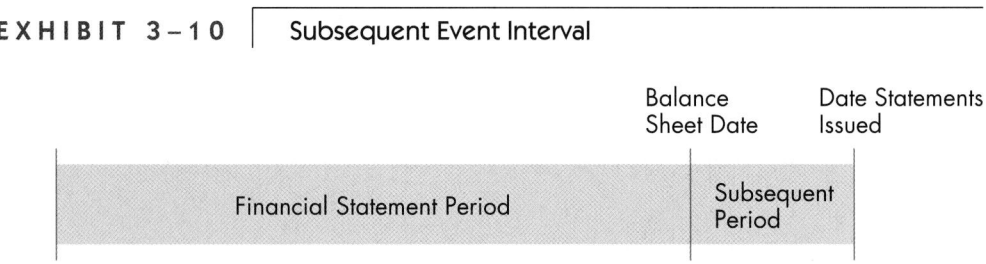

There are two different types of subsequent events that require consideration by management and evaluation by the independent auditor.[20]

- Those that require retroactive recognition and thus affect the amounts to be reported in the financial statements for the preceding accounting period
- Those that do not require recognition but should be disclosed in the notes to the financial statements

The first type of subsequent event usually provides additional information that affects the amounts included in the financial statements. The reported amounts in several accounts, such as Allowance for Doubtful Accounts, Warranty Liability, and Income Taxes Payable, reflect estimates of the expected value. These estimates are based on information available as of a given date. If a subsequent event provides new information that shows that the conditions existing as of the balance sheet date were different from those assumed when making the estimate, a change in the amount to be reported in the financial statements is required.

To illustrate this type of event, assume that a month after the balance sheet date it is learned that a major customer has filed for bankruptcy. This information was not known as of the balance sheet date, and only ordinary provisions were made in determining the Allowance for Doubtful Accounts. In all likelihood, the customer was already in financial difficulty at the balance sheet date, but it was not general knowledge. The filing of bankruptcy reveals that the conditions at the balance sheet date were different than those assumed in preparing the statements, and a further adjustment to both the balance sheet and income statement is indicated.

The second type of subsequent event does not reveal a difference in the conditions as of the balance sheet date but involves an event that is considered so significant that its disclosure is highly relevant to readers of the financial statements. These events will usu-

---

20 *AICPA Professional Standards, AU Section 560,* "Subsequent Events," Chicago: Commerce Clearing House, 1985, pars. .02–.05.

ally affect the subsequent year's financial statements and thus may affect decisions currently being made by users. Examples of such events include a casualty that destroys material portions of a company's assets, acquisition of a major subsidiary, sale of significant amounts of bonds or capital stock, and losses on receivables when the cause of the loss occurred subsequent to the balance sheet date. Information about this type of event is included in the notes to the financial statements and serves to notify the reader that the predictive value of the statements may be affected by the subsequent event.

The most common types of subsequent events reported by companies include events associated with debt refinancing, debt reduction, or incurring significant amounts of new debt; post-balance sheet developments associated with litigation; and changes in the status of a proposed merger or acquisition. There are, of course, many business events that occur during this subsequent period that are related only to the subsequent year and therefore have no impact on the preceding year's financial statements.

As an example of the types of disclosure associated with subsequent events, the following items were included in Note 15 to AT&T's financial statements dated December 31, 1998:

 Which of the five subsequent events disclosed by AT&T as occurring in 1999 would also require an adjustment to the 1998 financial statements?

- On March 9, 1999, AT&T exchanged approximately 439 million shares with the shareholders of TCI in order to effect a merger of the two companies.
- On January 8, 1999, AT&T announced a $4.0 billion share repurchase program, which was completed in March 1999.
- On February 1, 1999, AT&T announced the formation of a joint venture with TIME WARNER to offer AT&T-branded cable-telephony service to residential and small business customers over Time Warner's existing cable television systems in 33 states.
- On January 26, 1999, AT&T filed a registration statement with the SEC for the offering and sale of up to $10 billion of notes and warrants to purchase notes.
- On January 8, 1999, AT&T's board of directors announced the intention, following the completion of the TCI merger, to declare a 3-for-2 stock split of AT&T's common stock.

INTERNATIONAL ACCOUNTING FOR SUBSEQUENT EVENTS. The International Accounting Standards Committee (IASC) has released a standard, IAS 10, dealing specifically with the accounting for subsequent events. This standard, which was originally issued in September 1974 and was revised in March 1999, is essentially the same as the accounting employed in the United States. Specifically, IAS 10 requires that companies adjust the reported amounts of assets and liabilities if events occurring after the balance sheet date provide additional information about conditions that existed at the balance sheet date. In addition, IAS 10 requires that disclosure be made of significant subsequent events, even if those events do not impact the valuations reported in the balance sheet.

LIMITATIONS OF THE BALANCE SHEET

Understand the major limitations of the balance sheet.

Notwithstanding its usefulness, the balance sheet has some serious limitations. External users often need to know a company's worth. The balance sheet, however, does not generally reflect the current value of a business. A favorite ratio among followers of the stock market is the **book-to-market ratio,** computed as total book value of common equity divided by total market value of common equity. The book-to-market ratio reflects the difference between the balance sheet value of a company and the company's actual market value.[21] A company's book-to-market ratio is almost always less than one. This is because many assets are reported at historical cost, which is usually less than market value, and other assets are not included in the balance sheet at all. In addition, many intangible economic assets, such as a reputation for superior products or customer service, are not recognized in the balance sheet. Accordingly, the balance sheet numbers are often a very poor reflection of what a company is worth.

The graph in Exhibit 3–11 shows the average book-to-market ratio, from 1924 through 1998, of the 30 companies making up the Dow Jones Industrial Average. Note the steady decrease from an average book-to-market ratio of about 1.0 in 1980 to about 0.2 in 1998. This means that, in 1998, the accounting book value of the equity of the average company included in the Dow Jones Industrial Average was just 20% as large as the market value of the equity of that company. This low book-to-market ratio reflects the increasing importance of unreported, intangible assets as service and technology companies have become a more significant part of the U.S. economy.

EXHIBIT 3–11 | Average Book-to-Market Ratio of Companies Listed in the Dow Jones Industrial Average: 1924–1998

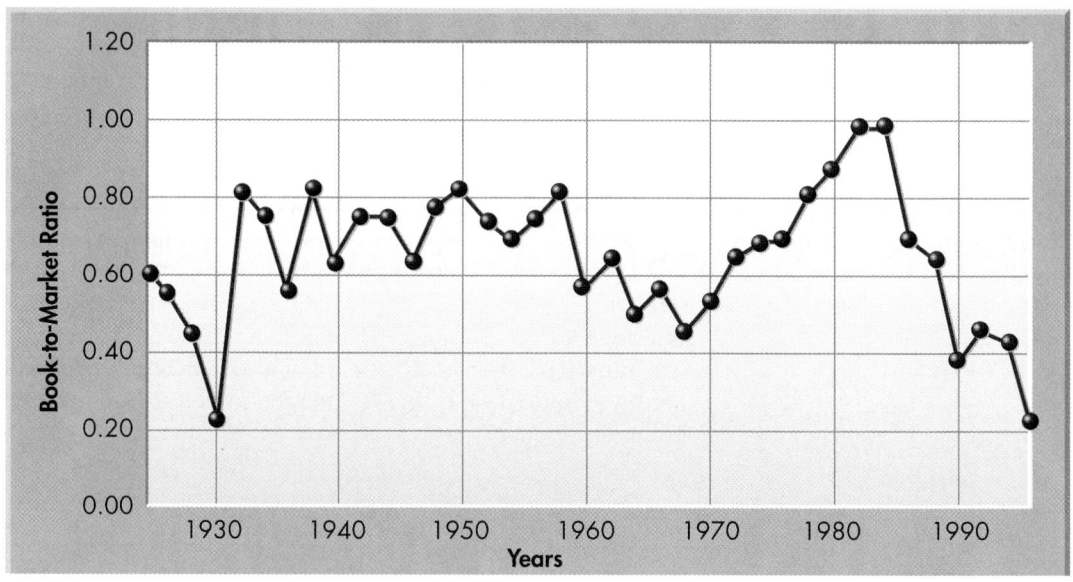

SOURCE: *The Wall Street Journal*, March 30, 1999, p. C14.

A related problem with the balance sheet is the instability of the dollar, the standard accounting measuring unit in the United States. Because of general price changes in the economy, the dollar does not maintain a constant purchasing power. Yet the historical costs of resources and equities shown on the balance sheet are not adjusted for changes in the purchasing power of the measuring unit. The result is a balance sheet that reflects assets, liabilities, and equities in terms of unequal purchasing power units. Some elements, for example, may be stated in terms of 1980 dollars and some in terms of current-year dollars. The variations in purchasing power of the amounts reported in the balance sheet make comparisons among companies, and even within a single company, less meaningful.

21 Research into the behavior of stock prices has found that firms with high book-to-market ratios tend to outperform the market in future years. See Eugene F. Fama and Kenneth R. French, "The Cross-Section of Expected Stock Returns," *The Journal of Finance*, June 1992, p. 427. No one is sure why high book-to-market-ratio firms outperform the market. One suggestion is that the accounting numbers partially reflect fundamental underlying value, and a high book-to-market ratio indicates that the market is currently undervaluing a company.

An additional limitation of the balance sheet, also related to the need for comparability, is that all companies do not classify and report all like items similarly. For example, titles and account classifications vary; some companies provide considerably more detail than others; and some companies with apparently similar transactions report them differently. Such differences make comparisons difficult and diminish the potential value of balance sheet analysis.

As mentioned above, some entity resources and obligations are not reported on the balance sheet. For example, as mentioned at the beginning of the chapter in connection with COCA-COLA, the company's network of bottling facilities is one of its most valuable resources; yet, it is not shown on the balance sheet, because its future service potential is not measurable in monetary terms. The assumptions of the traditional accounting model identified in Chapter 1, specifically the requirements of arm's-length transactions or events measurable in monetary terms, add to the objectivity of balance sheet disclosures but at the same time cause some information to be omitted that is likely to be relevant to certain users' decisions.

REVIEW OF LEARNING OBJECTIVES

1 **Describe the specific elements of the balance sheet (assets, liabilities, and owners' equity), and prepare a balance sheet with assets and liabilities properly classified into current and noncurrent categories.** A balance sheet is a listing of a company's assets, liabilities, and equities as of a certain point in time.

- Assets are probable future economic benefits obtained or controlled as a result of past transactions or events.
- Liabilities are probable future sacrifices of economic benefits arising from present obligations to transfer assets or provide services in the future as a result of past transactions or events.
- Equity is the net assets of an entity, that is, the amount that remains after total liabilities have been deducted from total assets.

For balance sheet reporting, assets and liabilities are often separated into current and noncurrent categories. Current items are those expected to be used or paid within one year, or within the normal operating cycle, whichever is longer.

When classifying assets and liabilities, the key considerations are how management intends to use an asset and when it expects to pay a liability.

Equity arises from owner investment, is increased by net income, and is decreased by losses and by distributions to owners. Equity is also impacted by stock repurchases, unrealized security gains and losses, and foreign exchange rate fluctuations.

2 **Identify the different formats used to present balance sheet data.** In most industries in the United States, assets and liabilities are listed in order of their liquidity, with current items first. For some industries, particularly those with large investments in long-term assets, current items are not listed first. In addition, in other countries, the format of the balance sheet can vary widely.

3 **Analyze a company's performance and financial position through the computation of financial ratios.** Balance sheet information is most often analyzed by looking at relationships between different balance sheet amounts and relationships between balance sheet and income statement amounts. Relationships between financial statement amounts are called financial ratios.

4 **Recognize the importance of the notes to the financial statements, and outline the types of disclosures made in the notes.** The information in the financial statements is supported by explanatory notes. The notes include a description of the accounting policies, details of summary totals, disclosure of significant items that fail to meet the recognition criteria, and supplemental information required by FASB and SEC standards.

Note disclosure also sometimes relates to subsequent events. Subsequent events are significant events occurring between the balance sheet date and the date the financial statements are issued. Subsequent events come in two varieties: those requiring immediate retroactive recognition in the financial statements and those requiring only note disclosure.

5 **Understand the major limitations of the balance sheet.** The balance sheet often does not provide an accurate reflection of the value of a business. Reasons for this include use of historical cost instead of current values, omission of some assets from the balance sheet, and failure to make adjustments for inflation. The balance sheet does not measure the market value of a company. The difference between balance sheet value and market value is captured in the book-to-market ratio (book value of equity divided by market value of equity), which is usually less than one.

KEY TERMS

Acid-test ratio 119
Additional paid-in capital 111
Asset 102
Asset mix 120
Asset turnover 121
Balance sheet 102
Book-to-market ratio 127
Callable obligation 108
Capital stock 111
Common stock 111
Contingent liability 110
Contributed capital 111
Corporation 111
Current asset 105
Current liability 107
Current ratio 119

Debt ratio 120
Deferred income tax asset 107
Deferred income tax liability 110
Deficit 112
Derivative 113
Equity 102
Estimated liability 110
Financial ratios 117
Leverage 120
Liability 102
Liquidity 117
Loan covenant 119
Objective acceleration clause 108
Other comprehensive income 112
Paid-in capital 111
Partnership 111

Post-balance sheet event 126
Preferred stock 111
Proprietorship 111
Quick ratio 119
Retained earnings 111
Return on assets 121
Return on equity 121
Sinking fund 107
Stockholders' (shareholders')
 equity 111
Subjective acceleration clause 108
Subsequent event 126
Trading securities 105
Treasury stock 112
Working capital 104

QUESTIONS

1. What three elements are contained in a balance sheet?
2. What is the importance of the term "probable" in the definition of an asset?
3. "Liabilities are obligations denominated in precise monetary terms." Do you agree or disagree? Explain.
4. What does the difference between current assets and current liabilities measure?
5. What criteria are generally used (a) in classifying assets as current? (b) in classifying liabilities as current?
6. Indicate under what circumstances each of the following can be considered noncurrent: (a) cash (b) receivables.
7. How can expected refinancing impact the classification of a liability?
8. (a) What is a subjective acceleration clause?
   (b) What is an objective acceleration clause?

(c) How do these clauses in debt instruments affect the classification of a liability?
9. Distinguish between contingent liabilities and estimated liabilities.
10. How do the equity sections of proprietorships, partnerships, and corporations differ from one another?
11. What are the three major categories in a corporation's equity section?
12. Under what circumstances may offset balances be properly recognized on the balance sheet?
13. In what order are assets usually listed in the balance sheet?
14. What are financial ratios?
15. Explain how the asset turnover ratio provides a measure of a company's overall efficiency.
16. What one financial ratio summarizes everything about the performance of a company? How is it computed?

17. What are the major types of notes attached to the financial statements?
18. How has the FASB used note disclosure as a tool of compromise?
19. What are some examples of supplementary information included in the notes to financial statements?

20. Under what circumstances does a subsequent event lead to a journal entry for the previous reporting period?
21. "The balance sheet does not reflect the value of a business." Do you agree or disagree? Explain.

DISCUSSION CASES

CASE 3–1

THE TEN LARGEST COMPANIES IN THE WORLD

Fortune annually provides a list of the most valuable companies in America. The top 10 most valuable companies, from the 1999 Fortune 500, are listed below.

(In millions of U.S. dollars)

Company Name	Industry	Market Value	Total Assets	Net Income
MICROSOFT	computers	$418,579	$ 22,357	$4,490
GENERAL ELECTRIC	electronics and machinery	360,251	355,935	9,296
WAL-MART	retailing	212,850	49,271	4,430
MERCK	pharmaceuticals	198,868	31,853	5,248
INTEL	computers	196,616	31,471	6,068
PFIZER	pharmaceuticals	182,211	18,302	3,351
AT&T	telecommunications	180,156	59,550	6,398
EXXON	energy	189,913	92,630	6,370
COCA-COLA	soft drinks	169,350	19,145	3,533
CISCO SYSTEMS	networking	166,616	8,917	1,350

As an analyst for a securities broker, you are asked the following questions concerning some of the figures.

1. Microsoft has total assets of $22 billion but a stock market value of $418 billion. How can a company be worth more than its total assets?
2. For each company, compute the ratio of total assets to total market value. What factors must the market be considering in valuing these companies that are not captured on the companies' balance sheets?
3. The price-earnings ratio, often called the P/E ratio, is defined as market price per share divided by earnings per share. Alternatively, the P/E ratio can be computed as total market value divided by net income. Compute the P/E ratios for the companies listed above. What factors do you think influence P/E ratios?

CASE 3–2

WE'VE GOT YOU NOW!

The Piedmont Computer Company has brought legal action against ATC Corporation for alleged monopolistic practices in the development of software. The claim has been pending for 2 years, with both sides accumulating evidence to support their positions. The case is now ready for trial. ATC Corporation has offered to settle out of court for $500,000, but Piedmont is asking for $5,000,000.

If financial statements must be issued prior to the court action, how should ATC reflect this contingent claim?

CASE 3–3

BUT WHAT IS OUR LIABILITY?

The Ditka Engineering Co. has signed a third-party loan guarantee for Liberty Company. The loan is from the National Bank of Illinois for $500,000. Liberty has recently filed for bankruptcy, and it is estimated by the company's auditors that creditors can expect to receive no more than 40% of their claims from Liberty. The treasurer of Ditka feels that because of the high uncertainty of final settlement, a liability should be recorded for the entire $500,000. The chief accountant, on the other hand, feels the 40% collection figure is reasonable and proposes that a $300,000 liability be recorded. The president of Ditka does not think a reasonable estimate can be made at this time and proposes that nothing be accrued for the contingent liability but that a note be added to the financial statements explaining the situation. As an independent outside auditor, what position would you take? Why?

CASE 3–4

AREN'T THE FINANCIAL STATEMENTS ENOUGH?

Excello Corporation's basic financial statements for the year just ended have been prepared in accordance with GAAP. During the current year, management changed the accounting method for computing depreciation, a major competitor constructed a new plant in the area, three separate lawsuits were brought against the corporation that are not expected to be settled for 2 years or more, and the corporation continued to use an acceptable revenue recognition principle that differs from that used by most other companies in the industry. Also, after the end of the year, but before the statements were issued, Excello issued additional shares of common stock.

Excello has recently applied for a large bank loan, and the bank has requested a copy of the financial statements. The auditors for Excello have prepared several notes, some quite lengthy, to accompany the financial statements, but Excello's management does not think the loan officer at the bank would understand them and therefore submits the statements without the notes. The bank accepts the statements as submitted.

Which of the events described above should be included in notes to the financial statements? Do you think it is acceptable to delete notes when submitting financial statements to third parties? Explain your position.

CASE 3–5

WHICH COMPANY IS WHICH?

Below are summaries of the balance sheets of five companies. The amounts are all stated as a percentage of total assets. The five companies are:

- D. BANKAMERICA, a large bank
- A. KELLY SERVICES, a firm that provides temporary employees
- C. YAHOO!, an Internet company
- E. MCDONALD'S, a fast-food company
- B. CONSOLIDATED EDISON, a utility serving New York City

	A	B	C	D	E
Receivables	59.1	4.0	4.0	62.9	3.1
Inventories	0.0	1.9	0.0	0.0	0.4
Other current assets	20.6	1.8	71.1	23.8	3.2
Land, buildings, and equipment	11.7	79.3	2.4	1.5	81.1
Other long-term assets	8.6	13.1	22.4	11.8	12.3
Short-term payables	42.1	6.6	12.9	26.8	8.5
Other current liabilities	0.0	1.3	0.0	57.8	4.1
Long-term liabilities	0.0	48.4	0.9	8.0	39.5
Equity	57.9	43.6	86.2	7.4	47.8

Match each balance sheet summary (A–E) with the appropriate company. Justify your choices.

CASE 3–6

HOW CAN WE LIVE WITH DEBT COVENANT REQUIREMENTS?

Bohr Company has a credit agreement with a syndicate of banks. In order to impose some limitations on Bohr's financial riskiness, the credit agreement requires Bohr to maintain a current ratio of at least 1.4 and a debt ratio of 0.55 or less.

The following summary data reflect a projection of Bohr's balance sheet for the coming year-end.

Current assets	$1,200,000
Long-term assets	1,800,000
Current liabilities	900,000
Long-term liabilities	800,000
Equity	1,300,000

The following information has also been prepared.

(a) If Bohr were to use FIFO instead of LIFO for inventory valuation, ending inventory would increase by $50,000.

(b) The amounts listed for long-term assets and liabilities include the anticipated purchase (and associated mortgage payable) of a building costing $100,000. Or Bohr can lease the building instead; the lease would qualify for treatment as an operating lease.

(c) Projected amounts include a planned declaration of cash dividends totaling $40,000 to be paid next year. Bohr has consistently paid dividends of equivalent amounts.

As a consultant to Bohr, you are asked to respond to the following two questions.

1. What steps can Bohr take to avoid violating the current ratio constraint?
2. What steps can Bohr take to avoid violating the debt ratio constraint? Of the steps that you propose, which ones do you think the banks had in mind when they imposed the loan covenants? If you had assisted the banks in drawing up the loan covenants, how would you have written them differently to avoid unintended consequences?

CASE 3–7

ARE CURRENT VALUES NECESSARY FOR VALUING INVESTMENT ASSETS?

First Federal Finance Co. has a large investment securities portfolio. In the "old days," First Federal was allowed to value these securities at the lower of cost or market. *Statement of Financial Accounting Standards (SFAS) No. 115* now requires current market valuation on the balance sheet for most securities. As a banker, you do not see current value reporting as being necessary. Indeed, you feel it unfairly harms your reported performance.

As a banker, why would current value accounting be threatening to you? How would you respond to these concerns if you were a member of the FASB?

CASE 3–8

WHAT SHOULD WE TELL THE STOCKHOLDERS?

Technology Unlimited, Inc., uses a fiscal year ending June 30. The auditors completed their review of the 2002 financial statements on September 8, 2002. They discovered the following subsequent events between June 30 and September 8.

1. Technology split its common stock 2 for 1 on August 15. Prior to the split, Technology had outstanding 100,000 shares of $1 par common stock.
2. A major customer, Diatride Company, declared bankruptcy on August 1. The customer owed Technology $75,000 on June 30. No payment has been received as of September 8. It is estimated that creditors will receive only 15% of outstanding claims.
3. Technology completed negotiations to purchase Liston Development Labs on July 18. The purchase price was $525,000 in cash and a 4-year, $250,000, 10% note.
4. A $750,000 lawsuit against Technology was filed on August 15. It is too early to measure the loss potential.
5. A general decline in stock market values for technology stocks occurred during the first week of September. Technology Unlimited's market value per share dropped from $42.50 to $28.00 in this week.

The auditors have requested that you prepare the "Subsequent Event" note that should accompany the financial statements for the year ending June 30, 2002. Only those events that require disclosure should be included in your note. Justify the exclusion of any events from your note.

CASE 3-9

WHAT DOES THIS BRITISH BALANCE SHEET MEAN?

Jonathan Atwood, a student from England, shows you the following balance sheet from his father's British company. Jonathan knows that you are studying accounting and asks you to look at the statement. You immediately recognize some differences between this statement and the ones you have been studying in your textbook.

	NOTES	Group 31 December 2002 £m	Group 31 December 2001 £m	Company 31 December 2002 £m	Company 31 December 2001 £m
Fixed Assets					
Intangibles	13	304.0	307.4	—	—
Tangible assets	14	978.8	822.5	16.8	16.2
Investments	15	16.7	25.2	938.9	679.3
		1,299.5	1,155.1	955.7	695.5
Current Assets					
Stock	16	328.2	334.8	—	—
Debtors	17	554.1	548.2	113.4	210.8
Investments—short-term loans and deposits		118.0	33.3	5.1	23.5
Cash at bank and in hand		62.6	57.4	—	—
		1,062.9	973.7	118.5	234.3
Creditors: amounts falling due within one year					
Borrowings	18	(136.3)	(133.7)	(175.0)	(74.6)
Other	19	(825.9)	(809.2)	(98.4)	(234.7)
Net current assets (liabilities)		100.7	30.8	(154.9)	(75.0)
Total assets less current liabilities		1,400.2	1,185.9	800.8	620.5
Other Liabilities					
Creditors: amounts falling due after more than one year					
Borrowings	18	(407.9)	(381.4)	(54.2)	(80.4)
Other	19	(12.0)	(8.5)	(26.4)	(42.1)
Provisions for liabilities and charges	20	(96.4)	(115.5)	0.5	1.2
		(516.3)	(505.4)	(80.1)	(121.3)
		883.9	680.5	720.7	499.2
Capital and Reserves					
Called-up share capital	21	174.7	173.6	174.7	173.6
Share premium account	22	381.6	217.4	381.6	217.4
Revaluation reserve	22	95.8	36.7	2.4	1.1
Profit and loss account	22	115.8	167.6	162.0	107.1
		767.9	595.3	720.7	499.2
Minority interests		116.0	85.2	—	—
		883.9	680.5	720.7	499.2

1. Identify the differences that exist between this British statement and those prepared using the standards and conventions of the United States.

2. Evaluate the differences, identifying strengths and weaknesses of each nation's approach.

CASE 3–10

ARE BANKS BACKWARD?

The following is an excerpt from an article dealing with accounting and banks in *The Wall Street Journal*:

> Congress deregulated the left side of the balance sheet [liabilities] by permitting thrifts to get into high-risk business but kept regulation and deposit insurance for the right side of the balance sheet [assets].

1. From an accounting perspective, what is wrong with this quote?
2. As a bank depositor, do you care about the balance sheet of the bank where you deposit your money? Why or why not? How might your attitude change if the U.S. federal government were to abolish deposit insurance?
3. Consider your account at a bank—does the bank view your account as an asset or as a liability?

EXERCISES

EXERCISE 3–11

BALANCE SHEET CLASSIFICATION

A balance sheet contains the following classifications:

(a) Current assets
(b) Investments
(c) Property, plant, and equipment
(d) Intangible assets
(e) Other noncurrent assets
(f) Current liabilities
(g) Long-term debt
(h) Other noncurrent liabilities
(i) Capital stock
(j) Additional paid-in capital
(k) Retained earnings

Indicate by letter how each of the following accounts would be classified. Place a minus sign (–) for all accounts representing offset or contra balances.

1. Discount on Bonds Payable *g –*
2. Stock of Subsidiary Corporation *b* *f*
3. 12% Bonds Payable (due in 6 months) *f*
4. U.S. Treasury Notes *a*
5. Income Taxes Payable *f*
6. Sales Taxes Payable *f*
7. Estimated Claims Under Warranties for Service and Replacements *h or f*
8. Par Value of Stock Issued and Outstanding *i*
9. Unearned Rent Revenue (6 months in advance) *f*
10. Long-Term Advances to Officers *e*
11. Interest Receivable *a*
12. Preferred Stock Retirement Fund *b*
13. Trademarks *d*
14. Allowance for Doubtful Accounts *a –*
15. Dividends Payable *f*
16. Accumulated Depreciation *c –*
17. Trading Securities *a*
18. Prepaid Rent *a*
19. Prepaid Insurance *a*
20. Deferred Income Tax Asset *e*

EXERCISE 3–12

BALANCE SHEET CLASSIFICATION

State how each of the following accounts should be classified on the balance sheet.

(a) Treasury Stock OE
(b) Retained Earnings OE
(c) Vacation Pay Payable CL
(d) Foreign Currency Translation Adjustment OE
(e) Allowance for Doubtful Accounts CA
(f) Liability for Pension Payments NCL
(g) Investment Securities (Trading) CA
(h) Paid-In Capital in Excess of Stated Value OE
(i) Leasehold Improvements PPE NCA
(j) Goodwill INTANGIBLE ASSET
(k) Receivables—U.S. Government Contracts CA
(l) Advances to Salespersons CA
(m) Premium on Bonds Payable
(n) Inventory CA
(o) Patents INTANGIBLE ASSET
(p) Unclaimed Payroll Checks CL
(q) Income Taxes Payable CL
(r) Subscription Revenue Received in Advance CL
(s) Interest Payable CL
(t) Deferred Income Tax Asset NCA
(u) Tools CA
(v) Deferred Income Tax Liability NCL

EXERCISE 3–13

ASSET DEFINITION

Using the definition of an asset from *FASB Concepts Statement No. 6,* indicate whether each of the following should be listed as an asset by DeBroglie Company.

(a) DeBroglie has legal title to a silver mine in a remote location. Historically, the mine has yielded over $100 million in silver. Engineering estimates suggest that no further minerals are economically extractable from the mine.
(b) DeBroglie is currently negotiating the purchase of an oil field with proven oil reserves totaling 2 billion barrels.
(c) DeBroglie employs a team of five geologists who are widely recognized as worldwide leaders in their field.
(d) DeBroglie claims ownership of a large piece of real estate in a foreign country. The real estate has a current market value of over $650 million. The country expropriated the land 35 years ago, and no representative of DeBroglie has been allowed on the property since.
(e) Several years ago, DeBroglie purchased a large meteor crater on the advice of a geologist who had developed a theory claiming that vast deposits of iron ore lay underneath the crater. The crater has no other economic use. No ore has been found, and the geologist's theory is not generally accepted.

EXERCISE 3–14

LIABILITY DEFINITION

Using the definition of a liability from *FASB Concepts Statement No. 6*, indicate whether each of the following should be listed as a liability by Pauli Company:

(a) Pauli was involved in a highly publicized lawsuit last year. Pauli lost and was ordered to pay damages of $125 million. The payment has been made.
(b) In exchange for television advertising services that Pauli received last month, Pauli is obligated to provide the television station with building maintenance service for the next 4 months.

(c) Pauli contractually guarantees to replace any of its stain-resistant carpets if they are stained and can't be cleaned.

(d) Pauli estimates that its total payroll for the coming year will exceed $35 million.

(e) In the past, Pauli has suffered frequent vandalism at its storage warehouses. Pauli estimates that losses due to vandalism during the coming year will total $3 million.

EXERCISE 3–15

BALANCE SHEET PREPARATION

From the following list of accounts, prepare a balance sheet showing all balance sheet items properly classified. (No monetary amounts are to be recognized.)

Accounts Payable
Accounts Receivable
Accumulated Depreciation—Buildings
Accumulated Depreciation—Equipment
Advertising Expense
Allowance for Doubtful Accounts
Bonds Payable
Buildings
Cash
Common Stock
Cost of Goods Sold
Deferred Income Tax Liability
Depreciation Expense—Buildings
Dividends
Doubtful Accounts Expense
Equipment
Estimated Warranty Expense Payable (current)
Gain on Sale of Investment Securities
Gain on Sale of Land
Goodwill
Income Tax Expense
Income Taxes Payable
Interest Receivable
Interest Revenue
Inventory
Investment in Subsidiary
Investment Securities (Trading)
Land
Loss on Purchase Commitments
Miscellaneous General Expense
Notes Payable (current)
Paid-In Capital from Sale of Treasury Stock
Paid-In Capital in Excess of Stated Value
Patents
Pension Fund
Premium on Bonds Payable
Prepaid Insurance
Property Tax Expense
Purchase Discounts
Purchases
Retained Earnings
Salaries Payable
Sales
Sales Salaries
Travel Expense

EXERCISE 3–16

COMPUTATION OF WORKING CAPITAL

From the following data, compute the working capital for Benson Equipment Co. at December 31, 2002.

Cash in general checking account	$ 20,000
Cash in fund to be used to retire bonds in 2006	50,000
Cash held to pay sales taxes	18,000
Notes receivable—due February 2004	100,000
Trade accounts receivable	125,000
Inventory	75,000
Prepaid insurance—for 2003 and 2004	15,000
Vacant land held as investment	300,000
Used equipment to be sold	25,000
Deferred tax asset—to be recovered in 2001	10,000
Trade accounts payable	60,000
Note payable—due July 2003	33,000
Note payable—due January 2004	10,000
Bonds payable—maturity date 2006	210,000
Salaries payable	20,000
Sales taxes payable	23,000
Goodwill	37,000

EXERCISE 3–17

PREPARATION OF CORRECTED BALANCE SHEET

The following balance sheet was prepared for Jared Corporation as of Dec. 31, 2002.

Jared Corporation
Balance Sheet
December 31, 2002

Assets		Liabilities and Owners' Equity	
Current assets:		**Current liabilities:**	
Cash	$ 12,500	Accounts payable	$ 3,400
Investment securities	8,000	Other current liabilities	2,000
Accounts receivable, net	21,350	Total current liabilities	$ 5,400
Inventory	31,000	Long-term liabilities	32,750
Other current assets	14,200	Total liabilities	$ 38,150
Total current assets	$ 87,050		
Noncurrent assets:		**Owners' equity:**	
Property, plant, and equipment, net	$ 64,800	Common stock	$ 50,000
Treasury stock	4,500	Retained earnings	81,800
Other noncurrent assets	13,600	Total owners' equity	$131,800
Total noncurrent assets	$ 82,900		
Total assets	$169,950	Total liabilities and owners' equity	$169,950

The following additional information relates to the December 31, 2002, balance sheet.

(a) Cash includes $4,000 that has been restricted to the purchase of manufacturing equipment (a noncurrent asset).

(b) Investment securities include $2,750 of stock that was purchased in order to give the company significant ownership and a seat on the board of directors of a major supplier.

(c) Other current assets include a $4,000 advance to the president of the company. No due date has been set.

(d) Long-term liabilities include bonds payable of $10,000. Of this amount, $2,500 represents bonds scheduled to be redeemed in 2003.

(e) Long-term liabilities also include a $7,000 bank loan. On May 15, the loan will become due on demand.

(f) On December 21, dividends in the amount of $15,000 were declared to be paid to shareholders of record on January 25. These dividends have not been reflected in the financial statements.

(g) Cash in the amount of $19,000 has been placed in a restricted fund for the redemption of preferred stock in 2003. Both the cash and the stock have been removed from the balance sheet.

(h) Property, plant, and equipment includes land costing $8,000 that is being held for investment purposes and that is scheduled to be sold in 2003.

Based on the information provided, prepare a corrected balance sheet.

EXERCISE 3–18

BALANCE SHEET RELATIONSHIPS

For each of the items (a) through (n) on the Faevero and Company Inc. balance sheet, indicate the amount that should appear on the balance sheet.

Faevero and Company Inc.
Consolidated Balance Sheet
December 31, 2002

Assets

Current assets:				
Cash			$ 23,185	
Investment securities			(a)	
Accounts and notes receivable	$	(b)		
Allowance for doubtful accounts and notes receivable		9,622	165,693	
Inventories			235,813	
Other current assets			10,419	
Total current assets				$ (c)
Noncurrent assets:				
Property, plant, and equipment	$771,604			
Accumulated depreciation		(d)	$419,418	
Other noncurrent assets			15,631	
Total noncurrent assets				435,049
Total assets				$895,312

Liabilities and Owners' Equity

Current liabilities:				
Accounts payable			$ (e)	
Payable to banks			32,858	
Income taxes payable			8,328	
Current installments of long-term debt			5,720	
Accrued expenses			6,610	
Total current liabilities				$ (f)
Noncurrent liabilities:				
Long-term debt			$ (g)	
Deferred income tax liability			40,406	
Minority interest in subsidiaries			3,309	
Total noncurrent liabilities				175,469
Total liabilities				$327,655
Contributed capital:				
Preferred stock, no par value (authorized 1,618 shares; issued 1,115 shares)	$ 16,596			
Common stock, $1 par value per share (authorized 60,000 shares; issued 25,939 shares)	(h)			
Additional paid-in capital	(i)		(j)	
Total contributed capital			$ (k)	
Retained earnings			504,744	
Total contributed capital and retained earnings			$ (l)	
Less: Treasury stock, at cost (1,236 shares)			26,688	
Total owners' equity				$ (m)
Total liabilities and owners' equity				$ (n)

EXERCISE 3–19

BALANCE SHEET SCHEDULES

In its annual report to stockholders, Crantz Inc. presents a condensed balance sheet with detailed data provided in supplementary schedules.

1. From the adjusted trial balance of Crantz, prepare the following sections of the balance sheet, properly classifying all accounts as to balance sheet categories:
   (a) Current assets
   (b) Property, plant, and equipment
   (c) Intangible assets
   (d) Total assets
   (e) Current liabilities
   (f) Noncurrent liabilities
   (g) Owners' equity
   (h) Total liabilities and owners' equity
2. Compute the current ratio and debt ratio for Crantz.

Crantz Inc.
Adjusted Trial Balance
December 31, 2002

	Debit	Credit
Cash	$ 33,900	
Investment securities (trading)	20,000	
Notes receivable—trade debtors	18,000	
Accrued interest on notes receivable	1,800	
Accounts receivable	88,400	
Allowance for doubtful accounts		$ 4,300
Inventory	56,900	
Prepaid expenses	6,100	
Accounts payable		31,500
Notes payable—trade creditors		16,000
Accrued interest on notes payable		800
Land	80,000	
Buildings	170,000	
Accumulated depreciation—buildings		34,000
Equipment	48,000	
Accumulated depreciation—equipment		7,600
Patents	15,000	
Franchises	10,000	
Bonds payable, 8%—issue 1 (mature 12/31/04)		50,000
Bonds payable, 12%—issue 2 (mature 12/31/08)		100,000
Accrued interest on bonds payable		8,000
Premium on bonds payable—issue 1		1,500
Discount on bonds payable—issue 2	10,500	
Mortgage payable		57,500
Accrued interest on mortgage payable		2,160
Capital stock, par value $1; 10,000 shares authorized; 4,000 shares issued		4,000
Additional paid-in capital		112,800
Retained earnings		139,440
Treasury stock—at cost (500 shares)	11,000	
	$569,600	$569,600

EXERCISE 3–20

COMPUTATION OF FINANCIAL RATIOS

The following data are from the financial statements of Borg Company.

Current assets	$ 70,000
Total assets	150,000
Current liabilities	30,000
Total liabilities	80,000
Net income	10,000
Sales	300,000

Compute Borg's current ratio, debt ratio, asset turnover, return on assets, and return on equity.

EXERCISE 3–21

COMPUTATION OF FINANCIAL RATIOS

Lwaxana Company has the following assets.

Cash	$ 15,000
Accounts receivable	50,000
Inventory	100,000
Property, plant, and equipment	200,000
Total assets	$365,000

Companies in Lwaxana's industry typically have the following asset mix: cash, 7%; accounts receivable, 15%; inventory, 18%; property, plant, and equipment, 60%.

Compared to other companies in its industry, Lwaxana has too much of one asset. Which one? Show your computations.

EXERCISE 3–22

CLASSIFICATION OF SUBSEQUENT EVENTS

The following events occurred after the end of the company's fiscal year but before the annual audit was completed. Classify each event as to its impact on the financial statements, that is, (1) reported by changing the amounts in the financial statements, (2) reported in notes to the financial statements, or (3) does not require reporting. Include support for your classification.

(a) Major customer went bankrupt due to a deteriorating financial condition.
(b) Company sustained extensive hurricane damage to one of its plants.
(c) Company lost a major lawsuit that had been pending for 2 years.
(d) Increasing U.S. trade deficit may have impact on company's overseas sales.
(e) Company sold a large block of preferred stock.
(f) Preparation of current year's income tax return disclosed an additional $25,000 is due on last year's return.
(g) Company's controller resigned and was replaced by an audit manager from the company's audit firm.

EXERCISE 3–23

REPORTING FINANCIAL INFORMATION

For each of the items below, indicate whether the item should be reflected in the 2002 financial statements for Rutherford Company. If the item should be reflected, indicate whether it should be reported in the financial statements themselves or by note disclosure.

(a) During 2002, the company had a gain on the sale of manufacturing assets.
(b) As of December 31, 2002, the company was in violation of certain loan covenants. The violation does not cause the loans to be callable immediately but does increase the interest charge by 1.5%.
(c) The company uses straight-line depreciation for all tangible, long-term assets.
(d) As of December 31, 2002, accounts receivable in the amount of $6.7 million are estimated to be uncollectible.
(e) The Environmental Protection Agency is investigating the company's procedures for disposing of toxic waste. Outside consultants have estimated that the company may be liable for fines of up to $8 million.
(f) The company's reported Provision for Income Taxes includes $3.6 million in current taxes and $7.3 million in deferred taxes.
(g) During 2002, a long-term insurance agreement was signed. The company paid 5 years of insurance premiums in advance.
(h) As of December 31, 2002, the company holds $11.2 million of its own stock that it purchased in the open market and is holding for possible reissuance.
(i) During 2002, the company hired three prominent research chemists away from its chief competitor.

(j) Reported long-term debt is composed of senior subordinated bonds payable, convertible bonds payable, junior subordinated bonds payable, and capital lease obligations.

(k) Early in 2003, a significant drop in raw material prices caused the company's stock price to rise in anticipation of sharply increased profits for the year.

EXERCISE 3–24

PREPARATION OF NOTES TO FINANCIAL STATEMENTS

The following information was used to prepare the financial statements for Delta Chemical Company. Prepare the necessary notes to accompany the statements.

Delta uses the LIFO inventory method on its financial statements. If the FIFO method were used, the ending inventory balance would be reduced by $50,000 and net income for the year would be reduced by $35,000 after taxes. Delta depreciates its equipment using the straight-line method. Revenue is generally recognized when inventory is shipped unless it is sold on a consignment basis. The current value of the equipment is $525,000, as contrasted to its depreciated cost of $375,000.

Delta has borrowed $350,000 on a 10–year note at 14% interest. The note is due on July 1, 2012. Delta's equipment has been pledged as collateral for the loan. The terms of the note prohibit additional long-term borrowing without the express permission of the holder of the note. Delta is planning to request such permission during the next fiscal year.

The board of directors of Delta is currently discussing a merger with another chemical company. No public announcement has yet been made, but it is anticipated that additional shares of stock will be issued as part of the merger. Delta's balance sheet will report receivables of $126,000. Included in this figure is a $25,000 advance to the president of Delta, $30,000 of notes receivable from customers, $10,000 in advances to sales representatives, and $70,000 of accounts receivable from customers. The reported balance reflects a deduction for anticipated collection losses.

PROBLEMS

PROBLEM 3–25

COMPUTING BALANCE SHEET COMPONENTS

Denton Equipment Inc. furnishes you with the following list of accounts.

Accounts Payable	$ 66,000
Accounts Receivable	40,000
Accumulated Depreciation	44,000
Advances to Salespersons	10,000
Advertising Expense	72,000
Allowance for Doubtful Accounts	10,000
Bonds Payable	80,000
Cash	22,000
Certificates of Deposit	16,000
Common Stock (par)	100,000
Deferred Income Tax Liability	46,000
Equipment	215,500
Inventory	55,000
Investment in Rowe Oil Co. Stock (40% of outstanding stock owned for control purposes)	76,500
Investment in Siebert Co. Stock (trading securities)	21,000
Paid-In Capital in Excess of Par	42,500
Premium on Bonds Payable	6,000
Prepaid Insurance	6,000
Rent Revenue	37,000
Rent Revenue Received in Advance (4 months)	12,000
Retained Earnings	97,500
Taxes Payable	10,000
Tools	52,000

Instructions:

1. From the preceding list of accounts, determine working capital, total assets, total liabilities, and owners' equity per share of stock (75,000 shares outstanding).
2. Assume net income of $20,000. Compute current ratio, debt ratio, and return on equity.

PROBLEM 3–26

CLASSIFIED BALANCE SHEET

Following is a list of account titles and balances for Zaldo Investment Corporation as of January 31, 2002.

Accounts Payable	$ 85,900
Accounts Receivable	153,100
Accumulated Depreciation—Buildings	151,700
Accumulated Depreciation—Machinery and Equipment	127,000
Additional Paid-In Capital—Common Stock	662,000
Allowance for Doubtful Notes and Accounts Receivable	16,500
Buildings	410,000
Cash Fund for Stock Redemption	17,500
Cash in Banks	9,120
Cash on Hand	97,300
Claim for Income Tax Refund	4,500
Common Stock, $1 par	50,000
Employees' Income Taxes Payable	4,780
Income Taxes Payable	29,200
Interest Payable	5,390
Interest Receivable	900
Inventory	211,300
Investment Securities (trading)	102,500
Investments in Undeveloped Properties	175,000
Land	188,000
Machinery and Equipment	145,000
Miscellaneous Supplies Inventory	6,200
Notes Payable (current)	58,260
Notes Payable (due in 2007)	38,000
Notes Receivable (current)	22,470
Preferred Stock, $5 par	320,000
Prepaid Insurance	3,500
Retained Earnings (debit balance)	11,740
Salaries and Wages Payable	9,400

Instructions:

1. Prepare a properly classified balance sheet.
2. Assume net income of $200,000 and sales of $5,000,000. Compute current ratio, debt ratio, and asset turnover.

PROBLEM 3–27

CLASSIFIED BALANCE SHEET—INCLUDING NOTES

Adjusted account balances and supplemental information for Brockbank Research Corp. as of December 31, 2002, are as follows:

Accounts Payable	$ 32,160
Accounts Receivable—Trade	57,731
Accumulated Depreciation—Leasehold Improvements and Equipment	579,472
Additional Paid-In Capital	265,000
Allowance for Doubtful Accounts	1,731
Automotive Equipment	132,800
Cash	25,600
Cash Fund for Bond Retirement	3,600
Common Stock	35,000
Deferred Income Tax Liability	45,000
Dividends Payable	37,500
Franchises	12,150
Furniture, Fixtures, and Store Equipment	769,000

Insurance Claims Receivable	$120,000
Inventories	201,620
Investment in Unconsolidated Subsidiary	80,000
Land	6,000
Leasehold Improvements	65,800
7½%–12% Mortgage Notes	200,000
Notes Payable—Banks (due in 2003)	12,000
Notes Payable—Trade	63,540
Patent Licenses	57,402
Prepaid Insurance	5,500
Profit Sharing, Payroll, and Vacation Payable	40,000
Retained Earnings	225,800

Supplemental information:

(a) Depreciation is provided by the straight-line method over the estimated useful lives of the assets.

(b) Common stock is $1 par, and 35,000 of the 100,000 authorized shares were issued and are outstanding.

(c) The cost of an exclusive franchise to import a foreign company's ball bearings and a related patent license are being amortized on the straight-line method over their remaining lives: franchise, 10 years; patents, 15 years.

(d) Inventories are stated at the lower of cost or market; cost was determined by the specific identification method.

(e) Insurance claims based on the opinion of an independent insurance adjustor are for property damages at the central warehouse. These claims are estimated to be two-thirds collectible in the following year and one-third collectible thereafter.

(f) The company leases all of its buildings from various lessors. Estimated fixed-lease obligations are $50,000 per year for the next 10 years. The leases do not meet the criteria for capitalization.

(g) The company is currently in litigation over a claimed overpayment of income tax of $13,000. In the opinion of counsel, the claim is valid. The company is contingently liable on guaranteed notes worth $12,000.

Instructions: Prepare a properly classified balance sheet. Include all notes and parenthetical notations necessary to properly disclose the essential financial data.

PROBLEM 3–28

CLASSIFICATION OF LIABILITIES

The accountant for Sierra Corp. prepared the following schedule of liabilities as of December 31, 2002.

Accounts payable	$ 65,000
Notes payable—trade	19,000
Notes payable—bank	80,000
Wages and salaries payable	1,500
Interest payable	14,300
Mortgage note payable—10%	60,000
Mortgage note payable—12%	150,000
Bonds payable	200,000
Total	$589,800

The following additional information pertains to these liabilities.

(a) All trade notes payable are due within 6 months of the balance sheet date.

(b) Bank notes payable include two separate notes payable to First Interstate Bank.

(1) A $30,000, 8% note issued March 1, 2000, payable on demand. Interest is payable every 6 months.

(2) A 1-year, $50,000, 11½% note issued January 2, 2002. On December 30, 2002, Sierra negotiated a written agreement with First Interstate Bank to replace the note with a 2-year, $50,000, 10% note to be issued January 2, 2003.

(c) The 10% mortgage note was issued October 1, 1999, with a term of 10 years. Terms of the note give the holder the right to demand immediate payment if the company fails to make a monthly interest payment within 10 days of the date the payment is due. As of December 31, 2002, Sierra is 3 months behind in paying its required interest payment.

(d) The 12% mortgage note was issued May 1, 1996, with a term of 20 years. The current principal amount due is $150,000. Principal and interest are payable annually on April 30. A payment of $22,000 is due April 30, 1993. The payment includes interest of $18,000.

(e) The bonds payable are 10-year, 8% bonds, issued June 30, 2003.

Instructions: Prepare the liabilities section of the December 31, 2002, classified balance sheet for Sierra Corp. Include notes as appropriate. Assume the interest payable accrual has been computed correctly.

PROBLEM 3–29

CORRECTED BALANCE SHEET
The following balance sheet was prepared by the accountant for Rowley Company.

Instructions: Prepare a corrected classified balance sheet using appropriate account titles.

Rowley Company
Balance Sheet
June 30, 2002

Assets

Cash	$ 25,500
Investment securities—Trading (includes long-term investment of $250,000 in stock of Oak Mountain Developers)	312,000
Inventories (net of amount still due suppliers of $85,000)	624,600
Prepaid expenses (includes a deposit of $10,000 made on inventories to be delivered in 18 months)	33,000
Property, plant, and equipment (excluding $60,000 of equipment still in use, but fully depreciated)	220,000
Goodwill (based on estimate by the president of Rowley Company)	70,000
Total assets	$1,285,100

Liabilities and Owners' Equity

Notes payable ($75,000 due in 2004)	$ 135,000
Accounts payable (not including amount due to suppliers of inventory—see above)	142,000
Long-term liability under pension plan	60,000
Retained earnings restricted for building expansion	105,000
Accumulated depreciation	73,000
Taxes payable	44,500
Bonds payable (net of discount of $10,000)	290,000
Deferred income tax liability	68,000
Common stock (10,000 shares, $1 par)	10,000
Additional paid-in capital	240,500
Unrestricted retained earnings	117,100
Total liabilities and owners' equity	$1,285,100

PROBLEM 3–30

CLASSIFIED BALANCE SHEET

The financial position of St. Charles Ranch is summarized in the following letter to the corporation's accountant.

Dear Dallas:

The following information should be of value to you in preparing the balance sheet for St. Charles Ranch as of December 31, 2002. The balance of cash as of December 31 as reported on the bank statement was $43,825. There were still outstanding checks of $9,320 that had not cleared the bank, and cash on hand of $10,640 was not deposited until January 4, 2003.

Customers owed the company $40,500 at December 31. We estimated 6% of this amount will never be collected. We owe suppliers $37,000 for poultry feed purchased in November and December. About 75% of this feed was used before December 31.

Because we think the price of grain will rise in 2003, we are holding 10,000 bushels of wheat and 5,000 bushels of oats until spring. The market value at December 31 was $3.50 per bushel of wheat and $1.50 per bushel of oats. We estimate that both prices will increase 15% by selling time. We are not able to estimate the cost of raising this product.

St. Charles Ranch owns 1,850 acres of land. Two separate purchases of land were made as follows: 1,250 acres at $200 per acre in 1985 and 600 acres at $400 per acre in 1990. Similar land is currently selling for $800 per acre. The balance of the mortgage on the two parcels of land is $250,000 at December 31; 10% of this mortgage must be paid in 2003.

Our farm buildings and equipment cost us $176,400 and on the average are 40% depreciated. If we were to replace these buildings and equipment at today's prices, we believe we would be conservative in estimating a cost of $300,000.

We have not paid property taxes of $5,500 for 2003 billed to us in late November. Our estimated income tax for 2002 is $18,500. A refund claim for $2,800 has been filed relative to the 2000 income tax return. The claim arose because of an error made on the 2000 return.

The operator of the ranch will receive a bonus of $9,000 for 2002 operations. It will be paid when the entire grain crop has been sold.

As you may recall, we issued 14,000 shares of $1 par stock upon incorporation. The ranch received $290,000 as net proceeds from the stock issue. Dividends of $30,000 were declared last month and will be paid on February 1, 2003.

The new year appears to hold great promise. Thanks for your help in preparing this statement.

Sincerely,

Frank K. Santiago
President—St. Charles Ranch

Instructions: Based on this information, prepare a properly classified balance sheet as of December 31, 2002.

PROBLEM 3–31

CORRECTED BALANCE SHEET

The bookkeeper for Dependable Computers, Inc. reports the following balance sheet amounts as of June 30, 2002.

Current assets	$244,050
Other assets	628,550
Current liabilities	138,600
Other liabilities	90,000
Owners' equity	644,000

A review of account balances reveals the following data.

(a) An analysis of current assets discloses:

Cash	$ 42,250
Investment securities—trading	60,000
Trade accounts receivable	56,800
Inventories, including advertising supplies of $2,000	85,000
	$244,050

(b) Other assets include:

Property, plant, and equipment:	
Depreciated book value (cost, $656,000)	$549,000
Deposit with a supplier for merchandise ordered for August delivery	2,150
Goodwill recorded on the books to cancel losses incurred by the company in prior years	77,400
	$628,550

(c) Current liabilities include:

Payroll payable		$ 7,150
Taxes payable		4,150
Rent payable		11,400
Trade accounts payable		
Total owed to suppliers on account	$101,400	
Less: 6-month note received from a supplier who purchased some used equipment on June 29, 2002	1,500	99,900
Notes payable		16,000
		$138,600

(d) Other liabilities include:

9% mortgage on property, plant, and equipment, payable in semiannual installments of $9,000 through June 30, 2007	$ 90,000

(e) Owners' equity includes:

Preferred stock: 19,000 shares outstanding ($20 par value)	$380,000
Common stock: 160,000 shares at $1 stated value	160,000
Additional paid-in capital	104,000
	$644,000

(f) Common shares were originally issued for $391,000, but the losses of the company for the past years were charged against additional paid-in capital.

Instructions: Using the account balances and related data, prepare a corrected balance sheet showing individual asset, liability, and owners' equity balances properly classified.

PROBLEM 3–32

CORRECTED BALANCE SHEET

The following balance sheet is submitted to you for inspection and review.

Appalachian Freight Company
Balance Sheet
December 31, 2002

Assets

Cash	$ 45,050
Accounts receivable	112,500
Inventories	204,000
Prepaid insurance	8,800
Property, plant, and equipment	376,800
	$747,150

Liabilities and Owners' Equity

Miscellaneous liabilities	$ 3,600
Loan payable	76,200
Accounts payable	75,250
Capital stock	134,000
Paid-in capital	458,100
	$747,150

In the course of the review, you find the following data.

(a) The possibility of uncollectible accounts on accounts receivable has not been considered. It is estimated that uncollectible accounts will total $4,800.

(b) $45,000 representing the cost of a large-scale newspaper advertising campaign completed in 2002 has been added to the inventories, because it is believed that this campaign will benefit sales of 2003. It is also found that inventories include merchandise of $16,250 received on December 31 that has not yet been recorded as a purchase.

(c) The books show that property, plant, and equipment have a cost of $556,800 with depreciation of $180,000 recognized in prior years. However, these balances include fully depreciated equipment of $85,000 that has been scrapped and is no longer on hand.

(d) Miscellaneous liabilities of $3,600 represent salaries payable of $9,500, less noncurrent advances of $5,900 made to company officials.

(e) Loan payable represents a loan from the bank that is payable in regular quarterly installments of $6,250.

(f) Tax liabilities not shown are estimated at $18,250.

(g) Deferred income tax liability arising from temporary differences totals $44,550. This liability was not included in the balance sheet.

(h) Capital stock consists of 6,250 shares of preferred 6% stock, par $20, and 9,000 shares of common stock, stated value $1.

(i) Capital stock had been issued for a total consideration of $283,600; the amount received in excess of the par and stated values of the stock has been reported as paid-in capital.

(j) Net income and dividends were recorded in Paid-In Capital.

Instructions: Prepare a corrected balance sheet with accounts properly classified.

PROBLEM 3–33

CORRECTED BALANCE SHEET
The accountant for the Delicious Bakery prepares the following condensed balance sheet.

Delicious Bakery
Condensed Balance Sheet
December 31, 2002

Current assets	$53,415
Less: Current liabilities	29,000
Working capital	$24,415
Add: Other assets	75,120
	$99,535
Less: Other liabilities	3,600
Investment in business	$95,935

A review of the account balances disclosed the following data.

(a) An analysis of the current asset grouping revealed:

Cash	$10,600
Trade accounts receivable (fully collectible)	12,500
Notes receivable (notes of customer who has been declared bankrupt and is unable to pay anything on the obligations)	1,000
Investment securities—trading, at cost (market value $2,575)	4,250
Inventory	20,965
Cash surrender value of insurance on officers' lives	4,100
Total current assets	$53,415

The inventory account was found to include supplies costing $425, a delivery truck acquired at the end of 2002 at a cost of $2,100, and fixtures at a depreciated value of $10,400. The fixtures had been acquired in 1999 at a cost of $12,500.

(b) The total for other assets was determined as follows.

Land and buildings at cost of acquisition, July 1, 2000	$92,000
Less balance due on mortgage, $16,000, and accrued interest on mortgage, $880 (mortgage is payable in annual installments of $4,000 on July 1 of each year together with interest for the year at that time at 11%)	16,880
Total other assets	$75,120

It was estimated that the land at the time of the purchase was worth $30,000. Buildings as of December 31, 2002, were estimated to have a remaining life of 17½ years.

(c) Current liabilities represented balances that were payable to trade creditors.

(d) Other liabilities consisted of withholding, payroll, real estate, and other taxes payable to the federal, state, and local governments. However, no recognition was given the accrued salaries, utilities, and other miscellaneous items totaling $350.

(e) The company was originally organized in 1998 when 5,000 shares of no-par stock with a stated value of $5 per share were issued in exchange for business assets that were recognized on the books at their fair market value of $55,000.

Instructions: Prepare a corrected balance sheet with the items properly classified.

PROBLEM 3–34

CLASSIFIED BALANCE SHEET

Tony Akea incorporated his concrete manufacturing operations on January 1, 2002, by issuing 10,000 shares of $1 par common stock to himself. The following balance sheet for the new corporation was prepared.

Cornish Corporation
Balance Sheet
January 1, 2002

Cash	$ 10,000
Accounts receivable	75,000
Inventory	75,000
Equipment	115,000
	$275,000
Accounts payable—suppliers	$ 45,000
Capital stock, $1 par	10,000
Additional paid-in capital	220,000
	$275,000

During 2002, Cornish Corporation engaged in the following transactions.

(a) Cornish Corporation produced concrete costing $270,000. Concrete costs consisted of the following: $200,000, raw materials purchased; $25,000, labor; and $45,000, overhead. Cornish Corporation paid the $45,000 owed to suppliers as of January 1 and $130,000 of the $200,000 of raw materials purchased during the year. All labor, except for $1,500, and recorded overhead were paid in cash during the year. Other operating expenses of $15,000 were incurred and paid in 2002.

(b) Concrete costing $290,000 was sold during 2002 for $380,000. All sales were made on credit, and collections on receivables were $365,000.

(c) Cornish Corporation purchased machinery (fair market value = $190,000) by trading in old equipment costing $50,000 and paying $140,000 in cash. There is no accumulated depreciation on the old equipment as it was revalued when the new corporation was formed.

(d) Cornish Corporation issued an additional 4,000 shares of common stock for $25 per share and declared a dividend of $3 per share to all stockholders of record as of December 31, 2002, payable on January 15, 2003.

(e) Depreciation expense for 2002 was $27,000. The allowance for doubtful accounts after year-end adjustments is $2,500.

Instructions: Prepare a properly classified balance sheet in account form for the Cornish Corporation as of December 31, 2002.

COMPETENCY ENHANCEMENT OPPORTUNITIES

▶ Deciphering Actual Financial Statements	▶ Ethical Dilemma
▶ Writing Assignment	▶ Cumulative Spreadsheet Analysis
▶ Research Project	▶ Internet Search
▶ The Debate	

Accounting is more than just doing textbook problems. This expanded competency material provides practice in critical thinking, oral and written communication, research, teamwork, and consideration of ethical issues.

▶ **DECIPHERING ACTUAL FINANCIAL STATEMENTS**

• Deciphering 3–1 (The Walt Disney Company)

The 1998 financial statements for THE WALT DISNEY COMPANY are included in Appendix A. Locate those financial statements and consider the following questions.

1. Compute a current ratio for Disney as of September 30, 1998. How does this ratio compare with the prior year's?
2. What method of inventory valuation does Disney use?
3. What method of depreciation does Disney use?
4. Disney's 1998 balance sheet reports Intangibles of $15,769 million. What amount of the Intangibles relates to Disney's acquisition of ABC?
5. What material commitments and contingencies does Disney report in the notes to its 1998 financial statements?
6. What percentage of Disney's 1998 operating income was generated in the United States?

• Deciphering 3–2 (Boston Celtics)

Refer to the June 30, 1995, balance sheet for the BOSTON CELTICS included on the next page.

Instructions:

1. From June 1994 to June 1995, the Celtics' total assets more than doubled, increasing from $103 million to $211 million. What assets accounted for most of the increase? Where did these assets come from (i.e., from borrowing, new investment, or retained profits)?
2. As of June 30, 1995, the Celtics have their NBA franchise recorded, net of amortization, at $4.3 million. What was the original value recorded for the NBA franchise? Over how many years is the NBA franchise being amortized? In what year was the NBA franchise originally recorded?
3. Partners' capital as of June 30, 1995, is a negative $15.7 million. How can partners' capital become negative?
4. The contracts of many players and coaches include agreements concerning deferred compensation. Interpret the changes from June 1994 to June 1995 in the reported amount of deferred compensation.

BOSTON CELTICS LIMITED PARTNERSHIP
and Subsidiaries
Consolidated Balance Sheets

	June 30, 1995	June 30, 1994
ASSETS		
CURRENT ASSETS		
Cash and cash equivalents	$ 39,563,015	$ 38,093,082
Marketable securities	45,132,667	22,205,099
Other short-term investments	67,558,465	
Accounts receivable (less allowance for doubtful accounts—$195,193 in 1995 and $407,544 in 1994)	16,236,108	11,828,640
Note receivable	4,444,444	
Program broadcast rights—current portion	7,301,340	7,084,177
Prepaid expenses	664,715	281,311
Other current assets and deferred charges	5,200,000	
TOTAL CURRENT ASSETS	186,100,754	79,492,309
PROGRAM BROADCAST RIGHTS—noncurrent portion	10,627,670	11,421,647
PROPERTY AND EQUIPMENT, net of depreciation of $3,647,208 in 1995 and $2,949,994 in 1994	2,504,354	2,544,234
NATIONAL BASKETBALL ASSOCIATION FRANCHISE, net of amortization of $1,850,880 in 1995 and $1,696,640 in 1994	4,318,701	4,472,941
NETWORK AFFILIATION AND OTHER INTANGIBLE ASSETS, net of amortization of $493,961 in 1995 and $393,043 in 1994	4,074,826	3,308,911
OTHER ASSETS	3,028,318	1,693,424
	$210,654,623	$102,933,466
LIABILITIES AND PARTNERS' CAPITAL (DEFICIT)		
CURRENT LIABILITIES		
Accounts payable and accrued expenses	$ 13,406,721	$ 8,758,022
Distribution payable	9,697,083	
Deferred revenues—current portion	6,645,562	
Ticket refunds payable	120,908	126,262
Program broadcast rights payable—current portion	6,048,649	6,023,495
Federal and state income taxes payable	5,163,158	100,000
Notes payable to bank—current portion	80,000,000	5,000,000
Deferred compensation—current portion	4,927,999	3,281,101
TOTAL CURRENT LIABILITIES	126,010,080	23,288,880
PROGRAM BROADCAST RIGHTS—noncurrent portion	9,061,781	8,566,453
DEFERRED REVENUES—noncurrent portion	1,440,612	
DEFERRED FEDERAL AND STATE INCOME TAXES	6,000,000	2,900,000
CONVERTIBLE SUBORDINATED NOTE PAYABLE	10,000,000	10,000,000
NOTES PAYABLE TO BANK—noncurrent portion	50,000,000	50,000,000
DEFERRED COMPENSATION—noncurrent portion	14,850,057	18,248,329
OTHER NONCURRENT LIABILITIES	4,023,750	850,000
MINORITY INTEREST IN BCBLP	4,988,790	1,909,304
PARTNERS' CAPITAL (DEFICIT)		
Boston Celtics Limited Partnership—		
General Partner	(160,255)	(127,387)
Limited Partners	(15,690,191)	(12,542,458)
	(15,850,446)	(12,669,845)
Celtics Limited Partnership—General Partner	(105,194)	(54,311)
Boston Celtics Communications Limited Partnership—General Partner	96,791	(122,686)
Boston Celtics Broadcasting Limited Partnership—Limited Partners	138,402	17,342
TOTAL PARTNERS' CAPITAL (DEFICIT)	(15,720,447)	(12,829,500)
	$210,654,623	$102,933,466

• Deciphering 3–3 (Diageo)

DIAGEO is a United Kingdom (UK) consumer products firm, best known in the United States for the following brand names: Smirnoff, Johnnie Walker, J&B, Gordon's, Guinness, Pillsbury, Haagen-Dazs, and Burger King. Diageo's 1998 balance sheet is shown below.

Diageo Consolidated Balance Sheet 30 June 1998 (In millions of pounds)		
Fixed assets		
Intangible assets		4,727
Tangible assets		3,006
Investments		1,244
		8,977
Current assets		
Stocks	2,236	
Debtors—due within one year	2,037	
Debtors—due after more than one year	999	
Debtors subject to financing arrangements (franchisee loans of £145 million, less nonreturnable proceeds of £127 million)	18	
Investments	484	
Cash at bank and in hand	2,503	
	8,277	
Creditors—due within one year		
Borrowings	(4,724)	
Other creditors	(3,524)	
	(8,248)	
Net current assets		29
Total assets less current liabilities		9,006
Creditors—due after more than one year		
Borrowings	(2,894)	
Other creditors	(243)	
		(3,137)
Provisions for liabilities and charges		(705)
		5,164
Shareholders' funds		
Equity share capital		1,034
Nonequity share capital		105
		1,139
Called-up share capital		
Share premium account	1,121	
Revaluation reserve	190	
Profit and loss account	2,179	
Reserves attributable to equity shareholders		3,490
		4,629
Minority interests		
Equity		169
Nonequity	366	
		535
		5,164

Instructions:

Re-create Diageo's June 30, 1998, balance sheet using U.S. terminology and a standard U.S. format. (Note: One of the reserve items has no counterpart in the United States. The revaluation reserve is the amount by which tangible assets have been written to reflect an increase in market value.)

• Deciphering 3–4 (Safeway, Albertsons, and A&P)

SAFEWAY operates 1,497 supermarkets in the United States and Canada. In the United States, Safeway is located principally in the Northwest, Rocky Mountain, Southwest, and Mid-Atlantic regions. ALBERTSONS operates 989 stores in 25 Western, Midwestern, and Southern states. THE GREAT ATLANTIC & PACIFIC TEA COMPANY (A&P) operates 988 stores in the Northeast and in Canada. Selected financial statement information for 1998 for these three companies is listed below (in millions of U.S. dollars).

	Safeway	Albertsons	A&P
Inventory	$ 1,856	$ 1,503	$ 882
Total current assets	2,320	1,834	1,217
Property, plant, and equipment	5,183	3,974	1,596
Total assets	11,390	6,234	2,995
Total current liabilities	2,894	1,379	955
Total liabilities	8,308	3,424	1,979
Sales	24,484	16,005	10,262
Cost of goods sold	17,360	11,622	7,327
Net income	807	567	63

Instructions:

1. For each of the three companies, compute the following ratios:
   a. Current ratio
   b. Debt ratio
   c. Asset turnover
   d. Return on equity
2. Which company uses its inventory most efficiently? Which company uses its property, plant, and equipment most efficiently?
3. What dangers might there be in making ratio comparisons without viewing the financial statement notes for the individual companies?

• Deciphering 3–5 (AT&T Corporation)

In the chapter we discussed a number of subsequent events that were detailed in AT&T CORPORATION's 1998 annual report. Now let's take a look at one of the largest subsequent events to affect the firm. In 1995 AT&T announced that it was splitting into three separate companies. The following note disclosure was provided in AT&T's 1995 annual report:

---

2. RESTRUCTURING OF AT&T

On September 20, 1995, we announced a plan to separate AT&T into three independent, publicly held, global companies that will each focus on serving certain core businesses: communications services (AT&T), communications systems and technology (Lucent Technologies Inc.), and transaction-intensive computing (NCR Corporation). We are planning an initial public offering of approximately 15% of Lucent Technologies Inc. (Lucent) common stock in the first half of 1996 with our remaining interest in Lucent and NCR Corporation (NCR) being spun off to AT&T shareowners by the end of 1996. The plan also includes our intention to pursue the sale of our remaining interest in AT&T Capital Corporation (AT&T Capital) in 1996. Our plan is subject to several conditions, including receipt of a favorable tax ruling and other approvals, and the absence of events or developments that would have a material adverse impact on AT&T or its shareowners.

Instructions:

1. In relation to AT&T's 1995 financial statements, is this proposed restructuring a subsequent event? Explain.
2. Assume that, instead of September 20, 1995, the announcement of the proposed restructuring occurred on January 20, 1996. Would the announcement have been a subsequent event? If so, would any revision of the 1995 financial statements have been required? Explain.
3. What accounting rationale is there for including this note in AT&T's 1995 financial statements?

▶ **WRITING ASSIGNMENT**

• Unrecorded assets should stay unrecorded.

You are a member of the most popular student club on campus, the Accounting Antidefamation Organization. Recently, the field of accounting was savagely attacked in an article written by a militant economics student group and published in the student newspaper. The article charged that the balance sheet is stupid, outdated, and useless and cited as an example the accounting practice of not recognizing many intangible assets. As a specific illustration, the article claimed that the name recognition, reputation, and goodwill of the COCA-COLA trademark are worth over $30 billion, but these assets are not recorded in Coca-Cola's balance sheet.

You have been asked by the editor of the student newspaper to respond in writing to this vicious assault by the economics students. Don't cave in to the pressure—argue persuasively why these unrecorded assets should stay unrecorded.

▶ **RESEARCH PROJECT**

• Why are the notes so long?

Your group is to report (either orally or in writing) on your examination of the makeup of a typical set of financial statement notes.

Choose 10 companies for which you can get a copy of a recent annual report. Using those annual reports, answer the following questions.

1. What is the average number of pages of notes?
2. Get a ruler and measure the length of each note. As your measurement number, use either the fraction of a page the note occupies or the number of column-inches in the note. Using information from all 10 annual reports, compile a list of the top five note topics in terms of average length.
3. In your opinion, which note topic consistently contains the most useful information? the least useful?
4. Are any note topics consistently labeled as "unaudited"? If so, what are the topics?
5. You looked at 10 sets of notes. What is the single most interesting piece of information you found?

▶ **THE DEBATE**

• Kill the notes!

The typical set of financial statements contains 4 or 5 pages of statements and 15 to 20 pages of notes. Without question, the note disclosure increases understanding of the statements. However, compiling the notes increases the cost of preparing the statements and delays their issuance.

Divide your group into two teams.

• One team is the "Statements Only" team. Prepare a 2-minute oral argument supporting the issuance of simplified financial statements with, at most, a single page of explanatory notes.

• The other team is the "Save the Notes" team. Prepare a 2-minute oral argument outlining the dangers of issuing financial statements without a complete set of notes.

► **ETHICAL DILEMMA**

• Dodging a loan covenant violation.

You are on the accounting staff of Chisos Manufacturing Company. Chisos has a $100 million loan with Rio Grande National Bank. One of the covenants associated with the loan is that Chisos must maintain a current ratio of greater than 1.5.

As of January 20, 2002, preliminary financial statement numbers for the year ended December 31, 2001, have been compiled. It looks like Chisos will violate the current ratio loan covenant. Violation could be very costly in two ways. First, Rio Grande National Bank has historically raised the interest rate one-half of a point on loans with covenant violations. Second, a violation will increase the perceived riskiness of Chisos and make future borrowing more costly.

The 2001 financial statement numbers are just preliminary, and the senior accounting staff of Chisos has discussed the following two options to avoid violation:

1. Reclassify "long-term investment property" as "short-term property held for sale." Doing this would require a statement from management that the intention is to sell the property within 1 year. Actually, Chisos intends to hold the property for several more years, and the property classification would be changed back to long-term next year when the threat of covenant violation has hopefully disappeared.

2. Reclassify certain short-term loans as long-term on the basis that Chisos will refinance the loans. Technically, this is true. However, Chisos has no formal refinancing commitment and will not have one until some time in June.

You have been chosen to present the findings of the accounting staff to the board of directors. What points will you emphasize in your presentation?

► **CUMULATIVE SPREADSHEET ANALYSIS**

This spreadsheet assignment is a continuation of the spreadsheet assignment given in Chapter 2. If you completed that assignment, you have a head start on this one.

1. Refer back to the financial statement numbers for Skywalker Enterprises for 2002 (given in part 1 of the Cumulative Spreadsheet Analysis assignment in Chapter 2). Revise those financial statements by making the following changes:
   • Change the paid-in capital amount from $150 to $200.
   • In the equity section of the balance sheet, insert a treasury stock amount of −$60. The remaining amount of the "other equity" mentioned in Chapter 2 is accumulated other comprehensive income.
   • Increase amount of long-term debt from $621 to $671.
   • In the asset section of the balance sheet, insert an intangible asset amount of $100.
   Using the revised balance sheet and income statement, create spreadsheet cell formulas to compute and display values for the following ratios.
   • Current ratio
   • Debt ratio
   • Asset turnover
   • Return on assets
   • Return on equity

2. Determine the impact of each of the following transactions on the ratio values computed in question 1. Treat each transaction independently, that is, before determining the impact of each new transaction you should reset the financial statement values to their original amounts. The transactions that follow are assumed to occur on December 31, 2002.
   a. Collected $60 cash from customer receivables.
   b. Purchased $90 in inventory on account.
   c. Purchased $300 in property, plant, and equipment. The entire amount of the purchase was financed with a mortgage. Principal repayment for the mortgage is due in 10 years.

d. Purchased $300 in property, plant, and equipment. The entire amount of the purchase was financed with new stockholder investment.

e. Borrowed $60 with a short-term loan payable. The $60 was paid out as a dividend to stockholders.

f. Received $60 as an investment from stockholders. The $60 was paid out as a dividend to stockholders.

g. The long-term debt amount of $671 includes $90 in short-term loans payable that Skywalker hopes to refinance. Skywalker has no explicit agreement with the bank to refinance the loan and doesn't expect to finalize the refinancing until the last quarter of 2003.

h. During the first week in January 2003, Skywalker learned that, of the $459 reported as inventory as of December 31, 2002, $45 is completely obsolete and worthless. The inventory had become obsolete during the last quarter of 2002, but the facts had not been verified until early 2003.

▶ **INTERNET SEARCH**

COCA-COLA's Web address is www.thecoca-colacompany.com. Once you've gained access to Coca-Cola's Web site, answer the following questions.

1. Write a brief description (step-by-step) outlining how to use Coca-Cola's home page to view a copy of Coca-Cola's most recent annual report.

2. Identify the components of Coca-Cola's accumulated other comprehensive income. Which item has changed the most over the past 3 years?

3. Call up the notes to Coca-Cola's most recent financial statements and find out what percentage of Coca-Cola's current-year revenue was generated in the United States.

4. Compute the average price at which Coca-Cola has sold its stock. Compute the average price at which Coca-Cola has repurchased its stock. Why the big difference? Is it a good idea for Coca-Cola to be repurchasing its own stock at a price so much higher than its original sales price?

chapter 4
The Income Statement

1

Define the concept of income.

2

Explain why an income measure is important.

3

Explain how income is measured, including the revenue recognition and expense-matching concepts.

4

Understand the format of an income statement.

5

Describe the specific components of an income statement.

6

Compute comprehensive income and prepare a statement of stockholders' equity.

7

Construct simple forecasts of income for future periods.

Eliza Grace Symonds was an accomplished pianist, a feat additionally notable because Eliza was deaf. Eliza met and married Melville Bell who was the son of a famous elocutionist, Alexander Graham Bell. Melville's career followed that of his father. Eliza and Melville had three sons, the second of whom was named Alexander Graham Bell after his paternal grandfather. Young Alexander Graham Bell demonstrated an early interest in speech. In 1871, Bell, at the age of 24, began teaching deaf children to speak at the Boston School for Deaf Mutes. Bell's approach was somewhat unorthodox because, at the time, it was common practice to teach deaf mutes only to sign, or to simply institutionalize them. Mabel Hubbard, who would become Bell's wife, was one of his students.

> **FYI:** Long after inventing the telephone, Bell continued his work with the deaf. In gratitude for his work, Helen Keller dedicated her autobiography to him.

His interest in speech caused Bell to try to develop what he called the "harmonic telegraph." Samuel Morse completed his first telegraph line in 1843, allowing communication using Morse code between two points, and Bell was interested in transmitting speech in a similar way.

At an electrical machine shop, Bell met Thomas Watson. At the time, Watson was a repair mechanic and model maker who was regularly assigned to work with inventors. As Watson learned more of Bell's "harmonic telegraph," the two formed a partnership. In 1876, Bell, while working on their invention, spilled some battery acid and uttered those now-famous words, "Mr. Watson, come here. I want you!" On March 7, 1876, Bell was issued patent number 174,465, covering: "the method of, and apparatus for, transmitting vocal or other sounds telegraphically . . . by causing electrical undulations, similar in form to the vibrations of the air accompanying the said vocal or other sounds."

The BELL TELEPHONE COMPANY immediately presented immense competition to the WESTERN UNION TELEGRAPH COMPANY, which was developing its own telephone technology. Western Union hired Thomas Edison to develop a competing system, forcing the Bell Company to sue Western Union for patent infringement—and win. The Bell Company would be forced in subsequent years to defend its patent in over 600 cases.

Alexander Graham Bell had little interest in the day-to-day operations of his company. Instead, he preferred studying science and nature. In 1888 he founded the National Geographic Society. Upon his death on August 2, 1922, in a tribute to their inventor, all the phones in the nation were silent for one minute.

The Bell Telephone Company was to become AMERICAN TELEPHONE AND TELEGRAPH COMPANY (AT&T) in 1899. AT&T first transmitted the human voice across the Atlantic Ocean in 1915, and in 1927, AT&T introduced commercial transatlantic phone service at a cost of $75 for five minutes. Numerous AT&T inventions followed, including the transistor (1947), the first microwave relay system (1950), the laser (1958), and the first communications satellite (1962).

AT&T functioned as a regulated monopoly until January 1, 1984, when after an eight-year legal battle with the U.S. federal government, AT&T agreed to get out of the local telephone service business by divesting itself of its regional Bell operating companies. On that day, AT&T shrunk from 1,009,000 employees to 373,000. On January 1, 1996, AT&T initiated a process of further divestiture, this time voluntarily, in order to create three focused operating companies. The old AT&T split into three separate companies: AT&T, LUCENT TECHNOLOGIES INC., and NCR CORPORATION. As shown in Exhibit 4–1, the companies that arose from the divestiture of AT&T, either government-mandated or voluntary, had an aggregate market value of $679.1 billion in February 1999. This is substantially more than the most valuable company in the world, MICROSOFT, which had a market value of approximately $400 billion during the same period.

All of this activity at AT&T has made it difficult to determine, from a look at the income statement, how the company is performing. For example, AT&T's 1998 income statement reports the following income numbers (in millions).

Operating income	$7,487
Income from continuing operations	5,235
Income before extraordinary loss	6,535
Net income	6,398

When analyzing a company such as AT&T, which measure of income is appropriate? When analysts refer to a company's results, which income measure are they referencing? And what are the differences between the various income measures?

EXHIBIT 4 – 1 | The Divestiture of AT&T

(in billions of dollars, as of February 1999)	Market Value
AT&T	$143.5
Lucent	113.5
NCR	4.1
Regional Bell Operating Companies:	
Ameritech (proposed acquisition by	
SBC Communications, 1999)	72.8
Bell Atlantic	93.1
Bell South	86.7
Nynex (acquired by Bell Atlantic, August 1997)	NA
Pacific Telesis (acquired by	
SBC Communications, April 1997)	NA
Southwestern Bell (renamed SBC Communications)	103.7
U S West (split into U S West and MediaOne	
in June 1998)	61.7
Total	$679.1

 net work exercise

For 1998, AT&T reported revenues of $53,223 million and net income of $6,398 million. Access the company's Web site at **www.att.com** and determine the amount reported in the most recent annual report for 1998 revenues and 1998 net income.

1. What events can cause the amount of revenue or net income originally reported for a given year to be altered in the financial reports of subsequent years?

I n this chapter, we address these and other questions by focusing on one of the primary financial statements—the income statement. By analyzing the various components of the income statement, you will understand how the performance of a business is reported to financial statement users and how reported performance can change over time as a company changes the nature of its operations. In addition, we will discuss the format of the income statement, its more common components, and how income statements from around the world differ in the information they contain and how that information is presented.

Define the concept of income.

INCOME—WHAT IT ISN'T AND WHAT IT IS

Individuals often confuse income with cash flows. Is income equal to the amount of cash generated from the successful operations of a business? No. For a variety of reasons, most of them related to accrual accounting, income and cash flows from operations will seldom be the same number. Because both income and cash flows provide measures of a firm's performance, which provides the best measure? The FASB, in its conceptual framework, stated that "information about earnings and its components measured by accrual accounting generally provides a better indication of enterprise performance than information about current cash receipts and payments."[1] Information regarding cash flows is important. In fact, Chapter 5 focuses entirely on the statement of cash flows. But research supports the FASB's assertion that the best indicator of a firm's performance is income.[2] So an understanding of income, what it measures, and its components is essential in understanding and interpreting a firm's financial situation.

So what is **income**? Although there are varying ways to measure income, all of them share a common basic concept: Income is a return over and above the investment. One of the more widely accepted definitions of income states that it is the amount that an entity could return to its investors and still leave the entity as well-off at the end of the period as it was at the beginning.[3] But what does it mean to be "as well-off," and how can it be measured? Most measurements are based on some concept of capital or ownership maintenance. Two concepts of capital maintenance were considered by the FASB in its conceptual framework: financial capital maintenance and physical capital maintenance.

Financial Capital Maintenance Concept of Income Determination

The **financial capital maintenance** concept assumes that an enterprise has income "only if the dollar amount of an enterprise's net assets (assets – liabilities, or owners' equity) at the end of a period exceeds the dollar amount of net assets at the beginning of the period after excluding the effects of transactions with owners."[4] To illustrate, assume that Kreidler, Inc., had the following assets and liabilities at the beginning and at the end of a period.

	Beginning of Period	End of Period
Total assets	$510,000	$560,000
Total liabilities	430,000	390,000
Net assets (owners' equity)	$ 80,000	$170,000

If there were no investments by owners or distributions to owners during the period, income would be $90,000, the amount of the increase in net assets. Assume, however, that owners invested $40,000 in the business and received distributions (dividends) of $15,000. Income for the period would be $65,000, computed as follows:

Net assets, end of period	$170,000
Net assets, beginning of period	80,000
Change (increase) in net assets	$ 90,000
Deduct investment by owners	(40,000)
Add distributions (dividends) to owners	15,000
Income	$ 65,000

Physical Capital Maintenance Concept of Income Determination

Another way of defining capital maintenance is in terms of **physical capital maintenance**. Under this concept, income occurs "only if the physical productive capacity of the enterprise at the end of a period . . . exceeds the physical productive capacity at the

1 *Statement of Financial Accounting Concepts No. 1,* "Objectives of Financial Reporting by Business Enterprises," Stamford, CT: Financial Accounting Standards Board, 1984, par. 44.

2 For example, see Gary C. Biddle, Robert M. Bowen, and James S. Wallace, "Does EVA® Beat Earnings? Evidence on Associations With Stock Returns and Firm Values," *Journal of Accounting and Economics,* December 1997, p. 301.

3 Although many economists and accountants have adopted this view, a basic reference is J. R. Hicks' widely accepted book, *Value and Capital,* 2nd edition, Oxford University Press, 1946.

4 *Statement of Financial Accounting Concepts No. 5,* "Recognition and Measurement in Financial Statements of Business Enterprises," Stamford, CT: Financial Accounting Standards Board, 1984, par. 47.

beginning of the same period, also after excluding the effects of transactions with owners."[5] This concept requires that productive assets (inventories, buildings, and equipment) be valued at current cost. Productive capital is maintained only if the current costs of these capital assets are maintained. Thus, if the beginning net asset value of $80,000 in the previous example rose to $100,000 by the end of the year because of rising prices, and new investments and dividends were as shown, income would be $45,000 rather than $65,000. The $20,000 difference would be the amount necessary to "maintain physical productive capacity" and would not be part of income.

The FASB considered carefully these two ways of viewing income, and it adopted the financial capital maintenance concept as part of its conceptual framework.

The acceptance of the financial capital maintenance concept rescued accountants from the difficult task of trying to measure productive capacity. But measuring income using the concept of financial capital maintenance still leaves the question of how the net asset balance should be valued. Many suggest that net assets should be measured at their unexpired historical cost values as is often done. Others feel that replacement values or disposal values should be used. Some would include as assets intangible resources, such as human resources, goodwill, and geographic location, that have been attained over time without specifically identified payments. Others feel that only resources that have been acquired in arm's-length exchange activities should be included.

 It would seem that the physical capital maintenance concept would provide the best theoretical measure of "well-offness." What difficulties would be encountered by a firm as it tried to turn theory into practice if the FASB had adopted the physical capital maintenance concept of measuring income?

Likewise, controversy has developed over the recognition and measurement of liabilities. Should future claims against the entity for items such as pensions, warranties, and deferred income taxes be valued at their discounted values, at their future cash flow values, or eliminated completely from the financial statements until events clearly define the existence of a specific liability? The reported income under the financial maintenance concept will vary widely depending on when and how the assets, liabilities, and changes in the valuation of assets and liabilities are measured. As it stands currently, a combination of historical costs, current values, present values, and other valuation measures are used to measure a firm's "well-offness."

WHY IS A MEASURE OF INCOME IMPORTANT?

Explain why an income measure is important.

The recognition, measurement, and reporting (display) of business income and its components are considered by many to be the most important tasks of accountants. The users of financial statements who must make decisions regarding their relationship with the company are almost always concerned with a measure of its success in using the resources committed to its operation. Has the activity been profitable? What is the trend of profitability? Is it increasingly profitable, or is there a downward trend? What is the most probable result for future years? Will the company be profitable enough to pay interest on its debt and dividends to its stockholders and still grow at a desired rate? These and other questions all relate to the basic question—What is income?

Information about the components of income is important and can be used to help predict future income and cash flows. Not only can this information be helpful to a specific user, but it is also of value to the economy. As discussed in Chapter 1, many groups utilize accounting information, and accountants play a key role in providing information that will assist in allocating scarce resources to the most efficient and effective organizations or groups.

In the United States, the FASB has specified that financial accounting information is designed with investors and creditors in mind, at the same time recognizing that many

5 Ibid.

other groups will find the resulting information useful as well. Of course, accrual-based financial accounting information is not suited for every possible use. For example, governments, both federal and state, rely heavily on income taxes as a source of their revenues. The income figure used for assessing taxes is based on laws passed by Congress and regulations applied by the IRS and various courts. The income determined for financial reporting, however, is determined by adherence to accounting standards (GAAP) developed by the accounting profession. Thus, the amount of income reported to creditors and investors may not be the same as the income reported for tax purposes. Many items are the same for both types of reporting, but there are some significant differences. Most of these differences relate to the specific purposes Congress has for taxing income. Governments use an income figure as a base to assess taxes, but they must use one that relates closely with the ability of the taxpayer to pay the computed tax. For example, accrual accounting requires companies to defer recognition of revenues that are received before they are earned. Income tax regulations, however, often require these unearned revenues to be reported as income as soon as they are received in cash.

As mentioned in previous chapters, the increasing globalization of business is providing the impetus for a movement toward a unified body of international accounting standards. However, because financial accounting information plays different roles in different countries, it is probably not reasonable to assume that one set of standards can fit the business, legal, and cultural settings of every country in the world. For example, countries can be separated, broadly speaking, into two groups—code law countries and common law countries.[6] In code law countries, such as Germany and Japan, accounting standards are set by legal processes. In such an environment, financial accounting numbers serve a variety of functions, including the determination of the amount of income tax and cash dividends to be paid. In a common law country, such as the United States or the United Kingdom, accounting standards are set in response to market forces. In a common law setting, financial accounting numbers are used more for informational purposes, not for deciding how the economic pie gets split among taxes, dividends, wages, and so forth. Given the significantly different roles played by financial accounting numbers in code law and common law countries, it may be unreasonable to expect one set of standards to work worldwide.

Accounting standards also play a different role in developing economies as compared to developed economies. In China, for example, the rudimentary state of the auditing and legal infrastructure makes the application of judgment-based accounting standards extremely problematic.[7] In a developing economy, it may be more important for financial reporting to satisfactorily fulfill its essential bookkeeping function rather than attempt to provide sophisticated investment information relevant for only a small set of companies trying to attract foreign investment. The fundamental question is this: How are accounting standards designed for use by international financial analysts going to help a domestic Chinese company with no plans to seek foreign investment and with a desire only to improve the monitoring of managers and the allocation of resources?

This text focuses on principles of accounting that are the supporting foundation for financial accounting and reporting as practiced in the United States. Income for tax purposes will be discussed, but only as it is used to determine the income tax expense and other tax-related amounts reported in the financial statements. Differences between U.S. and foreign accounting practices will be discussed where appropriate throughout the text.

---

6 Ray Ball, S. P. Kothari, and Ashok Robin, "The Effect of International Institutional Factors on Properties of Accounting Earnings," Working paper, University of Rochester, July 1998.
7 Bing Xiang, "Institutional Factors Influencing China's Accounting Reforms and Standards," *Accounting Horizons*, June 1998, p. 105.

Explain how income is measured, including the revenue recognition and expense-matching concepts.

HOW IS INCOME MEASURED?

Comparing the net assets at two points in time, as was done previously in introducing the concept of financial capital maintenance, yields a single net income figure. However, no detail concerning the components of income is disclosed. To provide this detail, accountants have adopted a **transaction approach** to measuring income that stresses the direct computation of revenues and expenses. As long as the same measurement method is used, income will be the same under the transaction approach as with a single income computation.

The transaction approach, sometimes referred to as the *matching method*, focuses on business events that affect certain elements of financial statements, namely, revenues, expenses, gains, and losses. Income is measured as the difference between resource inflows (revenues and gains) and outflows (expenses and losses) over a period of time. Definitions for the four income elements are presented in Exhibit 4-2 as an aid to the following discussion.

EXHIBIT 4-2 | Component Elements of Income

- **Revenues** are inflows or other enhancements of assets of an entity or settlements of its liabilities (or a combination of both) from delivering or producing goods, rendering services, or carrying out other activities that constitute the entity's ongoing major or central operations.

- **Expenses** are outflows or other "using up" of assets of an entity or incurrences of liabilities (or a combination of both) from delivering or producing goods, rendering services, or carrying out other activities that constitute the entity's ongoing major or central operations.

- **Gains** are increases in equity (net assets) from peripheral or incidental transactions of an entity and from all other transactions and other events and circumstances affecting the entity except those that result from revenues or investments by owners.

- **Losses** are decreases in equity (net assets) from peripheral or incidental transactions of an entity and from all other transactions and other events and circumstances affecting the entity except those that result from expenses or distributions to owners.

Source: *Statement of Financial Accounting Concepts No. 6,* "Elements of Financial Statements," Stamford, CT: Financial Accounting Standards Board, December 1985, p. x.

Why is it important to separately disclose revenues and gains? expenses and losses?

As can be seen from studying these definitions, by defining gains and losses in terms of changes in equity after providing for revenues, expenses, investments, and distributions to the owners, income determined by the transaction approach will be the same income as that determined under financial capital maintenance. However, by identifying intermediate income components, the transaction approach provides detail to assist in predicting future cash flows.

The key problem in recognizing and measuring income using the transaction approach is deciding when an "inflow or other enhancements of assets" has occurred and how to measure the "outflows or other 'using up' of assets." The first issue is identified as the revenue recognition problem, and the second issue is identified as the expense recognition, or expense-matching problem.

Revenue and Gain Recognition

The transaction approach requires a clear definition of when income elements should be recognized, or recorded, in the financial statements. Under the GAAP of accrual accounting, **revenue recognition** does not necessarily occur when cash is received. The FASB's conceptual framework identifies two factors that should be considered in deciding when revenues and gains should be recognized: realization and the earnings process. Revenues and gains are generally recognized when

1. they are realized or realizable, and
2. they have been earned through substantial completion of the activities involved in the earnings process.[8]

Put in simple terms, revenues are recognized when the company generating the revenue has provided the bulk of the goods or services it promised (substantial completion) for the customer and when the customer has provided payment or at least a valid promise of payment (realizable) to the company. That is, the company has lived up to its end of an agreement, and the customer has the intention of paying.

In order for revenues and gains to be realized, inventory or other assets must be exchanged for cash or claims to cash, such as accounts receivable. Revenues are realizable when assets held or assets received in an exchange are readily convertible to known amounts of cash or claims to cash. The earnings process criterion relates primarily to revenue recognition. Most gains result from transactions and events, such as the sale of land or a patent, that involve no earnings process. Thus, being realized, or realizable, is of more importance in recognizing gains.

Application of these two criteria to certain industries and companies within these industries has resulted in recognition of revenue at different points in the revenue-producing cycle. This cycle can be a lengthy one. For a manufacturing company, it begins with the development of proposals for a certain product by an individual or by the research and development department and extends through planning, production, sale, collection, and finally expiration of the warranty period. Consider, for example, the revenue-producing cycle for FORD MOTOR COMPANY. Engineers develop plans and create models and prototypes. Actual production of vehicles then occurs, followed by delivery to dealers for sale to customers. All new vehicles are warranted against defect, in some cases for several years. All of these steps, which can take over 10 years, are involved in generating sales revenue. If there is a failure at any step, revenue may be seriously curtailed or even completely eliminated. Yet, there is only one aggregate revenue amount for the entire cycle, the selling price of the product.

> **FYI:** Most firms specify their revenue recognition policies in the notes to the financial statements. For example, the notes to DISNEY's financial statements (Appendix A) disclose the corporation's revenue recognition policies for motion pictures, television licensing, video sales, and theme parks.

For a service company, the revenue-producing cycle begins with an agreement to provide a service and extends through the planning and performance of the service to the collection of the cash and final proof through the passage of time that the service has been adequately performed. As an example, consider the revenue-producing cycle of PRICEWATERHOUSECOOPERS (PWC), one of the Big 5 accounting firms. For a typical audit, much of the planning and preparation occurs before the actual on-site visit. The on-site visit is then followed by an accumulation of data and the preparation of an audit report. And with increasing legal actions being taken against professionals, such as doctors and accountants, one could argue that the revenue-producing cycle does not end until the possibility of legal claims for services performed is remote. Consider the case of PWC and one of its former clients, PHAR-MOR, detailed later in the chapter. In 1995, three years after the actual audit, PWC (actually a forerunner of PWC, COOPERS & LYBRAND) found itself being sued because of the audit conducted in 1992.

---

8 *Statement of Financial Accounting Concepts No. 5*, par. 83.

Construction contracts are an example of revenue that is recognized as services are performed.

Although some accountants have argued for recognizing revenue on a partial basis over these extended production or service periods, the prevailing practice has been to select one point in the cycle that best meets the revenue recognition criteria. Both of these criteria are generally met at the point of sale, which is generally when goods are delivered or services are rendered to customers and payment or a promise of payment is received. Thus, revenue for automobiles sold to dealers by Ford Motor Company will be recognized when the cars are shipped to the dealers. Similarly, PWC will record its revenue from audit and tax work when the services have been performed and billed. In both examples, the earnings process is deemed to be substantially complete, and the cash or receivable from the customer meets the realization criterion. Although the "point-of-sale" practice is the most common revenue recognition point, there are notable variations to this general rule.[9]

Earlier Recognition

1. If a market exists for a product such that its sale at an established price is practically assured without significant selling effort, revenues may be recognized at the point of completed production. Examples of this situation may occur with certain precious metals and agricultural products that are supported by government price guarantees.[10] In these situations, revenue is recognized when the mining or production of the goods is complete, because the earnings process is considered to be substantially complete and the existence of a virtually guaranteed purchaser provides evidence of realizability. An example of this method of revenue recognition is provided by a Canadian mining company, KINROSS GOLD CORPORATION; the appropriate note from Kinross' 1998 financial statements is reproduced in Exhibit 4-3. Kinross recognizes revenue prior to the point of sale with the expected sales price to be received being recorded in a current asset

STOP & THINK: Why do you think Kinross waits to recognize revenue from the sale of Kubaka gold until the gold is actually sold?

---

9 Accounting Principles Board, Statement No. 4, par. 152, "Basic Concepts in Accounting Principles Underlying Financial Statements of Business Enterprises," Oct. 1970.

10 While companies in these industries may recognize revenue prior to the point of sale, a survey of revenue recognition policies for companies in these industries reveals that the vast majority recognize revenue at the point of sale.

account, Bullion Settlements. Note that Kinross accounts for Kubaka bullion different than its other ores; revenue recognition for Kubaka bullion occurs when it is sold. The Kubaka gold is produced in eastern Russia.

EXHIBIT 4–3 | Kinross Gold Corporation Revenue Recognition Note Disclosure

Gold and silver poured, in transit and at refineries, are recorded at net realizable value and included in bullion settlements and other accounts receivable, with the exception of Kubaka bullion. The estimated net realizable value of Kubaka bullion is included in inventory until it is sold.

2. If a product or service is contracted for in advance, revenue may be recognized as production takes place or as services are performed, especially if the production or performance period extends over more than one fiscal year. The percentage-of-completion and proportional performance methods of accounting have been developed to recognize revenue at several points in the production or service cycle rather than waiting until the final delivery or performance takes place. This exception to the general point-of-sale rule is necessary if the qualitative characteristics of relevance and representational faithfulness are to be met. Construction contracts for buildings, roads, and dams, and contracts for scientific research are examples of situations where these methods of revenue recognition occur. In all cases where this revenue recognition variation is employed, a firm, enforceable contract must exist to meet the realizability criterion, and an objective measure of progress toward completion must be attainable to measure the degree of completeness. As an example of this type of revenue recognition, THE BOEING COMPANY indicates in its notes (see Exhibit 4–4) that a portion of its revenues are recognized prior to the point of sale.

EXHIBIT 4–4 | The Boeing Company Note on Revenue Recognition

For certain fixed-price contracts that require substantial performance over an extended period before deliveries begin, sales are recorded based on attainment of scheduled performance milestones.

Later Recognition

3. If collectibility of assets received for products or services is considered doubtful, revenues and gains may be recognized as the cash is received. The installment sales and cost recovery methods of accounting have been developed to recognize revenue under these conditions. Sales of real estate, especially speculative recreational property, are often recorded using this variation of the general rule. In these cases, although the earnings process has been substantially completed, the questionable receivable fails to meet the realization criterion. For example, RENTER'S CHOICE, also known as COLORTYME in some parts of the United States, operates rent-to-own stores where consumers can obtain furniture, televisions, and other consumer goods on a rent-to-own basis. A big concern for Renter's Choice is collecting the full amount of cash due under a rental contract. In fact, Renter's Choice states that fewer than 25% of its customers complete the full term of their agreement. With such a high likelihood of customers stopping payments on their rental agreements, Renter's Choice recognizes revenue from a specific contract only gradually as the cash is actually collected.

Caution! The term "realizable" is flexible in meaning. It may vary from meaning the same as "realized" (cash or claims to cash) to the probable ability to convert an asset to cash. The latter interpretation leads toward the increased use of current values to measure such assets as marketable securities and to recognize changes in market value as gains.

Losses from natural disasters, such as earthquakes, are recognized immediately.

The general point-of-sale rule will be assumed for examples in this text unless specifically stated otherwise. Variations on this rule are discussed fully in Chapter 7.

Expense and Loss Recognition

In order to determine income, not only must criteria for revenue recognition be established but the principles for recognizing expenses and losses must be clearly defined. Some expenses are directly associated with revenues and can thus be recognized in the same period as the related revenues. Other expenditures are not recognized currently as expenses because they relate to future revenues and therefore are reported as assets. Still other expenses are not associated with specific revenues and are recognized in the time period when paid or incurred. **Expense recognition**, then, is divided into three categories: (1) direct matching, (2) systematic and rational allocation, and (3) immediate recognition.

DIRECT MATCHING　Relating expenses to specific revenues is often referred to as the **matching** process. For example, the cost of goods sold is clearly a direct expense that can be "matched" with the revenues produced by the sale of goods and reported in the same time period as the revenues are recognized. Similarly, shipping costs and sales commissions usually relate directly to revenues.[11]

Direct expenses include not only those that have already been incurred but should also include anticipated expenses related to revenues of the current period. After delivery of goods to customers, there are still costs of collection, bad debt losses from uncollectible receivables, and possible warranty costs for product deficiencies. These expenses are directly related to revenues and should be estimated and matched against recognized revenues for the period.

SYSTEMATIC AND RATIONAL ALLOCATION　The second general expense recognition category involves assets that benefit more than one accounting period. The cost of assets such as buildings, equipment, patents, and prepaid insurance are spread across the periods of expected benefit in some systematic and rational way. Generally, it is difficult,

11 Statement of Financial Accounting Concepts No. 6, "Elements of Financial Statements," Stamford, CT: Financial Accounting Standards Board, December 1985, par. 144.

if not impossible, to relate these expenses directly to specific revenues or to specific periods, but it is clear that they are necessary if the revenue is to be earned. Examples of expenses that are included in this category are depreciation and amortization.

IMMEDIATE RECOGNITION   Many expenses are not related to specific revenues but are incurred to obtain goods and services that indirectly help to generate revenues. Because these goods and services are used almost immediately, their costs are recognized as expenses in the period of acquisition. Examples include most administrative costs, such as office salaries, utilities, and general advertising and selling expenses.

Immediate recognition is also appropriate when future benefits are highly uncertain. For example, expenditures for research and development may provide significant future benefits, but these benefits are usually so uncertain that the costs are written off in the period in which they are incurred.

Most losses also fit in the immediate recognition category. Because they arise from peripheral or incidental transactions, they do not relate directly to revenues. Examples include losses from disposition of used equipment, losses from natural catastrophes such as earthquakes or tornadoes, and losses from disposition of investments.

Understand the format of
an income statement.

FORM OF THE INCOME STATEMENT

All income statements prepared in accordance with GAAP report the same basic type of information and have certain common display features. Some sections of the income statement, especially irregular and extraordinary items, are specified by FASB pronouncements. Others have become standardized by wide usage.

Traditionally, the income from continuing operations category has been presented in either a single-step or a multiple-step form. With the **single-step form**, all revenues and gains that are identified as operating items are placed first on the income statement, followed by all expenses and losses that are identified as operating items. The difference between total revenues and gains and total expenses and losses represents income from operations. If there are no irregular or extraordinary items, this difference is also equal to net income (or loss). The income statements for NIKE, INC., in Exhibit 4–5 illustrate the

EXHIBIT 4–5 | Nike, Inc., Income Statements

NIKE, INC., CONSOLIDATED STATEMENTS OF INCOME			
	YEAR ENDED MAY 31,		
	1998	1997	1996
(In millions, except for per share data)			
Revenues	$9,553.1	$9,186.5	$6,470.6
Costs and expenses:			
Costs of sales	6,065.5	5,503.0	3,906.7
Selling and administrative	2,623.8	2,303.7	1,588.6
Interest expense (Notes 4 and 5)	60.0	52.3	39.5
Other income/expense, net (Notes 1, 10, and 11)	20.9	32.3	36.7
Restructuring charge (Note 13)	129.9	—	—
	8,900.1	7,891.3	5,571.5
Income before income taxes	653.0	1,295.2	899.1
Income taxes (Note 6)	253.4	499.4	345.9
Net income	$ 399.6	$ 795.8	$ 553.2
Basic earnings per common share (Notes 1 and 9)	$ 1.38	$ 2.76	$ 1.93
Diluted earnings per common share (Notes 1 and 9)	$ 1.35	$ 2.68	$ 1.88

single-step form. For 1998, Nike reported a 4% increase in sales while at the same time posting a 50% reduction in net income. The reasons for this drastic reduction in net income are an increase in recurring expenses of 11% and a one-time restructuring charge of $130 million. Note that income taxes are reported separately from other expenses, which is a common variation of the basic single-step form. Finally, notice the two earnings-per-share (EPS) figures—basic and diluted. Later in this chapter we discuss why companies report two EPS figures, and Chapter 19 is devoted entirely to earnings-per-share computations.

With the **multiple-step form**, the income statement is divided into separate sections (referred to as "intermediate components" in FASB Concepts Statement No. 5), and various subtotals are reported that reflect different levels of profitability. The income statement of IBM, Exhibit 4–6, illustrates a multiple-step income statement. With

EXHIBIT 4–6 | International Business Machines Income Statement

International Business Machines
Income Statement

(In millions, except per share amounts)

For the year ended December 31:	Notes	1998	1997	1996
Revenue:				
Hardware segment		$35,419	$36,630	$36,634
Global Services segment		28,916	25,166	22,310
Software segment		11,863	11,164	11,426
Global Financing segment		2,877	2,806	3,054
Enterprise Investments segment/Other		2,592	2,742	2,523
Total revenue		81,667	78,508	75,947
Cost:				
Hardware segment		24,214	23,473	22,888
Global Services segment		21,125	18,464	16,270
Software segment		2,260	2,785	2,946
Global Financing segment		1,494	1,448	1,481
Enterprise Investments segment/Other		1,702	1,729	1,823
Total cost		50,795	47,899	45,408
Gross profit		30,872	30,609	30,539
Operating expenses:				
Selling, general and administrative	R	16,662	16,634	16,854
Research, development and engineering	S	5,046	4,877	5,089
Total operating expenses		21,708	21,511	21,943
Operating income		9,164	9,098	8,596
Other income, principally interest		589	657	707
Interest expense	L	713	728	716
Income before income taxes		9,040	9,027	8,587
Provision for income taxes	Q	2,712	2,934	3,158
Net income		6,328	6,093	5,429
Preferred stock dividends		20	20	20
Net income applicable to common shareholders		$ 6,308	$ 6,073	$ 5,409
Earnings per share of common stock—basic	T	$ 6.75	$ 6.18	$ 5.12
Earnings per share of common stock—assuming dilution	T	$ 6.57	$ 6.01	$ 5.01

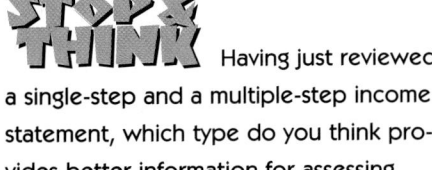

Having just reviewed a single-step and a multiple-step income statement, which type do you think provides better information for assessing a firm's performance?

the multiple-step form, the costs are partitioned so that intermediate components of income are presented. For example, IBM discloses gross profit, operating income, income before taxes, and net income in its income statements. Nike reports only income before taxes and net income.

For discussion purposes, we will use the multiple-step income statement for Techtronics Corporation (on page 172). This hypothetical income statement contains more categories and more detail than is usually found in actual published financial statements. It has become common practice to issue highly condensed statements (see Nike's income statement), with details and supporting schedules provided in notes to the statements. The potential problem with this practice is that the condensed statements may not provide as much predictive and feedback value as statements that provide more detail about the components of income directly on the statement.

The Techtronics income statement differs from most published statements in other ways. For example, to simplify the illustration of the various income components, only one year is presented for Techtronics. To comply with SEC requirements, income statements of public companies are presented in comparative form for three years (see Exhibits 4-5, and 4-6). **Comparative financial statements** enable users to analyze performance over multiple periods and identify significant trends that might impact future performance. Also note that the Techtronics income statement is for a single business entity, but public companies often present **consolidated financial statements** that combine the financial results of a "parent company," such as IBM, with other companies that it owns, called subsidiaries. All the actual company statements illustrated in this chapter, as well as THE WALT DISNEY COMPANY's statements in Appendix A, are consolidated statements.[12] In Chapter 14, we will discuss the preparation of consolidated financial statements and what the implications are for interpreting those statements.

COMPONENTS OF THE INCOME STATEMENT

5

Describe the specific components of an income statement.

In the following sections, the content of the income statement will be discussed and illustrated using the statement for Techtronics Corporation. Variations in current reporting practices will be examined and illustrated with income statements of actual companies. Subsequently, the requirement to supplement reported net income with a measure of comprehensive income will be discussed.

Income from Continuing Operations

The Techtronics Corporation income statement has two major categories of income: (1) income from continuing operations and (2) irregular or extraordinary items. **Income from continuing operations** includes all revenues and expenses and gains and losses arising from the ongoing operations of the firm. In the Techtronics example, income from continuing operations includes six separate sections as follows.

1. Revenue
2. Cost of goods sold
3. Operating expenses
4. Other revenues and gains
5. Other expenses and losses
6. Income taxes on continuing operations

12 Throughout this text, we will use many actual companies to illustrate financial reporting concepts and practices. You will observe many variations in statement titles, terminology, level of detail, and other aspects of reporting. As a result, you will develop an appreciation of the diversity in financial reporting and the ability to understand financial information presented in a wide variety of terms and formats.

Techtronics Corporation
Income Statement
For the Year Ended December 31, 2002

Revenue:			
Sales		$800,000	
Less: Sales returns and allowances		$ 12,000	
Sales discounts	8,000	20,000	$780,000
Cost of goods sold:			
Beginning inventory		$125,000	
Net purchases	$630,000		
Freight-in	32,000	662,000	
Cost of goods available for sale		$787,000	
Less ending inventory		296,000	491,000
Gross profit			$289,000
Operating expenses:			
Selling expenses:			
Sales salaries	$ 46,000		
Advertising expense	27,000		
Miscellaneous selling expenses	12,000	$ 85,000	
General and administrative expenses:			
Officers' and office salaries	$ 44,000		
Taxes and insurance	26,500		
Depreciation and amortization expense	30,000		
Doubtful accounts expense	8,600		
Miscellaneous general expense	9,200	118,300	203,300
Operating income			$ 85,700
Other revenues and gains:			
Interest revenue		$ 12,750	
Gain on sale of investment		37,000	49,750
Other expenses and losses:			
Interest expense		$ (18,250)	
Loss on sale of equipment		(5,250)	(23,500)
Income from continuing operations before income taxes			$111,950
Income taxes on continuing operations			33,585
Income from continuing operations			$ 78,365
Discontinued operations:			
Loss from operations of discontinued business segment (net of income tax savings of $10,500)		$ (24,500)	
Loss on disposal of business segment (net of income tax savings of $4,800)		(11,200)	(35,700)
Extraordinary gain from early debt extinguishment (net of income taxes of $7,620)			17,780
Cumulative effect of changing inventory method (net of income tax savings of $2,250)			(5,250)
Net income			$ 55,195
Translation adjustment		$ (2,450)	
Increase in unrealized gains on available-for-sale securities		1,180	(1,270)
Comprehensive Income			$ 53,925
Earnings per common share:			
Income from continuing operations			$1.57
Discontinued operations			(0.71)
Extraordinary gain			0.36
Cumulative effect of accounting change			(0.11)
Net income			$1.11

Also, a review of the Techtronics income statement discloses several subtotals in the income from continuing operations category. These subtotals are identified as follows:

1. Gross profit (Revenue – Cost of goods sold)
2. Operating income (Gross profit – Operating expenses)
3. Income from continuing operations before income taxes (Operating income + Other revenues and gains – Other expenses and losses)
4. Income from continuing operations (Income from continuing operations before income taxes – Income taxes on continuing operations)

Each of these major sections and related subtotals will be discussed separately as a way to better understand current practices in reporting income from continuing operations. Subsequently, we will examine the irregular and extraordinary components of income.

REVENUE   Revenue reports the total sales to customers for the period less any sales returns and allowances or discounts. This total should not include additions to billings for sales and excise taxes that the business is required to collect on behalf of the government. These billing increases are properly recognized as current liabilities. Sales returns and allowances and sales discounts should be subtracted from gross sales in arriving at net sales revenue. When the sales price is increased to cover the cost of freight to the customer and the customer is billed accordingly, freight charges paid by the company should also be subtracted from sales in arriving at net sales. Freight charges not passed on to the buyer are recognized as selling expenses.

COST OF GOODS SOLD   In any merchandising or manufacturing enterprise, the cost of goods relating to sales for the period must be determined. As illustrated in the Techtronics Corporation income statement, cost of goods available for sale is first determined. This is the sum of the beginning inventory, net purchases, and all other buying, freight, and storage costs relating to the acquisition of goods. (The net purchases balance is developed by subtracting purchase returns and allowances and purchase discounts from gross purchases, not shown.) Cost of goods sold is then calculated by subtracting the ending inventory from the cost of goods available for sale.

When the goods are manufactured by the seller, additional elements enter into the cost of goods sold. Besides material costs, a company incurs labor and overhead costs to convert the material from its raw material state to a finished good. A manufacturing company has three inventories rather than one: raw materials, goods in process, finished goods. Techtronics Corporation is a merchandising company. The cost of goods sold for a manufacturing company is illustrated in Chapter 8.

GROSS PROFIT   For most merchandising and manufacturing companies, cost of goods sold is the most significant expense on the income statement. Because of its size, firms pay particular attention to changes in cost of goods sold relative to changes in sales. **Gross profit** is the difference between revenue from net sales and cost of goods sold; **gross profit percentage**, computed by dividing gross profit by revenue from net sales, provides a measure of profitability that allows comparisons for a firm from year to year. For GENERAL MOTORS, gross profit is the difference between the cost to manufacture a car and the price GM charges to dealers who buy cars. In a supermarket, gross profit is the difference between retail selling price and wholesale cost.

Gross profit is an important number. If a company is not generating enough from the sale of a product or service to cover the costs directly associated with that product or service, that company will not be able to stay in that line of business for long. For example, if IBM sells a mainframe computer for $126,000 and the materials, labor, and overhead costs associated with producing that computer are $139,000, the gross profit of $(13,000) suggests that IBM is in serious difficulty. After all, with a negative gross profit,

► **POLLUTED ACCOUNTING**

The solid-waste disposal industry has gained much attention as cities and states wrestle with how to dispose of the thousands of tons of garbage produced daily by inhabitants. One "small but formidable player in the solid-waste industry" was CHAMBERS DEVELOPMENT COMPANY. Chambers went public in 1985 with three landfills and the capacity to handle 10 million tons of garbage per year. By 1992, Chambers owned

17 landfills with a capacity of 84 million tons of waste. Revenues grew at an annual rate of 51%—rising from $5 million in 1980 to $322 million in 1991.

But revenues weren't the only thing growing at Chambers Development Company. The gap between reported results and reality was increasing at an alarming rate. It seems that increasing pressure from top management to produce profitable results caused many within the company to ignore generally accepted accounting principles. Investigations by auditors from DELOITTE & TOUCHE revealed that after-tax income had been overstated by $362 million over a seven-year period. These overstatements were accomplished by incorrectly

capitalizing (i.e., recording items as assets instead of as expenses) such items as the costs of disposing of waste, interest costs, start-up costs, and certain intangible items.

On St. Patrick's Day 1992, Chambers Development announced that it had been engaging in improper accounting for years. Fear over what this announcement implied about Chambers' track record of steady earnings growth sent Chambers' stock price plunging by 62% in one day.

And where was the independent auditor when all of this was going on? The audit partner who signed off on Chambers' audits through 1990 joined the company

IBM would not be able to pay for advertising, executive salaries, interest expense, and so forth.

For example, using information from IBM's income statement in Exhibit 4–6, we can compute a gross profit percentage for each type of revenue.

IBM Corporation Gross Profit Percentage			
	1998	**1997**	**1996**
Hardware	31.6%	35.9%	37.5%
Global Services	26.9%	26.6%	27.1%
Software	80.9%	75.1%	74.2%
Global Financing	48.1%	48.4%	51.5%
Enterprise Investments/Other	34.3%	36.9%	27.7%
Overall gross profit	37.8%	39.0%	40.2%

This analysis reveals that IBM's overall gross profit percentage has decreased over the three-year period from 1996 to 1998. This decline can be attributed primarily to the decrease in the gross profit percentage of the hardware segment, which accounted for over 43% of IBM's 1998 revenues.

OPERATING EXPENSES   Operating expenses may be reported in two parts: (1) selling expenses and (2) general and administrative expenses. Selling expenses include such items as sales salaries and commissions and related payroll taxes, advertising and store displays, store supplies used, depreciation of store furniture and equipment, and delivery expenses. General and administrative expenses include officers' and office salaries and related payroll taxes, office supplies used, depreciation of office furniture and fixtures, telephone, postage, business licenses and fees, legal and accounting services, contributions, and similar items. For manufacturers, charges related jointly to production and

as chief financial officer later that same year. In addition, two other employees of the same audit firm were hired by Chambers to fill top finance positions. A new team of auditors from the same firm would not accept Chambers' accounting practices and refused to sign off on the audit report for 1991.

The accounting announcement on March 17, 1992, was just the beginning of troubles for Chambers Development. Continuing business problems eventually forced the board of directors of Chambers to put the company up for sale. Chambers was acquired by USA WASTE on June 30, 1995.

QUESTIONS:

1. How does capitalizing the costs of disposing of waste, interest costs, start-up costs, and certain intangible items affect the income statement? What journal entries would have been made by Chambers' accountant to capitalize these costs? What journal entries should have been made by the accountant?

2. A former consultant for Chambers stated that the president of Chambers "would not tolerate the presence of persons who would not give him the answers he wanted." As the accountant for Chambers Development Company, what would you have done if you had been asked to make these incorrect journal entries?

3. As a user of a firm's financial statements, would it have concerned you when the audit partner in charge of the independent audit became the chief financial officer for the company?

SOURCE:
Gabriella Stern, "Polluted Numbers: Audit Report Shows How Far Chambers Would Go for Profits," *The Wall Street Journal*, October 21, 1992, pp. A1, A8.

administrative functions should be allocated in an equitable manner between manufacturing overhead and operating expenses.

OPERATING INCOME   **Operating income** measures the performance of the fundamental business operations conducted by a company and is computed as gross profit minus operating expenses. A general rule of thumb is that all expenses are operating expenses *except* interest expense and income tax expense. Accordingly, another name for operating income is earnings before interest and taxes (EBIT).

Operating income tells users how well a business is performing in the activities unique to that business, separate from the financing and income tax management policies that are handled at the corporate headquarters level. For example, operating income allows you to evaluate WAL-MART's overall ability to choose store locations, establish pricing strategies, train and retain workers, and manage relations with its suppliers. Operating income does not tell you anything about the interest cost of Wal-Mart's loans or how successful Wal-Mart's tax planners have been at structuring and locating operations to minimize income taxes.

OTHER REVENUES AND GAINS   This section usually includes items identified with the peripheral activities of the company. Examples include revenue from financial activities, such as rents, interest, and dividends, and gains from the sale of assets such as equipment or investments. A gain reported on the income statement represents a net amount, that is, the difference between selling price and cost. This differs from revenues, which are reported in total separately from related expenses.

OTHER EXPENSES AND LOSSES   This section is parallel to the previous one but results in deductions from, rather than increases to, operating income. Examples include interest expense and losses from the sale of assets. Losses, like gains, are reported at their net amounts.

A particularly controversial type of loss arises when companies propose a restructuring of their operations. A restructuring typically causes some assets to lose value

► PHAR-MOR AND THE WORLD BASKETBALL LEAGUE

Michael "Mickey" Monus, former president of PHAR-MOR INC., a deep-discount drugstore chain, had a keen interest in sports. His interest was such that he purchased a share of the COLORADO ROCKIES major league baseball team and also founded the World Basketball League (WBL)—a league for players 6'7" and under. The Rockies did quite well financially, setting attendance records in their first season of play. Unfortunately,

Mr. Monus was forced to sell his interest in the Rockies because of financial difficulties touched off by the failure of the WBL. WBL players and referees rebelled in July 1992 because they hadn't been paid in two months. Monus tried to prop up the league, but it soon suspended operations.

During late July 1992, Phar-Mor received a tip that Monus had been transferring money from Phar-Mor to the WBL. Investigation revealed that the $10 million in Phar-Mor cash Monus had used in an attempt to sustain the WBL was just the tip of a large iceberg of accounting irregularities. Payments from large vendors to secure exclusive supply arrangements for a period of time were recorded as revenue at the time of receipt instead of being deferred and recognized over the period of the

arrangement. Inventory was overstated by $175 million by keeping items in the inventory records even after they had been sold and also by creating phantom inventory at selected stores. The stores were selected based on the auditor's plan to verify inventory at only a few stores—Mr. Monus and his accomplices allegedly found out which stores those were and made sure not to manipulate inventory in those stores. The resulting investigation resulted in Phar-Mor's filing for bankruptcy protection on August 17, 1992.

Monus faced a 129-count indictment filed by the U.S. attorney general's office. The first trial was declared a mistrial in June 1994. Monus was convicted on 109 felony counts in May 1995 and was sentenced to 20

FYI: In a speech given on September 28, 1998, Arthur Levitt, Chairman of the SEC, identified five popular areas of accounting "hocus-pocus" used by companies to manipulate reported earnings. Number one on that list was big bath restructuring charges.

because they no longer fit in a company's strategic plans. A restructuring also creates additional costs associated with the termination or relocation of employees. For example, in the notes to its financial statements, GENERAL MOTORS disclosed that its operating expenses for 1997 include a **restructuring charge** of $6.4 billion resulting from a series of three "Competitiveness Studies" that suggested a refocus of some operations. The controversy over restructuring charges stems from the fact that companies exercise considerable discretion in determining the amount of a restructuring charge. The fear is that companies can use this discretion as a tool for manipulating the amount of reported net income. For example, companies that are already faced with the prospect of poor reported performance for a year may intentionally overestimate the cost of a restructuring. The motivation for this so-called big bath approach is that, if a company is going to report poor results anyway, it makes sense to gather up all the bad news in the company and report it at the same time, thus diluting the effect of any single bad news item. If this approach is followed, reported performance in the years following the big bath year will appear much improved, in large part because the restructuring charge resulted in many expenses of future years being estimated and reported as one lump sum in the big bath year. Examples of companies reporting restructuring charges in recent years include EASTMAN KODAK ($1.290 billion in 1997), AT&T ($3.023 billion in 1995), and IBM ($445 million in 1997, $1.491 billion in 1996, and $2.119 billion in 1995).

INCOME FROM CONTINUING OPERATIONS BEFORE INCOME TAXES Subtracting other revenues and gains and other expenses and losses from operating income results in income from continuing operations before taxes.

INCOME TAXES ON CONTINUING OPERATIONS Income tax expense is the sum of all the income tax consequences of all transactions undertaken by a company during a year. Some of those tax consequences may occur in the current year, and some may occur

years in federal prison. In an interesting twist, the remaining management of Phar-Mor and Phar-Mor's auditor sued one another. Management claimed that the auditor was negligent. The auditor claimed that Phar-Mor's management should have detected Monus' fraudulent activities.

QUESTIONS:
1. How would overstating inventory and receivables inflate reported income? Why would someone want to inflate reported income?
2. Does the independent auditor have a responsibility for detecting these types of misstatements?

3. Observation of Monus' woes with the WBL may have given some indication that he was in need of cash. When performing an audit, what evidence should the auditor seek outside the financial records of the firm being audited?

SOURCES:
Lee Berton, "Inventory Chicanery Tempts More Firms, Fools More Auditors," *The Wall Street Journal*, December 14, 1992, p. A1.
Matt Murray, "Phar-Mor to Merge with Shopko Stores," *The Wall Street Journal*, September 10, 1996, p. A3.
Gabriella Stern and Clare Ansberry, "Fouling Out: A Founder Embezzled Millions for Basketball," *The Wall Street Journal*, August 5, 1992, p. A1.
Gabriella Stern, "Phar-Mor's Profit Growth Since 1989 May Have Been Inflated," *The Wall Street Journal*, August 28, 1992, p. A3.

Caution! Keep in mind that while a transaction may result in a gain or loss for one company, that same transaction may be treated differently for another. For example, if an office supplies store sells its delivery truck to a used car dealer, a gain or loss occurs for the office supplies store. However, when the used car dealer sells the delivery truck, the proceeds will be considered revenue. Why the different treatment? In the first instance, the sale of the truck is a peripheral activity. In the second case, the sale of the truck results from the dealer's ongoing operations.

in future years. When irregular or extraordinary items are reported, total taxes for the period must be allocated among the various components of income. One income tax amount is reported for all items included in the income from continuing operations category; it is presented as the last section in the category. In contrast, each item in the irregular or extraordinary items category is reported net of its income tax effect, referred to as "net of income tax." This separation of income taxes into different sections of the income statement is referred to as **intraperiod income tax allocation.**

For example, in 1998 IBM generated enough taxable income to require it to pay $1.9 billion in income taxes for the year. However, in 1998 IBM also entered into transactions creating tax liabilities that the company will pay in future years. Even though those taxes will not be paid until future years, they are recognized as an expense in the period in which they are incurred. So, as seen in Exhibit 4–6, IBM reports income tax expense for 1998 of $2.7 billion, which represents the net tax effects, both now and in the future, of all transactions entered into during the year.

In the Techtronics illustration, an income tax rate of 30% was assumed. Thus, the amount of income tax related to continuing operations is $33,585 ($111,950 × .30). The same tax rate is applied to all income components in the Techtronics example. In practice, however, intraperiod income tax allocation may involve different rates for different components of income. This results from graduated tax rates and special, or alternative, rates for certain types of gains and losses.

INCOME FROM CONTINUING OPERATIONS A key purpose of financial accounting is to provide interested parties with information that can be used to predict how a company will perform in the future. Therefore, financial statement users desire an income amount that reflects the aspects of a company's performance that are expected to continue into the future. This is labeled "Income from Continuing Operations." Income from continuing operations is computed by subtracting interest expense, income tax expense, and other gains and losses from operating income.

Irregular and Extraordinary Items

Components of income that are reported separately after income from continuing operations are sometimes called "below-the-line" items. They arise from transactions and events that are irregular or extraordinary and are material in amount. Reporting these items, and their related tax effects, separately from continuing operations provides more informative disclosure to users of financial statements. Three types of transactions and events are reported in this manner: (1) discontinued operations, (2) extraordinary items, and (3) cumulative effects of changes in accounting principles. In addition to these three items, the effects of changes in estimates and changing prices also influence the income statement and related disclosures. Each of these items is discussed in turn.

DISCONTINUED OPERATIONS An increasingly common irregular item involves the disposition of a major segment of a business either through sale or abandonment. The segment of the company disposed of may be a major line of business, a major class of customer, or a subsidiary company. To qualify as **discontinued operations** for reporting purposes, the assets and related activities of the segment must be clearly distinguishable from other assets, operating results, and general activities of the company, both physically and operationally, as well as for financial reporting purposes. For example, closing down one of three plants making the same product, eliminating part of a line of business, or shifting the production or marketing functions from one location to another would not be classified as discontinued operations.

There are many reasons why management may decide to dispose of a segment. For example:

- The segment may be unprofitable.
- The segment may not fit into the long-range plans for the company.
- Management may need funds to reduce long-term debt or to expand into other areas.
- Management may be fearful of a corporate takeover by new investors desiring to gain control of the company.

In the 1980s and 90s, management of many companies adopted antitakeover strategies to try to protect their companies. One of the more popular techniques was to sell peripheral operational segments, especially unprofitable ones, that had been acquired during earlier conglomerate years and to consolidate the company around its principal business operations. AT&T provides an example of this strategy. As mentioned at the beginning of this chapter, in 1996 AT&T decided to split itself into three publicly held companies. At that time AT&T also elected to divest itself of several other business segments. In 1996, AT&T sold its interest in AT&T CAPITAL CORPORATION. In 1997, the company sold its submarine systems business (SSI). Finally, in 1998 CITIBANK purchased AT&T UNIVERSAL CARD SERVICES INC. These three transactions resulted in a gain, on each sale, of $162 million, $66 million, and $1,290 million in 1996, 1997, and 1998, respectively. The relevant portion of AT&T's income statement and the related footnote are provided in Exhibit 4–7.

Regardless of the reason for a company's selling a segment, the discontinuance of a substantial portion of company operations is a significant event. Therefore, information about discontinued operations should be presented explicitly to readers of financial statements.

Reporting requirements for discontinued operations. When a company discontinues operating a segment of its business, future comparability requires that all elements that relate to the discontinued operation be identified and separated from continuing operations. Thus, in the Techtronics Corporation income statement illustrated earlier in

EXHIBIT 4-7 | AT&T Discontinued Operations—From the 1998 Income Statement and Related Note

(Dollars in millions)	1998	1997	1996
Income from continuing operations	$5,235	$4,249	$5,458
Discontinued operations			
Income from discontinued operations (net of taxes of $6, $50, and $353)	10	100	173
Gain on sale of discontinued operations (net of taxes of $799, $43, and $138)	1,290	66	162
Income before extraordinary loss	$6,535	$4,415	$5,793
Extraordinary loss (net of taxes of $80)	137	—	—
Net income	$6,398	$4,415	$5,793

NOTE

On October 1, 1996, AT&T sold its remaining interest in AT&T Capital Corp. for approximately $1.8 billion, resulting in an after-tax gain of $162, or $0.09 per diluted share.

On July 1, 1997, AT&T sold its submarine systems business (SSI) to Tyco International Ltd. for $850, resulting in an after-tax gain of $66, or $0.04 per diluted share.

On April 2, 1998, AT&T sold AT&T Universal Card Services Inc. (UCS) for $3,500 to Citibank. The after-tax gain resulting from the disposal of UCS was $1,290, or $0.72 per diluted share. Included in the transaction was a co-branding and joint marketing agreement. In addition, we received $5,722 as settlement of receivables from UCS.

The consolidated financial statements of AT&T have been restated to reflect the dispositions of Lucent, NCR, AT&T Capital Corp., SSI, UCS and certain other businesses as discontinued operations. Accordingly, the revenues, costs and expenses, assets and liabilities, and cash flows of these discontinued operations have been excluded from the respective captions in the Consolidated Statements of Income, Consolidated Balance Sheets and Consolidated Statements of Cash Flows, and have been reported through the dates of disposition as "Income from discontinued operations, net of applicable income taxes," as "Net assets of discontinued operations," and as "Net cash used in discontinued operations" for all periods presented. Gains associated with these sales are reflected as "Gain on sale of discontinued operations."

this chapter, the first category after income from continuing operations is discontinued operations. The category is further separated into two subdivisions: (1) the current-year income or loss from operating the discontinued segment, in this case a $24,500 loss, and (2) disclosure of the gain or loss on the actual disposal of the business segment, for Techtronics, a further $11,200 loss.

As previously indicated, the irregular items are all reported net of their respective tax effects. If the item is a gain, it is reduced by the tax on the gain. If the item is a loss, it is deductible against other income and thus its existence saves income taxes. The overall company loss can thus be reduced by the tax savings arising from being able to deduct the loss from otherwise taxable income.

The income statement for Techtronics Corporation discloses both of these subdivisions. The income tax rate is 30% on all items. Analysis of the income statement shows that the discontinued segment had an operating loss for the current year of $35,000, but that after a tax savings of $10,500 was deducted, only $24,500 is reported as a loss. The second item discloses that the segment was sold and a loss of $16,000 was experienced on the sale. Application of the income tax rate of 30% reduces this loss to $11,200. If comparative statements are prepared, the same separation between continued and discontinued operations for prior years should be made.

Often a company will decide on a particular date (the measurement date) to dispose of a business segment, but it will have a phase-out period between that date and the date the segment is actually sold (disposal date). The gain or loss on disposal will include any income or loss from operating the segment during the phase-out period. To illustrate, using Techtronics Corporation's income statement, assume the company decided on July 1, 2002, to phase out a segment of its operations. This date is the measurement date and marks the beginning of the phaseout period. Assume also that the segment was disposed of on November 17, 2002. The $11,200 loss on disposal reflects both the operating results during phaseout and the gain or loss on final disposal, net of income taxes. The $24,500 loss represents the operating loss (net of income tax savings of $10,500) for the period January 1, 2002, to July 1, 2002. The time line presented below uses the Techtronics example to illustrate the relevant time periods to be considered when accounting for discontinued operations.

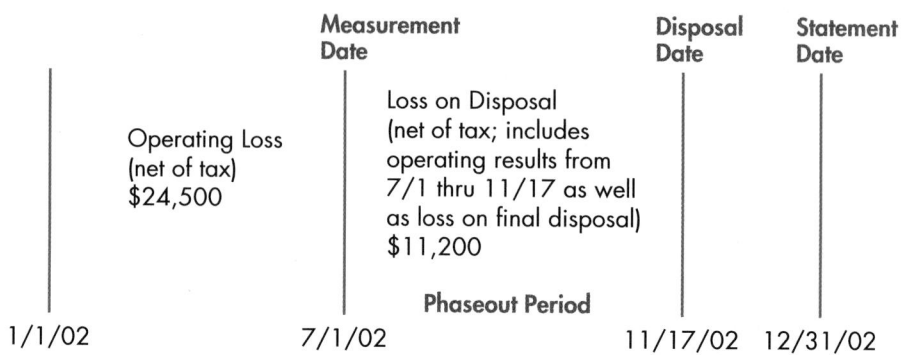

If the accounting year ends before the disposal is completed, estimates must be made of the expected operating results prior to disposal as well as the expected gain or loss from final disposal. If these computations indicate an overall expected net loss on disposal, the accounting constraint of conservatism dictates that the loss should be recognized in the current period, not in the later period when the loss is realized. If these computations indicate an overall expected gain on disposal, the gain will not be recognized until it is actually realized in the subsequent period. However, an expected gain on disposal in a subsequent period is recognized to the extent that it offsets a loss on disposal that has already occurred during the phase-out period in the current year. For example, if as of the end of 2002, Techtronics expected an additional gain on disposal of the discontinued segment in 2003 of $15,000 (in addition to the $11,200 loss on disposal realized in 2002), the overall reported loss on disposal reported in 2002 would be $0. Thus, a portion of the expected gain would be recognized to offset the realized loss, but the $3,800 ($15,000 − $11,200) additional gain would not be recognized until 2003 after it had been actually realized.

> **Caution!**   Don't forget that any income or loss earned after the measurement date but prior to the disposal date is included in the gain or loss on disposal, not in income or loss from operations of the discontinued segment. If financial statements are prepared between the measurement date and disposal date, expected future losses are recognized in the current period but expected future gains are not.

The AT&T income statement in Exhibit 4–7 illustrates how the two components of discontinued operations (income or loss from operating the segment and gain or loss on disposal) are reported. The first line in the discontinued operations section reports the operating income or loss, net of income taxes, for the discontinued operations for all three years. The separation of income from discontinued operations from regular income enhances the comparability of this year's results with those of prior years. The second line in the discontinued operations section indicates the estimated gain or loss (which includes estimated operating gains and losses) on disposal of the segments.

The reporting requirements for discontinued operations are contained in APB Opinion No. 30, "Reporting the Results of Operations."[13] The reporting of discontinued operations can become complex, and only a summary of the guidelines provided by APB Opinion No. 30 is covered here. Application of the guidelines requires judgment. The goal should be to report information that will assist external users in assessing future cash flows by clearly distinguishing normal recurring earnings patterns from those activities that are irregular, yet significant in assessing the total results of company operations.

---

13 *Opinions of the Accounting Principles Board No. 30*, "Reporting the Results of Operations," New York: American Institute of Certified Public Accountants, 1973, par. 20.

The reporting practices with respect to discontinued operations in the United Kingdom represent an interesting alternative to the U.S. approach. For example, in complying with Financial Reporting Standard (FRS) 3 of the Accounting Standards Board in the United Kingdom, British Telecommunications (BT) provided the following information in its 1998 profit and loss account (income statement).

(In millions of £)	1998
Total turnover (sales)	
Ongoing activities	£16,039
Discontinued activities	1,372
Total operating profit	
Ongoing activities	3,436
Discontinued activities	25

> **FYI:** According to International Accounting Standard (IAS) 35 (issued in June 1998), companies with discontinued operations must disclose the following: the amounts of revenue, expenses, and pretax profit or loss attributable to the discontinued operations and related income tax expense.

This approach provides more information to financial statement users than does the U.S. approach because it allows for a comparison of the relative size and operating profitability of the continuing and discontinued operations.

EXTRAORDINARY ITEMS According to APB Opinion No. 30, **extraordinary items** are events and transactions that are both unusual in nature and infrequent in occurrence. Thus, to qualify as extraordinary, an item must "possess a high degree of abnormality and be of a type clearly unrelated to, or only incidentally related to, the ordinary and typical activities of the entity . . . [and] be of a type that would not reasonably be expected to recur in the foreseeable future. . . ."[14]

The intent of the APB was to restrict the items that could be classified as extraordinary. The presumption of the Board was that an item should be considered ordinary and part of the company's continuing operations unless evidence clearly supports its classification as an extraordinary item. The Board offered examples of gains and losses that should *not* be reported as extraordinary items. These include:

- The write-down or write-off of receivables, inventories, equipment leased to others, or intangible assets.
- The gains or losses from exchanges or remeasurement of foreign currencies, including those relating to major devaluations and revaluations.
- The gains or losses on disposal of a segment of a business.
- Other gains or losses from sale or abandonment of property, plant, or equipment used in the business.
- The effects of a strike.
- The adjustment of accruals on long-term contracts.

The FASB has identified only one major item as extraordinary regardless of whether it meets the dual criteria: a gain or loss from early extinguishment of debt.[15] Because these gains and losses are actually quite common, many disagree with the FASB's rule mandating the reporting of these gains and losses as extraordinary items. For example, TIME WARNER reported "extraordinary" losses from early debt extinguishment three years in a row from 1995 through 1997. The extraordinary classification for these gains and losses is a result of the business environment at the time this rule was adopted. In 1975, high interest rates had caused a decline in the market value of bonds issued during the

---

14 Ibid.
15 Statement of Financial Accounting Standards No. 4, "Reporting Gains and Losses From Extinguishment of Debt," Stamford, CT: Financial Accounting Standards Board, 1975.

1960s. Many companies were retiring these bonds early in order to be able to report accounting gains on the retirement. To stop companies from including these gains as part of ordinary income from continuing operations, the FASB decreed that they be classified as extraordinary.

The portion of AT&T's 1998 income statement reproduced in Exhibit 4–7 provides an example of the disclosure required when debt is retired early. The accompanying note, found in Exhibit 4–8, details the nature of the extraordinary item.

EXHIBIT 4–8 | Note Disclosure from AT&T's 1998 Annual Report (dollars in millions)

> In August 1998, AT&T extinguished $1,046 of TCG debt. This early extinguishment of debt was recorded as an extraordinary loss and resulted in a $217 pretax loss. The after-tax impact was $137, or $.08 per diluted share. This debt reduction will produce significant savings in interest expense over time.

Besides early extinguishment of debt, companies have reported as extraordinary items litigation settlements, write-offs of assets in foreign countries where expropriation risks were high, and pension plan terminations.

Some items may not meet both criteria for extraordinary items but may meet one of them. Although these items do not qualify as extraordinary, they should be disclosed separately as part of income from continuing operations, either before or after operating income. Examples of these items include strike-related costs, obsolete inventory write-downs, and gains and losses from liquidation of investments.

CUMULATIVE EFFECTS OF CHANGES IN ACCOUNTING PRINCIPLES The last item included in the irregular category of the income statement is the effect of changing accounting principles. Although the profession has recognized the desirability of consistency in application of accounting principles, there are occasions where conditions justify a change from one principle to another. Sometimes this condition arises because the standard-setting body issues a new pronouncement requiring a change in principle. If GAAP is to be followed, the company has no choice but to change to conform with the new standard. The FASB has usually included in the standard the way these transition adjustments should be handled. Over time, the Board has leaned toward making the adjustment to net income rather than as a direct retained earnings adjustment.

The early 1990s involved numerous mandated changes in accounting principles related to such topics as postretirement benefits and deferred taxes. Such changes slowed to a trickle in the late 1990s and few if any companies were reporting cumulative effects of changes in accounting principles as this book went to press. An older example from DISNEY's 1993 financial statements indicated that the company changed its method of accounting for postretirement benefits other than pensions (SFAS No. 106), income taxes (SFAS No. 109), and pre-opening costs. The net effect of these three changes was to reduce income by $371.5 million in 1993.

Sometimes economic conditions change, and a company changes accounting principles so that reporting can be more representative of the actual conditions. For example, when there was double-digit inflation during the late 1970s, many companies changed their inventory methods to LIFO to reduce their income and thus reduce the actual cash payments for income taxes.

Depending on the type of change in accounting principle, the change may be implemented retroactively or it may be reflected only in the current and future periods. If the change arises because of a new FASB standard, the Board designates how the change must be implemented. If the change in accounting principle is made at management's discretion, however, the implementation decision is made by management using guidance provided by accounting standard setters. When there is a change in accounting method, a company is required to compute how much net income would have been different in past years if the new accounting method had been used all along. The Board has recognized two different ways to adjust current statements to reflect this **cumulative effect of a change in accounting principle:** (1) generally, income statements should report the cumulative effect of the change in the current year with no restatement of prior years' figures, (2) special cases require the restatement of financial statements presented for prior years. For example, in the general case, if a company decides to change its depreciation method from straight-line depreciation to declining balance for all existing assets, an entry is needed in the current year to adjust the statements for the cumulative effect of the change. In the special cases, such as a change from the LIFO to the FIFO inventory valuation method, the beginning balance of retained earnings for the current year reflects the cumulative effect of the prior years' changes. The Accounting Principles Board (APB) specified different criteria to help accountants determine which approach should be applied under what circumstances.

> **FYI:** GENERAL MOTORS (GM) has the distinction of having reported the largest cumulative effect of all time—a $20.8 billion reduction in net income in 1992 stemming from the adoption of SFAS No. 106, which mandated a change in the way GM accounts for its obligation to pay for the health care of retired workers. The $20.8 billion cumulative effect represents the total amount by which GM's net income in prior years would have been lower if SFAS No. 106 had always been in effect.

In the income statement illustrated earlier in the chapter, the Techtronics Corporation recorded a $5,250 cumulative loss due to changing inventory principles. The pretax loss to Techtronics was $7,500, but income tax savings reduced the reported loss by $2,250. If Techtronics had met one of the criteria identified by the APB as requiring restatement of the financial statements, the other method of reporting the cumulative effects of the change in accounting principles would have been used. There would have been no adjustment to income; instead, the loss would have been recorded by restating prior years' reported income and restating the beginning balance in Retained Earnings for the current year.

International Accounting Standard (IAS) 8 recommends a combination of the two methods described for reporting the cumulative effect of a change in accounting principle. IAS 8 does not require the restatement of prior years' net income and also does not require the cumulative effect to be reported as part of net income for the current year. Instead, the cumulative effect is reported as a direct adjustment to beginning retained earnings of the current year. This is a very simple and intuitive way to account for a change in accounting principle. This technique has the benefit of not retroactively changing earnings for prior years that have already been reported and also of not distorting the current year's income by including the cumulative effect of a change in accounting principle. The accounting for changes in accounting principles is discussed more fully in Chapter 19.

CHANGES IN ESTIMATES In reporting periodic revenues and in attempting to properly match those expenses incurred to generate current-period revenues, accountants must continually make judgments. The numbers reported in the financial statements reflect these judgments and are based on estimates of such factors as the number of years of useful life for depreciable assets, the amount of uncollectible accounts expected, or the amount of warranty liability to be recorded on the books. These and other estimates are made using the best available information at the statement date. However, conditions may subsequently change, and the estimates may need to be revised. Naturally, if either revenue or expense amounts are changed, the income statement is affected. The question is whether the previously reported income measures should be revised or whether the changes should impact only current and future periods.

The APB stated in Opinion No. 20 that changes in estimates should be reflected in the current period (the period in which the estimate is revised) and in future periods, if any, that are affected. No retroactive adjustments are to be made for a change in estimate.[16]

---

16 *Opinions of the Accounting Principles Board No. 20, "Accounting Changes,"* New York: American Institute of Certified Public Accountants, 1971, par. 31.

These changes are considered a normal part of the accounting process and not errors made in past periods. For example, as of July 1, 1998, DELTA AIR LINES increased the estimated useful life it uses in computing depreciation expense for selected new-generation aircraft from 20 years to 25 years.

To illustrate the computations for a change in estimate, assume that Springville Manufacturing Co., Inc., purchased a milling machine at a cost of $100,000. At the time of purchase, it was estimated that the machine would have a useful life of 10 years. Assuming no salvage value and that the straight-line method is used, the depreciation expense is $10,000 per year ($100,000/10). At the beginning of the fifth year, however, conditions indicated that the machine would be used for only three more years. Depreciation expense in the fifth, sixth, and seventh years should reflect the revised estimate, but depreciation expense recorded in the first four years would not be affected. Because the book value at the end of four years is $60,000 ($100,000 – $40,000, accumulated depreciation), annual depreciation charges for the remaining three years of estimated life would be $20,000 ($60,000/3). The following schedule summarizes the depreciation charges over the life of the asset.

Year	Depreciation
1	$ 10,000
2	10,000
3	10,000
4	10,000
5	20,000
6	20,000
7	20,000
Total (accumulated) depreciation	$100,000

EFFECTS OF CHANGING PRICES   The preceding presentation of revenue and expense recognition has not addressed the question of how, if at all, changing prices are to be recognized under the transaction approach. As indicated in Chapter 1, accountants have traditionally ignored this phenomenon, especially when gains would result from recognition. When an economy experiences high rates of inflation, users of financial statements become concerned that the statements do not reflect the impact of these changing prices. When the inflation rates are lower, this user concern decreases. When the price change rates are increasing, added pressure to adjust the financial statements is exerted by users of the income statement. Many foreign countries with high inflation rates require adjustments to remove the inflation effects. MCDONALD's addresses the effects of inflation in its 10-K, filed with the SEC. This note disclosure (included in Exhibit 4–9) indicates that McDonald's is able to deal with inflation through a quick turnover of inventory and by increasing prices in those locations where costs change rapidly.

EXHIBIT 4–9 | McDonald's—Note Disclosure

The Company has demonstrated an ability to manage inflationary cost increases effectively. This is because of rapid inventory turnover, the ability to adjust prices, cost controls and substantial property holdings—many of which are at fixed costs and partly financed by debt made cheaper by inflation. In hyperinflationary markets, menu board prices are typically adjusted to keep pace with inflation, mitigating the effect on reported results.

The FASB Statement No. 33 required certain large publicly held companies to disclose selected information about price changes on a supplemental basis. The Board did not require this recognition to be reported in the basic financial statements but in a supplemental note to the financial statements that did not have to be audited.

Subsequently, some of the disclosure requirements were eliminated in Statement No. 82, and all price-level disclosures were made voluntary with Statement No. 89.

Generally accepted accounting principles are still based primarily on historical exchange prices, and the transaction approach to income determination in most cases, with the exception of the accounting for investment securities, recognizes price changes only when losses in value are indicated.

Net Income or Loss

Income or loss from continuing operations combined with the results of discontinued operations, extraordinary items, and the cumulative effects of changes in accounting principles provides users with a summary measure of the firm's performance for a period—net income or net loss. This figure is the accountant's attempt to summarize in one number the overall economic performance of a company for a given period. In the absence of any irregular items, net income is the same as income from continuing operations.

From the discussion above, you can see that when someone makes a reference to a company's "income" or "profit," they could be referring to any one of a host of numbers—gross profit, operating income, income from continuing operations, or net income. It is important to learn to be very specific when discussing a company's income. After all, comparing one company's net income to another company's operating income would be like comparing apples to oranges.

In order to compare this period's results with prior periods or with the performance of other firms, net income is divided by net sales to determine the **return on sales**. This measurement represents the net income percentage per dollar of sales. For example, THE WALT DISNEY COMPANY (Appendix A) reported the following returns on sales.

	1998	1997	1996
Return on sales	8.1%	8.7%	6.5%

Compare these results with a sample of returns on sales from various companies in different industries, shown in Exhibit 4-10.

When computing the return on sales, keep in mind that net income may include extraordinary or irregular items that can distort the results and hamper comparability. Adjustments may be needed in the analysis to account for such items.

EXHIBIT 4-10 | Return on Sales

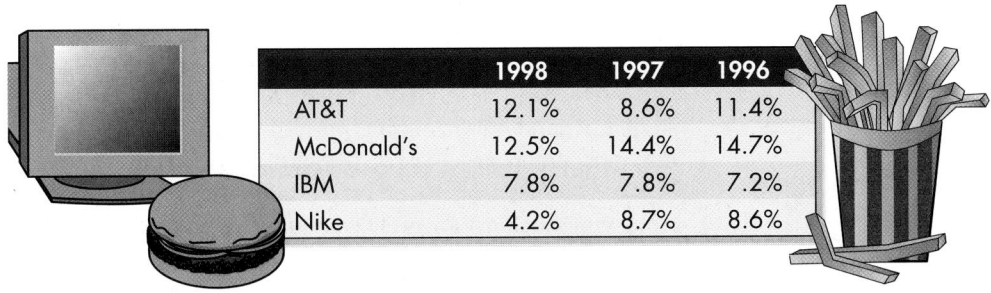

	1998	1997	1996
AT&T	12.1%	8.6%	11.4%
McDonald's	12.5%	14.4%	14.7%
IBM	7.8%	7.8%	7.2%
Nike	4.2%	8.7%	8.6%

EARNINGS PER SHARE An individual shareholder is interested in how much of a company's net income is associated with his or her ownership interest. As a result, the income statement reports **earnings per share (EPS)**, which is the amount of net income associated with each common share of stock. For example, in Exhibit 4-6 it can be seen that basic EPS for IBM in 1998 was $6.75. This means that an owner of 100 shares of IBM stock has claim on $675 ($6.75 EPS × 100 shares) of the $6.308 billion in IBM net income available to common shareholders for 1998.

Companies often disclose two earnings-per-share numbers. Basic EPS reports earnings based solely on shares actually outstanding during the year. Basic earnings per share is computed by dividing income available to common shareholders (net income less dividends paid to or promised to preferred shareholders) by the average number of common shares outstanding during the period.

Diluted earnings per share reflects the existence of stock options or other rights that can be converted into shares in the future. For example, in addition to having shares outstanding, a company can also have granted stock options that allow the option holders to buy shares of stock at some predetermined price. At present, the option holders don't own shares of stock, but they can acquire them from the company at any time. In other cases, a company might borrow money but also give the right to the lender to exchange the loan for shares of stock at some predetermined price. Diluted EPS is computed to give financial statement users an idea about the potential impact on EPS of the exercise of existing stock options or other rights to acquire shares.

IBM reports basic earnings per share and diluted earnings per share in 1998 of $6.75 and $6.57, respectively (see Exhibit 4-6). If all the options and other convertible items that are likely to be converted were in fact converted into shares of IBM stock, the effect on IBM's earnings per share would be to reduce it by $0.18. A small difference of $0.18 (less than 3% of basic EPS) indicates that IBM does not have a lot of options and convertible securities outstanding. On the other hand, there was a 5% difference between INTEL 's reported basic and diluted EPS in 1998 and a difference of 21% for YAHOO! These differences indicate that Intel and Yahoo! have a much larger percentage of stock options outstanding that could possibly dilute earnings per share.

Historically, the accounting rules in the United States governing the computation of EPS have been unnecessarily complex. In the mid-1990s, the FASB initiated a project, in conjunction with the IASC, to both improve U.S. accounting practice with respect to EPS and to increase international agreement on this important accounting issue. In 1997, the FASB and IASC issued almost identical standards prescribing the methods of computing the basic and diluted EPS numbers outlined above. Not only did this represent a big improvement in U.S. accounting practice but it also was a milestone in that it was the first time that the FASB and the IASC worked jointly to issue an accounting standard.

When presenting EPS figures, separate earnings-per-share amounts are computed by dividing income from continuing operations and each irregular or extraordinary item by the weighted average number of shares of common stock outstanding for the reporting period.[17]

For example, the Techtronics Corporation income statement shows earnings per common share of $1.57 for income from continuing operations, a $0.71 loss from discontinued operations, $0.36 for extraordinary gain, and a loss of $0.11 for the cumulative effect of a change in accounting principle, for a total of $1.11 for net income. These figures were derived by dividing each identified component of net income by 50,000 shares of common stock outstanding during the period. When a company has only common stock outstanding, computing EPS is very straightforward. The computations become more complex, however, when a company has certain types of securities outstanding, such as convertible stock and stock options. These and other types of securities are discussed in Chapter 11, and more detail on the computation of earnings per share is given in Chapter 19.

Earnings per share is often used to calculate a firm's **price-earnings (P/E) ratio.** This ratio expresses the market value of common stock as a multiple of earnings and allows investors to evaluate the attractiveness of a firm's common stock. The price-earnings ratio is computed by dividing the market price per share of common stock by

17 *Opinions of the Accounting Principles Board No. 15,* "Earnings Per Share," New York: American Institute of Certified Public Accountants, 1969, par. 47.

the annual basic EPS. Instead of using the average market value of shares for the period covered by earnings, the latest market value is normally used. *The Wall Street Journal* reports P/E ratios for most listed companies on a daily basis. Assuming Techtronics Corporation's stock closed with a market value of $14.25 per share on December 31, 2002, the P/E ratio would be computed as follows:

$$\text{P/E ratio} = \frac{\text{Market value per share}}{\text{Earnings per share}} \quad \frac{\$14.25}{\$1.11} = 12.8$$

To get an idea of how price-earnings ratios vary across time, consider the information contained in Exhibit 4–11. This exhibit summarizes data for thousands of companies over a 20-year period. The companies included in the analysis are the largest publicly-traded companies in the United States, determined each year by ranking all publicly-traded companies by market value and then computing the P/E ratios for the half with the largest market values. Note that, over this 20-year period, P/E ratios have tended to increase.

EXHIBIT 4–11 | P/E Ratios over Time for Large, Publicly-Traded U.S. Companies

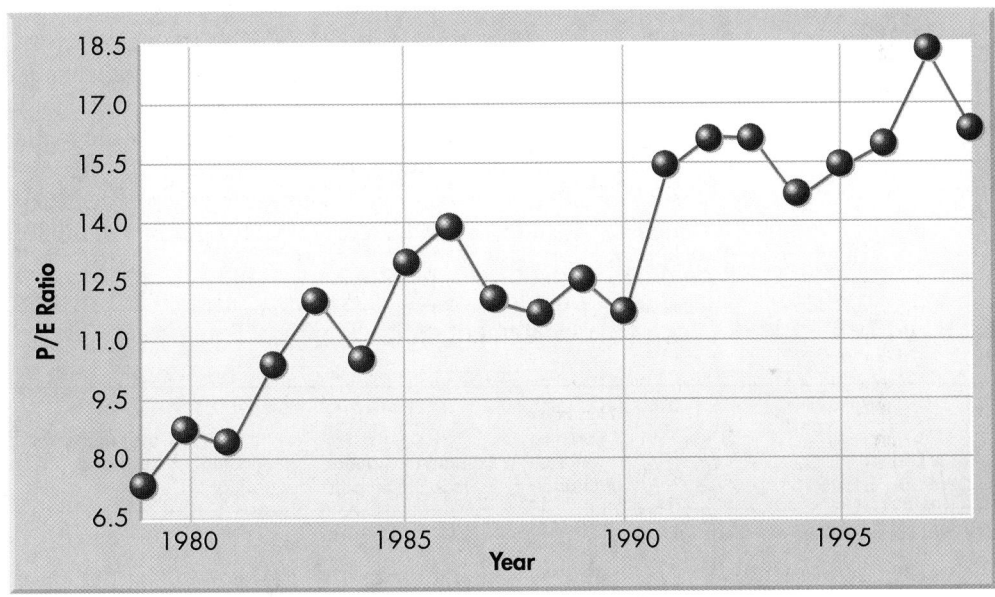

net work exercise

Yahoo! (**finance.yahoo.com**) offers Web services containing up-to-date stock quote information, including P/E ratios, for thousands of companies.

Net Work:
Find the P/E ratio for the following companies: Coca-Cola, PepsiCo, General Motors, Ford, Kmart, and Wal-Mart. What do the P/E ratios tell you?

6

Compute comprehensive income and prepare a statement of stockholders' equity.

COMPREHENSIVE INCOME AND THE STATEMENT OF STOCKHOLDERS' EQUITY

Recently, the FASB began requiring companies to provide an additional measure of income—comprehensive income. This measure of a company's performance includes items in addition to those included in net income. Companies can either provide this additional information in a separate financial statement or include it as a part of the statement of stockholders' equity. In this section, we discuss both comprehensive income and the statement of stockholders' equity.

Comprehensive Income

Recall from the beginning of this section that a general definition of income is the increase in a company's wealth during a period. The wealth of a company is impacted in a variety of ways that have nothing to do with the business operations of the company. For example, changes in exchange rates can cause the U.S. dollar value of a company's foreign subsidiaries to increase or decrease. **Comprehensive income** is the number used to reflect an overall measure of the change in a company's wealth during the period. In addition to net income, comprehensive income includes items that, in general, arise from changes in market conditions unrelated to the business operations of a company. These items are excluded from net income because they are viewed as yielding little information about the economic performance of a company's business operations. However, they are reported as part of comprehensive income because they do impact the value of assets and liabilities reported in the balance sheet.

The concept of comprehensive income was discussed by the FASB in its conceptual framework. However, it wasn't until 1998 that the concept was placed into practice with the issuance of FASB Statement No. 130. Exhibit 4–12 provides an example (COCA-COLA) of a statement of comprehensive income that is included as part of a statement of stockholders' equity. Three of the more common adjustments made in arriving at comprehensive income are: (1) foreign currency translation adjustments, (2) unrealized gains and losses on available-for-sale securities, and (3) deferred gains and losses on derivative financial instruments.

FOREIGN CURRENCY TRANSLATION ADJUSTMENT During 1998, there was an increase in the value of the currencies in the countries where COCA-COLA has foreign subsidiaries. Thus, the U.S. dollar value of the net assets of those subsidiaries increased $52 million during the year. This increase was not the result of good business performance by Coca-Cola; it was simply a function of the ebb and flow of the worldwide economy. This "gain" is not reported as part of net income but is included in the computation of comprehensive income. PEPSICO, Coca-Cola's major competitor, was exposed to slightly different market conditions during the year and reported a reduction in comprehensive income for foreign currency changes of $75 million.

EXHIBIT 4–12 | Coca-Cola's Statement of Stockholders' Equity for 1998

Year Ended December 31, 1998	Number of Common Shares Outstanding	Common Stock	Capital Surplus	Reinvested Earnings	Outstanding Restricted Stock	Accumulated Other Comprehensive Income	Treasury Stock	Total
(In millions except per share data)								
BALANCE DECEMBER 31, 1997	2,471	$861	$1,527	$17,869	$(50)	$(1,351)	$(11,582)	$7,274
COMPREHENSIVE INCOME:								
Net income	—	—	—	3,533	—	—	—	3,533
Translation adjustments	—	—	—	—	—	52	—	52
Net change in unrealized gain on securities	—	—	—	—	—	(47)	—	(47)
Minimum pension liability	—	—	—	—	—	(4)	—	(4)
COMPREHENSIVE INCOME								3,534
Stock issued to employees exercising stock options	16	4	298	—	—	—	—	302
Tax benefit from employees' stock option and restricted stock plans	—	—	97	—	—	—	—	97
Stock issued under restricted stock plans, less amortization of $5	1	—	47	—	(34)	—	—	13
Stock issued by an equity investee	—	—	226	—	—	—	—	226
Purchases of stock for treasury (22)		—	—	—	—	—	(1,563)	(1,563)
Dividends (per share — $.60)	—	—	—	(1,480)	—	—	—	(1,480)
BALANCE DECEMBER 31, 1998	2,466	$865	$2,195	$19,922	$(84)	$(1,350)	$(13,145)	$8,403

UNREALIZED GAINS AND LOSSES ON AVAILABLE-FOR-SALE SECURITIES In order to maintain a liquid reserve of assets that can be converted into cash if needed, most companies purchase an investment portfolio of stocks and bonds. For example, as of December 31, 1998, COCA-COLA owned $422 million in securities that had been classified as "available for sale," meaning Coca-Cola does not intend to actively trade the securities in this portfolio but they are available to be sold if the need for cash arises. These securities are reported in the balance sheet at their current market value. As the market value of these securities fluctuates, Coca-Cola experiences "unrealized" gains and losses. An "unrealized" gain or loss is the same as what is sometimes called a paper gain or loss, meaning that because the security has not yet been sold, the gain or loss is only on paper.

Because available-for-sale securities are not part of a company's operations, the associated unrealized gains and losses are excluded from the computation of net income and are instead reported as part of comprehensive income. During 1998, Coca-Cola recorded a $47 million loss on its available-for-sale portfolio; this amount was reported as a decrease in comprehensive income.

DEFERRED GAINS AND LOSSES ON DERIVATIVE FINANCIAL INSTRUMENTS Companies frequently use derivative financial instruments in order to hedge their exposure to risk stemming from changes in prices and rates. As prices and rates change, the value of a derivative based on that price or rate also changes. As with available-for-sale securities, these value changes give rise to unrealized gains and losses. In some cases, these unrealized gains and losses on derivatives are included in net income and offset against gains or losses on the items that were being hedged. In other cases, the reporting of the unrealized gains and losses on derivatives in net income is delayed until a subsequent year; in the meantime, the unrealized gains and losses are reported as part of comprehensive income. A further discussion of derivatives is given in Chapter 18.

A few other comprehensive income items exist in addition to the three described above. For example, in 1998 COCA-COLA reported a reduction in comprehensive income of $4 million stemming from an increase that was made to Coca-Cola's reported pension liability. The key point to remember is that these items represent changes in assets and liabilities reported in the balance sheet that are not deemed to reflect a company's own economic performance and are therefore excluded from the computation of net income. The net effect of each of these adjustments is to report a total comprehensive income of $3.534 billion, a net increase of $1 million over the reported amount of net income.

The Statement of Stockholders' Equity

Most companies include a report of comprehensive income as part of the statement of stockholders' equity. While this is not the required method of disclosure, it appears to be the disclosure chosen by most companies.

> **Caution!** When changes are made to retained earnings for prior-period adjustments, changes are also necessary to any prior-period income statements that are prepared in comparative format.

The statement of stockholders' equity also includes changes in equity other than those related to income. As the COCA-COLA example in Exhibit 4–12 illustrates, new share issues, treasury stock repurchases, dividends declared, and miscellaneous other transactions related to the equity of a company are disclosed in this statement. A more detailed discussion of the different types of equity transactions is included in Chapter 11.

Also included in this statement (or as a separate statement of retained earnings) are adjustments to retained earnings. There are two general types of retained earnings adjustments: (1) prior-period adjustments and (2) as indicated earlier, adjustments arising from some changes in accounting principles. **Prior-period adjustments** arise primarily when an error occurs in one period and is not discovered until a subsequent period.

7

Construct simple forecasts of income for future periods.

FORECASTING FUTURE PERFORMANCE

Financial statements report past results, but financial statement users are often interested in what will happen in the future. Therefore, an important skill for financial statement users to develop is using past financial statements to predict the future. This section gives a simple demonstration of how to use historical financial statement information to forecast a future income statement and balance sheet.

The key to a good financial statement forecast is identifying which underlying factors determine the level of a certain revenue or expense. For example, the level of cost of goods sold is closely tied to the level of sales, whereas the level of interest expense is only weakly tied to sales and is instead a direct function of the level of interest-bearing debt.

Most forecasting exercises start with a forecast of sales. The sales forecast indicates how fast the company is expected to grow and represents the general volume of activity expected in the company. This expected volume of activity influences the amount of assets that are needed to do business, which in turn determines the level of financing required. In short, for the resulting forecasted financial statements to be reliable, an accurate projection of sales is critical. The starting point for a sales forecast is last year's sales, with an addition for expected year-to-year growth based on the average sales growth experienced in previous years. This crude sales forecast should then be refined using as much company-specific information as is available. For example, in forecasting MCDONALD's sales, one should try to determine how many new outlets McDonald's expects to open during the coming year. The resulting sales forecast is the basis on which to forecast the remainder of the balance sheet, income statement, and statement of cash flow information.

Exhibit 4–13 contains financial statement information for the hypothetical Derrald Company. This information will be used as the basis for a simple forecasting exercise. The 2002 information for Derrald Company is historical information.

E X H I B I T   4 – 1 3 | Historical Financial Data for Derrald Company

Balance Sheet	2002
Cash	$ 10
Other current assets	250
Property, plant, and equipment, net	300
Total assets	$560
Accounts payable	$100
Bank loans payable	300
Total stockholders' equity	160
Total liabilities and stockholders' equity	$560

Income Statement	
Sales	$1,000
Cost of goods sold	700
Gross profit	$ 300
Depreciation expense	30
Other operating expenses	170
Operating profit	$ 100
Interest expense	30
Income before taxes	$ 70
Income taxes	30
Net income	$ 40

Analysis of Derrald's past history of sales growth, combined with a consideration of Derrald's strategic plans for 2003, suggests that sales for 2003 are likely to rise 40% to $1,400.

Forecast of Balance Sheet Accounts

Not all balance sheet accounts change according to the same process. Some items increase naturally as sales volume increases. Others increase only in response to specific long-term expansion plans. And other balance sheet items change only in response to specific financing choices made by management. How these different processes impact the forecast of a balance sheet is outlined below.

NATURAL INCREASE If Derrald Company plans to increase its sales volume by 40% in 2003, it seems logical to assume that Derrald will need about 40% more cash with which to handle this increased volume of business. In other words, the increased level of activity itself will create the need for more cash. The same is true of other current assets, such as accounts receivable and inventory, and of current operating liabilities, such as accounts payable and wages payable. In short, a planned 40% increase in the volume of Derrald's business means that, in the absence of plans to significantly change its methods of operation, Derrald will also experience a 40% increase in the levels of its current operating assets and liabilities. These forecasted natural increases are reflected in the forecasted balance sheet contained in Exhibit 4-14.

EXHIBIT 4-14 | Forecasted Balance Sheet and Income Statement for Derrald Company

Balance Sheet	2002	2003 Forecasted	Basis for Forecast
Cash	$ 10	$ 14	40% natural increase
Other current assets	250	350	40% natural increase
Property, plant, and equipment, net	300	500	
Total assets	$560	$864	
Accounts payable	$100	$140	40% natural increase
Bank loans payable	300	524	
Total stockholders' equity	160	200	
Total liabilities and stockholders' equity	$560	$864	

Income Statement	2002	2003 Forecasted	Basis for Forecast
Sales	$1,000	$1,400	40% increase
Cost of goods sold	700	980	70% of sales, same as last year
Gross profit	$ 300	$ 420	
Depreciation expense	30	50	10% of PPE, same as last year
Other operating expenses	170	238	17% of sales, same as last year
Operating profit	$ 100	$ 132	
Interest expense	30	52	10% of bank loans, same as last year
Income before taxes	$ 70	$ 80	
Income taxes	30	34	43% of pretax, same as last year
Net income	$ 40	$ 46	

LONG-TERM PLANNING Long-term assets, such as property, plant, and equipment, do not increase naturally as sales volume increases. Instead, the addition of a new factory building, for example, only occurs as the result of a long-term planning process. Thus, a business anticipating an increase of sales in the coming year of only 10% may expand its productive capacity by 50% as part of its long-term strategic plan. Similarly, a business forecasting 25% sales growth may plan to use existing excess capacity to handle the entire sales increase without any increase in long-term assets. In short, forecasting future levels of long-term assets requires some knowledge of a company's strategic expansion plan. For Derrald Company, it is assumed that we know that Derrald plans to increase its property, plant, and equipment from $300 in 2002 to $500 in 2003. This forecasted increase is reflected in Exhibit 4–14.

FINANCING CHOICES The levels of long-term debt and of stockholders' equity are determined by management's decisions on how to best obtain financing. In fact, management often uses forecasted financial statements, prepared under a variety of different financing scenarios, to help determine financing choices. Because detailed treatment of the field of corporate finance is beyond the scope of this discussion, we will merely assume that Derrald is planning to finance its operations in 2003 by increasing its bank loans payable from $300 to $524 and by increasing stockholders' equity from $160 to $200. These forecasted increases are shown in Exhibit 4–14. Notice that the forecasted balance sheet for 2003 has total assets of $864 and total liabilities and stockholders' equity of $864. The numerical discipline imposed by the structure of the balance sheet ensures that the forecasted asset increases are consistent with Derrald Company's plans for additional financing.

Forecast of Income Statement Accounts

The amount of some expenses is directly tied to the amount of sales for the year. Derrald Company's sales are forecasted to increase by 40% in 2003, so it is reasonable to predict that cost of goods sold will increase by the same 40%. Another way to perform this calculation is to assume that the ratio of cost of goods sold to sales remains constant from year to year. Thus, because cost of goods sold was 70% of sales in 2002 ($700/$1,000 = 70%), cost of goods sold should increase to $980 ($1,400 × .70) in 2003, as shown in Exhibit 4–14. Similarly, other operating expenses, such as wages and shipping costs, are also likely to maintain a constant relationship with the level of sales.

The amount of a company's depreciation expense is determined by how much property, plant, and equipment the company has. In 2002, Derrald Company had $30 of depreciation expense on $300 of property, plant, and equipment, that is, depreciation was 10% ($30/$300). If the same relationship holds in 2003, Derrald can expect to report depreciation expense of $50 ($500 × .10).

Interest expense depends on how much interest-bearing debt a company has. In 2002, Derrald Company reported interest expense of $30 with bank loans payable of $300. These numbers imply that the interest rate on Derrald's loans is 10% ($30/$300). Because the bank loans payable are expected to increase to $524 in 2003, Derrald can expect interest expense for the year of $52 ($524 × .10 = $52).

As shown in Exhibit 4–14, the assumptions made so far imply that Derrald's income before taxes in 2003 will total $80. Income tax expense is determined by how much pretax income a company has. And the most reasonable assumption to make is that a company's tax rate, equal to income tax expense divided by pretax income, will stay constant from year to year. Derrald's tax rate in 2002 was 43% ($30/$70), which when applied to the forecasted pretax income for 2003 of $80, implies that income tax expense in 2003 will total $34 ($80 × .43).

The complete forecasted income statement for 2003 indicates that Derrald Company's income for the year will be $46. The quality of this forecast is only as good as the assumptions that underlie it. In order to determine how much impact the assumptions can have, it is often useful to conduct a sensitivity analysis. This involves repeating the forecasting exercise using a set of pessimistic and a set of optimistic assumptions.

Thus, one can construct worst-case, standard-case, and best-case scenarios to use in making decisions with the forecasted numbers.

Financial statement forecasting is used to construct an estimate of how well a company will perform in the future. This forecasting exercise is useful for bankers worried about whether they can recover their money if they make a loan to a company and for investors who want to determine how much to invest in a company. Forecasted financial statements are also useful to company management for evaluating alternate strategies and determining whether the planned operating, investing, and financing activities appropriately mesh together. The Derrald Company example used in this chapter will also be used in Chapter 5 to illustrate how to forecast a company's statement of cash flows.

CONCLUDING COMMENTS

This chapter highlights the need for users of the income statement to use care with terminology. For example, income can mean gross profit, operating income, income from operations, net income, or comprehensive income. One must be very careful with accounting terminology.

The income statement summarizes a firm's performance in its primary business activities (operating income) as well as peripheral activities (income from operations). The income statement also includes three "below-the-line" items that are treated somewhat differently than other items included on the income statement. These are summarized in Exhibit 4-15.

The statement of stockholders' equity includes other changes in a company's equity and often includes comprehensive income. Comprehensive income is a relatively new operational measure, and it will be interesting to see how the financial community uses this information in making investment decisions.

EXHIBIT 4-15 | Summary of Procedures for Reporting Irregular, Nonrecurring, or Unusual Items*

Where Reported	Category	Description	Examples
Part of income from continuing operations.	Changes in estimates.	Normal recurring changes in estimating future amounts. Included in normal accounts.	Changes in building and equipment lives, changes in estimated loss from uncollectible accounts receivable, changes in estimate of warranty liability.
	Unusual gains and losses, not considered extraordinary.	Unusual or infrequent, but not both. Related to normal operations. Material in amount. Shown in other revenues and gains or other expenses and losses.	Gains or losses from sale of assets, investments, or other operating assets. Write-off of inventories as obsolete.
On income statement, but after income from continuing operations.	Discontinued operations.	Disposal of completely separate line of business. Include gain or loss from sale or abandonment.	Sale by conglomerate company of separate line of business, such as milling company selling restaurant segment.
	Extraordinary items.	Both unusual and infrequent. Not related to normal business operations. Material in amount.	Material gains and losses from early extinguishment of debt, from some casualties or legal claims if meet criteria.
	Changes in accounting principles—general case.	Change from one accepted principle to another.	Change from one method of inventory pricing to another; change in depreciation method.
As adjustments to retained earnings on the balance sheet	Prior-period adjustments and special case changes in accounting principles.	Material correction of errors; changes in accounting principles that require retroactive adjustment.	Failure to depreciate fixed assets; mathematical error in computing inventory balance; retroactive adjustment for new FASB standard.

*This chart describes the usual case. Exceptions to the descriptions occasionally do occur.

REVIEW OF LEARNING OBJECTIVES

1 **Define the concept of income. Income is a return over and above the investment of the owners.** It measures the amount that an entity could return to its investors and still leave the entity as well-off at the end of the period as at the beginning. Two concepts can be used to measure "well-offness": financial capital maintenance (the dollar amount of net assets) and physical capital maintenance (physical productive capacity). The FASB has chosen to use the financial capital maintenance concept in measuring income.

2 **Explain why an income measure is important.** The recognition, measurement, and reporting of income are considered by many to be among the most important tasks performed by accountants. Many individuals use this measure for business and economic decisions that result in the allocation of resources, which in turn contributes to the standard of living in society.

3 **Explain how income is measured, including the revenue recognition and expense-matching concepts.** Income is measured as the difference between resource inflows (revenues and gains) and outflows (expenses and losses) over a period of time. Revenues are recognized when (1) they are realized or realizable and (2) they have been earned through substantial completion of the activities involved in the earning process. Usually, this is at the point of sale of goods or services. Expenses are matched against revenues directly, in a systematic or rational manner, or are immediately recognized as a period expense.

4 **Understand the format of an income statement.** The income statement may be presented in a single-step or multiple-step form. With a single-step income statement, revenues and gains are grouped and disclosed together as are expenses and losses. The difference is income from continuing operations. The general format of a multiple-step income statement is to subtract cost of goods sold and operating expenses from operating revenues to derive operating income. Gains and losses are then included to arrive at income from continuing operations. Regardless of the format, irregular and extraordinary items are disclosed separately to determine net income.

5 **Describe the specific components of an income statement.** Most companies will report on some or all of the following specific components of an income statement.

- Revenue
- Cost of goods sold
- Gross profit
- Operating expenses
- Operating income
- Other revenues and gains
- Other expenses and losses
- Income from continuing operations before income taxes
- Income taxes on continuing operations
- Income from continuing operations
- Discontinued operations
- Extraordinary items
- Cumulative effects of changes in accounting principles

6 **Compute comprehensive income and prepare a statement of stockholders' equity.** The FASB, in its conceptual framework, suggests reporting comprehensive income, reflecting all changes in equity during a period except those resulting from investments by owners and distributions to owners. Comprehensive income is the number used to reflect an overall measure of the change in a company's wealth during the period. In addition to net income, comprehensive income includes items that, in general, arise from changes in market conditions unrelated to the business operations of a company. Most companies include a report of comprehensive income as part of the statement of stockholders' equity. The statement of stockholder's equity also includes changes in equity other than those related to income.

7 **Construct simple forecasts of income for future periods.** An important use of an income statement is to forecast income in future periods. Good forecasting requires an understanding of what underlying factors determine the level of a revenue or an expense. Most financial statement forecasting exercises start with a forecast of sales, which establishes the expected scale of operations in future periods. Some balance sheet items increase naturally as the level of sales increases; examples of such accounts are cash, accounts receivable, inventory, and accounts payable. Other balance sheet items, such as property, plant, and equipment, change in response to a company's long-term strategic plans. Finally, the amounts of the balance sheet items associated with financing, such as long-term debt and paid-in capital, are determined by the financing decisions made by a company's management.

Some income statement items, such as cost of goods sold, maintain a constant relationship with sales. Depreciation expense is more likely to be related to the amount of a company's property, plant, and equipment. Interest expense is tied to the balance in interest-bearing debt. Finally, income tax expense is typically a relatively constant percentage of income before taxes.

KEY TERMS

Comparative financial statements 170
Comprehensive income 188
Consolidated financial statements 170
Cumulative effect of a change in
    accounting principle 183
Discontinued operations 178
Earnings per share (EPS) 185
Expense recognition 168
Expenses 164
Extraordinary items 181
Financial capital maintenance 161

Gains 164
Gross profit 173
Gross profit percentage 173
Income 161
Income from continuing operations 170
Intraperiod income tax allocation 177
Losses 164
Matching 168
Multiple-step form 170
Operating income 175

Physical capital maintenance 161
Price-earnings ratio (P/E ratio) 186
Prior-period adjustments 189
Restructuring charge 176
Return on sales 185
Revenue recognition 165
Revenues 164
Single-step form 169
Transaction approach 164

QUESTIONS

1. FASB Concepts Statement No. 1 states, "The primary focus of financial reporting is information about an enterprise's performance provided by measures of earnings and its components." Why is it unwise for users of financial statements to focus too much attention on the income statement?

2. After the necessary definitions and assumptions have been made that support the determination of income, what are the two methods of income measurement that may be used to determine income? How do they differ?

3. What different measurement methods may be applied to net assets in arriving at income under the capital maintenance approach?

4. Income as determined by income tax regulations is not necessarily the same as income reported to external users. Why might there be differences?

5. What is the difference between a code law country and a common law country?

6. How are revenues and expenses different from gains and losses?

7. What two factors must be considered in deciding the point at which revenues and gains should be recognized? At what point in the revenue cycle are these conditions usually met?

8. Name three exceptions to the general rule that assumes revenue is recognized at the point of sale. What is the justification for these exceptions?

9. What guidelines are used to match costs with revenues in determining income?

10. What are some possible disadvantages of a multiple-step income statement and of a single-step statement?

11. Identify the major sections (components of income) that are included in a multiple-step income statement.

12. What are restructuring charges, and why do they generate controversy?

13. What is the meaning of "intraperiod" income tax allocation?

14. The Pop-Up Company has decided to sell its lid manufacturing division even though the division is expected to show a small profit this year. The division's assets will be sold at a loss of $10,000 to another company. What information (if any) should Pop-Up disclose in its financial reports with respect to this division?

15. Which of the following would *not* normally qualify as an extraordinary item?
    (a) The write-down or write-off of receivables.
    (b) Major devaluation of foreign currency.
    (c) Loss on sale of plant and equipment.
    (d) Gain from early extinguishment of debt.
    (e) Loss due to extensive flood damage to an asphalt company in Las Vegas, Nevada.
    (f) Loss due to extensive earthquake damage to a furniture company in Los Angeles, California.
    (g) Farming loss due to heavy spring rains in the Northwest.

16. Explain briefly the difference in accounting treatment of (a) a change in accounting principle and (b) a change in accounting estimate.

17. Under International Accounting Standards, how is the cumulative effect of a change in accounting principle reported?

18. What is the general practice in reporting earnings per share?

19. Define comprehensive income. How does it differ from net income?

20. What is the starting point for the preparation of forecasted financial statements?

21. Describe the process one should use in forecasting depreciation expense.

DISCUSSION CASES

CASE 4–1

ARE WE REALLY BETTER OFF?

The Plath Company board of directors finally receives the income statement for the past year from management. Board members are initially pleased to see that after 3 years of losses, the company will be reporting a profit for the current year. Further investigation reveals that depreciation expense is significantly lower than it was last year. Company management, concerned by the losses, decided to change its method of reporting depreciation from an accelerated to a straight-line method. If the depreciation method had not been changed, a loss would have resulted for the fourth consecutive year. When questioned by the board about the accounting change, management replied that the majority of companies in the industry use the straight-line depreciation method, and thus, the change makes Plath's income statement more comparable to other companies' statements.

Because comparability is an important qualitative characteristic of accounting information, should the board accept the explanation of management? How should the information about the change in the depreciation method be displayed in the financial statements?

CASE 4–2

HOW CAN MY COMPANY HAVE INCOME BUT NO CASH?

Max Stevenson owns a local drug store. During the past few years the economy has experienced a period of high inflation. Stevenson has had the policy of withdrawing cash from his business equal to 80% of the company's reported net income. As the business has grown, he has had a CPA prepare the company's financial statements and tax returns. The following is a summary of the company's income statement for the current year.

Revenue	$565,000
Cost of goods sold (drugs, etc.)	395,000
Gross profit on items sold	$170,000
Operating expenses (including taxes)	110,000
Net income	$ 60,000

Even though the business has reported net income each year, it has experienced severe cash flow shortages. The company has had to pay higher prices for its inventory as the company has tried to maintain the same quantity and quality of its goods. For example, last year's cost of goods sold had a historical cost of $250,000 and a replacement cost of $295,000. The current year's cost of goods sold has a replacement cost of $440,000. Stevenson's personal cash outflows have also grown faster than his withdrawals from the company due to increasing personal demands.

Stevenson asks you as a financial advisor how the company can have income of $60,000 yet he and the company still have a shortage of cash.

CASE 4–3

WHEN SHOULD REVENUE BE RECOGNIZED?

Stan Crowfoot is a renowned sculptor who specializes in Native American sculptures. Typically, a cast is prepared for each work to permit the multiple reproduction of the pieces. A limited number of copies are made for each sculpture, and the mold is destroyed after the number is reached. Limiting the number of pieces enhances the price, and most of the pieces have initially sold for $2,000 to $4,000. To encourage sales, Stan has a liberal return policy that permits customers to return any unwanted piece for a period of up to one year from the date of sale and receive a full refund.

Do you think Stan should recognize revenue: (1) when the piece is produced and cast in bronze, (2) when the goods are delivered to the customer, or (3) when the period of return has passed? Justify your answer in terms of the FASB conceptual framework.

CASE 4–4

THE REVENUE RECOGNITION PROCESS

You are engaged as a consultant to Skyways Unlimited, a manufacturer of satellite dishes for television reception. Skyways sells its dishes to dealers who in turn sell them to customers. As an inducement to carry sufficient inventory, the dealers are not required to pay for the dishes until they have been sold. There is no formal provision for return of the dishes by the dealers; however, Skyways has requested returns when a dealer's sales activity is considered to be too low. Overall, returns have amounted to less than 10% of the dishes sent to dealers. No interest is charged to the dealers on their balances unless they do not remit promptly upon the sale to a customer.

At what point would you recommend that Skyways recognize the revenue from the sale of dishes to the dealers?

CASE 4–5

WE JUST CHANGED OUR MINDS

Management for Marlowe Manufacturing Company decided in 2001 to discontinue one of its unsuccessful product lines. (The product line does not meet the definition of a business segment.) The planned discontinuance involved obsolete inventory, assembly lines, and packaging and advertising supplies. It was estimated that a loss of $250,000 would result from the decision, and this estimate was recorded as a loss in the 2001 income statement. In 2002, new management was appointed, and it was decided that maybe the unsuccessful product line could be turned around with a more aggressive marketing policy. The change was made, and indeed the product began to make money. The new management wants to reverse the adjustment made the previous year and remove the liability for the estimated loss.

How should the 2001 estimated loss be reported in the 2002 income statement? How should the 2002 reversal of the 2001 action be reported in the 2002 financial statements?

CASE 4–6

THE SURE-FIRE COMPUTER SOFTWARE

The Flexisoft Company has had excellent success in developing business software for microcomputers. Management has followed the accounting practice of deferring the development costs for the software until sufficient sales have developed to cover the software cost. Because of past successes, management feels it is improper to charge software costs directly to expense as current GAAP requires.

What are the pros and cons of deferring or expensing immediately these developmental costs?

CASE 4–7

DEFERRED INITIAL OPERATING LOSSES

Small loan companies often experience losses in the operation of newly opened branch loan offices. Such results usually can be anticipated by management prior to making a decision on expansion. It has been recommended by some accountants that the operating losses of newly opened branches should be reported as deferred charges during the first 12 months of operation or until the first profitable month occurs. Such deferred charges would then be amortized over a 5-year period.

Would you support this recommendation? Justify your answer.

CASE 4–8

WHAT WAS LAST YEAR'S INCOME?

The Walesco Corporation has decided to discontinue an entire segment of its business effective November 1, 2002. It hopes to sell the assets involved and convert the physical plant to other uses within the manufacturing division. The CPA auditing the books indicates that GAAP requires separate identification of the revenues and expenses related to the segment to be sold and their removal from the continuing revenue and expense amounts. The controller objects to this change. "We have already distributed last year's numbers. If we change them now, one year later, confidence in our financial statements will be greatly eroded."

What are the pros and cons of identifying separately the costs related to the discontinued segment?

CASE 4–9

ACCRUAL ACCOUNTING

The stock market crash of October 1987 caused many businesses to rethink the manner in which they operate. The crash caused at least one business to consider the way it recognized revenues and expenses. BOSTON COMPANY, INC., a money-managing unit of SHEARSON LEHMAN HUTTON HOLDINGS INC., reported that pretax profits for the first 9 months of 1988 had been overstated by an estimated 40%. Being a subsidiary of another company, Boston does not disclose separate earnings. However, the company admits that 1988 profits were overstated by $44 million.

In danger of not meeting corporate performance goals, top executives at Boston deferred many expenses "beyond accepted accounting norms, and revenue was inappropriately booked far in advance." These practices had the effect of "making the current quarter look more profitable." Boston Co. was hoping that a decline in short-term interest rates would provide additional profits to cover the deceptive accounting practices. (Boston Co. funds its long-term mortgages with short-term deposits in its banking units, so the firm benefits when short-term rates drop.)

SOURCES: George Anders, *The Wall Street Journal*, January 23, 1989; Christopher J. Chipallo and George Anders, *The Wall Street Journal*, January 30, 1989.

1. How are expenses deferred and revenues booked (recorded) in advance? What would the journal entries be?
2. Why would top executives encourage these misleading accounting practices?
3. None of the top executives who ordered the misstatements actually made the journal entries. If you were Boston Co.'s accountant, what would you have done?
4. Is Boston's independent auditor responsible for detecting these types of misstatements?

CASE 4–10

REVENUE RECOGNITION

A common method for inflating revenues and profits is to ship more inventory to customers than they order. *Business Week* illustrates two instances where the revenue recognition criteria may have been compromised. Using a practice known as "trade loading," RJR NABISCO, the second largest cigarette producer in America, would ship more inventory to wholesalers than the wholesalers could resell. The excess inventory would eventually be returned, but RJR would book the revenue and profit when the cigarettes were originally shipped. Management stopped this practice in 1988, and the result was a $360 million decrease in operating profits for 1989.

Another company, REGINA CO., took trade loading several steps further. In a hurried effort to compete in the upright vacuum cleaner market, Regina skipped proper testing of its product, the Housekeeper. The result: 40,000 units, or 16% of sales, were returned. Regina's solution: lease a building to store the returned items and make no entries to record the returns. In a continued effort to make Regina's stock attractive, the firm began to record sales when goods were ordered, not when they were shipped. Further, to ensure that projected sales figures were achieved for the fiscal year ending June 30, 1988, the company generated $5.4 million of fictitious sales invoices for the last 3 business days of the year.

SOURCES: Wafecia Konrad, "RJR Nabisco," *Business Week*, February 19, 1990; John A. Byrne, "Regina," *Business Week*, February 12, 1990.

1. Do the above transactions of RJR Nabisco and Regina satisfy the revenue recognition criteria as set forth by the FASB?
2. If RJR Nabisco has open contracts with distributors that require distributors to attempt to sell all inventory shipped to them, does trade loading violate the revenue recognition criteria?
3. Regina recorded revenue when goods were ordered rather than when the goods were shipped. Does it really make a difference when the journal entry is made?
4. As Regina's accountant, what would you do if the president of the company (who was fined $50,000 and sentenced to 1 year in jail) asked for your assistance in "cooking the books"?

CASE 4–11

FINANCIAL STATEMENT ANALYSIS—RATIOS

Shawn O'Neil owns two businesses: a drug store and a retail department store.

	Drug Store	Department Store
Net sales	$1,050,000	$670,000
Cost of goods sold	950,000	560,000
Other expenses	39,500	66,500

Which business earns more income? Which business has the higher gross profit percentage? return on sales? Which business would you consider more profitable?

EXERCISES

EXERCISE 4–12

CALCULATION OF NET INCOME

Changes in the balance sheet account balances for the Smite Sales Co. during 2002 are shown below. Dividends declared during 2002 were $25,000. Calculate the net income for the year assuming there were no transactions, other than the dividends, affecting retained earnings.

	Increase (Decrease)
Cash	$ 95,500
Accounts Receivable	92,000
Inventory	(30,000)
Buildings and Equipment (net)	190,000
Patents	(5,000)
Accounts Payable	(75,000)
Bonds Payable	150,000
Capital Stock	100,000
Additional Paid-In Capital	50,000

EXERCISE 4–13

REVENUE RECOGNITION

For each of the following transactions, events, or circumstances, indicate whether the recognition criteria for revenues and gains are met and provide support for your answer.

(a) An order of $25,000 for merchandise is received from a customer. Nothing
(b) The value of timberlands increases by $40,000 for the year due to normal growth. Nothing
(c) Accounting services are rendered to a client on account.
(d) A 1988 investment was made in land at a cost of $80,000. The land currently has a fair market value of $107,000. Nothing
(e) Cash of $5,600 is collected from the sale of a gift certificate that is redeemable in the next accounting period. Nothing Unearned Income
(f) Cash of $7,500 is collected from subscribers for subscription fees to a monthly magazine. The subscription period is 2 years. Nothing Unearned
(g) You owe a creditor $1,500, payable in 30 days. The creditor has cash flow difficulties and has agreed to allow you to retire the debt in full with an immediate payment of $1,200.

EXERCISE 4–14

REVENUE RECOGNITION

Indicate which of the following transactions or events gives rise to the recognition of revenue in 2002 under the accrual basis of accounting. If revenue is not recognized, what is the account, if any, that is credited?

(a) On December 15, 2002, Howe Company received $20,000 as rent revenue for the 6-month period beginning January 1, 2003.

(b) Monroe Tractor Co., on July 1, 2002, sold one of its tractors and received $10,000 in cash and a note for $50,000 at 12% interest, payable in 1 year. The fair market value of the tractor is $60,000.

(c) Oswald, Inc., issued additional shares of common stock on December 10, 2002, for $30,000 above par value.

(d) Balance Company received a purchase order in 2002 from an established customer for $10,200 of merchandise. The merchandise was shipped on December 20, 2002. The company's credit policy allows the customer to return the merchandise within 30 days, and a 3% discount is allowed if paid within 20 days from shipment.

(e) Gloria, Inc., sold merchandise costing $2,000 for $2,500 in August 2002. The terms of the sale are 15% down on a 12–month conditional sales contract, with title to the goods being retained by the seller until the contract price is paid in full.

(f) On November 1, 2002, Jones & Whitlock entered into an agreement to audit the 2002 financial statements of Lehi Mills for a fee of $35,000. The audit work began on December 15, 2002, and will be completed around February 15, 2003.

EXERCISE 4–15

EXPENSE RECOGNITION

For each of the following items, indicate whether the expense should be recognized using (1) direct matching, (2) systematic and rational allocation, or (3) immediate recognition. Provide support for your answer.

(a) Johnson & Smith, Inc., conducts cancer research. The company's hope is to develop a cure for the deadly disease. To date, its efforts have proven unsuccessful. It is testing a new drug, Ebzinene, which has cost $400,000 to develop.

(b) SEARS, ROEBUCK AND CO. warranties many of the products it sells. Although the warranty periods range from days to years, Sears can reasonably estimate warranty costs.

(c) Stocks Co. recently signed a 2-year lease agreement on a warehouse. The entire cost of $15,000 was paid in advance.

(d) John Clark assembles chairs for the Stone Furniture Company. The company pays Clark on an hourly basis.

(e) Hardy Co. recently purchased a fleet of new delivery trucks. The trucks are each expected to last for 100,000 miles.

(f) Taylor Manufacturing Inc. regularly advertises in national trade journals. The objective is to acquire name recognition, not to promote a specific product.

EXERCISE 4–16

CHANGE IN ESTIMATE

The Swalberg Corporation purchased a patent on January 2, 1997, for $450,000. The original life of the patent was estimated to be 15 years. However, in December of 2002, the controller of Swalberg received information proving conclusively that the product protected by the Swalberg patent would be obsolete within 3 years. Accordingly, the company decided to write off the unamortized portion of the patent cost over 4 years beginning in 2002. How would the change in estimate be reflected in the accounts for 2002 and subsequent years?

EXERCISE 4–17

CLASSIFICATION OF INCOME STATEMENT ITEMS

Where in a multiple-step income statement would each of the following items be reported?

(a) Purchase discounts *Cost of goods sold - nut purchases*
(b) Gain on early retirement of debt *Extraordinary item*
(c) Interest revenue *Other revenue + gains*
(d) Loss on sale of equipment *other expenses + losses*
(e) Casualty loss from hurricane *Extraordinary*
(f) Sales commissions *Operating expenses - selling expenses*
(g) Loss on disposal of segment *Discontinued operations*
(h) Income tax expense *taxes from income*
(i) Gain on sale of land *other revenue + gain*
(j) Sales discounts *Revenue - sales*
(k) Loss from long-term investments written off as worthless *other expenses + losses*
(l) Depletion expense *Cost of goods sold*
(m) Cumulative effect of change in depreciation method *Cumulative effect of change*
(n) Vacation pay of office employees *Operating*
(o) Ending inventory *Cost of goods sold*

EXERCISE 4–18

ANALYSIS AND PREPARATION OF INCOME STATEMENT

The selling expenses of Caribou Inc. for 2002 are 13% of sales. General expenses, excluding doubtful accounts, are 25% of cost of goods sold, but only 15% of sales. Doubtful accounts are 2% of sales. The beginning inventory was $136,000, and it decreased 30% during the year. Income from operations for the year before income taxes of 30% is $160,000. Extraordinary gain, net of tax of 30%, is $21,000. Prepare an income statement, including earnings-per-share data, giving supporting computations. Caribou Inc. has 130,000 shares of common stock outstanding.

EXERCISE 4–19

INTRAPERIOD INCOME TAX ALLOCATION

The Brigham Corporation reported the following income items before tax for the year 2002:

Income from continuing operations before income taxes	$210,000
Loss from operations of a discontinued business segment	50,000
Gain from disposal of a business segment	20,000
Extraordinary gain on retirement of debt	140,000

The income tax rate is 35% on all items. Prepare the portion of the income statement beginning with "Income from continuing operations before income taxes" for the year ended December 31, 2002, after applying proper intraperiod income tax allocation procedures.

EXERCISE 4–20

DISCONTINUED OPERATIONS

On June 30, 2002, top management of Garrison Manufacturing Co. decided to dispose of an unprofitable business segment. A loss of $110,000 associated with the segment was incurred during the first 6 months of 2002, prior to management's decision. Between July 1 and November 30, an additional $20,000 loss was incurred in phasing out the segment. The plant facilities associated with the business segment were sold on December 1, and a $15,000 gain was realized on the sale of the plant assets.

(a) Assuming a 30% tax rate, what will be the gain or loss from operating the discontinued segment?
(b) What will be the gain or loss on disposal of the business segment?
(c) Prepare the discontinued operations section of Garrison Manufacturing Co.'s income statement for the year ending December 31, 2002.
(d) What additional information about the discontinued segment would be provided by Garrison Manufacturing if it were reporting using the accounting standards of the United Kingdom?

EXERCISE 4–21

DISCONTINUED OPERATIONS

For the following independent cases, compute (1) the gain (loss) from operations of a discontinued segment, and (2) the gain (loss) from disposal of a discontinued segment. Ignore income taxes.

	Case A	Case B	Case C	Case D
Operating gain (loss) of discontinued segment to measurement date.	$1,000	$(3,000)	$(5,000)	$6,000
Operating gain (loss) of discontinued segment from measurement date to end of fiscal year or disposal date, whichever comes first.	2,000	1,000	6,000	(3,000)
Operating gain (loss) expected from discontinued segment in subsequent year until disposal date, if applicable.	1,000	NA	(4,000)	(5,000)
Expected or actual gain or (loss) on disposal of net assets.	(6,000)	2,500	3,000	(3,000)

EXERCISE 4–22

INTERNATIONAL

CHANGE IN ACCOUNTING PRINCIPLE

In 1988, SEARS, ROEBUCK AND CO. changed its method of accounting for income taxes. The FASB required the new principle to be applied retroactively, but prior years' financial statements were not required to be restated. The change decreased 1988 income from continuing operations by $177.6 million. However, the cumulative effect on prior years was a gain of $544.2 million (net of taxes).

(a) Assuming income from continuing operations for 1988 was $1,032.3 million, complete Sears' income statement for 1988, assuming no other irregular or extraordinary items. Assume 500 million shares of common stock were outstanding during the period.

(b) How would your answer in (a) differ if Sears were a non-U.S. company reporting using the provisions of IAS 8?

EXERCISE 4–23

REPORTING ITEMS ON FINANCIAL STATEMENTS

Under what classification would you report each of the following items on the financial statements?

(a) Revenue from sale of obsolete inventory.
(b) Loss on sale of the fertilizer production division of a lawn supplies manufacturer.
(c) Material penalties arising from early payment of a mortgage.
(d) Gain resulting from changing asset balances to adjust for the effect of excessive depreciation charged in error in prior years.
(e) Loss resulting from excessive accrual in prior years of estimated revenues from long-term contracts.
(f) Costs incurred to purchase a valuable patent.
(g) Net income from the discontinued dune buggy operations of a custom car designer.
(h) Costs of rearranging plant machinery into a more efficient order.
(i) Error made in capitalizing advertising expense during the prior year.
(j) Gain on sale of land to the government.
(k) Loss from destruction of crops by a hailstorm.
(l) Cumulative effect of changing depreciation method.
(m) Additional depreciation resulting from a change in the estimated useful life of an asset.
(n) Gain on sale of long-term investments.
(o) Loss from spring flooding.
(p) Sale of obsolete inventory at less than book value.

(q) Additional federal income tax assessment for prior years.

(r) Loss resulting from the sale of a portion of a line of business.

(s) Costs associated with moving an American business to Japan.

(t) Loss resulting from a patent that was recently determined to be worthless.

EXERCISE 4–24

MULTIPLE-STEP INCOME STATEMENT

From the following list of accounts, prepare a multiple-step income statement in good form showing all appropriate items properly classified, including disclosure of earnings-per-share data. (No monetary amounts are to be reported.)

Accounts Payable
Accumulated Depreciation—Office Building
Accumulated Depreciation—Office Furniture and Fixtures
Advertising Expense
Allowance for Doubtful Accounts
Cash
Common Stock, $1 par (10,000 shares outstanding)
Depreciation Expense—Office Building
Depreciation Expense—Office Furniture and Fixtures
Dividend Revenue
Dividends Payable
Dividends Receivable
Doubtful Accounts Expense
Extraordinary Gain (net of income taxes)
Federal Unemployment Tax Payable
Freight-In
Goodwill
Income Taxes Payable
Income Tax Expense
Insurance Expense
Interest Expense—Bonds
Interest Expense—Other
Interest Payable
Interest Receivable
Interest Revenue
Inventory
Loss from Discontinued Operations (net of income taxes)
Miscellaneous General Expense
Miscellaneous Selling Expense
Office Salaries Expense
Office Supplies
Officers' Salaries Expense
Office Supplies Expense
Property Taxes Expense
Purchase Discounts
Purchase Returns and Allowances
Purchases
Retained Earnings
Royalties Received in Advance
Royalty Revenue
Salaries and Wages Payable
Sales
Sales Discounts
Sales Returns and Allowances
Sales Salaries and Commissions
Sales Taxes Payable

EXERCISE 4–25

SINGLE-STEP INCOME STATEMENT AND STATEMENT OF RETAINED EARNINGS

The Pensacola Awning Co. reports the following for 2002:

Retained earnings, January 1	$ 444,500
Selling expenses	288,720
Sales revenue	1,380,000
Interest expense	13,390
General and administrative expenses	236,400
Cost of goods sold	765,000
Dividends declared this year	45,000
Tax rate for all items	40%
Average shares of common stock outstanding during the year	25,000

Prepare a single-step income statement (including earnings-per-share data) and a statement of retained earnings for Pensacola.

EXERCISE 4–26

CORRECTION OF RETAINED EARNINGS STATEMENT

M. Taylor has been employed as a bookkeeper at the Losser Corporation for a number of years. With the assistance of a clerk, Taylor handles all accounting duties, including the preparation of financial statements. The following is a statement of earned surplus prepared by Taylor for 2002.

Losser Corporation
Statement of Earned Surplus for 2002

Balance at beginning of year		$ 85,949
Additions:		
Change in estimate of 2002 amortization expense	$ 2,800	
Gain on sale of land	18,350	
Interest revenue	4,500	
Profit and loss for 2002	13,680	
Total additions		39,330
Total		$125,279
Deductions:		
Increased depreciation due to change in estimated life	$ 5,000	
Dividends declared and paid	10,000	
Loss on sale of equipment	3,860	
Loss from major casualty (extraordinary)	27,730	
Total deductions		46,590
Balance at end of year		$ 78,689

Instructions:

1. Prepare a schedule showing the correct net income for 2002. (Ignore income taxes.)
2. Prepare a retained earnings statement for 2002.
3. Explain why you have changed the retained earnings statement.

EXERCISE 4–27

STATEMENT OF COMPREHENSIVE INCOME

Svedin Incorporated provides the following information relating to 2002.

Net income	$17,650
Unrealized losses on available-for-sale securities	1,285
Foreign currency translation adjustment	287
Minimum pension liability adjustment	315

The foreign currency adjustment resulted from a weakening in the currencies of Svedin's foreign subsidiaries relative to the U.S. dollar. The minimum pension liability adjustment required an increase in the pension liability with a resulting decrease in equity. (Note: These items represent the results of events occurring during 2002, not the cumulative result of events in prior years.)

Instructions:

1. Determine the effect that each of these items would have when computing comprehensive income for 2002. Explain your rationale.
2. Prepare a statement of comprehensive income for Svedin Incorporated for 2002.

EXERCISE 4–28

FORECASTED INCOME STATEMENT

Han Company wishes to forecast its net income for the year 2003. Han has assembled balance sheet and income statement data for 2002 and has also done a forecast of the balance sheet for 2003. In addition, Han has estimated that its sales in 2003 will rise to $2,200. This information is summarized below.

Balance Sheet	2002	2003 Forecasted
Cash	$ 20	$ 22
Other current assets	500	550
Property, plant, and equipment, net	600	800
Total assets	$1,120	$1,372
Accounts payable	$ 200	$ 220
Bank loans payable	600	500
Total stockholders' equity	320	652
Total liabilities and stockholders' equity	$1,120	$1,372

Income Statement	2002	2003 Forecasted
Sales	$2,000	$2,200
Cost of goods sold	700	
Gross profit	$1,300	
Depreciation expense	120	
Other operating expenses	1,010	
Operating profit	$ 170	
Interest expense	90	
Income before taxes	$ 80	
Income taxes	30	
Net income	$ 50	

Instructions:

Prepare a forecasted income statement for 2003. Clearly state what assumptions you make.

EXERCISE 4–29

FORECASTED BALANCE SHEET AND INCOME STATEMENT

Ryan Company wishes to prepare a forecasted income statement and a forecasted balance sheet for 2003. Ryan's balance sheet and income statement for 2002 are given below.

Balance Sheet	2002
Cash	$ 10
Other current assets	250
Property, plant, and equipment, net	800
Total assets	$1,060
Accounts payable	$ 100
Bank loans payable	700
Total stockholders' equity	260
Total liabilities and stockholders' equity	$1,060

Income Statement	2002
Sales	$1,000
Cost of goods sold	750
Gross profit	$ 250
Depreciation expense	40
Other operating expenses	80
Operating profit	$ 130
Interest expense	70
Income before taxes	$ 60
Income taxes	20
Net income	$ 40

In addition, Ryan has assembled the following forecasted information regarding 2003.

(a) Sales are expected to increase to $1,500.

(b) Ryan expects to become more efficient at utilizing its property, plant, and equipment in 2003. Therefore, Ryan expects that the sales increase will not require any increase in property, plant, and equipment. Accordingly, the year 2003 property, plant, and equipment balance is expected to be $800.

(c) Ryan's bank has approved a new long-term loan of $200. This loan will be in addition to the existing loan payable.

Instructions:

Prepare a forecasted balance sheet and a forecasted income statement for 2003. Clearly state what assumptions you make.

PROBLEMS

PROBLEM 4–30

SINGLE-STEP INCOME STATEMENT

The Payette Co. on June 30, 2002, reported a retained earnings balance of $1,535,000. The books of the company showed the following account balances on June 30, 2002.

Sales	$2,380,000
Inventory: July 1, 2001	160,000
June 30, 2002	170,000
Sales Returns and Allowances	30,000
Purchases	1,497,000
Purchase Discounts	24,000
Dividends Declared	260,000
Selling and General Expenses	238,000
Interest Revenue	52,000
Income Taxes	262,800

Instructions:

Prepare a single-step income statement and a retained earnings statement. The Payette Co. has 325,000 shares of common stock outstanding.

PROBLEM 4–31

REVENUE RECOGNITION AND PREPARATION OF INCOME STATEMENT

The Richmond Company manufactures and sells robot-type toys for children. Under one type of agreement with the dealers, Richmond is to receive payment upon shipment to the dealers. Under another type of agreement, Richmond receives payments only after the dealer makes the sale. Under this latter agreement, toys may be returned by the dealer. The president of Richmond desires to know how the income statement would differ under these two methods over a 2-year period.

The following information is made available for making the computations.

Sales price per unit:	
If paid after shipment	$5
If paid after sale, with right of return	$6
Cost to produce per unit (assume fixed quantity of toys is produced)	$3
Expected bad debt percentage of sales if revenue recognized at time of shipment	5%
Expected bad debt percentage of sales if revenue recognized at time of sale	1/2%
Selling expenses—2002	$25,000
Selling expenses—2003	$15,000
General and administrative expenses—2002 and 2003	$22,000

Quantity Shipped and Sold	2003	2002
Units shipped to dealers	30,000	25,000
Units sold by dealers	22,000	14,000

Instructions:

1. Prepare comparative income statements for 2002 and 2003 for each of the two types of dealer agreements assuming the company began operations in 2002.
2. Discuss the implications of the revenue recognition method used for each of the dealer agreements.

PROBLEM 4–32

REVENUE AND EXPENSE RECOGNITION

On December 31, 2002, the Hadley Company provides the following pre-audit income statement for your review.

Sales	$185,000
Cost of goods sold	(94,000)
Gross profit	$ 91,000
Rent expense	(18,000)
Advertising expense	(6,000)
Warranty expense	(8,000)
Other expenses	(15,000)
Net income	$ 44,000

The following information is also available:

(a) Many of Hadley's customers pay for their orders in advance. At year-end, $18,000 of orders paid for in advance of shipment have been included in the sales figure.

(b) Hadley introduced and sold several products during the year with a 30–day, money-back guarantee. During the year, customers seldom returned the products. Hadley has not included in revenue or in cost of goods sold those items sold within the last 30 days that included the guarantee. The revenue is $16,000, and the cost associated with the products is $7,500.

(c) On January 1, 2002, Hadley prepaid its building rent for 18 months. The entire amount paid, $18,000, was charged to Rent Expense.

(d) On July 1, 2002, Hadley paid $24,000 for general advertising to be completed prior to the end of 2002. Hadley's management estimates that the advertising will benefit a 2-year period and, therefore, has elected to charge the costs to the income statement at the rate of $1,000 a month.

(e) Hadley has collected current cost information relating to its inventory. The cost of goods sold, if valued using current costing techniques, is $106,000.

(f) In past years, Hadley has estimated warranty expense using a percentage of sales. Hadley estimates future warranty costs relating to 2002 sales will amount to 5% of sales. However, during 2002, Hadley elected to charge costs to warranty expense as costs were incurred. Hadley spent $8,000 during 2002 to repair and replace defective inventory sold in current and prior periods.

Instructions:

1. For each item of additional information, identify the revenue or expense recognition issue.
2. Prepare a revised income statement using the information provided.

PROBLEM 4–33

INTRAPERIOD INCOME TAX ALLOCATION

The following information relates to Delaney Manufacturing Inc. for the fiscal year ended July 31, 2002. Assume there are no tax rate changes, a 30% tax rate applies to all items reported in the income statement, and there are no differences between financial and taxable income.

Taxable income, year ending July 31, 2002	$ 975,000
Nonoperating items included in taxable income:	
Extraordinary gain	101,000
Loss from disposal of a business segment	(140,000)
Prior-year error resulting in income overstatement	
for fiscal year 2001; tax refund to be requested	75,000
Retained earnings, August 1, 2001	2,750,000

Instructions:

Prepare the income statement for Delaney Manufacturing Inc. beginning with "Income from continuing operations before income taxes" and the retained earnings statement for the fiscal year ended July 31, 2002. Apply intraperiod income tax allocation procedures to both statements.

PROBLEM 4–34

REPORTING SPECIAL INCOME ITEMS

Radiant Cosmetics Inc. shows a retained earnings balance on January 1, 2002, of $620,000. For 2002, the income from continuing operations was $210,000 before income tax. Following is a list of special items.

Income from operations of a discontinued cosmetics division	$18,000
Loss on the sale of the cosmetics division	50,000
Gain on extinguishment of long-term debt	25,000
Correction of sales understatement in 2001 (net of income taxes of $21,000	
to be paid when amended 2001 return is filed)	39,000
Omission of depreciation charges of prior years (a claim has been filed	
for an income tax refund of $8,000)	20,000

Income taxes paid during 2002 were $82,000, which consisted of the tax on continuing operations, plus $8,000 resulting from operations of the discontinued cosmetics division and $10,000 from the gain from extinguishment of debt, less a $20,000 tax reduction for the loss on the sale of the cosmetics division. Dividends of $40,000 were declared by the company during the year (35,000 shares of common stock are outstanding).

Instructions:

Prepare the income statement for Radiant Cosmetics Inc. beginning with "Income from continuing operations before income taxes." Include an accompanying retained earnings statement.

PROBLEM 4–35

DISCONTINUED OPERATIONS IN PROCESS

In 2002, Laetner Industries decided to discontinue its Laminating Division, an identifiable segment of Laetner's business. The measurement date for the discontinuance is August 1. At December 31, Laetner's year-end, the division has not been sold. However, negotiations for the sale are progressing in a positive manner. Analysis of the records for the year disclosed the following relative to the Laminating Division.

Loss for period, January 1 to August 1, 2002	$38,600
Loss for period, August 1 to December 31, 2002	51,300
Expected loss in 2003 preceding disposal	25,000
Expected gain on disposal of division	20,000

Instructions:

1. Assuming a 35% tax rate, what will be the 2002 reported gain or loss from operating the discontinued division?
2. What will be the 2002 reported gain or loss from disposal of the division?
3. Prepare the discontinued operations section of Laetner Industries' income statement for the year ending December 31, 2002.

PROBLEM 4–36

FINANCIAL STATEMENT ANALYSIS—RATIOS

The following financial statement information for RoboCon Inc. is available.

(In thousands)	2002	2001	2000
Sales	$5,346	$5,127	$4,982
Cost of goods sold	2,780	2,461	2,292
Operating expenses	2,031	1,985	1,768
Income taxes	160	204	277

The following information relates to the firm's common stock for the same period.

	2002	2001	2000
Shares outstanding	1,000	1,000	1,000
Market value per share at year-end	$5.125	$8.625	$13.50

Instructions:

1. For each year compute:
   (a) Gross profit percentage.
   (b) Net profit percentage.
   (c) Price-earnings ratio.
2. Do you notice any significant trends as a result of this analysis?

PROBLEM 4–37

INCOME AND RETAINED EARNINGS STATEMENTS

Selected account balances of Connell Company for 2002 along with additional information as of December 31 are as follows.

Contribution to Employee Pension Fund	$ 190,000
Delivery Expense	425,000
Depreciation Expense—Delivery Trucks	29,000
Depreciation Expense-Office Building	25,000
Depreciation Expense—Office Equipment	10,000
Depreciation Expense—Store Equipment	25,000
Dividend Revenue	35,000
Dividends	150,000
Doubtful Accounts Expense	32,000
Freight-In	145,000
Gain on Sale of Office Equipment	8,000
Income Taxes, 2002	427,425
Interest Revenue	10,000
Inventory, January 1, 2002	775,000
Loss on Sale of Investment Securities	20,000
Loss on Write-Down of Obsolete Inventory	75,000
Miscellaneous General Expenses	45,000
Miscellaneous Selling Expenses	50,000
Officers' and Office Salaries	550,000
Property Taxes Expense	100,000
Purchase Discounts	47,700
Purchases	4,633,200
Retained Earnings, January 1, 2002	550,000
Sales	8,125,000
Sales Discounts	55,000

| Sales Returns and Allowances | 95,000 |
| Sales Salaries | 521,000 |

(a) Inventory was valued at year-end as follows:

Cost	$825,000
Write-down of obsolete inventory	75,000
	$750,000

(b) Number of Connell shares of stock outstanding: 60,000

Instructions:
Prepare a multiple-step income statement and statement of retained earnings for the year ended December 31, 2002.

PROBLEM 4–38

CORRECTED INCOME STATEMENT

The pre-audit income statement of Jericho Recreation Incorporated was prepared by a newly hired staff accountant for the year ending December 31, 2002.

Net revenues		$797,000
Cost of goods sold		320,800
Gross profit		$476,200
Expenses:		
Sales salaries and commissions	$160,000	
Officers' and office salaries	210,000	
Depreciation	56,000	
Advertising expense	13,400	
Other general and administrative expenses	38,800	
		478,200
Net loss from continuing operations		$ (2,000)
Discontinued operations:		
Gain on disposal of business segment		40,000
Income before income taxes		$ 38,000
Income taxes (30%)		11,400
Net income		$ 26,600
Earnings per common share (10,000 shares outstanding)		$ 2.66

The following information was obtained by Jericho's independent auditor.

(a) Net revenues in the income statement included the following items.

Sales returns and allowances	$ 9,500
Interest revenue	6,600
Interest expense	10,600
Loss on sale of short-term investment	3,000
Gain on early extinguishment of debt	16,000

(b) Jericho changed its method of inventory costing in 2002. The staff accountant correctly determined that the cumulative effect of the change, before any tax considerations, was a reduction in current-year income of $18,000. In preparing the income statement, the accountant added the $18,000 to cost of goods sold.

(c) Of the total depreciation expense reported in the income statement, 60% relates to stores and store equipment, 40% to office building and equipment.

(d) At the beginning of 2002, management decided to close one of Jericho's retail stores. The inventory and equipment were moved to another Jericho store, and the land and building were sold on July 1, 2002, at a pretax gain of $40,000. This amount has been reported under discontinued operations.

(e) The income tax rate is 30%.

Instructions:
Prepare a corrected multiple-step income statement for the year ended December 31, 2002.

PROBLEM 4–39

ANALYSIS OF INCOME ITEMS—MULTIPLE-STEP INCOME STATEMENT PREPARATION

On December 31, 2002, analysis of the Rollins Sporting Goods' operations for 2002 revealed the following.

(a) Total cash collections from customers, $107,770.

(b) December 31, 2001, inventory balance, $10,020.

(c) Total cash payments, $96,350.

(d) Accounts receivable, December 31, 2001, $20,350.

(e) Accounts payable, December 31, 2001, $9,870.

(f) Accounts receivable, December 31, 2002, $15,780.

(g) Accounts payable, December 31, 2002, $5,175.

(h) General and administrative expenses total 25% of sales. This amount includes the depreciation on store and equipment.

(i) Selling expenses of $11,661 total 20% of gross profit.

(j) No general and administrative or selling expense liabilities existed at December 31, 2002.

(k) Wages and salaries payable at December 31, 2001, $3,750.

(l) Depreciation expense on store and equipment total 12.0% of general and administrative expenses.

(m) Shares of stock issued and outstanding, 6,000.

(n) The income tax rate is 40%.

Instructions:

Prepare a multiple-step income statement for the year ended December 31, 2002.

PROBLEM 4–40

CORRECTED INCOME AND RETAINED EARNINGS STATEMENTS

Selected preadjustment account balances and adjusting information of Sunset Cosmetics Inc. for the year ended December 31, 2002, are as follows:

Retained Earnings, January 1, 2002	$440,670
Sales Salaries and Commissions	35,000
Advertising Expense	16,090
Legal Services	2,225
Insurance and Licenses	8,500
Travel Expense—Sales Representatives	4,560
Depreciation Expense—Sales/Delivery Equipment	6,100
Depreciation Expense—Office Equipment	4,800
Interest Revenue	700
Utilities Expense	6,400
Telephone and Postage Expense	1,475
Supplies Inventory	2,180
Miscellaneous Selling Expenses	2,200
Dividends	33,000
Dividend Revenue	7,150
Interest Expense	4,520
Allowance for Doubtful Accounts (Cr. balance)	370
Officers' Salaries Expense	36,600
Sales	495,200
Sales Returns and Allowances	11,200
Sales Discounts	880
Gain on Sale of Assets	18,500
Inventory, January 1, 2002	89,700
Inventory, December 31, 2002	20,550
Purchases	173,000
Freight-In	5,525
Accounts Receivable, December 31, 2002	261,000
Gain from Discontinued Operations (before income taxes)	40,000
Extraordinary Loss (before income taxes)	72,600
Shares of Common Stock Outstanding	39,000

Adjusting information:

(a) Cost of inventory in the possession of consignees as of December 31, 2002, was not included in the ending inventory balance. $33,600

(b) After preparing an analysis of aged accounts receivable, a decision was made to increase the allowance for doubtful accounts to a percentage of the ending accounts receivable balance. 3%

(c) Purchase returns and allowances were unrecorded. They are computed as a percentage of purchases (not including freight-in). 6%

(d) Sales commissions for the last day of the year had not been accrued. Total sales for the day... $3,600

Average sales commissions as a percent of sales........................... 3%

(e) No accrual had been made for a freight bill received on January 3, 2003, for goods received on December 29, 2002. .... $800

(f) An advertising campaign was initiated November 1, 2002. This amount was recorded as "prepaid advertising" and should be amortized over a 6-month period. No amortization was recorded. $1,818

(g) Freight charges paid on sold merchandise and not passed on to the buyer were netted against sales. Freight charge on sales during 2002......... $4,200

(h) Interest earned but not accrued.. $690

(i) Depreciation expense on a new forklift purchased March 1, 2002, had not been recognized. (Assume all equipment will have no salvage value and the straight-line method is used. Depreciation is calculated to the nearest month.)

Purchase price... $7,800

Estimated life in years... 10

(j) A "real" account is debited upon the receipt of supplies.

Supplies on hand at year-end $1,600

(k) Income tax rate (on all items) 35%

Instructions:
Prepare a corrected multiple-step income statement and a retained earnings statement for the year ended December 31, 2002. Assume all amounts are material.

PROBLEM 4–41

COMPREHENSIVE INCOME STATEMENT
The following information for the year ending December 31, 2002, has been provided for the Blacksburg Company.

Sales	$450,000
Cost of goods sold	263,000
Foreign translation adjustment (net of income taxes)	33,000 (cr.)
Selling expenses	63,900
Extraordinary gain (net of income taxes)	39,400
Correction of inventory error (net of income taxes)	28,680 (cr.)
General and administrative expenses	58,720
Cumulative effect of change in depreciation method (net of income tax savings)	18,380 (dr.)
Income tax expense	21,500
Gain on sale of investment	6,700
Proceeds from sale of land at cost	75,000
Dividends	8,900

Instructions:
Prepare a statement of comprehensive income for the Blacksburg Company.

PROBLEM 4–42

FORECASTED BALANCE SHEET AND INCOME STATEMENT

Lorien Company wishes to prepare a forecasted income statement and a forecasted balance sheet for 2003. Lorien's balance sheet and income statement for 2002 are given below.

Balance Sheet	2002
Cash	$ 40
Other current assets	350
Property, plant, and equipment, net	1,000
Total assets	$1,390
Accounts payable	$ 100
Bank loans payable	1,000
Paid-in capital	100
Retained earnings	190
Total liabilities and stockholders' equity	$1,390

Income Statement	2002
Sales	$1,000
Cost of goods sold	350
Gross profit	$ 650
Depreciation expense	200
Other operating expenses	250
Operating profit	$ 200
Interest expense	120
Income before taxes	$ 80
Income taxes	20
Net income	$ 60

In addition, Lorien has assembled the following forecasted information regarding 2003.

(a) Sales are expected to increase to $1,200.

(b) Lorien does not expect to buy any new property, plant, and equipment during 2003. (Hint: Think about how depreciation expense in 2003 will affect the net reported amount of property, plant, and equipment.)

(c) Because of adverse banking conditions, Lorien does not expect to receive any new bank loans in 2003.

(d) Lorien plans to pay cash dividends of $15 in 2003.

Instructions:

1. Prepare a forecasted balance sheet and a forecasted income statement for 2003. Clearly state what assumptions you make.

2. If you construct your forecasted balance sheet in (1) correctly, total forecasted paid-in capital for 2003 should be negative. Is this possible? Explain.

COMPETENCY ENHANCEMENT OPPORTUNITIES

▶ Deciphering Actual Financial Statements	▶ Ethical Dilemma
▶ Writing Assignment	▶ Cumulative Spreadsheet Analysis
▶ Research Project	▶ Internet Search
▶ The Debate	

Accounting is more than just doing textbook problems. This expanded competency material provides practice in critical thinking, oral and written communication, research, teamwork, and consideration of ethical issues.

▶ DECIPHERING ACTUAL FINANCIAL STATEMENTS
• Deciphering 4–1 (The Walt Disney Company)
Refer to the financial statements and related notes of THE WALT DISNEY COMPANY in Appendix A in answering the following questions.

1. Of Disney's three major segments—creative content, broadcasting, and, theme parks and resorts—which generated the most revenue in 1998? Which had the highest profit margin?
2. Disney's net income decreased from $1,966 million in 1997 to $1,850 million in 1998. Identify the major reasons for the decrease.
3. Does Disney generate most of its revenue within the United States or outside the United States? (Search the notes to the financial statements for additional information.)
4. How does Disney recognize revenue?
5. Does Disney expense its film and television costs using direct matching, systematic and rational allocation, or immediate recognition?
6. How does Disney expense its theme parks, resorts, and other property?

• Deciphering 4–2 (Compaq Computer Corporation)
COMPAQ COMPUTER provides income statement information on page 215.

Convert Compaq's income statement for 1996 through 1998 to percentages by dividing each component by total revenue for the year.

1. Compute Compaq's overall gross margin as well as its gross margin by segment for each of the 3 years. Which segment is the most profitable?
2. Can you determine what was the major cause of Compaq's net loss in 1998?
3. Are Compaq's research and development costs increasing or decreasing as a percentage of sales?
4. What do you think the account entitled "Purchased in-process technology" refers to? Is in-process technology an asset?

• Deciphering 4–3 (Wells Fargo & Company)
WELLS FARGO & COMPANY's consolidated statement of income is shown on page 216.

1. How is this income statement different from all the other income statements illustrated in this chapter?
2. For a merchandising firm, gross profit represents sales less cost of goods sold. For Wells Fargo, what component of the income statement would be similar to gross profit?
3. The market value of Wells Fargo's stock at the end of each year was $339.44, $269.75, and $216.00 for the years 1997, 1996, and 1995, respectively. Compute the firm's price-earnings ratio for each year. Is it increasing or decreasing over time?

COMPAQ COMPUTER CORPORATION
CONSOLIDATED STATEMENT OF INCOME

FOR THE YEARS ENDED DECEMBER 31 (IN MILLIONS, EXCEPT PER SHARE AMOUNTS)	1998	1997	1996
REVENUE:			
PRODUCT	$27,372	$24,122	$19,611
SERVICES	3,797	462	398
TOTAL REVENUE	31,169	24,584	20,009
COST OF SALES:			
PRODUCTS	21,383	17,500	14,565
SERVICES	2,597	333	290
TOTAL COST OF SALES	23,980	17,833	14,855
SELLING, GENERAL AND ADMINISTRATIVE EXPENSE	4,978	2,947	2,507
RESEARCH AND DEVELOPMENT COSTS	1,353	817	695
PURCHASED IN-PROCESS TECHNOLOGY	3,196	208	—
RESTRUCTURING AND ASSET IMPAIRMENT CHARGES	393	—	52
MERGER-RELATED COSTS	—	44	—
OTHER INCOME AND EXPENSE, NET	(69)	(23)	17
	9,851	3,993	3,271
INCOME (LOSS) BEFORE PROVISION FOR INCOME TAXES	(2,662)	2,758	1,883
PROVISION FOR INCOME TAXES	81	903	565
NET INCOME (LOSS)	$ (2,743)	$ 1,855	$ 1,318
EARNINGS (LOSS) PER COMMON SHARE:			
BASIC	$(1.71)	$1.23	$0.90
DILUTED	$(1.71)	$1.19	$0.87
SHARES USED IN COMPUTING EARNINGS (LOSS) PER COMMON SHARE:			
BASIC	1,608	1,505	1,472
DILUTED	1,608	1,564	1,516

• Deciphering 4–4 (The Reader's Digest Association, Inc.)

Reader's Digest is the most widely read monthly magazine in the world. But THE READER'S DIGEST ASSOCIATION does more than just sell a monthly magazine. Information relating to the company's business segments can be found in the company's annual report, an excerpt of which is reprinted at the top of page 217.

1. How does Reader's Digest generate most of its revenues? profits?

2. By dividing profits by assets, we can obtain a measure of the efficiency with which assets are being employed. Compute each segment's asset efficiency measure.

3. Based on your answers to questions 1 and 2, how critical is the *Reader's Digest* magazine to the firm's overall success? Before you answer this question, think about how the company is able to sell its books and home entertainment products.

WELLS FARGO & COMPANY AND SUBSIDIARIES
CONSOLIDATED STATEMENT OF INCOME

(IN MILLIONS)	FOR THE YEARS ENDED DECEMBER 31, 1997	1996	1995
INTEREST INCOME			
Federal funds sold and securities purchased under resale agreements	$ 18	$ 29	$ 4
Investment securities	732	779	599
Mortgage loans held for sale	—	—	76
Loans	6,094	5,688	3,403
Other	60	27	3
Total interest income	6,904	6,523	4,085
INTEREST EXPENSE			
Deposits	1,703	1,586	997
Federal funds purchased and securities sold under repurchase agreements	154	92	199
Commercial paper and other short-term borrowings	17	16	32
Senior and subordinated debt	315	302	203
Guaranteed preferred beneficial interests in company's subordinated debentures	101	6	—
Total interest expense	2,290	2,002	1,431
NET INTEREST INCOME	4,614	4,521	2,654
Provision for loan losses	615	105	—
Net Interest income after provision for loan losses	3,999	4,416	2,654
NONINTEREST INCOME			
Fees and commissions	946	740	433
Service charges on deposit accounts	861	868	478
Trust and investment services income	450	377	241
Investment securities gains (losses)	20	10	(17)
Sale of joint venture interest	—	—	163
Other	427	205	26
Total noninterest income	2,704	2,200	1,324
NONINTEREST EXPENSE			
Salaries	1,269	1,357	713
Incentive compensation	195	227	126
Employee benefits	332	373	187
Equipment	385	399	193
Net occupancy	388	366	211
Goodwill	326	250	35
Core deposit intangible	255	243	42
Operating losses	320	145	45
Other	1,079	1,277	649
Total noninterest expense	4,549	4,637	2,201
INCOME BEFORE INCOME TAX EXPENSE	2,154	1,979	1,777
Income tax expense	999	908	745
NET INCOME	$1,155	$1,071	$1,032
NET INCOME APPLICABLE TO COMMON STOCK	$1,130	$1,004	$ 990
EARNINGS PER COMMON SHARE	$12.77	$12.21	$20.37
EARNINGS PER COMMON SHARE—ASSUMING DILUTION	$12.64	$12.05	$20.06
DIVIDENDS DECLARED PER COMMON SHARE	$ 5.20	$ 5.20	$ 4.60

THE READER'S DIGEST ASSOCIATION, INC.

(IN MILLIONS)	YEARS ENDED JUNE 30,		
	1998	1997	1996
REVENUES			
READER'S DIGEST MAGAZINE	$ 712.3	$ 729.2	$ 739.8
BOOKS AND HOME ENTERTAINMENT PRODUCTS	1,635.0	1,850.5	2,099.4
SPECIAL INTEREST MAGAZINES	97.0	81.9	91.9
OTHER BUSINESSES	193.1	181.0	170.6
INTERSEGMENT	(3.7)	(3.6)	(3.6)
	$2,633.7	$2,839.0	$3,098.1
OPERATING PROFIT F1			
READER'S DIGEST MAGAZINE	$ 16.7	$ 42.7	$ 11.2
BOOKS AND HOME ENTERTAINMENT PRODUCTS	37.9	175.6	192.0
SPECIAL INTEREST MAGAZINES	1.7	0.4	(21.1)
OTHER BUSINESSES	19.9	22.5	(9.9)
CORPORATE EXPENSE	(46.0)	(48.4)	(62.9)
	$ 30.2	$ 192.8	$ 109.3
IDENTIFIABLE ASSETS			
READER'S DIGEST MAGAZINE	$ 380.4	$ 410.4	$ 358.3
BOOKS AND HOME ENTERTAINMENT PRODUCTS	853.6	881.8	981.1
SPECIAL INTEREST MAGAZINES	75.0	76.4	66.4
OTHER BUSINESSES	70.8	75.1	76.9
CORPORATE	184.2	200.1	421.4
	$1,564.0	$1,643.8	$1,904.1

• Deciphering 4–5 (Ford Motor Company)

The consolidated statement of income for FORD MOTOR COMPANY is presented on page 218:

1. What is the first thing you notice about the way revenues and expenses are partitioned?
2. Compute the profit margin for the 1998 Automotive and Financial Services divisions of Ford.
3. For the Financial Services Division, how do 1998 results compare with 1997? Why the difference?
4. Which of the company's two divisions seems to be performing better over time?
5. Is Ford a car company that finances automobiles or a finance company that makes cars?

▶ ## WRITING ASSIGNMENT

• Recognizing holding gains

For years, accounting standards have not allowed companies to recognize the increases in value that occur while a company holds an asset while awaiting its sale or use. However, in a recent pronouncement (FAS 115), the FASB allowed companies to recognize increases in the value of investment securities that are held for the purpose of earning a short-term return. The increases in value of these securities are reported in the current period's income. In 2 pages or less, answer the following questions:

1. Why have accounting standard setters been reluctant to allow firms to recognize holding gains?
2. Why would the FASB now allow investment securities held for trading purposes to be valued at fair market value?

FORD MOTOR COMPANY AND SUBSIDIARIES
CONSOLIDATED STATEMENT OF INCOME
FOR THE YEARS ENDED DECEMBER 31,

(IN MILLIONS, EXCEPT AMOUNTS PER SHARE)	1998	1997	1996
AUTOMOTIVE			
SALES (NOTE 1)	$119,083	$122,935	$118,023
COSTS AND EXPENSES (NOTES 1 AND 15):			
COSTS OF SALES	104,782	108,907	108,882
SELLING, ADMINISTRATIVE AND OTHER EXPENSES	7,616	7,082	6,625
TOTAL COSTS AND EXPENSES	112,398	115,989	115,507
OPERATING INCOME	6,685	6,946	2,516
INTEREST INCOME	1,331	1,116	841
INTEREST EXPENSE	829	788	695
NET INTEREST INCOME	502	328	146
EQUITY IN NET LOSS OF AFFILIATED COMPANIES (NOTE 1)	(38)	(88)	(6)
NET EXPENSE FROM TRANSACTIONS WITH FINANCIAL SERVICES (NOTE 1)	(191)	(104)	(85)
INCOME BEFORE INCOME TAXES—AUTOMOTIVE	6,958	7,082	2,571
FINANCIAL SERVICES			
REVENUES (NOTE 1)	25,333	30,692	28,968
COSTS AND EXPENSES (NOTE 1):			
INTEREST EXPENSE	8,036	9,712	9,704
DEPRECIATION	8,589	7,645	6,875
OPERATING AND OTHER EXPENSES	4,618	6,621	6,217
PROVISION FOR CREDIT AND INSURANCE LOSSES	1,798	3,230	2,564
ASSET WRITE-DOWNS AND DISPOSITIONS (NOTE 15)	—	—	121
TOTAL COSTS AND EXPENSES	23,041	27,208	25,481
NET REVENUE FROM TRANSACTIONS WITH AUTOMOTIVE (NOTE 1)	191	104	85
GAIN ON SPIN-OFF OF THE ASSOCIATES (NOTE 15)	15,955	—	—
GAIN ON SALE OF COMMON STOCK OF A SUBSIDIARY (NOTE 15)	—	269	650
INCOME BEFORE INCOME TAXES—FINANCIAL SERVICES	18,438	3,857	4,222
TOTAL COMPANY			
INCOME BEFORE INCOME TAXES	25,396	10,939	6,793
PROVISION FOR INCOME TAXES (NOTE 6)	3,176	3,741	2,166
INCOME BEFORE MINORITY INTERESTS	22,220	7,198	4,627
MINORITY INTERESTS IN NET INCOME OF SUBSIDIARIES	149	278	181
NET INCOME	$ 22,071	$ 6,920	$ 4,446
INCOME ATTRIBUTABLE TO COMMON AND CLASS B STOCK AFTER PREFERRED STOCK DIVIDENDS (NOTE 1)	$ 21,964	$ 6,866	$ 4,381
AVERAGE NUMBER OF SHARES OF COMMON AND CLASS B STOCK OUTSTANDING (NOTE 1)	1,211	1,195	1,179
AMOUNTS PER SHARE OF COMMON AND CLASS B STOCK (NOTE 1)			
BASIC INCOME	$18.14	$5.75	$3.72
DILUTED INCOME	$17.76	$5.62	$3.64
CASH DIVIDENDS	$1.72	$1.645	$1.47

3. Should these holding gains be reported on the income statement even though an arm's-length transaction has not occurred?

4. If the FASB allows holding gains to be recognized for certain investment securities, why doesn't the Board move to fair value accounting on other assets like equipment, patents, and land?

▶ **RESEARCH PROJECT**
• Reviewing actual income statements and associated notes

Your group is to obtain the annual reports of 10 companies. These annual reports can be obtained by contacting companies directly or by making use of the annual report distribution service referenced in *The Wall Street Journal*. Using these annual reports, your group is to report (either orally or in writing) the answers to the following questions.

1. What format of the income statement is used by the 10 companies—single-step or multiple-step?

2. Each income statement should have 3 years of information. Compute the percentage increase in revenues for the two latest years [e.g., (1999 revenues − 1998 revenues) / 1998 revenues] and compare the result with the percentage increase in net income for the same period of time. Search the income statements for possible explanations should significant differences result.

3. Review each firm's revenue recognition note. Do their revenue recognition policies make sense given the nature of their operation?

4. Determine if each annual report provides additional breakdown of revenues and net income. Common breakdowns are by business segment and by geographical location. Are the companies you are reviewing becoming more or less diversified in terms of sources of revenue and income? Are the companies becoming more or less international in terms of the revenue and income obtained from outside the United States?

5. Do any of the annual reports contain a below-the-line item? That is, are there any companies with discontinued operations, extraordinary items, or cumulative effects of changes in accounting principles? Review the notes to the annual reports to obtain detailed information as to the nature of the items.

▶ **THE DEBATE**
• What is accrual-basis income?

Most people understand the purpose of a balance sheet—it reports on a firm's resources and claims to those resources. Most people understand a statement of cash flows—it reports where a firm's cash comes from and where the cash goes. The concept of "income" is a little more difficult for many people to get a handle on. Is it cash? Is it retained earnings? Just what is it and what does it measure?

Divide your team into two groups.

• One team will argue for a cash-basis measure of income. That is, instead of measuring revenues, we should measure cash collected from customers. Instead of measuring cost of goods sold, we should measure cash paid for inventory, and so forth.

• The other team will argue for an accrual-basis measure of income.

In preparing your debate, consider things such as: Which measure of income would better predict the future performance of a company and why? Which measure of income is more easy to understand for the users of financial information?

▶ **ETHICAL DILEMMA**

Far from being an exact science, accounting involves estimation and judgment. Consider the case of Dwight Nelson, chief financial officer of Pilot Enterprises. Pilot is a relatively young, privately held company with thoughts of going public in the near future. The owners of the business would like to include in the prospectus (a document containing information about the company and its past performance) financial statements that support their assertion that Pilot is a successful company with a bright future.

And the problem is this—the income statement for the past year shows a slight decrease in income from the prior period. When Dwight presented this information to the board of directors of Pilot, he was told that the income statement would have to be revised. He was specifically counseled to review his estimates associated with bad debt expense, warranty expense, and estimated useful life of depreciable assets. He was invited to present his "revised" income statement to the board of directors when it showed a 5% increase over last period's net income—anything less would not do.

After reviewing the assumptions made regarding uncollectibles, warranties, and depreciation, Dwight found that he could revise his estimates and obtain the 5% target increase in income. But he did not feel that the revised income statement properly reflected the performance of Pilot for the period.

1. What are the risks to Dwight of revising the income statement to meet the target figure?
2. What are the risks to Dwight of not revising the income statement to meet the target figure?

CUMULATIVE SPREADSHEET ANALYSIS

This spreadsheet assignment is a continuation of the spreadsheet assignment given in Chapter 3. If you completed that assignment, you have a head start on this one.

Refer back to the instructions for preparing the revised financial statements for 2002 as given in part (1) of the Cumulative Spreadsheet Analysis assignment in Chapter 3. Clearly state any additional assumptions that you make.

Skywalker wishes to prepare a *forecasted* balance sheet and a *forecasted* income statement for 2003. Use the financial statement numbers for 2002 (given in part (1) of the Cumulative Spreadsheet Project assignment in Chapter 3) as the basis for the forecast, along with the following additional information.

(a) Sales in 2003 are expected to increase by 40% over 2002 sales of $2,100.
(b) In 2003, Skywalker expects to acquire new property, plant, and equipment costing $240.
(c) The $480 in operating expenses reported in 2002 breaks down as follows: $15 depreciation expense, $465 other operating expenses.
(d) No new long-term debt will be acquired in 2003.
(e) No cash dividends will be paid in 2003.
(f) New short-term loans payable will be acquired in an amount sufficient to make Skywalker's current ratio in 2003 exactly equal to 2.0.
(g) Skywalker does not anticipate repurchasing any additional shares of stock during 2003.
(h) Because changes in future prices and exchange rates are impossible to predict, Skywalker's best estimate is that the balance in accumulated other comprehensive income will remain unchanged in 2003.
(i) In the absence of more detailed information, assume that investment securities, long-term investments, other long-term assets, and intangible assets will all increase at the same rate as sales (40%) in 2003.
(j) In the absence of more detailed information, assume that other long-term liabilities will increase at the same rate as sales (40%) in 2003.

INTERNET SEARCH

We began this chapter with an introduction to AT&T. Let's now go to its Web site and find out more about the company and its financial status. Its Internet address is **www.att.com**.

Once you have accessed AT&T's Web site, complete the following exercises:

1. AT&T is in the technology business, which is constantly changing. For example, in 1999, AT&T announced major agreements with MICROSOFT and MEDIAONE. Search AT&T's site and identify other recent merger or partnership activities.
2. Find the location that gives the information on the financial side of AT&T. How did the company do in the most recent fiscal period? How does its performance compare with the previous year?

3. Find the Web site that discusses AT&T's stock. What is a share of AT&T stock being traded for on the New York Stock Exchange?

4. Locate the note in the annual report that discusses AT&T's revenue recognition policy. How does AT&T recognize revenue from its various sources?

chapter 5
The Statement

Karl Eller started out in the billboard business. After his company was acquired by GANNETT, he sat on the firm's board and was one of a group of directors who opposed Gannett's risky plan to start up the first U.S. national daily newspaper, USA TODAY. He left Gannett and went to COLUMBIA PICTURES where he was one of the driving forces behind the purchase of Columbia by COCA-COLA. (Columbia Pictures was subsequently purchased again, this time by SONY in one of the most overpriced Hollywood deals of all time. But that is another story.) In 1983, Mr. Eller went into the convenience store business and took on the challenge of transforming CIRCLE K from a regional 1,200-store convenience store chain centered in Arizona into the second-largest chain in the United States (behind 7-ELEVEN). At its peak, Circle K operated 4,685 stores in 32 states.

Circle K's rapid expansion was financed through long-term borrowing. Circle K's long-term debt increased from $41 million in 1983, when Mr. Eller took over, to $1.2 billion in 1990. The interest on this large debt, along with increased price competition from convenience stores operated by oil companies, combined to squeeze the profits of Circle K.[1] Net income dropped from a record high of $60 million in 1988 to $15 million in 1989. For the year ended April 30, 1990, Circle K reported a loss of $773 million. In May 1990, Circle K filed for Chapter 11 bankruptcy protection.

As illustrated in Exhibit 5–1, at the same time it was reporting the disastrous $773 million loss, Circle K was reporting a record high positive cash flow from operations of over $100 million. How could Circle K report positive cash flow at the same time it was reporting a record-breaking net loss? There are many causes for a difference between accrual net income and cash flow; these causes are discussed in this chapter. In Circle K's case, there were three primary contributing factors:

- Much of the reported loss was due to a $639 million restructuring charge. For example, goodwill previously recorded as a $300 million asset was written off. This drastically reduced net income but did not affect cash flow.
- Circle K added $75 million to its estimated liability for environmental cleanup charges resulting from leaky underground gasoline storage tanks. Again, this charge reduced income but did not involve an immediate cash outflow.
- Financial distress forced Circle K to make its operations more efficient. One result was that Circle K reduced its inventory by $65 million in 1990. This action increased cash flow because $65 million in cash was liberated that otherwise would have been tied up in the form of gasoline, beer, and Twinkies®.

In 1991, Circle K again showed positive cash flow from operations while reporting a large net loss. In an interesting twist, this positive cash flow was partially a result of the bankruptcy filing. When a company files for Chapter 11 bankruptcy, the courts allow the company to cease making interest payments on its old debts. During the fiscal year ended April 30, 1990, the year before the bankruptcy filing, Circle K paid over $100 million in interest. In

1 Roy J. Harris Jr., "Karl Eller of Circle K, Always Pushing Luck, Now Lives to Regret It." *The Wall Street Journal*, March 28, 1990. p. A1.

1

Describe the circumstances in which the cash flow statement is a particularly important companion of the income statement.

2

Outline the structure of and information reported in the three main categories of the cash flow statement: operating, investing, and financing.

3

Appreciate the historical process involved in the development of the modern statement of cash flows.

4

Compute cash flow from operations using either the direct or the indirect method.

5

Prepare a complete statement of cash flows and provide the required supplemental disclosures.

6

Understand the differences among cash flow statements prepared according to U.S. GAAP, U.K. GAAP, and International Accounting Standards.

7

Assess a firm's financial strength by analyzing the relationships among cash flows from operating, investing, and financing activities and by computing financial ratios based on cash flow data.

8

Use knowledge of how the three primary financial statements tie together in order to prepare a forecasted statement of cash flows.

EXPANDED MATERIAL

9

Use a T-account or work sheet approach to prepare a statement of cash flows.

EXHIBIT 5 – 1 | Circle K: Net Income vs. Cash Flow

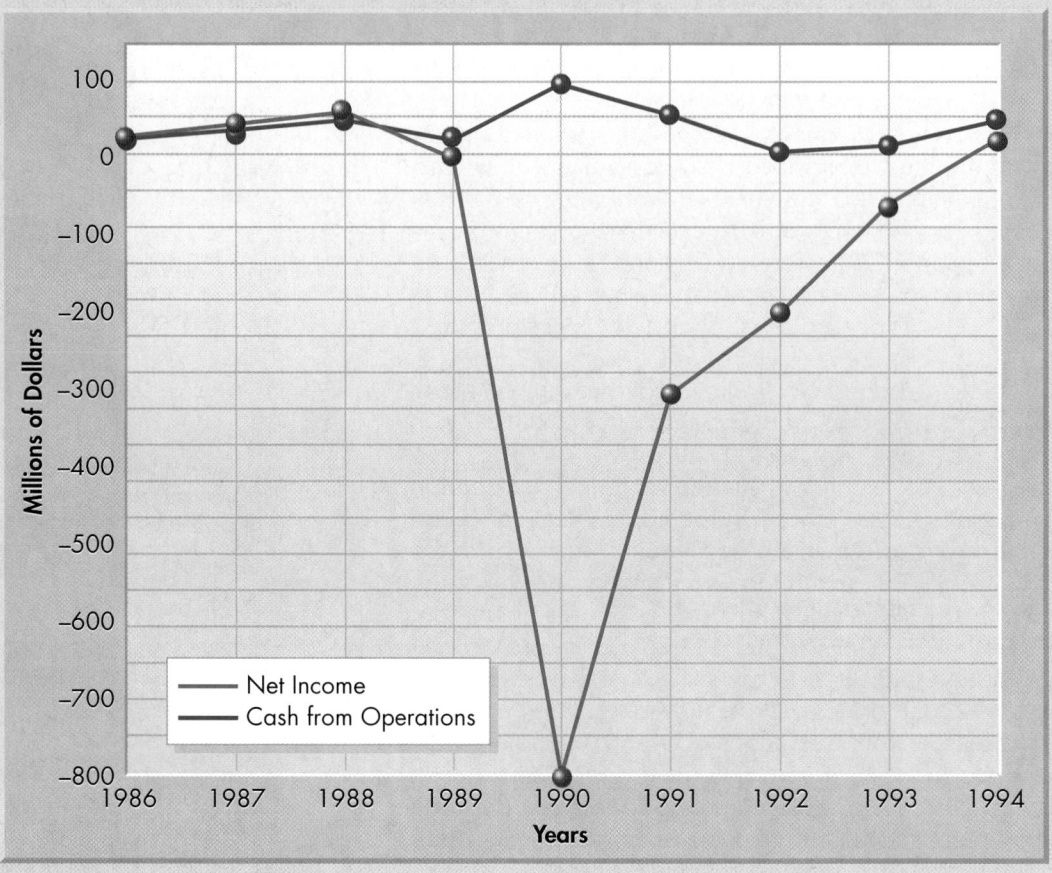

1991, after the filing, Circle K paid only $6 million in interest. In addition, the bankruptcy filing strengthened the willingness of suppliers to sell to Circle K on credit because bankruptcy laws place postbankruptcy lenders near the top of the creditor priority list. As a result, Circle K's accounts payable increased $80 million in 1991. This accounts payable increase freed up cash that otherwise would have been used to pay current bills.

Because of this positive cash flow from operations, Circle K was able to stay in business while its management devised a reorganization plan. As part of its bankruptcy restructuring, Circle K replaced Karl Eller as chief executive officer (CEO) in 1990. Following a lengthy debate among the creditors, Circle K's bankruptcy reorganization plan was formally approved by a federal bankruptcy court judge, and in 1993 Circle K was pur-

chased for $400 million by a diverse group of private investors from Barcelona, Kuwait, and Pittsburgh. Subsequently, Circle K was taken over by TOSCO, the largest independent refiner and marketer of petroleum products in the United States.[2]

And what about Mr. Eller, who started this whole thing? Well, you can't keep a good entrepreneur down. Karl Eller returned to his roots and became CEO of Eller Media, the largest billboard company in the United States.[3] On April 10, 1997, Eller Media was acquired by CLEAR CHANNEL COMMUNICATIONS, which has billboards across the United States and in the United Kingdom and operates radio and TV stations in the United States, Mexico, Australia, and New Zealand. Mr. Eller, in addition to continuing to run Eller Media, is also on the board of directors of Clear Channel. How is that for landing on your feet?

2 Jonathan Auerbach and Louise Lee, "Circle K Pact Gives Tosco Fuel Injection," *The Wall Street Journal,* February 20, 1996, p. A4. (Interestingly, Tosco's corporate headquarters are in Stamford, Connecticut, the same city where the FASB used to be located. Small world.)
3 William P. Barrett, "The Phoenix of Phoenix," *Forbes,* January 1, 1996, p. 44.

The Circle K case illustrates that cash flow data sometimes reveal aspects of operations not captured by earnings. In addition, recall that assessing the amounts, timing, and uncertainty of future cash flows is one of the primary objectives of financial reporting.[4] The statement that provides information needed to meet this objective is a statement of cash flows. This chapter provides an overview of reporting cash flows and outlines the techniques for preparing and analyzing a cash flow statement.

Describe the circumstances in which the cash flow statement is a particularly important companion of the income statement.

WHAT GOOD IS A CASH FLOW STATEMENT?

The key question is whether a cash flow statement tells us anything we don't already know from the balance sheet and income statement. This is a legitimate question, because the conceptual framework says that the primary focus of financial reporting is earnings, and earnings information is a better indicator of a firm's ability to generate cash in the future than is current cash flow information.

To answer the question: Yes, we need the cash flow statement. Some of the important reasons are discussed below.

- Sometimes earnings fail.
- Everything is on one page.
- It is used as a forecasting tool.

Sometimes Earnings Fail

There are situations in which net income does not give us an accurate picture of the economic performance of a company for a certain period. Three such scenarios are illustrated below by reference to actual company examples: (1) the Circle K scenario, (2) the Home Depot scenario, and (3) the KnowledgeWare scenario

THE CIRCLE K SCENARIO When a company reports large noncash expenses, such as write-offs, depreciation, and provisions for future obligations, earnings may give a more

For high-growth companies, positive earnings are no guarantee of sufficient cash flow. HomeDepot faced this problem in the mid-1980s.

4 *Statement of Financial Accounting Concepts No. 1,* "Objectives of Financial Reporting by Business Enterprises," Stamford, CT: Financial Accounting Standards Board, 1978, par. 37.

Caution! Note that the heading to this section says that "sometimes" earnings fail. In most cases, net income is the single best measure of a firm's economic performance.

gloomy picture of current operations than is warranted. As discussed in the opening scenario of the chapter, CIRCLE K reported record losses in the same years it was reporting record positive cash flow from operations. In such cases, cash flow from operations is a better indicator of whether the company can continue to honor its commitments to creditors, customers, employees, and investors in the near-term. Don't misunderstand this to mean that a reported loss is nothing to worry about as long as cash flow is positive; the positive cash flow indicates that business can continue for the time being, but the reported loss may hint at looming problems in the future.

THE HOME DEPOT SCENARIO Rapidly growing firms use large amounts of cash to expand inventory. In addition, cash collections on the growing accounts receivable often lag behind the need to pay creditors. In these cases, reported earnings may be positive, but operations are actually consuming rather than generating cash. This can make it difficult to service debt and satisfy investors' demands for cash dividends. For example, in the mid-1980s, HOME DEPOT was faced with a crisis as exponential sales growth necessitated operating cash infusions every year in spite of the fact that earnings were positive.[5] The lesson is this: For high-growth companies, positive earnings is no guarantee that sufficient cash flow is there to service current needs.

THE KNOWLEDGEWARE SCENARIO Accounting assumptions are the heart of accrual accounting. For companies entering phases where it is critical that reported earnings look good, those assumptions can be stretched—sometimes to the breaking point. Such phases include just before making a large loan application, just before the initial public offering of stock (when founding entrepreneurs cash in all those years of struggle and sweat), and just before being bought out by another company. In these cases, cash flow from operations, which is not impacted by accrual assumptions, provides an excellent reality check for reported earnings. For example, in 1994, KNOWLEDGEWARE, an Atlanta-based software company, was acquired by STERLING SOFTWARE. Negotiations over the purchase price were thrown into chaos when it was disclosed that KnowledgeWare had been overly optimistic with its revenue recognition assumptions. At the time, one accounting professor commented: "Cash from operations is the critical number investors should be looking at when evaluating one of these companies."[6]

Everything Is on One Page

As discussed in more detail later, the cash flow statement includes information on operating, investing, and financing activities. In essence, everything you ever wanted to know about a company's performance for the year is summarized in this one statement. How successful were operations for the year? Look at the operating activities section. What new investments were made in property, plant, and equipment? Look in the investing activities section. Where did the money come from this year to finance all this stuff? See the financing activities section. If you were stuck on a desert island and could receive only a single financial statement each year (by bottle floated in on the waves), you would probably choose the cash flow statement.

It Is Used as a Forecasting Tool

When forecasting the future, a cash flow statement is an excellent tool to analyze whether the operating, investing, and financing plans are consistent and workable. To do this, one constructs a pro forma, or projected, cash flow statement. A **pro forma cash**

---

5 The cash flow problems of Home Depot in 1985 are the subject of a very popular Harvard Business School case written by Professor Krishna Palepu.

6 Timothy L. O'Brien, "KnowledgeWare Accounting Practices Are Questioned," *The Wall Street Journal*, September 7, 1994, p. B2.

flow statement** is a prediction of what the actual cash flow statement will look like in future years if the operating, investing, and financing plans are implemented. For example, most lenders would be reluctant to loan money to a company to finance new investing activities when the pro forma cash flow statement indicates that there will be no positive operating cash flow to repay the loan. Construction of a pro forma cash flow statement is illustrated later in this chapter.

STRUCTURE OF THE CASH FLOW STATEMENT

2

Outline the structure of and information reported in the three main categories of the cash flow statement: operating, investing, and financing.

A **statement of cash flows** explains the change during the period in cash and cash equivalents. A **cash equivalent** is a short-term, highly liquid investment that can be converted easily into cash. To qualify as a cash equivalent, an item must be[7]:

1. Readily convertible to cash
2. So near to its maturity that there is insignificant risk of changes in value due to changes in interest rates

Generally, only investments with original maturities of three months or less qualify as cash equivalents. Original maturity in this case is determined from the date an investment is acquired by the reporting entity, which often does not coincide with the date the security is issued. For example, both a three-month U.S. Treasury bill and a three-year Treasury note purchased three months prior to maturity qualify as cash equivalents. However, if the Treasury note were purchased three years ago, it would not qualify as a cash equivalent during the last three months prior to its maturity.[8] In addition to U.S. Treasury obligations, cash equivalents can include such items as money market funds and commercial paper. Investments in marketable equity securities (common and preferred stock) normally would not be classified as cash equivalents because such securities have no maturity date.

Not all investments qualifying as cash equivalents need be reported as such. Management establishes a policy concerning which short-term, highly liquid investments are to be treated as cash equivalents. Once a policy is established, management should disclose which items are being treated as cash equivalents in presenting its cash flow statement. Any change in the established policy should be disclosed. For example, in 1993 GENERAL MOTORS disclosed that GMAC (GM's financing subsidiary) had changed its definition of cash equivalents to include short-term liquid investments. This change had the effect of increasing GM's reported cash and cash equivalents by 42%, or $3.3 billion.

Three Categories of Cash Flows

In the statement of cash flows, cash receipts and payments are classified according to three main categories:

- Operating activities
- Investing activities
- Financing activities

Exhibit 5-2 summarizes the major types of cash receipts and cash payments included in each category and includes the income statements and balance sheet accounts that are typically related to each category in the statement of cash flows.

OPERATING ACTIVITIES **Operating activities** include those transactions and events that enter into the determination of net income. Cash receipts from selling goods

---

7 *Statement of Financial Accounting Standards No. 95*, "Statement of Cash Flows," Stamford, CT: Financial Accounting Standards Board, November 1987, par. 8.
8 Ibid.

EXHIBIT 5–2 | Major Cash Receipts and Payments, by Category

Operating Activities

Cash receipts from:
    Sale of goods or services
    Sale of trading securities
    Interest revenue
    Dividend revenue

Cash payments for:
    Inventory purchases
    Wages and salaries
    Taxes
    Interest expense
    Other expenses (e.g., utilities, rent)
    Purchase of trading securities

Related items: income statement; current assets; current liabilities

Investing Activities

Cash receipts from:
    Sale of plant assets
    Sale of a business segment
    Sale of nontrading securities
    Collection of principal on loans

Cash payments for:
    Purchase of plant assets
    Purchase of nontrading securities
    Making loans to other entities

Related items: property, plant, and equipment; long-term investments; other long-term assets

Financing Activities

Cash receipts from:
    Issuance of stock
    Borrowing (e.g., bonds, notes, mortgages)

Cash payments for:
    Cash dividends
    Repayment of loans
    Repurchase of stock (treasury stock)

Related items: long-term debt; common stock; treasury stock; dividends

or from providing services are the major cash inflow for most businesses. Other cash receipts come from interest, dividends, and similar items. Major cash outflow includes payments to purchase inventory and to pay wages, taxes, interest, utilities, rent, and similar expenses. *The net amount of cash provided or used by operating activities is the key figure in a statement of cash flows.* In the same way that net income is used to summarize everything in an income statement, net cash from operations is the "bottom line" of the cash flow statement.

While cash inflows from interest or dividends logically might be classified as investing or financing activities, the FASB decided to classify them as operating activities. The guiding principle is that the operating activities section contains the cash flow effects of items included in the income statement.

INVESTING ACTIVITIES The primary **investing activities** are the purchase and sale of land, buildings, equipment, and other assets not generally held for resale. In addition, investing activities include the purchase and sale of financial instruments not intended for trading purposes, as well as the making and collecting of loans. These activities occur regularly and result in cash receipts and payments, but they are not classified as operating activities because they relate only indirectly to the central, ongoing operation of a business.

FINANCING ACTIVITIES **Financing activities** include transactions and events whereby cash is obtained from or repaid to owners (equity financing) and creditors (debt financing). For example, the cash proceeds from issuing stock or bonds would

Caution! Whether an activity is an operating activity depends upon the nature of the business. The purchase of machinery is an investing activity for a manufacturing business, but it is an operating activity for a machinery sales business.

be classified under financing activities. Similarly, payments to reacquire stock (treasury stock) or to retire bonds and the payment of dividends are considered financing activities.

The nature of financing activities is the same no matter what industry a company is in, but operating and investing activities differ considerably across industries. For example, the operating and investing activities of a supermarket chain are quite different from those of a sand and gravel company. However, for both companies, the process of borrowing money, selling stock, paying cash dividends, and repaying loans is almost the same.

CASH FLOW PATTERN The normal pattern of positive inflows or negative outflows of cash reported in the cash flow statement is as follows:

- Cash from operating activities, +
- Cash from investing activities, –
- Cash from financing activities, + or –

Most companies (over 70% in the U.S.) generate positive cash flow from operations. In fact, several periods of negative cash from operations is a sure indicator of financial trouble. In normal times, most companies use cash to expand or enhance long-term assets, so cash from investing activities is usually negative (about 85% of the time in the U.S.). A company with positive cash flows from investing activities is selling off its long-term assets faster than it is replacing them.

FYI: COCA-COLA is a classic example of a mature, successful, "cash cow" company. In 1997, Coca-Cola's operating cash flow of $4.033 billion was enough to pay for its investing activities ($500 million), repay debt ($596 million), pay cash dividends ($1.387 billion), and repurchase stock ($1.262 billion).

No general statements can be made about cash flows from financing activities; in healthy companies the number can be either positive or negative. As an example, positive cash flows from financing activities can be a sign of a young company that is expanding fast enough that operations cannot provide enough cash to finance the expansion. Hence, additional cash must come from financing. Negative cash flows from financing activities might be exhibited by a mature company that has reached a stable state and has surplus cash from operations that can be used to repay loans or to pay higher cash dividends. Accordingly, a company's cash flow pattern is a general reflection of where the company is in its life cycle. As shown in Exhibit 5-3, a young or rapidly growing company requires cash inflows from financing activities in order to pay for its capital expansion (investing activities) and also to subsidize negative operating cash flow resulting from a buildup in inventories and receivables. In a company that

EXHIBIT 5-3 | Cash Flow Patterns over the Life of a Company

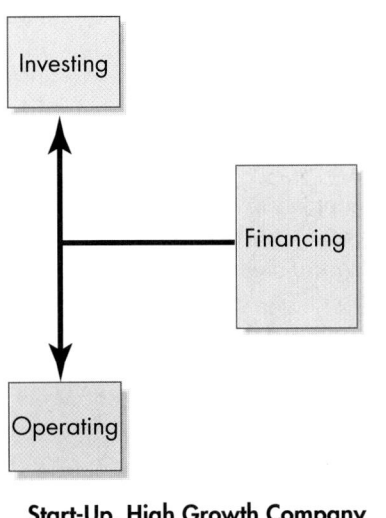

Start-Up, High Growth Company

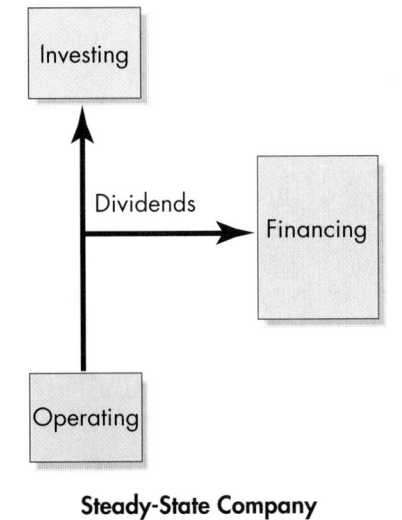

Steady-State Company

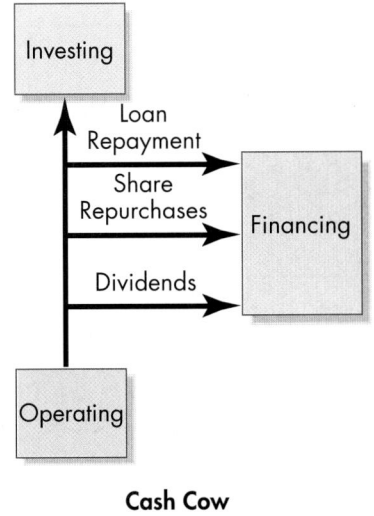

Cash Cow

has stopped growing and is focused on maintaining its position, cash from operations is sufficient enough to finance the replenishment of long-term assets and to pay dividends to the investors. Finally, a mature, successful company (sometimes called a "cash cow") generates so much cash from operations that it can pay for capital expansion and have cash left over to repay loans, pay cash dividends, and even repurchase shares of stock.

Further discussion of the interpretation of the cash flow pattern is found in a later section of this chapter.

Noncash Investing and Financing Activities

 The FASB specifies that a company's cash flow is to be summarized under three headings: operating activities, investing activities, and financing activities. Can you think of any alternatives to this three-way classification?

Some investing and financing activities affect an entity's financial position but not the entity's cash flow during the period. For example, equipment may be purchased with a note payable, or land may be acquired by issuing stock. Such **noncash investing and financing activities** should be disclosed separately, either in the notes to the financial statements or in an accompanying schedule, but not in the cash flow statement itself.[9] For example, in 1993, CHEVRON CORPORATION acquired a 50% interest in a joint venture with Kazakhstan to develop the Tengiz oil field. The $709 million deferred portion of the acquisition price was disclosed in the notes to Chevron's financial statements as a noncash transaction.

HISTORY OF THE CASH FLOW STATEMENT

Appreciate the historical process involved in the development of the modern statement of cash flows.

The balance sheet and income statement have been required statements for years, but the cash flow statement has only been formally required in the United States since 1988. However, cash flow statements, in some form or another, have a long history in the United States. In 1863, The NORTHERN CENTRAL RAILROAD issued a summary of its financial transactions that included an outline of its cash receipts and cash disbursements for the year.[10]

Because current assets can be thought of as those assets that are close to becoming cash and current liabilities as those liabilities that are close to being paid in cash, an alternative to focusing on cash flow is to examine the net change in working capital (current assets minus current liabilities). In some sense, working capital is equal to cash plus net short-term potential cash. In 1902, UNITED STATES STEEL CORPORATION produced a report that listed the major causes of the change in "funds" during the year, with funds being defined as current assets minus accounts payable. A working capital funds statement became increasingly popular after 1920.

FYI: During the 1970s, the "statement of changes in financial position" was not given great emphasis and was usually not even discussed in introductory financial accounting courses.

In 1971, the APB issued Opinion No. 19 officially requiring that a funds statement be included as one of the three primary financial statements in annual reports to shareholders and that it be covered by the auditor's report. Opinion No. 19 did not specify a single definition or concept of funds or a required format for the statement. This statement was called the "statement of changes in financial position."

During the early 1980s, the Financial Executives Institute (FEI) encouraged its members to adopt a cash emphasis in their statements of changes in financial position. In 1980, only 10% of the Fortune 500 companies used a cash focus; the other 90% reported net changes in working capital. By 1985, 70% used a cash focus. During this same period, the FASB issued Statement of Financial Accounting Concepts No. 5, which suggested that, conceptually, a cash flow statement should be part of a full set of financial statements. In late 1987, the FASB issued Statement No. 95,

---

9 *FASB Statement No. 95*, par. 32.

10 James H. Thompson and Thomas E. Buttross, "Return to Cash Flow," *The CPA Journal*, March 1988, pp. 30–40.

which superseded APB Opinion No. 19. Instead of allowing various definitions of funds, such as cash or working capital, and a variety of formats, the FASB called for a statement of cash flows to replace the more general statement of changes in financial position.

Because the required cash flow statement is relatively young (remember, double-entry accounting is 500 years old), it sometimes doesn't get the emphasis it deserves as one of the three primary financial statements. Many accounting textbooks still delay coverage of the cash flow statement until the end of the book. In addition, most of the age-old tools of financial statement analysis do not incorporate use of cash flow data. In fact, because the traditional analysis models were developed in an age when cash flow data were not available, analysts will go to great lengths to approximate cash flow numbers, seemingly unaware that since 1988 the actual numbers have been easily available in the cash flow statement. For example, a number often used in evaluating a company's health is earnings before interest, taxes, depreciation, and amortization—EBITDA. When pressed about why they use this number, an analyst will say, "EBITDA approximates operating cash flow." Why don't analysts use the real cash flow numbers? Because information from the cash flow statement is not yet ingrained in the analytical tradition. But it will be. In fact, one way to impress others that you are a modern, well-trained, future-looking professional is to become proficient in preparing and analyzing cash flow statements.

net work exercise

You can read a summary of FASB Statement No. 95 on the FASB's Web site (**www.fasb.org**).

Net Work:
According to the summary, Statement No. 95 became effective for fiscal years ending after what date?

4

Compute cash flow from operations using either the direct or the indirect method.

REPORTING CASH FLOW FROM OPERATIONS

Exhibit 5–4 illustrates the general format, with details and amounts omitted, for a statement of cash flows. The statement should report the net cash provided by or used in operating, investing, and financing activities and the net effect of total cash flow on cash and cash equivalents during the period. The information is to be presented in a manner that reconciles beginning and ending cash and cash equivalent amounts.[11]

EXHIBIT 5–4 | General Format for a Statement of Cash Flows

Cash provided by (or used in):	
Operating activities	$XXX
Investing activities	XXX
Financing activities	XXX
Net increase (decrease) in cash and cash equivalents	$XXX
Cash and cash equivalents at beginning of year	XXX
Cash and cash equivalents at end of year	$XXX

The preparation of the investing and financing activities sections of the statement of cash flows is straightforward. The operating activities section, however, is more complex. Operating cash flow is actually a simple concept—it is merely the difference between cash received and cash disbursed for operating activities. The computation of operating cash flow is difficult because accounting systems are designed to adjust cash

---

11   Additional disclosures are required in reconciling the change in cash and cash equivalents for a company that has foreign currency transactions. Such entities must report the equivalent of foreign currency cash flows and should show the effect of any exchange rate fluctuations on the cash balances as a separate item in the cash flow statement. Luckily, the complexities involved in reporting these foreign currency cash flows are considered beyond the scope of this text.

flow numbers to arrive at accrual net income. Computing operating cash flow requires undoing all the accrual accounting adjustments. This is illustrated in Exhibit 5-5.

EXHIBIT 5-5 | Relationship between Net Income and Operating Cash Flow

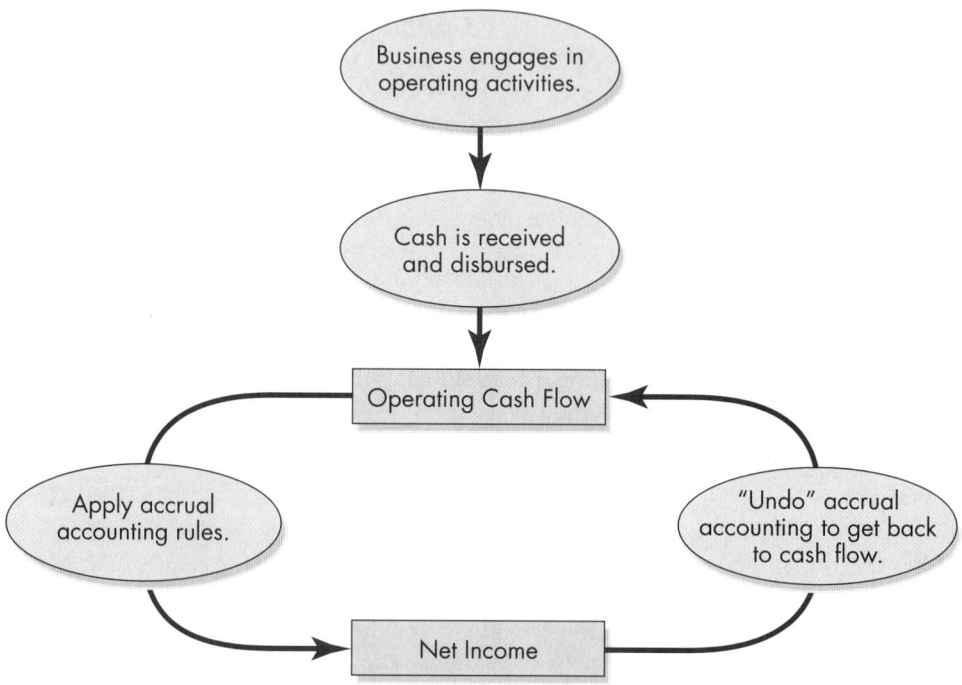

There are two methods that may be used in calculating and reporting the amount of net cash flow from operating activities: the indirect method and the direct method. The most popular method used in reported financial statements is the indirect method—it is used by approximately 95% of large U.S. corporations.

The **direct method** is essentially a reexamination of each income statement item with the objective of reporting how much cash was received or disbursed in association with the item. For example, for the item "sales" in the income statement, there is a corresponding item in the cash flow statement called "cash collected from customers." For "cost of goods sold," the corresponding item is "cash paid for inventory." To prepare the operating activities section using the direct method, one must adjust each income statement item for the effects of accruals.

The **indirect method** begins with net income as reported on the income statement and adjusts this accrual amount for any items that do not affect cash flow. The adjustments are of three basic types.

> **Caution!** The choice of the direct or indirect method is not a way to manipulate the amount of reported cash flow from operations. Both methods yield the same number.

- Revenues and expenses that do not involve cash inflow or outflow.
- Gains and losses associated with investing or financing activities.
- Adjustments for changes in current operating assets and liabilities that indicate non-cash sources of revenues and expenses.

Both methods produce identical results—that is, the same amount of net cash flow provided by (or used in) operations. The indirect method is favored and used by most companies because it is relatively easy to apply and it reconciles the difference between net income and the net cash flow provided by operations. The direct method is favored by many users of financial statements because it reports directly the sources of cash inflow and outflow without the potentially confusing adjustments to net income. The FASB considered the arguments for both methods, and although the Board favored the clarity of the direct method, they finally permitted either method to be used.[12]

The choice of the indirect or direct method affects only the operating activities section. The investing and financing activities sections are exactly the same regardless of which method is used to report cash flow from operations.

Operating Activities: Simple Illustration

The following data for Orchard Blossom Company is used to illustrate both the direct and the indirect methods.

Orchard Blossom Company
Selected Balance Sheet and Income Statement Data

	End of Year	Beginning of Year
Balance Sheet		
Cash	$ 25	$ 15
Accounts receivable	60	40
Inventory	75	100
Wages payable	10	7
Income Statement		
Sales	$150	
Cost of goods sold	(80)	
Wages expense	(25)	
Depreciation expense	(30)	
Net income	$ 15	

DIRECT METHOD The best way to do the direct method is to systematically go down the list of income statement items and calculate how much cash is associated with each item.

Sales and cash collected from customers. The beginning accounts receivable balance, along with sales for the year, constitutes potential collections from customers. The ending accounts receivable balance represents accounts not collected. Thus, cash collected from customers is computed as follows:

	Beginning accounts receivable	$ 40
+	Sales	150
=	Cash available for collection	$190
−	Ending accounts receivable	60
=	Cash collected from customers	$130

Note that a faster way to do this is to adjust the $150 sales amount by the $20 change in accounts receivable. The question is whether to add or subtract the $20. An increase in accounts receivable means less cash, so subtract the $20 increase ($150 − $20 = $130).

Cost of goods sold and cash paid for inventory. The ending inventory balance, along with cost of goods sold for the year, represents the total amount of inventory the company must have purchased some time in the past. The beginning inventory balance represents inventory purchased in prior years. Thus, inventory purchased this year is computed as follows:

	Ending inventory	$ 75
+	Cost of goods sold	80
=	Required inventory	$155
−	Beginning inventory	100
=	Inventory purchased this year	$ 55

Alternatively, adjust the $80 cost of goods sold amount by the $25 change in inventory. Should you add or subtract the $25? A decrease in inventory during the year means that you purchased less than you sold, so subtract the decrease in inventory ($80 − $25 = $55).

Note that in this simple illustration, all inventory is paid for in cash. A subsequent illustration in this chapter will show how to make adjustments for accounts payable.

Wages expense and cash paid for wages. The beginning wages payable balance, along with wages expense for the year, constitutes the total obligation to employees. The ending wages payable balance represents the amount of that obligation not yet paid. Thus, cash paid to employees for wages is computed as follows:

	Beginning wages payable	$ 7
+	Wages expense	25
=	Total obligation to employees	$32
−	Ending wages payable	10
=	Cash paid for wages	$22

This can also be computed by subtracting the $3 increase in wages payable from the $25 wages expense. You subtract the $3 increase because the increase represents wages that were not paid in cash during the year.

Depreciation expense. Here's a trick question: How much cash is paid for depreciation? None, because depreciation is a noncash expense.

The operating activities section of Orchard Blossom's cash flow statement, using the direct method, appears as follows:

Orchard Blossom Company
Statement of Cash Flows
Operating Activities: Direct Method

Cash collected from customers	$130
Cash paid for inventory	(55)
Cash paid for wages	(22)
Cash paid for depreciation	0
Net cash from operating activities	$ 53

Of course, in a proper cash flow statement, there would be no line for "Cash paid for depreciation." It is included here only to remind you that there is no cash paid for depreciation.

INDIRECT METHOD With the indirect method, we start with net income, which incorporates the net effect of all the income statement items, and then report the adjustments necessary to convert all the income statement items into cash flow numbers. Only the adjustments themselves are reported. As with the direct method, the best way to do the indirect method is to go right down the income statement, item by item.

Sales. What adjustment is necessary to convert this item to a cash flow number? The $20 increase in accounts receivable means that cash collected is $20 less than the $150 sales number indicates. So, the necessary adjustment to convert net income into cash flow is to subtract the $20 increase in accounts receivable.

Cost of goods sold. The $25 decrease in inventory means that although cost of goods sold of $80 is included in the income statement, less cash was used to purchase inventory than is suggested by the cost of goods sold number. Therefore, add the $25 inventory decrease to convert net income into cash flow.

Wages expense. The income statement includes a $25 subtraction for wages expense. However, the $3 increase in wages payable indicates that not all of that $25 wages expense was paid in cash. Accordingly, the $3 increase in wages payable is added to net income.

Depreciation expense. The $30 depreciation expense is a noncash expense. Because it was subtracted in computing net income, it must be added back to net income in computing cash flow. Add the $30 depreciation expense to net income.

The operating activities section of Orchard Blossom's cash flow statement, using the indirect method, appears as shown below.

Orchard Blossom Company
Statement of Cash Flows
Operating Activities: Indirect Method

Net income	$15
Plus: Depreciation	30
Less: Increase in accounts receivable	(20)
Plus: Decrease in inventory	25
Plus: Increase in wages payable	3
Net cash from operating activities	$53

Note that net cash from operating activities, commonly referred to as cash flow from operations, is the same, $53, whether the direct or the indirect method is used. Also note that depreciation is the first item listed after net income. This is the traditional presentation and is a holdover from the days of the "statement of changes in financial position." This ordering is unfortunate because it reinforces two wrong ideas.

- Depreciation is a source of cash. *Wrong.*
- Cash flow is equal to net income plus depreciation. *Wrong.*

> **FYI:** One advantage of the indirect method is that it highlights how cash flow can be improved in the short run by adjusting operating procedures. In the Orchard Blossom example, cutting back on inventory levels and slowing payments of wages both increased the amount of cash generated by operations.

Depreciation is *not* a source of cash.[13] Depreciation is added back to net income to offset the effect of subtracting depreciation expense in the original computation of net income. The net effect is to eliminate depreciation in the computation of cash flow.

The definition "cash flow equals net income plus depreciation" is widely used. But, a quick look at Orchard Blossom's indirect method operating activities section shows that the "net income plus depreciation" definition ignores all of the changes in current assets and current liabilities. Sometimes the changes in current items cancel (as they almost do in Orchard Blossom's case), so "net income plus depreciation" can be a good estimate of true cash from operations. However, many times, particularly with rapidly expanding firms, the current item changes do not cancel out. In those situations, true cash from operations is much lower than the "net income plus depreciation" definition would indicate. The "net income plus depreciation" definition is used widely in finance, and many finance professors believe it with all their hearts. Don't let them deceive you.

---

13 Depreciation is not a source of cash in a financial accounting context. However, when income taxes are considered, the depreciation tax deduction lowers the income tax liability. Thus, when analyzing the cash flow of a business or a project, the depreciation tax deduction is a source of cash to the extent that it lowers the amount of income taxes paid. This issue is covered in most textbook discussions of capital budgeting.

COMPARISON OF DIRECT AND INDIRECT METHODS The computations of Orchard Blossom's net income and operating cash flow are compared as follows:

Income Statement		Adjustments		Cash Flows from Operations	
Sales	$150	−20	(increase in accounts receivable)	$130	Cash collected from customers
Cost of goods sold	(80)	+25	(decrease in inventory)	(55)	Cash paid for inventory
Wages expense	(25)	+ 3	(increase in wages payable)	(22)	Cash paid for wages
Depreciation expense	(30)	+30	(not a cash flow item)	0	
Net income	$ 15	+38	net adjustment	$ 53	Cash flows from operations

With the direct method of reporting cash from operations, each of the individual cash flow items is reported. The operating activities section of a statement of cash flows prepared using the direct method is, in effect, a cash-basis income statement and involves reporting the shaded information from the worksheet below.

Income Statement		Adjustments		Cash Flows from Operations	
Sales	$150	−20	(increase in accounts receivable)	$130	Cash collected from customers
Cost of goods sold	(80)	+25	(decrease in inventory)	(55)	Cash paid for inventory
Wages expense	(25)	+ 3	(increase in wages payable)	(22)	Cash paid for wages
Depreciation expense	(30)	+30	(not a cash flow item)	0	
Net income	$ 15	+38	net adjustment	$ 53	Cash flows from operations

With the indirect method, only net income and the adjustments are reported. Therefore, the operating activities section of the statement of cash flows for Orchard Blossom would include the the shaded information for the table below.

Income Statement		Adjustments		Cash Flows from Operations	
Sales	$150	−20	(increase in accounts receivable)	$130	Cash collected from customers
Cost of goods sold	(80)	+25	(decrease in inventory)	(55)	Cash paid for inventory
Wages expense	(25)	+ 3	(increase in wages payable)	(22)	Cash paid for wages
Depreciation expense	(30)	+30	(not a cash flow item)	0	
Net income	$ 15	+38	net adjustment	$ 53	Cash flows from operations

Both methods of reporting operating cash flow have advantages. The primary advantage of the direct method is that it is very straightforward and intuitive. The primary advantage of the indirect method is that it highlights the factors that cause net income and cash from operations to differ. As mentioned earlier, almost all large U.S. companies use the indirect method. Some actual examples of the large differences that can exist between income and cash from operations are given in Exhibit 5-6.

5

Prepare a complete statement of cash flows and provide the required supplemental disclosures.

PREPARING A COMPLETE STATEMENT OF CASH FLOWS

In this section, we will work through a comprehensive problem in order to illustrate the preparation of a complete statement of cash flows. For this example, we will use financial statement and transaction information for CIRCLE K for fiscal year 1990.[14] Note that

---

14 To simplify the Circle K cash flow example, some accounts have been combined and some transactions slightly altered. Numbers are stated in millions.

EXHIBIT 5–6 | $10 Billion Differences between Income and Cash from Operations for the Year 1992 (in millions of U.S. dollars)

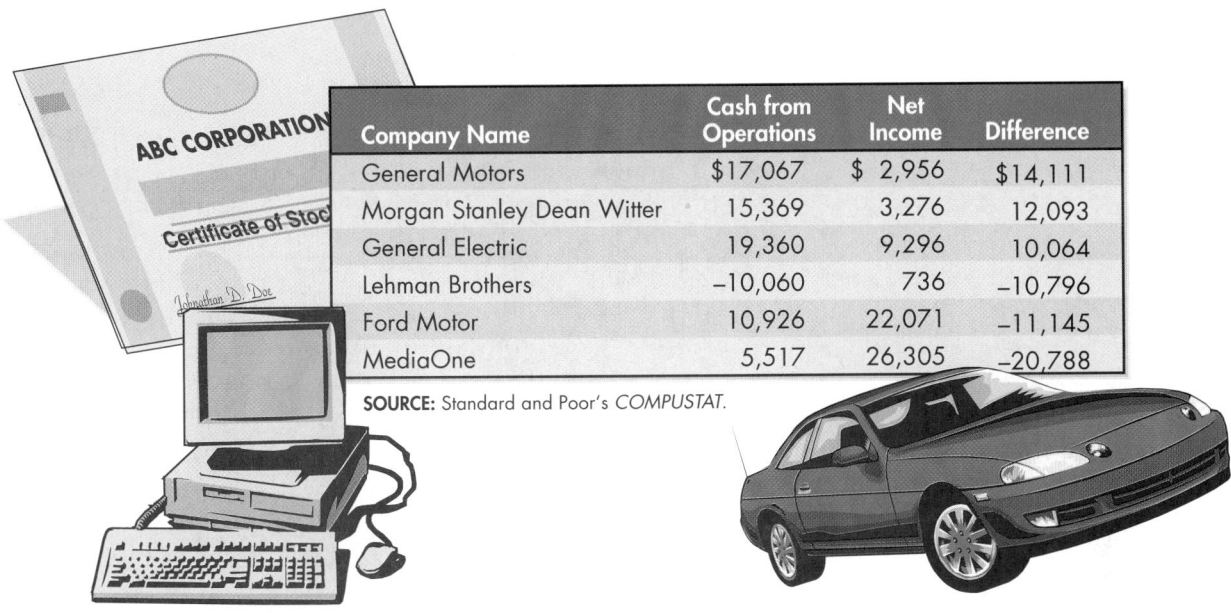

Company Name	Cash from Operations	Net Income	Difference
General Motors	$17,067	$ 2,956	$14,111
Morgan Stanley Dean Witter	15,369	3,276	12,093
General Electric	19,360	9,296	10,064
Lehman Brothers	–10,060	736	–10,796
Ford Motor	10,926	22,071	–11,145
MediaOne	5,517	26,305	–20,788

SOURCE: Standard and Poor's *COMPUSTAT.*

Circle K uses a fiscal year ending on April 30, so fiscal year 1990 extends from May 1, 1989, through April 30, 1990. During fiscal 1990, Circle K completed the following transactions (in summary form).

(1)   Sales on account, $3,737.
(2)   Collections on account, $3,735.
(3)   Received payments from customers in advance for services to be delivered in the future, i.e., unearned revenue, $13.
(4)   Collections on long-term receivables, $20.
(5)   Cost of goods sold, $2,797.
(6)   Purchased inventory on account, $2,732.
(7)   Paid accounts payable (all related to inventory), $2,755.
(8)   Purchased property, plant, and equipment for cash, $102.
(9)   Sold property, plant, and equipment for cash of $7 (original cost, $25; accumulated depreciation, $18).
(10) Paid long-term debt, $59.
(11) Borrowed additional long-term debt, $46.
(12) Issued stock, $1.
(13) Recorded depreciation expense on property, plant, and equipment and amortization expense on goodwill, $115 and $31, respectively.
(14) Paid interest on debt, $134.
(15) Incurred operating and administrative expenses (recorded in Other Current Liabilities), $772.
(16) Recorded additional environmental liability (recorded in Other Long-Term Liabilities), $109.
(17) Paid operating and administrative expenses for the period, $796. The incurrence of these expenses was recorded in (15).
(18) Recorded a tax benefit associated with the loss for the period, $62.
(19) Received an income tax refund, $45.
(20) Paid a dividend to shareholders, $8.
(21) Reclassified all of the current loan payable, $91, and $1,091 of long-term debt as liabilities subject to compromise.
(22) Wrote off $313 of property, plant, and equipment and $301 of goodwill as a restructuring charge.

A work sheet summarizing the beginning balances in Circle K's balance sheet accounts for fiscal 1990, the journal entries to record the 22 summary transactions for the year, and the ending preclosing account balances are given in Exhibit 5-7.

EXHIBIT 5–7 | Work Sheet Analyzing Circle K's Fiscal 1990 Transactions

Circle K Corporation
Work Sheet
December 31, 1990
(Amounts in millions)

	Account Title	Beginning Balance Debits	Beginning Balance Credits	Transactions During the Year Debits		Transactions During the Year Credits		Ending Balance Debits	Ending Balance Credits	
1	Cash	38		(2)	3,735	(7)	2,755	51		1
2				(3)	13	(8)	102			2
3				(4)	20	(10)	59			3
4				(9)	7	(14)	134			4
5				(11)	46	(17)	796			5
6				(12)	1	(20)	8			6
7				(19)	45					7
8	Accounts Receivable	36		(1)	3,737	(2)	3,735	38		8
9	Inventory	240		(6)	2,732	(5)	2,797	175		9
10	Property, Plant, and Equipment	1,558		(8)	102	(9)	25	1,322		10
11						(22)	313			11
12	Accumulated Depreciation		283	(9)	18	(13)	115		380	12
13	Long-Term Receivable	64				(4)	20	44		13
14	Goodwill	332				(13)	31	0		14
15						(22)	301			15
16	Accounts Payable		135	(7)	2,755	(6)	2,732		112	16
17	Current Portion of Long-Term Debt		91	(21)	91				0	17
18	Taxes Payable		41	(18)	62	(19)	45		24	18
19	Unearned Revenue		20			(3)	13		33	19
20	Other Current Liabilities		117	(17)	796	(15)	772		93	20
21	Liabilities Subject to Compromise		0			(21)	1,182		1,182	21
22	Long-Term Debt		1,158	(10)	59	(11)	46		54	22
23				(21)	1,091					23
24	Other Long-Term Liabilities		47			(16)	109		156	24
25	Common Stock		239			(12)	1		240	25
26	Retained Earnings		137					644		26
27										27
28	Dividends			(20)	8					28
29	Sales					(1)	3,737			29
30	Cost of Goods Sold			(5)	2,797					30
31	Depreciation and Amortization Expense			(13)	146					31
32	Interest Expense			(14)	134					32
33	Operating and Administrative Expenses			(15)	772					33
34				(16)	109					34
35	Income Tax Benefit					(18)	62			35
36	Restructuring Charge			(22)	614					36
37		2,268	2,268		19,890		19,890	2,274	2,274	37
38										38

From the work sheet in Exhibit 5-7, the information regarding the transactions impacting the cash account can be isolated. This is the information needed in order to construct the statement of cash flows for Circle K. A summary and categorization of all the transactions impacting cash is given in Exhibit 5-8.

As you can see, if one has access to the detailed transaction data from the cash account, preparing a statement of cash flows is easy. In fact, if transactions are properly coded as operating, investing, or financing when they are first input into an accounting system, the preparation of a statement of cash flows is no more complicated than a simple three-way sort of the transactions.

EXHIBIT 5–8 | Summary of Cash Transactions for Circle K for Fiscal 1990

Transaction Number	Cash Flows Relating to	Type of Activity	Amount of Cash Inflow	Amount of Cash Outflow
(2)	Collections on account	Operating	$3,735	
(3)	Collections in advance	Operating	13	
(4)	Collections on long-term receivable	Investing	20	
(7)	Paid for inventory	Operating		$2,755
(8)	Paid for PP&E	Investing		102
(9)	Sold PP&E	Investing	7	
(10)	Paid long-term debt	Financing		59
(11)	Borrowed long-term debt	Financing	46	
(12)	Issued stock	Financing	1	
(14)	Paid interest on debt	Operating		134
(17)	Paid operating and administrative expenses	Operating		796
(19)	Received a tax refund	Operating	45	
(20)	Paid a dividend to shareholders	Financing		8

Preparing a Statement of Cash Flows in the Absence of Detailed Transaction Data

In this section, we discuss how a statement of cash flows is prepared if one does not have ready access to detailed cash inflow and outflow information or if cash transactions are not coded as being operating, investing, or financing. A solid understanding of the process needed to construct a cash flow statement is important for several reasons. First, the majority of cash flow statements are prepared using the indirect method. Without a detailed understanding of how this type of statement is prepared, you are severely limited in your ability to understand and interpret the numbers. Second, an understanding of the intricacies of the statement of cash flows allows one to see how individual transactions can affect all of the financial statements. Thus, when we analyze the statement of cash flows, we are also looking at the income statement and the balance sheet. Finally, small companies that are not publicly traded frequently prepare only balance sheets and income statements, so external users of financial statements, such as banks and potential investors, are required to construct cash flow statements using partial information.

If one does not have access to detailed cash flow information, the preparation of a statement of cash flows involves analyzing the income statement and comparative balance sheets to determine how cash was generated and how cash was used by a business. A company's cash inflow and outflow can be determined through a careful analysis of each account contained in these statements. Our knowledge of the activities associated with each balance sheet and income statement account, coupled with our knowledge of the relationship between these two financial statements, allows us to infer the cash flow effects of the various transactions of a business during a period.

For example, consider the accounts receivable account. We know that an increase in Accounts Receivable is associated with a credit sale. Similarly, we know that a decrease in Accounts Receivable usually means that cash was collected. Accordingly, if you know the beginning and ending balances for the accounts receivable account (from comparative balance sheets) and you know sales for the period (from the income statement), you can then infer the cash collected from customers during the period.

To illustrate, consider the following information taken from CIRCLE K's beginning and ending balance sheets and income statement for fiscal 1990. Remember that we are assuming that the detailed transaction information is not available to us; we only have the summary information available in the resulting financial statements.

Beginning Accounts Receivable (initial amount owed to Circle K)		$ 36
+ Sales during the year		3,737
= Total amount owed to Circle K by customers		$3,773
− Ending Accounts Receivable (amount not yet collected)		38
= Cash collections for goods and services already provided		$3,735

In addition to cash collected from customers who have already received services, Circle K also received $13 from customers in advance of services being provided. This $13 must be added to the previous figure to arrive at total cash collections for the period.

Cash collections for goods and services already provided	$3,735
+ Increase in Unearned Revenue for the period	13
Total cash collections for the period	$3,748

Caution! Some students are skeptical of this analysis because it appears to exclude cash sales since they are never recorded as part of Accounts Receivable. Think of a cash sale as a credit sale with an extremely short collection period.

Because we know what was owed to Circle K at the start of the period, what was owed to them at the end of the period, and sales that were made during the period, we can infer the amount of cash that must have been collected during the period. As you can see from this analysis, we don't necessarily need the detailed cash account information to prepare a statement of cash flows. We can use our knowledge of business and accounting to infer those details.

A similar analysis is conducted for every balance sheet account. We use our knowledge of the relationship between the income statement and balance sheet accounts and couple it with our knowledge of what accounts are associated with operating, investing, and financing activities. Consider another example—Common Stock. First of all, we know that changes in the common stock account are considered to be financing activities. Second, we know that increases are associated with the issuance of shares of stock. Finally, we know that decreases to the common stock account are associated with the retirement of previously issued shares of stock. Using comparative balance sheet information for the common stock account of Circle K in fiscal 1990, we can infer the stock-related activities that occurred during the period.

	Beginning Balance	Ending Balance	Change
Common Stock	$239	$240	$1 Increase

From this information, it is reasonable to infer that Circle K issued stock in exchange for $1 million during the year. Of course, it is possible that Circle K issued more shares than this, and during the same year retired shares issued in prior years. If Circle K had done something such as this (which it didn't), that information would be disclosed somewhere in the financial statement notes and would be used to modify the analysis. By the way, note that we don't use information from the income statement in analyzing transactions impacting the common stock account because transactions in a company's own stock are not reflected in the income statement.

As one further illustration, consider Circle K's property, plant, and equipment (PP&E) account. The PP&E account is associated with investing activities—increases in property, plant, and equipment correspond to purchases of new PP&E and decreases relate to the sale of old PP&E. Circle K's financial statement notes reveal that equipment with an original cost of $25 million and with accumulated depreciation of $18 million was sold during 1990 for $7 million. Circle K's notes also tell us that $313 million in PP&E was written off during the year as part of the restructuring charge. Based on this information, and using information from the comparative balance sheets, we can infer that the following PP&E purchases were made during the period.

	Beginning PP&E balance	$1,558
+	Purchases during the period	?
−	Disposals during the period	(25)
−	PP&E written off because of restructuring	(313)
=	Ending PP&E balance	$1,322

Calculating reveals that the unknown amount is $102 million, which is the amount of PP&E purchased during fiscal 1990. Again, we see that we don't need the detail of the cash account to be able to infer the cash inflow and outflow for the company. Our knowledge of accounting allows us to do a little detective work and infer what transactions impacted Circle K's cash account.

A Six-Step Process for Preparing a Statement of Cash Flows

The following six-step process outlines a systematic method that can be used in analyzing the income statement and comparative balance sheets in preparing a statement of cash flows.

1. Compute how much the cash balance changed during the year. The statement of cash flows is not complete until the sum of cash from operating, investing, and financing activities exactly matches the total change in the cash balance during the year.
2. Convert the income statement from an accrual-basis to a cash-basis summary of operations. This is done in three steps.
   a. Eliminate expenses that do not involve the outflow of cash, such as depreciation expense.
   b. Eliminate gains and losses associated with investing or financing activities to avoid counting these items twice.
   c. Adjust for changes in the balances of current assets and current liabilities because these changes indicate cases in which the operating cash flow associated with an item does not match the revenue or expense reported for that item.
   The final result of these adjustments is that net income is converted into cash flow from operating activities.
3. Analyze the long-term assets to identify the cash flow effects of investing activities. Changes in property, plant, and equipment as well as in long-term investments may indicate that cash has either been spent or has been received.
4. Analyze the long-term debt and stockholders' equity accounts to determine the cash flow effects of any financing transactions. These transactions include borrowing or repaying debt, issuing or buying back stock, and paying dividends.
5. Make sure that the total net cash flow from operating, investing, and financing activities is equal to the net increase or decrease in cash as computed in Step 1. Then, prepare a formal statement of cash flows by classifying all cash inflows and outflows according to operating, investing, and financing activities. The net cash flows from each of the three main activities should be highlighted.
6. Prepare supplemental disclosure, including the disclosure of any significant investing or financing transactions that did not involve cash. This disclosure is done outside the cash flow statement itself. The types of transactions disclosed in this way include the purchase of land by issuing stock and the retirement of bonds by issuing stock. In addition, supplemental disclosure of cash paid for interest expense and taxes is required.

An Illustration of the Six-Step Process

We will illustrate this six-step process using the information from the CIRCLE K example presented earlier. Remember that we will prepare the statement of cash flows without reference to the detailed cash flow information. Thus, we are going to have to make inferences about cash flows by examining the balance sheet and income statement accounts.

STEP 1. COMPUTE HOW MUCH THE CASH BALANCE CHANGED DURING THE YEAR. Recall that Circle K began the year with a cash balance of $38 and ended with a cash balance of $51. Thus, our target in preparing the statement of cash flows is to explain why the cash account increased by $13 during the year.

STEP 2. CONVERT THE INCOME STATEMENT FROM AN ACCRUAL-BASIS TO A CASH-BASIS SUMMARY OF OPERATIONS. Recall that converting accrual net income into cash from operations involves eliminating noncash expenses, removing the effects of gains and losses, and adjusting for the impact of changes in current asset and liability balances. These adjustments are shown in the work sheet, Exhibit 5–9, and are explained below.

EXHIBIT 5–9 | Adjustments to Convert Circle K's Accrual Net Income into Cash from Operations—Work Sheet

	Income Statement		Adjustments		Cash Flows from Operations
Sales	$3,737	C1.	−2	(increase in accounts receivable)	$3,748
		C2.	+13	(increase in unearned revenue)	
Cost of goods sold	(2,797)	C3.	+65	(decrease in inventory)	(2,755)
		C4.	−23	(decrease in accounts payable)	
Operating and administrative expenses	(881)	C5.	−24	(decrease in other current liabilities)	(796)
		C6.	+109	(increase in other long-term liabilities)	
Depreciation and amortization expense	(146)	A1.	+146	(not a cash flow item)	0
Interest expense	(134)		0	No adjustment	(134)
Restructuring charge	(614)	A2.	+614	(not a cash flow item)	0
Tax benefit	62	C7.	−17	(decrease in taxes payable)	45
Net loss	$ (773)		+881	net adjustment	$ 108

Depreciation (adjustment A1). The first adjustment involves *adding* the amount of depreciation and amortization expense. Because this expense does not involve an outflow of cash and depreciation and amortization expense was initially subtracted to arrive at net income, this adjustment effectively eliminates depreciation and amortization from the computation of cash from operations. It can be seen in the far right column of the work sheet in Exhibit 5–9 that adjustment A1 results in a $0 (−$146 + $146 = $0) cash flow effect from depreciation and amortization. This adjustment is often the largest adjustment that is made. For example, in 1997 GENERAL MOTORS reported net income of $6.6 billion and cash flow from operations of $16.5 billion; its adjustment for depreciation and amortization involved adding $16.6 billion.

Restructuring charge (adjustment A2). The same analysis used for depreciation and amortization expense also applies to the restructuring charge. Recall from Chapter 4 that a restructuring charge is an accounting estimate of the decrease in value of some assets and the creation of future obligations as a result of the decision to restructure parts of a business. The important point to note is that this charge is an accounting estimate, not a cash payment. Accordingly, in computing cash from operating activities, a restructuring charge should be *added* back to net income. In Exhibit 5–9, this adjustment (A2) is shown as an addition of $614, resulting in a net cash flow effect of $0. As an example of this type of adjustment, in 1997 CAMPBELL SOUP reported a $216 million restructuring charge in its income statement. In its statement of cash flows, Campbell added the entire $216 million back to net income in arriving at cash flows from operations.

Gains and losses. Adjustment must also be made for any gains or losses included in the computation of net income. To illustrate the need for this type of adjustment, consider the case of a company that sells some equipment and records a gain on the sale. The cash flow effect of the equipment sale is shown in the investing activities section of the cash flow statement. To avoid counting this twice, the gain should be excluded from the operating activities section. However, the gain has already been added in the computation of net income. In order to exclude the gain from the operating activities section, it must be subtracted from net income. If there had been a loss on the equipment sale, that loss would be added back to net income in the operating activities section so that it would not impact cash flows from operations.

Because Circle K reported no gains or losses in 1990, no cash flow adjustments for gains or losses are necessary. Note that Circle K did sell property, plant, and equipment for $7 million during the year, but the sales price was equal to the book value of the PP&E so no gain or loss was reported. The proceeds from the sale, $7 million, is reported as cash from investing activities, as illustrated later. In 1989, Circle K did report a $19 million gain from the sale of its facilities for making convenience store fast-food items and for making ice. This sale was an investing activity, and the amount of the gain was subtracted in the computation of cash from operating activities.

Changes in current assets and liabilities. The remaining adjustments (C1–C7 in Exhibit 5-9) are needed because the computation of accrual net income involves reporting revenues and expenses when economic events occur, not necessarily when cash is received or paid. The timing differences between the receipt or payment of cash and the earning of revenue or the incurring of an expense are reflected in the shifting balances in the current assets and current liabilities that are related to operations. This is illustrated through a discussion of each of Circle K's current operating assets and liabilities accounts.

Accounts receivable (adjustment C1). Recall from our analysis earlier in the chapter that the amount of cash Circle K collected from customers in 1990 differed from sales for the period. In fact, sales exceeded collections by $2 million, which explains why the accounts receivable account increased by $2 million. In computing cash from operations, an adjustment must be made to decrease the accrual-basis sales figure to its cash-basis counterpart. The $2 million increase in accounts receivable is *subtracted,* as shown in Exhibit 5-9.

Unearned revenue (adjustment C2). In converting the accrual-based sales into cash collected from customers, we must also make an adjustment for cash received from customers in advance of its being earned. The unearned revenue account increased by $13 million (from $20 million to $33 million), representing cash received from customers in 1990 that won't be reflected in sales and included in the computation of net income until a subsequent year. The $13 million increase reflects an additional amount of cash not yet included in the computation of 1990 net income and is *added* in the computation of cash from operations, as shown in Exhibit 5-9.

Inventory (adjustment C3). The statement of cash flows should reflect the amount of cash paid for inventory during the year, which is not necessarily the same as the cost of inventory sold. Circle K's inventory decreased by $65 million (from $240 million to $175 million) during 1990, indicating that the amount of inventory purchased during 1990 was less than the amount of inventory sold. Accordingly, in the computation of cash from operations we must reduce the cost of goods sold number to reflect the fact that part of the inventory sold this period was actually purchased last period. To reduce cost of goods sold (which is subtracted in the computation of net income), the adjustment involves *adding* $65 million, as shown in Exhibit 5-9. As mentioned earlier in the chapter, the inventory increases experienced by rapidly growing companies result in a decrease in cash from operations because the cash is tied up in the form of inventory. In its 1998 cash flow statement, HOME DEPOT, the rapidly expanding chain of home handyman stores, reported a reduction in cash from operations of $885 million stemming from increased inventories.

Accounts payable (adjustment C4). The balance in Circle K's accounts payable account decreased by $23 million during 1990. This decrease occurred because Circle K paid for more than it bought from its suppliers during the year. The adjustment necessary to reflect this additional cash outflow is to *subtract* $23 million in computing cash from operations, shown as adjustment C4 in Exhibit 5–9. On the other hand, an increase in the accounts payable account results in more operating cash flow because cash that otherwise would have been used to pay bills is kept within the business. FORD MOTOR COMPANY, in its 1997 annual report, provides an example of just how significant this source of cash can be. In computing cash provided by the operations of its automotive division, Ford added $3.9 billion to reflect the effect of an increase in its accounts payable account balance.

Other current liabilities (adjustment C5). The other current liabilities account requires an adjustment similar to that done for Accounts Payable. The account began the year with a beginning balance of $117 million, and the ending balance was $93 million, indicating a decrease for the year of $24 million. Because the balance in the other current liabilities account decreased during the year, we know that the amount of cash paid for expenses exceeded the amount of expenses reported in the income statement. As a result, operating expenses must be increased to reflect the actual cash outflow for the period. Operating expenses are shown as a negative number in the work sheet (reflecting an expense), therefore, we make that number larger through an adjustment that *subtracts* an additional $24 million.

Other long-term liabilities (adjustment C6). In general, long-term liabilities are included in the financing section of the statement of cash flows. Changes in these liabilities are caused by the issuance or retirement of bonds, the borrowing and repaying of loans, and so forth. There are a few long-term liabilities, however, that are related to operations. For Circle K, the other long-term liabilities account reflects Circle K's obligation to pay for future environmental cleanup costs, primarily relating to underground gasoline storage tanks. Each year, Circle K makes an estimate of the increase in expected future cleanup costs caused by operations during the year, and this amount is reported as an expense in the income statement. Because the other long-term liabilities account balance increased by the same amount as the expense for the year, we can infer that Circle K

A company's statement of cash flows must reflect the amount of cash paid for inventory during the year. Thus, in the computation of cash from operations, Reebok must reduce the cost of goods sold number to reflect that part of the inventory sold in the current period was actually purchased in the prior period.

made no cash payments during the year to reduce its cleanup cost obligation. As a result, an adjustment (C6) must be made reflecting the fact that the reported amount of operating and administrative expenses is actually greater than the cash paid for those expenses. In Exhibit 5-9. the adjustment is to *add* $109 million. A similar adjustment to operating cash flow would be made for other selected long-term liabilities such as pensions (related to wages expense) and deferred taxes (related to income tax expense).

Interest expense. Because an interest payable account does not exist, we can safely assume that all interest expense was paid for in cash. Therefore, there is no need for an adjustment. If there were an interest payable account, the reasoning used when analyzing the accounts payable account would apply.

Tax benefit (adjustment C7). The tax benefit amount requires an adjustment to reflect the amount of cash received during the period relating to a tax refund. Circle K reported a tax benefit of $62 million relating to its loss for the year. A portion of this benefit was received in cash and the remainder was used to reduce the taxes payable relating to prior periods—this is how the taxes payable account *declined* by $17 million. The amount of cash received can be computed as follows:

Tax benefit for the period	$62
Amount applied to reduce payable balance (from $41 to $24)	17
Cash received relating to taxes	$45

FYI: The method used to illustrate the analysis associated with the operating activities section is called the simultaneous approach. That is, we simultaneously assemble the information needed to present operating cash flow using both the indirect and direct methods. Other methods are available such as the T-account approach and the work sheet approach. These two methods are illustrated in the expanded material section of this chapter.

The direct and indirect methods. The final task in reporting cash flows from operations relates to preparing the operating activities section of the statement of cash flows. Two alternative reporting methods are available—the indirect method and the direct method.

The indirect method begins with net income as reported in the income statement and then details the adjustments needed to arrive at cash flow from operations. Continuing the Circle K illustration, the indirect method involves reporting the information shown in the shaded segment of the work sheet in Exhibit 5-10. The actual format of the operating activities section of the cash flow statement, using the indirect method, is shown in Exhibit 5-11.

EXHIBIT 5-10 | Operating Cash Flow Items Reported under the Indirect Method—Work Sheet

	Income Statement	Adjustments			Cash Flows from Operations
Sales	$3,737	C1.	−2	(increase in accounts receivable)	$3,748
		C2.	+13	(increase in unearned revenue)	
Cost of goods sold	(2,797)	C3.	+65	(decrease in inventory)	(2,755)
		C4.	−23	(decrease in accounts payable)	
Operating and administrative expenses	(881)	C5.	−24	(decrease in other current liabilities)	(796)
		C6.	+109	(increase in other long-term liabilities)	
Depreciation and amortization expense	(146)	A1.	+146	(not a cash flow item)	0
Interest expense	(134)		0	No adjustment	(134)
Restructuring charge	(614)	A2.	+614	(not a cash flow item)	0
Tax benefit	62	C7.	−17	(decrease in taxes payable)	45
Net loss	$ (773)		+881	net adjustment	$ 108

EXHIBIT 5-11 | Cash from Operating Activities: Indirect Method

Cash flows from operating activities:		
Net loss		$(773)
Adjustments:		
Add Depreciation and amortization expense	$146	
Add Restructuring charge	614	
Subtract Increase in accounts receivable	(2)	
Add Increase in unearned revenue	13	
Add Decrease in inventory	65	
Subtract Decrease in accounts payable	(23)	
Subtract Decrease in other current liabilities	(24)	
Add Increase in other long-term liabilities	109	
Subtract Decrease in taxes payable	(17)	881
Net cash provided by operating activities		$108

Because understanding the adjustments made under the indirect method requires some practice, it is useful at this point to review the rationale behind each addition and subtraction reported in Exhibit 5-11:

- *Add the amount of depreciation and amortization expense and the restructuring charge.*   These amounts are added back to net income because no cash flow was associated with these expenses in the current period.
- *Subtract the increase in Accounts Receivable.*   The accounts receivable account increases when customers purchase more on account and pay out less cash for what they buy. Thus, Circle K has less cash than it would have if all sales were collected in cash.
- *Add the increase in Unearned Revenue.*   Unearned Revenue goes up when customers pay for goods or services in advance. Thus, an increase in Unearned Revenue represents extra cash collected, over and above the sales amount.
- *Add the decrease in Inventory.* By allowing the Inventory amount to decrease, Circle K has conserved cash that otherwise would have been used to purchased inventory.
- *Subtract the decreases in Accounts Payable, Other Current Liabilities, and Taxes Payable.*   Circle K paid extra cash to reduce the balances in Accounts Payable and Other Current Liabilities. The taxes payable account decreased because Circle K used some of the cash from its tax refund to pay down this liability.
- *Add the increase in Other Long-Term Liabilities.*   This liability increased because Circle K conserved its cash by not paying out any cash during the period to satisfy its long-term environmental cleanup obligation.

The direct method involves simply reporting the information contained in the last column of the adjustment work sheet, shown as the shaded portion in Exhibit 5-12. The resulting operating activities section is given in Exhibit 5-13.

Some rules of thumb for the indirect method.   Because the indirect method is the more commonly used of the two methods, and because the adjustments required under the indirect method are sometimes hard to understand, we outline below some simple rules to aid in your understanding.

Item	Direction of Change	Necessary Adjustment
Current asset	Increase	Subtract the increase
Current asset	Decrease	Add the decrease
Current liability	Increase	Add the increase
Current liability	Decrease	Subtract the decrease

EXHIBIT 5–12 | Operating Cash Flow Items Reported under the Direct Method

	Income Statement	Adjustments			Cash Flows from Operations
Sales	$3,737	C1.	−2	(increase in accounts receivable)	$3,748
		C2.	+13	(increase in unearned revenue)	
Cost of goods sold	(2,797)	C3.	+65	(decrease in inventory)	(2,755)
		C4.	−23	(decrease in accounts payable)	
Operating and administrative expenses	(881)	C5.	−24	(decrease in other current liabilities)	(796)
		C6.	+109	(increase in other long-term liabilities)	
Depreciation and amortization expense	(146)	A1.	+146	(not a cash flow item)	0
Interest expense	(134)		0	No adjustment	(134)
Restructuring charge	(614)	A2.	+614	(not a cash flow item)	0
Tax benefit	62	C7.	−17	(decrease in taxes payable)	45
Net loss	$ (773)		+881	net adjustment	$ 108

EXHIBIT 5–13 | Cash from Operating Activities: Direct Method

Cash flows from operating activities:	
Collections from customers	$3,748
Payments for inventory	(2,755)
Payments for operating and administrative expenses	(796)
Payments for interest	(134)
Cash received from tax refund	45
Net cash provided by operating activities	$ 108

More important than memorizing whether an increase is added or subtracted is understanding the business rationale for doing so. When a current asset increases, cash that otherwise would have been available for buying equipment or paying dividends is tied up in the form of that current asset. Thus, the current asset increase means a decrease in the cash generated by operations. As an example, an Accounts Receivable increase during the year means that cash that could be used for other purposes has not yet been collected from customers. On the other hand, an Accounts Receivable decrease means that, in addition to collecting all the cash from sales during the period, the business has also collected enough extra cash to reduce the outstanding balance in Accounts Receivable. In short, current assets represent cash tied up in noncash form; an increase in current assets means more cash tied up and a decrease means cash has been freed for other purposes.

In the case of current liabilities, an increase means that more cash is available to the business because the cash was not used to pay the liability. For example, an increase in Accounts Payable means that the amount of cash used to pay suppliers was less than the amount of purchases made during the period. This results in an increase in cash from operations because there is more cash available to be used for other purposes within the business. A decrease in Accounts Payable means that extra cash was paid to reduce the balance in the liability account; this extra cash is therefore not available for other uses in the business and represents a decrease in the cash generated by operating activities.

STEP 3. ANALYZE THE LONG-TERM ASSETS TO IDENTIFY THE CASH FLOW EFFECTS OF INVESTING ACTIVITIES. For example, Circle K reports three long-term asset accounts.

- Property, plant, and equipment (PP&E)
- Long-term receivable
- Goodwill

We will analyze each of these in turn to determine how much cash flow was associated with each during 1990.

The balance in Circle K's PP&E account decreased by $236 million during 1990. In the absence of any other information, this decrease would suggest that Circle K disposed of PP&E originally costing $236 million. In this case, additional information is available in the notes to Circle K's financial statements. Specifically, the notes tell us that PP&E costing $25 million was sold during the year for $7 million in cash; this amount is a cash inflow from investing activities. In addition, the recorded amount of PP&E was reduced by $313 million as part of the restructuring charge. When this information is combined with the fact that the beginning balance in PP&E was $1,558 million, we can make the following computation.

	Beginning PP&E	$1,558
−	PP&E sold during the year	(25)
−	PP&E reduction from restructuring	(313)
=	Ending PP&E *without* purchase of new PP&E	$1,220

The actual ending balance sheet for Circle K reports a PP&E balance of $1,322 million. We can therefore infer that Circle K purchased PP&E of $102 million ($1,322 − $1,220) to account for the difference. This $102 million purchase of PP&E represents cash used for investing activities.

The long-term receivable account was reduced by $20 million during the year, indicating that cash was collected in that amount. This represents a cash inflow from investing activities.

Finally, the goodwill account began the year with a $332 million balance and ended with a $0 balance. This dramatic decrease is accounted for as follows:

	Beginning Goodwill	$332
−	Goodwill amortization recognized during the year	(31)
−	Goodwill written off as part of the restructuring	(301)
=	Ending Goodwill	$0

Thus, there were no investing cash flow implications for the change in the Goodwill balance because no transactions creating new goodwill were completed during the year and the entire change in the Goodwill balance is explained by the two indicated items, which were discussed earlier.

The investing activities section of the statement of cash flows for Circle K is:

Cash flows from investing activities:	
Sold equipment	$ 7
Collections on long-term receivable	20
Purchased equipment	(102)
Net cash used by investing activities	$ (75)

This investing activities section, which we just prepared using balance sheet, income statement, and financial statement note information, would be identical to the one prepared earlier using the detailed cash transaction data. With a solid understanding of accounting, we can infer the cash flow effects of transactions without having access to all the details.

STEP 4. ANALYZE THE LONG-TERM DEBT AND STOCKHOLDERS' EQUITY ACCOUNTS TO DETERMINE THE CASH FLOW EFFECTS OF ANY FINANCING TRANSACTIONS.   Long-term debt accounts increase when a company borrows more money—an inflow of cash—and decrease when the company pays back the debt—an outflow of cash. In the case of Circle K, we observe that the company's long-term debt account (combining both the current and long-term portions) declined from $1,249 million ($91 + $1,158) to $54 million ($54 + $0) during 1990. Under normal circumstances, a decrease such as this would indicate the use of $1,195 million ($1,249 – $54) in cash to repay long-term debt.

The year 1990 was not a year of "normal circumstances" for Circle K. In fact, from the notes to Circle K's financial statements, it can be learned that only $59 million in long-term debt was repaid during the year. The large decrease in long-term debt resulted from Circle K's reclassifying $1,182 million of its long-term debt ($91 million current portion and $1,091 long-term portion) under the heading "Liabilities Subject to Compromise." This euphemistic title is associated with Circle K's bankruptcy filing, labeling this amount as being in question as to whether it will ever be repaid because of Circle K's financial difficulties. For purposes of the cash flow statement, this reclassification had no cash flow effect. With this information, we can compute the amount of cash acquired through new long-term borrowing during the year.

	Beginning Long-Term Debt (current + long-term)	$1,249
–	Reclassification of Long-Term Debt	(1,182)
–	Repayments	(59)
=	Ending Long-Term Debt *without* new borrowing	$ 8

Again, the actual ending balance in Long-Term Debt is $54 million; therefore, we can infer that Circle K borrowed an additional $46 million ($54 – $8) during 1990. This $46 million in new borrowing represents cash provided by financing activities.

As discussed earlier in the chapter, the $1 million increase in Circle K's common stock account during the year represents a cash inflow from the issuance of new shares of stock. This cash inflow is reported as part of cash from financing activities.

When companies repurchase some of their own common stock during the year, the price paid to repurchase the stock is shown as a reduction in stockholders' equity and is usually labeled "treasury stock." Thus, an increase in the treasury stock account would reflect a cash repurchase of the company's own shares. Circle K did not repurchase any of its own stock during 1990, and for good reason—imagine how creditors would have felt if Circle K had been using cash for stock repurchases instead of debt repayment on the eve of a bankruptcy declaration. To see an example of how a stock repurchase is reported in the cash flow statement, refer to DISNEY's cash flow statement in Appendix A: $30 million in cash was used to repurchase Disney shares, significantly lower than the $633 million in cash used to repurchase shares in 1997.

The retained earnings account increases from the recognition of net income (an operating activity), decreases as a result of net losses (also an operating activity), and decreases through the payment of dividends (a financing activity). In the absence of detailed information, it is possible to infer the amount of dividends paid by identifying the unexplained change in the retained earnings account balance. For Circle K, the computation is:

FYI: Companies will go to great lengths to continue making their dividend payments to shareholders. Thus, just nine months before declaring bankruptcy, Circle K still made its regular quarterly dividend payment during the first quarter of fiscal 1990.

	Beginning Retained Earnings	$137
–	Net loss for the year	(773)
=	Ending Retained Earnings *without* dividend payments	$(636)

The actual ending balance in Retained Earnings is a negative $644 million, or $(644). Thus, it appears that Circle K paid dividends of $8 million during 1990, a cash outflow from financing activities. Of course, it is usually the case that the amount of dividends paid is disclosed somewhere in the financial statements. However, you never know the level of detailed information to which you will have access. And, after all, it is a relatively simple (and fun!) analytical exercise.

The following information summarizes the cash flow effects of Circle K's financing activities during 1990.

Cash flows from financing activities:	
Issued stock	$ 1
Borrowed long-term debt	46
Paid dividends	(8)
Paid long-term debt	(59)
Net cash used by financing activities	$(20)

Again, and not surprisingly, this section of Circle K's statement of cash flows would be identical to the one prepared using the detailed cash information. Hopefully, you are convinced that if one knows enough about accounting, one can conduct some powerful analyses using very limited information.

STEP 5. PREPARE A FORMAL STATEMENT OF CASH FLOWS.   Based on our analyses of the income statement and balance sheet accounts, we have identified all inflows and outflows of cash for Circle K for 1990, and we have categorized those cash flows based on the type of activity. The resulting statement of cash flows (prepared using the indirect method, which is what Circle K actually used) is shown in Exhibit 5-14.

The FASB's decision to classify interest paid as part of operating activities was a controversial one. In fact, many users do not consider cash paid for either interest or income taxes to be part of operating cash flow. As a compromise, the FASB requires companies to separately disclose the amount of cash paid for interest and for income taxes during the year. This allows users to recast and reclassify the reported cash flow numbers into the format they think is most useful. When the direct method is used, the amounts of cash paid for interest and for income taxes are part of the operating activities section, so no additional disclosure is needed. When the indirect method is used, as in Exhibit 5-14, these amounts must be shown separately, either at the bottom of the cash flow statement, or in an accompanying note. For example, MCDONALD'S uses the indirect method and discloses separately at the bottom of its statement of cash flows that $407 million and $546 million were paid in 1998 for interest and taxes, respectively.

Remember, if one has access to the details of the cash account, a statement of cash flows can be easily prepared. Also, if operating cash flow is reported using the direct method, the cash flow statement can be easily understood. However, it is likely that at some point you will need to construct a cash flow statement using summary balance sheet and income statement data. In addition, most cash flow statements that you encounter will use the indirect method. The adjustments required to compute cash flow numbers can be confusing if one has no understanding of the "why" behind the adjustments. This section has covered the "gory" details of preparing a statement of cash flows to help you gain an understanding of why the adjustments are made.

STEP 6. PREPARE SUPPLEMENTAL DISCLOSURE.   Three categories of supplemental disclosure are associated with the statement of cash flows. These are:

- Cash paid for interest and income taxes
- Reconciliation schedule
- Noncash investing and financing activities

Cash paid for interest and income taxes.   As mentioned previously, FASB Statement No. 95 requires separate disclosure of the cash paid for interest and for income taxes during the year. When the direct method is used, the amounts of cash paid for inter-

EXHIBIT 5 – 14 | Statement of Cash Flows for Circle K for Fiscal 1990

Circle K
Statement of Cash Flows (Adapted)
For the Year Ended April 30, 1990

Cash flows from operating activities:		
Net loss		$(773)
Adjustments:		
Add Depreciation and amortization expense	$146	
Add Restructuring charge	614	
Subtract Increase in accounts receivable	(2)	
Add Increase in unearned revenue	13	
Add Decrease in inventory	65	
Subtract Decrease in accounts payable	(23)	
Subtract Decrease in other current liabilities	(24)	
Add Increase in other long-term liabilities	109	
Subtract Decrease in taxes payable	(17)	881
Net cash provided by operating activities		$ 108
Cash flows from investing activities:		
Sold equipment	$ 7	
Collections on long-term receivable	20	
Purchased equipment	(102)	
Net cash used by investing activities		(75)
Cash flows from financing activities:		
Issued stock	$ 1	
Borrowed long-term debt	46	
Paid dividends	(8)	
Paid long-term debt	(59)	
Net cash used by financing activities		(20)
Net increase in cash		$ 13
Beginning cash balance		38
Ending cash balance		$ 51

est and for income taxes are part of the operating activities section, so no additional disclosure is needed. When the indirect method is used, these amounts must be shown separately, either at the bottom of the cash flow statement, or in an accompanying note. In the case of Circle K, the supplemental information might be presented as:

Supplemental Disclosure:	
Cash paid for interest	$ 134,000
Cash received from tax refund	45,000

Reconciliation schedule. An important aspect of the indirect method is that it highlights the differences between net income and cash from operations. This comparison is absent when the direct method is used. The FASB concluded that this comparison is of such value to financial statement users that when the direct method is used, a schedule should be included that reconciles net income to cash from operations. Fortunately, we don't have to learn anything new because the schedule is the same as the operating activities section prepared using the indirect method (the middle column in our work

► BACKGROUND OF FASB STATEMENT NO. 95

The FASB cash flow pronouncement, Statement No. 95, illustrates that the setting of accounting standards is not a science, but is a "balancing act" with the differing opinions of users and preparers being weighed against one another and the considerations of cost of implementation being weighed against the potential benefits. Because standard setting is a balancing act, not all interested parties will agree on the final outcome. In fact, three of the seven FASB members dissented to the final version of Statement No. 95.

One area of disagreement involved the categorization of interest and dividend cash flows. Three of the Board members felt that interest and dividends paid are a cost of obtaining financing and each should be classified as a cash outflow from financing activities. But, in Statement No. 95, dividend payments are included in the financing activities section, while interest payments are classified as cash outflows from operating activities. Similarly, the three Board members felt that interest and dividends received are returns on investments and therefore should be classified as cash inflows from investing activities. Statement No. 95 includes both these items in the operating activities section.

A more significant disagreement related to the permissibility of both the indirect and the direct methods of reporting cash flow from operations. Before the issuance of the statement, a majority of the outside comments to the Board advocated requiring use of the direct method. Most of these comments were from commercial lenders who indicated that detailed cash flow information by category would help them to better assess a firm's ability to repay borrowing. Those opposed to this direct method requirement, and who instead advocated the permissibility of both methods, were mainly preparers

sheets). So, when a company uses the direct method, in essence it provides both operating cash flow computations: the direct method in the body of the cash flow statement and the indirect method as a supplemental schedule. When the indirect method is used, no additional reconciliation schedule is necessary.

Noncash investing and financing activities. If Circle K had had any significant noncash transactions, such as purchasing property, plant, and equipment by issuing debt or in exchange for shares of stock, these transactions would have been disclosed in the notes to the financial statements. In 1990, Circle K's most significant noncash transaction was the reclassification of long-term debt into the category of "Liabilities subject to compromise." As an example of this type of transaction, consider the TIME WARNER acquisition of the TURNER BROADCASTING SYSTEMS (TBS) in 1996. Nothing about the $6.2 billion acquisition appears in Time Warner's 1996 statement of cash flows. However, supplemental disclosure reveals that, among other things, 179.8 million shares of Time Warner stock were given to TBS shareholders as part of the acquisition price. The details of this significant noncash transaction are disclosed in the notes to Time Warner's financial statements.

Circle K purchased equipment for $102 million during fiscal 1990. In preparing the cash flow statement, we assumed that this $102 million was paid in cash. Consider how the statement of cash flows would differ if the equipment were purchased in exchange for the following:

- $52 million in cash.
- $30 million in long-term debt with the equipment as collateral.
- $20 million in Circle K stock.

Purchasing equipment in exchange for long-term debt and/or stock is an example of a significant noncash transaction. This kind of noncash transaction is not included in the body of the statement of cash flows but is disclosed separately. If Circle K actually did purchase the equipment for a combination of cash, debt, and stock, the investing and financing activities section of the cash flow statement would appear as follows:

and providers of financial statements. They argued that requiring use of the direct method would impose excessive implementation costs on some firms. They also argued that the indirect method provides more meaningful information because it is more similar to what has been used in the past. Statement No. 95 allows both methods, but does "encourage" use of the direct method.

The statement also describes major change in financial reporting as "an evolutionary process." Conceptual purity is balanced against feasibility and cost of implementation. While it is likely that the standards of cash flow reporting will be further improved in the future, Statement No. 95 represents a significant incremental improvement over prior practice.

QUESTIONS:

1. Interest and dividends paid are both costs of obtaining financing—interest is the cost of obtaining debt financing, and dividends are the cost of obtaining equity financing. Accordingly, some have advocated classifying both interest and dividends paid as cash outflows from financing activities. What arguments can you think of to support classifying interest paid as an operating cash outflow, as required by Statement No. 95?

2. Assume that you are a member of the FASB and that the Board is reconsidering the issue of whether both the direct and indirect methods should be allowed. What evidence would you look at to help you make your decision?

SOURCES:
Dennis R. Beresford, "The 'Balancing Act' in Setting Accounting Standards," *Accounting Horizons*, March 1988, pp. 1–7.
Statement of Financial Accounting Standards No. 95, "Statement of Cash Flows," Stamford, CT: Financial Accounting Standards Board, November 1987, pars. 88–90 and 106–121.

Circle K
Partial Statement of Cash Flows
For the Year Ended April 30, 1990

Cash flows from investing activities:		
Sold equipment	$ 7	
Collections on long-term receivable	20	
Purchased equipment	(52)	
Net cash used by investing activities		$ (25)
Cash flows from financing activities:		
Issued stock	$ 1	
Borrowed long-term debt	46	
Paid dividends	(8)	
Paid long-term debt	(59)	
Net cash used by financing activities		$ (20)
Supplemental Disclosure:		
Significant noncash transactions:		
Long-term debt issued in exchange for equipment		$30,000
Stock issued in exchange for equipment		20,000

Understand the differences among cash flow statements prepared according to U.S. GAAP, U.K. GAAP, and International Accounting Standards.

INTERNATIONAL CASH FLOW STATEMENTS

With the adoption of SFAS No. 95 in 1987, the FASB set the benchmark for cash flow reporting around the world. Before that time, cash flow reporting was either ignored or done using the antiquated "funds flow" approach. It wasn't until 1992 that the International Accounting Standards Committee (IASC) adopted a comparable cash flow standard, IAS 7. In this section, the provisions of IAS 7 are compared to those of SFAS No. 95. In addition, the United Kingdom's standard for cash flow reporting is also examined. As will be seen, the primary differences in cash flow reporting around the world relate to alternative classifications of selected cash transactions.

International Accounting Standard 7

IAS 7 closely matches the provisions of the U.S. cash flow reporting standard, with the primary difference being greater flexibility in classifying cash transactions as either operating, investing, or financing. The IASC opted to allow more company discretion in deciding how to classify items such as interest and dividends paid and received. Within the FASB, there was great debate about how these items should be classified, but the final version of SFAS No. 95 mandates that these items be classified as operating activities. The more flexible standard of the IASC is discussed below.

INTEREST AND DIVIDENDS RECEIVED   When SFAS No. 95 was adopted by the FASB in 1987, three of the seven Board members objected to the classification of interest and dividends received as operating activities. Those three Board members argued that interest and dividends received were investing activities since they represent returns on investments in debt and equity securities. Ultimately, the majority of the FASB decided that, because interest and dividends received are included in the computation of net income, they should be classified as operating activities. In IAS 7, the IASC acknowledges the merits of both sides of the philosophical debate over classifying interest and dividends received, as discussed earlier, and allows companies to classify them as either operating or investing activities.

INTEREST PAID   The same three FASB members also objected to the classification of interest paid as an operating activity. They contended that interest paid is the cost of obtaining financing and should be classified as a financing activity. Again, the majority of the FASB voted to classify interest paid as an operating activity because it is included in the computation of net income. The provisions of IAS 7 allow interest paid to be classified as either an operating activity or a financing activity; whichever classification is chosen, it should be applied on a consistent basis.

DIVIDENDS PAID   IAS 7 allows dividends paid to be classified as either a financing activity (as in the United States) or as an operating activity. The rationale for allowing dividend payments to be classified as operating activities is that this classification helps investors determine whether the operations of the business have the ability to generate enough cash to support the continued payment of dividends. This reasoning seems a little dubious and has led some to criticize IAS 7 of not being an effective accounting standard because it allows too much classification flexibility.

INCOME TAXES   According to IAS 7, the amount of income taxes paid should be reported as an operating activity, unless the income taxes can be specifically identified with a financing or investing activity. For example, if the disposal of equipment results in a gain on which income taxes are paid, those income taxes could be classified as a cash outflow from an investing activity. The FASB considered this approach and rejected it as being too complex and arbitrary and not worth the benefit that it might provide to financial statement users. No matter how income taxes are classified, IAS 7 requires separate disclosure of the total amount of income taxes paid for the period.

United Kingdom Cash Flow Standard—FRS I

The accounting standard setters in the United Kingdom first adopted a cash flow standard in 1991. In recognition of the fact that the cash flow statement has become an increasingly important addition to the set of primary financial statements, the U.K. Accounting Standards Board (ASB) revised its standard in 1996. The revised version of Financial Reporting Standard (FRS) 1 specifies eight different categories for classifying cash flow transactions and represents the most innovative and, probably, the most useful standard for cash flow reporting currently in existence in the world.

THE EIGHT CASH FLOW CATEGORIES   The eight cash flow categories specified in FRS 1 are as follows:

1. Operating activities
2. Returns on investments and servicing of finance
3. Taxation
4. Capital expenditure and financial investment
5. Acquisitions and disposals
6. Equity dividends paid
7. Management of liquid resources
8. Financing

The U.K. amount reported as cash from operating activities excludes items, such as interest and income taxes, that are included in the U.S. measure of operating cash flow but which are widely viewed as being nonoperating activities. As a result, the U.K. measure of "operating" cash flow is more precise than is the U.S. measure. For example, as described in the discussion of Statement No. 95, reasonable people can disagree about the classification of interest and dividends received and interest paid. In recognition of this fact, FRS 1 dictates that these items be reported in a separate category. Income taxes paid and dividends paid are also reported in their own separate categories. Finally, FRS 1 requires British companies to report an amount called "management of liquid resources," which summarizes the net amount of cash used to purchase and sell short-term investment securities—this amount would normally be included as part of operating activities in the United States.

net work exercise

Visit Diego's home page at (www.diageo.com).
Net Work:
1. In addition to the brand names mentioned in the text of the chapter, what other well-known brands does Diageo have?
2. Diageo prepares a Form 20-F, which is provided for the benefit of investors. Who requires that Diageo provide this Form 20-F?

EXAMPLE: DIAGEO   DIAGEO is a large British consumer products firm owning such brand names as Smirnoff, Johnnie Walker, J&B, Gordon's, Guinness, Pillsbury, Haagen-Dazs, and Burger King. Diageo's 1998 cash flow statement is reproduced in Exhibit 5-15. In addition to the eight cash flow categories listed above, Diageo also includes a separate category for dividends it has received from its associates (companies in which it has a significant but not a controlling interest). Also, Diageo reports two cash flow subtotals, titled "Free cash flow" and "Cash inflow before management of liquid resources and financing." The £1,415 million free cash flow subtotal tells financial statement users that this is the amount of excess cash generated by business operations, after paying for necessary capital expenditures. The second subtotal of £1,732 million is the amount of cash flow generated by Diageo before considering the actions of the corporate finance department in terms of external financing and management of short-term liquidity needs.

SUMMARY OF FRS 1   As seen in Diageo's cash flow statement, the provisions of FRS 1 require companies in the United Kingdom to provide a more detailed breakdown of the types of activities that create cash inflows and outflows than is required of U.S. companies. In terms of benefits to financial statement users, it appears that the focus on cash flow reporting that is required by FRS 1 makes the U.K. standard the premier cash flow standard in the world.

USING CASH FLOW DATA TO ASSESS FINANCIAL STRENGTH

7

Assess a firm's financial strength by analyzing the relationships among cash flows from operating, investing, and financing activities and by computing financial ratios based on cash flow data.

Various analytical techniques are used to assess a company's financial strength. Key variables are profitability, efficiency, leverage, and liquidity. By tradition, analysts have concentrated on the relationships captured in the income statement and the balance sheet. But more and more emphasis is now placed on cash flows and the relationships of data reported on the cash flow statement in conjunction with the income statement and the balance sheet.

EXHIBIT 5–15 | Statement of Cash Flows for Diageo for Fiscal 1998

Diageo
Consolidated Cash Flow Statement
For the 18-Month Period Ending 30 June 1998*
(In millions of £)

Operating activities:		
Operating profit	£2,168	
Exceptional operating costs	572	
Restructuring and integration payments	(230)	
Agreement with LVMH	(250)	
Merger transaction costs	(85)	
Acquisition and disposal provision payments	(77)	
Depreciation charge	484	
Increase in stocks	(54)	
Decrease in debtors	591	
Decrease in creditors and provisions	(36)	
Other items	(14)	
Net cash inflow from operating activities		£3,069
Dividends received from associates		162
Returns on investments and servicing of finance:		
Interest paid (net)	£ (435)	
Dividends paid to equity minority interests	(41)	(476)
Taxation		(834)
Capital expenditure and financial investment:		
Purchase of tangible fixed assets	£ (634)	
Sale of tangible fixed assets	128	(506)
Free cash flow		**£1,415**
Acquisitions and disposals:		
Purchase of subsidiaries	£ (66)	
Sale of subsidiaries and businesses	1,231	
Sale of associates	240	1,405
Equity dividends paid		(1,088)
Cash inflow before management of liquid resources and financing		**£1,732**
Management of liquid resources		(709)
Financing:		
Issue of share capital	£ 155	
Repurchase of shares	(2,970)	
Increase in borrowings excluding overdrafts	2,094	
Other financing inflow	75	(646)
Increase in cash in the period		£ 377

*Diageo's 1998 cash flow statement is for the 18-month period ended June 30, 1998. The predecessor companies of Diageo, Guinness, and Grand Metropolitan merged on December 17, 1997. The initial financial reports of the combined company covered an 18-month period in order to allow for the merger of the financial reporting systems of the predecessor companies, which had different fiscal reporting periods.

Cash Flow Patterns

It is possible to gain useful insights about a company by analyzing the relationships among the three cash flow categories. Exhibit 5–16 shows the eight different possible patterns. Patterns 1 and 8 are unusual. Pattern 1 might exist where a firm is experiencing positive cash flows from all three activities and is seeking to significantly increase its cash position for some strategic reason. Pattern 8 shows negative cash flows from all activities and could only exist, even in the short-term, if a company had existing cash reserves to draw upon. Patterns 2 through 4 show positive operating cash flows that are sufficient by themselves (pattern 2) or are supplemented by investing (pattern 3) or financing (pattern 4) activities to settle debt, pay owners, or expand the business. Patterns 5 through 7 are not healthy over the long term, because operating cash shortfalls have to be covered by selling long-term assets and/or by securing external financing.

EXHIBIT 5–16 | Analysis of Cash Flow Statement: Patterns

	CF from Operating	CF from Investing	CF from Financing	General Explanation
#1	+	+	+	Company is using cash generated from operations and from sale of assets and from financing to build up pile of cash—very liquid company—possibly looking for acquisition.
#2	+	–	–	Company is using cash flow generated from operations to buy fixed assets and to pay down debt or pay owners.
#3	+	+	–	Company is using cash from operations and from sale of fixed assets to pay down debt or pay owners.
#4	+	–	+	Company is using cash from operations and from borrowing (or from owner investment) to expand.
#5	–	+	+	Company's operating cash flow problems are covered by sale of fixed assets and by borrowing or by shareholder contributions.
#6	–	–	+	Company is growing rapidly but has shortfalls in cash flow from operations and from purchase of fixed assets financed by long-term debt or new investment.
#7	–	+	–	Company is financing operating cash flow shortages and payments to creditors and/or stockholders via sale of fixed assets.
#8	–	–	–	Company is using cash reserves to finance operation shortfall and pay long-term creditors and/or investors.

Source: Michael T. Dugan, Benton E. Gup, and William D. Samson, "Teaching the Statement of Cash Flows," *Journal of Accounting Education,* Vol. 9, 1991, p. 36.

FYI: Most courses in financial statement analysis still make only passing mention of cash flow ratios. Familiarity with the ratios discussed in this section is a quick and easy way to set yourself apart from the crowd.

These cash flow patterns stress the importance of operating cash flows. A positive operating cash flow allows a company to pay its bills, its creditors, and its shareholders and to grow and expand. A negative operating cash flow means a company has to look at other sources of cash, which eventually dry up if operations are not successful.

Cash Flow Ratios

Also, the data from a cash flow statement can be used to compute selected ratios that help determine a company's financial strength. If such ratios are compared for the same company over a period of time or with other companies in the same industry, they can be helpful in evaluating relative performance. To illustrate the computation of selected cash flow ratios, selected data from CIRCLE K's 1989 and 1988 financial statements (before Circle K's disastrous year in 1990) will be used (Exhibit 5–17).

EXHIBIT 5-17 | Selected Cash Flow Data for Circle K for 1988 and 1989

(In thousands of dollars)	1989	1988
Net income	$ 15,414	$ 60,411
Cash from operations	57,767	84,333
Cash paid for capital expenditures	193,338	233,087
Cash paid for acquisitions	68,139	147,500
Cash paid for interest	89,928	49,267
Cash paid for income taxes	11,233	28,439

CASH FLOW-TO-NET INCOME   Perhaps the most important cash flow relationship is the relationship between cash from operations and reported net income. **Cash flow-to-net income ratio** reflects the extent to which accrual accounting assumptions and adjustments have been included in computing net income. The formula is cash from operations divided by net income. For Circle K, computation of the cash flow-to-net income ratios is as follows:

	1989	1988
Cash from operations	$57,767	$84,333
Net income	÷15,414	÷60,411
Cash flow-to-net income ratio	3.75	1.40

In general, the cash flow-to-net income ratio will have a value greater than one because of the existence of significant noncash expenses (such as depreciation) that reduce reported net income but have no impact on cash flow. For a given company, the cash flow-to-net income ratio should remain fairly stable from year to year. A significant increase in the ratio, such as that reported by Circle K in 1989, indicates that accounting assumptions were instrumental in reducing reported net income. This ratio reveals that, from the standpoint of management concerned about being able to pay the bills and creditors concerned about timely repayment of loans, Circle K's performance in 1989 was actually somewhat better than indicated by just looking at net income. From the numbers reported earlier in the chapter, it is apparent that the same was true in 1990 when the reported net loss was $773 million but the cash generated by operations was $108 million.

CASH FLOW ADEQUACY   A "cash cow" is a business that is generating enough cash from operations to completely pay for all new plant and equipment purchases, with cash left over to repay loans or to distribute to investors. The **cash flow adequacy ratio,** computed as cash from operations divided by expenditures for fixed asset additions and acquisitions of new businesses, indicates whether a business is a "cash cow." Computation of the cash flow adequacy ratio for Circle K is as follows:

FYI: Cash paid for dividends is sometimes added to the denominator of the cash flow adequacy ratio. With this formulation, the ratio indicates whether operating cash flow is sufficient to pay for both capital additions and regular dividends to stockholders.

	1989	1988
Cash from operations	$ 57,767	$ 84,333
Cash paid for capital expenditures	$193,338	$233,087
Cash paid for acquisitions	68,139	147,500
Cash required for investing activities	261,477	380,587
Cash flow adequacy ratio	0.22	0.22

The calculations indicate that in both 1988 and 1989, Circle K's cash from operations fell well short of being able to pay for Circle K's expansion. This means that Circle K was forced to seek substantial amounts of external financing, either new debt or additional funds from investors, during both years.

CASH TIMES INTEREST EARNED   Because interest payments must be made with cash, an informative indicator of a company's interest-paying ability compares cash generated by operations to cash paid for interest. This **cash times interest earned ratio** is computed for Circle K as follows:

	1989	1988
Cash from operations	$ 57,767	$ 84,333
Cash paid for interest	89,928	49,267
Cash paid for income taxes	11,233	28,439
Cash before interest and taxes	$158,928	$162,039
Cash paid for interest	÷89,928	÷49,267
Cash times interest earned ratio	1.77	3.29

Pretax cash flow is used because interest is paid before any taxes are deducted. From this calculation, we can see that Circle K's creditors experienced a significant drop in security in 1989 because Circle K's operations generated only 1.77 times the amount of cash that was needed in order to make its required interest payments. Ultimately, the inability to continue making its interest payments forced Circle K into bankruptcy.[15]

Use knowledge of how the three primary financial statements tie together in order to prepare a forecasted statement of cash flows.

FORECASTED STATEMENT OF CASH FLOWS

The tools we developed and used in Chapter 4 for forecasting an income statement and a balance sheet are also useful in forecasting cash flows. In fact, we can prepare a forecasted statement of cash flows using the same data given in Chapter 4. Recall from Chapter 4 that we were provided with the 2002 balance sheet and income statement for the hypothetical Derrald Company. We then assumed that Derrald's sales would increase by 40% in 2003 and used our knowledge of the relationship among financial statement amounts, along with a few assumptions, to forecast an income statement and a balance sheet for Derrald for the year 2003. The resulting financial statements are reproduced in Exhibit 5–18.[16] Using the same six-step process for preparing a statement of cash flows that was described earlier in the chapter, we can use the data in Exhibit 5–18 to construct a forecasted statement of cash flows for Derrald Company for 2003.

15   For additional cash flow ratios, see Don E. Giacomino and David E. Mielke, "Cash Flows: Another Approach to Ratio Analysis," *Journal of Accountancy*, March 1993, p. 57.

16   In Chapter 4, accounts receivable and inventory were grouped under one heading, "other current assets," to simplify the analysis. These two accounts are shown separately here. In addition, "total stockholders' equity" has been split into its paid-in capital and retained earnings components.

EXHIBIT 5-18 | Forecasted Balance Sheet and Income Statement for Derrald Company

Balance Sheet	2002	2003 Forecasted	Basis for Forecast
Cash	$ 10	$ 14	40% natural increase
Accounts receivable	100	140	40% natural increase
Inventory	150	210	40% natural increase
Property, plant, and equipment, net	300	500	
Total assets	$ 560	$ 864	
Accounts payable	$ 100	$ 140	40% natural increase
Bank loans payable	300	524	
Paid-in capital	50	50	
Retained earnings	110	150	
Total liabilities and stockholders' equity ...	$ 560	$ 864	

Income Statement	2002	2003 Forecasted	Basis for Forecast
Sales	$1,000	$1,400	40% increase
Cost of goods sold	700	980	70% of sales, same as last year
Gross profit	$ 300	$ 420	
Depreciation expense	30	50	10% of PP&E, same as last year
Other operating expenses	170	238	17% of sales, same as last year
Operating profit	$ 100	$ 132	
Interest expense	30	52	10% of bank loan, same as last year
Income before taxes	$ 70	$ 80	
Income taxes	30	34	43% of pretax, same as last year
Net income	$ 40	$ 46	

STEP 1. COMPUTE THE CHANGE IN CASH. Cash is forecasted to increase by $4 ($14 – $10) from 2002 to 2003. Hence, we know that the sum of cash from operating, investing, and financing activities in the forecasted statement of cash flows must be $4.

STEP 2. CONVERT THE INCOME STATEMENT FROM AN ACCRUAL BASIS TO A CASH BASIS. Beginning with the forecasted income statement, the following adjustments are necessary.

	Income Statement	Adjustments	Cash Flows from Operations
Sales........................	$1,400	A. –40	$1,360
Cost of goods sold............	(980)	B. –60	(1,000)
		C. +40	
Depreciation expense..........	(50)	D. +50	0
Other operating expenses......	(238)	E. 0	(238)
Interest expense..............	(52)	F. 0	(52)
Income taxes.................	(34)	G. 0	(34)
Net income	$ 46		$ 36

Adjustment A. Accounts Receivable is forecasted to increase by $40 ($140 – $100) during 2003, indicating that more sales will be made during the year than will be collected in cash. To compute cash collected from customers, sales must be reduced by the amount of the $40 forecasted increase in Accounts Receivable.

Adjustment B. Inventory is forecasted to increase by $60 ($210 – $150), indicating that more inventory will be purchased than will be sold. This $60 Inventory increase represents an additional cash outflow.

Adjustment C. Accounts Payable is forecasted to increase by $40 ($140 – $100), signifying that not all inventory that will be purchased on account during 2003 will be paid for during 2003. Thus, Accounts Payable increase represents a cash savings.

Adjustment D. Forecasted depreciation expense of $50 does not involve cash and must be added back in computing cash from operating activities.

Adjustments E through G. For this example, we are assuming that the accounts payable account relates strictly to the purchase of inventory and that all other expenses involving the outflow of cash are paid for immediately. As a result, there are no payable accounts relating to other operating expenses, interest, or taxes. If payable accounts relating to these expenses were to exist, the analysis would be similar to that conducted for Accounts Payable—increases would be added (indicating a cash savings by allowing the payable to increase) and decreases would be subtracted (indicating an additional outflow of cash to reduce the payable balance).

The resulting operating section of the forecasted statement of cash flows indicates that Derrald Company will generate $36 from operations in 2003.

STEP 3.   ANALYZE THE LONG-TERM ASSET ACCOUNTS.   The only long-term asset account is Property, Plant, and Equipment (PP&E). PP&E is forecasted to increase from $300 to $500 in 2003. Note that the PP&E amount is reported "net," meaning that accumulated depreciation is subtracted from the reported PP&E amount rather than being shown as a separate amount. As result, the "net" PP&E amount can be affected by any of three events: purchase of new PP&E (an addition), sale of old PP&E (a subtraction), and depreciation of existing PP&E (a subtraction). Using the forecasted information, and assuming that no old PP&E will be sold during 2003, we can conclude the following.

	Beginning PP&E	$300
–	PP&E to be sold during the year	0
–	PP&E depreciation	(50)
=	Ending PP&E *without* purchase of new PP&E	$250

The fact that the projected ending PP&E balance is $500 implies that Derrald Company expects to purchase $250 ($500 – $250) in new PP&E during 2003. This $250 forecasted purchase represents cash to be used for investing activities.

STEP 4.   ANALYZE THE LONG-TERM DEBT AND STOCKHOLDERS' EQUITY ACCOUNTS.   Bank loans payable account is projected to increase from $300 to $524. This difference of $224 represents a cash inflow from financing. Because Paid-In Capital is projected to remain at $50, Derrald Company is not expecting to raise any new cash by issuing shares of stock during 2003.

The $40 ($150 – $110) projected increase in Retained Earnings must be analyzed in light of expected net income for 2003. Because Derrald Company is expected to have net income of $46 in 2003, it must also be expecting to pay dividends of $6 to result in the net increase in retained earnings of $40. The $6 forecasted dividend payment is reported as a cash outflow from financing activities.

STEP 5.   PREPARE THE STATEMENT OF CASH FLOWS.   All the information necessary to prepare the forecasted statement of cash flows is now assembled. The forecasted statement is shown in Exhibit 5–19, with forecasted operating cash flows being

EXHIBIT 5–19 | Forecasted Statement of Cash Flows for Derrald Company for 2003

**Derrald Company
Forecasted Statement of Cash Flows
For the Year Ended December 31, 2003**

Cash flows from operating activities:		
Net income		$ 46
Adjustments:		
Add depreciation	$ 50	
Increase in accounts receivable	(40)	
Increase in inventory	(60)	
Increase in accounts payable	40	
		(10)
Net cash provided by operating activities		$ 36
Cash flows from investing activities:		
Purchased	$(250)	
Net cash used in investing activities		(250)
Cash flows from financing activities:		
Borrowed (bank loan payable)	$224	
Paid dividends	(6)	
Net cash provided by financing activities		218
Net increase in cash		$ 4
Beginning cash balance		10
Ending cash balance		$ 14

reported using the indirect method. Note that the sum of the forecasted operating, investing, and financing cash flows ($36 – $250 + $218) is equal to the total forecasted change in cash of $4.

STEP 6.   DISCLOSE ANY SIGNIFICANT NONCASH ACTIVITIES.   Derrald Company does not anticipate any significant noncash activities during 2003, so the forecasted cash flow statement completely summarizes the important events that are expected to occur.

From the forecasted cash flow statement, we can see that Derrald's expected operating cash flow will not be anywhere near enough to pay for the additional PP&E Derrald expects to acquire during 2003. As a result, Derrald plans to make up the shortfall with a significant $224 increase in its bank loan payable account. When used internally, the projected statement of cash flows allows Derrald Company to plan ahead—Derrald can start investigating the likelihood of obtaining such a large new loan. Alternatively, Derrald may consider scaling back the expansion plans if obtaining the required financing doesn't appear feasible. An external user, such as a bank, can use the forecasted cash flow statement to see whether it seems likely that Derrald can continue to meet its existing obligations. An investor can use the projected cash flow statement to evaluate the likelihood that Derrald will be able to continue making dividend payments. In summary, construction of a full set of projected financial statements—a balance sheet, an income statement, and a statement of cash flows—allows the financial statement user to see whether a company's strategic plans concerning operating, investing, and financing activities are consistent with one another.

EXPANDED MATERIAL

Relax for a moment because you have a decision to make. The chapter illustrations presented thus far cover all the concepts you need to know for now. Cash flow complications relating to leases, bad debts, deferred taxes, and so forth, are treated in subsequent chapters as those topics are covered. The important point is that no new concepts are covered in this expanded material section. What the section does contain is a long cash flow example illustrating numerous different methods for analyzing financial statements to prepare a statement of cash flows when performing analyses with many accounts and adjustments. End-of-chapter problems that have solutions using these methods are marked as such. So, you decide—work through different methods, for example the T-account and work sheet approaches, now or go straight to the end-of-chapter summary.

9

Use a T-account or work sheet approach to prepare a statement of cash flows.

COMPREHENSIVE ILLUSTRATION OF STATEMENT OF CASH FLOWS

Examples in the preceding sections involved only a few accounts and were thus relatively simple. Ordinarily, however, more complex circumstances are encountered. In the pages that follow, we will examine a more complex example using several techniques. First, we will illustrate the simultaneous method described previously for preparing the operating activities section. Next, a comprehensive T-account approach for use with the indirect method is described. Preparing a statement of cash flows using a work sheet approach is then illustrated.

The illustrations and analyses that follow are based on the combined income and retained earnings statement and comparative balance sheet for Western Resources, Inc.

Western Resources, Inc.
Statement of Income and Retained Earnings
For the Year Ended December 31, 2002

Sales		$753,800
Cost of goods sold		524,100
Gross margin		$229,700
Expenses:		
Selling and general expenses	$146,400	
Depreciation and amortization expense	25,900	
Interest expense	3,600	175,900
Operating income		$ 53,800
Gain on sale of long-term investment		6,500
Income before income taxes		$ 60,300
Income tax expense		24,000
Net income		$ 36,300
Retained earnings, December 31, 2001		234,300
		$270,600
Cash dividends		25,100
Retained earnings, December 31, 2002		$245,500

Western Resources, Inc.
Comparative Balance Sheet
December 31, 2002 and 2001

	2002	2001
Assets		
Current assets		
Cash and cash equivalents	$ 46,300	$ 55,000
Available-for-sale securities	12,000	10,000
Accounts receivable	60,000	70,500
Inventories	75,000	76,500
Prepaid operating expenses	16,500	12,000
Total current assets	$209,800	$224,000
Investments (at cost)	$ 10,000	$106,000
Land, buildings, and equipment:		
Land	$183,500	$ 75,000
Buildings	290,000	225,000
Less: Accumulated depreciation	(130,600)	(155,000)
Machinery and equipment	132,000	120,000
Less: Accumulated depreciation	(58,800)	(43,500)
Total land, buildings, and equipment	$416,100	$221,500
Patents	$ 35,000	$ 40,000
Total assets	$670,900	$591,500
Liabilities		
Current liabilities		
Accounts payable	$ 91,000	$ 97,700
Income taxes payable	10,000	9,500
Dividends payable	4,400	—
Total current liabilities	$105,400	$107,200
Bonds payable	30,000	—
Total liabilities	$135,400	$107,200
Stockholders' Equity		
Common stock	$290,000	$250,000
Retained earnings	245,500	234,300
Total stockholders' equity	$535,500	$484,300
Total liabilities and stockholders' equity	$670,900	$591,500

Additional information:

- Securities that are classified as available-for-sale were purchased during the year at a cost of $2,000.
- A tornado totally destroyed a building costing $40,000 with a book value of $10,000. The insurance company paid $10,000 cash; a new building was then constructed at a cost of $105,000. Payment was made in cash.
- Long-term investments costing $96,000 were sold for $102,500.
- Land was acquired for $108,500, the seller accepting in payment $40,000 of common stock and $68,500 in cash.
- New machinery was purchased for $12,000 cash.
- The amortization of patent cost and depreciation expense on buildings and equipment were recorded as follows:

Depreciation—buildings	$ 5,600
Depreciation—machinery and equipment	15,300
Amortization—patents	5,000
Total depreciation and amortization	$25,900

- Ten-year bonds were sold at their face value of $30,000 at the beginning of the year.

Simultaneous Approach to Preparing the Operating Activities Section of the Statement of Cash Flows

As illustrated previously, we begin our analysis of operating activities with the income statement and adjust for noncash items, nonoperating activity items, and accrual items. This analysis is contained in Exhibit 5-20.

EXHIBIT 5-20 | Adjustments to Convert Western Resources' Accrual Net Income into Cash from Operations

	Income Statement	Adjustments		Cash Flows from Operations
Sales	$753,800	+10,500	(decrease in accounts receivable)	$764,300
Cost of goods sold	(524,100)	+1,500	(decrease in inventory)	
		−6,700	(decrease in accounts payable)	(529,300)
Selling and general expenses	(146,400)	−4,500	(increase in prepaid operating expense)	(150,900)
Depreciation expense	(20,900)	+20,900	(not a cash flow item)	0
Amortization expense	(5,000)	+5,000	(not a cash flow item)	0
Interest expense	(3,600)	0	No adjustment	(3,600)
Gain on sale of long-term investment	6,500	−6,500	(not an operating activity)	0
Income tax expense	(24,000)	+500	(increase in income taxes payable)	(23,500)
Net income	$ 36,300	20,700	net adjustment	$ 57,000

Each of the adjustments will be reviewed beginning with the adjustment to sales.

- Decrease in Accounts Receivable—To arrive at cash collected from customers, sales must be increased for the decrease in Accounts Receivable because that decrease reflects the fact that more cash was collected *this* period than was recorded in the sales account.
- Decrease in Inventories—The $1,500 decrease in inventories means that more inventory was sold this year than was purchased. The cash related to that purchase was expended *last* year—not this year.
- Decrease in Accounts Payable—Accounts Payable declines when we pay for more than we purchase during a period. Thus, purchases made *last* year are paid for this year. This $6,700 adjustment reflects that cash outflows for the period relating to Accounts Payable exceed the purchases made on account.
- Increase in Prepaid Operating Expense—An increase in Prepaid Operating Expense indicates that an asset was purchased *this* year to be used in future periods. This increase reflects a cash outflow.
- Depreciation and Amortization Expenses—Both of these items are expenses that do not involve the outflow of cash *this* period. The cash associated with these items was incurred when the land, buildings, and equipment and the patents were purchased.
- Gain on Sale—The sale of the long-term investments resulted in a cash flow this period. However, that cash flow is an investing activity. Thus, its effect must be removed from the operating activities section and reported in the investing activities section. The effect is removed through subtraction because the gain was initially added in computing net income.
- Increase in Income Taxes Payable—Income Taxes Payable increased during the period, representing the fact that expenses incurred this period will be paid for *next* period. The expense amount must be reduced to reflect the actual cash outflow for taxes this period.

With these adjustments to the income statement, we can now present the operating activities section of the statement of cash flows using either the direct or indirect methods. The indirect method would involve beginning with net income and adding or subtracting the adjustments (in the third column of the matrix) to arrive at cash flow from operations of $57,000. The direct method would simply detail the figures presented in the fourth column of the matrix. The formal cash flow statement, using the indirect method, is shown later in this section.

T-Account Approach to Preparing a Statement of Cash Flows—Indirect Method

With a comprehensive T-account approach, special "cash flow" T-accounts are established. These accounts are used to summarize cash flows from operations and from investing and financing activities during the period. They provide the basis for preparing the formal cash flow statement. Individual T-accounts are also established for Cash and all other balance sheet accounts.

During the process of analysis, the change in each account is explained as providing or using cash. In the three T-accounts summarizing cash flows from operating, investing, and financing activities, a debit represents an increase in cash, while a credit reflects a decrease. Once the changes in all balance sheet accounts have been reconciled and the cash flow T-accounts balanced, the formal cash flow statement can be prepared.

In preparing a cash flow statement for Western Resources, Inc., we begin by determining the change in the cash balance, in this case an $8,700 decrease. All noncash accounts may now be analyzed using the T-accounts illustrated on pages 268 and 269. As noted, the cash flow statement is prepared directly from the cash flow T-accounts and is illustrated following those T-accounts.

Generally, the most efficient approach to developing T-accounts for a statement of cash flows is to begin with an analysis of the change in Retained Earnings. After the change in Retained Earnings has been accounted for, the remaining noncash accounts should be reviewed in conjunction with the income statement and supplementary information to determine what additional adjustments are required. Operating income should be adjusted to determine the actual amount of cash provided or used by operations [items (e), (i), (j), and (l) – (p)]. Analysis must also be made to determine all other cash flows from investing and financing activities [items (b), (c), (d), (e), (f), (h), (k), and (q)] and to reflect significant investing and financing activities that have no effect on cash [item (g)].

Explanations for individual adjustments for Western Resources, Inc., follow. The letter preceding each explanation corresponds with that used in the T-accounts, which are presented on pages 268 and 269. Entries are presented to help explain the preparation of a statement of cash flows. They are *not* journal entries that would be recorded in the accounting records.

(a) Net income is recorded in the T-accounts as follows:

Cash Flows—Operating	36,300	
Retained Earnings		36,300

(b) The cash dividends declared and deducted from retained earnings are adjusted for the change in the dividends payable balance in arriving at the amount of dividends actually paid during the year. The entry would be:

Retained Earnings	25,100	
Dividends Payable		4,400
Cash Flows—Financing		20,700

(c) The destruction of the building and the subsequent insurance reimbursement have the effect of providing cash of $10,000, the proceeds from the insurance company. The entry would be:

Accumulated Depreciation—Buildings	30,000	
Cash Flows—Investing	10,000	
Buildings		40,000

(d) The buildings account was increased by the cost of constructing a new building, $105,000. The cost of the new building is reported separately as an investment of cash by the following entry:

| Buildings | 105,000 | |
| Cash Flows—Investing | | 105,000 |

(e) The sale of long-term investments was recorded by a credit to the asset account at cost, $96,000, and a credit to a gain on sale of investment account. At the end of the period, the gain account was closed to Retained Earnings as part of income from continuing operations. Because the effect of the sale was to provide cash of $102,500, this amount is reported as cash provided by investing activities. The investments account balance is reduced, and cash provided by operations is decreased by the amount of the gain. The following adjustment is made:

Cash Flows—Investing	102,500	
Investments		96,000
Cash Flows—Operating		6,500

(f) and (g) Land was acquired at a price of $108,500; payment was made in common stock valued at $40,000 and cash of $68,500. Two separate entries are made to segregate the cash and noncash components of this transaction:

(f) Land	68,500	
Cash Flows—Investing		68,500
(g) Land	40,000	
Common Stock		40,000

The issuance of common stock for land has no effect on cash, but it is a significant transaction that should be disclosed separately. Recall that the body of the cash flow statement reports only transactions affecting cash, in accordance with FASB Statement No. 95.

(h) Machinery costing $12,000 was acquired during the year. Payment was made in cash and is reported as cash used for investing purposes. The adjustment for the acquisition of machinery is:

| Machinery and Equipment | 12,000 | |
| Cash Flows—Investing | | 12,000 |

(i) and (j) The changes in the accumulated depreciation accounts and in the patents account result from the recognition of depreciation and amortization expenses for the period. These noncash expenses are added in computing cash flows from operations by the following adjustments:

(i) Cash Flows—Operating	20,900	
Accumulated Depreciation—Buildings		5,600
Accumulated Depreciation—Machinery and Equipment		15,300
(j) Cash Flows—Operating	5,000	
Patents		5,000

(k) During the year, bonds were issued at their face value of $30,000. The entry is:

| Cash Flows—Financing | 30,000 | |
| Bonds Payable | | 30,000 |

(l)–(p) In preparing a cash flow statement, operating income must be adjusted from an accrual basis to a cash basis, as explained earlier in the chapter. The entries (l) through (p) reflect that analysis for Western Resources, Inc.:

(l) Cash Flows—Operating	10,500	
Accounts Receivable		10,500
(m) Cash Flows—Operating	1,500	
Inventories		1,500
(n) Prepaid Operating Expenses	4,500	
Cash Flows—Operating		4,500
(o) Accounts Payable	6,700	
Cash Flows—Operating		6,700
(p) Cash Flows—Operating	500	
Income Taxes Payable		500

(q) As noted earlier in the chapter, available-for-sale securities are treated differently from other current assets in preparing a cash flow statement. The adjustment to reflect the purchase of $2,000 of available-for-sale securities would be:

Available-for-Sale Securities	2,000	
Cash Flows—Investing		2,000

(r) After all changes in account balances have been reconciled and the effects of the changes on cash flow have been recorded in the cash flows T-accounts, the balances of those T-accounts are determined and transferred to a Cash Flows Summary T-account as shown below. The excess of credits (decreases in cash) over debits (increases in cash) is equal to the net change in the cash balance for the period of $8,700. The following entry is made to reflect the net decrease in cash:

Net Decrease in Cash	8,700	
Cash		8,700

Cash Flows—Operating

(a)	36,300	(e)	6,500
(i)	20,900	(n)	4,500
(j)	5,000	(o)	6,700
(l)	10,500		
(m)	1,500		
(p)	500		

Net cash provided by operating activities   57,000

Cash Flows—Investing

(c)	10,000	(d)	105,000
(e)	102,500	(f)	68,500
		(h)	12,000
		(q)	2,000

Net cash used in investing activities   75,000

Cash Flows—Financing

(k)	30,000	(b)	20,700

Net cash provided by financing activities   9,300

Cash Flows Summary

Net cash provided—operating	57,000		75,000
Net cash used—investing			
Net cash provided—financing	9,300		
Net decrease in cash	(r) 8,700		
	75,000		75,000

Cash and Cash Equivalents

Beg. bal.	55,000	(r)	8,700
End. bal.	46,300		

Available-for-Sale Securities

Beg. bal.	10,000		
(q)	2,000		
End. bal.	12,000		

Accounts Receivable

Beg. bal.	70,500	(l)	10,500
End. bal.	60,000		

Inventories

Beg. bal.	76,500	(m)	1,500
End. bal.	75,000		

Prepaid Operating Expenses

Beg. bal.	12,000		
(n)	4,500		
End. bal.	16,500		

Investments

Beg. bal.	106,000	(e)	96,000
End. bal.	10,000		

Land

Beg. bal.	75,000		
(f)	68,500		
(g)	40,000		
End. bal.	183,500		

Buildings

Beg. bal.	225,000	(c)	40,000
(d)	105,000		
End. bal.	290,000		

Accumulated Depreciation—Buildings

(c)	30,000	Beg. bal.	155,000
		(i)	5,600
		End. bal.	130,600

Machinery and Equipment

Beg. bal.	120,000		
(h)	12,000		
End. bal.	132,000		

Accumulated Depreciation— Machinery and Equipment

		Beg. bal.	43,500
		(i)	15,300
		End. bal.	58,800

Patents

Beg. bal.	40,000	(j)	5,000
End. bal.	35,000		

Accounts Payable

(o)	6,700	Beg. bal.	97,700
		End. bal.	91,000

Income Taxes Payable

		Beg. bal.	9,500
		(p)	500
		End. bal.	10,000

Dividends Payable

		Beg. bal.	0
		(b)	4,400
		End. bal.	4,400

Bonds Payable

		Beg. bal.	0
		(k)	30,000
		End. bal.	30,000

Common Stock

		Beg. bal.	250,000
		(g)	40,000
		End. bal.	290,000

Retained Earnings

(b)	25,100	Beg. bal.	234,300
		(a)	36,300
		End. bal.	245,500

All T-accounts are now complete, and a statement of cash flows for Western Resources, Inc., can be prepared in an appropriate format, such as the one below.

Western Resources, Inc.
Statement of Cash Flows
For the Year Ended December 31, 2002

Cash flows from operating activities:		
Net income	$ 36,300	
Adjustments:		
Depreciation expense	20,900	
Amortization of patents	5,000	
Gain on sale of investments	(6,500)	
Decrease in accounts receivable	10,500	
Decrease in inventories	1,500	
Increase in prepaid operating expenses	(4,500)	
Decrease in accounts payable	(6,700)	
Increase in income taxes payable	500	
Net cash provided by operating activities		$57,000
Cash flows from investing activities:		
Involuntary conversion of building	$ 10,000	
Construction of building	(105,000)	
Sale of long-term investments	102,500	
Purchase of land	(68,500)	
Purchase of machinery and equipment	(12,000)	
Purchase of available-for-sale securities	(2,000)	
Net cash used in investing activities		(75,000)
Cash flows from financing activities:		
Issuance of bonds	$ 30,000	
Payment of cash dividends	(20,700)	
Net cash provided by financing activities		9,300
Net decrease in cash and cash equivalents		$ (8,700)
Cash and cash equivalents at beginning of year		55,000
Cash and cash equivalents at end of year		$46,300
Supplemental Disclosure:		
Cash payments for:		
Interest	$ 3,600	
Income taxes	23,500	
Noncash transaction:		
Land acquired by issuing common stock	40,000	

A reader analyzing the cash flow statement for Western Resources, Inc., can readily see that $57,000 cash was provided internally from operating activities. This amount was not sufficient to satisfy the investment needs of the company, and so additional cash was generated from external financing activities involving the issuance of bonds. The cash generated from operations clearly met the need for payment of cash dividends, but when other cash needs are considered, the total cash outflow exceeded the total inflow of cash for the period, causing the cash balance to decrease by $8,700, or 15.8%.

In addition to the formal statement of cash flows, supplemental disclosure is required for significant noncash investing and financing transactions. Thus, Western Resources would report the acquisition of land valued at $40,000 in exchange for common stock. When the indirect method is used to report operating activities, the amount of cash paid for interest and income taxes also must be disclosed. For Western Resources, the amount paid for interest, $3,600, is taken directly from the income statement because there is no interest payable at the beginning or end of the year. The amount paid for taxes is determined as follows:

Income tax expense (reported in the income statement)	$24,000
Deduct increase in income taxes payable	(500)
Amount of cash paid for income taxes	$23,500

In the Western Resources illustration, the supplemental disclosures are presented in a schedule accompanying the statement of cash flows. Alternatively, the information could be presented in the notes to the financial statements.

Work Sheet Approach to Preparing a Statement of Cash Flows—Indirect Method

This section illustrates a work sheet approach to preparing a statement of cash flows using the indirect method. As shown, this approach produces the same results as the T-account approach; only the format is different. To highlight the similarities in the two approaches, the information and account analysis used in the T-account illustration for Western Resources, Inc., will also be used for the work sheet illustration.

Using a work sheet, such as the one on page 272, facilitates the analysis of account changes when using the indirect method. The format of the work sheet is straightforward. The first amount column contains the beginning balances, then there are two columns for analysis of transactions to arrive at the ending balances in the fourth column.

In preparing a work sheet, accumulated depreciation balances, instead of being reported as credit balances in the debit (asset) section, may be more conveniently listed with liability and owners' equity balances in the credit section. Similarly, contra liability accounts and contra owners' equity balances may be separately recognized and more conveniently listed with assets in the debit section.

The lower portion of the work sheet shows the major categories of cash flows: operating, investing, and financing. A debit in the lower section means an increase in cash, while a credit is a decrease in cash. It is from the lower section of the work sheet that the formal statement of cash flows is prepared. In following the illustration, it may be helpful to refer to the detailed explanations for individual adjustments described on 266–268. Once the changes in all accounts have been reconciled and the work sheet is complete, the formal cash flow statement can be prepared, as illustrated on page 270.

CONCLUSION

This chapter has been an overview of the statement of cash flows. Along with the balance sheet and the income statement, the statement of cash flows is one of the three primary financial statements. However, because it is relatively new (required only since 1988), it sometimes does not receive the emphasis that it deserves. Cash flow variables and ratios are only now starting to make it into the mainstream of financial statement analysis. You are now a cash flow statement expert; be patient with those who learned their accounting back in the pre-1988 days of the statement of changes in financial position.

All the basic aspects of cash flow reporting and disclosure have been covered in this chapter. Additional complexities are introduced in later chapters as appropriate. An expanded illustration, incorporating these complexities, is provided in the last chapter of the text. You might start thinking now about how the cash flow statement will be affected by revenue recognition assumptions, FIFO and LIFO, capitalize or expense decisions, operating leases, bonds issued at a discount, stock splits and dividends. . . .

Western Resources, Inc.
Work Sheet for Statement of Cash Flows—Indirect Method
For the Year Ended December 31, 2002

Accounts	Balance Dec. 31, 2001	Adjustments Debit		Adjustments Credit		Balance Dec. 31, 2002
Debits						
Cash and Cash Equivalents	55,000			(r)	8,700	46,300
Available-for-Sale Securities	10,000	(q)	2,000			12,000
Accounts Receivable	70,500			(l)	10,500	60,000
Inventories	76,500			(m)	1,500	75,000
Prepaid Operating Expenses	12,000	(n)	4,500			16,500
Investments	106,000			(e)	96,000	10,000
Land			75,000	(f)	68,500	
		(g)	40,000			183,500
Buildings	225,000	(d)	105,000	(c)	40,000	290,000
Machinery and Equipment	120,000	(h)	12,000			132,000
Patents	40,000			(j)	5,000	35,000
	790,000					860,300
Credits						
Accumulated Depreciation—Buildings	155,000	(c)	30,000	(i)	5,600	130,600
Accumulated Depreciation—Machinery and Equipment	43,500			(i)	15,300	58,800
Accounts Payable	97,700	(o)	6,700			91,000
Income Taxes Payable	9,500			(p)	500	10,000
Dividends Payable	–0–			(b)	4,400	4,400
Bonds Payable	–0–			(k)	30,000	30,000
Common Stock	250,000			(g)	40,000	290,000
Retained Earnings	234,300	(b)	25,100	(a)	36,300	245,500
	790,000		293,800		293,800	860,300

	Debit		Credit	
Cash flows from operating activities:				
Net income	(a)	36,300		
Adjustments:				
Depreciation expense	(i)	20,900		
Amortization of patents	(j)	5,000		
Gain on sale of investments			(e)	6,500
Decrease in accounts receivable	(l)	10,500		
Decrease in inventories	(m)	1,500		
Increase in prepaid operating expenses			(n)	4,500
Decrease in accounts payable			(o)	6,700
Increase in income taxes payable	(p)	500		
Cash flows from investing activities:				
Involuntary conversion of building	(c)	10,000		
Construction of building			(d)	105,000
Sale of long-term investments	(e)	102,500		
Purchase of land			(f)	68,500
Purchase of machinery and equipment			(h)	12,000
Purchase of available-for-sale securities			(q)	2,000
Cash flows from financing activities:				
Issuance of bonds	(k)	30,000		
Payment of cash dividends			(b)	20,700
		217,200		225,900
Net decrease in cash	(r)	8,700		
		225,900		225,900

REVIEW OF LEARNING OBJECTIVES

1 **Describe the circumstances in which the cash flow statement is a particularly important companion of the income statement.** A cash flow statement is an important companion to the income statement. When noncash expenses are high, earnings gives an overly pessimistic view of a company's performance; cash flow from operations may give a better picture. In addition, the operations of rapidly growing companies can consume cash even when reported net income is positive. Finally, the cash flow statement provides a reality check in situations where companies have an incentive to bias the accrual accounting assumptions.

The cash flow statement offers a one-page summary of the results of a company's operating, investing, and financing activities for the period. A pro forma, or projected, cash flow statement is an excellent tool to analyze whether a company's operating, investing, and financing plans are consistent and workable.

2 **Outline the structure of and information reported in the three main categories of the cash flow statement: operating, investing, and financing.** The three sections of a cash flow statement are: operating, investing, and financing. Significant noncash investing and financing transactions must also be disclosed.

- Operating. For purposes of preparing a cash flow statement, operating activities are those activities that enter into the calculation of net income. Net cash provided by operating activities is the "bottom line" of the cash flow statement.
- Investing. The primary investing activities are the purchase and sale of land, buildings, equipment, and nontrading financial instruments.
- Financing. Financing activities involve the receipt of cash from and the repayment of cash to owners and creditors. An exception is that the payment of interest is considered an operating activity.
- Noncash investing and financing transactions include the purchase of long-term assets in exchange for the issuance of debt or stock.

3 **Appreciate the historical process involved in the development of the modern statement of cash flows.** The current structure of the statement of cash flows was mandated by the FASB in 1987. Before that, companies presented a "statement of changes in financial position" that did not focus strictly on cash flow. Because the statement of cash flows is relatively young, traditional models of financial statement analysis do not incorporate cash flow data.

4 **Compute cash flow from operations using either the direct or the indirect method.** There are two ways to present cash flow from operations: the direct method and the indirect method. The direct method is more intuitive; the indirect method emphasizes a reconciliation between net income and cash flow. Almost all companies use the indirect method.

The direct method is a recap of the income statement with the objective of reporting how much cash was received or disbursed in association with each income statement item.

The indirect method starts with net income and then reports adjustments for operating items not involving cash flow. The three types of adjustments are:

- Revenues and expenses that do not involve cash inflows or outflows
- Gains and losses associated with investing or financing activities
- Adjustments for changes in current operating assets and liabilities that indicate noncash sources of revenues and expenses

Net cash from operations is the same whether it is computed using the direct method or the indirect method.

5 **Prepare a complete statement of cash flows and provide the required supplemental disclosures.** Basic information to prepare the three sections of the cash flow statement comes from the following portions of the balance sheet and the income statement.

- Operating—income statement and current assets and liabilities
- Investing—long-term assets
- Financing—long-term liabilities and owners' equity

Preparation of a complete cash flow statement is not done until each income statement item has been considered, all changes in balance sheet items have been explained, and the net change in cash has been exactly reconciled.

Six steps to preparing a cash flow statement are:

1. Determine the change in cash (including cash equivalents). This is the target number.
2. Operating activities—analyze each income statement item and the changes in all current operating assets and current operating liabilities.
3. Investing activities—analyze the changes in all non-current assets as well as changes in all nonoperating current assets.

4. Financing activities—analyze the changes in all non-current liabilities, all owners' equity accounts, and all nonoperating current liabilities.

5. Prepare a formal statement of cash flows, reconciling the beginning and ending cash balances. If the sum of operating, investing, and financing activities does not equal the total balance sheet change in cash, something in the cash flow statement is wrong. Fix it.

6. Prepare supplemental disclosure, including the disclosure of any significant investing or financing transactions that did not involve cash.

6 **Understand the differences among cash flow statements prepared according to U.S. GAAP, U.K. GAAP, and International Accounting Standards.** The primary differences in cash flow reporting around the world relate to alternative classifications of selected cash transactions. IAS 7 closely matches the provisions of the U.S. cash flow reporting standard, with the difference being greater flexibility in classifying cash transactions such as interest and dividends paid and received and income taxes paid. In the United Kingdom, Financial Reporting Standard (FRS) 1 specifies eight different categories for classifying cash flow transactions and represents the most innovative and, probably, the most useful standard for cash flow reporting currently in existence in the world.

7 **Assess a firm's financial strength by analyzing the relationships among cash flows from operating, investing, and financing activities and by computing financial ratios based on cash flow data.** Patterns of positive and negative cash flow in the three categories of operating, investing, and financing yield insights into the health and current strategy of a business. Most companies have positive cash from operations and negative cash from investing activities.

Data from the cash flow statement can be used in conjunction with balance sheet and income statement data to compute financial ratios.

8 **Use knowledge of how the three primary financial statements tie together in order to prepare a forecasted statement of cash flows.** A projected cash flow statement can be constructed using information from a projected balance sheet and income statement. The cash flow projection allows a company to plan ahead as far as timing of new loans, stock issuances, long-term asset acquisitions, and so forth. Projected cash flow statements also allow potential lenders to evaluate the likelihood that the loan will be repaid and allow potential investors to evaluate the likelihood of receiving cash dividends in the future.

9 **Use a T-account or work sheet approach to prepare a statement of cash flows.** In the preparation of more complicated cash flow statements, the use of T-accounts or a work sheet provides a systematic, structured approach.

T-account approach:

- Special cash flow T-accounts are prepared, one each for the operating, investing, and financing sections, and one summary cash flow account.
- Memorandum journal entries are prepared summarizing the cash flow effect of net income and of all asset, liability, and owners' equity account changes. These are not real journal entries; they are only made to help in the preparation of the statement of cash flows.
- The memorandum journal entries are posted to a working set of T-accounts that includes the four special cash flow T-accounts and T-accounts containing the beginning balances of all asset, liability, and owners' equity accounts. When the posting is done, all computed ending balances for asset, liability, and owners' equity accounts should match actual ending balances.
- The statement of cash flows is prepared from items posted to the special cash flow T-accounts representing operating, investing, and financing sections.

Work sheet approach:

- The upper portion of the work sheet contains a column for beginning balances of all balance sheet accounts, two adjustment columns, and an ending balance column.
- The bottom portion of the work sheet contains sections for the operating, investing, and financing cash flow categories. Only the two adjustments columns are used here.
- The same memorandum journal entries used with the T-account approach are entered into the adjustments columns of the upper and lower portions of the work sheet.
- The formal cash flow statement is prepared from the lower portion of the work sheet.

KEY TERMS

Cash equivalent 227
Cash flow adequacy ratio 258
Cash flow-to-net income ratio 258
Cash times interest earned ratio 259
Direct method 232

Financing activities 228
Indirect method 232
Investing activities 228
Noncash investing and financing
    activities 230

Operating activities 227
Pro forma cash flow statement 226
Statement of cash flows 227

QUESTIONS

1. Under what circumstances does cash flow from operations offer a clearer picture of a company's performance than does net income?
2. What criteria must be met for an item to be considered a cash equivalent in preparing a statement of cash flows?
3. What are the three categories in a statement of cash flows? What types of items are included in each?
4. What is the normal pattern of cash flow (positive or negative) for operating, investing, and financing activities?
5. Prior to 1988, a "funds" statement was required instead of a cash flow statement. What was that "funds" statement called? How did it differ from a statement of cash flows?
6. Either the direct method or the indirect method may be used to report cash flows from operating activities. What is the difference in approach for the two methods?
7. Why do many users prefer the direct method? Why do the majority of preparers prefer the indirect method?
8. How is depreciation expense handled when the direct method is used? The indirect method?
9. What is wrong with the statement: "Cash flow is equal to net income plus depreciation"?
10. Why does the FASB in Statement No. 95 treat interest payments as an operating activity rather than as a financing activity?
11. When preparing a cash flow statement, what is the "target number"?
12. When using the direct method, what items must be considered in the calculation of cash paid for inventory purchases?
13. How is a loss on the sale of a long-term asset treated when using the direct method? The indirect method?
14. Is the purchase of securities an operating activity or an investing activity? Explain.
15. What supplemental disclosures are required by FASB Statement No. 95 if a company elects to use the direct method in preparing its statement of cash flows? What disclosures are required if the indirect method is used?
16. How are significant noncash investing and financing transactions reported in connection with a statement of cash flows?
17. Compare how interest paid is classified in a statement of cash flows under the provisions of FASB Statement No. 95 and IAS 7.
18. What is the difference between "cash from operating activities" as reported in the United States and in the United Kingdom?
19. On average, which number is larger—net income or cash from operations? Explain.
20. What does it mean when the value of a company's cash flow adequacy ratio is less than one?
21. A forecasted statement of cash flows allows management to plan ahead. What information is contained in the statement that can be used for planning purposes?
22. How can external users make use of a forecasted statement of cash flows?

23. What techniques can be used to simplify the preparation of a statement of cash flows when there are many accounts and transactions?

DISCUSSION CASES

CASE 5–1

IS DEPRECIATION A SOURCE OF CASH?

Brad Berrett and Jim Wong are roommates in college. Berrett is an accounting major, while Wong is a finance major. Both have recently studied the statement of cash flows in their classes. Wong's finance professor stated that depreciation is a major source of cash for some companies. Berrett's accounting professor indicated in class that depreciation cannot be a source of cash because cash is not affected by the recording of depreciation.

Berrett and Wong wonder which professor is correct. Explain the positions taken by both professors and indicate which viewpoint you support and why.

CASE 5–2

WHERE DOES ALL THE MONEY GO?

Price Auto Parts has hired you as a consultant to analyze the company's financial position. One of the owners, DeeAnn Price, is in charge of the financial affairs of the company. She makes all the deposits and pays the bills but has an accountant prepare a balance sheet and an income statement once a year. The business has been quite profitable over the years. In fact, 2 years ago Price opened a second store and is now considering a third outlet. However, the economy has slowed, and the cash position has become very tight. The company is having an increasingly difficult time paying its bills. DeeAnn has not been able to satisfactorily explain to her partners what is happening. What factors should you consider and what recommendations might you make to Price?

CASE 5–3

WHY DO WE HAVE MORE CASH?

Hot Lunch Delivery Service has always had a policy to pay stockholders annual dividends in an amount exactly equal to net income for the year. Joe Alberg, the company's president, is confused because the cash balance has been consistently increasing ever since Hot Lunch began operations 5 years ago, in spite of its faithful adherence to the dividend policy. Assuming no errors have been made in the bookkeeping process, explain why this situation might occur.

CASE 5–4

WHICH METHOD SHOULD WE USE: THE DIRECT OR THE INDIRECT METHOD?

As the assistant controller of Do-It-Right Company, you have been given the assignment to study FASB Statement No. 95 and make recommendations on how the company should prepare its statement of cash flows. Specifically, you are to indicate which method should be used in reporting cash flows from operating activities: the direct method or the indirect method. Which method do you recommend and why?

CASE 5–5

SOME KIND OF ACCOUNTANT YOU ARE!

Early in the year 2003, John Roberts, a recent graduate of Southeast State College, delivers the financial statements shown on page 277 to Laura Dennis of Dennis, Inc. After a quick review, Dennis exclaims, "What do you mean I had net income of $20,000? I borrowed $40,000 from the bank and my cash balance decreased by $2,000. I must have had a loss! Some kind of accountant you are!" How should Mr. Roberts answer Ms. Dennis?

CASE 5–6

HOW TO GENERATE CASH

Assume that you own and operate a small business. You have just completed your forecasts and budgets for next year and realize that you will need an infusion of $30,000 cash to get you through the year. You are reluctant to seek a partner because you do not want to dilute your control of the business. Preliminary talks with several lenders convince you that you probably won't be able to get a loan. What can you do to raise the $30,000 cash necessary to get you through the year?

Dennis, Inc.
Comparative Balance Sheet
December 31, 2002 and 2001

	2002	2001
Assets		
Cash	$ 3,000	$ 5,000
Accounts receivable	18,000	8,000
Inventory	20,000	15,000
Equipment (at cost)	52,000	20,000
Accumulated depreciation	(10,000)	(5,000)
Total assets	$83,000	$43,000
Liabilities and Stockholders' Equity		
Accounts payable	$ 4,000	$ 9,000
Notes payable—long-term	40,000	—
Common stock, $1 par	2,000	2,000
Additional paid-in capital	18,000	18,000
Retained earnings	19,000	14,000
Total liabilities and stockholders' equity	$83,000	$43,000

Dennis, Inc.
Combined Statement of Income and Retained Earnings
For the Year Ended December 31, 2002

Sales		$240,000
Cost of goods sold	$150,000	
Operating expenses (including depreciation of $5,000)	70,000	220,000
Net income		$ 20,000
Add: Retained earnings, January 1, 2002		14,000
Deduct: Dividends paid		(15,000)
Retained earnings, December 31, 2002		$ 19,000

CASE 5–7

CASH FLOW PER SHARE

In Statement No. 95, the FASB explicitly prohibited the reporting of "cash flow per share" in the financial statements. Cash flow per share is an amount often reported by firms outside the financial statements and also often included in financial analyses prepared by investment advisory services. Why do you think the FASB explicitly prohibited the inclusion of cash flow per share in the financial statements?

CASE 5–8

THE SECRET OF CASH FLOW PATTERNS

Kara Nemrow, a security analyst for Primer Mead & Co., asserts that she can tell more about a company's financial condition by looking at the trends of the negative or positive cash flows in the three categories than from other information found in the financial statements. She illustrates her theory with the following pattern of cash flows for Atlas Security over the past 3 years.

	2002	2001	2000
Net income	–	+	+
Cash flows from:			
Operating activities	–	–	+
Financing activities	+	+	+
Investing activities	+	+	+

How do you think Kara would analyze this pattern? Do you agree that analyzing cash flow patterns provides superior analytical information?

CASE 5–9

W. T. GRANT: WHAT IS "CASH FLOW"?

The case of W. T. GRANT is a classic in cash flow analysis. During the 1960s and 1970s, Grant was one of the largest retailers in the United States, with over 1,200 stores nationwide. Grant was a stable New York Stock Exchange firm that had paid cash dividends every year since 1907. However, the inability of Grant's operations to generate positive cash flow indicated the existence of serious problems. From 1966 through 1973, while Grant's net income was steady at about $35 million per year, cash flow from operations was negative in every year except 1968 and 1969, and even in those years the positive cash flow generated was insignificant in amount. The results for the fiscal year ended January 31, 1973, are the most striking. Net income for the year was $38 million. A frequently used measure of "cash flow" (net income and depreciation) suggested that W. T. Grant's operations generated $48 million in cash. However, actual cash flow generated by operations for the year was a negative $120 million. In October 1975, Grant filed for bankruptcy, and by early 1976, the company was liquidated and ceased to exist.

What might have caused the net income + depreciation measure of cash flow to be positive when in fact actual cash flow from operations was negative? Under what circumstances is the net income + depreciation measure of cash flow a good estimate of actual cash flow from operations? When is it a bad measure?

SOURCES: James A. Largay, III and Clyde P. Stickney, "Cash Flows, Ratio Analysis and the W. T. Grant Company Bankruptcy," *Financial Analysts Journal,* July/August 1980, pp. 51–54; and *Moody's Handbook of Common Stocks,* Second Quarterly 1973 Edition.

EXERCISES

EXERCISE 5–10

CLASSIFICATION OF CASH FLOWS

Indicate whether each of the following items would be classified as (1) an operating activity, an investing activity, or a financing activity, or (2) as a noncash transaction or noncash item.

- (a) Cash collected from customers.
- (b) Cash paid to suppliers for inventory.
- (c) Cash received for interest on a nontrade note receivable.
- (d) Cash received from issuance of stock.
- (e) Cash paid for dividends.
- (f) Cash received from bank on a loan.
- (g) Cash paid for interest on a loan.
- (h) Cash paid to retire bonds.
- (i) Cash paid to purchase stock of another company as a long-term investment.
- (j) Cash received from the sale of a business segment.
- (k) Cash paid for property taxes.
- (l) Cash received for dividend revenue.
- (m) Cash paid for wages.
- (n) Cash paid for insurance.
- (o) Preferred stock retired by issuing common stock.
- (p) Depreciation expense for the year.
- (q) Cash paid to purchase machinery.
- (r) Cash received from the sale of land.

EXERCISE 5–11

CASH FLOW ANALYSIS

State how each of the following items would be reflected on a statement of cash flows.

(a) Securities classified as available-for-sale were purchased for $5,000 INVESTING

(b) Buildings were acquired for $187,500, the company paying $50,000 cash and signing a 12% mortgage note, payable in 5 years, for the balance. JUST SHOW 50,000

(c) Cash of $62,500 was paid to purchase a business whose assets consisted of: merchandise, $22,500; furniture and fixtures, $7,500; land and buildings, $23,750; and goodwill, $8,750. INVESTING

(d) A cash dividend of $1,250 was declared in the current period, payable at the beginning of the next period.

(e) Accounts Payable shows a decrease for the period of $3,750.

EXERCISE 5–12

CASH RECEIPTS AND CASH PAYMENTS

The accountant for Alpine Hobby Stores prepared the following selected information for the year ended December 31, 2002.

	Dec. 31, 2002	Dec. 31, 2001
(a) Equipment	$35,000	$40,000
(b) Accumulated depreciation	11,000	9,500
(c) Long-term debt	13,000	20,000
(d) Common stock	20,000	15,000

Equipment with a book value of $20,000 was sold for $17,000 cash. The original cost of the equipment was $25,000.

Determine the cash inflows and outflows during 2002 associated with each of the accounts listed. Indicate how the cash flows for each item would be presented on the statement of cash flows.

EXERCISE 5–13

PREPARING THE OPERATING ACTIVITIES SECTION OF THE STATEMENT OF CASH FLOWS

Anakin, Inc. provides the following account balances for 2002 and 2001:

	Dec. 31, 2002	Dec. 31, 2001
Accounts Receivable	$ 18,700	$15,500
Inventory	25,440	27,200
Accounts Payable	21,650	22,400
Salaries Payable	1,500	1,350
Sales	278,700	
Cost of Goods Sold	197,000	
Depreciation Expense	16,700	
Salaries Expense	35,200	
Other Expenses	24,300	

Using the format presented in the chapter, prepare the operating activities section of the statement of cash flows and present that information using (a) the direct method and (b) the indirect method.

EXERCISE 5–14

PREPARING THE OPERATING ACTIVITIES SECTION OF A STATEMENT OF CASH FLOWS

Naboo Enterprises provides the following income statement for 2002.

Sales	$835,400
Cost of goods sold	454,500
Gross margin	$380,900
Depreciation expense	38,000
Salaries expense	121,350
Interest expense	12,200
Other expenses	87,500
Income taxes expense	56,000
Net income	$ 65,850

In addition, the following balance sheet information is available:

	Dec. 31, 2002	Dec. 31, 2001
Accounts receivable	$55,000	$47,500
Inventory	62,600	65,400
Prepaid other expenses	5,400	4,700
Accounts payable	48,700	45,250
Interest payable	800	1,200
Income taxes payable	2,850	3,200

Using the format presented in the chapter, prepare the operating activities section of the statement of cash flows and present that information using (a) the direct method and (b) the indirect method.

EXERCISE 5–15

FORMAT OF STATEMENT OF CASH FLOWS WITH INDIRECT METHOD

From the following information for the Carter Corporation, prepare a statement of cash flows for the year ended December 31, 2002, using the indirect method.

Amortization of patent	$ 4,000
Depreciation expense	7,000
Issuance of common stock	25,000
Issuance of new bonds payable	30,000
Net income	55,000
Payment of dividends	22,500
Purchase of equipment	33,200
Retirement of long-term debt	40,000
Sale of land (includes $6,000 gain)	35,000
Decrease in accounts receivable	2,100
Increase in inventory	1,200
Increase in accounts payable	1,500
Increase in cash	56,700
Cash balance, January 1, 2002	82,800

EXERCISE 5–16

CASH FLOW FROM OPERATIONS—INDIRECT METHOD

The following information was taken from the books of Tapwater Company. Compute the amount of net cash provided by (used in) operating activities during 2002 using the indirect method.

	Dec. 31, 2002	Dec. 31, 2001
Accounts receivable	$18,900	$16,750
Accounts payable	11,500	14,000
Accumulated depreciation (no plant assets retired during year)	29,000	22,000
Inventories	24,500	20,000
Other current liabilities	5,000	3,000
Prepaid insurance	1,200	2,000
Net income	35,500	—

EXERCISE 5–17

CASH FLOW FROM OPERATIONS—DIRECT METHOD

A summary of revenues and expenses for Stanton Company for 2002 follows:

Sales	$6,000,000
Cost of goods manufactured and sold	2,800,000
Gross profit	$3,200,000
Selling, general, and administrative expenses	2,000,000
Income before income taxes	$1,200,000
Income taxes	520,000
Net income	$ 680,000

Net changes in working capital accounts for 2002 were as follows:

	Debit	Credit
Cash	$104,000	
Trade accounts receivable	400,000	
Inventories		$ 60,000
Prepaid expenses (selling and general)	10,000	
Accrued expenses (75% of increase related to manufacturing activities and 25% to general operating activities)		32,000
Income taxes payable		48,000
Trade accounts payable		140,000

Depreciation on plant and equipment for the year totaled $600,000; 70% was related to manufacturing activities and 30% to general and administrative activities.

Prepare a schedule of net cash provided by (used in) operating activities for the year using the direct method.

EXERCISE 5–18

CASH FLOW FROM OPERATIONS—INDIRECT METHOD

The following information was taken from the comparative financial statements of Buttercup Corporation.

Net income for year	$ 90,000
Sales revenue	500,000
Cost of goods sold (except depreciation)	300,000
Depreciation expense for year	60,000
Amortization of goodwill for year	10,000
Interest expense on short-term debt for year	3,500
Dividends declared and paid during year	65,000

Selected account balances:

	Beginning of Year	End of Year
Accounts receivable	$43,000	$30,000
Inventory	42,000	50,000
Accounts payable	59,400	56,000
Interest payable	1,000	—

Using the indirect method, compute the net amount of cash provided by (used in) operating activities for the year.

EXERCISE 5–19

CASH FLOW FROM OPERATIONS—DIRECT METHOD

Based on the information given in Exercise 5-18 and using the direct method, compute the net amount of cash provided by (used in) operating activities for the year.

EXERCISE 5–20

CASH COMPUTATIONS

A comparative balance sheet, income statement, and additional information for the Xavier Metals Company are presented below.

Xavier Metals Company
Comparative Balance Sheet
December 31, 2002 and 2001

	2002	2001
Assets		
Current assets		
Cash	$ 119,000	$ 98,000
Available-for-sale securities	59,000	—
Accounts receivable	312,000	254,000
Inventory	278,000	239,000
Prepaid expenses	35,000	21,000
Total current assets	$ 803,000	$612,000
Property, plant, and equipment	$ 536,000	$409,000
Accumulated depreciation	(76,000)	(53,000)
	$ 460,000	$356,000
Total assets	$1,263,000	$968,000
Liabilities and Stockholders' Equity		
Current liabilities		
Accounts payable	$ 212,000	$198,000
Accrued expenses	98,000	76,000
Dividends payable	40,000	—
Total current liabilities	$ 350,000	$274,000
Notes payable—due 2004	125,000	—
Total liabilities	$ 475,000	$274,000
Stockholders' equity:		
Common stock	$ 600,000	$550,000
Retained earnings	188,000	144,000
Total stockholders' equity	$ 788,000	$694,000
Total liabilities and stockholders' equity	$1,263,000	$968,000

Xavier Metals Company
Condensed Comparative Income Statement
For the Years Ended December 31, 2002 and 2001

	2002	2001
Net sales	$3,561,000	$3,254,000
Cost of goods sold	2,789,000	2,568,000
Gross profit	$ 772,000	$ 686,000
Expenses	521,000	486,000
Net income	$ 251,000	$ 200,000

Additional information for Xavier:

(a) All accounts receivable and accounts payable relate to trade merchandise.

(b) The proceeds from the notes payable were used to finance plant expansion.

(c) Capital stock was sold to provide additional working capital.

Compute the following for 2002:

1. Cash collected from accounts receivable, assuming all sales are on account.
2. Cash payments made on accounts payable to suppliers, assuming that all purchases of inventory are on account.
3. Cash payments for dividends.
4. Cash receipts that were not provided by operations.
5. Cash payments for assets that were not reflected in operations.

EXERCISE 5–21

STATEMENT OF CASH FLOWS—INDIRECT METHOD
Below is information for Boswell Manufacturing Company:

(a) Long-term debt of $450,000 was retired at face value.
(b) New machinery was purchased for $48,000.
(c) Common stock with a par value of $120,000 was issued for $150,000.
(d) Dividends of $18,000 declared in 2001 were paid in January 2002, and dividends of $27,000 were declared in December 2002, to be paid in 2003.
(e) Net income was $320,800. Included in the computation were depreciation expense of $60,000 and goodwill amortization of $30,000.

	Dec. 31, 2002	Dec. 31, 2001
Current assets:		
Cash and cash equivalents	$187,100	$140,000
Accounts receivable	213,000	200,000
Inventory	192,000	162,000
Current liabilities:		
Accounts payable	51,000	85,800
Dividends payable	27,000	18,000
Interest payable	11,100	3,000
Wages payable	84,000	12,000

Prepare a statement of cash flows for the year ended December 31, 2002, using the indirect method.

EXERCISE 5–22

STATEMENT OF CASH FLOWS—INDIRECT METHOD
The Sunnyvale Corporation prepared for 2002 and 2001 the following balance sheet data.

	Dec. 31, 2002	Dec. 31, 2001
Cash and cash equivalents	$ 518,500	$ 675,000
Accounts receivable	360,000	345,000
Merchandise inventory	750,000	654,000
Prepaid insurance	4,500	6,000
Buildings and equipment	5,515,500	4,350,000
Accumulated depreciation—buildings and equipment	(2,235,000)	(1,995,000)
Total assets	$4,913,500	$4,035,000
Accounts payable	$ 613,500	$ 945,000
Salaries payable	75,000	105,000
Notes payable—bank (current)	150,000	600,000
Notes payable—bank (long-term)	1,500,000	—
Common stock	2,400,000	2,400,000
Retained earnings (deficit)	175,000	(15,000)
Total liabilities and stockholders' equity	$4,913,500	$4,035,000

75
−60
15 Accum (Debt

Cash needed to purchase new equipment and to improve the company's working capital position was raised by borrowing from the bank with a long-term note. Equipment costing $75,000 with a book value of $15,000 was sold for $18,000; the gain on sale was included in net income. The company paid cash dividends of $90,000 and reported earnings of $280,000 for 2002. There were no entries in the retained earnings account other than to record the dividend and net income for the year.

Prepare a statement of cash flows for 2002 using the indirect method.

EXERCISE 5–23

STATEMENT OF CASH FLOWS—INDIRECT METHOD

The following are financial statements for LaForge Company.

LaForge Company
Comparative Balance Sheet
December 31, 2002 and 2001
(Dollars in thousands)

Assets	2002	2001
Cash	$ 22	$ 16
Accounts receivable	200	250
Inventory	125	95
Prepaid general expenses	18	10
Plant assets	1,019	1,000
Accumulated depreciation—plant assets	(527)	(597)
Total assets	$ 857	$ 774

Liabilities and Stockholders' Equity		
Accounts payable	$ 75	$ 50
Interest payable	10	8
Income taxes payable	90	107
Bonds payable	117	77
Common stock	338	300
Retained earnings	227	232
Total liabilities and stockholders' equity	$ 857	$ 774

LaForge Company
Condensed Income Statement
For the Year Ended December 31, 2002
(Dollars in thousands)

Sales		$1,300
Cost of goods sold		880
Gross profit		$ 420
Operating expenses:		
Depreciation expense	$ 60	
General expenses	240	
Interest expense	15	
Income tax expense	35	350
Net income		$ 70

The following information is also available for 2002:

(a) Plant assets were sold for their book value of $200 during the year. The assets had an original cost of $330.
(b) Cash dividends totaling $75 were paid during the year.
(c) All accounts payable relate to inventory purchases.
(d) All purchases of plant assets were cash transactions.

Prepare a statement of cash flows for 2002 using the indirect method.

EXERCISE 5–24

STATEMENT OF CASH FLOWS—DIRECT METHOD
Using the information given in Exercise 5–23, prepare a statement of cash flows for 2002 for LaForge Company using the direct method.

EXERCISE 5–25

CASH FLOW RATIOS
Following are data from the financial statements for Choi Hung Company.

Choi Hung Company
Selected Financial Statement Data
For the Years Ended December 31, 2002 and 2001

	2002	2001
Net income	$32,000	$ 68,850
Cash from operating activities	25,500	155,030
Cash paid for purchase of fixed assets	35,000	178,000
Cash paid for interest	27,000	23,000
Cash paid for income taxes	20,000	40,430

Compute the following for both 2001 and 2002:

1. Cash flow-to-net income ratio
2. Cash flow adequacy ratio
3. Cash times interest earned ratio

EXERCISE 5–26

FORECASTED INCOME STATEMENT AND STATEMENT OF CASH FLOWS
(Note: This exercise uses the same information used in Exercise 4-28.) Han Company wishes to forecast its net income for the year 2003. In addition, for planning purposes Han intends to construct a forecasted statement of cash flows for 2003. Han has assembled balance sheet and income statement data for 2002 and has also done a forecast of the balance sheet for 2003. In addition, Han has estimated that its sales in 2003 will rise to $2,200 and does not anticipate paying any dividends in the coming year. This information is summarized below.

Balance Sheet	2002	2003 Forecasted
Cash	$ 20	$ 22
Other current assets	500	550
Property, plant, and equipment, net	600	800
Total assets	$1,120	$1,372
Accounts payable	$ 200	$ 220
Bank loans payable	600	500
Total stockholders' equity	320	652
Total liabilities and stockholders' equity	$1,120	$1,372

Income Statement	2002	2003 Forecasted
Sales	$2,000	$2,200
Cost of goods sold	700	
Gross profit	$1,300	
Depreciation expense	120	
Other operating expenses	1,010	
Operating profit	$ 170	
Interest expense	90	
Income before income taxes	$ 80	
Income taxes	30	
Net income	$ 50	

Instructions:

1. Prepare a forecasted income statement for 2003. Clearly state what assumptions you make.

2. Prepare a forecasted statement of cash flows for 2003. Use the indirect method of reporting cash from operating activities. (Hint: In computing cash paid to purchase new property, plant, and equipment, don't forget to consider the effect of depreciation expense in 2003.)

EXERCISE 5–27

FORECASTED BALANCE SHEET, INCOME STATEMENT, AND STATEMENT OF CASH FLOWS
(Note: This exercise uses the same information used in Exercise 4-29.) Ryan Company wishes to prepare a forecasted income statement, balance sheet, and statement of cash flows for 2003. Ryan's balance sheet and income statement for 2002 are given below:

Balance Sheet	2002
Cash	$ 10
Other current assets	250
Property, plant, and equipment, net	800
Total assets	$1,060
Accounts payable	$100
Bank loans payable	700
Total stockholders' equity	260
Total liabilities and stockholders' equity	$1,060

Income Statement	2002
Sales	$1,000
Cost of goods sold	750
Gross profit	$ 250
Depreciation expense	40
Other operating expenses	80
Operating profit	$ 130
Interest expense	70
Income before income taxes	$ 60
Income taxes	20
Net income	$ 40

In addition, Ryan has assembled the following forecasted information regarding 2003.

(a) Sales are expected to increase to $1,500.

(b) Ryan expects to become more efficient at utilizing its property, plant, and equipment in 2003. Therefore, Ryan expects that the sales increase will not require any overall increase in property, plant, and equipment. Accordingly, the year 2003 property, plant, and equipment balance is expected to be $800.

(c) Ryan's bank has approved a new long-term loan of $200. This loan will be in addition to the existing loan payable.

(d) Ryan Company does not anticipate paying any dividends in the coming year.

Instructions:

1. Prepare a forecasted balance sheet for 2003. Clearly state what assumptions you make.

2. Prepare a forecasted income statement for 2003. Clearly state what assumptions you make.

3. Prepare a forecasted statement of cash flows for 2003. Use the indirect method of reporting cash from operating activities. (Hint: In computing cash paid to purchase new property, plant, and equipment, don't forget to consider the effect of depreciation expense in 2003.)

PROBLEMS

PROBLEM 5–28

PREPARING THE OPERATING ACTIVITIES SECTION OF THE STATEMENT OF CASH FLOWS
Podracer Productions provides the following income statement for the year ended
December 31, 2002.

Sales	$1,530,600
Cost of goods sold	895,400
Gross margin	$ 635,200
General expenses	255,400
Depreciation expense	23,500
Salaries expense	114,300
Operating income	$ 242,000
Interest revenue	17,250
Interest expense	(12,500)
Loss on sale of equipment	(9,500)
Income before income taxes	$ 237,250
Income tax expense	85,500
Net income	$ 151,750

In addition, Podracer provides the following balance sheet information.

	Dec. 31, 2002	Dec 31, 2001
Accounts receivable	$250,400	$225,400
Interest receivable	2,100	2,250
Inventory	74,300	59,550
Prepaid general expenses	17,600	14,000
Accounts payable	39,500	46,300
Accrued general expenses	19,500	21,750
Interest payable	900	1,100
Income taxes payable	11,500	9,750
Salaries payable	9,850	5,400

Instructions: Using the simultaneous analysis matrix illustrated in the text, prepare
the operating activities section of the statement of cash flows using (1) the direct
method and (2) the indirect method.

PROBLEM 5–29

STATEMENT OF CASH FLOWS—INDIRECT METHOD
Comparative balance sheet data for the Amber Company are presented below and on
the following page. In addition, new equipment was purchased for $50,000, payment
consisting of $25,000 cash and a long-term note for $25,000. Proceeds from the short-
term notes payable were used for operating purposes. Cash dividends of $10,000 were
paid in 2002; all other changes to retained earnings were caused by the net income for
2002, which amounted to $83,500.

	Dec. 31, 2002	Dec. 31, 2001
Cash and cash equivalents	$ 41,000	$ 28,000
Accounts receivable	94,000	86,000
Inventory	110,000	100,000
Property, plant, and equipment	550,000	500,000
Accumulated depreciation—property, plant, and equipment	(277,500)	(250,000)
Total assets	$517,500	$464,000

	Dec. 31, 2002	Dec. 31, 2001
Short-term notes payable	$ —	$ 20,000
Accounts payable	105,000	80,000
Long-term notes payable	100,000	75,000
Bonds payable	50,000	100,000
Common stock, $1 par	20,000	20,000
Additional paid-in capital	155,000	155,000
Retained earnings	87,500	14,000
Total liabilities and stockholders' equity	$517,500	$464,000

Instructions: Prepare a statement of cash flows for the year ended December 31, 2002, using the indirect method.

PROBLEM 5–30

STATEMENT OF CASH FLOWS—INDIRECT METHOD
The following information was taken from the records of Alderman Produce Company for the year ended June 30, 2002.

Borrowed on long-term notes	$20,000
Issued capital stock	50,000
Purchased equipment	27,000
Net income	47,000
Purchased treasury stock	1,500
Paid dividends	30,000
Depreciation expense	12,000
Retired bonds payable	70,000
Goodwill amortization	2,000
Sold long-term investment (at cost)	5,000
Increase in cash	11,000
Decrease in inventories	8,000
Increase in accounts receivable	8,500
Increase in accounts payable	4,000
Cash balance, July 1, 2001	20,000

Instructions:

1. From the information given, prepare a statement of cash flows using the indirect method.
2. Briefly explain what an interested party would learn from studying the cash flow statement for Alderman Produce Company.

PROBLEM 5–31

STATEMENT OF CASH FLOWS—INDIRECT METHOD
The following information was obtained from analysis of selected accounts of Orlando Company for the year ended December 31, 2002.

Increase in long-term debt	$ 57,000
Purchase of treasury stock	52,000
Depreciation and amortization	197,000
Gain on sale of equipment (included in net income)	6,000
Proceeds from issuance of common stock	184,000
Purchase of equipment	434,000
Proceeds from sale of equipment	20,000
Payment of dividends	49,000
Net income	375,000
Increase (decrease) in working capital accounts:	
Cash	45,000
Accounts receivable	229,000
Inventories	275,000
Trade notes payable	167,000
Accounts payable	124,000
Income taxes payable	(34,000)
Cash balance, January 1, 2002	120,000

Instructions: From the information given, prepare a statement of cash flows using the indirect method.

PROBLEM 5–32

STATEMENT OF CASH FLOWS—DIRECT METHOD

Based on an analysis of the cash account and other accounts, the following information was provided by the controller of Lumbercamp, Inc., a manufacturer of wood-burning stoves, for the year 2002.

(a) Cash sales for the year were $150,000; sales on account totaled $180,000.
(b) Cost of goods sold was 50% of total sales.
(c) All inventory is purchased on account.
(d) Depreciation on equipment was $93,000 for the year.
(e) Amortization of goodwill was $6,000.
(f) Collection of accounts receivable was $114,000.
(g) Payments on accounts payable for inventory equaled $117,000.
(h) Rent expense paid in cash was $33,000.
(i) 60,000 shares of $10 par stock were issued for $720,000.
(j) Land was acquired by issuance of a $300,000 bond that sold for $318,000.
(k) Equipment was purchased for cash at a cost of $252,000.
(l) Dividends of $138,000 were declared.
(m) $45,000 of dividends that had been declared the previous year were paid.
(n) A machine used on the assembly line was sold for $36,000. The machine had a book value of $21,000.
(o) Another machine with a book value of $1,500 was scrapped and was reported as an ordinary loss. No cash was received on this transaction.
(p) The cash account had a balance of $87,000 on January 1, 2002.

Instructions: Use the direct method to prepare a statement of cash flows for Lumbercamp, Inc., for the year ended December 31, 2002.

PROBLEM 5–33

STATEMENT OF CASH FLOWS—INDIRECT METHOD

Comparative balance sheet data for the partnership of Young and Jones are presented below.

	Dec. 31, 2002	Dec. 31, 2001
Cash	$ 14,000	$ 10,500
Accounts receivable	22,000	25,500
Inventory	112,500	85,000
Prepaid expenses	3,500	4,250
Furniture and fixtures	64,500	42,000
Accumulated depreciation	(33,875)	(25,425)
Total assets	$182,625	$141,825
Accrued expenses	$ 7,000	$ 5,200
Accounts payable	19,425	28,875
Long-term note	17,700	—
Donna Young, capital	51,375	50,875
Diane Jones, capital	87,125	56,875
Total liabilities and stockholders' equity	$182,625	$141,825

Net income for the year was $43,000, and this was transferred in equal amounts to the partners' capital accounts. Further changes in the capital accounts arose from additional investments and withdrawals by the partners. The change in the furniture and fixtures account arose from a purchase of additional furniture; part of the purchase price was paid in cash and a long-term note was issued for the balance.

Instructions: Using the indirect method, prepare a statement of cash flows for 2002.

PROBLEM 5–34

STATEMENT OF CASH FLOWS—INDIRECT METHOD

Berclay Tile Company reported net income of $6,160 for 2002 but has been showing an overdraft in its bank account in recent months. The manager has contacted you as the auditor for an explanation. The comparative balance sheet was given to you for examination, along with the following information.

(a) Equipment was sold for $1,500, its cost was $2,500, and its book value was $500. The gain was reported as Other Revenue.

(b) Cash dividends of $4,500 were paid.

Berclay Tile Company
Comparative Balance Sheet
December 31, 2002 and 2001

		2002		2001
Assets				
Current assets:				
Cash		$ (960)		$ 4,780
Accounts receivable		4,000		1,000
Inventory		2,350		750
Prepaid insurance		70		195
Total current assets		$ 5,460		$ 6,725
Land, buildings, and equipment:				
Land		$12,500		$12,500
Buildings	$25,000		$25,000	
Less: Accumulated depreciation	(15,000)	10,000	(14,000)	11,000
Equipment	$37,250		$30,850	
Less: Accumulated depreciation	(22,500)	14,750	(18,400)	12,450
Total land, buildings, and equipment		$37,250		$35,950
Total assets		$42,710		$42,675
Liabilities and Stockholders' Equity				
Current liabilities:				
Accounts payable		$ 4,250		$ 3,500
Income taxes payable		1,400		2,350
Wages payable		750		1,675
Notes payable—current portion		1,500		3,500
Total current liabilities		$ 7,900		$11,025
Long-term liabilities:				
Notes payable		10,500		11,500
Stockholders' equity:				
Capital stock	$17,500		$15,000	
Retained earnings	6,810		5,150	
Total stockholders' equity		24,310		20,150
Total liabilities and stockholders' equity		$42,710		$42,675

Instructions: Prepare a statement of cash flows using the indirect method.

PROBLEM 5–35

STATEMENT OF CASH FLOWS—DIRECT METHOD

The table on the next page shows the account balances of Novations, Inc., at the beginning and end of the company's accounting period.

The following additional information is available.

(a) All purchases and sales were on account.

(b) Equipment costing $10,000 was sold for $3,000; a loss of $1,000 was recognized on the sale.

(c) Among other items, the operating expenses included depreciation expense of $7,000; interest expense of $2,800; and insurance expense of $2,400.

(d) Equipment was purchased during the year by issuing common stock and by paying the balance ($12,000) in cash.

(e) Treasury stock was sold for $4,000 less than it cost; the decrease in owners' equity was recorded by reducing retained earnings. No dividends were paid during the year.

Debits	Dec. 31, 2002	Jan. 1, 2002
Cash and Cash Equivalents	$176,400	$ 58,000
Accounts Receivable	32,000	26,600
Inventory	21,000	25,400
Prepaid Insurance	5,600	4,000
Long-Term Investments (at cost)	6,000	16,800
Equipment	80,000	66,000
Treasury Stock (at cost)	10,000	20,000
Cost of Goods Sold	368,000	
Operating Expenses	185,000	
Income Tax Expense	37,600	
Loss on Sale of Equipment	1,000	
Total debits	$922,600	$216,800

Credits	Dec. 31, 2002	Jan. 1, 2002
Accumulated Depreciation—Equipment	$ 19,000	$ 18,000
Accounts Payable	7,000	11,200
Interest Payable	1,000	2,000
Income Taxes Payable	12,000	8,000
Notes Payable—Long-Term	16,000	24,000
Common Stock	110,000	100,000
Paid-In Capital in Excess of Par	32,000	30,000
Retained Earnings	19,600*	23,600
Sales	704,000	
Gain on Sale of Long-Term Investments	2,000	
Total credits	$922,600	$216,800

*Preclosing balance.

Instructions:

1. Prepare a statement of cash flows for the year ended December 31, 2002, using the direct method of reporting cash flows from operating activities.

2. Comment on the lack of dividend payment. Does a "no dividend" policy seem appropriate under the current circumstances for Novations, Inc.?

3. Compute cash flow ratios for Novations, Inc. Comment on your analysis of the cash flow ratios.

PROBLEM 5–36

INCOME STATEMENT AND STATEMENT OF CASH FLOWS—INDIRECT METHOD
Refer to the data for Novations, Inc., in Problem 5-35.

Instructions:

1. Prepare an income statement for Novations, Inc., for the year ended December 31, 2002.

2. Prepare a statement of cash flows for the year ended December 31, 2002, using the indirect method.

PROBLEM 5–37

ANALYSIS OF CASH FLOW DATA

The following summary data are for Queue Company.

	2002	2001	2000
Cash	$ 75,000	$ 70,000	$ 60,000
Other current assets	450,000	400,000	370,000
Current liabilities	335,000	240,000	250,000
Depreciation expense	50,000	48,000	41,000
Net income	65,000	57,000	54,000

All current assets and current liabilities relate to operations.

Instructions:

1. Compute net cash provided by (used in) operating activities for 2001 and 2002.
2. How would the numbers you computed in (1) change if Queue had decided to delay payment of $50,000 in accounts payable from late 2001 to early 2002? This will increase both cash and accounts payable as of December 31, 2001; the December 31, 2002, amounts will be unaffected.
3. Ignore the change described in (2). How would the numbers you computed in (1) change if Queue had decided to delay purchase of $50,000 of inventory for cash from late 2001 to early 2002? This will increase cash but decrease inventory as of December 31, 2001; the December 31, 2002, amounts will be unaffected.
4. Can net cash from operations be manipulated? Explain your answer.

PROBLEM 5–38

DEFINITIONS OF CASH FLOW

The following summary information is for Data Company.

	2002	2001	2000	1999
Net income	$ 85	$ 85	$ 85	$ 85
Depreciation expense	30	30	30	30
Change in accounts receivable	+10	0	+20	+15
Change in inventory	+15	−30	0	−5
Change in accounts payable	+20	+25	−15	+10

Instructions:

1. Compute net cash provided by (used in) operating activities for Data Company for the years 1999 through 2002.
2. One definition of "cash flow" often used in financial analysis is net income + depreciation. Use this definition to compute "cash flow" for Data Company for the years 1999 through 2002.
3. Under what circumstances is the "net income + depreciation" measure of cash flow a good estimate of actual cash flow from operations? Under what circumstances is it a particularly misleading measure?

PROBLEM 5–39

CASH FLOW FROM OPERATIONS—DIRECT METHOD

The following combined income and retained earnings statement, along with selected balance sheet data, are provided for the Timberdale Company.

Timberdale Company
Combined Income and Retained Earnings Statement
For the Year Ended December 31, 2002

Revenues:
Net sales revenue		$170,000
Other revenues		9,000*
Total revenues		$179,000
Expenses:		
Cost of goods sold	$102,000	
Selling and administrative expenses	29,400	
Depreciation expense	6,400	
Interest expense	2,800	
Total expenses		140,600
Income before income taxes		$ 38,400
Income taxes		11,520
Net income		$ 26,880
Retained earnings, January 1, 2002		67,000
		$ 93,880
Dividends declared and paid		5,000
Retained earnings, December 31, 2002		$ 88,880

*Gain on sale of equipment (cost, $19,000; book value, $12,000; sales price, $21,000).

Balance Sheet Amounts

	Beginning of Year	End of Year
Accounts receivable	$21,000	$22,000
Inventory	38,600	36,000
Prepaid expenses	1,900	1,400
Accounts payable	14,400	16,000
Interest payable	3,000	2,000
Income taxes payable	1,000	5,000

Instructions:

1. Using the direct method, compute the amount of net cash provided by (used in) operating activities for Timberdale Company for 2002.
2. What is the impact of dividends paid on net cash from operations? Explain.

PROBLEM 5–40

CASH FLOW FROM OPERATIONS—COMPARISON OF INDIRECT AND DIRECT METHODS
The statement of cash flows for Riker Company (prepared using the indirect method) is shown on the next page. Consider the following additional information:

(a) Sales for the year totaled $812,350. Cost of goods sold was $500,000. Operating expenses were $100,000. Interest expense was $23,000. Income tax expense was $40,430.
(b) Of the decrease in accounts payable, 80% is related to inventory purchases; the remaining 20% related to operating expenses.
(c) Depreciation and amortization are period costs; they do not enter into the computation of cost of goods sold.

Instructions: Prepare the operating activities section of the statement of cash flows for Riker Company using the direct method.

Riker Company
Statement of Cash Flows (Indirect Method)
For the Year Ended December 31, 2002

Cash flows from operating activities:		
Net income		$ 68,850
Adjustments:		
Depreciation expense	$65,000	
Amortization expense	10,000	
Loss on sale of machine	7,400	
Gain on retirement of long-term debt	(2,330)	
Increase in accounts receivable	(8,600)	
Decrease in inventory	12,430	
Decrease in prepaid operating expenses	1,680	
Decrease in accounts payable	(2,400)	
Increase in interest payable	500	
Increase in income taxes payable	2,500	86,180
Net cash provided by operating activities		$155,030
Cash flows from investing activities:		
Sale of machine	$12,000	
Purchase of fixed assets	(78,000)	
Net cash used in investing activities		(66,000)
Cash flows from financing activities:		
Retirement of long-term debt	$(65,000)	
Payment of dividends	(27,000)	
Net cash used in financing activities		(92,000)
Net decrease in cash		$ (2,970)
Cash at beginning of year		5,320
Cash at end of year		$ 2,350

PROBLEM 5–41

PREPARATION OF INCOME STATEMENT USING BALANCE SHEET AND CASH FLOW DATA
The financial statements for Troi Company are shown below and on the next page.
Consider the following additional information:

(a) All the accounts payable relate to inventory purchases.
(b) Property, plant, and equipment sold had an original cost of $75,000 and a book value of $22,000.

Instructions: Prepare the income statement for Troi Company for the year ended December 31, 2002.

Troi Company
Comparative Balance Sheet
December 31, 2002 and 2001

	2002	2001
Assets		
Cash	$ 4,000	$ 3,400
Accounts receivable	25,000	18,000
Inventory	30,000	34,000
Prepaid general expenses	5,700	5,000
Property, plant, and equipment	305,000	320,000
Accumulated depreciation	(103,500)	(128,900)
Goodwill	36,000	40,000
Total assets	$302,200	$291,500

	2002	2001
Liabilities and Stockholders' Equity		
Accounts payable	$ 25,000	$ 22,000
Wages payable	12,000	10,300
Interest payable	2,800	4,000
Dividends payable	14,000	—
Income taxes payable	1,600	1,200
Bonds payable	100,000	120,000
Common stock	50,000	50,000
Retained earnings	96,800	84,000
Total liabilities and stockholders' equity	$302,200	$291,500

Troi Company
Statement of Cash Flows
For the Year Ended December 31, 2002

Cash flows from operating activities:			
Cash collected from customers			$685,300
Cash payments for:			
Inventory purchases	$300,000		
General expenses	102,000		
Wages expense	150,000		
Interest expense	11,000		
Income tax expense	23,900	586,900	
Net cash provided by operating activities			$ 98,400
Cash flows from investing activities:			
Sale of property, plant, and equipment	$ 27,200		
Purchase of property, plant, and equipment	(60,000)		
Net cash used in investing activities			(32,800)
Cash flows from financing activities:			
Retirement of bonds payable	$ (23,000)		
Payment of dividends	(42,000)		
Net cash used in financing activities			(65,000)
Net increase in cash			$ 600
Cash at beginning of year			3,400
Cash at end of year			$ 4,000

PROBLEM 5–42

CASH FLOW ANALYSIS

Below are data from the financial statements for Ping Shek Company.

Ping Shek Company
Selected Financial Statement Data
For the Years Ended December 31, 2002 and 2001
(In millions of dollars)

	2002	2001
Sales	$88,000	$74,000
Total assets	84,000	70,000
Stockholders' equity	22,000	20,000
Net income	7,200	4,800
Cash from operations	9,600	13,000
Cash paid for capital expenditures	8,900	6,600
Cash paid for acquisitions	2,500	200
Cash paid for interest	1,500	1,100
Cash paid for income taxes	4,100	4,000

Instructions:

1. Compute the following for 2001 and 2002.
   a. Return on sales
   b. Return on assets
   c. Return on equity
   d. Cash flow-to-net income ratio
   e. Cash flow adequacy ratio
   f. Cash times interest earned ratio
2. In which year did Ping Shek Company perform better: 2001 or 2002? Explain your answer.
3. Ping Shek Company intends to sell a large block of newly issued stock to the public in the first half of 2002. Given your computations in (1), what questions would you like to ask of Ping Shek's management before investing in the newly issued stock?

PROBLEM 5–43

FORECASTED BALANCE SHEET, INCOME STATEMENT, AND STATEMENT OF CASH FLOWS
(Note: This problem uses the same information used in Problem 4-42.) Lorien Company wishes to prepare a forecasted income statement, a forecasted balance sheet, and a forecasted statement of cash flows for 2003. Lorien's balance sheet and income statement for 2002 are given below.

Balance Sheet	2002
Cash	$ 40
Other current assets	350
Property, plant, and equipment, net	1,000
Total assets	$1,390
Accounts payable	$ 100
Bank loans payable	1,000
Paid-in capital	100
Retained earnings	190
Total liabilities and stockholders' equity	$1,390

Income Statement	2002
Sales	$1,000
Cost of goods sold	350
Gross profit	$ 650
Depreciation expense	200
Other operating expenses	250
Operating profit	$ 200
Interest expense	120
Income before income taxes	$ 80
Income taxes	20
Net income	$ 60

In addition, Lorien has assembled the following forecasted information for 2003.

(a) Sales are expected to increase to $1,200.
(b) Lorien does not expect to buy any new property, plant, and equipment during 2003. (Hint: Think about how depreciation expense in 2003 will affect the reported amount of property, plant, and equipment.)
(c) Because of adverse banking conditions, Lorien does not expect to receive any new bank loans in 2003.
(d) Lorien plans to pay cash dividends of $15 in 2003.

Instructions:

1. Prepare a forecasted balance sheet, a forecasted income statement, and a forecasted statement of cash flows for 2003. Clearly state what assumptions you make. Use the indirect method for reporting cash from operating activities.

2. If you have constructed your forecasted cash flow statement correctly, you will see that Lorien plans to distribute cash to shareholders through two different means in 2003. Which of these methods involves distributing an equal amount of cash for each share owned? Which of these methods channels the cash to shareholders who are the least optimistic about the prospects of the company?

PROBLEM 5–44

STATEMENT OF CASH FLOWS USING T-ACCOUNTS AND INDIRECT METHOD
The post-closing trial balances are provided for the Dallas Department Store. Credit balances are denoted with parentheses.

	Dec. 31, 2002	Dec. 31, 2001
Cash and Cash Equivalents	$ 28,800	$ 12,000
Accounts Receivable	24,000	36,000
Inventory	144,000	96,000
Prepaid Expenses	7,200	6,000
Plant Assets	624,000	480,000
Accumulated Depreciation—Plant Assets	(122,400)	(48,000)
Accounts Payable	(30,000)	(24,000)
Accrued Liabilities	(12,000)	(9,600)
Mortgage Payable	(84,000)	(60,000)
Bonds Payable	(240,000)	(240,000)
Common Stock	(210,000)	(180,000)
Capital in Excess of Par	(36,000)	(30,000)
Retained Earnings	(93,600)	(38,400)
Total	$ 0	$ 0

The following additional information was obtained from Dallas Department Store's accounting records.

- All accounts receivable were from sales to customers.
- The inventory and accounts payable were for merchandise purchased for resale.
- The prepaid expenses and accrued liabilities were for operating expenses.
- During the year, plant assets were purchased by paying $180,000 cash and signing a $24,000 mortgage.
- Plant assets with a cost of $60,000 and accumulated depreciation of $24,000 were sold for $48,000 cash.
- Depreciation expense for the year was included in operating expenses.
- Common stock was sold for $36,000 cash.
- Cash dividends of $12,000 were paid during the year.

Instructions: Using T-accounts, prepare a statement of cash flows for Dallas Department Store for the year ended December 31, 2002, using the indirect method.

PROBLEM 5–45

STATEMENT OF CASH FLOWS USING A WORK SHEET AND INDIRECT METHOD
Refer to the information for Dallas Department Store in Problem 5-44.

Instructions: Using a work sheet, prepare a statement of cash flows (indirect method) for the year ended December 31, 2002.

COMPETENCY ENHANCEMENT OPPORTUNITIES

▶ Deciphering Actual Financial Statements	▶ Ethical Dilemma
▶ Writing Assignment	▶ Cumulative Spreadsheet Analysis
▶ Research Project	▶ Internet Search
▶ The Debate	

Accounting is more than just doing textbook problems. This expanded competency material provides practice in critical thinking, oral and written communication, research, teamwork, and consideration of ethical issues.

▶ DECIPHERING ACTUAL FINANCIAL STATEMENTS

• Deciphering 5–1 (The Walt Disney Company)

The 1998 financial statements for THE WALT DISNEY COMPANY are included in Appendix A. Locate those financial statements and consider the following questions.

1. Does Disney use the direct method or the indirect method? Explain.
2. Analyze Disney's overall cash flow picture for 1996, 1997, and 1998 in light of the positive or negative cash flow patterns for the three categories of cash flows.
3. In the notes to the financial statements, Disney describes how it defines "cash and cash equivalents." What is that definition?
4. Disney had a large decrease in cash from the beginning of 1996 to the end of 1998 (from $1.077 billion down to $317 million). Why might a company decrease its cash balance so dramatically? (Hint: Look at Note 2 of Disney's financial statements.)

• Deciphering 5–2 (Diageo)

The June 30, 1998, statement of cash flows for DIAGEO is contained in Exhibit 5–15 on page 256. Diageo is a large British consumer products firm owning such brand names as Smirnoff, Johnnie Walker, J&B, Gordon's, Guinness, Pillsbury, Haagen-Dazs, and Burger King. Diageo's cash flow statement has been presented according to the provisions of FRS 1, which governs cash flow reporting by U.K. companies.

Instructions:

1. Refer to the data in Diageo's statement of cash flows. Apply the classification standards used in the United States and compute the following three quantities as they would be reported under U.S. GAAP.
   a. Net cash provided by (used in) operating activities.
   b. Net cash provided by (used in) investing activities.
   c. Net cash provided by (used in) financing activities.
2. With the information given in Diageo's cash flow statement, can you prepare the operating activities section of a cash flow statement according to U.S. GAAP using (a) the indirect method or (b) the direct method? Explain.

• Deciphering 5–3 (Caterpillar)

CATERPILLAR is a U.S.-based manufacturer of construction machinery and heavy-duty engines. In the last 5 years, Caterpillar has grown by 88 facilities, formed 17 joint ventures, acquired 20 companies, and introduced 244 new or improved products.

For the past several years, Caterpillar has elected not to include detailed financial statements in its annual report. The 1998 annual report included this explanation: "The following financial statements and notes have been condensed to make them more readable . . . . More comprehensive financial information is provided in the appendix to the proxy statement . . . ."

Below is Caterpillar's "condensed" comparative statement of cash flows for 1997 and 1998. All amounts are in millions of U.S. dollars.

	1998	1997
Profit	$1,513	$1,665
Depreciation and amortization	865	738
Changes in working capital—excluding cash & debt	(1,359)	(552)
Capital expenditures—excluding equipment leased to others	(925)	(824)
Expenditures for equipment leased to others	(203)	(144)
Dividends paid	(400)	(338)
Net free cash flow	$ (509)	$ 545
Other significant cash flow items:		
Treasury stock purchased	(567)	(706)
Net (increase) decrease in long-term finance receivables	(1,177)	(501)
Net increase (decrease) in debt	3,884	1,109
Investments and acquisitions	(1,428)	(59)
Prefunding of employee benefit plans	(200)	(200)
Other	65	(383)
Increase (decrease) in cash and short-term investments	$ 68	$ (195)

Instructions:

1. Prepare statements of cash flows for Caterpillar for 1997 and 1998 using the standard format. Assume that the "Prefunding of employee benefit plans" is an operating item and that "Other" is a financing activity.
2. What information is Caterpillar trying to convey in the term "Net free cash flow?"
3. Write a brief paragraph explaining why operating cash flow decreased so dramatically from 1997 to 1998.

• Deciphering 5–4 (Archer Daniels Midland)

ARCHER DANIELS MIDLAND (ADM) calls itself the "supermarket to the world." It is a leading processor, distributor, and marketer of agricultural products.

A copy of the consolidated statement of cash flows from ADM's 1998 annual report is shown at the top of page 300.

Instructions:

1. Identify the single major cause of the large decrease from 1997 to 1998 in ADM's cash flow from investing activities.
2. Identify the major causes for the increase from 1997 to 1998 in ADM's cash flow used in financing activities.
3. The financing activities section indicates consistent borrowing over the 3-year period. However, no new stock was issued during that period (in fact, significant stock was repurchased). Does this mean that ADM's debt ratio (total liabilities/total assets) was increasing during the period? Explain.

• Deciphering 5–5 (Coca-Cola)

The data at the bottom of page 300 were obtained from the cash flow statements (prepared using the indirect method) of the COCA-COLA COMPANY from 1995 through 1998. All amounts are in millions of U.S. dollars.

Archer Daniels Midland
Consolidated Statement of Cash Flows

	Year Ended June 30		
	1998	**1997** (In thousands)	**1996**
Operating Activities			
Net earnings	$ 403,609	$ 377,309	$ 695,912
Adjustments to reconcile to net cash provided by operations			
Depreciation and amortization	526,813	446,412	393,605
Deferred income taxes	28,659	(12,235)	72,673
Amortization of long-term debt discount	33,297	29,094	25,584
Gain on marketable securities transactions	(36,303)	(59,549)	(109,359)
Other	39,292	(40,758)	(33,243)
Changes in operating assets and liabilities			
Receivables	(294,407)	(23,225)	(183,569)
Inventories	(150,509)	23,046	(320,529)
Prepaid expenses	(27,275)	(18,760)	(1,683)
Accounts payable and accrued expenses	90,203	(110,653)	314,494
Total Operating Activities	$ 613,379	$ 610,681	$ 853,885
Investing Activities			
Purchases of property, plant and equipment	$ (702,683)	$ (779,508)	$ (754,268)
Net assets of businesses acquired	(370,561)	(429,940)	(28,612)
Investments in and advances to affiliates	(366,968)	(416,861)	(110,615)
Purchases of marketable securities	(1,202,662)	(966,203)	(816,401)
Proceeds from sales of marketable securities	1,007,373	1,607,631	1,260,710
Total Investing Activities	$(1,635,501)	$ (984,881)	$ (449,186)
Financing Activities			
Long-term debt borrowings	$ 441,464	$ 348,695	$ 42,066
Long-term debt payments	(55,972)	(115,853)	(22,233)
Net borrowings under line of credit agreements	774,033	421,046	—
Purchases of treasury stock	(81,154)	(312,525)	(259,980)
Cash dividends and other	(107,712)	(104,077)	(84,443)
Total Financing Activities	$ 970,659	$ 237,286	$ (324,590)
Increase (Decrease) In Cash And Cash Equivalents	$ (51,463)	$ (136,914)	$ 80,109

• Deciphering 5–5 (continued)

	1998	1997	1996	1995
Net income	$3,533	$4,129	$3,492	$2,986
Cash from operating activities	3,433	4,033	3,463	3,328
Cash from investing activities	(2,161)	(500)	(1,050)	(1,226)
Cash from financing activities:				
Issuances of debt	1,818	155	1,122	754
Payments of debt	(410)	(751)	(580)	(212)
Common stock issued	302	150	124	86
Purchases of common stock for treasury	(1,563)	(1,262)	(1,521)	(1,796)
Dividends	(1,480)	(1,387)	(1,247)	(1,110)

At January 1, 1995, the following items had the indicated balances:

Cash	$ 1,386
Paid-In Capital from Common Stock (includes par value and additional paid-in capital)	1,600
Retained Earnings	11,006
Treasury Stock	(7,073)

Instructions:

1. Using the information given, estimate the December 31, 1998, balances in the following accounts.
   a. Cash
   b. Paid-In Capital from Common Stock
   c. Retained Earnings
   d. Treasury Stock
2. Comment on the size of the December 31, 1998, balance in the paid-in capital from common stock account in relation to the balance in the treasury stock account.

• Deciphering 5–6 (Lockheed)

LOCKHEED MARTIN CORPORATION is a well-known producer of advanced aircraft, missiles, and space hardware. Lockheed Martin is most famous for its super-secret research and development division, nicknamed the "Skunk Works." Among the high-tech aircraft developed at the Skunk Works are the SR-71 Blackbird spy plane and the F-117A Stealth fighter.

The consolidated statement of cash flows from Lockheed Martin's 1998 annual report is reproduced on page 302.

When investors and analysts use the term "cash flow," they can mean a variety of things. Some common definitions of "cash flow" are:

a. Net income + depreciation
b. Cash flow from operating activities
c. Cash flow from operating activities + cash paid for interest + cash paid for income taxes
d. Cash flow from operating activities − capital expenditures − dividends

Instructions:

1. Using the data from Lockheed's statement of cash flows, compute values for the four measures of "cash flow" defined above for 1996, 1997, and 1998.
2. One of the definitions (a) through (d) is sometimes given the title "free cash flow" because it indicates the amount of discretionary cash generated by a business. Free cash flow is thought of as the amount of cash that an owner can remove from a business without harming its long-run potential. Which of the four definitions do you think is for "free cash flow"? Explain.
3. A leveraged buyout (LBO) is the purchase of a company using borrowed money. The idea behind an LBO is to borrow the money, buy the company, and then repay the loan using the cash flow generated by the purchased company. Which of the four definitions of "cash flow" do you think would be particularly useful to someone considering doing an LBO? Explain.

WRITING ASSIGNMENT
• Where is your statement of cash flows?

You are a senior credit analyst for Far West Bank. The president of Moran Auto Sales has asked you for a loan of $2,000,000. Moran's accountant has compiled and submitted a current balance sheet and income statement. Moran has had moderate income over the past 3 years but has found itself short of cash and therefore in need of the loan.

After receiving the statements, you call Moran's accountant and indicate that the financial statements are not complete; you need to see a statement of cash flows. The accountant argues, "Everything on a statement of cash flows comes from the other two statements. Why make me do the additional work? Just analyze what we sent."

Your task now is to write a memo to the president of Moran Auto Sales convincing her that a statement of cash flows is essential for you to properly evaluate Moran's loan application.

Lockheed Martin Corporation
CONSOLIDATED STATEMENT OF CASH FLOWS

(In millions)	Year ended December 31,		
	1998	**1997**	**1996**
Operating Activities			
Net earnings	$1,001	$1,300	$1,347
Adjustments to reconcile net earnings to net cash provided by operating activities:			
Depreciation and amortization	569	606	732
Amortization of intangible assets	436	446	402
Deferred federal income taxes	203	155	(251)
GE transaction	—	(311)	—
Materials transaction	—	—	(365)
Merger-related and consolidation payments	—	(68)	(244)
Changes in operating assets and liabilities:			
Receivables	809	(572)	(328)
Inventories	(1,183)	(687)	(125)
Customer advances and amounts in excess of costs incurred	329	1,048	544
Income taxes	189	(560)	(158)
Other	(322)	(149)	82
Net cash provided by operating activities	2,031	1,208	1,636
Investing Activities			
Expenditures for property, plant and equipment	(697)	(750)	(737)
Loral Transaction	—	—	(7,344)
Divestiture of L-3 companies	—	464	—
Divestiture of Armament Systems and Defense Systems	—	450	—
Other acquisition and divestiture activities	134	12	—
Other	108	9	52
Net cash (used for) provided by investing activities	(455)	185	(8,029)
Financing Activities			
Net (decrease) increase in short-term borrowings	(151)	(866)	1,110
Increases in long-term debt	266	1,505	7,000
Repayments and extinguishments of long-term debt	(1,136)	(219)	(2,105)
Issuances of common stock	91	110	97
Dividends on common stock	(310)	(299)	(302)
Dividends on preferred stock	—	(53)	(60)
Redemption of preferred stock	(51)	(1,571)	—
Net cash (used for) provided by financing activities	(1,291)	(1,393)	5,740
Net increase (decrease) in cash and cash equivalents	285	—	(653)
Cash and cash equivalents at beginning of year	—	—	653
Cash and cash equivalents at end of year	$ 285	$ —	$ —
Supplemental Disclosure Information			
Cash paid during the year for			
Interest	$ 856	$ 815	$ 655
Taxes	228	986	1,100

▶ **RESEARCH PROJECT**

• What is in a real cash flow statement?

Your group is to report (either orally or in writing) on what information you found in a search of actual cash flow statements.

Choose 10 companies for which you can get a copy of a recent annual report. Using those annual reports, answer the following questions.

1. How many of the 10 companies use the direct method?
2. How many of the 10 companies have the classic cash flow pattern: positive cash from operations and negative cash from investing activities?
3. How many of the 10 companies have cash from operations greater than net income?

4. For each of the 10 companies, identify the largest adjustment to net income (either positive or negative) in computing cash from operations. What item appears most frequently in your collection of the 10 largest adjustments?

5. Some investment strategists state that they will buy only the stocks of companies with positive "free cash flow." Free cash flow is defined as cash from operations minus capital expenditures minus cash dividend payments. How many of the 10 companies have positive free cash flow?

6. A naive definition of cash from operations is "net income plus depreciation." Compute this amount for each of the 10 companies. For your 10 companies, is "net income plus depreciation" a good estimate of actual cash from operations?

7. A very useful number for bankers and for corporate takeover specialists is sometimes called "operating cash flow" and is defined as cash from operations plus cash paid for interest plus cash paid for taxes. Compute "operating cash flow" for each of your 10 companies (sometimes you have to search the financial statement notes to find the amounts of cash paid for interest and taxes). How many of the 10 companies have "operating cash flow" greater than 15% of total assets?

8. One last thing. Somewhere in the annual report is a 5- or 10-year financial summary. How many of the 10 companies include any cash flow data in this financial summary?

▶ **THE DEBATE**
• **Give me the direct method or give me death!**

Three of the seven FASB members dissented to the issuance of FASB Statement No. 95 regarding the statement of cash flows. The two major areas of disagreement were:

- Direct method or indirect method?
- Interest paid: operating activity or financing activity?

  Divide your group into two teams.

- One team represents the FASB majority. Prepare a 2-minute oral argument supporting the allowance of both the direct and the indirect methods and the classification of interest paid as an operating activity.
- The other team represents the FASB minority. Prepare a 2-minute argument supporting the exclusive use of the direct method and the classification of interest paid as a financing activity.

▶ **ETHICAL DILEMMA**
• **Is the price right?**

You are a finance and accounting analyst for Bunscar Company and have been with the firm for 5 years. Bunscar is a closely held corporation—all of the shares are owned by the founder, Ryan Brown, and by other long-time employees. Bunscar is preparing to issue stock for the first time in an initial public offering (IPO). Of great interest is the initial selling price of the stock because that will determine how much Brown and the others will reap from the sale of their shares.

The board of directors has put together an analysis proposing that the initial selling price be set at $15 per share. Because Brown and the other insiders intend to sell 10 million shares, this price will bring them $150 million. The analysis relies heavily on the trend in Bunscar's earnings, which have grown sharply, particularly in the past year.

You have the reputation of possessing the best presentation skills in the company. The board of directors has asked you to present the $15-per-share proposal to the investment banking firm that will handle Bunscar's IPO. This is your big chance.

As you review the board's analysis in preparing your presentation, you notice that no mention is made of Bunscar's cash flow from operations (CFO). CFO has been fairly steady for the past few years; at the same time earnings have more than doubled. In the past year, when earnings increased 65%, CFO actually declined slightly. After some investigation, you find that Bunscar has become very loose in its assumptions about when revenue should be recognized. In fact, putting the revenue and cash flow numbers together, you conclude that most of Bunscar's earnings increase has come from questionable revenue that probably will never be collected in cash. It seems clear to you that Bunscar's accounting assumptions have been manipulated to make reported income look as good as possible to increase the IPO selling price.

Your presentation is scheduled for the day after tomorrow. What should you do?

► CUMULATIVE SPREADSHEET ANALYSIS

This spreadsheet assignment is a continuation of the spreadsheet assignments given in earlier chapters. If you completed those assignments, you have a head start on this one.

Refer back to the instructions for preparing the revised financial statements for 2002 as given in part (1) of the Cumulative Spreadsheet Analysis assignment in Chapter 3.

1. Skywalker wishes to prepare a *forecasted* balance sheet, a *forecasted* income statement, and a *forecasted* statement of cash flows for 2003. Use the financial statement numbers for 2002 as the basis for the forecast, along with the following additional information.
    (a) Sales in 2003 are expected to increase by 40% over 2002 sales of $2,100.
    (b) In 2003, Skywalker expects to acquire new property, plant, and equipment costing $240.
    (c) The $480 in operating expenses reported in 2002 breaks down as follows: $15 depreciation expense, $465 other operating expenses.
    (d) No new long-term debt will be acquired in 2003.
    (e) No cash dividends will be paid in 2003.
    (f) New short-term loans payable will be acquired in an amount sufficient to make Skywalker's current ratio in 2003 exactly equal to 2.0.
    (g) Skywalker does not anticipate repurchasing any additional shares of stock during 2003.
    (h) Because changes in future prices and exchange rates are impossible to predict, Skywalker's best estimate is that the balance in accumulated other comprehensive income will remain unchanged in 2003.
    (i) In the absence of more detailed information, assume that investment securities, long-term investments, other long-term assets, and intangible assets will all increase at the same rate as sales (40%) in 2003.
    (j) In the absence of more detailed information, assume that other long-term liabilities will increase at the same rate as sales (40%) in 2003.
    Note: The forecasted balance sheet and income statement were constructed as part of the spreadsheet assignment in Chapter 4; you can use that spreadsheet as a starting point if you have completed that assignment. In addition, assume the following:
    (k) The investment securities are classified as available-for-sale. Accordingly, cash from the purchase and sale of these securities is classified as an investing activity.
    (l) Transactions impacting other long-term assets and other long-term liabilities accounts are operating activities.
    Hint: Construction of the forecasted statement of cash flows for 2003 involves analyzing the forecasted income statement for 2003 along with the balance sheets for 2002 (actual) and 2003 (forecasted).
2. Repeat (1) with the following change in assumptions:
    (a) Sales growth in 2003 is expected to be 25%.
    (b) Sales growth in 2003 is expected to be 50%.
3. Comment on the forecasted values of cash from operating activities in 2003, assuming that sales will grow at 25%, 40%, and 50%.

► **INTERNET SEARCH**

We began this chapter with a discussion of CIRCLE K. Because financial information for Circle K is no longer available, let's take a look at Circle K's biggest competitor—7-ELEVEN. You can access 7-Eleven's web site at www.seveneleven.com.

Once you've gained access to 7-Eleven's Web site, answer the following questions:

1. 7-Eleven offers franchises to enterprising individuals. Use the company's Web site to determine what the typical initial cash payment is to purchase a 7-Eleven franchise.

2. There are 7-Elevens located throughout the world. Use the information relating to Global Licensing to determine how many 7-Elevens are owned by the company, how many are franchised, and how many are licensed. Where are the bulk of 7-Eleven's franchises located?

3. Access 7-Eleven's statement of cash flows. From the information contained therein, is the company financing its expansion through successful operations, borrowings, or a combination of the two?

4. From the statement of cash flows, identify the largest cash inflow and the largest cash outflow. What do these two items tell you about the company?

part 2

Primary Activities
of a Business

OPERATING ACTIVITIES

FINANCING ACTIVITIES

INVESTING ACTIVITIES

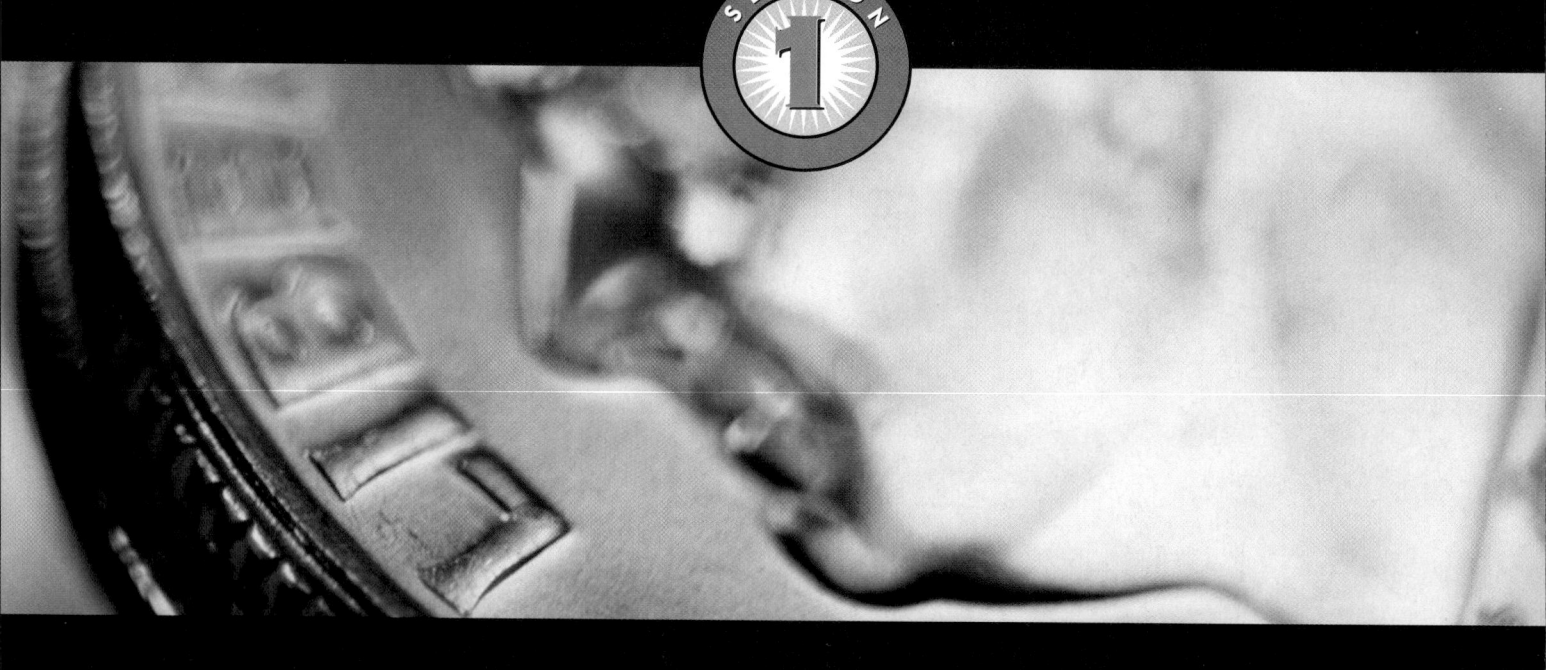

chapter 6
The Revenue/Receivables/

A. P. Giannini was born in 1870 in San Jose, California. When Giannini was seven, his father was killed. His mother remarried, and the family moved to San Francisco where Giannini's stepfather started a fruit wholesaling business. Giannini worked full-time in the business and by age 19 was made a junior partner in what was by then the most successful fruit wholesaling firm on the West Coast. He invested his profits in San Francisco real estate and by age 31 was financially secure enough to retire.

Giannini's retirement was an active one. He continued to manage his real estate portfolio, and he also was a member of the board of directors of COLUMBUS SAVINGS & LOAN ASSOCIATION, which was San Francisco's first Italian-owned bank. In spite of its immigrant roots, Columbus Savings followed the practice of the other area banks, lending only a portion of the deposits it took in to a few large local businesses and sending the rest to the money center banks in New York and Chicago. Giannini was disturbed to see that the farmers, merchants, and workers he was accustomed to dealing with were not able to get loans. When he was unable to get Columbus to change the policy, he quit the board and vowed to start his own bank. On October 17, 1904, A. P. Giannini, a man with no prior experience as a banker, embarked on a second career by opening the Bank of Italy in a converted saloon in San Francisco.

By April 1906, Giannini's bank was still an obscure little bank in the Italian section of town. On the morning of April 18, 1906, San Francisco was rocked by the worst earthquake in its history. About one-third of the town was destroyed and 500 people were killed. In the quake's aftermath, many local business and civic leaders advocated a slow rebuilding, with a moratorium on all building loans for six months. Giannini disagreed strongly: "Gentlemen, you are making a vital mistake. The time for doing business is right now. Tomorrow morning I am putting a desk on Washington Street wharf with a Bank of Italy sign over it. Any man who wants to rebuild San Francisco can come there and get as much cash as he needs to do it."

Giannini's little bank would eventually grow to become one of the largest banks in the world—BANK OF AMERICA. As of December 31, 1998, Bank of America reported total assets exceeding $617 billion, making it the second-largest company in the United States in terms of assets (behind CITIGROUP). The largest of Bank of America's assets is its loan portfolio, which totals $350 billion; Bank of America's loan portfolio alone is almost as large as GENERAL ELECTRIC'S entire asset base. As you can imagine, with a loan portfolio of this size, Bank of America is continually dealing with customers who don't pay. In 1998, Bank of America recognized an expense of almost $3 billion for loans that it does not expect its customers to repay.

LEARNING OBJECTIVES

1 Explain the normal operating cycle of a business.

2 Prepare journal entries to record sales revenue, including the accounting for bad debts and warranties for service or replacement.

3 Analyze accounts receivable to measure how efficiently a firm is using this operating asset.

4 Discuss the composition, management, and control of cash, including the use of a bank reconciliation.

5 Recognize appropriate disclosures for presenting sales and receivables in the financial statements.

EXPANDED MATERIAL

6 Explain how receivables may be used as a source of cash through secured borrowing or sale.

7 Describe proper accounting and valuation of notes receivable.

8 Understand the impact of uncollectible accounts on the statement of cash flows.

9 Use a petty cash fund.

O ur discussion of the income statement in Chapter 4 focused our attention on the importance of net income in the decisions made by investors and creditors. In this and the subsequent chapter, we focus on the event that begins the income-producing process—the sale. Because the financial statements are interrelated, a study of the measurement and recognition of the elements contained in the income statement is also a study of the measurement and recognition of changes in the elements contained in the balance sheet. So, in addition to discussing revenue, we will at the same time be discussing the resulting accounts receivable and/or cash side of the transaction.

Exhibit 6–1 illustrates the time line associated with the revenue/receivables/cash cycle. The chapter will begin with a discussion of the events relating to this time line. We will first discuss the journal entries that result from the sale of goods or services. With this background, we then introduce additional complexities associated with sales—sales discounts, sales returns and allowances, bad debts, and warranties—and their effect on the financial statements. As illustrated by the large amount of bad debt expense recognized by Bank of America in 1998, proper recognition of revenues and the valuation of receivables can have a very significant impact on the financial statements.

EXHIBIT 6 – 1 | Revenue/Receivables/Cash Time Line

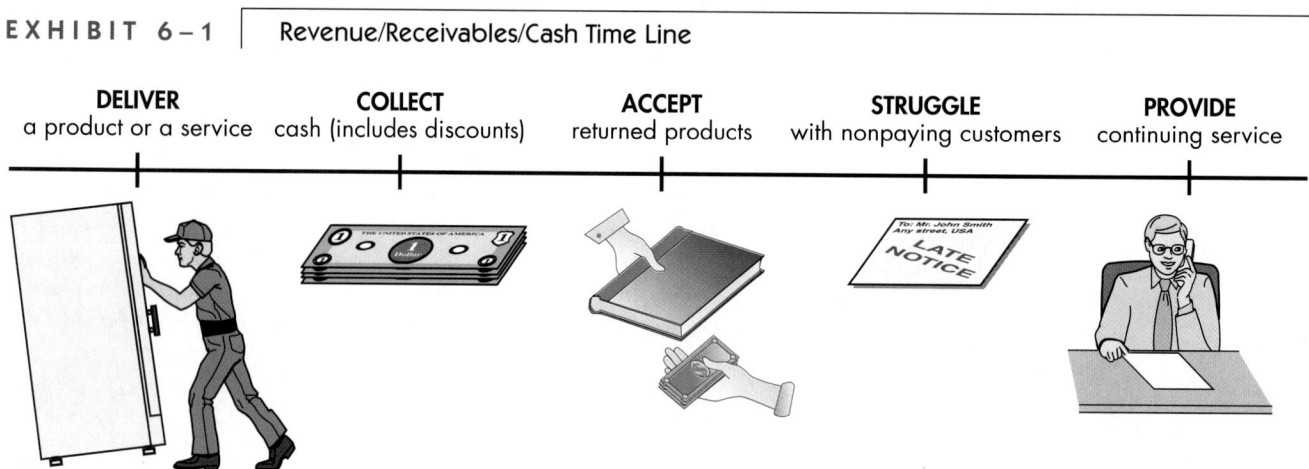

DELIVER	COLLECT	ACCEPT	STRUGGLE	PROVIDE
a product or a service	cash (includes discounts)	returned products	with nonpaying customers	continuing service

Once we discuss the events relating to the revenue/receivables/cash cycle, methods for monitoring accounts receivable, cash management and control, and the presentation of sales, receivables, and cash on the financial statements are also presented and discussed. In the expanded material section of this chapter, we discuss how receivables can be used as a source of cash. The chapter concludes with a discussion of the impact of bad debt expense on computing cash flows from operations. Chapter 7 addresses the more complex issues associated with revenue recognition.

THE OPERATING CYCLE OF A BUSINESS

1

Explain the normal operating cycle of a business.

The normal operating cycle of a business involves purchasing inventory (using either cash or credit), which is then sold, often on account. Once the receivable is collected, the cycle begins again. This cycle, illustrated in Exhibit 6–2, continually repeats itself and is the lifeblood of any business enterprise. An understanding of this operating cycle (which involves the recognition of revenue, the recording of a receivable, and the subsequent collection of cash) is critical if you are to understand how businesses operate and the role of accounting information in that business. Thus, we begin our detailed discussion of accounting with a look at the revenue/receivables/cash cycle.

EXHIBIT 6–2 | The Operating Cycle

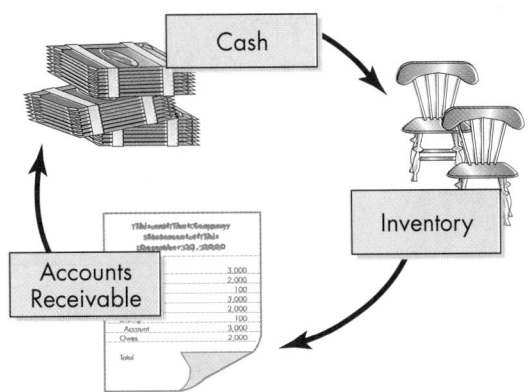

The recognition of **revenue** is generally related to the recognition of **accounts receivable.** Because revenues are generally recorded when the earning process is complete and a valid promise of payment (or payment itself) is received, it follows that a receivable arising from the sale of goods is generally recognized when title to the goods passes to a bona fide buyer. The point at which title passes may vary with the terms of the sale, therefore, it is normal practice to recognize the receivable when goods are shipped to the customer. It is at this point in time that the revenue recognition criteria are normally satisfied. Revenue should not be recognized for goods shipped on approval, where the shipper retains title until there is a formal acceptance, or for goods shipped on consignment, where the shipper retains title until the goods are sold by the consignee. Receivables for services to customers are properly recognized when the services are performed. The entry for recognizing revenue and a receivable from the sale of goods or services is:

FYI: When a company accepts another company's credit card (such as VISA, MasterCard, and American Express) as payment, a service fee is charged by the credit card company. This fee is recognized as an expense by the seller.

Accounts Receivable	XXX	
Sales		XXX

When the amount is collected, Accounts Receivable is credited and Cash is debited as follows:

Cash	XXX	
Accounts Receivable		XXX

For department stores and major oil and gas companies that have their own credit cards, a significant portion of revenues arises from sales using these credit cards. For example, there are over 55 million SEARS cardholders, and Sears reports that over 50% of its sales are from credit customers using the Sears card. The recognition of such revenue and the resulting receivables is similar to that illustrated above.

➤ ZZZZ BEST

Barry Minkow started operating his carpet-cleaning business out of the Minkow family garage when he was 15. At its peak six years later, the company, called ZZZZ BEST, had a market value of $211 million. On paper, Minkow himself was worth $109 million. Minkow was a celebrity. In February 1987, he was selected as one of the top 100 young entrepreneurs in the United States. He spoke of making ZZZZ Best the "General Motors"

of carpet cleaning. He talked of running for president one day. But, in a press release dated July 3, 1987, ZZZZ Best announced that Minkow had resigned as chief executive officer because of a "severe medical problem." Shortly thereafter, ZZZZ Best filed for Chapter 11 bankruptcy. The rapid growth of ZZZZ Best had been a fraud, and Barry Minkow was eventually sentenced to 25 years in prison.

The major aspect of the fraud involved reporting fictitious receivables and revenue from fire damage restoration jobs. For example, ZZZZ Best filed a registration statement with the Securities and Exchange Commission (SEC) in 1985 in which it claimed to have a con-tract for a $2.3 million restoration job on an eight-story building in Arroyo Grande, California. Unfortunately, Arroyo Grande, a town of 13,000 people and five traffic lights, had no buildings over three stories. On May 19, 1987, *The Wall Street Journal* reported that ZZZZ Best had received a $13.8 million restoration contract for a Dallas job. Again, the job was nonexistent. With bogus revenues and receivables like this, ZZZZ Best was able to report net income for the year ended April 30, 1987, of $5 million on revenue of $50 million, up from $900,000 net income on $4.8 million revenue the year before.

Why didn't the auditor uncover these irregularities?

 Why would a company consider selling on account in the first place? Why not just have a policy of "all sales are for cash"?

Before we move on and introduce some additional aspects of sales, let's take a moment and discuss the different types of receivables that are typical. In its broadest sense, the term receivables is applicable to all claims against others for money, goods, or services. For accounting purposes, however, the term is generally employed in a narrower sense to designate claims expected to be settled by the receipt of cash.

In classifying receivables, an important distinction is made between trade and nontrade receivables. **Trade receivables,** generally the most significant category of receivables, result from the normal operating activities of a business, that is, credit sales of goods or services to customers. Trade receivables may be evidenced

Companies must pay a fee for accepting another company's credit card. What do you think this fee is for?

Larry Gray, the partner in charge of auditing ZZZZ Best, did what he was supposed to do, but in this case he didn't do it well enough. When ZZZZ Best reported a $7 million contract to restore a building in Sacramento, Gray demanded to see the building. This was difficult because neither the building nor the job existed. However, officials of ZZZZ Best managed to get access to a large office building in Sacramento for a weekend, and Gray was allowed to tour the building to inspect the "finished work." On another occasion, ZZZZ Best reported an $8.2 million restoration contract in San Diego. Again, Gray demanded to see the job site. This time he was led through an unfinished building and told that the work was still ongoing. Things got very complicated for ZZZZ Best when Gray later requested to see the finished job. ZZZZ Best had to spend $1 million to lease the building and hire contractors to finish six of the eight floors in 10 days. Gray was led on another tour and wrote a memo saying, "Job looks very good." Gray has subsequently been faulted for looking only at what ZZZZ Best officials chose to show him without making independent inquiries.

QUESTIONS:

1. ZZZZ Best grossly inflated its operating results by reporting bogus revenue and receivables. What factors prevent a company from continuing to report fraudulent results indefinitely?

2. What could the auditor have done to uncover the ZZZZ Best fraud?

SOURCES:
Daniel Akst, "How Whiz-Kid Chief of ZZZZ Best Had, and Lost, It All," *The Wall Street Journal*, July 9, 1987, p. 1.
Daniel Akst, "How Barry Minkow Fooled the Auditors," *Forbes*, October 2, 1989, p. 126.

by a formal written promise to pay and classified as **notes receivable.** In most cases, however, trade receivables are unsecured "open accounts," often referred to simply as accounts receivable.

Accounts receivable represent an extension of short-term credit to customers. Payments are generally due within 30 to 90 days. The credit arrangements are typically informal agreements between seller and buyer supported by such business documents as invoices, sales orders, and delivery contracts. Normally trade receivables do not involve interest, although an interest or service charge may be added if payments are not made within a specified period. Trade receivables are the most common type of receivable and are generally the most significant in total dollar amount.

Nontrade receivables include all other types of receivables. They arise from a variety of transactions, such as: (1) the sale of securities or property other than inventory; (2) deposits to guarantee contract performance or expense payment; (3) claims for rebates and tax refunds; and (4) dividends and interest receivable. Nontrade receivables should be summarized in appropriately titled accounts and reported separately in the financial statements. Another way of classifying receivables relates to the current or short-term versus noncurrent or long-term nature of receivables. As indicated in Chapter 3, the "current assets" classification, as broadly conceived, includes all receivables identified as collectible within one year or the normal operating cycle, whichever is longer. Thus, for classification purposes, all trade receivables are considered current receivables; each nontrade item requires separate analysis to determine whether it is reasonable to assume that it will be collected within one year. Noncurrent receivables are reported under the "Investments" or "Other noncurrent assets" caption, or as a separate item with an appropriate description.

In summary, receivables are classified in various ways, for example, as accounts or notes receivable, as trade or nontrade receivables, and as current or noncurrent receivables. These categories are not mutually exclusive. For example, accounts receivable are trade receivables and are current; notes receivable may be trade receivables and therefore current in some circumstances, but they may be nontrade receivables, either current or noncurrent, in other situations. The classifications used most often in practice and throughout this book will be simply accounts receivable, notes receivable, and other receivables.

Prepare journal entries to record sales revenue, including the accounting for bad debts and warranties for service or replacement.

ACCOUNTING FOR SALES REVENUE

The amount of sales or revenues is always the largest item on the income statement (if it's not, the company has bigger problems to worry about than how to account for transactions), and accounts receivable is typically one of the largest current assets on a company's balance sheet. For example, retail companies such as SEARS, ROEBUCK AND CO. or J.C. PENNEY COMPANY, INC., typically have 50% to 70% of total current assets tied up in receivables. For some service-type businesses, the percentage is even higher. But the magnitude of these two account balances should not cause us to overlook some additional aspects of sales transactions. Though these items are significantly smaller when compared to sales and receivables, a knowledge of them is critical in properly accounting for the transactions of a company. The items we will examine in this section include:

- *Discounts*—Discounts are offered at the time of the sale or at the time of payment.
- *Sale Returns and Allowances*—Returns and allowances occur subsequent to the sale and can occur before or after payment has been made.
- *Accounting for Bad Debts*—Once a credit sale is made, the issue of collection remains. Bad debts must be accounted for once the expected payment period has lapsed.
- *Warranties for Service or Replacement*—Long after a sale occurs and collection is made, a warranty period associated with that sale may still be in place.

Discounts

Many companies bill their customers at a gross sales price less an amount designated as a **trade discount.** The discount may vary by customer, depending on the volume of business or size of order from the customer. In effect, the trade discount reduces the "list" sales price to the "net" sales price actually charged the customer. This net price is the amount at which the receivable and corresponding revenue should be recorded.

Another type of discount is a **cash (sales) discount** offered to customers by some companies to encourage prompt payment of bills. Cash discounts may be taken by the customer only if payment is made within a specified period of time, generally 30 days or less. Receivables are generally recorded at their gross amounts, without regard to any cash discount offered. If payment is received within the discount period, Sales Discounts (a contra account to Sales) is debited for the difference between the recorded amount of the receivable and the total cash collected. This method (called the *gross method*), which is simple and widely used, is illustrated as follows with credit terms of "2/10, n/30" (2% discount if paid within 10 days, net amount due in 30 days).

Cash (Sales) Discounts—Gross Method		
Sales of $1,000; terms 2/10, n/30:		
Accounts Receivable	1,000	
Sales		1,000
Partial payment of $300, received within discount period:		
Cash	294	
Sales Discounts	6	
Accounts Receivable		300
Payment of the remaining $700, received after discount period:		
Cash	700	
Accounts Receivable		700

The net method of accounting for sales discounts records the sale and the receivable net of the discount. Using the above example, the receivable and the sale would be recorded at $980 ($1,000 × .98). If payment is not made within the discount period, the additional amount paid by the customer through failure to take the sales discount would be recorded in a revenue account. The journal entries using the net method are illustrated below.

Cash (Sales) Discounts—Net Method		
Sales of $1,000; terms 2/10, n/30:		
Accounts Receivable	980	
Sales		980
Partial payment of $294, received within discount period:		
Cash	294	
Accounts Receivable		294
Payment of the remaining $700, received after discount period:		
Cash	700	
Sales Discounts Not Taken		14
Accounts Receivable ($700 × .98)		686

Sales Returns and Allowances

In the normal course of business, some goods will be returned by customers and some allowance will have to be made for such factors as goods damaged during shipment, spoiled or otherwise defective goods, or shipment of an incorrect quantity or type of goods. When an allowance is necessary, net sales and accounts receivable are reduced. To illustrate, assume that red sweaters costing $600 are sold to a customer for $1,000. The customer calls and states that green sweaters were ordered and should have been shipped. Rather than return the sweaters, the customer agrees to keep the sweaters in return for a reduction in the price—an allowance—of $200. The entry to record this sales allowance would be:

Sales Returns and Allowances	200	
Accounts Receivable		200

> **FYI:** Contra accounts are used because they often yield valuable information. For example, suppose Firm A and Firm B both have net sales of $10,000. Firm A has gross sales of $1,000,000 and sales returns of $990,000. Firm B has gross sales of $10,000 and no sales returns. Might this information affect decisions made about these two firms?

Although the charge could be made directly to Sales, the use of a separate contra account preserves information that may be useful to management.

Suppose that instead of an allowance, the customer elects to return the sweaters. The return would be recorded as:

Sales Returns and Allowances	1,000	
Accounts Receivable		1,000
Inventory	600	
Cost of Goods Sold		600

As will be discussed in Chapter 9, management must ensure that inventory is not recorded in the books at more than its current value. This lower-of-cost-or-market test is especially important for damaged inventory, as is often the case with returned inventory.

The Valuation of Accounts Receivable—Accounting for Bad Debts

Theoretically, all receivables should be valued at an amount representing the **present value** of the expected future cash receipts. Because accounts receivable are short term, usually being collected within 30 to 90 days, the amount of interest is small relative to the amount of the receivable. Consequently, the accounting profession has chosen to ignore the interest element for these trade receivables.[1]

Instead of valuing accounts receivable at a discounted present value, they are reported at their **net realizable value**, that is, their expected cash value. This means that accounts receivable should be recorded net of estimated uncollectible items and

---

1 See *Opinions of the Accounting Principles Board No. 21*, "Interest on Receivables and Payables," New York: American Institute of Certified Public Accountants, 1971, par. 3(a).

trade discounts. The objective is to report the receivables at the amount of claims from customers actually expected to be collected in cash.

UNCOLLECTIBLE ACCOUNTS RECEIVABLE Invariably, some receivables will prove uncollectible. The simplest method for recognizing the loss from these uncollectible accounts is to debit an expense account, such as Doubtful Accounts Expense, Bad Debt Expense, or Uncollectible Accounts Expense, and credit Accounts Receivable at the time it is determined that an account cannot be collected. This approach is called the direct write-off method and is often used by small businesses because of its simplicity. Although the recognition of uncollectibles in the period of their discovery is simple and convenient, this method does not provide for the matching of expenses with current revenues and does not report receivables at their net realizable value. Therefore, use of the **direct write-off method** is considered a departure from generally accepted accounting principles. The following sections describe the procedures used in estimating uncollectibles with the **allowance method,** which is required by GAAP.

Establishing an allowance for bad debts. When using the allowance method, the amount of receivables estimated to be uncollectible is recorded by a debit to Bad Debt Expense and a credit to Allowance for Bad Debts. The terminology for these account titles may vary somewhat. For example, other possibilities for Allowance for Bad Debts include Allowance for Uncollectible Accounts and Allowance for Doubtful Accounts. The expense account title usually is consistent with that of the allowance account.

The allowance for bad debts account is a contra asset account that is offset against Accounts Receivable, resulting in the accounts receivable balance being reported at its net realizable value. The credit side of the allowance account represents estimated future uncollectible accounts. The debit side of the account reflects verified uncollectible accounts. If a large credit balance builds up in the account over time, this is an indication that estimated bad debts are running higher than actual bad debts and that the estimation technique being used may need to be revised.

A typical entry to recognize bad debt expense, normally made as an end-of-the-period adjustment, would be as follows:

Bad Debt Expense	XXX	
Allowance for Bad Debts		XXX
To record estimated uncollectible accounts receivable for the period.		

The expense would be reported as a selling or general and administrative expense, and the allowance account would be shown as a deduction from Accounts Receivable, thereby reporting the net realizable amount of the receivables.

Writing off an uncollectible account under the allowance method. When positive evidence is available concerning the partial or complete worthlessness of an account, the account is written off by a debit to the allowance account, which was previously established, and a credit to Accounts Receivable. Positive evidence of a reduction in value is found in the bankruptcy, death, or disappearance of a debtor, failure to enforce collection legally, or barring of collection by the statute of limitations. Write-offs should be supported by evidence of the uncollectibility of the accounts from appropriate parties, such as courts, lawyers, or credit agencies. The entry to write off an uncollectible receivable is:

Allowance for Bad Debts	XXX	
Accounts Receivable		XXX
To record the write-off of an uncollectible account.		

Note that no entry is made to Bad Debt Expense at this time. That entry was made when the allowance was established. The expense was thus recorded in the period when the sale was made, not necessarily in the period when the account became uncollectible.

Occasionally an account that has been written off as uncollectible is unexpectedly collected. Entries are required to reverse the write-off entry and to record the collection. Assuming an account of $1,500 was written off as uncollectible but was subsequently collected, the following entries would be made at the time of collection.

Accounts Receivable	1,500	
Allowance for Bad Debts		1,500
To reverse the entry made to write off the account.		
Cash	1,500	
Accounts Receivable		1,500
To record collection of the account.		

For many companies, the issue of collection of accounts previously written off is not significant. But for companies in some industries, it is a multimillion dollar issue. For example, in 1998, BANK OF AMERICA recovered $583 million of loans and leases that had been previously written, or charged, off. Exhibit 6–3 provides the note from Bank of America's 1998 10-K filing, which illustrates that over the preceding three years, Bank of America recovered over $2 billion in accounts previously charged off.

EXHIBIT 6–3 | Bank of America's Note Disclosure Relating to Recoveries

(In millions)	1998	1997	1996
Balance on January 1	$ 6,778	$ 6,316	$ 6,222
Loans and leases charged off	(3,050)	(2,603)	(2,369)
Recoveries of loans and leases previously charged off	583	751	702
Net charge-offs	(2,467)	(1,852)	(1,667)
Provision for credit losses	2,920	1,904	1,645
Other, net	(109)	410	116
Balance on December 31	$ 7,122	$ 6,778	$ 6,316

Estimating uncollectibles based on percentage of sales. The estimate for uncollectible accounts may be based on sales for the period or the amount of receivables outstanding at the end of the period. When a sales basis is used, the amount of uncollectible accounts in past years relative to total sales provides a percentage of estimated uncollectibles. This percentage may be modified by expectations based on current experience. Because doubtful accounts occur only with credit sales, it is logical to develop a percentage of doubtful accounts based on credit sales of past periods. This percentage is then applied to credit sales of the current period. However, because extra work may be required in maintaining separate records of cash and credit sales or in analyzing sales data, the percentage is frequently developed in terms of total sales. Unless there is considerable periodic fluctuation in the proportion of cash and credit sales, the percentage-of-total-sales method will normally give satisfactory results.

To illustrate, if 2% of sales are considered doubtful in terms of collection and sales for the period are $100,000, the charge for Bad Debt Expense would be 2% of the current period's sales, or $2,000. Note that any existing balance in the allowance account resulting from past-period charges to Bad Debt Expense is ignored. The entry for this period would be simply:

> **FYI:** For a firm in a steady state, that is, one that has been in business for a number of years and has a stable level of accounts receivable, bad debt expense estimated on current year's credit sales will be approximately the same as actual write-offs.

Bad Debt Expense	2,000	
Allowance for Bad Debts		2,000
To record estimated bad debt expense for the period ($100,000 × .02 = $2,000).		

The percentage-of-sales method for estimating bad debts is widely used in practice because it is simple to apply. Companies often use this method to estimate bad debts periodically during the year and then adjust the allowance account at year-end in relationship to the accounts receivable balance, as explained in the next section.

Estimating uncollectibles based on accounts receivable balance. Instead of using a percentage of sales to estimate bad debts, companies may base their estimates on a percentage of total accounts receivable outstanding. This method emphasizes the relationship between the accounts receivable and the allowance for bad debts balances. For example, if total accounts receivable are $50,000 and it is estimated that 3% of those accounts will be uncollectible, then the allowance account should have a balance of $1,500 ($50,000 × .03). If the allowance account already has a $600 credit balance from prior periods, then the current-period adjusting entry would be:

Bad Debt Expense	900	
Allowance for Bad Debts		900
To record estimated bad debt expense for the period		
($1,500 required balance – $600 current balance =		
$900 adjustment).		

After posting this entry, the balance in the allowance account would be $1,500, or 3% of total accounts receivable. Note that this method adjusts the existing balance to the desired balance based on a percentage of total receivables outstanding. If, in the example, the allowance account had a $200 debit balance caused by writing off more bad debts than had been estimated previously, the adjusting entry would be for $1,700 in order to bring the allowance account to the desired credit balance of $1,500, or 3% of total receivables.

The most commonly used method for establishing an allowance based on outstanding receivables involves **aging receivables**. Individual accounts are analyzed to determine those not yet due and those past due. Past-due accounts are classified in terms of the length of the period past due. An analysis sheet used in aging accounts receivable is shown below.

ICO Products, Inc.
Analysis of Receivables
December 31, 2002

Customer	Amount	Not Yet Due	Not More Than 30 Days Past Due	31–60 Days Past Due	61–90 Days Past Due	91–180 Days Past Due	181–365 Days Past Due	More Than One Year Past Due
A. B. Andrews	$ 1,450			$1,450				
B. T. Brooks	300				$100	$200		
B. Bryant	200		$1,200					
L. B. Devine	2,100	$12,100						$1,200
K. Martinez	200						$1,200	
M. A. Young	1,400	1,000		100	300			
Total	$47,550	$40,000	$3,000	$1,200	$650	$500	$ 800	$1,400

Overdue balances can be evaluated individually to estimate the collectibility of each item as a basis for developing an overall estimate. An alternative procedure is to develop a series of estimated loss percentages and apply these to the different receivables classifications. ICO Products' calculation of the allowance on the latter basis is illustrated on the next page.

ICO Products, Inc.
Estimated Amount of Uncollectible Accounts
December 31, 2002

Classification	Balances	Uncollectible Accounts Experience Percentage	Estimated Amount of Uncollectible Accounts
Not yet due	$40,000	2%	$ 800
Not more than 30 days past due	3,000	5	150
31–60 days past due	1,200	10	120
61–90 days past due	650	20	130
91–180 days past due	500	30	150
181–365 days past due	800	50	400
More than one year past due	1,400	80	1,120
	$47,550		$2,870

Just as with the previous method based on a percentage of total receivables outstanding, Bad Debt Expense is debited and Allowance for Bad Debts is credited for an amount bringing the allowance account to the required balance. Assuming uncollectibles estimated at $2,870 as shown in the schedule above and a credit balance of $620 in the allowance account before adjustment, the following entry would be made:

Bad Debt Expense	2,250	
Allowance for Bad Debts		2,250
To record bad debt expense for the period		
($2,870 required balance – $620 current balance =		
$2,250 adjustment).		

The aging method provides the most satisfactory approach to the valuation of receivables at their net realizable amounts. Furthermore, data developed through aging receivables may be quite useful to management for purposes of credit analysis and control.

Corrections to allowance for bad debts. As previously indicated, the allowance for bad debts balance is established and maintained by means of adjusting entries at the close of each accounting period. If the allowance provisions are too large, the allowance account balance will be unnecessarily inflated and earnings and accounts receivable will be understated; if the allowance provisions are too small, the allowance account balance will be inadequate and both accounts receivable and earnings will be overstated.

Care must be taken to see that the allowance balance follows the credit experience of the particular business. The process of aging receivables at different intervals may be employed as a means of checking the allowance balance to be certain that it is being maintained satisfactorily. Such periodic reviews may indicate a need for a correction in the allowance as well as a change in the rate or in the method employed.

When the uncollectible accounts experience approximates the estimated losses, the allowance procedure may be considered satisfactory, and no adjustment is required. When it appears that there has been a failure to estimate uncollectible accounts accurately, resulting in an allowance balance that is clearly inadequate or excessive, an adjustment is in order. The effect of this change in accounting estimate would be reported in the current and future periods as an ordinary item on the income statement, usually as an addition to or subtraction from Bad Debt Expense.

The actual write-off of receivables as uncollectible by debits to the allowance account and credits to the receivables account may temporarily result

> **Caution!** The most common error when computing bad debt expense is to confuse the two methods—percentage of sales and percentage of receivables. Remember that when you are using the percentage-of-sales method, bad debt expense is computed and the balance in the allowance account is then determined. When you are using the percentage-of-receivables method, the balance in the allowance account is computed and then the amount of bad debt expense for the period is determined.

in a debit balance in the allowance account. A debit balance arising in this manner does not mean necessarily that the allowance is inadequate; debits to the allowance account simply predate the end-of-period adjustment for uncollectible accounts. Once an adjustment is made, the allowance account *will have* a credit balance. Think about what it would mean if, after adjustment, the allowance account still had a debit balance—when combined with the balance in accounts receivable—it would mean that you expect to receive more than you are owed, which is a very low probability event.

Warranties for Service or Replacement

FYI: Many companies that sell items such as electronics or appliances make large amounts of profits by selling "maintenance agreements." Because of the high profit margins associated with these agreements, salespersons are often given large incentives to sell them. Some consumer magazines have warned readers that these maintenance agreements are not cost-effective and should not be purchased.

As we have just read, bad debts must be estimated so that proper expenses can be matched with revenues in the period in which the revenues were earned. The same is true in the case of **warranties**. Many companies agree to provide free service on units failing to perform satisfactorily or to replace defective goods. When these agreements, or warranties, involve only minor costs, such costs may be recognized in the periods incurred. When these agreements involve significant future costs and when experience indicates that a definite future obligation exists, estimates of such costs should be made and matched against current revenues.

Such estimates are usually recorded by a debit to an expense account and a credit to a liability account. Subsequent costs of fulfilling warranties are debited to the liability account and credited to an appropriate account, for example, Cash or Inventory. As was the case with the allowance for bad debts account, the debit side of the estimated liability under warranties account tracks *actual* warranty costs, while the credit side of the account represents *estimated* costs.

To illustrate accounting for warranties, consider the following example. MJW Video & Sound sells compact stereo systems with a two-year warranty. Past experience indicates that 10% of all systems sold will need repairs in the first year, and 20% will need repairs in the second year. The average repair cost is $50 per system. The number of systems sold in 2001 and 2002 was 5,000 and 6,000, respectively. Actual repair costs were $12,500 in 2001 and $55,000 in 2002; it is assumed that all repair costs involved cash expenditures.

2001	Warranty Expense	75,000	
	Estimated Liability Under Warranties		75,000
	To record estimated warranty expense based on systems sold (5,000 × .30 × $50 = $75,000).		
	Estimated Liability Under Warranties	12,500	
	Cash		12,500
	To record cost of actual repairs in 2001.		
2002	Warranty Expense	90,000	
	Estimated Liability Under Warranties		90,000
	To record estimated warranty expense based on systems sold (6,000 × .30 × $50 = $90,000).		
	Estimated Liability Under Warranties	55,000	
	Cash		55,000
	To record cost of actual repairs in 2002.		

Periodically, the warranty liability account should be analyzed to see if the actual repairs approximate the estimate. Adjustment to the percentages used in estimating future warranty obligations will be required if experience differs materially from the estimates. These adjustments are changes in estimates and are reported prospectively, that is, in current and future periods. If sales and repairs in the preceding example are assumed to occur evenly through two years, analysis of the liability account at the end of 2002 shows that the ending balance of $97,500 ($75,000 + $90,000 − $12,500 − $55,000) is reasonably close to the predicted amount of $100,000 based upon the 10% and 20% estimates.

Computation:

2001 sales still under warranty for 6 months:		
$50 × [$5,000 (6/12 × .20)]		$ 25,000
2002 sales still under warranty for 18 months:		
$50 × [$6,000 (6/12 × .10) + $6,000 (12/12 × .20)]		75,000
Total		$100,000

On occasion, an estimate may differ significantly from actual experience. Misleading financial statements may result if an adjustment is not made. In those instances, an adjustment is made to the liability account in the current period. Continuing the previous example, assume that warranty costs incurred in 2002 were only $35,000. Then the ending balance of $117,500 would be much higher than the $100,000 estimate. If the $17,500 difference was considered to be material, an adjustment to warranty expense would be made in 2002 as follows:

Estimated Liability Under Warranties	17,500	
Warranty Expense		17,500
To record adjustment of estimate for warranty repairs.		

3

Analyze accounts receivable to measure how efficiently a firm is using this operating asset.

MONITORING ACCOUNTS RECEIVABLE

Managers as well as external users of financial information need to measure how efficiently a firm is utilizing its operating assets, particularly significant working capital elements such as receivables, inventories, and accounts payable. The most common relationship used to monitor receivables is the average collection period.

Average Collection Period

Average receivables are sometimes expressed in terms of the **average collection period,** which reflects the average number of days that elapse between the time that a sale is made and the time that cash is collected. Average receivables outstanding divided by average daily sales gives the average collection period. This measure is computed for the WS Corporation as illustrated below.

	2002	2001
Average receivables	$397,500	$354,250
Net sales	$1,425,000	$1,650,000
Average daily sales (net sales/365)	$ 3,904	$4,521
Average collection period (average receivables/average daily sales)	102 days	78 days

This same measurement can be obtained by dividing the number of days in the year by the receivables turnover. **Accounts receivable turnover** is determined by dividing net sales by the average trade accounts receivable outstanding during the year. In developing an average receivables amount, the average of the beginning-of-year and end-of-year balances is normally used; however, a better measure of the average balance can be obtained using quarterly or monthly balances.

Accounts receivable turnover rates for WS Corporation for 2002 and 2001 are computed as follows:

	2002	2001
Net sales	$1,425,000	$1,650,000
Net receivables:		
Beginning of year	$375,000	$333,500
End of year	$420,000	$375,000
Average receivables [(beginning balance + ending balance)/2]	$397,500	$354,250
Receivables turnover for year	3.6 times	4.7 times

The value computed for receivables turnover represents the average number of revenue/receivables/cash cycles completed by the firm during the year.

In some cases, instead of computing the average collection period for the entire year, it may be more useful to report the average collection period for the receivables existing at the end of the period. This information would be significant in evaluating current position and, particularly, the receivable position as of a given date. This information for the WS Corporation is computed as follows:

	2002	2001
Receivables at end of year	$420,000	$375,000
Average daily sales	$3,904	$4,521
Average collection period (end of year)	108 days	83 days

What constitutes a reasonable average collection period varies with individual businesses. For example, if merchandise is sold on terms of net 45 days, a 40-day average collection period would be reasonable, but if terms are net 30 days, a receivable balance equal to 40 days' sales would indicate slow collections. The average collection period for a number of companies is given in Exhibit 6–4. Notice the big difference between the 8.9-year average collection period of BANK OF AMERICA, a company that makes its money through creating and maintaining credit relationships, and the 6-day average collection period of HOME DEPOT, which emphasizes the sales of inventory and devotes relatively little effort to credit issues.

Sales activity just before the close of a period should be considered when interpreting accounts receivable measurements. If sales are unusually light or heavy just before the end of the fiscal period, this affects total receivables as well as the related measurements. When such unevenness prevails, it may be better to analyze accounts receivable according to their due dates, as was illustrated earlier in the chapter.

The problem of minimizing accounts receivable without losing desirable business is important. Receivables often do not earn interest revenue, and the cost of carrying them must be covered by the profit margin. The longer the accounts are carried without interest being earned, the smaller will be the percentage return realized on invested capital.

To attract business, credit frequently is granted for relatively long periods. The cost of granting long-term credit should be considered. Assume that a business has average daily sales of $5,000 and average accounts receivable of $250,000, which represents 50 days' sales. If collections and the credit period can be improved so that accounts receivable represent only 30 days' sales, then accounts receivable will be reduced to $150,000. Assuming a total cost of 10% to carry and service the accounts, the $100,000 decrease would yield annual savings of $10,000.

EXHIBIT 6–4 | Average Collection Period

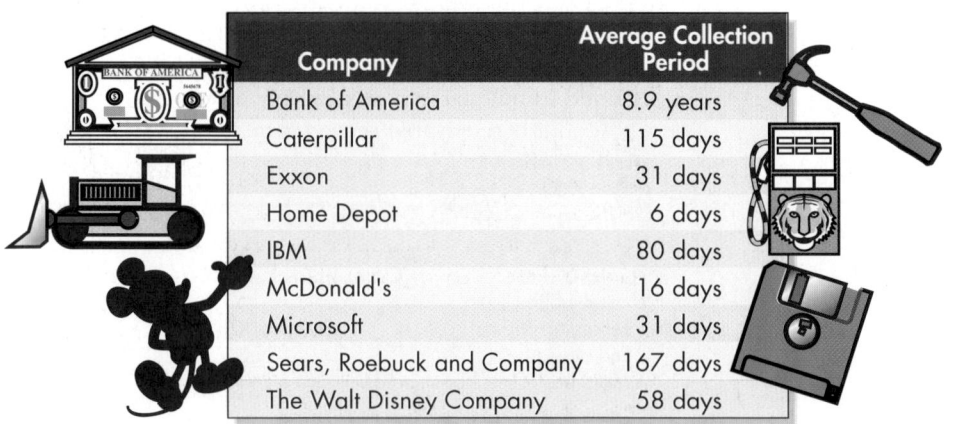

Company	Average Collection Period
Bank of America	8.9 years
Caterpillar	115 days
Exxon	31 days
Home Depot	6 days
IBM	80 days
McDonald's	16 days
Microsoft	31 days
Sears, Roebuck and Company	167 days
The Walt Disney Company	58 days

Discuss the composition, management, and control of cash, including the use of a bank reconciliation.

CASH MANAGEMENT AND CONTROL

To this point, our focus has been primarily on revenues and receivables. However, revenues and receivables have value because they will eventually be converted to cash. **Cash** is important because it provides the basis for measurement and accounting for all other items. Another reason why cash is so important is that individuals, businesses, and even governments must maintain an adequate liquidity position; that is, they must have a sufficient amount of cash on hand to pay obligations as they come due if they are to remain viable operating entities. In the early stages of its conceptual framework project, the FASB identified the need to report information on cash and liquidity as one of the key objectives of financial reporting. This emphasis eventually led to the requirement of providing a statement of cash flows as one of the primary financial statements.

In striking contrast to the importance of cash as a key element in the liquidity position of an entity is its unproductive nature. Because cash is the measure of value, it cannot expand or grow unless it is converted into other properties. Cash kept under a mattress, for example, will not grow or appreciate, whereas land may increase in value if held. Excessive balances of cash on hand are often referred to as idle cash. Efficient cash management requires available cash to be continuously working in one of several ways as part of the operating cycle or as a short-term or long-term investment. The management of cash is therefore a critical business function.

Because cash is the most liquid of all assets, it is also the one that needs to be safeguarded the most. Thus, we will spend some time discussing cash and its equivalents as well the most common safeguard—a bank reconciliation—often employed to ensure that cash is properly accounted for.

Composition of Cash

Cash is the most liquid of current assets and consists of those items that serve as a medium of exchange and provide a basis for accounting measurement. To be reported as "cash," an item must be readily available and not restricted for use in the payment of current obligations. A general guideline is whether an item is acceptable for deposit at face value by a bank or other financial institution.

Items that are classified as cash include coin and currency on hand and unrestricted funds available on deposit in a bank, which are often called **demand deposits**, because they can be withdrawn upon demand. Demand deposits include amounts in checking, savings, and money market deposit accounts. Petty cash funds or change funds and negotiable instruments, such as personal checks and cashiers' checks, are also items commonly reported as cash. The total of these items plus undeposited coin and currency is sometimes called cash on hand. In addition, many companies report investments in very short-term, interest-earning securities (such as three-month U.S. Treasury securities) as **cash equivalents** in the balance sheet. Deposits that are not immediately available due to withdrawal or other restrictions are sometimes referred to as **time deposits**. These deposits are sometimes separately classified as "temporary investments." Examples of time deposits include certificates of deposit (CDs) and money market savings certificates. CDs, for example, generally may be withdrawn without penalty only at specified maturity dates.

Deposits in foreign banks that are subject to immediate and unrestricted withdrawal generally qualify as cash and are reported at their U.S. dollar equivalents as of the date of the balance sheet. However, cash in foreign banks that is restricted as to use or withdrawal should be designated as receivables of a current or noncurrent nature and reported subject to appropriate allowances for estimated uncollectibles.

Some items do not meet the "acceptance at face value on deposit" test and should not be reported as cash. Examples include postage stamps (which are office supplies) and postdated checks, IOUs, and not-sufficient-funds (NSF) checks (all of which are, in effect, receivables).

Cash balances specifically designated by management for special purposes should be reported separately. An example would be cash set aside specifically for the purpose of retiring a bond issue in the future; this cash is called a sinking fund. Restricted cash should be reported as a current item only if it is to be applied to some current purpose or obligation. Classification of the cash balance as current or noncurrent should parallel the classification applied to the liability.

A credit balance in the cash account resulting from the issuance of checks in excess of the amount on deposit is known as a **cash overdraft** and should be reported as a current liability.

In summary, cash is a current asset comprised of coin, currency, and other items that (1) serve as a medium of exchange and (2) provide the basis for measurement in accounting. Most negotiable instruments (e.g., checks, bank drafts, and money orders) qualify as cash because they can be converted to currency on demand or are acceptable for deposit at face value by a bank. For many companies, the bulk of "cash" is held in the form of short-term, interest-earning securities. Components of cash restricted as to use or withdrawal should be disclosed or reported separately and classified as an investment, a receivable, or other asset. Exhibit 6–5 summarizes the classification of various items that have been discussed. The objective of disclosure is to provide the user of financial statements with information to assist in evaluating the entity's ability to meet obligations (i.e., its liquidity and solvency) and in assessing the effectiveness of cash management.

EXHIBIT 6–5 | Classification of Cash and Noncash Items

Item	Classification
Undeposited coin and currency	Cash
Unrestricted funds on deposit at bank (demand deposits)	Cash
Petty cash and change funds	Cash
Negotiable instruments, such as checks, bank drafts, and money orders	Cash
Company checks written but not yet mailed or delivered	Cash
Restricted deposits, such as CDs and money market savings certificates (time deposits)	Temporary Investment
Deposits in foreign banks:	
Unrestricted	Cash
Restricted	Receivables
Postage stamps	Office Supplies
IOUs, postdated checks, and not-sufficient-funds (NSF) checks	Receivables
Cash restricted for special purposes	Restricted Cash*
Cash overdraft	Current Liability

Separately reported as current or noncurrent asset depending on the purpose for which it is restricted.

Compensating Balances

In connection with financing arrangements, it is common practice for a company to agree to maintain a minimum or average balance on deposit with a bank or other lending institution. These **compensating balances** are defined by the SEC as "that portion of any demand deposit (or any time deposit or certificate of deposit) maintained by a corporation . . . which constitutes support for existing borrowing arrangements of the corporation . . . with a lending institution. Such arrangements would include both outstanding borrowings and the assurance of future credit availability."[2]

2 Securities and Exchange Commission, *Accounting Series Release No. 148,* "Disclosure of Compensating Balances and Short-Term Borrowing Arrangements," Washington, DC: U.S. Government Printing Office, 1973.

FYI: The effective interest rate on a loan can be thought of as interest/"take home" amount of loan. Because a compensating balance requirement reduces the amount of the loan that can be "taken home" while still requiring that interest be paid on the entire loan, it would increase the effective interest rate.

Compensating balances provide a source of funds to the lender as partial compensation for credit extended. In effect, such arrangements raise the interest rate of the borrower because a portion of the amount on deposit with the lending institution cannot be used. These balances present an accounting problem from the standpoint of disclosure. Readers of financial statements are likely to assume the entire cash balance is available to meet current obligations, when, in fact, part of the balance is restricted.

The solution to this problem is to disclose the amount of compensating balances. The SEC recommends that any "legally restricted" deposits held as compensating balances be segregated and reported separately. If the balances are the result of short-term financing arrangements, they should be shown separately among the "cash items" in the current asset section; if the compensating balances are in connection with long-term agreements, they should be classified as noncurrent, either as investments or "other assets." In many instances, deposits are not legally restricted, but compensating balance agreements still exist as business commitments in connection with lines of credit. In these situations, the amounts and nature of the arrangements should be disclosed in the notes to the financial statements, as illustrated in Exhibit 6-6 for ELK ASSOCIATES FUNDING, a small business lender whose primary customers are New York, Boston, Chicago, and Miami taxi drivers. This information is taken from the applicable portion of the note explaining notes payable and lines of credit.

EXHIBIT 6-6 | Elk Associates Funding—Disclosure of Compensating Balances

Pursuant to the terms of the [line of credit] agreements the Company is required to comply with certain terms, covenants and conditions. The Company pledged its loans receivable and other assets as collateral for the . . . lines of credit and since January 1998 was required to maintain compensating balances of 5%. During September 1998 the Company eliminated the compensating balance requirement with its banks. Prior to January 1998, the Company was required to maintain 10% compensating balances with each bank. At March 31, 1999, and June 30, 1998, average compensating balances of nil and $1,104,250, respectively, were maintained by the Company in accordance with these agreements.

Management and Control of Cash

As noted earlier, a business enterprise must maintain sufficient cash for current operations and for paying obligations as they come due. Any excess cash should be invested temporarily to earn an additional return for the shareholders. Effective cash management also requires controls to protect cash from loss by theft or fraud. Because cash is the most liquid asset, it is particularly susceptible to misappropriation unless properly safeguarded.

The system for controlling cash must be adapted to a particular business. It is not feasible to describe all the features and techniques employed in businesses of various kinds and sizes. In general, however, systems of cash control deny access to the accounting records to those who handle cash. This reduces the possibility of improper entries to conceal the misuse of cash receipts and cash payments. The probability of misappropriation of cash is greatly reduced if two or more employees must conspire in an embezzlement. Further, systems normally provide for separation of the receiving and paying functions. The basic characteristics of a system of cash control are:

1. Specifically assigned responsibility for handling cash receipts
2. Separation of handling and recording cash receipts
3. Daily deposit of all cash received
4. Voucher system to control cash payments
5. Internal audits at irregular intervals

► A CLASSIC BANK ACCOUNT MANIPULATION

From July 1980 through February 1982, E. F. HUTTON was able to create an extra $1 billion in available funds by aggressively manipulating and shuffling $10 billion in branch office bank accounts. These extra funds provided considerable interest revenue (or interest expense savings), because during that time period, short-term interest rates were often in the 18% to 20% range.

One technique used involved the intentional over-drafting of accounts held at small local banks. Large withdrawals, sometimes 10 times as much as the account balance, were made from small local banks, with the funds being deposited in Hutton's central bank account. The funds would earn interest in the central account until the local bank required the overdraft to be covered, a period often extending for several days.

Another abuse involved the overaggressive use of float in the local bank accounts. Float is extra money in a bank account, money that has already been spent by check, but that the bank has not yet deducted from the account because the check has yet to be presented at the bank for payment. For example, when a bank reconciliation is done, the total of the outstanding checks represents the amount of the float. Hutton intentionally opened accounts in small rural banks because the collection process of such banks is typically slower, allowing for more float. Hutton particularly liked doing business with banks in Watertown, New York, on the eastern shore of Lake Ontario, where heavy winter

6. Double record of cash—bank and books, with reconciliations performed by someone outside the accounting function

These controls are more likely to be found in large companies with many employees. Small companies with few employees generally have difficulty in totally segregating accounting and cash-handling duties. Even small companies, however, should incorporate as many control features as possible.

To the extent that a company can incorporate effective internal controls, it can reduce significantly the chances of theft, loss, or inadvertent errors in accounting for and controlling cash. Even the most elaborate control system, however, cannot totally eliminate the possibilities of misappropriations or errors. The use of periodic bank

Employees who are responsible for handling cash in a company should not be involved in accounting activities.

snowstorms could be expected to delay mail and thus slow down the check-clearing process. However, Hutton misused the process by creating chains of bank accounts and transferring funds from one to another by writing a check on one bank and depositing it in another. During the check-clearing interval, the funds would be earning interest in both banks.

This wasn't the first instance of overaggressive use of float. In October 1978, the SEC warned brokers to stop trying to extend the check-clearing period and thus increase the float by paying East Coast customers with checks drawn on West Coast banks, and vice versa. And in October 1979, a New York state judge assessed damages to MERRILL LYNCH for paying New York customers with California checks.

In May 1985, Hutton pleaded guilty to 2,000 counts

of mail and wire fraud and agreed to pay approximately $10 million in fines and restitution.

QUESTIONS:

1. What ethical issues are involved in using float as E. F. Hutton did?
2. How can manipulation, as described in this case, be controlled?

SOURCES:

Andy Pasztor, Bruce Ingersoll, and Daniel Hertzberg, "Hutton Unit Pleads Guilty in Fraud Case," *The Wall Street Journal*, May 3, 1985, p. 3.

Andy Pasztor and Scott McMurray, "E. F. Hutton Scheme Involved More Cash Than Disclosed, U.S. Prosecutor Says," *The Wall Street Journal*, May 6, 1985, p. 3.

Anthony Bianco and G. David Wallace, "What Did Hutton's Managers Know—And When Did They Know It?" *Business Week*, May 20, 1985, p. 110.

reconciliations can help identify any cash shortages or errors that may have been made in accounting for cash. Another common cash control, a petty cash fund, is discussed in the expanded material at the end of the chapter.

Bank Reconciliations

When daily receipts are deposited and payments are made by check, the bank's statement of its transactions with the depositor can be compared with the record of cash as reported on the depositor's books. A comparison of the bank balance with the balance reported on the books is usually made monthly by means of a summary known as a **bank reconciliation**. A bank reconciliation is prepared to disclose any errors or irregularities in either the records of the bank or those of the business unit. It is developed in a form that points out the reasons for discrepancies in the two balances. It should be prepared by an individual who neither handles nor records cash because if a person who was embezzling from the cash account also was in charge of the reconciliation, it would be too easy to cover his or her tracks.

When the bank statement and the depositor's records are compared, certain items may appear on one and not the other, resulting in a difference in the two balances. Most of these differences result from temporary timing lags and are thus normal. Four common types of differences arise in the following situations.

1. A deposit made near the end of the month and recorded on the depositor's books is not received by the bank in time to be reflected on the bank statement. This amount, referred to as a **deposit in transit**, has to be added to the bank statement balance to make it agree with the balance on the depositor's books.
2. Checks written near the end of the month have reduced the depositor's cash balance but have not cleared the bank as of the bank statement date. These **outstanding checks** must be subtracted from the bank statement balance to make it agree with the depositor's records.
3. The bank sometimes charges a monthly fee for servicing an account. The bank automatically reduces the depositor's account balance for this **bank service charge** and notes the amount on the bank statement. The depositor must deduct this amount from the recorded cash balance to make it agree with the bank statement balance.

> **Caution!** In preparing a bank reconciliation, it is essential to know how the bank handled a transaction (e.g., the entry made, if any, on an NSF check) so that a proper reconciliation can be made from the company's books' perspective.

The return of a customer's check for which insufficient funds are available, known as a **not-sufficient-funds (NSF) check**, is handled in a similar manner.

4. An amount owed to the depositor is paid directly to the bank by a third party and is added to the depositor's account. Upon receipt of the bank statement (assuming prior notification has not been received from the bank), this amount must be added to the cash balance on the depositor's books. Examples include a direct payroll deposit by an individual's employer and interest added by the bank on a savings account. Similarly, the depositor may have items deducted from the account by a third party (such as transfers to savings plans). These items must be deducted from the depositor's cash balance.

If, after considering the items mentioned above, the bank statement and the book balances cannot be reconciled, a detailed analysis of both the bank's records and the depositor's books may be necessary to determine whether errors or irregularities exist on the records of either party.

PREPARING A BANK RECONCILIATION   A common form of bank reconciliation is illustrated below. This form is prepared in two sections, the bank statement balance being adjusted to the corrected cash balance in the first section, and the book balance being adjusted to the same corrected cash balance in the second section. Any items not yet recognized by the bank (e.g., deposits in transit or outstanding checks) as well as any errors made by the bank are recorded in the first section. The second section contains any items the depositor has not yet recognized (e.g., direct deposits, NSF checks, or bank service charges) and any corrections for errors made on the depositor's books.

> **Caution!** Adjustments to the book balance should reflect new information learned upon receiving the bank statement. Adjustments to the bank balance should reflect checks written and deposits made that the bank doesn't know about yet.

The reconciliation of bank and book balances to a corrected balance has two important advantages: It develops a corrected cash figure, and it shows separately all items requiring adjustment on the depositor's books.

An alternative form of reconciliation would be to reconcile the bank statement balance to the book balance. This form would not develop a corrected cash figure, however, and would make it more difficult to determine the adjustments needed on the depositor's books.

Svendsen, Inc.
Bank Reconciliation
November 30, 2002

Balance per bank statement, November 30, 2002		$2,979.72
Add: Deposits in transit	$658.50	
Charge for interest made to depositor's account by bank in error	12.50	671.00
		$3,650.72
Deduct outstanding checks:		
No. 1125	$ 58.16	
No. 1138	100.00	
No. 1152	98.60	
No. 1154	255.00	
No. 1155	192.07	703.83
Corrected bank balance		$2,946.89
Balance per books, November 30, 2002		$2,952.49
Add: Interest earned during November	$ 98.50	
Check No. 1116 to Ace Advertising for $46 recorded by depositor as $64 in error	18.00	116.50
		$3,068.99
Deduct: Bank service charges	$ 3.16	
Customer's check deposited November 25 and returned marked NSF	118.94	122.10
Corrected book balance		$2,946.89

After preparing the reconciliation, the depositor should record any items appearing on the bank statement and requiring recognition on the company's books as well as any corrections for errors discovered on its own books. The bank should be notified immediately of any bank errors. The following entries would be required on the books of Svendsen, Inc., as a result of the November 30 reconciliation:

Cash	98.50	
Interest Revenue		98.50
To record interest earned during November.		
Cash	18.00	
Advertising Expense		18.00
To record correction for check in payment of advertising		
recorded as $64 instead of the actual amount, $46.		
Accounts Receivable	118.94	
Miscellaneous General Expense	3.16	
Cash		122.10
To record customer's uncollectible check and bank charges for November.		

Stop & Think Suppose that after employing the procedures outlined above, your bank and book balances are not the same. What types of errors might prevent your ability to get the balances to equal?

After these entries are posted, the cash account will show a balance of $2,946.89. If financial statements were prepared at November 30, this is the amount that would be reported as cash on the balance sheet. It should be noted that the bank reconciliation is not presented to external users. It is used as a control procedure and as an accounting tool to determine the adjustments required to bring the cash account and related account balances up to date.

5

Recognize appropriate disclosures for presenting sales and receivables in the financial statements.

PRESENTATION OF SALES AND RECEIVABLES IN THE FINANCIAL STATEMENTS

Companies often provide a breakdown of the sources of their revenues in the body of the income statement. For example, Note 11 of THE WALT DISNEY COMPANY'S financial statements (Appendix A) indicates three sources of revenues: creative content, broadcasting, and theme parks and resorts. As another example, MICROSOFT provides information in the notes to its financial statements partitioning revenues, operating income, and identifiable assets by geographical area (see Exhibit 6-7). This information is useful to users of the financial statements as they determine future sources of a firm's revenue. This information also allows users to determine how efficiently assets are being used to generate revenues and profits. In the case of Microsoft, we can compute the percentage of revenues generated from each geographical area and conclude that the percentage has remained constant over time. In computing the amount of sales dollars generated in the United States per dollar of assets, we note that the amount has steadily declined, from 0.82 in 1996 to 0.62 in 1998. That amount has also declined for Microsoft's European operations as well, from 0.97 in 1996 to 0.74 in 1998. With this analysis we can see that the European operations are generating more sales dollars per dollar of assets than are their American counterparts.

Receivables qualifying as current items may be grouped for presentation on the balance sheet in the following classes: (1) notes receivable—trade debtors, (2) accounts receivable—trade debtors, and (3) other receivables. Alternatively, trade notes and accounts receivable can be reported as a single amount. The detail reported for other receivables depends on the relative significance of the various items included. Valuation accounts are deducted from the individual receivable balances or combined balances to which they relate. Any long-term trade and nontrade receivables would be reported as "other noncurrent assets" on the balance sheet. A company should also disclose if restrictions have been placed on any receivables, such as when receivables have been set aside to satisfy a specific obligation or have been pledged as collateral on a loan. Finally, a company should disclose any significant concentrations of credit risk relating

EXHIBIT 6-7 | Microsoft's Note on Geographical Sources of Revenue

GEOGRAPHIC INFORMATION Year Ended June 30	1996	1997	1998
REVENUE			
U.S. operations	$ 6,739	$ 8,877	$11,331
European operations	2,215	2,770	3,719
Other international operations	1,267	1,757	1,776
Eliminations	(1,550)	(2,046)	(2,342)
Total revenue	$ 8,671	$11,358	$14,484
OPERATING INCOME			
U.S. operations	$ 2,118	$ 3,474	$ 4,591
European operations	649	1,013	1,470
Other international operations	297	469	423
Eliminations	(5)	(85)	(70)
Total operating income	$ 3,059	$ 4,871	$ 6,414
IDENTIFIABLE ASSETS			
U.S. operations	$ 8,193	$11,630	$18,294
European operations	2,280	3,395	5,052
Other international operations	1,042	705	1,113
Eliminations	(1,422)	(1,343)	(2,102)
Total identifiable assets	$10,093	$14,387	$22,357

to its receivables. For example, if a significant percentage of a company's sales (and corresponding receivables) are with one debtor, that would represent a concentration of credit risk and should be disclosed.

As is explained in the expanded material later in the chapter, when receivables have been sold or used as collateral for loans, the details associated with the sale or borrowing transaction should be disclosed. Disclosure would include such factors as the terms of the agreement, the value of the receivables involved, and the recourse available to the lender.

Accounts and notes receivable as presented by CATERPILLAR, INC. in its 1998 10-K filing are shown in Exhibits 6–8 and 6–9. Exhibit 6–8 presents the current asset portion of Caterpillar's balance sheet. Note that Caterpillar provides information relating to both trade and finance receivables and even provides detail as to which operating segments—machinery and engines or financial products—have generated the receivables. In Exhibit 6–9, Caterpillar's note disclosure relating to its finance receivables is presented. Information relating to maturity dates of receivables, residual values of leased equipment, and credit loss estimates are presented. Notice that Caterpillar's estimates for credit losses are significantly less than the actual write-offs over the three-year period presented ($150 million in estimates compared to $78 million in actual write-offs).

EXHIBIT 6-8 | Reporting Receivables—Caterpillar, Inc.

	Consolidated			Machinery and Engines			Financial Products		
	1998	1997	1996	1998	1997	1996	1998	1997	1996
Assets									
Current assets:									
Cash and short-term investments	$ 360	$ 292	$ 487	$ 303	$ 241	$ 445	$ 57	$ 51	$ 42
Receivables—trade and other	3,660	3,331	2,956	2,604	3,346	2,960	1,875	285	175
Receivables—finance (Note 5)	3,516	2,660	2,266	—	—	—	3,516	2,660	2,266
Deferred income taxes and prepaid expenses (Note 6)	1,081	928	852	1,081	935	876	18	9	15
Inventories (Notes 1D and 4)	2,842	2,603	2,222	2,842	2,603	2,222	—	—	—
Total current assets	11,459	9,814	8,783	6,830	7,125	6,503	5,466	3,005	2,498

(Header for the above table, spanning the Machinery and Engines and Financial Products groups: **Supplemental Consolidating Data**)

EXHIBIT 6-9 | Reporting Receivables—Note Disclosure

5. Finance receivables

Finance receivables are receivables of Cat Financial, which generally can be repaid or refinanced without penalty prior to contractual maturity. Total finance receivables reported in Statement 3 are net of an allowance for credit losses.

Contractual maturities of outstanding receivables:

	December 31, 1998			
Amounts Due In	**Installment Contracts**	**Financing Leases**	**Notes**	**Total**
1999	$ 917	$1,220	$ 850	$2,987
2000	645	862	553	2,060
2001	417	581	436	1,434
2002	221	288	203	712
2003	78	115	177	370
Thereafter	15	95	812	922
	2,293	3,161	3,031	8,485
Residual value	—	896	—	896
Less: Unearned income	197	487	13	697
Total	$2,096	$3,570	$3,018	$8,684

Allowance for credit loss activity:

	1998	**1997**	**1996**
Balance at beginning of year	$ 84	$ 74	$ 57
Provision for credit losses	70	39	41
Less: Net credit losses	38	19	21
Less: Other—net	6	10	3
Balance at end of year	$ 110	$ 84	$ 74

EXPANDED MATERIAL

In the first part of this chapter, we focused on the central activity of a business—selling a product or service and collecting the resulting receivable. We also discussed other events or activities related to this revenue/receivables/cash cycle. In this section of the chapter, we address the issue of using accounts receivable as a source of cash. Often, for a variety of reasons, a company will have an immediate need for cash. There are a number of methods available to a company to convert its receivables into cash without waiting for payment from the customer. The most common of those methods are discussed here. We also discuss notes receivable and how they are valued and used as a source of cash. The expanded material also includes a brief discussion of the impact of uncollectible accounts on the statement of cash flows. Finally, this chapter concludes with a discussion of the use and accounting for a petty cash fund.

6

Explain how receivables may be used as a source of cash through secured borrowing or sale.

RECEIVABLES AS A SOURCE OF CASH

As stated previously, receivables are a part of the normal revenue/receivables/cash operating cycle of a business. Frequently this cycle takes several months to complete. Sometimes companies need immediate cash and cannot wait for completion of the normal cycle. At other times companies are not in financial stress but want to accelerate the receivables collection process, shift the risk of credit and the effort of collection to someone else, or merely use receivables from customers as a source of financing.

Receivables financing was once looked upon as a desperate measure. In recent years, however, receivables financing has become quite popular for financing leveraged buyouts and for business expansion. As one executive put it, "receivables financing is no longer viewed as last-resort financing but as a legitimate business tool."[3]

Receivables may be converted to cash in one of two ways: as a sale (either with or without recourse) or as a secured borrowing. The FASB specified in Statement No. 125 the conditions that must be met if a transfer of receivables is to be accounted for as a sale. Those conditions are:

1. The transferred assets have been isolated from the transferor. That is, the transferor and its creditors cannot access the assets.
2. The transferee has the right to pledge or exchange the transferred assets.
3. The transferor does not maintain effective control over the assets through an agreement to repurchase them before their maturity.

If these three conditions are not met, then the transfer of receivables is accounted for as a secured borrowing. In the sections that follow, we discuss both the sale of receivables and their use as collateral in a borrowing arrangement.

Sale of Receivables Without Recourse

Certain banks, dealers, and finance companies purchase receivables from companies. In many cases, these purchases are done without *recourse*, meaning that the purchaser assumes the risks associated with the collectibility of the receivables. If the terms of the sale are with recourse, then if the receivables are not collected, the purchaser has the right to collect from the company that originally sold the receivable. A sale of accounts receivable without recourse[4] is commonly referred to as **accounts receivable factoring,** and the buyer is referred to as a "factor." Customers are usually notified that their bills are payable to the factor, and this party assumes the burden of billing and collecting accounts. The flow of activities involved in factoring is presented in Exhibit 6–10.

In many cases, factoring involves more than the purchase and collection of accounts receivable. Factoring frequently involves a continuing agreement whereby a financing institution assumes the credit function as well as the collection function. Under such an arrangement, the factor grants or denies credit, handles the accounts receivable records, bills customers, and makes collections. The business unit is relieved of all these activities, and the sale of goods provides immediate cash for business use. Because the factor absorbs the losses from bad accounts and frequently assumes credit and collection responsibilities, the charges associated with factoring generally exceed the interest charges on a loan with an assignment of receivables. Often the factor will charge a fee of 10% to 30% of the net amount of receivables purchased, except for credit card factoring where the rate is 3% to 5%. The

> **FYI:** Student loans are often factored to specialized loan servicing companies.

3 See "Factoring: A Flexible Borrowing Tool," *Small Business Report*, March 1987, p. 50. Also, Charles Batchelor, "Lenders of Last Resort," *Accountancy*, September 1992, p. 76.

4 Recourse is defined by the FASB as "the right of a transferee of receivables to receive payment from the transferor of those receivables for (a) failure of the debtors to pay when due, (b) the effects of prepayments, or (c) adjustments resulting from defects in the eligibility of the transferred receivables." *Statement of Financial Accounting Standards No. 77*, "Reporting by Transferors for Transfers of Receivables with Recourse," December 1983, p. 7.

EXHIBIT 6-10 | Flow of Activities Involved in Factoring

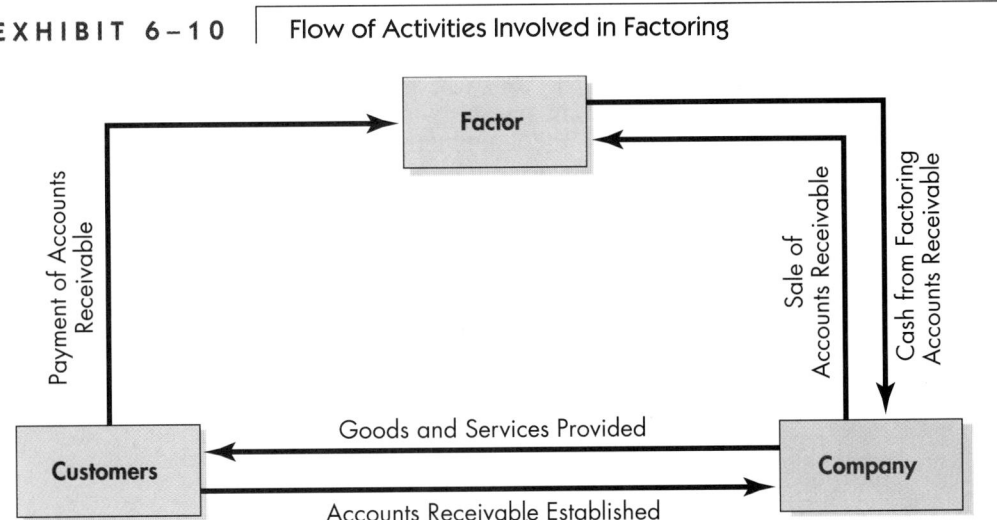

factor may withhold a portion of the purchase price for possible future charges for customer returns and allowances or other special adjustments. Final settlement is made after receivables have been collected.

When receivables are sold outright, without recourse, Cash is debited, receivables and related allowance balances are closed, and a loss account is debited for factoring charges. When part of the purchase price is withheld by the factor, a receivable from the factor is established pending final settlement. Upon receipt of the total purchase price from the bank or finance company, the factor receivable account is eliminated. To illustrate, assume that $10,000 of receivables are factored, that is, sold without recourse, to a finance company for $8,500. An allowance for bad debts equal to $300 was previously established for these accounts. This amount will need to be written off along with the accounts receivable being sold. The finance company withheld 5% of the purchase price as protection against sales returns and allowances. The entry to record the sale of the accounts is:

Cash	8,075	
Receivable From Factor	425	
Allowance for Bad Debts	300	
Loss From Factoring Receivables	1,200	
Accounts Receivable		10,000

To record the factoring of receivables. Computations:
Cash = $8,500 – $425 = $8,075; Factor receivable =
$8,500 × 5% = $425; Factoring loss = ($10,000 – $300)
– $8,500 = $1,200.

The loss from factoring is determined by comparing the book value of the receivables ($10,000 – $300) to the proceeds to be received ($8,500). Assuming there were no returns or allowances, the final settlement would be recorded as follows:

Cash	425	
Receivable From Factor		425

To record the final settlement associated with previously factored receivables.

Sale of Receivables With Recourse

Cash can be obtained by selling receivables with recourse. This is different from factoring, which generally is on a nonrecourse basis. **Selling receivables with recourse** means that a purchaser (bank or finance company) advances cash in return for receiv-

ables but retains the right to collect from the seller if debtors (seller's customers) fail to make payments when due.

With FASB No. 125, the seller is required to estimate the value of the recourse obligation and recognize that liability. That is, the seller must estimate the amount that will be paid to the purchaser as a result of default on the receivables that were sold. Continuing the previous example, assume that the receivables were sold with recourse and the recourse obligation has an estimated fair value of $500. In this instance, the loss to be recognized on the transaction is $1,700 and is computed as follows:

Cash received	$8,500
Estimated value of recourse obligation	(500)
Net proceeds	$8,000
Book value of the receivables	$9,700
Net proceeds to be received	(8,000)
Loss on sale of receivables	$1,700

The entry to record the sale of receivables with recourse would be as follows:

Cash	8,075	
Receivable From Factor	425	
Allowance for Bad Debts	300	
Loss on Sale of Receivables	1,700	
Accounts Receivable		10,000
Recourse Obligation		500

STOP & THINK Why would a company ever factor receivables with recourse when it could factor those same receivables without recourse? What might cause the company selling the receivables to allow the factor to have recourse?

If in the future the estimate of the recourse obligation turns out to have been incorrect, then the company will recognize income if the actual amount paid relating to the recourse obligation is less than $500 and will recognize an additional loss if the amount turns out to be greater than $500.

Secured Borrowing

Loans are frequently obtained from banks or other lending institutions by assigning or pledging receivables as security. The loan is evidenced by a written note that provides for either a general assignment of receivables or an assignment of specific receivables. With an **assignment of receivables**, there are no special accounting problems involved. The books simply report the loan (a debit to Cash and a credit to Notes Payable) and subsequent settlement of the obligation (a debit to Notes Payable and a credit to Cash). However, disclosure should be made on the balance sheet, by a parenthetical comment or a note, of the amount and nature of receivables pledged to secure the obligation to the lender.

The procedures involved are illustrated in the following example. It is assumed that the assignor (the borrower) collects the receivables, which is often the case.

On July 1, 2002, Provo Mercantile Co. assigns receivables totaling $300,000 to Salem Bank as collateral on a $200,000, 12% note. Provo Mercantile does not notify its account debtors and will continue to collect the assigned receivables. Salem assesses a 1% finance charge on assigned receivables in addition to the interest on the note. Provo is to make monthly payments to Salem with cash collected on assigned receivables. The entries shown on the next page would be made.

If in the preceding example Salem Bank assumes responsibility for collecting the assigned receivables, the account debtors would have to be notified to make their payments to the bank. Salem would then use a liability account (e.g., Payable to Provo Mercantile) to account for cash collections during the period. Because the receivables

Illustrative Entries for Assignment of Specific Receivables

Provo Mercantile Co.			Salem Bank		

Issuance of note and assignment of specific receivables on July 1, 2002:

Cash	197,000		Notes Receivable	200,000	
Finance Charge	3,000*		Finance Revenue		3,000*
Notes Payable		200,000	Cash		197,000

*(1% × $300,000)

Collections of assigned accounts during July, $180,000 less cash discounts of $1,000; sales returns in July, $2,000:

Cash	179,000		(No Entry)		
Sales Discounts	1,000				
Sales Returns and Allowances	2,000				
Accounts Receivable		182,000			

Paid Salem Bank amounts owed for July collections plus accrued interest on note to August 1:

Interest Expense	2,000*		Cash	181,000	
Notes Payable	179,000		Interest Revenue		2,000
Cash		181,000	Notes Receivable		179,000

*($200,000 × 12% × 1/12)

Collections of remaining assigned accounts during August less $800 written off as uncollectible:

Cash	117,200		(No Entry)		
Allowance for Bad Debts	800				
Accounts Receivable		118,000*			

*($300,000 – $182,000)

Paid Salem Bank remaining balance owed plus accrued interest on note to September 1:

Interest Expense	210*		Cash	21,210	
Notes Payable	21,000**		Interest Revenue		210*
Cash		21,210	Notes Receivable		21,000**

*($21,000 × 12% × 1/12)
**($200,000 – $179,000)

are still owned by Provo Mercantile, the bank would not record them as assets. Upon full payment of the note plus interest, the bank would remit to Provo Mercantile any cash collections in excess of the note, along with any uncollected accounts.

In summary, receivables provide an important source of cash for many companies. The transfer of receivables to third parties in return for cash generally takes the form of secured borrowing (borrowing with the receivables pledged as collateral) or factoring (a sale without recourse). The financing arrangements are often complex and may involve a transfer of receivables on a recourse basis. Each transaction must be analyzed carefully to see if in form and substance it is a borrowing transaction or a sales transaction, and treated accordingly.

NOTES RECEIVABLE

7

Describe proper accounting and valuation of notes receivable.

A **promissory note** is an unconditional written promise to pay a certain sum of money at a specified time. The note is signed by the maker and is payable to the order of a specified payee or bearer. Notes usually involve interest, stated at an annual rate and charged on the face amount of the note. Most notes are **negotiable notes** that are legally transferable by endorsement and delivery.

For reporting purposes, trade notes receivable should include only negotiable short-term instruments acquired from trade debtors and not yet due. Trade notes generally arise from sales involving relatively high dollar amounts where the buyer wants to extend payment beyond the usual trade credit period of 30 to 90 days. Also, sellers sometimes

request notes from customers whose accounts receivable are past due. Most companies, however, have relatively few trade notes receivable.

Nontrade notes receivable should be separately designated on the balance sheet under an appropriate title. For example, notes arising from loans to customers, officers, employees, and affiliated companies should be reported separately from trade notes.

Valuation of Notes Receivable

Notes receivable are initially recorded at their present value, which may be defined as the sum of future receipts discounted to the present date at an appropriate rate of interest.[5] In a lending transaction, the present value is the amount of cash received by the borrower. When a note is exchanged for property, goods, or services, the present value equals the current cash selling price of the items exchanged. The difference between the present value and the amount to be collected at the due date or maturity date is a charge for interest.

All notes arising in arm's-length transactions between unrelated parties involve an element of interest. However, a distinction as to form is made between interest-bearing and non-interest-bearing notes. An **interest-bearing note** is written as a promise to pay **principal** (or **face amount**) plus interest at a specified rate. In the absence of special valuation problems discussed in the next section, the face amount of an interest-bearing note is the present value upon issuance of the note.

A **non-interest-bearing note** does not specify an interest rate, but the face amount includes the interest charge. Thus, the present value is the difference between the face amount and the interest included in that amount, sometimes called the **implicit (or effective) interest**.

> **In light of the statement** that all arm's-length transactions that extend over time have elements of interest, what do you think about advertising slogans such as "Buy now, no interest and no payments for six months"?

> **FYI:**   Another name for Discount on Notes Receivable is Unearned Interest Revenue.

In recording receipt of a note, Notes Receivable is debited for the face amount of the note. When the face amount differs from the present value, as is the case with non-interest-bearing notes, the difference is recorded as a premium or discount and amortized over the life of the note. In the example to follow, a note receivable is established with credits to sales and discount on notes receivable accounts. The amount of discount is the implicit interest on the note and will be recognized as interest revenue as the note matures.

To illustrate, assume that High Value Corporation sells goods on January 1, 2002, with a price of $1,000. The buyer gives High Value a promissory note due December 31, 2003. The maturity value of the note includes interest at 10%. Thus, High Value will receive $1,210 ($1,000 × 1.21)[6] when the note is paid. The entries on the next page show the accounting procedures for an interest-bearing note and one written in a non-interest-bearing form.

At December 31, 2002, the unamortized discount of $110 on the non-interest-bearing note would be deducted from notes receivable on the balance sheet. If the non-interest-bearing note were recorded at face value with no recognition of the interest included therein, the sales price and profit to the seller would be overstated. In subsequent periods interest revenue would be understated. Failure to record the discount would also result in an overstatement of assets.

Although the proper valuation of receivables calls for the amortization procedure just described, exceptions may be appropriate in some situations due to special limitations or practical considerations. The Accounting Principles Board (APB) in Opinion No. 21 provided guidelines for the recognition of interest on receivables and payables and the accounting subsequently to be employed. However, the Board indicated that this process is not to be regarded as applicable under all circumstances.

---

5 See Appendix B, Time Value of Money, for a discussion of present-value concepts and applications.
6 The amount of $1 due in two years at an annual rate of 10% is $1.21. See Table I of Appendix B.

Illustrative Entries for Notes

Interest-Bearing Note Face Amount = Present Value = $1,000 Stated Interest Rate = 10%			Non-Interest-Bearing Note Face Amount = Maturity = $1,210 No Stated Interest Rate		

To record note received in exchange for goods selling for $1,000:

2002					
Jan. 1 Notes Receivable	1,000		Notes Receivable	1,210	
Sales		1,000	Sales		1,000
			Discount on Notes Receivable		210

To recognize interest earned for one year, $1,000 × .10:

Dec. 31 Interest Receivable	100		Discount on Notes Receivable	100	
Interest Revenue		100	Interest Revenue		100

To record settlement of note at maturity and recognize interest earned for one year, ($1,000 + $100) × .10:

2003					
Dec. 31 Cash	1,210		Cash	1,210	
Notes Receivable		1,000	Discount on Notes Receivable	110	
Interest Receivable		100	Notes Receivable		1,210
Interest Revenue		110	Interest Revenue		110

Among the exceptions are the following:

> . . . receivables and payables arising from transactions with customers or suppliers in the normal course of business which are due in customary trade terms not exceeding approximately one year.[7]

Accordingly, short-term notes and accounts receivable arising from trade sales may be properly recorded at the amounts collectible in the customary sales terms.

Notes, like accounts receivable, are not always collectible. If notes receivable comprise a significant portion of regular trade receivables, a provision should be made for uncollectible amounts and an allowance account established using procedures similar to those for accounts receivable already discussed.

Special Valuation Problems

APB Opinion No. 21 was issued to clarify and refine existing accounting practice with respect to receivables and payables. The opinion is especially applicable to nontrade long-term notes, such as secured and unsecured notes, debentures (bonds), equipment obligations, and mortgage notes. Examples are provided for notes exchanged for cash and for property, goods, or services.

NOTES EXCHANGED FOR CASH When a note is exchanged for cash and there are no other rights or privileges involved, the present value of the note is presumed to be the amount of the cash proceeds. The note should be recorded at its face amount, and any difference between the face amount and the cash proceeds should be recorded as a premium or discount on the note. The premium or discount should be amortized over the life of the note as illustrated previously for High Value Corporation. The total interest is measured by the difference in actual cash received by the borrower and the total amount to be received in the future by the lender. Any unamortized premium or discount on notes is reported on the balance sheet as a direct addition to or deduction from the face amount of the receivables, thus showing their net present value.

---

7 Opinions of the Accounting Principles Board, No. 21, "Interest on Receivables and Payables," New York: American Institute of Certified Public Accountants, 1971, par. 3(a).

► SELLING A NOTE RECEIVABLE: WHAT'S IT WORTH?

As discussed earlier in the chapter, accounts and notes receivable can be used as an immediate source of cash by selling them to a factor. When a note receivable is sold, the value of the receivable depends on several factors including the interest rate on the note, the interest rate charged by the factor, and the time period involved.

Suppose for a moment that you are a bank official. What factors will affect the amount you are willing to pay to a company who wants to discount (sell) a note? First and foremost will be the creditworthiness of the maker; a second factor will be the length of time you must wait to get the money, and a third factor will be how much money you are going to receive when the note matures. Each of these factors will be reflected in your computation of the present value of that note. The steps to determine the amount to be received by the bank (the proceeds) are as follows:

1. Determine the maturity value of the note.

   Maturity value = Face amount + Interest

   Interest = Face amount × Interest rate × Interest period

   Interest period = Date of note to date of maturity

   The maturity value is the amount you will receive when the note matures.

2. Determine the amount of discount.

   Discount = Maturity value × Discount rate × Discount period

   Discount period = Date of discount to date of maturity

NOTES EXCHANGED FOR PROPERTY, GOODS, OR SERVICES   When a note is exchanged for property, goods, or services in an arm's-length transaction, the present value of the note is usually evidenced by the terms of the note or supporting documents. There is a general presumption that the interest specified by the parties to a transaction represents fair and adequate compensation for the use of borrowed funds.[8] Valuation problems arise, however, when one of the following conditions exists:[9]

1. No interest rate is stated.
2. The stated rate does not seem reasonable, given the nature of the transaction and surrounding circumstances.
3. The stated face amount of the note is significantly different from the current cash equivalent sales price of similar property, goods, or services, or from the current market value of similar notes at the date of the transaction.

Under any of the preceding conditions, APB Opinion No. 21 requires accounting recognition of the economic substance of the transaction rather than the form of the note. The note should be recorded at (1) the fair market value of the property, goods, or services exchanged or (2) the current market value of the note, whichever is more clearly determinable. The difference between the face amount of the note and the present value is recognized as a discount or premium and is amortized over the life of the note.

> **Caution!**   Make sure you are comfortable with the time value of money concepts discussed in Appendix B before proceeding with this example.

To illustrate, assume that on July 1, 2002, Timberline Corporation sells a tract of land purchased three years ago at a cost of $250,000. The buyer gives Timberline a one-year note with a face amount of $310,000, bearing interest at a stated rate of 8%. An appraisal of the land prior to the sale indicated a market value of $300,000, which in this example is considered to be the appropriate basis for recording the sale as follows:

8 Ibid., par. 12.
9 Ibid.

Once the maturity value is determined, the second factor comes into play—how long you have to wait to get the money. This time period is termed the discount period. Finally, the creditworthiness of the maker enters into the equation. The riskier the maker, the higher the discount rate will be. Also affecting the discount rate are general economic variables.

3. Determine the proceeds.

Proceeds = Maturity value − Discount

Once the proceeds are determined, the transaction can be recorded, recognizing the applicable liability and net interest revenue or expense (if a borrowing transaction) or the gain or loss (if a sales transaction).

Consider the following example. Meeker Corporation received a 3 month, $5,000 10% note from a customer on September 1 to settle a past due accounts receivable. One month later the note is discounted at a bank at a discount rate of 15%. The amount received from the bank would be computed as follows:

Maturity value of the note = $5,000 + ($5,000 × .10 × 3/12) = $5,125

Amount of discount = $5,125 × .15 × 2/12 = $128.13

Proceeds = $5,125 − 128.13 = $4,996.87

In this instance, Meeker would recognize a loss of $3.13 ($5,000 − $4,996.87) as a result of discounting the note.

net work exercise

To learn more about the time value of money, visit the Financial Players Center Web site at **fpc.net66.com/**. You'll find all sorts of information, including a quiz and an on-line financial calculator.

Net Work:
Study the section called "Teach Me about Time Value of Money (TVM)." Then take the TVM quiz to see what you've learned.

```
2002
July 1  Notes Receivable.......................................................... 310,000
            Discount on Notes Receivable..........................                10,000
            Land................................................................              250,000
            Gain on Sale of Land.......................................               50,000
```

When the note is paid at maturity, Timberline will receive the face value ($310,000) plus stated interest of $24,800 ($310,000 × .08), or a total of $334,800. The interest to be recognized, however, is $34,800—the difference between the maturity value of the note and the market value of the land at the date of the exchange. Thus, the effective rate of interest on the note is 11.6% ($34,800/$300,000).

Assuming straight-line amortization of the discount and that Timberline's year-end is December 31, the following entries would be made to recognize interest revenue and to record payment of the note at maturity:

```
2002
Dec. 31  Interest Receivable................................................... 12,400*
             Discount on Notes Receivable .............................   5,000
                 Interest Revenue..............................................              17,400

         *$310,000 × .08 × 6/12 = $12,400


2003
June 30  Cash........................................................................ 334,800
             Discount on Notes Receivable .............................   5,000
                 Notes Receivable...............................................             310,000
                 Interest Receivable...........................................              12,400
                 Interest Revenue..............................................              17,400
```

The unamortized discount balance of $5,000 would be subtracted from Notes Receivable on the December 31, 2002, balance sheet.

IMPUTING AN INTEREST RATE   If there is no current market price for either the property, goods, or services, or the note, then the present value of the note must be determined by selecting an appropriate interest rate and using that rate to discount future receipts to the present. The **imputed interest rate** is determined at the date of the exchange and is not altered thereafter.

The selection of an appropriate rate is influenced by many factors, including the credit standing of the issuer of the note and prevailing interest rates for debt instruments of similar quality and length of time to maturity. APB Opinion No. 21 states:

> In any event, the rate used for valuation purposes will normally be at least equal to the rate at which the debtor can obtain financing of a similar nature from other sources at the date of the transaction. The objective is to approximate the rate which would have resulted if an independent borrower and an independent lender had negotiated a similar transaction under comparable terms and conditions with the option to pay the cash price upon purchase or to give a note for the amount of the purchase which bears the prevailing rate of interest to maturity.[10]

To illustrate the process of imputing interest rates, assume that Horrocks & Associates surveyed 800,000 acres of mountain property for the Mountain Meadow Ranch. On December 31, 2002, Horrocks accepted a $45,000 note as payment for services. The note is non-interest-bearing and comes due in three yearly installments of $15,000 each, beginning December 31, 2003. Assume there is no market for the note and no basis for estimating objectively the fair market value of the services rendered. After considering the current prime interest rate, the credit standing of the ranch, the collateral available, the terms for repayment, and the prevailing rates of interest for the issuer's other debt, a 10% imputed interest rate is considered appropriate. The note should be recorded at its present value and a discount recognized. The computation is based on Table IV, Present Value of an Ordinary Annuity, in Appendix B, as follows:

Face amount of note	$45,000
Less present value of note:	
$PV_n = R(PVAF \times 10\%)$	
$PV_n = \$15,000(2.4869)$	37,304*
Discount on note	$ 7,696

*Rounded to nearest dollar.

The entry to record the receipt of the note would be:

2002			
Dec. 31	Notes Receivable	45,000	
	Discount on Notes Receivable		7,696
	Service Revenue		37,304

To record a non-interest-bearing note receivable at its present value based on an imputed interest rate of 10% per year.

A schedule showing the amortization of the discount on the note follows. This type of computation is commonly referred to as the effective interest amortization method.

	(1) Face Amount Before Current Installment	(2) Unamortized Discount	(3) Net Amount (1) – (2)	(4) Discount Amortization 10% × (3)	(5) Payment Received
Dec. 31, 2003	$45,000	$7,696	$37,304	$3,730	$15,000
Dec. 31, 2004	30,000	3,966*	26,034	2,603	15,000
Dec. 31, 2005	15,000	1,363**	13,637	1,363	15,000
				$7,696	$45,000

*$7,696 – $3,730 = $3,966   **$3,966 – $2,603 = $1,363

10 Ibid., par. 13.

At the end of each year, an entry similar to the following would be made:

```
2003
Dec. 31  Cash.........................................................................  15,000
             Discount on Notes Receivable.................................  3,730
                 Interest Revenue....................................................          3,730
                 Notes Receivable....................................................        15,000
                 To record the first year's installment on notes receivable
                 and recognize interest earned during the period.
```

By using these procedures, at the end of the three years the discount will be completely amortized to interest revenue, the face amount of the note receivable will have been collected, and the appropriate amount of service revenue will have been recognized in the year it was earned. At the end of each year, the balance sheet will reflect the net present value of the receivable by subtracting the unamortized discount balance from the outstanding balance in Notes Receivable.

It is necessary to impute an interest rate only when the present value of the receivable cannot be determined through evaluation of existing market values of the elements of the transaction. The valuation and income measurement objectives remain the same regardless of the specific circumstances—to report notes receivable at their net present values and to record appropriate amounts of interest revenue during the collection period of the receivables.

8

Understand the impact of uncollectible accounts on the statement of cash flows.

IMPACT OF UNCOLLECTIBLE ACCOUNTS ON THE STATEMENT OF CASH FLOWS

As noted in Chapter 5, the amount of reported sales or net income on an accrual basis must be adjusted for the change in the accounts receivable balances to derive the corresponding amount of cash flow from operations. The establishment of a provision for bad debts with a corresponding allowance for bad debts and the subsequent writing off of uncollectible accounts will impact the adjustments made, depending on whether the analysis considers gross or net accounts receivable balances.

To this point, we have assumed that any decrease in accounts receivable represents a payment received on account. There are actually two possibilities associated with a decrease in receivables: Customers pay or customers never pay and the account is written off. Thus, a decrease in receivables may reflect a receipt of cash, or it may reflect the writing off of an account.

To illustrate the adjustments required for accounts receivable when preparing a statement of cash flows, consider the following information.

	Beginning Balances	Ending Balances
Accounts receivable	$20,000	$25,000
Allowance for bad debts	4,000	5,000
Net accounts receivable	$16,000	$20,000
Sales for the year	$1,000,000	
Net income for the year	100,000	
Bad debt expense for the year	2,000	
Write-off of uncollectible amounts for the year	1,000	
Cash expenses for the year	898,000	

In order to focus on the impact of uncollectible accounts, the illustration assumes that all operating expenses other than bad debt expense were paid in cash. Also, it is assumed that—with the exception of accounts receivable—there were no changes in the amounts of current assets and current liabilities.

In T-account form, the receivables account and the associated allowance account would appear as follows:

Accounts Receivable					Allowance for Bad Debts		
Beg. bal.	20,000					Beg. bal.	4,000
	1,000,000			1,000			2,000
		994,000					
		1,000				End. bal.	5,000
End. bal.	25,000						

The accounts receivable account increased from $20,000 to $25,000. Given sales of $1,000,000, credits to Accounts Receivable must have totaled $995,000. But this $995,000 does not relate entirely to cash collections. A portion of the decline, $1,000, relates to the fact that some cash will never be collected and is no longer an asset; it must be written off. Therefore, cash collections total $994,000.

How is this information reflected in the statement of cash flows? Using the format discussed in Chapter 5, we will begin with the income statement and make adjustments as follows:

Income Statement		Adjustments	Cash Flows From Operations	
Sales	$1,000,000	$ (5,000)	$995,000	Cash collected from customers
Bad debt expense	(2,000)	1,000	(1,000)	
Cash expenses	(898,000)	0	(898,000)	Cash paid for expenses
Net income	$ 100,000	$ (4,000)	$ 96,000	Cash from operations

The first adjustment of $(5,000) reflects the increase in the accounts receivable account resulting from sales (the debit side of the receivables account) exceeding cash collections (the credit side of the receivables account). The second adjustment converts the accrual-basis measure, the bad debt expense (the credit side of the allowance account), to its cash flow counterpart, actual bad debts (the debit side of the allowance account). These two adjustments, considered together, tell us that $994,000 ($995,000 – $1,000) was collected from customers during the period.

Using the above information, the net cash flow provided by operations during the period would be as follows:

Direct Method

Cash collected from customers	$ 994,000
Cash expenses	(898,000)
Net cash flow provided by operations	$ 96,000

Indirect Method

Net income	$ 100,000
Less: Increase in accounts receivable	(5,000)
Add: Increase in allowance for bad debts	1,000
Net cash flows provided by operations	$ 96,000

Often accounts receivable will be presented net of the bad debt expense. Take a look at the following T-account when "netting" occurs.

Accounts Receivable (net)

Beginning balance	16,000			
Sales	1,000,000			
		Collections	994,000	
		Bad debt expense	1,000	
Ending balance	20,000			

What happened to the $1,000 related to the amounts written off as uncollectible? Because that amount appeared as a credit in the receivables account and a debit in the allowance account, it will net out to $0 when the two accounts are combined.

The statement of cash flows, when net accounts receivable are presented, can be prepared from the following information.

Income Statement		Adjustments	Cash Flows From Operations	
Sales	$1,000,000	$ (4,000)	$996,000	⎱ Cash collected from customers
Bad debt expense	(2,000)	0	(2,000)	⎰
Cash expenses	(898,000)	0	(898,000)	Cash paid for expenses
Net income	$ 100,000	$ (4,000)	$ 96,000	Cash from operations

Sales is simply adjusted for the change in the net receivables account. Why is there no adjustment to bad debt expense in this case? Because the two accounts were netted together, all adjustments are netted together as well and result in the $4,000 adjustment.

Using net receivables, the net cash flows provided by operations during the period would be presented as follows:

Direct Method

Cash collected from customers	$ 994,000
Cash expenses	(898,000)
Net cash flows provided by operations	$ 96,000

Indirect Method

Net income	$ 100,000
Less: Increase in net accounts receivable	(4,000)
Net cash flows provided by operations	$ 96,000

In the vast majority of cases, net receivables are presented and the indirect method is used. In these instances, the only adjustment required relates to the change in the net accounts receivable balance.

PETTY CASH FUND

9

Use a petty cash fund.

Immediate cash payments and payments too small to be made by check may be made from a **petty cash fund.** Under an **imprest petty cash system**, the petty cash fund is created by cashing a check for the amount of the fund. In recording the establishment of the fund, Petty Cash is debited and Cash is credited. The cash is then turned over to a cashier or some person who is solely responsible for payments made out of the fund. The cashier should require a signed receipt for all payments made. These receipts may be printed in prenumbered form. Frequently, a bill or other memorandum is submitted when a payment is requested. A record of petty cash payments may be kept in a petty cash journal.

Whenever the amount of cash in the fund runs low and also at the end of each fiscal period, the fund is replenished by writing a check equal to the payments made. In recording replenishment, expenses and other appropriate accounts are debited for petty cash disbursements and Cash is credited. When the fund fails to balance, an adjustment is usually made to a miscellaneous expense or revenue account, sometimes called "Cash Short and Over." Unless theft is involved, this will usually involve only a nominal amount arising, for example, from errors in making change.

As noted above, a petty cash fund is usually replenished at the end of each fiscal period. If replenishment does not occur at year-end, however, an adjustment to Petty Cash is required to properly record all expenditures from the fund during the period. The debit entries would be the same as those to record replenishment; the credit entry would be to Petty Cash, reflecting a reduction in that account.

To illustrate the appropriate entries in accounting for petty cash, assume that Keat Company establishes a petty cash fund on January 1 in the amount of $500. The following entry would be made.

Petty Cash	500	
Cash		500
To establish a $500 petty cash fund.		

During the next six months, the person responsible for the fund made payments for office supplies ($245), postage ($110), and office equipment repairs ($25). Receipts for these items are maintained as evidence supporting the petty cash disbursements. On July 1 the fund is replenished. At that time the coin and currency in the fund totaled $115. The entry to record the expenses and replenish the fund would be:

Office Supplies Expense	245	
Postage Expense	110	
Repairs Expense	25	
Cash Short and Over (or Misc. Expenses)	5	
Cash		385
To record expenses and replenish the petty cash fund.		

After this entry, the fund would be restored to its original amount, $500. If Keat Company decided to reduce the fund to $400, an entry would be required as follows:

Cash	100	
Petty Cash		100
To reduce the petty cash fund from $500 to $400.		

The entry to increase a petty cash fund is the same as to establish the fund initially— a debit to Petty Cash and a credit to Cash. However, petty cash funds should only be large enough to cover small expenditures. Large amounts should be disbursed through an authorized voucher system

REVIEW OF LEARNING OBJECTIVES

1 **Explain the normal operating cycle of a business.** The operating cycle is the lifeblood of almost every business. The critical event for a business is the sale of goods or services. This sale often results in an account receivable being recorded. The account receivable is then collected, the resulting cash is reinvested in the business, and the cycle begins again.

2 **Prepare journal entries to record sales revenue, including the accounting for bad debts and warranties for service or replacement.** A sale is recorded with a credit to Sales Revenue and a debit to either Accounts Receivable or Cash. The matching principle requires that expenses associated with the sale be recorded in the period of the sale. As a result, items such as bad debts and warranties must be estimated and recorded.

Bad debts are estimated using one of two methods—percentage of sales or percentage of receivables. Each of these methods involves estimating the likelihood that some receivables will not be collected. The journal entry involves a debit to Bad Debts Expense and a credit to Allowance for Bad Debts. The allowance account is a contra asset account that, when offset against the accounts receivable account, values the asset at its net realizable value.

Warranties are quantified by estimating, based on past experience, the probable amount of future warranty costs and are recorded with a debit to Warranty Expense and a credit to a liability account. When the warranty claim is presented, the liability account is reduced and a credit is made to cash, parts, labor, and so forth.

3 **Analyze accounts receivable to measure how efficiently a firm is using this operating asset.** The effective management of accounts receivable is critical to the cash flows of any business. The most common tool used to monitor receivables is the average collection period, which reflects the average number of days that lapse between the time a sale is made and cash is collected. First, the accounts receivable turnover ratio is computed by dividing sales by average accounts receivable. The resulting number is divided into 365 (the number of days in a year) to compute the average collection period.

4 **Discuss the composition, management, and control of cash, including the use of a bank reconciliation.** Cash management and control is critical to the success of every business. Because cash is the most liquid of assets, safeguards must be in place to ensure that cash is properly handled and accounted for. A common control involves the use of a bank reconciliation. A bank reconciliation requires the accountant to reconcile the bank's balance for cash with the company's balance. Any discrepancies are identified and appropriate corrections are made.

5 **Recognize appropriate disclosures for presenting sales and receivables in the financial statements.** Disclosure of sales and receivables in the financial statements vary from company to company. In the body of the financial statements, sales are generally reported net of discounts and allowances. Receivables are often reported net of their allowance account with supplemental information provided in the notes to the financial statements.

6 **Explain how receivables may be used as a source of cash through secured borrowing or sale.** In most cases, a receivable is converted into cash when a customer, in the normal cycle of business, pays the company. However, companies can accelerate the cash collection process by using accounts receivable to assist in obtaining a loan. The method employed and the cost to the firm depend on the degree of risk to which the company wishes to expose itself. In the case of secured borrowing, the company is simply pledging the receivable as collateral on a loan. Receivables can also be sold to a third party, usually a bank or other financial institution. When a receivable is sold with recourse, the selling company must quantify the expected payout that will be made as a result of the recourse provision.

7 **Describe proper accounting and valuation of notes receivable.** Notes receivable represent a formal borrowing arrangement between two parties. A note receivable typically specifies an interest rate and a payment date. Notes receivable are valued using techniques that compute the present value of the principal and interest to be received. Problems can arise in the valuation of notes receivable when the note is exchanged for goods or services and the fair market value of those goods and services is difficult to determine. In some instances, an effective interest rate for the note must be imputed.

8 **Understand the impact of uncollectible accounts on the statement of cash flows.** The accounts Allowance for Bad Debts and Bad Debt Expense must be interpreted with care when determining the amount of cash flows related to receivables for a certain period. Different adjustments are made to the statement of cash flows, depending on whether the direct or indirect method is being used. The objective of these adjustments is to correctly identify cash collections from customers for the period.

9 **Use a petty cash fund.** A petty cash fund is used as a control for cash that is on hand in a business. The petty cash fund involves placing one person in charge of the cash on hand and employing a voucher system to account for expenditures from the fund.

KEY TERMS

Accounts receivable 311
Accounts receivable turnover 321
Aging receivables 318
Allowance method 316
Average collection period 321
Bank reconciliation 327
Bank service charge 327
Cash 323
Cash equivalents 323
Cash (sales) discount 314
Cash overdraft 324
Compensating balances 324
Demand deposits 323
Deposit in transit 327
Direct write-off method 316
Net realizable value 315
Nontrade receivables 313

Notes receivable 313
Not-sufficient-funds (NSF) check 328
Outstanding checks 327
Present value 315
Revenue 311
Time deposits 323
Trade discount 314
Trade receivables 312
Warranties 320

Accounts receivable factoring 332
Assignment of receivables 334

Implicit (effective) interest 336
Imprest petty cash system 343
Imputed interest rate 340
Interest-bearing note 336
Negotiable notes 335
Non-interest-bearing note 336
Petty cash fund 343
Principal (face amount)336
Promissory note 335
Selling receivables with recourse 333

QUESTIONS

1. Explain how each of the following factors affects the classification of a receivable: (a) the form of a receivable, (b) the source of a receivable, and (c) the expected time to maturity or collection.
2. (a) Describe the methods for establishing and maintaining an allowance for bad debts account.
   (b) How would the percentages used in estimating uncollectible accounts be determined under each of the methods?
3. In accounting for uncollectible accounts receivable, why is the allowance method, rather than the direct write-off method, required by GAAP?
4. An analysis of the accounts receivable balance of $8,702 on the records of Jorgenson, Inc., on December 31 reveals the following.

Accounts from sales of last 3 months (appear to be fully collectible)	$7,460
Accounts from sales prior to October 1 (of doubtful value)	1,312
Accounts known to be worthless	320
Dishonored notes charged back to customers' accounts	800
Credit balances in customers' accounts	1,190

   (a) What adjustments are required?
   (b) How should the various balances be shown on the balance sheet?
5. Why should a company normally account for product warranties on an accrual basis?

6. (a) How is accounts receivable turnover computed?
   (b) How is average collection period computed?
   (c) What do these two measurements show?
7. Why is cash on hand both necessary and yet potentially unproductive?
8. The following items were included as cash on the balance sheet for the Lawson Co. How should each of the items have been reported?
   (a) Demand deposits with bank
   (b) Restricted cash deposits in foreign banks
   (c) Bank account used for payment of salaries and wages
   (d) Cash in a special cash account to be used currently for the construction of a new building
   (e) Customers' checks returned by the bank marked "Not Sufficient Funds"
   (f) Customers' postdated checks
   (g) IOUs from employees
   (h) Postage stamps received in the mail for merchandise
   (i) Postal money orders received from customers and not yet deposited
   (j) Notes receivable in the hands of the bank for collection
   (k) Special bank account in which sales tax collections are deposited
   (l) Customers' checks not yet deposited

9. The Melvin Company shows in its accounts a cash balance of $66,500 with Bank A and an overdraft of $1,500 with Bank B on December 31. Bank B regards the overdraft as, in effect, a loan to the Melvin Company and charges interest on the overdraft balance. How would you report the balances with Banks A and B? Would your answer be any different if the overdraft arose as a result of certain checks that had been deposited and proved to be uncollectible and if the overdraft was cleared promptly by the Melvin Company at the beginning of January?

10. Mills Manufacturing is required to maintain a compensating balance of $15,000 with its bank to maintain a line of open credit. The compensating balance is legally restricted as to its use. How should the compensating balance be reported on the balance sheet and why?

11. (a) Give at least four common sources of differences between depositor and bank balances.
    (b) Which of the differences in (a) require an adjusting entry on the books of the depositor?

12. How are attitudes regarding the financing of accounts receivable changing? Why do you think this is so?

13. (a) Distinguish among the practices of (1) selling receivables and (2) using receivables as collateral for borrowing.
    (b) Describe the accounting procedures to be followed in each case.

14. According to FASB Statement No. 125, what three conditions must be met to record the transfer of receivables with recourse as a sale?

15. (a) When should a note receivable be recorded at an amount different from its face amount?
    (b) Describe the procedures employed in accounting for the difference between a note's face amount and its recorded value.

16. Explain what special accounting procedures are required when receivables are assigned as collateral for a secured loan.

17. What is meant by imputing a rate of interest? How is such a rate determined?

18. (a) What are the major advantages in using imprest petty cash funds?
    (b) What dangers must be guarded against when petty cash funds are used?

DISCUSSION CASES

CASE 6–1

SHOULD A COMPANY SELL ON CREDIT?

Olin Company currently makes only cash sales. Given the number of potential customers who have requested to buy on credit, Olin is considering allowing credit sales. What factors should Olin consider in making the decision whether to allow credit sales?

CASE 6–2

ACCOUNTING FOR POTENTIAL SALES RETURNS

Ultimate Corporation is a computer products supplier. Ultimate sells products to dealers who then sell the products to the end users. Most of the company's competitors require dealers to pay for shipments within 45 to 60 days. Ultimate has followed a more relaxed policy; in 2002 the average length of time it took the company to collect its receivables was 158 days. (This average collection period can be computed as average accounts receivable balance/average daily sales.) It has been suggested that in return for this lax collection policy, dealers allowed Ultimate to ship more product than the dealers needed, allowing Ultimate to recognize the excess shipments as sales. In 2003, Ultimate attempted to reduce the level of its accounts receivable by stepping up collection efforts. As a result, product returns from dealers increased significantly.

1. Assume that Ultimate's sales for the year were $1,000 with cost of sales being $600. For simplicity, also assume that all of the sales occurred on December 31, and that on

average, Ultimate expects about 15% of products sold to be returned by dissatisfied dealers or dealers who are unable to sell the products. What adjusting entry, if any, should be made at year-end to reflect the likelihood of future sales returns?

2. An allowance for sales returns is analogous to an allowance for bad debts. Most companies disclose an allowance for bad debts but very few disclose an allowance for sales returns. Why not?

3. What other more conservative accounting treatment is possible in regard to the potential sales returns?

CASE 6–3

ACCOUNTING FOR UNCOLLECTIBLES

During the audit of accounts receivable of Montana Company, the new CEO, Joe Frisco, asked why the company had debited the current year's expense for bad debts on the assumption that some accounts will become uncollectible next year. Frisco believes that the financial statements should be based on verifiable, objective evidence. In his opinion it would be more objective to wait until specific accounts become uncollectible before the expense is recorded. What accounting issues are involved? Which method of accounting for uncollectible accounts would you recommend and why?

CASE 6–4

CASH MANAGEMENT

Jack Wilson, manager of Expert Building Company, is a valued and trusted employee. He has been with the company from its start 2 years ago. Because of the demands of his job, he has not taken a vacation since he began working. He is in charge of recording collections on account, making the daily bank deposits, and reconciling the bank statement.

Early this year, clients began complaining to you, the president, about incorrect statements. As president, you check into this matter. Jack tells you there is nothing to worry about. He attests, "The problem is due to the slow mail; customers' payments and statements are crossing in the mail." However, because clients were not complaining last year, you doubt that the mail is the primary reason for the problem.

What might be some of the reasons for the delay? What are some other problems that might begin to occur? What can be done to remedy the problem? What should be done to make sure the problems are avoided in the future?

CASE 6–5

FLOAT MANAGEMENT

Bunsen Company's cash collections average $10,000 per day. Because Bunsen's customers are scattered across the country, the average interval between when a customer writes a check and when the check clears and the amount is credited to Bunsen's account is 7 days. Bunsen could reduce this to 3 days by implementing a lockbox system. With a lockbox system, a company makes arrangements with a bank to retrieve customer checks from a post office box and deposit them directly into the company's account.

Bunsen's cash payments also average $10,000 per day. Bunsen's checks are drawn on a bank located in a major metropolitan area, so the check-clearing time is very short—2 days. If Bunsen were to use a checking account in a small rural bank, the average check-clearing time would increase to 5 days.

1. How much would Bunsen's net interest income increase if it were to implement the lockbox system and switch its checking account to a small rural bank? Assume that the interest rate on checking accounts is 6% per annum based on the average daily balance.

2. What if the banking fee for operating the lockbox system were $4,000 per year—should the lockbox system be implemented?

CASE 6–6

ALLOCATION OF CASH AND NEAR-CASH ASSETS

Bruno Johnson, Chief Financial Officer of Tollerud Company, has determined that Tollerud should keep on hand $35 million in cash or near-cash assets in order to maintain proper liquidity. Bruno is now trying to determine how to allocate the $35 million among the checking account, certificates of deposit, and treasury notes. What factors should influence Bruno's decision?

CASE 6–7

DID I HIDE IT WELL ENOUGH?

Jonathan Mitchell is the accountant for the Mantua Service Company. Due to heavy investments in lottery tickets, Jonathan found himself short of cash and decided to "borrow" funds from Mantua. Jonathan received and deposited cash receipts, recorded the checks written in the cash disbursements journal, and reconciled the bank account. He made the reconciliation balance by manipulating outstanding checks in the bank reconciliation. Would this type of embezzlement be detected with a proper reconciliation of the checking account? Justify your answer.

CASE 6–8

ACCOUNTS RECEIVABLE AS A SOURCE OF CASH

Assume you are the treasurer for Fullmer Products Inc. and one of your responsibilities is to ensure that the company always takes available cash discounts on purchases. The corporation needs $150,000 within 1 week in order to take advantage of current cash discounts. The lending officer at the bank insists on adequate collateral for a $150,000 loan. For various reasons, your plant assets are not available as collateral, but your accounts receivable balance is $205,000. What alternatives would you consider for obtaining the necessary cash?

CASE 6–9

IS IT A SALE OR A BORROWING?

Caitlin Enterprises decides to finance its operations by transferring its receivables with recourse to Larsen Financial, Inc. The provisions of the agreement bar Caitlin and its creditors from claiming the receivables. In addition, Larsen Financial has the right to use the receivables in any way it wishes, and there is no agreement for Caitlin to repurchase the receivables. James McCabe, Caitlin's accountant, is not sure whether this arrangement should be recorded as a sale or as a borrowing. He is aware that the FASB has issued a standard covering this situation, but he isn't sure how this arrangement fits the standard. He approaches you, the company auditor, and asks for your opinion as to how the transaction should be recorded. He also asks you to describe how these two approaches would affect the basic financial statements.

CASE 6–10

ACCOUNTING FOR PETTY CASH

You have just accepted a job with Philodendron Co. Your duties include being cashier of the petty cash fund. Upon inspection of the fund, you find that it includes $143 in currency, $5 in postage stamps, $21 in IOUs, and $37 in various receipts. Because no written records are kept of the petty cash fund, you had to find out from the previous cashier that the approved amount of the fund is $215.

1. Discuss the elements of control necessary for effective maintenance of a petty cash fund.
2. Suggest changes that Philodendron Co. can make to improve the effectiveness of its petty cash fund.

EXERCISES

EXERCISE 6–11

CLASSIFYING RECEIVABLES

Classify each of the items listed below as: (A) Accounts Receivable, (B) Notes Receivable, (C) Trade Receivables, (D) Nontrade Receivables, or (E) Other (indicate nature of item). Because the classifications are not mutually exclusive, more than one classification may be appropriate. Also indicate whether the item would normally be reported as a current or noncurrent asset assuming a 6-month operating cycle.

1. MasterCard or VISA credit card sale of merchandise to customer
2. Overpayment to supplier for inventory purchased on account
3. Insurance claim on automobile accident

4. Charge sale to regular customer
5. Advance to sales manager
6. Interest due on 5-year note from company president, interest payable annually
7. Acceptance of 3-year note on sale of land held as investment
8. Acceptance of 6-month note for past-due account arising from the sale of inventory
9. Claim for a tax refund from last year
10. Prepaid insurance—4 months remaining in the policy period
11. Overpayment by customer of an account receivable

EXERCISE 6–12

COMPUTING THE ACCOUNTS RECEIVABLE BALANCE

The following information from Jumbo Company's first year of operations is to be used in testing the accuracy of Accounts Receivable. The December 31, 2002, balance is $33,500.

    (a) Collections from customers, $72,000.
    (b) Merchandise purchased, $98,000.
    (c) Ending merchandise inventory, $23,500.
    (d) Goods sell at 50% above cost.
    (e) All sales are on account.

Compute the balance that Accounts Receivable should show and determine the amount of any shortage or overage.

EXERCISE 6–13

SALES DISCOUNTS

On November 1, Magily Company sold goods on account for $5,000. The terms of the sale were 3/10, n/40. Payment in satisfaction of $2,000 of this amount was received on November 9. Payment in satisfaction of the remaining $3,000 was received on December 9.

1. How much cash did Magily Company collect from this $5,000 account?
2. Using the gross method, what journal entries would Magily make on November 9 and December 9?
3. Using the net method, what journal entries would Magily make on November 9 and December 9?

EXERCISE 6–14

SALES RETURNS

On July 23, Louie Company sold goods costing $3,000 on account for $4,500. The terms of the sale were n/30. Payment in satisfaction of $3,000 of this amount was received on August 17. Also on August 17, the customer returned goods costing $1,000 (with a sales price of $1,500). The customer reported that the goods did not meet the required specifications.

1. Make the journal entry necessary on July 23 to record the sale. Louie uses a perpetual inventory system.
2. Make the journal entry necessary on August 17 to record the cash collection.
3. Make the journal entry necessary on August 17 to record the return of the goods.
4. What question exists with respect to the valuation of the returned inventory?

EXERCISE 6–15

ESTIMATING BAD DEBTS

Accounts Receivable of the Drummond Manufacturing Co. on December 31, 2002, had a balance of $300,000. Allowance for Bad Debts had a $4,200 debit balance. Sales in 2002 were $1,690,000 less sales discounts of $14,000. Give the adjusting entry for estimated Bad Debt Expense under each of the following independent assumptions.

1. Of 2002 net sales, 1.5% will probably never be collected.
2. Of outstanding accounts receivable, 3% are doubtful.
3. An aging schedule shows that $11,000 of the outstanding accounts receivable are doubtful.

EXERCISE 6–16

JOURNAL ENTRIES FOR RECEIVABLE WRITE-OFFS

McGraw Medical Center has received a bankruptcy notice for Phillip Hollister. Hollister owes the medical center $1,350. The bankruptcy notice indicates that the medical center can't expect to receive payment of any of the $1,350.

1. Make the journal entry necessitated by receipt of the bankruptcy notice.
2. Six months after the medical center received the bankruptcy notice, Hollister appeared requesting medical treatment. He agreed to pay his old bill in its entirety. Make the journal entry or entries necessary to record receipt of the $1,350 payment from Hollister.

EXERCISE 6–17

AGING ACCOUNTS RECEIVABLE

Blanchard Company's accounts receivable subsidiary ledger reveals the following information.

Customer	Account Balance Dec. 31, 2002	Invoice Amounts and Dates	
Allison, Inc.	$8,795	$3,500	12/6/02
		5,295	11/29/02
Banks Bros.	5,230	3,000	9/27/02
		2,230	8/20/02
Barker & Co.	7,650	5,000	12/8/02
		2,650	10/25/02
Marrin Co.	11,285	5,785	11/17/02
		5,500	10/9/02
Ring, Inc.	7,900	4,800	12/12/02
		3,100	12/2/02
West Corp.	4,350	4,350	9/12/02

Blanchard Company's receivable collection experience indicates that, on the average, losses have occurred as follows:

Age of Accounts	Uncollectible Percentage
0–30 days	0.7%
31–60 days	1.4
61–90 days	3.5
91–120 days	10.2
Over 120 days	60.0

The Allowance for Bad Debts credit balance on December 31, 2002, was $2,245 before adjustment.

1. Prepare an accounts receivable aging schedule.
2. Using the aging schedule from (1), compute the Allowance for Bad Debts balance as of December 31, 2002.
3. Prepare the end-of-year adjusting entry.
4. (a) Where accounts receivable are few in number, such as in this exercise, what are some possible weaknesses in estimating bad debts by the aging method?
   (b) Would the other methods of estimating bad debts be subject to these same weaknesses? Explain.

EXERCISE 6–18

ANALYSIS OF ALLOWANCE FOR BAD DEBTS

The Transtech Publishing Company follows the procedure of debiting Bad Debt Expense for 2% of all new sales. Sales for 4 consecutive years and year-end allowance account balances were as follows:

Year	Sales	Allowance for Bad Debts End-of-Year Credit Balance
1999	$2,100,000	$21,500
2000	1,975,000	35,500
2001	2,500,000	50,000
2002	2,350,000	66,000

1. Compute the amount of accounts written off for the years 2000, 2001, and 2002.
2. The external auditors are concerned with the growing amount in the allowance account. What action do you recommend the auditors take?

EXERCISE 6–19

WARRANTY LIABILITY

In 2001 Hampton Office Supply began selling a new computer that carried a 2-year warranty against defects. Based on the manufacturer's recommendations, Hampton projects estimated warranty costs (as a percentage of dollar sales) as follows:

First year of warranty	3%
Second year of warranty	9%

Sales and actual warranty repairs for 2001 and 2002 are presented below.

	2002	2001
Sales	$625,000	$500,000
Actual warranty repairs	22,450	10,600

1. Give the necessary journal entries to record the liability at the end of 2001 and 2002.
2. Analyze the warranty liability account as of the year ended December 31, 2002, to see if the actual repairs approximate the estimate. Should Hampton revise the manufacturer's warranty estimate? (Assume sales and repairs occur evenly throughout the year.)

EXERCISE 6–20

WARRANTY LIABILITY

Modern Appliance Company's accountant has been reviewing the firm's past television sales. For the past 2 years, Modern has been offering a special service warranty on all televisions sold. With the purchase of a television, the customer has the right to purchase a 3-year service contract for an extra $60. Information concerning past television and warranty contract sales is given below.

Color-All Model II Television	2002	2001
Television sales in units	550	460
Sales price per unit	$500	$400
Number of service contracts sold	350	300
Expenses relating to television warranties	$9,630	$3,350

Modern's accountant has estimated from past records that the pattern of repairs has been 40% in the first year after sale, 36% in the second year, and 24% in the third year. Give the necessary journal entries related to the service contracts for 2001 and 2002. In addition, indicate how much profit on service contracts would be recognized in 2002. Assume sales of the contracts are made evenly during the year.

EXERCISE 6–21

ANALYZING ACCOUNTS RECEIVABLE

Trend Industries Company reported the following amounts on its 2001 and 2002 financial statements.

	2002	2001
Accounts receivable	$ 235,000	$ 210,000
Allowance for bad debts	12,000	8,000
Net sales	1,430,000	1,260,000
Cost of sales	1,067,000	856,000

1. Compute the accounts receivable turnover for 2002.
2. What is the average collection period during 2002? (Use 365 days.)

EXERCISE 6–22

REPORTING CASH ON THE BALANCE SHEET
1. Indicate how each of the items below should be reported using the following classifications: (a) cash, (b) restricted cash, (c) temporary investment, (d) receivable, (e) liability, or (f) office supplies.

(1)	Checking account at First Security	$ (20)
(2)	Checking account at Second Security	350
(3)	U.S. savings bonds	650
(4)	Payroll account	100
(5)	Sales tax account	150
(6)	Foreign bank account—restricted (in equivalent U.S. dollars)	750
(7)	Postage stamps	22
(8)	Employee's postdated check	30
(9)	IOU from president's brother	75
(10)	Credit memo from a vendor for a purchase return	87
(11)	Traveler's check	50
(12)	Not-sufficient-funds check	18
(13)	Petty cash fund ($16 in currency and expense receipts for $84)	100
(14)	Money order	36

2. What amount would be reported as unrestricted cash on the balance sheet?

EXERCISE 6–23

RESTRICTED CASH
CLUB MED, INC., operates Club Med resorts in the United States, Mexico, the Caribbean, Asia, the South Pacific, and the Indian Ocean Basin. Club Med routinely receives payment in advance from vacationers. In some countries, Club Med is required by law to deposit cash received as payment for future vacations in special accounts. Cash in these accounts is restricted as to its use.

Assume that on December 31 Club Med received cash totaling $6,000,000 as payment in advance for vacations at one of its resorts. The resort is in a country that requires that the cash be deposited in a special account.

1. Prepare the journal entry necessary to record receipt of the $6,000,000.
2. Explain how the $6,000,000 would be disclosed in the December 31 balance sheet.

EXERCISE 6–24

COMPOSITION OF CASH
Warfield Company had the following cash balances at December 31, 2002:

Undeposited coin and currency	$ 35,000
Unrestricted demand deposits	1,450,000
Company checks written (and deducted from the demand deposits amount) but not scheduled to be mailed until January 2	270,000
Time deposits restricted for use (expected use in 2003)	3,000,000

In exchange for a guaranteed line of credit, Warfield has agreed to maintain a minimum balance of $150,000 in its unrestricted demand deposits account. How much should Warfield report as "Cash" in its December 31, 2002, balance sheet?

EXERCISE 6–25

CORRECT CASH BALANCE
Sterling Company's bank statement for the month of March included the following information:

Ending balance, March 31	$28,046
Bank service charge for March	130
Interest paid by bank to Sterling for March	107

In comparing the bank statement to its own cash records, Sterling found the following:

Deposits made but not yet recorded by the bank	$3,689
Checks written and mailed but not yet recorded by the bank	6,530

In addition, Sterling discovered that it had erroneously recorded a check for $46 that should have been recorded for $64. What is Sterling's correct cash balance at March 31?

EXERCISE 6–26

CORRECT CASH BALANCE

Letterman Corporation's bank statement for the month of April included the following information:

Bank service charge for April	$130
Check deposited by Letterman during April was not collectible and has been marked "NSF" by the bank and returned	400

In comparing the bank statement to its own cash records, Letterman found:

Deposits made but not yet recorded by the bank	$1,324
Checks written and mailed but not yet recorded by the bank	987

All the deposits in transit and outstanding checks have been properly recorded in Letterman's books. Letterman also found a check for $350, payable to Letterman Corporation, that had not yet been deposited and had not been recorded in Letterman's books. Letterman's books show a bank account balance of $9,213 (before any adjustments or corrections). What is Letterman Corporation's correct cash balance at April 30?

EXERCISE 6–27

BANK RECONCILIATION AND ADJUSTING ENTRIES

The accounting department supplied the following data in reconciling the September 30 bank statement for Thalman Auto.

Ending cash balance per bank	$15,496.91
Ending cash balance per books	14,692.71
Deposits in transit	2,615.23
Bank service charge	25.00
Outstanding checks	3,079.51
Note collected by bank including $45 interest (Thalman not yet notified)	1,045.00
Error by bank—check drawn by Thalerman Corp. was charged to Thalman's account	617.08

A sale and deposit of $1,729.00 was entered in the sales journal and cash receipts journal as $1,792.00.

1. Prepare the September 30 bank reconciliation.
2. Give the journal entries required on the books to adjust the cash account.

EXERCISE 6–28

BANK RECONCILIATION—ANALYSIS OF OUTSTANDING CHECKS

The following information was included in the bank reconciliation for Rytton, Inc., for June. What was the total of outstanding checks at the beginning of June? Assume all other reconciling items are listed.

Checks and charges recorded by bank in June, including a June service charge of $30	$17,210
Service charge made by bank in May and recorded on the books in June	20
Total of credits to Cash in all journals during June	19,802
Customer's NSF check returned as a bank charge in June (no entry made on books)	100
Customer's NSF check returned in May and redeposited in June (no entry made on books in either May or June)	250
Outstanding checks at June 30	13,260
Deposits in transit at June 30	600

EXERCISE 6–29

ACCOUNTING FOR THE SALE OF ACCOUNTS RECEIVABLE

On July 15, Mann Company sold $600,000 in accounts receivable for cash of $500,000. The factor withheld 10% of the cash proceeds to allow for possible customer returns or account adjustments. An Allowance for Bad Debts of $80,000 had previously been established by Mann in relation to these accounts.

1. Make the journal entry necessary on Mann's books to record the sale of the accounts.
2. Make the journal entry necessary on Mann's books to record final settlement of the factoring arrangement. No customer returns or account adjustments occurred in relation to the accounts.

EXERCISE 6–30

ACCOUNTING FOR A NON-INTEREST-BEARING NOTE

Zobell Corporation sells equipment with a book value of $8,000, receiving a non-interest-bearing note due in 3 years with a face amount of $10,000. There is no established market value for the equipment. The interest rate on similar obligations is estimated at 12%. Compute the gain or loss on the sale and the discount on notes receivable, and make the necessary entry to record the sale. Also, make the entries to record the amortization of the discount at the end of the first, second, and third year using effective-interest amortization. (Round to the nearest dollar.)

EXERCISE 6–31

ACCOUNTING FOR AN INTEREST-BEARING NOTE

High Country, Inc., purchased inventory costing $50,000. Terms of the purchase were 5/10, n/30. In order to take advantage of the cash discount, High Country borrowed $40,000 from Downtown First National, signing a 2-month, 12% note. The bank requires monthly interest payments. Make the entries to record the following:

1. Initial purchase of inventory on account
2. Payment to the supplier within the discount period
3. Loan from the bank
4. First month's payment to the bank
5. Second and final payment to the bank

EXERCISE 6–32

RECEIVABLES AND THE STATEMENT OF CASH FLOWS

The following selected information is provided for Lynez Company. All sales are credit sales and all receivables are trade receivables.

Accounts receivable, Jan. 1 net balance	$125,000
Accounts receivable, Dec. 31 net balance	165,000
Sales for the year	800,000
Uncollectible accounts written off during the year	14,000
Bad debt expense for the year	24,000
Cash expenses for the year	681,000
Net income for the year	95,000

Using the format illustrated in the chapter and the above information, answer the following questions.

1. Using the *direct* method, compute the net cash flows from operations that Lynez Company would report in its statement of cash flows.
2. Assuming use of the *indirect* method, what adjustments to net income would be required in reporting net cash flows from operations?

EXERCISE 6–33

ACCOUNTING FOR PETTY CASH

An examination on the morning of January 2 by the auditor for the Santiago Appliance Company discloses the following items in the petty cash drawer.

Stamps		$ 43.00
Currency and coin		115.66
IOUs from members of the office staff		121.00
An envelope containing collections for a football pool, with office staff names attached		35.00
Petty cash vouchers for:		
Typewriter repairs	$13.00	
Stamps	70.00	
Telegram charges	28.50	
Delivery fees	12.00	123.50
Employee's check postdated January 15		225.00
Employee's check marked "NSF"		189.00
Check drawn by Santiago Appliance Company to Petty Cash		345.00
		$1,197.16

The ledger account discloses a $1,125 balance for Petty Cash. (1) What adjusting entries should be made so that petty cash is correctly stated on the balance sheet? (2) What is the correct amount of petty cash for the balance sheet? (3) How could the practice of borrowing by employees from the fund be discouraged?

PROBLEMS

PROBLEM 6–34

ACCOUNTING FOR RECEIVABLES—JOURNAL ENTRIES

The following transactions affecting the accounts receivable of Wonderland Corporation took place during the year ended January 31, 2002.

Sales (cash and credit)	$591,050
Cash received from credit customers, all of whom took advantage of the discount feature of the corporation's credit terms 4/10, n/30	303,800
Cash received from cash customers	210,270
Accounts receivable written off as worthless	5,250
Credit memoranda issued to credit customers for sales returns and allowances	63,800
Cash refunds given to cash customers for sales returns and allowances	13,318
Recoveries on accounts receivable written off as uncollectible in prior periods (not included in cash amount stated above)	8,290

The following two balances were taken from the January 31, 2001, balance sheet.

Accounts receivable	$95,842
Allowance for bad debts	9,740 (credit)

The corporation provides for its net uncollectible account losses by crediting Allowance for Bad Debts for 1.5% of net credit sales for the fiscal period.

Instructions:

1. Prepare the journal entries to record the transactions for the year ended January 31, 2002.
2. Prepare the adjusting journal entry for estimated uncollectible accounts on January 31, 2002.

PROBLEM 6–35

ACCOUNTING FOR CASH DISCOUNTS

Beebe Company sold goods on account with a sales price of $50,000 on August 17. The terms of the sale were 2/10, n/30.

Instructions:

1. Record the sale using the gross method of accounting for cash discounts.
2. Record the sale using the net method of accounting for cash discounts.

3. Assume that the payment is received on August 25. Record receipt of the payment using both the gross method and the net method.
4. Assume that payment is received on September 15. Record receipt of the payment using both the gross method and the net method. Is the account used for the net method an asset, liability, revenue, or expense?
5. Which method makes more theoretical sense—the gross method or the net method? Why? Why don't more firms use the net method?

PROBLEM 6–36

ESTIMATING BAD DEBT EXPENSE; SALES METHOD VS. RECEIVABLES METHOD

During 2002, Lacee Enterprises had gross sales of $247,000. At the end of 2002, Lacee had accounts receivable of $83,000 and a credit balance of $5,600 in Allowance for Bad Debts. Lacee has used the percentage-of-sales method to estimate the bad debt expense. For the past several years, the amount estimated to be uncollectible has been 3%.

Instructions:

1. Using the percentage-of-gross-sales method, estimate the bad debt expense and make any necessary adjusting entries.
2. Assuming that 6% of receivables are estimated to be uncollectible and that Lacee decides to use the percentage-of-receivables method to estimate the bad debt expense, estimate the bad debt expense and make any adjusting entries.
3. Which of the two methods more accurately reflects the net realizable value of receivables? Explain.

PROBLEM 6–37

ESTIMATING UNCOLLECTIBLE ACCOUNTS BY AGING RECEIVABLES

Rainy Day Company, a wholesaler, uses the aging method to estimate bad debt losses. The following schedule of aged accounts receivable was prepared at December 31, 2002.

Age of Accounts	Amount
0–30 days	$561,600
31–60 days	196,100
61–90 days	88,400
91–120 days	18,500
Over 120 days	9,600
	$874,200

The following schedule shows the year-end receivables balances and uncollectible accounts experience for the previous 5 years.

Year	Year-End Receivables	0–30 Days	31–60 Days	61–90 Days	91–120 Days	Over 120 Days
2001	$780,700	0.5%	1.0%	10.2%	49.1%	78.2%
2000	750,400	0.4	1.1	10.0	51.2	77.3
1999	681,400	0.6	1.2	11.0	51.7	79.0
1998	698,200	0.5	0.9	10.1	52.3	78.5
1997	723,600	0.4	1.0	8.9	49.2	77.6

The unadjusted allowance for bad debts balance on December 31, 2002, is $32,796.

Instructions: Compute the correct balance for the allowance account based on the average loss experience for the last 5 years and prepare the appropriate end-of-year adjusting entry.

PROBLEM 6–38

WARRANTY LIABILITY

High Fidelity Corporation sells stereos under a 2-year warranty contract that requires High Fidelity to replace defective parts and provide free labor on all repairs. During 2001, 1,050 units were sold at $900 each. In 2002, High Fidelity sold an additional 900 units at $925. Based on past experience, the estimated 2-year warranty costs are $20 for parts and $25 for labor per unit. It is also estimated that 40% of the warranty expenditures will occur in the first year and 60% in the second year. Actual warranty expenditures were as follows:

	2002	2003
Stereos sold in 2001	$18,300	$26,500
Stereos sold in 2002	—	18,100

Instructions: Assuming sales occurred on the last day of the year for both 2001 and 2002, give the necessary journal entries for the years 2001 through 2003. Analyze the warranty liability account for the year ended December 31, 2003, to see if the actual repairs approximate the estimate. Should High Fidelity revise its warranty estimates?

PROBLEM 6–39

WARRANTY LIABILITY

Monroe Corporation, a client, requests that you compute the appropriate balance of its estimated liability for product warranty account for a statement as of June 30, 2002.

Monroe Corporation manufactures television components and sells them with a 6-month warranty under which defective components will be replaced without charge. On December 31, 2001, Estimated Liability for Product Warranty had a balance of $510,000. By June 30, 2002, this balance had been reduced to $80,250 by debits for estimated net cost of components returned that had been sold in 2001.

The corporation started out in 2002 expecting 8% of the dollar volume of sales to be returned. However, due to the introduction of new models during the year, this estimated percentage of returns was increased to 10% on May 1. It is assumed that no components sold during a given month are returned in that month. Each component is stamped with a date at time of sale so that the warranty may be properly administered. The following table of percentages indicates the likely pattern of sales returns during the 6-month period of the warranty, starting with the month following the sale of components.

Month Following Sale	Percentage of Total Returns Expected
First	20%
Second	30
Third	20
Fourth through sixth—10% each month	30
	100%

Gross sales of components were as follows for the first 6 months of 2002:

Month	Amount	Month	Amount
January	$3,600,000	April	$2,850,000
February	3,300,000	May	2,000,000
March	4,100,000	June	1,800,000

The corporation's warranty also covers the payment of freight cost on defective components returned and on the new components sent out as replacements. This freight cost runs approximately 10% of the sales price of the components returned. The manufacturing cost of the components is roughly 80% of the sales price, and the salvage value of returned components averages 15% of their sales price. Returned components on hand at December 31, 2001, were thus valued in inventory at 15% of their original sales price.

Instructions: Using the data given, prepare a schedule for arriving at the balance of the estimated liability for product warranty account as of June 30, 2002, and give the proposed adjusting entry.

PROBLEM 6–40

JOURNAL ENTRIES AND BALANCE SHEET PRESENTATION
The balance sheet for the Itex Corporation on December 31, 2001, includes the following cash and receivables balances.

Cash—First Security Bank		$45,000
Currency on hand		16,000
Petty cash fund		1,000
Cash in bond sinking fund		15,000
Notes receivable (including notes discounted with recourse, $15,500)		36,500
Accounts receivable	$85,600	
Less: Allowance for Bad Debts	4,150	81,450
Interest receivable		525

Current liabilities reported in the December 31, 2001, balance sheet included:

Obligation on discounted notes receivable	$15,500

Transactions during 2002 included the following:

(a) Sales on account were $767,000.

(b) Cash collected on accounts totaled $576,500, including accounts of $93,000 with cash discounts of 2%.

(c) Notes received in settlement of accounts totaled $82,500.

(d) Notes receivable discounted as of December 31, 2001, were paid at maturity with the exception of one $3,000 note on which the company had to pay the bank $3,090, which included interest and protest fees. It is expected that recovery will be made on this note early in 2003.

(e) Customer notes of $60,000 were discounted with recourse during the year, proceeds from their transfer being $58,500. (All discounting transactions were recorded as loans.) Of this total, $48,000 matured during the year without notice of protest.

(f) Customer accounts of $8,720 were written off during the year as worthless.

(g) Recoveries of bad debts written off in prior years were $2,020.

(h) Notes receivable collected during the year totaled $27,000 and interest collected was $2,450.

(i) On December 31, accrued interest on notes receivable was $630.

(j) Uncollectible accounts are estimated to be 5% of the December 31, 2002, accounts receivable balance.

(k) Cash of $35,000 was borrowed from First Security Bank with accounts receivable of $40,000 being pledged on the loan. Collections of $19,500 had been made on these receivables [included in the total given in transaction (b)], and this amount was applied on December 31, 2002, to payment of accrued interest on the loan of $600, and the balance to partial payment of the loan.

(l) The petty cash fund was reimbursed (meaning that cash was removed from the bank account and placed in the petty cash fund) based on the following analysis of expenditure vouchers:

Travel expense	$112
Entertainment expense	78

Postage expense	$ 93
Office supplies expense	173
Cash short and over (a revenue account)	6

(m) Cash of $3,000 was added to a bond retirement fund.

(n) Currency on hand at December 31, 2002, was $12,000.

(o) Total cash payments for all expenses during the year were $680,000. Charge to General Expenses.

Instructions:

1. Prepare journal entries summarizing the transactions and information given above.
2. Prepare a summary of current cash and receivables for balance sheet presentation.

PROBLEM 6–41

COMPENSATING BALANCE AND EFFECTIVE INTEREST RATES

Krebsbach Company is negotiating a loan with FIS Bank. Krebsbach needs $900,000. As part of the loan agreement, FIS Bank will require Krebsbach to maintain a compensating balance of 15% of the loan amount on deposit in a checking account at the bank. Krebsbach currently maintains a balance of $50,000 in the checking account. The interest rate Krebsbach is required to pay on the loan is 12%; the interest rate FIS pays on checking accounts is 4%.

Instructions:

1. Compute the amount of the loan.
2. Determine the effective interest rate on the loan. (Hint: Compute the net interest paid on the loan per year and the "take-home" amount of the loan.)

PROBLEM 6–42

BANK RECONCILIATION

The cash account of Delta, Inc., disclosed a balance of $17,056.48 on October 31. The bank statement as of October 31 showed a balance of $21,209.45. Upon comparing the statement with the cash records, the following facts were developed.

(a) Delta's account was charged on October 26 for a customer's uncollectible check amounting to $1,143.

(b) A 2-month, 9%, $3,000 customer's note dated August 25, discounted on October 12, was dishonored October 26 and the bank charged Delta $3,050.83, which included a protest fee of $5.83.

(c) A customer's check for $725 was entered as $625 by both the depositor and the bank but was later corrected by the bank.

(d) Check No. 661 for $1,242.50 was entered in the cash disbursements journal at $1,224.50 and check No. 652 for $32.90 was entered as $329.00. The company uses the voucher system.

(e) Bank service charges of $39.43 for October were not yet recorded on the books.

(f) A bank memo stated that M. Sears' note for $2,500 and interest of $62.50 had been collected on October 29, and the bank charged $12.50. (No entry was made on the books when the note was sent to the bank for collection.)

(g) Receipts of October 29 for $6,850 were deposited November 1.

The following checks were outstanding on October 31:

No. 620	$1,250.00	No. 671	$ 732.50
No. 621	3,448.23	No. 673	187.90
No. 632	2,405.25	No. 675	275.72
No. 670	1,775.38	No. 676	2,233.15

Instructions:

1. Prepare a bank reconciliation as of October 31.
2. Give the journal entries required as a result of the preceding information.

PROBLEM 6–43

RECONCILIATION OF AN INDIVIDUAL'S BANK ACCOUNT

The following data was taken from Sylvester Krueger's check register for the month of April. Sylvester's bank reconciliation for March showed one outstanding check, check No. 78 for $43.00 (written on March 23), and one deposit in transit, deposit #10499 for $87.00 (made on March 30).

Date	Item	Checks	Deposits	Balance
2002				
April 1	Beginning Balance			$123.00
1	Deposit #10500		$523.34	646.34
1	Check #79	$ 5.00		651.34
4	Check #80	213.47		437.97
27	Deposit #10501		235.48	673.45
29	Check #81	264.35		409.80

The following is from Sylvester's bank statement for April:

April 1	Beginning Balance			$ 79.00
3	Check #79	$ 5.00		74.00
3	Deposit #10499		$ 87.00	161.00
5	Check #80	213.47		(52.47)
5	Automatic Loan		163.00	110.53
5	Deposit #10500		528.34	638.87
20	NSF Check	20.00		618.87
20	Service Charge	12.00		606.87
30	Interest		1.65	608.52

Instructions: Prepare a reconciliation of Sylvester's bank account as of April 30. Show both a corrected balance per bank and a corrected balance per books. Assume that any errors or discrepancies you find are Sylvester's fault, not the bank's.

PROBLEM 6–44

ACCOUNTING FOR ASSIGNMENT OF ACCOUNTS RECEIVABLE

On July 1, 2002, Balmforth Company used receivables totaling $200,000 as collateral on a $150,000, 16% note from Rocky Mountain Bank. The transaction is not structured such that receivables are being sold. Balmforth will continue to collect the assigned receivables. In addition to the interest on the note, Rocky Mountain also receives a 2% finance charge, deducted in advance on the $150,000 value of the note. Additional information for Balmforth Company is as follows:

(a) July collections amounted to $145,000, less cash discounts of $750.
(b) On August 1, paid bank the amount owed for July collections plus accrued interest on note to August 1.
(c) Balmforth collected the remaining accounts during August except for $550 written off as uncollectible.
(d) On September 1, paid bank the remaining amount owed plus accrued interest.

Instructions: Prepare the journal entries necessary to record the above information on the books of both Balmforth Company and Rocky Mountain Bank.

PROBLEM 6–45

ASSIGNING AND FACTORING ACCOUNTS RECEIVABLE

During its second year of operations, Shank Corporation found itself in financial difficulties. Shank decided to use its accounts receivable as a means of obtaining cash to continue operations. On July 1, 2002, Shank sold $75,000 of accounts receivable for cash proceeds of $69,500. No bad debt allowance was associated with these accounts. On December 17, 2002, Shank assigned the remainder of its accounts receivable, $250,000 as of that date, as collateral on a $125,000, 12% annual interest rate loan from

Sandy Finance Company. Shank received $125,000 less a 2% finance charge. Additional information is as follows:

Allowance for Bad Debts, 12/31/02	$3,200 (credit)
Estimated Uncollectibles, 12/31/02	3% of Accounts Receivable
Accounts Receivable (not including factored and assigned accounts), 12/31/02	$50,000
Loss Experience—Percentage of Uncollectible Accounts	
None of the assigned accounts had been collected by the end of the year.	

Instructions:

1. Prepare the journal entries to record the receipt of cash from (a) sale and (b) assignment of the accounts receivable.
2. Prepare the journal entry necessary to record the adjustment to Allowance for Bad Debts.
3. Prepare the accounts receivable section of Shank's balance sheet as it would appear after the above transactions.
4. What entry would be made on Shank's books when the sold accounts have been collected?

PROBLEM 6–46

SELLING RECEIVABLES

Freemont Factors provides financing to other companies by purchasing their accounts receivable on a nonrecourse basis. Freemont charges a commission to its clients of 15% of all receivables factored. In addition, Freemont withholds 10% of receivables factored as protection against sales returns or other adjustments. Freemont credits the 10% withheld to Client Retainer and makes payments to clients at the end of each month so that the balance in the retainer is equal to 10% of unpaid receivables at the end of the month. Freemont recognizes its 15% commissions as revenue at the time the receivables are factored. Also, experience has led Freemont to establish an Allowance for Bad Debts of 4% of all receivables purchased.

On January 4, 2002, Freemont purchased receivables from Detmer Company totaling $1,500,000. Detmer had previously established an Allowance for Bad Debts for these receivables of $35,000. By January 31, Freemont had collected $1,200,000 on these receivables.

Instructions:

1. Prepare the entries necessary on Freemont's books to record the above information. Freemont makes adjusting entries at the end of every month.
2. Prepare the entries on Detmer's books to record the above information.

PROBLEM 6–47

ACCOUNTING FOR A NON-INTEREST-BEARING NOTE

On January 1, 2002, Lost Valley Realty sold a tract of land to three doctors as an investment. The land, purchased 10 years ago, was carried on Lost Valley's books at a value of $125,000. Lost Valley received a non-interest-bearing note for $220,000 from the doctors. The note is due December 31, 2003. There is no readily available market value for the land, but the current market rate of interest for comparable notes is 10%.

Instructions:

1. Give the journal entry to record the sale of land on Lost Valley's books.
2. Prepare a schedule of discount amortization for the note with amounts rounded to the nearest dollar.
3. Give the adjusting entries to be made at the end of 2002 and 2003 to record the effective interest earned.

PROBLEM 6–48

NOTE WITH BELOW-MARKET INTEREST RATE

On January 1, 2002, the Denver Company sold land that originally cost $400,000 to the Boise Company. As payment, Boise gave Denver a $600,000 note. The note bears an interest rate of 4% and is to be repaid in 3 annual installments of $200,000 (plus interest on the outstanding balance). The first payment is due on December 31, 2002. The market price of the land is not reliably determinable. The prevailing rate of interest for notes of this type is 14%.

Instructions: Prepare the entries required on Denver's books to record the land sale and the receipt of each of the three payments. Use the effective-interest method of amortizing any premium or discount on the note.

PROBLEM 6–49

BAD DEBT EXPENSE—CASH FLOWS

Sage Company had a $300,000 balance in Accounts Receivable on January 1. The balance in Allowance for Bad Debts on January 1 was $36,000. Sales for the year totaled $1,700,000. All sales were credit sales. Bad debts expense is estimated to be 2% of sales. Write-offs of uncollectible accounts for the year were $28,000. The debit balance in Accounts Receivable on December 31 was $345,000. All receivables are trade receivables. Sage uses the direct method in preparing its statement of cash flows.

Instructions: What is the amount of cash collected from customers?

PROBLEM 6–50

ACCOUNTING FOR PETTY CASH

On December 1, 2002, LGA Corporation established an imprest petty cash fund. The operations of the fund for the last month of 2002 and the first month of 2003 are summarized as follows:

Dec. 1 The petty cash fund was established by cashing a company check for $2,000 and delivering the proceeds to the fund cashier.

21 A request for replenishment of the petty cash fund was received by the accounts payable department, supported by appropriate signed vouchers, summarized as follows:

Selling expenses	$ 324
Administrative expenses	513
Special equipment	176
Telephone, telegraph, and postage expense	48
Miscellaneous expenses	260
Total	$1,321

A check for $1,356 was drawn payable to the petty cash cashier.

31 The company's independent certified public accountant counted the fund in connection with the year-end audit work and found the following:

Cash in petty cash fund		$1,066
Employees' checks with January dates (postdated)		85
Expense vouchers properly approved as follows:		
Selling expenses	$146	
Administrative expenses	512	
Office supplies	28	
Telephone, telegraph, and postage expense	48	
Miscellaneous expenses	100	834
Total		$1,985

The petty cash fund was not replenished at December 31, 2002.

Jan. 15 The employees' checks held in the petty cash fund at December 31 were cashed and the proceeds retained in the fund.

31 A request for replenishment was made and a check was drawn to restore the

fund to its original balance of $2,000. The support vouchers for January expenditures are summarized below.

Selling expenses	$85
Administrative expenses	406
Telephone, telegraph, and postage expense	35
Miscellaneous expenses	220
Total	$746

Instructions: Record the transactions in general journal form.

COMPETENCY ENHANCEMENT OPPORTUNITIES

▶ Deciphering Actual Financial Statements   ▶ Ethical Dilemma

▶ Writing Assignment   ▶ Cumulative Spreadsheet Analysis

▶ Research Project   ▶ Internet Search

▶ The Debate

Accounting is more than just doing textbook problems. This expanded competency material provides practice in critical thinking, oral and written communication, research, teamwork, and consideration of ethical issues.

▶ **DECIPHERING ACTUAL FINANCIAL STATEMENTS**
• **Deciphering 6–1 (Disney)**
Use the information contained in Appendix A to answer the following questions:
1. Review DISNEY's note disclosure to determine how the company recognizes revenue from its various sources.
2. Based on what you know about The Disney Company, estimate what you think is the length of their average collection period. Once you have made that estimate, use the company's financial statements to compute the number. How does your estimate compare with the actual results?
3. Review the information relating to Disney's segment data. Which segment generates the most revenue for the company? Which segment's revenue growth is the highest? Which segment generates the most operating income?
4. Using information from the various financial statements, compute the amount of cash collected from customers for the 1998 fiscal year.
5. How does Disney define cash and cash equivalents?

• **Deciphering 6–2 (Sears, Roebuck and Co.)**
Using the information on the following page from SEARS, ROEBUCK AND CO.'s income statement and balance sheet:
1. Compute the company's 1998 average collection period (exclude from the computation "Credit revenues" on the income statement and "Retained interest in transferred credit card receivables" on the balance sheet). Does the resulting number seem a little high?
2. Find the company's bad debt expense on the income statement. Compare this number to the revenue the company makes by allowing such liberal credit terms. Assume the president of Sears was available to answer the question, "Is your company's average

collection period a little high?" What do you think would be the president's response? How would the president justify the answer?

SEARS, ROEBUCK AND CO.
Consolidated Statements of Income

MILLIONS, EXCEPT PER COMMON SHARE DATA	1998	1997	1996
REVENUES			
Merchandise sales and services	$36,704	$36,371	$33,751
Credit revenues	4,618	4,925	4,313
Total revenues	41,322	41,296	38,064
COSTS AND EXPENSES			
Cost of sales, buying and occupancy	27,257	26,779	24,889
Selling and administrative	8,318	8,322	8,059
Depreciation and amortization	830	785	697
Provision for uncollectible accounts	1,287	1,532	971
Interest	1,423	1,409	1,365
Reaffirmation charge	—	475	—
Impairment losses	352	—	—
Total costs and expenses	39,467	39,302	35,981
Operating income	1,855	1,994	2,083
ASSETS			
Current Assets			
Cash and invested cash	$ 495	$ 358	
Retained interest in transferred credit card receivables	4,294	3,316	
Credit card receivables	18,946	20,956	
Less: Allowance for uncollectible accounts	974	1,113	
	17,972	19,843	
Other receivables	397	335	
Merchandise inventories	4,816	5,044	
Prepaid expenses and deferred charges	506	517	
Deferred income taxes	791	830	
Total current assets	29,271	30,243	

- **Deciphering 6–3 (Wal-Mart Stores, Inc.)**

Using the financial information for Sears (from Deciphering 6–2) and the information from WAL-MART STORES, INC., given on page 366, answer the following questions.

1. For the most recent year given, compute each company's average collection period.
2. What percentage of total current assets are accounts receivable for both companies?
3. Determine the percentage of each firm's revenues that is derived from sources other than sales.
4. Given that these two companies are both in the retail business, how do you explain the dramatic difference in the two average collection period figures? For these two companies, what fundamental difference in the use of consumer credit can you infer from the above analysis?

WAL-MART STORES, INC. AND SUBSIDIARIES
Consolidated Statements of Income

(AMOUNTS IN MILLIONS)

Fiscal years ended January 31,	1999	1998	1997
Revenues:			
Net sales	$137,634	$117,958	$104,859
Other income—net	1,574	1,341	1,319
	139,208	119,299	106,178
Costs and Expenses:			
Cost of sales	108,725	93,438	83,510
Operating, selling and general and administrative expenses	22,363	19,358	16,946
Interest Costs:			
Debt	529	555	629
Capital leases	268	229	216
	131,885	113,580	101,301
Income Before Income Taxes,			
Minority Interest and Equity in Unconsolidated Subsidiaries	7,323	5,719	4,877
Provision for Income Taxes:			
Current	3,380	2,095	1,974
Deferred	(640)	20	(180)
	2,740	2,115	1,794
Income Before Minority Interest and Equity in Unconsolidated Subsidiaries	4,583	3,604	3,083
Minority Interest and Equity in Unconsolidated Subsidiaries	(153)	(78)	(27)
Net Income	$ 4,430	$ 3,526	$ 3,056

WAL-MART STORES, INC. AND SUBSIDIARIES
Consolidated Balance Sheets

(AMOUNTS IN MILLIONS)

January 31,	1999	1998
Assets		
Current Assets:		
Cash and cash equivalents	$ 1,879	$ 1,447
Receivables	1,118	976
Inventories:		
At replacement cost	17,549	16,845
Less LIFO reserve	473	348
Inventories at LIFO cost	17,076	16,497
Prepaid expenses and other	1,059	432
Total Current Assets	21,132	19,352

• **Deciphering 6–4 (Harley-Davidson Inc.)**

From the notes of the 1998 annual report for HARLEY-DAVIDSON INC., we find the following information relating to Allowance for Bad Debts.

Balance at the beginning of the year	$ 6,867
Provisions	10,338
Charge-offs	(7,227)
Balance at end of year	9,978

1. What do the terms "Provisions" and "Charge-offs" represent?
2. Reconstruct the journal entries that resulted in the above changes in Allowance for Bad Debts.
3. Why do you think there is such a difference between the amount being expensed for the period and the amount being written off?

▶ WRITING ASSIGNMENT

• Foreign loan write-offs

In July 1990, U.S. federal regulators ordered U.S. banks to write off 20% of their $11.1 billion in loans to Brazil and also 20% of their $2.9 billion in loans to Argentina. The action significantly affected the loan loss reserves, that is, Allowance for Bad Debts, of the banks. For example, CITICORP was ordered to write off loans totaling $780 million, compared to Citicorp's total loan loss reserve of $3.3 billion. However, it was reported that "the action won't automatically have any impact on bank earnings." Prepare a short report answering the following questions:

1. Why won't the ordered write-offs automatically impact bank earnings?
2. Might the ordered write-offs have an indirect impact on future bank earnings?
3. What effect would you expect to see on bank stock prices in response to this announcement?

SOURCE: Robert Guenther, "Federal Regulators Order Banks to Take Write-Offs on Loans to Brazil, Argentina," *The Wall Street Journal*, July 12, 1990, p. A3.

▶ RESEARCH PROJECT

• What is meant by "cash and cash equivalents"?

Obtain the annual reports for 10 companies. Using these annual reports, your group is to report (either orally or in writing) the answers to the following questions.

• How does each company define the term "cash and cash equivalents"?
• Where is the definition? In the notes? in the cash flow statement?
• Review Statement of Financial Accounting Standards (SFAS) No. 95, "Statement of Cash Flows." How does it define cash and cash equivalents?
• How many of the cash flow statements have items related to foreign exchange rate changes?
• Review SFAS No. 95 to determine how to interpret the foreign exchange rate numbers. What do they mean?

▶ THE DEBATE

• Estimating uncollectible accounts

It seems that whenever possible accountants have developed more than one way of accounting for things. Accounting for inventories, depreciation, and interest amortization and preparing a statement of cash flows are examples of instances where multiple methods have been developed. Another example is estimating uncollectible accounts expense. The percentage-of-sales method and the percentage-of-receivables method are both acceptable alternatives. Divide your group into two teams. This debate exercise actually involves two debates.

1. The first debate:
   • One team is to take the position that we should not allow multiple methods of accounting for uncollectible accounts. For comparability's sake, we should require all companies to use the same method to account for uncollectible accounts.
   • The other team is to support the position that allowing companies to select from multiple methods provides the best disclosure.
2. The second debate:
   • One team's task is to justify the percentage-of-sales method as preferable for estimating uncollectible accounts because it provides the best information.
   • The other team's task is to support the percentage-of-receivables method.

Each team should be prepared to present an oral summary of their reasoning to the class.

▶ **ETHICAL DILEMMA**

You recently graduated from college with your accounting degree. Your father's best friend is the director of the accounting department of a small manufacturing firm in the area, and you accepted a position on his staff. After a month on the job, you have noticed several deficiencies in the cash controls for the company. For example, the individual making the daily deposits at the bank is also in charge of updating accounts receivable. You also notice that the petty cash fund is under general control of everyone in the office (that means that no one person has ultimate responsibility) and that vouchers are seldom completed when cash is removed from the fund. You bring your concerns to the attention of your boss, your father's friend, and he makes the following comment.

I appreciate your concerns. I knew when we hired you that you were sharp, but you need to understand that not everything is done by the book here. We trust our employees. If we were to enforce rigid controls on cash, it would create a nontrusting work environment. We don't want that. Sure, a little money may turn up missing now and then, but it is a small price to pay. Now, don't you worry about it anymore.

What do you do now? Would you be comfortable working in an environment where there is a lack of control on cash? If a significant sum of money were to turn up missing, and the control system was unable to determine who was responsible, what would that do to the trusting work environment? And remember, big sums of money never turned up missing until you came to work at the company.

▶ **CUMULATIVE SPREADSHEET ANALYSIS**

This spreadsheet assignment is a continuation of the spreadsheet assignments given in earlier chapters. If you completed those assignments, you have a head start on this one.

Refer back to the instructions for preparing the revised financial statements for 2002 as given in part (1) of the Cumulative Spreadsheet Analysis assignment in Chapter 3.

1. Skywalker wishes to prepare a forecasted balance sheet, a forecasted income statement, and a forecasted statement of cash flows for 2003. Clearly state any additional assumptions that you make. Use the financial statement numbers for 2002 as the basis for the forecast, along with the following additional information.

   (a) Sales in 2003 are expected to increase by 40% over 2002 sales of $2,100.

   (b) In 2003, Skywalker expects to acquire new property, plant, and equipment costing $240.

   (c) The $480 in operating expenses reported in 2002 breaks down as follows: $15 depreciation expense, $465 other operating expenses.

   (d) No new long-term debt will be acquired in 2003.

   (e) No cash dividends will be paid in 2003.

   (f) New short-term loans payable will be acquired in an amount sufficient to make Skywalker's current ratio in 2003 exactly equal to 2.0.

   (g) Skywalker does not anticipate repurchasing any additional shares of stock during 2003.

   (h) Because changes in future prices and exchange rates are impossible to predict, Skywalker's best estimate is that the balance in accumulated other comprehensive income will remain unchanged in 2003.

   (i) In the absence of more detailed information, assume that investment securities, long-term investments, other long-term assets, and intangible assets will all increase at the same rate as sales (40%) in 2003.

   (j) In the absence of more detailed information, assume that other long-term liabilities will increase at the same rate as sales (40%) in 2003.

   Note: The forecasted balance sheet and income statement were constructed as part of the spreadsheet assignment in Chapter 4; you can use that spreadsheet as a starting point if you have completed that assignment. In addition, assume the following:

   (k) The investment securities are classified as available-for-sale. Accordingly, cash from the purchase and sale of these securities is classified as an investing activity.

(l) Transactions impacting other long-term assets and other long-term liabilities accounts are operating activities.

Hint: Construction of the forecasted statement of cash flows for 2003 involves analyzing the forecasted income statement for 2003 along with the balance sheets for 2002 (actual) and 2003 (forecasted).

For this exercise, the current assets are expected to behave as follows:

(m) Cash, investment securities, and inventory will increase at the same rate as sales.

(n) The forecasted amount of accounts receivable in 2003 is determined using the forecasted value for the average collection period (computed using the end-of-period accounts receivable balance). The average collection period for 2003 is expected to be 14.08 days.

2. Repeat (1), with the following changes in assumptions:
   a. Average collection period is expected to be 9.06 days.
   b. Average collection period is expected to be 20 days.

3. Comment on the differences in the forecasted values of cash from operating activities in 2003 under each of the following assumptions about the average collection period: 14.08 days, 9.06 days, and 20 days.

▶ **INTERNET SEARCH**

We began this chapter with a look at the beginnings of BANK OF AMERICA. Let's go to its Web site and learn more about this company. Its Web address is www.bofa.com. Once you have gained access to Bank of America's Web site, answer the following questions.

1. Bank of America has a "Fast Facts" page that lists some interesting information about the company. Locate that page and determine what major movie the bank helped finance in 1939, what bridge the company helped finance in the early 1930s, and what southern California major theme park the company helped finance.

2. In 1998, Bank of America merged with another major U.S. bank. Name the bank.

3. Access the company's income statement and balance sheet. Using information from both of those statements, compute the actual amount of bad debt that was written off for the last year. (Note: This will require you to use the balances in the allowance account from the balance sheet and the provision for credit losses from the income statement.)

SECTION

1

chapter 7
Complexities of
Revenue Recognition

The Wall Street Journal headlines seem to always be discussing the revenue recognition problems of one firm or another. For example, in 1999, TELXON CORP., a maker of wireless communication devices and computers, announced that it would restate its earnings for the prior three years after a review of its accounting procedures by its outside auditor, PRICEWATERHOUSECOOPERS. In 1998, CENDANT CORP. uncovered an accounting fraud that resulted in restating its earnings by $240 million for 1997. Cendant subsequently sued its auditor, ERNST & YOUNG, for failing to discover the problem during the course of its annual audit. Also, in 1998, ADAC LABORATORIES, a maker of medical devices and software, restated the results for its previous three fiscal years as a result of revenue recognition issues. A review by its auditors, PricewaterhouseCoopers, resulted in Adac's adopting a more conservative policy for recognizing revenue. Rather than recognizing revenue when the company booked a sale (as was previously the case), Adac will now wait to book revenue until the medical equipment is installed (which can be months later).

Auditing firms always seem to be closely associated with detecting and correcting a client's revenue recognition problems. Recently, however, one of the watchdog's revenue recognition policies was called into question. In 1996, several industry publications challenged the way in which the accounting firm of KPMG PEAT MARWICK reported its revenue. Peat Marwick reported revenues in fiscal 1995 of $2.3 billion. The accounting profession publications state that the figure should have been closer to $2.1 billion. The difference of $200 million related to the inclusion in revenue of expense reimbursements to subcontractors. For example, on projects requiring the installation of a computer system, Peat Marwick would contract out the electrical work and charge the client for the work done by electricians. Peat Marwick would then collect the money from the client and forward it to the electricians. These reimbursements were included as revenue and then deducted as an expense.

In addition, questions have arisen regarding Peat Marwick's computation of consulting revenue. According to trade publications, items previously included as tax or audit revenue were classified, beginning in fiscal 1995, as consulting revenue. This reclassification occurred, the publications imply, to portray a favorable comparison with increases being reported by other accounting firms.

Needless to say, KPMG Peat Marwick did not let these allegations go without a response. In a letter to the editor, Peat Marwick's chief financial officer, Joseph Heintz, asserted that *The Wall Street Journal* "tested the wrong information, used the wrong measures—and drew the wrong conclusions."[1]

net work exercise

KPMG Peat Marwick has a Web site specifically geared to college students (**www. kpmgcampus.com/**). Here you'll find company information, interviewing tips, and a description of a typical day of employment at KPMG.

Net Work:
1. What are KPMG's five lines of business?
2. What kind of training does KPMG provide for its employees?

1 "KPMG: You're Wrong, We're Positive," *The Wall Street Journal*, June 11, 1996.

1
Identify the primary criteria for revenue recognition.

2
Explain when revenue is appropriately recognized prior to delivery of goods or services through percentage-of-completion accounting.

3
Record journal entries for long-term construction-type contracts using percentage-of-completion and completed-contract methods.

4
Record journal entries for long-term service contracts using the proportional performance method.

5
Explain when revenue is recognized after delivery of goods or services through installment sales, cost recovery, and cash methods.

e/m

EXPANDED MATERIAL

6
Describe accounting for the transfer of assets prior to the recognition of revenue with the deposit method and consignment sales.

When public accounting firms, the very institutions charged with ensuring fairness in financial reporting, cannot agree on what is revenue and what isn't, one can quickly see that the issues associated with revenue recognition can get quite complicated. In Chapter 6 we addressed issues associated with recording revenue once it has met the criteria for revenue recognition. In this chapter we focus on the complexities associated with revenue recognition. We will discuss the various points at which revenue may be recognized and what factors drive the revenue recognition decision.

As discussed and illustrated in Chapter 4, both internal and external users of financial information focus considerable attention on how business activities affect the income statement. Because the financial statements are interrelated, a study of the measurement and recognition of the elements contained in the income statement is also a study of the measurement and recognition of changes in the elements contained in the balance sheet. Thus, while the focus in this chapter is on the recognition of revenue, it also relates to the recognition of assets and liabilities on the balance sheet.

REVENUE RECOGNITION

Identify the primary criteria for revenue recognition.

Recognition refers to the time when transactions are recorded on the books. The FASB's two criteria for recognizing revenues and gains were identified in Chapter 4 and are repeated here for emphasis. Revenues and gains are generally recognized when:

1.   They are realized or realizable.
2.   They have been earned through substantial completion of the activities involved in the earnings process.

> **FYI:**   "Realized" or "realizable" can be interpreted as having received cash or other assets or a valid promise of cash or other assets to be received at some future time.

Both of these criteria generally are met at the point of sale, which most often occurs when goods are delivered or when services are rendered to customers. Usually, assets and revenues are recognized concurrently. Thus, a sale of inventory results in an increase in Cash or Accounts Receivable and an increase in Sales Revenue. However, assets are sometimes received before these revenue recognition criteria are met. For example, if a client pays for consulting services in advance, an asset, Cash, is recorded on the books even though revenue has not been earned. In these cases, a liability, Unearned Revenue, is recorded. When the revenue recognition criteria are fully met, revenue is recognized and the liability account is reduced.

While the point-of-sale rule has dominated the interpretation of revenue recognition, there have been notable variations to this rule, especially in specific industries such as construction, real estate, and franchising. Special committees of the AICPA, and later the FASB, have studied these and other areas. For several years, these special studies were conducted under the direction of the AICPA, and publication of the committee's results appeared in the form of industry accounting guides, industry audit guides, or statements of position (SOPs). These publications have been studied by the FASB and, where deemed desirable, have been incorporated in the literature as Statements of Financial Accounting Standards.[2]

2 In the early 1980s, the FASB issued three research reports dealing with revenue recognition. These reports were used by the FASB in its deliberations leading to Concepts Statement No. 5 and several of the special industry standards. The reports were: (1) Yuji Ijiri, *Recognition of Contractual Rights and Obligations,* Stamford, CT: Financial Accounting Standards Board, 1980; (2) Henry R. Jaenicke, *Survey of Present Practice in Recognizing Revenues, Expenses, Gains and Losses,* Stamford, CT: Financial Accounting Standards Board, 1981; (3) L. Todd Johnson and Reed K. Storey, *Recognition in Financial Statements: Underlying Concepts and Practical Conventions,* Stamford, CT: Financial Accounting Standards Board, 1982.

Exhibit 7–1 illustrates the time line associated with revenue recognition. At the point of sale, both revenue recognition criteria are typically satisfied. That is, the company has provided a product or service (criterion #2), and the customer has provided payment or a valid promise of payment (criterion #1). But as pointed out in the exhibit, exceptions exist and revenue can be recognized before the point of sale; or in some conditions, the recognition of revenue may be deferred until after the point of sale.

EXHIBIT 7–1 | Revenue Recognition Time Line and Criteria

	Before the Point of Sale	Point of Sale	After the Point of Sale
	EXCEPTION: Revenue can be recognized prior to the point of sale *if:*	NORMALLY: Revenue is generally recognized at this point in time.	EXCEPTION: The recognition of revenue must be deferred *if:*
Criterion #1: Realized	Customer provides a valid promise of payment AND	Criterion #1 is typically satisfied at this point.	Customer does not provide a valid promise at time of receipt of product or service OR
Criterion #2: Substantially complete	conditions exist that contractually guarantee subsequent sale.	Criterion #2 is typically satisfied at this point.	significant effort remains on contract.

In general, revenue is not recognized prior to the point of sale because either (1) a valid promise of payment has not been received from the customer or (2) the company has not provided the product or service. An exception occurs when the customer provides a valid promise of payment and conditions exist that contractually guarantee the sale. The most common example of this exception occurs in the case of long-term contracts where the two parties involved are legally obligated to fulfill the terms of the contract. In this case, revenue (or at least a portion of the total contract price) may be recognized prior to the point of sale.

Another exception to the general rule occurs when *either* of the two revenue recognition criteria is not satisfied at the point of sale. In some cases, a product or service may be provided to the customer without receiving a valid promise of payment. In these instances, revenue is not recognized until payment or the valid promise is received. Now you are saying to yourself, "Why would anybody provide a product or service to a customer without receiving a valid promise of payment?" A common example would be physicians, who provide treatment first and then try to collect payment.[3] Also, if a customer provides payment yet substantial services must still be provided by the company, then the recognition of revenue must be postponed until those services are provided. In any case, if *both* of the two revenue recognition criteria are met prior to the point of sale, revenue may be recognized. If *either* of the two criteria is not met at the point of sale, then the recognition of revenue must wait.

FYI: The notes to WALT DISNEY's financial statements (see Appendix A) provide an example of how one firm might have several different revenue recognition policies, depending on what is being sold.

These exceptions will be the study of most of the chapter. This chapter will explore some of the more common variations in revenue recognition that have arisen over time. The focus of the presentation will be on the revenue recognition variations and not on

---

3 Anyone who has visited a doctor recently can attest to the fact that most medical personnel now do all they can to secure payment or a valid promise (generally through insurance) prior to providing the service. They have learned the hard way.

the detailed accounting procedures for a specific industry. The discussion focuses first on revenue recognition prior to delivery of goods or performance of services; second, on revenue recognition after delivery of goods or performance of services; and finally, on methods of accounting for cash receipts before revenue recognition occurs. The special industries referred to are construction, service, and franchising.

The International Standard for Revenue Recognition

The area of revenue recognition illustrates a general weakness of the set of International Accounting Standards (IAS) promulgated by the International Accounting Standards Committee (IASC)—it does not include specific guidance for applying broad accounting principles to the idiosyncrasies of various industries. In IAS 18 (Revenue), the IASC outlines the concept of revenue recognition, and companies purporting to use IAS in the preparation of their financial statements must figure out how to apply these general concepts to their operations. In contrast, U.S. GAAP includes literally scores of pronouncements regarding revenue recognition in specific industries such as insurance, franchising, cable television, motion pictures, retirement communities, and so forth.

The general guidelines of IAS 18 are outlined in this section. As you study the remainder of the chapter and learn some of the details of revenue recognition as applied under U.S. GAAP, consider the practical difficulties of applying the general revenue recognition concepts in IAS 18 to a variety of different business settings.

SALE OF GOODS Under IAS 18, a company should recognize revenue from the sale of goods when all of the following conditions have been satisfied:

- The significant risks and rewards of ownership of the goods have been transferred to the buyer and the selling company retains no effective control over what happens to the goods.
- Both the amount of the revenue and of the costs associated with the transaction can be reliably measured.
- It is probable that the economic benefits of the sale will flow to the selling company.

The combination of the ownership transfer and measurability conditions is comparable to the "earnings process substantially complete" criterion mentioned earlier. Similarly, the "realized or realizable" criterion mentioned earlier corresponds to the notion of the probability of a company's receiving the economic benefits of a sale.

RENDERING OF SERVICES When using IAS 18, a company should recognize revenue from the rendering of services when both of the following conditions have been satisfied.

- The total amount of the revenue, the total amount of the costs, and the stage of completion of the transaction can be reliably measured.
- It is probable that the economic benefits of the transaction will flow to the company rendering the services.

Note that in accounting for the revenue associated with services, the emphasis is on reliably measuring the total revenues and costs associated with the transaction; this measurement process can be quite difficult for service contracts extending over several accounting periods. (More details regarding this issue are discussed later in this chapter.)

REVENUE RECOGNITION PRIOR TO DELIVERY OF GOODS OR PERFORMANCE OF SERVICES

Explain when revenue is appropriately recognized prior to delivery of goods or services through percentage-of-completion accounting.

Under some circumstances, revenue can be meaningfully reported prior to the delivery of the finished product or completion of a service contract. Usually this occurs when the construction period of the asset being sold or the period of service performance is relatively long, that is, more than one year. In these cases, if a company waits until the production or service period is complete to recognize revenue, the income statement may not report meaningfully the periodic achievement of the company. Under this approach, referred to as the **completed-contract method,** all income from the contract is related to the year of completion, even though only a small part of the earnings may be attributable to effort in that period. Previous periods receive no credit for their efforts; in fact, they may be penalized through the absorption of selling, general and administrative, and other overhead costs relating to the contract but not considered part of the inventory cost.

before point of sale

  Percentage-of-completion accounting, an alternative to the completed-contract method, was developed to relate recognition of revenue on long-term construction-type contracts to the activities of a firm in fulfilling these contracts. Similarly, the **proportional performance method** has been developed to reflect revenue earned on service contracts under which many acts of service are to be performed before the contract is completed. Examples of such service contracts include contracts covering maintenance on electronic office equipment, correspondence schools, trustee services, health clubs, professional services such as those offered by attorneys and accountants, and servicing of mortgage loans by mortgage bankers. Percentage-of-completion accounting and proportional performance accounting are similar in their application. However, some special problems arise in accounting for service contracts. The discussion and examples in the following sections relate first to long-term construction-type contracts and then to the special problems encountered with service contracts.

STOP & THINK How would a contract's percentage of completion be measured? What methods can you come up with to determine how complete a contract is?

General Concepts of Percentage-of-Completion Accounting

Under the percentage-of-completion method, a company recognizes revenues and costs on a contract as it progresses toward completion, rather than deferring recognition of these items until the contract is completed. The amount of revenue to be recognized

Copier repair is accounted for using the proportional performance method, which allows for revenue of service contracts to be spread over the length of the contracts.

each period is based on some measure of progress toward completion. This requires an estimate of costs yet to be incurred. Changes in estimates of future costs arise normally, and the necessary adjustments are made in the year the estimates are revised. Thus, the revenues and costs to be recognized in a given year are affected by the revenues and costs already recognized. As work progresses on the contract, the actual costs incurred are charged to inventory. The amount of profit earned each period also is charged to this asset account. Thus, the inventory account is valued at its net realizable value—the sales (or contract) price less the cost to complete the contract and less the unearned profit on the unfinished contract. (See Chapter 9 for a review of the concepts and computations associated with net realizable value.) If a company projects a loss on the contract prior to completion, the full amount of the loss should be recognized immediately. This loss recognition results in a write-down of the asset to its estimated net realizable value. If only a percentage of the loss were recognized, the asset value would exceed the net realizable value. This would violate the lower-of-cost-or-market rule discussed earlier and more fully in Chapter 9.

Necessary Conditions to Use Percentage-of-Completion Accounting

Most long-term construction-type contracts should be reported using the percentage-of-completion method. The guidelines presently in force, however, are not specific as to when a company must use the percentage-of-completion method and when it must use the alternative completed-contract method. The accounting standards that still govern this area were issued by the Committee on Accounting Procedure in 1955.[4] In 1981, the Construction Contractor Guide Committee of the Accounting Standards Division of the AICPA issued Statement of Position 81-1, "Accounting for Performance of Construction-Type and Certain Production-Type Contracts." In this SOP, the committee strongly recommended which of the two common methods of accounting for these types of contracts should be required, depending on the specific circumstances involved. The committee further stated that the two methods should not be viewed as acceptable alternatives for the same circumstances. The committee identified several elements that should be present if percentage-of-completion accounting is to be used.[5]

> **FYI:** This area is a good example of one in which financial and tax accounting have come closer together, but for different reasons. Financial accounting prefers the percentage-of-completion method because of its representational faithfulness. Congress has pressed for the percentage-of-completion method because it accelerates the recognition of income and thus tax revenues.

1. Dependable estimates can be made of contract revenues, contract costs, and the extent of progress toward completion.
2. The contract clearly specifies the enforceable rights regarding goods or services to be provided and received by the parties, the consideration to be exchanged, and the manner and terms of settlement.
3. The buyer can be expected to satisfy obligations under the contract.
4. The contractor can be expected to perform the contractual obligation.

The completed-contract method should be used only when an entity has primarily short-term contracts, when the conditions for using percentage-of-completion accounting are not met, or when there are inherent uncertainties in the contract beyond the normal business risks.

In February 1982, the FASB issued Statement No. 56, designating the accounting and reporting principles and practices contained in SOP 81-1 and in the AICPA *Audit and Accounting Guide for Construction Contractors* as preferable accounting principles.[6] The Board indicated that it would consider adopting these principles as FASB standards after allowing sufficient time for the

---

4 *Committee on Accounting Procedure, Accounting Research Bulletin No. 45,* "Long-Term Construction-Type Contracts," New York: American Institute of Certified Public Accountants, 1955.

5 *Construction Contractor Guide Committee of the Accounting Standards Division, AICPA, Statement of Position 81–1,* "Accounting for Performance of Construction-Type and Certain Production-Type Contracts," New York: American Institute of Certified Public Accountants, 1981, par. 23.

6 *Statement of Financial Accounting Standards No. 56,* "Designation of AICPA Guide and Statement of Position (SOP) 81–1 on Contractor Accounting and SOP 81–2 Concerning Hospital-Related Organizations as Preferable for Purposes of Applying APB Opinion No. 20," Stamford, CT: Financial Accounting Standards Board, 1982.

principles to be used in practice so that a basis can be provided for determining their usefulness. A critical issue involved in this area is the clear preference in the SOP for using the percentage-of-completion method of accounting.

In 1992, the AICPA Auditing Standards Board issued SAS No. 69, "The Meaning of 'Present Fairly in Conformity With Generally Accepted Accounting Principles' in the Independent Auditor's Report." In SAS 69, the board detailed the hierarchy of acceptable accounting principles, which includes the AICPA Statements of Position. Following the issuance of SAS 69, the FASB issued FASB No. 111 that rescinded Statement No. 56 and stated that "the Board no longer needs to designate the specialized accounting and reporting principles and practices in AICPA Guides and SOPs" as GAAP.

For many years, income tax regulations permitted contractors wide latitude in selecting either the percentage-of-completion or completed-contract method. Beginning with the Tax Reform Act of 1986, the tax laws have limited the use of the completed-contract method and have required increased use of the percentage-of-completion method. This results in greater revenues from taxes without increasing the tax rates, and it also results in similar revenue recognition treatment for both taxes and financial reporting.

Measuring the Percentage of Completion

Various methods are currently used in practice to measure the earnings process. They can be conveniently grouped into two categories: input and output measures.

INPUT MEASURES   **Input measures** are made in relation to the costs or efforts devoted to a contract. They are based on an established or assumed relationship between a unit of input and productivity. They include the widely used cost-to-cost method and several variations of efforts-expended methods.

Cost-to-cost method.   Perhaps the most popular of the input measures is the **cost-to-cost method.** Under this method, the degree of completion is determined by comparing costs already incurred with the most recent estimates of total expected costs to complete the project. The percentage that costs incurred bear to total expected costs is applied to the contract price to determine the revenue to be recognized to date as well as to the expected net income on the project in arriving at earnings to date. Some of the costs incurred, particularly in the early stages of the contract, should be disregarded in applying this method because they do not relate directly to effort expended on the contract. These include such items as subcontract costs for work that has yet to be performed and standard fabricated materials that have not yet been installed. One of the most difficult problems in using this method is estimating the costs yet to be incurred. Engineers are often consulted to help provide estimates as to a project's percentage of completion. However difficult the estimation process may be, it is required in reporting income, regardless of how the percentage of completion is computed.

To illustrate, assume that in January 2001 Strong Construction Company was awarded a contract with a total price of $3,000,000. Strong expected to earn $400,000 profit on the contract, or in other words, total costs on the contract were estimated to be $2,600,000. The construction was completed over a three-year period, and the cost data and cost percentages shown on the next page were compiled during that time.

Note that the cost percentage is computed by dividing cumulative actual costs incurred by total cost, an amount that is estimated for the first two years.

Efforts-expended methods.   The **efforts-expended methods** are based on some measure of work performed. They include labor hours, labor dollars, machine hours, or material quantities. In each case, the degree of completion is measured in a way similar to that used in the cost-to-cost approach: the ratio of the efforts expended to date to the estimated total efforts to be expended on the entire contract. For example, if the measure of work performed is labor hours, the ratio of hours worked to date to the total estimated hours would produce the percentage for use in measuring income earned.

► # MICROSOFT CHARGED WITH ESTABLISHING COOKIE JAR RESERVES

In its June 30, 1998, balance sheet, MICROSOFT **reported an unearned revenue liability of almost $3 billion in association with its software sales. Microsoft disclosed that because significant elements of technical support are associated with the sale of products such as Windows and Office 97, not all of the revenue**

from a software product should be recognized at the time of sale. For Office 97, 20% of the sales price is reported as unearned revenue, which is then recognized as revenue over the estimated 18-month product life cycle. For Windows, 35% of the amount of retail sales is deferred and recognized as revenue over the subsequent 24 months.

In July 1999, Microsoft announced that this revenue deferral practice was being investigated by the SEC. The SEC probe was prompted by the concern that Microsoft was deferring too much revenue. When a company is doing very well, as Microsoft was in 1999, it can be

tempted to delay reporting all of its revenue in order to establish a so-called cookie jar reserve of revenue that can be recognized in the event that sales growth slows in subsequent years.

The Microsoft probe was part of an SEC crackdown that was formally kicked off in September 1998. At that time, Arthur Leavitt, Chairman of the SEC, gave a speech outlining five techniques of "accounting hocus-pocus" that companies use to manage earnings; one is the establishment of "cookie jar reserves" in order to "smooth" reported earnings. Leavitt also announced an SEC action plan intended to curtail the practice of earn-

Year	(1) Actual Cost Incurred	(2) Estimated Cost to Complete	(3) Total Cost (1) + (2)	(4) Cost Percentage (1)/(3)
2001	$1,040,000	$1,560,000	$2,600,000*	40
2002	910,000			
Total	$1,950,000	650,000	2,600,000*	75
2003	650,000			
Total	$2,600,000	0	2,600,000**	100

*Estimated total contract cost.
**Actual total contract cost.

OUTPUT MEASURES **Output measures** are made in terms of results achieved. Included in this category are methods based on units produced, contract milestones reached, and values added. For example, if the contract calls for units of output, such as miles of roadway, a measure of completion would be a ratio of the miles completed to the total miles in the contract. Architects and engineers are sometimes asked to evaluate jobs and estimate what percentage of a job is complete. These estimates are, in reality, output measures and usually are based on the physical progress made on a contract.

Record journal entries for long-term construction-type contracts using percentage-of-completion and completed-contract methods.

ACCOUNTING FOR LONG-TERM CONSTRUCTION-TYPE CONTRACTS

For both the percentage-of-completion and the completed-contract methods, all direct and allocable indirect costs of the contracts are charged to an inventory account. The difference in recording between the two methods relates to the timing of revenue and expense recognition; that is, when the estimated earned income is recognized with its

ings management.

The catalyst for the Microsoft investigation appeared to be the wrongful firing suit brought by former Microsoft internal auditor Charles Pancerzewski. Mr. Pancerzewski charged that he had been fired for uncovering a Microsoft plot to manipulate hundreds of millions of dollars in deferred revenues in order to smooth reported earnings. Mr. Pancerzewski offered as evidence an e-mail message by former Microsoft chief financial officer Mike Brown to chairman Bill Gates saying: "I believe we should do all we can to smooth our earnings and keep a steady state earnings model."

QUESTIONS:

1. In light of the two revenue recognition criteria, what theoretical justification exists for the deferral of revenue by Microsoft? What practical problems are associated with this deferral?

2. Why would a company's management wish to report smooth earnings?

3. In its response to the initial SEC charges, Microsoft stated that it has always been known as a company that is conservative in its application of accounting principles. Is revenue deferral a conservative accounting practice? Is conservative accounting necessarily good accounting?

SOURCES:
Arthur Leavitt, "The Numbers Game," Remarks delivered at the New York University Center for Law and Business, September 28, 1998.
Lee Gomes, "Microsoft Says SEC Probes Its Accounting," *The Wall Street Journal*, July 1, 1999, p. A3.
John Markoff, "Microsoft's Accounting Under Scrutiny," *The New York Times*, July 1, 1999, p. C1.

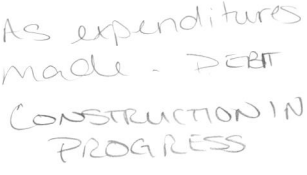

As expenditures made - DEBIT CONSTRUCTION IN PROGRESS

related effect on the income statement and the balance sheet. During the construction period, the annual reported income under these two accounting methods will differ. However, after the contract is completed, the combined income for the total construction period will be the same under each method of accounting. The balance sheet at the end of the construction and collection periods also will be identical.

Usually, contracts require progress billings by the contractor and payments by the customer on these billings. The billings and payments are accounted for and reported in the same manner under both methods. The amount of these billings usually is specified by the contract terms and may be related to the costs actually incurred. Generally, these contracts require inspection before final settlement is made. The billings are debited to Accounts Receivable and credited to a deferred account, Progress Billings on Construction Contracts, that serves as an offset to the inventory account, Construction in Progress. The billing of the contract thus transfers the asset value from inventory to receivables, but because of the long-term nature of the contract, the construction costs continue to be reflected in the accounts.

To illustrate accounting for a long-term construction contract, we will continue the Strong Construction Company example from pages 377–378. Recall that construction was completed over a three-year period and the contract price was $3,000,000. The direct and allocable indirect costs, billings, and collections[7] for 2001, 2002, and 2003 are as follows:

Year	Direct and Allocable Indirect Costs	Billings	Collections
2001	$1,040,000	$1,000,000	$ 800,000
2002	910,000	900,000	850,000
2003	650,000	1,100,000	1,350,000

7 As a protection for the customer, long-term contracts frequently provide for an amount to be retained from the progress payments. This retention is usually a percentage of the progress billings, for example, 10% to 20%, and is paid upon final acceptance of the construction. Thus, the amount collected is often less than the amount billed in the initial years of the contract.

The following entries for the three years would be made on the contractor's books under either the percentage-of-completion or the completed-contract method.

	2001		2002		2003	
Construction in Progress	1,040,000		910,000		650,000	
Materials, Cash, etc.		1,040,000		910,000		650,000
To record costs incurred.						
Accounts Receivable	1,000,000		900,000		1,100,000	
Progress Billings on Construction Contracts		1,000,000		900,000		1,100,000
To record billings.						
Cash	800,000		850,000		1,350,000	
Accounts Receivable		800,000		850,000		1,350,000
To record cash collections.						

> **FYI:** The reason these entries are the same under either revenue recognition method is because they are a function of the terms of the contract that specifies when payment will be made.

 Progress Billings on Construction Contracts is offset against the construction in progress account. What does the resulting net figure represent?

No other entries would be required in 2001 and 2002 under the completed-contract method. In both years, the balance of Construction in Progress exceeds the amount in Progress Billings on Construction Contracts; thus, the latter account would be offset against the inventory account in the balance sheet.

Before proceeding further, let's examine the relationship between the accounts Construction in Progress and Progress Billings on Construction Contracts. Amounts recorded in Construction in Progress represent the costs that have been incurred to date relating to a specific contract. If the customer has not been billed, then the entire cost represents a probable future benefit to the company and should be disclosed on the balance sheet as an asset. If, however, the customer has been billed for a portion of these costs, then the company has in effect traded one asset for another. In place of inventory, the company now has a receivable (or cash if the receivable has been paid).

Thus, if the balance in Construction in Progress exceeds the balance in Progress Billings on Construction Contracts, the excess represents the amount of the construction costs[8] for which the customer has *not* been billed. The amount for which the customer has been billed is included in either Accounts Receivable or Cash. If Progress Billings on Construction Contracts is greater than Construction in Progress, the difference represents a liability because the customer has been billed (and a receivable has been recorded) for more than the costs actually incurred.

Because the operating cycle of a company that emphasizes long-term contracts is usually more than one year, all of the preceding balance sheet accounts would be classified as current. The balance sheet at the end of 2002 under the completed-contract method would disclose the following balances related to the construction contract.

Current assets:		
Accounts receivable		$250,000
Construction in progress	$1,950,000	
Less: Progress billings on construction contracts	1,900,000	50,000

If the billings exceeded the construction costs, the excess would be reported in the current liability section of the balance sheet.

Under the completed-contract method, the following entries would be made to recognize revenue and costs and to close out the inventory and billings accounts at the completion of the contract, that is, in 2003.

---

8 As we will soon learn, under the percentage-of-completion method, Construction in Progress includes both costs and the portion of expected gross profit earned to date.

Progress Billings on Construction Contracts....................................	3,000,000	
Revenue From Long-Term Construction Contracts..................................		3,000,000
Cost of Long-Term Construction Contracts....................................	2,600,000	
Construction in Progress....................................		2,600,000

The first entry represents the billings on the contract that, at the end of the contract, equal the total revenue from the contract. The second journal entry transfers the inventoried cost from the contract to the appropriate expense account on the income statement. The income statement for 2003 would report the gross revenues and the matched costs, thus recognizing the entire $400,000 profit in one year.

Using Percentage-of-Completion Accounting: Cost-to-Cost Method

If the company used the percentage-of-completion method of accounting, the $400,000 profit would be spread over all three years of construction according to the estimated percentage of completion for each year. The information on page 378 details Strong's estimated cost to complete the contract at the end of 2001 and 2002 as well as the total actual costs at the end of 2003. Recall that the percentage of completion for each year, determined on a cost-to-cost basis, is as follows:

	2001	**2002**	**2003**
Percentage of completion to date..	40%	75%	100%

These percentages may be used to determine directly the gross profit that should be recognized on the income statement; that is, the income statement for 2001 would report only the gross profit from construction contracts in the amount of $160,000 (estimated gross profit—2001, $400,000 × 40% = $160,000). Preferably, the percentages should be used to determine both revenues and costs. The income statement will then disclose revenues, costs, and the resulting gross profit, a method more consistent with normal income statement reporting. The *AICPA Audit and Accounting Guide for Construction Contractors* recommended this proportional procedure, and the presentations in this chapter will reflect that recommendation.[9] The procedures are as follows:

1. Cumulative revenue to date should be computed by multiplying total estimated contract revenue by the percentage of completion. Revenue for the current period is the difference between the cumulative revenue at the end of the current period and the cumulative revenue recognized in prior periods.

> **Caution!** An instance in which the proportional cost will not equal actual costs incurred occurs when it is anticipated that the entire contract will result in a loss. This exception is discussed in the section "Reporting Anticipated Contract Losses."

2. Cumulative costs to date should be computed in a manner similar to revenue and should be equal to the total estimated contract cost multiplied by the percentage of completion on the contract. Cost for the current period is the difference between the cumulative costs at the end of the current period and the cumulative costs reported in prior periods.

3. Cumulative gross profit is the excess of cumulative revenue over cumulative costs, and the current period gross profit is the difference between current revenue and current costs.

If the cost-to-cost method is used to estimate earned revenue, the proportional cost for each period will typically equal the actual cost incurred.

To illustrate, for 2001, 40% of the fixed contract price of $3,000,000 would be recognized as revenue ($1,200,000) and 40% of the expected total cost of $2,600,000 would be reported as cost ($1,040,000). The following revenue recognition entries

---

9 *Construction Contractor Guide Committee of the Accounting Standards Division, AICPA,* "AICPA Audit and Accounting Guide for Construction Contractors," New York: American Institute of Certified Public Accountants, 1999.

would be made for each of the three years of the contract. These entries are in addition to the transaction entries illustrated on page 380.

	2001		2002		2003	
Cost of Long-Term Construction Contracts*	1,040,000		910,000		650,000	
Construction in Progress	160,000		140,000		100,000	
Revenue From Long-Term Construction Contracts		1,200,000		1,050,000**		750,000***

*Actual costs.
**($3,000,000 × .75) – $1,200,000 = $1,050,000.
***$3,000,000 – $1,200,000 – $1,050,000 = $750,000.

The gross profit recognized each year is added to the construction in progress account, thereby valuing the inventory on the books at its net realizable value. Note that the procedures used in recognizing revenue under the percentage-of-completion method do not affect the progress billings made or the amount of cash collected. These amounts are determined by contract and not by the accounting method used.

Because the construction in progress account contains costs incurred plus recognized profit (the two together equaling total revenues recognized to date), at the completion of the contract the balance in this account will exactly equal the amount in Progress Billings on Construction Contracts, because the progress billings account reflects the contract price (or total revenues). The following closing entry would complete the accounting process:

Progress Billings on Construction Contracts	3,000,000	
Construction in Progress		3,000,000

Using Percentage-of-Completion Accounting: Other Methods

If the cost-to-cost method is not used to measure progress on the contract, the proportional costs recognized under this method may not be equal to the actual costs incurred. For example, assume in 2001 that an engineering estimate measure was used, and 42% of the contract was assumed to be completed. The gross profit recognized would therefore be computed and reported as follows:

Recognized revenue (42% of $3,000,000)	$1,260,000
Cost (42% of $2,600,000)	1,092,000
Gross profit (42% of $400,000)	$ 168,000

Because some accountants believe that the amount of cost recognized should be equal to the costs actually incurred, an alternative to the preceding approach was included in SOP 81–1.[10] Under this actual cost approach, revenue is defined as the actual costs incurred on the contract plus the gross profit earned for the period on the contract. Using the data from the previous example, the revenue and costs to be reported on the 2001 income statement would be as follows:

Actual cost incurred to date	$1,040,000
Recognized gross profit (42% of $400,000)	168,000
Recognized revenue	$1,208,000

This contrasts with the $1,260,000 revenue using the proportional cost approach. Both approaches report gross profit as $168,000.

In a footnote to this discussion in the SOP, the committee made it clear that the actual cost approach and the proportional cost approach are equally acceptable. However,

10 SOP 81-1, pars. 80 and 81.

because the actual cost approach results in a varying gross profit percentage from period to period whenever the measurement of completion differs from that which would occur if the cost-to-cost method were used, the authors feel that the proportional cost approach is preferable. Unless a different method is explicitly stated, text examples and end-of-chapter material will assume the proportional cost approach.

Revision of Estimates

In the previous example, it was assumed that the estimated cost did not vary from the beginning of the contract. This rarely would be the case. As estimates change, catch-up adjustments are made in the year of the change. To illustrate the impact of changing estimates, assume that at the end of 2002, it was estimated that the remaining cost to complete the construction was $720,000 rather than $650,000. This would increase the total estimated cost to $2,670,000, reduce the expected profit to $330,000, and change the percentage of completion at the end of 2002 to 73% ($1,950,000/$2,670,000).

The following analysis shows how this change would affect the revenue and costs to be reported each year, assuming that the actual costs incurred in 2003 were $700,000.

	2001	2002	2003
Contract price	$3,000,000	$3,000,000	$3,000,000
Actual cost incurred to date	$1,040,000	$1,950,000	$2,650,000
Estimated cost to complete	1,560,000	720,000	0
Total estimated cost	$2,600,000	$2,670,000	$2,650,000
Total expected gross profit	$ 400,000	$ 330,000	$ 350,000
Percentage of completion to date	40%	73%	100%

	To Date	Recognized—Prior Years	Recognized—Current Year
2001:			
Recognized revenue ($3,000,000 × .40)	$1,200,000	0	$1,200,000
Cost (actual cost)	1,040,000	0	1,040,000
Gross profit	$ 160,000		$ 160,000
2002:			
Recognized revenue ($3,000,000 × .73)	$2,190,000	$1,200,000	$ 990,000
Cost (actual cost)	1,950,000	1,040,000	910,000
Gross profit	$ 240,000	$ 160,000	$ 80,000
2003:			
Recognized revenue	$3,000,000	$2,190,000	$ 810,000
Cost (actual cost)	2,650,000	1,950,000	700,000
Gross profit	$ 350,000	$ 240,000	$ 110,000

The entries to record revenue and cost for the three years, given the assumed estimate revision, would be as follows:

	2001		2002		2003	
Cost of Long-Term Construction Contracts	1,040,000		910,000		700,000	
Construction in Progress	160,000		80,000		110,000	
Revenue From Long-Term Construction Contracts		1,200,000		990,000		810,000

STOP & THINK What circumstances would give rise to a loss being reported on a profitable contract? In other words, what does a loss being reported for this period tell us about last year's profit?

In some cases, an increase in total estimated cost can result in recognition of a loss in the year of the increase. Revising the preceding example, assume that at the end of 2002 the estimated cost to complete construction was $836,000, and this was the actual cost incurred in 2003. The following analysis shows how this change in estimated cost would reduce the percentage of completion at the end of 2002 to 70%, and the cumulative profit at the end of 2002 to $150,000. Because $160,000 was already recognized as gross profit in 2001, a loss of $10,000 would be recognized in 2002.

	2001	2002	2003
Contract price	$3,000,000	$3,000,000	$3,000,000
Actual cost incurred to date	$1,040,000	$1,950,000	$2,786,000
Estimated cost to complete	1,560,000	836,000	0
Total estimated cost	$2,600,000	$2,786,000	$2,786,000
Total expected gross profit	$ 400,000	$ 214,000	$ 214,000
Percentage of completion to date	40%	70%	100%

	To Date	Recognized—Prior Years	Recognized—Current Year
2001:			
Recognized revenue ($3,000,000 × .40)	$1,200,000	0	$1,200,000
Cost (actual cost)	1,040,000	0	1,040,000
Gross profit	$ 160,000		$ 160,000
2002:			
Recognized revenue ($3,000,000 × .70)	$2,100,000	$1,200,000	$ 900,000
Cost (actual cost)	1,950,000	1,040,000	910,000
Gross profit (loss)	$ 150,000	$ 160,000	$ (10,000)
2003:			
Recognized revenue	$3,000,000	$2,100,000	$ 900,000
Cost (actual cost)	2,786,000	1,950,000	836,000
Gross profit	$ 214,000	$ 150,000	$ 64,000

The entries to record revenue and cost for the three years, given the assumed loss estimate in 2002, would be as follows:

	2001		2002		2003	
Cost of Long-Term Construction Contracts	1,040,000		910,000		836,000	
Construction in Progress	160,000			10,000	64,000	
Revenue From Long-Term Construction Contracts		1,200,000		900,000		900,000

Reporting Anticipated Contract Losses

In the example above, an increase in estimated total cost resulted in recognition of a loss in the year the estimate was revised; but overall, the contract resulted in a profit. In some cases, an increase in estimated total cost is so great that a loss on the entire contract is anticipated; that is, total estimated costs are expected to exceed the total revenue from the contract. When a loss on the total contract is anticipated, GAAP requires reporting the

Caution! Do not confuse a loss on an entire contract with a loss for a period on a profitable contract. The accounting for these two possibilities is entirely different.

loss in its entirety in the period when the loss is first anticipated. This is true under either the completed-contract or the percentage-of-completion method.

For example, assume that in the earlier construction example on page 384, the estimated cost to complete the contract at the end of 2002 was $1,300,000. Because $1,950,000 of costs had already been incurred, the total estimated cost of the contract would be $3,250,000 ($1,950,000 + $1,300,000), or $250,000 more than the contract price. Assume also that actual costs equaled expected costs in 2003.

	2001	**2002**	**2003**
Contract price	$3,000,000	$3,000,000	$3,000,000
Actual cost incurred to date	$1,040,000	$1,950,000	$3,250,000
Estimated cost to complete	1,560,000	1,300,000	0
Total estimated cost	$2,600,000	$3,250,000	$3,250,000
Total expected gross profit (loss)	$ 400,000	$ (250,000)	$ (250,000)
Percentage of completion to date	40%	60%	100%

Using this example, accounting for a contract loss is illustrated first for the completed-contract method and then for the percentage-of-completion method.

ANTICIPATED CONTRACT LOSS: COMPLETED-CONTRACT METHOD If the completed-contract method is used, the recognition of an anticipated contract loss is simple. The amount of the loss is debited to a loss account, and the inventory account, Construction in Progress, is credited by that amount to reduce the inventory to its expected net realizable value. To record the anticipated loss of $250,000 on the construction contract, the following entry would be made at the end of 2002:

FYI: Because the construction in progress inventory account is used to accumulate actual construction costs under the completed-contract method, this journal entry will ensure that at the end of the contract, the inventory account is not reported at an amount higher than the contract price.

Anticipated Loss on Long-Term Construction Contracts	250,000	
Construction in Progress		250,000

ANTICIPATED CONTRACT LOSS: PERCENTAGE-OF-COMPLETION METHOD Recognition of an anticipated contract loss under the percentage-of-completion method is more complex. To properly reflect the entire loss in the year it is first anticipated, the cumulative cost to deduct from cumulative recognized revenue cannot be the actual cost incurred but must be the cumulative recognized revenue plus the entire anticipated loss. Thus, continuing the construction contract example, the cumulative recognized revenue at the end of 2002 would be $1,800,000 (60% × $3,000,000), and the cumulative cost at the same date would be $2,050,000 ($1,800,000 + $250,000). Because the example assumes that $160,000 profit was recognized on this contract in 2001, the total loss to be recognized in 2002 is $410,000 ($160,000 + $250,000). The analysis that follows reflects the amounts to be reported for each of the three years of the contract life under the anticipated loss assumption.

The entry to record the revenue, costs, and adjustments to Construction in Progress for the loss in 2002 would be as follows:

Cost of Long-Term Construction Contracts	1,010,000	
Revenue From Long-Term Construction Contracts		600,000
Construction in Progress		410,000

	To Date	Recognized—Prior Years	Recognized—Current Year
2001:			
Recognized revenue ($3,000,000 × .40)........	$1,200,000	0	$1,200,000
Cost (actual cost)................................	1,040,000	0	1,040,000
Gross profit.....................................	$ 160,000		$ 160,000
2002:			
Recognized revenue ($3,000,000 × .60)........	$1,800,000	$1,200,000	$ 600,000
Cost (recognized revenue plus entire anticipated loss)................................	2,050,000	1,040,000	1,010,000
Gross profit (loss)...............................	$ (250,000)	$ 160,000	$ (410,000)
2003:			
Recognized revenue.............................	$3,000,000	$1,800,000	$1,200,000
Cost...	3,250,000	2,050,000	1,200,000
Gross profit (loss)...............................	$ (250,000)	$ (250,000)	$ 0

Note that the construction in progress account under both methods would have a balance of $1,700,000 at the end of 2002, computed as shown below.

**Completed-Contract Method
Construction in Progress**

2001 cost	1,040,000	2002 loss	250,000
2002 cost	910,000		
Balance	1,700,000		

**Percentage-of-Completion Method
Construction in Progress**

2001 cost	1,040,000	2002 loss	410,000
2001 gross profit	160,000		
2002 cost	910,000		
Balance	1,700,000		

Accounting for Contract Change Orders

Long-term construction contracts are seldom completed without change orders that affect both the contract price and the cost of performance. **Change orders** are modifications of an original contract that effectively change the provisions of the contract. They may be initiated by the contractor or the customer, and they include changes in specifications or design, method or manner of performance, facilities, equipment, materials, location site, and so forth. If the contract price is changed as a result of a change order, future computations are made with the revised expected revenue and any anticipated cost changes that will arise because of the change order. Change orders are often unpriced; that is, the work to be performed is defined, but the adjustment to the contract price is to be negotiated later. If it is probable that a contract price change will be negotiated to at least recover the increased costs, the increased costs may be included with the incurred costs of the period and the revenue may be increased by the same amount. Exhibit 7–2 provides an example from GENERAL DYNAMICS, producer of defense systems for the United States and its allies, of the typical note disclosure provided for long-term contracts.

Here, two technicians work on the first stage of a rocket for McDonnell Douglas. Since a rocket may take many years to build, McDonnell Douglas must account for this construction using the percentage-of-completion method.

EXHIBIT 7-2 | General Dynamics—Note Disclosure for Long-Term Contracts

SALES AND EARNINGS UNDER LONG-TERM CONTRACTS AND PROGRAMS. Defense programs are accounted for using the percentage-of-completion method of accounting. The combination of estimated profit rates on similar, economically interdependent contracts is used to develop program earnings rates for contracts that meet Statement of Position (SOP) 81-1 criteria. These rates are applied to contract costs, including general and administrative expenses, for the determination of sales and operating earnings. Program earnings rates are reviewed quarterly to assess revisions in contract values and estimated costs at completion. Based on these assessments, any changes in earnings rates are made prospectively.

Any anticipated losses on contracts or programs are charged to earnings when identified. Such losses encompass all costs, including general and administrative expenses, allocable to the contracts. Revenue arising from the claims process is not recognized either as income or as an offset against a potential loss until it can be reliably estimated and its realization is probable.

The International Standard for Construction Contracts—IAS 11

As mentioned earlier in the discussion of the general revenue recognition conditions of IAS 18, the most significant difference between IAS and U.S. GAAP is that U.S. GAAP includes vast amounts of guidance with respect to revenue recognition in specific industries whereas IAS only provides general principles. This same difference exists in the area of accounting for construction contracts. In fact, in a comparison of U.S. GAAP and IAS commissioned by the FASB, the biggest difference in the area of construction contracts is described as the lack of detailed guidance in IAS for determining the estimated cost to complete a contract; under U.S. GAAP, this guidance is part of AICPA SOP 81-1.[11]

11 "The IASC–U.S. Comparison Project: A Report on the Similarities and Differences between IASC Standards and U.S. GAAP," Norwalk, CT, Financial Accounting Standards Board, 1996, Chap. 11.

Another prominent difference between IAS and U.S. GAAP is that IAS 11 (Construction Contracts) does not allow the completed-contract method. Under the provisions of IAS 11, the percentage-of-completion method should be used whenever the outcome of a construction contract can be reliably estimated. In those cases in which this is not possible, a zero-profit approach is used. A zero-profit approach involves recognizing revenues equal to the amount of costs incurred during the period so that no net profit is recognized. But as soon as the ultimate outcome of a contract can be estimated, the percentage-of-completion method is applied. In the first year in which the percentage-of-completion method is applied, the cumulative revenues and costs recognized under the zero-profit approach are used in computing the revenues and costs to be recognized for the current period.

Record journal entries for long-term service contracts using the proportional performance method.

ACCOUNTING FOR LONG-TERM SERVICE CONTRACTS: THE PROPORTIONAL PERFORMANCE METHOD

Thus far, the discussion in this chapter has focused on long-term construction-type contracts. As indicated earlier, another type of contract that frequently extends over a long period of time is a service contract. An increasing percentage of sales in our economy is classified as sales of services as opposed to sales of goods. When the service to be performed is completed as a single act or over a relatively short period of time, no revenue recognition problems arise. The revenue recognition criteria previously defined apply, and all direct and indirect costs related to the service are charged to expense in the period the revenue is recognized. However, when several acts over a period of time are involved, the same revenue recognition problems illustrated for long-term construction-type contracts arise.

Unless the final act of service to be performed is so vital to the contract that earlier acts are relatively insignificant, for example, the packaging, loading, and final delivery of goods in a delivery contract, revenue should be recognized under the proportional performance method. Both input and output measures represent possible ways of measuring progress on a service contract. If a contract involves a specified number of identical or similar acts, for example, the processing of monthly mortgage payments by a mortgage banker, an output measure derived by relating the number of acts performed to the total number of acts to be performed over the contract life is recommended. If a contract involves a specified number of defined but not identical acts, such as a correspondence school that provides evaluation, lessons, examinations, and grading, a cost-to-cost input measurement percentage would be applicable. If future costs are not objectively determinable, output measures such as relating sales value of the individual acts to the total sales value of the service contract may be used. If no pattern of performance can be determined, or if a service contract involves an unspecified number of similar or identical acts with a fixed period for performance, for example, a maintenance contract for electronic office equipment, the straight-line method, that is, recognizing revenue equally over the periods of performance should be used. In Exhibit 7–3, Microsoft's revenue recognition note provides an example of how a company recognizes revenue for services when a lengthy time period is involved.

EXHIBIT 7–3 | Microsoft's Revenue Recognition Note—Partial

> Maintenance and subscription revenue is recognized ratably over the contract period. Revenue attributable to significant support (technical support and unspecified enhancements such as service packs and Internet browser updates) is based on the price charged or derived value of the undelivered elements and is recognized ratably on a straight-line basis over the product's life cycle.

Various measures can be used to determine what portion of the service contract fee should be recognized as revenue. Generally, the measures are only indirectly related to the pattern of cash collection; however, they are applicable only if cash collection is reasonably assured and if losses from nonpayment can be objectively determined.

The cost recognition problems of service contracts are somewhat different from those of long-term construction-type contracts. Most service contracts involve three different types of costs: (1) initial direct costs related to obtaining and performing initial services on the contract, such as commissions, legal fees, credit investigations, and paper processing; (2) direct costs related to performing the various acts of service; and (3) indirect costs related to maintaining the organization to service the contract, for example, general and administrative expenses. Initial direct costs generally are charged, that is, matched, against revenue using the same input or output measure used for revenue recognition. If the cost-to-cost method of input measurement is used, initial direct costs should be excluded from the cost incurred to date in computing the measure. Only direct costs related to the acts of service are relevant for this computation. Direct costs usually are charged to expense as incurred, because they relate directly to the acts for which revenue is recognized. Similarly, all indirect costs should be charged to expense as incurred. As is true for long-term construction-type contracts, any indicated loss on completion of the service contract is to be charged to the period in which the loss is first indicated. If collection of a service contract is highly uncertain, revenue recognition should not be related to performance but to the collection of the receivable using one of the methods described in the latter part of this chapter.

To illustrate accounting for a service contract using the proportional performance method, assume a correspondence school enters into 100 contracts with students for an extended writing course. The fee for each contract is $500, payable in advance. This fee includes many different services such as providing the text material, evaluating written assignments and examinations, and awarding of a certificate. The total initial direct costs related to the contracts are $5,000. Direct costs for the lessons actually completed during the first period are $12,000. It is estimated that the total direct costs of these contracts over all periods will be $30,000. The facts of this case suggest that the cost-to-cost method is applicable, and the following entries would be made to record these transactions:

> **Caution!** The initial direct costs are excluded from the percentage-of-completion percentage computation. However, the resulting percentage is used to allocate those initial direct costs. That can be confusing.

Cash..	50,000	
Deferred Course Revenue (liability account).................................		50,000
Deferred Initial Costs (asset account).........................	5,000	
Cash..		5,000
Contract Costs (expense account).................................	12,000	
Cash..		12,000
Deferred Course Revenue.................................	20,000*	
Recognized Course Revenue.................................		20,000
Contract Costs..	2,000**	
Deferred Initial Costs.................................		2,000

*Cost-to-cost percentage: $12,000/$30,000 = 40%; $50,000 × .40 = $20,000
**$5,000 × .40 = $2,000

The gross profit reported on these contracts for the period would be $6,000 ($20,000 – $12,000 – $2,000). The deferred initial cost and deferred course revenues would normally be reported as current balance sheet deferrals, because the operating cycle of a correspondence school would be equal to the average time to complete a contract or one year, whichever is longer.

Evaluation of the Proportional Performance Method

The FASB has not issued a standard on service industries. While the proportional performance method has theoretical support for its adoption, it tends to be extremely

> ## ► MCKESSON ACCOUNTING SCANDALS: 1937 AND 1999

On January 12, 1999, McKESSON CORPORATION, a large health care supply firm, paid $12 billion to acquire HBO & COMPANY, a leading producer of health care-related software. [*Note:* To avoid confusion, be aware that HBO & Company is not connected with HBO, the cable channel.] On April 22, 1999, the combined company, called McKESSON HBOC, announced that preliminary calculations indicated that income for the

year ended March 31, 1999, was $237.1 million. A few days later, a staff auditor from DELOITTE & TOUCHE, performing a routine confirmation of accounts receivable, was surprised to hear from a customer that a $20 million sale reported by the HBO division had never taken place. It was soon learned that $42 million in sales reported by HBO should not have been recognized. When this information was announced to the financial press by McKesson HBOC on April 28, 1999, the company's stock price dropped from $65⅝ to $34⅞ in one day; this 47.5% drop represented a market value loss of $8.8 billion.

Further investigation revealed that the accounting improprieties at McKesson HBOC were much more widespread than originally suspected. On May 25, 1999, the company revealed that further earnings restatements would be announced in the future. On July 14, 1999, when McKesson HBOC filed its 10-K with the SEC, it was revealed that net income for the year ended March 31, 1999, was not $237.1 million, as announced earlier, but was actually $84.9 million. The final amount of

overstated revenue in the HBO division was $327 million, which was spread over the preceding three years.

The HBO revenue overstatements, which appear to have been the work of top managers of HBO (five of whom were fired by McKesson HBOC on June 21, 1999), were accomplished in the following ways.

- *Side letters.* Great pressure was put on HBO salespeople in order for the company to meet its revenue targets. To get wavering customers to close deals, the salespeople would promise that the customer could cancel the deal in the future if they were unable to obtain financing, if their board of directors didn't approve, or even if they just changed their mind. The terms of these conditional agreements were written up in letters that were kept in files separate from the sales "orders."
- *Backdating.* In order to meet quarterly revenue targets, sales orders in the first couple of weeks of a new quarter were backdated so that they would boost reported revenue in the preceding quarter.

conservative, especially during a period of rapid growth in a company's revenues. Because no revenue is recognized until performance of the service has begun, the proportional performance method recognizes no revenue at the critical point of signing a service contract. Thus, in the growing years of a company, use of the proportional performance method will result in large losses being reported even though the operation might be very profitable over time. This can lead to the questionable conclusion that a company is no better off after service contracts are sold than it was before.

An alternative method of recognizing revenue for service contracts would be to recognize part of the revenue upon the signing of the contract and then spread the balance of the revenue over the contract life using the proportional performance concept. The decision as to how much revenue should be recognized at the beginning of the contract would depend on the nature and terms of the contract, including any forfeiture or cancellation provisions.

Explain when revenue is recognized after delivery of goods or services through installment sales, cost recovery, and cash methods.

REVENUE RECOGNITION AFTER DELIVERY
OF GOODS OR PERFORMANCE OF SERVICES

One of the FASB's two revenue recognition criteria, listed at the beginning of this chapter, states that revenue should not be recognized until the earnings process is substantially completed. Normally, the earnings process is substantially completed by the deliv-

- *Advanced recognition of future sales.* At the time of an original software sale, HBO would sometimes recognize revenue for both that sale and for all future revenue expected to be generated through software upgrades. Often, these expected future upgrades did not even exist at the time the revenue was recognized.

For accountants and auditors, the McKesson HBOC case stirs memories of the famous McKesson & Robbins fraud of 1937. For fiscal 1937, McKESSON & ROBBINS, the predecessor of McKesson HBOC, reported total assets of $87 million. It was later discovered that this $87 million included $10 million in nonexistent inventory and $9 million in fictitious receivables. The fraud was perpetrated by the top managers of McKesson & Robbins and involved phony purchases from and sales to dummy Canadian companies, which were actually just empty offices staffed by secretaries who forwarded mail.

The well-publicized McKesson & Robbins fraud spurred the auditing profession to adopt two auditing standards that are still followed today.

1. The physical existence of inventory must be confirmed through direct observation. This simple procedure applied in the McKesson & Robbins case would have revealed that the reported purchases from the Canadian suppliers were phony.

2. The existence and accuracy of reported receivables must be independently confirmed through contacting a sample of the parties who allegedly owe the money. Sixty-two years after the original McKesson & Robbins scandal, this simple procedure, applied by a staff auditor at Deloitte & Touche, uncovered the modern-day McKesson HBOC fraud.

QUESTIONS:

1. Why did McKesson HBOC's stock price drop so much (47.5%) upon release of the news on April 28, 1999, that sales in the HBO division had been overstated by $42 million?

2. This overstatement of revenue at HBO & Company coincided with the period in which the company was an acquisition target. Is this a coincidence? Explain.

3. What common aspect of both the 1937 McKesson & Robbins case and the 1999 McKesson HBOC case made it difficult to discover the frauds?

SOURCES:

Elizabeth McDonald, "The Ghost of Scandal Past," *The Wall Street Journal,* June 30, 1999, p. B1.

Ralph T. King, Jr., "McKesson Restates Income Again as Probe of Accounting Widens," *The Wall Street Journal,* July 15, 1999, p. A1.

10-K Filing of McKesson HBOC for the year ended March 31, 1999.

STOP & THINK If the collection of cash is uncertain, when and how should revenue and profits be recognized?

ery of goods or performance of services. Collection of receivables is usually routine, and any future warranty costs can be reasonably estimated. In some cases, however, the circumstances surrounding a revenue transaction are such that considerable uncertainty exists as to whether payments will indeed be received. This can occur if the sales transaction is unusual in nature or involves a customer in such a way that default carries little cost or penalty. Under these circumstances, the uncertainty of cash collection suggests that revenue recognition should await the actual receipt of cash.

There are at least three different approaches to revenue recognition that depend on the receipt of cash: installment sales, cost recovery, and cash. These methods differ as to the treatment of costs incurred and the timing of revenue recognition. They are summarized and contrasted with the full accrual method in the table on the following page.

These methods are really not alternatives to each other; however, the guidelines for applying them are not well defined. As the uncertainty of the environment increases, GAAP would require moving from the full accrual method to installment sales, cost recovery, and finally, a strict cash approach. The cash method is the most conservative approach, because it would not permit the deferral of any costs but would charge them to expense as those costs are paid. In the following pages, each of these revenue recognition methods will be discussed and illustrated.

Method	Timing of Revenue and/or Income Recognition	Treatment of Product Costs or Direct Costs Under Service Contracts
Full accrual	At point of sale.	Charge against revenue at time of sale or rendering of service.
Installment sales	At collection of cash. Usually a portion of the cash payment is recognized as income.	Defer to be matched against part of each cash collection. Usually done by deferring the estimated profit.
Cost recovery	At collection of cash, but only after all costs are recovered.	Defer to be matched against total cash collected.
Cash	At collection of cash.	Charge to expense as incurred.

> **Caution!** Do not confuse installment sales with the installment sales method of accounting. Remember that most installment sales are accounted for using accrual accounting. Only those sales with a high degree of uncertainty as to collection are accounted for using the installment sales method.

Installment Sales Method

Traditionally, the most commonly applied method for dealing with the uncertainty of cash collections has been the **installment sales method.** Under this method, profit is recognized as cash is collected rather than at the time of sale. The installment sales method is used most commonly in cases of real estate sales where contracts may involve little or no down payment, payments are spread over 10 to 30 or 40 years, and a high probability of default in the early years exists because of a small investment by the buyer in the contract and because the market prices of the property often are unstable. Application of the accrual method to these contracts frequently overstates income in the early years due to the failure to realistically provide for future costs related to the contract, including losses from contract defaults. The FASB considered these types of sales and concluded that accrual accounting applied in these circumstances often results in "front-end loading," that is, a recognition of all revenue at the time of the sales contract with improper matching of related costs. Thus, the Board has established criteria that must be met before real estate and retail land sales can be recorded using the full accrual method of revenue recognition. If the criteria are not fully met, then the use of the installment sales method, or in some cases the cost recovery or deposit methods, is recommended to reflect the conditions of the sale more accurately.[12] THE ROUSE COMPANY, a real estate development firm, provides disclosure, shown in Exhibit 7–4, relating to its revenue recognition policy. Note that Rouse uses one of three revenue recognition policies for its transactions, depending on whether or not the transaction meets established revenue recognition criteria.

EXHIBIT 7–4 | The Rouse Company's Revenue Recognition Note

> Gains from sales of operating properties and revenues from land sales are recognized using the full accrual method provided that various criteria relating to the terms of the transactions and any subsequent involvement by the Ventures with the properties sold are met. Gains or revenues relating to transactions which do not meet the established criteria are deferred and recognized when the criteria are met or using the installment or cost recovery methods, as appropriate in the circumstances.

Accounting for installment sales using the deferred gross profit approach requires determining a gross profit rate for the sales of each year and establishing an accounts receivable and a deferred gross profit account identified by the year of the sale. As

12 *Statement of Financial Accounting Standards No. 66,* "Accounting for Sales of Real Estate," Stamford, CT: Financial Accounting Standards Board, October 1982.

collections are made of a given year's receivables, a portion of the deferred profit equal to the gross profit rate times the collections made is recognized as income. To keep things relatively simple, the following examples of transactions and journal entries will illustrate the installment sales method assuming the sale of merchandise.

INSTALLMENT SALES OF MERCHANDISE Assume that the Riding Corporation sells merchandise on the installment basis and that the uncertainties of cash collection make the use of the installment sales method necessary. The following data relate to three years of operations. To simplify the presentation, interest charges are excluded from the example.

	2001	2002	2003
Installment sales	$150,000	$200,000	$300,000
Cost of installment sales	100,000	140,000	204,000
Gross profit	$ 50,000	$ 60,000	$ 96,000
Gross profit percentage	33.33%	30%	32%
Cash collections:			
2001 sales	$ 30,000	$ 75,000	$ 30,000
2002 sales		70,000	80,000
2003 sales			100,000

The entries to record the transactions for 2001 would be as follows:

During the Year:

Installment Accounts Receivable—2001	150,000	
Installment Sales		150,000
Cost of Installment Sales	100,000	
Inventory		100,000
Cash	30,000	
Installment Accounts Receivable—2001		30,000

End of Year:

Installment Sales	150,000	
Cost of Installment Sales		100,000
Deferred Gross Profit—2001		50,000
Deferred Gross Profit—2001	10,000*	
Realized Gross Profit on Installment Sales		10,000

*$30,000 × 33.33%

The sales and costs related to sales are recorded in a manner identical to the accounting for sales discussed in Chapter 6. At the end of the year, however, the sales and costs of sales accounts are closed to a deferred gross profit account rather than to Retained Earnings. The realized gross profit is then recognized by applying the gross profit percentage to cash collections. All other general and administrative expenses are normally written off in the period incurred.

For 2001, the income statement would begin with sales from which is subtracted deferred gross profit and to which is added realized gross profit for the year to arrive at a net figure. Cost of sales would then be subtracted along with other operating expenses (assumed to be $5,000 in this example) as illustrated below:

Sales	$150,000
Less: Deferred gross profit	(50,000)
Add: Realized gross profit	10,000
	$110,000
Less: Cost of installment sales	(100,000)
Other operating expenses	(5,000)
Operating income	$ 5,000

Entries for the next two years are summarized in the schedule below.

	2002		2003	
During the Year:				
Installment Accounts Receivable—2002	200,000			
Installment Accounts Receivable—2003			300,000	
Installment Sales		200,000		300,000
Cost of Installment Sales	140,000		204,000	
Inventory		140,000		204,000
Cash	145,000		210,000	
Installment Accounts Receivable—2001		75,000		30,000
Installment Accounts Receivable—2002		70,000		80,000
Installment Accounts Receivable—2003				100,000
End of Year:				
Installment Sale	200,000		300,000	
Cost of Installment Sales		140,000		204,000
Deferred Gross Profit—2002		60,000		
Deferred Gross Profit—2003				96,000
Deferred Gross Profit—2001	25,000*		10,000***	
Deferred Gross Profit—2002	21,000**		24,000****	
Deferred Gross Profit—2003			32,000*****	
Realized Gross Profit on Installment Sales		46,000		66,000

*$75,000 × 33.33% = $25,000
**$70,000 × 30% = $21,000
***$30,000 × 33.33% = $10,000
****$80,000 × 30% = $24,000
*****$100,000 × 32% = $32,000

> **Caution!** Note that a separate deferred gross profit account is kept for each year and that accounts receivable collections must be accounted for by year. This is to ensure that the appropriate gross profit percentage is applied to the cash collected.

STOP & THINK What does the $80,000 net amount represent?

If a company is heavily involved in installment sales, the operating cycle of the business is normally the period of the average installment contract. Thus, the currently accepted definition of current assets and current liabilities requires that the receivables and their related deferred gross profit accounts be reported in the current asset section of classified balance sheets. The deferred gross profit accounts should be reported as an offset to the related accounts receivable. Thus, at the end of 2001, the current asset section would include the following account balances:

Installment accounts receivable	$120,000	
Less: Deferred gross profit	40,000	$80,000

COMPLEXITIES OF INSTALLMENT SALES OF MERCHANDISE In the previous example, no provision was made for interest. In reality, installment sales contracts always include interest, either expressed or implied. The interest portion of the contract payments is recognized as income in the period in which cash is received, and the balance of the payment is treated as a collection on the installment sale. Thus, if in the example beginning on page 393, the $75,000 collection of 2001 sales in 2002 included interest of $40,000, only $35,000 would be used to compute the realized gross profit from 2001 sales. The resulting journal entries made in 2002 relating to the $75,000 collection of 2001 sales would be as follows:

Cash	75,000	
Interest Revenue		40,000
Installment Accounts Receivable—2001		35,000
Deferred Gross Profit—2001	11,666*	
Realized Gross Profit on Installment Sales		11,666

*$35,000 × 33.33% = $11,666

Additional complexities can arise in installment sales accounting in providing for uncollectible accounts. Because of the right to repossess merchandise in the event of nonpayment, the provision for uncollectible accounts can be less than might be expected. Only the amount of the receivable in excess of the current value of the repossessed merchandise is a potential loss. Accounting for repossessions is discussed in Chapter 9. Theoretically, a proper matching of estimated losses against revenues would require allocating the expected losses over the years of collection. Practically, however, the provision is made and charged against income in the period of the sale. Thus, the accounting entries for handling estimated uncollectible accounts are the same as illustrated in Chapter 6. However, normally the impact of accounting for bad debts with respect to installment sales is not great because revenue and receivables are not recognized until the probability of cash collection is quite high.

Cost Recovery Method

Under the **cost recovery method,** no income is recognized on a sale until the cost of the item sold is recovered through cash receipts. All cash receipts, both interest and principal portions, are applied first to the cost of those items sold. Then, all subsequent receipts are reported as revenue. Because all costs have been recovered, the recognized revenue after cost recovery represents income. This method is used only when the circumstances surrounding a sale are so uncertain that earlier recognition is impossible.

Using the information from the Riding Corporation example, assume that collections are so uncertain that the use of the cost recovery method is deemed appropriate. While the entries to record the installment sale, the receipt of cash, and the deferral of the gross profit are identical for both the installment sales and cost recovery methods, the entry for recognizing gross profit differs.

In 2001 no gross profit would be recognized, because the amount of cash collected ($30,000) is less than the cost of the inventory sold ($100,000). The cash collections in 2002 relating to 2001 sales result in total cash receipts exceeding the cost of sales ($30,000 + $75,000 > $100,000). Thus, in 2002 gross profit of $5,000 would be recognized on 2001 sales. The journal entry to recognize this gross profit in 2002 would be:

Deferred Gross Profit—2001	5,000	
Realized Gross Profit on Installment Sales		5,000

Because the cash collected in 2002 for 2002 sales ($70,000) is less than the cost of inventory sold ($140,000), no gross profit would be recognized in 2002 on 2002 sales. In 2003 the $30,000 collected in cash from the 2001 sales would all be recognized as gross profit. The cash collected relating to 2002 sales, $80,000, when added to the cash received in 2002, $70,000, exceeds the cost of the 2002 sales of $140,000. Thus, $10,000 of gross profit that was deferred in 2002 will be recognized in 2003. The journal entry to recognize gross profit in 2003 would be as follows:

Deferred Gross Profit—2001	30,000	
Deferred Gross Profit—2002	10,000	
Realized Gross Profit on Installment Sales		40,000

Comparing the amount of gross profit that is recognized using the various revenue recognition methods for the period 2001–2003 indicates how the income statement can be materially impacted by the method used.

	Gross Profit Recognized		
Revenue Recognition Method	**2001**	**2002**	**2003**
Full accrual	$50,000	$60,000	$96,000
Installment sales	10,000	46,000	66,000
Cost recovery	0	5,000	40,000

► SOFT REVENUE FOR SOFTWARE COMPANIES

The nature of the computer software industry presents several sticky revenue recognition issues. The installation of software and the promise of software upgrades require software companies to consider when the earnings process is substantially complete. Are the revenue recognition criteria satisfied at the point of sale? when the software is installed? or after promised upgrades are delivered?

Beginning in 1997, the AICPA required software companies to allocate revenue over the entire earnings process. A common practice at the time was to recognize all revenue associated with a sale at the point of sale. With the support of the SEC and the FASB, this new rule, SOP 97-2, requires software companies to attribute revenue from a sale to the various components of the sale. For example, if a software company sells a software package for $500 and agrees to install the software and deliver a free upgrade within a year, the AICPA requires the $500 selling price to be allocated over the software, the installation, and the upgrade.

Cash Method

If the probability of recovering product or service costs is remote, the **cash method** of accounting could be used. Seldom would this method be applicable for sales of merchandise or real estate, because the right of repossession would leave considerable value to the seller. However, the cash method might be appropriate for service contracts with high initial costs and considerable uncertainty as to the ultimate collection of the contract price. Under this method, all costs are charged to expense as incurred, and revenue is recognized as collections are made. This extreme method of revenue and expense recognition would be appropriate only when the potential losses on a contract cannot be estimated with any degree of certainty.

E X P A N D E D   M A T E R I A L

In addition to the revenue recognition methods discussed in this chapter, some sales arrangements involve an exchange of either goods or monetary assets, such as cash and notes receivable, prior to the point where the earnings process has been completed sufficiently to recognize revenue. Under these circumstances, special accounting procedures must be applied pending the finalization of the sale and subsequent application of one of the methods of revenue recognition. If monetary assets are received prior to finalization of a sale, the deposit method of accounting should be used. If inventory is exchanged in advance of a sale, consignment accounting procedures should be applied. Each of these methods will be discussed briefly.

Revenue would be recognized as each of these items or activities was delivered to the purchaser. Under the old rules, the entire $500 would be recognized at the point of sale.

As one might expect, not all software companies supported this new rule. But Microsoft, the biggest software publisher in the world, backed the reporting change.

QUESTIONS:

1. What difficulties might be associated with allocating a software package's purchase price over the entire earnings process?

2. Why might Microsoft be supportive of a rule that would cause software companies (like Microsoft) to slow the recognition of revenue?

SOURCE:

Elizabeth MacDonald, "Accounting Group Considers Forcing Software Companies to Defer Revenue," *The Wall Street Journal*, November 25, 1996.

Describe accounting for the transfer of assets prior to the recognition of revenue with the deposit method and consignment sales.

DEPOSIT METHOD: GENERAL

In some cases, cash is collected before a sales contract is sufficiently defined to recognize revenue. This situation frequently arises in real estate sales contracts. For these cases, a method of accounting referred to as the **deposit method** has been developed.[13] Pending recognition of a sale, the cash received from a buyer is reported as a deposit on the contract and classified among the liabilities on the balance sheet. The property continues to be shown as an asset of the seller, and any related debt on the property continues to be reported as debt of the seller. No revenue or income should be recognized until the sales contract is finalized. At that time, one of the revenue recognition methods illustrated in this chapter may be used, and the deposit account would be closed. If the deposit is forfeited, it should be credited to Miscellaneous Income. An interesting example of the application of the deposit method of accounting is provided in the notes to the financial statements of SERVICE CORPORATION INTERNATIONAL (SCI), as presented in Exhibit 7–5. SCI owns and operates funeral homes, cemeteries, and crematories. The company sells (and collects the cash for) funeral packages to individuals while the individuals are still alive. The revenue associated with these packages is then deferred until the earnings process is "substantially complete."

EXHIBIT 7–5 | Service Corporation International— ⁄ Deposit Method of Accounting

Unperformed price-guaranteed prearranged funeral contracts that are not funded through Company-owned insurance subsidiaries are included in the consolidated balance sheet as "Prearranged funeral contracts." This balance represents amounts due from trust funds, customer receivables, or third-party insurance companies. A corresponding credit is recorded to "Deferred prearranged funeral contract revenues." Amounts paid by a customer under prearranged funeral contract is recognized in funeral revenue at the time the funeral service is performed.

13 *Statement of Financial Accounting Standards No. 66*, pars. 65–67.

DEPOSIT METHOD: FRANCHISING INDUSTRY

A special application of the deposit method is found in the franchising industry, one of the fastest growing retail industries of recent years. Franchisers create faster growth by selling various rights to use a name and/or a product to operators (franchisees) who manage independent units as separate entrepreneurs from the franchiser.

Sales of franchises usually include several different services, products, and/or plant assets including: (1) intangible rights to use a trademark or name, (2) property owned by the franchiser, (3) pre-opening services such as helping locate suitable business sites, constructing a building, and training employees, and (4) ongoing services, products, and processes as the operations are carried out. Many revenue recognition problems are present in typical franchises; however, most of them may be solved if the elements are identified separately and accounted for in the same manner as they would be if the sale were a separate transaction. The most troublesome revenue recognition problem is the initial fee. Typically, the franchiser charges a substantial amount for the right to use the franchise name and to provide for pre-opening services. Sometimes these fees are payable immediately in cash, but typically they include a long-term note receivable. Frequently, liberal refund provisions are included in the agreement, especially in the period prior to opening.

In the early days of franchising agreements, franchisers often reported the initial fee as revenue when the monetary assets were received. Future estimated costs were provided as offsets to the revenue. However, this treatment often resulted in questionable front-end loading of revenue similar to that occurring in the real estate and retail land sale industries. As a result, the AICPA issued an *Industry Accounting Guide* in 1973 that established revenue recognition guidelines for the franchising industry.[14] The essentials of this guide were later incorporated into FASB Statement No. 45.[15] This standard specifies that no revenue is to be recognized prior to **substantial performance** of the services covered by the initial fee. Until that time, any monetary assets received should be offset by a deposit or deferred credit account, and any costs related to the services rendered should be deferred until revenue is recognized, except that such deferred costs shall not exceed anticipated revenue less estimated additional related costs. Once substantial performance is achieved, revenue should be recognized using the method that best reflects the probability of cash collection, for example, accrual, installment sales, or cost recovery method. The latter two methods "shall be used to account for franchise fee revenue only in those exceptional cases when revenue is collectible over an extended period and no reasonable basis exists for estimating collectibility."[16]

To illustrate, assume that a franchiser charges new franchisees a fee consisting of $10,000 payable in cash when the agreement is signed followed by four annual payments of $3,750 each. Assuming the franchisee could borrow money at 10%, the present value of the four annual payments is $11,887 ($3,750 × 3.1699).[17] The agreement provides that the franchiser will assist in locating the site for a building, conduct a market survey to estimate potential income, supervise the construction of a building, and provide initial training to employees.

If the down payment is refundable and no services have been rendered at the time the arrangement is made, the deposit method would be used as long as collection on the note is reasonably certain. The following entry would be made to record the transaction:

---

14   *Committee on Franchise Accounting and Auditing, AICPA, Industry Accounting Guide*, "Accounting for Franchise Fee Revenue," New York: American Institute of Certified Public Accountants, 1973.

15   *Statement of Financial Accounting Standards No. 45*, "Accounting for Franchise Fee Revenue," Stamford, CT: Financial Accounting Standards Board, March 1981.

16   Ibid., par. 6.

17   See Appendix B for a review of present value calculations.

net work exercise

The U.S. Small Business Association (SBA) offers an informational Web site on franchising (www.sba.gov/workshops/franchises).
Net Work:
1. Franchising makes up what percentage of retail sales?
2. What things should you consider if you are thinking about purchasing a franchise?

Cash	10,000	
Notes Receivable	11,887	
Deposit on Franchise (or Unearned Franchise Fee)		21,887

When the initial services are determined to be substantially performed, the revenue recognition method to be used and the resulting journal entries depend on the probability of future cash collection. If the collection of the note is reasonably assured, the full accrual method would be used. Assume that substantial performance of the initial services by the franchiser costs $14,000. The entries to record this event using the full accrual method would be as follows:

Cost of Franchise Fee Revenue	14,000	
Cash		14,000
Deposit on Franchise (or Unearned Franchise Fee)	21,887	
Franchise Fee Revenue		21,887

If the collection of the note is doubtful, the installment sales method could be used. In addition to the entries used under the full accrual method, the installment sales method requires the following entries:

Franchise Fee Revenue	21,887	
Cost of Franchise Fee Revenue		14,000
Deferred Gross Profit on Franchise		7,887
Deferred Gross Profit on Franchise	3,604*	
Realized Gross Profit on Franchise		3,604

*$7,887/$21,887 = 36.04% gross profit percentage; .3604 × $10,000 = $3,604

An example of financial statement disclosure provided by a franchise business is presented in Exhibit 7–6 for McDONALD'S CORPORATION.

EXHIBIT 7–6 | McDonald's Corporation Disclosure of Franchise Information

---

Franchise arrangements generally include a lease and a license and provide for payment of initial fees, as well as continuing rent, service fees and royalties to the Company, based upon a percentage of sales with minimum rent payments. Franchisees are granted the right to operate a McDonald's restaurant using the McDonald's system as well as the use of a restaurant facility, generally for a period of 20 years. Franchisees pay related occupancy costs including property taxes, insurance and maintenance. Beginning in 1998, franchisees in the U.S. generally have the option to own new restaurant facilities while leasing the land from McDonald's. In addition, franchisees outside the U.S. pay a refundable, noninterest-bearing security deposit.

CONSIGNMENT SALES

> **Caution!** The deposit method and consignment accounting are not revenue recognition methods. They are methods of accounting for assets prior to revenue recognition. When the point of revenue recognition is reached, the decision of which revenue recognition method to use must still be made.

Another method of accounting has developed for use when property is exchanged without a transfer of title and without a sales contract being completed. This type of arrangement is referred to as a **consignment.** Under a consignment, the potential seller, the **consignor,** delivers merchandise to another party, the **consignee,** who then acts as an agent for the consignor to sell the goods. Title to the merchandise continues to be held by the consignor until a sale is made, at which time title passes to the ultimate purchaser. The consignee usually is entitled to reimbursement for expenses incurred in relation to this arrangement and also is entitled to a commission if a sale is successfully made.

Because title to the merchandise is held by the consignor but physical possession is held by the consignee, special accounting records must be maintained by the consignor for control purposes. No revenue is recognized until a sale is made by the consignee. Upon shipment of the merchandise by the consignor, a special inventory account is established on the consignor's books to identify the consigned merchandise. Any consignment expenses paid by the consignor are added to the inventory balance as added costs. The consignee does not make an entry for receipt of the inventory in the general ledger; however, memorandum control records usually are kept. Any reimbursable expense paid by the consignee is charged to a receivable account by the consignee and added to the inventory balance by the consignor. When a sale is made, the consignor recognizes the sale as revenue according to one of the revenue recognition methods, and the consignee recognizes the commission as revenue on the transaction.

To illustrate consignment accounting entries, assume that Harrison Products Inc. sends $500,000 worth of goods on consignment to Benson Industries. Shipping costs of $5,000 are paid by Harrison, and reimbursable finishing costs of $20,000 are paid by Benson Industries. By the end of the year, one-half of the goods on consignment are sold for $400,000 cash. A 10% commission is earned by Benson Industries according to the terms of the consignment. The journal entries shown below would be made on the consignor's and consignee's books.

If the eventual sale had been on the installment basis, the installment sales entries illustrated earlier in this chapter could have been used by the consignor in place of the accrual entries illustrated.

Transaction	Entries on Consignor's Books (Harrison Products Inc.)		Entries on Consignee's Books (Benson Industries)	
(1) Shipment of goods on consignment	Inventory on Consignment .... 500,000 Finished Goods Inventory	500,000	No entry (memorandum control record)	
(2) Payment of expenses by consignor	Inventory on Consignment .... 5,000 Cash	5,000	No entry	

(3) Payment of expenses by consignee	Inventory on Consignment 20,000
	    Consignee Payable ....
		20,000	Consignor Receivable 20,000
			    Cash ....
				20,000

(4) Sale of merchandise	No entry		Cash .... 400,000 Consignor Payable	400,000

(5) Notification of sale to consignor and payment of cash due	Commission Expense 40,000
	 Cash 340,000
	 Consignee Payable 20,000
	    Consignment Sales Revenue ...
	
	 Cost of Goods Sold 262,500*
	    Inventory on Consignment ......
		
		400,000
		
		262,500
			Consignor Payable 400,000
			    Cash ....
			    Commission Revenue ......
			    Consignor Receivable ....
				340,000
				 40,000
				 20,000

*1/2($500,000 + $25,000) = $262,500

CONCLUDING COMMENTS

This chapter has explored some special problems that arise in recognizing revenue. Some industries such as franchising and construction have been used as illustrative of the types of problems that exist in applying the revenue recognition criteria included in currently accepted accounting standards. While recognizing revenue at the point of sale is still the most traditional method, accounting standards provide for flexibility when a different method of revenue recognition provides more meaningful information to users. Percentage-of-completion, proportional performance, installment sales, cost recovery, and deferral through the deposit methods are all part of GAAP under specified conditions.

REVIEW OF LEARNING OBJECTIVES

1 **Identify the primary criteria for revenue recognition.** Revenue is typically recognized and recorded when two criteria have been met. The first criterion is realizability, which means that the seller has received payment or a valid promise of payment from the purchaser. The second criterion is met when the earnings process is substantially complete. Substantial completion means that the seller has provided the product or service (or a large portion of the product or service) to the purchaser.

2 **Explain when revenue is appropriately recognized prior to delivery of goods or services through percentage-of-completion accounting.** In some instances, revenue may be recognized prior to the actual delivery of goods or services. The most common example of this is a long-term contract. In this case, revenue may be recognized prior to delivery if four criteria are met: (1) estimates can be made of the amount of work remaining, (2) a contract exists outlining each party's responsibilities, (3) the buyer can be expected to fulfill the contract, and (4) the seller can be expected to fulfill the contract. If these conditions are met, revenue may be recognized prior to the point of sale and the revenue recognition method is termed percentage of completion. With this method, revenue is recognized based on an estimate of the degree to which the contract is complete. Using the cost-to-cost method for estimating the degree of completion results in matching actual contract costs with estimated revenues.

3 **Record journal entries for long-term construction-type contracts using percentage-of-completion and completed-contract methods.** With long-term contracts, journal entries are required to record costs incurred, billings made to customers, and collections from customers. These entries would be the same for both the percentage-of-completion method and the completed-contract method. An additional journal entry is made each period under the percentage-of-completion method to record the recognition of revenue and related expenses for the period. The amount of revenue recognized is a function of the amount of costs incurred to date. With the completed-contract method, revenue is recognized only when the contract has been completed.

4 **Record journal entries for long-term service contracts using the proportional performance method.** With long-term service contracts, revenue can be recognized prior to completion based on the degree to which the contract is completed. Estimates of completion are made based on the ratio of actual costs incurred relative to total costs expected to be incurred. The amount of revenue to be recognized is computed by multiplying this ratio by the contract price.

5 **Explain when revenue is recognized after delivery of goods or services through installment sales, cost recovery, and cash methods.** In some cases, it is not appropriate to recognize revenue at the point of sale when a valid promise of payment has not been received. In these instances, the recognition of revenue is deferred until cash is actually received. Several methods exist for recognizing revenue. The installment sales method recognizes profit based on a gross profit percentage. Of every dollar collected, a portion is recorded as profit based on the gross profit percentage. With the cost recovery method, cash collections are first considered to be a recovery of the costs associated with the sale. Once costs are recovered, each subsequent dollar received is recorded as profit. When the cash method is employed, profit is determined by comparing the cash received from customers with the cash expended during the period relating to inventory or services.

6 **Describe accounting for the transfer of assets prior to the recognition of revenue with the deposit method and consignment sales.** On occasion, customers may prepay for a purchase. When this occurs, a liability is recorded on the books of the seller until services are provided to the customer. Once the service is provided, the liability is reduced and revenue is recorded.

Consignment sales occur when inventory is shipped to a vendor who holds the inventory for subsequent resale. Title to the inventory does not pass to the vendor (the consignee) but instead remains with the original holder of the inventory (the consignor). Once the inventory is sold by the vendor, the consignor is notified and makes the appropriate entries to record the sale.

KEY TERMS

Cash method 396
Change orders 386
Completed-contract method 375
Cost recovery method 395
Cost-to-cost method 377
Efforts-expended methods 377
Input measures 377
Installment sales method 392
Output measures 378
Percentage-of-completion accounting 375

Proportional performance method 375
Recognition 372

Consignee 399
Consignment 399

Consignor 399
Deposit method 397
Substantial performance 398

QUESTIONS

1. What are the two general revenue recognition criteria?
2. In what way does U.S. GAAP differ from IAS 18 in the area of revenue recognition?
3. Under what conditions is percentage-of-completion accounting recommended for construction contractors?
4. Distinguish between the cost-to-cost method and efforts-expended methods of measuring the percentage of completion.
5. Output measures of percentage of completion are sometimes preferred to input measures. What are some examples of commonly used output measures?
6. What is the relationship between the construction in progress account and the progress billings on construction contracts account? How should these accounts be reported on the balance sheet?
7. When a measure of percentage of completion other than cost-to-cost is used, the amount of cost charged against revenue using the percentage of completion usually will be different from the costs incurred. How do some AICPA committee members recommend handling this situation so that the costs charged against revenue are equal to the costs incurred?
8. The construction in progress account is used to accumulate all costs of construction. What additional item is included in this account when percentage-of-completion accounting is followed?
9. The gross profit percentage reported on long-term construction contracts often varies from year to year. What is the major reason for this variation?

10. How are anticipated contract losses treated under the completed-contract and percentage-of-completion methods?
11. What input and output measures usually are applicable to the proportional performance method for long-term service contracts?
12. Under the provisions of IAS 11, what revenue recognition approach should be used whenever the outcome of a construction contract can *not* be reliably estimated? Briefly describe this approach.
13. The proportional performance method spreads the profit over the periods in which services are being performed. What arguments could be made against this method of revenue recognition for newly formed service-oriented companies?
14. Distinguish among the three different approaches to revenue recognition that await the receipt of cash. How does the treatment of costs incurred vary depending on the approach used?
15. Under what general conditions is the installment sales method of accounting preferred to the full accrual method?
16. The normal accounting entries for installment sales require keeping a separate record by year of receivables, collections on receivables, and the deferred gross profit percentages. Why are these separate records necessary?
17. Installment sales contracts generally include interest. Contrast the method of recognizing interest revenue from the method used to recognize the gross profit on the sale.
18. Under what conditions would the cash method of recognizing revenue be acceptable for reporting purposes?

20. Consignment accounting is primarily a method of accounting for transfers of inventory prior to the point of revenue recognition. Describe the essential elements of this method from the standpoint of (a) the consignor and (b) the consignee.

19. What special recognition problems arise in accounting for franchise fees?

DISCUSSION CASES

CASE 7–1

RECOGNIZING REVENUE ON A PERCENTAGE-OF-COMPLETION BASIS

As the new controller for Enclave Construction Company, you have been advised that your predecessor classified all revenues and expenses by project, each project being considered a separate venture. All revenues from uncompleted projects were treated as unearned revenue, and all expenses applicable to each uncompleted project were treated as "work in process" inventory. Thus, the income statement for the current year includes only the revenues and expenses related to projects completed during the year.

What do you think about the use of the completed-contract method by the previous controller? What alternative approach might you suggest to company management?

CASE 7–2

LET'S SPREAD OUR LOSSES, TOO!

The Abbott Construction Company has several contracts to build sections of freeways, bridges, and dams. Because most of these contracts require more than 1 year to complete, the accountant, Dave Allred, has recommended use of the percentage-of-completion method to recognize revenue and income on these contracts. The president, Kathy Bahr, isn't quite sure how the accounting method works, and she indicates concern about the impact of this decision on income taxes. Bahr also inquires as to what happens when a contract results in a loss. When told by Allred that any estimated loss must be recognized when it is first identified, Bahr becomes upset. "If it is a percentage-of-completion method and we are recognizing profits in part as we go along, why shouldn't we be able to do the same for losses?"

How would you, as the accountant, answer Bahr's concerns?

CASE 7–3

WHAT IS THE DIFFERENCE BETWEEN COMPLETED-CONTRACT AND PERCENTAGE-OF-COMPLETION ACCOUNTING?

In accounting for long-term contracts (those taking longer than 1 year to complete), the two methods commonly followed are the percentage-of-completion method and the completed-contract method.

1. Discuss how earnings on long-term contracts are recognized and computed under these two methods.
2. Under what circumstances is it preferable to use one method over the other?
3. Why is earnings recognition as measured by interim billings not generally accepted for long-term contracts?

CASE 7–4

WHEN IS THE MEMBERSHIP FEE EARNED?

The Superb Health Studio has been operating for 5 years but is presently for sale. It has opened 50 salons in various cities in the United States. The normal pattern for a new opening is to advertise heavily and sell different types of memberships: 1-year, 3-year, and 5-year. For the initial membership fee, members may use the pool, exercise rooms, sauna, and other recreational facilities without charge. If special courses or programs are taken, additional fees are charged; however, members are granted certain privileges, and the fees are less than those charged to outsiders. In addition, $10-a-month dues are charged to all members. Nonmembers may use the facilities; however, they must pay a substantial daily charge for services they receive.

Your client, Dickson Inc., is considering purchasing the chain of health studios and asks you to give your opinion on its operations. You are provided with financial statements that show a growing revenue and income pattern over the 5-year period. The balance sheet shows that the physical facilities are apparently owned rather than leased. But you are aware that health studios, like all service institutions, have some challenging revenue recognition problems.

What questions would you want answered in preparing your report for Dickson?

CASE 7–5

WHEN IS IT REVENUE?

Hertzel Advertising Agency handles advertising for clients under contracts that require the agency to develop advertising copy and layouts and place ads in various media, charging clients a commission of 15% of the media cost as its fee. The agency makes advance billings to its clients of estimated media cost plus its 15% commission. Adjustments to these advances usually are small. Frequently, both the billings and receipt of cash from these billings occur before the period in which the advertising actually appears in the media.

A conference meeting is held between officers of the agency and the new firm of CPAs recently engaged to perform annual audits. In this meeting, consideration is given to four possible points for measuring revenue: (1) at the time the advanced billing is made, (2) when payment is received from the client, (3) in the month when the advertising appears in the media, and (4) when the bill for advertising is received from the media, generally in the month following its appearance. The agency has been following the first method for the past several years on the basis that a definite contract exists and the revenue is earned when billed. When the billing is made, an entry is prepared to record the estimated receivable and liability to the media. Estimated expenses related to the contract are also recorded. Adjusting entries are made later for any differences between the estimated and actual amounts.

As a member of the CPA firm attending this meeting, how would you react to the agency's method of recognizing revenue? Discuss the strengths and weaknesses of each of the four methods of revenue recognition and indicate which one you would recommend the agency follow.

CASE 7–6

WHICH METHOD IS APPROPRIATE?

Green Brothers Furniture sells discount furniture and offers easy credit terms. Its margins are not large, but it deals in heavy volume. Its customers are often low-income individuals who cannot obtain credit elsewhere. Green Brothers retains the title to the furniture until full payment is received, and it is not uncommon to have 20% of sales be uncollectible.

Green Brothers is considering expansion and has hired an independent auditor to review its financial statements prior to obtaining outside funding. The auditor questions the use of accrual accounting as a method for recognizing revenue and suggests that Green Brothers use the installment sales method. The auditor justifies this by stating that because of the high rate of uncollectibles, the earnings process is not substantially complete at the point of sale. Financial statements adjusted to the installment sales method result in a 17% decrease in net income for the fiscal year just ended.

The chief financial officer for Green Brothers counters that if uncollectibles can be estimated, even if that estimate is high, the use of the accrual method is appropriate. The accountant also notes that restated financial statements showing the lower net income figure will make obtaining external funding much more difficult.

Which method of revenue recognition would you argue that Green Brothers should use? Why? Remember that your decision could affect this company's ability to obtain favorable external financing.

CASE 7–7

A PROBLEM WITH ACCRUING REVENUES

MIDWESTERN COMPANIES, a firm specializing in the production and sale of ethanol plants, used accrual accounting to report revenues from the sale of the plants. However, details of the sale of an ethanol plant have left many questioning Midwestern's accounting practices.

An investor in a partnership would pay $15,000 and sign a note for $45,000. After the initial investment, investors were not required to pay any more money as the cash from the operations of the plant would be applied against the note. Midwestern promised that the plant would operate properly and that those purchasing the plant would be provided with customers.

While the firm reported $36.3 million in revenues from the sale of ethanol plants with costs of $12.2 million, they received only $10.8 million in cash. Thus, on a cash basis, the firm was actually operating at a loss for the period.

1. In selling an ethanol plant, identify the various points at which one could argue that the earnings process is substantially complete. At what point do you think Midwestern was recognizing revenue?
2. Did the use of accrual accounting accurately portray the financial performance of Midwestern?
3. In your opinion, what revenue recognition method should have been used by Midwestern?

SOURCE: "Up & Down Wall Street," *Barron's*, March 5, 1984.

CASE 7–8

THE SAVINGS & LOAN CRISIS

The cost to taxpayers to bail out failed savings and loan (S&L) companies in the late 1980s has been estimated as high as $500 billion. Reasons for the crisis included mismanagement of resources, management fraud, and unfavorable economic conditions. Another factor contributing to the S&L problems was their revenue recognition techniques.

When a loan was made, the associated loan origination fee, often as high as 6% of the loan principal, was recognized immediately as revenue. If a financial institution's objective was to increase income for the short term, one strategy would be to loan as much money as possible and collect large loan fees.

The president of one S&L, TEXAS' WESTERN SAVINGS, elected to follow this strategy. He enticed investors by promising high yields on certificates of deposit that were federally insured. His telephone operations often netted over $20 million in investments per day. Once the money was received from investors, the president would then loan the money to borrowers and collect loan fees as revenue. These fees and other income were the source of a $3 million dividend to the president over a 2-year period.

The problem for taxpayers was that the president was making poor-quality loans. Since investors' deposits were federally insured, the collectibility of loans was not a major issue for Western. Million-dollar loans were made with no required down payment. Loans were made for more than the full purchase price of properties. As an example, $64 million was loaned to purchase land that 2 years earlier had sold for $17.2 million. On this particular deal, Western, holding a sixth lien on the property, received $2 million in loan fees.

1. How can a savings and loan company justify recognizing immediately the loan origination fee as revenue rather than recognizing it over the life of the loan?
2. From an accounting point of view, what revenue recognition method should be used when dealing with high-risk loans?
3. Why would investors deposit their money in financial institutions that had lending practices like those illustrated in this case?
4. Do external auditors have a responsibility to evaluate the loan practices of the financial institutions that they audit?

SOURCE: "Easy Money," *The Wall Street Journal*, April 27, 1989.

CASE 7–9

COLLEGE BOUND WAS BANKRUPTCY BOUND

High school students know how important it is to perform well on the educational tests required by many colleges and universities as part of the admissions process. In fact, an entire industry has developed to prepare students to take these tests. One company in this industry was COLLEGE BOUND INC. It was a fast-growing company that claimed to be the largest educational counseling firm in the United States with 150 test centers nationally.

College Bound was founded by George and Janet Ronkin because they could not find a facility that, in their opinion, could adequately prepare their own son to take the college entrance exams.

The company went public in 1988 as a penny stock, and the price of the stock soared to a high of $24 per share in August 1991. In the early months of 1992, however, the SEC began to question many of College Bound's accounting practices. As a result of its investigations, the SEC determined that much of the rapid growth in revenues reported by College Bound came as a result of "churning bank accounts." This practice involved transferring funds from the home office's bank account to various test centers and then back to the home office. College Bound was recognizing as revenue the funds being transferred back from the test centers. The money used for the "churning" was obtained via a convertible note offering in Europe.

The result of these practices was to overstate pretax profits for the fiscal year ended August 1991 by 2.5 times, or $5.2 million. The SEC-alleged that the Ronkins were transferring large amounts of company money to their personal accounts. In addition to their compensation of $153,846 each, the Ronkins were said to have transferred over $500,000 to Swiss bank accounts during 1991. The court-appointed receiver, Joseph Del Raso, who was asked by the courts to monitor College Bound during bankruptcy proceedings, determined that most of the company's 150 test centers were not profitable by industry standards and closed over 100 centers in May 1992.

1. How would College Bound recognize revenue by simply transferring money from a test center to the home office? What would the journal entry be when the money was transferred from the test centers to the home office?

2. How would the accountant at the home office determine if money being received from a test center was to be recorded as revenue or as repayment of a loan?

SOURCES: Michael J. McCarthy, "College Bound Inc., Target of SEC Suit, Files for Bankruptcy Law Protection," *The Wall Street Journal,* April 30, 1992, p. A4; and Daniel Pearl, "U.S. Judge Freezes Assets of Founders of College Bound," *The Wall Street Journal,* April 24, 1992, p. C19.

CASE 7–10 **KEEP SHIPPING, WE NEED THE REVENUE.**

Datarite, a maker of computer hardware systems, sells its products to dealers who in turn sell to the final customer. Datarite offers very liberal credit terms and allows its dealers to take up to 90 days to pay. These terms allow dealers to hold larger inventories. As the end of the fiscal year nears, Datarite needs to increase its current ratio and decrease its debt-to-equity ratio in order to avoid violating its debt covenants. The president of the company has asked that all dealers be shipped extra inventory. This will increase both sales and accounts receivable, thereby allowing Datarite to remain in compliance with its debt covenants. The chief financial officer remarks that shipping inventory that has not been ordered should be accounted for as consigned inventory rather than revenue.

Should the inventory shipments be accounted for as sales or as consigned inventory? Debt covenants exist to protect the interests of creditors. In this instance, are debt covenants effective in monitoring the company's activities?

CASE 7–11 **WHEN IS THE INITIAL FRANCHISE FEE REALLY EARNED?**

Magleby Inn sells franchises to independent operators throughout the western part of the United States. The contract with the franchisee includes the following provisions.

a. The franchisee is charged an initial fee of $25,000. Of this amount, $5,000 is payable when the agreement is signed and a $4,000 non-interest-bearing note is payable at the end of each of the 5 subsequent years.

b. All the initial franchise fee collected by Magleby Inn is to be refunded and the remaining obligation canceled if, for any reason, the franchisee fails to open the franchise.

c. In return for the initial franchise fee, Magleby agrees to assist the franchisee in selecting the location for the business; negotiate the lease for the land; obtain financing and assist with the building design; supervise construction; establish accounting and tax records;

and provide expert advice over a 5-year period relating to such matters as employee and management training, quality control, and promotion.

d. In addition to the initial franchise fee, the franchisee is required to pay to Magleby Inn a monthly fee of 2% of sales for recipe innovations and the privilege of purchasing ingredients from Magleby Inn at or below prevailing market prices.

Management of Magleby Inn estimates that the value of the services rendered to the franchisee at the time the contract is signed amounts to at least $5,000. All franchisees to date have opened their locations at the scheduled time and none has defaulted on any of the notes receivable.

The credit ratings of all franchisees would entitle them to borrow at the current interest rate of 10%.

Given the nature of Magleby's agreement with its franchisees, when should revenue be recognized? Discuss the question of revenue recognition for both the initial franchise fee and the additional monthly fee of 2% of sales.

CASE 7–12

I THINK THEY'RE SALES!

The Rain-Soft Water Company distributes its water softeners to dealers upon their request. The contract agreement with the dealers is that they may have 90 days to sell and pay for the softeners. Until the 90-day period is over, any softeners may be returned at the dealer's expense and with no further obligation on the dealer's part. If the water softeners are damaged while in the hands of a dealer, Rain-Soft agrees to accept the return of the damaged softeners with no obligation to the dealer. Past experience indicates that 75% of all softeners distributed on this basis are sold by the dealer. In June, 100 units are delivered to dealers at an average billed price of $800 each. The average cost of the softeners to Rain-Soft is $600. Based on the expected sales, Rain-Soft reports profit of $15,000.

You are asked to evaluate the income statement for its compliance with GAAP. What recommendations would you make?

EXERCISES

EXERCISE 7–13

COMPLETED-CONTRACT METHOD

On December 1, 2002, bids were submitted for a construction project to build a new municipal building and fire station. The lowest bid was $3,980,000, submitted by the Jessop Construction Company. Jessop was awarded the contract. Jessop uses the completed-contract method to report gross profit. The following data are given to summarize the activities on this contract for 2002 and 2003. Give the entries to record these transactions using the completed-contract method.

Year	Cost Incurred	Estimated Cost to Complete	Billings on Contract	Collections of Billings
2002	$1,720,000	$2,060,000	$1,350,000	$ 950,000
2003	2,020,000	0	2,630,000	3,030,000

EXERCISE 7–14

PERCENTAGE-OF-COMPLETION ANALYSIS

Espiritu Construction Co. has used the cost-to-cost percentage-of-completion method of recognizing revenue. Tony Espiritu assumed leadership of the business after the recent death of his father, Howard. In reviewing the records, Espiritu finds the following information regarding a recently completed building project for which the total contract was $2,000,000.

	2001	2002	2003
Gross profit (loss)	$ 75,000	$140,000	$ (20,000)
Cost incurred	360,000	?	820,000

Espiritu wants to know how effectively the company operated during the last 3 years on this project and, because the information is not complete, has asked for answers to the following questions.

1. How much cost was incurred in 2002?
2. What percentage of the project was completed by the end of 2002?
3. What was the total estimated gross profit on the project by the end of 2002?
4. What was the estimated cost to complete the project at the end of 2002?

EXERCISE 7–15

PERCENTAGE-OF-COMPLETION ACCOUNTING

The Quality Construction Company was the low bidder on an office building construction contract. The contract bid was $7,000,000, with an estimated cost to complete the project of $6,000,000. The contract period was 34 months starting January 1, 2001. The company uses the cost-to-cost method of estimating earnings. Because of changes requested by the customer, the contract price was adjusted downward to $6,700,000 on January 1, 2002.

A record of construction activities for the years 2001–2004 is as follows:

Year	Actual Cost—Current Year	Progress Billings	Cash Receipts
2001	$2,500,000	$2,100,000	$1,800,000
2002	3,300,000	3,100,000	3,000,000
2003	410,000	1,300,000	1,000,000
2004			700,000

The estimated cost to complete the contract as of the end of each accounting period is:

2001	$3,500,000
2002	400,000
2003	0

Calculate the gross profit for the years 2001–2003 under the percentage-of-completion method of revenue recognition.

EXERCISE 7–16

PERCENTAGE-OF-COMPLETION ANALYSIS

Smokey International Inc. recently acquired the Kurtz Builders Company. Kurtz has incomplete accounting records. On one particular project, only the information below is available.

	2001	2002	2003
Costs incurred during year	$200,000	$250,000	380,000
Estimated cost to complete	450,000	190,000	0
Recognized revenue	220,000	20,000	370,000 ?
Gross profit on contract	20,000 ?	10,000	$(10,000)
Contract price	850,000		

Because the information is incomplete, you are asked the following questions assuming the percentage-of-completion method is used, an output measure is used to estimate the percentage completed, and revenue is recorded using the actual cost approach.

1. How much gross profit should be reported in 2001? 20,000
2. How much revenue should be reported in 2002? 260,000
3. How much revenue should be reported in 2003? 370,000
4. How much cost was incurred in 2003? 380,00 0
5. What are the total costs on the contract? 830,000
6. What would be the gross profit for 2002 if the cost-to-cost percentage-of-completion method were used rather than the output measure? (Hint: Ignore the revenue amount shown for 2001 and gross profit amount reported for 2002.)

EXERCISE 7–17

REPORTING CONSTRUCTION CONTRACTS

Tara Builders Inc. is building a new home for Margaret Mitchell at a contracted price of $120,000. The estimated cost at the time the contract is signed (January 2, 2002) is $97,000. At December 31, 2002, the total cost incurred is $59,000 with estimated costs to complete of $41,000. Tara has billed $70,000 on the job and has received a $45,000 payment. This is the only contract in process at year-end. Prepare the sections of the balance sheet and the income statement of Tara Builders Inc. affected by these events assuming use of (a) the percentage-of-completion method and (b) the completed-contract method.

EXERCISE 7–18

PERCENTAGE OF COMPLETION USING ARCHITECT'S ESTIMATES

Central Iowa Builders Inc. entered into a contract to construct an office building and plaza at a contract price of $10,000,000. Income is to be reported using the percentage-of-completion method as determined by estimates made by the architect. The data below summarize the activities on the construction for the years 2001–2003. For the years 2001–2003, what entries are required to record this information, assuming the architect's estimate of the percentage completed is used to determine revenue (proportional cost approach)?

Year	Actual Cost Incurred	Estimated Cost to Complete	Percentage Completed— Architect's Estimate	Project Billings	Collections on Billings
2001	$3,200,000	$6,000,000	25%	$3,300,000	$3,100,000
2002	4,300,000	1,600,000	75%	4,500,000	2,700,000
2003	1,550,000	0	100%	2,200,000	4,200,000

EXERCISE 7–19

COMPLETED-CONTRACT METHOD

On January 1, 2001, the Ishikawa Construction Company entered into a 3-year contract to build a dam. The original contract price was $18,000,000 and the estimated cost was $16,100,000. The following cost data relate to the construction period.

Year	Cost Incurred	Estimated Cost to Complete	Billings	Cash Collected
2001	$6,000,000	$10,000,000	$6,800,000	$6,000,000
2002	5,300,000	7,400,000	5,200,000	5,400,000
2003	7,650,000	0	6,000,000	6,600,000

Prepare the required journal entries for the 3 years of the contract, assuming Ishikawa uses the completed-contract method.

EXERCISE 7–20

PERCENTAGE-OF-COMPLETION METHOD WITH CHANGE ORDERS

The Build-It Construction Company enters into a contract on January 1, 2002, to construct a 20-story office building for $42,000,000. During the construction period, many change orders are made to the original contract. The following schedule summarizes the changes made in 2002.

	Cost Incurred—2002	Estimated Cost to Complete	Contract Price
Basic contract	$8,000,000	$28,000,000	$42,000,000
Change Order #1	50,000	50,000	125,000
Change Order #2	0	50,000	0
Change Order #3	300,000	300,000	Still to be negotiated; at least cost.
Change Order #4	125,000	0	100,000

Compute the revenues, costs, and gross profit to be recognized in 2002, assuming use of the cost-to-cost method to determine the percentage completed. (Round percentage to two decimal places.)

EXERCISE 7–21

SERVICE INDUSTRY ACCOUNTING

The Fitness Health Spa charges an annual membership fee of $600 for its services. For this fee, each member receives a fitness evaluation (value $100), a monthly magazine (value $32), and 2-hour's use of the equipment each week. The initial direct costs to obtain the membership are estimated to be $120. The direct cost of the fitness evaluation is $50, and the monthly direct costs to provide the other services are estimated to be $15 per person. In addition, the monthly indirect costs are estimated to average $8 per person. Give the journal entries to record the transactions in 2002 relative to a membership sold on April 1, 2002. The fitness evaluation is given in the first month of membership, and the initial direct cost is to be spread over all direct costs, including the fitness evaluation, using the proportional performance method. (Round percentage of performance to two decimal places and journal entries to the nearest dollar.)

EXERCISE 7–22

INSTALLMENT SALES ACCOUNTING

Denna Corporation had sales in 2001 of $210,000, in 2002 of $270,000, and in 2003 of $350,000. The gross profit percentage of each year, in order, was 25%, 29%, and 27%. Past history has shown that 10% of total sales are collected in the first year, 40% in the second year, and 30% in the third year. Assuming these collections are made as projected, give the journal entries for 2001, 2002, and 2003, assuming use of the installment sales method. Ignore provisions for doubtful accounts and interest.

EXERCISE 7–23

INSTALLMENT SALES ANALYSIS

Complete the following table.

	2001	2002	2003
Installment sales	$50,000	$80,000	$ (7)
Cost of installment sales	(1)	(5)	91,800
Gross profit	(2)	(6)	28,200
Gross profit percentage	(3)	25%	(8)
Cash collections:			
2001 sales	(4)	25,000	10,000
2002 sales		20,000	50,000
2003 sales			45,000
Realized gross profit on installment sales	1,100	$10,500	(9)

EXERCISE 7–24

COST RECOVERY METHOD

Bailey Bats Inc. had the following sales and gross profit percentages for the years 2001–2004.

	Sales	Gross Profit Percentage
2001	$47,000	45
2002	45,000	42
2003	58,000	47
2004	61,000	49

Historically, 55% of sales are collected in the year of the sale, 30% in the following year, 10% in the third year. Assuming collections are as projected, give the journal entries for the years 2001–2004, assuming the use of the cost recovery method. (Ignore provision for doubtful accounts.) Prepare a table comparing the gross profit recognized for 2001–2004 using the full accrual method and the cost recovery method.

EXERCISE 7–25

COST RECOVERY ANALYSIS

Johnson Enterprises uses the cost recovery method for all installment sales. Complete the following table.

	2001	2002	2003
Installment sales	$80,000	$95,000	$ (1)
Cost of installment sales	(2)	56,050	68,250
Gross profit percentage	38%	(3)	35%
Cash collections:			
2001 sales	25,600	46,400	15,600
2002 sales		22,800	(4)
2003 sales			32,550
Realized gross profit on installment sales	(5)	(6)	16,050

EXERCISE 7–26

FRANCHISE ACCOUNTING

On September 1, 2002, Jensen Company entered into franchise agreements with 3 franchisees. The agreements required an initial fee payment of $7,000 plus 4 $3,000 payments due every 4 months, the first payment due December 31, 2002. The interest rate is 12%. The initial deposit is refundable until substantial performance has been completed. The following table describes each agreement.

Franchisee	Probability of Full Collection	Services Performed by Franchiser at Dec. 31, 2002	Total Cost Incurred to Dec. 31, 2002
A	Likely	Substantial	$ 7,000
B	Doubtful	25%	2,000
C	Doubtful	Substantial	10,000

For each franchisee, identify the revenue recognition method that you would recommend for Jensen, considering the circumstances. What amount of revenue and income would be reported in 2002 for the method selected? Assume that $10,000 was received from each franchisee during the year.

EXERCISE 7–27

FRANCHISE ACCOUNTING

Starbrite Pizzas franchises its name to different people across the country. The franchise agreement requires the franchisee to make an initial payment of $12,000 and sign a $32,000 non-interest-bearing note on the agreement date. The note is to be paid in 4 annual payments of $8,000 each beginning 1 year from the agreement date. The initial payment is refundable until the date of opening. Interest rates are assumed to be 10%. The franchiser agrees to make market studies, find a location, train the employees, and perform a few other relatively minor services. The following transactions describe the relationship with Libby Loebig, a franchisee:

2002
July   1   Entered into a franchise agreement.
Sept.   1   Completed a market study at a cost of $8,000.
Nov.   15   Found suitable location. Service cost $1,900.

2003
Jan.   10   Completed training program for employees, cost $7,500.
       15   Franchise outlet opened.
July   1   Received first annual payment.

Give Starbrite Pizzas' journal entries in 2002–2003 to record these transactions, including any adjusting entries at December 31, 2002.

EXERCISE 7–28

CONSIGNMENT ACCOUNTING

In 2002, Rawlings Wholesalers transferred goods to a retailer on consignment. The transaction was recorded as a sale by Rawlings. The goods cost $45,000 and normally are sold at a 30% markup. In 2003, $12,000 (cost) of the merchandise was sold by the retailer at the normal markup, and the balance of the merchandise was returned to Rawlings. The retailer withheld a 15% commission from payment. Prepare the journal entry in 2003 to correct the books for 2002, and prepare the correct entries relative to the consignment sale in 2003.

PROBLEMS

PROBLEM 7–29

CONSTRUCTION ACCOUNTING

Zamponi's Construction Company reports its income for tax purposes on a completed-contract basis and income for financial statement purposes on a percentage-of-completion basis. A record of construction activities for 2002 and 2003 follows:

Project	Contract Price	Cost Incurred— 2002	Estimated Cost to Complete	Cost Incurred— 2003	Estimated Cost to Complete
A	$1,450,000	$840,000	$560,000	$480,000	$ 0
B	1,700,000	720,000	880,000	340,000	650,000
C	850,000	160,000	480,000	431,500	58,500
D	1,000,000			280,000	520,000

General and administrative expenses for 2002 and 2003 were $60,000 for each year and are to be recorded as a period cost.

Instructions:

1. Calculate the income for 2002 and 2003 that should be reported for financial statement purposes.
2. Calculate the income for 2003 to be reported on a completed-contract basis.

PROBLEM 7–30

CONSTRUCTION ACCOUNTING

The Rushing Construction Company obtained a construction contract to build a highway and bridge over the Snake River. It was estimated at the beginning of the contract that it would take 3 years to complete the project at an expected cost of $50,000,000. The contract price was $60,000,000. The project actually took 4 years, being accepted as completed late in 2003. The following information describes the status of the job at the close of production each year.

	2000	2001	2002	2003	2004
Actual cost incurred	$12,000,000	$18,160,000	$14,840,000	$10,000,000	$ 0
Estimated cost to complete	38,000,000	27,840,000	10,555,555	0	0
Collections on contract	12,000,000	13,500,000	15,000,000	15,000,000	4,500,000
Billings on contract	13,000,000	15,500,000	17,000,000	14,500,000	0

Instructions:

1. What is the revenue, cost, and gross profit recognized for each of the years 2000–2004 under (a) the percentage-of-completion method and (b) the completed-contract method?
2. Give the journal entries for each year assuming that the percentage-of-completion method is used.

PROBLEM 7–31

CONSTRUCTION ACCOUNTING

The Urban Construction Company commenced doing business in January 2002. Construction activities for the year 2002 are summarized in the following table.

Project	Total Contract Price	Contract Expenditures to Dec. 31, 2002	Estimated Additional Costs to Complete Contracts	Cash Collections to Dec. 31, 2002	Billings to Dec. 31, 2002
A	$ 310,000	$187,500	$ 12,500	$155,000	$155,000
B	415,000	195,000	255,000	210,000	249,000
C	350,000	310,000	0	300,000	350,000
D	300,000	16,500	183,500	0	4,000
	$1,375,000	$709,000	$451,000	$665,000	$758,000

The company is your client. The president has asked you to compute the amounts of revenue for the year ended December 31, 2002, that would be reported under the completed-contract method and the percentage-of-completion method of accounting for long-term contracts.

The following information is available:

(a) Each contract is with a different customer.
(b) Any work remaining to be done on the contracts is expected to be completed in 2003.
(c) The company's accounts have been maintained on the completed-contract method.

Instructions:

1. Prepare a schedule computing the amount of revenue, cost, and gross profit (loss) by project for the year ended December 31, 2002, to be reported under (a) the percentage-of-completion method and (b) the completed-contract method. (Round to two decimal places on percentages.)
2. Prepare a schedule under the completed-contract method, computing the amount that would appear on the company's balance sheet at December 31, 2002, for (a) costs in excess of billings and (b) billings in excess of costs.
3. Prepare a schedule under the percentage-of-completion method that would appear on the company's balance sheet at December 31, 2002, for (a) costs and estimated earnings in excess of billings and (b) billings in excess of costs and estimated earnings.

PROBLEM 7–32

CONSTRUCTION ACCOUNTING

The Kurtz Construction Corporation contracted with the City of Port Huron to construct a dam on the Erie River at a price of $16,000,000. Kurtz expects to earn $1,520,000 on the contract. The percentage-of-completion method is to be used, and the completion stage is to be determined by estimates made by the engineer. The following schedule summarizes the activities of the contract for the years 2001–2003.

Year	Cost Incurred	Engineer's Estimated Cost to Complete	Estimate of Completion	Billings on Contract	Collection on Billings
2001	$4,600,000	$9,640,000	31%	$5,000,000	$4,500,000
2002	4,500,000	5,100,000	58	6,000,000	5,400,000
2003	5,250,000	0	100	5,000,000	6,100,000

Instructions:

1. Prepare a schedule showing the revenue, cost, and the gross profit earned each year under the percentage-of-completion method, using the engineer's estimate as the measure of completion to be applied to revenues and costs.
2. Prepare all journal entries required to reflect the contract.
3. Prepare journal entries for 2003, assuming the completed-contract method is used.
4. How would the journal entries in (2) differ if the actual costs incurred were used to calculate cost for the period instead of the engineer's estimate?

PROBLEM 7–33

CONSTRUCTION ACCOUNTING

Jana Crebs is a contractor for the construction of large office buildings. At the beginning of 2002, 3 buildings were in progress. The following data describe the status of these buildings at the beginning of the year:

	Contract Price	Costs Incurred to Jan. 1, 2002	Estimated Cost to Complete as of Jan. 1, 2002
Building 1	$ 4,000,000	$2,070,000	$1,380,000
Building 2	9,000,000	6,318,000	1,782,000
Building 3	13,150,000	3,000,000	9,000,000

During 2002, the following costs were incurred.

Building 1 $930,000 (estimated cost to complete as of 12/31/02, $750,000)
Building 2 $1,800,000 (job completed)
Building 3 $7,400,000 (estimated cost to complete as of 12/31/02, $2,800,000)
Building 4 $800,000 (contract price, $2,500,000; estimated cost to complete as of 12/31/02, $1,200,000)

Instructions:

1. Compute the total revenue, costs, and gross profit in 2002. Assume that Crebs uses the cost-to-cost percentage-of-completion method. (Round to two decimal places for percentage completed.)
2. Compute the gross profit for 2002 if Crebs uses the completed-contract method.

PROBLEM 7–34

CONSTRUCTION ACCOUNTING

The Power Construction Company was the low bidder on a specialized equipment contract. The contract bid was $6,000,000 with an estimated cost to complete the project of $5,300,000. The contract period was 33 months, beginning January 1, 2001. The company uses the cost-to-cost method to estimate profits.

A record of construction activities for the years 2001–2004 follows:

Year	Actual Cost—Current Year	Progress Billings	Cash Receipts
2001	$3,400,000	$3,200,000	$3,000,000
2002	2,550,000	2,000,000	2,000,000
2003	200,000	800,000	600,000
2004	0	0	400,000

The estimated cost to complete the contract at the end of each accounting period is:

2001	$2,100,000
2002	150,000
2003	0

Instructions:

1. What is the revenue, cost, and gross profit recognized for each of the years 2001–2003 under the percentage-of-completion method?
2. Give the journal entries for each of the years 2001–2003 to record the information from (1).
3. Give the journal entries in 2004 to record any collections and to close out all construction accounts.

PROBLEM 7–35

CONSTRUCTION ACCOUNTING

Seattle Boatbuilders was recently awarded a $14,000,000 contract to construct a luxury liner for Cruiseliners Inc. Seattle estimates it will take 42 months to complete the contract. The company uses the cost-to-cost method to estimate profits.

The following information details the actual and estimated costs for the years 2001–2004.

Year	Actual Cost—Current Year	Estimated Cost to Complete
2001	$6,500,000	$6,800,000
2002	3,300,000	3,900,000
2003	2,400,000	1,900,000
2004	1,700,000	0

Instructions:

1. Compute the revenue, cost, and gross profit to be recognized for each of the years 2001–2004 under the percentage-of-completion method.
2. Give the journal entries for each of the years 2001–2004 to record the information from (1).

PROBLEM 7–36

INSTALLMENT SALES ACCOUNTING

London Corporation has been using the cash method to account for income since its first year of operation in 2002. All sales are made on credit with notes receivable given by the customers. The income statements for 2002 and 2003 included the following amounts:

	2002	2003
Revenues—collection on principal	$32,000	$50,000
Revenues—interest	3,600	5,500
Cost of goods purchased*	45,200	52,020

*Includes increase in inventory of goods on hand of $2,000 in 2002 and $8,000 in 2003.

The balances due on the notes at the end of each year were as follows:

	2002	2003
Notes receivable—2002	$62,000	$36,000
Notes receivable—2003	0	60,000
Unearned interest revenue—2002	7,167	5,579
Unearned interest revenue—2003	0	8,043

Instructions: Give the journal entries for 2002 and 2003 assuming the installment sales method was used rather than the cash method.

PROBLEM 7–37

INSTALLMENT SALES

Bain's Furniture sells furniture and electronic items. The majority of its business is on credit, and the following information is available relating to sales transactions for 2001, 2002, and 2003.

	2001	2002	2003
Installment sales (net of interest)	$104,000	$116,000	$121,000
Gross profit percentage	38%	41%	39%
Cash collections on installment sales:			
Principal—2001	$ 57,200	$ 29,120	$ 15,000
Principal—2002		71,920	26,680
Principal—2003			76,230
Interest—2001	9,780	17,870	3,030
Interest—2002		6,610	18,142
Interest—2003			6,378

Instructions: Prepare the journal entries for the years 2001–2003 assuming Bain's uses the installment sales method for revenue recognition and records receivables net of interest.

PROBLEM 7–38

REVENUE RECOGNITION ANALYSIS

The Wasatch Construction Company entered into a $4,500,000 contract in early 2002 to construct a multipurpose recreational facility for the city of Helper. Construction time extended over a 2-year period. The table below describes the pattern of progress payments made by the city of Helper and costs incurred by Wasatch Construction by semiannual periods. Estimated costs of $3,600,000 were incurred as expected.

Period	Progress Payments for Period	Progress Cost for Period
(1) Jan. 1–June 30, 2002	$ 750,000	$ 900,000
(2) July 1–Dec. 31, 2002	1,050,000	1,200,000
(3) Jan. 1–June 30, 2003	1,950,000	1,080,000
(4) July 1–Dec. 31, 2003	750,000	420,000
Total	$4,500,000	$3,600,000

The Wasatch Construction Company prepares financial statements twice each year, June 30 and December 31.

Instructions:

1. Based on the foregoing data, compute the amount of revenue, costs, and gross profit for the four semiannual periods under each of the following methods of revenue recognition.

(a) Percentage of completion

(b) Completed contract

(c) Installment sales (gross profit only)

(d) Cost recovery (gross profit only)

2. Which method do you feel best measures the performance of Wasatch on this contract?

PROBLEM 7–39 **CONSIGNMENT ACCOUNTING**

Tingey Industries sells merchandise on a consignment basis to dealers. Shipping costs are chargeable to Tingey, although in some cases the dealer pays them. The selling price of the merchandise averages 25% above cost of merchandise exclusive of freight. The dealer is paid a 10% commission on the sales price for all sales made. All dealer sales are made on a cash basis. The following consignment sales activities occurred during 2002.

Manufacturing cost of goods shipped on consignment		$250,000
Freight costs incurred:		
Paid by Tingey Industries	$15,000	
Paid by dealer	5,000	20,000
Sales price of merchandise sold by dealers		210,000
Payments made by dealers after deducting commission and freight costs		139,000

Instructions:

1. Prepare summary entries on the books of the consignor for these consignment sales transactions.

2. Prepare summary entries on the books of the dealer consignee, assuming there is only 1 dealer involved.

3. Prepare the parts of Tingey Industries' financial statements at December 31, 2002, that relate to these consignment sales.

COMPETENCY ENHANCEMENT OPPORTUNITIES

▶ Deciphering Actual Financial Statements	▶ Ethical Dilemma
▶ Writing Assignment	▶ Cumulative Spreadsheet Analysis
▶ Research Project	▶ Internet Search
▶ The Debate	

Accounting is more than just doing textbook problems. This expanded competency material provides practice in critical thinking, oral and written communication, research, teamwork, and consideration of ethical issues.

▶ **DECIPHERING ACTUAL FINANCIAL STATEMENTS**

• **Deciphering 7–1 (The Walt Disney Company)**

1. Locate DISNEY's note on revenue recognition. What is Disney's revenue recognition policy for the various business segments?

2. Relating to video sales, what other points in the revenue cycle (other than when videos are made widely available for sale by retailers) could Disney have used to recognize revenue?

3. Relating to motion pictures, what other points in the revenue cycle (other than when motion pictures are exhibited) could Disney have used to recognize revenue?

• Deciphering 7–2 (Siskon Gold Corporation)

Review the following note relating to revenue recognition for SISKON GOLD CORPORATION, a company "engaged in the business of exploring, acquiring, developing, and exploiting precious mineral properties, principally gold."

---

2. SIGNIFICANT ACCOUNTING POLICIES
Revenue recognition—Revenue from gold production is recognized when the finished product is poured based upon estimated weights and assays at current market prices.

---

1. What is the critical revenue recognition event for Siskon?
2. Is the company justified in recognizing revenue prior to the point of an actual sale? Why?
3. What potential risks exist when revenue is recognized prior to the point of sale?

• Deciphering 7–3 (Ben & Jerry's Homemade, Inc.)

Review the revenue recognition note for BEN & JERRY'S HOMEMADE, INC., an ice cream manufacturer.

Revenue Recognition
The Company recognizes revenue and the related costs when product is shipped. The Company recognizes franchise fees as income for individual stores when services required by the franchise agreement have been substantially performed and the store opens for business. Franchise fees relating to area franchise agreements are recognized in proportion to the number of stores for which the required services have been substantially performed. Franchise fees recognized as income and included in net sales were approximately $708,000, $553,000 and $301,000 in 1998, 1997 and 1996, respectively.

---

1. What is the critical event for Ben & Jerry's sale of ice cream?
2. What is the critical event for Ben & Jerry's recognition of franchise fee revenue? Note that Ben & Jerry's deals with two different types of franchise fees.

• Deciphering 7–4 (Lockheed Martin Corporation)

LOCKHEED MARTIN CORPORATION is "engaged in the design, manufacture, integration and operation of a broad array of products and services ranging from aircraft, spacecraft and launch vehicles to energy management, missiles, electronics, and information systems." As a result, Lockheed has a lot of long-term contracts. The note given below is taken from Lockheed's annual report and provides a good summary of the concepts associated with revenue recognition and long-term contracts.

Sales and earnings—Sales and anticipated profits under long-term fixed-price production contracts are recorded on a percentage of completion basis, generally using units of delivery as the measurement basis for effort accomplished. Estimated contract profits are taken into earnings in proportion to recorded sales. Sales under certain long-term fixed-price contracts which, among other things, provide for the delivery of minimal quantities or require a significant amount of development effort in relation to total contract value, are recorded upon achievement of performance milestones or using the cost-to-cost method of accounting where sales and profits are recorded based on the ratio of costs incurred to estimated total costs at completion.

Sales under cost-reimbursement-type contracts are recorded as costs are incurred. Applicable estimated profits are included in earnings in the proportion that incurred costs bear to total estimated costs. Sales of products and services essentially under commercial terms and conditions are recorded upon shipment or completion of specified tasks.

Amounts representing contract change orders, claims or other items are included in sales only when they can be reliably estimated and realization is probable. Incentives or penalties and awards applicable to performance on contracts are considered in estimating sales and profit rates and are recorded when there is sufficient information to assess anticipated contract performance. Incentive provisions which increase or decrease earnings based solely on a single significant event would generally not be recognized until the event has occurred.

When adjustments in contract value or estimated costs are determined, any changes from prior estimates are reflected in earnings in the current period. Any anticipated losses on contracts or programs in progress are charged to earnings when identified.

1. How does Lockheed measure its percentage of completion on most of its long-term contracts?
2. For the remaining long-term contracts, how does Lockheed recognize revenue and profits?
3. When a change in the contract is made, when is that change reflected in revenues?
4. In what periods are the changes in the company's estimated percentage of completion reflected?
5. If the company determines that the contract will result in a loss, when is that loss recognized?

▶ **WRITING ASSIGNMENT**
• **Credit terms and revenue recognition**
Many large electronics manufacturers offer very easy credit terms when a customer purchases their products. For example, MITSUBISHI often offers its customers a "$0 down, no payments for 12 months" payment option when purchasing a big-screen television. In a case such as this, when would Mitsubishi recognize revenue—at the point of sale, when payments are begun (in 12 months), or proportionally as payments are made? In no more than 2 pages, discuss the pros and cons of each possible revenue recognition point and provide a conclusion as to when you believe a company, like Mitsubishi in this example, should recognize revenue.

▶ **RESEARCH PROJECT**
• **Revenue recognition for the medical profession**
Contact the office managers of three local medical practices and ask them when revenue is recognized in their respective practices. Is it recognized when the service is provided to the customers or when payment is actually received from the customers or their insurance company? If revenue is recognized upon receipt of payment, ask them why the policy is to wait until that point.

Contact the accounting department of a local hospital (two hospitals if possible). Ask them what its revenue recognition policy is. Does it wait until payment is received or does it recognize revenue when the service is provided? Why might you expect the revenue recognition policies of a small medical practice and a large hospital to be different?

Summarize your findings and be prepared to give an oral report to the class.

▶ **THE DEBATE**
• **Health clubs and revenue recognition**
The decade of the 90s brought a renewed emphasis on health. Health clubs abound and, along with the clubs, accounting issues are being raised as well. As a client enrolls in a health

club, he/she typically pays an up-front registration fee and then a monthly membership fee. The major accounting issue is how to account for the up-front registration fee.

Divide your group into two teams, with one team representing current investors in a chain of health clubs looking to entice other investors and another team representing potential investors seeking to invest in the company as it expands.

- One team, the current investors, is to determine what method of revenue recognition would be most appropriate in accounting for the up-front fee as it seeks to get other investors to put their money into the business.
- The other team is to determine its preferred method of revenue recognition for the up-front fee. What method of accounting for the fee would provide potential investors with the most useful information?

Remember, you must be able to support your answers to the auditor.

▶ ETHICAL DILEMMA

You are the president and founder of Gold Strike Inc., a mining company that acquires land and mines gold. The success of your company is largely dependent on finding large deposits of gold. To do this requires expensive geological surveys and testing. You have used an engineering firm in the past that has proven quite reliable in its estimates of gold quality and quantity.

Because of recent events around the world, the price of gold has declined approximately 15% in the past 6 months. Accounting practice allows your company to recognize revenue when the gold is mined and processed rather than waiting until it is actually sold. Because of the recent unexpected decline in gold prices, you find that your revenue has suddenly declined even though the quality and quantity of the gold being produced have been maintained.

To avoid arousing investor concerns about your business's future, you consider the following option. The engineering firm assures you that, based on its tests, large amounts of gold still exist in your mines. Because you can recognize revenue when the gold is mined and you know it is in the ground (based on your engineer's assurances), could you recognize revenue for the gold that is in the ground but has not yet been mined? Now remember, you are not talking about accounting for fictitious gold. This gold does exist (again, based on your engineer's estimates).

▶ CUMULATIVE SPREADSHEET ANALYSIS

For the purpose of this spreadsheet assignment, assume that Skywalker is in the long-term construction business. As of the end of 2002, Skywalker has five active contracts (designated A through E). Information about each of the contracts, including forecasted information for 2003, is given below:

	A	B	C	D	E	Total
Contract price	$4,000	$1,000	$500	$1,500	$2,000	$9,000
Cumulative costs incurred, end of 2002	200	140	240	0	0	580
Estimated cost to complete, end of 2002	2,320	560	60	1,200	1,800	5,940
Estimated cost to be incurred during 2003	892	100	60	200	928	2,180
Cumulative progress billings, end of 2002	180	100	178	0	0	458
Estimated progress billings during 2003	1,300	130	120	240	966	2,756
Cumulative cash collected, end of 2002	170	80	127	0	0	377
Estimated cash to be collected during 2003	1,270	135	150	230	939	2,724

1. Using the information given, construct a spreadsheet that will compute the following. (Note: Skywalker uses the cost-to-cost method in estimating the percentage of completion.)
   a. Total accounts receivable, end of 2002

    b. Total inventory, end of 2002
    c. Total estimated revenue to be recognized in 2003
    d. Total estimated cost of goods sold to be recognized in 2003
    e. Total estimated accounts receivable, end of 2003
    f. Total estimated inventory, end of 2003

2. Repeat (1) with the following changes with respect to the estimated cost to be incurred in 2003.

	A	B	C	D	E	Total
Estimated cost to be incurred during 2003	$750	$120	$60	$200	$1,050	$2,180

3. Refer back to the original information in (1). Repeat (1) with the following changes with respect to the estimated progress billings during 2003.

	A	B	C	D	E	Total
Estimated progress billings during 2003	$1,270	$160	$140	$240	$946	$2,756

4. Refer back to (2) and (3). One of the changes results in a change in the estimated gross profit for 2003; the other change does not affect estimated gross profit for 2003. Explain this difference.

▶ **INTERNET SEARCH**

Revenue recognition issues such as those discussed in this chapter are unique to certain industries. Obviously, percentage-of-completion accounting is used by companies that deal in long-term contracts. Franchise fee issues are relevant only to those companies that deal with franchises. Let's take a look at a company that does a significant portion of its business using long-term contracts—BOEING COMPANY. Boeing is most famous for its commercial aircraft, but it also derives a significant amount of its revenue from other sources. One of its biggest customers is the U.S. government, which purchases helicopters, missiles, space stations, and military airplanes.

    Locate Boeing's Web site on the Internet at www.boeing.com. Once you have accessed Boeing's home page, answer the following questions.

1. Review Boeing's news releases for information relating to recently obtained long-term contracts. How many planes (or helicopters or missiles, etc.) has Boeing agreed to deliver? Over what period of time?
2. Locate Boeing's financial statements. What percentage of its revenue is obtained from commercial aircraft? from defense and space?
3. Find Boeing's note relating to revenue recognition and long-term contracts. How does the company recognize revenue?

chapter 8
Cost of Goods
Sold and Inventory:
Identification and Valuation

Let's go back to 1974. America was captivated by the Watergate investigation culminating in the resignation of President Nixon in August. In the spring, Hank Aaron hit his 715th career home run and broke Babe Ruth's long-standing record. Rock 'n' roll had fallen into the doldrums with best-selling songs for the year including forgettable numbers such as "Billy, Don't Be a Hero" by Bo Donaldson and the Heywoods and "Seasons in the Sun" by Terry Jacks. To add insult to injury, the first "disco" hit—"Rock the Boat" by The Hues Corporation—came out in 1974. At the movies, Americans were lining up to see disaster pictures such as *Earthquake* and *The Towering Inferno*.

From an accounting standpoint, 1974 was an interesting year because it was the first year since World War II in which consumer price inflation in the United States exceeded 10%. High inflation wreaks havoc on the reliability of historical cost financial statements. In fact, the high inflation experienced throughout the latter half of the 1970s caused the FASB to experiment with inflation-adjusted financial statements. But you'll have to wait until Chapter 21 to learn more about that.

High inflation also magnifies the difference between the FIFO (first in, first out) and LIFO (last in, first out) inventory methods. In times of rising prices, FIFO results in low cost of goods sold because the old, lower-cost inventory is assumed to be sold. Similarly, LIFO results in high cost of goods sold because the new, higher-cost inventory is assumed to be sold. This is illustrated in Exhibit 8–1. As an example of the FIFO/LIFO difference caused by the high inflation in 1974, the 1974 cost of goods sold of DUPONT was $600 million higher using LIFO than it would have been if DuPont had used FIFO.

By the way, 1974 happened to be the year that DuPont switched from FIFO to LIFO. DuPont was not alone—over 700 U.S. companies adopted LIFO in 1974. Why did these companies voluntarily adopt LIFO and subject themselves to higher cost of goods sold and lower reported profits? The one-word answer is *taxes*. The IRS requires firms using LIFO for income tax purposes to also use LIFO for financial reporting. So, if a company wants to get a reduction in taxes through higher LIFO cost of goods sold, the

EXHIBIT 8–1 | LIFO and FIFO in Times of Inflation

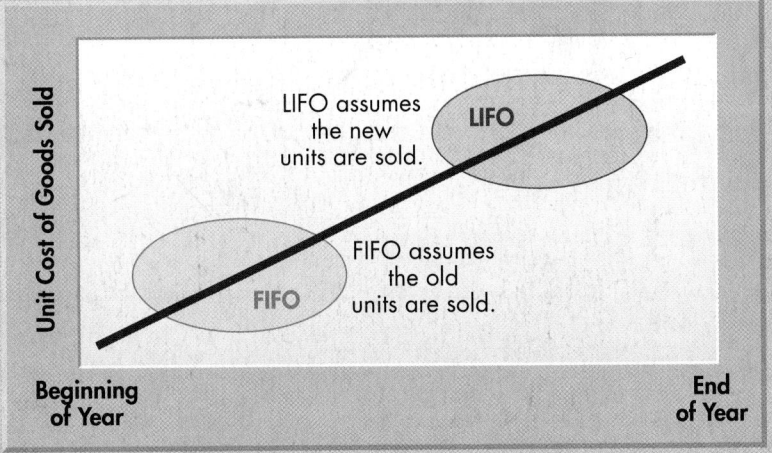

company must also accept a lower reported net income.[1] In DuPont's case, the adoption of LIFO in 1974 saved over $250 million in taxes but lowered DuPont's reported net income by over $300 million.

A question that has intrigued accounting researchers is whether investors viewed the 1974 LIFO adoptions as good news or bad news—good news because of the LIFO tax savings or bad news because of the reduction in reported net income. The answer to this question provides insight into whether investors are sophisticated in their knowledge of accounting. A sophisticated investor would view a LIFO adoption in a time of high inflation as good news, realizing that the adopting firm was focusing on real cash savings (lower taxes) and not worried about just looking good in the reported financial statements. An unsophisticated investor is fixated on reported earnings and would view LIFO adoption as bad news because it lowers net income.

In 1982, Professor William E. Ricks published a study suggesting that the LIFO adoptions were viewed as bad news, implying that investors back in 1974 were unsophisticated in their understanding of LIFO and FIFO.[2] He found that the market value of firms adopting LIFO dropped an average of 2% in the week surrounding the public announcement of 1974 earnings. Many studies have reexamined this result, and the overall conclusion is that it isn't clear exactly what caused this market value drop. After a careful analysis of competing explanations, Professor John R. M. Hand concluded: "[Negative] stock returns at 1974 LIFO adoption dates appear to reflect both sophisticated and unsophisticated responses to information on LIFO adopters. It is hard to disentangle the two responses. . . ."[3]

Your job is to study this chapter and make sure that your understanding of inventory accounting puts you in the set of sophisticated users of financial statements.

T he time line in Exhibit 8–2 illustrates the business issues involved with inventory. The accounting questions associated with the items in the time line are as follows:

- When is inventory considered to have been purchased—when it is ordered, when it is shipped, when it is received, or when it is paid for?

- Similarly, when is the inventory considered to have been sold?

- Many costs are associated with the "value-added" process—which of these costs are considered to be part of the cost of inventory and which are simply business expenses for that period?

- How should total inventory cost be divided between the inventory that was sold (cost of goods sold) and the inventory that remains (ending inventory)?

Determining what items should be included in inventory involves more than recognizing inventory when you see it. Some inventory that should be included in a company's balance sheet cannot be found in the company's warehouses but instead is in transit in trucks, trains, or ships or is temporarily in the custody of some other company. A proper physical determination of how much inventory a company owns as of a certain date is one of the most daunting tasks of an independent external auditor.

Attaching the proper costs to inventory is one of the primary functions of a cost accounting system. Advances made since 1980 in the practice of cost accounting have turned the sleepy topic of overhead allocation

1 This "LIFO conformity rule" is an exception—in most cases, the choice of a tax accounting method does not necessarily dictate the same choice for financial reporting. A brief history of LIFO is outlined in a boxed item later in the chapter.
2 William E. Ricks, "The Market's Response to the 1974 LIFO Adoptions," *Journal of Accounting Research,* Autumn 1982, p. 367.
3 John R. M. Hand, "1974 LIFO Excess Stock Return and Analyst Forecast Error Anomalies Revisited," *Journal of Accounting Research,* Spring 1995, p. 175.

EXHIBIT 8-2 | Time Line of Business Issues Involved With Inventory

BUY	**ADD**	**SELL**	**COMPUTE**	

| Raw Materials or Goods for Resale | Value | Finished Inventory | Ending Inventory | Cost of Goods Sold |

into a key element of product pricing and marketing focus. The important area of cost accounting is briefly covered in this chapter, but detailed treatment is left to a cost accounting course.

The majority of the chapter is devoted to the topic of inventory valuation. Almost all companies in the United States use one or more of three basic inventory valuation methods: FIFO (first in, first out), LIFO (last in, first out), and average cost. The objective of inventory valuation is to divide the total cost of goods available for sale during the period into two categories: the cost associated with goods that were sold (cost of goods sold) and the cost associated with goods that still remain (ending inventory). Coverage of the LIFO inventory valuation method takes up a large proportion of the chapter because the apparently simple assumption of last in, first out introduces all kinds of interesting twists into inventory accounting. Chapter 9 continues the discussion of inventory, covering the topics of inventory estimation and the accounting treatment required when the market value of inventory declines.

WHAT IS INVENTORY?

1

Define inventory for a merchandising business, and identify the different types of inventory for a manufacturing business.

The term **inventory** designates goods held for sale in the normal course of business and, in the case of a manufacturer, goods in production or to be placed in production. The nature of goods classified as inventory varies widely with the nature of business activities and in some cases includes assets not normally thought of as inventory. For example, land and buildings held for resale by a real estate firm, partially completed buildings to be sold in the future by a construction firm, and investment securities held for resale by a stockbroker are all properly classified as inventory by the respective firms in those industries.

For some businesses, inventory represents the most active element in business operations, being continuously acquired or produced and resold. A large part of a company's resources can be invested in goods purchased or manufactured. However, advances in information technology have made it possible for companies to more efficiently manage their inventory levels. As illustrated in Exhibit 8-3, inventory for the 50 largest companies in the United States declined steadily from 15.4% of total assets in 1987 to 7.4% of total assets in 1998. Actually, this trend is a combination of two factors: more efficient management of inventory and a decrease in the prominence of old-style smokestack industries that carried large inventories. Companies in the growth industries of service, technology, and information often have little or no inventory.

EXHIBIT 8–3 | How Much Inventory Do Companies Have?

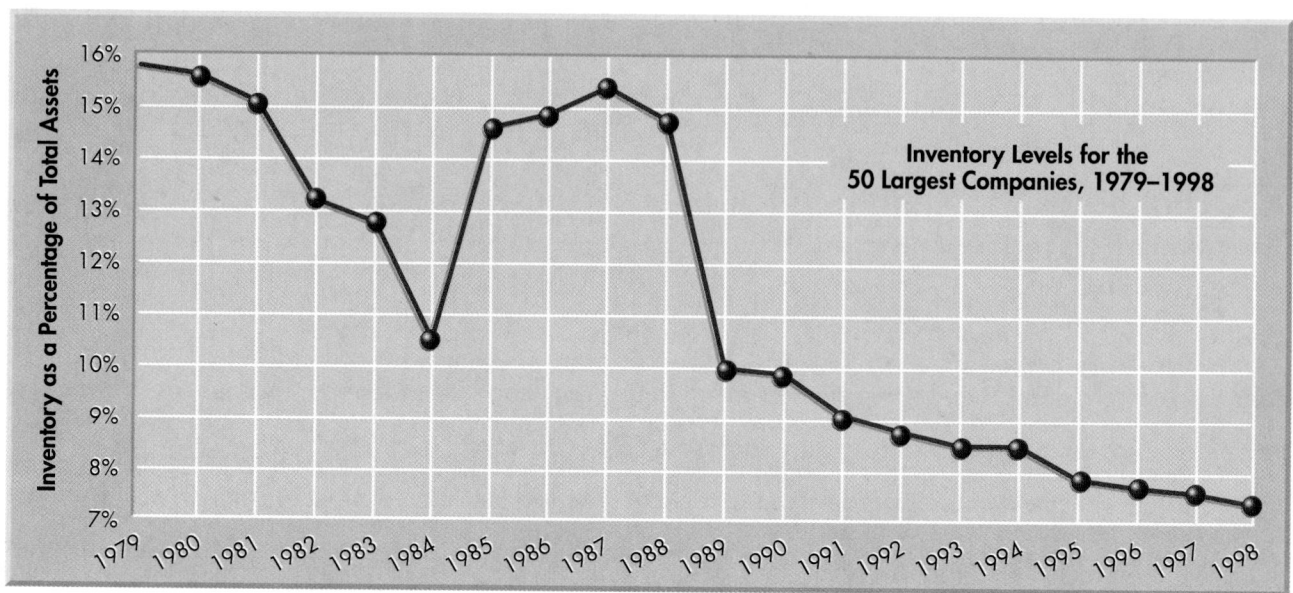

SOURCE: Standard and Poor's *COMPUSTAT*.

The term inventory (or merchandise inventory) is generally applied to goods held by a merchandising firm, either wholesale or retail, when such goods have been acquired in a condition for resale. The terms raw materials, work in process, and finished goods refer to the inventories of a manufacturing enterprise.

Raw Materials

Raw materials are goods acquired for use in the production process. Some raw materials are obtained directly from natural sources. More often, however, raw materials are purchased from other companies and represent the finished products of the suppliers. For example, high-quality acid-free paper (like that used for this book) is the finished product of a paper mill but represents raw material to a textbook publishing company.

Although the term raw materials can be used broadly to cover all materials used in manufacturing, this designation is usually restricted to materials that will be physically incorporated in the products being manufactured. Because these materials are used directly in the production of goods, they are frequently referred to as **direct materials**. The term **indirect materials** is then used to refer to auxiliary materials, that is, materials that are necessary in the production process but are not directly incorporated in the products. Oils and fuels for factory equipment, cleaning supplies, and similar items fall into this grouping because these items are not incorporated in a product but simply facilitate production.

Although indirect materials may be summarized separately, they should be reported as a part of a company's inventories since they ultimately will be consumed in the production process. Supplies purchased for use in the delivery, sales, and general administrative functions of the enterprise should not be reported as part of the inventories, but as selling and administrative supplies. Remember, inventory is the label given to assets to be sold in the normal course of business or to assets to be incorporated, directly or indirectly, into goods that are manufactured and then sold.

Work in Process

Work in process, alternately referred to as goods in process, consists of materials partly processed and requiring further work before they can be sold. This inventory includes three cost elements.

1. Direct materials—the cost of materials directly identified with goods in production
2. Direct labor—the cost of labor directly identified with goods in production
3. Manufacturing overhead—the portion of factory overhead assignable to goods in production

Manufacturing overhead consists of all manufacturing costs other than direct materials and direct labor. It includes factory supplies used and labor not directly identified with the production of specific products. It also includes general manufacturing costs such as depreciation, maintenance, repairs, property taxes, insurance, and light, heat, and power, as well as a reasonable share of the managerial costs other than those relating solely to the selling and administrative functions of the business.

Finished Goods

Finished goods are the manufactured products awaiting sale. As products are completed, the costs accumulated in the production process are transferred from Work in Process to the finished goods inventory account. The diagram in Exhibit 8–4 illustrates the basic flow of product costs through the inventory accounts of a manufacturer.

EXHIBIT 8–4 | Inventory Cost Flow

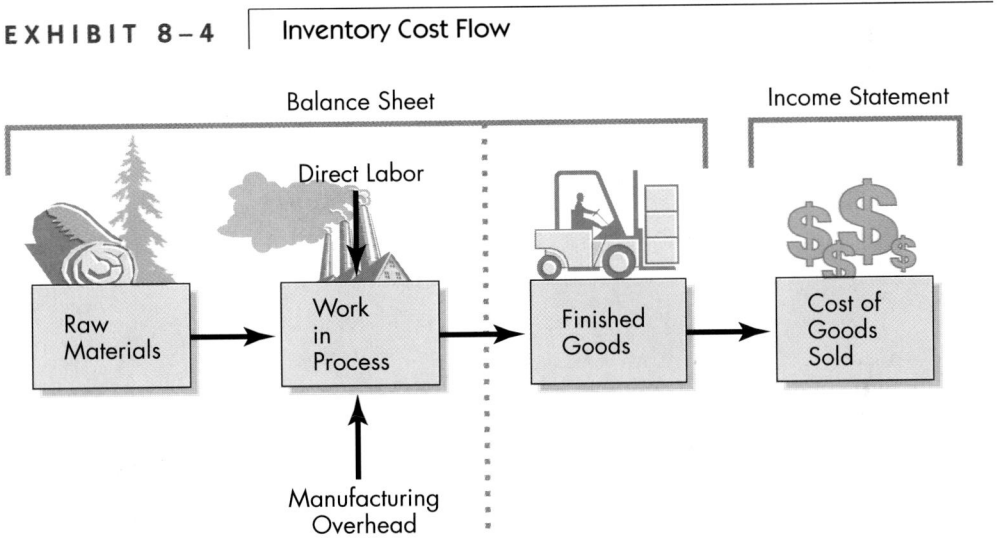

Note the vertical dotted line in Exhibit 8–4 separating Work in Process from Finished Goods. This line represents the factory wall. Historically, the rule of thumb was that costs incurred inside the factory wall were allocated to inventory, and costs incurred outside the factory wall (e.g., in the finished goods warehouse) were expensed as incurred. This simple rule doesn't always work because the IRS adopted inventory cost capitalization rules in 1986 that require some outside-the-factory costs to be capitalized as part of inventory cost. Although IRS rules do not govern financial accounting treatment, in this case some companies use the IRS rules for financial reporting to reduce the cost of maintaining separate records.[4]

STOP & THINK What was the motivation of the IRS in adopting the 1986 inventory cost capitalization rules described here?

---

4 The Emerging Issues Task Force (EITF) discussed whether the capitalization of an inventory cost for tax purposes requires that the same cost be included in inventory for financial reporting purposes. The EITF reached a consensus that the tax treatment should be considered but should not dictate the financial accounting treatment. See EITF 86-46, "Uniform Capitalization Rules for Inventory Under the Tax Reform Act of 1986," Stamford, CT: Financial Accounting Standards Board, 1986.

Explain the advantages and disadvantages of both periodic and perpetual inventory systems.

INVENTORY SYSTEMS

Consider the last time you made a purchase. Did the business where you made the purchase keep a record of what item they sold you, or did they just record the selling price? With a traditional cash register system, the seller records only the sales price; the seller has no record of how many units of a particular inventory item have been sold. Accountants call this type of system a **periodic inventory system** because the only way to verify what inventory has been sold and what remains is to do a periodic physical count.

The alternative to a periodic system is a **perpetual inventory system** in which both the selling price and the type of item sold are recorded for each sale. A bar code scanning system is an example of a perpetual inventory system. With a perpetual system, the seller knows the number of each item sold and the number that should still be in inventory. With a perpetual system, periodic physical inventory counts are useful in revealing the amount of inventory "shrinkage"—inventory lost, stolen, or spoiled.

To illustrate the differences between periodic and perpetual inventory systems, assume the following transactions occurred during the period for CyBorg Incorporated.

Beginning inventory	50 units @ $10	$500
Purchases during the period	300 units @ $10	3,000
Sales during the period	275 units @ $15	4,125
Ending inventory (physical count)	70 units @ $10	700

The journal entries to record these purchases and sales for both periodic and perpetual inventory systems are as follows:

Periodic Inventory System			Perpetual Inventory System		
Purchases during the period:			*Purchases during the period:*		
Purchases	3,000		Inventory	3,000	
Accounts Payable		3,000	Accounts Payable		3,000
Sales during the period:			*Sales during the period:*		
Accounts Receivable	4,125		Accounts Receivable	4,125	
Sales		4,125	Sales		4,125
			Cost of Goods Sold	2,750	
			Inventory		2,750

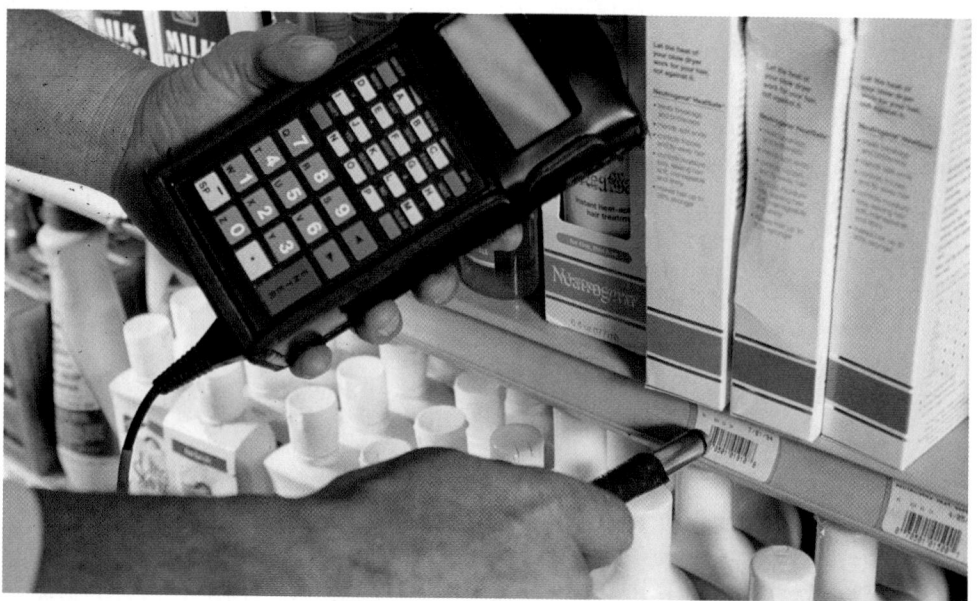

Most retail stores now use a scanning system that allows them to track inventory on a perpetual basis.

There are two differences between these two sets of journal entries. First, with a perpetual system an additional entry is made upon the sale of inventory to record the cost of goods sold. With a periodic system, cost of goods sold data are not known (or at least are not recorded) at the time of the sale. The second difference is that with the periodic system the debit for the inventory purchase is to Purchases instead of to Inventory. The purchases account is a temporary holding tank for inventory costs that are allocated between Inventory and Cost of Goods Sold at the end of the period. Under a periodic system, to debit Inventory directly for the amount of purchases during the period would yield misleading information about the level of inventory because the inventory account is not reduced for the cost of goods sold during the period. With a periodic system, the inventory account remains untouched until a physical inventory count is done at the end of the period.

When a perpetual inventory system is employed, the company knows how much inventory should be on hand at any point in time. Comparing the inventory records to the result of a physical count allows the company to track discrepancies in inventory totals. Thus, even when a perpetual system is employed, physical counts of units on hand should be made at least once a year to confirm the balances on the books. The frequency of physical inventories varies depending on the nature of the goods, their rate of turnover, and the degree of internal control.[5] A plan for continuous counting of inventory items on a rotation basis is frequently employed.

Variations may be found between the recorded amounts and the amounts actually on hand as a result of recording errors, shrinkage, breakage, theft, and other causes. The inventory accounts should be adjusted to agree with the physical count when a discrepancy exists. To illustrate, cost of goods sold in the CyBorg example is computed as follows:

	Periodic System	Perpetual System
Beginning inventory	$ 500	$ 500
+ Purchases	3,000	3,000
= Cost of goods available for sale	$3,500	$3,500
− Ending inventory	700 (count)	750 (records)
= Preliminary cost of goods sold	$2,800	$2,750 (records)
+ Cost of missing inventory	Unknown	50 ($750 − $700)
= Reported cost of goods sold	$2,800	$2,800

With the perpetual system, the accounting records contain amounts for ending inventory and cost of goods sold before the physical count is ever done. The physical count serves to verify the accounting records. And, in this case, it appears that CyBorg has lost $50 in inventory—the difference between the $750 inventory recorded in the books and the $700 physically counted. The entry to adjust the perpetual system inventory account for this **shrinkage** would be:

| Cost of Goods Sold | 50 | |
| Inventory | | 50 |

As indicated, this type of inventory adjustment for shrinkage and breakage would typically be included as part of cost of goods sold on the income statement.

With the periodic system, ending inventory is known only from the physical count. In addition, cost of goods sold can be computed only after the physical count is done. No

---

5 While paying for gas and soft drinks at a mini-convenience store, one of the authors noticed the cashier marking the soft drink purchases on an inventory sheet. Aha, thought the author, this place uses a perpetual inventory system. When asked how often a physical count was done to verify the inventory records, the cashier replied, "At the end of every shift." Obviously the store manager was using the combination of a perpetual inventory system and frequent physical counts to minimize shoplifting by customers and pilferage by employees.

shrinkage calculation is possible with a periodic system because the accounting records contain no indication of how much inventory should be found in the physical count. In fact, with a periodic system, the label "cost of goods sold" might be better replaced by "cost of goods sold, stolen, lost, and spoiled"—all that is known is that the goods are gone. For external reporting purposes, both the periodic and perpetual systems yield the same reported cost of goods sold. However, for internal purposes, the perpetual system divides that number into cost of goods sold and cost of inventory shrinkage.

 If perpetual inventory systems have so many clear advantages, why aren't they used by all companies?

Practically all large trading and manufacturing enterprises and many small organizations have adopted perpetual inventory systems. With the costs of computers and point-of-sale systems so low, perpetual inventory systems are now more economical and, in today's fast-moving world, almost a necessity. These systems offer a continuous check and control over inventories. Purchasing and production planning are facilitated, adequate on-hand inventories are ensured, and losses incurred through damage and theft are fully disclosed.

Determine when ownership of goods in transit changes hands and what circumstances require shipped inventory to be kept on the books.

WHOSE INVENTORY IS IT?

As a general rule, goods should be included in the inventory of the business holding legal title. The passing of title is a legal term designating the point at which ownership changes. When the rule of passing title is not observed, statements should include appropriate disclosure of the special practice followed and the factors supporting such practice. Application of the legal test under a number of special circumstances is described in the following paragraphs.

Goods in Transit

When goods are in transit from the seller to the buyer, who owns them? The answer depends on the terms of the sale. When terms of sale are **FOB (free on board) shipping point,** title passes to the buyer with the loading of goods at the point of shipment. Because title passes at the shipping point, goods in transit at year-end should be included in the inventory of the buyer even though the buyer hasn't received them yet.

When terms of a sale are **FOB destination,** legal title does not pass until the goods are received by the buyer. Because it can be difficult to determine whether goods have reached their destination by the end of the period, the seller may prefer to ignore the legal rule and remove goods from inventory as soon as they are shipped.

To summarize, when goods are shipped FOB shipping point, they belong to the buyer while they are in transit and should normally be included in the buyer's inventory while in transit. When goods are shipped FOB destination, they belong to the seller while in transit and are normally included in the seller's inventory. The impact of shipping terms on the ownership of goods in transit is summarized in Exhibit 8-5.

EXHIBIT 8-5 | Ownership Transfer for Goods in Transit

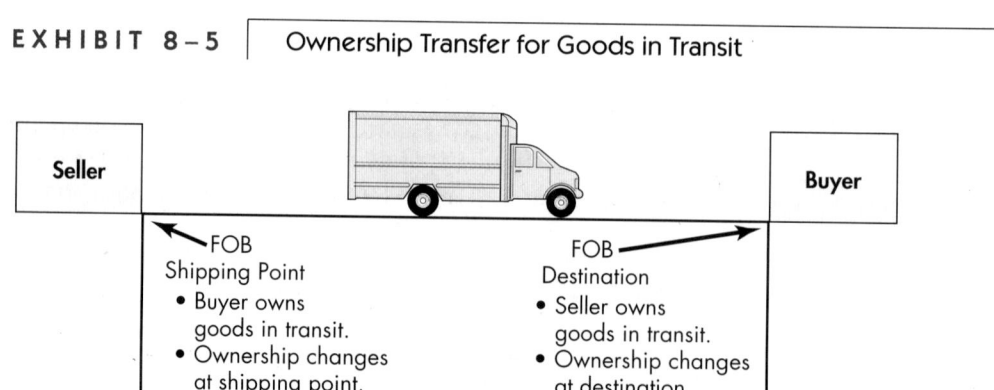

In some cases, title to goods may pass before shipment takes place. For example, if goods are produced on special customer order, they may be recorded as a sale as soon as they are completed and segregated from the regular inventory. If the sale is recognized upon segregation by the seller, the goods should be excluded from the seller's inventory. The buyer could recognize the goods as part of inventory as soon as they are separated.

Keep in mind that the shipping terms related to inventory are only an issue at the end of an accounting period. For most shipments, the goods will be shipped by the seller and received by the buyer in the same accounting period, thereby presenting no accounting problems.

Goods on Consignment

Goods are frequently transferred to a dealer or customer on a consignment basis. The shipper retains title and includes the goods in inventory until their sale or use by the dealer or customer. For example, NN BALL & ROLLER, a company that makes precision steel balls and rollers for use in manufacturing antifriction bearings, provides goods on consignment to some of its major customers. Through this arrangement, the customers are able to maintain low inventory levels. NN Ball & Roller benefits from this consignment arrangement because this added service improves customer satisfaction and, hopefully, increases sales. **Consigned goods** are properly reported by the shipper at the sum of their costs and the handling and shipping costs incurred in their transfer to the dealer or customer. The goods may be separately designated on the shipper's balance sheet as merchandise on consignment. Alternatively, the amount of inventory on consignment may be disclosed in the financial statement notes. For example, in the notes to its December 31, 1998, financial statements, NN Ball & Roller disclosed that $3.6 million of its $14.2 million in inventory was inventory on consignment. The dealer or customer does not own the consigned goods; hence, neither consigned goods nor obligations for such goods are reported on the dealer's or customer's financial statements. Recall that revenue recognition accounting for consignments was discussed in Chapter 7.

Other merchandise owned by a business but in the possession of others, such as goods in the hands of salespersons and agents, goods held by customers on approval, and goods held by others for storage, processing, or shipment also should be shown as a part of the ending inventory of the business that owns the goods.

> **FYI** Twenty years ago, when auditors got together, they exchanged "war stories" about difficult inventory audits. These days you are more likely to hear auditors complaining about lawsuits and nasty computer systems.

Auditing consigned inventory presents the auditor with a special set of problems. Inventory that is on the premises may not belong to the company because the company is holding it on consignment, yet inventory that is located with a vendor on consignment, hundreds of miles away, still belongs to the company. Imagine an auditor walking out into a warehouse and seeing row upon row of inventory. "That's not ours, we are just holding it on consignment," quips the warehouse manager. Then the warehouse manager leads the auditor to the shipping platform. "See that truck just leaving the gate? That truck and hundreds more just like it contain inventory that is still ours but has been shipped on consignment. Audit that!"

Conditional Sales, Installment Sales, and Repurchase Agreements

Conditional sales and installment sales contracts may provide for a retention of title by the seller until the sales price is fully recovered. Under these circumstances, the seller, who retains title, may continue to show the goods on its records, reduced by the buyer's equity in such goods as established by collections; the buyer, in turn, can report an equity in the goods accruing through payments made. However, in the usual case when the possibilities of returns and defaults are very low, the seller, anticipating completion of the contract and the ultimate passing of title, recognizes the transaction as a regular sale and removes the goods from reported inventory at the time of the sale; the buyer, intending to comply with the contract and acquire title, recognizes the transaction as a regular purchase. Revenue recognition accounting for installment sales also was discussed in Chapter 7.

As a creative way to obtain cash on a short-term basis, firms sometimes sell inventory to another company but at the same time agree to repurchase the inventory at some future date. The repurchase price typically includes the original selling price of the inventory plus finance and holding charges. In essence, the "selling" company has used inventory to secure a short-term loan but agrees to buy back the inventory later. For those familiar with such things, this is similar to how a pawnshop works. The FASB has decided that these arrangements should be accounted for according to their economic substance—no sale is recorded, the inventory is not removed from the selling company's balance sheet, and the seller must record a liability for the proceeds received in the "sale."[6]

Compute total inventory acquisition cost.

WHAT IS INVENTORY COST?

After the goods to be included as inventory have been identified, the accountant must assign a dollar value to the physical units. Both U.S. and international accounting standards agree that historical cost should normally be used in valuing inventory. Attention is directed in this section to identifying the elements that comprise inventory cost.

Items Included in Inventory Cost

Inventory cost consists of all expenditures, both direct and indirect, relating to inventory acquisition, preparation, and placement for sale. In the case of raw materials or goods acquired for resale, cost includes the purchase price, freight, receiving, storage, and all other costs incurred to the time goods are ready for sale. Certain expenditures can be traced to specific acquisitions or can be allocated to inventory items in some equitable manner. Other expenditures may be relatively small and difficult to allocate. Such items are normally excluded in the calculation of inventory cost and are recognized as expenses in the current period. These items are called **period costs.**

The charges to be included in the cost of manufactured products have already been mentioned. These costs are called **product** or **inventoriable costs.** Proper accounting for materials, labor, and manufacturing overhead items and their identification with goods in process and finished goods inventories are achieved through a cost accounting system. Certain costs relating to the acquisition or the manufacture of goods may be considered abnormal and may be excluded in arriving at inventory cost. For example, costs arising from idle capacity, excessive spoilage, and reprocessing are usually considered abnormal and are expensed in the current period. Only those portions of general and administrative costs that are clearly related to procurement or production should be included in inventory cost.

Inventory costing is important for financial reporting purposes, but it is absolutely critical for making production, pricing, and strategy decisions. For example, if competitive pressures dictate that a business can sell a product for no more than $10 per unit, it is essential to that business to know whether it costs $8 or $11 to produce the unit. As mentioned earlier in the chapter, recent advances in techniques for allocating manufacturing overhead have greatly improved cost accounting systems.

Traditionally, manufacturing overhead costs have been allocated to products based on the amount of direct labor required in production. This allocation scheme often fails because direct labor can be a small part of the cost of a product that actually causes a large amount of manufacturing overhead through requiring frequent machine maintenance, lots of invoice paperwork, heavy administrative supervision, and so forth. **Activity-based cost (ABC) systems** strive to allocate overhead based on clearly identified **cost drivers**—characteristics of the production process (e.g., number of required machine reconfigurations or

> **Caution!** One last warning—don't let the short coverage of overhead allocation here deceive you. This is a vital topic that has spawned arguments, textbooks, and lots of consulting revenue for the experts.

---

6 *Statement of Financial Accounting Standards No. 49,* "Accounting for Product Financing Arrangements," Stamford, CT: Financial Accounting Standards Board, 1981.

average frequency of production glitches requiring management intervention) that are known to create overhead costs. The real benefit of a good inventory costing system is seen in better information for internal decision making. As such, this important topic is covered fully in cost accounting courses.

A schedule of cost of goods manufactured is often prepared by manufacturing companies to illustrate how various costs affect inventories and, ultimately, cost of goods sold. An illustration of this schedule is presented in Exhibit 8-6.

In practice, companies take different positions in classifying certain costs. For example, costs of the purchasing department, costs of accounting for manufacturing activities, and costs of pensions for production personnel may be treated as inventoriable costs by some companies and period costs by others.

EXHIBIT 8-6 | Schedule of Cost of Goods Manufactured

Bartlett Corporation
Schedule of Cost of Goods Manufactured
For the Year Ended December 31, 2002

Direct materials:		
Raw materials inventory, January 1, 2002	$ 21,350	
Purchases	107,500	
Cost of raw materials available for use	$128,850	
Less: Raw materials inventory, December 31, 2002	22,350	
Raw materials used in production		$106,500
Direct labor		96,850
Manufacturing overhead:		
Indirect labor	$ 40,000	
Factory supervision	29,000	
Depreciation—factory buildings and equipment	20,000	
Light, heat, and power	18,000	
Factory supplies	15,000	
Miscellaneous manufacturing overhead	12,055	134,055
Total manufacturing costs		$337,405
Add: Work in process inventory, January 1, 2002		29,400
		$366,805
Less: Work in process inventory, December 31, 2002		26,500
Cost of goods manufactured		$340,305

Discounts as Reductions in Cost

Discounts associated with the purchase of inventory should be treated as a reduction in the cost assigned to the inventory. **Trade discounts** are the difference between a catalog price and the price actually charged to a buyer. Cost is defined as the list price less the trade discount. No record needs to be made of a trade discount, and the purchases should be recorded at the net price.

Cash discounts are discounts granted for payment of invoices within a limited time period. Cash discounts are usually stated as a certain percentage to be allowed if the invoice is paid within a certain number of days, with the full amount due within another time period. For example, 2/10, n/30 (two ten, net thirty) means that 2% is allowed as a cash discount if the invoice is paid within 10 days after the invoice date but the full or "net" amount is due within 30 days.

Theoretically, inventory should be recorded at the discounted amount, i.e., the gross invoice price less the allowable discount. This **net method** reflects the fact that discounts not taken are in effect a finance charge incurred for failure to pay within the discount period. Discounts not taken are recorded in the discounts lost account and reported as a separate item on the income statement. Discounts lost usually represent a relatively high rate of interest. To illustrate, assume a purchase of $10,000 provides for payment on a 2/10, n/30 basis. This purchase and the payment options are illustrated in Exhibit 8-7.

EXHIBIT 8–7 | Impact of Cash Discounts

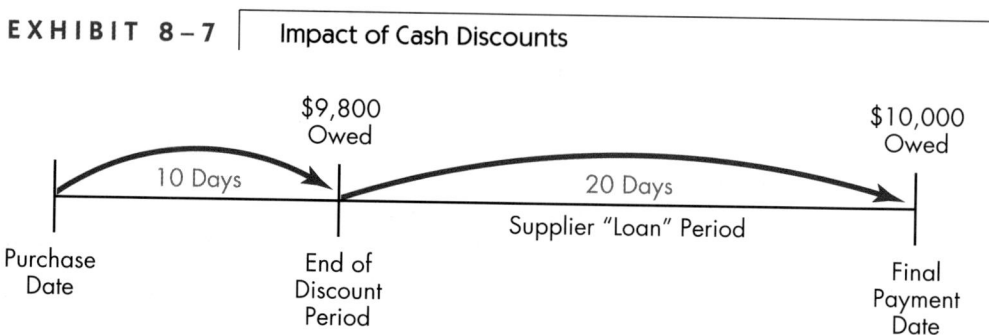

If the buyer pays for the purchase by the 10th day, only $9,800 must be paid. Twenty days later the full $10,000 is due. Thus, an additional $200 must be paid in exchange for delaying payment for an extra 20 days. In essence, this is a 20-day "loan" from the supplier to the purchaser. The effective interest rate on this 20-day "loan" is 2.04% ($200/$9,800). Because there are about eighteen 20-day periods in a year, the annual interest cost on this "loan" exceeds 36%, suggesting that missing a cash discount is a very costly mistake. Failure on the part of management to take a cash discount usually represents carelessness in considering payment alternatives. If cash discounts are accounted for using the net method, the $200 cost of a missed discount is not included as part of the inventory cost but is expensed immediately as a finance charge.

Under the **gross method,** cash discounts are booked only when they are taken. While the net method tracks discounts not taken, the gross method provides no such information and inventory records are maintained at the gross unit price. When a periodic system is used, cash discounts taken are reflected through a contra purchases account, Purchase Discounts. With a perpetual inventory system, discounts are credited directly to Inventory.

The net method of accounting for purchases is strongly preferred; however, many companies still follow the historical practice of recognizing cash discounts only as payments are made. The entries required for both the gross and net methods are illustrated in the following table. A perpetual inventory method is assumed.

Transaction	Purchases Reported *Net*		Purchases Reported *Gross*	

Purchase of merchandise priced at $10,000 along with a cash discount of 2%.	Inventory
	    Accounts Payable
		9,800
		9,800
			Inventory
			    Accounts Payable
				10,000
				10,000

(a) Assuming payment of the invoice within discount period.	Accounts Payable
	    Cash
		9,800
		9,800
			Accounts Payable
			    Inventory
			    Cash
				10,000
				200
				9,800

(b) Assuming payment of the invoice after discount period.	Accounts Payable
	Discounts Lost
	    Cash
		9,800
		200
		10,000
			Accounts Payable
			    Cash
				10,000
				10,000

(c) Required adjustment at the end of the period assuming that the invoice has not been paid and the discount period has lapsed.	Discounts Lost Accounts Payable	200 200	No entry required	

The difference in the two methods is that the net method shows the cost of missed discounts as a separate finance charge (Discounts Lost) whereas the gross method lumps this finance charge into the inventory cost. This result is the same if a periodic inventory system is used. The difference in journal entries with a periodic system is that Purchases, instead of Inventory, is debited to record the original purchase. In addition, Purchase Discounts, instead of Inventory, is credited under the gross method when payment occurs within the discount period.

Purchase Returns and Allowances

Adjustments to invoice cost are also made when merchandise either is damaged or is of a lesser quality than ordered. Sometimes the merchandise is physically returned to the supplier. In other instances, a credit is allowed to the buyer by the supplier to compensate for the damage or the inferior quality of the merchandise. A purchase allowance of $400 given for defective merchandise would be recorded as follows:

Periodic Inventory System			**Perpetual Inventory System**		
Accounts Payable	400		Accounts Payable	400	
Purchase Returns and Allowances		400	Inventory		400

Purchase Returns and Allowances is a contra purchases account.

The computation of total inventory acquisition cost is summarized as follows:

Invoice cost plus freight, storage, and preparation cost
− Cash discounts (only cash discounts *taken* if using the gross method)
− Purchase returns and allowances
= Inventory cost

INVENTORY VALUATION METHODS

Use the four basic inventory valuation methods: specific identification, average cost, FIFO, and LIFO.

At the end of an accounting period, total inventory cost must be allocated between inventory still remaining (to be reported on the balance sheet as an asset) and inventory sold during the period (to be reported on the income statement as the expense "Cost of goods sold"). Numerous methods have evolved to make this allocation between cost of goods sold and inventory. The most common methods are:

- Specific identification
- Average cost
- First-in, first-out (FIFO)
- Last-in, first-out (LIFO)

Caution! Although we call them inventory *valuation* methods, remember that they are actually methods for *allocating* total inventory acquisition cost between goods sold and goods remaining.

Each of these methods has certain characteristics that make it preferable under certain conditions. All four methods have in common the fact that inventory cost is allocated between the income statement and the balance sheet. Only the specific identification method determines the cost allocation according to the physical inventory flow. Unless individual inventory items, such as automobiles, are clearly definable, inventory items are exchangeable. Thus, the emphasis in inventory valuation usually is on the accounting cost allocation, not the physical flow.

FIFO is by far the most common inventory valuation method in the United States. Exhibit 8–8 reports the frequency of use of inventory valuation methods by U.S. companies in both 1979 and 1998. The percentages sum to more than 100%, indicating that many companies use more than one inventory method, applying different methods to different classes of inventory. Recall from the opening scenario of the chapter that LIFO generates income tax savings in times of inflation. The reduction in the rate of inflation in the United States from 1979 to 1998 is probably the cause of the overall decline in usage of LIFO. Finally, notice the difference in usage of LIFO between large and small firms. This is probably the consequence of the potentially sizable bookkeeping costs of maintaining a LIFO system.

EXHIBIT 8-8 | Frequency of Inventory Valuation Method Use

Frequency of Use of Inventory Valuation Methods
U.S. Companies
1979 and 1998

Inventory Method	1979 All Companies	1998 All Companies	1998 Large Companies
FIFO	75.6%	82.9%	72.6%
LIFO	25.8%	12.5%	33.0%
Average cost	20.8%	15.7%	30.0%
Specific identification	3.7%	3.2%	2.6%

SOURCE: Standard and Poor's *COMPUSTAT.*

There have been few guidelines developed by the profession to assist companies in choosing among these alternative inventory valuation methods. Some argue that cost flow should mirror the physical flow of goods. Others think that inventory valuation should concentrate on matching current costs with current revenues. Still others think that the emphasis should be on the proper valuation of inventory on the balance sheet. The following discussion of the allocation methods demonstrates how each method relates to these different viewpoints.

The four methods will be illustrated using the following simple example for Dalton Company. Dalton has no beginning inventory for 2002.

	Number of Units	Unit Cost	Total Cost
Purchases:			
January 1	200	$10	$ 2,000
March 23	300	12	3,600
July 15	500	11	5,500
November 6	100	13	1,300
Total purchases	1,100		$12,400
Sales:			

700 units at $15 per unit. For simplicity, assume that all sales occurred on December 31.

Specific Identification

Costs may be allocated between goods sold during the period and goods on hand at the end of the period according to the actual cost of specific units. This **specific identification method** requires a way to identify the historical cost of each individual unit of inventory. With specific identification, the flow of recorded costs matches the physical flow of goods.

From a theoretical standpoint, the specific identification method is very attractive, especially when each inventory item is unique and has a high cost. However, when inventory is composed of a great many items or identical items acquired at different times and at different prices, specific identification is likely to be slow, burdensome, and costly. Even a computer tracking system won't answer all these practical concerns. Consider the task of implementing a specific identification inventory system in a do-it-yourself hardware store with the requirement to specifically track all costs associated with each screwdriver, each bolt, each piece of lumber, and each can of paint.

Apart from practical concerns, when units are identical and interchangeable, the specific identification method opens the door to possible profit manipulation through the selection of particular units for delivery. Consider the Dalton Company example. If Dalton Company wants to minimize its cost of goods sold for 2002 (and thus maximize reported net income), it can strategically choose to ship the 700 units with the lowest cost. Cost of goods sold would be computed as follows:

Dalton Company
Specific Identification Method
Shipment of the Lowest Cost Units
Cost of Goods Sold (Computation)

	Number of Units	Unit Cost	Total Cost
Batch purchased on:			
January 1	200	$10	$2,000
July 15	500	11	5,500
Total cost of goods sold	700		$7,500

The specific identification method is the least common of the four methods discussed in this chapter. Exhibit 8-8 indicates that in 1998 it was used by only 3.2% of U.S. companies.

SERVICE CORPORATION INTERNATIONAL (SCI) provides an interesting example of a company that uses the specific identification method. SCI is the largest death care provider in the world. A popular method for increasing cash flows in this industry is to presell funeral packages. Exhibit 8-9 provides the company's note disclosure relating to its revenue recognition policies. It turns out that the company defers all revenues associated with presell funeral packages until the customers die and then specifically matches the costs associated with that individual with the cash received.

EXHIBIT 8-9 | Service Corporation International—Prearranged Funeral Accounting

The Company sells price guaranteed prearranged funeral contracts through various programs providing for future funeral services at prices prevailing when the agreements are signed. Payments under these contracts are placed in trust accounts (pursuant to applicable law) or are used to pay premiums on life insurance policies.

Revenues associated with sales of prearranged funeral contracts (which include accumulated trust earnings and increasing insurance benefits) are deferred until such time that the funeral services are performed.

Average Cost Method

The **average cost method** assigns the same average cost to each unit. This method is based on the assumption that goods sold should be charged at an average cost, with the average being weighted by the number of units acquired at each price. Using the cost data for Dalton Company, the weighted average cost of each unit would be computed as follows:

Total purchases: 1,100 units at a total cost of $12,400
Weighted average cost: $12,400 ÷ 1,100 units = $11.27 per unit (rounded)

Using the average cost method, cost of goods sold is simply the number of units sold multiplied by the average cost per unit: $7,890 (700 units × $11.27 per unit, rounded).

The average cost method can be supported as realistic and as paralleling the physical flow of goods, particularly where there is an intermingling of identical inventory units. Unlike the other inventory methods, the average cost approach provides the same cost for similar items of equal utility. The method does not permit profit manipulation. A limitation of the average cost method is that inventory values may lag significantly behind current prices in periods of rapidly rising or falling prices.

First-In, First-Out Method

The **first-in, first-out (FIFO) method** is based on the assumption that the units sold are the oldest units on hand. For Dalton Company, FIFO cost of goods sold is computed as follows:

Dalton Company
FIFO Method
Cost of Goods Sold Computation

	Number of Units	Unit Cost	Total Cost
Batch purchased on:			
January 1	200	$10	$2,000
March 23	300	12	3,600
July 15	200	11	2,200
Total cost of goods sold	700		$7,800

Note that only 200 units from the July 15 batch are assumed to be sold; the remaining 300 units from that batch are assumed to be in ending inventory.

FIFO can be supported as a logical and realistic approach to the flow of costs when it is impractical or impossible to achieve specific cost identification. FIFO assumes a cost flow closely paralleling the usual physical flow of goods sold. Expense is charged with costs considered applicable to the goods actually sold. FIFO affords little opportunity for profit manipulation because the assignment of costs is determined by the order in which costs are incurred. In addition, with FIFO the units remaining in ending inventory are the most recently purchased units, so their reported cost would most closely match end-of-period replacement cost.

Last-In, First-Out Method

The **last-in, first-out (LIFO) method** is based on the assumption that the newest units are sold. For Dalton Company, LIFO cost of goods sold is computed as follows:

Dalton Company
LIFO Method
Cost of Goods Sold Computation

	Number of Units	Unit Cost	Total Cost
Batch purchased on:			
November 6	100	$13	$1,300
July 15	500	11	5,500
March 23	100	12	1,200
Total cost of goods sold	700		$8,000

Caution! There is no required connection between the actual physical flow of goods and the inventory valuation method used.

Note that only 100 units from the March 23 batch are assumed to be sold; the remaining 200 units from that batch are assumed to be in ending inventory.

LIFO is frequently criticized from a theoretical standpoint. It does not match the usual flow of goods in a business (although it does unfortunately match the flow of food in and out of a college student's refrigerator—with nasty implications for "ending inventory"). As seen in the following sections, LIFO results in old values on the balance sheet and can yield very strange cost of goods sold numbers when inventory levels decline. However, LIFO is the best method at matching current inventory costs with current revenues. The difficulties and quirks of maintaining a LIFO inventory system are detailed later in the chapter.

Comparison of Methods: Cost of Goods Sold and Ending Inventory

Recall that the purpose of an inventory valuation method is to allocate total inventory cost between cost of goods sold and inventory. For Dalton Company, total inventory cost for 2002 is $12,400. The allocation of this cost between cost of goods sold and ending inventory is shown in Exhibit 8–10 for each of the four inventory valuation methods.

EXHIBIT 8–10 | Comparison of Inventory Valuation Methods

Dalton Company
Comparison of Four Inventory Valuation Methods
Cost of Goods Sold and Ending Inventory

	Unit Cost	Specific Identification	Average Cost*	FIFO	LIFO
Purchased on:					
January 1	$10	200	200	200	200
March 23	12	300	300	300	200 / 100
July 15	11	500	500	200 / 300	500
November 6	13	100	100	100	100

Units sold [ ]   Units remaining [ ]

Cost of goods sold (700 units):

Specific Identification	Average Cost*	FIFO	LIFO
200 × $10 = $ 2,000	700 × $11.27 = $ 7,890**	200 × $10 = $ 2,000	100 × $13 = $ 1,300
500 × $11 = 5,500		300 × $12 = 3,600	500 × $11 = 5,500
		200 × $11 = 2,200	100 × $12 = 1,200
$ 7,500	$ 7,890	$ 7,800	$ 8,000

Ending inventory (400 units):

Specific Identification	Average Cost*	FIFO	LIFO
300 × $12 = $ 3,600	400 × $11.27 = $ 4,510**	300 × $11 = $ 3,300	200 × $10 = $ 2,000
100 × $13 = 1,300		100 × $13 = 1,300	200 × $12 = 2,400
$ 4,900	$ 4,510	$ 4,600	$ 4,400

Total inventory cost:

Specific Identification	Average Cost*	FIFO	LIFO
$12,400	$12,400	$12,400	$12,400

*With the average cost method, no assumption is made about the sale of specific units. The average cost per unit is computed as follows: $12,400 ÷ 1,100 units = $11.27 per unit, rounded.
**Rounded.

Note that the average cost method differs from the other three methods in that no assumption is made about the sale of specific units. Instead, all sales are assumed to be of the hypothetical "average" unit at the average cost per unit.

Use of FIFO in a period of rising prices matches oldest low-cost inventory with rising sales prices, thus expanding the gross profit margin. In a period of declining prices, oldest high-cost inventory is matched with declining sales prices, thus narrowing the gross profit margin. Using average cost, the gross profit margin tends to follow a similar pattern in response to changing prices. On the other hand, use of LIFO in a period of rising prices relates current high costs of acquiring goods with rising sales prices. Thus, LIFO tends to have a stabilizing effect on gross profit margins.

In using FIFO, inventories are reported on the balance sheet at or near current costs. With LIFO, inventories are reported at the cost of the earliest purchases. If LIFO has been used for a long time, the disparity between current value of inventory and reported LIFO cost can grow quite large. Use of the average method generally provides inventory values similar to FIFO values, because average costs are heavily influenced by current costs. Specific identification can produce any variety of results depending on which particular units are chosen for shipment.

When the prices paid for merchandise do not fluctuate significantly, alternative inventory methods may provide only minor differences in the financial statements. However, in periods of steadily rising or falling prices, the alternative methods may produce material differences.

Complications With a Perpetual Inventory System

In the Dalton Company example, the simplifying assumption was made that all 700 units were sold on December 31. In essence, this is the assumption made when a periodic inventory system is used. Computation of average cost and LIFO under a perpetual system is complicated because the average cost of units available for sale changes every time a purchase is made, and the identification of the "last in" units also changes with every purchase. The complications of a perpetual system are illustrated in Exhibit 8–11, in which Dalton Company's cost of goods sold and ending inventory for 2002 are computed assuming that 300 units were sold on June 30 and 400 units were sold on December 31.

Examine Exhibit 8–11 and consider the following observations:

- Even in this more complicated example, the net result of each of the inventory valuation methods is to allocate the total inventory cost of $12,400 between cost of goods sold and ending inventory.
- For FIFO, cost of goods sold and ending inventory are the same whether a periodic system (all sales assumed to occur at year-end) or a perpetual system (sales occur throughout the year) is used. Compare Exhibits 8–10 and 8–11. This is because no matter when in the year the sales are assumed to occur, the oldest units (first in) are always the same ones.
- Because the newest units (last in) as of June 30 are not the same as the newest units on December 31, applying LIFO on a perpetual basis gives a different cost of goods sold and ending inventory than if a periodic system is used.
- Similarly, the average cost of units in inventory on June 30 ($11.20) is not the same as the average cost of all units purchased for the year ($11.27). Thus, applying average cost on a perpetual and a periodic basis yields different results.

Because of the unnecessary complications of perpetual LIFO and perpetual average cost, many businesses that use average cost or LIFO for financial reporting use a simple FIFO assumption in the maintenance of their day-to-day perpetual inventory records. These perpetual FIFO records are then converted to periodic average cost or LIFO for the financial reports.

EXHIBIT 8 – 11 | Inventory Valuation Methods and a Perpetual Inventory System

Dalton Company
Complications of a Perpetual Inventory System

	Unit Cost	Average Cost*	FIFO	LIFO

300 units sold on June 30:

Purchased on:

January 1	$10	200	200	200
March 23	12	300	100 / 200	300

Units sold ☐   Units remaining ☐

Cost of goods sold (300 units):

	Average Cost*	FIFO	LIFO
	300 × $11.20 = $3,360	200 × $10 = $2,000	300 × $12 = $3,600
		100 × $12 = 1,200	
	$3,360	$3,200	$3,600

Inventory on June 30 (200 units):

	200 × $11.20 = $2,240	200 × $12 = $2,400	200 × $10 = $2,000

	Unit Cost	Average Cost**	FIFO	LIFO

400 units sold on December 31:

Purchased on:

Inventory on June 30	—	200 × $11.20	200 × $12	200 × $10
July 15	$11	500	200 / 300	200 / 300
November 6	13	100	100	100

Units sold ☐   Units remaining ☐

Cost of goods sold (400 units):

	Average Cost**	FIFO	LIFO
	400 × $11.30 = $4,520	200 × $12 = $2,400	100 × $13 = $1,300
		200 × $11 = 2,200	300 × $11 = 3,300
	$4,520	$4,600	$4,600

Ending inventory (400 units):

	Average Cost**	FIFO	LIFO
	400 × $11.30 = $4,520	300 × $11 = $3,300	200 × $10 = $2,000
		100 × $13 = 1,300	200 × $11 = 2,200
	$4,520	$4,600	$4,200

Total inventory cost:

	Average Cost	FIFO	LIFO
Sold on June 30	$ 3,360	$ 3,200	$ 3,600
Sold on December 31	4,520	4,600	4,600
Total cost of goods sold	$ 7,880	$ 7,800	$ 8,200
Inventory on December 31	4,520	4,600	4,200
Total inventory cost	$12,400	$12,400	$12,400

*With the average cost method, no assumption is made about the sale of specific units. The average cost per unit is computed as follows:
  [(200 x $10) + (300 x $12)] ÷ 500 units = $11.20 per unit
**[(200 x $11.20) + (500 x $11) + (100 x $13)] ÷ 800 units = $11.30 per unit

Explain how LIFO inventory layers are created, and describe the significance of the LIFO reserve.

MORE ABOUT LIFO

In the simple Dalton Company example of the previous section, the LIFO calculations did not seem any more difficult than the calculations using the other three methods. In a more involved example, the complexities of LIFO become apparent. In this section, a multiyear example is used to illustrate LIFO layers and LIFO liquidation. The advantages of using LIFO pools and dollar-value LIFO to reduce the recordkeeping burden associated with LIFO are illustrated in the expanded material at the end of the chapter.

LIFO Layers

The following data are for Ryanes Company for the first three years of its existence.

	1999	2000	2001
Purchases	120 units @ $5	150 units @ $10	160 units @ $15
Sales	100 units @ $10	120 units @ $15	120 units @ $20

Caution! Pay close attention to this part of the chapter. You may think you understand LIFO, but until you work through the wrinkles and quirks presented here, you don't.

At the end of 1999, 20 units with a total cost of $100 (20 units × $5 per unit) remain in ending inventory. Are these units sold in 2000? If a FIFO assumption is made, the answer is yes. Under FIFO, the 120 units sold in 2000 are the oldest available units—the 20 units left over from 1999 plus 100 units purchased in 2000. However, if a LIFO assumption is made, the 20 units left over at the end of 1999 are *not* sold in 2000. Instead, the newest units are sold, and those are 120 of the units purchased in 2000. Using LIFO, cost of goods sold and ending inventory for each of the three years are as follows:

	1999	2000	2001
LIFO cost of goods sold	100 × $5 = $500	120 × $10 = $1,200	120 × $15 = $1,800
Ending inventory:			
Year Units Purchased			
1999	20 × $5 = $100	20 × $ 5 = $ 100	20 × $ 5 = $ 100
2000		30 × $10 = $ 300	30 × $10 = 300
2001			40 × $15 = 600
Ending inventory	20 units $100	50 units $ 400	90 units $1,000

Notice that each year in which the number of units purchased exceeds the number of units sold, a new **LIFO layer** is created in ending inventory. As long as inventory continues to grow, a new LIFO layer is created each year and the old LIFO layers remain untouched.

The creation of LIFO layers illustrates one of the drawbacks of LIFO in that after a few years, the LIFO assumption results in ending inventory containing old inventory at old prices. In the Ryanes example, 2001 ending inventory is assumed to contain inventory purchased back in 1999. And, because inventory costs have increased during the period, the $1,000 amount reported for 2001 ending inventory does not represent the current value of the 90 units of inventory. For example, if FIFO were used, the 90 units in 2001 ending inventory would be valued using the 2001 purchase price of $15 per unit, giving them a value of $1,350 (90 units × $15 per unit). The difference between the LIFO ending inventory amount and the amount obtained using another inventory valuation method (like FIFO or average cost) is called the **LIFO reserve.** In this example, the LIFO reserve is $350 ($1,350 FIFO ending inventory – $1,000 LIFO ending inventory).

Exhibit 8-12 contains the footnote disclosure of DUPONT's LIFO reserve from the company's 1998 annual report. Note that DuPont uses the average cost method for

EXHIBIT 8 – 1 2 | DuPont's LIFO Reserve Note

Inventories

December 31	1998	1997
Finished products	$2,209	$2,115
Semifinished products	836	827
Raw materials and supplies	749	659
Total	3,794	3,601
Less: Adjustment of inventories to a last-in, first-out (LIFO) basis	665	809
	$3,129	$2,792

Inventory values before LIFO adjustment are generally determined by the average cost method, which approximates current cost. Inventories valued under the LIFO method comprised 85 percent of consolidated inventories before LIFO adjustment at December 31, 1998 and 1997.

maintaining its accounting records during the year and then adjusts its inventory to the LIFO method for financial reporting purposes.

Many companies that use LIFO report the amount of their LIFO reserve, either as a parenthetical note in the balance sheet or in the notes to the financial statements. The size of the LIFO reserve for several large U.S. companies is given in Exhibit 8–13.

EXHIBIT 8 – 1 3 | Size of LIFO Reserve for Selected U.S. Companies

**U.S. Companies With the Largest LIFO Reserves
For the Year 1998
(in millions of U.S. dollars)**

Company Name	Reported LIFO Inventory	LIFO Reserve
General Motors	12,207	2,295
Caterpillar	2,842	1,978
Ford	5,656	1,200
Philip Morris	9,445	1,100
Deere & Co.	1,287	1,050
General Electric	12,216	1,011

These LIFO reserve disclosures can aid financial statement users in comparing companies that use different inventory valuation methods. The disclosures can be used to recalculate LIFO ending inventory and cost of goods sold on a FIFO or average cost basis. To illustrate, the following data can be used to calculate FIFO cost of goods sold for Ryanes for 2001.

► THE HISTORY OF LIFO—PART I

LIFO is an American invention, but the conceptual parent of LIFO, the base stock method, arose in the United Kingdom sometime in the late 1800s. The idea behind the base stock method is that a company must maintain a certain minimum quantity (base stock) of inventory in order to stay in business. This base stock will never be liquidated as long as the business is a going concern. Accordingly, the inventory base stock is similar in nature to a fixed asset and should be valued at the acquisition cost of the initial stock of inventory. Implementation of the base stock method requires management to designate how much of its inventory is base stock and what historical cost amount should be used to value the base stock.

In 1930, the U.S. Supreme Court ruled that the base stock method was not acceptable for tax purposes. (Those must have been exhilarating times for accountants—to have the merits of accounting methods debated before the Supreme Court!) The Supreme Court understood that the primary reason for a company to use the base stock method was not to more fairly reflect performance but to reduce income tax payments. LIFO was developed as an alternative to the base stock method that was not so dependent on arbitrary management designations of base stock quantities and prices. LIFO is beautiful in its definitional simplicity—the last goods in are the first goods out. And in practice, LIFO comes close to lowering taxes to the same extent as the base stock method.

Congress approved the use of LIFO for tax purposes in the Revenue Act of 1939, but it added an interesting stipulation known as the LIFO conformity rule: If you use

	2000	2001
LIFO ending inventory	$ 400	$1,000
LIFO reserve	100	350
LIFO cost of goods sold	1,200	1,800

The FIFO calculation can be done as follows:

	LIFO		FIFO	
$ 400	Beginning inventory	$ 500	($400 + $100 LIFO reserve)	
2,400	+ Purchases	2,400	(160 units × $15; same for LIFO and FIFO)	
$2,800	= Cost of goods available	$2,900		
1,000	− Ending inventory	1,350	($1,000 + $350 LIFO reserve)	
$1,800	= Cost of goods sold	$1,550		

 Verify by reference to the original data that FIFO cost of goods sold for 2001 is $1,550.

In this simple example, purchases can be computed from the original data. Alternatively, purchases can be inferred from the beginning inventory, ending inventory, and cost of goods sold amounts. The important insight is that purchases are the same whether LIFO or FIFO is used.

LIFO Liquidation

Continuing the Ryanes Company example, assume purchases and sales for 2002 are as follows:

Purchases	60 units @ $20
Sales	150 units @ $25

LIFO for income tax purposes, you must also use it for financial reporting. In no other accounting area is there a legally mandated correspondence between tax accounting and financial accounting. What was Congress' reasoning behind this LIFO conformity rule? Well, it is dangerous to try to fathom the intent of Congress. However, there is some belief that this condition was imposed in order to coerce auditors into being watchdogs for the IRS. The reasoning is as follows: In order to use LIFO for tax purposes, a company must also use it for financial reporting. The independent auditor must approve the financial statements and would not approve the use of LIFO if it didn't fairly reflect the performance of the company. Presumably, if a company wants to adopt LIFO strictly for the purpose of reducing income tax payments, the auditor would not approve. Hence, the auditor becomes the watchdog for the IRS.

Like many Congressional schemes, this grand design has not worked out. Although the LIFO conformity rule is still in place, since 1953 financial accounting standards have not included any meaningful constraints on a firm's choice among FIFO, LIFO, and average cost.

QUESTIONS:

1. If ending inventory levels are constant from one year to the next, is LIFO equivalent to the base stock method? How about if ending inventory levels are consistently growing from one year to the next?
2. If you were an accounting standard setter, what reasons would you give for banning LIFO? What if you were a government tax official?
3. Should Congress repeal the LIFO conformity rule?

SOURCE:
Harry Zvi Davis, "History of LIFO," *Accounting Historians Journal*, Spring 1982, p. 1.

Because the number of units purchased does not exceed the number sold, no new LIFO layer is added in 2002. In fact, because 2002 purchases are so low, inventory in the old LIFO layers must be sold. This is called **LIFO liquidation.** Computation of 2002 LIFO cost of goods sold is as follows:

Year	Units Purchased	
2002	60 units @ $20	$1,200
2001	40 units @ $15	600
2000	30 units @ $10	300
1999	20 units @ $ 5	100
Total	150 units	$2,200

A retail store such as Eddie Bauer must account for interim inventory reductions due to the seasonal fluctuation of inventory levels. This method is described on the following page.

LIFO liquidation causes old LIFO layer costs to flow through cost of goods sold, sometimes with bizarre results. In this example, if Ryanes had not reduced inventory during 2002, LIFO cost of goods sold would have been $3,000 (150 units × $20 per unit). Thus, the impact of reducing inventory levels and dragging old LIFO layers into cost of goods sold is to reduce reported cost of goods sold by $800 ($3,000 – $2,200). This LIFO liquidation effect would be disclosed in the notes to the financial statements.

Drastic inventory reductions can be caused by work stoppages, a slowdown in business, or financing problems. When a company has used LIFO during a period of rising prices (as illustrated in the Ryanes example), the odd result of an unfortunate inventory reduction is that LIFO liquidation causes cost of goods sold to go down and net income to go up. The potential for this LIFO liquidation effect is one reason given in some countries for banning the use of LIFO.

INTERIM LIFO LIQUIDATION   Frequently, a company experiences a decline in inventory at an interim reporting date but fully expects to replenish the inventory by the end of the fiscal year. This would be common, for example, in any business with seasonal fluctuations in inventory levels. For companies using LIFO, temporary interim inventory reductions are *not* viewed as the liquidation of LIFO layers. To maintain the recorded historical cost of the LIFO layers, a temporary provision account is established and then reversed when the inventory is replenished.[7]

To illustrate the appropriate journal entry, assume that the LIFO liquidation for Ryanes for 2002 had actually occurred at the end of the first quarter of 2002 and that the inventory was expected to be replenished by year-end. The $800 LIFO liquidation effect would be recorded as follows:

Cost of Goods Sold	800	
Provision for Temporary Decline in LIFO Inventory		800

The provision account represents a liability to replace the inventory at a cost exceeding its recorded LIFO amount. This provision account is recorded only for interim reports; a LIFO liquidation is recorded at the end of the fiscal year whether a year-end inventory decline is temporary or not.

LIFO and Income Taxes

> **Caution!**   LIFO is the exception! In every other case, companies are not required to use the same accounting methods in the financial statements as they use for income tax purposes. Therefore, a financial accounting decision usually has no impact on income taxes payable—LIFO is the exception.

The LIFO inventory method was developed in the United States during the late 1930s as a method of reducing income taxes during periods of rising prices. However, when Congress authorized the use of LIFO for income tax purposes, a unique provision was attached to the law. This provision has become known as the **LIFO conformity rule** and specifies that only those taxpayers who use LIFO for financial reporting purposes may use it for tax purposes. LIFO is the only accounting method that must be reported the same way for tax and book purposes. In the early years, the LIFO conformity rule was strictly applied, and companies were not permitted to report inventory values using any other method, either in the body of the financial statements or in the attached notes. In 1981, the IRS regulations were relaxed by permitting companies to provide supplemental non-LIFO disclosures (such as the LIFO reserve disclosures discussed previously) as long as the information is not presented on the face of the income statement.[8]

---

7 See *Opinions of the Accounting Principles Board No. 28*, "Interim Financial Reporting," New York: American Institute of Certified Public Accountants, May 1973, par. 14b.

8 The IRS LIFO conformity relaxation went so far as to state that, as far as the IRS is concerned, companies that use LIFO for tax purposes can prepare financial statements for external users using FIFO for inventory valuation on the balance sheet provided that LIFO cost of goods sold is reported on the income statement. However, this mismatch between the balance sheet and the income statement would be a violation of U.S. GAAP.

Prior to the relaxation of the LIFO conformity rule, the income tax regulations governed the detailed application of LIFO for financial reporting purposes as well. And in fact, the IRS rules are still very important in determining how companies apply LIFO for financial reporting. However, both the SEC and the AICPA have issued guidelines outlining how proper application of LIFO for financial reporting might differ from the IRS regulations concerning LIFO.[9] The FASB has never addressed the issue of LIFO, deciding that the AICPA and SEC guidelines on the topic are sufficient.

To illustrate how LIFO reduces taxes in times of inflation, refer back to the data for Ryanes Company. For simplicity, assume that cost of goods sold is the only expense and that the tax rate is 40%. Calculation of income taxes using both LIFO and FIFO is given in Exhibit 8–14.

EXHIBIT 8–14 | Ryanes Example: Comparison of Income Taxes Using LIFO and FIFO

LIFO:

	1999		2000		2001		2002	
Sales	100 @ $10	$1,000	120 @ $15	$1,800	120 @ $20	$2,400	150 @ $25	$3,750
Cost of goods sold	100 @ $5	500	120 @ $10	1,200	120 @ $15	1,800	60 @ $20	
							40 @ $15	
							30 @ $10	
							20 @ $5	2,200
Gross profit		$ 500		$ 600		$ 600		$1,550
Income taxes (40%)		$ 200		$ 240		$ 240		$ 620

FIFO:

	1999		2000		2001		2002	
Sales	100 @ $10	$1,000	120 @ $15	$1,800	120 @ $20	$2,400	150 @ $25	$3,750
Cost of goods sold	100 @ $ 5	500	20 @ $5		50 @ $10		90 @ $15	
			100 @ $10	1,100	70 @ $15	1,550	60 @ $20	2,550
Gross profit		$ 500		$ 700		$ 850		$1,200
Income taxes (40%)		$ 200		$ 280		$ 340		$ 480

From 1999 through 2001, with prices and inventory levels rising, the use of LIFO saves a total of $140 in income taxes [($280 - $240) + ($340 - $240)]. Because sales, collections, purchases, and payments are all the same whether LIFO or FIFO is used, the only cash flow difference between using LIFO and using FIFO is in cash paid for income taxes. Therefore, by the end of 2001, Ryanes will have additional cash of $140 (from tax savings) if LIFO is used.

Note also that this cumulative tax savings is exactly equal to the LIFO reserve at the end of 2001 (computed to be $350 in the previous section) multiplied by the tax rate

9 See *Issues Paper*, "Identification and Discussion of Certain Financial Accounting and Reporting Issues Concerning LIFO Inventories," New York: American Institute of Certified Public Accountants, 1984; and Staff Accounting Bulletin (SAB) 58 (Topic 5.L), Washington, DC: Securities and Exchange Commission, March 1985.

($350 × .40 = $140). Recall that the LIFO reserve represents the difference between the value of FIFO ending inventory and the value of LIFO ending inventory. Another way to think of the LIFO reserve is that it represents an inventory holding gain—an increase in the value of inventory because of price increases. In essence, when FIFO is used, this inventory holding gain becomes taxable income as it occurs, whereas with LIFO the inventory holding gain is not taxed until the inventory is liquidated, which happens in 2002 in this example.

The inventory liquidation in 2002 also illustrates that use of LIFO for tax purposes results in tax deferral, not tax reduction. But because many companies have a low probability of liquidating their inventories in the foreseeable future, use of LIFO can defer payment of taxes on inventory holding gains for a long time.

7

Choose an inventory valuation method based on the trade-offs among income tax effects, bookkeeping costs, and the impact on the financial statements.

OVERALL COMPARISON OF FIFO, LIFO, AND AVERAGE COST

The chart in Exhibit 8-15 gives a summary comparison of the advantages and disadvantages of FIFO and LIFO. Average cost can be viewed as being somewhere between these two.

So, which inventory valuation method should a company pick? Circumstances differ from firm to firm, and the decision would be based on an analysis of the following four factors.

- Income tax effects
- Bookkeeping costs
- Impact on financial statements
- Industry comparison

EXHIBIT 8-15 | Summary Comparison of FIFO and LIFO

	FIFO	LIFO
Income Statement	**Advantage:** • Usually corresponds with the physical flow of goods. **Disadvantages:** • Can cause older costs to be matched with current revenue. • Inventory holding gains and losses are included as part of gross profit.	**Advantages:** • Matches current costs with current revenues. • Excludes inventory holding gains and losses from gross profit. **Disadvantages:** • Usually does not correspond with the physical flow of goods. • Potential LIFO liquidation means old costs in LIFO layers can be drawn in to cost of goods sold.
Balance Sheet	**Advantage:** • Ending inventory balance agrees closely with current replacement cost.	**Disadvantage:** • Ending inventory balance is composed of old costs in LIFO layers and can be substantially lower than current replacement cost. This is partially offset by supplemental disclosure.
Income Taxes	**Disadvantage:** • Yields higher taxable income in times of inflation if inventory levels are stable or increasing.	**Advantage:** • Yields lower taxable income in times of inflation if inventory levels are stable or increasing. **Disadvantage:** • LIFO liquidation can result in greatly increased tax payments when inventory levels decline.

Income Tax Effects

If a company has large inventory levels, is experiencing significant inventory cost increases, and does not anticipate reducing inventory levels in the future, LIFO gives substantial cash flow benefits in terms of tax deferral. This is the primary reason for LIFO adoption by most firms. For the many firms with small inventory levels or with flat or decreasing inventory costs, LIFO gives little, if any, tax benefit. Such firms are unlikely to use LIFO.

Bookkeeping Costs

As seen in this chapter, the bookkeeping associated with LIFO is a bit more complicated than with FIFO or average cost. In dollars and cents, a LIFO system costs more to operate. For this reason, LIFO is less common among small firms where any LIFO tax benefits can be swamped by increased bookkeeping costs. However, with improved information technology and with the simplifications of LIFO pools and dollar-value LIFO (discussed in the expanded material at the end of this chapter), the incremental LIFO bookkeeping costs can be minimized.

 How about using LIFO for the income statement and FIFO for the balance sheet? Why wouldn't this work? Or would it?

Impact on Financial Statements

While LIFO gives tax benefits, it also gives reduced reported income and reduced reported inventory. These negative financial statement effects can harm a company by scaring off stockholders, potential investors, and banks. One way around this is to provide supplemental disclosure to allow users to see what the financial statements would look like if FIFO or average cost were used.

Industry Comparison

Although financial statement users should be sophisticated in their understanding of inventory accounting, they often are not. They ignore supplemental LIFO disclosures and just compare the unadjusted numbers. If other companies in an industry use FIFO, the reported performance of a LIFO company can look poor by comparison.

Inventory Accounting Changes

When a company changes its method of valuing inventory, the change is accounted for as a change in accounting principle. If the change is to average cost or FIFO, both the beginning and ending inventories can usually be computed on the new basis. Thus, the effect of changing inventory methods can be determined and reported in the financial statements, as explained in Chapter 20. If the change is to LIFO from another method, however, a company's records are generally not complete enough to reconstruct the prior years' inventory layers. Therefore, the base-year layer for the new LIFO inventory is the opening inventory for the year in which LIFO is adopted (also the ending inventory for the year before LIFO is adopted). There is no adjustment to the financial statements to reflect the change to LIFO. However, the impact of the change on income for the current year must be disclosed in a note to the statements. In addition, the note should explain why there is no effect on the financial statements. Required disclosures for a change to LIFO are illustrated in Exhibit 8–16 in a financial statement note from the 1998 annual report of GOLDEN STATE VINTNERS, a company that processes wine for and sells grapes to many of the well-known U.S. wineries.

   When inventories are a material item, a change in the inventory method by a company may impair comparability of that company's financial statements with prior years' statements and with the financial statements of other entities. Such changes require careful consideration and should be made only when management can clearly demonstrate the preferability of the alternative method. This position is emphasized in APB Opinion

No. 20: "The burden of justifying other changes rests with the entity proposing the change."[10]

EXHIBIT 8-16 | Golden State Vintners: Disclosure of Change to LIFO Method

---

INVENTORIES

The Company changed its method of costing wine inventories effective July 1, 1995 from the first-in, first-out ("FIFO") method, to the last-in, first-out ("LIFO") method. The Company also changed to the LIFO method for brandy inventory effective July 1, 1996. Management believes that the LIFO method matches current costs with current revenues and more clearly reflects the Company's results of operations. Inventories at June 30, 1997 and 1998 would have been higher by $1,694,299 (including $519,997 for brandy inventories) and $1,928,275 (including $866,774 for brandy inventories), respectively, had the Company used FIFO cost rather than LIFO cost for valuation of its inventories. The cumulative effect of these changes to the LIFO method on the operating results as of the beginning of 1996 and 1997 and the pro forma effects on the operating results of prior years have not been presented as the effects are not readily determinable.

Analyze inventory using financial ratios, and properly compare ratios of different firms after adjusting for differences in inventory valuation methods.

USING INVENTORY INFORMATION FOR FINANCIAL ANALYSIS

The inventory balances contained in the financial statements are often used to measure how efficiently the company is utilizing its inventory. The amount of inventory carried frequently relates closely to sales volume. The inventory position and the appropriateness of its size may be evaluated by computing the **inventory turnover.** The inventory turnover is measured by dividing cost of goods sold by average inventory [(beginning balance + ending balance) ÷ 2].

Consider the financial information relating to inventories for GENERAL MOTORS provided below.

General Motors Major Classes of Inventories (Dollars in millions)		
	1998	**1997**
Productive material, work in process, and supplies................	$ 7,287	$ 7,023
Finished product, service parts, etc.	7,215	7,347
Total inventories at FIFO...	14,502	14,370
Less LIFO allowance...	2,295	2,268
Total inventories (less allowances)..............................	$ 12,207	$12,102
Cost of goods sold..	$117,973	—

The inventory turnover rate for General Motors would be computed as follows:

$$\frac{\text{Cost of goods sold}}{\text{Average inventory*}} = \frac{\$117,973}{\$12,155} = 9.71 \text{ times}$$

Calculation:
*1998: ($12,207 + $12,102)/2 = $12,155

---

10 *Opinions of the Accounting Principles Board No. 20,* "Accounting Changes," New York: American Institute of Certified Public Accountants, 1971, par. 16.

Inventory turnover of 9.71 times means that if General Motors were to completely use up all of its inventory, and then instantaneously replace it, this process would be repeated 9.71 times during the year. The higher the inventory turnover number, the faster a company is using its inventory.

Using total inventory, this example has been simplified. If separate turnovers were computed for raw materials, work in process, and finished goods, the appropriate denominators for each computation would be raw materials used in production, cost of goods manufactured, and cost of goods sold, respectively. Note that total sales is *never* appropriate to use in inventory turnover calculations because sales numbers are stated in terms of selling prices, whereas inventory is stated in terms of acquisition or production cost. For example, in a retail setting, sales is a retail number and inventory is a wholesale number. Mixing them in the same calculation seriously impairs the interpretation of the inventory turnover ratio.[11]

General Motors uses LIFO. From note disclosure about GM's LIFO reserve, FIFO values for inventory and cost of goods sold can be calculated. If General Motors had used FIFO instead of LIFO, inventory turnover for 1998 would have been 8.17 (instead of 9.71 under LIFO), computed as follows:

$$\frac{\text{FIFO cost of goods sold*}}{\text{FIFO average inventory**}} \qquad \frac{\$117,946}{\$14,436} = 8.17 \text{ times}$$

Calculations:
*$117,973 + ($2,268 − $2,295) = $117,946
** [$14,502 + $14,370]/2 = $14,436

> **Caution!** Anyone can compute and compare a bunch of financial ratios. What sets you apart from someone without an accounting background is that you can clean up the accounting numbers, making adjustments for accounting method differences, before you compute the ratios.

This calculation illustrates that the ratios of two companies that are essentially the same will differ if one uses LIFO and the other uses FIFO. In any serious comparative ratio analysis, one must first make the necessary adjustments for differences in accounting methods to ensure that the accounting numbers are comparable.

Average inventories are sometimes expressed as number of days' sales in inventories. Information is thus provided concerning the average time it takes to turn over the inventory. The **number of days' sales in inventory** is calculated by dividing average inventory by average daily cost of goods sold. The number of days' sales in inventory also can be obtained by dividing the number of days in the year by the inventory turnover rate. The latter procedure for General Motors is illustrated below, using the originally reported LIFO numbers:

Inventory turnover for the year	9.71 times
Number of days' sales in inventory (365/inventory turnover)	37.6 days

Number of days' sales in inventory of 37.6 days means that, on average, General Motors has enough inventory to continue operations for 37.6 days using just its existing inventory.

With an increased inventory turnover, the investment necessary for a given volume of business is smaller, and consequently, the return on invested capital is higher. This assumes a company can acquire goods in smaller quantities (with more frequent orders) without paying a higher price. If merchandise must be bought in very large quantities to get favorable prices, then the savings on quantity purchases must be weighed against the savings of carrying lower inventory. Inventory investments and turnover rates vary among industries, and each business must be judged in terms of its financial structure and operations. Management must establish an inventory policy that avoids the extremes

---

11 In spite of the incomparability of sales and inventory, in practice many inventory turnover calculations are done using sales. Obviously, not everyone in the financial community has studied this textbook—yet.

► AS AMERICAN AS MOM, APPLE PIE, AND LIFO

As stated in the boxed item earlier in the chapter, LIFO is an American invention. Has LIFO caught on anywhere else in the world? Well, the response has been lukewarm. In a number of countries, such as Canada, LIFO use is minimal because, although LIFO is an allowable financial reporting option, it is prohibited for tax purposes. In Germany, the tax laws were changed in 1990 to allow the use of LIFO.

Apart from any income tax implications, LIFO is widely viewed with scorn by accounting theorists all over the world. In the United Kingdom, LIFO is allowable under British corporate law but is not acceptable according to professional accounting standards. Hong Kong accounting standards have this to say about LIFO:

LIFO [is] not usually appropriate . . . because [it]

may result in stocks [i.e., inventories] being stated in the balance sheet at amounts that bear little relationship to recent cost levels. . . . [T]here may be distortion of subsequent results if stock levels reduce and out of date costs are drawn into the profit and loss account [i.e., income statement].

The International Accounting Standards Committee (IASC) has waffled on its opinion about LIFO. In its initial

of a dangerously low stock, which may impair sales, and an overstocking of goods, which involves a heavy capital investment along with risks of spoilage, obsolescence, and price declines.

Exhibit 8-17 contains a listing of the number of days' sales in inventory of several large companies for 1998. As you can see, the numbers vary widely both across and within industries.

EXHIBIT 8-17 | Number of Days' Sales in Inventory for Selected Companies, 1998

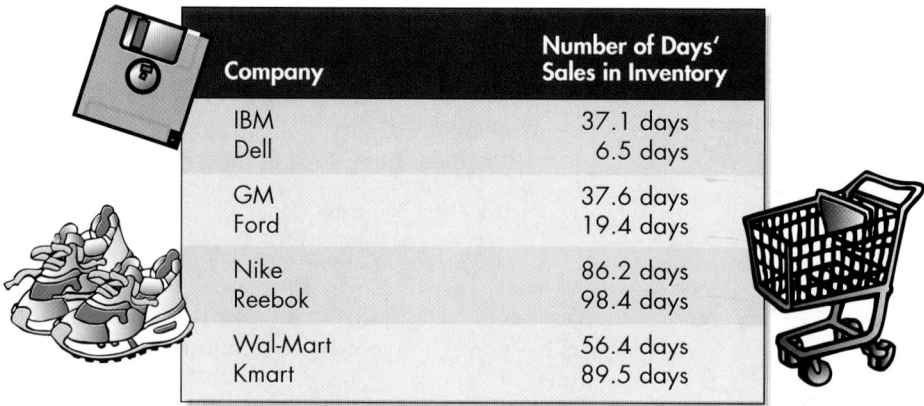

Company	Number of Days' Sales in Inventory
IBM	37.1 days
Dell	6.5 days
GM	37.6 days
Ford	19.4 days
Nike	86.2 days
Reebok	98.4 days
Wal-Mart	56.4 days
Kmart	89.5 days

E X P A N D E D   M A T E R I A L

With large and diversified inventories, application of LIFO procedures to specific goods can be extremely burdensome. In the extreme, a supermarket would have to maintain a record of several LIFO layers for each individual product—individual histories of LIFO layers for Heinz Ketchup, Wheaties, Kraft Macaroni and Cheese, and every

standard on inventory (IAS 2), the IASC identified LIFO, along with FIFO, average cost, and the base stock method, as allowable inventory valuation methods. In 1989, the IASC proposed eliminating the base stock method, and in 1991, it tentatively decided to eliminate both the base stock method and LIFO. Finally, in 1992, the IASC decided to officially endorse FIFO and average cost, to kill the base stock method, and to let LIFO live on as a second-class "allowed alternative treatment."

QUESTIONS:

1. Why are tax authorities reluctant to permit the use of LIFO?
2. The Hong Kong accounting standards claim that LIFO

can cause income statement distortion if inventory levels decline. What name is given to this phenomenon in the United States? Do you think the potential for this type of distortion is a valid reason for banning the use of LIFO for financial reporting purposes?
3. Because the IASC has now declared FIFO and average cost to be the preferred methods of inventory valuation, should LIFO be disallowed in the United States?

SOURCE:

Thomas G. Evans, Martin E. Taylor, and Oscar J. Holzmann, *International Accounting and Reporting*, 2nd ed., South-Western, Cincinnati, Ohio, 1994.

---

other product in the store. In addition, if LIFO layers are defined in terms of specific products, frequent LIFO liquidations can occur as demand for individual products declines. Two approaches have been developed to simplify the application of LIFO: LIFO pools and dollar-value LIFO.

LIFO POOLS

Use LIFO pools to simplify LIFO calculations.

As a means of simplifying the valuation process and extending its applicability to more items, the IRS developed the technique of establishing **LIFO inventory pools** of substantially identical goods. At the end of a period, the quantity of items in the pool is determined, and costs are assigned to those items. Units equal to the beginning quantity in the pool are assigned the beginning unit costs. If the number of units in ending inventory exceeds the number of beginning units, the additional units are regarded as an incremental layer within the pool.

To illustrate the formation of LIFO pools, the following data will be used for Elohar Company, a seller of fine neckties.

Beginning inventory:			
	Wide ties	1,000 units @ $10 =	$10,000
	Narrow ties	1,500 units @ $ 8 =	12,000
		2,500 units	$22,000
Purchases:			
January 16	Wide	800 units @ $13 =	$10,400
	Narrow	1,000 units @ $11 =	11,000
December 19	Wide	1,500 units @ $15 =	22,500
	Narrow	2,000 units @ $16 =	32,000
		5,300 units	$75,900
Sales:			
December 31	Wide	1,700 units	
	Narrow	3,200 units	
Ending inventory:			
	Wide	1,600 units	
	Narrow	1,300 units	

If the two types of neckties are accounted for separately, computations of LIFO ending inventory and cost of goods sold are as follows:

LIFO ending inventory:

Wide Ties			Narrow Ties	
1,000 units @ $10 =	$10,000		1,300 units @ $8 = $10,400	
600 units @ $13 =	7,800			
1,600 units	$17,800			

LIFO cost of goods sold:

	Wide Ties	Narrow Ties
Beginning inventory	$10,000	$12,000
+ Purchases	10,400	11,000
	22,500	32,000
= Cost of goods available	$42,900	$55,000
− Ending inventory	17,800	10,400
= Cost of goods sold	$25,100	$44,600

Total cost of goods sold: $25,100 + $44,600 = $69,700

Rather than account for the wide ties and narrow ties separately, they can be combined into one LIFO pool. This will simplify the accounting (as illustrated below) and also makes conceptual sense because the two types of ties form a natural business group. Similarly, a large appliance wholesaler might form a pool of all major kitchen appliances such as refrigerators, freezers, and ovens.

The data requirements for computing LIFO cost of goods sold with the two types of ties forming one LIFO pool are few. The three items below are all that are needed:

- Total beginning inventory: 2,500 units with a total cost of $22,000
- Number of units in the new LIFO layer: 400 units (2,900 ending − 2,500 beginning)
- Average cost per unit of ties purchased during the year: $14.32 ($75,900/5,300 units)

LIFO ending inventory using a LIFO pool is computed as follows:

Beginning inventory	2,500 units	=	$22,000
New LIFO layer	400 units @ $14.32	=	5,728
			$27,728

LIFO cost of goods sold is then:

	LIFO Pool
Beginning inventory	$22,000
+ Purchases	75,900
= Cost of goods available	$97,900
− Ending inventory	27,728
= Cost of goods sold	$70,172

Remember that the purpose of forming LIFO pools is to simplify the LIFO calculations associated with large numbers of products. The simplification results in an estimate of what cost of goods sold would be if LIFO were applied strictly and laboriously. In this example, the LIFO pool cost of goods sold estimate ($70,172) differs from the total of the individual LIFO calculations ($69,700) because of the simplifying assumption of using the average cost of purchases to value the new LIFO layer.[12]

LIFO pooling was originally developed as part of the IRS regulations but was quickly adopted as acceptable for financial reporting as well. Although it is not necessary for companies to use the same pools for tax and financial reporting purposes, most companies do, even when the IRS regulations require more pools than might be necessary for accounting purposes.[13]

Because companies can choose to have many LIFO pools or, in the extreme, just one pool, what factors determine the choice of the optimal number of pools? Focusing on the income tax effect, the conventional wisdom is that the fewer pools, the better, with one pool being the best of all. This is because lumping all inventories together into one LIFO pool allows decreases in the inventory of one product to be offset by increases in another product, making it less likely that a LIFO liquidation will result in a sudden increase in income taxes. This conventional wisdom emphasizes avoidance of LIFO liquidations but ignores the primary purpose of LIFO, which is the deferral of income taxes in normal times. Choosing the number of pools that gives maximum tax deferral in normal times (i.e., in times of steady or rising inventory levels) requires careful analysis and depends partly on whether different categories of inventory have different rates of price change.[14]

> **Caution!** Conceptually, each LIFO pool should contain substantially identical items. In practice, there is considerable leeway for defining acceptable pools within the IRS rules.

Compute ending inventory and cost of goods sold using dollar-value LIFO.

DOLLAR-VALUE LIFO

Even the grouping of substantially identical items into quantity pools does not produce all the benefits desired from the use of LIFO. For example, technological advances and marketing developments are constantly causing specific products to be phased out and replaced by something new that fills the market niche of the old product. The music store business has seen its inventory change from vinyl albums to eight-track tapes to cassettes to CDs in the past 30 years. The accounting question is whether old LIFO layers should be liquidated whenever a new product replaces an old one. To address this question, and also to further simplify the recordkeeping associated with LIFO, the **dollar-value LIFO** inventory method was developed. Under this method, LIFO layers are determined based on total dollar changes rather than quantity changes. The dollar-value method has become the most widely used adaptation of the LIFO concept. In a survey of LIFO users, Professors J. M. Reeve and K. G. Stanga found that 95% of the 206 companies responding to their survey used some version of the dollar-value method.[15]

With dollar-value LIFO, the unit of measurement is the dollar. All goods in the inventory pool to which dollar-value LIFO is to be applied are viewed as though they are identical items. To determine if the dollar quantity of inventory has increased during the year, it is necessary to value the ending inventory in a pool at base-year prices (i.e., those in effect when LIFO was first adopted by the company) and compare the total with that at the beginning of the year, also valued at base-year prices. If the end-of-year inventory at base-year prices exceeds the beginning-of-year inventory at base-year prices, a new LIFO layer is created. If there has been a decrease, the most recent LIFO layer (or layers) is reduced.

---

12   The unit cost assigned to the items in the new layer may be based on any one of the following measurements:
• The weighted average cost of acquisitions within the period
• Actual costs of earliest acquisitions within the period (LIFO)
• Actual costs of the latest acquisitions within the period (FIFO)

13   James M. Reeve and Keith G. Stanga, "The LIFO Pooling Decision: Some Empirical Results From Accounting Practice," *Accounting Horizons*, June 1987, p. 27.

14   For a full analysis, see William R. Cron and Randall B. Hayes, "The Dollar-Value LIFO Pooling Decision: The Conventional Wisdom Is Too General," *Accounting Horizons*, December 1989, p. 57.

15   Reeve and Stanga.

Dollar-value LIFO calculations are illustrated using the same Elohar Company example from the previous section.

First, the replacement cost of ending inventory is computed using prices prevailing at the end of the period. In this example, the end-of-period prices come from the December 19 purchases. For Elohar Company, the replacement cost of ending inventory is:

Ending inventory at ending prices:

Wide ties	1,600 units @ $15	=	$24,000
Narrow ties	1,300 units @ $16	=	20,800
			$44,800

Because beginning inventory was only $22,000, it appears that there was an increase in inventory during the period, suggesting that a new LIFO layer should be added. However, the increase in inventory may be a result of price increases rather than an actual increase in the quantity of inventory. To make this determination, computation is made of what the value of beginning inventory would be at ending prices:

Beginning inventory at ending prices:

Wide ties	1,000 units @ $15	=	$15,000
Narrow ties	1,500 units @ $16	=	24,000
			$39,000

After adjusting for price increases during the year, we can see that the dollar value of inventory increased by $5,800:

Ending inventory at ending prices	$44,800
− Beginning inventory at ending prices	39,000
Dollar value of new LIFO layer, at ending prices	$ 5,800

Finally, dollar-value LIFO ending inventory is computed as follows:

Beginning inventory, at base-year prices	$22,000
New LIFO layer, at ending prices	5,800
LIFO ending inventory	$27,800

This LIFO ending inventory is then used in the computation of LIFO cost of goods sold.

To summarize, the dollar-value LIFO computations are:

1. Compute ending inventory at ending prices.
2. Compute beginning inventory at ending prices.
3. Compute the difference. An increase represents a new LIFO layer.
4. LIFO ending inventory is beginning inventory at base-year prices plus the new LIFO layer.

> **Caution!** Stop here and make sure you know what is going on. The question is which prices should be used to value the new LIFO layer. Any of the three options mentioned is acceptable, but the one most consistent with the LIFO method is the valuation of the new LIFO layer using "first purchase prices."

In the example, the new LIFO layer was valued at ending prices. This is acceptable but is somewhat inconsistent with the LIFO assumption. In fact, this approach essentially results in the new layer being valued using a FIFO assumption. Alternatively, the new LIFO layer can be valued using average prices for the period or using the prices of the first purchases of the period. The only computational difference is that "ending prices" are replaced by "first purchase prices" or "average prices" in (1) and (2) above. The computations using first purchase prices to value the new LIFO layer are given below. The first purchase made during the period was on January 16.

Ending inventory at first purchase prices:

Wide ties	1,600 units @ $13	=	$20,800
Narrow ties	1,300 units @ $11	=	14,300
			$35,100

Beginning inventory at first purchase prices:

Wide ties	1,000 units @ $13 =	$13,000
Narrow ties	1,500 units @ $11 =	16,500
		$29,500

Ending inventory at first purchase prices	$35,100
– Beginning inventory at first purchase prices	29,500
Dollar value of new LIFO layer, at first purchase prices	$ 5,600
Beginning inventory, at base-year prices	$22,000
New LIFO layer, at first purchase prices	5,600
LIFO ending inventory	$27,600

Use of an Index

The dollar-value LIFO illustration just completed required a record of base-year prices and end-of-year prices for each individual inventory item. This technique is called the **double extension** method. Imagine how messy the computations would be with several thousand products. Recall that the purpose of LIFO pools and dollar-value LIFO is to reduce the bookkeeping costs associated with LIFO. Dollar-value LIFO is greatly simplified if a price index is used in place of the double extension method.

A **price index** is simply an overall measure of how much prices have increased during the year. A common example is the Consumer Price Index (CPI). The CPI measures how much consumer prices increase in the United States during a given period. If the CPI goes from 100 to 103 during a year, we say that prices for the year increased by 3%, or in other words, inflation for the year was 3%.

A price index in the Elohar Company example can be computed by comparing beginning inventory at beginning prices to beginning inventory at ending prices:

net work exercises

The U.S. Department of Labor's Bureau of Labor Statistics provides an excellent Web site on the CPI (**stats.bls.gov/cpihome.htm**).
Net Work:
1. What is the current CPI for All Urban Consumers (CPI-U)?
2. Write a one-page paper describing how the CPI is measured and used.

Beginning inventory at ending prices:

Wide ties	1,000 units @ $15 =	$15,000
Narrow ties	1,500 units @ $16 =	24,000
		$39,000

Beginning inventory at beginning prices:

Wide ties	1,000 units @ $10 =	$10,000
Narrow ties	1,500 units @ $ 8 =	12,000
		$22,000

End-of-year price index: $39,000/$22,000 = 1.77, or 177

With the beginning-of-year index being 100, an end-of-year-index of 177 means that prices increased an average of 77% during the year.[16] This index would be used in the following work sheet to compute ending inventory for Elohar Company using dollar-value LIFO.

Inventory at End-of-Year Prices		Year-End Price Index		Inventory at Base-Year Prices	Layers in Base-Year Prices		Incremental Layer Index		Dollar-Value LIFO Cost
$44,800	÷	1.77	=	$25,311	$22,000	×	1.00	=	$22,000
					3,311	×	1.77	=	5,860
					$25,311				$27,860

16 There are three acceptable techniques for developing a price index for use with dollar-value LIFO:
1. *Double extension index.* Uses a sample of inventory items; based on cumulative price changes since the base year.
2. *Link-chain index.* Uses a sample of inventory items; based on price changes for just the current year combined with the index from the previous year.
3. *Externally published index.* Examples of this type of index are the CPI and the Producer Price Index (PPI).

This ending inventory of $27,860 differs from the $27,800 computed earlier (with the new layer valued at ending prices) only because the index is rounded at 1.77 (instead of carrying it out to 1.7727272727 . . .).

Note that the index calculations in the work sheet result in the new layer being valued at ending prices. In order to value the new layer at first purchase prices, an additional index must be computed:

Beginning inventory at first purchase prices:

Wide ties	1,000 units @ $13 =	$13,000
Narrow ties	1,500 units @ $11 =	16,500
		$29,500

First purchase price index: $29,500/$22,000 = 1.34

The first purchase price index would be used to value the new LIFO layer as follows:

Inventory at End-of-Year Prices		Year-End Price Index		Inventory at Base-Year Prices	Layers in Base-Year Prices		Incremental Layer Index		Dollar-Value LIFO Cost
$44,800	÷	1.77	=	$25,311	$22,000	×	1.00	=	$22,000
					3,311	×	1.34	=	4,437
					$25,311				$26,437

To recap, the new LIFO layer can be valued using a year-end price index, a first purchase price index, or an average price index.[17]

Multiyear Example

One more illustration of dollar-value LIFO is given below. This example illustrates how dollar-value LIFO works when LIFO layers are liquidated.

Assume the index numbers and inventories at end-of-year prices for Hsu Wholesale Co. are as follows:

Date	Year-End Price Index*	Inventory at End-of-Year Prices
December 31, 1998	1.00	$38,000
December 31, 1999	1.20	$54,000
December 31, 2000	1.32	$66,000
December 31, 2001	1.40	$56,000
December 31, 2002	1.25	$55,000

*Many published indexes appear as percentages without decimals, e.g., 100, 120, 132, 140, 125.

The work sheet in Exhibit 8–18 shows the calculation of LIFO ending inventory for Hsu for each year.

---

17 Notice that the value of $26,437 arrived at using the first purchase price index differs substantially from the $27,600 computed using the double extension method with the first purchase price. This difference comes about because the prices of the two products in this simple example do not change at the same rate and because the mix of products in ending inventory differs from that in beginning inventory. The exact cause for the difference is not important. However, it does emphasize that dollar-value LIFO is a technique for *estimating* LIFO ending inventory, and the reliability of the estimate varies depending on circumstances.

EXHIBIT 8–18 | Dollar-Value LIFO: Multiyear Example

Date	Inventory at End-of-Year Prices		Year-End Price Index		Inventory at Base-Year Prices	Layers in Base-Year Prices		Incremental Layer Index		Dollar-Value LIFO Cost
December 31, 1998	$38,000	÷	1.00	=	$38,000	$38,000	×	1.00	=	$38,000
December 31, 1999	$54,000	÷	1.20	=	$45,000	$38,000	×	1.00	=	$38,000
						7,000	×	1.20	=	8,400
						$45,000				$46,400
December 31, 2000	$66,000	÷	1.32	=	$50,000	$38,000	×	1.00	=	$38,000
						7,000	×	1.20	=	8,400
						5,000	×	1.32	=	6,600
						$50,000				$53,000
December 31, 2001	$56,000	÷	1.40	=	$40,000	$38,000	×	1.00	=	$38,000
						2,000	×	1.20	=	2,400
						$40,000				$40,400
December 31, 2002	$55,000	÷	1.25	=	$44,000	$38,000	×	1.00	=	$38,000
						2,000	×	1.20	=	2,400
						4,000	×	1.25	=	5,000
						$44,000				$45,400

The following items should be observed in the example:

- *December 31, 1999*—With an ending inventory of $45,000 in terms of base prices, the inventory has increased in 1999 by $7,000; however, the $7,000 increase is stated in terms of base-year prices and needs to be restated in terms of 1999 year-end prices which are 120% of the base level.
- *December 31, 2000*—With an ending inventory of $50,000 in terms of base prices, the inventory has increased in 2000 by another $5,000; however, the $5,000 increase is stated in terms of base-year prices and needs to be restated in terms of 2000 year-end costs which are 132% of the base level.
- *December 31, 2001*—When the ending inventory of $40,000 (expressed in base-year dollars) is compared to the beginning inventory of $50,000 (also expressed in base-year dollars), it is apparent that the inventory has been decreased by $10,000 in base-year terms. Under LIFO procedures, the decrease is assumed to take place in the most recently added layers, reducing or eliminating them. As a result, the 2000 layer, priced at $5,000 in base-year terms, is completely eliminated, and $5,000 of the $7,000 layer from 1999 is eliminated. This leaves only $2,000 of the 1999 layer, plus the base-year amount. The remaining $2,000 of the 1999 layer is multiplied by 1.20 to restate it to 1999 dollars and is added to the base-year amount to arrive at the ending inventory amount of $40,400.
- *December 31, 2002*—The ending inventory of $44,000 in terms of the base-year prices indicates an inventory increase for 2002 of $4,000. This increase requires restatement in terms of 2002 year-end prices which are 125% of the base level.

STOP & THINK In the Hsu Wholesale Co. example, are new LIFO layers valued using a FIFO assumption, a LIFO assumption, or an average cost assumption?

In some cases, the index for the first year of the LIFO layers is not 1.00. This is especially true when an externally generated index is used. When this occurs, it is simpler to convert all inventories to a base of 1.00 rather than to use the index for the initial year of the LIFO layers. The computations are done in the same manner as in the previous

example except the inventory is stated in terms of the base year of the index, not the first year of the inventory layers. To illustrate, assume the same facts as stated earlier except that the base year of the external index is 1994; in 1998, the index is 1.20; and in 1999, it is 1.44. The schedule showing the LIFO inventory computations would be modified as follows for the first two years. Note that the inventory cost is the same under either situation.

EXHIBIT 8–19 | Dollar-Value LIFO: External Indexes

Date	Inventory at End-of-Year Prices		Year-End Price Index		Inventory at Base=1.00 (1994 Prices)	Layers in Base=1.00 (1994 Prices)		Incremental Layer Index		Dollar-Value LIFO Cost
December 31, 1998	$38,000	÷	1.20	=	$31,667	$31,667	×	1.20	=	$38,000
December 31, 1999	$54,000	÷	1.44	=	$37,500	$31,667	×	1.20	=	$38,000
						5,833	×	1.44	=	8,400
						$37,500				$46,400

REVIEW OF LEARNING OBJECTIVES

1 **Define inventory for a merchandising business, and identify the different types of inventory for a manufacturing business.** For a merchandising firm, inventory is the label given to assets sold in the normal course of business. The type of items included in the inventory of a merchandising company is determined by the nature of the business, not the nature of the item. For example, a truck is a fixed asset for an overnight mail delivery company but is inventory for a truck dealership.

For a manufacturing firm, there are three types of inventory.

- Raw materials are goods obtained for use in the manufacturing process. Direct materials are incorporated directly into the manufactured product (e.g., steel in an automobile, wood in furniture) and indirect materials are used to facilitate production (e.g., lubricant for factory equipment, factory cleaning supplies).
- Work in process consists of materials only partly processed that require further work before they can be sold. The three categories of costs that go into work in process are direct materials, direct labor, and manufacturing overhead.
- Finished goods are the manufactured products awaiting sale. Upon sale, the cost of finished goods becomes cost of goods sold. A rough rule of thumb is that costs incurred inside the factory are assigned to the cost of inventory, and costs incurred outside the

factory are classified as selling, general, or administrative expenses.

2 **Explain the advantages and disadvantages of both periodic and perpetual inventory systems.** The following chart summarizes the differences between periodic and perpetual inventory systems.

Periodic	Perpetual
Inventory	
Known only after an end-of-period physical count.	Known on a day-to-day basis.
Cost of Goods Sold	
Known only after an end-of-period physical count.	Known on a day-to-day basis.
Inventory Shrinkage	
Can't be calculated.	Can be calculated by comparing inventory records with physical count.
Journal Entries	
• No entry made to record cost of goods sold until the end of the period.	• Cost of goods sold entry made in association with each sale.
• Inventory purchases debited to a temporary purchases account.	• Inventory purchases debited directly to the inventory account.
Quality of Information Vs. Cost to Operate	
Lower quality of information but less costly to operate.	Higher quality of information but more costly to operate.

3 Determine when ownership of goods in transit changes hands and what circumstances require shipped inventory to be kept on the books. With a few exceptions, goods should be included in the reported inventory of the business that owns them, regardless of the physical location of the inventory.

- *Goods in transit.* Goods shipped FOB shipping point belong to the buyer while in transit. Goods shipped FOB destination belong to the seller while in transit.
- *Goods on consignment.* Goods on consignment should be included in the consignor's inventory. The consignee does not include the goods in inventory even though the consignee has physical possession of the goods.
- *Installment sales and conditional sales.* Even though the seller may retain legal title to the inventory until the end of the installment period, the seller should remove the goods from inventory at the time of sale if successful completion of the contract is anticipated.
- *Repurchase agreements.* When the seller promises to buy back goods at a specified price at a future date, the goods should not be removed from the seller's reported inventory. In addition, a liability is recorded for the "sales" proceeds.

4 Compute total inventory acquisition cost. For purchased goods, the recorded inventory amount includes all costs related to purchase, receipt, and preparation of the goods. For manufactured inventory, cost includes direct materials, direct labor, and manufacturing overhead.

The cost of purchased inventory is summarized as follows:

```
Invoice cost plus freight, storage, and preparation cost
  −   Cash discounts
  −   Purchase returns and allowances
  =   Inventory cost
```

The two ways to account for cash discounts are the net method and the gross method. With the net method, the cost of missed discounts is reported as a separate financing expense. With the gross method, missed cash discounts are included as part of the cost of inventory.

The most difficult part of computing the cost of manufactured inventory is allocating manufacturing overhead. Traditionally, overhead allocation has been proportioned on the amount of direct labor associated with a product. An activity-based cost (ABC) system allocates overhead based on clearly identified cost drivers—characteristics of the production process known to create overhead costs.

5 Use the four basic inventory valuation methods: specific identification, average cost, FIFO, and LIFO. Inventory valuation methods allocate total inventory cost between inventory remaining and inventory sold. The four most common methods are: specific identification, average cost, first-in, first-out (FIFO), and last-in, first-out (LIFO).

- *Specific identification.* The actual physical units sold are specifically identified and their aggregate cost is reported as cost of goods sold.
- *Average cost.* The same average cost is assigned to each unit. Cost of goods sold is computed by multiplying units sold by the average cost per unit.
- *FIFO.* The units sold are assumed to be the oldest units on hand.
- *LIFO.* The units sold are assumed to be the newest units on hand.

With a perpetual inventory system, computation of average cost and LIFO is more complicated because the average cost of goods available and the identification of the newest units change with each purchase and sale. In practice, perpetual records are usually maintained on a FIFO basis and then converted to average cost or LIFO for the financial reports.

6 Explain how LIFO inventory layers are created, and describe the significance of the LIFO reserve. A LIFO inventory layer is created in each year in which purchases exceed sales. The difference between LIFO inventory value and FIFO or average cost is called the LIFO reserve.

The LIFO assumption means that all sales are made from current purchases as long as purchases are greater than or equal to sales. Thus, inventory acquired in previous years remains on the books in LIFO layers.

When inventory levels decline, inventory in LIFO layers is sold, starting with the most recently created layer. In times of rising prices, these old LIFO layer costs are lower than current replacement cost. Consequently, LIFO liquidation often results in lower cost of goods sold and higher net income.

Companies using LIFO are allowed to disclose the difference between the inventory cost in old LIFO layers and the current replacement cost (approximated by FIFO or average cost inventory). These LIFO reserve disclosures can be used to compute what cost of goods sold and ending inventory would have been if the company had used FIFO (or average cost) instead of LIFO.

The primary motivation for a company to adopt LIFO is to defer payment of income taxes on inventory holding gains.

7 **Choose an inventory valuation method based on the trade-offs among income tax effects, bookkeeping costs, and the impact on the financial statements.**

FIFO

- *Advantages:* corresponds with physical flow of goods; ending inventory balance is close to current replacement cost
- *Disadvantages:* matches older costs with current revenues; inventory holding gains and losses are part of gross profit; no income tax deferral

LIFO

- *Advantages:* matches current costs with current revenues; excludes inventory holding gains from gross profit; income tax deferral
- *Disadvantages:* does not correspond with the physical flow of goods; potential LIFO liquidation can draw old costs into cost of goods sold; ending inventory balance can be much lower than current replacement cost

The cash flow benefits of LIFO income tax deferral must be weighed against increased bookkeeping costs and poorer reported financial statement performance. For firms with small inventory levels or low inventory cost increases, the tax deferral benefits of LIFO are probably insignificant.

8 **Analyze inventory using financial ratios, and properly compare ratios of different firms after adjusting for differences in inventory valuation methods.** Inventory ratios provide information on whether the level of inventory is appropriate for the volume of sales.

Inventory turnover is computed as cost of goods sold divided by average inventory, in which average inventory is usually the simple average of beginning and ending inventory. This ratio is the number of times a business completely uses and replaces its inventory during the year.

Number of days' sales in inventory is 365 divided by inventory turnover. This ratio is the number of days a firm can continue in business without buying/manufacturing additional inventory.

These ratios can differ significantly, depending on whether a company uses FIFO, LIFO, or average cost. Use the LIFO reserve disclosures to convert a company's LIFO numbers before comparing them to another company's FIFO or average cost numbers.

9 **Use LIFO pools to simplify LIFO calculations.** Use of LIFO pools simplifies LIFO by eliminating the need to keep detailed LIFO layer information on many different products. When the quantity of items in a LIFO pool increases during a year, a new LIFO layer is added. Decreases in the quantity of some items can be offset by increases in other items, reducing the frequency of LIFO liquidations. Choosing the correct number of LIFO pools to maximize the tax deferral benefits of LIFO involves analysis of the probability of LIFO liquidation and the comparative rate of price increases for different categories of inventory.

10 **Compute ending inventory and cost of goods sold using dollar-value LIFO.** Dollar-value LIFO further simplifies LIFO bookkeeping. With dollar-value LIFO, the dollar value of inventory (instead of the physical quantity) is the basic unit of measurement.

Dollar-value LIFO is applied as follows:

- Compute the value of ending inventory using ending prices.
- Convert this value to base-year prices by dividing by the end-of-period price index.
- Compare this number to the beginning inventory (in base-year prices) to determine whether a new LIFO layer has been added.
- All LIFO layers are then converted from base-year prices using the appropriate price index from the year in which the layer was created. New layers can be valued using an end-of-period price index (a FIFO assumption), an average price index (an average cost assumption), or a first purchase price index (a LIFO assumption).

KEY TERMS

Activity-based cost (ABC) system 432

Average cost method 437

Cash discount 433

Consigned goods 431

Cost driver 432

Direct materials 426

Finished goods 427

First-in, first-out (FIFO) method 438

FOB (free on board) destination 430

FOB (free on board) shipping point 430

Gross method 434

Indirect materials 426

Inventory 425

Inventory turnover 450

Last-in, first-out (LIFO) method 438

QUESTIONS

1. What four questions are associated with the accounting for inventory?
2. GENERAL MOTORS' finished goods inventory is composed primarily of automobiles. Are automobiles always classified as "inventory" on the balance sheets of all companies? Explain.
3. What is the difference between direct materials and indirect materials?
4. (a) What are the three cost elements entering into work in process and finished goods? (b) What items enter into manufacturing overhead?
5. What is the general rule for distinguishing between inventory-related costs that should be included in the cost of inventory and those that should be expensed as incurred?
6. A campus bookstore has a computerized inventory system. Is it more likely that the system is a periodic system or a perpetual system? Explain.
7. Would you expect to find a perpetual or a periodic inventory system used in each of the following situations?
   (a) Diamond ring department of a jewelry store
   (b) Computer department of a college bookstore
   (c) Candy department of a college bookstore
   (d) Automobile dealership—new car department
   (e) Automobile dealership—parts department
   (f) Wholesale dealer of small tools
   (g) A plumbing supply house—plastic fittings department
8. How is inventory shrinkage computed under a perpetual inventory system?
9. Under what conditions are goods in transit legally reported as inventory by the (a) seller? (b) buyer?
10. How should (a) consigned goods and (b) installment sales be treated in computing year-end inventory costs?
11. What is the appropriate way to account for inventory sold under a repurchase agreement?
12. What is an activity-based cost (ABC) system?

13. (a) What are the two methods of accounting for cash discounts? (b) Which method is generally preferred? Why?
14. What objections can be raised to the use of the specific identification method?
15. What advantages are there to using the average cost method of inventory valuation?
16. Which better matches the normal physical flow of goods—FIFO or LIFO? Which better matches current costs and current revenues?
17. Why are LIFO and average cost more complicated with a perpetual inventory system than with a periodic system?
18. Under what conditions is a LIFO layer created? What is meant by "LIFO reserve"?
19. (a) What is the LIFO conformity rule? (b) How has the rule changed since it was first adopted?
20. Assume there is no change in the physical quantity of inventory for the current accounting period. During a period of rising prices, which inventory valuation method (LIFO or FIFO) will result in the greater dollar value of ending inventory? The lower payment of income taxes?
21. What kind of companies would be least likely to use LIFO? Explain.
22. Company A has an inventory turnover ratio of 8.0 times. Company B has an inventory turnover ratio of 10.0 times. Both companies are in the same industry. Which company manages its inventory more efficiently? Explain.

23. What factors should a company consider in identifying the appropriate number of dollar-value LIFO pools?

24. What are the major advantages of dollar-value LIFO?

25. Indexes are used for two different purposes in computing the cost of LIFO layers with dollar-value LIFO. Clearly distinguish between these uses and describe how the indexes are applied.

26. Identify three different indexes that can be used in valuing a new LIFO layer with dollar-value LIFO. Which index is most consistent with the LIFO assumption?

DISCUSSION CASES

CASE 8–1

SHOULD WE ADOPT LIFO?

You are the controller of the Ford Steel Co. The economy enters a period of high inflation. Although profits are higher this year than last, you realize that the cost to replace inventory is also higher. You are aware that many companies are changing to the LIFO inventory method to save taxes in the current year, but you are concerned that what goes up will eventually come down, and when prices decline, the LIFO method will result in higher taxes. Because declining prices are usually equated with economic recession, it is likely that the higher taxes will have to be paid at a time when revenues are declining.

What factors should you consider before making a change to LIFO? Based on the above considerations, what would you recommend?

CASE 8–2

WHAT IS AN INVENTORIABLE COST?

You have been hired by Midwestern Products Co. to work in its accounting department. As part of your assignment, you have been asked to review the inventory costing procedures. In the past, the company has attempted to keep its inventory as low as possible to hedge against future declines in demand. One way of doing this has been to charge off as many costs as can be justified as expenses of the current period. Sales have declined, however, and the controller wants to include as many costs in ending inventory as possible in order to report a better income figure for the current year. Your study shows that the following costs have been consistently treated as period costs for financial reporting purposes.

Depreciation of plant
Fringe payroll benefits for factory personnel
Repairs of equipment
Salaries of foremen
Warehouse rental for storage of finished products
Pension costs for factory personnel
Training program—all employees
Cafeteria costs—all employees
Interest expense
Depreciation and maintenance of fleet of delivery trucks

Which items do you suggest could be included as part of inventory costs? Evaluate the wisdom and propriety of making the suggested changes.

CASE 8–3

WHICH METHOD SHALL WE USE?

The White Wove Corporation began operations in 2002. A summary of the first quarter appears below.

	Units	Total Cost
Purchases:		
January 2	250	$23,250
February 11	100	9,500
February 20	400	38,400
March 21	200	19,600
March 27	225	22,275

Other data:

	Sales in Units	Sales Price per Unit	Operating Expenses
January	200	$140	$ 9,575
February	225	142	7,820
March	350	145	7,905

The White Wove Corporation used the LIFO perpetual inventory method and correctly computed an inventory value of $38,300 at the end of the first quarter. Management is considering changing to a FIFO costing method. They have also considered using a periodic system instead of the perpetual system presently being used. You have been hired to assist management in making the decision. What would you advise?

CASE 8–4

CAN I USE BOTH LIFO AND FIFO?

Many countries around the world do not allow use of the LIFO method. The harmonization of accounting standards across countries may require a compromise on the use of LIFO concepts. Some accountants in the United States are suggesting the use of a LIFO/FIFO system that would use LIFO on the income statement and FIFO on the balance sheet. This method would not be a cost allocation method because in most cases it would not result in a clean allocation of cost of goods available for sale into ending inventory and cost of goods sold.

What theoretical arguments can be made in favor of this hybrid LIFO/FIFO system? One practical problem that would arise from using different methods for the income statement and the balance sheet is that the balance sheet wouldn't balance. How would you suggest solving this problem?

CASE 8–5

A NEW USE FOR BRICKS

In 1989 an investigation by the U.S. Department of Justice Criminal Division uncovered a massive fraud perpetrated by top management of MINISCRIBE CORPORATION. MiniScribe manufactured and sold computer disk drives. The investigation revealed the following practices.

- Recording inventory as being sold upon shipment from the Singapore factory even though the sales terms were FOB destination
- Recording sales when inventory was transferred from one warehouse to another
- Filling a disk drive box with bricks, shipping the bricks, and recording a disk drive sale
- Placing returned defective disk drives in with the regular inventory for reshipment to another customer

  How could an external auditor detect these fraudulent practices?

SOURCE: Andy Zipser, "Cooking the Books: How Pressure to Raise Sales Led MiniScribe to Falsify Numbers," *The Wall Street Journal*, September 11, 1989, p. A1.

CASE 8–6

BUT WE DO HAVE INVENTORY, AND IT DOES HAVE PROBLEMS.

The Mountain-Top Realty Company has decided to develop the mountain area around Hitown and has purchased several plots of mountainside property. In addition, the company acts as a realtor for existing homes in the area. Greg Hatch has recently graduated from school with an accounting degree and has been hired to work as Mountain-Top's accountant. Greg's favorite topic in intermediate accounting was inventory, and he's disappointed that he works for a firm without any inventory and its related problems. Marie Bowman, sales manager, overhears Greg mentioning this to a friend at lunch. "But we do have inventory, Greg, and I think you might be surprised at how many accounting problems a realtor can have with the inventory."

1. What is the nature of Mountain-Top's inventory?
2. What problems do you think Marie was referring to?
3. Other types of companies have "different" kinds of inventory. What is the strangest kind of "inventory" you have ever heard of?

CASE 8–7

SHOULD WE ACCEPT THE BASE STOCK INVENTORY METHOD?

Caitlin George, an accounting student at Rider College, is writing a research paper on inventories. She discovers that Accounting Research Study No. 13 on inventories was issued in the 1970s by the Accounting Principles Board. As she scans the report, she is surprised to find an inventory method referred to as the "base stock" method. She had not encountered this method in her intermediate accounting textbook. The research study identifies this method as one that defines a base quantity of inventory that is carried forward from year to year at its original cost. Deficiencies in quantity at year-end are considered temporary, and replacement of the deficiency in the next period is permitted. The method was used in the late 1800s and in the first part of the 20th century. When LIFO was accepted for income tax purposes, the base stock method was specifically disallowed for income tax use because LIFO was viewed as a substitute for base stock. Similarly, it was disallowed for financial statement purposes by the Committee on Accounting Procedures. The author of the research study concludes the discussion of the base stock method by recognizing its appropriateness to some industries and urging steps to remove the prohibitions against its use. Assume you are Caitlin George and wish to include in your report a support of the base stock method. Identify the principal positive arguments for recognizing the base stock method as a legitimate cost flow assumption. What are its advantages over the LIFO method?

CASE 8–8

HOW WELL AM I REALLY DOING?

Fay Stocks sells oriental rugs. She uses the FIFO method of inventory costing. The inventory available for sale for a particular style of rug is as follows:

Inventory Date	Current Inventory	Cost
June 14	4	@ $1,200 each
June 21	3	@ $1,500 each
July 5	6	@ $1,700 each

On July 31, a wealthy customer purchases 3 rugs paying $2,600 for each. Fay immediately replaces those rugs with 3 new rugs at a cost of $2,300 apiece. In addition, Fay immediately pays income tax on the sale at a rate of 40%. (Assume that she has no other expenses.) What is Fay's net income (after taxes) from the sale of the rugs? What is Fay's net cash flow from the sale of the rugs, the payment of income taxes, and the subsequent purchase of 3 new rugs? Why is there a substantial difference between net income and cash flow? What other circumstances can lead to differences like those illustrated in this case?

CASE 8–9

ARE INVENTORY SUMMARIES ENOUGH?

Harry Monst is presenting information to the board of directors relating to this year's annual financial statements. In discussing inventory, Mr. Monst argues, "There is no need to provide detail as to the components of inventory. A summary figure is all that investors and creditors require. Why should they care if inventory is in the form of raw materials, work in process, or finished goods?" Information relating to inventory is as follows:

	(In thousands $)	
	2002	2001
Raw materials	$162	$ 92
Work in process	60	65
Finished goods	53	93
Total	$275	$250

As a stockholder, which type of disclosure would you prefer? Why? What information is contained in the detailed inventory figures that cannot be inferred from the summary inventory figure?

CASE 8–10

THE WAR IN THE GULF

In August 1990, Iraq invaded Kuwait. For gasoline distributors, this meant that the price they paid for oil in the future could increase dramatically. For consumers, the effect was more immediate. Within a week, gasoline prices had jumped by as much as 20 cents per gallon. The American public accused gasoline distributors of ripping off consumers by raising the price on gas that was purchased prior to the Gulf Crisis. Distributors countered by stating that it is replacement cost, not historical cost, that dictates selling price.

1. Assuming FIFO costing of inventory, what would be the effect of an increased selling price on the income statement of a gasoline distributor?
2. What would be the effect on the distributor's statement of cash flows as the firm replaced the inventory with more expensive petroleum products?
3. Was the American public correct in claiming that gasoline distributors used the Gulf Crisis as an opportunity to increase profits?

CASE 8–11

THE STEEL INDUSTRY'S LIFO PROBLEM

In the early 1980s, the American steel industry was experiencing severe financial troubles. An increase in foreign competition as well as advancing technology combined to contribute to the decline of industry profits. The demand for domestic steel was down, and, as a result, many firms laid off workers. However, the use of the LIFO method of accounting for inventory distorted the actual financial position of many firms as illustrated by the following simple example.

USA STEEL CO. had the following LIFO inventory layers on January 1, 1982.

Layer 1 (oldest)	6,000 tons @ $10 per ton
Layer 2	5,000 tons @ $15 per ton
Layer 3 (newest)	8,000 tons @ $25 per ton

Assume steel sold for $50 per ton in 1983 and cost $35 per ton to produce. Because of a decrease in demand for domestic steel, USA Steel shut down its production facilities and elected to sell the inventory on hand rather than produce additional inventory.

1. If USA Steel Co. sold 15,000 tons of steel during 1983, what was the gross margin in this simplified example using LIFO?
2. What was USA Steel's gross margin if the 15,000 tons of steel had been calculated at the current cost of $35 per ton?
3. Does the LIFO gross margin accurately depict the financial situation of USA Steel Co.?
4. In order for the LIFO inventory method to accurately match current costs with current revenues, what sort of inventory policy must a company have regarding its LIFO layers?

CASE 8–12

SHOULD WE SWITCH TO DOLLAR-VALUE LIFO?

The Innovative Production Co. has used the LIFO method of valuing its inventories for several years. Layers for some of the inventory items are valued at amounts one-third to one-half of the current market price. The products manufactured and marketed by the company are subject to rapid technological obsolescence, and the company is continually developing new products and phasing out old ones. As items are discontinued and their LIFO layers liquidated, the company finds its income and taxes increasing as old costs are matched against current revenues. However, because new products must be produced at higher costs, it has been difficult to maintain a positive cash flow for the company. The president of Innovative Production, having heard a competitor mention dollar-value LIFO, approaches you, the chief accountant, with the following questions: "Would this help us? What differences are there between our LIFO system and dollar-value LIFO?"

EXERCISE 8–13

IDENTIFICATION OF INVENTORY COSTS AND CATEGORIES

The records of Burtone Company contain the following cost categories. Burtone manufactures exercise equipment and iron weights.

1. Cost of materials used to repair factory equipment
2. Depreciation on the fleet of salespersons' cars
3. Cost to purchase iron
4. Salaries of the factory supervisors
5. Cost of heat, electricity, and insurance for the company office building
6. Wages of the workers who shape the iron weights
7. Property taxes on the factory building
8. Cost of oil for the factory equipment
9. Salary of the company president
10. Pension benefits of workers who repair factory equipment

For each category, indicate whether the cost is an inventory cost (I) or if it should be expensed as incurred (E). For each inventory cost, indicate whether the cost is part of direct materials (DM), direct labor (DL), or manufacturing overhead (MOH).

EXERCISE 8–14

PERPETUAL AND PERIODIC INVENTORY SYSTEMS

The following inventory information is for Debo Company.

Beginning inventory	100 units @ $10
Purchases	500 units @ $10
Ending inventory	150 units

Sales for the year totaled $6,000. All sales and purchases are on account.

1. Make the journal entries necessary to record purchases and sales during the year assuming a periodic inventory system.
2. Assume that a periodic inventory system is used. Compute cost of goods sold.
3. Assume that a perpetual inventory system is used. The perpetual records indicate that the sales of $6,000 represent 400 units with a total cost of $4,000. Make the journal entries necessary to record purchases, sales, and inventory shrinkage for the year.

EXERCISE 8–15

COMPUTING CASH EXPENDITURE FOR INVENTORY

Using the following data, compute the total cash expended for inventory in 2002.

Accounts payable:	
January 1, 2002	$200,000
December 31, 2002	450,000
Cost of goods sold—2002	900,000
Inventory balance:	
January 1, 2002	300,000
December 31, 2002	200,000

EXERCISE 8–16

PASSAGE OF TITLE

The management of Kauer Company has engaged you to assist in the preparation of year-end (December 31) financial statements. You are told that on November 30, the correct inventory level was 150,000 units. During the month of December, sales totaled 50,000 units including 25,000 units shipped on consignment to Towsey Company. A letter received from Towsey indicates that as of December 31, it had sold 20,000 units and was still trying to sell the remainder. A review of the December purchase orders to various suppliers shows the following:

Purchase Order Date	Invoice Date	Quantity in Units	Date Shipped	Date Received	Terms
12/2/01	1/3/02	10,000	1/2/02	1/3/02	FOB shipping point
12/11/01	1/3/02	8,000	12/22/01	12/24/01	FOB destination
12/13/01	1/2/02	13,000	12/28/01	1/2/02	FOB shipping point
12/23/01	12/26/01	12,000	1/2/02	1/3/02	FOB shipping point
12/28/01	1/10/02	10,000	12/31/01	1/5/02	FOB destination
12/31/01	1/10/02	15,000	1/3/02	1/6/02	FOB destination

Kauer Company uses the "passing of legal title" for inventory recognition. Compute the number of units that should be included in the year-end inventory.

EXERCISE 8–17

PASSAGE OF TITLE

The Joliet Manufacturing Company reviewed its year-end inventory and found the following items. Indicate which items should be included in the inventory balance at December 31, 2002. Give your reasons for the treatment you suggest.

(a) A packing case containing a product costing $816 was standing in the shipping room when the physical inventory was taken. It was not included in the inventory because it was marked "Hold for shipping instructions." The customer's order was dated December 18, but the case was shipped and the customer billed on January 10, 2003.

(b) Merchandise costing $625 was received on December 28, 2002, and the invoice was recorded. The invoice was in the hands of the purchasing agent; it was marked "On consignment."

(c) Merchandise received on January 6, 2003, costing $720 was entered in the purchase register on January 7. The invoice showed shipment was made FOB shipping point on December 31, 2002. Because it was not on hand during the inventory count, it was not included.

(d) A special machine, fabricated to order for a particular customer, was finished and in the shipping room on December 30. The customer was billed on that date and the machine was excluded from inventory although it was shipped January 4, 2003.

(e) Merchandise costing $2,350 was received on January 3, 2003, and the related purchase invoice was recorded January 5. The invoice showed the shipment was made on December 29, 2002, FOB destination.

(f) Merchandise costing $1,100 was sold on an installment basis on December 15. The customer took possession of the goods on that date. The merchandise was included in inventory because Joliet still holds legal title. Historical experience suggests that full payment on installment sales is received approximately 99% of the time.

(g) Goods costing $1,500 were sold and delivered on December 20. The goods were included in inventory because the sale was accompanied by a repurchase agreement requiring Joliet to buy back the inventory in February 2003.

EXERCISE 8–18

COST OF GOODS MANUFACTURED SCHEDULE

The following quarterly cost data have been accumulated for Garrison Mfg. Inc.

Raw materials—beginning inventory (Jan. 1, 2002)	100 units @ $6.00
Purchases	85 units @ $7.00
	110 units @ $7.50

Transferred 215 units of raw materials to work in process:

Work in process—beginning inventory (Jan. 1, 2002)	56 units @ $13.50
Direct labor	$2,500
Manufacturing overhead	$3,250
Work in process—ending inventory (Mar. 31, 2002)	42 units @ $13.75

Garrison uses the FIFO method for valuing raw materials inventories. Prepare a cost of goods manufactured schedule for Garrison Mfg. Inc. for the quarter ended March 31, 2002.

EXERCISE 8–19

TRADE AND CASH DISCOUNTS

Olavssen Hardware regularly buys merchandise from Dawson Suppliers. Olavssen uses the net method to record purchases and discounts. On August 15, Olavssen Hardware purchased material from Dawson Suppliers. The invoice received from Dawson showed an invoiced price of $15,536 and payment terms of 2/10, n/30. Payment was sent to Dawson Suppliers on August 28. Prepare entries to record the purchase and subsequent payment assuming a periodic inventory system. (Round to nearest dollar.)

EXERCISE 8–20

NET AND GROSS METHODS—ENTRIES

On December 3, Hakan Photography purchased inventory listed at $8,600 from Mark Photo Supply. Terms of the purchase were 3/10, n/20. Hakan Photography also purchased inventory from Erickson Wholesale on December 10 for a list price of $7,500. Terms of the purchase were 3/10, n/30. On December 16, Hakan paid both suppliers for these purchases. Hakan does not use a perpetual inventory system.

1. Give the entries to record the purchases and invoice payments assuming that (a) the net method is used, (b) the gross method is used.
2. Assume that Hakan has not paid either of the invoices at December 31. Give the year-end adjusting entry if the net method is used.

EXERCISE 8–21

RECORDING PURCHASE RETURNS

On July 23, Pultneyville Company purchased goods on account for $5,000. Pultneyville later returned defective goods costing $300.

Record the purchase and the return of the defective goods assuming (1) a periodic inventory system, and (2) a perpetual inventory system.

EXERCISE 8–22

INVENTORY COMPUTATION USING DIFFERENT COST FLOWS

The Webster Store shows the following information relating to one of its products.

Inventory, January 1	300 units	@ $17.50
Sales, January 8	200 units	
Purchases, January 10	900 units	@ $18.00
Sales, January 18	800 units	
Purchases, January 20	1,200 units	@ $19.50
Sales, January 25	1,000 units	

What are the values of ending inventory under a periodic inventory system assuming a (1) FIFO, (2) LIFO, and (3) average cost flow? (Round unit costs to 3 decimal places.)

EXERCISE 8–23

INVENTORY COMPUTATION USING DIFFERENT COST FLOWS

Richmond Corporation had the following transactions relating to Product AB during September.

Date			Units	Unit Cost
September	1	Balance on hand	500 units	$5.00
	6	Purchase	100 units	4.50
	12	Sale	300 units	
	13	Sale	200 units	
	18	Purchase	200 units	6.00
	20	Purchase	200 units	4.00
	25	Sale	200 units	

Determine the ending inventory value under each of the following costing methods:

1. FIFO (perpetual)
2. FIFO (periodic)
3. LIFO (perpetual)
4. LIFO (periodic)

EXERCISE 8–24

COMPARISON OF INVENTORY METHODS

Spearman Truck Sales sells semitrailers. The current inventory includes the following 5 semitrailers (identical except for paint color) along with purchase dates and costs:

Semitrailer #	Purchase Date	Cost
1	April 4, 2002	$64,000
2	April 12, 2002	60,000
3	April 12, 2002	60,000
4	May 3, 2002	68,000
5	May 12, 2002	68,500

On May 20, 2002, a trucking firm purchases semitrailer #3 from Spearman for $79,000.

1. Compute the gross margin on this sale assuming Spearman uses:
   (a) FIFO inventory method
   (b) LIFO inventory method
   (c) Specific identification method
2. Which inventory method do you think Spearman should use? Why?

EXERCISE 8–25

LIFO INVENTORY COMPUTATION

White Farm Supply's records for the first 3 months of its existence show purchases of Commodity Y2 as follows:

	Number of Units	Cost
August	5,500	$28,050
September	8,000	41,600
October	5,100	27,030

The inventory of Commodity Y2 at the end of October using FIFO is valued at $36,390.

1. Assuming that none of Commodity Y2 was sold during August and September, what value would be shown at the end of October if LIFO cost was assumed?
2. If White Farm uses LIFO, what disclosure could it make in its October 31 quarterly report concerning the FIFO value of inventory?

EXERCISE 8–26

INVENTORY COMPUTATION FROM INCOMPLETE RECORDS

A flood recently destroyed many of the financial records of Riboldi Manufacturing Company. Management has hired you to re-create as much financial information as possible for the month of July. You are able to find out that the company uses an average cost inventory valuation system. You also learn that Riboldi makes a physical count at the end of each month in order to determine monthly ending inventory values. By examining various documents you are able to gather the following information:

Ending inventory at July 31 .... 50,000 units
Total cost of units available for sale in July $118,800
Cost of goods sold during July $99,000
Cost of beginning inventory, July 1 .... $0.35 per unit
Gross profit on sales for July $101,000

July purchases:

Date	Units	Unit Cost
July 5	60,000	$0.40
11	50,000	0.41
15	40,000	0.42
16	50,000	0.45

You are asked to provide the following information.

1. Number of units on hand, July 1
2. Units sold during July
3. Unit cost of inventory at July 31
4. Value of inventory at July 31

EXERCISE 8–27

COMPUTATION OF BEGINNING INVENTORY FROM ENDING INVENTORY
The Killpack Company sells Product N. During a move to a new location, the inventory records for Product N were misplaced. The bookkeeper has been able to gather some information from the sales records and gives you the data shown below.

July sales:
57,200 units at $10.00

July purchases:

Date	Quantity	Unit Cost
July 5	10,000	$6.50
9	12,500	6.25
12	15,000	6.00
25	14,000	6.20

On July 31, 16,000 units were on hand with a total value of $98,800. Killpack has always used a periodic FIFO inventory costing system. Gross profit on sales for July was $205,875. Reconstruct the beginning inventory (quantity and dollar value) for the month of July.

EXERCISE 8–28

IMPACT ON PROFIT OF FAILURE TO REPLACE LIFO LAYERS
Harrison Lumber Company uses a periodic LIFO method for inventory costing. The following information relates to the plywood inventory carried by Harrison Lumber.

Plywood inventory:

Date	Quantity	LIFO Costing Layers
May 1	600 sheets	300 sheets at $8.00
		225 sheets at $11.00
		75 sheets at $13.00

Plywood purchases:

May	8	115 sheets at $14.00
	17	95 sheets at $15.00
	29	200 sheets at $14.50

All sales of plywood during May were at $20 per sheet. On May 31, there were 360 sheets of plywood in the storeroom.

1. Compute the gross profit on sales for May, as a dollar value and as a percentage of sales.
2. Assume that because of a lumber strike, Harrison Lumber is not able to purchase the May 29 order of lumber until June 10. Assuming sales remained the same, recompute the gross profit on sales for May, as a dollar value and as a percentage of sales.
3. Compare the results of (1) and (2) and explain the difference.

EXERCISE 8–29

COMPUTATION OF BEGINNING INVENTORY

A note to the financial statements of Alpine Inc. at December 31, 2002, reads as follows:

> Because of the manufacturer's production problems for our Widget Limited line, our inventories were unavoidably reduced. Under the LIFO inventory accounting method currently being used for tax and financial accounting purposes, the net effect of all the inventory changes was to increase pretax income by $900,000 over what it would have been had the inventory of Widget Limited been maintained at the normal physical levels on hand at the start of the year.

The unit purchase price of the merchandise was $20 per unit during the year. Alpine Inc. uses the periodic inventory system. Additional data concerning Alpine's inventory were as follows:

Date	Physical Count of Inventory	LIFO Cost of Inventory
January 1, 2002	400,000 units	$?
December 31, 2002	300,000 units	$2,900,000

1. What was the unit average cost for the 100,000 units sold from the beginning inventory?
2. What was the reported value for the January 1, 2002, inventory?

EXERCISE 8–30

INCOME DIFFERENCES—FIFO VS. LIFO

First-in, first-out has been used for inventory valuation by the Atwood Co. since it was organized in 1999. Using the data that follow, redetermine the net incomes for each year on the assumption of inventory valuation on the last-in, first-out basis:

	1999	2000	2001	2002
Reported net income—FIFO basis	$15,500	$ 40,000	$ 34,250	$ 44,000
Reported ending inventories—FIFO basis	61,500	102,000	126,000	120,000
Inventories—LIFO basis	56,500	75,100	95,000	105,000

EXERCISE 8–31

GROSS MARGIN DIFFERENCES—FIFO VS. LIFO

Assume the Bullock Corporation had the following purchases and sales of its single product during its first 3 years of operation.

	Purchases		Sales	
Year	Units	Unit Cost	Units	Unit Price
1	10,000	$10	8,000	$14
2	9,000	12	9,000	17
3	8,000	15	10,000	18
	27,000		27,000	

Cost of goods sold is Bullock's only expense. The income tax rate is 40%.

1. Determine the net income (after tax) for each of the 3 years assuming FIFO historical cost flow.
2. Determine the net income (after tax) for each of the 3 years assuming LIFO historical cost flow.
3. Compare the total net income over the life of the business. How do the different cost flow assumptions affect net income and cash flows over the life of the business? From a cash flow perspective, which cost flow assumption is better? Explain.

EXERCISE 8–32

INVENTORY TURNOVER

The Boise Implement Company showed the following data in its financial statements.

	2002	2001
Cost of goods sold	$1,400,000	$1,200,000
Beginning inventory	200,000	150,000
Ending inventory	350,000	250,000

1. Compute the number of days' sales in average inventory for both 2001 and 2002. What can you infer from these numbers?
2. How would you interpret the answer to (1) if this company were in the business of selling fresh fruits and vegetables? What if this company sold real estate?

EXERCISE 8–33

COMPUTING INVENTORY USING LIFO POOLS

Miller Mfg. has one LIFO pool. Information relating to the products in this pool is as follows:

Beginning inventory, January 1	60 units @ $10 each
Purchase, February 12	45 units @ $12 each
Purchase, February 28	75 units @ $18 each
Purchase, March 15	65 units @ $12.50 each
Sales for the first quarter	135 units

Compute the ending LIFO inventory value for the first quarter assuming new layers are valued based on:

1. A FIFO assumption
2. A LIFO assumption
3. An average cost assumption

EXERCISE 8–34

DOLLAR-VALUE LIFO INVENTORY METHOD

The Johnson Manufacturing Company manufactures a single product. The managers, Ron and Ken Johnson, decided on December 31, 1999, to adopt the dollar-value LIFO inventory method. The inventory value on that date using the newly adopted dollar-value LIFO method was $500,000. Additional information is as follows:

Date	Inventory at Year-End Prices	Year-End Price Index
Dec. 31, 2000	$605,000	1.10
Dec. 31, 2001	597,360	1.14
Dec. 31, 2002	700,000	1.25

Compute the inventory value at December 31 of each year using the dollar-value LIFO method, assuming incremental layers are valued at year-end prices.

EXERCISE 8–35

DOLLAR-VALUE LIFO INVENTORY METHOD

Jennifer Inc. adopted dollar-value LIFO on December 31, 1999. Data for 1999–2002 follows:

Inventory and index on the adoption date, December 31, 1999:

Dollar-value LIFO inventory	$250,000
Price index at year-end (the base year)	1.00

Inventory information in succeeding years:

	Inventory at Year-End Prices	Year-End Price Index	Average Price Index
Dec. 31, 2000	$314,720	1.12	1.04
Dec. 31, 2001	$361,800	1.20	1.14
Dec. 31, 2002	$353,822	1.27	1.20

1. Compute the inventory value at December 31 of each year under the dollar-value LIFO method, assuming new layers are valued using the average price index.
2. Compute the inventory value at December 31, 2002, assuming that dollar-value procedures were adopted at December 31, 2000, rather than in 1999. The beginning layer is the December 31, 2000 balance.

EXERCISE 8–36

COMPUTING A PRICE INDEX

On December 31, 2002, the controller of Hardman Enterprises selected 6 items to use as a representative sample of the company's inventory. Information relative to these products was compiled and summarized in the following schedule:

	Products in Sample Inventory					
	1	2	3	4	5	6
January 1, 2002, price	$24	$51	$13	$60	$102	$ 71
December 31, 2002, price	$26	$55	$17	$62	$111	$ 78
December 31, 2002, quantity	300	530	60	180	780	330

The price index on January 1, 2002, is 1.00. Compute a price index for December 31, 2002.

EXERCISE 8–37

DOLLAR-VALUE LIFO INVENTORY AND PRICE INDEXES

LaRue's Fashion Clothing Store has hired you to assist with some year-end financial data preparation. The company's accountant quit 3 weeks ago and left many items incomplete. Summary information is given below.

	2000	2001	2002
Ending inventory (Dec. 31) at beginning-of-year prices	$155,000	?	$191,500
Ending inventory at end-of-year prices	?	$188,600	?
Price index at January 1	?	?	1.775
Percentage increase in price index during year	10%	6%	?
Price index at December 31	?	1.775	1.955

Determine the data that are missing from the table. Carry each index to 3 decimal places.

PROBLEMS

PROBLEM 8–38

COMPUTING COST OF GOODS SOLD FOR A MANUFACTURING FIRM

The following information is available for Woodfield Inc.

Products in Sample Inventory			
	2002	**2001**	**2000**
Raw materials:			
Beginning inventory	$ 117	$?	$ 100
Purchases	391	382	?
Materials available to use	$?	$?	$ 450
Ending inventory	121	?	?
Raw materials used	$?	$ 390	$ 325
Direct labor	325	?	300
Manufacturing overhead	405	411	?
Total manufacturing costs	$?	$1,118	$1,025
Work in process, January 1	85	?	55
	$1,202	$?	$?
Work in process, December 31	?	85	?
Cost of goods manufactured	$?	$?	$1,005
Finished goods, January 1	?	92	87
	$1,212	$?	$?
Finished goods, December 31	?	105	?
Cost of goods sold	$1,122	$1,095	$?

Instructions: Compute the missing amounts.

PROBLEM 8–39

WHOSE INVENTORY IS IT?

Streuling Inc. is preparing its 2002 year-end financial statements. Prior to any adjustments, inventory is valued at $76,050. The following information has been found relating to certain inventory transactions.

(a) Goods valued at $11,000 are on consignment with a customer. These goods are not included in the $76,050 inventory figure.

(b) Goods costing $2,700 were received from a vendor on January 5, 2003. The related invoice was received and recorded on January 12, 2003. The goods were shipped on December 31, 2002, terms FOB shipping point.

(c) Goods costing $8,500 were shipped on December 31, 2002, and were delivered to the customer on January 2, 2003. The terms of the invoice were FOB shipping point. The goods were included in ending inventory for 2002 even though the sale was recorded in 2002.

(d) A $3,500 shipment of goods to a customer on December 31, terms FOB destination, was not included in the year-end inventory. The goods cost $2,600 and were delivered to the customer on January 8, 2003. The sale was properly recorded in 2003.

(e) An invoice for goods costing $3,500 was received and recorded as a purchase on December 31, 2002. The related goods, shipped FOB destination, were received on January 2, 2003, and thus were not included in the physical inventory.

(f) Goods valued at $6,500 are on consignment from a vendor. These goods are not included in the year-end inventory figure.

(g) A $10,500 shipment of goods to a customer on December 30, 2002, terms FOB destination, was recorded as a sale in 2002. The goods, costing $8,200 and delivered to the customer on January 6, 2003, were not included in 2002 ending inventory.

Instructions:

1. Determine the appropriate accounting treatment for each of the above items. Justify your answers.
2. Compute the proper inventory amount to be reported on Streuling Inc.'s balance sheet for the year ended December 31, 2002.
3. By how much would net income have been misstated if no adjustments were made for the above transactions? Ignore income taxes.

PROBLEM 8–40

INVENTORY COMPUTATION USING DIFFERENT COST FLOWS

The Gidewall Corporation uses Part 210 in a manufacturing process. Information as to balances on hand, purchases, and requisitions of Part 210 is given in the following table.

Date	Quantities Received	Issued	Balance	Unit Purchase Price
January 8	—	—	200	$1.55
January 29	200	—	400	1.70
February 8	—	80	320	—
March 20	—	160	160	—
July 10	150	—	310	1.75
August 18	—	110	200	—
September 6	—	75	125	—
November 14	250	—	375	2.00
December 29	—	100	275	—

Instructions: What is the closing inventory under each of the following pricing methods? (Round unit costs to 3 decimal places.)

1. Perpetual FIFO
2. Periodic FIFO
3. Perpetual LIFO
4. Periodic LIFO
5. Perpetual average
6. Periodic average

PROBLEM 8–41

INVENTORY COMPUTATION USING DIFFERENT COST FLOWS

Records of the Schwab New Products Co. show the following data relative to Product C.

March	2	Inventory	325 units at $25.50
	3	Sale	300 units at $37.50
	6	Purchase	300 units at $26.00
	13	Purchase	350 units at $27.00
	20	Sale	200 units at $35.70
	25	Purchase	50 units at $27.50
	28	Sale	125 units at $36.00

Instructions: Calculate the inventory balance and the gross profit on sales for the month on each of the following bases.

1. Perpetual FIFO
2. Periodic FIFO
3. Perpetual LIFO
4. Periodic LIFO
5. Perpetual average (Carry calculations to 4 decimal places and round to 3.)
6. Periodic average

PROBLEM 8–42

INVENTORY CALCULATIONS—LIFO AND FIFO

The Zerbel Manufacturing Co. was organized in 2000 to produce a single product. The company's production and sales records for the period 2000–2002 are summarized below.

	Units Produced		Sales	
	No. of Units	Production Costs	No. of Units	Sales Revenue
2000	340,000	$153,000	200,000	$187,000
2001	310,000	161,200	290,000	230,000
2002	270,000	153,900	260,000	221,000

All units produced in a given year are assigned the same average cost.

Instructions: Calculate the gross profit for each of the 3 years assuming that inventory values are calculated in terms of:

1. LIFO
2. FIFO

PROBLEM 8–43

COMPUTATION OF INVENTORY FROM BALANCE SHEET AND TRANSACTION DATA

A portion of the Stark Company's balance sheet appears as follows:

	December 31, 2002	December 31, 2001
Assets:		
Cash	$353,300	$100,000
Notes receivable	0	25,000
Inventory	?	199,875
Liabilities:		
Accounts payable	?	75,000

Stark Company pays for all operating expenses with cash and purchases all inventory on credit. During 2002, cash totaling $471,700 was paid on accounts payable. Operating expenses for 2002 totaled $220,000. All sales are cash sales. The inventory was restocked by purchasing 1,500 units per month and valued by using periodic FIFO. The unit cost of inventory was $32.60 during January 2002 and increased $0.10 per month during the year. Stark sells only one product. All sales are made for $50 per unit. The ending inventory for 2001 was valued at $32.50 per unit.

Instructions:

1. Compute the number of units sold during 2002.
2. Compute the December 31, 2002, accounts payable balance.
3. Compute the beginning inventory quantity.
4. Compute the ending inventory quantity and value.
5. Prepare an income statement for 2002 (including a detailed cost of goods sold section and ignoring income taxes).

PROBLEM 8–44

IMPACT OF LIFO INVENTORY SYSTEM

The Manuel Corporation sells household appliances and uses LIFO for inventory costing. The inventory contains 10 different products, and historical LIFO layers are maintained for each of them. The LIFO layers for one of the products, Easy Chef, were as follows at December 31, 2001:

2000 layer	4,000 @ $90	1991 layer	1,000 @ $75
1995 layer	3,500 @ $85	1989 layer	3,000 @ $52

Instructions:

1. What was the value of the ending inventory of Easy Chefs at December 31, 2001?
2. How did the December 31, 2001, quantity of Easy Chefs compare with the December 31, 2000, quantity?

3. What is the value of the ending inventory of Easy Chefs at December 31, 2002, if there are 11,200 units on hand?
4. How would net income in (3) be affected if, in addition to the quantity on hand, 1,250 units were in transit to Manuel Corporation at December 31, 2002? The shipment was made on December 26, 2002, terms FOB shipping point. Total invoice cost was $131,250. Ignore income taxes.

PROBLEM 8–45

CHANGE FROM FIFO TO LIFO INVENTORY

The Greenriver Manufacturing Company manufactures two products: Raft and Float. At December 31, 2001, Greenriver used the FIFO inventory method. Effective January 1, 2002, Greenriver changed to the LIFO inventory method. The cumulative effect of this change is not determinable, and as a result, the ending inventory for 2001 for which the FIFO method was used is also the beginning inventory for 2002 for the LIFO method. Any layers added during 2002 should be costed by reference to the first acquisitions of 2002.

The information below was available from Greenriver inventory records for the 2 most recent years:

	Raft		Float	
	Units	Unit Cost	Units	Unit Cost
2001 purchases:				
January 7	5,000	$4.00	22,000	$2.00
April 16	12,000	4.50		
November 8	17,000	5.00	18,500	2.50
December 13	10,000	6.00		
2002 purchases:				
February 11	3,000	7.00	23,000	3.00
May 20	8,000	7.50		
October 15	20,000	8.00		
December 23			15,500	3.50
Units on hand:				
December 31, 2001	15,000		14,500	
December 31, 2002	16,000		13,000	

Instructions: Compute the effect on net income for the year ended December 31, 2002, resulting from the change from the FIFO to the LIFO inventory method. Ignore income taxes.

PROBLEM 8–46

INVENTORY TURNOVER ANALYSIS

The following information for Valdez Industries was taken from the company's financial statements (amounts in thousands).

	2002	2001	2000	1999
Sales	$24,000	$18,000	$15,000	$12,000
Cost of goods sold	19,600	13,900	10,200	7,200
Inventory	1,400	1,200	910	750
Accounts receivable	3,900	3,600	4,100	3,200
Accounts payable	2,300	1,200	1,500	1,800
Net income	560	320	510	430

Instructions:

1. Compute the inventory turnover and the number of days' sales in inventory for the years 2000–2002. Use average inventory in your calculations.
2. Evaluate Valdez's inventory turnover trend.

PROBLEM 8–47

COMPUTATION OF LIFO INVENTORY WITH LIFO POOLS

The Bergman Company sells 3 different products. Five years ago, management adopted the LIFO inventory method and established 3 specific pools of goods. Bergman values all incremental layers of inventory at the average cost of purchases within the period. Information relating to the 3 products for the first quarter of 2002 is given below.

	Product 400	Product 401	Product 402
Purchases:			
January	1,000 @ $12.00	500 @ $25	5,000 @ $5.30
February	1,500 @ $12.50	250 @ $26	4,850 @ $5.38
March	1,200 @ $12.25	—	3,500 @ $5.45
First quarter sales (units)	2,850	775	10,750
January 1, 2002, inventory	950 @ $11.50	155 @ $24	3,760 @ $5.00

Instructions: Compute the ending inventory value for the first quarter of 2002. (Round unit inventory values to the nearest cent and final inventory values to the nearest dollar.)

PROBLEM 8–48

DOLLAR-VALUE LIFO INVENTORY METHOD

Steve's Repair Shop began operations on January 1, 1997. After discussing the matter with his accountant, Steve decided dollar-value LIFO should be used for inventory costing. Information concerning the inventory of Steve's Repair Shop is shown below.

Date	Inventory at Year-End Prices	Year-End Index
Dec. 31, 1997	$20,500	1.00
Dec. 31, 1998	34,000	1.18
Dec. 31, 1999	55,600	1.36
Dec. 31, 2000	37,800	1.14
Dec. 31, 2001	72,250	1.72
Dec. 31, 2002	53,900	2.05

Instructions: Compute the inventory value at December 31 of each year under the dollar-value LIFO inventory method, assuming incremental layers are valued using the year-end price index.

PROBLEM 8–49

DOLLAR-VALUE LIFO INVENTORY METHOD

The Mietus Company manufactures a single product. The company adopted the dollar-value LIFO inventory method on December 31, 1997. More information concerning Mietus Company is shown below.

Inventory and index on the adoption date, December 31, 1997:
Dollar-value LIFO inventory $300,900
Price index at year-end (the base year) 1.18

Inventory information in succeeding years:

Date	Inventory at Year-End Prices	Year-End Price Index	Average Price Index
Dec. 31, 1998	$369,600	1.320	1.240
Dec. 31, 1999	420,206	1.420	1.368
Dec. 31, 2000	435,095	1.505	1.452
Dec. 31, 2001	417,073	1.543	1.515
Dec. 31, 2002	451,627	1.588	1.552

Instructions: Compute the inventory value at December 31 of each year under the dollar-value LIFO inventory method. New LIFO layers are valued using the average price index for the year.

PROBLEM 8–50   **LIFO INVENTORY POOLS—UNIT LIFO**

On January 1, 1998, Nolder Company changed its inventory cost flow method from FIFO to LIFO for its raw materials inventory. The change was made for both financial statement and income tax reporting purposes. Nolder uses the multiple-pools approach under which substantially identical raw materials are grouped into LIFO inventory pools; weighted average costs are used in valuing annual incremental layers. The composition of the December 31, 2000, inventory for the Class F inventory pool is as follows:

	Units	Weighted Average Units Cost	Total Cost
Base year inventory—1998	9,000	$10.00	$ 90,000
Incremental layer—1999	3,000	11.00	33,000
Incremental layer—2000	2,000	12.50	25,000
Inventory, December 31, 2000	14,000		$148,000

Inventory transactions for the Class F inventory pool during 2001 and 2002 were as follows:

2001
Mar. 1 4,800 units were purchased at a unit cost of $13.50 for $64,800.
Sept. 1 7,200 units were purchased at a unit cost of $14.00 for $100,800.

During 2001, 15,000 units were used for production.

2002
Jan. 10 7,500 units were purchased at a unit cost of $14.50 for $108,750.
May 15 5,500 units were purchased at a unit cost of $15.50 for $85,250.
Dec. 29 7,000 units were purchased at a unit cost of $16.00 for $112,000.

During 2002, 16,000 units were used for production.

Instructions:

1. Compute the inventory (unit and dollar amounts) of the Class F inventory pool at December 31, 2001.
2. Compute the cost of Class F raw materials used in production for the year ended December 31, 2001.
3. Compute the inventory (unit and dollar amounts) of the Class F inventory pool at December 31, 2002.

PROBLEM 8–51   **COMPUTING A PRICE INDEX**

Kristy's Cosmetics Supply is interested in generating price indexes for inventory. To aid in accomplishing this task, on December 31, 2002, the controller assembled information on various inventory items shown at the top of the next page. The controller indicated that 1999 is the base year.

Instructions: Compute the year-end price indexes at December 31, 2000, 2001, and 2002.

	Dec. 31, 1999	Dec. 31, 2000		Dec. 31, 2001		Dec. 31, 2002	
	Cost	Quantity	Cost	Quantity	Cost	Quantity	Cost
Bath oil	$ 8.00	2,000	$8.80				
Body lotion	4.50	1,000	4.80	1,500	$ 5.25		
Eye shadow	6.00	5,000	6.15	5,025	6.35		
Base makeup	5.50	3,000	5.70	3,200	5.90	3,500	$ 5.85
Blush	8.50	6,000	8.55	6,600	8.80	6,200	9.00
Facial cream	6.20	1,000	6.60	1,200	6.80	1,600	7.40
Carrying cases	14.00			2,000	14.80	2,200	15.75
Compacts	17.50					3,100	19.00
Mascara	3.25					5,500	3.95

PROBLEM 8–52 COMPUTING AND USING A PRICE INDEX

On December 31, 2002, Lelegren Architectural Supply took a statistical inventory of items for the sample of its inventory. The inventory revealed the following information.

	Dec. 31, 2000		Dec. 31, 2001		Dec. 31, 2002	
	Quantity	Cost	Quantity	Cost	Quantity	Cost
Pencil leads	2,000	$ 5.00	2,000	$ 5.50	2,200	$ 5.40
Masking tape	1,000	3.00	1,000	3.30	800	3.50
Pink erasers	5,000	4.00	5,000	4.40	5,500	4.75
Vellum paper	3,000	12.00	3,000	13.20	3,200	14.00
Sketch pads	6,000	8.00	6,000	8.80	5,000	9.00
Triangles	1,000	8.00	1,000	8.80	1,000	8.50
Cost of total inventory at year-end prices	$750,000		$950,000		$1,020,000	

Instructions:

1. Compute the year-end price index for Lelegren Architectural Supply at December 31, 2001, and 2002. The prices at December 31, 2000, are the base-year prices.
2. Compute the LIFO inventory at December 31, 2002. Assume the December 2000 LIFO inventory was $625,000. Incremental layers are valued using the year-end price index.

COMPETENCY ENHANCEMENT OPPORTUNITIES

▶ Deciphering Actual Financial Statements	▶ Ethical Dilemma
▶ Writing Assignment	▶ Cumulative Spreadsheet Analysis
▶ Research Project	▶ Internet Search
▶ The Debate	

Accounting is more than just doing textbook problems. This expanded competency material provides practice in critical thinking, oral and written communication, research, teamwork, and consideration of ethical issues.

▶ **DECIPHERING ACTUAL FINANCIAL STATEMENTS**

• Deciphering 8–1 (The Walt Disney Company)

The 1998 financial statements for THE WALT DISNEY COMPANY are included in Appendix A. Locate those financial statements and consider the following questions:

1. What inventory valuation method does Disney use?
2. How did the change in the level of inventory from September 1997 to September 1998 impact the statement of cash flows?
3. It isn't possible to compute the number of days' sales in inventory for Disney. Why not? Comment on the appropriateness of the level of detail presented in Disney's income statement.

• Deciphering 8–2 (Circle K)

CIRCLE K was once one of the largest convenience store chains in the United States. Circle K separated its products into two major categories: gasoline and merchandise (Twinkies, beef jerky, soda pop, etc.). Selected financial statement data for the year ended April 30, 1994, are given below. (Note: More current financial statement data are no longer available because Circle K is now a subsidiary of a larger company. See the opening scenario for Chapter 5.)

	Gasoline	Merchandise
Sales	$1,562.5 million	$1,710.3 million
Cost of goods sold	1,372.1 million	1,192.6 million
End-of-year inventory	26.6 million	93.9 million

1. Compute gross profit percentage for both gasoline and merchandise. Given these numbers, what do you think the attitude of convenience stores is toward automatic pump payment systems that eliminate the need to go into the store to pay for gas?
2. Compute inventory turnover (based on end-of-year inventory) for both gasoline and merchandise.
3. Compute number of days' sales in inventory for both gasoline and merchandise. Why do you think the number of days' sales in gasoline inventory is so much lower than for merchandise?

• Deciphering 8–3 (3M: Minnesota Mining and Manufacturing Company)

The 1998 10-K for MINNESOTA MINING AND MANUFACTURING COMPANY (3M) includes the following description of 3M's business:

> 3M's business has developed from its research and technology in coating and bonding for coated abrasives, the company's original product. Coating and bonding is the process of applying one material to another, such as abrasive granules to paper or cloth (coated abrasives), adhesives to a backing (pressure-sensitive tapes), ceramic coating to granular mineral (roofing granules), glass beads to plastic backing (reflective sheeting), and low-tack adhesives to paper (repositionable notes).

Familiar 3M products include Scotch tape and the ubiquitous Post-it notes.
Inventory data from 3M's 1998 10-K report are as follows (in millions of U.S. dollars):

	1998	1997
Cost of goods sold	$8,705	$8,580
Inventories:		
Finished goods	$1,161	$1,293
Work in process	613	605
Raw materials and supplies	445	501
Total inventories	$2,219	$2,399

1. Compute cost of goods manufactured for 1998.
2. Compute total manufacturing costs for 1998.
3. Compute number of days' sales in inventory for 1998 (use average inventory). Make the calculation using:
   a. Total inventory
   b. Finished goods inventory
4. Of the two numbers you computed in (3), which is more meaningful? Explain.

• Deciphering 8–4 (Caterpillar and Sara Lee)

SARA LEE (bakery goods and apparel) and CATERPILLAR (heavy equipment) both use the LIFO inventory valuation method. Caterpillar uses it for 90% of its inventories and Sara Lee for 19% of its inventories. Data from the 1998 10-K filings of these two companies are given below (in millions of U.S. dollars):

	Sara Lee	Caterpillar
Cost of goods sold	$12,331	$15,031
LIFO inventory, beginning	2,973	2,603
LIFO inventory, ending	2,882	2,842
LIFO reserve, beginning	32	2,067
LIFO reserve, ending	8	1,978

1. For both companies, as of the end of 1998, the existence of a LIFO reserve demonstrates that LIFO inventory is less than it would have been if FIFO had been used. For both companies, compute the ratio of LIFO inventory/FIFO inventory for 1998 ending inventory. Comment on the resulting numbers.
2. For both companies, compute what 1998 cost of goods sold would have been if FIFO had been used.
3. What might have caused Caterpillar's LIFO reserve to be so much larger than Sara Lee's?
4. If a company uses FIFO, can you use financial statement data to compute what its cost of goods sold would be using LIFO? Explain.

• Deciphering 8–5 (British Petroleum) Amoco

BRITISH PETROLEUM AMOCO (BP AMOCO) is one of the world's largest oil exploration, refining, and petrochemical firms. (British Petroleum and Amoco merged in December 1998.) The following data are adapted from BP Amoco's 1998 annual report. All numbers are in millions of U.S. dollars.

	1998	1997
Turnover (sales)	$68,304	$91,760
Replacement cost of sales (including production taxes)	56,958	75,235
Replacement cost gross profit	11,346	16,525
Stock holding gain (loss)	(1,391)	(939)
Historical cost gross profit	$ 9,955	$15,586

In the financial statement notes, BP Amoco explains that a stock holding gain is the difference between the replacement cost of inventory sold and the historical cost of inventory sold (calculated using FIFO). Replacement cost reflects the average cost of goods acquired during the year.

1. Consider the relationships among replacement cost of sales, LIFO cost of sales, and FIFO cost of sales. Estimate what BP Amoco's gross profit for 1998 and BP's gross profit for 1997 would be using FIFO. Explain your calculations.

2. Estimate what BP Amoco's gross profit for 1998 and the gross profit of BP for 1997 would be using LIFO. Explain your calculations.

▶ **WRITING ASSIGNMENT**
• **This is not the time for "just in time."**
You are the assistant controller of Duo-Therm Company and are in charge of preparation of the financial statements and tax returns. One of your colleagues, the assistant controller in charge of working capital management, has just returned from a 3-day seminar on "just-in-time" (JIT) inventory. JIT reduces inventory carrying costs by having arrangements with suppliers to deliver inventory just as it is needed for production or sale. Your colleague is excited to implement JIT, but you are concerned that not all factors are being considered. Your company has been using LIFO for about 25 years. Prepare a memo to the controller outlining why you think "just in time" might be a bad idea.

▶ **RESEARCH PROJECT**
• **Perpetual and periodic in the mall.**
Your group is to report (either orally or in writing) on your survey of the inventory practices in a local shopping mall.

Go to your favorite local shopping mall and choose 5 or 6 businesses to survey. Approach the store manager, identify yourself, briefly describe your project, and then determine the following.

- Does the business use a perpetual or a periodic inventory system? The store manager will probably not be familiar with the terms "perpetual" and "periodic," so plan to give a brief explanation.
- How often does the manager conduct a physical inventory count? During the count, is the store shut down or does business continue?
- If the store uses a computer system to register sales, how are transactions recorded when the computer goes down?

(Note: It might not be easy to find businesses that still use a periodic inventory system. In planning your survey, what type of business most likely would be still using a periodic system?)

▶ **THE DEBATE**
• **Americans, go home! And take LIFO with you!**
Use of LIFO outside the United States is quite limited. The International Accounting Standards Committee (IASC) has labeled LIFO an undesirable but "allowable" method whereas FIFO and average cost are the preferred "benchmark," according to IAS 2.

Divide your group into two teams.

- One team represents U.S. GAAP. Prepare a 2-minute oral argument seeking to persuade a foreign country's accounting standard-setting body to endorse the use of LIFO in the financial statements of companies in that country.
- The other team represents the anti-LIFO movement. This group is dedicated to the eradication of LIFO from the face of the earth. Prepare a 2-minute oral argument urging the foreign country's accounting standard setters to resist the temptation to allow LIFO.

For both teams, arguments must be based on financial accounting factors—discussion of income tax implications is not allowed.

▶ **ETHICAL DILEMMA**
• **LIFO and the strategic timing of inventory purchases.**
You have risen fast in Lam Tin Industries and are now in charge of purchasing for the entire company. Lam Tin is a privately held company, and negotiations are currently under way for Lam Tin to be acquired by Kwun Tong Company, a large publicly held firm. It is December, and the final negotiations with Kwun Tong, including the setting of the purchase price, will

take place in February after the release of Lam Tin's audited financial statements for the year ended December 31.

You are puzzling over a strange request you received earlier today from Lam Tin's vice president of finance. She visited your office and asked you to delay your normal December inventory purchases until the first week in January. You explained that this would result in a reduction of year-end inventories to less than half their normal year-end level. The vice president of finance seemed pleased with this information when she left your office.

This request seemed fishy, and you pulled out your copy of Lam Tin's annual report to check a hunch. Just as you suspected, Lam Tin has been using LIFO for many years and has built up a large LIFO reserve. If you delay the December purchases until January, Lam Tin will liquidate a large portion of its old LIFO layers, resulting in a big increase in reported profit for the year. It is possible that this artificial boost in Lam Tin's profits might increase the price offered by Kwun Tong in the purchase of Lam Tin.

Should you talk over your suspicions with the vice president of finance? with Lam Tin's independent auditors? with the negotiation team from Kwun Tong? Explain.

▶ CUMULATIVE SPREADSHEET ANALYSIS

This spreadsheet assignment is a continuation of the spreadsheet assignments given in earlier chapters. If you completed those assignments, you have a head start on this one.

Refer back to the instructions for preparing the revised financial statements for 2002 as given in (1) of the Cumulative Spreadsheet Analysis assignment in Chapter 3.

1. Skywalker wishes to prepare a *forecasted* balance sheet, a *forecasted* income statement, and a *forecasted* statement of cash flows for 2003. Use the financial statement numbers for 2002 as the basis for the forecast, along with the following additional information.
    a. Sales in 2003 are expected to increase by 40% over 2002 sales of $2,100.
    b. In 2003, Skywalker expects to acquire new property, plant, and equipment costing $240.
    c. The $480 in operating expenses reported in 2002 breaks down as follows: $15 depreciation expense, $465 other operating expenses.
    d. No new long-term debt will be acquired in 2003.
    e. No cash dividends will be paid in 2003.
    f. New short-term loans payable will be acquired in an amount sufficient to make Skywalker's current ratio in 2003 exactly equal to 2.0.
    g. Skywalker does not anticipate repurchasing any additional shares of stock during 2003.
    h. Because changes in future prices and exchange rates are impossible to predict, Skywalker's best estimate is that the balance in accumulated other comprehensive income will remain unchanged in 2003.
    i. In the absence of more detailed information, assume that the balances in the investment securities, long-term investments, other long-term assets, and intangible assets accounts will all increase at the same rate as sales (40%) in 2003.
    j. In the absence of more detailed information, assume that the balance in the other long-term liabilities account will increase at the same rate as sales (40%) in 2003.
    k. The investment securities are classified as available-for-sale securities. Accordingly, cash from the purchase and sale of these securities is classified as an investing activity.
    l. Assume that transactions impacting other long-term assets and other long-term liabilities accounts are operating activities.
    m. Cash and investment securities accounts will increase at the same rate as sales.
    n. The forecasted amount of accounts receivable in 2003 is determined using the forecasted value for the average collection period. The average collection period for 2003 is expected to be 14.08 days. To make the calculations less complex, this

value of 14.08 days is based on forecasted end-of-year accounts receivable rather than on average accounts receivable.

(Note: These forecasted statements were constructed as part of the spreadsheet assignment in Chapter 6; you can use that spreadsheet as a starting point if you have completed that assignment.)

For this exercise, add the following additional assumptions:

o. Skywalker will begin 2003 with an inventory of 918 units at a cost of $0.50 per unit. The estimated monthly purchases in 2003 are as follows:

Month of Forecasted Purchase	Estimated Units
January	200
February	200
March	200
April	300
May	300
June	400
July	200
August	200
September	200
October	600
November	1,000
December	326

The estimated purchase cost of the January units is $0.50. After that, it is expected that inflation will be quite high and that the cost per unit will increase by 2% each month. For example, the February units will cost $0.51 ($0.50 × 1.02) each; the March units will cost $0.5202 ($0.51 × 1.02) each; and so forth. In addition, assume that Skywalker uses the FIFO inventory valuation method and that the number of units expected to be sold in 2003 is 3,996.

Clearly state any additional assumptions that you make.

2. Repeat (1), assuming that Skywalker uses the LIFO inventory valuation method.
3. Which inventory valuation method, LIFO or FIFO, results in higher forecasted net income for Skywalker in 2003? Which results in higher forecasted cash from operating activities? Explain.
4. Repeat (1), (2), and (3), assuming that unit costs will increase by 3% per month rather than 2% per month. Comment on the impact that the higher rate has on the difference between the FIFO and LIFO numbers.

▶ **INTERNET SEARCH**

CATERPILLAR's Web address is www.caterpillar.com. Once you've gained access to Caterpillar's Web site, answer the following questions.

1. Who founded Caterpillar? When did Caterpillar form its joint venture with Mitsubishi?
2. Caterpillar sometimes ships goods on consignment to its dealers. Use Caterpillar's Web site to find the dealer nearest you.
3. Are Caterpillar's sales growing faster inside or outside the United States?
4. A key business indicator for Caterpillar is the quantity of inventory held by dealers. Excess inventory is a sign of a slump in sales. What does Caterpillar say about inventory levels in its most recent financial statement release?

chapter 9

Cost of Goods Sold and

In the early 1970s, Herbert Saffir and Robert Simpson developed the Saffir-Simpson damage potential scale used by the National Weather Service to assess the potential damage to be inflicted by a hurricane as it makes its way ashore. This five-point scale, ranging from "minimal" to "catastrophic," considers barometric pressure, wind speed, and water surge to predict damage. In the 20th century, only three storms have been classified as Category 5 hurricanes: the Labor Day hurricane of 1935 (before storms were named), Hurricane Camille from 1969, and Hurricane Mitch from 1998. A Category 5 hurricane is predicted to have wind speeds in excess of 155 miles per hour and is associated with the following property damage:

> Shrubs and trees blown down; considerable damage to roofs of buildings; all signs down. Very severe and extensive damage to windows and doors. Complete failure of roofs on many residences and industrial buildings. Extensive shattering of glass in windows and doors. Some complete building failures. Small buildings overturned or blown away. Complete destruction of mobile homes. Major damage to lower floors of all structures less than 15 feet above sea level within 500 yards or less of the shore. Low-lying escape routes inland cut by rising water 3 to 5 hours before hurricane center arrives. Massive evacuation of residential areas on low ground within 5 to 10 miles of shore possibly required.[1]

The damage done by these hurricanes is enormous. In 1998, for example, Hurricane Mitch, with sustained winds of 180 miles per hour and gusts of up to 200 miles per hour, stalled over Honduras and Nicaragua. The resulting flash floods and landslides caused billions of dollars in damage and the death toll was estimated to exceed 10,000 people. In addition to the tragic loss of human life, significant damage was done to homes and businesses.

In many cases, business property lost in floods or damaged by hurricanes is not covered by commercial insurance. Except for farm crops, most business inventory is not covered by flood insurance. In flood-prone areas, the insurance is expensive and hard to get; government disaster relief provides a form of backup coverage.

1

Apply the lower-of-cost-or-market (LCM) rule to reflect declines in the market value of inventory.

2

Use the gross profit method to estimate ending inventory.

3

Compute estimates of FIFO, LIFO, average cost, and lower-of-cost-or-market inventory using the retail inventory method.

4

Determine the financial statement impact of inventory recording errors.

e|m

EXPANDED MATERIAL

5

Combine the retail inventory method and dollar-value LIFO to compute ending inventory using the dollar-value LIFO retail method.

6

Account for the impact of changing prices on purchase commitments.

7

Record inventory purchase transactions denominated in foreign currencies.

---

1 The National Oceanic and Atmospheric Administration.

When an inventory casualty loss is covered by insurance, how does the insurance adjustor know how much inventory was destroyed? An unscrupulous business owner has an incentive to overstate the amount of inventory that was on hand when the disaster struck. And the claim often cannot be confirmed by physical evidence. In a flood, for example, the lost inventory has floated downstream. In the riots in Los Angeles in 1992, inventory had been burned and looted.[2]

On average, insurance companies spend about 10 cents verifying each dollar they pay out in claims. Adjustors use information from purchase invoices, bank deposits, and surviving accounting records. Inventory estimation techniques, like the gross profit and retail methods discussed in this chapter, are used to estimate the amount of missing inventory.

In addition to providing a means of determining the amount of inventory lost in a fire or flood, inventory estimation techniques are also used with periodic inventory systems to provide ending inventory estimates for preparing monthly or quarterly financial statements when a full physical inventory count is not feasible. Inventory estimates are also compared to perpetual inventory records to provide an early warning of unusual inventory shrinkage. Finally, external auditors and the IRS use inventory estimates to test the reasonableness of reported trends in cost of goods sold.

Insurance adjustors must use inventory estimation techniques to determine the value of inventory damaged or destroyed by a natural catastrophe.

2 Frederick Rose, "Adjusters Fan Out to Tackle Riot Claims," *The Wall Street Journal*, May 15, 1992, p. B1.

This chapter introduces two inventory estimation techniques—the gross profit and the retail inventory methods. The chapter also covers the valuation of inventory at the lower of cost or market. In the expanded material, dollar-value LIFO retail (the topic is even more fun than the name suggests), risk hedging for prices using purchase commitments, and foreign currency inventory transactions are discussed.

Apply the lower-of-cost-or-market (LCM) rule to reflect declines in the market value of inventory.

INVENTORY VALUATION AT OTHER THAN COST

The basic procedures for allocating total cost of goods available for sale between ending inventory and cost of goods sold were explained in the previous chapter. In some cases, these cost allocation procedures result in inventory cost that exceeds the current market value of the inventory. The following section discusses how to determine when inventory should be "written down" to reflect a decline in its market value. The section concludes with a discussion of inventory valuation when inventory is acquired in a nonmarket transaction (e.g., the return of defective merchandise) and a value must be assigned.

Lower of Cost or Market

One of the traditional concepts of accounting is conservatism, sometimes summarized as "when in doubt, recognize all unrealized losses, but don't recognize any unrealized gains." When applied to asset valuation, conservatism results in the rule of **lower of cost or market (LCM)**, meaning that assets are recorded at the lower of their cost or their market value.[3] LCM has the effect of recognizing unrealized decreases in the value of assets but not unrealized increases.[4]

In applying the lower-of-cost-or-market rule, the cost of the ending inventory, as determined under an appropriate cost allocation method, is compared with market value at the end of the period. If market is less than cost, an adjusting entry is made to record the loss and restate ending inventory at the lower value.[5]

WHAT IS "MARKET"? The term **market** in "lower of cost or market" is interpreted as meaning replacement cost, with potential adjustments for a ceiling and a floor value. **Replacement cost**, sometimes referred to as **entry cost**, includes the purchase price of the product or raw materials plus all other costs incurred in the acquisition or manufacture of goods. Replacement cost is frequently a good measure of the amount of future economic benefit embodied in inventory because declines in acquisition costs (entry cost) usually indicate a decline in selling prices (**exit value**). However, selling prices do not always respond immediately and in proportion to changes in replacement costs. Accordingly, the following ceiling and floor constraints are placed on the use of replacement cost as the measure of the market value of inventory[6]:

- **Ceiling.** The market value of inventory is not greater than the net realizable value of the inventory. Net realizable value (NRV) is equal to the estimated selling price of

---

3 Historically, investment securities, inventory, and property, plant, and equipment have all been recorded at the lower of cost or market. With the adoption of FASB Statement No. 115 in 1993, most investment securities are now recorded at their current market value whether that amount is lower or higher than cost.

4 For a time, the FASB required firms to make supplemental disclosure of the replacement cost of inventory. This requirement (FASB Statement No. 33) was a response to the high inflation of the late 1970s that frequently caused reported historical inventory cost to be much lower than current replacement cost. When inflation abated, interest in this supplemental disclosure waned and Statement No. 33 was repealed.

5 No adjustment to LIFO cost is permitted for tax purposes. Application of LCM to LIFO inventories for financial reporting purposes does not violate the "LIFO conformity" rule if IRS approval is obtained.

6 *Accounting Research and Terminology Bulletins—Final Edition, No. 43,* "Restatement and Revision of Accounting Research Bulletins," New York: American Institute of Certified Public Accountants, 1961, Ch. 4, Statement 6.

the inventory minus any normal selling costs. The reasoning behind this ceiling is that the market value of inventory could never reasonably be considered to be more than the net amount that can be received upon sale of the inventory.

- **Floor.** The market value of the inventory is not less than net realizable value minus a normal profit margin. If inventory is recorded below this floor amount, then the inventory can be sold in the future netting a return that is more than the normal profit margin.

In summary, market value of inventory is never less than the floor value, never more than the ceiling value, and is equal to replacement cost when replacement cost is between the floor and the ceiling. These relationships are summarized in Exhibit 9–1.

EXHIBIT 9–1 | Market Value Equals Replacement Cost, Constrained by the Ceiling and the Floor

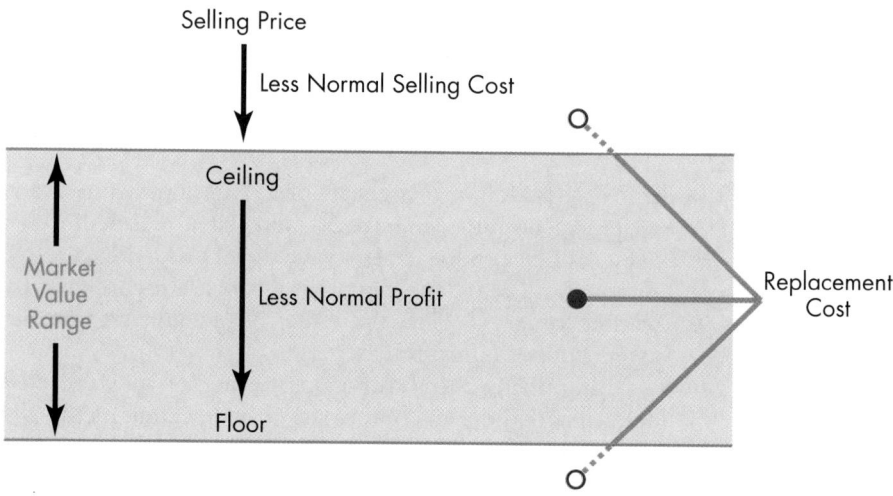

APPLYING THE LOWER-OF-COST-OR-MARKET METHOD Application of the LCM rule to determine the appropriate inventory valuation may be summarized in the following steps.

1. Define pertinent values: historical cost, floor (NRV – normal profit), replacement cost, ceiling (NRV).
2. Determine "market" (replacement cost as constrained by ceiling and floor limits).
3. Compare cost with market (as defined in step 2 above), and select the lower amount.

> **FYI:** A good way to apply the ceiling and floor rules is to remember that the market value will always be the *middle* value of these three—replacement cost and ceiling and floor amounts.

To illustrate these steps, assume that Fezzig Company sells six products identified with the letters A through F. For each product, the selling price per unit is $1, selling expenses are $0.20 per unit, and the normal profit is 25% of sales, or $0.25 per unit. The historical cost and the current replacement cost are different for each product. The lower-of-cost-or-market valuation for each product is shown on the next page with the appropriate "market" value highlighted.

For Products A and B, the replacement cost is between the floor and the ceiling, so the market value is the replacement cost. For Products C and D, replacement cost is below the floor, so the market value is the floor value. For Products E and F, replacement cost is greater than the ceiling, so the market value is the ceiling value.

To see the wisdom in using the floor and ceiling values in calculating market value, consider Products C and F. Without the floor, the market value for Product C would be $0.50 and the inventory would be written down from the cost of $0.65 to the

Item	Historical Cost	Floor	Replacement Cost	Ceiling	Market	Lower of Cost or Market
A.............	$.65	$.55	$ .70	$.80	$.70	$.65
B.............	.65	.55	.60	.80	.60	.60
C.............	.65	.55	.50	.80	.55	.55
D.............	.50	.55	.45	.80	.55	.50
E.............	.75	.55	.85	.80	.80	.75
F.............	.90	.55	1.00	.80	.80	.80

A: Market is equal to replacement cost; historical cost is less than market.
B: Market is equal to replacement cost; market is less than historical cost.
C: Market is equal to the floor; market is less than historical cost.
D: Market is equal to the floor; replacement and historical costs are less than market.
E: Market is equal to the ceiling; historical cost is less than market.
F: Market is equal to the ceiling; market is less than historical and replacement costs.

Caution! Don't get carried away—remember that an actual adjusting entry is made only if market value is less than historical cost. For Products A, D, and E, no LCM adjustment is needed.

market value of $0.50. But this $0.50 value is too low because it would result in extra profits being recorded next period when the inventory is sold. For example, selling price of $1.00 minus selling costs of $0.20 minus recorded inventory amount of $0.50 leaves a reported profit of $0.30 per unit, whereas the normal profit is just $0.25 per unit. Without the floor, Product C would be written down too much this period, resulting in unusually high profits next period.

For Product F, without the ceiling value the market value would be the $1.00 replacement cost. Because this exceeds the cost of $0.90, the inventory would continue to be recorded at cost. However, the ceiling amount suggests that the maximum that can be expected to be realized upon sale of units of Product F is the net realizable value of $0.80. In this case, the ceiling amount ensures that the inventory cost is written down so that reported inventory does not exceed the amount expected to be realized upon sale of the inventory.

The lower-of-cost-or-market method may be applied to each inventory item, to the major classes or categories of inventory items, or to the inventory as a whole. Application of LCM to the individual inventory items will result in the lowest inventory value because increases in the market value of some inventory items are not allowed to offset decreases in the value of other items.[7]

To illustrate the difference in valuation applications, assume that Fezzig Company's inventory includes 1,000 units each of Products A through F. The table on the following page illustrates how the lower-of-cost-or-market valuation of Fezzig's inventory would differ depending on whether the LCM rule is applied individually to each product or to the inventory as a whole.

If the individual product method is used, the lower-of-cost-or-market rule is applied separately to Products A through F, resulting in a total LCM inventory valuation of $3,850. If the LCM rule is applied to the inventory as a whole, the aggregate market value of $4,000 is compared to the aggregate cost of $4,100, and the inventory is recorded at $4,000.

7 The IRS requires application of the LCM rule to individual products. To reduce the burden of keeping two sets of inventory records, companies frequently use this same method for financial reporting purposes. Many disputes have arisen through the years between taxpayers and the IRS as to what constitutes a recognizable decline in inventory value. An important tax case in this area was settled by the U.S. Supreme Court in 1979. The taxpayer, THOR POWER TOOL CO., had followed the practice of writing down the value of spare parts inventories that were being held to cover future warranty requirements. Although the sales prices did not decline, the probability of the parts being sold, and thus their net realizable value, decreased as time passed. The write-down to reflect the current decline in value is consistent with the accounting principle of recognizing declines in value as they occur. The Supreme Court, however, ruled that for tax purposes the reduction must await the actual decline in the sales price for the parts in question.

Product	Number of Units	Total Cost	Total Market	Total LCM
A	1,000	$ 650	$ 700	$ 650
B	1,000	650	600	600
C	1,000	650	550	550
D	1,000	500	550	500
E	1,000	750	800	750
F	1,000	900	800	800
	6,000	$4,100	$4,000	$3,850

The journal entry to record the write-down of the inventory on an individual item basis is usually made as follows:

Loss From Decline in Value of Inventory 250
    Inventory 250
      ($4,100 – $3,850)

The loss on the decline in market value may be shown as a separate item on the income statement, or included as part of cost of goods sold. Separate reporting of the loss has the advantage of providing readers with increased information to forecast operations and cash flows. As an example, FLORSHEIM SHOES recognized an inventory write-down of $2,132,000 in 1998 in order to reduce the recorded amount of inventory in stores that it intended to close.[8]

Once an individual item is reduced to a lower market price, the new market price is considered to be the item's cost for future inventory valuations; cost reductions once made are not restored. Thus, inventory records must be adjusted to reflect the new values.

Rather than reducing the inventory directly, the inventory account can be maintained at cost, and an allowance for inventory decline can be used to record the decline in value. This method would generally be used when inventory is valued on a category or entire inventory basis. The entry to record the write-down on an entire inventory basis and using an allowance account would be as follows:

Loss From Decline in Value of Inventory 100
    Allowance for Decline in Value of Inventory 100
      ($4,100 – $4,000)

The allowance account would be reported as an offset to the inventory account on the balance sheet. The question then arises of what to do with this allowance in subsequent years. Assume that in the subsequent year, Fezzig Company sells its entire existing inventory of Products A through F. The allowance is no longer needed because the inventory to which the allowance applied has been sold. The adjusting entry necessary in the subsequent year is as follows:

Allowance for Decline in Value of Inventory 100
    Cost of Goods Sold 100

The credit is entered appropriately to Cost of Goods Sold, rather than to a gain, for the following reasons.

- The recorded cost of the old inventory sold during the year, $4,100, is an overstatement of the carrying amount of the inventory. The net carrying amount is only

8 According to Emerging Issues Task Force (EITF) 96-9, "Classification of Inventory Markdowns and Other Costs Associated with a Restructuring," inventory write-downs such as that made by Florsheim should be classified as an increase in cost of goods sold.

$4,000 ($4,100 cost minus $100 allowance), and Cost of Goods Sold has been overstated by the amount of the allowance.

- Recording a gain gives the misleading impression that recoveries of inventory market values are recognized as gains. On the contrary, once a particular inventory item or group of items is written down, no subsequent market value increases for those items are recognized.

> **Caution!** No gains are recorded on inventory market value recoveries.

The inventory at the end of the subsequent year is then evaluated to determine whether the establishment of a new Allowance for Decline in Value of Inventory is needed.[9]

Assigned Inventory Value: The Case of Returned Inventory

In some cases, the ceiling and floor values discussed provide guidance in assigning an appropriate inventory value when inventory cost is difficult to determine. As an illustration, consider the following data on defective inventory returned to Inigo Company by angry customers.

- Number of defective units returned: 1,000
- Selling price of normal units: $5
- Cost of normal units: $3
- Normal gross profit percentage: ($5 – $3)/$5 = 40%
- Scrap selling price of units returned as defective: $2
- For simplicity, assume that there are no extra expenses associated with the scrap sale of units that have been returned as defective.

In this case, it is clearly wrong to record the defective inventory units at their historical cost of $3 per unit because they can be sold for only $2 per unit. No replacement cost number can be used to determine the appropriate lower-of-cost-or-market write-down because no supplier will quote a price on entire batches of defective units. Thus, the appropriate inventory valuation is somewhere between the ceiling and the floor:

Ceiling: $2 selling price – $0 selling costs = $2 net realizable value

Floor: $2 net realizable value – $0.80 normal gross profit ($2 × 40%) = $1.20

If the inventory is written down to the ceiling value of $2, the loss on the write-down is $1,000 [($3 – $2) × 1,000 units]. If the inventory is written down to the floor value, the write-down loss is $1,800 [($3 – $1.20) × 1,000 units]. The write-down loss, and profit on subsequent scrap sale of defective units, is summarized as follows:

	Write-Down to Ceiling		Write-Down to Floor	
Loss on write-down		$(1,000)		$(1,800)
Scrap sales of defective units	$2,000		$2,000	
Cost of goods sold	2,000		1,200	
Gross profit on scrap sales		0		800
Total loss on defective units		$(1,000)		$(1,000)

In the absence of a reliable replacement cost number, should the returned inventory be recorded at the ceiling value, the floor value, or somewhere in between? Or does it make any difference? You might contend that it makes no difference because the total

---

9 The two adjusting entries eliminating the allowance from the previous year and creating a new allowance can be combined into one entry that merely changes the net balance in the allowance account. However, making the two entries separately greatly clarifies the reasoning underlying the entries.

FYI: These same issues arise when assigning values to used items given in trade for new items. For example, how does a car dealer value the used car inventory accepted in trade for new cars?

loss on defective units is $1,000 in all cases. However, if you are the manager in charge of scrap sales and your annual bonus is based on the profit generated by your department, which inventory valuation number would you prefer? You would prefer the floor value because this lowers your cost of goods sold and allows your department to show a profit. The general point of the illustration is this: When there is some leeway in the assigning of inventory values, the assigned value can be very important in determining how profits and losses associated with the inventory are allocated among different reporting units within the business.

In summary, the absence of a reliable measure of entry values (historical cost or replacement cost) means that an inventory value must be assigned based on exit values (net realizable value and normal selling profit). The decision of what inventory value to choose within the floor-to-ceiling interval can be an interesting exercise in intra-company bargaining as managers try to set the inventory values to maximize the reported profits in their departments and push losses off to other departments. This is the same issue that arises in the context of transfer pricing (assigning inventory values to goods "sold" from one division of a company to another) and is discussed at length in courses on cost accounting.[10]

Use the gross profit method to estimate ending inventory.

GROSS PROFIT METHOD

Inventory estimation techniques are used to generate inventory values when a physical inventory count is not practical and to provide an independent check of the validity of the inventory figures generated by the accounting system. The simplest inventory estimation technique is the gross profit method. The **gross profit method** is based on the observation that the relationship between sales and cost of goods sold is usually fairly stable. The gross profit percentage [(Sales – Cost of goods sold)/ Sales] is applied to sales to estimate cost of goods sold. This cost of goods sold estimate is subtracted from the cost of goods available for sale to arrive at an estimated inventory balance.

To be useful, the gross profit percentage used must be a reliable measure of current experience. In developing a reliable rate, reference is made to past rates, and these are adjusted for changes in current circumstances. For example, the historical gross profit percentage would be adjusted if the pricing strategy has changed (e.g., because of increased competition), if the sales mix has changed, or if a different inventory valuation method has been adopted (e.g., a switch from FIFO to LIFO).

To illustrate the application of the gross profit method, consider the following information for Rugen Company.

Beginning inventory, January 1	$25,000
Sales, January 1 through January 31	50,000
Purchases, January 1 through January 31	40,000
Historical gross profit percentages:	
Last year	40%
Two years ago	37%
Three years ago	42%

Rugen wishes to prepare financial statements as of January 31 and wants to use an estimate of ending inventory rather than performing a physical inventory count. Last year's gross profit percentage of 40% is considered to be a good estimate of the current gross profit percentage.

---

10 As illustrated, assigned inventory values can determine where within a company profits and losses are reported. Imagine how important this issue is in the context of tax reporting for multinational companies. Assigned inventory values determine whether a taxable profit is reported (and taxed) in a foreign subsidiary or in the U.S. parent company.

The inventory estimate is a two-step process: An assumed gross profit percentage is used to determine estimated gross profit, which then allows computation of estimated cost of goods sold. That number is then used to estimate ending inventory.

Sales (actual)	$50,000	100%
Cost of goods sold (estimate)	30,000	60%
Gross profit (estimate)	$20,000	40%
Beginning inventory (actual)	$25,000	
+ Purchases (actual)	40,000	
= Cost of goods available for sale (actual)	$65,000	
− Ending inventory (estimate)	35,000	
= Cost of goods sold (estimate)	$30,000	

This ending inventory estimate can now be used in the January 31 financial statements or can be compared to perpetual inventory records, if they exist, or can be used as the basis of an insurance reimbursement if the inventory on January 31 is destroyed in an accident. This two-step process is illustrated in Exhibit 9–2.

EXHIBIT 9–2 | The Gross Profit Method

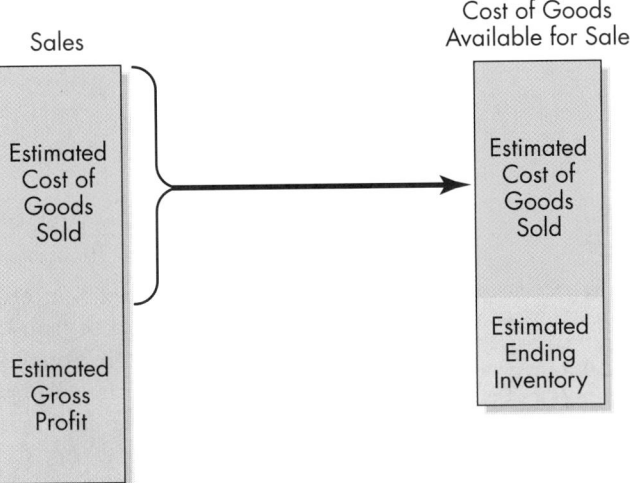

Assume that Rugen does a physical inventory count indicating that January 31 inventory is $32,000, compared to the $35,000 estimate computed above. Is this a reasonable difference, or is there reason for further investigation? One way to make this determination is to see what range of ending inventory estimates is possible given the differences observed in historical gross profit percentages. These calculations are given on the following page.

The range of estimates for January 31 inventory is from $33,500 to $36,000. The $32,000 value derived from the physical count is outside this range. Possible explanations are:

- This year's gross profit percentage is outside the historically observed range, suggesting that there has been a significant change in pricing strategy or product mix.
- Inventory shrinkage has occurred.
- Sales have been underreported. The IRS sometimes uses the gross profit method to detect underreporting of sales to avoid income taxes.

	Gross Profit Percentage		
	40%	37%	42%
Sales (actual)	$50,000	$50,000	$50,000
Cost of goods sold (estimate)	30,000	31,500	29,000
Gross profit (estimate)	$20,000	$18,500	$21,000
Beginning inventory (actual)	$25,000	$25,000	$25,000
+ Purchases (actual)	40,000	40,000	40,000
= Cost of goods available for sale (actual)	$65,000	$65,000	$65,000
− Ending inventory (estimate)	35,000	33,500	36,000
= Cost of goods sold (estimate)	$30,000	$31,500	$29,000

 STOP & THINK How exactly can inventory estimates be used to detect underreported sales?

Sometimes the hardest part of applying the gross profit method is deciphering language about the relationship between sales and cost of goods sold. In the example just completed, the sales/cost of goods sold relationship was summarized by saying that the gross profit percentage is 40%. The same relationship could be described in at least two other ways:

1. Sales are made at a markup of 40% of the selling price.
2. Sales are made at a markup of 66 2/3% of cost. (Gross profit/Cost = 66 2/3%)

Be careful.

RETAIL INVENTORY METHOD

3

Compute estimates of FIFO, LIFO, average cost, and lower-of-cost-or-market inventory using the retail inventory method.

The **retail inventory method** is widely employed by retail firms to arrive at reliable estimates of inventory position whenever desired. This method, like the gross profit method, permits the estimation of an inventory amount without the time and expense of taking a physical inventory or maintaining detailed perpetual inventory records. The retail inventory method is more flexible than the gross profit method in that it allows estimates to be based on FIFO, LIFO, or average cost assumptions, and it even permits estimation of lower-of-cost-or-market values. The retail inventory method also offers the advantage that when a physical inventory is actually taken for financial statement purposes, the inventory can be taken at retail and then converted to cost without reference to individual costs and invoices, thus saving time and expense.[11]

When the retail inventory method is used, records of goods purchased are maintained at two amounts—cost and retail. Computers have made it feasible to maintain cost records for the thousands of items normally included in a retail inventory. A **cost percentage** is computed by dividing the goods available for sale at cost by the goods available for sale at retail. This cost percentage can then be applied to the ending inventory at retail, an amount that can be readily calculated by subtracting sales for the period from the total goods available for sale at retail. This process is illustrated in Exhibit 9–3.

The computation of retail inventory at the end of January is illustrated with the example on the following page for Wesley Company.

The simple process illustrated on the next page is based on an average cost assumption because beginning inventory and purchases are lumped together to compute one cost percentage. FIFO and LIFO assumptions can be incorporated by computing different

---

11 The retail inventory method is acceptable for income tax purposes, provided the taxpayer maintains adequate and satisfactory records supporting inventory calculations and applies the method consistently on successive tax returns.

EXHIBIT 9-3 | The Retail Inventory Method

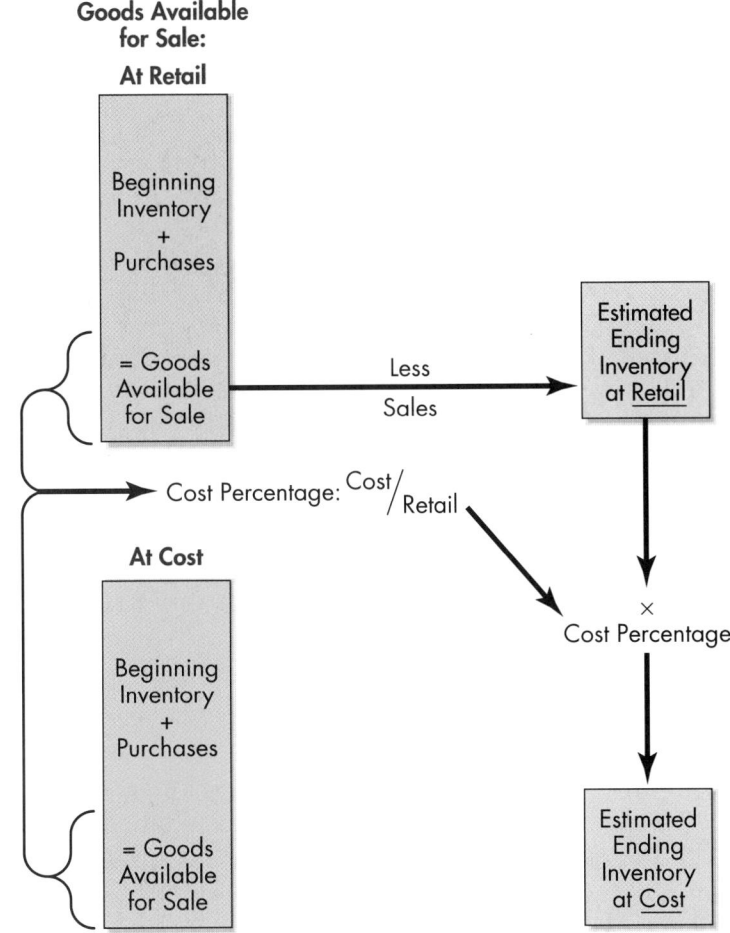

	Cost	Retail
Inventory, January 1	$30,000	$50,000
Purchases in January	30,000	40,000
Goods available for sale	$60,000	$90,000
Cost percentage ($60,000 ÷ $90,000) = 66.7%		
Deduct sales for January		65,000
Inventory, January 31, at retail		$25,000
Inventory, January 31, at estimated cost ($25,000 × 66.7%)	$16,675	

cost percentages for beginning inventory and purchases, as shown in the table on the next page.

With a FIFO assumption, the retail inventory is converted to cost using the cost percentage applicable to the most recently acquired goods (purchases). With a LIFO assumption, the retail-to-cost conversion for ending inventory is done using the old cost percentage (beginning inventory).[12]

---

12 A more complicated example of application of the retail inventory method using LIFO (with LIFO layers, changing prices, etc.) is given in the expanded material section of this chapter under the heading "Dollar-Value LIFO Retail Method."

► INVENTORY FRAUD AND INSTANT PROFITS

THE WALL STREET JOURNAL frequently reports on companies whose financial statements have been misstated through inventory manipulations. PHAR-MOR, LARIBEE WIRE, LESLIE FAY, and COMPTRONIX are a few examples that made the headlines in the 1990s because of alleged inventory fraud. Why is inventory such a common area for manipulation? The primary reason: Auditing inventory can be a difficult and complex process, so management is tempted into thinking that inventory fraud can be hidden.

For large companies, inventory is spread all across the United States. For example, Phar-Mor had over 300 stores in 30 states, yet the auditor visited only 5 stores. In the case of Laribee Wire Manufacturing Company, inventory was often transferred between plants—and recorded as inventory at each plant. Laribee's auditor did not inventory the plants simultaneously and as a result did not detect the fraud. In addition, Laribee continued carrying some copper wire inventory at its historical cost of $2.20 per pound, even after the selling price had fallen to $1.75 per pound. At apparel maker Leslie Fay, phantom inventory was created in order to lower reported cost of goods sold. A warning sign ignored by almost all outside observers was Leslie Fay's maintenance of stable reported gross profit percentages even while sales were plummeting.

	Cost	Retail
Inventory, January 1	$30,000	$50,000
Purchases in January	30,000	40,000
Goods available for sale	$60,000	$90,000
Cost percentage:		
Beginning inventory ($30,000 ÷ $50,000) = 60.0%		
Purchases ($30,000 ÷ $40,000) = 75.0%		
Deduct sales for January		65,000
Inventory, January 31, at retail		$25,000
Inventory, January 31, at estimated cost:		
FIFO ($25,000 × 75.0%)	$18,750	
LIFO ($25,000 × 60.0%)	$15,000	

Retail Inventory Method: Lower of Cost or Market

Frequently, retail prices change after they are originally set. The following terms are used to describe these changes.

- **Original retail**—the initial sales price, including the original increase over cost referred to as the **initial markup**.
- **Markups**—increases that raise sales prices above original retail.
- **Markdowns**—decreases that reduce sales prices below original retail.

To illustrate the use of these terms, assume that merchandise costing $4 a unit is marked to sell at $6, which is the original retail price. If the retail price is subsequently increased to $7.50, this represents a retail price markup of $1.50. If the goods originally marked to sell at $6 are reduced to a sales price of $5, this represents a markdown of $1.

Retail price changes can occur because of a change in pricing strategy or because of a change in the value of the underlying inventory. These two causes of retail price changes underlie two different methods of applying the retail inventory method. To illustrate, assume that, in addition to the information given earlier, Wesley Company had retail price markups of $30,000 and markdowns totaling $20,000 during the month of January.

The granddaddy of all inventory fraud cases is the famous Salad Oil Swindle. Tino DeAngelis rented a petroleum tank farm in Bayonne, New Jersey, and convinced auditors, investors, and investment bankers that the tanks contained over $100 million in valuable vegetable oil. Actually, the tanks were mainly filled with seawater. There was only a little vegetable oil, which Tino pumped from one tank to another, depending on his advance knowledge of the independent auditors' inventory verification plan. Tino was lucky that no one did any commonsense check on his inventory claims because, at one point, his Bayonne tank farm supposedly contained more vegetable oil than existed in the entire United States.

QUESTIONS:

1. How can inventory fraud create "instant profits"?
2. How does the focus on historical cost inventory valuation make it easier to perpetuate an inventory fraud?
3. In your opinion, what responsibilities should an auditor have for detecting inventory fraud?

SOURCES:

Lee Burton, "Convenient Fiction: Inventory Chicanery Tempts More Firms, Fools More Auditors," *The Wall Street Journal*, December 12, 1992, pp. A1, A5.

Lee Burton, "Audit Report Details Fraud at Leslie Fay," *The Wall Street Journal*, March 28, 1995, p. B1.

Norman C. Miller, *The Great Salad Oil Swindle*, New York: Howard McCann, 1965.

The markups and markdowns are incorporated into the retail inventory estimate as follows:

	Average Cost		Lower of Cost or Market	
	Cost	Retail	Cost	Retail
Inventory, January 1	$30,000	$ 50,000	$30,000	$ 50,000
Purchases in January	30,000	40,000	30,000	40,000
	$60,000	$ 90,000	$60,000	$ 90,000
Markups		30,000		30,000
Markdowns		(20,000)		—
		$100,000		$120,000
Cost percentage:				
Average cost: ($60,000 ÷ $100,000) = 60.0%				
Lower of cost or market: ($60,000 ÷ $120,000) = 50.0%				
Markdowns		—		(20,000)
Goods available for sale		$100,000		$100,000
Deduct sales for January		65,000		65,000
Inventory, January 31, at retail		$ 35,000		$ 35,000
Inventory, January 31, at estimated cost:				
Average cost: ($35,000 × 60.0%)	$21,000			
Lower of cost or market: ($35,000 × 50.0%)			$17,500	

Caution! The only difference between the average cost and the lower-of-cost-or-market estimates is in the treatment of markdowns.

Operationally, the simple difference between the two estimates is in when the markdowns are subtracted—before computation of the cost percentage or after. And this simple computational difference reflects the two different assumptions about the cause of markups and markdowns. Subtracting the markdowns before calculation of the cost percentage is equivalent to assuming that the markdowns result from a change in pricing strategy. Under this assumption, all markups and markdowns should be reflected in the computation of the cost percentage. The resulting calculation gives an estimate of the average cost of ending inventory.

Subtracting the markdowns after calculation of the cost percentage reflects the assumption that the markdowns are the result of a decline in the value of the inventory. As a result, markdowns do not affect the normal cost percentage but are instead reflected as a direct decline in the recorded value of inventory. This assumption yields an estimate of inventory at lower of cost or market.

The illustrations in this section demonstrate the flexibility of the retail inventory method. The retail inventory method can be used to estimate ending inventory using FIFO, LIFO, average cost, and lower of cost or market.

Freight, Discounts, Returns, and Allowances

When using the retail inventory method, the appropriate treatments for freight-in, discounts, returns, and allowances are as follows:

- Freight-in is added to the cost of purchases.
- Purchase discounts are subtracted from the cost of purchases.
- Purchase returns are subtracted from both the cost and retail amount of purchases.
- Purchase allowances are subtracted only from the cost of purchases unless a change in retail price is made as a result of the allowance.
- Sales returns are subtracted from retail sales.
- Sales discounts and sales allowances are *not* subtracted from retail sales in determining the estimated ending retail inventory. The deduction is not made because the sales price of an item is added into the computation of the retail inventory when it is purchased and deducted when it is sold, all at the gross sales price. Subsequent price adjustments included in the computation would leave a balance in the inventory account with no inventory on hand to represent it.

To illustrate the application of the rules outlined above, consider the following example. Docutron, Inc., had net purchases for the period as reported below. All inventory was sold with the exception of $4,000 in goods that were returned by the customer and subsequently returned by Docutron to the original supplier. In addition, sales discounts totaling $1,000 were taken by customers during the period. The cost percentage is determined as follows:

	Cost	Retail
Purchases	$ 50,000	$100,000
Freight-in	1,000	
Purchase discounts	(500)	
Purchase returns	(2,000)	(4,000)
Purchase allowances	(1,340)	
Goods available for sale	$ 47,160	$ 96,000
Cost percentage ($47,160 ÷ $96,000) = 49.1%		
Deduct: Sales	$100,000	
Less sales returns	4,000	96,000
Ending inventory at retail		$ 0

Because all inventory was sold during the period, ending inventory at retail is $0, as is ending inventory at cost. However, if sales discounts of $1,000 had been deducted, ending inventory at retail would have been $1,000 even though no inventory was on hand. Thus, use caution when dealing with returns, discounts, and allowances.

Retail Method With Varying Profit Margin Inventories

The calculation of a cost percentage for all goods carried in inventory is valid only when goods on hand can be regarded as representative of the total goods handled. Varying markup percentages and sales of high-margin and low-margin items in proportions that differ from purchases will require separate records and the development of separate cost percentages for different classes of goods. For example, assume that a store operates three departments and that for July the information below pertains to these departments.

Because of the range in cost percentages from 36% to 70% and the difference in mix of the purchases and ending inventory, the ending inventory balance, using an overall cost percentage, is $5,900 higher ($60,500 – $54,600) than when the departmental rates are used. When material variations exist in the cost percentages by departments, separate departmental rates should be computed and applied.

	Department A		Department B		Department C		Total	
	Cost	Retail	Cost	Retail	Cost	Retail	Cost	Retail
Beginning inventory	$20,000	$ 28,000	$10,000	$15,000	$16,000	$ 40,000	$ 46,000	$ 83,000
Net purchases	57,000	82,000	20,000	35,000	20,000	60,000	97,000	177,000
Goods available for sale	$77,000	$110,000	$30,000	$50,000	$36,000	$100,000	$143,000	$260,000
Cost percentage	70%		60%		36%		55%	
Sales		80,000		30,000		40,000		150,000
Inventory at retail		$ 30,000		$20,000		$ 60,000		$110,000
Inventory at cost		$ 21,000		$12,000		$ 21,600		$ 60,500

$54,600

EFFECTS OF ERRORS IN RECORDING INVENTORY

Determine the financial statement impact of inventory recording errors.

Failure to correctly report inventory results in misstatements on both the balance sheet and the income statement. The effect on the income statement is sometimes difficult to evaluate because of the different amounts that can be affected by an error. Analysis of the impact is aided by recalling the simple computation:

Beginning inventory
+ Purchases
= Goods available for sale
– Ending inventory
= Cost of goods sold

For example, an overstatement of the beginning inventory will result in an overstatement of goods available for sale and cost of goods sold. Because the cost of goods sold is deducted from sales to determine the gross profit, the overstated cost of goods sold results in an understated gross profit and finally an understated net income.

Sometimes an error may affect two of the amounts in such a way that they offset each other. For example, if a purchase in transit is neither recorded as a purchase nor included in the ending inventory, the understatement of purchases results in an understatement of goods available for sale; however, the understatement of ending inventory subtracted from goods available for sale offsets the error and creates a correct cost of goods sold, gross profit, and net income. Inventory and accounts payable, however, will be understated on the balance sheet.[13]

FYI: Because inventory errors reverse themselves in the following year, persons using inventory fraud to overstate income must create larger and larger amounts of fictitious inventory in succeeding years to maintain the bogus income growth. This escalation is often what causes the fraud to be detected.

---

13 This analysis is strictly true only if the FIFO inventory valuation method is used. With both LIFO and average cost, end-of-period purchases impact the calculation of cost of goods sold.

Because the ending inventory of one period becomes the beginning inventory of the next period, undetected inventory errors affect two accounting periods. If left undetected, the errors will offset each other under a FIFO or average method. Errors in LIFO layers, however, may perpetuate themselves until the layers are eliminated.

It is unwise to try to memorize the impact a particular type of inventory error has on the financial statements. It is preferable to analyze each situation. Analysis of the following three typical inventory errors provides further practice.

1. Overstatement of ending inventory through an improper physical count
2. Understatement of ending inventory through an improper physical count
3. Understatement of ending inventory through delay in recording a purchase until the following year

The impact of the three errors on the income statement and the balance sheet in the year of the error and the following year is summarized in Exhibit 9–4.

EXHIBIT 9–4 | Analysis of Inventory Errors

	#1 Overstatement of Ending Inventory		#2 Understatement of Ending Inventory		#3 Delay Recording Purchase	
	Error Year	Next Year	Error Year	Next Year	Error Year	Next Year
Beginning inventory	OK	over*	OK	under	OK	under
+ Purchases	OK	OK	OK	OK	under	over
= Goods available for sale	OK	over	OK	under	under	OK
– Ending inventory	over	OK	under	OK	under	OK
= Cost of goods sold	under	over	over	under	OK	OK
Income Statement:						
Cost of goods sold	under	over	over	under	OK	OK
Net income	over	under	under	over	OK	OK
Balance Sheet:						
Inventory	over	OK	under	OK	under	OK
Payables	OK	OK	OK	OK	under	OK
Retained earnings	over	OK	under	OK	OK	OK

*(Over) indicates overstatement, (under) indicates understatement, and (OK) indicates no effect.

STOP & THINK   Why would a manager risk his or her reputation by fraudulently overstating inventory in light of the fact that the resulting income increase is completely counterbalanced in the following year?

Error #1, overstatement of ending inventory, sometimes results when a company fraudulently manipulates its inventory count. As seen in Exhibit 9–4, this ending inventory overstatement reduces cost of goods sold and increases net income in the year of the error. A counterbalancing reduction in net income occurs in the following year because beginning inventory is overstated.

Error #2, understatement of ending inventory, is the opposite of Error #1 and results in a reduction in net income in the error year. As with Error #1, a counterbalancing error occurs in the following year.

Error #3, delay recording purchase or understatement of ending inventory and purchases, commonly occurs when a company fails to consider end-of-period goods in transit as part of purchases and inventory. As seen in Exhibit 9-4, this error has no impact on net income but does cause inventory and payables to be understated in the year of the error.

The correcting entry for each of these errors depends on when the error is discovered. If it is discovered in the current year, adjustments can be made to current accounts and the reported net income and balance sheet amounts will be correct. If the error is not discovered until the subsequent period, the correcting entry qualifies as a prior-period adjustment if the net income of the prior period was misstated. The error to a prior year's income is corrected through Retained Earnings. To illustrate these entries, assume that an incorrect physical count has resulted in an overstatement of ending inventory by $1,000 (Error #1). The correcting entry required, depending on when the error is discovered, would be as follows:

Error discovered in current year:

Cost of Goods Sold	1,000	
Inventory		1,000

Error discovered in subsequent year:

Retained Earnings	1,000	
Inventory		1,000

As an example of a recent inventory error (#1), EFI ELECTRONICS, a Salt Lake City–based manufacturer of industrial surge protection devices, was required to make a correction to its March 31, 1998, financial statements because of an error in valuing its inventories. This particular error involved a mistake in calculating the amount of overhead costs that should be added to manufactured inventory. Correction of the error caused EFI Electronics to reduce its reported inventory from $3,359,178 to $2,726,606 and to reduce its reported net income of $74,403 to a net loss of $245,751.

REQUIRED DISCLOSURES RELATED TO INVENTORIES

The balance sheet typically contains a single amount for a firm's inventory. For a manufacturing firm, the breakdown of inventory into raw materials, work in process, and finished goods is detailed in the financial statement notes. Merchandising firms also sometimes provide note disclosure of the quantities of major classes of inventory. The basis of valuation (such as cost or lower of cost or market), together with the inventory valuation method (LIFO, FIFO, average, or other method), must be disclosed either in a parenthetical note in the balance sheet or in the accompanying notes. A special note is included when a firm changes its valuation method. This note describes the change, the reason for the change, and the quantitative effect of the change on the financial statements.

The amount of write-downs of inventory to lower of cost or market is also disclosed in the notes. If such write-downs are material, the amount of the write-down should not be included in cost of goods sold but instead listed as a separate item in the income statement. If significant inventory price declines take place between the balance sheet date and the date the financial statements are issued, no adjustment of the financial statements is needed, but the declines should be disclosed as a subsequent event.

When inventories have been pledged as security on loans from banks, finance companies, or factors, the amounts pledged should be disclosed either parenthetically in the inventory section of the balance sheet or in the notes.

EXPANDED MATERIAL

The expanded material includes coverage of dollar-value LIFO retail, purchase commitments, and foreign currency transactions. The dollar-value LIFO retail method is the method most often used by retail companies for applying LIFO. The accounting for purchase commitments involves an interesting application of the lower-of-cost-or-market rule. The coverage of foreign currency transactions illustrates how movements in foreign exchange rates can cause gains or losses on inventory purchases transactions.

Combine the retail inventory method and dollar-value LIFO to compute ending inventory using the dollar-value LIFO retail method.

DOLLAR-VALUE LIFO RETAIL METHOD

The dollar-value LIFO procedures described in Chapter 8 can be combined with the retail inventory method described earlier in this chapter in developing LIFO inventory values.[14] With the **dollar-value LIFO retail method**, LIFO layers are stated in terms of retail values. After the LIFO retail layers have been identified and priced using a price index, a further adjustment is needed to state the inventory at cost. This is done by multiplying the retail inventory of each layer by the appropriate cost percentage.

Two things to keep in mind when computing cost percentages for the dollar-value LIFO retail method are:

1. Beginning inventory values are ignored. When LIFO is used, a new inventory layer is converted from retail to cost using the cost percentage applicable to current-year purchases.
2. Both markdowns and markups are included in the retail number used to compute the cost percentage. Earlier in the chapter, it was shown that excluding markdowns from the cost percentage calculation gives an inventory valuation estimate that approximates lower of cost or market. Because the write-down of LIFO inventory is not allowed for tax purposes, LIFO and lower-of-cost-or-market valuation traditionally have not been used together.

The following LIFO retail layer data for Miracle Max Department Store as of December 31, 2001, are used to illustrate the computations associated with the dollar-value LIFO retail method.

Layer Year	Year-End Price Index	Incremental Cost Percentage	Inventory at End-of-Year Retail Prices
1998	1.00	.60	$60,000
1999	1.05	.62	69,300
2000	1.10	.64	77,000
2001	1.12	.65	71,120

---

14 A survey of 195 U.S. retail companies using LIFO revealed that 95% used the dollar-value LIFO retail method. See James M. Reeve and Keith G. Stanga, "The LIFO Pooling Decision: Some Empirical Results from Accounting Practice," *Accounting Horizons*, June 1987, p. 27.

Assume that the 2002 year-end price index is 1.08.[15] The incremental cost percentage and 2002 ending inventory at end-of-year retail prices are computed as follows:

	Cost	Retail
Beginning inventory, December 31, 2001	—	$ 71,120
Purchases	$62,220	$ 98,000
Markups		8,000
Markdowns		(4,000)
Totals used to determine cost percentage applicable to new layer	$62,220	$102,000
Incremental cost percentage: ($62,220 ÷ $102,000) = 61%		
Goods available for sale		$173,120
Deduct: Sales		94,820
Ending inventory at retail (year-end prices)		$ 78,300

Caution! Don't get nervous—the dollar-value LIFO retail method is exactly the same as dollar-value LIFO. When you are finished identifying the LIFO layers, just remember to convert everything from retail to cost.

From these data, a work sheet similar to that illustrated in Chapter 8 for dollar-value LIFO can be constructed to determine the LIFO retail inventory layers. One additional column is necessary to record the incremental cost percentage that will convert the retail inventory to cost. It is important to note that the incremental cost percentage is used only if an incremental layer is added to the inventory in the current period. In the example, no layer was added in 2001, so the cost percentage applicable to purchases made in 2001 is not used. As seen with the dollar-value LIFO method in Chapter 8, when an inventory layer is eliminated, it is not reintroduced in subsequent years when layers are added. This is illustrated in the example when, in 2001, the $4,000 layer formed in 2000 is eliminated. In 2002, the 2000 $4,000 layer is not resurrected. Instead, the new layer is comprised of 2002 percentages.

Date	Inventory at End-of-Year Retail Prices		Year-End Price Index		Inventory at Base-Year Retail Prices	Layers	Incremental Layer Index		Incremental Cost Percentage		Dollar-Value LIFO Retail Cost
December 31, 1998	$60,000	÷	1.00	=	$60,000	$60,000 ×	1.00	×	.60	=	$36,000
December 31, 1999	$69,300	÷	1.05	=	$66,000	$60,000 ×	1.00	×	.60	=	$36,000
						6,000 ×	1.05	×	.62	=	3,906
						$66,000					$39,906
December 31, 2000	$77,000	÷	1.10	=	$70,000	$60,000 ×	1.00	×	.60	=	$36,000
						6,000 ×	1.05	×	.62	=	3,906
						4,000 ×	1.10	×	.64	=	2,816
						$70,000					$42,722
December 31, 2001	$71,120	÷	1.12	=	$63,500	$60,000 ×	1.00	×	.60	=	$36,000
						3,500 ×	1.05	×	.62	=	2,279*
						$63,500					$38,279
December 31, 2002	$78,300	÷	1.08	=	$72,500	$60,000 ×	1.00	×	.60	=	$36,000
						3,500 ×	1.05	×	.62	=	2,279*
						9,000 ×	1.08	×	.61	=	5,929*
						$72,500					$44,208

*Rounded to nearest dollar

[15] Recall from Chapter 8 that three acceptable options exist for converting a LIFO layer from base-year prices into current-year prices: a first purchase price index, an average price index, and an end-of-year price index. To keep this example simple, the end-of-year index is used.

To manage their risk, airlines often contract in advance to purchase fuel at a set price.

Account for the impact of changing prices on purchase commitments.

PURCHASE COMMITMENTS

Extreme fluctuations in the price of inventory purchases can expose a company to excessive risk. Of the different ways to manage this risk, the simplest is a **purchase commitment** that locks in the inventory purchase price in advance. For example, rather than being exposed to the ups and downs of oil prices, an airline can contract in advance to purchase its next month's fuel at a set price.

The first accounting issue raised by purchase commitments is whether the company committing to the future purchase should record an asset (for the inventory to be received) and a liability (for the payment obligation) at the commitment date. This type of contract is an exchange of promises about future actions and is known as an executory contract. Another example of an executory contract is an employment agreement in which a firm and an employee agree to employment terms for a future period. Accounting rules require some executory contracts to be recognized in the financial statements.[16]

With purchase commitments, no journal entry is required to record the commitment prior to delivery of the goods. However, in an adaptation of the lower-of-cost-or-market rule, when price declines take place subsequent to such a commitment and the commitment is outstanding at the end of an accounting period, the loss is recorded just as losses on goods on hand are recognized. A decline is recorded by a debit to a special loss account and a credit to either a contra asset account or an accrued liability account, such as Estimated Loss on Purchase Commitments. Acquisition of the goods in a subsequent period is recorded by a credit to Accounts Payable, a debit canceling the credit balance in the contra asset or accrued liability account, and a debit to Purchases for the difference.

To illustrate the accounting for purchase commitments, we'll use the following example. Rollins Oat Company entered into a purchase contract on November 1, 2001, for 100,000 bushels of wheat at $3.40 per bushel to be delivered in March 2002. At the end of 2001, the market price for wheat had dropped to $3.20 per bushel. The entries to record this decline in value and the subsequent delivery of the wheat would be as follows:

16 A lease is a good example of an executory contract. A lease is an exchange of promises about the future—the lessor promises to provide the use of an asset (like a building) and the lessee promises to pay for the use of the asset. As discussed in Chapter 15, some leases are recognized in the financial statements (capital leases) and some are not (operating leases).

2001			
Dec. 31	Loss on Purchase Commitments	20,000	
	Estimated Loss on Purchase Commitments		20,000
	(100,000 bushels × $0.20 per bushel)		

2002			
Mar. 31	Estimated Loss on Purchase Commitments	20,000	
	Purchases	320,000	
	Accounts Payable		340,000

The loss is thus assigned to the period in which the inventory price decline took place. Current loss recognition would not be appropriate when commitments can be canceled, when commitments provide for price adjustment, when hedging transactions prevent losses, or when declines do not suggest reductions in sale prices. If, prior to delivery, the market price increases, the estimated loss on purchase commitments account would be reduced and a gain would be recorded. The amount of gain to be recognized is limited to the amount of loss previously recorded.

7

Record inventory purchase transactions denominated in foreign currencies.

FOREIGN CURRENCY INVENTORY TRANSACTIONS

The discussion of inventories thus far has centered around the purchase and valuation of inventories in a domestic environment, that is, within the United States. As noted in Chapter 1, business has become increasingly global. Exports and imports of materials and finished goods are a significant part of many companies' purchases and sales. Depending on how a purchase transaction is structured, additional gains or losses may occur in foreign inventory transactions because of fluctuations in the currency exchange rates between two countries.

Not all international transactions involve foreign currency risk. Only transactions denominated in currencies other than the U.S. dollar are **foreign currency transactions** for U.S. companies. For example, if a U.S. company buys inventory from a German firm, the transaction is a normal purchase (for the U.S. company) if the inventory price is set in U.S. dollars. But, if the price is set in deutsche marks, the U.S. company is exposed to foreign currency exchange risk during the period the account payable is outstanding.

Caution! If the transaction contract is written in terms of U.S. dollars, there is *no* foreign currency risk whether the other company is based in Azerbaijan or Zimbabwe.

To illustrate the complexities associated with foreign currency transactions, assume that on November 1, 2001 Washington Company purchased inventory from France Company and that the invoice was denominated in francs with a purchase price of 50,000 francs. At the time of the purchase, the exchange rate was 5 francs per U.S. dollar. This rate is called the **spot rate**, the rate at which the two currencies can be exchanged right now. Washington Company would make the following journal entry to record the purchase:

2001			
Nov. 1	Inventory	10,000	
	Accounts Payable (fc)		10,000
	(50,000 francs ÷ 5 = $10,000)		

The (fc) designation is used for convenience to indicate those items that are denominated in a foreign currency. It is important to recognize, however, that the amounts in Washington's journal entry represent U.S. dollars.

The impact of a foreign currency inventory purchase is recognized when the liability is paid. If the terms call for payment of the liability on February 1, 2002, Washington Company will have to credit cash on that date, but for how much? Recall that the invoice requires payment in francs, not in dollars. Washington Company will have to purchase 50,000 francs from a foreign currency broker. How much will the company be required to pay the broker? The answer depends on the spot rate on that date. If the spot rate is

► HISTORY OF LIFO—PART II

When Congress approved the use of LIFO for income tax purposes in 1938, the approval was limited to just a few industries. Conceptually, LIFO was viewed as being appropriate only for inventories composed of identical units involved in a continuous production process. When LIFO was approved for use by all firms in 1939, retailers were uncertain about how LIFO should be applied to their inventories, which were made

up of many different products constantly being sold out and replaced by "new, improved" versions.

Despite the difficulties of implementing LIFO, retailers pressed ahead because of the potential income tax savings. They developed dollar-value LIFO retail, which uses two clever adaptations of the LIFO method. First, the inventory is viewed not as a collection of discrete units, but as one "pool" (or a set of pools) with a certain dollar value. The second adaptation is the maintenance of inventory records at retail values and use of

cost percentages to convert the numbers to LIFO cost. The IRS was not impressed by the elegance of the dollar-value LIFO retail method and rejected its use. Retailers fought back, and the dispute found its way to the Supreme Court in 1947. The Court ruled in favor of the retailers.

The IRS hasn't lost every battle over LIFO. Taxpayers and their accountants have argued that companies should be allowed to use the lower-of-cost-or-market rule in conjunction with LIFO. When the market value of

4.7 francs per U.S. dollar on February 1, 2002, then Washington Company will have to pay $10,638 (50,000 ÷ 4.7) to purchase 50,000 francs. The journal entry to record the payment to France Company is:

2002			
Feb. 1	Accounts Payable (fc)	10,000	
	Exchange Loss	638	
	Cash		10,638

Washington Company incurs a loss in this situation because it had a liability denominated in a currency (francs) that increased in value—the number of francs required to purchase one U.S. dollar declined. On November 1, 2001, Washington Company would have had to pay only $10,000 to purchase 50,000 francs. However, to purchase the same number of francs on February 1, 2002, requires $10,638. The exchange loss would be included as an expense in the income statement in the period incurred.

This situation could just as easily have resulted in an exchange gain for Washington Company. If the franc had weakened relative to the dollar, then fewer dollars would have been required to purchase 50,000 francs. Suppose the exchange rate for French francs had been 5.1 per U.S. dollar on February 1, 2002. Washington Company would have recorded the following journal entry and recognized an exchange gain:

2002			
Feb. 1	Accounts Payable (fc)	10,000	
	Exchange Gain		196
	Cash (50,000 francs ÷ 5.1)		9,804

STOP & THINK Have the authors picked realistic exchange rates for the U.S. dollar relative to the French franc? Check in *The Wall Street Journal*.

If a balance sheet date occurs while a foreign currency asset or liability is outstanding, the asset or liability is valued at the spot rate on the balance sheet date.[17] Continuing the initial example, suppose that Washington Company's fiscal year ends on December 31 and the exchange rate on December 31, 2001, is 4.8 francs per U.S. dollar. On that

---

17 *Statement of Financial Accounting Standards No. 52*, "Foreign Currency Translation," Stamford, CT: Financial Accounting Standards Board, 1981, par. 16b.

inventory falls below LIFO cost, a write-down of the balance sheet value is made for financial reporting purposes, along with recognition of an income statement loss. Inventory write-downs are also deductible for income tax purposes, except when LIFO is used. The IRS maintains that the concept behind LIFO is that unrealized gains on the base stock of inventory should not be taxed. Using the same reasoning, the IRS insists that unrealized losses on LIFO inventory should not be deductible. So, lower-of-cost-or-market write-downs of LIFO inventory are acceptable for financial reporting but not for income tax calculations.

QUESTIONS:

1. Conceptually, what makes LIFO appropriate for a con-

tinuous production process involving identical units?
2. What objections do you think the IRS had to the dollar-value LIFO retail method when it was first developed?
3. The combination of LIFO with the lower-of-cost-or-market rule has been nicknamed HIFO (highest in, first out). Consider two cases: a company facing rising inventory prices and a company facing falling inventory prices. Is the HIFO nickname appropriate for the combination of LIFO and lower of cost or market?

SOURCE:

Harry Zvi Davis, "History of LIFO," *Accounting Historians Journal,* Spring 1982, p. 1.

---

date, Washington Company would make the following adjusting entry to record the change in the amount of cash required to pay the liability:

2001			
Dec. 31	Exchange Loss	417	
	Accounts Payable (fc)		417
	[(50,000 francs ÷ 4.8) − $10,000 = $417]		

This journal entry adjusts the liability to its value of $10,417, given the balance sheet date spot rate, and allocates the exchange rate loss to the period in which the change in exchange rates occurred. When the liability is subsequently paid on February 1, 2002, and the spot rate is 4.7 francs per dollar, the journal entry would be:

2002			
Feb. 1	Accounts Payable (fc)	10,417	
	Exchange Loss	221	
	Cash (50,000 francs ÷ 4.7)		10,638

Note that the exchange losses of $417 and $221 recorded on December 31 and February 1, respectively, total $638, which is the same amount that is obtained if no adjusting entry is made. The adjusting entry simply allocates the exchange loss to the appropriate accounting periods.

An obvious question at this point is, why didn't Washington Company avoid the exchange loss and pay the liability early? If Washington knew that the franc was going to become more expensive, it probably would have. However, predicting the direction and amount of change in the exchange rate for a particular currency is as difficult as predicting whether the price of a specific stock on the New York Stock Exchange is going to rise or fall, and by how much.

Foreign currency exchange risk is another form of price risk. And, just like domestic price risk, foreign currency exchange risk can be hedged. Hedging involves contracting with a foreign currency broker to deliver or receive a specified foreign currency at a specified future date and at a specified exchange rate. A fully hedged transaction results in no exchange gain or loss to the company. The cost of hedging is the fee charged by the broker. For that fee, the broker assumes all of the risks associated with exchange rate changes. Accounting for foreign currency hedging is not that difficult, but it isn't covered

net work exercises

Olsen & Associates, a provider of advanced forecasting technology for financial markets, offers a currency converter on its Web site (www.olsen.ch/cgi-bin/exmenu). The converter lists daily exchange rates for 164 currencies, dating from January 1, 1990, to the present.

Net Work:

1. On January 1, 1999, one U.S. dollar equaled how many British pounds?
2. Convert one U.S. dollar to British pounds today. Did the value of the pound increase or decrease since January 1, 1999? How would this increase or decrease affect a U.S. company that had a liability denominated in British pounds?

in this text. We can't do *all* of the fun topics in intermediate accounting—we have to leave something for the advanced accounting class. For coverage of how multinational companies combine the financial statements of subsidiaries located in different countries, see Chapter 21.

REVIEW OF LEARNING OBJECTIVES

1 **Apply the lower-of-cost-or-market (LCM) rule to reflect declines in the market value of inventory.** The lower-of-cost-or-market (LCM) rule results in recognition of decreases in the market value of inventory. Applying the LCM rule requires careful specification of the "market" value. To use the lower-of-cost-or-market rule, the cost of the ending inventory is compared with its market value. If market is less than cost, ending inventory is written down to the market value.

The market value of inventory is equal to its replacement cost, subject to floor and ceiling constraints. The ceiling constraint is that the market value of inventory is not greater than net realizable value. The floor constraint is that the market value of the inventory is not less than net realizable value minus a normal profit margin. In summary, market value of inventory is never less than the floor value, never more than the ceiling value, and is equal to replacement cost when replacement cost is between the floor and the ceiling.

2 **Use the gross profit method to estimate ending inventory.** The gross profit method is a simple technique for estimating ending inventory. Inventory estimates are used to confirm the accounting records and to substitute for inventory counts when a physical count is not practical. The gross profit method is as follows:

- Estimate a gross profit percentage [(Sales – Cost of goods sold)/Sales] based on historical values adjusted for significant changes in pricing policy and sales mix.
- Apply the gross profit percentage to sales to estimate cost of goods sold.
- Subtract the cost of goods sold estimate from the cost of goods available for sale to arrive at an estimated ending inventory balance.

3 **Compute estimates of FIFO, LIFO, average cost, and lower-of-cost-or-market inventory using the retail inventory method.** When the retail inventory method is used, records of goods purchased are maintained at both cost and retail amounts.

A cost percentage is computed by dividing the goods available for sale at cost by the goods available for sale at retail. This cost percentage is then applied to the ending inventory at retail to get an estimate of the cost of ending inventory.

Variations on the computation of the cost percentage yield inventory estimates for a variety of valuation assumptions, such as:

- *FIFO.* The cost percentage is based on current purchases.
- *LIFO.* The cost percentage is based on beginning inventory, adjusted for the addition of any new LIFO layers.
- *Average cost.* The cost percentage is computed using both beginning inventory and current purchases and includes the effects of both markups and markdowns.
- *Lower of cost or market.* The cost percentage is computed using both beginning inventory and current purchases and includes the effects of markups but not of markdowns.

4 **Determine the financial statement impact of inventory recording errors.** Undetected inventory recording errors impact financial statements in both the year of the error and the subsequent year. Depending on the nature of the error, income can be understated or overstated.

Analysis of inventory errors is aided by recalling the simple computation:

Beginning inventory
+ Purchases
= Goods available for sale
- Ending inventory
= Cost of goods sold

Because the ending inventory of one period becomes the beginning inventory of the next period, undetected inventory errors affect two accounting periods. A common error is the overstatement of ending inventory. This error has the effect of reducing cost of goods sold and increasing net income in the year of the error. A counterbalancing reduction in net income occurs in the following year.

5 **Combine the retail inventory method and dollar-value LIFO to compute ending inventory using the dollar-value LIFO retail method.** Almost all retail companies that use LIFO employ the dollar-value LIFO retail method. The dollar-value LIFO retail method is used as follows:

- A cost percentage for the current year is computed using cost and retail information for current purchases.
- A price index is used to determine whether a new LIFO layer has been created.
- The retail values of all LIFO layers are converted to cost using the appropriate cost percentages.

6 **Account for the impact of changing prices on purchase commitments.** With a purchase commitment, a company locks in the cost of inventory before the inventory is actually purchased. The LCM rule is applied if prices decline between the commitment date and the purchase date. No journal entry is made to record the commitment. However, when price declines take place after a purchase commitment has been made, a loss is recorded in the period of the price decline.

7 **Record inventory purchase transactions denominated in foreign currencies.** Transactions denominated in currencies other than the U.S. dollar are foreign currency transactions for U.S. companies. Foreign currency transactions expose companies to exchange rate risk during the time between the purchase and the payment of the foreign currency obligation. Gains or losses resulting from exchange rate changes are recognized in the period in which the exchange rate changes occur.

KEY TERMS

Ceiling 491
Cost percentage 498
Entry cost 491
Exit value 491
Floor 492
Gross profit method 496
Initial markup 500
Lower of cost or market
  (LCM) 491

Markdown 500
Market (in "lower of cost or
  market") 491
Markup 500
Original retail 500
Replacement cost 491
Retail inventory method 498

Dollar-value LIFO retail method 506
Foreign currency transaction 509
Purchase commitment 508
Spot rate 509

QUESTIONS

1. The use of lower of cost or market is an unnecessary continuation of the tradition of conservative accounting. Comment on this view.
2. Why are ceiling and floor limitations on replacement cost considered necessary?
3. What differences result from applying lower of cost or market to individual inventory items instead of to the inventory as a whole?
4. Why would a manager care about the value assigned to inventory transferred in from another department?

5. What information is needed to develop a reliable gross profit percentage for use with the gross profit method?
6. What advantages does the retail inventory method have over the gross profit method?
7. How can FIFO and LIFO assumptions be incorporated into the retail inventory method?
8. (a) How are markdowns treated when estimating average cost using the retail inventory method? (b) How are markdowns treated when estimating lower of cost or market using the retail inventory method?

9. How are purchase discounts and sales discounts treated when using the retail inventory method?

10. State the effect of each of the following errors made by Clawson Inc. on the income statement and the balance sheet (1) of the current period and (2) of the succeeding period:

   a. The ending inventory is overstated as a result of a miscount of goods on hand.

   b. The company fails to record a purchase of merchandise on account, and the merchandise purchased is not recognized in recording the ending inventory.

   c. The ending inventory is understated as a result of a miscount of goods on hand.

11. When applying the dollar-value LIFO retail method: (a) How do beginning inventory values impact the computation of the cost percentage? (b) How are markdowns treated?

12. What journal entry is made when a purchase commitment is originally entered into? Explain.

13. Are all transactions with foreign companies classified as foreign currency transactions? If not, what determines if a transaction is a foreign currency transaction?

14. Why is an adjustment made on the balance sheet date to reflect exchange rate changes?

DISCUSSION CASES

CASE 9–1

HAVE WE REALLY HAD A LOSS?

The Destro Company is experiencing an unusual inventory situation. The replacement cost of its principal product has been declining, but because of a unique market condition, Destro has not had to reduce the selling price of the item. Eric Dona, company controller, is aware that GAAP requires the valuation of inventory at the lower of cost or market. He considers market to be replacement cost, and he is concerned that to reduce the ending inventory to replacement cost will improperly reduce net income for the current period. Has an inventory loss occurred? Discuss.

CASE 9–2

BUT THEY WON'T BUY DUCKS ANYMORE!

The Bright-Lite Shirt Company buys wholesale sweatshirts, nightshirts, T-shirts, and other clothing items and, using a novel four-color processing system, imprints hundreds of designs on the items. The printed shirts are marketed widely to sports stores, department stores, college campus outlets, variety stores, vacation shops, etc. Gordon Smith, marketing manager, likes to have a wide variety of products on hand so orders can be promptly met. As the number of designs has grown, so has the inventory. However, the designs often exhibit "fad" characteristics, and the demand for ducks, bears, flowers, or sports heroes can change fairly rapidly.

Beverly Patton, the controller, has expressed dismay at the growing inventory and especially the issue of inventory obsolescence. Beverly is now preparing for a meeting with Bright-Lite's external auditor. The auditor is sure to ask for a write-down of inventory to the lower of cost or market. Beverly has sent a report to Gordon urging him to reduce his inventory and change his production concept. Gordon is reluctant to change because Bright-Lite has developed an excellent reputation for meeting emergency requests for inventory.

As Bright-Lite's president, which position will you support: Gordon's or Beverly's? Explain.

CASE 9–3

WHAT VALUE SHOULD WE PLACE ON THE CLUNKER?

The Ritchie Automobile Agency is an exclusive agency for the sale of foreign sports cars. As part of its sales strategy, Ritchie allows liberal trade-in allowances on the sale of its new cars.

A used car division of the company sells these trade-ins at a separate location, usually at an amount significantly lower than the trade-in allowance. This division is continually showing large losses because the cars are charged to the division at their trade-in values. John Lund, manager of the used car division, has requested that the costing procedure be changed and that trade-ins be recorded at a price sufficiently below expected retail to allow a reasonable profit to his division. Janet Perry, controller of the agency, acknowledges that some adjustment needs to be made to the inflated trade-in values, but she feels that expected retail value should be used without allowance for a profit. What value should be used to record the trade-ins?

CASE 9–4

INVENTORY VALUATION WITHOUT RECORDS

The Ma & Pa Grocery Store has never kept many records. The proceeds from sales are used to pay suppliers for goods delivered. When the owners, Donald and Alicia Wride, need some cash, they withdraw it from the till without any record being made of it. The Wrides realize that eventually tax returns must be filed, but for 3 years, "they just haven't got around to it." Finally, the IRS catches up with the Wrides, and an audit of the company records is conducted. The auditor requests the general ledger, special journals, inventory counts, and supporting documentation—very little of which is available. Records of expenditures are extremely sketchy because most expenses are paid in cash. If you were the IRS auditor, what might you do to make a reasonable estimate of income for the company?

CASE 9–5

THE VERSATILITY OF THE RETAIL INVENTORY METHOD

Karen Stewart, president of Laronco, Inc., recently attended a seminar on effectively managing a business. One session of the seminar that particularly impressed Karen was the discussion of inventory management and the various types of inventory estimation methods available for producing interim financial statements. The seminar only highlighted the characteristics of the various methods, and Karen has come to you, the company's chief financial officer, and asked you to explain the retail inventory method in more detail. In particular, Karen wants you to explain how the retail inventory method can yield FIFO, LIFO, average cost, and lower-of-cost-or-market estimates. Outline a brief memo explaining the retail inventory method to Karen. Remember that she has a marketing background and doesn't know that much about accounting.

CASE 9–6

SALES ARE STILL INCREASING—OR ARE THEY?

Nu-Ware, Inc., sells cookware with a specialized coating that protects the product and prevents sticking better than other coatings on the market. The design of the cookware is also unique, and during the first 2 years of operations, Nu-Ware's sales increased dramatically. Inventory production increased continuously to meet the expanding demand. When the economy softened and sales started to level and even decline, Nu-Ware was caught with excessive inventory.

Shirley Morris, president of Nu-Ware, was concerned about the company's image. Investors had purchased stock with the expectation of continuing growth increases. Shirley contacted several customers and persuaded them to accept merchandise shipments that had not been ordered in case their needs were higher than anticipated. She assumed the risk for her customers by deferring payment for 6 months and agreeing to allow the return of any unsold goods after the end of the year. As a result of this arrangement, the company continued to show sales growth and the inventory levels were reduced. As the new year passed, the recession stubbornly held on, and many customers returned excess stock.

Assume you are assigned to audit Nu-Ware and know nothing of the above arrangements with customers. What analytical measures could suggest to you that the shipping and billing procedures had changed?

CASE 9–7

REGINA: IMAGINARY VACUUMS

REGINA, INC., was a fast-growing floor-care company that went public in 1985 and went bankrupt in 1988. Regina went from a one-product company with $60 million in sales in 1985 to a four-product company with $181 million in sales in 1988. Reported earnings climbed from $1.1 million in 1985 to $10.9 million in 1988.

Following the bankruptcy, investigations revealed a massive management fraud. It seems that in an effort to boost sales, sound business practices were changed and the accounting records were modified accordingly. For example, product quality testing was reduced or, in some cases, eliminated. As a result, Regina had many returned products. In fact, in one quarter more than 40,000 Housekeeper vacuum cleaners were returned. This volume of returns was so unexpected that a separate building had to be leased to store the defective products. These returns were not recorded on Regina's books. In addition, revenues were recorded when orders were received rather than when goods were shipped. This practice accelerated recognition of revenue beyond accepted norms. Finally, Regina modified its computer system to generate fictitious invoices. Approximately 200 invoices worth $5.4 million in sales were created during the last 3 business days of the fiscal year ended on June 30, 1988.

Uncovering the combined effect of these fraudulent activities led to restating 1988 income of $10.9 million to a loss of $16.8 million. Dan Sheelan, the president of Regina and the driving force behind these activities, was required to pay substantial fines and was eventually sentenced to serve time in prison.

How could an auditor have used the retail inventory method to detect that Regina was recording sales when orders were received rather than when goods were shipped?

CASE 9–8

SILVER'S UPS AND DOWNS

In 1979 and 1980, the Hunt brothers from Texas attempted to corner the world's silver market. Their hope was to own enough silver to be able to dictate world prices. They made purchase commitments, which locked in the price they would pay for silver. For a while, their plan worked. The price of silver rose, and the Hunt brothers used the silver they owned as collateral to purchase more silver.

Their plans were shattered when the price of silver started to decline. From a high in January 1980 of $50.35 an ounce, the price of silver fell to $10.80 in just 2 months. The silver they were using as collateral decreased in value, requiring the Hunt brothers to provide additional collateral. This collateral was in the form of oil, sugar, and real estate, each of which was faring poorly at the time of the silver crash. At the same time, the purchase commitments they had made required them to buy silver at prices higher than the current market value of silver. The Hunt brothers sought protection in bankruptcy court, and the scheme eventually cost them approximately $4 billion.

1. What are the risks associated with making purchase commitments?
2. Why do accounting standards require that price declines subsequent to the purchase commitment but prior to the actual purchase be recorded immediately?
3. Can firms take any action to reduce their exposure to changing prices?

CASE 9–9

CAN WE AVOID LOSSES FROM EXCHANGE RATE CHANGES?

Smith & Sons routinely purchases inventory from Matsutoshi Corp. Because of unpredictability in the foreign currency markets, transactions denominated in yen leave Smith & Sons exposed to the risks associated with exchange rate changes. Identify and discuss methods by which Smith & Sons can reduce its exposure to foreign currency losses.

EXERCISES

EXERCISE 9–10

LOWER-OF-COST-OR-MARKET VALUATION
Determine the proper carrying value of the following inventory items.

Item	Cost	Replacement Cost	Sales Price	Selling Expenses	Normal Profit
Product 561	$3.05	$3.00	$3.50	$0.35	$0.20
Product 562	0.69	0.72	1.00	0.30	0.04
Product 563	0.31	0.24	0.43	0.15	0.07
Product 564	0.92	0.70	1.05	0.27	0.05
Product 565	0.84	0.82	1.00	0.19	0.09
Product 566	1.19	1.25	1.43	0.13	0.09

EXERCISE 9–11

LOWER-OF-COST-OR-MARKET VALUATION
The following inventory data are available for Alpine Ski Shop at December 31.

	Cost	Market
Skis	$60,000	$65,000
Boots	37,500	35,000
Ski equipment	15,000	14,000
Ski apparel	9,500	13,500

1. Determine the value of ending inventory using the lower-of-cost-or-market method applied to (a) individual items and (b) total inventory.
2. Prepare any journal entries required to adjust the ending inventory if lower of cost or market is applied to (a) individual items and (b) total inventory.

EXERCISE 9–12

LOWER-OF-COST-OR-MARKET VALUATION
Newcomer, Inc., values inventories using the lower-of-cost-or-market method applied to total inventory. Inventory values at the end of the company's first and second years of operation are presented below.

	Cost	Market
Year 1	$58,000	$53,000
Year 2	75,000	73,800

1. Prepare the journal entries necessary to reflect the proper inventory valuation at the end of each year. (Assume Newcomer uses an inventory allowance account.)
2. For Year 1, assume sales were $510,000 and purchases were $440,000. What amount would be reported as cost of goods sold on the income statement for Year 1 if: (a) the inventory decline is reported separately and (b) the inventory decline is not reported separately?

EXERCISE 9–13

COMPARISON OF INVENTORY VALUATION METHODS
The Muhlstein Corporation began business on January 1, 2002. The following table shows information about inventories, as of December 31, for 3 consecutive years under different valuation methods. Assume that purchases are $50,000 each year. Using this information and assuming that the same method is used each year, you are to choose the phrase which best answers each of the questions that follow.

	LIFO	FIFO	Market	Lower of Cost or Market*
2002	$10,200	$10,000	$9,600	$8,900
2003	9,100	9,000	8,800	8,500
2004	10,300	11,000	12,000	10,900

*FIFO cost, item-by-item valuation.

1. Which inventory basis would result in the highest net income for 2002?
2. Which inventory basis would result in the highest net income for 2003?
3. Which inventory basis would result in the lowest net income for the 3 years combined?
4. For the year 2003, how much higher or lower would net income be on the FIFO cost basis than on the lower-of-cost-or-market basis?

EXERCISE 9–14

VALUATION OF RETURN

Wailea Inc. sells new equipment with a $3,900 list price. A dissatisfied customer returned one piece of equipment. Wailea determines that the returned equipment can be resold if it is reconditioned. The expected sales price of the reconditioned equipment is $3,500; the reconditioning expenses are estimated to be $500; and normal profit is 35% of the sales price.

1. Prepare the journal entry to record the sale of the reconditioned equipment for cash assuming that the floor value is used to record the returned equipment.
2. Prepare the journal entry to record the sale of the reconditioned equipment for cash assuming that the original list price is used to record the returned equipment.
3. Evaluate the entries.

EXERCISE 9–15

INVENTORY LOSS—GROSS PROFIT METHOD

On August 15, 2002, a hurricane damaged a warehouse of Rheinhart Merchandise Company. The entire inventory and many accounting records stored in the warehouse were completely destroyed. Although the inventory was not insured, a portion could be sold for scrap. Through the use of microfilmed records, the following data are assembled:

Inventory, January 1	$ 375,000
Purchases, January 1–August 15	1,385,000
Cash sales, January 1–August 15	225,000
Collection of accounts receivable, January 1–August 15	2,115,000
Accounts receivable, January 1	175,000
Accounts receivable, August 15	265,000
Salvage value of inventory	5,000
Gross profit percentage on sales	32%

Compute the inventory loss as a result of the hurricane.

EXERCISE 9–16

INVENTORY LOSS—GROSS PROFIT METHOD

On June 30, 2002, a flash flood damaged the warehouse and factory of Bend Corporation, completely destroying the work in process inventory. There was no damage to either the raw materials or finished goods inventories. A physical inventory taken after the flood revealed the following valuations.

Finished goods	$112,000
Work in process	0
Raw materials	52,000

The inventory on January 1, 2002, consisted of the following.

Finished goods	$120,000
Work in process	115,000
Raw materials	42,500
	$277,500

A review of the books and records disclosed that the gross profit margin historically approximated 34% of sales. The sales for the first 6 months of 2002 were $428,000. Raw materials purchases were $96,000. Direct labor costs for this period were $130,000, and manufacturing overhead has historically been applied at 60% of direct labor.

Compute the value of the work in process inventory lost on June 30, 2002.

EXERCISE 9–17

RETAIL INVENTORY METHOD

The Evening Out Clothing Store values its inventory using the retail inventory method. The following data are available for the month of November 2002.

	Cost	Retail
Inventory, November 1	$ 53,800	$ 80,000
Purchases	154,304	220,000
Sales		244,000

Compute the estimated inventory at November 30, 2002, assuming:

1. FIFO
2. LIFO
3. Average cost

EXERCISE 9–18

RETAIL INVENTORY METHOD

The Ivory Tower Bookstore recently received a shipment of accounting textbooks from the publisher. Following the receipt of the shipment, the FASB issued a major new accounting standard that related directly to the contents of one chapter of the text. Portions of this chapter became "obsolete" immediately as a result of the FASB's action. In order to sell the books, the bookstore marked down the selling price and offered a separate supplement covering the new standard, which was provided at no cost by the publisher. Information relating to the cost and selling price of the text for the month of September is given below.

	Cost	Retail
Beginning inventory	$ 1,500	$ 1,800
Purchases	24,000	33,760
Freight-in	1,100	
Markdowns		2,100
Sales		27,500

Based on the data given, compute the estimated inventory at the end of the month using the retail inventory method and assuming:

1. Lower-of-cost-or-market valuation
2. Average cost valuation

EXERCISE 9–19

RETAIL INVENTORY METHOD

Carmel Department Store uses the retail inventory method. On December 31, 2002, the following information relating to the inventory was gathered.

	Cost	Retail
Inventory, January 1, 2002	$ 26,550	$ 45,000
Sales		430,000
Purchases	309,000	435,000
Purchase discounts	4,200	
Freight-in	5,250	
Markups		30,000
Markdowns		40,000
Sales discounts		5,000

Compute the ending inventory value at December 31, 2002, using:

1. The average cost method
2. The lower-of-cost-or-market method

EXERCISE 9–20

CORRECTION OF INVENTORY ERRORS

Annual income for the Stoker Co. for the period 1998–2002 appears below. However, a review of the records for the company reveals inventory misstatements as listed. Calculate corrected net income for each year.

	1998	1999	2000	2001	2002
Reported net income (loss)	$18,000	$13,000	$2,000	$ (5,800)	$16,000
Inventory overstatement, end of year		5,500			3,600
Inventory understatement, end of year	4,500			10,500	

EXERCISE 9–21

EFFECT ON NET INCOME OF INVENTORY ERRORS

The Martin Company reported income before taxes of $370,000 for 2001 and $526,000 for 2002. A later audit produced the following information.

a. The ending inventory for 2001 included 2,000 units erroneously priced at $5.90 per unit. The correct cost was $9.50 per unit.

b. Merchandise costing $17,500 was shipped to the Martin Company, FOB shipping point, on December 26, 2001. The purchase was recorded in 2001, but the merchandise was excluded from the ending inventory because it was not received until January 4, 2002.

c. On December 28, 2001, merchandise costing $2,900 was sold to Deluxe Paint Shop. Deluxe had asked Martin to keep the merchandise for it until January 2, when it would come and pick it up. Because the merchandise was still in the store at year-end, the merchandise was included in the inventory count. The sale was correctly recorded in December 2001.

d. Craft Company sold merchandise costing $1,500 to Martin Company. The purchase was made on December 29, 2001, and the merchandise was shipped on December 30. Terms were FOB shipping point. Because the Martin Company bookkeeper was on vacation, neither the purchase nor the receipt of goods was recorded on the books until January 2002.

Assume that all amounts are material and a physical count of inventory was taken every December 31.

1. Compute the corrected income before taxes for each year.
2. By what amount did the total income before taxes change for the 2 years combined?
3. Assume all errors were found in February 2002, just after the books were closed for 2001. What journal entry would be made?

EXERCISE 9–22

CORRECTION OF LIFO INVENTORY

The Cardoza Products Company's inventory record appears below.

	Purchases		Sales
	Quantity	**Unit Cost**	**Quantity**
2000	9,000	$5.60	6,500
2001	9,500	5.75	10,000
2002	7,200	5.82	6,000

The company uses a LIFO cost flow assumption. It reported ending inventories as follows for its first 3 years of operations:

2000	$14,000
2001	11,600
2002	18,600

Determine if the Cardoza Products Company has reported its inventory correctly. Assuming that 2002 accounts are not yet closed, make any necessary correcting entries.

EXERCISE 9–23

DOLLAR-VALUE LIFO RETAIL METHOD

The Paradise Hardware Store began using the dollar-value LIFO retail method in 2001 for determining inventory values. In 2001, the cost percentage was computed at 62%. Information relating to the inventory for 2002 is given below.

	Cost	Retail
Inventory, January 1	$ 39,680	$ 64,000
Purchases	165,000	270,600
Purchase returns	11,200	18,368
Freight-in	26,000	
Sales		269,000
Markups		26,000
Markdowns		8,000

Price index:
2001—All year	1.00
2002—December 31	1.08

1. Compute the cost percentage for 2002. (Round percentage to 2 decimal places.)
2. Compute the inventory value to be reported at December 31, 2002, assuming incremental layers are costed at end-of-year prices.

EXERCISE 9–24

DOLLAR-VALUE LIFO RETAIL METHOD

On February 15, 2003, Rooker, Madras & Associates compiled the following information concerning inventory for five years. They used the dollar-value LIFO retail inventory method.

Date	Year-End Price Index	Incremental Layer Index	Incremental Cost Percentage	Inventory at Retail
Dec. 31, 1998	1.00	1.00	71%	$155,000
Dec. 31, 1999	1.04	1.02	72%	188,600
Dec. 31, 2000	1.14	1.09	64%	192,500
Dec. 31, 2001	1.12	1.11	63%	194,200
Dec. 31, 2002	1.16	1.12	67%	195,800

Compute the inventory cost at the end of each year under the dollar-value LIFO retail method. (Round all dollar amounts to the nearest dollar.)

EXERCISE 9–25

LOSS ON PURCHASE COMMITMENTS

On October 1, 2002, Gore Electronics Inc. entered into a 6-month, $520,000 purchase commitment for a supply of Product A. On December 31, 2002, the market value of this material had fallen to $421,500. Make the journal entries necessary on December 31, 2002, and on March 31, 2003, assuming that the market value of the inventory on March 31 is $390,000.

EXERCISE 9–26

FOREIGN CURRENCY PURCHASE

Guenther's, a German company that supplies your firm with a necessary raw material, recently shipped 10,000 units of the material to your production facility.

1. Prepare the necessary journal entries to record the purchase of the goods and the subsequent payment 30 days later if the selling price on the invoice is $2 per unit.
2. Prepare the necessary journal entries to record the purchase of the goods and the subsequent payment 30 days later if the selling price on the invoice is 4 German deutsche marks per unit. On the date of purchase, 1 German deutsche mark is worth $0.50, and the rate on the date of payment is $0.60.

EXERCISE 9–27

FOREIGN CURRENCY PURCHASE

Koreaco produces automobile transmissions, which are then sent to the United States where they are installed in domestically built cars. CarCo, a U.S. auto company, received a shipment of transmissions on December 15, 2001. The transmissions were subsequently paid for on January 30, 2002. The invoice was denominated in Korean won and totaled 5,000,000 won. The number of Korean won required to purchase 1 U.S. dollar fluctuated as follows:

	Exchange Rates
December 15, 2001	800
December 31, 2001	780
January 30, 2002	720

Provide the necessary journal entries for CarCo to record the above transactions assuming CarCo's fiscal year-end is December 31.

PROBLEMS

PROBLEM 9–28

LOWER-OF-COST-OR-MARKET VALUATION

Witte Inc. carries 4 items in inventory. The following per-unit data relate to these items at the end of 2002.

	Units	Cost	Replacement Cost	Estimated Sales Price	Selling Cost	Normal Profit
Category 1:						
Commodity A	3,000	$5.50	$5.25	$8.00	$0.90	$2.00
Commodity B	1,650	6.00	6.00	9.25	0.80	1.25
Category 2:						
Commodity C	5,000	2.50	2.00	4.20	0.95	0.50
Commodity D	3,250	7.00	7.50	7.50	1.20	1.75

Instructions:

1. Calculate the value of the inventory under each of the following methods.
   a. Cost
   b. The lower of cost or market applied to the individual inventory items
   c. The lower of cost or market applied to the inventory categories
   d. The lower of cost or market applied to the inventory as a whole

2. Prepare any journal entries necessary to reflect the proper inventory valuation assuming inventory is valued at:
   a. Cost
   b. The lower of cost or market applied to the individual inventory items
   c. The lower of cost or market applied to the inventory categories (Hint: Use valuation allowance.)
   d. The lower of cost or market applied to the inventory as a whole

PROBLEM 9–29

LOWER-OF-COST-OR-MARKET VALUATION

Oriental Sales Co. uses the first-in, first-out method in calculating cost of goods sold for 3 of the products that Oriental handles. Inventories and purchase information concerning these 3 products are given for the month of August.

		Product A	Product B	Product C
Aug. 1	Inventory	5,000 units at $6.00	3,000 units at $10.00	6,500 units at $0.90
Aug. 1–15	Purchases	7,000 units at $6.50	4,500 units at $10.50	3,000 units at $1.25
Aug. 16–31	Purchases	3,000 units at $8.00		
Aug. 1–31	Sales	10,500 units	5,000 units	4,500 units
Aug. 31	Sales price	$8.00 per unit	$11.00 per unit	$2.00 per unit

On August 31, Oriental's suppliers reduced their prices from the most recent purchase prices by the following percentages: Product A, 20%; Product B, 10%; Product C, 8%. Accordingly, Oriental decided to reduce its sales prices on all items by 10%, effective September 1. Oriental's selling cost is 10% of sales price. Products A and B have a normal profit (after selling costs) of 30% on sales prices, while the normal profit on Product C (after selling cost) is 15% of sales price.

Instructions:

1. Calculate the value of the inventory at August 31, using the lower-of-cost-or-market method (applied to individual items).
2. Calculate the FIFO cost of goods sold for August and the amount of inventory write-off due to the market decline.

PROBLEM 9–30

TRADE-INS AND REPOSSESSED INVENTORY

The Jamison Appliance Company began business on January 1, 2001. The company decided from the beginning to grant allowances on merchandise traded in as partial payment on new sales. During 2002 the company granted trade-in allowances of $64,035. The wholesale value of merchandise traded in was $40,875. Trade-ins recorded at $39,000 were sold for their wholesale value of $27,000 during the year. The following summary entries were made to record annual sales of new merchandise and trade-in sales for 2002.

Accounts Receivable	439,890	
Trade-In Inventory	64,035	
Sales		503,925
Cash	27,000	
Loss on Trade-In Inventory	12,000	
Trade-In Inventory		39,000

When a customer defaults on the accounts receivable contract, the merchandise is repossessed. During 2002 the following repossessions occurred:

	Original Sales Price	Unpaid Contract Balance
On 2001 contracts	$37,500	$15,600
On 2002 contracts	24,000	17,800

The wholesale value of these goods is estimated as follows:
a. Goods repossessed during year of sale are valued at 50% of original sales price.
b. Goods repossessed in later years are valued at 20% of original sales price.

Instructions:

1. At what values should Jamison Appliance report the trade-in and repossessed inventory at December 31, 2002?
2. Give the entry that should have been made to record the repossessions of 2002.
3. Give the entry that is required to correct the trade-in summary entries.

PROBLEM 9–31

INVENTORY TRANSACTIONS—JOURNAL ENTRIES

The Olsen Company values its inventory at the lower of FIFO cost or market. The inventory accounts at December 31, 2001, had the following balances.

Raw materials	$ 81,000
Work in process	131,520
Finished goods	205,200

The following are some of the transactions that affected the inventory of the Olsen Company during 2002.

Feb. 10   Olsen Company purchases raw materials at an invoice price of $25,000; terms 3/15, n/30. Olsen Company values inventory at the net invoice price.

Mar. 15   Olsen Company repossesses an inventory item from a customer who was overdue in making payment. The unpaid balance on the sale is $190. The repossessed merchandise is to be refinished and placed on sale. It is expected that the item can be sold for $300 after estimated refinishing costs of $85. The normal profit for this item is considered to be $40.

Apr. 1   Refinishing costs of $80 are incurred on the repossessed item.

    10   The repossessed item is resold for $300 on account, 20% down.

May 30   A sale on account is made of finished goods that have a list price of $740 and a cost of $480. A reduction of $100 off the list price is granted as a trade-in allowance. The trade-in item is to be priced to sell at $80 as is. The normal profit on this type of inventory is 25% of the sales price.

Dec. 31   The following information is available to adjust the accounts for the annual statements.
      a. The raw materials inventory account has a cost balance of $110,400. Current market value is $101,400.
      b. The finished goods inventory account has a cost balance of $177,600. Current market value is $189,000.

Instructions: Record this information in journal entry form, including any required adjusting entries at December 31, 2002.

PROBLEM 9–32

INVENTORY FIRE LOSS

Kimbell Manufacturing began operations 5 years ago. On August 13, 2002, a fire broke out in the warehouse destroying all inventory and many accounting records relating to the inventory. The information available is presented below. All sales and purchases are on account.

	January 1, 2002	August 13, 2002
Inventory	$143,850	
Accounts receivable	130,590	$128,890
Accounts payable	88,140	122,850
Collection on accounts receivable, January 1–August 13		753,800
Payments to suppliers, January 1–August 13		487,500
Goods out on consignment at August 13, at cost		52,900

Summary of previous years' sales:

	1999	2000	2001
Sales	$626,000	$705,000	$680,000
Gross profit on sales	187,800	183,300	231,200

Instructions: Determine the inventory loss suffered as a result of the fire.

PROBLEM 9–33

INTERIM INVENTORY COMPUTATION—GROSS PROFIT METHOD

The following information was taken from the records of the Prairie Company.

	Jan. 1, 2001–Dec. 31, 2001	Jan. 1, 2002–Sept. 30, 2002
Sales	$2,500,000	$1,500,000
Beginning inventory	420,000	785,000
Purchases	2,152,000	1,061,000
Freight-in	116,000	72,000
Purchase discounts	30,000	15,000
Purchase returns	40,000	13,000
Purchase allowances	8,000	5,000
Ending inventory	785,000	?
Selling and general expenses	450,000	320,000

Instructions: Using the gross profit method, compute the value to be assigned to the inventory as of September 30, 2002, and prepare an income statement for the 9-month period ending on this date.

PROBLEM 9–34

INVENTORY THEFT LOSS

In December 2002, Bullseye Merchandise Inc. had a significant portion of its inventory stolen. The company determined the cost of inventory remaining to be $31,100. The following information was taken from the records of the company.

	Jan. 1, 2002 to Date of Theft	2001
Purchases	$154,854	$185,375
Purchase returns and allowances	7,225	8,420
Sales	254,300	261,800
Sales returns and allowances	3,300	2,600
Salaries	9,600	10,800

	Jan. 1, 2002 to Date of Theft	2001
Rent	$ 6,480	$ 6,480
Insurance	1,160	1,178
Utilities	1,361	1,525
Advertising	5,100	3,216
Depreciation expense	1,506	1,536
Beginning inventory	69,923	64,040

Instructions: Estimate the cost of the stolen inventory.

PROBLEM 9–35

RETAIL INVENTORY METHOD

Soho Clothing Store values its inventory under the retail inventory method. The following data are available for 2002.

	Cost	Retail
Inventory, January 1	$ 46,053	$ 79,100
Markdowns		15,000
Markups		31,600
Purchases	142,390	221,600
Sales		251,500
Purchase returns	4,000	6,000
Sales discounts		12,000
Freight-in	14,600	

Instructions:

1. Compute the estimated inventory at December 31, 2002, using the retail inventory method to estimate inventory at lower of cost or market.
2. Prepare the summary accounting journal entries to record the above inventory data (include entries to record the purchases, sales, and closing of Inventory to Cost of Goods Sold).
3. What gross profit would be reported on the income statement for 2002?

PROBLEM 9–36

RETAIL INVENTORY METHOD

The following information was taken from the records of Trump Inc. for the years 2001 and 2002.

Instructions: Compute the value of the inventory at the end of 2001 and 2002 using the retail inventory method to estimate average cost.

	2002	2001
Sales	$128,600	$135,600
Sales discounts	1,840	1,200
Sales returns	2,100	1,600
Freight-in	4,000	3,640
Purchases (at cost)	78,000	68,560
Purchases (at retail)	100,500	92,480
Purchase discounts	4,155	1,000
Beginning inventory (at cost)		65,600
Beginning inventory (at retail)		87,520

PROBLEM 9–37

RETAIL INVENTORY METHOD

Johnson & Jones, a pharmaceutical company, uses the retail inventory method to estimate inventory at lower of cost or market. The limited information shown on the next page is available for the past 3 years.

	2002		2001		2000	
	Cost	Retail	Cost	Retail	Cost	Retail
Inventory, Jan. 1	$ 5,536	$?	$?	$?	$ 8,255	$ 14,000
Purchases	77,809	114,750	84,500	?	71,000	105,000
Markups		?		13,000		?
Goods available	$?	$133,780	$?	$?	$?	$?
Cost percentage	?		64.9%		?	
Deduct: Markdowns		7,750				?
Sales		?		132,450		110,000
Inventory, Dec. 31	$ 9,255	$?	$?	$ 8,530	$10,890	$ 18,000

Instructions: Compute the missing amounts from the information given.

PROBLEM 9–38

INVENTORY ERROR CORRECTION

The Sonntag Corporation has adjusted and closed its books at the end of 2001. The company arrives at its inventory position by a physical count taken on December 31 of each year. In March of 2002, the following errors were discovered.

a. Merchandise that cost $2,500 was sold for $3,400 on December 29, 2001. The order was shipped December 31, 2001, with terms of FOB shipping point. The merchandise was not included in the ending inventory. The sale was recorded on January 12, 2002, when the customer made payment on the sale.

b. On January 3, 2002, Sonntag Corporation received merchandise that had been shipped to them on December 30, 2001. The terms of the purchase were FOB shipping point. Cost of the merchandise was $1,750. The purchase was recorded and the goods included in the inventory when payment was made in January 2002.

c. On January 8, 2002, merchandise that had been included in the ending inventory was returned to Sonntag because the consignee had not been able to sell it. The cost of this merchandise was $1,200 with a selling price of $1,800.

d. Merchandise costing $750, located in a separate warehouse, was overlooked and excluded from the 2001 inventory count.

e. On December 26, 2001, Sonntag Corporation purchased merchandise costing $1,175 from a supplier. The order was shipped December 28 (terms FOB destination) and was still "in transit" on December 31. Because the invoice was received on December 31, the purchase was recorded in 2001. The merchandise was not included in the inventory count.

f. The corporation failed to make an entry for a purchase on account of $835 at the end of 2001, although it included this merchandise in the inventory count. The purchase was recorded when payment was made to the supplier in 2002.

g. The corporation included in its 2001 ending inventory merchandise with a cost of $1,350. This merchandise had been custom built and was being held until the customer could come and pick up the merchandise. The sale, for $1,825, was recorded in 2002.

Instructions: Give the entry in 2002 (2001 books are closed) to correct each error. Assume that the errors were made during 2001, all amounts are material, and the periodic inventory system is used.

PROBLEM 9–39

DOLLAR-VALUE LIFO RETAIL INVENTORY METHOD

In 1999, Van Hover Inc. adopted the dollar-value LIFO retail inventory method. The January 1, 1999, price index was 1.00. The data shown on the next page are available for the 4-year period ending December 31, 2002.

	Cost	Retail
1999:		
Inventory, January 1	$148,050	$235,000
Purchases	393,700	635,000
Sales		590,000
Year-end price index		1.12
2000:		
Purchases	$363,000	$550,000
Sales		579,170
Year-end price index		1.08
2001:		
Purchases	$377,000	$650,000
Sales		641,955
Year-end price index		1.09
2002:		
Purchases	$504,000	$800,000
Sales		762,500
Year-end price index		1.12

Instructions: Calculate the inventories to be reported at the end of 1999, 2000, 2001, and 2002. Incremental layers are costed at end-of-year prices.

PROBLEM 9–40

DOLLAR-VALUE LIFO RETAIL INVENTORY METHOD

The St. George Sports Shop values its inventory on the dollar-value LIFO retail basis. Incremental inventory layers are costed at end-of-year prices. At December 31, 2001, the inventory was valued as follows:

LIFO Layer Year	Cost	Year-End Retail	Year-End Price Index	Retail at Base of 1.00
1995	$14,760	$24,600	1.00	$24,600
1997	9,482	13,545	1.05	12,900
1999	13,442	26,884	1.03	26,100
2000	4,500	6,000	1.10	5,454
	$42,184	$71,029		$69,054

The December 31, 2001, inventory at 2001 retail prices was $77,340. Information relating to 2002 transactions is as follows:

Purchases—cost	$476,100
Purchases—selling price	673,845
Freight-in	9,900
Sales returns	11,220
Sales discounts	1,950
Markups	3,660
Markdowns	2,505
Gross sales	702,000
Year-end price index for 2002	1.08

Instructions: Based on the above information, compute the following:

1. 2002 cost ratio
2. Inventory amount that would be reported on the balance sheet on December 31, 2002

PROBLEM 9–41

PURCHASE COMMITMENTS

On November 17, 2002, Chaldees Airways entered into a commitment to purchase 3,000 barrels of aviation fuel for $165,000 on March 23, 2003. Chaldees entered into this purchase commitment to protect itself against the volatility in the aviation fuel market. By December 31, the purchase price of aviation fuel had fallen to $40 per barrel. However, by March 23, 2003, when Chaldees took delivery of the 3,000 barrels, the price of aviation fuel had risen to $60 per barrel.

Instructions:

1. Make the journal entry necessary on November 17, 2002, to record the purchase commitment.
2. Make any adjusting entry necessary on December 31, 2002.
3. What type of account (i.e., asset, liability, revenue, etc.) is "Estimated Loss on Purchase Commitments"?
4. Make the journal entry to record the purchase on March 23, 2003. Chaldees uses a periodic inventory system.

PROBLEM 9–42

FOREIGN CURRENCY TRANSACTIONS

Charles & Sons, a U.S. computer supplies firm, had the following transactions with foreign companies during December 2001.

a. Goldstar Co., Ltd., a South Korea–based firm, sold 5,000 computer hard drives to Charles & Sons for 100,000 won per drive on December 12, 2001. Charles & Sons paid the bill on January 13, 2002.

b. Charles & Sons sold 2,000 computer hard drives to a Swiss firm, Lockner Inc., on December 21, 2001. Lockner Inc. agreed to pay $135 per hard drive. Payment was received by Charles & Sons on February 4, 2002.

c. Charles & Sons sold 2,400 computer hard drives to Geopacific, Inc., a company with headquarters in Canada, on December 28, 2001. Geopacific was billed 148 Canadian dollars per drive. Payment was received on January 10, 2002.

d. Charles & Sons received 1,000 printers from Printco, a Japanese company, on December 28, 2001. Printco billed Charles & Sons 45,000 yen per printer. Charles & Sons paid the liability on January 14, 2002.

Exchange rates for the above transactions are as follows:

U.S. dollar value of 1 unit of foreign currency:

	As of Date of Sale or Purchase	As of Balance Sheet Date	As of Date of Payment or Receipt
South Korean won	$0.00103	$0.00112	$0.00115
Swiss franc	0.670	0.632	0.655
Canadian dollar	0.910	0.935	0.905
Japanese yen	0.0075	0.0069	0.0073

Instructions: Prepare the journal entries necessary for Charles & Sons to record each of the above transactions for the following: (1) date of the original transaction, (2) balance sheet date, and (3) date of payment or receipt of cash.

COMPETENCY ENHANCEMENT OPPORTUNITIES

▶ Deciphering Actual Financial Statements

▶ Writing Assignment

▶ Research Project

▶ The Debate

▶ Ethical Dilemma

▶ Cumulative Spreadsheet Analysis

▶ Internet Search

Accounting is more than just doing textbook problems. This expanded competency material provides practice in critical thinking, oral and written communication, research, teamwork, and consideration of ethical issues.

DECIPHERING ACTUAL FINANCIAL STATEMENTS
• Deciphering 9–1 (The Walt Disney Company)

The 1998 financial statements for THE WALT DISNEY COMPANY are included in Appendix A. The following numbers (in millions of dollars) have been taken from the financial statements and the notes.

Film and television costs, 12/31/97 .... $4,401
Film and television costs, 12/31/98 5,729
Amortization of film and television costs—1998 2,514

Disney accumulates the costs associated with its films and television on its balance sheet until revenue from those films and television programs is recognized on the income statement. At that time, costs are expensed to the income statement—much like inventory.

1. Compute the costs that were "inventoried" during 1998 associated with films and television programs.
2. Given revenues for Disney from its Creative Content segment (its film and television production business) of $10,302, compute the Creative Content segment's gross profit.

• Deciphering 9–2 (Circle K)

CIRCLE K is a large convenience store chain. Selected financial statement data for the years 1988 and 1993 are given below. All numbers are in millions of dollars.

	1993	1988
Sales:		
Gasoline	$1,504.1	$ 964.6
Merchandise	1,541.8	1,649.2
Cost of goods sold:		
Gasoline	1,354.5	862.4
Merchandise	1,054.5	1,030.8
Ending inventory—total	131.2	191.0

Note: More current comparable financial statement data are no longer available because Circle K is now a subsidiary of a larger company.

For 1994, Circle K had total sales of $3,272.8. Purchases for 1994 were $2,554.0.

1. Which set of numbers—1988 or 1993—is likely to give a better indication of the 1994 gross profit percentage? Explain.
2. Using the gross profit method, estimate Circle K's inventory as of the end of 1994.

• Deciphering 9–3 (Exxon)

On December 31, 1997, the aggregate replacement cost of all of EXXON's crude oil and natural gas inventory was approximately $7.4 billion. By December 31, 1998, the aggregate replacement cost of Exxon's inventory had fallen to $5.8 billion. This reduction in replacement cost was primarily the result of a decline in the price of crude oil. The average crude oil sales price per barrel was $11.03 in 1998, compared to $17.39 in 1997.

In spite of this $1.6 billion decline in the replacement cost of inventory, Exxon was not required to make a lower-of-cost-or-market adjustment in 1998. Why do you think this is so?

• Deciphering 9–4 (IBM)

In 1998, IBM reported that approximately 57% of its revenue were generated outside of the United States. The vast majority of that revenue were generated in a foreign currency. In addition, IBM noted that changing currency rates "resulted in an unfavorable impact on revenue of approximately 2 percent, 5 percent, and 3 percent, respectively, in 1998, 1997, and 1996."

To gain some insight into how IBM shields itself from the effects of currency fluctuations, consider the following example. On March 1, a company makes a sale, on account, for 100,000 Hong Kong dollars. On the same date, the company purchases inventory, on account, for 100,000 Hong Kong dollars. The spot rate on March 1 is 7.7 Hong Kong dollars per U.S. dollar. On July 1, when the receivable is collected and the payable is paid, the exchange rate is 8 Hong Kong dollars (HK$) per U.S. dollar.

After examining the journal entries necessary to record the foreign currency transactions described in the previous paragraph, discuss how multinational corporations such as IBM are able to minimize their exposure to currency rate fluctuation risk.

▶ WRITING ASSIGNMENT
• Where has all the inventory gone?

Main Street Department Store uses the retail inventory method. Periodically, a physical count is made of the inventory and compared with the book figure computed from the company sales and purchase records. This year the physical count resulted in a total inventory value 10% lower than the book figure. Jennifer Strack, the controller, is concerned by the variance. A 2% to 3% loss from shoplifting has been tolerated through the years. But 10% is too much.

You are the branch manager for Main Street Department Store and have been summoned to account for the discrepancy. You are confident that the apparent inventory shortage of 10% stems from errors related to the use of the retail inventory method and not from theft or fraud. Jennifer Strack has not been satisfied with your explanation and asks you to outline specifically what types of errors could have caused such a variance. Prepare a 1-page memo for Strack.

▶ RESEARCH PROJECT
• How much inventory is there in a supermarket?

Your group is to report (either orally or in writing) on your estimate of the total cost of inventory in a local supermarket.

1. Identify a large supermarket chain in your area.
2. Obtain a recent copy of the chain's annual report. Use the financial statement information to estimate the supermarket's gross profit percentage.
3. Go to one of the chain's local locations.
4. Estimate the total retail value of inventory located in the store. Don't take more than 30 minutes on this part of the project. Sample a few sections from some of the store aisles and extrapolate your estimate to the entire store.
5. Compute your estimate of the total inventory cost.
6. Describe the primary factors that might cause your inventory cost estimate to be in error.

▶ **THE DEBATE**

• Reported inventory should be accurate to the penny!

This chapter describes several techniques for estimating a firm's ending inventory. Both the retail inventory method and the dollar-value LIFO retail method are widely used by companies in preparing their quarterly and annual financial statements.

Divide your group into 2 teams.

- One team represents Precision. Prepare a 2-minute oral argument that exposes the evils of using inventory estimates in preparing financial statements. This group will be satisfied with nothing less than the physical counting of every single item in inventory.
- The other team represents Estimation. Prepare a 2-minute oral argument outlining the necessity of using inventory estimates for timely financial statement preparation and the idiocy of the insistence on precision.

▶ **ETHICAL DILEMMA**

• Just cut me the check!

You live in a small town and are the regional claims adjustor for a large commercial insurance company. Recently, a fire destroyed the hardware store of one of your clients (who is also a personal friend). A thorough arson investigation revealed that the fire was accidental, caused by an electrical surge.

Yesterday your friend gave you his estimate of the value of the inventory destroyed in the fire. Today you went to his office and told him that you thought the estimate was too high. After discussing the issue for 10 minutes or so, your friend summarized his view as follows:

- Yes, the estimate is a little high.
- The insurance company can afford to pay out a little extra.
- There is really no way to verify how much inventory was burned in the fire, so why not give the customer the benefit of the doubt?

How do you respond to your friend?

▶ **CUMULATIVE SPREADSHEET ANALYSIS**

This spreadsheet assignment is a continuation of the spreadsheet assignments given in earlier chapters. If you completed those assignments, you have a head start on this one.

Refer back to the instructions for preparing the revised financial statements for 2002 as given in (1) of the Cumulative Spreadsheet Analysis assignment in Chapter 3.

1. Skywalker wishes to prepare a *forecasted* balance sheet, a *forecasted* income statement, and a *forecasted* statement of cash flows for 2003. Use the financial statement numbers for 2002 as the basis for the forecast, along with the following additional information.

a. Sales in 2003 are expected to increase by 40% over 2002 sales of $2,100.

b. In 2003, Skywalker expects to acquire new property, plant, and equipment costing $240.

c. The $480 in operating expenses reported in 2002 breaks down as follows: $15 depreciation expense, $465 other operating expenses.

d. No new long-term debt will be acquired in 2003.

e. No cash dividends will be paid in 2003.

f. New short-term loans payable will be acquired in an amount sufficient to make Skywalker's current ratio in 2003 exactly equal to 2.0.

g. Skywalker does not anticipate repurchasing any additional shares of stock during 2003.

h. Because changes in future prices and exchange rates are impossible to predict, Skywalker's best estimate is that the balance in accumulated other comprehensive income will remain unchanged in 2003.

i.   In the absence of more detailed information, assume that the balances in the investment securities, long-term investments, other long-term assets, and intangible assets accounts will all increase at the same rate as sales (40%) in 2003.

j.   In the absence of more detailed information, assume that the balance in the other long-term liabilities account will increase at the same rate as sales (40%) in 2003.

k.   The investment securities are classified as available-for-sale securities. Accordingly, cash from the purchase and sale of these securities is classified as an investing activity.

l.   Assume that transactions impacting other long-term assets and other long-term liabilities accounts are operating activities.

m.   Cash and investment securities accounts will increase at the same rate as sales.

n.   The forecasted amount of accounts receivable in 2003 is determined using the forecasted value for the average collection period. The average collection period for 2003 is expected to be 14.08 days. To make the calculations less complex, this value of 14.08 days is based on forecasted end-of-year accounts receivable rather than on average accounts receivable.

(Note: These forecasted statements were constructed as part of the spreadsheet assignment in Chapter 6; you can use that spreadsheet as a starting point if you have completed that assignment.)

For this exercise, add the following additional assumptions.

o.   The forecasted amount of inventory in 2003 is determined using the forecasted value for the number of days' sales in inventory. The number of days' sales in inventory for 2003 is expected to be 107.6 days. To make the calculations easier, this value of 107.6 days is based on forecasted end-of-year inventory rather than on average inventory.

p.   The forecasted amount of accounts payable in 2003 is determined using the forecasted value for the number of days' purchases in accounts payable. The number of days' purchases in accounts payable for 2003 is expected to be 48.34 days. To make the calculations easier, this value of 48.34 days is based on forecasted end-of-year accounts payable rather than on average accounts payable.

Clearly state any additional assumptions that you make.

2.   Repeat (1), with the following changes in assumptions:
 a.   Number of days' sales in inventory is expected to be 66.2 days.
 b.   Number of days' sales in inventory is expected to be 150.0 days.

3.   Comment on the differences in the forecasted values of cash from operating activities in 2003 under each of the following assumptions about the number of days' sales in inventory: 107.6 days, 66.2 days, and 150.0 days.

4.   Is there any impact on the forecasted level of accounts payable when the number of days' sales in inventory is changed? Why or why not?

5.   What happens to the forecasted level of short-term loans payable when the number of days' sales in inventory is reduced to 66.2 days? Explain.

▶   **INTERNET SEARCH**

EXXON's Web address is **www.exxon.com**. Once you've gained access to Exxon's Web site, answer the following questions.

1.   When was Exxon founded? Who was the founder of Exxon? Exxon sometimes uses the brand name "Esso"—where and for what products?

2.   Oil exploration and transport exposes firms such as Exxon to potentially large costs from environmental contamination. What does Exxon's Web site say about Exxon's environmental policy?

3.   Exxon was one of the first U.S. multinational companies. In which South American and African countries is Exxon currently exploring for oil? producing oil?

137,000

140,000

89,678

117,451

chapter 10
Debt Financing

Analysis of the data gathered in the U.S. census of 1880 took almost 10 years. For the census of 1890, the U.S. government commissioned Herman Hollerith to provide data tabulation machines to speed up the process. This system of mechanized data handling saved the Census Bureau $5 million and slashed the data analysis time by two years. In 1924, Hollerith's company adopted the name INTERNATIONAL BUSINESS MACHINES CORPORATION (IBM). IBM became the largest office machine producer in the United States with sales of more than $180 million in 1949.

In 1950, there was great resistance to the idea of electronic computers at IBM. IBM's engineers were specialists in electro-mechanical devices and were uncomfortable working with vacuum tubes, diodes, and magnetic recording tapes. In addition, there were many questions about the customer demand for electronic computers. One IBM executive forecast that the size of the total worldwide market for computers was no more than five. However, following significant internal debate, IBM pressed forward with the production of its first electronic computer, the 701. Through the 1960s and 70s, with its aggressive leasing program, emphasis on sales and service, and continued investment in research and development, IBM established a dominant (some claimed a monopolistic) position in the mainframe computer market.

When the IBM personal computer was released in 1981, it quickly became the industry standard for PCs. By 1986, IBM held 40% of the PC market. Amid this success, IBM made what, in retrospect, was a crucial error—it chose to focus on producing and selling hardware and to leave software development, by and large, to others. In fact, IBM did not develop the operating system for its first PC, instead electing to use a system called DOS, licensed from a 32-person company named MICROSOFT. In the early 1990s, as profits of software developers such as Microsoft and NOVELL exploded, the profits of IBM slumped badly. In 1990, IBM reported an operating profit of $11 billion. Operating profit in 1991 fell to $942 million, and operations showed a loss of $45 million in 1992, which was IBM's first operating loss ever. As of December 31, 1992, the total market value of IBM stock was $29 billion, down from $106 billion in 1987 when IBM was the most valuable company in the world.

Interestingly, in the midst of these problems—decreasing market share, lower profit margins, and record losses—IBM found high demand for its record-setting bond issue. In 1993, IBM issued $1.25 billion of 7-year notes and $550 million of 20-year debentures. At the time, this was the largest U.S. bond issue in history. The stated interest rates were 6.375% for the notes and 7.50% for the bonds. On their issue date, these two bond issues provided investors with a yield just 0.7% above that provided by U.S. Treasury instruments with comparable maturity periods. Because of IBM's financial woes at the time, many thought that the difference would be much higher. Nonetheless, investors' concerns about IBM's future did increase the perceived risk associated with loaning money to the company. In January 1993, Standard & Poor's downgraded IBM's credit rating from the highest rating, AAA, to AA–. In March 1993, Moody's Investor's Service also lowered IBM's rating from A–1 to

1
Understand the various classification and measurement issues associated with debt.

2
Account for short-term debt obligations, including those expected to be refinanced, and describe the purpose of lines of credit.

3
Apply present value concepts to the accounting for long-term debts such as mortgages.

4
Understand the various types of bonds, compute the price of a bond issue, and account for the issuance, interest, and redemption of bonds.

5
Explain various types of off-balance-sheet financing, and understand the reasons for this type of financing.

6
Analyze a firm's debt position using ratios.

7
Review the notes to financial statements, and understand the disclosure associated with debt financing.

EXPANDED MATERIAL

8
Understand the conditions under which troubled debt restructuring occurs, and be able to account for troubled debt restructuring.

AA–2.[1] Prior to these downgrades, IBM was able to finance debt in the market at approximately 0.5% above the U.S. Treasury yield.[2]

In a bid to turn IBM around, the board of directors looked outside the company for a new CEO in 1993. They picked Louis V. Gerstner, Jr., who had been the CEO at RJR NABISCO for four years. In his 1997 address to IBM's shareholders, Mr. Gerstner looked back on the task that faced him when he took the reins in 1993. When he came aboard, he reports, IBM's board was considering dismantling the company, thinking that a collection of smaller, more nimble businesses would hopefully be worth more to IBM's shareholders than the lumbering, inefficient parent company. Mr. Gerstner changed the direction of the company, deciding to keep the company together and to rely on IBM's unique market position in terms of product breadth and strong customer ties. Under Mr. Gerstner's leadership, IBM has recovered, setting new revenue records in each year from 1995 through 1997. As of September 10, 1999, IBM's market value had climbed back up to $247.0 billion.

In addition to the routine notes and debentures issued by IBM in order to borrow $1.25 billion in 1993, a long list of more creative types of debt-financing instruments has been created by the U.S. financial industry. For years, we've had convertible bonds, junk bonds, zero-interest bonds, and commodity-backed bonds, to name a few. The objective of each of these debt instruments is to assist a company in raising needed funds for its business. In this chapter, we will discuss various methods available to companies for borrowing money. We begin with a quick review of liabilities—what they are and how they are measured. Then we will discuss short-term obligations and lines of credit. We then review the concept of present value and examine a mortgage to illustrate how present values apply to the accounting for long-term debt obligations. We then focus on the accounting for various types of bonds. Following our discussion of bonds, we will introduce some common methods that are used by companies to avoid disclosing debt on the financial statements. These methods are collectively referred to as off-balance-sheet financing. Once you have been exposed to various types of debt financing available to a company, we will talk about how one can analyze a firm's debt position as well as common note disclosures associated with debt.

In the expanded material section of the chapter, we discuss troubled debt restructuring. The topic of troubled debt restructuring covers those instances when a company is in poor financial condition and is in danger of defaulting on its debt payments. The negotiations between the bond issuer and the holders of the bonds (or troubled debt) often require journal entries to account for the concessions made on the part of the bondholders.

A time line illustrating the business issues associated with long-term financing is given in Exhibit 10–1. The first action is to choose the appropriate form of financing. For example, a company must decide whether to negotiate a private loan with a bank or to seek public financing through the issuance of bonds. After the debt is issued, it is usually serviced through periodic interest payments, although some forms of long-term debt defer

---

1 These bond rating scales have since been modified.
2 Thomas T. Vogel, Jr., and Leslie Scism, "Investors Snap Up $1.8 Billion of IBM Securities as Corporations Scramble to Best Higher Interest Rates," *The Wall Street Journal*, June 9, 1993, p. C16.

payment of all interest until the end of the loan period. An important part of issuing and monitoring long-term debt is the accounting for the specific features of the debt. As discussed in this chapter, bonds require specialized accounting procedures to ensure that the proper amount of interest expense is reported in the income statement and that the long-term debt obligation is reported at the appropriate amount in the balance sheet. Finally, the long-term debt is repaid, either as originally scheduled or, sometimes, in advance.

EXHIBIT 10–1 | Time Line of Business Issues Associated With Long-Term Debt

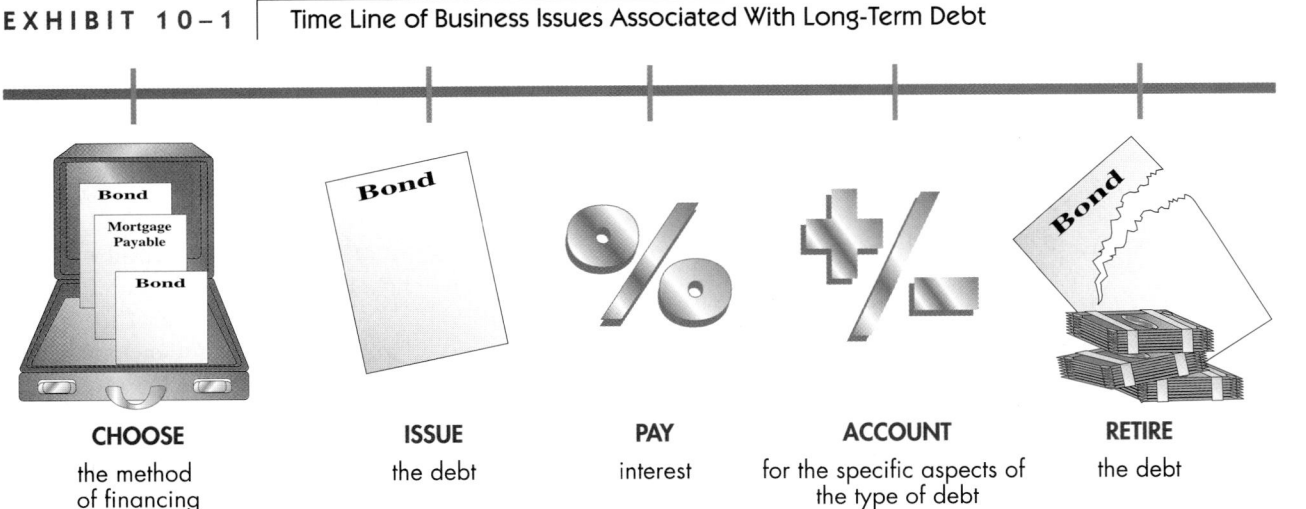

CHOOSE	ISSUE	PAY	ACCOUNT	RETIRE
the method of financing	the debt	interest	for the specific aspects of the type of debt	the debt

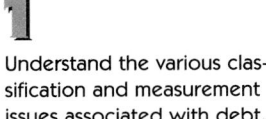

Understand the various classification and measurement issues associated with debt.

CLASSIFICATION AND MEASUREMENT ISSUES ASSOCIATED WITH DEBT

Before we get into the specifics of debt, let's first take a moment and review just what liabilities are and how they are classified and measured.

Definition of Liabilities

Liabilities have been defined by the FASB as "probable future sacrifices of economic benefits arising from present obligations of a particular entity to transfer assets or provide services to other entities in the future as a result of past transactions or events."[3] This definition contains significant components that need to be explained before individual liability accounts are discussed.

A liability is a result of *past transactions or events.* Thus, a liability is not recognized until incurred. This part of the definition excludes contractual obligations from an exchange of promises if performance by both parties is still in the future. Such contracts are referred to as executory contracts. Determining when an executory contract qualifies as a liability is not always easy. For example, the signing of a labor contract that obligates both the employer and the employee does not give rise to a liability in current accounting practice, nor does the placing of an order for the purchase of merchandise. However, under some conditions, the signing of a lease is recognized as an event that requires the current recognition of a liability even though a lease is essentially an executory contract.

3 *Statement of Financial Accounting Concepts No. 6,* "Elements of Financial Statements," Stamford, CT: Financial Accounting Standards Board, December 1985, par. 35.

A liability, such as a bank loan, has the following characteristics: (1) is a result of past transactions or events, (2) involves a probable future transfer of assets or services, and (3) is the obligation of a particular entity.

A liability must involve a *probable future transfer of assets or services.* Although liabilities result from past transactions or events, an obligation may be contingent upon the occurrence of another event sometime in the future. When occurrence of the future event seems probable, the obligation is defined as a liability. Although the majority of liabilities are satisfied by payment of cash, some obligations are satisfied by transferring other types of assets or by providing services. For example, revenue received in advance requires recognition of an obligation to provide goods or services in the future. Usually, the time of payment is specified by a debt instrument, for example, a note requiring payment of interest and principal on a given date or series of dates. Some obligations, however, require the transfer of assets or services over a period of time, but the exact dates cannot be determined when the liability is incurred, for example, obligations to provide parts or service under a warranty agreement.

A liability is the *obligation of a particular entity,* that is, the entity that has the responsibility to transfer assets or provide services. As long as the payment or transfer is probable, it is not necessary that the entity to whom the obligation is owed be identified. Thus, a warranty to make any repairs necessary to an item sold by an entity is an obligation of that entity even though it is not certain which customers will receive benefits. Generally, the obligation rests on a foundation of legal rights and duties. However, obligations created, inferred, or construed from the facts of a particular situation may also be recognized as liabilities. For example, if a company regularly pays vacation pay or year-end bonuses, accrual of these items as a liability is warranted even though no legal agreement exists to make these payments. For example, in its 1998 balance sheet, GENERAL MOTORS recognizes a liability of $38.1 billion associated with its promises to take care of the health care benefits of its retirees. However, in the notes to those same financial statements, GM is careful to state that even though it is recognizing this $38.1 billion liability, it does not admit or acknowledge in any way that this amount reflects a legally enforceable liability to the company.

Although the FASB's definition is helpful, the question of when a liability exists is not always easy to answer. Examples of areas in which there are continuing controversies include the problems associated with off-balance-sheet financing, deferred income taxes, leases, pensions, and even some equity securities, such as redeemable preferred stock. Once an item is accepted as having met the definition of a liability, there is still the need to appropriately classify, measure, and report the liability.

Classification of Liabilities

For reporting purposes, liabilities are usually classified as current or noncurrent. The distinction between current and noncurrent liabilities was introduced and explained in

Chapter 3, where it was pointed out that the computation of working capital is considered by many to be a useful measure of the liquidity of an enterprise.

As noted in Chapter 3, the same rules generally apply for the classification of liabilities as for assets. If a liability arises in the course of an entity's normal operating cycle, it is considered current if current assets will be used to satisfy the obligation within one year or one operating cycle, whichever period is longer. On the other hand, bank borrowings, notes, mortgages, and similar obligations are related to the general financial condition of the entity, rather than directly to the operating cycle, and are classified as current only if they are to be paid with current assets within one year.

When debt that has been classified as noncurrent will mature within the next year, the liability should be reported as a current liability in order to reflect the expected drain on current assets. However, if the liability is to be paid by transfer of noncurrent assets that have been accumulated for the purpose of liquidating the liability, the obligation continues to be classified as noncurrent.

The distinction between current and noncurrent liabilities is important because of the impact on a company's current ratio. This fundamental measurement of a company's liquidity is computed by dividing total current assets by total current liabilities.

The current ratio is a measure of an entity's ability to meet current obligations. Care must be taken to determine that proper items have been included in the current asset and current liability categories. Historically, the rule of thumb has been that a current ratio below 2.0 suggests the possibility of liquidity problems. However, advances in information technology have enabled companies to be much more effective in minimizing the need to hold cash, inventories, and other current assets. As a result, current ratios for successful companies these days are frequently less than 1.0. Current ratios for selected U.S. companies for 1998 are given in Exhibit 10–2. Note that, with the exception of MICROSOFT, all of the companies have current ratios substantially below the 2.0 historical benchmark, and the current ratio of DELTA AIR LINES is only .50.

EXHIBIT 10–2 | Current Ratios for Selected U.S. Companies for Fiscal 1998

$$\text{CURRENT RATIO} = \frac{\text{TOTAL CURRENT ASSETS}}{\text{TOTAL CURRENT LIABILITIES}}$$

	Current Ratio
Coca-Cola	.74
Delta Air Lines	.50
Dow Chemical	1.18
IBM	1.15
McDonald's	.52
Microsoft	2.32
Wal-Mart	1.26

A reasonable margin of current assets over current liabilities suggests that a company will be able to meet maturing obligations even in the event of unfavorable business

STOP & THINK The 1998 current ratio of McDonald's is only .52; does this mean that McDonald's will not be able to meet its current obligations as they come due? Explain.

conditions or losses on such assets as securities, receivables, and inventories. A current ratio of 1.4 means, for example, that a company could liquidate its total current liabilities 1.4 times using only its current assets.

Measurement of Liabilities

The distinction between current and noncurrent liabilities is also an important consideration in the measurement of liabilities. Obviously, before liabilities can be reported on the financial statements, they must be stated in monetary terms. The measurement used for liabilities is the present value of the future cash outflows to settle the obligation. Generally, this is the amount of cash required to liquidate the obligation if it were paid today.

If a claim isn't to be paid until sometime in the future, as is the case with noncurrent liabilities, either the claim should provide for interest to be paid on the debt or the obligation should be reported at the discounted value of its maturity amount. Current obligations that arise in the course of normal business operations are generally due within a short period, for example, 30 to 60 days, and normally are not discounted.[4] Thus, trade accounts payable are not discounted even though they carry no interest provision. However, this is an exception to the general rule; most nonoperating business transactions, such as the borrowing of money, purchasing of assets over time, and long-term leases, do involve the discounting process. The obligation in these instances is the present value of the future resource outflows. The use of present value concepts with long-term debt obligations is illustrated in detail later in the chapter.

For measurement purposes, liabilities can be divided into three categories:

1. Liabilities that are definite in amount
2. Estimated liabilities
3. Contingent liabilities

The measurement of liabilities always involves some uncertainty, because a liability, by definition, involves a future outflow of resources. However, for the first category above, both the existence of the liability and the amount to be paid are determinable because of a contract, trade agreement, or general business practice. An example of a liability that is definite in amount is the principal payment on a note.

The second category includes items that are definitely liabilities, that is, they involve a definite future resource outflow, but the actual amount of the obligation cannot be established currently. In this situation, the amount of the liability is estimated so that the obligation is reflected in the current period, even though at an approximated value. A warranty obligation that is recorded on an accrual basis is an example of an estimated liability.

Caution! A contingent liability results only when there is a high degree of uncertainty as to the outcome of the event associated with the potential liability. Recall from its definition that a liability involves a "probable future sacrifice. . . ." If the contingent event is probable, it meets the definition of a liability and should be recorded as such.

Generally, liabilities from both of the first two categories are reported on the balance sheet as claims against recorded assets, either as current or noncurrent liabilities, whichever is appropriate. However, items that resemble liabilities but are contingent upon the occurrence of some future event are not recorded until it is probable that the event will occur. Even though the amount of the potential obligation may be known, the actual existence of a liability is questionable, because it is contingent upon a future event for which there is considerable uncertainty. An example of a contingent liability is a pending lawsuit. Only if the lawsuit is lost or is settled out of court, will a liability be recorded. While not recorded in the accounts, some contingent liabilities should be disclosed in the notes to the financial statements as discussed and illustrated in Chapter 18.

4 *Opinions of the Accounting Principles Board No. 21, "Interest on Receivables and Payables,"* New York: American Institute of Certified Public Accountants, 1971, par. 3.

2

Account for short-term debt obligations, including those expected to be refinanced, and describe the purpose of lines of credit.

ACCOUNTING FOR SHORT-TERM DEBT OBLIGATIONS

As noted in the previous section, liabilities that have been classified as current are typically not discounted. They are reported on the balance sheet at their face value. Representative of this type of debt are accounts payable, notes payable, and miscellaneous operating payables including salaries, payroll taxes, property and sales taxes, and income taxes. Short-term obligations that are expected to be refinanced require special consideration. Problems that can arise in determining the balances to be reported for these various types of debt are described in the following sections.

Short-Term Operating Liabilities

Most goods and services in today's economic environment are purchased on credit. The term **account payable** usually refers to the amount due for the purchase of materials by a manufacturing company or merchandise by a wholesaler or retailer. Other obligations, such as salaries and wages, rent, interest, and utilities, are reported as separate liabilities in accounts descriptive of the nature of the obligation. Accounts payable are usually not recorded when purchase orders are placed but when legal title to the goods passes to the buyer. The rules for the customary recognition of legal passage of title were presented in Chapter 8. If goods are in transit at year-end, the purchase should be recorded if the shipment terms indicate that title has passed. This means that care must be exercised to review the purchase of goods and services near the end of an accounting period to ensure a proper cutoff and reporting of liabilities and inventory.

It is customary to report accounts payable at the expected amount of the payment. Because the payment period is normally short, no recognition of interest is required. As indicated in Chapter 8, if cash discounts are available, the liability should be reported net of the expected cash discount. Failure to use the net method in recording purchases usually results in reported liabilities being in excess of the payment finally made because most companies are careful to take advantage of available cash discounts.

Short-Term Debt

Companies often borrow money on a short-term basis for operating purposes other than for the purchase of materials or merchandise involving accounts payable. Collectively, these obligations may be referred to as short-term debt. In most cases, such debt is evidenced by a **promissory note,** a formal written promise to pay a sum of money in the future, and is usually reflected on the debtor's books as **Notes Payable.**

Notes issued to trade creditors for the purchase of goods or services are called **trade notes payable. Nontrade notes payable** are notes issued to banks or to officers and stockholders for loans to the company and those issued to others for the purchase of noncurrent operating assets. It is normally desirable to classify current notes payable on the balance sheet as trade or nontrade, because such information would reveal to statement users the sources of indebtedness and the extent to which the company has relied on each source in financing its activities.

The problems encountered in the valuation of notes payable are the same as those discussed in Chapter 6 with respect to notes receivable. Thus, a short-term note payable is recorded and reported at its present value, which is normally the face value of the note. This presumes that the note bears a reasonable stated rate of interest. However, if a note has no stated rate of interest, or if the stated rate is unreasonable, then the face value of the note would need to be discounted to its present value to reflect the effective rate of interest implicit in the note. This is accomplished by debiting Discount on Notes Payable when the note is issued and by writing off the discount to Interest Expense over the life of the note in the same manner as was illustrated for the discount on notes receivable in Chapter 6.

Discount on Notes Payable is a contra account to Notes Payable and would be reported on the balance sheet as follows:

Current liabilities:		
Notes payable	$100,000	
Less: Discount on notes payable	10,000	$90,000

Short-Term Obligations Expected to Be Refinanced

Misclassification of debt can create serious problems for users of financial statements. Because the "current" classification is reserved for those obligations that will be satisfied with current assets within a year, a short-term obligation that is expected to be refinanced on a long-term basis should not be reported as a current liability. This applies to the currently maturing portion of a long-term debt and to all other short-term obligations except those arising in the normal course of operations that are due in customary terms. Similarly, it should not be assumed that a short-term obligation will be refinanced, and therefore classified as a noncurrent liability, unless the refinancing arrangements are secure. Thus, to avoid potential manipulation, the refinancing expectation must be realistic and not just a mere possibility.

An example will illustrate this last point and show the importance of proper classification. Assume that a company borrows a substantial amount of money that it expects to pay back at the end of five years. The president of the company signs a six-month note, which the loan officer at the bank verbally agrees will be renewed "automatically" until the actual maturity date in five years. The only current obligation expected is payment of the accrued interest each renewal period. Under these circumstances, the company reports the obligation as noncurrent, except for the accrued interest obligation. Assume further that the loan officer leaves the bank and that the new bank official will not allow the short-term note to be refinanced. The financial picture of the company is now dramatically changed. What was considered a long-term obligation because of refinancing expectations is suddenly a current liability requiring settlement with liquid assets in the near future. This hypothetical situation is similar to what actually happened to PENN CENTRAL RAILROAD before it went bankrupt.

To assist with this problem, the FASB in 1975 issued Statement No. 6, which contains the authoritative guideline for classifying short-term obligations expected to be refinanced. According to the FASB, both of the following conditions must be met before a short-term obligation may be properly excluded from the current liability classification.[5]

1. Management must *intend to refinance* the obligation on a long-term basis.
2. Management must *demonstrate an ability to refinance* the obligation.
   Concerning the second point, an ability to refinance may be demonstrated by:
   (a) Actually refinancing the obligation during the period between the balance sheet date and the date the statements are issued.
   (b) Reaching a firm agreement that clearly provides for refinancing on a long-term basis.
   The terms of the refinancing agreement should be noncancelable as to all parties and extend beyond the current year. In addition, the company should not be in violation of the agreement at the balance sheet date or the date of issuance, and the lender or investor should be financially capable of meeting the refinancing requirements.

If an actual refinancing does occur before the balance sheet is issued, the portion of the short-term obligation that is to be excluded from current liabilities cannot exceed the proceeds from the new debt or equity securities issued to retire the old debt. For example, if a $400,000 long-term note is issued to partially refinance $750,000 of short-term obligations, only $400,000 of the short-term debt can be excluded from current liabilities.

An additional question relates to the timing of the refinancing. If the obligation is paid prior to the actual refinancing but before the balance sheet date, the obligation

5 *Statement of Financial Accounting Standards No. 6,* "Classification of Short-Term Obligations Expected to Be Refinanced," Stamford, CT: Financial Accounting Standards Board, 1975, pars. 10 and 11.

Seasonal businesses, such as toy stores like FAO Schwarz, often use lines of credit to handle temporary borrowing needs.

FYI: International Accounting Standard (IAS) 1 outlines the IASC's standard regarding the financial statement presentation of current assets and current liabilities, along with providing guidance about which items are to be classified as current. The provisions of IAS 1 are very similar to U.S. GAAP.

should be included in current liabilities on the balance sheet.[6] To illustrate, assume that the liabilities of CareFree Inc. at December 31, 2001, include a note payable for $200,000, due January 15, 2002. The management of CareFree intends to refinance the note by issuing 10-year bonds. The bonds are actually issued before the issuance of the December 31, 2001, balance sheet on February 15, 2002. If the bonds are issued prior to payment of the note, the note should be classified as noncurrent on the December 31, 2001, balance sheet. If payment of the note precedes the sale of the bonds, however, the note should be included in current liabilities.

Normally, classified balance sheets are presented showing a total for "Current liabilities." If a short-term obligation is excluded from that category due to refinancing expectations, disclosure should be made in the notes to the financial statements. The note should include a general description of the refinancing agreement.

Lines of Credit

Some companies have temporary borrowing needs necessitated by the seasonal nature of their business. TOYS "R" US is an example of this type of business. Even nonseasonal companies have predictable short-term funding needs that they prefer to arrange for in advance. A way to handle these temporary funding needs is to arrange lines of credit with banks. The lines of credit can be used for automatic borrowing as cash is needed, and then the loans can be repaid when cash is plentiful. For example, in 1998, Toys "R" Us had a $1 billion line of credit to finance seasonal inventory buildup and store construction costs. IBM also has lines of credit established with numerous banks that allow it to quickly borrow money. A **line of credit** is a negotiated arrangement with a lender in which the terms are agreed to prior to the need for borrowing. When a company finds itself in need of money, an established line of credit allows the company access to funds immediately without having to go through the credit approval process. IBM discloses the following in the notes to its 1998 financial statements.

6 FASB Interpretation No. 8, "Classification of a Short-Term Obligation Repaid Prior to Being Replaced by a Long-Term Security," Stamford, CT: Financial Accounting Standards Board, 1976, par. 3.

> I. Lines of Credit
>
> The company maintains a $10.0 billion committed global credit facility. Unused committed lines of credit from this global facility amounted to $8.8 billion and $9.2 billion at December 31, 1998 and 1997, respectively. The company's other committed and uncommitted lines of credit amounted to $5.2 billion at December 31, 1998 and 1997. The unused portion of those lines amounted to $4.3 billion and $3.9 billion at December 31, 1998 and 1997, respectively. Total unused lines of credit at December 31, 1998 and 1997, amounted to $13.1 billion.

The line of credit itself is *not* a liability. However, once the line of credit is used to borrow money, the company has a formal liability that will be reported as either a current or long-term liability, depending on the repayment terms of the agreement. A sample of U.S. companies with large unused lines of credit is given in Exhibit 10–3. Note especially that the lines of credit are quite large relative to the amount of outstanding debt; in the case of PHILIP MORRIS, use of the full amount of credit would increase its amount of outstanding debt by 75%. Details regarding the terms of the line of credit, for example, the used and unused portions and the applicable interest rates, are disclosed in the financial statement notes.

EXHIBIT 10–3 | Unused Lines of Credit—1997

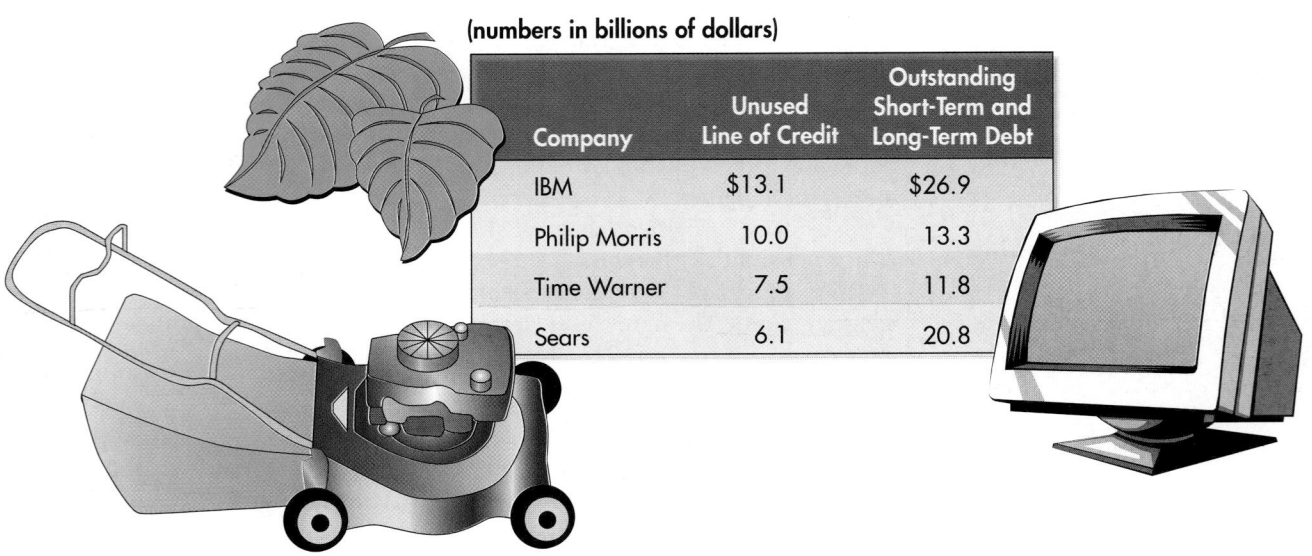

(numbers in billions of dollars)

Company	Unused Line of Credit	Outstanding Short-Term and Long-Term Debt
IBM	$13.1	$26.9
Philip Morris	10.0	13.3
Time Warner	7.5	11.8
Sears	6.1	20.8

PRESENT VALUE OF LONG-TERM DEBT

Apply present value concepts to the accounting for long-term debts such as mortgages.

The reporting of long-term debt obligations is more complex than for short-term obligations because the sum of the future cash payments to be made on a long-term debt is not a good measure of the actual economic obligation. For example, repaying a 30-year, $200,000 mortgage with a 7% interest rate will require monthly payments totaling $479,018 over the 30-year life of the mortgage. However, the entire obligation could be settled with one payment of $200,000 today. In reporting long-term debt obligations, the emphasis is on reporting what the real economic value of the obligation is today, not what the total debt payments will be in the future.

To illustrate the application of present value concepts to the accounting for long-term debt, a simple mortgage example will be used. A **mortgage** is a loan backed by an asset that serves as collateral for the loan. If the borrower cannot repay the loan, the lender has the legal right to claim the mortgaged asset and sell it in order to recover the loan amount. Mortgages are generally payable in equal installments; a portion of each payment represents interest on the unpaid mortgage balance and the remainder of the payment is designated as repayment of part of the principal of the loan. As an example, assume that on January 1, 2002, Crystal Michae purchases a house for $250,000 and makes a down payment of $50,000. The remaining $200,000 of the purchase price is financed through a mortgage on the house. The mortgage is payable over 30 years at a rate of $2,057 monthly. The interest rate is 12% compounded monthly, and the first payment is due on February 1, 2002. An interest rate of 12% compounded monthly is the same as 1% per month (12%/12 months). (See Appendix B for a review of present value concepts.)

As the mortgage payments are made, each monthly payment of $2,057 must be divided between principal and interest. The interest is based on 1% of the mortgage balance at the beginning of the month. On February 1, the interest is $2,000 ($200,000 × 1%), and the principal portion of the payment is $57 (or $2,057 - $2,000). In March, the interest is $1,999, 1% of $199,943 ($200,000 - $57), and this pattern continues monthly. The division of these payments into interest and principal components for the first five monthly payments is shown in Exhibit 10-4. It is called **loan** (or **mortgage**) **amortization**.

EXHIBIT 10-4 | Loan (Mortgage) Amortization Schedule

Date	(1) Payment Amount	(2) Interest Expense (4) × .01	(3) Amount Applied to Reduce Principal (1) – (2)	(4) Balance
January 1, 2002	—	—	—	$200,000
February 1, 2002	$2,057	$2,000	$57	199,943
March 1, 2002	2,057	1,999	58	199,885
April 1, 2002	2,057	1,999	58	199,827
May 1, 2002	2,057	1,998	59	199,768
June 1, 2002	2,057	1,998	59	199,709

If Crystal were to maintain a set of personal financial records, she would make the following journal entry on February 1:

Interest Expense	2,000	
Mortgage Payable	57	
Cash		2,057

As with other forms of long-term financing, a mortgage obligation is reported in a company's balance sheet at its present value, which approximates the cash amount that would fully satisfy the obligation today. So, for example, if Crystal were to prepare a quarterly balance sheet as of April 1, 2002 (after the third payment was made), she would show a mortgage liability of $199,827 (see Exhibit 10-4). Because most mortgages are payable in monthly installments, the principal payments for the next 12 months following the balance sheet date must be shown in the current liability section as the current portion of a long-term debt. The remaining portion is classified as a long-term liability.

A **secured loan** is similar to a mortgage in that it is a loan backed by certain assets as collateral. If the borrower cannot repay the loan, the lender can claim the securing assets. Secured loans are more common among firms experiencing financial difficulties. The fact that the loan is secured reduces the risk to the lender and therefore reduces the interest cost for the borrower. For example, TRANS WORLD AIRLINES (TWA) has experienced a variety of financial difficulties for a number of years. In its 1997 annual report, TWA disclosed the existence of several secured loans. One of the secured loan descriptions is given below:

> The 11½% Senior Secured Notes due 2004 were issued in December 1997 in the principal amount of $140.0 million. . . . The notes are secured by a lien on (i) a pool of aircraft spare parts, (ii) TWA's beneficial interest in 30 take-off and landing slots at Ronald Reagan Washington National Airport, and (iii) securities pledged to provide for the first three scheduled interest payments.

FINANCING WITH BONDS

4

Understand the various types of bonds, compute the price of a bond issue, and account for the issuance, interest, and redemption of bonds.

The long-term financing of a corporation is accomplished either through the issuance of **long-term debt** instruments, usually bonds or notes, or through the sale of additional stock. The issuance of bonds or notes instead of stock may be preferred by management and stockholders for the following reasons.

1. Present owners remain in control of the corporation.
2. Interest is a deductible expense in arriving at taxable income, while dividends are not.
3. Current market rates of interest may be favorable relative to stock market prices.
4. The charge against earnings for interest may be less than the amount of dividends that might be expected by shareholders.

There are, however, certain limitations and disadvantages of financing with long-term debt securities. Debt financing is possible only when a company is in satisfactory financial condition and can offer adequate security to creditors. Furthermore, interest obligations must be paid regardless of the company's earnings and financial position. If a company has operating losses and is unable to raise sufficient cash to meet periodic interest payments, secured debt holders may take legal action to assume control of company assets.

A complicating factor is that the distinction between debt and equity securities may become fuzzy. Usually, a debt instrument has a fixed interest rate and a definite maturity date when the principal must be repaid. Also, holders of debt instruments generally have no voting privileges. A traditional equity security, on the other hand, has no fixed repayment obligation or maturity date, and dividends on stock become obligations only after being formally declared by the board of directors of a corporation. In addition, common stockholders generally have voting and other ownership privileges. The problem is that certain convertible debt securities have many equity characteristics, and some preferred stocks have many of the characteristics of debt. This makes it important to recognize the distinction between debt and equity and to provide the accounting treatment that is most appropriate under the specific circumstances.

FYI: Often companies in poor financial condition can still obtain financing. However, the terms of the debt are typically very restrictive and the interest rate is very high. Bonds issued by high-risk companies are often classified as "junk bonds." Junk bonds are discussed later in this chapter.

Accounting for Bonds

Conceptually, bonds and long-term notes are similar types of debt instruments. There are some technical differences, however. For example, the **trust indenture,** i.e., the bond contract, associated with bonds generally provides more extensive detail than the contract terms of a note, often including restrictions on the payment of dividends or incurrence of additional debt. The length of time to maturity is also generally longer for bonds than for notes. Some bonds do not mature for 20 years or longer, while most notes mature in 1 to 5 years. Other characteristics of bonds and notes are similar. Therefore, although the discussion that follows deals specifically with bonds, the accounting principles and reporting practices related to bonds can also be applied to long-term notes.

There are three main considerations in accounting for bonds.

1. Recording the issuance or purchase.
2. Recognizing the applicable interest during the life of the bonds.
3. Accounting for the retirement of bonds either at maturity or prior to the maturity date.

Before these considerations are discussed, the nature of bonds and the determination of bond market prices will be reviewed.

Nature of Bonds

The power of a corporation to create bond indebtedness is found in the corporation laws of a state and may be specifically granted by charter. In some cases, formal authorization by a majority of stockholders is required before a board of directors can approve a bond issue.

Borrowing by means of bonds involves the issuance of certificates of indebtedness. **Bond certificates**, commonly referred to simply as "bonds," are frequently issued in denominations of $1,000, referred to as the **face value, par value**, or **maturity value** of the bond, although in some cases bonds are issued in varying denominations.

The group contract between the corporation and the bondholders is known as the **bond indenture**. The indenture details the rights and obligations of the contracting parties, indicates the property pledged as well as the protection offered on the loan, and names the bank or trust company that is to represent the bondholders.

Bonds may be sold by the company directly to investors, or they may be underwritten by investment bankers or a syndicate. The underwriters may agree to purchase the entire bond issue or that part of the issue not sold by the company, or they may agree simply to manage the sale of the security on a commission basis, often referred to as a "best efforts" basis.

Most companies attempt to sell their bonds to underwriters to avoid incurring a loss after the bonds are placed on the market. An interesting example of this occurred when IBM went to the bond market for the first time and issued a record $1 billion worth of bonds and long-term notes. After the issue was released by IBM to the underwriters, interest rates soared as the Federal Reserve Bank sharply increased its discount rate. The market price of the IBM securities fell, and the brokerage houses and investment bankers participating in the underwriting incurred a loss in excess of $50 million on the sale of the securities to investors.

ISSUERS OF BONDS   Bonds and similar debt instruments are issued by private corporations; the U.S. Government; state, county, and local governments; school districts; and government-sponsored organizations, such as the Federal Home Loan Bank and the Federal National Mortgage Association. At the end of 1998, the Federal Reserve estimated that the amount of outstanding bonds for corporations was $2.15 trillion.

The U.S. government's debt includes not only U.S. Treasury bonds but also U.S. Treasury bills, which are notes with less than one year to maturity date, and U.S. Treasury notes, which mature in one to seven years. According to the Treasury Department, outstanding U.S. government debt securities at the end of 1998 totaled $5.45 trillion.

Debt securities issued by state, county, and local governments and their agencies are collectively referred to as **municipal debt**. A unique feature of municipal debt is that the interest received by investors from such securities is exempt from federal income tax. Because of this tax advantage, "municipals" generally carry lower interest rates than debt securities of other issuers, enabling these governmental units to borrow at favorable interest rates. The tax exemption is in reality a subsidy granted by the federal government to encourage capital investment in state and local governments.

TYPES OF BONDS   Bonds may be categorized in many different ways, depending on the characteristics of a particular bond issue. The major distinguishing features of bonds are identified and discussed in the following sections.

Term versus serial bonds.   Bonds that mature on a single date are called **term bonds.** When bonds mature in installments, they are referred to as **serial bonds.** Serial bonds are much less common than term bonds.

Secured versus unsecured bonds.   Bonds issued by private corporations may be either secured or unsecured. **Secured bonds** offer protection to investors by providing some form of security, such as a mortgage on real estate or a pledge of other collateral. A first-mortgage bond represents a first claim against the property of a corporation in the event of the company's inability to meet bond interest and principal payments. A second-mortgage bond is a secondary claim ranking only after the claim of the first-mortgage bond or senior issue has been completely satisfied. A **collateral trust bond** is usually secured by stocks and bonds of other corporations owned by the issuing company. Such securities are generally transferred to a trustee, who holds them as collateral on behalf of the bondholders and, if necessary, will sell them to satisfy the bondholders' claim.

Unsecured bonds are not protected by the pledge of any specific assets and are frequently termed **debenture bonds, or debentures.** Holders of debenture bonds simply rank as general creditors along with other unsecured parties. The risk involved in these securities varies with the financial strength of the debtor. Debentures issued by a strong company may involve little risk; debentures issued by a weak company whose properties are already heavily mortgaged may involve considerable risk. Quality ratings for bonds are published by both Moody's and Standard & Poor's investor service companies. For example, Moody's bond ratings range from (Aaa), for prime or high-quality bonds to (C), for very high-risk bonds. Standard & Poor's range is from AAA, AA, A, BBB, and so forth to D.

Registered versus bearer (coupon) bonds.   **Registered bonds** call for the registry of the owner's name on the corporation books. Transfer of bond ownership is similar to that for stock. When a bond is sold, the corporate transfer agent cancels the bond certificate surrendered by the seller and issues a new certificate to the buyer. Interest checks are mailed periodically to the bondholders of record. **Bearer bonds, or coupon bonds,** are not recorded in the name of the owner; title to these bonds pass with delivery. Each bond is accompanied by coupons for individual interest payments covering the life of the issue. Coupons are clipped by the owner of the bond and presented to a bank for deposit or collection. The issue of bearer bonds eliminates the need for recording bond ownership changes and preparing and mailing periodic interest checks. But coupon bonds fail to offer the bondholder the protection found in registered bonds in the event the bonds are lost or stolen. In some cases, bonds provide interest coupons but require registry as to principal. Here, ownership safeguards are provided while the time-consuming routines involved in making interest payments are avoided. Bonds of recent issue are registered rather than coupon bonds.

Zero-interest bonds and bonds with variable interest rates.   In recent years, some companies have issued long-term debt securities that do not bear interest. Instead, these securities sell at a significant discount that provides an investor with a total interest payoff at maturity. These bonds are known as **zero-interest bonds** or **deep-discount bonds.** Another type of zero-interest bond delays interest payments for a period of time.

Because of potentially wide fluctuations in interest rates, some bonds and long-term notes are issued with variable (or floating) interest rates. Over the life of these obligations, the interest rate changes as prevailing market interest rates increase or decrease. A variable interest rate security reduces the risk to the investor when interest rates are rising and to the issuer when interest rates are falling.

Junk bonds. High-risk, high-yield bonds issued by companies that are heavily in debt or otherwise in weak financial condition are often referred to as **junk bonds.** These bonds are rated Ba or lower by Moody's and BB or lower by Standard & Poor's.[7] Junk bonds typically yield at least 12%, and some yield in excess of 20%. Some are zero-interest (deep-discount) bonds that pay no interest until maturity or pay no interest for the first few years. While junk bonds may not be an appropriate investment for individuals due to their high risk, they have been a significant segment of the corporate bond market in recent years.

Junk bonds are issued in at least three types of circumstances. First, they are issued by companies that once had high credit ratings but have fallen on hard times. Several companies in the steel industry are included in this category. Second, junk bonds are issued by emerging growth companies, such as AMAZON.COM that issued junk bonds priced at $275 million in 1998, that lack adequate cash flow, credit history, or diversification to permit them to issue higher grade (i.e., lower risk) bonds. The third circumstance is junk bonds issued by companies undergoing restructuring, often in conjunction with a leveraged buyout (LBO).

Convertible and commodity-backed bonds. Bonds may provide for their conversion into some other security at the option of the bondholder. Such bonds are known as **convertible bonds.** The conversion feature generally permits the owner of bonds to exchange them for common stock. The bondholder is thus able to convert the claim into an ownership interest if corporate operations prove successful and conversion becomes attractive; in the meantime, the special rights of a creditor are maintained. Bonds may also be redeemable in terms of commodities, such as oil or precious metals. These types of bonds are referred to as **commodity-backed bonds** or **asset-linked bonds.**

Callable bonds. Bond indentures frequently give the issuing company the right to call and retire the bonds prior to their maturity. Such bonds are termed **callable bonds.** When a corporation wishes to reduce its outstanding indebtedness, bondholders are notified of the portion of the issue to be surrendered, and they are paid in accordance with call provisions. Interest does not accrue after the call date.

Market Price of Bonds

The market price of bonds varies with the safety of the investment and the current market interest rate for similar instruments. When the financial condition and earnings of a corporation are such that payment of interest and principal on bond indebtedness is virtually assured, the interest rate a company must offer to sell a bond issue is relatively low. As the risk factor increases, a higher interest return is necessary to attract investors. The amount of interest paid on bonds is a specified percentage of the face value. This percentage is termed the **stated rate,** or **contract rate.** This rate, however, may not be the same as the prevailing or market rate for bonds of similar quality and length of time to maturity at the time the issue is sold. Furthermore, the market rate fluctuates constantly. These factors often result in a difference between bond face values and the prices at which the bonds actually sell on the market.

The purchase of bonds at face value implies agreement between the bond's stated rate of interest and the prevailing market rate of interest. If the stated rate exceeds the market rate, the bonds will sell at a premium; if the stated rate is less than the market rate, the bonds will sell at a discount. The **bond premium** or the **bond discount** is the amount needed to adjust the stated rate of interest to the actual market rate of interest or yield for that particular bond. Thus, the stated rate adjusted for the premium or the

7 Ben Weberman, "High-Grade Junk," *Forbes,* August 21, 1989, p. 115.

discount gives the actual rate of return on the bonds, known as the **market, yield,** or **effective interest rate**. A declining market rate of interest subsequent to issuance of the bonds results in an increase in the market value of the bonds; a rising market rate of interest results in a decrease in their market value.

Bond prices are quoted in the market as a percentage of face value. For example, a bond quotation of 96.5 means the market price is 96.5% of face value; thus, the bond is trading at a discount. A bond quotation of 104 means the market price is 104% of face value; thus, the bond is trading at a premium. U.S. government note and bond quotations are made in 32s rather than 100s. This means that a government bond selling at 98:16 is selling at 98½, or in terms of decimal equivalents, 98.5%.

The market price of a bond at any date can be determined by discounting the maturity value of the bond and each remaining interest payment at the market rate of interest for similar debt on that date. The present value tables in Appendix B can be used for computing bond market prices.

To illustrate the computation of a bond market price from the tables, assume 10-year, 8% bonds of $100,000 are to be sold on the bond issue date. Further assume that the effective interest rate for bonds of similar quality and maturity is 10%, compounded semiannually.

The computation of the market price of the bonds may be divided into two parts:

> **FYI:** The IBM example given previously illustrates how changing interest rates can materially affect the issue price of a bond.

> **Caution!** When the stated interest rate on a company's bonds is less than the market rate for similar bonds, investors will pay less than the face value of the bond because they are going to receive a lower interest payment. The amount paid below the face value is termed a discount. The reverse is true for a premium.

Part 1 Present value of principal (maturity value):

Maturity value of bonds after 10 years, or 20 semiannual periods	$100,000
Effective interest rate = 10% per year, or 5% per semiannual period; present value factor (PVF), Table II $\overline{20|}5$	× .3769
Present value of $100,000 discounted at 5% for 20 periods	$ 37,690

Part 2 Present value of 20 interest payments:

Semiannual payment, 4% of $100,000	$ 4,000
Effective interest rate, 10% per year, or 5% per semiannual period; present value of annuity factor (PVAF), Table IV $\overline{20|}5$	×12.4622
Present value of twenty $4,000 payments, discounted at 5%	$ 49,849
Total present value (market price) of bond	$ 87,539

The market price for the bonds would be $87,539, the sum of the present values of the two parts. Because the effective interest rate is higher than the stated interest rate, the bonds would sell at a $12,461 discount at the issuance date. It should be noted that if the effective rate on these bonds were 8% instead of 10%, the sum of the present values of the two parts would be $100,000, meaning that the bonds would sell at their face value, or at par. If the effective interest rate were less than 8%, the market price of the bonds would be more than $100,000, and the bonds would sell at a premium.

STOP & THINK In computing the market price for bonds, what is the only thing the stated rate of interest is used for?

The bonds of public corporations are traded on various bond exchanges, which are similar to stock exchanges. Exhibit 10–5 presents a selection of the New York Bond Exchange listings from *The Wall Street Journal* for bond trading occurring on March 1, 1999.

Notice that AT&T has more than one bond issue listed; the first listing is for bonds that mature in 2002, and the second listing is for bonds that mature in 2031. The current yield for the first AT&T bond listing is 6.8, which means that if the bonds were purchased at their closing price of 104¼, the interest payments would give the investor a 6.8% annual return. The notation "cv" listed in the Current Yield column for the Home Depot bond issue means that the bonds are convertible into HOME DEPOT stock; convertible bonds are discussed later in the chapter. The CANADIAN PACIFIC (CdnPc) bonds are listed as being perpetuities (perp), meaning that they have no maturity date; these unusual bonds pay 4% (4s) annual interest on their face value forever. The

EXHIBIT 10–5 | New York Bond Exchange Listing

Bonds	Bond Prices			
	Cur Yld	Vol	Close	Net Chg.
ATT 7⅛ 02...	6.8	89	104⅛	+ ¼
ATT 8⅝ 31...	7.7	50	112	+ 2⅛
BellsoT 5⅞ 09	5.9	75	99⅜	− ⅝
HomeDpt 3¼ 01	cv	10	255	− 1
IBM 8⅜ 19	7.1	25	118⅝	+ ¼
Lucent 6½ 28	6.6	25	99	−4 ½
CdnPc 4s perp...	5.4	31	73½	+ ½

Source: "New York Exchange of Bonds," *The Wall Street Journal*, March 2, 1999.

IBM bonds were trading at a significant premium, which means that the coupon rate on these bonds of 8.375% is significantly higher than was the market rate required on bonds of similar riskiness.

Issuance of Bonds

FYI: Banks were once the major source of debt financing for companies. With the development of the bond market, banks have found their profit margins significantly reduced because companies can obtain financing directly from investors rather than through a bank.

Bonds may be sold directly to investors by the issuer or they may be sold on the open market through securities exchanges or through investment bankers. Over 50% of bond issues are privately placed with large investors. Regardless of how they are placed, when bonds are issued (sold), the issuer must record the receipt of cash and recognize the long-term liability. The purchaser must record the payment of cash and the bond investment.

An issuer normally records the bond obligation at its face value—the amount that the company must pay at maturity. Hence, when bonds are issued at an amount other than face value, a bond discount or premium account is established for the difference between the cash received and the bond face value. The premium is added to or the discount is subtracted from the bond face value to report the bonds at their present value. Although an investor could also record the investment in bonds at their face value by using a premium or discount account, traditionally investors record their bond investments at cost, that is, the face value net of any premium or discount. Cost includes brokerage fees and any other costs incidental to the purchase.

Bonds issued or acquired in exchange for noncash assets or services are recorded at the fair market value of the bonds, unless the value of the exchanged assets or services is more clearly determinable. A difference between the face value of the bonds and the cash value of the bonds or the value of the property acquired is recognized as bond discount or bond premium. When bonds and other securities are acquired for a lump sum, an apportionment of such cost among the securities is required.

As indicated earlier, bonds may be issued at par, at a discount, or at a premium. They may be issued on an interest payment date or between interest dates, which calls for the recognition of accrued interest. Each of these situations will be illustrated using the following data: $100,000, 8%, 10-year bonds are issued; semiannual interest of $4,000 ($100,000 × .08 × 6/12) is payable on January 1 and July 1.

BONDS ISSUED AT PAR ON INTEREST DATE   When bonds are issued at par, or face value, on an interest date, there is no premium or discount to be recognized nor any accrued interest at the date of issuance. The appropriate entries for the first year on the issuer's books and on the investor's books, assuming the data in the preceding paragraph and issuance on January 1 at par value, would be:

► WILL MICKEY MOUSE BE AROUND IN 100 YEARS?

In July 1993, THE WALT DISNEY COMPANY began marketing 100-year bonds yielding 7.5%. The bonds have a face value of $150 million and will mature in 2093. Traditionally, bonds have had lives of 20 or 30 years, but in 1992, one company sold 50-year bonds—the first such issue in over a decade. Disney's issue of 100-year bonds was the first such issue since 1954. In 1954, CHICAGO AND EASTERN ILLINOIS, a railroad,

issued 100-year bonds with a stated rate of 5%. Investors of the Chicago and Eastern Illinois bonds have had marginal returns, especially during the late 1970s and early 1980s with double-digit inflation. An analysis of the Disney bonds prepared by Morgan Stanley indicates that even without factoring in the effects of inflation, if long-

	Issuer's Books				Investor's Books		
Jan. 1	Cash	100,000		Bond Investment	100,000	
	Bonds Payable		100,000	Cash		100,000
July 1	Interest Expense	4,000		Cash	4,000	
	Cash		4,000	Interest Revenue		4,000
Dec. 31	Interest Expense	4,000		Interest Receivable	4,000	
	Interest Payable		4,000	Interest Revenue		4,000

BONDS ISSUED AT DISCOUNT ON INTEREST DATE   Now assume that the bonds were issued on January 1 but that the effective rate of interest was 10%, requiring recognition of a discount of $12,461 ($100,000 – $87,539; see computations on page 550). The appropriate entries on January 1 are shown below. The interest entries on July 1 and December 31 are illustrated in a later section of this chapter that discusses the amortization of discounts and premiums.

	Issuer's Books				Investor's Books		
Jan. 1	Cash	87,539		Bond Investment	87,539	
	Discount on Bonds Payable	12,461		Cash		87,539
	Bonds Payable		100,000			

BONDS ISSUED AT PREMIUM ON INTEREST DATE   Again using the above data, assume that the bonds were sold at an effective interest rate of 7%. Using present value techniques, the bond will sell for a premium of $7,107. In this case, the entries on January 1 would be:

	Issuer's Books				Investor's Books		
Jan. 1	Cash	107,107		Bond Investment	107,107	
	Premium on Bonds Payable		7,107	Cash		107,107
	Bonds Payable		100,000			

BONDS ISSUED AT PAR BETWEEN INTEREST DATES   When bonds are issued between interest dates, an adjustment is made for the interest accrued between the last interest payment date and the date of the transaction. A buyer of the bonds pays the amount of accrued interest along with the purchase price and then receives the accrued interest plus interest earned subsequent to the purchase date when the next interest payment is made. This practice avoids the problem an issuer of bonds would have in trying to split interest payments for a given period between two or more owners of the

term yields were to rise by one point, the return for Disney bondholders would be –4.19% for the next year. However, if long-term bond yields were to drop one point, the return would exceed 22%. Comments from securities brokers range from "It's crazy" to "The Disney issue will turn out to be an 'historic artifact, a curiosity.'"

QUESTIONS:

1. What are the advantages to the issuer of using 50- or 100-year bonds?
2. What are the disadvantages to the issuer?
3. Why would investors purchase bonds with 100-year maturities?

SOURCE

Thomas T. Vogel, Jr., "Disney Amazes Investors With Sale of 100-Year Bonds," *The Wall Street Journal*, July 21, 1993, p. C1.

---

securities. To illustrate, if the bonds in the previous example were issued at par on March 1, the appropriate entries would be[8]:

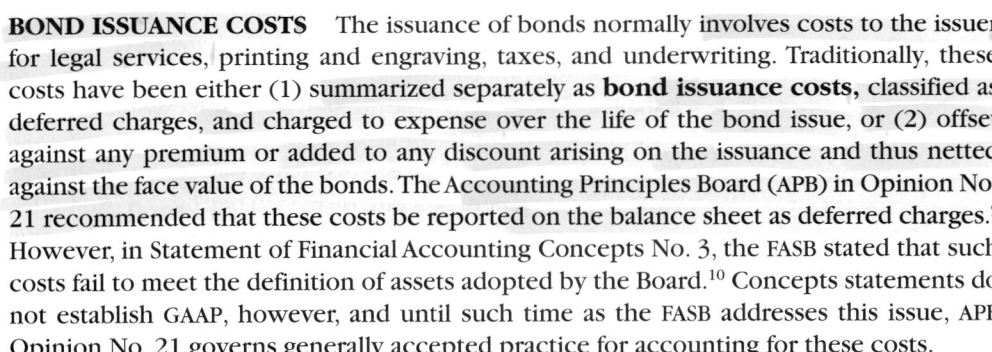

	Issuer's Books			Investor's Books		
Mar. 1	Cash	101,333		Bond Investment	100,000	
	Bonds Payable		100,000	Interest Receivable	1,333	
	Interest Payable		1,333*	Cash		101,333

*($100,000 × .08 × 2/12)

	Issuer's Books			Investor's Books		
July 1	Interest Expense	2,667*		Cash	4,000	
	Interest Payable	1,333		Interest Receivable		1,333
	Cash		4,000	Interest Revenue		2,667

*($100,000 × .08 × 4/12)

BOND ISSUANCE COSTS   The issuance of bonds normally involves costs to the issuer for legal services, printing and engraving, taxes, and underwriting. Traditionally, these costs have been either (1) summarized separately as **bond issuance costs,** classified as deferred charges, and charged to expense over the life of the bond issue, or (2) offset against any premium or added to any discount arising on the issuance and thus netted against the face value of the bonds. The Accounting Principles Board (APB) in Opinion No. 21 recommended that these costs be reported on the balance sheet as deferred charges.[9] However, in Statement of Financial Accounting Concepts No. 3, the FASB stated that such costs fail to meet the definition of assets adopted by the Board.[10] Concepts statements do not establish GAAP, however, and until such time as the FASB addresses this issue, APB Opinion No. 21 governs generally accepted practice for accounting for these costs.

Accounting for Bond Interest

With coupon bonds, cash is paid by the issuing company in exchange for interest coupons on the interest dates. Payments on coupons may be made by the company directly to bondholders, or payments may be cleared through a bank or other disbursing agent.

---

8 As an alternative, the accrued interest could be initially credited to Interest Expense by the issuer and debited to Interest Revenue by the investor. When the first interest payment is made, the debit to Interest Expense for the issuer, when combined with the initial entry, would result in the proper amount of interest expense being recognized. A similar procedure can be applied by the investor in determining interest revenue.

9 *Opinions of the Accounting Principles Board No. 21,* "Interest on Receivables and Payables," New York: American Institute of Certified Public Accountants, 1971, par. 16.

10 *Statement of Financial Accounting Concepts No. 3,* "Elements of Financial Statements of Business Enterprises," Stamford, CT: Financial Accounting Standards Board, December 1980, par. 161.

Subsidiary records with bondholders are not maintained, because coupons are redeemable by bearers. In the case of registered bonds, interest checks are mailed either by the company or its agent. When bonds are registered, the bonds account requires subsidiary ledger support. The subsidiary ledger shows holdings by individuals and changes in such holdings. Checks are sent to bondholders of record as of the interest payment dates.

When bonds are issued at a premium or discount, the market acts to adjust the stated interest rate to a market or effective interest rate. Because of the initial premium or discount, the periodic interest payments made over the bond's life by the issuer do not represent the total interest expense for the periods involved. An adjustment to the interest expense associated with the cash payment is necessary to reflect the effective interest being incurred on the bonds. This adjustment is referred to as bond premium or discount **amortization**. This periodic adjustment results in a gradual adjustment of the bond's carrying value toward the bond's face value.

A premium on issued bonds recognizes that the stated interest rate is higher than the market interest rate. Amortization of the premium reduces the interest expense below the amount of cash paid. A discount on issued bonds recognizes that the stated interest rate is lower than the market interest rate. Amortization of the discount increases the amount of interest expense above the amount of cash paid. In summary, the amortization of a discount or premium on bonds accomplishes two things: The bond's carrying value is gradually adjusted to be equal to the maturity value, and the periodic interest expense is adjusted to reflect the fact that the effective interest rate on the bonds is either higher (with a discount) or lower (with a premium) than the actual amount of cash paid each period.

Two main methods are used to amortize the premium or discount: (1) the straight-line method and (2) the effective-interest method. The straight-line method is explained first because the computations are simpler. This method is acceptable, however, only when its application results in periodic interest expense that does not differ materially from the amounts that would be reported using the effective-interest method.[11]

STRAIGHT-LINE METHOD   The **straight-line method** provides for the recognition of an equal amount of premium or discount amortization each period. The amount of monthly amortization is determined by dividing the premium or discount at purchase or issuance date by the number of months remaining to the bond maturity date. For example, if a 10-year, 10% bond issue with a maturity value of $200,000 was sold on the issuance date at 103, the $6,000 premium would be amortized evenly over the 120 months until maturity, or at a rate of $50 per month ($6,000/120). If the bonds were sold three months after the issuance date, the $6,000 premium would be amortized evenly over 117 months, or at a rate of $51.28 per month ($6,000/117). The amortization period is always the time from original sale to maturity. The premium amortization would reduce both interest expense on the issuer's books and interest revenue on the investor's books. A discount amortization would have the opposite results: Both accounts would be increased.

To illustrate the accounting for bond interest using straight-line amortization, consider again the earlier example of the $100,000, 8%, 10-year bonds issued on January 1. When sold at a $12,461 discount, the appropriate entries to record interest on July 1 and December 31 would be as follows:

Issuer's Books			Investor's Books		
July 1	Interest Expense	4,623		Cash	4,000	
	Discount on Bonds Payable		623*	Bond Investment	623	
	Cash		4,000**	Interest Revenue		4,623

*$12,461/120 × 6 months = $623 (rounded) discount amortization for six-month period
**$100,000 × .08 × 6/12 = $4,000 cash

11 *Opinions of the Accounting Principles Board No. 21*, par. 15.

Issuer's Books				**Investor's Books**		
Dec. 31	Interest Expense	4,623		Interest Receivable	4,000	
	Discount on Bonds Payable		623	Bond Investment	623	
	Interest Payable		4,000	Interest Revenue		4,623

Note that the discount amortization has the effect of increasing the effective interest rate over the life of the bond from the 8% stated rate to the 10% market rate of interest that the bonds were sold to yield. Over the life of the bond, the $12,461 discount will be charged to interest expense for the issuer and recognized as interest revenue by the investor.

To illustrate the entries that would be required to amortize a bond premium, consider again the situation in which the 8% bonds were sold to yield 7%, or $107,107. The $7,107 premium would be amortized on a straight-line basis as follows:

Issuer's Books				**Investor's Books**		
July 1	Interest Expense	3,645*		Cash	4,000	
	Premium on Bonds Payable	355*		Bond Investment		355
	Cash		4,000	Interest Revenue		3,645

*$7,107/120 × 6 months = $355 (rounded) premium amortization for six-month period

Dec. 31	Interest Expense	3,645		Interest Receivable	4,000	
	Premium on Bonds Payable	355		Bond Investment		355
	Interest Payable		4,000	Interest Revenue		3,645

The amortization of the premium has the effect of reducing the amount of interest expense or interest revenue over the life of the bond to the actual yield or market rate of the bonds, 7%.

Caution! Students often interchange the stated and market interest rates when computing interest expense for the period. Remember that the stated rate is used only once—to determine the amount of cash paid or received as interest. The market, or effective, rate is used to calculate the amount of interest expense or interest revenue.

EFFECTIVE-INTEREST METHOD The **effective-interest method** of amortization uses a uniform interest rate based on a changing loan balance and provides for an increasing premium or discount amortization each period. The mortgage (or loan) amortization schedule in Exhibit 10–4 on page 545 employs the effective-interest method. In order to use this method, the effective-interest rate for the bonds must be known. This is the rate of interest at bond issuance that discounts the maturity value of the bonds and the periodic interest payments to the market price of the bonds. This rate is used to determine the amount of revenue or expense to be recorded on the books.

To illustrate the amortization of a bond discount using the effective-interest method, consider once again the $100,000, 8%, 10-year bonds sold for $87,539, based on an effective interest rate of 10%. The discount amortization for the first six months using the effective-interest method would be computed as follows:

Investment balance (carrying value) at beginning of first period	$87,539
Effective rate per semiannual period	5%
Stated rate per semiannual period	4%
Interest amount based on carrying value and effective rate ($87,539 × .05)	$ 4,377
Interest payment based on face value and stated rate ($100,000 × .04)	4,000
Discount amortization—difference in interest based on effective rate and stated rate	$ 377

This difference between the amount paid (received) and the compound interest expense (revenue) is the discount amortization for the first period using the effective-interest method. For the second semiannual period, the bond carrying value increases by the amount of discount amortized. The amortization for the second semiannual period would be computed as follows:

Investment balance (carrying value) at beginning of second period ($87,539 + $377)	$87,916
Interest amount based on carrying value and effective rate ($87,916 × .05)	$ 4,396
Interest payment based on face value and stated rate ($100,000 × .04)	4,000
Discount amortization—difference in interest based on effective rate and stated rate	$ 396

The amount of interest to be recognized each period is computed at a uniform rate on an increasing balance. This results in an increasing discount amortization over the life of the bonds, which is graphically demonstrated and compared with straight-line amortization in Exhibit 10–6.

EXHIBIT 10–6 | Comparison of Straight-Line and Effective-Interest Amortization Methods

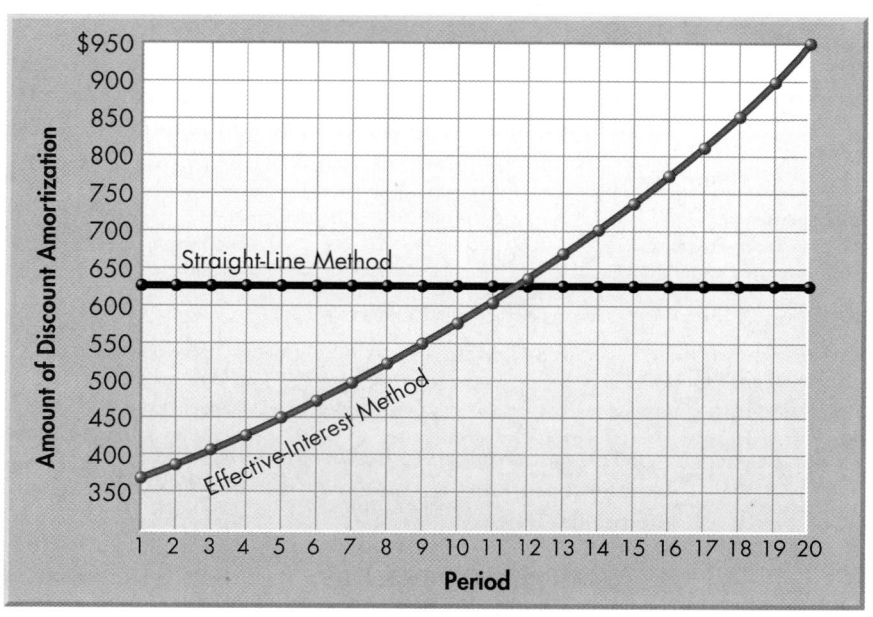

The entries for amortizing the discount would be the same as those shown for straight-line amortization; only the amounts would be different.

Premium amortization would be computed in a similar way except that the interest payment based on the stated interest rate would be higher than the interest amount based on the effective rate. For example, assume that the $100,000, 8%, 10-year bonds were sold on the issuance date for $107,107, thus providing an effective interest rate of 7%. The premium amortization for the first and second six-month periods would be computed as follows (amounts are rounded to the nearest dollar):

Investment balance (carrying value) at beginning of first period	$107,107
Effective rate per semiannual period	3.5%
Stated rate per semiannual period	4.0%
Interest payment based on face value and stated rate ($100,000 × .04)	$ 4,000
Interest amount based on carrying value and effective rate ($107,107 × .035)	3,749
Premium amortization—difference in interest based on stated rate and effective rate	$ 251
Investment balance (carrying value) at beginning of second period ($107,107 – $251)	$106,856
Interest payment based on face value and stated rate ($100,000 × .04)	$ 4,000
Interest amount based on carrying value and effective rate ($106,856 × .035)	3,740
Premium amortization—difference in interest based on stated rate and effective rate	$ 260

STOP & THINK When preparing a bond amortization schedule like the one illustrated at the top of the next page, there are certain numbers within that schedule that you know without having to do any elaborate computations. Identify what those numbers represent.

As illustrated, as the investment or liability balance is reduced by the premium amortization; the interest, based on the effective rate, also decreases. The difference between the interest payment and the effective interest amount increases in a manner similar to discount amortization. Bond amortization tables may be prepared to determine the periodic adjustments to the bond carrying value, that is, the present value of the bond. A partial bond amortization table is illustrated at the top of page 557.

Because the effective-interest method adjusts the stated interest rate to an effective interest rate, it is theoretically more accurate as an amortization method than is the straight-line method. Note that the total amortization over the life of the bond is the same under either method; only the interim amounts differ. Since the issuance of APB Opinion No. 21, the effective-interest method is the recommended amortization method. However, as stated previously, the straight-line method may be used by a company if the interim results of using it do not differ materially from the amortization using the effective-interest method.

Amortization of Bond Premium—Effective-Interest Method $100,000, 10-Year Bonds, Interest at 8% Payable Semiannually, Sold at $107,107 to Yield 7%

Interest Payment	A Interest Paid (.04 × $100,000)	B Interest Expense (.035 × Bond Carrying Value)	C Premium Amortization (A − B)	D Unamortized Premium (D − C)	E Bond Carrying Value ($100,000 + D)
				$7,107	$107,107
1	$4,000	$3,749 (.035 × $107,107)	$251	6,856	106,856
2	4,000	3,740 (.035 × $106,856)	260	6,596	106,596
3	4,000	3,731 (.035 × $106,596)	269	6,327	106,327
4	4,000	3,721 (.035 × $106,327)	279	6,048	106,048
5	4,000	3,712 (.035 × $106,048)	288	5,760	105,760

Cash Flow Effects of Amortizing Bond Premiums and Discounts

The amortization of a bond discount or premium does not involve the receipt or payment of cash and, like other noncash items, must be considered in preparing a statement of cash flows. Recall that when the indirect method is used to report cash flows from operating activities, net income is adjusted for noncash items. When a bond discount is amortized, interest expense reported on the income statement is higher than interest paid, and net income, on a cash basis, is understated. The appropriate adjustment is to add the amount of discount amortization back to net income. The reverse is true in the case of a bond premium. That is, the amount of bond premium amortization is subtracted from net income to arrive at cash flow from operations.

Using the direct method requires conversion of individual accrual-basis revenue and expense items to a cash basis. Thus, to convert interest expense to cash paid for interest, the expense reported on the income statement is decreased by the amount of discount amortization for the period or increased by the amount of premium amortization.

The following example illustrates the adjustments necessary when preparing a statement of cash flows. Consider the information used in the previous examples related to a bond discount—the company issues $100,000, 8%, 10-year bonds when the effective rate of interest is 10%. The bonds are issued at a price of $87,539. The calculations for the discount amortization during the first year are on page 555. The amount of discount amortized during the first year is $773 ($377 + $396). The amount of interest expense disclosed on the income statement for the year is $8,773 ($4,377 + $4,396), and the amount of cash paid to bondholders is $8,000. To keep the example simple, assume that the company reported net income for the year of $90,000 and that sales for the year (all cash) were $98,773, meaning that the $8,773 in interest expense was the only expense. An analysis of the cash flow impact of the discount amortization is included in the matrix below:

Income Statement		Adjustments	Cash Flows From Operations	
Sales	$98,773	None	$98,773	Cash collected from customers
Interest expense	(8,773)	+$773 (bond discount amortization; not a cash item)	(8,000)	Cash paid for interest
Net income	$90,000	+$773 net adjustment	$90,773	Cash flow from operations

Reporting using the indirect method, the amount of discount amortized ($773) is added back to net income. Reporting using the direct method, the amount of the discount is subtracted from reported interest expense to convert that amount to a cash basis as follows: $8,773 interest expense − $773 discount amortization = $8,000 cash paid for interest. In this case, in which only one bond issue is involved, cash paid for interest could instead be computed by multiplying the stated interest rate by the face value of the bonds ($100,000 × .08).

Retirement of Bonds at Maturity

In most cases, bonds include a specified termination or maturity date. At that time, the issuer must pay the current investors the maturity, or face, value of the bonds. When bond discount or premium and issuance costs have been properly amortized over the life of the bonds, bond retirement at maturity simply calls for elimination of the liability or the investment by a cash transaction, illustrated as follows assuming a $100,000 bond:

Issuer's Books			Investor's Books		
Bonds Payable	100,000		Cash	100,000	
Cash		100,000	Bond Investment		100,000

There is no recognition of any gain or loss on retirement, because the carrying value is equal to the maturity value, which is also equal to the market value of the bonds at that point in time.

Any bonds not presented for payment at their maturity date should be removed from the bonds payable balance on the issuer's books and reported separately as Matured Bonds Payable; these are reported as a current liability except when they are to be paid out of a bond retirement fund. Interest does not accrue on matured bonds not presented for payment. If a bond retirement fund is used to pay off a bond issue, any cash remaining in the fund may be returned to the cash account.

FYI: In 1975, high interest rates had caused a decline in the market value of bonds issued during the 1960s. Many companies were retiring these bonds early in order to be able to report accounting gains on the retirement. In order to stop companies from including these gains as part of ordinary income from continuing operations, the FASB decreed that they be classified as extraordinary.

Extinguishment of Debt Prior to Maturity

When debt is retired, or "extinguished," prior to the maturity date, a gain or loss must be recognized for the difference between the carrying value of the debt security and the amount paid to satisfy the obligation.[12] This gain or loss is classified as an **early extinguishment of debt** and, according to FASB Statement No. 4, is to be reported as an extraordinary item on the income statement.[13] Because these gains and losses are actually quite common, many disagree with the FASB's rule mandating the reporting of these gains and losses as extraordinary items. For example, TIME WARNER reported "extraordinary" losses from early debt extinguishment three years in a row (1995 through 1997).

The problems that arise in retiring bonds or other forms of long-term debt prior to maturity are described in the following sections. Bonds may be retired prior to maturity in one of the following ways.

1. Bonds may be *redeemed* by the issuer by purchasing the bonds on the open market or by exercising the call provision that is frequently included in bond indentures.
2. Bonds may be *converted*, that is, exchanged for other securities.

---

12 *Opinions of the Accounting Principles Board No. 26,* "Early Extinguishment of Debt," New York: American Institute of Certified Public Accountants, 1972, par. 20.

13 *Statement of Financial Accounting Standards No. 4,* "Reporting Gains and Losses from Extinguishment of Debt," Stamford, CT: Financial Accounting Standards Board, 1975, par. 8. Note than an exception to the extraordinary classification is made if the early termination is necessary to satisfy bond retirement (sinking) fund requirements within a one-year period; see *Statement of Financial Accounting Standards No. 64,* "Extinguishment of Debt Made to Satisfy Sinking-Fund Requirements," Stamford, CT: Financial Accounting Standards Board, 1982, par. 3.

3. Bonds may be *refinanced* (sometimes called "refunded") by using the proceeds from the sale of a new bond issue to retire outstanding bonds.

REDEMPTION BY PURCHASE OF BONDS IN THE MARKET Corporations frequently purchase their own bonds in the market when prices or other factors make such actions desirable. When bonds are purchased, amortization of bond premium or discount and issue costs should be brought up to date. Purchase by the issuer calls for the cancellation of the bond's face value together with any related premium, discount, or issue costs as of the purchase date.

> **CAUTION!** Note that a gain or loss is determined by comparing the carrying value of the bond to its fair market value. If a company can retire a bond for less than its carrying value, a gain results. If the company must pay more than the carrying value, the result is a loss.

To illustrate a bond redemption prior to maturity, assume that $100,000, 8% bonds of Triad Inc. are not held until maturity but are redeemed by the issuer on February 1, 2002, at 97. The carrying value of the bonds on both the issuer's and investor's books is $97,700 as of February 1. Interest payment dates on the bonds are January 31 and July 31. Entries on both the issuer's and investor's books at the time of redemption would be as follows:

Issuer's Books			Investor's Books		
Feb. 1 Bonds Payable	100,000		Cash	97,000	
Discount on Bonds Payable		2,300	Loss on Sale of Bonds	700	
Cash		97,000	Bond Investment—Triad Inc.		97,700
Gain on Bond Redemption		700*			

Computation:

*Carrying value of bonds, February 1, 2002	$97,700
Purchase (redemption) price	97,000
Gain on bond redemption	$ 700

If the redemption had occurred between interest payment dates, adjusting entries would have to be made to recognize the accrued interest and to amortize the bond discount or premium.

REDEMPTION BY EXERCISE OF CALL PROVISION A call provision gives the issuer the option of retiring bonds prior to maturity. Frequently the call must be made on an interest payment date, and no further interest accrues on the bonds not presented at this time. When only a part of an issue is to be redeemed, the bonds called may be determined by lot.

> **FYI:** Until the issuance of FASB Statement No. 125 in June 1996, early extinguishment of debt could also be accomplished through *in-substance defeasance*. This process involved transferring assets into an irrevocable trust, using those assets to satisfy the cash flow requirements of a certain debt obligation, and removing both the assets and the associated debt from the balance sheet. The provisions of Statement No. 125 require that the assets and debt in an in-substance defeasance arrangement still be reported in the balance sheet.

The inclusion of call provisions in a bond agreement is a feature favoring the issuer. The company is in a position to terminate the bond agreement and eliminate future interest charges whenever its financial position makes such action feasible. Furthermore, the company is protected in the event of a fall in the market interest rate by being able to retire the old issue from proceeds of a new issue paying a lower rate of interest. A bond contract normally requires payment of a premium if bonds are called. A bondholder is thus offered special compensation if the investment is terminated early.

When bonds are called, the difference between the amount paid and the bond carrying value is reported as a gain or a loss on both the issuer's and investor's books. Any interest paid at the time of the call is recorded as a debit to Interest Expense on the issuer's books and a credit to Interest Revenue on the investor's books. The entries to be made are the same as illustrated previously for the purchase (redemption) of bonds by the issuer.

CONVERTIBLE BONDS **Convertible debt securities** raise specific questions as to the nature of the securities, that is, whether they should be considered debt or equity securities, the valuation of the conversion feature, and the treatment of any gain or loss on conversion.

► THE LARGEST U.S. CORPORATE BOND ISSUE EVER

In July 1999, FORD issued $8.60 billion in bonds, the largest U.S. corporate bond issue in history, breaking the previous record of $8.00 billion set by AT&T in March 1999. Increased interest by corporations in raising money through the issuance of bonds was spurred by the decreased spread between the yield on U.S. Treasury securities and the yield on corporate bonds. For A-rated corporate bonds, the interest premium was 1.3% higher than U.S. Treasury securities during the first part of 1999.

A list of the top 10 U.S. corporate bond deals in history is follows.

QUESTIONS:

1. Why is the effective interest rate on U.S. corporate bonds higher than the rate on U.S. Treasury securities?
2. Why do investors buy bonds when they can buy stocks instead?
3. The bonds issued by RJR HOLDINGS in 1989 were junk bonds. What is a junk bond?

Issuer	Date	Amount (In billions)
Ford	July 9, 1999	$8.60
AT&T	March 23, 1999	8.00
RJR Holdings	May 12, 1989	6.11
WorldCom	August 6, 1998	6.10
Sprint	November 10, 1998	5.00
Assoc. Corp. of N. Amer.	October 27, 1998	4.80
Norfolk Southern	May 14, 1997	4.30
US West Capital	January 16, 1997	4.10
Conoco	April 15, 1999	4.00
Charter Communications	March 12, 1999	3.58

SOURCES

Gregory Zuckerman, "AT&T Issues Record $8 Billion of Bonds," *The Wall Street Journal*, March 24, 1999, p. C18.

Gregory Zuckerman, "Record Ford Issue May Spur Imitators," *The Wall Street Journal*, July 12, 1999, p. C1.

Convertible debt securities usually have the following features:[14]

1. An interest rate lower than the issuer could establish for nonconvertible debt
2. An initial conversion price higher than the market value of the common stock at time of issuance
3. A call option retained by the issuer

The popularity of these securities may be attributed to the advantages to both an issuer and a holder. An issuer is able to obtain financing at a lower interest rate because of the value of the conversion feature to the holder. Because of the call provision, an issuer is in a position to exert influence upon the holders to exchange the debt for equity securities if stock values increase; the issuer has had the use of relatively low interest rate financing if stock values do not increase. On the other hand, the holder has a debt instrument that, barring default, assures the return of investment plus a fixed return and, at the same time, offers an option to transfer his or her interest to equity capital should such transfer become attractive. Refer back to the bond listing in Exhibit 10–5. Among the bonds listed, the Home Depot bonds are convertible, as indicated by the "cv" in the Current Yield column. The value of Home Depot stock had increased substantially since the time these convertible bonds were issued; this fact is reflected in the high value (255% of face value) placed on these convertible bonds by investors in March 1999.

Many convertible bond issues place no restriction on when an issuer can call in bonds, and interest accrued on such bonds is sometimes absorbed in a conversion and not paid to the investor. Thus, a company can have the use of interest-free money as a result of calling in bonds prior to the first interest payment. Widespread use of early call

---

14 *Opinions of the Accounting Principles Board No. 14*, "Accounting for Convertible Debt and Debt Issued With Stock Purchase Warrants," New York: American Institute of Certified Public Accountants, 1969, par. 3.

provisions in the early 1980s led some investors to demand a provision restricting exercise of the call provision for a specified time period.[15]

Accounting for convertible debt issuance when the conversion feature is non-detachable.   Differences of opinion exist as to whether convertible debt securities should be treated by an issuer solely as debt or whether part of the proceeds received from the issuance of debt should be recognized as equity capital. One view holds that the debt and the conversion privilege are inseparably connected, and therefore the debt and equity portions of a security should not be separately valued. A holder cannot sell part of the instrument and retain the other. An alternate view holds that there are two distinct elements in these securities and that each should be recognized in the accounts: The portion of the issuance price attributable to the conversion privilege should be recorded as a credit to Paid-In Capital; the balance of the issuance price should be assigned to the debt. This would decrease the premium otherwise recognized in the debt or perhaps result in a discount.

These views are compared in the example that follows. Assume that 500 ten-year bonds, face value $1,000, are sold at 105, or a total issue price of $525,000 (500 × $1,000 × 1.05). The bonds contain a conversion privilege that provides for exchange of a $1,000 bond for 20 shares of stock, par value $1. The interest rate on the bonds is 8%. It is estimated that without the conversion privilege, the bonds would sell at 96. The journal entries to record the issuance on the issuer's books under the two approaches are as follows:

Debt and Equity Not Separated		
Cash	525,000	
Bonds Payable		500,000
Premium on Bonds Payable		25,000

Computations:
*Par value of bonds (500 × $1,000)		$500,000
Selling price of bonds without conversion feature ($500,000 × .96)		480,000
Discount on bonds without conversion feature		$ 20,000

Debt and Equity Separated		
Cash	525,000	
Discount on Bonds Payable	20,000*	
Bonds Payable		500,000
Paid-In Capital Arising From Bond Conversion Feature		45,000**

**Total cash received on sale of bonds		$525,000
Selling price without conversion feature		480,000
Amount applicable to conversion feature (equity portion)		$ 45,000

The periodic charge for interest will differ depending on which method is employed. To illustrate the computation of interest charges, assume that the straight-line method is used to amortize bond premium or discount. Under the first approach, the annual interest charge would be $37,500 ($40,000 paid less $2,500 premium amortization). Under the second approach, the annual interest charge would be $42,000 ($40,000 paid plus $2,000 discount amortization).

The APB stated that when convertible debt is sold at a price or with a value at issuance not significantly in excess of the face value, "no portion of the proceeds from the issuance ... should be accounted for as attributable to the conversion feature."[16]

The APB stated that greater weight for this decision was placed on the inseparability of the debt and the conversion option than upon the practical problems of valuing the separate parts. However, the practical problems are considerable. Separate valuation requires asking the question: How much would the security sell for without the conversion feature? In many instances, this question would appear to be unanswerable. Investment bankers responsible for selling these issues are frequently unable to separate the two features for valuation purposes; they contend that the cash required simply could not be raised without the conversion privilege.

15   Ben Weberman, "The Convertible Bond Scam," *Forbes*, January 19, 1981, p. 92.
16   *Opinions of the Accounting Principles Board No. 14*, par. 12.

On the other hand, there would seem to be strong theoretical support for separating the debt and equity portions of the proceeds from the issuance of convertible debt on the issuer's books. Despite these theoretical arguments, current practice follows APB Opinion No. 14, and no separation is usually made between debt and equity when the conversion feature of the debt is not detachable, or separately tradable, from the debt instrument itself. This is true even when separate values are determinable.

> **FYI:**   At an EITF meeting held on March 13, 1997, the SEC observer at the meeting announced that when a nondetachable conversion feature of convertible debt is "in the money" at issuance, the proceeds should be separated into debt and equity portions. An in-the-money conversion feature is one that would yield an instant return to investors if they were to convert immediately.

Accounting for convertible debt issuance when the conversion feature is detachable.   Sometimes bonds are issued in conjunction with stock warrants. The warrants allow the holder to buy shares of stock at a set price. The bonds and the warrants are issued as elements of a single security; in essence, the combination of the bonds and the stock warrants is economically equivalent to a convertible debt security. The practical difference is that investors can trade the stock warrants separately from the bonds themselves. In this case, the issuer of the bonds and the stock warrants is required to allocate the joint issuance price between the two instruments; the bonds are accounted for as debt, and the stock warrants are accounted for as part of paid-in capital as illustrated in the "Debt and Equity Separated" journal entry shown previously.[17] In a number of specific cases, the Emerging Issues Task Force (EITF) has confirmed this accounting for jointly issued but detachable debt and equity instruments.

Accounting for convertible debt issuance according to IAS 32.   IAS 32, "Financial Instruments: Disclosure and Presentation," does not differentiate between convertible debt with nondetachable and detachable conversion features. Instead, IAS 32 states that for all convertible debt issues, the issuance proceeds should be allocated between the debt and equity. Accordingly, the international standard mandates that in all cases the "Debt and Equity Separated" journal entry illustrated previously should be used.

Accounting for conversion.   When conversion takes place, a special valuation question must be answered: Should the market value of the securities be used to compute a gain or loss on the transaction? If the convertible security is viewed as debt, then the conversion to equity would seem to be a significant economic transaction, and a gain or loss would be recognized. If, however, the convertible security is viewed as equity, the conversion is really an exchange of one type of equity capital for another, and the historical cost principle would seem to indicate that no gain or loss would be recognized. In practice, the latter approach seems to be most commonly followed by both the issuer and investor of the bonds. No gain or loss is recognized either for book or tax purposes. The book value of the bonds is transferred to become the book value of the stock issued. However, this treatment seems inconsistent with APB Opinion No. 14, in which convertible debt is considered to be debt rather than equity.

If an investor views the security as debt, conversion of the debt could be viewed as an exchange of one asset for another. The general rule for the exchange of nonmonetary assets is that the market value of the asset exchanged should be used to measure any gain or loss on the transaction.[18] If there is no market value of the asset surrendered or if its value is undeterminable, the market value of the asset received should be used. The market value of convertible bonds should reflect the market value of the stock to be issued on the conversion, and thus the market value of the two securities should be similar.

To illustrate bond conversion for the investor recognizing a gain or loss on conversion, assume HiTec Co. offers bondholders 40 shares of HiTec Co. common stock, $1 par, in exchange for each $1,000, 8% bond held. An investor exchanges bonds of $10,000 (carrying value as brought up to date for both investor and issuer, $9,850) for 400 shares of common stock having a market price at the time of the exchange of $26 per share. The

---

17   *Opinions of the Accounting Principles Board No. 14*, par. 16.
18   *Opinions of the Accounting Principles Board No. 29*, "Accounting for Nonmonetary Transactions," New York: American Institute of Certified Public Accountants, 1973, par. 18.

exchange is completed at the interest payment date. The exchange is recorded on the books of the investor as follows:

Investment in HiTec Co. Common Stock	10,400	
Bond Investment—HiTec Co.		9,850
Gain on Conversion of HiTec Co. Bonds		550

If the investor chose not to recognize a gain or loss, the journal entry would be as follows:

Investment in HiTec Co. Common Stock	9,850	
Bond Investment—HiTec Co.		9,850

Similar differences would occur on the issuer's books depending on the viewpoint assumed. If the issuer desired to recognize the conversion of the convertible debt as a significant culminating transaction, the market value of the securities would be used to record the conversion. The HiTec example can be used to illustrate the journal entries for the issuer using this reasoning. The conversion would be recorded as follows:

Bonds Payable	10,000	
Loss on Conversion of Bonds	550*	
Common Stock, $1 par		400
Paid-In Capital in Excess of Par		10,000
Discount on Bonds Payable		150

Computation:		
*Market value of stock issued (400 shares at $26)		$10,400
Face value of bonds payable	$10,000	
Less unamortized discount	150	9,850
Loss to company on conversion of bonds		$ 550

If the issuer did not consider the conversion as a culminating transaction, no gain or loss would be recognized. The bond's carrying value would be transferred to the capital stock account on the theory that the company, upon issuing the bonds, is aware of the fact that bond proceeds may ultimately represent the consideration identified with stock. Thus, when bondholders exercise their conversion privileges, the value identified with the obligation is transferred to the security that replaces it. Under this assumption, the conversion would be recorded as follows:

Bonds Payable	10,000	
Common Stock, $1 par		400
Paid-In Capital in Excess of Par		9,450
Discount on Bonds Payable		150

The profession has not resolved the accounting issues surrounding convertible debt. Although the practice of not recognizing gain or loss on either the issuer's or the investor's books is widespread, it seems inconsistent with the treatment of other items that are transferred by an entity. The economic reality of the transaction would seem to require a recognition of the change in value at least at the time conversion takes place.

BOND REFINANCING   Cash for the retirement of a bond issue is frequently raised through the sale of a new issue and is referred to as **bond refinancing,** or refunding. Bond refinancing may take place when an issue matures, or bonds may be refinanced prior to their maturity when the interest rate has dropped and the interest savings on a new issue will more than offset the cost of retiring the old issue. To illustrate, assume that a corporation has outstanding 12% bonds of $1,000,000 callable at 102 and with a remaining 10-year term, and similar 10-year bonds can be marketed currently at an interest rate of only 10%. Under these circumstances it would be advantageous to retire the old issue with the proceeds from a new 10% issue, because the future savings in interest will exceed by a considerable amount the premium to be paid on the call of the old issue.

The desirability of refinancing may not be so obvious as in the preceding example. In determining whether refinancing is warranted in marginal cases, careful consideration must be given to such factors as the different maturity dates of the two issues, possible future changes in interest rates, changed loan requirements, different indenture provisions, income tax effects of refinancing, and legal fees, printing costs, and marketing costs involved in refinancing.

When refinancing takes place before the maturity date of the old issue, the problem arises as to how to dispose of the call premium and unamortized discount and issue costs of the original bonds. Three positions have been taken with respect to disposition of these items.

1. Such charges are considered a gain or loss on bond retirement.
2. Such charges are considered deferrable and are to be amortized systematically over the remaining life of the original issue.
3. Such charges are considered deferrable and are to be amortized systematically over the life of the new issue.

Although arguments can be presented supporting each of these alternatives, the APB concluded that "all extinguishments of debt. . . are fundamentally alike. The accounting for such transactions should be the same regardless of the means used to achieve the extinguishment."[19] The first position, immediate recognition of the gain or loss, was selected by the APB for all early extinguishment of debt. The FASB considered the nature of this gain or loss and defined it as being an extraordinary item requiring separate income statement disclosure, as indicated earlier.

OFF-BALANCE-SHEET FINANCING

5

Explain various types of off-balance-sheet financing, and understand the reasons for this type of financing.

A major issue facing the accounting profession today is how to deal with companies that do not disclose all their debt in order to make their financial position look stronger. This is often referred to as **off-balance-sheet financing.** Traditionally, leasing has been one of the most common forms of off-balance-sheet financing. (Accounting for leases is covered in detail in Chapter 15.) Other techniques that have been used to borrow money while keeping the debt off the balance sheet are:

1. Unconsolidated entities
2. Joint ventures
3. Research and development arrangements
4. Project financing arrangements

Unconsolidated Entities

In 1987, the FASB issued Statement No. 94 requiring all majority-owned subsidiaries to be consolidated.[20] Prior to the issuance of FASB Statement No. 94, subsidiaries involved in operations unrelated to the parent company's primary focus were not required to be consolidated. For example, IBM CREDIT CORPORATION, GE CAPITAL SERVICES, and GENERAL MOTORS ACCEPTANCE CORPORATION are each financing subsidiaries of their respective parent companies. The tremendous debt associated with these financing subsidiaries was not disclosed on the balance sheets of their parent companies prior to 1987 because the subsidiaries were involved in nonhomogeneous operations. However, with the issuance of Statement No. 94, even these subsidiaries are now consolidated. Thus, the FASB eliminated one opportunity that companies have used for off-balance-sheet financing.

However, companies are still able to avoid reporting debt associated with subsidiaries that are less than 50% owned by the company. As described in Chapter 14, unconsolidated subsidiaries using the equity method are those subsidiaries for which the

---

19　*Opinions of the Accounting Principles Board No. 26,* par. 19.
20　*Statement of Financial Accounting Standards No. 94,* "Consolidation of all Majority-Owned Subsidiaries," Stamford, CT: Financial Accounting Standards Board, 1987.

parent company owns between 20% and 50% of the outstanding shares. With this level of ownership, the presumption is that the parent influences but does not control the subsidiary. The equity method of accounting dictated for these subsidiaries provides that the parent reports, as an asset, its share of the net assets (assets minus liabilities) of the subsidiary; none of the individual liabilities of the subsidiary are reported in the parent company's balance sheet. Even with less than 50% ownership, a parent can often effectively control a subsidiary. For example, COCA-COLA owns just 44% of its major U.S. bottler, but Coca-Cola still effectively controls the operations of this bottler. But because Coca-Cola owns less than 50%, it is not required to report the liabilities of the bottler in its balance sheet. To illustrate the potential impact of unconsolidated subsidiaries on the reported amount of a company's debt, consider that Coca-Cola's reported liabilities as of December 31, 1998, were $10.7 billion, whereas the actual liabilities of Coca-Cola and its unconsolidated bottlers totaled $43.8 billion.

Joint Ventures

Companies will, on occasion, join forces with other companies to share the costs and benefits associated with specifically defined projects. These **joint ventures** are often developed to share the risks associated with high-risk projects. For example, *The Wall Street Journal* reported that in March 1999 drug companies were forming joint ventures to unravel the "biological blueprint for all human life." Their stated objective is that once they understand the complexities of human DNA they can develop personalized medical solutions. Start-up costs for this joint venture are estimated to be $100 million. By involving several pharmaceutical companies, these costs can be shared; the results can be shared as well.

Because the benefits of these joint ventures are uncertain, companies could incur substantial liabilities with few, if any, assets resulting from their efforts. As a result (as is sometimes the case with unconsolidated subsidiaries), a joint venture is sometimes carefully structured to ensure that its liabilities are not disclosed in the balance sheets of the companies that are partners.

A common form of a joint venture is a 50/50 partnership between two companies. For example, TEXACO has two 50/50 joint venture partnerships—one with CHEVRON and one with SAUDI REFINING, INC. The Chevron joint venture is called Caltex and engages in oil exploration, refining, and marketing in Africa, Asia, the Middle East, Australia, and New Zealand. The joint venture with Saudi Refining is called Star and markets gasoline in the eastern United States. The advantage of a 50/50 joint venture is that both companies can account for their investment using the equity method. Thus, joint ventures are often just a special type of unconsolidated subsidiary. For example, the Caltex and Star joint ventures have total long-term liabilities in excess of $3 billion, none of which are reported in Texaco's balance sheet.

Research and Development Arrangements

Another way a company may obtain off-balance-sheet financing is with research and development arrangements. These involve situations where an enterprise obtains the results of research and development activities funded partially or entirely by others. The main accounting issue is whether the arrangement is, in essence, a means of borrowing to fund research and development or if it is simply a contract to do research for others.[21] In deciding on the appropriate accounting treatment, a major consideration is whether the enterprise is obligated to repay the funds provided by the other parties regardless of the outcome of the research and development activities. If there is an obligation to repay, then the enterprise should estimate and recognize that liability and record the research and development expenses in the current year in accordance with FASB Statement No. 2. If the

---

21 *Statement of Financial Accounting Standards No. 68,* "Research and Development Arrangements," Stamford, CT: Financial Accounting Standards Board, 1982.

financial risk associated with the research and development is transferred from the enterprise to other parties and there is no obligation to them, then a liability need not be reported by the enterprise.

Research and development arrangements may take a variety of forms, including a limited partnership. For example, assume Kincher Company formed a limited partnership for the purpose of conducting research and development. Kincher is the general partner and manages the activities of the partnership. The limited partners are strictly investors. The question is—should Kincher record the research and development expenses and the obligation to the investors on its books? The answer depends on an assessment of who is at risk and if Kincher is obligated to repay the limited partners regardless of the results of the research and development. If the limited partners are at risk and have no guarantee or claim against Kincher Company for any of the funds contributed, the debt and related expenses need not be reported on Kincher's books.

> **FYI:** Many American automobile companies have formed joint ventures with foreign car companies to develop and manufacture cars. For example, FORD MOTOR CO. teamed up with MAZDA to produce numerous cars in the United States.

Project Financing Arrangements

At times, companies become involved in long-term commitments that are related to project financing arrangements. As an example, assume that Striker Corporation, a large construction company, has decided to establish a separate company, Paveway, in order to undertake a highway construction project. Paveway is to be organized as a separate legal entity, and all loans acquired by Paveway will specifically state that they are to be repaid from the cash flows of Paveway itself, with the assets of Paveway serving as collateral for the loans. It is likely that Striker would have a contingent obligation to satisfy the debt of Paveway even though the debt itself is intended to be repaid from Paveway cash flows. In this case, Striker would disclose this commitment in a note to the financial statements. This type of arrangement is another form of off-balance-sheet financing.[22]

Reasons for Off-Balance-Sheet Financing

There are several reasons why companies might use one of the preceding or other techniques to avoid including debt on the balance sheet. It may allow a company to borrow more than it otherwise could due to debt-limit restrictions. Also, if a company's financial position looks stronger, it will usually be able to borrow at a lower cost.

Whatever the reasons, the problems of off-balance-sheet financing are serious. Many investors and lenders aren't sophisticated enough to see through the off-balance-sheet borrowing tactics and therefore make ill-informed decisions. For example, in periods of economic downturn, a company with hidden debt may find it is not able to meet its obligations and, as a result, may suffer severe financial distress or, in extreme cases, business failure. In turn, unsuspecting creditors and investors may sustain substantial losses that could have been avoided had they known the true extent of the company's debt.

Analyze a firm's debt position using ratios.

ANALYZING A FIRM'S DEBT POSITION

Those parties considering investing in, or lending money to, a firm are particularly interested in that firm's obligations and capital structure. The term *leverage* refers to the relationship between a firm's debt and assets or its debt and stockholders' equity. A firm that is highly leveraged would have a large amount of debt relative to its assets or equity. A common measure of a firm's leverage is the **debt-to-equity ratio,** calculated by dividing total liabilities by total stockholders' equity. As an example, consider the following information from the 1998 annual report of IBM.

---

22 *Statement of Financial Accounting Standards No. 47,* "Disclosure of Long-Term Obligations," Stamford, CT.: Financial Accounting Standards Board, 1981.

(In millions)	1998	1997
Long-term debt	$15,508	$13,696
Total liabilities	66,667	61,683
Total stockholders' equity	19,433	19,816
Income before income taxes	9,040	9,027
Interest expense	713	728

IBM's debt-to-equity ratios for 1998 and 1997 would be:

1998: $66,667/$19,433 = 3.43
1997: $61,683/$19,816 = 3.11

A debt-to-equity ratio exceeding 1.0 indicates that the firm has more liabilities than stockholders' equity. For IBM, the debt-to-equity ratio has increased slightly from 1997 to 1998. IBM's total liabilities increased while its stockholders' equity decreased slightly. Investors generally prefer a higher debt-to-equity ratio to obtain the advantages of financial leverage, while creditors favor a lower ratio to increase the safety of their debt. Debt-to-equity ratios for a number of U.S. companies are presented in Exhibit 10-7.

EXHIBIT 10-7 | Debt-to-Equity Ratios for Selected U.S. Companies for Fiscal 1998 (In millions)

Company (Industry)	Total Liabilities	Total Equity	Debt-to-Equity Ratio
BankAmerica (banking)	$571,741	$45,938	12.45
Disney (entertainment)	21,990	19,388	1.13
General Electric (diversified industrial and financing)	312,780	38,880	8.04
McDonald's (fast food)	10,320	9,465	1.09
Merck (pharmaceuticals)	19,052	12,802	1.49
Microsoft (software)	5,730	16,627	0.34
Yahoo! (internet portal)	86	536	0.16

As these data illustrate, what constitutes an acceptable debt-to-equity ratio depends to a great extent upon the industry in which a company operates. For example, financial institutions, such as BANKAMERICA, typically have very high debt-to-equity ratios because the financial assets held by such institutions provide very good collateral for loans. Note that GENERAL ELECTRIC, which has a large amount of financial assets and liabilities in its GE CAPITAL SERVICES subsidiary, has a debt-to-equity ratio indicative of a financial institution. At the other end of the spectrum, companies with few tangible assets to offer as loan collateral typically have lower debt-to-equity ratios. The extreme example of this is YAHOO!, which has a debt-to-equity ratio of just 0.16.

Because there is no hard and fast rule for what is included in the term "debt," alternative definitions and interpretations of the debt-to-equity ratio have developed. For example, the ratio is often varied to include only long-term debt. If this definition were used for IBM, the debt-to-equity ratio for the two-year period would be:

1998: $15,508/$19,433 = 0.80
1997: $13,696/$19,816 = 0.69

Note that the debt-to-equity ratios differ dramatically depending on how "debt" is defined—the debt-to-equity ratio is 3.43 if debt is defined to include all liabilities, but is only .80 if debt is defined to include just long-term debt. Because there is no requirement for companies or analysts to compute ratios in particular ways, you are certain to encounter various different measures of the debt-to-equity ratio. The point to be remembered is this—make sure you understand the inputs to a ratio before you try and interpret the output. Debt to one person may not mean the same thing to another. Another common variation of the leverage measure is to compare total liabilities to total assets. This measure, frequently called the *debt ratio,* was introduced in Chapter 3 (see page 120).

Another measure of a company's performance relating to debt is the number of times interest is earned. This measure compares a company's interest obligations with its earnings ability. **Times interest earned** is calculated by adding a company's income before income taxes and interest expense and then dividing by the interest expense for the period. In the case of IBM, times interest earned for 1998 and 1997 is computed as follows:

1998: ($9,040 + $713)/$713 = 13.68
1997: ($9,027 + $728)/$728 = 13.40

The number of times interest is earned reflects the company's ability to meet interest payments and the degree of safety afforded the creditors. Note that in both 1997 and 1998, IBM offered creditors a very large margin of safety. In 1998, for example, IBM's operations generated more than 13 times the amount needed to be able to pay the company's interest obligation for the year.

Review the notes to financial statements, and understand the disclosure associated with debt financing.

DISCLOSING DEBT IN THE FINANCIAL STATEMENTS

In disclosing details about long-term debt in the notes to the financial statements, the nature of the liabilities, maturity dates, interest rates, methods of liquidation, conversion privileges, sinking fund requirements, borrowing restrictions, assets pledged, dividend limitations, and other significant matters should be indicated. The portion of long-term debt coming due in the current period should also be disclosed.

Bond liabilities are often combined with other long-term debt for balance sheet presentation, with supporting details disclosed in a note. An example of such a note taken from the 1998 annual report of IBM is presented in Exhibit 10–8. Note that IBM enters into long-term borrowing arrangements using a variety of different instruments and in a variety of different currencies. In U.S. dollars, IBM has both long-term debentures (unsecured bonds) and notes. The 7.125% debenture issue is interesting because it doesn't mature until 2096. IBM obtains loans denominated in foreign currencies for a variety of reasons. First, some countries are reluctant to allow large multinational corporations such as IBM to do business in their countries without using local financing. It helps IBM establish good local relations if it uses local financial institutions as much as possible. Also, some of IBM's foreign subsidiaries are relatively self-contained, meaning that almost all operating, investing, and financing activities are handled locally. Sometimes IBM gets foreign currency financing because the interest rate is low. (Look at the 3.1% average rate on the Japanese yen loans.) Finally, foreign currency financing is a way for IBM to hedge, or protect itself, again fluctuations in the value of foreign currencies. For example, if IBM has assets denominated in Thai baht, and the baht decreases in value, then IBM will have lost money. However, if IBM has an equal amount of loans denominated in Thai baht, the loss from the decrease in the value of the Thai baht assets will be offset by the gain from the decrease in value of the Thai baht liabilities. This is called a hedge and results in IBM being immune from the effects of exchange rate changes, up or down.

EXHIBIT 10-8 | IBM—Disclosure of Long-Term Debt

IBM—Disclosure of Long-Term Debt			
Long-Term Debt (Dollars in millions) At December 31:	**Maturities**	**1998**	**1997**
U.S. Dollars:			
Debentures:			
6.22%	2027	$ 500	$ 500
6.5%	2028	700	—
7.0%	2025	600	600
7.0%	2045	150	150
7.125%	2096	850	850
7.5%	2013	550	550
8.375%	2019	750	750
Notes: 6.7% average	2000–2013	2,695	2,674
Medium-term note			
program: 5.8% average	1999–2013	4,885	4,472
Other: 6.5% average	1999–2012	1,514	1,319
		13,194	11,865
Other currencies (average interest rate at December 31, 1998, in parentheses):			
Japanese yen (3.1%)	1999–2014	3,866	3,944
Canadian dollars (5.7%)	1999–2003	672	407
German marks (4.9%)	1999–2002	120	111
Swiss francs (2.5%)	2001	91	85
U.K. pounds (7.9%)	1999–2004	25	28
Other (11.9%)	1999–2026	221	235
		18,189	16,675
Less: Net unamortized discount		31	31
		18,158	16,644
Less: Current maturities		2,650	2,948
Total		$15,508	$13,696

Annual maturities in millions of dollars on long-term debt outstanding at December 31, 1998, are as follows: 1999, $2,650; 2000, $5,120; 2001, $1,491; 2002, $1,676; 2003, $1,116; 2004 and beyond, $6,136.

E X P A N D E D   M A T E R I A L

To this point in the chapter, we have covered the most common issues associated with debt—issuance, the payment of interest, and its retirement. In this expanded material, we will introduce and discuss an issue that does not occur frequently but, when it does occur, its impact is significant. The issue to be discussed is troubled debt restructuring—how to account for concessions made on the debt of firms in poor financial condition.

8

Understand the conditions under which troubled debt restructuring occurs, and be able to account for troubled debt restructuring.

FYI: Donald Trump, a player in the takeover mania of the 80s, experienced financial difficulties that were accompanied by significant troubled debt restructuring. The bondholders were able to force Trump to sell certain assets and were granted a voice in the management of his casinos in return for a forgiveness of interest payments.

ACCOUNTING FOR TROUBLED DEBT RESTRUCTURING

A significant accounting problem is created when economic conditions make it difficult for an issuer of long-term debt to make the cash payments required under the terms of the debt instrument. These payments include interest payments, principal payments on installment obligations, periodic payments to bond retirement funds, or even payments to retire debt at maturity. To avoid bankruptcy proceedings or foreclosure on the debt, investors may agree to make concessions and revise the original terms of the debt to permit the issuer to recover from financial problems. The revision of debt terms in such situations, referred to as **troubled debt restructuring,** can take many different forms. For example, there may be a suspension of interest payments for a period of time, a reduction in the interest rate, an extension of the maturity date of the debt, or even an exchange of assets or equity securities for the debt. The primary accounting question in these cases, on both the books of the issuer and the investor, is whether a gain or loss should be recognized upon the restructuring of the debt.

The issue became critical in the mid-1970s when several issues of municipal bonds, notably New York City bonds, were restructured due to the financial difficulties of the issuing organizations. Investors in the bonds were faced with interest and fund payments in arrears and a near bankrupt situation for New York City. Most investors felt the decline was only temporary and did not recognize any loss on their books. After considerable negotiation, the terms of the bonds were restructured. Changes included a moratorium on interest and fund payments and extended maturity dates. Other municipalities and private companies, such as CHRYSLER (before it merged with DAIMLER-BENZ) and MASSEY-FERGUSON, have experienced similar restructuring needs.

The FASB considered the area of debt restructuring carefully and issued Statement No. 15 in 1977. In this statement the Board defined troubled debt restructuring as a situation where "the creditor for economic or legal reasons related to the debtor's financial difficulties grants a concession to the debtor that it would not otherwise consider. That concession either stems from an agreement between the creditor and the debtor or is imposed by law or a court."[23]

The key word in this definition is concession. If a concession is not made by creditors, accounting for the restructuring follows the procedures discussed for extinguishment of debt prior to maturity.

The major issue addressed by the FASB in Statement No. 15 is whether a troubled debt restructuring agreement should be viewed as a significant economic transaction. It was decided that if it is considered to be a significant economic transaction, entries should be made on the issuer's books to reflect any gain or loss. If the restructuring is not considered to be a significant economic transaction, no entries are required. The accounting treatment thus depends on the nature of the restructuring. The FASB conclusions are summarized in the table on the following page.

For the issuer, each type of restructuring is discussed and illustrated in the following sections. For the investor, the procedures associated with an asset swap and an equity swap are discussed in this chapter. The complexities associated with a modification of terms from the point of view of the investor (or creditor) are discussed in Chapter 14 where we discuss the accounting for the impairment of a loan. Under FASB Statement No. 15, the accounting for troubled debt restructuring was similar for both the issuer and the investor. In 1993, however, the FASB issued Statement No. 114, "Accounting by Creditors for Impairment of a Loan," which drastically changed how the investor accounts for a modification of terms.

---

23 *Statement of Financial Accounting Standards No. 15,* "Accounting by Debtors and Creditors for Troubled Debt Restructuring," Stamford, CT: Financial Accounting Standards Board, 1977, par. 2.

Type	Restructuring Considered Significant Economic Transaction: Gain or Loss Recognized	Restructuring Not Considered Significant Economic Transaction: No Gain or Loss Recognized
Transfer of assets in full settlement (asset swap)	X	
Grant of equity interest in full settlement (equity swap)	X	
Modification of terms: Total payment under new structure exceeds debt carrying value		X
Modification of terms: Total payment under new structure is less than debt carrying value	X	

Transfer of Assets in Full Settlement (Asset Swap)

A debtor that transfers assets, such as real estate, inventories, receivables, or investments, to a creditor to fully settle a payable usually will recognize two types of gains or losses: (1) a gain or loss on disposal of the asset, and (2) a gain arising from the concession granted in the restructuring of the debt. The computation of these gains and/or losses is made as follows:

Carrying value of assets being transferred

Market value of asset being transferred

> Difference represents gain or loss on disposal

Carrying value of debt being liquidated

> Difference represents gain on restructuring

The gain or loss on disposal of an asset is usually reported as an ordinary income item unless it meets criteria for reporting it as an unusual or irregular item. However, the gain on restructuring is considered to arise from an early extinguishment of debt and must be reported as an extraordinary item.[24]

STOP & THINK How can there be a gain or loss on disposal but only a gain on restructuring?

An investor always recognizes a loss on the restructuring due to the concession granted unless the investment has already been written down in anticipation of the loss. The computation of the loss is made as follows:

Carrying value of investment liquidated

Market value of asset being transferred

> Difference represents loss on restructuring

The classification of this loss depends on the criteria being used to recognize irregular or extraordinary items. However, usually the loss is anticipated as market values of the investment decline, and it is recognized as an ordinary loss, either prior to the restructuring or as part of the restructuring.

To illustrate these points, assume that Stanton Industries is behind in its interest payments on outstanding bonds of $500,000 and is threatened with bankruptcy proceedings. The carrying value of the bonds on Stanton's books is $545,000 after deducting the unamortized discount of $5,000 and adding unpaid interest of $50,000. To settle the

---

24 Ibid., par. 21.

debt, Stanton transfers long-term investments it holds in Worth common stock with a carrying value of $350,000 and a current market value of $400,000 to all investors on a pro rata basis.

Assume Realty Inc. holds $40,000 face value of Stanton's bonds. Because of the troubled financial condition of Stanton Industries, Realty Inc. has previously recognized as a loss a $5,000 decline in the value of the debt and is carrying the investment at $35,000 on its books plus interest receivable of $4,000. The entries to record the asset transfer would be as follows:

Stanton Industries (Issuer)		
Interest Payable	50,000	
Bonds Payable	500,000	
Discount on Bonds Payable		5,000
Long-Term Investments—		
Worth Common Stock		350,000
Gain on Disposal of Worth		
Common Stock		50,000*
Gain on Restructuring of Debt		145,000*

*Carrying value of Worth common $350,000

$50,000 gain on disposal

Market value of Worth common $400,000

$145,000 gain from restructuring

Carrying value of debt liquidated $545,000

Realty Inc. (Investor)		
Long-Term Investments—		
Worth Common Stock	32,000**	
Loss on Restructuring of Debt	7,000	
Bond Investment—Stanton Industries		35,000
Interest Receivable		4,000

**Percentage of debt held by Realty Inc.: $40,000/$500,000 = 8%
Market value of long-term investment received in settlement of debt:
8% × $400,000 = $32,000

If an active market does not exist for the assets being transferred, estimates of the value should be made based on transfer of similar assets or by analyzing future cash flows from the assets.[25]

Grant of Equity Interest (Equity Swap)

A debtor that grants an equity interest to the investor as a substitute for a liability must recognize an extraordinary gain equal to the difference between the fair market value of the equity interest and the carrying value of the liquidated liability. A creditor (investor) must recognize a loss equal to the difference between the same fair market value of the equity interest and the carrying value of the debt as an investment. For example, assume that Stanton Industries transferred 20,000 shares of common stock to satisfy the $500,000 face value of bonds. The par value of the common stock per share is $1, and the market value at the date of the restructuring is $20 per share. Assume the other facts described in the preceding illustration of an asset swap are unchanged. The entries to record the grant of the equity interest on both sets of books are as follows:

Stanton Industries (Issuer)		
Interest Payable	50,000	
Bonds Payable	500,000	
Discount on Bonds Payable		5,000
Common Stock		20,000
Paid-In Capital in Excess of Par		380,000
Gain on Restructuring of Debt		145,000*

*Market value of common stock $400,000

$145,000 gain from restructuring

Carrying value of debt liquidated $545,000

Realty, Inc. (Investor)		
Long-Term Investments—Stanton		
Common Stock	32,000	
Loss on Restructuring of Debt	7,000	
Bond Investment—Stanton Industries		35,000
Interest Receivable		4,000

25 Ibid., par. 13.

The entry on Stanton's books for an equity swap differs from that made for the asset swap, because there can be no gain or loss on disposal of a company's own stock. However, the entry on Realty's books for an equity swap is identical to that for an asset swap except that the investment is in Stanton common stock.

Modification of Debt Terms

There are many ways debt terms may be modified to aid a troubled debtor. Modification may involve either the interest, the maturity value, or both. Interest concessions may involve a reduction of the interest rate, forgiveness of unpaid interest, or a moratorium on interest payments for a period of time. Maturity value concessions may involve an extension of the maturity date or a reduction in the amount to be repaid at maturity. Basically, the FASB decided that most modifications of debt did not result in a significant economic transaction for the issuer of the debt and thus did not give rise to a gain or loss at the date of restructuring. It argued that the new terms were merely an extension of an existing debt and that the modifications should be reflected in future periods through modified interest charges based on computed implicit interest rates. The only exception to this general rule occurs if the total payments to be made under the new structure, including all future interest payments, are less than the carrying value of the debt or the investment at the time of restructuring. Under this exception, the difference between the total future cash payments required and the carrying value of the debt or investment is recognized immediately as a gain on the debtor's books.

To illustrate the accounting for this type of restructuring, assume the interest rate on the Stanton Industries bonds (see page 572) is reduced from 10% to 7%, the maturity date is extended from three to five years from the restructuring date, and the past interest due of $50,000 is forgiven. The total future payments to be made after this restructuring are as follows:

Maturity value of bonds	$500,000
Interest—7% × $500,000 × 5 years	175,000
Total payments to be made after restructuring	$675,000

Because the $675,000 exceeds the carrying value of $545,000, no gain is recognized on the books of Stanton Industries at the time of restructuring.

However, if in addition to the preceding changes, $200,000 of maturity value is forgiven, the future payments would be reduced as follows:

Maturity value of bonds ($500,000 − $200,000)	$300,000
Interest—7% × $300,000 × 5 years	105,000
Total payments to be made after restructuring	$405,000

Now the carrying value exceeds the future payments by $140,000, and this gain would be recognized by Stanton as follows:

Interest Payable	50,000	
Bonds Payable	500,000	
Discount on Bonds Payable		5,000
Restructured Debt		405,000
Gain on Restructuring of Debt		140,000

When terms are modified, the amount recognized as interest expense or interest revenue in the remaining periods of the debt instrument's life is based on a computed implicit interest rate. The implicit interest rate is the rate that equates the present value of all future debt payments to the present carrying value of the debt or investment. The interest expense or interest revenue for each period is equal to the carrying value of the debt for the period involved times the implicit interest rate. The computation of the implicit interest rate can be complex and usually requires the use of a business calculator. However, approximations can be made by using a trial-and-error approach from the present value tables in Appendix B of the text.

To illustrate the computation of an implicit interest rate, the initial restructuring of Stanton Industries described on page 572 will be used. The question to be answered is what rate of interest will equate the total future payments of $675,000 to the present carrying value of $545,000. Trial-and-error use of Tables II and IV in Appendix B shows that the rate is between 4% and 6% per year. The computations are as follows:

	Interest Rate 6% (3% per Semiannual Period)	Interest Rate 4% (2% per Semiannual Period)
Present value of maturity value due in 5 years (10 semiannual periods)	.7441 × $500,000 = $372,050	.8203 × $500,000 = $410,150
Present value of $17,500 interest payments for 10 semi-annual periods	8.5302 × $17,500 = $149,279	8.9826 × $17,500 = $157,196
Total present value	$521,329	$567,346

Interpolation indicates that the present value of $545,000 lies almost exactly midway between the present values computed at 6% and 4%; therefore, the approximate interest rate is 5%. For purposes of the illustration, the 5% rate will be used, or 2½% per semiannual payment period.

Using this rate, the recorded interest expense for the first six months would be $13,625, or 2½% of $545,000. Because the actual cash payment for interest is $17,500, the carrying value of the debt will decline by $3,875 ($17,500 − $13,625). The interest expense for the second semiannual period will be less than for the first period because of the decrease in the carrying value of the debt [($545,000 − $3,875) × 2.5% = $13,528 interest expense]. These computations are the same as those required in applying the effective-interest method of amortization described on pages 555–557. If the exact implicit interest rate were used, continuation of the procedure for the 10 periods would leave a balance of $500,000, the maturity value, in the liability account of Stanton Industries. The entries to record the restructuring on Stanton's books and the first two interest payments would be as follows:

Bonds Payable	500,000	
Interest Payable	50,000	
Discount on Bonds Payable		5,000
Restructured Debt		545,000
Interest Expense	13,625	
Restructured Debt	3,875	
Cash		17,500
Interest Expense	13,528	
Restructured Debt	3,972	
Cash		17,500

The preceding discussion covers all situations when bond restructuring reflects a modification of terms except when the cash to be received after the restructuring is less than the carrying value of the debt. Under these conditions the implicit interest rate is negative. In order to raise the rate to zero, the carrying value must be reduced to the cash to be realized and a gain recognized for the difference. All interest payments in the future are offset directly to the debt account. No interest expense will be earned in the future because of the extreme concessions made in the restructuring. By charging all interest payments to the debt account, the balance remaining at the maturity date will be the maturity value of the debt.

Any combination of these methods of bond restructuring may be employed. Accounting for these multiple restructurings can become very complex and must be carefully evaluated. As stated previously, the accounting for a modification of terms by the creditor is discussed in Chapter 14.

REVIEW OF LEARNING OBJECTIVES

1 **Understand the various classification and measurement issues associated with debt.** Debt can be classified as either current or noncurrent. Debt is considered current if it will be paid within one year or the current operating cycle, whichever period is longer. Theoretically, all debt should be recorded at its present value. However, most current obligations arising in the normal course of business are not discounted. Some obligations cannot be measured with certainty. These obligations are estimated and recorded at an approximate amount.

2 **Account for short-term debt obligations, including those expected to be refinanced, and describe the purpose of lines of credit.** Short-term debt obligations can result from operations or from nonoperating activities. The most common example of a short-term obligation resulting from operations is accounts payable. Other short-term operating liabilities includes wages payable, interest payable, and taxes payable. Notes payable involve a more formal credit arrangement. These notes typically specify an interest rate and a payment date. Notes payable can be classified as trade or nontrade. Short-term obligations expected to be refinanced on a long-term basis should be classified as noncurrent if certain criteria are met.

Negotiating a line of credit allows a company to arrange the source of its financing in advance of the time that the funds are actually needed.

3 **Apply present value concepts to the accounting for long-term debts such as mortgages.** The present value of a long-term obligation is the amount of cash it would take today to completely satisfy the obligation. Mortgages and secured loans are loans that are backed by specific assets as collateral. These types of loans reduce the risk to the lender because the securing assets can be seized if the loan payments are not made. In accounting for the repayment of a mortgage obligation, each payment amount must be divided between the amount paid for interest and the amount paid for principal.

4 **Understand the various types of bonds, compute the price of a bond issue, and account for the issuance, interest, and redemption of bonds.** Bonds come in various shapes and sizes. They are issued by governments and corporations; they can be secured or unsecured, term or serial, registered or coupon—to name a few of the variations. But all bonds share one feature—they all involve the borrowing of money now with some form of repayment in the future.

Most bonds also involve periodic interest payments. The market price of a bond is determined using present value techniques that incorporate the market rate of interest and the stated rate of the bond. The difference between the market and stated rates will result in a premium or discount. This premium or discount is amortized over time.

When bonds are retired, the debt is removed from the books of the debtor when cash is paid. Bonds can be refinanced at or prior to maturity. Any gain on the early retirement of debt is disclosed as an extraordinary item on the income statement.

5 **Explain various types of off-balance-sheet financing, and understand the reasons for this type of financing.** Off-balance-sheet financing is a method companies employ to avoid disclosing obligations in the financial statements. Common examples of off-balance-sheet financing include unconsolidated entities, joint ventures, research and development arrangements, and project financing arrangements. Most areas involving off-balance-sheet financing have been addressed by the FASB, and disclosure associated with the financing arrangement is often required in the notes to the financial statements.

6 **Analyze a firm's debt position using ratios.** Ratios can be used to compare a firm's debt position over time or at the same time across companies. The most common measure of a firm's debt position is the debt-to-equity ratio. This ratio compares a firm's liabilities and its stockholders' equity. A common variation on this ratio is to include only long-term debt in the numerator. Times interest earned is another ratio often used to evaluate a company's debt position. This ratio is computed by dividing a firm's income before interest expense and taxes by interest expense for the period.

7 **Review the notes to financial statements, and understand the disclosure associated with debt financing.** Common disclosure associated with long-term debt includes information relating to maturities, interest rates, conversions privileges, and debt covenants. The portion of long-term debt coming due in the current period is also disclosed.

8 **Understand the conditions under which troubled debt restructuring occurs, and be able to account for troubled debt restructuring.** When a firm finds itself in financial trouble, options

used to alleviate some of the distress are to retire the debt at a reduced amount or to restructure the terms of its debt. Debt can be retired immediately at a reduced value with assets or by trading the debt for stock ownership. Gains realized with an asset swap or an equity swap are reported on the income statement as an extraordinary item. Another option for restructuring debt is to modify the terms of the debt. These modifications might include forgoing interest payments, reducing the interest rate on the debt, reducing the amount of the principal, or a combination of these options. If these modifications result in the total payments under the new structure being greater than the carrying value of the debt, no gain is recognized. A gain is recognized, however, if the total payments are less than the debt's current carrying value.

KEY TERMS

Accounts payable 541
Amortization 554
Bearer (coupon) bonds 548
Bond certificates 547
Bond discount 549
Bond indenture 547
Bond issuance costs 553
Bond premium 549
Bond refinancing 563
Callable bonds 549
Collateral trust bond 548
Commodity-backed (asset-linked) bonds 549
Convertible bonds 549
Convertible debt securities 559
Debt-to-equity ratio 566
Early extinguishment of debt 558
Effective-interest method 555

Face value, par value, or maturity value 547
Joint venture 565
Junk bonds 549
Liabilities 537
Line of credit 543
Loan (mortgage) amortization 545
Long-term debt 546
Market, yield, or effective interest rate 550
Mortgage 544
Municipal debt 547
Nontrade notes payable 541
Notes payable 541
Off-balance-sheet financing 564
Promissory note 541
Registered bonds 548
Secured bonds 548

Secured loan 545
Serial bonds 548
Stated (contract) rate 549
Straight-line method 554
Term bonds 548
Times interest earned 568
Trade notes payable 541
Trust indenture 546
Unsecured (debenture) bonds 548
Zero-interest (deep-discount) bonds 548

Troubled debt restructuring 570

QUESTIONS

1. Identify the major components included in the definition of liabilities established by the FASB.
2. (a) What is meant by an executory contract?
   (b) Do these contracts fit the definition of liabilities included in this chapter?
3. Distinguish between current and noncurrent liabilities. *CAN BE PAID IN 1 YEAR*
4. At what amount should liabilities generally be reported? *Present Value*

5. *Intend to refinance + the ability* Under what circumstances is a short-term loan classified among the long-term liabilities on the balance sheet?
6. What is a line of credit?
7. Why is it important to use present value concepts in properly valuing long-term liabilities?
8. When money is borrowed and monthly payments are made, how does one determine the portion of the payment that is interest and the portion that is principal?

9. Distinguish between (a) secured and unsecured bonds, (b) collateral trust and debenture bonds, (c) convertible and callable bonds, (d) coupon and registered bonds, (e) municipal and corporate bonds, and (f) term and serial bonds.

10. What is meant by market rate of interest, stated or contract rate, and effective or yield rate? Which of these rates changes during the lifetime of the bond issue?

11. What amortization method for premiums and discounts on bonds is recommended by APB Opinion No. 21? Why? When can the alternative method be used?

12. List three ways that bonds are commonly retired prior to maturity. How should the early extinguishment of debt be presented on the income statement?

13. What purpose is served by issuing callable bonds?

14. What are the distinguishing features of convertible debt securities? What questions relate to the nature of this type of security?

15. How does the accounting for convertible debt under IAS 32 differ from the accounting prescribed by U.S. GAAP?

16. The conversion of convertible bonds to common stock by an investor may be viewed as an exchange involving no gain or loss or as a transaction for which market values should be recognized and a gain or loss reported. What arguments support each of these views for the investor and for the issuer?

17. What is meant by refinancing or refunding a bond issue? When may refinancing be advisable?

18. Why is off-balance-sheet financing popular with many companies? What problems are associated with the use of this method of financing? *DONT WANT TO SHOW DEPT*

19. What is a joint venture, and how can a joint venture be a form of off-balance-sheet financing? *SPREAD DEBT OUT*

20. What distinguishes a troubled debt restructuring from other debt restructurings?

21. What is the recommended accounting treatment for bond restructurings effected as:
    (a) An asset swap?
    (b) An equity swap?
    (c) A modification of terms?

DISCUSSION CASES

CASE 10–1

WHAT IS A LIABILITY?

Professional athletes regularly sign long-term multimillion-dollar contracts in which they promise to play for a particular team for a specified time period. Owners of these teams often sign long-term leases for the use of playing facilities for a specified time period. GAAP often requires the leases to be booked as liabilities but does not require the obligations associated with pro athletes' contracts to be recorded.

Discuss the reasons for the differing treatment of these two seemingly similar events. Do you think the accounting treatment currently required by GAAP in these instances satisfies the needs of investors and creditors?

CASE 10–2

MEASURING LIABILITIES

Long-term leases and long-term debt are typically recognized in the financial statements at their discounted present values. This recognition practice acknowledges the time value of money. However, the standards related to accounting for deferred income taxes do not involve discounting expected future tax obligations.

Why do you suppose the FASB requires the use of discounting with some long-term liabilities and not with others? Should discounting be required for all long-term liabilities? Provide support for your answer.

CASE 10–3

LEAVE MY CURRENT RATIO ALONE!

Soto Inc., a closely held corporation, has never been audited and is seeking a large bank loan for plant expansion. The bank has requested audited financial statements. In conference with the president and majority stockholder of Soto, the auditor is informed that the bank looks very closely at the current ratio. The auditor's proposed reclassifications and adjustments include the following.

a. A note payable issued 4½ years ago matures in 6 months from the balance sheet date. The auditor wants to reclassify it as a current liability. The controller says no because "we are probably going to refinance this note with other long-term debt."

b. An accrual for compensated absences. Again the controller objects because the amount of the pay for these absences cannot be estimated. "Some employees quit in the first year and don't get vacation, and it is impossible to predict which employees will be absent for illness or other causes. Without being able to identify the employees, we can't determine the rate of compensation."

If you were the auditor, how would you respond to the controller?

CASE 10–4

ACCOUNTING FOR BONDS

Startup Company decided to issue $100,000 worth of 10%, 5-year bonds dated January 1, 2001, with interest payable semiannually on January 1 and July 1 of each year. Due to printing and other delays, Startup was not able to sell the bonds until July 1, 2001. The bonds were sold to yield 12% interest, and they are callable at 102 after January 1, 2003. The company expects interest rates to fall during the next few years and is planning to retire this bond issue and to replace it with a less costly one if the expected decline occurs.

Assume that you have just been hired as the accountant for Startup Company. The financial vice president would like you to identify the accounting issues involved with the bond transaction. You are also asked to explain why the company received less than $100,000 on the sale of the bonds and to compute the anticipated gain or loss on retirement of the bonds, assuming retirement on July 1, 2003, and use of straight-line amortization.

CASE 10–5

DISASTER BONDS

Natural disasters—they occur all too often. Californians worry about earthquakes. Residents of Florida worry about hurricanes. Folks along the Mississippi River worry about flooding. The Midwest has its twisters, and the Rocky Mountain states have wildfires. Insurance companies worry about them all. In simple terms, insurance companies make money by charging customers premiums that exceed the amount expected to be paid out in claims. And what are insurance companies doing? They are spreading the risks and costs across a lot of people. If your home is lost in a fire and you are not insured, you are responsible for paying to have your home rebuilt. But if you are insured, all the policyholders of your insurance company chip in, in effect, to rebuild your house.

In the case of a megadisaster, there is a risk that insurance companies will not have the resources to cover all losses of policyholders. The insurance industry estimates that a worst-case disaster would result in $50 billion in losses—enough to force many insurance companies out of business. If a disaster of this magnitude were to occur, many insurance companies wouldn't have enough policyholders over whom to spread the losses. So how do insurance companies deal with the enormous risks associated with "acts of God"? Disaster bonds!

Disaster bonds are a relatively new invention. These bonds allow insurance companies to share the risks of megadisasters with bondholders. In August 1996, MERRILL LYNCH & CO. began marketing the first major "act of God" bond issue. The bonds are issued by USAA, a car and home insurer based in San Antonio. These are the terms of the bonds: If USAA incurs over $1 billion in hurricane claims from a single storm over a 1-year period, investors in the disaster bonds will lose both interest and principal payments. Thus, if a huge hurricane hits the East Coast and claims from policyholders of USAA exceed $1 billion, USAA can use the money it would have paid to bondholders to pay policyholders. USAA is trying to do what insurance companies do best—spread the risk.

While yields for traditional bonds were around 8% in August 1996, the expected yield on disaster bonds was around 15%. Why do you think there is such a high premium on disaster bonds?

SOURCE: Suzanne McGee and Leslie Scism, "Disaster Bonds Have Investors 'Rolling the Dice with God,'" *The Wall Street Journal*, August 19, 1996.

CASE 10–6

IS THERE A LOSS ON CONVERSION?

Holton Co. recently issued $1,000,000 face value, 8%, 30-year debentures at 97. The debentures are callable at 103 upon 30 days' notice by the issuer at any time beginning 5 years after the date of issue. The debentures are convertible into $1 par value common stock of the company at the conversion price of $12.50 per share for each $500 or multiple thereof of the principal amount of the debentures ($500/$12.50 = 40 shares for each $500 of face value).

Assume that no value is assigned to the conversion feature at the date of issue of the debentures. Assume further that 5 years after issue, debentures with a face value of $100,000 and book value of $97,500 are tendered for conversion on an interest payment date when the market price of the debentures is 104 and the common stock is selling at $14 per share. J. K. Biggs, the company accountant, records the conversion as follows:

Bonds Payable	100,000	
Discount on Bonds Payable		2,500
Common Stock		8,000
Paid-In Capital in Excess of Par		89,500

Julie Robinson, staff auditor for the company's CPA firm, reviews the transaction and feels the conversion entry should reflect the market value of the stock. According to Robinson's analysis, a loss on the bond conversion of $14,500 should be recognized. Biggs objects to recognizing a loss, so Robinson discusses the problem with the audit manager, K. Ashworth. Ashworth has a different view and recommends using the market value of the debentures as a basis for recording the conversion and recognizing a loss of only $6,500.

Evaluate the various positions. Include in your evaluation the substitute entries that would be made under both Robinson's and Ashworth's proposals.

CASE 10–7

DEFERRED INTEREST AND INTEREST RATE RESETS

Corporations commonly incur debt in financing the acquisition of other companies or in fighting takeover attacks by competitors. Two strategies often employed involve deferring interest payments and incorporating interest rate resets. For example, INTERCO INC. incurred large amounts of debt in 1989 to make itself unattractive as a takeover target. The debt postponed interest payments until 1991 at which time interest was to be paid at 14%. Interco's strategy was to sell a portion of its business, ETHAN ALLEN INC., to redeem the debt. However, the sale netted $120 million less than expected.

WESTERN UNION incurred $500 million in debt that carried with it a reset provision. The provision called for increased interest rates if the bonds were not trading at a specified price. Western Union's reset provision increased interest rates from 16.5% to 19.25% in 1990. While interest expense rose, revenues dropped 28% from 1988 to 1989 as a result of fax machines making Western Union's telex service obsolete.

1. What is the significance of debt with respect to company acquisitions?
2. Why would corporations use deferred interest features and interest rate resets?
3. In the case of Interco, how would incurring large amounts of debt be an effective method for fighting a takeover?

CASE 10–8

CIRCLE K CORPORATION AND ITS DEBT COVENANTS

When companies raise money through the issuance of bonds or other long-term debt instruments, debt holders typically require the company to comply with certain conditions, or covenants. The notes to CIRCLE K's 1989 financial statements provide an example of debt covenants:

> The notes (Senior Secured Notes) required the Company to observe certain financial covenants, including covenants relating to maintenance of a minimum consolidated net worth, a fixed charge coverage ratio, limitations on dividends, purchases of capital stock and a requirement that any successor by merger or similar transaction to the Company have a comparable net worth and assume all the obligations under the notes.

In addition to using debt to finance expansion, Circle K financed many of its store acquisitions through sales and leaseback transactions. These types of transactions represent a form of long-term debt financing and often involve covenants as well. The notes to the 1989 financial statements detail the results of a violation of covenants:

> As of April 30, 1989, the Company was not in compliance with the fixed charge ratio of one of its sale and leaseback transactions involving 250 stores. Because of its noncompliance with such ratio, the Company is required to place $5 million per year into escrow.

1. What is the purpose of debt covenants?
2. What is the purpose of requiring an annual $5 million payment into escrow?
3. If Circle K's financial condition is such that it violates its financing covenants, will requiring the company to place $5 million in escrow help to ease the financial strains?

CASE 10–9

WHAT IS MEANT BY VALUING LIABILITIES AT CURRENT VALUES?

John Jex, CPA, had just delivered a keynote address to a banker's organization on the merits of valuing loan portfolio assets at market values that reflected changing interest rates. During the question-and-answer period he was asked why bank liabilities should not be valued using current interest rates if assets are to be revalued for interest rate changes. His answer did not seem to satisfy the banker, and the meeting soon adjourned. After the meeting, John was asked by a listener to explain the impact changing interest rates would have on liabilities if a revaluation were to occur. How would you respond to such a request?

CASE 10–10

LET'S GET THAT DEBT OFF THE BALANCE SHEET!

Both COCA-COLA CO. and MARRIOTT CORPORATION have improved the appearance of their parent company balance sheets by organizing separate companies and transferring significant amounts of debt to these entities. To avoid including these subsidiaries in their consolidated financial statements, they retained less than 50% of the outstanding common stock in them. You, as an intermediate accounting student, have the assignment to evaluate this action and consider its appropriateness in light of current GAAP. If GAAP is deficient, you are to suggest changes that will make the reporting more representative of economic reality. Prepare the report you would submit to fulfill this assignment.

CASE 10–11

IN-SUBSTANCE DEFEASANCE

Another form of early extinguishment of debt is referred to as in-substance defeasance, or economic defeasance. In-substance defeasance is a process of transferring assets, generally cash and securities, to an irrevocable trust, and using the assets and earnings therefrom to satisfy the long-term obligations as they come due. In some instances, the debt holders are not aware of these transactions and continue to rely on the issuer of the debt for settlement of the obligation. In other words, there has been no "legal defeasance" or release of the debtor from the legal liability.

Before FASB Statement No. 125 was issued in 1996, an in-substance defeasance was treated as an extinguishment of debt even though the debt is not actually repaid. The provisions of Statement No. 125 no longer allow debt to be removed from the balance sheet through in-substance defeasance.

Under Statement No. 125, what conditions must be satisfied for debt to be removed from the balance sheet? In what way do these conditions stop the use of in-substance defeasance as a way to remove debt from the balance sheet?

CASE 10–12

DO WE REALLY HAVE INCOME?

The Jefferson Corporation has $20,000,000 of 10% bonds outstanding. Because of cash flow problems, the company is behind in interest payments and in contributions to its bonds retirement fund. The market value of the bonds has declined until it is currently only 50% of the face value of the bonds. After lengthy negotiations, the principal bondholders have agreed to exchange their bonds for preferred stock that has a current market value of

$10,000,000. The accountant for Jefferson Corporation recorded the transaction by charging the bond liability for the entire $20,000,000, and crediting Preferred Stock for the same amount. This entry thus transfers the amount received by the company from debt to equity.

The CPA firm performing the annual audit, however, does not agree with this treatment. The auditors argue that this transfer represents a troubled debt restructuring due to the significant concessions made by the bondholders, and under these conditions, the FASB requires Jefferson to use the market value of the preferred stock as its recorded value. The difference between the $20,000,000 face value of the bonds and the $10,000,000 market value of the preferred stock is a reportable gain.

The controller of Jefferson, L. Rogers, is flabbergasted. "Here we are, almost bankrupt, and you tell us we must report the $10,000,000 as a gain. I don't care what the FASB says; that's a ridiculous situation. You can't be serious."

But the auditor in charge of the engagements is adamant, "We really have no choice. You have had a forgiveness of debt for $10,000,000. You had use of the money, and based on current conditions, you won't have to pay it back. That situation looks like a gain to me."

What position do you think should be taken? Consider the external users of the financial statements and their needs in your discussion.

EXERCISES

EXERCISE 10–13

ACCOUNTING FOR MORTGAGES

On January 1, 2002, Lily Company purchased a building for $800,000. The company made a 20% downpayment and took out a mortgage payable over 30 years with monthly payments of $5,616.46. The first payment is due February 1, 2002. The mortgage interest rate is 10%.

1. Determine how much of the first two mortgage payments would be applied to interest expense and how much would be applied to reducing the principal. (Note: The 10% interest rate is compounded monthly.)
2. Make the journal entry necessary to record the first mortgage payment on February 1, 2002.

EXERCISE 10–14

MORTGAGE AMORTIZATION SCHEDULE

On July 1, 2002, Gandalf Inc. borrowed $50,000 to finance the purchase of machinery. The terms of the mortgage require payments to be made at the end of every month with the first payment of $1,112 being due on July 31, 2002. The length of the mortgage is 5 years, and the mortgage carries an interest rate of 12% compounded monthly.

1. Prepare a mortgage amortization schedule for the last 6 months of 2002.
2. How much interest expense will be reported in 2002 in connection with this mortgage?
3. What amount will be reported in Gandalf's balance sheet as mortgage liability at the end of 2002?

EXERCISE 10–15

COMPUTATION OF MARKET VALUES OF BOND ISSUES

What is the market value of each of the following bond issues? (Round to the nearest dollar.)

(a) 10% bonds of $1,000,000 sold on bond issue date; 10-year life; interest payable semiannually; effective rate, 12%.
(b) 9% bonds of $200,000 sold on bond issue date; 5-year life; interest payable semiannually; effective rate, 8%.
(c) 8% bonds of $150,000 sold 30 months after bond issue date; 15-year life; interest payable semiannually; effective rate, 10%.

EXERCISE 10–16

SELLING BONDS AT PAR, PREMIUM, OR DISCOUNT

In each of the following independent cases, state whether the bonds were issued at par, a premium, or a discount. Explain your answers.

(a) Pop-up Manufacturing sold 1,500 of its $1,000, 8% stated-rate bonds when the market rate was 7%. PREMIUM

(b) Splendor, Inc., sold 500 of its $2,000, 8¾% bonds to yield 9%. DISCOUNT

(c) Cards Corporation issued 1,000 of its 9%, $100 face value bonds at an effective rate of 9½%. DISCOUNT

(d) Floppy, Inc., sold 3,000 of its 10% bonds with a face value of $2,500 at a time when the market rate was 9%. PREMIUM

(e) Cintron Co. sold 5,000 of its 12% contract-rate bonds with a stated value of $1,000 at an effective rate of 12%. PAR

EXERCISE 10–17

ZERO-COUPON BONDS

Allrite Inc. is considering issuing bonds to finance the acquisition of a nationwide chain of distributors of Allrite's products. Allrite is contemplating two different types of bonds to raise the required $50 million purchase price. The first is a traditional 10-year, 10% bond with semiannual interest payments. The second is a 10-year, zero-coupon bond.

Assuming the market rate of interest is 10%, compute the face value of the bond issuance and make the journal entries necessary to record the issuance if (a) a traditional bond is issued, and (b) a zero-coupon bond is issued.

EXERCISE 10–18

ISSUANCE AND REACQUISITION OF BONDS

On January 1, 2001, the Housen Company issued 10-year bonds of $500,000 at 102. Interest is payable on January 1 and July 1 at 10%. On April 1, 2002, the Housen Company reacquires and retires 50 of its own $1,000 bonds at 98 plus accrued interest. The fiscal period for the Housen Company is the calendar year.

Prepare entries to record (a) the issuance of the bonds, (b) the interest payments and adjustments relating to the debt in 2001, (c) the reacquisition and retirement of bonds in 2002, and (d) the interest payments and adjustments relating to the debt in 2002. Assume the premium or discount is amortized on a straight-line basis. (Round to the nearest dollar.)

EXERCISE 10–19

AMORTIZATION OF BOND PREMIUM OR DISCOUNT

On January 1, 2001, Terrel Company sold $100,000 of 10-year, 8% bonds at 92.5, an effective rate of 9%. Interest is to be paid on July 1 and December 31. Compute the premium or discount to be amortized in 2001 and 2002 using (a) the straight-line method and (b) the effective-interest method. Make the journal entries to record the amortization when the effective-interest method is used.

EXERCISE 10–20

BOND INTEREST AND PREMIUM OR DISCOUNT AMORTIZATION

Assume that $200,000 of Baker School District 6% bonds are sold on the bond issue date for $185,788. Interest is payable semiannually, and the bonds mature in 10 years. The purchase price provides a return of 7% on the investment.

1. What entries would be made on the investor's books for the receipt of the first 2 interest payments, assuming premium or discount amortization on each interest date by (a) the straight-line method and (b) the effective-interest method? (Round to the nearest dollar.)

2. What entries would be made on Baker School District's books to record the first 2 interest payments, assuming premium or discount amortization on each interest date by (a) the straight-line method and (b) the effective-interest method? (Round to the nearest dollar.)

EXERCISE 10–21

DISCOUNT AND PREMIUM AMORTIZATION

The Rolstone Corporation issued $200,000 of 8% debentures to yield 10%, receiving $184,556. Interest is payable semiannually and the bonds mature in 5 years.

1. What entries would be made by Rolstone for the first 2 interest payments, assuming premium or discount amortization on interest dates by (a) the straight-line method and (b) the effective-interest method? (Round to the nearest dollar.)
2. What entries would be made on the books of the investor for the first 2 interest receipts, assuming premium or discount amortization on interest dates and that one party obtained all the bonds and the straight-line method of amortization was used? (Round to the nearest dollar.)
3. If the sale is made to yield 6%, $217,062 being received, what entries would be made by Rolstone for the first 2 interest payments, assuming premium or discount amortization on interest dates by (a) the straight-line method and (b) the effective-interest method? (Round to the nearest dollar.)

EXERCISE 10–22

SALE OF BOND INVESTMENT

Jennifer Stack acquired $50,000 of Oldtown Corp. 9% bonds on July 1, 1999. The bonds were acquired at 92; interest is paid semiannually on March 1 and September 1. The bonds mature September 1, 2006. Stack's books are kept on a calendar-year basis. On February 1, 2002, Stack sold the bonds for 97 plus accrued interest. Assuming straight-line amortization and no reversing entry at January 1, 2002, give the entry to record the sale of the bonds on February 1. (Round to the nearest dollar.)

EXERCISE 10–23

RETIREMENT OF DEBT BEFORE MATURITY

The long-term debt section of Starr Company's balance sheet as of December 31, 2001, included 9% bonds payable of $200,000 less unamortized discount of $16,000. Further examination revealed that these bonds were issued to yield 10%. The amortization of the bond discount was recorded using the effective-interest method. Interest was paid on January 1 and July 1 of each year. On July 1, 2002, Starr retired the bonds at 103 before maturity.

Prepare the journal entries to record the July 1, 2002, payment of interest, including the amortization of the discount since December 31, 2001, and the early retirement on the books of Starr Company.

EXERCISE 10–24

RETIREMENT OF BONDS

The December 31, 2001, balance sheet of Worsham Company includes the following items:

9% bonds payable due December 31, 2010	$400,000
Premium on bonds payable	10,800

The bonds were issued on December 31, 2000, at 103, with interest payable on June 30 and December 31 of each year. The straight-line method is used for premium amortization.

On March 1, 2002, Worsham retired $100,000 of these bonds at 98, plus accrued interest. Prepare the journal entries to record retirement of the bonds, including accrual of interest since the last payment and amortization of the premium.

EXERCISE 10–25

RETIREMENT AND REFINANCING OF BONDS

Chiam Corporation has $300,000 of 12% bonds, callable at 102, with a remaining 10-year term, and interest payable semiannually. The bonds are currently valued on the books at $290,000, and the company has just made the interest payment and adjustments for amortization of any premium or discount. Similar bonds can be marketed currently at 10% and would sell at par.

1. Give the journal entries to retire the old debt and issue $300,000 of new 10% bonds at par.

2.   In what year will the reduction in interest offset the cost of refinancing the bond issue?

EXERCISE 10–26

ISSUANCE OF CONVERTIBLE BONDS

Ricardo Insurance decides to finance expansion of its physical facilities by issuing convertible debenture bonds. The terms of the bonds follow: maturity date 20 years after May 1, 2001, the date of issuance; conversion at option of holder after 2 years; 40 shares of $1 par value stock for each $1,000 bond held; interest rate of 12% and call provision on the bonds of 104. The bonds were sold at 101.

1.   Give the entry on Ricardo's books to record the sale of $1,000,000 of bonds on July 1, 2001; interest payment dates are May 1 and November 1.

2.   Assume the same condition as in (1) except that the sale of the bonds is to be recorded in a manner that will recognize a value related to the conversion feature. The estimated sales price of the bonds without the conversion feature is 98.

EXERCISE 10–27

CONVERTIBLE BONDS

Clarkston Inc. issued $1,000,000 of convertible 10-year, 11% bonds on July 1, 2001. The interest is payable semiannually on January 1 and July 1. The discount in connection with the issue was $9,500, which is amortized monthly using the straight-line basis. The debentures are convertible after 1 year into 5 shares of the company's $1 par common stock for each $1,000 of bonds.

On August 1, 2002, $100,000 of the bonds were converted. Interest has been accrued monthly and paid as due. Any interest accrued at the time of conversion of the bonds is paid in cash.

Prepare the journal entries on Clarkston's books to record the conversion, amortization, and interest on the bonds as of August 1 and August 31, 2002. (Round to the nearest dollar.)

EXERCISE 10–28   **TROUBLED DEBT RESTRUCTURING—ASSET SWAP**

The Buck Machine Company has outstanding a $150,000 note payable to the Ontario Investment Corporation. Because of financial difficulties, Buck negotiates with Ontario to exchange inventory of machine parts to satisfy the debt. The cost of the inventory transferred is carried on Buck's books at $90,000. The estimated retail value of the inventory is $140,000. Buck uses a perpetual inventory system. Prepare journal entries for the exchange on the books of both Buck Machine Company and Ontario Investment Corporation according to the requirements of FASB Statement No. 15.

EXERCISE 10–29   **TROUBLED DEBT RESTRUCTURING—EQUITY SWAP**

Southwest Enterprises is threatened with bankruptcy due to its inability to meet interest payments and fund requirements to retire $4,000,000 of long-term notes. The notes are all held by Imperial Insurance Company. In order to prevent bankruptcy, Southwest has entered into an agreement with Imperial to exchange equity securities for the debt. The terms of the exchange are as follows: 250,000 shares of $1 par common stock, current market value $8 per share, and 20,000 shares of $10 par preferred stock, current market value $70 per share. Prepare journal entries for the exchange on the books of both Imperial Insurance Company and Southwest Enterprises according to the requirements of FASB Statement No. 15.

EXERCISE 10–30

MODIFICATION OF DEBT TERMS

Moriarty Co. is experiencing financial difficulties. Income has exhibited a downward trend, and the company reported its first loss in company history this past year. The firm has been unable to service its debt and, as a result, has missed 2 semiannual interest payments. In an attempt to turn the company around, management has negotiated a modification of its debt terms with bondholders. These modified terms are effective January 1, 2002. The bonds are $10,000,000, 10-year, 10% bonds that were issued on

January 2, 1997, and currently have an unamortized premium of $210,000. Prepare the necessary journal entries on Moriarty's books for each of the following independent situations.

(a) Bondholders agree to forgive past-due interest and reduce the interest rate on the debt from 10% to 5%.
(b) Bondholders agree to forgive past-due interest and forgive $3,000,000 of the face amount of the debt.
(c) Bondholders agree to forgive past-due interest, reduce the interest rate on the debt from 10% to 6%, and forgive $2,000,000 of the face value of the debt.

PROBLEMS

PROBLEM 10-31

SHORT-TERM LOANS EXPECTED TO BE REFINANCED

The following information comes from the financial statements of Burton Davis Company.

Current assets	$ 75,000
Accounts payable	50,000
Short-term loan payable	60,000
Long-term debt	100,000
Total liabilities	300,000
Total stockholders' equity	200,000

Burton Davis has arranged with its bank to refinance its short-term loan when it becomes due in 3 months. The new loan will have a term of 5 years.

Instructions:

1. Compute the following ratio values.
   (a) Current ratio
   (b) Debt-to-equity ratio
   (c) Debt ratio
2. If you were the auditor of Burton Davis' financial statements, how would you convince yourself of the validity of the refinancing agreement?

PROBLEM 10–32

AMORTIZING A MORTGAGE AND THE EFFECT ON THE FINANCIAL STATEMENTS

On January 1, 2002, Picard Inc. purchased a new piece of equipment from LaForge Engineering to expand its production facilities. The equipment was purchased at a cost of $800,000. Picard financed the purchase with an $800,000 mortgage to be repaid in annual payments over 5 years at a rate of 10%. The mortgage was arranged through Pulaski Bank. The annual payments of $211,038 are to be made on December 31 of each year.

Instructions:

1. Prepare a mortgage amortization schedule for the 5-year life of the mortgage.
2. Assuming the equipment is expected to last for 5 years (with zero salvage value), determine the net amount at which the equipment will be reported on the balance sheet at the end of each year for its 5-year life using straight-line depreciation.
3. Compare the liability amount to be disclosed on the balance sheet at the end of each year for the 5-year mortgage term (1) with the asset amount to be disclosed at the end of the same years (2). Identify the primary reasons for the differences each year.

PROBLEM 10–33

BOND ISSUANCE AND ADJUSTING ENTRIES

On January 1, 2002, Bel Air Company issued bonds with a face value of $1,000,000 and a maturity date of December 31, 2011. The bonds have a stated interest rate of 10%,

payable on January 1 and July 1. They were sold to Mercur Company for $885,300, a yield of 12%. It cost Bel Air $30,000 to issue the bonds. This amount was deferred and amortized over the life of the issue using the straight-line method. Assume that both companies have December 31 year-ends and that Bel Air uses the effective-interest method to amortize any premium or discount and Mercur uses the straight-line method.

Instructions:

1. Make all entries necessary to record the sale and purchase of the bonds on each company's books.
2. Prepare the adjusting entries as of December 31, 2002, for both companies. Assume Mercur is carrying the bonds as a long-term investment.

PROBLEM 10–34

COMPUTATION OF BOND MARKET PRICE AND AMORTIZATION OF PREMIUM OR DISCOUNT

Signal Enterprises decided to issue $900,000 of 10-year bonds. The interest rate on the bonds is stated at 7%, payable semiannually. At the time the bonds were sold, the market rate had increased to 8%.

Instructions:

1. Determine the maximum amount an investor should pay for these bonds. (Round to the nearest dollar.)
2. Assuming that the amount in (1) is paid, compute the amount at which the bonds would be reported by the investor after being held for 1 year. Use 2 recognized methods of handling amortization of the difference in cost and maturity value of the bonds and give support to the method you prefer. (Round to the nearest dollar.)

PROBLEM 10–35

PREMIUM OR DISCOUNT AMORTIZATION TABLE

The Allen Co. acquired $20,000 of Locust Sales Co.'s 7% bonds, interest payable semiannually, bonds maturing in 5 years. The bonds were acquired at $20,850, a price to return approximately 6%.

Instructions:

1. Prepare tables to show the periodic adjustments to the investment account and the annual bond earnings, assuming adjustment by each of the following methods: (a) the straight-line method, and (b) the effective-interest method. (Round to the nearest dollar.)
2. Assuming use of the effective-interest method, prepare journal entries for each company.

PROBLEM 10–36

AMORTIZING DEFERRED INTEREST BONDS

R. J. Winter Co. recently issued $100,000, 10-year deferred interest bonds. The bonds have a stated rate of 10%, and interest is to be paid in 10 semiannual payments beginning in Year 6. The market rate of interest on the date of issuance was 8%.

Instructions:

1. Compute the maximum amount an investor should pay for these bonds. (Round to the nearest dollar.)
2. Prepare a bond amortization schedule for R.J. Winter assuming the effective-interest method is used. (Round to the nearest dollar.)

PROBLEM 10–37

CASH FLOW EFFECTS OF A BOND PREMIUM

On January 1, 2002, Datalink Inc. issued $100,000, 10%, 10-year bonds when the market rate of interest was 8%. Interest is payable on June 30 and December 31. The following financial information is available.

Sales	$300,000
Cost of sales	180,000
Gross profit	120,000
Interest expense	?
Depreciation expense	(14,500)
Other expenses	(82,000)
Net income	?

	Dec. 31, 2002	Jan. 1, 2002
Accounts receivable	$55,000	$48,000
Inventory	87,000	93,000
Accounts payable	60,000	58,000

All purchases of inventory are on account. Other expenses are paid for in cash.

Instructions:

1. Prepare the journal entry to record the issuance of the bonds on January 1, 2002.
2. Compute (a) the amount of cash paid to bondholders for interest during 2002, (b) the amount of premium amortized during 2002, assuming Datalink uses the straight-line method for amortizing bond premiums and discounts, and (c) the amount of interest expense for 2002.
3. Prepare the "Cash flows from operating activities" section of Datalink's statement of cash flows using (a) the direct method, and (b) the indirect method.

PROBLEM 10–38

BOND ENTRIES—ISSUER

On April 1, 1992, the Miromar Tool Company authorized the sale of $8,000,000 of 7% convertible bonds with interest payment dates of April 1 and October 1. The bonds were sold on July 1, 1992, and mature on April 1, 2012. The bond discount totaled $426,600. The bond contract entitles the bondholders to receive 25 shares of $1 par value common stock in exchange for each $1,000 bond. On April 1, 2002, the holders of bonds with total face value of $1,000,000 exercised their conversion feature. On July 1, 2002, the Miromar Tool Company reacquired bonds, face value $500,000, on the open market. The balances in the equity accounts as of December 31, 2001, were:

Common stock, $1 par, authorized 3 million shares, issued and outstanding, 250,000 shares	$ 250,000
Paid-in capital in excess of par	6,000,000

Market values of the common stock and bonds were as follows:

Date	Bonds (per $1,000)	Common Stock (per Share)
April 1, 2002	$1,220	$47
July 1, 2002	1,250	51

Instructions: Prepare journal entries on the issuer's books for each of the following transactions. (Use the straight-line amortization method for the bond discount.)

1. Sale of the bonds on July 1, 1992.
2. Interest payment on October 1, 1992.
3. Interest accrual on December 31, 1992, including bond discount amortization.
4. Conversion of bonds on April 1, 2002. (Assume that interest and discount amortization are correctly shown as of April 1, 2002. No gain or loss on conversion is recognized.)
5. Reacquisition and retirement of bonds on July 1, 2002. (Assume that interest and discount amortization are correctly reported as of July 1, 2002.)

PROBLEM 10–39

BOND ENTRIES—ISSUER

The Decker Company sold $3,000,000 of 9% first-mortgage bonds on October 1, 1994, at $2,873,640 plus accrued interest. The bonds were dated July 1, 1994; interest payable semiannually on January 1 and July 1; redeemable after June 30, 1999, to June 30, 2002, at 101, and thereafter until maturity at 100; and convertible into $1 par value common stock as follows:

- Until June 30, 1999, at the rate of 6 shares for each $1,000 bond.
- From July 1, 1999, to June 30, 2002, at the rate of 5 shares for each $1,000 bond.
- After June 30, 2002, at the rate of 4 shares for each $1,000 bond.

The bonds mature 10 years from their issue date. The company adjusts its books monthly and closes its books as of December 31 each year.

The following transactions occur in connection with the bonds.

2000
July 1 $1,000,000 of bonds were converted into stock, with no gain or loss recognized.

2001
Dec. 31 $500,000 face value of bonds were reacquired at 99¼ plus accrued interest. These were immediately retired.

2002
July 1   The remaining bonds were called for redemption and accrued interest was paid. For purposes of obtaining funds for redemption and business expansion, a $4,000,000 issue of 7% bonds was sold at 97. These bonds are dated July 1, 2002, and are due in 20 years.

Instructions: Prepare journal entries necessary for Decker Company in connection with the preceding transactions, including monthly adjustments, where appropriate, as of the following dates. Assume bond discount amortization is made using the straight-line method. (Round to the nearest dollar.)

1. October 1, 1994
2. December 31, 1994
3. July 1, 2000
4. December 31, 2001
5. July 1, 2002

PROBLEM 10–40

BOND ENTRIES—INVESTOR

On June 1, 2001, Sunderland Inc. purchased as a long-term investment 400 of the $1,000 face value, 8% bonds of Stateline Corporation for $369,150. The bonds were purchased to yield 10% interest. Interest is payable semiannually on December 1 and June 1. The bonds mature on June 1, 2007. Sunderland uses the effective-interest method of amortization. On November 1, 2002, Sunderland sold the bonds for $392,500. This amount includes the appropriate accrued interest. Sunderland intended to hold these bonds until they matured, so year-to-year market value fluctuations were ignored in accounting for the bonds.

Instructions: Prepare a schedule showing the income or loss before income taxes from the bond investment that Sunderland should record for the years ended December 31, 2001, and 2002.

PROBLEM 10–41

BOND ENTRIES—INVESTOR

On May 1, 1999, Desert Co. acquired $40,000 of Extel Corp. 9% bonds at 97 plus accrued interest. Interest on bonds is payable semiannually on March 1 and September 1, and bonds mature on September 1, 2002.

On May 1, 2000, Desert Co. sold bonds of $12,000 for 103 plus accrued interest. On July 1, 2001, bonds of $16,000 were exchanged for 2,250 shares of Extel Corp. common, no par value, quoted on the market on this date at $8. Interest was received on bonds to date of exchange.

On September 1, 2002, remaining bonds were redeemed and accrued interest was received.

Instructions: Give journal entries for 1999–2002 to record the foregoing transactions on the books for Desert Co., including any adjustments that are required at the end of each fiscal year ending on December 31. Assume bond premium or discount amortization is by the straight-line method. Ignore any potential impact of year-to-year market value changes on the accounting for the bonds.

PROBLEM 10–42

NOTE PAYABLE ENTRIES—INVESTOR AND ISSUER
Fitzgerald Inc. issued $750,000 of 8-year, 11% notes payable dated April 1, 1998. Interest on the notes is payable semiannually on April 1 and October 1. The notes were sold on April 1, 1998, to an underwriter for $720,000 net of issuance costs. The notes were then offered for sale by the underwriter, and on July 1, 1998, L. Baum purchased the entire issue as a long-term investment. Baum paid 101 plus accrued interest for the notes. On June 1, 2001, Baum sold the investment in Fitzgerald notes to J. Gott as a short-term investment. Gott paid 96 plus accrued interest for the notes as well as $1,500 for brokerage fees. Baum paid $1,000 brokerage fees to sell the notes. Gott held the investment until April 1, 2002, when the notes were called at 104 by Fitzgerald.

Instructions: Prepare all journal entries required: on the books of Fitzgerald Inc. for 1998 and 2002; on the books of Baum for 1998 and 2001; and on the books of Gott for 2001 and 2002. Assume each entity uses the calendar year for reporting purposes and that issue costs are netted against the note proceeds by Fitzgerald. Any required amortization is made using the straight-line method. Ignore any potential impact of year-to-year market value changes on the accounting for the notes by the investors.

PROBLEM 10–43

ADJUSTMENT OF BOND INVESTMENT ACCOUNT
In auditing the books for the Carmichael Corporation as of December 31, 2002, before the accounts are closed, you find the following long-term investment account balance.

Account: INVESTMENT IN BIG OIL 9% BONDS (MATURITY DATE, JUNE 1, 2006)

Date	Item	Debit	Credit	Balance Debit	Balance Credit
2002 Jan. 21	Bonds, $200,000 par, acquired at 102 plus accrued interest	206,550		206,550	
Mar. 1	Proceeds from sale of bonds, $100,000 par and accrued interest		106,000	100,550	
June 1	Interest received		4,500	96,050	
Nov. 1	Amount received on call of bonds, $40,000 par, at 101 plus accrued interest		41,900	54,150	
Dec. 1	Interest received		2,700	51,450	

Instructions:
1. Give the entries that should have been made relative to the investment in bonds, including any adjusting entries that would be made on December 31, the end of the fiscal year. (Assume bond premium or discount amortization is by the straight-line method and ignore any potential impact of year-to-year market value changes on the accounting for the bonds.)
2. Give the journal entries required at the end of 2002 to correct and bring the accounts up to date in view of the entries actually made.

PROBLEM 10–44

REACQUISITION OF BONDS
Guerra Company authorized the sale of $500,000 of 12%, 10-year debentures on January 1, 1997. Interest is payable on January 1 and July 1. The entire issue was sold on April 1, 1997, at 102 plus accrued interest. On April 1, 2002, $250,000 of the bond issue

was reacquired and retired at 99 plus accrued interest. On June 30, 2002, the remaining bonds were reacquired at 97 plus accrued interest and refunded with an issue of $400,000 of 9% bonds which were sold at 100.

Instructions: Give the journal entries for 1997 and 2002 (through June 30) on the Guerra Company books. The company's books are kept on a calendar-year basis. (Round to the nearest dollar. Assume straight-line amortization of the premium or discount. Ignore any potential impact of year-to-year market value changes on the accounting for the bonds.)

PROBLEM 10–45

DEFERRED INTEREST BONDS AND THE SELLING OF ASSETS

At the beginning of 2000, Wheel R. Dealer purchased the net assets of Consolidated Corp. by issuing 10-year, 10% bonds with a face value of $100,000,000, with semiannual interest payments made on June 30 and December 31 and no interest payments made until 2005. Dealer hopes to sell off assets of Consolidated and realize enough cash to buy back the bonds on the open market prior to interest payments becoming due in 2005. At the end of 2002, Dealer sold net assets with a carrying value of $85,000,000 for $70,000,000 and used the proceeds to retire the bond issue.

Instructions:

1. Prepare the journal entry to record the issuance of the bonds on January 2, 2000, assuming a market rate of 8%.
2. Prepare the journal entry to record the sale of the net assets.
3. Compute the market value of the bonds on January 3, 2003, the day of retirement, assuming a market rate of 14%.
4. Prepare the journal entry to record the retirement of the bond issue on January 3, 2003, assuming a carrying value of $96,000,000 and the market value as computed in (3) above.
5. Explain how Mr. Dealer can buy his bonds back 3 years after their initial sale for less than he originally sold them for and without ever having made an interest payment.
6. Should Mr. Dealer be able to reduce the liability to market value even if he does not retire the bonds?

PROBLEM 10–46

CONVERTIBLE BONDS

The Robison Co. issued $1,000,000 of convertible 10-year debentures on July 1, 2001. The debentures provide for 9% interest payable semiannually on January 1 and July 1. The discount in connection with the issue was $12,000, which is being amortized monthly on a straight-line basis.

The debentures are convertible after 1 year into 7 shares of the Robison Co.'s $1 par value common stock for each $1,000 of debentures.

On August 1, 2002, $100,000 of debentures were turned in for conversion into common stock. Interest has been accrued monthly and paid as due. Accrued interest on debentures is paid in cash upon conversion.

Instructions: Prepare the journal entries to record the conversion, amortization, and interest in connection with the debentures as of August 1, 2002, August 31, 2002, and December 31, 2002—including closing entries for year-end. No gain or loss is to be recognized on the conversion. (Round to the nearest dollar.)

PROBLEM 10–47

EARLY EXTINGUISHMENT AND CONVERSION OF BONDS

On January 1, 2001, Brewster Company issued 2,000 of its 5-year, $1,000 face value, 11% bonds dated January 1 at an effective annual interest rate (yield) of 9%. Interest is payable each December 31. Brewster uses the effective-interest method of amortization. On December 31, 2002, the 2,000 bonds were extinguished early through acquisition in the open market by Brewster for $1,980,000 plus accrued interest.

On July 1, 2001, Brewster issued 5,000 of its 6-year, $1,000 face value, 10% convertible bonds dated July 1 at an effective annual interest rate (yield) of 12%. Interest is payable every June 30 and December 31. The bonds are convertible at the investor's option into Brewster's common stock at a ratio of 10 shares of common stock for each bond. On July 1, 2002, an investor in Brewster's convertible bonds tendered 1,500 bonds for conversion into 15,000 shares of Brewster's common stock, which had a fair market value of $105 and a par value of $1 at the date of conversion.

Instructions:

1. Make all necessary journal entries for the issuer and the investor to record the issuance of both the 11% and the 10% bonds. Ignore any potential impact of year-to-year market value changes on the investor accounting for the bonds.
2. Make all necessary journal entries to record the early extinguishment of both debt instruments assuming:
   (a) Brewster considered the conversion to be a significant culminating event, and the investors considered their investment in convertible bonds to be debt rather than equity.
   (b) Brewster considered the conversion to be a nonculminating event, and the investors considered their investment in convertible bonds to be equity rather than debt.

PROBLEM 10–48

TROUBLED DEBT RESTRUCTURING—MODIFICATION OF TERMS
Risky Company, after having experienced financial difficulties in 2000, negotiated with 2 major creditors and arrived at an agreement to restructure its debts on December 31, 2000. The 2 creditors were M. Barboza and R. Janeiro. Barboza was owed principal of $300,000 and interest of $60,000 but agreed to accept equipment worth $60,000 and notes receivable from Risky Company's customers worth $250,000. The equipment had an original cost of $80,000 and accumulated depreciation of $40,000. Janeiro was owed $500,000 and agreed to extend the terms and to accept immediate payment of $100,000 and the remaining agreed-upon balance of $424,360 to be paid on December 31, 2002. All payments were made according to schedule.

Instructions: Prepare Risky's journal entries to record the restructuring on December 31, 2000, and the entries necessary to make the adjustments and record payments on December 31, 2001, and 2002.

PROBLEM 10–49

TROUBLED DEBT RESTRUCTURING—MODIFICATION OF TERMS
In the latter part of 2001, Caltex Company experienced severe financial pressure and was in default of meeting interest payments on long-term notes of $6,000,000 due on December 31, 2006. The interest rate on the debt was 11%, payable semiannually on June 30 and December 31. In an agreement with Modern Investment Corporation, Caltex obtained acceptance of a change in principal and interest terms for the remaining 5-year life of the notes. The changes in terms are as follows:

(a) A reduction of principal of $600,000.
(b) A reduction in the interest rate to 8%.
(c) Caltex agreed to pay on December 31, 2001, both the $660,000 of interest in arrears and the normal interest payment under the old terms.

Instructions:

1. Compute the total dollar difference in cash payments by Caltex over the 5-year period as a result of the restatement of terms.
2. Prepare the journal entries for the restructuring of the debt, payment of interest under the old terms, and the first two interest payments under the new terms that Caltex would make. (Assume an implicit interest rate of 6%.)

COMPETENCY ENHANCEMENT OPPORTUNITIES

▶ Deciphering Actual Financial Statements	▶ Ethical Dilemma
▶ Writing Assignment	▶ Cumulative Spreadsheet Analysis
▶ Research Project	▶ Internet Search
▶ The Debate	

Accounting is more than just doing textbook problems. This expanded competency material provides practice in critical thinking, oral and written communication, research, teamwork, and consideration of ethical issues.

▶ DECIPHERING ACTUAL FINANCIAL STATEMENTS

• Deciphering 10–1 (The Walt Disney Company)
Refer to Disney's 1998 annual report, shown in Appendix A at the back of the book.

1. What is the largest liability listed in DISNEY'S 1998 balance sheet?
2. By what percentage did Disney increase its total borrowings (current and long term) in 1998? The current portion of borrowings increased by 138% in 1998. What impact did this increase have on Disney's current ratio?
3. In the notes to the financial statements, Disney outlines how the company has borrowed money. What form of borrowing constitutes the greatest portion of Disney's total borrowing?

• Deciphering 10–2 (Boston Celtics)
On the following page is the liabilities and equity section of the balance sheet for the BOSTON CELTICS LIMITED PARTNERSHIP. Review the liability section of the balance sheet and answer the following questions.

1. What is "Deferred game revenues"? How would that liability have arisen?
2. What does the account "Deferred compensation" represent? Note that this account has both a current and noncurrent portion.
3. As of June 30, 1997, what did the Celtics report as total assets?

• Deciphering 10–3 (Hewlett-Packard & Compaq)
Review the balance sheets for HEWLETT-PACKARD (HP) (page 594) and COMPAQ COMPUTER (page 595) shown on the following pages and answer the following questions.

1. Compute each company's current ratio for 1998. Based on the result, which company appears to be more liquid?
2. Compute each company's debt-to-equity ratio for 1998. How did you define the debt part of that computation—long-term debt or total liabilities? Which company appears to have the most debt in relation to stockholders' equity?
3. Compare HP's largest single current liability in 1998 with Compaq's largest.
4. Why would HP have such a larger amount in retained earnings at the end of 1998 than Compaq?

• Deciphering 10–4 (Philip Morris)
Examine the partial balance sheet of PHILIP MORRIS shown on page 596 and answer the following questions.

1. Current assets for Philip Morris totaled $20,230 (in millions) at the end of 1998. Compute the company's current ratio.
2. Why would Philip Morris classify its liabilities into two different categories?

BOSTON CELTICS LIMITED PARTNERSHIP
LIABILITIES AND PARTNERS' CAPITAL (DEFICIT)

	June 30,	
	1997	1996
CURRENT LIABILITIES		
Accounts payable and accrued expenses	$12,877,723	$15,420,321
Deferred game revenues	5,584,848	4,629,704
Federal and state income taxes payable	-0-	539,325
Notes payable to bank—current portion	2,500,000	-0-
Notes payable	16,409,617	15,353,949
Deferred compensation—current portion	1,767,263	4,345,367
TOTAL CURRENT LIABILITIES	39,139,451	40,288,666
DEFERRED REVENUES—noncurrent portion	-0-	699,871
DEFERRED FEDERAL AND STATE INCOME TAXES	20,100,000	20,100,000
NOTES PAYABLE TO BANK—noncurrent portion	47,500,000	50,000,000
DEFERRED COMPENSATION—noncurrent portion	10,380,296	11,749,666
OTHER NONCURRENT LIABILITIES	9,870,000	5,875,000
PARTNERS' CAPITAL (DEFICIT)		
Boston Celtics Limited Partnership—General Partner	226,817	284,422
Limited Partners	(8,527,928)	15,688,456
	(8,301,111)	15,972,878
Celtics Limited Partnership—General Partner	(129,866)	(92,988)
Boston Celtics Communications Limited Partnership—General Partner	640,886	640,379
TOTAL PARTNERS' CAPITAL (DEFICIT)	(7,790,091)	16,520,269
	$119,199,656	$145,233,472

3. Compute Philip Morris' debt-to-equity ratio for 1998 (a) using only long-term debt and (b) using all liabilities in your computations. Why the huge difference in your answers? When interpreting a debt-to-equity ratio computed by someone else, what should be your first question?

• Deciphering 10–5 (H. J. Heinz Company)
Review the H. J. HEINZ CO. statement (page 597) relating to its debt and answer the following questions.

1. What is a "Eurodollar bond"?
2. Why would H. J. Heinz have debt denominated in English pounds, Italian lire, and Australian dollars?
3. In what year is H. J. Heinz going to have to come up with a lot of money to pay off its debt? What options might Heinz have for paying that debt off?

▶ ### WRITING ASSIGNMENT
I like these "no interest" bonds.

J. R. Chump, president of ProKeeper Industries, is contemplating the issuance of long-term debt to finance plant expansion and renovation. In the past, his company has issued traditional debt instruments that require regular interest payments and a retirement of the principal on the maturity date. However, he has noticed that several competitors have recently issued bonds that either do not require interest payments or defer interest payments for several years. He has asked you, as his chief financial officer, to prepare a short memo addressing the following questions.

Hewlett-Packard Company and Subsidiaries

Consolidated Balance Sheet

October 31
in millions except par value and number of shares

	1998	1997
Assets		
Current assets:		
Cash and cash equivalents	$ 4,046	$ 3,072
Short-term investments	21	1,497
Accounts receivable	6,232	6,142
Financing receivables	1,520	1,123
Inventory	6,184	6,763
Other current assets	3,581	2,350
Total current assets	21,584	20,947
Property, plant and equipment, net	6,358	6,312
Long-term investments and other assets	5,731	4,490
Total assets	**$33,673**	**$31,749**
Liabilities and shareholders' equity		
Current liabilities:		
Notes payable and short-term borrowings	$ 1,245	$ 1,226
Accounts payable	3,203	3,185
Employee compensation and benefits	1,768	1,723
Taxes on earnings	2,796	1,515
Deferred revenues	1,453	1,152
Other accrued liabilities	3,008	2,418
Total current liabilities	13,473	11,219
Long-term debt	2,063	3,158
Other liabilities	1,218	1,217
Shareholders' equity:		
Preferred stock, $1 par value		
(authorized: 300,000,000 shares; issued: none)	—	—
Common stock and capital in excess of $.01 par value (authorized: 4,800,000,000 shares; issued and outstanding: 1,015,403,000 in 1998 and 1,041,042,000 in 1997)	10	1,187
Retained earnings	16,909	14,968
Total shareholders' equity	16,919	16,155
Total liabilities and shareholders' equity	**$33,673**	**$31,749**

1. Why would a company issue bonds that require interest payments if bonds that do not require interest payments are being sold in the open market?
2. If the company were to issue 10-year bonds with a face value of $100,000 and the market rate of interest is 10%, what would be the proceeds from the sale if the bonds were zero-interest bonds? What would be the proceeds if the annual interest payments did not begin for 5 years and the stated rate of interest were 10%? What would be the proceeds if the bonds paid interest annually for 10 years at 10%?
3. What factors must a business consider when determining the interest terms associated with long-term debt?

▶ **RESEARCH PROJECT**
Foreign debt—why and how?
Almost every annual report of large multinational companies contains a note on debt. And many of these companies have debt denominated in a foreign currency. As an example, look back at Deciphering 10–5. H. J. Heinz has debt denominated in English pounds, Italian lire, and Australian dollars. Your research involves investigating the following issues and preparing a short report (either orally or in writing).

condensed consolidated balance sheet
Compaq Computer Corporation

Year ended December 31, (dollars in millions except par value)	1998	1997
ASSETS		
Current assets:		
Cash and cash equivalents	$ 4,091	$ 6,418
Short-term investments	—	344
Accounts receivable, less allowance of $318 and $243	6,998	2,891
Inventories	2,005	1,570
Deferred income taxes	1,602	595
Other current assets	471	199
Total current assets	15,167	12,017
Property, plant, and equipment, less accumulated depreciation	2,902	1,985
Deferred income taxes	1,341	—
Intangible and other assets	3,641	629
	$23,051	$14,631
LIABILITIES AND STOCKHOLDERS' EQUITY		
Current liabilities:		
Accounts payable	$ 4,237	$ 2,837
Income taxes payable	282	195
Accrued restructuring costs	1,110	—
Other current liabilities	5,104	2,170
Total current liabilities	10,733	5,202
Postretirement and other postemployment benefits	545	—
Commitments and contingencies (Note 13)		
Minority interest	422	—
Stockholders' equity:		
Preferred stock, $.01 par value (authorized: 10 million shares; issued: none)		
Common stock and capital in excess of $.01 par value: (authorized: 3 billion shares; issued and outstanding: 1,698 and 1,687 million shares, respectively, at December 31, 1998; and 1,519 million shares issued and outstanding at December 31, 1997)	7,270	2,096
Retained earnings	4,465	7,333
Treasury stock (at cost)	(384)	
Total stockholders' equity	11,351	9,429
	$23,051	$14,631

- Why would a company issue debt in another currency? Why didn't H. J. Heinz issue debt in American dollars?
- How would a company go about issuing debt in another currency? Who would buy it? (Hint: As you investigate these issues, you will need to find information about *hedging*; see Chapter 18. In addition, Chapter 9 contains some information about foreign currency transactions.)

▶ **THE DEBATE**
Rules for ratios
Five people could look at a set of financial statements for a company and get five different answers for the firm's debt-to-equity ratio, depending on how they defined debt and equity. Items such as mandatorily redeemable preferred stock, minority interest, and deferred taxes make computing a debt-to-equity ratio difficult.

Divide your group into two teams.

- One team is to represent the opinion that we should have standards to assist in computing ratios such as the debt-to-equity ratio. Prepare a short presentation supporting your position for having standard rules for the computation of ratios.
- The other team is to represent the view that ratios are user specific and that to mandate a certain set of ratios and computation standards might result in the needs of certain

PHILIP MORRIS COMPANIES

	1998	1997
Liabilities		
Consumer products		
Short-term borrowings	$ 225	$ 157
Current portion of long-term debt	1,822	1,516
Accounts payable	3,359	3,318
Accrued liabilities:		
Marketing	2,637	2,149
Taxes, except income taxes	1,408	1,234
Employment costs	968	1,083
Settlement charges	1,135	886
Other	2,608	2,894
Income taxes	1,144	862
Dividends payable	1,073	972
Total current liabilities	16,379	15,071
Long-term debt	11,906	11,585
Deferred income taxes	929	889
Accrued postretirement health care costs	2,543	2,432
Other liabilities	7,019	6,218
Total consumer products liabilities	38,776	36,195
Financial services		
Long-term debt	709	845
Deferred income taxes	4,151	3,877
Other liabilities	87	110
Total financial services liabilities	4,947	4,832
Total liabilities	43,723	41,027
Contingencies (Note 16)		
Stockholders' Equity		
Common stock, par value $0.33 1/3 per share (2,805,961,317 shares issued)	935	935
Earnings reinvested in the business	26,261	24,924
Accumulated other comprehensive earnings		
(including currency translation of $1,081 and $1,109)	(1,106)	(1,109)
Cost of repurchased stock ($375,426,742 and $380,474,028)	(9,893)	(9,830)
Total stockholders' equity	16,197	14,920
Total Liabilities and Stockholders' Equity	$59,920	$55,947

users being ignored. Prepare a short presentation defending the position of letting users compute ratios as needed.

▶ ETHICAL DILEMMA
Keeping our debt covenants

You are the chief financial officer of a local manufacturing company, Larsen Enterprises. This company is run by 2 brothers, Steve and John Larsen. The Larsen brothers have built this company up from a small 5-man shop to a company now employing over 200 people. The national economy has recently taken a turn for the worse and this has affected Larsen's business. In fact, the company's performance of late has been such that it is in jeopardy of violating several of its debt covenants (promises made to the lending institution). If the company violates these covenants, the bank has the option of calling the debt due immediately. If the debt is called, Larsen is not sure what will happen, but it will certainly not be good.

The covenant that is in jeopardy relates to the current ratio. If the current ratio drops below 2, Larsen Enterprises is considered in technical default on its debt. Steve and John

H. J. HEINZ CO.

Short-Term (Dollars in thousands)			1998	1997
Commercial paper			$ 79,841	$ 97,008
Bank and other borrowings			221,187	492,885
			$301,028	$589,893

Long-Term (Dollars in thousands)	Range of Interest	Maturity (Fiscal Year)	1998	1997
United States Dollars:				
Commercial paper	Variable%	2002	$1,337,574	$1,346,779
Senior unsecured notes	6.00–6.88%	2000–2008	797,791	749,681
Eurodollar bonds	5.75–7.50%	2000–2003	498,944	551,423
Revenue bonds	4.00–7.70%	1999–2027	18,342	16,121
Promissory notes	4.00–10.00%	1999–2005	47,157	49,220
Other	6.35%	1999–2006	6,337	7,072
			2,706,145	2,720,296
Foreign Currencies (U.S. Dollar Equivalents):				
Promissory notes:				
Pounds sterling	8.85%	1999–2006	27,272	41,260
Italian lire	3.9–12.55%	1999–2008	23,751	28,209
Australian dollars	5.21%	1999–2002	19,066	28,323
Other	5.19–24.00%	1999–2022	30,641	39,454
			100,730	137,246
Total long-term debt			2,806,875	2,857,542
Less portion due within one year			38,598	573,549
			$2,768,277	$2,283,993

have come to you and asked you to suggest ways in which the current ratio, which currently stands at 1.9, could be increased.

Take a moment and think of ways in which the current ratio might be manipulated. Identify specific actions that the Larsen brothers might take to increase the current ratio. Is it in the best interest of shareholders and lending institutions for Steve and John to make business decisions that have cosmetic effects on the financial statements?

▶ CUMULATIVE SPREADSHEET ANALYSIS

This spreadsheet assignment is a continuation of the spreadsheet assignments given in earlier chapters. If you completed those assignments, you have a head start on this one.

Refer back to the instructions for preparing the revised financial statements for 2002 as given in (1) of the Cumulative Spreadsheet Analysis assignment in Chapter 3.

1. Skywalker wishes to prepare a *forecasted* balance sheet, a *forecasted* income statement, and a *forecasted* statement of cash flows for 2003. Use the financial statement numbers for 2002 [given in (1) of the Cumulative Spreadsheet Project assignment in Chapter 3] as the basis for the forecast, along with the following additional information.
   a. Sales in 2003 are expected to increase by 40% over 2002 sales of $2,100.
   b. In 2003, Skywalker expects to acquire new property, plant, and equipment costing $240.
   c. The $480 in operating expenses reported in 2002 breaks down as follows: $15 depreciation expense, $465 other operating expenses.
   d. New long-term debt will be acquired in 2003 in accordance with (q) below.
   e. No cash dividends will be paid in 2003.

f.   New short-term loans payable will be acquired in an amount sufficient to make Skywalker's current ratio in 2003 exactly equal to 2.0.

g.   Skywalker does not anticipate repurchasing any additional shares of stock during 2003.

h.   Because changes in future prices and exchange rates are impossible to predict, Skywalker's best estimate is that the balance in accumulated other comprehensive income will remain unchanged in 2003.

i.   In the absence of more detailed information, assume that the balances in Investment Securities, Long-Term Investments, Other Long-Term Assets, and Intangible Assets will all increase at the same rate as sales (40%) in 2003.

j.   In the absence of more detailed information, assume that the balance in Other Long-Term Liabilities will increase at the same rate as sales (40%) in 2003.

k.   The Investment Securities are classified as available-for-sale. Accordingly, cash from the purchase and sale of these securities is classified as an investing activity.

l.   Assume that transactions impacting Other Long-Term Assets and Other Long-Term Liabilities are operating activities.

m.   Cash and Investment Securities will increase at the same rate as sales.

n.   The forecasted amount of accounts receivable in 2003 is determined using the forecasted value for the average collection period. The average collection period for 2003 is expected to be 14.08 days. To make the calculations simpler, this value is based on forecasted end-of-year accounts receivable rather than on average accounts receivable.

o.   The forecasted amount of inventory in 2003 is determined using the forecasted value for the number of days' sales in inventory. The number of days' sales in inventory for 2003 is expected to be 107.6 days. To make the calculations simpler, this value is based on forecasted end-of-year inventory rather than on average inventory.

p.   The forecasted amount of accounts payable in 2003 is determined using the forecasted value for the number of days' purchases in accounts payable. The number of days' purchases in accounts payable for 2003 is expected to be 48.34 days. To make the calculations simpler, this value is based on forecasted end-of-year accounts payable rather than on average accounts payable.

Note: These forecasted statements were constructed as part of the spreadsheet assignment in Chapter 9; you can use that spreadsheet as a starting point if you have completed that assignment.

For this exercise, add the following additional assumptions.

q.   New long-term debt will be acquired (or repaid) in an amount sufficient to make Skywalker's debt ratio (total liabilities divided by total assets) in 2003 exactly equal to .80.

r.   Assume an interest rate on short-term loans payable of 6.0% and on long-term debt of 8.0%. Only a half year's interest is charged on loans taken out during the year. For example, if short-term loans payable at the end of 2003 is $15 and given that short-term loans payable at the end of 2002 were $10, total short-term interest expense for 2003 would be $0.75 [($10 × .06) + ($5 × .06 × ½)].

2.   Repeat (1) with the following changes in assumptions.
   a.   The debt ratio in 2003 is exactly equal to .70.
   b.   The debt ratio in 2003 is exactly equal to .90.

3.   Comment on the differences in the forecasted values of cash from operating activities in 2003 under each of the following assumptions about the debt ratio: .70, .80, and .90. Explain exactly why a change in debt ratio has an impact on cash from operating activities.

▶ **INTERNET SEARCH**
Ford Motor Company
Let's look at FORD MOTOR COMPANY'S Web site at www.ford.com. Before we jump right into the financial information associated with Ford, take a minute and look around the Web

site. Ford gives career opportunities with the company, the history of how the company began, and Ford's worldwide public policy. Now on to the financial information. Locate the annual report information and answer the following questions.

1. Review the company's balance sheet. Most of the company's assets and liabilities are tied up in what segment or division?

2. Now take a look at the company's income statement. What part of the company appears to be making the most money—the Automotive division or Financial Services division?

3. Based on your answers to (1) and (2), would you consider Ford to be a finance company or a car company? Where does it make its money? Where are its assets?

4. Find the part of the annual report that provides a 10-year summary of the company. How has the company's debt load changed over the 10-year period? Again, what is causing this significant increase in debt—automotive or financial services?

5. Take a look at the note relating to debt. What information of interest do you find?

chapter 11
Equity Financing

Bill Gates is one of the two richest people in the United States. (The other one is mentioned further down—keep reading.) MICROSOFT, the company Bill Gates founded with partner Paul Allen in 1975, was originally best known for developing the first-generation DOS operating system used with IBM personal computers and their clones. Microsoft subsequently came to dominate (some would say monopolize) the software market with popular software packages such as Word, Excel, and PowerPoint, based on its Windows operating system.

In 1985, Microsoft decided to issue its stock publicly for the first time. Before this time, Microsoft had stock outstanding, but the stock was held by company officials and employees and was not publicly traded. A key consideration, of course, was what price to charge when issuing the shares. An initial price range of $16 to $19 per share was set, based on Microsoft's earnings per share and the price-earnings (P/E) ratios for similar firms that already had publicly traded stock. The large amount of interest in the Microsoft stock issue resulted in the final offering price being raised to $21 per share. On March 13, 1986, Microsoft shares were first publicly traded, and by the end of the first day of trading, the shares were at $27.75.[1] If you had purchased one of those initial shares for $21 in 1986, by March 1999 it would have been worth almost $13,000. (See Exhibit 11–1 on page 602.)

A share of Microsoft stock does not trade for $13,000 because, since 1986, Microsoft has split its stock several times. A split is like cutting a pie into more pieces—the number of shares is increased and the price of each share is reduced proportionately. Most firms use stock splits to maintain their per-share price in the range that is considered normal, usually between $20 and $80 per share in the United States.

A glaring exception to this price-per-share range is stock of BERKSHIRE HATHAWAY, which is headed by Warren Buffett, who annually vies with Bill Gates for the title of richest person in the United States. Buffett's company is involved in a number of diverse lines of business. Its largest operations are in property and casualty insurance. However, it also produces and sells KIRBY vacuums, SEE'S chocolates, and WORLD BOOK encyclopedias. In addition, Berkshire Hathaway has a substantial investment portfolio: It owns 11% of AMERICAN EXPRESS, 9% of GILLETTE, 8% of COCA-COLA, and 17% of the WASHINGTON POST.[2] In fact, a whole industry has built up around financial analysts who interpret the investment choices made by Warren Buffett.

Because Berkshire Hathaway has been very profitable, and because it has never split its stock, its price per share has risen higher than any other stock on the New York Stock Exchange. During 1999, Berkshire Hathaway shares traded for as much as $81,100 each.[3]

---

1 Bro Uttal, "Inside the Deal That Made Bill Gates $350,000,000," *Fortune*, July 21, 1986, p. 23.
2 From the 1998 10-K of Berkshire Hathaway.
3 In May 1996, the shareholders of Berkshire Hathaway approved the creation of a new class of shares, called Class B shares. Each of these shares has 1/30 the value of the original Class A shares. This action was taken to head off some investment companies that had started buying Berkshire Hathaway shares, carving them up, and selling shares of the shares.

1 Identify the rights associated with ownership of common and preferred stock.

2 Record the issuance of stock for cash, on a subscription basis, and in exchange for noncash assets or for services.

3 Use both the cost and par value methods to account for stock repurchases.

4 Account for the issuance of stock rights and stock warrants.

5 Explain the difference between the intrinsic value and fair value methods, and use both in accounting for a fixed stock option plan.

6 Distinguish between stock conversions that require a reduction in retained earnings and those that do not.

7 List the factors that impact the retained earnings balance.

8 Properly record cash dividends, property dividends, small and large stock dividends, and stock splits.

9 Explain the background of unrealized gains and losses recorded as direct equity adjustments, and list the major types of equity reserves found in foreign balance sheets.

10 Prepare a statement of changes in stockholders' equity.

EXPANDED MATERIAL

11 Eliminate a retained earnings deficit through a quasi-reorganization

12 Use both the intrinsic value and fair value methods to account for performance-based stock option plans and plans calling for a cash settlement.

By the way, in the October 1999 annual *Forbes* survey of America's richest people, Bill Gates ($85 billion) comfortably led Warren Buffett ($31 billion) as the richest person in the United States.[4]

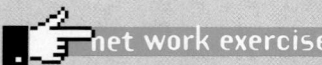

net work exercise

Go to Yahoo!'s financial Web site (**www.finance.yahoo.com**); using Microsoft's and Berkshire Hathaway's ticker symbols (a ticker symbol is the stock's abbreviated designation) to locate share information, answer the following questions.

Net Work:
1. What is Microsoft's (MSFT) current stock price? What is its P/E ratio? What does the P/E ratio tell you?
2. What is Berkshire Hathaway's (BRKa) current stock price? What was the stock's highest price during the past 52 weeks?

EXHIBIT 11-1 | Microsoft's Stock Value

Value of One Share From Microsoft Initial Public Offering

$12,500	
$5,500	
$5,000	
$4,500	
$4,000	
$3,500	
$3,000	
$2,500	
$2,000	
$1,500	
$1,000	
$500	
$21	

March 1986 March 1987 March 1988 March 1989 March 1990 March 1991 March 1992 March 1993 March 1994 March 1995 March 1996 March 1997 March 1998 March 1999

---

4 "The Forbes Four Hundred," *Forbes*, October 11, 1999. In the 1999 *Forbes* survey, Warren Buffett was actually only the third most wealthy person in the United States. The number two spot was held by Paul Allen ($40 billion), who was Bill Gates' partner in the founding of Microsoft.

The equity section of the balance sheet is the place where owner investment is reported. For example, the proceeds from Microsoft's initial public offering of stock were recorded in Microsoft's equity section. These invested funds are called contributed, or paid-in, capital. Owners also contribute funds to a company by allowing profits to be reinvested. In a corporation, these reinvested profits are called retained earnings. In sole proprietorships and partnerships, paid-in capital and retained earnings are lumped together into a single capital account. This chapter emphasizes the accounting for equity of corporations.

In a simple world, the equity section of a corporation's balance sheet would include just the two sections mentioned above—paid-in capital and retained earnings. However, the increasing complexity of worldwide business necessitates a number of other equity items. For example, unrealized gains or losses on some investment securities are shown in a separate equity category, as is the impact of foreign currency fluctuations on the equity of foreign subsidiaries. The items that can appear in the equity section are summarized in Exhibit 11–2 and are discussed in the remainder of the chapter.

EXHIBIT 11–2 | Equity Items

Stockholders' Equity

Contributed capital:
   Preferred stock
   Common stock
   Additional paid-in capital
Retained earnings
Less: Treasury stock
Accumulated other comprehensive income:
   Foreign currency translation adjustment
   Minimum pension liability adjustment
   Unrealized gains and losses on available-for-sale securities
Total stockholders' equity

Although the items that affect owners' equity are many, the major decisions associated with owner investment are illustrated in the time line in Exhibit 11–3. Note that many of the issues associated with transactions involving owners may or may not occur during any given period. Dividends may or may not be paid, options may or may not be granted. This chapter discusses many of the possible actions that may be taken by management that will affect owners' equity.

NATURE AND CLASSIFICATIONS OF PAID-IN CAPITAL

Identify the rights associated with ownership of common and preferred stock.

A corporation is a legal, artificial entity that has an existence separate from its owners and may engage in business within prescribed limits just as if it were a real person. The modern corporation makes it possible for large amounts of resources to be assembled under one management. These resources are transferred to the corporation by individual own-

EXHIBIT 11–3 | Time Line of Issues Associated With Owners' Equity

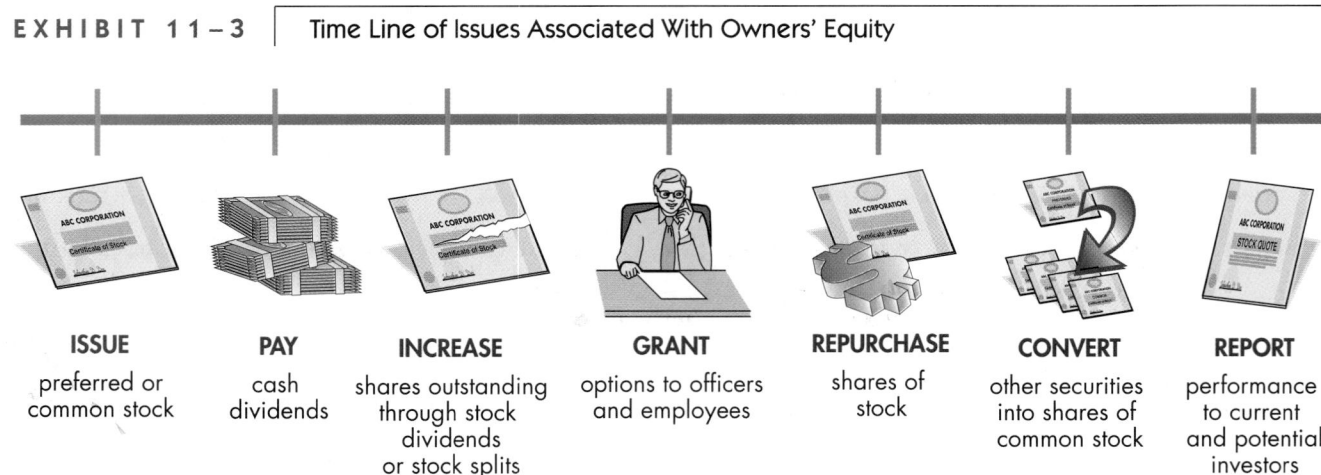

ISSUE	PAY	INCREASE	GRANT	REPURCHASE	CONVERT	REPORT
preferred or common stock	cash dividends	shares outstanding through stock dividends or stock splits	options to officers and employees	shares of stock	other securities into shares of common stock	performance to current and potential investors

ers, and, in exchange for these resources, the corporation issues stock certificates evidencing ownership interests.[5] Stockholders elect a **board of directors** whose members oversee the strategic and long-run planning for the corporation. The directors select managers who supervise the day-to-day operations of the corporation.

Corporations are typically created under the incorporating laws of one of the 50 states. Because the states do not follow a uniform incorporating act, the conditions under which corporations may be created and under which they may operate are somewhat varied. A large proportion of businesses are incorporated in Delaware because constraints on cash dividends are loose, and Delaware laws governing corporations are generally seen as being "pro business."

In theory, regulation of corporations is strictly a state matter falling outside the jurisdiction of federal authorities. However, in practice almost all issues of stock to the public fall under the jurisdiction of the federal Securities and Exchange Commission (SEC). Exceptions are made when an issue is small (less than $500,000 in any 12-month period), is made only to "accredited" investors (informed investors like banks, investment companies, issuing company officers, and individuals with net worth exceeding $1 million), or is made only to residents of a single state.

When a corporation is formed, a single class of stock, known as common stock, is usually issued. Corporations may later find that there are advantages to issuing one or more additional classes of stock with varying rights and priorities. Stock with certain preferences (rights) over common stock is called preferred stock.

> **FYI:** Boards of directors are composed of top managers of the company, top executives from other companies, prominent civic officials, and major shareholders. For example, the 1998 board of THE COCA-COLA COMPANY included Warren Buffett, a major Coca-Cola shareholder, and Peter Ueberroth, former head of the Los Angeles Olympics Committee and former commissioner of major league baseball.

Common Stock

The owners of the common stock of a corporation can be thought of as the true owners of the business. If the corporation does poorly, the common stockholders are likely to lose some or all of their investment because they can only receive cash from the corporation after the claims of all other parties (i.e., lenders, employees, government, preferred stockholders) are satisfied. On the other hand, if the corporation does well, the common stockholders reap the benefit because they own all assets in excess of those

---

5 Briefly, the advantages of organizing a business as a corporation instead of as a sole proprietorship or partnership are that the investors in a corporation have limited liability (they can only lose what they put in; their other personal assets are safe), and ownership interest is easily transferable (there is no need to get approval from the other shareholders before selling your shares). The primary disadvantage is that corporate income is taxed twice—once at the corporate level and again at the individual level when shareholders receive cash dividends.

needed to satisfy the fixed claims of others. In summary, the common stockholders bear the greatest risk, but they also stand to receive the highest return on their investment.

Unless restricted by terms of the articles of incorporation, certain basic rights are held by each common stockholder. These rights are as follows:

1. To vote in the election of directors and in the determination of certain corporate policies such as the management compensation plan or major corporate acquisitions.
2. To maintain one's proportional interest in the corporation through purchase of additional common stock if and when it is issued. This right is known as the *preemptive right* and ensures that a common stockholder's ownership percentage cannot be diluted against his or her will. In recent years, some states have eliminated the preemptive right.

<table>
<tr><td>

FYI: Outside the United States, corporations sometimes have different classes of shares for local investors and for foreign investors. For example, Chinese corporations can have two classes of shares that trade on the Shanghai and Shenzhen stock exchanges: A shares, which only Chinese citizens can own, and B shares, which can be purchased by foreigners. When Chinese B shares are traded on The Stock Exchange of Hong Kong, they are called H shares.

</td></tr>
</table>

Usually, each corporation has only one class of common stock. However, a recent phenomenon is the creation of multiple classes of common stock, each with slightly different ownership privileges. For example, BEN & JERRY'S, the premium ice cream company, has two classes of common stock. Ben & Jerry's Class B common is held almost exclusively by insiders, including Ben and Jerry themselves. Each share of Class B common has 10 votes in board elections, compared to one vote for each share of the publicly traded Class A common. With this share structure, Ben & Jerry's is able to raise equity funding through issuance of Class A shares without seriously diluting voting control. In fact, as of March 5, 1999, Ben, Jerry, and their associate Jeff Furman owned just 17% of the total common shares outstanding but held 46% of the shareholder voting power. Berkshire Hathaway, discussed in the opening scenario of this chapter, has recently created some Class B common shares that have 1/30 the value of the Class A shares—for those investors (like you and the authors) who might not have the $81,000 necessary to buy one share of Berkshire's Class A shares. However, to repeat, most corporations have only one class of common stock.

Some companies, like Ben & Jerry's, have two classes of stock. Class A stock is publicly traded, while Class B stock is held mostly by insiders of the company.

Par or Stated Value of Stock

The journal entry to record the issuance of common stock in exchange for cash frequently looks something like this:

Cash	xxx	
Common Stock (at Par Value)		xxx
Additional Paid-In Capital		xxx

> **FYI:** Legal capital constraints are not usually a limiting factor for payment of cash dividends. More frequently, payment of dividends is restricted by debt covenants imposed by lenders. A typical debt covenant might require maintenance of a debt-to-equity ratio below a certain amount.

Historically, **par value** was equal to the market value of the shares at issuance. Par value was also sometimes viewed by the courts as the minimum contribution by investors.[6] Accordingly, when corporate assets were insufficient to cover corporate liabilities, investors who had contributed less than par value were required to cover the shortfall. As a consequence, corporations began to issue shares with lower par values in order to protect investors. In addition, state incorporation laws were written to prevent payment of cash dividends whenever operating losses reduced corporate equity below total par value of shares issued. Lower par values allowed corporations more flexibility in their cash dividend policy.

Today, most stocks have either a nominal par value or no par value at all. No-par stock sometimes has a **stated value** that, for financial reporting purposes, functions exactly like a par value. In Exhibit 11–4, it can be seen that 84.0% of publicly traded stocks in the United States have par values of $1 or less.

EXHIBIT 11–4   Par Values of Publicly Traded Stocks

Par or Stated Values Publicly Traded Stocks in the United States For the Year 1998		
	All Firms	**Only Firms With Market Value Greater Than $1 Billion**
Less than $0.01	17.1%	12.2%
Exactly $0.01	40.6	30.9
Between $0.01 and $1.00	16.3	19.7
Exactly $1.00	10.0	17.0
Greater than $1.00	16.0	20.2

SOURCE: Standard & Poor's *COMPUSTAT.*

Preferred Stock

The title "preferred stock" is somewhat misleading because it gives the impression that preferred stock is better than common stock. Preferred stock isn't better; it's different. In fact, a useful way to think of preferred stock is that preferred stockholders give up many of the rights of ownership in exchange for some of the protection enjoyed by creditors.

The rights of ownership given up by preferred stockholders are

- *Voting.* In most cases, preferred stockholders are not allowed to vote for the board of directors. Voting rights can exist under circumstances specific to each preferred stock issue. For example, some preferred stockholders are granted corporate voting

6 For a more complete discussion of the legal significance of par value, see Philip McGough, "The Legal Significance of the Par Value of Common Stock: What Accounting Educators Should Know," *Issues in Accounting Education*, Fall 1988, pp. 330–350.

rights if the company fails to pay them cash dividends for, say, two consecutive quarters. When a company fails to pay preferred dividends, those dividends are said to have been "passed."

- *Sharing in success.* The cash dividends received by preferred stockholders are usually fixed in amount. Therefore, if the company does exceptionally well, preferred stockholders do not get to share in the success. As a result of this cap on dividends, the market value of preferred stock does not typically vary with the success of the company as does the price of common stock. Instead, the market value of preferred stock varies with changes in interest rates, in much the same way as bond prices change.

The protections enjoyed by preferred stockholders, relative to common stockholders, are

- *Cash dividend preference.* Preferred stockholders are entitled to receive their full cash dividend before any cash dividends are paid to common stockholders.
- *Liquidation preference.* If the company goes bankrupt, preferred stockholders are entitled to have their investment repaid, in full, before common stockholders receive anything.

The boxed item on page 610 discusses in a little more detail the securities, such as preferred stock, that share the characteristics of both debt and equity. As financial markets become more sophisticated, the line between debt and equity continues to blur and disclosure issues associated with these hybrid securities become even more important.

Preferred stock is generally issued with a par value. When preferred stock has a par value, the dividend is stated in terms of a percentage of par value. When preferred stock is no-par, the dividend must be stated in terms of dollars and cents. Thus, holders of 5% preferred stock with a $50 par value are entitled to an annual dividend of $2.50 per share before any distribution is made to common stockholders; holders of $5 no-par preferred stock are entitled to an annual dividend of $5 per share before dividends are paid to common stockholders.

A corporation may issue more than one class of preferred stock. For example, GENERAL MOTORS described four classes of preferred stock in the notes to its 1995 financial statements. The classes vary in terms of dividend rates, redemption requirements, convertibility, and other features.

CUMULATIVE AND NONCUMULATIVE PREFERRED STOCK When a corporation fails to declare dividends on **cumulative preferred stock**, such dividends accumulate and require payment in the future before any dividends may be paid to common stockholders.

For example, assume that Good Time Corporation has outstanding 100,000 shares of 9% cumulative preferred stock, $10 par. Dividends were last paid in 1999. Total dividends of $300,000 are declared in 2002 by the board of directors. The majority of this amount will be paid to the preferred shareholders as follows:

	Dividends to Preferred Shareholders	Dividends to Common Shareholders	Total Dividends
Cumulative dividend for 2000	$ 90,000	—	$ 90,000
Cumulative dividend for 2001	90,000	—	90,000
Dividends for 2002	90,000	$30,000	120,000
Total	$270,000	$30,000	$300,000

Dividends on cumulative preferred stock that are passed are referred to as **dividends in arrears.** Although these dividends are not a liability until declared by the

board of directors, this information is of importance to stockholders and other users of the financial statements. The amount of dividends in arrears is disclosed in the notes to the financial statements. For example, ENZON, a company based in Piscataway, New Jersey, and describing itself as a biopharmaceutical firm, disclosed in the notes to its June 30, 1999, financial statements that it had dividends in arrears on cumulative preferred stock totaling $18.54 per share.

With **noncumulative preferred stock,** it is not necessary to provide for passed dividends. A dividend omission on preferred stock in any one year means it is irretrievably lost. Dividends may be declared on common stock as long as the preferred stock receives the preferred rate for the current period. Thus, in the previous example, if the preferred stock were noncumulative, the 2002 dividends would be distributed as follows:

	Dividends to Preferred Shareholders	Dividends to Common Shareholders	Total Dividends
Dividend passed in 2000	—	—	—
Dividend passed in 2001	—	—	—
Dividends for 2002	$90,000	$210,000	$300,000
Total	$90,000	$210,000	$300,000

Preferred stock contracts normally provide for cumulative dividends. Also, courts have generally held that dividend rights on preferred stock are cumulative in the absence of specific provisions to the contrary.

PARTICIPATING PREFERRED STOCK   Dividends on preferred stock are generally of a fixed amount. However, **participating preferred stock** issues provide for additional dividends to be paid to preferred stockholders after dividends of a specified amount are paid to the common stockholders. A participative provision makes preferred stock more like common stock. Although once quite common, participating preferred stocks are now relatively rare.

CONVERTIBLE PREFERRED STOCK   Preferred stock is **convertible** when it can be exchanged by its owner for some other security of the issuing corporation. Conversion rights generally provide for the exchange of preferred stock into common stock. Conversion of preferred stock into common stock would be attractive when the company has done well, allowing the preferred shareholders to escape from the preferred dividend limits. In some instances, preferred stock may be convertible into bonds, thus allowing investors the option of changing their positions from stockholders to creditors. The journal entries required for stock conversions are illustrated later in the chapter.

CALLABLE PREFERRED STOCK   Many preferred issues are **callable,** meaning they may be called and canceled at the option of the corporation. The call price is usually specified in the original agreement and provides for payment of dividends in arrears as part of the repurchase price.

REDEEMABLE PREFERRED STOCK   **Redeemable preferred stock** is preferred stock that is redeemable at the option of the stockholder, or upon other conditions not within the control of the issuer (e.g., redemption on a specific date or upon reaching a certain level of earnings). This feature makes redeemable preferred stock somewhat like a loan in that the issuing corporation may be forced to repay the stock proceeds. The FASB currently requires disclosure of the extent of redemption requirements for all issues of preferred stock that are redeemable at fixed or determinable prices on fixed or determinable dates.[7] The SEC has ruled [in Financial Reporting Release (FRR) 1] that firms with publicly traded securities must not include mandatory redeemable preferred stock under the "Stockholders' equity" heading. Instead, mandatory redeemable preferred stock is listed above the equity section in a gray area between the liabilities and equities; this reporting of redeemable preferred stock as neither debt nor equity is often referred to as the *"mezzanine" treatment.*

Record the issuance of stock for cash on a subscription basis and in exchange for noncash assets or for services.

ISSUANCE OF CAPITAL STOCK

Stock can be issued in exchange for cash, on a subscription basis, in exchange for non-cash consideration, or as part of a business combination. The accounting for each of these possibilities is described on the following pages.

Capital Stock Issued for Cash

The issuance of stock for cash is recorded by a debit to Cash and a credit to Capital Stock for the par or stated value.[8] When the amount of cash received from the sale of stock is greater than the par or stated value, the excess is recorded separately as a credit to an **additional paid-in capital** account. This account is carried on the books as long as the stock to which it relates is outstanding. When stock is retired, the capital stock balance as well as any related additional paid-in capital balance is generally canceled.

To illustrate, assume that the Goode Corporation issued 4,000 shares of $1 par common stock on April 1, 2002, for $45,000 cash. The entry to record the transaction is:

2002			
April 1	Cash	45,000	
	Common Stock		4,000
	Paid-In Capital in Excess of Par		41,000

If, in the example, the common stock was no-par stock but with a $1 stated value, the entry would be the same except that the $41,000 would be designated Paid-In Capital in Excess of Stated Value. Generally, stock is assigned a par or a stated value. However, if there is no such value assigned, the entire amount of cash received on the sale of stock is credited to the capital stock account, and there is no additional paid-in capital account associated with the stock. Assuming Goode Corporation's stock was no-par common without a stated value, the entry to record the sale of 4,000 shares for $45,000 would be:

2002			
April 1	Cash	45,000	
	Common Stock		45,000

Capital Stock Sold on Subscription

Capital stock may be issued on a subscription basis. A **subscription** is a legally binding contract between the subscriber (purchaser of stock) and the corporation (issuer of stock). The contract states the number of shares subscribed, the subscription price, the terms of payment, and other conditions of the transaction. A subscription gives the corporation a legal claim for the contract price and also gives the subscriber the legal status of a stockholder unless certain rights as a stockholder are specifically withheld by law or by terms of the contract. Ordinarily, stock certificates evidencing share ownership are not issued until the full subscription price has been received by the corporation.

7 *Statement of Financial Accounting Standards No. 47*, "Disclosure of Long-Term Obligations," Stamford, CT: Financial Accounting Standards Board, 1981, par. 10c.

8 Capital stock is a general term; when it is used in account titles in the text, it represents either preferred stock or common stock. When an illustration is meant to apply specifically to preferred or common stock, the appropriate term is used in the account title.

▶ IS IT AN INVESTMENT OR IS IT A LOAN?

In the field of finance, a debt claim is one that entitles the debt holders to a fixed payment when company assets are sufficient to meet that payment; if company assets are below that amount, the debt holders get all the assets. An equity claim is one that entitles the equity holders to all company assets in excess of the debt holders' portion. The definitions of liabilities and equities given by the FASB in its Statement of

Accounting Concepts No. 6 embody similar notions—equity is defined as the residual amount of assets left after deducting the liability claims.

Although examples of pure equity (common stock) and pure debt (a bank loan) are easy to distinguish, many securities are in a middle ground and have characteristics of both debt and equity. For example, preferred stock is like debt in that the payments (both dividend and liquidation amounts) are capped, but it is also like equity because the payments aren't guaranteed and have lower priority than debt claims. As another example, convertible debt may be exchanged for equity if the issuing firm performs well, and thus as the performance of the issuing firm improves, the convertible

debt gradually changes in nature from debt to equity.

These examples illustrate that the line between a liability and an equity can be very unclear. The FASB performed a fundamental review of the accounting distinction between debt and equity. One suggestion for improved disclosure is to have a third category on the right side of the balance sheet where items with elements of both debt and equity would be reported. Mandatory redeemable preferred stock is already treated this way. Another possibility is to have no artificial division between liabilities and equities but instead list long-term sources of capital according to their mix of debt and equity characteristics—pure long-term debt could be listed first, common stock listed last, and the

---

The following entries illustrate the recording and issuance of capital stock sold on subscription.

November 1–30: Received subscriptions for 5,000 shares of $1 par common at $12.50 per share with 50% down, balance due in 60 days.

Common Stock Subscriptions Receivable	62,500	
Common Stock Subscribed		5,000
Paid-In Capital in Excess of Par		57,500
Cash	31,250	
Common Stock Subscriptions Receivable		31,250

[handwritten: NOT AN ASSET — CONTRA EQUITY ACCOUNT]

December 1–31: Received balance due on one-half of subscriptions and issued stock to the fully paid subscribers, 2,500 shares.

Cash	15,625	
Common Stock Subscriptions Receivable		15,625
Common Stock Subscribed	2,500	
Common Stock		2,500

Contributed capital would be reported in the stockholders' equity section of the December 31 balance sheet as follows:

Stockholders' Equity	
Contributed capital:	
Common stock, $1 par, 2,500 shares issued and outstanding	$ 2,500
Common stock subscribed, 2,500 shares	2,500
Paid-in capital in excess of par	57,500
	$62,500
Less: Common stock subscriptions receivable	15,625
Total contributed capital	$46,875

intermediate items listed in between. A committee of the American Accounting Association has recommended retaining the balance sheet distinction between debt and equity and using financial models to allocate the proceeds from the issuance of complex securities into their debt and equity components. The FASB has tabled the issue for now, but it will probably return to it in the future.

The IASC, on the other hand, addressed these issues in IAS 32 and determined that compound securities, that is, securities with features of both debt and equity, should be split into two components, and those components should be classified separately. Additionally, IAS 32 requires that mandatory redeemable preferred stock be classified as debt.

One thing is certain—as innovative securities continue to be introduced, drawing the accounting boundary between debt and equity will only become more difficult.

QUESTIONS:

1. As described above, it has been suggested that the artificial division between liabilities and equities be removed from the balance sheet. What implications would this have for the income statement?

2. Imagine two companies, A and B. Forty percent of A's financing comes from debt, the remainder comes from equity. B's financing is 99% debt and 1% equity. How does the debt of B differ from the debt of A?

SOURCES:

"Distinguishing Between Liability and Equity Instruments and Accounting for Instruments With Characteristics of Both," FASB Discussion Memorandum (August 21, 1990).

American Accounting Association's Financial Accounting Standards Committee, "Response to the FASB Discussion Memorandum 'Distinguishing Between Liability and Equity Instruments and Accounting for Instruments with Characteristics of Both,'" *Accounting Horizons*, September 1993, p. 105.

Capital Stock Subscriptions Receivable should normally not be shown as an asset but instead as an offset to equity.[9] This treatment is deemed appropriate because the legal penalty against subscribers who don't fully pay the contract price is often minimal, increasing the probability that the issuer of the stock may not fully collect on the subscriptions receivable. SEC rules allow subscription amounts receivable as of the balance sheet date to be shown as a current asset if the full contract price is collected prior to the date the financial statements are actually issued. For example, COVOL TECHNOLOGIES, a Lehi, Utah–based company that recycles industrial waste into briquettes for fuel, reported in its 1997 financial statements that it had recorded a $577,000 stock subscription receivable as an asset. Covol also reported that the $577,000 was collected in cash in the following year, before the 1997 financial statements were released.

SUBSCRIPTION DEFAULTS   If a subscriber defaults on a subscription by failing to make a payment when it is due, a corporation may (1) return to the subscriber the amount paid, (2) return to the subscriber the amount paid less any reduction in price or expense incurred on the resale of the stock, (3) declare the amount paid by the subscriber as forfeited, or (4) issue to the subscriber shares equal to the number paid for in full. The practice followed will depend on the policy adopted by the corporation within the legal limitations set by the state in which it is incorporated.

Capital Stock Issued for Consideration Other Than Cash

When capital stock is issued for consideration in the form of property other than cash or for services received, the fair market value of the stock or the fair market value of the property or services, whichever is more objectively determinable, is used to record the transaction. If a quoted market price for the stock is available, that amount should be used as a basis for recording the exchange. Otherwise, it may be possible to determine

---

9 Emerging Issues Task Force, *EITF Abstract 85–1*, "Classifying Notes Received for Capital Stock" Financial Accounting Standards Board, Norwalk, CT: 1985.

the fair market value of the property or services received, for example, through appraisal by a competent outside party.

To illustrate, assume that AC Company issues 200 shares of $0.50 par value common stock in return for land. The company's stock is currently selling for $50 per share. The entry on AC Company's books would be:

Land	10,000	
Common Stock		100
Paid-In Capital in Excess of Par		9,900

If, on the other hand, the land has a readily determinable market price of $12,000 but AC Company's common stock has no established fair market value, the transaction would be recorded as follows:

Land	12,000	
Common Stock		100
Paid-In Capital in Excess of Par		11,900

If no readily determinable value is available for either the stock or the property or services received, the accepted procedure is to have the value of the property or services independently appraised. If the transaction is material, the source of the appraisal should be disclosed in the financial statements.

When stock is issued in exchange for services, the journal entry is similar to that illustrated above. Assume that AC Company decides not to pay a key employee in cash but instead grants the employee 100 shares of $0.50 par common stock, with a market value of $50 per share, as payment of salary. The transaction would be recorded as follows:

Salary Expense	5,000	
Common Stock		50
Paid-In Capital in Excess of Par		4,950

This entry is interesting because it is so noncontroversial. However, if AC Company were to pay the employee with stock options instead of with actual shares of stock, the accounting would be very different and very controversial. Accounting for stock options given as employee compensation is discussed later in the chapter.

Issuance of Capital Stock in a Business Combination

Corporations often merge—the acquisition by MCI WORLDCOM of SPRINT CORP. in a $115 billion deal in 1999 is one recent example. The union of two corporations is called a **business combination.** The combination can be accomplished by one corporation paying cash to buy out the shareholders of the other, by an exchange of stock whereby all the shareholders of the two separate corporations become joint shareholders of the new combined company, or by a mixture of a cash buyout and a stock swap.

As of the beginning of 1999, there were two ways to account for a business combination. The **purchase method** assumes that one of the companies is dominant and is acquiring the other company. With this method, the assets of the company being acquired are revalued to their current market value. In addition, the acquiring company records goodwill if the value of the cash and stock given in the acquisition exceeds the market value of the net assets acquired. The **pooling-of-interests method** assumes a merger of equals; neither of the merging companies is thought of as purchasing the other. With a pooling of interests, the assets of both of the pooled companies remain recorded at their historical costs; no adjustment of the assets to market value is attempted, and no goodwill is recorded. During 1999, the FASB issued an Exposure Draft that proposed eliminating the pooling-of-interests method of accounting for business combinations. The Exposure Draft is likely to be adopted sometime during the year 2000.

Accounting for business combinations is discussed in detail in advanced accounting texts. Accounting for the acquisition of a business and any resulting goodwill is covered in Chapter 12.

Use both the cost and par value methods to account for stock repurchases.

STOCK REPURCHASES

For a variety of reasons, a company may find it desirable to reacquire shares of its own stock. For example, in the most aggressive stock buyback program to date, a number of years ago GENERAL ELECTRIC (GE) announced its intention to spend a total of $13 billion buying back its own shares. As of the end of 1998, GE had already exceeded this, spending a cumulative total of $18.7 billion for stock repurchases. In general, companies acquire their own stock to:

1. Provide shares for incentive compensation and employee savings plans.
2. Obtain shares needed to satisfy requests by holders of convertible securities (bonds and preferred stock).
3. Reduce the amount of equity relative to the amount of debt.
4. Invest excess cash temporarily.
5. Remove some shares from the open market in order to protect against a hostile takeover.
6. Improve per-share earnings by reducing the number of shares outstanding and returning inefficiently used assets to shareholders.
7. Display confidence that the stock is currently undervalued by the market.

Whatever the reason, a company's stock may be reacquired by exercise of call or redemption provisions or by repurchase of the stock in the open market. State laws normally prohibit the repurchase of stock if the repurchase would impair the ability of creditors to be repaid—in many states, the total amount spent to repurchase shares cannot exceed the sum of additional paid-in capital and retained earnings. In addition, share repurchases at prices that are exorbitant are banned because they dilute the stock value for the remaining shareholders.

In accounting for the reacquisition of stock, remember that reacquisitions do not give rise to income or loss. A company issues stock to raise capital; in reacquiring shares of its stock, the company is merely reducing its invested capital. Gains or losses arise from the operating and investing activities of the business, not from transactions with shareholders.

A company's stock may be reacquired for immediate retirement or be reacquired and held as treasury stock for subsequent disposition, either eventual retirement or reissuance. There are two methods of accounting for treasury stock transactions—the cost method and the par value method. After a short discussion on treasury stock, these methods will be discussed in detail.

Treasury Stock

> **Caution!** Reacquisition of shares may reduce retained earnings, but it can *never* increase retained earnings.

When a company's own stock is reacquired and held in the name of the company, it is referred to as **treasury stock.** Treasury shares may subsequently be reissued or formally retired. Before discussing how to account for treasury stock, three important features should be noted.

- Treasury stock should not be viewed as an asset; instead, it should be reported as a reduction in total owners' equity.[10]
- There is no income or loss on the reacquisition, reissuance, or retirement of treasury stock.
- Retained earnings can be decreased by treasury stock transactions but is never increased by such transactions.

Two methods for recording treasury stock transactions are generally accepted: (1) the **cost method,** where the treasury stock is recorded in a special equity account until

---

10 Occasionally, however, treasury stock is shown as an asset when shares are acquired in connection with an employee stock option plan. However, such instances are rare.

the shares are reissued or retired; and (2) the **par (or stated) value method,** where the purchase of treasury stock is accounted for as if the shares were being retired.

COST METHOD OF ACCOUNTING FOR TREASURY STOCK Under the cost method, the purchase of treasury stock is recorded by debiting a treasury stock account for the total amount paid to repurchase the shares. The treasury stock account is reported as a deduction from total stockholders' equity on the balance sheet.

The cost method of accounting for treasury stock transactions is illustrated in the following example:

2001—*Newly organized corporation issued 10,000 shares of common stock, $1 par, at $15:*

Cash	150,000	
Common Stock		10,000
Paid-In Capital in Excess of Par		140,000

Net income for the first year of business was $30,000.

2002—*Reacquired 1,000 shares of common stock at $40 per share:*

Treasury Stock	40,000	
Cash		40,000

2002—*Sold 200 shares of treasury stock at $50 per share:*

Because the treasury stock is reissued at a price greater than the $40 repurchase price, the excess is recorded in an additional paid-in capital account. *Note:* No gain is recorded.

Cash	10,000	
Treasury Stock (200 × $40)		8,000
Paid-In Capital From Treasury Stock		2,000

2002—*Sold 500 shares of treasury stock at $34 per share:*

Cash	17,000	
Paid-In Capital From Treasury Stock	2,000	
Retained Earnings	1,000	
Treasury Stock (500 × $40)		20,000

Because the treasury stock is reissued at a price less than the $40 repurchase price, retained earnings is debited for the difference, or, as in this example, any paid-in capital from prior treasury stock reissuances may first be debited.

2002—*Retired remaining 300 shares of treasury stock (3% of original issue of 10,000 shares):*

Common Stock	300	
Paid-In Capital in Excess of Par	4,200	
Retained Earnings [300 × ($40 − $15)]	7,500	
Treasury Stock (300 × $40)		12,000

Alternatively, the entire $11,700 difference between Common Stock and the cost to acquire the treasury stock may be debited to Retained Earnings.

It should be noted that in the example, all treasury stock was acquired at $40 per share. If several acquisitions of treasury stock are made at different prices, the resale or retirement of treasury shares must be recorded using the actual cost to reacquire the shares being sold or retired (specific identification) or using the basis of a cost flow assumption, such as FIFO or average cost.

PAR (OR STATED) VALUE METHOD OF ACCOUNTING FOR TREASURY STOCK If the par (or stated) value method is used, the purchase of treasury stock is regarded as a withdrawal of a group of stockholders. Similarly, the sale or reissuance of treasury stock, under this approach, is viewed as the admission of a new group of stockholders, requiring entries giving effect to the investment

FYI: The 1980s saw a large number of "greenmail" treasury stock transactions—a firm repurchased its shares from a troublesome shareholder at a price significantly greater than the market value. In many cases, the "greenmail" in excess of the market value of the repurchased shares must be expensed.

by this group. Thus, the purchase and sale are viewed as two separate and unrelated transactions.

Using the data given for the cost method illustration, the following entries would be made for 2002 under the par value method:

2002—Reacquired 1,000 shares of common stock at $40 per share:

Treasury Stock	1,000	
Paid-In Capital in Excess of Par	14,000	
Retained Earnings [1,000 × ($40 − $15)]	25,000	
Cash		40,000

Sold 200 shares of treasury stock at $50 per share:

Cash	10,000	
Treasury Stock		200
Paid-In Capital in Excess of Par		9,800

Sold 500 shares of treasury stock at $34 per share:

Cash	17,000	
Treasury Stock		500
Paid-In Capital in Excess of Par		16,500

Retired remaining 300 shares of treasury stock:

Common Stock	300	
Treasury Stock		300

If shares of stock are reacquired at par (or stated) value and then retired, the capital stock account is debited and the cash account is credited. However, if the purchase price of the stock exceeds the par value, the excess amount may be (1) charged to any paid-in capital balances applicable to that class of stock, (2) allocated between Paid-In Capital and Retained Earnings, or (3) charged entirely to Retained Earnings.[11] The alternative used depends on the existence of previously established paid-in capital amounts and on management's preference.

EVALUATING THE COST AND PAR VALUE METHODS Less than 10% of large U.S. companies use the par value method. Using the numbers from the example just given, the following comparison shows the impact on stockholders' equity of the two approaches after the original stock repurchases have occurred but prior to the reissuance or retirement of the treasury shares.

Comparison of Stockholders' Equity

	Cost Method	Par Value Method
Contributed capital:		
Common stock	$ 10,000	$ 10,000
Paid-in capital in excess of par	140,000	126,000
Total contributed capital	$150,000	$136,000
Retained earnings	30,000	5,000
Total contributed capital and retained earnings	$180,000	$141,000
Less: Treasury stock	40,000	1,000
Total stockholders' equity	$140,000	$140,000

---

11 *Opinions of the Accounting Principles Board No. 6*, "Status of Accounting Research Bulletins," New York: American Institute of Certified Public Accountants, 1965, par. 12a.

► **STRATEGIC TIMING OF STOCK REPURCHASES**

In the wake of the 508-point stock market crash on October 19, 1987, 645 companies announced stock repurchase plans totaling $77 billion. These buyback announcements were intended to inspire investor confidence and stop the slide in stock prices. Typical quotes from company executives were:

"It is an acknowledgment of confidence in our current and future value."

"It just underscores our financial stability and sends a signal that we believe in ourselves."

The controversy about these postcrash buyback announcements is that it subsequently became clear that at least some of the announcements had been made purely for their psychological effect and that the actual buybacks were not going to take place. One credit analyst characterized the buyback plans as representing "only a statement of faith intended to bolster shareholder confidence rather than a plan of action."

Companies also claim that they repurchase their shares when they think the market is undervaluing their

STOP & THINK After looking at this comparison, why do you think so few companies use the par value method?

Note that total stockholders' equity is the same regardless of which method is used. As shown by the example, however, there may be differences in the relative amounts of contributed capital and retained earnings reported. Note again that retained earnings may be decreased by treasury stock transactions but can never be increased by buying or selling treasury stock. Exhibit 11–5 lists the 10 largest companies in the United States (in terms of their March 1999 market value), and their stock repurchases, according to reported information. It is interesting to note that 5 of these 10 companies, including MICROSOFT and WAL-MART, use the par value method of accounting for their treasury stock purchases.

EXHIBIT 11–5 | Treasury Stock Purchases for the 10 Largest U.S. Companies

**Treasury Stock Purchases
for the 10 Largest U.S. Companies
(Numbers in millions)**

Company (Fiscal Year-End)	Repurchases During the Year	Balance Sheet Amount	Accounting Method
Microsoft (June 1999)	$2,950	$ 0	par value
General Electric (December 1998)	2,819	18,739	cost
Wal-Mart (January 1999)	1,202	0	par value
Merck (December 1998)	3,626	13,008	cost
Intel (December 1998)	6,785	0	par value
Pfizer (December 1998)	1,912	3,911	cost
AT&T (December 1998)	2,964	0	par value
Exxon (December 1998)	3,055	12,205	cost
Coca-Cola (December 1998)	1,563	13,145	cost
Cisco Systems (July 1999)	0	0	par value*

*Cisco Systems purchased treasury stock in 1997 and accounted for it using the par value method.
SOURCE: Identification of the 10 largest companies was made using the 1999 Fortune 500 listing, based on March 15, 1999, market values.

stock. Academic research has substantiated this motivation. A study of 1,239 stock repurchase announcements between 1980 and 1990 showed that the repurchasing firms outperformed a control group of companies by 12% over the next four years. Even more interesting is the finding that high book-to-market firms (i.e., those most frequently spoken of as being undervalued by the market) that announced stock repurchases outperformed nonrepurchasing high book-to-market firms by 45% over the next four years.

QUESTIONS:

1. Many companies engage in a stock buyback program without raising their debt-to-equity ratio (total liabilities/total equity). How is this possible?

2. Some companies claim that a stock repurchase will increase earnings per share. Do you agree?

SOURCES:

Jay Palmer, "Promises, Promises: Or What Happened to All Those Post-Crash Buybacks?" *Barron's*, April 25, 1988, p. 13.

D. Ikenberry, J. Lakonishok, and T. Vermaelen, "Market Underreaction to Open Market Stock Repurchases," *Journal of Financial Economics*, October 1995, pp. 181–208.

Account for the issuance of stock rights and stock warrants.

STOCK RIGHTS, WARRANTS, AND OPTIONS

A corporation may issue rights, warrants, or options that permit the purchase of the company's stock for a specified period (the exercise period) at a certain price (the exercise price). Although the terms rights, warrants, and options are sometimes used interchangeably, a distinction may be made as follows:

- **Stock rights**—issued to existing shareholders to permit them to maintain their proportionate ownership interests when new shares are to be issued. (Some state laws require this preemptive right.)
- **Stock warrants**—sold by the corporation for cash, generally in conjunction with the issuance of another security.
- **Stock options**—granted to officers or employees, usually as part of a compensation plan.

A company may offer rights, warrants, or options to raise additional capital, to encourage the sale of a particular class of securities, or as compensation for services received. The exercise period is generally longer for warrants and options than for rights. Warrants and rights may be traded independently among investors, whereas options generally are restricted to a particular person or specified group to whom the options are granted. The accounting considerations relating to stock rights, warrants, and options are described in the following sections.

Stock Rights

When announcing rights to purchase additional shares of stock, the directors of a corporation specify a date on which the rights will be issued. All stockholders of record on the issue date are entitled to receive the rights. Thus, between the announcement date and the issue date, the stock is said to sell *rights-on*. After the rights are issued, the stock sells *ex-rights*, and the rights may be sold separately by those receiving them from the corporation. An expiration date is also designated when the rights are announced, and rights not exercised by this date are worthless.

When rights are issued to stockholders, only a memorandum entry is made on the issuing company's books stating the number of shares that may be claimed under the outstanding rights. This information is required so the corporation may retain sufficient unissued or reacquired stock to meet the exercise of the rights. Upon surrender of the rights and the receipt of payments as specified by the rights, the stock is issued. At this time, a memorandum entry is made to record the decrease in the number of rights outstanding accompanied by an entry to record the stock sale. The entry for the sale is recorded the same as any other issue of stock, with appropriate recognition of the cash received, the par, or stated, value of the stock issued, and any additional paid-in capital. Information concerning outstanding rights should be reported with the corporation's balance sheet so that the effects of the future exercise of remaining rights may be determined.

Stock Warrants

> **FYI:** A company would include warrants to encourage investors to purchase the company's bonds. Of course, another way to encourage investors to purchase the bonds is to increase the interest rate paid on the bonds. Therefore, warrants can be viewed as decreasing the interest rate that must be paid.

Warrants may be sold in conjunction with other securities as a "sweetener" to make the purchase of the securities more attractive. For example, warrants to purchase shares of a corporation's common stock may be issued with bonds to encourage investors to purchase the bonds. A warrant has value when the exercise price is less than the market value, either present or potential, of the security that can be purchased with the warrants. Warrants issued with other securities may be detachable or nondetachable. **Detachable warrants** are similar to stock rights because they can be traded separately from the security with which they were originally issued. **Nondetachable warrants** cannot be separated from the security with which they were issued.

The Accounting Principles Board (APB) in Opinion No. 14 recommended assigning part of the issuance price of debt securities to any detachable stock warrants and classifying it as part of owners' equity.[12] The value assigned to the warrants is determined by the following equation:

$$\text{Value assigned to warrants} = \text{Total issue price} \times \frac{\text{Market value of warrants}}{\text{Market value of security without warrants} + \text{Market value of warrants}}$$

Although Opinion No. 14 is directed only to warrants attached to debt, it appears logical to extend the conclusions of that opinion to warrants attached to preferred stock. Thus, if a market value exists for the warrants at the issuance date, a separate equity account is credited with that portion of the issuance price assigned to the warrants. If the warrants are exercised, the value assigned to the common stock is the value allocated to the warrants plus the cash proceeds from the issuance of the common stock. If the warrants are allowed to expire, the value assigned to the warrants may be transferred to a permanent paid-in capital account.

> **FYI:** From an investor standpoint, both the preferred shares and the detachable warrants are recorded at their fair values.

Accounting for detachable warrants attached to a preferred stock issue is illustrated as follows. Assume the Stewart Co. sells 1,000 shares of $50 par preferred stock for $58 per share. As an incentive to purchase the stock, Stewart Co. gives the purchaser detachable warrants enabling holders to subscribe to 1,000 shares of $2 par common stock for $25 per share. The warrants expire after one year. Immediately following the issuance of the preferred stock, the warrants are selling at $3, and the fair market value of the preferred stock without the warrant attached is $57. The proceeds of $58,000 should be allocated by the Stewart Co. as follows:

$$\text{Value assigned to the warrants} = \$58,000 \times \frac{\$3}{\$57 + \$3} = \$2,900$$

---

12 *Opinions of the Accounting Principles Board No. 14,* "Accounting for Convertible Debt and Debt Issued with Stock Purchase Warrants," New York: American Institute of Certified Public Accountants, 1969, par. 16.

The entry on Stewart's books to record the sale of the preferred stock with detachable warrants is:

Cash	58,000	
Preferred Stock, $50 par		50,000
Paid-In Capital in Excess of Par—Preferred Stock		5,100
Common Stock Warrants		2,900

If the warrants are exercised, the entry to record the issuance of common stock would be:

Common Stock Warrants	2,900	
Cash	25,000	
Common Stock, $2 par		2,000
Paid-In Capital in Excess of Par—Common Stock		25,900

This entry would be the same regardless of the market price of the common stock at the issuance date.

If the warrants in the example were allowed to expire, the following entry would be made:

Common Stock Warrants	2,900	
Paid-In Capital From Expired Warrants		2,900

If warrants are nondetachable, the securities are considered inseparable, and no allocation is made to recognize the value of the warrant. The entire proceeds are assigned to the security to which the warrant is attached. Thus, for nondetachable warrants, the accounting treatment is similar to that for convertible securities, such as convertible bonds. Some accountants feel that this inconsistency is not justified because the economic value of a warrant exists, even if the warrant cannot be traded separately or "detached." This is essentially the same argument made for recognizing the conversion feature of a convertible security. Notwithstanding this argument, a separate instrument does not exist for a nondetachable warrant, and current practice in the United States does not require a separate value to be assigned to these warrants. However, this practice is both conceptually unsatisfactory and out of step with other standards around the world. For example, IAS 32 requires all compound financial instruments to be recorded as separate debt and equity components. During 1999, the FASB announced that it intended to issue an Exposure Draft that would propose separate recording of the debt and equity components of all financing instruments. Preliminary views were issued by the FASB for public comment in December 1999 as a step preceding the development of the Exposure Draft.

ACCOUNTING FOR STOCK-BASED COMPENSATION

5

Explain the difference between the intrinsic value and fair value methods, and use both in accounting for a fixed stock option plan.

During 1994, debate over the proper accounting for employee stock options escalated into a full-scale war, with the FASB pitted against the business community and, ultimately, the Congress of the United States. The FASB surrendered because "the debate threatened the future of accounting standard-setting in the private sector,"[13] meaning that Congress had suggested the possibility of abolishing the FASB if it didn't toe the line on stock option accounting.

Here is a sample of the public statements made during the debate.

- "U.S. entrepreneurial stalwarts, in this era of rapidly shrinking employment, are to be sacrificed on the altar of accounting principles by the high priests

13 *Statement of Financial Accounting Standards No. 123,* "Accounting for Stock-Based Compensation," Norwalk, CT: Financial Accounting Standards Boards, 1995, par. 60.

> **Caution!** Employee stock options are *not* the same as the call and put stock options traded on major exchanges. Traded option contracts can exist between any two parties. Call options entitle the owner to buy shares of a certain stock at a set "exercise" price. Put options entitle the owner to sell shares at a set price.

of the double-entry ledger."—T. J. Rodgers, President, CYPRESS SEMI-CONDUCTOR.[14]

- "[T]he FASB stock option proposal would be damaging to many companies in our Nation. . . . [I]t would be very damaging to California's nascent economic recovery. . . . If we need to legislate accounting rules, I am not going to walk away from that fight. . . ."—Senator Boxer from California.[15]

The subject of all the controversy is this: Should the fair value of stock options granted to employees be estimated and recognized as part of compensation expense? In his letter to the shareholders in BERKSHIRE HATHAWAY'S 1993 annual report, Warren Buffett, president, nicely summarized the position of accounting theorists:

> If options aren't a form of compensation, what are they? If compensation isn't an expense, what is it? And if expenses shouldn't go into the calculation of earnings, where in the world should they go?[16]

But, theoretical arguments aside, the vast majority of corporations in the United States opposed the FASB's attempt to require recognition of a stock option compensation expense. The reason for the opposition was simple: Recognition of a stock option compensation expense would reduce reported earnings. The surprising vigor of the opposition caused the FASB to reluctantly approve the following accounting treatment[17]:

- Companies are allowed to continue to use the **intrinsic value method** embodied in APB Opinion No. 25.[18] For most stock option plans, this means that no expense is recognized.
- Companies are encouraged, but not required, to adopt the **fair value method** for employee stock options. The fair value method results in compensation expense being recognized for almost all stock option plans.
- All companies, both those using the intrinsic value method and those using the fair value method, must disclose details of options outstanding, such as exercise price, length of contract period, fair value of options, and so forth.
- Those companies using the intrinsic value method must disclose what their net income would have been if they had used the fair value method.

The recognition and disclosure requirements for both the intrinsic value and the fair value methods are illustrated in the following simple example. A more comprehensive example is given in the expanded material portion of this chapter.

On January 1, 2000, the board of directors of the Neff Company authorized the grant of 10,000 stock options to supplement the salaries of certain employees. Each stock option permits the purchase of one share of Neff common stock at a price of $50 per share; the market price of the stock on January 1, 2000, is also $50 per share. The options vest, or become exercisable, beginning on January 1, 2003, and only if the employees stay with the company for the entire three-year vesting period. The options expire on December 31, 2003.

Under the intrinsic value method of APB Opinion No. 25, the value of a fixed stock option (one with a fixed exercise price) is equal to the difference between the option exercise price and the market price at the grant date. In the Neff example, each option has a value of $0 ($50 market price at grant date – $50 exercise price). This is typical of

---

14 "Taking Account of Stock Options," *Harvard Business Review*, January–February 1994, p. 27.

15 *Congressional Record*—Senate, May 3, 1994, pp. S5035—S5036. Quoted in Stephen A. Zeff and Bala G. Dharan, *Readings and Notes on Financial Accounting: Issues and Controversies*, 5th ed., New York: McGraw-Hill, 1997.

16 Berkshire Hathaway Annual Report—1993.

17 *FASB Statement No. 123.*

18 *Opinions of the Accounting Principles Board No. 25*, "Accounting for Stock Issued to Employees," New York: American Institute of Certified Public Accountants, 1972.

many actual stock option plans for real companies. For example, MICROSOFT, in its 1999 annual report, states that its board of directors sets the exercise price to be not less than the fair market value of the stock at the date of grant.

> **Caution!** Remember, if the exercise price is greater than or equal to the grant date stock price, the intrinsic value method results in *no* compensation expense.

The journal entry for Neff Company to record compensation expense under the intrinsic value method is quite easy: The options are assumed to have no value, so there is no compensation expense in any of the three years of the vesting period.

The following journal entry records the exercise of all 10,000 of the options on December 31, 2003, to purchase shares of Neff's no-par common stock:

2003			
Dec. 31	Cash (10,000 × $50)	500,000	
	Common Stock (no par)		500,000

This entry is the same no matter what the market value of Neff's stock is on the exercise date.

Under the fair value method, Neff is required to compute the fair value of the options as of the grant date. Clearly, each option has value because there is a chance that the stock price may increase above $50 during the three-year period and the options give the employees the right to buy the stock at the fixed exercise price of $50. Computation of the fair value of the options involves consideration of factors like the expected volatility of the stock price and the length of time the options are valid. For example, the higher the volatility of the stock price, the higher the value of the option because there is a bigger chance that the stock price will increase significantly. Of course, increased volatility also means that there is an increased probability that the stock price will decrease, but this doesn't negatively impact the option value because the employees can choose not to exercise the option if the share price drops below the option price of $50. Also, an option with a longer term has increased value because there is more chance of a significant stock price increase over a long time period than there is over a short one. Exact computation of option values involves formulas derived using stochastic calculus—and unfortunately we don't have time to cover stochastic calculus in this text. However, commercially available software packages make option valuation no more difficult than using a spreadsheet.

For the Neff Company example, assume that an option-pricing formula is used to estimate a grant date value of $10 for each of the employee stock options. Thus, the total fair value of the options granted is $100,000 (10,000 × $10) as of the grant date. Once the options granted have been valued, the remaining accounting problem is determining when the compensation expense should be recognized. The compensation should be charged to the periods in which the employees perform the services for which the options are granted. In the Neff example, no specific service period is mentioned, so compensation cost is allocated over the three-year period between the January 1, 2000, grant date and the January 1, 2003, vesting date. The journal entry to record the recognition of compensation expense for 2000 is as follows:

2000			
Dec. 31	Compensation Expense ($100,000/3 years)	33,333	
	Paid-In Capital From Stock Options		33,333

Similar entries would be made in 2001 and 2002. At the end of the three-year service period, the balance in the additional paid-in capital from stock options account is $100,000, which is equal to the grant date value of the options.

The journal entry to record the exercise of all 10,000 of the options on December 31, 2003, to purchase shares of Neff's no-par common stock would be as follows:

2003			
Dec. 31	Cash (10,000 × $50)	500,000	
	Paid-In Capital From Stock Options	100,000	
	Common Stock (no par)		600,000

If the options had been allowed to expire unexercised, the following journal entry would have been necessary on December 31, 2003, the end of the exercise period[19]:

2003			
Dec. 31	Paid-In Capital From Stock Options	100,000	
	Paid-In Capital From Expired Options		100,000

REQUIRED DISCLOSURE   Whether Neff uses the intrinsic value or fair value method, the following note disclosure (illustrated for 2000) is required each year:

Employee Stock Options		
	Shares	**Exercise Price**
Outstanding at January 1, 2000	0	—
Granted during 2000	10,000	$50
Exercised during 2000	0	—
Forfeited during 2000	0	—
Outstanding at December 31, 2000	10,000	$50
Options exercisable at December 31, 2000	0	
Weighted-average fair value of options granted during 2000	$10	

 Do financial statement users get the same information from disclosure of the fair value of employee stock options as they would get from recognition of the value of those options?

FYI: For the purpose of applying APB No. 25, the FASB has tentatively decided to define "employee" in the same way that term is used in common law. For example, an outside member of the board of directors is not considered to be an "employee" because the outside director does not spend the vast majority of his or her time working for the company.

Because the FASB is convinced that the fair value method is the more appropriate method for recognizing employee stock options, additional disclosures are required of those companies using the intrinsic value method. If Neff elected to use the intrinsic value method, the company would be required to disclose (in each year) what net income would have been if the fair value method had been used. In Appendix A, DISNEY presents extensive disclosure in its notes relating to its stock incentive plan. In its note on stock option plans, Disney states that had the fair value method been used, income for 1998 would have been $101 million lower.

Over time, many practical issues have arisen with respect to the application of APB No. 25. For example, are independent contractors employees of the company, in which case any stock options granted to them can be accounted for using the intrinsic value method of APB No. 25? Or are independent contractors considered to be "outsiders," in which case stock options granted to them must be accounted for using the fair value method? In 1999, the FASB released a proposed interpretation of APB No. 25 that addresses a number of these practical issues. The interpretation is expected to be formally adopted in the year 2000.

Distinguish between stock conversions that require a reduction in retained earnings and those that do not.

STOCK CONVERSIONS

As noted earlier, stockholders may be permitted by the terms of their stock agreement or by special action of the corporation to exchange their holdings for stock of other classes. No gain or loss is recognized by the issuer on these conversions, because it is an exchange of one form of equity for another. In certain instances, the exchanges may

---

19   The accounting for options voluntarily allowed to expire unexercised is the same under the intrinsic value method.

affect only corporate contributed capital accounts; in other instances, the exchanges may affect both capital and retained earnings accounts.

To illustrate the different conditions, assume that the capital of the Sorensen Corporation on December 31, 2002, is as follows:

Preferred stock, $50 par, 10,000 shares	$ 500,000
Paid-in capital in excess of par—preferred	100,000
Common stock, $1 par, 100,000 shares	100,000
Paid-in capital in excess of par—common	2,900,000
Retained earnings	1,000,000

Each preferred share is convertible into four common shares at any time at the option of the shareholder.

Case 1: One Preferred Share for Four Common Shares ($1 par)

On December 31, 2002, 1,000 shares of preferred stock are exchanged for 4,000 shares of common. The amount originally paid for the 1,000 preferred shares, $60,000, is now the consideration identified with 4,000 shares of common stock with a total par value of $4,000. The conversion is recorded as follows:

Preferred Stock, $50 Par	50,000	
Paid-In Capital in Excess of Par—Preferred	10,000	
Common Stock, $1 Par		4,000
Paid-In Capital in Excess of Par—Common		56,000

Case 1 is the usual case because par values for preferred stocks are typically high relative to par values of common stocks. This is because preferred stock par values are still approximately equal to the market value of the preferred stock at the issue date, whereas the par value of common stocks is usually set at some very low value (as discussed earlier in the chapter).

An example of a case of conversion in which the par values of both the preferred and common shares are small is given by PROBUSINESS SERVICES, a payroll and employee benefits outsourcing company based in Pleasanton, California. During fiscal 1998, ProBusiness converted 3.23 million preferred shares into 9.69 million common shares. The conversion was accomplished using the following journal entry (as reconstructed from the 1998 statement of stockholders' equity of ProBusiness):

Preferred Stock, at par	3,000	
Additional Paid-In Capital—Preferred	22,370,000	
Common Stock, at par		10,000
Additional Paid-In Capital—Common		22,363,000

Case 2: One Preferred Share for Four Common Shares ($20 par)

In Case 2, assume that the par value of the common shares is $20. In converting 1,000 shares of preferred for 4,000 shares of common, an increase in common stock at par of $80,000 (4,000 × $20) must be recognized, although it is accompanied by a decrease in the preferred equity of only $60,000. This type of conversion is generally recorded as follows:

Preferred Stock, $50 Par	50,000	
Paid-In Capital in Excess of Par—Preferred	10,000	
Retained Earnings	20,000	
Common Stock, $20 Par		80,000

The problems relating to the conversion of bonds for capital stock were described in Chapter 10.

For an investor, conversion of preferred stock for common stock often requires only a retitling of the investment account because both types of investment are carried at fair market value in the books of the investor. A special journal entry may be required if the conversion is also associated with a change in the investor's classification of the investment (e.g., from trading security to available-for-sale security). Investment reclassification is discussed in Chapter 14.

7

List the factors that impact the retained earnings balance.

FACTORS AFFECTING RETAINED EARNINGS

The retained earnings account is essentially the meeting place of balance sheet and income statement accounts. In successive periods, retained earnings are increased by income and decreased by losses and dividends. As a result, the retained earnings balance represents the net accumulated earnings of a corporation.

A number of other factors can affect retained earnings in addition to net income, losses, and dividends. These factors include prior-period adjustments for corrections of errors, quasi-reorganizations, stock dividends, and treasury stock transactions. The transactions and events that increase or decrease retained earnings may be summarized as follows:

Retained Earnings

Decreases	*Increases*
Error corrections	Error corrections
Some changes in accounting principle	Some changes in accounting principle
Net loss	Net income
Cash dividends	Quasi-reorganizations
Stock dividends	
Treasury stock transactions	
Stock conversions	

Net Income and Dividends

The primary source of retained earnings is the net income generated by a business. The retained earnings account is increased by net income and is reduced by net losses from business activities. When operating losses or other debits to Retained Earnings produce a debit balance in this account, the debit balance is referred to as a *deficit.*

Dividends are distributions to the stockholders of a corporation in proportion to the number of shares held by the respective owners. Distributions may take the form of cash, other assets, notes (in essence, these are deferred cash dividends), and stock dividends. Most dividends involve reductions in retained earnings. Exceptions include some large stock dividends, which involve a reduction in additional paid-in capital, and liquidating dividends, which represent a return of invested capital to stockholders and call for reductions in contributed capital.

Use of the term *dividend* without qualification normally implies the distribution of cash. Dividends in a form other than cash, such as property or stock dividends, should be designated by their special form. Distributions from a capital source other than retained earnings should carry a description of their special origin, for example, liquidating dividend or dividend distribution of paid-in capital.

Prior-Period Adjustments

In some situations, errors made in past years are discovered and corrected in the current year by an adjustment to the retained earnings account, referred to as a *prior-period adjustment.* There are several types of errors that may occur in measuring the results of operations and the financial status of an enterprise. Accounting errors can result from mathematical mistakes, a failure to apply appropriate accounting procedures, or a misstatement or omission of certain information. In addition, a change from an accounting

principle that is not generally accepted to one that is accepted is considered a correction of an error.[20]

Fortunately, most errors are discovered during the accounting period, prior to closing the books. When this is the case, corrections can be made by making correcting entries directly to the accounts. This is much better than error correction by prior-period adjustment because the error is fixed immediately and the error isn't advertised to the world through disclosure of a retained earnings adjustment.

Sometimes errors go undetected during the current period, but they are offset by an equal misstatement in the subsequent period. When this happens, the under- or overstatement of income in one period is counterbalanced by an equal over- or understatement of income in the next period. After the closing process is completed for the second year, the retained earnings account is correctly stated. If a counterbalancing error is discovered during the second year, however, it should be corrected at that time.

When errors of past periods are not counterbalancing, retained earnings will be misstated until a correction is made in the accounting records. If the error is material, a prior-period adjustment should be made directly to the retained earnings account. If an error resulted in an understatement of income in previous periods, a correcting entry would be needed to increase retained earnings; if an error overstated income in prior periods, then retained earnings would have to be decreased. These adjustments for corrections in net income of prior periods typically would be shown as a part of the total change in retained earnings as follows:

Retained earnings, unadjusted beginning balance	$XXX
Add or deduct prior-period adjustments	XX
Retained earnings, adjusted beginning balance	$XXX
Add current year's net income or deduct current year's net loss	XX
	$XXX
Deduct dividends	XX
Retained earnings, ending balance	$XXX

> **FYI:** The provisions of IAS 8 regarding prior-period adjustments are the same as those under U.S. GAAP. However, the IAS 8 handling of changes in accounting principle differs from U.S. GAAP. Chapter 20 will discuss those differences.

An example of a prior-period adjustment made to correct an error is in the June 1999 financial statements of WINCANTON CORPORATION, a company that now produces specialty vehicles but that at various times in the past has also dabbled in tree farming and in Australian real estate. In 1998, Wincanton was in financial difficulty and received a $371,000 loan in order to pay a legal settlement. It appears that $50,000 of this amount was recorded as revenue rather than as a loan. In 1999, this error was corrected by reducing the beginning retained earnings balance by $50,000.

Techniques for analyzing and correcting errors are covered in detail in Chapter 20. Chapter 20 also covers prior-period adjustments associated with changes in accounting principle. The cumulative effects of most changes in accounting principle are shown in current-period income. However, cumulative effects caused by the issuance of new FASB pronouncements are sometimes shown as a prior-period adjustment to retained earnings.

> **FYI:** Prior-period adjustments are more common in Canada than in the United States. Under Canadian GAAP, for example, payments of lawsuit settlements are accounted for as prior-period adjustments in the year that the payments are made. In the United States, estimates of such settlements are accrued as losses in the period in which the loss becomes "probable."

Other Changes in Retained Earnings

The most common changes in retained earnings result from earnings (or losses) and dividends. Other changes may result from treasury stock transactions (explained earlier in the chapter) or from a quasi-reorganization, which is affected only under special circumstances in which a business seeks a "fresh start." Quasi-reorganizations are covered in the expanded material section of this chapter.

20 *Opinions of the Accounting Principles Board No. 20, "Accounting Changes,"* New York: American Institute of Certified Public Accountants, 1971, par. 13.

Retained Earnings Restrictions

A company's retained earnings balance has historically served as a constraint on the payment of cash dividends and on the repurchase of treasury shares. For example, the General Corporation Law of the state of California states that

> Neither a corporation nor any of its subsidiaries shall make any distribution to the corporation's shareholders [unless]. . . the amount of the retained earnings of the corporation immediately prior thereto equals or exceeds the amount of the proposed distribution. (Division 1, Chapter 5, Section 500)

However, in most states this constraint is no longer absolute. California law allows the payment of cash dividends even if the above retained earnings provision is not satisfied, as long as the total equity and working capital of the corporation are at specified levels. Other states, with Delaware often being viewed as the leader, have even less restrictive laws.

This flexibility in state laws doesn't mean that the level of retained earnings is not important. Banks and other lenders often place retained earnings restrictions in their loan contracts. For example, OSMONICS, a Minnetonka, Minnesota-based company that sells products used in the filtration, separation, and processing of fluids, disclosed the following in its 1998 financial statements:

> The Company has issued promissory notes which contain a covenant limiting the payment of dividends to shareholders. At December 31, 1998, approximately $5,000,000 of retained earnings was restricted under this covenant.

In addition, industry regulations, such as banking code, can also restrict the amount of retained earnings that can be used to support dividend payments. This is illustrated in a note from the 1998 financial statements of MID PENN BANCORP, a bank that has been based in Pennsylvania since 1868.

> The Pennsylvania Banking Code restricts the availability of Bank retained earnings for dividend purposes. At December 31, 1998 and 1997, $17,181,000 and $14,147,000, respectively, was not available for dividends.

Retained earnings may also be restricted at the discretion of the board of directors. For example, the board may designate a portion of retained earnings as restricted for a particular purpose, such as expansion of plant facilities.

If restrictions on retained earnings are material, they are generally disclosed in a note to the financial statements. Occasionally, the restricted portion of retained earnings is reported on the balance sheet separately from the unrestricted amount that is available for dividends. The restricted portion may be designated as **appropriated retained earnings** and the unrestricted portion as unappropriated (or free) retained earnings. Whatever the form of disclosure, the main idea behind restrictions on retained earnings is to notify stockholders that some of the assets that might otherwise be available for dividend distribution are being retained within the business for specific purposes.

Properly record cash dividends, property dividends, small and large stock dividends, and stock splits.

ACCOUNTING FOR DIVIDENDS

Among the powers delegated by the stockholders to the board of directors is the power to control the dividend policy. Whether dividends shall or shall not be paid, as well as the nature and the amount of dividends, are matters that the board determines. In setting dividend policy, the board of directors must answer two questions:

1. Do we have the legal right to declare a dividend?
2. Is a dividend distribution financially advisable?

FYI: It has been recommended that the format of the stockholders' equity section in the balance sheet be changed to give emphasis to the specific legal restrictions on cash distributions to shareholders. See Roberts, Samson, and Dugan, "The Stockholders' Equity Section: Form Without Substance?" *Accounting Horizons,* December 1990, p. 35.

In answering the first question, the board of directors must observe the state incorporation laws governing the payment of dividends. The availability of capital as a basis for dividends is a determination to be made by the legal counsel and not by the accountant. The accountant must report accurately the sources of each capital increase or decrease; the legal counsel investigates the availability of such sources as bases for dividend distributions.

The board of directors must also consider the second question, i.e., does the payment of a dividend make financial sense? Literally thousands of research papers by finance professors have examined the issue of the "best" corporate dividend policy. Full discussion of this issue is a topic for a corporate finance class. Three general observations are made here:

- Old stable companies pay out a large portion of their income as cash dividends.
- Young growing companies pay out a small portion of their income as cash dividends. They keep the funds inside the company for expansion.
- Once a company has established a certain level of cash dividends, any subsequent reduction is seen as very bad news by investors. Accordingly, companies are quite cautious about raising their dividends, waiting until they are sure they can maintain the increased level permanently.

When a dividend is legally declared and announced, it cannot be revoked. The amount of the dividend is thereafter reported as a dividends payable liability until it is paid to the shareholders.

Recognition and Payment of Dividends

FYI: After the record date, stock no longer carries a right to dividends and sells at a lower price. Stock on the New York Stock Exchange is normally quoted ex-dividend (or ex-rights) several trading days prior to the record date because of the time required to deliver the stock and to record the stock transfers.

Three dates are essential in the recognition and payment of dividends: (1) date of declaration, (2) date of record, and (3) date of payment. Dividends are made payable to stockholders of record as of a date following the date of declaration and preceding the date of payment. The liability for dividends payable is recorded on the declaration date and is canceled on the payment date. No entry is required on the record date, but a list of the stockholders is made as of the close of business on this date. These are the persons who receive dividends on the payment date. For example, on November 20, 1998, THE WALT DISNEY COMPANY paid a quarterly cash dividend of $.0525 or 5.25 cents per share to shareholders of record as of October 9, 1998.

Cash Dividends

The most common type of dividend is a **cash dividend.** For the corporation, these dividends involve a reduction in retained earnings and in cash. For the investor, a cash dividend generates cash and is recognized as dividend revenue. Entries to record the declaration and payment of a $100,000 cash dividend by a corporation follow:

Declaration of Dividend:
Dividends (or Retained Earnings)	100,000	
Dividends Payable		100,000

Payment of Dividend:
Dividends Payable	100,000	
Cash		100,000

Property Dividends

A distribution to stockholders that is payable in some asset other than cash is generally referred to as a **property dividend.** Frequently the assets to be distributed are securities of other companies owned by the corporation. The corporation thus transfers to its stockholders its ownership interest in such securities. Property dividends occur most frequently in closely held corporations.

This type of transfer is sometimes referred to as a **nonreciprocal transfer to owners,** inasmuch as nothing is received by the company in return for its distribution to the stockholders. These transfers should be recorded using the fair market value (as of the day of declaration) of the assets distributed and a gain or loss recognized for the difference between the carrying value on the books of the issuing company and the fair market value of the assets.[21] Property dividends are valued at carrying value if the fair market value is not determinable.

To illustrate the entries for a property dividend, assume that the Bigler Corporation owns 100,000 shares in the Tri-State Oil Co., carrying value $2,700,000, current fair market value $3,000,000, or $30 per share, which it wishes to distribute to its stockholders. There are 1,000,000 shares of Bigler Corporation stock outstanding. Accordingly, a dividend of 1/10 of a share of Tri-State Oil Co. stock is declared on each share of Bigler Corporation stock outstanding. The entries for Bigler for the dividend declaration and payment are:

Declaration of Dividend:

Dividends (or Retained Earnings)	3,000,000	
Property Dividends Payable		2,700,000
Gain on Distribution of Property Dividends		300,000

Payment of Dividend:

Property Dividends Payable	2,700,000	
Investment in Tri-State Oil Co. Stock		2,700,000

Stock Dividends

A corporation may distribute to stockholders additional shares of the company's own stock as a stock dividend. A stock dividend involves no transfer of cash or any other asset to shareholders. In essence, a stock dividend results in the same pie (the company) being cut up into more pieces (shares outstanding), with each shareholder owning the same proportion of the pieces as before the stock dividend. From a shareholder's standpoint, receipt of a stock dividend is an economic nonevent.

Fear that investors were being deceived into thinking that receipt of a stock dividend actually represented income led to development of the rules governing how the issuing company must account for stock dividends. As described by Professor James Tucker, stock dividends acquired a shady reputation in the late 1800s because they were viewed as being similar to "stock watering."[22] Stock watering is the practice of issuing stock without receiving adequate compensation in return, thus diluting the value of the shares. In addition, in the 1920s and 1930s, accountants and regulatory authorities became concerned that companies issuing stock dividends were wrongly leading investors to believe that receiving a stock dividend was equivalent to receiving a cash dividend. This impression was particularly easy to convey when a company had a practice of issuing small, regular stock dividends (e.g., a 2.5% annual stock dividend). And, from the issuing company's standpoint, a stock dividend involved no cash outlay, and the standard accounting treatment required only a small reduction in retained earnings equal to the par value of the newly issued shares.

The Committee on Accounting Procedure (CAP) issued Accounting Research Bulletin (ARB) No. 11 in September 1941, which made it considerably more difficult for firms to issue small stock dividends by requiring a reduction in retained earnings equal

---

21   *Opinions of the Accounting Principles Board No. 29,* "Accounting for Nonmonetary Transactions," New York: American Institute of Certified Public Accountants, 1973, par. 18.

22   James J. Tucker III, "The Role of Stock Dividends in Defining Income, Developing Capital Market Research and Exploring the Economic Consequences of Accounting Policy Decisions," *The Accounting Historians Journal,* Fall 1985, pp. 73–94.

to the market value of the newly issued shares. To see what a difference this makes, recall that par values are typically around $1 per share, whereas market values usually range between $20 and $80 per share. Professor Stephen Zeff cites ARB No. 11 as one of the earliest examples of the economic consequences of accounting standards—in this case, the use of an accounting standard to reduce the incidence of small, regular stock dividends.[23]

SMALL VERSUS LARGE STOCK DIVIDENDS   In accounting for stock dividends, a distinction is made between a small and a large stock dividend.[24] Recall that the specific objective of the Committee on Accounting Procedures was to discourage regularly recurring small stock dividends. As a general guideline, a stock dividend of less than 20%–25% of the number of shares previously outstanding is considered a **small stock dividend.** Stock dividends involving the issuance of more than 20%–25% are considered **large stock dividends.**[25]

With a small stock dividend, companies must transfer from Retained Earnings to Capital Stock and Additional Paid-In Capital an amount equal to the fair market value of the additional shares issued. Such a transfer is consistent with the general public's view of a stock dividend as a distribution of corporate earnings at an amount equivalent to the fair market value of the shares received. The following example illustrates the entries for the declaration and issuance of a small stock dividend.

Assume that stockholders' equity for the Fuji Company on July 1 is as follows:

Common stock, $1 par, 100,000 shares outstanding	$ 100,000
Paid-in capital in excess of par	1,100,000
Retained earnings	750,000

The company declares a 10% stock dividend, or a dividend of 1 share of common for every 10 shares held. Before the stock dividend, the stock is selling for $22 per share. After the 10% stock dividend, each original share worth $22 will become 1.1 shares, each with a value of $20 ($22/1.1). The stock dividend is to be recorded at the market value of the new shares issued, or $200,000 (10,000 new shares at the postdividend price of $20). The entries to record the declaration of the dividend and the issuance of stock by Fuji Company are:

Declaration of Dividend:

Retained Earnings	200,000	
Stock Dividends Distributable		10,000
Paid-In Capital in Excess of Par		190,000

Issuance of Dividend:

Stock Dividends Distributable	10,000	
Common Stock, $1 par		10,000

If a balance sheet is prepared after the declaration of a stock dividend but before issue of the shares, Stock Dividends Distributable is reported in the stockholders' equity section as an addition to capital stock outstanding.

Because the focus of the CAP was on reducing the number of small stock dividends, the accounting requirements governing large stock dividends are less specific than those for small stock dividends. Accounting Research Bulletin No. 43, which summarizes all the preceding standards issued by the CAP, states the following about the accounting for large stock dividends:

23   Stephen A. Zeff, "Towards a Fundamental Rethinking of the Role of the 'Intermediate' Course in the Accounting Curriculum," in *The Impact of Rule-Making on Intermediate Financial Accounting Textbooks,* Daniel J. Jensen, ed., Columbus, Ohio: 1982, pp. 33–51.

24   See *Accounting Research and Terminology Bulletins—Final Edition, No. 43,* "Restatement and Revision of Accounting Research Bulletins," New York: American Institute of Certified Public Accountants, 1961, Ch. 7, Sec. B.

25   In *Accounting Series Release No. 124,* the SEC specified that for publicly traded companies, stock dividends of 25% or more should be accounted for as large stock dividends and those of less than 25% as small stock dividends.

". . . no transfer from earned surplus [i.e., Retained Earnings] to capital surplus or capital stock account is called for, other than to the extent occasioned by legal requirements." (Chapter 7B, para. 15)

In practice, this standard results in the par or stated value of the newly issued shares being transferred to the capital stock account from either the retained earnings or paid-in capital in excess of par accounts.[26] To illustrate, assume that Fuji Company declares a large stock dividend of 50%, or a dividend of one share for every two held. Legal requirements call for the transfer to Capital Stock of an amount equal to the par value of the shares issued. Entries for the declaration of the dividend and the issuance of the 50,000 new shares (100,000 × .50) are as follows:

Declaration of Dividend:

Retained Earnings	50,000	
Stock Dividends Distributable		50,000

OR

Paid-In Capital in Excess of Par	50,000	
Stock Dividends Distributable		50,000

Issuance of Dividend:

Stock Dividends Distributable	50,000	
Common Stock, $1 par		50,000

 You are hired as an accounting consultant by a company that is considering issuing either a 20% stock dividend or a 25% stock dividend. From an accounting standpoint, which would you recommend? The surprising answer is contained in the boxed item "Using Stock Dividends as Signals" in this chapter.

FRACTIONAL SHARE WARRANTS When stock dividends are issued by a company, it may be necessary to issue **fractional share warrants** to certain stockholders. For example, when a 10% stock dividend is issued, a stockholder owning 25 shares can be given no more than 2 full shares; however, the holdings in excess of an even multiple of 10 shares are recognized by issuing a fractional share warrant for one-half share. The warrant for one-half share may be sold, or a warrant for an additional half share may be purchased so that a full share may be claimed from the company. In some instances, the corporation may arrange for the payment of cash in lieu of fractional warrants, or it may issue a full share of stock in exchange for warrants accompanied by cash for the fractional share deficiency.

Assume that the Fuji Company, in distributing a stock dividend, issues fractional share warrants equivalent to 500 shares of $1 par common. The entry for the fractional share warrants issued would be as follows:

Stock Dividends Distributable	500	
Fractional Share Warrants Issued		500

Assuming 80% of the warrants are ultimately turned in for shares and the remaining warrants expire, the following entry would be made:

Fractional Share Warrants Issued	500	
Common Stock, $1 par		400
Paid-In Capital From Forfeitures of Fractional Share Warrants		100

STOCK DIVIDENDS VERSUS STOCK SPLITS A corporation may effect a **stock split** by reducing the par or stated value of each share of capital stock and proportionately increasing the number of shares outstanding. For example, a corporation with 1,000,000 shares of $3 par stock outstanding may split the stock on a 3-for-1 basis. After the split, the corporation will have 3,000,000 shares of $1 par stock outstanding, and each

---

26 Some large stock dividends are effected by reducing both paid-in capital in excess of par and retained earnings by a total of the par value of the newly issued shares.

stockholder will have three shares for every one previously held. However, each share now represents only one-third of the capital interest it previously represented; furthermore, each share of stock can be expected to sell for approximately one-third of its previous market price. From an investor's perspective, therefore, a stock split can be viewed the same as a stock dividend.

Although a stock dividend can be compared to a stock split from the investor's point of view, its effects on corporate capital differ from those of a stock split. A stock dividend results in an increase in the number of shares outstanding, and, because the par or stated value of each share is unchanged, the capital stock balance also increases. In contrast, a stock split merely divides the existing capital stock balance into more parts, with a reduction in the par or stated value of each share. Because a stock split does not involve any transfers among the capital accounts, no journal entry is necessary. Instead, the change in the number of shares outstanding, as well as the change in the par or stated value, may be recorded by means of a memorandum entry.

Exhibit 11–6 provides a comparative example of the effects of a 100% stock dividend and a 2-for-1 stock split.

EXHIBIT 11–6 | Comparative Example—Stock Dividend Versus Stock Split

Stockholders' Equity*	
Common stock, $5 par, 50,000 shares outstanding	$250,000
Paid-in capital in excess of par	400,000
Retained earnings	300,000
Total stockholders' equity	$950,000

*Prior to stock dividend or stock split.

Stockholders' Equity After 100% Stock Dividend		**Stockholders' Equity After 2-for-1 Stock Split**	
Common stock, $5 par, 100,000 shares outstanding	$500,000	Common stock, $2.50 par, 100,000 shares outstanding	$250,000
Paid-in capital in excess of par*	400,000	Paid-in capital in excess of par	400,000
Retained earnings	50,000	Retained earnings	300,000
Total stockholders' equity	$950,000	Total stockholders' equity	$950,000

*Some or all of the $250,000 transfer to common stock at par could have been made from paid-in capital in excess of par.

FYI: A reverse stock split is the consolidation of shares outstanding into a smaller number of shares. Conventional wisdom is that shares trading for less than $10 are viewed with some skepticism, and a reverse split can make the stock look more respectable. Whatever the conventional wisdom, a reverse stock split is almost always viewed as bad news by investors.

The simple example in Exhibit 11–6 illustrates that, from an accounting perspective, the effects of a large stock dividend can be very different from the effects of a stock split even though both result in the creation of the same number of new shares. The required transfer from retained earnings (or paid-in capital in excess of par) can significantly impact the stockholders' equity section of the balance sheet. For example, in the illustration in Exhibit 11–6, the 100% stock dividend may hinder the issuing firm's ability to pay future cash dividends because the retained earnings balance is so drastically reduced; no such constraint arises when the issuance of the new shares is accounted for as a 2-for-1 stock split.

Although stock splits and stock dividends are distinctly different in an accounting sense, the terms "stock split" and "stock dividend" are used inter-

► USING STOCK DIVIDENDS AS SIGNALS

The accounting treatment of stock dividends makes their declaration an interesting way of sending a good news signal to the market. The reasoning goes like this: Because cash dividend payments are often restricted to the amount of retained earnings, the reduction in Retained Earnings required in accounting for a stock dividend might make it more difficult to declare cash dividends in the future. Accordingly, only firms with favorable future prospects would be likely to declare stock dividends. These firms would be confident that future earnings would bolster the retained earnings balance, making up for the reduction required by the stock dividend declaration.

So, according to this reasoning, if you see a firm declaring a stock dividend, you can conclude that the management of that firm must be confident that future earnings will be adequate to cover future cash dividends. This signaling view of stock dividends is supported by the fact that stock prices of companies instantly go up when they announce plans to issue a stock dividend. The accompanying graph shows the size of the positive market reaction to a stock dividend announcement, based on the size of the stock dividend.

QUESTIONS:

1. Assume that there is validity to this signaling theory of stock dividends. Which would be a stronger signal a 20% stock dividend or a 25% stock dividend?

2. Again, assuming validity to the signaling theory, which would be a stronger signal, a 100% stock dividend or a 2-for-1 stock split?

changeably in the financial press and sometimes even in the issuing company's annual report. For example, *The Wall Street Journal's* description of a distribution as a split or dividend agrees with the actual accounting for the distribution only about 25% of the time.[27]

Liquidating Dividends

A **liquidating dividend** is a distribution representing a return to stockholders of a portion of contributed capital. Whereas a normal cash dividend provides a return on investment and is accounted for by reducing Retained Earnings, a liquidating dividend provides a return of investment. A liquidating dividend is accounted for by reducing Paid-In Capital.

To illustrate, assume the Stubbs Corporation declared and paid a cash dividend and a partial liquidating dividend amounting to $150,000. Of this amount, $100,000 represents a regular $10 cash dividend on 10,000 shares of common stock. The remaining $50,000 represents a $5-per-share liquidating dividend, which is recorded as a reduction to Paid-In Capital in Excess of Par. The entries would be:

Declaration of Dividend:

Dividends (or Retained Earnings)	100,000	
Paid-In Capital in Excess of Par	50,000	
Dividends Payable		150,000

Payment of Dividend:

Dividends Payable	150,000	
Cash		150,000

Stockholders should be notified as to the allocation of the total dividend payment, so they can determine the amount that represents revenue and the amount that represents a return of investment.

---

27   See Graeme Rankine and Earl K. Stice, "The Market Reaction to the Choice of Accounting Method for Stock Splits and Large Stock Dividends," *Journal of Financial and Quantitative Analysis,* 1997.

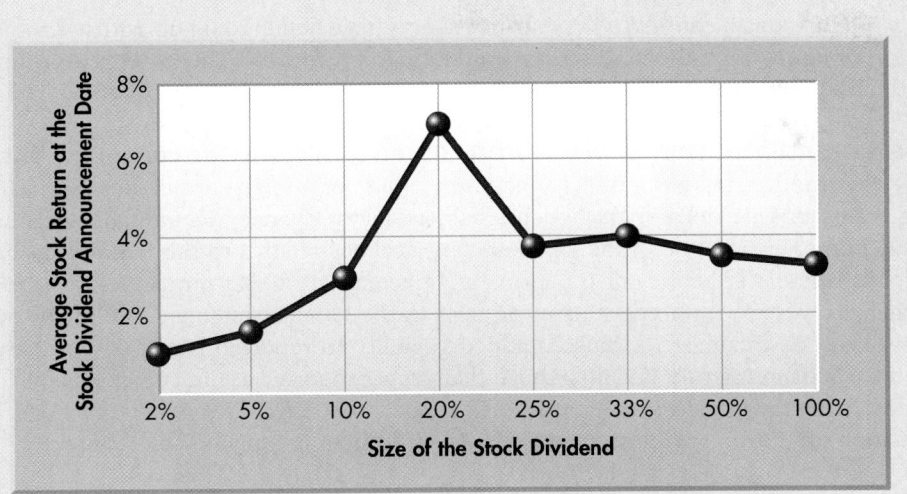

SOURCES:
Graeme Rankine and Earl K. Stice, "Accounting Rules and the Signaling Properties of 20% Stock Dividends," *The Accounting Review*, January 1997.
Graeme Rankine and Earl K. Stice, "The Market Reaction to the Choice of Accounting Method for Stock Splits and Large Stock Dividends," *Journal of Financial and Quantitative Analysis*, 1997.

OTHER EQUITY ITEMS

Explain the background of unrealized gains and losses recorded as direct equity adjustments, and list the major types of equity reserves found in foreign balance sheets.

In addition to the two major categories of contributed capital and retained earnings, the equity section of a U.S. balance sheet often includes a number of miscellaneous items. These items are gains or losses that bypass the income statement when they are recognized and are reported as part of accumulated other comprehensive income. A further discussion of these items is given below. In addition, the section below includes a discussion of equity reserves, which are common in the balance sheets of foreign companies that do not use U.S. accounting principles.

As discussed in Chapter 4, in 1997 the FASB issued Statement No. 130, "Reporting Comprehensive Income." This standard requires that all companies provide a statement of comprehensive income. An example of MICROSOFT's 1999 statement of comprehensive income is included in Exhibit 11-7. A discussion of the most common elements affecting comprehensive income follows:

EXHIBIT 11-7 | Microsoft's Statement of Comprehensive Income

Microsoft Statement of Comprehensive Income For the Year Ended June 30, 1999			
(In millions)	1999	1998	1997
Net income	$7,785	$4,490	$3,454
Other comprehensive income:			
Net unrealized investment gains	1,052	627	280
Translation adjustments and other	69	(124)	5
Comprehensive income	$8,906	$4,993	$3,739

Equity Items That Bypass the Income Statement and Are Reported as Part of Accumulated Other Comprehensive Income

Since 1980, the equity sections of U.S. balance sheets have begun to fill up with a strange collection of items, each the result of an accounting controversy. These items are summarized in the following sections.

FOREIGN CURRENCY TRANSLATION ADJUSTMENT The **foreign currency translation adjustment** arises from the change in the equity of foreign subsidiaries (as measured in terms of U.S. dollars) that occurs as a result of changes in foreign currency exchange rates. For example, if the Japanese yen weakens relative to the U.S. dollar, the equity of Japanese subsidiaries of U.S. firms will decrease, in dollar terms. Before 1981, these changes were recognized as losses or gains in the income statement. Multinational firms disliked this treatment because it added volatility to reported earnings. The FASB changed the accounting rule, and now these changes are reported as direct adjustments to equity, insulating the income statement from this aspect of foreign currency fluctuations.[28] Computation of this foreign currency translation adjustment is explained in Chapter 21.

MINIMUM PENSION LIABILITY ADJUSTMENT As you'll see when you get to Chapter 17, pension accounting is a complicated combination of tradition and compromise. Gains and losses are deferred, assets and liabilities are offset, and over all of this is imposed a minimum reported liability rule.[29] To briefly summarize, after all the pension calculations are completed, if the reported pension liability is not above a certain minimum amount, then an additional liability amount must be recognized. Conceptually, this **minimum pension liability adjustment** represents unrecognized pension expense. However, instead of being reported as an expense, the amount is shown as a direct reduction of equity.

UNREALIZED GAINS AND LOSSES ON AVAILABLE-FOR-SALE SECURITIES **Available-for-sale securities** are those that were not purchased with the immediate intention to resell but that a company also doesn't necessarily plan to hold forever. These securities, along with trading securities (those purchased as part of an active buying and selling program), are reported on the balance sheet at their current market values. The unrealized gains and losses from market value fluctuations in trading securities are included in the income statement, but the unrealized gains and losses from market value fluctuations in available-for-sale securities are shown as a direct adjustment to equity. When the FASB was considering requiring securities to be reported at their market values, companies complained about the income volatility that would be caused by recognition of changes in the market value of securities. The FASB made the standard more acceptable to businesses by allowing unrealized gains and losses on available-for-sale securities to bypass the income statement and go straight to the equity section.[30] Accounting for securities is covered in Chapter 14.

International Accounting: Equity Reserves

As discussed earlier in this chapter, state incorporation laws link the ability of a firm to pay cash dividends to the retained earnings balance. In other words, total equity is divided into two parts—the equity that is available to be distributed to shareholders and the equity that is not available for distribution. Restriction of the distribution of equity ensures that an equity "cushion" exists for the absorption of operating losses, thus increasing the chances of creditors to be fully repaid.

---

28 *Statement of Financial Accounting Standards No. 52*, "Foreign Currency Translation," Stamford, CT: Financial Accounting Standards Board, 1981.

29 *Statement of Financial Accounting Standards No. 87*, "Employers' Accounting for Pensions," Stamford, CT: Financial Accounting Standards Board, 1985.

30 *Statement of Financial Accounting Standards No. 115*, "Accounting for Certain Investments in Debt and Equity Securities," Norwalk, CT: Financial Accounting Standards Board, 1993.

Laws in foreign countries are often more explicit than U.S. state incorporation laws in linking the payment of cash dividends to the amount of distributable equity. Equity is divided among various **equity reserve** accounts, each with legal restrictions dictating whether it can be distributed to shareholders. In that type of legal environment, the accounting for equity accounts directly influences a firm's ability to pay dividends and thus becomes an important part of corporate financing policy.

A brief summary of accounting for equity reserves is given in the following sections. The discussion is based on equity accounting practice in the United Kingdom. Because of the worldwide British influence left over from the days of the British Empire, the U.K. model is widely used.

The major types of equity reserve accounts are illustrated in Exhibit 11–8. Remember that the most important distinction is whether the reserve is part of distributable or nondistributable equity.

EXHIBIT 11–8 | Equity Reserves

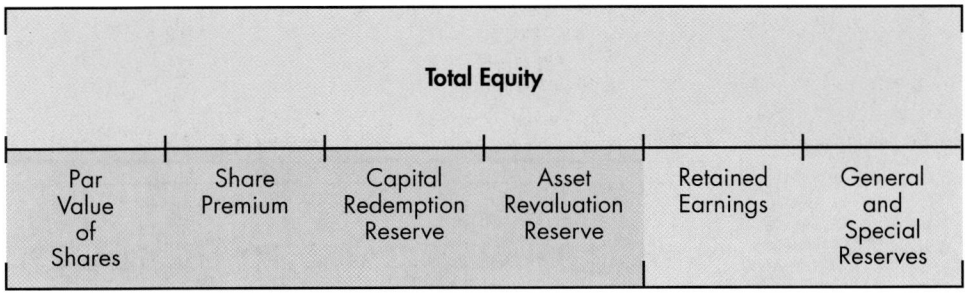

PAR VALUE AND SHARE PREMIUM These accounts correspond closely with U.S. practice, with the share premium account being the same as the paid-in capital in excess of par account. Usually, a country's laws restrict the ability of a firm to "refund" any of this paid-in capital, so these two accounts are part of nondistributable equity.

CAPITAL REDEMPTION RESERVE When shares are reacquired, total equity is reduced. To protect the ability of creditors to be fully repaid, these reductions are usually considered to be reductions in distributable equity. To reflect this fact in the accounts, an amount equal to the par value of the shares reacquired is transferred from Retained Earnings (part of distributable equity) to Capital Redemption Reserve (part of nondistributable equity).

ASSET REVALUATION RESERVE In many countries, property, plant, and equipment can be written up to its current market value. The recognition of this unrealized gain increases equity. The question is whether the additional equity can be used to support additional cash dividend payments. The answer is no. A revaluation reserve is established as part of nondistributable equity, and unrealized gains from increases in fixed asset market values are credited to the revaluation reserve.

FYI: One common reserve not discussed in this chapter is the goodwill reserve. As will be discussed in Chapter 12, in some foreign countries goodwill is not accounted for as an asset but instead as a negative equity reserve.

GENERAL AND SPECIAL RESERVES As discussed earlier, the board of directors can voluntarily restrict the use of retained earnings for the payment of cash dividends. These restrictions can later be rescinded. In the United States, these restrictions can be disclosed in a financial statement note or recognized as a formal appropriation of a portion of retained earnings. In many foreign countries, these restrictions are acknowledged by transferring part of retained earnings to a general or a special reserve account. Note that these reserves are still part of distributable equity—the board of directors can remove the restrictions at any time.

Some of the reserves mentioned above are illustrated with the accounts of SWIRE PACIFIC LIMITED shown in Exhibit 11–9. Swire Pacific Limited is based in Hong Kong and is one of the largest companies in the world. The primary operations of the company are in the regions of Hong Kong, China, and Taiwan where it has operated for over 125 years. Swire operates CATHAY PACIFIC AIRWAYS and has extensive real estate holdings in Hong Kong.

EXHIBIT 11–9 | Equity Section for Swire Pacific Limited

(All amounts are in millions of Hong Kong dollars)				
	Revenue Reserves	Property Valuation Reserve	Share Premium Account	Capital Redemption Reserve
At 31st December 1997	32,314	57,872	342	21
Retained profit for the year................	459			
Goodwill acquired	(68)			
Decrease in property valuation		(29,793)		
Exchange differences........................	17			
At 31st December 1998	32,722	28,079	342	21

Prepare a statement of changes in stockholders' equity.

DISCLOSURES RELATED TO THE EQUITY SECTION

In accounting for capital stock, it should be recognized that stock may be

- Authorized but unissued
- Subscribed for and held for issuance pending receipt of cash for the full amount of the subscription price
- Outstanding in the hands of stockholders
- Reacquired and held by the corporation for subsequent reissuance
- Canceled by appropriate corporation action

Thus, an accurate record of all transactions involving capital stock must be maintained by a corporation. Separate general ledger accounts are required for each source of capital including each class of stock. In addition, subsidiary records are needed to keep track of individual stockholders and stock certificates.

Contributed capital and its components should be disclosed separately from retained earnings on the balance sheet. Within the contributed capital section, it is important to identify the major classes of stock and the additional paid-in capital. Although it is common practice to report a single amount for additional paid-in capital, separate accounts should be provided in the ledger to identify the individual sources of additional paid-in capital, for example, paid-in capital in excess of par or stated value, paid-in capital from treasury stock, or paid-in capital from forfeited stock subscriptions.

For each class of stock, a description of the major features should be disclosed, such as par or stated value, dividend preference, or conversion terms. The number of shares authorized, issued, and outstanding should also be disclosed.

As an illustration, the stockholders' equity section from the balance sheet of IBM as of December 31, 1998, is presented in Exhibit 11–10. Many companies do not provide as much detail on the balance sheet as is illustrated for IBM. (For example, see the financial statements of THE WALT DISNEY COMPANY in Appendix A.)

Readers of financial statements should be provided with an explanation of the changes in individual equity balances during the period. When stockholders' equity is composed of numerous accounts, as in the preceding example, a **statement of changes**

in stockholders' equity is usually presented. The statement of changes in stockholders' equity for IBM for 1998 is illustrated in Exhibit 11–11.

EXHIBIT 11–10 | IBM's Stockholders' Equity Section

(Dollars in millions)	1998	1997
Stockholders' equity		
Preferred stock, par value $.01 per share...	$ 247	$ 252
Shares authorized: 150,000,000		
Shares issued (1998—2,546,011; 1997—2,597,261)		
Common stock, par value $.50 per share	10,121	8,601
Shares authorized: 1,875,000,000		
Shares issued (1998—926,869,052; 1997—969,015,351)		
Retained earnings	10,141	11,010
Treasury stock, at cost (shares: 1998—962,146; 1997—923,955)	(133)	(86)
Employee benefits trust (shares: 1998—10,000,000; 1997—10,000,000)	(1,854)	(860)
Accumulated gains and losses not affecting retained earnings	911	899
Total stockholders' equity...	$19,433	$19,816

EXHIBIT 11–11 | Statement of Stockholders' Equity for IBM

(Dollars in millions)	Preferred Stock	Common Stock	Retained Earnings	Treasury Stock	Employee Benefits Trust	Gains and Losses Not Affecting Retained Earnings	Total
1998							
Stockholders' equity, December 31, 1997	$252	$ 8,601	$11,010	$ (86)	$ (860)	$899	$19,816
Net income plus gains and losses not affecting retained earnings:							
Net income..................................			6,328				$ 6,328
Gains and losses not affecting retained earnings (net of tax):							
Foreign currency translation adjustments (net of tax benefit of $45)................						69	$ 69
Net unrealized losses on marketable securities (net of tax benefit of $36)..						(57)	(57)
Total gains and losses not affecting retained earnings.......................................							$ 12
Subtotal: Net income plus gains and losses not affecting retained earnings....................							$ 6,340
Cash dividends declared—common stock...........			(814)				(814)
Cash dividends declared—preferred stock..........			(20)				(20)
Common stock purchased and retired (56,996,818 shares)		(556)	(6,291)				(6,847)
Preferred stock purchased and retired (51,250 shares)	(5)						(5)
Common stock issued under employee plans (14,850,519 shares)		709	(1)				708
Purchases (4,163,057 shares) and sales (4,124,866 shares) of treasury stock under employee plans—net			(71)	(47)			(118)
Fair value adjustment of employee benefits trust..		1,002			(994)		8
Tax effect—stock transactions		365					365
Stockholders' equity, December 31, 1998	$247	$10,121	$10,141	$(133)	$(1,854)	$911	$19,433

EXPANDED MATERIAL

The expanded material for this chapter offers further coverage of the accounting for stock-based compensation. Stock-based compensation plans are widespread, and the recent debate over proper accounting for them has been explosive. The expanded material includes illustrations of performance-based plans and plans that call for cash settlements. The expanded material begins with coverage of quasi-reorganizations, also called "fresh-start" accounting.

Eliminate a retained earnings deficit through a quasi-reorganization.

QUASI-REORGANIZATIONS

As noted earlier, a debit balance in the retained earnings account is called a deficit. It may be the result of accumulated losses over a number of years or other significant debits to Retained Earnings. Sometimes a company with a large deficit is forced to discontinue operations and/or enter into bankruptcy proceedings. In some cases, however, where state laws permit, a company may eliminate a deficit through a restatement of invested capital balances. This provides, in effect, a fresh start for the company with a zero retained earnings balance. This is known as a **quasi-reorganization.** The advantage of a quasi-reorganization is that the procedure does not require recourse to the courts as in a formal reorganization or bankruptcy, and there is no change in the legal corporate entity or interruption of business activity.

Quasi-reorganizations are not common, but they may be appropriate for companies operating under circumstances that are quite different from those of the past, for example, a company with new management. Even if operated profitably, the company may take years to eliminate the deficit that was created under a prior management. In the meantime, the corporation generally cannot pay dividends to stockholders. With a quasi-reorganization, however, the accumulated deficit is eliminated. Performance from the reorganization date forward can then be measured and reported without having past mistakes and negative results reflecting unfavorably on the "new" company.

Normally in a quasi-reorganization, assets are revalued to reflect their current market values. This may require significant write-downs of assets against Retained Earnings, thus increasing the deficit. The total deficit is then written off (Retained Earnings is adjusted to a zero balance) against paid-in capital balances, giving the company a new capital structure.[31] The SEC requires that any anticipated accounting changes should be an integral part of the quasi-reorganization and that the reorganization should not result in a write-up of net assets of the company.[32]

To illustrate the nature of a quasi-reorganization, assume TSS Corporation has suffered operating losses for some time but is now operating profitably and expects to continue to do so. Current and projected income, however, will not be sufficient to eliminate the deficit in the near-term. It also appears that plant assets are overstated considering current prices and economic conditions. After receiving permission from state authorities and approval from the shareholders, the board of directors of TSS Corporation decides to restate company assets and paid-in capital balances in order to remove the deficit and make possible the declaration of dividends from profitable operations. A balance sheet for the company just prior to this action follows.

---

31   See *Accounting Research and Terminology Bulletins—Final Edition, No. 43*, Ch. 7, Sec. A.
32   *Staff Accounting Bulletin No. 78*, "Quasi-Reorganizations," Washington, DC: SEC, August 25, 1988.

TSS Corporation
Balance Sheet
June 30, 2002

Assets			Liabilities and Stockholders' Equity		
Current assets		$ 250,000	Liabilities...		$ 300,000
Property, plant,			Common stock, $10 par,		
and equipment.................................	$1,500,000		100,000 shares.................................	$1,000,000	
Less: Accumulated depreciation	600,000	900,000	Less: Deficit...	150,000	850,000
Total assets...		$1,150,000	Total liabilities and stockholders' equity ..		$1,150,000

The quasi-reorganization is to be accomplished as follows:

1. Property, plant, and equipment are to be reduced to their present fair market value of $600,000 by reducing the asset and accumulated depreciation balances by 33⅓%.
2. Common stock is to be reduced to a par value of $5; $500,000 in capital stock thus being converted into "additional paid-in capital."
3. The deficit of $450,000 ($150,000 as reported on the balance sheet increased by $300,000 arising from the write-down of property, plant, and equipment) is to be applied against the capital from the reduction of the par value of stock.

Entries to record the changes follow.

Transaction	Entry		
(1) To write down property, plant, and equipment and accumulated depreciation balances by 33⅓%.	Retained Earnings .... Accumulated Depreciation .... Property, Plant, and Equipment..........	300,000 200,000	 500,000

(2) To reduce the common stock balance from $10 par to $5 par and to establish the paid-in capital from reduction in stock par value account.	Common Stock, $10 par ....
	   Common Stock, $5 par ....
	   Paid-In Capital From Reduction
	   in Stock Par Value ....
		1,000,000	
			500,000
			
			500,000

(3) To apply the deficit after asset devaluation against the paid-in capital from reduction in stock par value account.	Paid-In Capital From Reduction in Stock Par Value .... Retained Earnings	 450,000	 450,000

The balance sheet after the quasi-reorganization is shown below.

TSS Corporation
Balance Sheet
June 30, 2002

Assets			Liabilities and Stockholders' Equity	
Current assets		$250,000	Liabilities..	$300,000
Property, plant, and equipment............	$1,000,000		Common stock, $5 par, 100,000 shares....................	500,000
Less: Accumulated depreciation	400,000	600,000	Paid-in capital from reduction in stock par value........	50,000
Total assets...		$850,000	Total liabilities and stockholders' equity......................	$850,000

After the quasi-reorganization, the accounting for the company's operations is similar to that for a new company. Earnings subsequent to the quasi-reorganization, however, should be accumulated in a **dated retained earnings** account. On future balance

sheets, retained earnings dated as of the time of account readjustment will inform readers of the date of such action and of the fresh start in earnings accumulation.

Exhibit 11–12 describes the quasi-reorganization undertaken by ILLINOVA, the holding company for Illinois Power.

E X H I B I T 1 1 – 1 2 | Illinova—Note Disclosure of Quasi-Reorganization

---

NOTE 2 — CLINTON IMPAIRMENT AND QUASI-REORGANIZATION

IP [Illinois Power] owns one nuclear generating station, Clinton, a 930-megawatt unit that represents approximately 20 percent of IP's generating capacity. Significant Clinton write-offs have weakened earnings and led to a 10-year decline in Illinova's and IP's retained earnings balances. Clinton has not operated since September 1996. In December 1998, Illinova's and IP's Boards of Directors voted to exit Clinton operations, resulting in an impairment of Clinton-related assets and accrual of exit-related costs. The impairment and accrual of costs resulted in a $1,327.2 million, net of income taxes, charge against earnings. Concurrent with the decision to exit Clinton, Illinova's and IP's Boards of Directors also voted to effect a quasi-reorganization, in which Illinova's consolidated accumulated deficit in retained earnings of $1,419.5 million was eliminated. . . . In conjunction with effecting its quasi-reorganization, IP reviewed its assets and liabilities to determine whether the book value of such items needed to be adjusted to reflect their fair value. IP determined that its fossil generation assets were not stated at fair value. With the help of a third-party consultant, management conducted an economic assessment of its fossil generation assets to determine their fair value. The assessment was based on projections of on-going operating costs, future prices for fossil fuels, and market prices of electricity in IP's service area. Management concluded that IP's fossil generation assets have a fair value of $2,867.0 million. This fair value was determined using the after-tax cash flows of the fossil assets. Prior to the quasi-reorganization, the fossil generation assets' book value, net of accumulated depreciation, was $631.7 million. The adjustment to fair value resulted in a write-up of $1,348.6 million, net of income taxes, which was recognized as an increase in retained earnings.

ACCOUNTING FOR STOCK-BASED COMPENSATION

12

Use both the intrinsic value and fair value methods to account for performance-based stock option plans and plans calling for a cash settlement.

The intrinsic value method of accounting for employee stock option plans results in inconsistency between the accounting for fixed stock option plans and performance-based option plans. A **fixed stock option plan** is one in which the plan terms (i.e., the option exercise price and the number of options granted) are fixed as of the date the options are granted. In a **performance-based stock option plan,** the plan terms are dependent on how well the individual or company performs after the date the options are granted. As illustrated earlier in the chapter, the intrinsic value method typically results in no compensation expense being recognized for fixed stock option plans. However, as shown below, compensation expense is usually recognized with performance-based plans when the intrinsic value method is used. As a result of this differential treatment, most U.S. companies have structured their stock compensation programs as fixed stock option plans to avoid recognizing any expense. This result has been particularly disturbing since a fixed stock option plan in some ways is more valuable to employees because the receipt of options under a fixed stock option plan is not contingent on the company or the employee meeting additional financial targets.

The fair value method eliminates the discrepancy between the accounting for fixed and performance-based option plans. This "leveling of the playing field" was a major reason for the FASB's reexamination of the accounting for stock-based compensation.

This section of the chapter covers the following topics, explaining the accounting for both the intrinsic and fair value methods:

- For performance-based plans
- For awards that call for cash settlement
- For broad-based plans

Accounting for Performance-Based Plans

In the fixed stock option plan of Neff Company that was illustrated earlier in the chapter, Neff's employees needed only to stay with the company for the entire three-year vesting period in order to receive the full value of the options. With a performance-based plan, the terms of the option depend on how well an employee performs or how well the company performs during the vesting period. To illustrate, assume that the terms of the Neff Company stock-based compensation plan are as follows:

- On January 1, 2000, the board of directors of the Neff Company authorized the grant of stock options to supplement the salaries of certain employees.
- Each stock option permits the purchase of one share of Neff common stock at a price of $50 per share; the market price of the stock on January 1, 2000, is also $50 per share.
- The options vest, or become exercisable, beginning on January 1, 2003, and only if the employees stay with the company for the entire three-year vesting period. The options expire on December 31, 2003.
- The number of options granted, instead of being fixed at 10,000 as in the earlier example, is contingent on Neff's level of sales for 2002. If Neff's sales for 2002 are less than $50 million, only the 10,000 options will vest. If Neff's 2002 sales are between $50 million and $80 million, an additional 2,000 options will vest, making a total of 12,000. Finally, if Neff's 2002 sales exceed $80 million, a total of 15,000 options will vest.
- Neff's share price changed as follows over the three-year vesting period:

January 1, 2000	$50
December 31, 2000	56
December 31, 2001	57
December 31, 2002	59

FAIR VALUE METHOD   For the Neff performance-based stock option plan, the computation of compensation expense is done by combining the value of the options on the grant date with the number of options that are expected to vest. As in the earlier example, application of an option valuation method results in a computed value for each option of $10 as of the grant date. The number of options expected to vest depends, of course, on the probable level of 2002 sales.[33] As of December 31, 2000, when compensation expense for the first year must be recorded, Neff forecasts that 2002 sales will be around $60 million, indicating that 12,000 options will vest. Recognition of compensation expense for 2000 involves recognizing one-third of the $120,000 (12,000 × $10) total estimated expense for the three-year service period. Note that the change in Neff's stock price during the year (from $50 to $56) does not affect the calculation. Under the fair value method, the options are valued once, at the grant date, and that value is used for the life of the options. The journal entry to recognize compensation expense is as follows:

2000
Dec. 31	Compensation Expense ($120,000/3 years)	40,000	
	Additional Paid-In Capital—Stock Options		40,000

Events in 2001 lead Neff to lower its forecast of 2002 sales. As of December 31, 2001, Neff expects 2002 sales to be only $40 million. Accordingly, it is estimated that only 10,000 options will vest on January 1, 2003. The new estimate for total compensation expense for the three-year service period is $100,000 (10,000 × $10). Because two-thirds of the service period has elapsed, aggregate compensation expense recognized should be $66,667 ($100,000 × ⅔). Because compensation expense of $40,000 was recognized in 2000, the necessary journal entry in 2001 is as follows:

---

33   *FASB Statement No. 123*, par. 29.

```
2001
Dec. 31  Compensation Expense ($66,667 – $40,000) .............................  26,667
              Additional Paid-In Capital—Stock Options .........................              26,667
```

Upon close examination, it can be seen that this computation of compensation expense differs from that typically encountered in situations with changing accounting estimates. Usually, the effects of changes in estimates are spread over current and future periods. In this case, such a procedure would result in 2001 compensation expense of $30,000, an allocation of the remaining compensation expense of $60,000 ($100,000 – $40,000) evenly over the remaining two years of the service period, 2001 and 2002. However, FASB Statement No. 123 requires a so-called catch-up adjustment when recognizing compensation expense related to performance-based option plans.[34] The catch-up adjustment makes the cumulative expense recognized equal to the amount it would have been had the updated estimate for 2002 sales been used all along.

Actual sales for 2002 are $85 million (Neff had a pretty good year). As a result, according to the terms of the performance-based plan, 15,000 options will vest as of January 1, 2003. Because the entire service period has elapsed, aggregate compensation expense recognized should be $150,000 (15,000 × $10). Because compensation expense of $66,667 ($40,000 + $26,667) has already been recognized in 2000 and 2001, the necessary journal entry in 2002 is as follows:

STOP & THINK Might Neff's performance-based stock option plan cause Neff's management (the ones who are receiving the stock options) to engage in some inappropriate revenue recognition practices?

```
2002
Dec. 31  Compensation Expense ($150,000 – $66,667) ..............  83,333
              Additional Paid-In Capital—Stock Options ................              83,333
```

The journal entry to record the exercise of all 15,000 of the options on December 31, 2003, to purchase shares of Neff's no-par common stock would be as follows:

```
2003
Dec. 31  Cash (15,000 × $50) ...........................................  750,000
         Additional Paid-In Capital—Stock Options .................  150,000
              Common Stock (no par) .......................................              900,000
```

INTRINSIC VALUE METHOD With the intrinsic value method, the total compensation expense for the service period for a performance-based plan is remeasured at the end of each year in response to changes in the variables used to compute the initial value. In the Neff example, the grant date estimate of total compensation expense for the three-year service period is $0 because the options have no "intrinsic value" on that date ($50 stock price – $50 exercise price). But, at December 31, 2000, an updated forecast of 2002 sales and the December 31, 2000, stock price are used to estimate total three-year compensation expense as $72,000 [12,000 options × ($56 stock price – $50 exercise price)].

This process differs substantially from the intrinsic value method of accounting for fixed stock option plans that was illustrated earlier in the chapter. With fixed stock options, changes in stock price occurring after the grant date are ignored. This significant difference in accounting between fixed plans and performance-based plans under the intrinsic value method is what caused the FASB to advocate the fair value method. However, as stated previously, most firms will continue to use the intrinsic value method because it usually results in no compensation expense for fixed plans.

The journal entry to recognize 2000 compensation expense using the intrinsic value method is as follows:

---

34 Total compensation expense is also affected by the number of options that employees forfeit, i.e., by leaving the firm before the vesting period is over. Under the fair value method, a forecast of forfeitures can be incorporated in the estimate of options to be exercised. Alternatively, the compensation expense each year can be computed based on the actual number of unforfeited options. Under the intrinsic value method, compensation expense each year is always computed based on the actual number of unforfeited options.

2000
Dec. 31   Compensation Expense ($72,000/3 years)................................   24,000
               Additional Paid-In Capital—Stock Options..............................   24,000

As of December 31, 2001, Neff expects that only 10,000 options will vest on January 1, 2003. In addition, the stock price on December 31, 2001, is $57 per share. The new estimate for total compensation expense for the three-year service period is $70,000 [10,000 × ($57 – $50)]. Because two-thirds of the service period has elapsed, aggregate compensation expense recognized should be $46,667 ($70,000 × ⅔). Because compensation expense of $24,000 was recognized in 2000, the necessary journal entry in 2001 is as follows:

2001
Dec. 31   Compensation Expense ($46,667 – $24,000)................................   22,667
               Additional Paid-In Capital—Stock Options..............................   22,667

This catch-up adjustment is exactly like that required with the fair value method.[35]

Actual sales for 2002 are $85 million, so 15,000 options will vest as of January 1, 2003. In addition, Neff's stock price is $59 per share on December 31, 2002. Because the entire service period has elapsed, aggregate compensation expense recognized should be $135,000 [15,000 × ($59 – $50)]. Because compensation expense of $46,667 ($24,000 + $22,667) has already been recognized in 2000 and 2001, the necessary journal entry in 2002 is as follows:

2002
Dec. 31   Compensation Expense ($135,000 – $46,667)................................   88,333
               Additional Paid-In Capital—Stock Options..............................   88,333

The Neff example illustrates why very few stock-based compensation plans in the United States are structured as performance-based plans. In the example, compensation expense in each year of the three-year vesting period was as follows:

2000................	$24,000
2001................	22,667
2002................	88,333

> **Caution!** Stock price changes after the grant date do *not* impact compensation expense under the fair value method. Under the intrinsic value method, stock price changes affect compensation expense for performance-based plans but not for fixed plans.

With a fixed stock option plan, total compensation expense for the vesting period is known as of the grant date (except for possible reductions stemming from option forfeitures). With Neff's performance-based plan, total compensation expense for the vesting period was not known until the end of the vesting period. Also, with the performance-based plan, Neff's compensation expense varied significantly among periods because of changes in the stock price and the forecasted level of the performance target. The intrinsic value method causes performance-based plans to yield more volatile amounts for compensation expense than do fixed option plans. Managers and investors have long shown a preference for smooth earnings. Consequently, the intrinsic value method has seriously hindered the adoption of performance-based stock option plans in the United States.

Accounting for Awards That Call for Cash Settlement

Neff Company's stock-based compensation plans discussed above stipulated that the compensation would be paid in the form of stock options. Because settlement of these stock options requires Neff to issue its own stock and does not require any transfer of assets, the stock options are considered to be equity instruments. When a stock-based compensation plan calls for a cash settlement or gives the employee the option of

---

35   *FASB Interpretation No. 28,* "Accounting for Stock Appreciation Rights and Other Variable Stock Option or Award Plans," Stamford, CT: Financial Accounting Standards Board, 1978.

choosing a cash settlement instead of receiving stock options, work by employees during the service period creates a liability for the firm because the firm is obligated to transfer assets (cash) in the future.

The accounting treatment for plans that call for settlement in cash is the same for both the intrinsic value and fair value methods. And the good news is that we don't need to learn anything new because the accounting is almost identical to that used for performance-based plans under the intrinsic value method. The reason is that a liability is created; therefore, the important accounting issue changes from measuring the value of options granted to estimating the amount of cash that will ultimately be paid out.

To illustrate the accounting for awards that call for settlement in cash, assume that Neff Company has decided that instead of granting its employees 10,000 stock options, it will grant an equal number of cash **stock appreciation rights (SARs)**. A cash SAR awards an employee a cash amount equal to the market value of the issuing firm's shares above a specified threshold price. Neff Company promises that after January 1, 2003, it will pay the exerciser of each cash SAR an amount equal to the excess of the share price on the exercise date over the $50 threshold price. The cash SARs vest beginning on January 1, 2003, only for the employees who stay with the company for the entire three-year vesting period. The cash SARs expire on December 31, 2003. From an employee's standpoint, this cash SAR plan is economically equivalent to the fixed option plan illustrated earlier in the chapter. However, from the standpoint of Neff's accounting treatment, the cash SAR plan is different because it creates a liability to transfer cash.

All journal entries to record compensation expense for 2000, 2001, and 2002 and for the redemption of the cash SARs on December 31, 2003, are given below. Remember that the accounting for plans requiring a cash settlement is the same for both the intrinsic value and fair value methods.

Assume the following information:

Neff share price:

January 1, 2000	$55
December 31, 2000	56
December 31, 2001	57
December 31, 2002	59
December 31, 2003	61

Just as with performance-based plans under the intrinsic value method, the forecast of the cash settlement amount is updated at the end of each period using current stock price information. This is true under both the intrinsic value and fair value methods.

As of December 31, 2000, because the stock price is $56, the best estimate of the amount of cash that will be transferred when the cash SARs are exercised is $60,000 [10,000 × ($56 – $50)]. The journal entry to recognize 2000 compensation expense using both the intrinsic value and fair value methods is as follows:

```
2000
Dec. 31   Compensation Expense ($60,000/3 years).....................................   20,000
                Cash SAR Payable ..................................................................           20,000
```

As of December 31, 2001, the stock price is $57 per share. The new estimate for total compensation expense for the three-year service period is $70,000 [10,000 × ($57 – $50)]. Because two-thirds of the service period has elapsed, aggregate compensation expense recognized should be $46,667 ($70,000 × ⅔). Because compensation expense of $20,000 was recognized in 2000, the necessary journal entry in 2001 is as follows:

```
2001
Dec. 31   Compensation Expense ($46,667 – $20,000).........................   26,667
                Cash SAR Payable ..................................................................           26,667
```

Except for the account titles, this catch-up adjustment is exactly like those illustrated previously.

Neff's stock price is $59 per share on December 31, 2002. Aggregate compensation expense for the three-year service period is $90,000 [10,000 × ($59 – $50)]. Because compensation expense of $46,667 ($20,000 + $26,667) has already been recognized in 2000 and 2001, the necessary journal entry in 2002 is as follows:

```
2002
Dec. 31  Compensation Expense ($90,000 – $46,667) ..........................    43,333
              Cash SAR Payable .....................................................              43,333
```

Between the time the cash SARs vest and the time they are exercised, the company's stock price can still move, affecting the ultimate amount of cash paid out for the cash SARs. The impact of these postvesting price movements on the cash SAR payable account are recognized as compensation expense in the year the price movements occur. The required entry in 2003, to reflect the increase in Neff's stock price to $61, is:

```
2003
Dec. 31  Compensation Expense [10,000 × ($61 – $59)] ..................    20,000
              Cash SAR Payable .....................................................              20,000
```

The entry to record the cash payments made to holders of the 10,000 cash SARs that vested on January 1, 2003, and were exercised on December 31, 2003, is as follows:

```
2003
Dec. 31  Cash SAR Payable ..........................................................   110,000
              Cash [10,000 × ($61 – $50)] .....................................             110,000
```

If the exercise period extended beyond 2003 and if cash SARs remained outstanding, an entry would be made at the end of each year to revise the estimated amount of the cash SAR liability. These revisions are recognized as part of compensation expense for the period.

Broad-Based Plans

Some employers grant employee stock options and employee stock purchase rights to substantially all employees. Common practice has been for companies to allow employees to purchase stock for as much as a 15% discount from the market price. Under APB Opinion No. 25, no compensation expense was recognized for these broad-based plans. Under FASB Statement No. 123, compensation expense is recognized if employees are allowed to purchase shares for more than a 5% discount from the market price. The rationale is that allowing employees to purchase stock for an excessive discount is just an alternative way to grant compensation.

REVIEW OF LEARNING OBJECTIVES

1 **Identify the rights associated with ownership of common and preferred stock.** Common stockholders are the true owners of the business. They are the first to lose their investment when a business does poorly, and they are the ones who get rich when a business does well. Common stockholders vote in the election of members of the board of directors.

Preferred stockholders usually cannot vote in director elections. Preferred stock dividends must be paid in full before any common stock dividends can be paid. Preferred stock can be cumulative, participating, convertible, callable, redeemable, or some combination of these.

Par values of common stocks are usually very low (less than $1). Par values of preferred stocks often approximate the issuance price.

2 **Record the issuance of stock for cash, on a subscription basis, and in exchange for non-cash assets or for services.** When stock is sold for cash, the amount of the proceeds is usually divided between par, or stated, value and additional paid-in capital.

When stock is sold on a subscription basis, any unpaid subscription amount (Stock Subscriptions Receivable) is reported as a subtraction from stockholders' equity.

When stock is issued in exchange for noncash assets or for services, the transaction is recorded using the fair market value of the assets or services or the fair market value of the stock, whichever is more objectively determinable.

3 **Use both the cost and par value methods to account for stock repurchases.** When capital stock is acquired and retired, the capital stock account is reduced, and retained earnings can be reduced for all or part of the excess over par value paid to reacquire the stock. Additional paid-in capital created at the issuance of the stock can also be reduced or eliminated when the stock is reacquired.

Treasury stock is stock reacquired but not immediately retired. When the par value method is used, the treasury shares are accounted for in a manner similar to a stock retirement. When the cost method is used, the entire cost to reacquire the treasury shares is shown in a contra equity account until the shares are reissued or retired.

4 **Account for the issuance of stock rights and stock warrants.** Stock rights are issued to existing shareholders to allow them to purchase sufficient shares to maintain their proportionate interest when new shares are issued. Only memorandum entries are needed to record the issuance of stock rights.

Stock warrants are issued in conjunction with other securities to make those other securities more attractive to investors. The proceeds of the security issuance are allocated between the security and a detachable stock warrant. No allocation is done for nondetachable warrants.

5 **Explain the difference between the intrinsic value and fair value methods, and use both in accounting for a fixed stock option plan.** With the intrinsic value method, total compensation expense for the option service period is equal to the number of options multiplied by the difference between the market price of the stock and the option exercise price as of the grant date. Usually, this results in no compensation expense.

With the fair value method, total compensation expense is the number of options multiplied by the fair value of each option as of the grant date. This expense is allocated over the service period.

The FASB recommends the fair value method, but most firms will probably continue to use the intrinsic value method. Firms that do so are required to disclose what net income would have been if they had used the fair value method.

6 **Distinguish between stock conversions that require a reduction in retained earnings**

and those that do not. When total paid-in capital (par value plus additional paid-in capital) associated with stock that is to be converted is less than the total par value of the postconversion shares, the retained earnings account is debited for the difference.

7 **List the factors that impact the retained earnings balance.** Retained earnings is reduced by the following.

- Some error corrections
- Some changes in accounting principle
- Net losses
- Cash dividends
- Stock dividends
- Treasury stock transactions
- Preferred stock conversions

Retained earnings is increased by the following.

- Some error corrections
- Some changes in accounting principle
- Net income
- Quasi-reorganizations

The retained earnings balance is often a constraint on the amount of cash dividends a firm can pay because of state incorporation law restrictions. In addition, a firm may voluntarily restrict the use of retained earnings.

8 **Properly record cash dividends, property dividends, small and large stock dividends, and stock splits.** A dividend payable is recorded on the dividend declaration date and is removed from the books when the dividend is distributed. When a property dividend is paid, a gain or loss is recorded on the declaration date to recognize the difference between the book value and fair value of the asset to be distributed as the property dividend.

A stock dividend is a distribution of additional shares to stockholders without receiving any cash in return. In essence, a stock dividend results in company ownership being divided into more pieces, with each stockholder owning a proportionately increased number of shares.

Stock dividends and stock splits are accounted for as follows:

- *Small stock dividend (less than 20–25%):* Retained Earnings is reduced by the market value of the new shares created.
- *Large stock dividend (more than 20–25%):* Retained Earnings and/or Additional Paid-In Capital is reduced by the par value of the new shares created.
- *Stock split:* No journal entry is made. A memorandum entry records the facts that the par value of each share is reduced and the number of outstanding shares is increased.

9 Explain the background of unrealized gains and losses recorded as direct equity adjustments, and list the major types of equity reserves found in foreign balance sheets. Unrealized gains and losses that bypass the income statement and are recognized as direct equity adjustments as part of accumulated other comprehensive income are as follows:

- *Foreign currency translation adjustment.* Changes in the equity of foreign subsidiaries resulting from foreign currency exchange rate fluctuations.
- *Minimum pension liability adjustment.* Additional pension expense that is recognized to make sure that the reported pension liability exceeds a minimum amount.
- *Unrealized gains and losses on available-for-sale securities.* Unrealized gains and losses from market value fluctuations of available-for-sale securities.

The equity sections of foreign balance sheets often include a number of equity reserves. These reserves are designed to carefully divide equity into the portion that is available for distribution to shareholders and the portion that is nondistributable. Some of these equity reserves are the capital redemption reserve, the asset revaluation reserve, and general and special reserves.

10 Prepare a statement of changes in stockholders' equity. A statement of changes in stockholders' equity outlines the changes during a given period in the different equity categories.

11 Eliminate a retained earnings deficit through a quasi-reorganization. A quasi-reorganization is used by a company that has reorganized itself after a period of financial difficulty. As part of a quasi-reorganization:

- Assets are written-down to reflect their fair market values.
- The par value of common stock is reduced, creating more additional paid-in capital.
- The additional paid-in capital of the firm is used to eliminate any retained earnings deficit.

After the quasi-reorganization, the retained earnings balance is dated to inform financial statement users about when the fresh start occurred.

12 Use both the intrinsic value and fair value methods to account for performance-based stock option plans and plans calling for a cash settlement.

Accounting for performance-based stock option plans:

- *Fair value method.* Total compensation expense for the service period is based on the number of options that ultimately vest multiplied by the fair value of the options on the grant date.
- *Intrinsic value method.* Total compensation expense is based on the number of options that vest multiplied by the difference between the market price of the stock and exercise price as of the date when both the number of options and the exercise price become measurable. This date is usually near the end of the service period. This approach differs significantly from the intrinsic value method treatment of fixed stock option plans.

Accounting for awards that call for cash settlement:

- *Both fair value and intrinsic value methods.* The obligation is recognized as a liability. The accounting is the same as for performance-based plans using the intrinsic value method.

KEY TERMS

Additional paid-in capital 609
Appropriated retained earnings 626
Available-for-sale securities 634
Board of directors 604
Business combination 612
Callable 608
Cash dividend 627
Convertible 608

Cost method 613
Cumulative preferred stock 607
Detachable warrants 618
Dividends in arrears 607
Equity reserve 635
Fair value method 620
Foreign currency translation
    adjustment 634

Fractional share warrants 630
Intrinsic value method 620
Large stock dividend 629
Liquidating dividend 632
Minimum pension liability
    adjustment 634
Noncumulative preferred stock 608
Nondetachable warrants 618

Nonreciprocal transfer to owners 628
Par value 606
Par (or stated) value method 614
Participating preferred stock 608
Pooling-of-interests method 612
Property dividend 627
Purchase method 612
Redeemable preferred stock 608
Small stock dividend 629

Stated value 606
Statement of changes in stockholders' equity 636/637
Stock options 617
Stock rights 617
Stock split 630
Stock warrants 617
Subscription 609
Treasury stock 613

Dated retained earnings 639
Fixed stock option plan 640
Performance-based stock option plan 640
Quasi-reorganization 638
Stock appreciation rights (SARs) 644

QUESTIONS

1. What basic rights are held by each common stockholder?
2. What is the historical significance of par value?
3. What rights of ownership are given up by preferred shareholders? What additional protections are enjoyed by preferred shareholders?
4. How is stock valued when it is issued in exchange for noncash assets or for services?
5. Why might a company purchase its own stock?
6. (a) What is the basic difference between the cost method and the par value method of accounting for treasury stock? (b) How will total stockholders' equity differ, if at all, under the two methods?
7. There is frequently a difference between the purchase price and the selling price of treasury stock. Why isn't this difference shown as a gain or a loss on the income statement?
8. Describe the difference in the accounting for detachable and nondetachable warrants.
9. What is the primary difference between the intrinsic value and fair value methods of accounting for stock-based compensation plans? Which method does the FASB recommend?
10. What types of disclosure are required in relation to stock-based compensation plans?
11. How are errors corrected when they are discovered in the current year? in a subsequent year?
12. How can retained earnings be restricted by law? In what other ways can retained earnings be restricted?
13. The following announcement appeared on the financial page of a newspaper:

> The Board of Directors of Benton Co., at its meeting on June 15, 2002, declared the regular quarterly dividend on outstanding common stock of $1.40 per share, payable on July 10, 2002, to the stockholders of record at the close of business June 30, 2002.

   (a) What is the purpose of each of the three dates given in the announcement?
   (b) When would the common stock of Benton Co. normally trade "ex-dividend"?

14. The directors of The Dress Shoppe are considering declaring either a stock dividend or a stock split. They have asked you to explain the difference between a stock dividend and a stock split, and the accounting for a small stock dividend versus a large stock dividend.
15. (a) What is a liquidating dividend? (b) Under what circumstances are such distributions made?
16. What three types of unrealized gains and losses are shown as direct equity adjustments (part of accumulated other comprehensive income), bypassing the income statement? Briefly explain each.
17. In accounting for the equity of foreign companies, what is the primary purpose of equity reserves?

18. (a) Why might a company seek a quasi-reorganization? (b) What are the steps in a quasi-reorganization?
19. Under the intrinsic value method, how does the accounting for a performance-based stock option plan differ from the accounting for a fixed stock option plan?
20. Under the intrinsic value method, how does the accounting for a performance-based stock option plan differ from the accounting for an award plan calling for cash settlements?

DISCUSSION CASES

CASE 11–1

SHOULD PAR VALUE DETERMINE THE AMOUNT OF CONTRIBUTED CAPITAL?

The Raton Company, in payment for services, issues 5,000 shares of common stock to persons organizing and promoting the company and another 20,000 shares in exchange for properties believed to have valuable mineral rights. The par value of the stock, $5 per share, is used in recording the consideration for the shares. Shortly after organization, the company decides to sell the properties and use the proceeds for another venture. The properties are sold for $265,000. What accounting issues are involved? How would you record the sale of properties and why?

CASE 11–2

STRATEGIC CONVERSION OF PREFERRED STOCK

Colter Corporation suspended dividend payments on all four classes of capital stock outstanding because of a downturn in the economy. The four classes of stock include: 7% preferred stock, cumulative, $50 par; 5% preferred stock, noncumulative, convertible, $35 par; 9% preferred stock, noncumulative, $80 par; and common stock. Fifteen thousand shares of each class of stock were outstanding. Dividends had been paid through 1999. Colter did not pay dividends in 2000 or 2001. In 2002, the economy improved and a proposal to pay a dividend of $1.50 per share of common stock was made.

You own 100 shares of the 5%, noncumulative, convertible preferred stock and have been thinking of converting those 100 shares to common stock at the existing conversion rate of 3 to 1 (3 shares of common for 1 share of preferred). The rate is scheduled to drop to 2 to 1 at the end of 2002. Because the price of common stock has been rising rapidly, you are trying to decide between retaining your preferred stock or converting to common stock before the price goes higher and the ratio is lowered.

Assuming there is no conversion of preferred stock, how much cash does Colter need to pay the proposed dividend? What are the merits of converting your stock at this time as opposed to waiting until after the dividend is paid and the conversion ratio decreases? Explain the issues involved.

CASE 11–3

SHOULD I THROW THE STOCK WARRANTS AWAY?

A stock warrant entitles the owner to buy a specified number of shares of stock at a specified price. Landon Davis owns 1,000 stock warrants. Each warrant entitles him to buy one share of Plum Street Company common stock for $50. The current market price of a share of Plum Street common is $40. Because the warrant price is higher than the current market price, Landon has decided that his warrants are worthless and is going to throw them away. Do the warrants have any value? How would you explain to Landon the factors that influence the value of a stock warrant?

CASE 11–4

WHICH KIND OF INCENTIVE PLAN WOULD YOU RECOMMEND?

Buzzyear Company is considering starting an employee incentive plan. One possibility is to make the plan a bonus plan in which employees receive bonuses based on the reported net income of the company. Another possibility is to give employees options to buy the company's stock. You are an expert in accounting and have been asked to evaluate these two types of plans, both in terms of the practical advantages and disadvantages of implementing each type of plan and also in terms of the impact on Buzzyear's reported net income.

CASE 11–5

TREASURY STOCK TRANSACTIONS—YOU CAN'T LOSE!

The following is adapted from an article appearing in *Forbes*:

> The board of HOSPITAL CORP. OF AMERICA authorized the buyback of 12 million of the firm's own shares at a total cost of $564 million. However, after the stock market crash of 1987, HCA's shares were trading at only 31 1/8. So, HCA was now out $190.5 million on its investment—right? Common sense

would answer yes, but beyond common sense lurks the logic of accounting. According to generally accepted accounting principles, HCA didn't lose a penny on the buyback. Call it a no-risk investment. In this era of stock market volatility, stock buybacks offer firms the opportunity to tell shareholders that they have a terrific investment—without ever having to own up to the bad news if it turns sour.

Consider the criticism in the paragraph above and evaluate the reasonableness of the accounting for treasury stock transactions.

SOURCE: Penelope Wang, "Losses? What Losses?" *Forbes*, February 8, 1988, p. 118.

CASE 11–6

HOW MUCH SHOULD OUR DIVIDEND BE?

Largo Corp. has paid quarterly dividends of $0.70 per share for the last 3 years and is trying to continue this tradition. Largo's balance sheet is as follows:

Largo Corp.
Balance Sheet
December 31, 2002

Assets		Liabilities	
Current assets:		Current liabilities:	
Cash	$ 50,000	Accounts payable	$ 520,000
Accounts receivable	450,000	Taxes payable	100,000
Inventory	1,200,000	Accrued liabilities	90,000
Total current assets	$1,700,000	Total current liabilities	$ 710,000
Investments	500,000	Bonds payable	1,500,000
Property, plant, and equipment (net)	1,600,000	Total liabilities	$2,210,000
		Stockholders' Equity	
		Common stock ($1 par, 69,000 shares outstanding)	$ 69,000
		Additional paid-in capital	621,000
		Retained earnings	900,000
		Total stockholders' equity	$1,590,000
Total assets	$3,800,000	Total liabilities and stockholders' equity	$3,800,000

Largo's net income in 2002 was $400,000. Should Largo continue its $0.70 per share quarterly dividend in the first quarter of 2003? Should Largo increase the cash dividend?

CASE 11–7

WHO GETS THE CASH DIVIDEND?

On March 23, 2002, the board of directors of Mycroft Company declared a quarterly cash dividend on its $1 par common stock of $0.50 per share, payable on May 10, 2002, to the shareholders of record on April 14, 2002. Before April 9, Mycroft's shares traded in the stock market "with dividend," meaning that the quoted stock price included the right to receive the dividend. After April 9, the shares traded "ex-dividend," meaning that the quoted price did not include the right to receive the dividend. Before April 9, Mycroft's shares were selling for $30 per share. What should happen to Mycroft's stock price on April 9, the ex-dividend date? What should happen to Mycroft's stock price on March 23, the dividend declaration date?

CASE 11–8

STOCK SPLIT OR STOCK DIVIDEND?

In early 2002, the $20 par common stock of Driftwood Construction Company was selling in the range of $100 to $130 per share, with 146,000 shares outstanding. On May 1, 2002, Driftwood's board of directors decided that, effective May 10, 2002, Driftwood stock would be split 2 for 1. Before making the public announcement, the board had to decide whether to do the split as a "true" stock split and reduce the par value per share to $10, or whether to accomplish the split through a 100% stock dividend.

Why does Driftwood's board of directors want to double the number of shares outstanding? What factors should Driftwood's board consider in deciding between a true 2-for-1 split and a 100% stock dividend?

CASE 11–9

OUT OF SIGHT, OUT OF MIND

In some countries, payments of bonuses to directors may be deducted directly from retained earnings rather than being charged to income of the year. Does this treatment make it more or less likely that bonuses will be paid to directors? Can accounting standards be neutral in their impact on economic decision making by companies? Should they be neutral?

EXERCISES

EXERCISE 11–10

ISSUANCE OF COMMON STOCK

The Verdero Company is authorized to issue 100,000 shares of $2 par value common stock. Verdero has the following transactions.

(a) Issued 20,000 shares at $30 per share; received cash.
(b) Issued 250 shares to attorneys for services in securing the corporate charter and for preliminary legal costs of organizing the corporation. The value of the services was $9,000.
(c) Issued 300 shares, valued objectively at $10,000, to the employees instead of paying them cash wages.
(d) Issued 12,500 shares of stock in exchange for a building valued at $295,000 and land valued at $80,000. (The building was originally acquired by the investor for $250,000 and has $100,000 of accumulated depreciation; the land was originally acquired for $30,000.)
(e) Received cash for 6,500 shares of stock sold at $38 per share.
(f) Issued 4,000 shares at $45 per share; received cash.

Make the journal entries necessary for Verdero Company to record the transactions above.

EXERCISE 11–11

DIVIDENDS—DIFFERENT CLASSES OF STOCK

Sun Spot Inc. began operations on June 30, 2000, and issued 40,000 shares of $1 par common stock on that date. On December 31, 2000, Sun Spot declared and paid $25,600 in dividends. After a vote of the board of directors, Sun Spot issued 24,000 shares of 6% cumulative, $12 par, preferred stock on January 1, 2002. On December 31, 2002, Sun Spot declared and paid $15,500 in dividends and again on December 31, 2003, Sun Spot declared and paid $32,660 in dividends. Determine the amount of dividends to be distributed to each class of stock for each of Sun Spot's dividend payments.

EXERCISE 11–12

PREFERRED STOCK—CUMULATIVE AND NONCUMULATIVE

The Anderson Company paid dividends at the end of each year as follows: 2000, $150,000; 2001, $240,000; 2002, $560,000. Determine the amount of dividends per share paid on common and preferred stock for each year, assuming independent capital structures as follows:

(a) 300,000 shares of no-par common; 10,000 shares of $100 par, 9% noncumulative preferred.

(b) 250,000 shares of no-par common; 20,000 shares of $100 par, 9% noncumulative preferred.

(c) 250,000 shares of no-par common; 20,000 shares of $100 par, 9% cumulative preferred.

(d) 250,000 shares of $1 par common; 30,000 shares of $100 par, 9% cumulative preferred.

EXERCISE 11–13

ISSUANCE OF CAPITAL STOCK WITH SUBSCRIPTIONS

The Timpview Company was incorporated on January 1, 2002, with the following authorized capitalization.

- 20,000 shares of common stock, stated value $5 per share
- 5,000 shares of 7% cumulative preferred stock, par value $15 per share

Give the entries required for each of the following transactions.

(a) Issued 12,000 shares of common stock for a total of $672,000 and 3,000 shares of preferred stock at $20 per share.

(b) Subscriptions were received for 2,500 shares of common stock at a price of $52. A 30% down payment is received.

(c) Collected the remaining amount owed on the stock subscriptions and issued the stock.

(d) The remaining authorized shares of common stock are sold at $61.00 per share.

EXERCISE 11–14

ACQUISITION AND RETIREMENT OF STOCK

The Steinbeck Company reported the following balances related to common stock as of December 31, 2001.

Common stock, $2 par, 100,000 shares issued and outstanding	$ 200,000
Paid-in capital in excess of par	1,900,000

The company purchased and immediately retired 5,000 shares at $26 on August 1, 2002, and 12,000 shares at $18 on December 31, 2002. Give the entries to record the acquisition and retirement of the common stock. (Assume all shares were originally sold at the same price.)

EXERCISE 11–15

TREASURY STOCK: PAR VALUE AND COST METHODS

The stockholders' equity of the Thomas Company as of December 31, 2001, was as follows:

Common stock, $1 par, authorized 275,000 shares;	
240,000 shares issued and outstanding	$ 240,000
Paid-in capital in excess of par	3,840,000
Retained earnings	900,000

On June 1, 2002, Thomas reacquired 15,000 shares of its common stock at $16. The following transactions occurred in 2002 with regard to these shares.

July 1   Sold 5,000 shares at $20.
Aug. 1   Sold 7,000 shares at $14.
Sept. 1   Retired 1,000 shares.

1. Using the cost method to account for treasury stock:
   (a) Prepare the journal entries to record all treasury stock transactions in 2002.
   (b) Prepare the stockholders' equity section of the balance sheet at December 31, 2002, assuming retained earnings of $1,005,000 (before the effects of treasury stock transactions).

2. Using the par value method to account for treasury stock:
   (a) Prepare the journal entries to record all treasury stock transactions in 2002.
   (b) Prepare the stockholders' equity section of the balance sheet at December 31, 2002, assuming retained earnings of $1,005,000 (before the effects of treasury stock transactions).

EXERCISE 11–16

STOCK RIGHTS

In 2002, Calton Inc. had 100,000 shares of $1.50 par value common stock outstanding. Calton issued 100,000 stock rights. Five rights, plus $50 in cash, are required to purchase one new share of Calton common stock. On the date the rights were issued, Calton common stock was selling for $55 per share.

What entries must Calton make to record the issuance of the stock rights?

EXERCISE 11–17

ACCOUNTING FOR STOCK WARRANTS

The Western Company wants to raise additional equity capital. After analysis of the available options, the company decides to issue 1,000 shares of $20 par preferred stock with detachable warrants. The package of the stock and warrants sells for $90. The warrants enable the holder to purchase 1,000 shares of $2 par common stock at $30 per share. Immediately following the issuance of the stock, the stock warrants are selling at $9 per share. The market value of the preferred stock without the warrants is $85.

1. Prepare a journal entry for Western Company to record the issuance of the preferred stock and the attached warrants.
2. Assuming that all the warrants are exercised, prepare a journal entry for Western to record the exercise of the warrants.
3. Assuming that only 70% of the warrants are exercised, prepare the journal entries for Western to record the exercise and expiration of the warrants.

EXERCISE 11–18

FIXED STOCK OPTIONS—INTRINSIC AND FAIR VALUE METHODS

On January 1, 2001, the Layton Hardware Company established a fixed stock option plan for its senior employees. A total of 90,000 options were granted that permit employees to purchase 90,000 shares of $2 par common stock at $48 per share. Each option had a fair value of $7 on the grant date. Options are exercisable beginning on January 1, 2004, and can be exercised anytime during 2004. The market price for Layton common stock on January 1, 2001, was $50.

Assume that all options were exercised on December 31, 2004. Prepare all entries required for the years 2001–2004 under the:

1. Fair value method
2. Intrinsic value method

EXERCISE 11–19

ACCOUNTING FOR STOCK OPTIONS—REQUIRED DISCLOSURE

Refer to the information in Exercise 11–18. Layton's income for 2001, before subtracting any compensation expense associated with the stock option plan, is $500,000. Layton is required to make supplemental note disclosure about its stock option plan. Prepare the required note for 2001 under the:

1. Fair value method
2. Intrinsic value method

EXERCISE 11–20

CONVERTIBLE PREFERRED STOCK

Stockholders' equity for the Yuri Co. on December 31 was as follows:

Preferred stock, $15 par, 30,000 shares issued and outstanding	$ 450,000
Paid-in capital in excess of par—preferred stock	90,000
Common stock, $10 par, 150,000 shares issued and outstanding	1,500,000
Paid-in capital in excess of par—common stock	750,000
Retained earnings	1,450,000

Preferred stock is convertible into common stock.

Give the entry made on Yuri Co.'s books assuming 4,000 shares of preferred are converted under each assumption listed:

1. Preferred shares are convertible into common on a share-for-share basis.
2. Each share of preferred stock is convertible into 4 shares of common.
3. Each share of preferred stock is convertible into 1.5 shares of common.

EXERCISE 11-21

REPORTING ERRORS FROM PREVIOUS PERIODS

Endicott Company's December 31, 2001, balance sheet reported retained earnings of $86,500, and net income of $124,000 was reported in the 2001 income statement. While preparing financial statements for the year ended December 31, 2002, Tom Dryden, accountant for Endicott Company, discovered that net income for 2001 had been overstated by $36,000 due to an error in recording depreciation expense for 2001. Net income for 2002 was $106,000, and dividends of $30,000 were declared and paid in 2002.

1. What effect, if any, would the $36,000 error made in 2001 have on the company's 2002 financial statements?
2. Compute the amount of retained earnings to be reported in Endicott Company's December 31, 2002, balance sheet.

EXERCISE 11-22

CASH DIVIDEND COMPUTATIONS

Consistent Company has been paying regular quarterly dividends of $1.50 and wants to pay the same amount in the third quarter of 2002. Given the following information, (1) what is the total amount that Consistent will have to pay in dividends in the third quarter in order to pay $1.50 per share, and (2) what is the total amount of dividends to be distributed during the year assuming no equity transactions occur after June 30?

2002
Jan.   1   Shares outstanding, 800,000; $2 par (1,500,000 shares authorized).
Feb. 15   Issued 50,000 new shares at $10.50.
Mar. 31   Paid quarterly dividends of $1.50 per share.
May   12 $1,000,000 of $1,000 bonds were converted to common stock at the rate of 100 shares of stock per $1,000 bond.
June 15   Issued an 11% stock dividend.
       30   Paid quarterly dividends of $1.50 per share.

EXERCISE 11-23

PROPERTY DIVIDENDS

Bradley Company distributed the following dividends to its stockholders.

(a) 400,000 shares of Shell Corporation stock, carrying value of investment, $1,500,000; fair market value, $2,700,000.
(b) 230,000 shares of Evans Company stock, a closely held corporation. The shares were purchased by Bradley 3 years ago at $5.60 per share, but no current market price is available.

Give the journal entries to account for the declaration and the payment of the dividends.

EXERCISE 11-24

Small FMV Big cost

STOCK DIVIDENDS

The balance sheet of the Carmen Corporation shows the following.

Common stock, $1 stated value, 80,000 shares issued and outstanding	$ 80,000
Paid-in capital in excess of stated value	1,120,000
Retained earnings	350,000

A 25% stock dividend is declared, with the board of directors authorizing a transfer from Retained Earnings to Common Stock at the stated value of the shares.

1. Give entries to record the declaration and issuance of the stock dividend.
2. What was the effect of the issuance of the stock dividend on the ownership equity of each stockholder in the corporation?
3. Give entries to record the declaration and issuance of the dividend if the board of directors had elected to declare a 15% stock dividend instead of 25%. The market value of the stock is $10 per share after the 15% stock dividend is issued.

EXERCISE 11–25

STOCK DIVIDENDS AND STOCK SPLITS

The capital accounts for Shop Right Market on June 30, 2002, are as follows:

Common stock, $5 par, 40,000 shares issued and outstanding	$ 200,000
Paid-in capital in excess of par	835,000
Retained earnings	2,160,000

Shares of the company's stock are selling at this time at $22. What entries would you make in each of the following cases?

(a) A 10% stock dividend is declared and issued.

(b) A 50% stock dividend is declared and issued.

(c) A 2-for-1 stock split is declared and issued.

EXERCISE 11–26

FRACTIONAL SHARE WARRANTS

Groton Company has 500,000 shares of $1 par value common stock outstanding. In declaring and distributing a 10% stock dividend, Groton initially issued only 46,000 new shares; the other stock dividend shares were not issued because some investors did not own Groton shares in even multiples of 10. To these stockholders, Groton issued fractional share warrants. Prepare all journal entries necessary to record the declaration and distribution of the stock dividend assuming that 90% of the fractional share warrants were ultimately turned in for shares. The market price of the shares is $25 per share after the 10% stock dividend is issued.

EXERCISE 11–27

LIQUIDATING DIVIDEND

Van Etten Company declared and paid a cash dividend of $3.25 per share on its $1 par common stock. Van Etten has 100,000 shares of common stock outstanding and total paid-in capital from common stock of $800,000. As part of the dividend announcement, Van Etten stated that retained earnings served as the basis for only $0.50 per share of the dividend; investors should consider the remainder to be a return of investment. Prepare the journal entries necessary on Van Etten's books to record the declaration and distribution of this dividend.

EXERCISE 11–28

CORRECTING THE RETAINED EARNINGS ACCOUNT

The retained earnings account for Gotfried Corp. shows the following debits and credits. Give all entries required to correct the account. What is the corrected amount of retained earnings?

Account: RETAINED EARNINGS

Date		Item	Debit	Credit	Balance Debit	Balance Credit
Jan.	1	Balance				263,200
(a)		Loss from fire	2,625			260,575
(b)		Write-off of goodwill	26,250			234,325
(c)		Stock dividend	70,000			164,325
(d)		Loss on sale of equipment	24,150			140,175
(e)		Officers' compensation related to income of prior periods—accrual overlooked	162,750		22,575	
(f)		Loss on retirement of preferred shares at more than issuance price	35,000		57,575	
(g)		Paid-in capital in excess of par		64,750		7,175
(h)		Stock subscription defaults		4,235		11,410
(i)		Gain on retirement of preferred stock at less than issuance price		12,950		24,360
(j)		Gain on early retirement of bonds at less than book value		7,525		31,885
(k)		Gain on life insurance policy settlement		9,500		41,385
(l)		Correction of prior-period error		25,025		66,410

EXERCISE 11–29

EQUITY ADJUSTMENTS

The data below are for Bypass Company.

Contributed capital and retained earnings	$700,000
Foreign currency translation adjustment	50,000
Minimum pension liability adjustment	95,000
Unrealized loss on available-for-sale securities	68,000

(Note: The currencies in the countries where Bypass has foreign subsidiaries have strengthened relative to the U.S. dollar.)

Compute total stockholders' equity for Bypass Company.

EXERCISE 11–30

ANALYSIS OF OWNERS' EQUITY

From the following information, reconstruct the journal entries that were made by the Rivers Corporation during 2002.

	Dec. 31, 2002		Dec. 31, 2001	
	Amount	**Shares**	**Amount**	**Shares**
Common stock	$175,000	7,000	$150,000	6,000
Paid-in capital in excess of par	54,250	—	36,000	—
Paid-in capital from treasury stock	1,000	200	—	—
Retained earnings	76,500*	—	49,000	—
Treasury stock	15,000	300	—	—

*Includes net income for 2002 of $40,000. There were no dividends. Assume that revenues and expenses were closed to a temporary account, Income Summary. Use this account to complete the closing process. There were 2,500 shares of common stock (issued when the company was formed) purchased at the beginning of 2002 and retired later in the year. The cost method is used to record treasury stock transactions.

EXERCISE 11–31

REPORTING STOCKHOLDERS' EQUITY

Kenny Co. began operations on January 1, 2001, by issuing at $15 per share one-half of the 950,000 shares of $1 par value common stock that had been authorized for sale. In addition, Kenny has 500,000 shares of $5 par value, 6% preferred shares authorized. During 2001, Kenny had $1,025,000 of net income and declared $237,500 of dividends.

During 2002, Kenny had the following transactions:

Jan.	10	Issued an additional 100,000 shares of common stock for $17 per share.
Apr.	1	Issued 150,000 shares of the preferred stock for $8 per share.
July	19	Authorized the purchase of a custom-made machine to be delivered in January 2003. Kenny restricted $295,000 of retained earnings for the purchase of the machine.
Oct.	23	Sold an additional 50,000 shares of the preferred stock for $9 per share.
Dec.	31	Reported $1,215,000 of net income and declared a dividend of $635,000 to stockholders of record on January 15, 2003, to be paid on February 1, 2003.

1. Prepare the stockholders' equity section of Kenny's balance sheet for December 31, 2001.
2. Prepare a statement of changes in stockholders' equity for 2002.
3. Prepare the stockholders' equity section of Kenny's balance sheet for December 31, 2002.

EXERCISE 11–32

QUASI-REORGANIZATION

Hard Luck Corporation has incurred losses from operations for many years. At the recommendation of the newly hired president, the board of directors voted to implement a quasi-reorganization, subject to stockholders' approval. Immediately prior to the quasi-reorganization, on June 30, 2002, Hard Luck's balance sheet was as follows:

Assets

Current assets	$ 275,000
Property, plant, and equipment (net)	675,000
Other assets	100,000
Total assets	$1,050,000

Liabilities & Stockholders' Equity

Total liabilities	$ 300,000
Common stock, $10 par	800,000
Paid-in capital in excess of par	150,000
Retained earnings	(200,000)
Total liabilities & stockholders' equity	$1,050,000

The stockholders approved the quasi-reorganization effective July 1, 2002, to be accomplished by a reduction in property, plant, and equipment (net) of $175,000, a reduction in other assets of $75,000, and a reduction in par value from $10 to $5.

1. Prepare the journal entries to record the quasi-reorganization on July 1, 2002.
2. Prepare a new balance sheet after the quasi-reorganization.

EXERCISE 11–33

ACCOUNTING FOR A PERFORMANCE-BASED STOCK OPTION PLAN

The Rhiener Corporation initiated a performance-based employee stock option plan on January 1, 2001. The performance base for the plan is net sales in the year 2003. The plan provides for stock options to be awarded to the employees as a group on the following basis:

Level	Net Sales Range	Options Granted
1	< $250,000	10,000
2	$250,000–$499,999	20,000
3	$500,000–$1,000,000	30,000
4	> $1,000,000	40,000

The options become exercisable on January 1, 2004. The option exercise price is $20 per share. On January 1, 2001, each option had a fair value of $9. The market prices of Rhiener stock on selected dates in 2001–2003 were as follows:

January 1, 2001	$25
December 31, 2001	30
December 31, 2002	35
December 31, 2003	32

Year 2003 sales estimates as of selected dates were as follows:

January 1, 2001	$400,000
December 31, 2001	450,000
December 31, 2002	550,000

Actual sales for 2003 were $700,000. Calculate the compensation expense Rhiener should report for the years 2001, 2002, and 2003 related to the stock option plan under the:

1. Fair value method
2. Intrinsic value method

EXERCISE 11–34

STOCK APPRECIATION RIGHTS

San Juan Corporation established a stock option plan that provides for cash payments to employees based on the appreciation of stock prices from an established option price. The plan was instituted on January 1, 2002, and provides benefits to employees who work for the succeeding 3 years. Cash payments to employees will be made on January 1, 2005, and will equal the excess of the stock price over the option price on that date. In total, 10,000 of these cash stock appreciation rights (SARs) were granted to employees.

The option price established for the stock is $10 per share. The market price of San Juan stock on selected dates in 2002–2004 was as follows:

January 1, 2002	$15
December 31, 2002	16
December 31, 2003	20
December 31, 2004	18

1. Prepare the journal entries on San Juan's books for the years 2002, 2003, 2004, and 2005 related to this plan. Use the intrinsic value method.
2. How would the entries differ if the fair value method were used?

PROBLEMS

PROBLEM 11–35

JOURNALIZING STOCK TRANSACTIONS

Vicars Company began operations on January 1. Authorized were 20,000 shares of $1 par value common stock and 4,000 shares of 10%, $100 par value convertible preferred stock. The following transactions involving stockholders' equity occurred during the first year of operations.

Jan. 1   Issued 500 shares of common stock to the corporation promoters in exchange for property valued at $17,000 and services valued at $7,000. The property had cost the promoters $9,000 3 years before and was carried on the promoters' books at $5,000.

Feb. 23   Issued 1,000 shares of convertible preferred stock with a par value of $100 per share. Each share can be converted to 5 shares of common stock. The stock was issued at a price of $150 per share, and the company paid $7,500 to an agent for selling the shares.

Mar. 10   Sold 3,000 shares of the common stock for $39 per share. Issue costs were $2,500.

Apr. 10   4,000 shares of common stock were sold under stock subscriptions at $45 per share. No shares are issued until a subscription contract is paid in full. No cash was received.

July 14   Exchanged 700 shares of common stock and 140 shares of preferred stock for a building with a fair market value of $51,000. The building was originally purchased for $38,000 by the investors and has a book value of $22,000. In addition, 600 shares of common stock were sold for $24,000 in cash.

Aug. 3   Received payments in full for half of the stock subscriptions and payments on account on the rest of the subscriptions. Total cash received was $140,000. Shares of stock were issued for the subscriptions paid in full.

Dec. 1   Declared a cash dividend of $10 per share on preferred stock, payable on December 31 to stockholders of record on December 15, and a $2-per-share cash dividend on common stock, payable on January 5 of the following year to stockholders of record on December 15. (No dividends are paid on unissued subscribed stock.)

     31   Paid the preferred stock dividend

     31   Received notice from holders of stock subscriptions for 800 shares that they would not pay further on the subscriptions because the price of the stock

had fallen to $25 per share. The amount still due on those contracts was $30,000. Amounts previously paid on the contracts are forfeited according to the agreements.

Net income for the first year of operations was $60,000. Assume that revenues and expenses were closed to a temporary account, Income Summary. Use this account to complete the closing process.

Instructions:
1. Prepare journal entries to record the preceding transactions on Vicars' books.
2. Prepare the stockholders' equity section of the balance sheet at December 31 for Vicars.

PROBLEM 11–36

STOCKHOLDERS' EQUITY TRANSACTIONS AND BALANCE SHEET PRESENTATION

The Pacific Basin Corporation was organized on September 1, 2002, with authorized capital stock of 200,000 shares of 9% cumulative preferred stock with a $40 par value and 1,000,000 shares of no-par common stock with a $3 stated value. During the balance of the year, the following transactions relating to capital stock were completed:

Oct. 1   Subscriptions were received for 300,000 shares of common stock at $42, payable $22 down and the balance in 2 equal installments due November 1 and December 1. On the same date, 16,500 shares of common stock were issued to Jan Smoot in exchange for her business. Assets transferred to the corporation were valued as follows: land, $210,000; buildings, $250,000; equipment, $50,000; merchandise, $110,000. Liabilities of the business assumed by the corporation were: mortgage payable, $41,000; accounts payable, $11,000; accrued interest on mortgage, $550. The fair value of the net assets is considered to be a reliable reflection of the value of the business; no goodwill is recognized.

    3   Subscriptions were received for 120,000 shares of preferred stock at $45, payable $15 down and the balance in 2 equal installments due November 1 and December 1.

Nov. 1   Amounts due on this date were collected from all common and preferred stock subscribers.

    12   Subscriptions were received for 480,000 shares of common stock at $44, payable $22 down and the balance in 2 equal installments due December 1 and January 1.

Dec. 1   Amounts due on this date were collected from all common stock and preferred stock subscribers, and stock fully paid for was issued.

Instructions:
1. Prepare journal entries to record the foregoing transactions.
2. Prepare the contributed capital section of stockholders' equity for the corporation as of December 31, including any equity offsets.

PROBLEM 11–37

RECONSTRUCTION OF EQUITY TRANSACTIONS

The Manti Company had the following account balances on its balance sheet at December 31, 2002, the end of its first year of operations. All stock was issued on a subscription basis.

Common stock subscriptions receivable	$150,000
Common stock, $1 par	3,000
Common stock subscribed	9,000
Paid-in capital in excess of par—common	348,000
8% preferred stock, $100 par	120,000
Paid-in capital in excess of par—8% preferred	60,000
10% preferred stock, $50 par	25,000
Retained earnings	10,000

The reported net income for 2002 was $55,000. Assume that revenues and expenses were closed to a temporary account, Income Summary. Use this account to complete the closing process.

Instructions: From the data given, reconstruct in summary form the journal entries to record all transactions involving the company's stockholders. Indicate the amount of dividends distributed on each class of stock.

PROBLEM 11–38

COMPREHENSIVE ANALYSIS AND REPORTING OF STOCKHOLDERS' EQUITY
The Lasser Company has 2 classes of capital stock outstanding: 9%, $20 par preferred and $1 par common. During the fiscal year ended November 30, 2002, the company was active in transactions affecting the stockholders' equity. The following summarizes these transactions:

Type of Transaction	Number of Shares	Price per Share
(a) Issue of preferred stock	10,000	$28
(b) Issue of common stock	35,000	70
(c) Reacquisition and retirement of preferred stock	2,000	30
(d) Purchase of treasury stock—common (reported at cost)	5,000	80
(e) Stock split—common (par value reduced to $0.50)	2 for 1	
(f) Reissuance of treasury stock—common (after stock split)	5,000	52

Balances of the accounts in the stockholders' equity section of the November 30, 2001, balance sheet were:

Preferred stock, 50,000 shares	$1,000,000
Common stock, 100,000 shares	100,000
Paid-in capital in excess of par—preferred	400,000
Paid-in capital in excess of par—common	8,100,000
Retained earnings	550,000

Dividends were paid at the end of the fiscal year on the common stock at $1.20 per share and on the preferred stock at the preferred rate. Net income for the year was $850,000.

Instructions: Based on the preceding data, prepare the stockholders' equity section of the balance sheet as of November 30, 2002. (Note: A work sheet beginning with November 30, 2001, balances showing transactions for the current year will facilitate the preparation of this section of the balance sheet.)

PROBLEM 11–39

ACCOUNTING FOR VARIOUS CAPITAL STOCK TRANSACTIONS
The stockholders' equity section of Webster Inc. showed the following data on December 31, 2001: common stock, $3 par, 300,000 shares authorized, 250,000 shares issued and outstanding, $750,000; paid-in capital in excess of par, $7,050,000; additional paid-in capital—stock options, $150,000; retained earnings, $480,000. The stock options were granted to key executives and provided them the right to acquire 30,000 shares of common stock at $35 per share. The stock was selling at $40 at the time the options were granted, and the company uses the intrinsic value method.

The following transactions occurred during 2002.

Mar. 31 Key executives exercised 4,500 options outstanding at December 31, 2001. The market price per share was $44 at this time.

Apr. 1 The company issued bonds of $2,000,000 at par, giving each $1,000 bond a detachable warrant enabling the holder to purchase 2 shares of stock at $40 for a 1-year period. Market values immediately following issuance of the bonds were: $4 per warrant and $998 per $1,000 bond without the warrant.

June 30   The company issued rights to stockholders (1 right on each share, exercisable within a 30-day period) permitting holders to acquire 1 share at $40 with every 10 rights submitted. Shares were selling for $43 at this time. All but 6,000 rights were exercised on July 30, and the additional stock was issued.

Sept. 30   All warrants issued with the bonds on April 1 were exercised.

Nov. 30   The market price per share dropped to $33 and options came due. Because the market price was below the option price, no remaining options were exercised.

Instructions:

1. Give entries to record the foregoing transactions.
2. Prepare the stockholders' equity section of the balance sheet as of December 31, 2002 (assume net income of $210,000 for 2002).

PROBLEM 11–40

ACCOUNTING FOR VARIOUS CAPITAL STOCK TRANSACTIONS

Pineview Co., organized on June 1, 2001, was authorized to issue stock as follows:

- 80,000 shares of preferred 9% stock, convertible, $100 par
- 250,000 shares of common stock, $2.50 stated value

During the remainder of the Pineview Co.'s fiscal year ended May 31, 2002, the following transactions were completed in the order given.

(a) 30,000 shares of preferred stock were subscribed for at $105, and 90,000 shares of common stock were subscribed for at $26. Both subscriptions were payable 30% upon subscription, the balance in one payment.

(b) The second subscription payment was received, except one subscriber for 6,000 shares of common stock defaulted on payment. The full amount paid by this subscriber was returned, and all the fully paid stock was issued.

(c) 15,000 shares of common stock were reacquired by purchase at $28. (Treasury stock is recorded at cost.)

(d) Each share of preferred stock was converted into 4 shares of common stock.

(e) The treasury stock was exchanged for machinery with a fair market value of $430,000.

(f) There was a 2-for-1 stock split, and the stated value of the new common stock is $1.25.

(g) Net income was $83,000. Assume that revenues and expenses have been closed to a temporary account, Income Summary.

Instructions:

1. Give the journal entries to record the foregoing transactions. (For net income, give the entry to close the income summary account to Retained Earnings.)
2. Prepare the stockholders' equity section as of May 31, 2002.

PROBLEM 11–41

ISSUANCE, REPURCHASE, AND RESALE OF CAPITAL STOCK

Tucker Company had the following transactions occur during 2002.

(a) Issued 8,000 shares of common stock to the founders for land valued at $450,000. Par value of the common stock is $1 per share.

(b) Issued 5,000 shares of $100 par preferred stock for cash at $110.

(c) Sold 1,000 shares of common stock to the company president for $60 per share.

(d) Purchased 400 shares of outstanding preferred stock issued in (b) for cash at par.

(e) Purchased 500 shares of the outstanding common stock issued in (a) for $55 per share.

(f) Reissued 150 shares of repurchased preferred stock at $102.

(g) Reissued 300 shares of reacquired common stock for $58 per share.

(h) Repurchased 100 shares of the common stock sold in (g) for $53 per share. These same 100 shares were later reissued for $50 per share.

Instructions:

1. Prepare the necessary entries to record the preceding transactions involving Tucker preferred stock. Assume that the par value method is used for recording treasury stock.
2. Prepare the necessary entries for the common stock transactions assuming that the cost method is used for recording treasury stock.

PROBLEM 11–42

TREASURY STOCK TRANSACTIONS

Transactions that affected Barter Company's stockholders' equity during 2002, the first year of operations, are given below.

(a) Issued 30,000 shares of 9% preferred stock, $20 par, at $26.
(b) Issued 50,000 shares of $3 par common stock at $33.
(c) Purchased and immediately retired 4,000 shares of preferred stock at $28.
(d) Purchased 6,000 shares of its own common stock at $35.
(e) Reissued 1,000 shares of treasury stock at $37.

No dividends were declared in 2002, and net income for 2002 was $185,000.

Instructions:

1. Record each of the transactions. Assume treasury stock acquisitions are recorded at cost.
2. Prepare the stockholders' equity section of the balance sheet at December 31, 2002.

PROBLEM 11–43

ACCOUNTING FOR STOCK OPTIONS

The board of directors of the Mellencamp Company adopted a fixed stock option plan to supplement the salaries of certain executives of the company. Options to buy common stock were granted as follows:

Date	Employee	Number of Shares	Exercise Price	Price of Shares at Date of Grant	Option Value at Date of Grant
Jan. 1, 1999	Q. L. Peck	75,000	$20	$21	$7
Jan. 1, 2000	A. G. Byrd	50,000	25	27	8
Jan. 1, 2001	K. C. Nelson	20,000	35	38	9

Options are nontransferable and can be exercised beginning 3 years after date of grant, providing the executive is still in the employ of the company. Stock options were exercised as follows:

Date	Employee	Number of Shares	Price of Shares at Date of Exercise
Dec. 31, 2002	Q. L. Peck	75,000	$45
Dec. 31, 2003	A. G. Byrd	50,000	36
Dec. 31, 2004	K. C. Nelson	20,000	38

Stock of the company has a $1 par value. The accounting period for the company is the calendar year.

Instructions:

1. Give all entries that would be made on the books of Mellencamp relative to the stock option plan for the period 1999 to 2004 inclusive. Use the intrinsic value method.

2. Repeat (1) using the fair value method.
3. Assume Mellencamp uses the intrinsic value method. Prepare the required note disclosure relative to the stock option plan for the year 2001 and for the year 2003.

PROBLEM 11–44

ANALYSIS OF STOCK TRANSACTIONS

You have been asked to audit the Greystone Company. During the course of your audit, you are asked to prepare comparative data from the company's inception to the present. You have determined the following.

(a) Greystone Company's charter became effective on January 2, 1998, when 2,000 shares of no-par common and 1,000 shares of 7% cumulative, nonparticipating, preferred stock were issued. The no-par common stock had no stated value and was sold at $120 per share, and the preferred stock was sold at its par value of $100 per share.

(b) Greystone was unable to pay preferred dividends at the end of its first year. The owners of the preferred stock agreed to accept 2 shares of common stock for every 50 shares of preferred stock owned in discharge of the preferred dividends due on December 31, 1998. The shares were issued on January 2, 1999. The fair market value was $100 per share for common on the date of issue.

(c) Greystone Company acquired all the outstanding stock of Booth Corporation on May 1, 2000, in exchange for 1,000 shares of Greystone common stock.

(d) Greystone split its common stock 3 for 2 on January 1, 2001, and 2 for 1 on January 1, 2002.

(e) Greystone offered to convert 20% of the preferred stock to common stock on the basis of 2 shares of common for 1 share of preferred. The offer was accepted, and the conversion was made on July 1, 2002.

(f) No cash dividends were declared on common stock until December 31, 2000. Cash dividends per share of common stock were declared as follows:

	June 30	Dec. 31
2000	—	$3.19
2001	$1.75	2.75
2002	1.25	1.25

Instructions: Compute the following.

1. The number of shares of each class of stock outstanding on the last day of each year from 1998 through 2002.
2. Total cash dividends applicable to common stock for each year from 2000 through 2002.

PROBLEM 11–45

ACCOUNTING FOR STOCK TRANSACTIONS

Morris Corporation is publicly owned, and its shares are traded on a national stock exchange. Morris has 16,000 shares of $2 stated value common stock authorized. Only 75% of these shares have been issued, and of the shares issued, only 11,000 are outstanding. On December 31, 2001, the stockholders' equity section revealed that the balance in Paid-In Capital in Excess of Stated Value was $416,000, and the retained earnings balance was $110,000. Treasury stock was purchased at an average cost of $37.50 per share.

During 2002, Morris had the following transactions:

Jan. 15 Morris issued, at $55 per share, 800 shares of $50 par, 5% cumulative preferred stock; 2,000 shares are authorized.

Feb. 1 Morris sold 1,500 shares of newly issued $2 stated value common stock at $42 per share.

Mar. 15 Morris declared a cash dividend on common stock of $0.15 per share, payable on April 30 to all stockholders of record on April 1.

Apr. 15 Morris reacquired 200 shares of its common stock for $43 per share. Morris uses the cost method to account for treasury stock.

30 Paid dividends.

30 Employees exercised 1,000 options granted in 1997 under a fixed stock option plan. When the options were granted, each option entitled the employee to purchase 1 share of common stock for $50 per share. The share price on the grant date was also $50 per share. On April 30, when the market price was $55 per share, Morris issued new shares to the employees. The fair value of the options at the grant date was $6. Morris uses the intrinsic value method.

May 1 Morris declared a 10% stock dividend to be distributed on June 1 to stockholders of record on May 7. The market price of the common stock was $55 per share on May 1 (before the stock dividend). (Assume treasury shares do not participate in stock dividends.)

31 Morris sold 150 treasury shares reacquired on April 15 and an additional 200 shares costing $7,500 that had been on hand since the beginning of the year. The selling price was $57 per share.

June 1 Distributed stock dividend.

Sept. 15 The semiannual cash dividend on common stock was declared, amounting to $0.15 per share. Morris also declared the yearly dividend on preferred stock. Both are payable on October 15 to stockholders of record on October 1.

Oct. 15 Paid dividends.

Net income for 2002 was $50,000. Assume that revenues and expenses were closed to a temporary account, Income Summary. Use this account to complete the closing process.

Instructions:

1. Compute the number of shares and dollar amount of treasury stock at the beginning of 2002.
2. Make the necessary journal entries to record the transactions in 2002 relating to stockholders' equity.
3. Prepare the stockholders' equity section of Morris Corporation's December 31, 2002, balance sheet.

PROBLEM 11–46

ACCOUNTING FOR STOCK TRANSACTIONS

Ellis Corporation was organized on June 30, 1999. After 2½ years of profitable operations, the equity section of Ellis' balance sheet was as follows:

Contributed capital:	
Common stock, $3 par, 600,000 shares authorized,	
200,000 shares issued and outstanding	$ 600,000
Paid-in capital in excess of par	6,000,000
Retained earnings	2,800,000
Total stockholders' equity	$9,400,000

During 2002, the following transactions affected stockholders' equity.

Jan. 31 10,000 shares of common stock were reacquired at $32; treasury stock is recorded at cost.

Apr. 1 The company declared a 30% stock dividend. (Applies to all issued stock.)

30 The company declared a $0.75 cash dividend. (Applies only to outstanding stock.)

June 1 The stock dividend was issued, and the cash dividend was paid.

Aug. 31 All treasury stock was sold at $35.

Instructions: Give journal entries to record the stock transactions.

PROBLEM 11–47

STOCK DIVIDEND AND CASH DIVIDEND

On January 1, 2002, Homer Company had 100,000 shares of $0.50 par value common stock outstanding. The market value of Homer's common stock was $22 per share. Homer's retained earnings balance on January 1 was $580,000. During 2001, Homer had declared and paid cash dividends of $0.70 per share. Net income for 2002 is expected to be $110,000. Homer has a large loan from Garth Bank; part of the loan agreement stipulates that Homer must maintain a minimum retained earnings balance of $400,000.

Homer's board of directors is debating whether to declare a stock dividend in addition to its $0.70 per share annual cash dividend. Three proposals have been presented: (1) no stock dividend, (2) a 10% stock dividend, and (3) a 25% stock dividend.

Instructions: As a shareholder in Homer Company, which of the 3 proposals do you favor? Support your answer.

PROBLEM 11–48

STOCKHOLDERS' EQUITY TRANSACTIONS

Seneca Inc. was organized on January 2, 2001, with authorized capital stock consisting of 50,000 shares of 10%, $200 par value preferred, and 200,000 shares of no-par, no stated value common. During the first 2 years of the company's existence, the following selected transactions took place.

2001

Jan.	2	Sold 10,000 shares of common stock at $16.
	2	Sold 3,000 shares of preferred stock at $216.
Mar.	2	Sold common stock as follows: 10,800 shares at $22; 2,700 shares at $25.
July	10	A nearby piece of land, appraised at $400,000, was acquired for 600 shares of preferred stock and 27,000 shares of common. (Preferred stock was recorded at $216, the balance being assigned to common.)
Dec.	16	The regular preferred dividend and a $1.50 common dividend were declared.
	28	Dividends declared on December 16 were paid.
	31	Assume that revenues and expenses were closed to a temporary account, Income Summary. The income summary account showed a credit balance of $450,000, which was transferred to Retained Earnings.

2002

Feb.	27	The corporation reacquired 12,000 shares of common stock at $19. The treasury stock is carried at cost. (State law requires that an appropriation of retained earnings be made for the purchase price of treasury stock. Appropriations are to be returned to Retained Earnings upon resale of the stock.)
June	17	Resold 10,000 shares of the treasury stock at $23.
July	31	Resold all of the remaining treasury stock at $18.
Sept.	30	The corporation sold 11,000 additional shares of common stock at $21.
Dec.	16	The regular preferred dividend and an $0.80 common dividend were declared.
	28	Dividends declared on December 16 were paid.
	31	The income summary account showed a credit balance of $425,000, which was transferred to Retained Earnings.

Instructions:
1. Give the journal entries to record the foregoing transactions.
2. Prepare the stockholders' equity section of the balance sheet as of December 31, 2002.

PROBLEM 11–49

ACCOUNTING FOR STOCKHOLDERS' EQUITY

A condensed balance sheet for Sharp Tax Inc. as of December 31, 1999, is shown below. Capital stock authorized consists of 750 shares of 8%, $100 par, cumulative preferred stock and 15,000 shares of $50 par common stock.

Information relating to operations of the succeeding 3 years follows the condensed balance sheet.

Sharp Tax Inc.
Condensed Balance Sheet
December 31, 1999

Assets		Liabilities and Stockholders' Equity	
Assets	$525,000	Liabilities	$120,000
		8% preferred stock, $100 par	75,000
		Common stock, $50 par	150,000
		Paid-in capital in excess of par	30,000
		Retained earnings	150,000
Total assets	$525,000	Total liabilities and stockholders' equity	$525,000

	2000	2001	2002
Dividends declared on Dec. 20, payable on Jan. 10 of the following year:			
Preferred stock	8% cash	8% cash	8% cash
Common stock	$1.00 cash	$1.25 cash	$1.00 cash
	50% stock		
Net income for year	$67,500	$39,000	$51,000

2001

Feb. 12   Accumulated depreciation was reduced by $72,000 following an income tax investigation. (Assume that this was an error that qualified as a prior-period adjustment.) Additional income tax of $22,500 for prior years was paid.

Mar. 3   Purchased 300 shares of common stock at $54 per share; treasury stock is recorded at cost, and retained earnings are appropriated equal to such costs.

2002

Aug. 10   All the treasury stock was resold at $59 per share and the retained earnings appropriation was canceled.

Sept. 12   By vote of the stockholders, each share of the common stock was exchanged by the corporation for 4 shares of no-par common stock with a stated value of $15.

Instructions:

1. Give the journal entries to record the foregoing transactions for the 3-year period ended December 31, 2002. (Assume that revenues and expenses were closed to a temporary account, Income Summary, at the end of each year. Use this account to complete the closing process.)

2. Prepare the stockholders' equity section of the balance sheet as it would appear at the end of 2000, 2001, and 2002.

PROBLEM 11–50

RETAINED EARNINGS AND THE STATEMENT OF CASH FLOWS

The following items relate to the activities of Cortland Company for 2002.

(a) Cash dividends declared and paid on common stock during the year totaled $80,000. In addition, on January 15, 2002, dividends of $15,000 that were declared in 2001 were paid.

(b) Retained earnings of $130,000 were appropriated during the year in anticipation of a major capital expansion in future years.

(c) Depreciation expense was $67,000.

(d) Equipment was purchased for $250,000 in cash.

(e) Early in the year, a 10% stock dividend was declared and distributed. This stock dividend resulted in the distribution of 50,000 new shares of $1 par common stock. The market value per share immediately after the stock dividend was $44.

(f) Cash revenues for the year totaled $617,000.

(g) Cash expenses for the year totaled $320,000.

(h) Old machinery was sold for its book value of $10,000.

(i) Near the end of the year, a 2-for-1 stock split was declared. The 550,000 shares of $1 par common stock outstanding at the time were exchanged for 1,100,000 shares with a par value of $0.50.

(j) Cash dividends totaling $35,000 were declared and paid on preferred stock.

(k) Land was acquired in exchange for 6,000 shares of $0.50 par value common stock. The land had a fair market value of $130,000.

(l) Assume no changes in current operating receivable and payable balances during the year.

Instructions: Prepare a statement of cash flows for Cortland Company for the year ended December 31, 2002. Use the indirect method for reporting cash flows from operating activities.

PROBLEM 11–51

REPORTING STOCKHOLDERS' EQUITY

The stockholders' equity section of Nilsson Corporation's balance sheet as of December 31, 2001, is as follows:

Common stock ($5 par, 500,000 shares authorized, 275,000 issued and outstanding)	$1,375,000	
Paid-in capital in excess of par	550,000	
Total paid-in capital		$1,925,000
Unappropriated retained earnings	$1,335,000	
Appropriated retained earnings	500,000	
Total retained earnings		1,835,000
Total stockholders' equity		$3,760,000

Nilsson Corporation had the following stockholders' equity transactions during 2002:

Jan. 15   Completed the building renovation for which $500,000 of retained earnings had been restricted. Paid the contractor $485,000, all of which is capitalized.

Mar. 3   Issued 100,000 additional shares of the common stock for $8 per share.

May 18   Declared a dividend of $1.50 per share to be paid on July 31, 2002, to stockholders of record on June 30, 2002.

June 19   Approved additional building renovation to be funded internally. The estimated cost of the project is $400,000, and retained earnings are to be restricted for that amount.

July 31   Paid the dividend.

Nov. 12   Declared a property dividend to be paid on December 31, 2002, to stockholders of record on November 30, 2002. The dividend is to consist of 35,000 shares of Hampton Inc. stock that are currently recorded in Nilsson's books at $9 per share. The fair market value of the stock on November 12 is $13 per share.

Dec. 31   Reported $885,000 of net income on the December 31, 2002, income statement. (Assume that revenues and expenses were closed to a temporary account, Income Summary. Use this account to complete the closing process.) In addition, the stock was distributed in satisfaction of the property dividend. The Hampton stock closed at $14 per share at the end of the day's trading.

Instructions:

1. Make all necessary journal entries for Nilsson to account for the transactions affecting stockholders' equity.
2. Prepare the December 31, 2002, stockholders' equity section of the balance sheet for Nilsson.

PROBLEM 11–52

AUDITING STOCKHOLDERS' EQUITY

You have been assigned to the audit of Belcore Inc., a manufacturing company. You have been asked to summarize the transactions for the year ended December 31, 2002, affecting stockholders' equity and other related accounts. The stockholders' equity section of Belcore's December 31, 2001, balance sheet follows:

Stockholders' Equity	
Contributed capital:	
Common stock, $2 par value, 500,000 shares authorized,	
90,000 shares issued, 88,790 shares outstanding	$ 180,000
Paid-in capital in excess of par	1,820,000
Paid-in capital from treasury stock	22,500
Total contributed capital	$2,022,500
Retained earnings	324,689
Total contributed capital and retained earnings	$2,347,189
Less: Cost of 1,210 shares of treasury stock	72,600
Total stockholders' equity	$2,274,589

You have extracted the following information from the accounting records and audit working papers.

2002

Jan. 15 Belcore reissued 650 shares of treasury stock for $40 per share. The 1,210 shares of treasury stock on hand at December 31, 2001, were purchased in one block in 2001. Belcore used the cost method for recording the treasury shares purchased.

Feb. 2 Sold 90, $1,000, 9% bonds due February 1, 2005, at 103 with one detachable stock warrant attached to each bond. Interest is payable annually on February 1. The fair market value of the bonds without the stock warrants is 97. The detachable warrants have a fair value of $60 each and expire on February 1, 2003. Each warrant entitles the holder to purchase 10 shares of common stock at $40 per share.

Mar. 6 Subscriptions for 1,400 shares of common stock were issued at $44 per share, payable 40% down and the balance by March 20.

20 The balance due on 1,200 shares was received and those shares were issued. The subscriber who defaulted on the 200 remaining shares forfeited the down payment in accordance with the subscription agreement.

Nov. 1 There were 55 stock warrants detached from the bonds and exercised.

Instructions: Give journal entries required to summarize the preceding transactions.

PROBLEM 11–53

QUASI-REORGANIZATION

The stockholders' equity of the Seasoned Lumber Co. on June 30, 2002, was as follows:

Contributed capital:

5% preferred stock, $50 par, cumulative, 30,000 shares issued, dividends 5 years in arrears	$1,500,000
Common stock, $30 par, 100,000 shares issued	3,000,000
	$4,500,000
Deficit from operations	(600,000)
Total stockholders' equity	$3,900,000

On July 1, the following actions were taken:

(a) Common stockholders turned in their old common stock and received in exchange new common stock, 1 share of the new stock being exchanged for every 4 shares of the old. New common stock was given a stated value of $60 per share.

(b) One-half share of the new common stock was issued on each share of preferred stock outstanding in liquidation of dividends in arrears on preferred stock.

(c) The deficit from operations was applied against the paid-in capital arising from the common stock restatement.

Transactions for the remainder of 2002 affecting the stockholders' equity were as follows:

Oct. 1   10,000 shares of preferred stock were called at $55 plus dividends for 3 months at 5%. Stock was formally retired.

Nov. 10 60,000 shares of new common stock were sold at $65.

Dec. 31 Net income for the 6 months ended on this date was $400,000. (Assume that revenues and expenses were closed to a temporary account, Income Summary. Use this account to complete the closing process.) The semiannual dividend was declared on preferred shares, and a $0.75 dividend was declared on common shares, dividends being payable January 20, 2003.

Instructions:

1. Record in journal form the foregoing transactions.
2. Prepare the stockholders' equity section of the balance sheet as of December 31, 2002.

PROBLEM 11–54

QUASI-REORGANIZATION

Kennington Copper has experienced several loss years and has plant assets on its books that are overvalued. Kennington plans to revalue its assets downward and eliminate the deficit. At December 31, 2002, the company owns the following plant assets:

	Cost	Accumulated Depreciation	Book Value	Market Value
Land	$ 600,000	—	$ 600,000	$300,000
Buildings	850,000	$350,000	500,000	250,000
Machinery and Equipment	450,000	250,000	200,000	150,000
	$1,900,000	$600,000	$1,300,000	$700,000

The balance sheet on December 31, 2002, reported the following balances in the stockholders' equity section:

Common stock, $25 par, 70,000 shares	$1,750,000
Paid-in capital in excess of par	300,000
Retained earnings (deficit)	(350,000)
Total	$1,700,000

As part of the reorganization, the common stock is to be canceled and reissued at $10 par.

Instructions:

1. Prepare the journal entries to record the quasi-reorganization.
2. Give the plant asset section and stockholders' equity section of the company's balance sheet as they would appear after the entries are posted.

PROBLEM 11–55

PERFORMANCE-BASED STOCK OPTIONS

Bauil Corporation, a new environmental control company, initiated a performance-based stock option plan for its management on January 1, 2001. The plan provided for the granting of a variable number of stock options to management personnel who worked for the entire 4-year period ending December 31, 2004, depending on the net income earned by the company in 2004. No options were granted for the first $50,000 of net income. Thereafter, the following options were available based on the performance measure of net income.

$50,000–$99,999	5,000 stock options
$100,000–$124,999	10,000 stock options
$125,000–$149,999	15,000 stock options
$150,000 or more	25,000 stock options

The exercise price for the $5 par common stock was $25 per share. The fair value of the options on the grant date was $7.

Assume the market price for the Bauil stock and Bauil's forecasted 2004 net income were as follows at each of the following dates:

	Stock Price	Forecasted 2004 Income
January 1, 2001	$27	$110,000
December 31, 2001	30	130,000
December 31, 2002	29	160,000
December 31, 2003	35	140,000
December 31, 2004	36	130,000 (actual)

Instructions:

1. Prepare journal entries related to the stock options of Bauil for the period 2001–2004 assuming that all available options are exercised on December 31, 2004. Use the intrinsic value method.
2. Repeat (1) using the fair value method.

COMPETENCY ENHANCEMENT OPPORTUNITIES

▶ Deciphering Actual Financial Statements	▶ Ethical Dilemma
▶ Writing Assignment	▶ Cumulative Spreadsheet Analysis
▶ Research Project	▶ Internet Search
▶ The Debate	

Accounting is more than just doing textbook problems. This expanded competency material provides practice in critical thinking, oral and written communication, research, teamwork, and consideration of ethical issues.

DECIPHERING ACTUAL FINANCIAL STATEMENTS

• Deciphering 11–1 (The Walt Disney Company)

The 1998 financial statements for THE WALT DISNEY COMPANY are included in Appendix A. Locate those financial statements and consider the following questions.

1. What is the par value of Disney's common stock? What was the average issuance price of Disney's common stock?
2. Does Disney use the cost method or the par value method of accounting for treasury stock? As of September 30, 1998, what was the average cost of the repurchased shares held in treasury?
3. Combining information from questions (1) and (2), estimate the decrease in Disney's retained earnings if all of the treasury shares were retired.
4. From Disney's foreign currency translation adjustment, deduce whether the foreign currencies got stronger or weaker in 1998 (relative to the U.S. dollar) in the countries where Disney has subsidiaries.
5. In the notes to Disney's financial statements, the accounting for stock options is summarized. Does Disney use the fair value or the intrinsic value method?

• Deciphering 11–2 (General Motors)

In 1993, GENERAL MOTORS paid cash dividends on 11 different classes of capital stock. Those classes of stock were:

	Dividends per Share	Total Dividends (in millions)
Preferred stock, $5.00 series	$1.68	$ 2.6
Preferred stock, $3.75 series	1.26	1.0
Preferred stock, E-I series	1.42	4.6
Preferred stock, Series A Conversion	3.31	59.0
Depositary Shares, Series B	2.28	101.1
Depositary Shares, Series C	3.25	103.6
Depositary Shares, Series D	1.98	31.1
Depositary Shares, Series G	2.34	53.8
$1⅔ par value common stock	0.80	565.8
Class E common stock	0.40	97.2
Class H common stock	0.72	64.1
Total		$1,083.9

1. The January 1, 1993, balance in General Motors' retained earnings was a negative $3.354 billion. The December 31, 1993, balance was a negative $2.003 billion. How is it possible that General Motors was able to pay cash dividends during 1993?
2. This question will require a little research. What is the difference in stockholder rights between General Motors' $1⅔ common stock and the Class E and Class H common shares? How did the Class E and Class H shares come into existence?
3. In May 1993, General Motors redeemed all of the $5.00 series and $3.75 series preferred stock. The board of directors stated that the redemption of these preferred shares would give the company more financial flexibility by eliminating certain covenants associated with the shares. Get a copy of GM's most recent annual report and find out how many of the 11 issues of General Motors capital stock outstanding in 1993 are still outstanding.

• Deciphering 11–3 (Swire Pacific Limited)

The equity categories for SWIRE PACIFIC LIMITED are illustrated in Exhibit 11–9, on page 636. Using the information in the exhibit, answer the following questions.

1. Recall that the primary purpose of defining different reserve categories is to distinguish between distributable and nondistributable equity. As of December 31, 1998, how much of Swire Pacific's equity is distributable?

2. What is the U.S. equivalent of Swire Pacific's Revenue reserve?
3. What do you think is the purpose of the capital redemption reserve?
4. As of December 31, 1998, Swire Pacific has a property valuation reserve of HK$28,079 million. Assume that this reserve is recognized as part of one big revaluation—what journal entry would be made? The property valuation reserve is not distributable—why not?
5. What happened to property values related to Swire's holdings during 1998?

• **Deciphering 11–4 (Microsoft)**
The following is extracted from the notes to the 1998 financial statements of MICROSOFT.

Employee stock purchase plan

The Company has an employee stock purchase plan for all eligible employ-ees. Under the plan, shares of the Company's common stock may be purchased at six-month intervals at 85% of the lower of the fair market value on the first or the last day of each six-month period. Employees may purchase shares having a value not exceeding 10% of their gross compensation during an offering period. During 1996, 1997, and 1998, employees purchased 3.6 million, 2.8 million, and 2.2 million shares at average prices of $18.86, $29.82, and $54.42 per share. At June 30, 1998, 36.8 million shares were reserved for future issuance.

Stock option plans

The Company has stock option plans for directors, officers, and employees, which provide for nonqualified and incentive stock options. The option exercise price is the fair market value at the date of grant. Options granted prior to 1995 generally vest over four and one-half years and expire 10 years from the date of grant. Options granted during and after 1995 generally vest over four and one-half years and expire seven years from the date of grant, while certain options vest over seven and one-half years and expire after 10 years. At June 30, 1998, options for 222 million shares were vested and 523 million shares were available for future grants under the plans.

Why doesn't Microsoft's plan allow employees to purchase common stock at a lower percentage of market value, e.g., at 80% of market price? Why doesn't Microsoft set the incentive option exercise price at less than the stock price on the grant date?

▶ **WRITING ASSIGNMENT**
• **Strategic accounting: par value or cost method?**
J. D. Michael Company has been very successful in recent years. Cash flow from operations is more than sufficient to cover the cost of all capital expenditures as well as regular cash dividends. J. D. Michael has decided to use some of its extra cash to begin a program of repurchasing its own shares in the open market. The shares will not be retired but will be held for potential reissue. Because J. D. Michael has never repurchased its own shares before, it has not had to make a choice between the par value and cost methods of account-ing for treasury stock.

As the resident expert on accounting in the company, you have been asked to draft a 1-page memo to the board of directors recommending either the cost method or the par value method of accounting for treasury stock. Your memo should address issues like the prevailing practice, the likely effect on the financial statements (particularly the equity sec-tion), and the potential impact of the treasury stock accounting treatment on the ability to maintain steady cash dividend payments in the future.

▶ **RESEARCH PROJECT**
• When do stock splits occur?
Your group is to report (either orally or in writing) on the results of the following stock market research project.

1. Identify 5 large companies that have been around for at least 10 years.
2. Find out which of the companies have declared stock splits or stock dividends in the past 10 years. The easiest way to find a history of a company's stock splits and stock dividends is to look in *Moody's Industrial Manual.* Some companies also give this information in their annual report or in their summary corporate history. You might be able to get this information from a company's Internet site.
3. Use historical stock price information to draw a line graph of each company's stock price movements over the past 10 years. Historical stock price information is often available in a company's annual report. Your library also has this information. *Make sure you adjust the stock price data for stock splits and stock dividends.*
4. From the stock price data, can you tell what price-per-share range companies find to be most desirable? For example, do companies split their shares when they get above $60 per share, or do they wait until the shares reach $150?
5. Describe any patterns you see in the line graphs. For example, do stock splits tend to follow periods of rapid price increases? And, most interestingly, do stock splits tend to be followed by periods of large price increases?

▶ **THE DEBATE**
• Stock-based compensation: The line in the sand!
In 1993 and 1994, the FASB was very nearly voted out of existence by the U.S. Congress. Congress (or, more accurately, business interests with influence in Congress) was upset by the FASB's proposal that companies be required to recognize the value of employee stock options as compensation expense on the income statement. The threat of Congressional legislation finally convinced the FASB to amend its proposal and require only disclosure, not recognition, of the cost of stock option compensation.

Divide your group into two teams.

• One team represents the "Truth in Accounting Coalition." Prepare a 2-minute presentation outlining the logic behind recognizing the value of employee stock options as an expense on the income statement.

• The other team represents "Save the Jobs!" Prepare a 2-minute presentation arguing that the FASB's proposal to recognize the value of employee stock options as an expense would have critically injured American industry, particularly high-tech industry where employee stock options are very common.

▶ **ETHICAL DILEMMA**
• Stock dividend instead of cash: The investors will never know!
Best Ski Manufacturer usually pays a cash dividend sufficient to give investors a dividend yield (annual dividend divided by stock price) of around 6%. Last quarter, Best Ski Manufacturer paid a quarterly cash dividend of $1 per share. Its stock price is currently at $65 per share.

In the current quarter, Best Ski has suddenly experienced a big slowdown in ski equipment orders. The vice president of finance unequivocally stated that Best Ski just didn't have the cash to pay another cash dividend of $1 per share. She suggested that Best Ski make a public announcement explaining the situation to shareholders. This suggestion infuriated the chief executive officer; he insisted that nothing be done to make the shareholders nervous or pessimistic about Best Ski's future prospects.

The controller (your boss) came to the rescue with an accounting solution to the problem. He proposed that Best Ski declare a 10% stock dividend in place of the regular quarterly cash dividend. He said that a stock dividend is merely a cosmetic increase in the number of shares, with no associated cash flow, either into or out of the company. However, he claimed that investors would never know the difference between a cash dividend and a stock dividend. The controller's suggestion was met with enthusiasm by the board of directors.

The shareholder relations department is drafting a press release to announce the 10% stock dividend. Because of your accounting expertise, you have been asked to help with the wording of the memo. What wording would you suggest?

▶ **CUMULATIVE SPREADSHEET ANALYSIS**

This spreadsheet assignment is a continuation of the spreadsheet assignments given in earlier chapters. If you completed those assignments, you have a head start on this one.

Refer back to the instructions for preparing the revised financial statements for 2002 as given in (1) of the Cumulative Spreadsheet Analysis assignment in Chapter 3.

1. Skywalker wishes to prepare a *forecasted* balance sheet, a *forecasted* income statement, and a *forecasted* statement of cash flows for 2003. Clearly state any additional assumptions that you make. Use the financial statement numbers for 2002 as the basis for the forecast, along with the following additional information.

    a. Sales in 2003 are expected to increase by 40% over 2002 sales of $2,100.
    b. In 2003, Skywalker expects to acquire new property, plant, and equipment costing $240.
    c. The $480 in operating expenses reported in 2002 breaks down as follows: $15 depreciation expense, $465 other operating expenses.
    d. New long-term debt will be acquired in 2003 in accordance with (q) below.
    e. Cash dividends will be paid in 2003 in accordance with (s) below.
    f. New short-term loans payable will be acquired in an amount sufficient to make Skywalker's current ratio in 2003 exactly equal to 2.0.
    g. Skywalker anticipates repurchasing additional shares of stock during 2003 in accordance with (t) below.
    h. Because changes in future prices and exchange rates are impossible to predict, Skywalker's best estimate is that the balance in Accumulated Other Comprehensive Income will remain unchanged in 2003.
    i. In the absence of more detailed information, assume that the balances in Investment Securities, Long-Term Investments, Other Long-Term Assets, and Intangible Assets will all increase at the same rate as sales (40%) in 2003.
    j. In the absence of more detailed information, assume that the balance in Other Long-Term Liabilities will increase at the same rate as sales (40%) in 2003.
    k. The Investment Securities are classified as available-for-sale. Accordingly, cash from the purchase and sale of these securities is classified as an investing activity.
    l. Assume that transactions impacting the other long-term assets and other long-term liabilities accounts are operating activities.
    m. Cash and investment securities will increase at the same rate as sales.
    n. The forecasted amount of accounts receivable in 2003 is determined using the forecasted value for the average collection period. The average collection period for 2003 is expected to be 14.08 days. To make the calculations simpler, this value of 14.08 days is based on forecasted end-of-year accounts receivable rather than on average accounts receivable.
    o. The forecasted amount of inventory in 2003 is determined using the forecasted value for the number of days' sales in inventory. The number of days' sales in inventory for 2003 is expected to be 107.6 days. To make the calculations simpler, this value of 107.6 days is based on forecasted end-of-year inventory rather than on average inventory.
    p. The forecasted amount of accounts payable in 2003 is determined using the forecasted value for the number of days' purchases in accounts payable. The number of days' purchases in accounts payable for 2003 is expected to be 48.34 days. To

make the calculations simpler, this value of 48.34 days is based on forecasted end-of-year accounts payable rather than on average accounts payable.

q. New long-term debt will be acquired (or repaid) in an amount sufficient to make Skywalker's debt ratio (total liabilities divided by total assets) in 2003 exactly equal to .80.

r. Assume an interest rate on short-term loans payable of 6.0% and on long-term debt of 8.0%. Only a half year's interest is charged on loans taken out during the year. For example, if short-term loans payable at the end of 2003 is $15 and given that short-term loans payable at the end of 2002 were $10, total short-term interest expense for 2003 would be $0.75 [($10 × .06) + ($5 × .06 × ½)].

(Note: These forecasted statements were constructed as part of the spreadsheet assignment in Chapter 10; you can use that spreadsheet as a starting point if you have completed that assignment.)

For this exercise, add the following additional assumptions:

s. Skywalker has decided to begin paying cash dividends in 2003. Skywalker intends to maintain a dividend payout ratio (cash dividends divided by net income) of 40%. (Note: Make sure you adjust your spreadsheet formula so that if net income happens to be negative, cash dividends are no lower than $0.)

t. Skywalker has decided to continue its stock repurchase program in 2003. Skywalker intends to spend $50 repurchasing shares during the year. Skywalker accounts for treasury stock purchases using the cost method.

2. According to the forecast for 2003, state whether Skywalker is expected to issue new shares of stock. Would your answer change if Skywalker were not to repurchase the shares as described in (t)?

3. Repeat (2), with the following changes in assumptions:
    a. The debt ratio in 2003 is exactly equal to .70.
    b. The debt ratio in 2003 is exactly equal to .95.

4. Comment on how it is possible for a company to have negative net paid-in capital when net paid-in capital is equal to paid-in capital minus treasury stock.

▶ **INTERNET SEARCH**

MICROSOFT's Web address is www.microsoft.com. Once you've gained access to Microsoft's Web site, answer the following questions.

1. Microsoft is a leader in using its Web site to sell its products. What software is Microsoft currently advertising on its home page?

2. Microsoft's corporate history is fascinating and has been the subject of many books. Find Microsoft's own summary of its history and ascertain when, and how, the name "Micro-soft" was first used? (Hint: It was in 1975.)

3. Microsoft's stock information gives a history of the company's stock splits. If you had purchased one share of Microsoft stock at the initial public offering (IPO) on March 13, 1986, how many shares would you have today?

4. Find Microsoft's most recent annual report. The notes to the financial statements contain a description of changes in the number of shares of common stock outstanding. Microsoft regularly repurchases its own shares. What reason is given?

5. The notes to the financial statements also describe Microsoft's employee stock option plan. Companies are required to disclose the weighted-average option price for options granted and exercised during the year. What are these weighted-average option prices for the most recent year for Microsoft, and why is the weighted-average option price for options granted larger than the price for options exercised?

chapter 12
Investments in

Jerry Jones didn't win many friends in Texas when one of his first acts after buying the DALLAS COWBOYS in 1989 was to fire Tom Landry, who had been the head coach of the Cowboys ever since the team entered the NFL. Jones became even less popular when the Cowboys lost 15 out of 16 games in their first year under new head coach Jimmy Johnson.[1] In those days, the Cowboys stunk as a football team but looked like a pretty shrewd business investment. When Jones, an Arkansas oil man, purchased the Cowboys for $140 million, he acquired a diverse array of assets. These assets included miscellaneous football equipment, stadium leases, radio and TV broadcast rights, cable TV rights, luxury stadium suites, player contracts, a lease on the Cowboys' luxurious Valley Ranch training facility, and the Cowboys' NFL franchise rights.

Allocation of the purchase price among these assets and defining their useful lives was a difficult and strategic task. When H. R. "Bum" Bright, Jones' predecessor, bought the Dallas Cowboys for $85 million in 1984, he was able to allocate half the purchase price to players' contracts. These were amortizable assets that, for tax purposes, were written off over four years.[2] Jones received a similar tax break when he acquired the Cowboys.

But entrepreneurs like Jerry Jones don't get rich by relying solely on depreciation tax breaks. Jones quickly set about putting the Cowboys' finances back in the black—in 1988 the Cowboys had lost $9.5 million. Jones encouraged the team's treasurer to look for ways to cut expenses—renegotiate insurance policy premiums, seek for competitive bids for printing tickets and providing training room supplies, and remove the floodlights from the parking lot of the training center. Jones also moved to increase revenues by signing leases for 99 unleased luxury boxes (generating an extra $8.5 million per year in revenue) and then building an additional 68 luxury boxes. By 1992, the Cowboys were again profitable with net income of $20.6 million.[3]

The on-field performance of the Cowboys matched their financial success. In 1990, the Cowboys improved their record to 7 and 9, and in 1991 they made the playoffs, advancing to the second round. The Cowboys' return to glory was capped in January 1993 when they returned to the Super Bowl for the first time since 1978 and routed the Buffalo Bills, 52–17. In 1995, the Cowboys became the first NFL franchise to win three Super Bowls in a four-year time period. The subsequent so-so on-field performance of the team (it has not been back to the Super Bowl since 1995 and missed the playoffs completely in 1997) has not seemed to hurt its financial performance. See Exhibit 12–1. In a 1999 estimate by *Forbes,* the Cowboys were rated the most valuable sports franchise in North America with an estimated value of $663 million.[4]

1 William P. Barrett, "Maybe They Should Let Jerry Play," *Forbes,* February 19, 1990, p. 140.
2 Hal Lancaster, "Football Team's Sale Is Strictly Business," *The Wall Street Journal,* April 18, 1989, p. B1.
3 David Whitford, "America's Owner," *Inc.,* December 1993, p. 102.
4 Daniel Fisher and Michael K. Ozanian, "Cowboy Capitalism," *Forbes,* September 20, 1999, p. 170.

LEARNING OBJECTIVES

1
Identify those costs to be included in the acquisition cost of different types of noncurrent operating assets.

2
Properly account for noncurrent operating asset acquisitions using various special arrangements, including deferred payment, self-construction, and acquisition of an entire company.

3
Separate costs into those that should be expensed immediately and those that should be capitalized, and understand the accounting standards for research and development and oil and gas exploration costs.

4
Discuss the pros and cons of recording noncurrent operating assets at their current values.

5
Use the fixed asset turnover ratio as a general measure of how efficiently a company is using its property, plant, and equipment.

e/m

EXPANDED MATERIAL

6
Evaluate the different ways to compute capitalized interest and properly incorporate midyear loans into the capitalized interest calculations.

EXHIBIT 12–1 | Time Line of the Dallas Cowboys' Franchise Value, 1991–1999

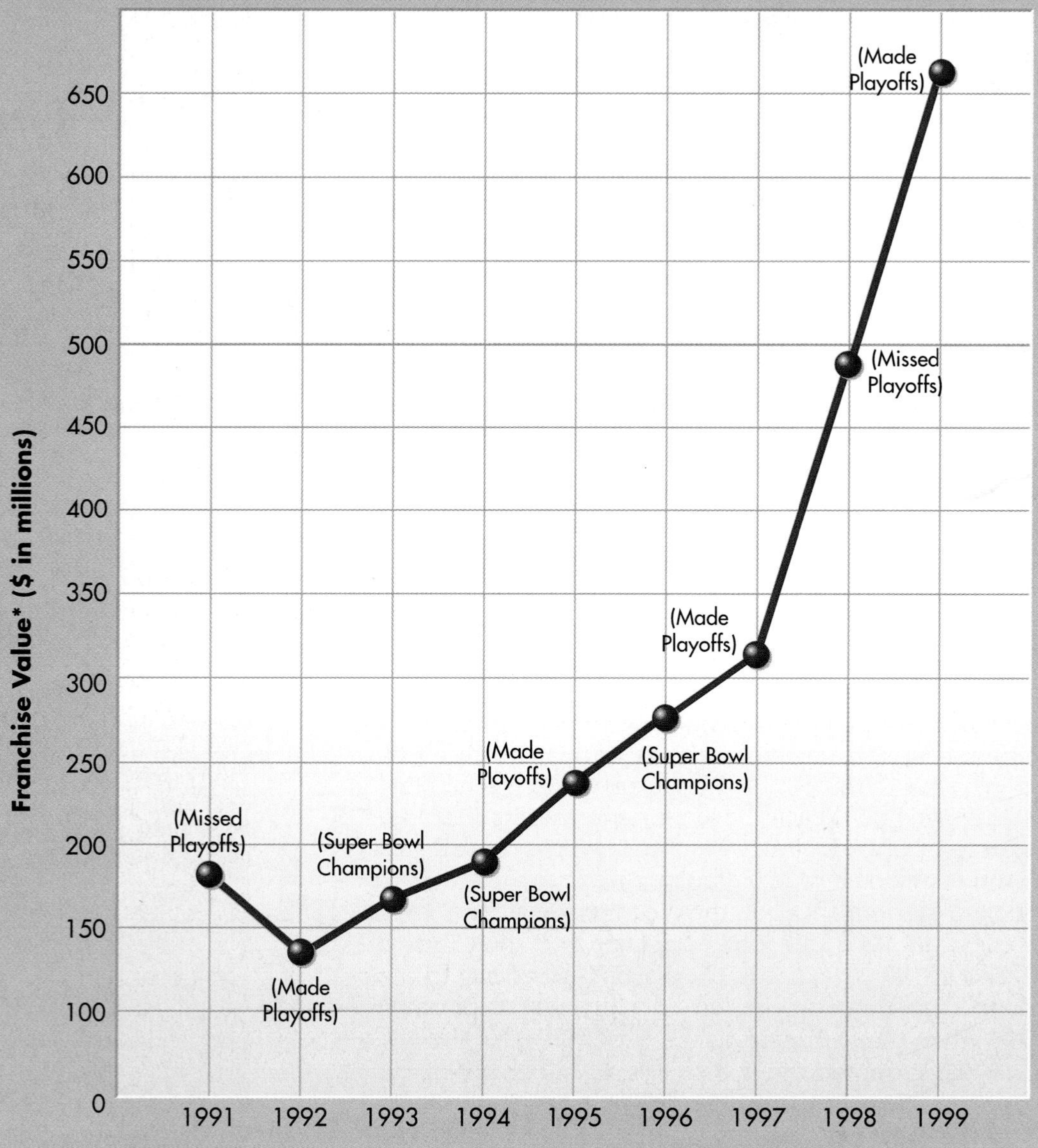

Franchise Value* ($ in millions)

650 —
600 —
550 —
500 — (Missed Playoffs)
450 —
400 —
350 —
300 — (Made Playoffs)
250 — (Made Playoffs) (Super Bowl Champions)
200 — (Missed Playoffs) (Super Bowl Champions)
150 — (Super Bowl Champions)
100 — (Made Playoffs)
0 —

(Made Playoffs)

1991 1992 1993 1994 1995 1996 1997 1998 1999

*Performance in the preceding season is shown in parentheses.

net work exercise

Visit the Dallas Cowboys' Web site at **www.dallascowboys.com**.
Net Work:
1. When did Texas Stadium open?
2. When did the Cowboys win their first Super Bowl? Which team did they beat? What was the score?

Many billions of dollars are invested each year in new property, plant, and equipment and increasingly in intangible assets as well. A time line of the business and accounting issues associated with property, plant, and equipment is shown in Exhibit 12–2.

One of the keys to successful business is correctly choosing which long-term assets to buy. Capital budgeting and discounted cash flow analysis are essential elements in making the best choices. In addition to the difficult financial decisions surrounding long-term assets, many accounting questions are introduced when long-term items are acquired. These accounting issues include:

- Which costs should be capitalized as assets and which ones should be expensed?
- What costs should be included in the acquisition cost of a long-term asset?
- At what amounts should long-term assets be recorded when the financing of the purchase is more complex than a simple cash payment?
- How should expenditures made subsequent to acquisition be recorded?
- What recognition should be given to changes in the market value of long-term assets?

This chapter discusses these general issues and describes many of the historic controversies that have led to changes in the accounting standards over the years. The chapter also discusses the controversial decision by the FASB to require all research and development costs to be expensed immediately (a decision that may soon be reversed), the embarrassing flip-flop the FASB was forced to make on oil and gas accounting, the historical roots of the capitalization of interest, and the question of historical cost vs. current cost. Chapter 13 will address the important issues of recognizing depreciation on long-term operating assets, recording impairment losses when asset values have significantly declined, and recording the disposal of long-term operating assets.

EXHIBIT 12–2 | Time Line of Business and Accounting Issues Involved With Long-Term Operating Assets

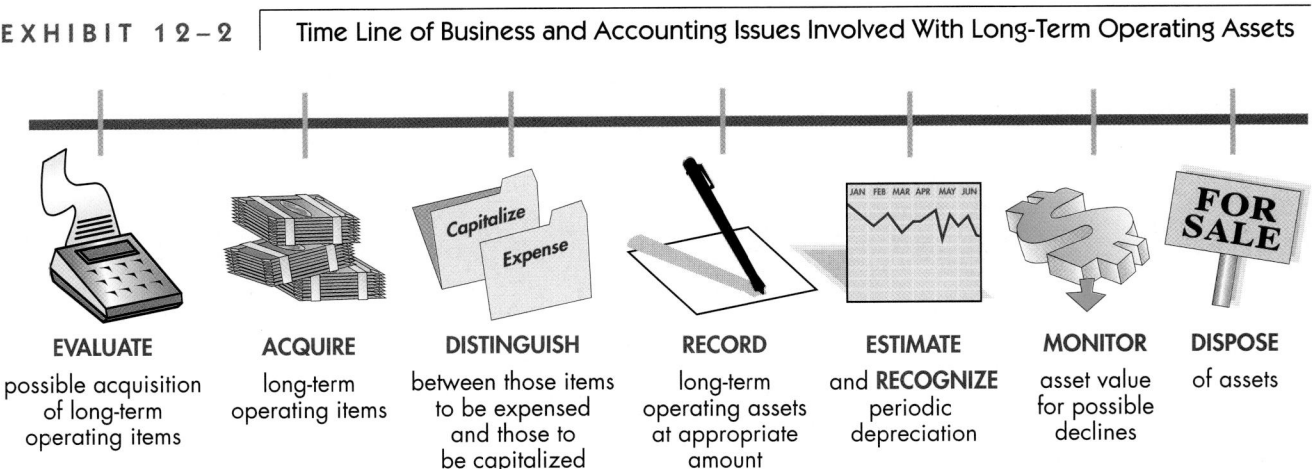

EVALUATE	**ACQUIRE**	**DISTINGUISH**	**RECORD**	**ESTIMATE**	**MONITOR**	**DISPOSE**
possible acquisition of long-term operating items	long-term operating items	between those items to be expensed and those to be capitalized	long-term operating assets at appropriate amount	and **RECOGNIZE** periodic depreciation	asset value for possible declines	of assets

Identify those costs to be included in the acquisition cost of different types of noncurrent operating assets.

WHAT COSTS ARE INCLUDED IN ACQUISITION COST?

Noncurrent operating assets are recorded initially at cost—the original bargained or cash sales price. In theory, the maximum price a company should be willing to pay for an operating asset is the present value of the net benefit the company expects to obtain from the use and final disposition of the asset. In a competitive economy, the market value or cost of an asset at acquisition is assumed to reflect the present value of its future benefits.

> **Caution!** Classification of an asset as a noncurrent operating asset depends on how management intends to use the asset. For example, land held for long-term investment purposes is not an operating asset; land held for resale within a year is a current asset.

The cost of property includes not only the original purchase price or equivalent value but also any other expenditures required in obtaining and preparing the asset for its intended use. Any taxes, freight, installation, and other expenditures related to the acquisition should be included in the asset's cost. Postacquisition costs, costs incurred after the asset is placed into service, are usually expensed rather than added to the acquisition cost. Exceptions to this general rule apply to some major replacements or improvements and will be discussed later in the chapter.

Although most noncurrent operating asset categories have similar acquisition costs, over time accounting practice has identified some specific costs that are included for different asset categories. Exhibits 12-3 and 12-4 summarize the types of costs normally included as acquisition costs for each major noncurrent asset category.

Land

**Five Largest Land Accounts[5]
1998 (in millions)**

Wal-Mart	$5,219
McDonald's	3,812
Home Depot	2,739
General Motors	2,680
United States Postal Service	2,286

Because land is a nondepreciable asset, costs assigned to land should be those costs that directly relate to land's unlimited life. Together with clearing and grading costs, costs of removing unwanted structures from newly acquired land are considered part of the cost to prepare the land for its intended use and are added to the purchase price of the land. Government assessments for water lines, sewers, roads, and other such items are considered part of the land's cost because maintenance of these items is the responsibility of the government; thus, to the landowner, they have unlimited life. These types of improvements are distinguished from similar costs for landscaping, parking lots, and interior sidewalks that are installed by the owner and must be replaced over time. The improvements owners are responsible for are generally classified as land improvements and are depreciated. *Improvements*

EXHIBIT 12-3 | Acquisition Costs of Tangible Noncurrent Operating Assets

Land	Realty used for business purposes.	**COST:** Purchase price, commissions, legal fees, escrow fees, surveying fees, clearing and grading costs, street and water line assessments.
Land Improvements	Items such as landscaping, paving, and fencing that improve the usefulness of property.	**COST:** Cost of improvements, including expenditures for materials, labor, and overhead.
Buildings	Structures used to house business operations.	**COST:** Purchase price, commissions, reconditioning costs.
Equipment	Assets used in the production of goods or in providing services. Examples include automobiles, trucks, machinery, patterns and dies, and furniture and fixtures.	**COST:** Purchase price, taxes, freight, insurance, installation, and any expenditures incurred in preparing the asset for its intended use, e.g., reconditioning and testing costs.

5 Source: Standard & Poor's COMPUSTAT.

EXHIBIT 12–4 | Acquisition Costs of Intangible Noncurrent Operating Assets

Patent	An exclusive right granted by the U.S. government that enables an inventor to control the manufacture, sale, or use of an invention. Legal life is 17 years.	**COST:** Purchase price, filing and registry fees, cost of subsequent litigation to protect right. Does not include internal research and development costs.
Copyright	An exclusive right granted by the U.S. government that permits an author to sell, license, or control his/her work. Copyright expires 50 years after the death of the author.	**COST:** Same as Patent.
Trademark and Trade Name	An exclusive right granted by the U.S. government that permits the use of distinctive symbols, labels, and designs, e.g., McDonald's golden arches, Levi's pocket patch, Chrysler's star. Legal life is virtually unlimited.	**COST:** Same as Patent.
Franchise	An exclusive right or privilege received by a business or individual to perform certain functions or sell certain products or services.	**COST:** Expenditures made to purchase the franchise. Legal fees and other costs incurred in obtaining the franchise.
Software Development Costs	Costs incurred in the development of computer software.	**COST:** Expenditures made after software is determined to be technologically feasible but before it is ready for commercial production.
Goodwill	Miscellaneous intangible resources, factors, and conditions that allow a company to earn above-normal income with its identifiable net assets. Goodwill is recorded only when a business entity is acquired by a purchase.	**COST:** Portion of purchase price that exceeds the sum of the current market value for all identifiable net assets.

Five Largest Building Accounts 1998 (in millions)

Wal-Mart	$16,061
United States Postal Service	15,123
McDonald's	14,576
General Motors	13,400
Alcan Aluminum	11,522

Five Largest Equipment Accounts 1998 (in millions)

General Motors	$99,341
GTE	51,489
General Electric	47,453
AT&T	44,806
IBM	32,691

Five Largest Total Intangible Asset Accounts 1998 (in millions)

General Electric	$23,635
Nabisco Group Holdings	18,715
Berkshire Hathaway	18,446
Philip Morris	17,566
Bank of America	17,084

Buildings

The cost of purchased buildings includes any reconditioning costs necessary before occupancy. Because self-constructed buildings have many unique costs, a separate discussion of self-constructed assets is included later in this chapter.

Equipment

Equipment costs include freight and insurance charges while the equipment is in transit and any expenditures for testing and installation. Costs for reconditioning purchased used equipment are also part of the asset cost.

Intangible Assets

Intangible assets also are generally recorded at cost; however, acquisition costs differ between externally purchased intangibles and those that are internally developed. Intangible assets arising from exclusive rights granted by the U.S. government, such as copyrights, patents, and trademarks, are recorded at their purchase price if externally obtained. Internal research and development costs incurred to generate the items subject to government license are generally expensed as incurred because of the uncertainty as to whether the work will result in a successful product. Only the actual legal and filing costs are included as part of the intangible asset cost for these internally developed items. Any costs to defend the rights in court are added to the intangible asset cost if successful. If not successful, all asset costs related to the rights would be written off as expenses.

Franchises

Franchise operations have become so common in everyday life that we often don't realize we are dealing with them. In fact, these days it is difficult to find a nonfranchise business in a typical shopping mall. When a business obtains a franchise, the recorded cost of the franchise includes any sum paid specifically for the franchise right as well as legal fees and other costs incurred in obtaining it. Although the value of a franchise at the time of its acquisition may be substantially in excess of its cost, the amount recorded should be limited to actual outlays. When a franchise is purchased from another company, the amount paid is recorded as the franchise cost. For an example of a recorded franchise, see the balance sheet for the THE COCA-COLA COMPANY in Chapter 3.

> **FYI:** The original Coca-Cola bottling franchise sold for $1.

Goodwill

Goodwill is the business contacts, reputation, functioning systems, staff camaraderie, and industry experience that make a business much more than just a collection of assets. Goodwill is recognized only when it is purchased as part of the acquisition of another company. In other words, a company's own goodwill, its homegrown goodwill, is not recognized. Goodwill will be discussed more in depth later in the chapter.

Organization Costs

In forming a corporation, certain organization costs are incurred, including legal fees, promotional costs, stock certificate costs, underwriting costs, and state incorporation fees. It can be argued that the benefits to be derived from these expenditures extend beyond the first fiscal period. However, the AICPA, with the approval of the FASB, has decided that organization costs (and the costs associated with other types of start-up activities) should be expensed as they are incurred. This pronouncement, which differs from prior practice, was released in 1998.[6]

Research and Development

Most research and development (R&D) expenditures are expensed as incurred. However, the FASB has made a special rule for computer software R&D. In brief, software

The recorded cost of a franchise includes the amount paid for franchise rights as well as legal fees and other associated costs. The amount recorded is limited to actual outlays, even though the franchise value may be substantially more than its cost.

6 Statement of Position 98-5, "Reporting on the Costs of Start-Up Activities," American Institute of Certified Public Accountants, April 3, 1998. This Statement of Position revised the practice with respect to organization costs as established in *SFAS No. 7*, "Accounting and Reporting by Development Stage Enterprises."

development costs incurred after a product has been shown to be technologically feasible are capitalized as an asset. In addition, controversy has recently flared over the accounting for R&D projects that are obtained as part of the acquisition of another business; this is called *acquired in-process R&D.* The accounting and reporting issues relating to research and development have a stormy history and are discussed in detail later in the chapter.

ACQUISITIONS OTHER THAN SIMPLE CASH TRANSACTIONS

2

Properly account for noncurrent operating asset acquisitions using various special arrangements, including deferred payment, self-construction, and acquisition of an entire company.

When an asset is purchased for cash, the acquisition is simply recorded at the amount of cash paid, including all outlays relating to its purchase and preparation for intended use. Assets can be acquired under a number of other arrangements, however, some of which present special problems relating to the cost to be recorded. The acquisition of assets is discussed under the following headings:

1. Basket purchase
2. Deferred payment
3. Leasing
4. Exchange of nonmonetary assets
5. Acquisition by issuing securities
6. Self-construction
7. Acquisition by donation or discovery
8. Acquisition of an entire company

Basket Purchase

> **FYI:** According to the IRS Code, Section 1056, no more than 50% of the purchase price of a sports franchise may be allocated to players' contracts, which are rapidly depreciable for income tax purposes.

In some purchases, a number of assets may be acquired in a **basket purchase** for one lump sum. For example, the opening scenario of this chapter described how Jerry Jones acquired football equipment, cable TV rights, player contracts, and the Cowboys' NFL franchise rights when he purchased the DALLAS COWBOYS. In order to account for the assets on an individual basis, the total purchase price must be allocated among the individual assets. When part of a purchase price can be clearly identified with specific assets, such a cost assignment should be made and the balance of the purchase price allocated among the remaining assets. When no part of the purchase price can be related to specific assets, the entire amount must be allocated among the different assets acquired.

Appraisal values or similar evidence provided by a competent independent authority should be sought to support the allocation.

To illustrate the allocation of a joint asset cost, assume that land, buildings, and equipment are acquired for $160,000. Assume further that a professional appraiser valued each of the assets at the acquisition date. The cost allocation is made as shown below.

	Appraised Values	Cost Allocation According to Relative Appraised Values	Cost Assigned to Individual Assets
Land	$ 56,000	56,000/200,000 × $160,000	$ 44,800
Buildings	120,000	120,000/200,000 × $160,000	96,000
Equipment	24,000	24,000/200,000 × $160,000	19,200
	$200,000		$160,000

The entry to record this acquisition, assuming a cash purchase, would be as follows:

Land	44,800	
Buildings	96,000	
Equipment	19,200	
Cash		160,000

It is important to recognize that this cost allocation of a basket purchase price is not merely a theoretical exercise. Some assets in the group may be depreciable, others nondepreciable. Depreciable assets may have different useful lives. Periodic depreciation expense can be significantly impacted by what proportion of the purchase price is allocated to assets with relatively long useful lives.

Deferred Payment

The acquisition of real estate or other property frequently involves deferred payment of all or part of the purchase price. The buyer signs a note or a mortgage that specifies the terms of settlement of the obligation. The debt contract may call for one payment at a given future date or a series of payments at specified intervals. Interest charged on the unpaid balance of the contract should be recognized as an expense.

To illustrate the accounting for a deferred payment purchase contract, assume that land is acquired on January 2, 2002, for $100,000; $35,000 is paid at the time of purchase, and the balance is to be paid in semiannual installments of $5,000 plus interest on the unpaid principal at an annual rate of 10%. Entries for the purchase and for the first payment on the contract are shown below.

> **Caution!** In this example, each semiannual payment declines, since the interest is calculated on a declining balance in notes payable. For example, on January 1, 2003, the total payment would be just $8,000 ($5,000 + $3,000 interest). Alternatively, a contract can provide for a constant payment, or annuity. With an annuity, the amount applied to the note principal increases (and the interest expense decreases) each period as the liability decreases.

Transaction	Entry		
January 2, 2002 Purchased land for $100,000, paying $35,000 down, the balance to be paid in semiannual payments of $5,000 plus interest at 10%.	Land Cash Notes Payable	100,000	35,000 65,000
June 30, 2002 Made first payment. Amount of payment: $5,000 + $3,250 (5% of $65,000) = $8,250	Interest Expense Notes Payable Cash	3,250 5,000	8,250

In the preceding example, the contract specified both a purchase price and interest at a stated rate on the unpaid balance. Sometimes, however, a contract may simply provide for a payment or series of payments without reference to interest or may provide for a stated interest rate that is unreasonable in relation to the market. In these circumstances, the note, sales price, and cost of the property, goods, or services exchanged for the note should be recorded at the fair market value of the property, goods, or services or at the current market value of the note, whichever value is more clearly determinable.[7] The following example illustrates the accounting by the purchaser in this circumstance.

Assume that certain equipment, which has a cash price of $50,000, is acquired under a deferred payment contract. The contract specifies a down payment of $15,000 plus seven annual payments of $7,189 each, or a total price, including interest, of $65,323. Although not stated, the effective interest rate implicit in this contract is 10%, the rate that discounts the annual payments of $7,189 to a present value of $35,000, the cash price less the down payment.[8] If the fair market value of the asset varies from the contract price

---

7 *Opinions of the Accounting Principles Board No. 21*, "Interest on Receivables and Payables," New York: American Institute of Certified Public Accountants, 1971.

8 As illustrated in Appendix B, the effective or implicit interest rate may be computed as follows:

$$PV_n = R(PVAF \, \overline{n}| \, i)$$
$$\$50,000 - \$15,000 = \$7,189(PVAF \, \overline{n}| \, i)$$
$$PVAF \, \overline{n}| \, i = \$35,000/\$7,189$$
$$PVAF \, \overline{n}| \, i = 4.8685$$

From Table IV, Appendix B, the interest rate for the present value of 4.8684 when $n = 7$ is 10%. Additional examples of computing an implicit rate of interest are presented in Appendix B. Implicit interest rates can also be computed using a business calculator.

because of delayed payments, the difference should be recorded as a discount (contra liability) and amortized over the life of the contract using the implicit or effective interest rate. Using the earlier example, the entries to record the purchase, the amortization of the discount for the first two years, and the first two payments would be as follows:

Transaction	Entry		
January 2, 2002	Equipment	50,000	
Purchased equipment with a cash price of	Discount on Notes Payable	15,323	
$50,000 for $15,000 down plus seven	Notes Payable		50,323
annual payments of $7,189 each, or a total	Cash		15,000
contract price of $65,323.			
December 31, 2002	Notes Payable	7,189	
Made first payment of $7,189.	Cash		7,189
Amortization of debt discount:			
$50,323 – $15,323 = $35,000	Interest Expense	3,500	
10% × $35,000 = $3,500	Discount on Notes Payable		3,500
December 31, 2003	Notes Payable	7,189	
Made second payment of $7,189.	Cash		7,189
Amortization of debt discount:			
10% × $31,311* = $3,131	Interest Expense	3,131	
	Discount on Notes Payable		3,131

*$50,323 – $7,189 = $43,134 Notes payable
$15,323 – $3,500 = <u>11,823</u> Discount on notes payable
<u>$31,311</u> Present value of notes payable at end of first year

> **Caution!** The account "Discount on Notes Payable" is a contra liability account and is reported as an offset to Notes Payable. It represents that portion of the remaining payments on the note that will be for interest.

When there is no established cash price for the property, goods, or services and there is no stated rate of interest on the contract, or the stated rate is unreasonable under the circumstances, an imputed interest rate must be used. The imputed interest rate is an estimate of what interest rate the borrowing company would have to pay on a loan, given its creditworthiness and current market interest rates.

Property is often acquired under a conditional sales contract whereby legal title to the asset is retained by the seller until payments are completed. The failure to acquire legal title may be disregarded by the buyer and the transaction recognized in terms of its substance—the acquisition of an asset and assumption of a liability. The buyer has the possession and use of the asset and must absorb any decline in its value; title to the asset is retained by the seller simply as a means of assuring payment on the purchase contract.

Leasing

A lease is a contract whereby one party (the lessee) is granted a right to use property owned by another party (the lessor) for a specified period of time for a specified periodic cost. Most leases are similar in nature to rentals. These leases are called **operating leases.** However, other leases, referred to as **capital leases,** are economically equivalent to a sale of the leased asset with the lessor allowing the lessee to pay for the asset over time with a series of "lease" payments. In these circumstances, the lease payments are exactly equivalent to mortgage payments. In such cases, the leased property should be recorded as an asset on the books of the company using the asset (the lessee), not on the books of the company that legally owns the asset (the lessor). The capital lease asset is recorded at the present value of the future lease payments. Because lease accounting is a complex area, an entire chapter (Chapter 15) is devoted to accounting for leases.

> **FYI:** In this text, the term "amortization" is used to refer to the periodic expensing of the cost of intangible assets and leasehold improvements; depreciation is used for tangible assets.

Even when a lease is not considered to be the same as a purchase and the periodic payments are recorded as rental expense, certain lease prepayments or improvements to the property by the lessee may be treated as capital expenditures. Because leasehold improvements, such as partitions in a building, additions, and attached equipment, revert to the owner at the expiration of the lease, they are properly capitalized on the books of the lessee and amortized over the remaining life of the lease. Some lease costs are really expenses of the period and should not be capitalized. These include improvements that are made in lieu of rent, for example, a lessee builds partitions in a leased warehouse for storage of its product, and the lessor allows the lessee to offset the cost against rental expense for the period. These costs should be expensed by the lessee.

Exchange of Nonmonetary Assets

In some cases, an enterprise acquires a new asset by exchanging or trading existing nonmonetary assets.[9] Generally, the new asset should be valued at its fair market value or at the fair market value of the asset given up, whichever is more clearly determinable.[10] If the nonmonetary asset is used equipment, the fair market value of the new asset is generally more clearly determinable and therefore used to record the exchange.

It should be observed that determining the fair market value of a new asset can sometimes be difficult. The quoted or list price for an asset is not always a good indicator of the market value and is often higher than the actual cash price for the asset. An inflated list price permits the seller to increase the indicated trade-in allowance for a used asset. The price for which the asset could be acquired in a cash transaction is the fair market value that should be used to record the acquisition.

To illustrate, assume the sticker on the window of a new car sitting in a dealer's showroom lists a total selling price of $23,500. The sticker includes a base price plus an itemized listing of all the options that have been added. If you, as a buyer, approached the dealer with your old clunker as a trade-in, you might be surprised to be offered $3,000 for a car you know is worth no more than $1,000. If you offered to pay cash for the new car with no trade-in, however, you could probably buy it for approximately $21,500 or the list price reduced by the inflated amount of allowance offered for the trade-in. The fair market value of the new asset is thus not the list price of $23,500 but the true cash price of $21,500.

If the nonmonetary asset given up to acquire the new asset is also property or equipment, a sale of property occurs simultaneously with the acquisition. When an exchange of a nonmonetary asset takes place, the use of fair market value results in a gain or loss on the disposal of the nonmonetary asset. Under some limited circumstances, a gain may be deferred and recognized over the life of the newly acquired asset. Because of the need to first discuss depreciation methods before explaining the accounting for the sale of assets, the full discussion of acquisition and disposal by exchange is covered in Chapter 13.

Acquisition by Issuing Securities

A company may acquire certain property by issuing its own bonds or stocks. When a market value for the securities can be determined, that value is assigned to the asset; in the absence of a market value for the securities, the fair market value of the asset acquired would be used. To illustrate, assume that a company issues 1,000 shares of $1 par common stock in acquiring land; the stock has a current market price of $45 per share. An entry should be made as follows:

Land	45,000	
Common Stock		1,000
Paid-In Capital in Excess of Par		44,000

9 Monetary assets are those assets whose amounts are fixed in terms of currency, by contract or otherwise. Examples include cash and accounts receivable. Nonmonetary assets include all other assets, such as inventories, land, buildings, and equipment.

10 *Opinions of the Accounting Principles Board No. 29*, "Accounting for Nonmonetary Transactions," New York: American Institute of Certified Public Accountants, 1973, par. 18.

When securities do not have an established market value, appraisal of the acquired assets by an independent authority may be required to arrive at an objective determination of their fair market value.

As discussed in Chapter 5, purchasing noncurrent assets in exchange for long-term debt and/or stock is an example of a significant noncash transaction. This kind of noncash transaction is not included in the body of the statement of cash flows as an investing or a financing activity. Instead, the transaction, if material, is disclosed separately.

Self-Construction

Sometimes buildings or equipment are constructed by a company for its own use. This may be done to save on construction costs, to utilize idle facilities, or to achieve a higher quality of construction.

SELF-CONSTRUCTED ASSETS Like purchased assets, these are recorded at cost, including all expenditures incurred to build the asset and make it ready for its intended use. Some considerations in determining the cost of self-constructed assets are discussed in the following sections.

OVERHEAD CHARGEABLE TO SELF-CONSTRUCTION All costs that can be related to construction should be charged to the assets under construction. There is no question about the inclusion of charges for material and labor directly attributable to the new construction. However, there is a difference of opinion regarding the amount of overhead properly assignable to the construction activity. Some accountants take the position that assets under construction should be charged with no more than the incremental overhead—the increase in a company's total overhead resulting from the special construction activity. Others maintain that overhead should be assigned to construction just as it is assigned to normal operations. This would call for the inclusion of not only the increase in overhead resulting from construction activities but also a pro rata share of the company's fixed overhead. Common practice is to allocate both variable overhead and a pro rata share of fixed overhead to self-construction projects. For example, in a 1998 filing with the SEC, TELESTRA, an Australian telecommunications company, revealed that it was changing its accounting policy for self-constructed assets. The change was designed to result in the capitalization of more overhead that is not directly attributable to self-construction projects. This change was made to align Telestra's accounting practices with other companies in the telecommunications industry.

SAVINGS OR LOSS ON SELF-CONSTRUCTION When the cost of self-construction of an asset is less than the cost to acquire it through purchase or construction by outsiders, the difference for accounting purposes is not a profit but a savings. The construction is properly reported at its actual cost. The savings will emerge as an increase in net income over the life of the asset as lower depreciation is charged against periodic revenue. Assume, on the other hand, the cost of self-construction is greater than bids originally received for the construction. There is generally no assurance that the asset under alternative arrangements might have been equal in quality to that which was self-constructed. In recording this transaction, just as in recording others, accounts should reflect those courses of action taken, not the alternatives that might have been selected. However, if there is evidence indicating cost has been materially excessive because of construction inefficiencies or failures, the asset should be evaluated for possible recording of an impairment loss. Recognition of impairment losses is discussed in Chapter 13.

INTEREST DURING PERIOD OF CONSTRUCTION When a construction company bids on a job, the bid includes a charge for interest that will be incurred on funds borrowed to finance the construction. The interest cost is viewed as being an integral part of the cost of construction, just like materials, labor, and equipment rental costs. In a similar way, when a company constructs an asset for its own use, long-standing accounting practice is for the company to capitalize the interest costs incurred to finance the construction.

Capitalization of interest first began with public utilities. Public utilities self-construct a large portion of their assets, so the capitalized interest amount can be very material. More importantly, public utility rates are frequently set by government bodies and are tied to the utility's rate base, which is the utility's book value of assets. The higher the rate base, the higher the utility rates. Accordingly, public utilities have a great incentive to include all possible costs, including **capitalized interest,** in the reported cost of their self-constructed assets.

Although capitalization of interest began with public utilities, it is now generally accepted accounting practice for all firms that construct assets for their own use. Remember, interest capitalization is not merely a ploy used by utilities to get higher rates; interest is a legitimate cost of construction, and the proper matching of revenues and expenses suggests that interest be deferred and charged over the life of the constructed asset. If buildings or equipment were acquired by purchase rather than by self-construction, a charge for interest during the construction period would be implicit in the purchase price.

Capitalization of interest is required for assets, such as buildings and equipment, that are being self-constructed for an enterprise's own use and assets that are intended to be leased or sold to others that can be identified as discrete projects. These are projects that can be clearly identified as to the assets involved. Interest should not be capitalized for inventories manufactured or produced on a repetitive basis, for assets that are currently being used, or for assets that are idle and are not undergoing activities to prepare them for use. Thus, land that is being held for future development does not qualify for interest capitalization.[11]

Once it is determined that the construction project qualifies for interest capitalization, the amount of interest to be capitalized must be determined. The following basic guidelines govern the computation of capitalized interest.

1. Interest charges begin when the first expenditures are made on the project and continue as long as work continues and until the asset is completed and actually ready for use.
2. The amount of interest to be capitalized is computed using the accumulated expenditures for the project, weighted based on when the expenditures were made during the year. Expenditures mean cash disbursements, not accruals.
3. The interest rates to be used in calculating the amount of interest to capitalize are, in order:
   (a) Interest rate incurred for any debt specifically incurred for funds used on the project.
   (b) Weighted-average interest rate from all other enterprise borrowings regardless of the use of funds.
4. If the construction period covers more than one fiscal period, accumulated expenditures include prior years' capitalized interest.

The maximum interest that can be capitalized is the total interest expense accrued for the year.

The following illustration demonstrates the application of these guidelines. Cutler Industries, Inc., has decided to construct a new computerized assembly plant. It is estimated that the construction period will be about 18 months and that the cost of construction will be approximately $6.4 million (excluding capitalized interest). A 12% construction loan for $2 million is obtained on January 1, 2002, at the beginning of construction.

---

11 *Statement of Financial Accounting Standards No. 34,* "Capitalization of Interest Cost," Stamford, CT: Financial Accounting Standards Board, 1979, par. 10.

In addition to the construction loan, Cutler has the following outstanding debt during the construction period:

5-year notes payable, 11% interest $3,000,000
Mortgage on other plant, 9% interest 4,800,000

The weighted-average interest rate on this general nonconstruction debt is computed as follows:

Nonconstruction Debt	Principal	Rate	Interest Cost
Notes Payable	$3,000,000	11%	$330,000
Mortgage	4,800,000	9%	432,000
	$7,800,000	9.8% *	$762,000

*Weighted-average rate = $762,000 ÷ $7,800,000 = 9.8% (rounded)

The following expenditures were incurred on the project during 2002:

January 1, 2002 .... $1,200,000
October 1, 2002 1,800,000

Computation of the amount of interest to be capitalized for 2002 is as follows:

Expenditure Date	Amount	Interest Capitalization Rate	Fraction of the Year Outstanding	Capitalized Interest
January 1, 2002	$1,200,000	12%	12/12	$144,000
October 1, 2002	800,000	12%	3/12	24,000
	1,000,000	9.8%	3/12	24,500
Total capitalized interest for 2002				$192,500

Notice first that capitalized interest is computed only for the amount of time the expenditures were outstanding. The January 1 expenditures caused increased borrowing costs for the entire year, but the October 1 expenditures were outstanding for only the final three months of the year. This approach results in an approximation of the amount of interest that could have been avoided if the expenditures had been used to repay debt instead of being used for the construction project.

This approach also assumes that the most avoidable interest is the interest on the borrowing specifically for the construction project. Accordingly, the interest rate of 12% on the specific construction borrowing is used. However, the amount of that loan is only $2,000,000—expenditures above this $2,000,000 amount could have been used to repay general company debt. Therefore, the October 1 expenditure of $1,800,000 has been split into two pieces—the first $800,000 could have been used to repay the balance of the construction loan ($800,000 = $2,000,000 - $1,200,000), so the amount of avoidable interest is computed using the 12% rate. The remaining $1,000,000 could have been used to repay general company debt, so the weighted-average rate of 9.8% on general borrowing is used.

Finally, recall that the amount of interest capitalized cannot exceed total interest incurred for the year. Total interest incurred during 2002 was:

 Is capitalized interest *extra* interest that the company has to pay? How would the financial statements be impacted if a company were to forget to capitalize interest?

Debt	Amount	Interest Rate	Annual Interest
Construction loan	$2,000,000	12%	$ 240,000
Notes payable	3,000,000	11%	330,000
Mortgage payable	4,800,000	9%	432,000
Total interest incurred			$1,002,000

► INTERESTED CAPITALIZATION: NOT EVERYONE AGREES

Not everyone agrees that interest on funds used to finance the self-construction of assets should be capitalized. In fact, the original FASB vote was only four to three in favor of *Statement No. 34*, which mandates the capitalization of interest.

Arguments advanced against interest capitalization are:

1. Cash is fungible; that is, it is difficult to follow cash once it is invested in a firm. Is the interest charge really related to the self-constructed asset, or is it a payment made to meet general financial needs? Even when a loan is made for specific purposes, it frees cash raised by other means to be used for other projects.

2. To be consistent, implicit interest on all funds used, both debt and equity, should be charged to the asset cost. Computing the cost of capital for internal

Because total interest incurred exceeds the computed amount of interest to be capitalized, the entire indicated amount of $192,500 is capitalized. The journal entry to record total interest incurred by Cutler Industries during 2002 (assuming that all interest was paid in cash) is as follows:

Construction in Progress	192,500	
Interest Expense ($1,002,000 – $192,500)	809,500	
Cash		1,002,000

Assume that further construction expenditures of $3,200,000 were made on February 1, 2003, and the project was completed on May 31, 2003.

The amount of interest to be capitalized for the year 2003 is:

Expenditure Date	Amount	Interest Capitalization Rate	Fraction of the Year Outstanding	Capitalized Interest
Accumulated in 2002	$2,000,000	12%	5/12	$100,000
	1,192,500	9.8%	5/12	48,694
February 1, 2003	3,200,000	9.8%	4/12	104,533
Total capitalized interest for 2003				$253,227

<table>
<tr><td>FYI: This is an unusual project indeed—it is finished ahead of schedule (in only 17 months), and the actual total cost of construction (excluding capitalized interest) is only $6.2 million, $200,000 less than forecasted.</td></tr>
</table>

Avoidable interest in 2003 includes interest on all the loans that could have been repaid with the construction expenditures made in 2002. These expenditures total $3,192,500 ($1,200,000 + $1,800,000 + $192,500) and include interest capitalized in 2002. Interest is capitalized only until May 31 (five months) when construction is completed and the building is ready for use.

Because $253,227 is less than the actual annual interest of $1,002,000, the entire indicated amount of $253,227 is capitalized in 2003.

Total recorded cost of the building on May 31, 2003, when it is put into service is $6,645,727, computed as follows:

Expenditures incurred in 2002	$3,000,000
Interest capitalized in 2002	192,500
Expenditures incurred in 2003	3,200,000
Interest capitalized in 2003	253,227
Total building cost, May 31, 2003	$6,645,727

equity funds is a very difficult and subjective task.

The changing stance of the International Accounting Standards Committee (IASC) perfectly illustrates the split view on interest capitalization. In its original standard on interest capitalization (IAS 23), the IASC said that a company may either capitalize (or capitalise, to use their spelling) interest or not, but the company should be consistent in its practice. In a 1989 exposure draft, the IASC then proposed establishing a benchmark treatment requiring interest capitalization. But the final standard issued in 1993 (revised IAS 23) says that all interest should be expensed, regardless of how the funds are used. So, if the notion of capitalization of interest seems strange to you, you are in good company.

QUESTIONS:

1. What practical difficulties would be involved with capitalizing implicit interest on equity funds?
2. Do you agree with the FASB (some interest should be capitalized) or with the IASC (all interest should be expensed as incurred)? Explain your position.

FASB Statement No. 34 requires disclosure of the total interest expense for the year and the amount capitalized. This disclosure can be made either in the body of the income statement or in a note to the statements.

To illustrate these two methods, assume that Cutler Industries reported the 2002 interest information on the income statement and the 2003 interest information in a note.

Cutler Industries, Inc.
Income Statement
For the Year Ended December 31, 2002

Operating income		$ XXX,XXX
Other expenses and losses:		
Total interest incurred	$1,002,000	
Less: Capitalized interest	192,500	809,500
Income before income taxes		$ XXX,XXX
Income taxes		XXX,XXX
Net income		$ XXX,XXX

Cutler Industries, Inc.
Financial Statement Notes
For the Year Ended December 31, 2003

Note X—Interest expense. Interest of $253,227 was capitalized in 2003 as part of the cost of construction for the computerized assembly plant in accordance with the requirements of FASB Statement No. 34.

The amount of capitalized interest reported for 1997 (except DISNEY, which is for 1998) by several large U.S. companies and its percentage of total interest expense reported by those companies are displayed in Exhibit 12-5. As you can see, GENERAL ELECTRIC reports that it capitalized only an insignificant amount of its $8,384 million in interest during 1997. On the other hand, EXXON capitalized more than half of its interest during 1997.

EXHIBIT 12–5 | Capitalized Interest for Several Large U.S. Companies (in millions of U.S. Dollars)

Company	Capitalized Interest	Interest Expense	Percentage of Capitalized Interest to Total Interest
General Electric*	$ 0	$8,384	0.0
General Motors	126	5,946	2.1
Exxon	494	415	54.3
McDonald's	23	364	5.9
The Walt Disney Company	139	685	16.9

*General Electric reports that it capitalized an insignificant amount of interest in 1997.

FYI: Valuation issues in transactions that are not arm's-length can be very difficult. SEC Staff Accounting Bulletin (SAB) No. 48 requires that when a corporation receives nonmonetary assets as an investment by a shareholder, the assets are recorded by the company at the shareholder's historical cost.

Acquisition by Donation or Discovery

When property is received through **donation,** there is no cost that can be used as a basis for its valuation. Even though certain expenditures may have to be made incidental to the gift, these expenditures are generally considerably less than the value of the property. Here, cost obviously fails to provide a satisfactory basis for asset valuation.

Property acquired through donation should be appraised and recorded at its fair market value. A donation is recognized as a revenue or gain in the period in which it is received.[12] To illustrate, Netty's Ice Cream Parlor is given a donation of land and a building by an eccentric ice cream lover. The entry on Netty's books, using the appraised values of the land and the building, is as follows:

Land	400,000	
Buildings	1,500,000	
Revenue or Gain		1,900,000

Depreciation of an asset acquired by gift should be recorded in the usual manner, the value assigned to the asset providing the basis for the depreciation charge.

If a gift is contingent upon some act to be performed by the recipient, no asset should be reported until the conditions of the gift have been met. At that time, both the increase in assets and the revenue or gain should be recognized in the accounts and in the financial statements.[13]

Occasionally, valuable resources are discovered on land already owned. The **discovery** greatly increases the value of the property. However, because the cost of the land is not affected by the discovery, it is common practice to ignore this increase in value. Similarly, the increase in value for assets that change over time, such as growing timber or aging wine, is ignored in common practice. Failure to recognize these discovery or

12 *Statement of Financial Accounting Standards No. 116,* "Accounting for Contributions Received and Contributions Made," Norwalk, CT: Financial Accounting Standards Board, 1993, par. 8. Statement No. 116 does not apply to the contribution of assets by governmental units to business enterprises. The accounting for such contributions often involves a credit to Donated Capital. Other options sometimes used to record contributions by governmental units are as a contra asset, as revenue for the period of the contribution, or as a deferred credit that is amortized to income over the life of the assets.

13 Ibid., par. 22.

Publicly traded oil and gas firms are required to disclose the quantity of their proven oil and gas reserves, as well as a forecast of the discounted value of future net cash flows expected to be generated by the reserves.

accretion values ignores the economic reality of the situation and tends to materially understate the assets of the entity. Nevertheless, asset write-ups are generally not allowable under U.S. accounting standards, although they are routine in some other countries. More information on asset write-ups is given later in the chapter.

One exception to the practice of ignoring the value of assets discovered is the supplemental disclosure required regarding oil and gas reserves. Publicly traded oil and gas firms are required to disclose the quantity of their proven oil and gas reserves, along with summary data on why the quantity of proven reserves changed during the period. In addition, the oil and gas firms are required to disclose a forecast of the discounted value of future net cash flows expected to be generated by the reserves.[14] The oil and gas firms are skeptical about the usefulness of this disclosure as illustrated by this quote from Exxon's 1998 annual report: "This [discounted value] measure may not necessarily match our view of the future cash flows from our proved reserves."

Acquisition of an Entire Company

Instead of buying selected assets from another firm, sometimes a company will buy the entire firm. This is called a business combination. There are two ways to account for a business combination. The easy way is called a pooling of interests. Conceptually, a pooling of interests is the joining of two equals. From an accounting standpoint, the ledgers of the two combining companies are merely added together.

The other way to account for a business combination is using the purchase method. Conceptually, the purchase method involves one company buying the other. The purchase method raises a number of accounting issues. The first, previously discussed, is how to allocate the purchase price to the various assets acquired. In general, when the purchase method is used, all acquired assets are recorded on the books of the acquiring company at their fair values as of the acquisition date.

net work exercise

Access Texaco's most recent annual report at **www.texaco.com**.
Net Work:
What were Texaco's worldwide net proven reserves at year-end?

14 *Statement of Financial Accounting Standards No. 69,* "Disclosures About Oil and Gas Producing Activities," Stamford: Financial Accounting Standards Board, 1982.

The question of purchase vs. pooling has been a major controversy in accounting. The dispute arises over the fact that in a purchase transaction, assets are recorded at their market values at the time of the transaction. Because this market value is typically greater than book value, the "step up" in recorded cost (including the cost of goodwill) would result in higher depreciation charges. Thus, a purchase transaction would result in lower reported earnings in subsequent years than would a pooling transaction. In 1999, the FASB issued an Exposure Draft that proposes the elimination of the pooling method.[15] The business community overwhelmingly opposes this proposal. However, the FASB has been able to push the proposal forward using the justification that eliminating the use of the pooling method puts U.S. GAAP more in line with international practice in this area. Specifically, members of the G4, which is composed of standard setters from the United States, the United Kingdom, Canada, Australia, New Zealand, have circulated a position paper among themselves proposing the elimination of the pooling method. It is interesting to note that the IASC still allows pooling accounting under the provisions of IAS 22 (which was last revised in 1998).

The second major accounting issue associated with a purchase is the recording of goodwill. **Goodwill** is often referred to as that intangible something that makes the whole company worth more than its individual parts. In general, goodwill represents all the special advantages, not otherwise identifiable, enjoyed by an enterprise, such as a good name, capable staff and personnel, high credit standing, reputation for superior products and services, and favorable location. These factors allow a business to earn above-normal income with the identifiable assets employed in the business.

FYI: In late 1998, the chairman of the SEC criticized acquiring companies for allocating too much of the acquisition cost to acquired in-process research and development, which is then written off immediately as an expense. This practice is discussed in a boxed item later in the chapter.

When a lump sum amount is paid for an established business, the identifiable net assets require appraisal, and the difference between the full purchase price and the value of identifiable net assets can be attributed to the purchase of goodwill. In appraising properties for this purpose, current market values should be sought rather than the values reported in the accounts. Receivables should be stated at amounts estimated to be realized. Inventories and securities should be restated in terms of current market values. Land, buildings, and equipment may require special appraisals in arriving at their present replacement or reproduction values. Intangible assets, such as patents and franchises, should be included at their current values whether or not they were recorded as assets on the books of the acquired company. Care should be taken to determine that liabilities are fully recognized.

To the extent possible, the amount paid for any existing company should be related to identifiable assets. If an excess does exist, it is recognized as an asset and called goodwill or "cost in excess of fair value of net assets acquired."

To illustrate the recording of the purchase of an ongoing business, assume that Airnational Corporation purchases the net assets of Speedy Freight Airlines for $875,000 in cash. A schedule of net assets for Speedy Freight at the time of acquisition is presented below.

Assets		
Cash	$ 37,500	
Receivables	246,000	
Inventory	392,000	
Land, buildings, and equipment (net)	361,200	$1,036,700
Liabilities		
Current liabilities	$ 86,000	
Long-term debt	183,500	269,500
Book value of net assets		$ 767,200

15 *Proposed Statement of Financial Accounting Standards,* "Business Combinations and Intangible Assets," Norwalk, CT: Financial Accounting Standards Board, September 7, 1999.

Analysis of the $107,800 difference between the purchase price ($875,000) and the net asset book value ($767,200) reveals the following differences between the recorded costs and market values of the assets.

	Cost	Market
Inventory	$392,000	$427,000
Land, buildings, and equipment	361,200	389,500
Patents	0	27,000
Totals	$753,200	$843,500

The identifiable portion of the $107,800 difference amounts to $90,300 ($843,500 − $753,200) and is allocated to the respective assets. The remaining difference of $17,500 is recorded as an intangible asset, goodwill.

The entry to record the purchase is as follows:

Cash	37,500	
Receivables	246,000	
Inventory	427,000	
Land, Buildings, and Equipment	389,500	
Patents	27,000	
Goodwill	17,500	
Current Liabilities		86,000
Long-Term Debt		183,500
Cash		875,000

After it is recognized, goodwill is amortized over a period not to exceed 20 years.[16]

STOP & THINK Companies prefer the pooling-of-interests method of accounting for business combinations. Look again at the Speedy Freight example, which uses the purchase method, and explain why companies don't like the purchase method.

Notice that the patent asset was not recorded on the books of Speedy Freight before the acquisition. This could be because the patent cost had been fully amortized or because the patent had been developed through in-house research and development and all of those costs had been immediately expensed. However, when Speedy Freight is acquired, all its identifiable economic assets are recognized. These nonrecorded assets can form a significant part of the value of the business. Exhibit 12–6 lists the estimated value of the 10 most valuable brand names in the world. For the most part, these valuable economic assets are not recognized on the balance sheets of the companies that own them. For example, the value of the Coca-Cola brand name as shown in Exhibit 12–6 is estimated to be $85.6 billion—this value is *not* recorded on Coca-Cola's balance sheet. However, the value of the Coca-Cola brand would add to the price that you or I would have to pay if we purchased THE COCA-COLA COMPANY, and we would report the Coke brand name on our balance sheet after the acquisition.

Because goodwill is recorded on the books only when another company is acquired, one must be careful in interpreting a company's reported goodwill balance. The reported goodwill balance does not reflect the company's own goodwill but the goodwill of other companies it has acquired. So, MICROSOFT goodwill is not recognized on Microsoft's balance sheet, nor is PEPSICO's goodwill shown on the balance sheet of PepsiCo. There is substantial goodwill on Pepsi's balance sheet, but that has arisen from the acquisitions of other companies, for example, FRITO LAY. Thus, companies with sizeable economic goodwill may have no recorded goodwill at all, and the goodwill that a company does report was developed by someone else. Current accounting principles may result in misleading users of financial statements as far as goodwill is concerned. On the other hand, to allow companies to place a value on their own goodwill and record this amount on the balance sheet would introduce a significant amount of added subjectivity to the financial statements.

16 According to the FASB Exposure Draft dated September 1999, the maximum goodwill amortization period is to be lowered from 40 years to 20 years. Goodwill amortization is discussed in Chapter 13.

EXHIBIT 12-6 | Ten Most Valuable Brands in the World for 1999

	Brand Value (in millions)
Coca-Cola	$85.6
Microsoft	57.8
IBM	44.7
General Electric	34.2
Ford	33.9
Disney	32.9
Intel	30.9
McDonald's	26.8
AT&T	24.7
Marlboro	21.5

SOURCE: "The Upwardly Mobile Nokia: Phone Makers Leap into Top Names List," *The Mirror*, June 23, 1999, p. 19.

NEGATIVE GOODWILL Occasionally, the amount paid for another company is less than the fair market value of the net assets of the acquired company. This condition can arise when the existing management of a company is using the assets in a suboptimal fashion. In cases like this, a bargain purchase is possible. The accounting profession has discussed from time to time how such **negative goodwill** should be recorded on the books of the acquiring company. In deciding the issue, the APB did not want the total assets to be recorded at an aggregate amount that exceeded cost. Therefore, the amount of negative goodwill is used to reduce the recorded amount of the acquired noncurrent assets (except for noncurrent marketable equity securities). If this allocation reduces the noncurrent assets to a zero balance, any remaining excess is credited to a negative goodwill account and amortized to revenue, increasing net income over the amortization period.[17]

To illustrate, assume that the Speedy Freight acquisition described earlier was for $400,000 instead of for $875,000. The market value of net assets for Speedy Freight is $857,500 ($767,200 book value plus $90,300 excess of fair value over book value of identifiable assets). If the purchase price is $400,000, the indicated negative goodwill is $457,500 ($857,500 – $400,000). The fair value of noncurrent assets totals $416,500 ($389,500 + $27,000). The acquisition is then recorded as follows:

Cash	37,500	
Receivables	246,000	
Inventory	427,000	
Land, Buildings, and Equipment	0	
Patents	0	
Negative Goodwill		41,000
Current Liabilities		86,000
Long-Term Debt		183,500
Cash		400,000

17 *Opinions of the Accounting Principles Board No. 16*, "Business Combinations," New York: American Institute of Certified Public Accountants, 1970, par. 91. Some accountants have suggested that in a negative goodwill transaction all acquired assets and liabilities should be recorded at their fair market values and that the entire excess of purchase price over net assets acquired be recorded as a one-time increase to stockholders' equity.

If the negative goodwill were less than the total fair value of the noncurrent assets, no negative goodwill would be recognized. Instead, the negative goodwill would be allocated to reduce the noncurrent assets based on their relative fair values.

CAPITALIZE OR EXPENSE?

Separate costs into those that should be expensed immediately and those that should be capitalized, and understand the accounting standards for research and development and oil and gas exploration costs.

The decision as to whether a given expenditure is an asset or an expense is one of the many areas in which an accountant must exercise judgment. Conceptually, the issue is straightforward: If an expenditure is expected to benefit future periods, it is an asset; otherwise, it is an expense.

In practice, the capitalize-or-expense question is much more difficult. To illustrate, look at the continuum in Exhibit 12–7.

EXHIBIT 12–7 | Expense/Asset Continuum

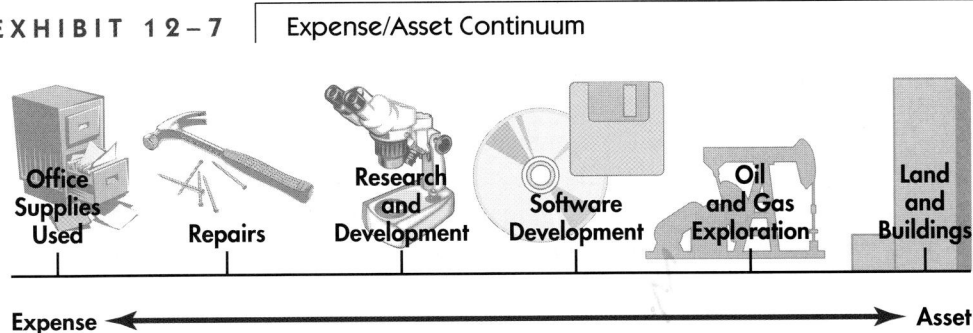

Office Supplies Used — Repairs — Research and Development — Software Development — Oil and Gas Exploration — Land and Buildings

Expense ←——————————————————————————————→ Asset

Few people would disagree with the claim that the cost of office supplies used is an expense. Once the supplies are used, the supplies offer no further future benefit. Similarly, the cost of a building clearly should be capitalized because the building will provide economic benefit in future periods. The endpoints of the continuum are easy, but it is the vast middle ground where accountants must exercise their judgment.

The difficulty with making capitalize-or-expense decisions is that many expenditures have some probability of generating future economic benefit, but there is uncertainty surrounding that benefit. Research and development expenditures are a good example. Companies spend money on research and development because they expect to reap future benefits. However, there is no guarantee that the benefits will materialize. The following sections examine several categories of expenditures in order to give you practice in analyzing the issues relevant to a capitalize-or-expense decision.

Before examining the conceptual issues, here is one practical note. Many companies establish a lower limit on amounts that will be considered for capitalization in order to avoid wasting time agonizing about the proper accounting for trivial amounts. Thus, any expenditure under the established limit is always expensed currently even though future benefits are expected from that expenditure. This practice is justified on the grounds of expediency and materiality. Of course, the amount of the limit varies with the size of the company. In the published financial statements of large corporations, for example, amounts are rounded to the nearest million. Detailed accounting for amounts smaller than this will have no impact on the reported numbers. This treatment is acceptable as long as it is consistently applied and no material misstatements arise due to unusual expenditure patterns or other causes.

Postacquisition Expenditures

Over the useful lives of plant assets, regular as well as special expenditures are incurred. Certain expenditures are required to maintain and repair assets; others are incurred to increase their capacity or efficiency or to extend their useful lives. Each expenditure requires careful analysis to determine whether it should be expensed or capitalized.

The terms maintenance, repairs, renewals, replacements, additions, betterments, improvements, and rearrangements are used in describing expenditures made in the course of asset use. These are described in the following sections. Exhibit 12–8 summarizes the accounting for these subsequent expenditures.

EXHIBIT 12–8 | Summary of Expenditures Subsequent to Acquisition

Type of Expenditure	Definition	Accounting Treatment
Maintenance and repairs	Normal cost of keeping property in operating condition.	Expense as incurred.
Renewals and replacements:		
1. No extension of useful life or increase in future cash flows.	Unplanned replacement. Expenditure needed to fulfill original plans.	Expense as incurred.
2. Extends useful life or increases future cash flows.	Improvement resulting from replacement with better component.	Record as an asset by one of two methods: 1. If cost of old component is known: Remove cost of old part and its accumulated depreciation, recognizing gain or loss. Defer cost of new component.
		2. If cost of old component is not known: Deduct cost of new component from accumulated depreciation.
Additions and betterments	Expenditures that add to asset usefulness by either extending life or increasing future cash flows. No replacement of component involved.	Add to the cost of an asset.

MAINTENANCE AND REPAIRS Expenditures to maintain plant assets in good operating condition are referred to as **maintenance.** Among these are expenditures for painting, lubricating, and adjusting equipment. Maintenance expenditures are ordinary, recurring, and do not improve the asset or add to its life; therefore, they are recorded as expenses when they are incurred.

Expenditures to restore assets to good operating condition upon their breakdown or to restore and replace broken parts are referred to as **repairs.** These are ordinary and recurring expenditures that benefit only current operations; thus, they also are charged to expense immediately.

RENEWALS AND REPLACEMENTS Expenditures for overhauling plant assets are frequently referred to as **renewals.** Substitutions of parts or entire units are referred to as **replacements.** If these expenditures are necessary to achieve the original plans and do not change the original estimates of useful life or cash flows, they should be expensed. If, however, these expenditures extend the life of the asset or increase the cash flows generated by the asset, they should be capitalized by either adding them to the asset value or deducting them from accumulated depreciation.

Theoretically, if a part is removed and replaced with a superior part, the cost and accumulated depreciation related to the replaced part should be removed from the accounts, a loss recognized for the undepreciated book value, and the expenditure for the replacement added to the asset value. Often it is not possible to identify the cost related to a specific part of an asset. In these instances, by debiting Accumulated Depreciation, the net book value is increased without creating a buildup of the gross asset value. When this entry is made, no immediate loss related to the removal of the old asset is recognized.

To illustrate replacements, assume the Mendon Fireworks Company replaces the roof of its manufacturing plant for $40,000 which extends the estimated life of the building by five years. Assume that the original cost of the building was $1,600,000 and it is three-fourths depreciated. If the original roof cost $20,000, the following entry could be made to remove the undepreciated book value of the old roof and record the expenditure for the new one.

Buildings (new roof)	40,000	
Accumulated Depreciation (old roof)	15,000	
Loss From Replacement of Roof	5,000	
Buildings (old roof)		20,000
Cash		40,000

If Mendon could not identify the cost of the old roof, the following entry would be made:

Accumulated Depreciation	40,000	
Cash		40,000

The book value of the building after the first entry is $435,000 ($1,600,000 – $1,200,000 + $40,000 – $5,000). Assuming the second entry is made, the book value would be $440,000 ($1,600,000 – $1,200,000 + $40,000). The $5,000 additional cost would be reflected in higher depreciation charges over the remaining life of the building.

ADDITIONS AND BETTERMENTS Enlargements and extensions of existing facilities are referred to as **additions.** Changes in assets designed to provide increased or improved services are referred to as **betterments.** If the addition or betterment does not involve a replacement of component parts of an existing asset, the expenditure should be capitalized by adding it to the cost of the asset. If a replacement is involved, it is accounted for as discussed in the Mendon roof example.

Research and Development Expenditures

Historically, expenditures for **research and development (R&D)** purposes were reported sometimes as assets and sometimes as expenses. The FASB inherited this problem from the Accounting Principles Board and made this area the subject of its first definitive standard.[18] The Board defined **research** activities as those undertaken to discover new knowledge that will be useful in developing new products, services, or processes or that will result in significant improvements of existing products or processes. **Development** activities involve the application of research findings to develop a plan or design for new or improved products and processes. Development activities include the formulation, design, and testing of products; construction of prototypes; and operation of pilot plants.

Because of the uncertainty surrounding the future economic benefit of R&D activities, the FASB concluded that research and development expenditures should be expensed in the period incurred. Among the arguments for expensing R&D costs is the frequent inability to find a definite causal relationship between the expenditures and future revenues. Sometimes very large expenditures do not generate any future revenue, while relatively small expenditures lead to significant discoveries that generate large revenues. The Board found it difficult to establish criteria that would distinguish between those research and development expenditures that would most likely benefit future periods and those that would not.

Research and development costs include those costs of materials, equipment, facilities, personnel, purchased intangibles, contract services, and a reasonable allocation of indirect costs that are related specifically to research and development activities and that have no alternative future uses. Such activities include:

18 *Statement of Financial Accounting Standards No. 2,* "Accounting for Research and Development Costs," Stamford, CT: Financial Accounting Standards Board, 1974.

- Research aimed at discovery of new knowledge
- Search for applications of research findings
- Search for possible product or process alternatives
- Design, construction, and testing of preproduction prototypes
- Design, construction, and operation of a pilot plant

Expenditures for certain items having alternative future uses, either in additional research projects or for productive purposes, can be recorded as assets and allocated against future projects or periods as research and development expenses. This exception permits the deferral of costs incurred for materials, equipment, facilities, and purchased intangibles, but only if an alternative use can be identified.

Computer Software Development Expenditures

The FASB's requirement that all R&D costs be expensed seemed particularly ill suited for the many software developers that sprang up in the early 1980s. The only economic assets owned by these firms were the software they developed, and strict application of Statement No. 2 dictated that all development costs be expensed. The FASB, with strong support from the SEC, reexamined the R&D issue in the context of software developers and in 1985 issued Statement No. 86, "Accounting for the Costs of Computer Software to Be Sold, Leased, or Otherwise Marketed."

The Board's conclusions concerning computer **software development costs** are summarized in Exhibit 12–9.

EXHIBIT 12–9 | Development of Successful Software

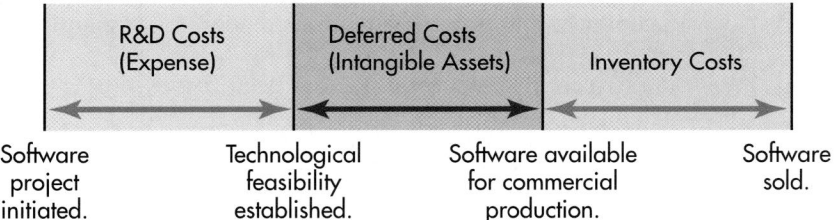

| Software project initiated. | Technological feasibility established. | Software available for commercial production. | Software sold. |

As demonstrated by Exhibit 12–9, all costs incurred up to the point where **technological feasibility** is established are to be expensed as research and development. These include costs incurred for planning, designing, and testing activities. In essence, the uncertainty surrounding the future benefits of these costs is so great that they should be expensed. After technological feasibility has been established, uncertainty about future benefits is decreased to the extent that costs incurred after this point can be capitalized. Capitalizable software development costs include the costs of coding and testing done after the establishment of technological feasibility and the cost to produce masters. Additional costs to actually produce software from the masters and package the software for distribution are inventoriable costs and will be expensed as part of cost of goods sold.

Considerable judgment is required to determine when technological feasibility has been established. At a minimum, technological feasibility is attained when an enterprise has produced either:[19]

- A detailed program design of the software, or
- A working model of the software

19 *Statement of Financial Accounting Standards No. 86*, "Accounting for the Costs of Computer Software to Be Sold, Leased, or Otherwise Marketed," Stamford, CT: Financial Accounting Standards Board, 1985, par. 4.

INTERNATIONAL ACCOUNTING FOR RESEARCH AND DEVELOPMENT: IAS 9
The IASC has established an R&D accounting rule that many think is superior to the FASB rule. IAS 9 requires research costs to be expensed and development costs to be capitalized. Research costs, as defined in this standard, are those R&D costs incurred before technological feasibility has been established, and development costs are those incurred after technological feasibility. As you can see, the FASB rule for the accounting for software development costs is the same as the IASC standard for all research and development costs.

THE FUTURE OF R&D ACCOUNTING IN THE UNITED STATES   In a press release dated July 28, 1999, the FASB announced its intention to revisit the standard of accounting for research and development costs. This broad reexamination was prompted by the desire to address the proper treatment of research and development acquired as part of a business acquisition. However, rather than merely address the narrow issue of acquired in-process R&D, the FASB plans to develop a comprehensive new standard on research and development accounting. It is likely that any new standard issued will be generally consistent with IAS 9—that is, research costs will be expensed and development costs will be capitalized. However, remember that, until then, U.S. GAAP requires that all R&D costs be expensed.

Oil and Gas Exploration Costs

The nature of oil exploration is that several dry wells are drilled for each "gusher" that is discovered. The accounting question is whether the cost of the dry holes should be expensed as incurred or whether the costs should be capitalized. Two methods of accounting have been developed to account for oil and gas exploratory costs. Under the **full cost method,** all exploratory costs are capitalized, the reasoning being that the cost of drilling dry wells is part of the cost of locating productive wells. Under the **successful efforts method,** exploratory costs for dry holes are expensed, and only exploratory costs for successful wells are capitalized. Most large, successful oil companies use the successful efforts method. Exhibit 12–10 contains a description of the successful efforts method given by EXXON in the notes to its 1998 financial statements.

For smaller companies, the full cost approach has been more popular. The claim is that the full cost method encourages small companies to continue exploration by not imposing the severe penalty of recognizing all costs of unsuccessful projects as immediate expenses. Exhibit 12–10 also contains an excerpt from the 1998 financial statements of UNITED HERITAGE, a small company based in Cleburne, Texas, which produces "lite" beef, and that also accounts for its oil and gas operations using the full cost method.

E X H I B I T   1 2 – 1 0 | Exxon Corporation and United Heritage—Exploration Costs

---

Exxon Corporation

The corporation's exploration and production activities are accounted for under the "successful efforts" method. Under this method, costs of productive wells and development dry holes, both tangible and intangible, as well as productive acreage are capitalized and amortized on the unit-of-production method. Costs of that portion of undeveloped acreage likely to be unproductive, based largely on historical experience, are amortized over the period of exploration.

United Heritage

The Company follows the full cost method of accounting for oil and gas properties. Accordingly, all costs associated with acquisition, exploration and development of oil and gas reserves are capitalized. When production commences all capitalized costs, including the estimated future costs to develop proved reserves, will be amortized on the unit-of-production method using estimates of proved reserves.

► **WHO SETS ACCOUNTING STANDARDS IN THE UNITED STATES? THE CASE OF ACQUIRED IN-PROCESS R&D**

In September 1998, Arthur Levitt, Chairman of the SEC, spoke out against accounting practices used by companies in order to manage earnings. One of the suspect practices identified by Chairman Levitt is labeled "creative acquisition accounting," and one specific technique involves the accounting for acquired

in-process research and development, that is, the amount of an acquisition price that is allocated to the value of R&D projects purchased as part of the acquisition.

Because FASB Statement No. 2 dictates that R&D costs be expensed immediately, any portion of an acquisition price designated as acquired in-process R&D is written off to expense in the year of the acquisition. On the face of it, this does not appear to be an attractive option because earnings in the acquisition year

are drastically reduced. However, the payoff comes in subsequent years through increased earnings, both relative to the artificially low earnings of the acquisition year and relative to the earnings that would have been reported if the acquired in-process R&D had been capitalized and then expensed over time.

In early 1999, the FASB considered promulgating a new standard for acquired in-process R&D but decided to delay any decision until it could undertake a compre-

The issue of how to account for exploratory costs in the oil and gas industry has attracted the attention of the FASB, the SEC, and even the U.S. Congress. When an apparent oil shortage developed in the 1970s, there was strong pressure placed on oil companies to expand their exploration to discover new sources of oil and gas. One provision of the Energy Policy and Conservation Act of 1975 was that the SEC establish accounting rules for U.S. firms engaged in the production of oil and gas. The SEC allowed the FASB to take the lead. In 1977, the FASB decided that the successful efforts method (i.e., expense the cost of dry holes) was the appropriate accounting treatment and issued FASB Statement No. 19, "Financial Accounting and Reporting by Oil and Gas Producing Companies."

FYI: In 1979, the SEC proposed a new method of accounting for oil and gas exploration called Reserve Recognition Accounting (RRA). RRA was a form of discovery accounting that would have recognized as an asset the value of the oil and gas discovered rather than the cost of the exploration efforts. A form of RRA lives on in the supplemental disclosures required by oil and gas firms.

The uproar over SFAS No. 19 was immediate and loud. Small independent oil exploration firms argued that using the successful efforts method would require them to expense costs that they had been capitalizing, resulting in lower profits, depressed stock prices, and more difficulty in getting loans. The Department of Energy held hearings and the Justice Department's antitrust division expressed concern. A bill was introduced in the Senate that would have made it *illegal* for the FASB to eliminate the full cost method. The SEC ran for cover and declared that in spite of the FASB standard, financial statements prepared using the full cost method would be acceptable to the SEC. In February 1979, the FASB succumbed to the pressure and issued SFAS No. 25, reinstating the full cost method.[20]

The oil and gas controversy is a perfect illustration of the difficulties surrounding the capitalize-or-expense decision. Conceptual arguments can usually be made on both sides of the issue. Some expenditures, such as research and development and oil and gas exploration costs, are covered by specific authoritative pronouncements. Other expenditures, such as repairs or renewals, require accounting judgment. Material in the cases at the end of the chapter allows you to test your judgment on such issues as the accounting for advertising and asbestos removal.

---

20 *Statement of Financial Accounting Standards No. 25,* "Suspension of Certain Accounting Requirements for Oil and Gas Producing Companies," Stamford, CT: Financial Accounting Standards Board, 1979.

hensive reexamination of the whole field of accounting for research and development. Interestingly, the SEC showed no reluctance in acting fast and made it known to companies filing financial statements that any allocation of an acquisition price to acquired in-process R&D would be looked at very carefully (and skeptically). As a result, the total amount of acquired in-process R&D written off in the first half of 1999 by U.S. companies was $2.8 billion, down from $8.3 billion in the first half of 1998. Thus, it appears that the SEC, through the threat of administrative enforcement, has greatly impacted an area in which the FASB has yet to voice an opinion. So, who sets the accounting standards in the United States?

QUESTIONS:

1. When the FASB does reconsider the accounting for research and development, what treatment do you think will be required for acquired in-process R&D? Explain.

2. Who sets the accounting standards in the United States? Explain.

SOURCES:

Elizabeth MacDonald, "Amount of Certain Corporate Write-Offs Falls 24% After SEC Battle on Abuses," *The Wall Street Journal,* September 13, 1999, p. A4.

Press Release, Norwalk, CT: Financial Accounting Standards Board, July 28, 1999.

Discuss the pros and cons of recording noncurrent operating assets at their current values.

VALUATION OF ASSETS AT CURRENT VALUES

Throughout this chapter, the valuation of assets has been based on historical costs. As discussed in Chapter 1, asset measurement is frequently a trade-off between relevance and reliability. Historical cost is a reliable number, but the current value of noncurrent assets can be more relevant.

The reduction in the recorded amount of noncurrent operating assets that have declined in value has long been part of generally accepted accounting principles. Writing down assets to recognize market value declines is a reflection of the conservative bias that is a fundamental part of accounting practice. The rules governing these impairment write-downs are discussed in Chapter 13. On the other hand, asset write-ups have not been generally accepted in recent times. Before the formation of the SEC in 1934, it was common for U.S. companies to report the upward revaluation of property and equipment. However, by 1940 the SEC had effectively eliminated this practice, not by explicitly banning it, but through informal administrative pressure. Much of the suspicion about asset revaluations stemmed from a Federal Trade Commission investigation, completed in 1935, that uncovered a number of cases in the public utility industry in which a utility had improperly revalued assets upward to boost its rate base. In the late 1980s, the absence of advance warning of the $500 billion collapse of the savings and loan (S&L) industry was blamed in part on the failure of S&Ls to report current market values of their loan portfolios. Reexamination of the accounting for financial institutions led to FASB Statement No. 115, which requires most investment securities to be reported at their current market values. It is likely that the continuing call by financial statement users for current value information will result in a reconsideration of the appropriateness of historical cost accounting for noncurrent operating assets. In fact, for a period of 10 years, the FASB required large companies to report the current value of noncurrent operating assets in a note to the statements. This requirement was rescinded in 1986 by FASB Statement No. 89.

In IAS 16, the IASC permits the inclusion of upward revaluations of noncurrent operating assets in the financial statements as an allowable alternative to reporting the historical cost of those assets. Because fair values are often based on subjective appraisals rather than objective historical cost, accountants and auditors have traditionally been concerned that companies might use upward asset revaluations in order to artificially

boost reported balance sheet and income statement values. This concern is reflected in the careful rules laid out in IAS 16, some of which are summarized below.

- If a company revalues its noncurrent operating assets to fair value, it must do so on a regular basis (not as a one-time event) and must revalue entire classes of assets rather than just picking and choosing certain assets in an effort to report the fair values of only those assets that have increased in value.
- Downward revaluations are recorded as a loss.
- Upward revaluations are recorded as a debit to the asset and a credit to a special "revaluation" equity account. This practice means that upward revaluations cannot be used to boost reported income. In addition, when an asset that has been revalued upward is subsequently sold, any associated balance in the special revaluation equity account is credited directly to retained earnings and is not reported as an income statement gain. The implication of this accounting treatment is that the choice to recognize the increase in the value of a noncurrent operating asset through an asset revaluation means that the increase will never be reported in the income statement as a gain, even when the asset is sold.

 Do you think it is likely that within the next 10 years the FASB or SEC will require companies to recognize the current value of noncurrent operating assets? Why or why not?

Asset revaluations are recorded quite frequently in the accounting records of companies based in the United Kingdom. One example can be found in the financial statements of DIAGEO, the British consumer products firm owning such brand names as Smirnoff, Johnnie Walker, J&B, Gordon's, Guinness, Pillsbury, Haagen-Dazs, and Burger King. As of June 30, 1998, the reported net amount of land and buildings for Diageo was £1.425 billion. This number is a mix of historical cost numbers and amounts obtained from professional revaluations. Without the revaluations, the net amount of land and buildings would have been £1.235 billion. Further explanation of the accounting for upward asset revaluations is given in Chapter 13.

Use the fixed asset turnover ratio as a general measure of how efficiently a company is using its property, plant, and equipment.

MEASURING PROPERTY, PLANT, AND EQUIPMENT EFFICIENCY

The result of proper capital budgeting analysis should be a level of property, plant, and equipment that is appropriate to the amount of sales a company is doing. As with any other asset, excess funds tied up in the form of property, plant, and equipment reduce a company's efficiency, increase financing costs, and lower return on equity.

In this section we discuss the **fixed asset turnover ratio,** which uses financial statement data to roughly indicate how efficiently a company is utilizing its property, plant, and equipment to generate sales. We also illustrate that careful interpretation of the fixed asset turnover ratio is necessary because the recorded book value of long-term operating assets can differ significantly from the actual value of those assets.

Evaluating the Level of Property, Plant, and Equipment

Fixed asset turnover ratio is computed as sales divided by average property, plant, and equipment (fixed assets) and is interpreted as the number of dollars in sales generated by each dollar of fixed assets. This ratio is also called *PP&E turnover.* The computation of the fixed asset turnover ratio for GENERAL ELECTRIC is given on the following page. (All financial statement numbers are in millions.)

The fixed asset turnover ratios suggest that General Electric was almost as efficient at using its fixed assets to generate sales in 1997 as it was in 1996. In 1997, each dollar of fixed assets generated $1.75 in sales, down just slightly from $1.76 in 1996.

	1997	1996
Sales	$53,404	$47,897
Property, plant, and equipment:		
Beginning of year	$28,795	$25,679
End of year	$32,316	$28,795
Average fixed assets [(beginning balance + ending balance) ÷ 2]	$30,556	$27,237
Fixed asset turnover ratio	1.75	1.76

Dangers in Using the Fixed Asset Turnover Ratio

As with all ratios, the fixed asset turnover ratio must be used carefully to ensure that erroneous conclusions are not made. For example, fixed asset turnover ratio values for two companies in different industries cannot be meaningfully compared. This point can be illustrated using the fact that General Electric is composed of two primary parts—General Electric, the manufacturing company, and GE Capital Services, the financial services firm. The fixed asset turnover ratio computed earlier was for both parts. Because GE Capital Services does not use property, plant, and equipment for manufacturing but instead leases assets to other companies to earn financial revenue, one would expect GE Capital Services' fixed asset turnover ratio to be quite unlike that for a manufacturing firm. In fact, as shown below, the fixed asset turnover ratio for the manufacturing segments of General Electric was 4.46 times in 1997, more than double the ratio value for the entire company.

Fixed Asset Turnover Ratio:
General Electric—Manufacturing Segments Only

	1997	1996
Sales	$48,952	$46,119
Property, plant, and equipment:		
Beginning of year	$10,832	$10,234
End of year	$11,118	$10,832
Average fixed assets [(beginning balance + ending balance) ÷ 2]	$10,975	$10,533
Fixed asset turnover ratio	4.46	4.38

Another difficulty in comparing values for the fixed asset turnover ratio among different companies is that the reported amount for property, plant, and equipment can be a poor indicator of the actual fair value of the fixed assets being used by a company. As discussed earlier, the accounting rules in the United States require fixed assets to be written down when their value is impaired, but do not allow the writing up of fixed asset amounts to reflect increases in fair value. This creates a comparability problem when one company has relatively new fixed assets, which are recorded at close to market value, and another company has older fixed assets, which are recorded at depreciated historical cost values that may significantly understate the real value of the assets.

A graphic illustration of this comparability problem is provided by SAFEWAY, the supermarket chain. Safeway was taken private in a leveraged buyout near the end of 1986. When the leveraged buyout occurred, Safeway became a new company, for accounting purposes at least, and Safeway's assets were restated to their current market values as of the leveraged buyout date. This provides a rare opportunity to see how significantly the fixed asset turnover ratio is impacted by whether a company has its fixed assets recorded at market values or at depreciated historical cost. On the following page are listed the cost, accumulated depreciation, and fixed asset turnover ratios for Safeway for 1985, just before the leveraged buyout, and 1986, just after the leveraged buyout.

Safeway had almost the same fixed assets in place at the end of 1986 as it had at the end of 1985; the difference in the reported num-

STOP & THINK Why did Safeway's accumulated depreciation decrease so dramatically from 1985 to 1986?

bers is due almost entirely to the revaluation that took place as part of the leveraged buy-out. Notice that the book value of Safeway's fixed assets increased by over $1 billion from 1985 to 1986. This increase reflects the impact of reporting the fixed assets at market value rather than at depreciated historical cost. Also, note the significant decline in the computed fixed asset turnover ratio—from 7.45 in 1985 to 5.44 in 1986. Actually, Safeway's use of its fixed assets was almost exactly the same in 1986 as it had been in 1985; the difference in the ratio is caused by the use of the artificially low depreciated cost numbers in 1985 to compute the ratio. In summary, the fixed asset turnover ratio can be significantly impacted by the difference between the market value of fixed assets and their reported depreciated cost. For some companies, this difference can be very large indeed.

	1986	1985
Cost	$3,854	$4,641
Less: Accumulated depreciation	120	2,004
Book value	$3,734	$2,637
Fixed asset turnover ratio	5.44	7.45

Another complication with analysis using the fixed asset turnover ratio is caused by leasing. As will be discussed in Chapter 15, many companies lease the bulk of their fixed assets, and as a result, many of these assets are not included in their balance sheets. This biases the fixed asset turnover ratio for these companies upward because the sales generated by the leased assets are included in the numerator of the ratio but the leased assets generating the sales are not included in the denominator.

EXPANDED MATERIAL

The capitalized interest example earlier in the chapter, although it probably seemed complicated enough, was simplified considerably by skirting two complexities. The expanded material section will illustrate an alternative method for computing capitalized interest and will demonstrate how to handle cases in which new borrowing occurs during the construction period.

CAPITALIZED INTEREST: COMPLEXITIES

6

Evaluate the different ways to compute capitalized interest and properly incorporate midyear loans into the capitalized interest calculations.

This section covers two complexities associated with computing the amount of capitalized interest.

1. An alternative method for computing the amount of capitalized interest, the **weighted average accumulated expenditure method,** yields a different number for capitalized interest than does the approach illustrated earlier in the chapter. The approach illustrated earlier will be called the **avoidable interest method.**
2. When new borrowings occur during the construction period, the interest capitalization computation must be adjusted to avoid capitalizing interest that was never incurred.[21]

21　These two complexities are also explained by Kathryn M. Means and Paul M. Karenski, "SFAS 34: A Recipe for Diversity," *Accounting Horizons,* September 1988, pp. 62–67.

Weighted Average Accumulated Expenditure Method

The same numbers from the Cutler Industries, Inc., example shown earlier in the chapter are used here. Recall that borrowings outstanding as of January 1, 2002, are as follows:

Construction loan, 12% interest	$2,000,000
5-year notes payable, 11% interest	3,000,000
Mortgage on other plant, 9% interest	4,800,000

The weighted-average interest rate on the general nonconstruction debt was computed earlier as 9.8%.

Expenditures on the project during 2002 were incurred as follows:

January 1, 2002	$1,200,000
October 1, 2002	1,800,000

Interest to be capitalized for 2002 was $192,500, computed using the avoidable interest method.

An alternative way to compute the amount of capitalized interest is to use the weighted average accumulated expenditure method. The amount of weighted average accumulated expenditures for 2002 is computed as follows:

Expenditure Date	Amount	Fraction of the Year Outstanding	Weighted Expenditures
January 1, 2002	$1,200,000	12/12	$1,200,000
October 1, 2002	1,800,000	3/12	450,000
Weighted average accumulated expenditures for 2002			$1,650,000

Using this technique, computation of the amount of interest to be capitalized for 2002 is as follows:

Weighted Average Expenditure Amount	Interest Capitalization Rate	Capitalized Interest
$1,650,000	12%	$198,000

> **Caution!** Don't be too hard on the average accumulated expenditure method. It is easy to use and gives a reasonable approximation of the value computed using the avoidable interest method.

If the weighted average accumulated expenditures had exceeded the $2,000,000 amount for the construction-specific loan, capitalized interest on the excess would have been computed using the 9.8% average rate on general debt.

The difference between the $198,000 computed using the weighted average accumulated expenditure method and the $192,500 computed using the avoidable interest method arises because the weighted average accumulated expenditure technique makes the simplifying assumption that the weighted average expenditure amount, and only that amount, was outstanding for the entire year. This assumption does not give as accurate an indication of the amount of interest cost that could have been avoided if the specific construction expenditures had been used to repay loans. However, both techniques are in accordance with the accounting standards.

New Borrowing During the Construction Period

Assume that the $2,000,000, 12% construction loan was obtained on July 1, 2002, rather than on January 1, 2002. Just as expenditures during the year are weighted to determine the average accumulated expenditures, loans obtained during the year can be weighted to compute a weighted average loan amount. The 2002 weighted average loan amount for the July 1, 2002, $2,000,000 construction loan is $1,000,000 ($2,000,000 × ½). The computation of interest eligible for capitalization for 2002, using the weighted average accumulated expenditure method, is as follows:

Weighted Average Expenditure Amount	Interest Capitalization Rate	Capitalized Interest
$1,000,000*	12%	$120,000
650,000**	9.8%	63,700
		$183,700

*Weighted average amount for the July 1 construction loan.
**$1,650,000 – $1,000,000. Recall that average accumulated expenditures for 2002 were $1,650,000.

The reason that only $183,700 would be capitalized in this case while $198,000 was capitalized in the original case is because, in the second case, the construction loan was not needed until six months after the beginning of the project. Predictably, with lower interest costs traceable to the project, the amount of interest capitalized is lower.

A similar calculation, though a little more complicated, can be done using the avoidable interest method, as follows:

Date	Amount	Interest Capitalization Rate	Fraction of the Year Outstanding	Capitalized Interest
January 1, 2002*	$1,200,000	9.8%	6/12	$ 58,800
July 1, 2002**	1,200,000	12%	6/12	72,000
October 1, 2002	800,000	12%	3/12	24,000
	1,000,000	9.8%	3/12	24,500
Total capitalized interest for 2002				$179,300

*Average rate on general debt of 9.8% is used for the first six months of the year because the 12% construction loan was not taken out until July 1.
**Reflects avoidable interest on the construction loan for the last six months of the year.

REVIEW OF LEARNING OBJECTIVES

1 **Identify those costs to be included in the acquisition cost of different types of noncurrent operating assets.** The cost of tangible noncurrent operating assets includes not only the original purchase price or equivalent value but also any other expenditures required in obtaining and preparing the asset for its intended use. For example, land cost includes surveying fees and the cost of removing old buildings. Equipment cost includes the costs of testing and installation.

Intangible noncurrent operating assets are also generally recorded at cost. The cost is the purchase price if copyrights, patents, or trademarks are purchased from another company. For internally generated intangibles, the cost often includes only the actual legal and filing costs, as well as any cost to successfully defend the rights in court.

2 **Properly account for noncurrent operating asset acquisitions using various special** arrangements, including deferred payment, self-construction, and acquisition of an entire company.

- *Basket purchase.* Acquisition cost is allocated to the various assets based on the relative fair values of the assets.
- *Deferred payment.* The acquisition is recorded at the discounted present value of the payments.
- *Leasing.* Property leased under a capital lease is recognized as an asset; property leased under an operating lease is not included in the balance sheet.
- *Exchange of nonmonetary assets.* The transaction is recorded at the fair value of the asset received or the asset given, whichever is more clearly determinable.
- *Acquisition by issuing securities.* The transaction is recorded at the fair value of the asset acquired or the securities issued, whichever is more clearly determinable.

- *Self-construction.* The cost of self-constructed assets includes an allocation of overhead and the cost of interest incurred to finance the construction. The amount of capitalized interest is an estimate of interest that could have been avoided if the construction expenditures had been used to repay loans instead.
- *Acquisition by donation or discovery.* Assets received as donations are recorded as revenue in an amount equal to the fair value of the assets. Discovered assets are not recognized.
- *Acquisition of an entire company.* In a business combination accounted for as a purchase, acquired assets are recorded at their fair values, and any excess is recognized as goodwill. Any negative goodwill amounts are first subtracted from the recorded amounts of acquired noncurrent assets and any remainder is accounted for as negative goodwill.

3 **Separate costs into those that should be expensed immediately and those that should be capitalized, and understand the accounting standards for research and development and oil and gas exploration costs.**

- *Postacquisition costs.* Repair and maintenance costs are expensed. Expenditures that add to the usefulness of the asset are capitalized.
- *Research and development costs.* In the United States, all general research and development expenditures are expensed as incurred. The FASB may reconsider this rule some time soon.
- *Software development costs.* In the United States, software development expenditures incurred before technological feasibility has been established are expensed; expenditures after technological feasibility has been established are capitalized.
- *Oil and gas exploration costs.* With the successful efforts method, costs of drilling dry wells are expensed immediately; with the full cost method these costs are capitalized.

4 **Discuss the pros and cons of recording noncurrent operating assets at their current values.** Recording noncurrent operating assets at their current values represents a trade-off between

relevance and reliability. In the United States, reliability concerns have resulted in the prohibition of asset write-ups. Under IAS 16, upward asset revaluations are an allowable alternative to reporting the historical cost of those assets.

5 **Use the fixed asset turnover ratio as a general measure of how efficiently a company is using its property, plant, and equipment.** The fixed asset turnover ratio is computed as sales divided by average property, plant, and equipment (fixed assets) and is interpreted as the number of dollars in sales generated by each dollar of fixed assets. Meaningful comparison of fixed asset turnover ratios can only be done between firms in similar industries. Another difficulty in comparing values for the fixed asset turnover ratio among different companies is that the reported amount for property, plant, and equipment can be a poor indicator of the actual fair value of the fixed assets being used by a company. This is true when fixed assets have increased in value, relative to their depreciated cost, and also when a significant number of assets have been leased and are not reported in the balance sheet.

6 **Evaluate the different ways to compute capitalized interest and properly incorporate mid-year loans into the capitalized interest calculations.**

- *Avoidable interest method.* This method approximates the interest that could have been avoided by using construction expenditures to repay loans. This method incorporates consideration of both the specific timing of expenditures and the specific periods that loans are outstanding.
- *Average accumulated expenditure method.* This method incorporates the simplifying assumption that the average expenditure amount was outstanding for the entire year. The appropriate interest rate is applied to this average balance.

KEY TERMS

QUESTIONS

1. On the balance sheets of many companies, the largest classification of assets in amount is noncurrent operating assets. Name the items, in addition to the amount paid to the former owner or contractor, that may be properly included as part of the acquisition cost of the following property items: (a) land, (b) buildings, and (c) equipment.

2. What acquisition costs are included in (a) copyrights, (b) franchises, and (c) trademarks?

3. What procedure should be followed to allocate the cost of a basket purchase of assets among specific accounts?

4. What special accounting problems are introduced when a company purchases equipment on a deferred payment contract rather than with cash?

5. (a) Why is the "list price" of an asset often not representative of its fair market value? (b) Under these conditions, how should a fair market value be determined?

6. Gaylen Corp. decides to construct a building for itself and plans to use existing plant facilities to assist with such construction. (a) What costs will enter into the cost of construction? (b) What two positions can the company take with respect to general overhead allocation during the period of construction? Evaluate each position and indicate your preference.

7. What characteristics must a construction project have before interest can be capitalized as part of the project cost?

8. The Parkhurst Corporation acquires land and buildings valued at $250,000 as a gift from a local philanthropist. The president of the company maintains that because there was no cost for the acquisition, neither the cost of the facilities nor depreciation needs to be recognized for financial statement purposes. Evaluate the president's position assuming (a) the donation is unconditional and (b) the donation is contingent upon the employment by the company of a certain number of employees for a 10-year period.

9. (a) Under what conditions may goodwill be reported as an asset? (b) The Roper Company engages in a widespread advertising campaign on behalf of new products, charging above-normal expenditures to goodwill. Do you approve of this practice? Why or why not?

10. Why do some companies expense asset expenditures that are under an established monetary amount?

11. Indicate the effects of the following errors on the balance sheet and the income statement in the current year and succeeding years.
    (a) The cost of a depreciable asset is incorrectly recorded as an expense.
    (b) An expense expenditure is incorrectly recorded as an addition to the cost of a depreciable asset.

12. Which of the following items would be recorded as expenses and which would be recorded as assets?
    (a) Cost of installing machinery *Capitalize*
    (b) Cost of unsuccessful litigation to protect patent *expense*
    (c) Extensive repairs as a result of a fire
    (d) Cost of grading land *Capitalize*
    (e) Insurance on machinery in transit *CAPITALIZE*
    (f) Interest incurred during construction period *CAP*
    (g) Cost of major unexpected overhaul on machinery *EXP*
    (h) New safety guards on machinery *CAP*
    (i) Commission on purchase of real estate *CAP*
    (j) Special tax assessment for street improvements *CAP*
    (k) Cost of repainting offices *EXP*

13. Why are some asset expenditures made subsequent to acquisition recorded as an increase in an asset account and others recorded as a decrease in Accumulated Depreciation?

14. (a) What type of activities are considered to be research and development activities? (b) Under what conditions, if any, are research and development costs capitalized?

15. Distinguish between the full cost and successful efforts methods of recording exploratory costs for oil and gas properties.

16. What argument is given for reporting noncurrent operating assets at their historical costs instead of at current values?

17. Under the provisions of IAS 16, what is the credit entry when noncurrent operating assets are written up to reflect an increase in market value?

18. How is the fixed asset turnover ratio calculated, and what does the resulting ratio measure?

19. Briefly describe the dangers to financial statement users inherent in the use of the fixed asset turnover ratio.

20. What two methods can be used to compute the amount of interest that should be capitalized? Which method is more theoretically correct?

DISCUSSION CASES

CASE 12–1

IS THERE ANY GOODWILL?

Fugate Energy Corp. has recently purchased a small local company, Gleave Inc., for $556,950 cash. The chief accountant of Fugate has been given the assignment of preparing the journal entry to record the purchase. An investigation disclosed the following information about the assets of Gleave Inc.:

(a) Gleave owned land and a small manufacturing building. The book value of the property on Gleave's records was $115,000. An appraisal for fire insurance purposes had been made during the year. The building was appraised by the insurance company at $175,000. Property tax assessment notices showed that the building's worth was five times the worth of the land.

(b) Gleave's equipment had a book value of $75,000. It is estimated by Gleave that it would take six times the amount of book value to replace the old equipment with new equipment. The old equipment is, on average, 50% depreciated.

(c) Gleave had a franchise to produce and sell solar energy units from another company in a set geographic area. The franchise was transferred to Fugate as part of the purchase. Gleave carried the asset on its books at $40,000, the unamortized balance of the original cost of $90,000. The franchise is for an unlimited time. Similar franchises are now being sold by the company for $120,000 per geographic area.

(d) Gleave had two excellent research scientists who were responsible for much of the company's innovation in product development. They are each paid $150,000 per year by Gleave. They have agreed to work for Fugate Energy at the same salary.

(e) Gleave held two patents on its products. Both had been fully amortized and were not carried as assets on Gleave's books. Gleave feels they could have been sold separately for $75,000 each.

Evaluate each of the above items and prepare the journal entry that should be made to record the purchase on Fugate's books. (Note: Gleave has no liabilities.)

CASE 12–2

HOW MUCH DOES A SELF-CONSTRUCTED MACHINE COST?

The Bakeman Co. decides to construct a piece of specialized machinery using personnel from the maintenance department. This is the first time the maintenance personnel have been used for this purpose, and the cost accountant for the factory is concerned as to the accounting for costs of the machine. Some of the issues raised by the maintenance department management are highlighted below.

(a) The supervisor of the maintenance department has instructed the workers to schedule work so all the overtime hours are charged to the machinery. Overtime is paid at 150% of the regular rate, or at a 50% premium.

(b) Material used in the production of the machine is charged out from the materials store-room at 125% of cost, the same markup used when material is furnished to subsidiary companies.

(c) The maintenance department overhead rate is applied on maintenance hours. No extra overhead is anticipated as a result of constructing the machine.

(d) The maintenance department personnel are not qualified to test the machine on the production line. This will be done by production employees.

(e) Although the machine will take about 1 year to build, no extra borrowing of funds will be necessary to finance its construction. The company does, however, have outstanding bonds from earlier financing.

(f) It is expected that the self-construction of the machinery will save the company at least $20,000.

What advice can you give the cost accountant to help in the determination of a proper cost for the machine? Address each individual issue.

CASE 12–3

BUT RESEARCH IS OUR ONLY ASSET!

Strategy, Inc., was organized by Elizabeth Durrant and Ramona Morales, two students working their way through college. Both Elizabeth and Ramona had used the Internet extensively while in high school and had become very proficient Web surfers. Elizabeth had a special ability for designing Web-based games that challenged the reasoning power of players. Ramona could see great potential in marketing Elizabeth's products to other Web users, and so the two began Strategy. Sales have exceeded expectations, and they have added 10 employees to their company to design additional products, debug new programs, and produce and distribute the final software products.

Because of its growing size, increased capital is needed for the company. The partners decide to apply for a $100,000 loan to support the growing cost of research. As part of the documentation to obtain the loan, the bank asks for audited financial statements for the past year. After some negotiation, Mark Dawson, CPA, is hired. Strategy had produced a preliminary income statement that reported net income of $35,000. After reviewing the statements, Dawson indicates that the company actually had a $10,000 loss for the year. The major difference relates to $45,000 of wage and material costs that Strategy had capitalized as an intangible asset but that Dawson determined should be expensed.

"It's all research and development," Dawson insisted.

"But we'll easily recoup it in sales next year," countered Ramona. "I thought you accountants believed in the matching principle. Why do you permit us to capitalize the equipment we're using, but not our Web development costs? We'll never look profitable under your requirements!"

What major issues are involved in this case? Which position best reflects generally accepted accounting principles?

CASE 12–4

I FOUND GOLD!!! CAN IT GO ON MY BALANCE SHEET?

The Ling Company owns several mining claims in Nevada and California. The claims are carried on the books at the cost paid to acquire them 10 years ago. At that time, it was estimated that the claims represented ore reserves valued at $250,000, and the price paid for the properties reflected this value. Subsequent mining and exploration activities have indicated values up to 4 times the original estimate. Additional capital is needed to pursue the claims, and Ling has decided to issue new shares of common stock. The company wants to report the true value of the claims in the financial statements in order to make the stock more attractive to potential investors. The accountant, Jennifer Harrison, realizes that the cost basis of accounting does not permit the recording of discovery values. On the other hand, she believes that to ignore the greatly increased value of the claims would be misleading to users. Isn't there some way the recorded asset values can be increased to better reflect future cash flows arising from the claims?

You are hired as an accounting consultant to assist Ling in obtaining additional capital. What recommendations can you make?

CASE 12–5

ACCOUNTING FOR GOODWILL: THE UNITED STATES AND THE UNITED KINGDOM

Sanford Pensler, a mergers and acquisitions investment banker writing on the editorial page of the *The Wall Street Journal,* said: "Would-be U.S. purchasers of U.S. firms are burdened by accounting rules that favor foreign buyers." Mr. Pensler was referring to the requirement that U.S. companies record goodwill acquired in a purchase as an asset and amortize the goodwill against earnings. This goodwill amortization can result in a very significant earnings reduction. Consider the case of the acquisition of KRAFT by PHILIP MORRIS. The purchase price was $12.9 billion, $11.6 billion of which was recorded as goodwill on Philip Morris' books. These numbers suggest a minimum annual goodwill amortization expense (using the 40-year amortization period that was accepted at the time) of $290 million; for comparison, Kraft's net income in 1987, the year before the purchase, was $489 million. A partner from ARTHUR ANDERSEN said: "Chief executives are compensated based on earnings per share. That makes them very wary about taking a big bite of goodwill."

In contrast, accounting standards in the United Kingdom have historically allowed goodwill to be recorded as a direct, one-time reduction in equity through the creation of "goodwill reserve." This goodwill reserve has been a very common item in equity notes of large U.K. firms. The conceptual justification for this treatment is consistency. Because companies are not allowed to recognize their own homegrown goodwill as a balance sheet asset, consistent treatment requires that purchased goodwill not be recognized as an asset either. The practical effect of the U.K. goodwill treatment is that with no goodwill asset recognized, there is no subsequent amortization and thus no effect on future earnings.

Many accountants in the United Kingdom disagree with the immediate writing off of goodwill against reserves. Because the IASC has recommended that goodwill be treated as an asset (IAS 22), the days of goodwill reserves in the United Kingdom may be numbered.

SOURCES: Jeannie D. Johnson and Michael G. Tearney, "Goodwill: An Eternal Controversy," *The CPA Journal,* April 1993, p. 58; Sanford Pensler, "Accounting Rules Favor Foreign Bidders," *The Wall Street Journal,* March 24, 1988, p. 30; and 1988 Annual Report of Philip Morris Companies Inc.

1. Examples such as this are cited as justification for working to arrive at a "harmonization" between the standards of different countries. How might representatives of different countries go about resolving such wide differences in practice?
2. Evaluate the rationale for immediately writing off goodwill against equity reserves.
3. How might the equity reduction method of accounting for goodwill give U.K. firms an advantage over U.S. firms?

CASE 12–6

WHY IS MY ROA LOWER THAN YOURS?

Terri Morton has been recently hired as a financial analyst. Terri's first assignment is to analyze why the reported return on assets (ROA) for Arnold Company is so much different from that of Baker Company. Arnold Company develops and markets innovative consumer products. Baker Company is a fabricator of heavy steel products. Both companies have net incomes of $1 million, but Arnold has reported total assets of only $3 million, compared to $6 million for Baker. Terri suspects her new boss is using this assignment to test her understanding of financial statements. Terri's boss did give her one cryptic clue: unrecorded assets. Prepare Terri's analysis.

CASE 12–7

THE ASBESTOS MUST GO, BUT WHERE DO WE CHARGE IT?

The FASB's Emerging Issues Task Force (EITF) considered the question of how the costs incurred in removing asbestos from buildings should be treated (Issue 89–13). This is a widespread issue because studies indicate that some 20% of buildings in the United States contain asbestos. The EITF considered the following specific questions.

1. If a company purchases a building with a known asbestos problem, should the removal costs be expensed or capitalized?
2. If a company discovers an asbestos problem in a building it already owns, should the removal costs be expensed or capitalized?

   If you had been on the task force, how would you have ruled on these two questions?

CASE 12–8

WHY ARE THE COSTS OF BUILDINGS DIFFERENT?

In FASB Statement No. 34, the FASB called for the capitalization of interest costs associated with projects involving the construction or development of assets extending over a significant time period. Interest capitalized is restricted to the amount of interest actually incurred.

Consider the case of the following 2 companies that each constructed a building with a total construction cost of $20 million but chose to finance the construction differently. The costs were incurred evenly over the course of a year—computationally, this is the same as assuming that the entire $20 million was paid halfway through the year.

	Company A	Company B
Total construction cost of building (excluding interest)	$20,000,000	$20,000,000
Company financing (outstanding at year-end):		
Construction loan (14%)	20,000,000	0
Common stock issue	0	20,000,000
Total construction loan interest during the year (based on average outstanding loan balance)	1,400,000	0

As the auditor for both companies, you are asked by your supervisor to prepare a report that calculates the total cost for each building that would be included in each company's financial statements. Because both companies had the option of purchasing the buildings from a contractor rather than constructing them, your report should include your estimate of the price the contractor would have charged and how you explain the discrepancy in the way cost was determined for the two buildings. Conclude your report by proposing a change in the accounting standards that could eliminate this discrepancy.

CASE 12–9

EXPENSING R&D: WILL IT KILL ME?

In 1974, as the FASB considered requiring the expensing of all in-house research and development expenditures, the Board received many comments predicting that if firms were required to expense R&D, they would significantly cut back on research expenditures to avoid hurting reported earnings. Subsequent to the adoption of FASB Statement No. 2, such an impact proved to be difficult to document. Elliott and coauthors summarized and extended conflicting prior research and concluded that R&D expenditures did decrease after the adoption of FASB Statement No. 2 but that the decrease may have been a function of the generally unfavorable economic conditions in the United States in the mid-1970s.

Would you expect that a rule requiring all firms to expense R&D outlays would cause R&D expenditures to decrease? Why or why not?

SOURCE: John Elliott, Gordon Richardson, Thomas Dyckman, and Roland Dukes, "The Impact of SFAS No. 2 on Firm Expenditures on Research and Development: Replications and Extensions," *Journal of Accounting Research*, Spring 1984, pp. 85–102.

CASE 12–10

BRAND VALUES ON THE BALANCE SHEET?

In 1996, *Financial World* magazine estimated and ranked the most valuable brand names in the world. Number 11 in the ranking was GILLETTE with an estimated value of $10.3 billion. *Financial World* explained its brand value estimation process for Gillette as follows:

- Estimate the amount of assets used in generating the brand sales. This estimation involves using industry sales-to-asset ratios. For Gillette, *Financial World* estimated that 1995 sales of $2.6 billion required the use of $988 million in assets.
- Compute excess return on assets. *Financial World* assumes that a generic brand name will generate a return on assets of 5%. Gillette's 1995 operating profit of $961 million exceeds this 5% return by $912 million [$961 million – ($988 million assets × .05)].
- Estimate after-tax return. *Financial World* puts Gillette's tax rate at 37%, yielding an after-tax excess return of $575 million [$912 million × (1 – .37)].
- Multiply the after-tax excess return by the brand's strength multiple. The strength multi-

ple takes into account the brand's leadership, stability, market size, internationality, trend, and legal protection. *Financial World* placed Gillette's strength multiple at 17.9 (quite high). This yields the final estimate of the brand value: $10.3 billion ($575 million excess after-tax return × 17.9).

Comment on the relevance and reliability of the $10.3 billion Gillette brand value calculated by *Financial World*. Under what circumstances would you be willing to recognize this value in the financial statements?

SOURCE: See "Behind the Numbers," *Financial World,* July 8, 1996, p. 54.

CASE 12–11

ASSET WRITE-UPS

The ROUSE COMPANY, a real estate developer, is well known as one of the few U.S. companies to report the current value of property and equipment in its financial statements. As mentioned in the text of the chapter, IAS 16 permits the inclusion of upward asset revaluations in the financial statements. However, rules enacted by national accounting standard-setting authorities vary greatly around the world.

In Germany, as in the United States, upward revaluations are not allowed. In fact, German rules are seen as encouraging write-downs, resulting in the creation of so-called hidden reserves, which constitute a systematic understatement of assets. In March 1993, DAIMLER-BENZ (one of the two companies that merged into DAIMLERCHRYSLER) disclosed that it had hidden reserves of $2.45 billion.

Asset revaluations occur quite frequently in the United Kingdom. As discussed in the text, one example can be found in the financial statements of DIAGEO, the British consumer products firm. The June 30, 1998 net amount of land and buildings for Diageo was reported at £1.425 billion, which is a mix of historical cost numbers and amounts obtained from professional revaluations. The net amount of land and buildings would have been £1.235 billion without the revaluations.

1. Why might real estate companies be among the leaders in encouraging the disclosure of the current value of property and equipment?
2. If German companies have "hidden reserves," why do you think Daimler-Benz chose to reveal the magnitude of its hidden reserves in March 1993? What is the advantage of having hidden reserves?
3. As an auditor, how would you feel about auditing the financial statements of a company that uses appraisal values instead of historical costs?

EXERCISES

EXERCISE 12–12

COST OF SPECIFIC PLANT ITEMS

The following expenditures were incurred by Lyon Enterprises Co. in 2002:

Purchase of land	$ 390,000
Land survey	5,200
Fees for search of title for land	600
Building permit	3,500
Temporary quarters for construction crews	10,750
Payment to tenants of old building for vacating premises	4,600
Razing of old building	47,000
Excavation of basement	10,000
Special assessment tax for street project	2,000
Dividends	5,000
Damages awarded for injuries sustained in construction (no insurance was carried)	8,400
Costs of construction	2,900,000
Cost of paving parking lot adjoining building	40,000
Cost of shrubs, trees, and other landscaping	33,000

What is the cost of the land, land improvements, and building?

EXERCISE 12–13

DETERMINING COST OF PATENT

Chen King Enterprises Inc. developed a new machine that reduces the time required to insert the fortunes into their fortune cookies. Because the process is considered very valuable to the fortune cookie industry, Chen King had the machine patented. The following expenses were incurred in developing and patenting the machine.

Research and development laboratory expenses	$25,000
Metal used in construction of the machine	8,000
Blueprints used to design the machine	3,200
Legal expenses to obtain patent	12,000
Wages paid for employees' work on the research, development, and building of the machine (60% of the time was spent in actually building the machine)	30,000
Expense of drawings required by the patent office to be submitted with the patent application	1,700
Fees paid to government patent office to process application	2,500

One year later, Chen King Enterprises Inc. paid $17,500 in legal fees to successfully defend the patent against an infringement suit by Dragon Cookie Co.

Give the entries on Chen King's books indicated by the above events. Ignore any amortization of the patent or depreciation of the machine.

EXERCISE 12–14

CORRECTING ORGANIZATION EXPENSES ACCOUNT

The Delta Products Co. was incorporated on January 1, 2002. In reviewing the accounts in 2003, you find that the organization costs account in the general ledger appears as follows:

Account: ORGANIZATION EXPENSES

			Balance	
Item	Debit	Credit	Debit	Credit
Incorporation fees	3,750		3,750	
Legal fees relative to organization	21,150		24,900	
Stock certificate cost	6,000		30,900	
Cost of repairing building acquired at end of 2002	165,600		196,500	
Advertising expenditures to promote company products in 2002	29,000		225,500	
Net loss for 2002	72,000		297,500	

Give the entry or entries required to correct the account.

EXERCISE 12–15

BASKET PURCHASE

The Allred Shipping Co. acquired land, buildings, and equipment at a lump sum price of $920,000. An appraisal of the assets at the time of acquisition disclosed the following values.

Land	$250,000
Buildings	600,000
Equipment	200,000

What cost should be assigned to each asset?

EXERCISE 12–16

BASKET PURCHASE

The Boswell Corporation purchased land, a building, a patent, and a franchise for the lump sum of $1,150,000. A real estate appraiser estimated the building to have a resale value of $400,000 (⅔ of the total worth of land and building). The franchise had no established resale value. The patent was valued by management at $250,000. Give the journal entry to record the acquisition of the assets.

EXERCISE 12–17

EQUIPMENT PURCHASE ON DEFERRED PAYMENT CONTRACT

Foley Industries purchases new specialized manufacturing equipment on July 1, 2002. The equipment cash price is $79,000. Foley signs a deferred payment contract that provides for a down payment of $10,000 and an 8-year note for $103,472. The note is to be paid in 8 equal annual payments of $12,934. The payments include 10% interest and are made on June 30 of each year, beginning June 30, 2003. Prepare the journal entries for 2002, 2003, and 2004 related to the equipment purchase and the contract. Foley's fiscal year ends on June 30.

EXERCISE 12–18

PURCHASE ON DEFERRED PAYMENT CONTRACT

HiTech Industries purchases new electronic equipment for its telecommunication system. The contractual arrangement specifies 10 payments of $8,600 each to be made over a 10-year period. If HiTech had borrowed money to buy the equipment, they would have paid interest at 9%. HiTech's accountant recorded the purchase as follows:

Equipment	86,000	
Notes Payable		86,000

Prepare the correcting acquisition entry, taking into consideration the implicit interest in the purchase.

EXERCISE 12–19

BASKET PURCHASE IN EXCHANGE FOR STOCK

On January 31, 2002, Cesarino Corp. exchanged 10,000 shares of its $1 par common stock for the following assets.

(a) A trademark valued at $145,000.
(b) A building, including land, valued at $650,000 (20% of the value is for the land).
(c) A franchise right. No estimate of value at time of exchange.

Cesarino Corp. stock is selling at $91 per share on the date of the exchange. Give the entries to record the exchange on Cesarino's books.

EXERCISE 12–20

PURCHASE OF BUILDING WITH BONDS AND STOCK

The Fellingham Co. enters into a contract with the Dice Construction Co. for construction of an office building at a cost of $710,000. Upon completion of construction, the Dice Construction Co. agrees to accept in full payment of the contract price Fellingham Co. 10% bonds with a face value of $300,000 and common stock with a par value of $100,000 and no established fair market value. Fellingham Co. bonds are selling in the market at this time at 106. How would you recommend the building acquisition be recorded?

EXERCISE 12–21

ACQUISITION OF LAND AND BUILDING FOR STOCK AND CASH

Valdilla's Music Store acquired land and an old building in exchange for 50,000 shares of its common stock, par $0.50, and cash of $80,000. The auditor ascertains that the company's stock was selling for $15 per share when the purchase was made. The following additional costs were incurred to complete the transaction:

Legal cost to complete transaction	$10,000
Property tax for previous year	30,000
Cost of building demolition	21,000
Salvage value of demolished building	(6,000)

What entry should be made to record the acquisition of the property?

EXERCISE 12–22

COST OF SELF-CONSTRUCTED ASSET

The Brodhead Manufacturing Company has constructed its own special equipment to produce a newly developed product. A bid to construct the equipment by an outside company was received for $1,200,000. The actual costs incurred by Brodhead to construct the equipment were as follows:

| Direct material | $320,000 |
| Direct labor | 200,000 |

It is estimated that incremental overhead costs for construction amount to 140% of direct labor costs. In addition, fixed costs (exclusive of interest) of $700,000 were incurred during the construction period and allocated to production on the basis of total prime costs (direct labor plus direct material). The prime costs incurred to build the new equipment amounted to 35% of the total prime costs incurred for the period. The company follows the policy of capitalizing all possible costs on self-construction projects.

In order to assist in financing the construction of the equipment, a $500,000, 10% loan was acquired at the beginning of the 6-month construction period. The company carries no other debt except for trade accounts payable. For simplicity, assume that all construction expenditures took place exactly midway through the project—that is, all expenditures took place with 3 months remaining in the construction period. Compute the cost to be assigned to the new equipment.

EXERCISE 12–23

CAPITALIZATION OF INTEREST

Lodi Department Stores, Inc., constructs its own stores. In the past, no cost has been added to the asset value for interest on funds borrowed for construction. Management has decided to change its policy and desires to include interest as part of the cost of a new store just being completed. Based on the following information, (1) how much interest would be added to the cost of the store in 2002? (2) in 2003?

Total construction expenditures:

January 2, 2002	$600,000
May 1, 2002	600,000
November 1, 2002	500,000
March 1, 2003	700,000
September 1, 2003	400,000
December 31, 2003	500,000
	$3,300,000

Outstanding company debt:

Mortgage related directly to new store; interest rate, 12%; term, 5 years from beginning of construction	$1,000,000
General bond liability:	
Bonds issued just prior to construction of store; interest rate, 10% for 10 years	$ 500,000
Bonds issued prior to construction; interest rate, 8%, mature in 5 years	$1,000,000
Estimated cost of equity capital	14%

EXERCISE 12–24

INTEREST CAPITALIZATION DECISION

For each of the situations described below, indicate when interest should be capitalized (C) and when it should not be capitalized (NC).

1. King Company is constructing a piece of equipment for its own use. Total construction costs are expected to be $5 million, and the construction period will be 1 month.
2. Ortegren Company is constructing a piece of equipment for sale. Total construction costs are expected to exceed $8 million, and the construction period will be about 10 months. This is a special order. Ortegren has never produced a piece of equipment like this before.
3. Lowe Company is constructing a piece of equipment for sale. Total construction costs are expected to exceed $8 million, and the construction period will be about 10 months. This particular piece of equipment is Lowe's best seller.
4. Nair Company is constructing a piece of equipment for its own use. Total construction costs are expected to be $1,000, and the construction period will be 10 months.

5. Rittenberg Company is constructing a piece of equipment for its own use. Total construction costs are expected to be $11 million, and the construction period will be about 2 years. The forecasted total construction cost is only a very rough estimate because Rittenberg has no system in place to accumulate separately the costs associated with this project.

6. LeClair Company is in the process of renovating its corporate office building. The project will cost $13 million and will take about 15 months. The building will remain in use throughout the project.

7. Ricketts Company owns a piece of undeveloped land. The land originally cost $27 million. Ricketts plans to hold onto the land for 3 to 4 years and then develop it into a vacation resort.

EXERCISE 12–25

PURCHASE OF A COMPANY

Hull Company purchased Heaston Company for $750,000 cash. A schedule of the market values of Heaston's assets and liabilities as of the purchase date is given below.

Heaston Company
Schedule of Asset and Liability Market Values

Assets

Cash	$ 5,000	
Receivables	78,000	
Inventory	136,000	
Land, buildings, and equipment	436,000	$655,000

Liabilities

Current liabilities	$ 80,000	
Long-term debt	120,000	200,000
Net asset market value		$455,000

1. Make the journal entry necessary for Hull Company to record the purchase.
2. Assume that the purchase price is $385,000 cash. Make the journal entry necessary to record the purchase.

EXERCISE 12–26

PURCHASE OF A COMPANY

Caruthers Inc. is considering purchasing K&M Properties, which has the following assets and liabilities.

	Cost	Fair Market Value
Accounts receivable	$240,000	$220,000
Inventory	240,000	250,000
Prepaid insurance	10,000	10,000
Buildings and equipment (net)	70,000	200,000
Accounts payable	(160,000)	(160,000)
Net assets	$400,000	$520,000

1. Make the journal entry necessary for Caruthers Inc. to record the purchase if the purchase price is $630,000 cash.
2. Assume that the purchase price is $300,000 cash. Make the journal entry necessary to record the purchase.

EXERCISE 12–27

POSTACQUISITION EXPENDITURES

Ash LaRue Company replaced some parts of its factory building during 2002:

(a) The outside corrugated covering on the factory walls was removed and replaced. The job was done by an expert crew from Marblehead Construction Company and will extend the life of the building by 4 years. The cost of the new wall was $63,000. The cost of the old wall is not known.

(b) Dust filters in the interior of the factory were replaced at a cost of $30,000. The new filters are expected to reduce employee health hazards and thus reduce wage and fringe benefit costs. The original filters cost $15,000. The building is ⅓ depreciated.

Prepare journal entries for the above information.

EXERCISE 12–28

RESEARCH AND DEVELOPMENT COSTS

In 2002 the Juarez Corporation incurred research and development costs as follows:

Materials and equipment	$130,000
Personnel	100,000
Indirect costs	50,000
	$280,000

These costs relate to a product that will be marketed in 2003. It is estimated that these costs will be recouped by December 31, 2006.

1. What is the amount of research and development costs that should be expensed in 2002?
2. Assume that of the above costs, equipment of $90,000 can be used on other research projects. Estimated useful life of the equipment is 5 years with no salvage value, and it was acquired at the beginning of 2002. What is the amount of research and development costs that should be expensed in 2002 under these conditions? Assume depreciation on all equipment is computed on a straight-line basis.

EXERCISE 12–29

WHAT ARE THE R&D COSTS?

Pringle Company has a substantial research department. Below are listed, in chronological order, some of the major activities associated with one of Pringle's research projects.

Project Started:
(a) Purchased special equipment to be used solely for this project.
(b) Purchased general equipment that will be usable in Pringle's normal operations.
(c) Allocated overhead to the project.

Technological Feasibility Established:
(d) Purchased more special equipment to be used solely for this project.
(e) Performed tests on an early model of the product.
(f) Allocated overhead to the project.

Product Becomes Ready for Production:
(g) Incurred direct production costs.
(h) Allocated overhead to the products.

1. For each activity (a) through (h), indicate whether the cost should be capitalized (C), expensed (E), or included in cost of inventory (I).
2. Repeat (1) assuming that Pringle is a computer software development company.

EXERCISE 12–30

FULL COST AND SUCCESSFUL EFFORTS

Playfair Company is an oil and gas exploration firm. During 2002, Playfair engaged in 67 different exploratory projects. Only 9 of these projects were successful. The total cost of this exploration effort was $16 million, $3 million of which was associated with the successful projects. As of the end of 2002, production had not yet begun at the successful sites.

1. Using the successful efforts method of accounting for oil and gas exploration costs, how much exploration expense would be shown in Playfair's income statement for 2002? How much of the exploration cost will be capitalized and shown as an asset on the company's balance sheet as of December 31, 2002?
2. Repeat (1) using the full cost method.

EXERCISE 12–31

CLASSIFYING EXPENDITURES AS ASSETS OR EXPENSES

One of the most difficult problems facing an accountant is the determination of which expenditures should be capitalized and which should be immediately expensed. What position would you take in each of the following instances?

(a) Painting of partitions in a large room recently divided into four sections.
(b) Labor cost of tearing down a wall to permit extension of assembly line.
(c) Replacement of motor on a machine. Life used to depreciate the machine is 8 years. The machine is 4 years old. Replacement of the motor was anticipated when the machine was purchased.
(d) Cost of grading land prior to construction.
(e) Assessment for street paving.
(f) Cost of tearing down a previously occupied old building in preparation for new construction; old building is fully depreciated.

EXERCISE 12–32

FIXED ASSET TURNOVER

Handy Corner Stores reported the following asset values in 2001 and 2002.

	2002	2001
Cash	$ 30,000	$ 20,000
Accounts receivable	400,000	300,000
Inventory	600,000	350,000
Land	200,000	150,000
Buildings	600,000	500,000
Equipment	300,000	200,000

In addition, Handy Corner had sales of $2,000,000 in 2002. Cost of goods sold for the year was $1,500,000.

Compute Handy Corner's fixed asset turnover ratio for 2002.

EXERCISE 12–33

INTEREST CAPITALIZATION

Refer to the information in Exercise 12-23.

1. Compute the amount of interest that should be capitalized in 2002 using both (a) the avoidable interest method, and (b) the average accumulated expenditure method.
2. Repeat (1), but this time assume that the mortgage loan specifically identified with the construction project was taken out on July 1, 2002, instead of at the beginning of the project.

PROBLEMS

PROBLEM 12–34

CORRECTING NONCURRENT OPERATING ASSET VALUATION

On December 31, 2002, the Lakeside Co. shows the following account for machinery it had assembled for its own use during 2002.

Account: MACHINERY (Job Order #1329)

Item	Debit	Credit	Balance Debit	Balance Credit
Cost of dismantling old machine	14,480		14,480	
Cash proceeds from sale of old machine		12,000	2,480	
Raw materials used in construction of new machine	76,000		78,480	
Labor in construction of new machine	49,000		127,480	
Cost of installation	11,200		138,680	
Materials spoiled in machine trial runs	2,400		141,080	
Profit on construction	24,000		165,080	
Purchase of machine tools	13,000		178,080	

An analysis of the details in the account disclosed the following:

(a) The old machine, which was removed before the installation of the new one, had been fully depreciated.

(b) Cash discounts received on the payments for materials used in construction totaled $3,000, and these were reported in the purchase discounts account.

(c) The factory overhead account shows a balance of $292,000 for the year ended December 31, 2002; this balance exceeds normal overhead on regular plant activities by approximately $16,900 and is attributable to machine construction.

(d) A profit was recognized on construction for the difference between costs incurred and the price at which the machine could have been purchased.

Instructions:

1. Determine the machinery and machine tools balances as of December 31, 2002.
2. Give individual journal entries necessary to correct the accounts as of December 31, 2002, assuming that the nominal accounts are still open.

PROBLEM 12–35

COST CLASSIFICATION FOR A GOLF COURSE

The accountant for Stansbury Development Company is uncertain how to record the following costs associated with the construction of a golf course.

(a) Building man-made lakes.
(b) Moving earth around to enhance the "hilliness" of the course.
(c) Planting fairway grass.
(d) Planting trees and shrubs.
(e) Installing an automatic sprinkler system.
(f) Installing golf cart paths.
(g) 50 wooden sand trap rakes (at $1 each).
(h) Paying attorneys' fees to prepare and file the land title.
(i) Demolishing an old house situated on the site planned for the clubhouse.

Instructions: Indicate which costs should be expensed (E), which should be capitalized and considered to be nondepreciable (CN), and which should be capitalized and depreciated (CD). Include explanations for each classification.

PROBLEM 12–36

ACQUISITION OF LAND AND BUILDINGS

The Castagno Corporation has decided to expand its operations and has purchased land in Grantsville for construction of a new manufacturing plant. The following costs were incurred in purchasing the property and constructing the building.

Land purchase price	$120,000
Payment of delinquent property taxes	35,000
Title search and insurance	6,500

City improvements for water and sewer	$ 18,000
Building permit	8,000
Cost to destroy existing building on land ($3,000 worth of salvaged material used in new building)	20,000
Contract cost of new building	1,650,000
Land improvements—landscaping	82,000
Sidewalks and parking lot	39,000
Fire insurance on building—1 year	18,000

The depreciated value of the old building on the books of the company from which the land was purchased was $26,000. The old building was never used by Castagno.

Instructions:

1. Determine the costs of the land and land improvements. Show clearly the elements included in the totals.
2. Determine the cost of the new building. Show clearly the elements included in the total.

PROBLEM 12–37

TRANSACTIONS INVOLVING PROPERTY

The following transactions were completed by the Space Age Toy Co. during 2002:

Mar. 1 Purchased real property for $628,250, which included a charge of $18,250 representing property tax for March 1–June 30 that had been prepaid by the vendor; 20% of the purchase price is deemed applicable to land and the balance to buildings. A mortgage of $375,000 was assumed by the Space Age Toy Co. on the purchase. Cash was paid for the balance.

2–30 Previous owners had failed to take care of normal maintenance and repair requirements on the building, necessitating current reconditioning at a cost of $29,600.

May 15 Garages in the rear of the building were demolished, $4,500 being recovered on the lumber salvage. The company proceeded to construct a warehouse. The cost of such construction was $67,600, which was almost exactly the same as bids made on the construction by independent contractors. Upon completion of construction, city inspectors ordered extensive modifications to the buildings as a result of failure on the part of the company to comply with the building safety code. Such modifications, which could have been avoided, cost $9,600.

June 1 The company exchanged its own stock with a fair market value of $40,000 (par $3,000) for a patent and a new toy-making machine. The machine has a market value of $25,000.

July 1 The new machinery for the new building arrived. In addition to the machinery, a new franchise was acquired from the manufacturer of the machinery to produce toy robots. Payment was made by issuing bonds with a face value of $50,000 and by paying cash of $18,000. The value of the franchise is set at $20,000, while the fair market value of the machine is $45,000.

Nov. 20 The company contracted for parking lots and landscaping at a cost of $45,000 and $9,600, respectively. The work was completed and paid for on November 20.

Dec. 31 The business was closed to permit taking the year-end inventory. During this time, required redecorating and repairs were completed at a cost of $7,500.

Instructions: Give the journal entries to record each of the preceding transactions. (Disregard depreciation.)

PROBLEM 12–38 **ACQUISITION OF LAND AND CONSTRUCTION OF PLANT**

The Crawford Corporation was organized in June 2002. In auditing their books, you find the land, buildings, and equipment account below.

Account: LAND, BUILDINGS, AND EQUIPMENT

Date		Item	Debit	Credit	Balance Debit	Balance Credit
2002						
June	8	Organization fees paid to the state	20,000		20,000	
	16	Land site and old building	315,000		335,000	
	30	Corporate organization costs	30,000		365,000	
July	2	Title clearance fees	18,400		383,400	
Aug.	28	Cost of razing old building	20,000		403,400	
Sept.	1	Salaries of Crawford Corporation executives	60,000		463,400	
	1	Cost to acquire patent for special equipment	60,000		523,400	
Dec.	12	Stock bonus to corporate promoters, 2,000 shares of common stock, $50/share market value	100,000		623,400	
	15	County real estate tax	14,400		637,800	
	15	Cost of new building completed and occupied on this date	1,750,000		2,387,800	

An analysis of this account and of other accounts disclosed the following additional information.

(a) The building acquired on June 16, 2002, was valued at $35,000.

(b) The corporation paid $20,000 for the demolition of the old building and then sold the scrap for $12,000 and credited the proceeds to Miscellaneous Revenue.

(c) The corporation executives did not participate in the construction of the new building.

(d) The county real estate tax was for the 6-month period ended December 31, 2002, and was assessed by the county on the land.

Instructions: Prepare journal entries to correct the books of the Crawford Corporation.

PROBLEM 12–39 **ACQUISITION OF INTANGIBLE ASSETS**

In your audit of the books of Dyer Corporation for the year ended September 30, 2002, you found the following items in connection with the company's patents account.

(a) The company had spent $120,000 during its fiscal year ended September 30, 2001, for research and development costs and debited this amount to its patents account. Your review of the company's cost records indicated the company had spent a total of $141,500 for the research and development of its patents, of which $21,500 spent in its fiscal year ended September 30, 2001, had been debited to Research and Development Expense.

(b) The patents were issued on April 1, 2001. Legal expenses in connection with the issuance of the patents of $14,280 were debited to Legal and Professional Fees Expense.

(c) The company paid a retainer of $15,000 on October 5, 2001, for legal services in connection with a patent infringement suit brought against it. This amount was debited to Deferred Costs.

(d) A letter dated October 15, 2002, from the company's attorneys in reply to your inquiry as to liabilities of the company existing at September 30, 2002, indicated that a settlement of the patent infringement suit had been arranged. The other party had agreed to drop the suit and to release the company from all future liabilities in exchange for $20,000. Additional fees due to the attorneys amounted to $1,260.

Instructions: From the information given, prepare correcting journal entries as of September 30, 2002.

PROBLEM 12–40

ACQUISITION OF INTANGIBLE ASSETS
Transactions during 2002 of the newly organized Menlove Corporation included the following.

Jan. 2 Paid legal fees of $15,000 and stock certificate costs of $8,300 to complete organization of the corporation.

15 Hired a clown to stand in front of the corporate office for 2 weeks and hand out pamphlets and candy to create goodwill for the new enterprise. Clown cost, $1,000; pamphlets and candy, $500.

Apr. 1 Patented a newly developed process with costs as follows:

Legal fees to obtain patent	$42,900
Patent application and licensing fees	6,350
Total	$49,250

It is estimated that in 6 years other companies will have developed improved processes, making the Menlove Corporation process obsolete.

May 1 Acquired both a license to use a special type of container and a distinctive trademark to be printed on the container in exchange for 600 shares of Menlove Corporation no-par common stock selling for $50 per share. The license is worth twice as much as the trademark, both of which may be used for 6 years.

July 1 Constructed a shed for $131,000 to house prototypes of experimental models to be developed in future research projects.

Dec. 31 Salaries for an engineer and chemist involved in product development totaled $175,000 in 2002.

Instructions:

1. Give journal entries to record the foregoing transactions. (Ignore amortization of intangible assets.)
2. Present the "Intangible assets" section of the Menlove Corporation balance sheet at December 31, 2002.

PROBLEM 12–41

BASKET PURCHASE OF NONCURRENT OPERATING ASSETS
The Wenatcher Wholesale Company incurred the following costs in 2002 for a warehouse acquired on July 1, 2002, the beginning of its fiscal year.

Cost of land	$ 90,000
Cost of building	510,000
Remodeling and repairs prior to occupancy	67,500
Escrow fee	10,000
Landscaping	25,000
Property tax for period prior to acquisition	15,000
Real estate commission	30,000

The company signed a non-interest-bearing note for $500,000 on July 1, 2002. The implicit interest rate is 10%. Payments of $25,000 are to be made semiannually beginning December 31, 2002, for 10 years.

Instructions: Give the required journal entries to record (1) the acquisition of the land and building (assume that cash is paid to equalize the cost of the assets and the present value of the note), and (2) the first 2 semiannual payments, including amortization of note discount.

PROBLEM 12–42

INCOME STATEMENT FOR COMPUTER SOFTWARE COMPANY

The Betterword Company is engaged in developing computer software for the small business and home computer market. Most of the computer programmers are involved in developmental work designed to produce software that will perform fairly specific tasks in a user-friendly manner. Extensive testing of the working model is performed before it is released to production for preparation of masters and further testing. As a result of careful preparation, Betterword has produced several products that have been very successful in the marketplace. The following costs were incurred during 2002:

Salaries and wages of programmers doing research	$235,000
Expenses related to projects prior to establishment of technological feasibility	78,400
Expenses related to projects after technological feasibility has been established but before software is available for production	49,500
Amortization of capitalized software development costs from current and prior years	26,750
Costs to produce and prepare software for sale	56,300
Additional data for 2002 include:	
Sales of products for the year	$515,000
Beginning inventory	142,000
Portion of goods available for sale sold during year	60%

Instructions: Prepare an income statement for Betterword for the year 2002. Income tax rate is 35%.

PROBLEM 12–43

VALUATION OF PROPERTY

At December 31, 2001, certain accounts included in the noncurrent operating assets section of the Salvino Company's balance sheet had the following balances:

Land	$150,000
Buildings	910,000
Leasehold improvements	500,000
Machinery and equipment	600,000

During 2002 the following transactions occurred.

(a) Land site #653 was acquired for $1,600,000. Additionally, to acquire the land, Salvino paid a $90,000 commission fee to a real estate agent. Costs of $25,000 were incurred to clear the land. During the course of clearing the land, timber and gravel were recovered and sold for $20,000.

(b) A second tract of land (site #654) with a building was acquired for $700,000. The closing statement indicated that the land value was $510,000 and the building value was $215,000. Shortly after acquisition, the building was demolished at a cost of $30,000. A new building was constructed for $600,000 plus the following costs.

Excavation fees	$35,000
Architectural design fees	19,000
Building permit fee	15,000
Imputed interest on funds used during construction	60,000

The building was completed and occupied on September 30, 2002.

(c) A third tract of land (site #655) was acquired for $600,000 and was put on the market for resale.

(d) Extensive work was done to a building occupied by Salvino under a lease agreement that expires on December 31, 2011. The total cost of work was $150,000, which consisted of the following.

Painting of ceilings	$ 10,000	(estimated useful life is 1 year)
Electrical work	60,000	(estimated useful life is 10 years)
Construction of extension to current working area	80,000	(estimated useful life is 30 years)
	$150,000	

The lessor paid half of the costs incurred in connection with the extension to the current working area.

(e) During December 2002, costs of $70,000 were incurred to improve leased office space. The related lease will terminate on December 31, 2004, and is not expected to be renewed.

(f) A group of new machines was purchased under a royalty agreement that provides for payment of royalties based on units of production for the machines. The invoice price of the machines was $90,000, freight costs were $2,000, unloading charges were $2,500, and royalty payments for 2002 were $13,000.

Instructions:

1. Prepare an analysis of the changes in each of the following balance sheet accounts for 2002. (Disregard the related accumulated depreciation accounts.)
   - Land
   - Buildings
   - Leasehold improvements
   - Machinery and equipment

2. List the items in the foregoing information that were not used to determine the answer to (1), and indicate where, if at all, these items should be included in Salvino's financial statements.

PROBLEM 12–44

ACQUISITION OF NONCURRENT OPERATING ASSETS

At December 31, 2001, Arnold Company's noncurrent operating asset accounts had the following balances:

Category	Cost
Land	$ 175,000
Buildings	1,500,000
Machinery and equipment	1,125,000
Automobiles	172,000
Leasehold improvements	216,000
Land improvements	0

Transactions for 2002 included the following:

Jan. 6 A plant facility consisting of land and a building was acquired from Jesco Corp. in exchange for 25,000 shares of Arnold's common stock. On this date, Arnold's stock had a market price of $50 a share. Current assessed values of land and building for property tax purposes are $187,500 and $562,500, respectively.

Mar. 25 New parking lots, streets, and sidewalks at the acquired plant facility were completed at a total cost of $192,000.

July 1 Machinery and equipment were purchased at a total invoice cost of $325,000, which included $14,000 of sales tax. Additional costs of $10,000 for delivery and $50,000 for installation were incurred.

Aug. 30 Arnold purchased a new automobile for $22,500.

Nov. 4 Arnold purchased for $350,000 a tract of land as a potential future building site.

Dec. 20 A machine with a cost of $17,000 and a remaining book value of $2,975 at date of disposition was scrapped without cash recovery.

Instructions: Prepare a schedule analyzing the changes in each of the noncurrent operating asset accounts during 2002. This schedule should include columns for beginning balance, increase, decrease, and ending balance for each of the noncurrent operating asset accounts.

PROBLEM 12–45

CAPITALIZATION OF INTEREST

Oceanwide Enterprises, Inc., is involved in building and operating cruise ships. Each ship is identified as a separate discrete job in the accounting records. At the end of 2001, Oceanwide correctly reported $5,400,000 as Construction in Progress on the following jobs.

Ship	Completion Date (end of month)	Accumulated Costs (including 2001 interest) December 31, 2001
#340	October 31, 2001*	$2,300,000
#341	June 30, 2002	1,150,000
#342	September 30, 2002	1,200,000
#343	January 31, 2003	750,000

*Ship #340 was completed and ready for use in October 2001 and will be placed in service May 1, 2002.

Construction costs for 2002, and the dates the expenditures were made, were as follows:

Ship	Date	Costs
#341	April 1, 2002	$1,200,000
#342	May 1, 2002	1,600,000
#343	July 1, 2002	2,200,000
#344	September 1, 2002	810,000
#345	November 1, 2002	360,000

Oceanwide had the following general liabilities at December 31, 2002.

12%, 5-year note (maturity date—2004)	$2,000,000
10%, 10-year bonds (maturity date—2007)	8,000,000

On January 1, 2002, Oceanwide borrowed $2,000,000 specifically for the construction of Ship #343. The loan was for 3 years with interest at 13%.

Instructions:

1. Compute the maximum interest that can be capitalized in 2002.
2. Compute the weighted-average interest rate for the general liabilities for 2002.
3. Compute the interest that Oceanwide should capitalize during 2002.

PROBLEM 12–46

SELF-CONSTRUCTION OF EQUIPMENT

American Corporation received a $400,000 low bid from a reputable manufacturer for the construction of special production equipment needed by American in an expansion program. Because its own plant was not operating at capacity, American decided to construct the equipment itself and recorded the following production costs related to the construction.

Services of consulting engineer	$ 10,000
Work subcontracted	20,000
Materials	200,000
Plant labor normally assigned to production	65,000
Plant labor normally assigned to maintenance	100,000
Total	$395,000

Management prefers to record the cost of the equipment under the incremental cost method. Approximately 40% of the corporation's production is devoted to government supply contracts, which are all based in some way on cost. The contracts require that any self-constructed equipment be allocated its full share of all costs related to the construction.

The following information also is available.

(a) The above production labor was for partial fabrication of the equipment in the plant. Skilled personnel were required and were assigned from other projects. The maintenance labor amount ($100,000) represents the cost of nonproduction plant employees assigned to the construction project. Had these workers not been assigned to construction, the $100,000 cost would still have been incurred for their idle time.

(b) Payroll taxes and employee fringe benefits are approximately 30% of labor cost and are included in manufacturing overhead cost. Total manufacturing overhead for the year was $5,630,000 including the $100,000 maintenance labor used to construct the equipment.

(c) Manufacturing overhead is approximately 50% variable and is applied on the basis of production labor cost. Production labor cost for the year for the corporation's normal products totaled $6,810,000.

(d) General and administrative expenses include $22,500 of executive salary cost and $10,500 of postage, telephone, supplies, and miscellaneous expenses identifiable with this equipment construction.

Instructions:

1. Compute the amount that should be reported as the full cost of the constructed equipment to meet the requirements of the government contracts.
2. Compute the incremental cost of the constructed equipment.
3. What is the greatest amount that should be capitalized as the cost of the equipment? Why?

PROBLEM 12–47

INTERNATIONAL

RECORDING GOODWILL

The Aurora Corp. acquired Payette Company on December 31, 2002. The following information concerning Payette's assets and liabilities was assembled on the acquisition date.

	Per Company's Books	As Adjusted by Appraisal and Audit
Assets		
Current assets	$307,000	$340,000
Land, buildings, and equipment (net)	179,200	260,000
	$486,200	$600,000
Liabilities		
Current liabilities	(25,000)	(25,000)
Long-term liabilities	(160,000)	(160,000)
Net assets	$301,200	$415,000

Instructions:

1. Make the journal entry necessary for Aurora Corp. to record the purchase assuming the purchase price was $1,500,000 in cash.
2. Why might Aurora be willing to pay such a high price for Payette?
3. Refer to Case 12-5. How might the transaction in (1) be recorded by a U.K. company? What is the rationale behind the U.K. treatment?
4. Repeat (1), assuming the purchase price is $350,000.
5. Repeat (1), assuming the purchase price is $150,000.

PROBLEM 12–48

SUMMARY ENTRIES FOR INTEREST PAYMENTS

Clarksville Company reported interest expense in 2002 and 2001 of $350,000 and $300,000, respectively. The balance in Accrued Interest Payable at the end of 2002, 2001, and 2000 was $30,000, $47,000, and $23,000, respectively. In addition, a note to Clarksville's 2002 financial statements included the following:

> Interest costs related to construction in progress are capitalized as incurred. The Company capitalized $500,000 and $200,000 of interest costs during the years 2002 and 2001, respectively.

Instructions:

1. What summary journal entries would be needed to record all information related to interest in 2002 and 2001?
2. How would interest paid be disclosed in Clarksville's statement of cash flows for 2002 and 2001? Clarksville uses the indirect method in reporting cash flow from operating activities.

PROBLEM 12–49

CLASSIFYING EXPENDITURES AS ASSETS OR EXPENSES

As of December 31, 2002, W. W. Cole Company's total assets were $325 million and total liabilities were $180 million. Net income for 2002 was $38 million. During 2002, W. W. Cole's chief executive officer had put extreme pressure on employees to meet the profitability goal the CEO had set for them. The goal was to achieve a return on stockholders' equity in 2002 of 25% (Net income/Stockholders' equity). The rumor among Cole's employees is that in order to meet this goal, the accounting for some items may have been overly "aggressive." The following items are of concern.

(a) Research and development costs totaling $18 million were capitalized. None of these costs related to items with alternative uses. The capitalized R&D was assigned a useful life of 6 years; $3 million was written off during 2002.
(b) During the year, a building was acquired in exchange for 5 million shares of Cole common stock. The building was assigned a value of $27 million by the board of directors. At the time of the exchange, Cole common stock was trading on the New York Stock Exchange for $3 per share.
(c) On December 31, equipment was purchased for $1 million in cash and an agreement to pay $3 million per year for the next 8 years—the first payment to be made in 1 year. The cost of the equipment was recorded at $25 million. The interest rate implicit in the contract was 12%.
(d) Interest of $7 million was capitalized during the year. The only items produced during the year by Cole were routine inventory items.

Instructions:

1. Ignoring any concerns raised by items (a) through (d), did W. W. Cole Company meet its profitability goal for the year?
2. After making any adjustments suggested by items (a) through (d), did W. W. Cole meet its profitability goal? (Ignore income taxes.)
3. What should prevent accounting abuses like those described above?

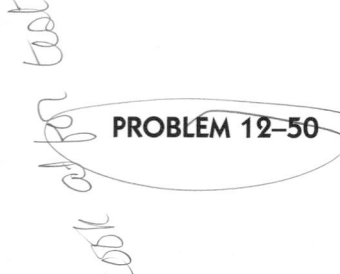

PROBLEM 12–50

CLASSIFYING EXPENDITURES AS ASSETS OR EXPENSES

The Rolitz Company completed a program of expansion and improvement of its plant during 2002. You are provided with the following information concerning its buildings account.

(a) On October 31, 2002, a 30-foot extension to the present factory building was completed at a contract cost of $329,000.
(b) During the course of construction, the following costs were incurred for the removal of the end wall of the building where the extension was to be constructed.

      (1) Payroll costs during the month of April arising from employees' time spent in removing the wall, $12,360.

      (2) Payments to a salvage company for removing unusual debris, $1,520.

(c) The cost of the original structure allocable to the end wall was estimated to be $26,400 with accumulated depreciation thereon of $11,100. Rolitz Company received $5,930 from the construction company for windows and other assorted materials salvaged from the old wall.

(d) The old floor covering was replaced with a new type of long-lasting floor covering at a cost of $5,290. Cost of old floor covering was not available.

(e) The interior of the plant was repainted in new bright colors for a contract price of $8,290.

(f) New and improved shelving was installed at a cost of $3,620. Cost of old shelving was not determinable.

(g) Old electrical wiring was replaced at a cost of $10,218. Cost of the old wiring was determined to be $4,650 with accumulated depreciation to date of $2,055.

(h) New electrical fixtures using fluorescent bulbs were installed. The new fixtures were purchased on the installment plan; the schedule of monthly payments showed total payments of $9,300, which included interest and carrying charges of $720. The old fixtures were carried at a cost of $2,790 with accumulated depreciation to date of $1,200. The old fixtures have no scrap value.

Instructions: Prepare journal entries for the foregoing information. Briefly justify the capitalize-or-expense decision for each item.

PROBLEM 12–51

LIMITATIONS OF THE FIXED ASSET TURNOVER RATIO

Waystation Company reported the following asset values in 2001 and 2002:

	2002	2001
Cash	$ 40,000	$ 30,000
Accounts receivable	500,000	400,000
Inventory	700,000	500,000
Land	300,000	200,000
Buildings	800,000	600,000
Equipment	400,000	300,000

     In addition, in 2002, Waystation had sales of $4,000,000; cost of goods sold for the year was $2,500,000.

     As of the end of 2001, the fair value of Waystation's total assets was $2,500,000. Of the excess of fair value over book value, $50,000 resulted from the fact that Waystation uses LIFO for inventory valuation. As of the end of 2002, the fair value of Waystation's total assets was $3,500,000, and Waystation's LIFO reserve was $100,000.

Instructions:

1. Compute Waystation's fixed asset turnover ratio for 2002.

2. Using the fair value of fixed assets instead of their book values, recompute Waystation's fixed asset turnover ratio for 2002. State any assumptions that you make.

3. Waystation's primary competitor is Handy Corner. Handy Corner's fixed asset turnover ratio for 2002, based on publicly available information, is 2.8. Is Waystation more or less efficient at using its fixed assets than Handy Corner? Explain your answer.

PROBLEM 12–52 **INTEREST CAPITALIZATION—VARIED LOAN DATES**

Assume the following information for Company A and Company B.

Company A
Expenditures for self-constructed asset:

April 1, 2002	$ 800,000
October 1, 2002	1,200,000

Interest-bearing instruments:
Construction loan:
$500,000, 10% loan issued on April 1, 2002
General debt:
$1,000,000, 8% bonds issued on June 30, 2001
$2,400,000, 12% note issued October 1, 2002

Company B
Expenditures for self-constructed asset:

January 1, 2002	$ 500,000
March 1, 2002	2,400,000
July 1, 2002	1,800,000

Interest-bearing instruments:
Construction loan:
$2,400,000, 11% loan issued on March 1, 2002
General debt:
$3,000,000, 10% bonds issued on July 1, 2002
$1,000,000, 9% note issued January 1, 2002

Instructions:

1. Compute the amount of interest that should be capitalized in 2002 for Company A and for Company B using the avoidable interest method.
2. Repeat (1) using the average accumulated expenditure method.
3. What makes the avoidable interest method harder to use than the average accumulated expenditure method?

C O M P E T E N C Y E N H A N C E M E N T O P P O R T U N I T I E S

▶ Deciphering Actual Financial Statements	▶ Ethical Dilemma
▶ Writing Assignment	▶ Cumulative Spreadsheet Analysis
▶ Research Project	▶ Internet Search
▶ The Debate	

Accounting is more than just doing textbook problems. This expanded competency material provides practice in critical thinking, oral and written communication, research, teamwork, and consideration of ethical issues.

▶ **DECIPHERING ACTUAL FINANCIAL STATEMENTS**
• **Deciphering 12–1 (The Walt Disney Company)**
The 1998 financial statements for THE WALT DISNEY COMPANY are included in Appendix A. Locate those financial statements and consider the following questions:

1. As illustrated in Exhibit 12–6, *The Mirror* estimates the value of the Disney brand name in June 1999 at $32.9 million. Search Disney's financial statements and notes—what is Disney's estimate of the value of the Disney name?
2. What summary journal entry did Disney make to record interest incurred during fiscal 1998? (Hint: Don't forget to distinguish between interest incurred and cash paid for interest.)

3. Find Disney's note about intangible assets. What is the amortization period for Disney's intangible assets? How often does Disney review the intangible assets to determine if their carrying values are recorded accurately?

4. In 1998, Disney included in its balance sheet long-term capitalized film and television costs of $2.5 billion. Historical cost of theme parks, resorts, and other property was $14.0 billion. On which of these two items—film costs or theme parks—did Disney have higher expenditures in 1998? Do you get different answers by looking at the statement of cash flows and the business segment information? Explain the difference.

• Deciphering 12–2 (Sierra On-Line)

SIERRA ON-LINE is a leading producer of computer games. Among its titles are King's Quest (3.8 million copies sold), Leisure Suit Larry (1.4 million copies sold), Space Quest (1.2 million copies sold), and Police Quest (1.2 million copies sold).

In 1992, Sierra was the object of an unfavorable *Forbes* magazine article (Roula Khalaf, "Accounting Adventure," *Forbes*, September 28, 1992, p. 116). The article claimed that Sierra was capitalizing too much of its software development costs. In its 1996 annual report, Sierra described its capitalization policy as shown below.

> Under the criteria set forth in SFAS No. 86, Accounting for the Costs of Computer Software to be Sold, Leased or Otherwise Marketed, capitalization of software development costs begins upon the establishment of technological feasibility of the product. The establishment of technological feasibility and the on-going assessment of the recoverability of costs require considerable judgment by management with respect to certain external factors, including, but not limited to, anticipated future gross product revenues, estimated economic life and changes in software and hardware technology. Amounts that have been capitalized under this statement, after consideration of the above factors, are amortized on either a straight-line basis over the estimated useful lives of the products (six to 24 months) or the ratio of current product revenues to the total revenues expected over the life of the product, whichever produces the greater expense.
>
> Amortization of software development costs decreased $8.8 million as the result of a decrease in costs qualifying for capitalization under the criteria set forth in SFAS No. 86, Accounting for the Costs of Computer Software to be Sold, Leased or Otherwise Marketed ("SFAS 86"). A number of significant changes in product development, including the use of more sophisticated development tools, the development of serial titles, and development for the Windows 95 operating system, have resulted in less cost meeting the definition of technological feasibility and accordingly not eligible for capitalization pursuant to SFAS 86.

The following data were extracted from Sierra On-Line's 1996 financial statements and notes:

	For the Year Ended March 31 (all amounts in millions)		
	1996	1995	1994
Income before taxes	$22,635	$18,857	$(8,551)
Research and development expense*	35,899	21,967	17,686
Amortization of capitalized software development costs	865	9,689	8,379
Software development costs capitalized	–0–	5,037	6,060

*Research and development expense reflects total research and development expenditures less capitalized software development costs.

1. On March 31, 1996, the balance in capitalized software development costs was $0. What was the balance on March 31, 1993?
2. What would income before taxes have been in fiscal 1996 if Sierra On-Line had capitalized the same proportion of total research and development expense as was capitalized in 1994? Ignore the possibility of same-year amortization of costs capitalized in 1996.
3. Evaluate Sierra On-Line's explanation for the decrease in the amount of capitalized software development costs in fiscal 1996.

• Deciphering 12–3 (3M: Minnesota Mining and Manufacturing)

The 1998 annual report of MINNESOTA MINING AND MANUFACTURING (3M) included the following information (all dollar amounts are in millions).

	1998	1997
From the balance sheet:		
Property, plant, and equipment (net)	$ 5,566	$ 5,034
From the statement of cash flows—operating:		
Depreciation	798	—
From the statement of cash flows—investing:		
Capital expenditures—outflow	(1,430)	—
Disposal of PP&E—inflow	25	—
From the notes to the financial statements:		
Property, plant, and equipment, at cost	13,397	12,098
Accumulated depreciation	7,831	7,064

1. Using the *net* PP&E figures, compute the book value of the property, plant, and equipment that was sold during the year.
2. Using the individual PP&E and accumulated depreciation accounts, estimate the gain or loss on the disposal of property, plant, and equipment during the year.

• Deciphering 12–4 (Kodak)

The 1998 annual report of the EASTMAN KODAK COMPANY (KODAK) included the following information (all dollar amounts are in millions):

	1998
Interest expense	$ 110
Earnings from continuing operations (before taxes)	2,106
Net property, plant, and equipment	5,914
Total assets	14,733
Total liabilities	10,745
Total equity	3,988
Net cash provided by operating activities	1,483
Net cash used in investing activities	(1,839)
Net cash provided by financing activities	77
Interest capitalized during the year	41

1. Recompute all the amounts given, assuming that all the capitalized interest for 1998 was expensed. Ignore income taxes and the possibility of same-year depreciation of interest capitalized in 1998.
2. Repeat (1) assuming that, of the $41 million of interest capitalized in 1998, Kodak had depreciated $3 million in that same year.

▶ ## WRITING ASSIGNMENT
• Is it an asset or not?

The Hunter Company has developed a computerized machine to assist in the production of appliances. It is anticipated that the machine will do well in the marketplace; however, the company lacks the necessary capital to produce the machine. Rosalyn Finch, the secretary-treasurer of the Hunter Company, has offered to transfer land to the company to be used as collateral for a bank loan. In exchange for the land transfer, Rosalyn will receive a 5-year employment contract and a percentage of any profits earned from sales of the new machine. The title to the land is to be transferred unconditionally. If Hunter defaults on the employment contract, a lump sum cash settlement for lost wages will be paid to Rosalyn.

The land transfer may be a good business move, but it has raised a number of sticky accounting issues. Hunter's controller has given you the task of writing a memo that summarizes the options available in accounting for the land transfer. Your memo should outline the arguments for and against recording the land as an asset on Hunter's books. Also discuss how the land should be valued if it is recorded as an asset.

▶ RESEARCH PROJECT
• Advertising costs: capitalize or expense?
Every year in the 2 weeks of hype preceding the Super Bowl, we hear about the incredible number of media people covering the event and about how much money advertisers are paying for a 30-second spot during the broadcast. We also hear a little bit about the football teams. With advertising costs running as high as $1,600,000 for 30 seconds, one has to believe that the advertisers expect some future economic benefit from the advertising. So, should advertising costs be capitalized or expensed?

Historically, there has been a diversity of practice regarding the accounting for advertising costs. This diversity led one accounting standard-setting body to prepare a statement on the reporting of advertising costs.

Search the accounting literature to find out what this standard is. (Hint: One good place to find announcements of new accounting pronouncements is the *Journal of Accountancy*. To find the answer to this question, you won't have to go back further than 1992.)

Your group is to report (either orally or in writing) on what the current U.S. accounting standard is in regard to the reporting of advertising costs.

▶ THE DEBATE
• R&D accounting will bring down the U.S. economy!

The debate over the proper accounting for research and development expenditures emphasized again that many people believe that accounting standards can have profound economic consequences for the companies subjected to those standards. The R&D debate was particularly acrimonious, with opponents of the FASB predicting that the rule would cripple the U.S. economy. Even though the debate took place in 1973 and 1974, many of the same arguments are still dragged out today when new accounting standards are considered.

Divide your group into two teams.

- One team represents "Economic Consequences." Prepare a 2-minute oral argument explaining exactly how the requirement to expense all R&D costs reduces the amount of actual research done by U.S. firms. Show how the U.S. rule puts U.S. companies at a competitive disadvantage relative to foreign companies that use the IASC's standards.
- The other team represents the "Efficient Market." Prepare a 2-minute presentation summarizing how the entire "Economic Consequences" claim is based on the erroneous assumption that bankers and investors are stupid and are completely trusting of any financial statements that the accountants choose to place in front of them. Argue that the accounting decision of whether R&D is capitalized or expensed has no impact on a company's underlying financial health and therefore has no impact on credit decisions or business valuation.

▶ ETHICAL DILEMMA
• Dumping costs into a landfill
On St. Patrick's Day 1992, CHAMBERS DEVELOPMENT COMPANY, one of the largest landfill and waste management firms in the United States, announced that it had been improperly capitalizing costs associated with landfill development. Chambers announced that it was immediately expensing over $40 million in executive salaries, travel expenses, and public relations costs that had been capitalized as part of the cost of landfills. Wall Street fear over

what this move meant for Chambers' track record of steady earnings growth sent Chambers' stock price plunging 62% in one day—total market value declined by $1.4 billion.

Imagine that it is early 1992 and you have just been assigned to work on the Chambers Development audit. In the course of your audit you find a number of irregular transactions, including the questionable capitalization of costs as described above. Chambers' accounting staff tells you that the company has always capitalized these costs. You do a little historical investigation and find that if all the questionable costs had been expensed as you think they should have been, the $362 million expense would completely wipe out all the profit reported by Chambers since it first went public in 1985. You are reluctant to approach your superior, the audit partner on the job, because you know that a large number of the financial staff working for Chambers are former partners in the audit firm you work for. However, you know that ignoring something like this can lead to a catastrophic audit failure.

Draft a memo to the audit partner summarizing your findings.

▶ **CUMULATIVE SPREADSHEET ANALYSIS**

This spreadsheet assignment is a continuation of the spreadsheet assignments given in earlier chapters. If you completed those assignments, you have a head start on this one.

Refer back to the instructions for preparing the revised financial statements for 2002 as given in (1) of the Cumulative Spreadsheet Analysis assignment in Chapter 3.

1. Skywalker wishes to prepare a *forecasted* balance sheet, a *forecasted* income statement, and a *forecasted* statement of cash flows for 2003. Clearly state any additional assumptions that you make. Use the financial statement numbers for 2002 as the basis for the forecast, along with the following additional information.
   a. Sales in 2003 are expected to increase by 40% over 2002 sales of $2,100.
   b. In 2003, new property, plant, and equipment acquisitions will be in accordance with the information in (u) below.
   c. The $480 in operating expenses reported in 2002 breaks down as follows: $15 depreciation expense, $465 other operating expenses.
   d. New long-term debt will be acquired in 2003 in accordance with (q) below.
   e. Cash dividends will be paid in 2003 in accordance with (s) below.
   f. New short-term loans payable will be acquired in an amount sufficient to make Skywalker's current ratio in 2003 exactly equal to 2.0.
   g. Skywalker anticipates repurchasing additional shares of stock during 2003 in accordance with (t) below.
   h. Because changes in future prices and exchange rates are impossible to predict, Skywalker's best estimate is that the balance in Accumulated Other Comprehensive Income will remain unchanged in 2003.
   i. In the absence of more detailed information, assume that the balances in Investment Securities, Long-Term Investments, Other Long-Term Assets, and Intangible Assets will all increase at the same rate as sales (40%) in 2003. The balance in Intangible Assets will change in accordance with item (v) below.
   j. In the absence of more detailed information, assume that the balance in Other Long-Term Liabilities will increase at the same rate as sales (40%) in 2003.
   k. The investment securities are classified as available-for-sale. Accordingly, cash from the purchase and sale of these securities is classified as an investing activity.
   l. Assume that transactions impacting the other long-term assets and other long-term liabilities accounts are operating activities.
   m. Cash and investment securities will increase at the same rate as sales.
   n. The forecasted amount of accounts receivable in 2003 is determined using the forecasted value for the average collection period. The average collection period for 2003 is expected to be 14.08 days. To make the calculations simpler, this value of 14.08 days is based on forecasted end-of-year accounts receivable rather than on average accounts receivable.
   o. The forecasted amount of inventory in 2003 is determined using the forecasted value for the number of days' sales in inventory. The number of days' sales in inven-

tory for 2003 is expected to be 107.6 days. To make the calculations simpler, this value of 107.6 days is based on forecasted end-of-year inventory rather than on average inventory.

p. The forecasted amount of accounts payable in 2003 is determined using the forecasted value for the number of days' purchases in accounts payable. The number of days' purchases in accounts payable for 2003 is expected to be 48.34 days. To make the calculations simpler, this value of 48.34 days is based on forecasted end-of-year accounts payable rather than on average accounts payable.

q. New long-term debt will be acquired (or repaid) in an amount sufficient to make Skywalker's debt ratio (total liabilities divided by total assets) in 2003 exactly equal to 0.80.

r. Assume an interest rate on short-term loans payable of 6.0% and on long-term debt of 8.0%. Only a half year's interest is charged on loans taken out during the year. For example, if short-term loans payable at the end of 2003 are $15 and given that short-term loans payable at the end of 2002 were $10, total short-term interest expense for 2003 would be $0.75 [($10 × .06) + ($5 × .06 × 1/2)].

s. Skywalker has decided to begin paying cash dividends in 2003. Skywalker intends to maintain a dividend payout ratio (cash dividends divided by net income) of 40%. (Note: Make sure you adjust your spreadsheet formula so that if net income happens to be negative, cash dividends are no lower than $0.)

t. Skywalker has decided to continue its stock repurchase program in 2003. Skywalker intends to spend $50 repurchasing shares during the year. Skywalker accounts for treasury stock purchases using the cost method.

(Note: These forecasted statements were constructed as part of the spreadsheet assignment in Chapter 11; you can use that spreadsheet as a starting point if you have completed that assignment.)

For this exercise, add the following additional assumptions.

u. The forecasted amount of property, plant, and equipment (PPE) in 2003 is determined using the forecasted value for the fixed asset turnover ratio. The fixed asset turnover ratio for 2003 is expected to be 3.518 times. To make the calculations simpler, this ratio of 3.518 is based on forecasted end-of-year gross property, plant, and equipment balance rather than on the average balance. (Note: For simplicity, ignore accumulated depreciation in making this calculation.)

v. Skywalker has determined that no new intangible assets will be acquired in 2003. For this assignment, ignore amortization of the existing intangible asset account balance.

2. Assume the same scenario as (1), and show where financial statements would be treated differently with the following changes in assumptions.
    a. Fixed asset turnover ratio is expected to be 4.500.
    b. Fixed asset turnover ratio is expected to be 2.500.

3. Comment on the differences in the forecasted values of cash provided by operating activities in 2002 under each of the following assumptions about the fixed asset turnover ratio: 3.518 times, 4.500 times, and 2.500 times. Explain how a change in the fixed asset turnover ratio impacts cash provided by operations.

▶ **INTERNET SEARCH**

NOVELL'S Web address is www.novell.com. Once you've gained access to Novell's Web site, answer the following questions.

1. Where is Novell's corporate headquarters located?
2. Like every other software company, Novell is in competition with MICROSOFT. Microsoft has been led by Bill Gates since its inception. Who is the current chairman of the board of directors of Novell? How long has he or she been with the company?
3. In a rapidly expanding industry such as computer software, sales growth is very important. What has been Novell's sales growth percentage for the past 4 years?
4. How does Novell account for its product development costs? What impact does FASB Statement No. 86 have on Novell's financial statements?

SECTION 3

chapter 13
Investments in Noncurrent Operating Assets— Utilization and Retirement

Garbage—that's how H. Wayne Huizenga made his first splash on the national scene. In the early 1960s, he started with one garbage truck in southern Florida. Huizenga went on to buy up hundreds of local garbage companies across the country, combining them into WASTE MANAGEMENT INC. (later changed to WMX TECHNOLOGIES), the largest trash hauler in the world.

After his retirement from the trash business in 1984, Huizenga's eye fell on a small, 20-store, video chain in Dallas called BLOCKBUSTER VIDEO.[1] By the end of 1987, Huizenga had acquired control of Blockbuster and had increased the number of stores to 130. Through a combination of aggressive expansion and the acquisition of existing video chains, Blockbuster soon became the nation's largest video chain. By the end of 1998, there were 6,380 Blockbuster Video stores, primarily located in the United States and Canada.

On May 8, 1989, a BEAR, STEARNS investment report was released that was critical of some of Blockbuster's accounting practices, particularly its depreciation policies. The report suggested that the 40-year life Blockbuster used for amortizing goodwill was much too long; to quote from the report: "Have you ever seen a 40-year-old videotape store?" Five years was suggested as a more reasonable amortization period. The report also criticized Blockbuster for increasing the depreciation period for videotapes from 9 months to 36 months.[2] Revising both these items to use the shorter amortization periods would have cut Blockbuster's 1988 net income almost in half—from $0.57 per share to $0.32 per share.

Release of the Bear, Stearns report caused Blockbuster's stock price to drop from $33.50 to $26.25 in two days, a 22% drop. (See Exhibit 13–1.) This represented a total decline in market value of approximately $200 million. Wayne Huizenga was livid. In a meeting with stock analysts, he showed a letter from the SEC ordering Blockbuster to use the longer videotape amortization

EXHIBIT 13–1 | Blockbuster Video Daily Stock Prices in May 1989

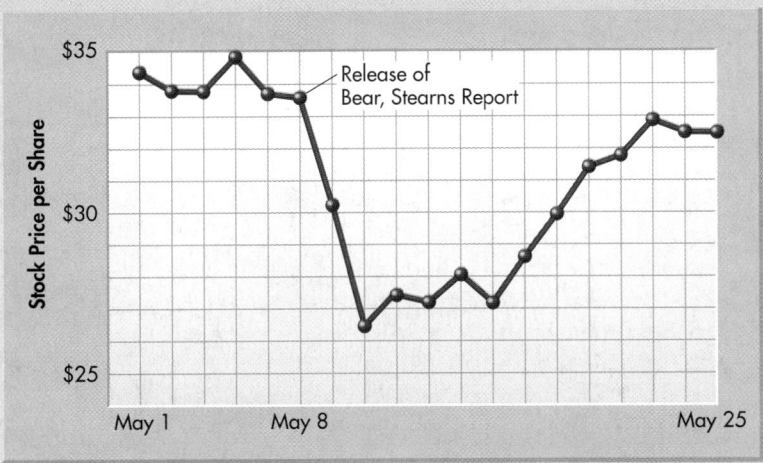

1 Eric Calonius, "Meet the King of Video," *Fortune*, June 4, 1990, p. 208.
2 Dana Weschsler, "Earnings Helper," *Forbes*, June 12, 1989, p. 15.

LEARNING OBJECTIVES

1 Use straight-line, accelerated, use-factor, and group depreciation methods to compute annual depreciation expense.

2 Discuss the issues impacting proper amortization of intangible assets.

3 Apply the productive-output method to the depletion of natural resources.

4 Incorporate changes in estimates into the computation of depreciation for current and future periods.

5 Identify whether an asset is impaired and measure the amount of the impairment loss, using both U.S. GAAP and international accounting standards.

6 Account for the sale of depreciable assets in exchange for cash and in exchange for other depreciable assets.

EXPANDED MATERIAL *e|m*

7 Compute depreciation for partial periods, using both straight-line and accelerated methods.

8 Understand the depreciation methods underlying the MACRS income tax depreciation system.

period. He criticized the Bear, Stearns researchers for not understanding his business and said that their report wasn't "worth the powder to blow it to hell."[3] Huizenga was vindicated when within two weeks of the release of the report, Blockbuster's stock had regained most of the 22% loss.

In 1994, Wayne Huizenga left Blockbuster after presiding over its acquisition by VIACOM in a deal valued at over $8 billion. This completed an incredible run by Huizenga—he had entered, dominated, and successfully exited two very different industries, garbage and video rentals. So, what was next? Selected as America's number 1 entrepreneur by *Success* magazine in 1995, it was certain that Wayne Huizenga would not just sit around and count his money (about $1.4 billion). At

one time he owned three professional sports teams in southern Florida: the Miami Dolphins (football), the Florida Marlins (baseball), and the Florida Panthers (hockey). His new company, REPUBLIC INDUSTRIES, is busy doing for auto dealerships (under the name AUTONATION USA) what Huizenga already did for garbage hauling and video stores—taking fragmented businesses across the country and consolidating them into a nationwide network. Currently, AutoNation USA is the single largest automotive retailer in the United States.

3 Duncan Maxwell Anderson and Michael Warshaw, "The #1 Entrepreneur in America," *Success*, March 1995, p. 32.

A fundamental task of accrual accounting is appropriately allocating the cost of long-lived assets to expense. If you are a Venetian shipmaster setting the price you will charge for the use of your ship on a spice-trading voyage to the Orient, you must somehow allocate the cost of the ship over the expected number of voyages the ship can complete. If you are a Silicon Valley research firm, proper measurement of annual income requires you to allocate the cost of your research patents over their expected economic life. Computing asset depreciation is an exercise in accounting judgment, and as illustrated in the Blockbuster/Bear, Stearns example, reasonable people can disagree, with huge implications for reported profits.

Three different terms are used to describe the process of allocating the cost of long-lived assets to periodic expense. The allocation of tangible property costs is referred to as **depreciation**. For minerals and other natural resources, the cost allocation process is called **depletion**. For intangible assets, such as patents, copyrights, and goodwill, the process is referred to as **amortization**. Sometimes amortization is used generically to encompass all three terms.

This chapter discusses what happens to a long-lived asset after acquisition. The first decision facing management relates to estimating and recognizing the expense associated with a long-lived asset's use. We will cover the common depreciation methods, the amortization of intangibles, and the depletion of natural resources. We will also address the issues associated with the proper treatment of changes in depreciation estimates. The chapter also describes when an impairment loss should be recognized and the proper accounting for the retirement of depreciable assets. The time line in Exhibit 13–2 illustrates the issues to be discussed. The expanded material at the end of the chapter offers more detail on depreciating assets acquired and retired in midyear and on the modified accelerated cost recovery system (MACRS), a depreciation system used for income tax purposes.

EXHIBIT 13-2 | Time Line of Business Issues Involved with Long-Term Operating Assets

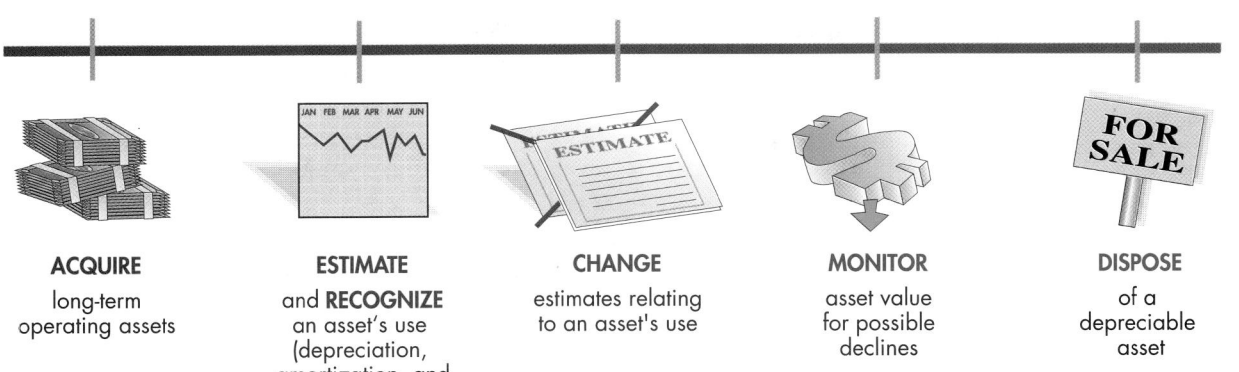

ACQUIRE	ESTIMATE	CHANGE	MONITOR	DISPOSE
long-term operating assets	and **RECOGNIZE** an asset's use (depreciation, amortization, and depletion)	estimates relating to an asset's use	asset value for possible declines	of a depreciable asset

DEPRECIATION

1

Use straight-line, accelerated, use-factor, and group depreciation methods to compute annual depreciation expense.

> **FYI:** Depreciation expense was not widely reported in income statements until the early 1900s. The passage of the Sixteenth Amendment in 1913, allowing the taxation of income, spurred companies to demand some depreciation deduction for the use of long-term assets.

Depreciation is *not* a process through which a company accumulates a cash fund to replace its long-lived assets. Depreciation is also *not* a way to compute the current value of long-lived assets. Instead, depreciation is the systematic allocation of the cost of an asset over the different periods benefited by the use of the asset. So, accumulated depreciation is not an asset replacement fund but is the sum of all the asset cost that has been expensed in prior periods. Similarly, the **book value** of an asset (historical cost less accumulated depreciation) is the asset cost remaining to be allocated to future periods and is not an estimate of the asset's current value.

Depreciation expense is the recognition of the using up of the service potential of an asset. The nature of depreciation expense is conceptually no different from the expenses that recognize the expiration of insurance premiums or prepaid rent—the practical difference is that noncurrent assets are depreciated over several years, whereas prepaid rent is usually expensed over a period of months.

Factors Affecting the Periodic Depreciation Charge

Four factors are taken into consideration in determining the appropriate amount of annual depreciation expense.

- Asset cost
- Residual or salvage value
- Useful life
- Pattern of use

ASSET COST   The cost of an asset includes all the expenditures relating to its acquisition and preparation for use as described in Chapter 12. The cost of property less the expected residual value, if any, is the depreciable cost or depreciation base, that is, the portion of asset cost to be expensed in future periods.

RESIDUAL OR SALVAGE VALUE   The **residual (salvage) value** of property is an estimate of the amount for which the asset can be sold when it is retired. The residual value depends on the retirement policy of the company as well as market conditions and other factors. If, for example, the company normally uses equipment until it is physically exhausted and no longer serviceable, the residual value, represented by the scrap or junk

net work exercise

As mentioned at the beginning of this chapter, Wayne Huizenga's latest business is AutoNation USA. AutoNation's Web site at **www.autonation.com** allows you to price new cars, find a dealership location, and also value your trade-in vehicle.

Net Work:

1. **Use AutoNation's link to the Kelley Blue Book guide to find out the retail value of the car that you (or a friend, if you don't drive) are currently driving.**

2. **How much has the car's economic value depreciated since you (or a friend) bought it?**

> **Caution!** Ignoring small residual values bothers some students who want to compute depreciation correctly to the penny. Remember that depreciation is an *estimate*—forget the pennies.

value that can be salvaged, may be quite small. But if the company normally replaces its equipment after a short period of use, the residual value, represented by the selling price or trade-in value, may be relatively high.

From a theoretical point of view, any estimated residual value should be subtracted from cost in arriving at the portion of asset cost to be charged to depreciation. In practice, however, residual values are frequently ignored in determining periodic depreciation charges. This practice is acceptable when residual values are relatively small or are not subject to reasonable estimation.

USEFUL LIFE Noncurrent operating assets other than land have a limited **useful life** as a result of certain physical and functional factors. The physical factors that limit the service life of an asset are (1) wear and tear, (2) deterioration and decay, and (3) damage or destruction. Everyone is familiar with the processes of wear and tear that render an automobile, a building, or furniture no longer usable. A tangible asset, whether used or not, also is subject to deterioration and decay through aging. Finally, fire, flood, earthquake, or accident may reduce or terminate the useful life of an asset.

The primary functional factor limiting the useful lives of assets is obsolescence. An asset may lose its usefulness when as a result of altered business requirements or technological progress, it no longer can produce sufficient revenue to justify its continued use. Although the asset is still physically usable, its inability to produce sufficient revenue has cut short its economic life. Look around—how many 286 personal computers are stored in corners, still perfectly operational, but unable to run the software that is currently being used?

Both physical and functional factors must be considered in estimating the useful life of a depreciable asset. This recognition requires estimating what events will take place in the future and requires careful judgment on the part of the accountant. Physical factors are more readily apparent than functional factors in predicting asset life. But when functional factors are expected to hasten the retirement of an asset, these also must be considered.

In practice, many companies as a matter of policy dispose of certain classes of assets after a predetermined period, without regard to the serviceability of individual assets within a class. Company automobiles, for example, may be replaced routinely every two or three years.

The useful life of a depreciable plant asset may be expressed in terms of either an estimated time factor or an estimated use factor. The time factor may be a period of

Computers have short useful lives due to the quick progress of technology.

months or years; the use factor may be a number of hours of service or a number of units of output. The cost of the asset is allocated in accordance with the lapse of time or extent of use. The rate of cost allocation may be modified by other factors, but basically depreciation must be recognized on a time or use basis.

PATTERN OF USE In order to match asset cost against revenues, periodic depreciation charges should reflect as closely as possible the pattern of use. If the asset produces a varying revenue pattern, then the depreciation charges should vary in a corresponding manner. When depreciation is measured in terms of a time factor, the pattern of use must be estimated. Because of the difficulty in identifying a pattern of use, several somewhat arbitrary methods have come into common practice. Each method represents a different pattern and is designed to make the time basis approximate the use basis. The time factor is employed in two general classes of methods: straight-line depreciation and accelerated depreciation. When depreciation is measured in terms of a use factor, the units of use must be estimated. The depreciation charge varies periodically in accordance with the services provided by the asset. The use factor is employed in service-hours depreciation and in productive-output depreciation.

Recording Periodic Depreciation

The general form of the journal entry used to recognize depreciation is as follows:

Depreciation Expense	xxx	
Accumulated Depreciation		xxx

In manufacturing operations, depreciation is sometimes charged to a production overhead account and then allocated to the cost of inventory. This merely extends the period of deferral—instead of going straight to an expense account, depreciation goes to inventory and then to expense (Cost of Sales).

The allowance account that is credited in recording periodic depreciation is commonly titled "Accumulated depreciation." The accumulation of expired cost in a separate account rather than crediting the asset account directly permits identification of the original cost of the asset and the accumulated depreciation. Companies are required to disclose both cost and accumulated depreciation for plant assets on the balance sheet or in the notes to the financial statements. This enables the user to estimate the relative age of plant assets and provides some basis for predicting future cash outflows for the replacement of plant assets.

Methods of Depreciation

There are a number of different methods for computing depreciation expense. The depreciation method used in any specific instance is a matter of judgment and, conceptually, should be selected to most closely approximate the actual pattern of use expected from the asset. In practice, most firms select one depreciation method, such as straight-line, and use it for substantially all their depreciable assets. The following methods are described in this section.

Time-Factor Methods
- Straight-line depreciation
- Accelerated methods
  - Sum-of-the-years'-digits depreciation
  - Declining-balance depreciation

Use-Factor Methods
- Service-hours depreciation
- Productive-output depreciation

Group and Composite Methods

The examples that follow assume the acquisition of a polyurethane plastic-molding machine at the beginning of 2002 by Schuss Boom Ski Manufacturing, Inc., at a cost of $100,000 with an estimated residual value of $5,000. The following symbols are used in the formulas for the development of depreciation rates and charges:

C = Asset cost

R = Estimated residual value

n = Estimated life in years, hours of service, or units of output

r = Depreciation rate per period, per hour of service, or per unit of output

D = Periodic depreciation charge

TIME-FACTOR METHODS The most common methods of cost allocation are related to the passage of time. A productive asset is used up over time, and possible obsolescence due to technological changes is also a function of time. Of the **time-factor depreciation** methods, straight-line depreciation is by far the most popular.

The use of **accelerated depreciation** methods is based largely on the assumption that there will be rapid reductions in a depreciable asset's efficiency, output, or other benefits in the early years of that asset's life. As assets age, they often require increased charges for maintenance and repairs. Charges for depreciation decline, then, as the economic advantages afforded through ownership of the asset decline. The most commonly used accelerated method is the declining-balance method; the sum-of-the-years'-digits method is also sometimes used.

> **FYI:** Straight-line depreciation is used for at least some assets by over 95% of publicly traded companies in the United States. For 75% of those companies, straight-line is the only depreciation method used.
>
> **SOURCE:** Standard & Poor's COMPUSTAT.

Straight-line depreciation. **Straight-line depreciation** relates depreciation to the passage of time and recognizes equal depreciation in each year of the life of the asset. The simple assumption behind the straight-line method is that the asset is equally useful during each time period, and depreciation is not affected by asset productivity or efficiency variations. In applying the straight-line method, an estimate is made of the useful life of the asset, and the depreciable asset cost (the difference between the asset cost and residual value) is divided by the useful life of the asset in arriving at the periodic depreciation amount.

Using data for the machine acquired by Schuss Boom Ski Manufacturing and assuming a five-year life, annual depreciation is computed as follows:

$$D = \frac{C - R}{n} \text{, or } \frac{\$100,000 - \$5,000}{5 \text{ years}} = \$19,000 \text{ per year}$$

A table summarizing annual depreciation for the entire life of the asset, using the straight-line method, follows:

End of Year	Computation		Depreciation Amount	Accumulated Depreciation	Asset Book Value
					$100,000
2002	$95,000 ÷ 5	=	$19,000	$19,000	81,000
2003	95,000 ÷ 5	=	19,000	38,000	62,000
2004	95,000 ÷ 5	=	19,000	57,000	43,000
2005	95,000 ÷ 5	=	19,000	76,000	24,000
2006	95,000 ÷ 5	=	19,000	95,000	5,000
			$95,000		

It was indicated earlier that residual value is frequently ignored when it is a relatively minor amount. If this were done in the above example, depreciation would be $20,000 per year instead of $19,000.

When assets are acquired or disposed of in the middle of a year, depreciation for the partial year should be recognized. The examples in this chapter assume that partial-year depreciation is recognized for the number of months an asset was held during the year.

There are a variety of other approaches to computing partial-year depreciation, and these are covered in the expanded material at the end of the chapter.

FYI: These days, very few companies use the sum-of-the-years'-digits method. GENERAL ELECTRIC is one of the few companies that does

Sum-of-the-years'-digits depreciation. The **sum-of-the-years'-digits depreciation** method yields decreasing depreciation in each successive year. The computations are done by applying a series of fractions, each of a smaller value, to depreciable asset cost. The numerator of the fraction is the number of years remaining in the asset life as of the beginning of the year. The denominator of the fraction is the sum of all the digits from one to the original useful life. There is no great conceptual insight behind this method—it is merely a clever arithmetic scheme that gives decreasing depreciation each year and results in the entire depreciable cost being allocated over the asset's useful life.

In the Schuss Boom example, the useful life is five years, so the denominator of the fraction is 15 $(1 + 2 + 3 + 4 + 5)$. Annual depreciation is computed as follows:

End of Year	Computation	Depreciation Amount	Accumulated Depreciation	Asset Book Value
				$100,000
2002	$95,000 × 5/15 =	$31,667	$31,667	68,333
2003	95,000 × 4/15 =	25,333	57,000	43,000
2004	95,000 × 3/15 =	19,000	76,000	24,000
2005	95,000 × 2/15 =	12,667	88,667	11,333
2006	95,000 × 1/15 =	6,333	95,000	5,000
		$95,000		

Note that under this method, annual depreciation expense declines by 1/15 of the depreciation asset base each year, or by $6,333 (by $6,334 in 2003 and 2006 due to effects of rounding).

When an asset has a long useful life, such as 20 years, computing the sum of the years' digits can be cumbersome. The following formula is a shortcut to computing the sum of the years' digits:

$$\frac{[n(n+1)]}{2} = (1 + 2 + 3 + \ldots + n)$$

FYI: The famous mathematician Carl Friedrich Gauss deduced this formula in 1878 during a test in school when he was 10 years old.

With a useful life of 20 years, the sum-of-the-years'-digits denominator, determined by the formula, is: $[20(20 + 1)] \div 2 = 210$. The fraction applied to depreciable cost in the first year would be 20/210, in the second year, 19/210, and so forth.

Declining-balance depreciation. The **declining-balance depreciation** methods provide decreasing charges by applying a constant percentage rate to a declining asset book value. The most popular rate is two times the straight-line rate, and this method is often referred to as **double-declining-balance depreciation**. The percentage to be used is double the straight-line rate, calculated for various useful lives as follows:

Estimated Useful Life in Years	Straight-Line Rate	2 Times Straight-Line Rate
3	33⅓%	66⅔%
5	20	40
7	14²⁄₇	28⁴⁄₇
8	12½	25
10	10	20
20	5	10

Residual value is not used in the computations under this method; however, it is generally recognized that depreciation should not continue once the book value is equal to the residual value. Depreciation using the double-declining-balance method for the Schuss Boom asset described earlier is summarized in the following table.

End of Year	Computation		Depreciation Amount	Accumulated Depreciation	Asset Book Value
					$100,000
2002	$100,000 × 40%	=	$40,000	$40,000	60,000
2003	60,000 × 40%	=	24,000	64,000	36,000
2004	36,000 × 40%	=	14,400	78,400	21,600
2005	21,600 × 40%	=	8,640	87,040	12,960
2006	12,960 × 40%	=	5,184	92,224	7,776
			$92,224		

> **Caution!** With both the straight-line and sum-of-the-years'-digits methods, the residual value is subtracted from the asset cost before calculating depreciation. Residual value is *not* subtracted when using the double-declining-balance method.

It should be noted that the rate of 40% is applied to the decreasing book value of the asset each year. This results in a declining amount of depreciation expense. In applying this rate, the book value after five years exceeds the residual value by $2,776 ($7,776 – $5,000). This condition arises whenever residual values are relatively low in amount. Companies usually switch to the straight-line method when the remaining annual depreciation computed using straight-line exceeds the depreciation computed by continuing to apply the declining-balance rate. In the Schuss Boom example, the depreciation expense for the year 2006 would be $7,960 if a switch was made from the double-declining-balance to the straight-line method. This would reduce the book value of the asset to its $5,000 residual value. In this example, the switch would be made in the last year of the asset's life, and the final year's depreciation expense is simply the amount necessary to reduce the asset's book value to its residual value. However, if the asset in the example had a lower residual value, the switch could have been made in the fourth year. For example, assume the asset is expected to have no residual value. The book value under the double-declining-balance method at the end of the third year as shown previously is $21,600, thus the straight-line depreciation for the fourth and fifth years would be $10,800 ($21,600 ÷ 2); because the straight-line depreciation of $10,800 exceeds the double-declining depreciation of $8,640, the straight-line amount would be used.

Evaluation of time-factor methods. Exhibit 13–3 illustrates the pattern of depreciation expense for the time-factor methods discussed in the preceding sections. Note that when the straight-line method is used, depreciation is a constant or fixed charge each period. When the life of an asset is affected primarily by the lapse of time rather than by the degree of use, recognition of depreciation as a constant charge is generally appropriate. However, when the straight-line method is used, net income measurements become particularly sensitive to changes in the volume of business activity. With above-normal activity, there is no increase in the depreciation charge; with below-normal activity, there is no decrease in the depreciation charge.

As mentioned, straight-line depreciation is the most widely used procedure for financial reporting purposes. It is readily understood and frequently parallels asset use. It has the advantage of simplicity and under normal conditions offers a satisfactory means of cost allocation. Normal asset conditions exist when (1) assets have been accumulated over a period of years so that the total of depreciation plus maintenance is comparatively even from period to period, and (2) service potentials of assets are being steadily reduced by functional as well as physical factors. The absence of either of these conditions may suggest the use of some depreciation method other than straight-line.

Accelerated methods can be supported as reasonable approaches to cost allocation when the annual benefits provided by an asset decline as it grows older. These methods, too, are suggested when an

STOP & THINK Imagine that at the beginning of 2002, Schuss Boom had five different machines—one brand new, and the others one year, two years, three years, and four years old. Which depreciation method—straight-line, sum-of-the-years'-digits, or double-declining-balance—would give the highest total depreciation expense in 2002?

EXHIBIT 13–3 | Time-Factor Methods: Depreciation Patterns Compared

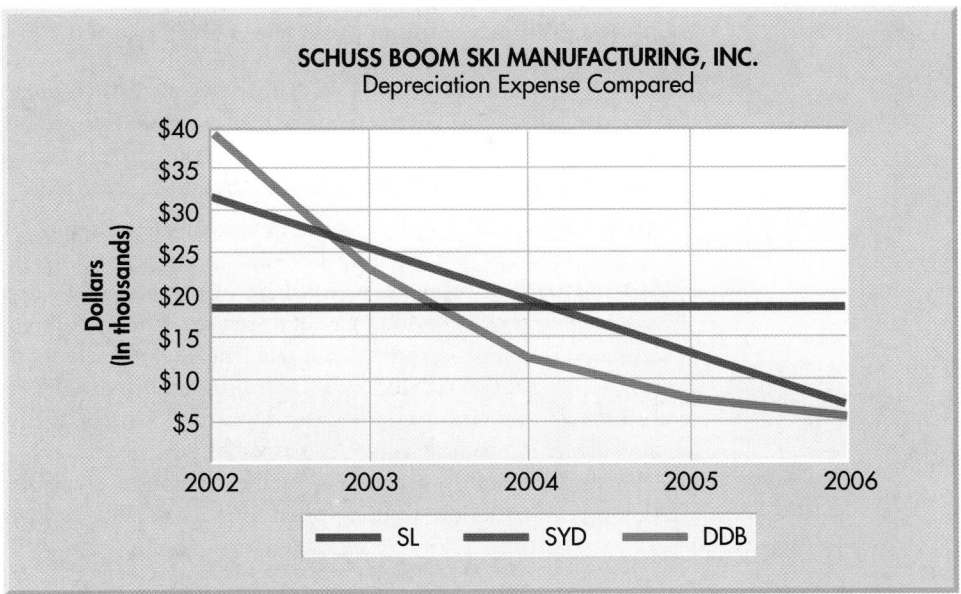

SCHUSS BOOM SKI MANUFACTURING, INC.
Depreciation Expense Compared

asset requires increasing maintenance and repairs over its useful life.[4] When straight-line depreciation is employed, the combined charges for depreciation, maintenance, and repairs will increase over the life of the asset; when an accelerated method is used, the combined charges will tend to be equalized. Exhibit 13–4 illustrates this relationship.

EXHIBIT 13–4 | Accelerated Depreciation and Repairs and Maintenance Expense

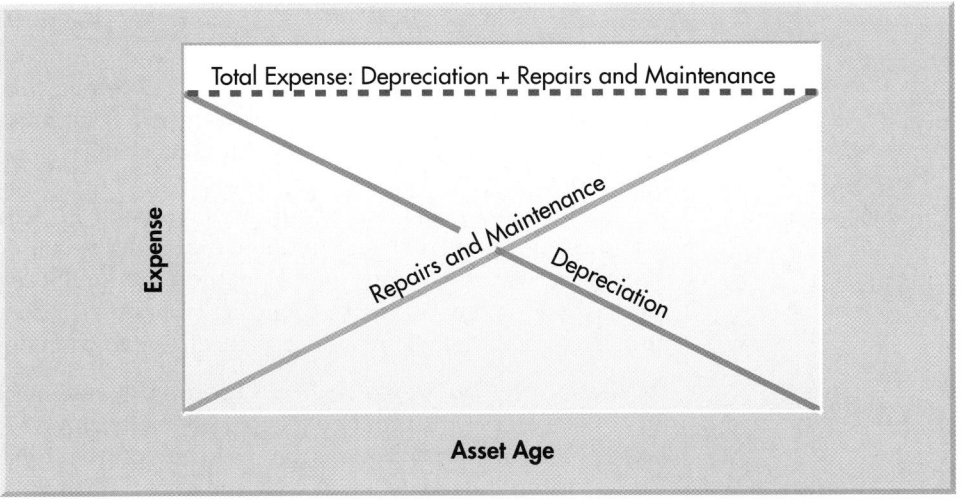

4 The AICPA Committee on Accounting Procedure stated, "The declining-balance method is one of those which meets the requirements of being 'systematic and rational.' In those cases where the expected productivity or revenue-earning power of the asset is relatively greater during the earlier years of its life or where maintenance charges tend to increase during the later years, the declining-balance method may well provide the most satisfactory allocation of cost." These conclusions apply to other accelerated methods, including the sum-of-the-years'-digits method, that produce substantially similar results. See *Accounting Research and Terminology Bulletins–Final Edition*, "No. 44 (Revised), Declining-Balance Depreciation," New York: American Institute of Certified Public Accountants, 1961, par. 2.

Other factors suggesting the use of an accelerated method include: (1) the anticipation of a significant contribution in early periods with the extent of the contribution to be realized in later periods being less definite; (2) the possibility that inadequacy or obsolescence may result in premature retirement of the asset.

USE-FACTOR METHODS **Use-factor depreciation** methods view asset exhaustion as related primarily to asset use or output and provide periodic charges varying with the degree of such service. Service life for certain assets can best be expressed in terms of hours of service; for others, in terms of units of production.

Service-hours depreciation. **Service-hours depreciation** is based on the theory that the purchase of an asset represents the purchase of a number of hours of direct service. This method requires an estimate of the life of the asset in terms of service hours. Depreciable cost is divided by total service hours in arriving at the depreciation rate to be assigned for each hour of asset use. The use of the asset during the period is measured, and the number of service hours is multiplied by the depreciation rate in arriving at the periodic depreciation charge. Depreciation charges against revenue fluctuate periodically according to how much the asset is used.

Using the Schuss Boom asset data previously given and an estimated service life of 20,000 hours, the rate to be applied for each service hour is determined as follows:

$$r \text{ (per hour)} = \frac{C-R}{n} \text{, or } \frac{\$100,000 - \$5,000}{20,000 \text{ hours}} = \$4.75 \text{ per hour}$$

Computation of annual depreciation is summarized in the following table.

End of Year	Service Hours	Computation		Depreciation Amount	Accumulated Depreciation	Asset Book Value
						$100,000
2200	3,000	3,000 × $4.75 =	$14,250	$14,250	85,750
2003	5,000	5,000 × $4.75 =	23,750	38,000	62,000
2004	5,000	5,000 × $4.75 =	23,750	61,750	38,250
2005	4,000	4,000 × $4.75 =	19,000	80,750	19,250
2006	3,000	3,000 × $4.75 =	14,250	95,000	5,000
	20,000			$95,000		

In this illustration, the original estimate of service hours is correct, and the asset is retired after 20,000 hours are reached in the fifth year. Such precise estimation would seldom be found in practice. Procedures for handling changes in estimates are discussed later in the chapter.

Recall that straight-line depreciation resulted in annual depreciation of $19,000 regardless of fluctuations in how much the asset was used. When asset life is affected directly by the degree of use and when there are significant fluctuations in such use, the service-hours method, which recognizes hours used instead of hours available for use, normally provides the more appropriate charge to operations.

Productive-output depreciation. **Productive-output depreciation** is based on the theory that an asset is acquired for the service it can provide in the form of production output. This method requires an estimate of the total unit output of the asset. Depreciable cost divided by the total estimated output gives the equal charge to be assigned for each unit of output. The measured production for a period multiplied by the charge per unit gives the charge to be made against revenue. Depreciation charges fluctuate periodically according to the contribution the asset makes in unit output.

FYI: The productive-output method approximates the technique used to depreciate the cost of producing a motion picture. This technique is discussed in Case 13–6.

Using the Schuss Boom asset data and an estimated productive life of 25,000 units, the rate to be applied for each unit produced is determined as follows:

$$r \text{ (per unit)} = \frac{C-R}{n} \text{, or } \frac{\$100,000 - \$5,000}{25,000 \text{ units}} = \$3.80 \text{ per unit}$$

A table for the productive-output method would be similar to that prepared for the service-hours method.

Evaluation of use-factor methods. When quantitative measures of asset use can be reasonably estimated, the use-factor methods provide highly satisfactory approaches to asset cost allocation. Depreciation as a fluctuating charge tends to follow the revenue curve: high depreciation charges are assigned to periods of high activity; low charges are assigned to periods of low activity. When the useful life of an asset is affected primarily by the degree of its use, recognition of depreciation as a variable charge is particularly appropriate.

However, certain limitations in applying the use-factor methods need to be pointed out. Asset performance in terms of service hours or productive output is often difficult to estimate. Measurement solely in terms of these factors could fail to recognize special conditions, such as increasing maintenance and repair costs, as well as possible inadequacy and obsolescence. Furthermore, when service life expires even in the absence of use, a use-factor method may conceal actual fluctuations in earnings; by relating periodic depreciation charges to the volume of operations, periodic operating results may be smoothed out, thus creating a false appearance of stability.

GROUP AND COMPOSITE METHODS It was assumed in preceding discussions that depreciation expense is associated with individual assets and is applied to each separate unit. This practice is called **unit depreciation**. From a practical standpoint, it often makes sense to compute depreciation for an entire group of assets as if the group were one asset. Group cost allocation procedures are referred to as **group depreciation** when the assets in the group are similar (e.g., all of a company's delivery vans) and **composite depreciation** when the assets in the group are related but dissimilar (e.g., all of a company's desks, chairs, and computers). In the discussion below, the term group depreciation will be used generically to refer to both methods.

The group depreciation procedure treats a collection of assets as a single group. Depreciation is accumulated in a single account, and the depreciation rate is based on the average life of assets in the group. Group depreciation is generally computed as an adaptation of the straight-line method, and the illustrations in this chapter assume this approach. A group rate is established by doing an initial analysis of the various assets or classes of assets in use and computing the depreciation as an average of the straight-line annual depreciation as follows:

Asset	Cost	Residual Value	Depreciable Cost	Estimated Life in Years	Annual Depreciation Expense (Straight-Line)
A	$ 2,000	$ 120	$ 1,880	4	$ 470
B	6,000	300	5,700	6	950
C	12,000	1,200	10,800	10	1,080
	$20,000	$1,620	$18,380		$2,500

Group depreciation rate to be applied to cost: $2,500 ÷ $20,000 = 12.5%
Average life of assets: $18,380 ÷ $2,500 = 7.352 years

The rate of 12.5% applied to the cost of the existing assets, $20,000, results in annual depreciation of $2,500. Annual depreciation of $2,500 will accumulate to a total of $18,380 in 7.352 years; hence, 7.352 years is the average life of the assets.

After the group rate of 12.5% has been set, it is used to compute annual depreciation for all assets subsequently included in the group. For example, if Asset D is acquired for $5,000, the total cost of the assets in the group becomes $25,000 ($2,000 + $6,000 + $12,000 + $5,000) and annual depreciation expense is $3,125 ($25,000 × .125). The group rate is ordinarily left the same in subsequent years in the absence of significant changes in the lives of assets included in the group. It is assumed that the assets are

---

► COLLEGE DEPRECIATION: FASB vs. GASB

Look carefully at the building where your accounting class is held—does it look as if it is depreciating? Probably so. Is your college or university recognizing this depreciation? Maybe not. In August 1987, the FASB issued Statement No. 93, which required all not-for-profit organizations, including public and private colleges and universities, to recognize depreciation in their external financial statements. Prior to the

issuance of the statement, more than 90% of colleges and universities had not reported depreciation and many questioned its usefulness. However, the FASB adopted Statement No. 93 with a unanimous vote.

Soon after Statement No. 93 was adopted, the Governmental Accounting Standards Board (GASB), which has responsibility for setting accounting standards for governmental bodies, issued Statement No. 8, which exempted public colleges and universities from the FASB's depreciation rule. A significant issue of comparability arose because public universities would now be reporting under a different set of standards from that of private universities. Some private universities threatened

to openly disregard the rule. Others declared their intention to ask Congress to force the FASB to back down. Bond-rating agencies promised not to lower the bond ratings of any institutions that refused to comply with the rule. In the face of all this opposition, the FASB issued Statement No. 99, delaying the effective date of the depreciation standard until January 1990.

The Financial Accounting Foundation (FAF), which oversees both the FASB and the GASB, was faced with a critical jurisdictional dispute. Clearly, the FASB had authority to set accounting standards for business entities. Clearly, the GASB had authority to set accounting standards for governmental entities. However, who had

---

replaced with similar assets when retired. The group rate should be reviewed periodically to confirm that it is still appropriate for the assets in the group.

Because the accumulated depreciation account under the group procedure applies to the entire group of assets, it is not related to any specific asset. Thus, no book value can be calculated for any specific asset, and there are no fully depreciated assets. No gains or losses are recognized at the time individual assets are retired. For example, if Asset B is sold for $3,500 after two years of use, the entry to record the sale using the group depreciation method would be as follows:

Cash	3,500	
Accumulated Depreciation	2,500	
Equipment		6,000

Because no gain or loss is recognized, the debit to Accumulated Depreciation is the difference between the cost of the asset and the cash received. Gains and losses due solely to normal variations in asset lives are not recognized.

In instances where assets in a group are continued in use after their cost has been assigned to operations, no further depreciation charges are recognized. On the other hand, where all the assets in a group are retired before their costs have been assigned to operations, a special charge related to such retirement would be recognized, either as a loss or as an addition to depreciation expense.

2

Discuss the issues impacting proper amortization of intangible assets.

AMORTIZATION OF INTANGIBLE ASSETS

The very nature of intangible assets makes estimating their useful lives a difficult problem. The useful life of an intangible asset may be affected by a variety of economic, legal, regulatory, and contractual factors. These factors, including options for renewal or extension, should be evaluated in determining the appropriate period over which the cost of the intangible asset should be allocated. A patent, for example, has a legal life of 17 years; but if the competitive advantages afforded by the patent are expected to terminate after 5 years, then the patent cost should be amortized over the shorter period.

authority to set the standards for those special entities whose ownership could be either public or private, such as hospitals and universities? The FAF originally considered giving jurisdiction over all these special entities to the FASB. This was deemed unacceptable by many governmental officials, and they threatened to withdraw their support from the FAF and establish their own independent body for setting governmental accounting standards. In late 1989, the FAF altered its position and gave the GASB authority over financial reporting by all governmental entities. For now, the comparability issue for special entities remains something that will have to be ironed out by the FASB and the GASB on a case-by-case basis. As to depreciation, private colleges and universities recognize it, and public ones usually don't. For example, in its 1997/98 statement of activities, STANFORD UNIVERSITY (a private school) reported depreciation expense for the year of $91.1 million, in comparison to total university revenue for the year of $1,524.2 million.

QUESTIONS:

1. What reasons are there for requiring colleges and universities to report depreciation? What arguments could be made against the requirement?
2. What dangers are there in jurisdictional disputes of this kind?
3. Are there any reasons that a college or university would *want* to recognize depreciation?

SOURCES:

Lee Berton, "Several Private Colleges May Ignore New Accounting Rule on Depreciation," *The Wall Street Journal*, February 4, 1988, p. 24.

Dennis M. Patten, "Battle of the Boards: Identifying the Political Nature of the Standard-Setting Controversies," *Government Accountants Journal*, Fall 1989, p. 3.

News Report, "FAF Alters Position on FASB-GASB Jurisdiction," *Journal of Accountancy*, January 1990, p. 13.

1997/98 Statement of Activities for Stanford University.

net work exercise

Consult the FASB's Web site (**www.fasb.org**) to determine the current status of this Exposure Draft.

Although the life of an intangible asset is to be estimated by careful analysis of the surrounding circumstances, APB Opinion No. 17 established a maximum life of 40 years for amortization purposes.

However, the issue of the appropriate amortization life for intangibles is currently being examined by the FASB. In 1999, an Exposure Draft was issued that, if adopted, would change the method by which intangibles are amortized.[5] The proposal requires that a determination first be made as to whether the intangible asset has a finite or infinite life. If it is determined that the asset has an infinite life and that a market exists in which that asset can be readily bought and sold, then the asset is not to be amortized until its life is determined to be finite.[6] An example of an intangible asset that can be readily traded and has an infinite life is a broadcast license, which includes an extension option that can be renewed indefinitely. If the intangible asset is determined to have a finite life, then the asset is presumed to have a useful life not exceeding 20 years unless persuasive evidence exists to the contrary.[7] Intangible assets are to be amortized by the straight-line method unless there is strong justification for using another method.

Amortization, like depreciation, may be charged as an operating expense of the period or allocated to production overhead if the asset is related directly to the manufacture of goods. In practice, the credit entry is often made directly to the asset account rather than to a separate accumulated amortization account. This practice is arbitrary, and there is no reason why charges for amortization cannot be accumulated in a separate account in the same manner as depreciation. Disclosure of both cost and accumulated depreciation is required for tangible assets, but similar disclosure is not required for intangible assets.

5 Proposed Statement of Accounting Standard, "Business Combinations and Intangible Assets," Norwalk, CT: Financial Accounting Standards Board, September 1999.

6 Ibid, par. 41.

7 Ibid, par. 40.

► BASEBALL ACCOUNTING

Football players in the NFL went on strike in 1982. In August 1994, major league baseball players went on strike for the eighth time in 20 years. This strike wasn't settled until the following April, resulting in the cancellation of the 1994 World Series. In 1998, the National Basketball Association experienced its first work stoppage in league history when the owners decided to lock out the players in order to force a renegotiation of the collective

bargaining agreement. And what was the underlying cause of each of these work stoppages? Accounting, of course.

During the baseball strike of 1994, the public was able to peer into the business side of baseball and get a look at the owners' accounting practices. The baseball team owners and the players had been arguing for years about how much money the owners were making. The owners claimed that they were losing millions; the players were skeptical. During a previous strike in 1985, George Sorter, a professor of accounting at New York University, was asked by the major league baseball team owners to estimate the aggregate profit or loss for the 26 major league teams for 1984. Professor Sorter identified the following three areas as being the most contentious from an accounting standpoint.

DEFERRED COMPENSATION

A standard player's contract might state that a player is to receive $3,000,000 for a season, $1,000,000 to be paid during the year and $2,000,000 to be deferred for 10 years. Most of the baseball teams failed to use the present value of the $2,000,000 deferred compensation when computing salary expense, overstating expenses.

INITIAL ROSTER DEPRECIATION

When a team changes hands, up to 50% of the purchase price is allocated to an asset called initial roster. This asset represents the value of the team, over and above the value of the individual players. The owners included $12 million of initial roster depreciation expense in their 1984 results. The troubling thing about this expense is that it is recorded only for teams that have changed hands recently. If a team is still owned by the original owner, the initial roster asset would still exist in an economic sense, but it would not be recognized in the accounting records. In addition, the reported profits of teams recognizing initial roster depreciation are hit twice for player development costs—player development expenditures for the current period are

DEPLETION OF NATURAL RESOURCES

Apply the productive-output method to the depletion of natural resources.

Natural resources, also called wasting assets, are consumed as the physical units representing these resources are removed and sold. The withdrawal of oil or gas, the cutting of timber, and the mining of coal, sulfur, iron, copper, or silver ore are examples of processes leading to the exhaustion of natural resources. Depletion expense is a charge for the "using up" of the resources.

Experts such as the person shown here have the difficult job of estimating the amount of natural resources available for economical removal from the land.

expensed along with initial roster depreciation, which represents the expensing of the capitalized value of past player development expenditures.

RELATED PARTY TRANSACTIONS

Professional sports teams are often owned as an integrated array of assets, and it is difficult, and sometimes misleading, to carve out and report the results of the sports operations separately. For example, the Atlanta Braves and the Chicago Cubs are owned by companies that also operate television "superstations" (TBS in Atlanta and WGN in Chicago, respectively), which broadcast Braves and Cubs games nationwide. It isn't clear that the fees "paid" by the superstations to the baseball teams reflect the value that those broadcast rights would command in an arm's-length transaction. It is widely suspected that related party transactions allow team owners to shift reported profits away from baseball operations.

Professor Sorter's final estimate was that the 26 major league baseball teams lost a total of $27 million in 1984—a diplomatic finding almost exactly halfway between the owners' claim of a $65 million loss and the players' claim of a $9 million profit. The same accounting issues that plagued the 1985 baseball negotiations

also arose in 1994 and still exist today. So when the next baseball strike occurs, remember that the underlying cause is accounting.

QUESTIONS:

1. All teams have an initial roster asset; however, the asset is recorded and depreciated only by those teams that have recently changed hands. Do other types of businesses (e.g., manufacturers, retailers) have assets similar in nature to baseball's initial roster asset? Explain.

2. The accounting treatment of the initial roster asset makes it difficult to compare the financial statements of a team that has never been sold to those of a team that has recently changed hands. Make a suggestion for a solution to this problem.

3. What incentives do owners of sports franchises have to understate profits?

SOURCES:

George H. Sorter, "Accounting for Baseball," *Journal of Accountancy*, June 1986, p. 126.

Timothy K. Smith and Erle Norton, "Throwing Curves: One Baseball Statistic Remains a Mystery—the Real Bottom Line," *The Wall Street Journal*, April 2, 1993, p. A1.

The computation of depletion expense is an adaptation of the productive-output method of depreciation. Perhaps the most difficult problem in computing depletion expense is estimating the amount of resources available for economical removal from the land. Generally, a geologist, mining engineer, or other expert is called upon to make the estimate, and it is subject to continual revision as the resource is extracted or removed.

Developmental costs, such as costs of drilling, sinking mine shafts, and constructing roads, should be capitalized and added to the original cost of the property in arriving at the total cost subject to depletion. These costs are often incurred before normal activities begin.

To illustrate the computation of depletion expense, assume the following facts: land containing mineral deposits is purchased at a cost of $5,500,000. The cost to restore the land to its original state after removal of the resources is estimated to be $200,000; the land can then be sold for $450,000, yielding a net residual value of $250,000 ($450,000 – $200,000). The natural resource supply is estimated at 1,000,000 tons. The unit-depletion charge and the total depletion charge for the first year, assuming the withdrawal of 80,000 tons, are calculated as follows:

Depletion charge per ton: ($5,500,000 – $250,000) ÷ 1,000,000 = $5.25
Depletion charge for the first year: 80,000 tons × $5.25 = $420,000

The following entries should be made to record these events:

Mineral Deposits	5,500,000	
Cash		5,500,000
Depletion Expense	420,000	
Accumulated Depletion (or Mineral Deposits)		420,000

If the 80,000 tons are sold in the current year, the entire $420,000 would be included as part of the cost of goods sold. If only 60,000 tons are sold, $105,000 is reported as part of ending inventory on the balance sheet.

When buildings and improvements are constructed in connection with the removal of natural resources and their usefulness is limited to the duration of the project, it is reasonable to recognize depreciation on such properties on an output basis consistent with the charges to be recognized for the natural resources themselves. For example, assume buildings are constructed at a cost of $250,000; the useful lives of the buildings are expected to terminate upon exhaustion of the natural resource consisting of 1,000,000 units. Under these circumstances, a depreciation charge of $0.25 ($250,000 ÷ 1,000,000) should accompany the depletion charge recognized for each unit. When improvements provide benefits expected to terminate prior to the exhaustion of the natural resource, the cost of such improvements should be allocated on the basis of the units to be removed during the life of the improvements or on a time basis, whichever is considered more appropriate.

4

Incorporate changes in estimates into the computation of depreciation for current and future periods.

CHANGES IN ESTIMATES OF COST ALLOCATION VARIABLES

The allocation of asset costs benefiting more than one period cannot be precisely determined at acquisition because so many of the variables must be estimated. Only one factor in determining the periodic charge for depreciation, amortization, or depletion is based on historical information—asset cost. Other factors—residual value, useful life or output, and the pattern of use or benefit—must be estimated. The question frequently facing accountants is how adjustments to these estimates, which arise as time passes, should be reflected in the accounts. A change in estimate is reported in the current and future periods rather than as an adjustment of prior periods. This type of adjustment is made for residual value and useful-life changes. However, a change in depreciation method (e.g., from double-declining-balance to straight-line) based on a revised expected pattern of use is a change in accounting principle and is accounted for retroactively. Changes in accounting principles are discussed in Chapter 20.

Change in Estimated Life

FYI: In 1998, a change in the estimated depreciation life for computer software increased the pretax income of TRANSPORT CORPORATION OF AMERICA by 6.7%. A 1987 change by GENERAL MOTORS in the estimated life of tools increased operating income by 93%.

To illustrate the procedure for a change in estimated life affecting allocation of asset cost, assume that a company purchased $50,000 of equipment and estimated a 10-year life. Using the straight-line method with no residual value, the annual depreciation would be $5,000. After four years, accumulated depreciation would amount to $20,000, and the remaining undepreciated book value would be $30,000. Early in the fifth year, a reevaluation of the life indicates only four more years of service can be expected from the asset. An adjustment must therefore be made for the fifth and subsequent years to reflect the change. A new annual depreciation charge is calculated by dividing the remaining book value by the remaining life of four years. This would result in an annual charge of $7,500 for the fifth through eighth years ($30,000 ÷ 4 = $7,500).

Year	Computation		Depreciation Amount	Accumulated Depreciation
1	$50,000 ÷ 10	=	$ 5,000	$ 5,000
2	$50,000 ÷ 10	=	5,000	10,000
3	$50,000 ÷ 10	=	5,000	15,000
4	$50,000 ÷ 10	=	5,000	20,000
5	($50,000 − $20,000) ÷ 4	=	7,500	27,500
6	($50,000 − $20,000) ÷ 4	=	7,500	35,000
7	($50,000 − $20,000) ÷ 4	=	7,500	42,500
8	($50,000 − $20,000) ÷ 4	=	7,500	50,000
			$50,000	

Note that no attempt is made to go back and "fix" the first four years. The $5,000 depreciation charge recognized in those years was computed using the best information available. When revised information becomes available in the fifth year, the impact is reflected in the current and future periods.

A change in the estimated life of an intangible asset is accounted for in the same manner, that is, the unamortized cost is allocated over the remaining life based on the revised estimate.

Change in Estimated Units of Production

Another change in estimate occurs in accounting for natural resources when the estimate of the recoverable units changes as a result of further discoveries, improved extraction processes, or changes in sales prices that indicate changes in the number of units that can be extracted profitably. A revised depletion rate is established by dividing the remaining resource cost balance by the estimated remaining recoverable units.

To illustrate, assume the facts used in the earlier depletion example. Land is purchased at a cost of $5,500,000 with estimated net residual value of $250,000. The original estimated supply of natural resources in the land is 1,000,000 tons. As indicated previously, the depletion rate under these conditions would be $5.25 per ton, and the depletion charge for the first year when 80,000 tons were mined would be $420,000. Assume that in the second year of operation, 100,000 tons of ore are withdrawn, but before the books are closed at the end of the second year, appraisal of the expected recoverable tons indicates a remaining tonnage of 950,000. The new depletion rate and the depletion charge for the second year would be computed as follows:

Cost assignable to recoverable tons as of the beginning of the second year:	
Original costs applicable to depletable resources	$5,250,000
Deduct: Depletion charge for the first year	420,000
Balance of cost subject to depletion	$4,830,000
Estimated recoverable tons as of the beginning of the second year:	
Number of tons withdrawn in the second year	100,000
Estimated recoverable tons as of the end of the second year	950,000
Total recoverable tons as of the beginning of the second year	1,050,000

Depletion charge per ton for the second year: $4,830,000 ÷ 1,050,000 = $4.60
Depletion charge for the second year: 100,000 × $4.60 = $460,000

Sometimes an increase in estimated recoverable units arises from additional expenditures for capital developments. When this occurs, the additional costs should be added to the remaining recoverable cost and divided by the number of tons remaining to be extracted. To illustrate this situation, assume in the preceding example that $525,000 of additional costs had been incurred at the beginning of the second year. The preceding computation of depletion rate and depletion expense would be changed as follows:

Cost assignable to recoverable tons as of the beginning of the second year:	
Original costs applicable to depletable resources	$5,250,000
Add: Additional costs incurred in the second year	525,000
	$5,775,000
Deduct: Depletion charge for the first year	420,000
Balance of cost subject to depletion	$5,355,000
Estimated recoverable tons as of the beginning of the second year (as stated previously)	1,050,000

Depletion charge per ton for the second year: $5,355,000 ÷ 1,050,000 = $5.10
Depletion charge for the second year: 100,000 × $5.10 = $510,000

Accounting is made up of many estimates. The procedures outlined in this section are designed to prevent the continual restating of reported income from prior years. Adjustments to prior-period income figures are made only if actual errors have occurred, not when reasonable estimates have been made that later prove inaccurate.

Identify whether an asset is impaired and measure the amount of the impairment loss, using both U.S. GAAP and international accounting standards.

FYI: In a final act of surrender, ELI LILLY sold its PCS division to RITE AID on January 22, 1999, for just $1.6 billion.

IMPAIRMENT

Events sometimes occur after the purchase of an asset and before the end of its estimated life that impair its value and require an immediate write-down of the asset rather than making a normal allocation of cost over a period of time. Until 1995, the authoritative accounting literature did not include a clear statement of accounting standards governing the recognition of asset **impairment**.

As an example, in 1994, ELI LILLY, a large pharmaceutical company, paid $4.1 billion to acquire PCS HEALTH SYSTEMS, a company that helps insurance companies and HMOs manage their prescription drug benefit plans. By the second quarter of 1997, it had become apparent that the PCS acquisition was not turning out as planned. The movement toward managed health care had not been as fast as Lilly had expected, and the the ominous possibility of increased government regulation of prescription drug benefit plans had tempered enthusiasm about PCS's prospects. In reviewing the acquisition, Eli Lilly decided that it should recognize a loss and reduce the recorded value of PCS's assets by $2.4 billion.

As illustrated by the Eli Lilly/PCS Health Systems case, whether to recognize the impairment of operating assets is not a simple decision. In addition, once the decision to recognize the impairment has been made, one is still faced with the question of the amount of the write-down. This section discusses the concepts and procedures associated with the recognition of an asset impairment.

Accounting for Asset Impairment

Guidance on the accounting for asset impairment, using U.S. GAAP, is provided in FASB Statement No. 121, issued in 1995, which addresses the following four questions[8]:
1. When should an asset be reviewed for possible impairment?
2. When is an asset impaired?
3. How should an impairment loss be measured?
4. What information should be disclosed about an impairment?

1. When should an asset be reviewed for possible impairment? Conducting an impairment review of every asset at the end of every year would be unlikely to provide sufficiently improved financial information to justify the cost of the reviews. Instead, companies are required to conduct impairment tests whenever there has been a material change in the way an asset is used or in the business environment. In addition, if management obtains information suggesting that the market value of an asset has declined, an impairment review should be conducted.

2. When is an asset impaired? According to the FASB, an entity should recognize an impairment loss only when the undiscounted sum of estimated future cash flows from an asset is less than the book value of the asset. Any recorded goodwill associated with the acquisition of an asset should be added to the book value of the asset in determining whether impairment exists. As illustrated in the following example, this is rather a strange impairment threshold—a more intuitive test would be to compare the book value to the fair value of the asset. Because the undiscounted cash flows do not incorporate the time value of money, the sum of undiscounted future cash flows will always be greater than the fair value of the asset.

3. How should an impairment loss be measured? The impairment loss is the difference between the book value of the asset and the fair value. The fair value can be

---

8 *Statement of Financial Accounting Standards No. 121,* "Accounting for the Impairment of Long-Lived Assets and for Long-Lived Assets to Be Disposed Of," Norwalk, CT: Financial Accounting Standards Board, March 1995.

> **Caution!** The existence of an impairment loss is determined using *undiscounted* future cash flows. The amount of the impairment loss is measured using fair value, or *discounted,* future cash flows.

approximated using the present value of estimated future cash flows from the asset. Any impairment loss amount should first be used to reduce the recorded value of goodwill associated with an asset purchase.

4. *What information should be disclosed about an impairment?* Disclosure should include a description of the impaired asset, reasons for the impairment, a description of the measurement assumptions, and the business segment or segments affected. An impairment loss should be included as part of income from continuing operations, and note disclosure of the amount should be made if the impairment loss is not shown as a separate income statement item.

Application of the impairment rules is illustrated with the following example. Guangzhou Company purchased a building five years ago for $600,000. The building has been depreciated using the straight-line method with a 20-year useful life and no residual value. Several other buildings in the immediate area have recently been abandoned, and Guangzhou has decided that the building should be evaluated for possible impairment. Guangzhou estimates that the building has a remaining useful life of 15 years, that net cash inflow from the building will be $25,000 per year, and that the fair value of the building is $230,000. No goodwill was associated with the purchase of the building.

Annual depreciation for the building has been $30,000 ($600,000 ÷ 20 years). The current book value of the building is computed as follows:

Original cost	$600,000
Accumulated depreciation ($30,000 × 5 years)	150,000
Book value	$450,000

The book value of $450,000 is compared to the $375,000 ($25,000 × 15 years) undiscounted sum of future cash flows to determine whether the building is impaired. The sum of future cash flows is less, so an impairment loss should be recognized. The loss is equal to the $220,000 ($450,000 – $230,000) difference between the book value of the building and its fair value. The impairment loss would be recorded as follows:

Accumulated Depreciation—Building	150,000	
Loss on Impairment of Building	220,000	
Building ($600,000 – $230,000)		370,000

The new recorded value of $230,000 ($600,000 – $370,000) is considered to be the cost of the asset. After an impairment loss is recognized, no restoration of the loss is allowed even if the fair value of the asset recovers.

Why do you think the FASB designated the undiscounted sum of future cash flows rather than the fair value as the threshold for determining whether an asset is impaired?

The odd nature of the undiscounted cash flow threshold can be seen if the facts in the Guangzhou example are changed slightly. Assume that net cash inflow from the building will be $35,000 per year, and that the fair value of the building is $330,000. With these numbers, no impairment loss is recognized, even though the fair value of $330,000 is less than the book value of $450,000, because the undiscounted sum of future cash flows of $525,000 ($35,000 × 15 years) exceeds the book value.

International Accounting for Asset Impairment: IAS 36

In June 1998, the IASC issued IAS 36, "Impairment of Assets." This international standard is, from a conceptual standpoint, superior to the impairment standard embodied in FASB Statement No. 121. The IASC standard requires that a company recognize an impairment loss whenever the "recoverable value" of an asset is less than its book value. Recoverable value is defined as the higher of the selling price of the asset or the discounted future cash flows associated with the asset's use. Both of these measures are based on the

FYI: Before the issuance of IAS 36 in 1998, the international standard for accounting for asset impairments was found in IAS 16. That standard allowed the use of either undiscounted or discounted cash flows in determining whether an impairment exists.

discounted value of the future cash flows from the asset, which means that the IASC has completely rejected the conceptually unappealing undiscounted cash flow threshold adopted by the FASB.

IAS 36 also differs from Statement No. 121 in that the international standard allows for the reversal of an impairment loss if events in subsequent years suggest the asset is no longer impaired. Therefore, if an asset has increased in value and is no longer deemed to be impaired, then the portion of the impairment loss that has been recovered should be reversed and recognized as a gain. Under the FASB standard, no subsequent recovery of an impairment loss is allowed.

Accounting for Upward Asset Revaluations: IAS 16

As mentioned in Chapter 12, an allowable alternative under IAS 16 is to recognize increases in the value of long-term operating assets. Because the accounting procedures associated with asset revaluation are similar to those used to recognize an asset impairment, they are illustrated in this section.

RECOGNIZING AN UPWARD ASSET REVALUATION Earlier, we used an example of a building purchased by Guangzhou Company to illustrate the accounting for an asset impairment. Recall that after five years, the book value of that building was as follows:

Original cost	$600,000
Accumulated depreciation ($30,000 × 5 years)	150,000
Book value	$450,000

Now assume that Guangzhou Company uses international accounting standards, the building's fair value is $540,000, and Guangzhou employs the allowable alternative under international standards, electing to recognize this increase in asset value. The journal entry to recognize the asset revaluation is as follows:

Accumulated Depreciation—Building	150,000	
Revaluation Equity Reserve		90,000
Building ($600,000 − $540,000)		60,000

Caution! Remember, the upward revaluation of long-term operating assets is an allowable alternative under international accounting standards but is *not* allowable under U.S. GAAP.

After the entry is posted, the balance in the accumulated depreciation account is $0, and the balance in the building account is $540,000 ($600,000 − $60,000), resulting in a net recorded amount of $540,000. As discussed in Chapter 11, the revaluation equity reserve is a separate category of equity and reflects the increase in the reported value of the total assets of the company stemming from increases in the market value of long-term operating assets. After the revaluation, annual depreciation expense is computed based on the revalued amount; the revalued amount is depreciated over the remaining estimated life of the asset.

RECORDING THE DISPOSAL OF A REVALUED ASSET An interesting twist in the provisions of IAS 16 makes it somewhat costly for a company to revalue its assets upward. To illustrate, assume that, immediately after revaluing its building to $540,000, Guangzhou Company sells the building for $540,000 in cash. This disposal would be recorded as follows:

Cash	540,000	
Building		540,000
Revaluation Equity Reserve	90,000	
Retained Earnings		90,000

Note that because Guangzhou chose to revalue the asset, the $90,000 "gain" from the increase in the value of the asset is never reported as a gain in Guangzhou's income statement.

The "gain" is initially reflected as an increase in the equity reserve; on disposal, the "gain" is transferred directly to Retained Earnings, bypassing the income statement completely. Thus, although IAS 16 gives companies the benefit of recognizing increases in the value of long-term operating assets, the provisions of IAS 16 also impose a cost in the sense that these increases are then never reflected as increases in earnings in the income statement.

ASSET RETIREMENTS

Account for the sale of depreciable assets in exchange for cash and in exchange for other depreciable assets.

Assets may be retired by sale, exchange, or abandonment. Generally, when an asset is disposed of, any unrecorded depreciation or amortization for the period is recorded to the date of disposition. A book value as of the date of disposition can then be computed as the difference between the cost of the asset and its accumulated depreciation. If the disposition price exceeds the book value, a **gain** is recognized. If the disposition price is less than the book value, a **loss** is recorded. As part of the disposition entry, the balances in the asset and accumulated depreciation accounts for the asset are canceled. The following sections illustrate the asset retirement process under varying conditions.

Asset Retirement by Sale

If the proceeds from the sale of an asset are in the form of cash or a receivable, the recording of the transaction follows the order outlined in the previous paragraph. For example, assume that on July 1, 2002, Landon Supply Co. sells for $43,600 machinery that is recorded on the books at cost of $83,600 with accumulated depreciation as of January 1, 2002, of $50,600. The company depreciates its machinery using a straight-line, 10% rate. In addition to recording the asset sale, a half-year of depreciation is recognized representing use of the asset for the first six months of the year.

The following entries would be made to record this transaction:

Depreciation Expense—Machinery	4,180	
Accumulated Depreciation—Machinery		4,180
To record depreciation for six months in 2002		
($83,600 × .10 × 6/12).		
Cash	43,600	
Accumulated Depreciation—Machinery	54,780	
Machinery		83,600
Gain on Sale of Machinery		14,780*
To record sale of machinery at a gain.		

*Sales price	$43,600
Book value ($83,600 – $54,780)	28,820
Gain on sale	$14,780

Asset Retirement by Exchange for Other Nonmonetary Assets

As indicated in Chapter 12, when operating assets are acquired in exchange for other nonmonetary assets, the new asset acquired is generally recorded at its fair market value or the fair market value of the nonmonetary asset given in exchange, whichever is more clearly determinable. However, if the assets are similar in nature and if the exchanging companies are in the same line of business, the asset received is sometimes recorded at the book value of the asset given.

The entries required to record the exchange of **dissimilar assets** are identical to those illustrated in the previous section except that a nonmonetary asset is received in exchange rather than cash or receivables. Gains and losses arising from these exchanges are recognized when the exchange takes place.

To illustrate, assume in the previous example that the retirement of the described asset was done by exchanging it for delivery equipment that had a market value of $43,600. The entries would be the same as illustrated except that instead of a debit to Cash, Delivery Equipment would be debited for $43,600. The gain would still be computed by comparing the book value of the machine and the market value of the asset acquired in the exchange. [Note: In the examples in this section, the entry to record depreciation expense for the first six months of the year will not be shown.]

Delivery Equipment	43,600	
Accumulated Depreciation—Machinery	54,780	
Machinery		83,600
Gain on Exchange of Machinery		14,780

If the machinery's fair market value were more clearly determinable than the value of the delivery equipment, the value of the machinery would be used to compute the gain or loss and to determine the value for the delivery equipment. Assume that the delivery equipment is used and has no readily available market price, but the machinery had a market value of $25,000. Under these circumstances, a loss of $3,820 ($28,820 – $25,000) would be indicated, and the entry to record the exchange would be as follows:

Delivery Equipment	25,000	
Accumulated Depreciation—Machinery	54,780	
Loss on Exchange of Machinery	3,820	
Machinery		83,600

Often the exchange of nonmonetary assets includes a transfer of cash, because the nonmonetary assets in most exchange transactions do not have equivalent market values. The cash part of the transaction adjusts the market values of the assets received to those of the assets given up. Thus, if in the previous example the exchange of delivery equipment were accompanied by the receipt of cash of $3,000, the loss would be reduced to $820 and the entry would be as follows:

Cash	3,000	
Delivery Equipment	25,000	
Accumulated Depreciation—Machinery	54,780	
Loss on Exchange of Machinery	820	
Machinery		83,600

In this example, the exchange involved assets that were dissimilar in nature: delivery equipment and machinery. If the exchange involved similar assets, for example, a used truck for a new one, the same accounting entries would be required unless the exchange is between two parties in the same line of business. This special case is discussed in the following section.

Asset Retirement by Exchange of Similar Assets

Not all exchanges of nonmonetary assets have the features to justify the recognition of a gain. Sometimes an exchange of **similar assets** is made to facilitate one of the parties to the exchange in making a sale to an ultimate consumer. For example, the Tri-City Cadillac dealership has a buyer for a blue Eldorado but has only a red one in stock. Another dealership in a nearby town has a blue Eldorado and is willing to exchange its car for Tri-City's red one. This exchange of similar assets is not intended to be an earnings transaction for either party and therefore should not reflect any gain, even if the market values of the cars have increased since they were originally acquired from the manufacturer. Another example of such an exchange would occur if two manufacturing companies exchanged similar equipment that both companies used in the production process.

In both of these illustrations, similar assets were transferred between parties in the same line of business. In the first instance, both parties were dealers of automobiles. In the second example, both parties were nondealers of machines being used in the production process. In neither case was the earnings process culminated. Proper accounting for the exchange of similar assets by companies in the same line of business depends on how much cash is exchanged as part of the transaction[9]:

- No cash: No gains are recognized.
- Cash less than 25% of the value of the transaction: Gain partially recognized if cash is received.
- Cash 25% or more of the value of the transaction: Recognize all gains.

Exhibit 13-5 summarizes the conditions under which indicated gains are to be recognized or deferred.

EXHIBIT 13-5 | Recognition of Indicated Gain When Assets Are Exchanged

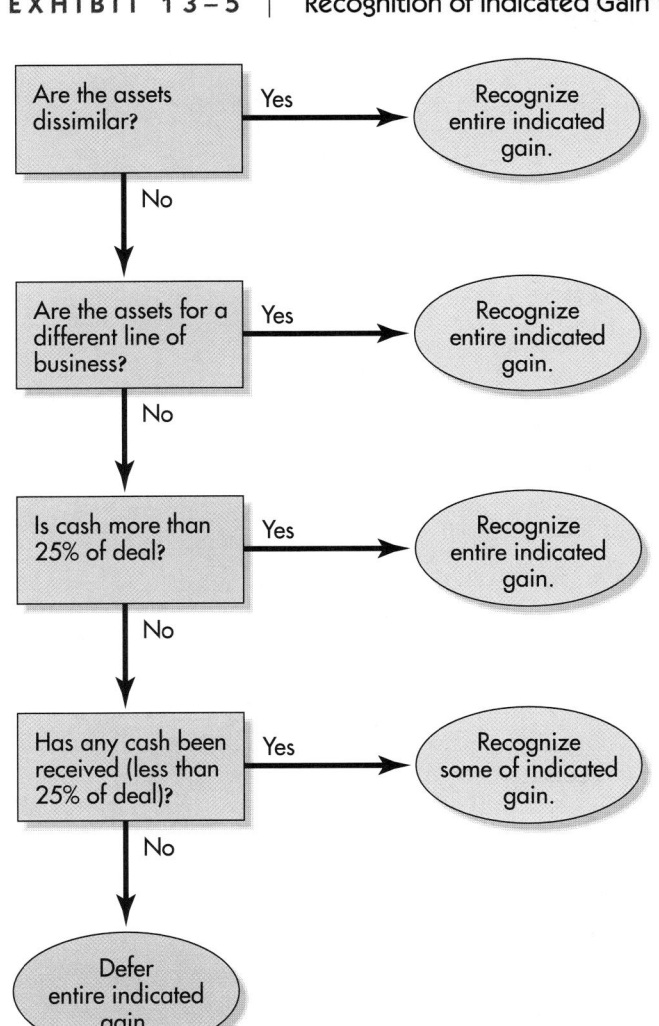

To illustrate the accounting for the exchange of similar assets, three examples follow. In the first example, no cash is involved in the exchange. In the second example, the

---

9 *Opinions of the Accounting Principles Board No. 29,* "Accounting for Nonmonetary Transactions," New York: American Institute of Certified Public Accountants, 1973, pars. 20–23. The "same line of business" test was added by the Emerging Issues Task Force in *Issue No. 86–29,* "Nonmonetary Transactions: Magnitude of Boot and the Exceptions to the Use of Fair Value."

exchange includes a "small" transfer of cash. In the third example, cash makes up 25% or more of the value of the transaction.

EXAMPLE 1—NO CASH INVOLVED The Republic Manufacturing Company owns a special molding machine that it no longer uses because of a change in products being manufactured. The machine still has several years of service remaining. Through discussions with other companies in the industry, Republic has located a buyer, Logan Square Company. However, Logan is low on funds and suggests an exchange for one of its machines that could be used in Republic's packaging department. It is decided that both machines meet the definition of being similar in use and have the same market values. The following cost and market data relate to the two machines:

	Republic	Logan
Costs of machines to be exchanged	$46,000	$54,000
Accumulated depreciation on machines to be exchanged	32,000	36,000
Book values of machines to be exchanged	14,000	18,000
Market values of machines to be exchanged	16,000	16,000

The entry on Republic's books to record the exchange is as follows:

Machinery (new)	14,000	
Accumulated Depreciation—Machinery (old)	32,000	
Machinery (old)		46,000

The entry on Logan's books to record the exchange is as follows:

Machinery	16,000	
Accumulated Depreciation—Machinery (old)	36,000	
Loss on Exchange of Machinery	2,000	
Machinery (old)		54,000

> **Caution!** Indicated losses are *always* recognized. Indicated gains are sometimes recognized and sometimes not.

Note that in Republic's entry, no gain is recognized even though there is an **indicated gain** because the market value of the asset received is $2,000 more than the book value of the asset given. The machines are similar, both parties in the exchange are in the same line of business, and no cash is involved, so no gain is recognized. The value assigned to Republic's newly acquired packaging machine is the book value of its old molding machine.

For Logan's entry, the market value of the asset exchanged is less than its book value, so there is an **indicated loss**. The loss is recognized, and the newly acquired molding machine is recorded on Logan's books at its market value. This is a good example of conservatism in accounting—losses are recognized as soon as they are objectively determinable; gains are not recognized until realized.

EXAMPLE 2—TRANSFER OF CASH LESS THAN 25% OF THE FAIR VALUE OF THE EXCHANGE Assume the same facts as in Example 1, except that it is agreed that Republic's machine has a market value of $16,000 and Logan's machine is worth $20,000. To make the exchange equal, Republic agrees to pay Logan $4,000 cash (20% of the fair value of the exchange). The entry on Republic's books for Example 2 is as follows:

Machinery (new)	18,000	
Accumulated Depreciation—Machinery (old)	32,000	
Machinery (old)		46,000
Cash		4,000

As was true for Example 1, Republic does not recognize any of the indicated gain. The market value of the assets surrendered ($16,000 + $4,000) exceeds their book values

($14,000 + $4,000), indicating a $2,000 gain. The machines are similar in use and the parties are both nondealers. The indicated gain, therefore, is deferred and not recognized. The new machine is recorded at $18,000, equal to the book value of the assets given in the exchange.

In Example 2, the book value of Logan's machine is less than the market value, indicating a $2,000 gain ($20,000 - $18,000). Because Logan received cash as part of the transaction, a portion of the $2,000 indicated gain should be recognized as having been earned. The amount to be recognized is computed using the following formula:

$$\text{Recognized gain} = \frac{\text{Cash received}}{\text{Cash received} + \text{Market value of acquired asset}} \times \text{Total indicated gain}$$

Using the figures from Example 2, Logan would recognize $400 of the indicated gain, computed as follows:

$$\frac{\$4,000}{\$4,000 + \$16,000} \times \$2,000 = \$400$$

The recorded value of the molding machine on Logan's books is $14,400, the book value of the packaging machine exchanged less the cash received plus the gain recognized, ($18,000 - $4,000 + $400). Another way of computing the recorded value is by deducting the **deferred gain** from the market value of the asset received ($16,000 - $1,600, or $14,400).

The entry on Logan's books to record the exchange is as follows:

Cash	4,000	
Machinery (new)	14,400	
Accumulated Depreciation—Machinery (old)	36,000	
Machinery (old)		54,000
Gain on Exchange of Machinery		400

The effect of this treatment is to defer a portion of the indicated gain and reduce the recorded book value of the new machinery.

STOP & THINK How is it possible for the companies on opposite sides of the deal to *both* show a gain on the same transaction?

EXAMPLE 3—TRANSFER OF CASH EXCEEDING 25% OF THE FAIR VALUE OF THE EXCHANGE Assume the same facts as in Example 2, except that it is agreed that Republic's machine has a market value of $15,000 and that Republic must pay $5,000 cash to make the exchange equal. In this case, the cash equals 25% of the fair value of the exchange ($20,000). When cash comprises a "large" part of the transaction (with "large" defined as 25% or more), the transaction is considered to be a monetary exchange, all gains and losses are recognized, and assets received are recorded at their market values. The entry on Republic's books would be:

Machinery (new)	20,000	
Accumulated Depreciation—Machinery (old)	32,000	
Machinery (old)		46,000
Cash		5,000
Gain on Exchange of Machinery		1,000

The entry on Logan's books would be:

Cash	5,000	
Machinery (new)	15,000	
Accumulated Depreciation—Machinery (old)	36,000	
Machinery (old)		54,000
Gain on Exchange of Machinery		2,000

E X P A N D E D   M A T E R I A L

The kind of depreciation that business people are most interested in is income tax depreciation. By lowering taxable income, tax depreciation reduces the payments for income taxes. The expanded material for this chapter shows how the MACRS income tax depreciation system is derived from the financial reporting depreciation methods illustrated earlier. An important part of MACRS is the depreciation computations for assets acquired or disposed of in the middle of the year. Accordingly, computation of depreciation for partial periods is also explained in more detail.

7

Compute depreciation for partial periods, using both straight-line and accelerated methods.

DEPRECIATION FOR PARTIAL PERIODS

Most of the illustrations in this chapter have assumed that assets were purchased on the first day of a company's fiscal period. In reality, of course, asset transactions occur throughout the year. When a time-factor method is used, depreciation on assets acquired or disposed of during the year may be based on the number of days the asset was held during the period. When the level of acquisitions and retirements is significant, however, companies often adopt a less burdensome policy for recognizing depreciation for partial periods. Some alternatives found in practice include the following.

1. Depreciation is recognized to the nearest whole month. Assets acquired on or before the 15th of the month are considered owned for the entire month; assets acquired after the 15th are not considered owned for any part of the month. Conversely, assets sold on or before the 15th of the month are not considered owned for any part of the month; assets sold after the 15th are considered owned for the entire month.

2. Depreciation is recognized to the nearest whole year. Assets acquired during the first six months are considered held for the entire year; assets acquired during the last six months are not considered in the depreciation computation. Conversely, no depreciation is recorded on assets sold during the first six months, and a full year's depreciation is recorded on assets sold during the last six months.

3. One-half year's depreciation is recognized on all assets purchased or sold during the year. A full year's depreciation is taken on all other assets. This approach is required for income tax purposes and is illustrated in the next section.

4. No depreciation is recognized on acquisitions during the year, but depreciation for a full year is recognized on retirements.

5. Depreciation is recognized for a full year on acquisitions during the year, but no depreciation is recognized on retirements.

> **Caution!** Remember that depreciation is an estimate, and computing depreciation for the exact number of days or months gives only an illusion of precision.

Alternatives 2 through 5 are attractive because of their simplicity. Alternative 1 makes the most intuitive sense, and its use is assumed in the examples and problems in the text unless otherwise noted.

If a company uses the sum-of-the-years'-digits method of depreciation and recognizes a partial year's depreciation on assets in the year purchased, the depreciation expense for

the second year must be determined by the following allocation procedure. To illustrate, the example used earlier in the chapter of the asset acquired by Schuss Boom Ski Manufacturing will be used. To repeat, the asset cost $100,000, has an estimated residual value of $5,000, and an estimated useful life of five years. Assume that the asset was purchased three-fourths of the way through the fiscal year. The computation of depreciation expense for the first two years, using sum-of-the-years'-digits depreciation, would be as follows:

First year:
Depreciation for full year ($95,000 × 5/15) $31,667
One-fourth year's depreciation ($31,667 ÷ 4) .... $ 7,917

Second year:
Depreciation for balance of first year ($31,667 – $7,917) $23,750
Depreciation for second full year ($95,000 × 4/15) $25,333
One-fourth year's depreciation ($25,333 ÷ 4) 6,333
Total depreciation—second year $30,083

From this point, each year's depreciation will be $6,333 less than the previous year's depreciation. This difference equals 1/15 of the original depreciable asset base of $95,000. A summary of the depreciation charges for the five-year period is as follows:

	Depreciation	Asset Book Value (Cost Less Accumulated Depreciation)
Year 1	$ 7,917	$92,083
Year 2	30,083	62,000
Year 3	23,750	38,250
Year 4	17,417	20,833
Year 5	11,083	9,750
Year 6	4,750	5,000
Total	$95,000	

Year 5 depreciation is $6,334 less than previous year due to effects of rounding.

Alternatively, depreciation for Years 2 through 6 can be computed using the standard sum-of-the-years'-digits computation with the numerator being the number of years remaining in the asset's useful life as of the beginning of the year. For Year 2, the number of years remaining in the asset's useful life at the beginning of the year is 4.75. The depreciation for Year 2 is: $95,000 × 4.75/15 = $30,083.

If a company uses a declining-balance method of depreciation, the computation of depreciation when partial years are involved is relatively straightforward. After Year 1's depreciation is computed, the remaining years are calculated in the same manner as illustrated earlier in the chapter; a constant percentage is multiplied by a declining book value. Again assuming a purchase three-fourths of the way through the fiscal year and the use of alternative 1, the double-declining-balance depreciation expense for the Schuss Boom asset would be as follows, assuming a switch to straight-line depreciation in Year 5.

Year	Computation		Depreciation Amount	Asset Book Value
1	$100,000 × .40 × 1/4	=	$10,000	$90,000
2	$90,000 × .40	=	36,000	54,000
3	$54,000 × .40	=	21,600	32,400
4	$32,400 × .40	=	12,960	19,440
5	($19,440 – $5,000) ÷ 1¾	=	8,251*	11,189
6	$11,189 – $5,000	=	6,189	5,000
			$95,000	

*Rounded.

8

Understand the depreciation methods underlying the MACRS income tax depreciation system.

The IRS Web site provides information on depreciation at **www.irs.ustreas.gov/prod/ tax_edu/teletax/tc704.html.**
Net Work:
1. What three tests must be met to depreciate an individual's tangible property?
2. When is it necessary to use MACRS depreciation?

FYI: Firms can choose MACRS for tax purposes and another method for financial reporting. Unlike LIFO elections, there is no necessary connection between income tax depreciation and depreciation for financial reporting.

INCOME TAX DEPRECIATION

The Economic Recovery Tax Act (ERTA) of 1981 introduced an adaptation of the declining-balance depreciation method to be used for income tax purposes. It is referred to as the **accelerated cost recovery system (ACRS)**. Subsequent revisions to the income tax laws have altered the original provisions. Because the Tax Reform Act of 1986 made several significant changes to ACRS, the new system is now referred to as the **modified accelerated cost recovery system (MACRS)**.

The term "cost recovery" was used in the tax regulations to emphasize that ACRS is not a standard depreciation method because the system is not based strictly on asset life or pattern of use. ACRS has largely replaced traditional depreciation accounting for income tax purposes. Its original purpose was to both simplify the computation of tax depreciation and provide for a more rapid write-off of asset cost to reduce income taxes and thus stimulate investment in noncurrent operating assets. Simplification was to be achieved by using one of three cost recovery periods for all assets rather than a specific useful life for each class of asset as previously prescribed by the income tax regulations. In addition, salvage values were to be ignored. A more rapid write-off was achieved by allowing companies to write off most machinery and equipment over 3 to 5 years, and all real estate over 15 years, even though previously prescribed income tax class lives were for much longer periods.

The subsequent modifications to ACRS by Congress have tended to dampen both of its original objectives, primarily because tightening tax depreciation rules is a way to increase tax revenues without increasing income tax rates.[10] The original three recovery periods have been replaced with six recovery periods for personal property, such as equipment, automobiles, and furniture, and two periods for real property, or land and buildings.[11] At the same time, the recovery periods for most assets have been extended so that less rapid write-off of asset cost is permitted.

Exhibit 13–6 illustrates the cost recovery periods and depreciation methods under MACRS. For personal property, the appropriate cost recovery period is determined by reference to the IRS class lives defined in the tax regulations. The real property recovery periods relate to the type of real property involved rather than class lives. ACRS initially provided for 150% declining-balance depreciation. The 1986 Reform Act increased the number of asset recovery periods and extended the recovery periods for most assets. The effects of these changes were partially offset by changing the method of depreciation for most personal property to the 200% (or double) declining-balance method.

The MACRS method for personal property also incorporates a **half-year convention**, meaning that one-half of a year's depreciation is recognized on all assets purchased or sold during the year. To illustrate, assume that office equipment is purchased for $100,000 on October 1, 2002. The office equipment has a $5,000 estimated residual value. The equipment is five-year property according to the IRS classification. Using the half-year convention, the double-declining-balance method, and ignoring the residual value, the MACRS depreciation for the equipment would be computed as follows:

Year	Computation		MACRS Depreciation Amount	Asset Book Value
1	$100,000 × .40 × ½	=	$ 20,000	$80,000
2	$80,000 × .40	=	32,000	48,000
3	$48,000 × .40	=	19,200	28,800
4	$28,800 × .40	=	11,520	17,280
5	$17,280 ÷ 1.5	=	11,520	5,760
6	Remaining book value	=	5,760	0
			$100,000	

10 For example, the Revenue Reconciliation Act of 1993 increased the recovery period for nonresidential real property from 31.5 years to 39 years. *RIA United States Tax Reporter, Tax Bulletin*, No. 33, August 12, 1993.

EXHIBIT 13-6 | MACRS Cost Recovery Periods and Depreciation Methods

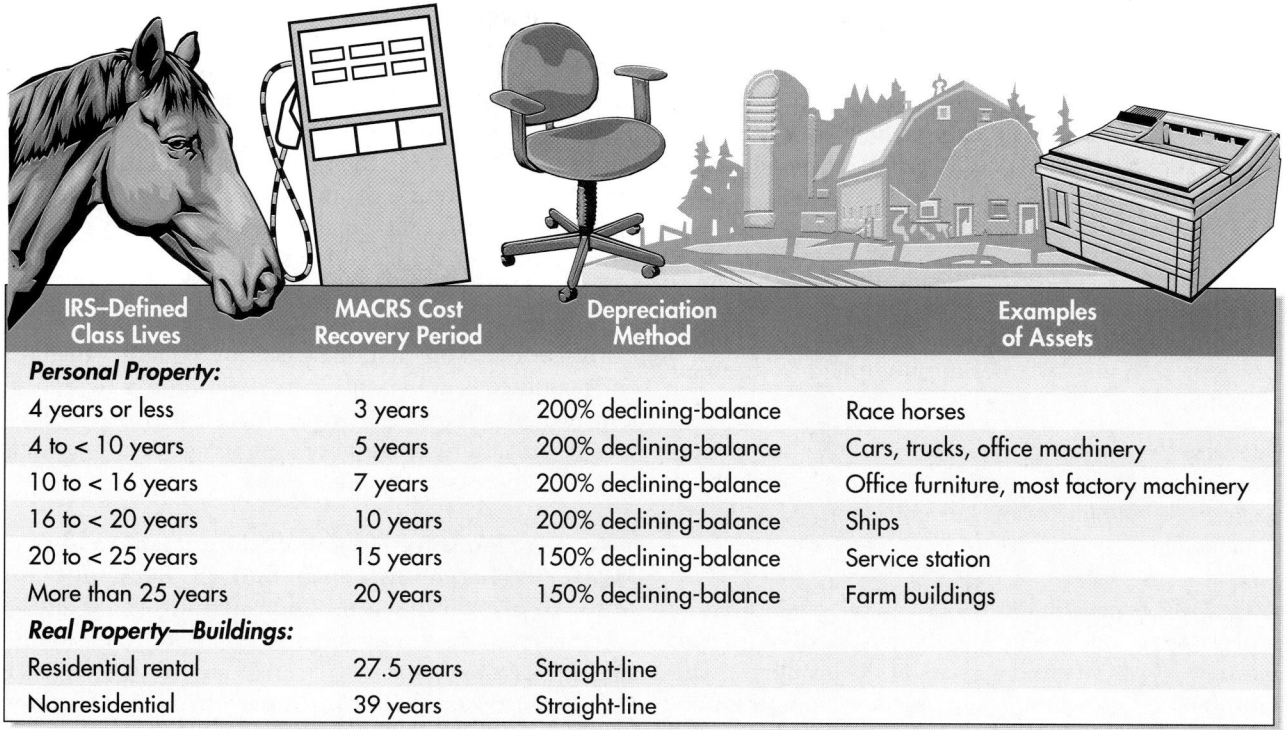

IRS–Defined Class Lives	MACRS Cost Recovery Period	Depreciation Method	Examples of Assets
Personal Property:			
4 years or less	3 years	200% declining-balance	Race horses
4 to < 10 years	5 years	200% declining-balance	Cars, trucks, office machinery
10 to < 16 years	7 years	200% declining-balance	Office furniture, most factory machinery
16 to < 20 years	10 years	200% declining-balance	Ships
20 to < 25 years	15 years	150% declining-balance	Service station
More than 25 years	20 years	150% declining-balance	Farm buildings
Real Property—Buildings:			
Residential rental	27.5 years	Straight-line	
Nonresidential	39 years	Straight-line	

FYI: Of course, regular taxpayers aren't prepared to do these calculations. The IRS has summarized the MACRS method in a series of tables listing the percentage of the original asset cost that should be depreciated each year.

Even though the asset was purchased three-fourths of the way through the year, for tax purposes $20,000 is reported as the cost recovery in the first year rather than $10,000 determined by computing depreciation to the nearest month. Note that a switch to the straight-line method was made in Year 5. If the double-declining-balance method had been applied to this year, only $6,912 ($17,280 × .40) would have been reported rather than $11,520 using straight-line for the remaining one and one-half years

11 Personal property is a general term that encompasses all property other than real property (land and buildings).

REVIEW OF LEARNING OBJECTIVES

1 Use straight-line, accelerated, use-factor, and group depreciation methods to compute annual depreciation expense. The four factors that are considered in computing annual depreciation are asset cost, residual (or salvage) value, useful life, and pattern of use. The most common methods for computing annual depreciation are:

Time-Factor Methods

- *Straight-line depreciation.* The difference between asset cost and residual value is divided by the useful life of the asset.
- *Accelerated methods*
  - *Sum-of-the-years'-digits depreciation.* The depreciable asset cost is multiplied by a fraction; the

numerator is the number of years remaining in the asset life as of the beginning of the year, and the denominator is the sum of all the digits from one to the original useful life.

- *Declining-balance depreciation.* The asset book value is multiplied by a constant percentage rate derived from the useful life. The most commonly used percentage is double the straight-line rate.

Use-Factor Methods

- *Service-hours depreciation.* Depreciable cost is divided by total expected lifetime service hours to compute a per-hour depreciation rate. The number of service hours in a period multiplied by the rate yields the periodic depreciation charge.

- *Productive-output depreciation.* Similar to service-hours depreciation, except the rate is based on expected number of output units during the life of the asset.

Group and Composite Methods. A collection of assets is depreciated as one group. A group rate, derived from an initial analysis of the type of assets in the group, is multiplied by the total cost of group assets to compute periodic depreciation expense. Gains and losses resulting from normal variations in asset lives are not recognized.

2 **Discuss the issues impacting proper amortization of intangible assets.** Intangible assets are to be amortized over their expected economic lives, not to exceed 20 years (assuming the changes proposed by the FASB in 1999 are implemented). The straight-line method is used unless there is strong justification for using another method.

3 **Apply the productive-output method to the depletion of natural resources.** The depletion rate is based on total development cost of the natural resource divided by the estimated amount of resource units to be removed. Periodic depletion expense is the depletion rate multiplied by the number of units removed during the period. Structures and improvements related specifically to removal of the natural resource should be depreciated based on the fraction of natural resources extracted during the period.

4 **Incorporate changes in estimates into the computation of depreciation for current and future periods.** A change in estimate impacts the current and future periods and is not used to adjust amounts reported in prior periods. The undepreciated book value is allocated over the remaining life based on the revised estimates.

5 **Identify whether an asset is impaired and measure the amount of the impairment loss, using both U.S. GAAP and international accounting standards.** Under U.S. GAAP, assets are reviewed for possible impairment whenever there is a significant change in operations or in the way an asset is used. An asset is impaired when the undiscounted sum of future cash flows from the asset is less than the reported book value (including goodwill associated with the purchase of the asset). An impaired asset is written down to its fair value. Associated goodwill amounts are written off before the asset book value itself is reduced.

International standards differ from U.S. GAAP in that the discounted sum of future cash flows—rather than the undiscounted sum—is used to determine whether an impairment loss exists. International standards also allow for the upward revaluation of long-term operating assets that have increased in value.

6 **Account for the sale of depreciable assets in exchange for cash and in exchange for other depreciable assets.** Indicated losses are always recognized. In cash transactions and in exchanges of dissimilar assets, indicated gains are recognized. If exchanged assets are similar, the parties in the transaction are in the same line of business, and cash comprises less than 25% of the value of the transaction, indicated gains are deferred:

- If no cash is received, indicated gains are fully deferred.

- If some cash is received, a portion of the indicated gain, proportional to the value of the cash received relative to the entire value of the assets exchanged, must be recognized.

7 **Compute depreciation for partial periods, using both straight-line and accelerated methods.** Depreciation is not always computed for the exact number of days or months an asset is owned. One common simplifying assumption is the half-year convention—one-half of a year's depreciation is recognized on all assets purchased or sold during the year.

8 **Understand the depreciation methods underlying the MACRS income tax depreciation system.** MACRS is based on the 200% declining-balance depreciation method with no residual value and a half-year convention. To streamline the system, the IRS has established six classes of assets with set depreciation lives.

KEY TERMS

Accelerated depreciation 744
Amortization 740
Book value 741
Composite depreciation 749
Declining-balance depreciation 745
Deferred gain 763
Depletion 740
Depreciation 740
Dissimilar assets 759
Double-declining-balance
   depreciation 745
Gain 759
Group depreciation 749

Impairment 756
Indicated gain 762
Indicated loss 762
Loss 759
Natural resources 752
Productive-output depreciation 748
Residual (salvage) value 741
Service-hours depreciation 748
Similar assets 760
Straight-line depreciation 744
Sum-of-the-years'-digits
   depreciation 745
Time-factor depreciation 744

Unit depreciation 749
Use-factor depreciation 748
Useful life 742

Accelerated cost recovery system
   (ACRS) 766
Half-year convention 766
Modified accelerated cost recovery
   system (MACRS) 766

QUESTIONS

1. Distinguish among depreciation, depletion, and amortization expenses.
2. What factors must be considered in determining the periodic depreciation charges that should be made for a company's depreciable assets?
3. What role does residual, or salvage, value play in the various methods of time-factor depreciation?
4. Distinguish between the functional and physical factors affecting the useful life of a tangible noncurrent operating asset.
5. Distinguish between time-factor and use-factor methods of depreciation.
6. Briefly describe group depreciation, and describe how asset retirements are recorded under this method.
7. What factors determine the period and method for amortizing intangible assets?
8. Historically, the maximum number of years for amortizing an intangible asset has been 40 years. How would this change under the 1999 FASB Exposure Draft?
9. Describe the proper accounting treatment for a change in estimated useful life.
10. What procedures must be followed when the estimate of recoverable natural resources is changed

due to subsequent development work?
11. Under U.S. GAAP, what test is used to determine whether an asset is impaired? How is an impairment loss measured?
12. How does the international accounting standard for asset impairment differ from the standard used in the United States?
13. If a non-U.S. company chooses to revalue a long-term operating asset upward in accordance with IAS 16, how is the unrealized "gain" on the revaluation recognized in the financial statements?
14. Under what circumstances is a gain recognized when a productive asset is exchanged for a similar productive asset? a loss?

15. Why isn't depreciation expense always computed for the exact number of days an asset is owned?
16. What were the original reasons for the development of the ACRS income tax depreciation method?

DISCUSSION CASES

CASE 13–1

WE DON'T NEED NO DEPRECIATION!

The managements of two different companies argue that because of specific conditions in their companies, recording depreciation expense should be suspended for 2002. Evaluate carefully their arguments.

(a) The president of Guzman Co. recommends that no depreciation be recorded for 2002 because the depreciation rate is 5% per year, and price indexes show that prices during the year have risen by more than this figure.

(b) The policy of Liebnitz Co. is to recondition its building and equipment each year so that they are maintained in perfect repair. In view of the extensive periodic costs incurred in 2002, officials of the company feel that the need for recognizing depreciation is eliminated.

CASE 13–2

WHY WRITE OFF GOODWILL?

The Nevada Corporation purchased the Stardust Club for $2,000,000, which included $500,000 for goodwill. Nevada Corporation incurs large promotional and advertising expenses to maintain Stardust Club's popularity. As the annual financial statements are being prepared, the CPA of the Nevada Corporation, Emily Teeson, insists that some of the goodwill be amortized against revenue. Teeson cites APB Opinion No. 17, which requires all intangible assets to be written off over a maximum life of 40 years. Mark Stevenson, the Nevada Corporation controller, feels that amortization of the purchased goodwill in the same periods as heavy expenses are incurred to maintain the goodwill in effect creates a double charge against income of the period. Stevenson argues that no write-off of goodwill is necessary and that goodwill has increased in value and, indeed, should even be increased on the books to reflect this improvement. Evaluate the logic of these two positions.

CASE 13–3

IS IT REALLY WORTH THAT MUCH?

Ferris Bueller, Inc., owns a building in Des Moines, Iowa, that was built at a cost of $5,000,000 in 1991. The building was used as a manufacturing facility from 1992 to 2001. However, economic conditions have made it necessary to consolidate Ferris Bueller's operations, and the building has been leased as of January 1, 2002, as a warehouse for 10 years at an annual rental of $240,000. Taxes, insurance, and normal maintenance costs are to be paid by the lessee. At the end of the 10-year period, Ferris Bueller may offer the lessee a renewal of the lease or again use the building in its operations. The building is being depreciated on a straight-line basis over a 40-year life.

In early 2002, Julie Ramos, a new staff accountant for Ferris Bueller, was assigned to review the building accounts and raised a question to Alison Crowther, her supervisor, concerning the carrying value of the Des Moines building. As of December 31, 2001, Julie feels the Des Moines building was impaired and should be written down in value. Alison is unsure about the current position of the FASB on this issue and invites Julie to prepare a memorandum recommending a specific write-down amount, with supporting justification. Prepare the memorandum, assuming current interest rates are 10%.

CASE 13–4

CREATE YOUR OWN DEPRECIATION METHOD.

In order to spark interest in choosing accounting as a major, the Accounting Students Association at South Willow University is sponsoring an accounting contest. Students across campus are invited to create their own time-factor depreciation methods. The straight-line, declining-balance, and sum-of-the-years'-digits methods are not allowable entries. Enter the contest by creating your own time-factor depreciation computation scheme. Does your method result in higher or lower depreciation in the first year than does the double-declining-balance method?

CASE 13–5

WHICH DEPRECIATION METHOD SHOULD WE USE?

The Atwater Manufacturing Company purchased a new machine especially built to perform one particular function on the assembly line. A difference of opinion has arisen as to the method of depreciation to be used in connection with this machine. Three methods are now being considered:

(a) The straight-line method
(b) The productive-output method
(c) The sum-of-the-years'-digits method

List separately the arguments for and against each of the proposed methods from both the theoretical and practical viewpoints.

CASE 13–6

HOW DO WE CHARGE THAT MOTION PICTURE COST TO REVENUE?

In today's high-tech, high-cost entertainment industry, motion pictures often have costs in the tens of millions of dollars. Of course, it is hoped that these movies will be box office winners and that the revenues will exceed the cost outlay. With first runs, reruns, video reprints, video rentals, and so forth, it has become increasingly difficult to determine how the initial cost should be amortized against the revenue. Considering this industry and its characteristics, what amortization method would you suggest for these movie production costs?

CASE 13–7

IS NOTHING SACRED?

FASB Statement No. 93 requires all not-for-profit organizations to compute and report depreciation expense in their external financial statements. Previously, many not-for-profits, including many religious institutions, did not report depreciation expense. Many users and preparers of financial statements for religious institutions were upset about the idea of depreciating churches. Robert Anthony, a well-known professor of accounting at Harvard University, was quoted as saying, "Depreciating cathedrals and churches is stupid." Monsignor Austin Bennett of Brooklyn claimed that the rule would cause "more trouble for American churches than all the sinners in their congregations." Robert K. Mautz in "Monuments, Mistakes and Opportunities," *Accounting Horizons*, June 1988, argued that buildings and monuments owned by governments and not-for-profit institutions may be more liabilities than assets because no revenue is generated from them, but they must be maintained.

Consider the following questions.

1. Why do churches prepare external financial statements?
2. It is claimed that requiring churches to record depreciation expense will increase the cost of a church's annual audit. How?
3. One person was quoted in *The Wall Street Journal* as saying, "As some . . . communities change in character, so does the value of the churches. Our depreciation values would have to change every year." Evaluate this comment.

SOURCE: Lee Berton, "Is Nothing Sacred? Churches Fight Plan to Alter Accounting," *The Wall Street Journal*, April 16, 1987, p. 1.

CASE 13–8

LET'S TAKE A BATH!

DeAngelo (1988) finds evidence suggesting that when the management of a company is ousted under fire, the new management tends to take an earnings "bath" after gaining control. A "bath" is a large reduction in earnings due to asset write-downs, reorganization charges, discontinuance of segments, and other extraordinary charges.

As an example, THE CIRCLE K CORPORATION declared Chapter 11 bankruptcy and also changed management during fiscal 1990. For the year, Circle K reported a reorganization and restructuring charge of $639 million, consisting primarily of write-downs of long-term assets. This contributed to a net loss for the year of $773 million, compared to average net income for the previous 4 years of about $40 million per year. Why might the new management of a company want to "take a bath" in its first year?

SOURCES:
Linda DeAngelo, "Managerial Compensation, Information Costs, and Corporate Governance," *Journal of Accounting and Economics* 10, January 1988, pp. 3–36.
1990 Annual Report of The Circle K Corporation.

CASE 13–9

BUT WHAT IS A REASONABLE LIFE FOR MY AIRPLANE?

Different airlines depreciate the same airplanes but using different useful-life and residual value assumptions. As an example, CONTINENTAL AIRLINES depreciates its aircraft over a period of 25 years, while DELTA AIR LINES has a policy of depreciating its aircraft, many of which are the same Boeing aircraft that Continental uses, over a period of 20 years with a 5% residual value. What might cause a firm to decide to increase the estimated useful life of a depreciable asset?

CASE 13–10  **SHOULD FINANCIAL REPORTING FOLLOW TAX LEGISLATION?**

During the 1960s and 1970s, the U.S. Congress used a tax measure known as the investment tax credit to encourage companies to expand their investment base. Under these provisions, companies received reductions of their tax liabilities based on a percentage of new investments in noncurrent operating assets. This approach was used in lieu of reducing tax rates as a stimulus to expansion. In 1981, the adoption of the ACRS method of cost allocation for noncurrent operating assets added further stimulation to the economy by permitting companies to write off the cost of their property over a shorter-than-normal period.

In 1986, Congress passed a massive Tax Reform Act that significantly reduced tax rates for all taxpaying entities. At the same time, the investment tax credit was eliminated and the ACRS legislation was replaced by a modified ACRS approach that lengthened the time period for the allocation. These latter provisions reduced the net impact of the reduced tax rates. Because elected government officials do not like to be identified with increased tax rates, there remains the possibility that further modifications to tax accounting for noncurrent operating assets will be made.

Should financial reporting for noncurrent operating assets be affected by tax legislation? Support your answer.

EXERCISES

EXERCISE 13–11

COMPUTATION OF ASSET COST AND DEPRECIATION EXPENSE

A machine is purchased at the beginning of 2002 for $36,000. Its estimated life is 6 years. Freight costs on the machine are $2,000. Installation costs are $1,200. The machine is estimated to have a residual value of $500 and a useful life of 40,000 hours. It was used 6,000 hours in 2002.

1. What is the cost of the machine for accounting purposes?
2. Compute the depreciation charge for 2002 using (a) the straight-line method and (b) the service-hours method.

EXERCISE 13–12

SERVICE-HOURS DEPRECIATION

Jen and Barry's Ice Milk Company used cash to purchase a new ice milk mixer on January 1, 2002. The new mixer is estimated to have a 20,000-hour service life. Jen and Barry's depreciates equipment on the service-hours method. The total price paid for the machine was $57,000. This price included $2,000 freight-in, $1,800 installation costs, and $3,000 for a 2-year maintenance contract.

During 2002, Jen and Barry's used the machine for 2,500 hours; in 2003, 3,000 hours. Prepare all related journal entries for the purchase of equipment, annual depreciation, and maintenance expense for 2002 and 2003.

EXERCISE 13–13

INFERRING USEFUL LIVES

The information that follows is from the balance sheet of Hampton Company for December 31, 2002, and December 31, 2001.

	Dec. 31, 2002	Dec. 31, 2001
Equipment—cost	$ 680,000	$ 680,000
Accumulated depreciation—equipment	(250,000)	(160,000)
Buildings—cost	2,450,000	2,450,000
Accumulated depreciation—buildings	(340,000)	(230,000)

Hampton did not acquire or dispose of any buildings or equipment during 2002. Hampton uses the straight-line method of depreciation. If residual values are assumed to be 10% of asset cost, what is the average useful life of Hampton's (1) equipment? (2) buildings?

EXERCISE 13–14

COMPUTATION OF DEPRECIATION EXPENSE

Ray Construction purchased a concrete mixer on July 15, 2002. Company officials revealed the following information regarding this asset and its acquisition.

Purchase price	$125,000
Residual value	$18,000
Estimated useful life	10 years
Estimated service hours	38,000
Estimated production in units	500,000 yards

The concrete mixer was operated by construction crews in 2002 for a total of 6,500 hours, and it produced 77,000 yards of concrete.

It is company policy to take a half-year's depreciation on all assets for which it used the straight-line or double-declining-balance depreciation method in the year of purchase.

Calculate the resulting depreciation expense for 2002 under each of the following methods, and specify which method allows the greatest depreciation expense.

1. Double-declining-balance
2. Productive-output
3. Service-hours
4. Straight-line

EXERCISE 13–15

PRODUCTIVE-OUTPUT DEPRECIATION AND ASSET RETIREMENT

Equipment was purchased at the beginning of 2000 for $100,000 with an estimated product life of 300,000 units. The estimated salvage value was $4,000. During 2000, 2001, and 2002, the equipment produced 80,000 units, 120,000 units, and 40,000 units, respectively. The machine was damaged at the beginning of 2003, and the equipment was scrapped with no salvage value.

1. Determine depreciation using the productive-output method for 2000, 2001, and 2002.
2. Give the entry to write off the equipment at the beginning of 2003.

EXERCISE 13–16

GROUP DEPRECIATION

Holdaway, Inc., a small furniture manufacturer, purchased the following assets at the end of 2001.

Description	Cost	Salvage	Life
Delivery truck	$24,000	$5,000	5 years
Circular saws	900	130	7 years
Workbench	320	—	8 years
Forklift	9,000	500	5 years

Compute the following amounts for 2002 using group depreciation on a straight-line basis:
(a) Depreciation expense
(b) Group depreciation rate
(c) Average life of the assets

EXERCISE 13–17

GROUP DEPRECIATION ENTRIES

Lundquist, Inc., uses the group depreciation method for its furniture account. The depreciation rate used for furniture is 21%. The balance in the furniture account on December 31, 2001, was $125,000, and the balance in Accumulated Depreciation—Furniture was $61,000. The following purchases and dispositions of furniture occurred in the years 2002-2004 (assume that all purchases and disposals occurred at the beginning of each year).

		Assets Sold	
Year	Assets Purchased—Cost (Cash)	Cost	Selling Price (Cash)
2002	$35,000	$27,000	$8,000
2003	27,600	15,000	6,000
2004	24,500	32,000	8,000

1. Prepare the summary journal entries Lundquist should make each year (2002-2004) for the purchase, disposition, and depreciation of the furniture.
2. Prepare a summary of the furniture and accumulated depreciation accounts for the years 2002-2004.

EXERCISE 13–18

DEPRECIATION OF SPECIAL COMPONENTS

Towsey Manufacturing acquired a new milling machine on April 1, 1997. The machine has a special component that requires replacement before the end of the useful life. The asset was originally recorded in two accounts, one representing the main unit and the other for the special component. Depreciation is recorded by the straight-line method to the nearest month, residual values being disregarded. On April 1, 2003, the special component is scrapped and is replaced with a similar component. This component is expected to have a residual value of approximately 25% of cost at the end of the useful life of the main unit, and because of its materiality, the residual value will be considered in calculating depreciation. Specific asset information is as follows:

Main milling machine:	
Purchase price in 1997	$62,400
Residual value	$4,400
Estimated useful life	10 years
First special component:	
Purchase price	$10,000
Residual value	$250
Estimated useful life	6 years
Second special component:	
Purchase price	$15,250

What are the depreciation charges to be recognized for the years (1) 1997, (2) 2003, and (3) 2004?

EXERCISE 13–19

ACCOUNTING FOR PATENTS

The Deep South Co. applied for and received numerous patents at a total cost of $30,345 at the beginning of 1997. It is assumed the patents will be evenly useful during their full legal life. At the beginning of 1999, the company paid $7,875 in successfully prosecuting an attempted infringement of these patent rights. At the beginning of 2002, $25,200 was paid to acquire patents that could make its own patents worthless; the patents acquired have a remaining life of 15 years but will not be used.

1. Give the entries to record the expenditures relative to patents.
2. Give the entries to record patent amortization for the years 1997, 1999, and 2002.

EXERCISE 13–20

DEPLETION EXPENSE

On January 2, 2001, Cynthia Foster purchased land with valuable natural ore deposits for $10 million. The estimated residual value of the land was $2 million. At the time of purchase, a geological survey estimated 2 million tons of removable ore were under the ground. Early in 2001, roads were constructed on the land to aid in the extraction and transportation of the mined ore at a cost of $750,000. In 2001, 50,000 tons were mined. In 2002, Cynthia fired her mining engineer and hired a new expert. A new survey made at the end of 2002 estimated 3 million tons of ore were available for mining. In 2002, 150,000 tons were mined. Assuming all the ore mined was sold, how much was the depletion expense for 2001 and 2002?

EXERCISE 13–21

CHANGE IN ESTIMATED USEFUL LIFE

Zierbel Corporation purchased a machine on January 1, 1997, for $400,000. At the date of acquisition, the machine had an estimated useful life of 15 years with no salvage value. The machine is being depreciated on a straight-line basis. On January 1, 2002, as a result of Zierbel's experience with the machine, it was decided that the machine had an estimated useful life of 10 years from the date of acquisition. What is the amount of depreciation expense on this machine in 2002 using a new annual depreciation charge for the remaining 5 years?

EXERCISE 13–22

CHANGE IN ESTIMATED USEFUL LIFE

Pierce Corporation purchased a machine on July 1, 1999, for $380,000. The machine was estimated to have a useful life of 10 years with an estimated salvage value of $10,000. During 2002, it became apparent that the machine would become uneconomical after December 31, 2006, and that the machine would have no scrap value. Pierce uses the straight-line method of depreciation for all machinery. What should be the charge for depreciation in 2002 under a new annual depreciation charge for the remaining life?

EXERCISE 13–23

RECORDING AN IMPAIRMENT LOSS

Della Bee Company purchased a manufacturing plant building 10 years ago for $1,300,000. The building has been depreciated using the straight-line method with a 30-year useful life and 10% residual value. Della Bee's manufacturing operations have experienced significant losses for the past 2 years, so Della Bee has decided that the manufacturing building should be evaluated for possible impairment. Della Bee estimates that the building has a remaining useful life of 15 years, that net cash inflow from the building will be $50,000 per year, and that the fair value of the building is $380,000. No goodwill was associated with the purchase of the building.

1. Determine whether an impairment loss should be recognized.
2. If an impairment loss should be recognized, make the appropriate journal entry.
3. How would your answer to (1) change if the fair value of the building was $560,000?

EXERCISE 13–24

RECORDING AN IMPAIRMENT LOSS WITH GOODWILL

Use the information given in Exercise 13–23, and also assume that in addition to the $1,300,000 cost assigned to the building, goodwill of $100,000 was associated with the purchase. The goodwill is being amortized over 20 years.

1. Determine whether an impairment loss should be recognized.
2. If an impairment loss should be recognized, make the appropriate journal entry.

EXERCISE 13–25

IMPAIRMENT AND REVALUATION UNDER INTERNATIONAL ACCOUNTING STANDARDS

Use the information given in Exercise 13–23 and also assume that Della Bee Company is located in Hong Kong and uses international accounting standards. Della Bee also has chosen to recognize increases in the value of long-term operating assets, in accordance with the allowable alternative under IAS 16.

1. Determine whether an impairment loss should be recognized.
2. If an impairment loss should be recognized, make the appropriate journal entry.
3. What journal entry would Della Bee make if the fair value of the building was $1,250,000?

EXERCISE 13–26

RECORDING THE SALE OF EQUIPMENT WITH NOTE

On December 31, 2002, Beckham Corporation sold for $10,000 an old machine having an original cost of $50,000 and a book value of $6,000. The terms of the sale were as follows: $2,000 down payment, $4,000 payable on December 31 of the next 2 years. The agreement of sale made no mention of interest; however, 10% would be a fair rate for this type of transaction. Give the journal entries on Beckham's books to record the sale of the machine and receipt of the 2 subsequent payments. (Round to the nearest dollar.)

EXERCISE 13–27

EXCHANGE OF MACHINERY

Assume that Coaltown Corporation has a machine that cost $52,000, has a book value of $35,000, and has a market value of $40,000. The machine is used in Coaltown's manufacturing process. For each of the following situations, indicate the value at which the company should record the new asset and why it should be recorded at that value.

    (a) Coaltown exchanged the machine for a truck with a list price of $43,000.

    (b) Coaltown exchanged the machine with another manufacturing company for a similar machine with a list price of $41,000.

    (c) Coaltown exchanged the machine for a newer model machine from another manufacturing company. The new machine had a list price of $62,000, and Coaltown paid cash of $15,000.

    (d) Coaltown exchanged the machine plus $3,000 cash for a similar machine from Newton Inc., a manufacturing company. The newly acquired machine is carried on Newton's books at its cost of $55,000 with accumulated depreciation of $42,000; its fair market value is $43,000. In addition to determining the value, give the journal entries for both companies to record the exchange.

EXERCISE 13–28

EXCHANGE OF TRUCK

On January 2, 2002, Bline Delivery Company traded with a dealer an old delivery truck for a newer model. Data relative to the old and new trucks follow:

Old truck:	
Original cost	$12,000
Accumulated depreciation as of January 2, 2002	9,000
New truck:	
List price	$15,000
Cash price without trade-in	14,000
Cash paid with trade-in	12,700

1.   Give the journal entries on Bline's books to record the purchase of the new truck.
2.   Give the journal entries on Bline's books if the cash paid was $10,700.

EXERCISE 13–29

COMPUTATION OF DEPRECIATION EXPENSE

The Feng Company purchased a machine for $180,000 on September 1, 2002. It is estimated that the machine will have a 10-year life and a salvage value of $18,000. Its working hours and production in units are estimated at 36,000 and 750,000, respectively. It is the company's policy to depreciate assets for the number of months they are held during a year. During 2002, the machine was operated 5,000 hours and produced 70,000 units. Which of the following methods will give the greatest depreciation expense for 2002? (1) double-declining-balance (2) sum-of-the-years'-digits (3) productive-output or (4) service-hours. (Show computations for all four methods.)

EXERCISE 13–30

COMPUTATION OF BOOK AND TAX DEPRECIATION

Midwest States Manufacturing purchased factory equipment on March 15, 2001. The equipment will be depreciated for financial purposes over its estimated useful life, counting the year of acquisition as a half-year. The company accountant revealed the following information regarding this machine:

Purchase price	$75,000
Residual value	$9,000
Estimated useful life	10 years

1. What amount should Midwest States Manufacturing record for depreciation expense for 2002 using the (a) double-declining-balance method? (b) sum-of-the-years'-digits method?

2. Assuming the equipment is classified as 7-year property under the modified accelerated cost recovery system (MACRS), what amount should Midwest States Manufacturing deduct for depreciation on its tax return in 2002?

EXERCISE 13–31  **MACRS COMPUTATION**

The Timpanogas Equipment Company purchased a new piece of factory equipment on May 1, 2002, for $26,500. For income tax purposes, the equipment is classified as a 7-year asset. Because this is similar to the economic life expected for the asset, Timpanogas decides to use the tax depreciation for financial reporting purposes. The equipment is not expected to have any residual value at the end of the 7 years. Prepare a depreciation schedule for the life of the asset using the MACRS method of cost recovery.

PROBLEMS

PROBLEM 13–32

TIME-FACTOR METHODS OF DEPRECIATION

A delivery truck was acquired by Navarro Inc. for $40,000 on January 1, 2002. The truck was estimated to have a 3-year life and a trade-in value at the end of that time of $10,000. The following depreciation methods are being considered.

    (a) Depreciation is to be calculated by the straight-line method.
    (b) Depreciation is to be calculated by the sum-of-the-years'-digits method.
    (c) Depreciation is to be calculated by the double-declining-balance method.

Instructions: Prepare tables reporting periodic depreciation and asset book value over a 3-year period for each assumption listed.

PROBLEM 13–33

DEPRECIATION UNDER DIFFERENT METHODS

On January 1, 1999, Ron Shelley purchased a new tractor to use on his farm. The tractor cost $100,000. Ron also had the dealer install a front-end loader on the tractor. The cost of the front-end loader was $7,000. The shipping charges were $600, and the cost to install the loader was $800. The estimated life of the tractor was 8 years and the estimated service-hour life of the tractor was 12,500 hours. Ron estimated that he could sell the tractor for $15,000 at the end of 8 years or 12,500 hours. The tractor was used for 1,725 hours in 2002. A full year's depreciation was taken in 1999, the year of acquisition.

Instructions: Compute depreciation expense for 2002 under each of the following methods.

1. Straight-line
2. Double-declining-balance
3. Sum-of-the-years'-digits
4. Service-hours

PROBLEM 13–34

MAINTENANCE CHARGES AND DEPRECIATION OF COMPONENTS

A company buys a machine for $25,400 on January 1, 1999. The maintenance costs for the years 1999–2002 are as follows: 1999, $1,500; 2000, $1,200; 2001, $7,300 (includes $6,100 for cost of a new motor installed in December 2001); 2002, $2,100.

Instructions:

1. Assume the machine is recorded in a single account at a cost of $25,400. No record is kept of the cost of the component parts. Straight-line depreciation is used, and the asset is estimated to have a useful life of 8 years. It is assumed there will be no residual value at the end of the useful life. What are the total expenses related to the machine for each of the first 4 years?

2. Assume the cost of the frame of the machine was recorded in one account at a cost of $19,600 and the motor was recorded in a second account at a cost of $5,800. Straight-line depreciation is used with a useful life of 10 years for the frame and 4 years for the motor. Neither item is assumed to have any residual value at the end of its useful life. What are the total expenses and losses related to the machine?

3. Evaluate the two methods.

PROBLEM 13–35

DEPRECIATION AND THE STEADY STATE

Lyell Company started a newspaper delivery business on January 1, 1999. On that date, the company purchased a small pickup truck for $14,000. Lyell planned to depreciate the truck over 3 years and assumed an $800 residual value. During 1999 and 2000, Lyell's business expanded. On January 1, 2000, Lyell purchased a second truck, identical to the first. On January 1, 2001, Lyell purchased a third truck, again identical to the first two. During 2001, Lyell's growth leveled off. However, on January 1, 2002, Lyell bought another truck to replace the one (purchased in 1999) that had just worn out. All trucks purchased cost the same amount as the first truck.

Instructions:

1. Compute depreciation expense for 1999, 2000, 2001, and 2002 using:
   a. Straight-line method
   b. Sum-of-the-years'-digits method

2. What general conclusions can be drawn from your calculations in (1)?

PROBLEM 13–36

GROUP DEPRECIATION AND ASSET RETIREMENT

The Wright Manufacturing Co. acquired 20 similar machines at the beginning of 1997 for a total cost of $75,000. The machines have an average life of 5 years and no residual value. The group depreciation method is employed in writing off the cost of the machines. They were retired as follows:

2 machines at the end of 1999
4 machines at the end of 2000
8 machines at the end of 2001
6 machines at the end of 2002

Assume the machines were not replaced.

Instructions: Give the entries to record the retirement of the machines and the periodic depreciation for the years 1997–2002 inclusive.

PROBLEM 13–37

GROUP DEPRECIATION

Machines are acquired by Siegel Inc. on March 1, 2002, as follows:

Machines	Cost	Estimated Residual Value	Estimated Life in Years
#301	$46,000	$6,000	5
#302	20,000	2,000	6
#303	20,000	4,000	8
#304	18,000	1,500	6
#305	26,000	None	10

Instructions:

1. Calculate the group depreciation rate for this group.
2. Calculate the average life in years for the group.
3. Give the entry to record the group depreciation for the year ended December 31, 2002.

PROBLEM 13–38

CHANGES IN ESTIMATES

The following independent cases describe facts concerning the ownership of racing bicycles.

(a) Maurizio Fondriest, winner of the 2000 Milan-San Remo cycling classic, purchased a new Colnago bicycle for $8,000 at the beginning of 2000. The bicycle was being depreciated using the straight-line method over an estimated useful life of 7 years, with a $1,000 salvage value. At the beginning of 2002, the Italian superstar paid $1,600 to upgrade the bicycle. As a result, the useful life of the bicycle was extended by 1 year. The salvage value remained $1,000.

(b) John Museeuw, winner of his country's own Tour of Flanders cycling classic in 2000, purchased a new Bianchi bicycle for $6,000 at the beginning of 1999. The bicycle was being depreciated using the double-declining-balance method over an estimated useful life of 5 years, with a $1,000 salvage value. At the beginning of 2000, when the Belgian superstar won at Flanders, the salvage value of his Bianchi (eventual selling price) jumped to $2,000.

(c) Gilbert Duclose-Lasalle, winner of the 1999 and 2000 Paris-Roubaix cycling classics, purchased a new Greg Lemond bicycle for $7,000 in 1998. The French superstar did not use his new bicycle during the 1998 season. However, in 1999 and 2000, Lasalle used his bicycle to win Paris-Roubaix and logged 6,000 and 8,000 kilometers, respectively, each year. Lasalle estimated that the bicycle had a productive life of 20,000 kilometers. He did not use the bike in 2001, but in 2002 he decided to upgrade the bike with $2,000 of new components, giving the bicycle an additional 10,000 kilometers of productive use. During the 2002 season, he logged 12,000 kilometers on the bike. The estimated salvage value of the bicycle is $1,000.

Instructions: In each case, compute the depreciation for 2002.

PROBLEM 13–39

ACCOUNTING FOR PATENTS

On January 3, 1994, the Masterson Company spent $96,000 to apply for and obtain a patent on a newly developed product. The patent had an estimated useful life of 10 years. At the beginning of 1998, the company spent $18,000 in successfully prosecuting an attempted infringement of the patent. At the beginning of 1999, the company purchased for $40,000 a patent that was expected to prolong the life of its original patent by 5 years. On July 1, 2002, a competitor obtained rights to a patent that made the company's patent obsolete.

Instructions: Give all the entries that would be made relative to the patent for the period 1994–2002, including entries to record the purchase of the patent, annual patent amortization, and ultimate patent obsolescence. (Assume the company's accounting period is the calendar year.)

PROBLEM 13–40

FINANCIAL STATEMENTS FOR MINING COMPANY

The Roscoe Corp. was organized on January 2, 2002. It was authorized to issue 74,000 shares of common stock. On the date of organization, it sold 20,000 shares at $50 per share and gave the remaining shares in exchange for certain land-bearing recoverable ore deposits estimated by geologists at 900,000 tons. The property is deemed to have a value of $2,700,000 with no residual value.

During 2002, purchases of mine buildings and equipment totaled $250,000. During the year, 75,000 tons were mined; 8,000 tons of this amount were unsold on December

31, the balance of the tonnage being sold for cash at $17 per ton. Expenses incurred and paid for during the year, exclusive of depletion and depreciation, were as follows:

Mining	$173,500
Delivery	20,000
General and administrative	19,500

Cash dividends of $2 per share were declared on December 31, payable January 15, 2003.

It is believed that buildings and sheds will be useful only over the life of the mine; hence, depreciation is to be recognized in terms of mine output.

Instructions: Prepare an income statement and a balance sheet for 2002. Ignore income taxes.

PROBLEM 13–41

DEPLETION EXPENSE

In 1998, the Kilbourne Mining Company purchased property with natural resources for $6,200,000. The property was relatively close to a large city and had an expected residual value of $1,500,000. However, $600,000 will have to be spent to restore the land for use.

The following information relates to the use of the property.

(a) In 1998, Kilbourne spent $400,000 in development costs and $300,000 in buildings on the property. Kilbourne does not anticipate that the buildings will have any utility after the natural resources are depleted.

(b) In 1999 and 2001, $300,000 and $800,000, respectively, were spent for additional developments on the mine.

(c) The tonnage mined and estimated remaining tons for years 1998–2002 are as follows:

Year	Tons Extracted	Estimated Tons Remaining
1998	0	5,000,000
1999	1,500,000	3,500,000
2000	1,800,000	2,000,000
2001	1,700,000	900,000
2002	900,000	0

Instructions: Compute the depletion and depreciation expense for the years 1998–2002.

PROBLEM 13–42

DEPLETION AND DEPRECIATION

In 1997, Sunbeam Corporation acquired a silver mine in eastern Alaska. Because the mine is located deep in the Alaskan frontier, Sunbeam was able to acquire the mine for the low price of $50,000. In 1998, Sunbeam constructed a road to the silver mine costing $5,000,000. Improvements to the mine made in 1998 cost $750,000. Because of the improvements to the mine and to the surrounding land, it is estimated that the mine can be sold for $600,000 when mining activities are complete.

During 1999, 5 buildings were constructed near the mine site to house the mine workers and their families. The total cost of the 5 buildings was $1,500,000. Estimated residual value is $250,000. In 1997, geologists estimated 4 million tons of silver ore could be removed from the mine for refining. During 2000, the first year of operations, only 5,000 tons of silver ore were removed from the mine. However, in 2001, workers mined 1 million tons of silver. During that same year, geologists discovered that the mine contained 3 million tons of silver ore in addition to the original 4 million tons. Improvements of $275,000 were made to the mine early in 2001 to facilitate the removal of the additional silver. Early in 2001, an additional building was constructed at a cost of $225,000 to house the additional workers needed to excavate the added silver. This building is not expected to have any residual value.

In 2002, 2.5 million tons of silver were mined and costs of $1,100,000 were incurred at the beginning of the year for improvements to the mine.

Instructions:
1. Compute the depreciation and depletion charges for 2000, 2001, and 2002.
2. Give the journal entries to record the depreciation and depletion charges for 2002.

PROBLEM 13–43
COMPUTATION OF DEPRECIATION AND DEPLETION
The following independent situations describe facts concerning the ownership of various assets.

(a) The Dewey Company purchased a tooling machine in 1992 for $60,000. The machine was being depreciated on the straight-line method over an estimated useful life of 20 years with no salvage value. At the beginning of 2002, when the machine had been in use for 10 years, Dewey paid $12,000 to overhaul the machine. As a result of this improvement, Dewey estimated that the useful life of the machine would be extended an additional 5 years.

(b) Emerson Manufacturing Co., a calendar-year company, purchased a machine for $65,000 on January 1, 2000. At the date of purchase, Emerson incurred the following additional costs:

Loss on sale of old machinery	$1,500
Freight cost	500
Installation cost	2,000
Testing costs prior to regular operation	400

The estimated salvage value of the machine was $5,000, and Emerson estimated that the machine would have a useful life of 20 years, with depreciation being computed using the straight-line method. In January 2002, accessories costing $4,860 were added to the machine in order to reduce its operating costs. These accessories neither prolonged the machine's life nor did they provide any additional salvage value.

(c) On July 1, 2002, Lund Corporation purchased equipment at a cost of $34,000. The equipment has an estimated salvage value of $3,000 and is being depreciated over an estimated life of 8 years under the double-declining-balance method of depreciation. For the 6 months ended December 31, 2002, Lund recorded one-half of a year's depreciation.

(d) The Aiken Company acquired a tract of land containing an extractable natural resource. Aiken is required by its purchase contract to restore the land to a condition suitable for recreational use after it has extracted the natural resource. Geological surveys estimate that the recoverable reserves will be 3,800,000 tons and that the land will have a value of $500,000 after restoration. Relevant cost information follows:

Land	$9,000,000
Estimated restoration costs	$1,000,000
Tons mined and sold in 2002	700,000

(e) In January 2002, Marcus Corporation entered into a contract to acquire a new machine for its factory. The machine, which had a cash price of $200,000, was paid for as follows:

Down payment	$ 30,000
Notes payable in 10 equal monthly installments, including interest at 10%	150,000
500 shares of Marcus common stock with an agreed-upon value of $70 per share	35,000
	$215,000

Prior to the machine's use, installation costs of $7,000 were incurred. The machine has an estimated useful life of 10 years and an estimated salvage value of $10,000. The straight-line method of depreciation is used.

Instructions: In each case, compute the amount of depreciation or depletion for 2002.

PROBLEM 13–44

DEPRECIATION AND THE CASH FLOW STATEMENT

Hutton Company is a manufacturing firm. Work-in-process and finished goods inventories for December 31, 2002, and December 31, 2001, are listed below.

	Dec. 31, 2002	Dec. 31, 2001
Work-in-process inventory (including depreciation)	$ 60,000	$ 63,000
Finished goods inventory (including depreciation)	131,000	120,000

Depreciation is a major portion of Hutton's overhead, and the inventories listed above include depreciation in the following amounts:

	Dec. 31, 2002	Dec. 31, 2001
Depreciation included in work-in-process inventory	$14,000	$13,000
Depreciation included in finished goods inventory	30,000	32,000

Hutton's net income for 2002 was $50,000. Cost of goods sold for the year included $16,000 in depreciation.

Instructions: Compute net cash flow from operating activities for Hutton Company for 2002. Assume that the levels of all current assets (except for inventories) and all current liabilities were unchanged from beginning of year to end of year.

PROBLEM 13–45

IMPAIRMENT

Deedle Company purchased 4 convenience store buildings on January 1, 1996, for a total of $22,000,000. The buildings have been depreciated using the straight-line method with a 20-year useful life and 5% residual value. As of January 1, 2002, Deedle has converted the buildings into Internet Learning Centers where classes on Internet usage will be conducted 6 days a week. Because of the change in the use of the buildings, Deedle is evaluating the buildings for possible impairment. Deedle estimates that the buildings have a remaining useful life of 10 years, that their residual value will be zero, that net cash inflow from each building will be $400,000 per year, and that the current fair value of each of the 4 buildings is $2,500,000. Goodwill of $4,000,000 was associated with the purchase of the buildings. The goodwill is being amortized over 20 years.

Instructions:

1. Make the appropriate journal entry, if any, to record an impairment loss as of January 1, 2002.
2. Compute total depreciation and amortization expense for 2002.
3. Repeat (1) and (2) assuming that the net cash inflow from each building is $550,000 per year. The fair value of each building is $3,000,000. (Note: There is no evidence suggesting that the useful life of goodwill has changed.)

PROBLEM 13–46

IMPAIRMENT: U.S. GAAP AND IAS

John Scott Snake Company purchased a building on January 1, 1998, for a total of $10,000,000. The building has been depreciated using the straight-line method with a 25-year useful life and no residual value. As of January 1, 2002, John Scott Snake is evaluating the building for possible impairment. The building has a remaining useful life of 15 years and is expected to generate cash inflows of $700,000 per year. The estimated fair value of the building on January 1, 2002, is $5,300,000.

Instructions:

1. Determine whether the building is impaired as of January 1, 2002. Make your determination using both the provisions of U.S. GAAP and the provisions of IAS 36. Compare your answers.

2. Assume that John Scott Snake uses U.S. GAAP. Compute depreciation expense for 2002. (Note: Don't forget the new information on the expected useful life of the building.)

3. Assume that John Scott Snake is a non-U.S. company and uses international accounting standards. Compute depreciation expense for 2002.

4. Assume that John Scott Snake is a non-U.S. company and uses international accounting standards. Further assume that the building has a fair value of $11,000,000 on January 1, 2002, and that John Scott Snake chooses to upwardly revalue its long-term operating assets when they increase in value. Compute depreciation expense for 2002.

PROBLEM 13–47

EXCHANGE OF ASSETS

A review of the books of Lakeshore Electric Co. disclosed that there were 5 transactions involving gains and losses on the exchange of fixed assets. The transactions were recorded as indicated in the following ledger accounts:

Cash				Buildings and Equipment			
(b)	5,000	(e)	1,000	(a)	10,000	(c)	118,000
(c)	6,000			(b)	25,000	(d)	850,000
				(d)	550,000		

Accum. Depr.—Buildings and Equipment				Intangible Assets			
(c)	110,000			(e)	1,000		
(d)	390,000						

Gain on Exchange of Buildings and Equipment				Loss on Exchange of Buildings and Equipment			
		(a)	10,000	(c)	2,000		
		(b)	30,000				
		(d)	90,000				

Investigation disclosed the following facts concerning these dealer-to-dealer transactions:

(a) Exchanged a piece of equipment with a $50,000 original cost, $20,000 book value, and $30,000 current market value for a piece of similar equipment owned by Highlite Electric, which had a $60,000 original cost, $10,000 book value, and a $30,000 current market value.

(b) Exchanged a machine—cost, $70,000; book value, $10,000; current market value, $40,000—for a similar machine—market value, $35,000—and $5,000 in cash.

(c) Exchanged a building—cost, $150,000; book value, $40,000; current market value, $30,000—for a building with market value of $24,000 plus cash of $6,000.

(d) Exchanged a factory building—cost, $850,000; book value, $460,000; current market value, $550,000—for equipment owned by Romeo Inc. that had an original cost of $900,000, accumulated depreciation of $325,000, and current market value of $550,000.

(e) Exchanged a patent—cost, $12,000; book value, $6,000; current market value, $3,000—and cash of $1,000 for another patent with market value of $4,000.

Instructions: Analyze each recorded transaction as to its compliance with generally accepted accounting principles. Prepare adjusting journal entries where required.

PROBLEM 13–48

EXCHANGE OF ASSETS

The Mutual Development Co. acquired the following assets in exchange for various nonmonetary assets.

2002

Mar. 15   Acquired from another company a computerized lathe in exchange for 3 old lathes. The old lathes had a total cost of $35,000 and a remaining book value of $14,000. The new lathe had a market value of $22,000, approximately the same value as the 3 old lathes.

June 1   Acquired 200 acres of land by issuing 3,000 shares of common stock with par value of $1 and market value of $90. Market analysis reveals that the market value of the stock was a reasonable value for the land.

July 15   Acquired a used piece of heavy, earth-moving equipment, market value, $120,000, by exchanging a used molding machine with a market value of $20,000 (book value, $8,000; cost, $40,000) and land with a market value of $110,000 (cost, $40,000). Cash of $10,000 was received by Mutual Development Co. as part of the transaction.

Aug. 15   Acquired a patent, franchise, and copyright for 2 used milling machines. The book value of each milling machine was $1,500, and each originally cost $10,000. The market value of each machine is $12,500. It is estimated that the patent and franchise have about the same market values, and the market value of the copyright is 50% of the market value of the patent.

Nov. 1   Acquired from a dealer a new packaging machine for 4 old packaging machines. The old machines had a total cost of $50,000 and a total remaining book value of $20,000. The new packaging machine has an indicated market value of $30,000, approximately the same value as the 4 machines.

Instructions: Prepare the journal entries required on Mutual Development Co.'s books to record the exchanges.

PROBLEM 13–49

COMPUTATION OF DEPRECIATION AND AMORTIZATION

Information pertaining to Hedlund Corporation's property, plant, and equipment for 2002 is presented below.

Account balances at January 1, 2002:

	Debit	Credit
Land	$ 150,000	
Buildings	1,200,000	
Accumulated Depreciation—Buildings		$263,100
Machinery and Equipment	900,000	
Accumulated Depreciation—Machinery and Equipment		250,000
Automotive Equipment	115,000	
Accumulated Depreciation—Automotive Equipment		84,600

Depreciation data:

	Depreciation Method	Useful Life
Buildings	150% declining-balance	25 years
Machinery and Equipment	Straight-line	10 years
Automotive Equipment	Sum-of-the-years'-digits	4 years
Leasehold Improvements	Straight-line	—

The salvage values of the depreciable assets are immaterial. Depreciation is computed to the nearest month.

Transactions during 2002 and other information are as follows:

(a) On January 2, 2002, Hedlund purchased a new car for $20,000 cash and trade-in of a 2-year-old car with a cost of $18,000 and a book value of $5,400. The new car has a cash price of $24,000; the market value of the trade-in is not known.

(b) On April 1, 2002, a machine purchased for $23,000 on April 1, 1997, was destroyed by fire. Hedlund recovered $15,500 from its insurance company.

(c) On May 1, 2002, costs of $168,000 were incurred to improve leased office premises. The leasehold improvements have a useful life of 8 years. The related lease terminates on December 31, 2008.

(d) On July 1, 2002, machinery and equipment were purchased at a total invoice cost of $280,000; additional costs of $5,000 for freight and $25,000 for installation were incurred.

(e) Hedlund determined that the automotive equipment comprising the $115,000 balance at January 1, 2002, would have been depreciated at a total amount of $18,000 for the year ended December 31, 2002.

Instructions:

1. Compute the total depreciation and amortization expense that would appear on Hedlund's income statement for the year ended December 31, 2002. Also compute the accumulated depreciation and amortization that would appear on the balance sheet at December 31, 2002.

2. Compute the total gain or loss from disposal of assets that would appear in Hedlund's income statement for the year ended December 31, 2002.

3. Prepare the noncurrent operating assets section of Hedlund's December 31, 2002, balance sheet.

PROBLEM 13–50

COMPREHENSIVE DEPRECIATION AND AMORTIZATION

At December 31, 2001, Martin Company's noncurrent operating asset and accumulated depreciation and amortization accounts had balances as follows:

Category	Cost of Asset	Accumulated Depreciation and Amortization
Land	$ 130,000	
Buildings	1,200,000	$265,400
Machinery and Equipment	775,000	196,200
Automobiles and Trucks	132,000	86,200
Leasehold Improvements	221,000	110,500

Category	Depreciation Method	Useful Life
Land Improvements	Straight-line	12 years
Buildings	150% declining-balance	25 years
Machinery and Equipment	Straight-line	10 years
Automobiles and Trucks	150% declining-balance	5 years
Leasehold Improvements	Straight-line	8 years

Depreciation is computed to the nearest month. The salvage values of the depreciable assets are immaterial.

Transactions during 2002 and other information are as follows:

(a) On January 6, 2002, a plant facility consisting of land and a building was acquired from Atlas Corp. for $600,000. Of this amount, 20% was allocated to land.

(b) On April 6, 2002, new parking lots, streets, and sidewalks at the acquired plant facility were completed at a total cost of $192,000. These expenditures had an estimated useful life of 12 years.

(c) The leasehold improvements were completed on December 31, 1998, and had an estimated useful life of 8 years. The related lease, which would have terminated on December 31, 2004, was renewable for an additional 4-year term. On April 29, 2002, Martin exercised the renewal option.

(d) On July 1, 2002, machinery and equipment were purchased at a total invoice cost of $250,000. Additional costs of $10,000 for delivery and $30,000 for installation were incurred.

(e) On August 30, 2002, Martin purchased a new automobile for $15,000.

(f) On September 30, 2002, a truck with a cost of $24,000 and a carrying amount of $8,100 on the date of sale was sold for $11,500. Depreciation for the 9 months ended September 30, 2002, was $2,352.

(g) On December 20, 2002, a machine with a cost of $17,000 and a carrying amount of $2,975 at date of disposition was scrapped without cash recovery.

Instructions: Compute total depreciation and amortization expense for the year ended December 31, 2002.

PROBLEM 13–51 **TAX DEPRECIATION METHODS AND THE TIME VALUE OF MONEY**

The following two depreciation methods are acceptable for tax purposes:

(a) Straight-line with a half-year convention. The half-year convention is the assumption that all assets are acquired in the middle of the year. Therefore, a half-year's depreciation is allowed in the first year.

(b) 200% declining-balance with a half-year convention. There is a switch to straight-line depreciation on the remaining cost when straight-line yields a larger amount than does 200% declining-balance.

On January 1, 2002, Burnet Company purchased a piece of equipment for $500,000. The equipment has an estimated useful life of 5 years and no estimated residual value.

Instructions:

1. For tax purposes, depreciation reduces taxes payable by reducing taxable income. If the tax rate is 40%, for example, a $100 depreciation deduction will reduce taxes by $40. Ignoring the time value of money, calculate the total reduction in taxes Burnet will realize through the recovery of the asset cost over the life of the equipment. Assume that the tax rate is 40%. Is the answer the same for each of the two acceptable depreciation methods?

2. For each of the acceptable methods, compute the present value (as of January 1, 2002) of the depreciation tax savings. Assume that the appropriate interest rate is 10% and that the tax savings occur at the end of the year.

3. Should a company be required to use the same depreciation method in its financial statements as it uses for tax purposes?

COMPETENCY ENHANCEMENT OPPORTUNITIES

▶ Deciphering Actual Financial Statements	▶ Ethical Dilemma
▶ Writing Assignment	▶ Cumulative Spreadsheet Analysis
▶ Research Project	▶ Internet Search
▶ The Debate	

Accounting is more than just doing textbook problems. This expanded competency material provides practice in critical thinking, oral and written communication, research, teamwork, and consideration of ethical issues.

▶ **DECIPHERING ACTUAL FINANCIAL STATEMENTS**

• **Deciphering 13–1 (The Walt Disney Company)**

The 1998 financial statements for THE WALT DISNEY COMPANY are included in Appendix A. Locate those financial statements and consider the following questions.

1. What depreciation method does Disney use for its theme parks and resorts? for its film and television costs?

2. Where do you have to look to find out that Disney's 1998 total depreciation and amortization expense is $3,754 million?

3. As of September 30, 1998, what percentage of film and television production costs are expected to be amortized within the next 3 years?
4. In 1996, Disney acquired ABC. The following information concerning the acquisition was provided in Disney's 1997 annual report:

> On February 9, 1996, the Company completed its acquisition of ABC. The aggregate consideration paid to ABC shareholders consisted of $10.1 billion in cash and 155 million shares of Company common stock valued at $8.8 billion based on the stock price as of the date the transaction was announced. The acquisition has been accounted for as a purchase and the acquisition cost of $18.9 billion was allocated to the assets acquired and liabilities assumed based on estimates of their respective fair values. Assets acquired totaled $4.0 billion (of which $1.5 billion was cash) and liabilities assumed were $4.3 billion. A total of $19.0 billion, representing the excess of acquisition cost over the fair value of ABC's net tangible assets, was allocated to intangible assets and is being amortized over forty years.

As seen in Note 10 to Disney's 1998 financial statements, the original cost associated with the ABC goodwill is only $14.248 billion as of September 30, 1998. What do you think is the explanation for this difference between the $19.0 billion originally recorded for goodwill and the $14.248 billion listed in 1998?

• Deciphering 13–2 (Delta Air Lines)

The following information is from the June 30, 1998, balance sheet for DELTA AIR LINES (all dollar amounts are in millions).

	1998	1997
Flight equipment	$11,180	$9,619
Less: Accumulated depreciation	3,895	3,510

Delta also included the following note to its financial statements:

> Depreciation and Amortization—Effective July 1, 1998, the Company increased the depreciable life of certain new generation aircraft types from 20 to 25 years. Owned flight equipment is depreciated on a straight-line basis to a residual value equal to 5% of cost.

Instructions:

1. Assume that all flight equipment will be affected by this change in policy. The new policy will not be reflected in the 1998 financial statements because the policy was changed on July 1, 1998. Estimate the total depreciation expense recognized by Delta on flight equipment for the year ended June 30, 1998 using the old 20-year life and the new 25-year life. Assume that there were no flight equipment retirements during the year and that new acquisitions are depreciated for half the year.
2. How reasonable is the assumption that there were no flight equipment retirements in 1998?

• Deciphering 13–3 (Ford Motor Company)

The information at the top of the next page comes from the 1998 financial statements of FORD MOTOR COMPANY (all dollar amounts are in millions).

Instructions:

1. Estimate the book value of property and equipment disposed of during 1998.
2. Assume that a half year's depreciation is taken on all assets acquired and disposed of during the year. Estimate the average depreciation life of Ford's property and equipment. Assume that none of the disposals was land, and eliminate the land balance when estimating the average depreciation life.
3. Estimate the average age of property and equipment (excluding land) owned by Ford as of December 31, 1998.

	1998	1997
Balance Sheet:		
Land..	$ 409	$ 393
Buildings and land improvements...	9,298	8,803
Machinery, equipment and other	43,562	41,510
Construction in progress	2,774	2,377
	$56,043	$53,083
Less: Accumulated depreciation and amortization	(26,840)	(26,004)
Net land, plant and equipment..	$29,203	$27,079
Statement of Cash Flows for 1998:		
Operating activities:		
Depreciation and amortization..	$ 5,740	
Investing activities:		
Capital expenditures...	$ 8,113	

• Deciphering 13–4 (AT&T Corporation)

The following information was extracted from the 1998 annual report of AT&T (all dollar amounts are in millions):

	1998	1997	1996	1995	1994	1993	1992	1991
Total revenues.....................................	$53,223	$51,577	$50,688	$79,609	$75,094	$69,351	$66,647	$64,455
Operating income	7,487	6,836	8,709	1,215	7,949	6,498	6,529	1,428
Net income...	6,398	4,415	5,793	139	4,710	(5,906)	3,442	171
Common shareowners' equity.........	16,949	18,910	17,320	17,274	17,921	13,374	20,313	17,973

- 1998 data reflect $2.5 billion of pretax business restructuring charges.
- 1995 data reflect $7.8 billion of pretax business restructuring and other charges.
- 1993 data reflect a $9.6 billion net charge for three accounting changes.
- 1991 data reflect $4.5 billion of pretax business restructuring and other charges.

Instructions:

1. For each year 1991–1998, calculate operating income as a percentage of total revenue, net income (loss) as a percentage of total revenue, and return on common equity (use end-of-year equity).
2. Repeat (1) after adding back the effects of the special charges in 1991, 1993, 1995, and 1998. For calculating net income, assume that the incremental income tax rate is 40%. (Note: The 1993 charge for the three accounting changes is shown net of tax.)
3. A large portion of the special charges in 1991 and 1995 were related to asset write-downs. These write-downs were recorded before FASB Statement No. 121 was issued, and thus there was more flexibility in determining when an asset was impaired. Comment on the impact of special charges on the usefulness of financial accounting data.

► WRITING ASSIGNMENT
• One depreciation method, please!

The FASB frequently receives recommendations about areas it should consider for study. Depreciation accounting has not been addressed as a separate topic by the FASB, and several alternative methods are used for recording this expense on the books. Assume that a group of financial analysts recommends to the FASB that a study be made of depreciation accounting with the objective of selecting one method as the only acceptable one. The analysts reason that only then will comparability in financial statements be achieved. You have recently been hired as a member of the FASB's research staff. Write a summary memo presenting the arguments for and against the FASB following the recommendation by the analysts.

▶ **RESEARCH PROJECT**
• How old are those assets?
Your group is to report (either orally or in writing) on the information you find in an examination of the depreciation disclosures of 5 actual companies. Proceed as follows:

1. Choose 5 companies for which you can get a copy of a recent annual report. If possible, choose each company from a different industry.
2. Find out current-year totals for gross property, plant, and equipment; accumulated depreciation; and depreciation expense.
3. Compute the average useful life of the assets included in the property, plant, and equipment category.
4. Compute the average age of the property, plant, and equipment assets in place as of the end of the current year.
5. Outline the assumptions you had to make in doing your computations. Do these assumptions seem reasonable?

▶ **THE DEBATE**
• The impairment standard is dumb!
As noted in the chapter, the recent accounting standard on the impairment of assets (Statement No. 121) includes a strange threshold value for the determination of whether an impairment loss has occurred. In addition, when the standard was adopted, it was opposed by 2 of the 7 members of the FASB for reasons other than this strange threshold value.

Divide your group into 2 teams.

- One team represents the the FASB Majority. Prepare a 2-minute oral argument explaining why the impairment standard in Statement No. 121 is good accounting.
- The other team represents the Anti-121 Coalition. Prepare a 2-minute presentation explaining why the impairment standard is dumb. The membership of this team will have diverse opinions—some will think that the FASB has not gone far enough in incorporating the current value of long-term assets into the impairment standard, and others will think that the FASB has gone too far.

▶ **ETHICAL DILEMMA**
• Profit manipulation during labor negotiations
You and your partner own a small data-entry company. You contract with businesses to manually enter data, such as library card catalogs and medical records, into a computer database. Your most significant physical assets are a large office building you own, along with the computer hardware and software necessary for operations. Your business has been running for five years and you now have 100 employees. Operating cash flow has always been healthy, and you and your partner have been able to withdraw significant amounts of cash from the business. Recently, you have seen growing discontent among your employees because of their low wages and lack of fringe benefits. You and your partner are preparing for the first meeting with an employee grievance committee.

Your partner has taken the responsibility of preparing the company's financial statements. You are embarrassed to admit that this is the first set of financial statements you have ever examined—you have never sought bank financing and all equity funding has come from you and your partner. You are surprised when you first review the statements because they reveal that the company has experienced significant losses in each of its 5 years of operation.

A closer look at the statements reveals that your partner has used the double-declining-balance method of depreciation for your office building and computer equipment. He has also assumed very short useful lives and zero residual values. Your calculations indicate that using the straight-line method with more realistic useful life and residual value assumptions would increase profits dramatically, even to the extent that substantial profits would be reported in each of the first 5 years of operation.

The meeting with the employee grievance committee is tomorrow. Your partner has been your friend since first grade. What, if anything, should you do?

▶ CUMULATIVE SPREADSHEET ANALYSIS

This spreadsheet assignment is a continuation of the spreadsheet assignments given in earlier chapters. If you completed those assignments, you have a head start on this one.

Refer back to the instructions for preparing the revised financial statements for 2002 as given in (1) of the Cumulative Spreadsheet Analysis assignment in Chapter 3.

1. Skywalker wishes to prepare a *forecasted* balance sheet, a *forecasted* income statement, and a *forecasted* statement of cash flows for 2003. Clearly state any additional assumptions that you make. Use the financial statement numbers for 2002 as the basis for the forecast, along with the following additional information.

    a. Sales in 2003 are expected to increase by 40% over 2002 sales of $2,100.
    b. In 2003, new property, plant, and equipment acquisitions will be in accordance with the information in (u) below.
    c. The $480 in operating expenses reported in 2002 breaks down as follows: $15 depreciation expense, $465 other operating expenses.
    d. New long-term debt will be acquired in 2003 in accordance with (q) below.
    e. Cash dividends will be paid in 2003 in accordance with (s) below.
    f. New short-term loans payable will be acquired in an amount sufficient to make Skywalker's current ratio in 2003 exactly equal to 2.0.
    g. Skywalker anticipates repurchasing additional shares of stock during 2003 in accordance with (t) below.
    h. Because changes in future prices and exchange rates are impossible to predict, Skywalker's best estimate is that the balance in Accumulated Other Comprehensive Income will remain unchanged in 2003.
    i. In the absence of more detailed information, assume that the balances in Investment Securities, Long-Term Investments, and Other Long-Term Assets will all increase at the same rate as sales (40%) in 2003. The balance in Intangible Assets will change in accordance with (v) below.
    j. In the absence of more detailed information, assume that the balance in Other Long-Term Liabilities will increase at the same rate as sales (40%) in 2003.
    k. The investment securities are classified as available-for-sale. Accordingly, cash from the purchase and sale of these securities is classified as an investing activity.
    l. Assume that transactions impacting Other Long-Term Assets and Other Long-Term Liabilities are operating activities.
    m. Cash and investment securities will increase at the same rate as sales.
    n. The forecasted amount of accounts receivable in 2003 is determined using the forecasted value for the average collection period. The average collection period for 2003 is expected to be 14.08 days. To make the calculations simpler, this value of 14.08 days is based on forecasted end-of-year accounts receivable rather than on average accounts receivable.
    o. The forecasted amount of inventory in 2003 is determined using the forecasted value for the number of days' sales in inventory. The number of days' sales in inventory for 2003 is expected to be 107.6 days. To make the calculations simpler, this value of 107.6 days is based on forecasted end-of-year inventory rather than on average inventory.
    p. The forecasted amount of accounts payable in 2003 is determined using the forecasted value for the number of days' purchases in accounts payable. The number of days' purchases in accounts payable for 2003 is expected to be 48.34 days. To make the calculations simpler, this value of 48.34 days is based on forecasted end-of-year accounts payable rather than on average accounts payable.
    q. New long-term debt will be acquired (or repaid) in an amount sufficient to make Skywalker's debt ratio (total liabilities divided by total assets) in 2003 exactly equal to .80.
    r. Assume an interest rate on short-term loans payable of 6.0% and on long-term debt of 8.0%. Only a half year's interest is charged on loans taken out during the year. For

example, if short-term loans payable at the end of 2003 is $15 and given that short-term loans payable at the end 'of 2002 were $10, total short-term interest expense for 2003 would be $0.75 [($10 x .06) + ($5 x .06 x 1/2)].

s. Skywalker has decided to begin paying cash dividends in 2003. Skywalker intends to maintain a dividend payout ratio (cash dividends divided by net income) of 40%. (Note: Make sure you adjust your spreadsheet formula so that if net income happens to be negative, cash dividends are no lower than $0.)

t. Skywalker has decided to continue its stock repurchase program in 2003. Skywalker intends to spend $50 repurchasing shares during the year. Skywalker accounts for treasury stock purchases using the cost method.

u. The forecasted amount of property, plant, and equipment (PP&E) in 2003 is determined using the forecasted value for the fixed asset turnover ratio. The fixed asset turnover ratio for 2003 is expected to be 3.518 times. To make the calculations simpler, this value is based on forecasted end-of-year GROSS property, plant, and equipment balance rather than on the average balance. (Note: For simplicity, ignore accumulated depreciation in making this calculation.)

v. Skywalker has determined that no new intangible assets will be acquired in 2003.

Note: These forecasted statements were constructed as part of the spreadsheet assignment in Chapter 12; you can use that spreadsheet as a starting point if you have completed that assignment.

For this exercise, add the following additional assumptions:

w. In computing depreciation expense for 2003, use straight-line depreciation and assume a 30-year useful life with no residual value. Gross PP&E acquired during the year is only depreciated for half the year. In other words, depreciation expense for 2003 is the sum of two parts: (1) a full year of depreciation on the beginning balance in PP&E, assuming a 30-year life and no residual value and (2) a half year of depreciation on any new PP&E acquired during the year, based on the change in the gross PP&E balance.

x. Skywalker assumes a 20-year useful life for its intangible assets. Assume that the $100 in intangible assets reported in 2002 is the original cost of the intangibles. Include the amortization expense with the depreciation expense in the income statement.

2. Assume the same scenario as (1), and show where financial statements would be treated differently with the following changes in assumptions:

a. Estimated useful life of property, plant, and equipment is expected to be 15 years.

b. Estimated useful life of property, plant, and equipment is expected to be 60 years.

3. Comment on the differences in the forecasted values of cash from operating activities in 2003 under each of the following assumptions about the estimated useful life of property, plant, and equipment: 15 years, 30 years, and 60 years. Explain exactly why a change in depreciation life has an impact on cash from operating activities.

▶ **INTERNET SEARCH**

VIACOM's Web address is www.viacom.com. Once you've gained access to Viacom's Web site, answer the following questions.

1. As mentioned in the opening scenario for the chapter, Viacom acquired BLOCKBUSTER VIDEO in 1994. In addition to Blockbuster, what other well-known businesses does Viacom operate?

2. Who is the chairman of the board of Viacom?

3. How does Viacom amortize its film and television production costs? Are capitalized film and television production costs reported as current or as noncurrent assets?

4. What method does Viacom use to depreciate its property and equipment?

chapter 14
Investments in
Debt and Equity Securities

Many companies invest in other companies. In some cases, the investor may own another company in its entirety—for example, THE WALT DISNEY COMPANY owns 100% of the AMERICAN BROAD-CASTING COMPANY (ABC). In other cases, the investor may own just a portion of another company as is the case with BERKSHIRE HATHAWAY, which owns over 8% of THE COCA-COLA COMPANY, 11% of AMERICAN EXPRESS, and over 7% of THE GILLETTE COMPANY. In other instances, investors may purchase debt rather than equity interests. Exhibit 14–1 lists selected U.S. companies with large investment account balances.

EXHIBIT 14–1 | Investment in Debt and Equity Securities—1998

Company	Total Investments (In billions)	Percentage of Total Assets
Berkshire Hathaway	$69.3	56.7%
Microsoft	13.9	63.2
Intel	11.0	34.8
MediaOne	9.8	34.6
Bell Atlantic	8.2	14.9
Texaco	7.2	25.2
Exxon	6.5	7.0
Coca-Cola	6.4	33.7

As the exhibit illustrates, company investment in other companies can be quite substantial. Berkshire Hathaway, a company whose major stockholder, Warren Buffett, is the third richest person in America, is a holding company that basically buys ownership in other companies. MICROSOFT, whose major stockholder, Bill Gates, is the richest person in America, makes more money than it can reinvest in its own company. As a result, it invests in other companies. But the magnitude of the securities investments by each of these companies pales in comparison to the investment holdings of COLLEGE RETIREMENT EQUITIES FUND (CREF), a company established to assist in the retirement plans for employees of nonprofit educational and research organizations. College professors and others have money withheld from their salaries and forwarded to CREF, which invests that money. As of December 31, 1998, CREF had over $146 billion, or 99% of the company's total assets, invested in the debt and equity securities of other companies. Exhibit 14–2 displays the asset portion of CREF's balance sheet as of December 31, 1998. How do companies like CREF, Berkshire Hathaway, and Microsoft account for their huge investments in securities? That topic is the focus of this chapter.

LEARNING OBJECTIVES

1
Determine why companies invest in other companies.

2
Understand the varying classifications associated with securities.

3
Account for the purchase of debt and equity securities.

4
Account for the recognition of revenue from investments.

5
Account for the change in value of securities.

6
Account for the sale of securities.

7
Record the transfer of securities between categories.

8
Explain the proper classification and disclosure of investments in securities.

9
Compare the accounting for securities under U.S. GAAP with the international standard in IAS 39.

e|m

EXPANDED MATERIAL

10
Account for changes to and from the equity method of accounting for securities.

11
Account for the impairment of a loan receivable.

EXHIBIT 14–2 | College Retirement Equities Fund Partial Balance Sheet

(In thousands)—1998 **Investments**	
Bonds	$ 12,401,904
Stocks	133,800,423
Cash and short-term investments	175,201
Investment income due and accrued	240,700
Other assets	934,164
TOTAL ASSETS	$147,552,392

A ccounting for investments in debt and equity securities has generated a great deal of interest over the past several years. The primary area of concern is the disclosure of changes in market value. Because the value of investment securities can change dramatically in a short period of time, accounting information that reflects this change in value is useful to businesses and financial statement users. To address the issue of valuation, the FASB issued Statement of Financial Accounting Standards No. 115, "Accounting for Certain Investments in Debt and Equity Securities." The major effect of this standard, issued in May 1993, is to require businesses to record many of their investment securities at fair market value. This position differs from previous standards in that increases, as well as decreases, in the value of certain securities are reported in the financial statements.

In this chapter, we discuss why and how companies invest in other companies. We will also address the accounting issues associated with investments in both debt and equity securities. Accounting for these investments involves several activities. These activities are summarized in Exhibit 14–3. Each of the issues presented in Exhibit 14–3 will be addressed in turn. Following the discussion of these issues, the Expanded Material section of the chapter discusses the reclassification of securities involving the equity method and the accounting for the impairment of a loan.

EXHIBIT 14–3 | Time Line of Business Issues Involved With Investment Securities

DETERMINE	CLASSIFY	PURCHASE	EARN AND RECOGNIZE	MONITOR	SELL	TRANSFER	DISCLOSE
purpose of investment	investments	securities	a return	changes in value	securities	securities between categories	status of portfolio at the end of the period

WHY COMPANIES INVEST IN OTHER COMPANIES

1

Determine why companies invest in other companies.

net work exercise

Microsoft (**www.microsoft. com**) has a history of purchasing companies that will enhance its business.
Net Work:
Name five companies that Microsoft has recently acquired.

Companies invest in the debt and equity securities of other companies for a host of reasons. Five of the more common reasons are discussed in this section.

Safety Cushion

MICROSOFT holds more cash and short-term investments than just about any company. As of June 30, 1998, Microsoft reported holding $13.927 billion in cash and short-term investments. Of this amount, only $195 million was actually composed of cash; the remainder was a mixture of certificates of deposit, U.S. Treasury securities, corporate notes and bonds, and other short-term interest-earning securities. In essence, Microsoft has stored a substantial amount of cash in the form of interest-earning loans to banks, governments, and other corporations. In *Time* magazine (January 13, 1997), it was reported that Bill Gates has a rule that Microsoft must always have a large enough liquid investment balance to operate for a year without any revenue. Thus, this large investment balance is a safety cushion to ensure that Microsoft can continue to operate even in the face of extreme adversity. Other companies have much smaller safety cushions, but the general principle is that investments are sometimes made in order to give a company a ready source of funds on which it can draw when needed.

Cyclical Cash Needs

Some companies operate in seasonal business environments that need cyclical inventory buildups requiring large amounts of cash, followed by lots of sales and cash collections. For example, the following is an excerpt from the January 31, 1998, 10-K filing of TOYS "R" US, the large retail toy chain:

> The seasonal nature of the business (approximately 45% of sales take place in the fourth quarter) typically causes cash to decline from the beginning of the year through October as inventory increases for the holiday selling season and funds are used for land purchases and construction of new stores, which usually open in the first ten months of the year.

The fluctuation in the cash balance for Toys "R" Us during 1997 and 1998 is shown in Exhibit 14-4. During those periods of time when excess cash exists for a company such as Toys "R" Us, the company can invest that money and earn a return. Of course, most companies are not satisfied with the low interest rates offered by bank deposits and turn to other investment alternatives. Investing in the stocks (equity) and bonds (debt) of other companies allows a firm to store its cyclical cash surplus and earn a higher rate of return by accepting a higher degree of risk.

Investment for a Return

Another reason that companies invest in the stocks and bonds of other companies is simply to earn money. Although companies owned by BERKSHIRE HATHAWAY employ 38,000 employees who provide a variety of products and services, Berkshire Hathaway is still commonly viewed as making its money through investments. This is because, as of December 31, 1998, Berkshire Hathaway had invested an average of $47,647 in stocks and bonds for each ownership share outstanding. In other words, with a share of Berkshire Hathaway stock selling for $70,000, substantially more than half of the amount required to buy a share of Berkshire Hathaway stock represents an indirect investment, through Berkshire Hathaway, in the stocks and bonds that Warren Buffett and Charlie Munger (Buffett's partner) have decided are good investments. Berkshire Hathaway's investment criteria, reprinted from the 1995 annual report, are listed in Exhibit 14-5.

Berkshire Hathaway is the exception; most U.S. corporations engage in only a small amount of investment solely for the purpose of earning a return. This is because those

EXHIBIT 14–4 | Cyclical Cash Balance: Toys "R" Us

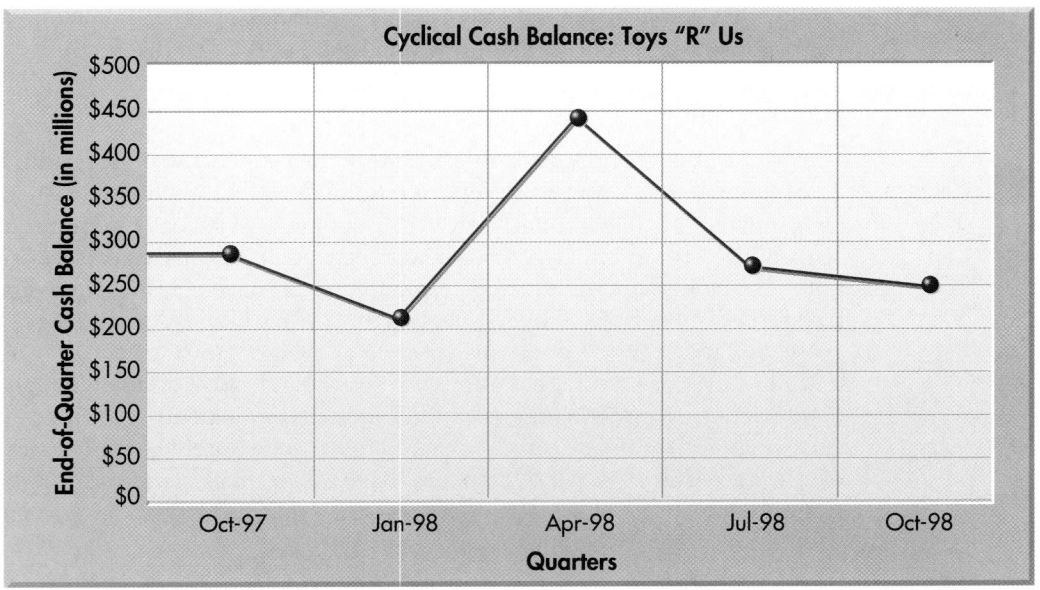

EXHIBIT 14–5 | Berkshire Hathaway's Acquisition Criteria

**BERKSHIRE HATHAWAY INC.
ACQUISITION CRITERIA**

1. Large purchases (at least $25 million of before-tax earnings),
2. Demonstrated consistent earning power (future projections are of no interest to us, nor are "turnaround" situations),
3. Businesses earning good returns on equity while employing little or no debt,
4. Management in place (we can't supply it),
5. Simple businesses (if there's lots of technology, we won't understand it),
6. An offering price (we don't want to waste our time or that of the seller by talking, even preliminarily, about a transaction when price is unknown).

companies, such as Microsoft, INTEL, and McDONALD'S, are not experts in investing. Instead, they are good at creating software, developing computer chips, and selling hamburgers. Thus, it makes sense for those companies to concentrate on operating decisions relative to their respective businesses rather than to spend management's valuable time trying to figure out the stock and bond markets.

Investment for Influence

For companies in which Berkshire Hathaway is a large shareholder, Warren Buffett is not content to be a passive investor. For example, he is on the board of directors of THE COCA-COLA COMPANY, THE GILLETTE COMPANY, and THE WASHINGTON POST COMPANY. In general, companies can invest in other companies for many reasons other than to earn a return, for example, the ability to ensure a supply of raw materials, to influence the board of directors, or to diversify their product offerings. For example, Coca-Cola does not bottle its own soft drinks; those bottling franchises are owned by independent bottlers all over the world. However, to ensure that the bottling segment of the soft drink supply chain remains predictably open to Coca-Cola, Coca-Cola owns sizeable portions of a number of the major bottlers of its soft drinks. Some of these bottlers, their location, and Coca-Cola's ownership percentage are listed in Exhibit 14–6.

Coca-Cola does not bottle its own soft drinks. However, it retains a significant percentage of ownership in several major bottlers to ensure that the bottling segment of the soft drink supply chain remains open to Coca-Cola.

To summarize, large investments in other companies are often made for business reasons such as to be able to exercise influence over the conduct of that company's operations.

EXHIBIT 14–6 | The Coca-Cola Company's Ownership Percentage of Major Bottlers of Its Products

Bottler	Location	Coca-Cola's Ownership Percentage
Coca-Cola Enterprises	United States (Largest bottler of Coca-Cola products in the world.)	44
Coca-Cola Amatil	Australia, New Zealand, Pacific Islands, Central and Eastern Europe	33
Panamco	Central and South America	24
Coca-Cola FEMSA	Mexico and Argentina	30

Purchase for Control

Warren Buffett first invested in GEICO insurance in 1951, soon after graduating from Columbia. He describes the company as his "first business love," partly stemming from his admiration of its basic strategy of being the low-cost provider of a necessary product. In 1976, Buffett decided that Berkshire Hathaway should buy a large number of GEICO shares. At the beginning of 1995, Berkshire Hathaway owned almost 50% of GEICO and obviously exercised significant influence over the operation of the company. In 1995, Buffett decided to buy the remaining shares of GEICO, making GEICO a wholly owned subsidiary of Berkshire Hathaway.

When a company purchases enough of another company to be able to control operating, investing, and financing decisions, different accounting treatment is required for that acquisition. For accounting purposes, a parent company is required to report the results of all of its subsidiaries of which it owns more than 50%—as if the parent and

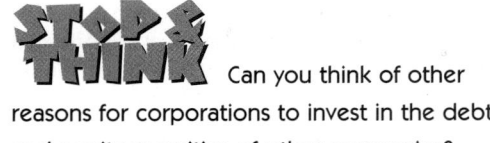

Can you think of other reasons for corporations to invest in the debt and equity securities of other companies?

subsidiaries were one company. For example, Berkshire Hathaway has a controlling interest in 76 different subsidiaries incorporated in 15 different states, ranging from Maine to California. The financial performances of these subsidiaries are included in the financial statements of Berkshire Hathaway. This is why the financial statements of most large corporations are called consolidated financial statements, because they include aggregated, or consolidated, results for both the parent and all of its majority-owned subsidiaries.

Understand the varying classifications associated with securities.

CLASSIFICATION OF SECURITIES

As mentioned previously, FASB Statement No. 115 was issued to address the valuation of securities. The statement applies to all debt securities and to equity securities for which a readily determinable fair value is available.[1] If, however, the investment in equity securities of a company is large enough, a different method of accounting for equity securities is applied.

Before we discuss the various classifications of securities associated with Statement No. 115, let's first review what debt and equity securities are:

Debt securities From Chapter 10 you will recall that debt securities are financial instruments issued by a company that typically have the following characteristics: (1) a maturity value, representing the amount to be repaid to the debt holder at maturity; (2) an interest rate (either fixed or variable) that specifies the periodic interest payments; and (3) a maturity date, indicating when the debt obligation will be redeemed.

Equity securities Equity securities represent ownership in a company. These shares of stock typically carry with them the right to collect dividends and to vote on corporate matters. In addition, equity securities are an attractive investment because of the potential for significant increases in the price of the security. Features of equity securities were covered in detail in Chapter 11.

Sophisticated trading markets for both debt and equity securities have developed over time, with the New York Stock Exchange, the New York Bond Exchange, and NASDAQ being the premier trading exchanges for stocks and bonds, respectively.

For accounting purposes, debt and equity securities falling under the scope of FASB 115 can be classified into one of four categories: held-to-maturity, available-for-sale, trading, and equity method. Exhibit 14–7 illustrates the major classifications of debt and equity securities.

EXHIBIT 14 – 7 | Classifications of Debt and Equity Securities

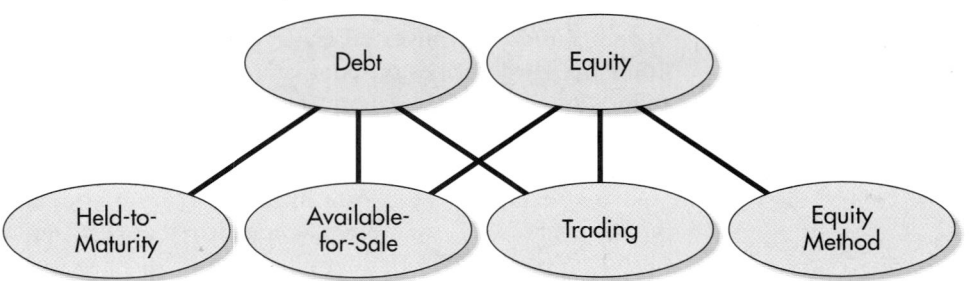

1 *Statement of Financial Accounting Standards No. 115*, "Accounting for Certain Investments in Debt and Equity Securities," Norwalk, CT: Financial Accounting Standards Board, 1993, par. 3.

Held-to-Maturity Securities

Held-to-maturity securities are debt securities purchased by a company with the intent and ability to hold those securities until they mature.[2] Note that this category includes only debt securities because equity securities typically do not mature. Note also that the company must have the intention of holding the security until it matures. Simply intending to hold a security for a long period of time does not qualify for inclusion in this category.

Available-for-Sale Securities

Debt securities that are not being held until maturity and are not classified as trading securities are considered, by default, to be "available-for-sale" securities.[3] **Available-for-sale securities** are also equity securities that are not considered trading securities and are not accounted for using the equity method.

Trading Securities

Trading securities are debt and equity securities purchased with the intent of selling them in the near future. Trading involves frequent buying and selling of securities, generally for the purpose of "generating profits on short-term differences in price."[4]

Equity Method Securities

Equity method securities are equity securities purchased with the intent of being able to control or significantly influence the operations of the investee. As a result, a large block of stock (presumed to be at least 20% of the outstanding stock unless there exists evidence to the contrary) must be owned to be classified as an equity method security. Because the intent associated with these securities is not simply to earn a return on an investment but instead includes being able to affect the operations of the investee, a different method of accounting has been developed for these securities.

The reason for these four distinct categories is that the FASB requires different accounting and disclosure, depending on the classification of the securities. Securities classified as trading securities are reported at their fair market value on the balance sheet with any unrealized holding gains or losses being reported on the income statement as part of net income. Securities classified as available-for-sale securities are also reported on the balance sheet at fair market value. However, any unrealized holding gains and losses associated with these securities are reported as a separate component of stockholders' equity and thus do not affect income for the period. Held-to-maturity securities are reported on the balance sheet at their amortized cost and are not reported at fair value. The accounting for held-to-maturity securities was discussed in Chapter 10. Equity method securities are not reported at their fair market value on the balance sheet. Instead, the investment account is increased or decreased as the net assets of the investee increase and decrease. The accounting for held-to-maturity and equity method securities remains relatively unchanged by FASB Statement No. 115. Exhibit 14–8 summarizes the accounting treatment for debt and equity securities.

Why the Different Categories?

Why does the FASB have these different categories for classifying securities? Why didn't they just make the rule that all increases and decreases in value go on the income statement? If you think about the classification scheme, it makes a lot of sense. Take, for example, held-to-maturity securities. Companies plan on holding these securities until

2 Ibid., par. 7.
3 Ibid., par. 12b.
4 Ibid., par. 12a.

EXHIBIT 14-8 | The Different Accounting Treatments for Debt and Equity Securities

Classification of Securities	Types of Securities	Disclosure on the Balance Sheet	Treatment of Temporary Changes in Value
Held-to-maturity	Debt	Amortized cost	Not recognized
Available-for-sale	Debt and equity	Fair market value	Reported in stockholders' equity
Trading	Debt and equity	Fair market value	Reported on the income statement
Equity method	Equity	Historical cost adjusted for changes in the net assets of the investee	Not recognized

they mature (hence the name). The company has no intention of realizing any changes in market value on these securities between the purchase date and the maturity date, so there is no reason to recognize any changes in value prior to the maturity date. Similarly, companies hold equity method securities, not to realize changes in the value of those securities but instead to maintain some level of influence over the investee. Thus, the market value of the investment is not of primary importance to the investor. In summary, because appreciation in price is not a major reason for holding held-to-maturity and equity method securities, adjustments for temporary changes in market value are not required.

Trading securities are purchased with the intent of realizing profits in the short term. Thus, changes in value are recorded in the period in which they occur, whether that change has been realized through an arm's-length transaction or not. Because an unrealized gain (or loss) can be turned into a realized gain (or loss) with a simple phone call to a broker, it makes sense to include the change in value on the income statement of the period in which the change occurs.

But what about available-for-sale securities? Why not treat increases and decreases in market value on this type of security similar to the treatment for trading securities? The answer lies in the probability of realizing those changes in value. With trading securities, it is likely that those changes in value will be realized sooner rather than later—that is why they are called trading securities. The same likelihood of realization is not as certain with available-for-sale securities. Because it is less certain that the changes in value of available-for-sale securities will actually be realized in the current period, the FASB elected to bypass the income statement and require these increases in value to be reported directly in the stockholders' equity section of the balance sheet as part of "Accumulated other comprehensive income." In addition, although these unrealized gains and losses are excluded from net income, they are included in the computation of comprehensive income.

> **Caution!** Who decides how a security is to be classified? Management does. Management's intent is the key factor in determining the reasons for holding certain securities. As you can guess, judgment plays a significant role in this classification.

Account for the purchase of debt and equity securities.

PURCHASE OF SECURITIES

The purchase of debt and equity securities is recorded at cost just like the purchase of any other asset. But because debt securities are bought and sold between interest payment dates, accounting for the amount of accrued interest since the last payment date adds a minor complexity.

Purchase of Debt Securities

The purchase of debt securities is recorded at cost, which includes brokerage fees, taxes, and other charges incurred in their acquisition. When debt securities are acquired between interest payment dates, the amount paid for the securities is increased by a charge for accrued interest to the date of purchase. This charge should not be reported as part of the investment cost. Two assets have been acquired—the security and the accrued interest receivable—and should be reported in two separate asset accounts. Upon receipt of the interest, Accrued Interest is closed and Interest Revenue is credited for the amount of interest earned since the purchase date. Instead of recording the interest as a receivable (asset approach), Interest Revenue may be debited for the accrued interest paid at the time of purchase. The subsequent collection of interest would then be credited in full to Interest Revenue. The latter procedure (revenue approach) is usually more convenient.

To illustrate the entries for the acquisition of debt securities, assume that $100,000 in U.S. Treasury notes are purchased at 104¼ (debt securities are normally quoted at a price per $100 face value), including brokerage fees, on May 1. Interest is 9% payable semiannually on January 1 and July 1. Accrued interest of $3,000 would thus be added to the purchase price. The debt securities are classified by the purchaser as trading securities because management will sell the securities if a change in the price will result in a profit. The entries to record the purchase of the notes and the subsequent collection of interest under the alternate procedures would be as follows:

Asset Approach:

May 1	Investment in Trading Securities		104,250	
	Interest Receivable		3,000	
	Cash			107,250
July 1	Cash		4,500	
	Interest Receivable			3,000
	Interest Revenue			1,500

Revenue Approach:

May 1	Investment in Trading Securities		104,250	
	Interest Revenue		3,000	
	Cash			107,250
July 1	Cash		4,500	
	Interest Revenue			4,500

The important point is that under either approach, the interest revenue recognized for the period is equal to the interest earned, not the amount received. In this case, the company earned $1,500, representing interest for the period May 1 to June 30.

Purchase of Equity Securities

Shares of stock are usually purchased for cash through stock exchanges (e.g., New York, American, or regional exchanges) and from individuals and institutional investors rather than from the corporations themselves. The investment is recorded at the amount paid, including brokers' commissions, taxes, and other fees incidental to the purchase price. Even when part of the purchase price is deferred, the full cost should be recorded as the investment in stock, with a liability account established for the amount yet to be paid. If stock is acquired in exchange for properties or services instead of cash, the fair market value of the consideration given or the value at which the stock is currently selling, whichever is more clearly determinable, should be used as the basis for recording the investment. If two or more securities are acquired for a lump sum price, the cost should be allocated to each security in an equitable manner, as explained in earlier chapters.

To illustrate the accounting for the purchase of equity securities, assume Gondor Enterprises purchased 300 shares of Boromir Co. stock at $75 per share plus brokerage fees of $800 and 500 shares of Faramir Inc. stock at $50 per share plus brokerage fees of $300. Gondor classifies the Boromir stock as a trading security because management has no intention of holding these securities for a long period of time and will sell them as soon as it is economically advantageous for the company. The Faramir stock is classified as available-for-sale. The journal entry to record the purchases would be as follows:

Stock purchased for cash through stock exchanges is recorded at the amount paid, including brokers' commissions, taxes, and other fees.

Investment in Trading Securities—Boromir Co.	23,300*	
Investment in Available-for-Sale Securities—Faramir Inc.	25,300**	
Cash		48,600

Computations:
*300 × $75 = $22,500 + $800 = $23,300
**500 × $50 = $25,000 + $300 = $25,300

RECOGNITION OF REVENUE FROM INVESTMENTS

Account for the recognition of revenue from investments.

A primary reason that companies invest in the debt or equity securities of other companies is to earn a return in the form of either interest or dividends. In the case of debt securities, the computation of that return is complicated because a difference often exists between the purchase price and the maturity value of the debt instrument. The resulting premium or discount can affect the amount of interest revenue recognized in each future period—depending on how the securities are classified when purchased. For equity securities, the recognition of revenue from an investment depends on the level of ownership in the investee. Each of these issues is discussed in the following sections.

Recognition of Revenue From Debt Securities

Recall from Chapter 10 that debt securities carry with them a stated rate of interest that when multiplied by the maturity value of the securities indicates the amount of cash to be received in interest each year. Often, interest is received on a semiannual basis. When interest is received, cash is debited and interest revenue is credited. However, when debt securities are acquired at a higher or lower price than their maturity value, and the debt securities are classified as held-to-maturity, periodic amortization of the premium or accumulation of the discount with corresponding adjustments to interest revenue is required. One could amortize a premium or discount associated with trading or available-for-sale securities. But recall that one of the primary reasons for this amortization process is to ensure that the carrying value of held-to-maturity securities is equal to its maturity value on the maturity date. If securities are not classified as being held-to-maturity, then the amortization process becomes less relevant.[5]

As explained in Chapter 10, a premium or discount results when the stated rate of interest and the market rate of interest on the date of acquisition of the debt security are different. If the stated rate of interest is higher than the prevailing market rate, investors will pay a higher price for the debt security (a premium) in order to receive the higher interest payments. When the market rate of interest is higher than the stated rate, investors will pay less than the face amount of the debt security, resulting in a discount.

> **Caution!** You will need to be comfortable with present value computations if you are to understand the calculations that follow. Appendix B contains an overview of the time value of money.

The present value computations associated with computing the value of a debt security were illustrated in Chapter 10 and an example is included here. Assume that on January 1, 2001, Silmaril Technologies purchased 5-year, 10% bonds with a face value of $100,000 and interest payable semiannually on January 1 and July 1. The market rate on bonds of similar quality and maturity is 8%. Silmaril computes the market price of the bonds as follows:

Present value of principal:		
Maturity value of bonds after 5 years	$100,000	
Present value factor, 10 periods, 4% semiannual market rate	× .6756	
Present value of $100,000 discounted at 4% for 10 periods		$ 67,560
Present value of interest payments:		
Semiannual payment, 5% of $100,000	$ 5,000	
Present value of annuity factor, 10 periods, 4%	× 8.1109	
Present value of 10 payments of $5,000 discounted at 4%		40,555
Total present value (market price) of the bonds (rounded)		$108,115

We will use two examples to illustrate the accounting for interest revenue. First, we will assume that Silmaril intends to sell the securities should the need for cash arise (thereby making them trading securities), and second, we will assume that Silmaril intends, and has the ability, to hold the bonds until they mature (making them held-to-maturity securities).

INTEREST REVENUE FOR DEBT SECURITIES CLASSIFIED AS TRADING Recall from Chapter 10 that the investor typically does not use a premium or discount account but instead records the investment at cost and nets the face value and any premium or discount. Silmaril would make the following journal entry to record the initial purchase of the bonds[6]:

Investment in Trading Securities	108,115	
Cash		108,115

When interest payments are received, the journal entry to record their receipt would be:

Cash	5,000	
Interest Revenue		5,000

---

5 In all the examples that follow as well as in the end-of-chapter material, we will assume that only premiums and discounts associated with held-to-maturity securities are amortized.

6 The journal entries would be similar had the security been classified as available-for-sale. The only difference would be in the account title.

INTEREST REVENUE FOR DEBT SECURITIES CLASSIFIED AS HELD-TO-MATURITY

The entry to record the initial purchase of the bonds had they been originally classified as held-to-maturity would be:

Investment in Held-to-Maturity Securities	108,115	
Cash		108,115

To determine the amount of premium to amortize each period, Silmaril would prepare an amortization table, as illustrated below. This table is based on the effective-interest method of amortization.[7]

Amortization of Bond Premium—Effective-Interest Method
$100,000, 5-Year Bonds, Interest at 10% Payable Semiannually,
Sold at $108,115 to Yield 8%

Interest Payment	A Interest Received (.05 × $100,000)	B Interest Revenue (.04 × Bond Carrying Value)	C Premium Amortization (A – B)	D Unamortized Premium (D – C)	Bond Carrying Value ($100,000 + D)
				$8,115	$108,115
1	$5,000	$4,325	$675	7,440	107,440
2	5,000	4,298	702	6,738	106,738
3	5,000	4,270	730	6,008	106,008
4	5,000	4,240	760	5,248	105,248
5	5,000	4,210	790	4,458	104,458
6	5,000	4,178	822	3,636	103,636
7	5,000	4,145	855	2,781	102,781
8	5,000	4,111	889	1,892	101,892
9	5,000	4,076	924	968	100,968
10	5,000	4,032*	968	0	100,000

*Rounding differences are adjusted with last entry.

When the first interest payment of $5,000 is received from the bond issuer, Silmaril would make the following journal entry:

Cash	5,000	
Interest Revenue		4,325
Investment in Held-to-Maturity Securities		675

STOP & THINK Theoretically, we should amortize the discount or premium associated with trading and available-for-sale debt securities just as we do with held-to-maturity securities. Why don't we?

Subsequent receipts of interest would be recorded with a similar journal entry, the only difference being that the amount amortized would differ depending on which interest payment was received.

Recognition of Revenue From Equity Securities

Once an equity security is purchased, one of two basic methods must be used to account for the revenue earned on that investment depending on the control or degree of influence exercised by the acquiring company (investor) over the acquired company (investee). In those instances where the level of ownership in the investee is such that the investor is able to control or significantly influence decisions made by the investee, use of the **equity method** is appropriate. The accounting procedures associated with the equity method are outlined in Accounting Principles Board Opinion No. 18. When the acquiring company does not exercise significant influence over the investee, the

---

7 As explained in Chapter 10, the straight-line method of interest amortization can be used when the results do not differ materially from effective-interest amortization. However, in all the examples that follow as well as in the end-of-chapter material, we will use the effective-interest method.

equity securities are classified as trading or available-for-sale and accounted for as FASB 115 securities.

The ability of the investor to exercise **significant influence** over such decisions as dividend distribution and operational and financial administration may be indicated in several ways: representation on the investee's board of directors, participation in policy-making processes, material intercompany transactions, interchange of managerial personnel, or technological dependency of investee on investor. Another important consideration is the extent of ownership by an investor in relation to the concentration of other stockholdings. While it is clear that ownership of over 50% of common stock virtually assures **control** by the acquiring company, ownership of 50% or less may give effective control if the remaining shares of the stock are widely held and no significant blocks of stockholders are consistently united in their ownership. In Opinion No. 18, the APB recognized that the degree of influence and control will not always be clear and that judgment will be required in assessing the status of each investment. To achieve a reasonable degree of uniformity in the application of its position, the APB set 20% as an ownership standard; the ownership of 20% or more of the voting stock of the company carries the presumption, in the absence of evidence to the contrary, that an investor has the ability to exercise significant influence over that company. Conversely, ownership of less than 20% leads to the presumption that the investor does not have the ability to exercise significant influence unless such ability can be demonstrated.[8]

In May 1981, the FASB issued Interpretation No. 35 to emphasize that the 20% criterion is only a guideline and that judgment is required in determining the appropriate accounting method in cases where ownership is 50% or less. Interpretation No. 35 lists five illustrative examples of circumstances that might indicate that the investor does not have significant influence, regardless of the percentage of ownership[9]:

1. Opposition by the investee, such as litigation or complaints to governmental regulatory authorities.
2. An agreement between the investor and investee under which the investor surrenders significant rights as a shareholder.
3. Majority ownership of the investee is concentrated among a small group of shareholders who operate the investee without regard to the views of the investor.
4. The investor needs or wants more financial information to apply the equity method than is available to the investee's other shareholders (for example, the investor wants quarterly financial information from an investee who publicly reports only annually), tries to obtain the information, and fails.
5. The investor tries and fails to obtain representation on the investee's board of directors.

While the FASB examples may be helpful in some cases, evaluating the degree of investor influence is often a very subjective process. As a result, the percentage-of-ownership criterion set forth in APB Opinion No. 18 has been widely accepted as the basis for determining the appropriate method of accounting for long-term investments in equity securities when the investor does not possess absolute voting control. If it is determined that control or significant influence exists, the equity method of accounting is applied to the investment. If not, then the securities are classified as either trading or available-for-sale. Note that because preferred stock is generally nonvoting stock and does not provide for significant influence, it is always classified as either trading or available-for-sale.

Before we move on to discuss the particulars of recognizing revenue on equity investments, an additional point should be made regarding controlling ownership.

8 *Opinions of the Accounting Principles Board No. 18,* "The Equity Method of Accounting for Investments in Common Stock," New York: American Institute of Certified Public Accountants, 1971.
9 *FASB Interpretation No. 35,* "Criteria for Applying the Equity Method of Accounting for Investments in Common Stock," Stamford, CT: Financial Accounting Standards Board, 1981, par. 4.

FYI: The FASB continues to examine the issue of control and consolidations. Ask your professor about the status of the FASB's deliberations.

When one company acquires a majority voting interest in another company through the acquisition of more than 50% of its voting common stock, the acquiring company has control over the acquired company. But, as noted, effective control may exist with less than 50% ownership. The FASB is examining the issue of control and has suggested that companies look beyond ownership percentage and examine other factors that may indicate control.[10] A couple of factors the FASB has highlighted include (1) owning a large minority voting interest (approximately 40%) with no other group owning a significant interest and (2) a company's domination of the election process for the investee's board of directors. Each of these events would suggest that control has been obtained and that consolidation would be appropriate.

In the case of consolidation, the investor and investee are referred to respectively as the **parent company** and the **subsidiary company.** Where control exists, preparation of consolidated financial statements is required. This means that the financial statement balances of the parent and subsidiary companies are combined, or consolidated, for financial reporting purposes even though the companies continue to operate as separate entities. In the consolidation process, any intercompany transactions are eliminated, for example, any sales and purchases between the parent and subsidiary companies. By eliminating all intercompany transactions, the combined balances or consolidated totals appropriately reflect the financial position and results of operation of the total economic unit. This treatment reflects the fact that majority ownership of common stock assures control by the parent over the decision-making processes of the subsidiary. The important point is this—the process of consolidation builds on the journal entries made when the equity method is applied. In fact, the equity method of accounting is often referred to as a "one-line consolidation." Accounting for consolidated entities is covered in advanced accounting texts.[11] COCA-COLA provides an example of an instance where the company owned a greater than 50% interest in a subsidiary and yet did not prepare consolidated financial statements for the subsidiary. Recall from our previous discussion of acquiring companies for influence that Coca-Cola owned 33% of COCA-COLA AMATIL, an Australian-based bottler. In past years, Coca-Cola's ownership interest in Coca-Cola Amatil exceeded 50%, yet the company did not consolidate. The reason Coca-Cola did not consolidate was because, as the company indicated in the notes to its financial statements, its control was considered temporary.

Caution! Remember, consolidation is not an alternative to the equity method. It constitutes procedures employed in addition to those used with the equity method.

Previous accounting standards allowed separate reporting for certain majority-owned subsidiaries if those subsidiaries had "nonhomogeneous" operations, a large minority interest, or a foreign location. Separate reporting by subsidiaries occurred most often when the operations of the subsidiary and parent were significantly different (i.e., nonhomogeneous). Typically, the subsidiary was engaged in finance, insurance, leasing, or real estate, while the parent company was a manufacturer or merchandiser. Examples include GENERAL MOTORS ACCEPTANCE CORPORATION (GMAC) and IBM CREDIT CORPORATION, which are finance companies that are wholly owned by GENERAL MOTORS CORP. and IBM CORP., respectively. Traditionally, the financial statements of these subsidiaries were not consolidated with those of their respective parent companies.

With the issuance of Statement of Financial Accounting Standards No. 94, the FASB currently requires the consolidation of all majority-owned subsidiaries unless control is temporary or does not rest with the majority owner (as, for instance, when the subsidiary is in legal reorganization or in bankruptcy) and is considering expanding the concept of control to encourage the consolidation of subsidiaries for which a parent company has

---

10 *Exposure Draft: Consolidated Financial Statements: Purpose and Policy,* Stamford, CT: Financial Accounting Standards Board, 1999.
11 See, for example, Paul Fischer, William Taylor, and Rita Cheng, *Advanced Accounting,* Seventh edition, Cincinnati, OH: South-Western College Publishing, 1999.

control even with a less-than-majority ownership interest.[12] Thus, even though a subsidiary has nonhomogeneous operations, a large minority interest, or a foreign location, it should be consolidated. The reporting entity is to be the total economic unit consisting of the parent and all its subsidiaries.

To summarize, in the absence of persuasive evidence to the contrary, equity securities are classified as trading or available-for-sale when ownership is less than 20%; the equity method is used when ownership is such that the investor has the ability to significantly influence or control the investee's operations; in those instances where control is deemed to exist, the equity method, along with additional consolidation procedures, is used. These relationships dealing with the effect of ownership interest and control or influence and the proper accounting method to be used are summarized in Exhibit 14–9. Note that the percentages are given only as guidelines. Subjective assessment of the ability of an investor to influence or control an investee should also be considered when determining the appropriate accounting for the investment.

EXHIBIT 14–9 | Effect of Ownership Interest and Control or Influence on Accounting for Long-Term Investments in Common Stocks

Ownership Interest	Control or Degree of Influence	Accounting Method	Applicable Standard
More than 50%	Control	Equity method and consolidation procedures	APB Opinion No. 18 FASB Exposure Draft
20 to 50%	Significant influence	Equity method	APB Opinion No. 18
Less than 20%	No significant influence	Account for as trading or available-for-sale	FASB Statement No. 115

> **FYI:** In the notes to its financial statements (see Appendix A), DISNEY details its guidelines for applying the equity method.

We will first discuss and illustrate the accounting and reporting issues associated with the recognition of revenue on trading and available-for-sale equity securities. The more complex equity method will then be discussed.

REVENUE FOR EQUITY SECURITIES CLASSIFIED AS TRADING AND AVAILABLE-FOR-SALE   When an investment in another company's stock does not involve either a controlling interest or significant influence, then it is classified as either trading or available-for-sale. Recall that equity securities cannot be classified as held-to-maturity. Revenue is recognized when dividends are declared (if the investor knows about the declaration) or when the dividends are received from the investee. Continuing a previous example, assume that Gondor Enterprises receives the following dividends from its investees:

Company	Classification	Number of Shares Held	Dividends Received per Share
Boromir Co.	Trading securities	300	$2.00
Faramir Inc.	Available-for-sale securities	500	$3.75

The journal entry to record receipt of the dividends would be:

Cash	2,475*	
Dividend Revenue		2,475

*[(300 × $2.00) + (500 × $3.75) = $2,475]

---

12 *Statement of Financial Accounting Standards No. 94*, "Consolidation of All Majority-Owned Subsidiaries," Stamford, CT: Financial Accounting Standards Board, 1987.

REVENUE FOR SECURITIES CLASSIFIED AS EQUITY METHOD SECURITIES The equity method of accounting for long-term investments in common stock reflects the economic substance of the relationship between the investor and investee rather than the legal distinction of the separate entities. The objective of this method is to reflect the underlying claim by the investor on the net assets of the investee company.

Under the equity method, the investment is initially recorded at cost, just like any other investment. However, with the equity method, the investment account is periodically adjusted to reflect changes in the underlying net assets of the investee. The investment balance is increased to reflect a proportionate share of the earnings of the investee company or decreased to reflect a share of any losses reported. If preferred stock dividends have been declared by the investee, they must be deducted from income reported by the investee before computing the investor's share of investee earnings or losses. When dividends are received by the investor, the investment account is reduced. Thus, the equity method results in an increase in the investment account when the investee's net assets increase; similarly, the investment account decreases when the investee records a loss or pays out dividends.

We will illustrate the equity method with a simple example. Assume that BioTech Inc. purchased all (100%) of the outstanding stock of Medco Enterprises on January 1 of the current year by paying $500,000. During the year, Medco reported net income of $50,000 and paid dividends of $10,000. BioTech would make the following journal entries during the year:

Investment in Medco Enterprises Stock	500,000	
Cash		500,000
To record the purchase of 100% of Medco stock.		
Investment in Medco Enterprises Stock	50,000	
Income From Investment in Medco Enterprises Stock		50,000
To record the recognition of revenue from investment in Medco.		
Cash	10,000	
Investment in Medco Enterprises Stock		10,000
To record the receipt of a dividend on Medco stock.		

Notice that Medco Enterprises' book value increased by $40,000 during the year ($50,000 in income less $10,000 dividend). BioTech's investment in Medco increased by the same amount. The equity method of accounting maintains a relationship between the book value of the investee and the investment account on the books of the investor. As the subsidiary's book value changes, so does the investment account on the books of the parent company. Had BioTech owned less than 100% of the stock of Medco, the journal entries to record revenue and dividends would have been reduced to reflect the percentage owned.

COMPARING FASB 115 WITH THE EQUITY METHODS To contrast and illustrate the accounting entries under various methods, assume that Powell Corporation purchases 5,000 shares of San Juan Company common stock on January 2 at $20 per share, including commissions and other costs. San Juan has a total of 25,000 shares outstanding; thus, the 5,000 shares represent a 20% ownership interest. We will illustrate the accounting differences in revenue recognition for equity securities by assuming that (1) the securities are classified as available-for-sale and accounted for using the cost method, and (2) the securities are classified as equity method securities and accounted for using the equity method. The appropriate entries under both assumptions are shown in Exhibit 14–10. The actual method used would depend on the degree of influence exercised by the investor as indicated by a consideration of all relevant factors, as well as the percentage owned. Exhibit 14–10 highlights the basic differences in accounting for investments using FASB 115 and the equity methods. Under both methods, the investment is originally recorded at cost. Dividends received are recognized as dividend revenue for the available-for-sale securities and as a reduction in the investment account under the equity method.

The investor's percentage of the earnings of the investee company are recorded as income and as an increase to the investment account under the equity method, whereas no entry is required for this event when the securities are classified as available-for-sale. If the securities had been classified as trading, the journal entries to recognize revenue would have been identical to those made for the available-for-sale securities.

EXHIBIT 14–10 | Journal Entries to Record Revenue Recognition Using FASB 115 and the Equity Method

Available-for-Sale (Cost Method)			Equity Method		
Jan. 2 Purchased 5,000 shares of San Juan Company common stock at $20 per share:					
Investment in Available-for-Sale Securities	100,000		Investment in San Juan Company Stock	100,000	
Cash		100,000	Cash		100,000
Oct. 31 Received dividend of $0.80 per share from San Juan Company ($0.80 × 5,000 shares):					
Cash	4,000		Cash	4,000	
Dividend Revenue		4,000	Investment in San Juan Company Stock		4,000
Dec. 31 San Juan Company announced earnings for the year of $60,000:					
No entry			Investment in San Juan Company Stock	12,000	
			Income From Investment in San Juan Company Stock (.20 × $60,000)		12,000

COMPLEXITIES UNDER THE EQUITY METHOD When a company is purchased by another company, the purchase price usually differs from the recorded book value of the underlying net assets of the acquired company. For example, assume Snowbird Company purchased 100% of the common stock of Ski Resorts International for $8 million, although the book value of Ski Resorts' net assets is only $6.5 million. In effect, Snowbird is purchasing some undervalued assets, above-normal earnings potential, or both.

As explained in Chapter 11, if the purchase price of an ongoing business exceeds the recorded value, the acquiring company must allocate this purchase price among the assets acquired using their current market values as opposed to the amounts carried on the books of the acquired company. If part of the purchase price cannot be allocated to specific assets, that amount is recorded as goodwill. If the purchase price is less than the recorded net asset value, the assets acquired must be recorded at an amount less than their carrying value on the books of the acquired company. Whether assets are increased or decreased as a result of the purchase, future income determination will use the new (adjusted) values to determine the depreciation and amortization charges.

When only a portion of a company's stock is purchased and the equity method is used to reflect the income of the partially owned company, an adjustment to the investee's reported income, similar to that just described, may be required. In order to determine whether such an adjustment is necessary, the acquiring company must compare the purchase price of the common stock with the recorded net asset value of the acquired company at the date of purchase. If the purchase price exceeds the investor's share of book value, the computed excess must be analyzed in the same way as described above for a 100% purchase. Although no entries to adjust asset values are made on the books of either company, an adjustment to the investee's reported income is required under the equity method for the investor to reflect the economic reality of paying more for the investment than the underlying net book value. If depreciable assets had been adjusted to higher market values on the books of the investee to reflect the price paid by the investor, additional depreciation would have been taken by the investee company. Similarly, if the purchase price reflected goodwill, additional amortization would have been required. These adjustments would have reduced the reported income of the investee. To reflect this condition, an adjustment is made by the investor to the income reported by the investee in applying the equity method. This adjustment serves to meet the objective of computing the income reported using the equity method in the same manner as would be done if the company were 100% purchased and consolidated financial statements were prepared.

To illustrate, assume that the book value of common stockholders' equity (net assets) of Stewart Inc. was $500,000 at the time Phillips Manufacturing Co. purchased 40% of its common shares for $250,000. Based on a 40% ownership interest, the market value of the net assets of Stewart Inc. would be $625,000 ($250,000/.40), or $125,000 more than the book value. Assume that a review of the asset values discloses that the market value of depreciable properties exceeds the carrying value of these assets by $50,000. The remaining $75,000 difference ($125,000 − $50,000) is attributed to goodwill. Assume further that the average remaining life of the depreciable assets is 10 years and that goodwill is amortized over 20 years. Phillips Manufacturing Co. would adjust its share of the annual income reported by Stewart Inc. to reflect the additional depreciation and the amortization of goodwill as follows:

Additional depreciation ($50,000 × 40%)/10 years =	$2,000
Goodwill amortization ($75,000 × 40%)/20 years =	1,500
	$3,500

Each year for the first 10 years, Phillips would make the following entry in addition to entries made to recognize its share of Stewart Inc.'s income and dividends:

Income From Investment in Stewart Inc. Stock	3,500	
Investment in Stewart Inc. Stock		3,500

To adjust share of income on Stewart Inc. common stock for proportionate depreciation on excess market value of depreciable property, $2,000, and for amortization of goodwill from acquisition of the stock, $1,500.

> **Caution!** If the fair market value of the assets had been less than their book value, the entry to adjust income would have resulted in increased income and an increase in the investment account.

After the 10th year, the adjustment would be for $1,500 until the goodwill amount is fully amortized.

To complete the illustration, assume that the purchase was made on January 2, 2002; Stewart Inc. declared and paid dividends of $70,000 to common stockholders during 2002, and Stewart Inc. reported net income of $150,000 for the year ended December 31, 2002. At the end of 2002, the investment in Stewart Inc. common stock would be reported on the balance sheet of Phillips Manufacturing Co. at $278,500, computed as shown below:

Investment in Stewart Inc. Common Stock

Acquisition cost	$250,000	
Add: Share of 2002 earnings of investee company ($150,000 × .40)	60,000	$310,000
Less: Dividends received from investee ($70,000 × .40)	$ 28,000	
Additional depreciation of undervalued assets	2,000	
Amortization of unrecorded goodwill	1,500	31,500
Year-end carrying value of investment (equity in investee company)		$278,500

This illustration assumes that the fiscal years of the two companies coincide and that the purchase of the stock is made at the first of the year. If a purchase is made at a time other than the beginning of the year, the income earned up to the date of the purchase is assumed to be included in the cost of purchase. Only income earned by the investee subsequent to acquisition should be recognized by the investor.

The adjustments for additional depreciation and goodwill amortization are needed only when the purchase price is greater than the underlying book value at the date of acquisition. If the purchase price is less than the underlying book value at the time of acquisition, it is assumed that specific assets of the investee are overvalued or that there is negative goodwill as discussed in Chapter 11. An adjustment is necessary to reduce the depreciation or amortization included in the reported income of the investee. The journal entry to reflect this adjustment is the reverse of the one illustrated previously. The computations would also be similar except that the adjustments for overvalued assets would be added to (instead of subtracted from) the carrying value of the investment.

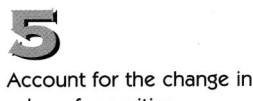

Account for the change in value of securities.

ACCOUNTING FOR THE CHANGE IN VALUE OF SECURITIES

The value of debt and equity securities can rise and fall on a daily basis. Some of these changes in value can be considered temporary while others might be of a more permanent nature. Prior to FASB Statement No. 115, if temporary price changes occurred, only declines (and their subsequent recovery) in value of securities were recognized in the financial statements. The new standard requires, for many types of debt and equity securities, both increases and decreases in value to be reflected in the financial statements. This section of the chapter deals with accounting for temporary changes in a security's value. We also briefly discuss the accounting for permanent declines in value.

Accounting for Temporary Changes in the Value of Securities

Recall from our previous discussion that all debt securities and those equity securities not being held with the intent to influence the investee are to be classified into one of three categories. Those categories and their required disclosures were summarized in Exhibit 14–8.

The following example will be used throughout this section to illustrate accounting for changes in fair value. Eastwood Incorporated purchased five different securities on March 1, 2002. A schedule showing the type and cost of each security, along with its fair value on December 31, 2002, is as follows:

Security	Classification	Cost	Fair Value Dec. 31, 2002
1	Trading	$ 8,000	$ 7,000
2	Trading	3,000	3,500
3	Available-for-sale	5,000	6,100
4	Available-for-sale	12,000	11,500
5	Held-to-maturity	20,000 [13]	19,000

The entry to record the initial purchase would be as follows:

Investment in Trading Securities	11,000	
Investment in Available-for-Sale Securities	17,000	
Investment in Held-to-Maturity Securities	20,000	
Cash		48,000

Securities 1 and 2 are classified by management as trading securities because management has no intention of holding these securities for a long period of time and will sell them as soon as it is economically advantageous for the company. Securities 3 and 4 are deemed by management to be available-for-sale securities. Management purchased Security 5 at face value and intends to hold it until it matures.

---

13 Security 5 was purchased at face value. If the security were purchased at a price other than face value, then the amortization procedures described previously would be employed.

> ## ► THE FASB VOTES TO PUT A STOP TO CHERRY-PICKING
>
> It was no small feat when the FASB finally issued Statement No. 115, "Accounting for Certain Investments in Debt and Equity Securities." The standard was strongly opposed by banks and insurance companies because of the anticipated negative effects on profits. The banking and insurance industries also objected to having to value the asset side of the balance sheet at market value while not being allowed to value the
>
> liability side at market as well. These debates were not restricted to the business world. Even on the Board there was a great deal of disagreement regarding the issue of marking securities to market value. At one time, the FASB thought they had the issues worked out only to have one Board member surprise his colleagues by changing his vote at the last minute. The member stated the "FASB should go back to the drawing board and take another look at this proposal."
>
> Meanwhile, the SEC continued to insist on a movement toward market value accounting. The SEC had desired market value disclosures as a means of providing financial statement users with more and better information regarding a firm's securities portfolio. The SEC was also concerned with a phenomenon known as *cherry-picking*. Cherry-picking occurs when securities whose prices have increased are sold, resulting in realized gains, while securities whose prices have

During an accounting period, the fair value of securities will rise and fall. Only at the end of the period, when financial statements are prepared, is a company required to account for any change in market value. At the end of the accounting period, the fair value of the portfolio of securities for certain categories is compared with the historical cost and an adjustment is made for the difference.

TRADING SECURITIES At the end of 2002, the value of the trading securities portfolio has decreased by $500 ($11,000 cost less $10,500 fair value). As a result, the following journal entry would be made:

Unrealized Loss on Trading Securities	500	
Market Adjustment—Trading Securities		500

> **Caution!** Once the adjusting entry is made, the trading securities account and the market adjustment account should always sum to the market value of the trading securities. The same is true for available-for-sale securities.

The loss of $500 reflects the fact that the value of the trading securities portfolio has declined during the period. The loss is classified as unrealized because these securities have not been sold. This entry introduces a valuation account, called "Market Adjustment—Trading Securities." This account is combined with Investment in Trading Securities and reported on the balance sheet. The use of a valuation account allows the company to maintain a record of historical cost. To determine realized and unrealized holding gains and losses, a record of historical cost is necessary. The unrealized loss on trading securities account would be reported on the income statement under "Other expenses and losses."

AVAILABLE-FOR-SALE SECURITIES For available-for-sale securities, similar adjustments to those illustrated for trading securities would be made; the only difference would be that instead of any unrealized gain or loss being disclosed on the income statement, it would be reported directly in stockholders' equity as part of "Accumulated other comprehensive income." Continuing the Eastwood example, at the end of 2002, its available-for-sale portfolio had increased from $17,000 to $17,600. This $600 increase in fair value of the securities above their cost would be recorded with the following journal entry:

Market Adjustment—Available-for-Sale Securities	600	
Unrealized Increase/Decrease in Value of Available-for-Sale Securities		600

declined are maintained at their historical cost. The issuance of FASB Statement No. 115 directly addressed this issue by requiring many securities to be valued at market.

Finally, in September 1993, the Board voted 5 to 2 to adopt Statement No. 115. The SEC quickly hailed the new standard, saying that it would "clarify the rules of the road" and lessen "enforcement actions."

QUESTIONS:

1. Should intense lobbying by certain industry groups be allowed to influence the standard-setting process?

2. The SEC has long urged the FASB to issue standards relating to market value accounting. Should pressure from the SEC be allowed to significantly influence the standard-setting process?

3. What is wrong with cherry-picking? If an investment's value has increased, why shouldn't a firm be allowed to record that increase?

SOURCES:
Lee Berton, "FASB Balks on Current-Market Rules for Banks as Member Switches His Vote," *The Wall Street Journal,* January 16, 1992, p. A3.
Lee Berton, "FASB Votes to Make Banks and Insurers Value Certain Bonds at Current Price," *The Wall Street Journal,* September 19, 1993, p. A3.

Note that the unrealized increase/decrease in value of available-for-sale securities account would serve to increase the amount of stockholders' equity, which is consistent with the fact that an asset has increased in value.

HELD-TO-MATURITY SECURITIES Security 5 has decreased in value from $20,000 to $19,000. However, because this security is classified as held-to-maturity, no adjustment is made for the difference between carrying value and fair market value. Exhibit 14–11 summarizes how the securities and the resulting increases and decreases in value would be disclosed in the financial statements of Eastwood Inc. for 2002.

EXHIBIT 14–11 | Financial Statement Disclosure of Securities

Eastwood Inc.
Balance Sheet (Partial)
December 31, 2002

Assets:			
Investment in trading securities, at cost	$11,000		
Less: Market adjustment—trading securities	(500)	$10,500	
Investment in available-for-sale securities, at cost	$17,000		
Add: Market adjustment—available-for-sale securities	600	17,600	
Investment in held-to-maturity securities, at amortized cost		20,000	$48,100
Stockholders' Equity:			
Add: Unrealized increase in value of available-for-sale securities		$ 600	

Eastwood Inc.
Income Statement (Partial)
For the Year Ended December 31, 2002

Other expenses and losses:		
Unrealized loss on trading securities		$ 500

At the end of 2003, similar adjustments must be made to reflect changes in fair value. Assume the following fair market values at the end of 2003:

Security	Classification	Cost	Fair Value Dec. 31, 2003
1	Trading	$ 8,000	$ 7,700
2	Trading	3,000	3,600
3	Available-for-sale	5,000	6,500
4	Available-for-sale	12,000	10,700
5	Held-to-maturity	20,000	20,700

By the end of 2003, the trading securities portfolio had increased to a value of $11,300 ($7,700 + $3,600). Comparing this amount to the historical cost of $11,000 indicates that Market Adjustment—Trading Securities should have a debit balance of $300. Because its current balance is a $500 credit (carried over from 2002), an adjusting entry must be made. The adjusting entry is as follows:

Market Adjustment—Trading Securities	800	
Unrealized Gain on Trading Securities		800

The balance in Market Adjustment—Trading Securities, which appears below in T-account form, would be added to Investment in Trading Securities and disclosed on the balance sheet.

Market Adjustment—Trading Securities

		12/31/02 Bal.	500
12/31/03 Adj.	800		
12/31/03 Bal.	300		

At the end of 2003, the value of the available-for-sale securities has decreased from $17,600 to $17,200. Because fair value now exceeds historical cost by $200, the market adjustment account should have a $200 debit balance. Its current balance, carried over from 2002, is $600 (debit). The journal entry made at the end of 2003 to adjust the account is as follows:

Unrealized Increase/Decrease in Value of Available-for-Sale Securities	400	
Market Adjustment—Available-for-Sale Securities		400

The effect on the market adjustment—available-for-sale securities account is reflected in the following T-account. Again, no adjustment is made for changes in the value of held-to-maturity securities.

Market Adjustment—Available-for-Sale Securities

12/31/02 Bal.	600		
		12/31/03 Adj.	400
12/31/03 Bal.	200		

The financial statements for Eastwood Inc. at the end of 2003 would include the effects of each of the above adjusting entries as shown in Exhibit 14–12.

EXHIBIT 14-12 | Financial Statement Disclosure of Securities

Eastwood Inc.
Balance Sheet (Partial)
December 31, 2003

Assets:

Investment in trading securities, at cost...................................	$11,000	
Add: Market adjustment—trading securities.............................	300	$11,300
Investment in available-for-sale securities, at cost....................	$17,000	
Add: Market adjustment—available-for-sale securities.............	200	17,200
Investment in held-to-maturity securities, at amortized cost		20,000 $48,500

Stockholders' Equity:

Add: Unrealized increase in value of available-for-sale securities	$ 200

Eastwood Inc.
Income Statement (Partial)
For the Year Ended December 31, 2003

Other revenues and gains:

Unrealized gain on trading securities..	$ 800

Accounting for Permanent Declines in the Value of Securities

Sometimes the fair value of investments declines due to economic circumstances that are unlikely to improve. For example, in the late 1980s the value of numerous savings and loan stocks decreased significantly without much expectation that they would ever recover. If a decline in the market value of an individual security is judged to be permanent, regardless of whether the security is debt or equity and regardless of whether it is being accounted for as a trading, available-for-sale, held-to-maturity, or equity method security, the cost basis of that security should be reduced by crediting the investment account rather than a market adjustment account. In addition, the write-down should be recognized as a loss and charged against current income. The new cost basis for the security may not be adjusted upward to its original cost for any subsequent increases in market value. If, however, the security is classified as a trading security or an available-for-sale security, a market adjustment account may be used to record future increases and decreases in value.

SALE OF SECURITIES

Account for the sale of securities.

When securities are sold, an entry must be made to remove the carrying value of the security from the investor's books and to record the receipt of cash. The difference between the carrying value and the cash received is a realized gain or loss. For trading and available-for-sale securities, the carrying value will be equal to the security's original cost. The carrying value of held-to-maturity and equity method securities will change as any premium or discount is amortized (in the case of held-to-maturity securities) or when the book value of the investee changes (in the case of equity method securities).

How does the market adjustment account come into play when a security is sold? Simply put—it does not. The market adjustment account is adjusted only at the end of each accounting period prior to the issuance of financial statements. The market adjustment account is used to reflect the fair value of the securities portfolio as of the end of the period; it is not to be associated with transactions that are measuring the amount of realized gains or losses. This approach makes practical sense if you think of a large company with an investment portfolio containing several hundred different securities. The significant effort required to associate a specific portion of the market adjustment account with each individual security (and to maintain this identification as hundreds or even thousands of securities are traded during the year) would not result in any improvement in the reported financial result.

At this point, it is important to distinguish between a realized and an unrealized gain or loss. A realized gain or loss occurs when an arm's-length transaction has occurred and a security has actually been sold. When the sale occurs, any difference between the carrying value of the security and the selling price is recognized on the income statement.

An unrealized gain or loss arises when the market value of a security changes, yet the security is still being held by the investor. As discussed previously, these unrealized gains and losses may or may not be recognized, depending upon the security's classification.

STOP & THINK What is the difference between realized and recognized?

In the case of a debt security, an entry must be made prior to recording the sale to record any interest earned to the date of the sale and to amortize any premium or discount. For example, continuing the Silmaril Technologies example from page 803, assume that the debt securities are sold on April 1, 2003, for $103,000, which includes accrued interest of $2,500. The carrying value of the debt securities on April 1, 2003, is $105,248. Interest revenue of $2,105 ($105,248 × .08 × $\frac{3}{12}$) would be recorded, and a receivable relating to interest of $2,500 would be established. The investment account would be reduced by $395 to reflect the amortization of the premium for the three-month period between January 1 and April 1.

Interest Receivable	2,500	
Investment in Held-to-Maturity Securities		395
Interest Revenue		2,105

A second entry would remove the book value of the investment from Silmaril's books, record the receipt of cash of $103,000, eliminate the Interest Receivable balance, and record a loss equal to the difference between the investment's carrying value and the amount of cash received (net of interest).

Cash	103,000	
Realized Loss on Sale of Securities	4,353	
Interest Receivable		2,500
Investment in Held-to-Maturity Securities		104,853

These two entries could easily be combined into a single journal entry:

Cash	103,000	
Realized Loss on Sale of Securities	4,353	
Investment in Held-to-Maturity Securities		105,248
Interest Revenue		2,105

7

Record the transfer of securities between categories.

TRANSFERRING SECURITIES BETWEEN CATEGORIES

On occasion, management will change its intentions with respect to holding certain securities. For example, a company may originally purchase securities for the purpose of making effective use of excess cash; subsequently, the company may decide to pursue a long-term business relationship with the investee. As a result, the company may reclassify the security from a trading security to an available-for-sale security. In addition, a company may initially purchase an equity security as a short-term investment and subsequently elect to increase its ownership interest to the point where the equity method is appropriate. This section of the chapter discusses the procedures employed when a security is transferred between categories as described in FASB Statement No. 115.

Transferring Debt and Equity Securities Between Categories

Under the provisions of FASB Statement No. 115, if a company reclassifies a security, the security is accounted for at the fair value at the time of the transfer.[14] Because these securities are maintained on the books at their historical cost, the historical cost of the securities must be removed from the "old" category, and the securities are recorded in the "new" category at their current fair value. The change in value that has occurred is accounted for differently depending on the category being transferred to and the category being transferred from. Exhibit 14–13 summarizes how these unrealized gains and losses are accounted for in each category.

EXHIBIT 14–13 | Accounting for Transfers of Securities Between Categories

Transferred	Treatment of the Change in Value
From Trading	Any unrealized change in value not previously recognized will be recognized in net income in the current period. Previously recognized changes in value are not to be reversed.
To Trading	Any unrealized change in value not previously recognized will be recognized in net income in the current period.
From Held-to-Maturity to Available-for-Sale	Recognize any unrealized change in value in a stockholders' equity account.
From Available-for-Sale to Held-to-Maturity	Any unrealized change in value recorded in a stockholders' equity account is to be amortized over the security's remaining life using the effective-interest method.[15]

To illustrate each type of transfer, we will use the data from the Eastwood Inc. example as of December 31, 2003 (page 814). Recall that on that date Eastwood Inc. had the following securities:

Security	Classification	Cost	Fair Value Dec. 31, 2003
1	Trading	$ 8,000	$ 7,700
2	Trading	3,000	3,600
3	Available-for-sale	5,000	6,500
4	Available-for-sale	12,000	10,700
5	Held-to-maturity	20,000	20,700

During 2004, Eastwood Inc. elects to reclassify certain of its securities. The category being transferred from and to along with the fair value for each security on the date of the transfer is as follows:

Security	Transferring From:	Transferring to:	Fair Value Date of Transfer
2	Trading	Available-for-sale	$ 3,800
3	Available-for-sale	Held-to-maturity	5,900
4	Available-for-sale	Trading	10,300
5	Held-to-maturity	Available-for-sale	20,400

The different types of reclassifications are illustrated in the following sections.

14 *Statement of Financial Accounting Standards No. 115,* par. 15.
15 Ibid., par. 15d.

FROM THE TRADING SECURITY CATEGORY Assume that Eastwood elects to reclassify Security 2 from a trading security to an available-for-sale security. The security's historical cost is removed from the trading security classification, along with the associated $600 market adjustment (as of December 31, 2003), and the security is recorded at its current fair market value as an available-for-sale security. The $200 difference between the fair value as of December 31, 2003, and the fair value at the date of transfer is recorded as an unrealized gain. The following journal entry illustrates this procedure:

Investment in Available-for-Sale Securities	3,800	
Market Adjustment—Trading Securities		600
Unrealized Gain on Transfer of Securities		200
Investment in Trading Securities		3,000

Alternatively, Eastwood could have recognized the $800 difference between fair value and historical cost as an unrealized gain at the time of the transfer and made an adjustment to the market adjustment—trading securities account at the end of the period. The net result of either approach would be the same. In the remainder of the examples that follow, we will adjust the market adjustment account on the date of the transfer.

INTO THE TRADING SECURITY CATEGORY Suppose Eastwood Inc. elects to reclassify Security 4 from an available-for-sale security to a trading security. Recall that unrealized holding gains and losses associated with available-for-sale securities are recorded in the stockholders' equity account: Unrealized Increase/Decrease in Value of Available-for-Sale Securities. The amount in this account associated with Security 4 is removed, and the security is recorded as a trading security at its current fair market value.

Investment in Trading Securities	10,300	
Market Adjustment—Available-for-Sale Securities	1,300	
Unrealized Loss on Transfer of Securities	1,700	
Unrealized Increase/Decrease in Value of Available-for-Sale Securities		1,300
Investment in Available-for-Sale Securities		12,000

With this journal entry, Security 4 is recorded as a trading security at its current fair market value of $10,300. The carrying value of Security 4 (historical cost less market adjustment) as an available-for-sale security is eliminated from the company's books. Because the security is now classified as a trading security, all changes in fair value should be reflected in the income statement. Thus, this journal entry transfers the unrealized changes in value from the stockholders' equity account to the income statement and recognizes the additional $400 decline in value since the last balance sheet date. The amount of the unrealized increase/decrease is determined by comparing the security's historical cost, obtained from subsidiary records, with its carrying value as of December 31, 2003. In this example, the unrealized decrease is $1,300 ($12,000 less $10,700). The final result of this journal entry is to reclassify the security and to record on the income statement the decline in fair value since the purchase of the security.

FROM THE HELD-TO-MATURITY TO THE AVAILABLE-FOR-SALE CATEGORY While transfers of debt securities from the held-to-maturity category should not occur often, they will happen on occasion. FASB Statement No. 115 includes a number of circumstances that might lead a firm to reclassify a held-to-maturity security.[16] In this instance, Eastwood Inc. has elected to reclassify Security 5 from a security being held until maturity to one that is available to be sold. Recall that Security 5's fair value on the date of the transfer is $20,400. The security is recorded as an available-for-sale security at its current fair value with any difference between its carrying cost and its fair value being recorded as an unrealized increase/decrease in value of available-for-sale securities. The following journal entry will accomplish these objectives:

16 Ibid., par. 8.

Investment in Available-for-Sale Securities	20,400	
Unrealized Increase/Decrease in Value of Available-for-Sale Securities		400
Investment in Held-to-Maturity Securities		20,000

Because Security 5 was originally classified as held-to-maturity, no adjustment has been made in prior periods to record any changes in value. Thus, there is no market adjustment account related to this transfer.

FROM THE AVAILABLE-FOR-SALE TO THE HELD-TO-MATURITY CATEGORY
Eastwood Inc. elects to reclassify Security 3 from one that is available to be sold to a security that will be held until maturity. Recall that Security 3 was originally purchased for $5,000, had a fair value on December 31, 2003, of $6,500, and has a fair value on the date of the transfer of $5,900. The following entry should be made:

Investment in Held-to-Maturity Securities	5,900	
Unrealized Increase/Decrease in Value of Available-for-Sale Securities	600	
Investment in Available-for-Sale Securities		5,000
Market Adjustment—Available-for-Sale Securities		1,500

The debit to Unrealized Increase/Decrease in Value of Available-for-Sale Securities reflects the fact that the security has declined in value by $600 since the last balance sheet date. The $1,500 credit to the market adjustment account removes the previously recorded increase in value for this security ($6,500 – $5,000) while it was classified as available-for-sale. The combination of these amounts illustrates that Security 3 has increased in value by $900 ($5,900 – $5,000) since its acquisition.

Once the security is classified as held-to-maturity, increases and decreases in its value will not be reflected in the financial statements. The treatment of the $900 unrealized increase in value (gain) existing at the transfer date is a bit of problem because, on the one hand, the gain can't be ignored because it occurred while the security was classified as available-for-sale, but, on the other hand, the gain would never have been recognized if the security had always been classified as held-to-maturity. FASB Statement No. 115 states that those unrealized increases and decreases in value that have been recorded to date (while the security has been available to be sold) must be amortized over the remaining life of the security using the effective-interest method and offset against (or added to) any interest revenue received on the debt security. The unamortized balance of an unrealized gain or loss continues to be reported as part of "Accumulated other comprehensive income" in the equity section of the balance sheet.[17] In addition, because the security is now classified as held-to-maturity, the company must also begin amortizing it down to its eventual maturity value. For example, if Security 3 has a maturity value of $4,500, then Eastwood Inc. must amortize, as a premium, the $1,400 difference between the security's carrying value and its maturity value ($5,900 less $4,500), as discussed previously. Thus, the interest revenue from Security 3 will be adjusted for two types of amortization: the unrealized gain (increasing interest revenue) that existed at the transfer date and the carrying value to the maturity value (reducing interest revenue).

 Based on having just read about how to transfer securities to and from each category, can you specify a set of rules that will apply to every transfer? For example, Rule #1 could be that every security being transferred is recorded at its current market value. What else?

Explain the proper classification and disclosure of investments in securities.

CLASSIFICATION AND DISCLOSURE

We have discussed the treatment of the gains and losses (both realized and unrealized) associated with selling, valuing, and/or reclassifying securities. Gains and losses from the sale of securities and unrealized gains and losses from changes in value while holding trading securities are disclosed on the income statement as "Other revenues and

17 Ibid., par. 15d.

expenses." Unrealized gains and losses on available-for-sale securities are disclosed in a separate account in stockholders' equity. As with any asset, significant permanent declines in the value of investments are recognized as a loss in the year they occur. BERKSHIRE HATHAWAY, for example, includes a one-line summary of all of its realized gains and losses for the year in its income statement and discloses further details in the notes. The relevant note disclosure for Berkshire Hathaway for 1998 is included in Exhibit 14–14. Note that Berkshire Hathaway has cumulative unrealized gains on its debt and equity investments of almost $29 billion. How is it possible that none of this unrealized amount shows up on Berkshire Hathaway's income statement? The company classifies its securities as either held-to-maturity (for debt) or available-for-sale (in the case of equity).

EXHIBIT 14–14 | Berkshire Hathaway–Note Disclosure Relating to Investments

(3) INVESTMENTS IN SECURITIES WITH FIXED MATURITIES

The amortized cost and estimated fair values of investments in securities with fixed maturities as of December 31, 1998 and 1997 are as follows (in millions):

December 31, 1998 Estimated	Amortized Cost	Gross Unrealized Gains	Gross Unrealized Losses	Fair Value
Bonds:				
U.S. Treasury securities and obligations of U.S. government corporations and agencies	$ 2,518	$10	—	$ 2,528
Obligations of states, municipalities and political subdivisions	9,574	73	—	9,647
Obligations of foreign governments	2,864	—	—	2,864
Corporate bonds	4,609	—	—	4,609
Redeemable preferred stocks	359	3	(7)	355
Mortgage-backed securities	1,235	8	—	1,243
	$21,159	$94	$(7)	$21,246

(4) INVESTMENTS IN EQUITY SECURITIES AND OTHER INVESTMENTS

Data with respect to the consolidated investment in equity securities and other investments are shown below. Amounts are in millions.

December 31, 1998	Cost	Unrealized Gains (Losses)	Fair Value
Common stock of:			
American Express Company	$ 1,470	$ 3,710	$ 5,180
The Coca-Cola Company	1,299	12,101	13,400
The Gillette Company	600	3,990	4,590
Other equity securities	5,889	9,062	14,951
Other investments	1,736	(96)	1,640
	$10,994	$28,767	$39,761

(5) REALIZED INVESTMENT GAINS (LOSSES)

Realized gains (losses) from sales and redemptions of investments are summarized below (in millions):

	1998	1997	1996
Equity securities and other investments—			
Gross realized gains	$2,087	$ 739	$2,379
Gross realized losses	(272)	(23)	(36)
Securities with fixed maturities —			
Gross realized gains	602	396	144
Gross realized losses	(2)	(6)	(3)
	$2,415	$1,106	$2,484

While the unrealized increases associated with the available-for-sale securities are not reported on the income statement, they are included in the computation of comprehensive income. Berkshire Hathaway's statement of comprehensive income is included in Exhibit 14–15.

EXHIBIT 14–15 | Berkshire Hathaway–Statement of Comprehensive Income for 1998

Net earnings		$2,830
Unrealized depreciation of investments	$ 3,011	
Reclassification adjustment for appreciation included in net earnings	(2,415)	
Income taxes and minority interests	(284)	
Other comprehensive income		312
Total comprehensive income		$3,142

Appropriate presentation of individual securities on the balance sheet depends on the intent of management. If management intends or is willing to sell the securities within one year or the current operating cycle, whichever is longer, the security is classified as a current asset. Because trading securities are short term by definition, they are always classified as current. Held-to-maturity securities are always classified as noncurrent unless they mature within a year. Available-for-sale securities are classified as current or noncurrent depending on the intentions of management. Because banks and other financial institutions do not present classified balance sheets, determining the current and noncurrent status of investments is not an issue.

Under previous accounting standards, the buying and selling of securities was classified as an investing activity on the statement of cash flows. However, with FASB Statement No. 115, cash flows associated with the purchase, sale, and redemption of trading securities are now reported as an operating activity.

In addition to the disclosure required in the income statement, balance sheet, and statement of cash flows, FASB Statement No. 115 requires disclosure in the notes to the financial statements. Specifically, FASB Statement No. 115 requires the following additional disclosures:

1. Trading securities:
   - The change in net unrealized holding gain or loss that is included in the income statement.
2. Available-for-sale securities:
   - Aggregate fair value, gross unrealized holding gains and gross unrealized holding losses, and amortized cost basis by major security type. For debt securities the company should disclose information about contractual maturities.
   - The proceeds from sales of available-for-sale securities and the gross realized gains and losses on those sales and the basis on which cost was determined in computing realized gains and losses.
   - The change in net unrealized holding gain or loss on available-for-sale securities that has been included in stockholders' equity during the period.
3. Held-to-maturity securities:
   - Aggregate fair value, gross unrealized holding gains and gross unrealized holding losses, and amortized cost basis by major security type. In addition, the company should disclose information about contractual maturities.
4. Transfers of securities between categories:
   - Gross gains and losses included in earnings from transfers of securities from available-for-sale into the trading category.

- For securities transferred from held-to-maturity, the company should disclose the amortized cost amount transferred, the related realized or unrealized gain or loss, and the reason for transferring the security.

This required disclosure is illustrated in Exhibit 14–16. In this exhibit, the note on investment securities taken from the 1998 annual report of WELLS FARGO & COMPANY, a major company in the banking industry, shows the cost, fair value, and unrealized gains and losses. In addition, the narrative discloses the realized gains and losses occurring during the year. Finally, Wells Fargo details the maturity and yields of its held-to-maturity securities portfolio.

EXHIBIT 14–16 | Wells Fargo—Note Disclosure for Investment Securities

NOTE 4 SECURITIES AVAILABLE FOR SALE

The following table provides the cost and fair value for the major components of securities available for sale carried at fair value (there were no securities held to maturity at the end of the last three years):

(in millions)

December 31,	1997				1998			
	Cost	Estimated unrealized gross gains	Estimated unrealized gross losses	Estimated fair value	Cost	Estimated unrealized gross gains	Estimated unrealized gross losses	Estimated fair value
Securities of U.S. Treasury and federal agencies	$ 3,260	$ 45	$18	$ 3,287	$ 3,594	$ 38	$ 6	$ 3,626
Securities of U.S. states and political subdivisions	1,683	115	4	1,794	1,652	76	2	1,726
Mortgage-backed securities:								
Federal agencies	20,539	293	28	20,804	18,203	369	20	18,552
Private collateralized mortgage obligations (1)	3,420	29	9	3,440	2,646	21	13	2,654
Total mortgage-backed securities	23,959	322	37	24,244	20,849	390	33	21,206
Other	1,879	41	21	1,899	729	18	3	744
Total debt securities	30,781	523	80	31,224	26,824	522	44	27,302
Marketable equity securities	386	396	9	773	308	265	3	570
Total	$31,167	$919	$89	$31,997	$27,132	$787	$47	$27,872

	December 31, 1996	
	Cost	Estimated fair value
Securities of U.S. Treasury and federal agencies	$ 3,998	$ 4,017
Securities of U.S. states and political subdivisions	928	962
Mortgage-backed securities:		
Federal agencies	19,694	19,834
Private collateralized mortgage obligations (1)	3,403	3,403
Total mortgage-backed securities	23,097	23,237
Other	844	844
Total debt securities	28,867	29,060
Marketable equity securities	374	692
Total	$29,241	$29,752

EXHIBIT 14–16 | **(continued)**

Proceeds from the sale of securities in the securities available for sale portfolio totaled $11.1 billion, $9.8 billion and $5.9 billion in 1998, 1997 and 1996.

For the year ended December 31, 1998, the sales of securities in the securities available for sale portfolio resulted in a realized net gain of $169 million, comprised of realized gross gains of $209 million and realized gross losses of $40 million. The sales of securities in the securities available for sale portfolio resulted in a realized net gain of $99 million and $12 million, comprised of realized gross gains of $168 million and $184 million,

and realized gross losses of $69 million and $172 million for the year ended December 31, 1997 and 1996, respectively.

The following table provides the remaining contractual principal maturities and yields (taxable-equivalent basis) of debt securities available for sale. The remaining contractual principal maturities for mortgage-backed securities were allocated assuming no prepayments. Expected remaining maturities will differ from contractual maturities because borrowers may have the right to prepay obligations with or without penalties.

(in millions)
December 31, 1998 Remaining contractual principal maturity

	Total amount	Weighted average yield	Within one year		After one year through five years		After five years through ten years		After ten years	
			Amount	Yield	Amount	Yield	Amount	Yield	Amount	Yield
Securities of U.S. Treasury and federal agencies	$ 3,287	5.76%	$1,241	5.91%	$1,109	5.93%	$ 872	5.38%	$ 65	5.05%
Securities of U.S. states and political subdivisions	1,794	6.54	79	5.58	423	6.58	293	6.94	999	6.49
Mortgage-backed securities:										
Federal agencies	20,804	6.88	454	6.37	1,448	6.62	1,092	6.59	17,810	6.93
Private collateralized mortgage obligations	3,440	6.71	274	6.28	843	6.54	644	7.12	1,679	6.71
Total mortgage-backed securities	24,244	6.86	728	6.34	2,291	6.59	1,736	6.79	19,489	6.91
Other	1,899	7.04	100	6.51	813	5.57	695	8.17	291	7.58
ESTIMATED FAIR VALUE OF DEBT SECURITIES (1)	$31,224	6.73%	$2,148	6.06%	$4,636	6.28%	$3,596	6.72%	$20,844	6.90%
TOTAL COST OF DEBT SECURITIES	$30,781		$2,086		$4,430		$3,576		$20,689	

Compare the accounting for securities under U.S. GAAP with the international standard in IAS 39.

FYI: IOSCO is currently reviewing the IASC's core standards. IOSCO expects to announce in early 2000 whether it will endorse the IASC standards for use in global markets. At that point, the SEC will have to decide whether to follow the lead of IOSCO and allow foreign companies to list their shares in the United States while issuing financial statements based on international standards rather than U.S. GAAP.

INTERNATIONAL ACCOUNTING FOR INVESTMENT SECURITIES

In 1993, the International Organization of Securities Commissions (IOSCO), of which the U.S. SEC is a member, identified a list of 40 core accounting standards that must be included in any set of standards being seriously considered as the universal standard for international use. In 1995, IOSCO publicly announced that if the International Accounting Standards Committee (IASC) were to complete work on this core set of standards, then IOSCO would consider endorsing the IASC as the accepted international standard setter. The IASC established a goal of completing work on this core set of standards by 1998. In December 1998, the IASC finished its standard on financial instruments, IAS 39, thus completing the last part of its core standards project.

The provisions of IAS 39 are very similar to the corresponding accounting treatment under U.S. GAAP. IAS 39 covers the accounting for investment securities, as discussed in this chapter, as well as the accounting for derivatives, which will be explained in Chapter 18. The key provisions of IAS 39 that relate to the accounting for investment securities are as follows:

- All financial assets and financial liabilities are initially measured at cost.
- Subsequent to initial recognition, all financial assets are to be remeasured to fair value except for (1) debt securities intended to be held until maturity and (2) financial assets whose fair value cannot be reliably determined.
- After acquisition, financial liabilities are to be measured at the original recorded amount, less repayments and amortization.

- A company can report unrealized gains and losses in one of two ways: (1) in net income of the period or (2) in net income for unrealized gains and losses on trading securities and as part of equity for "nontrading" securities.

Note that the only significant difference between the provisions of IAS 39 and those of FASB Statement No. 115 is in the reporting of unrealized gains and losses. Under IAS 39, a company can choose the same treatment required under Statement No. 115, in which unrealized gains and losses on trading securities are recognized as part of net income but those on available-for-sale securities are recognized as part of stockholders' equity, or a company can elect to recognize all unrealized gains and losses as part of net income. Thus, it appears that the provisions of Statement No. 115, adopted in the United States in 1993, have now become the accepted international benchmark.

EXPANDED MATERIAL

In this section of the chapter, we deal with two variations of topics previously discussed. While changes in the classification of securities associated with FASB Statement No. 115 might be common, changes to and from the equity method are less common—and can be more complex. We discuss the complexities in this expanded material. In addition, to this point in the chapter we have talked about securities for which there is a tradeable market. In some instances, a company may invest in another firm in the form of a nonmarketable security. The most common example of this type of security would be a loan. In this expanded material we deal with the most complex issue associated with these nonmarketable securities—impairment.

10

Account for changes to and from the equity method of accounting for securities.

CHANGES IN CLASSIFICATION INVOLVING THE EQUITY METHOD

Variations in percentage of ownership caused by additional purchases or sales of stock by the investor or by the additional sale or retirement of stock by the investee may require a change in accounting method. For example, if the equity method has been used but subsequent events reduce the investment ownership below 20%, a change should be made to account for the security using the cost method, as either an available-for-sale or trading security, effective for the year when the reduced ownership occurs. Similarly, if the security had been accounted for as a trading or available-for-sale security, that is, the cost method is being used, but subsequent acquisitions increase the investment owner-ship to 20% or more, a change should be made to the equity method. The required accounting is different depending on whether the change is from or to the equity method.

A Change From the Equity Method

If an investment in equity securities has been accounted for under the equity method but circumstances dictate that a change in the security's classification is necessary, no adjust-ment to the investment account is needed. At the time of change, the carrying amount of the investment, as determined by the equity method for prior years, becomes the new basis when reclassifying the security. From that time forward, the investment account would not be adjusted for a proportionate share of investee earnings nor would any adjustments be made for additional depreciation or amortization of undervalued or unrecorded assets. Dividends received would be credited to a revenue account, not the investment account. Thus, once the equity method is no longer appropriate, the security is reclassified and accounted for using the cost method, as either a trading or available-for-sale security.

A Change to the Equity Method

Accounting for a change to the equity method is more complex. A retroactive adjustment is required for prior years to reflect the income that would have been reported using the equity method. This adjustment modifies the carrying value of the investment, in effect restating it on an equity basis, as if the equity method had been used during the previous periods that the investment was held. The offsetting entry for the adjustment is to Retained Earnings. From the date of change forward, the equity method is applied normally.

To illustrate, assume that MTI Corporation acquired stock of Excellcior Inc. over the three-year period 2000–2002 and originally accounted for the stock as available-for-sale. Purchase, dividend, and income information for these years are as follows (the purchases were made on the first day of each year):

| | | | Excellcior Inc. | |
Year	Percentage Ownership Acquired	Purchase Price*	Dividends Paid Dec. 31	Income Earned
2000............	10	$ 50,000	$100,000	$200,000
2001............	5	30,000	120,000	300,000
2002............	15	117,000	180,000	400,000

*Purchase price is equal to underlying book value at date of purchase.

The following entries would be made on the books of MTI Corporation to reflect the securities being classified as available-for-sale for the years 2000 and 2001:

2000

Jan. 1   Investment in Available-for-Sale Securities...   50,000
       Cash...   50,000
       To record purchase of 10% interest.

Dec. 31   Cash..   10,000
       Dividend Revenue...   10,000
       To record receipt of dividends from Excellcior Inc.
       (10% × $100,000).

2001

Jan. 1   Investment in Available-for-Sale Securities...   30,000
       Cash...   30,000
       To record purchase of 5% interest. (Total ownership
       interest is now 15%.)

Dec. 31   Cash..   18,000
       Dividend Revenue...   18,000
       To record receipt of dividends from Excellcior Inc.
       (15% × $120,000).

The additional acquisition of stock at the beginning of 2002 increases ownership to 30%, and a retroactive adjustment to change to the equity method must be made at the time of acquisition. The adjustment is for the difference between the revenue reported using the cost method and that which would have been reported if the equity method had been used. The adjustment would be computed as follows:

Year	Percentage Ownership	Revenue Recognized— Cost Method	Revenue Recognized— Equity Method	Required Retroactive Adjustment
2000	10	$10,000	$20,000*	$10,000
2001	15	18,000	45,000**	27,000
			Total adjustment	$37,000

*$200,000 × 10%
**$300,000 × 15%

The following entries would be made on the books of MTI Corporation to reflect the equity method for 2002:

2002
Jan. 1   Investment in Excellcior Inc. Stock 197,000
    Cash 117,000
    Investment in Available-for-Sale Securities 80,000
      To record purchase of 15% interest and reclassify securities.
      (Total ownership interest is now 30%.)

Jan. 1   Investment in Excellcior Inc. Stock 37,000
    Retained Earnings 37,000
      To retroactively reflect revenue for 2000 and 2001 for
      investment in Excellcior Inc. as if the equity method had
      been used.

Dec. 31   Investment in Excellcior Inc. Stock 120,000
    Income From Investment in Excellcior Inc. Stock 120,000
      To record 30% of income earned by Excellcior Inc.
      using equity method.

Dec. 31   Cash 54,000
    Investment in Excellcior Inc. Stock 54,000
      To record receipt of dividend from Excellcior Inc. using
      equity method (30% × $180,000).

Note that in this example the retroactive adjustment restates the investment account to an equity basis. From that point on, the equity method is applied in a normal manner. For simplicity, the illustration assumed a purchase price equal to the underlying book value at date of purchase. If this were not the case, an adjustment to income for depreciation and amortization would be needed as discussed in an earlier section of this chapter.

11

Account for the impairment of a loan receivable.

ACCOUNTING FOR THE IMPAIRMENT OF A LOAN

A common example of an investment for which there might be no market value would be loan receivables. Accounting for loan receivables is straightforward except for impairment.[18] Loans may arise by a company lending money to a borrower or by selling inventory and assets in return for a receivable. An entry to Loans Receivable is thus offset by a credit to Sales, Cash, or a surrendered asset. Financial institutions engage in such loans on a regular basis. A critical issue with these loans is when cost should be abandoned as the valuation basis. Many people in the financial community believe that a failure to abandon cost soon enough was a major contributor to the savings and loans crisis of the late 1980s and early 1990s.

The FASB addressed the valuation issues concerning investments in loan receivables in Statement No. 114, issued in May 1993. Because it is assumed that no market exists for these loans, the market valuations prescribed by FASB Statement No. 115 cannot apply.

---

18   See Chapter 6 for discussion of notes receivable.

Loans receivable are thus carried at a cost valuation unless evidence exists of a probable impairment. Statement No. 114 defines impairment as follows:

> A loan is impaired when, based on current information and events, it is probable that a creditor will be unable to collect all amounts due according to the contractual terms of the loan agreement.[19]

All amounts due according to contractual terms include both interest and principal payments. The term "probable" is applied in accordance with FASB No. 5, an assessment that future collections will not be made. Troubled debt restructuring is direct evidence of impairment; however, impairment may occur even though a formal restructuring has not occurred. If sufficient write-down has not previously been made, the restructuring will give rise to an additional decrease in the value of the loan receivable.

Measurement of Impairment

FASB Statement No. 114 specifies that a creditor shall measure impairment for loans with no market value at the present value of expected future cash flows discounted at the loan's effective interest rate, that is, the rate implicit in the original loan contract. The impairment is recorded by creating a valuation allowance account and charging the estimated loss to Bad Debt Expense. Thus, accounting for loans receivable is similar to accounting for accounts receivable except that the measurement method is more specifically defined by the FASB.

If a loan agreement is restructured in a troubled debt restructuring, the interest rate to be used to discount the new modified contract terms is based on the original contract rate, not the rate specified in the restructuring agreement. The selection of the discount rate to use was one of the difficult issues addressed by the FASB. The continued use of the original loan rate is consistent with the historic cost principle. The estimate of future cash flows is based on the creditor's best estimate based on reasonable and supportable assumptions and projections. Any future changes in the estimates or timing of future cash flow result in a recalculation of the impairment and an adjustment of the receivable and valuation allowance accounts with a charge or credit to Bad Debt Expense. Income arising from the passage of time will be recognized as part of interest revenue in each respective reporting period.

> **Caution!** Again, you will need to be comfortable with present values if you are to understand the computations in this section. See Appendix B if you need a review.

Example of Accounting for Loan Impairment

Assume Malone Enterprises reports a loan receivable from Stockton Co. in the amount of $500,000. The initial loan's repayment terms include a 10% interest rate plus annual principal payments of $100,000 on January 1 each year. The loan was made on January 1, 2000. Stockton made the $50,000 interest payment in 2000 but did not make the $100,000 principal payment nor the $50,000 interest payment for 2001. Malone is preparing its annual financial statements on December 31, 2001. The loan receivable has a carrying value of $550,000 including the $50,000 interest receivable for 2001. Stockton is having financial difficulty, and Malone has concluded that the loan is impaired. Analysis of Stockton's financial conditions indicates the principal and interest currently due can probably be collected, but it is probable that no further interest can be collected. The probable amount and timing of the collections is determined to be as follows:

December 31, 2002	$175,000
December 31, 2003	200,000
December 31, 2004	175,000
	$550,000

---

19 *Statement of Financial Accounting Standards No. 114,* "Accounting by Creditors for Impairment of a Loan," Norwalk, CT: Financial Accounting Standards Board, 1993, par. 8.

The present value at December 31, 2001, of the expected future cash flows discounted at 10% is $455,851, calculated as follows:

Date	Payment	Time of Discount	Table Value	Present Value @ 10%
December 31, 2002	$175,000	1 year	.9091	$159,093
December 31, 2003	200,000	2 years	.8264	165,280
December 31, 2004	175,000	3 years	.7513	131,478
Present value at December 31, 2001				$455,851

The impairment loss to be reported for 2001 is $94,149 or the $550,000 carrying value less the present value of $455,851. The journal entry to record the impairment would be as follows:

```
2001
Dec. 31   Bad Debt Expense.........................................................   94,149
              Allowance for Loan Impairment.........................................        94,149
```

The allowance would be reported as an offset to the loan receivable account.

If Stockton makes the payments as projected, the accounting for the cash received and the recognition of interest revenue is computed by constructing an amortization schedule similar to that illustrated below.

Interest Revenue From Loan Impairment

Date	(1) Loan Receivable Before Current Payment	(2) Allowance for Loan Impairment	(3) Net Receivable (1) – (2)	(4) Interest Revenue 10% × (3)	(5) Payment Received
Dec. 31, 2002	$550,000	$94,149	$455,851	$45,585	$175,000
Dec. 31, 2003	375,000	48,564*	326,436	32,644	200,000
Dec. 31, 2004	175,000	15,920**	159,080	15,920***	175,000
				$94,149	$550,000

*$94,149 – $45,585 = $48,564
**$48,564 – $32,644 = $15,920
***Rounded to close allowance account.

FYI: If you look closely, you will realize that the computations being made in the table above are conceptually identical to those done in the bond amortization table on page 804.

The entries on December 31, 2002, to record the receipt of the 2002 loan payment and to recognize interest revenue for the year would be as follows:

```
2002
Dec. 31   Cash...............................................................   175,000
              Loan Receivable................................................        175,000

          Allowance for Loan Impairment.................................   45,585
              Interest Revenue*...............................................        45,585
```

*Alternatively, Statement No. 114 allows a company to show all changes in present value as an adjustment to Bad Debt Expense in the same manner in which impairment initially was recognized.[20]

The T-accounts for the loan receivable and allowance accounts for 2001 and 2002 would appear as follows:

---

20 Ibid., par. 17b.

Loan Receivable			Allowance for Loan Impairment		
Beg. Bal. 550,000					12/31/01 94,149
	12/31/02 175,000		12/31/02 45,585		
Bal. 375,000					Bal. 48,564

Similar entries would be made at the end of 2003 and 2004 using the amounts included in the above amortization schedule. Note that computation of the amortization of the allowance for loan impairment account is identical to the computation for the amortization of Discount on Notes Receivable used in Chapter 6. If all payments are made as scheduled, the loan receivable and allowance accounts will both be closed out as of December 31, 2004.

REVIEW OF LEARNING OBJECTIVES

1 **Determine why companies invest in other companies.** Companies invest in the debt and equity securities of other businesses for a variety of reasons. The most common reason is to earn a return on idle cash. Other reasons for investing in other companies include establishing a business relationship through ownership, diversifying seasonal or industry risk, or gaining access to a company's research or technology. The intended outcome of investing in other companies is to enhance the overall return to shareholders.

2 **Understand the varying classifications associated with securities.** Securities are classified based on management's intent in holding the securities. If a firm invests in the equity securities of another company with the intent of influencing or controlling the decisions and activities of that company, the investment is accounted for using the equity method. Investments in debt and equity securities where the intent is to sell those securities should the need for cash arise or to take advantage of increases in value are classified as trading securities. Debt securities that are intended to be held until they mature are classified as held-to-maturity securities. All remaining investment securities are classified as available-for-sale.

3 **Account for the purchase of debt and equity securities.** Debt and equity securities are accounted for at cost, which includes brokerage fees, taxes, and other charges incurred at acquisition. In the case of debt securities, accrued interest presents an additional complexity. The amount of interest accrued prior to the purchase date must be accounted for separately from the cost of the investment.

4 **Account for the recognition of revenue from investments.** The method for recognizing revenue from investments depends on how the investment was originally classified. For debt securities, the revenue recognized is termed interest revenue. For trading and available-for-sale debt securities, the amount of interest revenue is a function of the stated rate of interest associated with the debt interest. In the case of held-to-maturity securities, any premium or discount associated with the initial purchase must be amortized and offset against interest revenue. For equity securities classified as trading or available-for-sale, dividends declared by the investee are recorded as revenue. If an investment is accounted for using the equity method, then the amount of revenue recognized is a function of the percentage of ownership. The net income of the investee is multiplied by the ownership interest and recorded as revenue.

5 **Account for the change in value of securities.** Temporary changes in the value of debt and equity securities classified as trading or available-for-sale are accounted for through the use of a market adjustment account. The use of this account results in securities being valued at fair market value on the balance sheet. For trading securities, the increase or decrease in value is reported on the income statement. In the case of available-for-sale securities, the change in value is disclosed as a separate component of stockholders' equity. Temporary changes in value for held-to-maturity securities and equity method securities are not recognized. If a decline in the value of an investment is judged to be permanent, the amount of the decline is recorded in current period's income and the investment's cost basis is adjusted.

6 **Account for the sale of securities.** When an investment is sold, its carrying value is removed from the books and the difference between carrying value and the cash received is recorded as a realized gain or loss. In the case of debt securities, an adjustment may be required to record interest revenue earned but not received prior to the sale and to amortize any premium or discount.

7 **Record the transfer of securities between categories.** On occasion, management may elect to reclassify certain of its investment securities. If the reclassification involves a movement to or from the trading classification, any change in value not previously recognized in income is recorded in the current period. If the reclassification is from held-to-maturity to available-for-sale, changes in value since the investment's acquisition are recorded as a separate component of stockholders' equity. If an available-for-sale security is reclassified as a held-to-maturity security, all previously recorded changes in value are amortized over the remaining life of the investment.

8 **Explain the proper classification and disclosure of investments in securities.** Realized gains and losses on the sale of investment securities are disclosed on the income statement in the period of the sale. Unrealized gains and losses on trading securities are also disclosed on the income statement. Unrealized increases and decreases on securities being classified as available-for-sale are disclosed in the stockholders' equity section of the balance sheet. Additional note disclosure relating to investment securities is

required, and the appropriate disclosure varies depending on the classification of the security.

9 **Compare the accounting for securities under U.S. GAAP with the international standard in IAS 39.** The IASC's standard on accounting for financial instruments, IAS 39, is the final item in the IASC's core standards project. The provisions of IAS 39 are very similar to those of FASB Statement No. 115; the exception is that under IAS 39 a company can elect to recognize all unrealized gains and losses—both for trading and available-for-sale securities—in net income for the period.

10 **Account for changes to and from the equity method of accounting for securities.** No complexities are associated with reclassifying a security from the equity method to either a trading or available-for-sale security. The investment's adjusted basis is used in computing future increases and decreases in value. When a security is reclassified to the equity method, retroactive adjustments are required to account for the investment as though the equity method had been used since the original purchase.

11 **Account for the impairment of a loan receivable.** On some occasions, particularly in the case of investment in the debt of other companies, a market value may not exist for the investment. In these instances, the investor must regularly assess the collectibility of the investment, and if it is determined that an "impairment" exists, an adjustment to the value of the receivable must be made. Impairment is measured by comparing the present value of expected future cash flows with the carrying value of the investment.

KEY TERMS

Available-for-sale securities 799
Control 805
Debt securities 798
Equity method 804

Equity method securities 799
Equity securities 798
Held-to-maturity securities 799

Parent company 806
Significant influence 805
Subsidiary company 806

QUESTIONS

1. Why might a company invest in the securities of another company?
2. What securities fall under the scope of FASB Statement No. 115?
3. What criteria must be met for a security to be classified as held-to-maturity?
4. What criteria must be met for a security to be classified as a trading security?
5. When computing the price to be paid for a debt security, the stated rate of interest is used to determine what value? How does the market or effective rate affect a debt security's value?
6. How does one compute the interest revenue to be recognized on a debt security if the effective-interest method is being used?
7. What is the general rule used for determining the appropriate method of accounting for investments in equity securities when the investor does not possess absolute voting control?
8. (a) What factors may indicate the ability of an investor owning less than a majority voting interest to exercise significant influence on the investee's operating and financial policies?
   (b) What factors may indicate the investor's inability to exercise significant influence?
9. How are changes in value disclosed on the financial statements for trading securities? available-for-sale securities? held-to-maturity securities?
10. What type of account is Market Adjustment? How is it disclosed on the financial statements?

11. How is a permanent decline in the value of investments recorded?
12. When transferring securities between categories under the provisions of FASB Statement No. 115, how is the transfer accounted for? At what value are the securities recorded?
13. How are trading, available-for-sale, and held-to-maturity securities disclosed on the balance sheet—as current or long-term assets?
14. Where are the cash flow effects of purchases and sales of equity securities disclosed?
15. What additional disclosures are recommended under FASB Statement No. 115 for trading, available-for-sale, and held-to-maturity securities?
16. What is the only significant difference between the provisions of IAS 39 and those of FASB Statement No. 115?

17. What adjustment is needed when a company switches (a) from the equity method and (b) to the equity method of valuing securities?
18. Why is the impairment of a loan accounted for differently from the decline in value of a debt security?

DISCUSSION CASES

CASE 14–1

BUT DO WE REALLY HAVE "MARK TO MARKET" ACCOUNTING NOW?

The movement toward the use of market value for investments has been given the label "mark to market." Previously, marketable equity securities were valued at the lower of cost or market. The shift to market, whether higher or lower than cost, is a significant departure from the past. Even though all investments classified as trading or available-for-sale will now be valued at market values, only market changes for trading securities will affect the income statement. To many accounting theorists, this is indeed a cop-out on the part of the FASB. These accountants reason that if market changes are going to be recognized on the balance sheet, they should be recognized on the income statement as well. This position was held by the 2 FASB members who voted against the issuance of Statement No. 115.

Evaluate the rationale for this compromise position. What arguments for the two different approaches (income and equity) do you think are most persuasive and why? What future events could cause standard setters to revise this approach?

CASE 14–2

LET'S MAXIMIZE PROFITS THROUGH FASB STATEMENT NO. 115.

FASB Statement No. 115 is another example of the Board's emphasis on the balance sheet as contrasted with the income statement. As treasurer of Diamond Instrument, you desire to maximize income over the short run. Diamond has had excess cash, and you have chosen to invest it in both marketable debt and equity securities. What classification policy could you follow to maximize your investment's impact on net income? How would you justify this policy to your auditors?

CASE 14–3

I'M NOT A BANK, SO WHY MUST I WORRY ABOUT FASB STATEMENT NO. 115?

Accounting methods of financial institutions, such as savings and loan companies and banks, were the major reasons the FASB studied the valuation issues relating to investments. FASB Statement No. 115, however, affects all companies that invest in marketable debt and equity securities. As controller of a retailing company, you are concerned with the classification of "trading security." How can you decide if the investments you have are trading or available-for-sale securities? In discussing this issue with other controllers, you are surprised to hear some of them indicate that Statement No. 115 really doesn't affect the reported income of nonfinancial institutions and that all securities for these companies are considered available-for-sale securities. Other controllers were concerned by this statement because this reasoning would make accounting for investments less conservative than it was before FASB Statement No. 115. Do you agree with either of these points of view and why? In what way has FASB Statement No. 115 made accounting for investments less conservative?

CASE 14–4

WHY IS 49% OWNERSHIP ENOUGH?

In 1986, THE COCA-COLA COMPANY borrowed $2.4 billion to purchase several large soft drink bottling operations. Then a separate company, COCA-COLA ENTERPRISES, was formed to bottle and distribute Coke throughout the country. The Coca-Cola Company sold 51% of Coca-Cola Enterprises to the public and retained a 49% ownership. The $2.4 billion debt incurred to finance the purchase was transferred to the balance sheet of Coca-Cola Enterprises.

While 49% ownership does not guarantee control, it does give The Coca-Cola Company significant influence over the bottling company. For example, The Coca-Cola Company determines the price at which it will sell concentrate to Coca-Cola Enterprises and reviews Coca-Cola Enterprises' marketing plan. In addition, The Coca-Cola Company's chief operating officer is chairman of Coca-Cola Enterprises, and 6 other current or former Coca-Cola Company officials are serving on Coca-Cola Enterprises' board of directors.

SOURCE: *The Wall Street Journal,* October 15, 1986, pp. A1 and A12.

1. From an accounting standpoint, what is the significance of owning more than 50% of a company's stock?
2. Why would The Coca-Cola Company elect to own less than 50% of its distribution network?
3. In the consolidation process, the parent's and the subsidiary's individual asset and liability account balances are added together and reported on the consolidated financial statements, whereas with the equity method, the net investment is reported as an asset on the investor company's balance sheet. Why would The Coca-Cola Company want to avoid consolidation?

CASE 14–5

WHICH METHOD OF ACCOUNTING FOR INVESTMENTS IS APPROPRIATE?

International Inc. owns or owns the stock of companies in countries all over the world. International is reviewing its methods of accounting for those companies and has asked you to provide input as to whether the cost method, the equity method, or consolidation is appropriate for each of the following subsidiaries. Provide justification for your suggestions.

1. Subsidiary #1: This subsidiary, MEOil, is an oil company located in the Middle East. A growing anti-American sentiment in the country in which the company is located has led International to remove all non-native employees. There is a growing fear that the government may nationalize MEOil. International Inc. owns 75% of the oil company.

2. Subsidiary #2: Ecological Inc., a company that produces environmentally safe products, has production facilities in over 10 states. The ownership of the company is widely held, with International Inc. holding the largest block of stock. International has succeeded in placing its president and vice president in 2 of the 5 board of directors seats of Ecological Inc. International owns 15% of Ecological Inc.'s outstanding stock.

3. Subsidiary #3: International Inc. recently purchased 100% of the outstanding stock of Harmon National Bank. This subsidiary represents International's first purchase of a non-manufacturing facility, and management has expressed concern about the comparability of the different accounting methods used by financial institutions.

4. Subsidiary #4: International has been involved in a takeover battle with Beatrix Inc. involving Campton Soups. Beatrix recently purchased 50% of the stock of Campton. International has owned 30% of Campton's stock for 5 years.

CASE 14–6

WHAT IS THE DIFFERENCE IN ACCOUNTING BETWEEN THE COST AND EQUITY METHODS?

Logical Corporation, a producer of medical products, disclosed the following investments in affiliates in the notes to its July 31, 2002, financial statements:

	2002	2001
Investments, at cost	$ 822,188	$ 50,000
Investments, at equity	1,677,181	2,009,647

Discuss the factors that determine whether Logical uses the cost or the equity method in accounting for its investment in affiliates. What events are recorded when the security is accounted for as an available-for-sale security? What events are recorded when the equity method is used? What does the investment account represent when the security is classified as available-for-sale? What does it represent using the equity method?

CASE 14–7

HOW DIFFERENT ARE INTERNATIONAL STANDARDS?

You have been approached about doing a consulting job for Choi Hung Company, which is based in southern China. Choi Hung reports its financial results using international accounting standards (IAS). The consulting job involves sorting through Choi Hung's purchases and sales of investment securities for the past 3 years to make sure that the reported results are in conformity with IAS. An acquaintance has advised you not to take this consulting job because "you are trained in U.S. GAAP and don't know anything about IAS." How might you respond?

CASE 14–8

HOW DOES INCREASED OWNERSHIP IN ANOTHER COMPANY AFFECT OUR BOOKS?

For the past 3 years Mapleton Corp. has maintained an investment (properly accounted for and reported upon) in Johnson Co. reflecting a 15% interest in the voting common stock of Johnson. The purchase price was $800,000, and the underlying net equity in Johnson at the date of purchase was $660,000. On January 2 of the current year, Mapleton purchased an additional 10% (total ownership interest is now 25%) of the voting common stock of Johnson for $1,100,000; the underlying net equity of the additional investment on January 2 was $1,000,000. Johnson has been profitable and has paid dividends annually since Mapleton's initial acquisition.

Discuss how this increase in ownership affects the accounting for and reporting on the investment in Johnson. Include in your discussion the adjustments, if any, that must be made to the amount shown prior to the increase in investment to bring the amount into conformity with U.S. GAAP. Also include how current and subsequent periods would be reported on.

EXERCISES

EXERCISE 14–9

RECORDING SECURITIES TRANSACTIONS

The following transactions of Rexton, Inc., occurred within the same accounting period.

(a) Purchased $120,000 U.S. Treasury 8% bonds, paying 102.5 plus accrued interest of $1,500. In addition, Rexton paid brokerage fees of $590. Rexton uses the revenue approach to record accrued interest on purchased bonds. Rexton classified this security as a trading security.

(b) Purchased 1,000 shares of Agler Co. common stock at $175 per share plus brokerage fees of $1,200. Rexton classifies this stock as an available-for-sale security.

(c) Received semiannual interest on the U.S. Treasury bonds.

(d) Sold 150 shares of Agler at $185 per share.

(e) Sold $20,000 of U.S. Treasury 8% bonds at 102 plus accrued interest of $275.

(f) Purchased a $15,000, 6-month certificate of deposit. The certificate is classified as a trading security.

Prepare the entries necessary to record the above transactions.

EXERCISE 14–10

ACCOUNTING FOR THE PURCHASE AND SALE OF SECURITIES

During January 2002, Aragorn Inc. purchased the following securities.

Security	Classification	No. of Shares	Total Cost
Gimli Corporation stock	Trading	500	$ 9,000
Legolas International Inc. stock	Available-for-sale	1,000	22,000
Glorfindel Enterprises stock	Available-for-sale	2,500	42,500
Mirkwood Co. bonds	Held-to-maturity	—	24,000
U.S. Treasury bonds	Trading	—	11,000

During 2002, Aragorn received interest from Mirkwood and the U.S. Treasury totaling $3,630. Dividends received on the stock held amounted to $1,760. During November 2002, Aragorn sold 200 shares of the Gimli stock at $17 per share and 250 shares of the Glorfindel stock at $19 per share.

Give the journal entries required by Aragorn to record the (1) purchase of the debt and equity securities; (2) receipt of interest and dividends during 2002; and (3) sale of the equity securities during November.

EXERCISE 14–11

ACCOUNTING METHODS FOR EQUITY SECURITIES

For each of the following independent situations, determine the appropriate accounting method to be used: cost or equity. For cost method situations, determine whether the security should be classified as trading or available-for-sale. For equity method situations, determine if consolidated financial statements would be required. Explain the rationale for your decision.

1. ATV Company manufactures and sells four-wheel recreational vehicles. It also provides insurance on its products through its wholly owned subsidiary, RV Insurance Company.

2. Buy Right Inc. purchased 20,000 shares of Big Supply Company common stock to be held as a long-term investment. Big Supply has 200,000 shares of common stock outstanding.

3. Super Tire Manufacturing Co. holds 5,000 shares of the 10,000 outstanding shares of nonvoting preferred stock of Valley Corporation. Super Tire considers the investment as being long-term in nature.

4. Takeover Company owns 15,000 of the 50,000 shares of common stock of Western Supply Company. Takeover has tried and failed to obtain representation on

Western's board of directors. Takeover intends to sell the securities if it cannot obtain board representation at the next stockholders' meeting, scheduled in 3 weeks.

5. Espino Inc. purchased 50,000 shares of Independent Mining Company common stock. Independent has a total of 125,000 common shares outstanding. Espino has no intention to sell the securities in the foreseeable future.

EXERCISE 14–12

INVESTMENT IN EQUITY SECURITIES

On January 10, 2002, Booker Corporation acquired 20,000 shares of the outstanding common stock of Atlanta Company for $800,000. At the time of purchase, Atlanta Company had outstanding 80,000 shares with a book value of $4 million. On December 31, 2002, the following events took place.

(a) Atlanta reported net income of $180,000 for the calendar year 2002.
(b) Booker received from Atlanta a dividend of $0.75 per share of common stock.
(c) The market value of Atlanta Company stock had temporarily declined to $40 per share.

Give the entries that would be required to reflect the purchase and subsequent events on the books of Booker Corporation, assuming (1) the security is classified as available-for-sale; and (2) the equity method is appropriate.

EXERCISE 14–13

INVESTMENT IN EQUITY SECURITIES—UNRECORDED GOODWILL

Alpha Co. acquired 20,000 shares of Beta Co. on January 1, 2001, at $12 per share. Beta Co. had 80,000 shares outstanding with a book value of $800,000. There were no identifiable undervalued assets at the time of purchase. Beta Co. recorded earnings of $360,000 and $390,000 for 2001 and 2002, respectively, and paid per-share dividends of $1.60 in 2001 and $2.00 in 2002. Assuming a 20-year straight-line amortization policy for goodwill, give the entries to record the purchase in 2001 and to reflect Alpha's share of Beta's earnings and the receipt of the dividends for 2001 and 2002.

EXERCISE 14–14

INVESTMENT IN EQUITY SECURITIES—MARKET VALUE DIFFERENT FROM BOOK VALUE

On January 3, 2002, McDonald Inc. purchased 40% of the outstanding common stock of Old Farms Co., paying $128,000 when the book value of the net assets of Old Farms equaled $250,000. The difference was attributed to equipment, which had a book value of $60,000 and a fair market value of $100,000, and to buildings, with a book value of $50,000 and a fair market value of $80,000. The remaining useful life of the equipment and buildings was 4 years and 12 years, respectively. During 2002, Old Farms reported net income of $80,000 and paid dividends of $50,000.

Prepare the journal entries made by McDonald Inc. during 2002 related to its investment in Old Farms.

EXERCISE 14–15

AMORTIZATION OF A PREMIUM ON A DEBT SECURITY

On January 1, 2002, Wilcox Incorporated purchased $500,000 of 10-year, 11% bonds when the market rate of interest was 8%. Interest is to be paid on June 30 and December 31 of each year.

1. Prepare the journal entry to record the purchase of the debt security, classified as held-to-maturity.
2. Prepare the journal entry to record the receipt of the first 2 interest payments, assuming that Wilcox accounts for the debt security as held-to-maturity and uses the effective-interest method.

EXERCISE 14–16

AMORTIZATION OF A DISCOUNT ON A DEBT SECURITY

On January 1, 2002, Cougar Creations Inc. purchased $100,000 of 5-year, 8% bonds when the effective rate of interest was 10%, paying $92,277. Interest is to be paid on July 1 and December 31.

1. Prepare an interest amortization schedule for the bonds.
2. Prepare the journal entries made by Cougar Creations on July 1 and December 31 of 2002 to recognize the receipt of interest and to amortize the discount.

EXERCISE 14–17

VALUATION OF A DEBT SECURITY

Using the information from Exercise 14–16, provide the journal entry that would be necessary to properly value the debt security if, on December 31, 2002, the bond's fair value was $96,500. Assume the security was initially classified as:

1. A trading security
2. An available-for-sale security
3. A held-to-maturity security

EXERCISE 14–18

TRADING SECURITIES

During 2002, Litten Company purchased trading securities as a short-term investment. The costs of the securities and their market values on December 31, 2002, are listed below:

Security	Cost	Market Value Dec. 31, 2002
A	$ 65,000	$ 75,000
B	100,000	54,000
C	220,000	226,000

At the beginning of 2002, Litten had a zero balance in the market adjustment—trading securities account. Before any adjustments related to these trading securities, Litten had net income of $300,000.

1. What is net income after making any necessary trading security adjustments? (Ignore income taxes.)
2. What would net income be if the market value of Security B were $95,000?

EXERCISE 14–19

ACCOUNTING FOR TRADING SECURITIES

During 2001, Sunshine Inc. purchased the following trading securities.

Security	Cost	Market Value Dec. 31, 2001
Wexler Co. common	$12,000	$14,000
10% U.S. Treasury notes	18,000	11,000
TexCo bonds	25,000	27,000

At the beginning of 2001, Sunshine had a zero balance in Market Adjustment—Trading Securities.

1. What entry would be made at year-end assuming the above values?
2. What entry would be made during 2002 assuming one-half of the Wexler Co. common stock is sold for $7,000?
3. Give the entry that would be made at the end of 2002 assuming the following situations.
   a. The market value of remaining securities is $42,000.
   b. The market value of remaining securities is $47,000.
   c. The market value of remaining securities is $55,000.

EXERCISE 14–20

DEBT AND EQUITY SECURITIES

American Steel Corp. acquired the following securities in 2002.

Security	Classification	Cost	Market Value Dec. 31, 2002
A	Trading	$10,000	$12,000
B	Trading	16,000	10,000
C	Available-for-sale	12,000	15,000
D	Available-for-sale	20,000	15,000
E	Held-to-maturity	20,000	22,000

At the beginning of 2002, American Steel had a zero balance in each of its market adjustment accounts.

1. What entry or entries would be made at the end of 2002 assuming the above market values?
2. If net income before any adjustments related to marketable securities was $100,000, what would reported income be after adjustments? (Ignore income taxes.)

EXERCISE 14–21

TEMPORARY AND PERMANENT CHANGES IN VALUE

The securities portfolio for Hill Top Industries contained the trading securities listed below.

Securities (Common Stock)	Initial Cost	Market Value Dec. 31, 2001	Market Value Dec. 31, 2002
Randall Co.	$10,000	$12,000	$15,000
Streuling Co.	7,000	4,000	2,000
Santana Co.	21,000	18,000	22,000

1. Assuming all changes in fair value are considered temporary, what is the effect of the changes in value on the 2001 and 2002 financial statements? Give the valuation entries for these years assuming that the market adjustment account has a $0 balance at the beginning of the year.
2. Assume that at December 31, 2002, management believed that the market value of the Streuling Co. common stock reflected a permanent decline in the value of that stock. Give the entries to be made on December 31, 2002, under this assumption.

EXERCISE 14–22

RECLASSIFICATION OF SECURITIES

Surhako Inc. had the following portfolio of securities at the end of its first year of operations.

Security	Classification	Cost	Year-End Market Value
A	Trading	$13,000	$18,000
B	Trading	20,000	22,000

1. Provide the entry necessary to adjust the portfolio of securities to its market value.
2. After adjusting the securities to market, Surhako elects to reclassify Security B as an available-for-sale security. On the date of the transfer, Security B's market value is $21,500. Provide the journal entry to reclassify Security B.

EXERCISE 14–23

RECLASSIFICATION OF SECURITIES

Bicknel Technologies Inc. purchased the following securities during 2001.

Security	Classification	Cost	Market Value (12/31/01)
A	Trading	$ 2,000	$ 4,000
B	Trading	7,000	6,000
C	Available-for-sale	18,000	16,000
D	Available-for-sale	5,000	4,000
E	Held-to-maturity	14,000	15,000

At the beginning of 2001, Bicknel Technologies had a zero balance in each of its market adjustment accounts. During 2002, after the 2001 financial statements had been issued, Bicknel determined that Security B should be reclassified as an available-for-sale security and Security C should be reclassified as a trading security. The market values on the date of the transfer are $5,500 for Security B and $17,000 for Security C.

Prepare the journal entries to:

1. Adjust the portfolio of securities to its market value at December 31, 2001.
2. Reclassify Security B as an available-for-sale security in 2002.
3. Reclassify Security C as a trading security in 2002.

EXERCISE 14–24

VALUATION OF SECURITIES

Bridgeman Paper Co. reported the following selected balances on its financial statements for each of the 4 years 2000–2003.

	2000	2001	2002	2003
Market adjustment—Trading securities	$0	$5,500	$3,750	$ (1,200)
Market adjustment—Available-for-sale securities	$0	(1,300)	900	1,350

Based on these balances, reconstruct the valuation entries that must have been made each year.

EXERCISE 14–25

ACCOUNTING FOR SECURITIES

During 2001, the first year of its operations, Soelberg Industries purchased the following securities.

Security	Classification	Cost	Market Value Dec. 31, 2001	Market Value Dec. 31, 2002
A	Trading	$22,000	$14,000	$ 9,000
B	Trading	7,000	10,000	11,000
C	Available-for-sale	16,000	15,000	16,000
D	Available-for-sale	20,000	25,000	12,000

During 2002, Soelberg sold one-half of Security A for $10,000 and one-half of Security D for $13,000.

Provide the journal entries required to:

1. Adjust the portfolio of securities to its market value at the end of 2001.
2. Record the sale of Security A and Security D.
3. Adjust the portfolio of securities to its market value at the end of 2002.

EXERCISE 14–26

SECURITIES AND THE STATEMENT OF CASH FLOWS

Indicate how each of the following transactions or events would be reflected in a statement of cash flows prepared using the indirect method. Each transaction or event is independent of the others. For items (a) and (d), assume that the balance in the market adjustment account was zero at the beginning of the year.

(a) At year-end, the trading securities portfolio has an aggregate cost of $185,000 and an aggregate fair value of $150,000.

(b) During the year, trading securities and available-for-sale securities were purchased for $50,000 and $70,000, respectively. The securities were paid for in cash.

(c) Securities on hand at the beginning of the period (cost $40,000; fair market value [FMV] $40,000) were sold for $62,000 cash.

(d) At year-end, the trading securities portfolio has an aggregate cost of $170,000 and an aggregate fair value of $190,000.

EXERCISE 14–27

INVESTMENT IN COMMON STOCK—CHANGING FROM THE EQUITY METHOD

Porter Co. purchased 50,000 shares of Cannon Manufacturing Co. common stock on July 1, 2001, at $16.50 per share, which reflected book value as of that date. Cannon Manufacturing Co. had 200,000 common shares outstanding at the time of the purchase. Prior to this purchase, Porter Co. had no ownership interest in Cannon. In its second quarterly statement, Cannon Manufacturing Co. reported net income of $168,000 for the 6 months ended June 30, 2001. Porter Co. received a dividend of $21,000 from Cannon on August 1, 2001. Cannon reported net income of $360,000 for the year ended December 31, 2001, and again paid Porter Co. dividends of $21,000. On January 1, 2002, Porter Co. sold 20,000 shares of Cannon Manufacturing Co. common stock for $17 per share and reclassified the remaining stock as available-for-sale. Cannon reported net income of $372,000 for the year ended December 31, 2002, and paid Porter Co. dividends of $12,000. Give all entries Porter Co. would make in 2001 and 2002 in regard to the Cannon Manufacturing Co. stock. Assume that the market price remained constant throughout the 2-year period.

EXERCISE 14–28

INVESTMENT IN COMMON STOCK—CHANGING FROM THE EQUITY METHOD

On January 1, 2001, Medproducts Inc. purchased 50% of Electronico, paying $600,000. On that date, Medproducts' net assets had a book value of $1,100,000. The difference between fair value and book value is attributed to goodwill and is amortized over 20 years. On January 1, 2002, Medproducts sold 80% of its ownership in Electronico (40% of the outstanding stock) for $575,000 and elected to reclassify the remaining stock as available-for-sale. Net income and dividends for 2001 and 2002 for Electronico are given below.

	2001	2002
Net income	$85,000	$100,000
Dividends	20,000	30,000

Give the required journal entries made by Medproducts relating to its investment in Electronico for the years 2001 and 2002 assuming no change in market value during the 2-year period.

EXERCISE 14–29

INVESTMENT IN COMMON STOCK—CHANGING TO THE EQUITY METHOD

Peterson Inc. purchased 15% of the outstanding common stock of Sunspot Co. on January 1, 2002, when Sunspot's net assets had a book value and fair value of $400,000. Peterson Inc. paid $75,000. Any excess of fair value over cost is attributable to goodwill. Goodwill, when amortized, is amortized over a 20-year period. On January 1, 2003, Peterson purchased an additional 15% of the outstanding stock of Sunspot, paying another $75,000. (Assume net assets' book and fair values are still $400,000.) Sunspot's reported income and dividends for 2002 and 2003 are given on the next page.

	2002	2003
Net income	$30,000	$50,000
Dividends	30,000	40,000

Prepare the journal entries made by Peterson during 2002 and 2003 related to its investment in Sunspot Co., including the adjusting entries necessary to reflect the change from an available-for-sale security to the equity method.

EXERCISE 14–30

INVESTMENT IN COMMON STOCK—CHANGING TO THE EQUITY METHOD

Devers Corporation purchased 5% of the 100,000 outstanding common shares of Milo Inc. on January 1, 2000, for a total purchase price of $7,500. Devers considers the Milo Inc. stock as being available-for-sale. Net assets of Milo Inc. at the time had a book and fair value of $150,000. Net income for Milo Inc. for the year ended December 31, 2000, was $50,000. Devers received dividends from Milo during the year of $1,500. There was no change of Devers' ownership of Milo Inc. during 2001, and Milo reported net income of $70,000 for the year ended December 31, 2001. Devers received dividends of $2,000 from Milo for that year. On January 1, 2002, Devers purchased an additional 20% of Milo Inc.'s common stock (20,000 shares) for a total price of $40,000. Milo Inc.'s net asset book and fair value at the time of the purchase was $200,000. For the year ended December 31, 2002, Milo Inc. reported net income of $100,000; Devers received dividends from Milo Inc. totaling $10,000 for the year ended December 31, 2002.

Prepare journal entries for Devers Corporation to reflect the preceding transactions, including adjusting entries necessary to reclassify the security from available-for-sale to the equity method of accounting for Devers Corporation's investment in Milo Inc.

EXERCISE 14–31

ACCOUNTING FOR THE IMPAIRMENT OF A LOAN

Starship Enterprises loaned $100,000 to Pikkard Inc. on January 1, 2001. The terms of the loan require principal payments of $20,000 each year for 5 years plus interest at 8%. The first principal and interest payment is due on January 1, 2002. Pikkard made the required payments during 2002 and 2003. However, during 2003 Pikkard began to experience financial difficulties, requiring Starship to reassess the collectibility of the loan. On December 31, 2003, Starship determines that the remaining principal payments will be collected, but the collection of interest is unlikely.

1. Compute the present value of the expected future cash flows as of December 31, 2003.
2. Provide the journal entry to record the loan impairment as of December 31, 2003.
3. Provide the journal entries for 2004 to record the receipt of the principal payment on January 1 and the recognition of interest revenue as of December 31, assuming that Starship's assessment of the collectibility of the loan has not changed.

PROBLEMS

PROBLEM 14–32

ACCOUNTING FOR TRADING SECURITIES

Fox Company made the following transactions in the common stock of NOP Company.

July 10, 2000	Purchased 10,000 shares at $45 per share.
Sept. 29, 2001	Sold 2,000 shares for $51 per share.
Aug. 17, 2002	Sold 2,500 shares for $33 per share.

The end-of-year market prices for the shares were as follows:

December 31, 2000 $47 per share
December 31, 2001 $39 per share
December 31, 2002 $31 per share

Instructions: Prepare the necessary entries for 2000, 2001, and 2002 assuming the NOP stock is classified as a trading security.

PROBLEM 14–33

RECORDING AND VALUING TRADING SECURITIES

Myers & Associates reports the following information on its December 31, 2000, balance sheet.

Trading securities (at cost)	$225,850	
Less: Market adjustment—Trading securities	2,260	$223,590

Supporting records of Myers' trading securities portfolio show the following debt and equity securities.

Security	Cost	Market Value
200 shares Conway Co. common	$ 25,450	$ 24,300
$80,000 U.S. Treasury 7% bonds	79,650	77,400
$120,000 U.S. Treasury 7½% bonds	120,750	121,890
Total	$225,850	$223,590

Interest dates on the treasury bonds are January 1 and July 1. Myers & Associates uses the revenue approach to record the purchase of bonds with accrued interest. During 2001 and 2002, Myers & Associates completed the following transactions related to trading securities.

2001

Jan. 1 Received semiannual interest on U.S. Treasury bonds.

Apr. 1 Sold $60,000 of the 7½% U.S. Treasury bonds at 102 plus accrued interest. Brokerage fees were $200.

May 21 Received dividend of $0.25 per share on the Conway Co. common stock. The dividend had not been recorded on the declaration date.

July 1 Received semiannual interest on U.S. Treasury bonds and then sold the 7% bonds at 97½. Brokerage fees were $250.

Aug. 15 Purchased 100 shares of Nieman Inc. common stock at $116 per share plus brokerage fees of $50.

Nov. 1 Purchased $50,000 of 8% U.S. Treasury bonds at 101 plus accrued interest. Brokerage fees were $125. Interest dates are January 1 and July 1.

Dec. 31 Market prices of securities were: Conway Co. common, $110; 7½% U.S. Treasury bonds, 101¾; 8% U.S. Treasury bonds, 101; Nieman Inc. common, $116.75.

2002

Jan. 2 Recorded the receipt of semiannual interest on the U.S. Treasury bonds.

Feb. 1 Sold the remaining 7½% U.S. Treasury bonds at 101 plus accrued interest. Brokerage fees were $300.

Instructions:

1. Prepare journal entries for the foregoing transactions and to accrue interest on December 31, 2001. Ignore any amortization of premium or discount on U.S. Treasury bonds. Give computations in support of your entries.

2. Show how trading securities would be presented on the December 31, 2001, balance sheet.

PROBLEM 14-34

ACCOUNTING FOR DEBT AND EQUITY SECURITIES

During 2002, Merz Company purchased 3,000 shares of Silko Company common stock for $16 per share and 2,000 shares of Monroe Company common stock for $33 per share. These investments are intended to be held as ready sources of cash and are classified as trading securities.

Also in 2002, Merz purchased 3,500 shares of Barclay Company common stock for $29 per share and $40,000 of treasury notes at 101. These securities are classified as available-for-sale.

During 2002, Merz received the following interest and dividend payments on its investments:

Silko Company	$1 per share dividend
Monroe Company	$3 per share dividend
Barclay Company	$2 per share dividend
Treasury notes	6% annual interest earned for 6 months

Market values of the securities at December 31, 2002, were as follows:

Silko Company	$20 per share
Monroe Company	$22 per share
Barclay Company	$27 per share
Treasury notes	102

On March 23, 2003, the 2,000 shares of Monroe common stock were sold for $17 per share. On June 30, 2003, the treasury notes were sold at 100.5 plus accrued interest.

Market values of remaining securities at December 31, 2003, were as follows:

Silko Company	$19 per share
Barclay Company	$32 per share

Instructions:

1. Prepare all 2002 and 2003 journal entries related to these securities.
2. Describe how the following items would be treated on Merz Company's statement of cash flows for the year ended December 31, 2003. Merz uses the indirect method of reporting cash flows from operating activities.
   a. Proceeds from the sale of Monroe shares and any realized gain or loss from the sale.
   b. Proceeds from the sale of the treasury securities and any realized gain or loss from the sale.
   c. Any unrealized gain or loss on the remaining securities.

PROBLEM 14-35

JOURNAL ENTRIES AND BALANCE SHEET PRESENTATION FOR INVESTMENTS IN SECURITIES

On December 31, 2000, Durst Company's balance sheet showed the following balances related to its securities accounts.

Trading securities	$155,000	
Less: Market adjustment—trading securities	(7,250)	$147,750
Available-for-sale securities	$108,000	
Add: Market adjustment—available-for-sale securities	10,000	118,000
Interest receivable—NYC Water bonds		1,250

Durst's securities portfolio on December 31, 2000, was made up of the following securities.

Security	Classification	Cost	Market
1,000 shares Herzog Corp. stock	Trading	$75,000	$76,250
800 shares Taylor Inc. stock	Trading	55,000	52,825
10% New York City Water bonds (interest payable semiannually on January 1 and July 1)	Trading	25,000	18,675
1,000 shares Martin Inc. stock	Available-for-sale	59,000	65,000
2,000 shares Outdoors Unlimited Inc. stock	Available-for-sale	49,000	53,000

During 2001, the following transactions took place.

Jan. 3   Received interest on the New York City Water bonds.

Mar. 1   Purchased 300 additional shares of Herzog Corp. stock for $22,950, classified as a trading security.

Apr. 15   Sold 400 shares of the Taylor Inc. stock for $69 per share.

May 4   Sold 400 shares of the Martin Inc. stock for $62 per share.

July 1   Received interest on the New York City Water bonds.

Oct. 30   Purchased 1,500 shares of Cook Co. stock for $83,250, classified as a trading security.

The market values of the stocks and bonds on December 31, 2001, are as follows:

Herzog Corp. stock	$76.60 per share
Taylor Inc. stock	$68.50 per share
Cook Co. stock	$55.25 per share
New York City Water bonds	$20,555
Martin Inc. stock	$61.00 per share
Outdoors Unlimited Inc. stock	$27.00 per share

Instructions:

1. Make all necessary journal entries for 2001, including any year-end accrual or adjusting entries.
2. Show how the marketable securities would be presented on the balance sheet at December 31, 2001. Assume that the available-for-sale securities are classified as current assets.

PROBLEM 14–36

JOURNAL ENTRIES FOR TRADING SECURITIES

During 2002 and 2003, the Kopson Co. made the following journal entries to account for transactions involving trading securities.

2002

(a) Nov. 1   Investment in Trading Securities—10% U.S. Treasury Bonds 106,883

     Cash 106,883

        To record the purchase of $100,000 of U.S. Treasury bonds at 103¼. Brokerage fees were $300. Interest is payable semiannually on January 1 and July 1.

(b) Dec. 31   Unrealized Increase/Decrease in Value of Available-for-Sale Securities 4,283

     Market Adjustment—Trading Securities 4,283

        To record the decrease in market value of the current marketable securities based on the following data.

	Cost	Market	Market Adjustment
Fleming Co. stock	$ 25,250	$ 23,350	$1,900 Cr.
Dobson Co. stock	32,450	33,950	1,500 Dr.
10% U.S. Treasury bonds	106,883	103,000	3,883 Cr.
Total	$164,583	$160,300	$4,283 Cr.

The beginning balance in Market Adjustment—Trading Securities was a $500 credit. There were no other entries in 2002.

2003

(c) Jan. 1   Cash 5,000

     Interest Revenue 5,000

        To record interest revenue for 6 months.

(d) July 1   Cash 5,000

     Interest Revenue 5,000

        To record interest revenue for 6 months.

(e) Dec. 6   Investment in Available-for-Sale Securities—Fleming Co. 25,250
                   Investment in Trading Securities—Fleming Co.   25,250
                        To reclassify Fleming Co. stock from trading securities
                        to available-for-sale securities. Market price was
                        $24,500 at the date of reclassification.

(f) Dec. 31   Unrealized Increase/Decrease in Value of Available-for-
                   Sale Securities 3,483
                   Market Adjustment—Available-for-Sale Securities   300
                   Market Adjustment—Trading Securities...................................   3,183
                        To record the decrease in market value of available-
                        for-sale securities based on the following data.

	Cost	Market	Market Adjustment
Dobson Co. stock...	$ 32,450	$ 32,650	$ 200 Dr.
10% U.S. Treasury bonds	106,883	103,500	3,383 Cr.
Fleming Co. stock...	25,250	24,950	300 Cr.
Total...	$164,583	$161,100	$3,483 Cr.

There were no other entries in 2003.

Instructions: For each incorrect entry, give the entry that should have been made. Assume the revenue approach is used. Ignore any premium or discount amortization on U.S. Treasury bonds.

PROBLEM 14–37

VALUATION OF EQUITY SECURITIES

The investment portfolio of Morris Inc. on December 31, 2001, contains the following securities.

- Opus Co. common, 3% ownership, 5,000 shares; cost, $100,000; market value, $95,000; classified as a trading security.
- Garrod Inc. preferred, 2,000 shares; cost, $40,000; market value, $43,000; classified as a trading security.
- Sherrill Inc. common, 30% ownership, 20,000 shares; cost, $1,140,000; market value, $1,130,000; classified as controlling investment.
- Jennings Co. common, 15% ownership, 25,000 shares; cost, $67,500; market value, $50,000; classified as an available-for-sale security.

Instructions:

1. Give the valuation adjustment required at December 31, 2001, assuming all investments were purchased in 2001 and none of the indicated declines in market value are considered permanent.
2. Assume the Jennings Co.'s common stock market decline is considered permanent. Give the valuation entry required at December 31, 2001, under this change in assumption.
3. Assume the market values for the long-term investment portfolio at December 31, 2002, were as follows:

Opus Co. common...	$ 102,000
Garrod Inc. preferred...	43,000
Sherrill Inc. common..	1,115,000
Jennings Co. common	45,000

Give the valuation entries at December 31, 2002, assuming that the investment categories remain the same and that all declines in 2001 and 2002 are temporary except for the 2001 decline in Jennings Co. stock.

PROBLEM 14–38

INVESTMENTS IN COMMON STOCK

Arroyo Inc. and the Bell Corp. each have 100,000 shares of no-par common stock outstanding. Universal Inc. acquired 10,000 shares of Arroyo stock for $5 per share and 25,000 shares of Bell stock for $10 per share in 1999. Both securities are being held as long-term investments. Changes in retained earnings for Arroyo and Bell for 2001 and 2002 are as follows:

	Arroyo Inc.	Bell Corp.
Retained earnings (deficit), January 1, 2001	$200,000	$(35,000)
Cash dividends, 2001	(25,000)	—
	$175,000	$(35,000)
Net income, 2001	40,000	65,000
Retained earnings, December 31, 2001	$215,000	$ 30,000
Cash dividends, 2002	(30,000)	(10,000)
Net income, 2002	60,000	25,000
Retained earnings, December 31, 2002	$245,000	$ 45,000
Market value of stock: December 31, 2001	$ 7.00	$ 12.00
December 31, 2002	6.50	15.00

Instructions: Give the entries required on the books of Universal Inc. for 2001 and 2002 to account for its investments.

PROBLEM 14–39

LONG-TERM INVESTMENTS IN STOCK—EQUITY METHOD

On January 1, 2002, Compustat Co. bought 30% of the outstanding common stock of Freelance Corp. for $258,000 cash. Compustat Co. accounts for this investment by the equity method. At the date of acquisition of the stock, Freelance Corp.'s net assets had a carrying value of $590,000. Assets with an average remaining life of 5 years have a current market value that is $130,000 in excess of their carrying values. The remaining difference between the purchase price and the value of the underlying stockholders' equity cannot be attributed to any tangible asset. Compustat Co. has a policy of amortizing goodwill over 20 years. At the end of 2002, Freelance Corp. reports net income of $180,000. During 2002, Freelance Corp. declared and paid cash dividends of $20,000.

Instructions: Give the entries necessary to reflect Compustat Co.'s investment in Freelance Corp. for 2002.

PROBLEM 14–40

INVESTMENT IN COMMON STOCK

On July 1 of the current year, Melissa Co. acquired 25% of the outstanding shares of common stock of International Co. at a total cost of $700,000. The underlying equity (net assets) of the stock acquired by Melissa was only $600,000. Melissa was willing to pay more than book value for the International Co. stock for the following reasons.

(a) International owned depreciable plant assets (10-year remaining economic life) with a current fair value of $60,000 more than their carrying amount.

(b) International owned land with a current fair value of $300,000 more than its carrying amount.

(c) Melissa believed International possessed enough goodwill to justify the remainder of the cost. Melissa's accounting policy with respect to goodwill is to amortize it over 20 years.

International Co. earned net income of $540,000 evenly over the current year ended December 31. On December 31, International declared and paid a cash dividend of $105,000 to common stockholders. Market value of Melissa's share of the stock at December 31 is $750,000. Both companies close their accounting records on December 31.

Instructions:

1. Compute the total amount of goodwill of International Co. based on the price paid by Melissa Co.
2. Prepare all journal entries in Melissa's accounting records relating to the investment for the year ended December 31 under the cost method of accounting, classifying the securities as available-for-sale.
3. Prepare all journal entries in Melissa's accounting records relating to the investment for the year ended December 31 under the equity method of accounting.

PROBLEM 14–41

INVESTMENT IN COMMON STOCK—FAIR MARKET VALUE LESS THAN BOOK VALUE

MMM Inc. purchased 40% of XYZ Co. on January 4, 2002, for $250,000 when XYZ's book value was $630,000. On that day, the market value of the net assets of XYZ equaled their book values with the following exceptions:

	Book	Market
Equipment	$185,000	$160,000
Buildings	30,000	50,000

The equipment has a remaining useful life of 10 years, and the building has a remaining useful life of 20 years. XYZ reported the following related to operations for 2002 and 2003:

	Net Income (Loss)	Dividends
2002	$75,000	$10,000
2003	(15,000)	5,000

Instructions: Provide the entries made by MMM Inc. relating to its investment in XYZ for the years 2002 and 2003.

PROBLEM 14–42

RECLASSIFICATION OF SECURITIES

One Tree Incorporated had the following portfolio of securities on December 31, 2001.

Security	Classification	Cost	Market Value Dec. 31, 2001
A	Trading	$14,000	$17,000
B	Trading	22,000	31,000
C	Available-for-sale	7,000	9,000
D	Available-for-sale	18,000	20,500
E	Available-for-sale	21,000	15,000
F	Held-to-maturity	50,000	51,000

The balances in the market adjustment accounts as of January 1, 2001, were as follows:

Market Adjustment—Trading Securities	$8,000 Dr.
Market Adjustment—Available-for-Sale Securities	2,500 Cr.

During 2002, One Tree Inc. determined that certain securities should be reclassified. Those reclassifications are as follows:

Security	Old Classification	New Classification	Market Value at Date of Reclassification
A	Trading	Available-for-sale	$18,000
C	Available-for-sale	Trading	8,500
D	Available-for-sale	Held-to-maturity	21,000
F	Held-to-maturity	Trading	48,000

Instructions:
1. Make the necessary journal entries to adjust One Tree's portfolio of securities to market value as of December 31, 2001.
2. Make the necessary journal entries to reclassify the securities in 2002.

PROBLEM 14–43

ACCOUNTING FOR MARKETABLE EQUITY SECURITIES

The Trans America Trust Co. owns both trading and available-for-sale securities. The following securities were owned on December 31, 2001.

Trading Securities:

Security	Shares	Total Cost	Market Value Dec. 31, 2001	Market Adjustment
Albert Groceries, Inc.	600	$ 9,000	$11,500	$2,500 Dr.
West Data, Inc.	1,000	27,000	18,000	9,000 Cr.
Steel Co.	450	9,900	10,215	315 Dr.
Total		$45,900	$39,715	$6,185 Cr.

Available-for-Sale Securities:

Security	Shares	Total Cost	Market Value Dec. 31, 2001	Market Adjustment
Dairy Products	2,000	$ 86,000	$ 90,000	$ 4,000 Dr.
Vern Movies, Inc.	15,000	390,000	365,000	25,000 Cr.
Disks, Inc.	5,000	60,000	80,000	20,000 Dr.
Total		$536,000	$535,000	$ 1,000 Cr.

The following transactions occurred during 2002.

(a) Sold 500 shares of West Data, Inc. for $9,500.
(b) Sold 200 shares of Disks, Inc., for $3,000.
(c) Transferred all shares of Albert Groceries, Inc., to the available-for-sale portfolio when the total market value was $12,900.
(d) Transferred the remaining shares of Disks, Inc., to the trading securities portfolio when the market price was $20 per share. These shares were subsequently sold for $18 per share.

At December 31, 2002, market prices for the remaining securities were as follows:

Security	Market Price per Share
Albert Groceries, Inc.	$22
West Data, Inc.	15
Steel Co.	21
Dairy Products	42
Vern Movies, Inc.	28

Instructions: Prepare all journal entries necessary to record Trans America Trust Co.'s marketable equity securities transactions and year-end adjustments for 2002. Assume all declines in market value are temporary.

PROBLEM 14–44

ACCOUNTING FOR LONG-TERM INVESTMENTS

On January 2, 2000, Brozo Company acquired 20% of the 200,000 shares of outstanding common stock of Newberry Corp. for $30 per share. The purchase price was equal to Newberry's underlying book value. Brozo plans to hold this stock to influence the activities of Newberry.

The following data are applicable for 2000 and 2001.

	2000	2001
Newberry dividends (paid Oct. 31)	$20,000	$24,000
Newberry earnings	70,000	80,000
Newberry stock market price at year-end	32	31

On January 2, 2002, Brozo Company sold 10,000 shares of Newberry stock for $31 per share. During 2002, Newberry reported net income of $60,000, and on October 31, 2002, Newberry paid dividends of $10,000. At December 31, 2002, after a significant stock market decline, which is expected to be temporary, Newberry's stock was selling for $22 per share. After selling the 10,000 shares, Brozo does not expect to exercise significant influence over Newberry, and the shares are classified as available-for-sale.

Instructions:

1. Make all journal entries for Brozo Company for 2000, 2001, and 2002, assuming the 20% original ownership interest allowed significant influence over Newberry.
2. Make the year-end valuation adjusting entries for Brozo Company for 2000, 2001, and 2002, assuming the 20% original ownership interest did not allow significant influence over Newberry.

PROBLEM 14–45

ACCOUNTING FOR A CHANGE TO THE EQUITY METHOD

On January 1, 2001, Beans Inc. paid $400,000 for 10,000 shares of Keller Company's voting common stock, which was a 15% interest in Keller. At this date, the net assets of Keller totaled $2 million. The fair values of Keller's identifiable assets and liabilities were equal to their book values. Beans did not have the ability to exercise significant influence over the operating and financial policies of Keller. Beans received dividends of $0.70 per share from Keller on October 1, 2001. Keller reported net income of $250,000 for the year ended December 31, 2001. The stock was classified as available-for-sale. Market price for the 10,000 shares was $450,000.

On July 1, 2002, Beans paid $1,500,000 for 30,000 additional shares of Keller Company's voting common stock, which represents a 25% interest in Keller. The fair value of Keller's identifiable assets, net of liabilities, was equal to their book values of $4,600,000. As a result of this transaction, Beans has the ability to exercise significant influence over the operating and financial policies of Keller. Beans received a dividend of $0.80 per share from Keller on April 1, 2002, and $1.35 per share from Keller on October 1, 2002. Keller reported net income of $300,000 for the year ended December 31, 2002, and $100,000 for the 6 months ended December 31, 2002. Beans amortizes goodwill over a 20-year period.

Instructions:

1. Determine the amount of income from the investment in Keller Company common stock that should be reported in Beans' income statement for the year ended December 31, 2001.
2. Beans issues comparative financial statements for the years ended December 31, 2002, and 2001. Prepare schedules showing the income or loss that Beans should report from its investment in Keller Company for 2002 and 2001 (restated).

PROBLEM 14–46 **ACCOUNTING FOR THE IMPAIRMENT OF A LOAN**

Jayleen Associates loaned Norris Company $750,000 on January 1, 2000. The terms of the loan were payment in full on January 1, 2005, plus annual interest payments at 11%. The interest payment was made as scheduled on January 1, 2001; however, due to financial setbacks, Norris was unable to make its 2002 interest payment. Jayleen considers the loan impaired and projects the following cash flows from the loan as of December 31, 2002, and 2003. Assume that Jayleen accrued the interest at January 1, 2002, but did not continue to accrue interest due to the impairment of the loan.

Projected Cash Flows:

Date of Flow	Amount Projected as of Dec. 31, 2002	Amount Projected as of Dec. 31, 2003
Dec. 31, 2003	$ 50,000	$ 50,000
Dec. 31, 2004	100,000	150,000
Dec. 31, 2005	200,000	300,000
Dec. 31, 2006	300,000	250,000
Dec. 31, 2007	100,000	

Instructions:

1. Prepare the valuation adjusting entry at December 31, 2002.
2. Prepare the journal entry to record the $50,000 receipt on December 31, 2003.
3. Prepare the valuation adjusting entry at December 31, 2003.
4. Prepare the 2004 journal entries assuming receipt of $150,000 as scheduled; also assume that estimates for future cash flows remain the same as they were at the end of 2003.

COMPETENCY ENHANCEMENT OPPORTUNITIES

▶ Deciphering Actual Financial Statements	▶ Ethical Dilemma
▶ Writing Assignment	▶ Cumulative Spreadsheet Analysis
▶ Research Project	▶ Internet Search
▶ The Debate	

Accounting is more than just doing textbook problems. This expanded competency material provides practice in critical thinking, oral and written communication, research, teamwork, and consideration of ethical issues.

▶ **DECIPHERING ACTUAL FINANCIAL STATEMENTS**
• **Deciphering 14–1 (The Walt Disney Company)**
Use DISNEY's financial statements and related notes, located in Appendix A, to answer the following questions.

1. Locate Disney's note that discusses financial instruments. What is the amount of the investment portfolio classified as available-for-sale? Now look at Disney's balance sheet. What percentage of the investment account is available-for-sale securities? What types of securities constitute the balance in that account?

2. Locate Disney's note that discusses what types of securities are included in "Investments" of the balance sheet. Also examine the note that defines cash and cash equivalents. Are all of Disney's investment securities listed under Investments in the balance sheet?

3. Review the note on financial instruments to determine how the carrying value of investments compared to the fair value on September 30, 1998. Why is this number so much less than that reported as "Investments" on the balance sheet?

• Deciphering 14–2 (Archer Daniels Midland Company)

The investing activities section of the statement of cash flows of ARCHER DANIELS MIDLAND COMPANY (ADM), seller of agricultural commodities and products, is reproduced below. Based on the information given, answer the following questions.

Archer Daniels Midland Company
Consolidated Statements of Cash Flows

| | Year Ended June 30 | | |
	1998	1997	1996
	(In thousands)		
Investing Activities			
Purchases of property, plant and equipment	(702,683)	(779,508)	(754,268)
Business acquisitions	(370,561)	(429,940)	(28,612)
Investments in and advances to affiliates	(366,968)	(416,861)	(110,615)
Purchases of marketable securities	(1,202,662)	(966,203)	(816,401)
Proceeds from sales of marketable securities	1,007,373	1,607,631	1,260,710
Total Investing Activities	(1,635,501)	(984,881)	(449,186)

1. Based on all the buying and selling activity associated with ADM's marketable securities, how do you think the company classifies the bulk of its $3.0 billion portfolio of securities—as trading, available-for-sale, or held-to-maturity?

Now take a look at ADM's note relating to its classification of all of its marketable securities.

> **Marketable Securities** The Company classifies all of its marketable securities as available-for-sale. Available-for-sale securities are carried at fair value, with the unrealized gains and losses, net of income taxes, reported as a component of shareholders' equity.

2. Was your answer to (1) the same as ADM's classification policy? With the company selling one-third to one-half of its investment portfolio each year for the past 3 years, are the company's actions consistent with its classification policy?

Finally, take a look at a portion of ADM's consolidated statements of shareholders' equity from its 1998 annual report.

Archer Daniels Midland Company
Consolidated Statements of Shareholders' Equity

| | Common Stock | | Reinvested |
	Shares	Amount	Earnings
	(In thousands)		
Balance July 1, 1997	557,874	4,192,321	1,857,808
Net earnings	—	—	403,609
Cash dividends—$.19 per share	—	—	(111,551)
5% stock dividend	28,534	473,948	(473,948)
Treasury stock purchases	(3,767)	(81,154)	—
Common stock issued in purchase acquisition	13,953	298,244	—
Foreign currency translation	—	—	(108,551)
Change in unrealized net gains on marketable securities	—	—	1,187
Other	2,627	53,290	(291)
Balance July 1, 1998	$599,221	$4,936,649	$1,568,263

3. Did the company's portfolio of marketable securities experience an unrealized net gain or an unrealized net loss for the year? If these securities had been classified as trading, where would this amount have been reported?

• **Deciphering 14–3 (Ford Motor Company)**

The following note is taken from FORD's 1998 annual report.

NOTE 2. Marketable and Other Securities

Investments in available-for-sale securities at December 31, 1998 were as follows: (in millions)

	Amortized Cost	Unrealized Gains	Unrealized Losses	Fair Value
Available for sale securities				
Debt issued by the U.S.				
government and agencies	$153	$ 3	—	$156
Municipal securities	63	2	—	65
Debt securities issued by non-U.S. governments....	25	—	—	25
Corporate securities.............................	192	3	$2	193
Mortgage-backed securities....................	198	3	—	201
Equity securities.................................	35	56	1	90
Total available for sale securities........	$666	$67	$3	$730

Investments in available-for-sale securities at December 31, 1997 were as follows: (in millions)

	Amortized Cost	Unrealized Gains	Unrealized Losses	Fair Value
Available for sale securities				
Debt issued by the U.S.				
government and agencies	$ 385	$ 4	$1	$ 388
Municipal securities	13	—	—	13
Debt securities issued by non-U.S. governments....	36	—	—	36
Corporate securities.............................	489	7	1	495
Mortgage-backed securities....................	837	8	1	844
Other debt securities............................	14	—	—	14
Equity securities.................................	53	65	2	116
Total available for sale securities........	$1,827	$84	$5	$1,906

Proceeds from sales of available for sale securities were $2.1 billion in 1998, $2.9 billion in 1997 and $8.4 billion in 1996. In 1998, gross gains of $48 million and gross losses of $3 million were realized on those sales; gross gains of $98 million and gross losses of $8 million were realized in 1997 and gross gains of $43 million and gross losses of $21 million were realized in 1996.

---

1. What is the amount of gains and losses on available-for-sale securities that is reported in the 1998 income statement? How much is realized? How much is unrealized?

2. What is the amount of the net adjustment for unrealized holding gains and losses on available-for-sale securities as of the end of 1998?

3. In 1997, $6 million of equity securities were listed as not practicable to determine the fair value. What type of company could have issued this type of security?

• **Deciphering 14–4 (Seagram Company Ltd.)**
The following note information is taken from the annual report of SEAGRAM COMPANY LTD. Use it to answer the questions that follow.

Seagram
Notes to Consolidated Financial Statements

NOTE 4 **TIME WARNER INC. ("TIME WARNER") INVESTMENT**

On February 5, 1998, the Company sold 15 million shares of Time Warner common stock for pretax proceeds of $958 million. On May 27, 1998, the Company sold its remaining 11.8 million shares of Time Warner common stock for pretax proceeds of $905 million. The aggregate gain on the sale of the shares, included in interest, net and other on the consolidated statement of income, was $926 million ($602 million after tax).

NOTE 6 **ACQUISITION OF INTEREST IN UNIVERSAL HOLDING**

On June 5, 1995, the Company completed its purchase of an 80 percent interest in Universal Holding, the indirect parent of Universal, from Matsushita for $5.7 billion. Matsushita retained a 20 percent interest in Universal Holding. During the fiscal year ended June 30, 1998, Matsushita's ownership of Universal Holding was diluted to approximately 16 percent as described in Note 3.

NOTE 8 **INVESTMENTS IN UNCONSOLIDATED COMPANIES**

The Company has a number of investments in unconsolidated companies which are 50 percent or less owned or controlled and are carried in the consolidated balance sheet using the equity method.

Entertainment Segment Significant investments at June 30, 1998 include USANi LLC, primarily engaged in electronic retailing, network and first run syndication television production, domestic distribution of its and Universal's television production and operation of the USA Network and Sci-Fi Channel cable networks (45.8% equity interest); Loews Cineplex Entertainment Corporation, primarily engaged in theatrical exhibition of motion pictures in the U.S. and Canada (26 percent owned); United International Pictures, a distributor of theatrical product outside the U.S. and Canada (33 percent owned); Cinema International BV, primarily engaged in marketing of home video product outside the U.S. and Canada (49 percent owned); Cinema International Corporation and United Cinemas International, both engaged in theatrical exhibition of motion pictures in territories outside the U.S. and Canada (49 percent owned); Brillstein-Grey Entertainment (49.5 percent owned), which owns 50 percent of Brillstein-Grey Communications, a producer of network television series; Universal City Florida Partners, which owns Universal Studios Florida, a motion picture and television theme tourist attraction and production facility in Orlando, Florida (50 percent owned); Universal City Development Partners, which has begun development on land adjacent to Universal Studios Florida of an additional themed tourist attraction, Universal Studios Islands of Adventure, and commercial real estate (50 percent owned); USJ Co., Ltd., which has begun development of a motion picture themed tourist attraction, Universal Studios Japan, and commercial real estate in Osaka, Japan (24 percent owned); Port Aventura, a theme park located in Spain (37 percent owned); SEGA GameWorks, which designs, develops and operates location-based entertainment centers (27 percent owned); and Interplay Productions, an entertainment software developer (30 percent owned).

SPIRITS AND WINE SEGMENT Significant investments at June 30, 1998 include Seagram (Thailand) Limited, an importer and distributor of spirits and wines (49 percent owned) and Kirin-Seagram Limited, engaged in the manufacture, sale and distribution of distilled beverage alcohol and wines in Japan (50 percent owned).

---

1. How would Seagram account for its ownership in UNIVERSAL HOLDING? How would MATSUSHITA account for its 16% ownership of Universal Holding?
2. Determine the historical cost of the Time Warner stock that was sold in 1998.
3. From the information contained in Note 8, we see that Seagram has ownership in numerous entertainment and beverage concerns. As mentioned in the chapter, the FASB is considering changing the rules regarding control and consolidated financial statements. Which of the investments in Note 8, currently accounted for using the equity method, do you think would qualify for consolidation under the potential new FASB guidelines? What other information might you need in order to make a definitive answer?

▶ **WRITING ASSIGNMENT**

• Going around the income statement

In FASB Statement No. 115, there are two different treatments for unrealized gains and losses depending on whether the security is classified as trading or available-for-sale. Unrealized gains and losses for trading securities are reported on the income statement while unrealized gains and losses for available-for-sale securities are disclosed in stockholders' equity.

Your assignment is to develop an argument, in writing, for including unrealized gains and losses for available-for-sale securities on the income statement. Include in your paper reasons as to why the FASB might have chosen the disclosure rules that it did and be able to refute its reasoning.

▶ **RESEARCH PROJECT**

• Classification of securities

The objective of this exercise is to examine the classification practices for investments in debt and equity securities of several large companies. Your group is to obtain copies of recent annual reports for 5 large, publicly traded companies. Using these annual reports, examine their financial statements and note disclosures to answer the following questions.

1. How many of the 5 companies have investments in the securities of other firms?
2. For each of the companies that has investments, how does it classify those securities: as trading, available-for-sale, held-to-maturity, or a combination of the 3 categories?
3. Do the companies give any justification for the classification policy that they employ? That is, do the companies state how they determine if a security is to be classified as trading, available-for-sale, or held-to-maturity?
4. Examine the stockholders' equity section of each company's balance sheet (or a separate statement of stockholders' equity, if it is provided). Do the companies disclose any unrealized gains or losses relating to available-for-sale securities? Did the amount increase or decrease during the most recent year?
5. Can you draw any general conclusions based on your analysis of these 5 annual reports? For example, "Most companies classify their securities as available-for-sale" or "Most companies have experienced unrealized gains/losses on their portfolios of trading securities during the past year."

▶ **THE DEBATE**

• Control: What is it?

Accounting standards require companies to prepare consolidated financial statements that include the financial statements of those subsidiaries in which the parent company has a controlling interest. The trouble is, what constitutes a controlling interest? Historically, a controlling interest has been defined as ownership of more than 50% of a subsidiary's outstanding common stock. However, the FASB is reevaluating the 50% criterion to determine if there are other methods for determining control.

Divide your group into two teams.

• One team is to represent the status quo. That is, you are to defend the 50% criterion as being the best objective measure of determining control.

• The other team is to take the position that effective control can be obtained with a less than 50% ownership interest. You should suggest methods for measuring control other than stock ownership level.

▶ **ETHICAL DILEMMA**

• Reclassifying securities for gain

You are the chief financial officer of a large manufacturing company. As CFO you are responsible for investing excess cash in marketable securities and then handling the accounting for those securities. Your firm has a policy of classifying all securities as being available-for-sale. At the end of the year, preliminary financial results indicate that your company will be slightly below targeted net income. The board of directors has given you the task of determining how income might be increased without (and the board emphasized this point) going outside of the rules.

You determine that one method of increasing net income would be to reclassify all available-for-sale securities that have experienced an increase in market value as if they were purchased as trading securities.

1. Would this reclassification achieve the desired results?
2. Is this reclassification within the rules?
3. Is this reclassification consistent with the intent of FASB Statement No. 115?
4. If you were the company's external auditor, what questions might you have regarding this reclassification?

► CUMULATIVE SPREADSHEET ANALYSIS

This assignment is based on the spreadsheet prepared in (1) of the cumulative spreadsheet assignment for Chapter 13. Review that assignment for a summary of the assumptions made in preparing a forecasted balance sheet, income statement, and statement of cash flows for 2003 for Skywalker Company. This assignment involves changing assumption (h) in the Chapter 13 assignment.

Assume that Skywalker's investment securities portfolio contains the following available-for-sale securities as of December 31, 2002.

	Original Cost	Market Value 12/31/02
Security A	$10	$22
Security B	25	18
Security C	5	8
Security D	40	15
Security E	1	7
Total	$81	$70

(Note: These numbers imply that the accumulated other comprehensive income balance of $132 (credit) as of December 31, 2002, includes a debit amount of $11 ($81 − $70) from available-for-sale securities.)

As mentioned in the Chapter 13 assignment, Skywalker intends to invest another $28 in available-for-sale securities (Security F) in 2003 in order to increase the total value of the portfolio by 40% to $98 ($70 + $28).

Because Skywalker cannot predict future stock prices, the best forecast is that the market values of Securities A through E will remain the same during 2003 and that the market value of Security F, to be acquired in 2003 for $28, will remain at $28.

Revise the spreadsheet made in (1) of the Chapter 13 assignment in accordance with the above and following assumptions. In each case, any gains or losses expected to be realized in 2003 should be reported in a separate income statement line, "Investment income, net."

1. Skywalker intends to sell Security A in 2003 at an anticipated price of $22. That $22 will be used to buy Security G. Skywalker's best forecast is that the market value of Security G will remain at $22 through the end of 2003.
2. How does the sale of Security A in (1) impact expected cash from operating activities in 2003? Explain.
3. Repeat (1) and (2) assuming that, instead of selling Security A, Skywalker intends to sell Security D in 2003 at an anticipated price of $15, which will be used to buy Security G. Skywalker's best forecast is that the market value of Security G will remain at $15 through the end of 2003.

▶ **INTERNET SEARCH**

Let's take a look at the Web site for GENERAL ELECTRIC. The address is www.ge.com. Once you have gained access to General Electric's Web site, answer the following questions.

1. Use the GE History link to discover one of the major founders of the company that eventually became General Electric. Write a short bio of this person, including his contributions to GE.

2. Locate GE's financial statements and notes. What percentage of GE's total assets are invested in the securities of other companies?

3. Can you find the note that discloses how GE classifies its investment securities? If you can, what is the disclosure?

part 3

Additional Activities and Common Disclosures of a Business

chapter 15
Leases

While flying at 35,000 feet, have you ever wondered who owns the airplane in which you are riding? The chances are quite good that the plane isn't owned by UNITED, AMERICAN, or DELTA but instead by an aircraft leasing company such as INTERNATIONAL LEASE FINANCE CORP. OF CALIFORNIA, GPA GROUP OF IRELAND, or ANSETT WORLDWIDE AVIATION SERVICES OF AUSTRALIA. Aircraft leasing companies own about 40% of the passenger jets flying today. The leasing companies buy the jets from BOEING or AIRBUS and in turn lease them to an airline. Not one to let a good business opportunity slip away, Boeing has decided to enter the leasing business. In a move that is seen by many as putting itself in close competition with companies that already buy its planes and lease them to airlines, Boeing restructured Boeing Capital Corporation in 1999 in an effort to become a major player in the airplane financing business.[1]

Airlines use these leasing arrangements as an alternative to obtaining loans to buy the planes themselves. Large stable airlines typically sign long-term leases of 15 to 20 years. Smaller airlines trying to establish a market toehold are likely to sign more expensive short-term leases of four to eight years.[2]

Another question you might ask yourself while flying at 35,000 feet is whether or not an airline reports a leased plane as an asset on its balance sheet. The answer is: sometimes yes and sometimes no. In the case of Delta, a company that leased 226 airplanes (or 39% of its fleet) as of June 30, 1999, only 48 of those leased aircraft were reported on the company's balance sheet. The remaining 178 planes, for which Delta had made contractual promises to pay over $14.5 billion in the future, were not reported on the balance sheet as assets—nor were the future lease payments reported as a liability. The only financial statement indication that these planes even exist is buried in the lease note to Delta's financial statements.

So, when is a leased airplane an asset? Keep reading—that question is what this chapter is all about.

1 Jeff Cole, *The Wall Street Journal*, "Boeing Overhauls Financing Operation, Heightening Rivalry With Its Lessors," October 4, 1999, p. A3.
2 John H. Taylor, "Fasten Seat Belts, Please," *Forbes*, April 2, 1990, p. 84.

LEARNING OBJECTIVES

1
Describe the circumstances in which leasing makes more business sense than does an outright sale and purchase.

2
Understand the accounting issues faced by the asset owner (lessor) and the asset user (lessee) in recording a lease transaction.

3
Outline the types of contractual provisions typically included in lease agreements.

4
Apply the lease classification criteria in order to distinguish between capital and operating leases.

5
Properly account for both capital and operating leases from the standpoint of the lessee (asset user).

6
Properly account for both capital and operating leases from the standpoint of the lessor (asset owner).

7
Prepare and interpret the lease disclosures required of both lessors and lessees.

8
Compare the treatment of accounting for leases in the United States with the requirements of international accounting standards.

e/m

EXPANDED MATERIAL

9
Record a sale-leaseback transaction for both a seller-lessee and a purchaser-lessor.

10
Recognize the special characteristics of real estate leases.

A lease is a contract specifying the terms under which the owner of property, the **lessor**, transfers the right to use the property to a **lessee**. In this chapter, we will focus on how leases are accounted for from both the lessor's and the lessee's perspectives. We will discuss the issues associated with classifying a lease as a debt-financed purchase of property (capital lease) or as a rental (operating lease) and the disclosure issues associated with that classification. In addition, we will illustrate how businesses can have definite obligations to pay significant amounts of money in the future relating to operating lease obligations and yet not recognize those obligations as liabilities on the balance sheet.

Historically, a major challenge for the accounting profession has been to establish accounting standards that prevent companies from using the legal form of a lease to avoid recognizing future payment obligations as a lia-

> **FYI:** The CAP addressed the issue of leasing in 1949 with ARB No. 38. The APB, formed in 1959, issued four opinions on the subject. The FASB issued Statement No. 13 on leases in 1976 and has subsequently issued over a dozen amendments and interpretations of the lease accounting rules.

bility. "Off-balance-sheet financing" continues to be a perplexing problem for the accounting profession, and leasing is probably the oldest and most widely used means of keeping debt off the balance sheet. This chapter will discuss in detail and analyze the criteria established by the FASB in an attempt to bring more long-term leases onto the balance sheet as well as specific accounting procedures used for leased assets. In addition, we will discuss how international accounting standards differ from those in the U.S.

Describe the circumstances in which leasing makes more business sense than does an outright sale and purchase.

ECONOMIC ADVANTAGES OF LEASING

Before discussing the accounting treatment of leases, it is important to first consider the valid business reasons for entering into a lease agreement. It would be unfair and incorrect to imply that the only reason companies lease property is to avoid reporting the lease obligation in the financial statements. While the accounting ramifications are an important consideration in structuring a deal as a lease, other financial and tax considerations also play an important role in the leasing decision.

Every situation is different, but there are three primary advantages to the lessee of leasing over purchasing.

1. *No down payment.* Most debt-financed purchases of property require a portion of the purchase price to be paid immediately by the borrower. This provides added protection to the lender in the event of default and repossession. Lease agreements, in contrast, frequently are structured so that 100% of the value of the property is financed through the lease. This aspect of leasing makes it an attractive alternative to a company that does not have sufficient cash for a down payment or wishes to use available capital for other operating or investing purposes. Of course, many leases also require a down payment—as an example, look carefully at the fine print the next time you see a car lease advertisement on television.

2. *Avoid risks of ownership.* There are many risks accompanying the ownership of property. They include casualty loss, obsolescence, changing economic conditions, and physical deterioration. If the market value of a leased asset decreases dramatically, the lessee may terminate the lease, although usually with some penalty. On the other hand, if you own the asset, you are stuck with it when the market value declines.

3. ***Flexibility.*** Business conditions and requirements change over time. If assets are leased, a company can more easily replace assets in response to these changes. This flexibility is especially important in businesses where innovation and technological change make the future usefulness of particular equipment or facilities highly uncertain. A prime example of this condition in recent years has been in high-tech industries with rapid change in areas such as computer technology, robotics, and telecommunications. Flexibility is a primary reason for the popularity of automobile leasing. Car buyers like the flexibility of choosing a brand-new car every two or three years as their leases run out.

The lessor also may find benefits to leasing its property rather than selling it. Advantages of the lease to the lessor include the following:

1. ***Increased sales.*** For the reasons suggested in the preceding paragraphs, customers may be unwilling or unable to purchase property. By offering potential customers the option of leasing its products, a manufacturer or dealer may significantly increase its sales volume. For example, car prices have risen 69% over the last 10 years, while household incomes have not kept pace. The result is fewer and fewer Americans who can afford to purchase new cars. The automakers' response in order to maintain sales volume has been leasing. FORD leases about 20% of its cars and light trucks. About 49% of CADILLAC Sevilles, with a sticker price of $43,143, are leased. JAGUAR, a European-based car maker, leases approximately 70% of the cars it delivers to the United States.

2. ***Ongoing business relationship with lessee.*** When property is sold, the purchaser frequently has no more dealings with the seller of the property. In leasing situations, however, the lessor and lessee maintain contact over a period of time, and long-term business relationships often can be established through leasing.

3. ***Residual value retained.*** In many lease arrangements, title to the leased property never passes to the lessee. The lessor benefits from economic conditions that may result in a significant residual value at the end of the lease term. The lessor may lease the asset to another lessee or sell the property and realize an immediate gain. For example, new car leasing provides auto dealers with a supply of two- to three-year-old used cars, which can then be sold or leased again.

In summary, a leasing arrangement is often a sound business practice for both the lessee and the lessor. The remainder of the chapter discusses the intricate and interesting accounting implications of leases.

Caution! The sooner you get comfortable with the terms "lessee" and "lessor," the better. The lessor is the legal owner of the leased asset; the lessee is the party that will use the leased asset.

Car leasing provides increased sales for automakers while making payments more affordable for car owners.

Understand the accounting issues faced by the asset owner (lessor) and the asset user (lessee) in recording a lease transaction.

SIMPLE EXAMPLE

A simple example will be used to introduce the accounting issues associated with leases. Owner Company owns a piece of equipment with a market value of $10,000. User Company wishes to acquire the equipment for use in its operations. One option for User Company is to purchase the equipment from Owner by borrowing $10,000 from a bank at an interest rate of 10%. User can use the $10,000 to buy the equipment from Owner and can repay the principal and interest on the bank loan in five equal annual installments of $2,638.

Alternatively, User Company can lease the asset from Owner for five years, making five annual "rental" payments of $2,638. From User's standpoint, the lease is equivalent to purchasing the asset, the only difference being the legal form of the transaction. User will still use the equipment for five years and will still make payments of $2,638 per year. From Owner's standpoint, the only difference in the transaction is that now Owner is not just selling the equipment but is also substituting for the bank in providing financing.

With this lease arrangement, the key accounting issue for Owner Company is:

- On the date the lease is signed, should Owner Company recognize an equipment sale?

The correct answer to this question hinges on factors that have been discussed in previous chapters in connection with inventory sales and revenue recognition.

- Has effective ownership of the equipment been passed from Owner to User?
- Is the transaction complete, meaning does Owner have any significant responsibilities remaining in regard to the equipment?
- Is Owner reasonably certain that the five annual payments of $2,638 can be collected from User?

The key accounting issue for User Company is:

- On the date the lease is signed, should User recognize the leased equipment as an asset and the obligation to make the lease payments as a liability?

The correct answer to this question also hinges on whether effective ownership, as opposed to legal ownership, of the equipment changes hands when Owner and User sign the lease agreement.

Accounting for leases is a classic illustration of the accounting aphorism "substance over form." The legal form of the lease is that Owner Company maintains ownership of the equipment. But whether the lease transfers economic ownership of the asset from Owner to User depends on the specifics of the lease agreement. Consider the following four independent scenarios.

- The lease agreement stipulates that Owner is to maintain legal title to the equipment for the five-year lease period, but title is to pass to User at the end of the lease.
- The lease agreement stipulates that Owner is to maintain legal title to the equipment for the five-year lease period, but at the end of the lease period User has the option to buy the equipment for $1.
- The useful life of the equipment is just five years. Accordingly, when the lease term is over, the equipment can no longer be used by anyone else.
- Present value calculations suggest that payment of the five annual $2,638 lease payments is equivalent to paying $10,000 for the equipment on the lease signing date.

In each of these four scenarios, the economic substance of the lease is that the lease signing is equivalent to the transfer of effective ownership, and the fact that Owner retains legal title of the equipment during the lease period is a mere technicality. On the other hand, if the lease agreement does not provide for the transfer of the legal title at the end of the lease, if the lease covers only a fraction of the useful life of the equipment, and if the lease payments are not large enough to "pay" for the equipment, then economically the lease is just a rental, not a transfer of ownership.

For accounting purposes, leases are separated into two groups—capital leases and operating leases. Capital leases are accounted for as if the lease agreement transfers ownership of the asset from the lessor to the lessee. In the example above, if the lease is accounted for as a capital lease, Owner Company would recognize the sale of the equipment on the lease signing date and would also recognize earned interest revenue as the five annual lease payments are collected. On the lease signing date, User Company would recognize the leased asset, as well as the liability for the future lease payments, on its balance sheet.

Operating leases are accounted for as rental agreements, with no transfer of effective ownership associated with the lease. In the example above, if the lease is accounted for as an operating lease, Owner Company recognizes no sale on the lease signing date. Instead, lease rental revenue is recognized each year when the lease payment is collected. User Company recognizes no leased asset and no lease liability but reports only a periodic lease rental expense equal to the annual lease payments.

From this simple introduction, you may receive the misleading impression that accounting for leases is straightforward and noncontroversial. In fact, most companies using assets under lease agreements go to great lengths to ensure that they can account for the bulk of their leases as operating leases because it allows them to keep both the asset and the associated liability off the balance sheet. Keeping the asset off the balance sheet improves financial ratio measures of efficiency, and keeping the liability off the balance sheet improves measures of leverage. For companies that lease a large portion of the assets that they use, the accounting standards associated with leasing are the most critical accounting standards that they apply.

The following sections contain a more detailed description of the kinds of provisions found in lease agreements. In addition, the specific accounting rules used to distinguish between operating leases and capital leases will be explained.

Outline the types of contractual provisions typically included in lease agreements.

NATURE OF LEASES

Leases vary widely in their contractual provisions. Reasons for this variability include cancellation provisions and penalties, bargain renewal and purchase options, lease term, economic life of assets, residual asset values, minimum lease payments, interest rates implicit in the lease agreement, and the degree of risk assumed by the lessee, including payments of certain costs such as maintenance, insurance, and taxes. These and other relevant facts must be considered in determining the appropriate accounting treatment of a lease.

The many variables affecting lease capitalization have been given precise definitions that must be understood in order to account for the various types of leases found in practice. Each of these variables is defined and briefly discussed in the following sections.

Cancellation Provisions

Some leases are **noncancelable**, meaning that these lease contracts are cancelable only upon the outcome of some remote contingency or that the cancellation provisions and penalties of these leases are so costly to the lessee that, in all likelihood, cancellation will not occur. All cancelable leases are accounted for as operating leases; some, but not all, noncancelable leases are accounted for as capital leases.

Bargain Purchase Option

Leases often include a provision giving the lessee the right to purchase leased property at some future date. If the specified purchase option price is expected to be considerably

Caution! To determine if a bargain purchase option exists, the parties to the lease must be able to make a reasonable estimate as to what the fair market value of the leased asset will be at the end of the lease.

FYI: The lease term is an important concept in capital lease accounting for lessees because it determines the period over which the leased asset is depreciated.

less than the fair market value at the date the purchase option may be exercised, then the option is called a **bargain purchase option**. By definition, a bargain purchase option is one that is expected to be exercised. Accordingly, a lease agreement including a bargain purchase option is likely to result in the transfer of asset ownership from the lessor to the lessee. Noncancelable leases with bargain purchase options are accounted for as capital leases.

Lease Term

An important variable in lease agreements is the **lease term**, that is, the time period from the beginning to the end of the lease. The beginning of the lease term occurs when the leased property is transferred to the lessee. The end of the lease term is more flexible because many leases include provisions allowing the lessee to extend the lease period. For accounting purposes, the end of the lease term is defined as the end of the fixed noncancelable lease period plus all renewal option periods that are likely to be exercised. A **bargain renewal option** is one with such an attractive lease rate, or other favorable provision, that at the inception of the lease, it is likely that the lease will be renewed beyond the fixed lease period. If a bargain purchase option is included in the lease contract, the lease term includes any renewal periods preceding the date of the bargain purchase option but does not extend beyond the date of the bargain purchase option.

Residual Value

The market value of the leased property at the end of the lease term is referred to as its residual value. In some leases, the lease term extends over the entire economic life of the asset or the period in which the asset continues to be productive, and there is little, if any, residual value. In other leases, the lease term is shorter, and a significant residual value does exist. If the lessee can purchase the asset at the end of the lease term at a materially reduced price from its residual value, a bargain purchase option is present and it can be assumed that the lessee would exercise the option and purchase the asset.

Some lease contracts require the lessee to guarantee a minimum residual value. If the market value at the end of the lease term falls below the **guaranteed residual value**, the lessee must pay the difference. This provision protects the lessor from loss due to unexpected declines in the market value of the asset. For example, assume that the car you lease is expected to have a $15,000 residual value at the end of the lease term and that you guarantee that amount to the car dealership. However, at the end of the lease term, the residual value of the car is only $10,000. You are then obligated to pay the dealership the $5,000 difference because the dealership is, in effect, guaranteed the full amount of the residual value that was estimated at the beginning of the lease. You may buy the car for the $15,000 guaranteed amount, but the lease terms do not require the purchase.

Caution! The residual value risk for unguaranteed residual values is borne by the lessor; the residual value risk for guaranteed residual values is borne by the lessee.

If there is no bargain purchase option or guarantee of the residual value, the lessor reacquires the property at the end of the lease term and may offer to renew the lease, lease the asset to another lessee, or sell the property. The actual amount of the residual value is unknown until the end of the lease term; however, it must be estimated at the inception of the lease. The residual value under these circumstances is referred to as the **unguaranteed residual value**.

Minimum Lease Payments

The rental payments required over the lease term plus any amount to be paid for the residual value either through a bargain purchase option or a guarantee of the residual value are referred to as the **minimum lease payments**. Lease payments sometimes include charges for such items as insurance, maintenance, and taxes incurred for the leased property. These are referred to as **executory costs**, and they are not included as part of the minimum lease payments. In addition, building lease payments are often composed of a fixed minimum amount with additional payments made based on sales by the lessee. The additional payments are not considered part of the minimum lease payment.

To illustrate the computation of minimum lease payments, assume that Dorney Leasing Co. owns and leases road equipment for three years at $3,000 per month. Included in the lease payment is $500 per month for executory costs to insure and maintain the equipment. At the end of the three-year period, Dorney is guaranteed a residual value of $10,000 by the lessee.

Minimum lease payments:

Rental payments exclusive of executory costs ($2,500 × 36)...	$ 90,000
Guaranteed residual value..	10,000
Total minimum lease payments...	$100,000

How did Dorney decide that a $2,500 monthly lease payment would be sufficient? Calculation of the appropriate lease payment involves consideration of the fair value of the leased equipment, the guaranteed residual value, the lease term, and the appropriate interest rate. Dorney computed the $2,500 monthly lease payment by using an interest rate of 12% compounded monthly (1% per month) and a fair value of the road equipment of $82,258. The computation is as follows:

Present value of 36 monthly payments of $2,500 ($3,000 less executory costs of $500) at 1% interest (12% compounded monthly) paid at the end of each month:

$$PV_n = R(PVAF_{\overline{36}|1\%})$$
$$PV_n = \$2,500\ (30.1075) = \text{..}\quad \$75,269$$

Present value of $10,000 guaranteed residual value at the end of 3 years at 12% compounded monthly:

$$PV = A(PVF_{\overline{36}|1\%})$$
$$PV = \$10,000\ (0.6989) = \text{..}\quad \underline{6,989}$$

Present value of minimum lease payments $82,258

FYI: If the lessee cannot ascertain the lessor's implicit rate, the incremental borrowing rate is used in the lessee's present value calculations. Two reasons the lessee would not be able to compute the implicit rate are if the asset being leased does not have a readily determinable fair market value or if a reliable estimate of residual value cannot be obtained.

Of course, this computation is backwards—in actuality, Dorney would use the $82,258 fair value and the interest rate of 12% compounded monthly to compute the desired monthly lease payment of $2,500. The interest rate used is called the **implicit interest rate**—the rate used by the lessor in calculating the desired lease payment.

As discussed later in the chapter, the present value of the minimum lease payments is also an important quantity for the lessee. A complication arises because the implicit interest rate used by the lessor in calculating the lease payments may not be the appropriate discount rate for the lessee. For purposes of computing the present value of the minimum lease payments, the lessee uses the *lower* of the implicit interest rate used by the lessor and the lessee's own **incremental borrowing rate**. The lessee's incremental borrowing rate is the rate at which the lessee could borrow the amount of money necessary to purchase the leased asset, taking into consideration the lessee's financial situation and the current conditions in the marketplace.

The use of present value formulas and tables in discounting minimum lease payments is illustrated later in the chapter.

LEASE CLASSIFICATION CRITERIA

Apply the lease classification criteria in order to distinguish between capital and operating leases.

Leasing was one of the topics on the original agenda of the FASB, and in 1976 the Board issued Statement No. 13, "Accounting for Leases." The objective of the FASB in issuing Statement No. 13 was to reflect the economic reality of leasing by requiring that some long-term leases be accounted for as capital acquisitions by the lessee and sales by the lessor. To accomplish this objective, the FASB identified criteria to determine whether a lease is merely a rental contract (an operating lease) or is, in substance, a purchase of property (a capital lease). The lease classification criteria and their applicability to lessees and lessors are summarized in Exhibit 15-1.

EXHIBIT 15-1 | Lease Classification Criteria

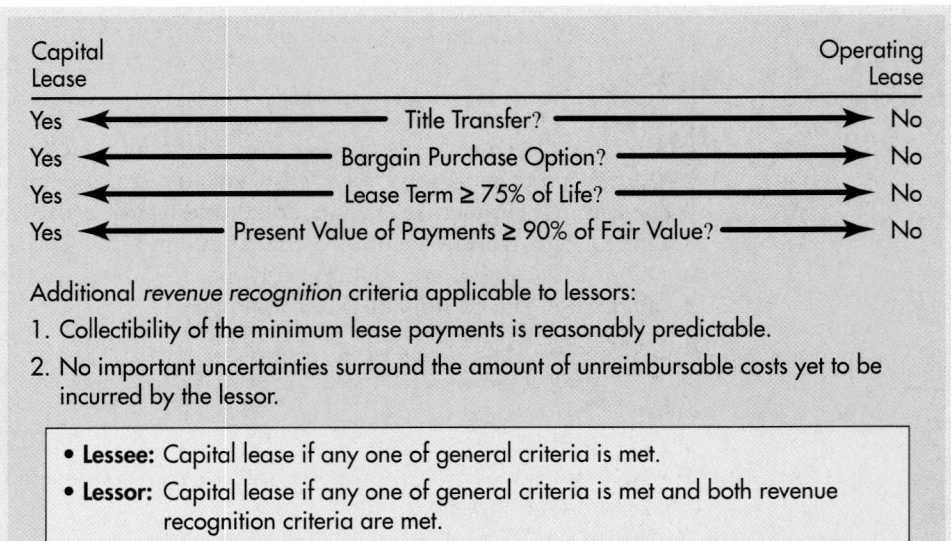

General Classification Criteria—Lessee and Lessor

The four general criteria that apply to all leases for both the lessee and lessor relate to transfer of ownership, bargain purchase options, economic life, and fair market value. The transfer of ownership criterion is met if the lease agreement includes a clause that transfers full ownership of the property to the lessee by the end of the lease term. Of all the classification criteria, transfer of ownership is the most objective and therefore the easiest to apply.

The second general criterion is met if the lease contains a bargain purchase option that makes it reasonably assured that the property will be purchased by the lessee at some future date. This criterion is more difficult to apply than the first criterion, because the future fair market value of the leased property must be estimated at the inception of the lease and compared with the purchase option price to determine if a bargain purchase is indeed indicated.

The third criterion relates to the economic life of the asset. This criterion is met if the lease term is equal to 75% or more of the estimated economic life of the leased property. As defined earlier, the lease term includes renewal periods if renewal seems assured. The economic life criterion is somewhat subjective because of the uncertainty of an asset's economic life. This criterion does not apply to land leases because land has an unlimited life.

The fourth general criterion focuses on the fair market value of the property in relation to the provisions of the lease. This criterion is met if, at the beginning of the lease term, the present value of the minimum lease payments equals or exceeds 90% of the fair market value of the leased asset. If the lessee is obligated to pay, in present value terms, almost all the fair market value of the leased property, the lease is in substance a purchase of the property. The key variable in this criterion is the discounted minimum lease payments.

The rate used to discount the future minimum lease payments is critical in determining whether the fair market value criterion is met. The lower the discount rate used, the higher the present value of the minimum lease payments and the greater the likelihood that the fair market value criterion of 90% will be met. As explained earlier, the FASB specified that the lessor should use the implicit interest rate of the lease agreement. The lessee also uses the lessor's implicit interest rate if it is known and if it is lower than the lessee's incremental borrowing rate. If the lessee cannot determine the lessor's implicit interest rate, the lessee must use its incremental borrowing rate.

STOP & THINK How exactly does using a higher incremental borrowing rate reduce the likelihood that a lessee will be required to account for a lease as a capital lease?

Because incremental borrowing rates are often higher than the implicit interest rates and because lessees generally do not want to capitalize leases, many lessees use the borrowing rate and do not attempt to estimate the implicit rate. In the 1980s, the FASB proposed tightening the capital lease criteria by requiring lessees to estimate the implicit interest rate in all cases. The FASB dropped the proposal when criticism of this proposed provision became widespread.

The four criteria outlined above represent the FASB's attempt to precisely delineate the difference between operating and capital leases. In practice, companies have become very skilled at structuring lease agreements according to whether they want to account for the lease as an operating or a capital lease. In essence, the precise nature of the FASB's four criteria provides a legalistic framework that firms easily circumvent through clever structuring of the lease. As a result, the goal of lease accounting that represents substance over form is not entirely met. An alternative to the FASB's precise framework is one that relies more on accounting judgment. For example, the international accounting standard on leases (IAS 17, "Accounting for Leases") states simply: "A lease is classified as a finance (i.e., capital) lease if it transfers substantially all the risks and rewards incident to ownership."[3] This type of standard places the responsibility of distinguishing between operating and capital leases on the accountant.

FYI: During World War II, the United Kingdom was in dire need of warships. The problem was it had no money, and U.S. law prohibited the United States to loan money to another country for purchasing ships. The solution: An 1892 statute that allowed the Secretary of War to lease U.S. military property. Thus was born the famous Lend-Lease Bill, which allowed the United States to provide warships to the United Kingdom.

Revenue Recognition Criteria—Lessor

In addition to meeting one of the four general criteria, a lease must meet two additional revenue recognition criteria in order to be classified by the lessor as a capital lease.[4] As indicated in Exhibit 15-1, the first of the two revenue recognition criteria relates to collectibility. Collection of the minimum lease payments must be reasonably predictable.

The second additional criterion requires substantial completion of performance by the lessor. This means that any unreimbursable costs yet to be incurred by the lessor under the terms of the lease are known or can be reasonably estimated at the lease inception date. If the leased asset is constructed by the lessor, this criterion is applied at the later of the lease inception date or the date construction is completed.

Application of General Lease Classification Criteria

To illustrate the application of the lease classification criteria, four different leasing situations are presented in Exhibit 15-2. A summary analysis of each lease also is presented in the exhibit. Following is a brief explanation of the analysis for each of the four leases.

---

3 *International Accounting Standard No. 17* (Accounting for Leases), International Accounting Standards Committee, January 1999.

4 *Statement of Financial Accounting Standards No. 13,* "Accounting for Leases," Stamford, CT: Financial Accounting Standards Board, 1976, par. 8. If the lease involves real estate, these revenue recognition criteria are replaced by a criterion that requires a transfer of title at the end of the lease term. *Statement of Financial Accounting Standards No. 98,* par. 22c.

EXHIBIT 15-2 | Application of Lease Classification Criteria to Lease Situations

Lease Provisions	Lease #1	Lease #2	Lease #3	Lease #4
Cancelable	No	No	No	Yes
Title passes to lessee	No	Yes	No	Yes
Bargain purchase option	No	No	Yes	No
Lease term	10 years	10 years	8 years	10 years
Economic life of asset	14 years	15 years	13 years	12 years
Present value of minimum lease payments as a percentage of fair market value—incremental borrowing rate	80%	79%	95%	76%
Present value of minimum lease payments as a percentage of fair market value—implicit interest rate	92%	91%	92%	82%
Lessee knows implicit interest rate	No	No	Yes	Yes
Rental payments collectible and lessor costs certain	Yes	Yes	No	Yes
Analysis of Leases:				
Lessee				
Treat as capital lease	No	Yes	Yes	No
Criteria met	None	Title	Bargain purchase, present value	Must be noncancelable
Lessor				
Treat as capital lease	Yes	Yes	No	No
First four criteria met	Present value	Title, present value	Bargain purchase, present value	Must be noncancelable
Lessor criteria met	Yes	Yes	No	—

Lease #1 will be treated as an operating lease by the lessee but as a capital lease by the lessor. The lease does not meet any of the first three general criteria. Because the lessee does not know the implicit interest rate of the lessor, the incremental borrowing rate is used to test for the present value criterion. The present value of the minimum lease payments using the incremental borrowing rate is less than 90% of the fair market value of the property; thus the present value criterion is not met for the lessee. Because the lessor uses the implicit interest rate, the present value criterion is met. The two additional criteria applicable to the lessor are also met.

Lease #2 will be treated as a capital lease by both the lessee and the lessor because title passes to the lessee at the end of the lease term and the additional lessor criteria are both met. Because of the difference in the present value calculations, if the title had not passed, Lease #2 would be treated as an operating lease by the lessee but as a capital lease by the lessor.

Lease #3 will be treated as a capital lease by the lessee but as an operating lease by the lessor. The bargain purchase option criterion is met as is the present value criterion. However, because there is some uncertainty as to the collectibility of the rental payments and the amount of lessor costs to be incurred, the lease fails to meet the revenue recognition criteria applicable to the lessor.

Lease #4 will be treated as an operating lease by both the lessee and the lessor. The lease is a cancelable lease, and even though title passes to the lessee at the end of the lease, it would be classified as a rental agreement.

Properly account for both capital and operating leases from the standpoint of the lessee (asset user).

ACCOUNTING FOR LEASES—LESSEE

All leases as viewed by the lessee may be divided into two types: operating leases and capital leases. If a lease meets any one of the four general classification criteria discussed previously, it is treated as a capital lease. Otherwise, it is accounted for as an operating lease.

Accounting for operating leases involves the recognition of rent expense over the term of the lease. The leased property is not reported as an asset on the lessee's balance sheet nor is a liability recognized for the obligation to make future payments for use of the property. Information concerning the lease is limited to disclosure in notes to the financial statements. Accounting for a capital lease essentially requires the lessee to report on the balance sheet the present value of the future lease payments, both as an asset and a liability. The asset is amortized as though it had been purchased by the lessee. The liability is accounted for in the same manner as would be a mortgage on the property. The difference in the impact of these two treatments on the financial statements of the lessee often can be significant, as illustrated below.

Accounting for Operating Leases—Lessee

Operating leases are considered to be simple rental agreements with debits being made to an expense account as the payments are made. For example, assume the lease terms for manufacturing equipment are $40,000 a year on a year-to-year basis. The entry to record the lease payment for a year would be:

Rent Expense	40,000	
Cash		40,000

Lease payments frequently are made in advance. If the lease period does not coincide with the lessee's fiscal year or if the lessee prepares interim reports, a prepaid rent account would be required to record the unexpired portion of the lease payment at the end of the accounting period involved. The prepaid rent account would be adjusted at the end of each period.

OPERATING LEASES WITH VARYING LEASE PAYMENTS Some operating leases specify lease terms that provide for varying lease payments over the lease term. Most commonly, these types of agreements call for lower initial payments and scheduled increases later in the life of the lease. They may even provide an inducement to prospective lessees in the form of a "rent holiday" (free rent). In some cases, however, the lease may provide for higher initial payments. In cases with varying lease payments, periodic expense should be recognized on a straight-line basis.[5]

When recording lease payments under these agreements, differences between the actual payments and the debit to expense would be reported as Rent Payable or Prepaid Rent, depending on whether the payments were accelerating or declining. For example, assume the terms of the lease for an aircraft by International Airlines provide for payments of $150,000 a year for the first two years of the lease and $250,000 for each of the next three years. The total lease payments for the five years would be $1,050,000, or $210,000 a year on a straight-line basis. The required entries in the first two years would be:

Rent Expense	210,000	
Cash		150,000
Rent Payable		60,000

---

5 Periodic lease expense is recognized on a straight-line basis "unless another systematic and rational basis is more representative of the time pattern in which use benefit is derived from the leased property, in which case that basis shall be used." *FASB Statement No. 13*, par. 15.

The entries for each of the last three years would be:

Rent Expense	210,000	
Rent Payable	40,000	
Cash		250,000

The portion of Rent Payable due in the subsequent year would be classified as a current liability.

As explained later in the chapter, a large amount of detail concerning operating leases is disclosed in the notes to the financial statements. This disclosure includes summary information about lease provisions and a schedule of future minimum lease payments associated with operating leases.

Accounting for Capital Leases—Lessee

Capital leases are considered to be more like a purchase of property than a rental. Consequently, accounting for capital leases by lessees requires entries similar to those required for the purchase of an asset with long-term credit terms. The amounts to be recorded as an asset and as a liability are the present values of the future minimum lease payments as previously defined. The discount rates used by lessees to record capital leases are the same as those used to apply the classification criteria previously discussed, that is, the lower of the implicit interest rate (if known) and the incremental borrowing rate. The minimum lease payments consist of the total rental payments, bargain purchase options, and lessee-guaranteed residual values.[6]

ILLUSTRATIVE ENTRIES FOR CAPITAL LEASES   Assume that Marshall Corporation leases equipment from Universal Leasing Company with the following terms:

- Lease period: 5 years, beginning January 1, 2002. Noncancelable.
- Rental amount: $65,000 per year payable annually in advance; includes $5,000 to cover executory costs.
- Estimated economic life of equipment: 5 years.
- Expected residual value of equipment at end of lease period: None.

Because the lease payments are payable in advance, the way to compute the present value of the lease is to add the amount of the first payment (made on the lease signing date) to the present value of the annuity of four remaining payments. Assuming Marshall Corporation's incremental borrowing rate and the implicit interest rate on the lease are both 10%, the present value for the lease would be $250,194 computed as follows[7]:

$$PVn = \$60,000 + [\$60,000(PVAF_{\overline{4}|10\%})]$$
$$PVn = \$60,000 + [\$60,000(3.1699)]$$
$$PVn = \$250,194$$

The journal entries to record the lease at the beginning of the lease term would be:

2002			
Jan. 1	Leased Equipment	250,194	
	Obligations Under Capital Leases		250,194
	To record the lease.		
1	Lease Expense	5,000	
	Obligations Under Capital Leases	60,000	
	Cash		65,000
	To record the first lease payment.		

6 An important exception to the use of the present value of future minimum lease payments as a basis for recording a capital lease was included by the FASB in Statement No. 13, par. 10, as follows: "However, if the amount so determined exceeds the fair value of the leased property at the inception of the lease, the amount recorded as the asset and obligation shall be the fair value." In this case, an implicit interest rate would have to be computed using the fair value of the asset.

7 All computations of present value in this chapter will be rounded to the nearest dollar. This will require some adjustment at times to the final figures in the tables to balance the amounts.

The term *lease expense* is used to record the executory costs related to the leased equipment, such as insurance and taxes. It is possible to record the lease liability at the gross amount of the payments ($300,000 = 5 × $60,000) and offset it with a discount account—Discount on Lease Contract. The net method is more common in accounting for leases by the lessee and will be used in this chapter.

> **FYI:** When a lease is capitalized, the asset is included on the balance sheet and written off over time. The term "amortization," instead of "depreciation," is typically used when describing the systematic expensing of the cost of a leased asset.

Once the leased asset and the lease liability are recorded, periodic entries must be made to recognize the gradual depreciation of the leased asset and the payment (with interest) of the lease liability. The asset value is amortized in accordance with the lessee's normal method of depreciation for owned assets. The amortization period to be used depends on which of the criteria is used to qualify the lease as a capital lease. If the lease qualifies under the ownership transfer or bargain purchase option criteria, the economic life of the asset should be used because it is assumed that the lessee will take ownership of the asset for the remainder of its useful life at the end of the lease term. If the lease fails to satisfy the ownership transfer or bargain purchase option criteria but does qualify under either the lease term or present value of minimum lease payments criteria, the length of the lease term should be used for amortization purposes. In the Marshall Corporation example, the equipment lease qualifies for capitalization under the lease term criterion because the lease period is equal to the economic life of the equipment. Accordingly, the equipment is amortized over the economic life of five years.

The recorded amount of the lease liability should be reduced each period as the lease payments are made. Interest expense on the unpaid balance is computed and recognized. The lessee's incremental borrowing rate, or the lessor's implicit interest rate if lower, is the interest rate that should be used in computing interest expense. Exhibit 15-3 shows how the $60,000 payments (excluding executory costs) would be allocated between payment on the obligation and interest expense. To simplify the schedule, it is assumed that all lease payments after the first payment are made on December 31 of each year. If the payments were made in January, an accrual of interest at December 31 would be required.

If the normal company depreciation policy for this type of equipment is straight-line, the required entry at December 31, 2002, for amortization of the leased asset would be as shown at the top of the next page.

EXHIBIT 15-3 | Schedule of Lease Payments [Five-Year Lease, $60,000 Annual Payments (Net of Executory Costs), 10% Interest]

Date	Description	Amount	Interest Expense*	Principal	Lease Obligation
1/1/02	Initial balance				$250,194
1/1/02	Payment	$ 60,000		$ 60,000	190,194
12/31/02	Payment	60,000	$19,019	40,981	149,213
12/31/03	Payment	60,000	14,921	45,079	104,134
12/31/04	Payment	60,000	10,413	49,587	54,547
12/31/05	Payment	60,000	5,453**	54,547	0
		$300,000	$49,806	$250,194	

*Preceding lease obligation × 10%.
**Rounded.

2002
Dec. 31 Amortization Expense on Leased Equipment 50,039*
        Accumulated Amortization on Leased Equipment 50,039

*Computation:
$250,194 ÷ 5 = $50,039

Similar entries would be made for each of the remaining four years. Although the credit could be made directly to the asset account, the use of a contra asset account provides the necessary disclosure information about the original lease value and accumulated amortization to date.

In addition to the entry recording amortization, another entry is required at December 31, 2002, to record the second lease payment, including a prepayment of 2003's executory costs. As indicated in Exhibit 15-3, the interest expense for 2002 would be computed by multiplying the incremental borrowing rate of 10% by the initial present value of the obligation less the immediate $60,000 first payment, or ($250,194 − $60,000) × .10 = $19,019.

2002
Dec. 31 Prepaid Executory Costs 5,000
        Obligations Under Capital Leases 40,981
        Interest Expense 19,019
           Cash 65,000

Because of the assumption that all lease payments after the first payment are made on December 31, the portion of each payment that represents executory costs must be recorded as a prepayment and charged to lease expense in the following year.

Based on the preceding journal entries and using information contained in Exhibit 15-3, the December 31, 2002, balance sheet of Marshall Corporation would include information concerning the leased equipment and related obligation as illustrated below.

Marshall Corporation
Balance Sheet (Partial)
December 31, 2002

Assets		Liabilities	
Current assets:		Current liabilities:	
Prepaid executory costs—		Obligations under capital	
leased equipment	$ 5,000	leases, current portion	$ 45,079
Land, buildings, and equipment:		Noncurrent liabilities:	
Leased equipment	$250,194	Obligations under capital	
Less: Accumulated amortization	50,039	leases, exclusive of $45,079	
Net value	$200,155	included in current liabilities	$104,134

Note that the principal portion of the payment due December 31, 2003, is reported as a current liability on the December 31, 2002, balance sheet.[8]

The income statement would include the amortization on leased property of $50,039, interest expense of $19,019, and executory costs of $5,000 as expenses for the period. The total expense of $74,058 exceeds the $65,000 rental payment made in the

8 There have been some theoretical arguments advanced against this method of allocating lease obligations between current and noncurrent liabilities. See Robert J. Swieringa, "When Current Is Noncurrent and Vice Versa," *The Accounting Review*, January 1984, pp. 123–130. Professor Swieringa identifies two methods of making the allocation: the "change in present value" (CPV) approach that is used in the example and the "present value of the next year's payment" (PVNYP) approach that allocates a larger portion of the liability to the current category. A later study shows that the CPV method is followed almost universally in practice. A. W. Richardson, "The Measurement of the Current Portion of Long-Term Lease Obligations—Some Evidence From Practice," *The Accounting Review*, October 1985, pp. 744–752. While there is theoretical support for both positions, this text uses the CPV method in chapter examples and problem materials.

EXHIBIT 15–4 | Schedule of Expenses Recognized—Capital and Operating Leases Compared

Year	Expenses Recognized—Capital Lease				Expenses Recognized—Operating Lease	Difference
	Interest	Executory Costs	Amortization	Total		
2002	$19,019	$ 5,000	$ 50,039	$ 74,058	$ 65,000	$9,058
2003	14,921	5,000	50,039	69,960	65,000	4,960
2004	10,413	5,000	50,039	65,452	65,000	452
2005	5,453	5,000	50,039	60,492	65,000	(4,508)
2006	0	5,000	50,038*	55,038	65,000	(9,962)
	$49,806	$25,000	$250,194	$325,000	$325,000	$ 0

*Rounded.

first year. As the amount of interest expense declines each period, the total expense will be reduced and, for the last two years, will be less than the $65,000 payments (Exhibit 15–4). The total amount debited to expense over the life of the lease will be the same regardless of whether the lease is accounted for as an operating lease or as a capital lease. If an accelerated depreciation method of amortization is used, the difference in the early years between the expense and the payment would be even larger.

In addition to the amounts recognized in the capital lease journal entries given above, a note to the financial statements would be necessary to explain the terms of the lease and future minimum lease payments in more detail.

ACCOUNTING FOR LEASES WITH A BARGAIN PURCHASE OPTION Frequently, the lessee is given the option of purchasing the property at some future date at a bargain price. As discussed previously, the present value of the bargain purchase option is part of the minimum lease payments and should be included in the capitalized value of the lease. Assume in the preceding example that there is a bargain purchase option of $75,000 exercisable after 5 years and the economic life of the equipment is expected to be 10 years. The other lease terms remain the same. The present value of the minimum lease payments would be increased by the present value of the bargain purchase amount of $75,000, or $46,568, computed as follows:

$$PV = \$75,000(PVF_{\overline{5}|10\%})$$
$$PV = \$75,000(0.6209)$$
$$PV = \$46,568$$

The total present value of the future minimum lease payments is $296,762 ($250,194 + $46,568). This amount will be used to record the initial asset and liability. The asset balance of $296,762 will be amortized over the asset life of 10 years because of the existence of the bargain purchase option; this makes the transaction, in reality, a sale. The liability balance will be reduced as shown in Exhibit 15–5.

At the date of exercising the option, the net balance in the leased equipment asset account and its related accumulated amortization account would be transferred to the regular equipment account. The entries at the exercise of the option would be:

2006			
Dec. 31	Obligations Under Capital Leases	68,183	
	Interest Expense	6,817	
	Cash		75,000
	To record exercise of bargain purchase option.		

EXHIBIT 15-5 | Schedule of Lease Payments [Five-Year Lease With Bargain Purchase Option of $75,000 After Five Years, $60,000 Annual Payments (Net of Executory Costs), 10% Interest]

Date	Description	Amount	Interest Expense	Principal	Lease Obligation
1/1/02	Initial balance				$296,762
1/1/02	Payment	$ 60,000		$ 60,000	236,762
12/31/02	Payment	60,000	$23,676	36,324	200,438
12/31/03	Payment	60,000	20,044	39,956	160,482
12/31/04	Payment	60,000	16,048	43,952	116,530
12/31/05	Payment	60,000	11,653	48,347	68,183
12/31/06	Payment	75,000	6,817*	68,183	0
		$375,000	$78,238	$296,762	

*Rounded.

FYI: In FASB Interpretation No. 26, the Board concluded that no gain or loss should be recognized when a leased asset is purchased (see footnote 9). As with the exchange of similar assets, the fair value of the equipment on the purchase date is ignored unless evidence of significant impairment exists. See Chapter 13.

Equipment	148,381*	
Accumulated Amortization on Leased Equipment	148,381	
Leased Equipment		296,762

To transfer remaining balance in leased asset account to equipment account.

*Computation:
Accumulated amortization: $296,762 ÷ 10 years = $29,676 per year (rounded);
5 years × $29,676 per year = $148,381 (rounded).

If the equipment is not purchased and the lease is permitted to lapse, a loss equal to the $73,381 difference ($148,381 – $75,000) between the equipment's remaining book value and the remaining balance in the lease liability account (including accrued interest) would have to be recognized by the following entry:

2006			
Dec. 31	Loss From Failure to Exercise Bargain Purchase Option	73,381	
	Obligations Under Capital Leases	68,183	
	Interest Expense	6,817	
	Accumulated Amortization on Leased Equipment	148,381	
	Leased Equipment		296,762

ACCOUNTING FOR LEASES WITH A LESSEE-GUARANTEED RESIDUAL VALUE If the lease agreement requires the lessee to guarantee a residual value, the lessee treats the guarantee similar to a bargain purchase option and includes the present value of the guarantee as part of the capitalized value of the lease. At the expiration of the lease term, the amount of the guarantee will be reported as a liability under the lease. In addition, the remaining book value of the leased asset will be equal to the guaranteed residual value. If the fair value of the leased asset is less than the guaranteed residual value, a loss is reported for the difference and the lessee must make up the difference with a cash payment.

ACCOUNTING FOR PURCHASE OF ASSET DURING LEASE TERM When a lease does not provide for a transfer of ownership or a purchase option, it is still possible that a lessee may purchase leased property during the term of the lease. Usually the purchase price will differ from the recorded lease obligation at the purchase date. No gain or loss should be recorded on the purchase, but the difference between the purchase price and the obligation still on the books should be charged or credited to the acquired asset's carrying value.[9]

To illustrate, assume that on December 31, 2004, rather than making the lease payment due, the lessee purchased the leased property in the Marshall Corporation example described on page 871 for $120,000. At that date, the remaining liability recorded on the lessee's books is $114,547 (lease obligation of $104,134 + interest payable of $10,413; see Exhibit 15-3) and the net book value of the recorded leased asset is $100,077, the original capitalized value of $250,194 less $150,117 amortization ($50,039 × 3). The entry to record the purchase on the lessee's books would be:

2004				
Dec. 31	Interest Expense		10,413	
	Obligations Under Capital Leases		104,134	
	Equipment		105,530	
	Accumulated Amortization on Leased Equipment		150,117	
	Leased Equipment			250,194
	Cash			120,000

The purchased equipment is capitalized at $105,530, which is the book value of the leased asset, $100,077, plus $5,453, the excess of the purchase price over the carrying value of the lease obligation ($120,000 - $114,547).

Treatment of Leases on Lessee's Statement of Cash Flows

Operating leases present no special problems to the lessee in preparing a statement of cash flows. The lease payments reduce, and thus require no adjustment to, net income under the indirect method except for accrued or prepaid rent expense. The cash payments would be reported as operating expense outlays under the direct method.

Adjustments for capital leases by the lessee, however, are more complex. The amortization of leased assets would be treated the same as depreciation, that is, added to net income under the indirect method and ignored under the direct method. The portion of the cash payment allocated to interest expense would require no adjustment under the indirect method and would be reported as part of the cash payment for interest expense under the direct method. The portion of the cash payment allocated to the lease liability would be reported as a financing outflow under either method. The signing of a capital lease would not be reported as either an investing or financing activity because it is a noncash transaction. The impact of a capital lease on the lessee's statement of cash flows is summarized in Exhibit 15-6.

EXHIBIT 15-6 | Impact of a Capital Lease on the Lessee's Statement of Cash Flows

Operating Activities (indirect)	**Operating Activities** (direct)
Net income (includes reduction for: Lease interest expense Lease amortization expense) + Amortization of leased asset	− Lease interest expense
Investing Activities No impact	
Financing Activities − Principal portion of lease payment	

---

9 *FASB Interpretation No. 26,* "Accounting for Purchase of a Leased Asset by the Lessee During the Term of the Lease," Stamford, CT: Financial Accounting Standards Board, 1978, par. 5.

► AVOIDING A LIABILITY

The effect on the financial statements of operating versus capital lease treatment can be significant. One study estimated that if MCDONALD's were required to capitalize all noncancelable leases that it currently classifies as operating, the company's debt-to-equity ratio would increase 30%. Examining firms in seven different industries, the same study concluded that for those firms that use leases extensively, the effect

on their return on assets and debt-to-equity ratios of capitalizing long-term operating leases would be even more significant. For those firms, the average decrease in the return on total assets would be 34%, while the debt-to-equity ratio would increase by 191%.

With the issuance of FASB Statement No. 13, it was thought that financial statements would reflect the economic reality of firms' lease agreements. However, the lease standard has been relatively ineffective in meeting its objective. Instead of complying with the spirit of the

standard, firms have gone to great lengths to structure leases that do not meet the criteria for balance sheet recognition. In an attempt to keep ahead of the clever manipulations employed by firms to avoid capital lease treatment, the FASB has had to amend and interpret the lease standard over a dozen times. Scanning the list of FASB pronouncements following the issuance of Statement No. 13, it can be seen that portions of Statement No. 13 have been amended or superseded by Statements 17, 22, 23, 26, 27, 28, 29, 34, 71, 77, 91,

ACCOUNTING FOR LEASES—LESSOR

Properly account for both capital and operating leases from the standpoint of the lessor (asset owner).

The lessor in a lease transaction gives up the physical possession of the property to the lessee. If the transfer of the property is considered temporary in nature, the lessor will continue to carry the leased asset as an owned asset on the balance sheet; the revenue from the lease will be reported as it is earned; and depreciation of the leased asset will be matched against the revenue. This type of lease is described as an operating lease, and cash receipts from the lessee are treated similar to the operating lease procedures described for the lessee. However, if a lease has terms that make the transaction similar in substance to a sale or a permanent transfer of the asset to the lessee, the lessor should no longer report the asset as though it were owned but should reflect the transfer to the lessee.

As indicated earlier, if a lease meets one of the four general lease classification criteria that apply to both lessees and lessors plus both of the revenue recognition criteria that apply to the lessor only (i.e., collectibility and substantial completion), it is classified by the lessor as a capital lease and recorded as either a direct financing lease or a sales-type lease.

FYI: The sale of new cars provides a good example of a sales-type lease. Each of the Big 3 automakers has a financing subsidiary to handle leasing. When a car is leased from a dealership, the auto company earns a profit on the lease as well as interest from the lease contract.

Direct financing leases involve a lessor who is primarily engaged in financing activities, such as a bank or finance company. The lessor views the lease as an investment. The revenue generated by this type of lease is interest revenue. **Sales-type leases**, on the other hand, involve manufacturers or dealers who use leases as a means of facilitating the marketing of their products. Thus, there are two different types of revenue generated by this type of lease: (1) an immediate profit or loss, which is the difference between the cost of the property being leased and its sales price, or fair value, at the inception of the lease, and (2) interest revenue earned over time as the lessee makes the lease payments that pay off the lease obligation plus interest.

For either an operating, direct financing, or sales-type lease, a lessor may incur certain costs, referred to as **initial direct costs**, in connection with

96, 98, 109, and 125. In addition, the FASB has released Interpretations 19, 21, 23, 24, 26, and 27 and issued 10 Technical Bulletins to clarify certain aspects of the lease standard. In spite of all this, firms still manage to treat the large majority of their long-term, noncancelable leases as off-balance-sheet operating leases.

QUESTIONS:

1. If a major objective of financial statement information is to provide useful information to investors and creditors, are those groups currently receiving financial statements that contain relevant and reliable information regarding leased assets?

2. Do you think that the FASB has achieved its objective of requiring leases that are economically equivalent to purchases to be recognized in the balance sheet?

3. It often seems that whenever the FASB provides detailed rules for applying a specific standard, companies spend a great deal of time looking for loopholes in those rules. What can the FASB do to get companies to comply with the intent of a standard?

4. If the FASB were to ask you for advice in revising its standard on leasing, what would your advice be?

SOURCE:

Imhoff, Lipe, and Wright, "Operating Leases: Impact of Constructive Capitalization," *Accounting Horizons*, March 1991, pp. 51–63.

obtaining the lease. These costs include the costs to negotiate the lease, perform the credit check on the lessee, and prepare the lease documents.[10]

Initial direct costs are accounted for differently depending on which of the three types of leases is involved. Exhibit 15-7 summarizes the accounting treatment for initial direct costs. These costs will be discussed further as each type of lease is presented.

EXHIBIT 15-7 | Accounting for Initial Direct Costs

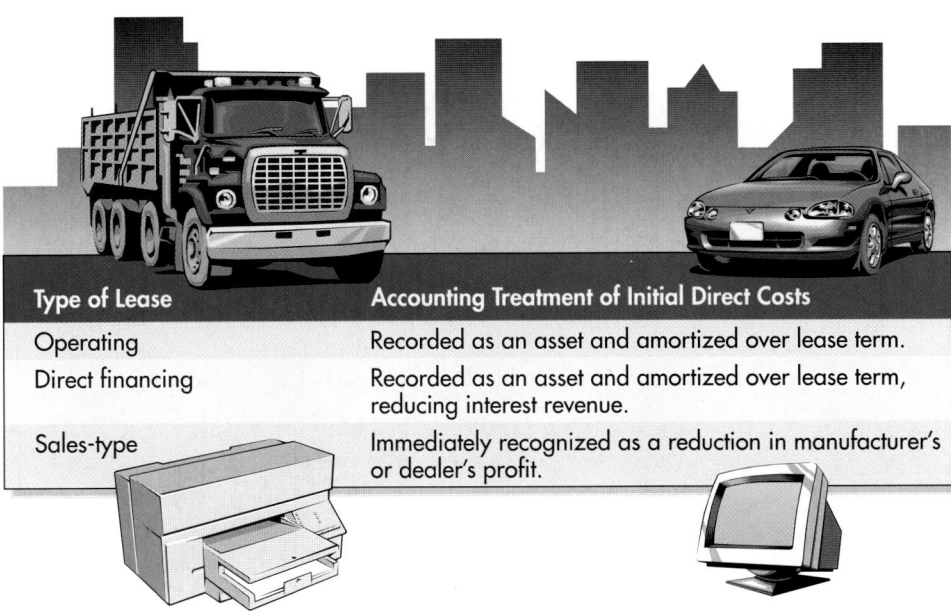

Type of Lease	Accounting Treatment of Initial Direct Costs
Operating	Recorded as an asset and amortized over lease term.
Direct financing	Recorded as an asset and amortized over lease term, reducing interest revenue.
Sales-type	Immediately recognized as a reduction in manufacturer's or dealer's profit.

10 *Statement of Financial Accounting Standards No. 91*, "Accounting for Nonrefundable Fees and Costs Associated With Originating or Acquiring Loans and Initial Direct Costs of Leases," Stamford, CT: Financial Accounting Standards Board, 1986, par. 24.

Accounting for Operating Leases—Lessor

Accounting for operating leases for the lessor is very similar to that described for the lessee. The lessor recognizes revenue as the payments are received. If there are significant variations in the payment terms, entries will be necessary to reflect a straight-line pattern of revenue recognition. Initial direct costs incurred in connection with an operating lease are deferred and amortized on a straight-line basis over the term of the lease, thus matching them against rent revenue.

To illustrate accounting for an operating lease on the lessor's books, assume that the equipment leased for five years by Universal Leasing Company to Marshall Corporation (page 870) on January 1, 2002, for $65,000 a year, including executory costs of $5,000 per year, had a cost of $400,000 to the lessor, Universal Leasing. Initial direct costs of $15,000 were incurred to obtain and finalize the lease. The equipment has an estimated life of 10 years, with no residual value. Assuming no purchase or renewal options or guarantees by the lessee, the lease does not meet any of the four general classification criteria and would be treated as an operating lease. The entries to record the payment of the initial direct costs and the receipt of the lease payments by Universal Leasing would be:

2002			
Jan. 1	Deferred Initial Direct Costs	15,000	
	Cash		15,000
1	Cash	65,000	
	Rent Revenue		60,000
	Executory Costs		5,000

The $5,000 payment received from the lessee to reimburse the executory costs may be reflected as a credit (reduction) to the executory costs account, as shown here, or as a credit to a separate revenue account against which the executory costs can be matched.

Assuming the lessor depreciates the equipment on a straight-line basis over its expected life of 10 years and amortizes the initial direct costs on a straight-line basis over the 5-year lease term, the depreciation and amortization entries at the end of the first year would be:

2002			
Dec. 31	Amortization of Initial Direct Costs	3,000	
	Deferred Initial Direct Costs		3,000
31	Depreciation Expense on Leased Equipment	40,000	
	Accumulated Depreciation on Leased Equipment		40,000

If the rental period and the lessor's fiscal year do not coincide or if the lessor prepares interim reports, an adjustment would be required to record the unearned rent revenue at the end of the accounting period. Amortization of the initial direct costs would be adjusted to reflect a partial year.

Accounting for Direct Financing Leases

Accounting for direct financing leases for lessors is very similar to that used for capital leases by lessees but with the entries reversed to provide for interest revenue rather than interest expense and reduction of a lease payment receivable rather than a lease liability. In practice, the lease payment receivable usually is recorded by the lessor at the gross amount of the lease payments with an offsetting valuation account for the unearned interest. Unearned interest revenue is computed as the difference between the total expected lease payments and the fair market value, or cost, of the leased asset. The difference between the total expected lease payments and the remaining unearned interest revenue is called the **net lease investment**.

ILLUSTRATIVE ENTRIES FOR DIRECT FINANCING LEASES   Referring to the lessee example on page 870, assume that the cost of the equipment to the Universal Leasing Company was the same as its fair market value, $250,194, and that the purchase by the lessor had been entered into Equipment Purchased for Lease. The entry to record the initial lease would be:

```
2002
Jan. 1   Lease Payments Receivable ...........................................   300,000
                Equipment Purchased for Lease .........................               250,194
                Unearned Interest Revenue ...............................                49,806
```

The first payment would be recorded as follows:

```
Jan. 1   Cash ............................................................................   65,000
                Lease Payments Receivable ...............................                60,000
                Executory Costs ..............................................                 5,000
```

The lessor is paying the executory costs but charging them to the lessee. The lessor can record the receipt of the executory costs by debiting Cash and crediting the executory costs expense account. As the lessor pays the costs, the expense account is debited. The lessor is serving as a conduit for these costs to the lessee and will have an expense only if the lessee fails to make the payments. Interest revenue will be recognized over the lease term as shown in Exhibit 15–8.

At the end of the first year, the following entries would be made to record receipt of the second lease payment, to recognize interest revenue for 2002, and to recognize the advance payment for next year's executory costs as a deferred credit.

```
2002
Dec. 31   Cash ...........................................................................   65,000
                Lease Payments Receivable ...............................                60,000
                Deferred Executory Costs (a liability) .................                 5,000
     31   Unearned Interest Revenue ......................................   19,019
                Interest Revenue ............................................                19,019
```

Notice that unlike the operating lease example, no annual depreciation expense is recorded by the lessor in association with an asset leased under a capital lease agreement. This is because the asset has been "sold" to the lessee and removed from the lessor's books.

EXHIBIT 15–8 | Schedule of Lease Receipts and Interest Revenue [Five-Year Lease, $60,000 Annual Payments (Exclusive of Executory Costs), 10% Interest]

Date	Description	Interest Revenue*	Payment Receipt	Lease Payments Receivable	Unearned Interest Revenue
1/1/02	Initial balance			$300,000	$49,806
1/1/02	Receipt		$ 60,000	240,000	49,806
12/31/02	Receipt	$19,019	60,000	180,000	30,787
12/31/03	Receipt	14,921	60,000	120,000	15,866
12/31/04	Receipt	10,413	60,000	60,000	5,453
12/31/05	Receipt	5,453**	60,000	0	0
		$49,806	$300,000		

*(Preceding lease payment receivable less unearned interest revenue) × 10%.
**Rounded.

Based on the journal entries, the asset portion of the balance sheet of the lessor at December 31, 2002, will report the lease receivable less the unearned interest revenue as follows:

Universal Leasing Company
Balance Sheet (Partial)
December 31, 2002

Assets

Current assets:		
Lease payments receivable	$ 60,000	
Less: Unearned interest revenue	14,921	$ 45,079
Noncurrent assets:		
Lease payments receivable		
(exclusive of $60,000 included in current assets)	$120,000	
Less: Unearned interest revenue	15,866	$104,134

If a direct financing lease contains a bargain purchase option, the amount of the option is added to the receivable and the interest component of the option amount (the difference between the option amount and its present value as of the lease signing date) is added to the unearned interest revenue account. The periodic entries and computations are made as though the bargain purchase amount was an additional rental payment.

LESSOR ACCOUNTING FOR DIRECT FINANCING LEASES WITH RESIDUAL VALUE

If leased property is expected to have residual value, the gross amount of the expected residual value is added to the receivable account. It does not matter whether the residual value is guaranteed or unguaranteed. If guaranteed, it is treated in the accounts exactly like a bargain purchase option. If unguaranteed, the lessor is expected to have an asset equal in value to the residual amount at the end of the lease term. The estimated residual value is added to the asset account, and the interest attributable to the unguaranteed residual value is added to the unearned interest revenue account.

To illustrate the recording of residual values, assume the same facts for the Universal Leasing Company as the example on pages 873–874 except that the asset has a residual value at the end of the five-year lease term of $75,000 (either guaranteed or unguaranteed) rather than a bargain purchase option. Assume the cost of the equipment to the Universal Leasing Company was again the same as its fair market value, $296,762.

The entries to record this lease and the first payment would be:

> **Caution!** The fair market value in this example ($296,762) is different from the fair market value in the previous example ($250,194) because, in the previous example, the asset was assumed to be worthless at the end of the lease term. In this example, the asset is estimated to have a residual value of $75,000. The present value of that $75,000, i.e., $46,568, accounts for the difference.

2002			
Jan. 1	Lease Payments Receivable	375,000	
	Equipment Purchased for Lease		296,762
	Unearned Interest Revenue		78,238
1	Cash	65,000	
	Lease Payments Receivable		60,000
	Executory Costs		5,000

The difference between the lease payments receivable of $375,000 and the cost of the equipment leased of $296,762 is the unearned interest revenue of $78,238. The amortization of the unearned interest revenue would be identical to the interest expense computation illustrated in Exhibit 15–5 for the lessee.

At the end of the first year, the lessor would make the following entries:

2002			
Dec. 31	Cash	65,000	
	Lease Payments Receivable		60,000
	Deferred Executory Costs		5,000

Dec. 31	Unearned Interest Revenue	23,676	
	Interest Revenue		23,676

At the end of the lease term, the lessor would make the following entry to record the recovery of the leased asset assuming the residual value was the same as originally estimated:

2006				
Dec. 31	Equipment		75,000	
	Unearned Interest Revenue		6,817	
	Lease Payments Receivable			75,000
	Interest Revenue			6,817

INITIAL DIRECT COSTS RELATED TO DIRECT FINANCING LEASES If the lessor incurs any initial direct costs in conjunction with a direct financing lease, those costs are recorded as a separate asset, increasing the net lease investment. Because the initial net lease investment is increased but the lease payments remain the same, the existence of initial direct costs results in a lower implicit interest rate earned by the lessor. Including initial direct costs as part of the initial net lease investment effectively spreads the initial costs over the lease term and reduces the amount of interest revenue that would otherwise be recognized.

Accounting for Sales-Type Leases—Lessor

Accounting for sales-type leases adds one more dimension to the lessor's revenue, an immediate profit or loss arising from the difference between the sales price of the leased property and the lessor's cost to manufacture or purchase the asset. If there is no difference between the sales price and the lessor's cost, the lease is not a sales-type lease. The lessor also will recognize interest revenue over the lease term for the difference between the sales price and the gross amount of the minimum lease payments. The three values that must be identified to determine these income elements, therefore, can be summarized as follows:

1. The minimum lease payments as defined previously for the lessee, that is, rental payments over the lease term net of any executory costs plus the amount to be paid under a bargain purchase option or guarantee of the residual value
2. The fair market value of the asset
3. The cost or carrying value of the asset to the lessor increased by any initial direct costs to lease the asset

The manufacturer's or dealer's profit is the difference between the fair market value of the asset and the cost or carrying value of the asset to the lessor. If cost exceeds the fair market value, a loss will be reported. The difference between the gross rentals and the fair market value of the asset is interest revenue and arises because of the time delay in paying for the asset as described by the lease terms. The relationship between these three values can be demonstrated as follows:

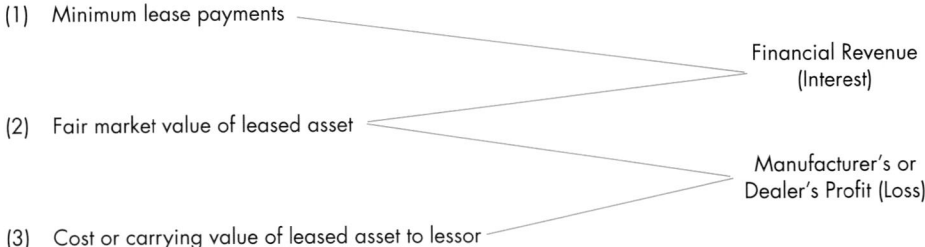

(1) Minimum lease payments

(2) Fair market value of leased asset

(3) Cost or carrying value of leased asset to lessor

Financial Revenue (Interest)

Manufacturer's or Dealer's Profit (Loss)

To illustrate this type of lease, assume the lessor for the equipment described on page 870 is American Manufacturing Company rather than Universal Leasing. The fair market value of the equipment is equal to its present value (the future lease payments discounted at 10%), or $250,194. This computation is reversed from what would happen in practice—normally, the fair market value is known, and the minimum lease payments are set at an amount that will yield the desired rate of return to the lessor.

Assume the equipment cost American Manufacturing $160,000 and initial direct costs of $15,000 were incurred. The three values and the related revenue amounts would be as follows:

(1)	Minimum lease payments: ($65,000 – $5,000) × 5	$300,000	$49,806 (Interest Revenue)
(2)	Fair market value of equipment	$250,194	
(3)	Cost of leased equipment to lessor, plus initial direct costs	$175,000	$75,194 (Manufacturer's Profit)

ILLUSTRATIVE ENTRIES FOR SALES-TYPE LEASES   The interest revenue ($49,806) is the same as that illustrated for a direct financing lease on page 878, and it is recognized over the lease term by the same entries and according to Exhibit 15–8. The manufacturer's profit is recognized as revenue immediately in the current period by including the fair market value of the asset as a sale and debiting the cost of the equipment carried in Finished Goods Inventory to Cost of Goods Sold. The initial direct costs previously deferred are recognized as an expense immediately by increasing Cost of Goods Sold by the amount expended for these costs. This reduces the amount of immediate profit to be recognized. The reimbursement of executory costs is treated in the same way as illustrated for direct financing leases.

The entries to record this information on American Manufacturing Company's books at the beginning of the lease term would be:

2002			
Jan. 1	Lease Payments Receivable	300,000	
	Unearned Interest Revenue		49,806
	Sales		250,194
1	Cost of Goods Sold	175,000	
	Finished Goods Inventory		160,000
	Deferred Initial Direct Costs		15,000
1	Cash	65,000	
	Lease Payments Receivable		60,000
	Executory Costs		5,000

> **Caution!**   The sales account is always credited for the present value of the minimum lease payments.

The first journal entry records the sale and recognizes a receivable, offset by the unearned interest that is included in the face amount of the receivable. The second journal entry simply removes the inventory and deferred direct costs from the books of the lessor and recognizes the cost of goods sold. The final entry records the first payment. The example does not show the payment for the initial direct costs. The deferred initial direct costs account would have been charged at the time these costs were paid.

The 2002 income statement would include the sales and cost of goods sold amounts yielding the manufacturer's profit of $75,194 and interest revenue of $19,019. A note to the statements would describe in more detail the nature of the lease and its terms.

ACCOUNTING FOR SALES-TYPE LEASES WITH A BARGAIN PURCHASE OPTION OR GUARANTEE OF RESIDUAL VALUE   If the lease agreement provides for the lessor to receive a lump sum payment at the end of the lease term in the form of a bargain purchase option or a guarantee of residual value, the minimum lease payments include these amounts. The receivable is thus increased by the gross amount of the future payment; the unearned interest revenue account is increased by the interest on the end-of-lease payment; and sales are increased by the present value of the additional amount.

To illustrate a sales-type lease with a bargain purchase option, assume American Manufacturing was the lessor on the lease described on page 873 and in Exhibit 15–5.

The initial entries when either a bargain purchase option or a guarantee of residual value of $75,000 is payable at the end of the five-year lease term would be:

2002			
Jan. 1	Lease Payments Receivable	375,000	
	Unearned Interest Revenue		78,238
	Sales		296,762
1	Cost of Goods Sold	175,000	
	Finished Goods Inventory		160,000
	Deferred Initial Direct Costs		15,000
1	Cash	65,000	
	Lease Payments Receivable		60,000
	Executory Costs		5,000

Because the lease now includes a bargain purchase option, Sales increases by $46,568 (present value of the bargain purchase amount) over the amount recognized in the previous example. The manufacturer's profit is also increased by this amount, and the difference between the $75,000 gross payment and the $46,568 increase in Sales is recorded as a $28,432 increase in Unearned Interest Revenue.

ACCOUNTING FOR SALES-TYPE LEASES WITH UNGUARANTEED RESIDUAL VALUE When a sales-type lease does not contain a bargain purchase option or a guaranteed residual value but the economic life of the leased asset exceeds the lease term, the residual value of the property will remain with the lessor. As indicated earlier, this is called an unguaranteed residual value. Because the sales account reflects the present value of the minimum lease payments, an unguaranteed residual value would not be included in the sales account. However, the cost of goods sold would be reduced by the present value of the unguaranteed residual value to recognize the fact that the lessor will be receiving back the $75,000 leased asset (worth a present value of $46,568) at the end of the lease term. The entry to record the initial lease described above with an unguaranteed residual value would be:

2002			
Jan. 1	Lease Payments Receivable	328,432	
	Unearned Interest Revenue		78,238
	Sales		250,194
1	Cost of Goods Sold	128,432	
	Finished Goods Inventory		113,432
	Deferred Initial Direct Costs		15,000
1	Lease Payment Receivable	46,568	
	Finished Goods Inventory		46,568

The only difference between accounting for an unguaranteed residual value and a guaranteed residual value or bargain purchase option is that rather than increasing Sales by the present value of the residual value, the present value of the unguaranteed residual value is deducted from the cost of the leased equipment sold. This reduction occurs because the portion of the leased asset represented by the unguaranteed residual value will be returned at the end of the lease term and therefore is not "sold" on the lease signing date. In essence, the $46,568 in inventory represented by the present value of the unguaranteed residual value has not been sold but has been exchanged for a receivable of equal amount.

Note that the gross profit on the transaction is the same regardless of whether the residual value is guaranteed or unguaranteed, as seen below:

	Guaranteed Residual Value	**Unguaranteed Residual Value**
Sales	$296,762	$250,194
Cost of goods sold	175,000	128,432
Gross profit	$121,762	$121,762

► LEASING STUD SERVICES

Today a business can lease cars, buildings, equipment, and machinery. You name it, you can probably lease it. Bill Roloson, a farmer from Canada, can verify that almost anything can be leased. Bill is in the horse racing and horse breeding businesses. When his stallion, Rebel Blue Chip, died in 1993, he began searching for a replacement to sire future winners. His search led him to the stallion Hunterstown, a horse that had

been put out to pasture in 1990 because of lameness. Roloson contacted Hunterstown's owner, Gertrude Seiling, and arranged to lease the horse for stud for five years.

Upon arrival at Prince Edward Island in Canada, the horse was given a workout. Much to Roloson's surprise,

Hunterstown's lameness seemed to have healed. Instead of using Hunterstown for breeding, Roloson wanted to begin racing the stallion again. The lease agreement with Seiling was renegotiated to cover race earnings, and Hunterstown began winning races. Roloson then faced the decision of continuing to race the horse or take the

THIRD-PARTY GUARANTEES OF RESIDUAL VALUE   When a lease is used by the seller as a means to provide financing to the buyer and to increase sales, the seller wants to account for the lease as a sales-type lease, not as an operating lease, so that the revenue from the sale can be recognized immediately. On the other hand, the buyer would prefer to account for the lease as an operating lease in order to keep the lease obligation off the balance sheet. A third-party guarantee of residual value is a clever trick that companies have devised to get around the accounting rules and allow the desires of both the seller-lessor and the buyer-lessee to be satisfied.

Consider the example just given in which the guaranteed residual value is $75,000. In this case, the fair value of the equipment on the lease signing date is $296,762. From the lessor's standpoint, the present value of the minimum lease payments, including the guaranteed residual value, is also $296,762. Accordingly, the lease meets the 90% of fair market value criterion, and the lease is accounted for as a sales-type lease.

Here is where the fun begins. The lessee, instead of guaranteeing the residual value itself, can pay an insurance company or investment firm to guarantee the residual value. For a fee, the insurance company bears the risk that the residual value of the leased asset might fall below the guaranteed residual value. If this happens, the insurance company, not the lessee, will make up the difference. By the purchase of this "insurance policy," the lessee removes the guaranteed residual value from its calculation of the present value of the minimum lease payments. Without the guaranteed residual value, the present value of the minimum lease payments is only $250,194, just 84% ($250,194 ÷ $296,762) of the fair value of the leased asset. As a result, the lessee accounts for the lease as an operating lease.

In summary, a third-party guarantee of residual value allows the seller-lessor to recognize the entire profit from the lease transaction immediately but also permits the buyer-lessee to treat the lease as an operating lease and keep the lease liability off the balance sheet.

Sale of Asset During Lease Term

If the lessor sells an asset to the lessee during the lease term, a gain or loss is recognized on the difference between the receivable balance, after deducting any remaining unearned interest revenue, and the selling price of the asset. Thus, if the leased asset described in Exhibit 15–8 is sold on December 31, 2004, for $140,000 before the $60,000 rental payment is made, a gain of $25,453 would be reported. The following journal entry

horse back to Prince Edward Island for stud duty. Roloson stated, "We'd planned to bring him back for at least a month . . . , but that's up in the air, depending on how he's racing."

QUESTIONS:

1. Can you capitalize the lease of an animal?
2. In this instance, what would be Hunterstown's expected useful life? Would your answer vary

depending upon whether Hunterstown was used for breeding or for racing?

3. When circumstances changed and the lease for the horse was renegotiated, could that affect whether or not the horse was capitalized? How?

SOURCE:
Paul Delean, "Hunterstown's Remarkable Return: Horse Returned to Racetrack After Three Years at Stud," *The Gazette* (Montreal), p. F7.

would be made to record the sale:

```
2004
Dec. 31   Unearned Interest Revenue ....................................... 15,866
          Cash ................................................................ 140,000
              Interest Revenue .......................................................        10,413
              Lease Payments Receivable ...........................................       120,000
              Gain on Sale of Leased Asset ........................................        25,453
```

Although the lessor does recognize a gain or loss on the sale, as mentioned earlier, the lessee accounts for the transaction as an exchange of similar assets and defers any gain or loss in the value placed on the purchased asset.

Treatment of Leases on Lessor's Statement of Cash Flows

Operating leases present no special problems to the lessor in preparing a statement of cash flows except for initial direct costs. Because initial direct costs are recognized as an asset when the lease is an operating lease, the payment of these costs would be reported as an investing cash outflow. Under the indirect method, the amortization of initial direct costs would be added to net income in the same way income is adjusted for depreciation. Under the direct method, the amortization would be ignored. The lease payment receipts would be reported as part of net income and would require no adjustment under the indirect method and would be reported as part of the revenue receipts under the direct method.

Capital leases must be analyzed carefully to determine their impact on the statement of cash flows. Financing leases would require adjustments similar to those made by the lessee for capital leases except that for the lender (lessor), the transaction is viewed as an investing activity rather than a financing activity as was the case for the borrower (lessee). The portion of the receipt that represents interest will be included in net income and requires no adjustment under the indirect method. It would be part of cash inflows from interest under the direct method. The portion of the lease payment representing the principal would be reported as a cash inflow from investing activities.

Under sales-type leases, the manufacturer's profit, net of initial direct costs, is reported in net income, but the cash inflow comes as the lease payments are received. Under the indirect method, this requires a deduction from net income for the manufacturer's profit at the inception of the lease. This would automatically occur as the changes in inventory, deferred initial costs, and net lease payments receivable are reflected in the operating section of the statement of cash flows. Because the transaction is being accounted for as a sale, all further receipts under the indirect method are reported as operating inflows either as interest revenue or as reductions in the net lease payments receivable. Under the direct method, the entire lease receipt would be included in cash flows from operating activities. A summary of the treatment of lease impact on the statement of cash flows is included in Exhibit 15-9.

DISCLOSURE REQUIREMENTS FOR LEASES

Prepare and interpret the lease disclosures required of both lessors and lessees.

The FASB has established specific disclosure requirements for all leases, regardless of whether they are classified as operating or capital leases. The required information supplements the amounts recognized in the financial statements and usually is included in a single note to the financial statements.

EXHIBIT 15–9 | Summary of Lease Impact on Statement of Cash Flows

| | Operating Activities | | Investing Activities | Financing Activities |
	Indirect Method	Direct Method		
Lessee:				
Operating lease payments	NI	– Cash		
Capital lease:				
Lease payments—interest	NI	– Cash		
Lease payments—principal				– Cash
Amortization of asset	+ NI	No impact		
Lessor:				
Operating lease:				
Initial direct costs (IDC)			– Cash	
Amortization of IDC	+ NI	No impact		
Lease receipts	NI	+ Cash		
Direct financing lease:				
Initial direct costs			– Cash	
Amortization of IDC	+ NI	No impact		
Lease receipts—interest	NI	+ Cash		
Lease receipts—principal			+ Cash	
Sales-type lease:				
Initial direct costs			– Cash	
Manufacturer's or dealer's profit (net of IDC)	– NI	No impact		
Lease receipts—interest	NI	+ Cash		
Lease receipts—principal	+ NI	+ Cash		

Key:
NI	=	Included in net income
+ NI	=	Added as an adjustment to net income
– NI	=	Deducted as an adjustment to net income
+ Cash	=	Reported as a receipt of cash
– Cash	=	Reported as a payment of cash

The following information is required for all leases that have initial or remaining noncancelable lease terms in excess of one year:

Lessee

1. Gross amount of assets recorded as capital leases, along with related accumulated amortization.
2. Future minimum rental payments required as of the date of the latest balance sheet presented in the aggregate and for each of the five succeeding fiscal years. These payments should be separated between operating and capital leases. For capital leases, executory costs should be excluded.
3. Rental expense for each period for which an income statement is presented. Additional information concerning minimum rentals, contingent rentals, and sublease rentals is required for the same periods.
4. A general description of the lease contracts, including information about restrictions on such items as dividends, additional debt, and further leasing.
5. For capital leases, the amount of imputed interest necessary to reduce the lease payments to present value.

Exhibit 15–10 presents a note accompanying the 1999 financial statements of DELTA AIR LINES, illustrating the required lessee disclosures for both operating and capital leases.

EXHIBIT 15–10 | Delta Air Lines—Lessee Disclosure

---

6. LEASE OBLIGATIONS

Our Company leases aircraft, airport terminal and maintenance facilities, ticket offices and other property and equipment. We record rent expense on a straight-line basis over the life of the lease. Rental expense for operating leases totaled $1.1 billion in fiscal 1999, $0.9 billion in fiscal 1998 and $0.9 billion in fiscal 1997. Amounts due under capital leases are recorded as liabilities, and our interests in assets acquired under capital leases are shown as assets on our Consolidated Balance Sheets.

The following table summarizes our minimum rental commitments under capital leases and operating leases with initial or remaining terms of more than one year as of June 30, 1999:

Year Ending June 30 (In Millions)	Capital Leases	Operating Leases
2000	$ 63	$ 1,020
2001	57	1,030
2002	57	1,040
2003	48	1,020
2004	32	980
After 2004	40	9,440
Total minimum lease payments	297	$14,530
Less: Amounts of lease payments which represent interest	62	
Present value of future minimum capital lease payments	235	
Less: Current obligations under capital leases	39	
Long-term capital lease obligations	$196	

As of June 30, 1999, we operated 208 aircraft under operating leases and 48 aircraft under capital leases. These leases have remaining terms ranging from 6 months to 18 years. Several municipalities and airport authorities have issued special facility revenue bonds to build or improve airport terminal and maintenance facilities that we lease. Under these operating lease agreements, we are required to make rental payments that are sufficient to pay principal and interest on these bonds.

A couple of points should be highlighted relating to Delta's lease disclosure. First, compare the minimum lease payments for Delta's capital leases to the payments to be made for its operating leases. The expected payments for operating leases exceed those for capital leases by a factor of almost 50. Note also that Delta discloses the portion of the minimum lease payments on its capital leases that represents interest. With the information in this note, we can approximate the impact that the obligations related to Delta's operating leases would have on its balance sheet if those leases were capitalized.

To approximate the present value of these future operating lease payments, we can make some simplifying assumptions:

- The appropriate interest rates for discounting future cash flows is 10%.
- The uneven stream of future operating lease payments by Delta is roughly equivalent to $1 billion per year for 15 years. This rough approximation stems from the fact that the payments in the first five years are around $1 billion per year and the total of the payments is $14.5 billion, which is roughly equal to $1 billion a year for 15 years.

Given these simplifying assumptions, it is easy to compute that the present value of an annuity of $1 billion per year for 15 years is $7.6 billion if the interest rate is 10%. This $7.6 billion approximates the economic value of Delta's obligations under its operating leases.

If Delta were required to report these future obligations as liabilities, there would be a significant impact on the company's reported debt-to-equity ratio, as shown below.

(In millions)	Total Debt	Total Equity	Debt-to-Equity Ratio
As reported	$11,183	$4,448	2.51
With operating leases capitalized	18,783	4,448	4.22

As you can see, the extent of Delta's leverage appears dramatically different when the operating leases are included as part of Delta's total debt. For this reason, companies go to great lengths to structure leases so that the leases can be classified as operating leases and the lease obligation can be excluded from the balance sheet.

Lessor

1. The following components of the net investment in sales-type and direct financing leases as of the date of each balance sheet presented:
   (a) Future minimum lease payments receivable with separate deductions for amounts representing executory costs and the accumulated allowance for uncollectible minimum lease payments receivable
   (b) Unguaranteed residual values accruing to the benefit of the lessor
   (c) Unearned revenue
   (d) For direct financing leases only, initial direct costs
2. Future minimum lease payments to be received for each of the five succeeding fiscal years as of the date of the latest balance sheet presented, including information on contingent rentals
3. The amount of unearned revenue included in income to offset initial direct costs for each year for which an income statement is prepared
4. For operating leases, the cost of assets leased to others and the accumulated depreciation related to these assets
5. A general description of the lessor's leasing arrangements

An example of lessor disclosure of sales-type and direct financing leases for INTERNATIONAL LEASE FINANCE CORP. of California, one of the major lessors of airplanes mentioned at the beginning of this chapter, is shown in Exhibit 15–11.

EXHIBIT 15-11 | International Lease Finance Corp. of California—Lessor Disclosure

NOTE C—NET INVESTMENT IN FINANCE AND SALES-TYPE LEASES
The following lists the components of the net investment in finance and sales-type leases:

	1998	1997
Total minimum lease payments to be received	$ 93,832	$109,615
Estimated residual values of leased flight equipment	19,949	19,993
Less: Unearned income	(23,877)	(31,582)
Net investment in finance and sales-type leases	$ 89,904	$ 98,026

Minimum future lease payments to be received for flight equipment on finance and sales-type leases at December 31, 1998 are as follows:

1999	$14,681
2000	16,095
2001	16,095
2002	16,035
2003	15,843
Thereafter	15,083
Total minimum lease payments to be received	$93,832

INTERNATIONAL ACCOUNTING OF LEASES

Compare the treatment of accounting for leases in the United States with the requirements of international accounting standards.

As mentioned earlier in the chapter, the international accounting standard on leases (IAS 17) relies on the exercise of accounting judgment to distinguish between operating and capital leases. IAS 17 states that a finance lease, which is the same as our capital lease, is "a lease that transfers substantially all the risks and rewards incident to ownership of an asset." This standard has been criticized because it leaves the classification of a lease as either operating or capital almost exclusively up to the accountant (subject to the approval of an external auditor). However, before finding fault with IAS 17, remember that the four lease classification criteria adopted as part of Statement No. 13 have not been successful in preventing U.S. companies from cleverly constructing most leases to be classified as operating.

A very interesting lease accounting proposal has been circulating among the members of the G4. (Recall that the G4 is composed of the national accounting standard setters of the United States, the United Kingdom, Canada, and Australia/New Zealand.)

> **FYI:** In applying the general provisions of IAS 17 in practice, accountants and auditors around the world often refer to the four lease criteria contained in FASB Statement No. 13.

The G4 has sponsored research projects and circulated proposed new accounting standards. One of these proposals, first discussed in 1996, is titled "Accounting for Leases: A New Approach." This proposal notes that current lease accounting standards fail in their objective of requiring companies to recognize significant rights and obligations as assets and liabilities in the balance sheet. It also suggests that the lease accounting rules be simplified as follows: All lease contracts longer than one year in length are to be accounted for as capital leases.

This proposal to capitalize all leases over one year in length is still in the discussion stage. At a meeting in September 1999, the G4 decided that each country's standard setters would invite comments on the proposal in their country. Thus, by the time you are reading this chapter, the FASB may be in the middle of such a discussion in the United States. Given the great efforts that U.S. companies now expend in order to keep leases off the balance sheet, a proposal to capitalize all leases with terms longer than one year is sure to touch off one of the largest accounting debates in the past 30 years.

EXPANDED MATERIAL

Lease agreements can be very complicated. Some of these complications have been specifically designed to circumvent the accounting rules and allow for favorable classification of leases. One example is the third-party guarantee of residual values mentioned earlier in the chapter. Another example is the sale-leaseback transaction described below—a transaction that usually has the effect of sweeping assets and liabilities right off a company's balance sheet even as those assets continue to be used exactly as they were before. Finally, this section briefly discusses the special rules associated with real estate leases—rules that primarily stem from the fact that land has an unlimited economic life.

Record a sale-leaseback transaction for both a seller-lessee and a purchaser-lessor.

SALE-LEASEBACK TRANSACTIONS

A common type of lease arrangement is referred to as a **sale-leaseback** transaction. Typical of this type of lease is an arrangement whereby one party sells the property to a second party, and then the first party leases the property back. Thus, the seller becomes a seller-lessee and the purchaser a purchaser-lessor.

The accounting problem raised by this transaction is whether the seller-lessee should recognize the profit from the original sale immediately or defer it over the lease term. The FASB has recommended that if the initial sale produces a profit, it should be deferred and amortized in proportion to the amortization of the leased asset if it is a capital lease or in proportion to the rental payments if it is an operating lease. If the transaction produces a loss because the fair market value of the asset is less than the undepreciated cost, an immediate loss should be recognized.[11]

 Why would a company sell an asset and then turn right around and lease that same asset back?

To illustrate the accounting treatment for a sale at a gain, assume that on January 1, 2002, Hopkins Inc. sells equipment having a carrying value of $750,000 on its books to Ashcroft Co. for $950,000 and immediately leases back the equipment. The following conditions are established to govern the transaction:

1. The term of the lease is 10 years, noncancelable. A down payment of $200,000 is required plus equal lease payments of $107,108 at the beginning of each year. The implicit interest rate is 10%.
2. The equipment has a fair value of $950,000 on January 1, 2002, and an estimated economic life of 20 years. Straight-line depreciation is used on all owned assets.
3. Hopkins has an option to renew the lease for $10,000 per year for 10 years, the rest of its economic life. Title passes at the end of the lease term.

---

11 *Statement of Financial Accounting Standards No. 28*, "Accounting for Sales With Leasebacks," Stamford, CT: Financial Accounting Standards Board, 1979, pars. 2–3. If only a minor portion of the asset is leased back, the sale and the leased back portions of the transaction are accounted for separately.

Analysis of this lease shows that it qualifies as a capital lease under both the lease term and present value of payments criteria. It meets the 75% of economic life criterion because of the bargain renewal option, which makes both the lease term and the economic life of the equipment 20 years. It meets the 90% of fair market value criterion because the present value of the lease payments is equal to the fair market value of the equipment ($950,000).[12] The journal entries for the first year of the lease for Hopkins, the seller-lessee, and Ashcroft, the purchaser-lessor, are shown below.

Hopkins Inc.

2002				
Jan. 1	Cash		950,000	
	Equipment			750,000
	Unearned Profit on Sale-Leaseback			200,000
	To record original sale of equipment.			
1	Leased Equipment		950,000	
	Obligations Under Capital Lease			642,892
	Cash			307,108
	To record lease of equipment, including down payment and first payment.			
Dec. 31	Amortization Expense on Leased Equipment		47,500	
	Accumulated Amortization on Leased Equipment			47,500
	To record amortization of equipment over 20-year period ($950,000 ÷ 20).			
31	Interest Expense		64,289	
	Obligations Under Capital Lease		42,819	
	Cash			107,108
	To record second lease payment (interest expense: $642,892 × 10% = $64,289).			
31	Unearned Profit on Sale-Leaseback		10,000	
	Revenue Earned on Sale-Leaseback			10,000
	To record recognition of revenue over 20-year life in proportion to the amortization of the leased asset.			

Ashcroft Co. (Purchaser-Lessor)

Jan. 1	Equipment		950,000	
	Cash			950,000
	To record purchase of equipment.			
1	Cash		307,108	
	Lease Payments Receivable		1,063,972	
	Equipment			950,000
	Unearned Interest Revenue			421,080
	To record direct financing sale-leaseback to Hopkins Inc. [total receivable = (10 × $107,108) + (10 × $10,000) = $1,171,080; $1,171,080 − $107,108 = $1,063,972].			
Dec. 31	Cash		107,108	
	Unearned Interest Revenue		64,289	
	Lease Payments Receivable			107,108
	Interest Revenue			64,289
	To record receipt of second lease payment (see computations for Hopkins Inc.).			

12 Computation of present value of lease:
   (a) Present value of 10 years' rentals:
       $107,108 + $107,108(PVAF $_{\overline{9}|10\%}$) = $107,108 + $107,108(5.7590) = $723,943.
   (b) Present value of second 10 years' rentals:
       $10,000 + $10,000(PVAF $_{\overline{9}|10\%}$) = $10,000 + $10,000(5.7590) = $67,590, present value at beginning of second 10 years' lease period.
       Present value at beginning of lease, 10 years earlier: A(PVF $_{\overline{10}|10\%}$) = $67,590 × 0.3855 = $26,056.
   (c) Total present value, $723,943 + $26,056 + $200,000 down payment = $950,000 (rounded).

► **A GROWING TREND TOWARD SALE-LEASEBACKS**

In the early 1970s, sale-leaseback transactions were popular because inflation was causing prices on real estate to skyrocket. Owners of real estate could realize the cash associated with those increasing prices and retain the use of the real estate through leasing.

The volume of sale-leaseback transactions increased in the late 1990s—not necessarily because of inflation but because of businesses' focus on core business assets. Consider, for example, the case of READER'S DIGEST. The company produces magazines and books, yet in 1999, more than 18% of the company's reported assets were invested in property, plant, and equipment. The company elected to sell its company headquarters and use the $100 million proceeds to develop new content and distribution channels. The company's

---

The amortization entries and recognition of the deferred gain on the sale for Hopkins Inc. would be the same each year for the 20-year lease term. The interest expense and interest revenue amounts would decline each year using the effective interest method of computation.

If the lease had not met the criteria, it would have been recorded as an operating lease. The gain on the sale would have been deferred and recognized in proportion to the lease payments. The yearly gain recognition amounts would closely parallel that illustrated above because both the amortization of a leased asset and the pattern of lease payments typically follow a straight-line process.

If the initial sale had been at a loss, an immediate recognition of the loss would have been recorded.

10

Recognize the special characteristics of real estate leases.

REAL ESTATE LEASES

A significant percentage of leases involve real estate. If the real estate includes both non-depreciable land and depreciable buildings and equipment, special problems arise in determining how the lease should be treated. Some of the criteria used to evaluate a lease do not apply to leases of land. The appropriate treatment of real estate leases is summarized in Exhibit 15–12 and in the following sections.

Leases Involving Land Only or Buildings Only

Leases of land should be classified as capital leases only if title to the land is certain to be transferred in the future or if transfer is reasonably assured based on the existence of a bargain purchase option. Thus, only the title transfer and bargain purchase option criteria apply to the classification of land leases. The lease term criterion cannot apply because land has an unlimited life. The present value of payments criterion is not considered to be applicable because under this criterion, no actual ownership transfer is contemplated. Ownership transfer is an important consideration because the residual value of the land to the lessor would be material, because there is no depreciation on land. Leases of land that meet either the title transfer or bargain purchase option criteria are capitalized on the lessee's books and treated as sales-type or direct financing leases on the lessor's books if both of the lessor's revenue recognition criteria also are met. Other leases of land are treated as operating leases.

No special problems arise when a lease involves only the building. The four general criteria for lessees and lessors and the two additional criteria for the lessor can be applied as discussed previously.

percentage of assets invested in PP&E dropped to 8.7%. Management then proceeded to lease the headquarters complex back.

As expected, Reader's Digest carefully structured the lease so that it would qualify as an operating lease, with total future minimum lease payments increasing from $68 million at the end of 1998 to $151 million at the end of 1999. None of this obligation is reflected on the liability side of Reader's Digest's balance sheet.

QUESTIONS:

1. Identify several advantages to a company of a sale-leaseback transaction.

2. What risks might the company face by entering into this type of transaction?

SOURCE:
Barbara Martinez, "Why Own? Sell It and Then Lease Back the Space," *The Wall Street Journal*, April 20, 1999, p. A2.

Leases Involving Land and Buildings

If a lease involves both land and buildings, the accounting treatment depends on which criteria the lease meets. If it meets either the title transfer or bargain purchase option criteria, both the land and the buildings should be classified as capital leases using the fair market values of the properties to allocate the capital value between them. The building lease portion will be amortized by the lessee, and the land will be left at originally allocated cost. The lessor treats the lease as a sale of a single unit and accounts for it as a sales-type or direct financing lease depending on the circumstances.

If the lease does not meet either of the title transfer or bargain purchase option criteria, then additional tests are prescribed by the FASB to determine if any portion should be capitalized. If the land fair market value is less than 25% of the total fair value, the lease is treated as a single unit and the lease term and present value of payments criteria are applied to the single unit to determine if it should be treated as an operating or a capital lease. The estimated economic life of the building is used in applying the lease term criterion. If the fair market value of the land exceeds 25% of the total fair value, the land portion is treated as an operating lease and the lease term and present value of payments criteria are applied to the building as a separate unit. If the test is met for the building, the building portion is classified as a capital lease; otherwise, it is treated as an operating lease.

Leases Involving Real Estate and Equipment

If a lease includes both real estate and equipment, the equipment is considered separately in determining the appropriate classification by the lessee and lessor and is accounted for separately over the term of the lease. The real estate portion of the lease is then classified and accounted for in accordance with the criteria applicable to leases of real estate.

Profit Recognition on Sales-Type Real Estate Leases

The provisions of profit recognition on sales of real estate have an impact on the lessor's classification of real estate leases. Under the guidelines for sales of real estate, a substantial down payment (approximately 25%) must be made before the profit on the sale can be recognized in full. The FASB amended Statement No. 13 to specify that leases that fail to meet the criteria for full and immediate profit recognition if the real estate had been sold should be classified as operating leases and no immediate profit should be recognized. This amendment does not apply to direct financing leases or sales-type leases where a loss is indicated.

EXHIBIT 15–12 | Flowchart for Treatment of Real Estate Leases

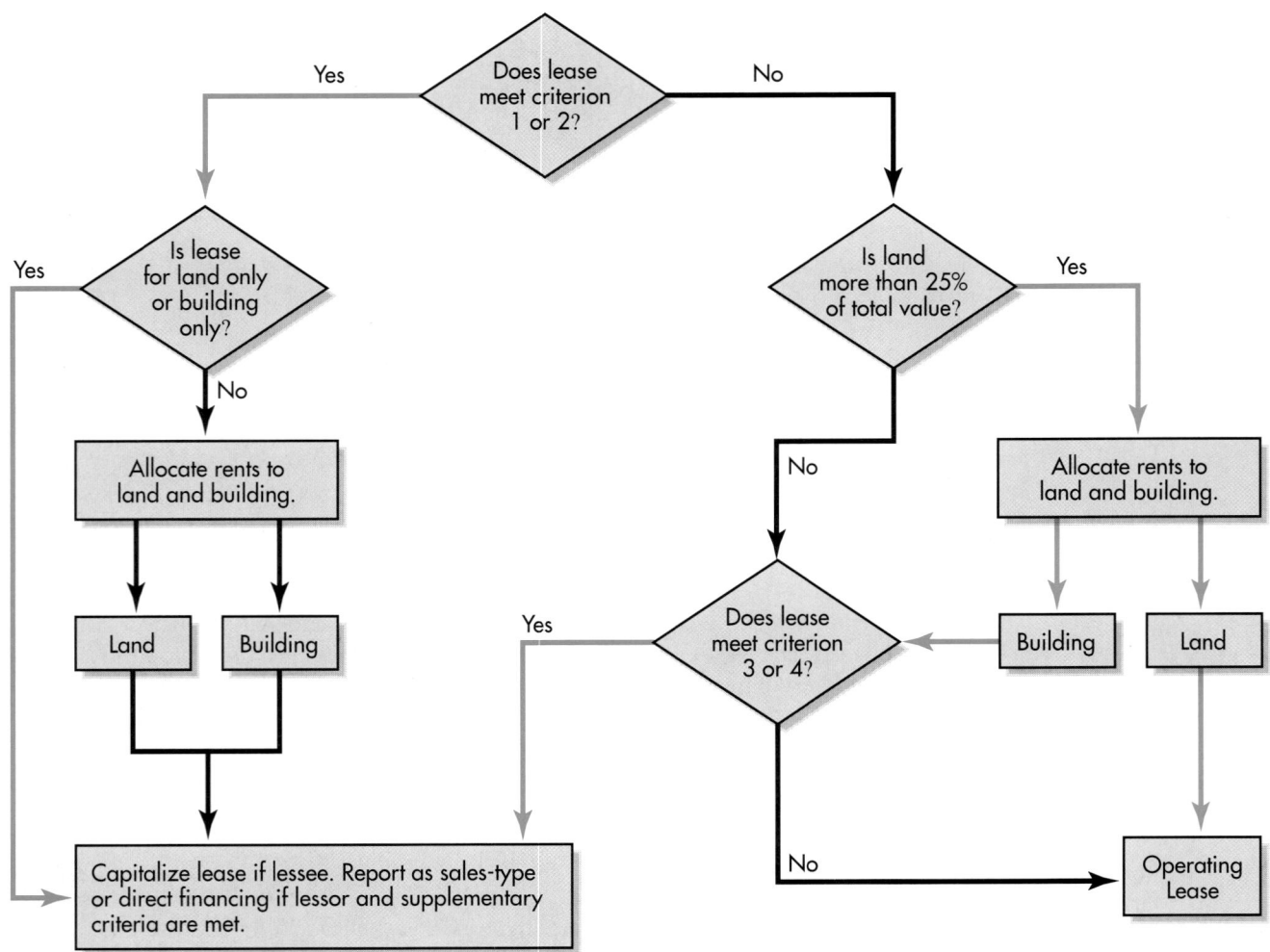

REVIEW OF LEARNING OBJECTIVES

1 **Describe the circumstances in which leasing makes more business sense than does an outright sale and purchase.** The three primary advantages to a lessee of leasing over purchasing are that a lease often involves no down payment, leasing avoids the risks of ownership, and leasing gives the lessee flexibility to change assets when technology or preferences change.

The economic advantages to a lessor include an increase in sales by providing financing to customers who might not otherwise be able to buy, establishment of an ongoing relationship with customers, and retention of the residual value of the leased asset after the lease term is over.

2 **Understand the accounting issues faced by the asset owner (lessor) and the asset user (lessee) in recording a lease transaction.** For the lessor, the key accounting issue is whether or not a sale should be recognized on the date the lease is signed. The proper accounting hinges on whether the lease signing transfers effective ownership of the leased asset, whether the lessor has any significant additional responsibilities remaining after the lease is signed, and whether payment collectibility is reasonably assured.

For the lessee, the key accounting issue is whether the leased asset and the lease payment obligation should be recognized on the balance sheet. Again, the proper accounting treatment depends on whether the lease signing transfers effective ownership of the leased asset.

Capital leases are accounted for as if the lease agreement transfers ownership of the leased asset from the lessor to the lessee. Operating leases are accounted for as rental agreements.

3 Outline the types of contractual provisions typically included in lease agreements.

- *Cancellation provisions.* A noncancelable lease agreement is one that can be canceled by the lessee only under very unusual circumstances. Only noncancelable leases can be classified as capital leases.

- *Bargain purchase option.* If the lessee has the option to purchase the leased asset in the future at an amount low enough such that exercise of the option is likely, a bargain purchase option exists.

- *Lease term.* The lease term includes the noncancelable lease period plus any periods covered by bargain renewal options that include favorable lease terms (e.g., low lease payments) that make it likely that the lessee will renew the lease.

- *Residual value.* The residual value is the value of the leased asset at the end of the lease term. Sometimes, the lease agreement requires that the lessee guarantee the residual value—if the residual value falls below the guaranteed amount, the lessee must pay the lessor the difference.

- *Minimum lease payments.* The minimum lease payments include the periodic lease payments plus any bargain purchase option amount or the amount of any guaranteed residual value. The lessor computes the present value of the minimum lease payments using the implicit interest rate. The lessee computes the present value using the lower of the implicit interest rate and the lessee's own incremental borrowing rate.

4 Apply the lease classification criteria in order to distinguish between capital and operating leases. The four general lease classification criteria, applicable to both lessors and lessees, are:

- *Transfer of ownership.* The lease includes a provision that title to the leased asset passes to the lessee by the end of the lease term.

- *Bargain purchase option.* A bargain purchase option exists that makes it reasonably assured that the lessee will acquire the asset.

- *75% of economic life.* The lease term is equal to 75% or more of the economic life of the leased asset.

- *90% of asset value.* The present value of the minimum lease payments is greater than or equal to 90% of the fair market value of the leased asset on the lease signing date.

If any one of these criteria is met, the lease is classified as a capital lease by the lessee. For the lessor, the lease is a capital lease if, in addition to one of the general criteria, both of the revenue recognition criteria are met:

- Collection of the minimum lease payments is reasonably assured.

- The lessor has substantially completed its obligations to the lessee as of the date of the lease signing; no significant work remains to be done.

5 Properly account for both capital and operating leases from the standpoint of the lessee (asset user). An operating lease is accounted for as a rental, with the lease payment amount being recognized as rent expense. With a capital lease, an asset and a liability are recognized on the lease signing date. The asset is subsequently amortized over the lease term or, if the ownership transfer or bargain purchase option criteria are met, over the economic life of the asset. The lease payments are recorded as reductions in the balance of the lease liability, with a part of the payment being classified as interest expense.

6 Properly account for both capital and operating leases from the standpoint of the lessor (asset owner). An operating lease is accounted for as a rental, with the lease payment amount being recognized as rent revenue. The lessor continues to depreciate the leased asset.

For a lessor, there are two types of capital leases: direct financing leases and sales-type leases. With a direct financing lease, a lease receivable is recognized on the lease signing date. Interest revenue on the receivable balance (net of unearned revenue) is recognized during the lease term. With a sales-type lease, in addition to interest revenue over the life of the lease, a profit is recognized on the lease signing date equal to the difference between the fair market value of the leased asset and its cost.

With operating leases and direct financing leases, initial direct costs are capitalized and amortized over the lease term. With a sales-type lease, initial direct costs are immediately recognized as a reduction in the sale profit.

7 Prepare and interpret the lease disclosures required of both lessors and lessees. Required disclosures for lessees include:

- Gross amount and accumulated amortization associated with assets leased under capital leases

- Rental expense associated with operating leases

- Schedule of future minimum lease payments for both capital and operating leases

Required disclosures for lessors include:

- Schedule of future minimum lease payments to be received for both capital and operating leases

- Cost and accumulated depreciation of assets leased to others under operating leases

8 **Compare the treatment of accounting for leases in the United States with the requirements of international accounting standards.** IAS 17 does not include specific lease classification criteria; instead, it states that a capital lease is "a lease that transfers substantially all the risks and rewards incident to ownership of an asset." The G4 is circulating a proposal that suggests that all leases longer than one year should be capitalized.

9 **Record a sale-leaseback transaction for both a seller-lessee and a purchaser-lessor.** A sale-leaseback is a transaction in which one party sells an asset to another, and then the first party immediately leases the asset back and continues to use it. Any gain realized on a sale-leaseback by the seller-lessee is deferred and amortized over the life of the lease. A loss on the sale is recognized immediately.

10 **Recognize the special characteristics of real estate leases.** A lease of land is classified as a capital lease only if the title transfers as part of the lease or if there is a bargain purchase option. If land and buildings are leased together, the lease is classified using the normal rules if the fair value of the land is less than 25% of the total fair value. If the land value is greater than 25%, the land portion of the lease and the building portion of the lease are classified separately as either operating or capital.

KEY TERMS

Bargain purchase option 864
Bargain renewal option 864
Direct financing leases 876
Executory costs 864
Guaranteed residual value 864
Implicit interest rate 865
Incremental borrowing rate 865
Initial direct costs 876

Lease 860
Lease term 864
Lessee 860
Lessor 860
Minimum lease payments 864
Net lease investment 878
Noncancelable 863
Sales-type leases 876

Unguaranteed residual value 864

Sale-leaseback 890

QUESTIONS

1. What are the principal advantages to a lessee in leasing rather than purchasing property?
2. What are the principal advantages to a lessor in leasing rather than selling property?
3. Conceptually, what is the difference between a capital lease and an operating lease?
4. What is a bargain purchase option?
5. How is the lease term measured?
6. (a) What discount rate is used to determine the present value of a lease by the lessee? (b) by the lessor?
7. What criteria must be met before a lease can be properly accounted for as a capital lease on the

books of the lessee?
8. In determining the classification of a lease, a lessor uses the criteria of the lessee plus two additional criteria. What are these additional criteria, and why are they included in the classification of leases by lessors?
9. What is the basic difference between an operating lease and a capital lease from the viewpoint of the lessee?
10. If an operating lease requires the payment of uneven rental amounts over its life, how should the lessee recognize rental expense?

11. What amount should be recorded as an asset and a liability for capital leases on the books of the lessee?

12. Why do asset and liability balances for capital leases usually differ after the first year?

13. A capitalized lease should be amortized in accordance with the lessee's normal depreciation policy. What time period should be used for lease amortization?

14. The use of the capital lease method for a given lease will always result in a lower net income than the operating lease method. Do you agree? Explain fully.

15. (a) How does a capital lease for equipment affect the lessee's statement of cash flows? (b) How would the treatment on the statement of cash flows differ if the contract was identified as a purchase of equipment with a down payment and a long-term note payable for the balance?

16. Distinguish a sales-type lease from a direct financing lease.

17. Unguaranteed residual values accrue to the lessor at the expiration of the lease. How are these values treated in a sales-type lease?

18. Under what circumstances are the minimum lease payments for the lessee different from those of the lessor?

19. Why is the principal portion of a lease receipt of a financing lease treated as an investment inflow on the lessor's books, while the principal portion of a lease payment is treated as a financial cash outflow on the lessee's books?

20. Describe the specific lease disclosure requirements for lessees.

21. What disclosures are required by the FASB for lessors under sales-type and direct financing leases?

22. How does the lease classification standard in IAS 17 differ from that in Statement No. 13?

23. What lease accounting proposal has been circulating among the members of the G4?

24. When should the profit or loss be recognized by the seller-lessee in a sale-leaseback arrangement?

25. Real estate leases can include land and/or buildings. Explain how the four criteria for determining lease capitalization are applied to the following:
    (a) Leases involving land only.
    (b) Leases involving land and buildings.
    (c) Leases involving buildings only.

DISCUSSION CASES

CASE 15–1

HOW SHOULD THE LEASE BE RECORDED?

Louise Corporation entered into a leasing arrangement with Wilder Leasing Corporation for a certain machine. Wilder's primary business is leasing, and it is not a manufacturer or dealer. Louise will lease the machine for a period of 3 years, which is 50% of the machine's economic life. Wilder will take possession of the machine at the end of the initial 3-year lease. Louise does not guarantee any residual value for the machine.

Louise's incremental borrowing rate is 10%, and the implicit rate in the lease is 8½%. Louise has no way of knowing the implicit rate used by Wilder. Using either rate, the present value of the minimum lease payments is between 90% and 100% of the fair value of the machine at the date of the lease agreement.

Louise has agreed to pay all executory costs directly, and no allowance for these costs is included in the lease payments.

Wilder is reasonably certain that Louise will pay all lease payments, and because Louise has agreed to pay all executory costs, there are no important uncertainties regarding costs to be incurred by Wilder.

1. With respect to Louise (the lessee), answer the following.
   a. What type of lease has been entered into? Explain the reason for your answer.
   b. How should Louise compute the appropriate amount to be recorded for the lease or asset acquired?
   c. What accounts will be created or affected by this transaction, and how will the lease or asset and other costs related to the transaction be matched with earnings?
   d. What disclosures must Louise make regarding this lease or asset?
2. With respect to Wilder (the lessor), answer the following:
   a. What type of leasing arrangement has been entered into? Explain the reason for your answer.

b. How should this lease be recorded by Wilder, and how are the appropriate amounts determined?

c. How should Wilder determine the appropriate amount of earnings to be recognized from each lease payment?

d. What disclosures must Wilder make regarding this lease?

CASE 15–2

SHOULD WE BUY OR LEASE?

The Meeker Machine and Die Company has learned that a sophisticated piece of computer-operated machinery is available to either buy or rent. The machinery will result in 3 employees being replaced, and quality of the output has been tested to be superior in every demonstration. There is no doubt that this machinery represents the latest in technology; however, new inventions and research make it difficult to estimate when the machinery will be made obsolete by new technology. The physical life expectancy of the machine is 10 years; however, the estimated economic life is between 2 and 5 years.

Meeker has a debt-to-equity ratio of .75. If the machine is purchased and the minimum down payment is made, the outstanding loan balance on the machine will cause the debt-to-equity ratio to increase to 1.1. The monthly payments if the machine is purchased are 20% lower than the lease payments if it is leased. The incremental borrowing rate for Meeker is 11%. The rate implicit in the lease is 12%. What factors should Meeker consider in deciding how to finance the acquisition of the machine?

CASE 15–3

HOW SHOULD THE LEASES BE CLASSIFIED AND ACCOUNTED FOR?

On January 1, Toronto Company, a lessee, entered into 3 noncancelable leases for new equipment, Lease J, Lease K, and Lease L. None of the 3 leases transfers ownership of the equipment to Toronto at the end of the lease term. For each of the 3 leases, the present value at the beginning of the lease term of the minimum lease payments is 75% of the fair value of the equipment to the lessor at the inception of the lease. This excludes that portion of the payments representing executory costs, such as insurance, maintenance, and taxes to be paid by the lessor, including any profit thereon.

The following information is peculiar to each lease:

(a) Lease J does not contain a bargain purchase option; the lease term is equal to 80% of the estimated economic life of the equipment.

(b) Lease K contains a bargain purchase option; the lease term is equal to 50% of the estimated economic life of the equipment.

(c) Lease L does not contain a bargain purchase option; the lease term is equal to 50% of the estimated economic life of the equipment.

1. How should Toronto Company classify each of the 3 leases and why? Discuss the rationale for your answer.

2. What amount, if any, should Toronto record as a liability at the inception of the lease for each of the 3 leases?

3. Assuming that the minimum lease payments are made on a straight-line basis, how should Toronto record each minimum lease payment for each of the 3 leases?

CASE 15–4

MORE LEASES MEAN LOWER PROFITS

Ultrasound, Inc., has introduced a new line of equipment that may revolutionize the medical profession. Because of the new technology involved, potential users of the equipment are reluctant to purchase the equipment, but they are willing to enter into a lease arrangement as long as they can classify the lease as an operating lease. The new equipment will replace equipment that Ultrasound has been selling in the past. It is estimated that a 25% loss of actual equipment sales will occur as a result of the leasing policy for the new equipment.

Management must decide how to structure the leases so that the lessees can treat them as operating leases. Some members of management want to structure the leases so that Ultrasound, as lessor, can classify the lease as a sales-type lease and thus avoid a further reduction of income. Others feel that they should treat the leases as operating leases and minimize the income tax liability in the short term. They are uncertain, however, as to how the financial statements would be affected under these two different approaches. They also are uncertain as to how leases could be structured to permit the lessee to treat the lease as an operating lease and the lessor to treat it as a sales-type lease. You are asked to respond to their questions.

CASE 15–5

STRUCTURING A LEASE TO AVOID LIABILITY RECOGNITION

Johnson Pharmaceuticals is in need of cash. One option being considered by the board of directors is to sell the plant facilities to a group of venture capitalists and then lease the facilities back for a long-term period with the option of repurchasing the plant facilities at the end of the lease.

The chairman has commented that this option will provide Johnson Pharmaceuticals with the needed cash but will result in a large lease liability on the balance sheet. As the chief financial officer, you comment that if the company carefully structures the terms of the lease agreement, it may be able to avoid recognizing the lease liability.

The chairman has asked you to prepare a memo discussing the specific ways in which a lease agreement can be structured so as to avoid recognizing the liability on the balance sheet.

CASE 15–6

RECOGNIZING A PROFIT FROM LEASING

In June 1988, BRITISH & COMMONWEALTH PLC (B&C) acquired ATLANTIC COMPUTERS, the world's third largest computer-leasing company. In April 1990, B&C placed Atlantic Computers into administrative receivership and wrote off its $900 million investment in the company. The reason for the write-off? Atlantic's method of accounting for leases.

Atlantic had developed what was called a "flexlease," which allowed customers to upgrade their computers at specified points during the lease period. The flexlease involved two separate contracts—one with a financing institution and the second with Atlantic. When customers elected to exercise their flex options, Atlantic would take back the equipment, pay off the remainder of the contract to the lender, and sell the equipment in the used computer market.

Even though the original lease arrangement did not meet the criteria for a sales-type lease, Atlantic was estimating the profits to be made from the sale of those computers that would be returned, assuming customers exercised their flex options, and was recognizing these sales profits when the original lease contract was signed.

1. Is there anything wrong with Atlantic's method of accounting for the profits to be made on the "flexleases"?
2. When would be the most appropriate time for Atlantic to recognize profits from the sale of a computer that was returned under a flex option?
3. Why would British & Commonwealth PLC get rid of Atlantic rather than simply change the accounting practice?

SOURCE: *Computerworld*, April 30, 1990, p. 99.

CASE 15–7

RECOGNIZING PROFITS ON A SALE-LEASEBACK TRANSACTION

John Carson, president of Carson Enterprises, recently arranged a financing deal with a group of foreign investors whereby he sold his movie company for $13,000,000 and immediately leased the company back, recognizing a $4,000,000 profit on the sale. Mr. Carson has just entered your office to tell you, his accountant, the good news.

After hearing the details of the transaction, you tell Mr. Carson that he must defer recognizing the gain immediately and instead recognize it piecemeal over the term of the lease agreement. Mr. Carson counters that if he had simply sold the company to the investors, he would be able to book the profits. He asks you: "What difference does it make if I lease the company back or not? Shouldn't the sale and the lease be treated as two separate transactions?" How do you respond?

EXERCISES

EXERCISE 15–8

CRITERIA FOR CAPITALIZING LEASES

Atwater Manufacturing Co. leases its equipment from Westside Leasing Company. In each of the following cases, assuming none of the other criteria for capitalizing leases are met, determine whether the lease would be a capital lease or an operating lease under FASB Statement No. 13. Your decision is to be based only on the terms presented, considering each case independently of the others.

(a) At the end of the lease term, the market value of the equipment is expected to be $20,000. Atwater has the option of purchasing it for $5,000.

(b) The fair market value of the equipment is $75,000. The present value of the lease payments is $67,000 (excluding any executory costs).

(c) Ownership of the property automatically passes to Atwater at the end of the lease term.

(d) The economic life of the equipment is 12 years. The lease term is 8 years.

(e) The lease requires payments of $9,000 per year in advance plus executory costs of $500 per year. The lease period is 3 years, and Atwater's incremental borrowing rate is 12%. The fair market value of the equipment is $28,000.

(f) The lease requires payments of $6,000 per year in advance, which includes executory costs of $500 per year. The lease period is 3 years, and Atwater's incremental borrowing rate is 10%. The fair market value of the equipment is $16,650.

EXERCISE 15–9

ENTRIES FOR LEASE—LESSOR AND LESSEE

The Doxey Company purchased a machine on January 1, 2002, for $1,250,000 for the express purpose of leasing it. The machine was expected to have a 9-year life from January 1, 2002, no salvage value, and to be depreciated on a straight-line basis. On March 1, 2002, Doxey leased the machine to Mondale Company for $300,000 a year for a 4-year period ending February 28, 2006. Doxey paid a total of $15,000 for maintenance, insurance, and property taxes on the machine for the year ended December 31, 2002. Mondale paid $300,000 to Doxey on March 1, 2002. Doxey retains title to the property and plans to lease it to someone else after the four-year lease period. Give all the 2002 entries relating to the lease on (1) Doxey Company's books and (2) Mondale Company's books. Assume both sets of books are maintained on the calendar-year basis.

EXERCISE 15–10

ENTRIES FOR OPERATING LEASE—LESSEE

Jonas Inc. leases some of the equipment it uses. The lease term is 5 years, and the lease payments are to be made in advance as shown in the following schedule.

January 1, 2002	$100,000
January 1, 2003	100,000
January 1, 2004	140,000
January 1, 2005	170,000
January 1, 2006	190,000
Total	$700,000

The equipment is to be used evenly over the 5-year period. For each of the 5 years, give the entry that should be made at the time the lease payment is made to allocate the proper share of rent expense to each period. The lease is classified as an operating lease by Jonas Inc.

EXERCISE 15–11

ENTRIES FOR LEASE—LESSEE

Bingham Smelting Company entered into a 15-year noncancelable lease beginning January 1, 2002, for equipment to use in its smelting operations. The term of the lease is

the same as the expected economic life of the equipment. Bingham uses straight-line depreciation for all plant assets. The provisions of the lease call for annual payments of $290,000 in advance plus $20,000 per year to cover executory costs, such as taxes and insurance, for the 15-year period of the lease. At the end of the 15 years, the equipment is expected to be scrapped. The incremental borrowing rate of Bingham is 10%. The lessor's computed implicit interest rate is unknown to Bingham.

Record the lease on the books of Bingham and give all the entries necessary to record the lease for its first year plus the entry to record the second lease payment on December 31, 2002. (Round to the nearest dollar.)

EXERCISE 15–12

ENTRIES FOR LEASE—LESSEE

On January 2, 2002, the Jacques Company entered into a noncancelable lease for new equipment. The equipment was built to the Jacques Company's specifications and is in an area where rental to another lessee would be difficult. Rental payments are $300,000 a year for 10 years, payable in advance. The equipment has an estimated economic life of 20 years. The taxes, maintenance, and insurance are to be paid directly by the Jacques Company, and the title to the equipment is to be transferred to Jacques at the end of the lease term. Assume the cost of borrowing funds for this type of an asset by Jacques Company is 12%.

1. Give the entry on Jacques' books that should be made at the inception of the lease.
2. Give the entries for 2002 and 2003 assuming the second payment and subsequent payments are made on December 31 and assuming double-declining-balance amortization.

EXERCISE 15–13

SCHEDULE OF LEASE PAYMENTS

Carter Construction Co. is leasing equipment from Vasquez Inc. The lease calls for payments of $50,000 a year plus $4,000 a year executory costs for 5 years. The first payment is due on January 1, 2002, when the lease is signed, with the other 4 payments coming due on December 31 of each year. Carter has also been given the option of purchasing the equipment at the end of the lease at a bargain price of $100,000. Carter has an incremental borrowing rate of 10%, the same as the implicit interest rate of Vasquez. Carter has hired you as an accountant and asks you to prepare a schedule showing how the lease payments will be split between principal and interest and the outstanding lease liability balance over the life of the lease.

EXERCISE 15–14

ENTRY FOR PURCHASE BY LESSEE

The Cordon Enterprise Company leases many of its assets and capitalizes most of the leased assets. At December 31, the company had the following balances on its books in relation to a piece of specialized equipment:

Leased Equipment	$80,000
Accumulated Amortization—Leased Equipment	49,300
Obligations Under Capital Leases	26,000

Amortization has been recorded up to the end of the year, and no accrued interest is involved. At December 31, Cordon decided to purchase the equipment for $32,000 and paid cash to complete the purchase. Give the entry required on Cordon's books to record the purchase.

EXERCISE 15–15

ENTRY FOR SALE BY LESSOR

Smithston Corporation leased equipment to Dayplanner Co. on January 1, 2002. The terms of the lease called for annual lease payments to be made at the first of each year. Smithston's implicit interest rate for the transaction is 12%. On July 1, 2004, Dayplanner purchased the equipment and paid $58,000 to complete the transaction. After the 2004 payment was made, the following balances relating to the leased equipment were on the books of Smithston as of January 1, 2004:

Lease Payments Receivable	$94,500
Unearned Interest Revenue	18,750

Prepare the journal entry that should be made by Smithston to record the sale, including the accrual of interest through July 1.

EXERCISE 15–16

COMPUTATION OF IMPLICIT INTEREST RATE

Tueller Leasing leases equipment to Tsoi Manufacturing. The fair market value of the equipment is $473,130. Lease payments, excluding executory costs, are $70,000 per year, payable in advance, for 10 years. What is the implicit rate of interest Tueller Leasing should use to record this capital lease on its books?

EXERCISE 15–17

DIRECT FINANCING LEASE—LESSOR

The Deseret Finance Company purchased a printing press to lease to the Quality Printing Company. The lease was structured so that at the end of the lease period of 15 years, Quality would own the printing press. Lease payments required in this lease were $190,000 (excluding executory costs) per year, payable in advance. The cost of the press to Deseret was $1,589,673, which is also its fair market value at the time of the lease.

1. Why is this a direct financing lease?
2. Give the entry to record the lease transaction on the books of Deseret Finance Company.
3. Give the entry at the end of the first year on Deseret Finance Company's books to recognize interest revenue.

EXERCISE 15–18

DIRECT FINANCING LEASE WITH RESIDUAL VALUE

The Massachusetts Casualty Insurance Company decides to enter the leasing business. It acquires a specialized packaging machine for $300,000 cash and leases it for a period of 6 years, after which the machine is returned to the insurance company for disposition. The expected unguaranteed residual value of the machine is $20,000. The lease terms are arranged so that a return of 12% is earned by the insurance company.

1. Calculate the annual lease payment, payable in advance, required to yield the desired return.
2. Prepare entries for the lessor for the first year of the lease assuming the machine is acquired and the lease is recorded on January 1, 2002. The first lease payment is made on January 1, 2002, and subsequent payments are made each December 31.
3. Assuming the packaging machine is sold by Massachusetts to the lessee at the end of the 6 years for $29,000, give the required entry to record the sale.

EXERCISE 15–19

TABLE FOR DIRECT FINANCING LEASE—LESSOR

The Pioche Savings and Loan Company acquires a piece of specialized hospital equipment for $1,500,000 that it leases on January 1, 2002, to a local hospital for $391,006 per year, payable in advance. Because of rapid technological developments, the equipment is expected to be replaced after 4 years. It is expected that the machine will have a residual value of $200,000 to Pioche Savings at the end of the lease term. The implicit rate of interest in the lease is 10%.

1. Prepare a 4-year table for Pioche Savings and Loan similar to Exhibit 15–8.
2. How would the table differ if the local hospital guaranteed the residual value to Pioche?

EXERCISE 15–20

CAPITAL LEASE WITH GUARANTEED RESIDUAL VALUE—LESSEE

The Mario Automobile Company leases automobiles under the following terms. A 3-year lease agreement is signed in which the lessor receives annual rental of $4,000 (in advance). At the end of the 3 years, the lessee agrees to make up any deficiency in residual value below $3,500. The cash price of the automobile is $13,251. The implicit interest rate is 12%, which is known to the lessee, and the lessee's incremental borrowing rate is 14%. The lessee estimates the residual value at the end of 3 years to be $4,200 and depreciates its automobiles on a straight-line basis.

1. Give the entries on the lessee's books required in the first year of the lease, including the second payment on April 30, 2003. Assume the lease begins May 1, 2002, the beginning of the lessee's fiscal year.
2. What balances relative to the lease would appear on the lessee's balance sheet at the end of year 3?
3. Assume that at the end of the 3 years, the automobile is sold by the lessee (with the permission of the lessor) for $3,800. Prepare the entries to record the sale and settlement with the lessor.

EXERCISE 15–21

SALES-TYPE LEASE—LESSOR

Salcedo Co. leased equipment to Erickson Inc. on April 1, 2002. The lease is appropriately recorded as a sale by Salcedo. The lease is for an 8-year period ending March 31, 2010. The first of 8 equal annual payments of $175,000 (excluding executory costs) was made on April 1, 2002. The cost of the equipment to Salcedo is $940,000. The equipment has an estimated useful life of 8 years with no residual value expected. Salcedo uses straight-line depreciation and takes a full year's depreciation in the year of purchase. The cash selling price of the equipment is $1,026,900.

1. Give the entry required to record the lease on Salcedo's books.
2. How much interest revenue will Salcedo recognize in 2002?

EXERCISE 15–22

SALES-TYPE LEASE—LESSOR

The Jacinto Leasing and Manufacturing Company uses leases as a means of financing sales of its equipment. Jacinto leased a machine to Hudson Construction for $22,000 per year, payable in advance, for a 10-year period. The cost of the machine to Jacinto was $108,000. The fair market value at the date of the lease was $120,000. Assume a residual value of $0 at the end of the lease.

1. Give the entry required to record the lease on Jacinto's books.
2. How much profit will Jacinto recognize initially on the lease, excluding any interest revenue?
3. How much interest revenue would be recognized in the first year? Round your estimate of the implicit interest rate to the nearest whole percent.

EXERCISE 15–23

EFFECT OF LEASE ON REPORTED INCOME—LESSEE AND LESSOR

On February 20, 2002, Topham Inc. purchased a machine for $1,200,000 for the purpose of leasing it. The machine is expected to have a 10-year life, no residual value, and is depreciated on the straight-line basis to the nearest month. The machine was leased to Lutts Company on March 1, 2002, for a 4-year period at a monthly rental of $22,000. There is no provision for the renewal of the lease or purchase of the machine by the lessee at the expiration of the lease term. Topham paid $60,000 of commissions associated with negotiating the lease in February 2002.

1. What expense should Lutts record as a result of the lease transaction for the year ended December 31, 2002?
2. What income or loss before income taxes should Topham record as a result of the lease transaction for the year ended December 31, 2002?

EXERCISE 15–24

CASH FLOW TREATMENT OF CAPITAL LEASES—LESSEE

The following information relates to a capital lease between Simpson Electric Co. (lessee) and Harris Manufacturing Inc. (lessor). The lease term began on January 1, 2002. Simpson capitalized the 10-year lease and recorded $110,000 as an asset. The annual lease payment, made at the beginning of each year, is $13,316 at 10% interest. Simpson uses the straight-line method to depreciate its owned assets. How will this lease be reported on Simpson's statement of cash flows for 2002 if the second lease payment is made on December 31, 2002, and Simpson uses the indirect method?

EXERCISE 15–25

LEASE DISCLOSURES—LESSEE

The following lease information was obtained by a staff auditor for a client, Kroller Inc., at December 31, 2002. Indicate how this information should be presented in Kroller's 2-year comparative financial statements. Include any notes to the statements required to meet generally accepted accounting principles. Lease payments are made on December 31 of each year.

Leased building; minimum lease payments per year; 10 years remaining life	$ 45,000
Executory costs per year	2,000
Capitalized lease value, 12% interest	343,269
Accumulated amortization of leased building at December 31, 2002	114,423
Amortization expense for 2002	22,885
Obligations under capital leases; balance at December 31, 2002	239,770
Obligations under capital leases; balance at December 31, 2001	254,259

EXERCISE 15–26

LEASE DISCLOSURE ON THE FINANCIAL STATEMENTS

Acme Enterprises leased equipment from Monument Equipment Co. on January 1, 2002. The terms of the lease agreement require 5 annual payments of $20,000 with the first payment being made on January 1, 2002, and each subsequent payment being made on December 31 of each year. Because the equipment has an expected useful life of 5 years, the lease qualifies as a capital lease for Acme. Acme does not know Monument's implicit interest rate and therefore uses its own incremental borrowing rate of 12% to calculate the present value of the lease payments. Acme uses the sum-of-the-years'-digits method for amortizing leased assets. The expected salvage value of the leased asset is $0.

1. Prepare a schedule that shows the lease obligation balance in each year of the lease.
2. Prepare an asset amortization schedule for the leased asset.
3. Compare the amount shown on the year-end balance sheet for the leased asset with that of the lease obligation for the years 2002 through 2006 and explain why the amounts differ.

EXERCISE 15–27

IMPACT OF CAPITALIZING THE VALUE OF OPERATING LEASES

The following information comes from the 2002 financial statements of Karlla Peterson Company:

Total liabilities	$100,000
Total stockholders' equity	80,000

In addition, Karlla Peterson has a large number of operating leases. The future payments on these operating leases are disclosed in the notes to the financial statements as follows:

Year	Payment
2003	$ 20,000
2004	20,000
2005	20,000
2006	20,000
2007	20,000
Thereafter	200,000

All of the above lease payments occur at the end of the year. The incremental borrowing rate of Karlla Peterson Company is 10%. This is also the implicit rate in all of the leases that Karlla Peterson signs.

1. Compute the debt-to-equity ratio (total liabilities/total equity).
2. Compute the debt ratio (total liabilities/total assets).

3. Assuming that Karlla Peterson's operating leases are accounted for as capital leases, compute the debt-to-equity ratio.

4. Assuming that Karlla Peterson's operating leases are accounted for as capital leases, compute the debt ratio.

EXERCISE 15–28

SALE-LEASEBACK ACCOUNTING

On July 1, 2002, Baker Corporation sold equipment it had recently purchased to an unaffiliated company for $570,000. The equipment had a book value on Baker's books of $450,000 and a remaining life of 5 years. On that same day, Baker leased back the equipment at $135,000 per year, payable in advance, for a 5-year period. Baker's incremental borrowing rate is 10%, and it does not know the lessor's implicit interest rate. What entries are required for Baker to record the transactions involving the equipment during the first full year, assuming the second lease payment is made on June 30, 2003? Ignore consideration of the lessee's fiscal year. The lessee uses the double-declining-balance method of depreciation for similar assets it owns outright.

EXERCISE 15–29

SALE-LEASEBACK TRANSACTION

Smalltown Grocers sold its plant facilities to United Grocers, Inc., for $813,487. United immediately leased the building back to Smalltown for 20 annual payments of $96,000 with the first payment due immediately. The terms of the lease agreement provide a bargain purchase option wherein Smalltown has the option of purchasing the building at the end of the lease term for $100,000. If United's implicit interest rate is 12% (lower than Smalltown's incremental borrowing rate), prepare the entries that should be made by United to record the purchase of the building and the receipt of the first 2 payments from Smalltown Grocers, assuming this leasing arrangement qualifies as a capital lease for United.

EXERCISE 15–30

ENTRIES FOR REAL ESTATE LEASE WITH RESIDUAL VALUE—LESSEE

Atlantus Corporation leases its land and buildings from an investment company. The terms of the lease are as follows:

(a) Lease term is 20 years, after which title to the property can be acquired for 25% of the market value at that date. The estimated remaining life of the building when the lease is executed is 30 years.

(b) Annual lease payments payable in advance are $250,000 (excluding executory costs). Expected residual value of the property in 20 years is $800,000.

(c) Assume the current market value of the combined land and buildings is $2,370,945, of which the market value of the land is $550,000. The implicit interest rate of the lease is 10%.

What entries would be required on Atlantus Corporation's books for the first year of the lease? Assume the second lease payment is made on the last day of the first year.

EXERCISE 15–31

LEASE OF REAL ESTATE—LESSEE

Maycomb Industries leases its land and buildings on a 10-year lease from E. L. Kimball. The property includes 10 acres of land that is used for parking and an amusement area. The market value of the leased land is $500,000, and the market value of the leased buildings is $1,200,000. The annual rent for the property, payable in advance, is $251,516. There is no provision in the lease for Maycomb to purchase the property at the conclusion of the lease. The buildings are estimated to have a 12-year remaining life and are depreciated on a straight-line basis.

1. Does the lease of Maycomb Industries qualify as a capital lease? If yes, what criteria apply?

2. Record the lease on Maycomb's books and give the entries for the first full year of the lease, assuming the first payment is made on January 1, 2002, and the second payment is made on December 31, 2002.

PROBLEMS

PROBLEM 15–32

ENTRIES FOR CAPITAL LEASE—LESSEE; LEASE CRITERIA

The Miner Company leased a machine on July 1, 2002, under a 10-year lease. The economic life of the machine is estimated to be 15 years. Title to the machine passes to Miner Company at the expiration of the lease, and thus, the lease is a capital lease. The lease payments are $83,000 per year, including executory costs of $3,000 per year, all payable in advance annually. The incremental borrowing rate of the company is 10%, and the lessor's implicit interest rate is unknown. The Miner Company uses the straight-line method of amortization and uses the calendar year for reporting purposes.

Instructions:

1. Give all entries on the books of the lessee relating to the lease for 2002.
2. Assume that the lessor retains title to the machine at the expiration of the lease, that there is no bargain renewal or purchase option, and that the fair market value of the equipment is $595,000 as of the lease date. Using the criteria for distinguishing between operating and capital leases according to FASB Statement No. 13, what would be the amortization expense for 2002?

PROBLEM 15–33

OPERATING LEASE—LESSEE AND LESSOR

Calderwood Industries leases a large specialized machine to the Youngstown Company at a total rental of $1,800,000, payable in 5 annual installments in the following declining pattern: 25% for each of the first 2 years, 22% in the third year, and 14% in each of the last 2 years. The lease begins January 1, 2002. In addition to the rent, Youngstown is required to pay annual executory costs of $15,000 to cover unusual repairs and insurance. The lease does not qualify as a capital lease for reporting purposes. Calderwood incurred initial direct costs of $15,000 in obtaining the lease. The machine cost Calderwood $2,100,000 to construct and has an estimated life of 10 years with an estimated residual value of $100,000. Calderwood uses the straight-line depreciation method on its equipment. Both companies report on a calendar-year basis.

Instructions:

1. Prepare the journal entries on Calderwood's books for 2002 and 2006 related to the lease.
2. Prepare the journal entries on Youngstown's books for 2002 and 2006 related to the lease.

PROBLEM 15–34

ENTRIES FOR CAPITAL LEASE—LESSEE

Aldridge Enterprises has a long-standing policy of acquiring company equipment by leasing. Early in 2002, the company entered into a lease for a new milling machine. The lease stipulates that annual payments will be made for 5 years. The payments are to be made in advance on December 31 of each year. At the end of the 5-year period, Aldridge may purchase the machine. Company financial records show the incremental borrowing rate to be less than the implicit interest rate. The estimated economic life of the equipment is 12 years. Aldridge uses the calendar year for reporting purposes and uses straight-line depreciation for other equipment. In addition, the following information about the lease is also available:

Annual lease payments	$55,000
Purchase option price	$25,000
Estimated fair market value of machine after 5 years	$75,000
Incremental borrowing rate	10%
Date of first lease payment	Jan. 1, 2002

Instructions:

1. Compute the amount to be capitalized as an asset for the lease of the milling machine.
2. Prepare a schedule that shows the computation of the interest expense for each period.
3. Give the journal entries that would be made on Aldridge's books for the first 2 years of the lease.
4. Assume that the purchase option is exercised at the end of the lease. Give the Aldridge journal entry necessary to record the exercise of the option. The actual fair market value of the milling machine at the end of the lease is $95,000. On the date the purchase option is exercised, the undiscounted sum of future cash flows expected from the machine is $125,000.

PROBLEM 15–35

ENTRIES FOR CAPITAL LEASE—LESSEE; GUARANTEED RESIDUAL VALUE

For some time, Balster Inc. has maintained a policy of acquiring company equipment by leasing. On January 1, 2002, Balster entered into a lease with Edgemont Fabricators for a new concrete truck that had a selling price of $265,000. The lease stipulates that annual payments of $52,500 will be made for 6 years. The first lease payment is made on January 1, 2002, and subsequent payments are made on December 31 of each year. Balster guarantees a residual value of $45,890 at the end of the 6-year period. Balster has an incremental borrowing rate of 13%, and the implicit interest rate to Edgemont is 12% after considering the guaranteed residual value. The economic life of the truck is 9 years. Balster uses the calendar year for reporting purposes and uses straight-line depreciation to depreciate other equipment.

Instructions:

1. Compute the amount to be capitalized as an asset on the lessee's books for the concrete truck. Balster knows that Edgemont's implicit interest rate is 12%.
2. Prepare a schedule showing the reduction of the liability by the annual payments after considering the interest charges.
3. Give the journal entries that would be made on Balster's books for the first 2 years of the lease.
4. Assume that the lessor sells the truck for $29,000 at the end of the 6-year period to a third party. Give the Balster journal entries necessary to record the payment to satisfy the residual guarantee and to write off the leased equipment accounts.

PROBLEM 15–36

ACCOUNTING FOR DIRECT FINANCING LEASE—LESSEE AND LESSOR

The Trost Leasing Company buys equipment for leasing to various manufacturing companies. On October 1, 2001, Trost leases a press to the Shumway Shoe Company. The cost of the machine to Trost was $196,110, which approximated its fair market value on the lease date. The lease payments stipulated in the lease are $33,000 per year in advance for the 10-year period of the lease. The payments include executory costs of $3,000 per year. The expected economic life of the equipment is also 10 years. The title to the equipment remains in the hands of Trost Leasing Company at the end of the lease term, although only nominal residual value is expected at that time. Shumway's incremental borrowing rate is 10%, and it uses the straight-line method of depreciation on all owned equipment. Both Shumway and Trost have fiscal years ending September 30, and lease payments are made on this date.

Instructions:

1. Prepare the entries to record the lease and the first lease payment on the books of the lessor and lessee assuming the lease meets the criteria of a direct financing lease for the lessor and a capital lease for the lessee.
2. Compute the implicit rate of interest of the lessor.
3. Give all entries required to account for the lease on both the lessee's and lessor's books for the fiscal years 2002, 2003, and 2004.

PROBLEM 15–37

LEASE COMPUTATIONS—LESSEE AND LESSOR

Computer Controls Corporation is in the business of leasing new sophisticated computer systems. As a lessor of computers, Computer Controls purchased a new system on December 31, 2002. The system was delivered the same day (by prior arrangement) to Edwards Investment Company, a lessee. The corporation accountant revealed the following information relating to the lease transaction:

Cost of system to Computer Controls	$550,000
Estimated useful life and lease term	8 years
Expected residual value (unguaranteed)	$40,000
Computer Controls' implicit rate of interest	12%
Edwards' incremental borrowing rate	14%
Date of first lease payment	Dec. 31, 2002

Additional information is as follows:

(a) At the end of the lease, the system will revert to Computer Controls.
(b) Edwards is aware of Computer Controls' rate of implicit interest.
(c) The lease rental consists of equal annual payments.
(d) Computer Controls accounts for leases using the direct financing method. Edwards intends to record the lease as a capital lease. Both the lessee and the lessor report on a calendar-year basis and elect to depreciate all assets on the straight-line basis.

Instructions:

1. Compute the annual rental under the lease. (Round to the nearest dollar.)
2. Compute the amounts of the lease payments receivable and the unearned interest revenue that Computer Controls should recognize at the inception of the lease.
3. What are the total expenses related to the lease that Edwards should record for the year ended December 31, 2003?

PROBLEM 15–38

SALES-TYPE LEASE—LESSOR

Aquatran Incorporated uses leases as a method of selling its products. In early 2002, Aquatran completed construction of a passenger ferry for use between Manhattan and Staten Island. On April 1, 2002, the ferry was leased to the Manhattan Ferry Line on a contract specifying that ownership of the ferry will transfer to the lessee at the end of the lease period. Annual lease payments do not include executory costs. Other terms of the agreement are as follows:

Original cost of the ferry	$1,500,000
Fair market value of ferry at lease date	$2,107,102
Lease payments (paid in advance)	$225,000
Estimated residual value	$78,000
Incremental borrowing rate—lessee	10%
Date of first lease payment	April 1, 2002
Lease period	20 years

Instructions:

1. Compute the amount of financial revenue that will be earned over the lease term and the manufacturer's profit that will be earned immediately by Aquatran.
2. Give the entry to record the lease on Aquatran's books. Compute the implicit rate of interest on the lease.
3. Give the journal entries necessary on Aquatran's books to record the lease for the first three years, exclusive of the initial entry. Aquatran's accounting period is the calendar year.
4. Indicate the balance of each of the following accounts at December 31, 2004: Unearned Interest Revenue and Lease Payments Receivable.

PROBLEM 15–39

SALES-TYPE LEASE—LESSOR

Universal Enterprises adopted the policy of leasing as the primary method of selling its products. The company's main product is a small jet airplane that is very popular among corporate executives. Universal constructed such a jet for Executive Transport Services (ETS) at a cost of $8,329,784. Financing of the construction was at a 13% rate. The terms of the lease provided for annual advance payments of $1,331,225 to be paid over 20 years with the ownership of the airplane transferring to ETS at the end of the lease period. It is estimated that the plane will have a residual value of $800,000 at that date. The lease payments began on October 1, 2002. Universal incurred initial direct costs of $150,000 in finalizing the lease agreement with ETS. The sales price of similar airplanes is $11,136,734.

Instructions:

1. Compute the amount of manufacturer's profit that will be earned immediately by Universal.
2. Prepare the journal entry to record the lease on Universal's books at October 1, 2002.
3. Prepare the journal entries to record the lease on Universal's books for the years 2002–2004 exclusive of the initial entry. Universal's accounting period is the calendar year.
4. How much revenue did Universal earn from this lease for each of the first 3 years of the lease?

PROBLEM 15–40

ENTRIES FOR CAPITAL LEASE—LESSEE AND LESSOR

The Alta Corporation entered into an agreement with Snowfire Company to lease equipment for use in its ski manufacturing facility. The lease is appropriately recorded as a purchase by Alta and as a sale by Snowfire. The agreement specifies that lease payments will be made on an annual basis. The cost of the machine is reported as inventory on Snowfire's accounting records. Because of extensive changes in ski manufacturing technology, the machine is not expected to have any residual value. Alta uses straight-line depreciation and computes depreciation to the nearest month. After 3 years, Alta purchases the machine from Snowfire.

Annual lease payments do not include executory costs. Other terms of the agreement are as follows:

Machine cost recorded in inventory	$3,700,000
Price at purchase option date	$3,250,000
Lease payments (paid in advance)	$710,000
Contract interest rate	10%
Contract date/first lease payment	Oct. 1, 2002
Date of Alta purchase	Oct. 1, 2005
Lease period	8 years

Instructions: Prepare journal entries on the books of both the lessee and the lessor as follows:

1. Make entries in 2002 to record the first lease payment, and make adjustments necessary at December 31, the end of each company's fiscal year.
2. Record all entries required in 2003.
3. Prepare the entry in 2005 to record the sale and purchase, assuming no previous entries have been made during the year in connection with the lease.

PROBLEM 15–41

ACCOUNTING FOR CAPITAL LEASE—LESSEE AND LESSOR

The Crosby Equipment Company both leases and sells its equipment to its customers. The most popular line of equipment includes a machine that costs $340,000 to manufacture. The standard lease terms provide for 5 annual payments of $130,000 each

(excluding executory costs), with the first payment due when the lease is signed and subsequent payments due on December 31 of each year. The implicit rate of interest in the contract is 10% per year. Dannell Tool Co. leases one of these machines on January 2, 2002. Initial direct costs of $17,000 are incurred by Crosby on January 2, 2002, to obtain the lease. Dannell's incremental borrowing rate is determined to be 12%. The equipment is very specialized, and it is assumed it will have no salvage value after 5 years. Assume the lease qualifies as a capital lease and a sales-type lease for lessee and lessor, respectively. Also assume that both the lessee and the lessor are on a calendar-year basis and that the lessee is aware of the lessor's implicit interest rate.

Instructions:

1. Give all entries required on the books of Dannell to record the lease of equipment from Crosby for the year 2002. The depreciation on owned equipment is computed once a year on the straight-line basis.
2. Give entries required on the books of Crosby to record the lease of equipment to Dannell for the year 2002.
3. Prepare the balance sheet section involving lease balances for both the lessee's and lessor's financial statements at December 31, 2002.
4. Determine the amount of expense Dannell will report relative to the lease for 2002 and the amount of revenue Crosby will report for the same period.

PROBLEM 15–42

ACCOUNTING FOR LEASES—LESSEE AND LESSOR WITH THIRD-PARTY GUARANTEE

Atwater Equipment Co. manufactures, sells, and leases heavy construction equipment. England Construction Company, a regular customer, leased equipment on July 1, 2002, that had cost Atwater $252,000 to manufacture. The lease payments are $63,161, beginning on July 1, 2002, and continuing annually with the last payment being made on July 1, 2006. If England were to purchase the equipment outright, the fair market value would be $291,881. Because of the heavy wear expected on construction equipment, the lease contains a guaranteed residual value clause wherein the lessee guarantees a residual value on June 30, 2007, of $65,000. England contracted with Weathertop Financial Services to serve as a third-party guarantor of the residual value. Atwater's implicit interest rate is 12%, which is lower than England's incremental borrowing rate of 14%.

Instructions:

1. Assuming that the equipment reverts to Atwater upon completion of the lease term and that the equipment has an expected useful life of 10 years, prepare the entries that should be made on the books of both Atwater and England in recording the lease on July 1, 2002. (Note: England knows the implicit interest rate for the lease.)
2. Prepare the journal entries that should be made by Atwater and England on July 1, 2003. Ignore fiscal year considerations.
3. What financial statement disclosure should be made by Weathertop in its role as a third-party guarantor?

PROBLEM 15–43

ACCOUNTING FOR LEASE—LESSEE AND LESSOR

Astle Manufacturing Company manufactures and leases a variety of items. On January 2, 2002, Astle leased a piece of equipment to Haws Industries Co. The lease is for 6 years with an annual amount of $33,500, payable in advance. The lease payment includes executory costs of $1,500 per year. The equipment has an estimated useful life of 9 years, and it was manufactured by Astle at a cost of $120,000. It is estimated that the equipment will have a residual value of $60,000 at the end of the 6-year lease term. There is no provision for purchase or renewal by Haws at the end of the lease term. However, a third party has guaranteed the residual value of $60,000. The equipment has a fair market value at the lease inception of $187,176. The implicit rate of interest in the contract is 10%, the same rate at which Haws can borrow money at its bank. All lease payments after the first one are made on December 31 of each year. Both companies use the straight-line method of depreciation.

Instructions:

1. Give all the entries relating to the lease on the books of the lessor and lessee for 2002.
2. Show how the lease would appear on the balance sheet of Astle Manufacturing Company and Haws Industries Co. (if applicable) as of December 31, 2002.
3. Assume Astle sold the equipment at the end of the 6-year lease for $85,000. Give the entry to record the sale, assuming all lease entries have been properly made.

PROBLEM 15–44

CASH FLOW TREATMENT OF CAPITAL LEASES—LESSOR

The following information relates to a capital lease between Bradshaw Electric Co. (lessee) and Smoot Manufacturing Inc. (lessor). The lease term began on January 1, 2002. Smoot recorded the lease as a sale and made the following entries related to the lease during 2002. Assume this was the only lease Smoot had during the year.

Jan. 1	Deferred Initial Direct Costs		4,000	
	Cash			4,000
1	Lease Payments Receivable		133,156	
	Sales			90,000
	Unearned Interest Revenue			43,156
1	Cost of Goods Sold		65,000	
	Inventory			61,000
	Deferred Initial Direct Costs			4,000
1	Cash		13,316	
	Lease Payments Receivable			13,316
Dec. 31	Cash		13,316	
	Lease Payments Receivable			13,316
31	Unearned Interest Revenue		7,666	
	Interest Revenue			7,666

Instructions:

1. Prepare the partial operating activities section of the statement of cash flows for 2002 for Smoot Manufacturing Inc. under the indirect method. Assume Smoot reported net income of $132,666 inclusive of the lease revenue in the above entries.
2. Prepare the partial operating activities section of the statement of cash flows for 2002 for Smoot Manufacturing Inc. under the direct method. Assume that cash provided by operating activities exclusive of the lease transactions is $100,000.

PROBLEM 15–45

DISCLOSURE REQUIREMENTS—OPERATING LEASES

Jaquar Mining and Manufacturing Company leases from Emory Leasing Company 3 machines under the following terms.

- Machine #1: Lease period—10 years, beginning April 1, 1996; Lease payment—$18,000 per year, payable in advance.
- Machine #2: Lease period—10 years, beginning July 1, 2000; Lease payment—$30,000 per year, payable in advance.
- Machine #3: Lease period—15 years, beginning January 1, 2001; Lease payment—$12,500 per year, payable in advance.

All the leases are classified as operating leases.

Instructions: Prepare the note to the 2002 financial statements that would be required to disclose the lease commitments of Jaquar Mining and Manufacturing Company. Jaquar uses the calendar year as its accounting period.

PROBLEM 15–46

CAPITALIZING THE VALUE OF OPERATING LEASES

The following information comes from the financial statements of Travis Campbell Company.

Total liabilities	$100,000
Total stockholders' equity	80,000
Property, plant, and equipment	110,000
Sales	500,000

In addition, Travis Campbell has a large number of operating leases. The payments on these operating leases total $30,000 per year for the next 10 years. All of these lease payments occur at the end of the year. The incremental borrowing rate of Travis Campbell Company is 10%. This is also the rate implicit in all of the leases that Travis Campbell signs.

Instructions:

1. Compute the following ratio values:
   a. Debt ratio (total liabilities/total assets).
   b. Debt ratio, assuming that Travis Campbell's operating leases are accounted for as capital leases.
   c. Asset turnover (sales/total assets).
   d. Asset turnover, assuming that Travis Campbell's operating leases are accounted for as capital leases.
2. Briefly describe how the accounting for assets used under operating leases distorts the values of financial ratios.

PROBLEM 15–47

SALE—LEASEBACK OF A BUILDING

On January 3, 2002, Juniper Inc. sold a building with a book value of $1,800,000 to Cedarcrest Industries for $1,757,340. Juniper immediately entered into a leasing agreement whereby Juniper would lease the building back for an annual payment of $260,000. The term of the lease is 10 years, the expected remaining useful life of the building. The first annual lease payment is to be made immediately, and future payments will be made on January 1 of each succeeding year. Cedarcrest's implicit interest rate is 10%.

Instructions:

1. Prepare the journal entries that should be made by both Juniper and Cedarcrest on January 3, 2002, relating to this sale-leaseback transaction.
2. Prepare the journal entries that should be made by both parties at the end of 2002 to accrue interest and to amortize the leased building. (Assume a salvage value of $0 and use of the straight-line method.)

COMPETENCY ENHANCEMENT OPPORTUNITIES

▶ Deciphering Actual Financial Statements	▶ Ethical Dilemma
▶ Writing Assignment	▶ Cumulative Spreadsheet Analysis
▶ Research Project	▶ Internet Search
▶ The Debate	

Accounting is more than just doing textbook problems. This expanded competency material provides practice in critical thinking, oral and written communication, research, teamwork, and consideration of ethical issues.

▶ DECIPHERING ACTUAL FINANCIAL STATEMENTS

• Deciphering 15–1 (The Walt Disney Company)

The 1998 financial statements for THE WALT DISNEY COMPANY are included in Appendix A. In Note 3 to the financial statements, Disney briefly outlines a rather complicated lease arrangement it has arranged in regard to the Disneyland Paris theme park assets of EURO DISNEY. To summarize:

- The theme park assets are owned by an unnamed party.
- A wholly owned subsidiary of Disney, called DISNEY SNC, has leased the theme park assets from the owner under a 12-year, noncancelable lease.
- Euro Disney has subleased the theme park assets from Disney SNC.
  1. With this leasing and subleasing, who will actually use the theme park assets?
  2. From the standpoint of Disney SNC, over the 12-year life of the lease, will there be a net cash inflow from the lease or a net cash outflow from the lease?
  3. Regarding the lease agreement between the owner of the assets and Disney SNC, does it appear that the lease includes a bargain purchase option?
  4. Why doesn't Euro Disney just lease the theme park assets directly from the owner? (Hint: Take a look at Euro Disney's financial performance for the past few years.)

• Deciphering 15–2 (Safeway)

SAFEWAY is a large U.S. supermarket chain. Safeway leases the majority of its store locations. Disclosure regarding these leases is reproduced at the top of the next page. From this information, answer the following questions:

1. Does Safeway have any leases that include bargain renewal options? Are these leases accounted for as capital leases?
2. At the beginning of 1998, Safeway's assets leased under capital leases had a recorded historical cost of $329.2 million. What average useful life is Safeway using to amortize its leased assets? Ignore the possibility of new capital leases signed or old capital leases expired during the year.
3. In addition to the minimum lease payments, Safeway must also make additional lease payments if store sales exceed certain specified amounts. Do these extra payments constitute a large portion of periodic operating lease expense?
4. Estimate the present value of the minimum lease payments for the operating leases. Use the following two techniques:
   - Assume that the same ratio between present value and total gross amount of future minimum lease payments that holds for the capital leases also holds for the operating leases.
   - Assume that the minimum operating lease payment stream can be approximated by a $230 million per year annuity for 13 years. Use a 10% discount rate.

   Comment on whether your two answers are in approximate agreement.

Safeway—Lessee Disclosures

Note D: LEASE OBLIGATIONS

Approximately two-thirds of the premises that the Company occupies are leased. The Company had approximately 1,400 leases at year-end 1998, including approximately 220 which are capitalized for financial reporting purposes. Most leases have renewal options, some with terms and conditions similar to the original lease, others with reduced rental rates during the option periods. Certain of these leases contain options to purchase the property at amounts that approximate fair market value. As of year-end 1998, future minimum rental payments applicable to non-cancelable capital and operating leases with remaining terms in excess of one year were as follows (in millions):

	Capital Leases	Operating Leases
1999	$ 87.9	$ 236.8
2000	84.5	231.5
2001	87.0	207.3
2002	70.1	210.7
2003	67.4	200.2
Thereafter	404.2	1,821.9
Total minimum lease payments	$801.1	$2,908.4
Less amounts representing interest	(351.4)	
Present value of net minimum lease payments	$449.7	
Less current obligations	(41.7)	
Long-term obligations	$408.0	

Future minimum lease payments under non-cancelable capital and operating lease agreements have not been reduced by minimum sublease rental income of $210.5 million. Amortization expense for property under capital leases was $22.3 million in 1998, $21.1 million in 1997 and $17.9 million in 1996. Accumulated amortization of property under capital leases was $136.1 million at year-end 1998 and $153.4 million at year-end 1997. The following schedule shows the composition of total rental expense for all operating leases (in millions). In general, contingent rentals are based on individual store sales.

	1998	1997	1996
Property leases:			
Minimum rentals	$208.7	$206.0	$138.2
Contingent rentals	19.2	12.3	9.9
Less rentals from subleases	(12.0)	(13.4)	(11.1)
	$215.9	$204.9	$137.0
Equipment leases	22.4	19.3	21.0
	$238.3	$224.2	$158.0

• Deciphering 15–3 (International Lease Finance Corporation of California)

As mentioned in the chapter, INTERNATIONAL LEASE FINANCE CORPORATION leases airplanes to airlines. Disclosure regarding International's leases is reproduced in Exhibit 15–11 in the text. In addition, information from the company's 1997 annual report is included below.

Minimum future lease payments to be received for flight equipment on finance and sales-type leases at December 31, 1997 are as follows:

1998	$ 15,783
1999	14,682
2000	16,095
2001	16,095
2002	16,035
Thereafter	30,925
Total minimum lease payments to be received	$109,615

1. By examining the stream of expected future lease payments from the 1997 and 1998 note disclosure, can you determine how much business in new capital leases the company generated during 1998?
2. Given your answer to (1), how much cash did the company collect during the year relating to: (a) interest earned on capital leases and (b) the principal balance on capital leases?
3. International's leasing revenues increased by 7% from 1997 to 1998 and net income increased by 9%. How can the company increase its revenues and net income when it is signing no new capital leases?

• Deciphering 15–4 (McDonald's Corporation)

The franchise arrangement between McDONALD's and its franchisees is summarized in the note from McDonald's 1998 annual report below.

McDonald's Corporation—Note to 1998 Annual Report

Franchise arrangements generally include a lease and a license and provide for payment of initial fees, as well as continuing rent, service fees and royalties to the Company, based upon a percentage of sales with minimum rent payments. Franchisees are granted the right to operate a McDonald's restaurant using the McDonald's system as well as the use of a restaurant facility, generally for a period of 20 years. Franchisees pay related occupancy costs including property taxes, insurance and maintenance. Beginning in 1998, franchisees in the U.S. generally have the option to own new restaurant facilities while leasing the land from McDonald's. In addition, franchisees outside the U.S. pay a refundable, noninterest-bearing security deposit. The results of operations of restaurant businesses purchased and sold in transactions with franchisees and affiliates were not material to the consolidated financial statements for periods prior to purchase and sale.

(In millions of dollars)	1998	1997	1996
Minimum rents	$1,440.9	$1,369.7	$1,350.7
Percent rent and service fees	2,026.9	1,836.3	1,689.7
Initial fees	58.7	66.3	75.4
Revenues from franchised and affiliate restaurants	$3,526.5	$3,272.3	$3,115.8

Future minimum rent payments due to the Company under franchise arrangements are:

(In millions of dollars)	Owned Sites	Leased Sites	Total
1999	$ 905.0	$ 670.6	$ 1,575.6
2000	887.8	660.3	1,548.1
2001	872.2	651.6	1,523.8
2002	854.1	638.0	1,492.1
2003	835.8	625.4	1,461.2
Thereafter	7,412.1	5,774.1	13,186.2
Total minimum payments	$11,767.0	$9,020.0	$20,787.0

From this information, answer the following questions:

1. McDonald's arrangement with its franchisees is that the franchisees agree to pay a minimum rent plus additional amounts if sales are above a certain level. How significant are these additional amounts?
2. Given the information in this franchise note, what is your forecast of McDonald's total franchise revenue for 1999?
3. As indicated in the franchise note, McDonald's owns some of its sites and leases others. An important comparison is the relationship between future minimum lease payments McDonald's must make and future minimum payments to be received from franchisees. The future payments (in millions of dollars) McDonald's must make on its leased sites are summarized on the following page:

1999	$ 625.2	$ 400.3
2000	598.0	392.7
2001	577.4	377.3
2002	549.7	359.0
2003	521.4	341.0
Thereafter	4,840.3	3,379.8
Total minimum payments	$7,712.0	$5,250.1

Comparing the payments to be made for leased sites and the minimum payments to be collected from franchisees for leased sites, it looks as if McDonald's is guaranteed to make money every year on its leased sites. What would have to happen for McDonald's to *lose* money on these leased sites?

▶ **WRITING ASSIGNMENT**
• All leases are sales-type leases!
You are the accountant for Clear Water Bay Company. Clear Water Bay is an equipment manufacturer. In order to help customers finance their purchases, Clear Water Bay often leases, rather than sells, the equipment. Clear Water Bay structures the lease agreements so that most of its equipment leases are classified as operating leases. This is because customers strongly prefer this treatment in order to keep the lease obligations off their balance sheets. This treatment does result in a delay in Clear Water Bay's ability to report profits from the sales, but this delay has been viewed as part of the cost of keeping customers happy.

The president of Clear Water Bay just returned from a week-long accounting and finance seminar at a prominent university. She is excited about the session she attended on the accounting for leases. She was told, or thinks she was told, that there is no need for Clear Water Bay to report its leasing arrangements as operating leases—according to U.S. GAAP, lessors can always classify a lease as a sales-type lease even when the lessee classifies the same lease as an operating lease. The president tells you to get to work restating Clear Water Bay's most recent financial statements to reflect reclassification of all Clear Water Bay's leases from operating leases to sales-type leases.

Write a memo to the president clarifying the accounting rules governing sales-type and operating leases. Carefully explain the circumstances in which the same lease can be classified as a sales-type lease by the lessor and an operating lease by the lessee.

▶ **RESEARCH PROJECT**
• Should you buy or lease that car?
These days, many new cars are leased instead of purchased. In order to find out when it makes sense to lease a car instead of buying, do the following:
1. Search a newspaper for an advertisement giving the terms of a car lease agreement. *The Wall Street Journal* often runs ads for luxury car leases.
2. Find out the values for the following aspects of the lease agreement:
   • Down payment (nonrefundable)
   • Deposit (refundable)
   • Monthly payments
   • Length of the lease
3. Find out the approximate cash price to purchase the same car.
4. Compute the present value (as of the lease signing date) of the lease payments. (Note: Use interest rates compounded monthly. For example, if you think that 12% compounded monthly is an appropriate interest rate, use 1% per month.)
5. Calculate the resale value that the car would have to have at the end of the lease term to make it financially smart to buy the car at the cash price rather than lease it.

After performing your analysis, your group is to report (either orally or in writing) on whether you think it makes more sense to lease a car or to buy a car. Make sure you outline your assumptions.

▶ **THE DEBATE**
• When classifying leases, just use common sense!
The four lease classification criteria were intended to get the majority of long-term non-cancelable leases onto the balance sheet by carefully defining the circumstances in which a lease must be accounted for as a capital lease. However, firms have treated the criteria as guidelines for constructing lease agreements that have many characteristics of a capital lease but that are still safely on the operating lease side of the dividing line.

Divide your group into two teams.

- One team represents Stricter Guidelines. Prepare a 2-minute oral argument explaining why the lease classification criteria should be reformulated and tightened so that more leases are classified as capital leases. In particular, the criteria should be designed to eliminate loopholes such as third-party guarantees of residual values. Operating leases are a tool for tricking financial statement users and hiding significant lease payment obligations.

- The other team represents Accounting Judgment. Prepare a 2-minute presentation explaining why no set of objective criteria can ever prevent firms from structuring leases to avoid balance sheet recognition. The solution is to put the classification decision squarely in the hands of the accountant—leases that smell like effective ownership transfers should be accounted for as capital leases, regardless of the specific numerical terms of the lease agreement.

▶ **ETHICAL DILEMMA**
• Using operating leases to fool the bank
You are the chief financial officer for RAM Solutions, a small but rapidly growing retail computer hardware chain. You are trying to figure out how to finance the new buildings that are scheduled to be purchased this year. The difficulty is that RAM has an existing loan with Commercial Security Bank (CSB) that requires RAM to maintain an interest coverage ratio (operating income/interest expense) of 2.0 or greater. Forecasts for next year are as follows:

Forecasted operating income	$15,000,000
Forecasted interest expense (assuming no new borrowing)	7,000,000
Cost of purchasing new buildings	50,000,000

If you borrow the $50 million needed to finance the new buildings, the increased interest expense will cause you to be in violation of the interest coverage constraint.

The controller has suggested an accounting solution to this dilemma: lease the new buildings, carefully constructing the lease agreements so that the leases will be accounted for as operating leases. The leasing arrangements will be economically similar to purchase of the buildings with borrowed money, but the annual payments will be reported as rent expense instead of interest expense. Accordingly, the interest coverage loan covenant will be completely sidestepped.

You personally negotiated the loan with Commercial Security Bank, and you know that the intent of the loan covenant was to prevent RAM from incurring large fixed obligations that might endanger the repayment of the CSB loan. Operating lease payments are fixed obligations, just like interest payments, and you are uneasy about using this accounting trick to get around the loan covenant. However, there does not seem to be any other solution. What should you do?

▶ **CUMULATIVE SPREADSHEET ANALYSIS**
This assignment is based on the spreadsheet prepared in (1) of the cumulative spreadsheet assignment for Chapter 13. Review that assignment for a summary of the assumptions made in preparing a forecasted balance sheet, income statement, and statement of cash flows for 2003 for Skywalker Company. This assignment involves revisiting assumptions (q) and (u) in the Chapter 13 assignment.

Skywalker would like to know how its forecasted financial statements would look if it decided to lease all new property, plant, and equipment under operating leases. Before

2003, all of Skywalker's property, plant, and equipment purchases had been 100% financed using long-term debt. This same assumption underlies the forecast prepared in (1) of the Chapter 13 assignment.

1. Using the same instructions given in (1) of the Chapter 13 spreadsheet assignment, forecast the following values for 2003:

   Forecasted balance sheet for 2003:
   a. Property, plant, and equipment
   b. Accumulated depreciation
   c. Long-term debt

   Forecasted income statement for 2003:
   d. Depreciation and amortization expense
   e. Other operating expenses
   f. Interest expense
   g. Income tax expense
   h. Net income

   Forecasted statement of cash flows for 2003:
   i. Cash from operating activities
   j. Cash from investing activities
   k. Cash from financing activities

   Financial ratios for 2003:
   l. Debt ratio (total liabilities/total assets)
   m. Asset turnover (sales/total assets)

2. Repeat (1), but now assume that all new property, plant, and equipment expected to be acquired during 2003 will be acquired under an operating lease arrangement. Assume that the annual operating lease payment for property, plant, and equipment is 15% of the purchase price of the asset and that the new property, plant, and equipment that Skywalker will lease in 2003 will be not all be leased at the start of the year but will be added evenly throughout the year. Mathematically, this is the same as assuming that new assets leased during the year are leased, on average, for half the year. (Note: Operating lease payments are classified in the income statement as "Other operating expenses.") Under this leasing arrangement, the forecasted balance in long-term debt at the end of 2003 should be the amount forecasted previously (assuming an 80% debt ratio), less the amount of recognized long-term debt that can be avoided through the leasing arrangement.

3. Comment on the differences between the numbers in (1) and (2).

▶ **INTERNET SEARCH**

DELTA AIR LINES' Web address is **www.delta-air.com**. Once you've gained access to Delta's Web site, answer the following questions:

1. Of course, Delta's Web site has lots of flight information. Use this information to find out whether Delta has any morning nonstop flights from Salt Lake City to Houston Intercontinental. Also, find out how long the flying time is from Portland, Oregon, to Seoul, Korea.

2. Find the notes to Delta's most recent set of financial statements. What rent expense was associated with operating leases in the most recent year?

3. Does Delta have more operating leases or more capital leases?

4. Does Delta purchase most of its flight and ground equipment, or does it lease most of this equipment?

chapter 16
Income Taxes

Accounting for deferred taxes has been a bit like a roller-coaster ride. In February 1992, the FASB issued Statement No. 109, "Accounting for Income Taxes," in response to five years of complaints and controversy surrounding the standard it superseded, FASB Statement No. 96. Statement No. 96 was so unpopular that some observers predicted it would result in an unraveling of public confidence in the FASB, with the possibility that the FASB would be replaced just as its two predecessor bodies, the CAP and the APB, had been. The two primary complaints against Statement No. 96 were that it was overly complicated and that it severely restricted the recognition of deferred tax assets.

Statement No. 96 was issued in 1987 and mandated that the deferred tax amounts reported on the balance sheet should be valued using enacted future tax rates. Previously, deferred tax items had been valued using tax rates in effect when the deferred taxes arose. This accounting change, coupled with the fact that the Tax Reform Act of 1986 had lowered the maximum corporate tax rate from 46% to 34%, caused significant downward revisions in the reported amounts of deferred taxes. For a firm with a deferred tax liability, the combined result was a decrease in the reported liability (a debit) and the recognition of a corresponding one-time gain (a credit). The business press of the period was full of articles warning investors of the large cosmetic accounting gains that companies were expected to report.[1] GENERAL ELECTRIC adopted Statement No. 96 in 1987; as a result, General Electric's finance subsidiary showed a gain of $518 million, increasing the subsidiary's net income by 106%. IBM adopted Statement No. 96 in 1988 and showed a gain of $315 million. EXXON made the adoption in 1989 and increased net income by 18% with a $535 million gain.

In response to one of the major criticisms of Statement No. 96, Statement No. 109, as explained more fully in this chapter, allows the recognition of most deferred tax assets. Once again, the business press warned investors to beware of firms reporting one-time accounting gains because of the change in accounting for deferred taxes.[2] These gains come about because previously unrecorded deferred tax assets are recognized (a debit), along with a corresponding gain (a credit). For example, on September 30, 1992, IBM announced that it would report a $1.9 billion gain as a result of adopting Statement No. 109. Interestingly, this gain was used to partially offset a $2.1 billion write-off of buildings and equipment.[3]

1 For an example, see Lee Berton, "FASB Is Expected to Issue Rule Allowing Many Firms to Post Big, One-Time Gains," *The Wall Street Journal*, November 4, 1987, p. 4.
2 See Mary Beth Grover, "Cosmetics," *Forbes*, March 30, 1992, p. 78.
3 See Michael W. Miller and Laurence Hooper, "IBM Announces Write-Off for Total of $2.1 Billion," *The Wall Street Journal*, September 30, 1992, p. A3.

LEARNING OBJECTIVES

1
Understand the concept of deferred taxes and the distinction between permanent and temporary differences.

2
Compute the amount of deferred tax liabilities and assets.

3
Explain the provisions of tax loss carrybacks and carryforwards, and be able to account for these provisions.

4
Schedule future tax rates, and determine the effect on tax assets and liabilities.

5
Determine appropriate financial statement presentation and disclosure associated with deferred tax assets and liabilities.

6
Comply with income tax disclosure requirements associated with the statement of cash flows.

7
Describe how, with respect to deferred income taxes, international accounting standards have converged toward the U.S. treatment.

e|m

EXPANDED MATERIAL

8
Perform intraperiod income tax allocation.

T his chapter begins with a discussion of the reasons for differences between financial reporting income and taxable income. This discussion leads into the topic of deferred taxes and how differences in the timing of the recognition of revenues and expenses for tax and financial reporting purposes cause differences between income tax payable and income tax expense for a period. Accounting for these deferred tax assets and liabilities comprises the bulk of this chapter. Additional topics covered include net operating loss carrybacks and carryforwards and their relationship to deferred taxes, the effect of deferred taxes on the statement of cash flows, and the disclosure requirements associated with deferred taxes. We will also discuss how the international standards for deferred tax accounting have become more similar to U.S. GAAP over the past few years. Finally, the expanded material section of this chapter discusses intraperiod tax allocation.

Understand the concept of deferred taxes and the distinction between permanent and temporary differences.

DEFERRED INCOME TAXES: AN OVERVIEW

When taking introductory financial accounting, many students are surprised to learn that corporations in the United States compute two different income numbers—**financial income** for reporting to stockholders and **taxable income** for reporting to the Internal Revenue Service (IRS). The existence of these two "sets of books" seems unethical to some, illegal to others. However, the difference between the information needs of the stockholders and the efficient revenue collection needs of the government makes the computation of the two different income numbers essential. The different purposes of these reporting systems were summarized by the U.S. Supreme Court in the Thor Power Tool case (1979):

> The primary goal of financial accounting is to provide useful information to management, shareholders, creditors, and others properly interested; the major responsibility of the accountant is to protect these parties from being misled. The primary goal of the income tax system, in contrast, is the equitable collection of revenue.

Corporations keep two "sets of books" to compute income—one for reporting financial income to stockholders, and the other for reporting taxable income to the IRS.

In summary, U.S. corporations compute income in two different ways, and rightly so. But, the existence of these two different numbers that can each be called "income before taxes" makes it surprisingly difficult to define what is meant by "income tax expense" and to compute an appropriate balance sheet value for income tax liabilities and prepaid income tax assets. This accounting difficulty stems from two basic considerations:

1. How to account for revenues and expenses that have already been recognized and reported to shareholders in a company's financial statements but will not affect taxable income until subsequent years.
2. How to account for revenues and expenses that have already been reported to the IRS but will not be recognized in the financial statements until subsequent years.

Accounting for deferred income taxes focuses on temporary differences between financial accounting income and taxable income. For example, the income tax rules allow companies to deduct depreciation faster than is typically done for the financial accounting books. Over the life of the asset, the amount of depreciation is the same for both sets of books. But *temporarily*, there is a difference between the cumulative depreciation deduction reported in the tax books and the amount of cumulative depreciation expense recognized in the financial accounting books. It is this temporary difference that results in deferred income taxes. The accounting for deferred taxes is summarized in Exhibit 16–1.

EXHIBIT 16–1 | A Summary of Temporary Differences and Deferred Income Taxes

Event occurs that creates a temporary difference between financial accounting income and taxable income.

If, in the initial year, taxable income is less than financial accounting income, then taxable income will be greater in subsequent years. The income tax expected to be paid on this future additional taxable income is recognized now as a deferred tax liability.

If, in the initial year, taxable income is greater than financial accounting income, then taxable income will be less in subsequent years. This expected income tax reduction is recognized now as a deferred tax asset. [*Note:* As explained later, realization of this deferred tax asset depends on the existence of taxable income in future years.]

Two simple examples will be used to illustrate the accounting issues resulting from this difference between financial accounting income and taxable income.

Example 1. Simple Deferred Income Tax Liability

In 2002, Ibanez Company earned revenues of $30,000. Ibanez has no expenses other than income taxes. Assume that in this case, the income tax law specifies that income is

FYI: Although accounting standard-setting bodies have not expressed interest in abandoning deferred income tax accounting, many writers through the years have suggested that basing income tax expense on the actual tax payments is the most practical way of reporting income taxes. If this solution were to become the standard, there would be no need for a chapter on income taxes in an intermediate accounting text. This would undoubtedly please authors, faculty, and students alike.

taxed when received in cash and that Ibanez received $10,000 cash in 2002 and expects to receive $20,000 in 2003. The income tax rate is 40%, and we will assume for the moment that the tax rate is expected to remain the same into the foreseeable future.

The two amounts to be determined are total income tax liability at the end of the year and total income tax expense for the year. Obviously, the income tax liability is at least $4,000 because that is how much the IRS is expecting based on Ibanez's reported taxable income of $10,000. In addition, it would be misleading to the shareholders not to tell them of the expected tax to be paid on the additional $20,000 to be received in cash in 2003. Remember, this $20,000 in income has been reported to the shareholders because it was earned in 2002, but it has not yet been reported to the IRS. The expected tax on the $20,000 is $8,000 ($20,000 × .40) and is called a *deferred tax liability*. It is a liability because it requires a payment in the future (hence the term deferred) as a result of a past transaction (the past transaction is the earning of the income). This liability can be thought of as the expected income tax on income earned but not yet taxed. The journal entries to record all the tax-related information for Ibanez for 2002 are as follows:

Income Tax Expense—Current	4,000	
Income Taxes Payable		4,000
Income Tax Expense—Deferred	8,000	
Deferred Tax Liability		8,000

It is important to recognize the difference between the two recorded liabilities. Income taxes payable is an existing legal liability that the IRS fully expects to collect by March 15, 2003 (corporations pay taxes at different times than do individuals). Deferred tax liability is not an existing legal liability—as far as the IRS is concerned, it doesn't exist. However, because Ibanez knows that $20,000 of the revenues earned in 2002 will be taxed in 2003, recognition of the deferred tax liability is necessary to ensure that all expenses associated with 2002 revenues are reported in the 2002 income statement and that all obligations are reported on the December 31, 2002, balance sheet.

As can be seen from the income tax journal entries for 2002, total income tax expense of $12,000 is the sum of the current and deferred tax expenses. The 2002 income statement for Ibanez Company is as follows:

Revenues		$30,000
Income tax expense:		
Current	$4,000	
Deferred	8,000	12,000
Net income		$18,000

Some have argued that reported income tax expense should just be the amount currently payable according to IRS rules. This type of disclosure would lead to a rude surprise in 2003 for the Ibanez shareholders—Ibanez will owe $8,000 in income tax in 2003 even if no new revenues are generated in 2003.

Example 2. Simple Deferred Tax Asset

In 2002, its first year of operations, Gupta Company generated service revenues totaling $60,000, all taxable in 2002. Gupta Company offers a warranty on its service. No warranty claims were made in 2002, but Gupta estimates that in 2003 warranty costs of $10,000 will be incurred for warranty claims relating to 2002 service revenues. The $10,000 estimated warranty expense is reported in the 2002 financial statements as required by GAAP. For tax purposes, however, assume that the IRS does not allow any tax deduction until the actual warranty services are performed. Also assume that the income tax rate is 40% and that Gupta Company had no expenses in 2002 other than warranty costs and income taxes.

Income taxes payable as of the end of 2002 is $24,000 ($60,000 × .40) because Gupta is required to report $60,000 in revenues to the IRS but is not allowed to take any warranty deduction until 2003. What about the $10,000 warranty deduction Gupta expects to take in 2003? Gupta can expect this deduction to lower the 2003 tax bill by $4,000 ($10,000 × .40). This $4,000 is called a *deferred tax asset* and represents the expected benefit of a tax deduction for an expense item that has already been incurred and reported to the shareholders but is not yet deductible according to IRS rules. In effect, Gupta is paying taxes this year in anticipation of lower taxes next year—a prepayment of taxes. The journal entries to record all the tax-related information for Gupta for 2002 are as follows:

Income Tax Expense—Current	24,000	
Income Taxes Payable		24,000
Deferred Tax Asset	4,000	
Income Tax Benefit—Deferred		4,000

Total income tax expense of $20,000 is the difference between the current tax expense and the deferred tax benefit. The 2002 income statement for Gupta Company is as follows:

Revenues		$60,000
Warranty expense		10,000
Income before taxes		$50,000
Income tax expense:		
Current	$24,000	
Deferred benefit	(4,000)	20,000
Net income		$30,000

As explained in detail later in the chapter, deferred tax assets can be much more complicated than this simple example indicates. The two most common complications revolve around: (1) the likelihood that a company will be able to realize the deferred tax asset in the future (a company that experiences repeated operating losses, for example, may not be able to take full advantage of the deferred tax asset) and (2) changing tax rates (a change in future tax rates affects the amount of deferred tax assets and liabilities). Dissatisfaction over the FASB's handling of these issues contributed to the demise of Statement No. 96 and the adoption of Statement No. 109.

Permanent and Temporary Differences

Before more detailed deferred tax examples are presented, some of the specific differences between financial accounting standards and tax rules will be described.

Some differences between financial and taxable income are **permanent differences.** These differences are caused by specific provisions of the tax law that exempt certain types of revenues from taxation and prohibit the deduction of certain types of expenses. Nontaxable revenues and nondeductible expenses are never included in determining taxable income, but they are included in determining financial income under GAAP. Permanent differences are created by political and social pressures to favor certain segments of society or to promote certain industries or economic activities. Examples of nontaxable revenues include proceeds from life insurance policies and interest received on municipal bonds. Examples of nondeductible expenses include fines for violation of laws and payment of life insurance premiums. Permanent differences do not create accounting problems. Because they are never included in the computation of taxable income, they have no impact on either current or future (deferred) tax obligations.

More commonly, differences between pretax financial income and taxable income arise from business events that are recognized for both financial reporting and tax purposes but in different time periods. In some cases, income tax payments are deferred to a period later than when the effect of the event on financial income is recognized. In other cases, income tax payments are required before the effect of the event on financial income is recognized. These differences are referred to as **temporary differences** because, over time, their impact on financial income and taxable income will be the same.

A common example of a temporary difference, and one that historically has been the most significant for U.S. companies, is the computation of depreciation. As indicated in Chapter 13, depreciation for federal income tax purposes is referred to as cost recovery and has varied over time as to the degree of acceleration in the recovery of asset costs. On the other hand, the most common depreciation method used to determine financial income is the straight-line method, which recognizes an even amount of depreciation expense each year the asset is in service. In the early years of asset life, straight-line depreciation reported on the income statement usually is less than the cost recovery deduction on the income tax return. In the latter portion of an asset's life, however, this pattern reverses; that is, the depreciation expense on the income statement exceeds the cost recovery deduction on the tax return.

There are many other temporary differences besides depreciation, and new income tax laws continue to create additional ones as income taxes are used to meet changing economic and policy objectives. Some examples of temporary differences are given in Exhibit 16–2. This list is just a sample of the differences between financial accounting standards and income tax laws that can create temporary differences between financial and taxable income.

EXHIBIT 16–2 | Examples of Temporary Differences

1. **Differences That Create Deferred Tax Liabilities for Future Taxable Amounts**
   (a) Revenues or gains are taxable *after* they are recognized for financial reporting purposes.
   - Installment sales method used for tax purposes but accrual method of recognizing sales revenue used for financial reporting purposes.
   - Completed-contract method of recognizing construction revenue used for tax purposes but percentage-of-completion method used for financial reporting purposes.
   (b) Expenses or losses are deductible for tax purposes *before* they are recognized for financial reporting purposes.
   - MACRS used for tax purposes but straight-line method of depreciation used for financial reporting purposes.
   - Intangible drilling costs for extractive industry written off as incurred for tax purposes but capitalized for financial reporting purposes.
2. **Differences That Create Deferred Tax Assets for Future Deductible Amounts**
   (a) Revenues or gains are taxable *before* they are recognized for financial reporting purposes.
   - Rent revenue received in advance of period earned recognized as revenue for tax purposes but deferred to be recognized in future periods for financial reporting purposes.
   - Subscription revenue received in advance of period earned recognized as revenue for tax purposes but deferred to be recognized in future periods for financial reporting purposes.
   (b) Expenses or losses are deductible for tax purposes *after* they are recognized for financial reporting purposes.
   - Warranty expense deductible for tax purposes only when actually incurred but accrued in the year of product sale for financial reporting purposes.
   - Marketable securities valued at cost for tax purposes but valued at market for financial reporting purposes.

The examples in the exhibit are presented in two major categories. The first category includes differences, called **taxable temporary differences,** that will result in taxable amounts in future years. Income taxes expected to be paid on future taxable amounts are reported on the balance sheet as a deferred tax liability. The second category includes

THINK How can a company have both deferred tax assets and deferred tax liabilities?

differences, called **deductible temporary differences,** that will result in deductible amounts in future years. Income tax benefits (savings) expected to be realized from future deductible amounts are reported on the balance sheet as a deferred tax asset. Exhibit 16–3 provides examples of deferred tax assets and deferred tax liabilities taken from the 1998 financial statements of several large U.S. companies. The large deferred tax liabilities of the capital-intensive companies listed in Exhibit 16–3 highlight the importance of deferred tax liabilities arising from depreciation. The $11,764 million deferred tax liability recognized by Berkshire Hathaway stems from its large investment portfolio. Increases in the value of investments are recognized for financial reporting purposes as they occur but are not taxed until the investments are sold; this gives rise to deferred tax liabilities.

EXHIBIT 16–3 | Selected Deferred Tax Assets and Deferred Tax Liabilities for 1998

(Numbers in millions)

Company	Deferred Tax Assets*	Deferred Tax Liabilities
Berkshire Hathaway	$ 1,008	$11,764
Exxon	3,696	16,756
Ford	14,086	14,196
General Electric	10,614	19,954
Union Pacific	1,929	7,993

*Where applicable, deferred tax assets are reported net of any associated valuation allowance. Valuation allowances are discussed later in the chapter.

Illustration of Permanent and Temporary Differences

To illustrate the effect of permanent and temporary differences on the computation of income taxes, assume that for the year ended December 31, 2002, Monroe Corporation reported income before taxes of $420,000. Assume this amount includes $20,000 of nontaxable revenues and $5,000 of nondeductible expenses, both permanent differences. In addition, assume that Monroe has one temporary difference: The depreciation (cost recovery) deduction on the 2002 income tax return exceeds depreciation expense on the income statement by $30,000. Assuming a corporate income tax rate of 35% for 2002, income taxes payable for the year would be computed as follows:

Caution! It is important that you be able to distinguish among the terms "pretax financial income," "pretax financial income subject to tax," and "taxable income." This simple illustration highlights these terms and will make the later discussion more clear. Where there are no permanent differences, pretax financial income and pretax financial income subject to tax are the same. Unless otherwise noted, the shorter term is used in the remainder of the chapter.

Pretax financial income (from income statement)		$420,000
Add (deduct) permanent differences:		
Nontaxable revenues	$(20,000)	
Nondeductible expenses	5,000	(15,000)
Financial income subject to tax		$405,000
Add (deduct) temporary differences:		
Excess of tax depreciation over book depreciation		(30,000)
Taxable income		$375,000
Tax on taxable income (income taxes payable):		
$375,000 × .35		$131,250

As illustrated, the permanent differences are not included in either the financial income subject to tax or the taxable income. In addition, because these permanent differences never reverse, they have no impact on income taxes payable in subsequent periods and are thus not associated with any deferred tax consequences. Temporary differences are the cause of the complexity and controversy in accounting for income taxes because they impact financial income and taxable income in different periods. In general, the accounting for temporary differences is referred to as **interperiod tax allocation.**

Compute the amount of deferred tax liabilities and assets.

ANNUAL COMPUTATION OF DEFERRED TAX LIABILITIES AND ASSETS

As illustrated with the earlier examples, the basic concepts underlying deferred tax accounting are fairly simple. The examples that follow introduce some of the complexities associated with the specific provisions of Statement No. 109. Before launching into these examples, take a moment to reflect on how lucky you are not to have taken this class a few years ago. At that time, this chapter was based on Statement No. 96, which was much more difficult to understand and to implement and was hated by practitioners, financial statement users, students, and professors alike.

As discussed in the boxed item on pages 936–937, FASB Statement No. 109 reflects the Board's preference for the **asset and liability method of interperiod tax allocation,** which emphasizes the measurement and reporting of balance sheet amounts. The major advantages of the asset and liability method of accounting for deferred taxes are as follows:

1. Because the assets and liabilities recorded under this method are in agreement with the FASB definitions of financial statement elements, the method is conceptually consistent with other standards.
2. The asset and liability method is a flexible method that recognizes changes in circumstances and adjusts the reported amounts accordingly. This flexibility may improve the predictive value of the financial statements.

One drawback of the asset and liability method is that in some ways, it is still too complicated (even after the significant simplification brought about by Statement No. 109). Many financial statement users claim that they ignore deferred tax assets and liabilities anyway, and thus, efforts devoted to deferred tax accounting are just a waste of time. For example, one financial statement analysis textbook reports that "because of the uncertainty over whether (and when) a deferred tax liability will be paid, some individuals elect to exclude deferred tax liabilities from liabilities when performing analysis."[4] On the other hand, research using stock market data suggests that investors compute values of companies as if the reported deferred tax liabilities are bona fide liabilities.[5]

The following list summarizes the procedure to be followed each year to compute the amount of deferred tax liabilities and assets to be included in the financial statements under the provisions of FASB Statement No. 109.[6]

1. Identify the types and amounts of existing temporary differences.
2. Measure the deferred tax liability for taxable temporary differences using applicable current and future tax rates.
3. Measure the deferred tax asset for deductible temporary differences using applicable current and future tax rates.

4 Charles H. Gibson, *Financial Statement Analysis: Using Financial Accounting Information*, 6th ed., Cincinnati, OH: South-Western Publishing Co., 1995, p. 321.
5 Dan Givoly and Carla Hayn, "The Valuation of the Deferred Tax Liability: Evidence from the Stock Market," *The Accounting Review*, April 1992, pp. 394–410.
6 *FASB Statement No. 109*, "Accounting for Income Taxes," Norwalk, CT: Financial Accounting Standards Board, 1992, par. 17.

4. Reduce deferred tax assets by a valuation allowance if it is more likely than not (a likelihood of more than 50%) that some portion or all of the deferred tax assets will not be realized. The valuation allowance should reduce the deferred tax asset to the amount that is more likely than not to be realized.

Several examples will illustrate the computation of deferred tax assets and liabilities under the provisions of Statement No. 109.

Example 3. Deferred Tax Liability

If a company has only deferred tax liabilities to consider, the accounting for deferred taxes is relatively straightforward. To illustrate, assume that Roland Inc. begins operations in 2002. For 2002, Roland computes pretax financial income of $75,000. The only difference between financial accounting income and taxable income is depreciation. Roland uses the straight-line method of depreciation for financial reporting purposes and an accelerated cost recovery method on its tax return. The depreciation amounts for existing plant assets for the years 2002 through 2005 are as follows:

Year	Financial Reporting	Income Tax Reporting
2002	$ 25,000	$ 40,000
2003	25,000	30,000
2004	25,000	25,000
2005	25,000	5,000
	$100,000	$100,000

The enacted tax rate for 2002 and future years is 40%. Roland's taxable income for 2002 is $60,000, computed as follows:

Financial income subject to tax	$75,000
Deduct temporary difference:	
Excess of tax depreciation over book depreciation	(15,000)
Taxable income	$60,000
Tax ($60,000 × .40)	$24,000

Thus, Roland records a current liability of $24,000. At the end of 2002, aggregate tax depreciation exceeds aggregate book depreciation by $15,000 ($40,000 – $25,000). This taxable temporary difference will result in a taxable amount of $15,000 in future years as the difference reverses. With the currently enacted 40% tax rate, income tax on this future taxable amount will total $6,000 ($15,000 × .40). Accordingly, a deferred tax liability of $6,000 will be reported on the December 31, 2002, balance sheet. Because the depreciable asset is a noncurrent operating asset, the associated deferred tax liability is also classified as noncurrent.

The journal entries to record Roland's income taxes for 2002 would be as follows:

Income Tax Expense—Current	24,000	
Income Taxes Payable		24,000
Income Tax Expense—Deferred	6,000	
Deferred Tax Liability—Noncurrent		6,000

Income taxes would be shown on Roland's 2002 income statement as follows:

Income before income taxes		$75,000
Income tax expense:		
Current	$24,000	
Deferred	6,000	30,000
Net income		$45,000

STOP & THINK How might the numbers for 2002 change if Roland expected tax rates in future periods to be 30% instead of 40%?

The December 31, 2002, balance sheet would report a current liability of $24,000 for income taxes payable and, as noted above, a noncurrent deferred tax liability of $6,000.

So as to not unnecessarily complicate this example, we will assume that Roland earns income of $75,000 in each of the years 2003 through 2005. In 2003, Roland reports taxable income of $70,000, computed as follows:

Financial income subject to tax	$75,000
Deduct temporary difference:	
Excess of tax depreciation over book depreciation	(5,000)
Taxable income	$70,000
Tax ($70,000 × .40)	$28,000

Roland's current taxes payable are $28,000. In each subsequent year following the initial deferral, the ending deferred tax liability is determined and compared with the beginning balance. The difference between the beginning and ending balance is recorded as an adjustment to the deferred tax liability account. At the end of 2003, aggregate tax depreciation exceeds aggregate book depreciation by $20,000 ($70,000 – $50,000). The deferred tax liability account, therefore, must be adjusted to a balance of $8,000 ($20,000 × .40). The amount of the adjustment is $2,000 ($8,000 less the beginning balance of $6,000). The following journal entries record the current payable and the adjustment to the deferred tax liability account:

Income Tax Expense—Current	28,000	
Income Taxes Payable		28,000
Income Tax Expense—Deferred	2,000	
Deferred Tax Liability—Noncurrent		2,000

Because the depreciation expense for tax and financial reporting purposes is the same for 2004, no adjustment to the deferred tax liability account would be necessary for that year. Income for tax purposes would be equal to financial accounting income, and tax expense and taxes payable would be recorded with the following journal entry:

Income Tax Expense—Current	30,000	
Income Taxes Payable		30,000
($75,000 × .40)		

For 2005, income for tax purposes would be equal to $95,000, computed as follows:

Financial income subject to tax	$75,000
Add reversal of temporary difference:	
Excess of book depreciation over tax depreciation	20,000
Taxable income	$95,000
Tax ($95,000 × .40)	$38,000

Therefore, current taxes payable would be $38,000. The accumulated difference of $20,000 in the deferred tax account reverses, and aggregate tax depreciation and aggregate book depreciation are the same ($100,000). Thus, the journal entries to record the current year's payable as well as to reduce the deferred tax liability to zero would be:

Income Tax Expense—Current	38,000	
Income Taxes Payable		38,000
Deferred Tax Liability—Noncurrent	8,000	
Income Tax Benefit		8,000

The income tax benefit reduces the current income tax expense for 2005.

EFFECT OF CURRENTLY ENACTED CHANGES IN FUTURE TAX RATES The example assumed a constant future tax rate of 40%. If changes in future tax rates have been enacted, the deferred tax liability (or asset) is measured using the enacted tax rate for the future years when the temporary difference is expected to reverse. To illustrate, assume that in 2002, Congress enacts legislation that reduces corporate tax rates for 2003 and subsequent years. In the Roland Inc. example, all the temporary difference reverses in 2005, and the deferred tax liability should be measured using the tax rate enacted for that year. If the enacted tax rate for 2005 is 35%, the deferred tax liability at the end of 2002 would be $5,250 ($15,000 × .35), rather than $6,000 as computed earlier. At the end of 2003, the deferred tax liability would be $7,000 ($20,000 × .35), and the required adjustment would be $1,750 ($7,000 – $5,250).

SUBSEQUENT CHANGES IN ENACTED TAX RATES   When rate changes are enacted after a deferred tax liability or asset has been recorded, FASB Statement No. 109 requires that the beginning deferred account balance be adjusted to reflect the new tax rate. Again using the Roland Inc. example, assume that the enacted tax rate for 2005 changed from 40% to 35% during 2003. The balance in the deferred tax liability at the beginning of 2003 is $6,000 ($15,000 × .40). The following adjusting entry would be made to reflect the newly enacted 35% tax rate for 2005:

Deferred Tax Liability—Noncurrent	750	
Income Tax Benefit—Rate Change		750
($15,000 × .05)		

> **Caution!**   The entire effect of a change in rates is reflected in tax expense on income from continuing operations even if some of the deferred tax balances relate to "below the line" or retained earnings items.

The income effect of the change is reflected in income tax expense. In this case, the effect is a tax benefit resulting from a lower tax rate and would be shown as a reduction in income tax expense on the 2003 income statement.

Example 4. Deferred Tax Asset

Assume that Sandusky Inc. begins operations in 2002. For 2002, Sandusky computes pretax financial income of $22,000. The only difference between financial and taxable income is the recognition of warranty expense. Sandusky accrues estimated warranty expense in the year of sale for financial reporting purposes but deducts only actual warranty expenditures for tax purposes. Accrued warranty expense for 2002 was $18,000; no actual warranty expenditures were made in 2002. Therefore, taxable income in 2002 is $40,000, computed as follows:

Financial income subject to tax	$22,000
Add temporary difference:	
Excess of warranty expense over warranty deductions	18,000
Taxable income	$40,000
Tax ($40,000 × .40)	$16,000

The difference in 2002 between warranty expense for financial reporting and tax purposes is a deductible temporary difference because it will result in future tax deductions of $18,000. The deferred tax asset implied by this difference is $7,200 ($18,000 × .40). Warranty expenditures for 2002 sales are expected to be $6,000 in each of the years 2003 through 2005. Because the underlying warranty obligation is assumed to be one-third current and two-thirds noncurrent, the associated deferred tax asset would be classified in the same ratio.

The future tax deduction of $18,000 will provide a tax benefit only if Sandusky has taxable income in future periods against which the deduction can be offset. Accordingly, in order to record a deferred tax asset, one must assume that sufficient taxable income will exist in future years. Conditions under which this assumption may or may not be reasonable are described later in the chapter in the section entitled "Valuation Allowance for Deferred Tax Assets."

Assuming that future taxable income will be sufficient to allow for full realization of the tax benefits of the $18,000 future tax deduction (and let's assume, just to keep things simple, that income is $22,000 in each of the next three years), the journal entries to record Sandusky's income taxes for 2002 would be as follows:

Income Tax Expense—Current	16,000	
Income Taxes Payable		16,000
Deferred Tax Asset—Current	2,400*	
Deferred Tax Asset—Noncurrent	4,800**	
Income Tax Benefit		7,200

*One-third of underlying warranty obligation is current (⅓ × $7,200).
**Two-thirds of underlying warranty obligation is noncurrent (⅔ × $7,200).

Sandusky's 2002 income statement would present income tax expense as follows:

Income before income taxes		$22,000
Income tax expense:		
Current	$16,000	
Deferred (benefit)	(7,200)	8,800
Net income		$13,200

Sandusky's December 31, 2002, balance sheet would report deferred tax assets of $2,400 under current assets and $4,800 under noncurrent assets. Income taxes payable for 2002 would be shown with current liabilities.

In subsequent periods, Sandusky's taxable income would be less than reported pretax financial income because the deductible temporary differences would begin to reverse. In the years 2003 through 2005, taxable income would be equal to $16,000, computed as follows:

Income subject to tax	$22,000
Reversal of temporary difference:	
Excess of warranty deductions over warranty expense	(6,000)
Taxable income	$16,000
Tax ($16,000 × .40)	$ 6,400

The amount of the deductible temporary difference would decline each year, affecting first the amount classified as noncurrent and finally eliminating the current portion of the deferred tax asset account. The following table illustrates the journal entries that would be made each year:

	2003		2004		2005	
Income Tax Expense—Current	6,400		6,400		6,400	
Income Taxes Payable		6,400		6,400		6,400
Income Tax Expense	2,400		2,400		2,400	
Deferred Tax Asset—Current		2,400		2,400		2,400
Deferred Tax Asset—Current	2,400		2,400			
Deferred Tax Asset—Noncurrent		2,400		2,400		

The first journal entry records the current period's tax liability. The second journal entry recognizes that the current portion of the deferred tax asset has expired. The final journal entry simply reclassifies the deferred tax asset from noncurrent to current, indicating that a portion of the deductible temporary difference will reverse in the upcoming period.

Example 5. Deferred Tax Liabilities and Assets

Hsieh Company began operation on January 1, 2002. For 2002, Hsieh reported pretax financial income of $38,000. As of December 31, 2002, the actual differences between Hsieh Company's financial accounting and income tax records for 2002 and the estimated differences for 2003 through 2005 are summarized as follows:

	Financial Reporting		Income Tax Reporting	
	Depreciation Expense	Warranty Expense	Depreciation Deduction	Warranty Deduction
2002 (actual)	$25,000	$18,000	$40,000	$ 0
2003 (estimated)	25,000	0	30,000	6,000
2004 (estimated)	25,000	0	25,000	6,000
2005 (estimated)	25,000	0	5,000	6,000

The enacted income tax rate for all years is 40% (note that Example 5 simply combines Examples 3 and 4). For 2002, taxable income would be computed as follows:

Financial income subject to tax	$38,000
Add (deduct) temporary differences:	
Excess of warranty expense over warranty deductions	18,000
Excess of tax depreciation over book depreciation	(15,000)
Taxable income	$41,000
Tax ($41,000 × .40)	$16,400

As of December 31, 2002, aggregate tax depreciation exceeds aggregate book depreciation by $15,000 ($40,000 – $25,000). As explained previously, this represents a future taxable amount. The income tax expected to be paid on this amount is $6,000 ($15,000 × .40). This $6,000 is a deferred tax liability as of December 31, 2002. Because the difference relates to a noncurrent item, the deferred tax liability is a noncurrent liability.

As of December 31, 2002, Hsieh has recognized an $18,000 warranty expense for financial accounting purposes, which it plans to deduct for tax purposes over the next three years. Assuming that future taxable income will be sufficient to allow the tax benefit of this deduction to be fully realized, this future deductible amount creates a deferred tax asset of $7,200 ($18,000 × .40). Because the underlying warranty liability is part current ($6,000) and part noncurrent ($12,000), the deferred tax asset would also be classified as part current ($2,400 = $6,000 × .40) and part noncurrent ($4,800 = $12,000 × .40). The journal entries to record Hsieh's current taxes payable as well as the deferred portion of Hsieh's 2002 income tax expense are as follows:

Income Tax Expense—Current	16,400	
Income Taxes Payable		16,400
Deferred Tax Asset—Current	2,400	
Deferred Tax Asset—Noncurrent	4,800	
Income Tax Benefit		1,200
Deferred Tax Liability—Noncurrent		6,000

Note that this journal entry is a combination of the journal entries associated with the deferred taxes from Examples 3 and 4. For reporting purposes, current deferred tax assets and current deferred tax liabilities are netted against one another and reported as a single amount. Similarly, noncurrent deferred tax assets and liabilities are netted and reported as a single amount.[7] In this example, the amounts to be reported on Hsieh's December 31, 2002, balance sheet are a $2,400 current deferred tax asset and a $1,200 noncurrent deferred tax liability ($6,000 liability – $4,800 asset). The income tax benefit would be shown as a $1,200 reduction of current income tax expense in the 2002 income statement.

Valuation Allowance for Deferred Tax Assets

A deferred tax asset represents future income tax benefits. But the tax benefits will be realized only if there is sufficient taxable income from which the deductible amount can be deducted. FASB Statement No. 109 requires that the deferred tax asset be reduced by a valuation allowance if, based on all available evidence, it is more likely than not that

7 FASB Statement No. 109, par. 42.

some portion or all the deferred tax asset will not be realized. As applied to deferred tax assets, more likely than not means a likelihood of more than 50%.[8] The **valuation allowance** is a contra asset account that reduces the asset to its expected realizable value. But before we get into the details of the valuation allowance, it is important for you to realize that for most companies, and for profitable companies in particular, the valuation allowance is not an issue. The valuation allowance becomes an issue in instances when future profitability is in doubt.

In the Hsieh Company example (Example 5 on page 932), it was assumed that there would be sufficient taxable income to allow for the full realization of the benefits from the $18,000 warranty deduction, and thus, no valuation allowance was established. Some possible sources of taxable income to be considered in evaluating the realizable value of a deferred tax asset are[9]:

1. Future reversals of existing taxable temporary differences.
2. Future taxable income exclusive of reversing temporary differences.
3. Taxable income in prior (carryback) years.

The first source of future taxable income, reversals of taxable temporary differences, can be identified without making assumptions about the profitability of future operations. In 2002, Hsieh Company has a $15,000 excess of aggregate tax depreciation over aggregate book depreciation, which will result in a future taxable amount. The reversal of this temporary difference will provide taxable income in the future against which the $18,000 warranty deduction can be offset. If it appears more likely than not that no other income will be available, then only $15,000 of the $18,000 warranty deduction is expected to be realized. Accordingly, the total deferred tax asset is $7,200 ($18,000 × .40), but the realizable amount is only $6,000 ($15,000 × .40). The $1,200 difference would be recorded as a valuation allowance, an offset to the reported deferred tax asset. For classification purposes, the valuation allowance is to be allocated proportionately between the current and noncurrent portions of the deferred tax asset.[10] In this example, because one-third of the deferred tax asset is current ($6,000/$18,000), one-third, or $400 ($1,200 × ⅓), of the valuation would be classified as current. The remaining $800 ($1,200 – $400) of the valuation allowance is noncurrent. The journal entry recording the deferred portion of income tax expense for 2002 is as follows:

Deferred Tax Asset—Current	2,400	
Deferred Tax Asset—Noncurrent	4,800	
Allowance to Reduce Deferred Tax Asset to Realizable Value—Current		400
Allowance to Reduce Deferred Tax Asset to Realizable Value—Noncurrent		800
Deferred Tax Liability—Noncurrent		6,000

In 2003 and subsequent years, the company should reconsider available evidence to determine whether the valuation account should be adjusted.

The other two sources through which the benefit of a deferred tax asset can be realized include taxable income expected from profitable operations in future years and taxable income in prior carryback years. This latter source relates to specific carryback provisions of the tax law, which are explained later in the chapter.

Statement No. 109 stipulates that both positive and negative evidence be considered when determining whether deferred tax assets will be fully realized.[11] Examples of negative evidence include cumulative losses in recent years, a history of the expiration of unused tax loss carryforwards, and unsettled circumstances that might cause a currently profitable company to report losses in future years. Positive evidence includes the existence of an order backlog sufficient to yield enough taxable income for the deferred tax asset to be realized, the existence of appreciated assets, and a strong earnings history.

---

8   Ibid., par. 17e.
9   Ibid., par. 21.
10 Ibid., par. 41.
11 Ibid., par. 20.

The FASB was very reluctant to allow firms to consider possible future taxable income when evaluating the realizability of deferred tax assets because, as stated in FASB Statement No. 96:

> Incurring losses or generating profits in future years are future events that are not recognized in financial statements for the current year. Those future events shall not be anticipated, regardless of probability, for purposes of recognizing and measuring a deferred tax liability or asset in the current year. The tax consequences of those future events shall be recognized and reported in the financial statements in future years when the events occur.[12]

However, because many firms complained that it was unfair to require them to report deferred tax liabilities but not allow them to report deferred tax assets, the FASB reconsidered and revised its position. Statement No. 109 explicitly allows a firm to consider potential future income in evaluating the realizability of deferred tax assets.

A few examples of U.S. companies with deferred tax asset valuation allowances are given in Exhibit 16-4. For example, a large portion of the $4.419 billion deferred tax asset reported by COMPAQ as of December 31, 1998, arose from the June 1998 acquisition of DIGITAL EQUIPMENT CORPORATION. As part of the acquisition, Compaq expensed $3.2 billion that was allocated to purchased in-process research and development; the IRS does not allow an immediate tax deduction for this amount, so a deferred tax asset was recognized. The deferred tax valuation allowance was recognized because Digital had experienced losses for a number of years and had some future tax deductions, which Compaq did not believe it would ever be able to use.

STOP & THINK Now that you have been introduced to deferred tax assets and liabilities, do you think the results of all the computations provide valuable information to current and potential investors and creditors?

EXHIBIT 16-4 | Example of Deferred Tax Asset Valuation Allowances (1998 and 1999)

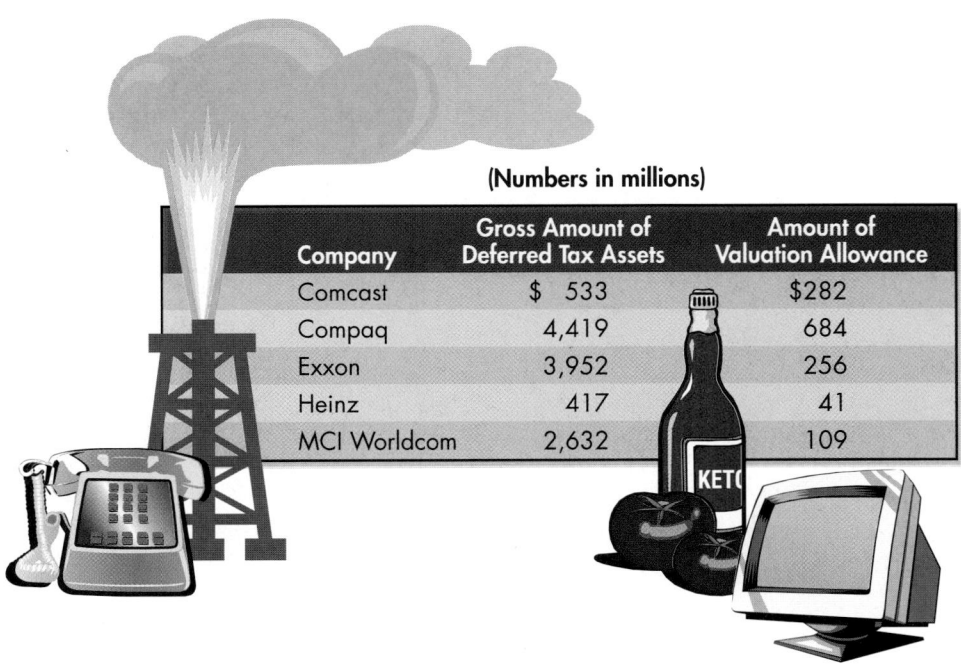

| | (Numbers in millions) | |
Company	Gross Amount of Deferred Tax Assets	Amount of Valuation Allowance
Comcast	$ 533	$282
Compaq	4,419	684
Exxon	3,952	256
Heinz	417	41
MCI Worldcom	2,632	109

12 FASB Statement No. 96, "Accounting for Income Taxes," Stamford, CT: Financial Accounting Standards Board, 1987, par. 15.

► HISTORY OF ACCOUNTING FOR DEFERRED TAXES

In the history of accounting standard setting, few issues have caused as much commotion as that of accounting for deferred income taxes. The debate began with a basic conceptual issue: Are income taxes paid by a business to be considered as expenses of doing business or as a distribution of income to government entities? If viewed as a distribution of income, the amount of income taxes paid each period could

be shown as the portion of financial income that is not available to the owners of the business. This amount would be determined by the tax laws in effect each period, and the existence of temporary differences would be of no consequence in the financial statements. If income taxes are considered to be business expenses, however, then the underlying concept of accrual accounting requires that the impact of temporary differences be reflected in the financial statements.

As the number of differences between pretax financial income and taxable income began to increase in the late 1940s and early 1950s, there were many articles in the accounting literature arguing the merits of these two positions. When the AICPA Committee on Accounting Procedures issued a consolidated set of accounting procedures in 1953, Accounting Research Bulletin (ARB) No. 43, it chose to consider income taxes as expenses, concluding that

> Income taxes are an expense that should be allocated, as other expenses are allocated. What the income statement should reflect under this head, as under any other head, is the expense properly allocable to the income included in the income statement for the year.[1]

Once the decision was made to classify income taxes as expenses, the next critical conceptual issues were how to measure income tax expense each period and then how to report the difference between the amount shown as income tax expense on the income statement and the amount of income taxes actually paid based on taxable income. No guidance on this issue was included in ARB No. 43, but in 1967, the Accounting Principles Board issued Opinion No. 11, "Accounting for Income Taxes," the standard that governed this area for over 20 years. Under APB Opinion No. 11, the deferred method was used in accounting for income taxes. Under this method, income tax expense is the amount of tax that would have been paid based on financial income and using the current year's tax rate. The deferred

method of allocation emphasizes the income statement—income tax expense is computed directly on the current year's financial income, and the deferred tax on the balance sheet (debit or credit) is a residual amount, the difference between the expense and the taxes payable for the period. Changes in future tax rates are not considered even though the actual tax effect will depend on the rates in effect when differences reverse. Thus, under the deferred method, over time deferred tax balances become meaningless as a measure of assets (future tax benefits) or liabilities (future tax payments).

The FASB expressed concern over the deferred method of reporting income taxes in Statement No. 3, "Elements of Financial Statements of Business Enterprises," issued in 1980. The Board concluded that deferred income tax amounts reported on the balance sheet did not meet the newly established conceptual framework definitions of assets and liabilities.[2] Other criticisms leveled against the deferred method included inconsistencies in the various accounting requirements, emphasis on procedures with little theoretical justification, and the excessive time and cost involved in applying APB Opinion No. 11 relative to the benefits.[3]

These concerns led the FASB to add income taxes to its agenda in 1982. For five years the Board issued Discussion Memorandums, held public hearings, and considered the many arguments. The Board was determined to make income tax accounting meet the asset and liability definitions of the conceptual framework. The result was the issuance in December 1987 of FASB Statement No. 96, which abandoned the deferred method of interperiod tax allocation in favor of the asset and liability method. The stated objectives of the asset and liability method are as follows:

> One objective of accounting for income taxes is to recognize the amount of taxes payable or refundable for the current year. A second objective is to recognize deferred tax liabilities and assets for the future tax conse-

quences of events that have been recognized in an enterprise's financial statements or tax returns.[4]

The second objective points out a fundamental difference between the asset and liability method and the deferred method. The asset and liability method emphasizes the reporting of balance sheet amounts that measure the future tax consequences of temporary differences. Deferred tax assets and liabilities are measured and recorded by applying currently enacted tax rates and laws that will be in effect when the differences reverse,[5] and the income tax expense reported on the income statement is a residual amount. Further, when tax rate changes are enacted in subsequent periods, deferred tax asset and liability balances are adjusted to reflect the impact of the changes.

After FASB Statement No. 96 was issued and before its mandatory implementation date, many companies became concerned when they began to see the effect the standard would have on their financial statements and the cost they would incur in implementing it. From a theoretical perspective, some opposed the inconsistent treatment of deferred tax liabilities and deferred tax assets. Others complained that because the deferred tax liability amount is not discounted to its present value and may never be paid anyway, it doesn't represent a true liability. Others argued that the FASB is fundamentally misguided in emphasizing deferred tax reporting on the balance sheet when historically the topic of deferred taxes arose in the context of proper reporting of tax expense on the income statement. Practitioners objected to the complex scheduling requirements and to the requirement to devise hypothetical tax strategies. One firm, CITICORP, estimated that it would cost $3,000,000 to implement the standard. The objections became so strong that the FASB postponed the implementation date from 1988 to 1989,[6] from 1989 to 1991,[7] and then from 1991 to 1992.[8]

In response to the issuance of Statement No. 96, the FASB "received (a) requests for about 20 different limited-scope amendments to Statement No. 96, (b) requests to change the criteria for recognition and measurement of deferred tax assets to anticipate, in certain circumstances, the tax consequences of future income,

and (c) requests to reduce the complexity of scheduling the future reversals of temporary differences and considering hypothetical tax-planning strategies."[9] These requests to amend FASB Statement No. 96 were considered at 41 public Board meetings and three Implementation Group meetings. On June 5, 1991, the FASB issued an Exposure Draft that proposed superseding FASB Statement No. 96 and several other accounting pronouncements. Finally, in February 1992, FASB Statement No. 109 was issued. Many hope that this whole area of accounting for deferred taxes has settled down.

QUESTIONS:

1. Many were concerned that the extended flap over deferred tax accounting hurt the credibility of the FASB. What dangers are there in a loss of prestige by the FASB?

2. Should pressure from practitioners be allowed to influence the FASB's deliberations?

3. In your opinion, were the time and resources spent in the area of deferred taxes by the FASB, practitioners, and other interest groups worth the benefits?

SOURCES:

1. *Accounting Research Bulletin No. 43*, "Income Taxes," New York: AICPA, 1953, Ch. 10, Section B, par. 4.

2. *Statement of Financial Accounting Concepts No. 3*, "Elements of Financial Statements of Business Enterprises," Stamford, CT: Financial Accounting Standards Board, 1980, par. 164.

3. Ibid.

4. *Statement of Financial Accounting Standards No. 96*, "Accounting for Income Taxes," Stamford, CT: Financial Accounting Standards Board, 1987, pars. 197–198.

5. Changes in tax rates and other provisions of the tax law often are legislated prior to the years in which they become effective. For example, the 1986 Tax Reform Act legislated a phased tax rate reduction over three years.

6. *Statement of Financial Accounting Standards No. 100*, "Accounting for Income Taxes—Deferral of the Effective Date of FASB Statement No. 96," Norwalk, CT: Financial Accounting Standards Board, 1988.

7. *Statement of Financial Accounting Standards No. 103*, "Accounting for Income Taxes—Deferral of the Effective Date of FASB Statement No. 96," Norwalk, CT: Financial Accounting Standards Board, 1989.

8. *Statement of Financial Accounting Standards No. 108*, "Accounting for Income Taxes—Deferral of the Effective Date of FASB Statement No. 96," Norwalk, CT: Financial Accounting Standards Board, 1992.

9. *Exposure Draft of Proposed Statement of Financial Accounting Standards*, "Accounting for Income Taxes," Norwalk, CT: Financial Accounting Standards Board, 1991, Appendix C, par. 266.

Explain the provisions of tax loss carrybacks and carryforwards, and be able to account for these provisions.

CARRYBACK AND CARRYFORWARD OF OPERATING LOSSES

Because income tax is based on the amount of taxable income reported, no tax is payable if a company experiences an operating loss. As an incentive to those businesses that experience alternate periods of income and losses, U.S. tax laws provide a way to ease the risk of loss years. This is done through a carryback and carryforward provision that permits a company to apply a net operating loss occurring in one year against income of other years. Specifically, the Internal Revenue Code provides for a 2-year carryback and a 20-year carryforward.[13]

Net Operating Loss (NOL) Carryback

If you were profitable in prior periods and, as a result, paid taxes, you can get a refund of some or all those tax payments in the period in which you incur an operating loss. A **net operating loss (NOL) carryback** is applied to the income of the two preceding years in reverse order, beginning with the second year and moving to the first year. If unused net operating losses are still available, they may be carried forward up to 20 years to offset any future income. Amended income tax returns must be filed for each year to which the carryback is applied to receive refunds of previously paid income taxes. Net operating loss carrybacks result in a journal entry establishing a current receivable for the tax refund claim. The benefit that arises from such refunds is used to reduce the loss in the current period. This treatment is supported in theory because it is the current year's operating loss that results in the tax refund.

To illustrate, assume that the Prairie Company had the following pattern of income and losses for the years 2001 through 2003.

Year	Income (Loss)	Income Tax Rate	Income Tax
2001	$10,000	35%	$3,500
2002	14,000	30%	4,200
2003	(19,000)	30%	0

The IRS provides a 2-year carryback and a 20-year carryforward provision that allows a company to apply a net operating loss occurring in one year against income of other years.

---

13   Before 1997, the carryback period was 3 years and the carryforward period was 15 years. Also, as an alternative, a taxpayer can elect to forgo the carryback and carry the entire loss forward for up to 20 years. This election is seldom made because carrybacks result in current refunds of taxes.

The $19,000 net operating loss in 2003 would be carried back to 2001 first and then to 2002. An income tax refund claim of $6,200 would be filed for the two years [$3,500 + .30 ($9,000)]. The entry to record the income tax receivable in 2003 would be:

Income Tax Refund Receivable	6,200	
Income Tax Benefit From NOL Carryback		6,200

The refund will be reflected on the income statement as a reduction of the operating loss as follows:

 These net operating loss carrybacks sound like a great feature of the tax law. However, what did the company have to do to take advantage of this aspect of the law?

Net operating loss before income tax benefit	$(19,000)
Income tax benefit from NOL carryback	6,200
Net loss	$(12,800)

The 2003 net operating loss reduces the 2001 taxable income to zero and the 2002 taxable income to $5,000 ($14,000 – $9,000). If another net operating loss occurs next year (in 2004), it may be carried back to the remaining $5,000 from 2002.

Net Operating Loss (NOL) Carryforward

If an operating loss exceeds income for the 2 preceding years, the remaining unused loss may be applied against income earned over the next 20 years as a **net operating loss (NOL) carryforward**. Under FASB Statement No. 109, a deferred tax asset is recognized for the potential future tax benefit from a loss carryforward. Full realization of the benefit, however, depends on the company having income equal to the carryforward in the next 20 years. As is true for other deferred tax assets, a valuation allowance is used to reduce the asset if it is more likely than not that some or all of the future benefit will not be realized.

To illustrate the carryforward provisions, let's continue the previous example and assume that in 2004 Prairie Company incurred an operating loss of $35,000. This loss would be carried back to the years 2002 and 2003 in that order. However, the only income remaining against which operating losses can be applied is $5,000 from 2002. After applying $5,000 to the 2002 income, $30,000 is left to carry forward against future income. The tax benefit from the carryback is $1,500 ($5,000 × .30). Assuming the enacted tax rate for future years is 30%, the potential tax benefit from the carryforward is $9,000 ($30,000 × .30). The entry in 2004 to record the tax benefits would be:

Income Tax Refund Receivable	1,500	
Deferred Tax Asset—NOL Carryforward	9,000	
Income Tax Benefit From NOL Carryback		1,500
Income Tax Benefit From NOL Carryforward		9,000

The deferred tax asset of $9,000 would be reported on the balance sheet as a current asset if it is expected to be realized in 2005. Any portion that is expected to be realized after 2005 would be classified as noncurrent. The $10,500 in tax benefits would be shown on the 2004 income statement as a reduction of the operating loss.

Assuming that Prairie becomes profitable in future periods, the deferred tax asset associated with the NOL carryforward would be used to offset any taxes payable resulting from profitable operations. As an example, assume that Prairie reports taxable income of $50,000 in 2005. Rather than pay $15,000 ($50,000 × .30) in taxes, Prairie would be allowed to offset the deferred tax asset against the liability. The journal entry made by Prairie associated with its tax liability would then be as follows:

Income Tax Expense	15,000	
Income Taxes Payable		6,000
Deferred Tax Asset—NOL Carryforward		9,000

FYI: Under certain conditions, a company may acquire another company's NOL carryforwards as part of an acquisition or merger. In some situations, these unused carryforwards are a company's most valuable "asset" to another company.

The journal entry recorded at the end of 2004 indicates that it is more likely than not that the carryforward benefit will be realized in full. If, however, it is more likely than not that some portion or all of the deferred tax asset will not be realized, a valuation allowance account is needed to reduce the asset to its estimated realizable value. For example, assume that Prairie Company's recent losses resulted from a declining market for its products and that the weight of available evidence indicates continuing losses in subsequent years. As a result, management believes it is more likely than not that none of the asset will be realized. In this case, the journal entry to record the carryback and carryforward would be:

Income Tax Refund Receivable	1,500	
Deferred Tax Asset—NOL Carryforward	9,000	
Income Tax Benefit From NOL Carryback		1,500
Allowance to Reduce Deferred Tax Asset to Realizable Value		
—NOL Carryforward		9,000

net work exercise

View the Coca-Cola Company's 1998 annual report by using EDGAR, the SEC's on-line database, at **www.sec.gov/edgarhp.htm**. Read through the notes to the consolidated financial statements to find the following information.
Net Work:
1. As of December 31, 1998, what were the total net operating loss carryforwards available for future years?
2. When do these carryforwards expire?

As a result of this entry, the net deferred tax asset is zero—the expected realizable value. If market conditions improve and the company does have taxable income in subsequent years, the valuation allowance account would be decreased (debited) and an income tax benefit account would be credited.

Under APB Opinion No. 11, future tax benefits from an NOL carryforward could be reported as an asset only if future income was "assured beyond reasonable doubt." Although such a criterion is not easily met, there have been cases in which NOL carryforward benefits were reported as an asset. In Statement No. 96, the FASB was even more restrictive and prohibited reporting income tax benefits from carryforwards as an asset under any circumstances. The adoption of the more-likely-than-not approach for deferred tax assets in FASB Statement No. 109 led the Board to conclude that a similar approach should be used for net operating loss carryforwards. That is, NOL carryforwards are reported as assets if it is more likely than not that future income will be sufficient to allow for the realization of the tax benefit. This is a significant change in accounting for NOL carryforwards. Under Statement No. 109, millions of dollars of previously unreported income tax carryforwards are now included in the assets of companies. For example, IBM indicated in the notes to its 1990 financial statements that in addition to $110 million of unrecognized deferred tax assets under FASB Statement No. 96, it had $700 million of unrecognized tax credit carryforwards. As reported at the beginning of the chapter, IBM announced in September 1992 that it would recognize a gain of $1.9 billion as a result of the deferred tax assets it would be able to recognize because of its adoption of Statement No. 109.

4

Schedule future tax rates, and determine the effect on tax assets and liabilities.

SCHEDULING FOR ENACTED FUTURE TAX RATES

Recall that the two major complaints about FASB Statement No. 96 were that it did not allow for the recognition of most deferred tax assets and that it was too complicated. The complaints about nonrecognition of deferred tax assets came primarily from companies and users of financial statements who thought the inconsistent treatment of deferred tax assets and liabilities was misleading and unfair. Complaints about the complexities of Statement No. 96 came primarily from preparers of financial statements. Those complaints focused on one topic—scheduling of the periods in which temporary differences are expected to reverse. Under the provisions of Statement No. 96, scheduling was required each year to determine which deferred tax assets could be realized because no future income could be assumed and these assets were realizable only through the carryback and carryforward provisions of the tax law. In addition, under the provisions of Statement No. 96, scheduling was necessary to determine how deferred tax assets and liabilities should be classified based on the expected period of their reversal.

Statement No. 109 eliminates much of the need for scheduling through the "more-likely-than-not" criterion for future income and because deferred tax assets and liabilities are classified according to the classification of the underlying items instead of according to the expected reversal period. However, scheduling is still required in a limited number of cases. One such case arises when differences in enacted future tax rates make it necessary to schedule the timing of a reversal in order to match that reversal with the tax rate expected to be in effect when it occurs.

Consider again the Hsieh Company example introduced on page 932. When that example was covered before, it was assumed that the enacted income tax rate was 40% for all periods. Assume now that the enacted tax rates are as follows: 2002, 40%; 2003, 35%; 2004, 30%; and 2005, 25%. As of December 31, 2002, using the 40% rate to value the deferred tax asset stemming from the future deductible amount of $18,000 and the deferred tax liability resulting from the future taxable amount of $15,000 would be misleading because it is known that the tax rate will not be 40% when those temporary differences reverse. A more accurate valuation can be obtained by applying tax rates expected to be in effect when the differences reverse, as follows:

	Enacted Tax Rate	Deductible Amount	Asset Valuation	Taxable Amount	Liability Valuation
2003	35%	$ 6,000	$2,100	$ 0	$ 0
2004	30%	6,000	1,800	0	0
2005	25%	6,000	1,500	15,000	3,750
Total		$18,000	$5,400	$15,000	$3,750

The noncurrent deferred tax liability is $3,750 ($15,000 × .25), which is the expected tax to be paid on the taxable amount when it is taxed in 2005. The current deferred tax asset is $2,100 ($6,000 × .35), and the noncurrent deferred tax asset is $3,300 [($6,000 × .30) + ($6,000 × .25)]. The journal entry to record the deferred portion of income tax expense for 2002 would be as follows:

Deferred Tax Asset—Current	2,100	
Deferred Tax Asset—Noncurrent	3,300	
Income Tax Benefit		1,650
Deferred Tax Liability—Noncurrent		3,750

In this example it was assumed that future income is more likely than not to be sufficient to allow for full deductibility of the $6,000 deductible amount each year. Accordingly, the tax benefit is computed as the deductible amount times the tax rate for that year. However, if the future income was not deemed sufficient to allow for offset of the deductible amounts and if the deferred tax asset could only be realized through the carryback provision of the tax law, the deferred tax asset would be valued using the tax rate in the carryback year. For example, if future income is unlikely but 2002 taxable income exceeds $18,000, then the deductible amounts will be realized only through carryback and offset against 2002 taxable income. If this is the case, the deferred tax asset would be valued using the tax rate in effect for 2002, the carryback year.

FINANCIAL STATEMENT PRESENTATION AND DISCLOSURE

5

Determine appropriate financial statement presentation and disclosure associated with deferred tax assets and liabilities.

On classified balance sheets, deferred tax assets and liabilities must be reported as either current or noncurrent. As discussed previously, FASB Statement No. 109 provides for some offsetting of deferred assets and liabilities. In order for offsetting to be acceptable, the asset and liability must both be current or both be noncurrent. A current asset cannot be offset against a noncurrent liability. Most companies are subject to state and municipal income taxes as well as federal income taxes. If a business enterprise pays income taxes in more than one tax jurisdiction, no offsetting is permitted across jurisdictions.

The income statement must show, either in the body of the statement or in a note, the following selected components of income taxes related to continuing operations[14]:

1. Current tax expense or benefit
2. Deferred tax expense or benefit
3. Investment tax credits
4. Government grants recognized as tax reductions
5. Benefits of operating loss carryforwards
6. Adjustments of a deferred tax liability or asset for enacted changes in tax laws or rates or a change in the tax status of an enterprise
7. Adjustments in the beginning-of-the-year valuation allowance because of a change in circumstances

The kind of disclosure typically made for income taxes is illustrated by an excerpt from the notes to the 1998 financial statements of GENERAL ELECTRIC, presented in Exhibit 16–5.

EXHIBIT 16–5 | General Electric—Disclosure for Provision for Income Taxes

(In millions)	1998	1997	1996
GE			
Estimated amounts payable	$2,227	$2,332	$2,235
Deferred tax expense (benefit) from temporary differences	590	(522)	60
	2,817	1,810	2,295
GECS			
Estimated amounts payable	815	368	164
Deferred tax expense from temporary differences	549	798	1,067
	1,364	1,166	1,231
CONSOLIDATED			
Estimated amounts payable	3,042	2,700	2,399
Deferred tax expense from temporary differences	1,139	276	1,127
	$4,181	$2,976	$3,526

The current portion of income tax expense (called "Estimated amounts payable" in the General Electric example) can be viewed as the one place in the financial statements where the financial accounting records and the tax records coincide. Roughly speaking, the $3.042 billion that General Electric reports as the consolidated current portion of income tax payable for 1998 is the same number that appears on General Electric's 1998 consolidated tax return under the heading of "Total Tax" for the year. Note that because of the existence of deferred taxes, the amount of reported income tax expense is significantly greater than the amount of income tax actually owed for the year.

As another example of disclosure, IBM reported in the notes to its 1998 financial statements that it had decreased the valuation allowance for its deferred tax assets by $1,675 million in 1998. This decrease had the effect of decreasing income tax expense for the year by the same amount. The reason given for the decrease was that "the company transferred certain intellectual property rights to several non-U.S. subsidiaries in December 1998. Since these strategies, including this transfer, result in the anticipated utilization of U.S. federal tax credit carryforwards, the company reduced the valuation allowance from that previously required." Relating to the remaining valuation allowance,

14 *FASB Statement No. 109, par. 45.*

IBM added that "The valuation allowance at December 31, 1998, principally applies to certain state and local and foreign tax loss carryforwards that, in the opinion of management, are more likely than not to expire before the company can utilize them."

In addition to the above disclosures, the reported amount of income tax expense related to continuing operations must be reconciled with the amount of income tax expense that would result from applying federal tax rates to pretax financial income from continuing operations. This reconciliation provides information to readers of the financial statements regarding how the entity has been affected by special provisions of the tax code such as permanent differences, tax credits, and operating loss carrybacks and carryforwards. For example, IBM reported in the notes to its 1998 financial statements that its effective tax rate for 1998 was 30%, significantly lower than the 35% U.S. federal statutory rate.

Firms also disclose the specific accounting differences between the financial statements and the tax return that give rise to deferred tax assets and deferred tax liabilities. The most common source of deferred tax items is depreciation. As an illustration, IBM provides significant disclosure as to the specific makeup of its deferred tax assets and liabilities. This disclosure is reproduced in Exhibit 16-6. Overall, as of December 31, 1998, IBM had $12.756 billion in deferred tax assets (net of a $488 million valuation allowance) and $9.841 billion in deferred tax liabilities.

EXHIBIT 16-6 | IBM—Disclosure for Deferred Tax Assets and Liabilities

The significant components of deferred tax assets and liabilities included on the balance sheet were as follows:

DEFERRED TAX ASSETS
(Dollars in millions)

At December 31:	1998	1997
Employee benefits	$ 3,909	$ 3,707
Bad debt, inventory and warranty reserves	1,249	1,027
Alternative minimum tax credits	1,169	1,092
Capitalized research and development	913	1,196
Restructuring charges	863	1,163
Deferred income	686	893
General business credits	555	492
Equity alliances	387	378
Foreign tax loss carryforwards	304	202
State and local tax loss carryforwards	212	203
Depreciation	201	132
Intracompany sales and services	182	235
Other	2,614	2,507
Gross deferred tax assets	13,244	13,227
Less: Valuation allowance	488	2,163
Net deferred tax assets	$12,756	$11,064

DEFERRED TAX LIABILITIES
(Dollars in millions)

At December 31:	1998	1997
Sales-type leases	$3,433	$3,147
Retirement benefits	2,775	2,147
Depreciation	1,505	1,556
Software costs deferred	287	420
Other	1,841	1,413
Gross deferred tax liabilities	$9,841	$8,683

Comply with income tax disclosure requirements associated with the statement of cash flows.

DEFERRED TAXES AND THE STATEMENT OF CASH FLOWS

FASB Statement No. 95, "Statement of Cash Flows," requires separate disclosure of the amount of cash paid for income taxes during a period. Statement No. 95 requires this separate disclosure for just two items—cash paid for income taxes and cash paid for interest. Financial statements are used to assess the amount and timing of future cash flows, and in the case of interest and income taxes, the FASB argued that this specific cash flow information should be readily available and easily disclosed by most firms.[15] As an example, DISNEY (see Appendix A) discloses in its financial statements that for the year ended September 30, 1998, it reported income tax expense of $1,307 million (on the income statement) and cash paid during the year for income taxes of $1,107 million (on the statement of cash flows).

Income taxes affect the operating activities section of the statement of cash flows.[16] When the direct method is used, cash paid for income taxes is shown as a separate line item. For example, STERLING CHEMICALS, a manufacturer of commodity petrochemicals based in Houston, Texas, reports "Income taxes received" of $3.1 million in the operating activities section (prepared using the direct method) of its 1997 statement of cash flows (the company had a taxable loss for 1997 and, as a result, received a tax refund). When the indirect method is used, the treatment of income taxes is a bit more complicated. Adjustments to convert net income into cash from operations are needed for changes in income taxes payable and receivable accounts and for changes in deferred tax asset and liability accounts. In addition, supplemental disclosure of the amount of cash paid for income taxes is required.

As an illustration of how income taxes are handled in the statement of cash flows, consider the following information for Collazo Company for 2002:

Revenue (all cash)		$30,000
Income tax expense:		
Current	$10,300	
Deferred	1,700	12,000
Net income		$18,000

Cash paid for income taxes during 2002 totaled $13,300. In addition, Collazo had the following balance sheet amounts at the beginning and end of the year:

	December 31, 2002	December 31, 2001
Income tax refund receivable	$2,000	$ 0
Income taxes payable	0	1,000
Deferred tax liability	9,700	8,000

Using the format developed in Chapter 5, we will analyze the income statement and convert the accrual basis number to the cash basis, as demonstrated in the following table:

---

15   *Statement of Financial Accounting Standards No. 95,* "Statement of Cash Flows," Stamford, CT: Financial Accounting Standards Board, November 1987, par. 121.

16   The FASB considered allocating income taxes paid among the operating, investing, and financing activities sections of the statement of cash flows. For example, any income tax effects from the disposal of equipment could be disclosed in the investing activities section. However, it was concluded that this allocation would be unnecessarily complex, with the cost of doing it outweighing the benefit. See *FASB Statement No. 95,* par. 92.

Income Statement		Adjustments	Statement of Cash Flows	
Revenue (all cash)	30,000	—	30,000	Cash collected from customers
Income Tax Expense – Current	(10,300)	–2,000—Increase in tax receivable –1,000—Decrease in taxes payable	(13,300)	Cash paid for taxes
Income Tax Expense – Deferred	(1,700)	+1,700—Increase in deferred tax liability	0	
Net Income	18,000	–1,300	16,700	Cash flow from operations

Using the resulting information, the operating activities section of Collazo's statement of cash flows is as follows if the direct method is used:

Cash collected from customers	$30,000
Income taxes paid	(13,300)
Cash provided by operating activities	$16,700

If the indirect method is used, the operating activities section is as follows:

Net income	$18,000
(Increase) decrease in income tax refund receivable	(2,000)
Increase (decrease) in income taxes payable	(1,000)
Increase (decrease) in deferred tax liability	1,700
Cash provided by operating activities	$16,700

In addition, if the indirect method is used, the amount of cash paid for income taxes, $13,300, must be separately disclosed either in the statement of cash flows or in the notes to the financial statements.

INTERNATIONAL ACCOUNTING FOR DEFERRED TAXES

Describe how, with respect to deferred income taxes, international accounting standards have converged toward the U.S. treatment.

In the past, accounting standards around the world differed substantially in the area of deferred taxes. However, if current trends continue it will soon be true that the U.S. approach to deferred tax accounting is used almost everywhere. This section discusses the different approaches that have been used around the world and also discusses recent developments in the international harmonization of deferred tax accounting.

The approach to deferred tax accounting used in the United States (and discussed in this chapter) is sometimes called the *comprehensive recognition approach* because it requires recognition of all temporary differences between financial accounting income and taxable income. At the other extreme, the *no-deferral approach* recognizes none of the differences. The *partial recognition approach,* which has been used in the United Kingdom, falls in between these two extremes. These three approaches are described in this section.

No-Deferral Approach

The simplest approach to accounting for differences between financial accounting and taxable income is to just ignore the differences and report income tax expense equal to the amount of tax payable for the year. Historically, this no-deferral approach was quite common around the world. And in countries where there is a close correspondence between financial accounting standards and tax rules, the no-deferral approach yields financial statement numbers that are not that much different from what would be generated using the full-blown deferred tax accounting practices used in the United States. The no-deferral approach has become much less common now as companies seek to converge to the prevailing international practice; the no-deferral approach has been formally frowned upon since the original issuance of International Accounting Standard (IAS) 12 in 1979.

Comprehensive Recognition Approach

The International Accounting Standards Committee (IASC) has embraced the comprehensive recognition approach to deferred tax accounting that underlies Statement No. 109 in the United States. The original version of IAS 12 required that deferred taxes be included in the computation of income tax expense and that deferred taxes be reported on the balance sheet, but it left open the method used to compute the deferred taxes. In 1996, the IASC revised IAS 12; the accounting required in the revised version is very similar to the deferred tax accounting practices that have been described throughout this chapter. The good news for U.S. accountants and accounting students is that the world appears to have come around to the United States' way of accounting for deferred taxes, so we don't have to learn very much in order to understand international accounting for deferred taxes.

Partial Recognition Approach

Historically, the United Kingdom has employed an innovative technique for accounting for deferred taxes that results in a deferred tax liability being recorded only to the extent that the deferred taxes are actually expected to be paid in the future. To use the U.K. terminology, deferred income taxes are recognized only if they are expected to "crystallise." An equivalent concept in the United States might be "realized." For example, if a company is growing and continually purchasing new assets, then as deferred taxes on the older assets reverse, they will be offset by taxes being deferred on the new assets. In cases like this, if the firm is assumed to be a going concern, the tax deferral may continue indefinitely as new assets replace old ones. In the United Kingdom, it is said that this type of deferred tax liability will not crystallise, and so it is not recognized. Only if it is expected that deferrals on new assets will not offset older assets will crystallisation occur—and then a deferred tax liability would be recognized. The reasoning behind the U.K. approach to deferred tax liabilities is actually quite interesting: If a liability is deferred indefinitely, then the present value of that liability is zero. This concept highlights a common criticism of U.S. deferred tax accounting—no accounting recognition is given to the fact that by deferring income tax payments, firms are decreasing the present value of their tax obligation. Despite its conceptual attractiveness, the U.K. partial recognition approach is on the verge of being dropped in the interest of international harmonization. On August 26, 1999, Sir David Tweedie, Chairman of the Accounting Standards Board (ASB) in the United Kingdom, said:

> The current proposals [to adopt the comprehensive recognition approach] reflect the Board's commitment to harmonising its standards with international ones. . . . [O]n deferred tax, we will not [be able to] shift international opinion back to partial provision. . . . We have concluded that deferred tax is not one of the areas where there are grounds for flying in the face of international practice."[17]

In summary, both the no-deferral and partial recognition approaches have been used around the world in the past, but IAS 12 now requires the comprehensive recognition approach that is employed in the United States. It appears that the international differences in accounting for deferred income taxes will be relatively small in future years.

---

17   See ASB PN 145 on FRED 19 "Deferred Tax," August 26, 1999, at www.asb.org.uk.

E X P A N D E D   M A T E R I A L

To this point, our discussion of income taxes has focused primarily on how timing differences result in deferred tax assets and liabilities. In this section of the chapter, we introduce the concept of intraperiod income tax allocation. This concept involves allocating income tax expense between income from continuing operations and below-the-line items such as extraordinary items, discontinued operations, and changes in accounting principles.

Perform intraperiod income tax allocation.

INTRAPERIOD TAX ALLOCATION

As discussed in Chapter 4, when a company reports irregular or extraordinary items (below-the-line items) on its income statement or when a prior-period adjustment affects retained earnings, **intraperiod tax allocation** is appropriate. Under this approach, the income tax effect of each of these special items is reported with the individual item rather than being included with the income tax expense related to current operations. It was assumed in Chapter 4 that a single rate was applied to each category of income and that no special tax limitations were present for any of the income categories. With this assumption, intraperiod income tax allocation is not difficult.

When this simplifying assumption is not realistic and different levels of income are taxed at varying rates, decision rules must be developed to make the allocation among the various categories of income. Paragraph 38 of FASB Statement No. 109 establishes the priority for intraperiod tax allocation.

In summary, a "with and without" approach is applied as follows[18]:

1. Income taxes are computed for current operations without any of the irregular or extraordinary items.
2. Income taxes are computed with all income items considered. The difference between (1) and (2) is the total tax allocation to irregular and extraordinary items.
3. Income taxes are computed on total income without irregular and extraordinary losses considered to determine the tax effect of all losses. If there are several losses, the incremental tax effect of each loss category is considered, and the total tax impact of all loss categories is allocated among the separate losses in the ratio of their separate incremental impacts.
4. The difference between the income tax benefit allocated to all losses and the total irregular and extraordinary allocation (2) is attributed to irregular and extraordinary gains. If there are several gains, the incremental tax effect of all gain categories is considered, and further allocation to gain items is made in the same manner as losses.

> **FYI:** Most tax rate structures are graduated. When a company's income from operations is in one tax rate level and the below-the-line items are at another level, the allocations described here apply.

An example will illustrate the application of these decision rules. Assume Marble Corp. reports the following pretax income components on its income statement.

---

18   To simplify the discussion of intraperiod income tax allocation, it is assumed that financial reporting income and taxable income are equal; thus, there are no deferred taxes. In many actual situations, deferred taxes may apply both to current operations and to irregular categories of income such as discontinued operations. The interplay of deferred taxes with intraperiod tax allocation adds another dimension of complexity not considered in this introductory presentation of accounting for income taxes.

Income from continuing operations	$75,600
Loss on disposal of business segment	(19,000)
Extraordinary gain on early extinguishment of debt	30,000
Extraordinary loss on litigation claim	(16,000)
Cumulative effect of change in depreciation method	15,000
Total income before considering income taxes	$85,600

Assume the tax department has applied the current tax regulations and rates to Marble's various income categories and computed the following tax information using the with-and-without concepts required for intraperiod tax allocation.

Tax on total income ($85,600)	$30,200
Tax on income from continuing operations ($75,600)	26,750
Tax on total income before considering all irregular and extraordinary losses ($85,600 + $19,000 + $16,000 = $120,600)	42,500

Based on this assumed tax information, the net income for the year is $55,400 ($85,600 – $30,200). The total intraperiod tax allocation is $3,450 tax expense ($30,200 – $26,750). The total tax benefit allocated to the two loss categories is $12,300 ($42,500 – $30,200), and the total tax expense allocated to the two gain categories is $15,750 ($12,300 + $3,450). This allocation can be shown graphically as follows:

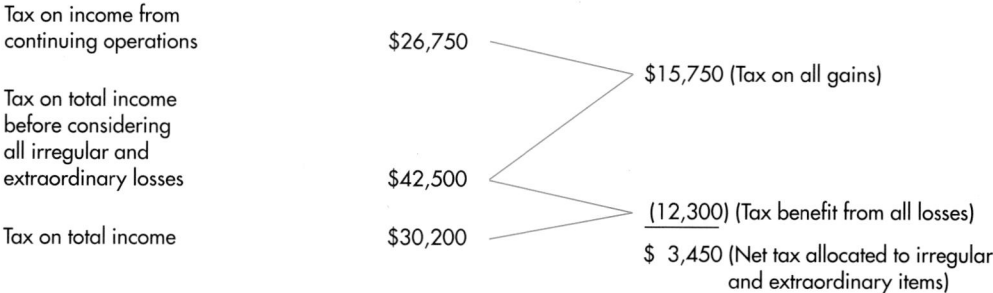

The loss and gain tax effects are further allocated to the specific gain and loss categories using the following assumed information also provided by the tax department. The incremental tax benefit or expense is determined by considering each component separately.

Incremental tax benefit—disposal loss	$ 9,000
Incremental tax benefit—extraordinary loss	6,000
Total tax benefits from losses	$15,000

Incremental tax expense—extraordinary gain	$10,200
Incremental tax expense—cumulative change	3,800
Total tax expense on gains	$14,000

Allocation of the $12,300 tax benefit to loss categories would be as follows:

Disposal loss ($9,000 ÷ $15,000) × $12,300	$ 7,380
Extraordinary loss ($6,000 ÷ $15,000) × $12,300	4,920
Total tax benefit	$12,300

Allocation of the $15,750 tax expense to gain categories would be as follows:

Extraordinary gain ($10,200 ÷ $14,000) × $15,750	$11,475
Cumulative change ($3,800 ÷ $14,000) × $15,750	4,275
Total tax expense	$15,750

The bottom portion of Marble Corp.'s income statement would be reported as follows:

Income from continuing operations before income taxes	$75,600
Income taxes	26,750
Income from continuing operations	$48,850
Loss on disposal of business segment (net of income tax benefit of $7,380)	(11,620)
Extraordinary gain from early extinguishment of debt (net of income taxes of $11,475)	18,525
Extraordinary loss on litigation claim (net of income tax benefit of $4,920)	(11,080)
Cumulative effect of change in depreciation method (net of income taxes of $4,275)	10,725
Net income	$55,400

If there are taxable direct entries to owners' equity accounts, the incremental approach is used to allocate tax benefits or tax expense to the equity accounts. For example, prior-period adjustments usually are affected by income taxes and must be shown in the statement of retained earnings net of the tax effect.

REVIEW OF LEARNING OBJECTIVES

1 **Understand the concept of deferred taxes and the distinction between permanent and temporary differences.** Deferred taxes result from the different objectives being used and applied for computing taxable income and income for financial reporting purposes. Because of differences between the tax code and GAAP, the accounting treatment for certain issues will differ. These differences can result in temporary timing differences that will eventually reverse or permanent differences that will not reverse. Temporary timing differences that result in taxable income in the future are termed taxable temporary differences and result in deferred tax liabilities. Those differences that result in expected deductible amounts in the future are termed deductible temporary differences and result in deferred tax assets.

2 **Compute the amount of deferred tax liabilities and assets.** Computing the amount of deferred tax assets and liabilities involves four steps: (1) identify the types and amounts of temporary timing differences, (2) compute the deferred tax liability associated with taxable temporary differences using current and future tax rates, (3) compute the amount of deferred tax asset associated with deductible temporary differences using current and future tax rates, and (4) reduce the amount of deferred tax asset if it is more likely than not that some or all of the asset may not be realized, using a valuation allowance account.

3 **Explain the provisions of tax loss carrybacks and carryforwards, and be able to account for these provisions.** Tax law requires corporations to pay taxes if they report taxable income. If a business reports a loss, the tax code allows that business to offset the loss against income in other years. The business is allowed to carry back its net operating losses up to

2 years to obtain a refund of taxes previously paid or to carry forward an operating loss up to 20 years in order to reduce the tax liability associated with future periods. A carryforward results in a deferred tax asset and may require the use of a valuation allowance account if it is more likely than not that the deferred asset may not be realized.

4 **Schedule future tax rates, and determine the effect on tax assets and liabilities.** Deferred tax assets and liabilities are recorded at the tax rates expected to be in effect in the periods of reversal. Thus, if Congress enacts rate changes or the corporation's taxable income level results in different expected future tax rates, these differing rates must be reflected in the valuation of deferred tax assets and liabilities.

5 **Determine appropriate financial statement presentation and disclosure associated with deferred tax assets and liabilities.** Deferred tax assets and liabilities are disclosed on the balance sheet as either current or noncurrent, based on the classification of the underlying asset or obligation. Additional disclosure is required relating to the tax expense (or benefit) for the period, deferred tax expense (or benefit), benefits associated with tax loss carryforwards, the effect of changes in tax rates, and adjustments associated with the valuation allowance account.

6 **Comply with income tax disclosure requirements associated with the statement of cash flows.** The amount of cash paid for income taxes must be disclosed using either the direct or indirect methods. With the direct method, the amount of cash paid for income taxes would be disclosed directly on the statement of cash flows. Under the indirect method, adjustments are made to net income for changes in receivable and payable balances associated with current and deferred tax assets and liabilities. Thus, with this method, the actual amount paid for taxes may not be disclosed in the body of the statement of cash flows. If this is the case, disclosure of cash paid for taxes is required in the notes to the financial statements or at the bottom of the statement of cash flows.

7 **Describe how, with respect to deferred income taxes, international accounting standards have converged toward the U.S. treatment.** Historically, companies around the world have used the no-deferral, the partial recognition, and the comprehensive recognition approaches to deferred tax accounting. With the revision of IAS 12 in 1996, it now appears that deferred tax accounting around the world will converge toward the comprehensive recognition approach employed in the United States.

8 **Perform intraperiod income tax allocation.** If a business has below-the-line income statement items, these items require intraperiod income tax allocation. If applicable tax rates are the same across all income levels, then intraperiod tax allocation is straightforward. In those instances where tax rates differ, a with-and-without decision rule is applied to allocate taxes for the period. This decision rule involves computing income taxes for current operations and income taxes on all income items. The difference between these two computations represents the amount of tax attributable to below-the-line items. The allocation of this amount involves first considering the effect of irregular and extraordinary gains and then considering losses.

KEY TERMS

asset and liability method of interperiod tax allocation 928
deductible temporary differences 927
financial income 922
interperiod tax allocation 928
net operating loss (NOL) carryback 938

net operating loss (NOL) carryforward 939
permanent differences 925
taxable income 922
taxable temporary differences 926
temporary differences 926
valuation allowance 934

intraperiod tax allocation 947

QUESTIONS

1. Accounting methods used by a company to determine income for financial reporting purposes frequently differ from those used to determine taxable income. What is the justification for these differences?

2. Distinguish between a nondeductible expense and a temporary difference that results in a taxable income greater than pretax financial income reported in the income statement.

3. Distinguish between taxable temporary differences and deductible temporary differences, and give at least two examples of each type.

4. One possibility for reporting income tax expense in the income statement for a given year is to merely report the amount of income tax payable in that year. What is wrong with this approach?

5. What are the major advantages of the asset and liability method?

6. What is a drawback of the asset and liability method?

7. Describe how a change in enacted future tax rates is

accounted for under the asset and liability method.

8. When is a valuation allowance necessary?

9. How does the FASB define the probability term "more likely than not" in Statement No. 109?

10. What are the sources of income through which the tax benefit of a deferred tax asset can be realized?

11. In applying the net operating loss carryback and carryforward provisions, what order of application is followed for federal tax purposes?

12. How is the classification of assets arising from NOL carryforwards determined under Statement No. 109?

13. Under what conditions would scheduling the temporary difference reversals be required under Statement No. 109?

14. What was the most significant change in accounting for income tax carryforwards made by FASB Statement No. 109?

15. How do changes in the balances of deferred income taxes affect the amount of cash paid for income taxes?

16. If a company experiences a current operating loss, it may carry the loss backward and forward. What impact do these carrybacks and carryforwards have on the reported operating loss? on the statement of cash flows?

17. What rules govern the netting of deferred tax assets and deferred tax liabilities?

18. Why is accounting for income taxes not as significant an issue in some foreign countries as it is in the United States?

19. In 1996, the IASC revised IAS 12. Did that revision make the international standard for deferred tax accounting more or less similar to the U.S. standard?

20. Briefly describe the partial recognition approach to accounting for deferred income taxes.

21. Describe the "with and without" approach of intraperiod tax allocation.

22. What is the proper sequence for computing intraperiod tax allocation?

DISCUSSION CASES

CASE 16–1

WHAT ARE DEFERRED INCOME TAXES?

Hurst Inc. is a new corporation that has just completed a highly successful first year of operations. Hurst is a privately held corporation, but its president, Byron Hurst, has indicated that if the company continues to do as well for the next 4 or 5 years, it will go public. By all indications, the company should continue to be highly profitable on both a short-term and a long-term basis.

The controller of the new company, Lori James, plans on using the MACRS method of depreciating Hurst's assets and using the installment sales method of recognizing income for tax purposes. For financial statement presentation, straight-line depreciation will be used and all sales will be fully recognized in the year of sale. There are no other differences between book and taxable income.

Hurst has hired your firm to prepare its financial statements. You are now preparing the income statement. The controller wants to show, as "Income tax expense," the amount of the tax liability actually due. "After all," James reasons, "that's the amount we'll actually pay, and in light of our plans for continued expansion, it's highly unlikely that the temporary differences will ever reverse."

Draft a memo to the controller outlining your reaction to the plan. Give reasons in support of your decision.

CASE 16–2

HOW DO DEFERRED TAXES WORK?

The Primrose Company appropriately uses the asset and liability method for interperiod income tax allocation. Primrose reports depreciation expense for certain machinery purchased this year using MACRS for income tax purposes and the straight-line basis for accounting purposes. The tax deduction is the larger amount this year.

Primrose received rent revenues in advance this year. These revenues are included in this year's taxable income. However, for accounting purposes, these revenues are reported as unearned revenues, a current liability.

1. What is the theoretical basis for deferred income taxes under the asset and liability concept as specified by FASB Statement No. 109?

2. How would Primrose determine and account for the income tax effect for depreciation and rent? Why?

CASE 16–3

WHY AREN'T DEFERRED TAXES DISCOUNTED?

Tyler Dee is the controller for Martinez Company. Martinez is a major employer in the area, and Tyler has just come from a meeting of a local civic group. The meeting was an opportunity for Tyler to present and explain Martinez's financial statements for the fiscal year recently ended. A significant amount of time was spent discussing the large deferred tax liability reported by Martinez. Several members of the civic group questioned Tyler about the nature of this liability. In particular, Tyler was asked why the liability wasn't discounted to reflect the time value of money. Tyler had no real answer, except to mumble something like, "That's just the way the standard is written."

How might Tyler have better explained the lack of discounting of deferred taxes?

CASE 16–4

RAISING TAX RATES: DOES IT HELP ME OR HURT ME?

When the corporate tax rate was lowered from 46% to 34% in 1986, most firms that had adopted the asset and liability method of deferred tax accounting reported one-time gains as a result of the revaluation of their deferred tax items. In fact, one writer claimed that this lowering of income tax rates "freed a large chunk of money that had been accumulated to pay deferred taxes at the former higher rate."

In early 1993, Congress was considering raising the corporate income tax rate. One proposal was to raise the top corporate rate from 34% to 36%. Accounting experts pointed out that the increase in the tax rate would cause some firms to report one-time losses and other firms to report one-time gains.

1. Why did the lowering of tax rates in 1986 result in most firms reporting gains, whereas an increase in tax rates in 1993 would cause some firms to report gains and some firms to report losses?

2. Comment on the writer's statement that the lowering of income tax rates "freed a large chunk of money."

SOURCES: Rick Wartzman, "Rise in Corporate Taxes Would Force Many Big Companies to Take Charges," *The Wall Street Journal*, February 11, 1993, p. A2; Lee Berton, "FASB Is Expected to Issue Rule Allowing Firms to Post Big, One-Time Gains," *The Wall Street Journal*, November 4, 1987, p. 4.

CASE 16–5

NO CARRYBACKS OR CARRYFORWARDS IN CARDASSIA

The president of Cardassia has recently been doing some recreational reading and came across an article on the adoption of FASB Statement No. 109 in the United States. The president liked the article so much that she has decided to adopt Statement No. 109 as the standard for deferred tax accounting in Cardassia.

You have been hired as the government minister in charge of accounting, taxation, and nuclear waste disposal for the country of Cardassia. It is your duty to figure out how to implement Statement No. 109. You note that the accounting rules and tax code in Cardassia are very similar to those in the United States, except that Cardassian income tax law does not allow the carryback or carryforward of net operating losses.

How will this difference in Cardassian tax law affect the accounting for deferred tax liabilities? deferred tax assets?

CASE 16–6

WHY DIFFERENT PROBABILITY TERMS FOR CONTINGENT ASSETS AND LIABILITIES?

Because you are an accounting student, one of your business major friends asks you to explain to him why the accounting profession records contingent liabilities only when their occurrence is probable but records deferred income tax assets as long as it is more likely than not that a future benefit will be realized from the deferral. He's confused by the probability terms used to record these items and wonders why the recognition of assets seems less conservative than the recognition of liabilities. How would you answer your friend?

CASE 16–7

IS A VALUATION ALLOWANCE NEEDED?

Assume that you go to work for one of the Big 5 accounting firms upon your graduation from college and that for your first assignment, you are asked to review the deferred income tax asset account to determine whether a valuation allowance seems to be warranted. You remember talking about deferred income taxes in your intermediate accounting class, but the problems always told you whether an allowance was required or not. Now you must examine the facts to help determine the need for an allowance. What factors would you consider in making your recommendation?

EXERCISES

EXERCISE 16–8

IDENTIFICATION OF TEMPORARY DIFFERENCES
Indicate which of the following items are temporary differences and which are nontaxable or nondeductible. For each temporary difference, indicate whether the item considered alone would create a deferred tax asset or a deferred tax liability.

(a) Tax depreciation in excess of book depreciation, $150,000.
(b) Excess of income on installment sales over income reportable for tax purposes, $130,000.
(c) Premium payment for life insurance policy on president, $95,000.
(d) Rent collected in advance of period earned, $75,000.
(e) Warranty provision accrued in advance of period paid, $40,000.
(f) Interest revenue received on municipal bonds, $30,000.

EXERCISE 16–9

CALCULATION OF TAXABLE INCOME
Using the information given in Exercise 16–8 and assuming pretax financial income of $3,100,000, calculate taxable income.

EXERCISE 16–10

DEFERRED TAX LIABILITY
Gideon Inc. began operating on January 1, 2002. At the end of the first year of operations, Gideon reported $750,000 income before income taxes on its income statement but only $620,000 taxable income on its tax return. Analysis of the $130,000 difference revealed that $70,000 was a permanent difference and $60,000 was a temporary tax liability difference related to a current asset. The enacted tax rate for 2002 and future years is 35%.

1. Prepare the journal entries to record income taxes for 2002.
2. Assume that at the end of 2003, the accumulated temporary tax liability difference related to future years is $110,000. Prepare the journal entry to record any adjustment to deferred tax liabilities at the end of 2003.

EXERCISE 16–11

DEFERRED TAX ASSET
Lofthouse Machinery Co. includes a 2-year warranty on its machinery sales. At the end of 2002, an analysis of the warranty records reveals an accumulated temporary difference of $120,000 for warranty expenses—book expenses related to warranties have exceeded tax deductions allowed. The enacted income tax rate for 2002 and future years is 40%. Management concludes that it is more likely than not that Lofthouse will have future income to realize the future tax benefit from this temporary difference. They also conclude that 20% of the warranty liability is current and 80% is noncurrent.

1. How would the deferred tax information be reported on the Lofthouse balance sheet at December 31, 2002?
2. If management assumed that only 70% of the tax benefit from the temporary difference could be realized, how would the deferred tax information be reported on the balance sheet at December 31, 2002? (Recall that the valuation allowance is allocated proportionately between the current and noncurrent portions of the deferred tax asset.)

EXERCISE 16–12

DETERMINANTS OF "MORE LIKELY THAN NOT"
Cobb Company computed a pretax financial loss of $10,000 for the first year of its operations ended December 31, 2002. This loss did not include $35,000 in unearned rent revenue that was recognized as taxable income in 2002 when the cash was received.

1. Prepare the journal entries necessary to record income tax for the year. The income tax rate is 40%. Assume it is more likely than not that future taxable income will be sufficient to allow for the full realization of any deferred tax assets and that unearned rent revenue is a current liability.

2. If future taxable income from operations was not expected to be sufficient to allow for the full realization of any deferred tax assets, what other sources of income may be considered to determine the need for a valuation allowance?

EXERCISE 16–13

DEFERRED TAX ASSET VALUATION ALLOWANCE

Rowberry Company computed a pretax financial loss of $5,000 for the first year of its operations ended December 31, 2002. Included in the loss was $28,000 in uncollectible accounts expense that was accrued on the books in 2002 using an allowance system based on a percentage of sales. For income tax purposes, deductions for uncollectible accounts are allowed when specific accounts receivable are determined to be uncollectible and written off. No accounts receivable have been written off as uncollectible in 2002.

1. Prepare the journal entries necessary to record income taxes for the year. The enacted income tax rate is 40% for 2002 and all future years. Assume that it is more likely than not that future taxable income will be sufficient to allow for the full realization of any deferred tax assets. Accounts Receivable and the related allowance account are reported under current assets on the balance sheet.
2. Repeat (1), assuming that it is more likely than not that future taxable income will be zero before considering the actual bad debt losses in future years.

EXERCISE 16–14

CHANGING TAX RATES

Goshute Company computed pretax financial income of $50,000 for the year ended December 31, 2002. Taxable income for the year was $15,000. Accumulated temporary differences as of December 31, 2001, were $120,000. A deferred tax liability of $48,000 was included on the December 31, 2001, balance sheet. Accumulated temporary differences as of December 31, 2002, are $155,000. The differences are related to noncurrent items.

1. Prepare the journal entries necessary to record income tax for 2002. The enacted income tax rate is assumed to be 40% for 2002 and future years.
2. On January 1, 2003, the income tax rate is changed to 32% for 2003 and all future years. Prepare the necessary journal entry, if any.

EXERCISE 16–15

DEFERRED TAX LIABILITY

The McCall Exploration Company reported pretax financial income of $596,500 for the calendar year 2002. Included in the "Other income" section of the income statement was $136,000 of interest revenue from municipal bonds held by the company. The income statement also included depreciation expense of $610,000 for a machine that cost $4,000,000. The income tax return reported $800,000 as MACRS depreciation on the machine.

The enacted tax rate is 40% for 2002 and future years. Prepare the journal entries necessary to record income taxes for 2002.

EXERCISE 16–16

DEFERRED TAX ASSET

Pro-Tech-Tronics Company computed pretax financial income of $35,000 for the first year of its operations ended December 31, 2002. Unearned rent revenue of $55,000 had been recognized as taxable income in 2002 when the cash was received but had not yet been recognized in the financial accounting records.

The unearned rent is expected to be recognized on the books in the following pattern.

2003	$15,000
2004	20,000
2005	12,000
2006	8,000
Total	$55,000

The enacted tax rates for this year and the next four years are as follows:

2002	34%
2003	34%
2004	30%
2005	30%
2006	37%

Prepare the journal entries necessary to record income taxes for 2002. Assume that there will be sufficient income in each future year to realize any deductible amounts.

EXERCISE 16–17

DEFERRED TAX ASSETS AND LIABILITIES

Fibertek, Inc., computed a pretax financial income of $40,000 for the first year of its operations ended December 31, 2002. Included in financial income was $25,000 of nondeductible expenses, $22,000 gross profit on installment sales that was deferred for tax purposes until the installments were collected, and $18,000 in doubtful accounts expense that had been accrued on the books in 2002.

The temporary differences are expected to reverse in the following patterns:

Year	Gross Profit on Collections	Bad Debt Write-Offs
2003	$ 5,000	$ 6,000
2004	7,000	12,000
2005	4,000	
2006	6,000	
Totals	$22,000	$18,000

The enacted tax rates for this year and the next four years are as follows:

2002	40%
2003	35%
2004	32%
2005	30%
2006	32%

Prepare the journal entries necessary to record income taxes for 2002. Assume that there will be sufficient income in each future year to realize any deductible amounts. For classification purposes, the bad debt write-offs are considered to be associated with a current asset and the receivable for installment sales is classified as both current and noncurrent, depending on the expected timing of the receipt.

EXERCISE 16–18

DEFERRED TAX ASSETS AND LIABILITIES

Energizer Manufacturing Corporation reports taxable income of $829,000 on its income tax return for the year ended December 31, 2002, its first year of operations. Temporary differences between financial income and taxable income for the year are:

Tax depreciation in excess of book depreciation	$ 80,000
Accrual for product liability claims in excess of actual claims (estimated product claims payable is a current liability)	125,000
Reported installment sales income in excess of taxable installment sales income (installments receivable is a current asset)	265,000

The enacted income tax rate is 40% for 2002 and all future years. Prepare the journal entries necessary to record income taxes for 2002.

EXERCISE 16–19

COMPUTATION OF DEFERRED ASSET AND LIABILITY BALANCES

Nashua Engineering reported taxable income of $20,000 for 2002, its first fiscal year. The enacted tax rate for 2002 is 40%. Enacted tax rates and deductible amounts for 2003–2005 are as follows:

	Enacted Tax Rate	Deductible Amount
2003	35%	$ 7,000
2004	32%	15,000
2005	30%	13,000

1. Prepare the journal entries necessary to record income taxes for 2002. Assume that there will be sufficient income in each future year to realize any deductible amounts. For classification purposes, assume that all deductible amounts relate to noncurrent items.
2. Repeat (1) assuming that it is more likely than not that taxable income for all future periods will be zero or less.

EXERCISE 16–20

COMPUTATION OF DEFERRED ASSET AND LIABILITY BALANCES

Dixon Type and Supply Company reported taxable income of $75,000 for 2002, its first fiscal year. The enacted tax rate for 2002 is 40%. Enacted tax rates and deductible amounts for 2003–2006 are as follows:

	Enacted Tax Rate	Deductible Amount
2003	35%	$14,000
2004	32%	24,000
2005	30%	16,000
2006	32%	40,000

1. Prepare the journal entries necessary to record income taxes for 2002. Assume that there will be sufficient income in each future year to realize any deductible amounts. For classification purposes, assume that all deductible amounts relate to noncurrent items.
2. Repeat (1) assuming it is more likely than not that taxable income for all future periods will be zero or less.

EXERCISE 16–21

NET OPERATING LOSS (NOL) CARRYBACK

The following historical financial data are available for the Bradshaw Manufacturing Company.

Year	Income	Tax Rate	Tax Paid
1999	$175,000	40%	$ 70,000
2000	230,000	42%	96,600
2001	310,000	35%	108,500

In 2002, Bradshaw suffered an $820,000 net operating loss due to an economic recession. The company elects to use the carryback provision in the tax law.

1. Using the information given, calculate the refund due arising from the loss carryback and the amount of the loss available to carry forward to future periods. Assume the enacted tax rate is 34% for 2002 and all future years.
2. Prepare the entry necessary to record the loss carryback and carryforward. Assume there will be sufficient taxable income in the carryforward period to realize all benefits from NOL carryforwards.
3. Using the answers from (1) and (2), prepare the bottom portion of the 2002 income statement, reflecting the effect of the loss carryback and carryforward.

EXERCISE 16–22

NOL CARRYFORWARD

The following historical financial data are available for the Terry Company.

Year	Income	Tax Rate	Tax Paid
1999	$300,000	30%	$90,000
2000	100,000	35%	35,000
2001	10,000	35%	3,500

In 2002 the Terry Company suffered a $1.5 million net operating loss. The company will use the carryback provision of the tax law.

1. Using the information given, calculate the refund due for the loss carryback and the amount of the loss available to carry forward to future periods. Assume the enacted tax rate for 2002 and all future years is 40%.
2. Prepare journal entries to record the loss carryback and carryforward. Assume it is more likely than not that future taxable income will be sufficient to allow for the full realization of any deferred tax assets.
3. Evaluate the reasonableness of the assumption in (2).

EXERCISE 16–23

CASH FLOW AND INCOME TAXES

Joyce Smithers Inc. reported the following amounts related to income taxes on its 2002 income statement.

Income tax expense—current	$32,000
Income tax expense—deferred	(8,000)

Smithers also reported the following amounts on its December 31, 2001 and 2002, balance sheets.

	2002	2001
Deferred tax liability	$26,000	$34,000
Income taxes payable	10,000	4,000

If Smithers uses the indirect method of reporting cash flows, what information concerning income taxes would Smithers include in its statement of cash flows and related disclosure?

EXERCISE 16–24

CASH FLOW AND INCOME TAXES

Owyhee Motors reported the following amounts related to income taxes on its 2002 income statement.

Income tax benefit from NOL carryback	$12,000
Income tax benefit from NOL carryforward	28,000

Owyhee also reported the following on its December 31, 2001 and 2002, balance sheets.

	2002	2001
Deferred tax asset—NOL carryforward	$28,000	$ 0
Income tax refund receivable	12,000	4,000

1. If Owyhee uses the indirect method of reporting cash flows, what information concerning income taxes would Owyhee include in its statement of cash flows and related disclosure?
2. If Owyhee uses the direct method of reporting cash flows, what information concerning income taxes would Owyhee include in its statement of cash flows and related disclosure?

EXERCISE 16–25

INTRAPERIOD INCOME TAX ALLOCATION

The Hughes Enterprise Company paid $360,000 in income taxes for the year ended December 31, 2002. Of these taxes, $20,000 related to an extraordinary gain that was taxed at 25%. Hughes discontinued one of its business segments during 2002 and realized a tax savings of $50,000 from the loss on disposition of the segment. The loss was treated for tax purposes as an ordinary loss and was deducted from ordinary income that was taxed at 40%. Included in the $360,000 tax payment was $10,000 resulting from a gain on the sale of equipment. The tax rate on the gain was 25%. All other income items were from normal operations and were taxed at 40%. Hughes had 40,000 shares of common stock outstanding.

Prepare the income statement for The Hughes Enterprise Company beginning with "Income from continuing operations before income taxes." Include the appropriate intraperiod tax allocation procedures.

PROBLEMS

PROBLEM 16–26

LIFE CYCLE OF A TEMPORARY DIFFERENCE

A. J. Johnson & Co. recorded certain revenues on its books in 2002 and 2003 of $15,400 and $16,600, respectively. However, such revenues were not subject to income taxation until 2004. Company records reveal pretax financial income and taxable income for the 3-year period as follows:

	Financial Income	Taxable Income
2002	$44,200	$28,800
2003	38,200	21,600
2004	21,100	53,100

Assume Johnson's tax rate is 40% for all periods.

Instructions: Prepare the journal entries necessary at the end of each year to record income taxes.

PROBLEM 16–27

DEFERRED TAX LIABILITY

Tristar Corporation reported taxable income of $1,996,000 for the year ended December 31, 2002. The controller is unfamiliar with the required treatment of temporary and permanent differences in reconciling taxable income to pretax financial income and has contacted your firm for advice. You are given company records that list the following differences.

Tax depreciation in excess of book depreciation	$275,000
Proceeds from life insurance policy upon death of officer	125,000
Interest revenue on municipal bonds	98,000

Instructions:

1. Compute pretax financial income.
2. Given an income tax rate of 40%, prepare the journal entry to record income taxes for the year.
3. Prepare a partial income statement beginning with "Income from continuing operations before income taxes."

PROBLEM 16–28

DEFERRED TAX LIABILITY

Timpany Motors, Inc., computed a pretax financial income of $75,000 for its first year of operations ended December 31, 2002. In preparing the income tax return for the year, the tax accountant determined the following differences between 2002 financial income and taxable income.

Nondeductible expenses	$30,000
Nontaxable revenues	12,500
Temporary difference—installment sales reported in financial income but not in taxable income	28,000

The temporary difference is expected to reverse in the following pattern as the cash is collected:

2003	$ 6,000
2004	13,500
2005	8,500
Total	$28,000

The enacted tax rates for this year and the next 3 years are as follows:

2002	40%
2003	36%
2004	34%
2005	30%

Instructions:

1. Prepare journal entries to record income taxes payable and deferred income taxes.
2. Prepare a partial income statement for Timpany Motors beginning with "Income from continuing operations before income taxes" for the year ended December 31, 2002.

PROBLEM 16–29

DEFERRED TAX ASSET

Davidson Gasket Inc. computed a pretax financial loss of $15,000 for the first year of its operations, ended December 31, 2002. Analysis of the tax and book bases of its liabilities disclosed $55,000 in unearned rent revenue on the books that had been recognized as taxable income in 2002 when the cash was received. Also disclosed was $20,000 in warranties payable that had been recognized as expense on the books in 2002 when product sales were made but that are not deductible on the tax return until paid.

These temporary differences are expected to reverse in the following pattern.

Year	Rent Earned on Books	Warranty Payments
2003	$13,000	$ 5,000
2004	25,000	8,000
2005	12,000	7,000
2006	5,000	
Totals	$55,000	$20,000

The enacted tax rates for this year and the next 4 years are as follows:

2002	38%
2003	36%
2004	32%
2005	30%
2006	30%

Instructions:

1. Prepare journal entries to record income taxes payable and deferred income taxes. Assume there will be sufficient income in each future year to realize any deductible amount.

2. Prepare the income statement for Davidson Gasket Inc. beginning with "Loss from continuing operations before income taxes" for the year ended December 31, 2002.

3. If future taxable income from operations was not expected to be sufficient to allow for the full realization of any deferred tax assets, what other sources of income may be used to avoid establishing a valuation allowance?

PROBLEM 16–30

DEFERRED TAX ASSETS AND LIABILITIES

As of December 31, 2002, its first year in business, Khaleeq Company had taxable temporary differences totaling $60,000. Of this total, $20,000 relates to current items. Khaleeq also had deductible temporary differences totaling $17,000, $5,000 of which relates to current items. Pretax financial income for the year was $100,000. The enacted tax rate for 2002 and all future years is 40%.

Instructions:

1. Prepare the journal entries to record income taxes for 2002.
2. Repeat (1), but assume that all the taxable temporary differences are noncurrent and that all the deductible temporary differences are current.

PROBLEM 16–31

NETTING OF DEFERRED TAX ASSETS AND LIABILITIES

Stratco Corporation computed a pretax financial income of $40,000 for the first year of its operations ended December 31, 2002. Included in financial income was $50,000 of nontaxable revenue, $20,000 gross profit on installment sales that was deferred for tax purposes until the installments were collected, and $50,000 in warranties payable that had been recognized as expense on the books in 2002 when product sales were made.

The temporary differences are expected to reverse in the following pattern.

Year	Gross Profit on Collections	Warranty Payments
2003	$ 5,000	$ 9,000
2004	7,000	16,500
2005	2,000	20,500
2006	6,000	4,000
Totals	$20,000	$50,000

The enacted tax rates for this year and the next 4 years are as follows:

2002	40%	2005	30%
2003	35%	2006	30%
2004	32%		

Instructions:

1. Prepare journal entries to record income taxes payable and deferred income taxes. Assume there will be sufficient income in each future year to realize any deductible amount.
2. Prepare the income statement for Stratco beginning with "Income from continuing operations before income taxes" for the year ended December 31, 2002.

PROBLEM 16–32

VALUATION ALLOWANCE

Cheng Company computed taxable income of $7,000 for the first year of its operations ended December 31, 2002. Tax depreciation exceeded depreciation for financial reporting purposes by $20,000. Receipt of $15,000 cash was reported as revenue for tax purposes but is reported as a current liability, Unearned Revenue, for financial reporting. The enacted tax rate for 2002 and all future years is 40%.

Instructions:

1. Prepare the journal entries to record income taxes for 2002. Assume that it is more likely than not that future taxable income will be sufficient to allow for the full realization of any deferred tax assets.
2. Repeat (1), assuming that it is more likely than not that future taxable income will be zero, exclusive of the expected reversal of the depreciation temporary difference.

PROBLEM 16–33

ADJUSTMENT FOR CHANGING TAX RATES

Moritz Company analyzed its temporary differences as of December 31, 2002. The enacted tax rate was 40% for 2002 and all future tax years.

The total amount of taxable temporary differences as of the end of 2002 was $110,000. All the temporary differences relate to noncurrent items.

Instructions:

1. Assume that in early 2003 the taxing authority changed the rates for 2003 and beyond to 34%. Prepare the 2003 journal entry to record the tax rate decrease.
2. Assume that instead of being decreased, the tax rate was increased to 46% in early 2003. Prepare the 2003 journal entry to record the tax rate increase.

PROBLEM 16–34

OPERATING LOSS CARRYBACK AND CARRYFORWARD

The following information is taken from the financial statements of Columbia Enterprises.

Year	Taxable and Pretax Financial Income	Income Tax Rate	Income Tax Paid
1998	$24,000	40%	$ 9,600
1999	27,400	40%	10,960
2000	31,500	34%	10,710
2001	21,240	34%	7,222
2002	(86,000)	36%	0

The company elects to use the carryback provisions of the tax law.

Instructions:

1. Given the information from the financial statements, compute the amount of income tax refund due as a result of the operating loss in 2002.
2. What is the amount, if any, of the operating loss carryforward? How would the operating loss carryforward be reflected in the financial statements?
3. Assume the foregoing information except:
   a. The loss in 2002 was $41,000. Calculate the refund due and prepare the journal entry to record the claim for income tax refund.
   b. In addition to (a), there was a loss in 2003 of $24,000. How much could be carried back and how much could be carried forward?

PROBLEM 16–35

NOL CARRYBACK AND CARRYFORWARD

The financial history on the following page shows the income and losses for Steele and Associates for the 10-year period 1993–2002.

Assume that no adjustments to taxable income are necessary for purposes of the NOL carryback and that the company elects to use the carryback provisions of the tax code.

Instructions:

1. Given the foregoing information, compute the amount of income tax refund for each year as a result of each NOL carryback and the amount of the carryforward (if any).

Year	Taxable and Pretax Financial Income (Before NOL)	Income Tax Rate	Income Tax Paid
1993	$ 8,800	50%	$ 4,400
1994	12,300	50%	6,150
1995	14,800	44%	6,512
1996	(24,250)	44%	0
1997	7,200	44%	3,168
1998	(21,750)	46%	0
1999	16,600	46%	?
2000	32,000	40%	12,800
2001	(58,700)	40%	0
2002	65,000	40%	?

2. How would the NOL carryforward as of December 31, 2001, be reflected in the 2001 financial statements?
3. Calculate the amount of income tax paid, showing the benefit of the NOL carryforward, for the years 1999 and 2002.
4. For 2002, give the entry (or entries) to record income taxes, assuming that the deferred tax asset stemming from the 2001 NOL carryforward was fully recognized in 2001.

PROBLEM 16–36 **INTRAPERIOD TAX ALLOCATION**

Assume Energy Corp. has the following income components on its income statement. Amounts are before tax.

Income from continuing operations	$37,500
Gain on disposal of business segment	19,000
Extraordinary gain on early extinguishment of debt	23,000
Extraordinary loss on property loss	(32,000)
Cumulative effect of change in depreciation method	(13,000)
Total income before considering income taxes	$34,500

Assume that the tax department has applied the current tax regulations and rates to Energy's various income categories and computed the following tax information using the "with and without" concept required for intraperiod tax allocation:

Tax on total income ($34,500)	$13,100
Tax on income from continuing operations ($37,500)	15,200
Tax on total income before considering all irregular and extraordinary losses	27,030

Instructions:

1. Compute the total tax to be allocated to all income components after income from continuing operations, the total tax benefit allocated to the two loss categories, and the total tax expense allocated to the two gain categories.
2. Assume the tax department has computed the following incremental tax benefits and expenses on each individual gain or loss component:

Incremental tax expense—gain components:	
Gain on disposal	$5,700
Extraordinary gain	6,500
Incremental tax benefit—loss components:	
Extraordinary loss	9,600
Cumulative effect	5,000

Allocate the total tax benefit and tax expense from (1) to the separate gain and loss components.

PROBLEM 16–37  **INTRAPERIOD TAX ALLOCATION CASES**

Assume the following intraperiod tax allocation information for Cases A, B, and C:

	Case A	Case B	Case C
Tax on income from continuing operations	$23,000	$57,000	$7,000
Tax on total income before considering all irregular and extraordinary losses	36,900	61,000	9,500
Tax on total income	32,000	46,000	7,000
Incremental tax expense—gains:			
Gain on disposal	4,300	1,700	800
Extraordinary gain—A	6,500	3,200	3,000
Extraordinary gain—B	3,900		
Incremental tax benefit—losses:			
Extraordinary loss	(2,500)	(12,500)	(1,600)
Cumulative effect of accounting changes	(3,000)	(6,000)	(900)

Instructions: Compute the tax expense and benefits in Cases A through C for all irregular and extraordinary items.

COMPETENCY ENHANCEMENT OPPORTUNITIES

▶ Deciphering Actual Financial Statements	▶ Ethical Dilemma
▶ Writing Assignment	▶ Cumulative Spreadsheet Analysis
▶ Research Project	▶ Internet Search
▶ The Debate	

Accounting is more than just doing textbook problems. This expanded competency material provides practice in critical thinking, oral and written communication, research, teamwork, and consideration of ethical issues.

▶ **DECIPHERING ACTUAL FINANCIAL STATEMENTS**

• **Deciphering 16–1 (The Walt Disney Company)**

Refer to the financial statements of THE WALT DISNEY COMPANY in Appendix A to answer the following questions.

1. Using the financial statements and information contained in the notes, determine how much income tax expense Disney reported for the fiscal year ended September 30, 1998.
2. Referring to the note on income taxes, how much of the tax expense relates to current items and how much relates to deferred items?
3. Disney notes that its effective income tax rate for 1998 was 41.4%. Using information from the income statement, determine how that number was computed.
4. Note that Disney has a valuation allowance of $50 million. In the journal entry establishing this allowance account, what would have been the debit and the credit?

• **Deciphering 16–2 (Sara Lee Corporation)**

SARA LEE CORPORATION owns the following brands: Ball Park franks, Sara Lee bakery goods, Kiwi shoe care products, Hanes and Hanes Her Way, L'eggs, and about a hundred other products. Information relating to its deferred taxes is shown on page 965. Based on that information, answer the following questions:

1. Provide the journal entry(ies) made by Sara Lee to record the current period's income tax expense of $80 million. Remember to allocate the expense between current and deferred.

2. Provide the journal entry made by Sara Lee to record the payment of income taxes during the year.

3. At the end of 1997, Sara Lee reported a net deferred tax asset of $41 million. At the end of 1998, the deferred tax asset had increased to $446 million. Can you identify the reasons for this increase?

• Deciphering 16–3 (Archer Daniels Midland Company)

ARCHER DANIELS MIDLAND COMPANY (ADM), the world's largest agricultural processor, is referred to as the "Supermarket to the World." Using the note information provided on page 966, answer the following questions regarding its taxes.

1. Compute the company's effective tax rate.
2. Provide the journal entry(ies) made by ADM to record income tax expense for 1999.
3. Provide the journal entry to record the payment of income taxes in 1999.
4. ADM's net deferred tax liability decreased by $42.728 million during 1999. Given your entry from (2) that increased the deferred tax account by a net amount of $23.750 million, what else must have happened in the deferred tax liability account? Provide the debit and the credit associated with the journal entry that adjusted the net deferred tax liability account.

• Deciphering 16–4 (Cadbury Schweppes)

CADBURY SCHWEPPES is a company based in the United Kingdom. It manufactures, markets, and distributes branded confectionary and beverage products internationally through wholesale and retail outlets. It is best known for its chocolates and bottled drinks. In 1995, the company acquired DR. PEPPER/SEVEN UP INC.

Although disclosure and terminology are a little different in the United Kingdom, we shall see that deferred taxes are similar around the world. Use the information on pages 967–968 to answer the following questions:

1. Cadbury Schweppes reported income before taxes in 1998 of 579 (in millions of pounds). Compute the company's effective tax rate. How does this rate compare to the applicable U.K. statutory rate in 1998 of 31%?

2. Provide the journal entry made by the company to record its tax expense for the year. Remember to allocate the expense between current and deferred.

3. Because Cadbury Schweppes is located in the United Kingdom, it has been using the partial recognition method of accounting for deferred income taxes. As of the end of 1998, what is the size of Cadbury Schweppes' deferred tax liability that is *not* recognized because it is not expected to "crystallise"?

4. In the spirit of giving financial statement users across the world useful information, Cadbury Schweppes had disclosed what its net deferred tax liability would be if it were to use U.S. GAAP. What is the net deferred tax liability using GAAP as of the end of 1998?

▶ WRITING ASSIGNMENT
• Crystallisation

As discussed in the chapter, deferred taxes in the United Kingdom have historically been computed in a slightly different manner than in the United States. The concept of crystallisation is introduced and the United Kingdom's conclusion is that if a liability is deferred indefinitely, then the present value of that liability is zero. No deferred tax liability is recognized if the accumulated deferred tax amount is expected to increase each year, thus delaying indefinitely the ultimate liquidation of this obligation.

In one page or less, address the following questions as they relate to crystallisation and accounts payable:

SARA LEE CORPORATION AND SUBSIDIARIES
Income Taxes

The provisions for income taxes computed by applying the U.S. statutory rate to income before taxes as reconciled to the actual provisions were:

	1998		1997		1996	
	Amount	**Percent**	**Amount**	**Percent**	**Amount**	**Percent**
(Loss) income before provision for income taxes						
United States	$(1,091)	(246.4)%	$ 742	50.0%	$ 638	46.3%
Foreign	648	146.4	742	50.0	740	53.7
	$ (443)	100.0%	$1,484	100.0%	$1,378	100.0%
Tax (benefit) expense at U.S. statutory rates	$ (155)	(35.0)%	$ 519	35.0%	$ 482	35.0%
State taxes, net of federal benefit	9	2.0	13	.9	15	1.1
Difference between U.S. and foreign rates	(76)	(17.1)	(85)	(5.7)	(68)	(5.0)
Nondeductible amortization	351	79.3	62	4.2	54	3.9
Other, net	(49)	(11.2)	(34)	(2.4)	(21)	(1.5)
Taxes at effective worldwide tax rates	$ 80	18.0%	$ 475	32.0%	$ 462	33.5%

Current and deferred tax provisions (benefits) were:

	1998		1997		1996	
	Current	**Deferred**	**Current**	**Deferred**	**Current**	**Deferred**
United States	$142	$(286)	$169	$12	$166	$25
Foreign	329	(118)	245	28	237	10
State	14	(1)	21	—	28	(4)
	$485	$(405)	$435	$40	$431	$31

Following are the components of the deferred tax (benefits) provisions occurring as a result of transactions being reported in different years for financial and tax reporting:

	1998	1997	1996
Depreciation	$ (3)	$ (2)	$ 22
Inventory valuation methods	6	37	(35)
Nondeductible reserves	(405)	53	77
Other, net	(3)	(48)	(33)
	$(405)	$ 40	$ 31
Cash payments for income taxes	$ 288	$340	$224

The deferred tax (assets) liabilities at the respective year-end were as follows:

	1998	1997	1996
Deferred tax (assets) liabilities:			
Restructuring reserves	$ (68)	$ —	$(89)
Reserves not deductible until paid	(287)	(295)	(253)
Pension, postretirement and other employee benefits	(12)	(42)	(35)
Net operating loss and other tax carryforwards	(15)	(1)	(2)
Property, plant and equipment	(4)	309	298
Other	(60)	(12)	—
Net deferred tax (assets)	$(446)	$(41)	$(81)

1. How might this same concept be applied to the recognition of a liability for accounts payable? That is, if accounts payable are expected to increase each year, should the crystallisation concept apply to this liability?
2. How reasonable does this approach seem?

Archer Daniels Midland
NOTES

Note 7—Income Taxes
For financial reporting purposes, earnings before income taxes includes the following components:

	1999	1998	1997
	(In thousands)		
United States	$327,489	$458,184	$563,086
Foreign	92,344	151,828	81,319
	$419,833	$610,012	$644,405

Significant components of income taxes are as follows:

	1999	1998	1997
	(In thousands)		
Current			
Federal	$ 74,040	$111,152	$216,641
State	12,787	20,879	29,440
Foreign	27,968	54,724	27,352
Deferred			
Federal	25,085	14,474	(5,357)
State	674	1,451	(2,910)
Foreign	(2,009)	3,723	1,930
	$138,545	$206,403	$267,096

Significant components of the Company's deferred tax liabilities and assets are as follows:

	1999	1998
	(In thousands)	
Deferred tax liabilities		
Depreciation	$527,833	$484,336
Unrealized gain (loss) on marketable securities	(2,117)	60,820
Bond discount amortization	58,286	52,645
Other	85,285	86,161
	669,287	683,962
Deferred tax assets		
Postretirement benefits	32,785	31,073
Other	107,772	81,431
	140,557	112,504
Net deferred tax liabilities	528,730	571,458
Current net deferred tax assets included in prepaid expenses	91,022	61,435
Non-current net deferred tax liabilities	$619,752	$632,893

The Company made income tax payments of $111 million, $225 million and $312 million in 1999, 1998 and 1997, respectively.

▶ **RESEARCH PROJECT**
- **Reviewing actual financial statements and associated notes**
  Your group is to obtain the annual reports of 5 companies. Using these annual reports, your group is to report (either orally or in writing) the answers to the following questions.

  - Determine each company's effective tax rate by dividing income tax expense by income before taxes. How do these rates compare across the 5 companies? Compare the rates over time for the same company to determine if effective tax rates are increasing or decreasing.
  - What percentage of each company's income tax expense is associated with current items and what percentage is associated with deferred tax items? How do these percentages compare across companies?
  - Determine each company's trend associated with its deferred tax assets and liabilities. Have those accounts gotten larger or smaller over the past 3 years? How many of the 5 companies have experienced increases in their deferred tax liability accounts?
  - For each company, locate the amount of cash paid for income taxes during the year. For the 5 companies, how many disclosed this on the statement of cash flows and how many required you to search the notes to the financial statements?
  - From the information contained in the notes, determine the largest component of deferred taxes for each company. For how many was the largest component related to property, plant, and equipment?

Cadbury Schweppes
17. Deferred taxation

The analysis of the deferred tax liabilities/(assets) included in the financial statements at the end of the year is as follows:

	Group		Company	
	1998	1997	1998	1997
	£m	£m	£m	£m
Accelerated capital allowance	2	4	—	—
Profit on sale of subsidiaries	—	95	—	100
Unutilised tax losses	(6)	—	—	—
Other timing differences	83	51	(6)	—
	79	150	(6)	100

The Group deferred taxation liability is included in provisions for liabilities and charges (see Note 16). Gross deferred tax assets at year end are £27m (1997: £25m). The Company deferred tax asset is included in debtors (see Note 14).

The potential liability for deferred taxation not provided comprised:

	Group		Company	
	1998	1997	1998	1997
	£m	£m	£m	£m
UK accelerated capital allowances	50	39	2	1
UK property valuations	5	6	1	1
Other timing differences	29	30	—	—
	84	75	3	2

To the extent that dividends from overseas undertakings are expected to result in additional taxes, appropriate amounts have been provided. No taxes have been provided for other unremitted earnings since these amounts are considered permanently reinvested by subsidiary undertakings and in the case of associated undertakings the taxes would not be material. Distributable earnings retained by overseas subsidiary undertakings and the principal associated undertakings totalled approximately £538m at 2 January 1999. The remittance of these amounts would incur tax at substantially lower than normal rates after giving effect to foreign tax credits.

Tax losses carried forward as at 2 January 1999 for offset against future earnings of overseas companies were approximately £111 million (1997: £171 million). The utilisation of losses is dependent upon the level of future earnings and other limiting factors within the countries concerned. Tax losses totalling £27 million have expiration periods in 1999 and 2000, tax losses of £33 million expire in 2001–2006, tax losses of £2 million expire in 2007–2011 and tax losses totalling £49 million have no expiry date.

The US GAAP analysis of the deferred tax liability is as follows:

	1998	1997
	£m	£m
Liabilities		
Fixed asset timing differences	84	77
Profit on sale of subsidiaries	—	95
Other timing differences	85	56
	169	228
Assets		
Operating losses carried forward	(40)	(61)
Less: Valuation allowance	34	61
	(6)	—
Net deferred tax liability	163	228

(continued)

NOTES TO THE ACCOUNTS
7. Tax on Profit on Ordinary Activities

	1998 Total £m	1997 Total £m
UK:		
Corporation tax at 31% (1997: 31.5%)	49	68
Double tax relief	(39)	(41)
Deferred tax	30	119
Associated undertaking	7	5
	47	151
Overseas:		
Tax payable	102	72
Deferred tax	39	43
Associated undertakings	4	3
	145	118
Over provision in previous years:		
-current tax	(5)	(6)
-deferred tax	(4)	(2)
	183	261

The charge of £183m (1997: £261m) has been decreased by £14m (1997: £4m increase) in respect of tax at the current year's rate on timing differences for which deferred tax has not been provided. No tax relief is expected to be available on the Exceptional items recorded in 1998 (see Note 3(d)).

▶ **THE DEBATE**
• Account for deferred taxes or not!
Some financial analysts argue that the information resulting from deferred tax computations is not worth the effort expended in performing the accounting calculations. In applying deferred tax accounting standards, accountants are required to factor in differences between U.S. GAAP and the Internal Revenue Code, changes in future tax rates, and estimated future profitability of a company to arrive at an estimate of deferred tax assets and liabilities.

Divide your group into two teams.

- One team will argue for no deferred taxes. The results of all those computations, assumptions, and estimates are not worth the costs.
- The other team will argue that it is essential that deferred taxes be accounted for in some fashion.

In this debate, you should be prepared not only to support your position but also to consider how you might rebut the points that will be made by the other team.

▶ **ETHICAL DILEMMA**
• The valuation allowance
You have just completed a preliminary draft of the year-end financial statements and notes and have distributed it to members of the board of directors for the upcoming board meeting. At the meeting, board members will have an opportunity to analyze, ask questions, and offer suggestions regarding the content of the statements and the accompanying notes.

According to your computations, the company will be reporting yet another loss—the third in as many years. The company has taken full advantage of the carryback provisions of the tax law. With this year's loss, the company will carry forward some of the loss. As a result, you have correctly recorded a deferred tax asset. However, because of continued losses, you have used a valuation allowance account to reduce the amount of the deferred tax asset.

At the board meeting, initial questions focus on the company's profitability or lack thereof. Following this discussion, an astute member of the board questions the use of a valuation allowance account. She asks for your reasoning as to why a valuation allowance account is being used. You explain that if losses continue, the entire amount of the deferred asset may not be realized and that it is your professional opinion that sufficient evidence exists to justify the use of a valuation allowance account.

Immediately the board begins to question your assumption of future losses. "Of course we will be profitable next year," says one board member. "We have a plan to turn this company around," says another. You overhear another whisper to his colleague, "If the accountants don't think we are going to make money in the future, why are they staying? They should get a job with a company that they think is going to be profitable."

You have heard this talk about a turnaround in prior years, yet management seems unsuccessful in implementing desired changes. In past years you have always had prior year's profits against which you could offset losses. But now the accounting department, of which you are the head, has openly questioned management's intentions to report profits in the future. Now the board is questioning your loyalty to the company as well as your judgment.

1. What other factors might be considered when valuing the deferred tax asset account?
2. As the accountant, is it your place to question management's ability to turn a company around?
3. What effect did the journal entry involving the valuation allowance account have on this year's income statement? Did net income go up or down? With this journal entry, are you contributing to the company's loss?

CUMULATIVE SPREADSHEET ANALYSIS

This assignment is based on the spreadsheet prepared in (1) of the cumulative spreadsheet assignment for Chapter 13. Review that assignment for a summary of the assumptions made in preparing a forecasted balance sheet, income statement, and statement of cash flows for 2003 for Skywalker Company. This assignment involves computations related to deferred income taxes and the amount of cash paid for income taxes.

Skywalker would like to estimate the amount of cash it will pay for income taxes in 2003. The only difference between financial accounting income and taxable income for Skywalker is in the area of depreciation. Skywalker uses straight-line depreciation for financial reporting purposes and an accelerated method for tax reporting. This difference has created a deferred tax liability, which is included in the "Other long-term liabilities" reported in Skywalker's balance sheet. The following information is available as of December 31, 2002.

Accumulated depreciation, financial accounting records	$27.00
Accumulated depreciation, tax records	$50.00
Expected future income tax rate	33.0%

Construct a spreadsheet that will allow you to answer the following questions.

1. Given this information, what is Skywalker's deferred tax liability as of December 31, 2002? (Carry calculations to two decimal places.)
2. In 2003, it is expected that depreciation expense for income tax purposes will be 1.5 times as much as depreciation expense computed for financial reporting purposes. Estimate the amount of cash that Skywalker will pay for income taxes in 2003. Report your answer with two decimal places, and assume the following.
   - Amortization expense is the same for book and for tax purposes.
   - All current income taxes are paid in cash during the year.

- These calculations do not impact the overall total forecast for "Other long-term liabilities" for 2003; the balance is still expected to increase at the same rate as sales.
3. Repeat (2), assuming the following:
   a. Depreciation expense for income tax purposes will be the same as depreciation expense computed for financial reporting purposes.
   b. Depreciation expense for income tax purposes will be 2.0 times as much as depreciation expense computed for financial reporting purposes.
4. Comment on what implicit assumption underlies your answer to (3b).

▶ **INTERNET SEARCH**
• Sprint

Let's take a look at SPRINT's Web site at www.sprint.com. Locate the section of Sprint's site that contains the annual report information (it might be easier to use its search feature), and answer the following questions.

1. What was Sprint's effective income tax rate for the most recent year?
2. Did the company's deferred tax asset and liability accounts increase or decrease for the year? (Hint: Go to the link for SEC filings to look at the company's 10-K to find the notes to the financial statements.)
3. Is the company using a valuation allowance account associated with its deferred tax assets? If so, search the notes to determine why a valuation allowance account is being used.

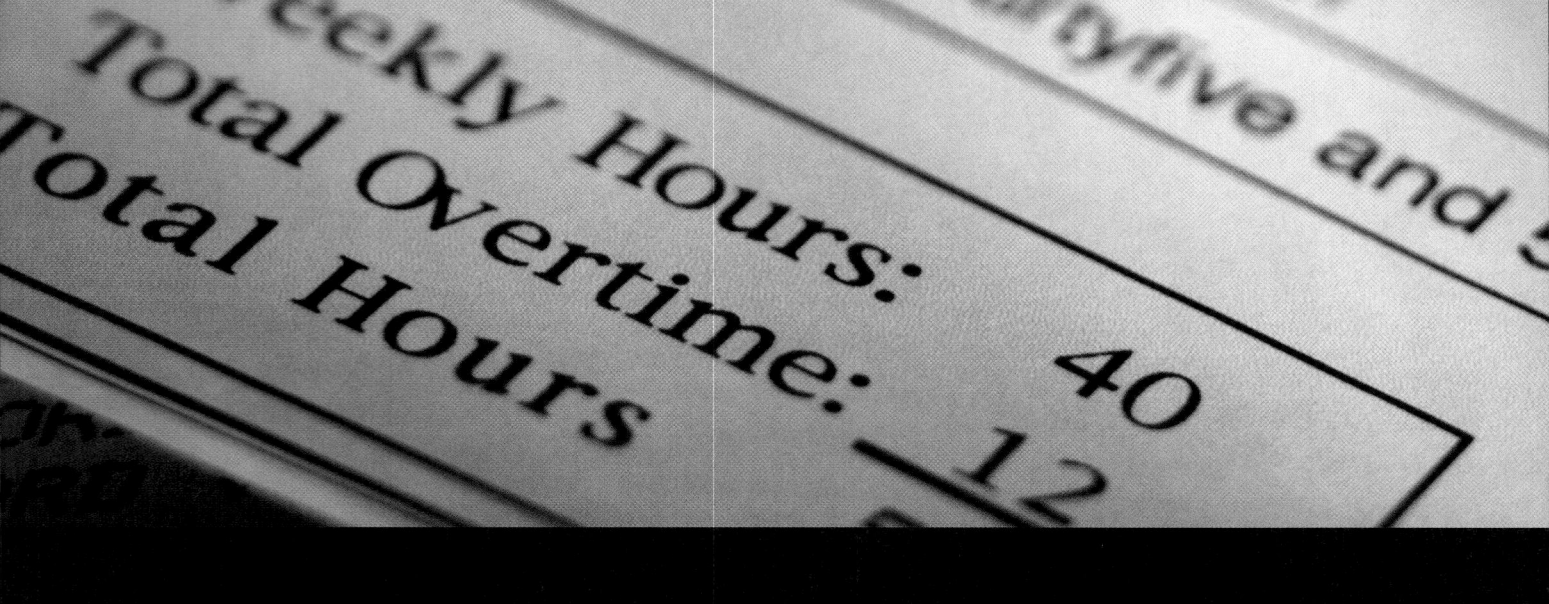

chapter 17

Employee Compensation—Payroll, Pensions, and Other Compensation Issues

Press reports in the United States often talk about the rising "national debt." As of September 30, 1998, borrowing from the public by the U.S. Treasury totaled $3.718 trillion. This obligation is the most publicized liability of the U.S. government, but it is not the only large one. As of the same date, the present value of the government liability under military and civilian pension plans and for veterans' benefits was $2.685 trillion.[1] These liabilities are certainly large (a trillion dollar bills laid end to end would stretch from the earth to the moon and back 197 times), but all other government liabilities are dwarfed by the social security pension obligation. Of course, in one sense it is not correct to view social security as a pension plan; it is a social insurance arrangement in which current workers pay for the benefits of past workers in the hopes that they (the current workers) will be supported by the contributions of future workers. With that qualification, it is still interesting to evaluate the status of social security as if it were a pension plan. As of September 30, 1998, the U.S. Treasury estimated that the present value of future benefits to existing workers exceeded the present value of expected future contributions from those workers and their employers by $3.802 trillion.

A widely recognized phenomenon of the 20th century has been the increasing life expectancy of people in almost all countries of the world. For example, in 1900 the average life expectancy of people in the United States was 49 years; by 1998 it had increased to 76.1 years.[2] As people live longer, they must deal with the problem of financing their extended retirement years. The magnitude of the problem in the United States will increase in the next 15 to 20 years as the "baby boomer" population of the 1940s and 1950s moves into retirement. It is estimated that the proportion of the U.S. population that is over 65 will increase from the current 13% to 20% by the year 2030.

1 *Financial Report of the United States Government—1998* (Department of the Treasury).
2 *Statistical Abstract of the United States—1998*, 118th Edition (U.S. Department of Commerce).

1

Account for payroll and payroll taxes, and understand the criteria for recognizing a liability associated with compensated absences.

2

Compute performance bonuses, and recognize the issues associated with postemployment benefits.

3

Understand the nature and characteristics of employer pension plans, including a detailed discussion of defined benefit plans.

4

Use the components of prepaid/accrued pension costs and changes in the components to compute the periodic expense associated with pensions.

5

Prepare required disclosures associated with pensions, and understand the accounting treatment for pension settlements and curtailments.

6

Describe the few remaining differences between U.S. pension accounting standards and the provisions of IAS 19.

e|m

EXPANDED MATERIAL

7

Explain the differences in accounting for pensions and postretirement benefits other than pensions, and be able to account for postretirement benefits other than pensions.

But complex accounting issues associated with employee compensation do not begin when an employee retires. As introduced in Chapter 11, stock compensation has become an increasingly complex and controversial issue. In addition, companies must address issues associated with the computation of performance bonuses and liabilities associated with sick and vacation pay. Finally, the compensation issues associated with payroll, such as the differing employee and employer payroll taxes, introduce added complexity to the topic of employee compensation.

The event line displayed in Exhibit 17–1 outlines the various issues associated with employee compensation. Naturally, immediate compensation for services provided is the issue with which we all are most familiar. The next issue on the event line relates to accruing for sick days, vacation days, and other types of compensated absences. These events accrue in the current period and are often related to the amount of time an employee has been employed. Stock options and other types of performance bonuses, which often are accounted for at the end of an accounting period, constitute the next event. In some instances, employees may leave an employer prior to retirement yet still are entitled to certain benefits. These benefits are known as postemployment benefits and are different from the final event listed—pensions and other postretirement benefits.

EXHIBIT 17–1 | Employee Compensation Event Line

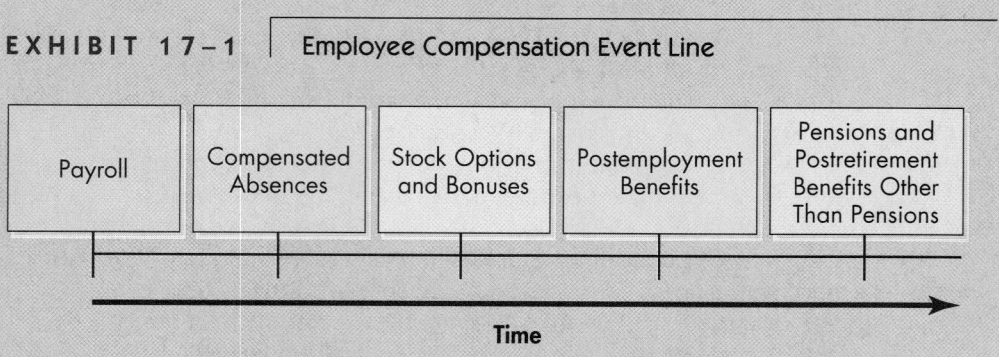

This chapter will proceed in the order of the employee compensation event line. We first focus on payroll, followed by issues related to compensated absences. Stock options and bonuses are then briefly discussed. Issues related to postemployment benefits are then reviewed, followed by a detailed discussion of pensions, including a discussion of the international standards for pension accounting. Postretirement benefits other than pensions are discussed in the expanded material section of this chapter.

ROUTINE EMPLOYEE COMPENSATION ISSUES

Account for payroll and payroll taxes, and understand the criteria for recognizing a liability associated with compensated absences.

In the area of employee compensation, the complexities associated with pensions have received a great deal of attention in recent years. But before we turn our attention to pensions, we will first discuss employee compensation issues associated with the current pay period. Along with accounting for current payroll issues, we will discuss issues associated with compensated absences, that is, sick pay, vacation pay, and so on.

Payroll and Payroll Taxes

In an ongoing entity, salaries and wages of officers and other employees accrue daily. Normally, no entry is made for these expenses until payment is made. A liability for unpaid salaries and wages is recorded, however, at the end of an accounting period when a more precise matching of revenues and expenses is desired. An estimate of the amount of unpaid wages and salaries is made, and an adjusting entry is prepared to recognize the amount due. Usually, the entire accrued amount is identified as salaries payable with no attempt to identify the withholdings associated with the accrual. When payment is made in the subsequent period, the amount is allocated between the employee and other entities such as government taxing units, unions, and insurance companies.

For example, assume that a company has 15 employees who are paid every two weeks. At December 31, four days of unpaid wages have accrued. Analysis reveals that the 15 employees earn a total of $1,000 a day. Thus the adjusting entry at December 31 would be:

Salaries and Wages Expense	4,000	
Salaries and Wages Payable		4,000

When payment is made, Salaries and Wages Payable will be debited for $4,000.

Social security and income tax legislation impose four taxes based on payrolls:

1. Federal old-age, survivors', disability, and hospital insurance (tax to both employer and employee).
2. Federal unemployment insurance (tax to employer only).
3. State unemployment insurance (tax to employer only).
4. Individual income tax (tax to employee only, but withheld and paid by employer).

FYI: Congress passed a law effective January 1991 wherein the medical hospital insurance portion of the FICA tax applies to a different wage base. The medical hospital insurance rate is 1.45% and is applied to all wages and self-employment income. Additional changes are expected due to pending health care reforms.

net work exercise

The Social Security Education Center (www.cas.muohio.edu/~security/) is a Web site devoted to the history and analysis of the social security system.

Net Work:
1. For every dollar paid in social security taxes, how is the dollar allocated?
2. Describe one of the potential social security reforms currently being considered. Do you support or oppose this reform? State your reasons.

FEDERAL OLD-AGE, SURVIVORS', DISABILITY, AND HOSPITAL INSURANCE The Federal Insurance Contributions Act (FICA), generally referred to as social security legislation, provides for FICA taxes from both employers and employees to provide funds for federal old-age, survivors', disability, and hospital insurance benefits for certain individuals and members of their families. At one time, only employees were covered by this legislation; however, coverage now includes most individuals who are self-employed.

Provisions of the legislation require an employer of one or more employees, with certain exceptions, to withhold FICA taxes from each employee's wages. The amount of the tax is based on a tax rate and wage base as currently specified in the law. The tax rate and wage base both have increased dramatically since the inception of the social security program in the 1930s. The initial rate of FICA tax was 1% in 1937; the rate in effect for 1999 was 7.65%.[3] During that same period, the annual wages subject to FICA tax increased from $3,000 to $76,200 (and for part of the tax, an unlimited amount). The taxable wage base is subject to yearly increases based on cost-of-living adjustments in social security benefits.

The employer remits the amount of FICA tax withheld for all employees, along with a matching amount, to the federal government. The employer is required to maintain complete records and submit detailed support for the tax remittance. The employer is responsible for the full amount of the tax even if employee contributions are not withheld.

FEDERAL UNEMPLOYMENT INSURANCE The Federal Social Security Act and the Federal Unemployment Tax Act (FUTA) provide for the establishment of unemployment insurance plans. Employers with insured workers employed in each of 20 weeks during a calendar year or who pay $1,500 or more in wages during any calendar quarter are affected.

Under present provisions of the law, the federal government taxes eligible employers on the first $7,000 paid to every employee during the calendar year. The rate of tax in effect since 1985 is 6.2%, but the employer is allowed a tax credit limited to 5.4% for taxes paid under state unemployment compensation laws. No tax is levied on the

---

3 For illustrative purposes and end-of-chapter exercises and problems, a rate of 7.65% will be used.

employee. When an employer is subject to a tax of 5.4% or more as a result of state unemployment legislation, the federal unemployment tax, then, is 0.8% of the qualifying wages.

Payment to the federal government is required quarterly. Unemployment benefits are paid by the individual states. Revenues collected by the federal government under the acts are used to meet the cost of administering state and federal unemployment plans as well as to provide supplemental unemployment benefits.

STATE UNEMPLOYMENT INSURANCE State unemployment compensation laws are not the same in all states. In most states, laws call for tax only on employers; but in a few states, taxes are applicable to both employers and employees. Each state law specifies the classes of exempt employees, the number of employees required or the amount of wages paid before the tax is applicable, and the contributions that are to be made by employers and employees. Exemptions are frequently similar to those under the federal act. Tax payment is generally required on or before the last day of the month following each calendar quarter.

Although the normal tax on employers may be 5.4%, states have merit rating or experience plans providing for lower rates based on employers' individual employment experiences. Employers with stable employment records are taxed at a rate in keeping with the limited amount of benefits required for their former employees; employers with less satisfactory employment records contribute at a rate more nearly approaching 5.4% in view of the greater amount of benefits paid to their former employees. Savings under state merit systems are allowed as credits in the calculation of the federal contribution, so the federal tax does not exceed 0.8% even though payment of less than 5.4% is made by an employer entitled to a lower rate under the merit rating system.

INCOME TAX Federal income taxes on the wages of individuals are collected in the period in which the wages are paid. The "pay as you go" plan requires employers to withhold income tax from wages paid to their employees. Most states and many local governments also impose income taxes on the earnings of employees that must be withheld and remitted by the employer. Withholding is required not only of employers engaged in a trade or business but also of religious and charitable organizations, educational institutions, social organizations, and governments of the United States, the states, the territories, and their agencies, instrumentalities, and political subdivisions. Certain classes of wage payments are exempt from withholding although these are still subject to income tax.

> **FYI:** Not all countries require employers to withhold income tax from employees. For example, in Hong Kong an employee is entirely responsible to accumulate sufficient funds to pay the 15% flat income tax due at the end of the year. Financial institutions are happy to arrange "tax loans" for those who forgot to set aside the money to pay their taxes.

An employer must meet withholding requirements under the law even if wages of only one employee are subject to such withholdings. The amounts to be withheld by the employer are developed from formulas provided by the law or from tax withholding tables made available by the government. Withholding is based on the length of the payroll period, the amount earned, and the number of withholding exemptions claimed by the employee. Taxes required under FICA (both employee and employer portions) and income tax that has been withheld by the employer are paid to the federal government at the same time. These combined taxes are deposited in an authorized bank quarterly, monthly, or several times each month depending on the amount of the liability. Quarterly and annual statements must also be filed providing a summary of all wages paid by the employer.

ACCOUNTING FOR PAYROLL TAXES To illustrate the accounting procedures for payroll taxes, assume that salaries for the month of January for a retail store with 15 employees are $16,000. The state unemployment compensation law provides for a tax on employers of 5.4%. Income tax withholdings for the month are $1,600. Assume FICA rates are 7.65% for employer and employee. Entries for the payroll and the employer's payroll taxes follow:

Salaries Expense	16,000	
FICA Taxes Payable		1,224
Employees Income Taxes Payable		1,600
Cash		13,176
To record payment of payroll and related employee withholdings.		
Payroll Tax Expense	2,216*	
FICA Taxes Payable		1,224
State Unemployment Taxes Payable		864
Federal Unemployment Taxes Payable		128
To record the payroll tax liability of the employer.		

*Computation:

Tax under FICA (7.65% × $16,000)	$ 1,224
Tax under state unemployment insurance legislation (5.4% × $16,000)	864
Tax under FUTA [0.8% (6.2% – credit of 5.4%) × $16,000]	128
Total payroll tax expense	$ 2,216

When tax payments are made to the proper agencies, the tax liability accounts are debited and Cash is credited.

    The employer's payroll taxes, as well as the taxes withheld from employees, are based on amounts paid to employees during the period regardless of the basis employed for reporting income. When financial reports are prepared on the accrual basis, the employer will have to recognize both accrued payroll and the employer's payroll taxes relating thereto by adjustments at the end of the accounting period.

    For example, assume that the salaries and wages accrued at December 31 were $9,500. Of this amount, $2,000 was subject to unemployment tax and $6,000 to FICA tax. Although the salaries and wages will not be paid until January of the following year, the concept of matching requires these costs to be allocated in the period in which they were incurred. This allocation is accomplished with an adjusting entry. The adjusting entry for the employer's payroll taxes would be as follows:

> **Caution!** Don't forget that in order to ensure the financial statements are properly stated, an adjusting entry is required at the end of an accounting period if salaries and wages are owed.

Payroll Tax Expense	583*	
FICA Taxes Payable		459
State Unemployment Taxes Payable		108
Federal Unemployment Taxes Payable		16
To accrue the payroll tax liability of the employer.		

*Computation:

Tax under FICA (7.65% × $6,000)	$459
Tax under state unemployment insurance legislation (5.4% × $2,000)	108
Tax under FUTA (0.8% × $2,000)	16
Total payroll tax expense	$583

    As was true with the adjusting entry for the salaries and wages discussed on page 975, the preceding entry may be reversed at the beginning of the new period, or the accrued liabilities may be debited when the payments are made to the taxing authorities.

    Agreements with employees may provide for payroll deductions and employer contributions for other items, such as group insurance plans, pension plans, savings bond purchases, or union dues. Such agreements call for accounting procedures similar to those described for payroll taxes.

Compensated Absences

Compensated absences include payments by employers for vacation, holiday, illness, or other personal activities. Employees often earn paid absences based on the time employed. Generally, the longer an employee works for a company, the longer the vacation allowed, or the more liberal the time allowed for illnesses. At the end of any given accounting period, a company has a liability for earned but unused compensated absences. The matching principle requires that the estimated amounts earned be charged against current revenue and a liability established for that amount.[4] The difficult part of this accounting treatment is estimating how much should be accrued. In Statement No. 43, the FASB requires a liability to be recognized for compensated absences that (1) have been earned through services already rendered, (2) vest or can be carried forward to subsequent years, and (3) are estimable and probable.

For example, assume that a company has a vacation pay policy for all employees. If all employees had the same anniversary date for computing time in service, the computations would not be too difficult. However, most plans provide for a flexible employee starting date. In order to compute the liability, a careful inventory of all employees must be made that includes the number of years of service, rate of pay, carryover of unused vacation from prior periods, turnover, and the probability of taking the vacation.

To illustrate the accounting for compensated absences, assume that S&N Corporation has 20 employees who are paid an average of $350 per week. During 2001, a total of 40 vacation weeks was earned by all employees, but only 30 weeks of vacation were taken that year. The remaining 10 weeks of vacation were taken in 2002 when the average rate of pay was $400 per week. The entry to record the accrued vacation pay on December 31, 2001, would be:

Wages Expense	3,500	
Vacation Wages Payable		3,500
To record accrued vacation wages ($350 × 10 weeks).		

The above entry assumes that Wages Expense has already been recorded for the 30 weeks of vacation taken during 2001. Therefore, the income statement would reflect the total wages expense for the entire 40 weeks of vacation earned during the period. On its December 31, 2001, balance sheet, S&N would report a current liability of $3,500 to reflect the obligation for the 10 weeks of vacation pay that are owed. In 2002, when the additional vacation weeks are taken and the payroll is paid, S&N would make the following entry:

Wages Expense	500	
Vacation Wages Payable	3,500	
Cash		4,000
To record payment at current rates of previously earned vacation time ($400 × 10 weeks).		

Because the vacation weeks are now used, the above entry eliminates the liability. An adjustment to Wages Expense is required because the liability was recorded at the rates of pay in effect during the time the compensation (vacation pay) was earned. However, the cash is being paid at the current rate, which requires an adjustment to Wages Expense. If the rate of pay for the 10 weeks of vacation taken in 2002 had remained the same as the rate used to record the accrual on December 31, 2001, there would not have been an adjustment to Wages Expense. The entry to record payment in 2002 would simply be a debit to the payable and a credit to Cash for $3,500.

An exception to the requirement for accrual of compensated absences, such as vacation pay, is made for sick pay. The FASB decided that sick pay should be accrued only if it *vests* with the employee, that is, the employee is entitled to compensation for a certain number of "sick days" regardless of whether the employee is actually absent for that period. Upon leaving the firm, the employee would be compensated for any unused sick time. If the sick pay does not vest, it is recorded as an expense only when actually paid.[5]

Although compensated absences are not deductible for income tax purposes until the vacation, holiday, or illness occurs and the payment is made, they are required by GAAP to be recognized as liabilities on the financial statements.

---

4 *Statement of Financial Accounting Standards No. 43*, "Accounting for Compensated Absences," Stamford, CT: Financial Accounting Standards Board, 1980, par. 6.

5 Ibid., par. 7.

2

Compute performance bonuses, and recognize the issues associated with postemployment benefits.

NONROUTINE EMPLOYEE COMPENSATION ISSUES

In addition to routine compensation issues that are addressed on a regular basis, there are several other compensation issues that arise, often at the end of the period. These issues, performance-based incentive plans either in the form of stock or bonus, are discussed in this section. We conclude this section with a discussion of the compensation issues that may arise following employment but prior to retirement.

Stock-Based Compensation and Bonuses

As discussed in Chapter 11, stock options are often a part of an employee's compensation package. While stock option compensation (particularly performance-based) is more common for upper management and directors, many companies have stock option plans available for all employees. The amount of compensation expense reported related to stock-based compensation is a function of the method under which the options are accounted—the intrinsic value method or the fair value method—and the type of option plan—fixed plans or performance-based plans. Recall that the intrinsic value method usually results in no compensation expense for option plans with a fixed exercise price. Both methods involve estimating the value of the option and accounting for the option value as compensation expense for the period over which the options are earned. The difference between the two methods is in how the option value is estimated. Refer back to Chapter 11 for a discussion of the details associated with stock-based compensation.

In addition to stock options, employees often earn bonuses based on a company's performance over a given period of time. This additional compensation should be recognized in the period in which it is earned. Bonuses are often based on some measure of the employer's income. For example, assume that Photo Graphics, Inc., gives its store managers a 10% bonus based on individual store earnings. The bonus is to be based on income after deduction for the bonus but before deduction for income taxes. Assume further that income for a particular store is $100,000 before charging any bonus or income taxes. The bonus would be calculated as follows:

$$B = .10 (\$100{,}000 - B)$$
$$B = \$10{,}000 - .10B$$
$$B + .10B = \$10{,}000$$
$$1.10B = \$10{,}000$$
$$B = \$9{,}091 \text{ (rounded)}$$

The bonus would be reported on the income statement as an operating expense, and the bonus payable would be shown as a current liability on the balance sheet, unless the bonus was paid immediately in cash. As an example of a bonus plan, EXXON disclosed in its 1997 proxy statement filed with the SEC that it has a management bonus plan targeted at 1,000 of its managers. The plan grants a certain number of award units to the managers; a manager is entitled to receive cash equal to Exxon's reported net earnings per share for each award unit held. For example, Exxon's CEO, Lee R. Raymond, received 325,000 of these award units in 1997. Exxon's earnings per share in 1997 was $3.41; therefore, these award units added $1,108,250 (325,000 units × $3.41) to Raymond's base salary of $1,750,000.

Postemployment Benefits

In a business world where downsizing has become commonplace, an employee cannot count on remaining with one employer for his or her entire career. In addition, employees are making job changes for such reasons as to facilitate career advancement and to enhance their family's quality of life. For these reasons and others, compensation issues following employment but preceding retirement have increased in magnitude. The FASB addressed the issue of postemployment benefits with the issuance of Statement No. 112,

"Employers' Accounting for Postemployment Benefits."[6] This statement amends Statement No. 43 relating to compensated absences that was discussed in a previous section. While Statement No. 43 requires the recognition of benefits that accrue to employees over time, such as sick and vacation pay, Statement No. 112 extends these recognition requirements to benefits that accrue to former or inactive employees after employment but before retirement. Examples of the types of benefits covered by Statement No. 112 include supplemental unemployment benefits, severance benefits, disability-related benefits, job training and counseling, and continuation of benefits such as health care benefits and life insurance coverage.[7]

 Compare the three criteria used in accounting for postemployment benefits with the FASB's definition of a liability. Does it appear that the definition of a liability as defined in the conceptual framework influenced Statement No. 43?

The same criteria used in accounting for compensated absences are applied to postemployment benefits. Those criteria were (1) the employer's obligation in the future relates to services already provided by the employee, (2) the employer's obligation relates to rights that vest, and (3) the payment of the liability is probable and the amount can be reasonably estimated.[8] If these criteria are met, then entries are made similar to those illustrated previously for compensated absences. To illustrate the magnitude of postemployment benefits, consider the disclosure provided by LEAR CORPORATION in the notes to its 1998 annual report, shown in Exhibit 17-2. (Lear is the largest maker of automobile interiors in the world and sells to FORD, GENERAL MOTORS, DAIMLERCHRYSLER, FIAT, VOLVO, SAAB, VOLKSWAGEN, and BMW.)

EXHIBIT 17-2 | Note Disclosure for Postemployment Benefits— Lear Corporation

---

Note 3

RESTRUCTURING AND OTHER CHARGES

In the fourth quarter of 1998, the Company began to implement a restructuring plan designed to lower its cost structure and improve the long-term competitive position of the Company. . . . The majority of the European countries in which the Company operates have statutory requirements with regards to the minimum severance payments that must be made to employees upon termination. The Company has accrued $37.7 million of severance costs for approximately 210 salaried and 1,040 hourly employees under SFAS No. 112, "Employers' Accounting for Postemployment Benefits," at December 31, 1998, as the Company anticipates this is the minimum aggregate severance payments that will be made in accordance with these statutory requirements.

3

Understand the nature and characteristics of employer pension plans, including a detailed discussion of defined benefit plans.

ACCOUNTING FOR PENSIONS

Financing retirement years is accomplished by establishing some type of **pension plan** that sets aside funds during an employee's working years so that at retirement the funds and earnings from investment of the funds may be returned to the employee in lieu of earned wages. In the United States, three major categories of pension plans have emerged:

1. Government plans, primarily social security
2. Individual plans, such as individual retirement accounts (IRAs)
3. Employer plans

6 *Statement of Financial Accounting Standards No. 112,* "Employers' Accounting for Postemployment Benefits," Stamford, CT: Financial Accounting Standards Board, 1992.
7 Ibid., par. 1.
8 Ibid., par. 6.

The third category, employer pension plans, involves several difficult and controversial accounting and reporting issues. In 1985, the FASB issued two new pension accounting standards, Statement No. 87, "Employers' Accounting for Pensions," and Statement No. 88, "Employers' Accounting for Settlements and Curtailments of Defined Benefit Pension Plans and for Termination Benefits." These standards, particularly Statement No. 87, significantly changed the way in which pension costs are determined and reported by employers.

A related issue to employer pension plans is the employer's accounting for **postretirement benefits other than pensions.** These benefits extend beyond the active years of employment and include such items as health care, life insurance, legal services, special discounts on items produced or sold by the employer, and tuition assistance. Historically, most companies recognized the costs of these benefits on a pay-as-you-go, or cash, basis. The FASB considered these postretirement benefits as a separate category and, in December 1990, issued FASB Statement No. 106, "Employers' Accounting for Postretirement Benefits Other Than Pensions." Generally, this standard requires companies to accrue the cost of postretirement benefits as deferred compensation and to disclose the nature of the company's future obligation for postretirement benefits.

Nature and Characteristics of Employer Pension Plans

The subject of employers' accounting for pensions is very complex, partly because of the many variations in plans that have been developed. Most pension plans are specifically designed for one employer and are known as **single-employer pension plans.** If several companies contribute to the same plan, it is called a multiemployer pension plan. This chapter, like the accounting standards, focuses on accounting for single-employer pension plans.

FUNDING OF EMPLOYER PENSION PLANS The basic purpose of all employer pension plans is the same—to provide retirement benefits to employees. A principal issue concerning pension plans is how to provide sufficient funds to meet the needs of retirees. The social security system of the federal government has frequently been criticized because it is not a "funded" plan. FICA taxes (contributions) paid by employers and employees in the current year are used to pay benefits to individuals who are currently retired. This means that the current employees must have faith that a future generation will do the same for them. Such a system creates much doubt and uncertainty.

Private plans are not permitted to operate in this way. Federal law, such as the Employee Retirement Income Security Act (ERISA) of 1974, requires companies to fund their pension plans in an orderly manner so that the employee is protected at retirement. Some pension plans are funded entirely by the employer and are referred to as **noncontributory pension plans.** In other cases, the employee also contributes to the cost of the pension plan, referred to as a **contributory pension plan.**[9] The amounts and timing of contributions depend on the particular circumstances and plan provisions. While the provisions of pension plans vary widely and in many cases are very complex, there are two basic classifications of pension plans: (1) defined contribution plans and (2) defined benefit plans.

DEFINED CONTRIBUTION PENSION PLANS **Defined contribution pension plans** are relatively simple in their construction and raise very few accounting issues for employers. Under these plans, a periodic contribution amount is paid by the employer into a separate trust fund, which is administered by an independent third-party trustee. The contribution may be defined as a fixed amount each period, a percentage of the

net work exercise

Northern Life Insurance Company offers a fun "Dream Retirement Game" at www.northernlifetsa.com/ calculate2.html. **Net Work:** Play the retirement game and see how you fare. How much money do you need to save per month to reach your dream retirement income?

---

9 Employee contributions are not considered in subsequent discussions and examples because the chapter is concerned with employers' accounting for pensions.

employer's income, a percentage of employee earnings, or a combination of these or other factors. As contributions to the fund are made, they are invested by the fund administrator. When an employee retires, the accumulated value in the fund is used to determine the pension payout to the employee. The employee's retirement income therefore depends on how the fund has been managed. If investments have been made wisely, the employee will fare better than if the investments were managed poorly. In effect, the investment risk is borne by the employee. The employer's obligation extends only to making the specified periodic contribution. This amount is charged to pension expense and no further accounting is required for the plan. As an example of this type of plan, many college professors belong to a defined contribution plan called TIAA/CREF. The college or university makes contributions on behalf of the professor who then must rely on the good judgment of the TIAA/CREF fund managers to ensure his or her retirement security. As of December 1998, TIAA/CREF was the largest private pension plan in the world with assets in excess of $146 billion.

> **FYI:** In a sense, all pension plans are funded completely by the employee. When considering an acceptable level of compensation, both the firm and the employee should consider total compensation—current salary, fringe benefits, and deferred compensation. A higher employer pension contribution presumably means lower current compensation.

DEFINED BENEFIT PENSION PLANS   **Defined benefit pension plans** are much more complex than defined contribution plans. Under defined benefit plans, the employee is guaranteed a specified retirement income often related to his or her number of years of employment and average salary over a certain number of years. The periodic amount of the employer's contribution is based on the expected future benefits to be paid to employees and is affected by a number of variables. Because the benefits are defined, the contributions (funding) must vary as conditions change. Exhibit 17–3 illustrates the basic nature of a defined benefit plan. A defined contribution plan could be illustrated in the same manner except that the contributions (rather than the benefits) would be defined. This difference, however, is significant and accounts for the complexity of defined benefit plans.

EXHIBIT 17–3 | Defined Benefit Pension Plans

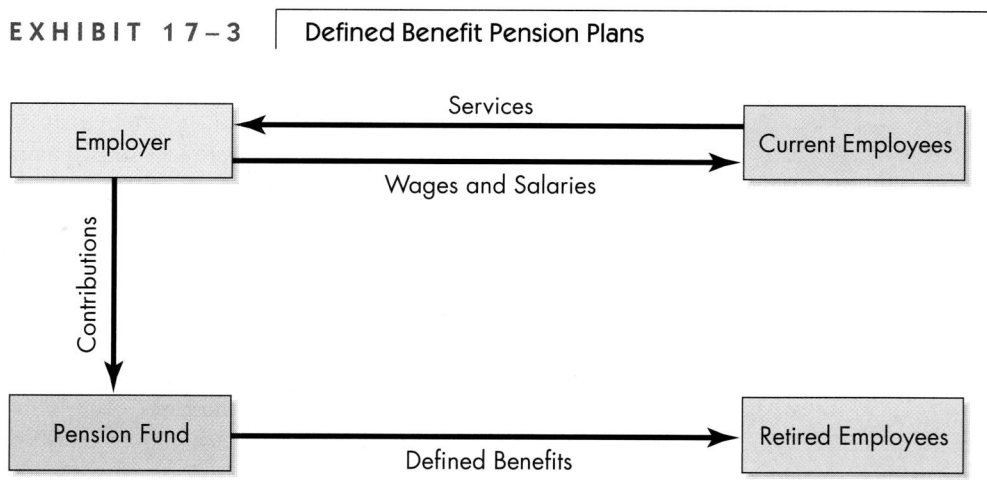

Under defined benefit plans, the investment risk is, in substance, borne by the employer. While a separate trust fund usually is maintained for contributions and investment earnings, the employer ultimately is responsible to ensure that employees receive the defined benefits provided by the plan. **Pension plan assets** may be viewed essentially as funds set aside to meet the employer's future pension obligation just as funds may be set aside for other purposes, for example, to retire bonds at maturity. One major difference, however, is that a future obligation to retire bonds is a definite amount, while the employer's future obligation for retirement benefits is based on many estimates and assumptions. In addition, U.S. federal law requires minimum pension plan funding, whereas sinking fund requirements are privately negotiated between the borrower and the bondholders.

Defined benefits Defined benefit pension plans provide for an increase in future retirement benefits as additional services are rendered by an employee. In effect, the employee's total compensation for a period consists of current wages or salaries plus deferred compensation represented by the right to receive a defined amount of future benefits. The amount of future benefits earned by employees for a particular period is determined by actuaries, not accountants. However, an understanding of the basic concepts used in measuring future retirement benefits is necessary for understanding the accounting issues relating to pensions.

The amount of future benefits earned for a period is based on the plan's benefit formula, which specifies how benefits are attributed (assigned) to years of employee service. Some plans attribute equal benefits to each year of service rendered, for example, a pension benefit of $20 per month for each year of employee service rendered. Thus an employee who retires after 30 years of service would be entitled to a monthly benefit of $600 ($20 per month × 30 years of service). The benefit attributed to each year of service would be $20 multiplied by the number of months of life expectancy after retirement. Some plans attribute different benefits to different years of service, for example, a pension benefit of $20 per month for each year of service up to 20 years and $25 per month for each additional year of service. Many plans include a benefit formula based on current or future employee earnings. For example, a plan might provide monthly benefits of 2% of an employee's average annual earnings for the five years preceding retirement.

The measurement of future benefits is highly subjective. The amount of benefits earned by employees for a period is based on many variables, including the average age of employees, length of service, expected turnover, vesting provisions, and life expectancy. Thus the actuaries must estimate how many of the current employees will retire and when they will retire, the number of employees who will leave the company prior to retirement, the life expectancy of employees after retirement, and other relevant factors.

> **FYI:** The issue of risk and who bears it is very important. With a defined benefit plan, the employee is not completely free of risk; receipt of the benefit payments might be in jeopardy if the employing firm goes bankrupt. To mitigate this risk, Congress created the PENSION BENEFIT GUARANTY CORPORATION (PBGC), a federally supported pension plan insurer. The PBGC collects insurance premiums from participating companies and is given a high-priority claim against company assets in case of bankruptcy.

As the uncertainty of other postretirement benefits increases, many companies are changing their plans from defined benefit to defined contribution. Why would employers do this?

Vesting of pension benefits A key element in all pension plans is the **vested benefits** provision. Vesting occurs when an employee has met certain specified requirements and is eligible to receive pension benefits at retirement regardless of whether the employee continues working for the employer. In early pension plans, vesting did not occur for many years. In extreme cases, vesting occurred only when an employee reached retirement. A major outcome of federal regulation is the much earlier vesting privileges for employees. Most pension plans provide for full vesting after 10 years of employment. Colleges and universities typically require professors to remain at the school for three to five years in order for pension contributions to vest. It is not uncommon for a professor to forfeit nonvested pension contributions when moving from one school to another.

Funding of defined benefit plans The periodic amounts to be contributed to a defined benefit plan by the employer are directly related to the future benefits expected to be paid to current employees. The methods of funding pension plans vary widely. Most defined benefit plans require periodic contributions that accumulate to the balance needed to pay the promised retirement benefits to employees. Some plans specify an even amount for each year of employee service. Others require a lower amount in the early years of employee service, with an accelerating schedule over the years. Still other plans provide for a higher amount at first, then a declining pattern of funding. The contribution amounts are determined by actuarial formulas and must be adjusted as estimates and assumptions are revised to reflect changing conditions.

All funding methods are based on present values. The additional future benefits earned by employees each year must be discounted to their present value, referred to as the **actuarial present value,** using an assumed rate of return on pension fund investments. In many cases, employers contribute an amount equal to the present value of future benefits attributed to current services. As noted above, however, funding patterns vary, and the amount contributed for a particular period may be less than or greater than the present value of the additional benefits earned for the period. Assume, for example, that the present value of future benefits earned in the current period is determined to be $30,000, using a discount rate of 10%. If the funding method requires a contribution of only $25,000 for the period, the employer has an unfunded obligation of $5,000. At the end of the following year, this obligation will have increased to $5,500 to reflect the interest cost of 10%. When contributions exceed the present value of the future benefits, lower contributions will be required in subsequent periods as a result of earnings on the "overfunded" amount.

The PENSION BENEFIT GUARANTY CORPORATION (PBGC) is charged with monitoring the funding status of defined benefit pension plans in the United States. The PBGC protects the retirement incomes of about one out of every three working Americans in more than 44,000 defined benefit pension plans. The PBGC provides federal insurance for participants in U.S. pension plans much as the FDIC provides insurance for bank depositors. The PBGC is not funded by general tax revenues but instead collects insurance premiums from employers, receives income on investments, and receives funds from pension plans that it takes over. In 1999, the PBGC was paying monthly retirement benefits to over 209,000 individuals.

Issues in Accounting for Defined Benefit Plans

Although the provisions of defined benefit pension plans can be extremely complex and the application of accounting standards to a specific plan can be highly technical, the accounting issues themselves are identified easily. Following is a list of these issues, all of which relate to accounting and reporting by employers.

1. The amount of net periodic pension expense to be recognized on the income statement.
2. The amount of pension liability to be reported on the balance sheet.
3. The amount of pension fund assets to be reported on the balance sheet.
4. Accounting for pension settlements, curtailments, and terminations.
5. Disclosures needed to supplement the amounts reported in the financial statements.

The issue of funding pension plans is purposely omitted from the list. Funding decisions are affected by tax laws, governmental regulations, actuarial computations, and contractual terms, not by accounting standards. They should not directly affect the amount that is reported as **net periodic pension expense** under the accrual concept.

The next section of the chapter illustrates the basic computational and accounting issues related to pensions in the context of a simple illustration. The simple example is then followed by a more complex illustration that introduces the intricacies for which pension accounting is famous.

Simple Illustration of Pension Accounting

Thakkar Company has established a defined benefit pension plan. As of January 1, 2002, only one employee, Lorien Bach, is enrolled in the plan. Some characteristics of the plan and of Bach as of January 1, 2002, are outlined as follows:

● Bach is 35 years old and has worked for Thakkar for 10 years.
● Bach's salary for 2001 was $40,000.
● Thakkar's pension plan pays a benefit based on an employee's highest salary. Pension payments begin after an employee turns 65, and payments are made at the

end of the year. The annual payment is equal to 2% of the highest salary times number of years with the company.

- Bach is an unusually predictable person; it is known with certainty that she will not quit, be fired, or die before age 65. Also, it is known with certainty that she will live exactly 75 years and will therefore collect 10 annual pension payments after she retires. Bach's benefits have already fully vested.
- In valuing pension fund liabilities, Thakkar uses a discount rate of 10%.
- As of January 1, 2002, Thakkar Company has a pension fund containing $10,000. During 2002, Thakkar made additional contributions to the fund totaling $1,500. Also, the fund earned a return of $350 during the year. Over the long run, Thakkar expects to earn an average return of 12% on pension fund assets.

ESTIMATION OF PENSION LIABILITY The first step in estimating Thakkar Company's pension liability is to compute the amount of the annual pension payment to be made to Bach when she retires. The amount of the payment depends on Bach's years of service and highest salary. As of January 1, 2002, Bach has put in 10 years of service and, assuming that her most recent salary of $40,000 is her highest salary to date, the forecasted amount of her annual pension payment can be computed as follows:

$$(2\% \times 10 \text{ years}) \times \$40,000 = \$8,000$$

It is known that Bach will live long enough after retirement at age 65 to collect 10 annual pension payments; thus, the total amount of pension benefits that Thakkar expects to pay to Bach is $80,000 (10 years × $8,000). However, $80,000 is an overstatement of the value of Thakkar's pension liability because the payments won't begin for another 30 years. To properly compute the present value of the payments to Bach, allowance must be made for the fact that the first payment won't be made until Bach is 66 years old (recall that pension payments are made at the end of the year), the payments are spread over 10 years, and Thakkar Company's discount rate is 10%. This discount rate can be thought of as the implicit rate of interest Thakkar would have to pay to a financial institution (such as an insurance company) to purchase annuity contracts settling the pension obligation to Bach.[10] In the appendix to this chapter, it is shown that, using the 10% discount rate, the present value of the expected pension payments to Bach is equal to $2,817.

> **FYI:** Over the past 10 years, *Job Rated Almanac* has rated being an actuary as one of the top jobs in America based on income, outlook, physical demands, stress, and security. How much do actuaries make? Starting salaries are around $40,000 with top salaries exceeding $130,000. What skills are needed to be a successful actuary? You need training in math, computers, communication, and business.

The $2,817 amount can be thought of as follows: If Thakkar Company deposited $2,817 on January 1, 2002, in a bank account yielding 10%, by the end of 30 years when Bach retires, that $2,817 will have accumulated to an amount large enough to support payments to Bach of $8,000 per year for the succeeding 10 years. The $2,817 is the actuarial present value of Thakkar's pension liability. An actuarial present value takes into account both time value of money considerations and actuarial assumptions (i.e., how long until Bach retires, how long Bach will live after retirement). In practice, such calculations are performed by professionals called actuaries. Financial accountants do not need to know how to perform the detailed actuarial present value calculations, but they should understand the general concepts underlying the calculations.

The $2,817 pension liability computed above is called the **accumulated benefit obligation (ABO).** The ABO is the actuarial present value of the expected future pension payments, using the current salary as the basis for forecasting the amount of the pension benefit payments. The ABO approach ignores the impact of expected future salary increases on the amount of the benefit payments. An alternative measure of the pension

---

10 *Statement of Financial Accounting Standards No. 87*, "Employers' Accounting for Pensions," Stamford, CT: Financial Accounting Standards Board, 1985, par. 44. The SEC has suggested that the appropriate discount rate is the return on highly rated fixed income debt securities. See EITF Topic D-36, Sept. 23, 1993.

liability that does consider the impact of future salary increases is called the **projected benefit obligation (PBO).**

To illustrate the difference between the PBO and the ABO, assume that Thakkar Company expects Bach's 2001 salary of $40,000 to increase 5% every year until retirement. As a result, Bach's salary is expected to increase to $172,876 by the year 2032, Bach's last year of employment.[11] The pension benefit payment based on this salary would be:

$$(2\% \times 10 \text{ years}) \times \$172,876 = \$34,575 \text{ (rounded)}$$

The PBO at January 1, 2002, is $12,176 (see the appendix to this chapter for details of the computation). This is the present value of the 10 future annual payments of $34,575 that Bach is expected to receive. The diagram in Exhibit 17–4 illustrates the relationship between the future payments and the PBO.

EXHIBIT 17–4 | Thakkar Company—Projected Benefit Obligation, January 1, 2002

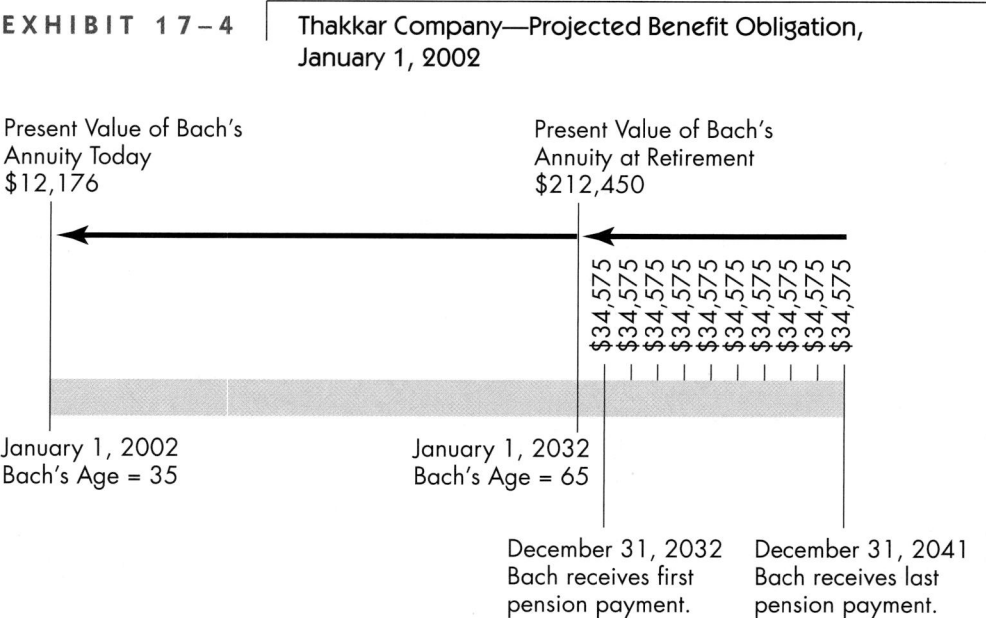

Both the PBO and the ABO computations are based on the amount of pension benefits that have already been earned—in this case, on the 10 years of service Bach has provided to Thakkar. The difference between the PBO and the ABO comes in the estimate of Bach's highest salary. The ABO computations ignore likely future salary increases; the PBO computations include estimates of those increases. The quantitative difference between these two approaches can be substantial. For Thakkar, the $2,817 ABO is substantially lower than the $12,176 value computed for the PBO.

The numerical relationship between the ABO and the PBO is often presented as follows:

Accumulated benefit obligation, Jan. 1, 2002	$ 2,817
Additional amounts related to projected pay increases	9,359
Projected benefit obligation, Jan. 1, 2002	$12,176

11 FV = P(FV $\overline{n|}$ i)
   = $40,000(Table I $\overline{30|}$ 5%)
   = $40,000(4.3219)
   = $172,876

So which is a better measure of a firm's pension obligation, the PBO or the ABO? FASB Statement No. 87 identifies the PBO as the measure appropriate for use in most calculations. The ABO is also disclosed and sometimes enters into the calculation of the reported pension liability (in a way that is explained later in the chapter). This choice of the PBO as the primary measure of a firm's pension obligation was not without some controversy.[12] It was argued that use of the PBO is not appropriate because it embodies future salary increases and the historical cost accounting model does not include recognition of future events. This argument was countered with the observation that use of a discount rate also results in recognition of future events because the discount rate includes a premium for expected future inflation. It was argued that to allow recognition of the impact of expected future inflation but not to allow consideration of expected salary increases would result in a gross understatement of the pension obligation in some cases. Hence, the PBO is the primary measure of a firm's pension obligation.

As of January 1, 2002, the pension obligation for Thakkar, as measured by the PBO, is $12,176, and from the information given at the beginning of the illustration, the total fair value of the pension plan assets is $10,000. One possible way to present this information on a balance sheet is to list the pension plan assets among the noncurrent assets and the pension liability as a noncurrent liability. However, FASB Statement No. 87 stipulates that these two items be offset against one another and a single net amount be shown as either a net pension asset or a net pension liability.[13] Thakkar would calculate the appropriate balance sheet amount in the following way:

ABO, Jan. 1, 2002	$ 2,817
Additional amounts related to projected pay increases	9,359
PBO, Jan. 1, 2002	$12,176
Plan assets at fair value, Jan. 1, 2002	10,000
Accrued pension liability, Jan. 1, 2002	$ 2,176

If the fair value of plan assets had exceeded the projected benefit obligation, the resulting net asset would have been labeled "Prepaid pension cost."

Why does Statement No. 87 require offsetting of pension liabilities and assets instead of separate recognition of each? The answer is, in one word, tradition. Accepted practice before Statement No. 87 was to offset pension liabilities and assets, and to avoid too great a change, the FASB decided to maintain that method. Statement No. 87 is viewed as an improvement over prior standards but not too different from those standards, in order to preserve the "gradual, evolutionary" nature of accounting standard setting.[14] The separate components of accrued pension liability and prepaid pension cost are disclosed in the notes to the financial statements in a manner similar to the table shown previously.

COMPUTATION OF PENSION EXPENSE FOR 2002   In the simple Thakkar Company example, measurement of pension expense[15] for the year involves consideration of three factors:

1. Implied interest on the beginning-of-the-period pension obligation (which increases the PBO).
2. New pension benefits earned by employees through service during the year (which increase the PBO).

---

12   Adoption of FASB Statement No. 87 was opposed by three of the seven members of the Board. A description of the dissenting views is included at the end of the primary text of the Statement (following paragraph 77).

13   *Statement of Financial Accounting Standards No. 87,* par. 35. In a more complicated example, other items would also be included in the computation of the net pension asset or liability. These items are discussed later in the chapter.

14   Ibid., par. 107.

15   To avoid confusion, the text discussion refers to pension expense instead of pension cost. Periodic pension cost may be expensed immediately or it may be capitalized as part of an asset such as inventory. In all of our examples, we will assume that pension costs are expensed immediately.

3. Investment return on the pension plan assets (which increases the fair value of plan assets).

These three factors will be considered in turn.

Interest cost The projected benefit obligation on January 1, 2002, is $12,176. This represents an amount owed by Thakkar to its employee, Bach. The 10% discount rate used in the computation of the PBO is called the **settlement interest rate** and can be viewed as the implied interest rate on this debt. In a sense, employees have agreed to loan the company money (by deferring the receipt of some of their compensation) to be repaid when they retire. As is the case with all loans, there is a charge for interest for the time period for which the money is loaned. Accordingly, one aspect of annual pension expense is the increase in the PBO resulting from implicit interest on this pension obligation, computed as follows:

PBO, beginning of period	×	Discount rate	=	Interest cost
$12,176	×	.10	=	$1,218 (rounded)

Service cost Bach's work for Thakkar Company during the year results in an increase in the forecasted annual pension benefit payments from Thakkar to Bach because those payments are now computed based on 11 years of service instead of 10 years. The impact of this extra year of service is to increase the December 31, 2002, projected benefit obligation by $1,339 over what it would have been if Bach had just vacationed for the entire year. (See the end-of-chapter appendix for the computations.) Therefore, the **service cost** element of pension expense for the year is $1,339. In practice, of course, service cost computations are very complex and are done by actuaries.

Return on pension plan assets Pension expense is reduced by the return on pension plan assets for the year. Just as liabilities and assets are offset to arrive at a net measure of accrued pension liability or prepaid pension cost, the return on pension plan assets is offset against interest and service costs to compute a single net pension expense number. Statement No. 87 indicates that instead of using the actual return, the expected long-term return should be used—more about why this number is used will be discussed shortly. This return is typically computed by multiplying the fair value of pension plan assets as of the beginning of the year by some estimate of the average rate of return the pension fund is expected to earn over the long run. For Thakkar Company, this long-term expected rate of return has been estimated to be 12%, and for this introductory example, we will assume that expected return and actual return are equal. Accordingly, for 2002, Thakkar's net pension expense is reduced by $1,200 ($10,000 × .12).

In addition to these changes in the PBO and the fair value of plan assets, two additional events are common when dealing with pension plans—contributions to the plan and benefits paid from the plan. Contributions increase the amount of assets in the pension fund; in this example, contributions of $1,500 were made during the year. Benefits paid from the plan have two effects—they reduce the amount of plan assets, and they also reduce the PBO. The reason the PBO is reduced is that if the benefits have been paid, they are no longer projected to be paid. In this simplified example, no benefits were paid during the year.

To review, the PBO is a present value measure of the future benefits expected to be paid to employees based on their employment to date but taking into consideration, if applicable, expected increases in wages that would affect their retirement benefits. The measurement is based on actuarial estimation of such factors as life expectancy, employee turnover, and interest rates. The projected benefit obligation increases each year as additional benefits are earned by employees through another year of service (service cost) and by the passage of time that brings employees one year closer to receiving their benefits (interest cost). The PBO decreases each year by the pension payments to retired employees. In addition, the obligation may increase or decrease by changes in any of the actuarial assumptions enumerated previously. These changes can be summarized as follows:

| Projected benefit obligation, beginning of year | + | Service cost and interest cost | − | Retirement benefits paid | ± | Change in actuarial assumptions | = | Projected benefit obligation, end of year |

The **fair value of pension plan assets** is based on the market value of pension plan assets at a given measurement date. The fair value of pension plan assets increases each year by employer contributions to the fund and decreases by the retirement benefits paid. The fair value also changes by the amount of earnings on the pension plan assets, including changes in the market value of the assets. These changes can be summarized as follows:

| Fair value of pension plan assets, beginning of year | + | Employer contributions | − | Retirement benefits paid | ± | Actual return on pension plan assets | = | Fair value of pension plan assets, end of year |

Exhibit 17–5 illustrates how service costs, interest costs, and return on assets change the PBO and the fair value of plan assets (FVPA) and how those changes are combined to be reflected on the income statement.

EXHIBIT 17–5 | Analysis of Pension Components

Pension Components	FVPA		PBO		Balance Sheet: Accrued Pension Cost	Income Statement: Pension Expense
Jan. 1 balance	$10,000	+	$(12,176)	=	$(2,176)	
Service costs			(1,339)			
Interest costs			(1,218)			$1,357
Expected return	1,200					
Contributions	1,500					
Benefits paid	0		0			
Dec. 31 balance	$12,700	+	$(14,733)	=	$(2,033)	

Net pension expense for 2002 for Thakkar is computed as follows:

Interest cost	$1,218
Service cost	1,339
Less: Expected return on plan assets	(1,200)
Net pension expense	$1,357

Note that benefits paid have no effect on the net pension liability as they reduce the FVPA and the PBO by the same amount. Also note that the amount of contributions to the pension fund is not reflected on the income statement. That amount would be disclosed as a cash outflow on the statement of cash flows.

The Thakkar Company illustration contains only the most basic elements of accounting for pensions. In more complex cases, pension expense is affected by amortization of deferred gains and losses from prior periods, amortization of the impact of a change in the terms of the pension plan, and amortization of the impact of changes in the actuarial assumptions. The accounting for these components of pension expense is illustrated in a subsequent example.

COMPUTATION OF ACCRUED PENSION LIABILITY   As of December 31, 2002, the PBO for Thakkar is $14,733 (see the appendix) and the total FVPA is $12,700 ($10,000 + $1,200 return + $1,500 new contributions). As illustrated previously, the PBO and the FVPA are offset to arrive at a single balance sheet amount. As of December 31, 2002, Thakkar Company would perform the following calculation:

ABO, Dec. 31, 2002	$ 3,578*
Additional amounts related to projected pay increases	11,155
PBO, Dec. 31, 2002	$14,733
Plan assets at fair value, Dec. 31, 2002	(12,700)
Accrued pension liability, Dec. 31, 2002	$ 2,033

*Based on the 2002 salary, which is assumed to be $42,000, representing a 5% increase over 2001.

The net accrued pension liability of $2,033 would be shown in the noncurrent liability section of Thakkar's balance sheet. The table above would be included in the notes to the financial statements.

BASIC PENSION JOURNAL ENTRIES   The basic accounting entries for pensions are straightforward. An entry is made to accrue the pension expense, and another entry is made to record the contribution to the pension fund. For convenience, a single account, the **prepaid/accrued pension cost** account, is used to reflect changes in the net pension asset or liability. Because Thakkar started the year with a credit balance of $2,176 in this account, it can be viewed as a liability account in this example. Thakkar Company would make the following journal entries for 2002:

Pension Expense	1,357	
Prepaid/Accrued Pension Cost		1,357
To record 2002 pension expense.		
Prepaid/Accrued Pension Cost	1,500	
Cash		1,500
To record 2002 contribution to pension plan.		

As a result of these entries, pension expense of $1,357 would be reported as an expense on the income statement. The combined effect of the two entries is to decrease Prepaid/Accrued Pension Cost liability by $143 ($1,500 – $1,357); the balance in Prepaid/Accrued Pension Cost is $2,033 ($2,176 beginning balance – $143 decrease).

KEY POINTS FROM THE THAKKAR COMPANY EXAMPLE   Before considering a more complicated example, take a moment now to review some important points illustrated with the Thakkar Company example.

- The actuarial computations are complicated, even in the simplest possible example. For proof, see the appendix at the end of the chapter. The good news is that in real life these computations are done by actuaries.
- The balance sheet and income statement amounts related to pensions are sensitive to the actuarial assumptions made. This is illustrated in the appendix.

- The balance sheet amount is a conglomeration of several items: the projected benefit obligation, the fair value of pension plan assets, and deferred items. The details of the computation are disclosed in the notes to the financial statements.
- Net pension expense is also a conglomeration of several items. The three main items are interest cost, service cost, and expected return on plan assets.

In the next section, the discussion of pension accounting continues with a more complex example. That example provides more detailed coverage of the treatment of deferred items and also introduces the minimum liability provisions that result in the messiest aspects of pension accounting. A work sheet approach is introduced that greatly simplifies the handling of complex pension situations.

COMPREHENSIVE PENSION ILLUSTRATION

4

Use the components of the prepaid/accrued pension costs and changes in the components to compute the periodic expense associated with pensions.

The Thakkar Company example included only three factors in the computation of pension expense. In a more general case, a company could recognize as many as six different components of net periodic pension expense. The six components are:

1. Service cost
2. Interest cost
3. Actual return on pension plan assets (if any)
4. Amortization of unrecognized prior service cost (if any)
5. Deferral of current period gain or loss and amortization of unrecognized net gain or loss
6. Effects (if any) of transition to Statement No. 87

The PBO and the FVPA are used extensively in computing pension cost. Because FASB Statement No. 87 permits the asset (FVPA) and the liability (PBO) to be offset against each other, they are not recorded in the employer's formal accounting system nor reported on the employer's balance sheet. However, informal memorandum records of these and other deferred pension balances must be maintained in order to compute pension cost. These memorandum records include accounts for the following five items:

1. PBO
2. FVPA
3. Deferred pension gains and losses
4. Unrecognized prior service cost
5. Unamortized transition gains or losses

Any reasonable recordkeeping method can be used to maintain these accounts. This chapter illustrates a pension work sheet that displays all accounts related to pensions, both formal and informal, in a side-by-side format.[16] An overview of that work sheet is provided in Exhibit 17–6.

Throughout the discussion of the components of pension expense, an illustration for a hypothetical company, Thornton Electronics, Inc., will be used.

Thornton Electronics—2002

Thornton's pension-related balances as of January 1, 2002, are as follows:

PBO	$1,500,000
FVPA	1,385,000
Unrecognized prior service cost	145,000
Unamortized transition gain	70,000
Accrued pension liability	40,000

---

16   This work sheet approach is based on an article by Paul B. W. Miller. See "The New Pension Accounting (part 2)," *Journal of Accountancy*, February 1987, pp. 84–94.

EXHIBIT 17–6 | Overview of Work Sheet Format

Dec. 1 Balance Sheet	PBO (–)	Fair Value of Plan Assets (+)	Deferred Gain/Loss (+/–)	Unamortized Transition Gain/Loss (+/–)	Unrecognized Prior Service Cost (+)
Income Statement	– Service Cost	+ Actual Return on Assets	+/– Difference Between Actual and Expected Return	+/– Amortization of Transition Gain/Loss	– Amortization of Prior Service Cost
	– Interest Cost		+/– Amortization of Gain/Loss		
	+ Benefits Paid	– Benefits Paid			
Statement of Cash Flows		+ Contributions			
Dec. 31 Balance Sheet	PBO (–)	Plan Assets (+)	Deferred Gain/Loss (+/–)	Unamortized Transition Gain/Loss (+/–)	Unrecognized Prior Service Costs (+)

Note: All signs are relative to the balance sheet. Positive amounts are debits; negative amounts are credits.

The PBO, the FVPA, and the net accrued pension liability have been explained previously. The two new items, unrecognized prior service cost and unamortized transition gain, are described below.

UNRECOGNIZED PRIOR SERVICE COST When a pension plan is initially adopted or amended to provide increased benefits, employees are granted additional benefits for services performed in years prior to the plan's adoption or amendment. The cost of these additional benefits to the employer is called **prior service cost.** The amount of prior service cost is determined by actuaries and represents the increase in the PBO arising from the adoption or amendment of the plan. Although prior service cost arises from services rendered in prior periods, there has been general agreement in the accounting profession that the cost should not be recognized at the plan's adoption or amendment date but rather should be amortized over future periods. This is based on the assumption that the employer will receive future economic benefits accruing from the plan's adoption or amendment in the form of improved employee morale, loyalty, and productivity.

STOP & THINK What is the relationship among unrecognized prior service cost, unamortized transition gains and losses, and the measurement of the PBO?

UNAMORTIZED TRANSITION GAIN OR LOSS The **transition gain or loss** is defined as the difference between the PBO and the FVPA at the time FASB Statement No. 87 was adopted by a company. For most companies, this occurred in their 1987 fiscal year. If the PBO was the larger of these two values at the transition date, the difference was a loss. If the FVPA was the larger value, the difference was a gain. The resulting transition gain or loss is not recorded on the books but is entered as a memorandum entry and is recognized by amortization over future periods. Transition gains and losses arise strictly from companies switching from an old accounting standard to FASB Statement No. 87. Because all companies have now made this switch, no new transition gains or losses are being created. However, amortization of existing transition items will still be part of many companies' pension expense until the year 2003.

The January 1, 2002, pension information for Thornton Electronics would appear in the pension work sheet as shown in Exhibit 17–7.

EXHIBIT 17–7 | Thornton Electronics, Inc.—Pension Work Sheet, January 1, 2002

	Formal Accounts			Memorandum Accounts				
	Net Pension Expense	Cash	Prepaid/ Accrued Pension Cost	Periodic Pension Expense Items	PBO	FVPA	Unamortized Transition Gain/Loss	Unrecognized Prior Service Costs
Balance, January 1, 2002			$(40,000)		$(1,500,000)	$1,385,000	$(70,000)	$145,000

Note: Positive amounts are debits; negative amounts are credits.   Components of Prepaid/Accrued Pension Cost

The work sheet is divided into two sections: the formal account section where the net effect of pension-related items on the balance sheet and income statement is shown, and the memorandum account section where detailed pension information, to be disclosed in the notes to the financial statements, is listed. The formal balance sheet account, Prepaid/Accrued Pension Cost, summarizes in one number all the asset and liability information contained in the memo records. When preparing a pension work sheet, make sure to confirm that the net balance in the formal prepaid/accrued pension cost account ($40,000 credit) is equal to the sum of the balances in the memo records ($1,500,000 credit – $1,385,000 debit + $70,000 credit – $145,000 debit). Note that if the transition item had been a deferred loss instead of a deferred gain, its balance would have been a debit instead of a credit. In the work sheet, a credit balance is indicated by parentheses.

Information summarizing the 2002 pension activity of Thornton Electronics is listed below:

Service cost as reported by actuaries	$ 75,000
Contributions to pension plan	115,000
Benefits paid to retirees	125,000
Fair value of pension plan assets at December 31, 2002	1,513,500
Settlement interest rate	11.0%
Long-term expected rate of return on pension plan assets	10.0%

The 2002 pension information has been entered in the pension work sheet shown in Exhibit 17–8. Each entry is explained below.

SERVICE COST   Recall that service cost is the present value of additional benefits earned by employees during the period. As explained earlier, service cost for the period is determined by actuaries based on the pension plan's benefit formula. Thornton Electronics' actuaries reported 2002 service cost of $75,000. This $75,000 is recorded in work sheet entry (a) as an increase in net periodic pension expense (a debit) and an increase to the PBO (a credit). This entry does not directly impact the formal accounting records. The indirect impact will be reflected in a year-end summary journal entry in the formal accounting records.

INTEREST COST   The interest cost represents the fact that the present value of Thornton's pension obligation is increased by the interest on the beginning PBO. The settlement interest rate is used to discount the PBO and is also used to compute the interest cost. The interest cost for 2002 is $1,500,000 × 11.0%, or $165,000. The interest cost is shown in entry (b) as a debit to net periodic pension expense and a credit to the PBO.

FYI: Many different interest rates are used throughout the accounting standards. The settlement rate can vary over time; thus, the computation of the benefit obligation may vary from one year to another as a result of the change in interest rates. An increase in the rate lowers the liability, while a decrease in the rate increases it. The FASB project of studying present values includes a study of the different rates currently in use.

EXHIBIT 17-8 | Thornton Electronics, Inc.—Pension Work Sheet for 2002

	Formal Accounts			Memorandum Accounts				
	Net Pension Expense	Cash	Prepaid/ Accrued Pension Cost	Periodic Pension Expense Items	PBO	FVPA	Unamor- tized Transition Gain/Loss	Unrecog- nized Prior Service Cost
Balance, January 1, 2002			$ (40,000)		$(1,500,000)	$1,385,000	$(70,000)	$145,000
(a) Service Cost				$ 75,000	(75,000)			
(b) Interest Cost				165,000	(165,000)			
(c) Actual Return on Assets				(138,500)		138,500		
(d) Benefits Paid					125,000	(125,000)		
(e) PSC Amortization				26,364				(26,364)
(f) Transition Amortization				(70,000)			70,000	
Summary Journal Entries								
(1) Annual Pension Expense Accrual	$57,864		(57,864)					
(2) Annual Pension Contribution		$(115,000)	115,000			115,000		
Balance, December 31, 1999			$ 17,136		$(1,615,000)	$1,513,500	$ 0	$118,636

Note: Positive amounts are debits; negative amounts are credits. Components of Prepaid/Accrued Pension Cost

ACTUAL RETURN ON PENSION PLAN ASSETS   The assets created by employer contributions to a pension plan usually earn a return that reduces the reported amount of annual pension expense. The return is composed of such elements as interest revenue, dividends, rentals, and changes in the market value of the assets. If a decline in the market value of the pension plan assets exceeds the earnings on the assets, the actual return will be a negative figure that would increase the pension expense rather than decrease it. The actual return can be computed by comparing the fair value of the pension plan assets at the beginning and end of the year. After adjusting for current-year contributions and benefits paid to retirees, any change is the **actual return on pension plan assets.** The actual return on pension plan assets for Thornton Electronics in 2002 is $138,500, computed as follows:

Fair value of pension plan assets December 31, 2002	$1,513,500
Fair value of pension plan assets January 1, 2002	1,385,000
Increase in fair value	$ 128,500
Add: Benefits paid	125,000
Deduct: Contributions made	(115,000)
Actual return on pension plan assets	$ 138,500

The actual return on pension plan assets is always computed in determining net periodic pension expense. However, as illustrated later, the actual return may be adjusted to the expected return when there is a difference between the two amounts. In this case, the actual return of $138,500 is equal to the expected return ($1,385,000 × .10).

The actual return of $138,500 is shown in entry (c) as a credit to net periodic pension expense (representing a decrease) and a debit to the fair value of pension assets (representing an increase). Note that benefits paid from fund assets do not reduce the formal account Cash—benefit payments are shown in entry (d) as a decrease in both plan assets and the remaining PBO. The entry to reduce cash because of contributions to the pension fund is shown later.

AMORTIZATION OF UNRECOGNIZED PRIOR SERVICE COST   Prior service cost (PSC) is the cost of benefits granted to employees for past service when a pension plan is adopted or amended. In some sense, prior service cost represents "pension goodwill" acquired by making the new or amended pension plan more attractive to existing employees. The accounting question is whether to expense prior service cost in the period of the plan's adoption or to amortize the cost over future periods.

FASB Statement No. 87 states that unrecognized prior service cost should be amortized by "assigning an equal amount to each future period of service of each employee active at the date of the amendment who is expected to receive benefits under the plan."[17] The future period of service is referred to as the **expected service period.** Because employees will have varying years of remaining service, this amortization method will result in a declining amortization charge.

When a company has many employees retiring or terminating in a systematic pattern, a method similar to the sum-of-the-years'-digits depreciation method can be used. The FASB included an illustration of how this computation would be made in Statement No. 87, Appendix B.[18] Assume that Thornton Electronics, Inc., has 150 employees who are expected to receive benefits for prior services under an amendment adopted at the end of 2001. Ten percent of the employees (15 employees) are expected to leave (either retire or quit with vesting privileges) in each of the next 10 years. Employees hired after the plan's amendment date do not affect the amortization. The formula for the sum-of-the-years'-digits depreciation method illustrated in Chapter 13 can be used with a slight modification to reflect the decreased number of employees each period. Thus, the total service years for Thornton Electronics, Inc., could be computed with the following formula:

$$\frac{N(N+1)}{2} \times D = \text{Total future years of service}$$

where
　　N = number of remaining years of service
　　D = decrease in number of employees working each year

Therefore

$$\frac{10(11)}{2} \times 15 = 825$$

The numerator would begin with the total employees at the time of the plan's amendment and decline by D each period. Under these assumptions, 825 service years will be rendered by the affected employees. The fraction used to determine the amortization has a numerator that declines by 15 employees each year and a denominator that is the sum of the service years, or 825. If the increase in the projected benefit obligation, or prior service cost, arising from the plan's amendment at the end of 2001 was $145,000, the amortization for 2002 would be 150/825 × $145,000, or $26,364. In the following two years, the amount amortized would be 135/825 × $145,000, or $23,727, and 120/825 × $145,000, or $21,091, respectively.

Although the FASB indicated a preference for this sum-of-the-years'-digits–type method of amortization, it also indicated that consistent use of an alternative amortization approach that more rapidly reduces the unrecognized prior service cost is acceptable.[19] As an example of such an alternative, a straight-line amortization of prior service cost over the average remaining service period of employees was presented in Statement No. 87, Appendix B.[20] To illustrate the straight-line approach using the Thornton

---

17　*Statement of Financial Accounting Standards No. 87*, par. 25.
18　Ibid., Appendix B, illustration 3.
19　Ibid., par. 26.
20　Ibid., Appendix B, illustration 3, Case 2.

Electronics example, the average remaining service life would be 5.5 years (825/150 employees), and $26,364 ($145,000/5.5) would be amortized for each full year.

A separate amortization schedule is necessary for each amendment of the plan. There is no need to alter the schedule for new employees, as they would not receive benefits from prior services. If the planned termination or retirement pattern does not occur, adjustments may be necessary later to completely amortize the prior service cost.

For the Thornton Electronics example, the amortization amount based on the number of service years remaining is used. For 2002, this amount is $26,364. In entry (e) of Exhibit 17–8, the $26,364 is shown as an increase in net periodic pension expense and a decrease in unrecognized prior service cost. This entry is analogous to the amortization of an intangible asset.

AMORTIZATION OF TRANSITION GAIN OR LOSS   The transition gain or loss created upon adoption of FASB Statement No. 87 is amortized on a straight-line basis over the average remaining service life of the participating employees as of the adoption date. Alternatively, if the average service life is less than 15 years, the employer is permitted to use a 15-year amortization period. Amortization of transition losses increases net periodic pension expense, while amortization of transition gains decreases net periodic pension expense.

Thornton Electronics made its transition to FASB Statement No. 87 on January 1, 1988[21] and its transition gain on that date was $1,050,000. Thornton elected to amortize this gain over 15 years, or $70,000 per year. Thus, the unamortized transition gain at January 1, 2002, is $70,000 [$1,050,000 − (14 × $70,000)]. Amortization for the year is recorded in work sheet entry (f) in Exhibit 17–8.

SUMMARY JOURNAL ENTRIES   The Thornton work sheet entries discussed to this point have impacted only the memorandum accounts. The net effect on the formal accounts is summarized in the two journal entries, (1) and (2), included at the bottom of the pension work sheet in Exhibit 17–8.

Using data from the memorandum records, pension expense for the year is computed to be $57,864. The journal entry to record net pension expense for the year is as follows:

Pension Expense... 57,864
    Prepaid/Accrued Pension Cost 57,864
        To record accrual of net pension expense for 2002.

The $57,864 increase in the reported accrued pension liability reflects the net effect of all the changes in the memorandum accounts—the projected benefit obligation (PBO), the pension fund, the unamortized transition gain, and the unrecognized prior service cost. Clearly, it is impossible to understand the events underlying this one number without seeing the notes to the financial statements. Because of the impact of the amortization of deferred items, this $57,864 amount should *not* be viewed as the increase in the pension obligation or unfunded pension obligation for the year.

The second formal journal entry records the cash contribution to the pension fund:

Prepaid/Accrued Pension Cost.. 115,000
    Cash... 115,000
        To record 2002 contribution to the pension plan.

Note that on the work sheet this entry includes two debit amounts and doesn't seem to follow the fundamental rule of double-entry accounting: debits equal credits. However, both debits are reflecting the same event, once in the memorandum accounts

21   Statement 87, par. 76, allowed certain small companies to adopt the new pension standard in 1988 instead of 1987. For purposes of this illustration, we will assume that Thornton took advantage of that exception.

and once in the formal accounts. One debit, the debit to the FVPA, reflects an increase in pension fund assets. The second debit, the debit to prepaid/accrued pension cost shown in the preceding formal journal entry, reflects the impact of this increase in the pension fund, a memorandum account, on the net pension liability, a formal account.

The closing balance in the prepaid/accrued pension cost account is a debit of $17,136. Accordingly, this amount is shown as an asset on Thornton's December 31, 2002, balance sheet. The pension work sheet illustrates that this $17,136 asset is much more complex than most assets or liabilities. The Prepaid/Accrued Pension Cost asset or liability contains elements of current market values (in both the PBO and the FVPA), a deferred gain (transition gain, now amortized to $0), and an intangible asset (unrecognized prior service cost).

Thornton Electronics—2003

The Thornton Electronics example continues with the information for 2003 shown below:

Service cost as reported by actuaries	$ 87,000
Contributions to pension plan	75,000
Benefits paid to retirees	132,000
Actual return on pension plan assets	26,350
Actuarial change increasing projected benefit obligation	80,000
Settlement interest rate	11.0%
Long-term expected rate of return on pension plan assets	10.0%

The pension work sheet to record the 2003 pension information is shown in Exhibit 17-9. Entries (a) through (e) are similar to those shown previously for 2002. Note that the amount of prior service cost (PSC) amortization has decreased because the remaining service years of the employees in place at the time of the plan amendment has declined; referring back to the earlier discussion, the amount is computed as follows: $135/825 \times \$145,000 = \$23,727$. Note also that the transition gain (f) is not amortized in 2003 because the transition period is over. Entries (g) and (h) relate to unrecognized gains and losses and are explained below.

DEFERRAL OF GAINS AND LOSSES Because pension costs include many assumptions and estimates, frequent adjustments must be made for variations between the actual results and the estimates or projections that were used in determining net periodic pension expense for previous periods. For example, the market value of pension plan assets may increase at a much higher or lower rate than anticipated, the employee turnover rate may differ from that projected in earlier periods, or changes in the interest rate may differ significantly from expectations. Such differences between expected results and actual experience give rise to a **pension gain or loss.**

Recognition of these pension gains and losses was a subject of controversy during the FASB's study of pensions. Immediate recognition was opposed by many accountants who were concerned about the volatility of pension expense. The FASB decided to minimize the volatility of net periodic pension expense by allowing deferral of some gains and losses and amortization over future periods rather than requiring recognition of gains and losses in the period they arise.[22] The FASB's position, as reflected in FASB Statement No. 87, represents a compromise and has created some unusual and complex accounting practices.

---

22 Alternatively, a company may elect to recognize all gains or losses immediately. If this election is made, the company must (1) apply the immediate recognition method consistently, (2) recognize all gains or losses immediately, and (3) disclose the fact that immediate recognition is being followed. Special Report, "A Guide to Implementation of Statement No. 87 on Employers' Accounting for Pensions—Questions and Answers," Stamford, CT: Financial Accounting Standards Board, 1986, p. 23. For purposes of this chapter, all illustrations and end-of-chapter material will assume that the deferred recognition method is used.

EXHIBIT 17-9 | Thornton Electronics, Inc.—Pension Work Sheet for 2003

		Formal Accounts	
	Net Pension Expense	Cash	Prepaid/Accrued Pension Cost
Balance, January 1, 2003			$ 17,136
(a) Service Cost..			
(b) Interest Cost			
(c) Actual Return on Assets....................................			
(d) Benefits Paid			
(e) PSC Amortization...			
(f) Transition Amortization....................................			
(g) Deferred Loss...			
(h) PBO change			
Summary Journal Entries			
(1) Annual Pension Cost Accrual...........................	$137,027		(137,027)
(2) Annual Pension Contribution		$(75,000)	75,000
Balance, December 31, 2003			$ (44,891)

Note: Positive amounts are debits; negative amounts are credits.

Although actuarial estimates may change for several reasons, only two will be considered in this illustration: (1) the current-year difference between the actual and expected return on pension plan assets and (2) actuarial changes in determining the PBO.

DEFERRAL OF CURRENT-YEAR DIFFERENCE BETWEEN ACTUAL AND EXPECTED RETURN ON PENSION PLAN ASSETS In estimating the return on pension plan assets, FASB Statement No. 87 indicates that the expected long-term rate of return on assets should be used rather than a more volatile short-term rate. Thus, in the short run, the actual return on pension plan assets usually will differ from the expected return. By deferring the difference between the expected return and the actual return, pension expense will tend to be reduced by the expected long-term rate of return rather than by the more volatile short-term return rates. If the actual return on pension plan assets exceeds the expected return, the difference is a deferred gain; if the expected return exceeds the actual return, the difference is a deferred loss.

The **expected return on pension plan assets** is computed by multiplying the market-related value of pension plan assets by the expected long-term rate of return. The FASB defines **market-related value of pension plan assets** as either (1) the fair market value of pension plan assets at the beginning of the current year or (2) a weighted-average value based on market values of pension plan assets over a period not to exceed five years.[23] If asset values have been increasing, the weighted-average value will be lower than the beginning fair market value, resulting in a lower expected return.

When the actual return on pension plan assets exceeds the expected return, the difference, a deferred gain, is added to the pension expense as part of the gain or loss component. When the actual return is less than the expected return, the difference, a deferred loss, is deducted from pension expense. Because the actual return on pension plan assets is deducted in computing pension expense, the net effect of the deferred pension gain or loss adjustment is that the expected return, rather than the actual return, is used to reduce pension expense, thus achieving a smoothing of pension expense over time.

23 Different methods of calculating market-related value may be used for different classes of assets. However, a company must apply the methods consistently from year to year.

Periodic Pension Cost Items	PBO	FVPA	Memorandum Accounts Unamortized Transition Gain/Loss	Unrecognized Prior Service Cost	Unrecognized Net Pension Gain/Loss
	$(1,615,000)	$1,513,500	$ 0	$118,636	$ 0
$ 87,000	(87,000)				
177,650	(177,650)				
(26,350)		26,350			
	132,000	(132,000)			
23,727				(23,727)	
0			0		
(125,000)					125,000
	(80,000)				80,000
		75,000			
	$(1,827,650)	$1,482,850	$(0)	$ 94,909	$205,000

Components of Prepaid/Accrued Pension Cost

To illustrate the computation of the pension gain or loss arising from differences between actual and expected return, assume Thornton Electronics computes the expected return on pension plan assets using the fair market value of pension plan assets at the beginning of the year. The expected return on pension plan assets for 2003 is $151,350 ($1,513,500 × .10). Because the actual return for the year is $26,350, the $125,000 difference is treated as a deferred pension loss and is subtracted in the computation of pension expense.

As mentioned above, combining the effects of the actual return and the unrecognized loss results in a net reduction in pension expense equal to the expected return of $151,350 (actual return of $26,350 + unrecognized loss of $125,000). The unrecognized loss is recorded in entry (g) in the 2003 pension work sheet as a credit (decrease) to annual pension expense and a debit to the memorandum account Unrecognized Net Pension Gain/Loss.

DIFFERENCES IN ACTUARIAL ESTIMATES OF PBO As indicated earlier, the actuarial computation of the projected benefit obligation involves many estimates, including future interest rates, life expectancy rates, and future salary rates. The effects of changing these estimates are deferred and accumulated for possible amortization to pension expense over future periods. During 2003, Thornton's actuaries reevaluated their actuarial assumptions in light of experience with Thornton's employees and calculated that the projected benefit obligation should be increased by $80,000. This increase is identified as a loss and is deferred to future periods. No adjustment is made to pension expense in the current period for this deferral as was necessary for the deferral of the difference in the return on pension plan assets. The deferred loss arising from the adjustment to the PBO becomes part of the **unrecognized net pension gain or loss** for future amortization.

This change in actuarial estimate is recorded in work sheet entry (h) as a credit (increase) to the PBO and a debit to the unrecognized net pension gain/loss. Note that the change has no impact on pension expense or on the reported accrued pension liability for 2003; only memorandum accounts are affected. However, the change will impact future years in two ways. First, because the PBO is higher, interest cost in future years will be higher. Second, depending on future developments, the deferred loss may be amortized to pension expense in future years. Circumstances under which deferred losses and gains are amortized are described later in the chapter.

From the work sheet in Exhibit 17–9, it can be seen that the summary journal entries for 2003 are as follows:

Pension Expense..	137,027	
Prepaid/Accrued Pension Cost		137,027
To record accrual of net pension expense for 2003.		
Prepaid/Accrued Pension Cost	75,000	
Cash		75,000
To record 2003 contribution to the pension plan.		

Thornton Electronics—2004

The Thornton Electronics pension information for 2004 is shown below:

Service cost as reported by actuaries	$ 115,000
Contributions to pension plan	80,000
Benefits paid to retirees	140,000
Actual return on pension plan assets	175,500
Settlement interest rate	11.0%
Long-term expected rate of return on pension plan assets	10.0%
Accumulated benefit obligation, December 31, 2004	1,763,350

This information is recorded in the 2004 pension work sheet shown in Exhibit 17–10. Entries (a) through (g) are similar to those made in 2003. Again, note that the prior service cost amortization amount is lower than in prior years, reflecting the continuing decline in the expected remaining service lives of those employees who were in place when the plan's amendment was initiated; the amount, as computed earlier, is $120/825 \times \$145,000 = \$21,091$. Entry (g) reflects the fact that the actual return on plan assets of $175,500 for the year exceeded the expected return of $148,285 ($1,482,850 \times

---

EXHIBIT 17–10 | Thornton Electronics, Inc.—Pension Work Sheet for 2004

	Formal Accounts			
	Net Pension Expense	Cash	Prepaid/ Accrued Pension Cost	Deferred Pension Cost
Balance, January 1, 2004			$ (44,891)	
(a) Service Cost............................				
(b) Interest Cost				
(c) Actual Return on Assets......................				
(d) Benefits Paid				
(e) PSC Amortization				
(f) Transition Amortization........................				
(g) Deferred Gain				
(h) Amort. of Deferred Loss				
Summary Journal Entries				
(1) Annual Pension Cost Accrual..............	$193,295		193,295	
(2) Annual Pension Contribution..............		$(80,000)	80,000	
(3) Minimum Liability Adjustment			(6,814)	$6,814
Balance, December 31, 2004...................			$(165,000)	$6,814

Note: Positive amounts are debits; negative amounts are credits.

.10). The excess of $27,215 is considered an unexpected gain and is credited to the unrecognized net pension gain/loss account in the memorandum records. The same amount is debited to net periodic pension expense.

Memorandum entry (h) and summary journal entry (3) relate to amortization of unrecognized pension gains and losses and to the minimum liability adjustment, respectively, and are explained below.

AMORTIZATION OF UNRECOGNIZED NET PENSION GAIN OR LOSS FROM PRIOR YEARS

Under certain conditions, an employer's net periodic pension expense will include the amortization of unrecognized net pension gain or loss. The unrecognized pension gain or loss from prior years is amortized over future years if it accumulates to more than an amount defined by the FASB as a **corridor amount.** Amortization is required only for an unrecognized net gain or loss that exceeds 10% of the greater of the PBO or the market-related value of the plan assets as of the beginning of the year. The Board indicated that any systematic method of amortization that equaled or exceeded the straight-line amortization over the remaining expected service years of the employees would be acceptable as long as the procedure is applied consistently to both gains and losses. The amortization of a deferred gain reduces the net periodic pension expense, while the amortization of a deferred loss increases the net periodic pension expense. It is important to remember that only unrecognized gains and losses from prior years are subject to amortization. Accordingly, the corridor comparison applies only to the beginning balances in the PBO, the FVPA, and the unrecognized net pension gain/loss accounts.

STOP & THINK How would a company find itself exceeding the corridor amount? If the company is constantly revising its estimated expected return, how often should the corridor amount come into play?

This corridor amortization is a compromise between immediate recognition of gains and losses (which is viewed as causing too much volatility in earnings) and permanent deferral. Permanent deferral makes sense as long as the gains and losses tend to cancel out, but it becomes less reasonable when a "large" deferred gain or loss accumulates. The corridor amount is simply an arbitrary definition of what amount of deferred gain or loss is considered "large."

To illustrate the computation of the corridor amount, Thornton would apply the 10% corridor threshold to the projected benefit

Periodic Pension Cost Items	PBO	FVPA	Unamortized Transition Gain/Loss	Unrecognized Prior Service Cost	Unrecognized Net Pension Gain/Loss
	$(1,827,650)	$1,482,850	$0	$94,909	$205,000
$115,000	(115,000)				
201,042	(201,042)				
(175,500)		175,500			
	140,000	(140,000)			
21,091				(21,091)	
0			0		
27,215					(27,215)
4,447					(4,447)
		80,000			
	$(2,003,692)	$1,598,350	$0	$73,818	$173,338

Components of Prepaid/Accrued Pension Cost

obligation at the beginning of the year because the PBO exceeds the market value of pension plan assets at the beginning of the year.[24] Thus, the corridor amount is $182,765 ($1,827,650 × .10). Because the unrecognized deferred loss at January 1, 2004, is $205,000, only the excess of $22,235 ($205,000 − $182,765) is subject to amortization. The average remaining employee service life on January 1, 2004, is assumed to be five years, so the 2004 amortization is $4,447 ($22,235/5). This amount represents amortization of a loss and is an addition to the other components in computing pension expense. The loss amortization is recorded in entry (h) in the 2004 pension work sheet as a debit to the net periodic pension expense and a credit to the unrecognized loss. Note the size of the loss amortization amount ($4,447) in relation to the size of the unrecognized loss itself ($205,000). Clearly, this deferral of gains and losses and subsequent corridor amortization accomplishes the goal of reducing volatility in annual pension expense.

MINIMUM PENSION LIABILITY The computation of the annual pension expense is based on the concept of accrual accounting. However, FASB Statement No. 87 allows companies to defer many gains and losses over an extended service period, thus minimizing the impact of these items on the financial statements. In formulating the pension standard, the FASB was concerned that the balance sheet would not disclose unfunded pension liabilities directly in the statement. To compensate for this omission, FASB Statement No. 87 identifies the concept of a **minimum pension liability** to reflect existing unfunded pension costs and establishes rules for an employer to apply in determining if an entry to record a minimum pension liability is required.

FASB Statement No. 87 requires the employer to report a minimum pension liability that is at least equal to the unfunded accumulated benefit obligation (ABO), which is determined as follows:

Unfunded ABO (minimum pension liability) = ABO − Fair value of pension plan assets

If the employer already has an accrued pension liability resulting from accrued pension costs in excess of the amount funded, no **additional pension liability** is recognized if the accrued pension cost is equal to or greater than the minimum pension liability (unfunded ABO). If accrued pension costs are less than the minimum liability, then an additional liability is recognized for the difference. In this situation, the additional pension liability equals the minimum pension liability minus the accrued pension cost.

In the case of Thornton, the company has a net pension liability of $158,186 ($44,891 + $193,295 − $80,000) prior to any consideration of an adjustment for the minimum pension liability. Comparing the ABO to the FVPA as of December 31, 2004, results in a minimum pension liability requirement of $165,000 ($1,763,350 − $1,598,350). Because the company's net pension liability is less than the minimum, an adjustment is required in the amount of $6,814 ($165,000 − $158,186). The journal entry required to make this adjustment is discussed in the next section.

If a prepaid pension cost balance exists because funding has exceeded the accrual, the total amount of the liability to be reported is the minimum pension liability (unfunded ABO) plus the prepaid balance reported as an asset. Thus, the net pension liability reported is the minimum pension liability. To illustrate, assume that the unfunded ABO at December 31 is determined to be $250,000 and that the accounts reflect prepaid pension cost of $36,000. The prepaid cost of $36,000 would be reported with the assets on the balance sheet, and a separate liability of $286,000 would be reported. The result is a net pension liability equal to the minimum pension liability of $250,000 required by Statement No. 87.

---

24 For simplicity, the fair market value of pension assets is used as the market-related value. Recall that an alternative measure is the weighted-average of the fair market value of pension assets from prior years.

Exhibit 17-11 illustrates the computation of the pension liability under four different conditions. The entries to record the liability are discussed and illustrated in the next section.

When the value of the pension plan assets is greater than the present value of the ABO, the pension plan is said to be overfunded. In this situation, however, no recognition of the net asset position on the balance sheet is permitted. The FASB's decision to exclude the reporting of net pension plan assets under these circumstances is another reflection of inconsistency in the interest of conservatism and reflects the intense pressure that was exerted on the Board by various groups. In Appendix A of Statement No. 87, the Board stated that it "believes that . . . an employer with . . . an overfunded pension obligation has an asset."[25] The Board concluded, however, that recognition of all changes in plan asset values and in the present value of the obligation would not be practical at the present time and would be too drastic a change from previous reporting practices.

EXHIBIT 17-11 | Pension Liability Computation

Case	(1) Accumulated Benefit Obligation	(2) Fair Value of Pension Plan Assets	(3) Minimum Pension Liability	(4) Prepaid Pension Cost	(5) Accrued Pension Cost	(6) Additional Pension Liability	(7) Total Pension Liability
1	$2,564,500	$1,685,600	$878,900		$125,000	$753,900	$878,900
2	2,564,500	2,480,000	84,500		125,000	0	125,000
3	2,150,000	2,480,000	0		125,000	0	125,000
4	2,564,500	2,480,000	84,500	$32,000		116,500	84,500

(1) Present value of future benefits attributable to service already rendered by employees. The measurement of future benefits is based on current, rather than future, salary levels.
(2) Fair market value of pension plan assets.
(3) The minimum amount of net pension liability to be reported on the balance sheet (ABO – Fair value of pension plan assets).
(4) Excess of pension contributions over accrued pension costs reported as an asset.
(5) Excess of accrued pension costs over pension contributions reported as a liability.
(6) Additional pension liability, if any, necessary to reflect the minimum liability required by FASB Statement No. 87.
(7) Total amount of pension liability to be reported on the balance sheet.

Deferred Pension Cost

If an employer is required to record an additional pension liability as a result of applying the minimum liability provisions, FASB Statement No. 87 indicates that the offsetting charge should be to a **deferred pension cost** account (intangible asset) to the extent of any unrecognized prior service cost or any unamortized transition loss. If the additional liability exceeds these unrecognized amounts, the excess should be recorded as a separate contra equity adjustment and the adjustment should be included as a component of "Other comprehensive income." The deferred account represents that portion of the additional liability that can be related to prior periods because of either the adoption of a plan or a plan's amendment or because of the transition to the new standards. These unrecognized costs will be recognized in future periods through the amortization procedures discussed earlier, and thus, the deferred account is not directly amortized. It is adjusted each period to reflect the increases or decreases in the recorded minimum liability.

The contra equity adjustment account represents that portion of the additional liability that reflects either changes in the value of pension plan assets or changes in the benefit obligation that are not related to unrecognized prior

FYI: Offsetting an additional pension liability with an intangible asset may seem counterintuitive. Remember that unrecognized prior service cost and unamortized transition loss can be thought of as unrecorded pension goodwill.

25 *Statement of Financial Accounting Standards No. 87,* par. 98.

service costs or to the transition adjustment. These unrecognized losses are recognized through the gains and losses component of pension expense. The contra equity account is also adjusted each period when the minimum liability is recorded, and this adjustment is disclosed as a component of "Other comprehensive income."

To illustrate accounting for the minimum liability and its offsetting asset or equity adjustment, assume the Clapton Corporation computes the following balances as of December 31, 2002:

Accumulated benefit obligation	$1,250,000
Fair value of pension plan assets	1,140,000
Accrued pension cost	16,000
Unrecognized prior service cost	80,000

The minimum pension liability is $110,000 ($1,250,000 − $1,140,000), and the recorded liability for accrued pension cost is only $16,000. An additional pension liability of $94,000 ($110,000 − $16,000) would be recorded as follows:

Deferred Pension Cost	80,000	
Excess of Additional Pension Liability Over Unrecognized Prior Service Cost	14,000	
Additional Pension Liability		94,000
To recognize additional pension liability.		

For reporting purposes, the $16,000 accrued pension cost and the $94,000 additional pension liability may be combined into one pension liability of $110,000 in the balance sheet. The "Excess of Additional Pension Liability Over Unrecognized Prior Service Cost"—$14,000—would be included in the computation of comprehensive income (a reduction).

The minimum liability is accounted for in subsequent periods in a similar manner. For example, assume that the computed minimum liability for Clapton Corporation at December 31, 2003, is $104,000 and that accrued pension cost at that date is $18,000. The balance in the additional pension liability account would be adjusted to $86,000 ($104,000 − $18,000). If the unrecognized prior service cost at December 31, 2003, has declined to $70,000, the deferred pension cost would be adjusted to $70,000. The excess of additional pension liability over unrecognized prior service cost would be adjusted to $16,000 ($86,000 − $70,000). The following journal entry would be made to adjust the accounts at the end of 2003:

Additional Pension Liability	8,000*	
Excess of Additional Pension Liability Over Unrecognized Prior Service Cost	2,000**	
Deferred Pension Cost		10,000***
To adjust additional pension liability and related asset and		
contra equity accounts.		

Computations:

	Beginning Balance	Ending Balance	Adjustment
*	$94,000 Cr.	$86,000 Cr.	$ 8,000 Dr.
**	14,000 Dr.	16,000 Dr.	2,000 Dr.
***	80,000 Dr.	70,000 Dr.	10,000 Cr.

The deferred pension cost balance of $70,000 (the amount of unrecognized prior service cost) would be reported on the balance sheet as an intangible asset. The contra equity account balance of $16,000 would be deducted in the stockholders' equity section as a component of "Accumulated other comprehensive income." The combined pension liability of $104,000 ($18,000 accrued pension cost + $86,000 additional pension liability) would be reported as a liability, usually under the noncurrent liabilities section.

If Clapton Corporation had an unamortized transition loss, that amount would be treated the same as unrecognized prior service cost in recording the minimum pension liability. The combined amount of any unrecognized prior service cost and unamortized transition loss determines the maximum amount of deferred pension cost. Unamortized transition gains are ignored in the computation of the maximum amount of deferred pension cost.

One of the more difficult aspects of the pension standards is identifying which obligation and asset values are used for the different pension amounts. It is important to note that the ABO is used only in determining the minimum pension liability. In all other determinations involving future benefits discussed in this chapter, the projected benefit obligation is used.

Applying the minimum liability computation to the December 31, 2004, data of Thornton Electronics yields work sheet entry (3) in Exhibit 17–10. The ABO of $1,763,350 exceeds the fair market value of the plan assets by $165,000 ($1,763,350 – $1,598,350). Because the preliminary balance in the accrued liability is only $158,186 ($44,891 + $193,295 – $80,000), an additional liability of $6,814 ($165,000 – $158,186) must be recorded. An intangible asset, Deferred Pension Cost, is recognized for the entire amount because unrecognized prior service cost of $73,818 exceeds the amount of the additional liability.

The formal journal entries to record pension-related data for 2004 are as follows:

Annual Pension Expense	193,295	
Prepaid/Accrued Pension Cost		193,295
To record accrual of net pension expense for 2004.		
Prepaid/Accrued Pension Cost	80,000	
Cash		80,000
To record 2004 contribution to the pension plan.		
Deferred Pension Cost (intangible asset)	6,814	
Prepaid/Accrued Pension Cost		6,814
To recognize additional pension liability.		

DISCLOSURE OF PENSION PLANS

Prepare required disclosures associated with pensions, and understand the accounting treatment for pension settlements and curtailments.

The disclosure requirements relating to pensions are discussed in FASB Statement No. 132, "Employers' Disclosures about Pensions and Other Postretirement Benefits." Originally the pension disclosure requirements were detailed in Statement No. 87. However, the Board revised the disclosure requirements to ensure that useful, consistent information relating to pensions and other postretirement benefits was being provided to financial statement users.

Statement No. 132 requires information similar to that presented in the work sheet that was used throughout the chapter for calculating pension costs. Specifically, the major disclosure requirements for most publicly traded companies are

1. A reconciliation between the beginning and ending balances for the projected benefit obligation.
2. A reconciliation between the beginning and ending balances in the fair value of plan assets.
3. A disclosure of the accumulated benefit obligation when the ABO exceeds the fair value of plan assets.
4. The funded status of the plans, the amounts not recognized in the balance sheet, and the amounts recognized in the balance sheet, including
   (a) the amount of unamortized prior service costs
   (b) the amount of unrecognized net gains or losses
   (c) the amount of any remaining unrecognized transition adjustment
   (d) the net pension asset or liability
5. The components of pension expense for the period
6. Any effects on the other comprehensive income section as a result of changes in the additional pension liability
7. The assumptions used relating to the following items

(a) discount rate

(b) rate of compensation increase

(c) expected long-term rate of return on plan assets

8. For postretirement benefits (which are discussed in the expanded material section of this chapter): assumed health care cost trend rates and their effect on service and interest costs and the ABO if the assumed health care cost trend rates were one percentage point higher.

As you can see, the work sheet used in this chapter provides the bulk of the information required for disclosure. In addition to specifying the disclosure requirement for defined benefit pension plans, Statement No. 132 added disclosure requirements for defined contribution plans as well. Specifically, an employer must disclose the amount of pension expense recognized for defined contribution plans separately from the amount of expense recognized for defined benefit plans. In addition, the nature and effect of any significant changes during the period should be disclosed.

For Thornton Electronics, most of the information needed for the disclosure of the details of the computation of annual pension expense and reconciliation of the funded status of the pension plan can be obtained from the 2004 pension work sheet in Exhibit 17–10. In addition, the ABO of $1,763,350 is disclosed.

Companies with more than one pension plan may combine the amounts of all pension plans. However, in those cases where the ABO exceeds the FVPA, that information must be disclosed separately in the notes. In addition, companies may combine the disclosure relating to their U.S. and non-U.S. plans unless the obligation associated with the non-U.S. plans is significant or the terms of the non-U.S. plans differ substantially from those of the U.S. plans. Statement No. 132 also allows firms to combine the disclosures relating to pensions and postretirement benefits other than pensions (these benefits are discussed in the expanded material section). This type of disclosure is illustrated in Exhibit 17–12 using an excerpt from the notes to the 1998 financial statements of General Motors.

EXHIBIT 17–12 | Note Disclosure for U.S. and Non-U.S. Pension Plans—General Motors

NOTE 13. Pensions and Other Postretirement Benefits

	U.S. Plans Pension Benefits		Non-U.S. Plans Pension Benefits		Other Benefits	
	1998	1997	1998	1997	1998	1997
(in millions)						
Change in benefit obligations						
Benefit obligation at beginning of year	$73,570	$72,501	$ 9,824	$9,526	$44,294	$41,387
Service cost	1,270	1,332	214	191	663	639
Interest cost	4,974	5,261	643	633	3,113	3,128
Plan participants' contributions	43	69	28	25	31	31
Amendments	208	25	81	—	—	—
Actuarial losses	1,973	4,443	92	710	1,622	1,819
Benefits paid	(5,196)	(5,408)	(349)	(331)	(2,287)	(2,174)
Curtailment charges and other	121	(4,653)	(250)	(930)	(90)	(536)
Benefit obligation at end of year	$76,963	$73,570	$10,283	$9,824	$47,346	$44,294

(continued)

| | U.S. Plans | | Non-U.S. Plans | | | |
| | Pension Benefits | | Pension Benefits | | Other Benefits | |
	1998	1997	1998	1997	1998	1997
Change in plan assets						
Fair value of plan assets at beginning of year	$72,280	$71,295	$ 6,075	$ 5,915	$ 3,000	—
Actual return on plan assets	6,438	10,882	328	756	249	—
Employer contributions	1,151	1,535	206	71	1,700	$ 3,000
Plan participants' contributions	43	69	28	25	—	—
Benefits paid	(5,196)	(5,408)	(349)	(331)	(375)	—
Settlement charges and other	291	(6,093)	(312)	(361)	—	—
Fair value of plan assets at end of year	$75,007	$72,280	$ 5,976	$ 6,075	$ 4,574	$ 3,000
Funded status	$ (1,956)	$ (1,290)	$(4,307)	$(3,749)	$(42,772)	$(41,294)
Unrecognized actuarial loss	10,368	8,632	1,880	1,773	2,209	689
Unrecognized prior service cost	7,064	8,103	764	824	(448)	(563)
Unrecognized transition (asset) obligation	(64)	(105)	48	10	—	—
Net amount recognized	$15,412	$15,340	$(1,615)	$(1,142)	$(41,011)	$(41,168)
Amounts recognized in the consolidated balance sheets consist of:						
Prepaid benefit cost	$ 6,448	$ 6,202	$ 898	$ 868	$ —	$ —
Accrued benefit liability	(4,361)	(3,595)	(3,814)	(3,463)	(41,011)	(41,168)
Intangible asset	5,961	7,071	504	602	—	—
Accumulated other comprehensive income	7,364	5,662	797	851	—	—
Net amount recognized	$15,412	$15,340	$(1,615)	$(1,142)	$(41,011)	$(41,168)

The projected benefit obligation, accumulated benefit obligation, and fair value of plan assets for the pension plans with accumulated benefit obligations in excess of plan assets were $56.7 billion, $56.0 billion and $47.8 billion, respectively, as of December 31, 1998 and $54.4 billion, $53.7 billion and $46.7 billion, respectively, as of December 31, 1997.

| | U.S. Plans | | | Non-U.S. Plans | | | | | |
| | Pension Benefits | | | Pension Benefits | | | Other Benefits | | |
	1998	1997	1996	1998	1997	1996	1998	1997	1996
(in millions)									
Components of expense									
Service cost	$1,270	$1,332	$1,208	$214	$191	$185	$ 663	$ 639	$ 668
Interest cost	4,974	5,261	4,777	643	633	653	3,113	3,128	2,980
Expected return on plan assets	(6,815)	(6,630)	(6,283)	(516)	(524)	(487)	(286)	—	—
Amortization of prior service cost	1,173	1,170	824	99	99	100	(116)	(116)	(116)
Amortization of transition asset	(44)	(85)	(63)	(17)	(20)	(18)	—	—	—
Recognized net actuarial loss	331	308	675	75	60	57	97	72	43
Curtailments, settlements and other	207	53	69	48	2	158	—	(2)	(3)
Net expense	$1,096	$1,409	$1,207	$546	$441	$648	$3,471	$3,721	$3,572
Weighted-average assumptions									
Discount rate	6.8%	7.0%	7.5%	6.4%	6.8%	7.3%	6.7%	7.2%	7.8%
Expected return on plan assets	10.0%	10.0%	10.0%	9.2%	9.2%	9.8%	10.0%	—	—
Rate of compensation increase	5.0%	5.0%	5.0%	3.5%	4.1%	4.2%	4.4%	4.4%	4.4%

For measurement purposes, a 6 percent annual rate of increase in the per capita cost of covered health care benefits was assumed for 1999. The rate was assumed to decrease on a linear basis to 5 percent through 2004 and remain at that level thereafter.

A one percentage point increase in the assumed health care trend rate would have increased the Accumulated Projected Benefit Obligation (APBO) by $5.5 billion at December 31, 1998 and increased the aggregate service and interest cost components of non-pension postretirement benefit expense for 1998 by $484 million. A one percentage point decrease would have decreased the APBO by $4.6 billion and decreased the aggregate service and interest cost components of non-pension postretirement benefit expense for 1998 by $377 million. A one percentage point increase in the weighted-average discount rate would have resulted in a $4.8 billion decrease in the APBO at December 31, 1998.

> # PENSION PLAN SETTLEMENTS

On June 11, 1985, UAL CORP., parent company of UNITED AIRLINES, announced its intention to settle some of its pension benefit obligations by purchasing annuity contracts and to convert the excess $962 million in pension fund assets to corporate use. As a result of this settlement, UAL recognized a gain of $137 million for the year 1985. This gain reduced UAL's 1985 net loss (before taxes) from $232 million to $95 million. The UAL pension plan settlement was only one of over 1,000 settlements initiated from 1980 through 1986. Asset reversion from excess pension fund assets exceeded $6 billion in 1985 alone.

Two questions that can be asked are why these firms settled the pension plans and what effect the settlements had on employee and corporate wealth. In addressing the question of why, Jacob K. Thomas identifies two major groups of firms settling overfunded pension plans: those that had experienced recent significant declines in cash flow from operations, and those that were in tight financial condition because of financial restructuring in the wake of a hostile takeover. Thus, the evidence suggests that while firms viewed settlement of an overfunded pension plan as one source of funds, in general this source was not used except by firms in extreme circumstances when other funding sources may have already been depleted.

H. Fred Mittelstaedt and Philip R. Regier summarize the research on what effect these excess asset reversions had on firms' stock prices. They confirm that firms' stock prices generally increased on announcement of an asset reversion but suggest that this result is primarily due to two factors:

1. Many asset reversions were announced in conjunction with other significant news (dividend increases, changes in corporate strategy, etc.), and these other items may have been responsible for the stock price increases.

Pension Settlements and Curtailments

If a pension plan is settled or the benefits are curtailed, a question arises as to how a resulting gain or loss should be treated by the employer. **Settlement of a pension plan** occurs when an employer takes an irrevocable action that relieves the employer of primary responsibility for all or part of the obligation. Examples of a settlement transaction include the purchase by the employer of an annuity from an insurance company that would cover employees' vested benefits or a lump sum cash payment to the employees in exchange for their rights to receive specified pension benefits. A **curtailment of a pension plan** arises from an event that significantly reduces the benefits that will be provided for present employees' future services. Curtailments include (1) the termination of employees' services earlier than expected, for example, as a result of closing a plant or discontinuing a segment of the business and (2) the termination or suspension of a pension plan so that employees do not earn additional benefits for future services.[26]

As discussed throughout this chapter, FASB Statement No. 87 provides for delayed recognition of pension gains and losses arising from the ordinary operations of the pension plan. In addition, the statement provides for delayed recognition of prior service cost and transition adjustments. Thus, at any given time, unrecognized gains, losses, and prior service cost usually exist.

The FASB felt it was clear that if a pension plan is completely terminated and all pension obligations are settled and plan assets are disbursed, then previously unrecognized pension amounts should be recognized. What wasn't clear, however, is what happens when partial settlements or curtailments take place. The FASB considered this issue and presented its recommendations in FASB Statement No. 88. The statement also addresses

---

26 *Statement of Financial Accounting Standards No. 88*, "Employers' Accounting for Settlements and Curtailments of Defined Benefit Pension Plans and for Termination Benefits," Stamford, CT: Financial Accounting Standards Board, 1985, par. 6.

2. The most significant stock price increases were for settlements prior to 1984. Before 1984, it was uncertain whether the courts would allow firms to keep excess pension fund assets. Accordingly, during that time period, financial analysts and investors were uncertain about who owned excess pension assets—the firm or the employees. By explicitly announcing a pension plan settlement and excess asset reversion, a firm increased the probability that it could claim the excess assets. As a result of this change in perception about whether the firm could claim the excess assets, the value of the firm went up and its stock price increased. After 1984, the legal environment was such that there was a strong presumption in the market that the excess assets did in fact belong to the firm. Thus, announcements in this period contained no new information and did not significantly impact stock prices.

Excess pension asset reversions have decreased dramatically since 1986, largely as a result of government action. These settlements were viewed by many as transfers of pension fund assets from employees to their employers. As a result, the Tax Reform Act of 1986 imposed a 10% excise tax on excess asset reversions. The excise tax was increased to 15% in 1988.

QUESTIONS:

1. Why would the announcement of a pension plan settlement and excess asset reversion have no impact on the announcing company's stock price?

2. Are there other less dramatic means a company can use to remove assets from an overfunded pension plan?

SOURCES:

H. Fred Mittelstaedt and Philip R. Regier, "Further Evidence on Excess Asset Reversions and Shareholder Wealth," *Journal of Risk and Insurance,* September 1990, p. 471.

Jacob K. Thomas, "Why Do Firms Terminate Overfunded Pension Plans?" *Journal of Accounting and Economics,* November 1989, p. 361.

the issue of termination benefits, that is, benefits provided to employees in connection with the termination of their employment.

SETTLEMENTS Pension plans occasionally become overfunded because a rising stock market causes the value of plan assets to exceed the pension obligation. To take advantage of this situation, companies sometimes settle their pension plans by purchasing annuity contracts from insurance companies for less than the amount in the pension fund. Subject to regulations such as ERISA, the excess funds can then be used for other corporate purposes.

The accounting issue surrounding settlements centers on whether the gain should be recognized immediately or deferred and recognized in future periods. Prior to Statement No. 88, settlement gains that were accompanied by asset withdrawals from the pension fund, referred to as "asset reversion transactions," were deferred and offset against future pension expenses. The Board, however, decided that if the settlement (1) was an irrevocable action, (2) relieved the employer of primary responsibility for the pension benefit obligation, and (3) eliminated significant risks related to the obligation and the assets used to effect the settlement, the previously unrecognized net gain or loss should be recognized in the current period. If only part of the projected benefit obligation (PBO) is settled, a pro rata portion of the gain should be recognized currently.[27]

CURTAILMENTS As indicated previously, a pension plan curtailment is an event that significantly reduces the expected years of future service of present employees or eliminates for a significant number of employees the accrual of defined benefits for their future services. Examples include termination of employees' services earlier than expected, such as occurs when a segment of the business is discontinued, or termination or suspension of a plan so that no further benefits are earned for future services.

Any unrecognized prior service cost or transition adjustment associated with years of service no longer expected to be rendered as a result of the curtailment is recognized as a loss. In addition, the projected benefit obligation of the pension plan may be changed as a result of the curtailment, giving rise to an additional gain or loss. The Board provided for offsetting previously unrecognized pension gains and losses against the gain or loss from changes in the projected benefit obligation and called the difference curtailment gains or losses. If the sum of all gains and losses attributed to the curtailment, including the write-off of unrecognized prior service cost, is a loss, it is recognized in the period when it is probable that the curtailment will occur and the effects are estimable. If the sum of all gains and losses attributed to the curtailment is a gain, it is recognized when the related employees are terminated or when the plan's suspension or amendment is adopted.[28]

INTERNATIONAL PENSION ACCOUNTING STANDARDS

6

Describe the few remaining differences between U.S. pension accounting standards and the provisions of IAS 19.

net work exercise

The Pension Benefit Guaranty Corporation (PBGC) is a government agency that insures private sector defined benefit pension plans. Access the PBGC's Web site at **www.pbgc.gov**.

Net Work:

1. Since 1975, almost half of the large firms that have declared bankruptcy and failed to pay promised pension benefits to employees have been from one particular industry. As of December 31, 1997, the PBGC had paid well over $1 billion to employees of these companies. What industry is this?

2. What single company bankruptcy has resulted in the highest claims paid by the PBGC?

3. The PBGC defines its "net position" as the difference between the PBGC's total assets and total liabilities. For the most recent year, is the PBGC in a net surplus or net deficit position? What is the largest net deficit ever reported by the PBGC?

Pension accounting has received more emphasis in U.S. GAAP than it has in other countries around the world because the system of private company pension plans is much more developed in the United States. The legal obligation of employers to fulfill pension promises made to employees is well established in U.S. law. In fact, as mentioned earlier in the chapter, the Pension Benefit Guaranty Corporation (PBGC) was established by Congress in 1974 to "ensure that participants in private sector defined benefit plans receive their pensions even if their plans terminate without sufficient assets to pay promised benefits." Accordingly, accounting recognition of pension obligations is a natural consequence of the legal environment in the United States.

The legal status of company pension obligations in other countries is not always as well defined as in the United States. This fact is acknowledged in the FASB requirement that U.S. multinational companies provide separate disclosure for their non-U.S. pension plans. In addition, pension accounting practices have varied substantially from country to country; IAS 19, "Retirement Benefit Costs," allowed significant variation in pension accounting standards. However, in January 1998, the standard was renamed "Employee Benefits" and now requires pension accounting that is quite similar to what has been required under U.S. GAAP since 1985. The revised version of IAS 19 is covered in this section, along with a brief discussion of an innovative pension accounting proposal that is currently being considered in the United Kingdom.

IAS 19: Old and New

One approach the "old" IAS 19 allowed was called the "accrued benefit method" and was similar to the approach followed in U.S. GAAP. Another widely used alternative approach was called the "projected benefit valuation method" and differed substantially from U.S. GAAP. This method emphasized the recognition of an equal amount of pension expense each year. Under this method, the total amount of funds needed to satisfy existing employees' pension benefits (both earned and not yet earned) was estimated and the annuity needed to accumulate to that amount was calculated. In practice, companies accounting for their pensions using this approach would use this procedure to calculate both annual pension expense and the annual required cash contribution to the pension fund. From a conceptual standpoint, this projected benefit method was deficient because it included unearned pension benefits in the computation of annual pension expense.

The revised version of IAS 19 eliminates this method and requires that a company's pension obligation be measured using the same approach as is used under U.S. GAAP. In

28 Ibid., pars. 12–14.

addition, the revised version of IAS 19 also incorporates the same 10% corridor amount (threshold) in calculating the amortization of deferred gains and losses. The two remaining major differences between IAS 19 and U.S. GAAP are as follows:

> **Caution!** Do not confuse the projected benefit valuation method with the projected benefit obligation discussed earlier in the chapter. They have nothing to do with one another.

- IAS 19 does *not* include any provision for the recognition of an additional minimum liability.
- IAS 19 does not allow the recognition of a net pension asset unless the amount is less than the discounted present value of any employee refunds to the company plus any anticipated reductions in future pension contributions. Thus, under this provision, a company cannot recognize a net pension asset under IAS 19 unless the company expects to be able to get its hands on the excess amount in the pension fund.

In summary, with the exception of the two items mentioned above, the revised version of IAS 19 has brought the international standard for pension accounting into close agreement with the provisions of U.S. GAAP.

New Proposal From the United Kingdom

Historically, accounting for pension benefits in the United Kingdom has followed the projected benefit valuation method described above. However, on November 4, 1999, the U.K. Accounting Standards Board (ASB) announced its intention to overhaul U.K. pension accounting. The ASB proposed adopting the revised version of IAS 19, however, with a different approach to dealing with deferred pension gains on losses. Recall that under both IAS 19 and U.S. GAAP, deferred pension gains and losses are accumulated and recognized as part of pension expense only after the aggregate amount exceeds the 10% corridor amount. The purpose of the deferral of gains and losses is to reduce the volatility in reported pension expense that would otherwise result from year-to-year differences from long-run expected trends. The ASB proposes to recognize these gains and losses immediately—but to recognize them as part of comprehensive income rather than as part of pension expense. The advantage of this approach is that the reported balance sheet amount would no longer include the confusing conglomeration of deferred items exhibited in the pension notes of most U.S. companies. In addition, reported annual pension expense would not be saddled with the amortization of deferred gains and losses that may have occurred years before. This proposal by the ASB offers a useful innovation to pension accounting that might be considered by the FASB for use in the United States in future years.

EXPANDED MATERIAL

In December 1990, five years after the pension standards were issued, the FASB issued a third major standard in the area of retirement benefits, FASB Statement No. 106, "Employers' Accounting for Postretirement Benefits Other Than Pensions." Although the standard's primary focus is on health care benefits, it also applies to other postretirement benefits, such as the cost of life insurance contracts, legal assistance benefits, and tuition assistance. The remainder of this chapter will address the issues associated with postretirement benefits other than pensions.

7

Explain the differences in accounting for pensions and postretirement benefits other than pensions, and be able to account for postretirement benefits other than pensions.

POSTRETIREMENT BENEFITS OTHER THAN PENSIONS

FASB Statement No. 106 relates only to single-employer defined benefit postretirement plans. The benefits are defined either in monetary amounts, such as a designated amount of life insurance, or as benefit coverage, such as specified coverage for hospital or doctor care.

The Board devoted several years to studying these postretirement benefits and after extensive exposure, hearings, and discussion agreed unanimously that, in general, the costs of the benefits should be accounted for by employers in the same way as pension costs, that is, on an accrual basis. However, as noted below, there are some important differences between pensions and other postretirement benefits.

Nature of Postretirement Health Care Plans

The Board spent much of its time considering the unique features of postretirement health care benefits as compared with pension benefits. Because the details of Statement No. 106 were affected by these features, they will be considered first before the differences between accounting for pensions and other postretirement benefits are discussed.

INFORMAL RATHER THAN FORMAL PLANS   Many company postretirement benefit plans are not written into formal contracts. Companies often begin paying for postretirement health care benefits as a continuation of health care coverage for active employees. In some cases, the practice becomes part of union contract bargaining, and informal plans are changed to formal, union-negotiated contractual plans. Even though a plan may be informal, and thus not legally binding, the courts have sometimes interpreted the informal plan as a contract and have required companies to honor the plan. General Motors has the largest postretirement benefit plan in the United States, with a nonpension postretirement obligation totaling $47.347 billion as of December 31, 1998. Interestingly, General Motors clearly indicates in its notes that although it is reporting a liability for these postretirement benefits, it does not recognize these benefits as a legal obligation. In the notes to the 1998 financial statements, the management of General Motors states:

> GM has disclosed in the consolidated financial statements certain amounts associated with estimated future postretirement benefits other than pensions and characterized such amounts as "accumulated postretirement benefit obligations," "liabilities," or "obligations." Notwithstanding the recording of such amounts and the use of these terms, GM does not admit or otherwise acknowledge that such amounts or existing postretirement benefit plans of GM (other than pensions) represent legally enforceable liabilities of GM.

NONFUNDED RATHER THAN FUNDED PLANS   Most company plans for postretirement benefits are not funded. Thus, companies rely on current revenues to meet current costs of the plan. Unlike pension contributions, postretirement benefit plan contributions usually are not deductible for income tax purposes. As discussed earlier, ERISA, a federal law, requires companies to fund their pension liability during an employee's working years. There has been no similar federal legislation to encourage funding of postretirement benefit costs. In some instances, a separate insurance carrier, such as Blue Cross, is used to cover the risk. But in many cases, especially for larger companies, a form of self-insurance has developed.

PAY-AS-YOU-GO ACCOUNTING RATHER THAN ACCRUAL ACCOUNTING
Because postretirement benefit plans usually are not funded, almost all companies previously charged these costs against revenue in the period the benefit costs were incurred

rather than in the period when the employee service was rendered. This policy results in uneven charges against revenue and does not recognize a liability for unfunded postretirement benefits. The total of unfunded postretirement benefits for all companies has been estimated to amount to over one trillion dollars.[29]

UNCERTAINTY OF FUTURE BENEFITS RATHER THAN CLEARLY DEFINED BENEFITS Defined benefit pension plans establish terms that make the amount of their future pension obligation measurable with reasonably high reliability. Salary trends, mortality tables, and discount rates are reasonably objective and have been used to implement FASB Statement Nos. 87 and 88. Health care costs, however, involve many variables that make accrual accounting difficult to implement. Over the years, factors such as longer life expectancy, improved medical treatment facilities, and early retirements have combined to cause health care costs for retired employees to increase dramatically. The amount of these costs absorbed by government Medicare programs has varied over time and will continue to vary as Congress works to bring government finances under control. As the Medicare plans cover fewer of these costs, employers and individuals are required to absorb higher costs.

Other variables that must be considered before an accrual entry can be made for postretirement benefits include age of retirees, geographic location of retirement, geographic differences in health costs, dependent coverage, sex of retiree, costs of new medical technology, emergence of new diseases, retirement dates, and so forth. Estimating future benefit costs based on these variables can be costly and time-consuming for companies. It was the magnitude of these recordkeeping costs, plus the impact of the accrual concept on the financial statements, that led many business groups to oppose this standard during its exposure period. Although the Board agreed to some compromises between the exposure draft and the final standard, the underlying theory of pension accounting introduced in FASB Statement No. 87 was retained.

NONPAY-RELATED RATHER THAN PAY-RELATED BENEFITS Most postretirement benefits are granted to employees after a certain number of service years or when an employee reaches a specified preretirement age. The amount of benefits to be received is usually unrelated to the level of compensation. The date when an employee becomes eligible for these benefits is known as the **full eligibility date**. No postretirement benefits are granted unless the employee meets this service or age requirement. After that date is reached, the employee is eligible to receive 100% of the postretirement benefits regardless of any future service or regardless of pay level reached. Thus, the period over which an employee earns postretirement benefits extends from the hire date to the full eligibility date.

In contrast, because most pension plans increase an employee's benefits for each additional year of service rendered and for salary increases, the employee continues to earn pension benefits until retirement. Accordingly, the period over which postretirement benefits are earned differs from that over which pension benefits are earned. There are, of course, many exceptions to this description of pensions and postretirement benefits. Some pension plans are nonpay-related and some health care postretirement benefit plans are pay-related. To avoid complicating the discussion, the more general situation of nonpay-related postretirement benefits will be assumed in the following analysis.

Overview of FASB Statement No. 106

Most companies adopted accrual accounting for postretirement benefits beginning with their 1993 financial statements. The same six components for net periodic pension expense listed on page 991 are required for net periodic postretirement benefit expense.

---

29 Lee Berton, "FASB Plan Would Make Firms Deduct Billions for Potential Retiree Benefits," *The Wall Street Journal*, August 17, 1988, p. 3.

e/m

► ACCOUNTING FOR POSTRETIREMENT BENEFITS OTHER THAN PENSIONS: COST VS. BENEFIT

Accounting standard setting always involves a trade-off between costs and benefits. A difficult aspect of standard setting is that the nature of the costs and benefits associated with a standard make them very hard to compare. The benefits from a new standard are typically difficult to quantify, and those benefits are spread over a large group (i.e., all financial statement users). On the other hand, the costs are usually easier to quantify and are concentrated on a smaller group, the firms preparing financial statements.

This asymmetry between costs and benefits makes disagreement and controversy almost inevitable. Predictably, such disagreement and controversy have surrounded the FASB's project on postretirement benefits other than pensions. In Statement No. 106, the FASB explicitly addresses the issue of costs and benefits to a greater extent than in any previous statement. The benefits of improved accounting disclosure and the increased costs of providing the data are certainly difficult to quantify, but the thorniest issues associated with the standard are actually nonaccounting ones: How will the standard impact the benefit packages offered by firms, and how will the standard influence government regulation?

Critics of the standard have offered evidence suggesting that firms have reduced retiree health benefits in order to lower the expense that will now have to be

---

Service cost and prior service cost are charged (attributed) to the years from the hire date to the full eligibility date rather than from the hire date to the retirement date as is true for pension expenses.[30] Any retirement benefit fund assets may be offset against retirement benefit obligations if the assets are clearly restricted for the payment of postretirement benefits. Under- or overfunding at the transition date must be computed and may be recognized immediately as a change in accounting principle, or it may be deferred and recognized over the remaining service life of the employees or 20 years, whichever is longer. As indicated on page 992, the transition gain or loss for pensions had to be deferred and written off over the remaining employee service life or 15 years, whichever is longer.

No minimum liability provision is required for postretirement health care benefits. Because most plans are nonfunded or only minimally funded, the amortization of the transition adjustment will increase postretirement costs and thus result in recognition of the liability over a reasonably short period of time. The disclosure required for postretirement benefit plans includes all the requirements for pension plans plus information about health cost trend assumptions and sensitivity analysis of how postretirement expenses and the postretirement obligation would vary if the health care costs trend rate were increased by 1%.

Components of Net Periodic Postretirement Benefit Cost

Because much of the accounting for postretirement health care costs parallels the accounting for pension costs presented in this chapter, only the major differences in accounting for the six components of net periodic postretirement costs will be explained further. Exhibit 17-13 summarizes the major differences in accounting for these two types of retirement benefits. Undoubtedly, application of this standard will reveal many other areas for clarification and possible exceptions.

---

30 If the period of service needed to earn the postretirement benefits does not include previous years, the attribution period will be from a later date, referred to as the beginning of the credited service period. *FASB Statement No. 106, par. 44.*

reported. Published comments such as the following are typical: "Some companies are reducing their health care costs for retirees to ease the effect of the FASB rule." In addition, firms have expressed fears that the explicit recognition of a liability for nonpension retirement benefits will increase the probability that government will mandate or regulate such plans. However, others have praised the FASB for forcing companies to seriously face the magnitude of the promises they have made to take care of retirees' health care and other postretirement benefits.

QUESTIONS:

1. List several reasons for a firm to reduce its retiree health benefits in response to the FASB's requirement

that such plans be accounted for on an accrual rather than a pay-as-you-go basis. Critically evaluate each reason.

2. In general, FASB Statement No. 106 results in firms reporting lower earnings and higher liabilities. Would you expect stock prices to decline for companies with large postretirement benefit plans? Would you expect it to be harder for these firms to obtain loans?

SOURCES:
Lee Berton, "FASB Issues Rule Change on Benefits," *The Wall Street Journal,* December 20, 1990, p. A3.
Statement of Financial Accounting Standards No. 106, "Employers' Accounting for Postretirement Benefits Other Than Pensions," Norwalk, CT: Financial Accounting Standards Board, December 1990, pars. 118–132.

EXHIBIT 17–13 | Major Differences in Accounting for Pensions and Other Postretirement Benefits

Item	Pension	Other Postretirement Benefits
Service cost	Present value of increased benefits coming from one additional year of service.	Present value of equal attribution of postretirement benefit costs for period from hiring date to full eligibility date.
Interest cost	Interest on beginning-of-year projected benefit obligation at settlement rate of interest.	Interest on beginning-of-year accumulated postretirement benefit obligation at assumed discount rate.
Total obligation	Projected benefit obligation or accumulated benefit obligation depending on component being measured.	Accumulated postretirement benefit obligation.
Minimum liability	Must be reported if accumulated benefit obligation exceeds the fair value of plan assets adjusted for prepaid and accrued pension costs.	No provisions for minimum liability.
Transition amortization period	Average remaining service life of employees or 15 years, whichever is longer.	Immediate recognition or delayed recognition over the remaining service life or 20 years, whichever is longer.
Disclosure requirements	Description of plan, detail of pension expense, rate assumptions, and reconciliation of funded status of the plan with amounts reported on the balance sheet.	Same as pensions with additional information about the health cost trend rate used and sensitivity information about effect of rate change.

SERVICE COST Service costs in most defined benefit pension plans are computed by measuring the cost to the employer of additional benefits earned during a period (see page 988). Because most postretirement benefits do not increase with length of service or level of pay, a different definition of service cost is required.

The FASB defined two new terms to describe the nature of service costs for postretirement benefits: **expected postretirement benefit obligation (EPBO)** and **accumulated postretirement benefit obligation (APBO)**. The expected postretirement benefit obligation is the actuarial present value as of a particular date of the postretirement benefits expected to be paid by the employer to or for the employee, the employee's beneficiaries, and any covered dependents pursuant to the terms of the plan. The amount of the EPBO for an employee in nonpay-related plans differs each year only by the discount factor unless the actuarial assumptions are changed.

The APBO as of a particular date is the actuarial present value of all future benefits attributed (charged) to an employee's service up to that date, assuming the plan remains in effect and all the assumptions about the future are fulfilled. Prior to an employee's full eligibility date, the APBO as of a specific date for an employee is the portion of the EPBO attributed to that employee's service rendered to that date; on and after the full eligibility date, the APBO and EPBO for an employee are the same.

To illustrate these definitions, assume that the Haymond Electrical Company has a postretirement benefit plan and that John Jenkins is hired as an employee at age 50. The plan provides for full benefits after age 60 and Jenkins plans to retire at age 65. The assumed discount rate to compute present values is 8%. The EPBO measurement for Jenkins at the full eligibility date (age 60) is $87,000. Exhibit 17–14 illustrates how the EPBO and APBO would be calculated for the 15 years of employment: 10 years to full eligibility and another 5 years to retirement. Note that the fraction of the EPBO included in the APBO increases by $\frac{1}{10}$ each year. After 10 years, the EPBO and APBO are the same.

Exhibit 17–15 is an expansion of Exhibit 17–14 to show the computation of the service and interest cost components of the net periodic postretirement benefit cost for the Haymond plan. The service cost for each year between the hire date and the full eligibility date is a portion of the expected postretirement benefit attributed to each year. Because Jenkins had 10 years before the full eligibility date, the present value of $\frac{1}{10}$ of the computed EPBO at the full eligibility date for each year is defined as the service cost. No service cost accrues after the 10th year. If Jenkins had been employed by Haymond at age 45 rather than age 50, the portion of EPBO each year allocated to service cost would be $\frac{1}{15}$ rather than $\frac{1}{10}$.

Pensions and other postretirement benefits represent a substantial liability for many companies.

EXHIBIT 17–14 | Computation of Expected and Accumulated Postretirement Benefit Obligations for John Jenkins

Year	Interest Factor—8%	EPBO	Portion	APBO
0	0.4632	40,298	0	0
1	0.5002	43,517	$\frac{1}{10}$	4,352
2	0.5403	47,006	$\frac{2}{10}$	9,401
3	0.5835	50,765	$\frac{3}{10}$	15,229
4	0.6302	54,827	$\frac{4}{10}$	21,931
5	0.6806	59,212	$\frac{5}{10}$	29,606
6	0.7350	63,945	$\frac{6}{10}$	38,367
7	0.7938	69,061	$\frac{7}{10}$	48,343
8	0.8573	74,585	$\frac{8}{10}$	59,668
9	0.9259	80,553	$\frac{9}{10}$	72,498*
10	1.0000	87,000	$\frac{10}{10}$	87,000
11	1.0800	93,960		93,960
12	1.1664	101,477		101,477
13	1.2597	109,594		109,594
14	1.3605	118,364		118,364
15	1.4693	127,829		127,829

*Computation example: $87,000 × .9259 = $80,553; $80,553 × $\frac{9}{10}$ = $72,498.

EXHIBIT 17–15 | Computation of Service Cost and Interest Cost for John Jenkins

Year	Interest Factor—8%	EPBO	Portion	APBO	Service Cost	Interest Cost
0	0.4632	40,298	0	0	0	0
1	0.5002	43,517	$\frac{1}{10}$	4,352	4,352	0
2	0.5403	47,006	$\frac{2}{10}$	9,401	4,701	348
3	0.5835	50,765	$\frac{3}{10}$	15,229	5,076	752
4	0.6302	54,827	$\frac{4}{10}$	21,931	5,483	1,218
5	0.6806	59,212	$\frac{5}{10}$	29,606	5,921	1,754
6	0.7350	63,945	$\frac{6}{10}$	38,367	6,395	2,368
7	0.7938	69,061	$\frac{7}{10}$	48,343	6,906	3,069
8	0.8573	74,585	$\frac{8}{10}$	59,668	7,459	3,867
9	0.9259	80,553	$\frac{9}{10}$	72,498	8,055*	4,773**
10	1.0000	87,000	$\frac{10}{10}$	87,000	8,700	5,800
11	1.0800	93,960		93,960	0	6,960
12	1.1664	101,477		101,477	0	7,517
13	1.2597	109,594		109,594	0	8,118
14	1.3605	118,364		118,364	0	8,768
15	1.4693	127,829		127,829	0	9,469
					63,048	64,781

*Computation example: $8,700 × .9259 = $8,055.
**Computation example: $59,668 × .08 = $4,773.
Note: The accumulated sum of service cost and interest cost equals the APBO.

In the above example, the EPBO at the full eligibility date for Jenkins was $87,000. Because this amount is attributed to the period between the hire date and the full eligibility date and because the Haymond plan provides for full benefits after a single date is reached, ¹⁄₁₀ of the $87,000, or $8,700, is attributed to each year of service between these dates. The service cost in any given year is the present value of this equal amount for that year. Thus, for Year 1 the service cost is $4,352 ($8,700 × .5002), and for Year 5, it is $5,921 ($8,700 × .6806). If the postretirement benefit plan provides for different percentages of benefits for different years of service, the service cost must be computed using the specific provisions of the plan.[31]

INTEREST COST   The interest cost component of the net periodic postretirement benefit is computed by applying an assumed discount (interest) rate to the beginning APBO. The assumed discount rate should reflect the rates of return on high-quality fixed income investments currently available whose cash flows match the timing and amount of expected benefit payments.[32] Thus, for Year 3 in Exhibit 17–15, the interest cost is $752 ($9,401 × 8%). Note that after the full eligibility date is reached, the interest cost component continues to grow even though service cost does not continue to accrue.

ACTUAL RETURN ON POSTRETIREMENT PLAN ASSETS   Because most plans in the past have not been funded, this offset against net periodic postretirement benefit expense will not be present for many employers until funding begins. As is true for pension accounting, the actual return is adjusted to the expected return through the gain or loss computation. If the fund holding the assets is a taxable entity, the actual return on plan assets shall reflect the tax expense or benefit for the period.

AMORTIZATION OF POSTRETIREMENT PRIOR SERVICE COSTS   These costs arise from plan initiations and amendments as they do for pensions. If the amendment includes provisions that count service years prior to the amendment date, the additional EPBO related to those years is calculated and amortized over the period from the date of the amendment to the full eligibility date. If the amendment provision only relates to future service periods, the additional costs are added to the service cost for the future years.

GAINS AND LOSSES ARISING FROM CHANGES IN THE APBO AND PLAN ASSETS
These gains and losses arise from experiences different from those assumed in initiating the plan or from changes in actuarial assumptions. They may be recognized immediately or deferred and amortized over future service periods if they exceed a "corridor" amount similar to that used for pensions. The corridor amount is 10% of the larger of the APBO or the market-related value of the postretirement plan assets as of the beginning of the year. Consistent treatment over the years is required.

AMORTIZATION OF TRANSITION ADJUSTMENT   As with pensions, a transition adjustment is computed when the postretirement standard is applied. The adjustment arises from over- or underfunded APBO for all the earned benefits of all plan participants at the transition date. The FASB decided to allow adopting companies to either recognize the transition asset or obligation immediately in the year the standard is applied or delay the recognition and amortize it over the average remaining service life of active participants or 20 years, whichever is longer.[33] If immediate recognition is selected, the offset to the asset or obligation is to be accounted for as a cumulative change adjustment to income in the transition year.[34]

---

31   See Appendix C of FASB Statement No. 106 for several illustrations of the computation of service cost under different assumed postretirement benefit plans.
32   *Statement of Financial Accounting Standards No. 106*, par. 31.
33   If most plan participants are inactive, for example, retired, amortization should be based on the life expectancy of the plan participants.
34   The adjustment to income would be net of any income tax effects. If the transition adjustment remains nondeductible for tax purposes, a timing difference deferred tax could result. See Chapter 16 for discussion of accounting for income taxes.

To illustrate, assume that Haymond Electrical Company had not funded nor recorded postretirement benefits but elected to make the transition to the accrual method at the end of Year 5. The transition obligation for John Jenkins as illustrated in Exhibit 17-14, would be $29,606. Haymond has the choice of immediately recognizing this amount as a postretirement obligation and a charge to the current income, to delay recognition over the 10 years to Jenkins' retirement ($2,961 per year), or to delay recognition over 20 years ($1,480 per year).

Disclosure of Postretirement Benefit Plans

The same work sheet reconciliation illustrated for pensions could be used for postretirement benefits. This information is part of the disclosure requirement of the standard. The health cost trend rate must be based on stated assumptions about the many variables discussed earlier. In most instances, the company must estimate the future variables. The one exception is future government regulations. The Board decided that anticipating federal legislation was too subjective, and it allowed companies to base its forecast of the government's activity on enacted legislation.

Appendix 17

Present Value Calculations—Thakkar Company

This appendix contains the detailed present value calculations underlying the pension liability numbers reported in the Thakkar Company example used in the body of the chapter. The tables referred to are in Appendix B.

Accumulated Benefit Obligation—January 1, 2002:

- Length of service: 10 years
- Highest salary: $40,000 (future salary increases ignored)
- Annual pension payment: $8,000 = [(2% × 10 years) × $40,000]
- Number of pension payments to be received after retirement: 10
- Length of time until retirement: 30 years
- Discount rate: 10%

The present value of the annuity stream of 10 $8,000 pension payments is computed as follows:

$$PVn = R(PVAF_{\overline{n}|i})$$

where:

$$R = \$8,000 \text{ annual payment}$$
$$n = 10 \text{ years}$$
$$i = 10\% \text{ discount rate}$$
$$PVn = \$8,000 \text{ (Table IV } _{\overline{10}|10\%})$$
$$PVn = \$8,000 \text{ (6.1446)}$$
$$PVn = \$49,157 \text{ (rounded to the nearest dollar)}$$

Recall from Appendix B that the formula for the present value of an annuity is derived under the assumption that the first annuity payment is made at the end of the first period. Viewed in another way, because the first pension payment to Bach is made on December 31, 2032, $49,157 is the present value of the stream of 10 payments as of January 1, 2032. Thakkar Company wishes to calculate the present value of the stream of payments as of January 1, 2002. This can be done by computing the present value of the lump sum of $49,157, as follows (see Exhibit 17-16):

$$PV = A(PVAF_{\overline{n}|i})$$

where:

$$A = \$49,157$$
$$n = 30 \text{ years (difference between 1/1/2032 and 1/1/2002)}$$
$$i = 10\% \text{ discount rate}$$
$$PV = \$49,157 \text{ (Table II } _{\overline{30}|10\%})$$
$$PV = \$49,157 \text{ (0.05731)*}$$
$$PV = \$2,817 \text{ (rounded to the nearest dollar)}$$

*This factor has been expanded to five decimal places to avoid rounding error.

Let's review the information and assumptions needed in arriving at the actuarial present value for Thakkar's pension liability.

1. How long has Bach worked for Thakkar?
2. What salary will Bach's pension benefit be based on? In this example, Bach's most recent salary was used as an indicator of the highest salary.
3. How long until Bach retires?

EXHIBIT 17–16 | Thakkar Company—Accumulated Benefit Obligation, January 1, 2002

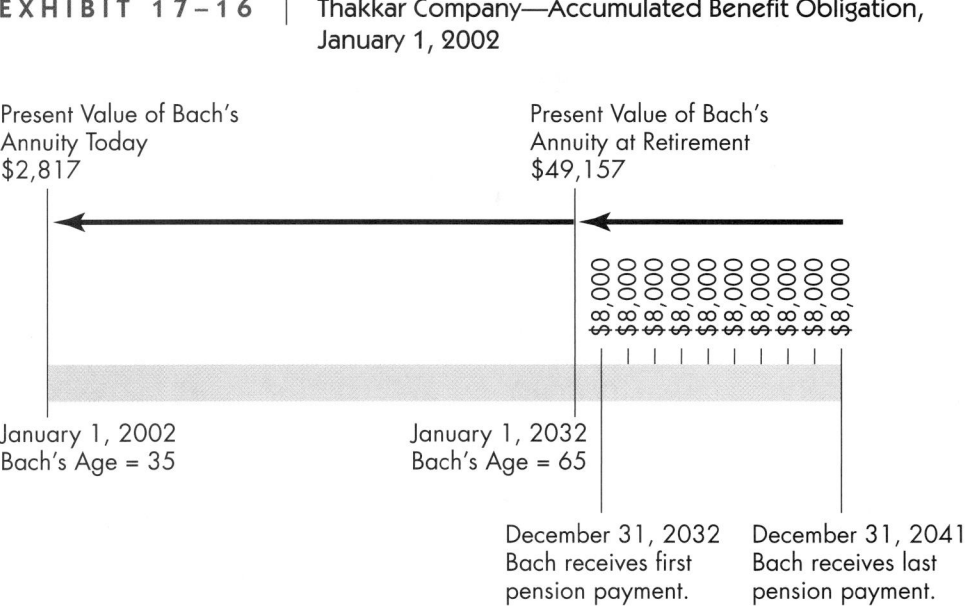

4. How long will Bach live after retirement?
5. What is the appropriate discount rate?

Under the assumptions made, the actuarial present value was $2,817. To illustrate how sensitive this calculation is to the assumptions made, the table below summarizes how the actuarial present value would change if different values for the discount rate and the length of Bach's life after retirement were used.

	Years of Life After Retirement				
Discount Rate	**5**	**10**	**15**	**20**	**25**
6%	5,867	10,252	13,528	15,976	17,806
8%	3,174	5,335	6,805	7,806	8,487
10%	1,738	2,817	3,487	3,903	4,162
12%	963	1,509	1,819	1,995	2,094
14%	539	819	964	1,040	1,079

As an illustration of the impact of the discount rate assumption on the magnitude of the ABO, restrict your attention to the 10-year column. Note that each 2% decrease in the discount rate nearly doubles the amount of the pension liability. The impact of changes in the discount rate assumption is particularly large in this Thakkar example because the expected pension payments are so many years in the future. However, the general point is valid with all computations of the actuarial present value of a pension liability—the final result is sensitive to the assumptions made.

Projected Benefit Obligation—January 1, 2002:

- Length of service: 10 years
- Estimated salary growth rate: 5%
- Length of time until retirement: 30 years
- Projected highest salary: $172,876 = $40,000 (Table I $_{\overline{30}|\,5\%}$) = $40,000 (4.3219)
- Annual pension payment: $34,575 = [(2% × 10 years) × $172,876]
- Number of pension payments to be received after retirement: 10
- Discount rate: 10%

The present value of the annuity stream of 10 $34,575 pension payments is computed as follows:

$$PV_n = R (PVAF_{\overline{n}|\,i})$$

where:
- R = $34,575 annual payment
- n = 10 years
- i = 10% discount rate
- PV_n = $34,575 (Table IV $_{\overline{10}|\,10\%}$)
- PV_n = $34,575 (6.1446)
- PV_n = $212,450 (rounded to the nearest dollar)

Compute the present value of the stream of payments as of January 1, 2002, as follows:

$$PV = A (PVAF_{\overline{n}|\,i})$$

where:
- A = $212,450
- n = 30 years (difference between 1/1/2032 and 1/1/2002)
- i = 10% discount rate
- PV = $212,450 (Table II $_{\overline{30}|\,10\%}$)
- PV = $212,450 (0.05731)
- PV = $12,176 (rounded to the nearest dollar)

As illustrated with the ABO computations and as shown in Exhibit 17–17, PBO actuarial present values are sensitive to the underlying assumptions. The additional assumption about future salary increases makes the PBO even more sensitive. The table below contains PBO values for different combinations of discount rate and salary growth rate assumptions, holding all other values constant.

Discount Rate	Salary Growth Rate					
	0%	**1%**	**3%**	**5%**	**7%**	**9%**
6%	10,252	13,818	24,884	44,307	78,039	136,017
8%	5,335	7,190	12,949	23,056	40,609	70,778
10%	2,817	3,797	6,838	12,176	21,444	37,376
12%	1,509	2,034	3,662	6,521	11,485	20,017
14%	819	1,104	1,988	3,540	6,235	10,866

The 0% column is equivalent to the ABO because it reflects the assumption of no future salary increases—it corresponds to the 10-year column in the earlier table of ABO values.

The range of discount rate and salary growth rate assumptions used in this hypothetical illustration is generally in line with what is observed for actual companies. In 1995, large U.S. corporations reported using discount rates ranging from 4.5% to 11.0% and salary growth rate assumptions from 1.0% to 10.0%. Extreme combinations of discount rate and salary growth rate assumptions are unlikely to occur in practice. For example, it is very unusual for the assumed salary growth rate to exceed the discount rate. The most typical case is for the discount rate to exceed the salary growth rate by 2% to 4%.

Computation of Service Cost for 2002

Service cost for 2002 is the increase in the PBO caused by the addition of one more service year in the computation of the expected amount of the pension benefit payments. The details of this computation for the Thakkar Company example are shown below.

Projected Benefit Obligation, Jan. 1, 2003, *with* an extra year of service:
Annual pension payment: $38,033 = [(2% × 11 years) × $172,876].

EXHIBIT 17–17 | Thakkar Company—Projected Benefit Obligation, January 1, 2002

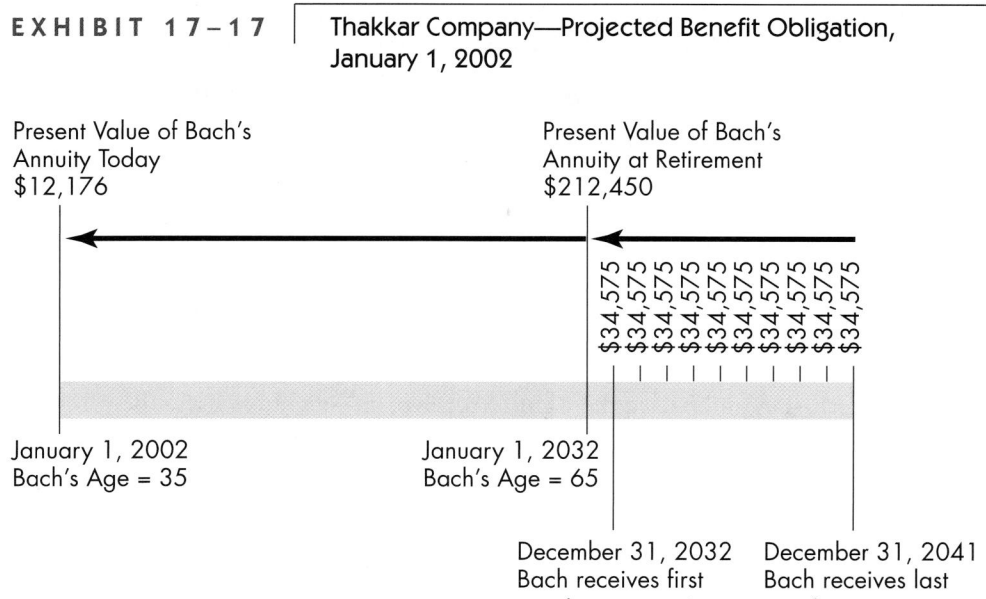

Computation of the present value of the annuity stream of 10 $38,033 payments:

PVn = $38,033 (Table IV $\overline{10}|_{10\%}$)
PVn = $38,033 (6.1446)
PVn = $233,698 (rounded to the nearest dollar)

Computation of the present value of the lump sum of $233,698:

PV = $233,698 (Table II $\overline{29}|_{10\%}$)
PV = $233,698 (0.06304)*
PV = $14,732 (rounded to the nearest dollar)

*This factor has been expanded to five decimal places to avoid rounding error.

Projected Benefit Obligation, January 1, 2003, *without* an extra year of service:

Annual pension payment: $34,575 = [(2% × 10 years) × $172,876].

Computation of the present value of the annuity stream of 10 $34,575 payments:

PVn = $34,575 (Table IV $\overline{10}|_{10\%}$)
PVn = $34,575 (6.1446)
PVn = $212,450 (rounded to the nearest dollar)

Computation of the present value of the lump sum of $212,450:

PV = $212,450 (Table II $\overline{29}|_{10\%}$)
PV = $212,450 (0.06304)
PV = $13,393 (rounded to the nearest dollar)

Service Cost for 2002:

PBO, 1/1/03, *with* an extra year of service	$14,732
PBO, 1/1/03, *without* an extra year of service	13,393
Increase in PBO resulting from 2002 service	$ 1,339

The interest cost and service cost for 2002 can be used to reconcile the change in the PBO between January 1, 2002, and January 1, 2003.

PBO, 1/1/02	$12,176
Interest cost ($12,176 × .10)	1,218
Service cost	1,339
Projected Benefit Obligation 1/1/03	$14,733*

*Difference due to rounding.

REVIEW OF LEARNING OBJECTIVES

1 **Account for payroll and payroll taxes, and understand the criteria for recognizing a liability associated with compensated absences.** Accounting for payroll and payroll taxes are routine events that occur at the end of every pay period. In addition to accounting for the taxes withheld from employees, care must be taken to ensure that employer payroll taxes are considered. Employers are responsible for FICA as well as state and federal unemployment taxes. As employees work, they often earn the right to receive, in the future, time off for sickness or vacation. These days are referred to as compensated absences and must be accounted for as expenses in the period in which the employee earns those rights.

2 **Compute performance bonuses, and recognize the issues associated with postemployment benefits.** In addition to regular payroll, employees may have the opportunity to receive additional compensation based on the achievement of performance goals. This additional compensation often takes the form of bonuses or stock options. The accounting for stock options requires estimates as to future value and can become quite complex. In some cases employees will leave a firm, either voluntarily or involuntarily. Benefits promised to these employees following employment but prior to retirement must be accounted for in a fashion similar to the accounting for compensated absences.

3 **Understand the nature and characteristics of employer pension plans, including a detailed discussion of defined benefit plans.** Pension plans can be structured as either defined benefit plans or defined contribution plans. With defined contribution plans, the employee receives, upon retirement, the funds that have accumulated over time. Accounting for defined contribution plans is straightforward. Defined benefit plans are more challenging in that the value of the benefits are often difficult to measure. These benefits are often a function of years of service, future salary levels, and life expectancy. Actuaries are employed to provide estimates as to projected future benefits.

4 **Use the components of the prepaid/ accrued pension costs and changes in the components to compute the periodic expense associated with pensions.** The prepaid/accrued pension account reflects the difference between the present value of the amount expected to be paid in the future (PBO) and the fair value of the plan assets (FVPA) set aside to meet that obligation. Additional factors can affect the pension account as well. These additional factors include transition gains/losses, prior service costs, and deferred gains/losses related to differences between expected and actual returns on plan assets.

Each year an assessment is made as to the additional benefits owed as a result of another year of service, the effects of being a year closer to paying out benefits, and the return received as a result of setting aside funds to meet these future obligations. The additional factors mentioned in the previous paragraph also affect the amount reported on the income statement in that they each may require adjustment over time.

5 **Prepare required disclosures associated with pensions, and understand the accounting treatment for pension settlements and curtailments.** Detailed disclosure is required relating to pensions. The assumptions made by actuaries relating to expected return on assets, discount rates, and projected increases in salaries are required to be disclosed. In addition, firms are required to disclose the components of the prepaid/accrued pension cost from the balance sheet as well as the periodic pension expense amount disclosed on the income statement. Most of the required disclosures can be provided through presentation of a work sheet such as those illustrated in the chapter.

In the event that the benefits associated with a pension plan are curtailed, any prior service cost associated with the curtailment is recognized as a loss and offset against adjustments required to the PBO. Pension settlements often give rise to gains or losses. The FASB determined that those gains and losses resulting from irrevocable actions by the company that relieved the company of future obligations were to be recognized immediately.

6 **Describe the few remaining differences between U.S. pension accounting standards and the provisions of IAS 19.** IAS 19 was revised in January 1998 and now requires that a company's pension obligation be measured using basically the same approach as is used under U.S. GAAP. IAS 19 does *not* include any provision for recognition of an additional minimum liability.

7 **Explain the differences in accounting for pensions and postretirement benefits other than pensions, and be able to account for**

postretirement benefits other than pensions. While many of the concepts used in accounting for pensions are similar to those used in accounting for postretirement benefits other than pensions, there are some important differences. A common difference, unrelated to the accounting for these benefits, relates to other postretirement benefits being largely unfunded by companies.

Other differences relate to other postretirement benefits often not being a function of salary levels and to the difficulty of measuring these other benefits. Finally, the accounting standard on other postretirement benefits (Statement No. 106) does not require recognition of a minimum liability as is the case with pensions.

KEY TERMS

Accumulated benefit obligation (ABO) 985
Actual return on pension plan assets 994
Actuarial present value 984
Additional pension liability 1002
Compensated absences 977
Contributory pension plan 981
Corridor amount 1001
Curtailment of a pension plan 1008
Deferred pension cost 1003
Defined benefit pension plans 982
Defined contribution pension plans 981
Expected return on pension plan assets 998
Expected service period 995

Fair value of pension plan assets 989
Market-related value of pension plan assets 998
Minimum pension liability 1002
Net periodic pension expense 984
Noncontributory pension plans 981
Pension gain or loss 997
Pension plan 980
Pension plan assets 982
Postretirement benefits other than pensions 981
Prepaid/accrued pension cost 990
Prior service cost 992
Projected benefit obligation (PBO) 986
Service cost 988
Settlement interest rate 988
Settlement of a pension plan 1007

Single-employer pension plans 981
Transition gain or loss 992
Unrecognized net pension gain or loss 999
Vested benefits 983

Accumulated postretirement benefit obligation (APBO) 1016
Expected postretirement benefit obligation (EPBO) 1016
Full eligibility date 1013

QUESTIONS

1. Gross payroll is taxed by both federal and state governments. Identify these taxes and indicate who bears the cost of the tax, the employer or the employee.
2. How should compensated absences be accounted for?
3. The sales manager for Off-Road Enterprises is entitled to a bonus equal to 12% of profits. What difficulties may arise in the interpretation of this profitsharing agreement?
4. Distinguish between (a) a defined benefit plan and a defined contribution plan, (b) a contributory plan and a noncontributory plan, (c) a multiemployer plan and a single-employer plan.
5. What is meant by the term vesting?
6. What factors must be considered by actuaries in determining the amount of future benefits under a defined benefit plan?

7. What five accounting issues were addressed by the FASB in relation to defined benefit plans?
8. Distinguish between the accumulated benefit approach and the projected benefit approach in determining the amount of future benefits earned by employees under a defined benefit pension plan.
9. List and briefly describe the six basic components of net periodic pension expense.
10. Explain how prior service costs arise (a) at the inception of a pension plan, and (b) at the time of a plan's amendment.
11. How is the service cost portion of net periodic pension expense to be measured according to FASB Statement No. 87?
12. Does pension cost include the actual return on plan assets or the expected return? Explain.
13. Because prior service cost is related to years of service already rendered, why is it considered to be a future pension expense?

14. (a) How is the transition gain or loss arising from adoption of FASB Statement No. 87 computed? (b) How is the unrecognized transition gain or loss amortized?

15. The FASB permits the use of an average market value of plan assets for some pension computations. In other cases, the fair market value at a specific measurement date must be used. Under what circumstances is the average market value permissible?

16. Why is a corridor amount identified in recognizing gain or loss from pension plans?

17. (a) Under what conditions does FASB Statement No. 87 provide for recording a contra equity account? (b) How is it adjusted from period to period? (c) How does this contra equity account affect net income?

18. What is the function of the pension disclosure requirement included in the pension standards?

19. Distinguish between a pension settlement and a pension curtailment.

20. Which international accounting standard governs the accounting for pensions? When was this standard last revised?

21. What are the two major differences between IAS 19 and U.S. GAAP?

22. What innovation in accounting for pensions is currently being considered in the United Kingdom?

23. What is meant by postretirement benefits, and what is the primary issue in accounting for their costs?

24. Describe the differences between pension plans and other postretirement benefit plans.

25. What is the full eligibility date, and why is it an important date in accounting for postretirement benefits?

26. Describe the major differences between the accounting for pensions and other postretirement benefits.

DISCUSSION CASES

CASE 17–1

WHY FIX SOMETHING THAT ISN'T BROKEN?

The FASB's study of pension accounting for employers generated considerable interest among business executives. During the extended discussion period, pressure was brought to bear against the FASB by several individuals and the companies they represented to leave pension accounting alone. These business executives felt that the existing standards (APB Opinion No. 8) were adequate and that further tinkering with the pension provisions was unnecessary. What are some of the factors that caused the FASB to "hold on to" the pension issue until a standard was released?

CASE 17–2

WHAT THEORETICAL SUPPORT IS THERE FOR THE PENSION STANDARDS?

The topic of pensions and other postretirement benefits was considered at length in an accounting theory class. The discussion centered on the following terms.

(a) Representational faithfulness
(b) Substance over form
(c) Verifiability
(d) Usefulness
(e) Present value
(f) Conservatism
(g) Adequate disclosure

How are these terms helpful in justifying the accounting for pension and other postretirement benefit plans on the employer's books? Based on your understanding of these terms, assess the treatment of pension and other postretirement benefit plans by the FASB in Statement Nos. 87, 88, and 106.

CASE 17–3

ARE THOSE POSTRETIREMENT BENEFITS REALLY ACCRUABLE?

George Logan, controller of Dyatine, Inc., has just finished reading a *Wall Street Journal* article about accounting for postretirement health costs. Dyatine has informally agreed to pay the medical costs of its retirees and their spouses for as long as they live. Because the company has a young workforce, very little has been paid under this program. Last year, an analysis of the potential liability indicated that there would not be significant risk of payment for at least 10 years. No liability for future benefits has been accrued on Dyatine's books. But according to the article, this must change under FASB Statement No. 106. George has always felt that Dyatine was being generous with its employees and that if economic circumstances changed, the plan easily could be altered or terminated. George calls his CPA, Debra Adams, to ask her how she feels about the FASB standard. He is surprised to learn that Debra is very supportive of the standard. He asks for reasons, and Debra, in turn, asks George to support his position. Prepare a summary of the pros and cons surrounding the implementation of FASB Statement No. 106.

CASE 17–4

DOES ACCOUNTING HAVE POLITICAL CONSEQUENCES?

C. B. Seabright, a U.S. congresswoman, has just received from her staff an analysis of FASB Statement No. 106, "Employers' Accounting for Postretirement Benefits Other Than Pensions." Seabright is very influential in the formation of tax legislation and also in federal regulation of employer-provided health care plans. How might FASB Statement No. 106 impact Seabright's legislative agenda?

CASE 17–5

LET THE USER BEWARE!

Joseph Hudson is a financial analyst. Hudson recently received the annual reports of Company A and Company B. Both Company A and Company B are in the same industry, one that Hudson specializes in. Hudson was interested to note that Company A had substantially lower earnings in the prior year than Company B, but Company A's earnings were slightly higher than B's in the current year. Hudson was ready to recommend Company A as a company on the rebound when he remembered that both Company A and Company B had substantial postretirement benefit plans other than pensions and both had adopted FASB Statement No. 106 in the prior year. What might explain the earnings trends for Companies A and B? Why do accounting standards allow like items to be accounted for differently by different firms? How can users of financial statements avoid confusion over the use of differing accounting methods by similar firms?

EXERCISES

EXERCISE 17–6

RECORDING PAYROLL AND PAYROLL TAXES

The Express Company paid one week's wages of $21,200 in cash (net pay after all withholdings and deductions) to its employees. Income tax withholdings were equal to 17% of the gross payroll, and the only other deductions were 7.65% for FICA tax and $160 for union dues. Give the entries that should be made on the books of the company to record the payroll and the tax accruals to be recognized by the employer, assuming that the company is subject to unemployment taxes of 5.4% (state) and 0.8% (federal). Assume all wages for the week are subject to FICA and unemployment taxes.

EXERCISE 17–7

MONTHLY PAYROLL ENTRIES

Aggie Co. sells agricultural products. Aggie pays its salespeople a salary plus a commission. The salary is the same for each salesperson, $1,000 per month. The commission varies by length of time of employment and is a percentage of the company's total gross sales. Each salesperson starts with a commission of 1.0%, which is increased an additional 0.5% for each full year of employment with Aggie, to a maximum of 5.0%. The total gross sales for the month of January were $120,000.

Aggie has 6 salespeople as follows:

	No. of Years Employment
Frank	10
Sally	9
Tina	8
Barry	6
Mark	3
Lisa	9 mos.

Assume the FICA rate is 7.65%, the FUTA rate is 6.2%, and the state unemployment rate is 5.4%. (Assume the federal government allows the maximum credit for state unemployment tax paid.) The federal income tax withholding rate is 30%. Compute the January salaries and commissions expense, and make any necessary entries to record the payroll transactions.

EXERCISE 17–8

COMPENSATED ABSENCE—VACATION PAY

The Merckx Company employs 6 people. Each employee is entitled to 2 weeks' paid vacation every year the employee works for the company. The conditions of the paid vacation are (a) for each full year of work, an employee will receive two weeks of paid vacation (no vacation accrues for a portion of a year), (b) each employee will receive the same pay for vacation time as the regular pay in the year taken, and (c) unused vacation pay can be carried forward. Based on the following data, compute the liability for vacation pay as of December 31, 2002.

Employee	Starting Date	Cumulative Vacation Taken as of December 31, 2002	Weekly Salary
Andy Hampsten	December 21, 1995	10 weeks	$475
Phil Anderson	March 6, 2000	2 weeks	600
Lance Armstrong	August 13, 2001	none	450
Steve Bauer	December 17, 2000	3 weeks	400
Sean Yates	March 29, 2002	none	500
Michele Fellows	May 31, 1994	14 weeks	700

EXERCISE 17–9

CALCULATION OF BONUS

Illinois Wholesale Company has an agreement with its sales manager whereby that individual is entitled to 7% of company earnings as a bonus. Company income for the calendar year before bonus and income tax is $350,000. Income tax is 30% of income after bonus.

1. Compute the amount of bonus if the bonus is calculated on income before deductions for bonus and income tax.
2. Compute the amount of bonus if the bonus is calculated on income after deduction for bonus but before deduction for income tax.

EXERCISE 17–10

COMPUTING DEFINED BENEFIT PENSION PAYMENTS

Francisco Company has established a defined benefit pension plan for its lone employee, Derrald Ryan. Annual payments under the pension plan are equal to 3% of Derrald's highest lifetime salary multiplied by the number of years with the company. Derrald's salary in 2001 was $75,000. Derrald is expected to retire in 20 years, and his salary increases are expected to average 4% per year during that period. As of the beginning of 2002, Derrald had worked for Francisco Company for 12 years.

1. What is the amount of the annual pension payment that should be used in computing Francisco's accumulated benefit obligation (ABO) as of January 1, 2002?
2. What is the amount of the annual pension payment that should be used in computing Francisco's projected benefit obligation (PBO) as of January 1, 2002?

EXERCISE 17–11

COMPUTATION OF PENSION SERVICE COST

Pension plan information for Springfield Metro Company is as follows:

January 1, 2002	PBO	$3,620,000
	ABO	2,850,000
During 2002	Pension benefits paid to retired employees	272,000
December 31, 2002	PBO	4,150,000
	ABO	3,125,000
Discount (settlement) rate		12%

Assuming no change in actuarial assumptions, what is the pension service cost for 2002?

EXERCISE 17–12

COMPUTING THE AMOUNT OF PREPAID/ACCRUED PENSION COST

Using the information given for the following 3 independent cases, compute the amount of prepaid/accrued pension cost that would be reported on the balance sheet. Clearly indicate whether the amount would be shown as an asset or as a liability.

	Case 1	Case 2	Case 3
Unamortized transition loss	$ 60	$ 130	$ 40
Unrecognized prior service cost	250	60	10
PBO	1,000	900	1,000
Unrecognized net pension gain	70	120	200
ABO	750	800	850
FVPA	700	1,300	900

EXERCISE 17–13

AMORTIZATION OF PRIOR SERVICE COST—PLAN AMENDMENT

Queensland Company has 5 employees belonging to its pension plan. One employee is expected to retire each year over the next 5 years.

On January 1, 2002, Queensland initiated an amendment to its pension plan that increased the PBO for the plan by $620,000. If Queensland amortizes the prior service cost of the pension plan using the sum-of-the-years'-digits method, determine the amortization for the each of the next 5 years.

EXERCISE 17–14

AMOUNT OF FUNDING AND AMORTIZATION OF PRIOR SERVICE COST

Stratosphere, Inc., has a workforce of 300 employees. A new pension plan is negotiated on January 1, 2002, with the labor union. Based on the provisions of the pension agreement, prior service cost related to the new plan amounts to $3,726,000. The cost is to be funded evenly with annual contributions over a 10-year period, with the first payment due at the end of 2002. The cost is to be amortized over the average remaining service life of the covered employees. The interest rate for funding purposes is 10%. It is anticipated that, on the average, 10 employees will retire each year over the next 30 years.

1. Compute the annual amount Stratosphere will pay to fund its prior service cost.
2. Compute the amount of amortization of prior service cost for 2002, 2004, and 2009.

EXERCISE 17–15

AMORTIZATION OF PRIOR SERVICE COST—STRAIGHT-LINE METHOD

Osvaldo Awning Co. has unrecognized prior service cost of $1,262,000 arising from a pension plan amendment. The board of directors decided to amortize this cost over the average remaining service period for its 45 employees on a straight-line basis. It is assumed that employees will retire at the rate of 3 employees each year over a 15-year period.

1. Compute the average remaining service life and the annual amortization of prior service cost for Osvaldo.

2. Assuming that pension expense other than amortization of prior service cost was $460,000 for the year and $520,000 was contributed by the employer to the pension fund, prepare the formal summary journal entries relating to the pension plan for the current year.

EXERCISE 17–16

COMPUTATION OF ACTUAL RETURN ON PLAN ASSETS

The Longlee Electrical Company maintains a fund to cover its pension plan. The following data relate to the fund for 2002.

January 1	FVPA	$875,000
	Market-related value of plan assets (5-year weighted average)	715,000
During year	Pension benefits paid	62,000
	Contributions made to the fund	70,000
December 31	FVPA	980,000
	Market-related value of plan assets (5-year weighted average)	730,000

Compute the 2002 actual return on plan assets for Longlee Electrical.

EXERCISE 17–17

RETURN ON PLAN ASSETS—EXPECTED AND ACTUAL

Tingey Originals has a pension plan covering its 75 employees. Tingey anticipates a 12% return on its pension plan assets. The fund trustee furnishes Tingey with the following information relating to the pension fund for 2002:

January 1	FVPA	$1,350,000
	Market-related value of pension plan assets (5-year weighted average)	1,100,000
During year	Actual return on pension plan assets	155,000
December 31	FVPA	1,470,000
	Market-related value of pension plan assets (5-year weighted average)	1,210,000

Compute the difference between the actual and expected return on plan assets. How should the difference be treated in determining pension expense for 2002, assuming Tingey bases expected return on the market-related value of the plan assets?

EXERCISE 17–18

AMORTIZATION OF UNRECOGNIZED GAIN ON PLAN ASSETS

Melba Enterprises has an unrecognized gain of $425,000 relating to its pension plan as of January 1, 2002. Management has chosen to amortize this deferral on a straight-line basis over the 10-year average remaining service life of its employees, subject to the limitation of the corridor amount. Additional facts about the pension plan as of January 1, 2002, are as follows:

PBO	$2,050,000
ABO	1,900,000
Fair value of pension plan assets	1,500,000
Market-related value of pension plan assets (5-year weighted average)	1,350,000

Compute the minimum amortization of unrecognized gain to be recognized by Melba in 2002.

EXERCISE 17–19

COMPUTATION OF GAIN OR LOSS COMPONENT

The gain or loss component of pension expense consists of (1) a deferral of the difference between actual and expected return on pension plan assets and (2) amortization of unrecognized pension gains and losses. Determine the proper addition (deduction) to pension expense related to the gain or loss component under each of the following independent conditions.

	A	B	C	D
(1) Actual return on pension plan assets	$200,000	$200,000	$ 500,000	$500,000
(2) Expected return on pension plan assets	$180,000	$230,000	$ 400,000	$550,000
(3) Unrecognized (gain) loss at beginning of year	$200,000	$275,000	$(100,000)	$ (75,000)
(4) Average service life of employees used for amortization	10 years	5 years	8 years	12 years
(5) Corridor amount	$100,000	$150,000	$ 50,000	$175,000

EXERCISE 17–20

COMPUTATION OF PENSION COST AND JOURNAL ENTRIES

The accountants for Bern Financial Services provide you with the following detailed information at December 31, 2002. Based on these data, prepare the journal entries related to the accrual and funding of pension expense for 2002.

Service cost	$45,000
Actual return on pension plan assets	75,000
Interest cost	52,000
Excess of expected return over actual return on pension plan assets	20,000
Amortization of deferred pension loss from prior years	15,000
Amortization of transition loss	8,000
Amortization of prior service cost	30,000
Contribution to pension fund	72,000

EXERCISE 17–21

PENSION COST COMPUTATION

Fredco's defined benefit pension plan had a PBO of $10,000,000 at the beginning of the year. This was based on a 10% discount rate (settlement interest rate). The fair value of pension plan assets at the beginning of the year was $10,400,000. These assets were expected to earn a long-term rate of return on the fair value of 8%. During the year, service cost was $750,000. At the date of transition to FASB Statement No. 87, a net pension asset of $375,000 existed. Of this amount, $25,000 remains, which will be amortized this period. There was no unrecognized prior service cost or unrecognized net pension gain (loss) at the beginning of the year. The actual return on pension plan assets for the year was $900,000. The ABO was $9,500,000 at the beginning of the year. Compute Fredco's net periodic pension expense for the year.

EXERCISE 17–22

PREPARING A PENSION WORK SHEET

The following information relates to the defined benefit pension plan of Mascare Company.

January 1, 2002:	
PBO	$ 9,000
FVPA	11,000
Expected return on plan assets	8%
Settlement discount rate	10%
For the year ended December 31, 2002:	
Service cost	$1,200
Benefit payments to retirees	500
Contributions to pension fund	100
Actual return on plan assets	1,500

Prepare a pension work sheet for Mascare Company for 2002.

EXERCISE 17–23

COMPUTING AND RECORDING MINIMUM PENSION LIABILITY

Tacoma Energy Corp. has had a retirement program for its employees for several years. It adopted FASB Statement No. 87 beginning January 1, 1989. The following information relates to the plan for 2002.

Balances at December 31, 2002:

PBO	$967,500
ABO	825,000
FVPA	790,000
Market-related value of pension plan assets (5-year weighted average)	750,000
Prepaid pension cost	27,000
Unamortized transition loss	76,000
Unrecognized prior service cost	80,000
Unrecognized net pension loss	42,500

In prior years, no additional liability was required. Compute the minimum pension liability, if any, for 2002, and prepare any necessary journal entries to record the liability.

EXERCISE 17–24

COMPUTING MINIMUM PENSION LIABILITY

Chateau Furniture and Cabinet Mfg. Co. computes the following balances for its defined benefit pension plan as of the end of its fiscal year.

	(In thousands)
PBO	$1,625
ABO	1,380
FVPA	1,460
Market-related value of pension plan assets (5-year weighted average)	1,336
Accrued pension cost	61
Unamortized transition loss	115
Unrecognized prior service cost	180
Unrecognized net pension (gain)	(191)

1. According to FASB Statement No. 87, what is the amount of additional liability, if any, required to reflect the minimum pension liability?
2. Some FASB members felt that the minimum pension liability should consider expected future salary levels rather than the current levels. If this approach had been adopted in the standard, what additional liability adjustment, if any, would have been required?

EXERCISE 17–25

RECONCILIATION OF FUNDING STATUS

From the following information for each of 3 independent cases, prepare the pension note disclosure that outlines the items that go into the computation of the net prepaid/accrued pension cost reported in the balance sheet.

	(In thousands)		
	Case 1	Case 2	Case 3
Projected Benefit Obligation	$12,500	$ 6,290	$ 890
Accumulated Benefit Obligation	9,700	4,100	750
Fair value of pension plan assets	15,300	4,200	650
Market-related value of pension plan assets	12,800	5,000	560
Unamortized transition (gain) or loss	(400)	1,200	(75)
Unrecognized net (gain) or loss from prior years	(200)	(850)	100
Unrecognized prior service cost	1,200	1,100	200
Recorded additional liability	0	0	85
Prepaid/(accrued) pension cost	3,400	(290)	(15)

EXERCISE 17–26

POSTRETIREMENT BENEFIT SERVICE COST AND INTEREST COST

Knox Company has a postretirement benefit plan. Employees are eligible for full benefits after working for the company for 10 years. On January 1, 2002, Knox hired Employee A. At the time of the hire, Knox estimated the expected postretirement benefit obligation (EPBO) at the full eligibility date for Employee A to be $100,000. On

January 1, 2004, Knox hired Employee B; the EPBO at the full eligibility date for Employee B was estimated to be $113,000. Knox uses a 10% discount rate in computing present values.

Prepare a schedule showing the service cost and interest cost associated with the postretirement benefits for Employees A and B for each of the years 2002–2014.

EXERCISE 17–27 **COMPUTATION OF POSTRETIREMENT BENEFIT COST**
Summary information for Lafe Company as of January 1, 2002, is listed as follows:

APBO	$800,000
FVPA	0
Unamortized transition loss	680,000
Remaining amortization period for transition loss	11 years

Postretirement benefit plan data for 2002 is listed below.

Service cost	$75,000
Contributions to plan	20,000
Benefits paid on behalf of retirees	14,000
Actual return on plan assets	300
Assumed discount rate	9.0%
Long-term expected rate of return on plan assets	8.5%

Lafe uses the fair market value of plan assets at the beginning of the year as the market-related value of plan assets.

Prepare the journal entries for recording net postretirement benefit expense and benefit plan funding for 2002.

EXERCISE 17–28 **COMPUTATION OF PREPAID/ACCRUED POSTRETIREMENT BENEFIT COST**
Orrin Company has an informal health benefit plan for its retirees. The following balances relate to the benefits from this plan as of December 31, 2002.

Unamortized transition loss	$650,000
Unrecognized net postretirement benefit gain	76,000
APBO	945,000
Unrecognized prior service postretirement cost	111,000
Fair value of postretirement plan assets	57,000

What amount should be shown on Orrin Company's December 31, 2002, balance sheet as "Prepaid/accrued postretirement benefit cost"?

EXERCISE 17–29 **DEFERRAL OF TRANSITION LOSS AND FINANCIAL STATEMENT EFFECT**
As of January 1, 1993, Jason Company adopted FASB Statement No. 106, "Employers' Accounting for Postretirement Benefits Other Than Pensions." On that date, Jason had $230,000 in its postretirement benefit fund. Jason computed its APBO as of January 1, 1993, to be $3,500,000. Jason elected to defer the transition loss and amortize it over 20 years. Jason reported net income of $4,000,000 for the year ended December 31, 1993; this represented an increase of approximately 10% compared to the prior year. What would net income have been if Jason had elected to recognize the transition loss immediately? How would Jason's December 31, 1993, balance sheet have been affected? (Ignore income taxes.)

PROBLEMS

PROBLEM 17–30   **ACCRUED PAYROLL AND PAYROLL TAXES**
Tomasso Clothiers' employees are paid on the 7th and 23rd of each month for the period ending the last day of the previous month and the 15th of the current month, respectively. An analysis of the payroll on Thursday, November 7, 2002, revealed the following data.

	Gross Pay	FICA	Federal Income Tax	State Income Tax	Insurance	Net Pay
Office staff salaries.....	$13,250	$ 624	$ 1,300	$ 550	$ 370	$10,406
Officer salaries..........	27,000	324	5,000	1,200	400	20,076
Sales salaries.............	22,000	812	3,800	770	410	16,208
Totals........................	$62,250	$1,760	$10,100	$2,520	$1,180	$46,690

It is determined that for the October 31 pay period, no additional employees exceeded the wage base for FICA purposes than had done so in prior pay periods. All the officer salaries, 80% of the office staff salaries, and 45% of the sales salaries for the payroll period ending October 31 were paid to employees who had exceeded the wage base for unemployment taxes. Assume the unemployment tax rates in force are as follows: federal unemployment tax, 0.8%, and state unemployment tax, 5.4%.

Instructions: Prepare the adjusting entries that would be required at October 31, the end of Tomasso's fiscal year, to reflect the accrual of the payroll and any related payroll taxes. Separate salaries and payroll tax expense accounts are used for each of the three employee categories: office staff, officer, and sales salaries.

PROBLEM 17–31

ACCOUNTING FOR PAYROLL

Bags, Inc., a manufacturer of suitcases, has 10 employees. Five of the employees are paid on a salary basis, and five are hourly employees. The employees and their compensation are as follows:

	Annual Salary
Ken Scott (president)...........	$91,500
Tatia Furgins......................	57,000
Jennifer Poulins..................	48,750
Robyn Meek........................	23,800
Kyle Roberts.......................	13,900

	Rate per Hour
Richard Dean (50 hours per week)...........	$14.00
Denise Ray (40 hours per week)...............	11.50
Dale Frank (40 hours per week)...............	9.75
Bryan Leslie (30 hours per week).............	4.50
Albert Lamb (20 hours per week).............	3.65

The salaried employees are covered by a comprehensive medical and dental plan. The cost of the plan is $45 per employee and is deducted from each paycheck. The hourly employees are covered only by a medical plan. The cost is calculated at 3.5% of gross pay and is deducted from each check. The FICA rate is 7.65%, and FUTA is 6.2%, with the maximum credit for state unemployment allowed. The state unemployment tax is 5.4%. No employee has reached the FICA, FUTA, or SUTA salary limits. In addition, each of the hourly employees, except Albert, belongs to the Suitcase Workers of America Union. Union dues are $5.65 per month and are deducted and paid on behalf of the hourly employees. The income tax withholding rate is 28% for employees with annual incomes above $29,500 and 15% for employees with annual incomes of $29,500 or less.

Hourly employees are paid weekly on Friday, January 6, 13, 20, and 27. Salaried employees are paid twice a month, on January 13 and 27. Assume that payroll taxes and all employee withholdings and deductions are paid on the 15th and the last day of each month.

Instructions: Make all entries related to Bags, Inc.'s, payroll for January 6, January 13, and January 15.

PROBLEM 17–32

COMPENSATED ABSENCES
Ludwig Electronics Inc. has a plan to compensate its employees for certain absences. Each employee can receive 5 days' sick leave each year plus 10 days' vacation. The benefits carry over for 2 additional years, after which the provision lapses on a FIFO flow basis. Thus, the maximum accumulation is 45 days. In some cases, the company permits vacations to be taken before they are earned. Payments are made based on current compensation levels, not on the level in effect when the absence time was earned.

Employee	Days Accrued Jan. 1, 2002	Daily Rate Jan. 1, 2002	Days Earned 2002	Days Taken 2002	Days Accrued Dec. 31, 2002	Daily Rate Dec. 31, 2002
A	20	$68	15	13	22	$70
B	15	74	15	15	15	76
C	25	62	7	32	0	Terminated, June 15— Rate = $64
D	–5	56	15	20	–10	$58
E	40	78	15	5	50	82
F	Hired July 1	60	8	2	6	60

Instructions:

1. How much is the liability for compensated absences at December 31, 2002?
2. Prepare a summary journal entry to record compensation absence payments during the year and the accrual at the end of the year. Assume the payroll liability account is charged for all payments made during the year for both sickness and vacation leaves. The average rate of compensation for the year may be used to value the hours taken except for Employee C, who took leaves at the date of termination. The end-of-year rate should be used to establish the ending liability.

PROBLEM 17–33

ENTRIES TO RECORD ACCRUAL AND FUNDING OF PENSION COSTS
The Allied Rental Company reported the following information related to its pension plan for the years 2002–2005. The fund is administered by a separate outside trustee.

Year	Pension Expense Accrual	Contribution	Benefit Payments to Retirees	Actual Return on Pension Plan Assets
2002	$560,700	$625,000	$300,000	$350,000
2003	725,000	670,000	300,000	400,000
2004	685,000	620,000	275,000	450,000
2005	726,500	625,000	400,000	525,000

Instructions:

1. Prepare the required summary journal entries for each year to record applicable pension items.
2. Assuming Allied had an accrued pension liability of $25,000 at January 1, 2002, compute the prepaid/accrued pension account balance at December 31, 2005.
3. Assuming that the fair value of the pension plan assets at January 1, 2002, was $2,600,000, compute the fair value of the pension plan assets at December 31, 2005.

PROBLEM 17–34

COMPUTATION OF PRIOR SERVICE COST FUNDING AND AMORTIZATION
The Staybrite Electronics Co. amended its pension plan effective January 1, 2002. The increase in the PBO occurring as a result of the plan amendment is $6,290,000.

Staybrite arranged to fund the prior service cost by equal annual contributions over the next 15 years at 10% interest. The first payment will be made December 31, 2002. The company decides to amortize the prior service cost on a straight-line basis over the average remaining service life of its employees. The company has 225 employees at January 1, 2002, who are entitled to the benefits of the amendment. It is estimated that, on the average, 15 employees will retire each year.

Instructions:

1. Compute the amount Staybrite will pay each year to fund the prior service cost arising from the plan's amendment.
2. Compute Staybrite's annual prior service cost amortization based on average remaining years of employee service.

PROBLEM 17–35

COMPUTATION OF GAIN OR LOSS COMPONENT

The Birnberg Equipment Co. has a defined benefit pension plan. As of January 1, 2002, the following balances were computed for the pension plan.

Unrecognized pension gain	$ 500,000
Fair value of pension plan assets	3,100,000
Market-related value of plan assets (5-year weighted average)	2,600,000
PBO	3,600,000
ABO	3,300,000

It was anticipated that the pension plan would earn 11% of the market-related value of plan assets in 2002. The actual return on pension plan assets was $275,000. The company has elected to amortize the unrecognized pension gains and losses over 10 years.

Instructions:

1. Compute the amount of gain or loss deferral for 2002.
2. Compute the amount of amortization of unrecognized pension gain or loss for 2002.
3. If net periodic pension expense, exclusive of the gain or loss component, is $626,000, what is the net periodic pension expense after including the gain or loss component?
4. What is the unrecognized pension gain or loss that Birnberg will carry forward to 2003 as a result of changes in the return on pension plan assets?

PROBLEM 17–36

COMPUTATION, RECORDING, AND FUNDING OF PENSION EXPENSE

Averon Industrial, Inc., computed the following components of pension expense for the years 2002–2004.

	(In thousands)		
Components of Pension Expense	**2002**	**2003**	**2004**
Service cost	$330	$415	$580
Interest cost	150	170	220
Actual return on pension plan assets	35	50	40
Expected return on pension plan assets	30	45	50
Amortization of unrecognized pension (gain) or loss— above corridor amount	(20)	(10)	18
Amortization of unrecognized prior service cost	90	105	105
Amortization of transition (gain) or loss	(20)	(15)	(15)
Amount contributed to fund	520	580	750

Instructions:

1. Compute the net periodic pension expense for the years 2002–2004.

2. Prepare the journal entries to record the computed pension expense in (1) and the funding of the pension plan.

3. If the prepaid pension cost balance at January 1, 2002, was $75,000, compute the balance of the prepaid/accrued pension cost account at December 31, 2004.

PROBLEM 17–37

COMPUTATION OF TRANSITION AMORTIZATION AND MINIMUM LIABILITY

The following information was provided relative to the pension plan for Atlas Wholesale Company for the years 2002–2004.

	January 1, 2002	December 31, 2002	December 31, 2003	December 31, 2004
Accrued pension cost	$ 985			
PBO	27,525	$29,700	$32,600	$39,000
ABO	22,900	23,800	29,300	37,000
Fair value of pension plan assets	23,600	24,200	27,900	31,500
Net pension expense exclusive of transition amortization		1,920	2,410	2,860
Contributions made to pension fund		2,970	2,510	2,410
Unrecognized net pension loss (gain)	2,520	1,145	1,445	3,795
Unrecognized net transition loss	420	0	0	0

Instructions:

1. Compute the amount of net periodic pension expense for each of the 3 years.
2. Prepare the journal entries for recording the net pension expense and the pension funding for the 3 years.
3. Compute any additional liability to be recorded for each of the 3 years under the minimum liability requirements of FASB Statement No. 87.
4. Identify the pension balance sheet accounts and their amounts as of December 31, 2004. There is no unrecognized prior service cost at this date.

PROBLEM 17–38

COMPUTING AND RECORDING ADDITIONAL PENSION LIABILITY

The following balances relate to the defined benefit pension plan of Cameron Industries.

	Dec. 31, 2002	Dec. 31, 2003
Fair value of pension plan assets	$149,000	$160,000
Market-related value of pension plan assets (5-year weighted average)	145,000	152,000
PBO	173,200	191,600
ABO	159,100	172,900
Prepaid/(accrued) pension cost	4,200	(1,950)
Unrecognized prior service cost	8,200	6,300
Unrecognized net pension loss	20,200	23,350

Instructions:

1. Determine the additional pension liability, if any, at December 31, 2002, and December 31, 2003.
2. Prepare journal entries for the additional pension liability adjustment, if any, at December 31, 2002, and December 31, 2003. Assume that the company had not previously recognized additional pension liability under FASB Statement No. 87.

PROBLEM 17–39

ADJUSTING ADDITIONAL PENSION LIABILITY

At the end of 2000, Adamson Corporation recorded an additional pension liability of $700,000 for the first time, the offset being charged to Deferred Pension Cost. Minimum pension liability computations for 2001–2004 indicated the following additional pension liability amounts:

December 31, 2001	$ 800,000
December 31, 2002	1,100,000
December 31, 2003	400,000
December 31, 2004	600,000

No plan amendments occurred during these years. The amount of the unrecognized prior service cost is as follows:

December 31, 2001	$1,000,000
December 31, 2002	750,000
December 31, 2003	500,000
December 31, 2004	250,000

Instructions: For each of the four years, prepare the journal entry to adjust the minimum pension liability account to the balance indicated above.

PROBLEM 17–40

JOURNAL ENTRIES AND MINIMUM PENSION LIABILITY
The following balances relate to the pension plan of Rienstem Transportation Co. at December 31, 2002 and 2003.

	(In thousands)	
	December 31, 2002	**December 31, 2003**
PBO	$3,075	$3,160
ABO	2,804	2,907
Fair value of pension plan assets	2,754	2,532
Market-related value of pension plan assets	2,550	2,750
Unrecognized prior service cost	240	215
Prepaid/(accrued) pension cost	15	(30)
Unrecognized net pension loss	96	383

Instructions:

1. Determine if a minimum pension liability adjustment is required at December 31, 2002 and 2003.
2. Prepare journal entries at December 31, 2002 and 2003, to record any additional liability.

PROBLEM 17–41

DISCLOSURE OF PENSION PLAN INFORMATION
The following information relates to the pension plan of Circle Manufacturing Company at December 31, 2002.

	(In thousands)
Balances at December 31, 2002:	
PBO	$11,750
Fair value of pension plan assets	10,800
ABO	9,900
Unrecognized transition loss	0
Unrecognized net pension loss (arose in 2002)	160
Accrued pension cost	790
2002 activity:	
Service cost	$ 875
Interest cost	1,100
Actual return on pension plan assets	1,250
Expected return on pension plan assets	1,310
Amortization of transition loss	75

Instructions: Prepare the pension note at December 31, 2002, that discloses the component parts of pension expense as well as the items that combine to yield the net amount reported in the balance sheet.

PROBLEM 17–42

PREPARING A PENSION WORK SHEET
The following data relate to the defined benefit pension plan of Haan Company.

Balances at January 1, 2002:

PBO	$3,500
Unamortized transition gain	50
Unrecognized prior service cost	200
Fair value of pension assets	3,000
ABO	2,800
Expected return on plan assets	7%
Settlement discount rate	10%

Activity for 2002:

Service cost	$ 400
Benefit payments to retirees	170
Contributions to pension fund	230
Actual return on plan assets	130
Prior service cost amortization	40
Transition gain amortization	50

Instructions: Prepare a pension work sheet for Haan Company for 2002.

PROBLEM 17–43

COMPREHENSIVE COMPUTATION OF PENSION COST COMPONENTS
The actuaries for Viewmont Cable Company provided Viewmont's accountants with the following information related to the company's pension plan.

	(In thousands)
December 31, 2000:	
Increase in PBO arising from plan's amendment	$732
January 1, 2001:	
PBO	$3,800
ABO	3,420
Fair value of pension plan assets	2,530
Market-related value of pension plan assets (5-year weighted average)	2,100
Accrued pension cost	532
Unamortized transition loss	66
Settlement discount rate	12%
Remaining life for amortization of transition loss	2 years
Average service life for amortization of gain and prior service costs	12 years
Unamortized pension gain—prior year	$60
Expected rate of return	10%
For Year 2001:	
Benefit payments to retirees	$185
Contributions to pension plan	300
December 31, 2001:	
PBO	$4,161
Fair value of pension plan assets	2,865

Instructions: Based on the data provided, prepare a pension work sheet for Viewmont Cable Company for 2001. The 5-year weighted average value of plan assets is used in computing the expected return.

PROBLEM 17–44

PENSION COST COMPONENTS AND RECONCILIATION OF FUNDED STATUS
As of January 1, 2002, information related to the defined benefit pension plan of Leffingwell Company was as follows:

PBO	$1,615,000
Fair value of pension assets	1,513,500
Unamortized transition gain	50,000
Unrecognized prior service cost	105,000
Unrecognized net pension gain or loss	0
Remaining amortization period for transition gain	1 year

Pension data for the years 2002 and 2003 are listed as follows:

2002 Pension plan information:

Service cost as reported by actuaries	$ 87,000
Contributions to pension plan	120,000
Benefits paid to retirees	132,000
Actual return on pension plan assets	26,350
Amortization of prior service cost	21,000
Actuarial change increasing PBO	80,000
Settlement interest rate	11.0%
Long-term expected rate of return on pension plan assets	10.0%
ABO, December 31, 2002	$1,530,000

2003 Pension plan information:

Service cost as reported by actuaries	$115,000
Contributions to pension plan	125,000
Benefits paid to retirees	140,000
Actual return on pension plan assets	180,000
Amortization of prior service cost	18,667
Settlement interest rate	11.0%
Long-term expected rate of return on pension plan assets	10.0%
ABO, December 31, 2003	$1,850,000

As of January 1, 2003, the remaining expected service life of employees was 5.0 years. Also, Leffingwell uses the fair market value of pension plan assets at the beginning of the year as the market-related value of pension plan assets.

Instructions:

1. For both 2002 and 2003, prepare the pension note that discloses the component parts of pension expense as well as the items that combine to yield the net amount reported in the balance sheet.
2. Prepare the journal entries for recording net pension expense and pension funding for 2002 and 2003.
3. Compute any additional liability to be recorded for each of the years. Prepare the necessary journal entry.

PROBLEM 17–45 **POSTRETIREMENT BENEFIT COST COMPONENTS AND RECONCILIATION OF FUNDED STATUS**

Summary information for Munson Company as of January 1, 2002, is listed below.

APBO	$1,200,000
Fair value of plan assets	170,000
Unamortized transition loss	875,500
Remaining amortization period for transition loss	11 years
Accrued postretirement cost	$154,500

Postretirement benefit plan data for the years 2002 and 2003 are listed below.

2002 Postretirement benefit plan information:

Service cost	$113,000
Contributions to plan	35,000
Benefits paid on behalf of retirees	35,000
Actual return (loss) on plan assets	(38,000)
Actuarial change increasing APBO	112,000
Assumed discount rate	10.0%
Long-term expected rate of return on plan assets	9.0%

2003 Postretirement benefit plan information:

Service cost	$121,000
Contributions to plan	100,000
Benefits paid on behalf of retirees	42,000
Actual return on plan assets	47,000
Assumed discount rate	10.0%
Long-term expected rate of return on plan assets	9.0%

As of January 1, 2003, the average remaining time to full benefit eligibility for Munson's employees was 6 years. Also, Munson uses the fair market value of plan assets at the beginning of the year as the market-related value of plan assets.

Instructions:

1. For both 2002 and 2003, prepare the note that discloses the component parts of postretirement benefit expense as well as the items that combine to yield the net amount reported in the balance sheet.
2. Prepare the journal entries for recording net postretirement benefit expense and benefit plan funding for 2002 and 2003.

COMPETENCY ENHANCEMENT OPPORTUNITIES

▶ Deciphering Actual Financial Statements	▶ Ethical Dilemma
▶ Writing Assignment	▶ Cumulative Spreadsheet Analysis
▶ Research Project	▶ Internet Search
▶ The Debate	

Accounting is more than just doing textbook problems. This expanded competency material provides practice in critical thinking, oral and written communication, research, teamwork, and consideration of ethical issues.

▶ DECIPHERING ACTUAL FINANCIAL STATEMENTS
• Deciphering 17–1 (The Walt Disney Company)
Review the information relating to pensions and other postretirement benefits found in THE WALT DISNEY COMPANY annual report in Appendix A and answer the following questions.

1. What is Disney's PBO in 1998?
2. By examining the change in Disney's "Unrecognized net loss," can you determine if Disney's actual return was greater than or less than its expected return?
3. What has Disney done to decrease its liability associated with postretirement medical benefits?
4. Disney's pension plan appears to be overfunded. Can you say the same about the status of its other postretirement benefits?

• Deciphering 17–2 (Litton Industries, Inc.)
LITTON INDUSTRIES is a leading aerospace/defense company. The company is involved in developing navigation, guidance and control, electronic warfare, and command, control and communications systems. Litton also builds combat ships for the U.S. Navy. Information relating to its "Pension and Other Postretirement Benefit Plans" is shown on page 1042. Based on that information, answer the following questions.

1. Is Litton's pension plan overfunded or underfunded? How can you tell?

Litton Industries, Inc.

A summary of the components of net periodic pension income (cost) for the U.S. defined benefit plans and costs for defined contribution plans and non-U.S. pension plans for fiscal years 1998, 1997 and 1996 are as follows:

(thousands of dollars)	Year Ended July 31		
	1998	**1997**	**1996**
Defined benefit plans			
Service cost—benefits earned during the period	$(31,758)	$(27,590)	$(25,235)
Interest cost on projected benefit obligation	(70,673)	(68,535)	(66,679)
Actual return on plan assets	238,045	168,775	159,459
Net amortization and deferral	(93,790)	(42,712)	(38,646)
Net periodic pension income	41,824	29,938	28,899
Defined contribution plans	(25,055)	(19,337)	(14,951)
Non-U.S. pension plans	(6,286)	(4,518)	(4,647)
Net pension income	$ 10,483	$ 6,083	$ 9,301

A reconciliation of the funded status of the U.S. defined benefit plans is as follows:

(thousands of dollars)	Year Ended July 31	
	1998	**1997**
Fair value of plan assets	$2,068,596	$1,616,205
Projected benefit obligation	(1,096,493)	(1,013,069)
Unrecognized net transition asset	(20,610)	(34,361)
Unrecognized net gain	(686,195)	(351,284)
Unrecognized prior service costs	22,126	24,194
Prepaid pension cost	$ 287,424	$ 241,685

2. Litton reports net pension income of almost $10.5 million for 1998. How is the company able to report income on its pension plans?

3. Analyze the company's PBO to determine the amount of pension benefits paid during the period. That is, consider the beginning and ending balances and the effect of service and interest costs to determine benefits paid.

4. Using your answer to (3), compute the amount Litton contributed to its pension fund in 1998.

• Deciphering 17–3 (Eli Lilly and Company)

ELI LILLY is a pharmaceutical company that is working to develop products to aid in the fight of cancer, diabetes, and other debilitating diseases. The company employs about 28,000 workers, many of whom are covered by the company's defined benefit retirement plans. Review Lilly's note disclosure on page 1043 on retirement benefits to answer the following questions.

1. Eli Lilly decreased its discount rate from 7.5% in 1997 to 6.9% in 1998. What effect would this have on net pension expense for 1998? What effect would it have on the prepaid/accrued pension cost reported in the balance sheet?

2. Overall, are Eli Lilly's pension plans overfunded or underfunded? How do you know?

3. Review the components of Eli Lilly's PBO to determine how accurate the actuaries were in estimating the PBO during 1997 and 1998.

4. Note that Eli Lilly's expected long-term rate of return on plan assets is 10.5%. Can you think of where the company might be investing its plan assets in order to receive a return that high? (Note that typical bank savings accounts pay about 3%.)

Eli Lilly

Net pension and retiree health benefit expense included the following components related to continuing operations:

	Defined Benefit Pension Plans			Retiree Health Benefits		
	1998	1997	1996	1998	1997	1996
Components of net periodic benefit cost:						
Service cost	$112.9	$ 86.3	$ 81.9	$12.8	$10.9	$11.4
Interest cost	184.2	178.0	166.3	34.3	31.5	28.7
Expected return on plan assets	(277.1)	(252.2)	(235.1)	(23.0)	(21.1)	(19.0)
Amortization of prior service cost (benefit)	9.7	9.2	8.8	(3.3)	(7.9)	(8.6)
Recognized actuarial loss	3.4	0.3	1.0	7.3	4.0	3.9
Net periodic benefit cost	$ 33.1	$ 21.6	$ 22.9	$28.1	$17.4	$16.4

The change in benefit obligation, change in plan assets, funded status and amounts recognized in the consolidated balance sheets at December 31 for the company's defined benefit pension and retiree health benefit plans were as follows:

	Defined Benefit Pension Plans		Retiree Health Benefits	
	1998	1997	1998	1997
Change in benefit obligation:				
Benefit obligation at beginning of year	$2,550.9	$2,303.5	$ 477.5	$ 412.1
Service cost	115.5	89.2	13.3	11.2
Interest cost	185.8	179.0	34.5	31.6
Actuarial loss	229.8	176.8	139.2	60.7
Benefits paid	(170.3)	(165.8)	(43.3)	(37.6)
Foreign currency exchange rate changes and other adjustments	(12.9)	(31.8)	0.3	(0.5)
Benefit obligation at end of year	2,898.8	2,550.9	621.5	477.5
Change in plan assets:				
Fair value of plan assets at beginning of year	2,923.2	2,629.2	228.1	200.1
Actual return on plan assets	286.4	407.7	33.8	30.1
Employer contribution	28.1	65.7	33.9	35.5
Benefits paid	(170.3)	(165.8)	(43.3)	(37.6)
Foreign currency exchange rate changes and other adjustments	2.2	(13.6)	—	—
Fair value of plan assets at end of year	3,069.6	2,923.2	252.5	228.1
Funded status	170.8	372.3	(369.0)	(249.4)
Unrecognized net actuarial (gain) loss	202.7	(13.8)	254.9	134.2
Unrecognized prior service cost (benefit)	130.5	118.0	(0.6)	(3.1)
Unrecognized net obligation at January 1, 1986	2.6	3.0	—	—
Net amount recognized	$ 506.6	$ 479.5	$(114.7)	$(118.3)

	Defined Benefit Pension Plans		Retiree Health Benefits	
	1998	1997	1998	1997
Amounts recognized in the consolidated balance sheet consisted of:				
Prepaid benefit cost	$ 612.3	$ 579.1	$ —	$ —
Accrued benefit liability	(192.3)	(131.6)	(114.7)	(118.3)
Intangible asset	37.9	14.1	—	—
Accumulated other comprehensive income before income taxes	48.7	17.9	—	—
Net amount recognized	$ 506.6	$ 479.5	$(114.7)	$(118.3)
Percents:				
Weighted-average assumptions as of December 31:				
Discount rate	6.9	7.5	7.0	7.5
Expected return on plan assets	10.5	10.5	10.5	10.5
Rate of compensation increase	4.0–8.0	4.0–8.0	—	—

• Deciphering 17–4 (General Motors)

Direct your attention to the company with perhaps the largest private pension plan in the world—GENERAL MOTORS. GM's note relating to its pension plan is included in Exhibit 17–12 on pages 1006–1007. Use that information to answer the following questions.

1. Compute GM's total PBO as of December 31, 1998. How much money has GM set aside to offset the PBO?
2. Now consider GM's postretirement benefits other than pensions. Add to the PBO from question (1) GM's accumulated postretirement benefit obligation (APBO). What is GM's estimated obligation related to pensions and other postretirement benefits?
3. Determine the assumption GM made regarding the rate at which health care costs would increase for 1999. If health care costs had risen at a faster rate, what effect did GM determine that would have had on the company's APBO?

▶ **WRITING ASSIGNMENT**

• Pensions in foreign countries

In the United States, accounting for pensions has received a great deal of attention. In other countries, pension accounting is given much less attention. In 1 page, examine the reasons that would explain why pension accounting is given much less emphasis in most foreign countries as compared to the emphasis it receives in the United States.

This assignment is not designed to require you to go to the library or to access international accounting standards. If you spend your time just thinking about the issue, the answers should become apparent.

▶ **RESEARCH PROJECT**

• Reviewing actual financial statements and associated notes

Your group is to obtain the annual reports of 5 companies. Using these annual reports, your group is to report (either orally or in writing) the answers to the following questions:

- Of the 5 companies, how many disclose information about pension plans? (Not all companies have large pension plans.) Of those that disclose information relating to their pension plans, how many are overfunded and underfunded?
- Of the companies disclosing information relating to pension plans, how many are still amortizing a transition gain or loss? How many are amortizing prior service cost?
- Do any of the companies report an additional minimum pension liability? If so, determine the difference between the ABO and the FVPA and compare that difference to the accrued pension liability before considering the additional minimum liability. Are the two numbers approximately the same? Should they be?
- Compare the actuarial assumptions across companies. What variance do you see in discount rates? future compensation levels? long-term rates of return? Do these assumptions seem reasonable to you?
- Review the annual reports for disclosure relating to postretirement benefits other than pensions. How many of the 5 companies report a liability associated with this obligation? How does the magnitude of this liability compare with the pension liability? In many cases, pension liabilities are funded to a greater extent than are other postretirement benefits. Why do you think that is the case?

▶ **THE DEBATE**

• The minimum pension liability

Accounting for pension liabilities seems to make a great deal of sense. A company estimates the present value of the amount it expects to pay in the future and offsets that against the amount of plan assets that have been set aside to meet that obligation. It would seem that this would be enough. This debate will focus on an additional step that is required—computation of the minimum pension liability.

Divide your group into 2 teams.

- One team will argue that there is no need to compute a minimum pension liability figure. Compute PBO, fair value of plan assets, offset the unamortized transition gain/loss, the unamortized prior service cost, and the amount of deferred gains and losses, and disclose the net amount in the balance sheet as prepaid/accrued pension cost. There is no need for a minimum liability computation.
- The other team will argue that the minimum liability computation ensures that the deferral features of Statement No. 87 prohibit a firm from not disclosing a liability when in fact one exists.

In this debate, you will need to thoroughly understand what features of FASB Statement No. 87 give rise to a minimum pension liability.

ETHICAL DILEMMA
• Actuarial assumptions

In a recent meeting of the board of directors, concern was expressed regarding the escalating balance in the Accrued Pension Liability and the liability associated with Postretirement Benefits Other Than Pensions. Following that meeting, you were asked to review the actuarial assumptions to determine if those balances and the expenses related to those balances can be reduced.

Part of your analysis included reviewing the financial statements and notes of other companies. In a review of the financial statements of GENERAL MOTORS, you noted that they provide some sensitivity analysis relating to actuarial assumptions.

Given the significant effect that a seemingly minor change can have on estimated obligations, you are tempted to contact the actuary and have her modify her original assumptions and recompute your company's future pension and other postretirement obligations with these new assumptions:

- Reduce the weighted average discount rate from 7% to 6%.
- Increase the expected long-term rate of return on plan assets from 10% to 11%.
- Decrease estimated increases in future compensation levels from 6% to 5%.
- Decrease estimated increases in future health care costs from 6% to 5%.
1. What effect would each of these changes have on the PBO associated with pensions or the APBO associated with the other postretirement benefits?
2. What effect would each of these changes have on the expense reported on the income statement associated with pensions and other postretirement benefits?
3. What constraints are there (or should there be) on a company's ability to influence actuarial assumptions?
4. While changing the assumptions may reduce the reported liabilities associated with pensions and other postretirement benefits, have the future obligations actually been reduced?
5. What factors would you need to consider before you placed the call to the actuary?

CUMULATIVE SPREADSHEET ANALYSIS

This assignment is a detailed examination of Skywalker's pension-related items. As of December 31, 2002, the $253 in "Other long-term liabilities" reported by Skywalker (see Chapter 13) included an amount for a net pension liability. In addition, Skywalker's $456 in "Other operating expenses" for 2002 included an amount for net pension expense.

The following information relates to Skywalker's pension plan as of December 31, 2002.

Fair value of pension fund assets	$200
Discount rate used in valuing the PBO	7%
Long-term expected rate of return on pension fund assets	9%
Total annual pension payment earned by Skywalker's employees so far	$50
Number of years that employees are expected to receive pension payments after retirement	30 years
Number of years until first pension payment is to be received	11 years

Construct a spreadsheet to answer the following.

1. Given the information above, compute the net pension liability that Skywalker will report as of December 31, 2002. (Note: Be careful in computing the PBO; remember that the standard annuity formula yields the present value of the annuity 1 year *before* the first payment is received.)

2. Compute a forecast of Skywalker's net pension liability as of December 31, 2003, and net pension expense for 2003 using the following information:
   - By working an extra year in 2003, the total annual pension payment earned by Skywalker's employees is expected to increase from $50 to $55.
   - Skywalker's employees will be 1 year closer to receiving the first pension payment.
   - No pension benefits are expected to be paid to employees in 2003.
   - Skywalker expects to contribute $50 to the pension plan during 2003.
   - Skywalker's best estimate is that the pension fund assets will earn in 2003 an amount equal to the long-term expected rate of return.

3. Repeat (1) and (2) using the following information:
   a. The discount rate is 8% and the long-term expected rate of return on the pension fund assets is 12%.
   b. The discount rate is 5% and the long-term expected rate of return on the pension fund assets is 11%.

▶ INTERNET SEARCH

• DaimlerChrysler Corporation

In 1998, CHRYSLER CORPORATION merged with DAIMLER-BENZ to create DAIMLER-CHRYSLER. Though DaimlerChrysler's pension plan is only about one-fifth the size of General Motors' plan (see Deciphering 17–4), it provides some interesting insight into accounting for pensions. Let's go to DaimlerChrysler's Web site and review its pension and other postretirement benefits notes. DaimlerChrysler's Web address is www.daimlerchrysler.com. Locate the annual report information, and answer the following questions.

1. Review the balance sheet to determine if DaimlerChrysler reports its pension plan as an asset or a liability.

2. What percent of total revenues are expenses relating to employee retirement benefits?

3. For the most recent fiscal year, did DaimlerChrysler's actual return exceed its expected return?

4. Locate the section of the notes that details the company's actuarial assumptions. Do those assumptions seem reasonable? How do they compare to assumptions made by other companies? (You may need to look at other companies' annual reports to answer this question.)

chapter 18
Derivatives, Contingencies, Business Segments, and Interim Reports

This chapter is a little different from the other chapters in the text. The chapter is composed of four modules: derivatives, contingencies, segment reporting, and interim reporting. Each of the modules is self-contained and can be studied independently. So, do as much or as little of this chapter as your instructor thinks best. Of course, you are free to sneak a look at any of the modules that your instructor does not assign.

1 DERIVATIVES
Understand the business and accounting concepts connected with derivatives and hedging activities.

2
Identify the different types of risk faced by a business.

3
Describe the characteristics of the following types of derivatives: swaps, forwards, futures, and options.

4
Define hedging, and outline the difference between a fair value hedge and a cash flow hedge.

5
Account for a variety of different derivatives and for hedging relationships.

6 CONTINGENCIES
Apply the accounting rules for contingent items to the areas of lawsuits and environmental liabilities.

7 SEGMENT REPORTING
Prepare the necessary supplemental disclosures of financial information by product line and by geographic area.

8 INTERIM REPORTING
Recognize the importance of interim reports, and outline the difficulties encountered when preparing those reports.

D E R I V A T I V E S

PROCTER & GAMBLE (P&G) is a sophisticated marketer of consumer products such as Tide, Pampers, Folgers, and Crest. Apparently this sophistication doesn't extend to P&G's understanding of derivative financial instruments. In November 1993, P&G agreed to buy a complex derivative that would give P&G lower current interest payments in exchange for an agreement to make higher payments in the future depending on the future level of interest rates.[1] When interest rates increased after the derivative was purchased, P&G learned a rough lesson relative to the risk associated with speculative derivatives. After the smoke had cleared, the increased interest payments from the derivative arrangement had cost P&G $195.5 million. A note written by former P&G chairman Edwin Artzt after this fiasco said that the officials who bought the derivative were like "farm boys at a country carnival."[2]

P rocter & Gamble is just one in a long list of organizations that have lost large amounts of money by trading in derivatives: GIBSON GREETINGS, BARINGS PLC, DELL COMPUTER, ORANGE COUNTY, ODESSA COLLEGE, and on and on. The combination of the complexity of derivatives, which are frequently misunderstood even by corporate treasurers and portfolio managers, and the lack of disclosure about derivatives created a dangerous environment in which users of financial statements could be completely unaware of huge company risks. This is exactly the type of situation the SEC was created to address. Accordingly, in recent years the FASB, with the blessing and prodding of the SEC, has significantly improved the accounting for and disclosure of derivative financial instruments. The first module in this chapter explains the general nature of derivatives, the types of risk faced by companies and how different types of derivatives can be used to hedge those risks, and the recent standards governing the accounting for derivatives.

 **net work exercise**

NumaWeb (**www.numa.com/**) is a Web site devoted entirely to derivatives.
Net Work:
1. What are derivatives?
2. What is the difference between derivatives and shares?

Understand the business and accounting concepts connected with derivatives and hedging activities.

SIMPLE EXAMPLE OF A DERIVATIVE

Assume that you are an employee of Nauvoo Software Solutions. On October 1, 2002, you purchase 100 shares of stock in the company at the market price of $50 per share, making the total purchase price $5,000. If you were to prepare a personal balance sheet, how would these shares be reported? Obviously, the 100 shares of Nauvoo stock would be reported as a $5,000 asset.

Now, assume that you are nervous about possible price fluctuations in the stock. On January 1, 2003, you need to make a college tuition payment of $5,000 on behalf of your daughter, and you must make certain that you have $5,000 on that date. You can't sell the

---

1 Kelley Holland, Linda Himelstein, and Zachary Schiller, "The Bankers Trust Tapes," *Business Week,* October 16, 1995, p. 106.
2 Carol J. Loomis, "Like Farm Boys at a Country Carnival," *Fortune,* November 27, 1995, p. 34.

Nauvoo shares now (and put the $5,000 cash under your mattress) because your employment contract states that any shares you purchase from the company must be held for at least three months before you can sell them. Your risk management dilemma is this: You must hold the Nauvoo shares as an asset for the next three months, but a downward movement in the stock price between now and January 1 would be disastrous for you.

The answer to your problem is the following agreement. If the price of Nauvoo stock is above $50 per share on January 1, you agree to pay a cash amount equal to that excess (multiplied by 100 shares) to John Bennett, a local stock speculator. If the price of Nauvoo stock goes below $50, John Bennett agrees to pay you a cash amount equal to the deficit (multiplied by 100 shares). As detailed later in the chapter, the broad name given to agreements such as this is a *derivative*. A derivative is a financial instrument or other contract that derives its value from the movement of the price, foreign exchange rate, or interest rate on some other underlying asset or financial instrument.

How does this derivative agreement solve your risk management dilemma? Look at the chart below:

	Stock Price on January 1		
	$45	$50	$55
Value of shares	$4,500	$5,000	$5,500
Receipt from (payment to) Bennett	500	0	(500)
Net amount	$5,000	$5,000	$5,000

Because of the structure of the agreement, you wind up with $5,000 on January 1 no matter what happens to the price of Nauvoo stock between now and then. After the fact, a derivative contract is sometimes a good deal and sometimes a bad one. If the price actually increases to $55, it would have been better had you not entered into the agreement. But because of the absolute necessity of having $5,000 on January 1, you are willing to trade off any stock profits you might make for the right to receive payments that will reimburse your stock losses.[3]

FYI: In the past, a derivative instrument like this was said to have "off balance sheet risk" because it could fluctuate in value after the initial agreement date, but these fluctuations would not be reflected in the balance sheet. As explained later, the accounting standards have been changed to bring these fluctuations onto the balance sheet.

How much money will change hands between you and John Bennett on October 1, the day you enter into the derivative contract? In other words, do you have to pay John Bennett anything up front to get him to sign the agreement? Or does he have to pay you? The valuation of derivatives is way beyond the scope of this book, but two of the factors that would be considered are the expected return on Nauvoo stock over the three-month period (on average, stock prices move up three or four percent per quarter) and the difference in the way you and John Bennett view risk. If you are very nervous about risk and John Bennett is not, he has the advantage in the bargaining and may be able to extract an up-front payment from you. For simplicity, the valuation assumptions made in this chapter will be very basic—for more advanced treatment you will need to talk to your finance professor. The simplest assumptions are that you and John Bennett have the same risk preferences and that the $50 price of the stock on October 1 is equal to the expected price on January 1. If these two assumptions hold, then the money exchanged at the signing of the agreement on October 1 is $0 because the probability of your being required to make a payment to Bennett on January 1 is equal to the probability that he will have to make a payment to you.

Another way to describe the arrangement between you and John Bennett is as follows: You have agreed, three months in advance, to sell 500 shares of Nauvoo stock to

---

3 Another question is why John Bennett, the speculator, would be willing to enter into this agreement. An arrangement such as this is one way for a speculator to make money if a price or rate moves in the direction he or she thinks it will. In this case, John Bennett's valuation analysis has led him to believe that the price of Nauvoo stock will move up in the next three months, and the derivative is a way for Bennett to make money if his analysis is correct.

John Bennett at a price of $50 per share. A forward sale such as this is similar to what the finance people call a short sale. To demonstrate that a forward sale is equivalent to the original exchange of cash payments you and John Bennett agreed to, consider the following:

> If the shares are worth, say, $5,500 on January 1, John Bennett will pay you $5,000 for the shares and then be able to immediately sell them for $5,500, netting a cash increase of $500. At the same time, you will have received $5,000, which is $500 less than you would have received if you had simply sold the shares in the market. In place of executing the forward sale, the same cash flow effects are achieved if you simply give John Bennett $500 in cash.

The same analysis could be done to show that requiring John Bennett to buy the shares for $5,000 when they are worth just $4,500 is equivalent to a simple cash transfer of $500 from John Bennett to you. A general characteristic of derivative arrangements is that although they are phrased in terms of the exchange of some underlying item (shares of stock, interest payments, pounds of orange juice concentrate, Japanese yen), they are often settled by a simple exchange of cash.

Now, let's talk about some accounting. What journal entry would you be required to make to recognize the signing of the agreement on October 1? The answer is that you make no journal entry. No cash changes hands; you and John Bennett have merely exchanged promises about some future action. This type of contract is called an **executory contract** and is very common in business. Another example of an executory contract is an operating lease—a promise to make payments in the future in exchange for the promise to receive the use of an asset in the future. And, like an operating lease, the derivative contract is "off balance sheet" on the day it is signed.

On December 31, 2002, the price of Nauvoo stock is $47 per share, making your investment in Nauvoo shares worth $4,700 ($47 × 100). The payment exchange with John Bennett is to be made on the following day. With the price per share at $47, it appears that you will receive a payment from Bennett of $300 [($50 – $47) × 100]. How should this information be reflected in the asset section of your December 31, 2002, balance sheet? Four possibilities are outlined below:

	Option #1	Option #2	Option #3	Option #4
Nauvoo stock	$5,000	$4,700	$5,000	$4,700
Derivative payment receivable	$0	$0	$300	$300
Valuation of stock	cost	fair value	cost	fair value
Recognition of derivative receivable?	No	No	Yes	Yes

Option #4 provides the best information because it reports the fair value of both the stock investment and the derivative payment receivable. Historically, the generally accepted treatment in the United States was Option #2, with some added disclosure about the derivative agreement.[4] The FASB has now adopted a standard that results in Option #4, the recognition of the fair value of derivatives in the financial statements.[5]

The remainder of this module details how derivatives are used to hedge risk and how information about derivatives should be reported in the financial statements.

---

4 *Statement of Financial Accounting Standards No. 119*, "Disclosure about Derivative Financial Instruments and Fair Value of Financial Instruments," Norwalk, CT: Financial Accounting Standards Board, 1994.

5 *Statement of Financial Accounting Standards No. 133*, "Accounting for Derivative Instruments and for Hedging Activities," Norwalk, CT: Financial Accounting Standards Board, 1998.

Identify the different types of risk faced by a business.

TYPES OF RISK

Most firms use derivatives as a tool for managing risk. Accordingly, before discussing the different types of derivatives, we will briefly outline the various types of risk.

Price Risk

Price risk is the uncertainty about the future price of an asset. It was uncertainty about the future price of Nauvoo Software Solutions stock that prompted the derivative contract in the preceding example. Firms can be exposed to price risk with existing assets, such as financial securities or inventory, or with assets to be acquired in the future, such as equipment to be purchased next month.

Credit Risk

Credit risk is the uncertainty that the party on the other side of an agreement will abide by the terms of the agreement. The most common example of credit risk is the uncertainty over whether a credit customer will ultimately pay his or her account. Banks are in the business of properly evaluating credit risk, and the success or failure of a bank depends largely on how good the bank's credit analysts are at identifying who will repay a loan and who won't. Credit risk analysis is a specialized skill, and many retail companies, through the acceptance of credit card purchases, have contracted their credit risk analysis to VISA, MASTERCARD, DISCOVER, or AMERICAN EXPRESS. In the Nauvoo stock and derivative contract example, the credit risk is the possibility that John Bennett, the party on the other side of the agreement, will not make the payments required under the agreement.

Interest Rate Risk

Interest rate risk is the uncertainty about future interest rates and their impact on future cash flows as well as on the fair value of existing assets and liabilities. A variable-rate mortgage is a good illustration of one type of interest rate risk. The periodic interest payments on the variable-rate mortgage will fluctuate in the future depending on the level of future interest rates. A fixed-rate mortgage is a good example of another type of interest rate risk. If interest rates decrease, then the present value of future fixed payments to be made under a fixed-rate mortgage will increase. Thus, the fair value of the mortgage liability increases—this is the downside of obligating yourself to a fixed stream of interest payments when there is a possibility that interest rates may go down in the future. In summary, interest rate risk exposes a firm to uncertainty about future cash flows as well as uncertainty about the fair value of assets and liabilities that have values tied to the level of interest rates.

Exchange Rate Risk

Exchange rate risk is the uncertainty about future U.S. dollar cash flows arising when assets and liabilities are denominated in a foreign currency. For example, many compensation packages for U.S. citizens working in foreign countries include an end-of-contract bonus payment if the employee sticks it out and stays on the foreign assignment for the entire length of the contract. If this bonus is denominated in the currency of the foreign country, then the employee knows with certainty the future amount of his or her foreign currency bonus, but the U.S. dollar value bonus depends on the exchange rate prevailing when the bonus is received. U.S. multinational firms face the same risk when sales, purchases, loans, and investments are denominated in foreign currencies.

Some degree of risk is an unwanted but common side effect of doing business. For example, the variation in the cost of jet fuel is a nuisance and a worry to the major airlines. Similarly, fluctuations in the U.S. dollar/Japanese yen exchange rate wreak havoc

FYI: Other types of risk include liquidity risk, theft risk, competitive risk, and business cycle risk. See Johnson and Swieringa, "Derivatives, Hedging and Comprehensive Income," *Accounting Horizons,* December 1996, p. 109.

on the competitive plans of both U.S. and Japanese car manufacturers. On the other hand, managing risk is the very reason for the existence of some businesses. Much of the revenue generated by a bank arises because the bank has expertise in evaluating and managing credit, interest rate, and exchange rate risk. The following sections discuss derivatives and hedging from the standpoint of a manufacturing, retailing, or service firm that is trying to use these techniques to reduce the risks that arise as part of doing business. Coverage of the more complicated risk management strategies of banks and financial institutions is outside the scope of this text.

Describe the characteristics of the following types of derivatives: swaps, forwards, futures, and options.

TYPES OF DERIVATIVES

Recall that a derivative is a financial instrument or other contract that derives its value from the movement of the price, exchange rate, or interest rate on some other underlying asset or financial instrument. In addition, a derivative does not require a firm to take delivery or make delivery of the underlying asset or financial instrument; in situations in which actual delivery is required, the underlying item can easily be converted into cash.[6] For example, you may have heard about the buying and selling of pork belly futures. These contracts (futures contracts are explained below) can qualify as derivatives because, fortunately, they do not require the holder to either deliver or take delivery of a truckload of pork bellies. Instead, these contracts are settled by cash payments, much as the Nauvoo stock derivative contract was settled, not with the delivery of any shares of stock, but by a cash payment.

The most common types of derivatives are swaps, forwards, futures, and options. Each type is explained below.

Swap

A **swap** is a contract in which two parties agree to exchange payments in the future based on the movement of some agreed-upon price or rate. A common type of swap is an interest rate swap. In an **interest rate swap**, two parties agree to exchange future interest payments on a given loan amount; usually, one set of interest payments is based on a fixed interest rate and the other is based on a variable interest rate. To illustrate, assume that Pratt Company has a good working relationship with a bank that issues only variable-rate loans. Pratt takes advantage of its relationship at the bank and on January 1, 2002, receives a two-year, $100,000 loan, with interest payments occurring at the end of each year. The interest rate for the first year is the prevailing market rate of 10%, and the rate in the second year will be equal to the market interest rate on January 1 of that year. Pratt is reluctant to bear the risk associated with the uncertainty about what the interest payment in the second year will be. So, Pratt enters into an interest rate swap agreement with another party (not the bank) whereby Pratt agrees to pay a fixed interest rate of 10% on the $100,000 loan amount to that party in exchange for receiving from that party a variable amount based on the prevailing market rate multiplied by $100,000. This is called a *pay-fixed, receive-variable swap.*

Instead of exchanging the entire amount of the interest payments called for under the swap contract, Pratt would probably settle the agreement by exchanging a small cash payment, depending on what has happened to interest rates. Accordingly, Pratt will receive an amount equal to [$100,000 × (Jan. 1, 2003, interest rate − 10%)] if the January 1, 2003, interest rate is greater than 10% and will pay the same amount if the rate is less than 10%. The interest swap payment will be made in 2003. To see the impact of this interest rate swap, consider the following table.

6 Ibid., par. 6c.

	Interest Rate on January 1, 2003		
	7%	10%	13%
Variable-rate interest payment	$ (7,000)	$(10,000)	$(13,000)
Receipt (payment) for interest rate swap	(3,000)	0	3,000
Net interest payment in 2003	$(10,000)	$(10,000)	$(10,000)

The interest rate swap agreement has changed Pratt's uncertain future interest payment into a payment of $10,000 no matter what the prevailing interest rates are in 2003. Why didn't Pratt just go out and get a fixed-rate loan in the first place? Sometimes, in this case because of Pratt's special relationship with the bank, it is easier to get one type of loan or investment security than another. A derivative instrument can effectively change the loan that you got into the loan that you want.

Forwards

A forward contract is an agreement between two parties to exchange a specified amount of a commodity, security, or foreign currency at a specified date in the future with the price or exchange rate being set now. To illustrate, assume that on November 1, 2002, Clayton Company sold machine parts to Maruta Company for ¥30,000,000 to be received on January 1, 2003. The current exchange rate is ¥120=$1. In order to be assured of the dollar amount that will be received, Clayton enters into a forward contract with a large bank, agreeing that on January 1 Clayton will deliver ¥30,000,000 to the bank and the bank will give U.S. dollars in exchange at the rate of ¥120=$1, or $250,000 (¥30,000,000/¥120 per $1). This forward contract guarantees the U.S. dollar amount that Clayton will receive from the receivable denominated in Japanese yen.

Operationally, this forward contract would usually be settled as follows. Given the exchange rate on January 1, 2003, if ¥30,000,000 is worth less than $250,000, the bank will pay Clayton the difference in cash (U.S. dollars). If ¥30,000,000 is worth more than $250,000, Clayton pays the difference to the bank in cash. Therefore, no yen need be delivered as part of the contract; the contract is settled with a U.S. dollar cash payment.

The impact of the forward exchange contract is shown in the following table.

> **Caution!** Don't forget that one of the characteristics of a derivative, whether it relates to yen, wheat, pork bellies, or stock index levels, is that it can be, and usually is, settled in the end with a cash payment instead of with actual delivery of the underlying item.

	Exchange Rate on January 1		
	¥118=$1	¥120=$1	¥122=$1
Value of ¥30,000,000	$254,237	$250,000	$245,902
Clayton receipt (payment) to settle forward contract	(4,237)	0	4,098
Net U.S. dollar receipt by Clayton	$250,000	$250,000	$250,000

If Clayton is nervous about exchange rate changes, why agree to denominating the transaction in Japanese yen in the first place? The answer is that some types of transactions and some products are routinely negotiated in terms of a certain currency. For example, almost all crude oil sales are denominated in U.S. dollars, regardless of the countries of the companies conducting the transaction. In addition, if denominating a sale in a certain currency will make the customer feel more comfortable, companies are likely to follow the policy that "the customer is always right."

In this simple example, the forward exchange rate of ¥120=$1 is equal to the prevailing exchange rate, called the spot rate, on the date the forward contract is signed. Usually, the forward rate would differ from the spot rate in order to compensate the bank for providing this risk-reduction service to Clayton. For example, a forward rate of

 Is there any credit risk with a forward contract?

¥121=$1 means that the bank would receive cash payments from Clayton whenever the dollar value of ¥30,000,000 was greater than $247,934 (¥30,000,000/¥121 per $1). With this lower threshold (instead of $250,000), it would be more likely that the bank would receive cash from Clayton to settle the forward contract. In this chapter, we will make the simplifying assumption that spot rates and forward rates are equal to one another.

Futures

A **futures contract** is a contract, traded on an exchange, that allows a company to buy a specified quantity of a commodity or a financial security at a specified price on a specified future date. A futures contract is very similar to a forward contract with the difference being that a forward contract is a private contract negotiated between two parties, whereas a futures contract is a standardized contract that is sponsored by a trading exchange and can be traded among different parties many times in a single day. So, with a forward contract, you know the party with whom you will be exchanging cash to settle the contract; with a futures contract, all these cash settlements are handled through the exchange and you never know, or care, who is on the other side of the contract.

As an example of the use of a futures contract, assume that Hyrum Bakery uses 1,000 bushels of wheat every month. On December 1, 2002, Hyrum decides to protect itself against price movements for its January 1, 2003, wheat purchase because long-term spring weather forecasts often come out in December, causing wide fluctuations in wheat prices. To protect against these fluctuations, Hyrum buys a futures contract on December 1 that obligates Hyrum to purchase 1,000 bushels of wheat on January 1, 2003, at a price of $4.00 per bushel (which is also the prevailing price of wheat on December 1). This is a standardized exchange-traded futures contract, so Hyrum has no idea who is on the other side of the agreement; that is, Hyrum doesn't know who is promising to deliver the wheat.

As with other derivatives, a wheat futures contract is usually settled by a cash payment at the end of the contract instead of by actual delivery of the wheat. Settlement of Hyrum's futures contract would be as follows. If the price of wheat is less than $4.00 per bushel on January 1, Hyrum will make a cash payment of that difference, multiplied by 1,000 bushels. If the price of wheat is greater than $4.00 per bushel on January 1, Hyrum will receive a cash payment equal to that difference multiplied by 1,000 bushels.[7] The effect of the futures contract is illustrated in the table below.

	Wheat Price on January 1		
	$3.80	**$4.00**	**$4.20**
Cost to purchase 1,000 bushels	$(3,800)	$(4,000)	$(4,200)
Hyrum receipt (payment) to settle futures contract	(200)	0	200
Net cost of January wheat	$(4,000)	$(4,000)	$(4,000)

Option

An **option** is a contract giving the owner the right, but not the obligation, to buy or sell an asset at a specified price any time during a specified period in the future. Options

---

7 For exchange-traded futures contracts, cash settlements usually are not deferred until the end of the contract but instead occur at the end of every day based on price movements during that day.

A wheat futures contract can protect the buyer from wide fluctuations in wheat prices.

come in two general types: call options and put options. A **call option** gives the owner the right to buy an asset at a specified price, and a **put option** gives the owner the right to sell an asset at a specified price. In exchange for the rights inherent in the option, the owner of the option pays an amount, in advance, to the party on the other side of the transaction, who is called the writer of the option. Like a futures contract, many options are standardized contracts that are traded on organized exchanges.

An option differs from the derivative instruments discussed previously because it protects the owner against unfavorable movements in prices or rates while allowing the owner to benefit from favorable movements. With the swaps, forwards, and futures discussed above, the protection from unfavorable movements was "paid for" by sacrificing the benefits from favorable movements. With an option, the protection is "paid for" with an up-front cash payment when the option is purchased.

Because of the asymmetrical nature of options, the owner of an option and the writer of an option are in very different positions. With a call option, for example, the owner of the option can buy the designated asset at a fixed price, no matter how high the market price of the asset goes. If the market price of the asset decreases, the option owner can just throw the option away because it is cheaper to buy the asset at the low market price. So, the maximum amount that the owner of an option can lose is the price paid to buy the option. On the other side of the transaction, the writer of the option has no such downside protection. No matter how high market prices increase, the writer of a call option must sell the asset at the fixed option price. So, there is no limit to the amount that a call option writer can lose.[8] Because this discussion of derivative instruments focuses on the use of derivatives for risk management and risk reduction, only buyers of options will be considered.

To illustrate the use of options in managing risk, assume that, on October 1, 2002, Woodruff Company decides that it will need to purchase 1,000 ounces of gold for use in its computer chip manufacturing process in January 2003. Gold is selling for $300 per ounce on October 1, 2002. For cash flow reasons, Woodruff plans to delay the purchase

8 The losses of the writer of a put option are limited to the full amount of the option price. Even if the asset becomes completely worthless, the put option writer must buy it at the option price.

of the gold until January 1, 2003, and is concerned about potential increases in the market price of gold between October 1, 2002, and January 1, 2003.

To reduce the price risk associated with the gold, Woodruff enters into a call option contract on October 1. The contract gives Woodruff the right, but not the obligation, to purchase 1,000 ounces of gold at a price of $300 per ounce. The option period extends to January 1, 2003, and Woodruff has to pay $8,000 to buy this option.[9] In exchange for this $8,000 payment, the option arrangement protects Woodruff from unfavorable movements in the price of gold but also allows Woodruff to benefit from favorable movements. This can be seen from the table below.

	Gold Price (per Ounce) on January 1		
	$280	$300	$320
Cost of 1,000 ounces of gold if:			
• Buy gold at January 1 price	$280,000	$300,000	$320,000
• Exercise option	$300,000	$300,000	$300,000
Will option be exercised?	No	Same either way	Yes
Cost of gold	$280,000	$300,000	$300,000

The existence of the option contract means that Woodruff will pay no more than $300,000 for the gold. And, because the option is a right and not an obligation, Woodruff can ignore it, as in the case above in which the January 1 price of gold is $280 per ounce, and just buy gold at the market price prevailing on January 1. Remember that this ability to enjoy protection from unfavorable price changes but to benefit from favorable price changes did not come for free—it cost Woodruff $8,000 at the beginning of the option period. As with the other derivative instruments, this option can be settled on January 1 by a direct cash payment from the option writer to Woodruff in place of the actual delivery of the gold. If the cost of 1,000 ounces of gold is greater than $300,000 on January 1, then the option writer pays Woodruff the difference.

> **Caution!** Remember that an option is a right, not an obligation. The owner of the option can always throw it away and forget the whole deal.

TYPES OF HEDGING ACTIVITIES

4

Define hedging, and outline the difference between a fair value hedge and a cash flow hedge.

The preceding illustrations of the different types of derivatives—swaps, forwards, futures, and options—also illustrated how these derivatives are used in hedging activities. Broadly defined, **hedging** is the structuring of transactions to reduce risk. Hedging occurs naturally as part of many business activities, examples of which follow.

- In the retail sale of gasoline, one risk to the gasoline retailer is that movement in worldwide oil prices will cause variation in the cost to purchase gasoline. This "cost of goods sold" risk is partially offset by the fact that the retail selling price of gasoline also goes up when oil prices rise. So, the increase in the cost is offset by the increase in the selling price.
- Banks are vulnerable to interest rate increases because this increases the amount they must pay to get the use of depositors' money. However, this risk is hedged because an interest rate increase also allows a bank to raise the rates it charges on its loans.
- Multinational companies can be impacted by changes in exchange rates. If a U.S. multinational has a subsidiary in France, then a decline in the value of the French

---

9 Computation of option values was outlined in Chapter 11, but a detailed treatment is beyond the scope of this text. Briefly, the price that must be paid to purchase a call option is higher when the option exercise price is lower, when the length of the option is longer, and when the movement of the price of the underlying asset (gold in this example) is more volatile.

franc will cause the dollar value of the subsidiary's franc-denominated assets to decline. But, this loss is partially offset because the dollar value of the subsidiary's franc-denominated liabilities will also decline.

Derivatives can be used in hedging activities through the acquisition of a derivative with the characteristic that changes in the value of the derivative are expected to offset changes in the value of the item being hedged. Let's review how derivatives were used as hedges in each of the derivative illustrations given in the preceding section.

> **FYI:** Historically, cash flow hedges have been very controversial. Firms have claimed to be using derivatives to hedge forecasted transactions when in fact the dollar value of supposed hedging activity has been far greater than any possible future transactions. Using a derivative in this way transforms the derivative from a hedging tool into a speculative investment.

- *Pratt swap.* The interest rate swap was structured to offset changes in the variable-rate interest payments.
- *Clayton forward.* The forward currency contract was entered into to offset changes in the dollar value of the receivable denominated in Japanese yen.
- *Hyrum future.* The wheat futures contract was acquired to offset movements in the expected purchase price of the following month's supply of wheat.
- *Woodruff option.* The gold call option was purchased to offset the negative impact on the cost of gold for production purposes of changes in the market price of gold.

The FASB has defined two of the broad categories of hedging activities as follows[10]:

- *Fair value hedges.* A **fair value hedge** is a derivative that offsets, at least partially, the change in the fair value of an asset or liability. A derivative can also serve as a hedge of the fair value of firm commitments even though the assets and liabilities associated with a firm commitment are not recognized until the actual transaction date.
- *Cash flow hedges.* A **cash flow hedge** is a derivative that offsets, at least partially, the variability in cash flows from forecasted transactions that are probable.

A third category of hedges related to foreign currency risk has also been identified by the FASB. Some of these hedges are fair value hedges, and some are cash flow hedges. In addition, some of these hedges relate to the foreign currency risk associated with the net investment in foreign subsidiaries. This category of hedges is covered in more detail in advanced accounting courses.

The next section illustrates the proper accounting for derivatives, particularly those designated as hedges.

Account for a variety of different derivatives and for hedging relationships.

ACCOUNTING FOR DERIVATIVES AND FOR HEDGING ACTIVITIES

Several factors combined in 1993 and 1994 to move the accounting for derivatives to the top of the FASB's agenda. First was the tremendous proliferation in the use of derivatives by U.S. businesses. Second was the derivative-related catastrophes experienced by companies such as PROCTER & GAMBLE. And third was the urging by the SEC for improvement in the accounting for derivatives. In October 1994, the FASB released Statement No. 119 with the main focus being on improved disclosure (not recognition) for the 1994 fiscal year. Statement No. 119 was viewed as a temporary stopgap standard.

In June 1996, the FASB released an Exposure Draft of a more comprehensive recognition standard for derivatives. The final standard, FASB Statement No. 133, was adopted in June 1998. The effective date of Statement No. 133 was subsequently delayed; it is now

10 *Statement of Financial Accounting Standards No. 133,* par. 18.

applicable for fiscal years beginning after June 15, 2000. The delay was motivated by two reasons—companies wanted more time to figure out how to implement the standard and companies did not want to implement the standard before January 1, 2000, because of "Y2K" concerns with their computer systems.[11]

Overview of Accounting for Derivatives and Hedging Activities

The accounting difficulty caused by derivatives is illustrated in the simple matrix below.

	Historical Cost	Subsequent Changes in Value
Traditional assets and liabilities	Focus	Frequently Ignored
Derivatives	Small or zero	Everything

As shown in the matrix, the historical cost focus of traditional accounting is misplaced with derivatives because derivatives often have little or no up-front historical cost. With derivatives, the subsequent changes in prices or rates is critical to determining the value of the derivative, and yet these changes are frequently ignored in traditional accounting.

Because derivatives do not mesh well with the traditional accounting model, the FASB has endorsed a different approach, based on two simple notions.

1. *Balance sheet.* Derivatives should be reported in the balance sheet at their fair value as of the balance sheet date. No other measure of value is relevant for derivatives.
2. *Income statement.* When a derivative is used to hedge risk, the gains and losses on the derivative should be reported in the same income statement in which the income effects on the hedged item are reported. This sometimes requires unrealized gains and losses being temporarily deferred in an accumulated other comprehensive income account that is reported as part of equity.

A consequence of this approach is that the appropriate treatment of changes in the fair value of a derivative depends on whether or not the derivative serves as a hedge, and the type of hedge, as follows:

- *No hedge.* All changes in the fair value of derivatives that are not designated as hedges are recognized as gains or losses in the income statement in the period in which the value changes. In a sense, a derivative that does not serve as a hedge can be thought of as a speculation about the direction of movement of some price or rate.
- *Fair value hedge.* Changes in the fair value of derivatives designated as fair value hedges are recognized as gains or losses in the period of the value change. These derivative gains or losses are offset (either in whole or in part) by the recognition of gains or losses on the change in fair value of the item being hedged. The net effect is that when gains or losses on derivatives designated as fair value hedges exceed the gains or losses on the item being hedged, the excess affects reported net income.
- *Cash flow hedge.* Changes in the fair value of derivatives designated as cash flow hedges are recognized as part of the accumulated other comprehensive income account. In effect, this treatment defers recognition of the gain or loss and classifies the deferred item as an equity adjustment. These deferred derivative gains and losses are recognized in net income in the period in which the hedged cash flow transaction was forecasted to occur.

---

11 See *Statement of Financial Accounting Standards No. 137,* "Accounting for Derivative Instruments and for Hedging Activities—Deferral of the Effective Date of FASB Statement No. 133," Norwalk, CT: Financial Accounting Standards Board, 1999.

An important aspect of this approach is that derivatives must be identified as hedges of specific items at the beginning of the hedging relationship. Firms cannot wait until after they see the results for the period to decide whether they want to designate certain derivatives as hedges. The designation of a derivative as a hedge should be supported with formal documentation.

In order to account for a derivative as a hedge, a company must define, in advance, how it will determine whether the derivative is functioning as an effective hedge. For the simple examples given in this chapter, hedge effectiveness is easy to assess because the terms of the derivatives have been constructed to exactly match the amount and timing of the underlying hedged item. Partial hedge ineffectiveness would occur if, for example, the derivative maturity date did not exactly match the date of a forecasted purchase. Similarly, hedge ineffectiveness occurs when the quantity in the derivative agreement (such as the number of units of foreign currency or of pounds of a commodity) is either more or less than the quantity of the underlying hedged item. Derivative gains or losses associated with hedge ineffectiveness are recognized in income immediately in the period in which they occur.

DISCLOSURE Companies are required to provide a description of their risk management strategy and how derivatives fit into that strategy. For both fair value and cash flow hedges, companies also must disclose the amount of derivative gains or losses that are included in income because of hedge ineffectiveness. Finally, for cash flow hedges, a company must describe the transactions that will cause deferred derivative gains and losses to be recognized in net income and disclose the amount of deferred gains or losses that are expected to be recognized in net income in the next 12 months.[12]

Another item that is often referred to in the business press is the notional amount of the derivative instrument. The **notional amount** is the total face amount of the asset or liability that underlies the derivative contract. For example, with a forward contract, the notional amount is the U.S. dollar value of the commodity or currency to be exchanged. The notional amount of derivative instruments is often reported and is frequently misleading. For example, the Clayton forward contract described earlier in the chapter has a notional amount of $250,000 (¥30,000,000/¥120 per $1) but has a fair value of $0 on the day the forward agreement is signed, and in the example, the total cash payment stemming from the derivative does not exceed $4,237. In summary, notional amounts grossly overstate both the fair value and the potential cash flows of derivatives.

> **FYI:** A favorite ploy of financial reporters is to report the notional amount of derivatives in order to exaggerate their importance.

The accounting for derivatives will be illustrated using the information from the previous four derivative examples.

Illustrations of Accounting for Derivatives and Hedging Activities

PRATT SWAP On January 1, 2002, Pratt Company received a two-year, $100,000, variable-rate loan and also entered into an interest rate swap agreement. The journal entry to record this information is:

2002			
Jan. 1	Cash	100,000	
	Loan Payable		100,000

No entry is made to record the swap agreement, because as of January 1, 2002, the swap has a fair value of $0. The value is zero because the interest rate on January 1, 2002, is 10%, and if it is assumed that the best forecast of the future interest rate is the current rate of 10%, it is expected that, on average, no payments will be exchanged under the swap agreement.[13]

---

12 *Statement of Financial Accounting Standards No. 133*, par. 45.

13 As mentioned earlier, detailed treatment of the valuation of derivatives is outside the scope of this text. Remember that the valuation assumptions used here represent a simplification.

> **Caution!** The interest rate swap asset is reported at its present value because the payment to be received under the swap agreement will not occur until the end of the year 2003.

Assume now that the actual market interest rate on December 31, 2002, is 11%. With the rate at 11%, Pratt will receive a $1,000 payment [$100,000 × (11% − 10%)] at the end of 2003 under the swap agreement. Accordingly, on December 31, 2002, Pratt has a $1,000 receivable under the swap agreement, and the receivable has a present value of $901 ($1,000 × PFV$_{\overline{1}|11\%}$). The impact of the change in interest rates on the interest rate swap and on reported interest expense is accounted for as follows:

	2002 Balance Sheet	2002 Income Statement
Underlying item	No change in the reported loan balance	No impact on 2002 interest expense; the impact will show up in 2003 interest expense
Derivative	Creation of a $901 receivable under the interest rate swap	Deferred gain of $901 on the interest rate swap; gain recognized in 2003 to offset increased interest expense

The interest rate swap asset is reported at its present value of $901 in the December 31, 2002, balance sheet. However, the $901 gain from the increase in the value of the swap is not included in the 2002 income statement. The swap is intended to offset changes in interest expense in 2003. Accordingly, the gain on the swap is deferred so that it can be offset against the increased interest expense to be reported in 2003. The deferral of the gain merely means that it is temporarily reported as an increase in equity under Other Comprehensive Income. The deferred gain would also be included as an addition in the statement of comprehensive income (but not in the normal income statement) for 2002.

The journal entry to record Pratt's 2002 interest payment, along with the adjusting entry to recognize the change in the fair value of the swap, is as follows:

```
2002
Dec. 31   Interest Expense..............................................    10,000
                Cash ($100,000 × .10)...............................             10,000

          Interest Rate Swap (asset)............................       901
                Other Comprehensive Income....................                901
```

The journal entries necessary in Pratt's books at the end of 2003 are as follows:

```
2003
Dec. 31   Interest Expense..............................................    11,000
                Cash ($100,000 × .11)...............................             11,000

          Cash (from swap agreement)........................     1,000
                Interest Rate Swap (asset)......................                901
                Other Comprehensive Income ($901 × .11; rounded)....          99

          Other Comprehensive Income.......................     1,000
                Interest Expense......................................              1,000

          Loan Payable..................................................   100,000
                Cash......................................................            100,000
```

The $99 credit to Other Comprehensive Income represents the increase in the value of the swap payment receivable stemming from the passage of time.

An important thing to notice in these journal entries is that net interest expense is $10,000 because of the hedging effect of the swap. Also, the value changes in a derivative designated as a cash flow hedge are deferred in comprehensive income and then reflected in earnings in the period when the hedged cash flow occurs.

CLAYTON FORWARD   On November 1, 2002, Clayton Company sold machine parts to Maruta Company for ¥30,000,000 to be received on January 1, 2003. On the same date, Clayton also entered a yen forward contract. The journal entry to record this information is:

```
2002
Nov. 1    Yen Receivable (¥30,000,000/¥120 per $1).........................................    250,000
              Sales.........................................................................................................              250,000
```

No entry is made to record the forward contract, because as of November 1, 2002, the forward has a fair value of $0. The value is zero because settlement payments are made under the contract only if the exchange rate on January 1, 2003, differs from ¥120=$1. If the current exchange rate of ¥120=$1 is assumed to be the best forecast of the future rate, it is expected that, on average, no payments will be exchanged under the forward contract.

Assume now that the actual exchange rate on December 31, 2002, is ¥119=$1. At this exchange rate, Clayton will have a loss on the forward contract and be required to make a $2,101 payment [(¥30,000,000/¥119 per $1) – $250,000] on January 1, 2003, to settle the forward contract. Accordingly, on December 31, 2002, Clayton has a $2,101 loss and payable under the forward contract. However, there is also an increase in the yen receivable and a corresponding gain on foreign exchange due to the change in yen value relative to the U.S. dollar. The impact of the change in the yen exchange rate on both the yen receivable and the value of the forward contract is accounted for as follows:

	2002 Balance Sheet	**2002 Income Statement**
Underlying item	Increase of $2,101 in the value of the yen receivable	Exchange gain of $2,101
Derivative	Creation of a $2,101 liability under the forward contract	Loss on forward contract of $2,101

The forward contract liability is reported at its fair value of $2,101 in the December 31, 2002, balance sheet. In addition, the $2,101 loss on the forward contract is included in the 2002 income statement, thus offsetting the gain reported from the increase in dollar value of the yen receivable. This accounting treatment accurately reflects the intent of the forward contract hedge; that is, unrealized gains and losses from changes in value of the forward contract are meant to offset similar changes in value in the item of concern, the yen receivable.

The adjusting entries to recognize the change in the fair value of the forward contract and in the U.S. dollar value of the yen receivable are as follows:

> **FYI:** These journal entries illustrate that, after the fact, hedging is not always a good idea. In the Clayton example, the forward contract hedge wipes out the gain on the increase in the value of the yen receivable. The advantage of a hedge is that it reduces volatility, but that sometimes means canceling out gains.

```
2002
Dec. 31   Loss on Forward Contract....................................................................    2,101
              Forward Contract (liability)..........................................................              2,101

          Yen Receivable.....................................................................................    2,101
              Gain on Foreign Currency...........................................................              2,101
```

The increase in the yen receivable reflects the $2,101 increased dollar value of the receivable after the change in the exchange rate to ¥119=$1. This gain is offset by the loss from the change in value of the forward contract. The forward contract is a fair value hedge of the value of the receivable, so both changes in value are recognized in earnings.

The journal entries necessary in Clayton's books on January 1, 2003, to record receipt of the yen payment and settlement of the yen forward contract are as follows:

```
2003
Jan. 1    Cash (¥30,000,000/¥119 per $1).....................................................    252,101
              Yen Receivable..........................................................................              252,101

          Forward Contract (liability) ...............................................................    2,101
              Cash (forward contract settlement)............................................              2,101
```

> **FYI:** By excluding derivatives associated with foreign currency assets and liabilities from the hedge accounting rules of Statement No. 133, the FASB has reduced the disclosure burden of companies who use such derivatives as hedges.

It should be noted that the Clayton forward contract does *not* qualify for hedge accounting under Statement No. 133. The FASB explicitly excluded foreign currency–denominated assets and liabilities from the set of items that can be considered as items underlying a hedge.[14] Thus, derivatives that serve as economic hedges of foreign currency assets and liabilities are accounted for as speculations, with all gains and losses recognized as part of income immediately. However, because the accounting standards (in Statement No. 52) already require that foreign currency assets and liabilities be revalued at current exchange rates at the end of each period, with the resulting exchange gains and losses recognized in income, the net effect is the same as if the foreign currency derivatives were accounted for as fair value hedges after all. This fact can be seen by reviewing the Clayton forward example—the gains and losses from both the foreign currency receivable and the yen forward contract are recognized in income immediately, effectively offsetting one another.[15]

HYRUM FUTURE On December 1, 2002, Hyrum Company decided to hedge against potential fluctuations in the price of wheat for its forecasted January 2003 purchases and bought a futures contract entitling and obligating Hyrum to purchase 1,000 bushels of wheat on January 1, 2003, for $4.00 per bushel. No entry is made to record the futures contract because, as of December 1, 2002, the future has a fair value of $0. The value is zero because settlement payments are made under the contract only if the price of wheat on January 1, 2003, differs from $4.00 per bushel. If the current price of $4.00 per bushel is assumed to be the best forecast of the future price, it is expected that, on average, no payments will be exchanged under the futures contract.

Assume that the actual price of wheat on December 31, 2002, is $4.40 per bushel. At this price, Hyrum will receive a $400 payment [1,000 bushels × ($4.40 - $4.00)] on January 1, 2003, to settle the futures contract. Accordingly, on December 31, 2002, Hyrum has a $400 receivable under the futures contract. The impact of the change in wheat prices on the wheat futures contract and on the anticipated cost of wheat purchases in January 2003 is accounted for as follows:

	2002 Balance Sheet	**2002 Income Statement**
Underlying item	No impact; the higher-priced wheat won't be purchased until January 2003	No impact on 2002 cost of goods sold; the impact will show up in 2003 cost of goods sold
Derivative	Creation of a $400 receivable under the wheat futures contract	Deferred gain of $400 on the wheat futures contract; gain recognized in 2003 to offset increased cost of goods sold

> **Caution!** It is *not* that derivative losses are reported immediately and derivative gains are deferred. If wheat prices had declined, Hyrum would have experienced a loss on the wheat futures contract,. which would have been deferred until 2003.

The wheat futures asset is reported at its fair value of $400 in the December 31, 2002, balance sheet. However, the $400 gain from the increase in the value of the futures contract is not included in the 2002 income statement. The futures contract is intended to offset changes in the purchase price of wheat in January 2003. Accordingly, the gain on the futures contract is deferred so that it can be offset against the increased cost of goods sold to be reported in 2003. As with the interest rate swap discussed above, the deferral of the gain means that it is temporarily reported as an increase in equity under Other Comprehensive Income.

---

14 *Statement of Financial Accounting Standards No. 133*, par. 21c.

15 As mentioned earlier, in this chapter we make the simplifying assumption that spot rates and forward rates are equal to one another. When this is not true, the foreign currency and derivative gains and losses will not exactly offset because foreign currency assets and liabilities are valued using the spot rate and derivative instruments are valued using the forward rate.

The adjusting entry to recognize the change in the fair value of the futures contract is as follows:

2002			
Dec. 31	Wheat Futures Contract (asset)..	400	
	Other Comprehensive Income		400

The gain from the increase in the value of Hyrum's futures contract is deferred as part of comprehensive income. The wheat futures contract is a cash flow hedge, with the futures contract payment intended to offset the increased amount that Hyrum will have to pay to make its forecasted purchase of 1,000 bushels of wheat on January 1, 2003.

The journal entries necessary in Hyrum's books on January 1, 2003, to record the purchase of 1,000 bushels of wheat in the open market and cash settlement of the wheat futures contract are as follows:

2003			
Jan. 1	Wheat Inventory..	4,400	
	Cash (1,000 bushels × $4.40)		4,400
	Cash (futures contract settlement)...	400	
	Wheat Futures Contract (asset)...		400
	Other Comprehensive Income	400	
	Gain on Futures Contract..		400

The gain on the futures contract is recognized in earnings on January 1, 2003, the forecasted date of the transaction that was hedged. To the extent that the wheat inventory is used to make bread and that bread is sold in 2003, the gain on the futures contract will offset the increased cost of goods sold arising from the increase in the price of wheat to $4.40 per bushel.

WOODRUFF OPTION   On October 1, 2002, Woodruff Company paid $8,000 to purchase a call option to buy 1,000 ounces of gold at a price of $300 per ounce some time before January 1, 2003. This option is intended to protect Woodruff against increases in the price of the gold that it needs for 2003. Because Woodruff paid cash for the gold call option, the following journal entry is made on October 1:

2002			
Oct. 1	Gold Call Option (asset)...	8,000	
	Cash		8,000

Assume that the actual price of gold on December 31, 2002, is $328 per ounce. At this gold price, Woodruff will receive a $28,000 payment [($328 × 1,000 ounces) – ($300 × 1,000 ounces)] on January 1, 2003, to settle the call option. Accordingly, on December 31, 2002, the call option is worth $28,000. The impact of the change in the price of gold on the gold call option and on the anticipated cost of gold purchases in January 2003 is accounted for as follows:

	2002 Balance Sheet	2002 Income Statement
Underlying item	No impact; the higher-priced gold won't be purchased until January 2003	No impact on 2002 cost of goods sold; the impact will show up in 2003 cost of goods sold
Derivative	Increase from $8,000 to $28,000 of the recorded value of the gold call option	Deferred gain of $20,000 on the gold call option; gain recognized in 2003 to offset increased cost of goods sold

The gold call option is reported at its fair value of $28,000 in the December 31, 2002, balance sheet. This represents a $20,000 increase ($28,000 – $8,000) over the amount originally paid for the option. However, the $20,000 gain from the increase in the value of the call option is not included in the 2002 income statement. The call option is intended to offset changes in the purchase price of gold in January 2003. Accordingly, the gain on the call option is deferred so that it can be offset against the increased production costs to be reported in 2003.

The adjusting entry to recognize the change in the fair value of the option is as follows:

2002			
Dec. 31	Gold Call Option ($28,000 – $8,000)	20,000	
	Other Comprehensive Income		20,000

> **Caution!** Stop a moment and consider the interesting impact of hedge accounting on this firm commitment. Generally, the obligation is not recognized; but in this case a portion is recognized to reflect the offsetting movements in the value of the hedge and the value of the underlying firm commitment obligation.

The journal entries necessary in Woodruff's books on January 1, 2003, to record the purchase of 1,000 ounces of gold and the cash settlement of the option contract are as follows:

2003			
Jan. 1	Gold Inventory	328,000	
	Cash (1,000 ounces × $328)		328,000
	Cash (gold call option settlement)	28,000	
	Gold Call Option (asset)		28,000
	Other Comprehensive Income	20,000	
	Gain on Gold Call Option		20,000

As mentioned previously, the gain from the increase in the value of the gold call option would be offset against the increased production costs in January 2003 resulting from the increase in the price of gold. The $20,000 gain does not completely offset the $28,000 increase in production costs because Woodruff had to pay $8,000 to purchase the gold call option in the first place.

SUMMARY

The centerpiece of accounting for derivatives and hedging activities is that derivatives are recognized as assets and liabilities and reported on the balance sheet at their fair values. For a derivative designated as a fair value hedge, changes in fair value are included in earnings and offset against changes in fair value of the hedged item. For a cash flow hedge, gains and losses are deferred in comprehensive income and recognized in earnings on the forecasted date of the hedged transaction. These provisions of Statement No. 133 codify and organize the recognition standards for derivatives and hedging activities. Statement No. 133 also improves on prior standards by bringing derivatives into the financial statements themselves instead of restricting them to note disclosure.

In formulating an international accounting standard for derivatives, the International Accounting Standards Committee (IASC) has drawn heavily on the work done by the FASB. The general provisions of IAS 39 are very similar to the provisions of Statement No. 133. As of this writing, neither standard has been applied in practice—SFAS No. 133 applies to fiscal years starting after June 15, 2000, and IAS 39 becomes effective for fiscal years beginning on or after January 1, 2001. It will be interesting to observe the refinements that are made to both standards as the accounting standard setters receive feedback from companies' attempts to implement the standards.

C O N T I N G E N C I E S

During 1983, PENNZOIL initiated negotiations for the acquisition of GETTY OIL. Before the Pennzoil-Getty deal could be closed, TEXACO swooped in and bought Getty right out from underneath Pennzoil's nose for $10.2 billion. Pennzoil immediately sued Texaco for $14 billion in damages caused by Texaco's interference in Pennzoil's attempted acquisition of Getty. In December 1985, a Houston jury awarded $10.5 billion to Pennzoil. The case was appealed in both 1986 and 1987, with judgment in each instance against Texaco. With the uncertainty of a multibillion dollar judgment hanging over its head, Texaco found it increasingly difficult to calm the fears of its suppliers and creditors. Texaco played its trump card

in April 1987 and declared Chapter 11 bankruptcy. This action forced Pennzoil to the bargaining table, and in December, 1987 the two companies negotiated a $3 billion payment to settle the case. Texaco made the payment on April 7, 1988.[16]

In addition to illustrating the strategic use of Chapter 11 bankruptcy, the Texaco-Pennzoil case serves as a classic example of the difficulties surrounding the accounting for contingencies. Among the interesting accounting questions here are: During the 4.5-year life of this lawsuit, when should Texaco have recognized a liability, and for what amount? At the same time, when should Pennzoil have recognized an asset for the receivable from Texaco?

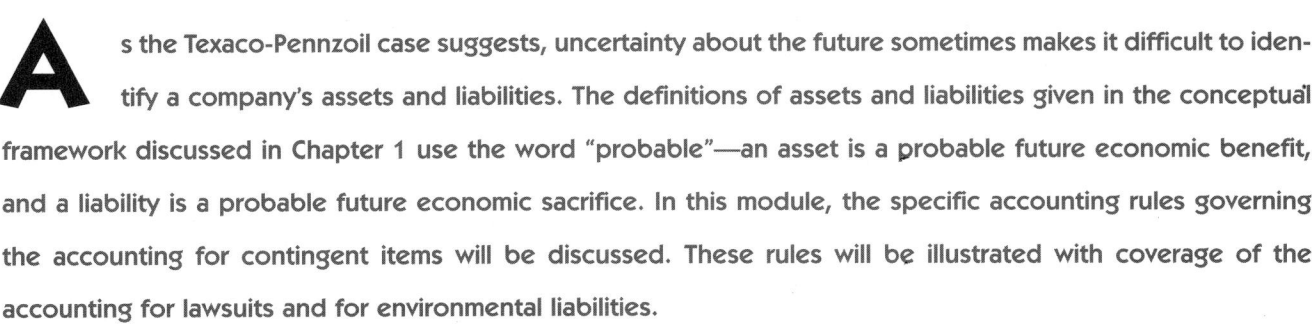

As the Texaco-Pennzoil case suggests, uncertainty about the future sometimes makes it difficult to identify a company's assets and liabilities. The definitions of assets and liabilities given in the conceptual framework discussed in Chapter 1 use the word "probable"—an asset is a probable future economic benefit, and a liability is a probable future economic sacrifice. In this module, the specific accounting rules governing the accounting for contingent items will be discussed. These rules will be illustrated with coverage of the accounting for lawsuits and for environmental liabilities.

Apply the accounting rules for contingent items to the areas of lawsuits and environmental liabilities.

ACCOUNTING FOR CONTINGENCIES: PROBABLE, POSSIBLE, AND REMOTE

A contingency is defined in FASB Statement No. 5 as:

> ". . . an existing condition, situation, or set of circumstances involving uncertainty as to possible gain . . . or loss . . . to an enterprise that will ultimately be resolved when one or more future events occur or fail to occur."[17]

As defined, contingencies may relate to either assets or liabilities and to either a gain or loss. The primary focus of this module is on **contingent losses** that might give rise to a liability, but the accounting for **contingent gains** is also discussed briefly.

Historically, when the existence of an obligation depended on the occurrence of a future event, recognition of the liability was deferred until the event occurred. This approach can fail to reflect the existence of significant obligations that are highly likely to materialize and that exist because of past transactions or events. For example, Texaco's contingent obligation to Pennzoil arose because of Texaco's interference in Pennzoil's attempted acquisition of Getty Oil, a past event. The future events determining whether

16 Edward B. Deakin, "Accounting for Contingencies: The Pennzoil-Texaco Case," *Accounting Horizons,* March 1989, p. 21.
17 *Statement of Financial Accounting Standards No. 5,* "Accounting for Contingencies," Stamford, CT: Financial Accounting Standards Board, 1975, par. 1.

Texaco would have to make payments to Pennzoil were the court verdicts. For Texaco to fail to record its liability until the day the $3 billion was actually paid to Pennzoil would be grossly misleading to users of the financial statements.

FASB Statement No. 5 specifies different accounting for contingent items based on the probability of the occurrence of the resolving future event. The likelihood of the event and the accounting actions recommended are shown in Exhibit 18–1.

EXHIBIT 18–1 | Accounting for Contingencies

Contingent Losses:

Likelihood	Accounting Action
Probable	Recognize a probable liability if the amount can be reasonably estimated. If not estimable, disclose facts in a note.
Reasonably possible	Disclose a possible liability in a note.
Remote	No recognition or disclosure unless contingency represents a guarantee. Then, note disclosure is required.

Contingent Gains:

Likelihood	Accounting Action
Probable	Recognize a probable asset if the amount can be reasonably estimated. If not estimable, disclose facts in a note.
Reasonably possible	Disclose a possible asset in a note, but be careful to avoid misleading implications. In practice, possible contingent gains are often not disclosed.
Remote	No recognition or disclosure.

SOURCE: *Statement of Financial Accounting Standards No. 5, pars. 3 and 17.*

If the occurrence of an event that would create a liability is probable and if the amount of the obligation can be reasonably estimated, the contingency should be recognized as a liability. Many estimated liabilities are in reality probable contingent liabilities, because the existence of the obligation is dependent on some future event occurring. For example, the estimated amount of warranty liability is a probable contingent liability because warranties are dependent on the need to provide future repairs or service. In addition, a pension obligation is dependent on employees staying with the company long enough to earn full pension benefits, and frequent-flier trips are contingent on whether customers accumulate enough miles for free trips and whether they actually claim their free trips.

If a contingent liability is reasonably possible, defined as more than remote but less than likely, it should be disclosed in a note to the financial statements. Probable gains are often not disclosed in order to avoid any misleading implications about the likelihood that the gain will eventually be realized. If a contingent item is remote, that is, the chance of occurrence is slight, there is no requirement that the item be disclosed, unless it is a contingent liability under a guarantee arrangement such as guaranteeing, or co-signing, the loan of another party.

The timing of the disclosures made in the Texaco-Pennzoil case illustrates the different treatment of contingent losses and contingent gains. As seen in Exhibit 18–2, the initial lawsuit was filed in early 1984, and Texaco was careful to mention the possibility of a loss in its 1984 and 1985 financial statements. Pennzoil made no mention of the contingent gain in its 1984 or its 1985 financial statements. In the body of the 1986 annual report, management of Texaco took two pages to discuss the Pennzoil litigation. In addition, the financial statements included another page in the notes discussing the case. Texaco's management concluded their discussion by stating that the Pennzoil litigation could materially affect Texaco. At the same time, the uncertainty surrounding Texaco's future, given the large judgment hanging over its head, caused Texaco's auditor to render a qualified audit opinion. While Texaco's financial statements were being drastically impacted by this contingent loss, Pennzoil's financial statements included just a brief note about the contingent gain. In 1987, Texaco formally recognized the $3 billion liability and also filed for Chapter 11 bankruptcy. Pennzoil did not recognize the gain until 1988 when the payment was actually received. This case nicely illustrates the asymmetry between the treatment of contingent losses and the treatment of contingent gains.

EXHIBIT 18–2 | Accounting Treatment in the Texaco-Pennzoil Case

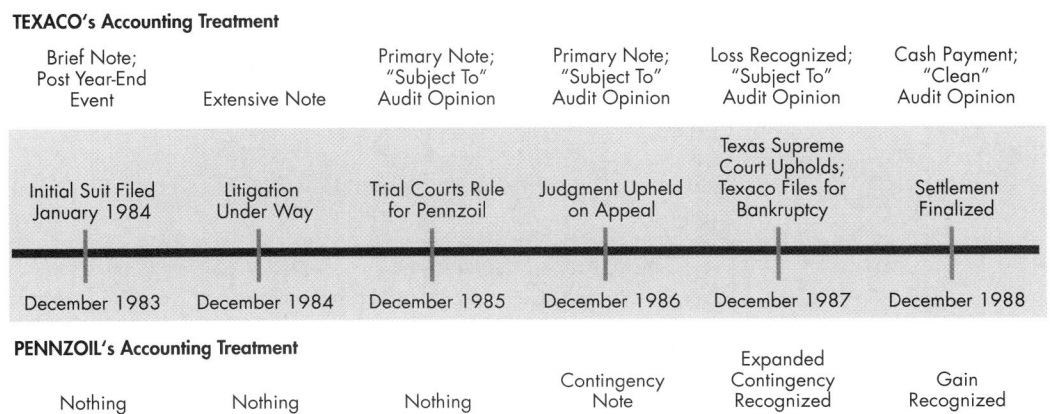

FASB Statement No. 5 does not provide specific guidelines as to how the terms probable, possible, and remote should be interpreted in terms of probability percentages. For example, is a 60% likelihood "probable" or just "possible"? Surveys made of statement preparers and users reveal a great diversity in the numerical interpretations of the probability terms used in Statement No. 5. Thus, the contingency standard that seems fairly easy to apply given the straightforward guidelines outlined in Exhibit 18–1 is actually very difficult to apply consistently in practice. This is illustrated below with a discussion of the accounting for lawsuits and for environmental liabilities.

> **FYI:** In the area of deferred taxes, the FASB has introduced a fourth probability term, "more likely than not," defined as a probability level of 50%. Use of the more-likely-than-not criterion is discussed in Chapter 16.

ACCOUNTING FOR LAWSUITS

America is the land of the lawsuit. Companies are sued by customers who claim they were injured by defective products, auditors are sued by stockholders who claim they were injured by defective financial statements, and parents are sued by children who claim they were injured by defective upbringing. Typically, a lawsuit takes a long time to wind its way through the courts. Even after a decision has been handed down by a lower court, there are many appeal opportunities available. Thus, both the amount and timing of a loss arising from litigation are generally highly uncertain. Some companies carry insurance to protect themselves against these losses, so the impact of the losses on the financial statements is minimized. For uninsured risks, however, a decision must be made as to when the liability for litigation becomes probable, and thus, a recorded loss. FASB

► FREQUENT-FLIER MILES

As individuals navigate the airways, they often earn frequent-flier miles that can be redeemed for free trips. During 1990 alone, nine U.S. airlines collectively gave 4.5 million free trips to members of frequent-flier programs. Rather than account for these bonus miles as they accumulate, airlines typically book a liability only after enough mileage has been accumulated to claim a free ticket. For example, in its 1998 annual

report, DELTA AIR LINES states that it "accrues the estimated incremental cost of providing free travel awards earned under its SkyMiles® frequent flier program when free travel award levels are achieved." Thus, while experts estimate that airlines have an existing obligation for 25 billion miles of free travel resulting from frequent-flier programs, airlines have recognized a liability for approximately only 30% of this amount, or 7.5 billion miles.

Some members of the accounting profession have argued that a portion of the revenue from each ticket should be deferred, as a "liability reserve," and matched against future periods when the bonus miles are redeemed. Following three years of debate within the accounting profession about whether and how airlines should account for this potential liability, the FASB ultimately decided not to pursue the issue. The SEC, however, is requiring airline companies to disclose

Statement No. 5 identifies several key factors to consider in making the decision. These include[18]:

1. The nature of the lawsuit.
2. Progress of the case in court, including progress between date of the financial statements and their issuance date.
3. Views of legal counsel as to the probability of loss.
4. Prior experience with similar cases.
5. Management's intended response to the lawsuit.

If analysis of these and similar factors results in the judgment that a loss is probable and the amount of the loss can be reasonably estimated, the liability should be recorded. A settlement after the balance sheet date but before the statements are issued would be evidence that the loss was probable at year-end, and it would result in reporting the loss in the current financial statements.

Another area of potential liability involves unasserted claims, that is, a cause of action has occurred but no claim has yet been asserted. For example, a person may be injured on the property of a company, but as of the date the financial statements are issued, no legal action has been taken. As another example, a violation of a government regulation may have occurred, but no federal action has yet been taken. If it is probable that a substantiated claim will be filed and upheld and the amount of the claim can be reasonably estimated, accrual of the liability should be made. If the amount cannot be reasonably estimated, note disclosure is required. If assertion of the claim is judged not to be at least reasonably possible, no accrual or disclosure is necessary.

As a practical matter, it should be noted that a company would be very unlikely to record a loss from unasserted claims or from pending litigation unless negotiations for a settlement had been substantially completed. When that is the case, the loss is no longer a contingency, but an estimated loss.

Some companies do not disclose any information regarding potential liabilities from lawsuits. Others provide a brief, general description of pending lawsuits. Sometimes companies provide fairly specific information about pending actions and claims. However, companies must be careful not to increase their chances of losing pending lawsuits, and they generally do not disclose dollar amounts of potential losses, which might

18 *FASB Statement No. 5*, par. 36.

information regarding frequent-flier programs in their 10-K reports.

The airline companies maintain that many of the free trips earned will not be taken. AMERICAN AIRLINES estimates 20% of its free trips will not be used; similarly, UNITED AIRLINES estimates 25% will go unused. Airlines are reducing their exposure to these liabilities by fixing deadlines to redeem miles for free trips and by raising the number of miles needed to qualify for certain trips.

QUESTIONS:

1. Do frequent-flier miles meet the definition of a liability?

2. If frequent-flier miles are a liability, can the liability be estimated at the time a ticket is sold?

3. When should frequent-flier miles be recorded on the books of the airlines: when tickets are sold or as bonus miles are redeemed?

4. If airlines are required to make a cumulative catch-up adjustment to account for their frequent-flier liabilities, the effects on the financial statements of many airlines could be catastrophic. Should this factor enter into the decision process of accounting rule makers?

SOURCES:

Penelope Wang, *Forbes*, June 13, 1988, p. 62.
"Accounting for Frequent Fliers," *USA Today*, May 22, 1991, p. 9B.

---

be interpreted as an admission of guilt and a willingness to pay a certain amount. As an illustration, EXXON disclosed the information in Exhibit 18-3 in its 1991 and 1997 annual reports in connection with lawsuits filed as a result of the Valdez oil spill. Note that, in 1991, Exxon sounds quite optimistic that it has settled the bulk of the claims related to the oil spill and that any further claims "will not have a materially adverse effect" upon the company. This optimistic disclosure is particularly interesting in light of the $5 billion adverse judgment discussed in the 1997 disclosure.

ACCOUNTING FOR ENVIRONMENTAL LIABILITIES

> **FYI:** Insurance companies have been particularly hard hit with environmental losses. For example, TRAVELERS CORPORATION took a $325 million charge in the third quarter of 1993. This charge was to provide "reserves" for expected environmental liabilities and litigation costs. John Snyder, Senior VP of AM BEST CO., estimates the insurance industry has paid $10 billion to settle asbestos cases alone, and the total cost for pollution losses will be "multiples of that amount." [*The Wall Street Journal*, Oct. 14, 1993, pp. A3–A4.]

An area that is receiving increasing attention in our society, both politically and from an accounting perspective, is the environment. The need to protect our environment, and in many instances to recover from past environmental abuses, is recognized by most citizens. What is not so obvious are the staggering costs associated with environmental liabilities. As but one example, current legislation in the United States mandates the cleanup of existing toxic waste sites. The Environmental Protection Agency (EPA) is empowered to clean up waste sites and then can charge the cleanup costs to those parties the EPA deems responsible. This can cost companies $25 to $100 million or more for each polluted site. The total environmental liability in the United States has been estimated to exceed $350 billion.[19]

Even though environmental costs are one of the critical issues facing businesses today, many, if not most, companies do not fully reflect those costs in their financial statements. The primary reason is that these loss contingencies often cannot be reasonably estimated. If a liability cannot be reasonably estimated, no amount can be recognized.

In addition, because FASB Statement No. 5 was intended as a broad contingency standard, it does not give specific guidance on the types of disclosure required when a loss contingency cannot be estimated. For this reason, disclosure in the notes to the financial statements often appears incomplete. For example, all that we can learn from Exxon's 1997 financial statements is that the company recognized an expense

---

19 Emily S. Plishner, "Environmental Financial Disclosure," *Chemical Week*, December 8, 1993.

After the Exxon Valdez oil spill in Prince William Sound, disclosure of the environmental liability was limited in the notes to the financial statements because it was difficult to estimate what the ultimate earnings impact would be.

of $140 million for 1997 as an estimate of the cost of cleaning up environmental damage caused during the year. This $140 million is part of Exxon's overall environmental cleanup liability of $2.5 billion as of December 31, 1997. No further details are given in the 1997 financial statements.

EXHIBIT 18–3 | Exxon—1991 and 1997 Disclosure Concerning Exxon Valdez Oil Spill

---

Disclosure in 1991 (in part)

On March 24, 1989, the Exxon Valdez, a tanker owned by Exxon Shipping Company, a subsidiary of Exxon Corporation, ran aground on Bligh Reef in Prince William Sound off the port of Valdez, Alaska, and released approximately 260,000 barrels of crude oil. More than 315 lawsuits, including class actions, have been brought in various courts against Exxon Corporation and certain of its subsidiaries.

On October 8, 1991, the United States District Court for the District of Alaska approved a civil agreement and consent decree. . . . These agreements provided for guilty pleas to certain misdemeanors, the dismissal of all felony charges and the remaining misdemeanor charges by the United States, and the release of all civil claims against Exxon. . . by the United States and the state of Alaska. The agreements also released all claims related to or arising from the oil spill by Exxon. . . .

Payments under the plea agreement totaled $125 million—$25 million in fines and $100 million in payments to the United States and Alaska for restoration projects in Alaska. Payments under the civil agreement and consent decree will total $900 million over a ten-year period. The civil agreement also provides for the possible payment, between September 1, 2002, and September 1, 2006, of up to $100 million for substantial loss or decline in populations, habitats, or species in areas affected by the oil spill which could not have been reasonably anticipated on September 25, 1991.

The remaining cost to the corporation from the Valdez accident is difficult to predict and cannot be determined at this time. It is believed the final outcome, net of reserves already provided, will not have a materially adverse effect upon the corporation's operations or financial condition.

Disclosure in 1997 (in part)

On September 24, 1996, the United States District Court for the District of Alaska entered a judgment in the amount of $5.058 billion in the Exxon Valdez civil trial that began in May 1994. The District Court awarded approximately $19.6 million in compensatory damages to fisher plaintiffs, $38 million in prejudgment interest on the compensatory damages and $5 billion in punitive damages to a class composed of all persons and entities who asserted claims for punitive damages from the corporation as a result of the Exxon Valdez grounding. The District Court also ordered that these awards shall bear interest from and after entry of the judgment. The District Court stayed execution on the judgment pending appeal based on a $6.75 billion letter of credit posted by the corporation. Exxon has appealed the judgment. The corporation continues to believe that the punitive damages in this case are unwarranted and that the judgment should be set aside or substantially reduced by the appellate courts. Since it is impossible to estimate what the ultimate earnings impact will be, no charge was taken in 1996 or 1997 related to these verdicts.

In recent years, accounting standard setters have issued several statements and Exposure Drafts designed to improve the environmental liability information reported in the financial statements and notes. The SEC staff has issued Staff Accounting Bulletin (SAB) No. 92, which sets forth the SEC's interpretation of GAAP regarding contingent liabilities, with particular applicability to companies having environmental liabilities. In 1996, the AICPA issued Statement of Position (SOP) 96-1, "Environmental Remediation Liabilities (Including Auditing Guidance)." SOP 96-1 outlines key events that can be used to determine whether an environmental liability is probable. For example, if a company acknowledges that it has some responsibility for environmental damage and if an initial cleanup feasibility study has been completed, it is reasonable to assume that the contingent liability is probable and the firm should recognize its share of the total cost. In addition, because a big part of dealing with the cleanup of an environmental site involves legal recovery of cleanup costs from other firms that initially refused to pay for their share of the cleanup, firms are allowed to recognize these potential recoveries as assets if they are probable.

The FASB has also done some preliminary work to improve the accounting for environmental remediation costs. The FASB began considering improved environmental accounting in the specific context of the accounting for the costs of decontaminating nuclear power plants. However, the project has now been renamed "Obligations Associated with the Retirement of Long-Lived Assets" to reflect a broader scope. The FASB has decided that an obligation associated with retiring an asset (such as the obligation to do environmental cleanup) should be recognized when it is incurred, should be measured using present value techniques, and the offsetting debit should be an addition to the cost of the associated asset. The FASB expects to release another Exposure Draft on this issue in early 2000.

As evidence of the increased importance of environmental liabilities and the need to account for them in the financial statements, several trends are noted. First, an increasing number of companies have established committees, often at the board of directors level, to oversee environmental compliance. Second, more companies now have written environmental accounting policies, which are disclosed in the accounting policies note to the financial statements. Finally, there is a heightened awareness of the need for improving environmental liability accounting. With the current regulatory environment and these trends, it is likely that there will be further accounting developments and increased financial disclosures of environmental liabilities in the future.

S E G M E N T   R E P O R T I N G

Who sells more soft drinks worldwide, COCA-COLA or PEPSICO? Coke sells more soft drinks worldwide, with a global market share of 46%, compared to 21% for Pepsi.[20] So, how is it that PepsiCo employs 141,000 people, whereas Coke employs just 29,000? The answer is that PepsiCo does a lot more than sell soft drinks. PepsiCo's revenue is split almost equally between its snack foods (Frito-Lay) and soft drink (Pepsi-Cola) segments. Which business strategy is more successful, the concentrated strategy of Coke or the diversified strategy of Pepsi? In recent years, the focused approach of Coke has been the clear winner—the March 1999 market value of The Coca-Cola Company was $169.4 billion, far greater than the $57.2 billion of PepsiCo.[21] An attempt at increased focus was behind the October 1997 strategic change of direction at PepsiCo involving the spinoff of its restaurant businesses (Pizza Hut, Taco Bell, and KFC) in order to focus more attention on soft drinks and snack foods.[22]

20 Patricia Sellers, "How Coke Is Kicking Pepsi's Can," *Fortune*, October 28, 1996, p. 70.

21 The Coca-Cola Company is also more successful internationally than is PepsiCo. Approximately 63% of Coke's revenues are generated outside North America, whereas revenues outside North America are only 26% of the total at Pepsi.

22 Lori Bongiorno, "Fiddling With the Formula at Pepsi?" *Business Week*, October 14, 1996, p. 42; and Nikhil Deogun, "Pepsi Has Had Its Fill of Pizza, Tacos, Chicken," *The Wall Street Journal*, January 24, 1997, p. B1.

Like PepsiCo, many businesses today are large, complex organizations engaged in a variety of activities that bear little relationship to each other. For example, a company might manufacture airplane engines, operate a real estate business, and manage a professional hockey team. Such companies, referred to as diversified companies, or **conglomerates,** operate in multiple industries and do not fit into any one specific industry category. The different segments of a diversified company often operate in distinct and separate markets, involve different management teams, and experience different growth patterns, profit potentials, and degrees of risk. In effect, the segments of the company behave almost like, and in some cases are, separate companies within an overall corporate structure. Yet, if only total company information is presented for a highly diversified company, the different degrees of risk, profitability, and growth potential for major segments of the company cannot be analyzed and compared.

Prepare the necessary supplemental disclosures of financial information by product line and by geographic area.

BUSINESS SEGMENTS

Historically, the United States has led the world in the quality and quantity of financial information required to be disclosed about business segments. In 1939, U.S. companies were encouraged to make separate disclosures concerning operations of foreign business segments because of the "disturbed conditions abroad"—polite language for World War II.[23] Increased creation of firms with many diverse lines of business in the 1960s caused the APB to issue a nonbinding statement encouraging diversified companies to provide summary business segment information to financial statement users. The segment disclosure rules were refined and made mandatory in 1976 with the issuance of Statement No. 14 by the FASB.[24]

Information to be disclosed in the financial statement notes under the provisions of FASB Statement No. 14 included revenues, operating profit, and identifiable assets for each significant industry segment of a company. Other provisions of Statement No. 14 required disclosure of revenues from major customers and information about foreign operations and export sales.

Although the disclosure required of U.S. companies under Statement No. 14 was more extensive than the segment disclosure required by the accounting standards of any other country in the world, financial statement users have consistently requested that firms be required to disclose more. The Association for Investment Management and Research (AIMR) has asked for increased segment disclosure in its annual evaluation of corporate reporting in each of the past 20 years. In 1994, the AICPA Special Committee on Financial Reporting (often called the Jenkins Committee) made the improvement of segment reporting its first recommendation. In response to this push for even better segment reporting, the FASB issued Statement No. 131 in June 1997.[25] In developing Statement No. 131, the FASB worked closely with the Accounting Standards Board (ACSB) in Canada and with the International Accounting Standards Committee (IASC). As a result, U.S. and

FYI: This was the first time the FASB worked directly with another national standard-setting body in the development of a standard.

23 The information in this historical review is adapted from the following source: Research Report (prepared by Paul Pacter), "Reporting Disaggregated Information," Norwalk, CT: Financial Accounting Standards Board, February 1993.
24 *Statement of Financial Accounting Standards No. 14,* "Financial Reporting for Segments of a Business Enterprise," Stamford, CT: Financial Accounting Standards Board, 1976.
25 *Statement of Financial Accounting Standards No. 131,* "Disclosures about Segments of an Enterprise and Related Information," Norwalk, CT: Financial Accounting Standards Board, 1997.

Canadian standards regarding segment reporting are nearly identical, and the international standard is very similar.

According to the provisions of FASB Statement No. 131, companies are required to disclose the following information concerning business segments.

1. Total segment operating profit or loss.
2. Amounts of certain income statement items such as operating revenues, depreciation, interest revenue, interest expense, tax expense, and significant noncash expenses.
3. Total segment assets.
4. Total capital expenditures.
5. Reconciliation of the sum of segment totals to the company total for each of the following items:
   - Revenues
   - Operating profit
   - Assets

In addition to these five items, companies must also disclose how operating segments are identified. Formerly, FASB Statement No. 14 required firms to identify "industry segments." Under the provisions of Statement No. 131, segments are to be identified using the same criteria, whatever they might be, used by management to distinguish business segments for internal reporting purposes. The objective of this requirement is to provide external users with the same type of information about business segments that is used internally. Some companies were concerned about this definition of reportable business segments because they have dozens or even hundreds of internally reportable segments. The FASB responded to this concern by retaining criteria from Statement No. 14 that specify how large a segment must be for separate disclosure to be required. Specifically, a segment is reportable if it meets any one of the three criteria as follows:

- *Revenue test:* A segment should be reported if its total revenue (both to external customers and to other internal segments) is 10% or more of the company's total revenue (external and internal).
- *Profit test:* A segment should be reported if the absolute value of its operating profit (or loss) is greater than 10% of the total of the operating profit for all segments that reported profits (or the total of the losses for all segments that reported losses).
- *Asset test:* A segment should be reported if it contains 10% or more of the combined assets of all operating segments.

The FASB also decided that segments can be combined for reporting purposes, even if they are treated as separate segments internally, if the segments have similar products or services, similar processes, similar customers, similar distribution methods, and are subject to similar regulations.

Companies typically define their business segments in terms of product lines or geographic areas. For those firms defining their segments along product lines, Statement No. 131 requires additional disclosure of revenues and long-lived assets for the company's home country and for all foreign operations combined. If one foreign country comprises a material portion of operations, separate revenue and long-lived asset disclosure should be made for that country. A company may consider also showing revenue and long-lived asset subtotals for "groups" of countries, such as for Europe or Asia.

For companies defining their business segments geographically, additional revenue information must be disclosed by product line. This product line information is provided on a companywide basis, however, not by geographic segment.

Companies are also required to disclose supplemental information about major customers. If revenues from any one customer are more that 10% of total revenue, this fact must be disclosed (although the name of the customer isn't disclosed) along with the amount of the revenue and the names of the operating segments in which the revenue is reported.

The primary difference between Statement No. 131 and Statement No. 14 is in the way that companies identify reportable segments—according to the designations used inside the firm instead of according to some arbitrary industry classification. In addition, Statement No. 131 requires, for the first time, that selected segment disclosure be included in interim reports.

To illustrate the type of business segment disclosure provided under FASB Statement No. 131, the segment information given in the 1998 annual report of PepsiCo will be used. PepsiCo discloses that it has five reportable segments, as follows:

- Pepsi-Cola North America (PepsiCo defines North America to be the United States and Canada.)
- Pepsi-Cola International
- Frito-Lay North America
- Frito-Lay International
- Tropicana

Exhibit 18–4 contains information on PepsiCo's sales and operating profit by segment.

EXHIBIT 18–4 | Net Sales and Operating Profit, By Reportable Segment, For PepsiCo

Net Sales:	1998	1997	1996
Pepsi-Cola			
North America	$ 8,266	$ 7,899	$ 7,788
International	2,385	2,642	2,799
Frito-Lay			
North America	7,474	6,967	6,628
International	3,501	3,409	3,122
Tropicana	722	—	—
	$22,348	$20,917	$20,337
Operating Profit:			
Pepsi-Cola			
North America	$1,211	$1,274	$1,428
International	(219)	(144)	(846)
Frito-Lay			
North America	1,424	1,388	1,286
International	367	318	346
Tropicana	40	—	—
Combined Segments	2,823	2,836	2,214
Corporate	(239)	(174)	(174)
	$2,584	$2,662	$2,040

Notice that the bulk of PepsiCo's sales occur in North America and that almost all of the operating profit is generated in North America. In addition to this sales and operating profit disclosure, PepsiCo also gives information, by segment, on total assets, amortization of intangibles, depreciation, and capital spending.

Application of accounting principles to individual segments of a business presents some unique problems. For example, if a firm uses LIFO and all the inventory is part of one LIFO pool for financial reporting purposes, how is LIFO to be applied in calculating cost of goods sold for individual segments? Another example is the allocation of income tax expense to different segments when the income tax return is prepared for the entire company as a whole. Because of difficulties such as these, FASB Statement No. 131 states that, for segment reporting purposes, firms are to report to external users using the same accounting practices that are used for internal purposes. What this means is that the financial data reported in the segment disclosures won't always conform with GAAP. The FASB views this as part of the price to be paid to reduce the incremental bookkeeping cost required for firms to provide segment information.

In summary, consider the question of how much segment information is enough. Of course, when asked whether they want more information or less, financial statement users will always reply that they want MORE. Ultimately, every user would like unlimited access to the accounting records of all companies. Understandably, companies are reluctant to disclose everything to everyone. The FASB must set segment reporting standards to balance users' desire for relevant data against firms' legitimate concern about disclosing proprietary information.

 How could The Coca-Cola Company use PepsiCo's reported segment information to aid it in formulating its competitive strategy?

I N T E R I M   R E P O R T I N G

The Business Roundtable is an organization of 200 CEOs of top U.S. corporations. On August 20, 1990, The Business Roundtable sent a letter to one of the commissioners of the SEC.[26] The letter was critical of the work of the FASB and suggested that FASB rules were burdening U.S. business "with a costly reporting infrastructure that overloads the user with data but provides very little insight into the economic condition or results of the enterprise." The Roundtable also complained that FASB rules were putting U.S. firms at a competitive disadvantage overseas where foreign accounting standard setters are more sympathetic to business concerns.

One of the specific problem areas identified by The Business Roundtable was quarterly reporting. The Roundtable described quarterly reports as being very costly in terms of preparation, and also counterproductive because they cause management to focus on short-term earnings rather than long-term growth. The Roundtable pointed out that many foreign companies (such as those in the United Kingdom) are required to report only semiannually.

This concern about the counterproductivity of quarterly reporting was echoed by Peter A. Magowan, CEO of SAFEWAY, the large supermarket chain based in Oakland, California. In November 1986, Safeway was taken private in a $5.3 billion leveraged buyout (LBO). In looking back on the success of the restructuring that followed the LBO, Magowan reported that one of the key advantages enjoyed by Safeway was that as a private company, it was no longer locked into the cycle of fixation on reported quarterly earnings. According to Magowan, this freedom from pressure to report ever-increasing quarterly profits made it possible for Safeway to institute aggressive pricing, store expansion, and increased spending for training and technology—all actions that would hurt reported profits in the short run but were for the long-term good of the company.[27]

I n spite of concerns that quarterly reports lead to a myopic focus on short-term profits by management, they are still required disclosure in the United States. Publicly traded firms must file quarterly financial statements with the SEC in a 10-Q filing within 45 days of the end of the quarter. An outline of the special problems associated with the preparation of interim reports is given in this module.

26 John S. Reed, Chairman, Accounting Principles Task Force of The Business Roundtable; letter dated August 20, 1990, addressed to Philip R. Lochner, Jr., Commissioner, Securities and Exchange Commission.
27 Peter A. Magowan, "The Case for LBOs: The Safeway Experience," *California Management Review*, Fall 1989, p. 9. In April 1990, Safeway again issued shares to the public.

INTERIM REPORTS

Statements showing financial position and operating results for intervals of less than a year are referred to as **interim financial statements.** Interim reports are considered essential in providing investors and others with timely information as to the position and progress of an enterprise. Notwithstanding the need for interim reports, there are significant difficulties associated with them. One problem is caused by the seasonal factors of certain businesses. For example, in some companies, revenues fluctuate widely among interim periods; in other businesses, significant fixed costs are incurred during a single period but are to benefit several periods. Not only must costs be allocated to appropriate periods of benefit, but they must be matched against the realized revenues for the interim period to determine a reasonable income measurement.

In preparing interim reports, adjustments for accrued items, generally required only at year-end, have to be considered at the end of each interim period. Because of the additional time and extra costs involved to develop complete information, many estimates of expenses are made for interim reports. The increased number of estimates adds an element of subjectivity to these reports. Another problem is that extraordinary items or the disposal of a business segment will have a greater impact on an interim period's earnings than on the results of operations for an entire year. In analyzing interim financial statements, special attention should be given to these and similar considerations.

Two prominent viewpoints exist in relation to the reporting of interim results. One viewpoint is that each reporting interval is to be recognized as a separate accounting period. Thus, the results of operations for each interim period are determined in essentially the same manner as for the annual accounting period. Under this approach, the same judgments, estimations, accruals, and deferrals are recognized at the end of each interim period as for the annual period.

The other viewpoint, and the one accepted by the APB in Opinion No. 28, is that the interim period is an integral part of the annual period.[28] Essentially, the revenues and expenses for the total period are allocated among interim periods on some reasonable basis, for example, time, sales volume, or productive activity. Under the **integral part of annual period concept,** the same general accounting principles and reporting practices employed for annual reports are to be utilized for interim statements, but modifications may be required so the interim results will better relate to the total results of operations for the annual period. As an example of the type of modification that may be required, assume a company uses the LIFO method of inventory valuation and encounters a situation where liquidation of the base period inventory occurs at an interim date but the inventory is expected to be replaced by the end of the annual period. Under these circumstances, the inventory reported at the interim date should not reflect the LIFO liquidation, and the cost of goods sold for the interim period should include the expected cost of replacing the liquidated LIFO base.

Another example of a required modification deals with a change in accounting principle during an interim period. In general, these changes should follow the provisions of APB Opinion No. 20 (see Chapter 20). However, the FASB concluded in Statement No. 3 that for any cumulative effect–type change, other than a change to LIFO, if the change is made "in other than the first interim period of an enterprise's fiscal year, the cumulative effect of the change on retained earnings at the beginning of that year shall be included in the determination of net income of the first interim period of the year of change."[29]

To illustrate the added insight that quarterly information can provide, quarterly data for the BOSTON CELTICS, a professional basketball team, are provided in Exhibit 18–5

---

28 *Opinions of the Accounting Principles Board No. 28*, "Interim Financial Reporting," New York: American Institute of Certified Public Accountants, 1973, par. 9.
29 *Statement of Financial Accounting Standards No. 3*, "Reporting Accounting Changes in Interim Financial Statements," Stamford, CT: Financial Accounting Standards Board, 1974, par. 4.

from its 1998 annual report. The basketball business is very seasonal, and this fact is reflected in the quarterly numbers for the Celtics. Reported revenue is at its maximum in the quarter ended March 31, which occurs in the heart of the basketball season. No revenue is recognized at all during July, August, and September, because the Celtics play no games during those three months. Anyone reading only the annual net income numbers of the Celtics misses the potentially valuable information contained in the wide variation in net income from quarter to quarter.

EXHIBIT 18–5 | Summary Quarterly Data for the Boston Celtics

Note M—Quarterly Results (Unaudited)
Numbers are in thousands of dollars.

	Quarter Ended				
	Sep. 30, 1997	Dec. 31, 1997	March 31, 1998	June 30, 1998	Total
Year Ended June 30, 1998:					
Revenues	$ 0	$25,274	$39,671	$10,735	$75,680
Net income (loss)	(3,866)	6,355	11,931	(2,153)	12,267

	Quarter Ended				
	Sep. 30, 1996	Dec. 31, 1996	March 31, 1997	June 30, 1997	Total
Year Ended June 30, 1997:					
Revenues	$ 0	$20,630	$33,865	$ 8,503	$62,998
Net income	(3,207)	4,544	10,006	(10,923)	420

 Will modern technology ever make it possible for firms to release *daily* financial statements to investors and creditors?

Notice that the Celtics' quarterly results are labeled "unaudited." Obviously, the small amount of information provided about each quarter does not "present fairly" the results of the Celtics' operations for that quarter. Accordingly, quarterly reports are almost always labeled "unaudited" because they do not fairly present a firm's operations, cash flows, and financial position in the same way as do the annual financial statements that are audited. Quarterly reports submitted to the SEC in the 10-Q filing are not required to be audited although they are to be prepared in accordance with GAAP.

REVIEW OF LEARNING OBJECTIVES

1 **DERIVATIVES Understand the business and accounting concepts connected with derivatives and hedging activities.** Uncertainty about the future fair value of assets and liabilities or about future cash flows exposes firms to risk. One way to manage this risk is through the use of derivatives. A derivative is a financial instrument or other contract that derives its value from the movement of prices, interest rates, or exchange rates associated with an underlying item. Many derivatives are executory contracts, meaning that they are not a transaction but are an exchange of promises about future actions.

2 **Identify the different types of risk faced by a business.** Of the many types of risk faced by a firm, four important types are:

- *Price risk.* Uncertainty about the future price of an asset.

- *Credit risk.* Uncertainty over whether the party on the other side of a transaction will abide by the terms of the agreement.
- *Interest rate risk.* Uncertainty about future interest rates and their impact on cash flows and the fair value of financial instruments.
- *Exchange rate risk.* Uncertainty about the future U.S. dollar cash flows stemming from assets and liabilities denominated in foreign currencies.

3 **Describe the characteristics of the following types of derivatives: swaps, forwards, futures, and options.**

- *Swap.* Contract in which two parties agree to exchange payments in the future based upon some price or rate. A good example is the exchange of a stream of variable-rate interest payments for a stream of fixed-rate payments. A swap can transform the stream of future cash flows that you have into the cash flow stream that you want.
- *Forwards.* Agreement between two parties to exchange a specified amount of a commodity, security, or foreign currency at a specified date with the price or rate being set now. Forward contracts are usually settled with cash payments instead of by actual delivery of the underlying asset.
- *Futures.* Very similar to a forward contract, with the difference being that a futures contract is a standardized instrument that is sponsored by and traded on an organized exchange.
- *Option.* Contract giving the owner the right, but not the obligation, to buy or sell an asset at a specified exercise price. A call option gives the owner the right to buy an asset; a put option gives the owner the right to sell an asset. The buyer of an option must pay cash in advance for the option; in exchange, the buyer is protected against unfavorable price or rate movements but can still benefit from favorable movements.

4 **Define hedging, and outline the difference between a fair value hedge and a cash flow hedge.** Hedging is the structuring of transactions to reduce risk. Much hedging occurs naturally in business as increases in costs or in the value of liabilities are offset by related increases in revenues or in the value of assets. Derivatives are also used for hedging. The FASB has identified two general types of hedges for which derivatives can be used:

- *Fair value hedge.* The change in the fair value of the derivative offsets changes in fair values of assets or liabilities.
- *Cash flow hedge.* Cash flows from the derivative offset variability in the cash flows from forecasted transactions.

5 **Account for a variety of different derivatives and for hedging relationships.** The fair value of all derivatives is to be recognized and reported in the balance sheet. Changes in fair value are reported as follows:

- *Derivative is not a hedge.* Changes in fair value are reported as gains or losses in the income statement.
- *Derivative is a fair value hedge.* Changes in fair value are reported as gains or losses in the income statement and are offset by gains or losses on changes in the fair value of the asset or liability being hedged.
- *Derivative is a cash flow hedge.* Changes in fair value are deferred and reported in comprehensive income (an equity adjustment). These deferred gains and losses are recognized in income on the forecasted date of the cash flows being hedged.

6 **CONTINGENCIES Apply the accounting rules for contingent items to the areas of lawsuits and environmental liabilities.** If a contingent liability is probable and can be reasonably estimated, it should be recognized in the financial statements. If a contingent liability is only possible, it should be disclosed in the financial statement notes. Contingent liabilities that are remote should not, in general, be disclosed. Contingent assets should not be disclosed unless they are probable.

In accounting for lawsuits, firms are usually reluctant to disclose specific amounts or to overestimate the likelihood of losing the suit because they don't want to increase their chances of losing the lawsuit or of paying a large judgment amount.

Accounting for environmental remediation liabilities is complicated by the fact that the future cost of the cleanup is very difficult to estimate. In addition, each cleanup project is surrounded by suits and countersuits between government agencies and the responsible firms and among the responsible firms themselves. The SEC requires substantial disclosure of the details of a firm's environmental cleanup projects.

7 **SEGMENT REPORTING Prepare the necessary supplemental disclosures of financial information by product line and by geographic area.** Historically, segment reporting in the U.S. has been more extensive than in any other country. Recently, the FASB has worked with the ACSB in Canada and with the IASC to improve segment reporting worldwide.

Under the provisions of FASB Statement No. 131, companies are required to disclose the following information for each business segment: revenues, operating profit, assets, capital expenditures, and certain income statement items such as depreciation and interest revenue and expense.

Companies are to define their reportable business segments using the same practice that is used internally. The objective of this requirement is to provide external users with the same type of segment information used inside the company.

8 INTERIM REPORTING Recognize the importance of interim reports, and outline the difficulties encountered when preparing those reports. In the United States, publicly traded firms are required to file quarterly summary financial statements with the SEC in a filing called a 10-Q. These interim financial statements are prepared using the "integral part of annual period" concept. Using this concept, each quarter is not viewed as a separate period; instead, each quarter is viewed as an integral part of the year, and estimates are used to appropriately allocate a share of the annual results to each quarter. Quarterly reports are typically not audited, but they still are to be prepared in accordance with GAAP.

KEY TERMS

Call option 1057
Cash flow hedge 1059
Conglomerates 1074
Contingent gains 1067
Contingent losses 1067
Credit risk 1053
Exchange rate risk 1053
Executory contract 1052

Fair value hedge 1059
Forward contract 1055
Futures contract 1056
Hedging 1058
Integral part of annual period
   concept 1078
Interest rate risk 1053
Interest rate swap 1054

Interim financial statements 1078
Notional amount 1061
Option 1056
Price risk 1053
Put option 1057
Swap 1054

QUESTIONS

DERIVATIVES

1. How does a derivative differ from other financial instruments and contracts?
2. Why is a derivative often an executory contract? Give another example of an executory contract.
3. Briefly describe the four types of risk discussed in the chapter.
4. Why would a company enter into an interest rate swap?
5. What is the difference between a forward contract and a futures contract?
6. How does an option differ from the other types of derivatives discussed in the chapter?
7. Describe the purpose of a cash flow hedge, and give an example of a cash flow hedge.
8. Why is traditional historical cost accounting inappropriate when accounting for derivative contracts?
9. When does partial hedge ineffectiveness occur?
10. Derivatives are to be reported in the balance sheet at their fair value on the balance sheet date. How are unrealized gains and losses on derivatives recognized in the financial statements?
11. What is the notional amount of a derivative? How can the notional amount be misleading?

12. A derivative used as an economic hedge of foreign currency risk associated with a foreign currency-denominated asset or liability is *not* accounted for as a hedge under the provisions of Statement No. 133. How are these derivatives accounted for?
13. What international standard governs the accounting for derivatives? How does this standard differ from Statement No. 133?

CONTINGENCIES

14. How should contingent liabilities that are reasonably possible of becoming liabilities be reported in the financial statements?
15. Describe the appropriate treatment of contingent gains.
16. What factors are important in deciding whether a pending lawsuit should be reported as a liability on the balance sheet?
17. Under what circumstances should the existence of an environmental liability be considered "probable"?

SEGMENT REPORTING

18. In what ways can segment information assist in the analysis of a company's financial statements?

19. How is a business segment defined under the provisions of FASB Statement No. 131?
20. How large must an internally defined segment be in order for separate financial statement disclosure to be required?
21. Is segment information prepared according to GAAP? Explain.

INTERIM REPORTING

22. Distinguish between the two primary viewpoints concerning the preparation of interim financial statements.
23. Why should investors be careful in interpreting interim reports?

DISCUSSION CASES

CASE 18–1

DERIVATIVES: WHAT RISKS DO WE FACE?

Palmer Equipment Company is a multinational firm that sells exercise equipment to fitness clubs and to individuals. When customers buy Palmer's equipment, they typically pay 20% down and pay the balance within 1 year. Palmer's primary market is the United States, where it makes 60% of its sales. Palmer makes 10% of its sales in Japan and 30% in Europe. All foreign sales are denominated in the local currencies.

All the equipment that Palmer sells is manufactured in southern China. The factories are not owned by Palmer; instead, Palmer contracts with various factory owners for the manufacture and delivery of equipment. Palmer's equipment purchase contracts are denominated in Hong Kong dollars.

Palmer has obtained its long-term debt financing from a mixture of U.S., Japanese, and German banks. About half of the loans from U.S. banks are variable-rate loans; the remainder of Palmer's bank loans have fixed rates.

Recently, Palmer has seen its earnings fluctuate wildly from one year to the next. As the recently appointed head of the corporate risk management committee, you have been asked by Jefferson Todd Palmer, CEO of Palmer Equipment, to briefly summarize the different types of risk faced by Palmer.

CASE 18–2

DERIVATIVES: HOW MANY BUSHELS SHALL WE HEDGE?

King Follett Foods produces premium tofu for the U.S. market. Sales are growing rapidly in the health-conscious United States, and King Follett expects sales in 2003 to be 30% more than sales in 2002.

A key ingredient in the making of tofu is soybeans. During 2002, King Follett has used approximately 10,000 bushels of soybeans per month. The cost of a bushel of soybeans has varied from a high of $9.00 to a low of $7.00.

In order to stabilize its production cost, in 2002 King Follett initiated a program of using forward contracts to lock in the cost of soybean purchases in advance. The 3 employees in the finance department who oversee this program are starting to get a pretty good feel for the way prices move in the soybean market. As of the end of 2002, these employees have purchased the following forward contracts for the first 3 months of 2003:

	Quantity	Forward Price
January 2003	20,000 bushels	$8.00 per bushel
February 2003	30,000 bushels	$8.50 per bushel
March 2003	30,000 bushels	$8.60 per bushel

In each case, if the market price on the first day of the month is greater than the forward price, King Follett collects the difference (multiplied by the number of bushels in the contract). In 2002, the forward contract purchase program netted a profit of $12,000 over and above the offsetting cost of goods sold increase from the effect of price increases on the cost of soybeans.

Comment on whether the 3 employees in the finance department have structured the forward contracts to properly hedge the risk of fluctuations in soybean prices.

CASE 18–3

DERIVATIVES: ARE DERIVATIVES JUST ANOTHER WAY TO GAMBLE?

Laurie Seals and Julie Winn are roommates at Upland State College. Laurie majors in political science and Julie is an accounting major. Recently, one of Laurie's political science classes has been discussing the impact of derivative trading losses on the finances of several public institutions in the United States, including city governments and public colleges. The political science class has decided that derivatives are nothing more than a sophisticated form of gambling and that the trading of derivatives in the United States should be banned.

What should Julie say to Laurie in explaining how derivatives serve a vital business purpose?

CASE 18–4

CONTINGENCIES: WHEN IS A LOSS A LOSS?

How should Newport Company report each of the following contingencies?

(a) A threat of expropriation exists for one of Newport's manufacturing plants located in a foreign country. Expropriation is deemed to be reasonably possible. Any compensation from the foreign government would be less than the carrying amount (book value) of the plant.

(b) Potential costs exist due to the discovery of a safety hazard related to one of Newport's products. These costs are probable and can be reasonably estimated.

(c) One of Newport's warehouses located at the base of a mountain can no longer be insured against rockslide losses. As of yet, no rockslide losses have occurred.

CASE 18–5

CONTINGENCIES: ACCOUNTING STANDARDS IN COURT

Judge Daniel H. Wells is currently deliberating over a suit filed by 3 stockholders against Transcontinental Corporation. The stockholders allege that Transcontinental's year-end balance sheet was misleading because it did not accurately reflect the financial position of the company at that date. The stockholders claim that they relied on the published financial statements and subsequently lost money on their investments in Transcontinental. The primary point at issue is that Transcontinental did not disclose anything about a contingent liability relating to a significant pending lawsuit with a supplier, which Transcontinental subsequently lost. The 3 stockholders contend that this information was material, relevant, and should have been disclosed.

Tomorrow, the accountant for Transcontinental will take the stand. Before the lawyers for the opposing parties begin their questioning of the accountant, Judge Wells intends to ask a few questions to determine whether Transcontinental was negligent in its accounting practices. What questions should Judge Wells ask?

CASE 18–6

CONTINGENCIES: IS "PROBABLE" ENOUGH?

One of the most difficult estimation questions in accounting is when contingent liabilities need to be recognized in a company's financial statements. The FASB indicated in Statement No. 5 that a liability and loss should be reported in the financial statements if it is probable that a loss will be incurred and the amount of the loss can be estimated. But what is the meaning of probable? Some accountants have interpreted this as meaning near certainty; others as being at a lesser percentage of certainty such as above 90%, 85%, or some other number.

In 1992, the FASB issued Statement No. 109, which requires reporting of deferred income tax assets if it is more likely than not that a company will have future income sufficient to realize the asset. The term "more likely than not" is defined as a percentage above 50%.

Because of the use of a new probability concept, some accountants have suggested that the definition of "probable" used in Statement No. 5 should be made more specific, perhaps even using the more-likely-than-not criterion for contingent liabilities. What are the arguments for and against this suggestion?

CASE 18-7

CONTINGENCIES: DO WE NEED SPECIFIC STANDARDS FOR ENVIRONMENTAL AND OTHER CONTINGENT LIABILITIES?

Many state and federal laws place possible future liabilities on companies as a result of environmental pollution, sexual discrimination, safety requirements, and other social responsibilities. In general, these items are part of those potential losses and liabilities covered by FASB Statement No. 5. Some companies are reporting these items as liabilities, while others are waiting for more specific guidelines by the FASB before reporting them. Should the FASB adopt specific guidelines for the reporting of these liabilities, or should the decision be left to companies based on the general conceptual guidelines of FASB Statement No. 5?

CASE 18-8

SEGMENT REPORTING: BY PRODUCT LINE OR BY COUNTRY?

Eliza Snow is the controller for Lorenzo Manufacturing. Lorenzo has 5 different product lines and conducts significant operations in 6 different countries. Lorenzo's internal organization is set up such that there is a division manager in each of the 6 different countries, with responsibility for sale of all 5 products in that country. Internal accounting reports are prepared based on this same organizational structure.

Snow has heard rumors that new FASB rules require Lorenzo to externally report summary segment information by product line. Snow is very upset because this is completely at odds with what Lorenzo does internally. Snow estimates that compiling segment information by product line will require at least a week's worth of work by her and her entire staff.

Does Snow have a correct understanding of the provisions of FASB Statement No. 131 on segment reporting? Explain.

CASE 18-9

INTERIM REPORTING: THE QUARTERLY REPORT MUST BE EXACTLY LIKE THE ANNUAL REPORT!

J. M. Grant has recently been elected to the board of directors of Montrose Company. The other directors of Montrose are beginning to regret this action. Grant has proved to be very opinionated, very stubborn, and quite old-fashioned. Every decision by the board members since Grant joined the board has taken two to three times as long as it should have, because Grant seems to disagree with everything that everyone else says.

The most recent crisis has arisen over the preparation of the quarterly report. Grant was shocked to learn that quarterly reports do not include the same detail as is contained in the annual report and that estimates and assumptions are used extensively in preparing the summary information that goes into the quarterly report. The last straw for Grant was when he learned that the quarterly report is not audited. Grant has absolutely refused to accept this slipshod method of quarterly reporting and has vowed that he will bottle up board action on all other decisions until the board agrees to the preparation of a quarterly report that contains the same detail, the same accounting practices, and the same type of audit opinion as the annual report.

You have been appointed by the board to reason with Grant. What will you tell him?

EXERCISES

EXERCISE 18-10

DERIVATIVES: IDENTIFYING A HEDGE

Yelrome Company manufactures candy. On September 1, Yelrome purchased a futures contract that obligates Yelrome to sell 100,000 pounds of sugar on September 30 at $0.24 per pound. Yelrome typically purchases 100,000 pounds of sugar per month to use as a raw material in the candy production process. Yelrome purchased the futures contract to hedge against movements in the price of sugar during the month of September.

In Yelrome's case, the sugar futures contract does *not* hedge against movements in the price of sugar. Demonstrate this by computing the net cost of the 100,000 pounds of sugar purchased in September under three sets of circumstances: when the price is $0.22, $0.24, and $0.26.

EXERCISE 18–11

DERIVATIVES: ACCOUNTING FOR SWAPS

On January 1, 2002, South Platte Company received a 2-year, $600,000 loan, with interest payments occurring at the end of each year and the principal to be repaid on December 31, 2003. The interest rate for the first year is the prevailing market rate of 8%, and the rate in 2003 will be equal to the market interest rate on January 1, 2003. In conjunction with this loan, South Platte enters into an interest rate swap agreement whereby South Platte will receive a swap payment (based on $600,000) if the January 1, 2003, interest rate is greater than 8% and will make a swap payment if the rate is less than 8%. The interest swap payment will be made on December 31, 2003.

Make all journal entries necessary on South Platte's books in 2002 and 2003 to record this loan and the interest rate swap. On January 1, 2003, the interest rate is 7%.

EXERCISE 18–12

DERIVATIVES: ACCOUNTING FOR FORWARD CONTRACTS

On September 1, 2002, Ramus Company purchased machine parts from Ho Man Tin Company for 6,000,000 Hong Kong dollars to be paid on January 1, 2003. The exchange rate on September 1 is HK$7.7=$1. On the same date, Ramus enters into a forward contract and agrees to purchase HK$6,000,000 on January 1, 2003, at the rate of HK$7.7=$1.

Make all journal entries necessary on Ramus' books on September 1, 2002, December 31, 2002, and January 1, 2003, to record this purchase and the forward contract. On December 31, 2002, and on January 1, 2003, the exchange rate is HK$8.0=$1. Ramus uses a perpetual inventory system.

EXERCISE 18–13

DERIVATIVES: ACCOUNTING FOR FUTURE CONTRACTS

Quincy Bottlers produces bottled orange juice. Orange juice concentrate is typically bought and sold by the pound, and Quincy uses 100,000 pounds of orange juice concentrate each month. On December 1, 2002, Quincy entered into an orange juice concentrate futures contract to buy 100,000 pounds of concentrate on January 1, at a price of $0.85 per pound, which is also the market price of concentrate on December 1. Quincy designates the futures contract as a hedge of the forecasted purchase of orange juice concentrate in January.

Make all journal entries necessary on Quincy's books on December 1, 2002, December 31, 2002, and January 1, 2003, to record this futures contract. On December 31, 2002, and on January 1, 2003, the market price of concentrate is $0.75 per pound.

EXERCISE 18–14

DERIVATIVES: ACCOUNTING FOR OPTIONS

Commerce Clothing Mills uses approximately 400,000 pounds of cotton each month to make the cotton fabric used in its patented no-wrinkle, short-sleeved white shirts. On December 1, 2002, Commerce purchased an option to buy 400,000 pounds of cotton on January 1, 2003, at a price of $0.75 per pound. The market price on December 1 is $0.75 per pound. Commerce had to pay $1,500 to purchase the cotton option. Commerce designated the option as a hedge against price fluctuations for its January purchases of cotton.

Make all journal entries necessary on Commerce's books on December 1, 2002, December 31, 2002, and January 1, 2003, to record this option and also to record the purchase of 400,000 pounds of cotton on January 1. On December 31, 2002, and on January 1, 2003, the market price of cotton is $0.60 per pound.

EXERCISE 18–15

DERIVATIVES: NOTIONAL AMOUNTS
Refer back to Exercises 18-12 and 18-13.

1. What is the notional value of the Hong Kong dollar forward contract described in Exercise 18-12? What is the fair value of the forward contract on December 31, 2002?
2. What is the notional value of the orange juice concentrate futures contract described in Exercise 18-13? What is the fair value of the futures contract on December 31, 2002?

EXERCISE 18–16

CONTINGENCIES: TYPES OF LIABILITIES
For each of the following scenarios, identify whether the event described is an actual liability, a contingent liability, or not a liability.

(a) Apple Inc. has used the toxic substance, iocaine powder, in its production process. Recently adopted federal regulations require companies to clean up any factory sites contaminated with iocaine. Apple has begun a preliminary investigation into the iocaine contamination at its factory sites.
(b) Banana Corp. financed its warehouse facilities with a long-term mortgage that calls for semiannual payments of $7,000. The mortgage's current outstanding balance is $98,000.
(c) Orange Company sells computer systems and supplies. It offers its customers a 1-year, money-back guarantee. In the past, approximately 10% of customers have exercised this return privilege.
(d) Kiwi Industries manufactures and distributes outdoor recreational equipment. An individual recently filed a lawsuit as a result of injuries sustained while using Kiwi equipment. Attorneys for Kiwi feel the chance of losing the case is minimal.
(e) Berry Incorporated, a newly formed company, has an unfunded pension plan that calls for retirement benefits to be paid to employees who retire after a minimum of 10 years of employment with the company.
(f) John Townson, a successful entrepreneur, has expressed a desire to establish university scholarships for disadvantaged youth in his community. He has been contacted by numerous universities, but as of yet, nothing firm has been established.

EXERCISE 18–17

CONTINGENCIES: DISCLOSURE OF CONTINGENCIES
Sound Wave, Inc., a manufacturer of electronic greeting cards, has had a lawsuit filed against it by Sounds Good, another manufacturer of electronic greeting cards. The suit alleges patent right infringements by Sound Wave and asks for compensatory damages. For the following possible situations, determine how Sound Wave should report the information concerning the lawsuit: recognize as a liability on the balance sheet, and if so, how much; disclose in a note; or do nothing. Give reasons for your answers.

(a) Sound Wave's legal counsel is convinced that the suit will result in a loss to Sound Wave but isn't sure of the dollar damages.
(b) Sound Wave's legal counsel believes an out-of-court settlement is probable and will cost Sound Wave approximately $600,000.
(c) Sound Wave's legal counsel believes it is reasonably possible that the case will result in a $2,000,000 loss to Sound Wave.
(d) Sound Wave's legal counsel believes it is probable that the case will result in an undeterminable loss to Sound Wave.
(e) Sound Wave's legal counsel believes there is a remote chance for a loss to occur.
(f) The suit hasn't been filed, but Sound Wave's legal counsel has informed management that an unintentional patent infringement has occurred.

EXERCISE 18–18

CONTINGENCIES: CONTINGENT LOSSES
Conrad Corporation sells motorcycle helmets. In 2002, Conrad sold 4 million helmets before discovering a significant defect in the helmet's construction. By December 31,

2002, 2 lawsuits had been filed against Conrad. The first lawsuit, which Conrad has little chance of winning, is expected to settle out of court for $750,000 in January 2003. Conrad's attorneys think the company has a 50-50 chance of winning the second lawsuit, which is for $400,000. What accounting treatment should Conrad give the pending lawsuits in the 2002 year-end financial statements? (Include any necessary journal entries.)

EXERCISE 18–19

CONTINGENCIES: CONTINGENT LIABILITIES

Bell Industries is a multinational company. In preparing the annual financial statements, the auditors met with Bell's attorneys to discuss various legal matters facing the firm. For each of the following independent items, determine the appropriate disclosure.

(a) Bell is being sued by a distributor for breach of contract. The attorneys feel there is a 30% chance of Bell's losing the suit.

(b) One of Bell's subsidiaries has been accused by a federal agency of violating numerous environmental laws. The company faces significant fines if found guilty. The attorneys feel that the subsidiary has complied with all applicable laws, and they therefore place the probability of incurring the fines at less than 10%.

(c) A subsidiary operating in a foreign country whose government is unstable was recently taken over by the government and nationalized. Bell is negotiating with representatives of that government, but company attorneys feel the probability of the company losing possession of its assets is approximately 90%.

EXERCISE 18–20

SEGMENT REPORTING: REPORTING SEGMENT INFORMATION

Putz Industries sells 5 different types of products. Internally, Putz is divided into 5 different divisions based on these 5 different product lines. Putz has prepared the following information to disclose to external users in the notes to its 2002 financial statements:

	Putz Industries Business Segment Information For the Year Ended December 31, 2002 (In millions of dollars)					
	Division 1	Division 2	Division 3	Division 4	Division 5	Total
Revenues	$ 577	$ 84	$ 93	$117	$ 96	$ 967
Operating profit	66	11	9	10	10	106
Total assets	2,124	298	328	314	353	3,417

According to the provisions of FASB Statement No. 131, what additional information must Putz provide?

EXERCISE 18–21

SEGMENT REPORTING: TYPES OF INFORMATION DISCLOSED BY BUSINESS SEGMENT

Companies are required to disclose selected results in the financial statements for significant business segments. This information often takes the form of industry segment reporting by diversified companies, but it also can be by geographic areas.

Refer to the annual report of THE WALT DISNEY COMPANY in Appendix A and identify what kind of segment disclosure is provided by Disney. Is this information useful to prospective investors? Why or why not?

EXERCISE 18–22

SEGMENT REPORTING: INTERIM INCOME STATEMENTS

The income statement for the year ended December 31, 2002, of Angus Technology Inc. is given at the top of the next page. Using the yearly income statement and the supplemental information, reconstruct the third-quarter interim statement for Angus.

Supplemental information:

(a) Assume a 40% tax rate.

(b) Third-quarter sales were 20% of total sales.

(c) For interim reporting purposes, a gross profit rate of 38% can be justified.

(d) Variable operating expenses are allocated in the same proportion as sales. Fixed operating expenses are allocated based on the expiration of time. Of the total operating expenses, $60,000 relate to variable expenses.

(e) The equipment was sold June 1, 2002.

(f) The extraordinary loss occurred September 1, 2002.

Angus Technology Inc.
Income Statement
For the Year Ended December 31, 2002

Sales	$900,000
Cost of goods sold	560,000
Gross profit on sales	$340,000
Operating expenses	96,000
Operating income	$244,000
Gain on sale of equipment	28,000
Income from continuing operations before income taxes	$272,000
Income taxes	108,800
Income from continuing operations	$163,200
Extraordinary loss (net of income tax savings of $40,000)	(52,000)
Net income	$111,200

EXERCISE 18–23

SEGMENT REPORTING: INTERIM LIFO LIQUIDATION

On December 31, 2001, Ryanes Company had LIFO ending inventory consisting of 500 units with a LIFO cost of $10 per unit. During the first quarter of 2002, Ryanes sold 1,000 units. As of March 31, 2002, the inventory of Ryanes is 400 units and the current purchase price of inventory is $32 per unit. The reduction in the level of inventory is temporary, and Ryanes fully expects inventory levels to be at or above 500 units by December 31, 2002. The recorded cost of goods sold for Ryanes for the first quarter of 2002 is $29,800 [(900 × $32) + (100 × $10)]. What adjusting entry, if any, should Ryanes make on March 31, 2002, in order to correctly apply LIFO to the reporting of quarterly results?

PROBLEMS

PROBLEM 18–24

DERIVATIVES: IDENTIFYING A HEDGE

Kanesville Company is still new at using derivatives to hedge business risk. Kanesville has entered into 5 derivative agreements in an attempt to hedge 5 specific items. The derivatives, and associated items, are briefly described below:

(a) *Deutsche mark futures contract.* If the U.S. dollar value of DM500,000 is greater than $300,000 on July 31, Kanesville must pay the difference; if the U.S. dollar value is less than $300,000, Kanesville receives the difference. This futures contract is intended to hedge a DM500,000 account payable due to be paid on July 31.

(b) *Copper forward contract.* If the price of copper is more than $1.10 per pound on August 31, Kanesville must pay the difference (multiplied by 100,000 pounds); if the price is less than $1.10, Kanesville receives the difference. This forward contract is intended to hedge Kanesville's expected purchases of copper (as a raw material) for the month of August.

(c) *Japanese yen futures contract.* If the U.S. dollar value of ¥10 million is greater than $90,000 on July 15, Kanesville receives the difference; if the U.S. dollar value is less than $90,000, Kanesville must pay the difference. This futures contract is intended to hedge Kanesville's expected purchase of some equipment from a Japanese company on July 15 for ¥5 million.

(d) *Interest rate swap.* If the interest rate on March 31 of next year is greater than 12%, Kanesville receives the difference (on a principal amount of $2,000,000); if the interest rate is less than 12%, Kanesville must pay the difference. This interest rate swap is intended to hedge a $2,000,000 variable-rate loan. The loan is expected to be fully repaid this year on May 10.

(e) *Call option on Williams Company stock.* If the price of a share of Williams Company stock is greater than $60 on September 24, Kanesville receives the difference (multiplied by 25,000 shares); if the price of the stock is less than $60, the option is worthless and will be allowed to expire. This call option is intended to hedge an investment in 25,000 shares of Williams Company stock.

Instructions: For each of the 5 pairs (derivative and associated item) above, state whether the derivative serves as an effective hedge. Explain your answer.

PROBLEM 18–25

DERIVATIVES: ACCOUNTING FOR SWAPS

On January 1, 2002, Kindall Company received a 5-year, $2,000,000 loan, with interest payments occurring at the end of each year and the principal to be repaid on December 31, 2006. The interest rate for the first year is the prevailing market rate of 10%, and the rate in each succeeding year will be equal to the market interest rate on January 1 of that year. In conjunction with this loan, Kindall enters into an interest rate swap agreement whereby, in each year of the loan starting with 2003, Kindall will receive a swap payment (based on $2,000,000) if the January 1 interest rate is greater than 10% and will make a swap payment if the rate is less than 10%. The swap payments are made at the end of the year.

On January 1, 2003, the interest rate is 12%, and on December 31, 2003, the interest rate is 9%.

Instructions: Make all journal entries necessary on Kindall's books in 2002 and 2003 to record this loan and the interest rate swap. For purposes of estimating future swap payments, assume that the current interest rate is the best forecast of the future interest rate.

PROBLEM 18–26

DERIVATIVES: ACCOUNTING FOR FORWARD CONTRACTS

Megan Rose Cuisine operates a chain of fine seafood restaurants. Megan Rose specializes in very detailed long-term planning. On October 1, 2002, Megan Rose determined that it would need to purchase 1,000,000 pounds of deluxe fish on January 1, 2004. Because of the fluctuations in the price of deluxe fish, on October 1 Megan Rose negotiated a special forward contract with Angela Investment Bank for Megan Rose to purchase 1,000,000 pounds of deluxe fish on January 1, 2004, at a price of $16,000,000. Angela Investment Bank has a staff of financial analysts who specialize in forecasting fish prices. These analysts are predicting a drop in worldwide fish prices between October 1, 2002, and January 1, 2004.

On December 31, 2002, the price of a pound of deluxe fish is $20. On December 31, 2003, the price of a pound of deluxe fish is $11. Also, the appropriate discount rate throughout this period is 10%.

Instructions: Make all journal entries necessary on Megan Rose's books in 2002, 2003, and 2004 to record the forward contract and the purchase of the fish. For purposes of estimating future settlement payments under the forward contract, assume that the current price of fish is the best forecast of the future price.

PROBLEM 18–27

DERIVATIVES: ACCOUNTING FOR FUTURES CONTRACTS

On January 1, 2002, Jessica Marie Company sold equipment to Gwang Ju Company for 20,000,000 Korean won, with payment to be received in 2 years on January 1, 2004. The exchange rate on January 1, 2002, is 800 won=$1. On the same date, Jessica Marie enters into a futures contract and agrees to sell 20,000,000 won on January 1, 2004, at the rate of 800 won=$1.

On December 31, 2002, the exchange rate is 790 won=$1. On December 31, 2003, the exchange rate is 830 won=$1. Also, the appropriate discount rate throughout this period is 10%.

Instructions: Make all journal entries necessary on Jessica Marie's books in 2002, 2003, and 2004 to record this sale, the futures contract, and the collection of the receivable. For purposes of estimating future settlement payments under the futures contract, assume that the current exchange rate is the best forecast of the future exchange rate. (Note: Don't forget to record the receivable at its present value.)

PROBLEM 18–28

DERIVATIVES: ACCOUNTING FOR OPTIONS

Orson Agriculture sells approximately 500,000 bushels of oats each month. On January 1, 2002, Orson purchased an option to sell 500,000 bushels of oats on January 1, 2004, at a price of $1.75 per bushel. The market price on January 1, 2002, is $1.75 per bushel. Orson had to pay $100,000 to purchase this oats put option. Orson designated the option as a hedge against price decreases for its January 2004 sales of oats.

On December 31, 2002, the price of oats is $2.00 per bushel. Because there is still time for the price of oats to potentially decrease below $1.75 per bushel before the option expires (thus making it advantageous to exercise the put option), the option has a value on December 31, 2002, of $30,000. (Note: This December 31, 2002, option value already takes into account an appropriate adjustment for the time value of money.) On December 31, 2003, the price of oats is $1.80 per bushel.

Instructions: Make all journal entries necessary on Orson's books in 2002, 2003, and 2004 to record this option and the sale of 500,000 bushels of oats in January 2004.

PROBLEM 18–29

DERIVATIVES: NOTIONAL AMOUNTS

Refer to Problems 18–26 and 18–27.

Instructions:

1. What is the notional value of the fish forward contract described in Problem 18–26? What is the fair value of the forward contract during its life?
2. What is the notional value of the Korean won futures contract described in Problem 18–27? What is the fair value of the futures contract during its life?

PROBLEM 18–30

CONTINGENCIES: CONTINGENT LIABILITIES

The Western Supply Co. has several contingent liabilities at December 31, 2002. The following brief description of each liability is obtained by the auditor.

(a) In May 2001, Western Supply became involved in litigation. In December 2002, a judgment for $800,000 was assessed against Western by the court. Western is appealing the amount of the judgment. Attorneys for Western feel it is probable that they can reduce the assessment on appeal by 50%. No entries have been made by Western pending completion of the appeal process, which is expected to take at least a year.

(b) In July 2002, Morgan County brought action against Western for polluting the Jordan River with its waste products. It is reasonably possible that Morgan County will be successful, but the amount of damages Western might have to pay should not exceed $200,000. No entry has been made by Western to reflect the possible loss.

(c) Western Supply has signed as guarantor for a $50,000 loan by Guaranty Bank to Midwest Parts Inc., a principal supplier to Western. At this time, there is a only a remote likelihood that Western Supply will have to make payments on behalf of Midwest Parts.

Instructions:

1. What amount should be reported as a liability on the December 31, 2002, balance sheet for each of the above items?
2. What note disclosure should be included as part of the balance sheet for each of the above items?
3. Prepare the journal entries necessary to adjust Western's books to reflect your answers in (1) and (2).

PROBLEM 18–31

CONTINGENCIES: ENTRIES AND DISCLOSURE

In the chapter, the legal history of the case between PENNZOIL and TEXACO was briefly outlined. Texaco was ordered to pay $10.5 billion to Pennzoil in 1985. Subsequent appeals in 1986 and 1987 affirmed the judgment against Texaco. The 2 companies agreed in late 1987 to a settlement of $3 billion, and in 1988 Texaco paid Pennzoil.

Instructions:

1. In 1984, when the lawsuit was initially filed, how should Texaco have disclosed the event? If a journal entry is required, prepare it.
2. In 1986, following the initial jury award and Texaco's failure to have the judgment reversed on appeal, how should Texaco have disclosed the event? If a journal entry is required, prepare it.
3. In 1987, following the $3 billion agreement between Texaco and Pennzoil, how should Texaco have disclosed the event? If a journal entry is required, prepare it.
4. Prepare the journal entry to record Texaco's settlement in 1988.
5. How should Pennzoil have disclosed this event during the years 1984 through 1987?

PROBLEM 18–32

CONTINGENCIES: ACCOUNTING FOR ENVIRONMENTAL LIABILITIES AND OTHER EVENTS

Asbestos Inc. manufactures heat shields for use in oil refineries. Management has prepared financial statements for the year ended 2002 for review by the auditors. The audit team has questioned several items contained in the financial statements and has asked for your advice concerning the proper treatment of these items. Each of the items being questioned is listed below.

(a) In November 2002, attorneys for current and former employees of Asbestos Inc. filed a class action lawsuit alleging that exposure to asbestos has caused significant medical problems. Attorneys for Asbestos Inc. are uncertain as to the outcome of the case. However, similar lawsuits against other firms in the asbestos industry have resulted in significant payments by the employer.

(b) On January 12, 2003, a fire at a production facility resulted in a number of adjacent buildings (owned by other businesses) being burned. Asbestos' insurance policy does not cover damage to the property of others. Insurance companies for those other businesses have billed Asbestos for the estimated cost of $2.4 million required to restore the damaged buildings.

(c) One of Asbestos' production plants is located on the shores of Lake Obewankanobe. The lake has been rising for a number of years, and the company has installed dikes to prevent flooding. The dikes are currently operating at or near capacity. Weather forecasters have predicted that the lake will rise another 8 inches this coming summer. If this occurs, significant damage will likely result from the dikes being stressed beyond capacity.

(d) A national magazine printed an article regarding the dangers of asbestos and specifically named Asbestos Inc. as a "killer of innocent victims." Attorneys for Asbestos filed suit for libel and were awarded $1.3 million in damages on December 16, 2002. The magazine has indicated it would appeal the verdict.

Instructions: Determine how each of the above events should be disclosed in the financial statements of Asbestos Inc. for the year ended December 31, 2002. Provide support for your position.

PROBLEM 18–33

SEGMENT REPORTING: **REPORTING SEGMENT DATA**

Abcom Industries operates in several different industries. Total sales for Abcom are $12,000,000, and total common costs are $6,000,000 for 2002. For internal reporting purposes, Abcom allocates common costs based on the ratio of a segment's sales to total sales. Additional information regarding the different segments is as follows:

	Segment 1	Segment 2	Segment 3	Segment 4	Other Segments
Contribution to total sales	23%	31%	28%	10%	8%
Costs specific to the segment	$800,000	$1,200,000	$1,000,000	$650,000	$350,000

Instructions:

1. Compute the operating profit that would be reported internally for each of the 4 segments.
2. Comment on whether it is appropriate for Abcom to report segment information in the external financial statements using the same common cost allocation method that is used for internal reports.

PROBLEM 18–34

SEGMENT REPORTING: **PRODUCT LINE AND COUNTRY DISCLOSURE**

Backenstos Company has 2 different product lines and makes significant sales in both the United States and Mexico. Backenstos has compiled the following information.

Instructions:

1. Assume that Backenstos has structured its company internally into divisions based on the two products, X and Y. Prepare the segment disclosure necessary under the provisions of FASB Statement No. 131.
2. Assume that Backenstos has structured its company internally into 2 divisions— one for operations in the U.S. and one for operations in Mexico. Prepare the segment disclosure necessary under the provisions of FASB Statement No. 131.

	Revenue	Operating Profit	Depr.	Plant & Equip.	Total Assets	Total Liab.	Capital Expend.
Product X/U.S.	$100	$20	$15	$ 50	$120	$ 70	$ 20
Product X/Mexico	150	40	20	60	140	60	40
Product Y/U.S.	400	50	80	250	600	400	100
Product Y/Mexico	200	20	50	150	400	200	30

PROBLEM 18–35

INTERIM REPORTING: **FORECASTING FOURTH-QUARTER SALES**

The Box-Jenkins Company sells toys, so its sales are heavily concentrated in the last quarter of the year because of holiday buying. Box-Jenkins reported total sales for the past 3 years as follows (all numbers are in thousands):

	Quarter Ending				
	Mar. 31	Jun. 30	Sep. 30	Dec. 31	Total
2000	$5,000	$5,000	$5,000	$10,000	$25,000
2001	6,000	6,000	6,000	12,000	30,000
2002	7,000	7,000	7,000	14,000	35,000

In order to make advance arrangements with suppliers, you have been asked to forecast Box-Jenkins' fourth-quarter sales for the year 2003.

Instructions:

1. Ignore the quarterly sales data given by Box-Jenkins. Forecast fourth-quarter 2003 sales using just the annual sales data. Describe your assumptions.
2. Repeat (1), but this time use the quarterly sales data.
3. Repeat (2), but also incorporate the fact that first-quarter sales in 2003 were $9,000.
4. Comment on the usefulness of quarterly data.

COMPETENCY ENHANCEMENT OPPORTUNITIES

▶ Deciphering Actual Financial Statements	▶ Ethical Dilemma
▶ Writing Assignment	▶ Cumulative Spreadsheet Analysis
▶ Research Project	▶ Internet Search
▶ The Debate	

Accounting is more than just doing textbook problems. This expanded competency material provides practice in critical thinking, oral and written communication, research, teamwork, and consideration of ethical issues.

▶ **DECIPHERING ACTUAL FINANCIAL STATEMENTS**

• Deciphering 18–1 (The Walt Disney Company)
The 1998 financial statements for THE WALT DISNEY COMPANY are included in Appendix A. Locate those financial statements and consider the following questions.

1. In Note 12 on financial instruments, Disney explains how the company manages interest rate risk and foreign exchange risk. What types of instruments does Disney use to manage foreign exchange risk? What currencies is Disney trying to hedge against? Does Disney speculate with its foreign currency transactions?
2. What interesting details about pending lawsuits does Disney include in the notes to the financial statements?
3. Disney has 3 primary business segments: Creative Content, Broadcasting, and Theme Parks and Resorts. Which of these 3 yields the highest return on assets (operating income/identifiable assets)? (Note: Use information from the financial statement notes.)
4. Find Disney's Quarterly Financial Summary. Do you detect any seasonal pattern in Disney's revenues? Explain.

• Deciphering 18–2 (DERIVATIVES: IBM)
In Note U to its 1998 financial statements, IBM includes disclosure about its derivatives as follows:

Derivative Financial Instruments

The following table summarizes the notional value, carrying value and fair value of the company's derivative financial instruments on and off the balance sheet. The notional value at year end provides an indication of the extent of the company's involvement in such instruments, but does not represent exposure to market risk.

(Dollars in millions)	Notional Amount	Carrying Value	Fair Value
At December 31, 1998:			
Interest rate and currency contracts	$31,484	$(485)	$(427)
Option contracts	9,021	67	45
Total	$40,505	$(418)	$(382)*
At December 31, 1997:			
Interest rate and currency contracts	$24,774	$ 29	$ 84
Option contracts	14,211	41	193
Total	$38,985	$ 70	$ 277*

Amounts in parentheses are liabilities.

*The estimated fair value of derivatives both on and off balance sheet at December 31, 1998 and 1997, consists of assets of $486 million and $581 million and liabilities of $868 million and $304 million, respectively.

Instructions:

1. In 1998, the fair value of IBM's interest rate and currency contracts is negative, indicating that these derivatives are liabilities. On the other hand, the option contracts are assets in both years. Are option contracts usually assets and interest rate and currency contracts usually liabilities?

2. IBM's note says that "the notional value at year end. . . does not represent exposure to market risk." Can you think of any disclosure that would give a good indication of the exposure to market risk?

• Deciphering 18–3 (CONTINGENCIES: DuPont)

In the late 1980s, DUPONT acknowledged that one of its products, a fungicide called Benlate, seemed to be at fault for damage to millions of acres of nurseries and fruit plantations. In 1992, after paying approximately $510 million in claims, the company concluded its product was not responsible for the damage and halted further damage payments. This set the stage for over 700 lawsuits. In the notes to its 1996 financial statements, DuPont disclosed the following about the Benlate lawsuits:

> During 1991, the company initiated a stop-sale and recall of Benlate® 50 DF fungicide. About 60 of the more than 700 cases filed against the company in connection with the recall remain, the rest having been disposed of by trial, dismissal or settlement.

Instructions:

1. In regard to the amount of the recognized liability for the Benlate lawsuits, DuPont discloses that the liability "is not reduced by the amounts of any expected insurance recoveries." Why isn't the amount of the liability reduced by the amount of expected insurance recoveries?

2. In regard to the recognition of liabilities for environmental cleanup, DuPont discloses the following: "Accrued liabilities are exclusive of claims against third parties and are not discounted." Does this policy increase or decrease the recognized amounts of the recorded liabilities? Explain.

3. Assume that DuPont spends $10 million cash on an environmental project. What is the appropriate journal entry, assuming that no liability for the environmental project had previously been recognized?

• **Deciphering 18–4 (SEGMENT REPORTING: PepsiCo)**

Refer to the 1998 segment information for PEPSICO given in Exhibit 18–4.

Instructions:

1. Compute operating profit margin (operating profit/sales) for 1998 for each of the following:
    a. Industry segments: Pepsi-Cola, Frito-Lay, and Tropicana.
    b. Regions: North America and International.
2. Given your calculations in (1), what is your analysis of the different segments of PepsiCo?

• **Deciphering 18–5 (INTERIM REPORTING: Toys "R" Us)**

TOYS "R" US is the biggest toy store chain in the United States, with significant operations outside the United States as well. Below are quarterly financial data from the 1999 annual report of Toys "R" Us.

	First Quarter	Second Quarter	Third Quarter	Fourth Quarter
Year Ended Jan. 30, 1999 (in Millions):				
Net Sales	$2,043	$2,020	$2,171	$4,936
Cost of Sales	1,417	1,390	1,831	3,553
Net Earnings	19	14	(475) (a)	310 (b)

(a) Third quarter results include restructuring and other charges of $678 ($495 net of tax benefits, or $1.86 per share).

(b) Fourth quarter results include provisions for legal settlements of $20 ($13 net of tax benefits, or $.05 per share).

	First Quarter	Second Quarter	Third Quarter	Fourth Quarter
Year Ended Jan. 31, 1998 (in Millions):				
Net Sales	$1,924	$1,989	$2,142	$4,983
Cost of Sales	1,326	1,355	1,455	3,574
Net Earnings	29	37	46	378

Instructions:

1. Does Toys "R" Us have any seasonal pattern in its sales?
2. Compute gross profit percentage [(Sales – Cost of sales)/Sales] for each quarter for fiscal years 1998 and 1999. Is the gross profit percentage in the fourth quarter substantially different from other quarters?
3. Assume that first-quarter sales for fiscal 2000 are $1,600 million. What is your prediction of fourth-quarter sales?

▶ **WRITING ASSIGNMENT**

• **The FASB Is an Eco-Villain!**

You are one of the seven members of the Financial Accounting Standards Board. The FASB was recently criticized in a cover story in a major newsmagazine. The topic was accounting for environmental liabilities. The main point of the article was that the accounting for potential environmental liabilities is governed by the obscure terms "probable, possible, and remote." In addition, the article claimed that firms could avoid recognizing a liability for future environmental cleanup costs by simply arguing that the costs cannot be "reasonably estimated."

Of course, the charges in the newsmagazine cover story were repeated in the network TV news programs. Various accounting academics appeared on the morning news shows to pontificate about the slowness of the FASB to address the vital area of environmental accounting. Environmental groups have started picketing outside FASB headquarters, shouting that the FASB is conspiring with Big Business to hide the corporate responsibility for cleaning up the environment.

You have been chosen to write the FASB's response to this criticism. Address your memo to the editor of the weekly newsmagazine and restrict it to 1 page or less.

(Note: This scenario is hypothetical—you are not a member of the FASB, the FASB's environmental accounting practices have not been the subject of a *Time* or *Newsweek* cover story, and environmental groups have not picketed the FASB. Yet.)

▶ RESEARCH PROJECT
• Survey of segment disclosures
Your group is to report (either orally or in writing) on your examination of the segment information given in a typical set of financial statement notes by a U.S. multinational firm.

Choose 5 large U.S. multinational companies for which you can get a copy of a recent annual report. Using those annual reports, answer the following questions.

1. On average, how many different business segments do the companies identify?
2. On average, how many countries or geographic regions are separately identified?
3. On average, what percentage of the companies' total sales are reported by U.S. operations? of total operating income?
4. For the 5 companies you examine, are U.S. operations more or less profitable than foreign operations? (Hint: Look at the difference between percentage of U.S. sales and percentage of U.S. operating profit.)

▶ THE DEBATE
• Keep derivatives off the balance sheet!
Historically, many, if not most, derivatives have not been recognized in the balance sheet because derivatives are often executory contracts involving only an exchange of promises. Because no exchange of resources takes place at the beginning of many derivative contracts, there is nothing to recognize. FASB Statement No. 133 requires that derivatives be brought into the balance sheet at their fair value as of the balance sheet date.

Divide your group into 2 teams.

• One team represents Recognize All Derivatives. Prepare a 2-minute oral argument explaining why it is important to include all derivatives in the balance sheet as either assets or liabilities and why it is misleading to fail to do so. Illustrate your argument with examples of the problems that can arise if derivatives remain off the balance sheet.

• The other team represents Recognize Transactions Only. Prepare a 2-minute presentation summarizing why derivatives should be disclosed but not recognized. Historical cost is the backbone of accounting, and most derivatives have a very small historical cost, sometimes zero. Critics of accounting are always advocating the inclusion of "fair values" in the financial statements, but the reliable historical cost model has worked well for years and will continue to work well.

▶ ETHICAL DILEMMA
• Once a hedge, always a hedge
You are the controller/treasurer for a small import-export company. You make all the finance and accounting decisions. Your company makes sales in Germany, Poland, and the Czech Republic. Historically, your German sales have been denominated in Deutsche marks. Early this year you decided to enter into some Deutsche mark futures contracts to protect against the effect of changes in the dollar/mark exchange rate on the cash flows from next year's sales in Germany. In accordance with proper accounting procedure, you formally designated the futures contracts as a cash flow hedge.

In December of this year, your customers in Germany notified you that they are nervous about the impact of European currency consolidation on the strength of the Deutsche mark, and they wish all future sales prices to be denominated in U.S. dollars. The good news is that this action removes the need to worry about the effect of exchange rate changes on German sales. The bad news is that you have already entered into the futures contracts and, at the end of the year, the futures have a fair value of $5 million (liability).

Your dilemma is this: The futures no longer serve as a hedge because future German sales will be denominated in U.S. dollars. However, if you account for the futures as speculative investments, you will be forced to recognize a loss in earnings this year of $5 million. This entire hedging operation was your idea, and you convinced the president of the company that you knew what you were doing and there was no chance of a major loss. If this loss is recognized, reported profits for the year will be wiped out, and the company will show a net loss for the first time in its history.

What should you do?

▶ CUMULATIVE SPREADSHEET ANALYSIS

This assignment is an exercise in simple derivative valuation. Skywalker is considering using derivative contracts in 2003 to hedge interest rate risk. However, before entering into any derivative contract agreements, the management of Skywalker wishes to better understand how the values of derivative financial instruments fluctuate.

For 2003, Skywalker is considering converting $600 of its long-term debt into 3-month renewable debt; by so doing, Skywalker will be able to receive various preferential privileges from its lender. However, Skywalker doesn't want to bear the associated interest rate risk that would arise from the interest rate on the debt being reset at the prevailing market interest rate every 3 months as the loan is renewed. As a result, Skywalker has inquired about entering into an interest rate swap with another financial institution. The terms of the swap would be as follows:

Loan amount $600
Swap interest rate 8%

Skywalker would pay a fixed amount of $12 ($600 × .08 × ³⁄₁₂) to the financial institution each quarter; in exchange, Skywalker would receive a variable amount equal to $600 multiplied by the current market interest rate (for a 3-month period). This is called a pay-fixed, receive-variable swap. Skywalker could then use the variable amount received to pay the variable interest amount on its 3-month renewable loan.

In practice, the swap will be settled by Skywalker's paying an amount equal to [$600 × (.08 − market interest rate) × ³⁄₁₂] when interest rates are below 8% and receiving the same amount when interest rates are above 8%.

The financial staff at Skywalker have done some research on the historical behavior of interest rates and have prepared the following table:

Interest Rate Expected to Prevail in 3 Months	Probability
Current rate + .5%	2%
Current rate + .4%	3%
Current rate + .3%	5%
Current rate + .2%	10%
Current rate + .1%	15%
Current rate	30%
Current rate − .1%	15%
Current rate − .2%	10%
Current rate − .3%	5%
Current rate − .4%	3%
Current rate − .5%	2%

The data in this table mean that if, for example, the current market interest rate is 8.0%, the probability that the market interest rate will still be 8.0% in 3 months is 30%. In addition, there is a 5% probability that the market rate will increase to 8.3% in 3 months, and a 3% probability that the market rate will decrease to 7.6% in 3 months.

Using this data, construct a spreadsheet to answer the following questions.

1. What is the value of the pay-fixed, receive-variable swap contract to Skywalker if there are 3 months remaining in the contract term and the current market interest rate is 8.0%? Be sure to indicate whether the swap contract is an asset or a liability for Skywalker.
2. Repeat (1) using the following assumptions about the current market interest rate:
   a. 7.2%
   b. 8.1%
   c. 9.0%
3. Comment on the relative sizes of the fair values of the derivative contract and the notional value of the contract.

▶ ### INTERNET SEARCH

PROCTER & GAMBLE's Web address is www.pg.com. Once you've gained access to P&G's Web site, answer the following questions.

1. What were the first products sold in 1837 by William Procter and James Gamble?
2. P&G is in the business of selling brand-recognized consumer products. Accordingly, the P&G Web site has lots of product information. In fact, many of P&G's products have their own Web sites. Check out one of these (such as www.mrclean.com) and describe what kind of information is there.
3. Find P&G's Environmental Progress Report and detail what P&G's goals are with respect to environmental responsibility.
4. Recall from the opening scenario of the chapter that P&G had some problems using derivatives to manage interest rate risk. Find the notes to P&G's most recent set of financial statements and relate what P&G currently says about its risk management activities.
5. In the most recent year, what were the major currencies that P&G hedged? What was the relationship between the notional amount and the fair value of foreign currency forward contracts?

part 4

Other Dimensions of Financial Reporting

chapter 19
Earnings Per Share

In the April 21, 1997, issue of *Business Week,* the FASB came under fire for its "dogged resistance to international accounting standards and its demand that foreign companies seeking to raise capital in the U.S. play by its rules."[1] This criticism maintains that the FASB does not consider the effect its standards might have on the ability of non-U.S. firms to comply with the FASB's standards and thereby gain access to the New York Stock Exchange. (Firms listing on the NYSE must comply with U.S. GAAP.) In an effort to combat such criticism, the FASB and the International Accounting Standards Committee (IASC) issued separate, but virtually identical, standards on earnings per share.[2] The only difference between the two standards relates to some additional disclosure required by the FASB but only encouraged by the IASC. The computations used in computing the earnings per share (EPS) amounts for both standards are identical. While the FASB is currently working with a number of accounting standard setters in other countries to develop standards, the issuance of FASB No. 128 represents the first instance where virtually identical standards have been issued simultaneously by the FASB and the IASC.

> **FYI:** While the standard on earnings per share was the first instance of the FASB working jointly with other standard-setting bodies, it is not the last. For example, the FASB and the Canadian Institute of Chartered Accountants worked together on a standard relating to segment disclosure. The FASB issued that standard (Statement No. 131) in June 1997.

Why the attention on EPS? How is this number used by investors and creditors? In the United States, stocks normally trade at between 10 and 30 times their reported EPS. (As you recall, the market value of a firm's stock divided by the firm's earnings per share is called the P/E ratio.) *The Wall Street Journal* reports P/E ratios on a daily basis because analysts consider this ratio when evaluating stocks. Exhibit 19–1 (on page 1102) illustrates how the average price-earnings ratio for the 30 companies making up the Dow Jones Industrial Average has changed during the past 70 years. While the market determines the ultimate trading price of stocks, the EPS figure provided by accountants can significantly influence a firm's perceived value.

1 Phillip L. Zweig and Dean Foust, "Corporate America Is Fed Up with FASB," *Business Week,* April 21, 1997, pp. 108–109.
2 *Statement of Financial Accounting Standards No. 128,* "Earnings per Share," Stamford, CT: Financial Accounting Standards Board, 1997; and *International Accounting Standard IAS 33,* "Earnings per Share," London: International Accounting Standards Committee, 1997.

LEARNING OBJECTIVES

1

Detail recent changes in accounting standards relating to earnings per share, and know why the changes were made and how these changes will affect computations relating to earnings per share.

2

Know the difference between a simple and a complex capital structure, and understand how dilutive securities affect earnings per share computations.

3

Compute basic earnings per share, taking into account the sale and repurchase of stock during the period as well as the effects of stock splits and stock dividends.

4

Use the treasury stock method to compute diluted earnings per share when a firm has outstanding stock options, warrants, and rights.

5

Use the if-converted method to compute diluted earnings per share when a company has convertible preferred stock or convertible bonds outstanding.

6

Factor into the diluted earnings per share computations the effect of actual conversion of convertible securities or the exercise of options, warrants, or rights during the period, and understand the antidilutive effect of potential common shares when a firm reports a loss from continuing operations.

7

Determine the order in which multiple potential dilutive securities should be considered in computing diluted earnings per share.

8

Understand the disclosure requirements associated with basic and diluted earnings per share computations.

9

EXPANDED MATERIAL

Make complex earnings per share computations involving multiple potentially dilutive securities.

1101

EXHIBIT 19 – 1 | Average Price-Earnings Ratio for the 30 Companies Included in the Dow Jones Industrial Average: 1928–1998

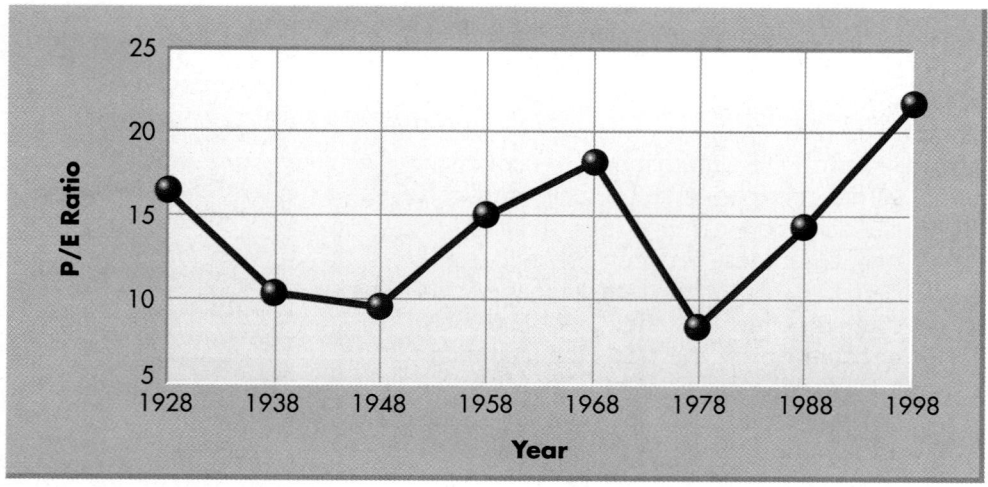

Source: *The Wall Street Journal*, March 30, 1999, p. C14.

A s indicated in Chapter 1, a primary objective of financial reporting is to provide information that is useful in making credit and investment decisions. Investors are interested in gauging how well a company is performing in comparison with other companies and with itself over time. When evaluating a company, it is not enough to know that net income is increasing or decreasing. Investors are concerned with how income is changing relative to their investment and to the current stock market valuation.

In an attempt to include both income and investment information in the same measurement, a computation known as EPS has been developed. While this measurement has some limitations, which will be discussed later in this chapter, its presentation on the income statement has been required by GAAP since 1969. Exhibit 19–2 provides examples of EPS figures for five companies. Note that a firm's net income does not necessarily correlate with its EPS. H. J. HEINZ, for example, reports the lowest net income of the group yet both DISNEY and WAL-MART report lower EPS. BERKSHIRE HATHAWAY doesn't have nearly the net income as that reported by MICROSOFT, yet Berkshire Hathaway's EPS is much higher. A firm's profitability takes on additional meaning when the number of shares outstanding (and the number of stock options outstanding in the case of diluted EPS) is taken into consideration.

Potential investors might use the EPS figure when choosing among different investment options. For example, if Company A earns $3 per share on common stock with a $21-per-share market price and Company B earns $6 per share on common stock with a $54-per-share market value, an investor can derive that Company A stock is selling at seven times earnings and Company B stock is selling at nine times earnings. Thus, investors as a

EXHIBIT 19-2 | Earnings per Share Figures for Selected Companies

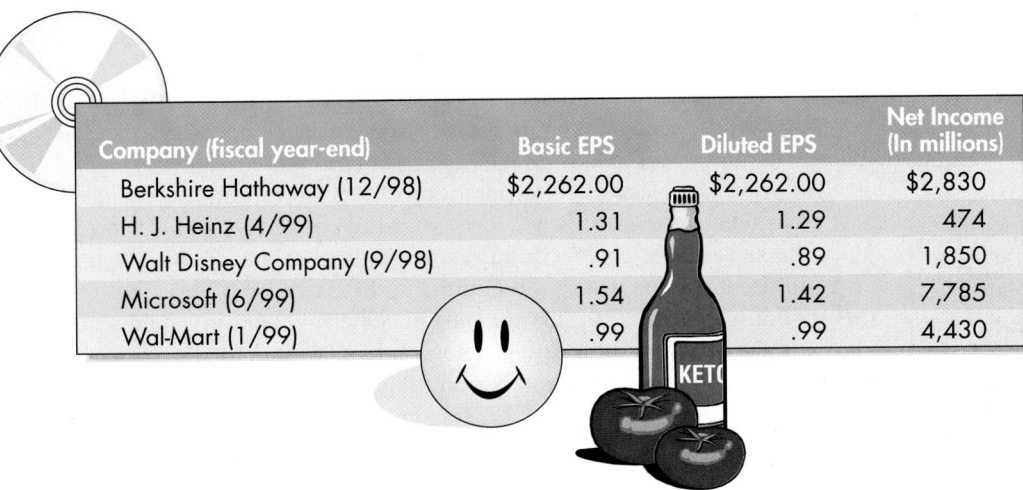

Company (fiscal year-end)	Basic EPS	Diluted EPS	Net Income (In millions)
Berkshire Hathaway (12/98)	$2,262.00	$2,262.00	$2,830
H. J. Heinz (4/99)	1.31	1.29	474
Walt Disney Company (9/98)	.91	.89	1,850
Microsoft (6/99)	1.54	1.42	7,785
Wal-Mart (1/99)	.99	.99	4,430

net work exercise

Fortune magazine lists its famous Fortune 500 on its Web site. *Fortune* also provides various lists of "Top Performers." One of the performance lists is based on 10-year growth in earnings per share. Go to *Fortune*'s Web site at **www.pathfinder.com/ fortune/fortune500/ perform9.html** to answer the following.
1. What company has experienced the most rapid EPS growth over the past 10 years?
2. Of the top 10 EPS growth performers over the past 10 years, how many are high-tech firms?

group may perceive Company B stock to have more growth potential than Company A. Alternatively, Company A stock may seem to be a better buy because of its lower market price relative to earnings.

Investors are also interested in dividends and can use EPS data to compute a *dividend payout ratio.* This ratio is computed by dividing earnings per share into dividends per share. Thus, if Company A in the previous example pays a dividend of $2 per share and Company B pays $3 per share, the dividend payout ratio would be 66⅔% for Company A and 50% for Company B.

Earnings per share data receive wide recognition in the annual reports issued by companies, in the press, and in financial reporting publications. As mentioned in the discussion of the P/E ratio, this measurement is frequently regarded as an important determinant of the market price of common stock.

EVOLUTION OF REQUIREMENTS FOR EARNINGS PER SHARE DISCLOSURE

1

Detail recent changes in accounting standards relating to earnings per share, and know why the changes were made and how these changes will affect computations relating to earnings per share.

Earnings per share figures were historically computed and used primarily by financial analysts. Sometimes the computation was disclosed in the unaudited section of the annual report along with a message from the company's president. However, because this measurement was not reviewed by an independent third party, figures used to develop EPS were often different from those attested to by the auditor. The situation became more complex when some companies and analysts began computing EPS not only on the basis of common shares actually outstanding but also on the basis of what shares would be outstanding if certain convertible securities were converted and if certain stock options were exercised. Usually the conversion or exercise terms were very favorable to the holders of these securities, and EPS would decline if common stock were issued upon conversion or exercise. This result, a reduced EPS, is referred to as a **dilution of earnings.** In some cases, however, the exercise of options or conversion of securities might result in an increased EPS. This result is referred to as an **antidilution of earnings.** Securities that would lead to dilution are referred to as **dilutive securities,** and those that would lead to antidilution are referred to as **antidilutive securities.** Rational investors would not convert or exercise antidilutive securities because they could do better by purchasing common stock in the marketplace.

These forward-looking computations of EPS attempted to provide information as to what future EPS might be, assuming conversions and exercises took place. Because these "as if" conditions were based on assumptions, they could be computed in several ways. Recognizing the diversity of reporting practices, the Accounting Principles Board (APB) became involved in establishing guidelines for the computation and disclosure of EPS figures. The result was the issuance in 1969 of APB Opinion No. 15, "Earnings per Share," which concluded:

> The Board believes that the significance attached by investors and others to earnings per share data, together with the importance of evaluating the data in conjunction with the financial statements, requires that such data be presented prominently in the financial statements. The Board has therefore concluded that earnings per share or net loss per share data should be shown on the face of the income statement. The extent of the data to be presented and the captions used will vary with the complexity of the company's capital structure. . . .[3]

In the process of establishing rules for computing earnings per share, the APB felt it necessary to be very specific about how future-oriented "as if" figures were to be computed. By 1971, 102 Accounting Interpretations of APB Opinion No. 15 had been issued with the intent of clarifying the computations for a variety of securities and under varied circumstances. In some areas, the rules became arbitrary and complex, and the resulting EPS computations have received much criticism as to their usefulness. Indeed, for companies with complex capital structures, the historical or basic EPS figure based on actual shares of common stock outstanding was not even reported. In its place, the APB substituted two earnings per share amounts: (1) **primary earnings per share,** based on the assumed conversion or exercise of certain securities identified as common stock equivalents, and (2) **diluted earnings per share,** based on the assumed conversions of all convertible securities or exercise of all stock options that would reduce or dilute primary EPS.

Although more than 30 years have passed since APB Opinion No. 15 was issued, little evidence to support the usefulness of these forward-type EPS figures has emerged. Indeed, many critical articles have been written suggesting this measurement be modified or eliminated from reporting.[4] Shortly after APB Opinion No. 15 was issued, the Canadian Institute of Chartered Accountants reviewed what the APB had done and concluded that only a historical or basic EPS and a diluted EPS had potential value. Many countries followed the Canadian lead, and thus internationally, two different approaches to measuring and reporting EPS emerged.

In an attempt to reduce the number of different reporting requirements of its constituent countries, the International Accounting Standards Committee (IASC) in 1993 appointed a steering committee to consider EPS. The committee concluded that the Canadian approach of a basic and diluted EPS was preferred to the American primary and diluted EPS.

3 *Opinions of the Accounting Principles Board, No. 15,* "Earnings per Share," New York: American Institute of Certified Public Accountants, 1969, par. 12.
4 For example, see R. David Mautz, Jr., and Thomas Jeffrey Hogan, "Earnings per Share Reporting: Time for an Overhaul?" *Accounting Horizons,* September 1989, pp. 21–27.

The earnings per share figure can significantly influence a firm's perceived value on the stock market.

In June 1993, the FASB issued a prospectus suggesting that a project be added to the FASB's agenda to consider the IASC position on EPS and to determine the wisdom of modifying APB Opinion No. 15. The prospectus suggested a wide range of options—from adopting the IASC position to reopening the entire subject of EPS with the objective of issuing a new standard to replace the old opinion. Finally, in February 1997 the FASB, working with the IASC, issued FASB Statement No. 128, "Earning per Share." This new standard eliminated primary EPS and replaced it with an historical-based basic EPS. A diluted EPS computation is also required for companies with a complex capital structure.

SIMPLE AND COMPLEX CAPITAL STRUCTURES

Know the difference between a simple and a complex capital structure, and understand how dilutive securities affect earnings per share computations.

The capital structure of a company may be classified as simple or complex. If a company has only common stock, or common and nonconvertible preferred stock outstanding and there are no convertible securities, stock options, warrants, or other rights outstanding, it is classified as a company with a **simple capital structure.** Earnings per share is computed by dividing income available to common shareholders by the weighted-average number of common shares outstanding for the period. No future-oriented "as if" conditions need to be considered. If net income includes extraordinary gains or losses or other below-the-line items, as discussed in Chapter 4, a separate EPS figure is required for each major component of income, as well as for net income. These historical EPS amounts are referred to as **basic earnings per share.**

Even if convertible securities, stock options, warrants, or other rights do exist, the capital structure may be classified as simple if there is no potential dilution to EPS from the conversion or exercise of these items. Potential EPS dilution exists if the EPS would decrease or the loss per share would increase as a result of the conversion of securities or exercise of stock options, warrants, or other rights based on the conditions existing at the financial statement date. A company with potential earnings per share dilution is considered to have a **complex capital structure.**

For those companies with a complex capital structure, the computation of both basic EPS and diluted EPS provides financial statement users with endpoints as to EPS. The basic EPS computation uses the results of actual transactions to determine both the numerator and the denominator in the EPS calculation. Diluted EPS is computed by making assumptions regarding transactions that did not occur. Now, why worry about transactions that did not occur? We can answer this question with an example. Suppose an individual is given stock options to purchase shares of stock in a company at $10 per share. The current market price for the company's stock is $15 per share. Why wouldn't the individual exercise the options and purchase the stock? The most likely reason is that the individual anticipates that the stock price will go even higher and waiting will result in an even better deal. Thus, even though the transaction (exercising the options) didn't occur, it could have occurred and it is likely that it will occur in the future. The FASB requires events like this to be included in the diluted EPS computation to disclose to financial statement users the effects of transactions that, although they did not occur, will likely occur in the future.

To summarize, the basic EPS computation uses the results of actual transactions and events to compute an EPS figure. Diluted EPS involves making assumptions about transactions relating to a company's stock that, based on information available now, will likely occur in the future. In other words, diluted EPS provides financial statement users with a "worst case" estimate as to EPS, assuming all events relating to the exercising of options or the conversion of securities that will likely occur in the future did in fact happen in the current period.

BASIC EARNINGS PER SHARE

3

Compute basic earnings per share, taking into account the sale and repurchase of stock during the period as well as the effects of stock splits and stock dividends.

The basic EPS computation presents no problem when only common stock has been issued and the number of shares outstanding has remained the same for the entire period. The numerator is the net income (loss) for the period, and the denominator is the number of shares outstanding for the entire period. Frequently, however, either the numerator, the denominator, or both must be adjusted because of the circumstances described in the following sections.

Issuance or Reacquisition of Common Stock

When common shares have been issued or have been reacquired by a company during a period, the resources available to the company have changed, and this change should affect earnings. To illustrate, suppose a company doubles the number of shares it has outstanding through the sale of additional stock. With the proceeds from the sale, one would expect the company to be able to invest in additional productive assets and thereby increase net income. Thus, income is not higher because the company suddenly became more profitable. Instead, income is higher because the company had more resources available for its use. This sale of stock must be factored into the EPS computation to provide a measure of per-share profitability given the resources available. Under these circumstances, a weighted average for shares outstanding should be computed.

The weighted-average number of shares may be computed by determining "month-shares" of outstanding stock and dividing by 12 to obtain the weighted average for the year. For example, if a company has 10,000 shares outstanding at the beginning of the year, issues 5,000 more shares on May 1, and reacquires 2,000 shares on November 1, the weighted-average number of shares would be computed as follows. Note that a separate period computation is required each time stock is sold or reacquired.

		Month-Shares
Jan. 1 to May 1	10,000 × 4 months...........................	40,000
May 1 to Nov. 1 (10,000 + 5,000)	15,000 × 6 months...........................	90,000
Nov. 1 to Dec. 31 (15,000 – 2,000)	13,000 × 2 months...........................	26,000
Total month-shares...........................		156,000
Weighted-average number of shares: 156,000/12		13,000

The same answer can be obtained by applying a weight to each period equivalent to the portion of the year since the last change in shares outstanding, as follows:

Jan. 1 to May 1	10,000 × 4/12 year...........................	3,333
May 1 to Nov. 1	15,000 × 6/12 year...........................	7,500
Nov. 1 to Dec. 31	13,000 × 2/12 year...........................	2,167
Weighted-average number of shares		13,000

If stock transactions occurred during a month, the weighted-average computation could be made either on a daily basis or to the nearest month. In examples and end-of-chapter material in this text, assume computations to the nearest month unless otherwise specified.

Stock Dividends and Stock Splits

When the number of common shares outstanding has changed during a period as a result of a stock dividend, a stock split, or a reverse split, a retroactive recognition of this change must be made in determining the weighted-average number of shares outstanding. To illustrate, assume that a company had 2,600 shares outstanding as of January 1 and the following events affecting common stock occurred during the year:

Date	Economic Event	Change in Shares Outstanding
Feb. 1	Exercise of stock option	+ 400
May 1	10% stock dividend (3,000 × 10%)...........................	+ 300
Sept. 1	Sale of stock for cash...........................	+ 1,200
Nov. 1	Purchase of treasury stock...........................	– 400
Dec. 15	3-for-1 stock split	+ 8,200

The computation of the weighted-average number of shares for the year would be as follows:

Dates	Shares Outstanding	Stock Dividend		Stock Split		Portion of Year		Average
Jan. 1 to Feb. 1 Feb. 1—option	2,600 400	× 1.10	×	3.0	×	1/12	=	715
Feb. 1 to May 1 May 1—stock dividend	3,000 300	× 1.10	×	3.0	×	3/12	=	2,475
May 1 to Sept. 1 Sept. 1—sale	3,300 1,200		×	3.0	×	4/12	=	3,300
Sept. 1 to Nov. 1 Nov. 1—treasury stock	4,500 (400)		×	3.0	×	2/12	=	2,250
Nov. 1 to Dec. 1 Dec. 1—split	4,100 8,200		×	3.0	×	1/12	=	1,025
Dec. 1 to Dec. 31	12,300				×	1/12	=	1,025
Weighted-average number of shares								10,790

Caution! As the example illustrates, stock splits and stock dividends must be incorporated to calculate weighted-average shares outstanding. This procedure must be applied for all periods included in the financial statements. Thus, the EPS figures computed in the current period may have to be changed in subsequent years if stock splits or stock dividends occur.

STOP & THINK Why must basic EPS associated with prior periods be adjusted for stock splits or stock dividends that occurred in the current period?

In the preceding illustration, the shares outstanding for January 1 to May 1 were multiplied by 1.10 to reflect the 10% stock dividend, and the shares outstanding for January 1 to December 1 were multiplied by 3 to reflect the 3-for-1 stock split. When comparative financial statements are presented, the common shares outstanding for all periods shown must be adjusted to reflect any stock dividend or stock split in the current period.

Only with the retroactive recognition of changes in the number of shares can EPS presentations for prior periods be stated on a basis comparable with the EPS presentation for the current period. Similar retroactive adjustments must be made even if a stock dividend or stock split occurs after the end of the period but before the financial statements are prepared; disclosure of this situation should be made in a note to the financial statements. As an example, consider the disclosure provided by MICROSOFT relating to its EPS: For the fiscal year ended June 30, 1998, the company reported EPS of $1.83. In its 1999 annual report, the company reported EPS for the fiscal year ended June 30, 1998, of just $0.92. In the notes accompanying its 1999 financial statements (shown in Exhibit 19–3), Microsoft explains the reason for the restatement of EPS for 1998—Microsoft split its shares 2-for-1 during fiscal 1999.

Preferred Stock Included in Capital Structure

Basic EPS reflects only income available to common stockholders and does not include preferred stock. It would be inappropriate to report EPS on preferred stock in view of the limited dividend rights of such stock. When a capital structure includes preferred stock, dividends on preferred stock should be deducted from income before extraordinary or other special items and from net income in arriving at the earnings related to common shares. If preferred dividends are not cumulative, only the dividends declared on preferred stock during the period are deducted. If preferred dividends are cumulative, the full amount of dividends on preferred stock for the period, whether declared or not, should be deducted from income in arriving at the earnings or loss balance related to the common stock. If there is a loss for the period, preferred dividends for the period, including any undeclared dividends on cumulative preferred stock, are added to the loss in arriving at the full loss related to the common stock.

To illustrate the computation of EPS at December 31, 2002, for a company with a simple capital structure for a comparative two-year period, assume the following data.

Summary of changes in capital balances:

	8% Cumulative Preferred Stock $100 Par		Common Stock No Par		Retained Earnings
	Shares	Amount	Shares	Amount	
Dec. 31, 2000, balances	10,000	$1,000,000	200,000	$1,000,000	$4,000,000
June 30, 2001, issuance of 100,000 shares of common stock			100,000	600,000	
June 30, 2001, dividend on preferred stock, 8%					(80,000)
June 30, 2001, dividend on common stock, $0.30					(90,000)
Dec. 31, 2001, net income for year, including extraordinary gain of $75,000					380,000
Dec. 31, 2001, balances	10,000	$1,000,000	300,000	$1,600,000	$4,210,000
May 1, 2002, 50% stock dividend on common stock			150,000	800,000	(800,000)
Dec. 31, 2002, net loss for year					(55,000)
Dec. 31, 2002, balances	10,000	$1,000,000	450,000	$2,400,000	$3,355,000

EXHIBIT 19-3 | Microsoft Note Disclosure Relating to Stock Splits

> STOCK SPLIT During March 1999, outstanding shares of common stock were split two-for-one. All share and per share amounts have been restated.

Because comparative statements are presented, the denominator of weighted-average shares outstanding for 2001 must be adjusted for the 50% stock dividend issued in 2002 as follows:

2001

Jan. 1–June 30	200,000 × 1.5 (50% stock dividend in 2002) × 6/12 year	150,000
July 1–Dec. 31	[200,000 + 100,000 (issuance of stock on June 30, 2001)]	
	× 1.5 (50% stock dividend in 2002) × 6/12 year	225,000
		375,000

2002

Jan. 1–May 1	300,000 × 1.5 (50% stock dividend in 2002) × 4/12 year	150,000
May 1–Dec. 31	450,000 (300,000 + 150,000) × 8/12 year	300,000
		450,000

Continuing the example, EPS for 2001 is shown separately for income from continuing operations, the extraordinary gain, and net income. The preferred dividends must be deducted from both income from continuing operations and net income in computing EPS for these income components. For 2002, the reported net loss must be increased by the full amount of the preferred dividend even though the dividend was not declared. If the preferred stock were noncumulative, no adjustment for the undeclared preferred dividend would be necessary in 2002. The adjusted income (loss) figures for computing basic EPS are determined as follows:

2001

Income from continuing operations	
($380,000 net income – $75,000 extraordinary gain)	$ 305,000
Less: Preferred dividend	80,000
Income from continuing operations identified with common stock	$ 225,000
Net income	$ 380,000
Less: Preferred dividend	80,000
Net income identified with common stock	$ 300,000

2002

Net loss	$ (55,000)
Less: Preferred dividend	(80,000)
Net loss identified with common stock	$(135,000)

The basic EPS amounts can now be computed as follows:

2001

Basic earnings per common share:	
Continuing operations ($225,000/375,000)	$ 0.60
Extraordinary gain ($75,000/375,000)	0.20
Net income per share ($300,000/375,000)	$ 0.80

2002

Basic loss per share [($135,000)/450,000]	$(0.30)

Use the treasury stock method to compute diluted earnings per share when a firm has outstanding stock options, warrants, and rights.

DILUTED EARNINGS PER SHARE— OPTIONS, WARRANTS, AND RIGHTS

When a company has a complex capital structure, additional information may be provided to users of the financial statements to reflect all potential dilution arising from the assumption that additional common stock is issued from exercise of options or conversion of convertible securities. FASB Statement No. 128 identifies this EPS figure as diluted, implying a maximum dilution that could occur. Dilution occurs if inclusion of a potentially dilutive security reduces the basic EPS or increases the basic loss per share. If the opposite results occur, the security is classified as an antidilutive security. If a company reports a below-the-line item (i.e., discontinued operations, an extraordinary item, or a cumulative effect of an accounting change), the "control number" used in determining whether a security is dilutive or not is "Income from continuing operations."[5] In general, securities classified as antidilutive are not included in computing diluted EPS.

The adjustment of the numerator and/or denominator of basic EPS to compute diluted EPS depends on the nature of the security and its terms. The adjustment process consists of a "what if" scenario. What would happen to the numerator and denominator if options had been exercised and convertible securities had been converted at the beginning of the year being evaluated. The two major types of potentially dilutive securities are (1) common stock options, warrants, and rights and (2) convertible bonds and convertible preferred stock. Because the purpose of a diluted EPS figure is to disclose how an exercise or conversion would affect future EPS, all computations of diluted EPS are made as if the exercise or conversion took place at the beginning of the company's fiscal year or at the issue date of the stock option or convertible security, whichever comes later. Thus, if a convertible bond has been outstanding the entire year, the diluted EPS computation will be made as if the conversion of the bonds took place at the beginning of the year. However, if the convertible bond is issued on May 1, and the fiscal year is the calendar year, all conversion computations will be made for eight months, or two-thirds of a year.

> **Caution!** You must continually remind yourself when dealing with diluted EPS that the events you are analyzing *did not* occur—bonds were not converted; options were not exercised; and so on. Diluted EPS is providing information *as if* these events occurred.

Stock Options, Warrants, and Rights

As explained in Chapter 11, stock options, warrants, and rights provide no cash yield to investors, but they have value because they permit the acquisition of common stock at specified prices for a certain period of time. As noted previously, options, warrants, and rights are included in the computation of diluted EPS for a particular period only if they are dilutive. If the price for which stock can be acquired (exercise price) is lower than the average market price during the period, the options, warrants, or rights probably would be exercised and their effect would be dilutive. If the exercise price is higher than the average market price, no exercise would take place; thus, there is no potential dilution from these securities. Why the average price instead of the market price at the end of the period? The Board addressed this issue by stating:

> The Board believes that the use of the average stock price is consistent with the objective of diluted EPS to measure earnings per share for the period based on period information and that the use of end-of-period data or estimates of the future is inconsistent with that objective. If purchases of treasury shares actually were to occur, the shares would be purchased at various prices, not at the price at the end of the period. In addition, use of an average stock price eliminates the concern that end-of-period fluctuations in stock price could have an undue effect on diluted EPS if an end-of-period stock price were required to be used.[6]

5 *Statement of Financial Accounting Standards No. 128*, par. 15.
6 Ibid., par. 107.

It is assumed that exercise of options, warrants, or rights takes place as of the beginning of the year or at the date they are issued, whichever comes later. Additional cash resources would thus have been available for the company's use. In order to compute diluted EPS when these types of securities exist, either net income must be increased to take into consideration the increase in revenue such additional resources would produce or the cash must be assumed to be used for some nonrevenue-producing purpose. The FASB selected the latter approach and recommended it be assumed that the cash proceeds from the exercise of options, warrants, or rights be used to purchase common stock on the market (treasury stock) at the average market price. It is further assumed that the shares of treasury stock are issued to those exercising their options, warrants, or rights, and the remaining shares required to be issued will be added as incremental shares to the actual number of shares outstanding to compute diluted EPS. This method of including warrants, options, and rights in the EPS computation is known as the **treasury stock method.**

To illustrate, assume that at the beginning of the current year, employees were granted options to acquire 5,000 shares of common stock at $40 per share. The average market price of the stock during the year is $50, so exercise is assumed and the effect will be dilutive. The proceeds received by the corporation from the issuance of stock to the employees would be $200,000 (5,000 shares × $40 exercise price). Because the average market price of the stock was $50, these proceeds would purchase 4,000 shares of treasury stock ($200,000/$50). If it is assumed that these 4,000 shares are issued to the employees, an additional 1,000 shares would have to be issued, and the number of shares of stock for computing diluted EPS would be increased by 1,000 shares.

Illustration of Diluted Earnings per Share With Stock Options

The use of the treasury stock method in computing diluted EPS is illustrated with the following data for the Rasband Corporation.

Summary of relevant information:	
Net income for the year	$ 92,800
Common shares outstanding (no change during year)	100,000
Options outstanding to purchase equivalent shares	20,000
Exercise price per share on options	$6
Average market price during the period for common shares	$10
Basic earnings per share:	
Net income for the year	$ 92,800
Actual number of shares outstanding	÷100,000
Basic EPS ($92,800/100,000)	$ 0.93
Application of proceeds from assumed exercise of options outstanding to purchase treasury stock:	
Proceeds from assumed exercise of options outstanding (20,000 × $6)	$120,000
Number of outstanding shares assumed to be repurchased with proceeds from options ($120,000/$10)	12,000
Number of shares to be used in computing diluted earnings per share:	
Actual number of shares outstanding	100,000
Incremental shares:	
Issued on assumed exercise of options	20,000
Less: Assumed repurchase of shares from proceeds of options	12,000	8,000
Total	108,000
Diluted EPS ($92,800/108,000)	$ 0.86

If the stock options had been issued to the company's employees on April 1 of the current year, the incremental shares would be three-fourths of 8,000, or 6,000 shares, and the diluted EPS would be $0.88 ($92,800/106,000).

If the market price of the company's stock is less than the option exercise price, the treasury stock computation would cause the EPS to increase when compared to basic EPS because the incremental shares would be negative rather than positive. To illustrate, assume the average market price for Rasband Corporation is $5 rather than $10. In this case, 24,000 shares could be purchased with the $120,000 proceeds from the stock options. Because only 20,000 shares would be issued on exercise of the options, the number of shares for computing diluted EPS would be 96,000 and the diluted EPS would be $0.97. When compared with basic EPS of $0.93, the result is antidilution.

Thus, the test for antidilution of stock options, warrants, and rights is simply to compare the average market price with the exercise price. If the market price exceeds the exercise price, the options are dilutive and would be included "as if" exercised in computing diluted EPS. If the average market price is less than the exercise price, the options are antidilutive and would not be used in computing diluted EPS.

5

Use the if-converted method to compute diluted earnings per share when a company has convertible preferred stock or convertible bonds outstanding.

DILUTED EARNINGS PER SHARE—CONVERTIBLE SECURITIES

In order to compute diluted EPS when convertible securities exist, adjustments must be made both to net income and to the number of shares of common stock outstanding. These adjustments must reflect what these amounts would have been if the conversion had taken place at the beginning of the current year or at the date of issuance of the convertible securities, whichever comes later. This method of including convertible securities in the EPS computation is referred to as the **if-converted method.** If the securities are bonds, net income is adjusted by adding back the interest expense, net of tax, to net income; the number of shares of common stock outstanding is increased by the number of shares that would have been issued on conversion.[7] Any amortization of initial premium or discount is included in the interest expense added back. If the convertible securities are shares of preferred stock, no reduction is made from net income for preferred dividends, as is done with the computation of basic EPS; the number of shares of common stock outstanding is increased by the number of shares that would have been issued upon conversion. Because preferred stock dividends are not deductible as an expense for tax purposes, no adjustment for tax effects is required. If the convertible securities were issued during the year, adjustments would be made for only the portion of the year since the issuance date.

In order to test for dilution, each potentially dilutive convertible security must be evaluated individually. If there is only one such security, comparison is made between EPS before considering the convertible security with the EPS after including it. As indicated earlier, if the EPS decreases or loss per share increases, the convertible security is defined as dilutive. Antidilutive securities are excluded from the computation of diluted EPS. We will now look at an example of the two most common types of dilutive securities—convertible bonds and convertible preferred stock.

Illustration of Diluted Earnings per Share With Convertible Securities

The following examples for the Reid Corporation illustrate the computation of diluted EPS when convertible securities exist.

Summary of relevant information:

8% convertible bonds issued at par	$500,000
Net income for the year	$83,000
Common shares outstanding (no change during year)	100,000
Conversion terms of convertible bonds—80 shares for each $1,000 bond	
Assumed tax rate	30%

Basic earnings per share:

Net income	$ 83,000
Actual number of shares outstanding	÷100,000
Basic EPS ($83,000/100,000)	$ 0.83

---

7 In addition to adjustments for interest, adjustments to net income for nondiscretionary or indirect items would have to be made in many situations. These items would include profit-sharing bonuses and other payments whose amount is determined by the net income reported. For simplicity, no indirect effects are illustrated in this chapter.

Diluted earnings per share:

Net income		$ 83,000
Add interest on convertible bonds, net of income tax:		
Interest ($500,000 × 8%)	$40,000	
Less: Income tax savings ($40,000 × 30%)	12,000	28,000
Adjusted net income		$111,000
Actual number of shares outstanding		100,000
Additional shares issued on assumed conversion of bonds (500 × 80)		40,000
Adjusted number of shares		140,000
Diluted EPS ($111,000/140,000)		$ 0.79

Computation of Diluted Earnings per Share for Securities Issued During Year

If the convertible bonds had been issued by Reid Corporation on June 30 of the current year, the adjustment would be made to reflect only the period subsequent to the issuance date, or one-half of a year.

Diluted earnings per share:

Net income		$83,000
Add interest on convertible bonds, net of income tax:		
Interest ($500,000 × 8% × ½ year)	$20,000	
Less: Income tax ($20,000 × 30%)	6,000	14,000
Adjusted net income		$97,000
Actual number of shares outstanding		100,000
Additional shares issued on assumed conversion of bonds (500 × 80 × ½)		20,000
Adjusted number of shares		120,000
Diluted EPS ($97,000/120,000)		$ 0.81

> **Caution!** Remember that with convertible preferred stock, preferred dividends were initially subtracted from income to arrive at income available to common shareholders. If we assume conversion, those dividends must be added back. Also remember that there is no tax effect associated with dividends.

Convertible preferred stock is treated in a similar manner to convertible debt securities (bonds). To illustrate application of the if-converted method to preferred stock, assume the same facts as given previously for Reid Corporation except that instead of 8% convertible bonds, the company has 8% preferred stock outstanding, par value $500,000, convertible into 40,000 shares of common stock. Note that because Reid would have no bond interest under the change in assumptions, the reported net income would be $111,000 ($83,000 + $28,000 bond interest net of tax savings). Assume the preferred stock was outstanding for the entire year.

Basic earnings per share:

Net income, without the deduction for interest on bonds	$111,000
Less: Preferred dividends	40,000
Net income identified with common stock	$ 71,000
Actual number of shares outstanding	÷100,000
Basic EPS ($71,000/100,000)	$ 0.71

Diluted earnings per share:

Net income assuming no payment of preferred dividends due to conversion	$111,000
Actual number of shares outstanding	100,000
Additional shares issued on assumed conversion of preferred stock	40,000
Adjusted number of shares	140,000
Diluted EPS ($111,000/140,000)	$ 0.79

In this example, diluted EPS ($0.79) is greater than basic EPS ($0.71). Thus, the convertible preferred stock is antidilutive and would not be considered in the computation of EPS. Assuming the corporation had no other potentially dilutive securities outstanding, only basic EPS would be presented on the income statement.

Shortcut Test for Antidilution

It is possible to determine if a convertible security is antidilutive without actually computing diluted EPS assuming conversion. If a company has net income rather than loss, the antidilutive test is performed by computing what the conversion contributes to per-share earnings. For example, if the 8% bonds are converted, net income to the common shareholders increases by $28,000 and the number of common shares outstanding increases by 40,000 shares. The contribution of this conversion to earnings is $0.70 ($28,000/40,000) per share. Because this amount is less than the preconversion basic EPS of $0.83, the bonds are dilutive. On the other hand, if the preferred stock is converted, the preferred dividends of $40,000 would no longer be deducted from net income in computing EPS and the number of common shares outstanding will increase by 40,000 shares. The contribution of this conversion to earnings is $1.00 ($40,000/40,000) per share. Because the preferred stock conversion contributes more per share than preconversion basic earnings of $0.71, the preferred stock is antidilutive.

Factor into the diluted earnings per share computations the effect of actual conversion of convertible securities or the exercise of options, warrants, or rights during the period, and understand the antidilutive effect of potential common shares when a firm reports a loss from continuing operations.

EFFECT OF ACTUAL EXERCISE OR CONVERSION

Recall that if additional shares are issued as a result of securities being converted, those newly issued shares would be included in the computation of the weighted-average number of shares outstanding for the period. In addition, however, an adjustment must be made to reflect what the EPS would have been if conversion or exercise had taken place at the beginning of the period or issuance date, whichever comes later. This adjustment is required for all securities *actually converted or exercised* during the period for computing diluted EPS whether dilutive or not.

When options or warrants are exercised, the adjustment for the period before exercise for diluted EPS uses the market price at exercise date. To illustrate the computation of diluted EPS when stock options are exercised during the year, assume the following data for Weatherby, Inc.

has terms indicating the purchaser is placing a premium on the conversion feature was also recognized as a common stock equivalent. Specifically, a convertible security was considered a common stock equivalent if, at the time of issuance, it had an effective yield of less than 66⅔% of the then-current average Aa-rated corporate bond yield.

Those convertible securities that did not meet the definition of dilutive common stock equivalents, while used to compute diluted EPS, were not used to compute primary EPS. Under APB Opinion No. 15, if a company with a complex capital structure computed a primary EPS number that was materially lower than the basic

EPS, the primary EPS was reported rather than the basic EPS. A diluted EPS figure was also required to be reported. Thus, APB Opinion No. 15 required a dual presentation of EPS, both assuming some conversion or exercise of potentially dilutive securities. Under APB Opinion No. 15, basic EPS was disclosed only for simple capital structures and for complex capital structures where the potentially dilutive securities are antidilutive.

QUESTIONS
1. What was primary EPS attempting to measure?
2. What was a common stock equivalent?
3. In your opinion, should the FASB have continued requiring primary EPS instead of basic EPS? Why?

Summary of relevant information:

Net income for the year	$2,300,000
Common shares outstanding at beginning of year	400,000
Options outstanding at beginning of year to purchase equivalent shares	100,000
Exercise price per share on options	$9.00
Proceeds from actual exercise of options on October 1 of current year	$900,000
Market price of common stock at exercise date, October 1	$15.00

Number of shares to be used in computing basic earnings per share:

Actual number of shares outstanding for full year	400,000
Weighted-average shares issued on October 1 (100,000 × ¼ year)	25,000
Weighted-average number of shares for basic EPS	425,000
Basic EPS ($2,300,000/425,000)	$5.41

Number of shares to be used in computing diluted earnings per share:

Weighted-average number of shares for basic EPS		425,000
Incremental shares if options had been exercised on January 1 (included whether dilutive or not):		
Issued on assumed exercise of options	100,000	
Less: Assumed repurchase of shares with proceeds ($900,000/$15)	60,000	
Incremental shares assumed to be issued	40,000	
Weighted average of incremental shares assumed to be issued (40,000 × ¾ year)		30,000
Weighted-average number of shares for diluted EPS		455,000
Diluted EPS ($2,300,000/455,000)		$5.05

STOP & THINK In the case of securities actually converted during the year, why must we assume conversion occurred at the beginning of the period when we know it did not?

Effect of a Loss From Continuing Operations on Earnings per Share

If a company reports a loss from continuing operations—referred to as the control number—no dual computation of EPS is necessary, because inclusion of stock options or convertible securities would decrease the loss per share and thus always would be antidilutive. This is the case even if, as a result of below-the-line items like discontinued operations, the firm reports net income. To illustrate this situation, assume the following data for the Boggs Co.

Summary of relevant information:

Loss from continuing operations	$(50,000)
Extraordinary gain	75,000
Net income	$ 25,000
Number of shares of stock outstanding—full year	100,000
Number of shares of convertible preferred stock	10,000
Conversion terms—2 shares of common for 1 share of preferred	
Dividends on preferred stock	$8,000

The computation of basic and diluted EPS would be as follows:

Basic loss per share:

Loss from continuing operations	$(50,000)
Dividends on preferred stock	(8,000)
Total loss to common shareholders	$(58,000)
Actual number of shares outstanding	100,000
Basic loss per share—from continuing operations [($58,000)/100,000]	$(0.58)
Basic EPS—extraordinary gain ($75,000/100,000)	0.75
Basic EPS—net income available to common shareholders ($17,000/100,000)	$0.17

Diluted loss per share:

Loss from continuing operations	$(50,000)
Actual number of shares outstanding	100,000
Incremental shares on assumed conversion of preferred stock	20,000
Adjusted number of shares	120,000
Diluted loss per share [($50,000)/120,000]	$(0.42)

Because the diluted loss per share from continuing operations is less than the basic loss per share from continuing operations, only information relating to basic EPS computations would be reported on the income statement. This is the case even though net income is positive. The comparison for determining dilution is made using the control number, income (or loss) from continuing operations, not net income.

Determine the order in which multiple potential dilutive securities should be considered in computing diluted earnings per share.

MULTIPLE POTENTIALLY DILUTIVE SECURITIES

The illustrations in the chapter thus far have dealt primarily with one type of potentially dilutive security at a time. For a company having several different issues of convertible securities and/or stock options and warrants, the FASB requires selection of the combination of securities producing the lowest possible EPS figure. To avoid having to test a large number of different combinations to find the lowest one, companies can compute the incremental EPS for each potentially dilutive security. Because the smaller the incremental computation, the greater the impact on basic EPS, the securities are then ranked in order from the smallest incremental EPS to the largest.[8] Then each security—beginning with the one having the smallest incremental EPS—is introduced into the computation until the EPS is lower than the next security's incremental computation. At that point, all remaining securities in the list would be antidilutive. Any dilutive stock options and warrants are considered first before introducing convertible securities into the computations.

To illustrate, assume a company had no stock options but did have four convertible securities that would have the following effects on diluted EPS if each were considered separately.

8 *Statement of Financial Accounting Standards No. 128*, par. 14.

	Effects of Assumed Conversion		
	Increase in Net Income	**Increase in No. of Shares**	**Incremental EPS**
Convertible Security A	$ 75,000	50,000	$1.50
Convertible Security B	150,000	60,000	2.50
Convertible Security C	110,000	20,000	5.50
Convertible Security D	600,000	100,000	6.00

Assume further that basic EPS was $6.50 ($2,275,000 income divided by 350,000 outstanding shares). Each of the four securities considered separately results in an incremental EPS figure lower than basic EPS and thus would be potentially dilutive. However, when considering all four securities together, only the first two (A and B) would be dilutive and therefore included in diluted EPS. This is determined by adding one security at a time to the basic EPS figure as follows:

	Net Income (Adjusted)	**No. of Shares (Adjusted)**	**Diluted EPS**
Simple capital structure	$2,275,000	350,000	$6.50
Convertible Security A	75,000	50,000	
	$2,350,000	400,000	5.88
Convertible Security B	150,000	60,000	
	$2,500,000	460,000	5.43
Convertible Security C	110,000	20,000	
	$2,610,000	480,000	5.44
Convertible Security D	600,000	100,000	
	$3,210,000	580,000	5.53

It would not be necessary to continue the computation beyond Security B, because the EPS at that point ($5.43) is lower than the incremental EPS impact of Security C ($5.50). Inclusion of Securities C and D would be antidilutive as the computations show.

When a company has multiple potentially dilutive convertible securities, an orderly approach to computing EPS is necessary. Exhibit 19-4 should prove helpful in understanding the above illustration and in solving complex EPS problems. The exhibit summarizes the steps in computing basic and diluted EPS.

EXHIBIT 19-4 | Steps in Computing Earnings per Share

1. Compute basic EPS using a weighted-average number of shares for common stock outstanding during the year.
2. For companies with complex capital structures, determine whether stock options, warrants, rights, and convertible securities are potentially dilutive.
   (a) Stock options, warrants, and rights: Dilutive if the exercise price is less than the average market price of the common stock.
   (b) Convertible securities: Compute incremental EPS for each security individually. Those with an incremental value greater than basic EPS after considering any stock options, warrants, or rights are antidilutive and are excluded.
3. Compute diluted EPS:
   (a) Include all dilutive stock options, warrants, and rights first. Apply proceeds using the treasury stock method at the average common stock market price during the period to compute incremental shares.
   (b) Include potentially dilutive convertible securities one at a time, beginning with the security that has the smallest incremental EPS. Compute a new EPS figure. Continue selecting and applying convertible securities until the next security in the list has an incremental EPS value greater than the last computed EPS. Discontinue the process at that point. All other securities in the list are antidilutive for purposes of computing the lowest possible diluted EPS figure.
4. Report basic and diluted EPS on the face of the income statement.

To illustrate the steps in Exhibit 19-4 for computing basic and diluted EPS, assume the following facts related to Wildwood, Inc.

Summary of relevant information:

Net income for the year	$136,000
Common shares outstanding (no change during the year)	125,000
Options outstanding to purchase equivalent shares	30,000
Exercise price per share on options	$10
Average market price for the period for common shares	$15
9% convertible bonds, issued at par	$600,000
Conversion terms for bonds, 100 shares for each $1,000 bond	
Tax rate	30%

Step 1—Compute basic earnings per share:

Net income for the year	$136,000
Actual number of shares outstanding	÷125,000
Basic EPS ($136,000/$125,000)	$ 1.09

Step 2—Determine whether stock options and convertible bonds are dilutive:
(a) Stock options: The options are dilutive because the exercise price is less than the average market price.
(b) Convertible bonds: The bonds are potentially dilutive because the EPS impact of $0.63, as computed below, is less than basic EPS of $1.09.

Net Income Impact	Number of Shares	EPS Impact
$600,000 × .09 × .70 = $37,800	60,000	$0.63

Step 3—Compute diluted earnings per share:

Description		Net Income	Number of Shares	EPS
Basic EPS		$136,000	125,000	$1.09
Options as if exercised at beginning of year:				
Number of shares assumed issued	30,000			
Less: Number of treasury shares assumed repurchased [(30,000 × $10)/$15]	(20,000)			
Incremental shares	10,000		10,000	
		$136,000	135,000	$1.01
9% Convertible bonds		37,800	60,000	
Diluted EPS		$173,800	195,000	$0.89

 Now that you are an expert in computing diluted EPS, elaborate on what information the measure is trying to convey, and explain whether the benefits exceed the costs.

FINANCIAL STATEMENT PRESENTATION

8

Understand the disclosure requirements associated with basic and diluted earnings per share computations.

Companies with a simple capital structure are required to present basic EPS on the face of the income statement. For those companies with a complex capital structure, both basic and diluted EPS for both income from continuing operations and net income are to be disclosed on the face of the income statement. When earnings of a period include income or loss from discontinued operations, extraordinary items, or a cumulative effect of a change in accounting principle, EPS amounts for these line items may be presented either on the face of the income statement or in the notes to the financial statements.

Firms are also required to provide the following disclosure items in the notes to the financial statements[9]:

1. A reconciliation of both the numerators and the denominators of the basic and diluted EPS computations for income from continuing operations. The example from Step 3 above illustrates the type of reconciliation required.
2. The effect that preferred dividends have on the EPS computations.
3. Securities that could potentially dilute basic EPS in the future that were not included in computing diluted EPS this period because those securities were antidilutive for the current period.
4. Disclosure of transactions that occurred after the period ended but prior to the issuance of financial statements that would have materially affected the number of common shares outstanding or potentially outstanding such as the issuance of stock options.

Earnings per share data should be presented for all periods covered by the income statement. If potential dilution exists in any of the periods presented, the dual presentation of basic and diluted EPS should be made for all periods presented.[10] If basic EPS and diluted EPS are the same amount, one amount can be presented on the income statement. Whenever net income of prior periods has been restated as a result of a prior-period adjustment, the EPS for these prior periods should be restated and the effect of the restatements disclosed in the current year.[11] Exhibit 19-5 illustrates the disclosure required when presenting earnings per share, using information from H.J. HEINZ's 1999 Annual Report.

EXHIBIT 19-5 | H. J. Heinz Note Disclosure Relating to Earnings per Share

---

13. NET INCOME PER COMMON SHARE

The following table sets forth the computation of basic and diluted earnings per share in accordance with the provisions of SFAS No. 128.

(Dollars in thousands, except per share data)	1999	1998	1997
Net income per share—basic:			
Net income	$474,341	$801,566	$301,871
Preferred dividends	30	37	43
Net income applicable to common stock	$474,311	$801,529	$301,828
Average common shares outstanding—basic	÷361,204	÷365,982	÷367,471
Net income per share—basic	$ 1.31	$ 2.19	$ 0.82
Net income per share—diluted:			
Net income	$474,341	$801,566	$301,871
Average common shares outstanding	361,204	365,982	367,471
Effect of dilutive securities:			
Convertible preferred stock	243	297	340
Stock options	6,383	6,674	6,233
Average common shares outstanding—diluted	367,830	372,953	374,044
Net income per share—diluted	$ 1.29	$ 2.15	$ 0.81

Stock options outstanding of 6.0 million, 2.0 million and 2.6 million as of April 28, 1999, April 29, 1998 and April 30, 1997, respectively, were not included in the above net income per diluted share calculations because to do so would have been antidilutive for the periods presented.

---

9   Ibid., par. 40
10 Ibid., par. 38.
11 Ibid., par. 18.

Note that Heinz adds back preferred dividends in computing basic EPS, includes the incremental number of shares associated with dilutive stock options, and does not include some options in the calculations because their effect would have been anitdilutive.

It is important that great care be exercised in interpreting EPS data regardless of the degree of refinement applied in the development of the data. These EPS figures are the products of the principles and practices employed in the accounting process and are subject to the same limitations found in the net income measurement reported on the income statement.

EXPANDED MATERIAL

In this expanded material we take the opportunity to combine most of the complexities associated with EPS computations into one example. In this example, we will review basic and diluted EPS computations and consider stock options, convertible preferred stock, and convertible debt. As you will see, care must be exercised in determining whether or not a security is dilutive.

9

Make complex earnings per share computations involving multiple potentially dilutive securities.

COMPREHENSIVE ILLUSTRATION USING MULTIPLE POTENTIALLY DILUTIVE SECURITIES

The steps outlined in Exhibit 19-4 (page 1117) for computing EPS for multiple securities will be used in the comprehensive problem that follows. The Circle West Transportation Company has the following outstanding stocks and bonds at January 1, 2002. All securities had been sold at par or face value.

Date of Issue	Type of Security	Par or Face Value	No. of Shares or Total Face Value	Conversion Terms
1990–2001	Common stock	$ 0.25	200,000	None
May 1, 1996	12% debentures	1,000	$750,000	None
Jan. 1, 2000	6% cumulative preferred stock	100	40,000	4 shares of common for each preferred share
Jan. 1, 2001	6% debentures	1,000	$1,000,000	15 shares of common for each $1,000 debenture
June 30, 2001	10% debentures	1,000	$600,000	30 shares of common for each $1,000 debenture
Dec. 31, 2001	8% cumulative preferred stock	50	12,500	None

Circle West also had stock options outstanding at January 1, 2002, for the purchase of 20,000 shares of common. During 2002, options were granted for an additional 40,000 shares. The terms of these stock options are as follows:

Date of Issue	Exercisable Date	Exercise Price	Number of Options
Jan. 1, 1999	Oct. 1, 2002	$30	20,000
Oct. 1, 2002	June 30, 2004	60	40,000

Common stock market prices for 2002 were as follows:

Average for year	$61
Average for first 9 months of year	55
Oct. 1 price	62
Dec. 31 price	65

During 2002, Circle West issued the following common stock:

Apr. 1   30,000 shares sold at $56.
Oct. 1   20,000 shares issued from exercise of Jan. 1, 1999, options.

On December 1, 2002, Circle West paid a full year's dividend on the 6% preferred stock and on the 8% preferred stock. Assume that the company had net income of $1,026,000 in 2002, all from income from continuing operations. The income tax rate is 30%.

The steps for computing EPS will be applied to the data for Circle West Transportation Company to compute the various EPS amounts.

Step 1—Compute basic earnings per share:

Net income			$1,026,000
Less: Preferred dividends:			
6% stock (40,000 × $100 × .06)		$240,000	
8% stock (12,500 × $50 × .08)		50,000	290,000
Net income identified with common stock			$ 736,000
Weighted-average number of shares:			
Jan. 1 to Apr. 1	200,000 × ¼	50,000	
Apr. 1 to Oct. 1 (200,000 + 30,000)	230,000 × ½	115,000	
Oct. 1 to Dec. 31 (230,000 + 20,000)	250,000 × ¼	62,500	
Total weighted-average number of shares		227,500	
Basic earnings per share ($736,000/227,500)			$ 3.24

Step 2—Determine whether options and convertible securities are dilutive:
(a)   Stock options: Both stock options are dilutive, because the exercise prices ($30 and $60) are less than the applicable ending market prices ($62 on October 1 for the exercised options and $61 average market price for the year for the unexercised options).
(b)   Convertible securities:

	Net Income Impact	Number of Shares	Incremental EPS
6% preferred stock	$240,000	160,000	$1.50
10% debentures	42,000*	18,000	2.33
6% debentures	42,000**	15,000	2.80

*$600,000 × .10 × .70
**$1,000,000 × .06 × .70

All three convertible securities are potentially dilutive, because their impact on EPS is less than the $3.24 basic EPS.

Step 3—Compute diluted earnings per share:

Description	Net Income	Number of Shares	Part of Year	Weighted Average	EPS
Basic earnings per share	$ 736,000			227,500	$3.24
Jan. 1, 1999, options—exercised Oct. 1, as if exercised Jan. 1, 2002:					
Number of shares assumed issued		20,000			
Less: Number of treasury shares assumed repurchased [(20,000 × $30)/$62]		(9,677)			
Incremental shares		10,323	¾	7,742	
June 30, 2002, options:					
Number of shares assumed issued		40,000			
Number of treasury shares assumed repurchased [(40,000 × $60)/$61]		(39,344)			
Incremental shares		656	½	328	
	$ 736,000			235,570	$3.12
6% preferred stock	240,000	160,000	1	160,000	
	$ 976,000			395,570	$2.47
10% debentures	42,000			18,000	
Diluted EPS	$1,018,000			413,570	$2.46

6% debentures: Because incremental EPS value of $2.80 exceeds latest EPS of $2.46, the debentures are antidilutive and not included in diluted EPS.

Under FASB No. 128, Circle West would report basic EPS of $3.24 and diluted EPS of $2.46. In addition, Circle West would provide note information similar to that developed in Step 3.

REVIEW OF LEARNING OBJECTIVES

1 **Detail recent changes in accounting standards relating to earnings per share, and know why the changes were made and how these changes will affect computations relating to earnings per share.** In 1997, the FASB issued Statement No. 128, which provides new requirements associated with EPS computations and disclosure. The IASC issued a similar EPS standard. The result of FASB No. 128 is to require two EPS computations—basic and diluted. Dilution relates to those convertible securities and stock options that, if exercised, would result in a decrease in EPS.

2 **Know the difference between a simple and a complex capital structure, and understand how dilutive securities affect earnings per share computations.** A simple capital structure exists when a company has only common stock, or common and nonconvertible bonds outstanding, and there are no convertible securities, stock options, warrants, or other rights outstanding. A company with convertible securities or stock options that would, if exercised, result in a dilution in EPS is considered to have a complex capital structure.

3 **Compute basic earnings per share, taking into account the sale and repurchase of stock during the period as well as the effects of stock splits and stock dividends.** Basic EPS is computed by dividing income available to common shareholders by the weighted-average number of common shares outstanding. If a company splits its stock or declares a stock dividend, a retroactive recognition of this change must be made in determining the weighted-average number of shares outstanding. When comparative financial statements are presented, the common shares outstanding for all periods shown must be adjusted to reflect any stock dividend or stock split in the current period.

4 **Use the treasury stock method to compute diluted earnings per share when a firm has outstanding stock options, warrants, and rights.** If a firm has stock options, warrants, or rights outstanding, a determination must be made as to their potential effects on EPS. If the exercise price is less than the average market price for the period, the option, warrant, or right is considered dilutive and would be included in computing diluted EPS. The treasury stock method involves determining the number of incremental shares that would be issued assuming the options, warrants, or rights were exercised and the proceeds used to buy treasury shares on the market.

5 **Use the if-converted method to compute diluted earnings per share when a company has convertible preferred stock or convertible bonds outstanding.** A company with convertible securities may be required to adjust both the numerator and the denominator in computing diluted EPS if those convertible securities are determined to be potentially dilutive. In the case of convertible bonds, interest expense (net of tax) must be added back to the numerator, and the number of shares that would be issued upon conversion would be included in the denominator. For convertible preferred stock, preferred dividends must be added back to income available to common shareholders, and the denominator would be increased by the number of shares that would be issued upon conversion.

6 **Factor into the diluted earnings per share computations the effect of actual conversion of convertible securities or the exercise of options, warrants, or rights during the period, and understand the antidilutive effect of potential common shares when a firm reports a loss from continuing operations.** If conversion actually takes place during a period, an adjustment must be made to reflect what the EPS would have been if conversion or exercise had taken place at the beginning of the period or issuance date, whichever comes later. In the case of a firm reporting a loss from continuing operations, no dual presentation of EPS is required because inclusion of stock options or convertible securities would decrease the loss per share and thus always would be antidilutive.

7 **Determine the order in which multiple potential dilutive securities should be considered in computing diluted earnings per share.** In those instances where a firm has multiple potentially dilutive securities, the FASB requires a systematic procedure for determining the order in which the various securities are considered. The individual effect of each security is computed, and the securities are considered in turn beginning with the security with the least favorable effect on basic EPS. The procedure is repeated until the diluted EPS figure is lower than the next security's incremental impact.

8 **Understand the disclosure requirements associated with basic and diluted earnings per share computations.** Basic and diluted EPS are required to be disclosed on the face of the income statement for those companies with a complex capital structure. Firms reporting below-the-line items on their income statement may report the per-share effects of these items either on the face of the income statement or in the notes. In addition, a schedule reconciling both the

numerator and the denominator for the basic and diluted per-share computations must be provided in the notes to the financial statements.

9 **Make complex earnings per share computations involving multiple potentially dilutive securities.** For firms with stock options, warrants, rights, convertible preferred stock, and/or convertible bonds, the computations associated with diluted EPS can become quite complex. For those items that are dilutive or potentially dilutive, considering them in the proper sequence will ensure that diluted EPS is properly calculated.

KEY TERMS

Antidilution of earnings 1104
Antidilutive securities 1104
Basic earnings per share 1105
Complex capital structure 1106

Diluted earnings per share 1104
Dilution of earnings 1104
Dilutive securities 1104
Dividend payout ratio 1103

If-converted method 1112
Primary earnings per share 1104
Simple capital structure 1105
Treasury stock method 1111

QUESTIONS

1. Earnings per share computations have received increased prominence on the income statement. How would an investor use such information in making investment decisions?

2. What limitations should be recognized in using EPS data?

3. Why are EPS figures computed on the basis of common stock transactions that have not yet happened rather than on the basis of strictly historical common stock data?

4. What distinguishes a simple capital structure from a complex capital structure?

5. An enterprise split its common stock 3 for 1 on July 1. Its accounting year ends December 31. Prior to the split, there were 10,000 shares of common stock outstanding. What is the weighted-average number of shares that should be used to compute EPS in the current and preceding years?

6. Why are EPS figures adjusted retroactively for stock dividends, stock splits, and reverse stock splits?

7. What is meant by "dilution of EPS"?

8. What is an antidilutive security? Why are such securities generally excluded from the computation of EPS?

9. What is the treasury stock method of accounting for outstanding stock options, warrants, and rights in computing diluted EPS?

10. Convertible debt that is dilutive requires an adjustment to income. What is the nature of the adjustment?

11. What is the meaning of the if-converted method of computing EPS?

12. If stock options are actually exercised during the year, how is diluted EPS affected?

13. Why are all convertible securities and options antidilutive when a company is operating at a loss?

14. If a company has multiple potentially dilutive securities, how are the computations made to ensure obtaining the lowest EPS figure?

DISCUSSION CASES

CASE 19–1

BUT WHY IS EPS DIFFERENT IF INCOME IS THE SAME?

Fredrica Brown has $200,000 that she plans to invest in growth common stock. She has narrowed her choices to 2 companies in the same industry, White Inc. and Adam Inc. Each company has a documented history of growth and an established, strong position within the industry. Last year, each company reported net income of $10 million and a return on owners' investment of 17%; however, White reported EPS of $10, while Adam reported EPS of $20.

Fredrica requests that you explain why the EPS differs when other measures of activity and profitability are similar. What factors contribute to and limit the comparability of these data?

CASE 19–2

BUT LET'S MAINTAIN EARNINGS PER SHARE.

On January 1, 2000, Farnsworth Company had 1,000,000 shares of common stock and 100,000 shares of $8 cumulative preferred stock issued and outstanding. A principal goal of Farnsworth's management is to maintain or increase EPS.

On January 1, 2001, Farnsworth Company retired 50,000 shares of the preferred stock with excess cash and additional funds provided from the sale of a subsidiary.

At the beginning of 2002, the company borrowed $5,000,000 at 10% and used the proceeds to retire 200,000 shares of common stock. Operating income, before interest and income taxes (income tax rate is 30%), is as follows:

	2002	2001	2000
Operating income	$6,500,000	$7,000,000	$7,500,000

Did Farnsworth Company maintain its EPS even though income declined? What was the impact of the preferred and common stock transactions on EPS?

CASE 19–3

ARE WE IN TROUBLE OR NOT?

Tolman Yacht Company has just completed its determination of EPS for the year. As a result of issuing convertible securities during the year, the capital structure of Tolman is now defined as being complex. The basic EPS for this year is $2.90, but the diluted EPS is only $2.50; both figures are down from the prior year's $3.25 basic EPS figure.

Sung Wong and Martha Chou, 2 stockholders, have received their financial statements from Tolman and are discussing the EPS figures over lunch. The following dialogue ensues.

Wong: "I guess Tolman must be having trouble. I see its earnings per share is down significantly."

Chou: "Maybe so, but this year there are two figures, where before there was only one."

Wong: "Something to do with the convertible bonds and preferred stock issued during the year making it a complex capital structure. But both of the earnings per share figures are lower than the single figure the year before."

Chou: "That's true. But income for the current year is higher than last year. I'm confused."

Enlighten the stockholders.

CASE 19–4

HOW DOES A COMPLEX CAPITAL STRUCTURE AFFECT EPS?

Big Horn Construction Company has gradually grown in size since its inception in 1919. The third generation of Jensens who now manage the enterprise are considering selling a large block of stock to raise capital for new equipment purchases and to help finance several big projects. The Jensens are concerned about how the EPS information should be presented on the income statement and have many questions concerning the nature of EPS.

1. Discuss the EPS presentation that would be required if Big Horn Construction has (a) a simple capital structure or (b) a complex capital structure. What factors determine whether a capital structure is simple or complex?
2. Assume Big Horn Construction Company has a complex capital structure. Discuss the effect, if any, of each of the following transactions on the computation of EPS.
    a. The firm acquires some of its outstanding common stock to hold as treasury stock.
    b. The firm pays a dividend of $0.50 per common stock share.
    c. The firm declares a dividend of $0.75 per share on cumulative preferred stock.
    d. A 3-for-1 common stock split occurs during the year.
    e. Retained earnings are appropriated for a disputed construction contract that may be litigated.

CASE 19–5

WHAT IS DILUTION?

You have just finished presenting a summary of this year's financial results to the board of directors. Included in your presentation was an income statement including both basic and diluted EPS figures. One of the board members comments that he understands basic EPS but has no clue as to what diluted EPS is referring to. He actually wondered aloud if this diluted EPS computation was part of some "full-employment for accountants" project. He asks you to explain the concept of dilution and what diluted EPS is trying to measure.

CASE 19–6

ONCE DILUTIVE, ALWAYS DILUTIVE!

As you know, a firm with multiple potentially dilutive securities must individually determine the effect of each security's incremental per-share contribution and include those securities with the smallest incremental contribution to the point where diluted EPS is less than the next security's incremental contribution. At that point, the remaining potentially dilutive securities become antidilutive because including them would cause diluted EPS to increase.

Another option would be to (1) determine if a security is potentially dilutive and then (2) include the effects of all potentially dilutive securities. While including those convertible securities that would have a large positive effect on EPS may cause diluted EPS to increase, at least one would not have to worry about a potentially dilutive security suddenly becoming antidilutive.

Is there merit to this alternative? What reasons can you think of as to why the FASB does not allow this approach?

EXERCISES

EXERCISE 19–7

WEIGHTED-AVERAGE NUMBER OF SHARES

Compute the weighted-average number of shares outstanding for Troy Company, which has a simple capital structure, assuming the following transactions in common stock occurred during the calendar year.

Date	Transactions in Common Stock	Number of Shares $10 Par Value
Jan. 1	Shares outstanding	44,000
Feb. 1	Issued for cash	56,000
May 1	Acquisition of treasury stock	(25,000)
Aug. 1	25% stock dividend	25% of shares outstanding
Sept. 1	Resold part of treasury stock shares	10,000
Nov. 1	Issued 3-for-1 stock split	

EXERCISE 19–8

WEIGHTED-AVERAGE NUMBER OF SHARES

Transactions involving the common stock account of the Higrade Gas Company during the 2-year period 2002 to 2003 were as follows:

2002

Jan.	1	Balance 200,000 shares of $10 par common stock.
Apr.	1	$2,500,000 of convertible bonds were converted with 50 shares issued for each $1,000 bond.
July	1	A 10% stock dividend was declared.
Oct.	1	Option to purchase 7,000 shares for $20 a share was exercised.

2003

Apr.	1	A 2-for-1 stock split was declared.
Oct.	1	170,000 shares were sold for $30 a share.

From the information given, compute the comparative number of weighted-average shares outstanding for 2002 and 2003 to be used for basic EPS computations at the end of 2003.

EXERCISE 19–9

WEIGHTED-AVERAGE NUMBER OF SHARES

Assume the following transactions affected owners' equity for Cervantes Inc. during 2002.

Feb.	1	30,000 shares of common stock were sold in the market.
Apr.	1	Purchased 5,000 shares of common stock to be held as treasury stock. Paid cash dividends of $0.50 per share.
May	1	Split common stock 3 for 1.
July	1	35,000 shares of common stock were sold.
Oct.	1	A 5% stock dividend was issued.
Dec.	31	Paid a cash dividend of $0.75 per share. The total amount paid for dividends on December 31 was $511,875.

Compute the weighted-average number of shares to be used in computing basic EPS for 2002. Because no beginning share figures are available, you must work backward from December 31, 2002, to compute shares outstanding.

EXERCISE 19–10

BASIC EARNINGS PER SHARE—SIMPLE CAPITAL STRUCTURE

At December 31, 2002, the Munter Corporation had 50,000 shares of common stock issued and outstanding, 30,000 of which had been issued and outstanding throughout the year and 20,000 of which had been issued on October 1, 2002. Operating income before income taxes for the year ended December 31, 2002, was $753,200. In 2002 and 2003, a dividend of $80,000 was paid on 80,000 shares of 10% cumulative preferred stock, $10 par.

On April 1, 2003, there were 30,000 additional shares issued. Total income before income taxes for 2003 was $527,000, which included an extraordinary gain before income taxes of $37,000. Assuming a 30% tax rate, what is Munter's basic earnings per common share for 2002 and for 2003, rounded to the nearest cent? Show computations in good form.

EXERCISE 19–11

BASIC EARNINGS PER SHARE—SIMPLE CAPITAL STRUCTURE

The income statement for the Fignon Co. for the year ended December 31, 2002, reported the following.

Income from continuing operations before income taxes	$35,000
Income taxes	14,000
Income from continuing operations	$21,000
Loss from disposal of segment (net of income taxes)	(4,200)
Net income	$16,800

Compute basic EPS amounts for 2002 under each of the following assumptions (consider each assumption separately):

(a) The company has only one class of common stock with 20,000 shares outstanding.

(b) The company has shares outstanding as follows: preferred 8% stock, $15 par, cumulative, 5,000 shares; common, $12 par, 20,000 shares. Only the current year's preferred dividends are unpaid.

(c) Same as (b) except Fignon Co. also has preferred 7% stock, $10 par, noncumulative, 2,000 shares, and only $3,000 in dividends on the noncumulative preferred has been declared.

EXERCISE 19–12

DILUTIVE SECURITIES

The Claney Corporation has basic earnings per common share of $2.09 for the year ended December 31, 2002. For each of the following examples, decide whether the convertible security would be dilutive or antidilutive in computing diluted EPS. Consider each example individually. The tax rate is 30%.

(a) 8½% debentures, $1,000,000 face value are convertible into common stock at the rate of 25 shares for each $1,000 bond.

(b) $5 preferred stock (no par) is convertible into common stock at the rate of 2 shares of common stock for 1 share of preferred stock. There are 50,000 shares of preferred stock outstanding.

(c) Options to purchase 200,000 shares of common stock are outstanding. The exercise price is $25 per share. Average market price is $30 per share.

(d) $400,000 of 10% debentures are convertible at the rate of 25 shares of common stock for each $1,000 bond.

(e) Preferred 6% stock, $100 par, 5,000 shares outstanding is convertible into 3 shares of common stock for each share of preferred stock.

EXERCISE 19–13

NUMBER OF SHARES—STOCK OPTIONS

On January 1, 2002, Wander Corporation had 68,000 shares of common stock outstanding that did not change during 2002. In 2001, Wander Corporation granted options to certain executives to purchase 9,000 shares of its common stock at $7 each. The average market price of common was $10.50 per share during 2002. Compute the number of shares to be used in computing diluted EPS for 2002.

EXERCISE 19–14

NUMBER OF SHARES—STOCK OPTIONS

Barone Company has employee stock options outstanding to purchase 40,000 common shares at $14 per share. All options were outstanding during the entire year. The average price of the company's common stock during the year was $20. Compute the incremental shares that would be used in arriving at diluted EPS. Barone has 80,000 shares outstanding at the date the option is granted.

EXERCISE 19–15

DILUTED EARNINGS PER SHARE—CONVERTIBLE BONDS

On January 2, 2002, Saftner Co. issued at par $30,000 of 10% bonds convertible in total into 2,000 shares of Saftner's common stock. No bonds were converted during 2002. Throughout 2002, Saftner had 5,000 shares of common stock outstanding. Saftner's 2002 net income was $55,000. Saftner's tax rate is 30%.

No other potentially dilutive securities other than the convertible bonds were outstanding during 2002. For 2002, compute Saftner's basic and diluted EPS.

EXERCISE 19–16

DILUTED EARNINGS PER SHARE—CONVERTIBLE BONDS

The Delgado Manufacturing Company reports long-term liabilities and stockholders' equity balances at December 31, 2002, as follows:

Convertible 5% bonds (par)	$ 800,000
Common stock, $25 par, 100,000 shares issued and outstanding	2,500,000

Additional information is determined as follows:

Conversion term of bonds—50 shares for each $1,000 bond

Operating income—2002	$199,800
Extraordinary gain (net of tax)	43,520
Net income—2002	$243,320

Compute the basic and diluted EPS for the company for 2002, assuming that the income tax rate is 30%. No changes occurred in the debt and equity balances during 2002.

EXERCISE 19–17

EARNINGS AND LOSS PER SHARE—CONVERTIBLE PREFERRED STOCK, OPERATING LOSS
During all of 2002, Malone Inc. had outstanding 100,000 shares of common stock and 5,000 shares of $7 preferred stock. Each share of the preferred stock is convertible into 4 shares of common stock. For 2002, Malone had a $230,000 loss from operations; no dividends were paid or declared.

Compute the basic and diluted earnings (loss) per share for Malone assuming (1) the preferred stock is noncumulative, and (2) the preferred stock is cumulative.

EXERCISE 19–18

EARNINGS PER SHARE WITH ACTUAL CONVERSION
Atlas, Inc., has the following capital structure at January 1, 2002.

	Outstanding
Common stock, $10 par	800,000 shares
11% stated interest rate convertible bonds issued at par; each $1,000 bond is convertible into 80 shares of common stock	$5,000,000

During 2002, Atlas had the following stock transactions:

May 1   Issued 50,000 shares of common stock for $30 per share.
Aug. 1   Purchased 100,000 shares of treasury stock at $35 per share.
Oct. 1   Converted $2,000,000 of bonds.

Net income for 2002 was $950,000. The income tax rate was 30%. Compute basic and diluted EPS for Atlas for 2002.

EXERCISE 19–19

EARNINGS PER SHARE—FASB NO. 128
At December 31, 2002, the books of Yorke Corporation include the following balances:

Long-term liabilities:	
Bonds payable, 8%, each $1,000 bond is convertible into 50 shares of common stock; bonds sold at par and were issued November 3, 2001	$ 500,000
Stockholders' equity:	
Preferred stock, 7%, $50 par, cumulative, nonconvertible, 10,000 shares outstanding	500,000
Paid-in capital in excess of par, preferred stock	300,000
Common stock, $10 par, authorized 300,000 shares; 199,500 shares outstanding	1,995,000
Paid-in capital in excess of par, common stock	450,000
Retained earnings	519,000

The records of Yorke reveal the following additional information.

(a) 150,000 shares of common stock were outstanding January 1, 2002.
(b) 40,000 shares of common stock were sold for cash on April 30, 2002.
(c) Issued 5% stock dividend on July 1, 2002.
(d) Operating income before extraordinary items (after tax) was $715,000.
(e) Extraordinary loss (net of tax), $16,000.

(f) Income tax rate, 30%.
(g) Bond indenture does not provide for increase in shares at conversion due to stock dividends declared subsequent to the bond issue date.
    1. Is this a simple or complex capital structure?
    2. Compute EPS amounts as required by FASB No. 128. How should EPS data be presented under this statement?

EXERCISE 19–20

EARNINGS PER SHARE—CONVERTIBLE SECURITIES

Information relating to the capital structure of the Roninger Corporation at December 31, 2001 and 2002, is as follows:

	Outstanding
Common stock	120,000 shares
Convertible preferred stock noncumulative (issued in 2000)	18,000 shares
7.5% convertible bonds (issued in 2001)	$1,200,000
Stock options to purchase 20,000 shares at $15. Market price of Roninger stock was $22 at December 31, 2002, and averaged $20 during the year	

Roninger Corporation paid dividends of $5 per share on its preferred stock. The preferred stock is convertible into 40,000 shares of common stock. The 7.5% convertible bonds are convertible into a total of 35,000 shares of common stock. The net income for the year ended December 31, 2002, is $640,000. Assume that the income tax rate is 30%. Compute basic and diluted EPS for the year ended December 31, 2002.

PROBLEMS

PROBLEM 19–21

WEIGHTED-AVERAGE NUMBER OF SHARES

Inman's Wholesale Products Inc. had 75,000 shares of common stock outstanding at the end of 2001. During 2002 and 2003, the following transactions took place.

2002

Mar.	31	Sold 5,000 shares at $27.
Apr.	26	Paid cash dividend of $0.50 per share.
July	31	Paid cash dividend of $0.25 per share, and issued a 10% stock dividend.
Nov.	1	Sold 7,000 shares at $30.

2003

Feb.	28	Purchased 5,000 shares of common stock to be held in treasury.
Mar.	1	Paid cash dividend of $0.50 per share.
Apr.	30	Issued 3-for-1 stock split.
Nov.	1	Sold 6,000 shares of treasury stock.
Dec.	20	Declared cash dividend of $0.25 per share.

Inman's Wholesale Products Inc. has a simple capital structure.

Instructions: Compute the weighted-average number of shares for 2002 and 2003 to be used in the EPS computation at the end of 2003.

PROBLEM 19–22

BASIC EARNINGS PER SHARE—SIMPLE CAPITAL STRUCTURE

The following condensed financial statements for the Tomac Corporation were prepared by the accounting department.

Tomac Corporation
Income Statement
For the Year Ended December 31, 2002

Sales		$12,000,000
Cost of goods sold		10,000,000
Gross profit on sales		$ 2,000,000
Expenses:		
Selling expense	$500,000	
Administrative expense	340,000	
Interest expense	24,000	864,000
Income from continuing operations before income taxes		$ 1,136,000
Income taxes		446,000
Income from continuing operations		$ 690,000
Extraordinary loss, net of tax savings		(60,000)
Net income		$ 630,000

Tomac Corporation
Balance Sheet
December 31, 2002

Assets	$5,300,000
Liabilities:	
Current liabilities	$1,450,000
6% bonds, due December 31, 2006	900,000
Stockholders' equity:	
Common stock, $10 par, 200,000 shares authorized, issued and outstanding	2,000,000
Additional paid-in capital	600,000
Retained earnings	350,000
Total liabilities and stockholders' equity	$5,300,000

Instructions: Compute the basic EPS under each of the following separate assumptions (the company has a simple capital structure).

1. No change in the capital structure occurred in 2002.
2. On December 31, 2001, there were 120,000 shares outstanding. On May 1, 2002, 60,000 shares were sold at par, and on October 1, 2002, 20,000 shares were sold at par.
3. On December 31, 2001, there were 160,000 shares outstanding. On July 1, 2002, the company issued a 25% stock dividend.

PROBLEM 19–23

BASIC EARNINGS PER SHARE—SIMPLE CAPITAL STRUCTURE
Great Northern Inc. reported the following comparative information in the stockholders' equity section of its 2003 balance sheet.

	Dec. 31, 2003	Dec. 31, 2002	Dec. 31, 2001
12% preferred stock, $50 par	$ 82,500	$ 67,500	$ 50,000
Paid-in capital in excess of par—preferred	13,400	9,200	5,000
Common stock, $5 par*	410,600	399,600	325,000
Paid-in capital in excess of par—common	64,300	58,800	35,000
Paid-in capital from treasury stock	1,800	800	800
Retained earnings	471,200	396,460	290,200
Total stockholders' equity	$1,043,800	$932,360	$706,000

*Par value after June 1, 2003, stock split.

In addition, company records show that the following transactions involving stockholders' equity were recorded in 2002 and 2003.

2002

May	1	Sold 4,500 shares of common stock for $12, par value $10.
June	30	Sold 350 shares of preferred stock for $62, par value $50.
Aug.	1	Issued an 8% stock dividend on common stock. The market price of the stock was $15.
Sept.	1	Declared cash dividends of 12% on preferred stock and $1.50 on common stock.
Dec.	1	Income from operations for the year totaled $316,200. In addition, Great Northern had an extraordinary gain of $12,500, net of tax.

2003

Jan.	31	Sold 1,100 shares of common stock for $15.
May	1	Sold 300 shares of preferred stock for $64.
June	1	Issued a 2-for-1 split of common stock, reduced par value to $5.
Sept.	1	Purchased 500 shares of common stock for $9 to be held as treasury stock.
Oct.	1	Declared cash dividends of 12% on preferred stock and $2 per share on outstanding common stock.
Nov.	1	Sold 500 shares of treasury stock for $11.
Dec.	31	Net income for the year included an extraordinary loss, net of income tax, of $19,000.

Instructions: Compute the basic EPS amounts for 2002 and 2003 to be presented in the income statement for 2003.

PROBLEM 19–24

DILUTED EARNINGS PER SHARE—STOCK OPTIONS

The records of Mountain Crest Company reveal the following capital structure as of December 31, 2001.

$10 preferred stock, $80 par, 7,500 shares issued and outstanding	$ 600,000
Additional paid-in capital on preferred stock	90,000
Common stock, $10 par, 200,000 shares issued and outstanding	2,000,000
Additional paid-in capital on common stock	350,000
Retained earnings	886,000

To stimulate work incentive and to bolster trade relations, Mountain Crest on May 1, 2002, issued stock options to select executives, creditors, and others allowing the purchase of 26,000 shares of common stock for $28 a share. Market prices for the stock at various times during 2002 were:

Option issuance date	$25
Average, May 1 to Dec. 31	75

A dividend on preferred stock was paid during the year, and there are no dividends in arrears at year-end. There are no other capital transactions during the year. Net income for 2002 was $631,000.

Instructions: Compute basic and diluted EPS for 2002.

PROBLEM 19–25

DILUTED EARNINGS PER SHARE—STOCK OPTIONS

The Ugrumov Technology Co. provides the following data at December 31, 2002.

Operating revenue	$1,120,000
Operating expenses	$600,000
Income tax rate	30%
Common stock outstanding during the entire year	26,000 shares

On January 1, 2002, there were options outstanding to purchase 15,000 shares of common stock at $25 per share. The average market price during the year was $35 per share. The balance sheet reports $240,000 of 7% nonconvertible bonds at December 31, 2002. (Interest expense is included in operating expenses.)

Instructions:

1. Compute for 2002 basic EPS.
2. Compute diluted EPS for 2002.

PROBLEM 19–26

DILUTED EARNINGS PER SHARE WITH EXERCISE OF STOCK OPTIONS

As of January 1, 2002, the Bayer Corporation had 30,000 shares of $5 par common stock outstanding. The company had issued stock options in 2000 to its management personnel permitting them to acquire 6,000 shares of common stock at $9 per share. At the time of the issuance, common stock was selling for $9 per share. The market price of common stock was $23 on September 1, 2002, and the average price for 2002 was $25. Income from operations for 2002 was $131,700. The company also had an extraordinary gain of $25,000, net of taxes. Terms of the options make them currently exercisable. On September 1, 2002, options to acquire 2,000 shares were exercised. The other 4,000 options are still outstanding at December 31, 2002.

Instructions: Compute basic and diluted EPS for the year ended December 31, 2002.

PROBLEM 19–27

DILUTED EARNINGS PER SHARE—CONVERSION OF DEBENTURES

The following information relates to the December 31, 2001, balance sheet for Chiapucci Incorporated.

6% convertible 10-year debentures issued at par	$1,000,000
Common stock, $12 par, 110,000 shares issued and outstanding	$1,320,000
Retained earnings	842,000
Total stockholders' equity	$2,162,000

The convertible debentures include terms stating that each $1,000 bond can be converted into 30 shares of common stock.

The following events occurred during 2002.

(a) On August 31, 2002, the complete issue of convertible debentures was converted into common stock.

(b) Chiapucci reported net income of $540,000 in 2002. The company's income tax rate was 30%.

(c) No other common stock transactions took place during the year other than the debenture conversion.

Instructions:

1. Compute basic and diluted EPS for the year ended December 31, 2002.
2. Assume Chiapucci had a net loss of $220,000. Show why the convertible debentures are antidilutive under loss conditions.

PROBLEM 19–28

DILUTED EARNINGS PER SHARE—COMPLEX CAPITAL STRUCTURE

Carrizo Corporation's capital structure is as follows:

	December 31,	
	2003	**2002**
Outstanding shares of:		
Common stock	336,000	280,000
Nonconvertible, noncumulative preferred stock	10,000	10,000
10% convertible bonds	$1,000,000	$1,000,000

The following additional information is available.

(a) On September 1, 2003, Carrizo sold 56,000 additional shares of common stock.

(b) Net income for the year ended December 31, 2003, was $860,000.

(c) During 2003, Carrizo declared and paid dividends of $5 per share on its preferred stock.

(d) The 10% bonds are convertible into 40 shares of common stock for each $1,000 bond.

(e) Unexercised options to purchase 30,000 shares of common stock at $22.50 per share were outstanding at the beginning and end of 2003. The average market price of Carrizo's common stock during 2003 was $36 per share.

(f) Warrants to purchase 20,000 shares of common stock at $38 per share were attached to the preferred stock at the time of issuance. The warrants, which expire on December 31, 2008, were outstanding at December 31, 2003.

(g) Carrizo's effective income tax rate was 30% for 2002 and 2003.

Instructions:

1. For the year ended December 31, 2003, compute basic EPS.
2. Compute diluted EPS for 2003.

PROBLEM 19-29

EARNINGS PER SHARE—COMPLEX CAPITAL STRUCTURE

The stockholders' equity section of Alta Company's balance sheet as of December 31, 2002, contains the following:

$2 cumulative preferred stock, $25 par, convertible, 1,600,000 shares authorized, 1,400,000 shares issued, 750,000 converted to common, 650,000 shares outstanding	$16,250,000
Common stock, $0.25 par, 15,000,000 shares authorized, 8,800,000 shares issued and outstanding	2,200,000
Additional paid-in capital	32,750,000
Retained earnings	40,595,000
Total stockholders' equity	$91,795,000

Included in the liabilities of Alta Company are 9% convertible subordinated debentures, face value $20,000,000, issued at par in 2001. The debentures are due in 2010 and, until then, are convertible into the common stock of Alta Company at the rate of 60 shares of common stock for each $1,000 debenture. To date, none has been converted.

On April 2, 2002, Alta Company issued 1,400,000 shares of convertible preferred stock at $40 per share. Quarterly dividends to December 31, 2002, have been paid on these shares. The preferred stock is convertible into common stock at the rate of 2 shares of common for each share of preferred. On October 1, 2002, 150,000 shares and on November 1, 2002, 600,000 shares of the preferred stock were converted into common stock.

During July 2001, Alta Company granted options to its officers and key employees to purchase 500,000 shares of the company's common stock at a price of $20 per share. No options were exercised in 2002.

During 2002, dividend payments for the Alta common stock were as follows.

	Dividend per Share
First quarter	$0.10
Second quarter	0.15
Third quarter	0.10
Fourth quarter	0.15

The average market price for the company's common stock during the year was $25. Alta Company's net income for the year ended December 31, 2002, was $12,750,000. The provision for income tax was computed at a rate of 30%.

Instructions: Compute basic and diluted EPS for the year ended December 31, 2002.

PROBLEM 19–30   **EARNINGS PER SHARE—COMPLEX CAPITAL STRUCTURE**

At December 31, 2002, the Norbalco Company had 400,000 shares of common stock outstanding. Norbalco sold 100,000 shares on October 1, 2003. Net income for 2003 was $2,565,000; the income tax rate was 30%. In addition, Norbalco had the following debt and equity securities on its books at December 31, 2002.

(a) 20,000 shares of $100 par, 10% cumulative preferred stock.

(b) 30,000 shares of 8% convertible cumulative preferred stock, par $100, sold at 110. Each share of preferred stock is convertible into 2 shares of common stock.

(c) $2,000,000 face value of 8% bonds sold at par.

(d) $3,000,000 face value of 6% convertible bonds sold to yield 7%. Unamortized bond discount is $100,000 at December 31, 2002. Each $1,000 bond is convertible into 20 shares of common stock.

Also, options to purchase 10,000 shares of common stock were issued May 1, 2003. Exercise price is $30 per share; market value at date of option was $29; average market value May 1 to December 31, 2003, $40.

Instructions: For the year ended December 31, 2003, compute basic and diluted EPS.

PROBLEM 19–31   **EARNINGS PER SHARE—MULTIPLE CONVERTIBLE SECURITIES**

Data for the Dwight Powder Company at the end of 2003 are listed below. All bonds are convertible as indicated and were issued at their face amounts.

Description of Bonds	Amount	Date Issued	Conversion Terms
10-year, 6½% convertible bonds	$ 700,000	Jan. 1, 1997	100 shares of common for each $1,000 bond
20-year, 7% convertible bonds	1,000,000	Jan. 1, 1998	50 shares of common for each $1,000 bond
25-year, 10½% convertible bonds	1,600,000	June 30, 2002	32 shares of common for each $1,000 bond
Additional information:			
Common shares outstanding at December 31, 2002			700,000
Net income for 2003			$1,406,000
Income tax rate			30%

Instructions:

1. Compute basic and diluted EPS for 2003, assuming that no additional shares of common stock were issued during the year.

2. Compute basic and diluted EPS assuming that the 10-year bonds were converted on July 1, 2003, and that net income for the year was $1,421,925 (reflects reduction in interest due to bond conversion).

PROBLEM 19–32   **EARNINGS PER SHARE—MULTIPLE CONVERTIBLE SECURITIES**

Sawyer Company had the following capital structure at December 31, 2002 and 2003:

	2003	2002
Shares of stock outstanding:		
Common stock	756,000	600,000
$6 convertible preferred stock	10,000	20,000
Bonds outstanding:		
8½%, 10-year convertible bonds	$1,500,000	$2,000,000

The following additional information is available.

(a) The conversion terms of the preferred stock and bonds at January 1, 2003, were as follows: Preferred stock, 5 shares of common for each share of preferred; convertible bonds, 40 shares of common for each $1,000 bond. These terms are to be adjusted for any issued stock dividends or stock splits.

(b) On May 1, 2003, Sawyer sold an additional 50,000 shares of common stock, and on August 1, 2003, a 5% stock dividend on common shares was declared.

(c) On October 1, 2003, 10,000 shares of preferred stock were converted to 52,500 shares of common stock (5.25 shares common for each share of preferred). The preferred stock was issued at $100 par in 1999.

(d) On December 1, 2003, 25% of the convertible bonds were converted. The bonds were issued at par in 2002.

(e) On December 31, 2003, Sawyer declared and paid a $6-per-share dividend on outstanding preferred stock. Income for the year was $1,400,000.

(f) Stock options (issued and unexercised) to purchase 60,000 shares of common stock at $25 per share were outstanding at the beginning of 2003. Average market price for 2003 was $48.

(g) Stock warrants to purchase 40,000 shares of common stock at $46 per share were attached to the preferred stock. The warrants expire on December 31, 2007, and were outstanding at December 31, 2003.

(h) The effective tax rate was 30% for both years.

(i) On February 1, 2004, before the 2003 financial statements were issued, Sawyer split its common stock 2 for 1.

Instructions: For the year ended December 31, 2003, compute basic and diluted EPS.

COMPETENCY ENHANCEMENT OPPORTUNITIES

▶ Deciphering Actual Financial Statements	▶ Ethical Dilemma
▶ Writing Assignment	▶ Cumulative Spreadsheet Analysis
▶ Research Project	▶ Internet Search
▶ The Debate	

Accounting is more than just doing textbook problems. This expanded competency material provides practice in critical thinking, oral and written communication, research, teamwork, and consideration of ethical issues.

▶ **DECIPHERING ACTUAL FINANCIAL STATEMENTS**
• **Deciphering 19–1 (The Walt Disney Company)**
Review the information relating to EPS found in THE WALT DISNEY COMPANY income statement and notes to the financial statements in Appendix A. Answer the following questions.

1. Using the information provided on the face of the income statement relating to net income and average number of shares outstanding, verify the reported EPS figure.

2. From its statement of cash flows, we see that Disney paid dividends of $412 million. Using the average number of shares outstanding from the EPS computation in (1), compute the approximate dividends paid per share. Using this number, compute the dividend payout ratio for Disney.

3. Search the notes to determine if Disney had any stock splits in 1998. How do stock splits affect the presentation of the prior year's information?

• Deciphering 19-2 (McDonald's Corporation)

MCDONALD'S is in the business of—wait, we all know what McDonald's does. Take a look at the company's income statement and an accompanying note relating to its computation of EPS to answer the following questions.

1. Using the information from the income statement, compute the average number of shares outstanding used in McDonald's computation of net income per common share for 1998 and 1997. Compare this number with the weighted-average shares of common stock outstanding from the note. What is the most likely reason that the results of your computations and the numbers provided by McDonald's do not agree?
2. Compute McDonald's dividend payout ratio for 1996 through 1998. Has the ratio increased or decreased by a significant amount over the 3-year period?
3. What transactions occurred in 1996–1999 related to the company's stock that affected the computation of EPS?
4. As stated in the note, a stock split occurred on March 5, 1999. If the split occurred in 1999, why have the per-common-share amounts been restated?

McDonald's Corporation
Consolidated Statement of Income

(In millions of dollars, except per common share data)	Years ended December 31, 1998	1997	1996
Revenues			
Sales by Company-operated restaurants	$ 8,894.9	$ 8,136.5	$ 7,570.5
Revenues from franchised and affiliated restaurants	3,526.5	3,272.3	3,115.8
Total revenues	12,421.4	11,408.8	10,686.5
Operating costs and expenses			
Company-operated restaurants			
Food and packaging	2,997.4	2,772.6	2,546.6
Payroll and employee benefits	2,230.3	2,025.1	1,909.8
Occupancy and other operating expenses	2,043.9	1,851.9	1,706.8
	7,261.6	6,649.6	6,163.2
Franchised restaurants—occupancy expenses	678.0	613.9	570.1
Selling, general, and administrative expenses	1,458.5	1,450.5	1,366.4
Made-for-you costs	161.6		
Special charges	160.0		72.0
Other operating (income) expense	(60.2)	(113.5)	(117.8)
Total operating costs and expenses	9,659.5	8,600.5	8,053.9
Operating income	2,761.9	2,808.3	2,632.6
Interest expense—net of capitalized interest of $17.9, $22.7 and $22.2	(413.8)	(364.4)	(342.5)
Nonoperating income (expense)—net	(40.7)	(36.6)	(39.1)
Income before provision for income taxes	2,307.4	2,407.3	2,251.0
Provision for income taxes	757.3	764.8	678.4
Net income	$ 1,550.1	$ 1,642.5	$ 1,572.6
Net income per common share	$ 1.14	$ 1.17	$ 1.11
Net income per common share—diluted	1.10	1.15	1.08
Dividends per common share	$ .18	$ .16	$ .15

The accompanying Financial Comments are an integral part of the consolidated financial statements.

Capital stock
Per common share information

Income used in the computation of per common share information was reduced by preferred stock cash dividends (net of applicable tax benefits) of $25.3 million in 1997 and $27.6 million in 1996. The Company retired its remaining Series E Preferred Stock in December 1997. Diluted net income per common share includes the dilutive effect of stock options. Weighted average shares were 1,365.3, 1,378.7, and 1,396.4 in 1998, 1997, and 1996, respectively.

On January 26, 1999, the Board of directors declared a two-for-one stock split of the Company's common stock, effected in the form of a stock dividend paid on March 5, 1999. As a result of this action, 830.3 millions shares were issued to shareholders of record as of February 12, 1999. Par value of the stock remains at $.01 per share and accordingly, $8.3 million was transferred from additional paid-in capital to common stock. All references to the number of common shares and per common share amounts have been restated to give retroactive effect to the stock split for all periods presented.

• Deciphering 19-3 (Cadbury Schweppes)

CADBURY SCHWEPPES is a company that manufactures beverages and confectionary candies. Because the company is based in the United Kingdom, it is not required to comply with U.S. GAAP. However, the standards relating to EPS under which Cadbury Schweppes prepared its 1998 annual report are similar to the requirements of FASB No. 128. Review Cadbury Schweppes note disclosures and answer the following questions.

Cadbury Schweppes
9. Earnings per Ordinary Share

(a) Basic EPS is calculated on the weighted average of 1,015 million shares (1997: 1,006 million shares; 1996: 996 million shares) in issue during the year.

(b) The reconciliation between Basic EPS and Underlying EPS , and between the earnings figures used in calculating them, is as follows:

	1998	1997	1996
Earnings..	£355	£691	£340
Adjust for:			
Exceptional items..	68	—	—
Profit on sale of subsidiaries and investments,			
net of tax and minority interests............................	(23)	(317)	—
Underlying earnings...	£400	£374	£340

(c) Diluted EPS has been calculated based on the Basic EPS Earnings amount above. A reconciliation between the shares used in calculating Basic and Diluted EPS is as follows:

	1998	1997	1996
Average shares used in Basic EPS calculation...........................	1,015	1,006	996
Dilutive share options outstanding..	15	10	9
Shares used in Diluted EPS calculation	1,030	1,016	1,005

Share options not included in the diluted calculation because they were anti-dilutive in the period totalled 4.2 million in 1998 (1997: 4.6 million; 1996: 5.5 million).

Note 1 (i).
Earnings per Ordinary Share

The Group has adopted FRS 14 "Earnings per Share" for the 1998 financial statements and presentation of earnings per share for prior periods has been amended to comply with this new standard. Basic Earnings per Ordinary Share is calculated by dividing the profit on ordinary activities after taxation, minority interests and preference dividends by the weighted average number of shares in issue during the year. Diluted EPS is calculated by dividing profit on ordinary activities after taxation, minority interests and preference dividends by the weighted average number of shares in issue during the year increased by the effects of all dilutive potential ordinary shares (primarily share options).

Underlying EPS represents Basic EPS, adjusted to exclude exceptional items and gains and losses on disposals of subsidiaries and investments.

1. Is Cadbury Schweppes accounting for EPS according to U.S. GAAP? If not, what are the differences? What is Underlying EPS? Does U.S. GAAP require something similar to Underlying EPS?

2. Based on the information given, calculate Cadbury Schweppes basic EPS, diluted EPS, and underlying EPS for 1998.

▶ **WRITING ASSIGNMENT**
• U.S. and international accounting standards

FASB Statement No. 128 represents the first time in which the FASB has worked directly with the IASC in issuing a major accounting standard. The FASB is now working with several

accounting standard-setting bodies from around the world to address other accounting issues.

In 2 pages or less, address the following questions: Is it important for the FASB to consider the impact of its accounting standards on the international community? If so, why? If not, why not? In answering these questions, consider how the FASB's pronouncements might affect businesses operating outside of the United States.

▶ RESEARCH PROJECT
• Reviewing actual financial statements and associated notes

Your group is to obtain the annual reports of 5 companies. Using these annual reports, your group is to report (either orally or in writing) the answers to the following questions.

- Of the 5 companies, how many disclose both basic and diluted EPS on the face of their income statement? How many provide detailed information about their computation of EPS in the notes to the financial statements?
- Of the 5 companies, determine how many have the following:
- preferred stock
- convertible preferred stock
- convertible bonds
- stock options

    For each of these items, determine how it would affect both basic and diluted EPS.

- For those companies with stock options, can you determine if the options were dilutive? How?
- For those companies with complex capital structures, how large (on a percentage basis) is the effect of considering potential dilutive securities?

▶ THE DEBATE
• Speculating about the future

The standard on EPS requires companies to provide EPS information relating to transactions that have not (and may not) occur. Accountants computing diluted EPS are required to consider the effect on both net income and shares outstanding of events that may or may not come to pass. The objective of this debate is to consider the value of the information provided in the diluted EPS figure.

Divide your group into 2 teams.

- Team One will argue that accountants should not be involved in speculating about the possible exercise of stock options or the conversion of securities in the future. Basic EPS is based on historical information and should be the only EPS information provided in the financial statements.
- Team Two will take the position that forward-looking information about possible conversion of securities or the exercise of stock options provides valuable information to investors and creditors.

ETHICAL DILEMMA
• Are there other options?

After computing the current period's basic and diluted EPS figures, you notice that while basic EPS continues its upward trend, diluted EPS has dropped slightly. In discussions with your manager regarding reasons for the decline, you identify numerous potentially dilutive securities that were considered in computing diluted EPS. Because the company has multiple dilutive securities, those securities were considered in turn, beginning with the convertible security that had the least favorable impact on EPS. As a result of considering the potentially dilutive securities in this order, convertible bonds that were potentially dilutive were not included in the computations because they became antidilutive after considering the effect of other convertible securities.

Your manager takes the position that if a security is dilutive when compared to basic EPS, it should be included in the diluted EPS computations. He maintains that each dilutive security should be considered independently of the others. Including these convertible bonds in the diluted EPS computations would result in maintaining an upward trend for diluted EPS.

1. Is there merit to your manager's position? That is, does the approach he is advocating make some sense?
2. Do the accounting standards allow for this flexibility in interpretation?
3. Prepare your defense for when your manager insists that diluted EPS be computed using his approach. What will you say to him to convince him that his approach is not acceptable?

CUMULATIVE SPREADSHEET ANALYSIS

This assignment is an exercise in computing diluted EPS. In prior years, Skywalker has had a simple capital structure. That may change in 2003; Skywalker is considering the following actions at the beginning of 2003.

- Issue options granting top-level managers the opportunity to purchase a total of 2,000,000 shares of Skywalker common stock for $25 per share.
- Exchange $600 million in existing long-term debt (with an interest rate of 8%) for $600 million in 8% convertible bonds (600,000 bonds, each with a $1,000 face value).

Without these changes, Skywalker expects to have net income of $15,890,000 in 2003; the net income forecast reflects the expectation that Skywalker will be subject to a 33% tax rate in 2003. (Note: This $15,890,000 forecasted net income for 2003 comes from the assumptions outlined in Chapter 13; all numbers in Chapter 13 are in millions of dollars.) As of the end of 2002, Skywalker had 10,000,000 common shares outstanding.

Using this data, construct a spreadsheet to answer the following questions.

1. What is Skywalker's basic EPS expected to be in 2003?
2. What is Skywalker's diluted EPS expected to be in 2003 if the options and convertible bonds are issued on January 1, 2003, the average stock price is expected to be $20 per share during 2003, and each bond is convertible into 40 shares of common stock?
3. What is Skywalker's diluted EPS expected to be in 2003 if the options and convertible bonds are issued on January 1, 2003, the average stock price is expected to be $40 per share during 2003, and each bond is convertible into 35 shares of common stock?
4. Assuming that Skywalker issues the options and convertible bonds on January 1, 2003, complete the following table.

DILUTED EARNINGS PER SHARE in 2003

		Forecasted average market price		
		$20	$30	$40
	20			
Common Shares per Bond	35			
	40			

INTERNET SEARCH

Everybody loves chocolate, and HERSHEY'S FOODS is the largest chocolate manufacturing company in the world. Hershey's Web address is www.hersheys.com. Let's take a look at the company's Web site. Answer the following questions.

1. Rather than go straight to the financial information, take a look at Hershey's history page. Read about the Milton Hershey School and describe what Mr. Hershey did with money he made from the chocolate business.
2. Next, turn your attention to the financial information. Locate Hershey's income statement to determine its EPS. Does Hershey's have a simple or a complex capital structure? What numbers are disclosed related to EPS?
3. Read the note disclosure relating to EPS. What information does Hershey's provide relating to dilutive securities? Did these dilutive securities have a large impact on EPS?

chapter 20
Accounting Changes
and Error Corrections

The last major accounting standard to significantly affect corporate income statements was Statement of Financial Accounting Standards No. 106, "Employers' Accounting for Postretirement Benefits Other Than Pensions," issued in 1992. The overall impact of this standard on corporate profits established a record for a new accounting rule and was estimated to result in a decrease in the profits of major U.S. companies by as much as $1 trillion.[1] As an example of the effect, GENERAL MOTORS created a liability relating to other postretirement benefits and took a one-time charge of $33 billion. The after-tax effect of this charge was to decrease earnings by $21 billion and decrease earnings per share (EPS) by $33.38. Although the standard gave companies the option of spreading the charge over 20 years, many companies chose to take the "big hit" in one year rather than to have it negatively impact earnings for 19 additional years. The impact for a few companies that elected the one-time change method is shown in Exhibit 20–1 (on page 1142).

As the experience of these companies illustrates, the financial statements sometimes report significantly different results from year to year. This may be due to changes in economic circumstances, but it also may be due to changes in accounting methods or corrections of errors in recording past transactions.

Changing the accounting methods used can have a dramatic impact on the financial statements of a company. Because of this impact, one can argue that accounting changes detract from the informational characteristics of comparability and consistency discussed in Chapter 1. So why are these accounting changes made? The main reasons for such changes may be summarized as follows:

1. A company, as a result of experience or new information, may change its estimates of revenues or expenses—for example, the estimate of uncollectible accounts receivable or the estimated service lives of depreciable assets.
2. Due to changes in economic conditions, companies may need to change methods of accounting to more clearly reflect the current economic situation.
3. Accounting standard-setting bodies may require the use of a new accounting method or principle, such as new reporting requirements for postretirement benefits.
4. The acquisition or divestiture of companies, which was prevalent in the 1980s and early 1990s, may cause a change in the reporting entity.
5. Management may be pressured to report profitable performance. Making accounting changes can often result in higher net income, thereby reflecting favorably on management.

1
Understand the three different types of accounting changes that have been identified by accounting standard setters.

2
Recognize the difference between a change in accounting estimate and a change in accounting principle, and know how a change in accounting estimate is reflected in the financial statements.

3
Determine if a change in accounting principle requires a cumulative adjustment relating to its effect or a restatement of prior periods' financial statements, and be able to compute the necessary adjustment.

4
Determine when a change in reporting entity has occurred, and understand the disclosure requirements associated with this change.

5
Recognize the various types of errors that can occur in the accounting process, understand when errors counterbalance, and be able to correct errors when necessary.

6
Describe the differences between the U.S. approach to accounting changes and error corrections and the international approach found in IAS 8.

1 Lee Berton and Robert J. Brennan, "New Medical-Benefits Accounting Rule Seen Wounding Profits, Hurting Shares," *The Wall Street Journal*, April 22, 1992, p. C1.

EXHIBIT 20–1 | Effect of FASB Statement No. 106

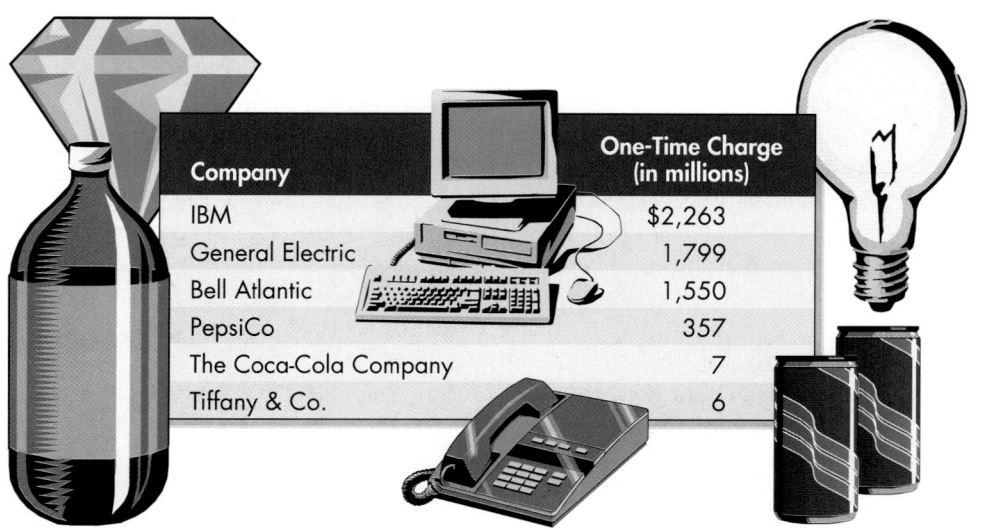

Company	One-Time Charge (in millions)
IBM	$2,263
General Electric	1,799
Bell Atlantic	1,550
PepsiCo	357
The Coca-Cola Company	7
Tiffany & Co.	6

Whatever the reason, accountants must keep the primary qualitative characteristic of usefulness in mind. They must determine if the reasons for accounting changes are appropriate and then how best to report the changes to facilitate understanding of the financial statements.

The detection of errors in accounting for past transactions presents a similar problem. The errors must be corrected and appropriate disclosures made so that readers of the financial statements will clearly understand what has happened. The purpose of this chapter is to discuss the different types of accounting changes and error corrections and the related accounting procedures that should be used.

Understand the three different types of accounting changes that have been identified by accounting standard setters.

ACCOUNTING CHANGES

The accounting profession has identified three main categories of **accounting changes**[2]:

1. Change in accounting estimate
2. Change in accounting principle
3. Change in reporting entity

As pointed out in Chapter 1, a major objective of published financial statements is to provide users with information to help them predict, compare, and evaluate future earning power and cash flows of the reporting entity. When a reporting entity adjusts its past estimates of revenues earned or costs incurred, changes its accounting principles from one method to another, or changes its nature as a reporting entity, it becomes more difficult for a user to predict the future from past historical statements. The basic accounting issue is whether accounting changes should be reported as adjustments of the prior

2 *Opinions of the Accounting Principles Board No. 20*, "Accounting Changes," New York: American Institute of Certified Public Accountants, 1971.

periods' statements (thus increasing their comparability with current and future statements) or whether the changes should affect only the current and future years.

Several alternatives have been suggested for reporting accounting changes.

1. Restate the financial statements presented for prior periods to reflect the effect of the change. Adjust the beginning retained earnings balance of the current period for the cumulative effect of the change.
2. Make no adjustment to statements presented for prior periods. Report the cumulative effect of the change in the current year as a direct entry to Retained Earnings.
3. Same as (2), except report the cumulative effect of the change as a special item in the income statement instead of directly to Retained Earnings.
4. Report the cumulative effect in the current year as in (3), but also present limited pro forma information for all prior periods included in the financial statements reporting "what might have been" if the change had been made in the prior years.
5. Make the change effective only for current and future periods with no catch-up adjustment.

Each of these methods for reporting an accounting change has been used by companies in the past, and arguments can be made for each of the various approaches. For example, some accountants argue that accounting principles should be applied consistently for all reported periods. Therefore, if a new accounting principle is used in the current period, the financial statements presented for prior periods should be restated so that the results shown for all reported periods are based on the same accounting principles. Other accountants contend that restating financial statements may dilute public confidence in those statements. Principles applied in earlier periods were presumably appropriate at that time and should be considered final. The only exception would be for changes in a reporting entity. In addition, restating financial statements is costly, requires considerable effort, and is sometimes impossible due to lack of data.

Consider the GENERAL MOTORS (GM) example at the beginning of this chapter. How should the liability and the effect on earnings have been reported? Specifically, what would have been the appropriate journal entry? Obviously, GM would recognize a liability of $33 billion. Because GM will not receive a tax deduction for the other postretirement benefits until those expenses are actually paid, GM would also recognize a deferred tax asset of $12 billion. This deferred tax asset would be recognized because GM expensed the cost of the benefits now for financial accounting purposes but does not expect to receive the tax deduction for those expenses until they are paid in the future —recall from Chapter 16 that this would result in taxable income being higher than financial income in the current period, resulting in a deferred tax asset. As a result, the journal entry would appear as follows:

Deferred Tax Asset	12 billion	
????	21 billion	
Other Postretirement Benefits Liability		33 billion

What account should replace the question marks? Should it be an income statement account, a balance sheet account, or some other type of account? In the United States, most companies elected to expense the amount immediately. For example, General Motors debited Cumulative Effect of an Accounting Change and reported the $21 billion reduction in earnings as a below-the-line item on the income statement. International practice is different with respect to the handling of this type of accounting change. Under the provisions of International Accounting Standard (IAS) 8 (discussed later in this chapter), companies would debit the beginning balance in the retained earnings account, reasoning that the adjustment was related to prior periods and the income from those prior periods had been previously closed to the retained earnings account.

The change in the accounting method for postretirement benefits is an illustration of just one type of accounting change. In the United States, there

FYI: Recall from Chapter 4 that the three types of below-the-line items are (1) extraordinary items, (2) results of discontinued operations, and (3) cumulative effects of changes in accounting principle.

historically was a significant amount of diversity in the way that companies accounted for the effects of a change in accounting. Because of the diversity of practice and the resulting difficulty in user understandability of the financial statements, the Accounting Principles Board (APB) issued Opinion No. 20. The APB's objective was to bring increased uniformity to reporting practice. Evidence of compromise exists in the final opinion, as the APB attempted to reflect both its desire to increase comparability of financial statements and to improve user confidence in published financial statements. Depending on the type of accounting change, different accounting treatment is required, as explained in the following sections.

2

Recognize the difference between a change in accounting estimate and a change in accounting principle, and know how a change in accounting estimate is reflected in the financial statements.

FYI: Jerry's Famous Deli, Inc., operates New York deli-style restaurants, primarily in Southern California. On July 1, 1998, the company changed the estimated useful lives of certain restaurant equipment and furniture and fixtures from a five-year to an eight-year useful life. The change lowered depreciation expense by $420,000, increasing income from operations by 52.1%.

Change in Accounting Estimate

Contrary to what many people believe, accounting information cannot always be measured and reported precisely. Also, to be reported on a timely basis for decision making, accounting data often must be based on estimates of future events. The financial statements incorporate these estimates, which are based on the best professional judgment given the information available at that time. At a later date, however, additional experience or new facts sometimes make it clear that the estimates need to be revised to more accurately reflect the existing business circumstances. When this happens, a **change in accounting estimate** occurs.

Examples of areas where changes in accounting estimates often are needed include:

1. Uncollectible receivables
2. Useful lives of depreciable or intangible assets
3. Residual values for depreciable assets
4. Warranty obligations
5. Quantities of mineral reserves to be depleted
6. Actuarial assumptions for pensions or other postemployment benefits
7. Number of periods benefited by deferred costs

Exhibit 20-2 provides examples of disclosure relating to estimates contained in the 1998 annual reports of two companies: H. J. HEINZ COMPANY and MCDONALD'S. Even though the companies had different auditors (COOPERS & LYBRAND and ERNST & YOUNG, respectively), it is surprising how similar the note disclosures are.

Accounting for a change in estimate has already been discussed in Chapter 4 and throughout the text in areas where changes in estimates are common. By way of review, all changes in estimates should be reflected either in the current period or in

---

EXHIBIT 20-2 | H.J. Heinz Company and McDonald's—Disclosure Relating to Estimates

---

NOTES TO CONSOLIDATED FINANCIAL STATEMENTS
H. J. Heinz Company and Subsidiaries
I. Significant Accounting Policies   *Use of Estimates:* The preparation of financial statements in conformity with generally accepted accounting principles requires management to make estimates and assumptions that affect the reported amounts of assets and liabilities, the disclosure of contingent assets and liabilities at the date of the financial statements, and the reported amounts of revenues and expenses during the reporting period. Actual results could differ from these estimates.

McDonald's Corporation Financial Comments
Summary of significant accounting policies

Estimates in financial statements
The preparation of financial statements in conformity with generally accepted accounting principles requires management to make estimates and assumptions that affect the amounts reported in the financial statements and accompanying notes. Actual results could differ from those estimates.

 If a change in estimate required restatement of prior periods' financial statements, how often would financial statements be restated? How much reliability would financial statement users be willing to place on this period's statements when odds are that the numbers will change? Does it make sense that changes in accounting estimates are accounted for the way they are?

current and future periods. No retroactive adjustments or pro forma (as if) statements are to be prepared for a change in accounting estimate. Changes in estimates are considered to be part of the normal accounting process and not corrections or changes of past periods. However, disclosures such as the one in Exhibit 20-3, reported by DELTA AIR LINES, are useful in helping readers of financial statements understand the impact of changes in estimates.

EXHIBIT 20-3 | Delta Air Lines—Disclosure of Change in Estimate

NOTES TO FINANCIAL STATEMENTS (in part)
As of July 1, 1998, we increased the depreciable lives of certain aircraft types from 20 to 25 years. The change in estimate reduced depreciation expense by $92 million ($0.64 basic and $0.60 diluted earnings per share) for fiscal 1999.

Change in Accounting Principle

 Determine if a change in accounting principle requires a cumulative adjustment relating to its effect or a restatement of prior periods' financial statements, and be able to compute the necessary adjustment.

A **change in accounting principle** involves a change from one generally accepted principle or method to another.[3] A change in principle, as defined in APB Opinion No. 20, does not include the initial adoption of an accounting principle as a result of transactions or events that had not occurred (or were immaterial) in previous periods. Also, a change from a principle that is not generally accepted to one that is generally accepted is considered to be an error correction rather than a change in accounting principle.

If an asset is affected by both a change in principle and a change in estimate during the same period, APB Opinion No. 20 requires that the change be treated as a change in estimate rather than a change in principle.[4] For example, if a company changes its depreciation method at the same time it recognizes a change in estimated asset life, this would

By increasing the depreciable lives of certain aircraft types, Delta Air Lines reduced depreciation expense by $92 million for fiscal 1999.

3 The classification "change in accounting principle" includes changes in methods used to account for transactions. No attempt was made by the APB in Opinion No. 20 to distinguish between a principle and a method.
4 *Opinions of the Accounting Principles Board No. 20*, par. 32.

involve both a change in method and a change in estimate. According to APB Opinion No. 20, such circumstances would be treated as a change in estimate.

As indicated in previous chapters, companies may select among alternative accounting principles to account for business transactions. For example, for financial reporting purposes, a company may depreciate its buildings and equipment using the straight-line depreciation method, the double-declining-balance method, the sum-of-the-years'-digits method, or any other consistent and rational allocation procedure. Long-term construction contracts may be accounted for by the percentage-of-completion method or the completed-contract method. Inventory may be accounted for using FIFO, LIFO, or other acceptable methods. These alternative methods are often equally available to a given company, but in most instances, criteria for selection among the methods are inadequate. As a result, companies have found it rather easy to justify changing from one accounting principle or method to another.

CURRENT RECOGNITION OF CUMULATIVE EFFECT OF CHANGE IN PRINCIPLE

The APB concluded that, in general, companies should not change their accounting principles from one period to the next. "Consistent use of accounting principles from one period to another enhances the utility of financial statements to users by facilitating analysis and understanding of comparative accounting data."[5] A company may change its accounting principles, however, if it can justify a change because of a new pronouncement by the authoritative accounting standard-setting body or because of a change in its economic circumstances. Just what constitutes an acceptable change in economic circumstances is not clear. It presumably could include a change in the competitive structure of an industry, a significant change in the rate of inflation in the economy, a change resulting from government restrictions due to economic or political crisis, and so forth.

In general, the effect of a change from one accepted accounting principle to another is reflected by reporting the cumulative effect of the change in the income statement in the period of the change. This cumulative adjustment is shown as a separate item on the income statement after extraordinary items and before net income. When a change in accounting principle occurs, the financial statements for all prior periods reported for comparative purposes with the current year's financial statements are presented as previously reported. To enhance trend analysis, however, pro forma information also is required to reflect the income before extraordinary items and net income that would have been reported if the new accounting principle had been in effect for the respective prior years. Pro forma EPS figures also should be reported.

FYI: In fiscal 1998, WALGREENS, America's largest drugstore retailer, changed the way it accounts for business process reengineering costs. Formerly, Walgreens had capitalized these costs; they are now expensed in accordance with EITF 97-13. The cumulative effect of this accounting change was a reduction in net income of $26 million, or 4.8%.

To illustrate the general treatment of a change in accounting principle, assume Telstar Company, a high-power telescope sales and manufacturing firm, elected in 2002 to change from the double-declining-balance (DDB) method of depreciation to the straight-line method to make its financial reporting more consistent with the majority of its competitors. For tax purposes, assume Telstar had elected to use the straight-line method and will continue to do so. Assume further that Telstar presents comparative income statements for three years and that the past difference in book and tax depreciation is the only difference in accounting treatment impacting Telstar's financial and taxable income.

These and other assumptions are necessary because, in most instances, a change in accounting principle involves temporary differences between book and tax income, creating the need for interperiod tax allocation. The exact amounts of any deferred income tax liabilities or potential deferred income tax assets are dependent on several factors,

---

5 Ibid., par. 15.

net work exercise

Go to Walgreens' Web site (**www.walgreens.com**) and access its most recent annual report.

Net Work:

Determine whether the 1998 cumulative effect is still shown in Walgreens' comparative income statement. Also, determine whether the change is still described in the notes to the financial statements.

such as current tax laws and current and future tax rates. Therefore, in this chapter, including the end-of-chapter material, the impact of income tax either is ignored or the assumed amounts are provided to simplify the illustrations and focus on the effects of accounting changes and error corrections.

For Telstar, the change to straight-line depreciation for reporting purposes means that tax and book depreciation will be the same in future years. It is assumed, however, that the greater depreciation charged on the books in prior years, as compared to the tax depreciation taken, resulted in a previously recorded deferred tax asset. This and other relevant information for Telstar is presented next.

The data indicate that depreciation expense for the years prior to 2002 would have been $131,000 ($288,000 – $157,000) less if the straight-line method had been used. Thus, income would have been $131,000 higher, less the applicable assumed income

Year	Double-Declining-Balance Depreciation	Straight-Line Depreciation	Depreciation Difference	Assumed Tax Effects	Effects on Income (Net of Taxes)
Prior to 2000	$163,000	$ 90,000	$ 73,000	$21,900	$51,100
2000	60,000	32,000	28,000	8,400	19,600
2001	65,000	35,000	30,000	9,000	21,000
	$288,000	$157,000	$131,000	$39,300	$91,700

taxes of $39,300. Based on these data, the journal entry to record the cumulative effect adjustment and to eliminate the previously recorded deferred tax asset is as follows:

Accumulated Depreciation	131,000	
Deferred Tax Asset		39,300
Cumulative Effect of Change in Accounting Principle		91,700

The $131,000 debit to Accumulated Depreciation represents the excess depreciation charged to the books in prior years. The $39,300 credit would eliminate the previously established deferred tax asset amount. The $91,700 after-tax cumulative effect would be reported as additional income in the income statement for 2002, the year of the change.

Continuing the Telstar example, assume that net income for the two preceding years as originally reported was $450,000 in 2000 and $500,000 in 2001 and that all net income in both years was from continuing operations. Using the new depreciation method, in 2002 Telstar reported $560,000 income from continuing operations and an extraordinary gain of $70,000 net of income taxes of $30,000. Following is a partial income statement for 2002 with comparative information for 2001 and 2000.

Telstar Company
Partial Comparative Income Statement
For the Years Ended December 31

	2002	2001	2000
Income from continuing operations	$560,000	$500,000	$450,000
Extraordinary gain (net of income taxes of $30,000)	70,000		
Cumulative effect on prior years of change in accounting principle—change to the straight-line method of depreciation from double-declining-balance method (net of income taxes of $39,300)	91,700		
Net income	$721,700	$500,000	$450,000

Note that in 2002 the cumulative effect is shown net of tax and as a separate item after the extraordinary item. As explained in Chapter 4, all below-the-line items, such as extraordinary gains or losses and the cumulative effect of a change in accounting principle, are to be reported net of related income taxes. This is referred to as intraperiod tax allocation. With this disclosure technique, the appropriate amount of income taxes is associated with income from continuing operations and with the individual below-the-line items reported separately. Also note that the amounts of income from continuing operations for the two prior years are presented as originally reported. In addition, the disclosure of pro forma income for the prior years is required and would be shown on the face of the income statement (using the assumed data) as follows:

Pro forma income data:

	2001	2000
Net income from continuing operations as previously reported	$500,000	$450,000
Effect of change in accounting principle (net of tax)	21,000	19,600
Pro forma income (restated)	$521,000	$469,600

STOP & THINK Dow Chemical does not report any cumulative effect in association with its change from accelerated to straight-line depreciation methods. Read the note in Exhibit 20–4 and determine why there is no cumulative effect from this accounting change.

Pro forma EPS amounts reflecting the revised income figures also would be presented.

In 1997, DOW CHEMICAL changed its method of depreciation from an accelerated method to the straight-line method. Exhibit 20–4 provides the company's note disclosure explaining why Dow Chemical made the switch.

EXHIBIT 20–4 | Dow Chemical—-Disclosure Relating to a Change in Depreciation Method

DOW CHEMICAL
NOTES TO CONSOLIDATED FINANCIAL STATEMENTS
Note B (in part): Accounting Change

For property released to operations beginning January 1, 1997, the Company has changed from an accelerated method to the straight-line method of depreciation. The change reflects improvements in the Company's engineering and maintenance practices which result in property not being subject to high maintenance costs or substantially reduced productivity in the later years of its useful life. In addition, the change to the straight-line method conforms to predominant industry practice. This change did not have a material effect on 1997 income.

In a few cases, past records are inadequate to prepare pro forma statements for individual years. This fact should be disclosed when applicable. For example, a change to the LIFO method of inventory valuation is usually made effective with the beginning inventory in the year of change rather than with some prior year because of the difficulty in identifying prior-year layers or dollar-value pools. Thus, the beginning inventory in the year of change becomes the same as the previous inventory valued using another costing method, and this becomes the base LIFO layer. No cumulative effect adjustment is required. Exhibit 20–5 illustrates note disclosure from three different companies that switched to LIFO during fiscal 1998. Note both the similarities and differences in the justification for the change by each company.

EXHIBIT 20-5 | Disclosure From Three Companies Relating to a Change to LIFO

GENLYTE GROUP (designs, manufactures, markets, and sells lighting fixtures):
During 1998, the Company changed its method of accounting for certain inventories from the FIFO method to the LIFO method. This change, applied prospectively from the date of the change, was made to have a consistent method throughout the U.S. operations because the Thomas Lighting U.S. inventories, now consolidated with Genlyte through the Genlyte Thomas Group LLC, are valued using the LIFO method. This change increased net income by $507 or $.04 per diluted share.

M.A. HANNA COMPANY (produces specialized rubber and plastic compounds):
Effective January 1, 1998, the Company changed its method of accounting for all domestic inventories to the LIFO cost method. The change in accounting was made to better match acquisition costs against sales, conform to the LIFO election made for income tax purposes and to provide greater consistency in inventory valuations across domestic business units. The effect of this change was not significant to 1998 reported results.

FLOWSERVE (manufactures industrial pumps, valves, and mechanical seals):

	1998	1997
Percent of inventory accounted for by LIFO	61%	43%
Percent of inventory accounted for by FIFO	39%	57%

The percentage of inventory accounted for by the last-in first-out (LIFO) method increased in 1998 as the U.S. operations of the former BW/IP changed its method of accounting for inventories to LIFO during the year. Because the December 31, 1997, BW/IP inventory valued at FIFO is the opening LIFO inventory, there is neither a cumulative effect to January 1, 1998, nor pro forma amounts of retroactively applying the change to LIFO. The effect of the change in 1998 was not significant.

RESTATEMENT OF PRIOR PERIODS FOR CHANGE IN PRINCIPLE If a change in accounting principle is caused by a new pronouncement by an authoritative accounting body, the cumulative effect may be reported retroactively or currently, depending on the instructions contained in the pronouncement. The APB generally favored the reporting procedures described in the previous section, that is, current recognition of the cumulative effect. However, it identified the following four specific changes as being of such a nature that the "advantages of retroactive treatment in prior periods' reports outweigh the disadvantages."[6]

1. A change from LIFO method of inventory pricing to another method.
2. A change in the method of accounting for long-term construction contracts.
3. A change to or from the full cost method of accounting used in extractive industries.
4. Changes made at the time of an initial distribution of company stock.[7]

STOP & THINK Do these four exceptions have anything in common with one another that might have caused the APB to treat them differently? Think big.

In addition to these exceptions, several FASB statements require retroactive restatement.

In those cases where retroactive restatement is required, the cumulative effect of the change is recorded directly as an adjustment to the beginning retained earnings balance for the earliest year presented. Income statement data reported for comparative purposes also must be adjusted to reflect the new principle.

To illustrate the procedures required for restatement, assume that in 2002 the Forester Company changed from the LIFO inventory costing method to the FIFO method for both financial reporting and income tax purposes. There are no deferred tax consequences because both the old and new methods apply to both financial and tax reporting. However, additional taxes will be payable for prior years

---

6 Ibid., par. 27.

7 Ibid., par. 29. This exception is available only once for a company, and it may be used for (a) obtaining additional equity capital from investors, (b) effecting business combinations, or (c) registering securities, whenever a company first issues financial statements.

► THE CHANGE FROM FIFO TO LIFO

In 1974, more firms switched their inventory to LIFO than in any other year. As noted in Chapter 9, if LIFO is used for tax purposes, it must also be used for financial reporting purposes. In periods of rising prices, as was the case in 1974, LIFO results in a lower reported net income figure for both financial and tax purposes. Thus, the use of LIFO can result in significant tax savings.

Given these potential savings, one author wondered why more firms didn't switch. Professor Gary Biddle examined 105 firms that did not switch to LIFO during 1974 and estimated that those firms paid, on average, $12 million each in additional taxes simply because they used FIFO rather than LIFO. He concludes by stating, "It is puzzling why so many firms in so many industries have continued to use FIFO." Biddle's research results were questioned by two other professors, who surveyed the controllers of 380 corporations and asked them why they didn't switch from FIFO to LIFO. These controllers provided a number of reasons, among them the claim that "the recordkeeping requirements of LIFO are burdensome and costly," presumably costly enough to

as a result of the change in inventory method used for tax purposes. The following data are applicable, and a tax rate of 30% is assumed for all years.

Year	Pretax Income		Pretax Income Difference	Income Tax Effect (30%)	Effect on Income (Net of Tax)
	FIFO	LIFO			
Prior to 2000	$190,000	$160,000	$30,000	$ 9,000	$21,000
2000	110,000	75,000	35,000	10,500	24,500
2001	120,000	100,000	20,000	6,000	14,000
Totals—beginning of 2002	$420,000	$335,000	$85,000	$25,500	$59,500
2002 results	$125,000	$100,000	$25,000	$ 7,500	$17,500

The entry in 2002 to record the prior-period effects of the change in accounting principle would be:

Inventory	85,000	
Income Taxes Payable		25,500
Retained Earnings		59,500

The $85,000 debit to Inventory adjusts the beginning 2002 inventory to its FIFO cost. The $59,500 reflects the after-tax effect on cost of goods sold in years prior to 2002. Cost of goods sold would have been lower using FIFO and pretax income would have been higher, resulting in additional taxes of $25,500. Assumed comparative income statement data, restated for 2001 and 2000, would be presented as follows:

Forester Company
Partial Comparative Income Statement
For Years Ended December 31

	2002	2001	2000
Income before income taxes	$125,000	$120,000	$110,000
Income taxes (30%)	37,500	36,000	33,000
Net income	$ 87,500	$ 84,000	$ 77,000
Earnings per share (10,000 shares outstanding)	$ 8.75	$ 8.40	$ 7.70

outweigh the $12 million in potential tax savings identi-fied by Biddle. Biddle responded to these survey results by writing: "A follow-up questionnaire would provide welcome evidence on this hypothesis (and may reveal some lucrative employment opportunities for cost accountants)."

QUESTIONS

1. If inventory costing $100 is purchased by a firm, how much is paid for that inventory if the FIFO inventory method is used? How much if the LIFO method is used?

2. Why might firms elect not to switch to LIFO given the tax savings they could receive?

3. How is a change to LIFO reported in the financial statements?

SOURCES:

Gary C. Biddle, "Paying FIFO Taxes: Your Favorite Charity," *The Wall Street Journal,* January 19, 1981.
Michael H. Granof and Daniel G. Short, "For Some Companies, FIFO Accounting Makes Sense," *The Wall Street Journal,* August 30, 1982.
Gary C. Biddle, "Taking Stock of Inventory Accounting Choices," *The Wall Street Journal,* September 15, 1982.

> **Caution!** Note that ending retained earnings is derived directly from adjusted beginning retained earnings rather than from retained earnings as previously reported. This format is different from what you have studied in earlier chapters.

The adjustment for the cumulative effect of the change in principle would be reported in Forester Company's statement of retained earnings. Assuming a beginning retained earnings balance in 2000 of $351,000 and no dividends, a comparative retained earnings statement would appear as shown below.

Note that no pro forma information is required with the retroactive approach because the statements for prior years are restated directly. If prior years' income statements cannot be presented because of inadequate data, that fact should be disclosed. Under those circumstances, the cumulative effect would be reported only in the retained earnings statement.

Forester Company
Comparative Statement of Retained Earnings
For Years Ended December 31

	2002	2001	2000
Retained earnings at beginning of year, as previously reported	$473,500	$403,500	$351,000
Add adjustment for cumulative effect on prior years of retroactively applying the FIFO method of inventory costing (see Note A)	59,500	45,500	21,000
Adjusted retained earnings, beginning of year	$533,000	$449,000	$372,000
Net income	87,500	84,000	77,000
Retained earnings, end of year	$620,500	$533,000	$449,000

Note A Change in Accounting Principle Forester Company has changed its inventory costing method from last-in, first-out (LIFO) to first-in, first-out (FIFO), effective January 1, 2002. The new inventory method was adopted to better reflect company earnings and inventory values. The financial statements have been restated to apply the new method retroactively. Because income tax laws permit the use of LIFO for tax purposes only if it is also used for financial reporting, the FIFO method has also been adopted for income tax reporting. As a result, an additional tax liability of $25,500 was incurred for years prior to 2002. The effect of the accounting change on income in 2002 (net of taxes of $7,500) was an increase of $17,500, or $1.75 per share. The effect in 2001 (net of taxes) was an increase of $14,000, and in 2000, an increase of $24,500. The retained earnings balances for 2002, 2001, and 2000 have been adjusted to reflect the cumulative effect of retroactively applying the new method of inventory costing, net of applicable taxes.

Determine when a change in reporting entity has occurred, and understand the disclosure requirements associated with this change.

Change in Reporting Entity

Companies sometimes change their structures or report their operations in such a way that the financial statements are, in effect, those of a different reporting entity. Specifically, a **change in reporting entity** includes (a) presenting consolidated or combined statements in place of statements of individual companies, (b) changing specific subsidiaries comprising the group of companies for which consolidated statements are presented, (c) changing the companies included in combined financial statements, and (d) a business combination accounted for as a pooling of interests.[8]

Because of the basic objective of comparability, the APB required that financial statements be adjusted retroactively to disclose what the statements would have looked like if the current entity had been in existence in the prior years. Thus, previous years' financial statements presented for comparison with the current year (the year of change) must be restated to reflect results of operations, financial condition, and cash flows as if the current reporting entity had been in existence in those years. Also, in the period of the change, the financial statements should disclose the nature of, and reasons for, the change, as illustrated in the note included in PACIFIC BELL's 1998 annual report, as shown in Exhibit 20-6. Pacific Bell provides landline telecommunications services to about 18 million lines in California.

The statements also should disclose the effect of the change on income from continuing operations, net income, and the related EPS amounts for all periods presented. Subsequent years' statements do not need to repeat the disclosure.[9] Changes in reporting entities are covered in more depth in advanced accounting texts.

> **FYI:** The issuance of FASB Statement No. 94, "Consolidation of All Majority-Owned Subsidiaries," resulted in hundreds of large companies having to provide revised financial statements. Examples include IBM, GENERAL MOTORS, FORD, and GENERAL MILLS.

EXHIBIT 20-6 | Pacific Bell—Disclosure of Change in Reporting Entity

Basis of Presentation—The consolidated financial statements include the accounts of Pacific Bell (PacBell, which also includes its subsidiary Pacific Bell Information Services). PacBell is a wholly-owned subsidiary of Pacific Telesis Group (PAC), a wholly-owned subsidiary of SBC Communications Inc. (SBC). PacBell operates in the telecommunications industry providing landline services in California. On March 31, 1998, PacBell distributed the shares of Pacific Bell Directory, Pacific Bell Mobile Services, Pacific Bell Internet Services and PB COMM Switches, Inc. to PAC. PacBell has accounted for this distribution as a change in reporting entity. The financial statements of all periods presented have been restated to show financial information for the new reporting entity.

The following information was extracted from the 1997 and 1998 10-K filings by Pacific Bell. (Numbers are in millions.)

	1997 Results as Originally Reported	1997 Results as Restated
Net operating revenues	$9,938	$8,726
Net income	350	345
Total assets	15,503	14,339

---

8 Ibid., par. 12.
9 Ibid., par. 35.

Recognize the various types of errors that can occur in the accounting process, understand when errors counterbalance, and be able to correct errors when necessary.

ERROR CORRECTIONS

Error corrections are not considered accounting changes, but their treatment is specified in APB Opinion No. 20 and reaffirmed in FASB Statement No. 16.[10] In effect, **accounting errors** made in prior years that have not already been "counterbalanced" or reversed are reported as prior-period adjustments and recorded directly to Retained Earnings. Examples of errors include mathematical mistakes, improper application of accounting principles, or omissions of material facts.

Kinds of Errors

There are a number of different kinds of errors. Some errors are discovered in the period in which they are made, and these are easily corrected. Others may not be discovered currently and are reflected on the financial statements until discovered. Some errors are never discovered; however, the effects of these errors may be counterbalanced in subsequent periods, and after this takes place, account balances are again accurately stated. Errors may be classified as follows:

1. *Errors discovered currently in the course of normal accounting procedures.* Examples of this type of error are clerical errors, such as an addition error, posting to the wrong account, misstating an account, or omitting an account from the trial balance. These types of errors usually are detected during the regular summarizing process of the accounting cycle and are readily corrected.
2. *Errors limited to balance sheet accounts.* Examples include debiting Accounts Receivable instead of Notes Receivable, crediting Interest Payable instead of Notes Payable, or crediting Interest Payable instead of Salaries Payable. Another example is not recording the exchange of convertible bonds for stock. Such errors are frequently discovered and corrected in the period in which they are made. When such errors are not found until a subsequent period, corrections must be made at that time and balance sheet data subsequently restated for comparative reporting purposes.
3. *Errors limited to income statement accounts.* The examples and correcting procedures for this type of error are similar to those in (2). For example, Office Salaries may be debited instead of Sales Salaries. This type of error should be corrected as soon as it is discovered. Even though the error would not affect net income, the misstated accounts should be restated for analysis purposes and comparative reporting.
4. *Errors affecting both income statement accounts and balance sheet accounts.* Certain errors, when not discovered currently, result in the misstatement of net income and thus affect both the income statement accounts and the balance sheet accounts. The balance sheet accounts are carried into the succeeding period; hence, an error made currently and not detected will affect earnings of the future. Such errors may be classified into two groups:
   (a) *Errors in net income that, when not detected, are automatically counterbalanced in the following fiscal period.* Net income amounts on the income statements for two successive periods are inaccurately stated; certain account balances on the balance sheet at the end of the first period are inaccurately stated, but the account balances in the balance sheet at the end of the succeeding period are accurately stated. In this class are errors such as the misstatement of inventories and the omission of adjustments for prepaid and accrued items at the end of the period.
   (b) *Errors in net income that, when not detected, are not automatically counterbalanced in the following fiscal period.* Account balances on successive

---

10 *Statement of Financial Accounting Standards No. 16*, "Prior-Period Adjustments," Stamford, CT: Financial Accounting Standards Board, 1977, p. 5.

balance sheets are inaccurately stated until such time as entries are made compensating for or correcting the errors. In this class are errors such as the recognition of capital expenditures as revenue expenditures and the omission of charges for depreciation and amortization.

When errors affecting income are discovered, careful analysis is necessary to determine the required action to correct the account balances. As indicated, most errors will be caught and corrected prior to closing the books. The few material errors not detected until subsequent periods and those that have not already been counterbalanced must be treated as prior-period adjustments.

The following sections describe and illustrate the procedures to be applied when error corrections require prior-period adjustments. It is assumed that each of the errors is material. Errors that are discovered usually affect the income tax liability for a prior period. Amended tax returns are usually prepared either to claim a refund or to pay any additional tax assessment. For simplicity, the examples on the following pages and in the exercises and problems at the end of the chapter ignore the income tax effects of errors.

Illustrative Example of Error Correction

> **Caution!** Errors (1) through (6) provide examples of errors that will counterbalance over two periods. However, errors that will "fix themselves" still result in misstated financial statements for the two-year period. Investors and creditors may make ill-advised decisions based on those misstated financial statements.

Assume Supply Master, Inc., began operations at the beginning of 2000. An auditing firm is engaged for the first time in 2002. Before the accounts are adjusted and closed for 2002, the auditor reviews the books and accounts and discovers the errors summarized on pages 1156 and 1157. Effects of these errors on the financial statements, before any correcting entries, are indicated as follows: A plus sign (+) indicates an overstatement; a minus sign (–) indicates an understatement. Each error correction is discussed in the following paragraphs.

(1) UNDERSTATEMENT OF MERCHANDISE INVENTORY It is discovered that the merchandise inventory as of December 31, 2000, was understated by $1,000. The effects of the misstatement were as follows:

	Income Statement	Balance Sheet
2000:	Cost of goods sold overstated (ending inventory too low)	Assets understated (inventory too low)
	Net income understated	Retained earnings understated
2001:	Cost of goods sold understated (beginning inventory too low)	Balance sheet items not affected, retained earnings understatement for 2000 being
	Net income overstated	corrected by net income overstatement for 2001

Because this type of error counterbalances after two years, no correcting entry is required in 2002.

> **Caution!** This entry is made only if the error is identified at the end of 2001.

If the error had been discovered in 2001 instead of 2002, an entry would have been made to correct the account balances so that operations for 2001 would be reported accurately. The beginning inventory for 2001 would have been increased by $1,000, the amount of the asset understatement, and Retained Earnings would have been credited for this amount, representing the income understatement in 2000. The correcting entry in 2001 would have been:

Merchandise Inventory	1,000	
Retained Earnings		1,000

(2) FAILURE TO RECORD MERCHANDISE PURCHASES It is discovered that purchase invoices as of December 28, 2000, for $850 were not recorded until 2001. The goods were included in the inventory at the end of 2000. The effects of failure to record the purchases were as follows:

	Income Statement	Balance Sheet
2000:	Cost of goods sold understated (purchases too low) Net income overstated	Liabilities understated (accounts payable too low) Retained earnings overstated
2001:	Cost of goods sold overstated (purchases too high) Net income understated	Balance sheet items not affected, retained earnings overstatement for 2000 being corrected by net income understatement for 2001

Because this is a counterbalancing error, no correcting entry is required in 2002.

If the error had been discovered in 2001 instead of 2002, a correcting entry would have been necessary. In 2001, Purchases was debited and Accounts Payable credited for $850 for merchandise acquired in 2000 and included in the ending inventory of 2000. Retained Earnings would have to be debited for $850, representing the net income overstatement for 2000, and Purchases would have to be credited for the same amount to reduce the balance in 2001. The correcting entry in 2001 would have been:

Retained Earnings	850	
Purchases		850

(3) FAILURE TO RECORD MERCHANDISE SALES It is discovered that sales on account for the last week of December 2001 for $1,800 were not recorded until 2002. The goods sold were not included in the inventory at the end of 2001. The effects of the failure to report the revenue in 2001 were:

	Income Statement	Balance Sheet
2001:	Revenue understated (sales too low) Net income understated	Assets understated (accounts receivable too low) Retained earnings understated

When the error is discovered in 2002, Sales is debited for $1,800 and Retained Earnings is credited for this amount, representing the net income understatement for 2001. The following entry is made:

Sales	1,800	
Retained Earnings		1,800

(4) FAILURE TO RECORD ACCRUED EXPENSE Accrued sales salaries of $450 as of December 31, 2000, were overlooked in adjusting the accounts. Sales Salaries is debited for salary payments. The effects of the failure to record the accrued expense of $450 as of December 31, 2000, were as follows:

	Income Statement	Balance Sheet
2000:	Expenses understated (sales salaries too low) Net income overstated	Liabilities understated (accrued salaries not reported) Retained earnings overstated
2001:	Expenses overstated (sales salaries too high) Net income understated	Balance sheet items not affected, retained earnings overstatement for 2000 being corrected by net income understatement for 2001

No entry is required in 2002 to correct the accounts for the failure to record the accrued expense at the end of 2000—the misstatement in 2000 having been counterbalanced by the misstatement in 2001. If the error had been discovered in 2001, an entry would have been required to correct the accounts for the failure to record the accrued expense at the end of 2000 if the net income for 2001 is not to be misstated. If accrued expenses are to be properly recorded at the end of 2001, Retained Earnings would be

Analysis Sheet to Show Effects

	At End of 2000			
	Income Statement		Balance Sheet	
	Section	Net Income	Section	Retained Earnings
(1) Understatement of merchandise inventory of $1,000 on December 31, 2000.	Cost of Goods Sold +	−	Current Assets −	−
(2) Failure to record merchandise purchases on account of $850 in 2000; purchases were recorded in 2001.	Cost of Goods Sold −	+	Current Liabilities −	+
(3) Failure to record merchandise sales on account of $1,800 in 2001. (It is assumed that the sales for 2001 were recognized as revenue in 2002.)				
(4) Failure to record accrued sales salaries of $450 on December 31, 2000; expense was recognized when payment was made.	Selling Expense −	+	Current Liabilities −	+
(5) Failure to record prepaid taxes of $275 on December 31, 2000; amount was included in Miscellaneous General Expense.	General Expense +	−	Current Assets −	−
(6) Failure to record accrued interest on notes receivable of $150 on December 31, 2000; revenue was recognized when collected in 2001.	Other Revenue −	−	Current Assets −	−
(7) Failure to record unearned service fees of $225 on December 31, 2001; amount received was included in Miscellaneous Revenue.				
(8) Failure to record depreciation of delivery equipment. On December 31, 2000, $1,200.	Selling Expense −	+	Noncurrent Assets +	+
On December 31, 2001, $1,200.				

debited for $450, representing the net income overstatement for 2000, and Sales Salaries would be credited for the same amount, representing the amount to be subtracted from salary payments in 2001. The correcting entry made in 2001 would be:

Retained Earnings	450	
Sales Salaries		450

(5) FAILURE TO RECORD PREPAID EXPENSE It is discovered that Miscellaneous General Expense for 2000 included taxes of $275 that should have been deferred in adjusting the accounts on December 31, 2000. The effects of the failure to record the prepaid expense were as follows:

	Income Statement	Balance Sheet
2000:	Expenses overstated (miscellaneous general expense too high) Net income understated	Assets understated (prepaid taxes not reported) Retained earnings understated
2001:	Expenses understated (miscellaneous general expense too low) Net income overstated	Balance sheet items not affected, retained earnings understatement for 2000 being corrected by net income overstatement for 2001

Because this is a counterbalancing error, no entry to correct the accounts is required in 2002.

of Errors on Financial Statements

| At End of 2001 | | | | At End of 2002 | | | |
| Income Statement | | Balance Sheet | | Income Statement | | Balance Sheet | |
Section	Net Income	Section	Retained Earnings	Section	Net Income	Section	Retained Earnings
Cost of Goods Sold −	+						
Cost of Goods Sold +	−						
Sales −		Accounts Receivable −	−	Sales +	+		
Selling Expense +	−						
General Expense −	+						
Other Revenue +	+						
Other Revenue +	+	Current Liabilities −	+	Other Revenue −	−		
		Noncurrent Assets +	+			Noncurrent Assets +	+
Selling Expense −	+	Noncurrent Assets +	+			Noncurrent Assets +	+

If the error had been discovered in 2001 instead of 2002, a correcting entry would have been necessary. If prepaid taxes were properly recorded at the end of 2001, Miscellaneous General Expense would have to be debited for $275, the expense relating to operations of 2001, and Retained Earnings would have to be credited for the same amount, representing the net income understatement for 2000. The correcting entry in 2001 would have been:

Miscellaneous General Expense...	275	
Retained Earnings		275

(6) FAILURE TO RECORD ACCRUED REVENUE Accrued interest on notes receivable of $150 was overlooked in adjusting the accounts on December 31, 2000. The revenue was recognized when the interest was collected in 2001. The effects of the failure to record the accrued revenue were:

	Income Statement	**Balance Sheet**
2000:	Revenue understated (interest revenue too low) Net income understated	Assets understated (interest receivable not reported) Retained earnings understated
2001:	Revenue overstated (interest revenue too high) Net income overstated	Balance sheet items not affected, retained earnings understatement for 2000 being corrected by net income overstatement for 2001

Because the balance sheet items at the end of 2001 were correctly stated, no entry to correct the accounts is required in 2002.

If the error had been discovered in 2001 instead of 2002, an entry would have been necessary to correct the account balances. If accrued interest on notes receivable had been properly recorded at the end of 2001, Interest Revenue would have to be debited for $150, the amount to be subtracted from receipts of 2001, and Retained Earnings would have to be credited for the same amount, representing the net income understatement for 2000. The correcting entry in 2001 would have been:

Interest Revenue	150	
Retained Earnings		150

(7) FAILURE TO RECORD UNEARNED REVENUE Fees of $225 received in advance for miscellaneous services as of December 31, 2001, were overlooked in adjusting the accounts. Miscellaneous Revenue had been credited when fees were received. The effects of the failure to recognize the unearned revenue of $225 at the end of 2001 were as follows:

	Income Statement	Balance Sheet
2001:	Revenue overstated (miscellaneous revenue too high)	Liabilities understated (unearned service fees not reported)
	Net income overstated	Retained earnings overstated

> **Caution!** Error (8) does not counterbalance. Thus, financial statements have the potential to be misstated for several years. In this example, the error could continue until the account is written off.

An entry is required to correct the accounts for the failure to record the unearned revenue at the end of 2001 if the net income for 2002 is not to be misstated. If the unearned revenue were properly recorded at the end of 2002, Retained Earnings would be debited for $225, representing the net income overstatement for 2001, and Miscellaneous Revenue would be credited for the same amount, representing the revenue that is to be identified with 2002. The correcting entry is:

Retained Earnings	225	
Miscellaneous Revenue		225

(8) FAILURE TO RECORD DEPRECIATION Delivery equipment was acquired at the beginning of 2000 at a cost of $6,000. The equipment has an estimated five-year life, and depreciation of $1,200 was overlooked at the end of 2000 and 2001. The effects of the failure to record depreciation for 2000 were as follows:

	Income Statement	Balance Sheet
2000:	Expenses understated (depreciation of delivery equipment too low)	Assets overstated (accumulated depreciation of delivery equipment too low)
	Net income overstated	Retained earnings overstated
2001:	Expenses not affected	Assets overstated (accumulated depreciation of delivery equipment too low)
	Net income not affected	Retained earnings overstated

It should be observed that the misstatements arising from the failure to record depreciation are not counterbalanced in the succeeding year.

Failure to record depreciation for 2001 affected the statements as follows:

	Income Statement	Balance Sheet
2001:	Expenses understated (depreciation of delivery equipment too low)	Assets overstated (accumulated depreciation of delivery equipment too low)
	Net income overstated	Retained earnings overstated

When the omission is recognized, Retained Earnings must be decreased by the net income overstatements of prior years and Accumulated Depreciation must be increased by the depreciation that should have been recorded. The correcting entry in 2002 for depreciation that should have been recognized for 2000 and 2001 is as follows:

Retained Earnings...	2,400	
Accumulated Depreciation—Delivery Equipment		2,400

Required Disclosure for Prior-Period Adjustments

STOP & THINK In addition to the depreciation example, can you identify other types of errors that would not counterbalance?

If an error is discovered that affected a prior period, the nature of the error, its effect on previously issued financial statements, and the effect of its correction on current period's net income and EPS should be disclosed in the period in which the error is corrected.[11]

An example of the disclosure provided when an error correction is made through a prior-period adjustment is given in Exhibit 20–7; the error correction was made in 1998 by IMAGE SOFTWARE, which develops and markets a software product for electronic document image management and retrieval.

EXHIBIT 20–7 | Image Software—Disclosure of Error Correction

11. PRIOR PERIOD ADJUSTMENT

In prior years, the Company recognized an asset for the cash value build-up in an officer's life insurance policy. The recording of this asset was subsequently determined to be an error, which resulted in both the overstatement and the understatement of previously reported other assets and operating expenses. This error was retroactively corrected in 1998, resulting in the following changes to retained earnings as of December 31, 1997 and 1996, and the related statements of operations for the years ended December 31, 1997 and 1996. The effect on loss per common share is negligible.

	Accumulated Deficit	Net Loss
As previously reported, December 31, 1996	$(5,470,944)	$ (89,074)
Correction for years ended prior to December 31, 1996	(31,601)	—
Removal of recorded cash value build-up in officers' life insurance	(7,086)	(7,086)
As adjusted, December 31, 1996	$(5,509,631)	$ (96,160)
As previously reported, December 31, 1997	$(5,946,203)	$(475,259)
Correction for years ended prior to December 31, 1997	(38,687)	—
Removal of recorded cash value build-up in officer's life insurance	(8,824)	(8,824)
As adjusted, December 31, 1997	$(5,993,714)	$(484,083)

SUMMARY OF ACCOUNTING CHANGES AND ERROR CORRECTIONS

The summary on the following page presents the appropriate accounting procedures applicable to each of the four main categories covered in APB Opinion No. 20. Naturally, accountants must apply these guidelines with judgment and should seek to provide the most relevant and reliable information possible.

---

11 *Opinions of the Accounting Principle Board No. 20, par. 37.*

Summary of Procedures for Reporting Accounting Changes and Error Corrections

Category	Accounting Procedures
I. Change in estimate	1. Adjust either current-period results or current- and future-period results. 2. No separate cumulative adjustment or restated financial statements. 3. No pro forma disclosure needed.
II. Change in accounting principle A. Current recognition of cumulative effect	1. Adjust for cumulative effect, i.e., a "catch-up" of adjustment in current period as special item in income statement. 2. No restated financial statements. 3. Pro forma data required showing income and EPS information for all periods presented.
B. Restatement of prior periods	1. Direct cumulative adjustment to beginning retained earnings balance of earliest year presented in the financial statements. 2. Restate financial statements to reflect new principle for comparative purposes. 3. No pro forma information required because prior-periods' statements are changed directly.
III. Change in reporting entity	1. Restate financial statements as though new entity had been in existence for all periods presented.
IV. Error corrections	1. If detected in period error occurred, correct accounts through normal accounting cycle adjustments. 2. If detected in a subsequent period, adjust for effect of material errors by making prior-period adjustments directly to retained earnings balance for the years affected by those errors. If the error relates to a year that is not presented in the financial statements, then the retained earnings balance for the earliest year presented is adjusted. 3. Once an error is discovered in previously issued financial statements, the nature of the error, its effect on the financial statements, and its effect on the current period's income and EPS should be disclosed.

Describe the differences between the U.S. approach to accounting changes and error corrections and the international approach found in IAS 8.

ACCOUNTING CHANGES AND ERROR CORRECTIONS UNDER IAS 8

The primary difference between the U.S. approach to accounting changes and error corrections and the provisions of IAS 8 is that the international standard allows alternative treatments that differ from U.S. GAAP. The provisions of IAS 8 and its significant differences from U.S. GAAP are discussed below.[12]

Change in Accounting Estimate

According to IAS 8, a change in an accounting estimate is reflected in the current and future periods; this treatment is consistent with U.S. GAAP. A difference in application is seen in accounting for a change in depreciation method, such as from an accelerated method to a straight-line method. Under IAS 8, a change in depreciation method is classified as a change in estimate; such a change is classified as a change in accounting principle under U.S. GAAP.

Change in Accounting Principle

Under IAS 8, the recommended approach for accounting for a change in accounting principle is that results from prior periods should be restated; a cumulative adjustment is

---

12 IAS 8 does not include any provisions for accounting for a change in reporting entity.

reported in the beginning retained earnings balance of the earliest period presented. As discussed earlier in the chapter, this approach is followed under U.S. GAAP for only a small set of accounting changes. As an allowable alternative to this approach, IAS 8 also allows a change in accounting principle to be accounted for by reflecting the cumulative effect of the change in the income of the current period without restating prior-period results. This allowable alternative is the same as the most commonly used approach in the United States. This alternative is included in IAS 8 because the laws of some countries do not allow companies to retroactively restate financial results that have already been formally submitted to the government.

Error Corrections

The benchmark treatment for accounting for a significant error correction under IAS 8 is the same as that required under U.S. GAAP—the effect of the error is reflected as an adjustment to the beginning retained earnings balance of the earliest period presented, and all past periods presented are restated to correct for the impact of the error. As with a change in accounting principle, IAS 8 includes an alternative that allows the error correction to be accounted for by reflecting the effect of the error correction in income of the period in which the error was discovered without restating previously reported results.

As seen in the accounting for accounting changes and for error corrections, IAS 8 reflects a preference for restating prior results to improve comparability of financial statements. U.S. GAAP requires restatement for error corrections but not for most accounting changes.

REVIEW OF LEARNING OBJECTIVES

1 **Understand the three different types of accounting changes that have been identified by accounting standard setters.** The accounting profession has identified three different types of accounting changes: change in accounting estimate, change in accounting principle, and change in reporting entity. The distinction among the three is important, as different accounting treatment and disclosure is required for each type of accounting change.

2 **Recognize the difference between a change in accounting estimate and a change in accounting principle, and know how a change in accounting estimate is reflected in the financial statements.** A change in accounting estimate does not involve a restatement of prior periods' financial statements. Instead, the effects of these types of changes are reflected in the current and future periods. Previous chapters discussed the accounting for common areas involving changing estimates. Examples include bad debts expense (Chapter 6), depreciation (Chapter 12), and actuarial assumptions (Chapter 17).

3 **Determine if a change in accounting principle requires a cumulative adjustment relating to its effect or a restatement of prior-periods' financial statements, and be able to compute the necessary adjustment.** Changes in accounting principle can be one of two types. The more general case involves reporting a cumulative adjustment on the income statement in the period of the change. Pro forma information is also provided in the notes, disclosing the effect on net income in prior periods of the new accounting method. In certain cases, a change in accounting principle is accounted for by adjusting the beginning retained earnings balance for the earliest year being reported and then restating the income statement for each year being reported to reflect the new accounting method.

4 **Determine when a change in reporting entity has occurred, and understand the disclosure requirements associated with this change.** A change in reporting entity includes preparing consolidated financial statements for the first time, significantly changing specific subsidiaries included in consolidated financial statements, or accounting for a business combination as a pooling of interests. In these instances, prior years' financial statements are restated to reflect the results of operations as if the current reporting entity had been in existence for the entire reporting period.

5 Recognize the various types of errors that can occur in the accounting process, understand when errors counterbalance, and be able to correct errors when necessary. Numerous errors can occur in the accounting process. Many of those errors will be discovered and corrected in the normal course of business. Some errors will be detected after the books have been closed for an accounting period, thereby requiring an adjustment to the retained earnings

balance. Most errors that go undetected counterbalance over a two-year period, but those that do not often require a cumulative adjustment once they are detected.

6 Describe the differences between the U.S. approach to accounting changes and error corrections and the international approach found in IAS 8. Under IAS 8, the recommended approach for accounting for both an accounting change and an error correction is that results from prior periods should be restated; a cumulative adjustment is reported in the beginning retained earnings balance of the earliest period presented. In both cases, allowable alternative treatments allow the effect of the change or the error to be included in current income with no restatement of prior results.

KEY TERMS

Accounting changes 1142

Accounting errors 1153

Change in accounting estimate 1144

Change in accounting principle 1145

Change in reporting entity 1152

QUESTIONS

1. How do accounting changes detract from the informational characteristics of comparability and consistency as described in FASB Concepts Statement No. 2?

2. List the three categories of accounting changes and explain briefly why such changes are made.

3. What alternative procedures have been suggested as solutions for reporting accounting changes?

4. (a) List several examples of areas where changes in accounting estimates are often made. (b) Explain briefly the proper accounting treatment for a change in estimate. (c) Why is this procedure considered proper for recording changes in accounting estimates?

5. (a) List several examples of changes in accounting principle that a company may make. (b) Explain briefly the proper accounting treatment for recognizing currently a change in accounting principle.

6. What information should pro forma statements include?

7. Why does a change in accounting principle require justification?

8. (a) When should the effects of a change in accounting principle be reported as a restatement of prior periods? (b) Although no justification was given by the APB for selecting certain items for special treatment, what might be a possible reason?

9. The Dallas Company purchased a delivery van in 1999. At the time of purchase, the van's service life was estimated to be 7 years with a salvage value of $500. The company has been using the straight-line method of depreciation. During 2002, the company determined that because of extensive use, the van's service life would be only 5 years with no salvage value. Also, the company has decided to change the depreciation method used from straight-line to the sum-of-the-years'-digits method. How would these changes be treated?

10. (a) List the four types of changes in reporting entities that might occur. (b) How are these changes treated? (c) What assumption does the treatment of a change in reporting entity make?

11. Describe the effect on current net income, beginning retained earnings, individual asset accounts, and contra asset accounts when:

    (a) Depreciation is changed from the straight-line method to an accelerated method.

    (b) Depreciation is changed from an accelerated method to the straight-line method.

    (c) Income on construction contracts that had been reported on a completed-contract basis is now reported on the percentage-of-completion basis.

(d) The valuation of inventories is changed from a FIFO to a LIFO basis.

(e) It is determined that warranty expenses in prior years should have been 5% of sales instead of 4%.

(f) The valuation of inventories is changed from a LIFO to a FIFO basis.

(g) Your accounts receivable clerk has learned that a major customer has declared bankruptcy.

(h) Your patent lawyer informs you that your rival has perfected and patented a new invention making your product obsolete.

12. (a) How are accounting errors to be treated? (b) What are counterbalancing errors?

13. The Mendez Manufacturing Company failed to record accrued interest for 1999, $800; 2000, $700; and 2001, $950. What is the amount of overstate- ment or understatement of the retained earnings account at December 31, 2002?

14. Goods purchased FOB shipping point were shipped to Merkley & Co. on December 31, 2002. The pur- chase was recorded in 2002, but the goods were not included in ending inventory. (a) What effect would this error have had on reported income for 2002 had it not been discovered? (b) What entry should be made on the books to correct this error assum- ing the books have not yet been closed for 2002?

15. How does the accounting for a change in deprecia- tion method differ under IAS 8 from the approach used under U.S. GAAP?

16. How does the accounting for a change in account- ing principle differ under IAS 8 from the approach used under U.S. GAAP?

DISCUSSION CASES

CASE 20–1

ACCOUNTING CHANGES

Situation A: Tucker Corporation has determined that the depreciable lives of several operat- ing machines are too long and therefore do not fairly match the cost of the assets with the revenues produced. Tucker therefore decides to reduce the depreciable lives of these machines by 3 years.

Situation B: Trent Company decides that at the beginning of the year, it will adopt the straight-line method of depreciation for plant equipment. The straight-line method will be used for new acquisitions as well as for the previously acquired plant equipment, which had been accounted for using an accelerated depreciation method.

What types of accounting changes are involved in the 2 situations? Describe the method of reporting the changes under current GAAP. Where applicable, explain how the reported amounts are computed.

CASE 20–2

CHANGE IN ACCOUNTING PRINCIPLE OR CHANGE IN ACCOUNTING ESTIMATE?

Jill Stanton, president of Central Company, is confused about why your accounting firm has recommended that she report certain events as changes in principle instead of changes in estimate, which is what Jill thought they should be. She has asked you for an explanation. Describe a change in an accounting principle and a change in accounting estimate. Explain how each would be reported in the income statement of the period of change.

CASE 20–3

WHY DO THEY MAKE THE CHANGE?

An interesting phenomenon can sometimes occur when companies are in danger of not meeting their projected earnings goals. Management suddenly realizes that they have been far too conservative in their previous estimates associated with bad debts, estimated useful lives of equipment, and residual values, to name a few. With this newfound realization, management proceeds to revise these estimates to, as is often stated, "more closely reflect economic reality."

What is the primary difference in financial statement disclosure between a change in estimate and a change in principle? Why do you think managers who are in danger of not meeting their goals would prefer to revise an accounting estimate rather than change an accounting principle?

CASE 20–4

CONTINUING THAT UPWARD TREND

Hornberger Company has demonstrated a consistently increasing earnings trend over the past 10 years. Stockholders have come to expect this steady increase, and management has gone to great lengths to emphasize the smooth growth pattern associated with Hornberger's earnings.

At the year-end board of directors meeting, you, as the chief financial officer, present to the board the preliminary results for the year just ended. These results indicate a slight decline in both income from operations and net income when compared to the previous year. The chairman of the board quickly reviews the firm's earnings history and then suggests the following items for consideration.

(a) Increase the estimated useful life of the company's plant facilities from 15 to 25 years.
(b) Change the firm's estimate of bad debts from 4% of credit sales to 2.5% of credit sales.
(c) Change the firm's amortization period for goodwill from the industry average of 10 years to the maximum allowed by GAAP of 40 years.

These changes will result in income for the period that is slightly higher than that reported for the past year and will continue the upward trend. The board votes on the proposed changes and instructs you to revise the income statement to reflect the changed estimates.

How would each of the above changes be reported in the current year's annual report to shareholders? Why would the chairman of the board suggest changing accounting estimates rather than accounting principles? As the accountant, do you have a responsibility to review management's estimates for reasonableness and to evaluate the motives behind management's decision to change an accounting estimate?

CASE 20–5

HOW LONG CAN AIRPLANES FLY?

In 1994, DELTA AIR LINES depreciated its airplanes over a 15-year period and estimated a salvage value of 10% of the cost of the plane. At the same time, PAN AM depreciated identical airplanes over a 25-year period and provided for a 15% salvage value. These different assumptions resulted in markedly different operating results. For example, if one Boeing 727 costs $10 million, Delta would depreciate $260,000 more per year for 15 years than would Pan Am.

Which company's estimate of useful life more closely reflects reality? Would you feel comfortable as a passenger in an airplane that is 25 years old? Does the fact that Pan Am subsequently went out of business provide any information as to why its estimates were so substantially different from those of financially sound Delta?

CASE 20–6

CAN YOU FOOL THE MARKET?

During the 1980s, BLOCKBUSTER ENTERTAINMENT became one of the largest national video rental chains in the United States. With its rapid growth came significantly increased stock prices. Then, in 1988, Blockbuster changed the amortization period for its videotapes from 9 months to 36 months. Why do you think Blockbuster changed its estimate of the useful life of its videotapes? What do you think happened to Blockbuster's market value?

EXERCISES

EXERCISE 20–7

CHANGE IN ACCOUNTING ESTIMATE AND IN ACCOUNTING PRINCIPLE

Manchester Manufacturing purchased a machine on January 1, 1998, for $50,000. At the time, it was determined that the machine had an estimated useful life of 10 years and an estimated residual value of $2,000. The company used the double-declining-balance method of depreciation. On January 1, 2002, the company decided to change its depreciation method from double-declining-balance to straight-line. The machine's remaining useful life was estimated to be 5 years with a residual value of $500.

1. Give the entry required to record the company's depreciation expense for 2002.
2. Give the entry, if any, to record the effect of the change in depreciation methods.

EXERCISE 20–8

CHANGE IN ACCOUNTING ESTIMATE

The Curtis Company purchased a machine on January 1, 1999, for $1,500,000. At the date of acquisition, the machine had an estimated useful life of 6 years with no residual value. The machine is being depreciated on a straight-line basis. On January 1, 2002, Curtis determined, as a result of additional information, that the machine had an estimated useful life of 7 years from the date of acquisition with no residual value.

1. Give the journal entry, if any, to record the cumulative effect on prior years of changing the estimated useful life of the machine.
2. What is the amount of depreciation expense on the machine that should be charged to Curtis Company's income statement for the year ended December 31, 2002?

EXERCISE 20–9

CHANGE IN ACCOUNTING ESTIMATE

Albrecht Inc. began business in 1999. An examination of the company's allowance for bad debts account reveals the following.

	Estimated Bad Debts	Actual Bad Debts
1999	$11,000	$4,500
2000	13,000	6,800
2001	16,500	8,950
2002	No adjustment yet	9,500

In the past, the company has estimated that 3% of credit sales will be uncollectible. The accountant for Albrecht Inc. has determined that the percentage used in estimating bad debts has been inappropriate. She would like to revise the estimate downward to 1.5%. The president of the company has stated that if the previous estimates of bad debt expense were incorrect, the financial statements should be restated using the more accurate estimate.

1. Assuming credit sales for 2002 are $650,000, provide the adjusting entry to record bad debt expense for the year.
2. What catch-up entry, if any, would be made to correct the inaccurate estimates for previous years?
3. How would you respond to the president's request to restate the prior years' financial statements?

EXERCISE 20–10

CHANGE IN ACCOUNTING ESTIMATE

On January 1, 2002, management of Micro Storage Inc. determined that a revision in the estimates associated with the depreciation of storage facilities was appropriate. These facilities, purchased on January 5, 2000, for $600,000, had been depreciated using the straight-line method with an estimated salvage value of $60,000 and an estimated useful life of 20 years. Management has determined that the storage facilities' expected remaining useful life is 10 years and that they have an estimated salvage value of $80,000.

1. How much depreciation was recognized by Micro Storage in 2000 and 2001?
2. How much depreciation will be recognized by Micro Storage in 2002 as a result of the changes in estimates?
3. What journal entry is required to account for the changes in estimates at the beginning of 2002?

EXERCISE 20–11

CHANGE IN ESTIMATE OF NATURAL RESOURCES

Western Mining Company purchased a tract of land with estimated silver ore deposits totaling 400,000 tons. The purchase price for the land was $1.5 million. During the first year of operation, Western mined 50,000 tons of ore. During the second year, Western mined 110,000 tons of ore. At the beginning of the third year, new geological engineering estimates determined that a total of 300,000 tons of silver ore remained. During Year 3, 150,000 tons of ore were mined.

1.   What was the original depletion rate used by Western in Years 1 and 2?
2.   Make the accounting entries for depletion expense for Western Mining Company at the end of Years 1 and 2.
3.   What is the depletion rate for Year 3, and what accounting entry should be made to reflect the change in accounting estimate in Year 3?

EXERCISE 20–12

CHANGE IN ACCOUNTING PRINCIPLE

Modern Lighting Inc. has, in the past, depreciated its computer hardware using the straight-line method assuming a 10% salvage value and an expected useful life of 5 years. As a result of the rapid obsolescence associated with the computer industry, Modern Lighting has determined that it receives most of the benefit from its computer systems in the first few years of ownership. Therefore, Modern Lighting proposes changing to the sum-of-the-years'-digits method for depreciating its computer hardware. The following information is available regarding all of Modern Lighting's computer purchases:

	Cost
1999	$45,000
2000	25,000
2001	30,000

1.   Compute the depreciation taken by Modern Lighting during 1999, 2000, and 2001. Assume all purchases were made at the beginning of the year.
2.   Compute the amount of depreciation expense for 1999–2001, assuming sum-of-the-years'-digits had been used.
3.   Prepare the journal entry required to adjust the accounts on January 1, 2002. (Ignore income tax effects.)

EXERCISE 20–13

CHANGE IN ACCOUNTING PRINCIPLE

High Quality Construction Company has used the completed-contract method of accounting since it began operations in 1999. In 2002, for justifiable reasons, management decided to adopt the percentage-of-completion method.

The following schedule, reporting income for the past 3 years, has been prepared by the company.

	1999	2000	2001
Total revenues from completed contracts	$500,000	$1,200,000	$1,080,000
Less: Cost of completed contracts	350,000	925,000	760,000
Income from operations	$150,000	$ 275,000	$ 320,000
Extraordinary loss	0	0	(65,000)
Income	$150,000	$ 275,000	$ 255,000

Analysis of the accounting records disclosed the following income by projects, earned in the years 1999–2001 using the percentage-of-completion method.

	1999	2000	2001
Project A	$150,000		
Project B	100,000	$175,000	
Project C	70,000	280,000	$ 10,000
Project D		10,000	60,000
Project E			(40,000)

Give the journal entry required in 2002 to reflect the change in accounting principle. (Ignore income tax effects.)

EXERCISE 20–14

CHANGE IN ACCOUNTING PRINCIPLE

Diversified Manufacturing Company decides to change from an accelerated depreciation method it has used for both reporting and tax purposes to the straight-line method for reporting purposes. From the following information, prepare the income statement for the year ended December 31, 2002.

Year	Net Income as Reported	Excess of Accelerated Depreciation Over Straight-Line Depreciation	Income Effect (Net of Tax)
Prior to 1999		$12,500	$ 7,500
1999	$62,500	6,250	3,750
2000	54,500	7,500	4,500
2001	78,000	11,250	6,750
		$37,500	$22,500

In 2002, net sales were $190,000; cost of goods sold, $92,500; selling expenses, $47,500; and general and administrative expenses, $14,000. The income tax on operating income was $14,400. In addition, Diversified had a tax-deductible extraordinary loss of $16,000, net of $11,200 income tax savings.

EXERCISE 20–15

CHANGE IN ACCOUNTING PRINCIPLE INVOLVING LIFO

Assume the change in net income as shown in Exercise 20–14 is the result of a change from the LIFO method of inventory pricing to another method. During 2002, dividends of $17,500 were paid. Based on this information, prepare the retained earnings statement for 2002. The December 31, 2001, retained earnings balance as reported was $260,000.

EXERCISE 20–16

CHANGES IN ACCOUNTING ESTIMATES AND ACCOUNTING PRINCIPLES

Due to changing economic conditions and to make its financial statements more comparable to those of other companies in its industry, the management of Kelsea Inc. decided in 2002 to review its accounting practices.

On January 1, management decided to change its allowance for doubtful accounts from 2% to 3½% of its outstanding receivables balance.

On July 1, Kelsea decided to begin using the straight-line method of depreciation on its mainframe computer instead of the sum-of-the-years'-digits method. The change will be effective as of January 1, 2002. Based on further information, it also was decided that the computer has 10 more years of useful life as of January 2, 2002. Kelsea bought the computer on January 1, 1992, at a cost of $550,000. At that time, Kelsea estimated it would have a 15-year useful life. The computer has no expected salvage value. Prior years' depreciation is as follows:

Year	Amount	Year	Amount
1992	$68,750	1997	$45,833
1993	64,167	1998	41,250
1994	59,583	1999	36,667
1995	55,000	2000	32,083
1996	50,417	2001	27,500

On October 1, Kelsea determined that starting with the current year, it would depreciate the company's printing press using hours of use as the depreciation base. The press, which had been purchased on January 1, 1989, at a cost of $930,000, was being depreciated for 25 years using the straight-line method. No salvage value was anticipated. It is estimated that this type of press provides 200,000 total hours of use and, as of January 1, 2002, it had been used 76,000 hours. At the end of 2002, the plant manager determined that the press had been run 6,250 hours during the year. Ignore income taxes relating to this change.

1. Evaluate each of the foregoing changes and determine whether it is a change in estimate or a change in accounting principle.
2. Give the journal entries required at December 31, 2002, to account for the above changes. Kelsea's receivable balance at December 31, 2002, was $345,000. Allowance for Bad Debts carried a $1,000 debit balance before adjustment.

EXERCISE 20–17

ACCOUNTING ERRORS

The following errors in the accounting records of the Reed & Kinsey Partnership were discovered on January 10, 2002.

Year of Error	Ending Inventories Overstated	Depreciation Understated	Accrued Rent Revenue Not Recorded	Accrued Interest Expense Not Recorded
1999	$20,000		$ 6,000	
2000		$5,000	22,000	
2001	24,000			$2,000

The partners share net income and losses as follows: 40%, Reed; 60%, Kinsey.

1. Prepare a correcting journal entry on January 10, 2002, assuming that the books were closed for 2001.
2. Prepare a correcting journal entry on January 10, 2002, assuming that the books are still open for 2001 and that the partnership uses the perpetual inventory system.

EXERCISE 20–18

ANALYSIS OF ERRORS

State the effect of each of the following errors made in 2001 on the balance sheets and the income statements prepared in 2001 and 2002.

1. The ending inventory is understated as a result of an error in the count of goods on hand.
2. The ending inventory is overstated as a result of the inclusion of goods acquired and held on a consignment basis. No purchase was recorded on the books.
3. A purchase of merchandise at the end of 2001 is not recorded until payment is made for the goods in 2002; the goods purchased were included in the inventory at the end of 2001.
4. A sale of merchandise at the end of 2001 is not recorded until cash is received for the goods in 2002; the goods sold were excluded from the inventory at the end of 2001.
5. Goods shipped to consignees in 2001 were reported as sales; goods in the hands of consignees at the end of 2001 were not recognized for inventory purposes; sale of such goods in 2002 and collections on such sales were recorded as credits to the receivables established with consignees in 2001.
6. The total of 1 week's sales during 2001 was credited to Gain on Sale—-Machinery.
7. No depreciation is taken in 2001 for equipment sold in April 2001. The company reports on a calendar-year basis and computes depreciation to the nearest month.
8. No depreciation is taken in 2001 for equipment purchased in October 2001. The company reports on a calendar-year basis and computes depreciation to the nearest month.
9. Customer notes receivable are debited to the accounts receivable account.

EXERCISE 20–19

ERROR AND CHANGE IN ACCOUNTING PRINCIPLE

Comparative statements for Bodie Corporation are as follows:

Bodie Corporation Income Statements and Statement of Retained Earnings For the Years Ended December 31		
	2001	2000
Sales	$4,600,000	$4,350,000
Cost of goods sold	2,346,000	2,305,500
Gross profit	$2,254,000	$2,044,500
Expenses	1,598,000	1,533,000
Net income	$ 656,000	$ 511,500
Beginning retained earnings	$1,441,000	$1,077,500
Net income	656,000	511,500
Dividends	(157,000)	(148,000)
Ending retained earnings	$1,940,000	$1,441,000

In 2001, Bodie Corporation discovers that ending inventory for 2000 was understated by $11,000. In addition, Bodie decides to change its depreciation method from double-declining-balance to straight-line. The differences in the 2 depreciation methods for the assets involved are as follows:

	2001	2000
Double-declining-balance	$358,400	$448,000
Straight-line	350,000	350,000

Expenses in the income statements presented above include depreciation based on the double-declining-balance method.

Prepare comparative income and retained earnings statements for 2000 and 2001. Ignore income tax effects, and assume the 2001 books have not been closed.

EXERCISE 20–20

JOURNAL ENTRIES TO CORRECT ACCOUNTS

The first audit of the books for the Calienti Corporation was made for the year ended December 31, 2002. In reviewing the books, the auditor discovered that certain adjustments had been overlooked at the end of 2001 and 2002 and also that other items had been improperly recorded. Omissions and other failures for each year are summarized as follows:

	December 31,	
	2001	2002
Sales Salaries Payable	$1,300	$1,100
Interest Receivable	325	215
Prepaid Insurance	450	300
Advances From Customers	1,750	2,500
(Collections from customers had been included in sales but should have been recognized as advances from customers, because goods were not shipped until the following year.)		
Equipment	1,400	1,200
(Expenditures had been recognized as repairs but should have been recognized as cost of equipment; the depreciation rate on such equipment is 10% per year, but depreciation in the year of the expenditure is to be recognized at 5%.)		

Prepare journal entries to correct revenue and expense accounts for 2002 and record assets and liabilities that require recognition on the balance sheet as of December 31, 2002. Assume the nominal accounts for 2002 have not yet been closed into the income summary account.

EXERCISE 20–21

ERROR ANALYSIS

In early 2001, while reviewing Huffman Inc.'s 2000 financial records, Huffman's accountant discovered several errors. For each of the errors listed below, indicate the effect on net income (i.e., understatement, overstatement, or no effect) for both 2000 and 2001, assuming no correction is made and the company uses a periodic system for inventory.

1. Certain items of ending inventory were accidentally not counted at the end of 2000.
2. Machinery was sold in May 2000, but the company continued to deduct depreciation for the remainder of 2000, although the asset was removed from the books in May.
3. The 2000 year-end purchases of inventory were not recorded until the beginning of 2001, although the inventory was correctly counted at the end of 2000.
4. Goods sold on account in 2000 were not recorded as sales until 2001.
5. Insurance costs incurred but unpaid in 2000 were not recorded until paid in 2001.
6. Interest revenue in 2000 was not recorded until 2001.
7. The 2000 year-end purchases were not recorded until the beginning of 2001. The inventory associated with these purchases was omitted from the ending inventory count in 2000.
8. A check for January 2001 rent was received and recorded as revenue at the end of 2000.
9. Interest accrued in 2000 on a note payable was not recorded until it was paid in 2001.

PROBLEMS

PROBLEM 20–22

CHANGE IN ACCOUNTING PRINCIPLE

Yuki, Inc., acquired the following assets on January 3, 1999.

Equipment, estimated useful life 5 years; residual value $13,000	$513,000
Building, estimated useful life 40 years; no residual value	900,000

The equipment has been depreciated using the sum-of-the-years'-digits method for the first 3 years. In 2002, the company decided to change the method of depreciation to straight-line. No change was made in the estimated service life or residual value. The company also decided to change the total estimated useful life of the building from 40 to 45 years with no change in the estimated residual value. The building is depreciated on the straight-line method. The company has 200,000 shares of capital stock outstanding. Partial results of operations for 2002 and 2001 are as follows:

	2002	2001
Income before cumulative effect of change in computing depreciation for 2002; depreciation for 2002 was computed on a straight-line basis for equipment and building*	$890,000	$856,000
Earnings per share before cumulative effect of change in computing depreciation for 2002	$4.45	$4.28

*The computations for depreciation expense for 2002 and 2001 for the building were based on the original estimate of useful life of 40 years.

Instructions:

1. Compute the cumulative effect of the change in accounting principle to be reported on the income statement for 2002, and prepare the journal entry to record the change. (Ignore income tax effects.)
2. Present comparative data for the years 2001 and 2002, starting with income before cumulative effect of accounting change. Prepare pro forma data. (Ignore income tax effects).

PROBLEM 20–23

ACCOUNTING CHANGES

Barney Corporation has released the following condensed financial statements for 2000 and 2001 and has prepared the following proposed statements for 2002:

Barney Corporation
Comparative Balance Sheets
December 31

	2002	2001	2000
Assets			
Current assets	$249,000	$219,000	$165,000
Land	60,000	45,000	30,000
Equipment	150,000	150,000	150,000
Accumulated depreciation—equipment	(45,000)	(30,000)	(15,000)
Total assets	$414,000	$384,000	$330,000
Liabilities and Stockholders' Equity			
Current liabilities	$177,000	$177,000	$147,000
Common stock	60,000	60,000	60,000
Retained earnings	177,000	147,000	123,000
Total liabilities and stockholders' equity	$414,000	$384,000	$330,000

Barney Corporation
Comparative Income Statements
For the Years Ended December 31

	2002	2001	2000
Sales	$315,000	$300,000	$255,000
Cost of goods sold	$240,000	$225,000	$189,000
Other expenses except depreciation	30,000	36,000	33,000
Depreciation expense—equipment	15,000	15,000	15,000
Total costs	$285,000	$276,000	$237,000
Net income	$ 30,000	$ 24,000	$ 18,000

Barney Corporation acquired the equipment for $150,000 on January 1, 2000, and began depreciating the equipment over a 10-year estimated useful life with no salvage value, using the straight-line method of depreciation. The double-declining-balance method of depreciation, under the same assumptions, would have required the following depreciation expense:

2000	20% × $150,000 = $30,000
2001	20% × $120,000 = $24,000
2002	20% × $96,000 = $19,200

Instructions: In comparative format, prepare a balance sheet and a combined statement of income and retained earnings for 2002, giving effect to the following changes. (Ignore any income tax effect.) Barney Corporation has 10,000 shares of common stock outstanding. The following situations are independent of each other.

1. For justifiable reasons, Barney Corporation changed to the double-declining-balance method of depreciation in 2002. The effect of the change should be included in the net income of the period in which the change was made.
2. During 2002, Barney Corporation determined that the equipment was fast becoming obsolete and decided to change the estimated useful life from 10 years to 5 years. The books for 2002 had not yet been closed.
3. During 2002, Barney Corporation found that additional equipment, also acquired on January 1, 2000, costing $24,000, had been recorded in the land account and had not been depreciated. This error should be corrected using straight-line depreciation over a 10-year period.

PROBLEM 20–24

CHANGE IN ACCOUNTING ESTIMATE AND PRINCIPLE

The following information relates to depreciable assets of Brillantez Electronics.

(a) Machine A was purchased for $30,000 on January 1, 1997. The entire cost was expensed in the year of purchase. The machine had a 15-year useful life and no residual value.
(b) Machine B cost $105,000 and was purchased January 1, 1998. The straight-line method of depreciation was used. At the time of purchase, the expected useful life was 12 years with no residual value. In 2002, it was estimated that the total useful life of the asset would be only 8 years and that there would be a $5,000 residual value.
(c) Building A was purchased January 1, 1999, for $600,000. The straight-line method of depreciation was originally chosen. The building was expected to be useful for 20 years and to have zero residual value. In 2002, a change was made from the straight-line depreciation method to the sum-of-the-years'-digits method. Estimates relating to the useful life and residual value remained the same.

Income before depreciation expense was $520,000 for 2002. Depreciation on assets other than those described totaled $50,000. Net income for 2001 was $415,000.

Instructions: (Ignore all income tax effects.)

1. Prepare all entries for 2002 relating to depreciable assets.
2. Prepare partial income statements for 2001 and 2002. Begin with income before the cumulative effects of any accounting changes. Show all computations.

PROBLEM 20–25

CHANGE IN ACCOUNTING ESTIMATE AND ACCOUNTING PRINCIPLE

Johnston Doors began operations on January 4, 1999. During the first month, Johnston purchased the following assets, all of which were depreciated using the straight-line method.

Equipment: Cost, $48,000; estimated salvage value, $5,000; estimated useful life, 10 years.
Building: Cost, $85,000; estimated salvage value, $15,000; estimated useful life, 15 years.

At the end of 2003, Johnston reviewed its accounting records and determined that the building should have a total useful life of 20 years. In addition, because of significant wear on the equipment, Johnston proposes changing to the sum-of-the-years'-digits method for depreciating equipment.

Johnston also has found that its estimated bad debt expense has been consistently higher than actual bad debts. Management proposes lowering the percentage from 3% of credit sales to 2%. If 2% had been used since 1999, the balance in Allowance for Bad Debts at the beginning of 2003 would have been $3,200 rather than $6,900. Credit sales for 2003 totaled $250,000, and accounts written off as uncollectible during 2003 totaled $5,500.

Instructions: (Ignore income tax effects.)

1. What is the proper accounting treatment for each of the proposed changes?
2. Prepare the journal entry necessary to record the cumulative adjustment associated with changing depreciation methods. The change is effective as of January 1, 2002.

3. Prepare the journal entries necessary to record the depreciation expense for 2003 for both the equipment and the building.
4. Prepare the journal entry to record the write-off of accounts deemed uncollectible during 2003 and the adjusting entry at year-end to record the bad debt expense for the period.
5. What adjustment is made to the allowance account at the beginning of 2003 as a result of changing the bad debt estimate percentage?

PROBLEM 20-26

REPORTING ACCOUNTING CHANGES

Listed below are three independent, unrelated sets of facts concerning accounting changes.

- *Case 1:* The Runyon Development Company determined that the amortization rate on its patents is unacceptably low due to current advances in technology. The company decided at the beginning of 2002 to increase the amortization rate on all existing patents from 10% to 20%. Patents purchased on January 1, 1997, for $3,000,000 had a book value of $1,500,000 on January 1, 2002.
- *Case 2:* Cartwright Corporation decided on January 1, 2002, to change its depreciation method for manufacturing equipment from an accelerated method to the straight-line method. The straight-line method is to be used for new acquisitions as well as for previously acquired equipment. It has been determined that the excess of accelerated depreciation over straight-line depreciation for the years 1999 through 2001 totals $343,000.
- *Case 3:* On December 31, 2001, Enterprise Inc. owned 35% of the Packard Company and reported its investment using the equity method. During 2002, Enterprise increased its ownership in Packard by 25%. Accordingly, Enterprise is planning to prepare consolidated financial statements for Enterprise and Packard for the year ended December 31, 2002.

Instructions: For each of the cases:

1. Identify the type of accounting change.
2. Explain how the accounting change should be reported in 2002. Where applicable, prepare the journal entries to record the accounting change. (Ignore income tax effects.)
3. Explain the effect of the change on the December 31, 2002, balance sheet and the 2002 income statement.

PROBLEM 20-27

CHANGE IN ACCOUNTING PRINCIPLE

During 2002, All Seasons Company changed its method of depreciating equipment from an accelerated depreciation method to the straight-line method. The following information shows the effect of this change.

Year	Net Income as Reported	Excess of Accelerated Depreciation Over Straight-Line Depreciation	Assumed Tax Effects
Prior to 2000		$68,000	$27,200
2000	$190,000	14,000	5,600
2001	210,000	17,000	6,800

Instructions:

1. Compute the effect of the change in accounting principle on income (net of tax).
2. Prepare a partial income statement for 2002, assuming income before extraordinary items was $225,000 and an extraordinary loss of $21,600 (net of $14,400 income tax reduction) was incurred. Assume 100,000 shares of common stock are outstanding.

3. Present pro forma income data for the years 2000–2002. Assume 100,000 shares of common stock were outstanding in all years.

PROBLEM 20–28

CHANGE IN ACCOUNTING ESTIMATE

On January 3, 2001, Sandy's Fashions, a clothing chain selling moderately priced women's clothing, purchased a large quantity of personal computers. The cost of these computers was $120,000. On the date of purchase, Sandy's management estimated that the computers would last approximately 5 years and would have a salvage value at that time of $12,000. The company used the double-declining-balance method to depreciate the computers.

During January 2002, Sandy's management realized that technological advancements had made the computers virtually obsolete and that they would have to be replaced. Management proposed changing the estimated useful life of the computers to 2 years.

Instructions: Prepare the journal entry necessary at the end of 2002 to record depreciation on the computers.

PROBLEM 20–29

CHANGE IN ACCOUNTING PRINCIPLE—LIFO TO FIFO

On January 1, 2002, Overland Inc. decided to change from the LIFO method of inventory costing to the FIFO method. The reported income for the 4 years Overland had been in business was as follows:

1998	$250,000	2000	$310,000
1999	$260,000	2001	$330,000

Analysis of the inventory records disclosed that the following inventories were on hand at the end of each year as valued under both the LIFO and FIFO methods.

	LIFO Method	FIFO Method
January 1, 1998	$ 0	$ 0
December 31, 1998	228,000	256,000
December 31, 1999	240,000	238,000
December 31, 2000	270,000	302,000
December 31, 2001	288,000	352,000

The income tax effect of the change in inventory method is assumed to be as follows:

1998	$ 11,200	2000	$13,600
1999	$(12,000)	2001	$12,800

Instructions:

1. Compute the restated net income for the years 1998–2001.
2. Prepare the retained earnings statement for Overland Inc. for 2002 if the 2001 ending balance had been previously reported at $600,000, 2002 net income using the FIFO method is $360,000, and dividends of $200,000 were paid during 2002.

PROBLEM 20–30

CHANGE IN PRINCIPLE—INVENTORY METHODS

Shoestring, Inc., had the following pretax net income under three different inventory methods.

Year	FIFO	LIFO	Average Cost
Prior to 1999	$331,000	$264,000	$282,000
1999	117,000	108,000	114,000
2000	129,000	114,000	123,000
2001	133,000	126,000	129,000

Assume that the following independent changes are made during 2001:

1. Shoestring, Inc., changes its inventory method from FIFO to LIFO.
2. Shoestring, Inc., changes its inventory method from LIFO to FIFO.
3. Shoestring, Inc., changes its inventory method from FIFO to average cost.

Instructions: For each of the changes described above, prepare the journal entries necessary to account for the change. Also show the appropriate pro forma or restated comparative income statement and/or statement of retained earnings for the years 1999 through 2001. Assume a tax rate of 40% for all years, a beginning retained earnings balance of $483,200 in 1999, and no payments for dividends.

PROBLEM 20–31

CORRECTION OF ERRORS

Hiatt Textile Corporation is planning an expansion of its current plant facilities. Hiatt is in the process of obtaining a loan at City Bank. The bank has requested audited financial statements. Hiatt has never been audited before. It has prepared the following comparative financial statements for the years ended December 31, 2002 and 2001.

Hiatt Textile Corporation
Comparative Balance Sheets
December 31, 2002 and 2001

	2002	2001
Assets		
Current assets:		
Cash	$ 602,500	$ 400,000
Accounts receivable	980,000	740,000
Allowance for bad debts	(92,500)	(45,000)
Inventory	517,500	505,000
Total current assets	$2,007,500	$1,600,000
Plant assets:		
Property, plant, and equipment	$ 417,500	$ 423,750
Accumulated depreciation	(304,000)	(266,000)
Total plant assets	$ 113,500	$ 157,750
Total assets	$2,121,000	$1,757,750
Liabilities and Stockholders' Equity		
Liabilities:		
Accounts payable	$ 303,500	$ 490,250
Stockholders' equity:		
Common stock, par value $25; authorized, 30,000 shares;		
issued and outstanding, 26,000 shares	$ 650,000	$ 650,000
Retained earnings	1,167,500	617,500
Total stockholders' equity	$1,817,500	$1,267,500
Total liabilities and stockholders' equity	$2,121,000	$1,757,750

Hiatt Textile Corporation
Comparative Income Statements
For the Years Ended December 31, 2002 and 2001

	2002	2001
Sales	$2,500,000	$2,250,000
Cost of goods sold	1,075,000	987,500
Gross margin	$1,425,000	$1,262,500
Operating expenses	$ 575,000	$ 512,500
General and administrative expenses	300,000	262,500
	$ 875,000	$ 775,000
Net income	$ 550,000	$ 487,500

The following facts were disclosed during the audit.

(a) On January 20, 2001, Hiatt had charged a 5-year fire insurance premium to expense. The total premium amounted to $15,500.

(b) Over the last 2 years, the amount of loss due to bad debts has steadily decreased. Hiatt has decided to reduce the amount of bad debt expense from 2% to 1½% of sales, beginning with 2002. (A charge of 2% has already been made for 2002.)

(c) The inventory account (maintained on a periodic basis) has been in error the last 2 years. The errors were as follows:

> 2001: Ending inventory overstated by $37,750
> 2002: Ending inventory overstated by $49,500

(d) A machine costing $75,000, purchased on January 4, 2001, was incorrectly charged to operating expense. The machine has a useful life of 10 years and a residual value of $12,500. The straight-line depreciation method is used by Hiatt.

Instructions:

1. Prepare the journal entries to correct the books at December 31, 2002. The books for 2002 have not been closed. (Ignore income taxes.)

2. Prepare a schedule showing the computation of corrected net income for the years ended December 31, 2001 and 2002, assuming that any adjustments are to be reported on the comparative statements for the 2 years. Begin your schedule with the net income for each year. (Ignore income taxes.)

PROBLEM 20–32

ANALYSIS AND CORRECTION OF ERRORS

A CPA is engaged by the Alpine Corp. in 2002 to examine the books and records and to make whatever corrections are necessary. An examination of the accounts discloses the following.

(a) Dividends had been declared on December 15 in 1999 and 2000 but had not been entered in the books until paid.

(b) Improvements in buildings and equipment of $4,800 had been debited to expense at the end of April 1998. Improvements are estimated to have an 8-year life. The company uses the straight-line method in recording depreciation and computes depreciation to the nearest month.

(c) The physical inventory of merchandise had been understated by $1,500 at the end of 1999 and by $2,150 at the end of 2000.

(d) The merchandise inventories at the end of 2000 and 2001 did not include merchandise that was then in transit and to which the company had title. These shipments of $1,900 and $2,750 were recorded as purchases in January of 2001 and 2002, respectively.

(e) The company had failed to record sales commissions payable of $1,050 and $850 at the end of 2000 and 2001, respectively.

(f) The company had failed to recognize supplies on hand of $600 and $1,250 at the end of 2000 and 2001, respectively.

The retained earnings account appeared as shown on the following page on the date the CPA began the examination.

Instructions:

1. Journalize the necessary corrections.

2. Prepare a statement of retained earnings covering the 3-year period beginning January 1, 1999. The statement should report the corrected retained earnings balance on January 1, 1999, the annual changes in the account, and the corrected retained earnings balances as of December 31, 1999, 2000, and 2001.

3. Set up an account for retained earnings before correction, and post correcting data to this account for (1). Balance the account, showing the corrected retained earnings as of January 1, 2002.

Account: RETAINED EARNINGS

Date	Item	Debit	Credit	Balance Debit	Balance Credit
1999					
Jan. 1	Balance				40,500
Dec. 31	Net income for year		9,000		49,500
2000					
Jan. 10	Dividends paid	7,500			42,000
Mar. 6	Stock sold—excess over par		16,000		58,000
Dec. 31	Net loss for year	5,600			52,400
2001					
Jan. 10	Dividends paid	7,500			44,900
Dec. 31	Net loss for year	6,200			38,700

PROBLEM 20–33

ACCOUNTING CHANGES AND CORRECTION OF ERRORS

Stevens Company is in the process of adjusting its books at the end of 2002. Stevens' records reveal the following information:

(a) Stevens failed to accrue sales commissions at the end of 2000 and 2001 as follows:

2000 .... $27,000
2001 15,333

The sales commissions were paid in January of the following year.

(b) On December 31, 2002, Stevens changed its depreciation method for machinery from double-declining-balance to the straight-line method. Stevens has already recorded the 2002 depreciation using the double-declining-balance method. The following information also was provided:

	Double-Declining-Balance Depreciation	Straight-Line Depreciation	Depreciation Difference
Prior to 2002	$233,333	$133,333	$100,000
2002	40,000	33,333	6,667

(c) Errors in ending inventories for the last 3 years were discovered to be as follows:

2000 .... $43,333 understated
2001 .... 56,667 understated
2002 .... 10,000 overstated

The incorrect amount has already been recorded for 2002.

(d) Early in 2002, Stevens changed from the percentage-of-completion method of accounting for long-term construction contracts to the completed-contract method. The income for 2002 was recorded using the completed-contract method. The following information also was available:

	Pretax Income Percentage of Completion	Pretax Income Completed Contract
Prior to 2002	$583,333	$166,667
2002	200,000	66,667

Instructions:

1. Prepare the necessary journal entries at December 31, 2002, to record the above information. Assume the books are still open for 2002. Ignore all income tax effects.

2. Assuming income from continuing operations before taxes of $500,000, taxes of $150,000 on operating income, and no applicable taxes on the cumulative effect of changing depreciation methods, prepare a partial income statement (beginning with income from continuing operations before taxes) for Stevens Company for 2002. (Ignore EPS.)

3. Assuming the retained earnings balance at the beginning of 2002 was $1,985,000 and that dividends of $125,000 were declared during 2002, prepare a statement of retained earnings for Stevens Company, reflecting appropriate adjustments from (1). Assume no applicable taxes on the cumulative effect of changing to the completed-contract method.

COMPETENCY ENHANCEMENT OPPORTUNITIES

▶ Deciphering Actual Financial Statements	▶ Ethical Dilemma
▶ Writing Assignment	▶ Cumulative Spreadsheet Analysis
▶ Research Project	▶ Internet Search
▶ The Debate	

Accounting is more than just doing textbook problems. This expanded competency material provides practice in critical thinking, oral and written communication, research, teamwork, and consideration of ethical issues.

▶ **DECIPHERING ACTUAL FINANCIAL STATEMENTS**

• Deciphering 20–1 (The Walt Disney Company)

Review THE WALT DISNEY COMPANY's annual report in Appendix A and answer the following questions.

1. Review the income statement and related notes and determine if the company had any accounting changes for any of the years reported. What did those changes relate to?
2. How large of an effect did the changes identified in (1) have on Disney's EPS?
3. Did any of the changes identified in (1) have associated cash flow effects?

• Deciphering 20–2 (Campbell Soup)

Use the information at the top of the following page taken from CAMPBELL SOUP's 1999 annual report to answer the questions below.

1. What are business process reengineering costs?
2. Provide the journal entry to record the change in accounting principle.
3. What happens to the financial statements for prior periods when a change in accounting principle occurs?

• Deciphering 20–3 (Bausch & Lomb Inc.)

BAUSCH & LOMB, maker of eye-care products, found itself in the news because of certain procedures that were outside accepted accounting and business practices. The note on the following page from its 1995 annual report provides information about the company's problems. Review this information to answer the questions that follow.

1. What exactly was the company doing that was wrong?
2. Compare the "As Reported" and "As Restated" columns to determine what income was included in both categories over the combined 2-year period. What did the company gain?
3. If this error had been uncovered in 1994 after the 1993 reporting year had been closed, what journal entry would have been made to correct the error?
4. When this error was uncovered in 1995 after the 1994 reporting year had been closed, what journal entry was made to correct the error?

CAMPBELL SOUP
CONSOLIDATED STATEMENTS OF EARNINGS

In Millions, Except per Share Data	Fiscal Year Ended		
	1999	1998	1997
Earnings from Continuing Operations	724	689	634
Earnings (Loss) from Discontinued Operations	—	(18)	79
Cumulative Effect of Change in Accounting Principle	—	(11)	—
Net Earnings	$724	$660	$713
Per Share—Basic:			
Earnings from continuing operations	$ 1.64	$ 1.52	$ 1.34
Earnings (Loss) from discontinued operations	—	(.04)	.17
Cumulative effect of change in accounting principle	—	(.02)	—
Net Earnings	$ 1.64	$ 1.46	$ 1.51
Weighted average shares outstanding—basic	441	454	472

4. Cumulative Effect of Change in Accounting Principle
In 1998, the company adopted the provisions of the Emerging Issues Task Force consensus ruling on Issue 97-13, "Accounting for Costs Incurred in Connection with a Consulting Contract that Combines Business Process Reengineering and Information Technology Transformation." The unamortized balance of previously capitalized business process reengineering cost was written off as a cumulative effect of a change in accounting principle of $11 or $.02 per share, net of an income tax benefit of approximately $7.

Prior Period Adjustment

BAUSCH & LOMB INCORPORATED (DEC)
NOTES TO FINANCIAL STATEMENTS

Note 2. Restatement of Financial Information
The Company has restated its financial statements for the years ended December 31, 1994 and December 25, 1993. This action was taken as a result of an ongoing investigation which identified uncertainties surrounding the execution of a fourth quarter 1993 contact lens sales program and the improper recording of 1993 sunglass sales in Southeast Asia. In the fourth quarter of 1993 a marketing program was initiated to implement a business strategy to shift responsibility for the sale and distribution of a portion of the U.S. traditional contact lens business to optical distributors. Subsequently, this strategy proved unsuccessful and, in the 1994 third quarter, led to the implementation of a new pricing policy for traditional contact lenses and a decision to accept on a one-time basis returns from these distributors. The investigation of this marketing program disclosed instances where unauthorized terms may have been or were offered which were inconsistent with the stated terms and conditions of the program. The resulting uncertainties relating to the execution of this marketing program led to a decision to restate the 1993 financial statements to account for shipments under the program as consigned inventory and to record revenues when the products were sold by the distributors to their customers and to reverse the effect of subsequent product returns and pricing adjustments related to this program which had been previously recognized in 1994. The investigation of Southeast Asia sunglass sales disclosed that in certain instances distributor transactions recorded as revenues in 1993 had not actually resulted from a sale to those customers, and thus were improperly recorded. The 1993 financial statements have been restated to reverse the improperly recorded sales with a corresponding restatement of the 1994 financial statements to reverse the effect of sales returns previously recognized in that period. In the opinion of management, all material adjustments necessary to correct the financial statements have been recorded. The impact of these adjustments on the Company's financial results as originally reported is summarized below:

Dollar Amounts in Thousands (Except Per Share Data)	1994		1993	
	As Reported	As Restated	As Reported	As Restated
Net Sales:				
Healthcare	$1,227,648	$1,249,923	$1,191,467	$1,169,192
Optics	622,904	642,763	680,717	660,858
Total	$1,850,552	$1,892,686	$1,872,184	$1,830,050
Business Segment Earnings:				
Healthcare	$ 73,466	$ 91,541	$ 210,393	$ 192,318
Optics	64,148	72,075	87,456	79,529
Total	$ 137,614	$ 163,616	$ 297,849	$ 271,847
Net Earnings	$ 13,478	$ 31,123	$ 156,547	$ 138,902
Net Earnings Per Share	$ 0.23	$ 0.52	$ 2.60	$ 2.31
Retained Earnings At End of Year	$ 846,245	$ 846,245	$ 889,325	$ 871,680

• Deciphering 20–4 (Cendant Corporation)

CENDANT CORPORATION was created through the merger of CUC INTERNATIONAL, INC. and HFS INCORPORATED. The company provides travel service, real estate services, and membership-based consumer services. In April 1998, Cendant discovered several accounting irregularities relating to the CUC segment. Widespread fraud had been occurring in that segment. The 1997, 1996, and 1995 financial statements were restated as shown below. Review the information presented and answer the questions that follow.

3. RESTATEMENT (Partial)

As publicly announced on April 15, 1998, the Company discovered accounting irregularities in certain business units of CUC. The Audit Committee of the Company's Board of Directors initiated an investigation into such matters (See Note 17). As a result of the findings of the Audit Committee investigation and Company investigation, the Company has restated previously reported annual results including the 1997, 1996 and 1995 financial information set forth herein. The 1997 annual results have also been restated for a change in accounting, effective January 1, 1997, related to revenue and expense recognition for memberships.

While management has made all adjustments considered necessary as a result of the investigation into accounting irregularities and the preparation and audit of the restated financial statements for 1997, 1996 and 1995, there can be no assurances that additional adjustments will not be required as a result of the SEC investigation.

The following statements of operations and balance sheets reconcile previously reported and restated financial information.

	Year Ended December 31, 1997	
	As Previously Reported	Accounting Adjustments for Errors, Irregularities, and Accounting Change
Net revenues	$ 5,314.7	$ (432.5)
Expenses:		
Operating	1,555.5	115.9
Marketing and reservation	1,266.3	(114.2)
General and administrative	727.2	7.4
Depreciation and amortization	256.8	16.3
Interest-net	66.3	(0.2)
Merger-related costs and other unusual charges	1,147.9	(409.9)
Total expenses	5,020.0	(384.7)
Income from continuing operations before income taxes, extraordinary gain and cumulative effect of accounting change	294.7	(47.8)
Provision for income taxes	239.3	(47.1)
Income from continuing operations before extraordinary gain and cumulative effect of accounting change	55.4	(0.7)
Loss from discontinued operations, net of taxes	—	—
Income before extraordinary gain and cumulative effect of accounting change	55.4	(0.7)
Extraordinary gain, net of tax	—	11.2
Income before cumulative effect of accounting change	55.4	10.5
Cumulative effect of accounting change, net of tax	—	(283.1)
Net income (loss)	$ 55.4	$ (272.6)

IMPROPER REVENUE RECOGNITION

The Company made adjustments to correct the misapplication of generally accepted accounting principles resulting in improper revenue recognition. These errors include: the understatement of estimated membership fees to be refunded to members; the immediate recognition of revenue which should have been deferred and recognized over the membership term; the recording of fictitious revenue; other accounting errors.

IMPROPER REVERSAL OF MERGER LIABILITIES

The Company recorded adjustments to correct the reduction of liabilities previously established primarily for merger transactions and a corresponding inappropriate entry to record revenue.

REVENUE ASSOCIATED WITH POOLED ENTITIES—NOT PREVIOUSLY RECORDED

The Company recorded adjustments to consolidate the financial statements of acquired entities which were accounted for as poolings of interest as required by generally accepted accounting principles. Previous consolidated financial statements did not reflect certain acquired company financial statements for periods required.

ELIMINATION OF INTERCOMPANY TRANSACTIONS AND CONTRA-REVENUE

The Company made adjustments to eliminate intercompany revenue not previously eliminated and properly classify certain expenses as contra-revenue resulting in reductions to revenue.

1. Under the heading "Improper Revenue Recognition," the company identifies three ways in which revenue was overstated. What would have been the journal entries that were made (or weren't made) to overstate revenues?
2. Determine the amount that should have been reported as "Income from continuing operations before income taxes, extraordinary gain and cumulative effect of accounting change." How did this result differ from what was initially reported? Why was net income so much less than income from continuing operations?
3. From the information given here, can you tell what the accounting change was? How does the accounting change relate to Cendant's accounting errors?

▶ **WRITING ASSIGNMENT**
• Counterbalancing errors

As stated in the chapter, most accounting-related errors are detected and corrected in the current period. However, some errors may go undetected. Of those that go undetected, some will fix themselves over 2 periods, while other errors may remain undetected for years.

The objective of this writing assignment is to have you think about what it is that is different between those errors that will counterbalance and those that carry over from period to period. In a short memo, identify these differences considering such issues as whether the accounts involved are balance sheet and/or income statement accounts, and whether they are current and/or noncurrent accounts, and whether they involve revenue or expense accounts. Finally, provide a systematic method for analyzing an error to determine if it counterbalances or if a journal entry is necessary to correct the books.

▶ **RESEARCH PROJECT**
• Reviewing actual financial statements and associated notes

By the time you use this book, companies will have begun adopting FASB Statement No. 133, "Accounting for Derivative Instruments and for Hedging Activities." The objective of this research project is to examine how firms disclose information relating to the adoption of this standard.

Your group is to obtain the annual reports of 5 companies. Using these annual reports, your group is to report (either orally or in writing) the answers to the following questions:
- Of the 5 companies, how many have a line item on the income statement relating to the adoption of this standard? How many discuss the standard in the notes to the financial statements?
- For the companies that are affected by Statement No. 133, what is the impact on income for the period the standard is adopted? That is, on a percentage basis, what is the effect on income? What balance sheet effects are disclosed?

▶ **THE DEBATE**
• Restating prior years' financial statements

This chapter began with an illustration of the impact that Statement No. 106 had on the earnings of several companies. Recall that GENERAL MOTORS reported a $33 billion decline in income in 1992. One-time "hits" such as this can make comparison of financial statements and ratios over time difficult.

This debate relates to the different methods for dealing with changes in accounting principle by either making a cumulative adjustment or restating the financial statements.

Divide your group into 2 teams.
- One team will argue that when a new standard is issued, all prior years' financial statements being disclosed with the current year's information should be restated to comply with the new standard. That is, the financial results of previous periods should be restated to reflect the new standard.
- The other team will argue that a cumulative adjustment that summarizes the new standard's effect on prior periods is sufficient.

▶ **ETHICAL DILEMMA**
• Changing a change in principle

Your company has recently decided to change its method of depreciating long-term assets to be consistent with major competitors. While your company has used the straight-line method in the past, most other companies in the industry use a declining-balance method. Preliminary computations indicate that the cumulative effect of changing this accounting principle will reduce EPS by about 10%. Naturally, those to whom you report would like to know if there is any way to lessen the impact of this change.

You seem to recall from your college days that APB No. 20, the accounting standard dealing with accounting changes, required that when an asset is affected by both a change in principle and a change in estimate, the change is accounted for as a change in estimate—meaning that no cumulative adjustment is made for prior periods and instead the changes are reflected in the current and future periods. You reason that if the estimated useful life of all long-term assets is reassessed with minor modifications being made to these estimated lives, then switching the depreciation method can be treated as a change in estimate and earnings will not be decreased this period.

1. Will the plan of reassessing the estimated lives of long-term assets achieve the desired result of allowing the firm to account for the change in depreciation method as a change in estimate?
2. Will the firm have a higher cash inflow as a result of either the change in principle or the change in estimate?
3. Do you agree with the position that when an asset is affected by both a change in principle and a change in estimate that the change in estimate should prevail? Why or why not?

▶ **CUMULATIVE SPREADSHEET ANALYSIS**

This spreadsheet assignment is an extension of the spreadsheet assignment given in Chapter 13, (1). Refer back to the instructions given in Chapter 13. If you completed the spreadsheet assignment for Chapter 13, that spreadsheet can form the foundation for this assignment.

1. In addition to preparing forecasted financial statements for 2003, Skywalker also wishes to prepare forecasted financial statements for 2004. All assumptions applicable to 2003 are assumed to be applicable to 2004. Sales in 2004 are expected to be 40% higher than sales in 2003. (Clearly state any additional assumptions that you make.)
2. Assume that Skywalker expects the number of days' sales in inventory in both 2003 and 2004 to be 60 days instead of 107.6 days. This change should make the forecasted level of the short-term loans payable in your spreadsheet negative for both 2003 and 2004.
   a. Explain why this change causes negative short-term loans payable.
   b. Because a negative amount of short-term loans payable is not possible, adjust your spreadsheet so that the value of short-term loans payable cannot be less than zero. What is the forecasted current ratio for 2003 and 2004 after you make this adjustment?

▶ **INTERNET SEARCH**

BESTFOOD markets a broad range of consumer food brands including Knorr (soups), Skippy (peanut butter), Karo (syrups), and Mazola (corn and canola oils). Go to Bestfood's Web site, www.bestfoods.com, and answer the following questions.

1. How many countries does Bestfoods operate in?
2. Did Bestfoods have any changes in accounting principles recently? (Hint: Look at the 1998 annual report.) If so, what did the change(s) relate to?
3. What was the effect on EPS of the change(s) in accounting principle?

chapter 21
Analysis of
Financial Statements

HOME DEPOT is the leading retailer in the do-it-yourself home handyman market. In January 1999, Home Depot had 707 stores in the United States and Canada. With each store averaging 105,000 square feet (and an additional 25,000 square feet in the outside garden center), that is a lot of shelf space filled with paint, lumber, hardware, and plumbing fixtures. If plumbing fixtures don't seem very exciting to you, consider this: Home Depot is the 24th largest company in the United States (in terms of market value), with a 1999 market value of $95.5 billion.[1] And if lumber and hardware seem obsolete in this high-tech world, consider that for the past 10 years, Home Depot's growth in earnings per share (EPS) has averaged 31% per year, close to the 39% annual growth in EPS experienced by high-flying MICROSOFT during the same period. In fiscal 1998, Home Depot's sales reached $30.22 billion.[2]

But Home Depot's prospects weren't always so rosy. Back in 1985, when sales were only $700 million, Home Depot experienced severe profitability problems that threatened to terminate Home Depot's expansion in its infancy. For example, Home Depot's gross profit percentage (gross profit ÷ sales) had decreased from 27.3% to 25.9%. This decrease of 1.4 percentage points doesn't seem like much until you calculate that this decrease, with sales of $700 million, caused a gross profit reduction of $9.8 million ($700 million × .014) and reduced total operating profit by 34%. Overall, Home Depot's net income in 1985 was only $8.2 million, down by 42% from the year before.

Home Depot also experienced cash flow problems, in large part due to rapid increases in the level of inventory. Part of this inventory increase was the natural result of Home Depot's expansion. But Home Depot stores were also starting to fill up with excess inventory because of lax inventory management. In 1983, the average Home Depot store contained enough inventory to support average sales for 75 days. By 1985, the number of days' sales in inventory had increased to 83 days. Combined with Home Depot's rapid growth, this inventory inefficiency caused total inventory to increase by $69 million in 1985, and this increase in inventory was instrumental in Home Depot's negative cash from operations of $43 million. Driven by this declining profitability and negative cash flow, Home Depot's stock value took a dive in 1985, and the beginning of 1986 found Home Depot wondering where it would find the investors and creditors to finance its aggressive expansion plans.

But in 1986, Home Depot pulled off an incredible turnaround. Gross profit percentage went back up to 27.5%, operating income almost tripled compared to 1985, and net income increased from $8.2 million to $23.9 million. A computerized inventory management program was instituted, and the number of days' sales in inventory dropped to 80 days. Improved profitability and more efficient management of inventory combined to transform the

1 1999 Fortune 500 listing. This list can be viewed by accessing FORTUNE's Web site at www.fortune.com.
2 1999 10-K filing of The Home Depot, Inc.

LEARNING OBJECTIVES

1
Organize a systematic financial ratio analysis using common-size financial statements and the DuPont framework.

2
Recognize the potential impact that differing accounting methods can have on the financial ratios of otherwise essentially identical companies.

3
Understand how foreign companies report their financial results to U.S. investors.

4
Adjust reported financial statement numbers for the impact of inflation and for changes in the market values of specific assets.

e|m

EXPANDED MATERIAL

5
Convert foreign currency financial statements into U.S. dollars using the translation method.

6
Incorporate material from the entire text into the preparation of a statement of cash flows.

negative $43 million operating cash flow in 1985 into positive cash from operations of $66 million in 1986. Home Depot even used a clever sale-leaseback arrangement to get $32 million of debt off its balance sheet.[3]

The Home Depot example illustrates how financial statement information can be used to evaluate the health of a business and identify specific areas that need improvement. This final chapter in the textbook covers financial statement analysis and reinforces that the entire purpose of preparing financial statements is so that the statements can be used. This chapter summarizes the discussions of financial ratios that have appeared throughout the text and presents a coherent framework in which ratios can be systematically analyzed. The chapter also illustrates how differing accounting assumptions impact the values of financial ratios. In addition, the chapter discusses how reporting practices vary around the world and introduces Form 20-F, required by the SEC when a foreign corporation lists on a U.S. stock exchange. The chapter also describes the impact that inflation can have on financial statements and outlines techniques for clearly presenting the financial effects of changing prices. The expanded material for this chapter includes a brief discussion of how the financial statements of a company's foreign subsidiaries are converted into U.S. dollars. The final section in the textbook contains a comprehensive cash flow example that brings together many of the topics covered in the text.

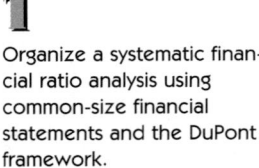

Organize a systematic financial ratio analysis using common-size financial statements and the DuPont framework.

FRAMEWORK FOR FINANCIAL STATEMENT ANALYSIS

Financial statement analysis is the examination of both the relationships among financial statement numbers and the trends in those numbers over time. One purpose of financial statement analysis is to use the past performance of a company to predict its future profitability and cash flows. Another purpose of financial statement analysis is to evaluate the performance of a company with an eye toward identifying problem areas. For example, the HOME DEPOT numbers from 1985 indicated that Home Depot had an inventory management problem that was severely reducing cash from operations. Home Depot's management used this information to spur inventory management improvements, and Home Depot's investors and creditors used the information in forecasting cash from operations for subsequent years. In summary, financial statement analysis is both diagnostic, identifying where a firm has problems, and prognostic, predicting how a firm will perform in the future.

Most pieces of information are meaningful only when they can be compared to some benchmark. For example, if you ask your friend how she feels, and she says, "42," you will have some difficulty interpreting the information. But, if you know that she felt "48" yesterday and that the happiest people you know are between "39" and "41," then you can reasonably infer that your friend was unhappy yesterday but is feeling much better today. Similarly, the informativeness of financial ratios is greatly enhanced when they are compared with past values and with values for other firms in the same industry.

---

3 The troubles of Home Depot in 1985 are the subject of a popular Harvard Business School case: Professor Krishna Palepu, "*The Home Depot, Inc.*," Harvard Business School, 9-188-148.

Financial statement analysis helped Home Depot identify and fix inventory management problems.

FYI: Financial information is almost always compared to what was reported the previous year. For example, when THE WALT DISNEY COMPANY publicly announced on July 22, 1999, that its third-quarter revenues were $5.5 billion, the press release also stated that this amount represented a 5% increase over the prior year.

To enhance users' ability to do time-series comparisons, the SEC requires comparative financial reporting. Annual statements, for example, must include income and cash flow statements for three years and balance sheets for two years. These are minimum standards. Many companies include comparative statistics for 10 to 20 years in their annual reports.

Industry comparisons can be done by comparing financial statements for specific companies in an industry and also by comparing a company's ratios with overall industry averages. The *COMPUSTAT* database from which the information in many of the exhibits in this text has been extracted is one source of industry data. Other well-known commercial sources for industry benchmark ratios include VALUELINE and DUN & BRADSTREET.

The Accounting Principles Board stated that comparisons between financial statements are most informative and useful under the following conditions[4]:

1. The presentations are in good form; that is, the arrangement within the statements is identical.
2. The content of the statements is identical; that is, the same items from the underlying accounting records are classified under the same captions.
3. Accounting principles are not changed, or, if they are changed, the financial effects of the changes are disclosed.
4. Changes in circumstances or in the nature of the underlying transactions are disclosed.

Caution! This chapter presents only an introduction to financial statement analysis. A good source for further information is Palepu, Bernard, and Healy, *Business Analysis and Valuation*, South-Western, Cincinnati, Ohio, 2000.

To the extent that the foregoing criteria are not met, comparisons may be misleading. Consistent practices and procedures are also important, especially when comparisons are made for a single enterprise. The potential impact of accounting differences on financial ratio comparisons is illustrated in a later section in this chapter.

Financial statement analysis is sometimes wrongly viewed as just the computation of a bunch of financial ratios—take every financial statement number and divide it by every other number. This is a very inefficient and ineffective approach to analyzing a set of financial statements. This shotgun approach

---

4 *Statement of the Accounting Principles Board No. 4,* "Basic Concepts and Accounting Principles Underlying Financial Statements of Business Enterprises" (New York: American Institute of Certified Public Accountants, 1970), pars. 95–99.

usually fails to lead to any concrete conclusions. This section of the chapter will introduce the DuPont framework, which is one useful way to structure the analysis of financial ratios. In addition, this section explains the use of common-size financial statements, which are easy to prepare, easy to use, and should be the first step in any comprehensive financial statement analysis.

Common-Size Financial Statements

The first problem encountered when using comparative data to analyze financial statements is that the scale, or size, of the numbers is usually different. If a firm has more sales this year than last year, it is now a larger company and the levels of expenses and assets this year can't be meaningfully compared to the levels last year. In addition, if a company is of medium size in its industry, how can its financial statements be compared to those of the larger firms? The quickest and easiest solution to this comparability problem is to divide all financial statement numbers for a given year by sales for the year. The resulting financial statements are called **common-size financial statements,** with all amounts for a given year being shown as a percentage of sales for that year.

Exhibit 21–1 contains a common-size income statement for Colesville Corporation, a hypothetical example. To illustrate the usefulness of a common-size income statement, consider the question of whether Colesville's gross profit in 2002 is too low. In comparison to the gross profit of $1,280,000 in 2000, the $1,700,000 gross profit for 2002 looks pretty good. But sales in 2002 are higher than sales in 2000, so the absolute levels of gross profit in the two years cannot be compared. But looking at the common-size information, it is seen that gross profit is 33.7% of sales in 2000, compared to 29.8% in 2002. The common-size information reveals something that was not apparent in the raw numbers—in 2000, an item selling for one dollar yielded an average gross profit of 33.7 cents; in 2002, an item selling for one dollar yielded an average gross profit of 29.8 cents. Is this good or bad? Well, in 2002, Colesville made less gross profit from each dollar of sales than in 2000, so this is bad news. The good news is that gross profit as a percentage of sales is improved in 2002 relative to 2001 (27.3%).

EXHIBIT 21–1 | Common-Size Income Statement

	2002	%	2001	%	2000	%
Colesville Corporation						
Comparative Income Statements						
For the Years Ended December 31						
Net sales	$5,700,000	100.0	$6,600,000	100.0	$3,800,000	100.0
Cost of goods sold	4,000,000	70.2	4,800,000	72.7	2,520,000	66.3
Gross profit on sales	$1,700,000	29.8	$1,800,000	27.3	$1,280,000	33.7
Selling expenses	$1,120,000	19.6	$1,200,000	18.2	$ 960,000	25.3
General expense	400,000	7.0	440,000	6.7	400,000	10.5
Total operating expenses	$1,520,000	26.6	$1,640,000	24.9	$1,360,000	35.8
Operating income (loss)	$ 180,000	3.2	$ 160,000	2.4	$ (80,000)	(2.1)
Other revenue (expense)	80,000	1.4	130,000	2.0	160,000	4.2
Income before taxes	$ 260,000	4.6	$ 290,000	4.4	$ 80,000	2.1
Income taxes	80,000	1.4	85,000	1.3	20,000	0.5
Net income	$ 180,000	3.2	$ 205,000	3.1	$ 60,000	1.6

Minor adjustments to the percentage computations have been made to counteract the cumulative effect of rounding.

Each item in the income statement can be analyzed in the same way. In 2002, bottom-line net income was 3.2% of sales, compared to just 1.6% in 2000. How can gross profit be better in 2000 while net income is worse? The answer lies in an examination of the remaining income statement items. Total operating expenses were 35.8% of sales in 2000, compared to just 26.6% in 2002. With a common-size income statement, each of the income statement items can be examined in this way, yielding much more information value than just looking at the raw income statement numbers.

A full analysis of Colesville's common-size income statement requires a comparison to industry averages. Assume that for companies in Colesville's industry, gross profit averages 31.5% of sales. Combined with the information previously discussed, this suggests that Colesville was outperforming its industry in 2000, suffered serious gross profit problems in 2001, and has started a slow comeback in 2002.

At this point, you should be saying to yourself: "Yes, but what is the exact explanation for Colesville's drop in gross profit percentage from 2000? And how was Colesville able to reduce operating expenses?" These questions illustrate the usefulness and the limitation of financial statement analysis. Our analysis of Colesville's income statement has pointed out two areas in which Colesville has experienced significant income statement change in the past two years. But the only way to find out *why* these financial statement numbers changed is to gather information from outside the financial statements—ask management, read press releases, talk to financial analysts who follow the firm and/or read industry newsletters. In short, financial statement analysis may not give you all the final answers, but it can guide you toward which questions you should be asking.

A common-size balance sheet also expresses each amount as a percentage of sales for the year. As an illustration, a comparative balance sheet for Colesville Corporation with each item expressed in both dollar amounts and percentages is shown in Exhibit 21–2.

EXHIBIT 21–2 | Common-Size Balance Sheet

Colesville Corporation
Comparative Balance Sheets
December 31

	2002	%	2001	%	2000	%
Assets						
Current assets	$ 855,000	15.0	$ 955,500	14.5	$ 673,500	17.7
Land, building, and equipment (net)	1,275,000	22.4	1,075,000	16.3	925,000	24.4
Intangible assets	100,000	1.8	100,000	1.5	100,000	2.6
Other assets	48,000	0.8	60,500	0.9	61,500	1.6
Total assets	$2,278,000	40.0	$2,191,000	33.2	$1,760,000	46.3
Liabilities and Stockholders' Equity						
Current liabilities	$ 410,000	7.2	$ 501,000	7.6	$ 130,000	3.4
Noncurrent liabilities	400,000	7.0	600,000	9.1	400,000	10.5
Total liabilities	$ 810,000	14.2	$1,101,000	16.7	$ 530,000	13.9
Paid-in capital	$1,100,000	19.3	$ 800,000	12.1	$1,000,000	26.3
Retained earnings	368,000	6.5	290,000	4.4	230,000	6.1
Total stockholders' equity	$1,468,000	25.8	$1,090,000	16.5	$1,230,000	32.4
Total liabilities and stockholders' equity	$2,278,000	40.0	$2,191,000	33.2	$1,760,000	46.3

Minor adjustments to the percentage computations have been made to counteract the cumulative effect of rounding.

FYI: A common-size balance sheet can also be prepared using total assets to standardize each amount instead of using total sales. If this is done, the asset percentages are a good indication of the company's asset mix.

The most informative section of the common-size balance sheet is the asset section, which can be used to determine how efficiently a company is using its assets. For example, compare total assets for Colesville in 2001 and 2002. Colesville has total assets of $2,278,000 in 2002. Is Colesville managing its assets more efficiently than in 2001 when total assets were $2,191,000? Comparing the raw numbers cannot give a clear answer because Colesville's level of sales is different in the two years. The common-size balance sheet indicates that each dollar of sales in 2001 required assets of 33.2 cents, whereas each dollar of sales in 2002 required assets of 40.0 cents. So, in which of the two years is Colesville more efficient at using its assets to generate sales? In 2001, when each dollar of sales required a lower level of assets. Examination of the individual asset accounts suggests that the primary reason for less efficient total asset usage in 2002 is land, building, and equipment—a dollar of sales in 2001 required only 16.3 cents of land, building, and equipment, compared to 22.4 cents in 2002.

DuPont Framework

As discussed in Chapter 3, return on equity (net income ÷ equity) is the single measure that summarizes the financial health of a company. Return on equity can be interpreted as the number of cents of net income an investor earns in one year by investing one dollar in the company. As a very rough rule of thumb, return on equity (ROE) consistently above 15% is a sign of a company in good health; ROE consistently below 15% is a sign of trouble. Return on equity for Colesville Corporation for the years 2002 and 2001 is computed below.

	2002	2001
Net income	$ 180,000	$ 205,000
Stockholders' equity	$1,468,000	$1,090,000
Return on equity	12.3%	18.8%

So, what can we say about Colesville's overall performance in 2002? It was bad relative to the rough ROE benchmark of 15%, and it was bad relative to ROE in 2001 of 18.8%. But how do we pin down the exact reason(s) for the poor performance in 2002? That's what this section is about.

The **DuPont framework** (named after a system of ratio analysis developed internally at DUPONT around 1920) provides a systematic approach to identifying general factors causing ROE to deviate from normal. The DuPont system also provides a framework for computation of financial ratios to yield more in-depth analysis of a company's areas of strength and weakness. The insight behind the DuPont framework is that ROE can be decomposed into three components as shown in Exhibit 21–3.

EXHIBIT 21–3 | Analysis of ROE Using the DuPont Framework

Return on Equity	=	Profitability	×	Efficiency	×	Leverage
	=	Return on Sales	×	Asset Turnover	×	Assets-to-Equity Ratio
	=	$\dfrac{\text{Net Income}}{\text{Sales}}$	×	$\dfrac{\text{Sales}}{\text{Assets}}$	×	$\dfrac{\text{Assets}}{\text{Equity}}$

For each of the three ROE components—profitability, efficiency, and leverage—there is one ratio that summarizes a company's performance in that area. These ratios are as follows:

- Return on sales is computed as net income divided by sales and is interpreted as the number of pennies in profit generated from each dollar of sales.
- Asset turnover is computed as sales divided by assets and is interpreted as the number of dollars in sales generated by each dollar of assets.
- Assets-to-equity ratio is computed as assets divided by stockholders' equity and is interpreted as the number of dollars of assets a company is able to acquire using each dollar invested by stockholders.

The DuPont analysis of Colesville's ROE for 2002 and 2001 is as follows:

Return on Equity	=	$\dfrac{\text{Net income}}{\text{Sales}}$	×	$\dfrac{\text{Sales}}{\text{Assets}}$	×	$\dfrac{\text{Assets}}{\text{Equity}}$
2002 12.3%	=	$\dfrac{\$180,000}{\$5,700,000}$	×	$\dfrac{\$5,700,000}{\$2,278,000}$	×	$\dfrac{\$2,278,000}{\$1,468,000}$
	=	3.16%	×	2.50	×	1.55
2001 18.8%	=	$\dfrac{\$205,000}{\$6,600,000}$	×	$\dfrac{\$6,600,000}{\$2,191,000}$	×	$\dfrac{\$2,191,000}{\$1,090,000}$
	=	3.11%	×	3.01	×	2.01

The results of the DuPont analysis suggest that Colesville's ROE is lower in 2002, not because of a decrease in profitability of sales but because of the following.

1. In 2002, assets are used less efficiently to generate sales. Each $1 of assets generated $3.01 in sales in 2001 but only $2.50 in sales in 2002.
2. In 2002, Colesville is less effective at leveraging stockholders' investment. By use of borrowing, Colesville was able to turn each $1 of invested funds in 2001 into $2.01 of assets, which is more than the $1.55 in assets in 2002.

This preliminary DuPont analysis is only the beginning of a proper ratio analysis. If a DuPont analysis suggests problems in any of the three ROE components, there are further ratios in each area that can shed more light on the exact nature of the problem. A sampling of those ratios is discussed below. Many of these ratios were introduced in prior chapters.

PROFITABILITY RATIOS If the DuPont calculations had shown that Colesville had a profitability problem in 2002, then a common-size income statement could have been used to identify which expenses were causing the problem. Referring back to the common-size income statement in Exhibit 21–1, cost of goods sold as a percentage of sales is lower in 2002 than in 2001 (70.2% vs. 72.7%). This positive development is partially offset by higher 2002 selling expenses (19.6% vs. 18.2%) and higher general expenses (7.0% vs. 6.7%). To summarize, the return on sales gives an overall indication of whether a firm has a problem with the profitability of each dollar of sales; the common-size income statement can be used to pinpoint exactly which expenses are causing the problem.

EFFICIENCY RATIOS The asset turnover ratio suggests that Colesville is less efficient at using its assets to generate sales in 2002 than it was in 2001. But which assets are causing this problem? One way to get a quick indication is to review the common-size balance sheet in Exhibit 21–2. The common-size balance sheet numbers indicate that in 2002, Colesville has a much larger amount of land, buildings, and equipment as a percentage of sales (22.4%) than in 2001 (16.3%), suggesting that Colesville is using its land, buildings, and equipment less efficiently in 2002. If the individual current assets were listed on the balance sheets (only total current assets are reported on the balance sheets in Exhibit 21–2), a similar analysis could be done with each individual current asset account.

In addition to the common-size balance sheet, specific financial ratios have been developed to indicate whether a firm is holding too much or too little of a particular asset. A selection of the most common of these ratios is discussed next. Many of the detailed asset balances used in the following calculations are not listed in Colesville's summary balance sheets contained in Exhibit 21-2.

Accounts Receivable Turnover   The amount of receivables usually bears a close relationship to the volume of credit sales. The appropriateness of the level of receivables may be evaluated by computing the accounts receivable turnover. This ratio is computed by dividing sales by the average accounts receivable for the year. The computations for Colesville Corporation for 2001 and 2002 are illustrated below.

	2002	2001
Sales	$5,700,000	$6,600,000
Net receivables:		
Beginning of year	$ 375,000	$ 333,500
End of year	$ 420,000	$ 375,000
Average receivables		
[(beginning balance + ending balance) ÷ 2]	$ 397,500	$ 354,250
Accounts receivable turnover	14.3 times	18.6 times

Receivables turnover represents the average number of sales/collection cycles completed by the firm during the year. The higher the turnover, the more rapid is a firm's average collection period for receivables. The numbers indicate that Colesville collected its receivables more rapidly in 2001 (18.6 times) than in 2002 (14.3 times).

> **Caution!**   If sales occur seasonally, the ending balance in receivables may be unusually large (if many sales occur near the end of the year) or small (if the year-end occurs during a natural business lull). Averaging the beginning and ending balance will not correct for seasonality because the same thing happens each year. If quarterly data are available, the average of the quarterly balances can be used to correct for seasonality.

The average accounts receivable balance is used in the calculation because of the desire to compare sales, which were made throughout the year, with the average level of receivables outstanding throughout the year. The ending balance in receivables may not be a good reflection of the normal receivable balance prevailing during the year. For example, if a business grows significantly during the year, the ending balance in the receivables account is greater than the average prevailing balance during the year. The opposite is true if the business shrinks during the year. Using the average receivables balance is a way to adjust for changes in the size of a business during the year. Similar adjustments are made with other ratios that compare end-of-year balance sheet amounts to sales made or expenses incurred throughout the year.

Average Collection Period   Average receivables are sometimes expressed in terms of the average collection period, which shows the average time required to collect receivables. Average receivables outstanding divided by average daily sales gives the average collection period. This measure is computed for Colesville as illustrated below.

	2002	2001
Average receivables	$ 397,500	$ 354,250
Sales	$5,700,000	$6,600,000
Average daily sales (sales ÷ 365)	$ 15,616	$ 18,082
Average collection period		
(average receivables ÷ average daily sales)	25.5 days	19.6 days

This same measurement can be obtained by dividing the number of days in a year by the receivables turnover.

What constitutes a reasonable average collection period varies with individual businesses. For example, if the credit sale contract gives customers 60 days to pay, then a 40-day average collection period would be reasonable. But if customers are supposed to pay in 30 days, a 40-day average collection period would indicate slow collections.

Inventory Turnover   The amount of inventory carried relates closely to sales volume. The inventory position and the appropriateness of its size may be evaluated by computing the inventory turnover. The inventory turnover is computed by dividing cost of goods sold by average inventory. Inventory turnover for Colesville is computed as follows:

	2002	2001
Cost of goods sold	$4,000,000	$4,800,000
Inventory:		
Beginning of year	$ 330,000	$ 125,000
End of year	$ 225,000	$ 330,000
Average inventory [(beginning balance + ending balance) ÷ 2]	$ 277,500	$ 227,500
Inventory turnover	14.4 times	21.1 times

Inventory turnover sometimes is computed using sales instead of cost of goods sold. This is not entirely correct, because sales is a retail number and both cost of goods sold and inventory are wholesale numbers. However, when it comes to ratios, people are free to perform the calculations any way they wish. The most important thing is that the computation is made the same way and is compared with other values computed in the same way.

Number of Days' Sales in Inventory   Average inventories are sometimes expressed as the number of days' sales in inventory. Information is thus afforded concerning the average time it takes to turn over the inventory. The number of days' sales in inventory is calculated by dividing average inventory by average daily cost of goods sold. The number of days' sales also can be obtained by dividing the number of days in the year by the inventory turnover rate. The latter procedure for Colesville is illustrated below.

Caution!   Be careful when using ratios computed by someone else or extracted from a published source. Make sure you know exactly what formula was used to compute the ratio.

	2002	2001
Inventory turnover for year	14.4 times	21.1 times
Number of days' sales in inventory (365 ÷ inventory turnover)	25.3 days	17.3 days

Colesville is holding a 25-day supply of inventory in 2002, compared to a 17-day supply in 2001. Is the 2002 level too high? The important thing with inventory, receivables, cash, and all other assets is for a company to hold just enough, but not too much. For example, the 17-day supply of inventory in 2001 might be too low, exposing Colesville to the risk of running out of inventory. As mentioned earlier, drawing meaningful conclusions requires that the ratio values be compared to an industry benchmark to find out what level of inventory is normal for Colesville's industry.

   You have probably heard of just-in-time inventory systems. What would a just-in-time system do to a company's number of days' sales in inventory?

Fixed Asset Turnover   In addition to analyzing the level of the individual current assets, ratios can be used to determine whether the level of long-term assets is appropriate. As mentioned previously, the common-size balance sheet indicates that in 2002 Colesville has a much larger amount of land, buildings, and equipment, as a percentage of sales (22.4%), than in 2001 (16.3%). An alternate way to represent this same information is to compute the fixed asset turnover. Fixed asset turnover is computed as sales divided by average long-term assets and is interpreted as the number of dollars in sales generated by each dollar invested in fixed assets. The computation for Colesville is given below.

	2002	2001
Sales	$5,700,000	$6,600,000
Land, buildings, and equipment:		
Beginning of year	$1,075,000	$ 925,000
End of year	$1,275,000	$1,075,000
Average fixed assets [(beginning balance + ending balance) ÷ 2]	$1,175,000	$1,000,000
Fixed asset turnover	4.85 times	6.60 times

As suggested by the common-size balance sheet, Colesville is less efficient at using its fixed assets to generate sales in 2002 than it was in 2001.

Other Measures of Activity The efficiency ratios just outlined are not the only ratios that can be used to evaluate how efficiently a company is using its resources. For example, in its 1999 annual report, HOME DEPOT reports that its average weekly sales per store is $844,000 and its annual sales per square foot of store space is $409.79. The key thing to remember with ratios is that there are no rules limiting the ratios that can be computed—users and managers are free to calculate and use any ratios they think will aid their understanding of the company.

Margin vs. Turnover Profitability and efficiency combine to determine a company's return on assets. Return on assets is computed as net income divided by total assets and is the cents amount of net income generated by each dollar of assets. The return on assets is impacted by both the profitability of each dollar of sales and the efficiency of using assets to generate sales. Return on assets for Colesville is computed as follows:

	2002	2001
Net income	$ 180,000	$ 205,000
Total assets:		
Beginning of year	$2,191,000	$1,760,000
End of year	$2,278,000	$2,191,000
Average total assets [(beginning balance + ending balance) ÷ 2]	$2,234,500	$1,975,500
Return on assets	8.1%	10.4%

Even though profitability, as measured by return on sales, is approximately the same in 2002 and 2001, the return on assets is higher in 2001 because in that year Colesville was more efficient at using assets to generate sales.

The profitability of each dollar in sales is sometimes called a company's **margin**. The degree to which assets are used to generate sales is called **turnover**. The nature of business is that some industries, such as the supermarket industry, are characterized by low margin but high turnover. Other industries, such as the jewelry store business, are characterized by high margin but low turnover. The important point to remember is that companies with a low margin can still earn an acceptable level of return on assets if they have a high turnover. This is illustrated with the information for selected U.S. companies given in Exhibit 21-4. Notice the wide variation in return on sales, ranging from 3.2 % for WAL-MART to 12.5% for MCDONALD'S. But also notice that the variation in return on assets is less. The return on assets varies only between 4.5% and 12.0%. The companies with a high return on sales (Disney and McDonald's) have a low asset turnover, whereas those with a low return on sales (Home Depot, SAFEWAY, and Wal-Mart) have a high turnover. Margin isn't everything and turnover isn't everything—the important thing is how they combine to generate return on assets.

EXHIBIT 21-4 | Return on Sales and Asset Turnover for Selected U.S. Companies in 1998

Company	Return on Sales	Asset Turnover	Return on Assets
Disney	8.1%	.56	4.5%
Home Depot	5.3	2.24	12.0
McDonald's	12.5	.63	7.8
Safeway (supermarket)	3.3	2.15	7.1
Wal-Mart	3.2	2.78	8.9

LEVERAGE RATIOS   Leverage ratios are an indication of the extent to which a company is using other people's money to purchase assets. Leverage is borrowing so that a company can purchase more assets than the stockholders are able to pay for through their own investment. The assets-to-equity ratios for Colesville for 2001 and 2002 indicate that leverage was higher in 2001. Higher leverage increases return on equity through the following chain of events.

- More borrowing means that more assets can be purchased without any additional equity investment by stockholders.
- More assets mean that more sales can be generated.
- More sales means that net income should increase.

Investors generally prefer high leverage in order to increase the size of their company without increasing their investment, but lenders prefer low leverage to increase the safety of their loans. The field of corporate finance deals with how to optimally balance these opposing tendencies and choose the perfect capital structure for a firm. As a general rule of thumb, most large U.S. companies borrow about half the funds they use to purchase assets.

Two common leverage ratios, debt ratio and debt-to-equity ratio, are explained below.

> **FYI:**   Thomas Selling and Clyde Stickney have documented the trade-off between margin and turnover described on page 1194. They report that industries with high levels of fixed costs and other barriers to entry are characterized by a low asset turnover and high profit margins. Industries with low fixed costs and commodity-like products have a high asset turnover and low profit margins. See *Financial Analysts Journal* (January–February 1989), p. 43.

Debt Ratio   Debt ratio is computed as total liabilities divided by total assets and can be interpreted as the percentage of total funds, both borrowed and invested, that a company acquires through borrowing. Debt ratios for Colesville for 2001 and 2002 are computed below.

	2002	2001
Total liabilities	$810,000	$1,101,000
Total assets	$2,278,000	$2,191,000
Debt ratio	35.6%	50.3%

Debt-to-Equity Ratio Another common way to measure the level of leverage is the debt-to-equity ratio, computed as total liabilities divided by total equity. This ratio is computed for Colesville as follows.:

	2002	2001
Total liabilities	$810,000	$1,101,000
Stockholders' equity	$1,468,000	$1,090,000
Debt-to-equity ratio	0.55	1.01

STOP & THINK Company Z has an assets-to-equity ratio of 2.5. What are its debt and debt-to-equity ratios?

The assets-to-equity ratio used in the DuPont framework, the debt ratio, and the debt-to-equity ratio all measure the same thing—the level of borrowing relative to funds (borrowing and investment) used to finance the company. The most important thing to remember, as stated before, is that you use comparable ratios when analyzing a company. It doesn't matter whether you use debt ratio or debt-to-equity ratio, but make sure you don't compare one company's debt ratio to another company's debt-to-equity ratio.

To illustrate the impact of financial leverage on stockholders, assume that Company A has stockholders' equity of $500,000 and has no liabilities. The company estimates that its income before income taxes will be $80,000 without any borrowed capital. Income taxes are estimated to be 30% of income; therefore, net income is estimated to be $56,000 [$80,000 – (.30 × $80,000)]. This would result in a return on equity of 11.2% ($56,000 ÷ $500,000).

Exhibit 21–5 illustrates the effects of borrowing an extra million dollars at 12% interest under (1) the assumption that the $1,000,000 in additional assets earn a before-tax return on assets of 15%, more than the cost of the borrowed funds, and (2) the assumption that the additional assets earn a before-tax return of 5%, less than the cost of the borrowed funds. In the first case, because the company can earn a higher return from the new $1,000,000 in assets than it must pay to use the borrowed money, return on equity increases from 11.2% to 15.4%. In essence, the stockholders get to keep the difference between what they can earn from the assets and what they must pay the lender in order to borrow the money. On the other hand, the risk of financial leverage can be seen under the second assumption as the return on equity decreases from 11.2% to 1.4%.

EXHIBIT 21–5 | The Positive and Negative Aspects of Financial Leverage

	Assumption 1: Borrowed Capital Earns 15%	Assumption 2: Borrowed Capital Earns 5%
Income before interest and taxes:		
Without borrowed funds	$ 80,000	$ 80,000
On $1,000,000 borrowed	150,000	50,000
	$230,000	$130,000
Interest (12% × $1,000,000)	120,000	120,000
Income before taxes	$110,000	$ 10,000
Income taxes (30%)	33,000	3,000
Net income	$ 77,000	$ 7,000
Stockholders' equity	$500,000	$500,000
Return on equity	15.4%	1.4%

Times Interest Earned A measure of the debt position of a company in relation to its earnings ability is the number of times interest is earned. The times interest earned calculation is made by dividing income before any charges for interest or income taxes by the interest requirements for the period. The resulting figure reflects the company's ability to meet interest payments and the degree of safety afforded the creditors. The times interest earned ratio for Colesville is computed as follows.

	2002	2001
Income before income taxes	$260,000	$290,000
Add interest: 10% of long-term debt		
$400,000 × .10	40,000	
$600,000 × .10		60,000
Earnings before interest and taxes	$300,000	$350,000
Times interest earned	7.5 times	5.8 times

Pretax income was used in the computation, because income tax applies only after interest is deducted, and it is pretax income that protects creditors. The times interest earned ratio indicates that Colesville's creditors are happier in 2002 because their interest requirements are covered 7.5 times, offering a larger margin of safety than in 2001. However, this high times interest earned value might also indicate that Colesville has not properly leveraged its investment capital in 2002. Again, the appropriate level of times interest earned represents a balancing of the desire of investors to leverage their investment with the desire of creditors for safety concerning the collection of their loans.

A computation similar to times interest earned, but more inclusive, is the fixed charge coverage. Fixed charges include such obligations as interest on bonds and notes, lease obligations, and any other recurring financial commitments. The number of times fixed charges are covered is calculated by adding the fixed charges to pretax income and then dividing the total by the fixed charges.

Other Common Ratios

Not all commonly used ratios fit into the DuPont framework. Ratios for measuring liquidity, cash flow, dividend payments, and stock price performance are outlined in this section.

Current Ratio An important concern about any company is its liquidity, or ability to meet its current obligations. If a firm cannot meet its obligations in the short run, it may not be around to enjoy the long run. The most commonly used measure of liquidity is the current ratio. Current ratio is computed by dividing total current assets by total current liabilities. For Colesville, current ratios for December 31, 2001, and December 31, 2002, are computed as follows:

	2002	2001
Current assets	$855,000	$955,500
Current liabilities	$410,000	$501,000
Current ratio	2.09	1.91

Historically, the rule of thumb has been that a current ratio below 2.0 suggests the possibility of liquidity problems. However, advances in information technology have enabled companies to be much more effective in minimizing the need to hold cash, inventories, and other current assets. As a result, current ratios for successful companies these days are frequently less than 1.0. As mentioned previously in relation to other ratios, the best way to interpret a current ratio is to compare the value to the current ratio for the same firm in previous years and to different companies in the same industry. Current ratios for selected U.S. companies are given in Exhibit 21-6.

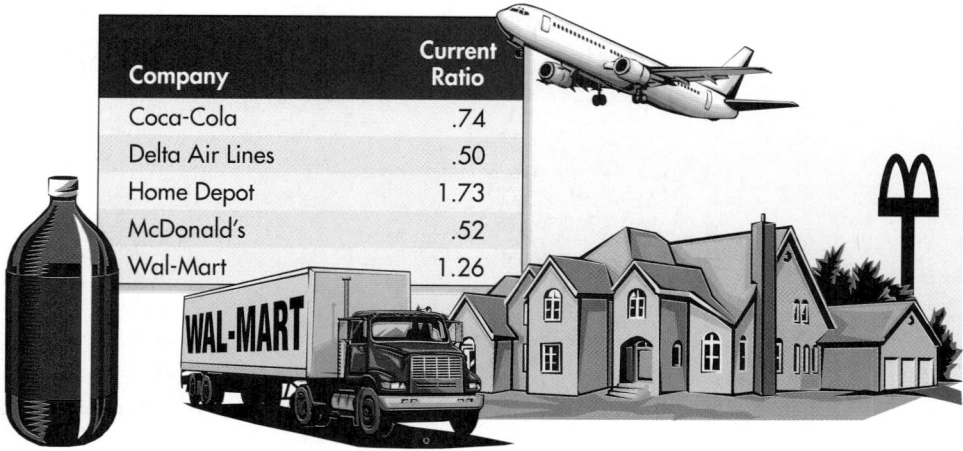

EXHIBIT 21–6 | Current Ratios for Selected U.S. Companies in 1998

Company	Current Ratio
Coca-Cola	.74
Delta Air Lines	.50
Home Depot	1.73
McDonald's	.52
Wal-Mart	1.26

Cash Flow Adequacy Ratio The current ratio is an indirect measure of a company's ability to meet its upcoming obligations. Ratios based on cash flow from operations give a more direct indication of a company's ability to generate sufficient cash to satisfy predictable cash requirements. One overall indicator of cash flow sufficiency is the cash flow adequacy ratio.[5] This ratio is computed by dividing cash flow from operating activities by the total primary cash requirements, defined as the sum of dividend payments, long-term asset purchases, and long-term debt repayments. The following information for Colesville Corporation is needed to compute this ratio.

	2001	2000
Net income	$180,000	$205,000
Depreciation expense	100,000	80,000
(Increase) Decrease in noncash current assets	60,000	(231,500)
Increase (Decrease) in current liabilities	(91,000)	371,000
Cash from operating activities	$249,000	$424,500
Long-term asset purchases	$300,000	$230,000
Long-term debt repayments	200,000	0
Dividends paid	102,000	145,000
Total primary cash requirements	$602,000	$375,000

Note that long-term asset purchases in 2002 and 2001 were enough to offset the depreciation of assets for the year and increase the level of net land, buildings, and equipment.

The computation of the cash flow adequacy ratio is as follows:

	2002	2001
Cash from operating activities	$249,000	$424,500
Total primary cash requirements	$602,000	$375,000
Cash flow adequacy ratio	0.41	1.13

---

5 See Chapter 5 for a summary of other cash flow ratios.

Because the cash flow adequacy ratio in 2002 is less than one, Colesville was not able to satisfy its primary cash requirements with cash generated by operations. A look at Colesville's balance sheets in Exhibit 21-2 indicates that the shortfall has been partially compensated by the issuance of additional stock in 2002. One study has shown that for a sample of Fortune 500 companies, the cash flow adequacy ratio averaged 0.88.[6]

Earnings Per Share   Earnings per share (EPS) is such a fundamental number that we usually forget that it is a financial ratio. The necessary adjustments for dilutive securities and so forth were covered fully in Chapter 19 and are not repeated here. For Colesville, EPS for 2002 and 2001 is computed as follows:

	2002	2001
Net income	$180,000	$205,000
Weighted shares outstanding	90,000	75,000
Earnings per share	$2.00	$2.73

Dividend Payout Ratio   All net income belongs to the stockholders. Cash dividends are the portion of net income paid to the stockholders in the form of cash. An important ratio in analyzing a firm's dividend policy is the dividend payout ratio, computed as dividends divided by net income. Colesville's dividend payout ratios for 2002 and 2001 are computed as follows:

	2002	2001
Dividends	$102,000	$145,000
Net income	$180,000	$205,000
Dividend payout ratio	56.7%	70.7%

In general, high-growth firms have low dividend payout ratios (Microsoft has never paid a cash dividend to its common stockholders in its history), and low-growth stable firms have higher dividend payout ratios.

> **FYI:**   Finance and accounting professors often prefer to compute the inverse of the P/E ratio, called the earnings-price (EP) ratio. There are some interesting econometric reasons why EP is better than P/E. But so far the business press and most businesspeople have stuck with the P/E ratio.

Price-Earnings Ratio   The market price of a share of stock is often expressed as a multiple of earnings to indicate how attractive the market views the stock as an investment. This ratio is called the price-earnings ratio, or P/E ratio, and is computed by dividing the market price per share of stock by the EPS. In the United States, P/E ratios typically range between 5 and 30. Assuming market values per share of Colesville stock at the end of 2002 of $29 and at the end of 2001 of $60, P/E ratios would be computed as follows:

	2002	2001
Market value per share	$29	$60
Earnings per share	$2.00	$2.73
Price-earnings ratio	14.5	22.0

High P/E ratios are generally associated with firms for which strong growth is predicted in the future.

Book-to-Market Ratio   The ratio of book value to market value, called the book-to-market ratio, is frequently used in investment analysis. The book-to-market ratio reflects

---

6 Don E. Giacomino and David E. Mielke, "Cash Flows: Another Approach to Ratio Analysis," *Journal of Accountancy,* March 1993, pp. 55–58.

the difference between the balance sheet value of a company and the company's actual market value. A company's book-to-market ratio is almost always less than one. This is because many assets are reported at historical cost, which is usually less than market value and other assets are not included in the balance sheet at all. Research has shown that firms with high book-to-market ratios tend to have high stock returns in future years.[7] One possible reason for this is that the accounting book value reflects fundamental underlying value and a high book-to-market ratio indicates that the market is currently undervaluing a company. For Colesville Corporation, the book-to-market ratio is computed as follows:

	2002	2001
Book value of stockholders' equity	$1,468,000	$1,090,000
Year-end shares outstanding	100,000	70,000
Market value per share	$29	$60
Total market value of equity	$2,900,000	$4,200,000
Book-to-market ratio	0.51	0.26

A summary of the financial ratios discussed in this section is presented in Exhibit 21–7. This overview of financial ratios is intended to emphasize the point that the preparation of the financial statements by the accountant is not the end of the process but just the beginning. Those financial statements are then analyzed by investors, creditors, and management to detect signs of existing deficiencies in performance and to predict how the firm will perform in the future. As repeated throughout this section, proper interpretation of a ratio depends on comparing the ratio value to the value for the same firm in previous years and to values for other firms in the same industry. In addition, diversity or inconsistency in accounting practice can harm the comparability of ratio values. This point is illustrated in the next section.

IMPACT OF ALTERNATIVE ACCOUNTING METHODS

This section illustrates the impact of accounting method differences on reported financial statement numbers and the resulting financial ratios. The balance sheets and income statements for 2002 for two hypothetical companies, Sai Kung Company and Tuen Mun Limited, both of which started business on January 1, 2002, are shown on page 1202. To keep things simple, there are no income taxes in the example.

The following additional information relates to Sai Kung and Tuen Mun.

1. Sai Kung and Tuen Mun both purchased investment securities for $275. In both cases, the fair value of the securities dropped to $200. Sai Kung classifies the securities as trading; Tuen Mun classifies them as available-for-sale.
2. Sai Kung uses LIFO, and Tuen Mun uses FIFO. If Sai Kung had used FIFO, ending inventory would have been $1,000.
3. Both companies purchased similar buildings and equipment for $3,000 at the start of the year. Sai Kung assumes a 10-year useful life; Tuen Mun uses a 30-year life.
4. Both companies leased additional buildings and equipment at the beginning of the year. The annual lease payment is $150. The present value of the lease obligation on the lease signing date was $1,000. The terms of the leases are very similar. Sai Kung classifies its lease as a capital lease; Tuen Mun classifies its lease as an operating lease.

net work exercise

Visit The Gap's Web site (www.gap.com) and view its most recent consolidated financial statements. Then take a trip to The Limited's Web site (www.limited.com) and find its most recent annual report.

Net Work:

Compute the following financial ratios for each company for the most recent year and compare the results. Which company is doing better based on your analysis?

1. Return on equity
2. Return on assets
3. Asset turnover
4. Debt ratio
5. Current ratio

Recognize the potential impact that differing accounting methods can have on the financial ratios of otherwise essentially identical companies.

---

7 See Eugene F. Fama and Kenneth R. French, "The Cross-Section of Expected Stock Returns," *The Journal of Finance,* June 1992, p. 427.

EXHIBIT 21-7 | Summary of Selected Financial Ratios

| (1) | Return on equity | $\dfrac{\text{Net income}}{\text{Stockholders' equity}}$ | Number of pennies earned during the year on each dollar invested. |

DuPont Framework

(2)	Return on sales	$\dfrac{\text{Net income}}{\text{Sales}}$	Number of pennies earned during the year on each dollar of sales.
(3)	Asset turnover	$\dfrac{\text{Sales}}{\text{Total assets}}$	Number of dollars of sales during the year generated by each dollar of assets.
(4)	Assets-to-equity	$\dfrac{\text{Total assets}}{\text{Stockholders' equity}}$	Number of dollars of assets acquired for each dollar of funds invested by stockholders.

Efficiency:

(5)	Accounts receivable turnover	$\dfrac{\text{Sales}}{\text{Average accounts receivable}}$	Number of sales/collection cycles completed during the year.
(6)	Average collection period	$\dfrac{\text{Average accounts receivable}}{\text{Average daily sales}}$	Average number of days that elapse between sale and cash collection.
(7)	Inventory turnover	$\dfrac{\text{Cost of goods sold}}{\text{Average inventory}}$	Number of purchase/sale cycles completed during the year.
(8)	Number of days' sales in inventory	$\dfrac{\text{Average inventory}}{\text{Average daily cost of goods sold}}$	Average number of days of sales that can be made using only the supply of inventory on hand.
(9)	Fixed asset turnover	$\dfrac{\text{Sales}}{\text{Average fixed assets}}$	Number of dollars of sales during the year generated by each dollar of fixed assets.

Leverage:

(10)	Debt ratio	$\dfrac{\text{Total liabilities}}{\text{Total assets}}$	Percentage of funds needed to purchase assets that were obtained through borrowing.
(11)	Debt-to-equity ratio	$\dfrac{\text{Total liabilities}}{\text{Stockholders' equity}}$	Number of dollars of borrowing for each dollar of equity investment.
(12)	Times interest earned	$\dfrac{\text{Earnings before interest and taxes}}{\text{Interest expense}}$	Number of times that interest payments could be covered by operating earnings.

Other Financial Ratios

(13)	Return on assets	$\dfrac{\text{Net income}}{\text{Total assets}}$	Number of pennies of income generated by each dollar of assets.
(14)	Current ratio	$\dfrac{\text{Current assets}}{\text{Current liabilities}}$	Measure of liquidity; number of times current assets could cover current liabilities.
(15)	Cash flow adequacy ratio	$\dfrac{\text{Cash flow from operations}}{\begin{array}{c}\text{(Purchases of long-term assets +}\\\text{Repayments of long-term debt +}\\\text{Cash dividend payments)}\end{array}}$	Number of times that cash from operations can cover predictable cash requirements.
(16)	Earnings per share	$\dfrac{\text{Net income}}{\text{Weighted number of shares outstanding}}$	Dollars of net income attributable to each share of common stock.
(17)	Dividend payout ratio	$\dfrac{\text{Cash dividends}}{\text{Net income}}$	Percentage of net income paid out to the stockholders as dividends.
(18)	Price-earnings ratio	$\dfrac{\text{Market price per share}}{\text{Earnings per share}}$	Amount investors are willing to pay for each dollar of earnings; indication of growth potential.
(19)	Book-to-market ratio	$\dfrac{\text{Stockholders' equity}}{\text{Market value of shares outstanding}}$	Number of dollars of book equity for each dollar of market value.

► MARKET EFFICIENCY

An efficient market is one in which information is reflected rapidly in prices. For example, if the real estate market in a city is efficient, then news of an impending layoff at a major employer in the city should result quickly in lower housing prices because of an anticipated decrease in demand. The major stock exchanges in the United States often are considered to be efficient markets in the sense that information about

specific companies or about the economy in general is reflected almost immediately in stock prices. One implication of market efficiency is that because current stock prices reflect all available information, future movements in stock prices should be unpredictable.

It seems clear that capital markets in the United States are efficient in a general sense, but accumulated evidence suggests the existence of a number of puzzling "anomalies" in the form of predictability in the pattern of stock returns. For example, prices tend to continue to drift upward for weeks or months after favorable earnings news is released. In addition, prices continue to climb for at least a year after a stock split is announced.

From an accounting standpoint, market efficiency relates to the usefulness of so-called "fundamental

	Sai Kung	Tuen Mun
Cash	$ 100	$ 100
Investment securities	200	200
Accounts receivable	500	500
Inventory	700	1,000
Total current assets	$1,500	$1,800
Buildings and equipment (net)	2,700	2,900
Capital lease assets	900	0
Total assets	$5,100	$4,700
Current liabilities	$1,000	$1,000
Long-term debt	1,500	1,500
Capital lease obligations	950	0
Total liabilities	$3,450	$2,500
Paid-in capital	$1,500	$1,500
Retained earnings	150	775
Other equity	0	(75)
Total equities	$1,650	$2,200
Total liabilities and equities	$5,100	$4,700
Sales	$6,000	$6,000
Cost of goods sold	4,000	3,700
Gross profit	$2,000	$2,300
Depreciation expense	(400)	(100)
Lease expense	0	(150)
Other operating expenses	(1,125)	(1,125)
Operating income	$ 475	$ 925
Interest expense:		
Long-term debt ($1,500 × .10)	(150)	(150)
Capital lease ($1,000 × .10)	(100)	0
Loss on investment securities	(75)	0
Net income	$ 150	$ 775

A careful comparison of the financial statements for Sai Kung and Tuen Mun reveals that the companies are economically identical. The differences between the two sets of financial statements are caused by differences in accounting treatment. Consider the following:

analysis." Fundamental analysis is the practice of using financial data to calculate the underlying value of a firm and using this underlying value to identify over- and underpriced stocks. The notion of fundamental analysis is in conflict with market efficiency, because the analysis works only if current stock prices do not fully reflect all available accounting information. For this reason, fundamental analysis frequently has been regarded with skepticism by academics. However, some research has suggested that accounting data may be useful in predicting future stock returns. Ou and Penman (1989) and Holthausen and Larcker (1992) demonstrate that financial ratios derived from publicly available financial

statements can be used to successfully forecast stock returns for the coming year.

QUESTION:

Why might accountants be interested in whether stock prices fully reflect the information contained in the financial statements?

SOURCES:

Jane A. Ou and Stephen H. Penman, "Financial Statement Analysis and the Prediction of Stock Returns," *Journal of Accounting and Economics*, November 1989, p. 295.

Robert W. Holthausen and David F. Larcker, "The Prediction of Stock Returns Using Financial Statement Information," *Journal of Accounting and Economics*, June 1992, p. 373.

1. Both companies have a $75 economic loss on investment securities. Sai Kung recognizes this loss in its income statement; Tuen Mun recognizes the loss as an equity adjustment.
2. If both companies had used FIFO, ending inventory, cost of goods sold, and gross profit would have been the same for both.
3. The purchased buildings and equipment are similar; the difference is that Sai Kung recognized $300 ($3,000 ÷ 10) of depreciation in 2002, whereas Tuen Mun assumed a longer life and recognized depreciation of $100 ($3,000 ÷ 30).
4. The leased buildings and equipment are also similar, as are the terms of the lease contracts. Because Sai Kung accounts for the lease as a capital lease, it recognizes depreciation expense of $100 ($1,000 ÷ 10 years) and interest expense of $100 ($1,000 × .10). Tuen Mun accounts for the lease as an operating lease and reports lease expense equal to the annual lease payment of $150.

In this example, these four accounting differences cause significant differences between the financial statements of two otherwise essentially identical companies. To illustrate the impact of these accounting differences on the financial ratios of the two companies, ratios (1) through (14) in Exhibit 21–7 are computed and compared for Sai Kung and Tuen Mun. Where required, end-of-year amounts are used in place of average balances.

		Sai Kung	Tuen Mun
(1)	Return on equity	9.1%	35.2%
(2)	Return on sales	2.5%	12.9%
(3)	Asset turnover	1.18	1.28
(4)	Assets-to-equity	3.09	2.14
(5)	Accounts receivable turnover	12.0	12.0
(6)	Average collection period	30.4	30.4
(7)	Inventory turnover	5.71	3.7
(8)	Number of days' sales in inventory	63.9	98.6
(9)	Fixed asset turnover	1.67	2.07
(10)	Debt ratio	67.6%	53.2%
(11)	Debt-to-equity ratio	2.09	1.14
(12)	Times interest earned	1.90	6.17
(13)	Return on assets	2.9%	16.5%
(14)	Current ratio	1.5	1.8

The differences in accounting method have made Tuen Mun appear to be a superior company on almost every dimension. Tuen Mun has better return on equity, better profitability, and better overall efficiency. In addition, Tuen Mun looks like a less risky company because its leverage is lower and its liquidity, as indicated by the current ratio, is higher.

The point of this example is that ratio comparisons can yield misleading implications if the ratios come from companies with differing accounting practices. Frequently, financial ratios from companies are compared without adjusting for underlying accounting differences. Be careful.

Understand how foreign companies report their financial results to U.S. investors.

FOREIGN REPORTING TO U.S. INVESTORS

Companies of all sizes and types are operating in the international environment. Well-conceived global financing strategies are an important part of successful international operations. For a U.S. firm, these strategies might include a stock listing on a foreign exchange, such as the Tokyo Stock Market or the London Stock Exchange; selling bonds and other debt securities in countries other than or in addition to the United States; and borrowing from non-U.S. financial institutions. For example, as disclosed in Appendix A, Disney has significant loan amounts denominated in Japanese yen, Australian dollars, and Italian lira.

Similarly, to raise debt or equity capital, many non-U.S. firms, such as SONY, BRITISH AIRWAYS, and FIAT, list their securities on U.S. exchanges and borrow from U.S. financial institutions. For example, DAIMLERCHRYSLER lists its shares on 21 different stock exchanges around the world, including stock exchanges in New York, Frankfurt, Paris, London, and Tokyo. The number of non-U.S. companies listed on the New York Stock Exchange (NYSE) has increased substantially in recent years. As detailed in Exhibit 21–8, 452 foreign share issues were trading on the NYSE as of March 10, 1999, including 74 from Canadian companies and 64 from British companies.

EXHIBIT 21–8 | Number of Foreign Companies Listed on the New York Stock Exchange by Country of Origin

Country of Origin	Number of Listed Companies
Argentina	11
Australia	12
Bermuda	9
Brazil	24
Canada	74
Cayman Islands	15
Chile	23
China	9
France	16
Germany	9
Hong Kong	10
Italy	15
Japan	12
Mexico	31
Netherlands	17
Spain	14
United Kingdom	64
Others (representing 31 countries)	87
Total	452

SOURCE: www.nyse.com. List is current as of March 10, 1999.

Firms such as Disney must produce financial statements for users not only in their own countries but also in other countries.

International financing strategies impose a variety of financial reporting standards on these multinational corporations. Firms such as DaimlerChrysler and Disney must produce financial statements for users not only in their own countries but also in other countries. The significant differences in accounting standards that exist throughout the world complicate both the preparation of financial statements and the understanding of these financial statements by users.

The significant difference in accounting standards around the world is illustrated by the case of DAIMLER-BENZ. In fall 1993, Daimler-Benz became the first German company to list its shares on the NYSE. Companies listed on the NYSE must provide financial information prepared according to U.S. GAAP. For 1993, Daimler-Benz reported a profit of DM615 million using German accounting principles. For the same year, the net *loss* for Daimler-Benz was DM1,839 million according to U.S. GAAP. As you can see, potentially significant differences can exist between reported results using U.S. and foreign GAAP. As a result, the Securities and Exchange Commission (SEC) requires foreign companies with shares traded in the United States to report and reconcile the differences in their reported net income to what their net income would have been using U.S. GAAP. This reconciliation is provided in what is called a Form 20F, and this form is filed with the SEC. A sample of this reconciliation for Daimler-Benz for 1993, included in SEC Form 20F, appears in Exhibit 21–9.

A close look at Exhibit 21–9 reveals why Daimler-Benz might have been reluctant to report income using U.S. GAAP. The DM2,454 million reduction in net income in converting from German GAAP to U.S. GAAP is caused primarily by a removal from income of DM4,262 million in "appropriated retained earnings." This innocent-sounding adjustment actually represents the removal of some income manipulation that is allowable under German GAAP. In good years, German companies often overstate their expenses by creating provisions (liability accounts such as "Provision for future environmental cleanup costs") and reserves (separate categories of equity, as described in Chapter 11) or by writing

FYI: In 1998, DAIMLER-BENZ and CHRYSLER combined forces to become—in terms of 1998 combined revenues, ($132.7 billion—the fourth-largest company in the world—Daimler-Chrysler.

down the value of assets. Created in good years, these so-called hidden reserves can be reversed in bad years, thus increasing income. In 1993, Daimler-Benz took advantage of German GAAP and reversed DM4,262 million in hidden reserves, thus increasing reported net income and covering up an operating loss. Under the more restrictive standards of U.S. GAAP, this huge reversal of hidden reserves was not allowable, necessitating the large adjustment shown in Exhibit 21–9.

EXHIBIT 21–9 | Daimler-Benz's Form 20F Reconciliation for 1993

(In millions of DM) Consolidated net income in accordance with German HGB (Commercial Code)	**615**
– Minority interest	(13)
Adjusted net income under German GAAP	602
– Changes in appropriated retained earnings:provisions, reserves and valuation differences	(4,262)
	(3,660)
Additional adjustments:	
Long-term contracts	78
Goodwill and business acquisitions	(287)
Pensions and other postretirement benefits	(624)
Foreign currency translation	(40)
Financial instruments	(225)
Other valuation differences	292
Deferred taxes	2,627
Consolidated loss in accordance with U.S. GAAP	(1,839)

As illustrated in Daimler-Benz's 1993 reconciliation, the divergent national accounting practices around the world can have an extremely significant impact on reported financial statements. And with the increasing integration of the worldwide economy, such as the merger of Daimler-Benz and Chrysler, these accounting differences have become impossible to ignore.

The Daimler-Benz example points out that some of the differences between U.S. GAAP and GAAP of other countries can change a profit under one country's set of GAAP to a loss under another country's. A comprehensive comparison of different countries' accounting methods probably would exceed the length of this textbook. The good news is that, as discussed in this section, the demands of international financial statement users are forcing companies to provide disclosure so that users can recognize and reconcile the differing accounting standards. In addition, as illustrated in previous chapters, International Accounting Standards (IAS) and U.S. GAAP are becoming increasingly similar.

Meeting the Needs of International Investors

A growing number of multinational firms are responding to the needs of the international investment community by preparing specialized financial statements and annual reports designed for international users. These statements are specialized in one or more of the following ways: (1) translated into the language of the target user, (2) denominated in the target user's currency, or (3) partially or fully restated to the set of accounting principles familiar to the target user. Another approach is the mutual recognition of financial statements in which the regulators of country A simply accept the financial statements prepared under the accounting standards of country B for stock listing purposes. Finally, there is a growing interest in preparing financial statements according to IAS.

STATEMENTS TRANSLATED INTO THE LOCAL LANGUAGE   Some multinational firms respond to users in other countries simply by taking their financial statements or annual reports and translating them into the language of the user. For example, German-based BAYERISCHE MOTOREN WERKE (BMW) manufactures and sells sport and luxury automobiles. Its annual report distributed to U.S. stockholders is translated into English. The financial statements are prepared according to German GAAP and are denominated in deutsche marks.

STATEMENTS DENOMINATED IN THE LOCAL CURRENCY   Another response to the needs of international users is to denominate the financial statements in the currency of the country where the financial statements will be used. The income statements prepared by TOYOTA are an example of this type of statement. They are prepared in English and denominated in both Japanese yen and in U.S. dollars. A selection from the notes to Toyota's financial statements, reproduced below, explains the basis for the presentation of these financial statements.

> The accompanying consolidated financial statements have been prepared in accordance with the accounting principles generally accepted in Japan. . . . The Consolidated Statements of Cash Flows have been prepared for inclusion in these consolidated financial statements, though those statements are not required in Japan. Relevant notes have been added, and certain reclassifications of the accounts in the basic financial statements published in Japan have been made to present them in a form more familiar to readers outside Japan. These reclassifications do not affect the values of total assets, shareholders' equity, net sales, or net income.
>
> The financial statements presented here are expressed in yen. Solely for the convenience of the reader, they have been translated into U.S. dollars at the rate of 132 yen = US$1, the approximate exchange rate on the Tokyo Foreign Exchange Market on March 31, 1998. These translations should not be construed as representations that the yen amounts have been or could be converted into U.S. dollars at the rate used here or at any other rate.

Although Toyota's financial statements are still useful to U.S. readers, it must be remembered that there are important differences between U.S. and Japanese GAAP that are not clearly set forth. A reader or user of these financial statements would have to be familiar with both U.S. and Japanese GAAP to comprehend fully these statements. However, the similarities in financial statements around the world still outweigh the differences, and one can get a reasonable idea of Toyota's performance by using the techniques of financial statement analysis discussed in this chapter.

STATEMENTS PARTIALLY OR FULLY RESTATED   Some multinationals partially or completely restate their financial statements to the accounting principles of the financial statement users' country. That is, a multinational might prepare a supplemental schedule reconciling the net income prepared under the firm's home country's accounting principles with the net income based on the accounting principles of the users' home country. Daimler-Benz's Form 20F for 1993 shown in Exhibit 21–9 is an example of one such reconciliation.

The degree of restatement can be limited or comprehensive. Most of the companies that provide such statements only include reconciliations between the accounting standards of interest and the GAAP under which the financial statements were prepared. For example, the POLYGRAM GROUP, an entertainment company based in the Netherlands that is involved in the music and film industry, provides U.S. financial statement users with a reconciliation for net income as well as for stockholders' equity. The reconciliation of stockholders' equity is included in Exhibit 21–10. The primary difference relates to goodwill. Recall that goodwill is the amount paid to acquire a company that is in excess of the net identifiable assets of that company. In the United States, this excess is presumed to represent the value of an intangible asset called goodwill. In the

Netherlands, an allowable alternative treatment for goodwill is to record it as a reduction in stockholders' equity. The rationale behind this approach is one of consistency—because homegrown goodwill is never recognized as an asset, purchased goodwill should not be recognized either. The practical effect of this goodwill treatment is that the stockholders' equity of PolyGram has been greatly reduced through the immediate write-off of purchased goodwill. As shown in Exhibit 21-10, the reconciliation to U.S. GAAP requires that this negative equity amount stemming from purchased goodwill be added back in order to match the U.S. treatment.

EXHIBIT 21-10 | PolyGram Group's Reconciliation of Shareholders' Equity to U.S. GAAP

(All amounts are expressed in millions of Netherlands Guilders)	December 31	
	1996	1997
Shareholders' equity as per consolidated balance Sheets of the PolyGram Group..	3,302	4,143
Adjustments to reported equity:		
a. goodwill	1,021	1,110
b. intangible fixed assets other than goodwill.............................	(549)	(739)
c. other	(14)	(28)
d. tax effects of U.S. GAAP adjustments.....................................	116	197
Approximate shareholders' equity in accordance with U.S. GAAP............	3,876	4,683

FYI: The other large reconciling item in Exhibit 21–10 is a subtraction for intangible fixed assets other than goodwill. PolyGram has increased its reported assets (and equity) by estimating values for homegrown brand names and other intangibles and recognizing them in its balance sheet. This practice is not allowed under U.S. GAAP.

Instead of partial restatement or reconciliation, a company can completely restate its financial statements to conform to the accounting principles used in the country of the target financial statement users. For example, NIPPON TELEGRAPH AND TELEPHONE (NTT) maintains its formal accounting records in accordance with Japanese GAAP. However, in order to aid U.S. financial analysts in evaluating its shares that trade on the NYSE, NTT also prepares a separate set of financial statements using U.S. GAAP.

Financial statements, either partially or fully restated, provide a level of information to international users that is not found in the language or currency translations. Obviously, there are substantial costs involved in restating financial statements to the various accounting principles of users in many different countries; for this reason, preparation of restated financial statements has been limited historically. However, the practice is increasing as companies seek to communicate with providers of capital all over the world.

Perhaps the best example of restated financial statements using the accounting principles from various countries comes from Microsoft. At www.microsoft.com, you can find Microsoft's U.S. GAAP net income converted into net income computed under the accounting rules of the following countries:

Australia
Canada
Germany
France
Japan
United Kingdom

In each case, Microsoft provides a reconciliation explaining why there is a difference between the income reported in the United States and the income that would be reported if the accounting standards of a selected country were used. Exhibit 21-11 illustrates specific differences in Microsoft's net income based on Australian GAAP, Canadian GAAP, and U.K. GAAP.

EXHIBIT 21-11 | Microsoft's 1998 Net Income Computed According to Australian, Canadian, and U.K. GAAP

AUSTRALIA

In Australian (AUD) dollars; AUD$1 = US $0.6763.

Operating profit after income tax—Australian GAAP	8,935
Preferred stock dividends provided for or paid	(41)
Tax benefit of stock options	(2,296)
Net Income—U.S. GAAP	6,598

CANADA

In Canadian (C) dollars; C$1 = US $0.7046.

Net income—Canadian GAAP	8,817
Acquired in-process technology	(280)
Tax benefit of stock options	(2,204)
Net Income—U.S. GAAP	6,333

UNITED KINGDOM

In British (BP) pounds; BP1 = US $1.6474.

Profit for the financial year—U.K. GAAP	3,650
Tax benefit of stock options	(943)
Net income per published U.S. financial statements	2,707

FYI: The London Stock Exchange practices a form of unilateral recognition. Domestic British companies are required to abide by U.K. GAAP, but foreign companies can use U.K. GAAP, U.S. GAAP, IAS, or the standards of any European Union country.

MUTUAL RECOGNITION Mutual recognition is another alternative to what some consider the costly translation or conversion of financial statements from one set of accounting principles to another. As noted, in its simplest case, mutual recognition involves country A accepting the financial statements of country B and country B accepting the financial statements of country A for all regulatory purposes (that is, listing on stock exchanges, filing annual reports, and so forth). The importance of such bilateral mutual recognition is fading. The global accounting community is focusing more on the process of convergence to a worldwide set of accounting principles that will be acceptable in all countries.

Adjust reported financial statement numbers for the impact of inflation and for changes in the market values of specific assets.

IMPACT OF CHANGING PRICES ON THE FINANCIAL STATEMENTS

Financial statements in the United States generally do not incorporate the impact of changing prices on the reported numbers. These statements are often referred to as historical cost/**nominal dollar,** or simply historical cost, statements, meaning statements reporting unadjusted original dollar amounts. The justification for reporting original dollar amounts is objectivity. Historical costs generally are based on arm's-length transactions that are considered to measure appropriate exchange values at the transaction date.

The problem is that historical cost statements do not reflect the impact of price changes subsequent to the transaction date. When market prices for assets increase significantly or when high inflation reduces the ability to compare dollar amounts from one

► HOW DO FOREIGN COMPANIES LIST STOCK IN THE UNITED STATES?

Foreign companies can choose among several alternative ways to have their shares traded in U.S. stock markets. The most straightforward approach is to simply agree to comply with all SEC rules that apply to domestic U.S. companies. For accounting purposes, this means providing U.S. investors with a complete

set of financial statements prepared according to U.S. GAAP. This is the approach followed by DaimlerChrysler and, because of the similarity between U.S. and Canadian GAAP, by most Canadian companies listing in the United States.

The most common technique used by foreign companies for listing in the United States is an American Depository Receipt (ADR). With an ADR, a foreign company deposits a number of its shares with a bank. The bank then issues certificates, the ADRs, which are

tradable and which represent ownership of a certain number of foreign shares. The accounting requirement for ADRs is that the foreign company must annually file a Form 20F net income reconciliation and a stockholders' equity reconciliation, such as those shown for Daimler-Benz and PolyGram, respectively, earlier in the chapter.

Two options exist that allow for foreign listings in the United States with no additional accounting disclosure beyond the company's local GAAP financial statements.

year with dollar amounts from another, traditional historical cost/nominal dollar financial statements can be seriously deficient.

Accounting standards in the United States allow for some current value accounting (e.g., for investment securities), but inflation-adjusted accounting is not currently part of GAAP. However, the concepts of current value and inflation-adjusted accounting are still important in understanding the deficiencies of U.S. practice and also in understanding financial statements from other countries where current value and inflation-adjusted accounting exist. This section explains some basic concepts related to changing prices and provides simple examples to illustrate the procedures involved in accounting for changing prices.

Alternative Reporting of the Effects of Changing Prices

Two kinds of price changes have been identified. The first deals with changes in the general price level for all commodities and services. The second kind of price change relates to changes in prices of specific items. Prices for individual items may fluctuate up or down and by differing magnitudes; the average of all specific price changes determines the change in the general price level. With respect to terminology, accounting for the first kind of price change is referred to as **constant dollar accounting,** or general price level–adjusted accounting. Accounting for the second kind of price change is referred to as **current cost accounting,** or current value accounting.

The major financial reporting alternatives, including the currently used historical cost/nominal dollar basis, may be classified as follows:

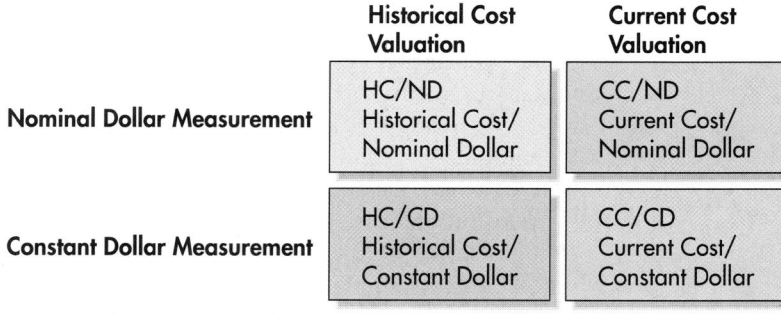

	Historical Cost Valuation	Current Cost Valuation
Nominal Dollar Measurement	HC/ND Historical Cost/ Nominal Dollar	CC/ND Current Cost/ Nominal Dollar
Constant Dollar Measurement	HC/CD Historical Cost/ Constant Dollar	CC/CD Current Cost/ Constant Dollar

Under Regulation 144A, a foreign company's shares can be traded in the United States but can be sold only to qualified institutional investors. The presumption with regulation 144A listings is that sophisticated institutional investors do not need additional accounting disclosures. Finally, companies listing in the United States for the first time can have their shares traded in the OTC "Pink Sheet" market. The presumption with these listings is that the buyer is on his or her own with respect to figuring out the foreign GAAP financial statements.

QUESTIONS:

1. Why does the SEC insist, in most cases, that foreign companies provide U.S. GAAP financial data in order to list their shares in the United States?

2. Why don't all foreign companies list their shares in the United States?

3. With both Regulation 144A and OTC "Pink Sheet" listings, no accounting data beyond local GAAP financial statements are required by the SEC. What are the rationales for these exceptions?

SOURCE: Irene Karamanou and Jana Smith Raedy, "Financial Analysts and the Usefulness of Form 20F Reconciliations and Disclosures," Working paper, Pennsylvania State University and University of North Carolina—Chapel Hill, January 1999.

The two distinct aspects of changing prices are highlighted by the matrix: the change in the unit of measurement (nominal and constant dollars) and the change in basis of valuation (historical and current costs). As an illustration, assume that a piece of land was purchased for investment purposes in 1972 for $10,000. At the end of 2002, the land has a market value of $100,000. In addition, the effect of inflation over the 30 years from 1972 to 2002 has diluted the purchasing power of the dollar such that it takes $4.30 in 2002 to have the same purchasing power as $1.00 in 1972. How should this land be reported in the December 31, 2002, balance sheet? The four options, following the matrix given above, are:

	Historical Cost	Current Cost
Nominal dollars	$10,000	$100,000
Constant dollars	$43,000	$100,000

STOP & THINK Which number is the best measure of the real economic gain from the investment in the land—$33,000, $57,000, or $90,000? Explain.

The $10,000 historical cost/nominal dollar number is the number that is reported under the traditional accounting model. It was objective and relevant in 1972, but the passage of time and the changing of prices have rendered it almost meaningless. The $43,000 historical cost/constant dollar number includes the impact of the change in purchasing power in the 30 years from 1972 to 2002. However, this inflation adjustment ignores the impact of the change in the specific price of the land to $100,000, which is reported under both the current cost/nominal dollar approach and the current cost/constant dollar approach. As explained more fully later, the difference between the two current cost approaches is that the $90,000 ($100,000 - $10,000) increase in the value of the land is attributed entirely to the increase in the land value under the current cost/nominal dollar approach. With the current cost/constant dollar approach, the $90,000 increase is divided between the $33,000 ($43,000 - $10,000) increase resulting from inflation and the $57,000 ($100,000 - $43,000) increase over and above inflation.

Constant Dollar Accounting

Recording transactions in terms of the number of nominal dollars exchanged ignores the fact that the dollar is not a stable monetary unit. As a unit of measurement, the dollar has significance only in reference to a particular price level. Thus, nominal dollar measurements represent diverse amounts of purchasing power. To illustrate, consider Global Trading Company, which is attempting to calculate its year-end cash balance. Global has made the following preliminary calculation based on the amount of cash on hand (all amounts are in millions):

U.S. dollars	$40
Japanese yen	¥100
British pounds sterling	£25
Deutsche marks	DM30
Hong Kong dollars	HK$80
Total cash on hand	275

Of course, this total is completely meaningless—the different currencies cannot be added together because each unit of currency represents a different amount of purchasing power. In the same way, adding unadjusted historical costs incurred in different years is misleading because inflation causes a dollar spent in one year to represent a different amount of purchasing power than a dollar spent in another year.

PRICE INDEXES The value or purchasing power of a monetary unit is related to the goods or services for which it can be exchanged. To measure changes in the general price level, a sample of commodities and services is selected and the current prices of these items are compared with their prices during a base period. The prices during the base period are assigned a value of 100, and the prices of all other periods are expressed as percentages of this amount. The resulting series of numbers is called a price index.

To illustrate how a price index is constructed, consider a simple case involving the following representative products and prices.

	Dec. 31, 2001	Dec. 31, 2002
Spaghetti (one case)	$12.00	$12.50
One movie ticket	8.00	10.00
One gallon of bathroom cleaner	6.00	5.00
Total	$26.00	$27.50

The three products comprise a hypothetical "market basket" of goods. For this market basket, price inflation during 2002 is 5.8% ($1.50 increase ÷ $26.00). But several factors can cause this measure of inflation to be a poor indicator of the actual inflation faced by a particular individual or company.

1. *Not everyone purchases the market basket.* Some people don't restrict their purchases to spaghetti, movie tickets, and bathroom cleaner. For those people, this 5.8% inflation rate may be irrelevant. A price index is only an accurate measure of inflation if the sample market basket matches the buying patterns of the individual or company using the index.
2. *Purchase mix.* The buying patterns of individuals and companies change. A price index based on goods normally purchased by people in 1965 will not be applicable to individuals now because we buy different kinds of things. For example, videotape rentals and computer software purchases comprised a fairly small percentage of the "market basket" in 1965.
3. *Product improvements.* The most difficult aspect of compiling a price index is controlling for changes in product quality. For example, what is automobile price inflation when car prices increase by 5% but the new cars are safer, more fuel-efficient, and more comfortable?

Although there is no perfect way to measure the changing value of the dollar, indexes have been developed that provide reasonable estimates of changes in the dollar's general purchasing power. Among these are the Consumer Price Index (CPI) and the Wholesale Price Index, both provided by the Bureau of Labor Statistics, and the GNP (Gross National Product) Implicit Price Deflator provided by the Department of Commerce. The CPI is probably the most widely used. Changes in the level of the CPI over the past 50 years are summarized in Exhibit 21-12. By the way, the biggest interest in inflation-adjusted financial statements in the United States arose in the 1970s; from Exhibit 21-12 it can be seen that the reason for this is that inflation in the 1970s was higher than at any other time in the past 50 years.

EXHIBIT 21-12 | Changes in the U.S. Consumer Price Index: 1940–1998

	Level of CPI-U (1982–1984 = 100)	Annual Inflation Rate*
1940	14.0	—
1950	24.1	5.6%
1960	29.6	2.1%
1970	38.8	2.7%
1980	82.4	7.8%
1990	130.7	4.7%
1991	136.2	4.2%
1992	140.3	3.0%
1993	144.5	3.0%
1994	148.2	2.6%
1995	152.4	2.8%
1996	156.9	3.3%
1997	160.5	1.7%
1998	163.0	1.6%

*For the 10-year periods, the rate is the average annual rate for the preceding decade. For the one-year periods, the rate is the inflation rate for that year.
SOURCE: U.S. Bureau of the Census, *Statistical Abstract of the United States: 1999* (119th edition), Washington, D.C., 1999.

MECHANICS OF CONSTANT DOLLAR RESTATEMENT Constant dollar accounting requires that nominal dollar amounts be restated to equivalent purchasing power units, for example, constant dollars. The general formula for restatement is:

$$\text{Nominal dollar amount} \times \frac{\text{Price index converting } \textit{to}}{\text{Price index converting } \textit{from}} = \text{Constant dollar amount}$$

To illustrate the conversion process, assume that a company purchased inventory for $50,000. Further assume that the current end-of-year price index is 105 and that the inventory purchase took place when the general price index was 100. The company holds inventory during the year without engaging in any other activities. A conventional balance sheet prepared at the end of the year will show the inventory at its nominal amount of $50,000. In preparing a constant dollar balance sheet at the end of the year, however, the reported inventory amount would be adjusted as follows:

$$\$50,000 \times \frac{\text{Index converting to (105)}}{\text{Index converting from (100)}} = \$52,500$$

FYI: The procedures used in converting nominal dollars to constant dollars are similar to the procedures illustrated in Chapter 9 when dealing with foreign currency transactions. Recall that these transactions require a company to convert an invoice denominated in a foreign currency, French francs for example, into U.S. dollars using a specified exchange rate.

FYI: If money is invested and earns a return less than the rate of inflation, a purchasing power loss results. For example, if you invest $1,000 in a certificate of deposit and receive interest of 8% for the year while at the same time the price index rises 10%, you would suffer a purchasing power loss equal to the 2% difference.

A year-end price index is used to adjust balance sheet accounts for the effects of a change in the general price level because balance sheet amounts reflect year-end balances. When adjusting income statement amounts, usually an average price index for the year would be used because revenues and expenses occur evenly throughout the year.

PURCHASING POWER GAINS AND LOSSES To illustrate the concept of purchasing power gain or loss, assume that a person placed $1,000 cash under the mattress for "safekeeping" when the price index was 100. If the price index were to rise to 110 a year later, the individual would have suffered a purchasing power loss because it would require $1,100 to purchase the same amount of goods that $1,000 would have bought a year ago. On the other hand, a debt of $1,000 payable a year later, again assuming an increase in the price index from 100 to 110, would result in a purchasing power gain. The equivalent purchasing power of the money borrowed would be $1,100, yet the debt can be settled for the fixed amount of $1,000.

Monetary items are assets, liabilities, and equities whose balances are fixed in terms of numbers of dollars regardless of changes in the general price level. Monetary assets include cash, items such as accounts and notes receivable, and marketable debt securities, such as bonds, that are expected to be held to maturity and redeemed at a fixed number of dollars. Regardless of changes in the general price level, these balances are fixed and provide for the recovery of neither more nor less than the stated number of dollars. Monetary liabilities include such items as accounts and notes payable and long-term debt. Regardless of changes in the price level, these balances are fixed and call for the payment of neither more nor less than the stated amounts.

The difference between a company's monetary assets and its monetary liabilities is referred to as its **net monetary position.** With the number of dollars relating to monetary items remaining fixed and reflecting current dollars regardless of the change in the price level, purchasing power gains and losses arise as prices change. In any given period, the gain or loss from holding monetary assets is offset by the loss or gain from maintaining monetary liabilities. The net gain or loss for a period, therefore, depends on whether a company's position in net monetary items is positive—monetary assets exceed monetary liabilities—or negative—monetary liabilities exceed monetary assets. Gains and losses are associated with a company's net monetary position as follows:

	Rising Prices	**Declining Prices**
Positive Net Monetary Position	Loss	Gain
Negative Net Monetary Position	Gain	Loss

FYI: The offsetting of purchasing power gains on monetary assets and losses on monetary liabilities is an illustration of a natural hedging relationship as discussed in Chapter 18.

ARGUMENTS FOR AND AGAINST CONSTANT DOLLAR ACCOUNTING
Proponents of constant dollar accounting maintain that meaningful comparisons of accounting data are not possible unless the measuring units are comparable. They argue that the purchasing power of the dollar is not stable, fluctuating with changes in the general price level. Constant dollar accounting corrects this deficiency by measuring transactions in terms of equivalent purchasing power units, thus giving proper recognition to changes in the general price level. Those in favor of constant dollar accounting also point out that recognition of purchasing

power gains and losses highlights the impact of inflation with respect to monetary assets, liabilities, and equities. They conclude that constant dollar information is relevant to decision makers and can be provided on a reliable basis without undue cost.

Those opposed to constant dollar accounting note that it reflects only changes in the general price level. It ignores many underlying reasons for specific price changes—for example, those due to improvements in quality and specialized industry circumstances. In addition, the general price index used may not be relevant to particular industries. Constant dollar opponents also point out that price indexes are based on statistical averages and have many weaknesses. They question the reliability of the data, especially if used indiscriminately. Many accountants also question whether the benefits exceed the costs of providing constant dollar data. They fear companies will incur substantial costs only to have users of the data be confused by or uninterested in the information.

Current Cost Accounting

The objective of current cost accounting is different from constant dollar accounting. Constant dollar accounting seeks to use comparable measuring units to reflect equivalent purchasing power for a specified general price level. Current cost accounting attempts to measure the current values of assets, liabilities, and equities. The current values may be measured in nominal dollars or in constant dollars, but they are intended to represent the current exchange prices of goods or services, not historical costs.

HOLDING GAINS OR LOSSES   Current cost accounting makes it possible to isolate any gains or losses resulting from holding nonmonetary assets. Traditionally, accountants have recognized income at the point of sale, measuring the difference between the sales price and the historical cost of the item sold. Under current cost accounting, changes in asset values during a period are recognized whether the assets are sold or not. The recognition of holding gains or losses is therefore an essential ingredient of current cost accounting.

Two types of gains and losses from holding assets need to be accounted for. **Realized holding gains and losses** indicate the differences between the current costs and the historical costs of assets sold or used during a period. **Unrealized holding gains and losses** are increases (or decreases) in the current values of assets held during a period but not sold or used. To illustrate the concept of holding gains or losses, assume that Current Value Company made a sale of $100,000. The cost of goods sold was $65,000, and the cost to replace the inventory sold was $80,000. The total gross profit recognized under historical cost accounting is $35,000 (sales price minus historical cost of inventory sold). However, the $35,000 includes an operating gross profit of $20,000 (sales price minus current cost of inventory sold) and an inventory holding gain of $15,000. The realized holding gain of $15,000 represents the difference between the historical cost and the replacement cost of the inventory sold. This may be illustrated as follows:

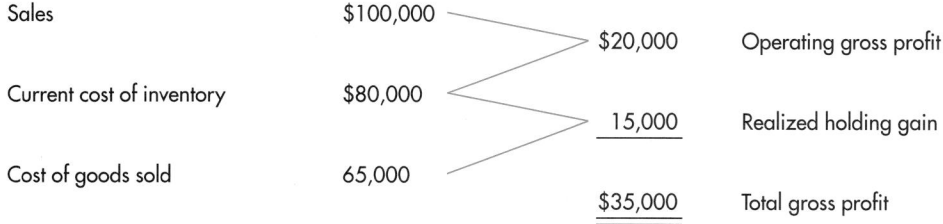

Sales	$100,000	$20,000	Operating gross profit
Current cost of inventory	$80,000	15,000	Realized holding gain
Cost of goods sold	65,000	$35,000	Total gross profit

If, in the example, Current Value Company had additional inventory that was not sold but that had a change in value, it would have an unrealized holding gain or loss. Assume inventory that was not sold cost $50,000 and had a replacement cost of $75,000. There would be a $25,000 unrealized holding gain on the inventory.

Current cost accounting has two primary impacts. First, realized holding gains are reported separately. With historical cost accounting, Current Value Company would report a total gross profit of $35,000 without separating the gross profit into operating

► **THE FASB EXPERIMENT**

There is a long history of concern in the United States over the impact of changing prices on historical cost financial statements. In the 1920s and 1930s, constant dollar accounting was advocated under the names of "stabilized" or price-level accounting. In fact, the creation of LIFO in the late 1930s was largely an effort to remove inflation-induced holding gains from reported profits.

In the 1960s, both the AICPA and the APB released statements advocating the supplemental disclosure of general price level–adjusted information. In the 1970s, when double-digit inflation hit the United States, the FASB and the SEC engaged in a little tug-of-war over accounting for changing prices. The FASB initially proposed supplemental disclosure of only inflation-adjusted information. But the SEC decided to instead require companies to disclose current cost information. The FASB retreated, temporarily. In 1979, after careful evaluation, the FASB decided to experiment with alternative ways of reporting the impact of changing prices by issuing Statement No. 33, "Financial Reporting and Changing Prices." This statement required large companies to disclose supplemental information for selected items on both a constant dollar and a current cost basis. The SEC modified its requirements to match this comprehensive standard.

The business community complained long and loud about Statement No. 33. They complained that it was very costly to prepare the supplemental information, especially the current cost data. They claimed that no one used the information. And they claimed that the information was worse than useless because it could lead to confusion among financial statement users. When Statement No. 33 was issued, the FASB indicated that it

gross profit and holding gain components. The second impact of current cost accounting is the recognition of unrealized holding gains. Traditionally, accountants have preferred to defer the recognition of a gain until it is realized. However, in recent years accountants have begun to recognize unrealized gains and losses on financial instruments (see Chapter 14) and derivatives (see Chapter 18). The FASB has not shown any indication that it will soon apply the concept of current cost accounting to inventory and to property, plant, and equipment.

ARGUMENTS FOR AND AGAINST CURRENT COST ACCOUNTING Proponents of current cost accounting argue that historical cost financial statements, even if adjusted for general price-level changes, do not adequately reflect the economic circumstances of a business. The balance sheet is deficient because only historical costs are presented, and these measurements do not reflect the current financial picture of an enterprise. The income statement is deficient because charges against revenues are based on historical costs that may differ from current costs. Also, increases in net asset values are not recognized at the time of a change in asset value but must await realization at time of sale. Under current cost accounting, assets are reported at their current values, thus more closely reflecting the actual financial position of a business. Expenses are based on the expiration of current costs of assets utilized, thus providing a more meaningful income measure, and changes in values of assets held are recognized as they occur.

Opponents of current cost accounting argue that determining current values is too subjective. For example, the current cost of a particular item may not be readily available and may have to be determined by appraisal or estimation. It may be difficult or impossible to even find an identical replacement item to consider its replacement cost. If an identical asset is not used, a subjective adjustment for differences in the quality of a similar but not identical item would have to be made. Another disadvantage is the increased subjectivity of the income measurement if changes in current values are recognized as income prior to transactions that confirm arm's-length exchange values. Additional arguments against current cost accounting include the lack of understanding of current cost financial statements; the question of whether the benefits are worth the extra costs involved;

would review the results of the reporting requirements after five years. The Board completed that review and concluded in 1986 that the "great experiment" in accounting for changing prices should be stopped. In FASB Statement No. 89, the FASB stated that supplementary inflation-adjusted and current cost disclosures should be encouraged but not required. Very few companies currently provide this supplemental disclosure.

The decision of the FASB to rescind Statement No. 33 was a split decision. Three of the seven Board members argued that instead of dropping Statement No. 33, its requirements should be expanded. These three Board members suggested using the experiment with Statement No. 33 data to design a more comprehensive system for accounting for the effects of changing prices. One dissenting Board member stated that "accounting for the interrelated effects of general and specific price changes is the most critical set of issues that the Board will face in this century."

QUESTIONS:

1. Interest in inflation-adjusted financial statements grows and shrinks depending on the inflation rate. Should GAAP be dictated by macroeconomic conditions?
2. What evidence is there that, although interest in inflation-adjusted financial statements is quite low right now, interest in current cost, or fair value, accounting is quite high?

SOURCES:

Henry W. Sweeney, *Stabilized Accounting*, New York: Harper & Brothers, 1936.

Statement of Financial Accounting Standards No. 33, "Financial Reporting and Changing Prices," Stamford, CT: Financial Accounting Standards Board, 1979.

Statement of Financial Accounting Standards No. 89, "Financial Reporting and Changing Prices," Stamford, CT: Financial Accounting Standards Board, 1986.

and the uncertainty of whether financial statement users will be better served by current cost accounting.

CURRENT COST/CONSTANT DOLLAR ACCOUNTING A number of accountants argue against both constant dollar and current cost accounting, pointing out that each approach solves only one of the problems of accounting for changing prices. Constant dollar accounting adjusts for general price changes; current cost accounting recognizes the impact of specific price changes. Current cost/constant dollar accounting combines both approaches and reflects current cost valuation on a constant dollar basis. Such an approach recognizes that adjustments for specific and general price changes are neither mutually exclusive nor competing alternatives. Conceptually, this is the best reporting alternative if the objective is to give full effect to the impact of changing prices on business enterprises. Its primary disadvantage, in addition to the shortcomings ascribed to the other approaches considered separately, is its complexity.

To illustrate current cost/constant dollar accounting, assume that land has an historical cost of $20,000, an inflation-adjusted value of $41,600, and a current cost of $60,000. The $60,000 current cost/constant dollar land amount is $40,000 higher than the $20,000 reported under the historical cost/nominal dollar approach. As explained earlier, this is an unrealized holding gain. However, only part of the $40,000 total unrealized holding gain is real; a portion of it is an inflationary component or fictitious holding gain due to changes in the general purchasing power of the dollar. This concept can be illustrated by the following diagram:

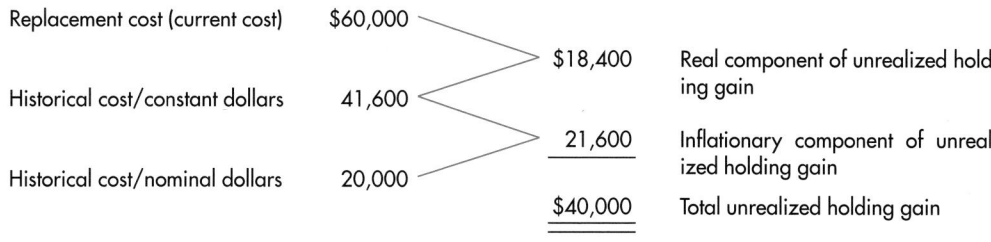

Replacement cost (current cost)	$60,000	
		$18,400 — Real component of unrealized holding gain
Historical cost/constant dollars	41,600	
		21,600 — Inflationary component of unrealized holding gain
Historical cost/nominal dollars	20,000	
		$40,000 — Total unrealized holding gain

This example shows the impact of both general and specific price changes on only one item. It is indeed a complex problem to determine and report such information for all items on a balance sheet as well as to trace the impact of real and inflationary and realized and unrealized holding gains and losses through the income statement.

Summary

For now, financial statements in the United States do not include any adjustment for inflation. Many items, particularly inventory and property, plant, and equipment, are not reported at their current values. The preceding section has given a brief overview of some of the concepts involved with the accounting for changing prices and has illustrated the factors that can cause historical cost to be a misleading number. In conducting an analysis of a company's financial statements, realize that many reported numbers do not reflect current values. When examining a company's sales trend over time, remember that the sales numbers have not been adjusted for inflation. And especially be aware that the distorting impact of changing prices does not impact all companies equally—a company with older property, plant, and equipment has financial statement numbers that differ more from current values than does a company with newer assets.

EXPANDED MATERIAL

Financial statements of a U.S. company's foreign subsidiaries must be converted into U.S. dollars before they can be consolidated with the financial statements of the U.S. parent. This expanded material outlines how this conversion is done and how the resulting foreign currency translation adjustments arise. The expanded material also includes a comprehensive cash flow example that brings together many of the topics covered throughout the text.

FOREIGN CURRENCY FINANCIAL STATEMENTS

5

Convert foreign currency financial statements into U.S. dollars using the translation method.

In Chapter 9 (inventory purchases) and Chapter 18 (derivatives), the issues associated with foreign exchange rates and their impact on accounting for transactions were introduced. In this section, the concepts associated with foreign currency are extended to include entire foreign currency financial statements. Foreign currency financial statements are financial statements prepared in a currency other than the U.S. dollar. For example, IBM has many European subsidiaries whose internal financial statements are prepared in French francs, deutsche marks, and so forth. Those financial statements, when submitted to IBM headquarters in Armonk, New York, must be converted into U.S. dollars. There are two methods for converting foreign currency financial statements—translation and remeasurement. **Translation** is used when the foreign subsidiary is a relatively self-contained unit that is independent from the parent company's operations. **Remeasurement** is appropriate when the subsidiary does not operate independently of the parent company. The translation process simply converts the foreign currency financial statements into U.S. dollars for consolidation with the parent company's statements, while remeasurement involves remeasuring the financial statements as though the transactions had been originally recorded in U.S. dollars.

To determine the correct method of conversion, the **functional currency** of the foreign subsidiary must first be determined. In most instances, the functional currency is

the currency in which most of the subsidiary's transactions are denominated.[8] If the functional currency is the local currency, the subsidiary is considered to be self-contained and its financial statements are translated into U.S. dollars. If the functional currency is the U.S. dollar, the subsidiary is considered to be just a branch office of the parent and the financial statements are remeasured into U.S. dollars. Most foreign entities are self-contained and use their local currency as the functional currency; thus, their financial statements are converted into U.S. dollars by translation. Therefore, this chapter discusses the translation process. Coverage of remeasurement is left to an advanced accounting course.

Translation

Translation involves converting financial statement information from a subsidiary's functional currency to the parent company's reporting currency using the current exchange rate. The specifics are listed below.

- Assets and liabilities are translated using the current exchange rate prevailing as of the balance sheet date.
- Income statement items are translated at the average exchange rate for the year.
- Dividends are translated using the exchange rate prevailing on the date the dividends were declared.
- Capital stock is translated at the historical rate, that is, the rate prevailing on the date the subsidiary was acquired or the stock was issued.
- Retained earnings is translated in the first year using historical rates, but in subsequent years, it is computed by taking the balance in retained earnings from the prior period's translated financial statements, adding translated net income, and subtracting translated dividends.

Double-entry accounting works the same for foreign subsidiaries as it does for U.S. companies—when a local currency trial balance is prepared, debits equal credits. However, as a result of the translation process, debits in the translated U.S. dollar trial balance typically will not equal credits. The balancing figure is called a **translation adjustment** and is recognized as part of the U.S. parent company's stockholders' equity.

To illustrate the translation process, consider the following example. USA Company purchased French Inc. on January 1, 2002, for 50,000 francs. On that date, the exchange rate for 1 French franc was $0.25, so the acquisition price was equivalent to $12,500. On December 31, 2002, the following trial balance for French Inc. is available. The current exchange rate is $0.28, and the average exchange rate for the year was $0.27. Dividends were declared and paid when the exchange rate was $0.275.

Cash	10,000	francs	Accounts Payable	50,000	francs
Accounts Receivable	35,000		Long-Term Debt	80,000	
Inventory	65,000		Capital Stock	30,000	
Equipment	90,000		Retained Earnings	20,000	
Cost of Goods Sold	60,000		Sales	120,000	
Expenses	30,000				
Dividends	10,000				
Total debits	300,000	francs	Total credits	300,000	francs

If French Inc. determines its functional currency to be the French franc, translation is required to convert the financial statements into U.S. dollars for consolidation with USA Company's financial statements. As stated previously, the current rate is used to translate assets and liabilities, and the average rate is used to translate income statement items. The translation process is as follows:

8 *Statement of Financial Accounting Standards No. 52*, "Foreign Currency Translation," Stamford, CT: Financial Accounting Standards Board, 1981, Appendix A.

December 31, 2002	Trial Balance (In French francs)	Exchange Rate	Trial Balance (In U.S. dollars)
Cash	10,000	$0.28	$ 2,800
Accounts Receivable	35,000	0.28	9,800
Inventory	65,000	0.28	18,200
Equipment	90,000	0.28	25,200
Cost of Goods Sold	60,000	0.27	16,200
Expenses	30,000	0.27	8,100
Dividends	10,000	0.275	2,750
	300,000		$83,050
Accounts Payable	50,000	$0.28	$14,000
Long-Term Debt	80,000	0.28	22,400
Capital Stock	30,000	0.25	7,500
Retained Earnings	20,000	0.25	5,000
Sales	120,000	0.27	32,400
Translation Adjustment			1,750
	300,000		$83,050

FYI: For comparison, remeasurement uses historical rates in converting assets such as equipment and land. The historical rate is also used for converting the associated depreciation expense.

FYI: With remeasurement, the adjustment needed to balance the foreign subsidiary's U.S. dollar trial balance is recognized as a foreign currency gain or loss and is included in the income statement of the U.S. parent company.

In this example, French Inc. requires an additional credit of $1,750 to balance the U.S. dollar trial balance. This translation adjustment can be thought of as a deferred gain. USA Company invested 50,000 francs in French Inc. when one franc was worth $0.25. By year-end, each franc was worth $0.28, suggesting that USA Company had experienced a gain of approximately $1,500 [50,000 francs × ($0.28 – $0.25)]. The reason the deferred gain is not exactly equal to $1,500 is that the investment just didn't sit there during the year—transactions occurred (sales, expenses, and dividends) that impacted the amount of USA Company's net franc investment.

The U.S. dollar amounts for the French Inc. financial statement items are added to USA Company's amounts as part of the consolidation process. In addition, the translation adjustment is shown as a separate item in USA Company's equity section. The translation adjustment is recognized as a deferred gain (or loss) rather than as an income statement gain or loss because the only way the foreign currency gain can be realized is through liquidation of all the assets and liabilities of the foreign subsidiary. If the foreign subsidiary is a self-contained going concern, as it is assumed to be when the functional currency is the local currency and translation is used, it makes sense to defer the translation gain (or loss) because actual liquidation and conversion of the foreign subsidiary's net assets into U.S. dollars is not expected any time soon.

Incorporate material from the entire text into the preparation of a statement of cash flows.

EXPANDED ILLUSTRATION OF STATEMENT OF CASH FLOWS

The basic techniques for preparing a statement of cash flows were explained in Chapter 5. More complex circumstances have been addressed as the topics have come up in subsequent chapters. Here we present an expanded problem that illustrates many of the cash flow issues that have been treated in the text.

The comparative balance sheet on the following page is for December 31, 2002, and December 31, 2001, is for Willard Company.

Additional information includes:

1. Net income for the year ended December 31, 2002, was $175,300. There were no extraordinary items.
2. During 2002, uncollectible accounts receivable of $43,000 were written off. Bad debt expense for the year was $32,000.

Willard Company
Comparative Balance Sheet
December 31, 2002 and 2001

	2002	2001
Assets		
Cash and cash equivalents	$ 42,400	$ 180,000
Investment securities (net)	47,000	0
Accounts receivable	400,000	345,000
Allowance for bad debts	(20,000)	(31,000)
Inventories	680,000	643,000
Property, plant, and equipment	810,500	743,400
Accumulated depreciation	(229,000)	(228,000)
Total assets	$1,730,900	$1,652,400
Liabilities and Stockholder's Equity		
Accounts payable	$ 46,000	$ 103,000
Short-term notes payable	100,000	120,000
Accrued liabilities	76,500	48,000
Bonds payable	250,000	278,000
Discount on bonds payable	(19,600)	(20,800)
Deferred income tax liability	108,000	97,000
Total liabilities	$ 560,900	$ 625,200
Common stock, $10 par	$ 840,000	$ 790,000
Paid-in capital in excess of par	52,000	20,000
Retained earnings	301,000	217,200
Other equity	(23,000)	0
Total stockholders' equity	$1,170,000	$1,027,200
Total liabilities and stockholders' equity	$1,730,900	$1,652,400

3. During 2002, machinery and land were purchased at a total cost of $115,100.
4. Machinery with a cost of $48,000 and a book value of $4,200 was sold for $3,600.
5. The bonds payable mature at the rate of $28,000 every year.
6. In January 2002, the company issued an additional 1,000 shares of its common stock at $14 per share.
7. In May 2002, the company declared and issued a 5% stock dividend on its outstanding stock; there were 80,000 shares of stock outstanding at the time, and the market value per share after the stock dividend was issued was $17.
8. During the year, cash dividends of $20,000 were paid on the common stock.
9. In November 2002, 1,000 shares of treasury stock were purchased for $20 per share. Willard uses the cost method.
10. The notes payable relate to operating activities.
11. During 2002, a prior-period adjustment was made to correct an understatement of depreciation on equipment. The amount of the adjustment was $3,500 after taxes.
12. During the year, investment securities were purchased for $50,000. As of December 31, 2002, the securities have a market value of $47,000. The securities are classified as available-for-sale securities.
13. Depreciation expense for the year totaled $41,300.

The preparation of the statement of cash flows will be illustrated using the indirect method of determining cash flows from operations. The analysis uses T-accounts. The T-accounts are shown on page 1224. Explanations for the individual adjustments and the related entries that are recorded in the T-accounts are presented below and on subsequent pages. Recall that these entries are only presented to aid in the preparation of the statement of cash flows; they are not actually posted to the accounts. The letter preceding each explanation corresponds with that used in the T-accounts.

(a) Net income is recorded as follows:

Cash Flows—Operating	175,300	
Retained Earnings		175,300

(b) Cash dividends paid are recorded as follows:

Retained Earnings	20,000	
Cash Flows—Financing		20,000

(c) The 5% stock dividend results in a transfer of Retained Earnings to Common Stock at Par and to Paid-In Capital in Excess of Par. However, the stock dividend has no effect on cash. The amount of the transfer is the number of new shares (80,000 × .05 = 4,000) multiplied by the market value of the new shares ($17):

Retained Earnings	68,000	
Common Stock, $10 par		40,000
Paid-In Capital in Excess of Par		28,000

(d) The recognition that depreciation had been understated in prior periods is recorded by a debit to Retained Earnings and a credit to Accumulated Depreciation. This correction of earnings of prior periods has no effect on cash:

Retained Earnings	3,500	
Accumulated Depreciation		3,500

(e) The purchase of the treasury shares is a financing activity and, because the cost method is used, is recorded as follows:

Other Equity	20,000	
Cash Flows—Financing		20,000

(f) The purchase of the machinery and land is recorded as follows:

Property, Plant, and Equipment	115,100	
Cash Flows—Investing		115,100

(g) The amount of cash received in the sale of machinery was $3,600, and this is shown as cash provided by investing activities. The sale involved a loss of $600. Because this loss reduced net income but involved no cash effects beyond the $3,600 received, the $600 must be added to cash flows from operating activities to avoid understating the cash effect of the transaction:

Cash Flows—Investing	3,600	
Accumulated Depreciation	43,800	
Cash Flows—Operating	600	
Property, Plant, and Equipment		48,000

(h) Depreciation reduces net income but does not involve cash, so the following adjustment to cash flows is necessary:

Cash Flows—Operating	41,300	
Accumulated Depreciation		41,300

(i) The purchase of investment securities that are available-for-sale or held-to-maturity is an investing activity; purchase of trading securities is an operating activity. The necessary entry is:

Investment Securities—Available-for-Sale	50,000	
Cash Flows—Investing		50,000

(j) A decline in the market value of the investment securities caused them to be written down. Because the securities are classified as available-for-sale, the $3,000 write-down reduced equity but did not impact net income; no cash is involved:

| Other Equity | 3,000 | |
| Investment Securities—Available-for-Sale | | 3,000 |

(k) Bonds retired for $28,000 during the year resulted in an outflow of cash for financing activities:

| Bonds Payable | 28,000 | |
| Cash Flows—Financing | | 28,000 |

(l) The amortization of bond discount represents another item that reduced net income but did not involve cash. The necessary adjustment to cash flows is as follows:

| Cash Flows—Operating | 1,200 | |
| Discount on Bonds Payable | | 1,200 |

(m) The $11,000 increase in Deferred Income Tax Liability is added back to cash flows provided by operating activities because it represents income taxes recognized as an expense of the current period for which no cash was paid:

| Cash Flows—Operating | 11,000 | |
| Deferred Income Tax Liability | | 11,000 |

(n) The issuance of new common stock is shown as an increase in cash from financing activities:

Cash Flows—Financing	14,000	
Common Stock, $10 par		10,000
Paid-In Capital in Excess of Par		4,000

Cash flows from operating activities must be adjusted for changes in the levels of current assets and current liabilities. These adjustments are as follows:

(o) The simplest way to handle bad debt expense and account write-offs is to make the adjustment using the net receivable balance. If this is done and the indirect method is used, no special adjustments are required:

| Accounts Receivable (net) | 66,000 | |
| Cash Flows—Operating | | 66,000 |

(p) | Inventories | 37,000 | |
| Cash Flows—Operating | | 37,000 |

(q) | Accounts Payable | 57,000 | |
| Cash Flows—Operating | | 57,000 |

(r) | Short-Term Notes Payable | 20,000 | |
| Cash Flows—Operating | | 20,000 |

(s) | Cash Flows—Operating | 28,500 | |
| Accrued Liabilities | | 28,500 |

After all changes in account balances for the year have been reconciled, the balances in the three cash flows T-accounts are transferred to a summary account. The $137,600 excess credit amount in this summary account represents a net decrease in cash for the year. The final entry records this decrease in the cash account and completes the analysis:

(t) | Net Decrease in Cash | 137,600 | |
| Cash and Cash Equivalents | | 137,600 |

The formal statement of cash flows is prepared using the data in the three cash flows T-accounts.

Cash Flows—Operating			
(a)	175,300	(o)	66,000
(g)	600	(p)	37,000
(h)	41,300	(q)	57,000
(l)	1,200	(r)	20,000
(m)	11,000		
(s)	28,500		
	77,900		

Cash Flows—Investing			
(g)	3,600	(f)	115,100
		(i)	50,000
			161,500

Cash Flows—Financing			
(n)	14,000	(b)	20,000
		(e)	20,000
		(k)	28,000
			54,000

Cash Flows—Summary		
	77,900	
		161,500
		54,000
(t)	137,600	
	215,500	215,500

Operating
Investing
Financing
Net Decrease in Cash

Cash and Cash Equivalents			
Beg. bal.	180,000	(t)	137,600
End bal.	42,400		

Investment Securities (net)			
Beg. bal.	0	(j)	3,000
(i)	50,000		
End. bal.	47,000		

Accounts Receivable (net)		
Beg. bal.	314,000	
(o)	66,000	
End. bal.	380,000	

Inventories		
Beg. bal.	643,000	
(p)	37,000	
End. bal.	680,000	

Property, Plant, and Equipment			
Beg. bal.	743,400	(g)	48,000
(f)	115,100		
End. bal.	810,500		

Accumulated Depreciation			
(g)	43,800	Beg. bal.	228,000
		(d)	3,500
		(h)	41,300
		End. bal.	229,000

Accounts Payable			
(q)	57,000	Beg. bal.	103,000
		End. bal.	46,000

Short-Term Notes Payable			
(r)	20,000	Beg. bal.	120,000
		End. bal.	100,000

Accrued Liabilities			
		Beg. bal.	48,000
		(s)	28,500
		End. bal.	76,500

Bonds Payable			
(k)	28,000	Beg. bal.	278,000
		End. bal.	250,000

Discount on Bonds Payable			
Beg. bal.	20,800	(l)	1,200
End. bal.	19,600		

Deferred Income Tax Liability			
		Beg. bal.	97,000
		(m)	11,000
		End. bal.	108,000

Common Stock, $10 par			
		Beg. bal.	790,000
		(c)	40,000
		(n)	10,000
		End. bal.	840,000

Paid-In Capital in Excess of Par			
		Beg. bal.	20,000
		(c)	28,000
		(n)	4,000
		End. bal.	52,000

Retained Earnings			
(b)	20,000	Beg. bal.	217,200
(c)	68,000	(a)	175,300
(d)	3,500		
		End. bal.	301,000

Other Equity			
Beg. bal.	0		
(e)	20,000		
(j)	3,000		
End. bal.	23,000		

Willard Company
Statement of Cash Flows
For the Year Ended December 31, 2002

Cash flows from operating activities:		
Net income	$ 175,300	
Adjustments:		
Loss on sale of machinery	600	
Depreciation expense	41,300	
Amortization of bond discount	1,200	
Increase in deferred income tax liability	11,000	
Increase in net accounts receivable	(66,000)	
Increase in inventories	(37,000)	
Decrease in accounts payable	(57,000)	
Decrease in short-term notes payable	(20,000)	
Increase in accrued liabilities	28,500	
Net cash provided by operating activities		$ 77,900
Cash flows from investing activities:		
Purchase of machinery and land	$(115,100)	
Sale of machinery	3,600	
Purchase of investment securities	(50,000)	
Net cash used in investing activities		(161,500)
Cash flows from financing activities:		
Payment of cash dividends	$ (20,000)	
Purchase of treasury stock	(20,000)	
Retirement of bonds payable	(28,000)	
Issuance of common stock	14,000	
Net cash used in financing activities		(54,000)
Net decrease in cash		$ (137,600)
Cash and cash equivalents, beginning of year		180,000
Cash and cash equivalents, end of year		$ 42,400

REVIEW OF LEARNING OBJECTIVES

1 Organize a systematic financial ratio analysis using common-size financial statements and the DuPont framework. Financial statement analysis is used to predict a company's future profitability and cash flows from its past performance and to evaluate the performance of a company with an eye toward identifying problem areas. The informativeness of financial ratios is greatly enhanced when they are compared with past values and with values for other firms in the same industry.

Common-size financial statements are computed by dividing all financial statement amounts for a given year by sales for that year. A common-size income statement reveals the number of pennies of each expense for each dollar of sales. The asset section of a common-size balance sheet tells how many pennies of each asset are needed to generate each dollar of sales.

The DuPont framework decomposes return on equity (ROE) into three areas:

- *Profitability.* Return on sales is computed as net income divided by sales and is interpreted as the number of pennies in profit generated from each dollar of sales.

- *Efficiency.* Asset turnover is computed as sales divided by assets and is interpreted as the number of dollars in sales generated by each dollar of assets.

- *Leverage.* Assets-to-equity ratio is computed as assets divided by equity and is interpreted as the number of dollars of assets a company is able to acquire using each dollar invested by stockholders.

If a company has a profitability problem, the common-size income statement is the best tool for detecting which expenses are responsible. Financial ratios for detailed analysis of a company's efficiency and leverage have been developed—a number of them are summarized in Exhibit 21–7.

Margin is the profitability of each dollar in sales, and turnover is the degree to which assets are used to generate sales. Companies with a low margin can still earn an acceptable level of return on assets if they have a high turnover.

2 **Recognize the potential impact that differing accounting methods can have on the financial ratios of otherwise essentially identical companies.** Ratio comparisons can yield misleading implications if the ratios come from companies with differing accounting practices. Adjustments for accounting differences should be made before financial ratios are compared.

3 **Understand how foreign companies report their financial results to U.S. investors.** The divergent national accounting practices around the world can have an extremely significant impact on reported financial statements. Multinational companies have responded to the needs of the international investment community by preparing specialized financial statements that are: (1) translated into the language of the target user; (2) denominated in the currency of the target user; or (3) partially or fully restated to the set of accounting principles familiar to the target user. For foreign companies with shares traded on a U.S. stock exchange, filing of SEC's Form 20F provides reconciliation between net income and stockholders' equity reported under foreign GAAP with what would have been reported under U.S. GAAP.

4 **Adjust reported financial statement numbers for the impact of inflation and for changes in the market values of specific assets.** Historical cost financial statements do not reflect the impact of price changes subsequent to the transaction date. When market prices for assets increase significantly or when high inflation reduces the ability to compare dollar amounts from one year with dollar amounts from another, traditional historical cost/nominal dollar financial statements can be seriously deficient.

Accounting for the change in the general price level of all commodities and services is referred to as constant dollar accounting, or general price level–adjusted accounting. Accounting for the changes in prices of specific items is referred to as current cost accounting, or current value accounting.

The general formula for restatement of nominal dollar amounts into constant dollar amounts is:

$$\text{Nominal dollar amount} \times \frac{\text{Price index converting } \textit{to}}{\text{Price index converting } \textit{from}} = \text{Constant dollar amount}$$

Monetary items are those assets and liabilities, such as accounts receivable and accounts payable, that are denominated in terms of a specific number of dollars, no matter what happens to the general price level. With the number of dollars relating to monetary items remaining fixed, purchasing power gains and losses arise as the general price level changes. The net purchasing power gain or loss for a period depends on a company's net monetary position.

Under current cost accounting, changes in asset values during a period are recognized whether the assets are sold or not. Realized holding gains and losses indicate the differences between the current costs and the historical costs of assets sold or used during a period. Unrealized holding gains and losses are increases (or decreases) in the current values of assets held during a period but not sold or used.

5 **Convert foreign currency financial statements into U.S. dollars using the translation method.** A foreign subsidiary's functional currency is the currency in which most of the subsidiary's transactions are denominated. If the functional currency is the local currency, the subsidiary is considered to be self-contained and its financial statements are converted into U.S. dollars through a process called translation. The financial statements of most foreign subsidiaries of U.S. companies are translated as follows:

- Assets and liabilities are translated using the current exchange rate prevailing as of the balance sheet date.
- Income statement items are translated at the average exchange rate for the year.
- Dividends are translated using the exchange rate prevailing on the date the dividends were declared.
- Capital stock is translated at the historical rate, that is, the rate prevailing on the date the subsidiary was acquired or the stock was issued.
- Retained earnings is translated in the first year using historical rates, but in subsequent years, it is computed by taking the balance in retained earnings from the prior period's translated financial statements, adding translated net income, and subtracting translated dividends.

The translation adjustment is a balancing figure and can be thought of as a deferred gain or loss stemming from the impact of exchange rate changes on the value of the U.S. parent's investment in the foreign subsidiary. The translation adjustment is recognized as a separate component of the U.S. parent company's stockholders' equity.

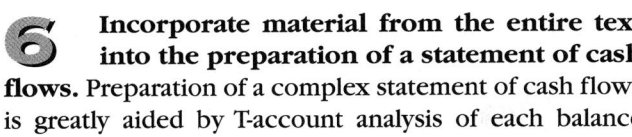 **Incorporate material from the entire text into the preparation of a statement of cash flows.** Preparation of a complex statement of cash flows is greatly aided by T-account analysis of each balance sheet account. Once the cash flow implications of each balance sheet account change have been categorized, the formal statement of cash flows can be prepared from the summary T-accounts for operating, investing, and financing activities.

KEY TERMS

Common-size financial
    statements 1188
Constant dollar accounting 1210
Current cost accounting 1210
DuPont framework 1190
Financial statement analysis 1186
Margin 1194
Monetary items 1214

Net monetary position 1214
Nominal dollar 1209
Realized holding gains and
    losses 1215
Turnover 1194
Unrealized holding gains and losses
    1215

Functional currency 1218
Remeasurement 1218
Translation 1218
Translation adjustment 1219

QUESTIONS

1. Financial statement analysis can be used to identify a company's weak areas so that management can work toward improvement. Can financial statement analysis be used for any other purpose? Explain.
2. Why are comparative financial statements considered more meaningful than statements prepared for a single period? What conditions increase the usefulness of comparative statements?
3. "An analysis of a company's financial ratios reveals the underlying reasons for profitability and efficiency problems." Do you agree or disagree? Explain.
4. What is meant by a common-size statement? What are its advantages?
5. What is the purpose of the DuPont framework?
6. (a) How is the inventory turnover computed? (b) What precautions are necessary in arriving at the inventory number to be used in the turnover calculation? (c) How would you interpret a rising inventory turnover rate?
7. Indicate how each of the following measurements is calculated and appraise its significance.
   (a) Times interest earned
   (b) Return on equity
   (c) Earnings per share
   (d) Price-earnings ratio
   (e) Dividend payout ratio

   (f) Book-to-market ratio
8. Explain how the turnover of assets can affect return on assets.
9. Under what conditions is the return on assets equal to the ROE?
10. How do accounting differences impact the usefulness of financial ratio comparisons?
11. What are the advantages and disadvantages of each of the following types of special-purpose financial statements?
    (a) Statements translated into the local language.
    (b) Statements denominated in the currency of the target users.
    (c) Statements that are partially or fully restated to the accounting principles most frequently used by the target user.
    (d) Statements prepared according to International Accounting Standards (IAS).
12. What is meant by mutual recognition? Is mutual recognition a feasible solution to the issue of allowing foreign companies to register on the stock exchanges of other countries?
13. (a) Why have accountants traditionally preferred to report historical costs rather than current costs in conventional statements? (b) What are some limitations of historical cost statements?

14. What are the three alternatives to reporting historical cost/nominal dollar financial statements, and how do they differ from conventional reporting practice?

15. (a) How are general price indexes computed? (b) What are some of their limitations?

16. If equipment was purchased for $85,000 at the beginning of the year when the Consumer Price Index (CPI) was 160, how would the equipment be recorded on a constant dollar end-of-year balance sheet if the year-end CPI was 180?

17. Indicate whether a company sustains a gain or loss in purchasing power under each of the following conditions.

    (a) A company maintains an excess of monetary assets over monetary liabilities during a period of increasing general price levels.

    (b) A company maintains an excess of monetary liabilities over monetary assets during a period of increasing general price levels.

    (c) A company maintains an excess of monetary assets over monetary liabilities during a period of decreasing general price levels.

    (d) A company maintains an excess of monetary liabilities over monetary assets during a period of decreasing general price levels.

18. (a) Distinguish between realized and unrealized holding gains and losses. (b) Distinguish between the real and inflationary components of total holding gains and losses.

19. A foreign subsidiary's functional currency determines whether its financial statements should be translated or remeasured. Identify the primary factor in determining a subsidiary's functional currency. What other factors can influence management's determination as to the subsidiary's functional currency?

20. When financial statements are translated, which exchange rate is used for translating assets and liabilities? Which exchange rate is used for translating common stock? Which exchange rate is used for translating income statement items?

21. When financial statements are translated, what is the difference between the resulting debits and credits called? Where is this difference disclosed on the balance sheet?

DISCUSSION CASES

CASE 21–1

ARE INTERNATIONAL RATIOS COMPARABLE?

As the world economy becomes more integrated, one question facing financial analysts is whether financial ratios can be compared across national boundaries. For example, at one time the average P/E ratio for Japanese companies was around 60, while the average for U.S. companies was between 15 and 20. (A P/E ratio in excess of 30 is considered quite high in the United States.) This dramatic variation was a result of differences in the two national economies and in their accounting methods. One of the accounting differences is that Japanese companies generally depreciate their fixed assets over shorter lives than do U.S. companies.

In addition to differences in accounting methods, what other challenges are faced by financial analysts in comparing the financial ratios of a U.S. company to those of a Japanese, German, or British company?

CASE 21–2

ANALYZING EARNINGS

Royer Donahoe owns two businesses: a drug store and a retail department store.

	Drug Store	Department Store
Net sales	$1,050,000	$670,000
Cost of goods sold	1,000,000	600,000
Average total assets	50,000	200,000
Other expenses	39,500	36,500

Which business is more profitable? Which business is more efficient? Overall, which business would you consider to be a more attractive investment?

CASE 21–3

CAN A RATIO BE TOO GOOD?

Tony Christopher is analyzing the financial statements of Shaycole Company and has computed the following ratios.

	Shaycole	Industry Comparison
Current ratio	4.7	1.9
Inventory turnover	14.8 times	6.1 times
Accounts receivable turnover	27.4 times	8.7 times
Debt-to-equity ratio	.117	.864

Andy Martinez, Tony's colleague, tells Tony that Shaycole looks great. Andy points out that although Shaycole's ratios deviate significantly from the industry norms, all the deviations suggest that Shaycole is doing better than other firms in its industry. Is Andy right?

CASE 21–4

EVALUATING ALTERNATIVE INVESTMENTS

Judy Snow is considering investing $10,000 and wishes to know which of 2 following companies offers the better alternative.

The Hoffman Company earned net income of $63,000 last year on average total assets of $280,000 and average stockholders' equity of $210,000. The company's shares are selling for $100 per share; 6,300 shares of common stock are outstanding.

The McMahon Company earned $24,375 last year on average total assets of $125,000 and average stockholders' equity of $100,000. The company's common shares are selling for $78 per share; 2,500 shares are outstanding.

Which stock should Snow buy?

CASE 21–5

FEAR OF REPORTING UNDER U.S. GAAP

You are on the board of directors of a large German corporation. For several years, the board has been discussing the possibility of listing the company's shares on the New York Stock Exchange. The CEO has approached the SEC several times asking for permission to list in the United States without also being required to reconcile its reported income to U.S. GAAP. So far the SEC has refused to compromise. As a result, the CEO has decreed that the company will not list its shares in the United States.

You know that the reason the CEO is so vehemently opposed to reporting net income under U.S. GAAP is that doing so would reveal the income manipulation that your company has engaged in during the past few years. Historically, your company has overstated expenses, thereby creating a large amount of "hidden reserves." During the past 2 years, those hidden reserves have been reversed, increasing reported income and covering up mounting operating losses.

You are fearful of the survivability of the company in the long run as long as operating losses are being covered up instead of addressed head on. The board of directors meets tomorrow, and one of the items on the agenda is yet another proposal to list shares on the New York Stock Exchange. What points should you bring up during that discussion?

CASE 21–6

WHICH REPORTING ALTERNATIVE IS BEST?

At a recent executive committee meeting, the officers of Celebrar Corporation entered into a lively discussion concerning changing prices in the economy and financial reporting. Kyle Jones, the controller, argued that something must be done to reflect price changes caused by inflation. The economic analyst, Marie Colton, argued strongly for a current cost approach. Colton had little good to say about "irrelevant" historical costs, even if adjusted to constant dollars. On the other hand, Ted Starley, the marketing V.P., felt comfortable with historical cost data. Starley understands that approach and has confidence in the objectivity of the numbers reported. As president of the company, what position do you take?

CASE 21–7

CONSTANT DOLLAR THEORY

Published financial statements of U.S. companies are currently prepared on a "stable dollar" assumption, even though inflation causes the general purchasing power of the dollar to decline considerably over the years. To account for this changing value of the dollar, many accountants suggest that financial statements should be adjusted for general price-level changes. Two independent statements regarding constant dollar financial statements follow. Each statement contains some faulty reasoning.

1. *Statement 1:* The accounting profession has not seriously considered constant dollar financial statements before because the rate of inflation usually has been so small from year to year that the adjustments would have been immaterial in amount. Constant dollar financial statements represent a departure from the historical cost basis of accounting. Financial statements should be prepared from facts, not estimates.

2. *Statement 2:* If financial statements were adjusted for general price-level changes, depreciation charges in the earnings statement would permit the recovery of dollars of current purchasing power and thereby equal the cost of new assets to replace the old ones. Constant dollar–adjusted data would yield balance sheet amounts closely approximating current values. Furthermore, management can make better decisions if constant dollar financial statements are published.

Evaluate each of the independent statements, identify the areas of faulty reasoning in each, and explain why the reasoning is incorrect.

CASE 21–8

CURRENT VALUATION OF ASSETS

The financial statements of a business entity could be prepared by using historical cost or current value as a measurement basis. In addition, the basis could be stated in terms of unadjusted dollars or dollars restated for changes in purchasing power. The various combinations of these two separate and distinct areas are shown in the following matrix:

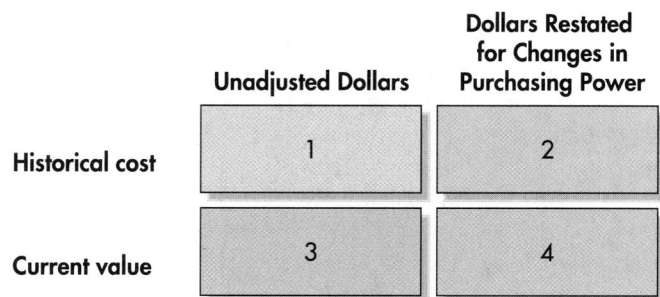

	Unadjusted Dollars	Dollars Restated for Changes in Purchasing Power
Historical cost	1	2
Current value	3	4

Block 1 of the matrix represents the traditional method of accounting for transactions wherein the absolute (unadjusted) amount of dollars given up or received is recorded for the asset or liability obtained. Amounts recorded in the method described in block 1 reflect the original cost of the asset or liability and do not take into account any change in value of the unit of measure. This method assumes the validity of the accounting concepts of going concern and stable monetary unit. Any gain or loss (including holding and purchasing power gains or losses) resulting from the sale or repayment of amounts recorded under this method is deferred in its entirety until sale or repayment.

For each of the remaining matrix blocks, what is the theoretic justification for using each method? Limit your discussion to nonmonetary assets only.

CASE 21–9

TRANSLATION OR REMEASUREMENT?

As the chief financial officer for Harvestors Inc., you are responsible for preparing the consolidated financial statements for Harvestors. Your first problem is how to consolidate the French subsidiary it purchased during the past year. You have recently received the subsidiary's year-end financial statements and find that they are stated in French francs. Before you can consolidate the financial statements, you must first convert them from French francs to U.S. dollars. You know that foreign financial statements can be either translated or remeasured, and you must now determine which method is appropriate.

What factors should you consider in determining whether the financial statements should be translated or remeasured? Who has the final say in determining which method is used? What are the major differences between translation and remeasurement?

EXERCISES

EXERCISE 21–10

COMMON-SIZE INCOME STATEMENTS

Comparative income statements for Long Pond Company for 2002 and 2001 are given below.

	2002	2001
Sales	$800,000	$450,000
Cost of goods sold	510,000	240,000
Gross profit	$290,000	$210,000
Selling and general expenses	80,000	60,000
Operating income	$210,000	$150,000
Interest expense	40,000	30,000
Income before income taxes	$170,000	$120,000
Income taxes	51,000	36,000
Net income	$119,000	$ 84,000

1. Prepare common-size income statements for Long Pond Company for 2002 and 2001.

2. Return on sales for Long Pond is lower in 2002 than in 2001. What expense or expenses are causing this lower profitability?

EXERCISE 21–11

COMMON-SIZE BALANCE SHEETS

The following data are taken from the comparative balance sheets prepared for the McCabe Resources Company.

	2002	2001
Cash	$ 34,000	$ 25,000
Accounts receivables (net)	43,000	40,000
Inventories	68,000	30,000
Property, plant, and equipment (net)	111,000	55,000
Total assets	$256,000	$150,000

Sales for 2002 were $1,000,000. Sales for 2001 were $800,000.

1. Prepare the asset sections of common-size balance sheets for McCabe Resources Company for 2002 and 2001.

2. Overall, McCabe is less efficient at using its assets to generate sales in 2002 than in 2001. What asset or assets are responsible for this decreased efficiency?

EXERCISE 21–12

DUPONT FRAMEWORK

Using the data presented below, estimate the return on equity (ROE) for the following industries.

	Assets-to-Equity Ratio	Asset Turnover	Return on Sales
Retail jewelry stores	1.578	1.529	0.040
Retail grocery stores	1.832	5.556	0.014
Electric service companies	2.592	0.498	0.069
Legal services firms	1.708	3.534	0.073

EXERCISE 21–13

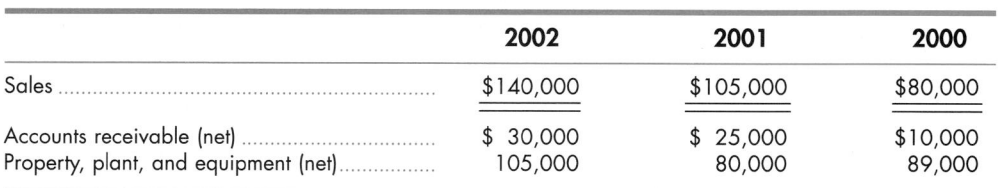

RATIOS FOR RECEIVABLES AND FIXED ASSETS

The financial statement data below are for Ridge Road Company.

	2002	2001	2000
Sales	$140,000	$105,000	$80,000
Accounts receivable (net)	$ 30,000	$ 25,000	$10,000
Property, plant, and equipment (net)	105,000	80,000	89,000

For 2001 and 2002, compute:

- Accounts receivable turnover
- Average collection period
- Fixed asset turnover

Use the average of the beginning and ending asset balances in computing the ratios.

EXERCISE 21–14

ANALYSIS OF INVENTORY

Income statements for the Eldermon Sales Company are shown below.

Analyze the inventory position at the end of each year as well as the profitability of inventory sales in each year. What conclusions would you make concerning the inventory trend?

	2002	2001	2000
Sales	$125,000	$100,000	$75,000
Cost of goods sold:			
Beginning inventory	$ 30,000	$ 25,000	$ 5,000
Purchases	105,000	80,000	85,000
	$135,000	$105,000	$90,000
Ending inventory	45,000	30,000	25,000
	$ 90,000	$ 75,000	$65,000
Gross profit	$ 35,000	$ 25,000	$10,000

EXERCISE 21–15

EFFECT OF LEVERAGE

The Vijay Corporation estimates that pretax earnings for the year ended December 31, 2002, will be $200,000 if it operates without borrowed capital. Income tax is 30% of earnings. Average stockholders' equity for 2002 is $750,000. Assuming that the company is able to borrow $1,200,000 at 12% interest, indicate the effects on net income and return on equity if borrowed capital earns (1) 18%, and (2) 10%. Explain the cause of the variations.

EXERCISE 21–16

MARGIN AND TURNOVER

The following information is obtained from the primary financial statements of two retail companies. One company markets its merchandise in a resort area; the other company is a discount household goods store. Neither company has any debt. By analyzing these data, indicate which company is more likely to be the gift shop and which is the discount household goods store. Support your answer.

	Company A	Company B
Revenue	$6,000,000	$6,000,000
Average total assets	1,200,000	6,000,000
Net income	125,000	600,000

EXERCISE 21–17

EQUITY RATIOS

Fargo Paint Corp. reported the following information.

	2002	2001	2000
10% bonds payable	$ 600,000	$ 600,000	$ 600,000
Common stock, $1 par	200,000	150,000	150,000
Additional paid-in capital	1,750,000	1,250,000	1,250,000
Retained earnings	300,000	100,000	50,000
Net income	280,000	130,000	70,000
Dividends	100,000	80,000	50,000
Year-end stock price per share	21	24	10

Compute the following for each year, 2000–2002.

1. Return on equity
2. Times interest earned (ignore income taxes)
3. Earnings per share
4. Dividend payout ratio
5. Price-earnings ratio
6. Book-to-market ratio

EXERCISE 21–18

DEBT COVENANTS AND FINANCING ALTERNATIVES

Chasebry Company is in need of another factory building. The building will cost $100,000. Chasebry is considering the following possible financing alternatives to acquire the building.

(a) Lease the building under an operating lease.
(b) Issue common stock in the amount of $100,000.
(c) Negotiate a long-term bank loan for $100,000.
(d) Negotiate a long-term bank loan for $60,000 and also increase short-term borrowing by $40,000.

Currently, Chasebry has current assets of $150,000, noncurrent assets of $325,000, current liabilities of $60,000, and noncurrent liabilities of $140,000. Under existing loan covenants, Chasebry must maintain a current ratio of 2.0 or more and a debt-to-equity ratio of less than .80. Which, if any, of the financing alternatives will allow Chasebry to avoid violating the loan covenants?

EXERCISE 21–19

ANALYSIS OF FINANCIAL DATA

The December 31, 2002, balance sheet of Copepper's Inc. and additional information are presented below. These are the only accounts on Copepper's balance sheet.

Amounts indicated by a question mark (?) can be calculated from the additional information given.

Assets		Liabilities and Stockholders' Equity	
Cash	$ 25,000	Accounts payable	$?
Accounts receivable (net)	?	Income taxes payable (current)	25,000
Inventory	?	Long-term debt	?
Property, plant, and		Common stock	300,000
equipment (net)	294,000	Retained earnings	?
	$432,000		$?

Additional information:

Current ratio (at year-end)	1.5 to 1
Total liabilities divided by total stockholders' equity	.8
Inventory turnover based on sales and ending inventory	15 times
Inventory turnover based on cost of goods sold and ending inventory	10.5 times
Gross margin for 2002	$315,000

1. What was Copepper's December 31, 2002 balance in accounts payable?
2. What was Copepper's December 31, 2002 balance in retained earnings?
3. What was Copepper's December 31, 2002 balance in inventory?

EXERCISE 21–20

MEETING THE NEEDS OF FOREIGN INVESTORS

Lyle Hollenbeck is the controller of the KPM Corporation, a small U.S. multinational. KPM has a number of non-U.S. stockholders, and Lyle is considering preparing a special annual report to provide them with information about KPM. Give Lyle some suggestions for such a report.

EXERCISE 21–21

DIFFERING ACCOUNTING STANDARDS

Fortune magazine lists the world's largest corporations by several categories including sales and profitability (profits according to the financial statements). When ranked by 1998 sales, 4 U.S. companies, 5 Japanese companies, and 1 Dutch company are in the top 10 as follows (all numbers are in millions of U.S. dollars):

Rank	Company	Revenues
1	General Motors Corporation	$178,174
2	Ford Motor Company	153,627
3	Mitsui & Co., Ltd.	142,688
4	Mitsubishi Corporation	128,922
5	Royal Dutch/Shell Group	128,142
6	Itochu Corporation	126,632
7	Exxon Corporation	122,379
8	Wal-Mart Stores, Inc.	119,299
9	Marubeni Corporation	111,121
10	Sumitomo Corporation	102,395

When ranked by profits, 7 of the top 10 are U.S. companies (no Japanese company appears in the top 20).

Other than economic factors, what could cause this difference in rankings between sales and reported profits?

EXERCISE 21-22

PREPARATION OF A FORM 20F RECONCILIATION

The following financial information is for MEBA Company, a non-U.S. firm with shares listed on a U.S. stock exchange.

Net income, computed according to home country GAAP	$ 12,000
Stockholders' equity, computed according to home country GAAP	100,000
Goodwill, recorded as a subtraction from equity rather than as an asset (occurred 5 years ago)	80,000
Market value of investment securities acquired this year, reported at cost of $3,000	4,700

If MEBA was following U.S. GAAP, goodwill would have been recorded as an asset and amortized over a period of 40 years and the investment securities would have been classified as available-for-sale and reported in the balance sheet at their current market value.

1. Prepare a reconciliation of MEBA's stockholders' equity of $100,000 to U.S. GAAP.
2. Reconcile MEBA's net income of $12,000 to U.S. GAAP.

EXERCISE 21-23

PREPARATION OF A FORM 20F RECONCILIATION

The following financial information is for Gwang Ju Company, a non-U.S. firm with shares listed on a U.S. stock exchange.

Net income, computed according to home country GAAP	$ 500,000
Stockholders' equity, computed according to home country GAAP	4,700,000
Brand names developed in house and recorded as both an increase in assets and an increase in equity	2,000,000
Obligation for postretirement medical care that is not reported as a liability in the balance sheet	1,500,000
Development costs capitalized at the end of the year	400,000

If Gwang Ju was following U.S. GAAP, the brand names would not have been recorded in the financial statements. In addition, the development costs would not have been capitalized but would have been expensed immediately. Finally, the postretirement medical care obligation would be reported as a liability according to U.S. GAAP. The additional postretirment medical care expense that would have been recognized for the year under U.S. GAAP is $230,000.

1. Prepare a reconciliation of Gwang Ju's reported stockholders' equity of $4,700,000 to U.S. GAAP.
2. Reconcile Gwang Ju's reported net income of $500,000 to U.S. GAAP.

EXERCISE 21-24

CONSTANT DOLLAR RESTATEMENT OF BALANCE SHEET

Comparative asset data for Fletch Inc. are presented below. The general price level during the 2-year period went up steadily; index numbers expressing the general price-level changes are listed after the asset data. Restate both sets of asset data in terms of constant dollars at the end of the second year.

	End of First Year	End of Second Year
Cash	$ 90,000	$ 75,000
Receivables	60,000	84,000
Land, buildings, and equipment (net)*	156,000	113,000
	$306,000	$272,000

*Acquired at the beginning of the first year.

General Price Index	
Beginning of first year	106
End of first year	120
End of second year	130

EXERCISE 21–25

COMPUTING PURCHASING POWER GAINS OR LOSSES

On January 1, 2002, Camden Corporation had monetary assets of $5,000,000 and monetary liabilities of $1,500,000. During 2002, Camden's monetary inflows and outflows were relatively constant and equal so that it ended the year with net monetary assets of $3,500,000.

Assume that the CPI was 200 on January 1, 2002, and 220 on December 31, 2002. In end-of-year constant dollars, what is Camden's purchasing power gain or loss for 2002?

EXERCISE 21–26

CURRENT COST INCOME

On January 1, 2002, Outerspace Corp. purchased 1,000 robots at $25 per robot. As of December 31, 2002, Outerspace had sold three-fourths of the robots at $32 per robot and the robot manufacturer (supplier) was selling to retailers (Outerspace) at $27 per robot.

Compute the operating gross profit for 2002 on a current cost basis. Also identify the amount of realized holding gain and unrealized holding gain. Ignore income taxes.

EXERCISE 21–27

CONSTANT DOLLAR AND CURRENT COST ADJUSTMENTS

Gifford Company purchased land for $150,000 in 2001 when the price index was 150. At the end of 2002 when the price index was 175, the land had a fair market value of $192,000. How would the land be reported on the balance sheet under each of the following approaches?

1. Historical cost/nominal dollar
2. Historical cost/constant dollar
3. Current cost/nominal dollar
4. Current cost/constant dollar (year-end dollars)

EXERCISE 21–28

CURRENT COST/CONSTANT DOLLAR BALANCE SHEET

The current cost/nominal dollar balance sheet for the Josh Corporation at December 31, 2002, is shown below. The equipment and land were purchased at year-end. The inventory is valued at year-end current prices. The capital stock was issued when the CPI was 240. The CPI at December 31, 2002, was 255. Prepare a current cost/constant dollar balance sheet for the Josh Corporation at December 31, 2002, stated in end-of-year constant dollars.

Balance Sheet
December 31, 2002
(Current Cost/Nominal Dollar Basis)

Assets		Liabilities and Stockholders' Equity	
Cash	$ 10,000	Accounts payable	$ 20,000
Accounts receivable	15,000	Interest payable	10,000
Inventory	30,000	Total liabilities	$ 30,000
Equipment (net)	50,000	Capital stock	$ 80,000
Land	45,000	Retained earnings	40,000
		Total stockholders' equity	$120,000
		Total liabilities and	
Total assets	$150,000	stockholders' equity	$150,000

(Note: Retained earnings is the residual amount after everything else has been adjusted to a current cost/constant dollar basis.)

EXERCISE 21–29

TRANSLATING FOREIGN CURRENCY FINANCIAL STATEMENTS

On January 3, 2002, Pecos Yo Company purchased International Metals, a Canadian company. On the day of the purchase, the exchange rate for 1 Canadian dollar was $0.79 (U.S.). International Metals' balance sheet on the date of the purchase is presented below.

(In Canadian dollars)	
Assets	
Cash	$ 58,000
Accounts receivable	112,500
Inventory	91,800
Plant assets	145,400
Total assets	$407,700
Liabilities and Equity	
Accounts payable	$165,600
Long-term debt	98,000
Capital stock	65,100
Retained earnings	79,000
Total liabilities and equity	$407,700

Prepare a translated balance sheet as of January 3, 2002.

EXERCISE 21–30

TRANSLATING FOREIGN CURRENCY FINANCIAL STATEMENTS

The following trial balance for International Data Products, a Japanese subsidiary of National Data Products, is available.

	(In Japanese yen)
Cash	¥ 6,000,000
Accounts Receivable	18,500,000
Inventory	21,250,000
Equipment	27,700,000
Cost of Goods Sold	36,000,000
Expenses	15,500,000
Dividends	5,000,000
Total debits	¥129,950,000
Accounts Payable	¥ 24,000,000
Long-Term Debt	12,000,000
Capital Stock	20,000,000
Retained Earnings	15,950,000
Sales	58,000,000
Total credits	¥129,950,000

The exchange rate when the subsidiary was purchased was $0.0055. The current exchange rate is $0.007, the average exchange rate for the year is $0.0065, and the exchange rate on the date dividends were declared and paid was $0.0067. The computed retained earnings balance from the previous year's translated financial statements was $105,000.

1. Prepare a translated trial balance for International Data Products using the information provided.
2. Prepare a combined income and retained earnings statement and a balance sheet for International Data Products using the information contained in the translated trial balance.

PROBLEMS

PROBLEM 21–31

COMMON-SIZE INCOME STATEMENTS
Operations for the Gordo Company for 2001 and 2002 are summarized below.

	2002	2001
Net sales	$480,000	$440,000
Cost of goods sold	350,000	240,000
Gross profit	$130,000	$200,000
Selling and general expenses	100,000	120,000
Operating income	$ 30,000	$ 80,000
Other expenses	35,000	30,000
Income (loss) before income taxes	$ (5,000)	$ 50,000
Income taxes (refund)	(2,000)	20,000
Net income (loss)	$ (3,000)	$ 30,000

Instructions:

1. Prepare common-size income statements for 2002 and 2001.
2. Comment on Gordo's profitability in 2002 relative to 2001.

PROBLEM 21–32

COMMON-SIZE BALANCE SHEETS
As of December 31, 2002, balance sheet data for the Stay-Trim Company and the Tone-Up Company are as follows:

	Stay-Trim Company	Tone-Up Company
Assets		
Current assets	$ 51,000	$ 240,000
Long-term investments	5,000	280,000
Land, buildings, and equipment (net)	48,000	520,000
Intangible assets	6,000	100,000
Other assets	5,000	60,000
Total assets	$115,000	$1,200,000
Liabilities and Stockholders' Equity		
Current liabilities	$ 15,000	$ 180,000
Long-term liabilities	25,000	300,000
Deferred revenues	5,000	70,000
Total liabilities	$ 45,000	$ 550,000
Preferred stock	$ 5,000	$ 100,000
Common stock	30,000	200,000
Additional paid-in capital	25,000	185,000
Retained earnings	10,000	165,000
Total stockholders' equity	$ 70,000	$ 650,000
Total liabilities and stockholders' equity	$115,000	$1,200,000

Instructions:

1. Prepare comparative common-size balance sheets for these 2 companies using total assets.
2. What conclusions can be drawn from these comparative common-size balance sheets?

PROBLEM 21–33

DUPONT ANALYSIS OF THREE COMPANIES

Financial information (in thousands of dollars) relating to 3 different companies follows.

	Company A	Company B	Company C
Net sales	$ 60,000	$28,000	$21,000
Net income	9,600	1,850	360
Total assets	155,400	21,500	3,200
Total equity	61,000	11,300	1,690

Instructions:

1. Compute the following ratios:
   a. Return on sales
   b. Asset turnover
   c. Assets-to-equity ratio
   d. Return on assets
   e. Return on equity
2. Assume the 3 companies are (a) a large department store, (b) a large grocery store, and (c) a large utility. Based on the above information, identify each company. Explain your answer.

PROBLEM 21–34

ANALYSIS OF INVENTORY AND RECEIVABLES

Inventory and receivable balances and gross profit data for Balboa Arrow Company are given below.

	2002	2001	2000
Balance sheet data:			
Inventory, December 31	$100,000	$ 90,000	$ 80,000
Accounts receivable, December 31	55,000	50,000	20,000
Income statement data:			
Net sales	$320,000	$260,000	$250,000
Cost of goods sold	215,000	200,000	180,000
Gross profit	$105,000	$ 60,000	$ 70,000

Instructions: Compute the following ratios for 2002 and 2001.

1. Accounts receivable turnover
2. Average collection period (Use the receivables balance at the end of the year.)
3. Inventory turnover
4. Number of days' sales in inventory (Use the inventory balance at end of year.)

PROBLEM 21–35

INVENTORY TURNOVER

The following data are taken from the Clayburgh Corporation records for the years ended December 31, 2002, 2001, and 2000.

	2002	2001	2000
Finished goods inventory	$ 60,000	$ 40,000	$ 30,000
Goods in process inventory	60,000	65,000	60,000
Raw materials inventory	60,000	40,000	35,000
Sales	400,000	340,000	300,000
Cost of goods sold	225,000	230,000	210,000
Cost of goods manufactured	260,000	250,000	200,000
Raw materials used in production	150,000	130,000	120,000

Instructions:
1. Compute turnover rates for 2002 and for 2001 for the following:
   a. Finished goods
   b. Goods in process
   c. Raw materials
2. Analyze the turnover results as to reasonableness and the message they send to a statement reader.

PROBLEM 21–36

COMPARATIVE RATIO ANALYSIS

The following are comparative data for Sunshine State Equipment, Inc., for the 3-year period 2000–2002.

Income Statement Data			
	2002	**2001**	**2000**
Net sales	$1,400,000	$1,100,000	$1,220,000
Cost of goods sold	760,000	600,000	610,000
Gross profit on sales	$ 640,000	$ 500,000	$ 610,000
Selling, general, and other expenses	340,000	280,000	250,000
Income before taxes	$ 300,000	$ 220,000	$ 360,000
Income taxes	120,000	89,000	152,000
Net income	$ 180,000	$ 131,000	$ 208,000
Dividends paid	155,000	150,000	208,000
Net increase (decrease) in retained earnings	$ 25,000	$ (19,000)	$ 0

Balance Sheet Data			
	2002	**2001**	**2000**
Assets			
Cash	$ 50,000	$ 40,000	$ 75,000
Accounts receivable (net)	300,000	320,000	250,000
Inventory	380,000	420,000	350,000
Prepaid expenses	30,000	10,000	40,000
Land, buildings, and equipment (net)	760,000	600,000	690,000
Intangible assets	110,000	100,000	125,000
Other assets	70,000	10,000	20,000
	$1,700,000	$1,500,000	$1,550,000
Liabilities and Stockholders' Equity			
Accounts payable	$ 120,000	$ 185,000	$ 220,000
Wages, interest, and dividends payable	25,000	25,000	25,000
Income tax payable	29,000	5,000	30,000
Miscellaneous current liabilities	10,000	4,000	10,000
8% bonds payable	300,000	300,000	250,000
Deferred revenues	10,000	10,000	25,000
No-par common stock, $10 stated value	500,000	400,000	400,000
Additional paid-in capital	510,000	400,000	400,000
Retained earnings	196,000	171,000	190,000
	$1,700,000	$1,500,000	$1,550,000

Instructions:
1. From the foregoing data, calculate financial ratios for the 3 years 2000–2002 as follows (for all ratios using balance sheet amounts, use the end-of-year balance):

a. Return on equity
b. Return on sales
c. Asset turnover
d. Assets-to-equity ratio

e. Return on assets
f. Current ratio
g. Dividend payout ratio

2. Based on the ratios calculated in (1), evaluate Sunshine State Equipment, Inc., in 2002 as compared with 2001.

PROBLEM 21–37

COMPARATIVE RATIO ANALYSIS

Use the comparative data for Sunshine State Equipment, Inc., as given in Problem 21–36. In addition, the year-end price per share of Sunshine's stock was $50 for 2000, $25 for 2001, and $35 for 2002.

Instructions:

1. Compute financial ratios for the 3 years 2000–2002 as follows (for ratios normally using average balances, assume 1999 figures are the same as 2000):
   a. Accounts receivable turnover
   b. Average collection period
   c. Inventory turnover
   d. Number of days' sales in inventory
   e. Fixed asset turnover
   f. Debt ratio
   g. Debt-to-equity ratio
   h. Times interest earned (assume Bonds Payable is the only interest-bearing liability)
   i. Earnings per share
   j. Price-earnings ratio
   k. Book-to-market ratio

2. Based on the ratios calculated in (1), evaluate Sunshine State Equipment, Inc., in 2002 as compared with 2001.

PROBLEM 21–38

ACCOUNTING DIFFERENCES AND RATIO ANALYSIS

The following 3 ratios have been computed using the financial statements for the year ended December 31, 2002, for Mikemath Company:

$$
\begin{aligned}
\text{Current ratio} &= \text{(Current assets/Current liabilities)} \\
&= \$80{,}000 \div \$43{,}000 \\
&= 1.86 \\
\text{Debt-to-equity ratio} &= \text{(Total liabilities/Stockholders' equity)} \\
&= \$110{,}000 \div \$125{,}000 \\
&= .88 \\
\text{Return on sales} &= \text{(Net income/Sales)} \\
&= \$45{,}000 \div \$400{,}000 \\
&= .11
\end{aligned}
$$

The following additional information has been assembled:

(a) Mikemath uses the LIFO method of inventory valuation. Beginning inventory was $36,000 and ending inventory was $43,000. If Mikemath had used FIFO, beginning inventory would have been $48,000 and ending inventory would have been $58,500.

(b) Mikemath's sole depreciable asset was purchased on January 1, 1999. The asset cost $120,000 and is being depreciated over 12 years with no estimated salvage value. Although the 12-year life is within the acceptable range, most firms in Mikemath's industry depreciate similar assets over 7 years.

(c) For 2002, Mikemath decided to recognize an $18,000 liability for future environmental cleanup costs. Most other firms in Mikemath's industry have similar environmental cleanup obligations but have decided that the amounts of the obligations are not reasonably estimable at this time; on average, these firms recognized only 5% of their total environmental cleanup obligation.

Instructions:

1. How would the values for the 3 ratios computed above differ if Mikemath had used FIFO, depreciated the asset over 7 years, and recognized only 5% of its environmental cleanup obligation? Do not think of these as accounting changes; compute how the financial statements would differ if the alternate accounting methods had been used to begin with. Ignore any income tax effects.
2. What dangers are there in comparing a company's financial ratios with summary industry ratios?

PROBLEM 21–39

PREPARATION OF A FORM 20F RECONCILIATION

The following financial information is for HKUST Company, a non-U.S. firm with shares listed on a U.S. stock exchange.

Net income, computed according to home country GAAP	33,000
Stockholders' equity, computed according to home country GAAP	146,000
Minority interest, recorded as an addition to stockholders' equity	25,000
Market value of investment securities acquired this year that were reported at cost of 3,000	4,700
Interest on the financing of self-constructed assets	5,000

If HKUST were following U.S. GAAP, the minority interest would have been classified as a liability instead of as part of stockholders' equity. In addition, minority interest income of 4,100 for the year would have been excluded from the computation of net income. Under U.S. GAAP, the investment securities would have been classified as trading securities. Also, under U.S. GAAP the interest on the financing of self-constructed assets would have been capitalized rather than expensed.

Instructions:

1. Prepare a reconciliation of HKUST's reported stockholders' equity of 146,000 to U.S. GAAP.
2. Reconcile HKUST's reported net income of 33,000 to U.S. GAAP.
3. Compute ROE using both HKUST's home country GAAP financial statement numbers and the U.S. GAAP numbers. In this case, ROE is higher for HKUST using U.S. GAAP. Are there reasons that a company might not wish to reconcile its reported numbers to U.S. GAAP, even when doing so would result in higher ROE? Explain.

PROBLEM 21–40

PREPARATION OF A FORM 20F RECONCILIATION

Delpie Company, a non-U.S. firm with shares listed on a U.S. stock exchange, reports the following financial information.

Net income, computed according to home country GAAP	400,000
Stockholders' equity, computed according to home country GAAP	4,000,000
Possible obligation for severance benefits to be paid to employees in future years, recognized this year	1,500,000
Goodwill recorded as a subtraction from equity rather than as an asset (occurred 3 years ago)	1,600,000

If Delpie was following U.S. GAAP, the goodwill would have been recorded as an asset and amortized over a period of 20 years. According to U.S. GAAP, the possible obligation for severance benefits would not be recognized until it had become probable.

Instructions:

1. Prepare a reconciliation of Delpie's reported stockholders' equity of 4,000,000 to U.S. GAAP.
2. Reconcile Delpie's reported net income of 400,000 to U.S. GAAP.
3. Delpie has reported income averaging 350,000 per year for the past 5 years. During the current year, sale of investment property created an unusual gain of 1,600,000. Why do you think that Delpie chose to recognize the obligation for possible future severance benefits this year rather than waiting to recognize the obligation in a future year?

PROBLEM 21–41

USING A PRICE INDEX
Sales for Leung Mfg. Company and a price index constructed specifically for its industry are as follows:

	2002	2001	2000	1999	1998
Sales of Leung Mfg. Company	$8,850	$8,385	$7,735	$7,280	$7,000
Industry price index (1998 = 100)	121	114	108	105	100

Instructions:

1. Compute price index–adjusted sales for 1998–2002 for Leung Mfg. Company. State sales in terms of 2002 dollars.
2. Prepare a short report for the management of Leung Mfg. Company summarizing your findings.

PROBLEM 21–42

CONSTANT DOLLAR ADJUSTMENTS AND REPLACEMENT COSTS
Valuation to reflect constant dollar adjustments yields differing amounts on a firm's financial statements compared to replacement costs.

Transactions regarding one asset of a company that operates on a calendar-year basis are as follows:

2000   Purchased land for $48,000 cash on December 31. Replacement cost at year-end was $48,000.

2001   Held land all year. Replacement cost at year-end was $62,400.

2002   December 31—sold land for $81,600.

General price-level index at December 31, 2000, was 120; at December 31, 2001, was 132; and at December 31, 2002, was 144.

Instructions: Based on the foregoing transactions, compute the amounts needed to complete the following chart. Express all constant dollar amounts in year-end dollars. Do not distinguish between realized and unrealized holding gains.

	Historical Cost		Replacement Cost	
	Nominal Dollar	Constant Dollar	Unadjusted for Inflation	Adjusted for Inflation
Valuation of land:				
December 31, 2000	_____	_____	_____	_____
December 31, 2001	_____	_____	_____	_____
Gain on income statement:				
2000	_____	_____	_____	_____
2001	_____	_____	_____	_____
2002	_____	_____	_____	_____
Total	======	======	======	======

PROBLEM 21–43

RESTATEMENT OF BALANCE SHEET TO CONSTANT DOLLARS
The Layton Company began operations in 1971. At the end of 2002 the company decided to furnish stockholders with a balance sheet restated in terms of constant 2002 dollars as a supplement to the conventional financial statements. This is the first time such a statement was prepared. The following balance sheet was prepared in conventional form at the end of 2002.

Layton Company
Balance Sheet
December 31, 2002

Assets		Liabilities and Stockholders' Equity	
Cash	$ 187,600	Accounts payable	$ 379,900
Accounts receivable	342,400	Mortgage note payable	450,000
Inventory	742,300	Bonds payable	1,250,000
Land	1,720,000	Capital stock	1,000,000
Building	2,115,000	Additional paid-in capital	200,000
Less: Accumulated			
depreciation	(705,000)	Retained earnings	1,122,400
		Total liabilities and	
Total assets	$4,402,300	stockholders' equity	$4,402,300

All the stock was issued in 1971. Land was purchased subject to a mortgage note of $1,000,000 at the time the company was formed. The present building is being depreciated on a straight-line basis with a 30-year life and no salvage value. The bonds were issued in 1981. The company uses the FIFO method in pricing inventories.

Instructions: Prepare a balance sheet for Layton Company restated in terms of 2002 constant dollars. Use the following indexes in making adjustments; assume the index for each year is regarded as representative of the price level for the entire year.

Year	Price Index	Year	Price Index
1971	54.9	1999	160.1
1981	70.7	2000	168.0
1991	93.0	2001	178.6
1993	100.0	2002	185.2
1998	146.5		

PROBLEM 21–44

CONSTANT DOLLAR INCOME STATEMENT
The historical cost income statement for the Colorado Company is presented below.

Colorado Company
Income Statement
For the Year Ended December 31, 2002

Sales		$180,000
Cost of goods sold:		
Beginning inventory	$ 20,000	
Purchases	140,000	
Goods available for sale	$160,000	
Ending inventory	50,000	
Cost of goods sold		110,000
Gross profit		$ 70,000
Operating expenses:		
Depreciation expense	$ 10,000	
Other expenses	20,000	30,000
Net income		$ 40,000

The following additional information is provided:

(a) Sales, purchases, and other expenses were incurred evenly over the year.

(b) The beginning inventory was purchased when the price index was 180.
Assume the ending inventory was acquired when the price index was 220.

(c) Price indexes were as follows:

Beginning of year 200
Average for year..................... 220
End of year............................ 240

(d) The equipment on which the depreciation expense is computed was purchased when the price index was 110.

Instructions: Prepare a statement showing net income in 2002 average-year constant dollars.

PROBLEM 21–45

CURRENT COST ACCOUNTING

Hastings Inc. adopted a current cost system in its first year of operation. At the start of the first year, 2002, the company purchased $168,000 of inventory. At the end of the year, it had an inventory of $100,800 on a historical cost basis and $164,500 on a current cost basis. At the time the inventory was sold, the current cost of the inventory was $107,800. Sales for the year were $182,000. Ignore all tax effects, and assume that there was no inflation during 2002. Other expenses were $8,400 on both historical cost and current cost bases.

Instructions: Prepare a current cost income statement, separately listing realized and unrealized holding gains.

PROBLEM 21–46

TRANSLATING FOREIGN CURRENCY FINANCIAL STATEMENTS

Crab Beach Systems, a U.S. multinational producer of computer hardware, has subsidiaries located throughout the world. The company recently received year-end financial statements from its French subsidiary, Doghead Technology. Doghead was purchased by Crab Beach on January 1, 2001. Doghead's financial statements are prepared and submitted to Crab Beach company headquarters in French francs. The accountant in charge of translating the financial statements has been unable to locate last year's translated financial statements. Instead, all that is available from last year is the financial statements prepared in francs. Doghead's adjusted trial balances as of December 31, 2001 and 2002, in French francs, are as follows:

	Trial Balance Dec. 31, 2002	Trial Balance Dec. 31, 2001
Cash	925,000	750,000
Accounts Receivable	1,875,000	1,215,000
Inventory	2,115,000	1,850,000
Equipment	1,025,000	975,000
Cost of Goods Sold	7,985,000	6,505,000
Expenses	4,234,000	3,156,000
Dividends	900,000	500,000
Total debits	19,059,000	14,951,000
Accounts Payable	2,100,000	1,825,000
Long-Term Debt	1,000,000	1,125,000
Capital Stock	1,200,000	1,200,000
Retained Earnings (balance at beginning of year)	640,000	301,000
Sales	14,119,000	10,500,000
Total credits	19,059,000	14,951,000

Relevant exchange rates for 2002 and 2001 are as follows:

	2002	2001
January 1	$0.196	$0.175
Date of dividend payment	0.205	0.188
Average rate for the year	0.210	0.178
December 31	0.228	0.196

Instructions: Using the information given, prepare a translated income and retained earnings statement and balance sheet, in U.S. dollars, for Doghead Technology for 2002.

PROBLEM 21–47

TRANSLATING FOREIGN CURRENCY FINANCIAL STATEMENTS

Renecko Corp., a company with headquarters in London, England, is a fully owned subsidiary of South Kaibab Inc. The accountant for South Kaibab just received Renecko's financial statements and must translate them from British pounds into U.S. dollars in order to prepare consolidated financial statements. Income statement and balance sheet data for the year just ended, along with relevant exchange rates, are as follows:

	(In Pounds)
Revenues	£350,000
Cost of goods sold	218,000
Gross margin	£132,000
Other expenses	74,000
Net income	£ 58,000
Cash	£ 55,000
Accounts receivable	113,000
Inventory	89,000
Plant and equipment	121,000
Total assets	£378,000
Current liabilities	£167,000
Long-term debt	48,000
Common stock	100,000
Retained earnings	63,000
Total liabilities and equity	£378,000

Exchange rates are:

On date of purchase	$2.15
Average rate for the year	1.98
On the balance sheet date	1.94
On date of dividend payment	1.97

In addition, dividends of 40,000 pounds were paid during the year.

Renecko's translated financial statements at year-end result in a translation adjustment with a debit balance of $55,000.

Instructions: Determine Renecko's retained earnings balance, in U.S. dollars, at the beginning of the year.

PROBLEM 21–48

COMPREHENSIVE STATEMENT OF CASH FLOWS

The schedule below shows the account balances of the Beneficio Corporation at the beginning and end of the fiscal year ended October 31, 2002.

Debits	October 31, 2002	October 31, 2001
Cash and Cash Equivalents	$ 222,000	$ 50,000
Investment Securities—Trading	10,000	40,000
Accounts Receivable	148,000	100,000
Inventories	291,000	300,000
Prepaid Insurance	2,500	2,000
Land and Building	195,000	195,000
Equipment	305,000	170,000
Discount on Bonds Payable	8,500	9,000
Treasury Stock (at cost)	5,000	10,000
Cost of Goods Sold	539,000	
Selling and General Expenses	287,000	
Income Taxes	35,000	
Loss on Write-Down of Investment Securities	4,000	
Loss on Sale of Equipment	1,000	
Total debits	$2,053,000	$876,000

Credits	October 31, 2002	October 31, 2001
Allowance for Bad Debts	$ 8,000	$ 5,000
Accumulated Depreciation—Building	26,250	22,500
Accumulated Depreciation—Equipment	39,750	27,500
Accounts Payable	55,000	60,000
Notes Payable—Current	70,000	20,000
Miscellaneous Expenses Payable	18,000	8,700
Taxes Payable	35,000	10,000
Unearned Revenue	1,000	9,000
Notes Payable—Long-Term	40,000	60,000
Bonds Payable—Long-Term	250,000	250,000
Deferred Income Tax Liability	47,000	53,300
Common Stock, $2 par	359,400	200,000
Retained Earnings Appropriated for Possible Building Expansion	43,000	33,000
Unappropriated Retained Earnings	34,600	112,000
Paid-In Capital in Excess of Par Value	116,000	5,000
Sales	898,000	
Gain on Sale of Investment Securities	12,000	
Total credits	$2,053,000	$876,000

The following information was also available:

(a) All purchases and sales were on account.

(b) Equipment with an original cost of $15,000 was sold for $7,000.

(c) Selling and general expenses include the following:

Building depreciation	$ 3,750
Equipment depreciation	25,250
Bad debts expense	4,000
Interest expense	18,000

(d) A 6-month note payable for $50,000 was issued toward the purchase of new equipment.

(e) The long-term note payable requires the payment of $20,000 per year plus interest until paid.

(f) Treasury stock was sold for $1,000 more than its cost.

(g) During the year, a 30% stock dividend was declared and issued. At the time, there were 100,000 shares of $2 par common stock outstanding. However, 1,000 of these shares were held as treasury stock at the time and were prohibited from participating in the stock dividend. Market price was $10.00 per share after the stock dividend was issued.

(h) Equipment was overhauled, extending its useful life at a cost of $6,000. The cost was debited to Accumulated Depreciation—Equipment.

Instructions: Prepare a statement of cash flows for the year ended October 31, 2002, using the indirect method of reporting cash flows from operations.

COMPETENCY ENHANCEMENT OPPORTUNITIES

▶ Deciphering Actual Financial Statements	▶ Ethical Dilemma
▶ Writing Assignment	▶ Cumulative Spreadsheet Analysis
▶ Research Project	▶ Internet Search
▶ The Debate	

Accounting is more than just doing textbook problems. This expanded competency material provides practice in critical thinking, oral and written communication, research, teamwork, and consideration of ethical issues.

▶ DECIPHERING ACTUAL FINANCIAL STATEMENTS
• Deciphering 21–1 (The Walt Disney Company)
The 1998 financial statements for THE WALT DISNEY COMPANY are included in Appendix A. Locate those financial statements and consider the following questions.

1. Disney has 3 primary business segments: Creative Content, Broadcasting, and Theme Parks and Resorts. Which of these 3 has the best 1998 profitability as measured by return on sales?
2. Which of Disney's 3 segments has the best overall asset efficiency in 1998 as measured by asset turnover?
3. Which of Disney's 3 segments best combines margin and turnover in 1998 to yield the highest return on assets?
4. Discuss why ROE cannot be computed for each segment. What is Disney's overall ROE in 1998?
5. From Disney's foreign currency translation adjustment, deduce whether the foreign currencies got stronger or weaker in 1998 (relative to the U.S. dollar) in the countries where Disney has subsidiaries.

• Deciphering 21–2 (McDonald's)
At the top of the page 1249 are comparative income statements for MCDONALD's for 1996, 1997, and 1998.

Instructions:

1. There are two kinds of McDonald's restaurants—restaurants that McDonald's itself owns, and restaurants owned by McDonald's franchisees. For each of the 3 years, prepare a mini income statement for McDonald's containing the following items:

	Sales by company-operated restaurants
Less:	Food and packaging
Less:	Payroll and employee benefits
Less:	Occupancy and other operating expenses
=	Operating income from company-operated restaurants

2. From the mini income statements prepared in (1), prepare common-size income statements for McDonald's company-operated restaurants for the 3 years 1996–1998.

3. Comment on the common-size income statements prepared in (2).
4. Where does McDonald's get more of its total operating income—from company-owned restaurants or from franchise operations?

McDonald's Comparative Income Statements
(In Millions of U.S. Dollars)

Years ended December 31,	1998	1997	1996
REVENUES			
Sales by Company-operated restaurants	$ 8,894.9	$ 8,136.5	$ 7,570.7
Revenues from franchised and affiliated restaurants	3,526.5	3,272.3	3,115.8
TOTAL REVENUES	12,421.4	11,408.8	10,686.5
OPERATING COSTS AND EXPENSES			
Company-operated restaurants:			
Food and packaging	2,997.4	2,772.6	2,546.6
Payroll and employee benefits	2,230.3	2,025.1	1,909.8
Occupancy and other operating expenses	2,043.9	1,851.9	1,706.8
	7,271.6	6,649.6	6,163.2
Franchised restaurants—occupancy expenses	678.0	613.9	570.1
Selling, general, and administration expenses	1,458.5	1,450.5	1,366.4
Made for You costs	161.6		
Special charges	160.0		72.0
Other operating (income) expense—net	(60.2)	(113.5)	(117.8)
TOTAL OPERATING COSTS AND EXPENSES	9,659.5	8,600.5	8,053.9
OPERATING INCOME	2,761.9	2,808.3	2,632.6
Interest expense—net of capitalized interest of $17.9, $22.7 and $22.2	(413.8)	(364.4)	(342.5)
Nonoperating income (expense)—net	(40.7)	(36.6)	(39.1)
Income before provision for income taxes	2,307.4	2,407.3	2,251.0
Provision for income taxes	757.3	764.8	678.4
NET INCOME	$ 1,550.1	$ 1,642.5	$ 1,572.6

• Deciphering 21–3 (Coke vs. Pepsi)

The following information is from the 1998 annual reports of THE COCA-COLA COMPANY and of PEPSICO (all amounts are in millions of U.S. dollars).

	PepsiCo		Coca-Cola	
	Overall	Beverages	Overall	Beverages
Sales	$22,348	$10,651	$18,813	$18,636
Net income	1,993	992	3,533	5,447
Total assets	22,660	10,805	19,145	10,665
Total equity	6,401	—	8,403	—

For the Beverage segment information, net income is the operating income for the segment and total assets are the assets that are identifiable with the Beverage segment.

Instructions:

1. Using the overall data, compute return on equity, return on sales, asset turnover, and assets-to-equity ratio for both PepsiCo and Coca-Cola.
2. Using the Beverage segment data, compute return on sales, asset turnover, and return on assets for both PepsiCo and Coca-Cola.

3. Some writers have claimed that The Coca-Cola Company has outperformed PepsiCo in recent years because Coke has concentrated on the profitable soft drink business, whereas PepsiCo has diversified into snack foods. Evaluate this claim in light of your calculations in (1) and (2).

• **Deciphering 21–4 (The Rouse Company)**

THE ROUSE COMPANY is a real estate development firm with ownership of shopping malls, office buildings, hotels, and undeveloped land throughout the United States. In 1996, Rouse paid $549 million to purchase Las Vegas real estate from the heirs of billionaire Howard Hughes.

The Rouse Company is well known in accounting circles because it is one of the few firms that provides a current value balance sheet in addition to the traditional historical cost balance sheet. Rouse included the following note in its 1996 annual report:

CURRENT VALUE REPORTING

The Company's interests in operating properties, land held for development and sale and certain other assets have appreciated in value and, accordingly, their aggregate current value substantially exceeds their aggregate cost basis net book value determined in conformity with generally accepted accounting principles. The current value basis financial statements present information about the current values to the Company of its assets and liabilities and the changes in such values. The current value basis financial statements are not intended to present the current liquidation values of assets or liabilities of the Company or its net assets taken as a whole.

Management believes that the current value basis financial statements more realistically reflect the underlying financial strength of the Company. The current values of the Company's interests in operating properties, including interests in unconsolidated real estate ventures, represent management's estimates of the value of these assets primarily as investments. These values will generally be realized through future cash flows generated by the operation of these properties over their economic lives. The current values of land held for development and sale represent management's estimates of the value of these assets under long-term development and sales programs.

The asset section of Rouse Company's balance sheet as of December 31, 1996, is as follows:

The Rouse Company and Subsidiaries
CONSOLIDATED COST BASIS AND
CURRENT VALUE BASIS BALANCE SHEETS
[Asset Section only]
December 31, 1996 (in thousands)

	Current Value Basis (note 1)	Cost Basis
Property (notes 5, 9, 16 and 17):		
Operating properties:		
Property and deferred costs of projects	$4,662,590	$3,374,976
Less accumulated depreciation and amortization	–0–	552,201
	4,662,590	2,822,775
Properties in development	181,368	176,060
Properties held for sale	73,080	73,080
Investment land and land held for		
development and sale	322,136	244,117
Total property	5,239,174	3,316,032
Prepaid expenses, deferred charges and other assets	196,952	187,689
Accounts and notes receivable (note 6)	92,369	92,369
Investments in marketable securities	3,596	3,596
Cash and cash equivalents	43,766	43,766
Total assets	$5,575,857	$3,643,452

Instructions:

1. Examine the asset section of The Rouse Company's 1996 balance sheet and answer the following questions:
   a. Why is there no accumulated depreciation on operating properties under the current value basis?
   b. The total difference between the current value of Rouse's assets and the cost basis of those assets is $1,932,405 ($5,575,857 − $3,643,452). Compute the difference for just the current assets. Comment.
   c. Is it possible for the current value basis of Rouse's total assets to be *less* than the cost basis? Explain.
2. What characteristic of The Rouse Company has caused it to voluntarily emphasize its current value disclosures to the extent that those supplemental disclosures are given equal prominence with the cost-basis balance sheet numbers?
3. Assume that The Rouse Company is required to make a journal entry to convert "Property and deferred costs of projects" from the net cost basis of $2,822,775 to the current value basis. Make the necessary journal entry. Also, discuss whether there are any income tax issues that should be considered in making the journal entry.
4. The Rouse Company does not include current value basis financial statements as part of its quarterly financial statements. Why do you think this is so?
5. The current value basis balance sheet is not in conformity with GAAP in the United States. As such, those statements are not included within the scope of the standard auditor's opinion. How can The Rouse Company give financial statement users some credible assurance that the current value numbers are reliable?

• Deciphering 21–5 (Safeway)

Below are sales data, in nominal dollars, for SAFEWAY, the supermarket chain, from 1981 through 1998 (in millions of U.S. dollars). In addition, the Consumer Price Index (CPI) for each year is given (1982–1984 = 100).

Year	Sales	CPI	Year	Sales	CPI
1981	$16,580	90.9	1990	$14,874	130.7
1982	17,633	96.5	1991	15,119	136.2
1983	18,585	99.6	1992	15,152	140.3
1984	19,642	103.9	1993	15,215	144.5
1985	19,651	107.6	1994	15,627	148.2
1986	20,312	109.6	1995	16,398	152.4
1987	18,301	113.6	1996	17,269	156.9
1988	13,612	118.3	1997	22,484	160.5
1989	14,325	124.0	1998	24,484	163.0

Instructions:

1. Use the CPI to restate all the Safeway sales numbers in terms of 1998 dollars.
2. In terms of nominal dollar sales, Safeway's sales have been growing steadily since 1988. Does the constant dollar sales data give the same picture? Explain.
3. In the latter part of 1986, Safeway underwent a leveraged buyout and began to get rid of a number of its stores. Is there any evidence of this in the nominal dollar sales data? in the constant dollar sales data?

WRITING ASSIGNMENT
• Choosing the functional currency

You are on the accounting staff at Jeff Pong Company. Jeff Pong is based in California and has recently acquired a subsidiary, Mak Hung Enterprises, located in Guangzhou, China. The board of directors of Jeff Pong is curious about how the Chinese currency (yuan) financial statements of Mak Hung will be consolidated with Jeff Pong's U.S. dollar financial statements. Yesterday, your boss, the controller, made a presentation to the board explaining the adjustments that will be made to Mak Hung's financial statements to restate them from international accounting standards to U.S. GAAP.

The controller has asked you to write a memo to the board explaining how the yuan financial statements, once restated to be in conformity with U.S. GAAP, will be converted into U.S. dollars. The controller has decided that Mak Hung's functional currency is the yuan. Make sure you explain to the board what a functional currency is, how it is determined, and what implications it has for the way financial statements are converted into U.S. dollars.

▶ **RESEARCH PROJECT**
• **Finding sources for industry ratios**
Your group is to report (either orally or in writing) on your examination of a published source of ratio values for use as industry benchmarks.

Go to your library and find a publication that provides summary ratio values by industry group. Using the information in this publication, answer the following questions:

1. What is the sample of firms used to compile the industry averages?
2. How are the industry groups defined?
3. Look at the definitions of the ratios. Are there any that are defined differently from the definitions given in the textbook? Are any ratios given different names from the ones used in the textbook?
4. Look at the list of industries and choose 3 different industries that you think will have different values for return on sales: an industry with a very low value, an industry with a medium value, and one with a very high value. Explain what factors of these 3 industries caused you to choose them. Check the actual return on sales for these 3 industries and see how well you did with your predictions.

▶ **THE DEBATE**
• **We need standards for ratios!**
Financial ratios can be computed using many different formulas. The formulas used to compute ratios such as debt ratio and inventory turnover differ from one source to another. In addition, there is no required set of ratios for companies to provide in the annual report—companies report whatever ratios they choose. Because financial ratios are an important part of the financial reporting environment, should the FASB become involved in identifying common formulas and ratios that would be included in all financial statements?

Divide your group into 2 teams.

• One team represents Standardized Ratios. Prepare a 2-minute oral argument explaining why it is imperative that the FASB establish standards for the computation and reporting of financial ratios. The freedom that currently exists contributes to investor confusion, waste of time, and potential information manipulation as firms choose to report only those ratio values that are favorable.

• The other team represents Ratio Freedom. Prepare a 2-minute presentation summarizing why the standardization of ratios is counterproductive. The needs of users differ, so different sets of ratios are applicable to different sets of users. Any attempt to define a standard list of "accepted" ratios will necessarily favor the needs of one group of users over others.

▶ **ETHICAL DILEMMA**
• **Does the bonus plan reward the right thing?**
Roaring Springs Booksellers is a mail-order book company. Customers choose their purchases from a catalog and send in their order by mail, fax, phone, or e-mail. Roaring Springs then assembles the books from its warehouse inventory, packs the order, and ships it to the customer within 3 working days. This rapid turnaround time on orders requires Roaring Springs to have a large warehouse staff; wage expense averages almost 20% of sales.

Each member of the top management of Roaring Springs receives an annual bonus equal to 1% of his or her salary for every 0.1% that Roaring Springs' return on sales exceeds

5.0%. For example, if return on sales is 5.3%, each top manager would receive a bonus of 3% of salary. Historically, return on sales for Roaring Springs has ranged from 4.5% to 5.5%.

The management of Roaring Springs has come up with a plan to dramatically increase return on sales, perhaps to as high as 6.5% to 7.0%. The plan is to acquire a sophisticated, computerized packing machine that can receive customer order information, mechanically assemble the books for each individual order, box the order, print an address label, and route the box to the correct loading dock for pickup by the delivery service. Acquisition of this machine will allow Roaring Springs to lay off 100 warehouse employees, resulting in a significant savings in wage expense. Top management intends to acquire the machine using new investment capital from stockholders. In this way, there will be no increase in interest expense. Because the depreciation expense on the new machine will be much less than the savings in reduced wage expense, return on sales will increase.

All top managers of Roaring Springs are excited about this plan: It could increase their bonuses to as much as 20% of salary. As assistant to the chief financial officer of Roaring Springs, you have been asked to prepare a briefing for the board of directors explaining exactly how this new packing machine will increase return on sales. As part of your preparation, you decide to examine the impact of the machine acquisition on the other two components of the DuPont framework—efficiency and leverage. You find that even with the projected increase in return on sales, the decrease in asset turnover and in the assets-to-equity ratio will cause total ROE to decline from its current level of 18.0% to around 14.0%.

Your presentation is scheduled for the next board of directors meeting in 2 weeks. What should you do?

CUMULATIVE SPREADSHEET ANALYSIS

This spreadsheet assignment is an extension of the spreadsheet assignment given in Chapter 20, (1) and (2). Refer back to the instructions given in Chapter 20. If you completed the spreadsheet assignment for Chapter 20, that spreadsheet can form the foundation for this assignment.

1. In addition to preparing forecasted financial statements for 2003 and 2004, Skywalker also wishes to prepare forecasted financial statements for 2005, 2006, and 2007. All assumptions applicable to 2003 and 2004 are assumed to be applicable to the subsequent years. Refer back to Chapter 13, (1), for an explanation of each of the assumptions. Sales in each year are expected to be 40% higher than sales in the year before. (Note: For this part of the assignment, use the original 107.6-day value for the number of days' sales in inventory; ignore the change assumed in (2) of the Chapter 20 assignment.) Clearly state any additional assumptions that you make.

2. As a company matures, it expects to generate enough cash from its operating activities to pay for a significant portion of its investing activities. Comment on whether it appears that Skywalker will reach that condition between 2002 and 2007.

3. Repeat (1), with the following changes in assumptions:

Average collection period	9.06 days
Number of days' sales in inventory	66.23 days
Fixed asset turnover	3.989 times
Gross profit percentage	27.55%
Other operating expenses/sales	19.86%
Number of days' purchases in accounts payable	50.37 days

(Note: After making these changes in ratio values, your spreadsheet may have negative amounts for Short-term Loans Payable. This is impossible. Adjust your spreadsheet so that Short-term Loans Payable is never less than zero. This will require a relaxation of the requirement that the current ratio be at least 2.0.)

4. Discuss why Skywalker has a projected current ratio of less than 2.0 in some years when using the ratios in (3).

5. Which company would you rather loan money to: a company with the projected financial statements prepared in (1) or a company with the projected financial statements prepared in (3)? Explain your answer.

▶ **INTERNET SEARCH**

FORTUNE magazine's Web address is www.fortune.com. Once you've gained access to Fortune's Web site, answer the following questions.

1. Who is the editor-in-chief of *Fortune* magazine? What is Fortune's parent company?
2. In addition to the famous Fortune 500, an annual listing of the 500 largest companies in the United States, Fortune also periodically compiles other lists. What other lists does Fortune compile?
3. Look at the Fortune 500 listing, and for the largest 5 firms (Fortune ranks them in terms of total revenues), extract the following information:
   - Total revenues
   - Net profits
   - Total assets
   - Stockholders' equity
   - Total market value of stock

   For each of these 5 companies, compute the following:
   a. Return on sales
   b. Asset turnover
   c. Assets-to-equity ratio
   d. Return on equity
   e. Book-to-market ratio
4. Fortune ranks the 500 largest firms by Revenues. Do you think this is the best measure of size? Explain.

Appendix A

the Walt Disney Company 1998 Annual Report

$\mathscr{F}$INANCIAL HIGHLIGHTS

The Walt Disney Company and Subsidiaries

(In millions of dollars, except per share data)	1998	1997	1996	CAGR
Revenues	$22,976	$22,473	$18,739	11%
Operating income[1]	4,015	4,312	3,333	10%
Net income[1][2]	1,850	1,886	1,534	10%
Diluted earnings per share[1][2]	0.89	0.92	0.83	4%
Cash flow from operations	5,115	5,099	3,707	17%
Stockholders' equity	19,388	17,285	16,086	10%
Book value per share	9.46	8.59	7.96	9%

[1]The 1997 amounts exclude the impact of a $135 million gain on the sale of KCAL and
the 1996 amounts exclude the impact of a $300 million non-cash charge for the
SFAS 121 accounting change

[2]The 1996 amounts exclude the impact of $225 million of acquisition-related costs

1

$\mathcal{L}$ ETTER TO $\mathcal{S}$ HAREHOLDERS

To Disney Owners and Fellow Cast Members:

I am looking out the window and can see the seasons change (yes, the seasons do change in Los Angeles – the eucalyptus leaves droop more and the sprinklers go on less often). I am reminded that our rhythms are set by the seasons and that any number of human endeavors are ruled by the calendar. Such as this annual report. Every 12 months we compile it, and every 12 months I sit down to write you this letter.

There's just one problem with this annual exercise: It implies that businesses can be run in neat 12-month chunks of time. Unfortunately, the business cycle has its own seasons, which are not ruled by the orderly and predictable orbit of the earth around the sun. Indeed, at Disney, we live by a 60-month calendar. We set our goals over rolling five-year timelines. In this context, each year is more like a season. Some are sunny and some are overcast, but each is merely a period of passage and not a destination. Our five-year calendars force us to think long-term. They make us devise strategies that add value, not squeeze profits.

But this is an *annual* report, not a quinquennial report. Our fiscal year earnings were roughly the same as they were in

the previous 12 months. This flat performance probably doesn't come as a surprise to you, given the metaphorical way I opened this letter, trying to ease gently into a discussion of what appears to be our twice-a-decade problem.

I'll call it "semi-decadal" because in many ways 1998 reminds me of 1991, a year that also featured languishing earnings. But I believe that there is a more important similarity between 1998 and 1991 ... namely, that both were years of key strategic investments and significant new initiatives.

In 1991, our initiatives included three new hotels at Walt Disney World; Hyperion Books; Discover Magazine; the Disney Vacation Club; Fantasmic! and the CarToon Spin at Disneyland and Muppet 3D at the Disney-MGM Studios.

In 1998, the list of major new initiatives was even longer, with Disney's Animal Kingdom; DisneyQuest; the Disney Cruise Line; ESPNZone; *ESPN-The Magazine*; *Jane* magazine; new Disney Channels in Italy and Spain; Downtown Disney and the All-Star Movies Resort at Walt Disney World; Radio Disney; the ESPN Classic sports channel; Toon Disney on cable; the new Tomorrowland at Disneyland; the refurbishment of Anaheim Stadium; the acquisition of

Starwave; the investment in Infoseek and the creation of the Go Network™. In 1998, I also saw the *end* of an initiative begun five years ago and subsequently accomplished in midnight-to-2 a.m. shifts, namely my book, *Work in Progress*. At long last, it is finally done! It turned out to be a book about the challenges of running a creative company, utilizing examples from my personal experience. It did not destroy my marriage, it was reviewed reasonably well, despite some criticism for not being "a kiss and tell," and it has yet to be read by my three sons – who fortunately have their own lives and have heard enough stories from their father.

As with our 1991 initiatives, our 1998 efforts are all designed to further Disney's overall corporate mission – to offer quality entertainment that people will seek out. Consider what this really means. About 2,300 years ago, the Greek philosopher Theophrastus said, "Time is the most valuable thing a man can spend." It still is. At Disney, we are dedicated to creating entertainment of such excellence that people will choose to spend some of their valuable time with us. All of our 1998 initiatives are geared toward this goal. Given their high quality and given the evidence that people all over the world will be enjoying more and more disposable time (a horrible phrase, considering time's preciousness)

in the years ahead, these investments have the potential to create significant growth down the road. Unfortunately, like all investments that create theoretical opportunities in the future, they cost *real* money right now. Consequently, during the fiscal season that was 1998, they helped drag down our net income. But that's the short-run story. In the long run (which is the run that really matters), we believe they will enrich our company.

Not only do all of these initiatives represent wonderful ways to spend one's time, but they also reflect a tremendous range of experience. Some, like Disney's Animal Kingdom, the new Tomorrowland and the expansion of the Disney Channel, are extensions of established forms of Disney entertainment. Others, like DisneyQuest, the Disney Cruise Line and the Go Network, encompass forms of entertainment that are new to us. They reflect our belief that developments such as regional entertainment, the cruise business and the Internet relate directly to our core business and are opportunities that will help lead us to the future.

The future was very much on our minds this past October, when we held a senior management retreat at my parents' apple orchard in Vermont. Although we were a week late for "cow appreciation day" in Woodstock, we were not too late to cruise Sam's Army and Navy Store (recently renamed Sam's Outfitters for political correctness) or to meet and hike, communicate and get excited and organized about the seasons and years and decade ahead. We pondered the ecological environment and the economic environment, which a few weeks earlier the pundits had proclaimed was teetering on the brink of recession. Lately, they seem to be saying "never mind."

While we didn't find a crystal ball at Sam's Outfitters, we did crystallize a Disney methodology for weathering any economic storms that may lie ahead. That methodology can be stated quite simply: "Put the creative process first and while we're at it, try to make sure not to lose money." At its heart, ours is a creative company, and creativity of all kinds – artistic, financial and administrative – holds the key to prospering as the new century approaches, whatever surprises it may bring with it. By the way, this methodology is nothing new. Throughout its 75-year history, creativity has been the hallmark of our company and has driven its remarkable success.

On October 16, we honored this legacy of creativity during our 75th anniversary celebration. On this occasion, we inducted another 19 people as Disney Legends, including two especially legendary individuals. The first was Virginia Davis, who starred in the Alice Comedies, the very first films produced by the Disney Brothers Cartoon Studio. The second was Roy E. Disney, who is vice chairman of our Board of Directors and chairman of Feature Animation. If it weren't for Roy, the Disney legacy would have ended at its 60th anniversary. It was in 1984 that he provided crucial leadership in fending off corporate raiders intent on breaking the company apart. Roy is also a record-setting international yachtsman, which I mention because, when he's not on the high seas, he continues to be an invaluable rudder and stabilizer for our company. You need look no further than his name to see why Roy understands better than anyone the

essence of Disney ... an essence, I might add, that was remarkably evident in those very first Alice Comedies.

Two individuals who are also legends in their own right are Card Walker and Dick Nunis, who have announced their retirement as members of our Board of Directors, with Dick also stepping down as chairman of Walt Disney Attractions. Between them, these two men have dedicated 103 years to our company! Card first joined Disney in 1938 and ultimately served as chairman and chief executive officer, while Dick started in 1955 and went on to head our Attractions division. They may be retiring, but I will continue to rely on their wisdom and insights about all things Disney.

And, while I'm recognizing legends, I want to mention the Singing Cowboy, Gene Autry, who died this year. He was not only a Hollywood legend and a brilliant businessman, but also a good friend of our company, dating back to the days of Walt, who served on the original board of directors of Gene's Angels baseball team. I am sure Gene is somewhere smiling at the Angels' acquisition of Mo Vaughn, a quality star who completely fits into Gene's Cowboy Code, especially Code #6: "He must help people in distress."

The weekend following our 75th anniversary celebration, we conducted the Disney VoluntEARS Global Celebration of Children. During these two days, nearly 11,000 Disney cast members volunteered in 212 cities in 44 states, five Canadian provinces, 24 countries, on five continents. Our goal was to further celebrate our 75th anniversary by helping 75,000 children around the globe. This was one more way to honor the Disney heritage of making the world a better and happier place.

Toward the end of the year, action was taken in Washington that should help us further protect and build on our heritage. Congress passed and the President signed an extension of the copyright law, assuring that Mickey Mouse's home will continue to be exclusively at The Walt Disney Company.

One important way that we're continuing to make Mickey and his friends feel right at home is a new initiative for 1999, tentatively called *MouseWorks*. We are producing brand new cartoon shorts featuring everyone's favorite mice, ducks and dogs – Mickey, Minnie, Donald, Daisy, Pluto and Goofy (yes, Goofy is a dog). Some of these shorts will initially appear with Disney theatrical and video releases. After that, they will form the basis of a television series that will appear initially in the United States and eventually around the world. In recent decades, these Disney stars have remained incredibly popular despite the fact they've rarely ventured away from their residences in Toon Town. Now they are going to be put back to work doing what they do best – entertaining their fans on the big and little screen.

One other parallel between 1998 and 1991 was the bad news/good news of our live-action movie business. The bad news is that 1998 was a tough year for us. As in 1991, we succumbed to the overall industry trend of paying more and more for talent in front of and behind the camera. Of course, we had our successes, such as the number one film of the summer, *Armageddon*, and the remake of *The Parent Trap*. We also had some highly regarded films such as *The Horse Whisperer* and *Beloved*. And Miramax enjoyed the commercially and artistically successful *Good Will Hunting*. But, in too many instances, profits did not materialize from the revenues achieved by our films. Stated more bluntly, either the films and marketing cost too much, or the audience rejected our ideas. Whatever the reason, we're glad fiscal '98 is over in this area.

Which brings me to the good news. Fiscal '99 has started off like gangbusters for our movie division. I know this is last year's annual report, but I am not about to wait a year to report on *A Bug's Life*, *Enemy of the State* and *The Waterboy*, which were three of the top four films during Thanksgiving weekend. I go for the good news wherever and whenever I can. And it is good news indeed when the first two months of the new fiscal year bring break-out hits.

In an effort to improve our odds for continued success in the live-action film business, we are implementing a strategy that calls for the making of a higher percentage of Disney-labeled films ... a strategy that, needless to say, could only be undertaken by our studio. Disney continues to be the only brand name in the entertainment industry. For 75 years, it has earned the trust of the public. Under our new strategy, we hope to build on this trust with a renewed emphasis on Disney family films.

Another area that is getting our strategic attention is broadcasting. All three of the once-dominant networks have seen audience erosion, and the ABC network has been no exception. But the fact is that ABC's prime-time ratings receive too much emphasis as a measure of our broadcasting division's performance. The entire ABC network – daytime, prime-time, news and late night – continues to comprise less than 10 percent of broadcasting's operating income. This is a primary reason that we opted, in 1995, to purchase Cap Cities/ABC rather than one of the other networks that was then available. Not only were we getting one of the major broadcast networks, which is still a completely unique entertainment asset in its enormous audience reach, but we were also getting some of the rising brands on the cable spectrum, such as ESPN, A&E, Lifetime and The History Channel, as well as some of the strongest owned-and-operated stations in the country. To be sure, the days of total dominance by just three networks are over. But with our wide range of broadcast assets, which also include the Disney Channel here and abroad, we are well positioned to play a strong role in the ongoing evolution of the incredible medium that is television.

O.K., I have now dutifully stated a rational, mature, restrained and, I hope, intelligent overview of the broadcast and cable landscape. Now, please allow me to succumb to my more native impulses by simply saying, "Watch *Sports Night* on ABC!" It is fantastic and it is one of the building blocks we are putting together to eventually make ABC number one, irrespective of the new competition! (There, now I feel better.)

In much the same way we have invested in cable television, we have also invested in another growing area of home entertainment that is drawing eyes to screens – the Internet. Under the management of our Buena Vista Internet Group, we were already reaping benefits from the Internet, thanks to Disney.com, the web's most-visited entertainment site; ESPN.com, the most-visited sports site, and ABCNews.com, the fastest growing news site. In recognition of the immense opportunity that the Internet poses, we took three important steps this year to move from being a major participant on the Internet to becoming a true leader. First, we purchased Starwave, one of the top Internet technology companies. Then, we sold Starwave to Infoseek in exchange for a 43 percent stake in this popular search engine. With these two partners in place, we announced the creation of the Go Network, which will be launched in the spring and, we believe, be something of a next step in the development of the world wide web. Once Internet users enter the Go Network, they will find a wealth of integrated services just a click away, all of which offer content from units of The Walt Disney Company, plus access to every other destination on the world wide web.

The opportunity posed by the Internet is both very new and very old. As I've expressed before in these letters, I firmly believe that Disney is ruled by the royalty of King Content and Queen Creativity. Serving as their advancing army is Technology. This is as it has always been. Creativity gave birth to the Content we call Mickey Mouse. And, look where Technology has led him – onto movie screens and television screens, videotape and theme park attractions, T-shirts and toys, CD-ROM's and video games. Every one of these technological venues has offered a new way for Mickey to engage audiences and gain fans. Now Mickey is encountering the opportunities of the Internet.

But, beyond Mickey, this new medium is wonderfully suited for the development of *new* characters, and it is on the backs of new characters that our Internet business will grow. These characters can also be coordinated with our parks and consumer products and co-produced with our broadcast and cable entities. For example, Zoog Disney on the Disney Channel has created the new characters that also appear on the Disney.com and the ZOOGDisney.com sites.

Just as the Buena Vista Internet Group is providing a new venue for Disney content *inside* the home, Disney Regional Entertainment is providing new venues for Disney content *outside* the home. We have developed three lines of business, each of which has an inherent potential for growth. Club Disney came first, offering a richly themed play space for young children and their parents (adults without children may not enter!). Then came the first DisneyQuest, an interactive entertainment zone within one giant 100,000-square-foot building that offers a whole new way for families to enjoy the Disney experience. One month later, we opened the first ESPNZone, a lively extension of the ESPN brand that gives fans a place to talk sports, eat sports, watch sports and play sports. Over the coming years, more Club Disneys, DisneyQuests and ESPNZones will be established in cities across America. If the concepts are successful, as we anticipate, then they should be readily exportable overseas. The closest model for these efforts is the Disney Stores and our new ESPN Stores, which owe their great popularity not just to the merchandise but to the fact that people like being able to step inside a Disney-designed environment close to home. Now we'll be providing three significant new ways for guests to enter the world of Disney and, judging from the early results, the appeal and the potential are great.

It should be emphasized that the new venues of Disney Regional Entertainment are designed to complement the Disney theme park experience, not replace it. Indeed, we suspect they may whet more than a few appetites for a trip to Orlando or Anaheim. Fortunately, lots of trips to Orlando and Anaheim are already being taken. Our Attractions division had a spectacular year in 1998. For the fourth consecutive year, park attendance and hotel occupancy were up across the board, partly because there were more parks to attend and more hotel rooms to occupy. Disney's Animal Kingdom was filled to capacity for much of the summer, and the new Coronado Springs Resort was an instant hit. Disneyland's new Tomorrowland was also a big draw, and the All-Star Movies Resort recently opened to sell-out business.

We plan to build on this success by continuing to improve our parks in little ways and big ways. Among the big ways, there are the additions of major attractions, such as the GM Test Track, Downtown Disney and the Rock'n' Roller Coaster at Walt Disney World, Disneyland's new Tomorrowland and the Asia section of Disney's Animal Kingdom. And then there are the *really* big ways: the creation of entirely new theme parks. Currently under way are Disney's California Adventure in Anaheim and Tokyo DisneySea in Japan. Until now, Disneyland and Tokyo Disneyland have been wonderful single-day venues that most families visit during one rising and setting of the sun. With the addition of these new adjacent parks, they will be transformed into true resort destinations.

In the fall, I traveled to Japan to participate in the groundbreaking for Tokyo DisneySea. I generally don't get nervous appearing before large groups of people, even in foreign lands ... but participating in a Shinto ceremony, for which I had to memorize the exacting customs of a religious tradition that has been nurtured over thousands of years, did test my ability to maintain my professional aplomb. Also participating in the event were our partners from the Oriental Land Company. OLC is actually paying for the construction and will own the park. Disney will receive licensing and management fees. This will result in a strong cash flow starting with opening day. Oriental Land Company's willingness to make such a huge investment in this new park reflects the Japanese people's underlying confidence in the future, and the enormous potential upside that exists in Japan and throughout the currently depressed economies of Asia.

Following my visit to Japan, I went on to meet with leaders in China and be exposed to more of this extraordinary nation. I saw a number of exotic sights, but there was one recurring sight that, given where I was traveling, seemed especially exotic to me – the golden arches of McDonald's. I am completely confident that the Chinese people love Mickey no less than Big Mac. I plan to have lunch with Jack Greenberg, the CEO of McDonald's, to ask him how they managed to make the fries taste just as good in Shanghai as on Sunset Blvd. As evidenced by the popularity of McDonalds, we could be getting close to the time for a major Disney attraction in the world's most populous nation.

Our efforts in China underscore the growing importance of the international market in general. The coming century will not be the American Century, it will be the World Century. It used to be that in order for a company to be successful, it had to devise strategies that would work in Maine, Montana and Missouri. Now, the list includes all the nations of the world. Outside the United States, we must still remember we are guests, and not just export our American product, but produce locally created entertainment that reflects local cultures as well. This makes our work more challenging, but it also makes it vastly more exciting as we can see possibilities anywhere we spin the globe.

Of course, China already had a markedly favorable impact on our company this year, since it supplied the folktale around which we built our 36th animated film – *Mulan*. *Mulan* just won 10 first place awards presented by the International Animated Film Society. The film's commercial and artistic success was all the more remarkable since it was the first feature to come from our new Florida animation studio. It provided one more example of the incredible ability of our Feature Animation group to marry an emotional story to an artistic vision. Would it be too much like a father to dreamingly say nobody does it as well, that no one comes close to this level of work? Probably!

1999 will be a historic year for Walt Disney Feature Animation. For the first time in the 75 years that Disney has been animating movies, we will be releasing three feature-length animated films in a single year – *Tarzan*®, *Toy Story 2* and, to close out the year, *Fantasia 2000*. In addition, from our growing TV Animation group, we have the terrific shows being produced for ABC's *One Saturday Morning*, which has become the top-rated Saturday morning show for kids 2 to 11. Then there's our made-for-video product line, the latest of which, *The Lion King II: Simba's Pride*, is performing exceptionally well. Next year, we will have four made-for-video films, including *Mickey's Once Upon a Christmas*. Another development that may or may not have an impact on our animation business is the digital video disk. I say "may not" because, over time, it may simply replace videotape. Therefore, I will restrain my enthusiasm for the potential of this new format, which of course is difficult for me. In 1998, we began releasing our films onto DVD. We are hopeful that, in the coming decade, this technology will grow to the point

where we can profitably release more of our animated library titles in this format.

We will be greeting the new decade, the new century and the new millennium with *Fantasia 2000*, a film that hearkens directly to our creative roots even as it leads the way into a new era. *Fantasia 2000* will be part of a year-long millennial celebration that will be centered at Epcot and will include entertainment spectaculars, special welcoming ceremonies and exhibits from around the globe. To further memorialize the millennium, we have commissioned two symphonies by the world-renowned composers Michael Torke and Aaron Jay Kernis.

Of course, every CEO in every annual report this year will feel obliged to talk in grand and expansive terms about the millennium. And, at Disney we will be firing off more than our share of fireworks when the calendar turns. But, personally, I think the year 2000 will offer a quiet moment to reflect on the past, present and future of our company (once all the bugs are out of our computers, and I am assured that we are ahead of schedule in this effort). To put it mildly, the little business that Walt and Roy founded 75 years ago grew to have an important and positive impact throughout the 20th century. Now, it is up to all of us, the 120,000 cast members of The Walt Disney Company, to make sure that this heritage is honored and built upon in a new century.

To be sure, the years of the 21st century will include ups and downs, just as did the years of the 20th. But, through all our fiscal seasons, I am confident that, over the long term, Disney will continue to be a leader in offering creative new ways – and creative old ways – for people to spend their most precious possession: their time.

Sincerely,

Michael D. Eisner
Chairman and CEO
December 8, 1998

FINANCIAL REVIEW

The Walt Disney Company strives to maximize value to its shareholders by leveraging the strength of its brand, character and entertainment franchises through a commitment to creative excellence and guest service coupled with strict financial discipline. The company evaluates its existing businesses and new initiatives based on their ability to contribute to Disney's long-term cash flow and earnings growth and to provide returns that exceed Disney's cost of capital.

1998 was a year that highlighted Disney's commitment to continued value-creating investment in the company's branded attractions, entertainment and consumer products offerings. Creating value through investment in existing businesses and new initiatives has been an ongoing focus for the company since Michael Eisner joined Disney nearly 15 years ago. This year, investment in future growth opportunities was higher than in any previous year.

OVERVIEW

The company delivered record revenues and solid earnings in 1998. Nonetheless, the year presented a number of challenges, including increasing cost pressures in the filmed entertainment and broadcasting businesses and turbulent international market conditions. These challenges led to lower-than-expected earnings growth for the year. As a result, the company has begun and will continue to take steps to reduce costs and investment where appropriate while positioning itself for future growth.

Disney delivered record revenues of just under $23 billion in fiscal year 1998. Disney's revenues have grown substantially over time, registering average annual growth of 21% over the last 15 years.

The company generated operating income of $4 billion in 1998, with contributions in nearly equal measure from Disney's individual business segments. Creative Content generated 35% of the company's total operating income, with 33% coming from Broadcasting and 32% from Theme Parks and Resorts.

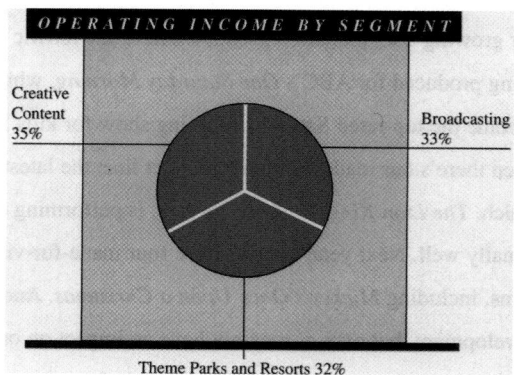

With the exception of Theme Parks and Resorts, growth in operating income in 1998 lagged historical trends, due in part to increased external cost pressures from such things as higher costs for key sports programming rights and increased industry-wide live-action film production costs. Difficult international economic conditions also impacted 1998 results.

Net income increased 4% over the prior year's pro forma results to $1.9 billion in 1998, while diluted earnings per share increased 3% to 89 cents. Over the past 15 years, Disney's earnings per share have grown by a factor of nearly 15 times for a compound annual growth rate of 20%. While earnings growth in 1998 fell short of historical growth, the company believes that its core franchises coupled with recent investments are capable of generating long-term earnings increases.

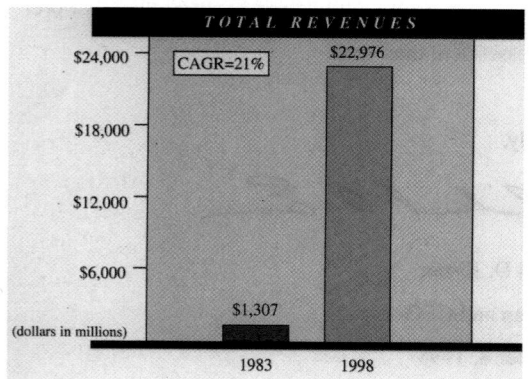

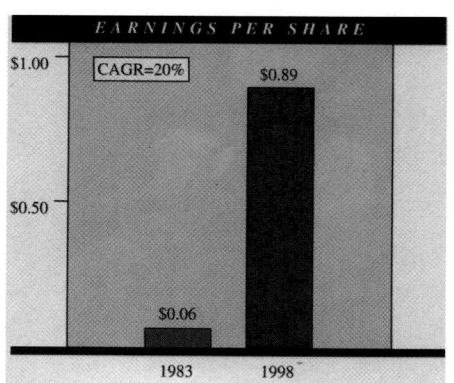

Amortization of intangible assets, including the goodwill associated with the acquisition of ABC, amounted to 21 cents per share in 1998. For those who prefer to look at earnings before this non-cash charge, diluted earnings per share excluding this amortization was $1.10 in the fiscal year just ended.

INTERNATIONAL

In 1998, revenues from international sources, including U.S. exports, totaled almost $5 billion, or 21% of total company revenues.

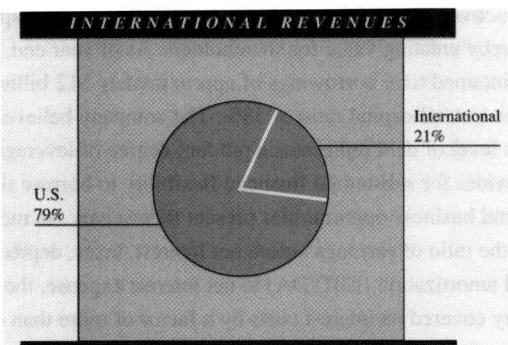

1998 was a year of volatile economic conditions that challenged Disney to become ever more cost-conscious, as is evidenced by the strategic downsizing in certain of the company's international operations, primarily in Asia. Nonetheless, the company believes there are opportunities for significant growth in international revenues over the long term. For instance, the United States, Japan and the four largest countries in Europe constitute just over 10% of the world's population, yet they accounted for approximately 80% of Disney's licensed merchandise sales in 1998. Additionally, The Disney Store opened more new stores outside the U.S. than within the U.S. for the first time. In television, the international expansion of the Disney Channel and other Disney programming helps expand and deepen market awareness of the company's brands and products around the world, thereby paving the way for future growth. Thus, while dramatic economic growth in other parts of the world may take some time to develop, Disney continues to position itself to capitalize on long-term international growth opportunities.

CASH FLOW

In addition to exceptional long-term earnings growth, Disney strives to achieve increasing cash flow from its operations. Over the past three years Disney has generated cumulative after-tax cash flow from operations of nearly $14 billion. 1998's after-tax cash flow from operations totaled over $5 billion.

Disney's primary priority for use of its cash flow continues to be investment for attractive shareholder returns in new and existing businesses. When appropriate, Disney also seeks to efficiently return capital to shareholders through repurchase of the company's shares.

INVESTMENT IN GROWTH INITIATIVES AND NEW BUSINESSES

In allocating its discretionary capital to projects around the company, Disney assesses and then continuously monitors each project's return on investment versus required returns (i.e., the cost of capital). By this mechanism, Disney strives to maximize the shareholder value created by its investments. In 1998, the company's total cash flow exceeded $6 billion.* Of this total cash flow, approximately $700 million or 12% was spent to maintain existing assets. The company allocated another $5.2 billion in capital spending toward projects to fuel Disney's future growth. The majority of this spending was in businesses that capitalize on and help to expand the company's core *Disney*, **ESPN** and abc brand franchises. Disney believes this allocation of capital to its key global brands is an important driver of long-term shareholder value.

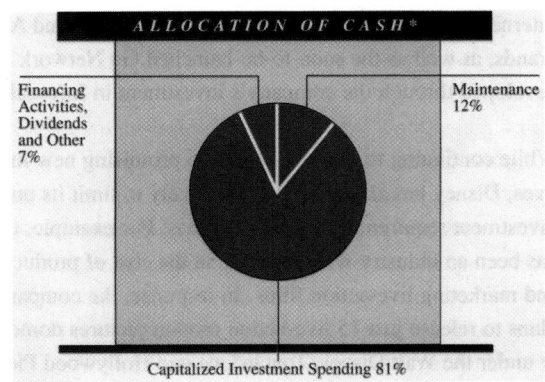

*Total cash flow includes after-tax cash flow from operations, borrowings and proceeds from the exercise of stock options and asset dispositions.

In addition to the capital investment cited above, 1998 results reflected the absorption of start-up costs and operating losses associated with new initiatives that the company believes can generate significant incremental value and growth for Disney shareholders within the next four to five years and beyond. These initiatives include Disney's Animal Kingdom theme park; the Disney Cruise Line; international expansion of the Disney Channel in Italy and Spain; new Toon Disney cable programming; RadioDisney; DisneyQuest; Club Disney; ESPN Classic sports network; ESPNZone restaurants/entertainment centers; ESPN-The Magazine; and a variety of

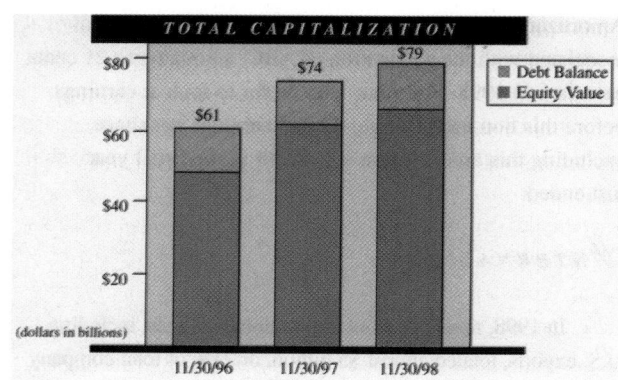

Disney's solid balance sheet allows the company to borrow at attractive rates, helping to reduce the overall cost of capital and thereby creating value for shareholders. As of year end, Disney maintained total borrowings of approximately $12 billion and a debt-to-total-capital ratio of 38%. The company believes that this level of debt represents a prudent degree of leverage, which provides for substantial financial flexibility to borrow should sound business opportunities present themselves. As measured by the ratio of earnings before net interest, taxes, depreciation and amortization (EBITDA) to net interest expense, the company covered its interest costs by a factor of more than eight times for the year ended September 30.

Internet-related activities under the Disney, ESPN and ABC brands, as well as the soon-to-be-launched Go Network developed through the company's investment in Infoseek.

While continuing to allocate capital to promising new initiatives, Disney has also moved aggressively to limit its ongoing investment requirements in certain areas. For example, there has been an industry-wide increase in the cost of producing and marketing live-action films. In response, the company plans to release just 15 live-action motion pictures domestically under the Walt Disney, Touchstone and Hollywood Pictures labels in calendar 1999 compared to 18 live-action releases in calendar 1998. This move allows Disney to reduce its overall investment and overhead spending in live-action films, while still focusing on the highest-potential motion picture projects. As a result, the company believes it can increase its return on investment in the live-action film business.

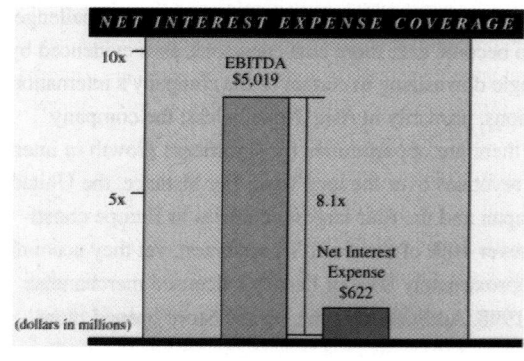

The company monitors its cash flow, interest coverage and its debt-to-total-capital ratio with the long-term goal of maintaining a strong single-A or better credit rating. Standard & Poor's/Moody's rates Disney's long-term debt A/A2 and its short-term debt A1/P1. Additionally, as part of its overall risk management program, the company evaluates and seeks to manage its exposure to changes in interest rates and currency exchange rates on an ongoing basis.

*C*APITALIZATION

At fiscal year end, Disney had a total capitalization of $65 billion, placing it among the 40 largest corporations in the United States. Measured as of November 30, 1998, the company's total capitalization was even higher, at $79 billion.

*S*HAREHOLDER PAYOUT

The company distributes value to shareholders through dividends and share repurchase.

Over time, Disney has returned significant amounts of capital to shareholders through cash dividends. In January, Disney's board of directors voted to raise the company's dividend by 19%, to just over 20 cents per share. As a result, the company paid over $400 million in dividends to Disney shareholders in 1998. Later in the year, the company's board decided that all shareholder dividends will be paid on an annual rather than a quarterly basis beginning in fiscal 1999. This change will reduce costs and vastly simplify payments to a shareholder base that includes a great number of small investors. Annual dividends will be paid in November each year as approved by the board of directors.

Through share repurchase, Disney has both returned capital to its shareholders and created significant shareholder value. Since 1983, Disney has invested $3.1 billion to buy back 480 million shares at an average price of approximately $6.50 per share. Measured as of November 30, these shares were worth $15.5 billion for an annualized return of 20%, exceeding the stock market return of 14% as measured by the Standard & Poor's 500 index over the same time. As of November 30, Disney had authorization from its board of directors to repurchase an additional 400 million shares.

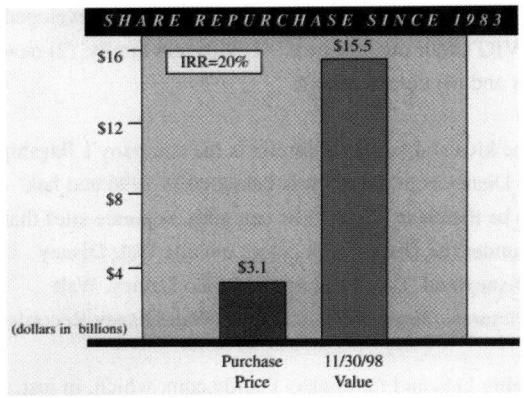

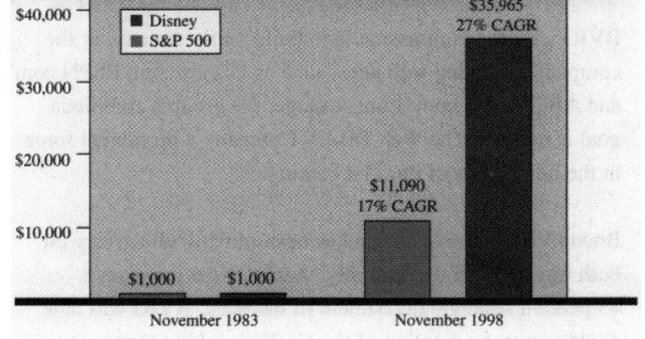

𝒯OTAL RETURN TO INVESTORS

As a result of Disney's financial performance over time, driven by expansion and extension of existing brands and businesses, investment in new businesses and share repurchase, the return to long-term investors in Disney stock has surpassed the return delivered by the market overall. An investment of $1,000 in Disney stock on November 30, 1983, including reinvestment of dividends, was worth $35,965 on November 30, 1998, providing a 27% compound annual return over the ensuing 15-year period. A similar investment in the Standard & Poor's 500 would have been worth $11,090 over the same time, representing a 17% annual return to investors.

Disney split its stock 3-for-1 on July 9, the seventh stock split since the company went public in 1940. As evidence of the ongoing strength of the Disney franchise, 100 shares of Disney stock purchased for $2,500 in the company's initial public offering would have equaled 250,233 shares worth approximately $8 million as of November 30, a compound annual growth rate of nearly 15% over the last 58 years. Through the patient pursuit of earnings growth and an intense focus on managing and investing to create shareholder value, the company strives to continue providing superior returns for its shareholders.

MANAGEMENT'S DISCUSSION AND ANALYSIS OF FINANCIAL CONDITION AND RESULTS OF OPERATIONS

RESULTS OF OPERATIONS

The company acquired the operations of ABC, Inc. ("ABC") on February 9, 1996. During 1997, the company sold KCAL, a Los Angeles television station, completed its final ABC purchase price allocation and determination of the related intangible assets and disposed of certain ABC publishing assets. To enhance comparability, certain information for 1997 and 1996 is presented on a "pro forma" basis, which assumes that these events occurred at the beginning of 1996. The pro forma results are not necessarily indicative of the combined results that would have occurred had these events actually occurred at the beginning of 1996.

CONSOLIDATED RESULTS

(in millions, except per share data)	As reported 1998	As reported 1997	As reported 1996	Pro forma (unaudited) 1997	Pro forma (unaudited) 1996
Revenues:					
Creative Content	$10,302	$10,937	$10,159	$10,098	$ 9,564
Broadcasting	7,142	6,522	4,078	6,501	6,009
Theme Parks and Resorts	5,532	5,014	4,502	5,014	4,502
Total	$22,976	$22,473	$18,739	$21,613	$20,075
Operating income: [1]					
Creative Content	$ 1,403	$ 1,882	$ 1,561	$ 1,693	$ 1,435
Broadcasting	1,325	1,294	782	1,285	1,084
Theme Parks and Resorts	1,287	1,136	990	1,136	990
Gain on sale of KCAL	—	135	—	—	—
Accounting change	—	—	(300)	—	(300)
Total	4,015	4,447	3,033	4,114	3,209
Corporate activities and other	(236)	(367)	(309)	(367)	(249)
Net interest expense	(622)	(693)	(438)	(693)	(698)
Acquisition-related costs	—	—	(225)	—	—
Income before income taxes	3,157	3,387	2,061	3,054	2,262
Income taxes	(1,307)	(1,421)	(847)	(1,282)	(988)
Net income	$ 1,850	$ 1,966	$ 1,214	$ 1,772	$ 1,274
Earnings per share: [3]					
Diluted	$ 0.89	$ 0.95	$ 0.65	$ 0.86	$ 0.62
Basic	$ 0.91	$ 0.97	$ 0.66	$ 0.88	$ 0.63
Net income excluding non-recurring items [2]	$ 1,850	$ 1,886	$ 1,534	$ 1,772	$ 1,457
Earnings per share excluding non-recurring items: [2][3]					
Diluted	$ 0.89	$ 0.92	$ 0.83	$ 0.86	$ 0.70
Basic	$ 0.91	$ 0.93	$ 0.84	$ 0.88	$ 0.72
Amortization of intangible assets included in operating income	$ 431	$ 439	$ 301	$ 413	$ 413
Average number of common and common equivalent shares outstanding: [3]					
Diluted	2,079	2,060	1,857	2,060	2,067
Basic	2,037	2,021	1,827	2,021	2,037
[1]Includes depreciation and amortization (excluding film costs) of:					
Creative Content	$ 219	$ 222	$ 186	$ 187	$ 145
Broadcasting	543	508	382	521	521
Theme Parks and Resorts	444	408	358	408	358
	$ 1,206	$ 1,138	$ 926	$ 1,116	$ 1,024

[2]The 1997 results include a $135 million gain from the sale of KCAL. See Note 2 to the Consolidated Financial Statements. The 1996 results include two non-recurring charges. The company adopted Statement of Financial Accounting Standards No. 121 *Accounting for the Impairment of Long-Lived Assets and for Long-Lived Assets to be Disposed Of,* which resulted in the company recognizing a $300 million non-cash charge. In addition, the company recognized a $225 million charge for costs related to the acquisition of ABC. See Notes 2 and 11 to the Consolidated Financial Statements.

[3]Earnings per share and average shares outstanding have been adjusted to give effect to the three-for-one split of the company's common shares in June 1998.

The following discussion of 1998 versus 1997 and 1997 versus 1996 performance includes comparisons to pro forma results for 1997 and 1996. The company believes pro forma results represent a meaningful comparative standard for assessing net income, changes in net income and earnings trends because the pro forma results include comparable operations in each year presented. The discussion of the Theme Parks and Resorts segment does not include pro forma comparisons, since the pro forma adjustments did not impact this segment.

CONSOLIDATED RESULTS

1998 vs. 1997 Compared to 1997 pro forma results, revenues increased 6% to $23 billion, driven by growth in all business segments. Net income and diluted earnings per share increased 4% and 3% to $1.9 billion and $.89, respectively. These results were driven by a reduction in net expense associated with corporate activities and other and lower net interest expense, partially offset by decreased operating income. The reduction in net expense associated with corporate activities and other was driven by improved results from the company's equity investments, including A&E Television and Lifetime Television, and a gain on the sale of the company's interest in Scandinavian Broadcasting System. Decreased net interest expense reflected lower average debt balances during the year. Lower operating income was driven by a decline in Creative Content results, partially offset by improvements from Theme Parks and Resorts and Broadcasting.

As reported revenues increased 2% and net income and diluted earnings per share decreased by 6%. The as reported results reflect the items described above as well as the impact of the disposition of certain ABC publishing assets and the sale of KCAL in 1997.

In April 1997, the company purchased a significant equity stake in Starwave Corporation ("Starwave"), an internet technology company. In connection with the acquisition, the company was granted an option to purchase substantially all the remaining shares of Starwave. The company exercised the option during the third quarter of 1998. Accordingly, the accounts of Starwave have been included in the company's September 30, 1998 consolidated financial statements. On June 18, 1998, the company reached an agreement for the acquisition of Starwave by Infoseek Corporation ("Infoseek"), a publicly-held internet search company, pursuant to a merger. On November 18, 1998, the shareholders of both Infoseek and Starwave approved the merger. As a result of the merger and the company's purchase of additional shares of Infoseek common stock pursuant to the merger agreement, the company owns approximately 43% of Infoseek's outstanding common stock. In addition, pursuant to the merger agreement, the company purchased warrants enabling it, under certain circumstances, to achieve a majority stake in Infoseek. These warrants vest over a three-year period and expire in five years. Effective as of the November 18, 1998 closing date of the transaction, the company will record a significant non-cash gain, a write-off for purchased in-process research and development costs and an increase in investments, reflecting the company's share of the fair value of Infoseek's intangible assets. The company is currently performing the necessary valuations to determine the gain, the research and development write-off and the amount of and amortization period for the intangible assets. Thereafter, the company will account for its investment in Infoseek under the equity method. The merger is not expected to have a material effect on the company's financial position.

1997 vs. 1996 Compared to 1996 pro forma results, pro forma revenues increased 8% to $21.6 billion, reflecting growth in all business segments. Pro forma net income and diluted earnings per share, excluding non-recurring items, increased 22% and 23% to $1.8 billion and $.86, respectively. These results were driven by increased operating income across all business segments, partially offset by an increase in corporate activities and other driven by certain non-recurring items in both years. 1997 reflects settlements with former senior executives and 1996 reflects certain gains at ABC, primarily related to the sale of an investment in a cellular communications company.

As reported revenues increased 20%, reflecting increases in all business segments and the impact of the acquisition of ABC. Net income, excluding the non-recurring items discussed above, increased 23%, driven by increased operating income for each business segment. Diluted earnings per share, excluding the non-recurring items, increased 11%, reflecting net income growth, partially offset by the impact of additional shares issued in connection with the acquisition. Results for 1997 included a full period of ABC's operations.

BUSINESS SEGMENT RESULTS

CREATIVE CONTENT

1998 vs. 1997 Revenues increased 2% or $204 million to $10.3 billion compared with pro forma 1997, driven by growth of $204 million in television distribution, $136 million in the Disney Stores, $54 million in domestic publishing and $51 million in domestic character merchandise licensing. These increases were partially offset by declines in worldwide home video and theatrical motion picture distribution of $330 million. Growth in television distribution revenue was driven by higher volume of television programming and theatrical releases distributed to the worldwide television market. Increased revenues at the Disney Stores reflected an increase in comparable store sales in North America and Europe and continued worldwide expansion, partially offset by a decrease in comparable store sales in Asian markets. The increase in domestic publishing revenues resulted from the success of book titles such as *Don't Sweat the Small Stuff* and the launch of ESPN *The Magazine*. Character merchandise licensing growth was driven primarily by the continued strength of *Winnie the Pooh* in the domestic market, partially offset by declines internationally, primarily due to softness in Asian markets. Lower worldwide home video revenues reflected difficult comparisons to the prior year, which benefited from the strength of *Toy Story, The Hunchback of Notre Dame* and *101 Dalmatians,* compared to the current year release of *Lady & the Tramp, Hercules* and *The Little Mermaid,* as well as economic weaknesses in Asian markets. In worldwide theatrical motion picture distribution, while current year revenues reflected successful box-office performances of *Armageddon,* Disney's highest-grossing live-action film, and *Mulan,* its most recent animated release, revenues were lower overall due to difficult comparisons to the prior year, which benefited from the strong performances of *101 Dalmatians, Ransom* and *The English Patient.*

On an as reported basis, revenues decreased $635 million or 6%, reflecting the items described above, as well as the impact of the disposition of certain ABC publishing assets in the prior year.

Operating income decreased 17% or $290 million to $1.4 billion compared with pro forma 1997 results, reflecting declines in worldwide theatrical motion picture distribution and international home video. These declines were partially offset by growth in television distribution, increases in domestic merchandise licensing, Disney Store growth in North America and Europe and improved results in domestic home video, driven by the success of *The Little Mermaid, Lady & the Tramp* and *Peter Pan.* Costs and expenses, which consist primarily of production cost amortization, distribution and selling expenses, product costs, labor and leasehold expenses, increased 6% or $494 million. The increase was driven by increased writedowns related to domestic theatrical live-action releases and an increase in production costs for theatrical and television product, as well as an increase in the number of shows produced for network television and syndication. Production cost increases are reflective of industry trends: as competition for creative talent has increased, costs within the industry have increased at a rate significantly above inflation. Cost and expense increases were also due to increased activity related to internet start-up businesses. In addition, current year costs and expenses reflected charges totaling $64 million related to strategic downsizing in the Company's consumer product business, particularly in response to Asian economic difficulties, and consolidation of certain studio operations in its filmed entertainment business. Increased expenses for the year were partially offset by declines in distribution and selling expenses in the home video and domestic theatrical motion picture distribution markets reflecting lower volume, declines within television distribution due to the termination of a network production joint venture and a decrease in development and other operating expenses at Disney Interactive.

On an as reported basis, operating income decreased $479 million or 25%, reflecting the items described above, as well as the impact of the disposition of certain ABC publishing assets in the prior year.

1997 vs. 1996 Pro forma revenues increased 6% or $534 million to $10.1 billion compared with pro forma 1996, driven by growth of $210 million in the Disney Stores, $143 million in character merchandise licensing, $104 million in television distribution and $88 million in home video. Growth at the Disney Stores reflected continued worldwide expansion with 106 new stores opening in 1997. Increases in character merchandise licensing reflected the strength of *Winnie the Pooh* and *Toy Story* domestically, and standard characters and *101 Dalmatians* worldwide. The increase in television revenues was driven by an increase in the distribution of film and television product in the international television market. Home video results reflected the successful performance of *Toy Story, The Hunchback of Notre Dame* and *101 Dalmatians* worldwide and *Bambi* and *Sleeping Beauty* domestically.

On an as reported basis, revenues increased $778 million or 8%, reflecting the items described above, as well as increased revenues from ABC's publishing assets up to the date of disposition. Additionally, 1997 included a full period of revenues from certain ABC Television production operations.

Pro forma operating income increased 18% or $258 million to $1.7 billion compared with pro forma 1996, reflecting improved results for theatrical distribution, character merchandise licensing and television distribution, partially offset by a reduction in home video results. Costs and expenses, increased 3% or $276 million, reflecting increased amortization in the home video market and continued expansion of the Disney Stores, offset by a reduction in distribution costs in the domestic theatrical market and the write-off of certain theatrical development projects in the prior year.

On an as reported basis, operating income increased $321 million or 21%, reflecting the items described above as well as higher operating income from ABC's publishing assets up to the date of disposition.

BROADCASTING

1998 vs. 1997 Revenues increased 10% or $641 million to $7.1 billion compared with pro forma 1997 results, reflecting a $427 million increase at ESPN and the Disney Channel, a $110 million increase at the television network and an $81 million increase at the television stations. A strong advertising market resulted in increased revenues at ESPN and the television stations and subscriber growth contributed to revenue increases at ESPN and the Disney Channel. Television network growth was driven by higher sports advertising revenues, primarily attributable to the 1998 soccer World Cup.

On an as reported basis, revenues increased $620 million or 10%, reflecting the items described above, partially offset by the impact of the sale of KCAL in the prior year.

Operating income increased 3% or $40 million to $1.3 billion compared with pro forma 1997 results reflecting increased revenues at ESPN, the Disney Channel and the television stations, partially offset by lower results at the television network and start-up and operating losses from new business initiatives. Results at the television network reflected the impact of lower ratings and increased costs and expenses. Costs and expenses, which consist primarily of programming rights and amortization, production costs, distribution and selling expenses and labor costs, increased 12% or $601 million, reflecting increased programming and production costs at ESPN, higher program amortization at the television network, reflecting a reduction in benefits from the ABC acquisition, increased costs related to the NFL contract (see discussion below) and start-up and operating costs related to new business initiatives.

On an as reported basis, operating income increased $31 million or 2%, reflecting the items described above, partially offset by the impact of the sale of KCAL in the prior year.

The company has continued to invest in its existing cable television networks and in new cable ventures to diversify and expand the available distribution channels for acquired and company programming. During 1998, the company acquired the Classic Sports Network, a cable network devoted to memorable sporting events, invested in a number of international cable ventures and continued its international expansion of the Disney Channel.

The company's cable operations continue to provide strong earnings growth. The company's results for 1998 reflect an increase in pretax income of $148 million or 18% for mature cable properties compared with 1997 results, including the company's share of earnings from ESPN, the Disney Channel, A&E Television and Lifetime Television. These increases were partially offset by the company's recognition of its proportionate share of losses associated with start-up cable ventures. Start-up cable ventures are generally operations that are in the process of establishing distribution channels and a subscriber base and that have not reached their full level of normalized operations. These include various domestic and international ESPN and Disney Channel start-up cable ventures. The company's pretax income reflected an increase of 20% from all cable properties.

The financial results of ESPN and the Disney Channel are included in Broadcasting operating income. The company's share of all other cable operations and the ESPN minority interest deduction are reported in "Corporate activities and other" in the Consolidated Statements of Income.

There has been a continuing decline in viewership at all major broadcast networks, including ABC, reflecting the growth in the cable industry's share of viewers. In addition, there have been continuing increases in the cost of sports and other programming.

During the second quarter of 1998, the company entered into a new agreement with the National Football League (the "NFL") for the right to broadcast NFL football games on the ABC Television Network and ESPN. The contract provides for total payments of approximately $9 billion over an eight-year period, commencing with the 1998 season. The programming rights fees under the new contract are significantly higher than those required by the previous contract and the fee increases exceed the estimated revenue increases over the contract term. The higher fees under the new contract reflect various factors, including increased competition for sports programming rights and an increase in the number of games to be broadcast by ESPN. The company is pursuing a variety of strategies, including marketing efforts, to reduce the impact of the higher costs. The contract's impact on the company's results over the remaining contract term is dependent upon a number of factors, including the strength of the advertising markets, effectiveness of marketing efforts and the size of viewer audiences.

The cost of the NFL contract is charged to expense based on the ratio of each period's gross revenues to estimated total gross revenues. Estimates of total gross revenues can change significantly and accordingly, they are reviewed periodically and amortization is adjusted if necessary. Such adjustments could have a material effect on results of operations in future periods.

1997 vs. 1996 Pro forma revenues increased 8% or $492 million to $6.5 billion compared with pro forma 1996, driven by increases of $336 million at ESPN and the Disney Channel, and $74 million at the television network. The increases at ESPN and the Disney Channel were due primarily to higher advertising revenues and affiliate fees due primarily to expansion, subscriber growth and improved advertising rates. Growth in revenues at the television network was primarily the result of improved performance of sports, news and latenight programming, partially offset by a decline in primetime ratings.

On an as reported basis, revenues increased $2.4 billion or 60%, reflecting a full period of ABC's broadcasting operations in 1997.

Pro forma operating income increased 19% or $201 million to $1.3 billion compared with pro forma 1996, reflecting increases in revenues at ESPN and the Disney Channel, as well as improved results at the television stations, partially offset by decreases at the television network. Results at the television network reflected the impact of lower ratings, partially offset by benefits arising from the period's sporting events, improvements in children's programming, continued strength in the advertising market and decreased program amortization. Costs and expenses increased 6% or $291 million. This increase reflected increased programming rights and production costs, driven by international growth at ESPN and increases at the television network, partially offset by benefits arising from reductions in program amortization and other costs at the television network, primarily attributable to the acquisition.

On an as reported basis, operating income increased $512 million or 65%, reflecting a full period of ABC's broadcasting operations in 1997.

The company's results for 1997 reflect an increase in pretax income of $182 million or 28% for mature cable properties compared with 1996 results. These increases were partially offset by the company's recognition of its proportionate share of losses associated with start-up cable ventures. Overall, the company's pretax income increased 29% in 1997 from all cable properties.

THEME PARKS AND RESORTS

1998 vs. 1997 Revenues increased 10% or $518 million to $5.5 billion, driven by growth at the Walt Disney World Resort, reflecting contributions of $256 million, from increased guest spending and record attendance, growth of $106 million from higher occupied room nights and $76 million from Disney Cruise Line. Higher guest spending reflected strong per capita spending, due in part to new food, beverage and merchandise offerings throughout the resort, and higher average room rates. Increased occupied room nights reflected additional capacity resulting from the opening of Disney's Coronado Springs Resort in August 1997. Record theme park attendance resulted from growth in domestic and international tourist visitation due to the opening of the new theme park, Disney's Animal Kingdom. Disneyland's revenues for the year increased slightly as higher guest spending was largely offset by reduced attendance driven primarily by difficult comparisons to the prior year's Main Street Electrical Parade farewell season and construction of New Tomorrowland in the first half of 1998.

Operating income increased 13% or $151 million to $1.3 billion, resulting primarily from higher guest spending, increased occupied room nights and record attendance at the Walt Disney World Resort, partially offset by start-up and operating costs associated with Disney's Animal Kingdom and Disney Cruise Line. Costs and expenses, which consist principally of labor, costs of merchandise, food, and beverages sold, depreciation, repairs and maintenance, entertainment and marketing and sales expenses, increased 9% or $367 million. Increased costs and expenses were driven by higher theme park attendance, start-up and operating costs at the new theme park and Disney Cruise Line.

1997 vs. 1996 Revenues increased 11% or $512 million to $5.0 billion, reflecting growth at the Walt Disney World Resort, which celebrated its 25th Anniversary. Growth at the resort included $272 million from greater guest spending, $111 million from increased occupied rooms and $97 million due to record theme park attendance. Higher guest spending reflected increased merchandise and food and beverage sales, higher admission prices and increased room rates at hotel properties. Increased merchandise spending reflected sales of the 25th Anniversary products and the performance of the World of Disney, the largest Disney retail outlet, which opened in October 1996. The increase in occupied rooms reflected higher occupancy and a complete year of operations at Disney's BoardWalk Resort, which opened in the fourth quarter of 1996. Occupied rooms also increased due to the opening of Disney's Coronado Springs Resort in August 1997.

Record theme park attendance resulted from growth in domestic tourist visitation. Disneyland's revenues for the year were flat due to higher guest spending offset by reduced attendance from the prior-year's record level.

Operating income increased 15% or $146 million to $1.1 billion, resulting primarily from higher guest spending, increased occupied rooms and record theme park attendance at the Walt Disney World Resort. Costs and expenses increased 10% or $366 million. Increased operating costs were associated with growth in theme park attendance and occupied rooms, higher guest spending and increased marketing and sales expenses primarily associated with Walt Disney World Resort's 25th Anniversary celebration. Additional cost increases resulted from theme park and resort expansions including Disney's Animal Kingdom and Disney Cruise Line, which both began operations in 1998.

*L*IQUIDITY AND CAPITAL RESOURCES

The company generates significant cash from operations and has substantial borrowing capacity to meet its operating and discretionary spending requirements. Cash provided by operations was comparable to the prior year, at $5.1 billion.

In 1998, the company invested $3.3 billion to develop and produce film and television properties and $2.3 billion to design and develop new theme park attractions, resort properties, real estate developments and other properties. 1997 investments totaled $3.1 billion and $1.9 billion, respectively.

The $246 million increase in investment in film and television properties was primarily driven by higher live-action and animation spending. Live-action production spending was driven by increases at Miramax and higher animation spending reflected an increase in the number of films in production.

The $392 million increase in investment in theme parks, resorts and other properties resulted primarily from initiatives including Disney's California Adventure and Disney Cruise Line. Capital spending is expected to increase in 1999, driven by increased spending for Disney's California Adventure.

The company acquires shares of its stock on an ongoing basis and is authorized as of September 30, 1998 to purchase up to an additional 400 million shares. This amount reflects an increase in the repurchase authorization and the three-for-one split of the company's common shares, both effected in June 1998. During 1998, a subsidiary of the company acquired approximately 1.1 million shares of the company's common stock for approximately $30 million. The company also used $412 million to fund dividend payments during the year.

During 1998, total borrowings increased to $11.7 billion. The company borrowed approximately $1.8 billion in 1998, with effective interest rates, including the impact of interest rate swaps, ranging from 5.2% to 6.8% and maturities in fiscal 1999 through fiscal 2008. Certain of these financing agreements are denominated in foreign currencies, and the company has entered into cross-currency swap agreements effectively converting these obligations into U.S. dollar denominated LIBOR-based variable rate debt instruments. In August 1998, the company filed a new U.S. registration statement, which replaced the existing U.S. shelf registration statement, and provides for issuance of up to $5.0 billion of debt. As of September 30, 1998, the company had the ability to borrow under the U.S. shelf registration statement and a euro medium-term note program, which collectively permitted the issuance of up to approximately $5.8 billion of additional debt. In addition, the company has $5.2 billion available under bank facilities to support its commercial paper activities.

The company's financial condition remains strong. The company believes that its cash, other liquid assets, operating cash flows and access to capital markets, taken together, provide adequate resources to fund ongoing operating requirements and future capital expenditures related to the expansion of existing businesses and development of new projects.

OTHER MATTERS

YEAR 2000

The Y2K Problem. The company is devoting significant resources throughout its business operations to minimize the risk of potential disruption from the "year 2000 ('Y2K') problem." This problem is a result of computer programs having been written using two digits (rather than four) to define the applicable year. Any information technology ("IT") systems that have time-sensitive software may recognize a date using "00" as the year 1900 rather than the year 2000, which could result in miscalculations and system failures. The problem also extends to many "non-IT" systems; that is, operating and control systems that rely on embedded chip systems. In addition, like every other business enterprise, the company is at risk from Y2K failures on the part of its major business counterparts, including suppliers, distributors, licensees and manufacturers, as well as potential failures in public and private infrastructure services, including electricity, water, gas, transportation and communications.

System failures resulting from the Y2K problem could adversely affect operations and financial results in all of the company's business segments. Failures may affect security, payroll operations or employee and guest health and safety, as well as such routine but important operations as billing and collection. In addition, the company's business segments face more specific risks. For example:

The company's Theme Parks and Resorts operations could be significantly impeded by failures in hotel and cruise line reservation and operating systems; in theme park operating systems, including those controlling individual rides, attractions, parades and shows; and in security, health and safety systems.

In the Creative Content segment, Y2K failures could interfere with critical systems in such areas as the production, duplication and distribution of motion picture and home video product and the ordering, distribution and sale of merchandise at the company's retail stores and catalog operations.

In the Broadcasting segment, at-risk operations include satellite transmission and communication systems. Y2K failures in such systems could adversely affect the company's television and radio networks, including cable services, as well as its owned and operated stations.

Addressing the Problem. The company has developed a six-phase approach to resolving the Y2K issues that are reasonably within its control. All of these efforts are being coordinated through a senior-level task force chaired by the company's Chief Information Officer ("CIO"), as well as individual task forces in each major business unit. As of September 30, 1998, approximately 400 employees were devoting more than half of their time to Y2K efforts, in addition to approximately 400 expert consultants retained on a full-time basis to assist with specific potential problems. The CIO reports periodically to the Audit Review Committee of the Board of Directors with respect to the company's Y2K efforts.

The company's approach to and the anticipated timing of each phase are described below.

Phase 1 – Inventory. The first phase entails a worldwide inventory of all hardware and software (including business and operational applications, operating systems and third-party products) that may be at risk, and identification of key third-party businesses whose Y2K failures might most significantly impact the company. The IT system inventory process has been completed, and the inventories of key third-party businesses and of internal non-IT systems are expected to be completed by December 31, 1998.

Phase 2 – Assessment. Once each at-risk system has been identified, the Y2K task forces assess how critical the system is to business operations and the potential impact of failure, in order to establish priorities for repair or replacement. Systems are classified as "critical," "important" or "non-critical." A "critical" system is one that, if not operational, would cause the shutdown of all or a portion of a business unit within two weeks, while an "important" system is one that would cause such a shutdown within two months. This process has been completed for all IT systems, resulting in the identification of nearly 600 business systems that are "critical" to continued functioning and more than 1,000 that are either "important" or are otherwise being monitored. The assessment process for internal non-IT systems and for key third-party businesses is expected to be completed by mid-1999. Systems that are known to be critical or important are receiving top priority in assessment and remediation.

Phase 3 – Strategy. This phase involves the development of appropriate remedial strategies for both IT and non-IT systems. These strategies may include repairing, testing and certifying, replacing or abandoning particular systems (as discussed under Phases 4 and 5 below). Selection of appropriate strategies is based upon such factors as the assessments made in Phase 2, the type of system, the availability of a Y2K-compliant replacement and cost. The strategy phase has been completed for all IT systems. For some non-IT embedded systems, strategy development is continuing. At the company's theme parks, the majority of ride and show control systems have been tested and certified. A strategy for addressing embedded systems in office buildings is being developed in concert with building managers and systems vendors and should be completed by spring 1999. The process of analysis, certification or replacement or "workaround" for embedded systems in office buildings is expected to consume the first half of 1999. Strategies for other embedded systems, such as satellite communications systems, are being developed and are also expected to be complete by mid-1999.

Phase 4 – Remediation. The remediation phase involves creating detailed project plans, marshalling necessary resources and executing the strategies chosen. For IT systems, this phase is approximately 75% complete for critical and important systems, and is expected to be completed (including certification) by July 31, 1999. For non-critical systems, most corrections are expected to be completed by December 31, 1999. For those systems that are not expected to be reliably functional after January 1, 2000, detailed manual workaround plans will be developed prior to the end of 1999.

Phase 5 – Testing and Certification. This phase includes establishing a test environment, performing systems testing (with third parties if necessary), and certifying the results. The certification process entails having functional experts review test results, computer screens and printouts against pre-established criteria to ensure system compliance. The company expects all critical and important IT systems to be certified by July 31, 1999. Testing for non-IT systems has been initiated; however, due to the company's reliance on many third-party vendors for these systems, the company cannot estimate precisely when this phase will be completed. The majority of embedded systems at the company's theme parks are expected to be certified by December 31, 1998. The company's target for all critical and important non-IT systems is July 1999.

The company has initiated written and telephonic communications with key third-party businesses, as well as public and private providers of infrastructure services, to ascertain and evaluate their efforts in addressing Y2K compliance. It is anticipated that the majority of testing and certification with these entities will occur in 1999.

Phase 6 – Contingency Planning. This phase involves addressing any remaining open issues expected in 1999 and early 2000. As a precautionary measure, the company is currently developing contingency plans for all systems that are not expected to be Y2K compliant by March 1999. A variety of automated as well as manual fallback plans are under consideration, including the use of electronic spreadsheets, resetting system dates to 1972, a year in which the calendar coincides with that of 2000, and manual workarounds. The company estimates that all of these plans will be completed by December 1999.

Costs. As of September 30, 1998, the company had incurred costs of approximately $136 million related to its Y2K project, of which $82 million has been capitalized. The estimated additional costs to complete the project are currently expected to be approximately $125 million, of which $60 million is expected to be capitalized. A significant portion of these costs have not been incremental, but rather reflect redeployment of internal resources from other activities. The company does not expect these redeployments to have a material adverse effect on other ongoing business operations of the company and its subsidiaries, although it is possible that certain maintenance and upgrading processes will be delayed as the result of the priority being given to Y2K remediation. All of the costs of the Y2K project are being borne out of the company's operating cash flow.

Based upon its efforts to date, the company believes that the vast majority of both its IT and its non-IT systems, including all critical and important systems, will remain up and running after January 1, 2000. Accordingly, the company does not currently anticipate that internal systems failures will result in any material adverse effect to its operations or financial condition. During 1999, the company will also continue and expand its efforts to ensure that major third-party businesses and public and private providers of infrastructure services, such as utilities, communications services and transportation, will also be prepared for the year 2000, and to develop contingency plans to address any failures on their part to become Y2K compliant. At this time, the company believes that the most likely "worst-case" scenario involves potential disruptions in areas in which the company's operations must rely on such third parties whose systems may not work properly after January 1, 2000. In addition, the company's international operations may be adversely affected by failures of businesses in other parts of the world to take adequate steps to address the Y2K problem. While such failures could affect important operations of the company and its subsidiaries, either directly or indirectly, in a significant manner, the company cannot at present estimate either the likelihood or the potential cost of such failures.

The nature and focus of the company's efforts to address the Year 2000 problem may be revised periodically as interim goals are achieved or new issues are identified. In addition, it is important to note that the description of the company's efforts necessarily involves estimates and projections with respect to activities required in the future. These estimates and projections are subject to change as work continues, and such changes may be substantial.

CONVERSION TO THE EURO CURRENCY

On January 1, 1999, certain member countries of the European Union are scheduled to establish fixed conversion rates between their existing currencies and the European Union's common currency ("euro"). The company conducts business in member countries. The transition period for the introduction of the euro will be between January 1, 1999 and June 30, 2002. The company is addressing the issues involved with the introduction of the euro. The more important issues facing the company include: converting information technology systems; reassessing currency risk; negotiating and amending licensing agreements and contracts; and processing tax and accounting records.

Based upon progress to date the company believes that use of the euro will not have a significant impact on the manner in which it conducts its business affairs and processes its business and accounting records. Accordingly, conversion to the euro is not expected to have a material effect on the company's financial condition or results of operations.

FORWARD-LOOKING STATEMENTS

The Private Securities Litigation Reform Act of 1995 (the "Act") provides a safe harbor for forward-looking statements made by or on behalf of the company. The company and its representatives may from time to time make written or oral statements that are "forward-looking," including statements contained in this report and other filings with the Securities and Exchange Commission and in reports to the company's stockholders. All statements that express expectations and projections with respect to future matters, including the launching or prospective development of new business initiatives; anticipated motion picture or television releases; internet or theme park and resort projects; "Year 2000" remediation efforts; and preparations for the introduction of the euro, are forward-looking statements within the meaning of the Act. These statements are made on the basis of management's views and assumptions, as of the time the statements are made, regarding future events and business performance. There can be no assurance, however, that management's expectations will necessarily come to pass.

Factors that may affect forward-looking statements. For an enterprise as large and complex as the company, a wide range of factors could materially affect future developments and performance, including the following:

Changes in company-wide or business-unit strategies, which may result in changes in the types or mix of businesses in which the company is involved or chooses to invest;

Changes in U.S., global or regional economic conditions, which may affect attendance and spending at the company's theme parks and resorts, purchases of company-licensed consumer products and the performance of the company's broadcasting and motion picture operations;

Changes in U.S. and global financial and equity markets, including significant interest rate fluctuations, which may impede the company's access to, or increase the cost of, external financing for its operations and investments;

Increased competitive pressures, both domestically and internationally, which may, among other things, affect the performance of the company's theme park, resort and regional

entertainment operations and lead to increased expenses in such areas as television programming acquisition and motion picture production and marketing;

Legal and regulatory developments that may affect particular business units, such as regulatory actions affecting environmental activities, consumer products, broadcasting or internet activities, or the protection of intellectual properties, the imposition by foreign countries of trade restrictions or motion picture or television content requirements or quotas, and changes in international tax laws or currency controls;

Adverse weather conditions or natural disasters, such as hurricanes and earthquakes, which may, among other things, impair performance at the company's theme parks and resorts;

Technological developments that may affect the distribution of the company's creative products or create new risks to the company's ability to protect its intellectual property;

Labor disputes, which may lead to increased costs or disruption of operations in any of the company's business units; and

Changing public and consumer taste, which may affect the company's entertainment, broadcasting and consumer products businesses.

This list of factors that may affect future performance and the accuracy of forward-looking statements is illustrative, but by no means exhaustive. Accordingly, all forward-looking statements should be evaluated with the understanding of their inherent uncertainty.

MARKET RISK

The company is exposed to the impact of interest rate changes, foreign currency fluctuations and changes in the market values of its investments.

Policies and Procedures In the normal course of business, the company employs established policies and procedures to manage its exposure to changes in interest rates and fluctuations in the value of foreign currencies using a variety of financial instruments.

The company's objective in managing its exposure to interest rate changes is to limit the impact of interest rate changes on earnings and cash flows and to lower its overall borrowing costs. To achieve its objectives, the company primarily uses interest rate swaps to manage net exposure to interest rate changes related to its portfolio of borrowings. The company maintains fixed rate debt as a percentage of its net debt between a minimum and maximum percentage, which is set by policy.

The company's objective in managing the exposure to foreign currency fluctuations is to reduce earnings and cash flow volatility associated with foreign exchange rate changes to allow management to focus its attention on its core business issues and challenges. Accordingly, the company enters into various contracts that change in value as foreign exchange rates change to protect the value of its existing foreign currency assets, liabilities, commitments and anticipated foreign currency revenues. The company uses option strategies that provide for the sale of foreign currencies to hedge probable, but not firmly committed, revenues. The principal currencies hedged are the Japanese yen, French franc, German mark, British pound, Canadian dollar and Italian lira. By policy, the company maintains hedge coverage between minimum and maximum percentages of its anticipated foreign exchange exposures for periods not to exceed five years. The gains and losses on these contracts offset changes in the value of the related exposures.

It is the company's policy to enter into foreign currency and interest rate transactions only to the extent considered necessary to meet its objectives as stated above. The company does not enter into foreign currency or interest rate transactions for speculative purposes.

Value At Risk The company utilizes a "Value-at-Risk" ("VAR") model to determine the maximum potential one-day loss in the fair value of its interest rate and foreign exchange sensitive financial instruments. The VAR model estimates were made assuming normal market conditions and a 95% confidence level. There are various modeling techniques which can be used in the VAR computation. The company's computations are based on the interrelationships between movements in various currencies and interest rates (a "variance/co-variance" technique). These interrelationships were determined by observing interest rate and foreign currency market changes over the preceding quarter for the calculation of VAR amounts at year-end and over each of the four quarters for the calculation of average VAR amounts during the year. The model includes all of the company's debt as well as all interest rate and foreign exchange derivative contracts. The values of foreign exchange options do not change on a one-to-one basis with the underlying currencies, as exchange rates vary. Therefore, the hedge coverage assumed to be obtained from each option has been adjusted to reflect its respective sensitivity to changes in currency values. Anticipated transactions, firm commitments and receivables and accounts payable denominated in foreign currencies, which certain of these instruments are intended to hedge, were excluded from the model.

The VAR model is a risk analysis tool and does not purport to represent actual losses in fair value that will be incurred by the company, nor does it consider the potential effect of favorable changes in market factors. (See Note 12 to the Consolidated Financial Statements regarding the company's financial instruments at September 30, 1998 and 1997.)

The estimated maximum potential one-day loss in fair value, calculated using the VAR model, follows (in millions):

	Interest Rate Sensitive Financial Instruments	Currency Sensitive Financial Instruments	Combined Portfolio
VAR as of September 30, 1998	$32	$29	$56
Average VAR during the year ended September 30, 1998	$21	$26	$32

The higher VAR combined portfolio exposure at September 30, 1998 is primarily due to the volatile financial market environment existing at year end. Since the company utilizes currency sensitive derivative instruments to hedge anticipated foreign currency transactions, a loss in fair value for those instruments is generally offset by increases in the value of the underlying anticipated transactions.

New Accounting Guidance. In June 1998, the Financial Accounting Standards Board (the "FASB") issued Statement No. 133, *Accounting for Derivative Instruments and Hedging Activities* ("SFAS 133"), which the company is required to adopt effective October 1, 1999. SFAS 133 will require the company to record all derivatives on the balance sheet at fair value. Changes in derivative fair values will either be recognized in earnings as offsets to the changes in fair value of related hedged assets, liabilities and firm commitments or for forecasted transactions, deferred and recorded as a component of other stockholders' equity until the hedged transactions occur and are recognized in earnings. The ineffective portion of a hedging derivative's change in fair value will be immediately recognized in earnings. The impact of SFAS 133 on the company's financial statements will depend on a variety of factors, including future interpretative guidance from the FASB, the future level of forecasted and actual foreign currency transactions, the extent of the company's hedging activities, the types of hedging instruments used and the effectiveness of such instruments. However, the company does not believe the effect of adopting SFAS 133 will be material to its financial position.

CONSOLIDATED STATEMENTS OF INCOME

The Walt Disney Company and Subsidiaries

(In millions, except per share data)	1998	1997	1996
	Year Ended September 30		
Revenues	$ 22,976	$ 22,473	$ 18,739
Costs and expenses	(18,961)	(18,161)	(15,406)
Gain on sale of KCAL	—	135	—
Accounting change	—	—	(300)
Operating income	4,015	4,447	3,033
Corporate activities and other	(236)	(367)	(309)
Net interest expense	(622)	(693)	(438)
Acquisition-related costs	—	—	(225)
Income before income taxes	3,157	3,387	2,061
Income taxes	(1,307)	(1,421)	(847)
Net income	$ 1,850	$ 1,966	$ 1,214
Earnings per share			
Diluted	$ 0.89	$ 0.95	$ 0.65
Basic	$ 0.91	$ 0.97	$ 0.66
Average number of common and common equivalent shares outstanding			
Diluted	2,079	2,060	1,857
Basic	2,037	2,021	1,827

See Notes to Consolidated Financial Statements

CONSOLIDATED BALANCE SHEETS

The Walt Disney Company and Subsidiaries

	September 30	
(In millions)	**1998**	1997
Assets		
Current Assets		
Cash and cash equivalents	**$ 127**	$ 317
Receivables	**3,999**	3,329
Inventories	**899**	853
Film and television costs	**3,223**	2,186
Deferred income taxes	**463**	482
Other assets	**664**	486
Total current assets	**9,375**	7,653
Film and television costs	**2,506**	2,215
Investments	**1,814**	1,914
Theme parks, resorts and other property, at cost		
Attractions, buildings and equipment	**14,037**	11,787
Accumulated depreciation	**(5,382)**	(4,857)
	8,655	6,930
Projects in progress	**1,280**	1,928
Land	**411**	93
	10,346	8,951
Intangible assets, net	**15,769**	16,011
Other assets	**1,568**	1,753
	$41,378	$38,497
Liabilities and Stockholders' Equity		
Current Liabilities		
Accounts and taxes payable and other accrued liabilities	**$ 4,767**	$ 4,748
Current portion of borrowings	**2,132**	897
Unearned royalties and other advances	**635**	631
Total current liabilities	**7,525**	6,276
Borrowings	**9,562**	10,171
Deferred income taxes	**2,488**	2,161
Other long term liabilities, unearned royalties and other advances	**2,415**	2,604
Stockholders' Equity		
Preferred stock, $.01 par value		
Authorized — 100 million shares		
Issued — none		
Common stock, $.01 par value		
Authorized — 3.6 billion shares		
Issued — 2.1 billion shares and 2.0 billion shares	**8,995**	8,548
Retained earnings	**10,981**	9,543
Cumulative translation and other	**13**	(12)
	19,989	18,079
Treasury stock, at cost, 29 million shares and 24 million shares	**(593)**	(462)
Shares held by TWDC Stock Compensation Fund, at cost — 0.4 million shares and 13 million shares	**(8)**	(332)
	19,388	17,285
	$41,378	$38,497

See Notes to Consolidated Financial Statements

ℭONSOLIDATED STATEMENTS OF CASH FLOWS

The Walt Disney Company and Subsidiaries

(In millions)	Year Ended September 30		
	1998	1997	1996
Net Income	**$ 1,850**	$ 1,966	$ 1,214
Items Not Requiring Cash Outlays			
Amortization of film and television costs	**2,514**	1,995	1,786
Depreciation	**809**	738	672
Amortization of intangible assets	**431**	439	301
Gain on sale of KCAL	**—**	(135)	—
Accounting change	**—**	—	300
Other	**(75)**	(15)	22
Changes In			
Receivables	**(664)**	(177)	(297)
Inventories	**(46)**	8	(13)
Other assets	**179**	(441)	(399)
Accounts and taxes payable and accrued liabilities	**218**	608	56
Film and television costs — television broadcast rights	**(447)**	(179)	58
Deferred income taxes	**346**	292	(78)
Investments in trading securities	**—**	—	85
	3,265	3,133	2,493
Cash Provided by Operations	**5,115**	5,099	3,707
Investing Activities			
Film and television costs	**(3,335)**	(3,089)	(2,760)
Investments in theme parks, resorts and other property	**(2,314)**	(1,922)	(1,745)
Acquisitions	**(213)**	(180)	—
Proceeds from sales of marketable securities and other investments	**238**	31	409
Purchases of marketable securities	**(13)**	(56)	(18)
Investment in and loan to E! Entertainment	**(28)**	(321)	—
Proceeds from disposal of publishing operations	**—**	1,214	—
Acquisition of ABC, net of cash acquired	**—**	—	(8,432)
Proceeds from disposal of KCAL	**—**	387	—
	(5,665)	(3,936)	(12,546)
Financing Activities			
Borrowings	**1,830**	2,437	13,560
Reduction of borrowings	**(1,212)**	(4,078)	(4,872)
Repurchases of common stock	**(30)**	(633)	(462)
Dividends	**(412)**	(342)	(271)
Exercise of stock options and other	**184**	180	85
Proceeds from formation of REITs	**—**	1,312	—
	360	(1,124)	8,040
(Decrease) Increase in Cash and Cash Equivalents	**(190)**	39	(799)
Cash and Cash Equivalents, Beginning of Year	**317**	278	1,077
Cash and Cash Equivalents, End of Year	**$ 127**	$ 317	$ 278
Supplemental disclosure of cash flow information:			
Interest paid	**$ 555**	$ 777	$ 379
Income taxes paid	**$ 1,107**	$ 958	$ 689

See Notes to Consolidated Financial Statements

CONSOLIDATED STATEMENTS OF STOCKHOLDERS' EQUITY

The Walt Disney Company and Subsidiaries

(In millions, except per share data)	Shares	Common Stock	Retained Earnings	Cumulative Translation and Other	Treasury Stock	TWDC Stock Compensation Fund	Total
Balance at September 30, 1995	1,573	$1,240	$ 6,976	$ 38	$(1,603)	$ —	$ 6,651
Impact of ABC acquisition	464	7,206	—	—	1,603	—	8,809
Exercise of stock options, net	9	144	—	—	—	—	144
Common stock repurchased	(24)	—	—	—	(462)	—	(462)
Dividends ($.14 per share)	—	—	(271)	—	—	—	(271)
Cumulative translation and other	—	—	—	1	—	—	1
Net income	—	—	1,214	—	—	—	1,214
Balance at September 30, 1996	2,022	8,590	7,919	39	(462)	—	16,086
Exercise of stock options, net	15	(42)	—	—	—	301	259
Common stock repurchased	(24)	—	—	—	—	(633)	(633)
Dividends ($.17 per share)	—	—	(342)	—	—	—	(342)
Cumulative translation and other	—	—	—	(51)	—	—	(51)
Net income	—	—	1,966	—	—	—	1,966
Balance at September 30, 1997	2,013	8,548	9,543	(12)	(462)	(332)	17,285
Common stock issued	4	160	—	—	—	—	160
Exercise of stock options, net	34	287	—	—	(131)	354	510
Common stock repurchased	(1)	—	—	—	—	(30)	(30)
Dividends ($.20 per share)	—	—	(412)	—	—	—	(412)
Cumulative translation and other	—	—	—	25	—	—	25
Net income	—	—	1,850	—	—	—	1,850
Balance at September 30, 1998	2,050	$8,995	$10,981	$13	$ (593)	$ (8)	$19,388

See Notes to Consolidated Financial Statements

NOTES TO CONSOLIDATED FINANCIAL STATEMENTS

The Walt Disney Company and Subsidiaries

(Tabular dollars in millions, except per share amounts)

NOTE 1. DESCRIPTION OF THE BUSINESS AND SUMMARY OF SIGNIFICANT ACCOUNTING POLICIES

The Walt Disney Company, together with its subsidiaries (the "company"), is a diversified international entertainment organization with operations in the following businesses.

CREATIVE CONTENT

The company produces and acquires live-action and animated motion pictures for distribution to the theatrical, home video and television markets. The company also produces original television programming for the network and first-run syndication markets. The company distributes its filmed product through its own distribution and marketing companies in the United States and most foreign markets.

The company licenses the name "Walt Disney," as well as the company's characters, visual and literary properties and songs and music, to various consumer manufacturers, retailers, show promoters and publishers throughout the world. The company also engages in direct retail distribution principally through the Disney Stores, and produces books and magazines for the general public in the United States and Europe. In addition, the company produces audio and computer software products for the entertainment market, as well as film, video and computer software products for the educational marketplace.

Buena Vista Internet Group ("BVIG") coordinates the company's internet initiatives. BVIG develops, publishes and distributes content for narrow-band on-line services, the interactive software market, interactive television platforms, internet web sites, including Disney.com, Disney's Daily Blast, ESPN.com, ABCNews.com and the Disney Store Online, which offers Disney-themed merchandise over the internet.

BROADCASTING

The company operates the ABC Television Network, which has affiliated stations providing coverage to U.S. television households. The company also owns television and radio stations, most of which are affiliated with either the ABC Television Network or the ABC Radio Networks. The company's cable and international broadcast operations are principally involved in the production and distribution of cable television programming, the licensing of programming to domestic and international markets and investing in foreign television broadcasting, production and distribution entities. Primary domestic cable programming services, which operate through subsidiary companies and joint ventures, are ESPN, the A&E Television Networks, Lifetime Entertainment Services and E! Entertainment Television. The company provides programming for and operates cable and satellite television programming services, including the Disney Channel and Disney Channel International.

THEME PARKS AND RESORTS

The company operates the Walt Disney World Resort® in Florida, and Disneyland Park,® the Disneyland Hotel and the Disneyland Pacific Hotel in California. The Walt Disney World Resort includes the Magic Kingdom, Epcot, Disney-MGM Studios and Disney's Animal Kingdom, thirteen resort hotels and a complex of villas and suites, a retail, dining and entertainment complex, a sports complex, conference centers, campgrounds, golf courses, water parks and other recreational facilities. In addition, the resort operates Disney Cruise Line from Port Canaveral, Florida. Disney Regional Entertainment designs, develops and operates a variety of new entertainment concepts based on Disney brands and creative properties, operating under the names Club Disney, ESPN Zone and DisneyQuest. The company earns royalties on revenues generated by the Tokyo Disneyland® theme park near Tokyo, Japan, which is owned and operated by an unrelated Japanese corporation. The company also has an investment in Euro Disney S.C.A., a publicly-held French entity that operates Disneyland Paris. The company's Walt Disney Imagineering unit designs and develops new theme park concepts and attractions, as well as resort properties. The company also manages and markets vacation ownership interests in the Disney Vacation Club. Included in Theme Parks and Resorts are the company's National Hockey League franchise, the Mighty Ducks of Anaheim, and its ownership interest in the Anaheim Angels, a Major League Baseball team.

SIGNIFICANT ACCOUNTING POLICIES

Principles of Consolidation The consolidated financial statements of the company include the accounts of The Walt Disney Company and its subsidiaries after elimination of intercompany accounts and transactions.

Accounting Changes During the first quarter, the company adopted Statement of Financial Accounting Standards No. 128 *Earnings Per Share* ("SFAS 128"), which specifies the method of computation, presentation and disclosure for earnings per share ("EPS"). SFAS 128 requires the presentation of two EPS amounts, basic and diluted. Basic EPS is calculated by dividing net income by the weighted average number of common shares outstanding for the period. Diluted EPS includes the dilution that would occur if outstanding stock options and other dilutive securities were exercised and is comparable to the EPS the company has historically reported. The diluted EPS calculation excludes the effect of stock options when their exercise prices exceed the average market price over the period.

During 1997, the company adopted SFAS 123 *Accounting for Stock-Based Compensation* ("SFAS 123"), which requires disclosure of the fair value and other characteristics of stock options (see Note 9). The company has chosen under the provisions of SFAS 123 to continue using the intrinsic-value method of accounting for employee stock-based compensation in accordance with Accounting Principles Board Opinion No. 25 *Accounting for Stock Issued to Employees* ("APB 25").

During 1996, the company adopted SFAS 121 *Accounting for the Impairment of Long-Lived Assets and for Long-Lived Assets to be Disposed Of* ("SFAS 121") (see Note 11).

Use of Estimates   The preparation of financial statements in conformity with generally accepted accounting principles requires management to make estimates and assumptions that affect the amounts reported in the financial statements and footnotes thereto. Actual results could differ from those estimates.

Revenue Recognition   Revenues from the theatrical distribution of motion pictures are recognized when motion pictures are exhibited. Revenues from video sales are recognized on the date that video units are made widely available for sale by retailers. Revenues from the licensing of feature films and television programming are recorded when the material is available for telecasting by the licensee and when certain other conditions are met.

Broadcast advertising revenues are recognized when commercials are aired. Revenues from television subscription services related to the company's primary cable programming services are recognized as services are provided.

Revenues from participants and sponsors at the theme parks are generally recorded over the period of the applicable agreements commencing with the opening of the related attraction.

Cash and Cash Equivalents   Cash and cash equivalents consist of cash on hand and marketable securities with original maturities of three months or less.

Investments   Debt securities that the company has the positive intent and ability to hold to maturity are classified as "held-to-maturity" and reported at amortized cost. Debt securities not classified as held-to-maturity and marketable equity securities are classified as either "trading" or "available-for-sale," and are recorded at fair value with unrealized gains and losses included in earnings or stockholders' equity, respectively. All other equity securities are accounted for using either the cost method or the equity method. The company's share of earnings or losses in its equity investments accounted for under the equity method is included in "Corporate activities and other" in the consolidated statements of income.

Inventories   Carrying amounts of merchandise, materials and supplies inventories are generally determined on a moving average cost basis and are stated at the lower of cost or market.

Film and Television Costs   Film and television costs are stated at the lower of cost, less accumulated amortization, or net realizable value. Television broadcast program licenses and rights and related liabilities are recorded when the license period begins and the program is available for use.

Film and television production and participation costs are expensed based on the ratio of the current period's gross revenues to estimated total gross revenues from all sources on an individual production basis. Television network and station rights for theatrical movies and other long-form programming are charged to expense primarily on accelerated bases related to the usage of the programs. Television network series costs and multi-year sports rights are charged to expense based on the ratio of the current period's gross revenues to estimated total gross revenues from such programs.

Estimates of total gross revenues can change significantly due to a variety of factors, including the level of market acceptance of film and television products, advertising rates and subscriber fees. Accordingly, revenue estimates are reviewed periodically and amortization is adjusted if necessary. Such adjustments could have a material effect on results of operations in future periods.

Theme Parks, Resorts and Other Property   Theme parks, resorts and other property are carried at cost. Depreciation is computed on the straight-line method based upon estimated useful lives ranging from three to fifty years.

Intangible/Other Assets   Intangible assets are amortized over periods ranging from two to forty years. The company continually reviews the recoverability of the carrying value of these assets using the methodology prescribed in SFAS 121. The company also reviews long-lived assets and the related intangible assets for impairment whenever events or changes in circumstances indicate the carrying amounts of such assets may not be recoverable. Recoverability of these assets is determined by comparing the forecasted undiscounted net cash flows of the operation to which the assets relate, to the carrying amount, including associated intangible assets, of such operation. If the operation is determined to be unable to recover the carrying amount of its assets, then intangible assets are written down first, followed by the other long-lived assets of the operation, to fair value. Fair value is determined based on discounted cash flows or appraised values, depending upon the nature of the assets.

Risk Management Contracts   In the normal course of business, the company employs a variety of off-balance-sheet financial instruments to manage its exposure to fluctuations in interest and foreign currency exchange rates, including interest rate and cross-currency swap agreements, forward, option, swaption and spreadlock contracts and interest rate caps.

The company designates and assigns the financial instruments as hedges of specific assets, liabilities or anticipated transactions. When hedged assets or liabilities are sold or extinguished or the anticipated transactions being hedged are no longer expected to occur, the company recognizes the gain or loss on the designated hedging financial instruments.

The company classifies its derivative financial instruments as held or issued for purposes other than trading. Option premiums and unrealized losses on forward contracts and the accrued differential for interest rate and cross-currency swaps to be received under the agreements are recorded in the balance sheet as other assets. Unrealized gains on forward contracts and the accrued differential for interest rate and cross-currency swaps to be paid under the agreements are included in accounts and taxes payable and other accrued liabilities. Realized gains and losses from hedges are classified in the income statement consistent with the accounting treatment of the items being hedged. The company accrues the differential for interest rate and cross-currency swaps to be paid or received under the agreements as interest and exchange rates shift as adjustments to net interest expense over the lives of the swaps. Gains and losses on the termination of swap agreements, prior to their original maturity, are deferred and amortized to net interest expense over the remaining term of the underlying hedged transactions.

Cash flows from hedges are classified in the statements of cash flows under the same category as the cash flows from the related assets, liabilities or anticipated transactions (see Notes 5 and 12).

Earnings Per Share Diluted earnings per share amounts are based upon the weighted average number of common and common equivalent shares outstanding during the year. Common equivalent shares are excluded from the computation in periods in which they have an anti-dilutive effect. The difference between basic and diluted earnings per share, for the company, is solely attributable to stock options. For the years ended September 30, 1998, 1997 and 1996, options for 18 million, 15 million and 39 million shares, respectively, were excluded from diluted earnings per share.

Earnings per share amounts have been adjusted, for all years presented, to reflect the three-for-one split of the company's common shares effective June 1998 (see Note 8).

Reclassifications Certain reclassifications have been made in the 1997 and 1996 financial statements to conform to the 1998 presentation, including the change in format from an unclassified balance sheet to a classified balance sheet, which separately presents the current and non-current portions of assets and liabilities. Consistent with the classification of television broadcast rights as current assets, payments for such rights are now reclassified as operating cash flows.

NOTE 2. ACQUISITION AND DISPOSITIONS

On February 9, 1996, the company completed its acquisition of ABC. The aggregate consideration paid to ABC shareholders consisted of $10.1 billion in cash and 155 million shares of company common stock valued at $8.8 billion based on the stock price as of the date the transaction was announced.

As a result of the ABC acquisition, the company sold its independent Los Angeles television station, KCAL, during the first quarter of 1997 for $387 million, resulting in a gain of $135 million.

The company completed its final purchase price allocation and determination of related goodwill, deferred taxes and other accounts during the second quarter of 1997.

During the third and fourth quarters of 1997, the company disposed of most of the publishing businesses acquired with ABC to various third parties for consideration approximating their carrying amount. Proceeds consisted of $1.2 billion in cash, $1.0 billion in debt assumption and preferred stock convertible to common stock with a market value of $660 million.

The unaudited pro forma information below presents results of operations as if the acquisition of ABC in 1996 and the sale of KCAL, the finalization of purchase price allocation and the disposition of certain ABC publishing assets in 1997 had occurred at the beginning of the respective years presented. The unaudited pro forma information is not necessarily indicative of the results of operations of the combined company had these events occurred at the beginning of the years presented, nor is it necessarily indicative of future results.

	Year Ended September 30,	
	1997	1996[a]
Revenues	$21,613	$20,075
Net income	1,772	1,274
Earnings per share		
Diluted	$ 0.86	$ 0.62
Basic	$ 0.88	$ 0.63

[a] 1996 includes the impact of a $300 million non-cash charge related to the initial adoption of a new accounting standard (see Note 11). The charge reduced diluted earnings per share by $.09 for the year.

NOTE 3. INVESTMENT IN EURO DISNEY

Euro Disney S.C.A. ("Euro Disney") operates the Disneyland Paris theme park and resort complex on a 4,800-acre site near Paris, France. The company accounts for its 39% ownership interest in Euro Disney using the equity method of accounting. As of September 30, 1998, the company's recorded investment in Euro Disney was $340 million. The quoted market value of the company's Euro Disney shares at September 30, 1998 was approximately $452 million.

In connection with the financial restructuring of Euro Disney in 1994, Euro Disney Associés S.N.C. ("Disney SNC"), a wholly-owned affiliate of the company, entered into a lease arrangement with a noncancelable term of 12 years (the "Lease") related to substantially all of the Disneyland Paris theme park assets, and then entered into a 12-year sublease agreement (the "Sublease") with Euro Disney. Remaining lease rentals at September 30, 1998 of FF 8.3 billion ($1.5 billion) receivable from Euro Disney under the Sublease approximate the amounts payable by Disney SNC under the Lease. At the conclusion of the Sublease term, Euro Disney will have the option to assume Disney SNC's rights and obligations under the Lease. If Euro Disney does not exercise its option, Disney SNC may purchase the assets, continue to lease the assets or elect to terminate the Lease, in which case Disney SNC would make a termination payment to the lessor equal to 75% of the lessor's then outstanding debt related to the theme park assets, estimated to be $1.1 billion; Disney SNC could then sell or lease the assets on behalf of the lessor to satisfy the remaining debt, with any excess proceeds payable to Disney SNC.

Also as part of the restructuring, the company agreed to arrange for the provision of a 10-year unsecured standby credit facility of approximately $201 million, upon request, bearing interest at PIBOR. As of September 30, 1998, Euro Disney had not requested that the company establish this facility. The company also agreed, as long as any of the restructured debt is outstanding, to maintain ownership of at least 34% of the outstanding common stock of Euro Disney until June 1999, at least 25% for the subsequent five years and at least 16.67% for an additional term thereafter.

$\mathscr{N}$OTE 4. FILM AND TELEVISION COSTS

	1998	1997
Theatrical film costs		
Released, less amortization	$2,035	$1,691
In-process	2,041	1,855
	4,076	3,546
Television costs		
Released, less amortization	374	276
In-process	589	279
	963	555
Television broadcast rights	690	300
	5,729	4,401
Less: current portion	3,223	2,186
Non-current portion	$2,506	$2,215

Based on management's total gross revenue estimates as of September 30, 1998, approximately 82% of unamortized film and television costs (except in-process) are expected to be amortized during the next three years.

$\mathscr{N}$OTE 5. BORROWINGS

The company's borrowings at September 30, 1998 and 1997, including interest rate swaps designated as hedges, are summarized below.

1998

	Balance	Stated Interest Rate[e]	Interest rate and cross currency swaps[f] Pay Float	Pay Fixed	Effective Interest Rate[g]	Swap Maturities
Commercial paper due 1999[a]	$ 2,225	5.5%	$ —	$2,225	6.2%	1999
U.S. dollar notes and debentures due 1999–2093[b]	6,321	6.6%	2,886	675	6.4%	1999–2012
Dual currency and foreign notes due 1999–2003[c]	1,678	5.8%	1,678	—	5.4%	1999–2003
Senior participating notes due 2000–2001[d]	1,195	2.7%	—	—	n/a	n/a
Other due 1999–2027	266	5.2%	—	—	n/a	n/a
	11,685	5.8%	—	—	6.2%	
Less current portion	2,123					
Total long-term borrowings	$ 9,562		$4,564	$2,900		

1997

	Balance	Stated Interest Rate[e]	Interest rate and cross currency swaps[f] Pay Float	Pay Fixed	Effective Interest Rate[g]	Swap Maturities
Commercial paper due 1998[a]	$ 2,019	5.8%	$ —	$950	6.2%	1999
U.S. dollar notes and debentures due 1998–2093[b]	5,796	6.7%	2,086	—	6.5%	1998–2012
Dual currency and foreign notes due 1998–2001[c]	1,854	5.2%	1,812	—	5.4%	1998–2001
Senior participating notes due 2000–2001[d]	1,145	2.7%	—	—	n/a	n/a
Other due 1998–2027	254	8.2%	—	—	n/a	n/a
	11,068	5.9%	—	—	6.3%	
Less current portion	897					
Total long-term borrowings	$10,171		$3,898	$950		

(a)The company has established bank facilities totaling $5.2 billion which expire in one to four years. Under the bank facilities, the company has the option to borrow at various interest rates. Commercial paper is classified as long-term since the company intends to refinance these borrowings on a long-term basis through continued commercial paper borrowings supported by available bank facilities.

(b)Includes $771 million in 1998 and $821 million in 1997 representing minority interest in a real estate investment trust established by the company.

(c)Denominated principally in U.S. dollars, Japanese yen, Australian dollars and Italian lira.

(d)The average coupon rate is 2.7% on $1.3 billion face value of notes. Additional interest may be paid based on the performance of designated portfolios of films. The effective interest rates at September 30, 1998 and 1997 were 6.8% and 6.3%, respectively.

(e)The stated interest rate represents the weighted average coupon rate for each category of borrowings. For floating rate borrowings, interest rates are based upon the rates at September 30, 1998 and 1997; these rates are not necessarily an indication of future interest rates.

(f)Amounts represent notional values of interest rate swaps.

(g)The effective interest rate reflects the effect of interest rate and cross-currency swaps entered into with respect to certain borrowings as indicated in the "Pay Float" and "Pay Fixed" columns.

Borrowings, excluding commercial paper and minority interest, have the following scheduled maturities:

1999	$2,123
2000	2,074
2001	2,054
2002	—
2003	92
Thereafter	2,346

The company capitalizes interest on assets constructed for its theme parks, resorts and other property, and on theatrical and television productions in process. In 1998, 1997 and 1996, respectively, total interest costs incurred were $824 million, $841 million and $545 million, of which $139 million, $100 million and $66 million were capitalized.

NOTE 6. INCOME TAXES

	1998	1997	1996
Income before income taxes			
Domestic (including U.S. exports)	$3,114	$3,193	$1,822
Foreign subsidiaries	43	194	239
	$3,157	$3,387	$2,061
Income tax provision			
Current			
Federal	$ 698	$1,023	$ 389
State	119	203	101
Foreign (including withholding)	139	190	235
	956	1,416	725
Deferred			
Federal	303	21	106
State	48	(16)	16
	351	5	122
	$1,307	$1,421	$ 847

Components of Deferred Tax Assets and Liabilities	1998	1997
Deferred tax assets		
Accrued liabilities	$(1,051)	$(1,257)
Other, net	(61)	(89)
Total deferred tax assets	(1,112)	(1,346)
Deferred tax liabilities		
Depreciable, amortizable and other property	2,396	2,413
Licensing revenues	249	193
Leveraged leases	313	279
Investment in Euro Disney	129	90
Total deferred tax liabilities	3,087	2,975
Net deferred tax liability before valuation allowance	1,975	1,629
Valuation allowance	50	50
Net deferred tax liability	$ 2,025	$ 1,679

Reconciliation of Effective Income Tax Rate	1998	1997	1996
Federal income tax rate	35.0%	35.0%	35.0%
Nondeductible amortization of intangible assets	4.4	4.4	5.1
State taxes, net of federal income tax benefit	3.4	3.6	3.7
Other, net	(1.4)	(1.0)	(2.7)
	41.4%	42.0%	41.1%

In 1998, 1997 and 1996, income tax benefits attributable to employee stock option transactions of $327 million, $81 million and $44 million, respectively, were allocated to stockholders' equity.

NOTE 7. PENSION AND OTHER BENEFIT PROGRAMS

The company maintains pension plans and postretirement medical benefit plans covering most of its domestic employees not covered by union or industry-wide plans. Employees hired after January 1, 1994 are not eligible for the postretirement medical benefits. Pension benefits are generally based on years of service and/or compensation. The following chart summarizes the balance sheet impact, as well as the benefit obligations, assets, funded status and rate assumptions associated with the pension and postretirement medical benefit plans.

	Pension Plans		Postretirement Benefit Plans	
	1998	1997	**1998**	1997
Reconciliation of funded status of the plans and the amounts included in the company's consolidated balance sheets:				
Projected benefit obligations				
Beginning obligations	**$(1,438)**	$(1,402)	**$(293)**	$(271)
Service cost	**(71)**	(73)	**(11)**	(10)
Interest cost	**(109)**	(106)	**(22)**	(21)
Actuarial gains (losses)	**(247)**	9	**(2)**	5
Benefits paid	**63**	62	**10**	9
Other	**9**	72	**(3)**	(5)
Ending obligations	**(1,793)**	(1,438)	**(321)**	(293)
Fair value of plans' assets				
Beginning fair value	**1,726**	1,442	**162**	138
Actual return on plans' assets	**294**	304	**26**	22
Employer contributions	**75**	110	**7**	—
Participants' contributions	**1**	1	**—**	11
Benefits paid	**(63)**	(62)	**(10)**	(9)
Expenses	**(15)**	(9)	**—**	—
Other	**(4)**	(60)	**—**	—
Ending fair value	**2,014**	1,726	**185**	162
Funded status of the plans	**221**	288	**(136)**	(131)
Unrecognized net gain (loss)	**(80)**	(219)	**(30)**	(20)
Unrecognized prior service benefit (cost)	**(11)**	(2)	**1**	(34)
Other	**33**	28	**—**	—
Net balance sheet asset (liability)	**$ 163**	$ 95	**$(165)**	$(185)

	Pension Plans		Postretirement Benefit Plans	
	1998	1997	**1998**	1997
Rate Assumptions				
Discount rate	**6.8%**	7.8%	**6.8%**	7.8%
Rate of return on plans' assets	**10.5%**	10.5%	**10.5%**	10.5%
Salary increases	**4.4%**	5.4%	**n/a**	n/a
Annual increase in cost of benefits	**n/a**	n/a	**6.4%**	6.7%

The projected benefit obligations and accumulated benefit obligations for the pension plans with accumulated benefit obligations in excess of plan assets were $96 million and $74 million for 1998, and $79 million and $50 million for 1997.

The annual increase in cost of postretirement benefits is assumed to decrease .3 percentage points per year until reaching 4.9%.

Assumed health care cost trend rates have a significant effect on the amounts reported for the postretirement medical benefit plans. The effects of a one percentage point decrease in the assumed health care cost trend rates on total service and interest cost components and on postretirement benefit obligations are $9 million and $70 million, respectively. The effects of a one percentage point increase in the assumed health care cost trend rates on total service and interest cost components and on postretirement benefit obligations are ($7) million and ($53) million, respectively.

The company's accumulated pension benefit obligations at September 30, 1998 and 1997 were $1.6 billion and $1.3 billion, of which 97.7% and 97.8% were vested, respectively.

The income statement costs of the pension plans for 1998, 1997 and 1996 totaled $12 million, $45 million and $58 million, respectively. The discount rate, rate of return on plan assets and salary increase assumptions for the pension plans were 7.8%, 10.0% and 5.6%, respectively, in 1996. The income statement credits for the postretirement benefit plans for 1998, 1997 and 1996 were $13 million, $18 million and $16 million, respectively. The discount rate, rate of return on plan assets and annual increase in cost of postretirement benefits assumptions were 7.8%, 10.0% and 7.0%, respectively, in 1996.

The market values of the company's shares held by the pension plan master trust as of September 30, 1998 and 1997 were $71 million and $75 million, respectively.

NOTE 8. STOCKHOLDERS' EQUITY

In June 1998, the company effected a three-for-one split of the company's common stock, by means of a special stock dividend. Stockholders' equity has been restated to give retroactive recognition to the stock split in prior periods by reclassifying from retained earnings to common stock the par value of additional shares issued pursuant to the split. In connection with the common stock split, the company amended its corporate charter to increase the company's authorized common stock from 1.2 billion shares to 3.6 billion shares. The Board of Directors also approved an increase in the company's share repurchase authorization to 133.3 million shares of common stock pre-split or 400 million post-split. All share and per share data included herein have been restated to reflect the split.

In 1996, the company established the TWDC Stock Compensation Fund pursuant to the repurchase program to acquire shares of the company for the purpose of funding certain stock-based compensation. Any shares acquired by the fund that are not utilized must be disposed of by December 31, 1999.

The company has a stockholder rights plan, expiring June 30, 1999, which becomes operative upon certain events involving the acquisition of 25% or more of the company's common stock by any person or group in a transaction not approved by the company's Board of Directors. Upon the occurrence of such an event, each right, unless redeemed by the Board, entitles its holder to purchase for $350 an amount of common stock of the company, or in certain circumstances the acquirer, having a $700 market value. In connection with the rights plan, 7 million shares of preferred stock were reserved.

Note 9. STOCK INCENTIVE PLANS

Under various plans, the company may grant stock options and other awards to key executive, management and creative personnel at exercise prices equal to or exceeding the market price at the date of grant. In general, options become exercisable over a five-year period from the grant date and expire 10 years after the date of grant. In certain cases for senior executives, options become exercisable over periods up to 10 years and expire up to 15 years after date of grant. Shares available for future option grants at September 30, 1998, totaled 119 million.

The following table summarizes information about stock option transactions (shares in millions):

	1998		1997		1996	
	Shares	**Weighted Average Exercise Price**	Shares	Weighted Average Exercise Price	Shares	Weighted Average Exercise Price
Outstanding at beginning of year	**183**	**$17.44**	189	$15.84	105	$11.20
Awards canceled	**(10)**	**20.98**	(18)	19.32	(6)	17.10
Awards granted	**27**	**33.07**	27	25.64	96	19.63
Awards exercised	**(37)**	**9.06**	(15)	11.14	(9)	10.53
Awards transferred (ABC)	**—**		—		3	11.05
Outstanding at September 30	**163**	**$21.70**	183	$17.44	189	$15.84
Exercisable at September 30	**51**	**$16.34**	63	$11.77	51	$ 9.40

The following table summarizes information about stock options outstanding at September 30, 1998 (shares in millions):

	Outstanding			Exercisable	
Range of Exercise Prices	Number of Options	Weighted Average Remaining Years of Contractual Life	Weighted Average Exercise Price	Number of Options	Weighted Average Exercise Price
$ 2–$ 5	**2**	**0.28**	**$ 5.71**	**2**	**$ 5.71**
$ 5–$10	**7**	**2.19**	**8.55**	**6**	**8.58**
$10–$15	**20**	**5.01**	**13.41**	**14**	**13.27**
$15–$20	**24**	**6.72**	**18.33**	**16**	**18.44**
$20–$25	**60**	**7.79**	**21.54**	**11**	**21.33**
$25–$30	**26**	**9.10**	**26.48**	**2**	**26.64**
$30–$35	**9**	**8.82**	**31.76**	**—**	**—**
$35–$40	**12**	**9.56**	**38.02**	**—**	**—**
$40–$45	**3**	**8.01**	**42.21**	**—**	**—**
	163			**51**	

During 1997, the company adopted SFAS 123 and pursuant to its provision elected to continue using the intrinsic-value method of accounting for stock-based awards granted to employees in accordance with APB 25. Accordingly, the company has not recognized compensation expense for its stock-based awards to employees. The following table reflects pro forma net income and earnings per share had the company elected to adopt the fair value approach of SFAS 123:

	1998	1997	1996
Net income:			
As reported	**$1,850**	$1,966	$1,214
Pro forma	**1,749**	1,870	1,185
Diluted earnings per share:			
As reported	**0.89**	0.95	0.65
Pro forma	**0.84**	0.91	0.64

These pro forma amounts may not be representative of future disclosures since the estimated fair value of stock options is amortized to expense over the vesting period, and additional options may be granted in future years.

The weighted average fair values of options at their grant date during 1998, 1997 and 1996, where the exercise price equaled the market price on the grant date, were $10.82 and $9.09, and $7.67, respectively. The weighted average fair values of options at their grant date during 1998 and 1996, where the exercise price exceeded the market price on the grant date, were $8.55 and $6.20, respectively. No such options were granted during 1997. The estimated fair value of each option granted is calculated using the Black-Scholes option-pricing model. The weighted average assumptions used in the model were as follows:

	1998	1997	1996
Risk-free interest rate	**5.4%**	6.4%	6.2%
Expected years until exercise	**6.0**	6.1	7.1
Expected stock volatility	**23%**	23%	23%
Dividend yield	**.71%**	.71%	.69%

NOTE 10. DETAIL OF CERTAIN BALANCE SHEET ACCOUNTS

	1998	1997
Current Receivables		
Trade, net of allowances	$ 3,447	$ 3,002
Other	552	327
	$ 3,999	$ 3,329
Accounts and taxes payable and other accrued liabilities		
Accounts payable	$ 3,792	$ 3,560
Income taxes payable	—	383
Payroll and employee benefits	853	684
Other	122	121
	$ 4,767	$ 4,748
Intangible assets		
Cost in excess of ABC's net assets acquired	$14,248	$14,307
Trademark	1,100	1,100
FCC licenses	1,100	1,100
Other	474	211
Accumulated amortization	(1,153)	(707)
	$15,769	$16,011

NOTE 11. SEGMENTS

Business Segments	1998	1997	1996
Revenues			
Creative Content	$10,302	$10,937	$10,159
Broadcasting	7,142	6,522	4,078
Theme Parks and Resorts	5,532	5,014	4,502
	$22,976	$22,473	$18,739
Operating income			
Creative Content	$ 1,403	$ 1,882	$ 1,561
Broadcasting	1,325	1,294	782
Theme Parks and Resorts	1,287	1,136	990
KCAL gain	—	135	—
Accounting change	—	—	(300)
	$ 4,015	$ 4,447	$ 3,033
Capital expenditures			
Creative Content	$ 221	$ 301	$ 359
Broadcasting	245	152	113
Theme Parks and Resorts	1,693	1,266	1,196
Corporate	155	203	77
	$ 2,314	$ 1,922	$ 1,745
Depreciation expense			
Creative Content	$ 209	$ 187	$ 163
Broadcasting	122	104	104
Theme Parks and Resorts	444	408	358
Corporate	34	39	47
	$ 809	$ 738	$ 672

Business Segments (continued)	1998	1997	1996
Identifiable assets			
Creative Content	$ 9,509	$ 8,832	$ 8,837
Broadcasting	20,099	19,036	19,576
Theme Parks and Resorts	9,214	8,051	7,066
Corporate	2,556	2,578	1,862
	$41,378	$38,497	$37,341
Supplemental revenue data			
Creative Content			
Theatrical product	$ 5,085	$5,595	$5,472
Consumer products	3,452	3,076	2,518
Broadcasting			
Advertising	5,287	4,937	3,092
Theme Parks and Resorts			
Merchandise, food and beverage	1,780	1,754	1,555
Admissions	1,739	1,603	1,493

Geographic Segments			
Revenues			
United States	$18,106	$17,868	$14,422
United States export	1,036	874	746
Europe	2,215	2,073	2,086
Rest of world	1,619	1,658	1,485
	$22,976	$22,473	$18,739
Operating income			
United States	$ 3,468	$ 3,712	$ 2,229
Europe	369	499	633
Rest of world	390	397	382
Unallocated expenses	(212)	(161)	(211)
	$ 4,015	$ 4,447	$ 3,033
Identifiable assets			
United States	$39,462	$36,706	$35,477
Europe	1,468	1,275	1,495
Rest of world	448	516	369
	$41,378	$38,497	$37,341

During the second quarter of 1996, the company implemented SFAS 121. This accounting standard changed the method that companies use to evaluate the carrying value of such assets by, among other things, requiring companies to evaluate assets at the lowest level at which identifiable cash flows can be determined. The implementation of SFAS 121 resulted in the company recognizing a $300 million non-cash charge related principally to certain assets included in the Theme Parks and Resorts segment.

$\mathcal{N}$OTE 12. FINANCIAL INSTRUMENTS

Investments As of September 30, 1998 and 1997, the company held $126 million and $137 million, respectively, of securities classified as available for sale. In 1998, 1997 and 1996, realized gains and losses on available-for-sale securities, determined principally on an average cost basis, and unrealized gains and losses on available-for-sale securities were not material.

Interest Rate Risk Management The company is exposed to the impact of interest rate changes. The company's objective is to manage the impact of interest rate changes on earnings and cash flows and on the market value of its investments and borrowings. The company maintains fixed rate debt as a percentage of its net debt between a minimum and maximum percentage, which is set by policy.

The company uses interest rate swaps and other instruments to manage net exposure to interest rate changes related to its borrowings and to lower its overall borrowing costs. Significant interest rate risk management instruments held by the company at September 30, 1998 and 1997 included pay-floating and pay-fixed swaps, interest rate caps and swaption contracts. Pay-floating swaps effectively converted medium-term obligations to LIBOR-based or commercial paper variable rate instruments. These swap agreements expire in one to fourteen years. Pay-fixed swaps and interest rate caps effectively converted floating rate obligations to fixed rate instruments. These instruments expire within one year. Swaption contracts were designated as hedges of floating rate debt and expired in 1998.

The following table reflects incremental changes in the notional or contractual amounts of the company's interest rate contracts during 1998 and 1997. Activity representing renewal of existing positions is excluded.

	September 30, 1997	Additions	Maturities/ Expirations	Terminations	September 30, 1998
Pay-floating swaps	$2,086	$ 950	$ (50)	$(100)	**$2,886**
Pay-fixed swaps	950	6,000	(4,050)	—	**2,900**
Interest rate caps	—	3,100	(2,000)	—	**1,100**
Swaption contracts	300	—	(300)	—	**—**
	$3,336	$10,050	$(6,400)	$(100)	**$6,886**

	September 30, 1996	Additions	Maturities/ Expirations	Terminations	September 30, 1997
Pay-floating swaps	$1,520	$2,479	$ —	$(1,913)	$2,086
Pay-fixed swaps	900	850	(200)	(600)	950
Swaption contracts	—	1,100	—	(800)	300
Option contracts	—	593	—	(593)	—
Spreadlock contracts	—	470	(470)	—	—
	$2,420	$5,492	$(670)	$(3,906)	$3,336

The impact of interest rate risk management activities on income in 1998, 1997 and 1996, and the amount of deferred gains and losses from interest rate risk management transactions at September 30, 1998 and 1997 were not material.

Foreign Exchange Risk Management The company transacts business in virtually every part of the world and is subject to risks associated with changing foreign exchange rates. The company's objective is to reduce earnings and cash flow volatility associated with foreign exchange rate changes to allow management to focus its attention on its core business issues and challenges. Accordingly, the company enters into various contracts which change in value as foreign exchange rates change to protect the value of its exiting foreign currency assets and liabilities, commitments and anticipated foreign currency revenues. By policy, the company maintains hedge coverage between minimum and maximum percentages of its anticipated foreign exchange exposures for periods not to exceed five years. The gains and losses on these contracts offset changes in the value of the related exposures.

It is the company's policy to enter into foreign currency transactions only to the extent considered necessary to meet its objectives as stated above. The company does not enter into foreign currency transactions for speculative purposes.

The company uses option strategies which provide for the sale of foreign currencies to hedge probable, but not firmly committed, revenues. While these hedging instruments are subject to fluctuations in value, such fluctuations are offset by changes in the value of the underlying exposures being hedged. The principal currencies hedged are the Japanese yen, French franc, German mark, British pound, Canadian dollar and Italian lira. The company also uses forward contracts to hedge foreign currency assets, liabilities and foreign currency payments the company is committed to make in connection with the construction of a cruise ship (see Note 13). Cross-currency swaps are used to hedge foreign currency-denominated borrowings.

At September 30, 1998 and 1997, the notional amounts of the company's foreign exchange risk management contracts, net of notional amounts of contracts with counterparties against which the company has a legal right of offset, the related exposures hedged and the contract maturities are as follows:

	Notional Amount	Exposures Hedged	Fiscal Year Maturity
1998			
Option contracts	**$2,966**	**$1,061**	**1999–2000**
Forward contracts	**2,053**	**1,773**	**1999–2000**
Cross-currency swaps	**1,678**	**1,678**	**1999–2003**
	$6,697	**$4,512**	
1997			
Option contracts	$3,460	$1,633	1998–1999
Forward contracts	2,284	1,725	1998–1999
Cross-currency swaps	1,812	1,812	1998–2001
	$7,556	$5,170	

Gains and losses on contracts hedging anticipated foreign currency revenues and foreign currency commitments are deferred until such revenues are recognized or such commitments are met, and offset changes in the value of the foreign currency revenues and commitments. At September 30, 1998 and 1997, the company had deferred gains of $245 million and $486 million respectively, and deferred losses of $118 million and $220 million, respectively, related to foreign currency hedge transactions. Deferred amounts to be recognized can change with market conditions and will be substantially offset by changes in the value of the related hedged transactions. The impact of foreign exchange risk management activities on operating income in 1998 and in 1997 was a net gain of $227 million and $166 million, respectively.

Fair Value of Financial Instruments At September 30, 1998 and 1997, the company's financial instruments included cash, cash equivalents, investments, receivables, accounts payable, borrowings and interest rate and foreign exchange risk management contracts.

At September 30, 1998 and 1997, the fair values of cash and cash equivalents, receivables, accounts payable and commercial paper approximated carrying values because of the short-term nature of these instruments. The estimated fair values of other financial instruments subject to fair value disclosures, determined based on broker quotes or quoted market prices or rates for the same or similar instruments, and the related carrying amounts are as follows:

	1998		1997	
	Carrying Amount	Fair Value	Carrying Amount	Fair Value
Investments	$ 686	$ 765	$ 769	$ 1,174
Borrowings	$(10,914)	$(11,271)	$(10,313)	$(10,290)
Risk management contracts:				
Foreign exchange forwards	$ 49	$ 18	$ 43	$ 93
Foreign exchange options	58	178	177	367
Interest rate swaps	30	181	20	54
Cross-currency swaps	25	(89)	17	(77)
	$ 162	$ 288	$ 257	$ 437

Credit Concentrations The company continually monitors its positions with, and the credit quality of, the financial institutions which are counterparties to its financial instruments and does not anticipate nonperformance by the counterparties. The company would not realize a material loss as of September 30, 1998 in the event of nonperformance by any one counterparty. The company enters into transactions only with financial institution counterparties which have a credit rating of A– or better. The company's current policy regarding agreements with financial institution counterparties is generally to require collateral in the event credit ratings fall below A– or in the event aggregate exposures exceed limits as defined by contract. In addition, the company limits the amount of credit exposure with any one institution. At September 30, 1998, financial institution counterparties posted collateral of $83 million to the company, and the company was not required to collateralize its financial instrument obligations.

The company's trade receivables and investments do not represent significant concentration of credit risk at September 30, 1998, due to the wide variety of customers and markets into which the company's products are sold, their dispersion across many geographic areas, and the diversification of the company's portfolio among instruments and issuers.

New Accounting Guidance In June 1998, the Financial Accounting Standards Board ("the FASB") issued Statement No. 133, *Accounting for Derivative Instruments and Hedging Activities* ("SFAS 133"), which the company is required to adopt effective October 1, 1999. SFAS 133 will require the company to record all derivatives on the balance sheet at fair value. Changes in derivative fair values will either be recognized in earnings as offsets to the changes in fair value of related hedged assets, liabilities and firm commitments or, for forecasted transactions, deferred and recorded as a component of other stockholders' equity until the hedged transactions occur and are recognized in earnings. The ineffective portion of a hedging derivative's change in fair value will be immediately recognized in earnings. The impact of SFAS 133 on the company's financial statements will depend on a variety of factors, including future interpretive guidance from the FASB, the future level of forecasted and actual foreign currency transactions, the extent of the company's hedging activities, the types of hedging instruments used and the effectiveness of such instruments. However, the company does not believe the effect of adopting SFAS 133 will be material to its financial position.

Note 13. COMMITMENTS AND CONTINGENCIES

Pursuant to an agreement with a shipyard for the construction of a cruise ship for its Disney Cruise Line, the company is committed to make payments totaling approximately $290 million in 1999.

The company is committed to the purchase of broadcast rights for various feature films, sports and other programming aggregating approximately $14.7 billion as of September 30, 1998. This amount is substantially payable over the next six years.

The company has various real estate operating leases including retail outlets for the distribution of consumer products and office space for general and administrative purposes. Future minimum lease payments under these non-cancelable operating leases totaled $2 billion at September 30, 1998, payable as follows:

1999	$272
2000	259
2001	236
2002	214
2003	183
Thereafter	819

Rental expense for the above operating leases during 1998, 1997 and 1996, including overages, common-area maintenance and other contingent rentals, was $321 million, $327 million and $233 million, respectively.

The company, together with, in some instances, certain of its directors and officers, is a defendant or co-defendant in various legal actions involving copyright, breach of contract and various other claims incident to the conduct of its businesses. Management does not expect the company to suffer any material liability by reason of such actions, nor does it expect that such actions will have a material effect on the company's liquidity or operating results.

Note 14. SUBSEQUENT EVENT

In April 1997, the company purchased a significant equity stake in Starwave Corporation ("Starwave"), an internet technology company. In connection with the acquisition, the company was granted an option to purchase substantially all the remaining shares of Starwave, which the company exercised during the third quarter of 1998. Accordingly, the accounts of Starwave have been included in the company's September 30, 1998 consolidated financial statements. On June 18, 1998, the company reached an agreement for the acquisition of Starwave by Infoseek Corporation ("Infoseek"), a publicly-held internet search company, pursuant to a merger. On November 18, 1998, the shareholders of both Infoseek and Starwave approved the merger. As a result of the merger and the company's purchase of additional shares of Infoseek common stock pursuant to the merger agreement, the company owns approximately 43% of Infoseek's outstanding common stock. In addition, pursuant to the merger agreement, the company purchased warrants enabling it, under certain circumstances, to achieve a majority stake in Infoseek. These warrants vest over a three-year period and expire in five years. Effective as of the November 18, 1998 closing date of the transaction, the company will record a significant non-cash gain, a write-off for purchased in-process research and development costs and an increase in investments, reflecting the company's share of the fair value of Infoseek's intangible assets. The company is currently performing the necessary valuations to determine the gain, the research and development write-off and the amount of and amortization period for the intangible assets. Thereafter, the company will account for its investment in Infoseek under the equity method. The merger is not expected to have a material effect on the company's financial position.

$\mathcal{Q}$UARTERLY FINANCIAL SUMMARY

(In millions, except per share data) (Unaudited)	December 31	March 31	June 30	September 30
1998				
Revenues	$ 6,339	$ 5,242	$ 5,248	$ 6,147
Operating income	1,492	849	923	751
Net income	755	384	415	296
Earnings per share[1]				
Diluted	0.37	0.18	0.20	0.14
Basic	0.37	0.19	0.20	0.14
Dividends per share	0.04	0.05	0.05	0.05
Market price per share				
High	33	38^{19}/$_{64}$	42^{3}/$_{8}$	39^{7}/$_{8}$
Low	25^{59}/$_{64}$	31^{31}/$_{64}$	35^{1}/$_{64}$	24^{7}/$_{16}$
1997				
Revenues	$ 6,278	$ 5,481	$ 5,194	$ 5,520
Operating income	1,562	864	1,060	961
Net income	749	333	473	411
Earnings per share[1]				
Diluted	0.36	0.16	0.23	0.20
Basic	0.37	0.16	0.23	0.20
Dividends per share	0.04	0.04	0.04	0.04
Market price per share				
High	25^{21}/$_{64}$	26^{3}/$_{64}$	28^{11}/$_{64}$	26^{63}/$_{64}$
Low	20^{53}/$_{64}$	22^{29}/$_{64}$	23^{45}/$_{64}$	25^{1}/$_{16}$

[1]Amounts have been adjusted to give effect to the three-for-one split of the company's common shares effective June 1998. See Note 8 to the Consolidated Financial Statements.

𝒮ELECTED FINANCIAL DATA

The Walt Disney Company and Subsidiaries

(In millions, except per share data)	1998	1997	1996	1995	1994
Statements of income					
Revenues	$22,976	$22,473	$ 18,739	$12,151	$10,090
Operating income	4,015	4,447	3,033	2,466	1,972
Net income	1,850	1,966	1,214	1,380	1,110
Per share					
Earnings					
Diluted	$ 0.89	$ 0.95	$ 0.65	$ 0.87	$ 0.68
Basic	0.91	0.97	0.66	0.88	0.69
Dividends	0.20	0.17	0.14	0.12	0.10
Balance sheets					
Total assets	$41,378	$38,497	$ 37,341	$14,995	$13,110
Borrowings	11,685	11,068	12,342	2,984	2,937
Stockholders' equity	19,388	17,285	16,086	6,651	5,508
Statements of cash flows					
Cash provided by operations	$ 5,115	$ 5,099	$ 3,707	$ 3,510	$ 2,808
Investing activities	(5,665)	(3,936)	(12,546)	(2,288)	(2,887)
Financing activities	360	(1,124)	8,040	(332)	(97)
Other					
Stockholders at year end	658,000	588,000	564,000	508,000	459,000
Employees at year end	117,000	108,000	100,000	71,000	65,000

Management's Responsibility for Financial Statements

Management is responsible for the preparation of the company's consolidated financial statements and related information appearing in this annual report. Management believes that the consolidated financial statements fairly reflect the form and substance of transactions and that the financial statements reasonably present the company's financial position and results of operations in conformity with generally accepted accounting principles. Management also has included in the company's financial statements amounts that are based on estimates and judgments which it believes are reasonable under the circumstances.

The independent accountants audit the company's consolidated financial statements in accordance with generally accepted auditing standards and provide an objective, independent review of the fairness of reported operating results and financial position.

The Board of Directors of the company has an Audit Review Committee composed of seven non-management Directors. The Committee meets periodically with financial management, the internal auditors and the independent accountants to review accounting, control, auditing and financial reporting matters.

Report of Independent Accountants

To the Board of Directors and Stockholders of
The Walt Disney Company

In our opinion, the consolidated balance sheets (page 60) and the related consolidated statements of income (page 59), of cash flows (page 61) and of stockholders' equity (page 62) present fairly, in all material respects, the financial position of The Walt Disney Company and its subsidiaries (the "company") at September 30, 1998 and 1997, and the results of their operations and their cash flows for each of the three years in the period ended September 30, 1998, in conformity with generally accepted accounting principles. These financial statements are the responsibility of the company's management; our responsibility is to express an opinion on these financial statements based on our audits. We conducted our audits of these statements in accordance with generally accepted auditing standards which require that we plan and perform the audits to obtain reasonable assurance about whether the financial statements are free of material misstatement. An audit includes examining, on a test basis, evidence supporting the amounts and disclosures in the financial statements, assessing the accounting principles used and significant estimates made by management, and evaluating the overall financial statement presentation. We believe that our audits provide a reasonable basis for the opinion expressed above.

PricewaterhouseCoopers LLP

Los Angeles, California
November 19, 1998

Supplemental Information

STOCK EXCHANGES

The Common Stock of the company is listed for trading on the New York (principal market) and Pacific Stock Exchanges. Certain debt securities of the company are listed on the Luxembourg and Swiss Stock Exchanges.

REGISTRAR AND STOCK TRANSFER AGENT

The Walt Disney Company
611 N. Brand Boulevard, Suite 6100
Glendale, California 91203
(818) 553-7200

INDEPENDENT ACCOUNTANTS

PricewaterhouseCoopers LLP, Los Angeles

OTHER INFORMATION

A copy of the company's annual report to the Securities and Exchange Commission (Form 10-K) will be furnished without charge to any stockholder upon written request.

A copy of the company's quarterly reports will be furnished without charge to any stockholder upon written or telephone request.

All written requests should be sent to Shareholder Services, The Walt Disney Company, 500 South Buena Vista Street, Burbank, California 91521-9722. Telephone requests can be made to (818) 553-7200.

Appendix B

Time Value of Money

The concept of the time value of money is very important in today's business world. No doubt you have studied this concept previously in basic accounting, finance, and business math classes. This appendix is intended as a review of the subject and includes illustrations of common applications.

THE TIME-VALUE-OF-MONEY CONCEPT

Decision makers, whether sports figures, entertainers, business executives, or home makers, must try to adjust for the impact of interest and changing economic prices. Consider the following illustrative situations:

- You are in the market for a used car. A newspaper advertisement offers the vehicle you want with two payment options. You can choose between an immediate cash price of $12,500 or a 6% financing option with payments over two years of $532 at the end of each month. Which alternative purchase plan should you choose?
- You intend to provide income for your retirement. If you are 20 years old, how much must you invest now in order to establish a fund large enough to pay for your retirement in 45 years?
- Every month, millions of individuals make mortgage payments on their homes. Because part of each payment is interest, and therefore tax-deductible, a method is needed for calculating the interest portion of each payment. What are the procedures for determining the interest and principal portions of each payment over the life of the mortgage?

In each of the preceding situations, decisions must be made regarding inflows and outflows of money over an extended period of time. Making correct financial decisions requires that the time value of money be taken into account. This means that dollars to be received or paid in the future must be "discounted" or adjusted to their **present value**. Alternatively, current dollars may be "accumulated" or adjusted to their **future values** so that comparisons of dollar amounts at different time periods can be meaningful.

In the first example, you must decide whether to pay $12,500 cash now or make 24 monthly payments of $532. Assuming you have sufficient cash, wouldn't it be better to pay $12,500 for the car now instead of $12,768 (24 payments of $532) under the time-payment plan? The answer to that question is, "Not necessarily." This decision requires that the alternatives be made comparable in terms of the time value of money, that is, the two alternatives must be stated at their respective present values.

The present value of the first alternative, the cash purchase, is simply the amount of cash to be paid currently, or $12,500. The present value of the second alternative is equal to the present value of each of the 24 payments, as illustrated below.

The total present value of the 24 payments of $532 each discounted to the date of purchase at 6% interest is approximately $12,003.[1] This amount is less than the $12,500 cash price the dealer is willing to accept. Therefore, assuming no other factors are relevant to your decision, you should purchase the car on the time-payment plan. This conclusion and the other examples in the chapter ignore any tax implications, which may modify the decision in actual practice.

---

1 As will be explained later, the $12,003 is determined by discounting an annuity of $532 for 24 months at an annual interest rate of 6%.

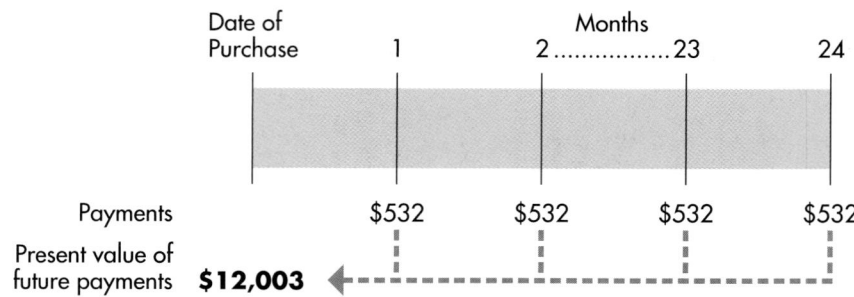

There are many business situations where present or future value techniques must be used in making financial decisions. Common applications in accounting include the following categories:

1. Valuing long-term notes receivable and payable where there is no stated rate of interest or where the stated rate does not reflect existing economic conditions.
2. Determining bond prices and using the effective-interest method for amortizing bond premiums or discounts.
3. Determining appropriate values for long-term capital leases and measuring the amount of interest expense and principal applicable to the periodic lease payments.
4. Accounting for pension funds, including interest accruals and amortization entries.
5. Analyzing investment alternatives.
6. Establishing amortization schedules for mortgages and measuring periodic payments on long-term purchase contracts.
7. Determining appropriate asset, liability, and equity values in mergers and business combinations.

Since future and present value techniques are commonly used in business and have become increasingly important for accountants, this appendix explains these techniques and provides several illustrations of their use. The emphasis in the appendix is on present value techniques, since most applications in accounting require future amounts to be discounted to the present. Before future and present value techniques can be explained, however, the concept of interest must first be reviewed.

COMPUTING THE AMOUNT OF INTEREST

Money, like other commodities, is a scarce resource and a payment for its use is generally required. This payment (cost) for the use of money is **interest**. For example, if $100 is borrowed, whether from an individual, a business, or a bank, and $110 is paid back, $10 in interest has been paid for the use of the $100. Thus, interest represents the excess cash paid or received over the amount of cash borrowed or loaned, as illustrated below.

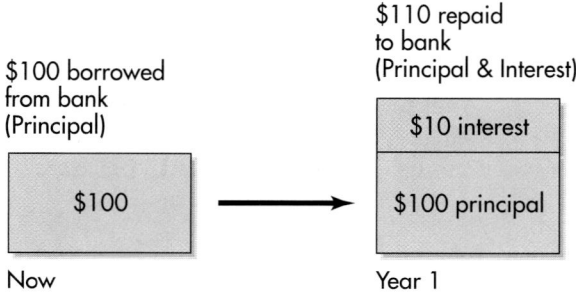

Simple Interest

Generally, interest is specified in terms of a percentage rate for a period of time, usually a year. For example, interest at 8% means the annual cost of borrowing an amount of money, called the **principal**, is equal to 8% of that amount. If $100 is borrowed for a period of one year at 8% annual interest, the total to be repaid is $108—the amount of the principal, $100, and the interest for a year, $8 ($100 × .08 × 1). Interest on a $1,000 note for 6 months at an annual rate of 8% is $40 ($1,000 × .08 × 6/12). In this case, the annual rate of 8% is multiplied by 6/12 (or 1/2 year) because interest is being computed for less than one year. Thus, the formula for computing **simple interest** is:

$$i = p \times r \times t,$$

where:
i = Amount of simple interest
p = Principal amount
r = Interest rate (per period)
t = Time (number of periods)

The Difference Between Simple and Compound Interest

The preceding formula applies to the computation of simple interest. Most transactions, however, involve **compound interest**. This means that the amount of interest earned for a certain period is added to the principal for the next period. Interest for the subsequent period is computed on the new amount, which includes both principal and accumulated interest.

The difference between simple and compound interest can be quite significant, particularly over a long period of time. Consider, for example, the case of Christopher Columbus. On October 12, 1492, Columbus landed in the Americas and (although this is not well known) his first action was to deposit $100 in the First Bank of the Americas. The annual interest rate was 5%. On October 12, 1992, Columbus' heirs went to the bank to check the status of their ancestor's account. The bank manager informed them that certain records had been lost, and it was unknown whether Mr. Columbus had selected a simple or compound interest account. The heirs were given the option of making that choice now. After a few calculations, the heirs elected compound interest. Why? Using simple interest, the balance in Columbus' account had increased by $5 per year ($100 × .05) to a current total of $2,600 ($100 principal + $2,500 interest). Using compound interest, the money in Columbus' account (which had been earning interest on the interest) totaled $3,932,000,000,000, or approximately $4 trillion.

COMPUTING COMPOUND INTEREST To illustrate the computation of compound interest, assume $100 is deposited in a bank and left for two years at 6% annual interest. At the end of the first year, the $100 has earned $6 interest ($100 × .06 × 1). At the end of the second year, $6 has been earned for the first year, plus another $6.36 interest (6% on the $106 balance at the beginning of the second year). Thus, the total interest earned is $12.36 rather than $12 because of the compounding effect. The table below, based on the foregoing example, illustrates the computation of simple and compound interest for four years.

	Simple Interest			Compound Interest		
Year	Computation	Interest	Total	Computation	Interest	Total
1	($100 × .06)	$6	$106	($100.00 × .06)	$6.00	$106.00
2	($100 × .06)	6	112	($106.00 × .06)	6.36	112.36
3	($100 × .06)	6	118	($112.36 × .06)	6.74	119.10
4	($100 × .06)	6	124	($119.10 × .06)	7.15	126.25

THE EFFECT OF COMPOUNDING PERIODS The interest rate used in compound interest problems is the **effective rate of interest** and is generally stated as an annual rate, sometimes called "per annum." However, if the compounding of interest is for periods other than a year, the stated rate of interest must be adjusted. A comparable adjustment must be made to the number of periods. The interest rate per period equals the stated interest rate divided by the number of compounding per period. And the number of periods equals the number of years times the number of compoundings per year. Thus, the adjustments required to the interest rate (i) and to the number of periods (n) for semiannual, quarterly, and monthly compounding of interest are as follows:

Example	Annual Compounding	Semiannual Compounding	Quarterly Compounding	Monthly Compounding
1.	$i = 6\%, n = 10$	$i = 3\%, n = 20$	$i = 1.5\%, n = 40$	$i = .5\%, n = 120$
2.	$i = 12\%, n = 5$	$i = 6\%, n = 10$	$i = 3\%, n = 20$	$i = 1\%, n = 60$
3.	$i = 24\%, n = 3$	$i = 12\%, n = 6$	$i = 6\%, n = 12$	$i = 2\%, n = 36$

As shown in the table, the semiannual compounding of interest requires the annual interest rate to be reduced by half and the number of periods to be doubled. Quarterly compounding of interest requires use of one-fourth the annual rate and 4 times the number of periods, and so forth. Because of this compounding effect, more interest is earned by an investor with semiannual interest than with annual interest, and more is earned with quarterly compounding than with semiannual compounding. Monthly compounding of interest is even better than quarterly compounding, from an investor's perspective.

FUTURE- AND PRESENT-VALUE TECHNIQUES

Since money earns interest over time, $100 received today is more valuable than $100 received one year from today. Future and present value analysis is a method of comparing the value of money received or expected to be received at different time periods.

Analyses requiring comparisons of present dollars and future dollars may be viewed from one of two perspectives, the future or the present. If a future time frame is chosen, all cash flows must be *accumulated* to that future point. In this instance, the effect of interest is to increase the amounts or values over time so that the future amount is greater than the present amount. For example, $500 invested today will accumulate to a future value of $1,079 (rounded) in 10 years if 8% annually compounded interest is paid on the investment.

If, on the other hand, the present is chosen as the point in time at which to evaluate alternatives, all cash flows must be *discounted* from the future to the present. In this instance, the discounting effect reduces the amounts or values. To illustrate, if an investor is earning 10% annual interest on a note receivable that will pay $10,000 in 3 years, what might the investor accept today in full payment, i.e., what is the present value of that note? The amount the investor should be willing to accept, assuming a 10% interest rate is satisfactory and that other considerations are held constant, is $7,513 (rounded), which is the discounted present value of the note. The rationale for the investor is that if the $7,513 could be invested at 10%, compounded annually, it would accumulate to $10,000 in 3 years.

As just illustrated, the future and present value situations involving single payments are essentially reciprocal relationships, and both future and present values are based on the concept of interest. Thus, if interest can be earned at 8% per year, the future value of $100 one year from now is $108. Conversely, assuming the same rate of interest, the present value of a $108 payment due in one year is $100[$108 ÷ (1 + .08)]. Similarly,

$100 to be received in one year, at an 8% annual interest rate, is worth $92.59 today ($100 ÷ 1.08), because $92.59 invested at 8% will grow to $100 in one year.

Use of Formulas

There are four common future and present value situations, each with a corresponding formula. Two of the situations deal with one-time, single payments or receipts[2] (either future or present values), and the other two involve annuities (either future or present values). An **annuity** consists of a series of equal payments over a specified number of equal time periods. For example, a contract calling for three annual payments of $3,000 each would be an annuity. However, a similar contract requiring three annual payments of $2,000, $3,000, and $4,000, respectively, would not be an annuity since the payments are not equal.

Without going into the derivations, the formulas for the four common situations are as follows:

1. Future Value of a Single Payment: $FV = P(1 + i)^n$ where:

   FV = Future value
   P   = Principal amount to be accumulated
   i   = Interest rate per period
   n   = Number of periods

   Example. To calculate the future value of $1,500 to be accumulated at 10% annual interest for 5 years.

   $FV = \$1,500 (1 + .10)^5$
   $FV = \underline{\$2,416}$ (rounded)

2. Present Value of a Single Payment: $PV = A\left[\dfrac{1}{(1 + 1)^n}\right]$ where:

   PV = Present value
   A   = Accumulated amount to be discounted
   i   = Interest rate per period
   n   = Number of periods

   Example. To calculate the present value of $2,416 to be discounted at 10% annual interest for 5 years.

   $PV = \$2,416\left[\dfrac{1}{(1 + .10)^5}\right]$
   $PV = \underline{\$1,500}$ (rounded)

3. Future Value of an Annuity: $FV_n = R\left[\dfrac{(1 + i)^n - 1}{i}\right]$ where:

   FV_n = Future value of an annuity
   R   = Annuity payment to be accumulated
   i   = Interest rate per period
   n   = Number of periods

   Example. To calculate the future value of annuity of $2,000 for 10 years to be accumulated at 12% annual interest.

   $FV_n = \$2,000\left[\dfrac{(1 + .12)^{10} - 1}{.12}\right]$
   $FV_n = \underline{\$35,097}$ (rounded)

---

2 Hereafter in this appendix, the terms *payments* and *receipts* will be used interchangeably. A payment by one party in a transaction becomes a receipt to the other party and vice versa.

4. Present Value of an Annuity: $PV_n = R \left[\dfrac{1 - \dfrac{1}{(1 + i)^n}}{i} \right]$ where:

PV_n = Present value of an annuity
R = Annuity payment to be discounted
I = Interest rate per period
n = Number of periods

Example. To calculate the present value of an annuity of $5,000 for 3 years to be discounted at 11% annual interest.

$PV_n = \$5,000 \left[\dfrac{1 - \dfrac{1}{(1 + .11)^3}}{.11} \right]$

$PV_n = \$12,219$ (rounded)

Use of Tables

In the previous examples, formulas were used to make the computations. This is easily accomplished with most modern-day calculators or with personal computers. Without such tools, however, use of the formulas is time-consuming. Because of this, future and present value tables have been developed for each of the four situations. These tables, such as those provided on pages B–20 to B–25, are based on computing the value of $1 for various interest rates and periods of time. Consequently, future and present value computations can be made by multiplying the appropriate table value factor for $1 by the applicable single payment or annuity amount involved in the particular situation. Thus, the formulas for the four situations may be rewritten as follows:

1. Future Value of a Single Payment:

FV = $P(1 + i)^n$ or FV = $P(FVF_{\overline{n}|i})$ or simply
FV = P(Table I factor)

where:

$FVF_{\overline{n}|i}$ = Future value factor for a particular interest rate (i) and for a certain number of periods (n) from Table I.

Example. (from example 1, previously illustrated)

FV = $1,500 (1.6105 = Factor from Table I; n = 5; i = 10%)
FV = $2,416 (rounded)

2. Present Value of a Single Payment:

PV = $A \left[\dfrac{1}{(1 + i)^n} \right]$ or PV = $A(PVF_{\overline{n}|i})$ or simply

PV = A (Table II factor)

where:

$PVF_{\overline{n}|i}$ = Present value factor for a particular interest rate (i) and for a certain number of periods (n) from Table II.

Example. (from example 2, previously illustrated):

PV = $2,416 (0.6209 = Factor from Table II; n = 5; i = 10%)
PV = $1,500 (rounded)

3. Future Value of an Annuity:

$FV_n = R \left[\dfrac{(1 + i)^n - 1}{i} \right]$ or $FV_n = R(FVAF_{\overline{n}|i})$ or simply

$$FV_n = R \text{ (Table III factor)}$$

where:

FVAF $_{\overline{n}|i}$ = Future value annuity factor for a particular interest rate (i) and for a certain number of periods (n) from Table III.

Example. (from example 3; previously illustrated)

$$FV_n = \$2,000 \ (17.5487 = \text{Factor from Table III}; n = 10; i = 12\%)$$
$$FV_n = \underline{\$35,097} \text{ (rounded)}$$

4. Present Value of an Annuity:

$$PV_n = R \left[\frac{(1 - \frac{1}{(1 + i)^n})}{i} \right] \text{ or } PV_n = R(PVAF \ _{\overline{n}|i}) \text{ or simply}$$

$$PV_n = R \text{ (Table IV factor)}$$

where:

PVAF $_{\overline{n}|i}$ = Present value annuity factor for a particular interest rate (i) and for a certain number of periods (n) from Table IV.

Example. from example 4, illustrated previously)

$$PV_n = \$5,000 \ (2.4437 = \text{Factor from Table IV}; n = 3; i = 11\%)$$
$$PV_n = \underline{\$12,219} \text{ (rounded)}$$

Note that the answers obtained in the examples by using the tables are the same as those obtained using the formulas with a calculator or personal computer.

Business Applications

The following examples demonstrate the application of future and present value computations in solving business problems. Additional applications are provided in later sections as well as in the exercises at the end of the appendix.

EXAMPLE 1—FUTURE VALUE OF A SINGLE PAYMENT

Marywhether Company loans its president, Celia Phillips, $15,000 to purchase a car. Marywhether accepts a note due in 4 years with interest at 10% compounded semiannually. How much cash does Marywhether expect to receive from Phillips when the note is paid at maturity?

Solution. This problem involves a single payment to be accumulated 4 years into the future. In many present and future value problems, a time line is helpful in visualizing the problem:

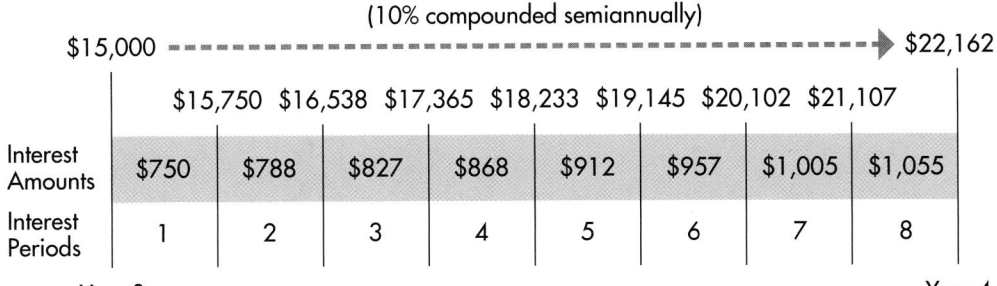

The $15,000 must be accumulated for 4 years at 10% compounded semiannually. Table I may be used, and the applicable formula is:

$$FV = P(FVF_{\overline{n}|i})$$

where:

FV = The future value of a single payment
P = $15,000
n = 8 periods (4 years × 2)
i = 5% effective interest rate per period (10% ÷ 2)

FV = $15,000 (Table I $_{\overline{8}|5\%}$)
FV = $15,000 (1.4775)
FV = $22,162 (rounded)

In 4 years, Marywhether will expect to receive $22,162, consisting of $15,000 principal repayment and $7,162 interest.

EXAMPLE 2—PRESENT VALUE OF A SINGLE PAYMENT

Edgemont Enterprises holds a note receivable from a regular customer. The note is for $22,000, which includes principal and interest, and is due to be paid in exactly 2 years. The customer wants to pay the note now, and both parties agree that 10% is a reasonable annual interest rate to use in discounting the note. How much will the customer pay Edgemont Enterprises today to settle the obligation?

Solution. The single future payment must be discounted to the present value at the agreed upon annual rate of interest of 10%. Since this involves a present-value computation of a single payment, Table II is used, and the applicable formula is:

$$PV = A(PVF_{\overline{n}|i})$$

where:

PV = The present value of a single payment
A = $22,000
n = 2 periods
i = 10% effective interest rate per period

PV = $22,000 (Table II $_{\overline{2}|10\%}$)
PV = $22,000 (0.8264)
PV = $18,181 (rounded)

The customer will pay approximately $18,181 today to settle the obligation.

EXAMPLE 3—PRESENT VALUE OF SERIES OF UNEQUAL PAYMENTS

Casper Sporting Goods Co. is considering a $1 million capital investment that will provide the following expected net receipts at the *end* of each of the next six years.

Year	Expected Net Receipts
1	$195,000
2	457,000
3	593,000
4	421,000
5	95,000
6	5,000

Casper will make the investment only if the rate of return is greater than 12%. Will Casper make the investment?

Solution. A series of unequal future receipts must be compared with a present single-payment investment. For such a comparison to be made, all future cash flows must be discounted to the present.

If the rate of return on the investment is greater than 12%, then the total of all yearly net receipts discounted to the present at 12% will be greater than the amount invested. Since the future receipts are not equal, this situation does not involve an annuity. Each receipt must be discounted individually. Table II is used, and the applicable formula is: $PV = A(PVF_{\overline{n}|i})$ where:

(1) Year = n	(2) A (Net Receipts)	(3) Table II $_{\overline{n}|12\%}$	(2) × (3) = (4) PV (Discounted Amount)
1	$195,000	.8929	$ 174,116
2	457,000	.7972	364,320
3	593,000	.7118	422,097
4	421,000	.6355	267,546
5	95,000	.5674	53,903
6	5,000	.5066	2,533
			Total $1,284,515 (Rounded)

The total discounted receipts are greater than the $1 million investment; thus, the rate of return is more than 12%. Therefore, other things being equal, Casper will invest.

EXAMPLE 4—FUTURE VALUE OF AN ANNUITY

Boswell Co. owes an installment debt of $1,000 per quarter for 5 years. The creditor has indicated a willingness to accept an equivalent single payment at the end of the 5-year period instead of the series of equal payments made at the end of each quarter. If the money is worth 16% compounded quarterly, what is the equivalent single payment at the end of the contract period?

Solution. The equivalent single payment can be found by accumulating the quarterly $1,000 payments to the end of the contract period. Since the payments are equal, this is an annuity. Table III is used, and the applicable formula is:

$$FV_n = R(FVAF_{\overline{n}|i})$$

where:

FV_n = The unknown equivalent lump-sum payment
R = $1,000 quarterly installment to be accumulated
n = 20 periods (5 years × 4 quarters)
i = 4% effective interest rate per period (16% ÷ 4)

FV_n = $1,000 (Table III $_{\overline{20}|4\%}$)
FV_n = $1,000 (29.7781)
FV_n = $29,778 (rounded)

The $29,778 paid at the end of 5 years is approximately equivalent to the 20 quarterly payments of $1,000 each plus interest.

EXAMPLE 5—PRESENT VALUE OF AN ANNUITY

Mary Sabin, proprietor of Sabin Appliance, received two offers for her last deluxe-model refrigerator. Jerry Sloan will pay $650 in cash. Elise Jensen will pay $700 consisting of a down payment of $100 and 12 monthly payments of $50. If the installment interest rate is 24% compounded monthly, which offer should Sabin accept?

Solution. In order to compare the two alternative methods of payment, all cash flows must be accumulated or discounted to one point in time. As illustrated by the time line, the present is selected as the point of comparison.

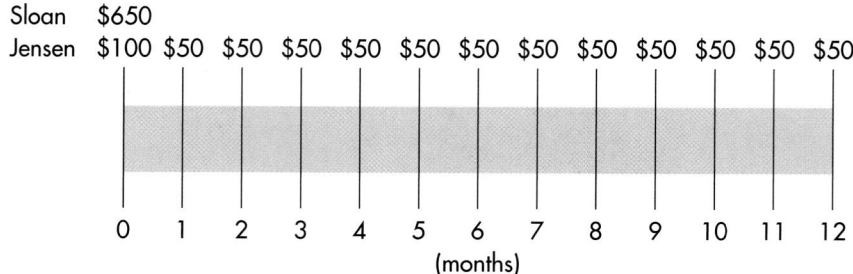

Sloan's offer is $650 today. The present value of $650 today is $650. Jensen's offer consists of an annuity of 12 payments, plus $100 paid today, which is not part of the annuity. The annuity may be discounted to the present by using Table IV and the applicable formula:

$$PV_n = R(PVAF_{\overline{n}|i})$$

where:

PV_n = Unknown present value of 12 payments
R = $50 monthly payment to be discounted
n = 12 periods (1 year × 12 months)
i = 2% effective interest rate per period (24% ÷ 12)

PV_n = $50 (Table IV $_{\overline{12}|2\%}$)
PV_n = $50 (10.5753)
PV_n = $529

Present value of Jensen's payments	$529
Present value of Jensen's $100 down payment	100
Total present value of Jensen's offer	$629

Therefore, Sloan's offer of $650 cash is more desirable than Jensen's offer.

Determining the Number of Periods, the Interest Rate, or the Amount of Payment

So far, the examples and illustrations have required solutions for the future or present values, with the other three variables in the formulas being given. Sometimes business problems require solving for the number of periods, the interest rate,[3] or the amount of payment instead of the future or present value amounts. In each of the formulas, there are four variables. If information is known about any three of the variables, the fourth (unknown) value can be determined. The following examples illustrate how to solve for these other variables.

EXAMPLE 6—DETERMINING THE NUMBER OF PERIODS

Rocky Mountain Survey Company wants to purchase new equipment at a cost of $100,000. The company has $88,850 available in cash but does not want to borrow the other $11,150 for the purchase. If the company can invest the $88,850 today at an interest rate of 12% compounded quarterly, how many years will it be before Rocky Mountain will have the $100,000 it needs to buy the equipment?

Solution. As illustrated below, Rocky Mountain Survey Company can invest $88,850 now at 12% interest compounded quarterly and needs to know how long it will take for this amount to accumulate to $100,000.

---

3 When the interest is not known, it is properly called the **implicit rate of interest**, that is, the rate of interest implied by the terms of a contract or situation. (See Examples 7 and 10 in this appendix.)

$88,850 $100,000

i = 12% compounded quarterly
n = ?

Present   Future
Value   Value

In this situation, involving both present values and future values, either Table I or Table II may be used. If Table I is used, the applicable formula is:

$$FV = P(FVF_{\overline{n}|i})$$
$$FV = P\ (\text{Table I factor})$$

The problem may be solved as follows:

$$\frac{FV}{P} = \text{Table I factor}$$

$$\frac{\$100,000}{\$88,850} = 1.1255$$

Reading down the 3% column (12% ÷ 4) in Table I, the factor value of 1.1255 is shown for n = 4. Therefore, it would take 4 periods (quarters) or 1 year for Rocky Mountain to earn enough interest to have $88,850 accumulate to a future value of $100,000.

If Table II is used, the applicable formula is:

$$PV = A\ (PVF_{\overline{n}|i})$$
$$PV = A\ (\text{Table II factor})$$

Solving,

$$\frac{PV}{A} = \text{Table II factor}$$

$$\frac{\$88,850}{\$100,000} = .8885$$

Reading down the 3% column in Table II, the factor of 0.8885 corresponds with n = 4 (quarters) or 1 year. This illustrates again the reciprocal nature of future and present values for single payments.

EXAMPLE 7—DETERMINING THE INTEREST RATE

The Hughes family wishes to purchase a used grand piano. The cost of the piano one year from now will be $5,800. If the family can invest $5,000 now, what annual interest rate must they earn on their investment to have $5,800 at the end of one year?

Solution. The Hughes family can invest $5,000 now and needs it to accumulate to $5,800 in one year. The rate of annual interest they need to earn can be computed as shown below.

If Table I is used, the applicable formula is:

$$FV = P\ (FVF_{\overline{n}|i})$$
$$FV = P\ (\text{Table I factor})$$

$$\frac{FV}{P} = \text{Table I factor}$$

$$\frac{\$5,800}{\$5,000} = 1.1600$$

Reading across the n = 1 row, the factor value 1.1600 corresponds to an annual effective interest rate of 16%. Therefore, the Hughes family would have to earn 16% annual interest to accomplish their goal. The same result is obtained if Table II is used to solve this problem.

EXAMPLE 8—DETERMINING THE AMOUNT OF PAYMENT

Provo 1st National Bank is willing to lend a customer $75,000 to buy a warehouse. The note will be secured by a 5-year mortgage and carry an annual interest rate of 12%. Equal payments are to be made at the end of each year over the 5-year period. How much will the yearly payment be?

Solution. This is an example of an unknown annuity payment. Since the present value ($75,000) is known, as well as the interest rate (12%) and the number of periods (5), the annuity payment can be determined using Table IV. The applicable formula is:

$$PV_n = R \, (PVAF \; _{\overline{n}|i})$$
$$PV_n = R \, (\text{Table IV factor})$$
$$\$75,000 = R \, (3.6048) \; (\text{for } n = 5 \text{ and } i = 12\%)$$

$$\frac{\$75,000}{3,6048} = R$$

$$\underline{\$20,806} \, (\text{rounded}) = R$$

The payment on this 5-year mortgage would be approximately $20,806 each year.

Ordinary Annuity vs. Annuity Due

The illustrations up to this point have been fairly straightforward. In practice, however, complexities can arise that make it somewhat more difficult to use the future and present value tables. One of these complexities involves converting ordinary annuity tables to annuity-due factor values.

Annuities are of two types: ordinary annuities (annuities in arrears) and annuities due (annuities in advance). The periodic receipts or payments for an **ordinary annuity** are made at the *end of each period*, and the last payment coincides with the end of the annuity term. The periodic receipts or payments for an **annuity due** are made at the *beginning of the period*, and one period of the annuity term remains after the last payment. These differences are illustrated below.

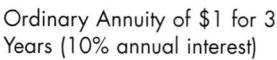
Ordinary Annuity of $1 for 3 Years (10% annual interest)

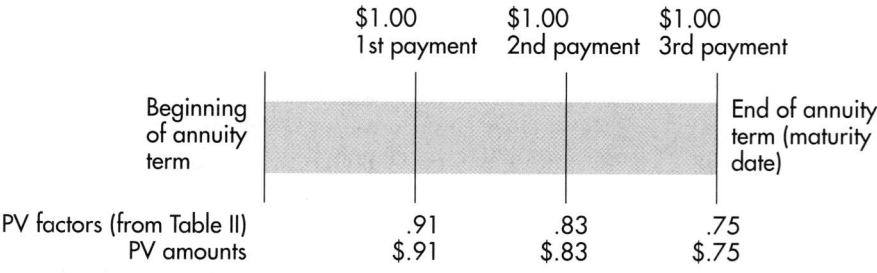

Therefore, assuming a 10% annual interest rate, the present value of an annuity of $1 per year to be received at the end of each of the next 3 years is $2.49 ($.91 + $.83 + $.75). Notice that the last $1 is received on the maturity date, or the end of the annuity term.

Again assuming a 10% annual interest rate, the present value of an annuity of $1 per year to be received at the beginning of each of the next 3 years is $2.74 ($1.00 + $.91 + $.83). Notice here that the last payment is received 1 year prior to the maturity date.

Annuity Due of $1 for 3 Years
(10% annual interest)

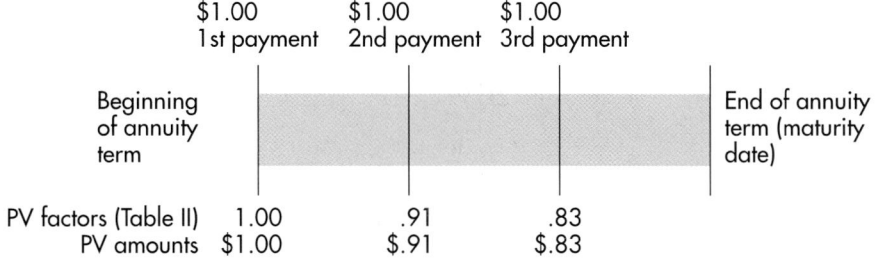

The difference in the two annuities is in the timing of the payments, and, therefore, how many interest periods are involved. As shown below, both annuities require 3 payments. However, the ordinary annuity payments are at the end of each period, so there are only 2 periods of interest accumulation; the annuity-due payments are in advance or at the beginning of the period, so there are 3 periods of interest accumulation.

Accumulation of Ordinary
Annuity for 3 Years

Accumulation of Annuity Due
for 3 Years

The preceding situation is exactly reversed when viewed from a present-value standpoint. The ordinary annuity has 3 interest or discount periods, while the annuity due has only 2 periods, as shown below.

Present Value of Ordinary
Annuity for 3 Years

Present Value of Annuity Due
for 3 Years

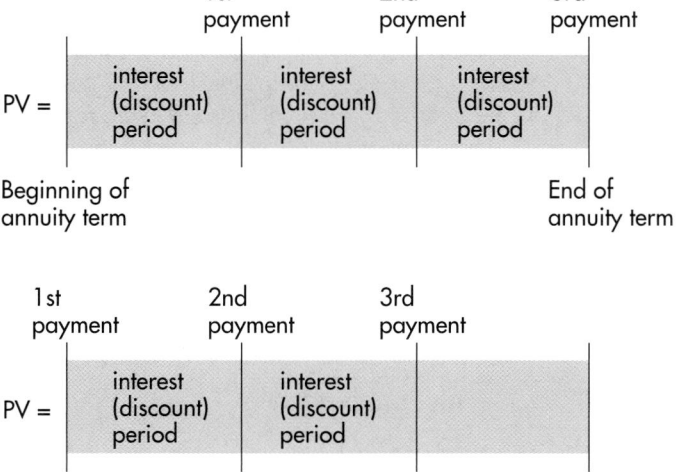

Even though most future- and present-value annuity tables are computed for ordinary annuities (payments at the end of the periods), these tables can be used for solving annuity-due problems where the payments are in advance. However, the following adjustments will be required:

1. To find the **future value of an annuity due** using ordinary annuity table values (Table III), select the appropriate table value for an ordinary annuity for one additional period (n + 1) and subtract the extra payment (which is 1.0000 in terms of the table value for $1.00). The formula is:

$$FV_n = R(FVAF_{\overline{n+1}|i} - 1)$$

2. To find the **present value of an annuity due** using ordinary annuity table values (Table IV), select the appropriate table value for an ordinary annuity for one less period (n − 1) and add the extra payment (1.0000). The formula is:

$$PV_n = R(PVAF_{\overline{n-1}|i} + 1)$$

By making the above adjustments, when payments are in advance, ordinary annuity tables may be used for all annuity situations. For example, the table value (Table III) for the future amount of an annuity due for 3 periods at 10% is:

(1) Factor for future value of an ordinary annuity of $1 for 4 periods (n + 1) at 10%	4.6410
(2) Less one payment	1.0000
(3) Factor for future value of an annuity due of $1 for 3 periods at 10%	3.6410

The table value (Table IV) for the present value of an annuity due for 3 periods at 10% is:

(1) Factor for present value of an ordinary annuity of $1 for 2 periods (n − 1) at 10%	1.7355
(2) Plus one payment	1.0000
(3) Factor for present value of an annuity due of $1 for 3 periods at 10%	2.7355

As noted, ordinary annuity tables can be converted for use with annuity-due situations. There are annuity-due tables available, however, that make these conversions unnecessary. Table V and Table VI are provided for annuity-due factor values. Note that these table values are the same as those for Tables III and IV if annuity-due adjustments are made, as previously described.

The following examples illustrate the application of annuity-due table values.

EXAMPLE 9—USING ANNUITY-DUE TABLE VALUES FOR FUTURE AMOUNTS

The Porter Corporation desires to accumulate funds to retire a $200,000 bond issue at the end of 15 years. Funds set aside for this purpose can be invested to yield 8%. What annual payment, starting immediately, would provide the needed funds?

Solution. Annuity payments of an unknown amount, to be paid in advance, are to be accumulated toward a specific dollar amount at a known interest rate. Because the first payment is to be made immediately, all payments will fall due at the beginning of each period and an annuity due is used. Therefore, Table V is used. The appropriate formula is the same as that presented previously for an ordinary annuity, the only difference being the table in which the annuity factor is found.

$$FV_n = R(FVAF_{\overline{n}|i})$$

where:

FV_n = $200,000
R = Unknown annual payment

n   =   15 periods
i   =   8% annual interest
$200,000 = R(Table V $\overline{15|}$ 8%)
$200,000 = R(29.3243)

$$\frac{\$200,000}{29.3243} = R$$

$\underline{\$6,820}$ = R

Porter Corporation must deposit $6,820 annually, starting immediately, to accumulate $200,000 in 15 years at 8% annual interest.

EXAMPLE 10—USING ANNUITY-DUE TABLE VALUES FOR PRESENT VALUES

Utah Corporation has completed negotiations to lease equipment with a fair market value of $45,897. The lease contract specifies semiannual payments of $3,775 for 10 years beginning immediately. At the end of the lease, Utah Corporation may purchase the equipment for a nominal amount. What is the implicit annual rate of interest on the lease purchase?

Solution. This is a common application of an annuity-due situation in accounting since most lease contracts require payments in advance, i.e., at the beginning of the period rather than at the end of the period. The implicit interest rate must be computed for the present value of an annuity due. The present value is the fair market value of the equipment, and the payment is the lease payment. Table VI is used, and the applicable formula is:

PV_n =   R(PVAF $\overline{n|}$ i)

where:

PV_n = $45,897
R   = $3,775
n   = 20 periods (10 years × 2 payments per year)
i   = The unknown semiannual interest rate
$45,897 = $3,775 (Table VI $\overline{20|}$ i)

$$\frac{\$45,897}{\$3,775} = 12.1581 = \text{Table VI } \overline{20|} \text{ i}$$

i   =   6%

Examination of Table VI for 20 periods and a factor of 12.1581 shows i = 6%. The implicit annual interest rate is twice the semiannual rate, or 2 × 6% = 12%.

CONCLUDING COMMENT

As noted in Chapter 1, the FASB's conceptual framework allows for various measurement attributes, one of which is discounted present values. This measurement attribute is receiving additional attention from the FASB. In October 1988, the FASB added to its agenda a project to consider the use of present values and interest in accounting measurements. In December 1990 the FASB issued a Discussion Memorandum entitled, "Present-Value-Based Measurements in Accounting." A public hearing was held in August 1991, and a Special Report entitled "The FASB Project on Present-Value-Based Measurements, an Analysis of Deliberations and Techniques" was published in February 1996.

The work of the FASB on this topic is in response to the need for a comprehensive study of present-value-based measurements. The FASB is addressing: (1) under what circumstances an amount should be recognized in financial statements based on the present value of estimated future cash flows; (2) when is it appropriate to use the effective interest method in accounting allocations over the life of an asset or liability; and (3) when the interest element involved with present-value-based measurements should be recognized as interest revenue or expense. The project will also explore related implementation issues.

This appendix has illustrated a few of the many business applications of present- and future-value measurement techniques. As the FASB continues to debate issues with long-term financial impact, e.g., deferred income taxes and postretirement employment benefits, the importance of the time-value-of-money concept will no doubt increase.

KEY TERMS

Annuity B–5
Annuity due B–12
Compound interest B–3
Effective rate of interest B–4

Future value B–1
Future value of annuity due B–14
Interest B–2
Ordinary annuity B–12

Present value B–1
Present value of annuity due B–14
Principal B–3
Simple interest B–3

EXERCISES

EXERCISE B–1

SIMPLE AND COMPOUND INTEREST
Dietrick Corporation borrowed $30,000 from its major shareholder, the president of the company, at an annual interest rate of 12%.

1. Assuming simple interest,
    (a) How much will Dietrick have to pay to settle its obligation if the loan is to be repaid in 12 months?
    (b) How much of the payment is interest?
    (c) How much will Dietrick have to pay if the loan is due in 18 months?
2. If the loan is paid off in 18 months and interest is compounded annually, how much will the company have to pay?
3. Compare the answers for (1c) and (2) and explain why they differ.

EXERCISE B–2

RECIPROCAL RELATIONSHIPS: FUTURE AND PRESENT VALUES
Determine the amount that would accumulate for the following investments:
    (a) $10,050 at 10% per annum, compounded annually for 6 years.
    (b) $650 at 12% per annum, compounded quarterly for 10 years.
    (c) $5,000 at 16% per annum, compounded annually for 4 years, and then reinvested at 16% per annum, compounded semiannually for 4 more years.
    (d) $1,000 at 8% per annum, compounded semiannually for 5 years, an additional $1,000 added and then the entire amount reinvested at 12% per annum, compounded quarterly for 3 more years.

EXERCISE B–3

RECIPROCAL RELATIONSHIPS: FUTURE AND PRESENT VALUES
Determine the amount that must be deposited now at compound interest to provide the desired sum for each of the following:
    (a) Amount to be invested for 10 years at 6% per annum, compounded semiannually, to equal $17,000.
    (b) Amount to be invested for 2½ years at 8% per annum, compounded quarterly, to equal $5,000.

(c) Amount to be invested for 15 years at 12% per annum, compounded semiannually, then reinvested at 16% per annum, compounded quarterly, for 5 more years to equal $25,000.

(d) Amount to be invested at 8% per annum, compounded semiannually for 3 years, then $5,000 more added and the entire amount reinvested at the same rate for another 3 years, compounded semiannually, to equal $12,500.

EXERCISE B–4

CHOOSING BETWEEN ALTERNATIVE INVESTMENTS

Heather Company has $10,000 to invest. One alternative will yield 10% per year, compounded annually for 4 years. A second alternative is to deposit the $10,000 in a bank that will pay 8% per year, compounded quarterly. Which alternative should Heather select?

EXERCISE B–5

UNKNOWN ANNUITY AMOUNT

Ryan Henry wants to buy his son a car for his 21st birthday. If Ryan's son is turning 16 today, and interest is 8% per annum, compounded semiannually, what would Ryan's semiannual investment need to be if the car will cost $26,000 and the first payment is made six months from today?

EXERCISE B–6

UNKNOWN INVESTMENT PERIODS

Determine the number of periods for which the following amounts would have to be invested, under the terms specified, to accumulate to $10,000. Convert the number of periods to years.

(a) $5,051 at 10% per annum, compounded semiannually.

(b) $5,002 at 8% per annum, compounded annually.

(c) $5,134 at 16% per annum, compounded quarterly.

EXERCISE B–7

UNKNOWN INTEREST RATES

Determine the annual interest rate that is needed for the following investments to accumulate to $50,000.

(a) $10,414 for 20 years, interest compounded semiannually.

(b) $7,102 for 10 years, interest compounded quarterly.

(c) $33,778 for 10 years, interest compounded annually.

EXERCISE B–8

UNKNOWN INVESTMENT PERIODS—ANNUITIES

Determine the number of periods for which the following annuity payments would have to be invested to accumulate to $20,000. Assume payments are made at the end of each period. Convert the number of periods to years.

(a) Annual payments of $5,927 at 12% per annum, compounded annually.

(b) Semiannual payments of $3,409 at 16% per annum, compounded semiannually.

(c) Quarterly payments of $4,640 at 20% per annum, compounded quarterly.

EXERCISE B–9

UNKNOWN INTEREST RATES—ANNUITIES

Determine the annual interest rate that is needed for the following annuities to accumulate to $25,000. Assume payments are made at the end of each period.

(a) Annual payments of $4,095 for 5 years, interest compounded annually.

(b) Semiannual payments of $5,715 for 2 years, interest compounded semiannually.

(c) Quarterly payments of $1,864 for 3 years, interest compounded quarterly.

EXERCISE B–10

DETERMINING ORDINARY ANNUITY PAYMENTS

Determine the amount of the periodic payments needed to pay off the following purchases. Payments are made at the end of the period.

(a) Purchase of a waterbed for $1,205. Monthly payments are to be made for 1 year with interest at 24% per annum, compounded monthly.

(b) Purchase of a motor boat for $26,565. Quarterly payments are to be made for 4 years with interest at 8% per annum, compounded quarterly.

(c) Purchase of a condominium for $65,500. Semiannual payments are to be made for 10 years with interest at 10% per annum, compounded semiannually.

EXERCISE B–11

DETERMINING UNKNOWN QUANTITIES

Determine the unknown quantity for each of the following independent situations using the appropriate interest tables:

1. Jeff and Nancy want to start a trust fund for their newborn son, Mark. They have decided to invest $5,000 today. If interest is 8% compounded semiannually, how much will be in the fund when Mark turns 20?

2. Nixon Corporation wants to establish a retirement fund. Management wants to have $1,000,000 in the fund at the end of 40 years. If fund assets will earn 12%, compounded annually, how much will need to be invested now?

3. How many payments would Star, Inc., need to make if it purchases a new building for $100,000 with annual payments made at the end of each year of $16,401.24 and interest of 16%, compounded annually?

4. An investment broker indicates that an investment of $10,000 in a CD for 10 years at the current interest rate will accumulate to $21,589. What is the current annual rate of interest if interest is compounded annually?

EXERCISE B–12

DETERMINING UNKNOWN QUANTITIES

Determine the unknown quantity for each of the following independent situations using the appropriate interest tables:

1. Sue wants to have $10,000 saved when she begins college. If Sue enters college in 4 years and interest is 8% compounded annually, how much will Sue need to save each year assuming equal deposits at the end of each year?

2. XYZ Company has obtained a bank loan to finance the purchase of an automobile for one of its executives. The terms of the loan require monthly payments at the end of each month of $585. If the interest rate is 18% compounded monthly and the car costs $15,850, for how many months will XYZ have to make payments?

3. Diaz Company is offering the following investment plan. If deposits of $250 are made semiannually for the next 9 years, $7,726 will accrue. If interest is compounded semiannually, what is the approximate annual rate of interest on the investment?

4. Jack wants to buy a rental unit. For how many periods will he have to make annual deposits of $5,000 in order to accumulate $50,445, the price of the rental unit, if interest is 12% compounded annually? Assume deposits are made at the end of each year.

EXERCISE B–13

DETERMINING THE IMPLICIT INTEREST RATE

Valley Technical College needs to purchase some computers. Because the college is short of cash, Computer Sales Company has agreed to let Valley have the computers now and pay $2,500 per computer 6 months from now. If the current cash price is $2,404, what is the rate of interest Valley would be paying?

EXERCISE B–14

CHOOSING BETWEEN PURCHASE ALTERNATIVES

Foot Loose, Inc., needs to purchase a new shoelace-making machine. Machines Ready has agreed to sell them the machine for $22,000 down and 4 payments of $5,700 to be paid in semiannual installments for the next 2 years. Do-It-Yourself Machines has offered to sell Foot Loose a comparable machine for $10,000 down and 4 semiannual payments of $9,000. If the current interest rate is 16%, compounded semiannually, which machine should Foot Loose purchase?

EXERCISE B–15

CHOOSING BETWEEN RENT PAYMENT ALTERNATIVES

Park City Construction is building a new office building, and management is trying to decide how rent payments for the office space should be structured. The alternatives are:

(a) Annual payment of $15,000 at the end of each year.
(b) Monthly payments of $1,200 at the end of each month.

Assuming an interest rate of 12% compounded monthly, which payment schedule should Park City use?

EXERCISE B–16

COMPUTING MORTGAGE PAYMENTS WITH THE USE OF FORMULAS

George and Barbara Shrub would like to purchase a large white house and are evaluating their financing options. Bank A offers a 10-year mortgage at 12% annual interest, compounded monthly, with payments made at the end of each month. Bank B is offering a 10-year mortgage at 13% annual interest, compounded annually, with payments made at the end of each year. The purchase price of the white house is $250,000.

1. Use formulas to compute the following amounts:
   (a) The monthly payment for the Bank A mortgage.
   (b) The annual payment for the Bank B mortgage.
2. Which financing alternative would you advise the Shrubs to select?

EXERCISE B–17

CHOOSING AMONG ALTERNATIVE PAYMENT PLANS

The following payment plans are offered on the purchase of a new freezer:

(a) $375 cash.
(b) 8 monthly payments of $55.
(c) $100 cash down and 6 monthly payments of $50.

Which payment plan would you choose if interest is 24% annually, compounded monthly, if you are the purchaser? if you are the seller? (Assume ordinary annuities where applicable.)

EXERCISE B–18

DETERMINING PURCHASE PRICE

Big Company purchased a machine on February 1, 2000, and will make 7 semiannual payments of $14,000 beginning 5 years from the date of purchase. The interest rate will be 12%, compounded semiannually. Determine the purchase price of the machine.

Table I Future Value of a Single Payment

	1%	2%	3%	4%	5%	6%	7%	8%	9%	10%	11%	12%	14%	16%	20%
1	1.0100	1.0200	1.0300	1.0400	1.0500	1.0600	1.0700	1.0800	1.0900	1.1000	1.1100	1.1200	1.1400	1.1600	1.2000
2	1.0201	1.0404	1.0609	1.0816	1.1025	1.1236	1.1449	1.1664	1.1881	1.2100	1.2321	1.2544	1.2996	1.3456	1.4400
3	1.0303	1.0612	1.0927	1.1249	1.1576	1.1910	1.2250	1.2597	1.2950	1.3310	1.3676	1.4049	1.4815	1.5609	1.7280
4	1.0406	1.0824	1.1255	1.1699	1.2155	1.2625	1.3108	1.3605	1.4116	1.4641	1.5181	1.5735	1.6890	1.8106	2.0736
5	1.0510	1.1041	1.1593	1.2167	1.2763	1.3382	1.4026	1.4693	1.5386	1.6105	1.6851	1.7623	1.9254	2.1003	2.4883
6	1.0615	1.1262	1.1941	1.2653	1.3401	1.4185	1.5007	1.5869	1.6771	1.7716	1.8704	1.9738	2.1950	2.4364	2.9860
7	1.0721	1.1487	1.2299	1.3159	1.4071	1.5036	1.6058	1.7138	1.8280	1.9487	2.0762	2.2107	2.5023	2.8262	3.5832
8	1.0829	1.1717	1.2668	1.3686	1.4775	1.5938	1.7182	1.8509	1.9926	2.1436	2.3045	2.4760	2.8526	3.2784	4.2998
9	1.0937	1.1951	1.3048	1.4233	1.5513	1.6895	1.8385	1.9990	2.1719	2.3579	2.5580	2.7731	3.2519	3.8030	5.1598
10	1.1046	1.2190	1.3439	1.4802	1.6289	1.7908	1.9672	2.1589	2.3674	2.5937	2.8394	3.1058	3.7072	4.4114	6.1917
11	1.1157	1.2434	1.3842	1.5395	1.7103	1.8983	2.1049	2.3316	2.5804	2.8531	3.1518	3.4785	4.2262	5.1173	7.4301
12	1.1268	1.2682	1.4258	1.6010	1.7959	2.0122	2.2522	2.5182	2.8127	3.1384	3.4985	3.8960	4.8179	5.9360	8.9161
13	1.1381	1.2936	1.4685	1.6651	1.8856	2.1329	2.4098	2.7196	3.0658	3.4523	3.8833	4.3635	5.4924	6.8858	10.6993
14	1.1495	1.3195	1.5126	1.7317	1.9799	2.2609	2.5785	2.9372	3.3417	3.7975	4.3104	4.8871	6.2613	7.9875	12.8392
15	1.1610	1.3459	1.5580	1.8009	2.0789	2.3966	2.7590	3.1722	3.6425	4.1772	4.7846	5.4736	7.1379	9.2655	15.4070
16	1.1726	1.3728	1.6047	1.8730	2.1829	2.5404	2.9522	3.4259	3.9703	4.5950	5.3109	6.1304	8.1372	10.7480	18.4884
17	1.1843	1.4002	1.6528	1.9479	2.2920	2.6928	3.1588	3.7000	4.3276	5.0545	5.8951	6.8660	9.2765	12.4677	22.1861
18	1.1961	1.4282	1.7024	2.0258	2.4066	2.8543	3.3799	3.9960	4.7171	5.5599	6.5436	7.6900	10.5752	14.4625	26.6233
19	1.2081	1.4568	1.7535	2.1068	2.5270	3.0256	3.6165	4.3157	5.1417	6.1159	7.2633	8.6128	12.0557	16.7765	31.9480
20	1.2202	1.4859	1.8061	2.1911	2.6533	3.2071	3.8697	4.6610	5.6044	6.7275	8.0623	9.6463	13.7435	19.4608	38.3376
21	1.2324	1.5157	1.8603	2.2788	2.7860	3.3996	4.1406	5.0338	6.1088	7.4002	8.9492	10.8038	15.6676	22.5745	46.0051
22	1.2447	1.5460	1.9161	2.3699	2.9253	3.6035	4.4304	5.4365	6.6586	8.1403	9.9336	12.1003	17.8610	26.1864	55.2061
23	1.2572	1.5769	1.9736	2.4647	3.0715	3.8197	4.7405	5.8715	7.2579	8.9543	11.0263	13.5523	20.3616	30.3762	66.2474
24	1.2697	1.6084	2.0328	2.5633	3.2251	4.0489	5.0724	6.3412	7.9111	9.8497	12.2392	15.1786	23.2122	35.2364	79.4968
25	1.2824	1.6406	2.0938	2.6658	3.3864	4.2919	5.4274	6.8485	8.6231	10.8347	13.5855	17.0001	26.4619	40.8742	95.3962
26	1.2953	1.6734	2.1566	2.7725	3.5557	4.5494	5.8074	7.3964	9.3992	11.9182	15.0799	19.0401	30.1666	47.4141	114.4755
27	1.3082	1.7069	2.2213	2.8834	3.7335	4.8223	6.2139	7.9881	10.2451	13.1100	16.7386	21.3249	34.3899	55.0004	137.3706
28	1.3213	1.7410	2.2879	2.9987	3.9201	5.1117	6.6488	8.6271	11.1671	14.4210	18.5799	23.8839	39.2045	63.8004	164.8447
29	1.3345	1.7758	2.3566	3.1187	4.1161	5.4184	7.1143	9.3173	12.1722	15.8631	20.6237	26.7499	44.6931	74.0085	197.8136
30	1.3478	1.8114	2.4273	3.2434	4.3219	5.7435	7.6123	10.0627	13.2677	17.4494	22.8923	29.9599	50.9502	85.8499	237.3763
35	1.4166	1.9999	2.8139	3.9461	5.5160	7.6861	10.6766	14.7853	20.4140	28.1024	38.5749	52.7996	98.1002	180.3141	590.6682
40	1.4889	2.2080	3.2620	4.8010	7.0400	10.2857	14.9745	21.7245	31.4094	45.2593	65.0009	93.0510	188.8835	378.7212	1469.7716

Table II   Present Value of a Single Payment

	1%	2%	3%	4%	5%	6%	7%	8%	9%	10%	11%	12%	14%	16%	20%
1	0.9901	0.9804	0.9709	0.9615	0.9524	0.9434	0.9346	0.9259	0.9174	0.9091	0.9009	0.8929	0.8772	0.8621	0.8333
2	0.9803	0.9612	0.9426	0.9246	0.9070	0.8900	0.8734	0.8573	0.8417	0.8264	0.8116	0.7972	0.7695	0.7432	0.6944
3	0.9706	0.9423	0.9151	0.8890	0.8638	0.8396	0.8163	0.7938	0.7722	0.7513	0.7312	0.7118	0.6750	0.6407	0.5787
4	0.9610	0.9238	0.8885	0.8548	0.8227	0.7921	0.7629	0.7350	0.7084	0.6830	0.6587	0.6355	0.5921	0.5523	0.4823
5	0.9515	0.9057	0.8626	0.8219	0.7835	0.7473	0.7130	0.6806	0.6499	0.6209	0.5935	0.5674	0.5194	0.4761	0.4019
6	0.9420	0.8880	0.8375	0.7903	0.7462	0.7050	0.6663	0.6302	0.5963	0.5645	0.5346	0.5066	0.4556	0.4104	0.3349
7	0.9327	0.8706	0.8131	0.7599	0.7107	0.6651	0.6227	0.5835	0.5470	0.5132	0.4817	0.4523	0.3996	0.3538	0.2791
8	0.9235	0.8535	0.7894	0.7307	0.6768	0.6274	0.5820	0.5403	0.5019	0.4665	0.4339	0.4039	0.3506	0.3050	0.2326
9	0.9143	0.8368	0.7664	0.7026	0.6446	0.5919	0.5439	0.5002	0.4604	0.4241	0.3909	0.3606	0.3075	0.2630	0.1938
10	0.9053	0.8203	0.7441	0.6756	0.6139	0.5584	0.5083	0.4632	0.4224	0.3855	0.3522	0.3220	0.2697	0.2267	0.1615
11	0.8963	0.8043	0.7224	0.6496	0.5847	0.5268	0.4751	0.4289	0.3875	0.3505	0.3173	0.2875	0.2366	0.1954	0.1346
12	0.8874	0.7885	0.7014	0.6246	0.5568	0.4970	0.4440	0.3971	0.3555	0.3186	0.2858	0.2567	0.2076	0.1685	0.1122
13	0.8787	0.7730	0.6810	0.6006	0.5303	0.4688	0.4150	0.3677	0.3262	0.2897	0.2575	0.2292	0.1821	0.1452	0.0935
14	0.8700	0.7579	0.6611	0.5775	0.5051	0.4423	0.3878	0.3405	0.2992	0.2633	0.2320	0.2046	0.1597	0.1252	0.0779
15	0.8613	0.7430	0.6419	0.5553	0.4810	0.4173	0.3624	0.3152	0.2745	0.2394	0.2090	0.1827	0.1401	0.1079	0.0649
16	0.8528	0.7284	0.6232	0.5339	0.4581	0.3936	0.3387	0.2919	0.2519	0.2176	0.1883	0.1631	0.1229	0.0930	0.0541
17	0.8444	0.7142	0.6050	0.5134	0.4363	0.3714	0.3166	0.2703	0.2311	0.1978	0.1696	0.1456	0.1078	0.0802	0.0451
18	0.8360	0.7002	0.5874	0.4936	0.4155	0.3503	0.2959	0.2502	0.2120	0.1799	0.1528	0.1300	0.0946	0.0691	0.0376
19	0.8277	0.6864	0.5703	0.4746	0.3957	0.3305	0.2765	0.2317	0.1945	0.1635	0.1377	0.1161	0.0829	0.0596	0.0313
20	0.8195	0.6730	0.5537	0.4564	0.3769	0.3118	0.2584	0.2145	0.1784	0.1486	0.1240	0.1037	0.0728	0.0514	0.0261
21	0.8114	0.6598	0.5375	0.4388	0.3589	0.2942	0.2415	0.1987	0.1637	0.1351	0.1117	0.0926	0.0638	0.0443	0.0217
22	0.8034	0.6468	0.5219	0.4220	0.3418	0.2775	0.2257	0.1839	0.1502	0.1228	0.1007	0.0826	0.0560	0.0382	0.0181
23	0.7954	0.6342	0.5067	0.4057	0.3256	0.2618	0.2109	0.1703	0.1378	0.1117	0.0907	0.0738	0.0491	0.0329	0.0151
24	0.7876	0.6217	0.4919	0.3901	0.3101	0.2470	0.1971	0.1577	0.1264	0.1015	0.0817	0.0659	0.0431	0.0284	0.0126
25	0.7798	0.6095	0.4776	0.3751	0.2953	0.2330	0.1842	0.1460	0.1160	0.0923	0.0736	0.0588	0.0378	0.0245	0.0105
26	0.7720	0.5976	0.4637	0.3607	0.2812	0.2198	0.1722	0.1352	0.1064	0.0839	0.0663	0.0525	0.0331	0.0211	0.0087
27	0.7644	0.5859	0.4502	0.3468	0.2678	0.2074	0.1609	0.1252	0.0976	0.0763	0.0597	0.0469	0.0291	0.0182	0.0073
28	0.7568	0.5744	0.4371	0.3335	0.2551	0.1956	0.1504	0.1159	0.0895	0.0693	0.0538	0.0419	0.0255	0.0157	0.0061
29	0.7493	0.5631	0.4243	0.3207	0.2429	0.1846	0.1406	0.1073	0.0822	0.0630	0.0485	0.0374	0.0224	0.0135	0.0051
30	0.7419	0.5521	0.4120	0.3083	0.2314	0.1741	0.1314	0.0994	0.0754	0.0573	0.0437	0.0334	0.0196	0.0116	0.0042
35	0.7059	0.5000	0.3554	0.2534	0.1813	0.1301	0.0937	0.0676	0.0490	0.0356	0.0259	0.0189	0.0102	0.0055	0.0017
40	0.6717	0.4529	0.3066	0.2083	0.1420	0.0972	0.0668	0.0460	0.0318	0.0221	0.0154	0.0107	0.0053	0.0026	0.0007

Table III   **Future Value of an Ordinary Annuity**

	1%	2%	3%	4%	5%	6%	7%	8%	9%	10%	11%	12%	14%	16%	20%
1	1.0000	1.0000	1.0000	1.0000	1.0000	1.0000	1.0000	1.0000	1.0000	1.0000	1.0000	1.0000	1.0000	1.0000	1.0000
2	2.0100	2.0200	2.0300	2.0400	2.0500	2.0600	2.0700	2.0800	2.0900	2.1000	2.1100	2.1200	2.1400	2.1600	2.2000
3	3.0301	3.0604	3.0909	3.1216	3.1525	3.1836	3.2149	3.2464	3.2781	3.3100	3.3421	3.3744	3.4396	3.5056	3.6400
4	4.0604	4.1216	4.1836	4.2465	4.3101	4.3746	4.4399	4.5061	4.5731	4.6410	4.7097	4.7793	4.9211	5.0665	5.3680
5	5.1010	5.2040	5.3091	5.4163	5.5256	5.6371	5.7507	5.8666	5.9847	6.1051	6.2278	6.3528	6.6101	6.8771	7.4416
6	6.1520	6.3081	6.4684	6.6330	6.8019	6.9753	7.1533	7.3359	7.5233	7.7156	7.9129	8.1152	8.5355	8.9775	9.9299
7	7.2135	7.4343	7.6625	7.8983	8.1420	8.3938	8.6540	8.9228	9.2004	9.4872	9.7833	10.0890	10.7305	11.4139	12.9159
8	8.2857	8.5830	8.8923	9.2142	9.5491	9.8975	10.2598	10.6366	11.0285	11.4359	11.8594	12.2997	13.2328	14.2401	16.4991
9	9.3685	9.7546	10.1591	10.5828	11.0266	11.4913	11.9780	12.4876	13.0210	13.5795	14.1640	14.7757	16.0853	17.5185	20.7989
10	10.4622	10.9497	11.4639	12.0061	12.5779	13.1808	13.8164	14.4866	15.1929	15.9374	16.7220	17.5487	19.3373	21.3215	25.9587
11	11.5668	12.1687	12.8078	13.4864	14.2068	14.9716	15.7836	16.6455	17.5603	18.5312	19.5614	20.6546	23.0445	25.7329	32.1504
12	12.6825	13.4121	14.1920	15.0258	15.9171	16.8699	17.8885	18.9771	20.1407	21.3843	22.7132	24.1331	27.2707	30.8502	39.5805
13	13.8093	14.6803	15.6178	16.6268	17.7130	18.8821	20.1406	21.4953	22.9534	24.5227	26.2116	28.0291	32.0887	36.7862	48.4966
14	14.9474	15.9739	17.0863	18.2919	19.5986	21.0151	22.5505	24.2149	26.0192	27.9750	30.0949	32.3926	37.5811	43.6720	59.1959
15	16.0969	17.2934	18.5989	20.0236	21.5786	23.2760	25.1290	27.1521	29.3609	31.7725	34.4054	37.2797	43.8424	51.6595	72.0351
16	17.2579	18.6393	20.1569	21.8245	23.6575	25.6725	27.8881	30.3243	33.0034	35.9497	39.1899	42.7533	50.9804	60.9250	87.4421
17	18.4304	20.0121	21.7616	23.6975	25.8404	28.2129	30.8402	33.7502	36.9737	40.5447	44.5008	48.8837	59.1176	71.6730	105.9306
18	19.6147	21.4123	23.4144	25.6454	28.1324	30.9057	33.9990	37.4502	41.3013	45.5992	50.3959	55.7497	68.3941	84.1407	128.1167
19	20.8109	22.8406	25.1169	27.6712	30.5390	33.7600	37.3790	41.4463	46.0185	51.1591	56.9395	63.4397	78.9692	98.6032	154.7400
20	22.0190	24.2974	26.8704	29.7781	33.0660	36.7856	40.9955	45.7620	51.1601	57.2750	64.2028	72.0524	91.0249	115.3797	186.6880
21	23.2392	25.7833	28.6765	31.9692	35.7193	39.9927	44.8652	50.4229	56.7645	64.0025	72.2651	81.6987	104.7684	134.8405	225.0256
22	24.4716	27.2990	30.5368	34.2480	38.5052	43.3923	49.0057	55.4568	62.8733	71.4027	81.2143	92.5026	120.4360	157.4150	271.0307
23	25.7163	28.8450	32.4529	36.6179	41.4305	46.9958	53.4361	60.8933	69.5319	79.5430	91.1479	104.6029	138.2970	183.6014	326.2369
24	26.9735	30.4219	34.4265	39.0826	44.5020	50.8156	58.1767	66.7648	76.7898	88.4973	102.1742	118.1552	158.6586	213.9776	392.4842
25	28.2432	32.0303	36.4593	41.6459	47.7271	54.8645	63.2490	73.1059	84.7009	98.3471	114.4133	133.3339	181.8708	249.2140	471.9811
26	29.5256	33.6709	38.5530	44.3117	51.1135	59.1564	68.6765	79.9544	93.3240	109.1818	127.9988	150.3339	208.3327	290.0883	567.3773
27	30.8209	35.3443	40.7096	47.0842	54.6691	63.7058	74.4838	87.3508	102.7231	121.0999	143.0786	169.3740	238.4993	337.5024	681.8528
28	32.1291	37.0512	42.9309	49.9676	58.4026	68.5281	80.6977	95.3388	112.9682	134.2099	159.8173	190.6989	272.8892	392.5028	819.2233
29	33.4504	38.7922	45.2189	52.9663	62.3227	73.6398	87.3465	103.9659	124.1354	148.6309	178.3972	214.5828	312.0937	456.3052	984.0680
30	34.7849	40.5681	47.5754	56.0849	66.4388	79.0582	94.4608	113.2832	136.3075	164.4940	199.0209	241.3327	356.7868	530.3117	1181.8816
35	41.6603	49.9945	60.4621	73.6522	90.3203	111.4348	138.2369	172.3168	215.7108	271.0244	341.5896	431.6635	693.5727	1120.7130	2948.3411
40	48.8864	60.4020	75.4013	95.0255	120.7998	154.7620	199.6351	259.0565	337.8824	442.5926	581.8261	767.0914	1342.0251	2360.7572	7343.8578

Table IV   Present Value of an Ordinary Annuity

n	1%	2%	3%	4%	5%	6%	7%	8%	9%	10%	11%	12%	14%	16%	20%
1	0.9901	0.9804	0.9709	0.9615	0.9524	0.9434	0.9346	0.9259	0.9174	0.9091	0.9009	0.8929	0.8772	0.8621	0.8333
2	1.9704	1.9416	1.9135	1.8861	1.8594	1.8334	1.8080	1.7833	1.7591	1.7355	1.7125	1.6901	1.6467	1.6052	1.5278
3	2.9410	2.8839	2.8286	2.7751	2.7232	2.6730	2.6243	2.5771	2.5313	2.4869	2.4437	2.4018	2.3216	2.2459	2.1065
4	3.9020	3.8077	3.7171	3.6299	3.5460	3.4651	3.3872	3.3121	3.2397	3.1699	3.1024	3.0373	2.9137	2.7982	2.5887
5	4.8534	4.7135	4.5797	4.4518	4.3295	4.2124	4.1002	3.9927	3.8897	3.7908	3.6959	3.6048	3.4331	3.2743	2.9906
6	5.7955	5.6014	5.4172	5.2421	5.0757	4.9173	4.7665	4.6229	4.4859	4.3553	4.2305	4.1114	3.8887	3.6847	3.3255
7	6.7282	6.4720	6.2303	6.0021	5.7864	5.5824	5.3893	5.2064	5.0330	4.8684	4.7122	4.5638	4.2883	4.0386	3.6046
8	7.6517	7.3255	7.0197	6.7327	6.4632	6.2098	5.9713	5.7466	5.5348	5.3349	5.1461	4.9676	4.6389	4.3436	3.8372
9	8.5660	8.1622	7.7861	7.4353	7.1078	6.8017	6.5152	6.2469	5.9952	5.7590	5.5370	5.3282	4.9464	4.6065	4.0310
10	9.4713	8.9826	8.5302	8.1109	7.7217	7.3601	7.0236	6.7101	6.4177	6.1446	5.8892	5.6502	5.2161	4.8332	4.1925
11	10.3676	9.7868	9.2526	8.7605	8.3064	7.8869	7.4987	7.1390	6.8052	6.4951	6.2065	5.9377	5.4527	5.0286	4.3271
12	11.2551	10.5753	9.9540	9.3851	8.8633	8.3838	7.9427	7.5361	7.1607	6.8137	6.4924	6.1944	5.6603	5.1971	4.4392
13	12.1337	11.3484	10.6350	9.9856	9.3936	8.8527	8.3577	7.9038	7.4869	7.1034	6.7499	6.4235	5.8424	5.3423	4.5327
14	13.0037	12.1062	11.2961	10.5631	9.8986	9.2950	8.7455	8.2442	7.7862	7.3667	6.9819	6.6282	6.0021	5.4675	4.6106
15	13.8651	12.8493	11.9379	11.1184	10.3797	9.7122	9.1079	8.5595	8.0607	7.6061	7.1909	6.8109	6.1422	5.5755	4.6755
16	14.7179	13.5777	12.5611	11.6523	10.8378	10.1059	9.4466	8.8514	8.3126	7.8237	7.3792	6.9740	6.2651	5.6685	4.7296
17	15.5623	14.2919	13.1661	12.1657	11.2741	10.4773	9.7632	9.1216	8.5436	8.0216	7.5488	7.1196	6.3729	5.7487	4.7746
18	16.3983	14.9920	13.7535	12.6593	11.6896	10.8276	10.0591	9.3719	8.7556	8.2014	7.7016	7.2497	6.4674	5.8178	4.8122
19	17.2260	15.6785	14.3238	13.1339	12.0853	11.1581	10.3356	9.6036	8.9501	8.3649	7.8393	7.3658	6.5504	5.8775	4.8435
20	18.0456	16.3514	14.8775	13.5903	12.4622	11.4699	10.5940	9.8181	9.1285	8.5136	7.9633	7.4694	6.6231	5.9288	4.8696
21	18.8570	17.0112	15.4150	14.0292	12.8212	11.7641	10.8355	10.0168	9.2922	8.6487	8.0751	7.5620	6.6870	5.9731	4.8913
22	19.6604	17.6580	15.9369	14.4511	13.1630	12.0416	11.0612	10.2007	9.4424	8.7715	8.1757	7.6446	6.7429	6.0113	4.9094
23	20.4558	18.2922	16.4436	14.8568	13.4886	12.3034	11.2722	10.3711	9.5802	8.8832	8.2664	7.7184	6.7921	6.0442	4.9245
24	21.2434	18.9139	16.9355	15.2470	13.7986	12.5504	11.4693	10.5288	9.7066	8.9847	8.3481	7.7843	6.8351	6.0726	4.9371
25	22.0232	19.5235	17.4131	15.6221	14.0939	12.7834	11.6536	10.6748	9.8226	9.0770	8.4217	7.8431	6.8729	6.0971	4.9476
26	22.7952	20.1210	17.8768	15.9828	14.3752	13.0032	11.8258	10.8100	9.9290	9.1609	8.4881	7.8957	6.9061	6.1182	4.9563
27	23.5596	20.7069	18.3270	16.3296	14.6430	13.2105	11.9867	10.9352	10.0266	9.2372	8.5478	7.9426	6.9352	6.1364	4.9636
28	24.3164	21.2813	18.7641	16.6631	14.8981	13.4062	12.1371	11.0511	10.1161	9.3066	8.6016	7.9844	6.9607	6.1520	4.9697
29	25.0658	21.8444	19.1885	16.9837	15.1411	13.5907	12.2777	11.1584	10.1983	9.3696	8.6501	8.0218	6.9830	6.1656	4.9747
30	25.8077	22.3965	19.6004	17.2920	15.3725	13.7648	12.4090	11.2578	10.2737	9.4269	8.6938	8.0552	7.0027	6.1772	4.9789
35	29.4086	24.9986	21.4872	18.6646	16.3742	14.4982	12.9477	11.6546	10.5668	9.6442	8.8552	8.1755	7.0700	6.2153	4.9915
40	32.8347	27.3555	23.1148	19.7928	17.1591	15.0463	13.3317	11.9246	10.7574	9.7791	8.9511	8.2438	7.1050	6.2335	4.9966

Table V Future Value of an Annuity Due

	1%	2%	3%	4%	5%	6%	7%	8%	9%	10%	11%	12%	14%	16%	20%
1	1.0100	1.0200	1.0300	1.0400	1.0500	1.0600	1.0700	1.0800	1.0900	1.1000	1.1100	1.1200	1.1400	1.1600	1.2000
2	2.0301	2.0604	2.0909	2.1216	2.1525	2.1836	2.2149	2.2464	2.2781	2.3100	2.3421	2.3744	2.4396	2.5056	2.6400
3	3.0604	3.1216	3.1836	3.2465	3.3101	3.3746	3.4399	3.5061	3.5731	3.6410	3.7097	3.7793	3.9211	4.0665	4.3680
4	4.1010	4.2040	4.3091	4.4163	4.5256	4.6371	4.7507	4.8666	4.9847	5.1051	5.2278	5.3528	5.6101	5.8771	6.4416
5	5.1520	5.3081	5.4684	5.6330	5.8019	5.9753	6.1533	6.3359	6.5233	6.7156	6.9129	7.1152	7.5355	7.9775	8.9299
6	6.2135	6.4343	6.6625	6.8983	7.1420	7.3938	7.6540	7.9228	8.2004	8.4872	8.7833	9.0890	9.7305	10.4139	11.9159
7	7.2857	7.5830	7.8923	8.2142	8.5491	8.8975	9.2598	9.6366	10.0285	10.4359	10.8594	11.2997	12.2328	13.2401	15.4991
8	8.3685	8.7546	9.1591	9.5828	10.0266	10.4913	10.9780	11.4876	12.0210	12.5795	13.1640	13.7757	15.0853	16.5185	19.7989
9	9.4622	9.9497	10.4639	11.0061	11.5779	12.1808	12.8164	13.4866	14.1929	14.9374	15.7220	16.5487	18.3373	20.3215	24.9587
10	10.5668	11.1687	11.8078	12.4864	13.2068	13.9716	14.7836	15.6455	16.5603	17.5312	18.5614	19.6546	22.0445	24.7329	31.1504
11	11.6825	12.4121	13.1920	14.0258	14.9171	15.8699	16.8885	17.9771	19.1407	20.3843	21.7132	23.1331	26.2707	29.8502	38.5805
12	12.8093	13.6803	14.6178	15.6268	16.7130	17.8821	19.1406	20.4953	21.9534	23.5227	25.2116	27.0291	31.0887	35.7862	47.4966
13	13.9474	14.9739	16.0863	17.2919	18.5986	20.0151	21.5505	23.2149	25.0192	26.9750	29.0949	31.3926	36.5811	42.6720	58.1959
14	15.0969	16.2934	17.5989	19.0236	20.5786	22.2760	24.1290	26.1521	28.3609	30.7725	33.4054	36.2797	42.8424	50.6595	71.0351
15	16.2579	17.6393	19.1569	20.8245	22.6575	24.6725	26.8881	29.3243	32.0034	34.9497	38.1899	41.7533	49.9804	59.9250	86.4421
16	17.4304	19.0121	20.7616	22.6975	24.8404	27.2129	29.8402	32.7502	35.9737	39.5447	43.5008	47.8837	58.1176	70.6750	104.9306
17	18.6147	20.4123	22.4144	24.6454	27.1324	29.9057	32.9990	36.4502	40.3013	44.5992	49.3959	54.7497	67.3941	83.1407	127.1167
18	19.8109	21.8406	24.1169	26.6712	29.5390	32.7600	36.3790	40.4463	45.0185	50.1591	55.9395	62.4397	77.9692	97.6032	153.7400
19	21.0190	23.2974	25.8704	28.7781	32.0660	35.7856	39.9955	44.7620	50.1601	56.2750	63.2028	71.0524	90.0249	114.3797	185.6880
20	22.2392	24.7833	27.6765	30.9692	34.7193	38.9927	43.8652	49.4229	55.7645	63.0025	71.2651	80.6987	103.7684	133.8405	224.0256
21	23.4716	26.2990	29.5368	33.2480	37.5052	42.3923	48.0057	54.4568	61.8733	70.4027	80.2143	91.5026	119.4360	156.4150	270.0307
22	24.7163	27.8450	31.4529	35.6179	40.4305	45.9958	52.4361	59.8933	68.5319	78.5430	90.1479	103.6029	137.2970	182.6014	325.2369
23	25.9735	29.4219	33.4265	38.0826	43.5020	49.8156	57.1767	65.7648	75.7898	87.4973	101.1742	117.1552	157.6586	212.9776	391.4842
24	27.2432	31.0303	35.4593	40.6459	46.7271	53.8645	62.2490	72.1059	83.7009	97.3471	113.4133	132.3339	180.8708	248.2140	470.9811
25	28.5256	32.6709	37.5530	43.3117	50.1135	58.1564	67.6765	78.9544	92.3240	108.1818	126.9988	149.3339	207.3327	289.0883	566.3773
26	29.8209	34.3443	39.7096	46.0842	53.6691	62.7058	73.4838	86.3508	101.7231	120.0999	142.0786	168.3740	237.4993	336.5024	680.8528
27	31.1291	36.0512	41.9309	48.9676	57.4026	67.5281	79.6977	94.3388	111.9682	133.2099	158.8173	189.6989	271.8892	391.5028	818.2233
28	32.4504	37.7922	44.2189	51.9663	61.3227	72.6398	86.3465	102.9659	123.1354	147.6309	177.3972	213.5828	311.0937	455.3032	983.0680
29	33.7849	39.5681	46.5754	55.0849	65.4388	78.0582	93.4608	112.2832	135.3075	163.4940	198.0209	240.3327	355.7868	529.3117	1180.8816
30	35.1327	41.3794	49.0027	58.3283	69.7608	83.8017	101.0730	122.3459	148.5752	180.9434	220.9132	270.2926	406.7370	615.1616	1418.2579
35	42.0769	50.9944	62.2759	76.5983	94.8363	118.1209	147.9135	186.1021	235.1247	298.1268	379.1644	483.4631	790.6729	1300.0270	3538.0094
40	49.3752	61.6100	77.6633	98.8265	126.8398	164.0477	213.6096	279.7810	368.2919	486.8518	645.8269	859.1424	1529.9086	2738.4784	8812.6294

Table VI   Present Value of an Annuity Due

	1%	2%	3%	4%	5%	6%	7%	8%	9%	10%	11%	12%	14%	16%	20%
1	1.0000	1.0000	1.0000	1.0000	1.0000	1.0000	1.0000	1.0000	1.0000	1.0000	1.0000	1.0000	1.0000	1.0000	1.0000
2	1.9901	1.9804	1.9709	1.9615	1.9524	1.9434	1.9346	1.9259	1.9174	1.9091	1.9009	1.8929	1.8772	1.8621	1.8333
3	2.9704	2.9416	2.9135	2.8861	2.8594	2.8334	2.8080	2.7833	2.7591	2.7355	2.7125	2.6901	2.6467	2.6052	2.5278
4	3.9410	3.8839	3.8286	3.7751	3.7232	3.6730	3.6243	3.5771	3.5313	3.4869	3.4437	3.4018	3.3216	3.2459	3.1065
5	4.9020	4.8077	4.7171	4.6299	4.5460	4.4651	4.3872	4.3121	4.2397	4.1699	4.1024	4.0373	3.9137	3.7982	3.5887
6	5.8534	5.7135	5.5797	5.4518	5.3295	5.2124	5.1002	4.9927	4.8897	4.7908	4.6959	4.6048	4.4331	4.2743	3.9906
7	6.7955	6.6014	6.4172	6.2421	6.0757	5.9173	5.7665	5.6229	5.4859	5.3553	5.2305	5.1114	4.8887	4.6847	4.3255
8	7.7282	7.4720	7.2303	7.0021	6.7864	6.5824	6.3893	6.2064	6.0330	5.8684	5.7122	5.5638	5.2883	5.0386	4.6046
9	8.6517	8.3255	8.0197	7.7327	7.4632	7.2098	6.9713	6.7466	6.5348	6.3349	6.1461	5.9676	5.6389	5.3436	4.8372
10	9.5660	9.1622	8.7861	8.4353	8.1078	7.8017	7.5152	7.2469	6.9952	6.7590	6.5370	6.3282	5.9464	5.6065	5.0310
11	10.4713	9.9826	9.5302	9.1109	8.7217	8.3601	8.0236	7.7101	7.4177	7.1446	6.8892	6.6502	6.2161	5.8332	5.1925
12	11.3676	10.7868	10.2526	9.7605	9.3064	8.8869	8.4987	8.1390	7.8052	7.4951	7.2065	6.9377	6.4527	6.0286	5.3271
13	12.2551	11.5753	10.9540	10.3851	9.8633	9.3838	8.9427	8.5361	8.1607	7.8137	7.4924	7.1944	6.6603	6.1971	5.4392
14	13.1337	12.3484	11.6350	10.9856	10.3936	9.8527	9.3577	8.9038	8.4869	8.1034	7.7499	7.4235	6.8424	6.3423	5.5327
15	14.0037	13.1062	12.2961	11.5631	10.8986	10.2950	9.7455	9.2442	8.7862	8.3667	7.9819	7.6282	7.0021	6.4675	5.6106
16	14.8651	13.8493	12.9379	12.1184	11.3797	10.7122	10.1079	9.5595	9.0607	8.6061	8.1909	7.8109	7.1422	6.5755	5.6755
17	15.7179	14.5777	13.5611	12.6523	11.8378	11.1059	10.4466	9.8514	9.3126	8.8237	8.3792	7.9740	7.2651	6.6685	5.7296
18	16.5623	15.2919	14.1661	13.1657	12.2741	11.4773	10.7632	10.1216	9.5436	9.0216	8.5488	8.1196	7.3729	6.7487	5.7746
19	17.3983	15.9920	14.7535	13.6593	12.6896	11.8276	11.0591	10.3719	9.7556	9.2014	8.7016	8.2497	7.4674	6.8178	5.8122
20	18.2260	16.6785	15.3238	14.1339	13.0853	12.1581	11.3356	10.6036	9.9501	9.3649	8.8393	8.3658	7.5504	6.8775	5.8435
21	19.0456	17.3514	15.8775	14.5903	13.4622	12.4699	11.5940	10.8181	10.1285	9.5136	8.9633	8.4694	7.6231	6.9288	5.8696
22	19.8570	18.0112	16.4150	15.0292	13.8212	12.7641	11.8355	11.0168	10.2922	9.6487	9.0751	8.5620	7.6870	6.9731	5.8913
23	20.6604	18.6580	16.9369	15.4511	14.1630	13.0416	12.0612	11.2007	10.4424	9.7715	9.1757	8.6446	7.7429	7.0113	5.9094
24	21.4558	19.2922	17.4436	15.8568	14.4886	13.3034	12.2722	11.3711	10.5802	9.8832	9.2664	8.7184	7.7921	7.0442	5.9245
25	22.2434	19.9139	17.9355	16.2470	14.7986	13.5504	12.4693	11.5288	10.7066	9.9847	9.3481	8.7843	7.8351	7.0726	5.9371
26	23.0232	20.5235	18.4131	16.6221	15.0939	13.7834	12.6536	11.6748	10.8226	10.0770	9.4217	8.8431	7.8729	7.0971	5.9476
27	23.7952	21.1210	18.8768	16.9828	15.3752	14.0032	12.8258	11.8100	10.9290	10.1609	9.4881	8.8957	7.9061	7.1182	5.9563
28	24.5596	21.7069	19.3270	17.3296	15.6430	14.2105	12.9867	11.9352	11.0266	10.2372	9.5478	8.9426	7.9352	7.1364	5.9636
29	25.3164	22.2813	19.7641	17.6631	15.8981	14.4062	13.1371	12.0511	11.1161	10.3066	9.6016	8.9844	7.9607	7.1520	5.9697
30	26.0658	22.8444	20.1885	17.9837	16.1411	14.5907	13.2777	12.1584	11.1983	10.3696	9.6501	9.0218	7.9830	7.1656	5.9747
35	29.7027	25.4986	22.1318	19.4112	17.1929	15.3681	13.8540	12.5869	11.5178	10.6086	9.8293	9.1566	8.0599	7.2098	5.9898
40	33.1630	27.9026	23.8082	20.5845	18.0170	15.9491	14.2649	12.8786	11.7255	10.7570	9.9357	9.2330	8.0997	7.2309	5.9959

Appendix C

Index of References to APB and FASB Pronouncements

The following list of pronouncements by the Accounting Principles Board and the Financial Accounting Standards Board (as of December 1, 1999) is provided as an overview of the standards issued since 1962 and to reference these standards to the relevant chapters in this book. Some of the pronouncements by the Committee on Accounting Procedure are still authoritative; most of these are summarized in Accounting Research Bulletin No. 43 issued in June 1953. A number of the APB and FASB pronouncements have been superseded; these pronouncements are labeled "superseded" in the Chapter References column of the list.

Accounting Principles Board Opinions

Date Issued	Opinion Number	Title	Chapter References
Nov. 1962	1	New Depreciation Guidelines and Rules	superseded
Dec. 1962	2	Accounting for the "Investment Credit"; addendum to Opinion No. 2—Accounting Principles for Regulated Industries	16
Oct. 1963	3	The Statement of Source and Application of Funds	superseded
Mar. 1964	4	Accounting for the "Investment Credit"	16
Sep. 1964	5	Reporting of Leases in Financial Statements of Lessee	superseded
Oct. 1965	6	Status of Accounting Research Bulletins	11
May 1966	7	Accounting for Leases in Financial Statements of Lessor	superseded
Nov. 1966	8	Accounting for the Cost of Pension Plans	superseded
Dec. 1966	9	Reporting the Results of Operations	4
Dec. 1966	10	Omnibus Opinion—1966	7
Dec. 1967	11	Accounting for Income Taxes	superseded
Dec. 1967	12	Omnibus Opinion—1967	10, 13
Mar. 1969	13	Amending Paragraph 6 of APB Opinion No. 9, Application to Commercial Banks	N/A
Mar. 1969	14	Accounting for Convertible Debt and Debt Issued with Stock Purchase Warrants	10, 11
May 1969	15	Earnings per Share	superseded
Aug. 1970	16	Business Combinations	12
Aug. 1970	17	Intangible Assets	12, 13
Mar. 1971	18	The Equity Method of Accounting for Investments in Common Stock	14
Mar. 1971	19	Reporting Changes in Financial Position	superseded
July 1971	20	Accounting Changes	20
Aug. 1971	21	Interest on Receivables and Payables	6, 10
Apr. 1972	22	Disclosures of Accounting Policies	3
Apr. 1972	23	Accounting for Income Taxes—Special Areas	16
Apr. 1972	24	Accounting for Income Taxes—Investments in Common Stock Accounted for by the Equity Method (Other than Subsidiaries and Corporate Joint Ventures)	superseded
Oct. 1972	25	Accounting for Stock Issued to Employees	11
Oct. 1972	26	Early Extinguishment of Debt	4, 10
Nov. 1972	27	Accounting for Lease Transactions by Manufacturer or Dealer Lessors	superseded
May 1973	28	Interim Financial Reporting	18
May 1973	29	Accounting for Nonmonetary Transactions	11, 12, 13
June 1973	30	Reporting the Results of Operations	4, 20
June 1973	31	Disclosures of Lease Commitments by Lessees	superseded

Financial Accounting Standards Board
Statements of Financial Accounting Standards

Date Issued	Statement Number	Title	Chapter References
Dec. 1973	1	Disclosure of Foreign Currency Translation Information	superseded
Oct. 1974	2	Accounting for Research and Development Costs	12
Dec. 1974	3	Reporting Accounting Changes in Interim Financial Statements	N/A
Mar. 1975	4	Reporting Gains and Losses from Extinguishment of Debt	4, 10
Mar. 1975	5	Accounting for Contingencies	18
May 1975	6	Classification of Short-Term Obligations Expected to be Refinanced	3
June 1975	7	Accounting and Reporting by Development Stage Enterprises	12
Oct. 1975	8	Accounting for the Translation of Foreign Currency Transactions and Foreign Currency Financial Statements	superseded
Oct. 1975	9	Accounting for Income Taxes—Oil and Gas Producing Companies	superseded
Oct. 1975	10	Extension of "Grandfather" Provisions for Business Combinations	N/A
Dec. 1975	11	Accounting for Contingencies—Transition Method	20
Dec. 1975	12	Accounting for Certain Marketable Securities	superseded
Nov. 1976	13	Accounting for Leases	15
Dec. 1976	14	Financial Reporting for Segments of a Business Enterprise	superseded
June 1977	15	Accounting by Debtors and Creditors for Troubled Debt Restructurings	10
June 1977	16	Prior Period Adjustments	11, 20
Nov. 1977	17	Accounting for Leases—Initial Direct Costs	superseded
Nov. 1977	18	Financial Reporting for Segments of a Business Enterprise—Interim Financial Statements	superseded
Dec. 1977	19	Financial Accounting and Reporting by Oil and Gas Producing Companies	12
Dec. 1977	20	Accounting for Forward Exchange Contracts	superseded
Apr. 1978	21	Suspension of the Reporting of Earnings Per Share and Segment Information by Nonpublic Enterprises	superseded
June 1978	22	Changes in the Provisions of Lease Agreements Resulting from Refunding of Tax-Exempt Debt	N/A
Aug. 1978	23	Inception of the Lease	15
Dec. 1978	24	Reporting Segment Information in Financial Statements That Are Presented in Another Enterprise's Financial Report	superseded
Feb. 1979	25	Suspension of Certain Accounting Requirements for Oil and Gas Producing Companies	12
Apr. 1979	26	Profit Recognition on Sales-Type Leases of Real Estate	superseded
May 1979	27	Classification of Renewals or Extensions of Existing Sales-Type or Direct Financing Leases	15
May 1979	28	Accounting for Sales with Leasebacks	15
June 1979	29	Determining Contingent Rentals	15
Aug. 1979	30	Disclosures of Information About Major Customers	superseded
Sep. 1979	31	Accounting for Tax Benefits Related to U.K. Tax Legislation Concerning Stock Relief	superseded
Sep. 1979	32	Specialized Accounting and Reporting Principles and Practices in AICPA Statements of Position and Guides on Accounting and Auditing Matters	superseded
Sep. 1979	33	Financial Reporting and Changing Prices	superseded
Oct. 1979	34	Capitalization of Interest Cost	12
Mar. 1980	35	Accounting and Reporting by Defined Benefit Pension Plans	17
May 1980	36	Disclosure of Pension Information	superseded
July 1980	37	Balance Sheet Classification of Deferred Income Taxes	16

Date Issued	Statement Number	Title	Chapter References
Sep. 1980	38	Accounting for Preacquisition Contingencies of Purchased Enterprises	N/A
Oct. 1980	39	Financial Reporting and Changing Prices: Specialized Assets—Mining and Oil and Gas	superseded
Nov. 1980	40	Financial Reporting and Changing Prices: Specialized Assets—Timberlands and Growing Timber	superseded
Nov. 1980	41	Financial Reporting and Changing Prices: Specialized Assets—Income-Producing Real Estate	superseded
Nov. 1980	42	Determining Materiality for Capitalization of Interest Costs	12
Nov. 1980	43	Accounting for Compensated Absences	17
Dec. 1980	44	Accounting for Intangible Assets of Motor Carriers	N/A
Mar. 1981	45	Accounting for Franchise Fee Revenue	7
Mar. 1981	46	Financial Reporting and Changing Prices: Motion Picture Films	superseded
Mar. 1981	47	Disclosure of Long-Term Obligations	10
June 1981	48	Revenue Recognition When Right of Return Exists	7, 8
June 1981	49	Accounting for Product Financing Arrangements	N/A
Nov. 1981	50	Financial Reporting in the Record and Music Industry	N/A
Nov. 1981	51	Financial Reporting by Cable Television Companies	N/A
Dec. 1981	52	Foreign Currency Translation	21
Dec. 1981	53	Financial Reporting by Producers and Distributors of Motion Picture Films	N/A
Jan. 1982	54	Financial Reporting and Changing Prices: Investment Companies	superseded
Feb. 1982	55	Determining Whether a Convertible Security Is a Common Stock Equivalent	superseded
Feb. 1982	56	Designation of AICPA Guide and Statement of Position (SOP) 81-1 on Contractor Accounting and SOP 81-2 Concerning Hospital-Related Organizations as Preferable for Purposes of Applying APB Opinion 20	superseded
Mar. 1982	57	Related Party Disclosures	N/A
Apr. 1982	58	Capitalization of Interest Cost in Financial Statements That Include Investments Accounted for by the Equity Method	N/A
Apr. 1982	59	Deferral of the Effective Date of Certain Accounting Requirements for Pension Plans of State and Local Governmental Units	superseded
June 1982	60	Accounting and Reporting by Insurance Enterprises	N/A
June 1982	61	Accounting for Title Plant	N/A
June 1982	62	Capitalization of Interest Cost in Situations Involving Certain Tax-Exempt Borrowings and Certain Gifts and Grants	N/A
June 1982	63	Financial Reporting by Broadcasters	N/A
Sep. 1982	64	Extinguishments of Debt Made to Satisfy Sinking-Fund Requirements	10
Sep. 1982	65	Accounting for Certain Mortgage Banking Activities	N/A
Oct. 1982	66	Accounting for Sales of Real Estate	7
Oct. 1982	67	Accounting for Costs and Initial Rental Operations of Real Estate Projects	N/A
Oct. 1982	68	Research and Development Arrangements	10
Nov. 1982	69	Disclosures About Oil and Gas Producing Activities	12
Dec. 1982	70	Financial Reporting and Changing Prices: Foreign Currency Translation	superseded
Dec. 1982	71	Accounting for the Effects of Certain Types of Regulation	N/A
Feb. 1983	72	Accounting for Certain Acquisitions of Banking or Thrift Institutions	N/A
Aug. 1983	73	Reporting a Change in Accounting for Railroad Track Structures	N/A
Aug. 1983	74	Accounting for Special Termination Benefits Paid to Employees	superseded

Date Issued	Statement Number	Title	Chapter References
Nov. 1983	75	Deferral of the Effective Date of Certain Accounting Requirements for Pension Plans of State and Local Governmental Units	superseded
Nov. 1983	76	Extinguishment of Debt	superseded
Dec. 1983	77	Reporting by Transferors for Transfers of Receivables with Recourse	superseded
Dec. 1983	78	Classification of Obligations That Are Callable by the Creditor	3, 10
Feb. 1984	79	Elimination of Certain Disclosures for Business Combinations by Nonpublic Enterprises	N/A
Aug. 1984	80	Accounting for Future Contracts	superseded
Nov. 1984	81	Disclosure of Postretirement Health Care and Life Insurance Benefits	superseded
Nov. 1984	82	Financial Reporting and Changing Prices: Elimination of Certain Disclosures	superseded
Mar. 1985	83	Designation of AICPA Guides and Statement of Position on Accounting by Brokers and Dealers in Securities, by Employee Benefit Plans, and by Banks as Preferable for Purposes of Applying APB Opinion 20	superseded
Mar. 1985	84	Induced Conversion of Convertible Debt	10
Mar. 1985	85	Yield Test for Determining Whether a Convertible Security Is a Common Stock Equivalent	superseded
Aug. 1985	86	Accounting for the Costs of Computer Software to Be Sold, Leased, or Otherwise Marketed	12
Dec. 1985	87	Employers' Accounting for Pensions	17
Dec. 1985	88	Employers' Accounting for Settlements and Curtailments of Defined Benefit Pension Plans and for Termination Benefits	17
Dec. 1986	89	Financial Reporting and Changing Prices	21
Dec. 1986	90	Regulated Enterprises—Accounting for Abandonments and Disallowances of Plant Costs	N/A
Dec. 1986	91	Accounting for Nonrefundable Fees and Costs Associated with Originating or Acquiring Loans and Initial Direct Costs of Leases	15
Aug. 1987	92	Regulated Enterprises—Accounting for Phase-In Plans	N/A
Aug. 1987	93	Recognition of Depreciation by Not-for-Profit Organizations	13
Oct. 1987	94	Consolidation of All Majority-Owned Subsidiaries	14
Nov. 1987	95	Statement of Cash Flows	5
Dec. 1987	96	Accounting for Income Taxes	superseded
Dec. 1987	97	Accounting and Reporting by Insurance Enterprises for Certain Long-Duration Contracts and for Realized Gains and Losses from the Sale of Investments	N/A
May 1988	98	Accounting for Leases: • Sale-Leaseback Transactions Involving Real Estate • Sales-Type Leases of Real Estate • Definition of the Lease Term • Initial Direct Costs of Direct Financial Leases	15
Sep. 1988	99	Deferral of the Effective Date of Recognition of Depreciation by Not-for-Profit Organizations	13
Dec. 1988	100	Accounting for Income Taxes—Deferral of the Effective Date FASB Statement No. 96	superseded
Dec. 1988	101	Regulated Enterprises—Accounting for the Discontinuation of Application of FASB Statement No. 71	N/A
Feb. 1989	102	Statement of Cash Flows—Exemption of Certain Enterprises and Classification of Cash Flows from Certain Securities Acquired for Resale	N/A
Dec. 1989	103	Accounting for Income Taxes—Deferral of Effective Date of FASB Statement No. 96	superseded
Dec. 1989	104	Statement of Cash Flows—Net Reporting of Certain Cash Receipts and Cash Payments and Classification of Cash Flows from Hedging Transactions	N/A

Date Issued	Statement Number	Title	Chapter References
Mar. 1990	105	Disclosure of Information about Financial Instruments with Off-Balance-Sheet Risk and Financial Instruments with Concentrations of Credit Risk	superseded
Dec. 1990	106	Employers' Accounting for Postretirement Benefits Other Than Pensions	17
Dec. 1991	107	Disclosures about Fair Value of Financial Instruments	14
Dec. 1991	108	Accounting for Income Taxes—Deferral of the Effective Date of FASB Statement No. 96	superseded
Feb. 1992	109	Accounting for Income Taxes	16
Aug. 1992	110	Reporting by Defined Benefit Pension Plans of Investment Contracts	N/A
Nov. 1992	111	Recision of FASB Statement No. 32 and Technical Corrections	1
Nov. 1992	112	Employers' Accounting for Postemployment Benefits	17
Dec. 1992	113	Accounting and Reporting for Reinsurance of Short-Duration and Long-Duration Contracts	N/A
May 1993	114	Accounting by Creditors for Impairment of a Loan	14
May 1993	115	Accounting for Certain Investments in Debt and Equity Securities	14
June 1993	116	Accounting for Contributions Received and Contributions Made	11, 12
June 1993	117	Financial Statements of Not-for-Profit Organizations	N/A
Oct. 1994	118	Accounting by Creditors for Impairment of a Loan-Income Recognition and Disclosures—an amendment of FASB Statement No. 114	14
Oct. 1994	119	Disclosure about Derivative Financial Instruments and Fair Value of Financial Instruments	superseded
Jan. 1995	120	Accounting and Reporting by Mutual Life Insurance Enterprises and by Insurance Enterprises for Certain Long-Duration Participating Contracts—an amendment of FASB Statements 60, 97, and 113 and Interpretation No. 40	N/A
Mar. 1995	121	Accounting for the Impairment of Long-Lived Assets and for Long-Lived Assets to Be Disposed Of	13
May 1995	122	Accounting for Mortgage Servicing Rights—an amendment of FASB Statement No. 65	superseded
Oct. 1995	123	Accounting for Stock-Based Compensation	11
Nov. 1995	124	Accounting for Certain Investments Held by Not-for-Profit Organizations	14
June 1996	125	Accounting for Transfers and Servicing of Financial Assets and Extinguishments of Liabilities	10, 14
Dec. 1996	126	Exemption from Certain Required Disclosures about Financial Instruments for Certain Nonpublic Entities—an amendment to FASB Statement No. 107	N/A
Dec. 1996	127	Deferral of the Effective Date of Certain Provisions of FASB Statement No. 125—an amendment to FASB Statement No. 125	N/A
Feb. 1997	128	Earnings per Share	19
Feb. 1997	129	Disclosure of Information about Capital Structure	19
June 1997	130	Reporting Comprehensive Income	4,14,17,18
June 1997	131	Disclosures about Segments of an Enterprise and Related Information	18
February 1998	132	Employers' Disclosures about Pensions and Other Postretirement Benefits	17
June 1998	133	Accounting for Derivative Instruments and Hedging Activities	18
October 1998	134	Accounting for Mortgage-Backed Securities Retained After the Securitization of Mortgage Loans Held for Resale by a Mortgage Banking Enterprise	N/A
February 1999	135	Rescission of FASB Statement No. 75 And Technical Corrections	N/A

Date Issued	Statement Number	Title	Chapter References
June 1999	136	Transfers of Assets to a Not-for-Profit Organization or Charitable Trust that Raises or Holds Contributions for Others	N/A
June 1999	137	Accounting for Derivative Instruments and Hedging Activities—Deferral of the Effective Date of FASB Statement No. 133	18

Financial Accounting Standards Board
Statements of Financial Accounting Concepts

Date Issued	Statement Number	Title	Chapter References
Nov. 1978	1	Objectives of Financial Reporting by Business Enterprises	1
May 1980	2	Qualitative Characteristics of Accounting Information	1
Dec. 1980	3	Elements of Financial Statements of Business Enterprises	superseded
Dec. 1980	4	Objectives of Financial Reporting by Nonbusiness Organizations	N/A
Dec. 1984	5	Recognition and Measurement in Financial Statements of Business Enterprises	1
Dec. 1985	6	Elements of Financial Statements	1

Appendix D

Glossary

A

accelerated cost recovery system (ACRS) Adaptation of the declining-balance depreciation method introduced for tax purposes in 1981 and subsequently modified.

accelerated depreciation Method of computing depreciation that yields higher annual depreciation in the early years of an asset's life than in later years.

account A record used to classify and summarize the effects of transactions.

account payable The amount due for the purchase of materials by a manufacturing company or merchandise by a wholesaler or retailer.

accounting A service activity whose "function is to provide quantitative information, primarily financial in nature, about economic entities that is intended to be useful in making economic decisions—in making reasoned choices among alternative courses of action" (*Statement of the Accounting Principles Board* No. 4, par. 40).

accounting changes A general term used to describe the use of different estimates or accounting principles or reporting entities from those used in a prior year.

accounting errors Incorrect accounting treatment resulting from mathematical mistakes, improper application of accounting principles, or omissions of material facts.

accounting periods The time intervals used for financial reporting; due to the need for timely information, the life of a business or other entity is divided into specific accounting periods for external reporting purposes. One year is the normal reporting period, although most large U.S. companies also provide quarterly statements.

Accounting Principles Board (APB) A board of the AICPA that issued Opinions establishing accounting standards during the period 1959–1973.

accounting process The procedures used for analyzing, recording, classifying, and summarizing the information to be presented in accounting reports; also referred to as the *accounting cycle.*

accounting system The procedures and methods used, including use of data processing equipment, to collect and report accounting data.

accounts receivable Trade receivables that are not evidenced by a formal agreement or "note"; accounts receivable are usually unsecured "open accounts" and represent an extension of short-term credit to customers.

accounts receivable factoring The sale of receivables without recourse for cash to a third party, usually a bank or other financial institution.

accounts receivable turnover An analytical measurement of how rapidly customers' accounts are being collected. The net accounts receivable turnover formula is net sales divided by average trade accounts receivable for a period.

accrual accounting A basic assumption that revenues are recognized when earned and expenses are recognized when incurred, without regard to when cash is received or paid.

accumulated benefit obligation (ABO) The actuarial present value of pension benefits based on the plan formula for employee service earned to date using the existing salary structure. It is used to compute the minimum liability.

accumulated postretirement benefit obligation (APBO) The actuarial present value of all future postretirement benefits earned by employees as of a certain date, assuming that the benefit plan remains in effect and that assumptions about the future are fulfilled.

acid-test ratio A financial ratio used as a measure of short-term liquidity. Also called quick ratio.

activity-based cost (ABC) system Cost system that allocates overhead based on clearly identified characteristics of the production process that are known to create overhead costs.

actual return on pension plan assets A component of net periodic pension expense measured by the difference between the fair value of pension plan assets at the end of the period and the fair value at the beginning of the period, adjusted for contributions and payments of benefits during the period.

actuarial present value The present value of pension obligations determined by using stated actuarial assumptions and estimates.

additional paid-in capital The investment by stockholders in excess of the amounts assignable to capital stock as par or stated value, as well as invested capital from other sources, such as sale of treasury stock.

additional pension liability An additional liability reported for underfunded pension plans. It is computed as the difference between the minimum pension liability and accrued pension cost or as the sum of the minimum pension liability and the prepaid pension cost.

adjunct account An account used to record additions to a related account.

adjusting entries Entries required at the end of each accounting period to update the accounts as necessary and to fully recognize, on an accrual basis, revenues and expenses for the period.

aging receivables The most commonly used method for establishing an allowance for bad debts account based on outstanding receivables. This method involves analyzing individual accounts to determine those not yet due and those past due. Past-due accounts are classified in terms of length of the period past due.

allowance method A method of recognizing the estimated losses from uncollectible accounts as expenses during the period in which the sales occur; this method is required by GAAP.

American Accounting Association (AAA) An organization primarily for accounting professors. The AAA's role in establishing accounting standards includes research projects to help the FASB and a forum for representing different points of view on various issues.

American Institute of Certified Public Accountants (AICPA) A professional organization for CPAs. Membership in the AICPA is voluntary. It publishes a monthly journal, the *Journal of Accountancy.*

amortization An adjustment to interest expense (for either a premium or a discount) to reflect the effective interest being incurred on bonds. This periodic adjustment results in the carrying value of a bond converging to its face value over time.

antidilution of earnings Assumed conversion of convertible securities or exercise of stock options that results in an increase in earnings per share (or decrease in loss per share).

antidilutive securities Securities whose assumed conversion or exercise results in an antidilution of earnings per share.

appropriated retained earnings Amount of retained earnings restricted (i.e., made unavailable for dividend payments) at the discretion of the board of directors.

arm's-length transactions Exchanges between parties who are independent of each other; a traditional assumption in accounting is that recorded transactions and events are executed between independent parties, each of whom is acting in its own best interest.

asset A resource of an entity.

asset and liability method of interperiod tax allocation A method of income tax allocation that determines deferred tax assets or tax liabilities based on scheduling future expected temporary difference reversals. If tax rates change, the asset or liability balances are adjusted to reflect the tax rates legislated to be in effect in the year when reversal is expected to occur.

asset turnover Financial ratio measuring how efficiently a company uses its assets to generate sales. The ratio formula is total sales divided by total assets.

assignment of receivables The borrowing of money with receivables pledged as security on the loan.

auditor An external public accountant hired by a company to independently examine the company's financial records and issue an opinion about the fairness of the financial statements.

auditor's opinion Report about the fairness of a company's financial statements, issued by an auditor after reviewing the company's financial records.

available-for-sale securities Investment securities not intended for immediate trading but also, in the case of debt securities, not intended to be held until maturity.

average collection period Average number of days that lapse between the time that a sale is made and the time that cash is collected. Computed by dividing average receivables outstanding by average daily sales.

average cost method An inventory valuation method that assigns the same average cost to each unit sold and to each item in the inventory.

B

balance sheet A statement that reports, as of a given point in time, the assets, liabilities, and owners' equity of a business.

bank reconciliation A process that identifies differences between the cash balance on the depositor's books and the balance reported on the bank statement. The reconciliation provides information needed to adjust the book balance to a corrected cash amount.

bank service charge Monthly fee sometimes charged by a bank to service the depositor's account.

bargain purchase option A lease provision that allows for the purchase of a leased asset in the future by the lessee at a price so low that the lessee is almost certain to exercise the option.

bargain renewal option A lease provision that allows for renewal of the lease by the lessee at significantly reduced lease payments from the original lease. The bargain terms strongly imply that the lease will be renewed.

basic earnings per share An earnings per share computation that considers only common stock issued and outstanding. It is computed as the net income less preferred dividends divided by the weighted-average common shares outstanding for the period.

basket purchase The purchase of a number of assets for one lump sum purchase price.

bearer (coupon) bonds Bonds whose ownership is determined by possession and for which interest is paid to the holder (bearer) of an interest coupon.

board of directors Group elected by the shareholders to oversee the strategic and long-run planning for the corporation.

bond certificates Certificates of indebtedness issued by a company or government agency guaranteeing payment of a principal amount at a specified future date plus periodic interest; usually issued in denominations of $1,000.

bond discount The difference between the face value and the sales price when bonds are sold below their face value.

bond indenture The contract between the issuing entity and the bondholders specifying the terms, rights, and obligations of the contracting parties.

bond issuance costs Costs incurred by the issuer for legal services, printing and engraving, taxes, and underwriting in connection with the sale of a bond.

bond premium The difference between the face value and the sales price when bonds are sold above their face value.

bond refinancing Issuing new bonds to replace outstanding bonds either at maturity or prior to maturity.

book value The long-term asset cost remaining to be allocated to future periods; computed as historical cost less accumulated depreciation.

book-to-market ratio A financial ratio measuring the deviation between accounting book value of equity and market value of equity. The ratio formula is book equity divided by market equity.

business combination The combining of two businesses; accomplished through the exchange of cash or an exchange of stock.

business (or source) document Business record used as the basis for analyzing and recording transactions; examples include invoices, check stubs, receipts, and similar business papers. Also referred to as source documents.

C

call option Contract giving the owner the right, but not the obligation, to buy an asset at a specified price.

callable A security, such as a bond or a preferred stock, that can be redeemed and canceled at the option of the issuing company.

callable bonds Bonds for which the issuer reserves the right to pay the obligation prior to the maturity date.

callable obligation A debt instrument that is (1) payable on demand or (2) has a specified due date but is payable on demand if the debtor defaults on the provisions of the loan agreement.

capital lease A lease that is economically equivalent to the purchase of the leased asset.

capital stock The portion of the amount invested by stockholders that is designated as par or stated value.

capitalized interest Interest incurred during the self-construction of an asset that is considered to be part of the asset cost.

cash Coin, currency, and other items that are acceptable for deposit at face value; serves as a medium of exchange and provides a basis of measurement for accounting.

cash-basis accounting A system of accounting in which revenues and expenses are recorded as they are received and paid.

cash (sales) discount A reduction in the selling price, allowed if payment is received within a specified period, usually offered to customers to encourage prompt payment.

cash dividend The payment of cash to shareholders in proportion to the number of shares owned.

cash equivalents Short-term, highly liquid investments that can be converted easily to cash. Generally, only investments that on the day of acquisition have less than three months remaining to maturity qualify as cash equivalents.

cash flow hedge Derivative that offsets the variability in cash flows from forecasted transactions that are probable.

cash flow–to–net income ratio Financial ratio used to analyze the cash flow relationship between cash from operations and reported net income; computed as cash from operations divided by net income.

cash method The method of accounting under which all costs are charged to expense as incurred and revenue is recognized as collections are made.

cash overdraft A credit balance in the cash account; results from checks being written for more than the cash amount on deposit; should be reported as a current liability.

cash times interest earned ratio A measure used to indicate a company's interest-paying ability; computed as pretax cash flow divided by cash paid for interest.

ceiling The net realizable value; used as an upper limit in defining market when valuing inventory at the lower of cost or market.

Certified Public Accountant (CPA) An accountant who has met specified professional requirements established by the AICPA and local and state societies. A CPA often does not work for a single business enterprise but rather provides a variety of professional services for many different individual and business clients. A key service provided by CPAs is the performance of independent audits of financial statements.

change in accounting estimate A specific type of accounting change that modifies predictions of future events, for example, the useful life of a depreciable asset; changes in estimates are to be reflected in current and future periods.

change in accounting principle A specific type of accounting change that uses a different accounting principle or method from that used previously, for example, using straight-line depreciation instead of the declining-balance method; generally, changes in principle require the reporting of a cumulative effect of the change in the current year's income statement, as well as pro forma information.

change in reporting entity A specific type of accounting change that reflects financial statements for a different unit of accountability, for example, after a business merger; a change in reporting entity requires restatement of the financial results of prior periods so as to provide comparative data.

chart of accounts A systematic listing of all accounts used by a particular business entity.

closing entries Entries that reduce all temporary accounts to a zero balance at the end of each accounting period, transferring the preclosed balances to a permanent account.

collateral trust bond Bonds that are secured by the stocks and bonds of other corporations owned by the issuer but held in trust for the benefit of the bondholders.

commodity-backed (asset-linked) bonds Bonds that may be redeemed in terms of commodities, such as oil or precious metals.

common-size financial statements Financial statements standardized by a measure of size, either sales or total assets. All amounts are stated in terms of a percentage of the size measure.

common stock The class of stock issued by corporations that represents the basic ownership of the company; allows shareholders the right to vote and to receive dividends if declared, although the right to dividends is generally secondary to that of preferred stockholders.

comparability A quality of useful accounting information based on the premise that information is more useful when it can be related to a benchmark or standard, such as data for other firms within the same industry.

comparative financial statements Financial statements reflecting data for two or more periods.

compensated absences Payments by employers for vacation, holiday, illness, or other personal activities.

compensating balances The portion of a demand deposit that must be maintained as support for existing borrowing arrangements.

completed-contract method An accounting method that recognizes revenues and expenses on long-term construction contracts only when completed.

complex capital structure A corporate structure that includes convertible securities and/or stock options, warrants, or rights that could result in the issuance of additional common stock through exercise or conversion.

composite depreciation Computation of depreciation on an entire group of related but dissimilar assets as if the group were one asset.

comprehensive income A concept of income measurement and reporting that includes all changes in owners' equity except investments by and distributions to owners.

conceptual framework A theoretical foundation underlying accounting standards and practice. The framework established by the FASB encompasses the objectives, fundamental concepts, and implementation guidelines described in FASB Concepts Statement Nos. 1–6.

conglomerates Complex companies that operate in multiple industries.

conservatism The notion that when doubt exists concerning two or more reporting alternatives, users should select the alternative with the least favorable impact on reported income, assets, and liabilities.

consigned goods Inventory that is physically located at a dealer; however, ownership is retained by the shipper until the dealer sells the inventory.

consignee An entity that acts as an agent for another party (the consignor) by holding the consignor's inventory in an attempt to sell it. Title to the inventory is retained by the consignor even though physical possession is held by the consignee.

consignment A transfer of property without a transfer of title and risk of ownership. The recipient of the property (consignee) acts as a selling agent on behalf of the owner (consignor).

consignor A seller that ships merchandise to a third party (the consignee) but retains title until the inventory is sold by the third party. When the merchandise is subsequently sold, the consignee is typically paid a commission on the sale with the balance from the sale being remitted to the seller.

consistency A quality of useful accounting information requiring that accounting methods be followed consistently from one period to the next.

consolidated financial statements Financial statements that combine the financial results of a parent company and its subsidiaries.

constant dollar accounting Accounting for the impact of inflation, or the change in the general level of prices.

contingent gains Circumstances involving potential gains that will not be resolved until some future event occurs.

contingent liability A potential obligation, the existence of which is uncertain because it is dependent on the outcome of a future event, such as a pending lawsuit. The amount of the potential obligation may or may not be determinable.

contingent losses Circumstances involving potential losses that will not be resolved until some future event occurs.

contra account An account used to record subtractions from a related account. Also called an offset account.

contributed capital The portion of corporate capital that represents investments by the stockholders. Also referred to as paid-in capital.

contributory pension plan A pension plan in which employees make contributions to the plan and thus bear part of the cost.

control The ability of an investor to decisively influence the operating, investing, and financing decisions made by an investee.

control account A general ledger account that summarizes the detailed information in a subsidiary ledger.

convertible Securities, such as bonds and preferred stock, whose terms permit the holder to convert the investment into common stock of the issuing company.

convertible bonds Bonds that provide for conversion into common stock at the option of the bondholder.

convertible debt securities Securities, such as bonds and preferred stock, whose terms permit the holder to convert the investment into common stock of the issuing companies.

corporation A business entity that is a separate legal entity owned by its shareholders.

corridor amount An amount established as a minimum before amortization of pension gains and losses is required. Only amortization of unrecognized pension gains and losses that exceed 10% of the greater of the projected benefit obligation or the market-related asset value as of the beginning of the period is included in the net periodic pension expense. Any systematic method of amortization that exceeds the minimum may be used as long as it is consistently applied to both gains and losses and it is disclosed in the statements.

cost driver Characteristic of the production process that is known to create overhead costs.

cost method Method of accounting for treasury stock purchases in which the entire cost of the treasury stock is shown as a subtraction from equity.

cost percentage Percentage reflecting the relationship between cost values and retail values; used with the retail inventory method.

cost recovery method A revenue recognition method that requires recovery of the total cost (investment) prior to the recognition of revenue.

cost-to-cost method A method for determining the percentage of completion for long-term construction contracts using a ratio of the actual cost incurred to date to the estimated total costs.

credit An entry on the right side of an account.

credit risk Uncertainty that the party on the other side of an agreement will abide by the terms of the agreement.

creditors Outside parties who are owed money by a company.

cumulative effect of a change in accounting principle An account that summarizes the net effect on the balance sheet of changing from one accounting principle to another. The effect is disclosed on the income statement as an irregular item net of tax.

cumulative preferred stock Preferred stock that has a right to receive current dividends as well as any dividends in arrears before common stockholders receive any dividends.

current asset Cash or assets that are reasonably expected to be converted into cash during the normal operating cycle of a business or within one year, whichever period is longer.

current cost accounting Accounting for the impact of changes in the prices of specific items.

current liability Obligations that are reasonably expected to be paid within one year.

current market value The cash equivalent price that could be obtained currently by selling an asset in an orderly liquidation.

current ratio Current assets divided by current liabilities.

current replacement cost The cash equivalent price that would be paid currently to purchase or replace goods or services.

curtailment of a pension plan An event that significantly reduces the expected years of future services of present employees or eliminates for a significant number of employees the accrual of defined benefits for their future services.

D

dated retained earnings The amount of retained earnings accumulated subsequent to a quasi-reorganization.

debit An entry on the left side of an account.

debt ratio A financial ratio used to measure the degree of leverage of a company. The debt ratio formula is total liabilities divided by total assets.

debt securities Financial instruments issued by a company that typically have the following characteristics: (1) a maturity value, (2) an interest rate (either fixed or variable) that specifies the periodic interest payments, and (3) a maturity date.

debt-to-equity ratio A ratio that measures the relationship between the debt and equity of an entity. The debt-to-equity formula is total debt divided by total stockholders' equity.

declining-balance depreciation Computation of periodic depreciation expense with a decreasing amount of depreciation recognized in each successive period, based on depreciation of a fixed percentage of a declining book value.

deductible temporary differences Differences between financial and taxable income that will result in deductible amounts in future years; expected benefits (tax savings) are reported on the balance sheet as deferred tax assets.

deferred gain A gain for which accounting recognition is delayed until a future period.

deferred income tax asset Expected future benefits from tax deductions that have been recognized as expenses in the income statement but not yet deducted for income tax purposes.

deferred income tax liability Expected future income taxes to be paid on income that has been recognized in the income statement but not yet taxed. Deferred income tax liabilities often arise from the temporary tax shielding provided by accelerated depreciation.

deferred pension cost A noncurrent asset resulting from recognition of an additional pension liability for underfunded pension plans. The balance in this account should not exceed the sum of any unrecognized transition loss plus prior service cost.

deficit A negative retained earnings balance caused by an excess of dividend payments and losses over net income.

defined benefit pension plans Pension plans that define the benefits that employees will receive at retirement. In these plans, it is necessary to determine what the contribution should be to meet the future benefit requirements. FASB Statement No. 87 deals primarily with this type of pension plan.

defined contribution pension plans Pension plans that specify the employer's contributions based on a formula that includes such factors as age, length of service, employer's profits, and compensation levels. FASB Statement No. 87 does not deal with these types of plans except for disclosure requirements. The pension expense is the amount funded each year.

demand deposits Funds deposited in a bank that can be withdrawn upon demand.

depletion Process of allocating the cost of mineral and other natural resource assets to periodic expense.

deposit in transit A deposit made near the end of the month and recorded on the depositor's books but is not received by the bank in time to be reflected on the bank statement.

deposit method An accounting method that recognizes the receipt of cash and the unearned revenue prior to the completion of a contract.

depreciation Process of allocating the cost of tangible long-term assets to periodic expense.

detachable warrants Stock warrants that can be traded separately from the security with which they were originally issued.

diluted earnings per share The amount of current earnings per share reflecting the maximum dilution that would have resulted from conversions, exercises, and other contingent issuances of stock that individually would have decreased earnings per share and in the aggregate would have had a dilutive effect.

dilution of earnings A reduction in earnings per share (or increase in loss per share) resulting from the assumption that convertible securities have been converted or that options and warrants have been exercised or other shares have been issued upon the fulfillment of certain conditions.

dilutive securities Securities whose assumed exercise or conversion results in a reduction in earnings per share (or increase in loss per share).

direct financing leases A lease in which the lessor is primarily engaged in financial activities and views the lease as an investment.

direct materials Materials used directly in the production of goods; the primary physical materials making up the final product.

direct method An approach to calculating and reporting cash flow from operating activities that itemizes the major operating cash receipt and cash payment categories.

direct write-off method A method of recognizing the actual losses from uncollectible accounts as expenses during the period in which the receivables are determined to be uncollectible; this method is not in accordance with GAAP.

disclosure Reporting the details of a transaction in the notes to the financial statements. Disclosure is sometimes used in place of recognition; that is, instead of including the results of a transaction in the financial statements themselves, it is disclosed in the notes.

discontinued operations The disposal of a major segment of a business either through sale or abandonment. The segment may be a product line, a division, or a subsidiary company. The assets and related activities of the segment must be clearly distinguishable from other activities of the company, both physically and operationally.

discovery The finding of valuable resources located on property that is already owned.

discussion memorandum A document issued by the FASB that identifies the principal issues involved with financial accounting and reporting topics. It includes a discussion of the various points of view as to the resolution of issues but does not reach a specific conclusion.

dissimilar assets Assets that differ in their physical nature or mode of use.

dividend payout ratio Dividends per share divided by earnings per share.

dividends in arrears Dividends on cumulative preferred stock that are passed or not paid. Dividends in arrears must be paid before any dividends can be paid to common stockholders.

dollar-value LIFO An adaptation of LIFO that measures inventory by total dollar amount rather than by individual units. LIFO incremental layers are determined based on total dollar changes.

dollar-value LIFO retail method A combination of dollar-value LIFO and the retail inventory method. Retail values are converted to base-year amounts by use of index numbers, LIFO incremental layers are determined based on incremental dollar changes, and retail values are converted to cost using a cost percentage.

donation The receipt of assets without being required to give goods or services in return.

double extension A method of determining the valuation of inventory using the dollar-value LIFO method by computing all inventory dollar values twice: once at a base-year cost and once at current-year cost.

double-declining-balance depreciation Computation of periodic depreciation expense with depreciation equal to double the straight-line rate multiplied by a declining book value.

double-entry accounting A system of recording transactions in a way that maintains the equality of the accounting equation: Assets = Liabilities + Owners' Equity.

DuPont framework Systematic approach to identifying general factors impacting return on equity; decomposes return on equity into profitability, efficiency, and leverage components.

E

early extinguishment of debt The retirement of debt prior to the maturity date of the obligation; any gain or loss arising from early extinguishment of debt must be classified as an extraordinary item on the income statement.

earnings per share (EPS) Income for the period reported on a per-share-of-common-stock basis. The presentation of earnings per share on the income statement is required by generally accepted accounting principles. Separate EPS amounts are required for income from continuing operations and for each irregular or extraordinary component of reported income.

economic entity A specific reporting unit, separate and distinct from its owners or other entities.

effective-interest method An amortization method that provides for recognition of an equal rate of amortization of bond premium or discount each period; uses a constant interest rate times a changing investment balance.

efforts-expended methods Methods for determining the percentage of completion for long-term construction contracts using an estimate of work or service performed. The estimates may be based on labor hours, labor dollars, or estimates of experts.

Emerging Issues Task Force (EITF) A task force of representatives from the accounting profession and industry created by the FASB to take timely action on emerging issues of financial reporting. The EITF identifies significant emerging issues and develops consensus positions when possible.

entry cost The acquisition cost of an asset.

equity The residual interest in the assets of an entity that remains after deducting its liabilities; sometimes referred to as net assets.

equity method The method of accounting for long-term investments in the stock of another company where significant influence exists (generally, 20%–50% ownership); the initial investment is recorded at cost but is increased by a proportionate share of investor's income and decreased by dividends and a proportionate share of losses to reflect the underlying claim by the investor on the net assets of the investee company.

equity method securities Equity securities purchased with the intent of being able to control or significantly influence the operations of the investee.

equity reserve A partition of total equity common in the financial statements of foreign companies. Each equity reserve has specific legal restrictions dictating whether it can be distributed to shareholders.

equity securities Equity securities represent ownership in a company. These shares of stock typically carry with them the right to collect dividends and to vote on corporate matters.

estimated liability A liability for an indefinite amount that must be estimated.

exchange rate risk Uncertainty about future U.S. dollar cash flows arising when assets and liabilities are denominated in a foreign currency.

executory contract An exchange of promises to engage in a transaction in the future.

executory costs Costs to maintain leased property such as repairs, insurance, and taxes.

exit value The value received for an asset when sold.

expected postretirement benefit obligation (EPBO) The actuarial present value, as of a certain date, of all future postretirement benefits to be paid to employees.

expected return on pension plan assets An amount calculated as a basis for determining the extent of delayed recognition of the effects of changes in the fair value of pension plan assets. The expected return on pension plan assets is determined based on the expected long-term rate of return on pension plan assets and the market-related value of pension plan assets.

expected service period Estimated number of years an employee will work before receiving pension benefits. Can be estimated as the average computed life based on the total expected future years of service divided by the number of employees. The expected future years of service may be computed by the formula $[N(N + 1) \div 2] \times D$, where N equals the number of years over which service is to be performed and D is the decrease in number of employees through retirement or termination of services per year.

expense recognition The process of determining the period in which expenses are to be recorded. Expense recognition is divided into three categories: (1) direct matching, (2) systematic and rational allocation, and (3) immediate recognition.

exposure draft A preliminary statement of a standard that includes specific recommendations made by the FASB. Reaction to the Exposure Draft is requested from the accounting and business communities, and the comments received are carefully considered before a final Statement of Financial Accounting Standards is issued.

external users Users of a company's financial statements who are outside the company.

extraordinary items Gains or losses resulting from events and transactions that are both unusual in nature and infrequent in occurrence or otherwise defined as an extraordinary item per accounting standards.

F

face value, par value, or maturity value The amount that will be paid on a bond at the maturity date.

fair value hedge Derivative that offsets the change in the fair value of an asset or liability.

fair value method Method of accounting for stock-based compensation in which the fair value of options granted is used to measure compensation expense.

fair value of pension plan assets The amount that could be received from the sale of plan assets in a current sale between a willing buyer and seller. Fair value is used to determine the minimum liability and the transition amount.

feedback value A key ingredient of relevant accounting information; helps to confirm or change a decision maker's beliefs based on whether the information matches what was expected.

financial accounting The activity associated with the development and communication of financial information for external users.

Financial Accounting Foundation (FAF) An organization responsible for selecting members of the FASB, GASB, and their advisory councils.

Financial Accounting Standards Board (FASB) Responsible for studying accounting issues and establishing accounting standards to govern financial reporting in the United States.

financial capital maintenance A concept under which income is defined as the excess of net assets at the end of an accounting period over the net assets at the beginning of the period, excluding effects of transactions with owners.

financial income Income reported on the financial statements as opposed to taxable income that is reported to taxing authorities in accordance with tax regulations.

financial ratios Mathematical relationships between financial statement amounts, used to quantify various characteristics of a company's performance such as efficiency and profitability.

Financial Reporting Release (FRR) SEC statement dealing with reporting and disclosure requirements in documents filed with the SEC.

financial statement analysis Examination of the relationships among financial statement numbers and the trends in those numbers over time.

financing activities One of three major categories included in a statement of cash flows; includes transactions and events whereby cash is obtained from or repaid to owners and creditors.

finished goods Manufactured products for which the manufacturing process is complete.

first-in, first-out (FIFO) method An inventory valuation method that assumes that the units sold are the first ones purchased or manufactured.

fixed stock option plan A plan in which terms, such as option exercise price and the number of options granted, are fixed on the date the options are granted.

floor The net realizable value less a normal profit; used as a lower limit in defining market when valuing inventory at the lower of cost or market.

FOB (free on board) destination Terms of sale under which title of goods passes to the purchaser at the point of destination.

FOB (free on board) shipping point Terms of sale under which title of goods passes to the purchaser at the point of shipment.

foreign currency transaction For a U.S. company, a transaction denominated in a currency other than the U.S. dollar.

foreign currency translation adjustment Equity item arising from the change in the equity of foreign subsidiaries resulting from changes in foreign currency exchange rates.

forward contract Agreement between two parties to exchange a specified amount of a commodity, security, or foreign currency at a specified date with the price being set now.

fractional share warrants Share warrants issued in conjunction with a stock dividend to shareholders who hold an irregular number of shares not entitling them to an exact number of stock dividend shares.

full disclosure principle A basic accounting concept that requires that all relevant information be presented in an unbiased, understandable, and timely manner.

full eligibility date The date at which an employee attains full eligibility for the benefits that employee is expected to earn under the terms of a postretirement benefit plan.

functional currency Currency in which most of a foreign subsidiary's transactions are denominated.

futures contract Contract, traded on an exchange, that allows a company to buy a specified quantity of a commodity or a financial security at a specified price on a specified future date.

G

gain Amount by which the proceeds from disposing of an asset exceed the book value of the asset.

general journal An accounting record used to record all business activities for which a special journal is not maintained.

general ledger A collection of all the accounts used by a business that could appear on the financial statements.

Generally Accepted Accounting Principles (GAAP) Accounting standards recognized by the accounting profession as required in the preparation of financial statements for external users. Currently, the FASB is the principal issuer of generally accepted accounting principles.

general-purpose financial statements A balance sheet, income statement, and statement of cash flows.

going concern An entity that is expected to continue in existence for the foreseeable future.

Governmental Accounting Standards Board (GASB) An independent private organization responsible for establishing standards in state and local governmental areas.

gross method A method of inventory accounting that records inventory cost before considering cash discounts.

gross profit Revenue from net sales minus cost of goods sold.

gross profit method An inventory estimation technique based on the relationship between gross profit and sales. The gross profit percentage is used to estimate cost of goods sold, which in turn, is used to estimate the value of the inventory not yet sold.

gross profit percentage on sales A measure of the profitability of sales in relation to the cost of the goods sold. The gross profit percentage formula is the gross profit for a financial period divided by revenue from net sales for the same period.

gross profit percentage Gross profit divided by sales; a measure of the profitability of sales in relation to the cost of the goods sold.

group depreciation Computation of depreciation on an entire group of similar assets as if the group were one asset.

guaranteed residual value A guarantee by lessee of a minimum value for the residual value of a leased asset. If the residual value is less than the guarantee, the lessee must pay the difference to the lessor.

H

half-year convention Assumption sometimes used in computing depreciation; one-half of a year's depreciation is recognized for assets acquired or disposed of during a year.

hedging Structuring of transactions to reduce risk.

held-to-maturity securities Debt securities purchased by a company with both the intent and ability to hold the securities to maturity.

historical cost The cash equivalent price of goods or services at the date of acquisition.

I

if-converted method A method used to adjust the earnings per share computation to consider the impact of the possible conversion of convertible securities. Under this method, the earnings per share computation is made as if the convertible securities were converted at the beginning of the year or the date the convertible security was issued, whichever is later.

impairment Reduction in the expected cash flow to be generated by a long-term asset sufficient to warrant reducing the recorded value of the asset.

implicit (effective) interest The actual interest rate earned or paid on a note, bond, or similar instrument.

implicit interest rate The interest rate that would discount the minimum lease payments to the fair market value of the leased asset at the lease signing date.

imprest petty cash system A petty cash fund in which all expenditures are documented by vouchers or vendor receipts or invoices.

imputed interest rate A rate of interest assigned to a note when there is no current market price for either the property, goods or services, or the note. The assigned rate of interest is used to discount future receipts or payments to the present in computing the present value of the note.

income A measure of a company's "well-offness." It is often defined as the amount that an entity could return to its investors and still be as well-off at the end of the period as it was at the beginning.

income from continuing operations A measure of the profitability of a firm's operations. The number is obtained by subtracting expenses and losses from revenues and gains. Income from continuing operations is always disclosed after taxes have been subtracted.

income statement A statement that reports a company's net income for a certain period.

incremental borrowing rate The interest rate at which the lessee could borrow the amount of money necessary to purchase the leased asset, taking into consideration the lessee's financial situation and the current conditions in the marketplace.

indicated gain The excess of the market value over the book value of the asset given up in an exchange of assets.

indicated loss The excess of the book value over the market value of the asset given up in an exchange of assets.

indirect materials Materials that are necessary to facilitate the production process but are not directly incorporated in the final product.

indirect method An approach to calculating and reporting cash flow from operating activities that reconciles net income with operating cash flow; net income is adjusted for noncash revenues and expenses, for any gains or losses associated with investing financing activities, and for changes in current operating assets and liabilities that indicate noncash sources of revenues and expenses.

initial direct costs Costs such as commissions, legal fees, and preparation of documents that are incurred by the lessor in negotiating and completing a lease transaction.

initial markup The difference between the initial retail price of merchandise and the original historical cost.

input measures Measures of the earnings process in percentage-of-completion accounting based on cost or efforts devoted to a contract.

installment sales method A revenue recognition method that recognizes revenue and related expenses as cash is received.

in-substance defeasance A process involving the transfer of assets (generally cash and securities) to a trust and the use of the assets and earnings there-from to satisfy long-term obligations as they come due; a gain or loss is recognized as an extraordinary item and the debt is removed from the balance sheet at the time of transfer.

intangible assets Legal or economic rights controlled by a company that are expected to generate future economic benefits.

integral part of annual period concept Concept guiding the preparation of interim statements; accounting practices may be slightly modified to make sure the interim results relate properly to the annual results.

interest rate risk Uncertainty about future interest rates and their impact on future cash flows as well as on the fair value of existing assets and liabilities.

interest rate swap Contract in which two parties agree to exchange future interest payments on a given loan amount; usually, one set of interest payments is fixed and the other is variable.

interest-bearing note A note written in a form in which the maker promises to pay the face amount plus interest at a specified rate; in this form, the face amount is usually equal to the present value upon issuance of the note.

interim financial statements Statements showing financial position and operating results for an interval of less than a year.

Internal Revenue Service (IRS) U.S. government agency responsible for administering U.S. income tax rules.

internal users Parties within a company who use accounting information to make operating decisions.

International Accounting Standards Committee (IASC) International group, based in London, representing accounting bodies in over 100 countries formed to develop accounting standards that can serve as the basis for harmonizing conflicting national standards.

interperiod tax allocation An accounting method that recognizes the tax effect of temporary differences between financial and taxable income in the financial statements rather than reporting as tax expense the actual tax liability in each year. The allocation may be made either by the (1) deferred method or (2) the asset and liability method. The latter method is currently required by GAAP.

intraperiod income tax allocation A method of income statement presentation of irregular or extraordinary items in which the tax effect of each of these special items is reported with the individual item rather than in the income tax expense related to current operations.

intraperiod tax allocation A method of income statement presentation of irregular or extraordinary items in which the tax effect of each of these special items is reported with the individual item rather than in the income tax expense related to current operations.

intrinsic value method Method of accounting for stock-based compensation in which the difference between the exercise price and the market price per share at the grant date is used to measure compensation expense.

inventory Assets held for sale in the normal course of business; also, assets held to be used as materials in a production process.

inventory turnover Measured by dividing cost of goods sold by average inventory; used to evaluate whether the level of inventory is appropriate, given the volume of business.

investing activities One of three major categories included in a statement of cash flows; primarily includes purchases and sales of noncurrent assets like land, buildings, and nontrading financial instruments.

investors Owners and potential owners of a company.

J

joint venture A separate economic entity created when companies join forces with other companies to share the costs and benefits associated with a specifically defined project.

journals Accounting records in which transactions are first entered, providing a chronological record of business activity.

journal entry A recording of a transaction where debits equal credits; it usually includes a date and an explanation of the transaction.

junk bonds High-risk, high-yield bonds issued by companies in a weak financial condition.

L

large stock dividend A stock dividend of 25% or more of the shares outstanding.

last-in, first-out (LIFO) method An inventory valuation method that assumes that the units sold are the most recent ones purchased or manufactured.

lease A contract specifying the terms under which the owner of the property, the lessor, transfers the right to use the property to a lessee.

lease term The noncancelable period of a lease designated in the lease contract plus the period of any bargain renewal periods over which the lease is likely to be renewed.

ledger A collection of accounts maintained by a business.

lessee The party using property that is owned by another party (lessor).

lessor The owner of leased property who transfers the right to use the property to a second party (lessee).

leverage The degree to which a company uses borrowed funds instead of invested funds. By adding borrowed funds to their own capital, owners are said to "leverage" their investment.

leveraged buy-out (LBO) An acquisition of a company where a substantial amount of the purchase price, often 90 percent or more, is debt-financed.

liabilities The claims of creditors against an entity's resources: technically defined by the FASB as "probable future sacrifices of economic benefits arising from present obligations of a particular entity to transfer assets or provide services to other entities in the future as a result of past transactions or events."

liability The claim of creditors against an entity's resources.

LIFO conformity rule A federal tax regulation that requires the use of LIFO for financial reporting purposes if LIFO is used for income tax purposes.

LIFO inventory pool A group of inventory items having common characteristics and assumed to be the same when applying LIFO.

LIFO layer An incremental group of LIFO inventory items created in any year in which the quantity of units purchased or produced exceeds the quantity sold.

LIFO liquidation Reduction or elimination of old LIFO layers because total purchases or production in the current period is less than sales.

LIFO reserve The difference between LIFO ending inventory and the amount obtained using another method such as FIFO or average cost.

line of credit A negotiated arrangement with a lender in which the terms are agreed to prior to the need for actual borrowing.

liquidating dividend A distribution to stockholders representing a return of a portion of their contributed capital.

liquidity The ability of a company to pay its short-term obligations.

loan (mortgage) amortization The process by which payments on a loan are allocated between principal and interest components.

loan covenant Provision of a loan contract restricting the actions of the borrower or allowing for some monitoring of the borrower's actions.

long-term debt Obligations that are not expected to be paid in cash or other current assets within one year or the normal operating cycle.

loss Amount by which the proceeds from disposing of an asset are less than the book value of the asset.

lower of cost or market (LCM) Generally accepted method for valuation of inventories in which assets are recorded at the lower of their cost or market value; this method can be applied to inventories on an aggregate or individual item basis.

M

management accounting The activity associated with financial reporting for internal users.

manufacturing overhead All manufacturing costs other than direct materials and direct labor.

margin Profitability of each dollar in sales; another term for return on sales.

markdown Decrease that reduces sales price below original retail price.

market (in "lower of cost or market") The replacement cost adjusted for an upper and lower limit that reflects the estimated net realizable value.

market adjustment A valuation account used to record trading and available-for-sale securities at their fair market values on the balance sheet.

market, yield, or effective interest rate The actual rate of interest earned or paid on a bond.

market-related value of pension plan assets Value of pension plan assets used in computing the expected return. Either of the following can be used as the market-related value: (1) the fair market value of pension plan assets as of the beginning of the year or (2) a weighted average value based on the market value of plan assets over a preceding period not exceeding five years.

markup Increase that raises sales price above original retail price.

matching A basic accounting concept that is applied to determine when expenses are recognized (recorded). Under this principle, expenses for a period are determined by associating or "matching" them with specific revenues over a particular time period.

materiality An important constraint underlying the reporting of accounting information; it relates to how large an item is in terms of dollar amount. Accounting standards do not need to be applied to items that are considered to be immaterial.

minimum lease payments The lease payments required over the lease term plus any amount to be paid for the residual value either through a bargain purchase option or a guarantee of residual value.

minimum pension liability The net amount of pension liability that must be reported when a plan is underfunded. The minimum liability is measured as the difference between the accumulated benefit obligation and the fair value of the pension plan assets.

minimum pension liability adjustment Negative equity item resulting from the adjustment to pension liability to ensure that at least a minimum pension liability is reported.

modified accelerated cost recovery system (MACRS) Modification of the ACRS tax depreciation method that is based on declining-balance depreciation, fixed cost recovery periods, and no residual values.

monetary items Assets, liabilities, and equities whose values and settlement amounts are fixed in terms of numbers of dollars.

mortgage A loan backed by an asset with the asset title pledged to the lender.

multiple-step form A format of the income statement that lists operating revenues and expenses first, resulting in operating income. From this figure, gains and losses are then added or subtracted to arrive at income from continuing operations. Irregular and extraordinary items are then added or subtracted to arrive at net income.

municipal debt Debt securities issued by state, county, and local governments and their agencies.

N

natural resources Products of the earth, such as oil, gold, and timber. Also called wasting assets.

negotiable notes Notes that are legally transferable by endorsement and delivery.

net lease investment The carrying value of a lease on the lessor's books; equals the difference between total lease payments receivable (gross investment) and unearned interest revenue.

net method A method of inventory accounting that records inventory net of any cash discounts.

net monetary position Difference between a company's monetary assets and its monetary liabilities.

net operating loss (NOL) carryback The amount of operating loss that can be carried back and offset against the income of earlier profitable years to obtain a refund of previously paid income taxes.

net operating loss (NOL) carryforward The amount of operating loss that can be carried forward and offset against income of future profitable years to reduce the tax liability for those years.

net periodic pension expense The amount recognized in an employer's financial statements as an expense of a pension plan for a period. Components of net periodic pension expense are service cost, interest cost, actual return on plan assets, pension gain or loss, amortization of unrecognized prior service cost, and amortization of unrecognized transition gain or loss.

net realizable value The amount of cash expected to be received from the conversion of assets in the normal course of business; net realizable value equals selling price less normal selling costs for inventory and equals gross receivables less the allowance for bad debts for accounts receivable.

neutrality A key ingredient of reliable accounting information requiring that information be presented in an unbiased manner; neutrality relates to the concept of fairness to users.

nominal accounts Accounts that are closed to a zero balance at the end of an accounting period.

nominal dollar A dollar that has not been adjusted for the impact of inflation.

noncancelable A lease contract that can be canceled only under very unlikely circumstances or with extremely expensive penalties to the lessee.

noncash investing and financing activities Investing and financing transactions that affect a company's financial position but not the cash flows during the period; an example would be the purchase of land by issuing stock.

noncontributory pension plans Plans in which the employer bears the total cost of the plan.

noncumulative preferred stock Preferred stock that has no claim on any prior year dividends that may have been "passed."

noncurrent operating assets Assets used in the normal course of business that are expected to have a useful life exceeding one year, or one operating cycle, whichever is longer.

nondetachable warrants Stock warrants that cannot be traded separately from the security with which they were originally issued.

non-interest-bearing note A note written in a form in which the face amount includes an interest charge; in this form, the difference between the face amount and the present value of the note is the implicit or effective interest.

nonreciprocal transfer to owners Transfer of cash or property to shareholders in which nothing is received by the company in return.

nontrade notes payable A note issued to nontrade creditors for purposes other than to purchase goods or services.

nontrade receivables Any receivables arising from transactions that are not directly associated with the normal operating activities of a business.

notes payable A formal written promise to pay a sum of money in the future. Notes payable are generally evidenced by a promissory note.

notes receivable Receivables that are evidenced by a formal written promise to pay a certain sum of money at a specified date.

notes to the financial statements Supplemental information that outlines the accounting assumptions and estimates.

notional amount Total face amount of the asset or liability that underlies a derivative contract.

not-sufficient-funds (NSF) check A check that is not honored by a bank because of insufficient cash in the maker's account.

number of days' sales in inventory Measured by dividing average inventory by average daily cost of goods sold; used to evaluate whether the level of inventory is appropriate, given the volume of business.

O

objective acceleration clause A clause in a debt agreement that identifies specific conditions that will cause the debt to be callable immediately.

off-balance-sheet financing Procedures used by companies to avoid disclosing all their debt on the balance sheet in order to make their financial position look stronger.

operating activities One of three major categories included in a statement of cash flows; includes transactions and events that normally enter into the determination of net income, including interest and taxes.

operating income A measure of the performance of a company's business operations. The formula is revenues minus cost of goods sold and operating expenses. Also called earnings before interest and taxes.

operating lease A lease that is economically equivalent to the rental of the leased asset.

option Contract giving the owner the right, but not the obligation, to buy or sell an asset at a specified price any time during a specified period.

original retail The initial sales price, including the original increase over cost referred to as the initial markup.

output measures Measures of the earnings process in percentage-of-completion accounting based on units produced, contract milestones reached, or values added.

outstanding checks Checks written near the end of the month that have reduced the depositor's cash balance but have not yet cleared the bank as of the bank statement date.

P

paid-in capital The portion of corporate capital that represents investments by the stockholders. Also referred to as contributed capital.

par (or stated) value method Method of accounting for treasury stock purchases in which the repurchased shares are accounted for as if they were being retired.

par value A nominal value that is assigned to stock by the terms of a corporation's charter.

parent company A company that exercises control over another company, known as a subsidiary, through majority ownership (more than 50%) of the subsidiary's voting stock.

participating preferred stock Preferred stock that provides for additional dividends to be paid to preferred stockholders after dividends of a specified amount are paid to common stockholders.

partnership A business entity owned by two or more people.

pension gain or loss A component of net periodic pension expense that is the sum of (a) the difference between the actual return on plan assets and the expected return on plan assets and (b) the amortization of the unrecognized net gain or loss arising in a prior period from a change in the value of either the projected benefit obligation or the plan assets because of an experience different from that assumed or from a change in an actuarial assumption.

pension plan An agreement, usually written, that provides for benefits to employees upon retirement from active employment. The plan usually includes provisions as to how the benefits are to be funded, who receives benefits, the amount of benefits to be paid, and restrictions on investments of pension plan assets.

pension plan assets Assets arising from contributions to the pension plan. Generally comprised of cash and investments that have been segregated and designated for use of the pension plan only.

percentage-of-completion accounting An accounting method for long-term construction contracts that recognizes revenue and related expenses prior to delivery of the goods. Recognition is based on either an input or output measure of the earning process.

performance-based stock option plan A plan with terms (option exercise price, number of options, etc.) that depend on how well the individual or company performs after the options are granted.

period cost Cost that is recognized as an expense during the period in which it is incurred; not included as part of inventory cost.

periodic inventory system A method of accounting for inventory in which cost of goods sold is determined and inventory is adjusted to the proper balance at the end of the accounting period. Purchases are recorded in the purchases account, and ending inventory is determined by a physical count.

permanent differences Nondeductible expenses or nontaxable revenues that are recognized for financial reporting purposes but that are never part of taxable income.

perpetual inventory system A method of accounting for inventory in which detailed records of each inventory purchase and sale are maintained. This system provides a current record of inventory on hand and cost of goods sold to date.

perpetual inventory system Inventory system in which detailed records of each inventory purchase and sale are maintained. Purchases are recorded in the inventory account.

petty cash fund A small amount of cash kept on hand for the purpose of making miscellaneous payments.

physical capital maintenance A concept under which income is defined as the excess of physical productive capacity at the end of an accounting period over the physical productive capacity at the beginning of the period, excluding the effects of transactions with owners.

pooling-of-interests method A method of accounting for a business combination whereby all the asset, liability, and owners' equity values are combined at their book values; no goodwill is recognized.

post-balance sheet event Event occurring between the balance sheet date and the date financial statements are issued and made available to external users. Also called a subsequent event.

post-closing trial balance A list of all real accounts and their balances after the closing process has been completed.

posting The process of summarizing transactions by transferring amounts from the journals to the ledger accounts.

postretirement benefits other than pensions Benefits other than pensions provided by an employer to former employees. Includes health insurance, life insurance, and disability payments. Current standards require these benefits to be accrued in a manner similar to pension costs.

predictive value Helps a decision maker predict future consequences based on information about past transactions and events.

preferred stock A class of stock that usually confers dividend and liquidation rights that take precedence over those of common stock; preferred stockholders usually aren't allowed to vote in the selection of the board of directors.

prepaid/accrued pension cost The difference between annual pension contributions and annual pension costs. If contributions exceed costs, the balance is reported as an asset on a company's balance sheet. If costs exceed contributions, the difference is reported as a liability.

present (or discounted) value The amount of net future cash inflows or outflows discounted to their present value at an appropriate rate of interest.

price-earnings (P/E) ratio A measure of the relationship between the market price of a company's stock and its profitability. The formula is the market price per share of common stock divided by the earnings per share of common stock.

price index Overall measure of how much prices have increased over a period of time. Prices are expressed as some percentage of the prices prevailing during a base period.

price risk Uncertainty about the future price of an asset.

primary earnings per share The amount of earnings attributable to each share of common stock outstanding, including common stock equivalents.

principal (face amount) The amount, excluding interest, that the maker of a note or the issuer of a bond agrees to pay at the maturity date; this amount is printed on the note or bond contract.

prior-period adjustment An adjustment made directly to the retained earnings account to correct errors made in prior accounting periods.

prior service cost The present value of the increased benefits granted by a pension plan's amendment (or initial adoption of a plan). Recognized as a component of net periodic pension expense through amortization over the future service life of the covered employees.

pro forma cash flow statement A forecast or projection of the amounts that will be in the cash flow statement in a future period.

product (inventoriable) cost Costs included in the total cost of manufactured inventory.

productive-output depreciation Computation of periodic depreciation expense based on how many units of output were produced during the period relative to estimated total lifetime output units.

projected benefit obligation (PBO) The actuarial present value of pension benefits using the benefits/years of service approach that requires assumptions about future compensation levels, such as increases over time by interest, amendments to plan, additional service years, and changes in actuarial assumptions.

promissory note A formal written promise to pay a certain amount of money at a specified future date.

property dividend A dividend paid in the form of some asset other than cash.

proportional performance method An accounting method for recording service revenue and related expenses prior to completion of a service contract.

proprietorship A business entity owned by one person.

purchase commitment An advance commitment to purchase inventory in the future at a set price.

purchase method A method of accounting for a business combination whereby the asset and liability values of the purchased company are recorded at their market values; goodwill is recognized.

put option Contract giving the owner the right, but not the obligation, to sell an asset at a specified price.

Q

quasi-reorganization A procedure by which a company eliminates a deficit in Retained Earnings by restating its invested capital balance.

quick ratio A financial ratio used as a measure of short-term liquidity. Also called acid-test ratio.

R

raw materials Inventory acquired by a manufacturer for use in the production process.

real accounts Accounts that are not closed to a zero balance at the end of each accounting period.

realized holding gains and losses Differences between the current costs and the historical costs of assets sold or used during a period.

recognition The process of formally recording an item in the accounting records and eventually reporting it in the financial statements; includes both the initial recording of an item and any subsequent changes related to that item.

redeemable preferred stock Preferred stock that may be redeemed at the option of the holder, or at a fixed price on a specific date, or upon other conditions not solely within the control of the issuer.

registered bonds Bonds for which the bondholders' names and addresses are kept on file by the issuing company.

relevance One of two primary qualities inherent in useful accounting information; essentially, information is relevant if it will affect a decision. The key ingredients of relevance are feedback value, predictive value, and timeliness.

reliability One of two primary qualities inherent in useful accounting information; to be reliable, information must contain the key ingredients of verifiability, neutrality, and representational faithfulness.

remeasurement Method of converting a foreign subsidiary's financial statements into U.S. dollars; used when most of the subsidiary's transactions are denominated in U.S. dollars.

replacement cost The cost that would be required to replace an existing asset.

representational faithfulness A key ingredient of reliable accounting information requiring that the amounts and descriptions reported in the financial statements reflect the actual results of economic transactions and events.

residual (salvage) value Estimate of the amount for which an asset can be sold when it is retired.

restructuring charge An estimate of the costs expected to be incurred as a result of a plan to significantly modify a company's operations.

retail inventory method A procedure that converts the retail value of inventory to an estimation of cost by using a cost percentage that reflects the relationship of inventory available for sale valued at retail and cost.

retained earnings The portion of owners' equity that represents the net accumulated earnings of a corporation; generally, equal to total owners' equity less contributed capital.

return on assets A financial ratio used to measure the degree to which assets have been used to generate profits. The return on assets formula is net income divided by total assets.

return on equity A financial ratio used to measure the degree to which funds invested by owners have been used to generate profits. The return on equity formula is net income divided by total equity.

return on sales A measure of the profitability of a company that relates net income to the sales of the company. The formula is net income divided by net sales.

revenue recognition A basic accounting concept that is applied to determine when revenue should be recognized (recorded). Generally, under this principle, revenues are recognized when two criteria are met: The earnings process is substantially complete, and the revenues are realized, or realizable.

revenues Inflows or other enhancements of assets of an entity or settlements of its liabilities (or a combination of both) from delivering or producing goods, rendering services, or other activities that constitute the entity's ongoing major or central operations.

S

sale-leaseback An arrangement in which one party sells an asset and then immediately leases back and uses the same asset. The seller becomes the seller-lessee and the purchaser is the purchaser-lessor.

sales-type leases A lease in which the lessor is a manufacturer or dealer utilizing the lease to facilitate the sale of goods.

secured bonds Bonds for which assets are pledged to guarantee repayment.

secured loan A loan backed by certain assets as collateral.

Securities and Exchange Commission (SEC) A U.S. government agency created to regulate the issuance and trading of securities in the United States. As part of this function, the SEC is vitally interested in financial accounting and reporting standards. While the SEC has the legal authority to establish accounting standards, it has historically relied heavily on the private sector to perform this function.

serial bonds Bonds that mature in a series of installments at future dates.

service cost A component of net periodic pension expense representing the actuarial present value of benefits accruing to employees for services rendered during that period.

service-hours depreciation Computation of periodic depreciation expense based on how many hours of service were used during the period relative to estimated total lifetime service hours.

settlement interest rate The interest rate used to compute the interest component of net periodic pension expense and the interest rate used to discount projected and accumulated benefit obligations to their present values. It is the rate at which pension plan obligations could be effectively settled; that is, the rate implicit in the current prices of annuity contracts that could be purchased to settle the benefits owed to employees.

settlement of a pension plan An irrevocable action taken by an employer that relieves the employer of primary responsibility for all or part of the pension obligation. Examples include purchasing from an insurance company an annuity that would cover employees' vested benefits or a lump sum payment to employees in exchange for their rights to receive specified pension benefits.

shrinkage The amount of inventory that is lost, stolen, or spoiled.

significant influence The ability of an investor to impact the operating, investing, and financing decisions of an investee but not absolutely determine those decisions.

similar assets Assets that are the same in their physical nature and mode of use.

simple capital structure A corporate structure that includes only common and nonconvertible preferred stock and has no convertible securities, stock options, warrants, or other rights outstanding.

single-employer pension plans Pension plans established for a single employer. FASB Statement No. 87 primarily refers to this type of plan.

single-step form A format of the income statement that combines revenues and gains and subtracts from them expenses and losses, resulting in income from continuing operations. Irregular and extraordinary items are then added or subtracted to arrive at net income.

sinking fund Assets that have been accumulated in order to repay a loan.

small stock dividend A stock dividend of less than 25% of the shares outstanding.

special journal An accounting record used to record a particular type of frequently recurring transaction.

specific identification method Inventory valuation method that assigns the actual cost of inventory items sold to cost of goods sold.

spot rate The exchange rate at which currencies can be traded immediately.

stable monetary units An accounting assumption that the measuring unit maintains constant purchasing power; based on this assumption, U.S. financial statements have traditionally reported items in nominal dollars without adjustment for changes in purchasing power.

Staff Accounting Bulletin (SAB) Accounting interpretations made by the staff of the SEC. SABs do not necessarily represent official positions of the SEC.

stakeholders All parties interested in the performance of a company.

stated (contract) rate The rate of interest printed on the bond.

stated value A nominal value that may be assigned to no-par stock by the board of directors of a corporation; similar in concept to par value.

statement of cash flows One of the three primary financial statements. The cash flow statement provides information about the cash receipts (inflows) and cash payments (outflows) of a company during a period of time. The statement is separated into cash flows from operating, investing, and financing activities.

statement of changes in owners' equity A report that shows the total changes in all owners' equity accounts during a period of time; provides a reconciliation of the beginning and ending owners' equity amounts.

statement of changes in stockholders' equity A report that summarizes the reasons for the changes in all equity accounts during a period of time.

Statements of Financial Accounting Concepts A set of guidelines established by the FASB to provide a conceptual framework for establishing and administering accounting standards.

Statements of Financial Accounting Standards The official statements of the FASB that govern external financial reporting.

stock appreciation rights (SARs) The right for the holder, typically an employee, to receive an amount equal to the excess of the market value of the issuing company's common stock above a specified price.

stock options Rights granted to officers or employees as part of a compensation plan; the options allow for the purchase of shares at a specified exercise price.

stock rights Rights issued to existing shareholders to buy shares of stock in order to maintain their proportionate ownership interests.

stock split A reduction in the par or stated value of stock accompanied by a proportionate increase in the number of shares outstanding.

stock warrants Rights to purchase shares of stock; warrants are generally issued in conjunction with the issuance of another security.

stockholders' (shareholders') equity Total owners' equity of a corporation.

straight-line depreciation Computation of periodic depreciation expense with an equal amount of depreciation recognized in each year.

straight-line method An amortization method that provides for recognition of an equal amount of bond premium or discount amortization each period.

subjective acceleration clause A clause in a debt agreement that identifies general conditions that can cause the debt to be callable immediately, but violation of the conditions cannot be determined objectively.

subscription A contract between the purchaser of stock and the issuer in which the purchaser promises to buy shares of the issuing company's stock.

subsequent event Event occurring between the balance sheet date and the date financial statements are issued and made available to external users. Also called a post-balance sheet event.

subsidiary company A company that is owned or controlled by another company, known as the parent company.

subsidiary ledgers A grouping of supporting accounts that in total equal the balance of a control account in the general ledger.

substantial performance A criterion for recognizing revenue from a franchising agreement that requires that all provisions of the contract agreement be substantially complete before revenue and related expenses may be recognized.

sum-of-the-years'-digits depreciation Computation of periodic depreciation expense with a decreasing amount of depreciation recognized in each successive period, based on a fraction derived from the sum of the digits from one to the asset's original useful life.

swap Contract in which two parties agree to exchange payments in the future based on the movement of some agreed-upon price or rate.

T

taxable income Income as defined by income tax regulations as the basis for determining the income tax liability for a given entity.

taxable temporary differences Differences between financial and taxable income that result in future taxable amounts; income taxes expected to be paid on future taxable amounts are reported in the balance sheet as a deferred tax liability.

temporary differences Differences between pretax financial income and taxable income arising from business events that are recognized for both financial and tax purposes, but in different time periods. For example, it is common for a temporary difference to result from depreciation expense on equipment.

term bonds Bonds that mature in one lump sum at a specified future date.

time deposits Funds deposited in a bank that legally require prior notification before they can be withdrawn.

time-factor depreciation Computation of periodic depreciation expense based on the passage of time.

timeliness Quality of information that is provided on a timely basis.

times interest earned An indicator of a company's ability to meet interest payments; calculated as income before income taxes plus interest expense divided by interest expense for the period.

trade discount A reduction in the "list" sales price of an item to the "net" sales price actually charged the customer; trade discounts are generally dependent on the volume of business or size of order from the customer.

trade notes payable A note issued to trade creditors for the purchase of goods or services.

trade receivables Receivables associated with the normal operating activities of a business, e.g., credit sales of goods or services to customers.

trading securities Debt and equity securities that are purchased with the intent of selling them in the near future to generate profits from short-term changes in market prices.

transaction approach A method of determining income by defining the financial statement effects of certain events classified as revenues, gains, expenses, and losses. Also known as the matching method, this is the traditional accounting approach to measuring and defining income.

transactions Exchanges of goods or services between two or more entities or some other event having an economic impact on a business enterprise.

transition gain or loss The difference between the projected benefit obligation and the fair value of pension fund assets existing at the time FASB Statement No. 87 is adopted, adjusted by any accrued pension cost or prepaid pension cost at the time of transition. This gain or loss is amortized over the average remaining service life of employees. If average service life is less than 15 years, the employer may use 15 years for amortization purposes.

translation Method of converting a foreign subsidiary's financial statements into U.S. dollars; used when most of the subsidiary's transactions are denominated in the local (foreign) currency.

translation adjustment Balancing figure to equate a foreign subsidiary's U.S. dollar debits and credits; can be thought of as an unrealized gain or loss from the impact of exchange rate changes on the U.S. dollar value of a foreign subsidiary's equity.

treasury stock Stock issued but subsequently bought back by the same company and held for possible future reissuance or retirement.

treasury stock method A method of recognizing the use of proceeds that would be obtained upon exercise of options and warrants in computing earnings per share. It assumes that any proceeds would be used to purchase common stock at current market prices.

trial balance A list of all accounts and their balances.

troubled debt restructuring A situation involving a concession by creditors to allow debtors to eliminate or significantly modify debt obligations due to the debtor's financial difficulties.

trust indenture A legal agreement specifying how a bond fund should be administered by its trustees.

turnover Degree to which assets are used to generate sales.

U

unguaranteed residual value A residual value of leased property that reverts to the lessor at the end of the lease term. Because there is no guarantee of the residual value, market factors and asset condition determine the value of the leased asset at the end of the lease.

unit depreciation Computation of depreciation on an individual asset as a separate unit.

unrealized holding gains and losses Increases or decreases in the current values of assets held during a period but not sold or used.

unrecognized net pension gain or loss The cumulative net pension gain or loss that has not been recognized as a part of net periodic pension expense.

unsecured (debenture) bonds Bonds for which no specific collateral has been pledged.

use-factor depreciation Computation of periodic depreciation expense based on how much the asset is used during the period.

useful life Length of time over which a long-term asset is forecasted to provide economic benefits.

V

valuation allowance A contra asset account that reduces an asset to its expected realizable value. This type of account is used, for example, in valuing accounts receivable and deferred tax assets.

verifiability A key ingredient of reliable accounting information; reported information should be based on objectively determined facts that can be verified by other accountants using the same measurement methods.

vested benefits The amount of pension benefits an employee will retain if employment with the employer is terminated.

voucher system A system that provides for the control of purchases and cash disbursements. Business documents are used to prepare vouchers in support of all payments by check. The voucher identifies the person authorizing the expenditure, explains the nature of the transaction, and names the affected accounts. Checks are written in payment for each individual voucher.

W

warranties Obligations of a company to provide free service on units failing to perform satisfactorily or to replace defective goods.

work in process Inventory of a manufacturer that is partly processed and requires further work before it can be sold.

work sheet A columnar schedule used to summarize accounting data; often used to facilitate the preparation of adjusting entries and financial statements.

working capital Current assets less current liabilities; a measure of liquidity.

Z

zero-interest (deep-discount) bonds Bonds that do not bear interest but instead are sold at significant discounts, providing the investor with a total interest payoff at maturity.

Appendix E

Check Figures

Chapter 1

E1-16	5. False
E1-17	2. e, k, n
E1-19	4. a, d, g, 1

Chapter 2

E2-7	Dividends = $33,750 (Debit)
E2-8	1. (d) Prepaid Rent = $1,800 (Debit)
E2-9	(c) Receivable from Insurance Company = $6,500 (Debit)
E2-10	1. Insurance Expense = $1,700 (Debit)
E2-11	1. Sales Commissions Payable = $5,900 (Credit)
E2-12	f. Other Assets = $15,000 (Debit)
E2-14	b. Purchases = $120,000 (Credit)
E2-15	b. Adjustment = $3,900
E2-16	2. Interest Revenue = $2,400 - $650 + $1,800 = $3,550
E2-17	1. (q) Retained Earnings; Balance Carried Forward
E2-18	c. Dividends = $32,500 (Credit)
E2-19	Total Credit = $136,000
E2-20	Net Income Increase for 2001 = $4,000
E2-22	Total Credits to Accounts Payable = $23,390
E2-23	Total Debits to Payroll = $10,000
E2-24	Total Debits to Cash = $22,874
P2-25	1. May 18 Accounts Receivable = $21,000 (Debit)
P2-27	1. (e) Sales Revenue = $6,800 (Debit)
P2-28	c. Mar. 1 Cash = $5,400 (Debit)
P2-29	c. Discount on Notes Payable = $1,100 (Debit)
P2-30	1. (d) Utilities Expense = $2,700 (Debit)
P2-31	2. (d) Selling Expenses = $3,840 (Debit)
P2-32	1. (a) No adjustment needed
P2-34	2. (b) Doubtful Accounts Expense = $1,850 (Debit)
P2-35	e. Purchases = $5,000 (Debit)
P2-36	Total Debits to Cash = $7,338
P2-37	Total Credits to Cash = $44,847

Chapter 3

E3-11	7. (f) or (h)
E3-16	Working Capital = $142,000
E3-17	Total Current Assets = $84,300
E3-18	i. $47,066
E3-19	1. (a) Inventory = $56,900
E3-20	ROE = 14.29%
E3-21	Inventory Industry Asset Mix = 18.0%
E3-23	b. Note Disclosure
P3-25	1. Total Current Liabilities = $88,000
P3-26	Total Liabilities = $230,930
P3-27	Total Assets = $956,000
P3-28	Bonds Payable = $200,000
P3-29	Total Liabilities and Owners' Equity = $1,227,100
P3-30	Total Liabilities = $344,500
P3-31	Total Corrections Debits = $1,980,700
P3-32	Retained Earnings = $179,650
P3-33	Total Liabilities = $49,830
P3-34	Total Current Liabilities = $113,500

Chapter 4

E4-12	Net Income = $142,500
E4-18	Selling Expenses = $208,000
E4-19	Income from Continuing Operations = $136,500
E4-22	Earnings per Common Share: Net Income = $3.15 (in millions of dollars)
E4-25	Income Taxes = $30,596
E4-26	1. Corrected Net Income = $2,740
E4-27	Comprehensive Income = $15,763
E4-28	Forecasted Net Income 2003 = $52
E4-29	Forecasted Total Liabilities and Stockholders' Equities 2003 = $1,190
P4-30	Net Income = $438,200
P4-31	1. Income Statement—Time of Sale: 2003 Gross Profit = $66,000
P4-32	2. Net Income = $21,350
P4-33	Retained Earnings, July 31, 2002 = $3,380,000
P4-34	Net Income = $121,000
P4-36	1. (b) Net Profit Percentage on Sales for 2000 = 12.9%
P4-37	Net Income = $823,075
P4-38	Net Income = $26,600
P4-39	Net Income = $12,506
P4-40	Net Income = $87,874
P4-41	Net Income = $70,600

Chapter 5

E5-10	j. Investing Activity
E5-13	Net Cash Provided by Operating Activities = $20,160
E5-14	Net Cash Provided by Operating Activities = $101,150
E5-15	Cash Balance at End of Year = $139,500
E5-16	Net Cash Provided by Operating Activities = $36,150
E5-17	Cash from Operating Activities = $1,150,000
E5-18	Net Cash Provided by Operating Activities = $160,600
E5-19	Net Cash Provided by Operating Activities = $160,600
E5-20	1. Cash collected in 2002 = $3,503,000
E5-21	Net Increase in Cash and Cash Equivalents = $47,100
E5-22	Cash & Cash Equivalents at End of Year = $518,500
E5-23	Cash & Cash Equivalents at End of Year = $22
E5-24	Net Increase in Cash and Cash Equivalents = $6
E5-25	3. 2002: 2.69

E5–26	Net Income Forecasted 2003 = $52
E5–27	1. Total Liabilities and Stockholders' Equity for 2003 = $1,190
P5–28	2. Net Cash Provided by Operating Activities = $138,500
P5–29	Cash and Cash Equivalents at End of Year = $41,000
P5–30	Cash Balance at End of Year = $31,000
P5–31	Net Increase in Cash = $45,000
P5–32	Cash Balance at End of Year = $660,000
P5–33	Cash & Cash Equivalents at End of Year = $14,000
P5–34	Net Decrease in Cash & Cash Equivalents = $(5,740)
P5–35	1. Net Increase in Cash & Cash Equivalents = $118,400
P5–36	2. Cash & Cash Equivalents at End of Year = $176,400
P5–37	1. Net Cash from Operating Activities for 2001 = $65,000
P5–38	1. Net Income for 2002 = $85
P5–39	1. Net Cash Provided by Operating Activities = $30,980
P5–40	Net Cash Flow Provided by Operating Activities = $155,030
P5–41	Net Income = $68,800
P5–42	1. Cash Flow-to-Net Income Ratio 2002 = 1.33%
P5–43	1. Net Income Forecasted 2003 = $120
P5–44	Net Increase in Cash & Cash Equivalents = $16,800

Chapter 6

E6–11	7. B, D, Noncurrent Asset
E6–13	Total Cash Collected = $4,940
E6–14	Sales Returns and Allowances = $1,500
E6–15	1. Bad Debt Expense = $25,140
E6–16	2. Cash = $1,350 (Debit)
E6–17	2. Total = $2,642.87
E6–18	1. Accounts Written Off for 2000: $25,500
E6–19	2. Balance in Liability Account at end of 2002: $101,950
E6–20	Profit from Service Contracts in 2002 = $1,410
E6–21	Net Credit Sales = $1,430,000
E6–22	1. (11) (a)
E6–23	1. Restricted Cash = $6,000,000 (Debit)
E6–26	Correct Balance = $9,033
E6–27	Corrected Book Balance = $15,649.71
E6–28	Outstanding Checks at the Beginning of June = $10,558
E6–29	1. Cash = $450,000
E6–30	End of Third Year, Interest Revenue = $1,071 (Credit)
E6–31	3. Notes Payable = $40,000 (Credit)
E6–32	1. Cash Flows from Operating Activities = $55,000
E6–33	Cash Short and Over = 5.84 (Debit)
P6–34	2. Bad Debt Expense = $4,565 (Debit)
P6–35	1. Gross Method: Sales = $50,000 (Credit)

P6–36	Bad Debt Expense = $7,410
P6–37	Balance for Estimated Uncollectible = $30,490
P6–38	Balance in Liability Account at end of 2003 = $24,850
P6–39	Required Adjustment to Liability Account = $395,250
P6–40	(i) Interest Revenue = $630 (Credit)
P6–42	1. Corrected Book Balance = $15,751.32
P6–43	Corrected Book Balance = $536.65
P6–44	Rocky Mountain Bank: (b) Cash = $146,250 (Debit)
P6–45	1. (b) Cash = $122,500 (Debit)
P6–46	2. Jan. 31, Receivable from Factor = $120,000 (Credit)
P6–47	1. Gain on Sale of Land = $56,808 (Credit)
P6–48	Total Discounted Value = $503,105
P6–49	Cash Collected from Customers = $1,627,000
P6–50	Jan. 31, 2003, Cash = $1,595 (Credit)

Chapter 7

E7–13	Construction in Progress for 2003 = $3,740,000 (Credit)
E7–14	4. Estimated Cost to Complete Contract as of End of 2002 = $656,667
E7–15	2003 (100% Completed) Gross Profit Recognized in Current Year = $22,150
E7–16	3. $370,000
E7–17	a. Balance Sheet: Construction in Progress = $70,800
E7–18	2002 Cost of Long-Term Construction Contracts = $4,525,000
E7–19	2002 Construction in Progress = $700,000 (Credit)
E7–20	Gross Profit to be Recognized in 2002 = $1,366,185
E7–21	Dec. 31 Contract Costs = $97 (Debit)
E7–22	Deferred Gross Profit—2003 = $9,450 (Debit)
E7–23	7. $120,000 ($91,800 + $28,200)
E7–24	Realized Gross Profit 2002 = $14,100 (Credit)
E7–25	Realized Gross Profit 2002 = $22,400
E7–27	July 1, 2003, Cash = $8,000 (Debit)
E7–28	Consignee Receivable = $15,600
P7–29	1. Net Income 2003 = $178,500
P7–30	1. a. (4) 2003 = $55,000,000
P7–31	1. a. (9) Gross Profit for Project D = $8,250
P7–32	4. Revenue from Long-Term Construction Contracts 2003 = $5,856,000 (Credit)
P7–33	2. Adjusted Gross Profit = $832,000
P7–34	1. (1) 2003 = $6,150,000
P7–35	1. 2004 = 100%
P7–37	Deferred Gross Profit—2001 = $21,736 (Debit)
P7–38	1. (b) Gross Profit = $900,000
P7–39	1. Cost of Consignment Goods Sold = $181,440 (Debit)

Chapter 8

E8–13	6. I, DL
E8–14	1. Purchases = $5,000 (Debit)
E8–15	Cash Expended for Inventory—2002 = $550,000

E8-16	Ending Inventory Quantity as of Dec. 31 = 126,000 units
E8-17	d. Excluded
E8-18	Cost of Goods Manufactured = $7,348
E8-19	Aug. 15 Purchases = $15,225 (Debit)
E8-20	1. a. Dec. 10 Purchases = $7,275 (Debit)
E8-21	2. Inventory = $5,000 (Debit)
E8-22	b. LIFO Oldest Costs = $5,250
E8-23	1. Ending Inventory Value = $1,400
E8-24	1. a. $15,000
E8-25	1. FIFO Inventory, Oct. 31 = $36,390
E8-26	Purchases: Total Cost = $83,800
E8-27	Quantity Available for Sale = 73,200 units
E8-28	1. Gross Profit as a Percent of Sales = 32.88% of Sales
E8-29	2. Jan. 1, 2002 Inventory = $4,000,000
E8-30	Net Income—LIFO Basis, 2002 = Debit $75,000
E8-31	1. Net Income Total = $70,200
E8-33	2. $1,230
E8-34	Dec. 31, 2002 Dollar Value LIFO Cost = $571,400
E8-35	2. Dollar Value LIFO Cost at 12/31/02 = $312,032
E8-36	Total Extended Year-End = $161,450
E8-37	(2) (b) $210,842
P8-38	Cost of Goods Sold 2000 = $1,000
P8-39	2. Total = $92,050
P8-40	3. Dec. 29 Balance = $493.75
P8-41	1. Mar. 28 Balance = $10,825.00
P8-42	2. Gross Profit on Sales = $80,800
P8-43	4. Ending Inventory Value = $192,950
P8-44	1. 1989 Layer = $156,000
P8-46	2000 Inventory Turnover = 12.29
P8-47	Product 401, Ending Inventory Units = 130
P8-48	12/31/98 Dollar Value LIFO Cost = $30,311
P8-49	12/31/02 Dollar Value LIFO Cost = $341,755
P8-50	Inventory 12/31/01 = 11,000 Units
P8-51	12/31/01 End-of-Year Cost = $154,504
P8-52	12/31/01 End-of-Year Cost = $137,500

Chapter 9

E9-10	Product 563, LCM = .24
E9-11	1. a. $118,500
E9-12	2. b. Cost of Goods Sold = $387,000
E9-13	2. Cost of Goods Sold, LCM = $50,400
E9-14	2. Cash = $3,500 (Debit)
E9-15	Total Sales = $2,430,000
E9-16	Work-in-Process Inventory Lost = $135,020
E9-17	3. Average Cost % = 69.37%
E9-18	2. Ending Inventory at Retail = $5,960
E9-19	2. Cost Percentage: $336,600/$510,000 = 66%
E9-20	Corrected Net Income for 2002 = $1,900
E9-21	3. Inventory for Feb. 28 = $23,300
E9-22	Overstated Inventory for 2002 = $416
E9-23	2. Ending Inventory at Retail = $65,232
E9-24	12/31/02 Dollar Value LIFO Retail Cost = $120,180
E9-25	Mar. 31 Accounts Payable = $520,000 (Credit)
E9-26	2. Cash = $24,000 (Credit)
E9-27	Jan. 30, 2002 Exchange Loss = $534 (Debit)

P9-28	1. d. $61,650
P9-29	2. Total Cost of Goods Sold = $120,800
P9-30	3. Trade-In Inventory = $11,160 (Credit)
P9-31	Dec. 31 (b) No Adjustment Required
P9-32	2001 = 34%
P9-33	Net Income = $85,000
P9-34	Cost of Stolen Inventory = $20,792
P9-35	3. Gross Profit = $76,935
P9-36	Ending Inventory at Retail, 2002 = $20,000
P9-37	Inventory Dec. 31, 2002 Retail = $14,856
P9-38	g. Retained Earnings = $475 (Credit)
P9-39	Dec. 31, 2001 Inventory at End-of-Year Retail Prices = $258, 875
P9-40	2. Dec. 31, 2001 Year-End Price Index: 1.12
P9-41	4. Mar. 23, 2003 Purchases = $165,000 (Debit)
P9-42	2. Printco: Exchange Gain = $27,000 (Credit)

Chapter 10

E10-13	2. Mortgage Payable = 283.13 (Debit)
E10-14	2. Interest Expense 2002 = $2,907
E10-15	a. Market Price = $885,295
E10-18	c. Interest Expense = $25 (Credit)
E10-19	a. $750
E10-21	1. a. Discount on Bonds Payable = $1,544 (Credit)
E10-24	Gain on Early Retirement of Bonds = $4,650 (Credit)
E10-25	1. Loss on Early Retirement of Debt = $16,000 (Debit)
E10-26	1. Interest Payable = $20,000 (Credit)
E10-27	8/1/02 Discount on Bonds Payable = $847 (Credit)
E10-28	Gain on Restructuring of Debt = $10,000
E10-29	Imperial Loss on Restructuring of Debt = $600,000
E10-30	a. Total Payments = $12,500,000
P10-31	c. Debt Ratio = .60
P10-32	2. Book Value 2003 = $480,000
P10-34	1. Maximum Amount Investor Should Pay = $838,854
P10-36	1. $73,037
P10-37	2. c. $8,641
P10-39	1. Accrued Interest = $67,500
P10-40	2002 Income before Taxes = $33,795
P10-45	1. Market Value = $73,037,000
P10-47	2. a. Gain on Bond Retirement, Brewster = $121,190
P10-48	Imputed Interest Rate = 3%

Chapter 11

E11-10	e. Paid-In Capital in Excess of Par = $234,000 (Credit)
E11-12	a. Common Stock for 2002 = $1.57
E11-13	c. Common Stock Subscribed = $12,500 (Debit)
E11-14	Dec. 31 Cash = $216,000 (Credit)
E11-15	1. b. Total Stockholders Equity = $5,043,000
E11-17	1. Paid-In Capital in Excess of Par—Preferred = $61,383 (Credit)
E11-18	2. Common Stock = $180,000 (Credit)

E11-19   1. Outstanding at 12/31/01 = 90,000 shares
E11-21   2. Retained Earning 12/31/02 = $126,500
E11-22   2. $6,020,250
E11-24   1. Retained Earnings = $20,000 (Debit)
E11-25   b. Retained Earnings = $100,000 (Debit)
E11-27   Paid-In Capital in Excess of Par = $275,000 (Debit)
E11-28   a. Fire Loss = $2,625 (Debit)
E11-32   2. Total Assets = $800,000
E11-33   1. 2003 Compensation Expense = $90,000
E11-34   2003 Compensation Expense = $46,667 (Debit)
P11-35   1. Mar. 10 Paid-In Capital = $111,500 (Credit)
P11-38   Total Stockholders' Equity = $13,107,600
P11-39   Apr. 1 Discount on Bonds Payable = $8,000 (Debit)
P11-40   1. c. Treasury Stock = $420,000 (Debit)
P11-41   1. f. Treasury Stock, Preferred = $15,000 (Credit)
P11-42   1. (e) Treasury Stock, Common = $35,000 (Credit)
P11-43   1. 12/31/99 Compensation Expense = $25,000 (Debit)
P11-45   1. $37,500
P11-46   8/31 Cash = $455,000 (Debit)
P11-48   1. 3/2/01 Cash = $305,100 (Debit)
P11-49   1. 12/31/00 Income Summary = $67,500 (Debit)
P11-50   Net Cash Used in Financing Activities = $(130,000)
P11-51   1. 5/18/02 Dividends Payable = $562,500 (Credit)
P11-52   1/15/02 Treasury Stock = $39,000 (Credit)
P11-54   1. Buildings = $425,000 (Credit)
P11-55   1. 2002 Compensation Expense = $31,250

Chapter 12

E12-12   Total Land = $449,400
E12-13   R & D Expense = $37,000 (Debit)
E12-15   Cost Assigned to Land = $219,048
E12-16   Land = $200,000 (Debit)
E12-17   2004 Int. Exp. = $6,297 (Debit)
E12-18   Disc. on N/P = $30,808 (Debit)
E12-19   Value Assigned to Franchise = $115,000
E12-20   Premium on Bonds Payable = $18,000 (Credit)
E12-22   Interest Charges Capitalized = $25,000
E12-23   a. Total Capitalized Interest for 2002 = $122,850
E12-25   1. Goodwill = $295,000 (Debit)
E12-26   2. Negative Goodwill = $20,000 (Credit)
E12-28   2. Total = $208,000
E12-30   2. Exploration Expense = $0
E12-33   1. a. Total Capitalized Interest for 2002 = $122,850
P12-34   1. Raw Materials = $73,000
P12-36   1. Total Cost of Land = $196,500
P12-37   Mar. 2-30 Buildings = $29,600 (Debit)
P12-38   Organization Expenses = $150,000 (Debit)
P12-39   b. Patents = $14,280 (Debit)
P12-40   1. Jan. 2 Org. Exp. = $23,300 (Debit)
P12-41   Building Cost = $624,250
P12-42   Net Income = $43,270
P12-44   Land Increase = $312,500

P12-45   1. Total Interest Accrued = $1,300,000
P12-47   1. Goodwill = $1,085,000 (Debit)
P12-49   1. ROE = 26.2%
P12-50   b. Loss on Removal of Wall = $13,880 (Debit)
P12-52   1. Total Capitalized Interest for 2002 = $90,000

Chapter 13

E13-11   Machine Cost = $39,200
E13-12   Dec. 31, 2002 Deprec. Exp. = $6,750 (Debit)
E13-13   1. 6.8 Years
E13-14   1. = $12,500
E13-15   1. Depreciation Rate = $320
E13-16   a. $5,650
E13-18   a. $5,930
E13-19   2. 2002 Amort. Exp. = $4,410
E13-21   2002 Deprec. Exp. = $53,333
E13-22   Charge for 2002 = $57,500
E13-23   1. Book Value = $910,000
E13-24   1. Book Value = $50,000
E13-25   3. Building = $50,000
E13-26   Gain on Sale of Equipment = $2,942
E13-28   2. Gain on Trade-In of Truck = $300 (Credit)
E13-29   4. = $22,500
E13-30   1. a. $13,500
E13-31   2004 Cost Recovery Amount = $4,635
P13-33   1. $11,675
P13-38   a. 2002 Depreciation = $1,100
P13-40   (h) Cost of Ending Inv. = $44,728
P13-41   1999 Cost Subject to Depletion = $6,000,000
P13-42   2000 Depreciation Per Ton = $1,550
P13-43   a. Deprec. Exp. = $2,800
P13-49   2002 Deprec. & Amort. Exp. = $200,789

Chapter 14

E14-9   c. Int. Revenue = $4,800 (Credit)
E14-10   3. Realized Loss on Sale of Securities = $200 (Debit)
E14-13   Annual Amortization = $2,000
E14-15   1. Investment in Held-to-Maturity Securities = $601,933 (Debit)
E14-17   1. Unrealized Gain on Trading Securities = $2,964 (Credit)
E14-18   2. Total Cost = $385,000
E14-19   2. Realized Gain on Sale of Securities = $1,000 (Credit)
E14-20   2. Adj. N/I = $96,000
E14-22   1. Unrealized Gain on Trading Securities = $7,000 (Credit)
E14-23   2. Unrealized Loss on Transfer of Securities = $500 (Debit)
E14-25   3. Unrealized Gain on Trading Securities = $7,000 (Credit)
E14-31   2. Bad Debt Expense = $4,336 (Debit)
P14-32   Dec. 31, 2002 Unrealized Loss on Trading Securities = $29,000 (Debit)
P14-33   1. Jan. 1, 2001 Cash = $7,300 (Debit)
P14-36   b. Market Adjustment—Trading Securities = $450 (Credit)
P14-38   2001 Dividend Revenue = $2,500 (Credit)

P14-39   Net Annual Adj. to Income = $9,900
P14-40   1. Goodwill = $40,000
P14-41   Diff. Between FV & BV = $(2,000)
P14-43   c. Unreal. Gain = $1,400 (Credit)
P14-44   2. 2002 Adjustment Required = $280,000
P14-46   1. PV = $529,405

Chapter 15

E15-10   Debit Rent Exp. each year = $140,000
E15-11   PV = $2,426,343
E15-12   PV = $1,898,460
E15-13   12/31/03 Interest Exp. = $19,264
E15-14   Cost of Owned Equip. = $36,700
E15-15   Interest Revenue = $4,545 (Credit)
E15-16   Interest Rate = 10%
E15-17   3. Interest Rate = 10%
E15-18   1. $62,949
E15-19   1. 12/31/04 Interest Revenue = $52,077
E15-20   2. Net Balance = $4,200
E15-21   2. Interest Revenue Recognized = $63,893
E15-22   3. Implicit Int. Rate = 17%
E15-23   2. Income from Operating Lease = $107,500
E15-25   2002 Noncurrent Liabilities = $223,542
E15-26   3. Dec. 31, 2004 Book Value of Asset = $16,150
E15-29   Interest Revenue = $86,098
E15-30   Interest Exp. = $212,095
E15-31   2. Dec. 31 Int. Exp. = $102,246 (Debit)
P15-32   2. Amortization for Period = $27,036
P15-33   2. 2006 Cash = $267,000 (Credit)
P15-34   2. 12/31/04 Int. Exp. = $11,424
P15-35   1. PV of Lease = $265,000
P15-36   2. Int. Rate = 11%
P15-37   1. PV of Residual Value = $16,156
P15-38   1. Manufacturer's Profit = $607,102
P15-39   1. Manufacturer's Profit = $2,656,950
P15-40   3. Int. Exp. = $201,858
P15-41   1. Dec. 31 Amortization Exp. = $108,417 (Debit)
P15-42   1. PV of Guaranteed Residual Value = $36,881
P15-43   1. Lease Payments Rec. = $252,000
P15-44   1. Cash Provided by Operating Activities = $122,632
P15-45   Future Minimum Rental Payments = $446,000

Chapter 16

E16-9   Taxable Inc. = $3,000,000
E16-10   1. Income Tax Exp.—Deferred = $21,000 (Debit)
E16-11   1. Current Deferred Tax Asset = $9,600
E16-12   1. Inc. Tax Benefit = $14,000 (Credit)
E16-13   1. Inc. Tax Benefit = $11,200 (Credit)
E16-14   1. Inc. Tax Exp.—Current = $6,000 (Debit)
E16-15   Inc. Taxes Payable = $108,200 (Credit)
E16-16   Inc. Tax Benefit = $17,660 (Credit)
E16-17   Inc. Taxes Pay. = $24,400 (Credit)
E16-18   Net Deferred Tax Liability = $56,000
E16-19   2. Inc. Tax Benefit = $3,150 (Debit)
E16-20   1. Inc. Taxes Pay = $30,000 (Credit)
E16-21   1. 2001 Refund Due = $108,500
E16-22   1. Refund Due = $38,500
E16-23   Increase in Income Tax Pay. = $6,000

E16-24   2. $4,000
E16-25   Net Income = $585,000
P16-26   2004 Inc. Tax Benefit = $12,800 (Credit)
P16-27   1. Pretax Financial Income = $2,494,000
P16-28   1. Taxable Income = $64,500
P16-29   2. Net Loss = $(13,560)
P16-30   2. Inc. Tax Exp.—Current = $22,800 (Debit)
P16-31   2. Net Income = $41,390
P16-32   1. Def. Tax Asset—Current = $6,000 (Debit)
P16-33   1. Inc. Tax Benefit—Rate Change = $6,600 (Credit)
P16-34   1. Tax Refund Due Columbia = $17,932
P16-35   1. Inc. Tax Refund Due in 1996 = $11,408
P16-36   1. Total Tax Benefit to Be Allocated = $2,100
P16-37   Case A Tax Exp. on Gains = $13,900

Chapter 17

E17-6   FICA Taxes Payable = $2,169 (Credit)
E17-7   Salaries & Comm. Expense = $33,000 (Debit)
E17-8   Total Liability for Vacation Pay = $5,800
E17-9   1. $24,500
E17-10   1. $27,000
E17-11   Pension Service Expense = $367,600
E17-12   Case 1, Acc. Pension Liability = $60
E17-13   2002 Amortization Amount = $206,667
E17-14   1. $606,386
E17-15   1. $157,750
E17-16   Actual Return on Plan Assets = $97,000
E17-17   Difference = $23,000
E17-18   Amortization = $22,000
E17-20   Pension Expense = $55,000
E17-21   Pension Expense = $893,000
E17-23   Additional Pension Liability = $62,000
E17-24   Add. Pension Liability = $104
E17-25   Case 1 Prepaid Pension Cost = $3,400
E17-27   Actual Return = $(300)
E17-28   Unamortized Transition Loss = $650,000
E17-29   Loss Amortization = $163,500
P17-30   Salaries Payable = $62,250 (Credit)
P17-31   Jan. 6 Payroll Tax Exp. = $243.48 (Debit)
P17-32   1. Total Accrued = $6,150
P17-33   1. 2002 Cash = $625,000 (Credit)
P17-34   2. 8 years
P17-35   1. Difference = $(11,000)
P17-36   1. 2002 Interest Cost = $150
P17-37   3. 2003 Add. Pension Liability = $1,145
P17-38   1. 2002 Add. Pension Liability = $14,300
P17-39   2002 Prior Service Cost = $750,000
P17-40   1. 2002 Add. Pension Liability = $65
P17-41   2002 Net Pension Expense = $740
P17-43   f. Amort. of Prior Service Cost = $61
P17-44   2002 Net Pension Expense = $84,300
P17-45   2002 Interest Cost = $120,000

Chapter 18

E18-10   Net Cost @ $.24 = $(24,000)
E18-11   Dec. 31, 2002 Int. Exp. = $48,000 (Debit)
E18-12   Dec. 31, 2002 Gain on Foreign Currency = $29,221 (Credit)

E18-13 Dec. 31, 2002 Futures Contract = $10,000 (Credit)

E18-14 Dec. 31, 2002 Cotton Call Option = $1,500 (Credit)

E18-22 Gross Profit = $68,400

E18-23 COGS = $2,200 (Debit)

P18-24 b. Net Cost on Aug. 31 @ $1.00 = $(90,000)

P18-25 Dec. 31, 2002 Interest Rate Swap = $121,492 (Debit)

P18-27 Dec. 31, 2002 Int. Revenue = $2,066 (Credit)

P18-28 Jan. 1, 2002 Oats Put Option = $100,000 (Debit)

P18-30 1. (c) $0

P18-33 1. Segment 2 Operating Profit = $660,000

Chapter 19

E19-7 Weighted Avg. Shares Outstanding = 305,000

E19-8 Weighted Avg. # of Common Shares, 2003 = 771,500

E19-9 Weighted Avg. Shares, 2002 = 660,188

E19-10 2002 EPS = $12.78

E19-11 (c) Income From Continuing Operations = $0.60

E19-12 e. $2.00

E19-13 Total Shares = 71,000

E19-14 Incremental Shares = 12,000

E19-15 Basic EPS = $11.00

E19-16 Basic EPS = $2.43

E19-17 1. Basic Loss per Share = $(2.30)

E19-18 Basic EPS = $1.14

E19-19 Basic EPS = $3.58

E19-20 Basic EPS = $4.58

P19-21 2002 Weighted Avg. # of Shares = 263,375

P19-22 1. Net Income = $630,000

P19-23 Basic EPS = $4.18

P19-24 Basic EPS = $2.78

P19-25 1. Basic EPS = $14.00

P19-26 Basic EPS = $5.11

P19-27 2. Basic Loss per Share = $(1.83)

P19-28 1. Basic EPS = $2.71

P19-29 Basic EPS = $1.46

P19-30 1. Basic EPS = $5.00

P19-31 1. Basic EPS = $2.01

P19-32 Basic EPS = $0.985

Chapter 20

E20-7 Book Value, Jan. 1, 2002 = $20,480

E20-8 2. Depreciation to Date = $750,000

E20-9 1. Bad Debts Exp. = $9,750

E20-10 1. $27,000 per Year

E20-11 1. $3.75 per Ton

E20-12 1. 2001 Depreciation = $18,000

E20-13 Increase in Retained Earnings for 1999-2001 = $70,000

E20-14 Net Income = $28,100

E20-15 Retained Earnings, Dec. 31, 2002 = $270,600

E20-16 2. Bad Debts Expense = $13,075 (Debit)

E20-17 1. Reed, Capital = $12,400 (Debit)

E20-19 2000 COGS = $2,294,500

E20-20 2001 Depreciation = $70

P20-22 1. Acc. Depreciation—Equip. = $100,000 (Debit)

P20-23 Retained Earnings Dec. 31, 2002 (3) = $169,800

P20-24 1. (a) Acc. Dep.—Mach. = $10,000 (Credit)

P20-25 2. $4,300 per Year

P20-26 2. Patents = $600,000 (Credit)

P20-27 3. 2001 EPS = $2.20

P20-28 2001 Dep. Expense = $48,000

P20-29 1. 1998 Restated Net Income = $266,800

P20-30 2. 2001 Net Income = $79,800

P20-31 1. (c) Retained Earnings = $37,750 (Debit)

P20-32 2. Retained Earnings Dec. 31, 2001 = $25,700

P20-33 1. (a) Retained Earnings = $15,333 (Debit)

Chapter 21

E21-10 2002 Net Income = $119,000

E21-11 2002 Sales = $1,000,000

E21-12 Electric Services Companies ROE = 8.9%

E21-13 2002 A/R Turnover = 5.09 times

E21-14 2002 Inventory Turnover—Average = 2.4

E21-15 W/O Borrowed Capital, Net Income = $140,000

E21-16 Company A, Return on Sales = 2.08%

E21-17 2002 ROE = 12.4%

E21-18 Operating Lease, Debt-to-Equity Ratio = 0.73

E21-19 1. Current Liabilities = $92,000

E21-22 Net Income with U.S. GAAP = $10,000

E21-23 Stockholders' Equity = $800,000

E21-24 HC/CD (End of 2nd Year) Cash = $97,500

E21-25 Purchasing Power Loss = $350,000

E21-26 Unrealized Holding Gain = $500

E21-27 4. Current Cost/Constant Dollar = $192,000

E21-28 Capital Stock = $85,000

E21-29 Total Assets (American Dollars) = $322,083

E21-30 Total Debits (American Dollars) = $882,400

P21-32 Stay-Trim Total Liabilities = 39%

P21-33 Company A, Asset Turnover = 0.39

P21-34 1. 2002 Avg. Receivables = $52,500

P21-35 2002 Raw Materials Turnover = 3

P21-36 1. (a) 2002 ROE = 14.9%

P21-37 b. 2001 Avg. Collection Period = 94.6 days

P21-38 1. (a) Beg. Retained Earnings Increases by $12,000

P21-39 3. Return on Equity—Home Country = 22.6%

P21-40 2. Net Income with U.S. GAAP = $1,820,000

P21-41 1. 2001 Price-Index Adjusted Sales = $8,900

P21-42 2002 Gain Adjusted for Inflation = $13,527

P21-43 HC/CD Total Assets = $4,402,300

P21-44 COGS = $114,444

P21-45 Current Cost Net Income = $170,100

P21-46 Ending Retained Earnings = $322,517

P21-47 Ending Retained Earnings = $156,220

P21-48 Net Cash Provided by Operating Activities = $83,000

Indexes

Subject Index

Indexes

Company and Internet Site Index

Y

Z